Library
Western Wyoming Community College

FOR REFERENCE

Do Not Take
From This Room

Contemporary Literary Criticism

Guide to Gale Literary Criticism Series

When you need to review criticism of literary works, these are the Gale series to use:

If the author's death date is: **You should turn to:**

After Dec. 31, 1959
(or author is still living)

CONTEMPORARY LITERARY CRITICISM

for example: Jorge Luis Borges, Anthony Burgess,
William Faulkner, Mary Gordon,
Ernest Hemingway, Iris Murdoch

1900 through 1959

TWENTIETH-CENTURY LITERARY CRITICISM

for example: Willa Cather, F. Scott Fitzgerald,
Henry James, Mark Twain, Virginia Woolf

1800 through 1899

NINETEENTH-CENTURY LITERATURE CRITICISM

for example: Fedor Dostoevski, George Sand,
Gerard Manley Hopkins, Emily Dickinson

1400 through 1799

LITERATURE CRITICISM FROM 1400 TO 1800
(excluding Shakespeare)

for example: Anne Bradstreet, Pierre Corneille,
Daniel Defoe, Alexander Pope,
Jonathan Swift, Phillis Wheatley

SHAKESPEAREAN CRITICISM

Shakespeare's plays and poetry

Gale also publishes related criticism series:

CONTEMPORARY ISSUES CRITICISM

Presents criticism on contemporary authors writing on current issues. Topics covered include the social sciences, philosophy, economics, natural science, law, and related areas.

CHILDREN'S LITERATURE REVIEW

Covers authors of all eras. Presents criticism on authors and author/illustrators who write for the preschool to junior-high audience.

Volume 28

Contemporary Literary Criticism

Excerpts from Criticism of
the Works of Today's Novelists,
Poets, Playwrights, Short Story
Writers, Filmmakers, Scriptwriters,
and Other Creative Writers

Jean C. Stine
Editor

Bridget Broderick
Daniel G. Marowski
Associate Editors

Gale Research Company
Book Tower
Detroit, Michigan 48226

STAFF

Jean C. Stine, *Editor*

Bridget Broderick, Daniel G. Marowski, *Associate Editors*

Robyn V. Young, *Senior Assistant Editor*

Lee Fournier, Roger Matuz, Jane E. Neidhardt, Lisa M. Rost,
Jane C. Thacker, Marjorie Wachtel, Debra A. Wells, *Assistant Editors*

Sharon R. Gunton, Thomas Ligotti,
Phyllis Carmel Mendelson, *Contributing Editors*

Robert J. Elster, Jr., *Production Supervisor*
Lizbeth A. Purdy, *Production Coordinator*
Denise Michlewicz, *Assistant Production Coordinator*
Eric F. Berger, Paula J. DiSante, Amy T. Marcaccio, *Editorial Assistants*

Linda M. Pugliese, *Manuscript Coordinator*
Donna Craft, *Assistant Manuscript Coordinator*
Rosetta Irene Simms Carr, Colleen M. Crane, Maureen A. Puhl, *Manuscript Assistants*

Karen Rae Forsyth, *Research Coordinator*
Jeannine Schiffman Davidson, *Assistant Research Coordinator*
Kevin John Campbell, Victoria Cariappa, Robert J. Hill, Harry Kronick,
James A. MacEachern, Kyle Schell, Valerie Webster, *Research Assistants*

L. Elizabeth Hardin, *Permissions Supervisor*
Filomena Sgambati, *Permissions Associate*
Janice M. Mach, *Permissions Coordinator*
Patricia A. Seefelt, *Assistant Permissions Coordinator, Illustrations*
Susan D. Nobles, *Senior Permissions Assistant*
Margaret A. Chamberlain, Mary M. Matuz, Joan B. Weber, *Permissions Assistants*
Sandra C. Davis, Dorothy J. Fowler, Kathy Grell, Josephine M. Keene,
Virgie T. Leavens, Diane M. Platzke, Mabel E. Schoening, *Permissions Clerks*

Frederick G. Ruffner, *Publisher*
James M. Ethridge, *Executive Vice President/Editorial*
Dedria Bryfonski, *Editorial Director*
Christine Nasso, *Director, Literature Division*
Laurie Lanzen Harris, *Senior Editor, Literary Criticism Series*

Copyright © 1984 by Gale Research Company

Library of Congress Catalog Card Number 76-38938
ISBN 0-8103-4402-5
ISSN 0091-3421

Contents

Preface 7
Authors Forthcoming in *CLC* 9
Appendix 475
Cumulative Index to Authors 481
Cumulative Index to Critics 521

Jeffrey Archer 1940- 11	Denise Levertov 1923- 238
Juan Benet 1927- 15	Mina Loy 1882-1966 245
Louise Bennett 1919- 26	Norman Mailer 1923- 255
Doris Betts 1932- 32	David Malouf 1934- 265
William Boyd 1952- 37	Bobbie Ann Mason 1940- 271
James M. Cain 1892-1977 43	Thomas McGrath 1916- 275
Taylor Caldwell 1900- 55	John Mortimer 1923- 281
Bruce Chatwin 1940- 70	R. K. Narayan 1906- 290
Walter Van Tilburg Clark 1909-1971 76	Gloria Naylor 1950- 304
	Pablo Neruda 1904-1973 306
Padraic Colum 1881-1972 85	Marsha Norman 1947- 317
Michael Cristofer 1946- 94	Clifford Odets 1906-1963 322
Peter Davison 1928- 99	Toby Olson 1937- 342
Peter De Vries 1910- 105	Cynthia Ozick 1928- 346
William Dickey 1928- 116	Bette Pesetsky 1932- 357
John Gregory Dunne 1932- 120	Robert Phillips 1938- 361
Umberto Eco 1932- 130	Katha Pollitt 1949- 366
William Faulkner 1897-1962 134	Manuel Puig 1932- 369
Roy Fuller 1912- 147	James Purdy 1923- 376
John Gardner 1933-1982 160	Ruth Rendell 1930- 383
Andrew M. Greeley 1928- 169	M. L. Rosenthal 1917- 389
Edward Hoagland 1932- 179	Mari Sandoz 1896-1966 399
Hugh Hood 1928- 187	Peter Straub 1943- 408
M. M. Kaye 1909?- 197	Jun'ichirō Tanizaki 1886-1965 413
William Kennedy 1928- 203	Paul Theroux 1941- 422
Tadeusz Konwicki 1926- 207	Anne Tyler 1941- 429
Richard Kostelanetz 1940- 212	Miriam Waddington 1917- 436
Maxine Kumin 1925- 220	René Wellek 1903- 441
John le Carré 1931- 226	Charles Wright 1935- 456
Elmore Leonard 1925- 233	James Wright 1927-1980 461

Preface

Literary criticism is, by definition, "the art of evaluating or analyzing with knowledge and propriety works of literature." The complexity and variety of the themes and forms of contemporary literature make the function of the critic especially important to today's reader. It is the critic who assists the reader in identifying significant new writers, recognizing trends in critical methods, mastering new terminology, and monitoring scholarly and popular sources of critical opinion.

Until the publication of the first volume of *Contemporary Literary Criticism (CLC)* in 1973, there existed no ongoing digest of current literary opinion. *CLC,* therefore, has fulfilled an essential need.

Scope of the Work

CLC presents significant passages from published criticism of work by today's creative writers. Each volume of *CLC* includes excerpted criticism on about 65 authors who are now living or who died after December 31, 1959. Since the series began publication, more than 1,700 authors have been included. The majority of authors covered by *CLC* are living writers who continue to publish; therefore, an author frequently appears in more than one volume. There is, of course, no duplication of reprinted criticism.

Authors are selected for inclusion for a variety of reasons, among them: the publication of a critically acclaimed new work, the reception of a major literary award, or the dramatization of a literary work as a movie or television screenplay. For example, the present volume includes Katha Pollitt and William Kennedy, who each recently won a National Book Critics Circle Award; John le Carré, who added *The Little Drummer Girl* to the list of his popular and critically acclaimed espionage novels; and Norman Mailer, whose long-awaited novel *Ancient Evenings* received much critical attention. Perhaps most importantly, authors who appear frequently on the syllabuses of high school and college literature classes are heavily represented in *CLC*. William Faulkner, Denise Levertov, and Clifford Odets are examples of writers of this stature in the present volume. Attention is also given to several other groups of writers—authors of considerable public interest—about whose work criticism is often difficult to locate. These are the contributors to the well-loved but nonscholarly genres of mystery and science fiction, as well as writers who appeal specifically to young adults and writers for the nonprint media, including scriptwriters, lyricists, and cartoonists. Foreign writers and authors who represent particular ethnic groups in the United States are also featured in each volume.

Format of the Work

Altogether there are about 750 individual excerpts in each volume—with an average of about eleven excerpts per author—taken from hundreds of literary reviews, general magazines, scholarly journals, and monographs. Contemporary criticism is loosely defined as that which is relevant to the evaluation of the author under discussion; this includes criticism written at the beginning of an author's career as well as current commentary. Emphasis has been placed on expanding the sources for criticism by including an increasing number of scholarly and specialized periodicals. Students, teachers, librarians, and researchers frequently find that the generous excerpts and supplementary material provided by the editors supply them with all the information that they need to write a term paper, analyze a poem, or lead a book discussion group. However, complete bibliographical citations facilitate the location of the original source as well as provide all of the information necessary for a term paper footnote or bibliography.

A *CLC* entry consists of the following elements:

- The **author heading** consists of the author's full name, followed by birth date, and death date when applicable. The portion of the name outside the parentheses denotes the form under which the author has most commonly published. If an author has written consistently under a pseudonym, the pseudonym will be listed in the author heading and the real name given on the first line of the biocritical introduction. Also located at the beginning of the biocritical introduction are any important name variations under which an author has written. Uncertainty as to a birth or death date is indicated by a question mark.

- A **portrait** of the author is included when available.

- A brief **biocritical introduction** to the author and his or her work precedes the excerpted criticism. However, *CLC* is not intended to be a definitive biographical source. Therefore, *cross-references* have been included to direct the user to other useful sources published by the Gale Research Company: *Contemporary Authors* now includes detailed biographical and bibliographical sketches of nearly 76,000 authors; *Children's Literature Review* presents excerpted criticism on the works of authors of children's books; *Something about the Author* contains heavily illustrated biographical sketches on writers and illustrators who create books for children and young adults; *Contemporary Issues Criticism* presents excerpted commentary on the nonfiction works of authors who influence contemporary thought; and *Dictionary of Literary Biography* provides original evaluations of authors important to literary history. Previous volumes of *CLC* in which the author has been featured are also listed.

- The **excerpted criticism** represents various kinds of critical writing—a particular essay may be normative, descriptive, interpretive, textual, appreciative, comparative, or generic. It may range in form from the brief review to the scholarly monograph. Essays are selected by the editors to reflect the spectrum of opinion about a specific work or about an author's writing in general. The excerpts are presented chronologically, adding a useful perspective to the entry. All titles by the author featured in the entry are printed in boldface, which enables the user to readily ascertain the work being discussed.

- A complete **bibliographical citation** designed to help the student find the original essay or book follows each excerpt. An asterisk (*) at the end of a citation indicates the essay is on more than one author.

Other Features

- An **Appendix** lists the sources from which material has been reprinted in a volume. Many other sources have also been consulted during the preparation of the volume.

- A **Cumulative Index to Authors** lists all the authors who have appeared in *Contemporary Literary Criticism, Twentieth-Century Literary Criticism, Nineteenth-Century Literature Criticism,* and *Literature Criticism from 1400 to 1800,* along with cross-references to other Gale series: *Children's Literature Review, Authors in the News, Contemporary Authors, Dictionary of Literary Biography, Something about the Author,* and *Yesterday's Authors of Books for Children.* Users will welcome this cumulated author index as a useful tool for locating an author within the various series. The index, which lists birth and death dates when available, will be particularly valuable for those authors who are identified with a certain period but whose death date causes them to be placed in another, or for those authors whose careers span two periods. For example, F. Scott Fitzgerald is found in *Twentieth-Century Literary Criticism,* yet a writer often associated with him, Ernest Hemingway, is found in *Contemporary Literary Criticism.*

- A **Cumulative Index to Critics** lists the critics and the author entries in which their work appears.

- A list of **Authors Forthcoming in *CLC*** previews the authors to be researched for future volumes.

Acknowledgments

The editors wish to thank the copyright holders of the excerpted articles included in this volume for permission to use the material and the photographers and individuals who provided photographs for us. We are grateful to the staffs of the following libraries for making their resources available to us: Detroit Public Library and the libraries of Wayne State University, the University of Michigan, and the University of Detroit. We also wish to thank Jeri Yaryan for her assistance with copyright research.

Suggestions Are Welcome

The editors welcome the comments and suggestions of readers to expand the coverage and enhance the usefulness of the series.

Authors Forthcoming in *CLC*

With the publication of *Contemporary Literary Criticism,* Volume 12, the series expanded its scope to encompass songwriters, filmmakers, cartoonists, scriptwriters, producers, and other creative writers whose work is often evaluated from a literary perspective. These writers take their place with the novelists, poets, dramatists, and short story writers who will continue to be the primary focus of *CLC.* Volume 29 will include criticism on a number of authors not previously listed and will also feature criticism on newer works by authors included in earlier volumes. Material in Volume 30 will be selected to be of special interest to young adult readers.

To Be Included in Volume 29

Van Wyck Brooks (American literary critic and historian)—One of the foremost critics of the early twentieth century, Brooks won the 1937 Pulitzer Prize in history for *The Flowering of New England.*

Noël Coward (English dramatist, short story writer, poet, essayist, and editor)—Recent publication of *The Collected Short Stories of Noel Coward* and *The Noel Coward Diaries* has renewed popular and critical interest in this prolific writer.

Leon Edel (American biographer and literary critic)—His five-volume biography of Henry James has been praised by Joseph Epstein as "the single greatest work of biography produced in our century."

John Guare (American dramatist)—He is highly regarded for such theatrically innovative plays as *House of Blue Leaves* and *Lydie Breeze.* Guare has been compared with Edward Albee for his ability to combine farce with poignant social commentary.

David Hare (English dramatist)—A left-wing political playwright whose works focus on post-World War II Britain, Hare has gained popular and critical recognition in the United States for his play *Plenty.*

Jack Kerouac (American novelist and poet)—He was a central figure of the Beat Movement, and his life and work have generated a significant amount of new biographical and critical material.

Charles R. Larson (American novelist, short story writer, essayist, critic, and editor)—A renowned scholar of African, Indian, and other third world literatures, Larson recently published his third novel, *Arthur Dimmesdale.*

William Least Heat Moon (American travel writer)—Moon's first book, *Blue Highways: A Journey into America,* recounts his travels along the backroads of the United States in search of his Indian and American roots.

Judith Rossner (American novelist)—Her recent best-selling novel, *August,* is a story of the relationship between a middle-aged New York psychoanalyst and her teenage client.

William Stafford (American poet, editor, and critic)—A prolific writer of calm, understated verse, Stafford continues to create a uniquely American style of contemporary poetry in his recent volume, *A Glass Face in the Rain.*

Richard Tillinghast (American poet and critic)—Tillinghast's recent collection, *The Knife and Other Poems,* reinforces his growing reputation as an important contemporary poet.

Michel Tremblay (French-Canadian dramatist and novelist)—One of Canada's most widely known dramatists writing in French, he has recently written his first novel, *The Fat Lady Next Door Is Pregnant.*

Amos Tutuola (Nigerian novelist)—One of the earliest Nigerian writers to achieve international recognition, he recently published his first book in fourteen years, *The Witch Herbalist of the Remote Town.*

Christa Wolf (East German novelist, short story writer, and essayist)—Her recently translated novel, *A Model Childhood,* reflects Wolf's moral impetus to understand her country's past and how it affects the present. Criticism will also be included on another recent book, *Kein Ort, Nirgends.*

To Be Included in Volume 30

Charles Addams (American cartoonist)—His macabre cartoon characters have delighted readers of *The New Yorker* for many years and were the basis for the popular 1960s television series *The Addams Family*.

Robert Cormier (American novelist and short story writer)—Best known for the realistic and sensitive young adult works *The Chocolate War* and *I Am the Cheese*, Cormier has recently written two more novels and a collection of short fiction.

Jacques Cousteau (French oceanographer, author, and filmmaker)—The books and films of his undersea explorations have helped foster a greater understanding, appreciation, and respect for the marine environment.

Ernest Hemingway (American novelist, short story writer, dramatist, poet, and essayist)—Hemingway's short stories form a vital part of his body of work and will be the focus of the criticism in his entry.

S. E. Hinton (American novelist)—Her well-known novel *The Outsiders* was written when she was only sixteen. Several of Hinton's novels, including *Rumble Fish*, have found renewed popularity through their screen adaptations.

Zora Neale Hurston (Black American novelist and folklorist)—Long neglected by critics, Hurston is now considered a leading writer of the Harlem Renaissance.

Steve Martin (American comedian, writer, and actor)—One of the most popular contemporary comedians, Martin has recorded several albums, has written a book entitled *Cruel Shoes*, and is pursuing a career as an actor.

Paul McCartney (English songwriter)—Among the most successful songwriters, McCartney has sustained much of the acclaim he enjoyed as a member of the Beatles. Criticism will focus on his work as a solo artist and as leader of his band, Wings.

Carl Sagan (American nonfiction writer)—In addition to his well-received television series, *Cosmos*, Sagan has written many books concerning the universe and the origins of life on earth.

Zoa Sherburne (American novelist, short story writer, and poet)—Sherburne's novels portray problems commonly encountered by contemporary adolescents. Her best-known work, *Too Bad about the Haines Girl*, is one of the first young adult novels to address the problem of unwanted pregnancy.

Stephen Sondheim (American lyricist)—His lyrics for Broadway musicals, including *West Side Story* and *A Little Night Music*, have entertained audiences for over twenty-five years.

Scott Spencer (American novelist)—His critically acclaimed novel *Endless Love*, the story of a teenager's obsessive love, was the basis for a major motion picture.

Erich von Daeniken (Swiss nonfiction writer)—In *Chariots of the Gods?* he explores the possibility that earth may have been visited by extraterrestrial beings thousands of years ago.

T. H. White (Indian-born English novelist)—His fantasy tales such as *The Once and Future King*, many of which are based on the legends of Camelot, are popular among readers of all ages.

Tennessee Williams (American dramatist)—Criticism in his entry will focus on the classic play *A Streetcar Named Desire*, a favorite of many young adults.

Jeffrey (Howard) Archer
1940-

English novelist and short story writer.

A former member of the British Parliament, Archer is the author of several best-selling novels. He wrote his first novel, *Not a Penny More, Not a Penny Less* (1976), after being a victim of a million-dollar swindle similar to the one described in that novel. *Shall We Tell the President?* (1977) is an imaginary account of the presidency of Edward M. Kennedy and was faulted for the sensationalism of the plot, which ends in Kennedy's death. Archer's most popular works, *Kane and Abel* (1979) and its sequel *The Prodigal Daughter* (1982), are sagas of two business rivals and their children.

(See also *Contemporary Authors*, Vols. 77-80.)

© Jerry Bauer

A. J. ANDERSON

[*Not a Penny More, Not a Penny Less*] has about as much substance as a soap bubble, but it is quite entertaining. It has to do with the efforts of four men—a professor, a doctor, an art gallery owner, and an English Lord—to retrieve from a slippery con man, who has all the charm of a pailful of hissing snakes, the million dollars they invested in his nonexistent oil company in the North Sea. . . . The book forces us to accept the most outrageous unlikelihoods of plot, but, by the same token, it doesn't put us under the slightest cerebral strain.

> A. J. Anderson, in a review of "Not a Penny More, Not a Penny Less," in Library Journal (*reprinted from* Library Journal, *May 1, 1976; published by R. R. Bowker Co. (a Xerox company); copyright © 1976 by Xerox Corporation*), Vol. 101, No. 9, May 1, 1976, p. 1141.

CHARLES J. KEFFER

[*Not a Penny More, Not a Penny Less*] is fascinating. . . . The story contains some interesting character development, a clear and plausible story line, and its share of suspense. Even the ending is not completely expected. Perhaps the reason it all works out so well in the telling is that Mr. Archer really has his heart in it—the book jacket relates that he wrote the book after being bilked of a million dollars in a stock deal. For his first effort, it is well done. Who knows, he may recover *his* million from the book.

> Charles J. Keffer, in a review of "Not a Penny More, Not a Penny Less," in Best Sellers (*copyright © 1976 Helen Dwight Reid Educational Foundation*), Vol. 36, No. 4, July, 1976, p. 106.

E. S. TURNER

[Archer] has written a tale [*Not a Penny More, Not a Penny Less*] about four men who, collectively, are cheated out of a million dollars and who resolve to steal back the money from the swindler. There could be a moral here for other public figures who have seen their financial dreams dissolve. We have had plenty of "inside" political novels, by Douglas Hurd and others, so why not the inside business novel?

Jeffrey Archer's ingenious plot, with its echoes of Edgar Wallace and vintage Sexton Blake, is the sort to take the public fancy. The novel has a curious racy innocence all its own. It is told with that name-dropping and logging of train times that is thought to lend authenticity. . . . There are walk-on parts for people as diverse as Lord Lichfield, Linda Lovelace and Harold Macmillan. Yet sophisticated it is not. . . .

The pace is quick, but would have been quicker if the author had not lingered to tell us irrelevant facts about the staffing of *The Times*, the square footage of the American embassy in London and so on. The reader has time to strain at gobbets he might otherwise have swallowed. . . .

> E. S. Turner, "Four Unjust Men," in The Times Literary Supplement (© *Times Newspapers Ltd. (London) 1976; reproduced from* The Times Literary Supplement *by permission*), No. 3887, September 10, 1976, p. 1098.

GENE LYONS

["*Shall We Tell the President?*"] is a commonplace thriller whose main interest lies in its political predictions and whose main flaw is that its premise—nicely tricked up to appeal to the vaguely liberal instincts of the people who turn novels into movies—is utterly fanciful and politically absurd.

It is 1981. Edward M. Kennedy has been elected President, with Dale Bumpers of Arkansas as his Vice President. . . . Here is part of his inaugural address: "My fellow Americans, as I take office the problems facing the United States across the world are vast and threatening. In South Africa, pitiless civil war rages between black and white; in the Middle East the ravages of last year's war are being repaired, but . . ." So much for the interesting part; the rest is written in prose almost as scintillating. Why [the publisher] thinks anybody will lay out $8.95 when he can read the newspapers for 20 cents is beyond me. Some of it is even duller, blow by blow automatic writing: "The light turned green, but a car ahead of Marc and Barry in the inside lane wanted to make a left turn on First Street. For the moment, the two impatient F.B.I. men were trapped in a line of traffic." As if getting stuck in traffic were not tiresome enough, Archer thinks we want to read about it.

For all of that, if you can swallow the premise, suspend a good deal of disbelief and tolerate the prose, **"Shall We Tell the President?"** is rather ingeniously plotted and does provide a certain amount of suspense. It may be fairly described as a page turner. (pp. 36-7)

It is giving away nothing of the plot to tell you that the would-be assassins are Southern arms merchants who have in mind eliminating the President as their only means of preventing a Gun Control Bill that is all but assured of passage, and about which Kennedy is to address the Senate on the day of his killing, which is to take place on the steps of the Capitol. One feels dirtied by the necessity of pointing out that such a killing at such a time would in fact do more than anything else to insure the passage of the law. If you wonder whether there is a writer greedy enough to try making a buck by killing off Edward Kennedy, read the book and find out. (p. 37)

Gene Lyons, "Four Novels," in The New York Times Book Review *(copyright © 1977 by The New York Times Company; reprinted by permission), October 23, 1977, pp. 15, 36-7.*

CHARLES WHEELER

[Archer's] use of living politicians, presumably intended to distinguish his [**Shall We Tell the President?**] from the common run of post-Watergate whodunnits, backfires. The plot is implausible, the senators are shadows. Edward Kennedy is little more than a name on the dustcover. Even so, Mr. Archer has deeply offended the two Kennedy widows, who know that their brother-in-law still receives threats from anonymous letter writers, are aware of the special nature of the risk he will run if he ever seeks the Presidency, and must wonder whether this kind of sensationalism might not increase that risk. At all events, it was a sick idea—and the result is a silly, imperceptive book.

Charles Wheeler, "Gunning for Office," in The Times Literary Supplement *(© Times Newspapers Ltd. (London) 1977; reproduced from* The Times Literary Supplement *by permission), No. 3944, October 28, 1977, p. 1258.*

VALENTINE CUNNINGHAM

Jeffrey Archer's [**Shall We Tell the President?**] creaks with keenness to straighten out for you every fact in his dossiers.

Here's a plot to shoot President Edward Kennedy, and plausible enough it's made, especially if you like watching repeats of old movies. There's even a nicely developed if obvious set of parallels with Julius Caesar—man and drama. But it's the manner of the author's address to his narrative that irks most. He's a swot who will show off his busyness about the Washington street-map, constitutional amendments, FBI history and the layout of the Senate. Naturally, the FBI agent who unravels the plot spends his time posing as a student doing research, for what else has his author been doing? Index cards and their dimensions keep getting mentioned: sure signs of an outsider's story. And good novels are inside stories.

Valentine Cunningham, "Lacklust," in New Statesman *(© 1977 The Statesman & Nation Publishing Co. Ltd.), Vol. 94, No. 2433, November 4, 1977, p. 625.*

JOHN NAUGHTON

Kane and Abel is . . . [about survival over a long time-span] involving two principals—a Boston banker named William Kane, and a Polish immigrant to the US, one Abel Rosnovski. . . . Inhabitants of different social worlds, their paths cross initially when Kane's bank withdraws crucial support for the first American who gave Abel a break, thereby triggering off the benefactor's suicide. For this, Kane is never forgiven, and is thereafter pursued by the Pole through thick and thin in a vendetta which sets Wall Street alight.

If you detect in all this a whiff of schmaltz, then your senses are in good working order. No doubt it will sell well in its blockbusting way; but so does Kentucky fried chicken. It's the recipe that counts. (p. 355)

John Naughton, "Marooned in France" (© British Broadcasting Corp. 1979; reprinted by permission of John Naughton), in The Listener, *Vol. 102, No. 2628, September 13, 1979, pp. 354-55.*

KIRKUS REVIEWS

A Boston-Brahmin banker. A rags-to-riches immigrant hotel-king. Two intermittently interesting, mostly clichéd life stories (1906-1967)—which unsubtle Archer (**Shall We Tell the President?**) has linked up [in **Kane and Abel**] using coincidences that belong only in Italian opera and plot secrets that only Dickens could get away with (and did). . . . So how do these two heroes—both of them tiresomely brilliant and decent—hook up? Well, there's a brief teasing glimpse of waiter Abel serving William at the Plaza Hotel. But the real connection is made after Abel has become the indispensable right-hand man of a midwest hotelier: when the 1929 Crash comes, Abel and his boss need help from William's bank, William refuses, and Abel's beloved boss commits suicide. So Abel vows vengeance on William while—with aid from a mysterious anonymous backer(!)—he manages to salvage the hotel chain and achieve tycoon-dom. And with World War II the Abel/William contacts really start hopping. Even the most indulgent readers will surely gag when Abel just happens to save William's life on the battlefield (neither of them recognizing the other!). And next . . . what else but a coincidental meeting between William's son and Abel's daughter? (The two fall madly in love and marry over both fathers' protests.) Abel continues to try to destroy William, however. . . . Finally, after William dies, Abel—who apparently hasn't read *Great Expectations* or *Our*

Mutual Friend—learns that William was his anonymous backer all those years ago.... Obviously inspired by Hollywood's corniest movies and Howard Fast as well as the great Boz, Archer works hard to put in every known commercial grabber (except, thankfully, gratuitous hard-core sex); but, though a few individual scenes have some melodramatic snap, the ludicrous plotting and cardboard characterization make [*Kane and Abel*] a long, ragged trek—for the most undiscriminating saga-seekers only.

> A review of "Kane and Abel," in Kirkus Reviews (copyright © 1980 The Kirkus Service, Inc.), Vol. XLVIII, No. 2, January 15, 1980, p. 74.

MARTIN LEVIN

["**Kane and Abel**"] is a family saga that is overweight but undernourished. Jeffrey Archer, a former British M.P., is a writer unskilled at showing you how things are. He merely tells you what they are. (Florentyna "put on the prettiest dress." Anne Kane "enjoyed a light lunch.") Descriptions that don't describe contribute an air of staleness to the atmosphere. In this thin climate, Abel crosses the sea to America and becomes a hotel baron. (He names each hotel The Baron because his father was one.) Kane takes over the family bank and has occasion to incur Abel's enmity. It's really a big misunderstanding, but there isn't enough life in either of these parties to make you care if they ever make up. (pp. 9, 15)

> Martin Levin, "Five Novels," in The New York Times Book Review (copyright © 1980 by The New York Times Company; reprinted by permission), July 6, 1980, pp. 9, 15.*

ROBERT HEWISON

With the exception of a sad tale of adultery in New York, [the dozen stories in *A Quiver full of Arrows*] could all have been written at any time since 1910—there is a bow to Somerset Maugham and a cricketing story straight out of *Boy's Own Paper*. The only sign of modernity is the use of names: ever since Ian Fleming brand names have been used as a substitute for authenticity, and Archer names faces as well as brands, asserting that all the stories but one are based on known incidents....

Jeffrey Archer has knocked about a bit, and it is interesting to see what themes concern this man of the world. There is clearly a nostalgia for the social securities of Oxford and Cambridge and cricket, and the business world is presented as, if not wholly corrupt, then hardly playing the game. Wealth is one obsession, and writers, or the idea of being a writer, are another; but if Archer truly wants to be a good writer he should avoid repeating himself within the narrow confines of twelve stories. There are two characters of extreme punctuality, and two stories concerning corruption, the construction industry and developing countries. Only the last story, "**Old Love**" shows very much feeling or ingenuity of invention. *A Quiver full of Arrows* is eminently readable, easily forgettable.

> Robert Hewison, "Naming Names," in The Times Literary Supplement (© Times Newspapers Ltd. (London) 1980; reproduced from The Times Literary Supplement by permission), No. 4051, November 21, 1980, p. 1313.

NORA JOHNSON

"**Kane & Abel**," Jeffrey Archer's previous best seller, chronicled the blood feud of two powerful men. In this sequel, ["**The Prodigal Daughter**,"] Abel's daughter, Florentyna Rosnovski, marries Kane's son and then goes on to the Vice Presidency.

Florentyna is so flawless she makes other flawless heroines look as faulty as rhinestones. By the time of her birth, Abel, once a poor immigrant, is a rich hotel baron and can buy her anything she wants or needs.... [When] she meets and marries Richard Kane (handsome, rich, brilliant, charming, etc.) the two feuding fathers won't speak to the young couple and cut them off without a cent. Never mind, this perfect pair can do anything....

Mr. Archer substitutes tons of information for characterization and a breakneck pace for insights. It's all impossible: I longed for something to go wrong with Florentyna's Wonder Woman life, but hardly anything did. Still, for the most part I was very much behind Florentyna and will certainly vote for her. (p. 27)

> Nora Johnson, "Men and Women and Trouble," in The New York Times Book Review (copyright © 1982 by The New York Times Company; reprinted by permission), July 11, 1982, pp. 14, 27.*

BETTY LUKAS

If you're expecting another prodigal son parable here, forget it.

Although separation and reunion are part of this multifaceted contemporary novel [**"The Prodigal Daughter"**] by the English author of **"Kane and Abel,"** they are but a minor part. And other themes—just as those other themes in the biblical parable—are more provocative.

Through his primary character, Florentyna Rosnovski, Archer probes such intriguing topics as power, politics, pride, parochialism and prejudice. He also deals with some old-fashioned virtues—fidelity, honor and integrity as they affect this only child of a Polish immigrant who has amassed a huge fortune by hard work and canny—but mostly honest—business strategy....

Given that background, you say, the novel must be pure romance. Romance it is. Don't knock it.

There is pain, of course, but it heals; there is failure, but it pales; there is estrangement, but it passes. And there is love, honor and fidelity. And you'll lap it up. Florentyna's husband is so stalwart, so devoted, so enduringly loving that he teeters on the brink of dullness. Their children—with the exception of one little slip by Annabel—are models of deportment (probably because of their nanny).

If you're not already aching with jealousy—if you're a woman, that is—let me rub a little salt in the wound. Florentyna wants to be the first woman President. Quite logically she approaches her goal by being elected to Congress. Then she moves on to the Senate. She's admired and respected by her colleagues. How could it be otherwise, given our ingredients?

And, as she moves toward the presidency with the courage of a Clarence Darrow, Archer creates so much suspense in the dialogue that the usual chase scene seems like a turtle race. Does Florentyna get what she wants? Settle into the blankets and find out for yourself. It's that kind of novel.

Betty Lukas, "A Probe of Power, Pride, Politics," in Los Angeles Times Book Review (copyright, 1982, Los Angeles Times; reprinted by permission), October 24, 1982, p. 10.

JACKIE CASSADA

[*A Quiver Full of Arrows*] relies more on ironic twists and carefully constructed surprises for its overall effect than on plot or character development. In the single standout, **"Old Love"**—in which a married couple's intense rivalry continues up to the very moment of their deaths—Archer's desultory, almost impersonal style is displayed to greatest advantage, brilliantly understating the strength of the bonds of love; the other stories have the vaguely unsatisfying feel of anecdotes embellished to story length. Taken together, they make for a passably entertaining unit, though separately they more resemble flimsy darts instead of the "arrows" of the collection's title. (pp. 2107-08)

Jackie Cassada, in a review of "A Quiver Full of Arrows," in Library Journal *(reprinted from* Library Journal, *November 1, 1982; published by R. R. Bowker Co. (a Xerox company); copyright © 1982 by Xerox Corporation), Vol. 107, No. 19, November 1, 1982, pp. 2107-08.*

MICHAEL MEWSHAW

After the enormous commercial success of his recent novels, **"Kane and Abel"** and **"The Prodigal Daughter,"** one can easily understand why Jeffrey Archer and his publisher would bring out a collection of his short stories. But it is difficult to comprehend what conceivable enjoyment readers will derive from the sophomoric fictions in **"A Quiver Full of Arrows,"** which suggest the author is unaware that the genre has made strides since the days of O. Henry.

In a prefatory note, Mr. Archer writes, "Of these eleven short stories, ten are based on known incidents. . . . Only one is totally the result of my own imagination. **'The Luncheon'** was inspired by W. Somerset Maugham." While it is worth wondering who, if anyone, knows these "known incidents" and whether these stories have ever appeared elsewhere, there's little point in trying to puzzle out which work is totally the product of Mr. Archer's imagination since they all display the same slack language and slick, manipulative style.

Although the settings range from New York to Nigeria and from London to Mexico, Mr. Archer makes no effort to distinguish one place from another. Similarly, he shows little interest in giving his characters distinctive qualities. Instead he recycles the same tired material. In **"The Chinese Statue"** a punctilious 19th-century diplomat, Sir Alexander Heathcote, "rose at seven o'clock every morning, joined his wife at breakfast to eat one boiled egg cooked for precisely four minutes and two pieces of toast with one spoonful of Cooper's marmalade and drink one cup of China tea." A hundred years, and four stories later, in **"Broken Routine,"** Septimus Horatio Cornwallis follows a similar regimen. . . . (pp. 12, 27)

These two humdrum gentlemen are triumphs of complexity, however, compared to others who remember names "in the nick of time," cast "baleful glare(s)" and grow "chilled . . . to the very marrow." A mandarin actually remains "inscrutable," and there's a cipher named Victor Perez, a grubby Mexican middleman in **"A Matter of Principle,"** who not only dresses in jeans and a T-shirt just like Manuel Rodriguez in **"The Coup"** but grins "from ear to ear" twice in two pages. **"The Nativity,"** retold from the point of view of Pontius Pilate as a child, is apparently Mr. Archer's idea of irony.

To grant credit where it's due, **"Old Love"** is an amusing account of a couple of Oxford graduates whose intellectual competitiveness becomes the basis for marriage, and **"The Hungarian Professor"** is a poignant depiction of a Shakespearean scholar isolated in Budapest. The rest of this collection, however, collapses as Jeffrey Archer tries to wrestle each story toward a trick ending or punch line. (p. 27)

Michael Mewshaw, "A Novel and Some Stories," in The New York Times Book Review *(copyright © 1982 by The New York Times Company; reprinted by permission), November 28, 1982, pp. 12, 27.*

Juan Benet
1927-

Spanish novelist, short story writer, essayist, dramatist, and poet.

Benet is a major contributor to the Spanish New Wave literary movement, which has developed alternatives to the realistic literature characteristic of post-Civil War Spain. Although his highly esoteric and complex fiction has only recently gained international recognition, Benet is considered by many to be one of Spain's best contemporary authors. Many elements of his fiction are compared to similar aspects in the work of Marcel Proust and William Faulkner. *Una meditación* (1970; *A Meditation*), Benet's second novel, has recently been translated into English and has evoked considerable critical debate. Some critics contend that the enigmatic and unconventional nature of his work detracts from its overall impact, yet others cite Benet's mastery of language and literary technique.

Although Benet is chronologically a member of the "Generation of 1950," his literary views differ from the principles of this Spanish movement. The "Generation of 1950"—which includes such important authors as Camilo José Cela and Juan Goytisolo—believes that literature should be simple, direct, and grounded in the specific realities of postwar Spain in order to increase awareness of the country's devastation and its need for reform. Benet's writing expresses a similar concern with the social and cultural effects of the Civil War, yet its similarity to the "Generation of 1950" ends there. Whereas the "Generation of 1950" emphasizes content over style, Benet strongly adheres to the "art for art's sake" approach to literature. He considers style of paramount importance, while discernible plots and conventional structures are of lesser significance in his fiction.

While Benet has written plays, poetry, and short fiction, his novels are generally considered his most significant works. His first novel, *Volverás a Región* (1968), remained virtually unknown to both critics and readers until the success of *A Meditation*. The enthusiastic reception to Benet's second novel generated substantial retrospective interest, and *Volverás a Región* is now largely regarded as being as important as *A Meditation*, although it has yet to be translated into English.

Like the majority of Benet's novels and many of his short stories, *A Meditation* is set in a fictional location called Región. As with Faulkner's Yoknapatawpha County and Gabriel García Márquez's Macondo, Región both forms the background for the novels and assumes a significance of its own. Acting as a microcosm for Spain in particular and contemporary civilization in general, Región symbolizes the mythical, multilayered complexity of reality within which Benet's characters struggle to define themselves and their surroundings. Benet achieves his effects largely through the mysterious, suggestive manner in which he reveals the reality of Región. In spite of the large amount of concrete, objective information supplied regarding the topography, geology, and vegetation, an aura of despair, destruction, and decay is also portrayed. The mythical complexity assigned to the atmosphere of Región resembles and symbolizes the enigmatic and perplexing nature of the characters' reality.

Photograph by Layle Silbert; © copyright 1983

The themes of *A Meditation* include the destructive nature of the past, the surreal, dreamlike nature of the present, and the fatalistic immutability of the future. This preoccupation with time adds to the abstruse nature of the novel: not only does the past haunt the present, and the future offer no relief, but the temporal construction is based on the protagonists' perceptions and remembrances, which are of questionable validity. Through the subjective use of memory, reflection, and speculation, the narrative flows freely through time, often leaving the reader uncertain as to the actual chronology of events. The elusiveness of Benet's fictional world is further enhanced by a juxtaposition of realistic details and surrealistically ambiguous motivations, by the suggestive but undefined significance of recurring symbols, and by Benet's prose style. Devoid of conventional syntax, a typical sentence runs from page to page, overflowing with digressions within digressions. The end result is a novel which some describe as overwhelming, others praise highly, and many agree is "the most imposing, challenging, and radically intransigent" novel to emerge from contemporary Spanish literature.

DAVID K. HERZBERGER

Volverás a Región clearly represents . . . a significant departure from the neorealistic novel of the 1950's and early 1960's. It exhibits several characteristics which, when analyzed in depth, exemplify an innovative approach to the novel in Spain. (p. 43)

What has traditionally been called the "plot" of a novel does not exist in *Volverás a Región*. Instead, the novel consists of a complex framework of third person narration and pseudo-dialogues between the two principal characters, Dr. Sebastián and Gamallo's daughter. Daniel Sebastián is an aging doctor who has been living in solitude for nearly a quarter of a century in Región, with little else to do but drink, remember and care for a child driven insane by the absence of his mother. One evening he is visited by a woman—who we know only as Gamallo's daughter—and throughout the night the two characters carry on a soliloquy-like dialogue in which they evoke their past and examine their destinies. . . . Through the memories of Dr. Sebastián and his visitor, and with the additional comments of the third person narrator, we are able to reconstruct the fragmented history of the ruination of Región and its inhabitants.

One of the most distinctive aspects of *Volverás a Región,* and an important element in all of Benet's novels, is the physical setting in which the action takes place. Similar to Rulfo's Comala, García Márquez's Macondo or Faulkner's Yoknapatawpha County, Benet's mythical Región plays a central role in the creation of his novelistic reality. Benet's private narrative universe—Región—can be described in many ways. From one point of view it is the aggregate of characters, events and social themes which, in Benet's opinion, compose Spain at the time of the Civil War. However, more important than the social background is the enigmatic reality of Región itself. Benet carefully constructs the spatial and physical existence of the town on different levels of complexity. From one perspective, he portrays Región and the surrounding area with scientific preciseness. (pp. 43-4)

On a second, and more complex level of reality, Benet portrays Región in a full state of decadence, surrounded by hostile landscapes and immersed in a threatening temperate zone. For example, one of the recurring images associated with Región is the labyrinth. If on the one hand Benet describes the [surrounding] mountains with scientific objectivity, on the other he portrays the area as a menacing maze of streams. . . . (p. 45)

Benet paints a very complex portrait of Región, composed of contrastive descriptions and subtle complexities. For example, the desert—hot, lonely, hostile—is contrasted with luxuriant valleys nearby. . . . Yet despite their differences in vegetation, the desert and the valleys represent the same impenetrable and hostile environment. . . . [Throughout] the early part of his novel Benet carefully constructs an ambience in which he underscores the hostile and contrasting elements of the physical environment: desert-luxuriant vegetation; hot-cold; mountains-valley; rivers-dried up streams; life-death.

On a third level of comprehension, the description of Región stresses the mysterious and enigmatic elements which pervade the novel. . . . In *Volverás a Región* Benet utilizes his style to break the barriers imposed by the normal perception of reality, and portrays a novelistic climate replete with mystery and ambiguity.

One of the most significant ways in which Benet creates an aura of mystery around Región is by juxtaposing antithetical elements in his description of the countryside. Whereas he meticulously describes the geological formation of a mountain or valley, he contrasts the scientific description with personification. . . . The mountains are alive, and can therefore witness the tragedy which unfolds both around and within them. Similarly, the rivers which flow through the valleys of Región display lifelike characteristics. . . . Since the landscape is "alive," it not only serves as the spatial background of the novel, but also becomes an active character. Benet's descriptions of the landscape transcend the literal preciseness of the words because of their suggestive powers. The physical environment actively asserts its will and penetrates the lives of the people who live within it.

Another way in which Benet portrays the enigmatic milieu of Región is through the use of *realismo mágico*. . . . In *Volverás a Región* Benet clearly intends to capture the mysterious elements which lie beneath surface reality. He achieves this goal in two significant ways: 1) by the juxtaposition of "real" and "unreal" elements in his description of Región; 2) through the use of specific symbolic objects which recur in the narrative, and which clearly pertain to the world of magical realism.

One of the most striking elements involved in the use of magical realism is the red flower which grows wild in the mountains of Región. . . . [Not] only does the flower suggest a legendary past of violence, but it also plays a central role in the lives of the people who live near it. . . . (pp. 46-8)

Another instance of the use of magical realism in the description of Región involves a mysterious red light, an inexplicable sound, and a painful sting, all which emanate from an unknown source. According to the narrator, for some mysterious reason—which Benet never reveals—the traveler who attempts to penetrate the Mantuan forest begins to hear the nearby explosions of a combustion engine. Although he hunts for the source of the noise, the traveler succeeds only in exhausting himself as he frantically searches about. The same night, the tired traveler is unexpectedly awakened from his restless sleep by a bright red light. Terrified, he stares at the light, and is suddenly struck by a spear-like object which buries itself in his back and causes him great pain. . . . Benet explains neither the origin nor the ultimate result of such occurrences, because in fact there is no explanation. It is only one aspect of the total enigmatic reality which envelops Región and, when combined with other puzzling events, completes the intricate spatial and temporal labyrinth which Benet carefully constructs in his novel.

The psychological and physical atmosphere of Región consists of a pervasive desolation, ruin and overwhelming fatalism. The hostile and enigmatic nature of the town permeates the inhabitants through a process of antipathetic osmosis. Similar to Juan Rulfo's Comala, there exists in Región a direct relationship between the geographical location, climatic conditions and physical ruin of the town and the ultimate abrogation of human existence. In addition, the destructive fatalism of the inhabitants of Región parallels the tragic acceptance of destiny by the people of Faulkner's Yoknapatawpha County. Both Benet and Faulkner submerge their characters in the damnatory atmosphere of moribund towns, and the result is a physical and moral human destructiveness which eventually causes complete ruination. (pp. 48-9)

Another aspect of the theme of decay entails the moral disintegration brought about by increasing materialistic influences in the twentieth century. Benet vacillates on the critical point concerning the source of corruption: is it part of human nature, or does it lie within man's political and economic institutions? Although he offers no definitive answer, Benet nonetheless criticizes the importance of money and investment in modern society. (p. 50)

The presentation of time, and the correlative elements of destiny and fatalism, are inextricably bound to the principal theme of ruin in *Volverás a Región.* Although the chronological duration of the novel is only one night . . . , the psychological time spans nearly four decades, from 1925 to the unspecified present sometime during the 1960's. Through the memory of Dr. Sebastián and Gamallo's daughter we examine the past of Región and its inhabitants. However, our view of the past is not structured chronologically, but rather follows certain impulses and emotions of the characters.

Many of the great twentieth-century writers—Proust, Joyce, Dos Passos, Faulkner, Gide, Woolf—have attempted, each in his own way, to mutilate time. Like many of these authors, Benet divides the temporal structure of his novel into several complex segments which must be reconstructed by the reader. To achieve this effect Benet frequently employs the time-shift technique, in which the temporal focus continually shifts. He deliberately fuses time periods so that the past is felt not as distinct from the present, but included in it and permeating it. In effect, past is present in *Volverás a Región.* For Benet's characters time is a fusion of present and past in which the latter is predominant. The present constantly becomes the past, while the future does not exist. In a sense, the future is decapitated by an overwhelming sense of fatalism. (pp. 51-2)

Memory is a patently destructive concept in *Volverás a Región,* both for the individual characters and the people of Región as a whole. For the latter, the past causes a radical devastation of their illusions, of which memory is a constant reminder. . . . Memory is . . . equally destructive for the individuals of the novel. It creates only solitude and despair. . . .

The concept of isolation or insulation from the world outside of Región, and therefore from time, is also an important element in the temporal construction of the novel. For the inhabitants of Región, and particularly for Dr. Sebastián, days, months and years lose their independent value and fuse into an infinite void in which time ceases to exist. (p. 53)

The concept of time in *Volverás a Región,* like that of memory, is associated with decadence [and] ruination. . . . During some moments the people of Región seem to exist in a temporal vacuum, while during others they live oppressed by the omnipresent power of time. . . . In effect, the people of Región (and particularly Dr. Sebastián and Gamallo's daughter) are so completely overwhelmed by the effects of time that the present ceases to exist and the future is merely a reflection of the past. . . . The Doctor and his visitor possess a past that "was not." That is, there exists nothing (or very little) from their previous life which can be remembered in a positive sense. Therefore, since their present life consists of an accumulation of past events, then in effect, there can be no hope for the future. Like the characters in Faulkner's *The Sound and the Fury,* nothing can happen to these people because everything has already happened. As one of the children declares in Faulkner's novel, "I am not is, I am was." The elusive present and non-existent future are helpless before the character's past. (pp. 54-5)

Benet's attitude toward time is also reflected in the form of his novel. A large portion is written in the first person, either from the point of view of Dr. Sebastián or Gamallo's daughter. In many twentieth-century novels written in the first person, there is no concept of "past" as such, but rather only a growing present. . . . Benet, however, achieves the opposite effect with his first-person narration. His characters do not grow as a result of the fusion of past and present, but rather become stagnant. They exist to fulfill a future destiny previously determined by a ruined past. (p. 55)

The principal reason for the impossibility of future fulfillment for the inhabitants of Región lies in their fatalistic concept of a ruinous, predetermined destiny. Similar to both Proust and Faulkner, Benet eliminates the dimension of free choice and action for his characters by engulfing them in an atmosphere of naturalistic positivism. Dr. Sebastián and his visitor form only one link in a chain of historical degeneration. . . . (p. 56)

On one level Benet's treatment of destiny connotes a kind of nineteenth-century positivism in which the characters cannot escape from their *race, moment* and *milieu.* On another level, however, Benet's concept of destiny serves to intensify the mysterious world of Región and the author's attitude toward magical realism. Previously we have seen the manner in which Benet creates the complex and enigmatic ambience of Región by using certain magical elements, such as the red flower, the strange light and the bee-like sting. When treating the problem of destiny, Benet once again utilizes magical realism and, by doing so, transcends the limitations imposed by purely positivistic influences. As a result, he is able to stress the mysterious and undefinable forces at work in the decadence of Región. (p. 57)

Concerning the literary style of William Faulkner, Warren Beck has written: "If Faulkner's sentences sometimes soar and circle involved and prolonged, if his scenes become halls of mirrors repeating tableaux in a progressive magnification, if echoes multiply into dissonance of infinite overtones, it is because the meanings his stories unfold are complex, mysterious, obscure and incomplete." The preceding quote by Beck is . . . equally appropriate in our discussion of Benet's style in *Volverás a Región.* Form and content are tightly interwoven in Benet's novel and, taken together, form the complex reality of Región and its inhabitants.

In *Volverás a Región* Benet employs two dissimilar styles of writing. In his portrayal of the Civil War, or in the scientific descriptions of Región, he utilizes a straightforward, direct prose which manifests a concern for detail and accuracy. Each geological explanation or description of the *flora* and *fauna* is carefully expressed, and Benet displays an intimate knowledge of scientific terminology. In contrast, when describing the enigmatic elements of Región, and especially in the lengthy soliloquys of Dr. Sebastián or Gamallo's daughter, Benet utilizes a very complex, highly metaphorical language which in many ways resembles the style of Faulkner. Frequently Benet's complicated syntax is as impenetrable as the mysterious mountains of Mantua. (pp. 65-6)

[Benet's] sentences are frequently the length of a full page or more, and include parentheses, parentheses within parentheses and subordinate clauses which unite to form a syntactical webwork. Benet's style is, in fact, a persistent maze of obstacles replete with complex obtrusions, delays, ambiguous interpolations and confusions. Benet's purpose in creating such difficulties is two-fold, depending upon the narrative point of view. When used by the third person narrator, for example, the baroque-like sentences increase the enigmatic nature of the reality he is attempting to create. The mere length of the sentences seems to be part of a deliberate plan to withhold the meaning he hopes to convey: the partial or delayed disclosure of the central idea of a sentence often occurs near the end, thus keeping the reader intrigued (and confused) until the last instant.

Because of his peculiar style of writing Benet's characters are essentially stylized creations. The monologues of Dr. Sebastián and Gamallo's daughter are the antithesis of realistic speech patterns, and serve to dehumanize the characters. The use of esoteric vocabulary and, conversely, the total lack of common word choice, further diminishes the realistic nature of the characters. Nevertheless, Benet overcomes the shortcomings of stylized characters by stressing the tragic human problems which consume them. Benet's ability at psychological analysis is in no way undermined by his style. On the contrary, the depth of his characters is enhanced by the complexity of their monologues and the details of their descriptions. . . . [The] ideas or emotions which the characters express are so complex that a single noun or short descriptive phrase is rejected in favor of a more peripatetic pattern of speech. The result is a highly artificial soliloquy in which Benet nonetheless achieves psychological depth. (p. 66)

Although [Benet's second novel, *Una meditación*,] displays certain stylistic and philosophical characteristics evident in *Volverás a Región*, it represents a more ambitious undertaking than Benet's first novel. Written in the first person, *Una meditación* is precisely what the title suggests: a meditation on the past which covers a time span of nearly fifty years from 1920 to the present. Although the novel is composed of an artistically manipulated structure (i.e., not a loosely formed stream of consciousness), the events and characters which are presented do not appear in a specific, chronological arrangement. Instead, the narrator evokes a succession of fragmented memories which frequently remain vague and incomplete. . . . Utilizing a Proustian memory and a Faulknerian style, the narrator scrutinizes the past in an attempt to recover and understand the nature of his family, friends and previous existence in the vicinity of Región.

The traditional use of plot, which in *Volverás a Región* is reduced to a minimum, regains significance in *Una meditación*. However, there is no dramatic development and subsequent denouement, and the novel could easily be rearranged without detracting from the intrinsic interest of the events themselves. As the narrator's mind wanders through the past, certain incidents and characters are summoned into consciousness and placed in view of the reader. No single event or character, however, is presented in its entirety during a specific moment in the novel. Instead, Benet creates a complex labyrinth of interpenetrating segments which represent the narrator's voluntary and involuntary memory and the desire for a "remembrance of things past."

Since Benet presented the geographic formation of Región in great detail in his first novel, there was no need to repeat the process in *Una meditación*. However, the reader who is familiar with *Volverás a Región* cannot help but be influenced by his previous knowledge of Región upon reading *Una meditación*. In the same way that our familiarity with Yoknapatawpha County influences our reaction to the novels of William Faulkner, our knowledge of the mythical Región affects our reading of subsequent novels which take place in the same location. (pp. 71-2)

Although Benet does not discuss the Civil War in great detail in *Una meditación*, the conflict nonetheless plays an important role in the prevailing atmosphere of ruin and decay. When the narrator returns to Región in 1939, the destructive effects of the war are everywhere manifest. . . . Several of the narrator's memories concern events which take place after the war, and the country is described in terms of a diseased body which has unsuccessfully attempted to cure itself. . . . Thus from a social perspective, which most critics incorrectly find completely absent from Benet's novels, Franco's government has magnified certain economic and social problems but more importantly, has infused Spanish society with a paralytic state of mind in which the inability to think or to act has resulted in the continual deterioration of the nation's spiritual and physical condition. (pp. 72-4)

Benet's use of a first person narrator in *Una meditación* creates several structural and temporal problems in the development of the narrative. (p. 74)

The "I" of *Una meditación* infrequently discusses his own personality and rarely indulges in self-analysis. Nonetheless, the personality of the "I" is implicit in everything that he relates. First of all, the "I" plays an important role in the theme of "the return," which is explicit in the title of Benet's first novel, and is underscored in *Una meditación* by the return to Región of several of the characters: Mary, Carlos, Leo and the narrator himself. All the characters have returned to Región in search of something, and the narrator is no exception. . . . The whole narrative method of the "I" takes root in his desire to recapture the past (i.e., to return psychologically to Región) as a means of explaining the present. Each major event which he relates is followed (or interrupted) by a lengthy digression on the subject at hand. (p. 75)

The "I" of *Una meditación* is what Wayne C. Booth would categorize as a "narrator-observer," and therefore is conscious of his role as the conveyor of information within a preconceived narrative structure. Frequently, the "I" intrudes in the narrative in order to express his control over the telling of the story and the order of events. . . . [The] "I" is conscious of his fallibility as a narrator. Since he experiences a strong desire to tell the truth . . . he readily admits that he cannot remember certain events. . . . The narrator, therefore, expresses his concern for accuracy of description and confesses his shortcomings as a recorder of past events.

Despite the efforts of the "I" to define his limitations . . . the descriptions and analyses of characters in *Una meditación* frequently reflect the view of a third person omniscient narrator who relates the thoughts and motives of his characters. . . . [In] contrast to the usual limitations of the first person narrator, the "I" of *Una meditación* becomes the center of consciousness not only for external, observable occurrences, but also for the psychological development of the other characters. The frequency with which the "I" presents glimpses into the consciousness and private lives of the characters introduces an artificial note into the narrative, and detracts from the verisimilitude of the entire "meditation." (pp. 77-8)

Occasionally Benet demonstrates a preoccupation with expanding his narrative point of view. Instead of depending upon the "I" for a paraphrase or opinion, Benet inserts the viewpoint of the original source. For example, when discussing the reactions of the people of Región to the early days of the Civil War, the narration switches to the direct discourse of Tío Ricardo. . . . By means of this lengthy monologue Benet achieves a new perspective in the novel without resorting to first person omniscience. (p. 80)

Benet's treatment of time and memory in *Una meditación* clearly resembles the temporal concerns evident in *Volverás a Región*. In both novels time plays an integral part in the psychological and physical ruin of Región and its inhabitants, and serves as a point of departure for philosophical speculation. In *Una med-*

itación, however, the reflections on time by the first person narrator are actually reflections on the writing of the novel itself. Since the novel consists of the recollection and subsequent expression of past events, any kind of temporal speculation must necessarily reflect on the construction of the work. Thus time and recollection, which form the intrinsic essence of *Una meditación,* play an equal role in both the form and content of the novel. (pp. 80-1)

Eros and sexual desire constitute a recurrent topic of concern in *Una meditación,* and are treated both in the abstract during the philosophical digressions of the "I," and concretely through the portrayal of several of the characters. Love and sex furnish the motivating forces behind many of the occurrences in the novel, and Freudian influence can be noted throughout. . . . In *Una meditación* Benet . . . intensifies the sexual desires of his characters to such a degree that eros and frustrated emptiness become synonymous with sex and life itself. (p. 86)

If sexual gratification eludes the characters of *Una meditación* as a means of obtaining permanent satisfaction, the sexual act itself provides a temporary liberation from the obstacles which prevent fulfillment. The most important of these is the constant oppression of time. . . . [The] chronological time of the sexual act (i.e., the discharge of instinctual psychic energy) creates a psychological period of escape during which time exercises no influence. In effect, sex conquers time, but only temporarily. (pp. 87-8)

Benet's style of writing in *Una meditación,* although similar to that of *Volverás a Región,* is much more complex. Written in a single paragraph which extends for 329 pages, the novel demands the reader's active participation in penetrating the baroque syntax and untangling the complicated system of images. Although *Una meditación* resembles Proust's *A la Recherche du Temps Perdu* in terms of narrative structure and technique, the influence of Faulkner remains predominant in Benet's complex style of writing. Like the American writer, Benet frequently amasses words in a manner which has caused some critics to charge him with prolixity. Indeed, many of Benet's sentences cover several pages, and it becomes a difficult task to remain attentive to the assorted ideas contained in one of the narrator's thought patterns. On the other hand, Benet's peripatetic style can be justified because of its intimate association with the content and structure of the novel. . . . Like Faulkner's, Benet's sentences are perhaps best described as "saturated solutions" in which diverse images and topics are juxtaposed in order to create complex and enigmatic realities.

One of the recurring characteristics of Benet's style in *Una meditación* is his presentation of opposed or contradictory suggestions within a single context. Similar to Faulkner's use of oxymoronic or near oxymoronic terms in many of his novels, Benet utilizes the contradictory statements to maintain his novel in a state of flux or suspension, thereby keeping the reader confused and uncertain in his response. The oxymoronic descriptions which Benet employs are constructed by the simultaneous suggestions of disparate or opposed elements, and therefore create a sharp polarity or tension. (pp. 91-3)

Walter Slatoff's conclusion that full coherence in Faulkner's novels is something the author hoped to avoid can also be applied to Benet's *Una meditación.* The distorted time sequences, the juxtaposition of largely independent stories and the unsyntactical marathon sentences all indicate an eagerness to avoid order and coherence. Benet constantly imposes obstacles to the complete and rational comprehension of events by his experiments with both style and content. He chooses to suggest complex, enigmatic realities rather than define circumstances which are orderly and unequivocal. (p. 93)

Benet's use of animalistic imagery to describe some of his characters, coupled with the stylized manner of narration and dialogue and the ambitious nature of much of the action, combine to create essentially dehumanized and abstract characters. . . . [However], the problems with which they are associated are palpably real: sex, the escape from time, memory, despair. Thus Benet's "dehumanized" characters struggle with "human" problems characteristic of all mankind. (pp. 95-6)

By means of his complex style Benet invents a reality which is more obscure and enigmatic than the realities external to his novel. He refuses to remove the obstacles which, once eliminated, would clarify the mysteries of his work. The events of *Una meditación* are maintained in a constant flux, and therefore many aspects of the novel remain paradoxical and intentionally insoluble. (p. 100)

Una tumba (1971) represents a significant departure from Juan Benet's first two novels in terms of style and narrative technique. It is by far the most easily understood and least complex of any of Benet's novels written to date. In contrast to the peripatetic narration of *Volverás a Región* and *Una meditación,* in which the concern with plot and dramatic development is only of secondary importance, *Una tumba* suggests Benet's preoccupation with a more traditional novelistic structure and plot formation. (p. 101)

At the outset of the Civil War a "niño" (whose name we are never told), is left with an elderly couple charged with overseeing a mansion which the child will apparently inherit one day. During the course of the novel the niño fulfills a mysterious destiny in which he gains a kind of diabolical power from both his ancestors (whom we learn about through retrospective action) and the mansion he is to inherit. However, it is the ambience of the novel, and not the plot, which creates the primary interest and establishes the main tensions. As in his previous two novels, Benet carefully constructs the psychological and physical environment and creates a symbiotic relationship between his characters and their surroundings. (p. 102)

Una tumba forms a unique part of Benet's novelistic repertory by virtue of its contracted length, the supplementary use of photographs and, above all, due to its relative simplicity. Nonetheless, the novel possesses several characteristics found in both *Volverás a Región* and *Una meditación:* the historical background of the Civil War, the recurring themes of solitude and decay and the mysterious environment of Región are portrayed in varying degrees of intensity in each of these novels. Furthermore, although *Una tumba* is stylistically a much less complex work, it shares with the other two novels such features as baroque-like sentences, the dehumanization of the characters, the deliberate withholding of meaning and the suggestive, rather than the precise use of language to create the overall novelistic reality. (p. 113)

The physical and psychological atmosphere of *Una tumba* reflects Benet's most characteristic manner of writing. Enhanced by the use of magical realism and the portrayal of fear and superstition, a sensation of mystery and destruction pervades the novel. Within this ambience the niño-protagonist awaits the fulfillment of his destiny. Like the principal characters of both *Volverás a Región* and *Una meditación,* the child is overcome by a predetermined future, against which it is impossible to struggle....

Although *Una tumba* has not received the critical acclaim granted *Volverás a Región* and *Una meditación,* it nonetheless constitutes an important part of Benet's novelistic art. It reveals a certain willingness (or desire) on the part of Benet to participate in an esthetic endeavor quite distinct from that which is normally involved in the writing of a novel. The result . . . [is] a work which is relatively penetrable, yet which remains characteristically abstruse and deceptive. (p. 114)

The complex, dense style of writing which characterizes *Volverás a Región* and *Una meditación,* reappears in Benet's fourth novel, *Un viaje de invierno* (1972). . . . Once again the reader is forced to penetrate a world which consists of marathon sentences, a complex framework of recurring images, an ambiguous temporal structure and an interrelated series of events which remains essentially unexplained in terms of motivation and ultimate resolution. (p. 115)

As José Domingo has pointed out, *Un viaje* represents Benet's maximum effort to eliminate plot as an integral part of the novel. . . . [The] characters of *Un viaje,* which perhaps can be described more accurately as "apparitions," are never brought into clear focus, but instead remain obscured in a dense fog. As a result, Benet succeeds in creating a mysterious world of shadowy figures who approach a destiny which, although never explicitly defined, is suggested by the title of the novel: a winter's journey or, more precisely, a journey toward death.

In addition to stylistic and thematic elements . . . , *Un viaje* shares important temporal and spatial characteristics with Benet's earlier novels. In the first place, the spatial background of *Un viaje* consists of the area in and around Región. . . . Although not described in detail, the oppressive, ruinous atmosphere of Región appears in *Un viaje* as an important component of the physical and psychological environment. (pp. 115-16)

Although the temporal setting of the novel remains vague, the Civil War and the post-war period are mentioned several times as a symbol of the past ruin which continues to influence the lives of the characters. . . . In *Un viaje* . . . , as in Benet's first three novels, the destructive power of the Civil War continues to gnaw at the heart of Spain and results in a negation of the life force through which the characters strive for meaning and fulfillment. (p. 117)

The fatalistic concept of destiny which is portrayed in each of Benet's first three novels reaches its fullest and most critical development in *Un viaje.* As he does in his other novels, Benet eliminates the dimension of free choice for his characters by infusing them with a fatidical acceptance of their destiny. (p. 122)

A large part of Benet's style of writing in *Un viaje* seems to be based upon the desire to avoid translating sensation into perception. A cognitive knowledge of something, be it of a character, an object or a particular ambience, is of secondary importance to the awareness of a situation in terms of pure consciousness of it. In this sense, Benet can be viewed as an idealist: since our consciousness seizes nothing but manifestations, reality is very illusory. When reading *Un viaje,* we sense that we are before the dream of reality, instead of reality itself. Indeed, much of Benet's style supports this point of view. (p. 127)

Benet's style of writing in *Un viaje* is similar to that of both *Volverás a Región* and *Una meditación.* In characteristic fashion he utilizes page-length sentences, complicated syntax, parentheses and parentheses within parentheses. However, Benet seems to exert a control over the flow of his prose in *Un viaje* which is absent from his previous full-length novels: he exercises restraint in the length of his sentences and paragraphs, and eliminates many of the subordinate clauses which characterize much of his earlier writing. In addition, he places many of his typical digressions in the margins of the page in reduced-size print instead of within the narrative itself. As a result, the more condensed nature of his prose appears less peripatetic than usual. Nonetheless, Benet's style continues to evolve as a complex webwork of language replete with delays and confusions. (p. 130)

Until now, the similarities between the novels of Faulkner and Benet are manifest primarily in terms of style: recurring motifs, oxymoronic constructions, ruptured syntax and peripatetic sentences appear repeatedly in the works of both authors. . . . In *La otra casa de Mazón* (1973), . . . Faulknerian influence extends well beyond stylistic similarities. As in the American's *Requiem for a Nun* (1951), Benet's novel consists of interwoven sections of narrative and dramatic dialogue in the form of a play. However, whereas Faulkner's work consists of three acts, each of which is preceded by a lengthy prose introduction describing the historical background of the events, *La otra casa* consists of five sections each of prose and dialogue (including stage directions) which are intimately related by plot and thematic similarities. Indeed, a large portion of the drama serves either to clarify the ambiguity which characterizes the prose sections, or to enhance the themes of physical and psychological ruin which pervade the novel.

There is no plot in *La otra casa* in the traditional sense. Instead, the novel consists of a carefully selected series of events from the past and present which represent the decadence of the Mazón family. The house . . . which is mentioned in the first sentence and recurs throughout the novel, forms the setting for both the drama and prose sections, and therefore provides spatial unity and serves to intensify the themes of physical and psychological destructiveness. . . . [The] narrative segments serve as an informational background to the play, allow Benet to introduce his thematic concerns by portraying the decadence of a once wealthy family and, primarily due to his style, enable him to create the ambience of despair and ruin which forms the essence of all of his novels. (pp. 137-38)

Benet has so far set the action of all of his novels in or around Región. In *La otra casa,* although the area bears the name El Auge, the geographic similarities between it and Región (which is also mentioned in the novel) clearly indicate that Benet wishes the reader to associate the two towns as part of the same spatial background. This fact is underscored by reference to several incidents, characters and geographic locations which have appeared before in Benet's novels. (p. 139)

Similar to the novels of Faulkner in which the history of such famous literary families as the Compsons, Sutpens, Sartoris and Snopes is related in detail, the Mazón family tree becomes the subject for study and analysis by Benet. However, in contrast to Faulkner, who generally develops several family members to a high degree of complexity, Benet concentrates on only one character, Cristino Mazón, who appears as the central figure in the play and also merits detailed attention in the narrative. The other family members, however, appear and disappear throughout the novel and never gain full development as real human beings. Cristino, then, becomes the symbol of the entire Mazón family and personifies the theme of "ruin-in-life" which dominates the novel. (pp. 142-43)

The differences in style between the prose and dialogue segments of *La otra casa* could not be more pronounced. The play, which consists of five sections of dialogue, is characterized by a straightforward and succinct manner of speech which is highly realistic in terms of syntax and word usage. In contrast, the dense, circumlocutory style of writing which marks each of Benet's previous novels appears in the narrative segments of *La otra casa* with characteristic intensity and complexity.

One of the principal achievements of Benet's style lies in the author's ability to draw the reader into the flow and rhythm of his words as they interanimate. In *La otra casa,* Benet frequently amasses words in order to describe as accurately as possible the complex reality which he portrays at any particular moment. Most commonly, he compounds words into groups of three, and thereby gives depth and multiformity to his descriptions. (pp. 150-51)

[In conclusion, like] the French new novelists, Benet writes complex novels which are the antithesis of the popular "novels of consumption." Indeed, he intentionally writes for a minority of people. . . . (p. 155)

The fundamental question persists, however, as to what genuinely distinguishes Benet as a writer for the elite; a writer whose novels are difficult to read, let alone understand. . . .

In short, what is the figure which Benet is weaving in his still incomplete carpet? In the first place, the extreme difficulty of Benet's works stems from . . . the enigmatic and inexplicable nature of nearly all of his novels. . . . Like Faulkner, Benet offers obstacles, obtrusions and confusing digressions in his novels which discourage the passive reader but challenge the active one. However, one pronounced difference between the novels of Benet and Faulkner reveals an underlying contrast in their approach to writing. Whereas a novel of Faulkner may be extremely difficult to untangle, the intelligent reader will be able to overcome the obstacles in his path and understand the work because Faulkner furnishes (albeit indirectly) all the necessary information. Benet, on the other hand, not only imposes barriers, but by means of delaying or partially disclosing certain incidents and ideas, he in effect forecloses the possibility of total understanding of his work. . . . [A score of questions] remain unanswered in Benet's novels, primarily, I believe, because they represent the author's view that many facets of our existence defy rational cognition. (pp. 155-56)

David K. Herzberger, in his The Novelistic World of Juan Benet *(copyright © 1976 by The American Hispanist, Inc.), American Hispanist, 1976, 174 p.*

KESSEL SCHWARTZ

[Juan Benet, in his novel *Saúl ante Samuel*,] repeats his standard themes of ruin, disintegration, solitude, guilt, time, life, and death involving the Spanish Civil War and his mythical Región. In the author's examination of the State, revenge, and avarice as exemplified by the various characters, he seems to conclude that no answers exist for their multiple human motivations and concomitant problems.

The author deliberately obfuscates the slowly developing plot. The novel opens in an abandoned house where a solitary figure has been waiting twenty years for the return of a traveler fixed and frozen in time by the memory of events. The scene shifts to that past and to a Republican convoy, one of whose officers is the younger son of the owner of the house, asked by his father to take on a Republican role to protect his family, Nationalist supporters, from the consequences of their political beliefs. The convoy, on its way to Región, is held up by an accident and various war strategies. The older brother's wife has an adulterous affair with her brother-in-law. After a suspenseful delay and disquisitions on the meaning of guilt and responsibility, we learn of the older brother's execution, the death of the younger brother, and the death or disappearance of all the other principal actors, except for the solitary survivor in the ruined and abandoned home. Acting as biographer, a cousin, also in love with the adulteress, plays out his tragic role. Indeed, as the fortune-telling cards of the grandmother convey, all of the protagonists, the jealous unloved young brother, the incompetent father, the arrogant older brother, are actors in a tragic play, serving at the same time as symbolic multiple representations of a decadent Spain.

The author dwells on destiny as a "mysterious arrangement of merciless logic for futile purpose," with events predestined rather than aleatory, though the disordered cards, one of the leitmotifs, seem to reflect the destructive forces and chaos of life, the repetition and reversal of mutually compensating roles, and life's dualities and antinomies. Benet governs a time frame in which events seem atemporal, with little difference between real and imaginery trips, possible or probable futures. He examines the intellectual thought processes, determining that memory, capable of detailing precisely fixed mnemonic cross sections of past events, may also change and deceive.

Divided into three parts and five chapters, filled with baroque sentences of more than one page, interspersed with French, German, and English, the novel builds up its mosaic with nuances, fragmentary allusions, and repetitious references to the same scenes or events. . . . Sharing his creative force with his characters, Benet enlightens the reader as to the "what" and the "why" of the plot while at the same time mystifying him concerning the "who" and the "how" of events through the use of a spectrum of subtleties and simultaneous time frames.

In the final analysis, as the long interpolations testify, the novelist reveals his predilection for the philosophical and psychological over the novelistic in this latest fictional elaboration. (pp. 478-79)

Kessel Schwartz, in a review of "Saúl ante Samuel," in Hispania *(© 1981 The American Association of Teachers of Spanish and Portuguese, Inc.), Vol. 64, No. 3, September, 1981, pp. 478-79.*

JAMES H. ABBOTT

Using the style and tone of traditional fables, Juan Benet turns the formula into a contemporary art form to serve his own artistic and ideological purposes [in *Trece fábulas y media*]. While some of the short tales end with morals concerning traditional concepts of destiny and death—i.e., each man's destiny is his alone and man voluntarily or involuntarily seeks his own death—others end with reversals of traditional ideas or with no moral at all. . . . [One of the fables, for example,] tells of a general who overlooks one decisive detail in his preparations for war. The fable has alternate endings: one in which the general's troops win, and another which shows the enemy triumphant. Readers may choose. (p. 308)

Religious themes are at the core of two of the tales: one deals with Abraham, who refuses to sacrifice Isaac and states that he owes explanations to nobody for sacrificing and eating a lamb with his son; another revolves around God's idea that man creates a god unlike God, and ends with His statement, "I am the error and the life." While death is depicted in a traditional way in at least two of the fables, the twelfth one departs somewhat from the usual presentation when a gentleman invites Lady Death to his tomb and she flees, seeing that she too might die.

The simple, clear language of the "thirteen-and-one-half fables" is not an indication of a simple and clear purpose. Since satire is often implicit in parody, even the seemingly traditional morals become suspect, and the whole collection, viewed in this light, becomes a travesty of both form and content. (p. 309)

James H. Abbott, in a review of "Trece fábulas y media," in World Literature Today *(copyright 1982 by the University of Oklahoma Press), Vol. 56, No. 2, Spring, 1982, pp. 308-09.*

KATHRYN KILGORE

Juan Benet has been called the Spanish Proust. He is one of Spain's most important and controversial modernists. His style, strongly influenced by Central and South American writers, has in turn influenced the post-Franco generation. *A Meditation* is the second novel in a trilogy and the first to be translated into English. . . . It contains echoes of Faulkner and Hardy, as well as the clear footprints of Mr. Proust. It is crammed with references to Plato, Nietzsche, Kafka, Rilke, Schopenhauer, and the Bible.

It has no paragraphs. It has sentences that sometimes run on for a couple of pages, full of digressions in dashes and parentheses, then digressions inside the digressions, and negatives, then double negatives, qualifying the original (if you can find it) premise. It is written in language which is usually left alone in the dictionary and which sounds, frequently, like this: "Not even in the spacious narthex in the portico of which a reduced semi-ellipse of rachitic turf came to mark the limit of the transgressions of solar rays within the chthonic kingdom."

The book is a reader's nemesis. The effort of staggering through this kind of stuff, the work needed to understand its point, can easily release either the vengeful urge to belittle the book's value, or the urge to brag that you ate the whole thing, and to expound upon its infinite virtues. But there's something numbing about this accomplished novel. It feels like one of those dinner-party conversations in which your partner discourses so elaborately and at such length on a topic that you find you have no reply, not necessarily because nothing was said but because how it was said so smothers the content that its emotional import is dead on arrival.

The slow wide river of Benet's style carries along the broken pieces of a rather simple narrative about a group of friends who come to maturity after the Spanish civil war. Family stories drift into some funny, and some spooky, side-plots, in the leisurely interweaving currents of abstract meditations on the nature of power, reason, time, knowledge and belief, fear, love, memory, and morality. Some whirls of the philosophizing are interesting and beautiful, some are full of junk, some instantly evaporate in the mind. The themes of time (because it is linked to the story of a clock that finally focuses the whole novel), and memory (because the demonstration of Benet's theories on memory is in how he tells the story), and love (because of a few vivid scenes involving rats and other non-romantic images) are slowly built to complex conclusions. Other themes that are not so concretely tied down to the narrative may make the whirls wheel in pretty circles, but anybody with a background in philosophy can also spin the ABC's of these in their sleep, and yawn at some of them. . . .

The style of the novel creates an intentionally weird, deadpan world, in which the wretched lives of the characters seem not quite emotionless, but only melancholic, wry, and too flat in tone to be human. Besides creating a mood for an unhealthy era, this tone exists because the stories are told from the perspective of memory, in which "the death of a blood aunt can be much less a reason for concern than the loss of a cigarette lighter; because it is the interest and the capacity for passion that fade away and it isn't memory that commands." And because memory does not command, some of reality has grown to be myth and fable. . . .

Gradually most of the narratives come to include Cayetano Corral, the spokesperson for this madness, who comments, "Notice . . . how during times of peace like these the historical content decreases and the sociological increases. War resolves the past and peace the future, just halfway, because only disasters and passions are capable of fixing time."

I won't quite accept Cayetano's disclaimer on times of peace. It's unfortunate that there's so little said about postwar politics. The author leaves the characters isolated, floating amid his abstract examinations of morality and power, and this is slightly insidious; we can't see enough of how Benet judges the specific morality of the times, or what political position he's taking, since his focus on abstractions leads us to believe it's the abstractions themselves that comfort or disturb him, and not the human activities, the acts in the name of which all abstractions are invariably used, or misused.

Since there's so little factual or real context for Benet's characters, it's difficult to care about them in the end. They seem too deracinated. While this is in fact a point being made by the author about the period, the bloodlessness is also the result, and the major weakness, of this modernist style. It's too bad that Spanish writers continue to elaborate on South and Central American style; the transplantation doesn't seem to have taken root. It's dried up, full of cerebralized formalizations which lack juice, action, and passion. . . .

One major point *A Meditation* makes over and over is that things always fall apart. When Cayetano finally fixes his clock and sets it ticking so imperfectly that after a few days its vibrations (which start time moving again in Region) begin to cause cracks, fissures, chaos, and change for miles around. I felt relieved. The flow of time was stopped for a bit too long while the narrator stooped to tie his shoelace, and the sheer weight of all that accumulating prose, while impressive, finally overwhelms everything else.

Kathryn Kilgore, "Modernism As a Second Language," in VLS *(copyright © 1982 News Group Publications, Inc.), No. 7, May, 1982, p. 9.*

ALLEN JOSEPHS

Juan Benet is sometimes called the Proust of Spain, sometimes the Faulkner. Neither label is correct. He is best described as the Juan Benet of Spain, the most imposing, challenging and radically intransigent novelist writing in Spanish (or perhaps in any language) today.

"A Meditation" may be the most demanding novel I've ever read....

What really binds this almost unimaginably dense novel together is not Benet's sense of character or of scene but his brilliant, overarching and fascinatingly difficult style.... His figures of speech are so elaborated and extended that it's easy to forget what they are illustrating. You must struggle with the text, rereading sentence after sentence, many of which could be called, depending on your point of view, acts of literary defiance, slaps in the reader's face or brilliant inquisitions. (p. 13)

Unlike novelists who attempt to interpret the world around them, Benet has created his own autonomous and parallel world that is less an interpretation of reality than an analogue for it. He is not creating order in fiction out of the chaos of reality; he is inventing a fictional chaos with the same consistency of enigma, illusion, paradox and half-truth we face in ordinary reality.

Benet does not write about things we can know; he writes about what we can never fully comprehend, about what he calls repeatedly the "zones of shadow" that lie beyond the ken of the rational mind. His convolutions and circumlocutions—his symphonically arranged style—give **"A Meditation"** a fidelilty to the movements of consciousness unique in the modern novel. Beyond the pale of conventional realism, Benet has become a kind of mythic realist, guardian . . . of the irreducibility of the sacred grove of human consciousness. . . .

If you are a true aficionado of the modern novel, if you think the novel is the ultimate puzzle to be reconstructed by the reader, you will consider Benet a great discovery and another rung up the Gnostic ladder begun by the likes of Proust and Faulkner and Lowry. If you have the stamina and the patience, you may find that Benet's deliberately obfuscated narration creates a new bridge—or no man's land—between the double solipsisms of reader and writer. His ironic meditation, his universal story of time and memory and ruin, is also one more gauntlet thrown down by Spanish-language novelists in the arena of world literature. (p. 42)

<blockquote>Allen Josephs, "Onward Goes the Paragraph," in The New York Times Book Review (copyright © 1982 by The New York Times Company; reprinted by permission), May 23, 1982, pp. 13, 42.</blockquote>

VINCENTE CABRERA

Benet's six novelettes are chronologically scattered throughout his entire career: from his first and seminal four-work collection, *Nunca llegarás a nada* [You Will Never Get Anywhere], dating back to the 1950s, up to his latest legend, **"Numa,"** published in 1978 as part of *Del pozo y del Numa (un ensayo y una leyenda)* [Of the Well and Numa (an essay and a legend)]. In between, two important pieces were published: *Una tumba* [A Tomb] in 1971 and **"Sub Rosa"** in 1973, the latter being included in a book of short stories bearing the same title. The novelettes as a whole clearly reveal Benet's poetic imagination and narrative versatility.

You Will Never Get Anywhere is Benet's first formal step into literary creation, a collection of four novelettes written between 1958 and 1961, when the group was published. . . . They are well-built, well-written pieces that, had Benet not written anything else, by themselves would have placed him among the most original narrators in Spanish Literature. But most important, *You Will Never Get Anywhere* is in many respects Benet's seminal work. Many stylistic and thematic characteristics prevalent in his later works are visible in these early novelettes. Of special importance are his typical long, exhausting sentences, the enigmatic nature of characters, the consistent minimization of plot, the emergence of his mythical Región along with its ruins and overwhelming solitude, and man's inevitable failure embodied in one of Benet's most important images, that of the journey, which man must begin, even if he knows it will lead nowhere. The novelettes of *You Will Never Get Anywhere* are "Nunca llegarás a nada" [You Will Never Get Anywhere], "Baalbec, una mancha" [Baalbec, a Stain], "Duelo" [Mourning], and "Después" [Afterwards]. (pp. 31-2)

Juan, the protagonist [of the title novelette], recounts a trip taken in the past with Vicente, his wealthy friend, through northern Europe: France, Germany, Denmark, and other unspecified countries. His recollection covers the period of preparation and the trip itself. The mystery which clouds the story is progressively intensified with the detailed and introspective description of events. This description, however, is carried out not because of the events as such, but rather because of their metaphysical implications which enable Juan to evolve and elucidate his own conception of life and his vision of the world. The plot of the work, therefore, does not rest on the dynamic sequence of those events in time, but instead on their inner human value that motivates the character's search for himself and for his place in the world. Thus, the trip to northern Europe is a symbol of man's odyssey into himself. The more detailed it is, the more complete his concept of life becomes. Taking into account the development of the plot, this short story is a novelette that opens with what structurally constitutes its conclusion: the sketch of a drunken Englishman and what he says about the two traveling friends. After asking them why they force themselves to continue traveling aimlessly, he says that they are poor humans trying in vain to survive, "trying to rise again." . . . Acknowledging the truth of these statements (after the journey, but at the beginning of the narrative), remarks which when they were made had no meaning to either of them, Juan says somewhat regretfully that "we ignored him." . . . In the closing pages, the reader learns that the Englishman also said (consistent with what he has already stated about man) that "this common body, like to a vagabond flag upon the stream, goes to and back, lackeying the varying tide, to rot itself with motion." . . . The part of the English sentence which impressed Juan the most was "to rot itself with motion." He is not sure about the construction of the enigmatic language in which, he felt later, the truth was hidden. So in order to reveal it, measure its scope, as if impelled by the inner desire for self-definition, he must start the recollection of his symbolic journey. It should be realized that what his anonymous friend had to say is reproduced defectively, thus emphasizing the fallibility and the efforts to grasp the truth embodied in the English statement.

The artistic complexity derived from the Englishman's statements is unique and important to the total structure of the work, for the following reasons. (1) From a novelistic point of view, Juan recalls his journey and thus this novelette is created. He knows where and when it started and ended. From a metaphysical point of view, he is in the same situation as the reader; he is about to embark and does not know his destination. It is the tension between these two realities that enhances the artistic beauty of the work. . . . The reader knows from the Englishman that man's voyage in life will lead nowhere, yet he insists on reading the work, that is, binding himself to continue with Juan's self-discovery, which is also his own. (2) Thus, the reader and the protagonist, who shows him the way to nothingness, at the end become the drunken Englishman, both able to reach the same conclusion about themselves. (3) Juan and the reader follow in the footsteps of the Englishman, whom they unfortunately ignored and whose words—"you will never get anywhere"—they did not heed. (4) Ironically, the truth given at the beginning is the truth found and experienced at the end. In addition, that same loose truth of the beginning becomes at the end the unifying element which circularly structures the work, which is seemingly formless. This circular structure is aesthetically satisfying since the idea of an odyssey is developed. The actual destination of both the character and the reader becomes their point of departure: nothingness. One may say that if they reached nothingness, philosophically, they got somewhere. But that somewhere, in the poetic context of the work, means nothingness, which in the final analysis is nowhere, and hence the title of the work. This thematic and artistic vicious circle is another aspect that makes Benet's literature an essentially enigmatic experience. (pp. 32-3)

Benet's preoccupation with the traditional concepts of time and character in **"You Will Never Get Anywhere"** is minimal. These two technical elements are subject to the total vision of the work revealed through the inner reality of Juan. Character and time, rather than ends in themselves, are only means to the end of novelistic architecture. . . This is one of the reasons why the reader may experience difficulty in following the trend of thought and reflection wrought by the dense narration of the story. (p. 34)

It is enlightening to examine together the main thematic and technical characteristics of *You Will Never Get Anywhere* as a whole, that is, as a work of art in which its parts, although independent from each other, comprise a total structural unity embodying a specific vision of life. The four works underline man's nothingness in time and space. An individual, a family, a generation, or an entire era is rooted in nothingness to bear, in turn, nothingness. This pessimistic cyclical pattern makes of the characters in all these novelettes not so much individuals developed according to traditional tenets of depiction, as symbolic shadows whose *raison d'etre* is subject to the total vision of the work. That is, character is not subjugated to any ideal of realistic consistency, but to the effectiveness of the system of expression. . . . The same conviction of artistic independence from the traditional concept of the novel is also perceptible in the author's skillful engineering of plot and handling of time. With the possible exception of the first two novelettes, where "something happens," plot is minimal, almost nonexistent. Events, stripped of their realistic apparel, do not stand for themselves as signs of chronological sequence, but are almost imperceptible references in the midst of the characters' (or the narrators') flow of reflections. The events are there not for the plot's sake, but for the elucidation of the characters' conceptions of the world. The order in which they are arranged is determined by the characters' patterns of reflection rather than by a chronology of occurrence decided by the author, which explains why juxtaposition of past, present, and future is found throughout the collection. The fragmentation of Benet's typically long sentence through repeated subordinate clauses containing past, present, and future becomes the symbolic microcosm of the organic juxtaposition in the plot of the work, which in turn is the composite image of man's labyrinthine existence.

Other important technical modes common in the collection are (1) the use of symbols to infuse a variety of levels of reality and to give structural unity to the work, since these symbols are developed and transformed into extended metaphors; (2) the careful elaboration of mystery, paralleling life's enigma in which characters and readers are trapped and must find their way out through an interpretation of man's destiny; (3) the implementation of irony and absurdity in the character's thoughts and actions, which inevitably lead him to nowhere; and (4) the persistent recurrence of uncertainty regarding the distinction between reality and fantasy, between the natural and the supernatural, as in the case of the flying cups of **"Afterwards."** Benet's approach to reality, to conventional reality, recalls that of García Márquez, yet there are no grounds for implying influences from the latter upon the former, for this collection appeared six years before Márquez's *One Hundred Years of Solitude*. (pp. 39-40)

"Numa" is Benet's latest novella, published as part of his book *Del Pozo y del Numa (un ensayo y una leyenda)* **[Of Pozo and Numa (an essay and a legend)**, 1978]. It deals with the mysterious and ubiquitous guard Numa, already in Benet's fiction a legend in his own right. He is charged with watching over the sacred forest, a forest menaced in vain and persistently by an anonymous outsider or intruder. The mystery of both Numa and the intruder, and their instinctive desire to protect and tread upon the forest, is successfully sustained throughout the entire narrative discourse in the same way it is sustained in Benet's other major works. But unlike these works, this "legend" contains a deceptive intention and a special narrative method which the author employs to create—for the first time—a complete and comprehensive account of Numa. The reader is led to believe that this is the opportunity to grasp fully the elusive nature, personality, character, intentions, and intuitions of the legendary Numa. To this purpose Benet incessantly accumulates a variety of information concerning these vital aspects of Numa. (pp. 47-8)

Every bit of information ironically both creates and destroys the objectivity of the legend. This is important to emphasize here because this literary piece, this legend, is supposedly the most thorough and complete portrayal of Numa in Benet's fictional world. And the reader sees that, indeed, it is complete but at the same time, and paradoxically, helps very little to clarify the mystery of the character. The brilliant and persuasive reasonings handled by the objective narrator in the exposition of his material make him appear as a very reliable instrument for the discovery of the inner truth about the two opposing and irreconcilable forces (Numa-intruder) and motivations that make up the legend or history of Numa's domain—or, one may say, of Franco's Spain. One understands the narrator's lucid statements. He says (and it is simple, just like Numa's mind) that he, Numa, knows exactly what his mission is: the protection of the forest. His consolation is that he has this limited function in life, which he needs as it needs him. (pp. 48-9)

As suggested earlier, this legend is, among other things, an extended metaphor of Franco's Spain. Unlike Benet's other works, here the reference to Spanish historical reality is more subtle. Between the lines, one finds allusions to the traditional confict between Republicans and Nationalists, allusions to Juan Carlos as the young and timid successor of Franco, allusions to Franco's semidivine right to rule Spain in death as well as in life. The substructure of meaning, of course, does not undermine the universality of the conflict implicit in the narration. Instead it enriches and enhances its ambiguity: it is one thing and also another, both at the same time.

As in Benet's major long works of fiction, in this legend plot is reduced to a minimum, making the narrative an immobile body of discourse. The confrontation at the end, between Numa and the unknown intruder who, more than a real person, seems to be a recalcitrant shadow in Numa's paranoid mind, is the only spark of action in the whole legend. It is not a plot in the traditional sense of the word, but rather an epilogue or appendix, attached to the end in order to show in action the conflict reasoned in the discourse of the text. The intruder seems to die by two shots, one in the buttock and the other in the face. For the reader's momentary relief, or better yet, for his further confusion and exhaustion, Benet resorts—as he does in his other works—to some recurrent symbols: the cloud of dust and the gray lamina of water wherein the two protagonists of history or legend must remain forever. Numa's legend (forest) is as eternal as the change of the seasons or as certain as the intruder's hopes that will turn inevitably into failure.

Benet's use of the third-person narrative point of view is effective. He does not allow Numa or the intruder to speak to the reader or to each other. They are confined to their corners of silence and solitude, there to live, fermenting mutual hatred and hostility, with no hope for communication or possible reconciliation. As they are mysterious to each other, so are they both to the reader and to the narrator. The language Benet uses to build this mysterious legend is consistently technical, cold, and precise. His clauses are extensive and broken in his usual fashion, with parentheses, hyphens, and commas, all contributing to make the text purposely an inflexible, alienating, and exhausting narrative discourse. (pp. 49-50)

To the present, Benet has published two major collections of short stories: *5 narraciones y 2 fábulas* [**5 Tales and 2 Fables**] and *Sub Rosa,* that is, a total of fifteen short stories and two very brief, witty fables. As in the case of the novelettes, these two collections reveal Benet's artistic unity within a narrative variety. Enigma and futility continue to be the central forces of artistic creation and life, in Región or New York, among the young and the old, in situations of love, lust, greed, ambition, or death. Benet's short fiction, including the novelettes, is a gallery of enigmas incarnating passions that cover "a large part of human behavior's complex spectrum." (p. 51)

Vincente Cabrera, in his Juan Benet *(copyright © 1983 by Twayne Publishers; reprinted with the permission of Twayne Publishers, a Division of G. K. Hall & Co., Boston), Twayne, 1983, 152 p.*

Louise (Simone) Bennett
1919-

(Also known as Louise Simone Bennett-Coverley and Miss Lou) Jamaican poet.

Bennett's poetry develops out of the Jamaican culture. She has been called "the voice of the people." Relying heavily on the native dialect and the natural rhythms of the spoken language, Bennett preserves what has largely been an oral tradition by transforming the myths, stories, and songs of her people into written form. Her ability to make people laugh is one of her most prominent characteristics. Claiming she "believes in laughter," she crafts her poems with a light and comic touch.

Although Bennett is popular in her own country—mainly due to her public readings, which border on theatrical performances—many critics do not take her seriously, labelling her a comedian or entertainer not worthy of in-depth critical attention. Others, however, find underneath the comic surface of her poems an intricate understanding of the native dialect and sensibility, which is essential in order to grasp the subtlety of her writing and the underlying depth of her concerns.

(See also *Contemporary Authors*, Vols. 97-100.)

Courtesy of The Gleaner Company Limited

MERVYN MORRIS

. . . I do not believe that Louise Bennett is a considerable poet. But a poet, and, in her best work, a better poet than most other Jamaican writers she certainly is. She does not offer her readers any great insight into the nature of life or human experience, but she recreates human experience vividly, delightfully and intelligently. She is rarely pretentious—the most common fault in West Indian poetry; she is not derived from other poets—she has her own interesting voice; and she is invariably sane.

. . . The form most often chosen by Miss Bennett is dramatic monologue. This is hardly surprising in a poet who often performs her work. She writes for the voice and the ear, and when her poems are expertly performed something more, movement, is added. (pp. 137-38)

As in a Browning monologue, the entire dramatic situation [of Bennett's poem **'Candy Seller'**] is made clear without the direct intervention of the author. The whole poem convinces; it has a vitality that seems perfectly to match the imagined context. The images focus on war because the poem was written in wartime and it was perfectly natural that the first abuse that came to mind should relate to war. If anyone doubts the precise suitability of the images—wedge-heel boot like submarine, clothes like black-out, and so on—he should be disarmed by the dramatic context. This could all well be said by a candy-seller in this situation. Rhythm and rhyme are used effortlessly, the pauses coming where the dramatic sense demands them. There is no constriction, no monotony. The poem has the oneness, the wholeness, of a completely realized experience. What more does literary taste ask for?

Several other of Louise Bennett's dramatic monologues could survive detailed examination: for example, **'Street Boy'**, in which a youngster, held by a policeman for swearing, pleads with passersby to beg for him, appeals to the policeman's memory of his own young days, thanks him extravagantly when he lets him go, and then, once out of reach, gloats: 'Ah get weh doah, yuh brut!' **'Parting'**, where the situation is a platform farewell, and **'South Parade Pedlar'** are other outstanding monologues of this type.

Sometimes the situation is presented through the poet as storyteller rather than directly through characters. A good example of this is **'Dry Foot Bwoy'**, in which the affected speech of a boy just home from England is dramatically contrasted with the story-teller's Jamaican dialect. . . . (p. 139)

In some of her poems Louise Bennett is not just a story-teller but is herself the central character. **'Television'** is an example of this. . . . Perhaps there is a trace of falsity here: one is not entirely convinced of the ordinariness of this performer. The milieu is wrong. She can convince us that she is a peasant or a maid or a market-woman or a street-boy, but somehow the television studio reminds us too forcibly that Miss Bennett is a trained performer; dialect seems imposed on the situation.

. . . I have claimed that Louise Bennett is a very sane poet and that she has generosity of spirit. She is always attacking pretension by laughter, and sometimes by hard logic. An example of logic would be **'Back to Africa'** in which an argument is ruthlessly followed through. . . . It takes a shape very eighteenth-century in its careful balance, the balance helping to point the strictly logical operation of a keen intelligence. Louise Bennett's sanity takes her straight to a fact that too many intellectuals, evidently, find too simple for their acceptance: the central fact of our identity: that we are Jamaicans because Jamaica is where we come from.

Miss Bennett's irony is sometimes easy and cheap; but it is also sometimes important and illuminating [as in her poem **'Independence'**]. . . . (pp. 140-42)

Often the pretensions attacked are minor or topical pretensions, but not always. Look for example at **'Po' Ting'** in which a common, and no doubt eternal, human pretension is ridiculed, unwillingness to face the fact of age. . . . (p. 142)

There is a good deal of simple plain fun in Louise Bennett. Sometimes it is fun in the situation, as in, say, **'De Bathsuit And De Cow'**, an excellent little dialect ballad. Sometimes the fun is an intoxication with language which she manipulates or invents with infectious delight. . . .

I think [Miss Bennett's] most central difficulty is choice of subject. Many of her poems are a sort of comic-verse-journalism. . . .

[And] Miss Bennett is sometimes false to her medium. (p. 143)

[Nevertheless, to] trace Louise Bennett's development is interesting. She develops, I think, from the high-spirited monologuist to a more purposeful thinker writing in dialect: it is not for nothing that the mature irony of **'Independence'** or the logic of **'Back to Africa'** are recent, and the best dramatic monologues are early. Or, compare the tone of **'Gay Paree'** (an earlyish poem in which there is a childlike peasant delight in the strangeness of French) with the tone of **'Touris'** (much later, in which the poet sees herself ironically, with a certain sophistication). (p. 144)

In between these two stages of development Miss Bennett spent some years in England; when she returned she wrote what I consider some of her worst pieces. The dialect was forced and untrue. . . . She made some metrical experiments she would have done well to keep out of print. A fair example is the internal jingle of **'Pedestrian Crossin'**, a jingle which seems to have no function. The rapidity of her normal stanza form is lost, and, it seems, nothing is gained. . . . (p. 145)

Living in Jamaica again, Miss Bennett seemed to grow into dialect again, though she never regained her early innocent vitality. I think that accounts for the greater pervasiveness of acute intelligence in the later poems and the decreasing inclination to rumbustious dramatic monologue. Miss Bennett's own development seems to show that her use of dialect is involved with real feeling, as is any poet's use of language.

A weakness, particularly in the early poems, is for direct and unsubtle moralising. In the later poems any sentimentality or tendency to moralise is usually redeemed by irony or wit. . . . [For instance, in] **'Homesickness'** Miss Bennett gives a sentimental list of things she misses while in England; the list does name things we can recognise as part of a real Jamaica: bullas, sugar and water, dumplings; but is nevertheless a sentimental selection in its total effect. . . . [Yet there is a final irony in the last three stanzas which] redeems the poem. It gives a guarantee that there is a mind alive behind it all. (pp. 145-46)

Louise Bennett uses dialect more or less as we can believe the normal speakers of dialect might use it, if they were skilled enough; [some of our other West Indian poets] . . . borrow dialect for the literary middle class. The image 'smile black as sorrow' [in Dennis Scott's 'Uncle Time'] is too abstract for the eminently concrete medium of dialect. It must be said, however, that this poem has a careful exquisite beauty that I cannot claim for anything in Louise Bennett.

Louise Bennett . . . is a poet of serious merit, although like all poets, she has her limitations. Like most poets she is, I have tried to show, developing. And she is so much more rewarding a poet than many to whom we in Jamaica give the name, that it seems reasonable to expect more of those who claim an interest in poetry to give her more attention. She is sane; throughout, her poems imply that sound common sense and generous love and understanding of people are worthwhile assets. Jamaican dialect is, of course, limiting (in more senses than one); but within its limitations Louise Bennett works well. Hers is a precious talent. . . . (pp. 147-48)

> Mervyn Morris, "On Reading Louise Bennett, Seriously" (1963; reprinted by permission of the author), in Jamaica Journal, Vol. 1, No. 1, December, 1967 (and reprinted as "The Dialect Poetry of Louise Bennett," in Critics on Caribbean Literature: Readings in Literary Criticism, edited by Edward Baugh, St. Martin's Press, 1978, pp. 137-48).

THE TIMES LITERARY SUPPLEMENT

To bring a colonial society to a recognition of its own distinctive voice is always a difficult, slow but necessary task. A real literature of place can only begin when that recognition is complete. Louise Bennett, outstanding composer and performer of dialect ballads over the past twenty-five years, has contributed enormously to this process in Jamaica.

Nothing once caused so much uneasiness and actual rage in polite Jamaican society as the admission that the whole island had a distinctive way of communing with itself—"Jamaica Talk". Now comes a collection of Louise Bennett's ballads [*Jamaica Labrish*] ranging from early wartime to the late 1950s. Throughout these years she has unerringly summed up a certain national mood, unerringly satirized the more obvious pretensions of the colour-snob, the returned traveller with his carefully cultivated Yankee twang or Oxford drawl. . . .

In print these ballads are like a phonetic libretto for performance, but they cannot recreate for us the performance itself. Not merely something, but too much, is lost. Only the most devoted and nostalgic admirer will read this volume through, though many will wish they could hear Miss Bennett fill out the text with the richness of her voice, presence, personality and humour. This is not to suggest that there is no place for dialect in printed poetry. Rather, a reading of these poems forces a recognition that to write dialect poems for publication is a very different exercise from vernacular recitation. The poem on the page must offer its riches to the reader through a verbal, even at times typographical wit, rather than a vocal one. Also, an art so essentially popular as Miss Bennett's is inevitably limited in its perceptions to what is popularly perceived.

> "Jamaica Talk," in The Times Literary Supplement (© Times Newspapers Ltd. (London) 1966; reproduced from The Times Literary Supplement by permission), No. 3381, December 15, 1966, p. 1173.*

REX NETTLEFORD

The work of Louise Bennett is unique. Whether in the field of the Jamaican theatre where she has found form and living purpose, or in the field of literature where she is yet an unheralded guest among some of the literary establishment, she presents problems—problems of classification and of description. This in a way is her greatest asset, for she is original and of her own kind. (p. 9)

[In a quarter of a century she] has carved designs out of the shapeless and unruly substance that is the Jamaican dialect—the language which most of the Jamaican people speak most of the time—and has raised the sing-song patter of the hills and of the towns to an art level acceptable to and appreciated by people from all classes in her country. Yet not all are agreed on just what she is or stands for on the cultural scene. . . . [There are some] who would feel it improper to endow her with the name of poet, though they would generously crown her as the leading entertainer in Jamaica's comedy-lore whether on stage, television, or radio. And those who indulge her rumbustious abandon and spontaneous inducement of laughter will sometimes forget that behind the exuberance and carefree stance, there are years of training—formal and informal—as well as this artist's own struggles to shape an idiom whose limitations as a bastard tongue are all too evident. Then there is the view, sometimes barely conceded, that Miss Bennett has given to Jamaica "valid social documents reflecting the way we think and feel and live".

All these views are themselves valid and serve to delineate the role of Miss Bennett in the cultural development of the infant life of a nation. (pp. 9-10)

As poet Miss Bennett must first be seen against the background of her society. This is imperative. . . . Miss Bennett went to the basics and grasped the fact that she lived in an oral tradition where people talked and listened, cross-talked and reported and possess, almost to a fault, a high propensity for words—"bad" words, new words, archaic words, "big", long and sonorous words. The Bible, the Sankey hymnal, the folksong and the memory gems form the background to these propensities. To Louise Bennett who had the benefit of schooling, the ballad-form, the oldest form of English poetry, would probably have come as the nearest basis of comparison and in her early years it could even have been a conscious model. . . . Indeed, most of Miss Bennett's stanzas do take the conventional structure of iambic quatrains with an *abab* rhyme scheme and with stresses of 4 and 3 in alternating lines. But even the iambic rhythms are natural to the Jamaican drawl. Conscious aping of a poetic form is no guarantee of success, however, and one must look to Miss Bennett's own individual use of balladic and other poetic attributes to measure her success.

Like the ballad form, Miss Bennett's writing suffers from not having had a tradition of criticism. . . . This is, however, not surprising. The absence of more serious literary analysis is a commentary on the prevailing ignorance that envelops the subject of the Jamaican dialect. (pp. 10-11)

[And yet it] is to the form and nature of the language that one must . . . turn to find explanation for some of what could be mistaken as metrical aberrations in some of [Miss Bennett's] poems. . . . [Frederic] Cassidy's famous example of how the word "can" can be made to mean "can't" depending on pitch is a case in point. Miss Bennett has used the flexibilities to advantage and at an early stage she departed, consciously or unconsciously, from the normal iambic rhythm to variations such as were later developed and sustained in a poem like *Pedestrian Crosses*. Far from being a functionless jingle, this poem illustrates the propriety of metric form, language and rhythm for a subject-matter which deals with the nervous anxieties of a pedestrian who must now co-ordinate with the newly-introduced traffic control system. The racy monologue takes on the breathless gallop of the anapaestic rhythm and conveys effectively the plight of that simple, fearful fellow on the sidewalk over there. . . . This [poem] is technically successful, and the form is complete. Read at the proper pace the poem becomes almost a tongue-twister, thus heightening the confusion that exists in the mind of the pedestrian. (p. 13)

Terseness and brevity of expression are . . . the strength of her characterisation. . . . The hypocrisy and lovable rascality of the character from the poem, *Roas Turkey*, is at once portrayed. The sturdy independence of the Jamaican spirit, sometimes regarded as aggressiveness, is neatly summed up in . . . [a single] stanza from her poem *Independence*. . . . She is able to make incisive comments on situations without flourish or undue explanation. . . . And Jamaica's postures as a full-fledged nation are briskly put into realistic light in the poem *Jamaica Elevate*. . . . (pp. 14-15)

It is in poems like [*Jamaica Elevate*] that Louise Bennett tells the truth about us and tells it wickedly. The "wickedness" is not at all malicious. Rather, it is rooted in her developed sense of irony, her clear insight into the limitations which are often set on any given human situation and the inevitable comedy which underlies much of the sad outcome. She allows certain devastating facts to speak for themselves, and like her Jamaican compatriots she can "tek bad tings mek laugh". When accused once of not being prepared to subject her art to the rigours of the tragic experiences which plague the human condition, Louise Bennett in one of her few "serious" moments replied, "I believe in laughter." This is borne out by the satiric content of many of her political poems and of her pieces commenting on the foibles of Jamaicans. There is in this something of an analogy with the phenomenon usually found among an emergent group like the American negro community. In seeking its identity the emergent group seems very often to explore its problems and its times through the ambivalence of a comic sense coming to grips with an essentially or potentially tragic situation. . . . The comedy contains the tragedy and even overpowers it in complex forms of expression. This is why the straight-forward simplicity of Louise Bennett's iambic quatrains is often deceptive. *Colonisation In Reverse* is a classic of her brand of satire and the biting irony of the situation is brought out even more forcibly when Miss Bennett recites this with her peculiar relish and clean fun.

For Miss Bennett is a performer, accomplished and unrivalled. If on the printed pages her poems appear to be dated frozen jingles, in the renditions she gives of them they take on vitality and meaning—capturing all the spontaneity of the ordinary Jamaican's joys and even sorrows, his ready poignant and even wicked wit, his religion and his philosophy of life. *Miss Bennett is indeed a poet of utterance*. With her experience and skill she exploits the complex intonation contours of the Jamaican dialect and turns out pieces which are at once fresh, vital and entertaining. . . . What she sometimes does is to manipulate the tonal range of the language, setting the poems almost to music as she patters along. The punch-line technique of music-hall comedy is liberally utilised. . . . Her play on the infinite nuances of meanings of a single word or phrase reminds us that she is involved in the art of words. . . . (pp. 15-16)

But to those who believe that all that [her] poems need are stentorian vocals and tireless gusto, the truth is soon revealed. For they are capable of subtle interpretation and demand the careful modulation of tones and pitch in order to communicate honestly and vividly. Above all, they demand an understanding of and a feel for the language. For understanding and feeling are among Miss Bennett's greatest attributes, resulting in the delightful intermingling of "those qualities of head and heart which we term wit and humour—wit which illuminates and humour which reveals", as Philip Sherlock once aptly put it. (pp. 16-17)

It is through her performances that she has proven herself relevant to the society about which she writes, and it is through her performances that the sanity and generosity of spirit which Mervyn Morris commends [see excerpt above] becomes evident. This sanity and generosity of spirit is the occasion, not the cause, of her artistry. For as a poet of utterance, she has had to be sane and generous for the nightly confrontation which a live and living audience demands of any performing artist. The safe distance of the published writer she never enjoyed. But, in any case, she was using the normally *spoken* language, not the normally *written* tongue.

What was she speaking about? The question finds an answer in her role as social commentator and as such the poems in [*Jamaica Labrish*] tell not one, but many stories. Together they bear testimony to her keen sense of observation. . . . She is at once involved in and detached from the experiences, and she uses her peculiar position to very great advantage.

City Life, the first section, vividly describes aspects of life in Kingston of an earlier period. The picturesque street scenes are enhanced by such characters as the street-peddlar in South Parade crying out her wares or the candy-seller soliciting patronage from passers-by. We come to know something about the passers-by, but most of all we come to know about the candy-seller and her kind. (p. 17)

Some of her liveliest works are . . . about the city transport. For many, Kingston of the forties was Kingston of the "old palam-pam of the tram-cars" and when these were replaced by a trans-urban bus system, Kingston seemed to be no longer the same. The city grew fast in the decade after the war and with it the traffic—hence the plight of that pedestrian in the piece *Pedestrian Crosses.* . . .

Her *War Time* poems will undoubtedly be dated by their topicality but she did have something to say in them. When Britain went to war, the then colony of Jamaica went to war as well. But how many of the ordinary people understood the issues sufficiently to be emotionally involved in what has now come to be regarded as the great struggle against totalitarianism? Young middle-class intellectuals and working-class leaders were more concerned with achieving the goal of the nationalist movement—self-government, or the objectives of the social revolution—better wages and living conditions. Miss Bennett comments accurately on the early non-involvement in the poem *Perplex*. The second poem, *Obeah Win de War*, would suggest that neither Miss Bennett nor her countrymen took the events seriously. The third and fourth stanzas, however, indicate that Jamaicans soon developed an interest in a war which sought to defeat, *inter alia*, the excesses of racism. (p. 18)

The aftermath of war brought much suffering and countless problems. Not least among these were the war-babies—the offspring of war. With a full knowledge of attitudes in her society, Louise Bennett in *White Pickney* gives "sound" advice to a Jamaican on what to do with her offspring or "souvenir", as she called the little ones in another war-time poem, *Solja Work*.

Politics (the third section) fascinated Miss Bennett. Almost from the beginning she caught the political temper of the times and her capacity to comment succinctly on the paradoxes of politics and the whims of politicians stayed with her and even matured right down to the time of Independence. The first five poems in this section recapture the crises of the late thirties and early forties, the emergence of labour leaders, the advent of the Moyne Commission and the persistence of hard times. . . . (p. 19)

The fourth section represents a collection of poems dealing with a variety of topics that are of general interest and relevance to life in the Jamaican community in the past and to-day. True, there are allusions which put some in a strict historical context but they also deal with the wandering Jamaican—the migrant. . . . The travelling Jamaican (in these cases Louise Bennett herself) continues to be a phenomenon in his display of a capacity to cope with any situation, whether it be the endless anti-colonial conferences of well-meaning Fabians (*Poor Gum*) or the carryings-on of a Welsh Eisteddfod (*Eena Wales*).

Back home, the litigiousness of the tenement and some peasant life (*House O'Law*) is sometimes the result of the unending yard quarrels or "tracing-matches" between people (*Kas-Kas* and *Cuss-Cuss*). Pugnacious maidservants who defy a rising and sometimes conscienceless middle-class are a force to be reckoned with (*Me Bredda* and *Seeking a Job*), and the persistent superstitions in Jamaican folklore with its oil-o-love me, duppies (ghosts), signs of the end and rolling calves are worthy of Bennettian comment.

The poem *Po' Sammy* caricatures the love for pets, while the two following poems recapture the Anancy spirit everywhere evident in the ease with which people will turn someone's misfortunes to their own advantage. The street urchin and "corpie" (policeman), the exuberance of love-making and the Jamaican's predisposition to preachments are dealt with in *Street Boy, Love Letta, Uriah Preach* and *Amy Son* respectively. Then comes the series dealing with the understandably conscious acquisition of a foreign tongue or accent as a status symbol—an all too common occurrence among Jamaicans returning from "foreign" or visiting a place like *Gay Paree*. When one chap returns from America with no trace of linguistic influence, Miss Bennett rues the situation in *Noh Lickle Twang*. Yet another status symbol, that of colour, comes in for sharp comment in *Colour Bar* and *Pass Fe White*. And for those who insist on being black, *Back To Africa* offers some sane advice about this particular shade of identity.

The section ends with three poems which take as their subject matter the very substance of Miss Bennett's art. *Mash Flat* is a commentary on the flexibility of the Jamaican language, even if it leads to confusion in communication. The poem *Proverbs* consciously utilises the epigrams of folk-speech, which are a distillation of a folk's collective experience. And *Bans O' Killing* stands on its own as a kind of declaration of Miss Bennett's belief in the strength and inner consistency of the language which she has chosen for her art. . . . [Jamaica has] seen many crusaders against "bad speaking" ever since it was established that a command of "Standard English" was a passport to status and class in the island. There has developed genuine academic interest in the Jamaican dialect, which has been carefully studied by reputable scholars, but it is still the target of middle-class snobbery. Although it has been accepted for entertainment largely through the efforts of people like Louise Bennett, and even though its literary merit is conceded by some, it still carries with it the stigma of ignorance and nonsophistication. Louise Bennett has often been the target of attack and the fact that **Bans O' Killing** was written in 1944 near the beginning of her career, gives the reader some insight into Miss Bennett's early sense of purpose and literary courage. That the earlier criticisms are far less applicable today is to the credit of Louise Bennett, who has never doubted the power of the language she uses to express the essential passions of her people's hearts.

Her inspiration came, and still comes, from the everyday happenings around her. She is acutely sensitive to these occurrences and finds in them a thousand wonders—wonders easily concealed from those of us who have been too long conditioned to seeing the worth of human experience only in the deeds of kings and conquerors. She may not have bothered to ask in explicit terms about the ends of existence. Nor did she labour on the fears that men have about their inevitable mortality. Instead she concentrated on the immediacy of the task of having to survive. An uprooted, poor, but proud people are primarily concerned about surviving, having found themselves alive. They make the best of it with an intelligent optimism which is the occasion of Miss Bennett's bright-side-of-life humour. Humour becomes, as it were, the expression of a people's will to live and Miss Bennett recaptures this will with understanding, compassion and truth. (pp. 21-4)

> Rex Nettleford, in an introduction to Jamaica Labrish by Louise Bennett (© Louise Bennett 1966), Sangster's Book Stores, 1966, pp. 9-24.

LOUIS JAMES

Any discussion of Caribbean popular culture must notice the work of the Jamaican Louise Bennett. Her unique gift is that she is both a folk-lore scholar and a brilliant popular entertainer, and while the qualities of Caribbean popular culture are evanescent before the recording of the conventional researcher, Miss Bennett is able to physically recreate her findings in performances that reveal the idiom, the gestures, the stress and the flow of the personalities and private dramas of the people. Her use of dialect can be amusing, but it is not necessarily so. In **'Bans o' Killing'** she places herself, along with Burns and the European dialect writers, in the tradition of poets who have used dialect for serious purposes, as the straightest route to the inner life of the ordinary people. Miss Bennett would not claim either the depth of feeling or the lyrical impulse of the greatest dialect poets, and in a volume the length of her first major book of collected poems, **Jamaica Labrish** . . . , there was inevitably some weak material. On the other hand her claim that dialect be taken seriously is not only valid, it is borne out by many of her own successful pieces. Through dialect she catches conversational tones that illuminate both individual and national character. (pp. 15-16)

Because Miss Bennett uses essentially the natural speech idiom of the people, and because she is guarded from pretention by self-critical folk wit, she can, as Mervyn Morris points out [see excerpt above], cover a range of subjects unrivalled by more conventional poets, without striking a false note. Further, her verse is a valuable aid to the social historian. Her selection of themes reflects the concerns of Jamaican life; the public ones—Federation, street peddlers, body-building contests, Paul Robeson's visit to Jamaica, emigration or an infuriating telephone system; and the private—the yard gossip or the death of a pet turkey watched by a hungry neighbour. More important, she approaches her theme by way of the attitude an ordinary person feels towards it, and it is this that makes an historical event meaningful. This is particularly important in the West Indies, where the private attitudes behind public events are so complex, a tension between national pride and self-satire, between knowledge, ignorance and common-sense. This complexity of attitude comes through a light piece like **'Votin' Ink'**, which tells more about the first public elections than a volume of pretentious occasional pieces. (pp. 16-17)

> Louis James, in an introduction to The Islands in Between: Essays on West Indian Literature, edited by Louis James (© Oxford University Press 1968; reprinted by permission of Oxford University Press), Oxford University Press, London, 1968, pp. 1-49.*

CAROLYN COOPER

In a 1968 interview with the Jamaican poet Dennis Scott, Louise Bennett describes how her use of Jamaican Creole as poetic language disqualified her from membership in the Jamaican Poetry League: ". . . I have been set apart by other creative writers a long time ago because of the language I speak and work in. From the beginning nobody ever recognized me as a writer. 'Well, she is doing dialect'; it wasn't even writing you know. Up to now a lot of people don't even think I write. They say 'Oh, you just stand up and say these things!'" But the very characteristic of Bennett's style that had alienated her from the literati—the vivacious immediacy of her Jamaican Creole rhythms—has been recognized in contemporary reassessments of her poetry as its strength. (p. 322)

The poems in Bennett's collection **Jamaica Labrish**, spanning approximately twenty-five years, cover a broad spectrum of dramatic personalities and events. The poems are classified in four groups: City Life, War-Time, Politics, and Jamaica—Now An' Then. Some of the subject matter is so topical that not all historical details are easily accessible to the contemporary reader. But the majority of poems constitute a kind of comedy of manners in which those recurring rascals of Caribbean societies—social climbers, petty crooks, displaced colonials, to name a few—come decidedly to grief.

One kind of social climber whom Bennett satirizes ruthlessly—for obvious reasons—is the character who feels impelled to deny any connections with the Creole culture. Several poems in the collection poke fun at this character type with varying degrees of gentleness. **"Dry Foot Bwoy"** satirizes a Jamaican of peasant stock who has travelled to England, perhaps to study, and has returned with an English accent and a bad case of linguistic amnesia. He can no longer converse with his former acquaintances, much to their annoyance, for he disclaims knowledge of Jamaican Creole. . . . (pp. 322-23)

Similarly the poem **"Noh Lickle Twang"** makes fun of a woman who is embarrassed because her son, newly returned from the States after six months abroad, doesn't have even the slightest trace of an American accent. He cannot, therefore, be shown off to the discriminating neighbours, who, once he opens his mouth will think that he's merely been to "Mocho"—the archetypal Jamaican village that epitomizes social gaucheness. The depth of the young man's failure must be measured against his sister's success in acquiring the semblance of an American accent after having had only one week's exposure to American expatriates. The fact that her parents cannot understand her is the proof of her sophistication. (pp. 323-24)

In some poems in which Bennett confronts the demeaning poverty of the Jamaican worker—more often, non-worker—the comic vision seems inadequate to express the sustained pathos of intense poverty. The pain of deprivation cannot always be sublimated in laughter. The pair of poems that I shall now consider, **"Me Bredda"** and **"My Dream,"** demonstrate the differences of tone that Bennett can employ in examining the same subject matter. In both poems the persona is that of a female domestic servant, who, in Jamaica, has been an ubiquitous symbol of middle-class exploitation of cheap peasant labour. But whereas **"Me Bredda,"** in true comic spirit, vigorously affirms the supremacy of Good over Evil, **"My Dream"** articulates the burgeoning political engagement of the oppressed in colonial Jamaica.

In **"Me Bredda,"** the servant manages to outwit her prospective employer, a middle-class housewife who, on a whim, has threatened not to hire her for the day's work even though she had previously arranged to do so. The servant, refusing to be intimidated by her opponent's adamant stance, vociferously demands that expectant onlookers summon her brother to avenge her. The housewife, for fear of the inevitable brawl with the irate maid—plus her brother—succumbs to the demands of propriety. The maid's final repartee as she smugly departs with two week's wages and her reimbursed taxi fare is:

> You would like fe know me bredda?
> Me kean help you eena dat
> Me hooda like know him meself
> For is me one me parents got. . . .

The vivacious maid is the clever rogue, who both dupes the housewife and manages to convince us of the rightness of her actions. She is a type of Anansi-figure—that recurring hero-rascal of Caribbean folk culture—for whom the end—survival—justifies the means—deception.

"My Dream" is an allegorical poem in which the class struggle of **"Me Bredda"** is transformed into the nationalistic struggles of Jamaica against colonial England. The servant—Jamaica—is compelled by malevolent cousin Rose—England—to launder a bottomless tub of soiled clothes. The exploited servant, powerless to openly antagonize cousin Rose, resorts to displacing her aggression on the laundry. . . . The undercurrent of rebellion that the action of displacement reveals is an insidious political force—akin to the cunning of the Anansi-figure—that is celebrated in the proverb, the traditional repository of folk wisdom:

> Dog a-sweat but long hair hide i',
> Mout a-laugh, but heart a-leap!
> Everything wha shine noh gole piece. . . .
>
> (pp. 324-25)

The strength of Bennett's poetry then is the accuracy with which it depicts and attempts to correct through laughter the absurdities of Jamaican society. Its comic vision affirms a norm of common sense and good-natured decorum. The limitations of the poetry are partially the inevitable consequences of having used Jamaican Creole as a poetic medium. For what the experiments in Creole—whether St. Lucian, Trinidadian, or Barbadian, for example—have indicated is that there are subtle nuances of thought and feeling that are at times best expressed in Creole, at times in English. The poet who relies exclusively on either medium reduces the expressive range of his/her art.

Louise Bennett, having chosen to write exclusively in Jamaican Creole, cannot easily answer the charge of parochialism and insularity. But what she loses in universality she gains in vivid particularity. In her own words: "You know, one reason I persisted writing in dialect in spite of all the opposition was because nobody else was doing so and there was such rich material in the dialect that I wanted to put on paper some of the wonderful things that people say in dialect. You could never say 'look here' as vividly as 'kuyah.'" (pp. 325-26)

Carolyn Cooper, "Caribbean Poetry in English: 1900-1976," in World Literature Written in English (© copyright 1978 WLWE-World Literature Written in English), Vol. 17, No. 1, April, 1978, pp. 317-27.

Doris (Waugh) Betts
1932-

American novelist, short story writer, and journalist.

Betts's work has inspired some critics to define her as a regional or Southern writer because of her realistic descriptions of small-town life in the South and her emphasis on familial relationships. However, Betts's themes of love and responsibility and her thoughtful characterizations have a universal appeal. Although Betts has received substantial critical attention, her work has not gained the public acknowledgment some critics feel she deserves.

Many critics consider Betts's short story collections to be her most powerful work. These stories are highly praised for their sensitive prose style and realistic dialogue. The humanistic studies of love, pain, loneliness, and death found in *The Gentle Insurrection* (1954) are particularly noteworthy. *The Astronomer and Other Stories* (1966) has also gained favorable critical attention. The title story, which some critics maintain is Betts's finest work, tells of a recently retired widower whose sole interest in life is studying astronomy. His solitary existence is interrupted when he boards a young couple who involve him in their troubled relationship. Betts's inventive use of the cosmos as a guide to the actions of her characters in this story is an important motif.

Betts has also written four novels. *Tall Houses in Winter* (1957) is a poignant depiction of a man struggling to decide whether to undergo surgery that could possibly save his life. Although some critics find the book sentimental, others cite Betts's well-crafted characterizations and skillful use of recollections through which the protagonist confronts his past mistakes and is better able to assess his future.

Betts's third novel, *The River to Pickle Beach* (1972), is a story of the power of bigotry and ignorance. Set in a coastal North Carolina town in the summer of 1968, following the assassinations of Robert Kennedy and Martin Luther King, Jr., a prejudiced man directs his hatred and anxiety toward a retarded woman and her son and instills fear and violence into the rest of the community. The use of the Kennedy and King assassinations as an omnipresent element serves as an indirect influence on the tragic events in the novel and typifies the national malaise of the time.

Literary authorities generally acknowledge that Betts emerges as a powerful and sensitive novelist in *Heading West* (1981). Considered by some to be her most ambitious novel, it introduces into her work a setting outside the South, the theme of the value of independence, and a more complex plot structure. The book is a psychological drama about a passive woman whose life is controlled by her family until she is kidnapped. Her physical imprisonment while being taken across the country results in the gradual realization both of her need to live as an independent person and her potential for further growth.

(See also *CLC*, Vols. 3, 6; *Contemporary Authors*, Vols. 13-16, rev. ed.; *Contemporary Authors New Revision Series*, Vol. 9; and *Dictionary of Literary Biography Yearbook: 1982*.)

© 1981 Mark Morrow

ROBERT TALLANT

In her first book ["**The Gentle Insurrection**"], a collection of twelve short stories, Doris Betts, a young North Carolinian, proves herself to be already a sturdy professional writer, a master of the short story form, and a candidate for an important position among those concerned with serious and perceptive reporting in literary form of the Southern small town and Southern people. Mrs. Betts is concerned with a universal problem: the difficulty of achieving real understanding between people. In all the stories this theme becomes more important than background and region. One seems to hear Mrs. Betts cry out: "If only we could talk to each other! If only we could understand each other! Then we could be almost happy!"

Outside the unity of theme the stories are unalike: the characters, all alive and very believable, are varied, leading different kinds of lives and having different kinds of troubles. Yet, basically, it is their inability to understand or to be understood that is their tragedy. . . .

Most of Mrs. Betts' people are sad people, but they are rarely morbid. She writes of them with insight and pity, but never with bathos. Her small Southern town is not sordid or decadent, but outwardly at least normal, clean and average.

Robert Tallant, "The Sad People," in The New York Times Book Review *(copyright © 1954 by The New*

York Times Company; reprinted by permission), May 30, 1954, p. 4.

SYLVIA STALLINGS

Those who found much to admire in Doris Betts' **"The Gentle Insurrection"** . . . will be gratified to learn that **"Tall Houses in Winter,"** her second book and first novel, shows her talent to have matured and clarified. She has a sensitive response to persons and situations and a natural sense of timing.

"Tall Houses in Winter" turns on the simplest of devices, a man's appraisal of his past. Ryan Godwin, returning after ten years to the small Southern town where he had been born and from which he had several times fled, faced an operation which might or might not arrest a malignancy in his throat. Even for his own satisfaction, he could not explain the reasons for first taking one more look at Stoneville. Only three people living and two dead connected him with it: his grim spinster sister, Asa; Lady Malveena, the Negro woman who had raised all the Godwin children, and twelve-year-old Fen, the son of the woman whom Ryan had loved. Jessica Godwin herself had lain for those ten years on Methodist Hill beside her husband, Ryan's dull brother Avery. They had been killed together in an automobile crash when Fen was barely two and without Jessica's ever admitting that the boy, as Ryan suspected, was his son.

Mrs. Betts creates with infinite subtlety the character of Stoneville, as it appeared to Ryan while he was growing up and hating its smugness, its small-mindedness, and its total lack of imagination, and as it seems to Ryan at forty-eight, after a successful career teaching in a New England college.

He had loved Jessica and she had refused to go away with him, clinging to Stoneville for the very reasons that he hated it: its predictability, its dullness, its lack of menace. Their affair was concealed successfully from everyone but Lady Malveena, who knew "the undersides of the centuries" and who steals scene after scene of the book. . . .

[As] the weeks in Stoneville passed he came to love Fen for the boy's own sake, not as a possible extension of himself, and to make his peace with the town on both his and its terms. A second level of meaning underlies the overt turn of events in the Godwin family: the history of a young man's rebellion against conformity and his gradual attainment of a humility which can accept it.

It is too bad that Mrs. Betts has made her professed Christians into such straw figures, to set against Ryan's very appealing agnosticism. Asa's priggishness, the Reverend Mr. Barnes' maddening affability, and the simpers of church-minded old ladies may be all that Stoneville had to offer, but surely, once he was out in the world, Ryan Godwin would have encountered some men in whom ordination did not preclude intelligence.

Mrs. Betts has set herself a demanding task and fulfilled it with skill and imagination. As in her earlier book, she has also showed that regionalism can become a universal as well as a travesty. Whatever external influences may in the future fall across her writing, she has no need to question a literary instinct as sound as it is gifted.

> Sylvia Stallings, "'Old Times There Are Not Forgotten'," in New York Herald Tribune Book Review (© I.H.T. Corporation; reprinted by permission), March 3, 1957, p. 6.

BORDEN DEAL

Considering the excellence of its ingredients, it is difficult to state precisely why **"Tall Houses in Winter"** is a disappointing novel. Somehow, it reads like an exercise instead of an inspiration. The background detail is heavy-handed, too careful, too much sieved through other novels instead of deriving from life. The minor characters are carefully eccentric, just enough to make them stick in the reader's mind, and they utter too many casually significant remarks. The well-engineered flashbacks come precisely when and how expected, never surprising the reader. Just once—in the long flashback detailing the love between Ryan and Jessica—do the book, the writing and the characters come to life. Here Miss Betts gets her teeth into her story and writes absorbingly, inventively and all too briefly of a beautiful and doomed love. But thereafter, as before, her loaded dice invariably turn up the expected numbers.

Miss Betts has mastered all the necessary technical tools, and it is obvious that a great deal of thought and work has gone into her books. But there is a feeling that she writes from a deep conscientiousness rather than from a deep conviction; it is as though the novel had been written for a master's thesis, hand-tailored to the known whims of a capricious professor. If she can learn to absorb her technique instead of exploiting it and if, most of all, she can grow into recklessness and commitment, she may go far indeed. But **"Tall Houses in Winter"** is a novel that promises and disappoints.

> Borden Deal, "Some Things to Do Before Dying," in The New York Times Book Review (copyright © 1957 by The New York Times Company; reprinted by permission), March 3, 1957, p. 4.

WILLIAM PEDEN

Doris Betts's third book follows a plot line that has produced some great fiction along with an avalanche of artistically contemptible but commercially successful novels and film scripts: the material rise and spiritual decline of a family of sharply contrasted individuals. **The Scarlet Thread** falls somewhere between the two extremes.

The scene is Greenway, a small town in the North Carolina piedmont; the time is 1897 and a few years thereafter. The novel begins auspiciously with the effective presentation of the Allen family of Greenway: imaginative, attractive Esther Allen and her brothers Thomas and David; their hardheaded father who is as crooked as a dog's hind leg; their Bible-quoting mother with her recurring recollections of her family's scarlet thread of abnormality, and their feisty grandfather, soon to die of a heart attack, who dominates the early chapters and is a first-rate literary achievement.

Complications soon develop with the plans to bring a cotton mill to Greenway, and Mrs. Betts's firm and admirable opening chapters at times degenerate into almost a burlesque of the "scrambled-genes" school of regional writing. We are presented with: a "romantic"—and doomed—love affair between Esther and the Yankee imported to supervise the mill; "social significance," centering around the discontented Negro Jube (as one might expect, the Klan rides again in what seems to me the most contrived sequences of the novel); sensationalism, provided by, among others, Miss Bethesda, a Negro "sorceress" whom Thomas disposes of in one of the many acts of violence, which include rape, sudden death, and the blowing up of the mill; sex (see Thomas); perversion (see Thomas); cruelty (see Thomas); artistic aspiration (see David); madness (see Miss Rosa, Mrs. Allen's sister); alcoholism (see Rosa's husband); folklore (see Miss Bethesda).

To all of this Mrs. Betts adds an often unwieldy level of Biblical symbol, allusion, reference, and parallel. . . .

This is a shame, because Mrs. Betts is very talented, as she demonstrates time and again throughout *The Scarlet Thread* and *Gentle Insurrection*. . . . She is still a young writer. With the Gothic excesses of *The Scarlet Thread* behind her, she may yet become a very good one.

> William Peden, "Myth, Magic, and a Touch of Madness," in Saturday Review (© 1965 Saturday Review Magazine Co.; reprinted by permission), Vol. XLVIII, No. 6, February 6, 1965, p. 32.

THE VIRGINIA QUARTERLY REVIEW

[In *The Astronomer and Other Stories*] Mrs. Betts once again reveals those qualifications which place her among the finest writers of contemporary fiction. For, as in her previous short stories and novels, she continues to demonstrate not only her great powers of observation and imagination, her feeling for time, place, and character, but also a wonderful sense of form and structure without which writers seldom achieve lasting distinction in their creative work. . . . [In the title story of this collection] Mrs. Betts introduces an originality, a depth and richness of content, not possible in shorter pieces. In this beautifully structured narrative in which the relationship between an elderly man retired from the world and a young couple who bring him back into it develops into a story of absorbing interest, Mrs. Betts explores or touches on many themes: the loneliness of old age, the nature of love, the problem of forgiveness, even the relative importance of Biblical and classical reference as a guide to conduct in our own time. If Mrs. Betts's shorter pieces are less original and provocative, they are just as carefully wrought. With one exception the background of stories and novella is the small-town South which Mrs. Betts knows so well both as geography and as state of mind and treats with such understanding and affection.

> A review of "The Astronomer and Other Stories," in The Virginia Quarterly Review (copyright, 1966, by The Virginia Quarterly Review, The University of Virginia), Vol. 42, No. 2 (Spring, 1966), p. xlviii.

JONATHAN YARDLEY

Among those Southern women who have contributed so vigorously to postwar American fiction, Doris Betts has never quite got her due. She is a tough, wise and compassionate writer, her last book, **"The Astronomer and Other Stories,"** is among the best collections of short fiction of the 1960's, but outside her native North Carolina her audience has been small.

"The River to Pickle Beach" may change that. It has the ingredients of good popular fiction, and it is also a serious, provocative novel. Set in the summer of 1968, against the background of the King and Kennedy assassinations, the novel is about Jack and Bebe Sellars. A childless couple in their forties, they take over the management of an isolated North Carolina beach. Very different people—she is ebullient and outgoing; he is quiet and inward—they are bound by a deep, understanding affection and a strong sexual attraction.

Their summer is disrupted when a retarded woman and her illegitimate son, also retarded, come to the beach; their presence revives Jack's boyhood fears of derangement and murder. Then a third visitor arrives: Mickey McCane, an old Army buddy of Jack's, who lusts openly after Bebe, parades his racial prejudices, and outfits himself with an arsenal of firearms.

The author's ambitious attempt to depict McCane's violence as a microcosm of national violence is rather strained, and the novel is too long. But the portraits of Bebe and Jack are first-rate. . . .

Mrs. Betts is a writer with a firm hold on what we in the South call "home truths." She has a splendid prose style, and she deserves to be read.

> Jonathan Yardley, in a review of "The River to Pickle Beach," in The New York Times Book Review (copyright © 1972 by The New York Times Company; reprinted by permission), May 21, 1972, p. 12.

STEVEN E. ALFORD

Whenever I hear the terms "women's novel" or "Southern fiction," a strange transformation overcomes me. In company, my eyes widen (a careful observer would suspect a thyroid condition) and my smile jacks up several degrees. Alone, an irrepressible torpor sets in, and my body seeks a place to recline, preferably in a cork-lined enclosure. . . . Consequently, when I learned that I would be reviewing a new novel by one of the more charming and accomplished female Southern writers, Doris Betts, I began pricing cork at the hardware stores around Chapel Hill. Having finished reading her fine new work, *Heading West,* I am happy to say that this novel is not Southern Women's Fiction, but an amusing and humane work about one person coming of age.

Nancy Finch is in a rut. Unmarried at thirty-four, she is edging imperceptibly into that Scholastic category of Spinster. In Greenway, North Carolina, for the past fifteen years she has lived with and cared for her hypochondriacal kvetch of a mother and her retarded brother. She is a librarian at the Stone County Library . . . and an alto in the Presbyterian choir. Living in Greenway, she seems poised to become another Evaline Sample, "whose small nervous breakdowns had each been shocked back together by small jolts of electrotherapy. Awed tenth-grade girls had warned one another that spinsterhood had driven Evaline Sample crazy, that older women needed 'sex juice' to stay normal." Nancy has had lovers, (unbeknownst to her mother), three by her count, though her first love, unconsummated, had become more important to her than the subsequent, dissatisfying affairs. Her relationship with this man, Oliver Newton, was, in her words, "the last time . . . that by doing nothing I did something right."

Mired in her passivity, she had planned on going on a sea cruise, praying that she would find a man to take her away; instead she found herself on a car trip through the Carolina mountains with her sister Faye and Faye's husband, Eddie Rayburn. On this trip, at Wiseman's Point overlooking Linville Gorge, she finds a man to take her away—not Prince Charming, but a twenty-nine year old kidnapper, Dwight Anderson. . . . Thus begins the action of this novel, a journey from North Carolina to the Grand Canyon and back again.

One of the exemplary instances of Sam Peckinpah's Neanderthal view of women occurs in *Straw Dogs,* wherein The Wife is raped by The Old Boyfriend, whom she at first resists; but then she Begins to Love It. In *Heading West,* we have a similar psychological situation, in which the kidnapped woman doesn't really want to escape; but Ms. Betts's treatment of this situation teaches us something about the complexity of human response. During her physical and mental battle with Dwight, Nancy is wrenched out of her passivity, and she finds a strength of character which had been buried under the drudgery and boredom of her life in Greenway. The Germans would call this novel a *Bildungsroman,* and that is one generic classification that I would go along with.

West has always been a special direction for Americans (vide Frederick Jackson Turner, John Wayne). By heading West, Nancy discovers the Self buried under the moribund persona of the Spinster Librarian. There is, however, a navigational metaphor buried in the title—Heading: West. Both at sea and in the air (and nautical and aerial metaphors abound in this work), one finds one's direction through triangulation. Nancy's attempts at finding her own proper direction involve a remarkable number of triangular relationships, and these bear watching throughout the novel. She leaves for her vacation trip with Faye and Eddie; her trip West is with Dwight and Judge Jolly; the Stone County Library has two permanent residents, Miss Boykin and Evaline Sample; her home life is dominated by her mother and brother; her brief friendship with J. Waldo Foster included his son, Benjy, and her discovery of Dwight's brother led her to a further triangular relationship with Dwight. Finally, the real events of Nancy's life are constantly juxtaposed between the memories and fantasies that pervade her inner life, and we could see her *Bildung* as consisting of striking a balance between the limiting *and* liberating qualities of memory and fantasy. (pp. 93-4)

From the height of Wiseman's Point to the depths of the Grand Canyon, Nancy emerged from this relationship not a new or a changed person, but one finally in touch with herself as a person, and not an extension of everyone else's expectations. *Heading West* is the story of a Southern woman written by a Southern woman, but in its careful and intelligent composition, psychological insight, humor, and, above all, its humanity, it transcends its regional boundaries and shows itself to be an exceptional work of fiction. (p. 94)

<blockquote>Steven E. Alford, in a review of "Heading West," in Carolina Quarterly (© copyright 1981 Carolina Quarterly) Vol. XXXIV, No. 2, Fall, 1981, pp. 93-4.</blockquote>

JONATHAN YARDLEY

Perhaps the best news about *Heading West* is that it should liberate Doris Betts from the relative obscurity in which she has labored for most of her career. . . . Those coming to her work for the first time will find that she writes clear, vivid prose, creates distinct and interesting characters, and is a master at conveying the nuances of psychological conflict; she is a serious writer whose books are unfailingly intelligent and readable.

But for those who have followed Betts' work over the years, *Heading West* is not unalloyed good news. It may be her "breakthrough" book in a commercial sense, but it is not an artistic breakthrough. She is one of the best writers of fiction in the country, and a very important figure among those Southern writers who have come to prominence since the '60s, but she has yet to demonstrate a firm grasp on the structural complexities of the novel; in *Heading West,* as in her previous novels, she reveals herself to be a short-story writer who is uncomfortable going long distance.

In fact she is a writer with two careers, or two personalities. As a writer of short stories she is in the tradition of Flannery O'Connor, though very much herself; these stories appear in literary magazines, mainly Southern ones, and have earned her a reputation as a craftsman and stylist worthy of comparison with O'Connor, Peter Taylor, Eudora Welty and other American masters of short fiction. But as a novelist she reaches for a larger audience; her novels are not exactly "commercial," inasmuch as that term has acquired negative overtones that do not apply to any of her work, but they do tend to be overlong and overplotted.

Heading West is actually two novels. The first, which ends on page 215, is quite brilliant; it is the story of a woman who, idly yearning for "a new and freer life," suddenly finds herself sucked into a journey of prolonged fear and gradual self-discovery. It is followed, unfortunately, by a second novel in which the same woman is nursed back to health, falls in love, and returns home to accomplish her final liberation; this novel might be described as superior women's-magazine fiction. . . .

Betts, who in her short stories knows exactly what to leave out, continues the story for another 144 pages. Certainly she satisfies the reader's natural desire to learn how everything comes out; she even supplies a happy ending. Yet after 215 pages of tension and psychological ambiguity, all of it strongly sustained, *Heading West* comes to a halt; the animosity between Nancy and Dwight, and the sexual tension, and the growing bonds between them—these are the cement that holds the novel together, and without that cement the novel has no core, no unifying center.

To be sure, *Heading West* is about solid, provocative themes: the clash between independence and family loyalties, the relationship of art and life, the randomness of fate, the mystery of love, the allure of evil. And heaven knows the novel is beautifully written, in prose that impresses itself on the mind without calling attention to itself. But its structural difficulties diminish its many accomplishments; the short story remains the form in which Doris Betts is most comfortable and successful.

<blockquote>Jonathan Yardley, "The Librarian and the Highwayman," in Book World—The Washington Post (© 1981, The Washington Post), November 29, 1981, p. 3.</blockquote>

BETH GUTCHEON

"Heading West" is the story of a young spinster librarian who is kidnapped from a picnic at Linville Falls, N.C., in much the same sense that Flannery O'Connor's "A Good Man Is Hard to Find" is the story of a Southern family's vacation trip to Florida being interrupted by a gunman known as the Misfit. In fact, a character not unlike the Misfit interrupts Nancy Finch and her sister and brother-in-law just as they are beginning their ham sandwiches. The kidnapper then carries Nancy off with something like the Misfit's pointless malevolence, and she remains his hostage all the way to the Grand Canyon. Although the publisher promises the reader "suspense" and "terror" on the dust jacket and says the novel "winds to a fierce pitch"—probably assuming that readers no longer value, or perhaps notice, any but stupendously obvious emotions—

the pleasures of **"Heading West"** are infinitely more subtle, complex and memorable than being scared in your armchair.

Certain recent novelists have been content to place fictive events within their cultural and historical context merely by providing a sound track, telling you what pop song is playing in the background of a scene. Ignorance of the recent recordings of, say, Blondie or Linda Ronstadt is enough to bar a reader from grasping all larger significance beyond plot in the works of such writers. Doris Betts . . . may or may not be familiar with Blondie, but without doubt she is deeply familiar with the Bible, Flannery O'Connor and William Faulkner, Freud, Darwin, Konrad Lorenz, Navajo mythology and the doctrine of Manifest Destiny. She is also capable of thinking and writing about more than one thing at once, and so, just as the horizontal progress of the Colorado River cuts vertically through stratum after stratum of rock in the canyon that is the central image of the novel, she tells a story that is taut and linear and compelling while simultaneously she cuts through layer after layer of different kinds of meaning.

The novel is divided into four parts. In the first, Nancy's problem is the same as a novelist's: how to persuade people that in the middle of a perfectly familiar scene, something extraordinary is happening. If suspense and terror were the point, Mrs. Betts could certainly have filled this section with tears, mad dashes and cries for help. Instead, she shows you a heroine who is wry, intelligent and sane, who wants to be free but for good reasons may not exactly want to go home. And Mrs. Betts makes you understand that what Nancy—or you—would really do at a coffee shop while in the custody of an armed man with faulty moral faculties is order your breakfast and eat it quietly. (pp. 12, 28)

In Part 2, farther west and into another stratum of meaning, images and associations switch from literary to biblical, from Robin Hood and Kafka to the prodigal son and thy brother's keeper. In Part 3, the characters actually enter the canyon, and as its rock wall shows striations formed before human life, so questions of blame and accountability are deftly interlarded with talk of wolves, eugenics, and the possibility that good and evil are simply traits carried in the cells, with no larger moral implications at all. And in Part 4, after Nancy has decisively ended her own victimization, the question of whether or not you can go home again emerges, as well as the possibility of transformation.

This last section is especially rich in echoes of the best of Southern literature. A character like William Faulkner's Benjy, awful relatives like those in Eudora Welty, and grotesque creatures akin to Flannery O'Connor's characters appear both as flesh and metaphor. Mrs. Betts can evoke them all, the wry, comic, familiar voices, without a quiver of lost timbre, and in addition to her marvelous ear there's her own droll vision. . . .

"Heading West" is a book of great delights. (p. 28)

Beth Gutcheon, "Willing Victim," in The New York Times Book Review *(copyright © 1982 by The New York Times Company; reprinted by permission), January 17, 1982, pp. 12, 28.*

William Boyd
1952-

Ghanian-born English novelist, short story writer, and critic.

Boyd impressed critics with his first works of fiction, which display a strong command of language and a fine sense of comedy. His first novel, *A Good Man in Africa* (1981), centers on the farcical mishaps of Morgan Leafy, a pale, fat British diplomat in West Africa who despite his bumbling prevails in most situations. The novel, which portrays comic misadventures, yet makes serious observations on the behavior of transplanted English people and their relations with native Africans, is considered both amusing and poignant. Boyd's focus on embarrassment and uncertainty in the character of Leafy, who makes disparaging asides about almost everyone he meets, has drawn favorable comparison with the title character of Kingsley Amis's novel *Lucky Jim*.

Boyd's short stories in *On the Yankee Station* (1981) often feature disenchanted protagonists and display the wry humor that distinguished his successful first novel. While many critics feel they lack the overall polish and completeness of *A Good Man in Africa*, these stories are more experimental than his novel and are considered to represent the work of a young, talented writer developing his craft.

An Ice Cream War (1982), Boyd's second novel, was numbered among the best books of the year by many prominent literary reviews. A historical novel, *An Ice Cream War* is more complex than *A Good Man in Africa*, principally because of Boyd's use of multiple narrative voices. Set in Africa during the outbreak of World War I, the novel focuses on the effects of war on a remote African town, where simple, happy people are suddenly caught up in a foreign conflict. The novel has been applauded for its historical accuracy, its human drama, and for Boyd's unflinching insights into the waste and chaos of war.

Photograph by Mark Gerson

ALAN HOLLINGHURST

Overwriting is the only thing that occasionally spoils *A Good Man in Africa*, William Boyd's first novel, and one which is in every other respect highly controlled; Boyd is clearly a comic writer with a very successful career ahead of him. The comedy is of an Amisian cast, focusing on embarrassment and disaster, social, sexual and political. There is no room for sentiment or for the finer feelings, and social manners and political pressures only just manage to clothe and contain feelings of naked revulsion and contempt between the principal characters. The novel has a sweaty tropical setting in which dead bodies rapidly become unapproachable and live ones, even if lusted for, have a certain grotesquery. The protagonist, Morgan Leafy, is pale and fat, and in public and private life (he is First Secretary to a Deputy High Commission) he undergoes a herculean series of labours with varying degrees of failure. Boyd knows his West Africa and recreates it in full and interesting detail.

The middle part of the story, chronologically, is told first, though this seems an unnecessary fidelity to the *in medias res* catastrophe managed with such virtuosity. Everything that can go awry for Leafy does, and no screw is left unturned. This great thoroughness in pursuing the comic objective has potential disadvantages, and Boyd's manner at times allows extravagance and hyperbole to become automatic. . . . On the other hand the strong physical identification of the characters displays the more serious gift of using a comic shorthand at the same time as going beyond it to suggest a confusion of feelings, particularly between disgust and lust. The pampered, powdered whiteness of Leafy's boss's wife is viewed with an ambiguous fascination, which explodes in the bizarre final pages of the novel.

Alan Hollinghurst, "Wordy Wisdom," in New Statesman (© 1981 The Statesman & Nation Publishing Co. Ltd.), Vol. 101, No. 2602, January 30, 1981, p. 19.*

D.A.N. JONES

This engaging novel [*A Good Man in Africa*] about a damn-fool Englishman doing everything wrong in West Africa (Nigeria, lightly disguised) will give pleasure, both malicious and humane, to all Old Coasters. It is stiff with the British tribalism of expats. The hero, Morgan Leafy, is a junior diplomat with the inverted snobbery of an early Amis hero. A lower-middle Southerner, he is infuriated by the mannerisms of his bosses, the upper-middle Southerners. "Good *man*!" the book begins.

"Oh, good *man*!" The compliment comes from a newly arrived young poshocrat who, Morgan fears, will get on better with the boss and the boss's daughter than Morgan can. "Good man"—like "old boy", "mate", "colonel", "sir" and "squire"—is an endearment used by British males to wound, as often as not. The real meaning of "a good man" is, however, illustrated indirectly, in parenthesis. . . .

Also disliked and punished by Morgan is a pleasingly hearty Welsh paterfamilias called Denzil Jones who slaps his back in the Europeans' club and calls him "Boyo!" Then there is Dr Murray, a righteous Scotsman of the type often called Calvinist in the South, even when neither Scot nor Sassenach has read a word of Calvin. Morgan has to go to Dr Murray when he gets the clap from his African girlfriend, he even tries to jump the queue—and Dr Murray's righteousness is quite hellish. Morgan hates him. Dr Murray is the sort of "good man in Africa" that makes Morgan want to be bad.

His boss, Arthur Fanshawe, is the sort of man who grows daily more interested and expert in his previous posting—rather as British generals are alleged to be constantly preparing for the last war. The Fanshawes have much to tell Morgan about the wisdom of Asia: they have got up their house as a cross between a Buddhist temple and a Chinese restaurant, they teach Morgan Siamese toasts—but they cannot be doing much with Nigeria, its gods and its politicians. It is Morgan who must deal with the priests, Morgan who must worm his way into the Kinjanjan National Party (thus making it unpopular, as "a British puppet"). His vitality is however rewarded by the advances of both Fanshawe's daughter and his wife.

Morgan's dealings with Africans are not quite so plausible. There is a politician and university professor called Chief Sam Adekunle who compels Morgan to make friends with Dr Murray, even to play golf with him. This is true to life, so far: by virtue of their royal charisma, West African chiefs can easily persuade British expatriates to make friends with one another. But it is improbable that a skilful politician like Adekunle would attempt to bribe a man as guid as Dr Murray and still more improbable that he would use an ass like Morgan as his intermediary.

More convincing is Morgan's affair with Adekunle's English wife. She reminds us first of Monica Faseyi in Wole Soyinka's novel, *The Interpreters*. But then we notice a more obvious literary allusion. Mrs Adekunle's name is Celia and she lives in Kinjanja. Celia in *The Cocktail Party* was crucified in Kinkanja . . . This novel contains many other literary allusions and poetic ambiguities, but they do not impede the pace of the narrative. Nor do the terse impressions of West African landscapes and people, some of them magically evocative, even through the unenthusiastic *Lucky Jim*-like spectacles of Morgan.

Some of the writing, though, is not good. "Celia and Morgan knelt naked facing each other on the towel-draped back seat. This seemed to be the point to which all their conversations and meetings had inevitably been heading. There was a sense of something final in the air, of something ended, reached. . . . Morgan fumed inwardly. . . . Morgan repeated, nonplussed . . .". The author is better at describing bathing costumes, "horrible oozings from the body", or Dr Murray making Morgan strip for medical purposes: "Aye. Breeks down, the lot." Such descriptions are relevant to an underlying thesis about the different ways in which West Africans and British react to their bodies. . . .

It is amusing to contrast this very British book with the work of the best Nigerian novelists. If we do not know the properties of the god Ogun, it is no fault of Wole Soyinka's; but William Boyd's Shango is merely a romantic menace, known by hearsay. Soyinka, in *The King's Horseman,* makes the British very shrewd in their understanding of Nigeria, very grand in their preparations for a royal visit, while Mr Boyd makes them absurd. There are no poetic proverbs from wise old chiefs: Mr Boyd sends up this Nigerian convention. The only chief is crooked Sam Adekunle—and we would like to know more about him. Here we miss the acuteness of Chinua Achebe, portraying the virtues and vices of the type in his valuable novel *A Man of the People*.

D.A.N. Jones, "The Language of the Tribe," in The Times Literary Supplement *(© Times Newspapers Ltd. (London) 1981; reproduced from* The Times Literary Supplement *by permission), No. 4061, January 30, 1981, p. 106.*

ANDREW MOTION

"If any one theme can be said to emerge from the stories in **On The Yankee Station** it is a concern with narrative in its varying guises and modes, approaches and methods." William Boyd's publishers are keen to make him hot property—not simply by bringing out this collection hard on the heels of his successful first novel [*A Good Man in Africa*], but by implying that he is an innovator: a post-modernist trouble-shooter. Boyd himself provides some justification for this enrolment into the avant-garde. His concluding story tricksily exploits the methods by which life becomes art. Its speaker, William (Boyd? or who?), loses his girlfriend to an older brother and compensates for the actual loss in a fictional retaliation. He pushes—or does he?—his brother over a waterfall. Boyd encourages us to admire his playfulness: "You write fiction and what are you doing?", his namesake asks, "You're telling lies, pal, that's all". But as the book's other stories testify, it is very far from being all; neither is it true to say that Boyd's main concern is with the processes and resources of narrative. **On The Yankee Station** is a collection of eminently readable, entertaining and deeply traditional stories, in which the inclination to fabricate is not self-consciously or modernistically investigated as a problem of the "novel", but granted to characters as a sign of emotional or (usually) sexual uncertainty.

"Hardly Ever", one of the most engaging stories, makes the point comically. A group of public school boys volunteer to sing in *H.M.S. Pinafore,* not for any musical reason, but because it gives them a chance to meet girls from the local grammar school. Although pairings do quickly occur, one of the boys, Niles, is conspicuously less active in fact than he is in imagination. Every innocent meeting with the girl of his choice is subsequently embroidered and recast for the benefit of his dormitory companions. . . . When Niles and his partner come to what is meant to be the crunch, after the last performance of *Pinafore,* he humiliates himself by falling asleep beside her in the squash courts, but sets off back to the dormitory, intent on giving his listeners what they expect. His tale-telling is an exploitative compensation for his own ineptitude; he turns the girl from a sympathetic individual into a sex-object. . . .

"On the Yankee Station", characteristically, is an immaculately constructed story. It is more gripping than it is elegant or profound, but Boyd imagines the location and recreates the necessary details with impressive efficiency. There is, though, a tendency for the very tightness of his plots to inhibit their effect. Each one snaps shut with a well-timed satisfying exactitude, in rather the same way as, say, Somerset Maugham's do. Like Maugham, Boyd does not show his characters receiving impressions in what Virginia Woolf famously called "an incessant shower of innumerable atoms". They exist primarily in terms of narrative event: for all the frequency with which circumstances conspire against them, they seldom form a speculative or philosophical attachment to their worlds. The greatest virtue of this narrative method is a certain kind of readability—Boyd's stories race along, confident and competent. The disadvantage, though, is a degree of sameness: in spite of the prodigiously various settings—America, France and Africa, not to mention Vietnam—the individuals in these stories play persistently luckless, passive, sexually clumsy roles. Even when Boyd allows his characters to be more active, as he does in the two stories featuring the hero of his novel, Morgan Leafy, the result is little different: Leafy's efforts to exert himself are quickly and relentlessly satirized. He is made submissive, in fact, to Boyd's unwavering conviction of human unsuccess, and to an accompanying reluctance to create resonant psychological complexities.

> Andrew Motion, "The Secret of Unsuccess," in The Times Literary Supplement (© Times Newspapers Ltd. (London) 1981; reproduced from The Times Literary Supplement by permission), No. 4085, July 17, 1981, p. 803.

PAUL ABLEMAN

[*On The Yankee Station* comprises] short stories which are, with one exception, formidably accomplished. Like William Boyd's first novel, *A Good Man in Africa,* they reveal no sign of beginner's fumbling. Several of them have already appeared in various magazines and it is likely that they represent Mr Boyd's literary apprenticeship. Apart from the exception already mentioned, all the tales are assured and expert. The feeling of apprentice work derives not from their quality but from their variety. They include a psychological thriller, a touching story of sexual initiation, a sickening (because of its flawless evocation) study of a napalm-happy American pilot in the Vietnam war and the mechanic who hates him, several pieces about unpleasant fat Englishmen sweating in post-colonial Africa, a first-person memoir (in as seamless an American vernacular as Salinger at his best) by a sometime child star on the skids and several others. The impression they convey is of an aspiring author exploring his talent by setting it a variety of literary challenges. So far, so good, and there is no doubt that Mr Boyd, not yet 30, is set fair for a dazzling career. And yet there is something about these stories that disturbs me. They are imbued with a fashionable sense of disenchantment. The author appears to be blasé before he has lived long enough to be genuinely disillusioned. This does not seem a pose but rather the product of that kind of precocity often associated with a public school education. There is no sense of a questing mind grappling anew with experience.

This applies to 12 of the stories. The ominous thirteenth is another matter. It seems an authentically early work. It has an experimental format and is entitled, not very happily, '**Long Story Short**'. It is both too confused and confusing to be reviewed with any clarity but basically it is an attempt to explore the relationship between reality and its literary representation. The author sets up a scene and then destroys it by telling you that the characters 'really' had different names and even qualities.... This process is accompanied by sly authorial comments on the author's function and powers.... (pp. 21-2)

The relationship between the world and its literary representation is not only a valid but a vital subject for literature. Borges is perhaps the major artist to tackle it in our age although Nabokov, Beckett and Joyce have at least glanced at it. But the impulse inspiring Mr Boyd seems less a mature concern with the problem than the kind of 'settling in' process which all young writers pass through. '**Long Story Short**' is really a mediocre example of immature writing of the kind that is best left to gather dust. Possibly it has been included because the collection is a relatively short one. What is interesting about it is that beneath its experimental format a conventional thriller is struggling to get out. The piece ends with a murder which echoes several in the more mature stories in the collection. It is as if Mr Boyd, after a single attempt to probe the nature of his vocation, had brushed aside all such tiresome speculation and charged into full-scale commercial production. Now, no sensible critic knocks the market. Many of the world's masterpieces have been thoroughly commercial productions, but only produced after their authors had investigated their own talent and the craft it was to inherit. Mr Boyd's tales are not derivative but they follow well-trodden literary paths and there seems a danger that he will never explore and then colonise his own literary territory. This would be a great pity because he is bursting at the seams with raw ability.

Particularly impressive is his effortless mastery of the technologised environment. Most English, and even American writers, perhaps as a result of an 'arts' education, despise technology and apparently regard scientific knowledge as debased. They affect, even as they jet round the world and join movements to avert thermo-nuclear annihilation, to regard the world as essentially unchanged since Roman times. In fact, of course, technology is the most significant and challenging process in the world to-day. Mr Boyd, more than many Science Fiction writers, appreciates this truth. He could be the first of a new wave of authors to explore profoundly the dynamics of human experience in the 20th century. (p. 22)

> Paul Ableman, "Settling In," in The Spectator (© 1981 by The Spectator; reprinted by permission of The Spectator), Vol. 247, No. 7987, August 8, 1981, pp. 21-2.

FRANCIS KING

This second novel by William Boyd [*An Ice Cream War*] confounds but does not disappoint the expectations raised by his first. Heartlessly farcical, *A Good Man in Africa* was the brightest work of fiction to emerge from the dark continent since Waugh's *Black Mischief*. Although it was in no way messy in shape or sloppy in writing, it was one of those books which, products of exuberant improvisation rather than of rigorous planning, seem, like Waugh's own early novels, to have spurted from their creators' imaginations in a single, glittering jet.

In contrast, *An Ice Cream War* obviously could not have been written without a vast amount of patient digging for information. Prefacing it, there are first a letter written from Nairobi by a member of the East African Railway Volunteer Force to his sister in October 1914 and then a map of the area of East Africa, stretching from Lake Victoria to Lake Nyasa and from Lake Tanganyika to the Indian Ocean, in which much of the action takes place. Mr Boyd knows Africa, having been born in Ghana; but clearly he could not have known much about the obscure, four-year war which dragged on in this corner of the world while a far more momentous war was raging in Europe, and, in order to achieve so much authenticity in his descriptions of battles, living-conditions and terrain, he must have had to read widely and deeply.

For example, one of his six chief characters is a corpulent, lively American settler, Temple Smith, who has a farm on the borders of British and German East Africa, just on the British side. Temple Smith's most prized possession is a decorticator for his sisal crop; and when, after he has been ejected from his farm, this giant machine vanishes, either removed or destroyed by the Germans, he feels its loss with all the bitterness and grief of a man bereaved by the war of a son or a brother. Until reading this book, I had little idea of what a decorticator was or of how a farmer in East Africa at that period would have set about making a living. Mr Boyd at once makes both things clear. (pp. 23-4)

Seesawing between two continents, the book is at its most vivid and enthralling when it touches down on Africa. This may be because novels like *Death of a Hero* have already described in terms no less harshly relentless the noble sacrifices and the mean hypocrisies of the 1914-18 war in Europe, but from the war in Africa no comparable novels have ever emerged. When Mr Boyd deals with events back at home, he often seems to be patiently reconstructing; when he deals with events in Africa, his imagination takes off with a powerful upsurge, like a hawk too long mewed.

The commanders, German or English, in East Africa worked on the assumption that their victories were the result of elaborate plans succeeding and their failures the result of those same plans being frustrated by the enemy; but, like Stendhal and Tolstoy, Mr Boyd shows how most military engagements are, literally and figuratively, a bloody mess and most victories and defeats are fortuitous.

From time to time Mr Boyd has lapses from authenticity. For example, at that period members of a family like the Cobbs would have asked for 'some sherry' or 'a glass of sherry', not for 'a sherry'; Carson was an opponent, not a proponent, of Home Rule for Ireland; and in Bombay before World War I the term 'taxi-cab' could surely not have come into use, even if by then cars plied for hire. But whether writing of the armaments, the family prayers or the methods of contraception of the period, Mr Boyd generally convinces. (p. 24)

Francis King, "Bookerabile?" in The Spectator *(© 1982 by* The Spectator; *reprinted by permission of* The Spectator*), Vol. 249, No. 8044, September 11, 1982, pp. 23-4.*

BLAKE MORRISON

Inside every comic fat man there's a serious thin man trying to get out. William Boyd's **'A Good Man in Africa'** may not have been the novel for the Eighties it was hailed as (in tone it was a novel of the Fifties), but its flabby, red-haired, heavily perspiring British diplomat, Morgan Leafy, was a memorably funny creation. His second novel, **'An Ice Cream War'** (again rather old-fashioned, again compulsively readable), takes as its central figure the slim, nervous, dark-haired would-be aesthete Felix Cobb, who barely raises a smile.

Boyd's subject is the 1914-18 War, his venue the little-known East African front, where German-British hostilities follow a parochial, disorganised but violent course. Those caught up include Temple Smith, an American with a farm near Kilimanjaro; the German couple Erich and Liesl von Bishop; and Felix's brother, the simple, carthorse-like Gabriel, drafted out during his honeymoon. Back home Felix finds solace during his unhappy guilt-ridden career at Oxford through an affair with Gabriel's wife, Charis, but eventually he too finds himself journeying into the heart of darkness.

It's not that there aren't some comic moments: Felix's exasperation with his mad, blimpish father; minor characters like the mean Nigel Bathes and indecipherable Scotsman Gilzean; Temple Smith's botched schemes to get rich quick in the colonies. But Felix is the book's presiding spirit and he brings out a more sombre, reflective side of Boyd.

'An Ice Cream War' is a nice, clean read, almost Victorian in the way it introduces each character with a head-to-toe physical description. Its lack of modernist fizz evidently worries the publishers (and, I suspect, Boyd himself), whose blurb speaks of conventions being subverted and of assumptions challenged. No doubt this refers to the marginal shift away from realism in the novel's bleak finale, and to the point this reinforces about the First World War being a turning point in English life: bathing in ponds and romantic love during the summer of 1914 give way to death, betrayal and adultery. But this is hardly novel or subversive. Boyd's strengths should be accepted for what they are—old-fashioned ones, but no less admirable for that.

Blake Morrison, "Old Fashioned Virtues," in The Observer *(reprinted by permission of The Observer Limited), September 12, 1982, p. 32.*

T. J. BINYON

"After Evelyn Waugh came Kingsley Amis; after Amis, Tom Sharpe; after Sharpe, William Boyd": so enthused one reviewer over William Boyd's first novel, *A Good Man in Africa*. The dust-jacket of his new, second novel, *An Ice Cream War*—also set in Africa—places him as a term in a very different and much more old-fashioned progression. "Boyd has taken some of the story-telling and narrative conventions of the novel of colonial adventure—as practised by P. C. Wren, John Buchan and Rider Haggard—and used them for his own subversive ends." In other words, he has changed his spots and has followed a satire by a historical novel, set against the background of the East African campaign of the First World War, when a British army chased a German army commanded by von Lettow-Vorbeck up and down East Africa for four years without achieving any particular success. . . .

The place and time put the novel, of course, into *African Queen* territory. But as a more modern and more objective author than Forester, Boyd doesn't allow his characters any display of valour, heroism or even mild bravery. The military are relentlessly presented as inefficient, incompetent, disorganized and undisciplined; officers are bone-headed, obstinate, arrogant and often drunk; other ranks idle, shambolic and demoralized. At the unsuccessful British landing at Tanga, between Mombasa and Dar-es-Salaam, in 1914, Cobb wanders through the battle as even more of an ignorant innocent than Pierre at Borodino or Fabrice at Waterloo, until he is wounded and taken prisoner. Strangely enough the German army is treated with much more respect, revealed, in the glimpses we have of it, as a model of discipline and efficiency.

The author's subversive intent is demonstrated only too obviously by his constant care to keep his readers' noses firmly in touch with those human functions which his more delicate predecessors would have passed by in silence. Characters retire frequently into the bush to lower their trousers and squat; Temple Smith returns to his farm to find that the Germans have left a noticeable trace of their occupation. . . . Even this, however, becomes a symbol for German efficiency: "It looked as if a battalion had marched in, lowered their trousers and, on the given command, had shat where they stood." Charis's prophylactic methods against childbirth are described with ruthless realism, as are Felix and Temple Smith's encounters with prostitutes—both unsuccessful—in Bloomsbury and downtown Dar-es-Salaam respectively.

Subversion, however, like patriotism, is not enough; though it is not easy to see what other aim the author has in mind. In the end, with all due respect to the sage of the dust-jacket, the comparison to earlier novelists fails. The book's interest is fragmented among too many characters for it to have the narrative thrust of their less self-conscious tales. It is not the story of a quest, like *Prester John*, of one man's fate, like *Beau Geste*, or even of a historical episode, as Rider Haggard's *Finished* narrates the events of the Zulu war of 1879.

Individual episodes are effective—some highly so—in creating the African atmosphere, while others are no less comic. Yet the comedy always seems artificially imposed, brought on by the introduction of a character fabricated solely for that purpose, whereas in *A Good Man in Africa* it was undeniably organic and all-embracing. Though each chapter, in the annoying habit originally established by bad thrillers, is headed by a day, a date and a place-name, no impression of cohesion, tension or movement is achieved: incidents are oddly disconnected, and the conclusion is less than dramatic. Hidden beneath the high glaze of the surface a message is perhaps struggling to get out. But its efforts are no more than tentative, and the script in which it is written remains indecipherable.

> T. J. Binyon, "Rubbing Noses in It," in The Times Literary Supplement (© Times Newspapers Ltd. (London) 1982; reproduced from The Times Literary Supplement by permission), No. 4146, September 17, 1982, p. 993.

MICHIKO KAKUTANI

With "**A Good Man in Africa**," William Boyd made a precocious debut. Though somewhat derivative of Evelyn Waugh and Kingsley Amis, this story of a British diplomat's hapless adventures in Africa was told with brio and generous helpings of black humor, and it marked the start of a promising career. Now, only a year later, Mr. Boyd has more than fulfilled the bright promise of the first novel. "**An Ice-Cream War**" is more ambitious in scope and theme than "**Good Man**," and it represents Mr. Boyd's discovery of his own voice—an elastic voice that is capable not only of some very funny satire but also of seriousness and compassion.

Played out against the backdrop of World War I, "**An Ice-Cream War**" examines the consequences of that conflict, which would so fundamentally change the British state of mind. The setting is marginal as far as the main theatre of war is concerned—most of the action takes place in British and German East Africa—and the characters, too, tend to be people caught on the sideline of history. Somewhat selfish and not particularly introspective, they are ordinary people who regard the war not as a political conflict calling for heroics, but as a noisy, somewhat messy interruption in their daily lives. . . .

In the course of "**An Ice-Cream War**," the war is seen from the point-of-view of . . . [several] central characters, for unlike "**Good Man**"—which was filtered entirely through the mind of the hero, Morgan Leafy—this book boasts a rich, expansive tableau. Using an almost cinematic technique, Mr. Boyd cuts back and forth between the exploits of different characters, building narrative suspense with brisk assurance. So what if the convergence of the various story lines is contrived, if some of the characters' hijinks are faintly ridiculous—Mr. Boyd is such a good story teller that we don't really mind.

The only real problem is that Mr. Boyd's narrative fluency lets him get away with a handful of characters, who seem like two-dimensional exiles from an old English comic novel. Charis, the woman with whom both Gabriel and Felix fall in love, for example, never becomes much more than a pretty plot device; and the boys' father remains a parody of old Empire clichés.

Felix, however, is one of those characters who insidiously grows in the reader's mind as he, himself, matures. When we first meet him, he is the sort of young aristocrat who carries around Kropotkin's "Social Anarchy" in hopes that working-class youths will see him reading it and appreciate his proletarian sympathies. He makes a fool of himself with the tarted-up sister of a friend and thinks it amusing to run about an Oxford courtyard bashing rats on the head with a hockey stick. The war, of course, quickly changes all this.

Having initially joined up for essentially selfish reasons—he wants to find his brother who has been captured by the Germans and also find out if Gabriel knows about his wife's affair—Felix finds himself afflicted by boredom and loneliness, emotions that only too soon are replaced by a visceral apprehension of the consequences of war. Mr. Boyd has modulated the brittle satire of "**Good Man**," and the outrageous, "M*A*S*H"-like events that Felix and Gabriel witness early on—an invasion routed by swarms of bees, an accident with a bomb-gun—give way to more sobering glimpses of brutality. By the end of this fine novel, death is no longer merely comic, but terrible and senseless and suddenly very personal as well.

> Michiko Kakutani, in a review of "An Ice-Cream War," in The New York Times (copyright © 1983 by The New York Times Company; reprinted by permission), April 5, 1983, p. C13.

ROBERT TOWERS

Boyd's first novel, *A Good Man in Africa* . . . , won three distinguished British literary prizes: the Whitbread, the Somerset Maugham, and the John Llewellyn Rhys awards—a reception that must have seemed dazzling to Boyd and that makes at least one American reader wonder about the state of the competition in England. *A Good Man in Africa* is cleverly and intricately constructed, its various strands pulled together and knotted with aplomb; it is also sexy, nasty, and intermittently funny. But the book seems to me so heavily imitative, in tone and farcical incident, of the early novels of Kingsley Amis that it might well be called *Lucky Jim Goes to Africa* or *One Fat Englishman in Nkongsamba*. Boyd makes his anti-hero, Morgan Leafy, too abjectly contemptible to win even the sneaking sympathy we regularly accord to rogues; one derives little exhilaration from his mischief-making and small satisfaction from his repeated humiliations. The postcolonial British officials and their women are remarkably like the academic types that Amis earlier skewered in both British and American settings, and the rascality of the natives is exactly what we expect.

Stylistically, the novel is heavy-handed, especially in the way in which nearly every recorded moment of Leafy's baleful consciousness is underlined. He is always laughing "harshly to himself," remembering "the most achingly embarrassing moments of his life," thinking "shamefacedly," and even, in a burst of adverbial excess, reflecting "sour grapily" on his ex-girlfriend's prominent nose. Did none of the British reviewers or prize givers feel oppressed by this weight of redundancy and cliché?

An Ice-Cream War also comes to us accompanied by transatlantic applause—applause which, though still excessive in my view, seems far more justifiable than that lavished upon *A Good Man in Africa*. Boyd's second novel is neither inventive nor profound, but it is a substantial, satisfying work of fiction. Its style is that of a writer confident enough of his effects to refrain from belaboring the obvious. Instead of being directly imitative, *An Ice-Cream War* is evocative, bringing to mind a generation of writers whose subject matter was the late afternoon of the Edwardian upper-middle class and its abrupt descent into the most devastating war the Western world has yet experienced. Though perhaps a third of the book takes place in an England made familiar to us by scores of novels, memoirs, plays, and films, Boyd's chief concern is with the haphazard, often farcical conduct of the war on a remote stage: the East African colonies of Great Britain and Germany. (p. 42)

Elaborate in its construction, *An Ice-Cream War* is straightforward and graphic in its narration. The scenes and characters shift with admirable dispatch, aided by dates and locations given in capital letters. . . . I sometimes had the feeling that I was watching the master of ceremonies in a fast-moving review as he calls the various performers to the footlights to do their turns. A large supporting cast includes fire-breathing English officers, foppish asses, missionaries, assorted Germans, and native troops who routinely defile any occupied building with their excrement. The episodes in which they participate range widely in their emotional impact—some are funny, some touching to the point of pain, some so gruesome that one can barely stomach them. All display the narrator's firm hand and a style that is not distinctive but eminently workable and lively. War, the book seems to say, is as foolish and confusing as it is hellish, and the English are not very good at waging it.

Boyd's panoramic approach involves certain shortcuts in characterization that preclude any real subtlety or inwardness. Whatever is ultimately mysterious or unpredictable in the human personality is largely missing—and yet we hardly notice its absence, so effective are the strong, quick outlines he provides. *An Ice-Cream War* is essentially an extroverted book, a saga of British imperialism in its next-to-last phase. (pp. 42-3)

Robert Towers, "Closing Time," in The New York Review of Books *(reprinted with permission from* The New York Review of Books; *copyright © 1983 Nyrev, Inc.), Vol. XXX, No. 9, June 2, 1983, pp. 42-3.**

James M(allahan) Cain
1892-1977

American novelist, short story writer, screenwriter, journalist, and dramatist.

Cain was the author of *The Postman Always Rings Twice* (1934) and other novels which explore America's obsession with sex, violence, and money. His theme, the American dream-turned-nightmare, is complemented by stylistic directness and relentless action. Cain's so-called "hard-boiled" style of writing has put him in the company of Dashiell Hammett and Raymond Chandler. However, one notable difference between Cain's work and theirs is that Cain used the point of view of the criminal rather than the detective. Cain's plots and characters are based on a simple formula: a "low life" character expresses a wish (likened by Cain to opening Pandora's box) and the fulfillment of the wish thrusts him upon the "love rack" as he becomes enmeshed in illegal and immoral activities. As Edmund Wilson pointed out, Cain's characters carry their own precipices with them and, in consequence of their passions, they eventually fall over, clutching the remains of their dreams.

Cain pursued several careers before the publication of his first and best-known novel, *The Postman Always Rings Twice*. He developed his writing skills as a journalist in the employ of such luminaries as H. L. Mencken, Walter Lippmann, and Harold Ross. Many critics attribute Cain's terse, unembellished style to the restrictions of that profession. Although a number of Cain's stories were made into films—among them *The Postman, Mildred Pierce, Double Indemnity, The Embezzler,* and *The Baby in the Icebox*—Cain's career as a screenwriter was unsuccessful, and he was not involved in the films made from his books. Although the cinematic quality of his work is often noted, he denied having written anything but *Love's Lovely Counterfeit* (1942) with the movies in mind. He did, however, admit that the camera's-eye-view he used helped him maintain the dispassionate appraisal and swift movement characteristic of his work. Perhaps because of these elements, Cain called himself a writer of the "pure novel," one in which the author does not intrude. Cain does, however, use omission, suggestion, and dialogue to manipulate the pace and to involve the reader in situations which might otherwise not be acceptable. Cain handles such controversial subjects as incest, prostitution, homosexuality, and pedophilia nonjudgmentally, causing some critics to complain about his refusal to condemn his immoral characters.

At one point, Cain decided that he had exhausted his formula. In an effort to diversify, he used a picaresque tale instead of a crime story in *The Moth* (1948), he turned to the past for the settings of *Past All Dishonor* (1946) and *Mignon* (1962), and he gave *The Root of His Evil* (1951) an uncharacteristically happy ending. These and other later works, such as *Galatea* (1953) and *The Magician's Wife* (1965), disappointed critics. Towards the end of his career, Cain was unable to find a publisher for several of his manuscripts. While *The Institute* (1976) and *Rainbow's End* (1975) have been published in recent years, two other books, announced for publication, were quietly dropped.

Photograph by Slinkman Studio

Cain's realism gives a stark account of American life as he observed it. He described the frustrations and anxieties of the Depression era without analyzing the society about which he wrote. Despite the tendency of some critics to discount his work as sensational and superficial, his early work was held in high regard by European intellectuals, among them Albert Camus, who acknowledged *The Postman* as his inspiration for *The Stranger*. Cain himself believed that posterity is the only critic of importance. He stated that his purpose as an author was to write a good story that would be bought and read. He often remarked that he never felt a sense of artistic accomplishment in his life, yet the continued appeal of his novels and the growing scholarly interest in his early work indicate that Cain has achieved posthumously the success he valued.

(See also *CLC*, Vols. 3, 11; *Contemporary Authors*, Vols. 17-20, rev. ed., Vols. 73-76 [obituary]; and *Contemporary Authors New Revision Series*, Vol. 8.)

FRANKLIN P. ADAMS

Mr. Cain has written the most engrossing, unlaydownable book that I have any memory of. . . .

"The Postman Always Rings Twice" is so continuously exciting that if you can put it down before you've finished it, you are not the reader I think you are.... To my mind, its style, which some will compare with Hemingway's, is better than most of Hemingway's, and as good as the Hemingway of "Twenty Grand." It is as tightly written, and as vernacularly dictaphonic as Lardner. And, like Lardner, it is slangless, though so intensely colloquial that to many readers it will give the effect of slang. I can't detect a stylistic flaw in the book.

It is, in addition to being a first-rate story from its beginning to its surprise—though not tricky—ending, thrilling, credible, humorous, heart-breaking, romantic, and realistic. I could say that it was unsentimental, too. But that is debatable....

This is neither a detective nor a mystery story. It is the breathlessly moving tale of Frank Chambers, the narrator; Nick Papadakis, the Greek proprietor of the Twin Oaks Tavern; and Cora Papadakis, his wife. They are a tough, lustful, selfish, sadistic, drinking, suspicious, double-crossing, two-timing trio. And in spite of it, or maybe on account of it, they are people that I liked, for the author liked them. He liked them, it seemed to me, with the scornful compassion that a man has who hates most members of the human race, but loves humanity....

This is a book, in the story and the telling of it, that I praise without reservation.

> Franklin P. Adams, "Hardboiled and Exciting," in New York Herald Tribune Books (© I.H.T. Corporation; reprinted by permission), February 18, 1934, p. 7.

HAROLD STRAUSS

Every so often a writer turns up who forces us to revalue our notions of the realistic manner, for, no less than reality itself, it is relative and inconstant, depending on the period, the fashion, the point of view. There is the feeling of realism, of intense realism, in James M. Cain's work, and yet he cannot be compared to such diverse types of realists as Zola, Ibsen, Sandburg, Dreiser, or Hemingway. It is the hard-boiled manner that has been heralded for some time, and is now upon us. It is the manner that James T. Farrell has been attempting in an inadequate way, that Dashiell Hammett has stumbled on, even that Tiffany Thayer has used to his own deplorable ends. But Cain is to be compared to none of these, for where Farrell loses the strands of his story, Cain rushes forward like a hound on a hot scent; where Hammett's people act tough mostly out of boredom, Cain's are toughness itself; and where Thayer achieves his sensationalism by gaudy overstatement, Cain achieves his by the most telling sort of understatement. In short, Cain has developed the hard-boiled manner as a perfect instrument of narration....

Cain is an old newspaper man who learned his reporting well, so well that he makes Hemingway look like a lexicographer and Caldwell like a sob sister at her first eviction.... ["**The Postman Always Rings Twice**"] is a third as long as most novels, and its success is due entirely to one quality: Cain can get down to the primary impulses of greed and sex in fewer words than any writer we know of. He has exorcised all the inhibitions; there is a minimum of reason, of complexity, of what we commonly call civilization, between an impulse and its gratification. In the broadest sense he is no asset as yet to American literature, for he adds nothing in breadth, but only in intensity, to our consciousness of life. But we want to see more of his work. Meanwhile, we defy anyone who has broached that remarkable first sentence to put his book down without finishing it.

> Harold Strauss, "A Six-Minute Egg," in The New York Times Book Review (copyright © 1934 by The New York Times Company; reprinted by permission), February 18, 1934, p. 8.

WILLIAM SOSKIN

Mr. James M. Cain rings twice. This time it is with a story called "**Serenade**," one that will give the I-couldn't-put-it-downers and the stayers-up-into-the-wee-hours and the hair-turning-white-over-night industry something to do.

Critical readers who want to know whether "**Serenade**" and "**The Postman Always Rings Twice**" are art will have to dope it out for themselves.... "**Serenade**" whizzes by too fast for any such judgment and yet it leaves the impression that there is a good deal of mature realistic wisdom in its careening, sirening, screeching journey from a Mexican bordello to Hollywood to the Metropolitan Opera House and the penthouse heights of New York's most *chi chi* set—back to the *ole's* and the tequila-soaked simplicity of Mexico.

A glittering murder is thrown in for good measure and some of the most toro passion and spine-shaking amor there's been around this sedate neighborhood since love retreated to the tabloid papers. All of this is set down with the hard concreteness, the repertorial genius that give James Cain's stories a unique specific gravity....

He can somehow compound elements of curiosity, adventure between alien races and temperaments, frenzied physical appeal and the desperate beauty of love excommunicated by conventional society—into a tremendously stirring romance.

The affair between Juana Montes and the singer is a most satisfying illustration of this....

By a dizzy pyramiding of fortunate events, entirely improbable in fiction but quite probable in terms of Hollywood careers, John becomes a Number One singing star on the screen. Then he goes to the Metropolitan, in New York only to meet an orchestral conductor, a wealthy patron of music who has been part of John's past—a homosexual.

It turns out, then, that John is something of a split personality in this respect, and Mr. Cain thus presents us with an unusual triangle....

I would have been happy if the tale had not involved this problem, for the simple reason that no one, Mr. Cain included, seems to be able to write well on the subject of homosexuality.... When Mr. Cain pits his direct, honest, almost sadistically passionate account of John and Juana's love against the perfumed and lisping fantasia of ... homosexuals, I think he does himself an injury.

Fortunately, however, the rococo design of "**Serenade**" is able to contain these chapters quite comfortably, and they lead to the murder of the patron, Winston, by Juana. This is negotiated in as melodramatic a fashion as the gaudiest of "movie" directors could demand, and Mr. Cain's denouement is appropriately swift and tragic.

In some of the interesting musical obiter dicta of the novel Mr. Cain displays refreshing sympathy with and understanding of the less ponderous composers' work—Rossini's overtures, for example, and his shining musical theatricality. There is something of that quality in the writing of **"Serenade"**—a gaudy, rhapsodic, Lisztian quality, a magical concoction of complex suspense and recurring climax that leaves the reader wilted—and hugely entertained.

> William Soskin, "Like His Postman, Mr. Cain Rings Twice," in New York Herald Tribune Books (© I.H.T. Corporation; reprinted by permission), December 5, 1937, p. 4.

STANLEY EDGAR HYMAN

[**"Mildred Pierce"**] has about three books worth of plot: financial ups and downs, everyone in bed with everyone else, six punchy trick endings one after another. Yet it has many good things. Cain makes no pretensions whatsoever to being a social novelist, but the scenes of Mildred looking for a job, Mildred waiting on table, and Mildred talking to the rich mother of the boy who got Veda into [James T.] Farrell's favorite condition, are bitter, incisive and unquestionably authentic. Cain's talent is the hare to Farrell's tortoise. He is a slick and accomplished writer, with a genius for effective, sparse dialogue and tight, neat plots with trick endings, preferably ringing twice. Like Farrell, he has been kidded out of the worst of his excesses, . . . but unlike Farrell he has now become readable.

And yet, for all of Farrell's weakness and Cain's competence, **"Mildred Pierce"** is essentially a more minor work than "Ellen Rogers." Weak and unimportant as the Farrell book is, it at least deals with believable people living in a real world, in a tangible city with streets in it. Cain deals with ciphers, picturesque cardboard characters whom he cuts into attractive designs. He has certain specified knowledges that he draws on in all of his novels: the workings of the law, the inside of the restaurant business and the world of music. . . . He has a few favorite themes: fate, the relationship of art and sex, and particularly the relationship of sex and violence. All his books give the sense of having been pieced together skillfully out of these shiny bits of glass, having no organic existence or internal necessity. The blurb speaks of Cain as a "first-rate storyteller," which is so unconsciously fair and exact an estimate of his ability as well as his limitations that no reviewer can add more, except to say that **"Mildred Pierce"** doesn't seem to be so shocking as either **"The Postman Always Rings Twice"** or **"Serenade,"** his first two. (p. 442)

> Stanley Edgar Hyman, "The Tortoise and the Hare," in The New Republic, Vol. 105, No. 14, October 6, 1941, pp. 441-42.*

WILLIAM DuBOIS

The title of [**"Love's Lovely Counterfeit"**] is all too descriptive. Bang it on your chair-arm when you have finished, and it will ring false as a plugged quarter. But if you can stomach the first chapter, it will hold you to the end—even if the aftereffect is comparable to a morning at the reptile-house in the zoo. (pp. 6-7)

Mr. Cain's new novel is conceived in sin; like [his] others, it proves that the wages of sin is death. But **"Love's Lovely Counterfeit"** can hardly be compared to his earlier work. In fact, it is redeemed from sheer pulp melodrama only by his spine-tingling treatment of "big" scenes, his wonderfully accurate ear for the rhythms of dialogue. The plot is as trite as most Grade B movies, with the same awkward transitions, the same contrived crises. Every character, including the protagonist, is a hundred-per cent heel. . . . "When you come right down to it," says one stir-happy gunman, "nobody isn't so hot. Not really they're not. But if they're buddies, they can generally figure an angle." If this novel has a philosophy, it may well be summarized in these lines.

The story deals with political racketeering in a Midwestern city. . . .

"Love's Lovely Counterfeit" is packed with enough material for a dozen novels, but most of it is tossed away in shilling-shocker theatrics. It's a pity, for Mr. Cain's talent for creating horrific images is very real. Yet the people of this fictional world are cardboard bogey-men, warped at creation. In this novel, at least, he seems content to be a comicstrip Doré.

> William DuBois, "The Racketeers," in The New York Times Book Review (copyright © 1942 by The New York Times Company; reprinted by permission), October 11, 1942, pp. 6-7.

J.M.C.

These novels [**Double Indemnity, Career in C Major,** and **The Embezzler,** collected in **Three of a Kind**], though written fairly recently, really belong to the Depression, rather than the War, and make interesting footnotes to an era. They also make, to anybody who finds me interesting, an interesting commentary on my own development as a novelist, and as I am probably the most mis-read, mis-reviewed, and misunderstood novelist now writing, this may be a good place to say a word about myself, my literary ideals, and my method of composition. I have had, since I began writing, the greatest difficulties with technique, or at any rate fictive technique. . . . [For] ten years [I] resigned myself to the conviction that I couldn't write a novel. I tried plays with no success, and short stories with very little success, but with a curious discovery. What had made the novel so hopeless was that I didn't seem to have the least idea where I was going with it, or even which paragraph should follow which. But my short stories, which were put into the mouth of some character, marched right along, for if I in the third person faltered and stumbled, my characters in the first person knew perfectly well what they had to say. Yet they were very homely characters, and spoke a gnarled and grotesque jargon that didn't seem quite adapted to long fiction; it seemed to me that after fifty pages of ain'ts, brungs, and fittens, the reader would want to throw the book at me. But then I moved to California and heard the Western roughneck: the boy who is just as elemental inside as his Eastern colleague, but who has been to high school, completes his sentences, and uses reasonably good grammar. Once my ear had put this on wax, so that I had it, I began to wonder if *that* wouldn't be the medium I could use to write novels. This is the origin of the style that is usually associated with me, and that will be found, in a somewhat modified form, in this book. No writer would be telling the truth if he said he didn't think about style, for his style is the very pattern and weave and dye of his work. Yet I confess I usually read comments on this style with some surprise, for I make no conscious effort to be tough, or hard-boiled, or grim, or any of the things I am usually called. I merely try to write as the character would write, and I never forget that the average man, from the fields, the streets, the bars, the offices, and even the gutters of his country, has acquired a vividness of speech that goes beyond anything I could invent, and that if I stick to this heritage, this *logos* of the American countryside, I shall attain a maximum of effectiveness with very little effort. In general my style is rural rather than urban; my ear seems to like fields better than streets. I am glad of this, for I think language loses a bit of its bounce the moment its heels touch concrete.

About the time I was having these meditations on style, I fell under the spell of a man named Vincent Lawrence. You probably associate him with the writing credits of a good many movies, and no doubt have seen his plays; but his influence in Hollywood goes considerably beyond the scripts he has written, admirable as some of them have been. He has laid down principles that are pretty generally incorporated into pictures by now, and for that reason, as well as personal idiosyncrasies that are to say the least of it odd, has become something of a legend. (pp. vii-ix)

[When] this wight got me by the lapel, and talked technique at me, I was a little hostile. Until then, my ideal of writing, as well as I can recall it, was that the story correspond with life, mirror it, give a picture whose main element was truth. Lawrence had no objection to this, but insisted that truth was not all. He said if truth were the main object of writing, I would have a hard time competing with a $3 camera. He said if truth were what a writer really worshipped, he would write, not a novel, but a case history. Then he recalled for me Dreiser's play, The Hand of the Potter. He pointed out that this play was truthful enough, but utterly pointless, since it made a plea for a degenerate, without ever once attempting to get you interested in that degenerate.

Writing, narrative writing, whether in the theatre, a book, or a picture house, he said, must first make you *care* about the people whose fortunes you follow. Then he expounded to me the principle of the *love-rack,* as he calls it;—I haven't the faintest idea whether this is a rack on which the lovers are tortured, or something with pegs to hold the shining cloak of romance, or how the word figures in it;—and as it is this which has had such an effect on Hollywood picture writing, I shall give in a little detail what he had to say about it: "O.K., Cain, it's Romeo and Juliet, they're out on the balcony, it's the worst love scene in the world, but anyway it's some kind of love scene, and what makes it? The balcony, lad, that piece of wood that's shoved on just before the curtain goes up. If she ever knocks it over some night, and that guy can really climb up there, it'll lay an egg so bad the Department of Health will move in. In this true story you think you want to write, they meet, they have lunch, they talk, they like each other, they fall in love. That's how it does happen. But I don't pay $5.50 for that. It may be love, but it's not a play. I don't *feel* anything, and making me feel it is what you're after. . . . Before you can interest me in story, you got to interest me in *them.*"

All this, as I write it now, seems obvious enough, but it didn't seem obvious then, either to me or the picture business. . . . I began talking to him, instead of listening to him talk to me. I wanted to know why the whole thing couldn't be a love-rack. I wanted to know why, if the main situation was pregnant, if it was such as to create an emotional area in which a man and woman lived, there had to be such special attention to an isolated scene in which they fell in love. I wanted to know why every episode in the story couldn't be invented and moulded and written with a view to its effect on the love story. Lawrence saw no particular objection, and then I somewhat hesitantly revealed what was in my mind. Murder, I said, had always been written from its least interesting angle, which was whether the police would catch the murderer. I was considering, I said, a story in which murder was the love-rack, as it must be to

any man and woman who conspire to commit it. But, I said, they would commit the perfect murder. It wouldn't go, of course, quite as they planned it. But in the end they would get away with it, and then what? They would find, I said, that the earth is not big enough for two persons who share such a dreadful secret, and eventually turn on each other. He was enthusiastic, and I wrote it as planned, with no love-rack in the Lawrence sense. He has always quarreled with me for the first scene between the lovers in that novel, insisting it is commonplace. A commonplace scene was just what I wanted. They were that kind of people, and I still proposed to be true to my ideal of truth, something theatrical people are inclined to be a little perfunctory about. But after this scene, as the dreadful venture became more and more inevitable, I strove for a rising coefficient of intensity, and even hoped that somewhere along the line I would graze passion. The whole thing corresponded to a definition of tragedy I found later in some of my father's writings: that it was the "force of circumstances driving the protagonists to the commission of a dreadful act." I didn't, however, know of that definition at this time. Lawrence liked it, and even gave me a title for it. We were talking one day, about the time he had mailed a play, his first, to a producer. Then, he said, "I almost went nuts. I'd sit and watch for the postman, and then I'd think, 'You got to cut this out,' and then when I left the window I'd be listening for his ring. How I'd know it was the postman was that he'd always ring twice." (pp. x-xiii)

Although only one of [the novels in **Three of a Kind**] is about murder, these three novels embody this theory of story-building, for they all concern some high adventure on which a man and woman embark. (p. xiii)

Reading these stories over, I get quite a surprise. I would have said, on the basis of how I felt after finishing them, that I liked **Double Indemnity** best, **Career in C Major** next, and **The Embezzler** least. Now my preference is quite the reverse. In **The Embezzler** I find writing that is much simpler, much freer from calculated effect, than I find in the other two. And for long stretches I find the story quite free of what Clifton Fadiman, writing about me, once called "the conscious muscle-flexing." The muscle-flexing is often there, all right, and it is real, but it is not, as so many assume, born of a desire to be tough. I had acquired, I suspect as a result of my first fiasco at novel-writing, such a morbid fear of boring a reader that I certainly got the habit of needling a story at the least hint of a letdown. This bothered Edmund Wilson, too, in an article he wrote about me: he attributed these socko twists and surprises to a leaning toward Hollywood, which is not particularly the case. Recently, I have made steady progress at the art of letting a story secrete its own adrenalin, and I have probably written the last of my intense tales of the type that these represent. The trouble with that approach is that you have to have a "natural," as it is called, before you can start, and a natural is not to be had every day. If what you start with is less, if you shoot at passion and miss by ever so little, you hit lust, which isn't pretty, or even interesting. Again, the whole method, if the least touch of feebleness gets into it, lends itself to what is perilously close to an etude in eroticism. Again, love is not all of life, and I confess that lately, having got past the stymie of style that bothered me for so many years, I want to tell tales of a little wider implication than those which deal exclusively with one man's relation to one woman. In the future, what was valid in the technical organization of my first few novels will be synthetized, I hope, into a somewhat larger technique. What was bad will continue to drop off the cart until in the end most of it will be bounced out. (pp. xiv-xv)

> J.M.C. [James M. Cain], "Preface" (1942), in his Three of a Kind (copyright 1943 and renewed 1971 by James M. Cain; reprinted by permission of Alfred A. Knopf, Inc.), Knopf, 1943 (and reprinted by The Blackiston Company, 1944), pp. vii-xv.

MAX LERNER

Cain is known as a novelist of the "hard-boiled" school, but the designation strikes me as covering too many other diverse writers and not saying anything about Cain's essential quality. **Double Indemnity** was published last year along with two other Cain stories in a volume called **Three of a Kind.** To that volume Cain has contributed a revealing preface on how he came to write the sort of fiction he does, and what sort he thinks it is [see excerpt above]. It makes some sense, as a writer's self-scrutiny often does. But Cain is too apologetic to see himself and his America whole.

Whatever the characters and plots of Cain's novels, there is always pretty much the same theme running through them. It is the theme of love and death coiled up with each other like fatal serpents. It is love-in-death and death-and-rebirth-in-love. Cain's idea as a writing technician is that if you mix a potion of love with the powerful ingredient of murder, then you get the strongest light possible shed on the love story. It is what he calls "murder as the love-rack." And in both **Double Indemnity** and in his minor classic, **The Postman Always Rings Twice,** you get the same theme: of a man and woman, powerfully drawn to each other, who commit murder for love and money, and then "find that the earth is not big enough for two persons who share such a dreadful secret, and eventually turn on each other." Thus, more than any other contemporary writer, Cain has become the novelist-laureate of the crime of passion in America.

He takes his task seriously, and aims at getting his characters caught in the same grip of fatality that the Greek tragedians did. If he fails it is partly because of the phony tensions in a Cain story. The mills of the Greeks' gods ground slowly, but terribly. Cain thunders ahead like a movie of an express train rounding a series of curves at full speed. He has, he confesses, "the habit of needling a story at the least hint of a letdown." Which explains why reading one of his stories is like taking a hypo of adrenalin.

Cain bridles a bit at Edmund Wilson's accusation that he has the Hollywood touch. In one sense Wilson is right—in terms of pace and shock and formula writing. But the formula is, in Cain's case, generally too stiff a dose for Hollywood. It is a bit hard to think of other Cain books in the movies. The love-amidst-death story in **The Postman** would scarcely get by the Hays-Breen office. Cain's characters have a way of celebrating their love in ghoulish surroundings. That applies in **Love's Lovely Counterfeit,** which is a story of love, politics, racketeering, and murder in a Midwestern city. And it applies, with a curious twist, to the best of Cain's novels—**Serenade,** where one of the high spots is a church scene that would pull Hollywood's pillars down on any director that ventured it. And it is equally hard to think of filming the mother-daughter mixup in **Mildred Pierce.**

In the end, however, no matter how much excitement a Cain story furnishes me, I am left not enriched, but with a sense of emptiness. I think it is because Cain always aims at getting a story that is a "natural." That is to say, something perfect for his "love-rack" formula. But the formula by itself won't do. While the characters are racked, I am not. Their motivations leave me baffled, and their love turns out to be sawdust.

That may be why, at the end of his preface, Cain seems to be saying farewell to this sort of story, and promises that he will turn to "tales of a little wider application." I shall be waiting for them. (pp. 47-8)

> Max Lerner, "Cain in the Movies" (originally published in PM, September 21, 1944), in his Public Journal: Marginal Notes on Wartime America (copyright © 1943, 1944, 1945 by Max Lerner; reprinted by permission of the author), The Viking Press, 1945, pp. 46-8.

STEPHEN STEPANCHEV

In the preface to his new novel ["**The Butterfly**"] James M. Cain lashes back at Eastern critics who have accused him of imitating Ernest Hemingway and of writing with the movies in mind. To the first charge he replies that he is older than Hemingway and that the essential characteristics of his swift, lean prose were evident in his short story "**Pastorale**" written in 1927 before he had seen any of Hemingway's work. To the second charge he replies that although he has learned technically from the movies he has written only one novel, "**Love's Lovely Counterfeit,**" with the screen in mind. . . .

One must concede that Mr. Cain has good reason for anger. In their passion for simplicity and order some critics have been detecting the influence of Hemingway in any dialogue that has a resemblance to American speech as it is spoken. What they forget is that Hemingway is not alone in possessing a pair of ears. What they forget about Mr. Cain, in particular, is that though his dialogue resembles Hemingway's in sharpness and lifelikeness, the basic rhythms of his prose are quite different. Any one who will take the trouble to compare the dialogue in Mr. Cain's new novel with the talk in, say, "A Farewell to Arms" will recognize the difference at once.

As for the effect of the movies on Mr. Cain's writing, it would be idiotic to suppose that "**Serenade**" "**Double Indemnity**" or "**The Butterfly**" were written expressly for the screen. On the other hand, the selectivity apparent in these novels and their photographic emphases undoubtedly owe something to camera-eye movement. This technical indebtedness Mr. Cain himself acknowledges. . . .

What makes Mr. Cain's preface especially valuable to readers of his novels is that he reveals there his basic preoccupation as an artist. He writes, he says, of "the wish that comes true, for some reason a terrifying concept, at least to my imagination." His men and women are Pandora-like creatures who passionately want something that happens to be forbidden. He shows them opening the tabooed box, realizing their terrible wishes, and then suffering the consequences. . . .

["**The Butterfly**"] is concerned once again with a forbidden wish. This time it is incestuous.

The story is told with Mr. Cain's usual expertness. Every chapter is measured and ordered and serves functionally to advance the plot. Every page of the way it is clear that Mr. Cain knows exactly where he is going and that he is going to get there by the most direct route. The language, too, is strictly functional; there are no purple passages, no luxuriating excesses anywhere; every word counts. It is a clean, bare prose that cleaves tightly to the hard outline of the plot skeleton.

That the novel is contrived is, of course, true. But unless I am greatly mistaken, you are likely to enjoy the neatly packaged violence of **"The Butterfly."**

Stephen Stepanchev, "Packaged Violence," in New York Herald Tribune Weekly Book Review, January 26, 1947, p. 4.

JAMES MacBRIDE

Merely by hefting this full-size volume [**"The Moth"**] the Cain addict will sense instantly that it is the Malibu maestro's most ambitious effort to date. . . . Unlike all of Mr. Cain's previous books, it is both full-bodied and chronological, taking a boy from boyhood to maturity, and doing its honest best to give that protagonist a third dimension. The present reader . . . can only report, in sorrow, that Mr. Cain's most ambitious novel is also his dullest. . . .

When you've closed **"The Moth"** you may know just how to crack a cash register—or earn your living as a fruit-tramp. Jack Dillon remains a vaguely glimpsed stranger who has talked you to death, and beyond. And Mr. Cain's famous sense of pace, his knack with the wages-of-sin pattern, are lost in verbiage.

James MacBride, "Mr. Cain, Jumbo Size," in The New York Times Book Review (copyright © 1948 by The New York Times Company; reprinted by permission), July 11, 1948, p. 5.

EDMUND WILSON

Let us begin with Mr. Cain and his school. ***The Postman Always Rings Twice*** came out in 1934; and Mr. Cain's second novel, ***Serenade***, in 1937. They were followed by other similar novels which apparently derived from Mr. Cain. The whole group stemmed originally from Hemingway, but it was Hemingway turned picaresque; and it had its connections also with the new school of mystery writers of the type of Dashiell Hammett.

Mr. Cain remained the best of these novelists. (pp. 19-20)

The hero of the typical Cain novel is a good-looking down-and-outer, who leads the life of a vagrant and a rogue. He invariably falls under the domination—usually to his ruin—of a vulgar and determined woman from whom he finds it impossible to escape. In the novels of McCoy and Hallas, he holds our sympathy through his essential innocence; but in the novels of Cain himself, the situation is not so simple. Cain's heroes are capable of extraordinary exploits, but they are always treading the edge of a precipice; and they are doomed, like the heroes of Hemingway, for they will eventually fall off the precipice. But whereas in Hemingway's stories, it is simply that these brave and decent men have had a dirty deal from life, the hero of a novel by Cain is an individual of mixed unstable character, who carries his precipice with him like Pascal.

His fate is thus forecast from the beginning; but in the meantime he has fabulous adventures—samples, as it were, from a *Thousand and One Nights* of the screwy Pacific Coast: you have jungle lust in roadside lunch-rooms, family motor-trips that end in murder, careers catastrophically broken by the vagaries of bisexual personality, the fracas created by a Mexican Indian introduced among the phonies of Hollywood. (pp. 20-1)

Cain himself is particularly ingenious in tracing from their first beginnings the tangles that gradually tighten around the necks of the people involved in those bizarre and brutal crimes that figure in the American papers, and is capable even of tackling—in ***Serenade***, at any rate—the larger tangles of social interest from which these deadly little knots derive. Such a subject might provide a great novel: in *An American Tragedy,* such a subject did. But as we follow, in a novel by Mr. Cain, the development of one of his plots, we find ourselves more and more disconcerted at knocking up—to the destruction of illusion—against the blank and hard planes and angles of something we know all too well: the wooden old conventions of Hollywood. Here is the Hollywood gag: the echo of the murdered man's voice reverberating from the mountains when the man himself is dead, and the party in ***Serenade,*** in which the heroine stabs the villain under cover of acting out a bull-fight; the punctual Hollywood coincidence: the popping-up of the music-loving sea-captain, who is the *deus ex machina* of ***Serenade;*** the Hollywood reversal of fortune: the singer who loses his voice and then gets it back again, becoming famous and rich in a sequence that lasts about three minutes. (p. 21)

All the things that have been excluded by the Catholic censorship: sex, debauchery, unpunished crime, sacrilege against the Church—Mr. Cain has let them loose in these stories with a gusto as of pent-up ferocity that the reader cannot but share. . . .

In the meantime, ***Serenade*** is a definite improvement on ***The Postman***. It, too, has its trashy aspect, its movie foreshortenings and its too-well oiled action; but it establishes a surer illusion. ***The Postman*** was always in danger of becoming unintentionally funny. Yet even there brilliant moments of insight redeemed the unconscious burlesque; and there is enough of the real poet in Cain—both in writing and in imagination—to make one hope for something better than either. (p. 22)

Edmund Wilson, "The Boys in the Back Room," in his Classics and Commercials: A Literary Chronicle of the Forties (reprinted by permission of Farrar, Straus and Giroux, Inc.; copyright 1950 by Edmund Wilson; copyright renewed © 1978 by Elena Wilson), Farrar, Straus and Giroux, 1950, pp. 19-56.*

DAVID DEMPSEY

One must read James M. Cain on his own terms. He is something more than a whodunit writer, something less than a serious novelist; but within the zone of psychological cheekiness that he has staked out for exploration, he is a master craftsman. In **"Galatea,"** which is southern Maryland, rather than southern California, Cain edges a little closer to the method of Graham Greene. His characters are endowed with a self-awareness of guilt, purged of their sins through violence rather than good deeds. There is even a word or two in favor of God. **"Galatea"** is a tender book, built around a grotesque situation, with only a few of the old Cainine snarls in evidence. (p. 4)

[The heroine] is in imminent danger of death by overeating, a terminal condition plotted by her husband as a means of getting her inheritance. Since this consists of a very profitable chain of restaurants, the inheritance is at once the means of destruction and the reason for it.

She is rescued, of course, by Pygmalion—in this case a young prizefight trainer who has taken weight off of some of the most gluttonous boxers in the business. By means of a wonder diet . . . he transforms his Galatea into a lissome and Junoesque creature indeed.

Shaw's version of this legend underscored the point that one must provide for a soul that one has brought into being just as one must provide for a child to which he has given birth. Cain reverses this situation. . . . Both the boxer and the husband, who eventually fight for possession of Galatea, are haunted by symbols of evil, neatly evoked as a solution to the murder that forms the book's dénouement.

In carving his statue out of a mountain of flesh, Pygmalion discovers a bit of soul of his own. Even so, **"Galatea"** is better entertainment than mythology, which is no doubt what Mr. Cain intended. His style is as lean and spare as ever—like the heroine when she has finished cutting out the starches and fats. (pp. 4, 15)

David Dempsey, "Eat Hearty and Die!" in The New York Times Book Review (copyright © 1953 by The New York Times Company; reprinted by permission), August 16, 1953, pp. 4, 15.

MARTIN LEVIN

["**Mignon**"], James M. Cain's first novel in a decade, is nominally about the Civil War: period costumes aside, it barrels along like a private-eye escapade. Into New Orleans in the year 1864 comes Bill Cresap, invalided out of the Union Army and on the lookout for a stake. Before you can say Raymond Chandler, a Creole damsel in distress named Mignon Landry has appeared at Cresap's hotel room door, with a heartrending plea to get her daddy out of a military prison, where he has been sent for trading with the enemy. From this point on Mr. Cain never looks back, pulling onstage one gaudy character after another, including a sporting lady (gambling) who vies with Mignon for Cresap's heart—and involving one and all in some get-rich-quick trading in confiscated cotton. There's enough blood and lust in all this to satisfy the author's public. However, one nostalgic admirer of **"The Postman Always Rings Twice"** would prefer Mr. Cain in modern dress—where the blood he lets seems redder and the dialogue truer.

Martin Levin, in a review of "Mignon," in The New York Times Book Review (copyright © 1962 by The New York Times Company; reprinted by permission), May 6, 1962, p. 31.

GRANVILLE HICKS

[*The Magician's Wife*], Cain's first novel in some time, follows in all essentials, as the publisher candidly admits, the pattern he developed more than thirty years ago. There is a minor variation in that the hero is not a more or less disreputable drifter but an up-and-coming executive of a meat-packing company. . . . This man, Clay Lockwood, stops for lunch at one of a chain of restaurants with which his firm does business, and is immediately impressed by the hostess. . . . After lunch he says, "Sally, I've fallen for you," and, as every reader of Cain knows, the only question is how long it will take them to get into bed together. . . .

But, like other Cain heroines, she has a husband she would like to get rid of—Alexis, a magician, son of "a fabulously rich man." She wants, Clay suspects, to dispose of the father-in-law, too, and he decides to have nothing more to do with her. . . . But no experienced reader will believe it for a moment.

There are many complications. . . .

It is unfair to reveal too much of the plot of a novel of this sort, and I do not intend to do so; but no one will be surprised to learn that Clay kills Alexis; otherwise, of course, there would be no story. Clay's murder, however, is nowhere near the climax of the novel; all sorts of things happen after that—a marraige, a trial, another murder, and so on. (p. 27)

Edmund Wilson in 1940 hoped that Cain might go on to do something better, but he didn't, and here, in this production of his later years, he has merely repeated himself. There is as much trash as ever. . . .

That Cain was at one time taken seriously is hard to understand. He has always known how to keep a story moving, and in *The Magician's Wife* action follows action with such speed that the reader may temporarily overlook the faults. But at best it is only a diversion, and there are better diversions on the market. (p. 28)

Granville Hicks, "The Hard-Boiled School," in Saturday Review (© 1965 Saturday Review Magazine Co.; reprinted by permission), Vol. XLVIII, No. 33, August 14, 1965, pp. 27-8.

TOM WOLFE

Cain was one of those writers who first amazed and delighted me when I was old enough to start looking around and seeing what was being done in American literature. Steinbeck, Farrell, Saroyan, Faulkner, and Thomas Wolfe were some of the others. But Cain—*momentum* was something he had a patent on. Or maybe acceleration is the word. Picking up a Cain novel was like climbing into a car with one of those Superstockers who is up to forty by the time your right leg is in the door. Today, twenty years later, I have read *The Postman Always Rings Twice*, *Double Indemnity*, and *Mildred Pierce* again . . . and I am still amazed and delighted . . . partly because I can now see how complex Cain's famous "fast-paced," "hard-boiled" technique really is. . . .

Cain was a bit notorious in the 1930's and 1940's as a novelist of "sex and violence." I can remember that myself. I suppose a lot of critics never got beyond that notion. *The Postman Always Rings Twice* was the reigning *hot*, *taboo* novel before *Forever Amber*. It was banned in Canada; the old Hays Office blocked MGM's first efforts to bring it out as a movie—and so on. God knows how many concupiscent young men stole hornily to pages 71 and 72 of the original edition, to the "Rip Me" scene, in which a man and a woman are trying to make a murder look like an automobile accident. . . . (pp. v-vi)

One of Cain's secrets is that he never uses a detail, sexual or otherwise, in a gratuitous way. (p. vi)

Likewise with Cain's handling of violence. *The Postman Always Rings Twice* and *Double Indemnity* are both about murders, but Cain takes no relish in the brutality. In *Double Indemnity* he passes up the blow-by-blow description almost completely, telling the reader, in effect, "The guy breaks the man's neck—O.K.? Fill in the gasps, gurgles, hyoid snaps, and blue bloat any way you like. . . ." Yet you come away feeling like you have been through a long and extremely violent experience. Cain's trick here—well, it is no trick. It is a feat, one that dates back at least as far as *Crime and Punishment*.

Namely, in book after book Cain puts you inside the skin of one utterly egocentric heel after another, losers who will stop at nothing—and makes you care about them. Sympathy runs along shank to flank with the horror and disgust. It's strange stuff! Perhaps he has touched the Universal Heel in everybody . . . I don't know. . . . The sin Cain likes to play on is not murder or sadism but betrayal. You come away from *Mildred Pierce,* for example, feeling like you have been through something more murderous than *Double Indemnity.* The only physical violence in the book, however, is one choking . . . that doesn't even come close to killing the little bitch. . . . (pp. vi-vii)

Cain lets nothing get in the way of the pace. Instead, everything gets swept along for the ride. He is in a class with Chandler when it comes to re-creating the atmosphere of Stucco Rococo, Lay-Away Plan, and Low-Rent California . . . but he does it with amazingly few details . . . a few yards of department-store Ferdinand Spanish drapes hanging from Konkistador Spear rods . . . and you can conjure it all up, right up to the 8-foot-6-inch bungalow ceiling with the two-story mortgage over it. He is in a class with Hemingway when it comes to immersing the reader in the secrets of various arcane arts, like short-order cooking, insurance investigation, operatic concerts, all sorts of things—and yet you get all this scenery and setting and atmosphere at a cool hundred miles an hour . . . Cain is a master of the change of pace when he wants to be, as in the opening pages of *Mildred Pierce.* Three pages of a man bracing trees, pruning twigs, and otherwise coddling and fussing over his suburban lawn—and he has set you up for a very nice sucker punch. But the pure Cain momentum is the thing, and I recommend . . . the opening of *The Postman Always Rings Twice.* It starts off:

"They threw me off the hay truck about noon. . . ."

Take a look . . . and hang on . . . for you and me the joyride is just beginning. . . . (pp. vii-viii)

> Tom Wolfe, "Introduction" (reprinted by permission of International Creative Management; copyright © 1969 by Tom Wolfe), in Cain x 3: Three Novels by James M. Cain, Alfred A. Knopf, Inc., 1969, pp. v-viii.

TOM S. RECK

The literary reputation of James M. Cain is evidence of justice denied, a classic example of scholarly myopia toward the man whose novel *The Postman Always Rings Twice* (and we have Camus's word for this) was a model for *The Stranger.* Critics offer some begrudging admissions about Cain's power but mainly they only patronize his work. Typical comments say things like "good writing on less than good material," "a bath in sensationalism," or "hard-boiled hocus-pocus." They piously suggest that "the nearest architectural analogy . . . is a mile high outdoor juke box" or that "all the research necessary . . . could have been gathered in an afternoon at a third rate movie house."

Some of the depreciation has nothing to do with Cain per se. His large (and largely "illiterate") audience renders him suspect, as does his "easiness." The Puritan ethic, at work among the very cognoscenti who satirize it in the bourgeois, works against him: anything as much fun as *The Postman* must be questioned. Although we have moved a long way from banning a book like *Postman,* the feeling that Cain appeals to our prurience still prevails and causes us to adopt an attitude of either silly defensiveness or postured superiority.

Students of fiction often appraise Cain at face value, adjudge his "modesty" to be "simplemindedness," take him no more seriously than is absolutely required, as opposed to what might be possible. He adamantly refuses to dress up his fiction in order to make himself more and the novel less. The language seems more like wisecracks than literary similes, and we do not trust our instincts about it: we dislike it because it is so easy to like. Ordinarily, realistic novels bring in colloquial vocabulary by way of dialogue, but Cain includes it in the narrative proper, and he does not snobbishly establish his superiority to it by the usual signs of satire or patronization.

Furthermore, Cain's narrative technique (first person confessionals, stair-stepped progressions) deliberately makes the reader an accomplice to the crimes which are his subjects, a commitment some are unwilling to make, much as they are unable to accept murder as proper subject for serious consideration unless the raw impact of the act itself is muted by philosophy (as in *Crime and Punishment*) or by metaphor (as in *Intruder in the Dust*). Cain recognizes this prejudice in his introduction to *Three of a Kind* (a collection of three of his novellas), where he contends that murder has "always been written from its most uninteresting angle; which was whether the police would catch the murderer." With the mystery removed, Cain prefers to concentrate on the effect and the excitement.

As for the charge that Cain is "commonplace," . . . Cain also has the right answer: "A commonplace scene was just what I wanted." He explains that "many of life's most moving things are banal. . . . I try in using a cliche to set it up so perhaps it gains its own awkward pathetic eloquence." If it is correct that the French think about writing as writing and that Anglo Saxons think first of subject matter and second, if at all, of the delivery, then it is not surprising that Cain's reputation with the French has been comparatively more secure for some time, since they would not ignore the presentation because of antagonisms over the content.

The argument that popular fiction can tell us more about "ordinary" people than so-called serious fiction usually has more to do with sociology than with literature. In other words, the lesson that Harold Robbins teaches is separate from his fiction and contingent upon his appearance on best-seller listings and on what that means. In Cain's case, however, the insights into "ordinary" people occur within the fiction itself and not by virtue of its being widely read, thereby creating his proletarian content.

The typical Cain character is a common man trying to get along but without the brains or the personality to either obtain happiness or keep out of trouble. As such, he creates a kind of proletarian fiction, and in it Cain is actually more direct and accurate than such acknowledged proletarian fictionists as John Steinbeck or Upton Sinclair. Cain never makes ordinary people quaint as Steinbeck does in *Tortilla Flat. Mildred Pierce* is in ways a better chronicle of the Depression than *Grapes of Wrath* because its characters are not sentimentalized, glamorized, or passed off as similes. Cain is never moved to justify his people, patronize them, or use them for sociological and political intellectualizing. The result is that they are baptized with a dry if grim irony, which is appropriate to their environment. He leaves them intact, tawdry, and true to themselves and their milieu. (pp. 375-77)

Against the charge that reading Cain is reactionary anti-intellectualism or defiant slumming, we have Cain's statements about his theory of the novel to verify his serious intent. He writes what he calls "the pure novel." He says that he has a story to tell and believes that all energy should be expended toward telling it. His respect for "nothing but the facts" may stem from his journalistic background; it results in the typical Cain novel being about one-third as long as most novels.

For Cain the novel should refer to nothing outside itself. For example, in *The Postman Always Rings Twice* we are allowed to view the two people only in terms of the experience at hand, with no extraneous information. Cain dispenses with any Jamesean psychological analysis of the inner life of the characters. He does not want the reader to view them in respect to any values except the one experience of their lives he is examining. So it is that we get action, narrative, and character in one clean thrust. Still it is more than his personal preference, for the pruning lets him discard the irrelevancies and get down to the primary impulses of sex and greed; and by avoiding psychological analysis, he can spotlight psychological mythology. For example, through *Double Indemnity*'s refusal to offer any reason for Walter Huff to steal and murder, the novel lets human depravity alone to stand or to fall on itself without either condemnation or justification.

Cain has remarkable detachment—not from the characters or the incidents necessarily, but from judging them. Despite whatever conscious will is exercised to maintain objectivity, most writers cannot avoid a moral judgment. Cain feels the characters, but he does not feel for or against them; he does not moralize, ridicule, or lament. The events are piteously portrayed, but without malice.

As for Cain's subject, he himself has written, "I write of the dream come true, for some reason a terrifying concept." Why the wish-become-real turns invariably into nightmare has to do with a combination of mysticism, fatality, and psychology. It is a compliment to the definition of madness as being waking nightmare, which says that since "dream" is ordinarily related to "unconsciousness," when it becomes "reality," it becomes also "nightmare." In Cain when the dream-wish evolves to actuality, it not only fails to live up to its potential, it moves headlong into the opposite direction of fearsomeness. The Cain heroes lean over the precipice for a better look at the wish. The recurring pattern of the Cain vision is for the hero to "get the girl" and "get the money" and "get away with" the various transgressions and then, and only then, to fall into the precipice. (pp. 377-78)

The Cain people seldom pay legally. Instead they set in motion a series of circumstances which cause the destruction. They are "doomed" much as Hemingway's characters are, except that Cain does not use the tricks that might make them tragic. Hemingway is careful always to make his doomed decent and brave and sensitive, but Cain just lets them alone to be their awful selves. If Fitzgerald knew that the dream fulfilled was the dream destroyed, Cain knows the dream fulfilled is the dream perverted. To Fitzgerald reality fails to live up to the majesty of the dream. To Cain reality pushes the dream one more step—to the nightmare. Or if we choose to apply Freud, it is less that the secret is dreadful than that the sharing of it is, as if one character (they always come in twos in Cain) serves as mirror for the other, to reflect and magnify the shared horror until the image must be smashed.

On the surface in psychological terms it is paranoia. Or in the colloquialism of the characters it is only "ditching" the partner in crime for a bigger share or for safety. Yet, Cain makes it considerably more. (pp. 378-79)

The confessionals that serve as a framework for *The Postman Always Rings Twice, Double Indemnity, Serenade, Past All Dishonor, Butterfly,* and *Galetea* are strictly Christian and place the reader automatically in a position of Father-Confessor, a role for which at least the first instinct is to offer absolution. Cain conducts, then, a kind of grim trick by letting you forgive people by virtue of narrative structure for acts you really do not condone at all. Although the narrator-confessor writes down his story, the style is always as if he were telling it; and so since you are being addressed rather personally, your politeness and your sentimentality win out over morality.

From a sociological point of view, the Cain patterns of self-imposed disaster just at the point of final safety belong to a syndrome that an American anthropologist might call the mystique of our lower classes, which ties the novels in with their value as proletarian fiction. It is characterized by self-defeatist patterns of masochistic anger, adultery, violence, crimes of assorted natures, acts that are nothing if not stupid in their transparency that they will lead to catastrophe. Cain's world view manifests itself best in *The Postman Always Rings Twice, Double Indemnity,* and *Mildred Pierce,* since they contain the aspects of Cain that work best. They are concise "pure" novels about Los Angeles "proletariates" whose dreams have become nightmares.

The Postman Always Rings Twice, Cain's most famous novel and his definitive work, is lean. . . . In the first three pages of Cain's novel you have it all. The characters—Frank, Cora, and Cora's husband, Nick. You have the impetuses, namely sexuality and money. You feel that you know what will happen and how it will come out; you have only to go through the emotions of the experience with the characters. The novel's opening sentence, "They threw me off the hay truck about noon," gives in nine words the necessary information about Frank's past, present, a clue to his future, a social comment relating to the economic period, and a taste of the violence that is to shape the novel.

Although the novel's sexuality is in its straightforwardness often mistaken for schmaltz, it is exactly right for the subject and characters. . . . The words match the simplicity and the coarseness of the acts. Frank's initial reaction to Cora is, "Her lips stood out in a way that made me want to mash them in for her." As an image of passion, it lacks any Keatsian aestheticism or Lawrencian religiosity. It not only refuses to dress up the sex impulse with high-sounding phrases, it also refuses to dress it down with descriptive eroticism to let it work as titillation. It is a perfect semantic correlative to the emotion at hand. (pp. 379-80)

The setting is a roadside business with a "Luncheon Part," a "House Part," and a half dozen shacks behind it called an "Auto Court." . . . The "Auto Court" is the grand-daddy that in sublime innocence sired the country's great plastic motel system, which tells everything we need to know about the American Dream gone awry. (p. 380)

Like *Postman,* Cain's less known novel *Double Indemnity* resists middle-class analysis of human behavior. There is no preparation or rationale for the love affair between the insurance agent and the wife of one of his clients. . . . And the decision to murder is offered with Walter's simple declaration, "You are going to do it and I am going to help you." (p. 382)

As for the Cain business of the wish-coming-true, the perfect murder inexplicably goes sour and Walter is soon saying, "I would have to kill her. . . . The world isn't big enough for two people once they've got something like that on each other." Cain's hero, in fact, states his theme more directly than does Frank in *Postman:* "I was standing on the deep end, peeping over the ledge, and all the time I was trying to pull myself away; there was something in me that kept edging a little closer, trying to get a better look." It is Nietzche looking out over the void.

In addition to the rewards we can always count on in Cain, *Double Indemnity* provides an extra metaphor in its analysis of the insurance combine that serves as backdrop for the sex and violence. (p. 383)

Cain's special vision of the insurance business suggests not only amorality, irony, and absurdity, but a mystical cause-effect relationship as well. . . .

Mildred Pierce also contains the usual Cain trappings of adultery and violence. It has the wish-coming-true, as an ordinary woman rises to become a restaurant magnate; and it has the dream going horrible as a series of tawdry disasters ensue. It exposes the ugly underside of Southern California. (p. 384)

As a proletarian chronicle of the Great Depression, *Mildred Pierce* does not use Steinbeckian economic extremes to represent an era of suffering or equate the fall of Wall Street with that of a rich American family. We get a documentation of the Depression's ravages on the average lower middle-class family of the period. The dream-gone-bad is so entangled with tenants of the American Dream that the book is not only a historical novel of the American 1930s but a comment on this country's aspirations and failures generally. The symbol of the American fetish with work/money/success is female in gender to suggest the bitch-goddess. Mildred's devotion to work is the novel's running theme. When her husband leaves her, "the only clear thought in her head was that now she had no way to deliver the cakes." As she consummates an advantageous seduction, she does not open the love gift of a bottle of Scotch because "she might be able to get $6.00 for it somewhere." When her daughter lies mortally ill in the hospital, she does not stay because she has to "deliver pies, pay off the painters, contract the chickens" for her restaurant business. (pp. 384-85)

The first symbol of her success with work, her automobile, pumps "something into her veins, something of pride, of self-interest, that no love could give." (p. 385)

In *Mildred Pierce* Cain also captures the very odd attitude that lower-class Americans manifested toward the rich during the period, a Gatsbyish adoration that causes Mildred to remark of her wealthy lover: "His loafing wasn't a weakness. It was a way of life." (p. 386)

Cain has tried enlarging his field of vision. He has travelled to Mexico (*Serenade*), to New York (*Career in C Major*), to the Civil War (*Mignon*), and to the American West in the 1800s (*Past All Dishonor*). But in these he has never managed the firm grasp on his material that he demonstrates in *The Postman Always Rings Twice, Double Indemnity,* and *Mildred Pierce,* his "L.A. Novels." That these three have similar settings, themes, characterizations, and imagery proves that their content is his proper milieu. (pp. 386-87)

We may not "like" any of the characters from Cain (our conditioning may not let us do that), but we "like" to read about them, because through them we are also leaning over the precipice for that better look at the wish. (p. 387)

Tom S. Reck, "J. M. Cain's Los Angeles Novels," in The Colorado Quarterly (copyright, 1974, by the University of Colorado, Boulder, Colorado), Vol. XXII, No. 3, Winter, 1974, pp. 375-87.

KEVIN STARR

If you have the courage, take a look this summer at [*Cain x 3*]. . . . Courage is needed because of an entire generation of tough-guy writers—Dashiell Hammett, Raymond Chandler, B. Traven, Horace McCoy and others of the Southern California school—James M. Cain is possessed of the most brutal, elemental, and intrinsically pessimistic view of human events and possibilities. Only another Californian, Robinson Jeffers, working up the coast at Big Sur and in another genre, narrative poetry, matches Cain's abysmal bleakness.

Something happened in Southern California during the 1930s. Some new vision of evil rushed in upon the American consciousness. . . .

It was a demicivilization of expatriates, and James M. Cain was part of it, brought there, like Fitzgerald and Faulkner, to write for the movies. . . . Yet Cain looked around himself, noted what he saw, and in 1934, after more than a decade of trying to write fiction, published *The Postman Always Rings Twice,* one of the finest moments of depression literature. (p. 31)

A Cain story rushes forward with the headlong pace of a writer who has left everything save narrative on the cutting room floor. Yet we put Cain down with a conviction of social density and accomplished experience; for he triggers in us an act of imaginative cooperation. Convinced that Cain's fables of lust, murder and money are true to the epistructure of life in the urban-industrial complex, the reader amplifies and visualizes the details, like a director working from the bare bones of a story line. . . . Hollywood transformed Cain's cinematic narratives into great movies, and the movies in turn conferred upon the Cain canon a more ample and substantial life than it would have had on its own. Reading Cain, then, is a mixed media event. . . . (pp. 31-2)

Cain is primarily a writer of the 1930s and the 1940s. Cain's *The Magician's Wife* (1965), for instance, suffers from an element of time displacement, the characters moving and acting in a psychological calculation outside of anything having to do with the 1960s, either as a matter of motivation or ambience.

But then again all of Cain's best work has an element of laconic timelessness. The depression addicted certain writers to ideology. Many of them wrote great—and talky—novels. Writers like Cain, Chandler, Hammett and McCoy went in the opposite direction. Rather than explicitly analyze the breakdown of the machinery of the *polis*, they funded the anxieties of the collapse into moments of pure experience: moments that existed beyond the consolations of style, thought or symbol. Here, they said, face it straight and draw your own conclusions. Cain and the others did this partly because, possessed of solid commercial instincts, they knew that unadorned sex and violence had been on the bestseller list since the Bible and the Greeks. But they did it this way also because they realized that, in rendering what was evil and tragic in human affairs, it was often better to keep your mouth shut because most of what you would be saying was not what you meant at all, not what you meant at all. They turned themselves into tough guys because that seemed the best moral and esthetic posture with which to face a time of collapse and lost meaning. (p. 32)

Kevin Starr, "It's Chinatown," in The New Republic (reprinted by permission of The New Republic;

© 1975 The New Republic, Inc.), Vol. 173, No. 4, July 26, 1975, pp. 31-2.

GARY GIDDINS

James M. Cain was a caustic writer of newspaper editorials who published his first novel at 42 and his 18th at 84. His short, squalid thrillers made him as famous as Hemingway in the '30s; often more purple than *noir,* they creaked with ludicrous plot contrivances and panting dialogue, but how the pages crackled! From the first sentence, pitching the reader headlong behind the headlines of tabloid murders, to the last irony, which sounded a note more in keeping with Puritan tribunals than the requisites of hard-boiled realism, Cain drummed his trashy American fairy tales with relentless drive. By 1950, however, his tempo enfeebled partly by his own literary ambition, his audience headed for sleazier pastures. His once enthusiastic critics were silent, his later books ignored. Cain receded into the past, a relic of the Depression frequently bracketed with contemporaries in the hard-boiled schools (detective and proletariat divisions), and his lingering admirers resorted to indirection in praising him—hoisting the flags of existentialism and sociology. . . .

Yet a few of Cain's novels have been successfully reprinted every decade or so, and the biggest groundswell in 30 years has slowly taken shape in the years since his death in 1977. . . .

What's more, there is Cain's much touted rediscovery by Hollywood, where he labored for years as a scriptwriter and consultant, though not on the adaptations of his own books. . . .

It can't be merely Cain's rotgut lubricity that keeps his reputation bobbing along the surface. . . .

If Cain was a tough-guy writer, he was also the first American novelist to explore bisexuality (*Serenade*) and incest (*The Butterfly*), while asserting the connection between motiveless violence and sentimentality (*Postman*) and acknowledging a confused religiosity that, especially in his later works, assumes a born-again arrogance. Unlike Hammett and Chandler, Cain did not dispatch saints to patrol our mean streets, nor did he posit a balance sheet of good and evil. He was mesmerized by evil; it animates his most luminous images—Frank making the blood spurt from Cora's lips, Kady daring her father to lick the milk off her lips. His theme was the ugliness underlying American dreams, which he found more arbitrary and consequently more terrifying than Ragged Dick's desire for riches, or Jay Gatsby's for social standing. Cain saw the American dream as a childish demand for gratification at any cost, accompanied by a haunted desire for moral retribution. Cain is often considered a chronicler of California's lower depths, but he documented those dreams in all the classes of a class-bound society, from the poverty of Appalachia (*Butterfly*) and Mexico (*Serenade*), to the lower (*Postman*), middle (*Mildred*), and upper (*Double Indemnity*) classes of California, to the filthy rich in New York (*Career in C Major*). In each instance, a wish is granted, a futile delusion realized, and, in Dr. Johnson's words, "fate wings with every wish the afflicted dart."

Cain handled the variety of human wishes in tragedies and comedies—terms loosely used here, for convenience. In the tragedies, the protagonists scribble their confessions in the final moments before certain death; hell is a yawning pit waiting to engulf them and there's no possibility of escape. . . . In the comedies, which might be subdivided as dark (*Mildred Pierce, Galatea*) and light (*Career in C Major, Sinful Woman, Rainbow's End*), the protagonists are ultimately forgiven their sins and permitted to survive and perhaps prosper. Cain thought himself a funny man, and even his most doom-laden stories have sly moments that border on comic madness; yet his comedies, though often amusing, are invariably undermined by mawkish, disingenuous conclusions. Perhaps Cain couldn't bring himself to believe that there really was a way out.

In his most celebrated triumph, *The Postman Always Rings Twice,* the Cain mannerisms are sharpened to a steely glint. . . .

Time is of the essence in Cain's first-person narratives, particularly when the protagonist faces death. Non-Freudians all, these characters have no desire to explain or justify themselves, only to tell how they got trapped. Plot is fate, and Cain will not have his victims worrying about motivation at the expense of terse, honest, unemotional accounts that carry the warning: here but for fortune, reader, goes you. (p. 34)

Perhaps what's most terrifying about Cain's outcasts is their self-righteous certainty. Cainland is out of whack with any objective moral system, but it isn't sad—it's bleak and absurd, but not forlorn. Sometimes it's almost slapstick funny.

Career in C Major (1940) is an underrated comical variation on the opera world glimpsed in *Serenade,* in which singing is the sword in a wittily sadistic duel of the sexes, and is used to wound instead of kill. . . . Singing also plays a major part in *Mildred Pierce,* which Cain narrated from a woman's point of view. But though there are brilliant bits, the novel is a rather one-sided chess game in which the diabolical daughter, Veda, finds countless ways to make Mildred's life unbearable, until Cain brings it to an arbitrary, exhausted close by sending her out of town. . . .

In 1942, Cain published his dreadful gangster saga, *Love's Lovely Counterfeit,* a book that yellows and crinkles in the very presence of Dashiell Hammett's *Red Harvest*. . . . After a three-year silence, he produced a clever historical novel, *Past All Dishonor,* that made use of Virginia mining areas he knew from his boyhood.

Its successor, *The Butterfly,* recaptured the tremor and pace of Cain's early work and gave a new wrinkle to his Oedipal obsession. The maddeningly unpredictable mountain girl, Kady Tyler, who is salacious, innocent, loyal, or murderous from one page to the next, is bent on seducing her father. . . . *The Butterfly* is more poignant than its predecessors in that Jess resents his fate; his meticulous account (he's killed mid-sentence) is as much a justification as a confession. He knows he's in hell, but can't quite comprehend the events that brought him so low.

The Butterfly was Cain's last success, though five other novels quickly followed, including the three Avons, each of which was worked up from an earlier idea. *Sinful Woman,* a play he couldn't get produced, was altered into a funny poke at Hollywood. . . . Unfortunately, Cain undermines his own mischief with a cynical finish dumber than any B-movie he may have thought he was satirizing. . . .

Galatea (1953) is Cain's strangest story, an all but incomprehensible variation on *Postman,* in which the sentimental flashes of religion experienced by Frank and Cora assume righteous, protective fervor. (p. 35)

Cain was 61 when he wrote *Galatea,* and nine years passed before he brought out the historical drama, *Mignon* (1962), followed by *The Magician's Wife* (1965). Then, after another decade, he found the energy for two final testaments, *Rainbow's End* (1975) and *The Institute* (1976), of which the former is most characteristic. Like his early work, it was fueled by newspaper headlines, the D. B. Cooper skyjacking, but as a backdrop for another joust with unrequited incest. The skyjacker falls dead into the front yard of a Li'l Abner type who is forever kicking Mammy Yokum out of his bed. At long last, Cain wrote an authentic dirty-old-man novel, in which sorry attempts at humor are grounded in constant references to round fannies and heaving cleavage, but the moral purview of *Galatea* is extended: the money is a jinx on them that stole it, and a blessing from heaven for the goodhearted hero, his mom, and his Daisy Mae.

In chronicling an arc that begins in the blank acceptance of Depression hopelessness and ends with the kind of moral imperviousness that made Vietnam possible, Cain may be said to have kept a close watch on the pulse of America's steadily increasing conviction that God is on her side. But it didn't help his art. In *Galatea* and *Rainbow's End,* dreams come true and everyone lives happily after. Cain became an old optimist, flabby though still leering, willing to sacrifice the metallic glint that made his early work austere and vital. He said his favorite stories were Cinderella and Pandora, wicked analogies for an age that woke up from an opulent ball to discover broken pumpkin shells and mice. At his best, he applied those fearful stories to probe more than most of his contemporaries the dirty little secrets dreamed by a desperate America and he prepared them with tabloid gusto and pitiless irony. The Augustinian confessions enhanced his rhythmic velocity, and the avenging twists of fate tightened the grip of his web, but they are not the source of Cain's immediacy, nor do they suggest the nature of his originality. . . . Rather it's the blank menace in his tone, the naked vitality of his craftsmanship, the unblinking willingness to follow his scamps and lowlifes to a predestined edge that keeps him shuddery and compelling. The dirty little secrets haven't changed that much, the dreams are still terrifying. Even trash has its own dominion, where greasy Prousts are valued, and in that realm, no one squats more imposingly than James M. Cain. (pp. 35, 104)

Gary Giddins, "James M. Cain Rings Again" (reprinted by permission of The Village Voice and the author; copyright © News Group Publications, Inc., 1981), in The Village Voice, Vol. XXVI, No. 15, April 8-14, 1981, pp. 34-5, 104.

JOE FLAHERTY

There is nothing in ["**The Baby in the Icebox and Other Short Fiction**"] that will enhance Cain's reputation or seduce new readers. . . .

[The editor] tells us that one of Cain's themes is the doom of joint guilt: When two people engage in an evil act, they cannot share their terrible secret and live on the same earth—they turn on each other. But to me, the theme that purrs in the engine of Cain's best work . . . is the proposition that love is dangerous. For Cain, when the lower regions start to percolate, there is sure to be a burnout in the brain. Cain is not a man for meaningful relationships and marriage contracts; for him the libido levels logic every time. . . .

The pieces in the first part of this collection smack of cracker-barrel cuteness and mawkishness. Cain himself claimed that many of them were conscious imitations of Ring Lardner. But fidelity to regional language is not enough, without the writer's adding bottom, as did Twain and Faulkner. Without that substance Cain becomes indistinguishable from Titus Moody of Pepperidge Farm.

In this collection, the short stories and the magazine serial, "**The Embezzler,**" are interesting for the formative wisps we find in them of Cain's later themes and style. When he moves to California from the East, we hear the stirrings of the later polished Cain voice, and we can see Cain's facility for delivering more information in one good paragraph than most writers do in a chapter. Amazingly, these beautiful paragraphs are never cluttered. . . .

In "**The Embezzler**" there is some pure Cain, even though the polished Cain would have dismissed the ending as drivel. . . .

The most interesting thread running through many of these stories is Cain's obsession with hobos and drifters. This might not have led to the dazzling heights of "**Postman**" if Cain had remained on the East Coast; but in the California of the 30's and 40's, Frank Chambers and Cora, the Des Moines beauty-contest winner, could be viewed as integral parts of a landscape that used to beckon emotional drifters (and, for that matter, still does). Cain realized that California was the only place in America where one could jettison personal history without being questioned, since nearly everyone else was in on the same scam. . . .

This collection does offer some nuggets: early clues to style and substance, dialogue that breaks off in the teeth and descriptions as snappy as the brim of a fedora. But there is not enough.

Joe Flaherty, "Raising Cain," in The New York Times Book Review (copyright © 1981 by The New York Times Company; reprinted by permission), December 13, 1981, p. 12.

(Janet Miriam) Taylor (Holland) Caldwell
1900-

(Also wrote under pseudonyms of Max Reiner and Marcus Holland) English-born American novelist.

Since the publication of her first novel, *Dynasty of Death*, in 1938, Caldwell has written over thirty internationally best-selling romance novels. Many of her works are long, multi-generational sagas featuring immigrant protagonists who struggle for wealth and power. Caldwell has also written religious fiction, notably *Dear and Glorious Physician* (1959) and *I, Judas* (1977). These novels received favorable reviews for their attempt to demystify Saint Luke and Judas Iscariot. *Testimony of Two Men* (1968) and *Captains and the Kings* (1972) were serialized for television.

Critics generally agree that Caldwell's greatest strength as a novelist lies in her narrative ability. Her novels exhibit extensive historical research, thus providing a realistic sense of place. It is conceded, however, that much of her writing is formulaic, with stock characters and contrived plots. In addition, critics fault her didactic tendency. Still, Caldwell provides a "good read" and her enduring popularity ensures her a dominant place in the romance genre.

(See also *CLC*, Vol. 2; *Contemporary Authors*, Vol. 5-8, rev. ed.; and *Contemporary Authors New Revision Series*, Vol. 5.)

Courtesy of The Putnam Publishing Group

GEORGE DANGERFIELD

The armaments industry is a subject which fiction does well to take up; and Mrs. Caldwell's attack [in *Dynasty of Death*] is handled with the patience and skill of a prosecuting attorney. In order to establish her case she builds up a careful background, introducing a number of facts and side-issues which a defense attorney would probably characterize—and an impartial judge perhaps disallow—as irrelevant, incompetent, and all the rest of it. But when the whole picture is complete, you have to admit that she has been handling with considerable ability several interacting and at times rather refractory themes. . . .

One's chief criticism of this novel is that it pays the industry a compliment which, though backhanded and unconscious, is none the less a compliment. The author assumes that the industry requires, as its representative, something rather terrific in the way of a man. In all the pages, and they are 797, in which she deals with Ernest Barbour, she never quite reduces him to human stature. Ernest is a devil, the personification of a great industrial evil; and when a devil goes about the devil's work, something is missing. What we miss in this instance is the ultimate historical irony: on the one hand, the traffic in murder; on the other, a trafficker who is just as muddled and petty and able to compound with his conscience as the rest of us. Only a genius could in a novel of this sort create or maintain such an ironical contrast. Mrs. Caldwell has chosen the safer way; she provides her industry with a superman, surrounded by a lesser group of supermen and superwomen, all living on a plane just a little removed from our own.

Fiction, of course, cannot avoid super-reality, which it is its business to attain. But the plane upon which these people live is not one of super-reality, but of slight but consistent fantasy. We have to accept them, or the novel would collapse; and it is pleasant to record that they are not at all difficult to accept. They move easily in and out of the narrative, and are adequate to the narrative, though not to the author's intention. Had they been *that*, this would have been a great novel. As it is, few readers will, I think, deny that it is a thoroughly good one, soundly constructed and in a sound tradition.

> George Dangerfield, "Traffic in Murder," in The Saturday Review of Literature (© 1938, copyright renewed © 1965, Saturday Review Magazine Co.; reprinted by permission), Vol. XVIII, No. 21, September 17, 1938, p. 7.

HALFORD E. LUCCOCK

[In *Dynasty of Death* the] author avoids one ready pitfall of the long family-history novel, that of sacrificing everything to breadth and length. There is a stretch of a hundred years and a cast of actors running into many score. Yet there is intensity of interest, full detail and characterization at each period.

The most noticeable weakness of the novel is that the villains are too darkly and consistently villainous and the good people too obviously equipped with a halo. This is seen in the sharp black-and-white woodcut contrast between Ernest Barbour, the Napoleon of the firm, and his brother Martin, a sort of Pennsylvania St. Francis of Assisi. Ernest is a terribly integrated person—completely integrated about the dollar. He is relentless, cruel, endowed with satanic skill and all the other gifts and graces necessary to make a well rounded devil. His brother Martin gives his life in the effort to relieve the terrible slavery into which Ernest has plunged his workers. This gives an unreal effect, for real life is far more complex and perplexing. The typical munitions king or industrial grand duke is likely to be not an inhuman monster, but rather a person deserving of the classic tribute to a pirate, "as mild-mannered a man as ever scuttled a ship."

This is a novel of sustained interest, done with care and skill, notable for its picture of the unfolding industrial life of America, particularly of the steel industry. (p. 1338)

> Halford E. Luccock, "One of the Sixty Families," in The Christian Century (copyright 1938 Christian Century Foundation; reprinted by permission from the November 2, 1938 issue of The Christian Century), Vol. LV, No. 44, November 2, 1938, pp. 1337-38.

HAROLD STRAUSS

["**The Eagles Gather**"] continues the saga of the Bouchard family, the great armaments clan whose fortunes were first set forth in "**Dynasty of Death**." The Bouchards are ruthless, self-willed men, and their women are pawns of their overweening lust for power. One recalls how, in the earlier novel, the Bouchards together with the Barbours founded a small powder and arms factory in Pennsylvania in the middle of the last century. One recalls how they gradually outstripped and exterminated their competitors, how they created a gigantic munitions monopoly with interests extending into affiliated industries, and how these merchants of death learned to manipulate public opinion and to provoke wars when business was dull. . . .

Tradition is a powerful motor force in human behavior. When we first met the Bouchards they seemed shocking and unreal. It was difficult to accustom oneself to the irresponsible violence and unmotivated hatreds with which "**Dynasty of Death**" was peppered. But now violence and treachery have come to have the force of tradition in the Bouchard family, and one accepts their monstrous behavior with more credence. By that measure "**The Eagles Gather**" . . . emerges as a much stronger book than its predecessor. We might also add that its narrative has much more unity, and its drama is much more concentrated. "**Dynasty of Death**" spread out from 1837 to 1910, and its texture, for all its 400,000 words, seemed a little thin. The new novel lavishes a quarter of a million words on the period from 1917 to 1929. There is a difference in pace that produces a marked improvement in effectiveness. . . .

No review can suggest all the ramifications of the plot. The net of intrigue spreads into Wall Street and into the capitals of Europe and South America. To Taylor Caldwell the Bouchards are the font of all the evil in the world, the fomenters of war, the financiers of fascism, the catalysts of depressions, the oppressors of labor and the masters of public opinion in all lands. As primitive tribes place all unaccountable natural phenomena upon the doorstep of an anthropomorphic god, so Taylor Caldwell traces all perilous social phenomena to the Bouchards. She is unable to go beyond the Bouchards, to see what makes them behave as they do. But throughout history mankind has been expert at passing the buck to the devil, so that perhaps we must allow Taylor Caldwell her political naïveté. It is a little more difficult to overlook her careless writing, which admits not only stylistic blunders but also factual inconsistencies. . . . Nevertheless, in spite of these deficiencies, "**The Eagles Gather**" is an undeniably powerful novel. The pace is swift, and dramatic scene follows upon dramatic scene.

> Harold Strauss, "'The Eagles Gather' and Other New Works of Fiction," in The New York Times Book Review (©1939 by The New York Times Company; reprinted by permission), December 31, 1939, p. 7.

CLIFTON FADIMAN

Taylor Caldwell's "**Dynasty of Death**" succeeded in making munitions manufacturers seem considerably more dramatic than they probably are in actuality. "**The Eagles Gather**," a sequel, is more of the same, only not as good. For one thing, perhaps Taylor Caldwell can keep her Bouchards clear and separate, but there are just too many of them for this simple mind. After a while you lose count, and after you lose count you lose interest. As a matter of fact, I think I lost interest before I lost count, because the characterization in "**The Eagles Gather**" is so definitely melodramatic that it makes the whole long, crowded, and painstaking narrative a bit unconvincing. Also, while I'm perfectly willing to credit anything evil I read about munitions people, I cannot believe that they alone manipulate history, start and stop wars, plan in advance what we shall think, etc. They're powerful, no doubt, but they're not gods. The view of current history on which "**The Eagles Gather**" is based seems to me rather too simplified.

Those who like complicated family chronicles with a raft of sinister villains will, I think, take to Taylor Caldwell's latest installment of Bouchards. My own feeling is that her message could have been projected in half the length and with half the characters. The book would have been about twice as effective, too. (pp. 52-3)

> Clifton Fadiman, "Three Novels" (copyright © 1940 by The New Yorker Magazine, Inc.; copyright renewed © 1969 by The New Yorker Magazine, Inc.; reprinted by permission of Lescher & Lescher, Ltd., as literary agents for the author), in The New Yorker, Vol. XV, No. 47, January 6, 1940, pp. 52-3.*

RICHARD A. CORDELL

["**Dynasty of Death**" and its recently-published sequel, "**The Eagles Gather**,"] have the same theme—the titanic struggle between ruthlessness, greed, opportunism, selfishness, and dishonesty on the one side (the munitions barons blandly lump together all such practices as "realism"), and altruism, justice, love, and self-sacrifice on the other side. The victor in this internecine war is not announced, for the war is still raging—perhaps more fiercely today than ever before.

"**The Eagles Gather**" is a depressing, almost terrifying book. It hurls formidable charges against the powers of evil that shape our personal and national destinies, and although the book is fiction, its insinuations and implications are disturbing and sometimes alarming. . . .

Under the impact of these allegations we find difficulty in responding always to the deep human demands of the story, but human interest is here. For these men of greed, these "realists," do not hesitate to sacrifice friends, brothers, children, and parents in their ruthless battle for power. The various narratives of the novel deal with death-struggles between Machiavellism and human decency. Although the author is not an absolute cynic, she is no facile optimist, and to resolve these conflicts she does not conjure up the comfortable old saw that right makes might.

One fault of the novel, less annoying than in **"Dynasty of Death,"** is the confusing legion of characters. . . . The author does not exercise her artist's privilege to select, but presents to us in detail, often amusing, the whole clan. Possibly, too, the novel is weakened by a glut of guile and hate. Nearly everyone loathes and despises nearly all the other members of the family—brothers hate brothers, parents and children abominate one another—there is hardly a page which does not contain "hate" or "detest" or "nauseate" or "despise" or some such ill-tempered verb. Everything considered, **"The Eagles Gather"** is a full-blooded book, provocative and haunting.

> *Richard A. Cordell, "War of the Vultures," in* The Saturday Review of Literature *(© 1940, copyright renewed © 1967, Saturday Review Magazine Co.; reprinted by permission), Vol. XXI, No. 11, January 6, 1940, p. 5.*

CLIFTON FADIMAN

Taylor Caldwell's **"The Earth Is the Lord's"** . . . reminds one less of a novel than it does of a particularly grandiloquent opera. All the characters talk in a kind of recitative, the psychology is always grand to the point of inflation, and all the action seems to be accompanied by full orchestra, with percussion instruments dominating. The net effect, too, is operatic, for you feel that while all this blood and thunder verges on the silly, it never really *is* silly but, on the contrary, is perversely, if only momentarily, fascinating.

Those who remember Taylor Caldwell's munitions melodramas, **"Dynasty of Death"** and **"The Eagles Gather"**—her taste in titles runs to the garish—will recall her penchant for the colossally evil, for the *tyrannosaurs* of the human species. In Temujin she has an unbeatable subject, for this Mongol barbarian, born with a clot of dried blood in his tiny hand, was a perfect beyond-good-and-evil type—in other and less romantic words, a conscienceless killer whose extraordinary abilities enabled him to commit his murders wholesale. Such types bob up every few centuries, and it is damning evidence of human stupidity that we do not recognize them until it is too late.

Taylor Caldwell's story carries Temujin to only one of the summits of his career. When her book ends, he is ready to begin his conquest of southern and central China but has not yet done so. Her main interest lies in Temujin's relations with his wife, his mother, his beloved mistress, and his brothers, as well as in the manner by which he forcibly confederated the Mongol tribes of the steppes and began to elaborate his vision of a universal slave empire. Now, for all I know, the author's melodramatic reconstruction of the character of Temujin may be accurate, or it may be a smooth piece of fakery. There's no way of telling, Mongol memoirs not being very numerous. All you can say with any certainty is that she has fashioned a vigorous yarn, full of seductions, assassinations, lurid visions, tortures, mass murders, battles, ambushes, and high-flown speeches.

From this you derive considerable entertainment of a high-grade penny-dreadful variety. Of the historical significance of Temujin you learn precisely nothing. . . .

If you say that the author is writing fiction, not history, I can only reply that to my mind she is not even writing fiction but, rather, that what she is producing is non-musical opera. And, of its sort, pretty good. (p. 58)

> *Clifton Fadiman, "Temujin—Richard Aldington" (copyright © 1941 by The New Yorker Magazine, Inc.; copyright renewed © 1969 by The New Yorker Magazine, Inc.; reprinted by permission of Lescher & Lescher, Ltd., as literary agents for the author), in* The New Yorker, *Vol. XVI, No. 48, January 11, 1941, pp. 58, 60.**

LOUISE MAUNSELL FIELD

For the background of her new novel, **"The Strong City,"** Taylor Caldwell has chosen the town of "Nazareth," Pa., and the steel industry as it was during the latter years of the past century. That was the time when men worked twelve hours a day six days a week, when unions were struggling for existence and many employers regarded the "Knights of Labor" with considerable disfavor and even more suspicion. Immigrants were then swarming into the United States, and it is from among these immigrants and their immediate descendants that the author has chosen most of her characters. First in importance is Franz Stoessel, a foreman in the Schmidt Mills when the novel begins. . . .

The first part of the book is by all odds the most interesting. The account of the great steel mills and of the men who worked there, men from all countries with "sullen and desperate faces," whom Franz drove mercilessly, hating them "with a purity of hatred undisturbed by considerations of family or fear of hunger," has real vitality. This first part is largely dominated by the young Englishman, Tom Harrow, who was "ignorant and clever, philosophical and vulgar," trying to organize a union, "boiling with an infuriated sense of outrage and injustice" done, not to him, but to all his fellow-workers, something Franz was utterly unable to understand. Tom's speech to the workers at the labor meeting, Jan's denunciation of Franz at Tom's funeral are the most dramatic moments in the book. Next to Tom in interest come Emmi, the disappointed idealist, and Hans Schmidt, the gross peasant who by some unexplained means had succeeded in marrying Frances Bradhurst, an "American aristocrat" he loathed because she was timid and weak and sickly, and had borne him a crippled son, but whimpered and sobbed over after she was dead. The novel is extremely wordy and could have been much improved by drastic cutting and editing. It is over-written, the author analyzing and reanalyzing her characters interminably, while the tacit duel between Franz and Baldur has become tedious long before it ends. Yet the book has power; the opening part is very interesting, and the picture of the steel industry as it once was is worth careful consideration, especially at the present time.

> *Louise Maunsell Field, in her review of "The Steel Makers," in* The New York Times Book Review *(© 1942 by The New York Times Company; reprinted by permission), April 12, 1942, p. 16.*

HERBERT GORMAN

While **"The Arm and the Darkness"** by Taylor Caldwell is primarily a long narrative of the physical and spiritual struggles of a young nobleman during the conflicts between the Catholic reaction and the Huguenots in France in the time of Louis XIII and Cardinal Richelieu, it is also an adumbration of the emergence of the Common Man into history and his opening battles for liberty, enlightenment and justice. The real villain of this novel is the corrupt hierarchy of the Roman Catholic Church and the real hero is that urge toward liberation that expressed itself in the Huguenot movement. Of course, the line between good and evil is not drawn quite so definitely as that, for Miss Caldwell makes it plain that there were good Catholics and corrupt Huguenots; but, all the same, the protagonists are reaction and progress and their other names were Rome and Luther. To express all this Miss Caldwell has created Arsène de Richepane, at first a devil-may-care young swashbuckler and then a brooding and disillusioned man. (p. 6)

She has employed every ingredient that Alexander Dumas *père* ever used but with a difference. Here are the clash of swords, racing horses on night roads, hunted men pursued through dark alleys, conspirators in closed cabinets, rendezvous and passionate meetings, burning chateaux, enraged mobs, battle and siege, haughty noblemen and jackal sycophants, terrifying priests and gentle old abbés, duels, revenge and love and death. Here, too, out of history are Richelieu, Father Joseph, Louis XIII, Anne of Austria, de Bouillon, Rohan, Guiton and Gaston d'Orléans. And not out of history we have the two de Richepane brothers and their father, Cecile and Francois Grandjean, de Vitry and his false Antoinette and a dozen others. It is a vast bubbling mixture but it is stirred by a capable hand. The difference is in the unifying idea. The action is not for the action alone, as in so much of Dumas, but rather to emphasize the spiritual struggle of man, his better self fighting his worse self in an area when all the powers of reaction, repression and mental and physical tyranny seemed invincible. (pp. 6, 12)

History, on the whole, is well handled in the novel although there appears to be some telescoping in the chapters concerned with the siege of La Rochelle. Richelieu and the King were at the siege long before the assassination of the Duke of Buckingham and Denbigh's British fleet made its weak and fleeting approach and retreat off the beleaguered town before that tragedy. But these are minor matters. Miss Caldwell was writing fiction and not history and her sense and presentation of the complex period with all its color and violence are admirable and convincing. Her concern with the deeper spiritual and philosophical implications of the period, too, raises the novel from a mere cloak-and-sword romance to the plane of the novel of ideas. One may read for pleasure (for a world of action is here) and one may read to think as well. **"The Arm and the Darkness"** is in the best tradition and somewhat more than that. (p. 12)

> Herbert Gorman, "The France of Richelieu," in The New York Times Book Review (© 1943 by The New York Times Company; reprinted by permission), March 14, 1943, pp. 6, 12.

THE TIMES LITERARY SUPPLEMENT

Miss Taylor Caldwell casts her net wide in search of themes and periods for the sort of elaborate fiction she favours.... Nobody need or should despise the amount of work which has gone into the quarter of a million words or so of [**"The Arm and the Darkness"**]. Regretfully, however, one cannot but wish it had a little more life, a little real substance or individuality. Here, it must be confessed, is rather too much of the stale perfume of historical romance, too much of the faded tinsel, altogether too much of the conventional rhetoric.... Miss Caldwell, though extreme facility has always been her failing, has written better books than this....

The tale, and with it the personality of Richelieu, is much overwritten. Miss Caldwell presents a line of seventeenth-century Protestant criticism that in point of fact is very much out of its time, and she does not hesitate to round off a generally improbable fiction with a similarly post-dated greeting to the American future.

> A review of "The Arm and the Darkness," in The Times Literary Supplement (© Times Newspapers Ltd. (London) 1943; reproduced from The Times Literary Supplement by permission), No. 2179, November 6, 1943, p. 533.

NONA BALAKIAN

[In] **"The Wide House"** Miss Caldwell has begun to question her formula. She has discovered that "a man might find some kindliness * * * in men who were avowedly rascals * * * and find nothing but mercilessness * * * in those who had the approval of God." But though she has given the matter some thought, her old habits persist.

When the curtain rises on the buzzing young town of Grandeville, N.Y., in the Eighteen Fifties, we meet in Stuart Coleman the robust, full-blooded hero of costume drama. A rebellious Irishman with a weakness for women, he deviates from type in his passionate love for a house. Though only a small shopkeeper, he has built himself a great white castle that stands in marked contrast to the ugly dark buildings around him. For a reason which we learn much later, "he would fight to death for it * * *. In an odd way it had so completed him that he felt no need for any woman to share it with him." But when his rich, widowed cousin, the cruel and ugly Janie Cauder, arrives with her four children, Stuart wastes no time in making her his mistress and in gaining control of her wealth to marry the daughter of his worst enemy.

But if you think you know Stuart by now, you underrate Miss Caldwell. You haven't yet watched him grow misty-eyed over Janie's pathetic, maltreated children; you haven't heard him plan with his wise old friend, Sam, to establish a refuge on River Island for the persecuted Jews of Europe; nor heard him philosophizing over a weekly game of poker with a doughty, Barry Fitzgerald type of priest, who never forgets to remind Stuart that he's a "good man" though an "eternal child." In the end this adventurer, who admits he was always "afraid of life," becomes a public-spirited figure, building schools and convents.

This is not to imply that **"The Wide House"** is unreadable. Like the late Elizabethan, Mrs. Caldwell holds her audience by the sheer power to mystify. She loads her sentences with explosive words (at the least provocation her characters writhe, curse, foam, shriek, pant). She adds flavor and probability to her incidents by giving them a superficial historical setting and interspersing her novel with lofty passages (like the ones here on racial prejudice) which have the ring of contemporary truths. There's no denying that these are good tricks which should fool some of the people some of the time.

> Nona Balakian, "Standard Melodrama," in The New York Times Book Review (© 1945 by The New York

Times Company; reprinted by permission), April 8, 1945, p. 6.

RICHARD A. CORDELL

Taylor Caldwell's long, turbulent narratives—one appears every year with the regularity of the almanac or year-book—are very much alike. From **"Dynasty of Death"** (1938) down to [her new novel **"This Side of Innocence"**] the ingredients vary only slightly; a family or two of wealth and power, most of their members despising one another and engaging in callous and unscrupulous business enterprise; intra-family love duels; intimate details of high finance and industrial backgrounds; meticulous attention to *Godey's Lady's Book* and other sources of information for details of costumes and interior decoration in the Gilded Age. The prolific Buffalo novelist puzzles the discriminating reader of fiction: the books are too long and cry out for the blue pencil, particularly the obvious comments on situations that speak for themselves; the dialogue is often stilted and prolix, but perhaps no more unrealistic than Hemingway's, which is stilted and too bare; and in spite of outbursts of melodrama and frequent nebulous characterization, she nearly always avoids sentimentality and downright banality. These energetic, surging stories proceed with a poise and stateliness which, many believe, the author could elevate into a sort of grandeur if she cared to do so. The novels sometimes have a power and magnitude out of all proportion to their content. . . .

Faithful readers of Taylor Caldwell—and they are legion—will be grateful that [in **"This Side of Innocence"**] she has only a modest cast of characters, and not the bewildering regiments of Bouchards who march through the pages of the horrifying trilogy of the munitions family. This novel gains in intensity by the simplification and also from the skilful, Ibsenish manner in which the characters work out their destinies without resort to outside aid or deus ex machina.

Richard A. Cordell, "Mrs. Caldwell's Latest Annual," in The Saturday Review of Literature (© 1946 Saturday Review Magazine Co.), Vol. XXIX, No. 19, May 11, 1946, p. 36.

MARY McGRORY

Will **"There Was a Time"** cause a rift between Taylor Caldwell and her everloving public? Will that public . . . mind that she has slapped their wrists in this semi-autobiographical novel about a young writer who forsakes thunderous chronicles of villainous financiers to write from his heart? The answer to these questions must be a resounding no. . . .

Miss Caldwell's desertion of the titans who stomp through her previous output has in no wise affected her approach or her prose—which still throbs with passion, sags with adjectives and overflows into royal-purple rapture. As of old, her characters, wading ankle-deep in malevolence, are locked in unequal contest with compound, overpowering emotions. To be sure, sex has taken a holiday here: her Frank Clair, although shamefully cavalier with his muse, is faithful in his fashion to the girl who took his beauty-starved heart when he was a lad. But anyone who thinks that the literary life is without melodrama need only be referred to the scene in which Frank's stifled human compassion breathes again at the sight of a prostitute nursing her fatherless babe. . . .

[The] book really began for this reader when Frank is finally established at his typewriter—battling nausea to produce the bon-bon romances editors wanted at the height of the depression, and working exultantly at his first *real* novel on the side. These passages are rich with scorn. Miss Caldwell divides her vitriol equally between a public which demands raw melodrama—and critics who are "annoyed and disconcerted by heroic and ruthless writing, by reality." She seems to be of two minds here, torn between renouncing her works and defending them. Even in books you can't have your cake and eat it, too.

Being the novel she evidently yearned to write all the while she was turning out those other enormously popular opera, **"There Was a Time"** will doubtless rank as the author's favorite. . . . Unreconstructed reviewers may mulishly decide that Miss Caldwell has proved to be the exception to the rule about writing what one knows best. **"There Was a Time"** comes no closer than her other books to literature or to life. With her astonishing powers of invention she would perhaps do best to leave the soul-searching to others.

Mary McGrory, "The Pin-Up Girl of the Lending Libraries," in The New York Times Book Review (© 1947 by The New York Times Company; reprinted by permission), May 11, 1947, p. 20.

WILLIAM SOSKIN

Taylor Caldwell realizes full well the limitations and stupidities of her Melissa [the heroine of Caldwell's **"Melissa"**], daughter of a philosophic writer who has deliberately made a mess of her out of his villainous desire to dominate her and make her subject to his psychologically poisonous whims. But the author never intended that we should become painfully bored and irritated with the beautiful creature; and that miscarriage of Taylor Caldwell's purpose must be attributed to the apparent hurry, the lack of careful organization, the adjectival and prolifically adverbial style in which the novel is written. The author of **"Dynasty of Death"** and other best sellers seems to be writing too fast and too much. Even those who have regarded her strong, often lusty stories as good examples of intelligent, popular drama will be disturbed at her present work.

This novel of a passionately idealistic and fanatically narrow-minded girl who is married to an urbane, broad-minded publisher in the post-Civil-War period, is written in Taylor Caldwell's deepest purple. On almost any page the heroine palpitates, shivers, trembles, chokes, aches, weeps, denunciates, lies rigid and cold in her hard bed, clenches every muscle, wrings her handkerchief, has to clutch at furniture to keep from falling in a faint, feels her breast rising and falling with anguish and outrage, her body shaking with denial and horror and with fear.

Heroines of the ten-twenty-thirty theatre of the 1880's used to behave in this violent manner. Our Melissa has something more in common with those lurid ladies of the stage: she is sinned against and plotted against in a disgraceful manner. Her father ruined her spirit and destroyed her mind in his scheme to make her his creature. Her sister Phoebe plotted against her and helped to disrupt her marriage. Her husband's sister shamed her, betrayed her, made it appear she was unfaithful to her husband, humiliated her before his rich and fashionable friends. . . .

Occasionally Taylor Caldwell takes a flyer in philosophic or social criticism to indicate that she is quite well aware of values beyond the melodramatic. Thus when the gentlemanly publisher has finally weaned Melissa away from her fanaticism and her terrifying innocence, he tells her that she must discard any fixed notions about the world, any idea that its values are immutable. An intelligent human being, he tells his Melissa, passes constantly from old worlds to new, and mind, no less than external nature, is always in flux.

This is a large and dynamic theme. It seems a pity that Taylor Caldwell has derived so trifling a novel from it.

> William Soskin, "Terrifying Innocence," in The Saturday Review of Literature (© 1948, copyright renewed © 1976, Saturday Review Magazine Co.; reprinted by permission), Vol. XXXI, No. 27, July 3, 1948, p. 15.

CHARLES LEE

What will America be like in 1970? Miss Caldwell's [apocalyptic **"The Devil's Advocate"**] makes Spengler seem cheerful by comparison. In this novel of fierce prophecy she sees a Communist conspiracy in control in Washington. The courts and the Constitution have been outlawed; family life is directed by the Government; the fifth world war is about to erupt (this one against South America, the rest of the world being subject and in ruins). Tipping her political hand, she offers as her trump of horrors the fact that the Republican party has been banned as of 1958....

[The story] that follows is full of nightmare complexities and melodramatic suspense. Unfortunately, it is also full of repetitions, distortions, contradictions, and downright offenses to common sense. For example, we are told that in the monstrous third and fourth world wars only the United States used atomic weapons—and was itself untouched by a single bomb.

Worse still, however, is the author's hysterical antipathy for the New Deal. Instead of the great depression, we are offered America of 1932 as a country that lived by a code of honor, freedom, individualism, dignity, and self-responsibility. Then "the misguided people elected a man to the Presidency whose twisted mind stands out against the black background of history like a conflagration." Arguments can assuredly be mounted against Welfareism, and Miss Caldwell's legerdemain as queen of the lending library is well-known. But this time she has simply outpunched herself. The fury of her interpretations of history vitiates whatever merit certain of her criticisms may contain—and gives to the shrill story illustrating them all the weight of a comic-strip.

> Charles Lee, "Minute Men of 1970," in The New York Times Book Review (© 1952 by The New York Times Company; reprinted by permission), May 4, 1952, p. 24.

RILEY HUGHES

Up to now Miss Caldwell has been in the habit of simplifying the past, of building her plot and bullying her characters around one idea.... In *The Devil's Advocate* she presents a simplification of recent past and proximate future both. Her scene is the slave America of the 1970's, the seeds of whose destruction were sown in the 1930's.

America's downward slide into a Communist state "had begun with a loathsome use of the word 'security.' And in the name of that fantasy, that dream-filled myth, American pride, responsibility, grandeur and strength, had been systematically murdered." ... Thus by 1970 the Republic had become "The Democracy," and the President was the captive of The Military and The Farmers, and the people were everywhere in chains.

Miss Caldwell's own fantasy concerns a "Minute Man" named Durant, a Catholic (who goes to confession before a dangerous "subversive" mission which requires much butchery on his part), who takes the name of Major Curtiss to be *gauleiter* of the Philadelphia area. Ostensibly a loyal servant of "The Democracy," Durant-Curtiss has the secret mission of goading the people to rebellion by his outrageous cruelty. The cops and robbers stuff Miss Caldwell handles with exemplary skill, but the rest is unfunny, and quite dangerous, nonsense. (pp. 313-14)

> Riley Hughes, in his review of "The Devil's Advocate," in Catholic World (copyright 1952 by The Missionary Society of St. Paul the Apostle in the State of New York; used by permission), Vol. CLXXV, No. 1048, July, 1952, pp. 313-14.

GRANVILLE HICKS

If critics took the author of **"Never Victorious, Never Defeated"** as seriously as she takes herself, articles would have long since appeared on "The World of Taylor Caldwell." Fourteen of the sixteen novels she has published in less than two decades portray important aspects of American life in the period from the middle of the nineteenth century to the present time, most of them concerned with families of great wealth and power. Three of the novels, beginning with **"Dynasty of Death,"** have to do with the Barbour-Bouchard family and the manufacture of munitions. In other novels she has done steel, textiles and lumber, and now she has turned to railroading....

If someone were to repeat to Miss Caldwell Scott Fitzgerald's famous statement that the very rich are different from the rest of us, she would doubtless reply, "Yes, they are more interesting." And there are millions of readers who obviously agree with her. What she thinks about the wealthy is not easy to say, for her opinions, never perfectly clear, have shifted more than once since she began writing. But she has always been fascinated by the way they get their money and the way they spend it. There are more of the very rich in her novels than in Fitzgerald's or Dreiser's or Dos Passos' or even Upton Sinclair's.

Of the four authors mentioned, Upton Sinclair is the one with whom Miss Caldwell has most in common. Both are belated Victorians, addicted to a full canvas, with bold outlines, high color and massive details. In one of Miss Caldwell's novels a publisher speaks of "passion, single-mindedness, colorfulness, gift of storytelling and sincerity" as the great gifts for a successful writer. She has the gift of storytelling.

Her characters, who are constantly involved in sensational intrigues and stormy struggles for power, are sharply defined, and she is explicit about them: they are good or they are bad, and if, as does happen, they are something of both, she gives the reader fair warning. They speak as no human being ever spoke, but their way of talking befits her conception of them. They live in her world, and if you can admit the existence of that world, you can admit their existence too.

It may be objected that, even if she and Upton Sinclair are alike in their methods of writing fiction, he is a novelist with a message, whereas she is simply a manufacturer of popular fiction; but this is not fair to Miss Caldwell. She must be given credit for passion, single-mindedness and sincerity. Not only is the kind of novel she writes the kind of novel she admires; she preaches the lesson that seems to her at the moment to be needed.

Currently Miss Caldwell is warning against a world-wide conspiracy of frustrated intellectuals, who are seeking to subordinate the individual to the state. One may doubt whether she has accurately diagnosed the evils of our time. But one cannot doubt that she believes whatever she happens to be saying.

> Granville Hicks, "With a Zest for the Rich and Mighty," in The New York Times Book Review (© 1954 by The New York Times Company; reprinted by permission), May 2, 1954, p. 5.

HARRISON SMITH

[Taylor Caldwell] has pursued through sixteen novels almost every aspect of the rise of those multi-millionaire families in the United States Theodore Roosevelt called malefactors of great wealth. The fact that her great-uncle once owned all of the railroads in Scotland and that her grandmother was half Irish has had a great deal to do with the subject of her newest book, **"Never Victorious, Never Defeated."** This long and absorbing novel is by no means a pursuit of a wornout vein; the author has discovered a new gold mine in the intramural conflicts of four generations of a prolific family of Pennsylvania railroad builders fighting to extend their lines north and west. It is a complex story involving more than twenty principal characters, as well as striking theories on immigration, labor unions, socialism, and war. . . .

In the background of this tumultuous railroad novel there is the history of eighty years of conflict, change, and war through which the author's beliefs constantly come to the surface. "All men are instinctively tyrannous and dangerous," she writes. "The impoverishment of men and the earth in the act of preparing for war will lead to the slow erosion of our liberties. . . . Idealists have a secret contempt for the self-made men while they prate of the majesty of labor and the nobility of toil. . . . Who ever trusted another man?"

For 550 pages Taylor Caldwell succeeds in the astonishing feat of maintaining the reader's interest in the creation of a great railroad, the changing history of America from the Civil War through the Roosevelt administration, the political and economic philosophy of the time, and an intense and colorful account of the fortunes and the emotional and financial crises of the relatives, descendants, and friends of the family of Aaron DeWitt of Portersville, Pa. It is a feat which few writers could, or would attempt to accomplish today.

> Harrison Smith, "Pittsburgh Epic," in The Saturday Review, New York (© 1954 Saturday Review Magazine Co.), Vol. XXXVII, No. 23, June 5, 1954, p. 32.

JANE COBB

It is impossible to read anything of Taylor Caldwell's without being reminded of the old gag, "He don't sing good, but he sings loud." Miss Caldwell doesn't write well, to be sure—but her books are infused with a sort of wild, anything-goes vitality which can hardly be ascribed to Henry James. Not that **"The Sound of Thunder"** is a good book. It isn't. But Miss Caldwell has managed to stay sufficiently within the bounds of educated standards to make the reader feel rewarded for panting after her as she free-wheels through this long, complicated chronicle.

The central character is Edward Enger, a hard worker who was sent to help in his father's delicatessen at 14 so that his three brothers and one sister—the geniuses—could become, respectively, a pianist, a painter, a writer and a theatrical producer. That, at least, was his mother's idea, but it didn't quite work out. Eddie, we discover, is something of a genius himself. He works day and night, makes a fabulous amount of money and asks nothing of his family except that they turn out to be geniuses, as advertised.

Inevitably, they aren't geniuses at all. (pp. 48-9)

One of the chief assets of the book is Miss Caldwell's account of Eddie's career in the delicatessen business and her ability to make it fascinating. It is easy to believe that her documentation here is accurate. When she gets into the field of world politics, she is somewhat less than reliable. She is also a bit tedious when she gets on the theme "the power to tax is the power to destroy," as she does at fairly regular intervals. Understandably, Miss Caldwell is even crosser with the Bureau of Internal Revenue than most of us.

As noted, **"The Sound of Thunder"** is not, in any academic sense of the word, a successful novel. But it has pace, drama—and more characters than a suburban phone book. Readers who enjoy stories of this kind will get their money's worth. (p. 49)

> Jane Cobb, "The Man behind the Geniuses," in The New York Times Book Review (© 1957 by The New York Times Company; reprinted by permission), October 27, 1957, pp. 48-9.

VIRGINIA KIRKUS' SERVICE

In choosing to put emphasis on the early life of Luke the physician, Taylor Caldwell has presented [in **Dear and Glorious Physician**] quite a different picture from that Frank Slaughter has given in The Road to Bithynia. . . . It is—she tells her readers—a subject on which she has worked most of her life. The result shows an immense amount of research, a dedication to her subject. Luke emerges as a whole man—and most readers will find the biographical aspects of her story—up to the time when she gears it into the Gospel record—far more moving and convincing than the final chapters, when Luke approaches what has been, at times unwittingly, his life goal, an identification with the "unknown god" of his youth. It makes an extraordinarily authentic picture of the Greek and Roman world, with the scene shifting from Alexandria to Rome to other parts of the Roman Empire; peopled by individuals who made up that world, in their relation to each other, the conquerors and the conquered, the victims and the slaves, the masters, the rulers. . . . It is a wonderful story, drawn from many sources, most of them apocryphal, and it builds up to the crucifixion—at second hand—the coming to the land of Israel—the weaving into his Gospel the story told by many, and finally the culmination in the meeting with Mary.

> A review of "Dear and Glorious Physician," in Virginia Kirkus' Service, Vol. XXVII, No. 1, January 1, 1959, p. 17.

CAROLINE TUNSTALL

St. Luke, author of the third Gospel and of the Acts, was with St. Paul in Rome and is referred to by him as "the beloved physician." According to tradition he was a gentile Greek. The shadowy figure evoked by these few phrases bursts forth technicolored and Toddeoscale in Taylor Caldwell's ["**Dear and Glorious Physician**"]....

Aside from any religious conviction, the scholar will deplore the book's heavy-handed reproduction of the period, while any lover of English will cringe at its lush overwriting. The depiction of Luke, Mary and Jesus as Nordic blondes has all the dignity and restraint of a theater poster. No doubt **"Dear and Glorious Physician"** will be a best-seller and will be bought by Hollywood for an "epic" production at an epic price.

> Caroline Tunstall, "Taylor Caldwell's St. Luke," in New York Herald Tribune Book Review (© I.H.T. Corporation; reprinted by permission), March 15, 1959, p. 14.

CHARLES LEE

Spacious, alive with the bustle of ancient times and places, and illumined by flashes of genuine lyrical intensity, **"Dear and Glorious Physician"** is the product of an obsession that has challenged Miss Caldwell's talents for more than forty years....

Armed both with insight and erudition, she movingly reconstructs St. Luke's search for God, universalizing his anguish for troubled men everywhere. With her we live his childhood, meet his family and friends, participate in his extraordinary education, admire his Apollonian beauty and his athletic prowess. We discover the amazing world of ancient medicine; we see him suffer evil and loss, and then, in torments of rage and pity, arrive at an affirmation of faith. In Miss Caldwell's resurrective prose St. Luke lives in his journeys both inward and outward; he lives as physician, son, wanderer, lover—and as a maker of miracles, all of them palpitatingly described. Finally, and this is the author's ultimate purpose, he lives as a tower of spiritual strength.

Miss Caldwell's novel hums with the activities of the older world.... The one serious complaint that many readers are likely to make is that the author's political observations are too strident, too frequent and too loaded with contemporary implications. But none can deny that she has written with unusual passion and success.

> Charles Lee, "Inspired Apostle," in The New York Times Book Review (© 1959 by The New York Times Company; reprinted by permission), March 15, 1959, p. 34.

RILEY HUGHES

On page 572 (the final page) [of *Dear and Glorious Physician*] Miss Caldwell adds this sentence (in parentheses) after her own final sentence of the novel: "Continued in the Holy Bible, Gospel of St. Luke, and Acts I and II." There is something awesome in assurance like that, something that defies comment. Lucanus (St. Luke) is a very pedestrian fellow who finally comes to some faint understanding of God.

Lucanus strikes this reader, at least, as a rather dimwitted figure, unable to account for his miraculous powers of healing and, even in his attraction to the new religion, a man who acts remarkably like a twentieth-century agnostic. If Christianity is Pickwickian and shadowy in *Dear and Glorious Physician,* the decadent, pagan Roman world is not. What with licentiousness and "the disturbing mysticism of the Jews," poor Lucanus has, over these interminable pages, an unhappy career of it. As for his career as evangelist, Miss Caldwell, voluble on all else, remains staunchly mum.

> Riley Hughes, in his review of "Dear and Glorious Physician," in Catholic World (copyright 1959 by The Missionary Society of St. Paul the Apostle in the State of New York; used by permission), Vol. 189, No. 1133, August, 1959, p. 402.

CHARLES LEE

Taylor Caldwell is an angry woman. She tells us so in a candid foreword to her curious new novel [**"The Listener"**]. Man does not need a new religion, she says. He does not require better bombs and missiles. He does not have to travel to the moon. What he really needs is someone to listen to his hurts and bewilderments. Of course, that Someone is the not very mysterious "Listener" of her book.

The role of **"The Listener"** is dramatized in fifteen chapters that successively feature troubled "Souls," each numbered and tagged, as, for example, Soul One, The Confessed; Soul Two, the Underprivileged; Soul Three, The Despised and Rejected. A troubled Soul repairs to a two-room marble sanctuary that is open to the public. Once there, the Soul begins to talk. In every instance, the supplicants receive unspoken guidance or undergo sudden conversions that produce admirably ethical solutions to their problems.

The fact that no one is ever interrupted in his soliloquy suggests that few actually make use of the sanctuary—though it is conveniently located in the heart of a big city. It is also, even more conveniently, located in the heart of the individual Soul. Since Souls are always made better for the expedience of the sanctuary, Miss Caldwell has a right to be angry. It is a righteous anger that has been shared down the centuries.

Using her fifteen chapters as a platform and her wide assortment of Souls as mouthpieces, the author attacks a hundred vulgarizations of our spiritual sterility, our assembly-line populace, our intellectual sloth—in short, our collectivized cretinism.

Few will quarrel with the main thesis of this book or its motivations. Nevertheless, many will find **"The Listener"** a tediously contrived series of over-didacticized testimonies lacking tension and persuasion.... One cannot help wondering why she did not listen to her own foreword and write polemically to the point, with fist instead of fancy.

> Charles Lee, "Unspoken Guidance," in The New York Times Book Review (© 1960 by The New York Times Company; reprinted by permission), October 9, 1960, p. 56.

RILEY HUGHES

The Listener is not exactly a novel; it is rather a series of related episodes or tales held together by a slender string of place. The protagonists of these episodes come to a sanctuary built through the aid of a bequest left by the lawyer John Godfrey. Some are scoffing and defiant; others are hurt and humble; all are seeking peace. Some push the button which opens the curtains to reveal "The Man Who Listens" patiently. Others tell their story without caring to learn the identity of the man. Gradually, as one episode succeeds another, it is implied from the guarded language used that (in some way not made clear) "The Man Who Listens" is Christ.

Religious novels such as this one have their greatest appeal for those who share the subordinate ideas and who relish the style of the author. For example, the client called "The Pharisee," we are told, "hated the inelegant, the openly enjoyed." (p. 197)

Some readers may have difficulty in seeing all this as a serious indictment. But even Alexander Damon, an esthete and an alcoholic, is humbled by his experience in the late John Godfrey's sanctuary. His parting remark is "The ancient Greeks poured out wine in a libation to God. Would you mind very much if I poured out my whiskey in a libation?"

The slick ease with which Miss Caldwell cures alcoholism, ends racial tensions and irons out life's chief problems is sufficient explanation of the low critical status which the religious novel, so-called, enjoys.

Those individuals who bring maturity to the life of the spirit and the life of art will be well advised to give *The Listener* the widest possible berth. (p. 198)

> *Riley Hughes, in his review of "The Listener," in* Catholic World *(copyright 1961 by The Missionary Society of St. Paul the Apostle in the State of New York; used by permission), Vol. 193, No. 1155, June, 1961, pp. 197-98.*

MARTIN LEVIN

When love comes to Caroline Ames Sheldon in Taylor Caldwell's **"A Prologue to Love"** . . . , it is page 553, and there are only sixty pages or so to tidy things up: change a few bequests, do a little benevolent blackmailing, engage a brain surgeon, and otherwise try to alter the course of a lifetime of bitchery.

Bitchery comes naturally to the wretched billionairess, since the father Miss Caldwell has devised for her is a marvelous nineteenth-century monster of a dad who has everything but fangs. Shut up in a rotting old country house for most of her childhood, schooled in niggardliness by her miserly parent, Caroline comes to womanly estate so terrified of poverty that she is incapable of conducting human relationships. In this block-buster of misery that blasts lives from the Franco-Prussian War to World War I, there are human relationships aplenty, most of them stemming from the fact that shifty old John fathered dual dynasties—one with his wife and another with his mistress, Cynthia, who happened to be the wife's twin sister. What a mess! . . .

A dependable performer, Miss Caldwell delivers what her readers have come to expect of her: a no-nonsense view of character, a convincing belief in moral absolutes, and a relish for detail that would have been appreciated by Hieronymus Bosch. If cavilers find **"A Prologue to Love"** a bit lacking in credibility—well, you can't have everything.

> *Martin Levin, in his review of "A Prologue to Love," in* The New York Times Book Review *(© 1961 by The New York Times Company; reprinted by permission), November 19, 1961, p. 60.*

ANNETTE T. ROTTENBERG

The natural perversity of students can sometimes be turned to good account, as when a student asks (apropos of a discussion about reading habits), "But isn't it necessary to read bad books in order to recognize good ones?" and the teacher replies, "Yes, it is." The attempt to implement this proposition can be unexpectedly rewarding.

My own experience grew out of a class in American Literature since the Civil War, which had just concluded a study of *The American* and "The Art of Fiction." There would surely be few better opportunities for applying the criteria of the master craftsman to a work which takes itself seriously but must renounce any claim to artistic importance.

The "bad" book had to meet several not very stringent requirements; it had to belong to the realistic tradition in order to afford closer comparison with the novels read during the course; it had to be widely read or at least the product of an author who is widely read; it had to be full enough to contain most of the elements worth discussing, but not too long; and it had to violate, but perhaps not too openly, most of the rules laid down by James and others. Finding such a book is, fortunately for our purposes, very easy. Half an hour spent at the racks of a paperback collection yielded two prizes: *The Final Hour* and *Your Sins and Mine*, both by Taylor Caldwell. A hundred other novels might have done as well. For several reasons, however, the Caldwell books turned out to be a happy choice. Not only do Miss Caldwell's books dwell consistently on the best-seller lists, but they diffuse an atmosphere of moral earnestness which, spurious though it is, misleads the unwary student into believing that he is now in the presence of a work of art. Many of her novels, in addition, seem full of the results of zealous scholarship and attention to the disorders of our time. Their themes are portentous, their canvases huge. But, above all, for the purposes of this study, they partake delightfully of the characteristics of *kitsch*, as Gilbert Highet describes it, "obviously bad; so bad that you can scarcely understand how any human being would spend days and weeks making it . . ." (p. 496)

Perhaps it ought to go without saying that the creation of characters who enter into the context of our lives is the ultimate test of the novel. The student, however, will often take for granted the ease with which characters can be brought to life—until he has compared the creations of Henry James with those of Taylor Caldwell. The latter, a prodigious race much larger than life, inhabit a world which resembles a mental hospital; the ordinary reactions of our fellow-creatures do not exist here. The characters live in an eternally manic state where passion and anguish (there is very little joy) exert themselves in towering eruptions which no mortal could ever hope to survive. (This is even more apparent in *The Final Hour*.) Oddly enough, despite the violent manifestations which accompany the recurrent bouts of suffering, there is no real pain, simply because each bereavement, each sacrifice, must lead (inevitably, in this best of all possible worlds) to higher levels of happiness. (p. 497)

The student can profitably speculate on one aspect of the relationship between theme and characterization in the treatment of which good and bad fiction differ profoundly, and this is that, although both kinds explore reality versus appearance, morality versus disorder, light versus darkness, the bad novel tends to translate the conflict into grandiose, even metaphysical, terms, while the good novel reduces the struggle to a strictly existential proposition, not a conflict between forces, but between people, or their own impulses, expressed through their ordinary pursuits of love, marriage, peace of mind, freedom, money, success. It has not been emphasized enough that the great novel does, in fact, deal with the most commonplace preoccupations of the human condition.

Perhaps not so obvious as characterization is the importance of setting, on which may devolve the total reality of the illusion to be maintained. In second-rate fiction there are two familiar approaches to the treatment of background. One is a glassy-eyed attention to detail which apparently satisfies the reader whose appetite for such trivia is insatiable. In the stories appearing in popular women's magazines we are often treated to catalogues of the meals which are eaten (even the recipes for the meals!), the dresses which are worn, the furniture which is purchased, but unlike the detail in the good novel, these painfully transcribed descriptions are generally irrelevant to the essential movement of the story and only interrupt its development. While their function is ostensibly to impart reality to the background, they exist instead as lumpy and unassimilated substitutes for reality. . . . In the kind of didactic novel represented by **Your Sins and Mine,** however, the treatment is quite the opposite. Attention to thesis appropriates all the author's energies, and the background remains meager and unrealized—a line drawing compared to what ought to be a genre painting. To put it differently, the events could occur anywhere. But this is hardly the same thing as creating events of universal significance. (pp. 497-98)

The inability or unwillingness of an author to observe, in James' words, "the look of things, the look that conveys their meaning, to catch the colour, the relief, the expression, the surface, the substance of the human spectacle," is symptomatic of a much greater failure—a failure of the creative intelligence. One can imagine the author protesting that there are more important things to do than furnish the stage. But for a realistic novel, one which professes to explore the mores of a particular class in a particular place at a particular time, the fact that a set of events does not belong to any recognizable universe can be fatal. The backgrounds of the novels we remember, no matter what their deficiencies—let the student think of *Sister Carrie* or *The Great Gatsby* or *Look Homeward, Angel*—have in common the lavish accumulation of myriad strokes which render the drawing-rooms, the houses, the streets, the towns and cities more familiar than those we walk in every day. Better too many strokes than too few. And if the author does not see the shapes and colors, or hear the sounds, of multifarious life around him, he will probably see very little else—neither the people nor the meaning of the world they inhabit. He must, in fact, be one of those on whom nothing is lost. (p. 498)

[It] is precisely in the treatment of the setting and the characters that minor writers often distinguish themselves, a fact which makes clear that the great novel is much more than a sum of its parts. James chided Besant for his failure to realize that the elements of the novel cannot be separated into distinct categories. And in evaluating these works by Taylor Caldwell, we came upon a curious dislocation affecting the whole, a suspension of the laws governing time and space, cause and effect, and suggesting a general distortion of the relationship which ought to exist between the parts of the novel as they reflect the relationships in the real world.

In the first place, the objective world has no perceptible influence on the subjective experience of the characters. The world of these novels is not real, and where it is symbolic—in **Your Sins and Mine,** universal drought and infestation to represent moral blight, a blazing cross in the sky to signal God's forgiveness—the imagery is patently mechanical, trite, or extrinsic. One of the most obvious symptoms of this imbalance is the speed with which the characters respond to any change in the environment. If the author is not really contemplating life but promoting a thesis, he will be reckless of orderly development and of the slow accommodation of our understanding to the events. Let the crops on the farm show signs of failing, and the hero says, "You're being avenged, Ed." (Ed has been blinded in war.) "The whole world forgot you, but God has remembered." Let the sky be darkened by an unpredicted eclipse, and the protagonist knows intuitively the meaning of the phenomenon. He is already prepared to receive the significance of any event at any moment. No, more than prepared—prophetic, in fact, knowledgeable before the event. Indeed, he appears to serve no other dramatic purpose than to interpret the evidence. His readiness is a kind of perversion of the cause and effect which exist in the world we know as inhabited by human beings of limited understanding. If Miss Caldwell were a stand-up comedian, we should say that her timing was off. In addition, all but the most unsophisticated readers resent the directness of the approach and the author's unwillingness to allow the exercise of any judgment but her own.

For the same reason—the artificiality of the objective world—the sudden conversions in which these novels abound are never produced by any real happening. They generate spontaneously out of a crude culture composed of the author's assumptions and certain familiar psychological clichés. (pp. 498-99)

In the special limbo of **Your Sins and Mine,** the speeches and actions of the characters, no matter how private, are never revelatory of any truth about themselves, since they are not real people. The great contributions of the modern novel have been not only the faithful rendition of manners but also the exploration of psychology in depth. . . . Almost any reader with a sense of the ridiculous can match Miss Caldwell and her counterparts at this game. And because these novels are extraordinarily simple (the only complications are those of incident) and incapable of exploring the sources of our human conflicts, there is, despite the great number of *happenings,* no real *action*.

In fact, one sees three levels functioning at once, but independently of each other. At the lowest, a world of spurious newspaper headlines which substitute for objective events, above this a world of people whose attempts to behave like human beings bear no relationship either to the world they live in or to the characters they profess to be, and finally, a nominalistic world inhabited only by the ideas and opinions of the author, having no connection with either of the two worlds below. (pp. 499-500)

What else characterizes the serious bad novel? Not surprisingly, a lack of humor and wit. In their absence we endure the self-righteousness of the unreconstructed preacher. We miss the ironic view of life, and those elements of concealment and mystery in the human creature which give savor to experience as well as to literature. The student can learn to associate this failure of ironic perception with something else—the quality of the intelligence that informs the pretended work of art and that sees life, not as a heroic tragedy which arouses our pity and our terror, but as a comedy, sure to come out right in the end after we have executed all the required motions.

Not the least of the rewards for the student is the incomparable satisfaction of joining that select group whose passport is the authority to look down on those who enjoy *kitsch* for the wrong reasons. Morally not very defensible, perhaps, but, as we all suspect of each other, more often than not the beginning of taste. (p. 500)

Annette T. Rottenberg, "Obviously Bad," in English Journal (copyright © 1963 by the National Council of Teachers of English; reprinted by permission of the publisher), Vol. LII, No. 7, October, 1963, pp. 496-500.

EDITH FARR RIDINGTON

[*A Pillar of Iron*] is a long and pretentious novel about Cicero which I found extremely annoying both because of its many inaccuracies (I made note as I read of some forty questionable statements) and because it builds up a picture of Cicero that seemed to me to be very far removed from the Cicero most classicists know. For a novelist to deliberately alter historical fact for artistic purposes, and to tell the reader that he is doing so, as Thornton Wilder did in his *Ides of March,* is one thing. But to set oneself up as a model of research and scholarship, as Miss Caldwell does in her Foreword, and then to present a Roman like Cicero as longing for the coming of the Jewish Messiah, and having visions of a nuclear holocaust, is quite another. The book has some interesting scenes; its picture of Julius Caesar is rather lively; and the early part is better than the later; but it drags interminably, and misses completely the real flavor of Cicero.

> Edith Farr Ridington, in her review of "A Pillar of Iron," in The Classical World, Vol. 59, No. 3, November, 1965, p. 75.

WILLIAM B. HILL

[*A Pillar of Iron* is an] astonishingly powerful novel based on the life of Cicero. Miss Caldwell obviously admires the great orator, practically making him a pre-Christian Christian; she glosses over his faults, extols his virtues. Had she shortened some of the scenes and in general been less wordy, she might have had room for a more comprehensive treatment of Cicero's entire life. But even so, she has made his stirring times real.

> William B. Hill, in his review of "A Pillar of Iron," in America (reprinted with permission of America Press, Inc.; © 1965; all rights reserved), Vol. 113, No. 22, November 27, 1965, p. 688.

ANTHONY BOUCHER

["Dialogues with the Devil"] is an exercise in moral indignation without the mechanics of fiction that customarily camouflage Miss Caldwell's opinions. Thus, in an exchange of letters between Beelzebub and the Archangel Michael, we are made directly aware of a catalogue of modern scourges beloved of the devil: egalitarianism, water pollution, Freud, masculine women, insubordinate children, climate control and deodorants for men. (Miss Caldwell doesn't say how the letters are delivered, but I suspect that Lucifer has a hell of a lot to do with the U.S. Post Office.) . . .

The author is certainly on the side of the angels—but she is guilty of a couple of misdemeanors not mentioned by the devil, namely, Prolixity and Sententiousness. Her celestial visions, ornamented with "alabaster bowls of fruit" and "limbs like carved white stone" evoke Maxfield Parrish and worse. A proper novel is a far more effective vehicle for ideas than a mere jeremiad, however deeply felt.

> Anthony Boucher, in his review of "Dialogues with the Devil," in The New York Times Book Review (© 1967 by The New York Times Company; reprinted by permission), June 11, 1967, p. 43.

THE TIMES LITERARY SUPPLEMENT

A conversation with the Devil presents a fairly obvious literary temptation, especially perhaps to a Christian, but to anyone who plans to discuss the painful evil of the modern world, its false values or its misdirected aims, C. S. Lewis comes immediately to mind. He knew that the Devil himself would be difficult to catch, so very cleverly he avoided the problem by composing a series of letters from one of Hell's staff to a junior Tempter on his first assignment in the world. . . . [In *Dialogues with the Devil*] Miss Caldwell attempts something much more exacting, for she presents Lucifer himself, and, as though that were not problem enough, puts him into correspondence with the Archangel Michael. She is an experienced novelist, but it must be said that the two contestants use [styles that are] disconcertingly alike. Possibly it is because both are angels even though one of them is "fallen", but by the close of the book the heavy style has begun to pall. One misses the verve, and the wit, of Lewis.

But the real fault of the book is that it lacks bite, roaming too widely over unknown planets. Lucifer would have done better, and set Gabriel a tougher problem, had he been allowed to stick to Miss Caldwell's home ground. He might have preened himself on the success with which he had made a bogy of communism and with it had engulfed a great nation in a prolonged and dreadful war. He might have had much more to say about the skill with which he had exalted wealth into the predominant human aim. He could, one would think, have made nice use of his handling of the race problem, its ignoring of the fact of "coloureds", and its attractive list of murders. But he has sex on his mind and the idea of wholesale destruction on planet after planet, and undervalues his detailed successes, so that he becomes faintly ridiculous and Michael has too easy a task. Lucifer, it seems, has fallen from heaven into a pit of generalizations.

> "Dear Devil," in The Times Literary Supplement (©Times Newspapers Ltd. (London) 1968; reproduced from The Times Literary Supplement by permission), No. 3470, August 29, 1968, p. 926.

PUBLISHERS WEEKLY

No question, [Taylor Caldwell] . . . can tell an engrossing story. She proves it once again in ["**Captains and the Kings**," a] gigantic novel about the Armagh family, closest, perhaps, in structure to her first big success, **Dynasty of Death**." As an Irish immigrant, Joseph Armagh arrives via steerage in the 1850s. Upon the death of both his parents, Joseph, at 13, is left with a baby sister and small brother, whom he leaves with nuns near Pittsburgh. He sets out to support them and to survive. He becomes tough, ruthless and proud, and eventually makes an immense fortune that gives him a part in international currency manipulation, in politics, and the waging of wars. Joseph marries, lovelessly, has children and ambitions for them, grooming one son for the presidency. . . . Through all this saga one cannot help but find some parallels with the Kennedy saga, set back to the period 1850-1915. Portraits of some characters, rather bitterly slanted, are certainly more than coincidental. Underlying the magnetic plot is the author's deeply felt view of the world's manipulation by international moneymen, the conspiracy of a few to wield power over the many, economically, politically, militarily. It is not a point of view that will please some liberals among us.

> *A review of "Captains and the Kings," in* Publishers Weekly *(reprinted from the February 14, 1972 issue of* Publishers Weekly, *published by R. R. Bowker Company, a Xerox company; copyright © 1972 by Xerox Corporation), Vol. 201, No. 7, February 14, 1972, p. 66.*

DUNCAN FALLOWELL

Until about three quarters of the way through [*Captains and the Kings*] I more or less knew what I should be writing about. Now I am not so sure. It seemed to be one of those capacious dramatic tales of the American dollar dream in the tradition of *The Magnificent Ambersons, The Great Gatsby* or *Citizen Kane*. 'Joseph Francis Xavier Armagh was thirteen years old when he first saw America through the dirty porthole on the steerage deck of *The Irish Queen*. It was the early 1850's and he was a penniless immigrant, an orphan cast on a hostile shore to make a home for himself and his younger brother and infant sister.' And he does, although the brother turns out to be a homosexual concert tenor and the sister a nun. Joseph's childhood humiliation makes him bitter and his bitterness makes him cruelly determined. His mania to reach the top devours him and all who cross his path, excepting his mistress. With his ruthless disregard for other people which is always necessary in accumulating great wealth, he does grow vastly rich, from oil and newspapers, gunrunning and brothels, and he grows very brutal in his use of that frightening political power which will obviously accompany it. Private riches on this lurid scale can and must buy everything which is of this every-day world, including Washington. This is the ultimate trophy Armagh covets for his son. The Presidency of a country which once spat upon him. . . . The story is rich in incident and character, complex in structure, and written with a strong narrative urgency which carries one forward without wasting breath. If the above outline should appear off-putting I ask you to ignore it because this is a solid and awesome book, worth anybody's time. . . .

Captains and the Kings should become known as an addition to epic American literature—it has all the qualifications, muscularity above all—but its intentions go far beyond this and only become truly apparent towards the end. And it has unnerved me. Frightened me, I could say. This is a persuasive realist novel which draws you in and makes you believe in its fiction. When towards the end it moves, we are assured, into the region of fact that belief carries on through, and what it has to say is disturbing. When was the last time you read a novel which *explicitly* tries to save the world? (p. 105)

As Joseph Armagh's riches increase he moves in more and more powerful circles. He becomes a member of the Scardo Society, an alliance in the USA of intellectuals and rich capitalists who between them plan to run the system for their own benefit. This is scarcely the top, however. Not even the President is that. Right at the very top on this planet of ours is The Committee for Foreign Studies, a kind of super-sophisticated mafia group of the most powerful world bankers based in Europe and their biggest customers. It is they who control the global purse strings, who can make or break a President (Rory Armagh is ditched in favour of Woodrow Wilson), because the world fiscal system has reduced nations and governments to the status of pawns in the hands of international financiers. We all know that we live in a world of self-effacing intrigue, spying and conspiracy, official secrets and back-room deals, the grey faceless men controlling our destinies, popular participation in the process merely an illusion. But previously this conspiracy had been presented in involuntary abstract terms. Now it is revealed in concrete terms, in the conscious will at the very top of the pyramid. Its aficionados are beyond questions like the East-West conflict. It is all the same to them. Money is totally amoral, that is its beauty and its danger. . . . But the human species has an instinctive long-term awareness of what is best for it and a courageous minority rebels. The young, of course. Only they still have enough freedom of mind left to see what is wrong and the courage to express their distrust or contempt. It is no coincidence that those who attack or drop out of the system are harassed mercilessly by the majority whose minds—even the old lady next door—are blinded by the greed born of seductive material promises from above. It is no coincidence that the industrial political power blocks pay out huge sums to smaller governments to evict hippies, to develop the 'underdeveloped nations' more inescapably into the system (all the talk about giving the Third World enough to eat conceals a less attractive motive: the maxim that in this world you never get something for nothing holds good even here), to stamp out psychedelic drugs but not heroin which is very profitable and kills people's minds whereas the psychedelics *do* alter the consciousness and so frequently expose the fraud simply by altering one's point of observation and increasing its sensitivity (in consequence, as far as they are concerned, Timothy Leary is a far more dangerous man than, say, Eldridge Cleaver who is merely competing for power, hence Leary must be tracked down in Afghanistan then confined). By chance a book I reviewed two months ago, Enzensberger's *Smut,* drew very similar parallels between capitalism (not opposed to Communism), power and dirt. Humans have been made into dirt in their own world and are manipulated by financier despots. Humans are conditioned in their needs by heavy advertising and propaganda because conformity facilitates trade and profits. The entire system will probably collapse from its own cancerous gluttony, which is one of the few things the Committee did not bank on, but not before widespread misery has been created. We might mention the population explosion. It is patently vital for the future of the people that this be drastically reduced. Unfortunately, however, the system demands that it increase and so it does because the system has the power. The only people with nothing to lose meantime are the bankers because they deal in the central illusion only. Money. Which is ultimately nothing at all. They have no responsibility, they only collect and about that they are ruthless. No corpses can ever be laid at their door. As [*Captains and the Kings*] illustrates, when you pursue wealth to its limits your mind divorces itself from all humanity. In the world of pure finance, people and what happens to them never have to enter your calculations at all. (pp. 105-06)

> *Duncan Fallowell, in his review of "Captains and the Kings" (© copyright Duncan Fallowell 1973; reprinted with permission), in* Books and Bookmen, *Vol. 18, No. 8, May, 1973, pp. 105-06.*

BEST SELLERS

Big, wordy, sprawling, [**"Captains and the Kings"**] is probably a thesis novel; there is some loose association with the Kennedy family, though in this instance all of the tragedy is the result of a curse imposed by a ruthlessly destroyed statesman and the time ranges from around 1860 to the second decade of this century; but the theme of an Irish immigrant, raised up to wealth by his own driving passion and bent on making his son President, is finally made secondary to the theme of an international cabal that controls the press and statesmen throughout the world, plans wars, determines international destinies. No one coming new to the book but familiar with the author will be surprised to find that the beginning of all tyranny is the income tax. It is hard to believe that anybody could take seriously the conferences of this cabal; this aspect of the work, some looseness of construction and carelessness about details—Taylor Caldwell never seems aware that the Molly Maguires were associated with anthracite coal—are harmful but many readers have worked their way through this much too long book, and doubtless many others will do so....

A review of "Captains and the Kings," in Best Sellers *(copyright 1973, by the University of Scranton), Vol. 33, No. 11, September 1, 1973, p. 259.*

MARTIN LEVIN

Return with Taylor Caldwell to ancient Greece [in **"Glory and the Lightning"**], where characters in desperation are wont to cry: "Wine, in the name of the gods." At an Athenian dinner party, you can hear the architect Phidias say: "Ah, yes, Pericles, I am at your service. I have the sketches drawn, for the Parthenon." Puts you right into the classic picture, where the Acropolis, in its day, was a bigger provocation than the Albany Mall.

There are other social parallels, if you look for them, in the spectacle of a high but weakened civilization being overwhelmed by a determined force of hairies, the Spartans. And there are stirrings of feminism, too, even in the fifth century B.C., the heyday of the brainy courtesan, Aspasia.... A dormitory student at a school for courtesans, Aspasia confounds her math teacher, science teacher and gym teacher: ("... suddenly all was fire and shuddering transports beyond description").

After a tour of duty with a Mede satrap, whom she cures of the flux, Aspasia leaves for Athens an heiress, to start her famous school and to do her own thing. The rest is history.... The plague from which, according to the author, Aspasia's healing arts succor Pericles—at least temporarily. And the ubiquitous Spartans. All of which is enrobed in the author's familiar verbosity, which can leave you crying for wine in the name of the gods.

Martin Levin, in his review of "Glory and the Lightning," in The New York Times Book Review *(© 1974 by The New York Times Company; reprinted by permission), December 15, 1974, p. 14.*

MARTIN LEVIN

"But you can't marry me! You are—Jeremy Porter—a rich man and a lawyer, and I am only a servant girl!" So says Ellen Watson, a beautiful but dreadfully downtrodden housemaid in turn-of-the-century Pennsylvania. Ellen is actually the illegitimate daughter of one of Philadelphia's first families, but this doesn't matter to Jeremy one way or another. He marries Cinder-Ellen when she is 17, and their life together, according to Taylor Caldwell, becomes a microcosm of the American apocalypse....

Caldwell's [**"Ceremony of The Innocent"**] finds her at the top of her form as a storyteller and as a vendor of the ideas that have surfaced in her novels since **"Dynasty of Death."** The story is pure melodrama, rich in characters you love to hate. And the ideology, in the light of the current conspiracy explosion, is beginning to seem less exotic.

Martin Levin, in his review of "Ceremony of the Innocent," in The New York Times Book Review *(© 1976 by The New York Times Company; reprinted by permission), October 31, 1976, p. 41.*

BARBARA SICHERMAN

Ceremony of the Innocent is well written, but the plot remains unconvincing. This time the notion of a small group secretly controlling the world is implausible. The book may be of some interest because of its autobiographical insights. Miss Caldwell disavows autobiographical intent but also states that [the heroine] Ellen Porter's "thoughts have been my thoughts and her experiences mine also." The author would be well advised to seek another theme the next time.

Barbara Sicherman, in her review of "Ceremony of the Innocent," in Best Sellers *(copyright © 1977 Helen Dwight Reid Educational Foundation), Vol. 36, No. 11, February, 1977, p. 346.*

PUBLISHERS WEEKLY

The prolific and best selling Caldwell collaborates with [Jess Stearn in *I, Judas*], retelling the Judas Iscariot story from an angle that's unusual if not new. In what might almost be called The Gospel According to St. Judas, the protagonist describes how, loving Jesus more than the other disciples and having more faith in him, he "betrays" him only that Jesus may prove his messiahship and liberate both Israel and humankind. Judas tries to show, moreover, that it was really *he* who was betrayed.... The authors follow the events of the New Testament drama closely, give it a setting of some historical authenticity, and recreate, with middling success, its major participants, including John the Baptist, Caiaphas, Pilate, Mary Magdalene, Lazarus, the Apostles and of course Jesus. Their Judas isn't particularly convincing, though, and their whole narrative lacks subtlety and fire. It is, however pleasantly entertaining.

A review of "I, Judas," in Publishers Weekly *(reprinted from the July 11, 1977 issue of* Publishers Weekly, *published by R. R. Bowker Company, a Xerox company; copyright © 1977 by Xerox Corporation), Vol. 212, No. 2, July 11, 1977, p. 74.*

GLENN MAYER

The collaboration of Taylor Caldwell and Jess Stearn on their second novel, *I, Judas,* has resulted in an exceptionally interesting work....

Judas is depicted not as a poor thief, but as the educated son of a wealthy aristocrat. He sacrificed a large inheritance to follow Christ. We learn from Judas' actions that he is somewhat of an elitist, as he speaks of "another bleak Galilean fishing village with country clods in evidence wherever we went," a chauvinist, "for anybody who knows about women recognizes that they are the most devious and self-centered of creatures," but above all, a patriot devoted to freeing Israel from the tyranny of Rome. Caldwell and Stearn portray the character of Judas so effectively that we are forced to consider him as a human being with strengths and frailties, not as the archetypal betrayer.

After we accept Judas's humanity we find that perspective becomes a crucial issue. Caldwell and Stearn demonstrate well that reality itself is highly dependent upon perspective. Viewing Judas without taking his motivation into consideration, we see that it was he who caused Jesus to be brought to trial. . . . When we consider, however, that Judas was promised by the Sanhedrin, the Jewish Supreme Court, that Jesus would be acquitted, our view is somewhat altered. His devotion to Israel and belief in Jesus as the Messiah who could lead his oppressed country against Rome also influenced Judas' actions. Judas believed so strongly in Jesus that he knew Jesus could, at any time, save himself. Judas hoped that by causing a confrontation between the Messiah and the Romans, Jesus would be forced to assume the role of king of the Jews and lead them in revolt against the tyranny of Rome. From Judas' perspective, he had not betrayed Christ, but had shown more belief in Jesus as the Son of God than had anyone else.

Caldwell and Stearn have dealt brilliantly with the issue of perspective and therein lies the value of their work. To himself, Judas was the strongest of believers in Christ. To others, his name was synonymous with betrayer. Which in fact was true is entirely a matter of perspective.

> Glenn Mayer, in his review of "I, Judas," in Best Sellers (copyright © 1977 Helen Dwight Reid Educational Foundation), Vol. 37, No. 7, October, 1977, p. 195.

PAT GOLD

[Taylor Caldwell's *Bright Flows the River*] is anti-establishment, anti-feminist, anti-democracy, anti-family, anti-power, anti-duty, and in fact anti almost everything save the right and the need of the individual to make the correct choice and philosophy of a way of life that is not counter to his very basic, personal tenets. Caldwell's prose is, most of the time, majestic and almost poetic. The characters, mostly men and four or five of the women, who she has peopled this—her thirty-second book—with, though not realistic or believable to me, are indeed unique.

The plot of the book itself is fascinating and easy to follow. Guy Jerald is a man who has gone after the American Dream of rags to riches and has triumphed. He has taken 900 acres of barren and almost worthless farmland and has built an empire. But is triumph success? Jerald, a man one would think has everything to live for, tries to kill himself in a most violent manner one night, and he is confined to a luxurious sanitarium. (pp. 34-5)

Through flashbacks we are introduced to Tom Jerald, Guy's father, the quintessential philosopher who has made the choice of being happily poor rather than being a professor, and his mistress—old, earthy Sal. We meet Guy's mother, whose gods are duty and money, his vapid wife, Lucey, his vacuous, greedy children, his brother-in-law, Hugh, with a wife the equal of Guy's, who has a mistress to make his life happy. The only women who stand out in this book are the various mistresses of Tom, Guy, Dr. Meyer and Hugh. The wives, according to Taylor Caldwell, are all silly, grasping, near to illiterate, creatures that can only strangle, never create. The author has a running diatribe against women who dare to think that they are more than a servant to the moods of the male or more than a nursemaid to keep the children away from the male until he deigns to want their company. At some point in the book, Caldwell points out that woman was made out of Adam's rib and therefore made for him.

Unfortunately, Taylor Caldwell often becomes woefully redundant on the subject of women and her fear that Communistic Facism is taking over the entire world. I find lengthy sermons that are pounded over and over again to be soporific, whether or not I agree or disagree with them. She also deals with power and power brokers, conformity, the right of the individualist in society and a host of other topics usually in an interesting and stimulating manner. . . .

Bright Flows the River is not simply a story, it is a controversy. Taylor Caldwell, for all of that, is a stimulating, sometimes irritating, well-versed writer who knows well how to weave a tale, put over her point of view and hold the reader's attention. (p. 35)

> Pat Gold, in a review of "Bright Flows the River," in West Coast Review of Books (copyright 1979 by Rapport Publishing Co., Inc.), Vol. 5, No. 1, January, 1979, pp. 34-5.

ANNE MARIE STAMFORD

After thirty-two novels it's good to see that Taylor Caldwell hasn't lost her touch. Her superb style of storytelling turns the ordinary theme of *Bright Flows the River* into an extraordinary and memorable novel. . . .

The only reservation that I have is that some of the characters border on clichés, but this somehow did not detract from my enjoyment. In a novel in which most of the action takes place in the minds on the characters, Caldwell manages to sustain the suspense of an adventure story. I think that this is a relevant and thought-provoking book.

> Anne Marie Stamford, in her review of "Bright Flows the River," in Best Sellers (copyright © 1979 Helen Dwight Reid Educational Foundation), Vol. 38, No. 11, February, 1979, p. 337.

KIRKUS REVIEWS

Although there's no dearth here of Caldwell's portable sermonettes on such evils as soft living, [*Answer As a Man*, a] turn-of-the-century Pennsylvania tale of rags to riches and love tangles, has the ease and zip of the author's earlier period. The hero and true M-A-N of the title is Jason Garrity, only approved kin of his grandfather, Bernard. Bernard is another true M-A-N, plumping for solid male strength and putting a fist in the face of the flabby, whining, slimy world. As for wimmin: "they should niver have the rearing of men children." So Jason has enough gumption to survive childhood and youth in a shantytown house with his widowed mother, his fatuously religious brother John, his dazzlingly beautiful, crippled, vindictive sister Joan; and then, through shrewd business sense and hard work, he begins to stake out his territory, profit-wise. Eventually he'll even be manager of a Pocono summer hotel, the Ipswich House, and he'll use his inheritance of some land to demand shares in the business. But Jason flunks the mating test, marrying whiny, snobbish, slightly stupid Patricia Mulligan by whom he has (he thinks) three children: son Sebastian is really the offspring of wily, charming chum Lionel Nolan. Then Lionel marries Joan; and Molly, the spirited, sensible girl Jason *should* have married, marries agreeable lawyer Daniel Dugan, nephew of Jason's genial father-in-law Pat. So it takes some years of domestic and fiscal turmoil before Molly and Jason at last entwine hearts. . . . Finally Patricia and Daniel conveniently expire, and there's a happy fade-out. Still the old Rand-wagon, but less preachment than usual and more gossipy goin's on—so the always-solid-selling Caldwell should really climb the charts with this one.

> *A review of "Answer As a Man," in* Kirkus Reviews *(copyright © 1980 The Kirkus Service, Inc.), Vol. XLVIII, No. 21, November 1, 1980, p. 1408.*

RICHARD FREEDMAN

Taylor Caldwell is a shining exemplar of Grey Power, still churning out highly successful novels in which she loftily pretends the 20th century—at least in fiction—never happened.

Millions of readers must agree that the narrative innovations of Proust and Joyce, to say nothing of Beckett and Borges, were all a mistake; that old-fashioned linear realism is still the best mode for fiction. So her ["**Answer as a Man**"] reads the way the works of Arnold Bennett or Theodore Dreiser would read if they hadn't been geniuses. On a certain level, Miss Caldwell steadfastly insists on providing a "good read."

This time her hero is Jason Garrity, born at the end of the 19th century to a desperately poor family of Irish immigrants in the grim little town of Belleville, Pa. . . .

Miss Caldwell presents [Jason] as a contemporary Job, a heavy burden for a character compounded largely of Horatio Alger and pasteboard.

Like Archibald MacLeish's "J.B." and most other modern parallels to the Job story, "**Answer as a Man**" reduces the biblical account of a good man's suffering at the hands of an autocratic God to something closely resembling soap. But it's first-class soap, vastly superior to the suds you get on television, if not comparable to the tough-minded—and far more compact—Bible story.

> *Richard Freedman, in his review of "Answer As a Man," in* The New York Times Book Review *(© 1981 by The New York Times Company; reprinted by permission), March 1, 1981, p. 29.*

(Charles) Bruce Chatwin
1940-

English novelist and travel writer.

Each of Chatwin's books depicts a different world, consistently evoking the strangeness of place and people in a style termed "powerfully visual and aural" by the *New Yorker*. His acclaimed travel book, *In Patagonia* (1977), contains historical data and insightfully delineates people and places he encountered on a journey through the tip of South America. His first novel, *The Viceroy of Ouidah* (1980), was originally intended to be a biography but became instead an imaginative reconstruction of the nineteenth-century slave trade set within the former West African country of Dahomey. Horror and grotesque humor combine in this novel to depict the world and mentality of a Brazilian slave trader. Most critics praised the novel, although a few objected to the sensational subject matter.

Chatwin's second novel, *On the Black Hill* (1982), shifts locale once more. In this novel Chatwin delves into the lives of identical twins living in rural Wales. The important events in the story are confined to the family farm; the peculiarities and limited perspectives of that existence emerge through a series of compact, keenly observed episodes. Most critics praised the novel and Chatwin's compressed style. John Updike observed that Chatwin gave a sense "of the immensity of time a human life spans, a span itself dwarfed by the perspectives of history."

(See also *Contemporary Authors*, Vols. 85-88.)

Photograph by Paul Kasmin

MAURICE RICHARDSON

Bruce Chatwin is an original: laconic, wistful, sweet and sour, detached and sympathetic, with a sharp eye for the curious. [In the travel book *In Patagonia*, he] writes very well indeed in a clear, streamlined, educated cis-Atlantic style that reminds you a little of Evelyn Waugh. He has a special gift for catching the *genius loci* of this strange springboard into the Void. (p. 550)

> Maurice Richardson, "Walkabout," in New Statesman *(© 1977 The Statesman & Nation Publishing Co. Ltd.), Vol. 94, No. 2431, October 21, 1977, pp. 550-51.*

MALCOLM DEAS

Bruce Chatwin's *In Patagonia* is . . . concerned with the human agents who have failed to transform the *ambiente* there in the past hundred years or so. It is a work of travel, of observation and accident, but also of learning, reflection and art, and can stand in the curiously distinguished literary company that Patagonia has touched. . . .

Frequently on the journey south from Buenos Aires the author walked. In ninety-seven passages of from a few lines to a few pages he covers the distance, and much else besides. . . . Bruce Chatwin's success in this short book is the more interesting because it is so exceptional.

It is a book about isolated people, but of very diverse origins; the reader must reflect that any man might be a Patagonian. . . . As [William Henry] Hudson hinted, human weakness and oddity will show up more sharply against this background than against any other. *In Patagonia* resists the temptation of exploiting this natural advantage to excess. Chatwin can convey a person's eccentricity and absurdity without giving the reader that uneasy sense that a life is being reduced to a *trouvaille*. With persons as they appear in Patagonia, this requires an unusual exercise of rapport and restraint. . . .

Mr Chatwin's encounters are always interesting because his episodic method allows him to leave all the others out entirely, and to cut each recorded encounter to just what it will bear. He relieves the eccentric with the ordinary, but the ordinary are just as finely conveyed. . . . He describes individuals, and not types, with the economy of the sketch, not the caricature.

In Patagonia is also the work of a learned man, not of the sort of traveller who thinks that reading will blunt rather than heighten sensibility. The author has read deeply in the extensive bibliography of the region, from the earliest discoverers through Darwin and Hudson to the Argentine writers of the present day. . . . Historically, it is the shade of Darwin that haunts the book most frequently. . . .

In Patagonia is that most enviable achievement, a minor classic.

Malcolm Deas, "The Sands of the Deep South," in The Times Literary Supplement *(© Times Newspapers Ltd. (London) 1977; reproduced from* The Times Literary Supplement *by permission), No. 3950, December 9, 1977, p. 1444.*

HILTON KRAMER

It has taken some 85 years, but it looks as if Patagonia has now acquired another English laureate of remarkable literary powers in the person of Bruce Chatwin, who reversed [W. H.] Hudson's journey, traveling from London to the remote corners of "the accursed land," as it is called in Buenos Aires, and coming away with a book that is a little masterpiece of travel, history and adventure. It is called, simply, **"In Patagonia"** . . . ; it is short—199 pages; and it is a wonderful read.

For Mr. Chatwin is a marvelous storyteller—a miniaturist who packs dozens of odd tales, bizarre characters and unforgettable scenes into the 97 succinct chapters of his book, many of them scarcely a page in length. Like Hudson, he has a sharp and sympathetic eye for natural history, and his book abounds in vivid pictorial glimpses of the landscape, but it is in his accounts of the human history of Patagonia that he is most absorbing. About everything from the legendary exploits of Butch Cassidy and the Sundance Kid to the coming of kosher butchers from Israel to anarchist uprisings to grim Boer settlements, Mr. Chatwin has something memorable to tell us. And if the imagery of Patagonia has found its way into the poetry of Donne and Coleridge or the prose of Edgar Allan Poe, he knows exactly how it got there, and he tells us that too. He is not only a hearty traveler, capable of enduring the most awful discomforts and the most terrible food without complaint, but he has done his homework too, and he writes about all of it—the past and the present, the mythical and the historical, the land and the people—in a style that is alternately grave and comical but always precise and pictorial. (p. 3)

Mr. Chatwin's Patagonia is in many ways . . . a long way from Hudson's "solitary wilderness . . . remote from civilization," yet in other ways it is the same place, and it is in his gift for conjuring up these contrasts—for writing about both society and nature with an equally informed and distinguished eye—that his book is so impressive, and so pleasurable to read. **"In Patagonia"** is a book that in the beginning seems to promise an escape from the modern world but in the end leaves us with an even deeper sense of it. (p. 16)

Hilton Kramer, "Patagonia Revisited," in The New York Times Book Review *(copyright © 1978 by The New York Times Company; reprinted by permission), July 30, 1978, pp. 3, 16.*

ALASTAIR REID

Since tourists took over from travellers, the times have not been kind to those few, rare writers who have always seen the world well for us—who filter unknown landscapes through the screen of their curiosity, who travel at a human pace, and who keep notes that allow us to take armchair journeys after them. . . .

The English, perhaps because they look on strangenesses with a piercingly cool eye, have turned up a steady stream of enlightening travellers. . . . But such writings have dwindled over the last two decades, giving way to more massive studies, which sum up countries and tell us everything about them except what they are like. . . . Yet there are endless alluring unknowns, lacking only a traveller with time to take them in, with an uncommitted curiosity and an unjudging eye, and with an appropriate prose manner. These qualities come brilliantly together in Bruce Chatwin, whose **"In Patagonia"** . . . takes travelling back to its magic roots. . . .

[Mr. Chatwin] remains rigorously true to the tradition of the traveller's tale—the oldest form of storytelling—and never once intrudes himself self-consciously into the narrative. We know nothing about him at the book's end except that he has been ears, eyes, and memory to us—not impersonal but unpersonal. He is less a traveller than a wanderer, for he has few express intentions. His journey, through the startling landscapes of Patagonia and Tierra del Fuego, is thoroughly externalized, in sharp physical detail. He has the power of compressing place and character into small and vivid compass. . . . (p. 186)

[Clear-cut] cameos seem almost surreal separated from the thread of the narrative, but so do the scenes and characters in the book, for they loom like outposts of human existence against the empty landscape of the Patagonian desert. Since Patagonia has been settled largely in this century, the figures that Mr. Chatwin meets . . . have come from other lives, each with the tale of a journey, and the encounters become small inset narratives—as do tracks of history, for the past intrudes regularly as anecdote and memory into the journey. . . . Mr. Chatwin is as close to travellers' tales of the past and to the travellers whose paths he is crossing as he is to the landscape and its present inhabitants. What he shares with all of them is a sense of strangeness on the earth's surface, an awed sense of separation from anything fixed. He even sets himself up with a mock quest as a whimsical excuse for his journey. During his English childhood, his grandmother kept as a sacred relic a piece of what she insisted was brontosaurus skin, with coarse red hairs, brought back from Patagonia by her cousin, a sea captain called Charley Milward. It was unceremoniously thrown out on her death, but it serves Mr. Chatwin as a kind of Grail. . . . His journey is toward the enfabled Patagonia of his childhood.

Patagonia suits Mr. Chatwin admirably well, given his disposition toward wonders, both past and present. It is virtually only since 1877, when sheep farming was profitably introduced, that the region has attracted settlers from various parts of Europe, and their remote stations are often repositories of a pre-Patagonian existence. Each case of exile is a different story, entered into for distinct reasons, and each of the characters who punctuate the journey is an incarnation of a separate past. (pp. 186, 188)

"In Patagonia" jogs us with the realization that what we have come to regard as travel is no more than geographical transference, where hardly anything changes, where map and guidebook obliterate the landscape, where journeys are taken for the purpose of summing up, of reaching a conclusion—the very opposite of a wonder voyage. The book is of infinitely more value than cheap air fares, and we must look with enormous anticipation to wherever Mr. Chatwin goes for us next, for his prose is honed to bare and moving essentials. (pp. 188, 190)

Alastair Reid, "The Giant Ground Sloth and Other Wonders," in The New Yorker *(© 1978 by The New Yorker Magazine, Inc.), Vol. LIV, No. 34, October 9, 1978, pp. 186, 188, 190.*

EVE AUCHINCLOSS

[*In Patagonia*] is a travel book of sorts, containing a lot of well-digested history of that strange southerly part of Argentina where so many oddly assorted people have turned up: Magellan, Drake, Darwin, Butch Cassidy and the Sundance Kid, Spanish revolutionaries, Scotch sheep farmers, Jewish merchants, a colony of dour Welshmen, and the author's grandmother's cousin, a shipwrecked sea captain. As he travels south from Buenos Aires, much of the way on foot, Chatwin gives us Patagonia in charged fragments: anecdotes, etymology, landscape, characters, poetry, towns, Patagonian literature, tragic sea stories. The style is the man: detached, humorous, succinct, wry, feeling, energetic, self-effacing: he catches the essence and gives just that, not a word more. *In Patagonia* may bring to mind *The Great Railway Bazaar,* but it is a less showoff book: absolutely original, perfectly poised, wise, an unclassifiable classic.

Eve Auchincloss, in a review of "In Patagonia," in Book World—The Washington Post (© 1978, The Washington Post), December 3, 1978, p. E14.

BRIAN MARTIN

[*The Viceroy of Ouidah* shows that] Chatwin has a gift for remarkably vivid imagery: 'Virgins were broken at Simbodji with the ease of bursting seedpods', and on the way to Dahomey, 'women pointed up a tree to where a crucified man croaked for water in a library of sleeping fruit bats.' Reading Chatwin's descriptions of life in Brazil and West Africa is like reading the early history of Greene-land. It is a sad, barbaric, decadent story told beautifully and brilliantly. Admirers of Conrad and Malcolm Lowry will relish it: and to most palates, it is curiously original, like 'the shock of aguardiente on the tongue'.

Brian Martin, "Slave Coast," in New Statesman (© 1980 The Statesman & Nation Publishing Co. Ltd.), Vol. 100, No. 2590, November 7, 1980, p. 29.

MARY HOPE

[*The Viceroy of Ouidah* is an] extraordinary fictional treatment of the life of a Brazilian slave-trader who ended his days in Dahomey, flamboyant, ruined, flawed, the god-like ancestor of generations of darker and darker-skinned descendants whom the author discovered when he was trying to write a factual history. His information was patchy and he decided to turn the story into fiction, which he has triumphantly done. From early 19th-century Brazil, he follows Francisco Manoel de Silva to Dahomey (now Benin) where the farouche hero sets up a sub kingdom, is patronised and then rejected by the fearsome king, saved by the king's half brother, and dies sadly, surrounded by his teeming offspring forever exiled from the Brazil he longs for.

It is flawed as fiction but has such an obsessional quality, such vigour and exactitude in the description of life beyond conventional boundaries that it is intensely powerful stuff. Chatwin is fascinated by flamboyant savagery, the barbarity of the African kings matched only by the barbarity of the Christian slave-traders who deal with them. It should not be missed.

Mary Hope, in a review of "The Viceroy of Ouidah," in The Spectator (© 1980 by The Spectator; reprinted by permission of The Spectator), Vol. 245, No. 7949, November 15, 1980, p. 21.

VICTORIA GLENDINNING

The Viceroy of Ouidah is far more fantastic than most novels, while being far closer to fact. The unbelievable brutality of the slave trade, and the smell of blood, are overpowering. . . .

Extravagant though all [the details] . . . may seem, it is the discipline with which this book is written that is the most striking thing about it. Every temptation . . . to interpret, explain, embroider, enlarge, has been resisted. Bruce Chatwin's literary manner is stark and staccato. But his material is so baroque and suggestive that his short book seems longer and denser than it really is. It verges on being excessively 'decadent', hideously and ludicrously camp, a glittering sado-masochistic drag-act performed to the beat of the black man's drum. It is held back from the brink by strict compression—there must have been some hard-headed cutting—and by the sad and moral marriage the author makes between historic and poetic truth. . . .

The overriding impression is of clashing cultural myths, all of them with death at their centre, that lie rotting one on top of another in a dreadful, comic compost—and not only, if one thinks about it, in Dahomey.

Victoria Glendinning, "Death in Dahomey" (© British Broadcasting Corp. 1980; reprinted by permission of Victoria Glendinning), in The Listener, Vol. 104, No. 2689, November 27, 1980, p. 733.

JOHN HEMMING

[Dahomey] makes a strange setting for the second book of an author whose *In Patagonia* enjoyed much critical praise. The story [of *The Viceroy of Ouidah*] evidently appealed to Chatwin not because of any prurient interest in the scandal of the slave trade, but because it took place in backwaters of Africa and South America. There is almost nothing in this book about the sufferings of the slaves or the mechanics or dimensions of the slave trade. But there are brilliant descriptions of the dusty poverty of the Brazilian interior and of the rot and decay of the humid coast. Almost every page contains marvellously concise observations by someone who has travelled in these remote places and who revels in the outlandish or the exotic. The strength of the book lies in the wealth of detail, the meticulous depiction of everything from the look of a man burnt alive in a brushfire to a tree full of "a library of sleeping fruit bats", or to the pictures and termite-riddled furnishings of a Benin house.

Chatwin reserves his most careful descriptions for anything connected with religion or superstition. He compares the power of a blood-thirsty Dahomean king, surrounded by prostrate subjects and the skulls of his victims, and that of a *poderoso do sertão*, a mighty cattle baron of the Brazilian north-east. He notices every custom or ritual that surrounds marriage, child-birth, or particularly death in those two regions. He loves to catalogue the curios and relics kept by old people—by Francisco da Silva after his eventual decline, or by his daughter.

The Viceroy of Ouidah is remarkably short for a novel that covers the rise and fall of a trading dynasty and spans a century and a half in time. But it is none the less powerful despite its brevity. It tells of amazing adventures in wild places and makes compelling reading.

John Hemming, "A Trader from the Badlands," in The Times Literary Supplement (© Times Newspapers Ltd. (London) 1980; reproduced from The Times

Literary Supplement *by permission*), No. 4053, December 5, 1980, p. 1380.

JOHN THOMPSON

Bruce Chatwin's travel book **"In Patagonia"** . . . earned wide praise and distinguished awards. In it he yielded only occasionally to the urge for novelistic invention that overcame him this time [in **"The Viceroy of Ouidah"**]. He set out to write a biography of a Brazilian slaver in Dahomey, but he was arrested in Cotinou and something happened—he doesn't say what—that made him decide not to go back for more research. Thus he wrote this "work of the imagination." How can we object? None of us has seen these things. No doubt Dahomey was and is something special. We read today of Uganda. Still, others have found or imagined other primitive Africas. One could mention Graham Greene's "Journey Without Maps" or, for a work of the imagination based on somewhat less horrendous events, Chinua Achebe's "Arrow of God." That novel of West Africa has violence enough, and cruel superstition too, yet it is suffused with the common humanity of which I find not one dried drop in **"The Viceroy of Ouidah."** (p. 28)

> John Thompson, "The Hero Was a Slaver," in The New York Times Book Review (*copyright © 1980 by The New York Times Company; reprinted by permission*), December 14, 1980, pp. 7, 28.

RICHARD HALL

There is no denying the brilliance of Bruce Chatwin's book. The prose coruscates, so that many images from this African horror story linger disturbingly in the mind.

Yet you are left wondering what to make of **The Viceroy of Ouidah.** The tale's bare bones (a fitting metaphor) concern a young Brazilian who set himself up on the slave coast of Dahomey in the early 19th century and grew rich from the many human cargoes he shipped back to South America, until the dark continent wreaked its dreadful revenge upon him.

This may be taken as a superb, impressionistic piece of historical reconstruction, although Chatwin carefully calls it "a work of imagination." . . .

So the way to approach this brief, splendid book is to put aside any agonizing about truth (even the Aristotelian sort) and treat it as an "entertainment," in Graham Greene's use of the word.

The story begins in the present, at the requiem held every year for the long-dead Dom Francisco. His many descendants, darker with every generation, and now "numberless as grasshoppers," gather to honor him. After the mass, the voodoo, as a sweating procession weaves through the African town to the ant-ridden ancestral home. Beside the Goanese four-poster a bottle of Gordon's gin is always ready, for when the great man awakes. Near the praying plaster statue of St. Francis of Assisi stands a curious object covered in blood and feathers: a Dahomean altar of the dead.

From this moment you are in thrall. The word-pictures pile up, haunting and horrific, in paragraphs often only a short sentence in length. On every page they compete to be quoted. . . .

But there is much sardonic humor in the story too. As the slave-trader succumbs to Africa, its people pay him back for his old ways in a fashion which is terrible, yet somehow clownish and affectionate.

The structure of the book is adroit. It works backwards in time, telling of the slave-trader's amber-eyed daughter, forever lost in love for a young English lieutenant who came to Ouidah, danced with her, then sailed away.

A third of the way through you are told about the childhood of Francisco in the backlands of Brazil. This section has quite a different texture from the African chapters which surround it: but the author of the much-praised **In Patagonia** also has a keen sense of South America's past, so the spell is never broken. You know, although he does not, that Francisco's destiny and doom lie across the Atlantic. . . .

Just as Francisco can be remembered as not one man, but several, so the story may be given many interpretations. This is one of those enigmatic books which might be handed to several friends who could afterwards be lured together for a diverting evening, when each declares what the message is.

> Richard Hall, "Nightmare in the Darkness of Dahomey," in Book World—The Washington Post (© *1981, The Washington Post*), January 4, 1981, p. 4.

ANNE DUCHÊNE

[**On the Black Hill**] disconcerts expectation; something one imagines by now this author very much enjoys doing. After the harshly and brilliantly exotic expanses of **In Patagonia** and **The Viceroy of Ouidah,** [Chatwin] has elected to study a few square miles of hill-farm in Radnorshire, and the lives of the twin brothers who farm it.

The writing has the emblematic self-sufficiency of the late David Garnett's. The sense of place is flawlessly invoked, usually in paragraphs of only a few lines . . . ; but the necessary presence of the practical is never neglected. . . .

The mixture of the possible and the unlikely with the laconically lyrical is very much in David Garnett's peculiar vein. So is the humour, which gets in everywhere . . . ; and so is the author's amusing himself by pretending to be a loyal slave of the accidental, while in fact he is magisterially pulling all the strings. Anyone who enjoyed being bullied in this way by Garnett will enjoy this book too.

Benjamin and Lewis, the brothers, who are identical twins, are shown over a period of eighty years sharing their work, and also their bed, noncommittally, and sharing each other's pains when the other is in danger or distress; Lewis's nose bleeds too when Benjamin, rejected in 1914 as a conscientious objector, is beaten up in the Army.

They do not invariably share each other's pleasures—Lewis several times broaches relationships, always abortive, with women—but often they do, as when their mother gives them each a Hercules bicycle on their thirty-seventh birthday, on which they make archaeological forays into Wales. Unhappily rebuffed in these, they keep the more closely to their farm—which is called The Vision, as if challenging reviewers to make too much of the fact—but they never become recluses; their friends include members of the local gentry, the local hippie, and numerous crumbling neighbours, chiefly female, who are often difficult to distinguish under the caked grime and dung.

The book is "about" such concrete, arbitrary details as those suggested here. It may give a fine insight into the feuding and tolerance of a small community, and even a series of incidental comments on British social history in this century, but these are certainly not its motives. Its intention is to paint a picture of two men's lives in a particular place. What happens is not really the author's business, Chatwin implies. Love may occur, or violence, or sadness, but his concern is to show the continued existence of the brothers in their parents' house. Sentiment is always checked, anticipation always baffled, by events. . . . The charitable, if slightly distended eye suspends judgment, and Radnorshire is seen as every bit as full of banked-down human madness as Patagonia. Where on earth, one wonders, will Bruce Chatwin go next?

Anne Duchêne, "Doubling the Vision," in The Times Literary Supplement (© Times Newspapers Ltd. (London) 1982; reproduced from The Times Literary Supplement by permission), No. 4148, October 1, 1982, p. 1063.

FRANCIS KING

Geographically, the claustrophobic world inhabited for 80 years by Lewis and Benjamin Jones [in *On the Black Hill*] is close to that of Mary Webb's novels; thematically it is even closer. . . . Mr Chatwin is a better, because more fastidious, writer than Mary Webb; but the elements which are finest in her novels are also to be found in his: an ability to evoke country lives flowing, strong, dark and deep, through their narrow channels; a poetic sensitivity to landscapes changing with each change of season; and the born storyteller's knack of convincing one that these characters scraped their precarious livings, carried on their embittered feuds, triumphed or (more often) were thwarted in their violent passions, and had their momentary epiphanies of glory in precisely this manner and no other. . . .

There are passages in the book when Mr Chatwin edges perilously near to the cliff-edge of sentimentality and bathos. . . .

But, in general, the book tells its strange, moving story of these two intertwined lives, each supporting and choking the other, two halves, male and female, of single, larger nature, with honesty, dignity and conviction.

Francis King, "Ties of Blood," in The Spectator (© 1982 by The Spectator; reprinted by permission of The Spectator), Vol. 249, No. 8047, October 2, 1982, p. 24.

LORNA SAGE

'On the Black Hill' experiments with themes [Chatwin] has made his own as a travel writer—the improbable and bizarre completeness of worlds on the margins of consciousness, and the ready-made fiction you can find, if you look, in the accidents of history and geography. **'On the Black Hill'** surveys twentieth-century life from the vantage-point of a small mountain in Radnorshire, where time arranges itself in slow layers, and you can observe the frenzy of large events through the wrong end of the telescope.

Eccentricity is the order of things, and the book's beginning, describing the curious, crotchety routines of twin bachelor brothers perched on their hill . . . has the same sort of imaginative effrontery as the opening of Mervyn Peake's 'Gormenghast.' You're plunged into a pattern of life that refers only to itself.

Chatwin, unlike Peake, is interested in the way his characters' insulated and conventionally crazy existence is, against all odds, a good recipe for survival. Lewis and Benjamin preserve an innocence that satirizes the world outside. By the original accident of their twinhood they've never learned to be 'individuals,' never tried to take possession of their destinies. In their musty, communal consciousness the things that happen—the First World War, their father's murder of their pet pig, the excavation of the tomb of Tutankhamun in the *News of the World*—repose innocently side by side, rather as the aged twins do in bed, making no sense and doing no harm. . . .

This is shameless nostalgia that recognises itself as such, and one of the novel's charms is its gently mocking perspective on the fashionable themes of conservation and self-sufficiency. Mr Chatwin's twin Joneses achieve self-sufficiency through mother, and having very small egos. That said, though, the book is in the end disappointing because the characters—as opposed to their setting—aren't, after their first appearance, invented thoroughly enough. I suspect Mr Chatwin finds truth stranger than fiction. This novel leaves one with the sense that for him fact is, to date, more imaginatively liberating than fantasy.

Lorna Sage, "Bachelor Sanctuary," in The Observer (reprinted by permission of The Observer Limited), October 3, 1982, p. 33.*

V. S. PRITCHETT

After the excellent book on his travels, *In Patagonia,* it is at first surprising to find Bruce Chatwin writing a novel about the small sheep farmers at home on the hills of the Welsh Border country of England. Sheep farming is, of course, the common link. In the nineteenth century large numbers of tough, poor, and exalted Welsh peasants migrated to Patagonia as if drawn to the isolation, the rains, the snows and hard conditions they knew at home and where they would be free of the mocking gaze and rule of the Sassenach conquerors. The people of *On the Black Hill* are part of the sturdy remnant who toiled and haggled at home.

But if the novel is a watchful traveler's journey through peasant life during the first eighty years of this century, its characters are strong and strange enough to burst the bonds of parish record. They are by nature self-dramatizing. They are carrying with them the ancient inner life of their race. *On the Black Hill* has been compared to works like Thomas Hardy's *The Woodlanders* or *Tess of the D'Urbervilles*, because it comes so close to the skin of rural life, but the comparison is misleading. Chatwin dispenses with grand tragic plot and Hardy's dire use of coincidence. Above all there is no President of the Immortals indifferent to human fate, there is no Victorian atheism and pessimism. . . .

Strangeness plainly stated is the key to Mr. Chatwin's plotless chronicle, the mixing of outward and inner life. The story is dominated by two bachelor brothers who are identical twins. They are thrifty farmers who slave for eighty years on poor mountainy land in an isolated farm. . . . (p. 6)

There is rural murder in the novel and suicide and there is a rotting corpse when a farm is isolated in a bad winter. We are watching the behavior of raw people as they fight their way fiercely and sometimes comically through their lives: they are neither the poeticized people of towny nostalgic novels about peasant life, nor are they crude and Zolaesque. They are far from decadent; they take their sexuality whole-heartedly. Mr. Chatwin is not an erotic novelist but he does convey the ruling sexual willingness. There is a robust account of a lusty Welsh fair where Lewis, who is after the girls, makes Benjamin take a spin on the Wall of Death. Benjamin has to face the intolerable sight of girls with their dresses flying over their faces and sees bare flesh. Benjamin staggers into the street and vomits into the gutter but the girls cannot get Lewis from him.

Mr. Chatwin's writing is simple and direct. He has learned from the Russians "to make it strange," which is second nature to the Welsh; he is quietly true to changes of sky and landscape and is remarkable in his power to bring human feeling to the sight by some casual action. (pp. 6, 8)

The whole book is at once grave, sparkling, and ingeniously contrived. Even the German psychiatrist who appears to explain the pathology of twinship is assimilated into the story without turning it into a case history. (p. 8)

V. S. Pritchett, "Make It Strange," in The New York Review of Books *(reprinted with permission from* The New York Review of Books; *copyright © 1983 Nyrev, Inc.), Vol. XXIX, Nos. 21 & 22, January 20, 1983, pp. 6, 8.*

JOHN UPDIKE

[Bruce Chatwin] writes a clipped, lapidary prose that compresses worlds into pages. **"In Patagonia,"** an account of his wanderings in southern Argentina, won high praise five years ago for its witty obliquity, elegantly economical descriptions, wealth of curious historical and paleontological data, and perky word portraits of the drunken gauchos and homesick Scotsmen he encountered in this vast, raw region. The one virtue **"In Patagonia"** did not conspicuously possess, it seemed to me, was momentum; the traveller so deliberately minimized his personality and obscured his motives that the prose seemed to travel on ghostly legs of its own, snacking on scenery and bits of dialogue where it pleased, and hopping about so airily between past and present, between experienced incident and researched document, that the exotic reality was half-eclipsed by the willful manners of the invisible guide. Mr. Chatwin writes in such short paragraphs that he seems to be constantly interrupting himself. His narratives must be savored in short takes, like collections of short stories. His third book and second novel, **"On the Black Hill"** . . . , also skips, scintillatingly, across a vast terrain—a stretch of time: the eighty years that the Jones twins, Lewis and Benjamin, have lived in Radnorshire, a rural county of Wales bordering that of Hereford, in England. (p. 126)

The author lays out this tale of country narrowness in a mosaic of wonderfully sharp and knowing small scenes. Though Mr. Chatwin was born in 1940, the details of daily life early in the century seem an open book to him. . . . [He] re-creates the past out of what seem not paper souvenirs but living memories, with an understated mastery of period detail and a loving empathy into the inner lives such detail adorned. (pp. 126-27)

The Jones twins are his centerpiece, and the mysterious, infrangible connection between them somehow his moral. From toddlerhood on, they share the same sensations, and Lewis, the older and stronger, feels the pain that mishaps inflict upon Benjamin. Their earliest memories are identical, and even in old age they can dream the same dream. (p. 128)

Now, Mr. Chatwin, a demon researcher, must have a basis for these supernatural connections that the twins enjoy and suffer; but there is something creepy here, and perhaps allegorical, that strains belief. Their twinship is in fact a homosexual marriage, with Benjamin the feminine partner and Lewis the masculine. . . . Mr. Chatwin's ingenuity at posing obstacles and long blank intervals is fully needed to suppress our wonder that a robust and prosperous male goes eighty years with no more than a few scratchy and aborted romances. (pp. 128-29)

Nevertheless, the apparition of the linked twins chimes with much else that is slightly fabulous in their Welsh surround; we seem to see through them into a hilly, antique landscape drenched in flowers—dozens and dozens of botanical specifics are woven into the text—and overshadowed by dramatic clouds. . . . A sense has been conveyed—and this only a novel to some degree "historic" can do—of the immensity of time a human life spans, a span itself dwarfed by the perspectives of history. . . . It is a measure of Mr. Chatwin's compression that **"On the Black Hill"** achieves it in less than two hundred and fifty pages. His studied style—with something in it of Hemingway's chiselled bleakness, and something of Lawrence's inspired swiftness—touches on the epic. (pp. 129-30)

John Updike, "The Jones Boys" (© 1983 by John Updike), in The New Yorker, *Vol. LIX, No. 5, March 21, 1983, pp. 126-30.*

Walter Van Tilburg Clark
1909-1971

American novelist, short story writer, essayist, and poet.

Clark's stories of the American West are among the finest ever written. Unlike other Western novels that focus on stereotypic masculine heroes, Clark's work features male characters who are three-dimensional and portrays such basic human emotions as fear and insecurity. His themes, often bordering on the mystical, are universal. He examines the conflict between good and evil, adolescence and maturity, and the predatory relationship between humanity and nature.

Clark's first novel, *The Ox-Bow Incident* (1940), is his most popular work. The book, described by L. L. Lee as "a superior cowboy story," explores the implications of vigilante "justice." Clark wrote *The Ox-Bow Incident* as a warning against fascism and demagoguery. Most critics read the novel as a powerful social and political allegory. *The Ox-Bow Incident* was made into a critically acclaimed motion picture in 1943.

Many critics were disappointed with Clark's second work, *The City of Trembling Leaves* (1945). This book is a semiautobiographical account of a sensitive boy growing up in Reno, Nevada. Told in a lyrical prose style, critics found the book too lengthy and rambling.

The Track of the Cat (1949) is a symbolic psychological novel that is similar in many ways to Melville's *Moby Dick*. In this book, which some critics believe is Clark's best work, the pursuit of a mountain lion evokes different reactions in each character. Clark's prose realistically conveys their tension and terror. Critics consider Clark's use of dreams in predicting each character's fate an effective motif. *The Watchful Gods and Other Stories* (1950) was Clark's last published work. The title story, with its depiction of a young boy's painful initiation into the world of good and evil, reflects Clark's perception of nature. The remaining stories in the book contain many themes covered in Clark's earlier writing.

(See also *Contemporary Authors*, Vols. 9-12, rev. ed., Vols. 33-36, rev. ed. [obituary]; *Something about the Author*, Vol. 8; and *Dictionary of Literary Biography*, Vol. 9.)

Special Collections, University of Nevada Library

CLIFTON FADIMAN

Walter Van Tilburg Clark's **"The Ox-Bow Incident"** is your correspondent's unwavering choice for the year's finest first novel. It has many of the elements of an old-fashioned horse opera—monosyllabic cowpunchers, cattle rustlers, a Mae Western lady, barroom brawls, shootings, lynchings, a villainous Mexican. But it bears about the same relation to an ordinary Western that "The Maltese Falcon" does to a hack detective story. Not to put too fine a point on it, I think it's sort of what you might call a masterpiece. . . .

"The Ox-Box Incident" is not so much a story about a violent happening as a mature, unpitying examination of what causes men to love violence and to transgress justice. What lends the book an unusual touch—almost a touch of genius—is the way in which everything that is important in it revolves around the most profound moral issues and is presented only in terms of the tensest melodrama. Each of the characters—there are a score of them and they are realized with almost over-elaborate precision—bears a special relation to the problem of violence, from the sadistic Tetley to Davies, the saint *manqué*. But none of them figures merely as a spokesman for an idea or even a feeling; each one, you sense, is a whole life of which only a facet is presented in this particular episode.

In addition to being the inventor of a plot whose convolutions you will follow popeyed and goose-pimpled, Mr. Clark is the commander of a completely adult style, all bone and sinew, without a trace of the affectation of oversimplicity. If he has a fault, it is that of understatement, for which he will be freely forgiven.

On the basis of **"The Ox-Bow Incident,"** I don't think you can make any predictions about Mr. Clark. The thing is so darned perfect that it seems to deny the possibility of growth on the part of the author. . . . There's a kind of cabinet-worker precision about **"The Ox-Bow Incident;"** everything—characters, plot, style, rhythm, even the title, so cool and complete—falls into place not mechanically but organically, as if the final effect had been calculated shrewdly and patiently, with nothing left to improvisation. Such a book can never be followed up by another of the same kind; it stands by itself.

But whether or not Mr. Clark publishes a single line in the future, he's a writer, here and now. (p. 84)

> Clifton Fadiman, "Make Way for Mr. Clark—The O'Neill Family Afloat and Ashore" (copyright © 1940, 1968 by The New Yorker Magazine, Inc.; reprinted by permission of Lescher & Lescher, Ltd.), in The New Yorker, Vol. XVI, No. 35, October 12, 1940, pp. 84-5.*

EDMUND WILSON

["**The City of Trembling Leaves**"] is a book of which the faults and the virtues are combined in an unusual way and which may baffle or give pause to the reviewer.... It is a long history of a young composer growing up in Reno, Nevada, and it manages to be undramatic with a consistency that seems to be not deliberate but the result of a complete indifference to the ways in which stories are conventionally built (the author *can* tell a good story when it happens to work out that way, as is demonstrated by the chapter on the track meet). Mr. Clark takes us, episode by episode, through the protracted adolescence of his hero with what, aside from the literary proficiency, would seem almost the innocence of adolescence itself.... [We] are led to believe—since the author seems to know what he is doing—that [the lengthy account of Tim Hazard's youth] is eventually to be justified by being invested with significance in the light of what is afterward to happen. Yet when we glance back at the first part from the end, it still looks like a youthful diary full of ambitions, obsessions, and tempests that seem absurdly out of proportion to their causes. (p. 75)

You decide, when you are approaching the close, that the whole book is a first installment of one of those long biographical novels, an American "Jean-Christophe," and that the themes are to be further developed and the ultimate judgments conveyed in a succession of later volumes. But this turns out to be not the case.... [The] reader is left rather blank. He had assumed that the author was preparing for Tim some bitter ordeal or frustration or some unexpected self-fulfillment. But the suspense has been entirely an illusion created by the reader himself. The author has not been leading up to anything except the reversion of the hero to his origins, and not even this is made dramatic, as it might conceivably be, by showing that the Tim who returns has seen the world and found that what is in it is no different from his home town—because Tim has not known the world, and he has not even had the gumption to make any determined play for his ideal woman, Rachel.

This is so far an unpromising account of "**The City of Trembling Leaves**," and you may think that you will not want to read it. Yet long though it is and immature though it is and unskillfully managed though it is—the author is always impeding his own progress with flashbacks which last so long that they become confused with the present, and crowding out his human beings with mountain landscapes that cover pages—in spite of all this, if you start the novel, you are likely to read it through without skipping, for the author has got what it takes to make the reader become involved in his imaginative experience and to keep him under the spell of his writing. The real triumph of Mr. Clark is that he makes you accept his story of coming of age in Reno entirely on its own terms. You so completely live the life of these young people that you hardly think to question their importance or the meaning of what they are doing. Above all, you enjoy their life: the camping trips and mountain walks and musical evenings at Carmel and nights of drinking in lonely bars are all made so enchanting or so amiable that we rarely become impatient at being compelled to take part in so many of them. What the book lacks in point and intensity it more or less makes up for in felicity—a felicity of both spirit and style.

For "**The City of Trembling Leaves**" is not, as my description may suggest, a book like the novels of Thomas Wolfe, in which the author pours out streams of language in a lava that is always amorphous and that may or may not be incandescent. The writing of Mr. Clark's novel, though it sometimes gives an effect of dilution, of needing to be compressed and trimmed, has a literary sureness and a purity of taste rather rare in American fiction; it is natural without being colloquial in the conventional Hemingway manner—quite free from either self-consciousness or effort. He slips sometimes, as if without knowing the difference, into images that are insipid or banal, but he can more often set flowing phrases which are at once precise and fresh. The paragraphs are fluid and pellucid, full of day and of cold Nevada shade—a little thin, a little lightheaded, like the air in the Sierras itself, but exhilarating and almost exalting. (pp. 75-6)

> Edmund Wilson, "White Peaks and Limpid Lakes: A Novel about Nevada" (© 1945 by The New Yorker Magazine, Inc.; reprinted by permission of Farrar, Straus and Giroux, Inc.), in The New Yorker, Vol. XXI, No. 15, May 26, 1945, pp. 75-7.

MARK SCHORER

"**The Track of the Cat**" is one of the great American novels of "place." Something of its nobility should be suggested by the fact that one cannot bring to mind a similar novel of its kind that is quite worthy of comparison. One thinks of the best in the genre, even of such works as Elizabeth Madox Roberts' "The Time of Man" and Willa Cather's "My Antonia," and they come to seem, by comparison, more than ever like miniature studies of special manners, more than graceful surely, yet without grandeur. Mr. Clark's new novel likewise transcends his own earlier books, being larger in scope than his tight drama of a lynching, "**The Ox-Bow Incident**," and more controlled than the loosely constructed, personal chronicle, "**The City of Trembling Leaves**." "**The Track of the Cat**" may well be the achievement that twentieth-century American regionalism has needed to justify itself....

[The] narrative, simple to the point of being stark, is not in itself the major interest of the book. It is almost as if Mr. Clark had written his novel around an archetypal, universally known fable. The major interest is the manner in which he sustains that simple narrative, and that is an achievement nothing less than extraordinary. It returns us, too, to the essence of the novel, which is the scene—a landscape, an atmosphere, an experienced segment and quality of earth and weather, magnificently realized and therefore continually thrilling. To this atmosphere the plot is subsidiary, as the characters are subsidiary. They exist, they have their reality in terms of their place.

The characterization is simple and direct, each person sharply, even baldly, differentiated from the others (one might, in fact, complain that Mr. Clark tends to underline these simple characterizations too heavily), and they operate in the narrative almost like gears when they mesh, each in his relationships with others still isolate in his unyielding identity. At the same time, that identity is in every case diminished by the scene, by the mute vastness of mountains and the mystery of familiar places and the eerie elusiveness of the wild spirit that haunts it, as one by one each of the brothers makes his detailed confrontation with these.

And what is the cat, the object of the hunt? There will no doubt be cries of "Moby Dick" and "the spirit of evil," yet the fact is that Mr. Clark presses no symbolism and this novel is a novel without metaphysical overtones. (p. 1)

There are, of course, two cats—the real one, which kills cattle and is finally found and killed by men, and the other one, the black one, which is only real in dreams, whether they are the day-dreams of Arthur or the savage visions of the primitive Joe Sam, or the final, terrorized dreams of the balked "realist," Curt. The dreamed panther is not apprehended. It is, I should say, quite simply, the spirit of the place, the untrackable wildness of mountains and the melancholy mystery of human experience in its solitude.

For one reader, at any rate, this is the real beauty of Walter Clark's masterful prose—its wonderful capacity to evoke from the homeliest circumstances the quality of grief and loneliness that exists deep in or under every human effort. The sharp visual clarity and the consequent fulness of evocation in scene after scene—many of them sustained in the most lavish detail for page after page—are a constant delight. . . . And under all is the same deep strain of melancholy that shares in the elegiac character of most epic effort. (pp. 1, 16)

If Walter Clark uses his scene for purposes greater than its own greatness, he does so because the power of his prose can create from the scene a perfect symbolization of those qualities in the life of man which make him a tragic being: his solitary engagement with a moral destiny. And that is why he has here given stature and beauty to what has often seemed little more than a dogged movement in contemporary literary history. (p. 16)

> *Mark Schorer, "An Eloquent Novel of 'Place'," in* The New York Times Book Review *(copyright © 1949 by The New York Times Company; reprinted by permission), June 5, 1949, pp. 1, 16.*

HARVEY SWADOS

Mr. Clark appears in this collection of his short stories ["**The Watchful Gods and Other Stories**"] as a sensitive and cultivated writer, as much at home with knowledgeable outdoor men and their natural world as with intellectuals and academicians whose connection to the earth on which they live is only that of a man to his city apartment.

This unlikely but graceful combination seems to be responsible for a prose style that is wiry, masculine, and mature, and that has produced almost by its own evocative power—without the aid of complex structuring—a number of interesting stories, and one at least that is really superb. **The Wind and the Snow of Winter** brings a lonely and addled old prospector to the terrible realization of his own senility, as he plods slowly across the bleak Western landscape with the dreamlike cinematic movement of the cowboys in Mr. Clark's fine first novel, "**The Ox-Bow Incident.**" (p. 317)

But this is the high point of Mr. Clark's collection. When he attempts to utilize his remarkable feeling for the quality of man's relation to the natural elements—a matter of concern to few important American writers other than Faulkner—in order to assert a philosophical generalization, he is merely banal, as in **Why Don't You Look Where You're Going?** which counterposes the effete travelers on a luxury steamship to a hero crossing the ocean alone in a small boat. And in **The Portable Phonograph**, in which a group of cave-dwelling survivors of War Number Three (or Four) attempt to warm their hearts with the memories of an extinct culture preserved in a few phonograph records, Mr. Clark has recourse to a snapper, or punch line, in the final sentence in order to drive home his point— an unnecessary device if the survivors had been individuals instead of stereotypes selected to reflect Mr. Clark's attitude. (pp. 317-18)

[In the title story] a boy is given a twenty-two rifle for his twelfth birthday. He shoots a little rabbit, is tortured with remorse, and finally buries his first prize. The minute descriptions, not only of the boy's mental processes but of his physical surroundings, begin by trying our patience and end by boring us, and we are left with the feeling that Mr. Clark has expended 115 pages on the exploration of a theme which might better have been encompassed in 15, if he had been under the compulsion to adapt this story, like the others in the collection, to the exigencies of magazine fiction. . . .

Surely a writer is entitled to indulge himself with a glittering tour deforce like **Hook,** which describes the life cycle of a hawk with the cold brilliance of a documentary nature film, and which leaves us with much the same feelings of awe and admiration for the skill and patience of the seeing eye. But when in 306 pages of short stories perhaps only 15 contain any dialogue, aside from people talking to animals, one must inevitably consider the extent of their relevance to the human situation, and one must wonder whether the writer's horizons are not bounded on the one hand by the hawk and on the other by the boy with the twenty-two. (p. 318)

> *Harvey Swados, "Hawks and Men," in* The Nation, *Vol. 171, No. 15, October 7, 1950, pp 317-18.*

VERNON YOUNG

In all of Clark's fiction his exceptionally acute observations of outdoor sound, light, smell, mass, texture and relationship are superior to his understanding of the human psyche in any but a decivilised area of operation. There is no living American writer of fiction who can type a richer page of landscape but no writer of equal talent is more endangered by the inability to enrich his human types. The Man on Clark's natural stage is never sufficiently conscious of his position to turn that position into one of tragedy. Curt, in **The Track of the Cat,** is almost an exception, but it seems to me we do not intimately understand him so much as we pity him, and we are spellbound by the absorbing depersonalized emotions of the hunt fracturing into fear and superstition. Clark's genius in this novel lay in his dramatic and symbolic disposition of forces operating through rather thin characters, just as in **The Ox-Bow Incident** he left us with a stronger impression of The Incident than of the callow males involved in it. This disparity is only in part the result of selection. The simple souls whom Clark generally chooses for his protagonists are, besides being, often, indigenous to his scene, the most convenient effigies for his limited psychological imagination. When he actually frees his material sufficiently to include beings with a higher potential for perception (as he did with Arthur in **The Track of the Cat** and with the intelligentsia of **The Portable Phonograph**) he fails to render the interesting complexity we anticipate. Always, his most vivid presentation is of inhuman nature; the drama presides in the forces at work which he, as author, is obliged to explain, not in the awareness of the differentiated ego involved in this drama.

All this may be simply another way of defining Clark's teleology, of inferring that his strength lies in relating Experience as Ritual rather than in Experience as Photographic Analysis. His strength may but his intention clearly does not. His dessicated humans are inducted by his one-sided knowledge, not by his aesthetic wisdom. Tentatively, he is essaying an American myth but up to now it is a myth in which the gods are more clearly construed than the heroes. The myth is therefore magnificent in synopsis but less satisfactory in the page-to-page experience. The hallucinations in *The Track of the Cat* and in [his latest volume] *The Watchful Gods* have more substance than the victims who suffer them. (pp. 111-12)

Clark's style, in itself, is still the most arresting topic of scrutiny in his work. It is the gauge of his points of reference and the key to his personal fluctuation between fact and myth. Up to now, the liberation of his talent has come from his imagination when it relaxes into the *im*personal consciousness which easily produces the symbolic. There, overpowering whatever self-consciousness may show up when he is paying homage to observed manners, lies his warmth and his flexibility. Crippling takes place either when he adopts a stringently intellectual attitude toward his material or when he fails to rise above the childhood sensitivity to which he is painfully in thrall. It is often thus with American fiction: the inability to trust maturity or the puritanical forcing of it by an act of will imposed on the style. These failures are two sides of the coin; they reveal the prevailing insecurity of the American artist who is, like the adolescent, between two worlds, neither of which he can accept, reject or find median terms for. (pp. 112-13)

[The] writer of the great moments in *The Track of the Cat,* the superb geographer who has given us the subsensory life of desert and coastline, endangers his development by . . . lapses into small-town talk and viewpoint. Whatever democratic strength may derive from small town, it cannot be a permanent asset to an artist; it is this aspect which nobody takes seriously in Hemingway or Stegner, to name two contemporaries in Clark's company who are always just about to "make it." If Clark's intelligence should not be indicated by reference to his rationalizations, we can fairly deplore his precariously infantile story, *The Fish Who Could Close His Eyes,* an unintentional and certainly unnecessary parody of the late—can one say?—John Steinbeck. It seems hardly possible that the hand that wrote this jejeune nonsense could also have authored the virtuoso power of **"Hook,"** the mastered undertones of **"Wind and Snow of Winter"** or, insofar as its mythic structure is concerned—vision, deed, flight and immersion—that wonderful "ceremony of innocence," soured periodically by a sentimental pitch, **"The Watchful Gods."**

One is hard on Clark because one fears for the failure of his freshening strength and intuitive wisdom. The short stories in his latest volume predate *The Track of the Cat* but if *The Watchful Gods,* itself, is indeed a new production, it is warning that Clark is not yet out of the household woods. When he cuts free from the apron-strings of his obligation to teen-age wistfulness which, let us face it, is a boring and relatively worthless drag on the responsibility of a grown-up teller of tales; when he enters into the hidden life of cruelty and sublimity which infests nature (as well as man, but he hasn't quite caught up with that), he can soar like the veriest hawk. He knows *how* to write, that is sure. He need not worry himself into professorial traps on the subject of process in order to console teachers of composition. He knows *what* to write but he does not yet risk leaving, without a backward glance, the tennis courts of his suburban youth for the deserts of the soul which open before us in those [stories] . . . where his truly enchanting interfusions of mystery and phenomena take place. . . . (pp. 116-17)

> Vernon Young, "Gods without Heroes: The Tentative Myth of Van Tilburg Clark," in Arizona Quarterly (copyright © 1951 by the Arizona Quarterly), Vol. 7, No. 2, Summer, 1951, pp. 110-19.

L. L. LEE

"The fat dream," Arthur Bridges calls it in *The Track of the Cat*. . . . Explicitly, Arthur is talking about that American dream of conquering the American land in order to create the good, i.e., the abundantly material life—the dream indeed not just of American capitalism but of "modern" man. But Arthur is also speaking of other dreams, of the American Dream, and for the moment he is his creator's, Walter Van Tilburg Clark's, voice.

What one means by the American Dream depends, of course, upon the speaker. But in every man's definition and in every artist's realization of the Dream must appear the American land, sometimes a new Eden, sometimes something very near to Hell, sometimes mother and destroyer both, almost always a great ambiguity. Moreover, in every definition, the question of what man, or rather the white man, has to do with the mystery of nature must be asked and explored. And, finally, one must say what man has to do with man as they live together in that land. (p. 164)

Clark's work is a criticism of the American Dream—not directly, through satire, and not entirely, for Clark accepts much of that dream, but indirectly by giving a statement of value of his own. He is, despite his surface simplicity and occasional sentimentality, a notable ironist.

At bottom, Clark is a moralist. But he does not preach a social system, unless a kind of anarchy be a social system. He addresses himself to the individual: we must love one another, and nature, or die. Nature must not be considered only as something to be overcome and made useful; it is for men to live in, to be *alive* in. The orthodoxies of America, the Puritan Jehovah or the god of money, are anti-life. . . .

All men as living creatures are equal, Clark has agreed (*The Oxbow Incident* is a bitter indictment of social inequality as well as of injustice). But men are good, and so valuable, only if they live in the right way. That right way is to live almost as a holy fool with high moral courage in and with the natural world and with other men. Above all, man's way with man corresponds to his way with nature. This statement is, I suggest, the key theme of Clark's fiction: one side of it may be more important than the other for any one work, but both sides are in every work.

But if Clark is a moralist, he is also a realist. . . . The good men of Clark's fiction are not the new Adam; Clark is not so innocent as to believe that the American can remain innocent nor does he believe that the world has been reborn in America. He says, rather simply, that man should be good but that evil exists.

And evil can be anywhere. For Clark, the natural world is usually a good, but is also a mystery, a sometimes terrifying mystery. The natural world can offer images to live by; it can give and restore human integrity; it can be fulfillment if one comes to it as a worshipper, with love but also with awareness. I use the word "worshipper" deliberately. Clark's fiction is filled with the gods of nature who are to be recognized as gods. They are not the devices of bad poetry or mere abstractions; they are true images of man's sense of the real powers of nature. (p. 165)

It is in some of the short stories, in the novelette **"The Watchful Gods,"** and in *The Track of the Cat* that Clark most clearly presents his view of the ambiguity of the American landscape. Now, it would be untrue to insist that Clark is talking only about man's relationship with nature in these works; the gods, the good and the evil, are often obviously within the characters. But it would be equally untrue to say that the natural world is nothing but a stage, for the natural world *is*, it is an actual being as well as a subjective symbol. . . .

The actual mountain lion is an insane killer: it slaughters the cattle without need for food; it kills Arthur Bridges with a cold cunning. It is, then, an aspect of nature as non-human, indifferent to human values. In a way, it is one side of the actual American land. (p. 166)

But if nature, the American land, represents horror and threat, i.e., death, it also represents life. As Harold, the youngest of the good Bridges (Clark perhaps too neatly balances three Bridges against three) observes Gwen Williams, the young woman he is going to marry, he thinks of her as a priestess of life, a priestess of the God of Life as opposed to the God of Death. And "she wants what Arthur wanted." What Arthur wanted was the unspoiled natural world. Too, Gwen embodies the principle of fertility; she and Harold will carry on life.

In *The City of Trembling Leaves*, Clark gives this other side of nature a fuller exposition. Nature here is usually benign, beautiful, solacing, and alive. . . . [Tim Hazzard believes] that excessive intellectualism is an anti-life orthodoxy. One must experience nature, not use it only as symbol and idea. (p. 167)

It is the white man, the builder of cities, living usually as the outsider on the land, who is most endangered by the powers of nature. The white man is the man of organization, of groups, not yielding himself to the natural world. He is not a true individual, despite all his shouting about individualism. . . . Clark illustrates these contradictions in the American position on individualism when he speaks of "dreamers, or, as Tim would call them, primary realists, and factualists, or secondary realists. . . ." The dreamers are the real individuals, the others are simply members of the mob.

It is this lack of real individualism in the white man that has most disturbed Clark. The white man has acted only to gain power in his group and to gain power over things: this is a violent and false ethic. It is what has led to the rape of the land and to the cruelty of one man to another. From Tetley in *Oxbow* through the corrupt Briasi in *Leaves* to Curt Bridges in *Cat* and perhaps the father in **"The Watchful Gods"** runs the line of his destroyers, both of land and of other men.

On the other hand, the true individual is not a seeker after power. It is only by opposing the American dream of success, by cutting oneself off from the crowd and the crowd's values, from the hunt for money, that one can be really complete. The individual, then, is likely to be a lonely man; he does not fit into the social organization. Sometimes Clark presents him as the artist, always a figure on the fringes of the community. (In an odd way, Clark's artist is a conservative; he wants to hold on to the still unravaged land and the human values of the past, if not to the nineteenth-century American capitalism that is destroying them.) The true individual has only the power of his integrity—which does not always suffice; he needs, also, moral and physical courage. (pp. 168-69)

The Oxbow Incident is Clark's best known novel; it is also the one most directly concerned with man as a political animal, that is, man as member of a community. And nature seems almost ignored except as setting, as stage. But stages, certainly, are always symbolic, for they can suggest the attitude of the author of the drama. The stage does so here; nature functions as a symbolic comment upon men's actions. The novel begins in the sunlight, in the beginning warmth of spring, but the main action takes place at night and in the cold. Nature, and so, Life, in a sense withdraws. The cold and the darkness symbolize the lynchers' being outside of nature as well as their own inner coldness and darkness. The hanging at dawn, then, is not just a simple reversal, i.e., death occurring just as the day is reborn, but is also a deliberate assault by the lynchers against the continuing processes of nature.

Oxbow is also the most ambiguous of Clark's treatments of the American scene: not in its protest against injustice, certainly not in its obvious protest against racism. But it is ambiguous in that it is concerned with ambiguities: how does one arrive at justice—and can man arrive at justice anyway?

What is justice to be based upon? Davies answers that it comes from the law, and that the law is based upon the majority will. This is good American doctrine. But every reader will note that Tetley goes through certain forms: he holds a kind of trial, and the decision is based upon the votes of the majority. That majority, though, is not of a group of individuals, but of a "pack" (as young Tetley calls them), men more afraid of being thought physically afraid than they are afraid of committing an injustice. And the action they perform is manifestly unjust, that is, it is wrong. The men are hanged to satisfy Tetley's lust for power, and the group of "rugged individualists" surrenders to him.

Clark is indeed talking about more than a Western lynch mob; he is talking about the whole American society or, rather, the whole human society. And the horror lies in the irony: it is far easier to understand and forgive the brutal actions of slaves than it is to understand and forgive the brutal actions of men who think themselves free and act as slaves. Here is Clark's most explicit criticism of the American Dream: the forms of law will not suffice if they are not based upon true individualism. And these Americans are not individuals nor are they concerned with individuals. (pp. 169-70)

In short, Clark is saying that man will not have justice until certain external codes, the killing hand of the past that denies the individuality of each person, are forgotten (man must not, of course, reject those elements of the past that raise the spirit). And justice will only exist when it is exercised by individuals, not by packs. The individual is one who understands others and his natural world and is willing to live and to let live. Stated this baldly, Clark's themes are romantic, romantic in a way that has been under considerable attack these past fifty years. But he does not present them as simply answers. Evil does exist; but man should not surrender just because he may not win. One certainly should not accept the death of the spirit merely because such a death is an order, a material order. For, if the fat dream is ended, there are other dreams. (pp. 170-71)

L. L. Lee, "Walter Van Tilburg Clark's Ambiguous American Dream" (copyright © 1965 by the National Council of Teachers of English; reprinted by permission of the publisher and the author), in College English, Vol. 26, No. 5, February, 1965 (and reprinted in Critical Essays on the Western American Novel, edited by William T. Pilkington, G. K. Hall & Co., 1980, pp. 164-71).

WALLACE STEGNER

Civilization is Walter Clark's theme; the West is only his raw material. What else is the burden of *The Ox-Bow Incident*? That novel is a long way from being a simple reversal of the vigilante stereotype or an ironic questioning of vigilante justice. It is a probing of the whole blind ethics of an essentially false, imperfectly formed, excessively masculine society, and of the way in which individuals, out of personal inadequacy, out of mistaken loyalties and priorities, out of a fear of seeming to be womanish, or out of plain cowardice, let themselves be pushed into murder. . . . Evil has courage, good is sometimes cowardly, reality gets bent by appearances. And the book does not end with the discovery that the hanged men are innocent and that lynch law is a mistake. It goes on examining how *profound* a mistake. The moral ambiguities reverberate through the town. We begin to know the good guys from the bad guys by the way they deal with their own complicity in a tragic error. (pp. 126-27)

I suspect that *The Ox-Bow Incident*'s unchallenged place on the shelf of Western classics is due not to its being fully appreciated and comprehended but to its persistently being misread as the kind of mythic Western Walt Clark was actually all but parodying. . . . [To the publishers and readers] it is a novel of excitement and suspense and nervous trigger fingers. They do not read it as the report of a failure of individual and social conscience and nerve, an account of wrong sanctioned and forced by the false ethics of a barbarous folk culture. They do not read it as a lamentable episode of a civilization in the throes of being born.

Clark's adaptation of the Western makes use of its machinery but substitutes a complex and ambiguous moral problem for the blacks and whites of the genre. His version of the *Kunstroman* is equally desimplified. I call *The City of Trembling Leaves* . . . a *Kunstroman* rather than a spiritual autobiography because, though there are unquestionably autobiographical elements in it, Clark has taken evasive action: has made Tim Hazard's family entirely unlike his own and has kept himself in the book, by name, as a commentator. . . . (p. 127)

[*The City of Trembling Leaves*] belongs in the pigeonhole with *A Portrait of the Artist as a Young Man; Look Homeward, Angel; Wilhelm Meister; The Hill of Dreams,* and some more somber books such as *Jude the Obscure,* and especially some western American portraits of the artist such as *The Song of the Lark*. It chronicles the development of a sensitive adolescent into an artist. It is focused on the relation between art and life, that obsessive theme of Thomas Mann's, and it explores that relation not only through Tim's music and through the painting and sculpture of Lawrence Black but also through the several variations on artistic adjustment made by Tim's musician friends in Carmel. It reveals a skinless sensibility in its mystical feeling for Pyramid Lake, the Sierra, and the desert. . . . These are all fairly standard elements of a literary genre at least a hundred years old before Walter Clark took hold of it—a genre, one should note, often favored by self-obsessed romantics at war with their surroundings.

But if Tim Hazard is romantic, his book is not. It is steadily cauterized by irony. And the element of repudiation and compulsive self-exile, almost standard among spiritual autobiographies, is absolutely missing. Tim Hazard, this sensitive youth with musical aspirations and a high cultural potential, grows up in Reno, Nevada, and is never at war with it. . . . He accepts—and so did I—the standards of his time and place, and tries to star in what they value; and if he can't accept them he ignores them. (pp. 127-28)

Most important, the end of his long struggle to be an artist is not exile or flight, as in so many lives and books, but reconciliation with his town and himself. . . . Ultimately he simply incorporates the divergences of taste between himself and his town. Some things he outgrows, as he outgrows his adolescent adorations and excesses, but they have strengthened rather than harmed him. And that makes *The City of Trembling Leaves* unique in its genre. Clark has not justified himself at the expense of his surroundings, if we may take Tim to represent Clark. He has tried to use them to grow from, and in.

One must admit flaws in this novel. For me, at least, there is an excess of philosophical abstraction. And in trying to present Tim's adolescent adorations sympathetically but ironically, and at the same time not be ironic about the seriousness of Tim's efforts to make a unity of his divided heritage, Clark is sometimes overlong and unduly detailed, as if he feared the realistic boy might get lost under the symbolic artist. (pp. 128-29)

In *The Ox-Box Incident,* Clark had suggested that the values of the frontier society were narrow, half formed, and in large measure false, and in the mind of the sensitive cowpuncher who was one of the lynchers, he had planted a civilizing seed of conscience and doubt and unrest, and hence growth. In *The City of Trembling Leaves* he proposed that a native western boy, given talent and motivation, might become an artist even in the unlikely arena of The Biggest Little City on Earth, and might make commonplace origins serve art. In *The Track of the Cat,* his third novel, he came in quite another way at the theme of civilization, the evil of the exploitative and profane white culture, and the possibility of reconciliation between that culture's energies and the watchful gods of the earth. (pp. 129-30)

[The characters are symbolic], but for the most part persuasively real, too. There is a real lion loose in the mountains, but the black painter of evil lives in the ranch house. He lives in Curt, as dominating and arrogant as the worst of the Ox-Bow lynchers; and in Curt's mother, harshly pious, capable of suffering but invulnerable to understanding; and to a lesser extent in Curt's weak and evasive father. Their evil has already defeated the gentle brother, Arthur, long before Curt finds Arthur's broken-necked body in the snow. The same family evil—an evil that we soon recognize as a regional evil, a social evil, an evil of attitude and spirit like the cowardice and mob impulse in *The Ox-Bow Incident*—has completely destroyed the sister, Grace. The only one capable of resisting it, the only one of them, besides the defeated Arthur, who can make contact with the primitive survivor Joe Sam, is Hal, the youngest son. Most readers will identify themselves with Hal and feel his role as their own. It is hard to resist the temptation to be a culture hero. It is important to notice that Hal's position, his hopeful stance as combiner and reconciler, is the essential stance of Art Croft, too, and of Tim Hazard, and of Walter Clark.

I am perhaps eccentric in responding less to Curt's disintegration—evil destroying itself—than to the slow, tense drama of the ranch house. I feel Curt's disaster as a necessity of the plot rather than as a realistic probability. My experience with the Curts of the world does not lead me to think that either as persons or as symbols they are ever touched by the primal gods, that they ever comprehend good and evil, that they are very often visited by poetic justice. Curt at the end of this novel is something out of Eugene O'Neill, an Emperor Jones in chaps, where the others, heightened or not, are authentic. (pp. 131-32)

All of Walter Clark's novels were written from ideas, I believe, especially from a preoccupation with problems of good and evil within the context of the real West. He was a little like Hawthorne in knowing all the time what he wanted to say. The characters he created to say it through, whether historical or contemporary, have most of the time a solidity and realism that are altogether admirable. If he had a weakness, it was that sometimes his ideas outran their realistic base, and he steered his people, or talked about them, instead of letting them act. Not often. And when the symbolic larger meanings emerge, as they do so often, from realities as solid as logs, when we meet and recognize the substance before we are asked to contemplate the shadow, then I follow him with my hat in my hand. He wasn't quite, like Hawthorne, trying to develop a usable past, or not that alone. He was trying, rather, to marry sensitivity and ideas to the half-primitive western life he knew. (pp. 132-33)

[Walter Clark's] books are on the permanent shelf, and I don't mean the shelf of mythic, easy, deluding Westerns. His theme was civilization, and he recorded, indelibly, its first steps in a new country. He naturalized the struggle between good and evil in Nevada as surely as Robinson Jeffers naturalized tragedy on the Big Sur coast. (pp. 134-35)

> Wallace Stegner, "Walter Clark's Frontier" (copyright © 1973 by Wallace Stegner; reprinted by permission of Doubleday & Company, Inc.), in his *One Way to Spell Man*, Doubleday, 1982, pp. 124-35.

JOHN R. MILTON

Walter Clark has come to be known through the years as the essential Western novelist, the one who did perhaps more than anyone else to define (in his fiction) the mode of perception, the acquisition of knowledge, and the style which we tend to call Western. . . . [His] prose style is imagistic, symbolic (or metaphoric), and direct, tapping the subconscious but staying in touch with the real world. (His style is not unlike that of Harvey Fergusson, but it is more forceful and more frequently evocative, probably because of his stronger concern with a sacred as well as a profane world.) His perception of reality rests heavily on dualities and contrasts, in imagery as well as in characterization, and he assumes that knowledge acquired through the intellect or the conscious mind is, at best, incomplete. He searches for unity, and while the distinctions or contrasts of experience are not resolved openly—as they might be for a mystic—they are joined by implication. Through intuitive recognition of the relationships between the two sides of dualities, there is also recognition of likeness (perhaps sameness) of the real, observable, personal world and the mythic or unconscious world of origins—this latter world at least approximating the primal world.

Not a pantheist, Clark nevertheless sees "likeness through all creation" and an alliance between man and nature as well as with the eternal. But these likenesses are often seen as, and stated as, opposites. Whatever fusion of elements is possible must often be implied, must be seen in the point of tension between the opposites, as though between the intellectual and the intuitive means of perception. . . . In particular, Clark is interested in unity—of things, of past and present, of man and nature—and in the circle of life, whose image is the symbol of unity or completeness. Yet on the surface—considering structure superficially—it does not appear that Clark's novels arrive at a point of definite completion. *The Ox-Bow Incident* opens and closes with the somewhat hopeful song of the meadowlark and with the presence of two characters—Art Croft and Gil Carter—who are spectators to the action of the novel more than they are participants in it. Theoretically, this kind of circular structure does not prohibit development along the way. It does not destroy the linear. It simply turns the line back on itself, to a new beginning as it were. (pp. 197-99)

Quite apart from philosophical considerations, *The Ox-Bow Incident* expresses unity in its construction. Clark was knowledgeable in the area of classical literature and it is not surprising to find the Aristotelian unities of time, place, and action in *The Ox-Bow Incident*. . . . Thematically, the unity is not as obvious, relying on suggestion and implication, whereas in *The City of Trembling Leaves* it is more apparent in the theme than in the structure, and in *The Track of the Cat* these two approaches are modified and brought together in what Clark must have considered the most meaningful way of getting at his truest statement of life. What I am suggesting is that the intuitional (supported by the reasonable) motivation toward ultimate unity as expressed by the circle is not superficially neat but is built into structure, texture, symbol, action, and characterization in different degrees and at different times. When "the circle closes" it does not cut off all further discussion; it brings a cycle to the conclusion which is then another beginning. Despite an increasing emphasis upon intuitional beliefs in the unity of life, the major Western novels are open-ended. Furthermore, although some of them point to a link between the images of our world and the images of an ancient, even primordial, world, this is not the romanticism of Plato's ideal world. It is the reality of the unconscious linked to the reality of origins. It is archetypal and Jungian. And yet, each novel has a consciously real, human, and dramatic base, so that it can be read on several levels: (1) as a story which can be accepted literally, (2) as a representation of common types of people and actions, and (3) as a symbolic or mythic or archetypal recognition of the deeper significance of the unconscious and its ability to reveal a link between man and the universe. (pp. 199-200)

Serious Western novels had been written before 1940, but it was *The Ox-Bow Incident* that brought dramatically to the public's attention the nonromantic cowboy and the unresolved Western conflict that boldly defied the conventional patterns of the shoot-out and the clear-cut victory of good over evil. Contrary to the comforting predictability of the mass-produced Western novel, the situation in *Ox-Bow* is discouragingly real. After three innocent men have been lynched by a posse of assorted cowhands and townspeople, Davies, an elderly man beset with the ghosts of conscience, judges himself harshly in terms that apply not only to the necessary violence of the traditional Western story but also to the world's political conditions at the time the novel was written.... What characterizes *The Ox-Bow Incident,* however, is the lack of the strong will and the fast gun. No one comes forward to accept the role of hero and savior, even though it might have been done rather easily. Davies confesses further that he was glad he did not have a gun, implying that without it he was at least partly excused from attempting to stop Tetley and the crowd. Davies is not alone. There are no "superior" characters in this crowd; even Tetley, the leader, is ultimately shamed into suicide, although his shame centers on his son rather than on the lynching which he ordered. These are real people, exasperating in their plausibility.... And so the circumstances lead to a lynching by a group of average men, first aroused by the notion that one of their friends has been murdered, then spurred on by the talkers in the crowd, later hesitant to act but equally hesitant to back out, and finally chagrined and perhaps shamed by the knowledge of the victims' innocence. (pp. 201-02)

It has been suggested often that *The Ox-Bow Incident* is not really a Western novel, that the lynching could have occurred anywhere. (Attesting, perhaps, to the fact that *Ox-Bow,* like any good regional novel, transcends its locale.) Yet, it is not the lynching itself that is important but the motives and pressures—the specific human behavior—which lead to the lynching or allow it to happen. What causes injustice? The answer to that question seems to stand as an indictment of man and is reminiscent of the charges against man made by Fisher in *The Testament of Man:* irrationality, prejudice, racism, emotionalism, ambition, passion, lust, bestiality, latent primitive desires, lack of love and consideration and compassion, frustration and compensation, perverted love (as for the "victim"), and groupism (as opposed to individuality). As Manfred implied in *Lord Grizzly,* man has not yet reached a spiritual stage in the evolutionary process, even though he occasionally seems to be moving toward it. (pp. 206-07)

The sense of innocent wonder pervading [*The City of Trembling Leaves*] perhaps offends the intellectuals and the sophisticates, but the capacity for wonder is an integral part of Clark's view of the world and the renewal of this wonder is essential to Western literature in general. Renewal itself is the major characteristic of the natural world, and recognition of this fact is vital to anyone who thinks in cyclical rather than linear terms, who seeks unity rather than diffusion, and who accepts death as a part of the cycle rather than fearing it because it marks the termination of the individual linear lifeline.... *Leaves* admits of a variety of tones, attitudes, and styles. Clark, however, is neither careless nor confused. Courageously, he establishes as much variation as he can in his pursuit of unity, this being the honest and realistic way of conducting the pursuit. Furthermore, if there is a style which can be called western, it is not one limited to a single voice. It is generally lyrical, but it is laced with irony, concrete realism, metaphor, straightforward narration, and natural symbols. It may seem pastoral because the images are usually taken from the natural world rather than from a man-made world, but it is not governed by nostalgia. It is strong in rhythms, corresponding in varying degrees with the rhythms of the land. To the extend that there may be a Western style, its origins are in the land, in the natural cycles, in the primitive two-handed beat stressed by Mary Austin, and in the search for and recognition of an underlying unity in the natural life. (pp. 211-13)

The artist, like any man, must of necessity be grounded in the earth, in the multiple confusion of the literal or physical aspects of life; but his job is to unify, to seek the organizing principle, to reach for the sky—or the primal sources of life. His work must have roots in the land first of all, and this characteristic is strong in Western regional literature. However, out of the earthly context must spring an awareness of and a search for the ultimate unity which transcends the multiple object. Bound up in this process is what I call "the Western attitude," an attitude which Walter Van Tilburg Clark exemplifies perhaps better than anyone else. (p. 215)

The Track of the Cat, Clark's major novel, reveals his philosophy most clearly and makes the most effective use of his western materials. It has the fullness, and almost the length, of *The City of Trembling Leaves,* and maintains much of the unity and clarity of *The Ox-Bow Incident.* ... It is carefully grounded upon a Western ranch with all of its literal details, and yet it operates consistently upon a symbolic level. The natural symbols are this time an organic part of each consciousness, and each character serves as a facet of Clark's view of the world. A shifting point of view enables Clark to make the most of his situation and his group of characters. Yet strict unities of time, place, and purpose give the entire work the impact of immediacy and emotional reality. (pp. 216-17)

[Clark] is concerned with universal themes—good and evil, adolescence and maturity, man and nature—which he objectifies with the materials of the American West. He cannot, as do eastern and southern writers, probe into family relationships and traditions over many generations. The West is young and does not have lengthy family or social traditions, and so the Western regional writer must concentrate on man in nature to a large extent. In addition, of course, nature is more directly important in a practical way in an area devoted to ranching and farming than it is in a metropolitan or industrial area. The traditions which the Western writer has to work with are first directly in nature itself, then in the cultural and spiritual history of the American Indian, and only finally in the more recent traditions of the Western white man. As these traditions come together in *The Track of the Cat,* Clark does not try to cement them intellectually. Again, there are more questions than answers, not only in relation to theme but also concerning method, or techniques. To what extent is the cat—and the entire narrative—symbolic? Does Clark rely too heavily on symbolism? What is the function of the dream sequences? Is the black-and-white imagery as obvious a device as it seems? And can Clark be accused of stereotyping all of his characters? The very presence of these questions partially explains the richness of the novel as well as exemplifying the open-endedness of Clark's method.

Clark's characters do not have the faddish or curious eccentricities that some novelists (especially nonwestern) give their characters in order to make them appear original, startling, or real. Without these artificial quirks, Clark's characters often seem to be either thematic or typical—not stereotypes (although a few come close), not always archetypes (although some are), but representatives of not uncommon kinds of people. To the extent to which they are representative, they foster the ideal of unity. As individuals, however, they interact with each other and with the environment with full psychological and emotional plausibility, so that Clark is a psychological realist even while he is also an intuitionist and very nearly a visionary. A mystic he is not, because his quest for oneness is firmly rooted in the earth and in people who are not in the least disembodied. Particularly in *The Track of the Cat,* the characters seem to belong to a deliberate scheme, with each person playing a role within discussions of good and evil, of man and the cosmos, of attitudes toward the land, and of archetypal meanings which do not yield to examination in terms of reason, science, or the so-called rational Freudian psychology. Clark, like Jung, is willing to tap the ancient mysteries, to find archetypal meanings in the unconscious. Freudians, presumably more empirical, look into the unconscious for repressions which have been forced from the conscious mind and which must be dealt with in order to make the conscious mind healthy. . . . What makes Clark's novels—and especially *The Track of the Cat*—seem either confusing or overly symbolic to many critics and readers is that the novels may be examined from the Freudian viewpoint as well as from the Jungian. All this proves, I think, is that the characters are so true to life that they are susceptible to routine Freudian analysis. Yet they are much more than that. In time, perhaps, Clark will be cherished for his psychological perceptions and his skill at creating characters, while his theme of unity will be accepted as an undercurrent (and a vital one) rather than as the surface significance.

I have said earlier that the Western novel seems to lie within the sphere of Jungian influence. However difficult it may be to offer indisputable proof, there is certainly a tendency (seen perhaps most strongly in Clark and in *The Track of the Cat*) to avoid intellectual judgment and to engage in the experience of the unconscious. Because Jung said that it was extremely difficult for the occidental to have this kind of experience, it has often been assumed that at least some Western novels have been influenced by oriental thought. . . . Yet, the connection is not obvious, and it is more likely that American Indian religion and the special relationship which the Westerner has with his land have been the major influences. (pp. 224-26)

None of this is so obvious in *The Track of the Cat* that it endangers either characterization or narrative. Reference to Freud and Jung might even be unnecessary were it not for the dream sequences, and there is a strong possibility that the dreams were included precisely to draw attention to the Jungian attitudes underlying the narrative, for these dreams are not the kind to be studied for repressions and guilt complexes—they are projections, not signals of repression barriers. They are revelations of inner truths and realities; they point to inner and outer dangers and may even suggest the solutions. Therefore, a relationship exists between the individual's dreams and his waking state, or between his unconscious and conscious minds, or, to push it further, between his own unconscious experiences and those of archetypal figures from the dawn of time to the present. Curiously, these dreams are saturated with color imagery, the dominating colors being black and white (one of which is devoid of color, and the other a dense mixture of all colors), imagery which appears in almost all of Clark's writing but which is used more profusely in *The Track of the Cat*. The obvious symbolism of black and white is the religious one of evil and good, and it is this use of the image which is dominant in the hundreds of formula Westerns. Although it is possible to make the same application to *Cat,* it is more likely that Clark is concerned with all dualities, not just one: good and evil, the sacred and the profane, intellect and intuition, lightness (enlightenment) and darkness (ignorance), and so on. He then implies the ultimate necessity of a fusion in each case. He does not bring the black and the white together, but he lets them stand in juxtaposition. The unconscious mind brings them together, just as the conscious mind (mistakenly) maintains their separation. (p. 227)

> John R. Milton, "The Western Attitude: Walter Van Tilburg Clark," in Critique: Studies in Modern Fiction *(reprinted by permission of Heldref Publications, a publication of the Helen Dwight Reed Educational Foundation), Vol. II, No. 3, Winter, 1959 (and reprinted in an enlarged form as "Walter Van Tilburg Clark: The Western Attitude," in his* The Novel of the American West, *University of Nebraska Press, 1980, pp. 195-229).*

Padraic Colum
1881-1972

Irish-born American dramatist, poet, novelist, essayist, biographer, children's writer, and editor.

Colum was a central figure in the Irish Literary Renaissance. He first gained recognition in 1902 as one of the founders of the Irish National Theatre, later known as the Abbey Theatre. Unlike William Butler Yeats and Lady Gregory, who were also co-founders of the Abbey, Colum rejected intellectual treatment of Irish issues and believed that Ireland would be most accurately represented by the dialect and lifestyle of its peasantry. Colum and John M. Synge are regarded by many critics as the company's most important nationalistic playwrights because of their emphasis on the speech and the attitudes of the common Irishman.

Colum's first plays, *Broken Soil* (1903), *The Land* (1905), and *Thomas Muskerry* (1910), were among the most popular of the Abbey's early productions. However, Colum left the company because of a disagreement in policy and wrote little subsequent drama, becoming instead a poet of modest reputation. While his poetry is largely narrative and free of obscure symbolism, it is also lyrical and illustrates the musical dimension of the peasant dialect. *Wild Earth,* a volume published in 1907, contains many of Colum's best poems.

Colum moved with his wife to the United States in 1914, and lived there for the rest of his life. However, the themes of his work remained as devoted to the Irish people as when he lived in Ireland. Colum's first novel, *Castle Conquer* (1923), has a poetic quality and focuses on the rural folkways which are so prominent in his poetry. The late novel, *The Flying Swans* (1957), is a *bildungsroman* which resembles James Joyce's *Stephen Hero* and *Portrait of the Artist as a Young Man.*

Throughout his career Colum wrote many books for children; these stories and tales are rich in mythology and Irish folklore. Through these works, as well as his factual chronicles, Colum sought to expand international recognition and appreciation of Irish literature. Colum's entire *oeuvre* is dedicated to the importance of Irish tradition and the beauty of Ireland's speech and history.

(See also *Contemporary Authors,* Vols. 73-76, Vols. 33-36, rev. ed. [obituary]; *Something about the Author,* Vol. 15; and *Dictionary of Literary Biography,* Vol. 19.)

ALICE CORBIN HENDERSON

Padraic Colum is one of the most gifted, if not the most gifted, of the younger Irish poets. . . . Some of the other younger Irish poets have seemed to echo Mr. W. B. Yeats, as was indeed quite natural; but Mr. Colum by no means wears the mantle of the older poet. Whereas Mr. Yeats' own dreams are usually reflected in his poems representing peasant life, or whereas Mr. Yeats almost always sees the peasant through the glamour of "old mythologies," Mr. Colum gives us the peasant as nearly as possible in the peasant's own terms, and with a direct, concrete touch. Of course the distinction is not watertight, nor meant to be. Mr. Yeats' old woman making the fire

Reproduced by Permission of Padraic and Mary Colum Estate

at dawn, when "the seed of the fire gets feeble and low," is as direct as possible; and Mr. Colum's poems are not untouched by the glamour of tradition and "the thought of white ships and the King of Spain's daughter." How else could it be, and he a poet?

However, the reader who turns to Mr. Colum's poems [in *Wild Earth and Other Poems*] with this distinction in mind will realize something of his artistic method. He has identified himself with his subject, and his own personality is not obtruded except as it is incidentally revealed. This is the method of genuine "folk" poetry—be it Greek or Irish or of any race at all. Such poetry has the solidity of life, of the hills or of the earth itself, and the title *Wild Earth* is indeed appropriate. (pp. 105-06)

I do not mean to indicate by what I have said that Mr. Colum's poems are entirely objective, or that, being objective in method, they do not serve to convey subjective and personal emotions. There are many beautiful poems in the book that give us the sense of personal vision and passion. *The Wayfarer* . . . is one of these. There is much primal feeling—I know no other way to name it—in all that this poet writes. His poems take hold of earth and do not let go. This is a feeling which does not recognize division between nature and man or between man and man. (p. 106)

Mr. Colum is an artist with the conscientiousness of a thorough craftsman, and his touch is always authentic. I have not mentioned his humor, which makes him doubly sympathetic—of course there is no real sympathy without humor; but that goes without saying. His work is a definite contribution to Irish literature; it is a permanent contribution to English poetry. (pp. 107-08)

Alice Corbin Henderson "That Wilder Earth" (© 1917 by the Modern Poetry Association; reprinted by permission of the Editor of Poetry *and the Literary Estate of Alice Corbin Henderson), in* Poetry, *Vol. X, No. 11, May, 1917, pp. 105-08.*

THE DIAL

[*Mogu, the Wanderer*] is fantastic and full of authentic oriental color. It moves in a world, both physically and psychologically remote, where Fate, though never actually present to the eye, is really the chief actor. It is a world intrinsically democratic where, by Fate's intervention, a beggar and his daughter may serve as lofty a purpose as a king. There Fate makes all, least and greatest, but the puppets of its will. The actors suffer and rejoice, and believe themselves to be acting freely, but he is most wise and content who realizes that he is only the servant of a higher power. To the occidental believer in the power of the will, there is something too humiliating in this belief, an indefinable something too spineless, too resigned and weak. To some, however, the mystic idea of self-immolation is lofty and beautiful. To these, the yielding of will and responsibility only makes man the more free in his actions. Mogu, the beggar, made vizier for a brief time, plays both parts with the proper gestures, returning to beggardom gracefully. The working out of his destiny is necessarily accompanied by a grim humor with suggestive, comic high-lights that make the play very readable. Mr. Colum displays his talent as a dramatist in the ordered and economical use of few materials and in his easy familiarity with stage technique. (pp. 445-46)

A review of "Mogu, the Wanderer," in The Dial, *Vol. LXII, No. 742, May 17, 1917, pp. 445-46.*

ERNEST BOYD

Padraic Colum was the first of the peasant dramatists, in the strict sense of the word; he was, that is to say, the first to dramatise the realities of rural life in Ireland. Where Synge's fantastic intuition divined human prototypes, Colum's realistic insight revealed local peasant types, whose general significance is subordinate to the immediate purpose of the dramatist. Together they define the limits within which our folk-drama has developed, for none of the later playwrights has added anything to the tradition initiated by Padraic Colum and J. M. Synge. With rare exceptions, which will be noticed, their successors have failed to give personality to their work, contenting themselves with certain general formulae, whose elaboration leaves them as far from the restraint of Colum as from the flamboyancy of Synge. For, it is interesting to note, the former dramatist is the direct antithesis of the latter, nor has he been at all influenced by him, in spite of the disparity of their respective successes. Synge's fame and work made resistance difficult for all but the most original of his young contemporaries. But Colum has remained, at the cost of popular recognition, faithful to the spirit of *Broken Soil,* whose almost simultaneous appearance [in 1903] with Synge's first play precluded any possibility of imitation. (pp. 335-36)

The Land, although his second play, was published in 1905 prior to *Broken Soil,* which did not appear in book form until its material had been recast as *The Fiddler's House,* two years later. It is at once more logical and more significant that Padraic Colum's published writings should begin with that "agrarian comedy," for there he handles the central and fundamental fact of peasant life, the call of the land. The struggle between town and country to hold the people, the problem of rural life, which is at last receiving serious attention, is the leading note of *The Land.* In Ireland it is against the attraction of the United States, no less than against the lure of urban civilisation, that resistance must be strengthened, and the dramatist shows us the drain upon the countryside resulting from the emigration of the young and vigorous. (p. 337)

The Fiddler's House is a study of another aspect of peasant life. Having shown us the peasant face to face with the fundamental problem of his existence, in his relation to the land, the dramatist now portrays him in his spiritual and artistic manifestations. The ties of the soil are, of course, a part of the drama, for Conn Hourican is the peasant as artist, and the essential factor of that condition is not wanting. But while the land hunger finds its expression in his child Anne, the father is primarily a study in temperament. The old fiddler, for all his attachment to home, carries within him the yearning for change and freedom, the inability to remain settled, which we associate with the nature of genius. The trait which unites the artist and the vagabond brings Conn Hourican somewhat nearer to the symbolic types of Synge than is usual with the carefully realised figures of Colum's drama. . . . The deep distrust entertained by respectable peasants towards the unattached man of the roads, the concern of Conn's daughters at his desire to resume his vagabondage, are the fitting background against which to set this fine old figure. The sympathy and realism which have gone to the portrayal of Conn Hourican make of him the personification of that element of our peasant life to which folk-art and folk-poetry owe their existence and preservation.

With the exception of the specifically agrarian problem, which was the point of departure of *The Land,* there is no question more vital than the patriarchal family system which obtains throughout rural Ireland. In selecting this theme for *Thomas Muskerry* Padraic Colum displayed his characteristic feeling for those situations and aspects of life which present themselves most readily to the mind of a people mainly composed of the peasant class. The sacrifice of the individual to the family unit is a tradition preserved most carefully in the agricultural communities of Western Europe. . . . It is strange that no writer of Irish fiction has given us an equivalent to Henry Bordeaux's *Les Roquevillard.* But all through the work of Colum the sense of family life is evident. We have the problem suggested in *The Land,* where the revolt of the younger generation is, in part, accounted for by the exigencies of paternal authority. In *Thomas Muskerry* the full significance of the system is revealed.

Instead of illustrating his subject by the elaboration of those hints at revolt which are noticeable in the earlier plays, the dramatist has preferred to reverse the process. It is not the children who feel the restraints of family duty, but the old father, Thomas Muskerry, who dies a pauper in the workhouse of which he once was master, after being cruelly exploited by his relations. This middle-class family in a country town is aptly chosen for the development of such a theme. Being just one remove from the soil, they retain all the worst traits of their immediate peasant forerunners and serve best to emphasise the evils to which the exaggerated sense of domestic obligations may lead. The kindness and generosity of Muskerry have for years encouraged his children and their dependents to exercise their cupidity and unscrupulousness at his expense. When they find him no longer profitable, they cease to play upon the family relationship, and frankly abandon him, having robbed him of his good name, his dignity and his money. The tragic end of this victim of the claims of kinship is the culminating event in a grim story of petty meannesses and sordid motives, all rising out of the exploitation of kindness in the name of family solidarity. There are few writers who have disclosed with such insight the under-currents of existence in our provincial towns, where the virtues of the peasant are lost in the indirect contact with the ambitions and practises of urban civilisation. (pp. 339-41)

It would be misleading to leave the dramatic work of Padraic Colum without making clear his innocence of any avowedly didactic purpose. A brief analysis of his plays involves the use of phrases which are perhaps more convenient than accurate. *The Land* and *Thomas Muskerry* envisage certain phases of Irish life which constitute the "problems" of our sociologists, but the latter need not suspect him of any intention to anticipate their conclusions. The effort of the dramatist is not to propound or solve social questions, but is directed, as he says, "towards the creation of situations." "For character conceived as a psychological synthesis he has only a secondary concern." In thus defining the attitude of the playwright, Colum clearly demonstrates the character of his own work. The three plays that have been mentioned are primarily attempts to situate the Irish peasant in such circumstances as to bring out the essential drama of rural life. Coming from the Midlands, and viewing the world from the standpoint of the peasantry, he saw at once the naturally dramatic situations in which they revealed themselves most characteristically. These restrained and faithful pictures, from which every exaggerated or adventitious element is eliminated, have a quality which recalls Ibsen in their almost purely intellectual action. Colum even avoids the melodramatic *dénouements* which the author of *Hedda Gabler* did not disdain.

In this last respect, but in that only, the later peasant playwrights approach more closely to Ibsen. The majority, indeed, show so marked an affection for violent effects and purely external drama, that the local setting of their work seems fortuitous. The drama of Padraic Colum, on the other hand, is peculiarly Irish, and has its very basis in peasant conditions. One cannot imagine Conn Hourican, Murtagh Cosgar or Thomas Muskerry transplanted to another soil. . . . The greater part of our pseudo "peasant" drama is merely melodrama with an Irish accent. The situations are not inherent in, or peculiar to, our national life, but are adapted. . . . Even where the national and literary quality of the work done by his successors is beyond dispute, the achievement of Padraic Colum only gains by comparison. Without any predecessors of importance, he shares with Synge the right to be considered the most original of our folk-dramatists. (pp. 341-43)

> Ernest Boyd, "The Dramatic Movement: Third Phase," in his Ireland's Literary Renaissance (reprinted by permission of The American Play Company, Inc.), revised edition, Alfred A. Knopf, 1922 (and reprinted by Barnes & Noble, Inc., 1968), pp. 335-43.

BROOM

The material [of *Castle Conquer*] is rich and interesting: a feudal Ireland for a background; a plot of political conspiracy and peasant revolt; a love tale; Irish tenant farmers, peddlers, soldiers, landowners; Irish songs, frolics, dancing, fairs. The prose is fresh and easy-flowing. And a music comes into it by way of lovely Irish names and the peculiar Irish-English dialog. Nor, given the peasant rhythm, can one seriously object to the book's slow movement, or to the somewhat episodic way in which it unfolds. What, then, is wrong? This: for some reason, perhaps because Mr. Colum has placed too much reliance upon his content, upon its inherent soil-ness and lyricism, upon the general interest in Ireland's struggle for political autonomy, because he has given himself too sparingly unto his work, the poetry of the material and the poetry of the prose fail to achieve a mutually transforming contact. There is no sustained interchange between them. There is no complete intersaturation. . . . Hence *Castle Conquer,* for all its fresh loveliness and health, misses that living beauty which one somehow expects from it.

> A review of "Castle Conquer," in Broom, Vol. 5, No. 1, August, 1923, p. 53.

ERNEST BOYD

Those who have followed the work of Padraic Colum from its beginnings in **"Wild Earth"** have always looked forward to the novel which one felt he could and would write. That anticipation is not disappointed in **"Castle Conquer."** In spite of the years that have slipped by since he gave us that first book of poems, since **"The Land," "The Fiddler's House,"** and **"Thomas Muskerry"** established him in an unassailable position in the Irish Theater, this book betrays nothing of the changed life, the varied activities that have since been his. **"Castle Conquer"** belongs to the period preceding his hegira, and the perfume of Irish earth clings about it as unmistakably as it breathed out of every page of his early plays and poems. This prose has all the simple charm, the fresh tang that made the poetry of **"Wild Earth"** irresistible.

The story centers about Francis Gillick, the returned student from the Irish College in Salamanca, who has given up his studies for the priesthood and come to settle down among his own people. As a "spoilt priest" he is too greatly handicapped in the immediate circle of his own friends and relatives, so he goes to another part of the country to work on the farm of Honor Paralon, whose daughters Oona and Brighid befriend him, until inevitably both girls are more deeply involved by their affections than mere friendship. It is to Brighid that Francis pledges himself, and their love is drawn by the author in scenes of a whispered and passionate intensity which contrast curiously with the mawkish sentimentality, on the one hand, and the pathological realism, on the other, which are an essential feature of the average novel of today. In the relations of these two there is a tender shyness, charmingly rendered, which is as characteristic, in its way, as the brutalities of James Joyce, who, too, has described one phase of the Irish attitude in matters of sex. But Colum shows how this idyll, like so many other normal human impulses, is overshadowed in Ireland by the figure of Kathleen ni Houlihan, into whose mouth W. B. Yeats has put words that are not forgotten: "It is hard service they take that help me. Many that are red-cheeked now will be pale-cheeked; many that have been free to walk the hills and the bogs and the rushes will be sent to walk hard streets in far countries . . . and for all that they will think they are well paid.''

In such service Francis Gillick gradually finds himself enrolled and in his adventures we watch the beginning of the Land War in Ireland, and see how inevitably the land and the nation became identical in the eyes of many generations. The evolution of Gillick, the pressure of innumerable little circumstances which transform him into a "rebel" in the eyes of the British authorities, and finally, the accusation which lands him in jail—all these elements inseparable from the life of the period are skilfully woven into Mr. Colum's narrative. His great skill lies in the unostentatious way in which he develops this main theme, without ever insisting upon it. This is not just the story of a young Irishman's revolt, for the individual hero is merely the focusing-point of an era and a people. **"Castle Conquer"** is a true microcosm of Irish country life, the Ascendancy minority, harsh, always insecure and baffled, with its servitors drawn from the people, and then the people themselves, with their own life and traditions, sustained by a definite hope and the will to survive. Padraic Colum knows the Irish countryside, its physical aspects at all seasons, the customs and beliefs of the peasantry, the striking characters who may be found by those who know how to seek them. . . . (pp. 299-300)

One lays down a book of this caliber with a regret for all the cheap sentimentalities and trivial humor which make up the usual popular novel of Irish life, against which one wishes to set a **"Castle Conquer,"** or such a work as Seumas O'Kelly's "The Weaver's Grave." The manner of the telling is a delight in itself, a style full of poetry and tenderness and color, touched with laughter which does not depend upon verbal caricature, that great stock in trade of the manufacturers of "Irish" fiction for export. With his first novel Padraic Colum has enhanced the distinction of his already valuable contribution to Anglo-Irish literature, his work as poet and dramatist. (p. 300)

Ernest Boyd, "Romantic Ireland," in The Nation *(copyright 1923* The Nation *magazine, The Nation Associates, Inc.), Vol. CXVII, No. 3037, September 19, 1923, pp. 299-300.*

WALTER PRICHARD EATON

["**Balloon**"] is a four-act comedy in prose. The jacket says "it is the first play to be based on modern philosophical ideas. The action takes place in a 'Spenglerian' world in which life has become externalized and where the idea of height and distance is dominant.'' Perhaps that is the matter with it. Or perhaps that is the matter with me. I have only the haziest notion of what a "Spenglerian" world is, and the ideas of height and distance become dominant in my life only when I climb a mountain. . . .

Caspar, the hero of **"Balloon,"** invites people to take a peep at the moon through his telescope outside the Hotel Daedalus, the glittering skyscraper pile where the sophisticated of the world gather. . . . Along comes the architect of the hotel, world weary, and pays Caspar a large sum for his telescope, so off goes Caspar into the hotel. . . . He tries to make a balloon ascent from the roof with a famous movie actress, but she calls off the stunt when she learns there are to be no papers printed the next day. However, when he encounters a dancer whom he had loved as a wandering gypsy girl and she wants him to take her up in the balloon he funks and proposes a ferry ride. She goes up instead with the architect, who has got tired of contemplating the moon, and poor Caspar stands brokenhearted on the roof, persuaded that one of his kind does not belong in the Hotel Daedalus. But there is a happy ending. The girl drops by a parachute back to the roof, hitting it exactly. She couldn't hear what the architect said to her in the higher altitude, so she and Caspar take the elevator down, presumably to hit the gypsy trail together.

All this is fantastic, preposterous. . . . Caspar, the telescope man, and the rest in **"Balloon"** have no reality, and hence can arouse no dramatic emotion. It is not necessary to make them characters out of "Street Scene." But within their fantastic and symbolic world they must function with feeling, they must have three dimensions, they must possess sufficient specific gravity to make us take them seriously. Of course, in a world "where the idea of height and distance is dominant" no doubt specific gravity is a drawback, but in a comedy on the stage the lack of it certainly makes for the other kind. **"Balloon"** is singularly unfunny.

Yet there is in this fantasy the makings of a wistful and significant comedy. What it needs is less Spengler and more Barrie. . . . But that would mean the development of . . . scenes along the lines of tested human emotional reactions, as all dramatists have done since drama was, and as they will all have to continue to do even in a Spenglerian world.

Walter Prichard Eaton, "Spenglerian," in New York Herald Tribune Books *(© I.H.T. Corporation; reprinted by permission), July 14, 1929, p. 14.*

HAROLD CLURMAN

[Though] **"Balloon"** cannot be regarded as an "intellectual" play, it is none the less true that its writing must have first been impelled by a general idea. To put it briefly, Mr. Colum purports to show that a man's acts are significant only as they are expressions of his own inner being, and that a world where action becomes a value in itself is a ludicrous and empty show.

But this is the world we live in; and in the play it is represented by the great hotel in Megalopolis. Here are gathered all the heroes of the earth, the moral and literal acrobats whose astonishing and useless feats make the daily spectacle of our civilization. Here athletic actresses, esthetic millionaires, erudite sportsmen and lettered politicans pass in a fleeting and colorful pageant. And on the square outside the hotel stands Mr. Colum's little hero, Casper, who, like all of us, yearns to be part of the glory he beholds but cannot share. If the opportunity offered itself, he wonders, could he too not accomplish some overwhelming deed to place him with these fabulous creatures? Fortune favors him, and he is enabled to take a room in the hotel for a day. Because he is a person simple enough to be extraordinary he wins a momentary notoriety. But he soon learns that the most beautiful woman in the hotel is a girl he once knew when he was traveling with a sort of circus, the most companionable man, an old clown of the same company. More than one opportunity for the "great" deed is offered him—the most sensational being the chance to steal away in a balloon with his girl—but he seems inadequate to all of them. At last he renounces the idea of doing things he didn't want to do in the first place and, with his girl, returns to the square, his trade and the open road.

With such material, a satire or a philosophic parable might have been written. But though **"Balloon"** may be said to include elements of both, it is neither one nor the other. The quality of Mr. Colum's talent is not for these forms. His comedy is essentially a fairy-tale. When we have seized its spirit we discover that the locale of its action is not so much the great hotel which the stage directions indicate, as a comic wonderland peopled by elves and sprites created in the image of journalism, opera-singers, ambassadors and prize-fighters! Mr. Colum's gift has a happy ambiguity, a peculiar and adorable unconsciousness that lends these figures their original charm. They seem to have been conceived in all seriousness, even, if one could credit Mr. Colum with such candor, as realistic characters. They are utterly unaware of their doll-like and puckish absurdity. They wear their little masks very gravely, and with incongruous suddenness perform their grandiose and impossible little gestures. They behave according to a logic of their own. They are poised, reasonable and unexpectedly perverse. We might, at first, mistake them for bodies of flesh and blood, but soon we note that there is something awry in everything they do. They are puppets whom the author believes in as people. The protagonists alone are sufficiently developed to have emotions, and, in them, emotion is only a kind of wistfulness.

To use a facile critical formula, **"Balloon"** is a minor treatment of a major theme. But it has nevertheless a significance that exceeds its own individual scope. For a retrospective summary will show us that Mr. Colum has succeeded in doing what most of the expressionists, in an entirely different mood and more deliberately, have really been trying to do. He has taken a socially vital subject and has presented it in theatrical terms that are both universal and immediately relevant. If there is a tendency in the modern theater, this is it. This is what the contemporary dramatist is groping for; a form that will create new myths and new symbols to express in the most general and complete manner the preoccupations of our day.

Mr. Colum has succeeded in this crucial artistic task not through any theory or awareness of our esthetic needs, but because he is a poet. Because he is a poet his plot and nearly all its details are deeply right. . . . These details, moreover, are not merely static literary metaphors. They are admirable *theatrical* images: the man of the theater can work with them.

Here, then, is a paradox, a paradox with a moral. A poet has written a play that has greater theatrical than literary interest. This suggests that, were they encouraged to do so, the poets and other creative literary artists might be more apt to provide our theater with fresh themes and new impulses than the hacks and showmen now engaged in the profession. (pp. 266-67)

To do their part in the theater, however, the poets cannot, of course, remain outside it. With more intimate knowledge of the art, they will learn that the largely contemplative attitude of the literary man is wrong for the playwright. Like everyone else in the theater, he must, in a psychological sense, be himself an actor. He must consider the play not as something he watches and listens to, but something he himself *acts*. In this respect **"Balloon"** betrays its literary derivation. The writing of some of the speeches and very frequently their ordering reveal Mr. Colum as still innocent of any sure theatrical instinct. (p. 267)

Harold Clurman, "A Poet Writes a Play," in The New Republic, Vol. LIX, No. 764, July 24, 1929, pp. 266-67.

MELVIN MADDOCKS

Written over the past 10 years, [**"The Flying Swans"**] lacks momentum, as works extended over a period of time often do. It sprawls rather than drives through a 538-page account of the childhood and youth of Ulick O'Rehill. The narrative is a series of jerky jumps from scene to scene. The numerous characters dragged in and out of the action tend to be flat when they are not blurred.

But as a nineteenth-century Irish pastoral, **"The Flying Swans"** is an evocative book. In the earlier chapters when Ulick is in the country, there is an almost physical sense of well-groomed horses prancing across fields in early morning; of fresh cream and sweet butter in the dairy; of corn crakes singing in the meadow grass at twilight. When Ulick moves to the town of Cairnthual, there are mellowed scenes in an old-fashioned candy shop, at the village fair, and along the sea wall.

But the golden haze of nostalgia that bathes these Irish remembrances of things past makes them seem part of a dream, and the charming, sad people who move against these backgrounds in generally picturesque but often inept postures do not engage a reader's concern as less fey, more substantial characters might. The women, curiously remote and unhappy, suffer passively through mistaken marriages, from Ulick's mother Saba to his sweetheart Christine. The men live on a thin margin of slowly vanishing hopes and . . . stumble to disaster "with bowed heads making their way through a desolate country."

The story ends with Ulick, in early manhood, reunited with his younger brother Breasal and determined to continue in his apprenticeship to a stonecutter with the prospect of art school in the offing. But since this has been largely a backward-looking story, it is largely a story of loss. Ulick's father's fall, not Ulick's anticipated climb, makes the dominant curve. . . .

Against this motif of faded better days the fresh green background of Ireland seems vivid to too little purpose.

Melvin Maddocks, "Morgan and Colum with Novels of Italy and Ireland: 'The Flying Swans'," in The Christian Science Monitor (reprinted by permission from The Christian Science Monitor; © 1957 The Christian Science Publishing Society; all rights reserved), June 20, 1957, p. 11.*

VIVIAN MERCIER

A broad plain, frequently accented by little hills, would certainly form an appropriate metaphor to describe the effect of Padraic Colum's new novel [*The Flying Swans*]. . . .

I would not recommend this contemplative book to the kind of reader who expects a novel to give him a roller-coaster ride, on which, once pinned down by the safety bar, he is swept breathless up dizzy heights and hurtled screaming down dizzier depths, until the vehicle deposits him, retching and staggering, on firm ground once more. This is rather the kind of book that one lays aside from time to time in order to daydream over one's own youth. (p. 404)

In the long run, when this novel's characters and incidents have faded from the reader's mind, one abiding influence will remain with him—its style. Perhaps it would be more correct to call it a language rather than a style, that collective language of the first generation of the Irish literary revival. The most recent generation of Irish writers seem to have lost it completely. To them Gaelic is Gaelic, English is Oxford or Hollywood, and Irish English is a bastard dialect never spoken off the stage of the Abbey Theatre. As a result, their novels and plays are unreadable, their poems readable but not speakable.

But here, with scarce-diminished vigor, the sinewy style rides once more, giving—in narrative as well as dialogue—the old sense of a language reborn, of an English grafted on Gaelic, almost every phrase of which has been formed, not by pen or typewriter, but on the living lips of men. (pp. 404-05)

> Vivian Mercier, "Sinewy Style of the Irish Literary Revival," in Commonweal (copyright © 1957 Commonweal Publishing Co., Inc.; reprinted by permission of Commonweal Publishing Co., Inc.), Vol. LXVI, No. 16, July 19, 1957, pp. 404-05.

WILLIAM TURNER LEVY

Padraic Colum has been acknowledged as a master of the Irish faerie: the quaint and leprechaunish peasants have been celebrated by him in prose and verse. This is simply not true. His tales for children include fairy stories, but Colum is the vigorous, hard-headed spokesman of the true peasant, the recorder of the historic fate of Ireland; and even in the books for the young he has never talked down but has sought to hand down both the historic and mythic past. As poet and playwright and essayist—and now as novelist—he speaks the true spirit of his nation and has the versatility of a scholar-poet. Most important, he has written poems that would astonish those who know only the set anthology pieces—"**The Plougher**," "**A Drover**," and "**An Old Woman of the Roads**." . . . [*The Collected Poems of Padraic Colum*] is a proud book, and it ranks its begetter among the authentic poets of Ireland. (p. 493)

In 1903 with *Broken Soil* (later rewritten as *The Fiddler's House*), [Colum] created the peasant play. It was a felicitous moment, with Yeats and Synge and Lady Gregory and Æ all striving in the National Theatre Movement, which centered around the Abbey Theatre in Dublin. (pp. 493-94)

Colum's next play, *The Land,* was the Abbey's first success. Together with *Thomas Muskerry,* these two plays have been called second only to Synge's. With no predecessor of importance, young Colum wrote of the call of the land, the struggle between town and country to hold people (a people also attracted to America), peasant conditions, and the revolt of the young against the patriarchal system which embodied the authority of the older generation. He was the first to do the peasant on his own level and in the speech of the field and marketplace. . . .

Before long, Colum was writing poems, and it is not unnatural that this should have been so. Æ said, "There is probably no poetry published for generations which sank so deeply into the affections of Irish readers . . ." Confronted with the statement, Colum replied that it was really not surprising, for all that he was doing was giving back to the people what he had taken from them. He considers himself fortunate that as a child in his grandmother's house, which was a folk household, he had been able to hear the story tellers and the ballad singers. (p. 494)

Colum's verse has been widely translated, and into languages like Albanian and Ukranian as well as the more familiar; it is not surprising, for his subjects are universal for all their particularity—with gravity and simplicity he communicates the dignity of a people without material gifts, the changing beauty of natural things and the timeless surroundings of farm and cottage; the dependence of the landless, the skill of the craftsman, the peasant mixture of realism and fantasy—he knows—and man's fight for freedom, and man's haunting interest in animals, especially the shy, neglected, or exotic ones. (pp. 499-500)

If his most original contribution was the form of the dramatic lyric, his continuous sense of history and an alert curiosity of eye as well as mind, account for the chief qualities of his work. Out of the language and dramatic situations of the theatre he conceived dramatic lyrics like "**A Drover**," "**A Poor Scholar of the 'Forties**" and the splendid "**Dermott Donn MacMorna**." Browning was an influence, but Douglas Hyde's "The Love Songs of Connacht" gave the pattern and the language. . . . (p. 500)

Colum's dramatic sense can be measured against Tennyson's, say, if one compares the over-romantic, dramatically conceived "Ulysses" with "**The Burial of Saint Brendan**." The canny saint has decided none will thwart his will to be buried at Cluan, so his words arise out of a necessary situation. They are perfect—as is the poem—felt, not conceived, and, unlike Browning, arrogantly unself-conscious. Colum understands his saints. In "**A Saint**" he paints the gala day . . . , but then he probes the cost to the saint in denial and strife and work in order that his name might sanctify those who did not welcome him. And he understands their Master, too, as he proves in his verses for the Stations of the Cross.

In view of his nation and the state of the nation, his fascinated study of history is not surprising. It everywhere enriches the scope of his work. . . . (p. 501)

Which poem is his finest? "**The Bird of Jesus**." But it is a collection of poems, not one, that he offers us. In their honesty, richness, and variety, they produce in us a reverence for what has been done by the poet:

> A song is more lasting than the voice of the birds!
> A word is more lasting than the riches of the world!
> (p. 504)

> William Turner Levy, "Padraic Colum, Poet," in The Literary Review (copyright © 1958 by Fairleigh Dickinson University), Vol. 1, No. 4, Summer, 1958, pp. 493-504.

ZACK BOWEN

It is wholly proper that Padraic Colum is best known as poet, for his poems are his most significant contribution to literature. . . . To dismiss Colum's style as merely straightforward, accurate, or simple, as many critics have done, is to do the craftsmanship of the poetry a considerable disservice. The way Colum says things is very often beautiful and his poetic scenes and the characters as delightful as they are unassuming and familiar. His language is unpretentious and his verse forms are predominantly lyrical and rhyming with heavily accentuated iambs and tripping anapests, the sort of poems that on first reading tend to inspire song rather than thought. . . . I suspect the forthrightness of the poet's style has been the principal cause of the dearth of literary criticism about his poetry, since the fashionable critics are now more explicative than descriptive.

Colum's subject matter and conclusions reflect the same directness. His subjects are generally common people and common sights, commemorated without bravado in their own language and terms. (p. 25)

Colum thinks of himself as one of the few authentic national poets of Ireland because his upbringing is rural and Catholic, as opposed to the Protestant ascendency backgrounds of poets like Yeats, AE and Lady Gregory, whose links with the peasant people are at best studied and vicarious. Much of Colum's poetry retains its roots in the Catholic peasantry of the Irish Republic, dealing occasionally with the joys and aspirations of the people but far more with their sorrows, hopelessness and disintegration. Always, however, his people are uncomplicated and readily understandable and his language sparse and accurate.

Colum cannot be considered typical of any particular modern tradition. Hailed as a poet of the Irish Renaissance, his poems lacked the nationalistic didacticism which plagued other Irish poets, whose vision of things was colored by recollections of an unblemished past and the certainty of a utopian future. . . . [Colum] is perfectly at home in the world as it "appears," that is, presents itself to his senses. The tendency in modern poetry is to seek the truth behind what we see, to get a meaning of the world by interpreting the objects and events around us as symbols or indicators of the truth which lies behind and above. For Colum, however, the truth of things resides in the accurate perception of them. . . . His poetry is designed to enhance perception by clear delineation and description. (pp. 26-7)

The chief characteristic of Colum's work . . . lies in his insistence that the ultimate truth of things does in fact lie in the world of appearances, in how they look and in what they say. Things cry out only to be observed, digested, and understood. Colum's philosophy—that the depth of understanding of the essential qualities of nature and people is accessible by merely letting down the artificial barriers to perception—is reminiscent of Thoreau's. . . .

Colum's continual marveling at shapes and colors is a main facet of his poetry about plants and animals. Two sizeable collections, *Creatures* (1927) and *The Vegetable Kingdom* (1954), abound in a breathless description of color and appearance. (p. 28)

The direct, honest manifestations of experience in Colum's poetry are at one time his source of excellence and the source of frustration to a literary critic attempting to deal with his work. (p. 29)

The most marked aspect of Colum's poetry is unquestionably its lyrical quality. This becomes apparent through his use of meter and rhyme as well as his heavy utilization of the ballad stanza and refrain line. Only the narrative poems, such as *The Story of Lowry Maen* and the introductions to several of the sections of *Poet's Circuits,* are not essentially strong and regular in meter. (p. 30)

If Padraic Colum's principal poetic technique is lyric, the content of his poetry can best be described as romantic. He is preoccupied with such romantic subjects as the remote, the ancient, the supernatural, the pathetic, the exiled and the passionate. Because he is an Irish romantic poet, he is inescapably concerned also with nationalism and elegiac veneration of Irish heroes. His love of nature and all living creatures is still another aspect of his romanticism. Yet for all the passionate intensity his subjects would seem to provide, they are all made to seem familiar, natural and unpretentious.

Colum's penchant for things and stories of ancient times and remote places was destined to build an international reputation for him as a legend collector and folklorist. It is really only a short step from his ballads and folk poems to the legends of antiquity, and his poems constantly reflect this kinship between the past and present. (pp. 44-5)

Another major romantic tendency in Colum's poetry is an underlying sense of the pathetic: of poverty and hopeless love, of past deeds and glories which can never be duplicated, and of old people hopelessly resigned and young people grown old before their time. Even the poems which are not essentially about a particular calamity have a gentle air of pathos about them. (p. 48)

I do not mean to imply that all of the poetry is sad or resigned. There are moments of passion, though admittedly few, to rival any in romanticism's *sturm und drang* movement. (p. 51)

Like most Irish poets and romantic poets, Colum has written his share of poems of exile. His longest poem *Lowry Maen* combines folklore and antiquity with exile in a long narrative about a young prince who, after years of trial and planning, returns to his country at the head of a mighty alien army to recover his usurped throne. Some poems, like **"Ishmael the Archer"** . . . , glory in the pride and strength of the outcast, while others stress the loneliness and isolation of the exile. (p. 52)

For an author whose earlier plays were in the nationalistic tradition, who was referred to from the very early days as a spokesman for the Irish people and peasantry, there are surprisingly few poems devoted to the didacticism and propaganda which were so prevalent in the patriotic pieces of Lady Gregory and Yeats. (p. 53)

Colum's elegies are, in a sense, his most nationalistic poems. If they lack militancy, they are no less indicative of national pride and patriotism. Veneration of departed heroes, while a universal trait, is a particularly Irish preoccupation, and Colum's elegies have been reprinted with additions in Dublin every two or three years since 1958. These poems are gaining considerable stature as an increasingly significant part of his work. They are described in the volume *Irish Elegies* as being less elegies than memorabilia, and indeed it is the quality of the poet's having known these men intimately as friends as well as great men of Ireland that has given many of the poems their personal charm and significance. (pp. 53-4)

· · · · ·

Most students of Irish literature know Padraic Colum as a poet, a dramatist and perhaps even a writer of children's stories. It may come as a surprise that he has written a considerable number of short stories, two novels, two biographies and four books of essays, as well as contributions and prefaces for fifty-one books and pieces of various sorts for more than sixty newspapers and periodicals. . . .

Almost all of Colum's fiction grows out of its Irish milieu, and similarly most of his nonfiction is an elaboration on the country, its people and its customs. (p. 90)

Just as his subject matter is predominantly Irish, his style can also be generally described as familiar and colloquial. His most characteristic stylistic trait is his abundant use of the present tense narration in fiction as well as nonfiction. This together with a first person narrator places him in the role of a storyteller sitting by a turf fire spinning out tales of things familiar to him and wondrous to his audience. This posture that Colum tries to maintain in his work is one he is well suited to. The particular criteria of excellence in evaluating Colum's work are not the normal currency of contemporary literary critics, because few other serious writers attempt what he is doing, and our appreciation of it has fallen into disrepair through disuse. (p. 91)

Colum's greatest achievement as a fiction writer was not to come until . . . [late] in his life with the publication of the second of his two novels, *The Flying Swans*. Because the first, which enjoyed far more critical acclaim when it was printed, afforded a necessary preparation for the second, it should be given some consideration here.

Castle Conquer has all of the flaws one would expect from a writer who had never before attempted a long piece of fiction. It is a romance set in the late 1870's and early 80's having as its background the struggle against the oppressive landholders who preceded the uprisings of the early twentieth century. The young protagonists, Brighid Moynagh and Francis Gillick, must undergo the torments of their own youthful temperaments and community censure as well as the persecution of a tyrannical system. . . . [The] reader feels more and more the encroachments of Irish nationalistic propaganda altering the motivations of the couple and the artistic integrity of the book.

Although Colum's accurate ear for Irish speech is as apparent in *Castle Conquer* as it is in *The Flying Swans,* I will defer a fuller discussion of this aspect of style until the discussion of the latter novel. Colum also includes such typically Irish literary devices as the indispensable informer, the occult mysticism of the road people, and a plethora of dreams and omens.

Further, *Castle Conquer* affords the first example of what was to become a favorite format of the author in such later works as *The Flying Swans* and the Noh plays: the relationship of recurring action to a place. The plot of *Castle Conquer* centers around the castle itself and around O'Failey's tower, which Gillick's ancestor built and which is the site of the protagonist's commitment to the Irish militant movement. (pp. 93-4)

Francis Gillick was obviously intended to be one of Ireland's deliverers from these evils, and if Colum has not succeeded in casting him as an epic hero, the author has not left him wholly without credentials for his role as emancipator. He is a member of the ancient Irish aristocracy. Family ties and bloodlines hence become a major motif of the book. This theme, which is to recur as a main motif of *The Flying Swans,* is to its heritage minded author part of the heroic idea.

The other major aspect of Colum's concept of heredity is that of the natural dignity and nobility of the common Irish people. This motif is implicit in all of Colum's work, but nowhere is it spelled out as explicitly as in *Castle Conquer*. . . .

The political aspects of the novel are based upon another theme central to the Colum canon, one which we have seen before in his plays: the love for the land. *Castle Conquer* represents the tyranny of the land usurping establishment, and Francis Gillick's enmity is aroused by the plight of a peasant, Martin Jordan, who is about to be evicted. . . .

[*Castle Conquer* is] by no means an uninteresting book. The love story is poignant, the action for the most part absorbing and realistic, and the characters believable. Despite its flaws the book did produce a number of themes and characters which Colum was later able to employ in such widely diversified works as *The Flying Swans* and *Poet's Circuits*. (p. 97)

[*The Flying Swans*] is well constructed, written in a language which is always striking and often beautiful, and searching in its themes. It is a *Bildungsroman* influenced by those Irish sagas dealing with expulsion and return of the Irish heroes and by *The Mabinogion,* the series of Welsh romances concerning the youthful exploits of various Celtic heroes. The novel traces its protagonist, Ulick O'Rehill, from his birth to young adulthood.

Though Colum was writing fairy stories as his main source of income during the more than ten years that *The Flying Swans* was in progress, there is little of the childlike fantasy which was to make his children's books so popular. The world he describes in his book is realistic, if undatable. His Irish countryside is populated with lifelike characters who are unique even if their identities as types of Irish peasantry seem familiar.

One of the most remarkable things about Colum's fiction as well as his drama and poetry is his ability to reproduce so accurately the nuances of Irish speech, particularly the midland dialect. *The Flying Swans* is no exception to this rule. In both narration and dialogue the novel abounds in such Irish expressions as *bychild* for *bastard, behindhand* for *behind,* and *fornenst* for *in front of*. Other more usual Irish expressions like *myself, himself* and *herself* as direct objects also appear in the narration and dialogue, but these are not uncommon in Irish letters.

If many writers use the Irish idiom, none do it so completely as Colum and few so well. He conveys the Irish lilt not only in his choice of words, but also in his ordering of them. For example he very often reverses past participle and verb (''when he had a sup taken'') and subject and predicate adjective (''Oh, very poor was the boy's mother''). This produces the downward cadence and tone of voice at the end of the phrase or sentence which is characteristic of Irish speech. Colum also enriches the rhythms of his prose by occasionally repeating words, especially polysyllabic words, for no apparent reason beyond the sensuous quality of the sound (''On this day pigs were grunting and grunting in its street''). Often these word repetitions give the narrative a fairy-tale aspect. . . . Because the inverted syntax, the cadenced speech and the word and phrase repetition are all indigenous to poetry, it is not surprising to find that a good deal of *The Flying Swans* sounds much like a poem. Colum's prosodic style helps capture in his peasant characters the natural dignity their counterparts possess in life.

Colum lends to the formality of his narrative by frequently giving formal introductions to various narrative segments and stories the characters relate. . . . The device is one used extensively in Colum's children's stories to make them appear more magnificent and meaningful in the eyes of their audience. While American readers may at first find this particularly Irish use of words and word order a bit disconcerting, the devices wear well and are easy to accept after a few chapters of *The Flying Swans*.

Though the narrative perspective of the novel is third person, it parallels fairly closely the impressions and feelings of the protagonist. The events that make the greatest impression on the youngster, like the death and funeral of his grandfather, Breasal O'Breasal, are given predominance. Colum followed the pattern Joyce set in *A Portrait of the Artist* by constructing a novel of impressions as well as events. (pp. 98-100)

Colum divided his novel into ten sections, each consisting of from seven to seventeen chapters. The smaller divisions deal with specific scenes and events while the larger correspond to various stages of Ulick's and Breasal's life and maturity. The novel begins in the market town of Dooard and follows the travels and fortunes of the family of Robert O'Rehill throughout Ireland until it comes full cycle back to Dooard and history begins again. The cyclical aspect of the book can be largely attributed, as can a number of other scenes and devices, to Joyce, to whom, along with James Stephens, the novel is dedicated. (pp. 105-06)

Though *The Flying Swans,* like the bulk of Colum's work, is striking on first reading, principally for its cadenced Irish language and its realistic images and description, this novel also has the depth and durability of structure, theme and characterization that withstand and reward repeated reading. It is a book which deserves far more critical attention than it has received. (p. 109)

Zack Bowen, in his Padraic Colum: A Biographical-Critical Introduction *(copyright © 1970 by Southern Illinois University Press; reprinted by permission of Southern Illinois University Press), Southern Illinois University Press, 1970, 162 p.*

Michael Cristofer
1946-

(Pseudonym of Michael Procaccino) American dramatist and actor.

A highly regarded actor, Cristofer earned respect as a skillful and stimulating dramatist for his candid treatment of terminal illness in his first major work, *The Shadow Box* (1975). He has been praised for his use of techniques which are purely dramatic, rather than literary or novelistic. One way in which Cristofer effectively exploits the set's potential as a theatrical device in *The Shadow Box* is by placing onstage three cottages, which physically separate the dying characters and serve to individualize their common plight. Other important aspects of Cristofer's play are the overall complexity of language and the innovative use of cross-cut and chorally arranged dialogue. *The Shadow Box* won both the Pulitzer Prize in drama and a Tony Award in 1977.

After *The Shadow Box* Cristofer continued to explore provocative themes, but with less successful results. *Ice* (1976), an expressionistic play about basic human instincts, was criticized as both pointlessly obscene and symbolically trite, while *Black Angel* (1978), which concerns Nazism, vigilantism, and the degree to which evil actions are forgivable, received little critical attention.

(See also *Contemporary Authors,* Vol. 110 and *Dictionary of Literary Biography,* Vol. 7.)

STEPHEN FARBER

During the last few years, Los Angeles theater audiences have come to know Michael Cristofer as one of the most gifted actors of his generation. As a dramatist Cristofer is not yet on the same level, but the intelligence and compassion that make him such a versatile actor are also visible in his new play "**The Shadow Box.**" . . .

"**The Shadow Box**" covers one 24-hour period and concentrates on three terminally ill patients (all presumably dying of cancer, though this is not specified) living in private cottages on the grounds of a progressive hospital. Joe, a middle-aged working man, has to break the news to his wife and teen-age son. Brian, a failed writer who has completed four autobiographies since learning he is going to die, is living with his homosexual lover when his ex-wife stops in for a visit. In the third cottage a salty old woman named Felicity is being tended by her unmarried daughter, Agnes. The people in the three cottages never meet; their stories unfold simultaneously, and they are adroitly interwoven in Cristofer's text. . . . When the play begins, the dying patients have already resigned themselves to the inevitable. The drama in each case grows from the struggle of the patients' families to come to terms with death.

Cristofer has a weakness for rhetorical effects—for example, a long, flashy speech about the taste of "yellow, putrid death"—that are awkward and self-conscious. He is best at straight naturalistic writing; his dialogue is witty and idiomatic, flavored with tart flashes of gallows humor, and he has a feeling for dramatic interplay.

Keith Meyers/NYT PICTURES

Unfortunately, some of the characters in "**The Shadow Box**" are stock figures. Joe and Maggie, the lower-middle-class couple from New Jersey, are textbook examples of a working class couple. Cristofer's most memorable characters are the most idiosyncratic. The amateur philosopher Brian . . . , chattering compulsively about metaphysical mysteries, is alternately foolish and dignified, posturing and self-mocking; he is funny, quirky, unpredictable.

At the end of "**The Shadow Box**" the characters all come to accept death, and in the final reconciliations between the dying and their families or lovers, there is meant to be a tentative feeling of consolation tempering the despair. Cristofer never gets much beyond prosaic home truths on the subject of living and dying, but his genuine feeling for the people gives the play its pathos. . . .

In sum, "**The Shadow Box**" does not really rise much above the level of good television drama of the "Playhouse 90" school, but it is always intelligent, enterprising and affecting.

Stephen Farber, "Prosaic Truths on the Subject of Dying," in The New York Times *(copyright © 1975 by The New York Times Company; reprinted by permission), November 30, 1975 (and reprinted in* The New York Times Theater Reviews: 1975-1976, *The New York Times Company & Arno Press, 1977, p. 184).*

MEL GUSSOW

In "**The Shadow Box,**" ... Michael Cristofer has written a play about dying that also deals with living. ...

"**The Shadow Box,**" treating a serious and important subject with great perspicacity and compassion, is a courageous drama. At times it is also funny, which makes it even more moving. ...

[Mr. Cristofer] has created characters throbbing with humanity and has placed them on the scalpel-edge of survival. ...

"**The Shadow Box**" is three separate stories, each taking place on the same set. Occasionally dialogue overlaps, but the stories never inter-act except in our minds. We are so caught up that it comes as something of a surprise at the curtain call to realize that most of the characters have not met in the course of the play—although they inhabit the same space, emotionally as well as physically. (p. 16)

The play is about [three] terminal cases, their anxieties, their changes of mind, their determination to avoid coming down with "a bad case of the hopes." It is also about those who will survive them. How do they react—with love or revulsion, or a mixture of both? Mr. Cristofer suggests that some of these lives, perhaps all of them, are less than living. ...

We can never really know these people until we change places with them, which in a sense is what we do while watching "**The Shadow Box.**" (p. 17)

> *Mel Gussow, in a review of "The Shadow Box," in* The New York Times *(copyright © 1977 by The New York Times Company; reprinted by permission), January 25, 1977 (and reprinted in* The New York Times Theater Reviews: 1977-1978, *The New York Times Company & Arno Press, 1979, pp. 16-17).*

WALTER KERR

I don't know that I have ever before found myself faulting a play for becoming more dramatic than it ought to have been, but that's the situation I was caught in by the time Michael Cristofer's "**The Shadow Box**" lowered its last lights on a collage of solo voices, all of them softly lamenting the oncoming cloak of death. Death is the exclusive subject of the intelligently written, lustrously performed work ..., and during its entire first half I felt myself deeply committed to the restive but intensely realistic victims living out their limited lives in private cottages scattered about the grounds of a hospital.

"**The Shadow Box**" might easily seem a sociological tract, making the pitch it does for permitting terminal cases to spend their days as normally as possible, taking care of themselves in the company of relations and friends, if it weren't possessed of a psychological vigor that compels us to focus on its tart, talkative, undefeated people rather than its thesis. ...

[Brian] is not all last-ditch dynamism. He will stop for wryness, for reflection: when a probing doctor tells him there's no hurry about answering a question, he remarks swiftly but simply "Not for you maybe; some of us are on a tighter schedule." And we grow to understand that the fever pitch at which he thinks and speaks is not entirely born of desperation. He was always as he is now, he's just put his foot a bit more firmly on the accelerator. ...

[Felicity], nearly senile in a wheelchair, is still able to list with a rapid cackle all of the organs that have been snatched from her, one by one. Does her elder daughter—never her favorite—quietly sing hymns as she cares for her? On one lung, she can drown her out lustily with the bawdiest song she remembers. And you feel there are others in reserve.

Of the three who are simply waiting for the known, yet unpredictable, end, [Joe] is the least ebullient, though not the least sturdy. He's come to terms with himself, he flips back the peaked baseball cap he wears as though he were listening to a coach rather than a medical man, he is ready for total candor any time he can persuade his rattled wife to listen. But [his] wife ... has willfully, helplessly made herself obtuse. It is plain to her that he is growing better daily, she will not set foot in the bungalow that is surely stealing him from her, she has fussed and fussed to bring him all sorts of delicacies—though his refrigerator is stocked with the same hams, the same fruits. She has brought the unnecessary because it is the only thing she can bring.

At first glance one might consider these introductions to the condemned undramatic, mere character-sketches; the dying, after all, have no external enemy they can meet in an arena, fairly and squarely. There is, however, a fierce interior struggle going on in each case, whatever mask may be worn, whatever energy displayed. And we are aware of the psychic battle that produces an overlay of sassiness, of genuine humor, of unself-pitying facing-up. The evening's first half is warm and arresting.

Then, much to my surprise, I realized that I was resisting precisely those things in the second half that I normally look for, even demand: open clash, fierce exchange, heat. [Brian's] onetime wife, an inveterate playgirl with a party cap, a horn to toot and a collection of bangles and brooches to account for every affair she's ever had, arrives to discover that [Brian's] present companion is a homosexual. There is a slugging match, a face-slapping contest. And each of the flare-ups ... rings quite false. As does the ultimate effort of [Joe] to force [his wife] into opening her eyes and mind to the facts; here there is no violence but an undue sentimentality, a begging for tears when begging is the last thing required. ... [The] second act acquires a facade of theatricality that denies, or at least damages, the sensitivity of the first.

I think I see why. Until intermission, the play is centered on the dying; their internal struggles interest us and move us and we ask for no more. After intermission, playwright Cristofer turns his attention to the others concerned, the wives and companions standing by. But there is no drama in which these people can reasonably engage; they can *only* stand by, suffer, offer solace. Sensing this, and not wanting simply to repeat his first act, the author has forced dramatic postures upon the visitors, invented angers and recriminations out of whole cloth. His salute to courage and to common sense is diminished by the gratuitous imposition. He remains, nonetheless, a writer of perception and much promise. (p. 26)

> *Walter Kerr, "'The Shadow Box' Gets Too Dramatic for Its Own Good," in* The New York Times *(copyright © 1977 by The New York Times Company; reprinted by permission), February 6, 1977 (and reprinted in* The New York Times Theater Reviews: 1977-1978, *The New York Times Company & Arno Press, 1979, pp. 26-7).*

CLIVE BARNES

["**The Shadow Box**"] is a bright, occasionally even funny, play about [a] dark subject. One wonders gently what the title means—"**The Shadow Box.**" Perhaps the author is suggesting the final training before the ultimate bout—as one character says, "If you are told you are going to die, it means you are not yet dead!"—or perhaps he is merely thinking of a space, where shadows inexorably take over from former realities, until the shadows themselves are no longer cast, but exist in the vaguer outer penumbra of memory. Yet this is not a gloomy play—it merely faces a serious answer with serious questions. . . .

The play is far from perfect. The author permits a mild undercurrent of unreality to wash over the proceedings. Indeed he does not just permit it—he bathes in it. This is not a play about death in the way Edward Albee's magnificent "All Over" is a play about death. Despite its moments of savagery, this play takes a more amenable view of the process, and also a more sentimental view. It is still an important, touching and courageous play. You do not write about death for either fun or money. And Mr. Cristofer writes with the compassion of the undamned. . . .

[Are the dying characters common] folks on the brink? Not really. An O'Neill or a Tennessee Williams would have given their bleeding hearts a touch more blood and a touch less heart, and the surgery would have been beneficial. But there is enough of the palatable truth here to make an extraordinarily good Broadway play, decently crafted—the antiphonal ending is outstanding—and with meaty roles for actors, and a fine vehicle for directing.

Clive Barnes, "Final Taxi Ride," in The New York Times *(copyright © 1977 by The New York Times Company; reprinted by permission), April 1, 1977 (and reprinted in* The New York Times Theater Reviews: 1977-1978, *The New York Times Company & Arno Press, 1979, p. 62).*

BRENDAN GILL

In the plotting of ["**The Shadow Box**"], Mr. Cristofer has skillfully threaded together what amount to three variations on a single theme. His patients have it in common that they are about to die and that neither they nor anyone around them is able to behave "naturally;" their emotion is that of the ancient Latin refrain *"Timor mortis conturbat me,"* which the intellectual would no doubt translate to his unlettered lover as "Fear of death gives me the willies." Hard as it may be to credit, "**The Shadow Box**" is by no means a gloomy affair; again and again it astonishes us by being hilarious. Moreover, something like joy enters into the final moments of the play, when Mr. Cristofer abandons the realistic mode in favor of a chorus of chanted lyrical affirmations by the entire company. Seize this moment, the company adjures us, and then, if you are lucky, you may be able to seize the next as well; whatever death may be, life is a fine thing and well worth the living.

Brendan Gill, "Timor Mortis," in The New Yorker *(© 1977 by The New Yorker Magazine, Inc.), Vol. LIII, No. 8, April 11, 1977, p. 85.*

JULES AARON

While [Michael Cristofer's] first play, *The Shadow Box,* was concerned with a group of people faced literally with death, *Ice* deals with the equally terrifying *living* death of contemporary man's "frozen" existence. Murph, an impotent, talkative male model, leaves the pressures of city living for Alaska, where he buys a cabin surrounded by acres of barren land. He desperately befriends an alcoholic ex-teacher, Ray, and a sexy "free soul," Sunshine; the three live together and create a shifting network of relationships that end with Sunshine's violent death and Murph's and Ray's reversal of personalities.

Cristofer has an actor's feel for the visceral poetic rhythms of good theatre. Although influences of Beckett, Pinter, and Shepard are evident, he is an original talent. The play suffers from some overt symbolism—the metaphoric story of "winterkill" and Murph confronting himself dead in a cake of ice—and from some easy one-liner laughs. However, the majority of the play is a rich barrage of tragicomic repartée and self-realization by people submerged in "a hole filled with water," desperately trying to gasp for air through interpersonal "connections." . . .

Ice is the "love story" that Cristofer labels it; however, its love is as ironic, haunting, evasive, and frightening as twentieth-century life. The play, like its title, is crystal-sharp, resonating theatre: intellectual yet visceral, continually comic yet ultimately moving. (p. 264)

Jules Aaron, in a review of "Ice," in Educational Theatre Journal *(© 1977 University College Theatre Association of the American Theatre Association), Vol. 29, No. 2, May, 1977, pp. 264-65.*

JOHN SIMON

[The] pathetic state of Broadway theater—and, for that matter, regional theater, . . . is epitomized by the case of **The Shadow Box**. This alleged drama by the actor-playwright Michael Cristofer won both the Pulitzer Prize and Tony Award, and made a more than respectable showing in the voting for the third major award, given by the New York drama critics. It takes place in three cottages for the terminally ill on the grounds of a large hospital, in each of which an allegedly archetypal patient is dying in his or her own quirky way. To make things jazzier, one cottage represents all three cottages, the characters from one being largely confined to the porch; from the second, to the living room; from the third, to the kitchen. But there is also some actual interpenetration of the same space by all three groups, a device invented by Alan Ayckbourn in *How the Other Half Loves,* which may have worked once in a particular farce, but which is showing signs of undue proliferation. . . . (p. 147)

The author could have more appropriately named these cottages—instead of One, Two, and Three—Miller, Albee, and Williams Cottage. But perhaps his nomenclature was right after all, for this is certainly playwriting by the numbers. Not only is the action in each cottage a full-blown piece of eclecticism, but also the very dialogue is at best derivative, at worst garishly ostentatious. Moreover, the mentality displayed is unpleasantly misogynistic, what with the central female character in each cottage a bit of a beast, and the two principal men extremely decent fellows, joined at last in goodness even by the redeemed male whore. Mostly, though, the problem is that none of this rings true. The good are too good, the bitchy too bitchy, and I, for one, did not for a moment believe that the author has really comprehended the effect of oncoming death on any of his characters. He has made everything even more grandiose—and faintly obscene—by introducing The Interviewer, who is intended as a sort of cross between a staff psychiatrist and God.

This character, who apparently listens in simultaneously on all three bugged cottages, is always there interrogating either the dying or their next-of-kin, sometimes over a loudspeaker, sometimes in person. The concept is doubly odious: first, because it is clearly a shabby shortcut for the author to draw out the characters in an essentially nondramatic way; secondly, because it suggests a hospital that surpasses even actual hospitals in inhumanity with a Big Brother always listening, watching, pestering with prying questions. . . .

[A] shoddy play meretriciously designed to strike critics and audiences dumb with awe before its Great Theme did not begin to do justice to its subject. If *The Shadow Box* is the best dramatic fare it has to offer, Broadway deserves to die in whichever cottage it chooses. (p. 148)

> John Simon, in a review of "The Shadow Box," in The Hudson Review (copyright © 1978 by The Hudson Review, Inc.; reprinted by permission), Vol. XXXI, No. 1, Spring, 1978, pp. 147-48.

LEONARD GROSS

[Michael Cristofer's play] **"Black Angel"** concerns the efforts of a former German officer to receive judgment—either death or forgiveness—for his crimes during World War II. Part of the controversy, in the press and public alike, stems from Cristofer's sympathetic portrayal of the leading character. The remainder arises from Cristofer's suggestion that the very tendencies toward obedience and conformity that destroyed this man exist in all of us, and that our judgment of him must be tempered by the knowledge.

Martin Engel, once a hero in his own country, was tried, convicted and sentenced to death for ordering the extermination of 247 inhabitants of a French village. Released after 13 years because of technical imperfections in his trial, he had returned to a childhood haunt in France, a town where he'd courted his German wife, to construct their dream house. . . . Engel uses his real name. He refuses to hide or, once his identity is disclosed, to run. He is anchored by his conscience, a man, as Cristofer has put it, more concerned with the manner of survival than with survival itself.

The dramatic question is this: should the sensitive, introspective, conscience-ridden man Engel has become be punished for the crimes of the mindlessly loyal militarist he had been 35 years before? The Mayor of the village thinks not. Its vigilantes think yes. They prevail.

The anger the play aroused was aimed at precisely this point. Cristofer, said one critic, has treated the villain of the play with loving care and the Frenchmen opposed to his presence as clichés. Another wrote: "Engel and his admirers are all eloquent charmers; his enemies are all vulgar chumps."

But praise—some of it bordering ecstasy—far outweighed the anger. . . . The finest accolade came from William Murray writing in New West: "The hope with this play . . . is that . . . the playwright will continue to refine it and reconsider various aspects of the implications it raises until he may at last succeed in creating the masterpiece he has very nearly achieved." Even Variety, which felt that the play had been presented before its holes had been plugged and its scenes properly stacked, called **"Black Angel"** a "potentially powerful (and possibly even great) play. This could be a modern classical tragedy." . . .

Cristofer's inquiries are never simple, but they *are* basic. In **"The Shadow Box,"** he used the clarity developed by dying people to ask questions about life. In **"Black Angel,"** he is wondering about the source of evil.

> Leonard Gross, "Michael Cristofer Writes 'A Play of Questions'," in The New York Times (copyright © 1978 by The New York Times Company; reprinted by permission), June 25, 1978, p. 9.

MEL GUSSOW

Clearly [in **"Ice"**] Mr. Cristofer has intended to write an archetypical drama about vagrant people, who, through force of circumstance, have become more animal than human. However, the result is unfocused and unsavory—a self-parody whose best feature is its brevity.

The owner of the cabin . . . begins as a clean-cut outdoorsman. Inexplicably, he invites a scrofulous derelict to share his quarters, and talks to him as if he might be an old buddy from high school, instead of a filthy, crab-infested stranger. By the end of the play, the derelict . . . is sober, shaven and even articulate—with cleanliness comes good speech. On the other hand, [the owner] is chattering to himself like a deranged parrot. The switch in roles is as obvious as it is farfetched. (pp. 187-88)

Sunshine is loose-talking and promiscuous, aggressively available to one man and another. The men in the play are usually passive when it comes to sex, although in other respects they can be whirligigs of energy, charging into the night to walk four cold miles to stand alone at the nearest bar. . . .

Perhaps [**"Ice"**] should be regarded as the equivalent of a successful novelist's failed second novel—something to be forgotten. (p. 188)

> Mel Gussow, "Cabin Fever," in The New York Times (copyright © 1979 by The New York Times Company; reprinted by permission), November 2, 1979 (and reprinted in The New York Times Theater Reviews: 1979-1980, The New York Times Company & Arno Press, 1981, pp. 187-88).

JOHN SIMON

[*Ice*] enjoys the one distinction of managing, in a much shorter compass, to be about as offensive as [*Losing Time*]. In fact, *Ice* recalls *Losing Time* with a similar wallowing in obscenity and scatology, a like reveling in human vileness, violence, and abjection equally unconvincingly portrayed, and in an almost identical inconsistency of characterization. But Cristofer adds his own brand of insufferable pseudo-poetry and obfuscatory symbolism that symbolizes nothing, as well as a highly developed pretentiousness to which the author of *Losing Time* can as yet only aspire.

Ice concerns Murph, a young man who has bought a shack and some land in Alaska, where he proposes to lead a pure and authentic life close to nature and laced with quart bottles of whiskey. He takes in, first, a tongue-tied wino, Ray, then a pretty female drifter, Sunshine. The former promptly becomes an articulate, indeed voluble, pseudo-philosopher; the latter, a tragicomic nymphomaniac. Each first shares Murph's bed, then proceeds to cuckold him with the other, preferably while Murph can listen to their moans and grunts through a thin partition. Sample dialogue from Murph: "You may look like a piece of shit, you may smell like a piece of shit, but inside you're beautiful." From Ray: "The color of my urine is near perfection; I fart only after meals, upwind . . ." and "Love makes an arsehole taste like a fudge sundae." From Sunshine (about her mother's warning that she might get raped and murdered): "I could be murdered and not raped, and that would be worse" and "I'd screw my brains out all day and night, and the next day I'd wake up horny—not even depressed, just horny. . . ."

To make things a little less appetizing yet, Cristofer douses them with profundities, conundrums, symbols: Seemingly dead men rise from the ice, a man hallucinates that someone is undressing him and masturbating him exclusively with his or her teeth, an ax is used indiscriminately to slice a cake and chop up the floorboards, and someone will say, "You want nothing from me, and nothing is what you won't get—nothing is too much to ask." Entire scenes consist of actions or inaction whose sole purpose seems to be to flagellate the audience as much as the characters torture one another. *Ice* is the kind of play that requires not public performance but immediate close confinement.

I am both sorry and pleased to say that the contriver of this morass is the Pulitzer- and Tony-award-winning author of *The Shadow Box,* which my colleagues extolled and to which I, in a heated moment on television, applied one of Mr. Cristofer's own favorite epithets. Let the lovers of *The Shadow Box* re-examine that play in the light of this one (which, under a slightly cooler surface, it closely resembles); they may now find themselves unable to muster enough love to make either work taste like a fudge sundae. (pp. 130-31)

John Simon, "Sugar and Spite," in New York Magazine *(copyright © 1984 by News Group Publications, Inc.; reprinted with the permission of* New York Magazine*), Vol. 12, No. 44, November 12, 1979, pp. 130-31.**

Peter Davison
1928-

American poet and editor.

Davison's first book, *The Breaking of the Day* (1964), won the Yale Series of Younger Poets Award. It contains themes and subjects which recur throughout much of his poetry: death, depression, spiritual isolation, and loss. The volume includes tributes to members of the confessional school of poetry with whom Davison was acquainted early in his career. A number of poems concern the late poet Sylvia Plath, with whom Davison was once romantically involved. In *Half Remembered* (1973), an autobiographical account of his unhappy childhood and his self-discovery through psychoanalysis and poetry, Davison provides insight into the psychosocial dynamics which shaped many young poets of the confessional movement after World War II. Critics have commended this volume for its intelligent and representational, rather than self-absorbed, stance.

Walking the Boundaries: Poems 1957-1974 contains a chronological arrangement of Davison's best poetry during this period. Critics note a discernible shift in his style and thematic emphasis. His earlier verse leans toward rigid formality and didacticism, while his later work is more meditative. Robert Frost is often mentioned as having the strongest influence on Davison's work. From Frost's poetry Davison learned to use nature as an apt metaphor for an ideal, harmonious human society. Davison's recent volume *Barn Fever and Other Poems* (1982) is considered by many critics to be his best collection. Much of the formality of his early poetry has been replaced by a more relaxed and confident association with the subject matter and an increasingly skillful use of nature imagery.

(See also *Contemporary Authors*, Vols. 9-12, rev. ed.; *Contemporary Authors New Revision Series*, Vol. 3; and *Dictionary of Literary Biography*, Vol. 5.)

Courtesy of Peter Davison

JAMES SCHEVILL

The way in which young poets are using autobiography meaningfully to extend the range of their subject matter is shown in two fine sequences in Peter Davison's first book, *The Breaking of the Day*. . . . The first sequence, **"Not Forgotten,"** contains five poems about his mother's death from cancer. Since the sequence focuses on a real protagonist, the mother, the poet has the advantage of a dramatic relationship, which he expresses with rare compassion and powerful imagery. . . . The second sequence, **"The Breaking of the Day,"** derives from Genesis, the story of Jacob wrestling with the Angel. The subject is the poet's search for identity and faith after his conflict with his Christian father and his Jewish mother. Again, the characters are presented with compassion and understanding and no self-pity. In these poems Davison uses a direct, colloquial style that he makes uniquely his own. In other poems his subjects and techniques are often more conventional, sometimes revealing the rather strange, combined influence of Robert Frost and Robert Lowell. Nevertheless, in such poems as **"To a Mad Friend"** and **"After a Nightmare"** he shows that ability to move deeply into an experience and transform it with brilliant technical control that is the mark of the real poet. This is a strong first book, and Peter Davison takes his place with the important young poets in the country. (p. 30)

James Schevill, "Poets Ascend the Technical Trend," in Saturday Review (© 1963 Saturday Review Magazine Co.; reprinted by permission), Vol. XLVII, No. 27, July 4, 1963, pp. 30-3.*

DUDLEY FITTS

The title of Peter Davison's book [*The Breaking of the Day*] is taken from the Old Testament story of Jacob wrestling with the Angel. Specifically, the symbol illuminates the internal *agôn* of the seven concluding poems, a severe and perilously poised act of introspection. The agonist self is engaged with itself, and the contest ends—if it can be said to end at all—with the equivocal blessing of recognition: 'And Jacob called the name of the place Peniel: for I have seen God face to face.' Each of us moves towards his own Peniel in one way or another, and we shall probably agree that Mr. Davison's use of the metaphor is as right as it is impressively climactic. Nevertheless, it is with a minor and more diffuse application of it that I am concerned in this prefatory note. Encounter and struggle are figured here not only in the great perplexities of religion, of race, of love; they are constantly recurring as variations, seriously parodic, to cast new light and shadow upon the contours of the main design. In nearly all of these poems there is an encounter, a question, more often implied than stated; and there is an ambiguous answer. It was the delicate management of this counterpointing that attracted me on my first reading of the manuscript, and my pleasure in it has grown with each rereading.

There are two principal tones of composition here, both of them, in a sense, rhetorics. The first, and the less frequently employed, is declamatory and hard; the second is relaxed and fluid, muted, at times risking real audacities of throw-away and understatement. As the book stands, the one mode could hardly work effectively without the other, and at the highest moments they combine, as in the final section. (p. vii)

I should admire Mr. Davison if for no other reason than that he knows how to make poems speak. All good verse is artifice, and it must be so before it can be anything else. In the second place, neither of these poems is simply an exercise in technic. True, each exemplifies an extreme of the poet's style, and the pieces are to this extent rhetorical; but here is even less reason for rejecting either as a working element in a body of verse. These extremes enclose the book, inform it; they are the poles that make its motion possible. (p. ix)

Whether in the five-part elegy of the first section or the balancing group of the last, in the circumstantial horror of **'After a Nightmare'**, or the scaled-down trailing off of **'To a Mad Friend'**, or the chilling salacities of **'The Peeper'** and **'Summer School'**—one is impressed by the range and the depth of these poems, and by the generous human candor that speaks in them. There is torment, too, and irony, and ambiguity unresolved; for these things are proper to wrestling with an Angel, and the name of the place is Peniel. (p. x)

> *Dudley Fitts, "Foreword" (copyright © 1958, 1959, 1960, 1961, 1963, 1964 by Peter Davison; reprinted by permission of Peter Davison and Mrs. Dudley Fitts), in* The Breaking of the Day and Other Poems *by Peter Davison, Yale University Press, 1964, pp. vii-x.*

JOSEPHINE JACOBSEN

There is a preoccupation with death in *The Breaking of the Day.* Of the best poems in the book—and the best are good—a number are concerned with the implications and act of dying, this concern being illustrated in ways totally different by *Not Forgotten* (a sequence of five poems), *The Suicide, Finale: Presto,* and *The Massacre of the Innocents.* The foregoing poems are—basically—narrative, and in the narrative poem Mr. Davison moves extremely well; it is his forte. (p. 203)

The more introspective or abstract poems are very uneven. They range from the excellent—as in *At the Site of Last Night's Fire,* and *North Shore*—to the unsatisfactory—as in *Jenny* and *Out of Tune,* poems with good fragments but which in their final lines have a horrid patness. The apparent necessity to write a poem about Robert Frost, and The Bomb (not necessarily in that order), is so rampant today that one should be grateful to find here a better-than-fifty-fifty break: Mr. Davison's poem on Frost is agreeable, and his poem on The Bomb achieves the startling success of making its reader forget while he reads it that others have been written. It is a potent and moving poem. (p. 204)

> *Josephine Jacobsen, "Five Poets" (© 1964 by The Modern Poetry Association; reprinted by permission of the Editor of* Poetry *and the author), in* Poetry, *Vol. CV, No. 3, December, 1964, pp. 201-06.**

PHOEBE-LOU ADAMS

Expertly made, varied in technique, superficially concerned with topics ranging from an eclipse of the sun to misfiled papers, the poems [in *The City and the Island*] are in fact all part of an examination of the differences between the public world and the private one. The island is a protean territory, shifting from individual imagination to the practice of art to the general graveyard of history; it is always lonely and sometimes terrifying. The city is no less alarming but not so chameleon in habit.... Both city and island are full of unexpected images and meanings that turn into other meanings, unforeseeable until Mr. Davison casually lifts a rug or a rock.

> *Phoebe-Lou Adams, in a review of "The City and the Island," in* The Atlantic Monthly *(copyright © 1966, by The Atlantic Monthly Company, Boston, Mass.; reprinted with permission), Vol. 218, No. 6, December, 1966, p. 160.*

DAVID GALLER

I have little to say of Peter Davison's second book of poems [*The City and the Island*], except that it is pretty much on a par with his first of two years ago. He is still "all promise", with few fulfilled poems. His chief faults are an average imagination and lapses in tone within a given poem, both amply illustrated in *Eurydice in Darkness* and *One of the Muses.* These poems are also among those which continue to search his chief thematic concern: the minds of women. Writing on this theme, he has written more evenly but also more dully, as in *Lucifer Ashore, Intacta,* and *Mary Magdalene at Easter.*

Davison has, however, a considerable virtue, especially nowadays: his constant, however precarious, involvement with craft is evident throughout his book; and the result, when not burdened with tonal lapses, is an open, simple, declarative diction wholly without pretentiousness—which deserves congratulation. The question is whether complicated material can become successfully absorbed into this casual language. And also whether Davison can resist putting this asset to work in his lighter pieces, such as *Letter from a City Dweller, Galop,* and *In Season.* Too often still, a Frostian simplicity of language is vying with either psychological material not wholly understood or with post-Auden lighter social ironies. I respect Davison's mode; enjoy my belief that eventually he may gain both more analytical depth and more tonal control.

> *David Galler, in a review of "The City and the Island" (© 1967 by The Modern Poetry Association; reprinted by permission of the Editor of* Poetry *and the author), in* Poetry, *Vol. CX, No. 4, July, 1967, p. 269.*

VICTOR HOWES

Peter Davison is not one poet, he is an anthology of poets. By turns he can sound like Auden, like Randall Jarrell, like Thomas Hardy, like Frost, like Roethke, like, even, would you believe Tennyson? . . .

Make no mistake, [in *Pretending to Be Asleep*] Mr. Davison is not writing parodies. He does not, like the parodist, zero in on a writer's mannerisms, and hammer them into absurdity. Nor is he writing imitation, lifeless ventriloquist's dummies fashioned on well-known models. He seems rather to be pacing himself against his masters, attempting to bring off new and original poems in traditional modalities. And, amazingly, the experiment works.

Though now he alludes to Yeats, now modifies a phrase from Sir Thomas Wyatt, now employs an epigraph from Coleridge, the effect Mr. Davison achieves is not "literary" in the pejorative sense. In poem after poem he at once transcends his sources, and at the same time offers new insight into the poetic tradition.

If pressed to explain how he gets away with it, how he succeeds, in fact, at a most dangerous game, I should suggest that he succeeds because he is a poet with something to say. Unlike the parrot, or the parodist, who deals only in echoes of things overheard, Peter Davison reads like a man talking to men. He writes about life-and-death concerns, about being aware (awake), and about being unaware (asleep), and about pretending to be asleep when you are really awake....

Peter Davison's third book of poems is the virtuoso performance of a man trying on a variety of poetic hats in an effort to find one that fits. Fits, that is, for everyday and for all days in all kinds of weathers. His problem may come when he has to choose among the hats that fit.

> Victor Howes, "A Poet Who Writes Like an Anthology," in The Christian Science Monitor (reprinted by permission from The Christian Science Monitor; © 1970 The Christian Science Publishing Society; all rights reserved), June 4, 1970, p. 7.

ROBERT B. SHAW

I find it difficult to form a clear opinion of Peter Davison's *Pretending to Be Asleep.* There are a few excellent poems and a few major embarrassments (as when he compares himself and his father to Telemachus and Odysseus). But the collection is not vividly memorable for either its faults or its virtues. It is basically competent but basically unexciting. Perhaps Davison simply has not found any theme which can exercise to the utmost his imagination and his moderate but genuine talent. I was most attracted by *A Word in Your Ear on Behalf of Indifference,* which is sensible and funny; *Afterwards,* which has a Herbert-like simplicity to its music; and *Stumps,* which deals nicely with those "amputations / Too short to see, too tall to be mown over."... I do not feel that the 14-poem title sequence captures, except in a very few places, the strangeness of the borderlines between sleep and waking, dream and reality. The best parts are those written for other voices (especially *Third Voice: the Widower* and *Fourth Voice: the Grandmother*); this suggests that Davison has a flair for the dramatic monologue, and one hopes that he will attempt further poems in this form. The distinguished quality of a handful of these poems heightens my disappointment with the book for its general lack of energy. (p. 229)

> Robert B. Shaw, "Poets in Midstream" (© 1971 by The Modern Poetry Association; reprinted by permission of the Editor of Poetry and the author), in Poetry, Vol. CXVIII, No. 4, July, 1971, pp. 228-33.*

HELEN BEVINGTON

[In "**Half Remembered**" Peter Davison] has written a personal history indeed. The stern candor of it makes one wonder at first if he is to be linked with the confessional writers—the Robert Lowells, Sylvia Plaths—who have walked naked before us these years in bitter anger and resentment, accusing and hating their fathers, finding life worth revealing only in its guilts and humiliations, its appalling failures. But of Peter Davison this is far from true. If his search is, like theirs, a search for identity, unlike them he has escaped self-pity; he has made the impossibly difficult journey from resentment to compassion. And he has found himself....

The tale is a familiar one, of course, as all personal histories are familiar. The remarkable impact of Peter Davison's tale lies in the telling—in the depth of recognition, for one thing, that a person can never escape by turning away. He can only grow up somehow from the unforgiving child, the accuser, the judge rebuking the flaws and failure in others, to the man who must learn to judge and define himself.

The scrutiny is close, the story is clearly true, of a life more than half remembered: it was lived, it is relived in all its flounderings, all the random searchings for answer to the conundrum of self....

Peter Davison can almost name the hour he began to write poetry, at 29. Suddenly he wrote, teaching himself the craft, trying to hear not his father's voice but his own. Gradually the wheel turned; he began to accept his parents as human beings, his scars began to fade. "Poetry was my way of keeping alive," and it was not too late.

But it is a final discovery from this long exploration and quest that delights me most, learned as it was at the feet of Robert Frost, who was his parents' friend, then Peter's own. "Two roads diverged in a wood," wrote Frost in his famous poem, "and I—, / I took the one less traveled by." Only one of the roads could be taken, the poet said, the choice must be made between them, "And that has made all the difference." In a splendid burst of independence, in a flash of insight, Peter Davison rejected this statement of dilemma as false. On the contrary, the traveler may take both roads if he will; and the world, I think, should be advised of this comforting fact. Peter Davison has had the courage to take both roads.

> Helen Bevington, "Answer to the Conundrum of Self," in The New York Times Book Review (copyright © 1973 by The New York Times Company; reprinted by permission), September 16, 1973, p. 6.

ALISON LURIE

The 'confessional poetry' which is now being produced in such quantity, especially in America, has been received, especially in Britain, with a good deal of affectionate mockery, if not with hostile jeering. There is likely to be a similar reception for the latest development in the genre, the Poet's Confession in book-length prose, of which Peter Davison's *Half Remembered* is a prime example. What do I care about the details of Mr Davison's schoolboy masturbation experiences, reviewers are going to say, or the interpretation of his nightmares? Why does he feel obliged to tell me all this, either in verse or in prose?

One answer at least is that Davison, like many of his contemporaries, held it all in so long—spent so many years not telling anyone anything. When he was at Harvard just after World War Two, the correct models for a poet were Eliot, Stevens, Empson, and Winters. The approved poem was an elegant machine, a sort of jewelled watch whose regular metric ticking ought to have only the most subtle relation, if any, to the uneven and bloody beat of the poet's heart. The approved life was equally contrived and artificial....

He was saved, again like so many of his contemporaries, by psychoanalysis. **Half Remembered** centres on the analytic experience, which seems to have been, within its limits, extremely successful, freeing Davison from a classic Oedipal neurosis and making it possible for him, for the first time, to love and to write. In many ways the book reads like a case history, though it is much more intelligent and infinitely better written than most.

Perhaps it is for this reason that the first three-quarters of the book are so much better than the final section. Before psychoanalysis the neurotic person is like a man with a dirty sack tied tightly over his head and arms.... Analysis cuts the rope and lets him out of the sack, but it does not tell him in what direction to walk, or at what speed. I was left at the end of **Half Remembered** with a feeling of joy at Peter Davison's release, but without any clear idea of where he is going now.

Moreover, I think he is rather hard on his past self, like so many of the twice-born.... It is easier for me to see him as a representative man of his time, and his autobiography as a capsule of recent American literary history. In his account of his childhood, low-key but moving descriptions of solitary landscape experiences alternate with scenes of violent domestic conflict—as it were, Frost with O'Neill....

A false answer to his problems is provided by the academic-literary establishment invoked at the start of this review, and a true solution through self-discovery and confession in the manner of Ginsberg and Lowell. Almost all the elements in his story have parallels either in my own experience or that of my friends and relatives; and this, of course, is both the real achievement of **Half Remembered** and, on a higher level, its failure. A good writer, like Peter Davison, faithfully and courageously reflects his age; only a great writer creates it.

> Alison Lurie, "Out of the Sack," in New Statesman (© 1974 The Statesman & Nation Publishing Co. Ltd.), Vol. 87, No. 2249, April 26, 1974, p. 591.

JOHN FULLER

Walking the Boundaries is a substantial selection from the work of an American poet . . . who has not been published over here before. What an assured talent is here unveiled! There seems to be little that Davison can't accomplish within the Frost/Jarrell tradition he is largely working in. The earlier poems have a fine singing line, sure-footed rhythms and a well-directed variety of form. There are monologues, confessions, ratiocinations, erotic mythologies, much sympathy and intelligence and surprising imaginative leaps. He can create characters and situations with facility, and later develops a descriptive power much in evidence in the rustic-symbolic landscapes of the four title-poems. There are a few bad poems (one about the stages of sexual experience and another about the Kennedy clan) but they are only bad in the degree to which they do not achieve the reader's assent. Davison's strategy is generally attractive. One reads on and on, in curiosity—a reading hunger unusual in poetry. It is a splendidly accessible body of work. (p. 22)

> John Fuller, "Personal Columns," in New Statesman (© 1974 The Statesman & Nation Publishing Co. Ltd.), Vol. 88, No. 2259, July 5, 1974, pp. 22-3.*

JAMES ATLAS

Walking the Boundaries is subtitled **Poems 1957-1974,** and collects what [Davison] considers to be the best from his previous three volumes, as well as an ample selection of new poems. Arranged more or less chronologically, **Walking the Boundaries** moves from the decorous formal modes of an educated, rather inhibited practitioner of poetry to more meditative autobiographical poems that demonstrate a gathering of confidence in the narrative possibilities his own experience can yield. With few exceptions, the earlier poems are stylized, overly literary, grandiose, their subject cautious and generalized.... There is an element of pathetic fallacy to Davison's imagination; his efforts to imbue situations with a larger significance than they seem really to have for him contributes to what is in the end a conflict between abstract language and specific emotion. It is this, perhaps, that accounts for the awkwardness of the speaker's voice, which, even when intended to represent someone else, sounds always the same. Moreover, there is a kind of rhetorical convention to these poems, whatever their actual subject.... (pp. 299-300)

[In **Dark Houses,** a meditative memoir to his father,] and in the four poems, each given a direction (**North by the Creek, West by the Road,** and so on), that make up the book's title, Davison achieves an expansiveness of tone that allows him to widen his discourse, taking in more of experience than was available to him in the set pieces of his previous collections. **Dark Houses** follows his father's life backwards through time, from his death in New York to Pennsylvania, Colorado, and his university days in Cambridge, England, then his boyhood; a final section returns to the present, where, his ashes scattered at sea, he becomes

> part of the land at last, land of his children,
> Where the gray ungiving stone can always stand
> For fathers, thrusting up above the fields
> Not ever his own, though dearer than the land
> That gave him birth but never knew his name.

Davison's progression from sentimental, unfocussed speech to a less nervously refined, more direct intervention of the speaker has obviously served him well. (p. 300)

> James Atlas, "Autobiography of the Present" (© 1975 by The Modern Poetry Association; reprinted by permission of the Editor of Poetry and the author), in Poetry, Vol. CXXV, No. 5, February, 1975, pp. 295-302.*

VERNON YOUNG

I first encountered Davison on the page about ten years ago in the appropriately titled multisequence poem, **"Not Forgotten."** I was impressed beyond measure by the dexterity with which . . . the poet had juxtaposed orders of emotion and simile so discrete as to imply, if this had been proposed and not yet actualized, a feat unlikely or impossible to achieve.... The present selection of his verse [**Walking the Boundaries: Poems 1957-1974**] surpasses the most confident expectations I had meanwhile formed. And the essential character of his art—its character, not its full range nor its scale of intonations—is trenchantly illustrated . . . [in] the almost instinctive reference to creatures of the wild, the unstinting concern with mortality, the sardonic revision of knowledge unbearably somber. (pp. 80-1)

Davison's poems may not invariably begin in delight; they always end in wisdom; or they incorporate a parenthesis of invincible candor that robs us of our slumbering complacency (or should) for hours at a time. (pp. 81-2)

Davison's poetry would be indefinable without undue emphasis on last rites; *not* inconceivable—he can write about anything (so he encourages us to believe); but indefinable *centrally*, since it is through his kinship with the Imperious Subject [Death] . . . that he rivets our attention—over all, by the several perspectives from which he conducts an inquest. He is inside the phenomenon, outside it, acting the victim (to say nothing of the perpetrator), mocking (sometimes) the ceremonies by which it is exalted, setting it to copious rhythms, rising easily or uneasily above its gross accompaniments, regarding it as a practical consequence of glandular dissolution, as an awesome mystery in the face of which we devise impotent exorcisms, or as an absurd anticlimax to a third act which the ego had pathetically thought of as its crowning and perpetual structure. Hence, **"Walking the Boundaries"**—which, in the four poems sharing that title, summons (ineffably) the seasons and the points of the compass, the infinities of underleaf and tidal life that annihilate and transform the natural world and leave their reflection in the anima of the poet—becomes the governing metaphor subsuming each and every poem. Everyone walks the boundary of himself that daily shrinks or which he fails to locate, "pretending to be asleep," living in dementia—or camouflaged like our latest tribe of Necropolitans for whom Davison has surely written the last testament. (p. 83)

I would seriously falsify Davison, however, if I promoted him exclusively as an historian of *memento mori*. He is, besides, as I have amply hinted, a poet who explores and interrogates; one who by empathy can inhabit his grandmother, his father, Robert Frost and Eurydice (clearly bored by Orpheus); who controls a notable auxiliary subject—the city and the island, bridged by an Odysseus ironically modified; who demonstrates for James Dickey, forever trying to become an owl or a whale or a feathered armadillo, that this can be arranged with far less literalism or labor-and-lather (note **"Standing Fast: Fox into Hedgehog"**); who, finally—I mean with finality—is among the superlative modern witnesses to the intricate poetry of topographical change. (pp. 83-4)

[Peter Davison] is one of the few poets of the first order writing in English today. And this cancels no encomia I may have written last year nor inhibits my praise of another poet three months from now. While I'm reading Davison, only his kind of excellence exists and I believe that it is an excellence endurably safe from trespassers with admirable talent of another order. (p. 84)

> Vernon Young, "Raptures of Distress," in Parnassus: Poetry in Review *(copyright © Poetry in Review Foundation), Vol. 3, No. 2, Spring-Summer, 1975, pp. 75-89.*

ANNE STEVENSON

A Voice in the Mountain is a pleasant, intelligent collection by one who obviously wants to be understood. There is much that is elegant here, but it is an elegance tempered with urbanity and a good narrative technique. Peter Davison has obviously learnt much from Robert Frost. **"Making Much of Orioles"**, a tale about saving orioles from a felled elm, is written in competent Frostian iambics and it ends in a predictably Frostian moral. . . . To write like Frost but not quite as well as Frost is the risk this poet seems willing to take to get himself in trim, as it were, for writing poems which are not at all like Frost but wholly his own. Mr Davison is at his best when he is least self-conscious and allows his talents as a critic and satirist full rein. . . . There are so many good poems in *A Voice in the Mountain* that a few minor, over-academic failures are scarcely noticed.

> Anne Stevenson, "Well under Control," in The Times Literary Supplement *(© Times Newspapers Ltd. (London) 1978; reproduced from* The Times Literary Supplement *by permission), No. 3959, February 10, 1978, p. 160.*

JAY PARINI

A Voice in the Mountain is Peter Davison's sixth book of poetry. His last collection, *Walking the Boundaries: Poems 1957-1974*, established him as one of America's finest contemporary poets, one whose sharpness of vision and candor left the reader breathless. . . . Davison offered his world in a language chill as mountain water. He wrote with intensity about his struggle for identity, with all of its attendant complications. . . . With an eerie detachment, he traced the lineaments of himself and catalogued his passions. He faced directly the Medusa, memory, refusing, like Perseus, to deflect his vision with a mirroring shield. . . . Davison remembered his life selectively, as a poet must, plotting the co-ordinates of self, family, landscape, and society. Writing in a voice characterized by its civil tone, he proved himself capable of giving what Thoreau asked of everyone: a true account of himself.

One poem coming toward the end of *Walking the Boundaries,* called **"Ground,"** prepares us for the new book: "This stuff is what we are born from. Before my eyes / and between my fingers—grainy, sticky, chalky— / the provisions lie at hand for life to burst out of." It is this life which bursts from *A Voice in the Mountain,* a book which displays the wide range of Davison's talents. His personae, to begin with, vary enormously. He can be urban (and urbane) as in **"Circolo Della Caccia"** or **"La Bocca Della Verità,"** or satirical, as in **"Gratified Desires,"** or bucolic, as in **"Day of Wrath"** or **"Cross Cut."** What unifies these diverse tones is, obviously, not subject matter; instead, Davison radiates a confidence, an assuredness, an equipoise which lends to his work an unmistakable unity. Like a Tiffany lamp, whose shade glimmers a range of colors illuminated by a single lamp, these poems reveal a poet whose center is a constant flame. (pp. 765-66)

Like many of Frost's best poems, **"Cross Cut"** focuses on a natural symbol; the poet disallows abstract comment, letting the image stand for itself, concretely, resonant. **"Cross Cut"** will stand up favorably, I think, beside its counterpart in Frost, "The Wood-Pile."

Another important poem in this bucolic mode is **"Haskell's Mill,"** a descendant of Frost's "Directive." One finds here a strong moral tone reminiscent of Wendell Berry. . . . In this poem, as in most of the poems Davison writes, one finds a wealth of natural observation, minute particulars of the landscape at the back of his mind. . . . (p. 767)

What Davison possesses in abundance, and Berry seems devoid of, is a sense of humor. **"The Hanging Man,"** for instance, betrays an impish wit. . . . Even his "serious" poems display a civilized wit, and this contributes to the profound sense of balance, of equilibrium, which makes these poems worth reading....

[Davison] is one of our truest poets, one whose fundamental sanity and intelligence are more than welcome in a time of cultural disarray. (p. 768)

> Jay Parini, "In the Presence of What Is There: Wendell Berry and Peter Davison," in The Virginia Quarterly Review (copyright, 1978, by The Virginia Quarterly Review, The University of Virginia), Vol. 54, No. 4 (Autumn, 1978), pp. 762-68.*

JAMES FINN COTTER

[*Barn Fever and Other Poems*, Davison's] seventh book of poems, demonstrates his steady growth as a reporter of life fashioned close to the land and the thoughts that arise from such a life. Drawing on his own experiences of living on a farm in Gloucester, Mass., he describes in the title poem the 200-year story of the barn he now owns: "Time and some care have spared this barn, a sign / of the work a farm does to keep itself a farm." Deliberate echoes of Robert Frost reverberate in these country verses—a debt that goes back to family friendship—but Davison is his own man with his peculiar approach and idiom. He writes about cows and sheep, pasture and planting, with the specific knowledge that rural life demands through toil and weather. The poet explores other themes as well: the return of Odysseus, a Jewish heritage, memories of his father and the love of his wife. There is a series of poems on Colorado—dedicated to Reg Saner—which recalls boyhood in Boulder, climbing Cheyenne Mountain, a visit to the National Center for Atmospheric Research (really a fine piece) and a return to Boulder. In its praise for "all those who learned the secret / that the seed must be buried to live," the poem affirms the theme of "gift" which appears as the epigraph for each of the book's four parts. Davison also shows humor in exposing his inability to learn to play the piano and to master the Palmer method of handwriting. **"My Lady the Lake"** both graphically pictures an actual lake and suggests the Jungian anima: "Whatever we cast in, it will accept, / and in such lakes within the lake we drown." *Barn Fever* is like that—like all good poetry—it drops us to the bottom of our selves. (p. 37)

> James Finn Cotter, "Five Poets" (reprinted with permission of America Press, Inc. and the author; © 1981; all rights reserved), in America, Vol. 145, No. 2, July 18-25, 1981, pp. 36-7.*

STEPHEN SANDY

No one would accuse Peter Davison of failing to address large themes. *Barn Fever* is Davison's strongest book to date; in conjunction with it his previous collection, *A Voice in the Mountain,* reads like a loquacious staging area in which momentum builds for this vibrant array of poems, at once more passionate and more knowing than earlier sequences. Writing outside the clamors of poetryland, in urbane "exile and cunning," Davison is a poet with a fortunate gift. He takes himself seriously and is afraid of nothing, not even Meaning—whether found in a barnyard or at a dinner-party, the span of occasions for these poems. Davison has long been pegged either as a "nature poet" or as a mere disciple of his master, Frost; *Barn Fever* successfully liberates him (if he ever knew the shackles) from these silly and (for many) opprobrious labels. In a host of poems—among them **"Il Se Sauve"** and the precise sequence, **"Wordless Winter"**—Davison makes his case.

The poet's natural descriptions are both accurate and euphonious:

> Yielding far more than we had ever sown—
> lushness of fescue laced with grapevine
> and poison ivy, raspberries loud with bees—
> the land flowed with milkweed and honeysuckle . . .

Anyone who has ever tried to hold back a New England farm from repossession by the roots of 19th-century raspberry or grape and of the original fescue or poison ivy will appreciate these lines. But such lush rosettes are only embroideries on a fabric of larger purpose, wit, and precision; the land flowed with milkweed and honeysuckle as well as with milk and honey. There is a grandeur in Davison's conception of poetry which one finds in few of his contemporaries; this strongly felt sense of its possibilities is matched by the poet's innate sense of entitlement and power; indeed, of commission. Embedded in nearly every poem is an allusion to—or quotation from—scripture. In **"Fawn,"** the barn in which a dazed fawn is "settled" and nursed to health recalls the stable at Bethlehem. In **"My Lady The Lake,"** a finely turned variation on the Narcissus myth, we hear a psalmic echo, "By its waters I have sat down and wept."

Davison finds a mission in his poesies, to make a treaty—both personal and of public dimensions—with the Judaeo-Christian tradition, which (from his first collection in 1964) he has quietly but tenaciously suggested it is his charge to undertake. (pp. 299-300)

In a remarkable poem, **"The Ram Beneath the Barn,"** we find Davison's themes and devices at work in a tightly organized dramatic whole depicting a passionate but suspended encounter between man and beast. . . . The theme of this poem is the fall of libido in grief; the collocation of symbolic readings at its closure shower the little drama with radiant meanings. (pp. 300-01)

> Stephen Sandy, "Experienced Bards" (© 1982 by The Modern Poetry Association; reprinted by permission of the Editor of Poetry and the author), in Poetry, Vol. CXL, No. 5, August, 1982, pp. 293-305.*

Peter De Vries
1910-

American novelist, short story writer, and essayist.

De Vries is one of America's best comic writers. His work provides the reader with a critical view of modern society. De Vries's main themes—marriage, love, religion, and conformity—are explored in darkly humorous ways. Using a combination of puns, parodies, epigrams, and burlesques, he shows modern men and women to be both absurd and strangely brave in their endless struggle to make sense of their lives and the confusing, unpredictable world that surrounds them.

De Vries is unconcerned with complex characterizations, relying instead on character types and incident. His protagonists are usually middle or upper middle-class young men from strict religious families who embark on a quest for the "real" self as marriage, family, and careers close in on them. These men reject the faith of their parents, avoid or abandon marriage, and often seek meaning in wild illusions and promiscuous sex. Most of them, however, revert to "normalcy." They become, if not formally religious, then humanistically agnostic, and they return to their wives or resolve to marry. Convention and conformity, De Vries seems to say, allow us to survive the chaos of modern life even as they limit and inhibit us.

While lacking the depth and sophistication of his later works, De Vries's early novels, *But Who Wakes the Bugler?* (1940), *The Handsome Heart* (1943), and *Angels Can't Do Better* (1944), introduce the themes and characterizations that recur throughout the rest of his work. In *The Tunnel of Love* (1954), *Comfort Me with Apples* (1956), and *The Mackerel Plaza* (1958), De Vries's "verbal wizardry," keen sense of life's ironies, and shrewd social observations are effectively and enjoyably combined. These three novels are among De Vries's best known and most acclaimed works.

With *The Cat's Pajamas* (1968) and many of the novels that follow it, a strain of cynicism and black humor not previously evident appears in De Vries's work. In general, critics found these books less successful than the earlier work, but most admired De Vries's skill in manipulating language to comic effect. *Consenting Adults* (1980), *Sauce for the Goose* (1982), and *Slouching towards Kalamazoo* (1983) are more optimistic and lightly humorous. In these works, De Vries seems again willing to accept and even relish life in spite of its darker sides and inexplicability.

(See also *CLC*, Vols. 1, 2, 3, 7, 10; *Contemporary Authors*, Vols. 17-20, rev. ed.; *Dictionary of Literary Biography*, Vol. 6; and *Dictionary of Literary Biography Yearbook: 1982*.)

CHRISTOPHER CERF

QUESTION: Is it possible to cram into a novel every joke the theme and plot will allow, then add a couple of hundred more for good measure, and still maintain, from first page to last, a graceful, elegant and, above all, seemingly effortless prose style? ANSWER: Absolutely—but probably only if you're Peter De Vries. And in his latest comedy ["**Consenting Adults:**

© Kelly Wise

Or, The Duchess Will Be Furious"] Mr. De Vries once again demonstrates his unique ability to blend a motley array of absurd aphorisms, one-sentence character sketches, running gags, cosmological musings and inspired word games into a coherent—well, almost coherent—and hugely enjoyable book.

The narrator of "**Consenting Adults**" is Ted Peachum, the youthful product of a Pocock, Ill., furniture-moving family who, in his ambition to rise above his station, studies nihilist philosophy, discovers that everything he's "been so glibly spouting may very well be true" and promptly suffers a nervous collapse. Fortunately, Burwash, the "highly advanced" college Peachum chose when he failed to get into Harvard, allows him to take full academic credit for his crack-up, with the simple provision that he document the experience "to the satisfaction of the Psychology and English departments." Despite a B+ on his breakdown, Peachum soon decides that the pleasures of the flesh offer the only escape from his overwhelming feelings of nonexistence, and it is with his resulting picaresque adventures that "**Consenting Adults**" principally concerns itself.

The gulf between Peachum's metaphysical and erotomaniacal pretensions, and the reality of everyday life in Pocock . . . provides Mr. De Vries with a perfect opportunity to dispense his own patented brand of irony, and he seizes it with awesome gusto. (pp. 1, 22)

Scarcely an event is allowed to occur unless it measures up to the standards of De Vriesian irony. A house burns down; we learn the fire started in the smoke-alarm system. A chiropractor throws his back out while ministering to a patient. And Mrs. d'Amboise's virginal daughter, Columbine—an island of innocence in the steamy sea of Peachum's sex life—is revealed to have been molested, as a tot, by a department-store Santa Claus: "He was a disgrace to his uniform," blusters Mrs. d'.

Of all the characters who wander through the landscape of **"Consenting Adults"**—and there are dozens of them, consenting and otherwise—Mrs. d'Amboise is the author's triumph. We first encounter her when she discovers Peachum affecting a "supine" posture in a high school play, invites him to pose for her sculpture of the drowned Shelley found washed up on the shore of the Gulf of Spezia, and informs him he must save himself for Columbine (then 10 years old and otherwise known as "the bijou"). Thus, she immediately establishes herself as the embodiment of the higher (by Pocock standards) social levels to which Ted Peachum aspires and the guardian of his rapidly eroding sexual conscience: indeed, she's the Alice-in-Wonderland "Duchess" of the novel's subtitle. Also a delight is Peachum's father, a bear of a man who actually hibernates every winter until—irony of ironies!—he develops insomnia.

Then there are the bit players, most of them introduced, one suspects, solely to allow the author to get off a few more of his matchless one-liners. . . .

As for Peachum himself, his penchant for peripatetic monologues makes him, above all else, a vehicle ("runaway Mack truck" might be a more apt phrase) for the author's own tongue-in-cheek epigrams. Such a protagonist has served Mr. De Vries well before: Chick Swallow, the hero of **"Comfort Me With Apples,"** was, for example, the "official aphorist" for a newspaper called The Picayune Blade. And in general, Peachum, too, is a success—especially when his periodic attacks of moral ambivalence lead him to outpourings of oxymoronic self-analysis. ("I'm a self-pitying stoic," he tells us at the beginning of the book; by novel's end he's also a "jilted Narcissus": "I have this crush on myself—but the feeling is not returned.") Less effective, however, are several longer Peachum digressions on everything from Aristotle and the semanticists to the geometric felicity of planks. In a novel whose characters are seldom more than one-dimensional symbols and in which there is little real suspense, these passages seem overlong and not a little self-indulgent.

Which brings us, finally, to the plot: If I've shown little concern for the subject thus far, so, for the most part, has Mr. De Vries, who, incidentally, once wrote that every novel should have "a beginning, a muddle and an end." One can easily summarize the basic conflicts of **"Consenting Adults"** in a single short paragraph; in fact, the author does just this near the middle of the book, but it would be unfair to spoil the story by quoting him. Is this a serious flaw? Well, that depends on how much unadulterated japery—albeit ingenious—one can tolerate at a single sitting. Many, I suspect, will find **"Consenting Adults"** a book they can—and will—put down. But they will almost surely pick it up again, refreshed and ready to enjoy more magic from one of the true masters of humorous style the past half-century has produced. (p. 22)

> Christopher Cerf, "Peter De Vries in Form," in The New York Times Book Review (copyright © 1980 by The New York Times Company; reprinted by permission), August 17, 1980, pp. 1, 22.

T. JEFF EVANS

Tunnel of Love [1954] uses most of the components of the enduring De Vries pattern: the world is suburbia, USA, and its characters the middle or upper-middle class who are materially advanced but are psychically and comically somewhat in arrears. Here, he introduced marriage—its demands and the flights from it—as one of his central subject matters; as well, De Vries discovers his comic narrator, who so often ostensibly observes the bizarre antics of his fellows but then finds himself gradually drawn into the events and a chagrining self-discovery and revelation. . . .

Tunnel of Love is early, vintage De Vries and was followed in quick succession by a series of adept comic novels with alternating shades of darker tragicomedy. In *Comfort Me With Apples* (1956) and *Tents of Wickedness* (1959), he unwinds the complicated affairs of Chick Swallow, who, feeling confined and repressed by marriage, is drawn to the seeming comforts of adultery and role-playing. Typically, the overall movement of De Vries' novels is first a reaction against and then a comic acceptance of the adult community of marriage, and Swallow ends the second book by refusing the tempting offer of a tryst with an old girlfriend, "Thanks just the same . . . but I don't want any pleasures interfering with my happiness." *Tents of Wickedness* interests by its style, too: each chapter is a technical tour de force, written in the style of one or another 20th century writer—from James Joyce to James Jones—whose language and plots De Vries parodies.

Among the funniest of the novels are *The Mackerel Plaza* (1958) and *Let Me Count the Ways* (1965). Both reveal another central De Vries subject, religion, and especially the plights we face when traditional faiths and beliefs no longer serve us. Surely there is no more absurd picture of a contemporary clergy than the ludicrously liberal Rev. Andrew Mackerel with his split-level church. It is this present expense of spirit that creates the schizophrenic Tom Waltz of *Let Me Count the Ways*, offspring of an evangelical mother, who gives hand-tooled Bible belts as gifts, and an atheistic father. The result? "You want to raise him as a believer . . . I want to raise him as an atheist. O.K. we'll compromise. We'll bring him up an agnostic." Tom is finally saved by journeying to the religious shrine at Lourdes; miraculously, here he catches an unknown disease that reunites him with his estranged wife. A third novel, *Blood of the Lamb* (1961), is a moving tragicomic study of the possibility of faith in face of personal tragedy, the death of a child.

Reuben, Reuben (1964) is De Vries' attempt at a blockbuster. Its three-part structure and triple narration are meant to underscore the difficulty and complexity of its subject, modern love. Its characters include Spofford, a septuagenarian Yankee chicken farmer who becomes co-opted by the suburbia he mercilessly ridicules, and Owen McGland, easily the most damning portrait of Dylan Thomas ever sketched. *Reuben, Reuben,* to a degree, but much more *Cat's Pajamas* and *Witch's Milk* (1968)—two short novels published together—undercut or temper the essential comic tone of De Vries. Integral to De Vries' structures is a plot where the individual moves away from conformity and institutions in order to discover the repressed self. What he typically discovers, however, is that the self is false or distorted outside its community; the novels generally then return the individual to society through reconciliation. But not so *Cat's Pajamas*, which may be De Vries' most radical vision while still positing a comic world. At the end of the novel Hank Tattersall dies grotesquely, his head pinned in the kitchen side of a doggie door, his torso freezing in the winter storm outside. His Doppelganger, the social conscience that has followed him throughout the book, chidingly envisions the absurdly literal and figurative fate of the De Vries character who resists communal responsibility, "Well, your end is in sight, Tattersall."

With occasional flashes, the eight works after *Cat's Pajamas* and *Witch's Milk* . . . fall off. The characters, never especially believable, become somewhat unlikeable. The essentially optimistic universe is replaced by a more grimly black humorous one. As De Vries' smile freezes into a grimace, love is replaced by empty lust. However, *Mrs. Wallop* (1970) is interesting for its use of narrative frames and its playful travesty of Philip Roth's wildly successful *Portnoy's Complaint*. *I Hear America Swinging* (1976), returns to the Midwest where De Vries grew up in its attempt to deal with archetypal American materials. And *Madder Music* (1977) compels by its macabre world and its identification and manipulation of two of our bizarre cultural custodians, Groucho Marx and W. C. Fields.

His newest novel, *Consenting Adults*, (1980), continues De Vries' comic investigation of our cultural experience: "If we can think of this great country of ours as polarized between two sets of James brothers . . . Frank and Jesse at one end and Henry and William at the other, why, we begin to get some sense of the enormous spectrum in between." Ted Peachum, De Vries' protagonist, thus acknowledges a divergence in our cultural heritage and somewhat schizophrenically tries to live up to both directions of it. If we can take Peachum at his many words, we see the conflicts that tug at this typical De Vries character. Peachum is coming of age in contemporary America, and the cultural elitism represented by the William/Henry James branch attracts the impressionable Peachum, whose early goal is "The society of people who did not ask for ketchup in public restaurants." Naturally, among the characters Peachum is seeking to rise above are his parents, a father who gains national notoriety by hibernating through the winters and a mother who is widely believed throughout the neighborhood (and beginning to believe herself) to be a Turk.

Peachum's method of American upward mobility is to attach himself to various women, this romantic individualism identifying him with the Frank and Jesse James ilk. (pp. 14-15)

A little religion, a good deal of sexual warfare and then victory-making, a cast of unbelievable but effective satiric characters all go toward fleshing out *Consenting Adults*. De Vries' major theme remains constant too. One of the characters says "We must sooner or later be trundled into surgery for . . . an illusionectomy," and in investigating human relations and the relations the individual must have with those institutions around him, De Vries has composed his latest novelistic lesson on the text of growing up in modern America, on the necessity of separating workable illusions from those that defeat the individual. "I must find my own idiom," Peachum begins the book, and search he does, through lust, love, and De Vries' rich language to find a compatible way the self can exist in today's world. Like many De Vries characters, he modishly adopts different philosophical poses and stances in an attempt to discover the romantic self. But variously Existentialism, Causality, and Absurdism fail him, and he finally gives in to the lush variety he finds in contemporary life. By the end of the novel he has comically defined himself as a "jilted Narcissist," and with this paradox we are together forced back to the James brothers metaphor that De Vries has insisted tantalizingly represents the comic variance in American experience today.

Although the novel has De Vries' traditional touches—including a certain plot looseness—there are a few differences as well. The characters, while at times farcical, are pleasant and humane, as opposed to the cold and somewhat hostile characters who have frequented his books beginning roughly with *Into Your Tent I'll Creep* (1971). And the book ends touchingly, perhaps forewarningly, as Peachum envisions his deathbed scene. The elegiac note here might remind us that De Vries is himself seventy years old, that perhaps here in Peachum's comic acceptance of the cosmos with all its flux and paradox is also De Vries' own, that De Vries, like Prospero, may soon be ready to give up his particular brand of magic. Like the world of De Vries' early and masterful fictions, the world of Peachum is comic and positive rather than darkly absurd as in De Vries' later novels, a world that, with all its confusion and chaos, as Peachum learns, beckons commitment, not avoidance.

Taken together, the novels of Peter De Vries form a fascinating investigation into the mores of America over the last thirty years. We tend to neglect De Vries' artistry and insight because of the sheer wealth of his comic virtuosity—a typical De Vries novel contains enough wit for other authors to salt judiciously throughout their canons. But the exuberent comic display masks the unity of comic vision and technique. De Vries' most serious comic devices—fallible narrators, character role-playing, stylistic parody and burlesque, and word play—typically serve dual purposes. They entertain—at times almost overwhelmingly so—but they also reinforce and support his major theme of the illusion-making propensities of the individual, especially when rebelling against tradition or institution. There is a purposeful confluence, then, between idea and form in De Vries' work, a deft union of language, style, wit, and theme that creates an enduring comic vision of the way we live. (pp. 15-16)

T. Jeff Evans, "Peter De Vries: A Retrospective," in American Humor: An Interdisciplinary Newsletter, *Vol. 7, No. 2, Fall, 1980, pp. 13-16.*

STUART SUTHERLAND

Kingsley Amis once remarked of Peter De Vries: "I would rate him the funniest serious writer on either side of the Atlantic." De Vries's humour derives not just from his remarkable capacity for word play, but from his ability to invent situations that invert the natural order of things. . . . De Vries's puns are ingenious enough to justify the elaborate situations often needed to set them up: in an early novel, for example, he has someone throwing stones at seabirds in order that, on being asked what he is doing, he can remark "I'm leaving no tern unstoned". Some of De Vries's aphorisms are worthy of Oscar Wilde, and his characters are never short of repartee. The ultramodern young clergyman of *Mackerel Plaza* is caught staring at a girl's legs; "Stop looking at my legs", she says, to which he replies "Don't worry, ma'am, my thoughts were on higher things". Of twentieth-century novelists, only P. G. Wodehouse and Evelyn Waugh have De Vries's capacity to make the reader laugh out loud.

De Vries is also a serious satirist of the American way of life, having savaged, among others, clergymen who rely on Madison Avenue methods to enlarge their flocks, psychiatrists whose treatments change the form but not the quality of their patients' madness, and artists for whom the novelty of a gimmick makes up for its lack of meaning. He gently exposes middle class snobbery and acquisitiveness, but sympathizes with the dreams of youth that end in disillusion. Even his characters' love of verbal pyrotechnics is only a means of distracting themselves from the pointlessness of much human existence: as he puts it in his latest novel, *Consenting Adults,* "One was a stick of bone and a strand of gut riding for a piteous splinter of eternity on a speck of astral foot. A fresh gust from Aldebaran at my heels, I ran upstairs two at a time and pulled the covers over my head. Thus began my nervous breakdown."

Consenting Adults is rarely serious and only occasionally does it evoke pathos. It is more of a fun novel than a funny one—a literary romp. It reverts to a device so effectively used in some of De Vries's earlier novels, such as *Comfort Me With Apples:* the narrator, Ted Peachum, is a young boulevardier whose plebeian parents, both of whom are furniture removers, are a source of embarrassment. Peachum is a home-spun philosopher who collects around him a crowd of devotees. . . . He also claims, and indeed exhibits, "an imaginative gift for metaphor", but for the most part he eschews puns, an act of self-restraint which will disappoint De Vries's aficionados. Like his predecessors, Peachum lacks the touch of greatness needed in a hero, and is not nasty enough to be an anti-hero: he is more of an anti-anti-hero.

The plot of *Consenting Adults* is typically diffuse, consisting mainly of a string of isolated episodes held together by the reader's knowledge that the main character is progressing through youthful glory to a conventional marriage and the tedium of suburbia. . . .

De Vries's narrator has a fondness for literary parody, unusual words, pranks, bizarre philosophical arguments, and the misuse of psychoanalytic concepts. The jokes or parodies that do not quite come up to scratch are his responsibility, and they help to establish his character; the author can take the credit for the better quips. Perhaps conscious that when he was writing *Consenting Adults* he was not consistently at the peak of his aphoristic powers, De Vries has Peachum going through a bad patch in which his lost touch drives away his disciples. . . . It is only when Peachum is reduced to remarks like "It is not true that some people need less sleep. They only sleep faster" that we become convinced that neither Peachum's nor De Vries's powers are at full stretch. That is also true even of some of the literary allusions. "We got lost on a motor jaunt to Marrakesh, when a pagan suckled in a creed outworn misdirected us somewhere along the line. . . ."—fun, but not funny.

The jokes made by De Vries's characters are of course not always intentional and he retains his mastery of the ill-turned phrase. Ted Peachum's father, impressed by his son's exegesis on anal eroticism, says "Anal, my ass, but keep talking like that it'll get you into Harvard". . . .

In *Consenting Adults* De Vries also does well with the contrariety of situations. A fire starts in a fire alarm; a chiropractor dislocates his own back while manipulating a patient; and a mad prophet warns Ted Peachum to "Beware of those who go down to the sea in ships": since he never goes to sea, he feels quite safe until his car collides with a twenty-five foot ketch being towed behind a station-wagon. Of more consequence in the novel's development is Peachum's attempt to convince himself that Columbine's nymphet-like attractions mean nothing to him. Meeting another young girl in a public park, he tests his power to resist temptation by patting her on the head: despite his repeated self-reassurances ("the pleasure that went through me at the realization that I felt absolutely nothing—this would put rout to all knowing suspicions"), he is caught by a policeman while searching for a frisbee with her in a thicket of bushes. . . .

Moving with the times, De Vries provides lubricious but accurate descriptions of the sexual act, but he transforms them by adding the bathos of the banal events that precede, follow, or, too often, accompany the ecstasy. Like many of his characters, De Vries never quite knows whether to take himself seriously: his descriptions—which include three (appropriately enough) of Ted Peachum's performances with his triplets—can be read either as genuinely erotic or as parody.

De Vries retains his eye for commonplace events. He provides a splendid account of a beer-swilling, pretzel-crunching family reunion of emigré American Germans; he captures the slang and antics of furniture removers; and he describes the wearing of new shoes that have to be trodden with care since the owner cannot decide whether or not they should be returned to the shop.

Consenting Adults only occasionally attempts to capture life's pathos: its main characters may not achieve all their ambitions, but they remain largely unscathed. The most touching episode is when Peachum's mother bundles up his father's prized collection of children's comics and throws them out. The father exclaims "Do you know how much these things are *worth*? Thousands". Peachum then describes his mother's reaction. . . . De Vries displays here his most original knack—the capacity to convey simultaneously absurdity and sadness. . . .

Consenting Adults may not be De Vries's best novel since it lacks any new ingredient, yet it retains the sharp contrarieties of his writing style. His prose is entirely his own—which is to say a mixture of the styles of others larded with biblical English and modern slang, and with metaphors drawn from such everyday happenings as the freezer unthawing. Anyone unfortunate enough never to have read him might do better to start with an earlier novel such as *Comfort Me With Apples,* but unlike Ted Peachum, he is in no danger of driving away his devotees. If *Consenting Adults* only barely justifies Kingsley Amis's claim that he is today's funniest serious writer, it is nevertheless pure fun to read.

Stuart Sutherland, "The Comedy of the Commonplace," *in* The Times Literary Supplement *(© Times Newspapers Ltd. (London) 1981; reproduced from* The Times Literary Supplement *by permission), No. 4061, January 30, 1981, p. 107.*

PETER ANDREWS

"Sauce for the Goose" establishes once again that even a weak Peter De Vries novel is fun to read. Many of Mr. De Vries's major faults are brought into sharp focus in his latest comedy of manners for our troubled times. The plotting, something that has never been close to his heart, is unusually skimpy: A feminist writer, seeking to write an exposé of sexual harassment in the business world, falls into traditional love with the boss and they get married. Mr. De Vries uses such a light satiric pen in spinning out this contemporary fairy tale that it is sometimes difficult to know exactly what it is he is making fun of. Women's Lib would seem an inviting-enough target, but Mr. De Vries is so gentlemanly that his thrusts have little effect. What might have been an ironic view of feminism is often no more than a pedestrian story of some women who are not very good at their jobs.

Although often a genuinely witty author, Mr. De Vries sometimes reaches too far for funny lines in **"Sauce for the Goose."** I myself am prepared to go to almost any lengths to get a laugh, but it seems to me that a malaprop black cleaning lady who describes a woman dressed in mannish tweeds as "one dem 'lezibethians" is really the sort of comic characterization that should be stored away wherever it is they keep old "Amos 'n' Andy" scripts. But you can't stay irritated with Peter De Vries for long. If you don't like the page you are reading at the moment, stick around because a terrific one is coming along right behind it.

Mr. De Vries has made his considerable reputation as a wide-ranging social commentator willing to take on everybody from social workers to Episcopal bishops. But he is perhaps best at creating slightly off-center characters who lead lives that are forever going askew. In this novel there is Mr. Dobbin, who once tried to asphyxiate himself in the garage, but his car ran out of gas. There is Dog Bokum, the office wolf, who once broke up with a lady of stunning meticulousness on the perfectly reasonable grounds that "you can't be happy with a woman who pronounces both d's in Wednesday."

Then there is one of my favorite characters in modern fiction. Mr. Shrubsole appears on exactly one page, and his sole function is to leave a suburban luncheon party early with the excuse, "I have premises to keep and miles to mow before I sleep."

I felt a kind of reverential awe that the novelist would construct a gag like that. Of course, Peter De Vries is not only a gag man. He uses the gag to create a situation. Mr. Shrubsole's *mot juste* lays a good sized omelet because his hostess doesn't get the Frostian reference. Mr. Shrubsole, who had planned for weeks to have his sally be the conversational high point of the afternoon, retreats hurriedly, feeling the fool in a manner only someone who is too clever for his good can know. Peter De Vries is like that. He rattles along, and you start to feel he is doing nothing more than being amusing and then he hits you with a small scene of social embarrassment that lingers in the mind long after you have used all of his best lines at dinner parties.

The main story of **"Sauce for the Goose"** concerns the love affair between Daisy Dobbin [and Dirk Dolfin]. . . . Daisy and Dirk are nice, amiable people and deserve to have a good relationship. I wish I liked their story more than I did, but I have come to expect a great deal from Peter De Vries. I kept waiting for him to do something interesting with their situation, to give us some fresh, slightly distorted image of romance. But this time he seems content with the standard version.

When Peter De Vries is not writing about sex with humor, he writes with what is called "restraint," a quality that has all but disappeared from contemporary novels. I have reached the point where I simply cannot absorb one more piece of technical information regarding sexual matters, and I will remain in Mr. De Vries's debt for not offering me any. Also, I particularly enjoyed the fact that Daisy and Dirk eventually find tumultuous happiness together chiefly because they earn a great deal of money and live extremely well. It is a situation that, I suspect, is closer to reality than many serious novelists would lead us to believe. (pp. 14-15)

Peter Andrews, "Standard Fun," in The New York Times Book Review *(copyright © 1981 by The New York Times Company; reprinted by permission), September 20, 1981, pp. 14-15.*

ANTHONY BURGESS

Peter De Vries's old habit, sustained through twenty novels, of larding his narrative with *mots,* wisecracks, and malapropisms has been regarded by some as a vitiation of an art comic enough without external embellishments. And it is true that he gives us the impression of storing nuggets or nugacities until he has enough to decorate a book; then comes the secondary task of deciding what the book shall be about. But he has made the technique his own—a mixture of social comedy and vaudeville—and for him it works. Take the ending of [*Sauce for the Goose*]. There is a party, and a man we have not met before and will never meet again says, "I don't for the life of me understand why people keep insisting marriage is doomed. All five of mine worked out."

There are not only cracks; there are supererogatory situations inserted just for laughs and the hell with the structure. In Grand Rapids, where a Babylonian "New Ferment" swirls, there is the annual Meatloaf Writers Conference and also street theater. A couple of actors sit in rocking chairs, the woman reading *Dorian Gray* and the man *The Skin of Our Teeth*. She says, "You've driven me Wilde," and he, "You've driven me Wilder."

Seriously, though, there is an admirable story going on under the coruscations. (p. 63)

Dirk Dolfin, one of the ten best-dressed men, who has his entire wardrobe gutted by Vandalic breakers-in, is an admirable creation. So is Daisy. Mr. De Vries is staunchly resisting the feminist allegation that men cannot create women (and yet what woman has not at some time or other modeled herself on Emma Bovary or Anna Karenina?). Men, he says, best give pleasure to women when they are taking it. Dangerous, but does any woman know enough about men to deny it?

This is not only a gentle satire on feminist extremism; it is an only slightly exaggerated picture of crazy America. America remains her own best satirist. . . . Holland is pretty crazy, too. (Daisy goes with Dirk thither on their honeymoon.) The language is crammed with diminutives, and even their flight back on KLM is a *vluchtje*, or flightling. Back to New York and restaurants with waitresses on roller skates and the marketing of a disastrous stain remover (it removes stains but leaves itself behind) called Out Damn Spot!

Which brings me to the intense literary allusiveness of Mr. De Vries. He is one of the few novelists we have left who are joyfully aware of the books others have written. The new American way, perhaps initiated by Mr. Pynchon, is to pretend that literature has given way to the mythology of junk, but hardly a line goes by in *Sauce for the Goose* without an echo from the immense heritage of civilized reading. A bookish man, Mr. De Vries does not drop books on our toes: He is aware, as Joyce was, of the relish to be squeezed from the demotic. He is also immensely intelligent without ramming intelligence down our gorges. And he has a fine ear. All this adds up to the conclusion that he is a major stylist, and he expends his major style on materials that would have shocked Henry James.

This major style once met a major theme in *The Blood of the Lamb,* a poignant novel about the death of a child that brought to the surface another of Mr. De Vries's preoccupations—the mysterious agonies of theology. There is theology here, too, with Dirk dissertating on infralapsarianism and Arminianism in the languor of after-love. Nothing is alien to the De Vries humanity, or Dutch humanism (Erasmic is also the name of a shaving soap), and readers will be wise if they look deeper than the cracks. As somebody once said about something else, the whole of life is here. (p. 64)

Anthony Burgess, in a review of "Sauce for the Goose" (copyright © 1981 by Anthony Burgess; reprinted by permission of the author), in New York *Magazine, Vol. 14, No. 38, September 28, 1981, pp. 63-4.*

RHODA KOENIG

"She would be sitting at the window, eating fruit out of the hubcap." That's the kind of sentence you run across in a Peter De Vries novel—if one can give that name to an extended prose work that has no plot (just situations) and no characterizations (just tics and funny lines). De Vries's books are like giant towers of nougat—agglutinations of puns, metaphors, literary allusions, old songs, snapshots of people behaving, by their lights, in a perfectly reasonable manner. On this page, you hit on a tasty bit with a soft liquid center; on another, you chip off a piece of your mind. (p. 38)

For De Vries, a story is just an excuse to pour on the jokes, lots of thick sauce over a little bit of meat. But most of the jokes are pretty good. . . .

[In *Sauce for the Goose* De Vries occasionally] bruises our ribs with his elbow (I got the one about Domblémy the *first* time, I got it, I got it), and some of his conceits reach so far they're stretched out of shape, but most of them hit home. Even better than his fancy dancing like such little tricks as backward sentences, discontented descriptions (a restaurant table "the size of a throat lozenge"), and well-designed fretwork ("Men could be so illegible," Daisy sighs). This crazy quilt of rhetoric and randiness, language and ladies turned upside down, is stitched together with De Vries's comic despair. "The episode had offered a fitting accompaniment to the sense of her own life being blown sky-high—or hell-deep," Daisy muses after a burglary. . . .

De Vries himself is versus anybody who makes the relations between the sexes even worse than they are, or who lays large, greasy hands on his heroine-in-distress, the beautiful English language. So feminism is a handy target for him, though one wonders why he waited ten years after the tumult and shouting. Perhaps at the time he was too angry to laugh. Apparently, the subject still gets his back up higher than a humorist's should be. His digs about "dikes" and "lezzies" have a sour note, and remarks such as a feminist's "beating off men who weren't trying to get to her" (for once this is not a double entendre) sound flat and self-righteous. Offering the blissful sex between Daisy and her sportive publisher as evidence, De Vries hauls out the old one about a man being able to give a woman pleasure only by taking it. I'm not going to disagree with the statement itself, but I don't like the tone. This old chestnut is usually dropped by a man who explains, oh, so reasonably, "I won't do that thing because I don't like it, therefore you won't either." The solution for the woman is not to nod and roll over, but to go and find a man who likes more things. Trying to make sense out of the craziness shifting slowly over us all, De Vries sometimes crosses the line between sanity and smugness.

In the earliest days of the movies, there was something called Hale's Tours. People sat in theaters got up to look like railroad cars, and while their seats bounced gently, motion pictures of scenery unreeled. Reading *Sauce for the Goose* is a little like that. De Vries never gets you anywhere, but the wheels spin, and the sparks fly. (p. 39)

Rhoda Koenig, "A Satire on Feminism," in The New Republic *(reprinted by permission of* The New Republic, Inc.*), Vol. 185, No. 15, October 14, 1981, pp. 38-9.*

JAMES WOLCOTT

[Peter De Vries] has been taking his cuts in the batting cage for quite a spell now, turning out twenty books of fiction in the last four decades. But a writer—particularly a comic writer—who's unflamboyantly industrious and accomplished runs the risk of being taken for granted, and the release of a new De Vries has never been taken as occasion for carting out the pastries. Yet De Vries's work may very well outlast that of his noisier contemporaries. In an essay on P. G. Wodehouse, Wilfrid Sheed observed that Wodehouse's whimsical creations "have the sturdiness of Japanese No theater, while Thomas Wolfe's 'feelings' expire like a scream."

De Vries's novels aren't as neatly plotted as Wodehouse's, and his range of follies is smaller . . . , but his best novels too have a well-hammered sturdiness, and may be standing long after the more fashionable funks of John Irving and Joseph Heller splinter like matchsticks. (p. 61)

The true comedy in De Vries's novels is that his characters flit so far out of themselves that [their] scissoring of consciousness into Commentator, Performer, and Spectator leads to a mad, dizzying tangle. Personalities are slipped on and off like dimestore disguises. In *Madder Music,* the protagonist roams the grounds of a sanitarium in a Groucho Marx slouch, peppering the staff with puns and sallies . . . ; in *Forever Panting,* the protagonist uses his spare time to polish up his impressions, occasionally lurching about in the cellar as Boris Karloff. . . . And in *The Tents of Wickedness,* a novel now regrettably out of print, De Vries really trots out the ventriloquial tricks, parodying the prose of (among others) Proust, Faulkner, and Dreiser as he traces the capricious life of a poetic lass named Sweetie Appleyard—"a half-daft girl with vine leaves in her hair, who hears the horns of elfland faintly blowing." With so many pretensions to imitate and mock, with so many voices crowding for attention, it's small wonder that De Vries's heroes often long to click off their minds and silence all this tape hiss and babble. Language is not only their trampoline, but the ceiling on which they bump their heads.

It's this acute attention to excess and inflection that makes De Vries's novels triumphs of screwy nuance. Dr. Johnson chided Shakespeare for haring after quibbles, but De Vries's quibbles are usually worth the chase. . . . Puns, fluffs, fumbled epigrams, wheezes of fustian, snorts of damning indignation, none of it escapes De Vries's notice, and from these faint swishes of nuance larger notions of style and paradox can be built. When the hero of *The Tents of Wickedness* is introduced to a haughty number named Mrs. Bickerstaffe, he registers: "She was unmistakably British. In her voice rustled the thin paper on which the air editions of the better English journals are printed, in America used for wiping eyeglasses and binding cigarettes. Perhaps the Americans saw too clearly to have vision? They lacked the touch of fog responsible for the mysticism that made English poetry great." . . . Now, every time I peel off the wrapper of the *Manchester Guardian Weekly,* I can hear Romantic poets sneezing in the mists. (pp. 61-2)

[Linguistic] and erotic connoisseurship go hand in glove in De Vries. Love and language alike sound lightly on the tongue. In De Vries's earlier novels, his suburban tomcats and kitlings chased each other like foolhardy cheats out of John O'Hara, with a curtain of discretion falling over their adulterous couplings. But in the swinging freedom of the post-*Portnoy* era, De Vries has been able to draw back the curtain and give his erotic imagination its full striding romp. In **Consenting Adults,** the action is so wild and frantic that the bedsprings come shooting out of the mattress. After more conventional boudoir gymnastics, De Vries's hero strikes acquaintance with a handful of triplets called the Peppermint Sisters, whose thumping erotic finesse scatters pigeons from the windowsill and brings down the wallpaper in a swooning wilt. "Such travels on cusp and curve and hollow, such ceaselessly ranging bliss," sighs De Vries's hero, himself swoonily awilt.

It's been said of Henry Miller's writing that when ol' Henry parted the sheets for a goaty go of it, the reader could feel the crumbs on the pillowcases, the moles on the chippie's upper lip. The lovemaking in De Vries's novels—all that choreographic slapstick—is brushed clean of this naturalistic grit. Even with their imperfections (a chipped tooth, a crooked toe), the women in De Vries seem buffed and dimpled, not so much idealized as mock-idealized. They're earth angels with a few discolored feathers. If De Vries's sexual comedies have a flaw, it's that De Vries is locked too tightly into his heroes' prowling lusts—he's so in tune with the hoofbeats of his satyrs that he never quite zeroes in on the needy, naughty appetites of the nymphs to whom they give chase.

No Geoffrey Chaucer he. But this is a small kick to make against a writer who has given us twenty spry, funny glimpses into the bulging tents of wickedness. (p. 62)

James Wolcott, "Naughty Old Men," in Harper's *(copyright © 1982 by* Harper's Magazine; *all rights reserved; reprinted from the October, 1982 issue by special permission), Vol. 265, No. 1589, October, 1982, pp. 60-3.**

JONATHAN YARDLEY

It goes without saying that Peter De Vries is terrifically amusing in this, his 21st work of fiction. As in many of his recent books, he tells in **Slouching Towards Kalamazoo** the instructive tale of a young person from the heartland who encounters the sexual revolution in all its baffling glory and who pays the price for its pleasures: "What a mess! What a shambles I had made of my life just for an ankle down the old primrose path!" It is a tale of innocence and carnality, a mix both explosive and hilarious, and the wily De Vries milks it for every available laugh; but it is also a tale of sober and sobering aspects, and these too De Vries explores with characteristic subtlety.

The innocent of the tale is Anthony Thrasher, a.k.a. Tony, a.k.a. Biff, who as the story begins is a 15-year-old eighth grader, a classic and chronic underachiever, residing in "my North Dakota home town, which I will call Ulalume." His teacher, Miss Maggie Doubloon, is a luscious peach soon to turn 30, in whom "I seemed to sense a burning wish to Live, certainly to enjoy a life far richer than she was now, a self-realization for which getting the hell out of Ulalume would be only the beginning." As part of her curriculum Miss Doubloon decides to teach *The Scarlet Letter,* and soon enough she goes ahead and lives it. As a consequence of a one-night stand she enjoys with Tony while tutoring him in history and biology she becomes pregnant; with that, De Vries is off and running into this highly irreverent modernization of Hawthorne's scandalous classic.

To say that one thing leads to another is, to put it mildly, an understatement; orderly plotting is not among De Vries' strong points, and he permits *Slouching Towards Kalamazoo* to drift in any direction it chooses. Thank goodness. With De Vries the rule is serendipity, not structure. Characters wander in and out not in order to contribute to the overall movement of events but so that De Vries can get this observation or that off his chest....

In *Slouching Towards Kalamazoo* as in so much of his previous work, questions of faith lurk beneath the frolic and fun. When the great debate between the minister and the atheist causes each to convert to the other's credo, and then when a second confrontation further muddles matters, De Vries is left to observe: "Voltaire was right. If there were no God, it would be necessary to invent one. And invent Him mankind jolly well had, to see him through this vale of tears." It is not an original observation, but this in no way diminishes its profundity....

No doubt it is because Peter De Vries so acutely understands the sadness of this vale of tears, and the capacity of hope and illusion to ease our passage through it, that he is our finest contemporary chronicler of the human comedy. If it is true that there is no funnier novelist now writing in America, it is equally true that there is no kinder one. This, in the end, is why we read him.

Jonathan Yardley, "Laughing and Laughing in a Widening Gyre," in Book World—The Washington Post *(© 1983, The Washington Post), July 17, 1983, p. 3.*

MICHIKO KAKUTANI

"I seem to bear my share of responsibility, for the chuckles and chortles, all of them naturally nervous and not a few hideously forced, that went around our dinner table." This admission by Anthony Thrasher, the narrator-hero of **"Slouching Towards Kalamazoo,"** could well be mistaken as an authorial plea for indulgence on the part of Peter De Vries. When not "hideously forced," most of *his* jokes seem silly or simply pointless. Still, in a novel that is devoid of believable characters, compelling narrative and moral resonance, the jokes are probably the best thing to be had.

Certainly, Mr. De Vries is capable of more. Though critical comparisons to the likes of P. G. Wodehouse, Max Beerbohm and Evelyn Waugh have always been overdrawn—his apotheosis is perhaps a reflection of how impoverished American humor truly is—Mr. De Vries has proved, in the past, that he can be a masterly entertainer and social satirist, acutely observant of how our edifice of morals has slowly crumbled and decayed. His sensitivity to language and its inflections has made him a gifted parodist, and at his best, he uses his wacky, compulsive humor to illuminate our vanities and pretensions.

Instead of developing as a novelist, however, Mr. De Vries has continued, over the years, to produce novels that are remarkably the same: most of them feature narrator-heroes—much like Anthony Thrasher—who suffer from a conflict between their spirits and their bodily desires; most explore the tension between Eastern sophistication and Middle Western provincialism, and most boast preposterous, gag-filled narratives, in which one absurd event is followed by another.

"Slouching Towards Kalamazoo" is no exception.... The main purpose of [the action], of course, is to provide an armature for Mr. De Vries's jokes—jokes that often seem all too familiar as well. For instance, the novel's central, continuing gag—in which Hawthorne's Hester Prynne earns an A-plus for her sexual abilities, instead of an A for adultery—is borrowed from the author's **"Reuben, Reuben,"** and the young hero's penchant for parodying T. S. Eliot's "Love Song of J. Alfred Prufrock" recalls a sendup of the same poem in his **"Madder Music."**

As for the other comic routines in **"Slouching Towards Kalamazoo,"** there are the usual De Vries mixture of puns, [aphorisms and riddles]. . . . The jokes about birth control and dandruff, though stale, are harmless enough; but others, made at the expense of women and small-town residents, have a nasty, prejudicial edge. To make matters worse, these jokes simply tend to sit there on the page as lumpy, unalloyed one-liners; they serve no larger comic vision and are never integrated into the drama.

Nearly all the characters in **"Slouching Towards Kalamazoo,"** in fact, share Mr. De Vries's sense of humor. At least they all talk in the same self-conscious, pun-filled language, and they all have the same annoying penchant for turning conversations into games of verbal one-upmanship, dropping literary quotations and allusions as though they had recently memorized Bartlett's.

As a consequence, the exchanges between Miss Doubloon and Anthony, between Anthony and his father—between almost any two of the characters, for that matter—sound very much alike, and the tension that usually arises from the clash of differing viewpoints never gets developed. It is as though Mr. De Vries were reading a play aloud and performing each of the parts in his own monotonous voice—a curious lapse, given his ear for the nuances of slang. For the reader, it makes for very tedious reading indeed.

Michiko Kakutani, in a review of "Slouching towards Kalamazoo," in The New York Times *(copyright © 1983 by The New York Times Company; reprinted by permission), July 22, 1983, p. C23.*

THOMAS MEEHAN

[**"Slouching Towards Kalamazoo"**] is vintage De Vries, a perfect example of the sort of hilarious and expertly crafted comic novel that he amazingly seems to be able to turn out annually. "Don't you think the important thing when you're freezing to death is to keep your cool?" asks Mr. De Vries's hero near the beginning of the novel, and you immediately know that you are cheerfully once again in the hands of America's master of comic wordplay.

The time of **"Slouching Towards Kalamazoo"** is the early 1960's, shortly before the onset of the sexual revolution and other major American upheavals, and the place is an unnamed North Dakota town that the novel's off-the-wall first-person narrator, a 15-year-old junior high school student named Anthony Thrasher, chooses to refer to as Ulalume. Young Anthony, who is spending his second year in the eighth grade, is an academic underachiever if there ever was one. But he is no dope. Like most of Mr. De Vries's heroes, he has a paradoxical problem—Anthony spends all of his time reading Joyce, Eliot, Dylan Thomas and other literary masters on the sly when he should instead be memorizing the chief products of Venezuela. And so it appears that he is never going to get out of the eighth grade, much less ever make it to college. Anthony is turned over for private tutoring to his eighth-grade teacher, Miss Maggie Doubloon, a 29-year-old free spirit who has shocked the local townsfolk by assigning "The Scarlet Letter" to her teen-aged students.

One thing leads outrageously to another, as it inevitably does in a novel by Mr. De Vries, and Anthony succeeds both in graduating from the eighth grade and in impregnating Miss Doubloon, who goes back home to Kalamazoo, Mich., in disgrace, although blithely unrepentant and determined to have her out-of-wedlock child. And thus, in a comically distorted rewriting of recent history, Mr. De Vries slyly suggests that the sexual revolution and the women's liberation movement were begun in 1961 in small-town North Dakota.

The second half of the novel takes place over a period of several years and mainly in Kalamazoo, to which Anthony, a lovesick rough beast, slouches in hot pursuit of Maggie, out of whom he has nobly resolved to make an honest woman. But Maggie, who has delivered herself of a bouncing baby boy named Ahab, has considerably cooled toward Anthony, who, in any event, is soon smitten by Ahab's baby sitter, a nubile teen-ager, Bubbles Breedlove. And Anthony's first encounter with Bubbles prompts a description of her by Mr. De Vries that is both one of the most delightful passages in the book and also perhaps a first-rate example of his comic style. . . . (pp. 7, 20)

The final chapters of the novel follow Anthony as he grows up, goes to Northwestern University, ultimately marries Bubbles and ends up as a fund-raiser for a crackpot religion known as the First Church of Christian Atheists. All of the above, however, is merely the bare bones of the fairly old-fashioned plot that serves as a structural skeleton for the book. Mr. De Vries doesn't simply turn out mindless comedies that have no point, and at the heart of **"Slouching Towards Kalamazoo"** there is, in the guise of comedy, a serious theological discussion—on whether or not rational man can rationally believe in Christianity. And the resolution of the discussion, or argument, is the founding of Anthony's church, an organization of highly ambivalent worshipers who don't for a moment believe in Christianity but who—like Mr. De Vries himself, one suspects—figure that Christianity is better than nothing.

If you've somehow never read Mr. De Vries, you should, starting . . . with **"Slouching Towards Kalamazoo"** and working your way back to **"The Tunnel of Love"** and **"Comfort Me With Apples,"** for such highly intelligent literary pleasures as he has to offer are rare indeed to come upon these days. Besides, life is too short for one to waste his time reading any but our best writers, for as Mr. De Vries himself puts it in the present book: "We're all like the cleaning woman. We come to dust." (p. 20)

Thomas Meehan, "Travels of a Lovesick Beast," in The New York Times Book Review *(copyright © 1983 by The New York Times Company; reprinted by permission), August 14, 1983, pp. 7, 20.*

J. H. BOWDEN

[*But Who Wakes the Bugler?*, De Vries's first published novel,] has a certain charm as a product of its time. And it *is* dated: not only is there a stage Negro, Jubal, who speaks in a thick dialect, but it's the man—Mr. Thwing—not his fiancée Hermina, who can't face up to matrimony. Now it's women who fear stifling. (p. 11)

The novel is essentially formless, but there is some pattern supplied by Mr. Thwing's attempt to solve an apparent murder in the Chicago rooming house he owns: a Dutch sea captain, Jehoiachim, who gives his age at 106, is found dead at the foot of the stairs after a large report is heard, and at the same time a Chinese is caught by Mr. Thwing while in the act of stealing a vase of great value from Jehoiachim's room. But Jehoiachim isn't killed till page 124, and the main issue is whether Thwing will marry Hermina. (pp. 11-12)

A stolen Ming vase (there also is a dog named Ming), taken by a stage Chinaman, Hang Lee, is lifted only because Jehoiachim died owing him for laundry, and Chinese like such art. Still, Thwing gets a threatening phone call from his brother-in-law, Hang Moy. Nothing comes of that either. But a thunderstorm and lightning in the room brings Jubal to confess that he traded the vase—given him by a drunken Thwing—for a blue sash Jehoiachim had. So there was no theft at all, except Thwing's of the vase, while drunk, and there was no murder; a suspicious bump on the sea captain's head was the result of a mosquito bite, his death caused by an accidental fall. Hermina becomes more and more nervous until Thwing marries her. That ends things.

Is this proto-De Vries, or a trying out that was later abandoned? Both. Insofar as style goes, the future brilliance shows in the quips and little gems of description sparkling here and there. . . . (pp. 13-14)

One line that De Vries does develop—clumsily—for the next few novels, before dropping it, is the Mystery Story motif. Since the New Testament can be seen to be the prototypal Mystery Story and since so many overtly religious people have used the genre . . . , it might be that this tack shows a streak not usually identified with De Vries, one that he later either erased, or camouflaged.

The custom of creating characters for the sake of a joke is one he has never abandoned (Hermina's brother Ludwig, editor of a digest of digests); nor has he changed his habit of throwing out tantalizing turns of plot, turns that lead to blank walls (either Hecuba or Lola would have served as the failed-sex-pot type, but he has them both). (pp. 14-15)

[Another] characteristic motif of De Vries's, not overwhelming in *But Who Wakes the Bugler?*, although covertly present . . . [is] the man of sensibility, damned to life among the mundane. Perhaps this distaste for the ordinary comes from a reaction to Calvinism—a system complete unto itself and intellectually rigorous enough, but lacking in the aesthetic: in short, it offers the theological gourmet a casserole. . . . [De Vries's] people are aristocrats of the soul condemned to suffer the calumny of the bourgeois who own the culture, but who accept him not.

Either it is that way, or it is that way turned inside out; someone who is basically a clod somehow finds himself living among the elect, often causing embarrassment of which he is himself unaware. In large part this situation is developed for the sake of humor, but it is significant that in either case it is the juxtaposition of the widely differing outlooks that makes the drama happen. And this is incipient in De Vries's first book.

More fully developed is his Weltanschauung. George Thwing, spokesman here for De Vries, is an agnostic, basing his opinion on the light-in-the-ice-box analogy: "You could never know if there was an after life till you were there, never knew upon what your eyes might rest after death, until you died yourself. But he was equally skeptical of the atheist." . . . In response to this he takes a Humanist stance, adopting a wait-and-see attitude. . . . (pp. 15-16)

In nearly four decades of novel-writing, that outlook has not been much modified.

In the biographical sketch on De Vries in the *Wilson Library Bulletin*, the *Saturday Review* is quoted on *Bugler*: "It may well be that this book will become known . . . as the first wild bleat of a young voice which was soon to blossom. . . ." It didn't happen that way, though: "His next two novels . . . had only a small public and dubious critical reception." Is that why De Vries never went back to the sort of prose fiction that usually passes for "serious"? No, it was the comparatively successful *But Who Wakes the Bugler?* that was zany, and it is to that sort of writing that he has never returned.

The big difference is simply that he got married. The out-of-print books all end with marriage; from *The Tunnel of Love* on they pretty much begin with it. This is a generally un-American situation, writing about married love. In fact, the only way it seems possible to do so seriously is by lacing the work generously with levity: this is what De Vries does. It may be significant that these first three novels, thought by De Vries to be "not good enough," he dislikes because he is too mature for them. Their "dubious critical reception" may be due to lack of maturity elsewhere.

Although we are told of funny things done by Brian Carston in the past, none of them happens during the course of *The Handsome Heart*, of which he is the central intelligence. (pp. 16-17)

[Edith Bracken is] in love with Brian, whom she has met while visiting her Uncle Edgar at a state hospital somewhere in Michigan. Brian has hitched a ride back to town with her and her aunts, having passed himself off as an orderly. Grimsberg [a psychiatrist at the asylum from which Brian has escaped] tells Edith that Brian has delusions his brother Charles is plotting to take away his money and put him in an institution. Edith asks whether it isn't pretty much the truth that Charles *is* plotting that way, a possibility Grimsberg apparently had not considered.

In addition to this setting, which invites consideration of the phenomenon of mental instability, there also occurs incest, murder, and suicide, as well as a walk through the halls of high finance. Obviously, it is a very serious novel. And although suffering from the usual De Vries vagaries—characters popping in and out, a plot that meanders—it is also one of his best works, for a number of reasons. For one thing, it is told not just from one person's point of view. We hear it mainly from Brian, but also in part from Charles, and also from Edith. This provides a rich mixture of attitudes, suggesting a more unbiased look at the world than what we usually are served by De Vries. For another, there are fewer gratuitous personalities; and, lastly, no one is patronized—all cultural levels are present and treated humanely.

Mainly it is a study of neuroticism, one of the ghosts De Vries had to exorcise. In *The Handsome Heart* he does so fairly well although there is no novel of his in which someone doesn't have to be put away or in which there is not at least mention of such a possibility. Some things you never get rid of, and in this instance it may be as well for his readers since the initial analysis of the problem seems also to be De Vries's enduring analysis of the problem: Brian, discussing instability with Edith's aunts, is asked by one of them, "How shall we explain that fascination madness has for us?" Her sister says "Maybe we laugh at it to protect ourselves, otherwise it would be too horrible." . . . That explanation will do as well as any, both for the fascination with madness and the humorous treatment of it. But De Vries doesn't glamorize such people, as certain other writers have, claiming that insanity is an appropriate reaction to a cruel world. . . . (pp. 17-18)

[After his escape, Brian sleeps in an empty cabin in the woods]. Awakened by the owner, a rough but vain man, he is allowed to stay. He claims to work for a leftish journal, the *Southpaw*, and goes on inventing tales till the uninterested man cuts him off. The man eats heavily: "Toilers are never epicures." . . . Such throw-away lines and situations do two things: after more basic literary matters are attended to—plot and characterization, say—the quality of writing is classified most easily by these "lines between the lines"; and they portend greater things to come. This ability is shown also as Brian thinks of his sister-in-law in his brother's nest, "purring among the furs and silverware, face smooth as ivory, breasts like cups of cream, the thousand little veins crying for conception." . . . (p. 19)

[It] seems every author early on has to write something about incest; but before Brian can get to Irene he kills a man who is trying to kill the cabin owner who took him in. Both have been working at moving corpses to make way for a road project when a fight breaks out over gold supposedly hidden in the bottom of one of the coffins. The digging itself suggests an abortive sort of resurrection and, in this case, an attempt to bury the murdered Novak fails when the night watchman makes a spot check. There was no gold, anyway. . . . (pp. 19-20)

As for the sister-in-law, Irene, she is a type common enough in the American novel—the highly desirable bad girl with whom the hero has fun but doesn't marry. In this case, that of Brian as parvenu, she embodies the delicious possibilities of life at the top—rather like Daisy Buchanan for Jay Gatsby. Like Daisy, Irene proves to be amoral, and looking out for Number One.

Woodie, a fellow inmate, similarly escaped, joins Brian in Chicago. Previously unmentioned, Woodie appears suddenly, functioning as someone for Brian to talk to; and at one critical point he posts a letter to Edith, to get her to come save his friend from Irene. (p. 20)

[It] appears to be a fairly typical romantic novel, having a troubled hero and a fair and a dark heroine, culminating in marriage.

Grimsberg the psychiatrist advises a plea of insanity, even though Brian is sane, because he's uncertain of what the prosecution may pull in the trial over Novak. The trial is a bit long; we see too much of the gravediggers Judo and Morgan, and new personalities appear and are developed even in these waning pages. This last is a habit that De Vries has never changed, and although it does lend a touch of *tranche de vie* it is not ultimately successful: the "slice of life" style supposedly is valuable for creating verisimilitude, an atmosphere of reality. But this atmosphere doesn't develop in De Vries's novels because he does not use the other techniques or attitudes of that school: his characters are not naturalistic, and there is a general progression—albeit a meandering one—from beginning to end. In short, a plot.

It is, therefore, disconcerting to find new people popping up in the last fifth of the novel. That's the portion of the book where we expect to see a summing up, with a giving of the lesson. Which—a lesson—there happens to be in this book. In this case, Grimsberg gives it. Telling Brian to claim insanity at the trial, he says:

> Perjure yourself? That's all relative. What Truth is or whether there is any such thing in an absolute sense or personified in a God, or what have you, I don't know—and neither do you. But there is a scale of human values by which man lives, a hierarchy so to speak, within which there is much uncertainty and great variation, in the light of each individual case. . . .
>
> (p. 22)

Grimsberg, as a psychiatrist, is an acceptable person to give such a summation, and since he at least has been introduced early on, his appearance does not seem *deus ex machina*, and his philosophy is credible. It is De Vries's philosophy, of course, and his later works repeat it.

The Handsome Heart ends on the farm, with Beevers conducting his orchestra, an orchestra invisible to the rest of us. Grimsberg says Beevers thinks he's Toscanini, but adds that so does every small-town conductor: that's what makes the small-town conductor's existence possible. The only difference is that Beevers has taken a shortcut.

Indeed, the same could be said of De Vries in choosing as his persona Brian Carston, an escapee from an insane asylum who turns out to be quite sane. It would have been a far stronger work had Brian not been so stable after all; for why else are we started off in the milieu of the unstable? So, readable though ***The Handsome Heart*** is, it seems largely to be a missed opportunity. The subject—confusion about reality—ultimately is kept at arm's length. By and large the illusions are perceived as being what they are, illusions. But an illusion perceived is an option no longer but only an illusion, and we are left with dull reality, commonplace, mundane. (pp. 22-3)

Grimsberg, whose job consists of the sorting out of illusions, comments on the serviceability of some of them:

> Falling in love, for instance, is embracing an illusion, the illusion that one's woman is the most wonderful creature in the world. This is a serviceable delusion, and indispensable to society, which would of course abruptly come to an end without it. So marriage, our number-one social institution, begins with an illusion. . . .
>
> (p. 23)

Maybe it does, and maybe it doesn't. (Notice that it is the *man* who is deluded, above, not the woman: do females know better, and merely go along with men's delusions, or are they the prestidigitators who create the delusions? A bit of both, thinks De Vries.) Whether marriage is based on an illusion or whether it is a mystery makes some difference, obviously, as to how one will write about it. One more novel, and De Vries would be willing to consider the subject seriously. Humorously, of course, but seriously. (pp. 23-4)

Angels Can't Do Better begins with a prefaced quotation from James Thurber's *One Is a Wanderer*: "Just shut up and get married, just get married and shut up." And it is a good introduction since this, too, is the story of a young man's finding himself and then marrying (De Vries's women would seem to find themselves through marrying), giving up meanwhile the world of politics. It is a much less schizophrenic novel than its two predecessors. Although Peter Topp is somewhat divided, he's less split than Mr. Thwing; and he has no double, as Brian Carston has with his Charles. He is simply a young man who knows that if he chooses the option of marriage he'll be closing the door on a number of other possibilities; it's not a matter of having a theoretical complaint against the institution as such. Marriage is simply seen as female victory and male capitulation—a view he would later modify and speak to at some length.

In [*Angels Can't Do Better*] . . . absurdity is as usual in the saddle and riding mankind. But unlike the absurdities of writers like Kafka, the logic is not that of the nightmare: Peter Topp (whose name we first learn on page 60) is quite aware that he is being ridden. Thus the absurdity is perceived for being an illusion, and we can relax a little. An illusion perceived is an option no longer. We are, in fact, told at the outset that absurdity is the topic when De Vries defines it as "the gulf between intention and appearance." . . . (p. 24)

[The] De Vries cocktail can make you giddy, but there's always the acrid lemon twist of sanity that keeps it from making the drinker sick. In *Angels Can't Do Better* the town, Chicago, is jammed with birds—starlings—or at least the ward Topp lives in is. Since Topp is the ward-heeler, this is a matter of some importance. This was in 1936, and when the book ends, early in World War II, they still are there. Inbetween times, Topp has to decide whether to follow his father (and grandfather before him) into the ancestral chair of Political Science at Lebanon College, nearby, or whether to go into politics. Contractors who put up inferior buildings at Lebanon do so by paying off politicians, and he decides to try to stop it. So it's politics, with academics in tandem: "I saw life as blurred, scrambled, patternless. Morons with earlaps eating up all your ham sandwiches, key men of great institutions dying at inopportune moments, people electing thieves to rob them, and one's father dancing indifferently in the hall" . . . , Peter comments.

What he means is that no one came to his political organizing meeting except one fellow who ate all the sandwiches, the president of Lebanon College is dying, the councilman who likely will defeat him is a crook, and his father absurdly slaps his mittens together in the hall to keep warm. Pastor De Bruin also shows up at the party-formation meeting, although mainly in order to "labor" with the elder Topp; the pastor is the sort who won't let a man quit the church. Rather he must be excommunicated. The father's unbelief—matched by the son's—doesn't prevent their Dutch-fashion throwing of proof-texts at each other, each gobbet wildly out of context. Neither the father nor De Bruin, however, is of much importance to the progress of the novel.

Rago is. An old-time politician-racketeer, he has torpedoes who do his dirty work for him. He "seemed hard at the same time that his body seemed soft; he was not at all fat yet his flesh was of the kind that if you poke it it stays poked." . . . His secretary, Judy Marsh, eyes like "blue jumping beans," becomes a romantic interest of Peter's, malapropping as she goes: asked if she's hungry, she says she's ravished. Also there is Lucy Mayhew, daughter of a Lebanon alumnus whose construction company (with Rago's connivance) will bilk the college. He fears her: *"She would be forever doing things for my own good."* . . . But he cannot separate himself from her before his Lebanon appointment comes through. Also there is Bessie Murdock, left over from undergraduate days, a girl who for good reason owned many sweaters.

With Bessie he goes to restaurants, where she lets it drop that they're newly wed; free drinks and dinner invariably follow. She rationalizes the imposture on the grounds that it lifts out of the humdrum the lives of the buyers, too, gives them a chance to celebrate. But the word marriage immobilizes Topp: better to be free but lonely, or companioned but in-lawed? He can't face it. . . . [He] pleads that the world is "uncertain." Bessie informs him that it has ever been so.

The campaign progresses; he has a cousin throw rocks through his windows, notes wrapped around them warning him to lay off his crackdown on gambling. But the campaign is not terribly important in the novel. Blessedly, it is not a Political Novel, one of those works of art designed to get salami taxed at the Brenner Pass instead of somewhere else. Politics, to be sure, was an early interest of De Vries—so it furnishes in part the background structure of *Angels Can't Do Better*—but he knows well enough to use it for the sake of his art, not the reverse. (pp. 25-6)

Birds function throughout as a leitmotiv, one pathetic starling in particular. . . . (p. 26)

Whenever Peter can't face up to marriage with Bessie, he focuses his telescope on the starling. When the bird seems to crack up finally and attack the window of the room where Topp is, he realizes it's only his own reflection that the starling is fighting. Even so with himself. . . . The election is lost; the war is on. Pfau, a sage old man from an apartment down the hall, recommends, finally, marriage—although he suggests that the partners "should live together for several months, maybe a year, before marriage, *without congress.*" . . . Peter Topp says that's asking a lot, and Pfau agrees. Writers (and perhaps the rest of humanity, too) tend to assume their own problems of the moment to be those of the world as well.

And the world has troubled them: "Half the world is nervous," Peter tells Pfau, "and it's spreading to the animal kingdom. We must try to love one another." . . . But he will face up to marriage, to war: "Civilization is the record and result of man's not scramming . . ." . . . As he is driven off on the bus to army camp he waves goodbye to Bessie, his "version of the Woman who haunts, in some fashion, the dreams of every man apart: the immortal She who taunts and blesses, the gift of the covenant, the treasure where the heart is." . . . (pp. 26-7)

J. H. Bowden, in his Peter De Vries *(copyright © 1983 by Twayne Publishers; reprinted with the permission of Twayne Publishers, a Division of G. K. Hall & Co., Boston), Twayne, 1983, 179 p.*

William Dickey
1928-

American poet.

Perhaps the most important element in Dickey's poetry is its diversity. Reminiscent in its sophisticated precision of W. H. Auden, Dickey's poems are noted for their many different moods and voices. Not preoccupied with the pursuit of a single theme or question, Dickey varies the subjects of his verse greatly. In one poem he may write of loss and despair; in another, the subject might be some whimsical act or thing that once captured his attention. Accordingly, his verse is variously light and deeply contemplative.

W. H. Auden selected *Of the Festivity* **(1959), Dickey's first collection, for inclusion in the Yale Series of Younger Poets. In the Foreword to** *Of the Festivity***, Auden describes his three criteria for good poetry: the lines of a poem must have "the power to speak," the poet a "capacity to notice," and an original and personal vision. Dickey, Auden declares, meets these three requirements.**

Dickey's two recent collections, *The Rainbow Grocery* **(1978) and** *The Sacrifice Consenting* **(1982), are characteristic of the majority of his works in their fluctuation between humorous and serious observations on many aspects of life. Here, as elsewhere, Dickey employs several different forms in the creation of his verse, including dramatic monologues, lyrical portraits, and comic parodies. Both books have received generally favorable critical reception. Critics who find fault with Dickey's work nonetheless seem to admire his wit and vitality.**

(See also *CLC,* **Vol. 3;** *Contemporary Authors,* **Vols. 9-12, rev. ed.; and** *Dictionary of Literary Biography,* **Vol. 5.)**

Photograph by Warren Marcus

W. H. AUDEN

Few people, on retiring from a position [such as editor of the Yale Series of Younger Poets] can resist offering advice to their successors, who probably do not want it and will not heed it. Accordingly, I shall pass on to mine, for his imaginary benefit, a description of my procedure upon receiving in the spring a heavy parcel of manuscripts by names unknown to me.

The first time I go through them, I try to exclude from my mind any such considerations as originality, style, taste, or even sense, while I look for one thing only, *lines* of poetry. By this I mean a line which speaks itself, which, as it were, no longer needs its author's help to exist.

Thus, in my first reading of Mr. Dickey, I came upon lines like

> Spinning and smiling as the world diminished

> . . . . .

> That showed him whole, when we had gone away

> . . . . .

> Their husbands carve the dressing and the bird,
> The day, the napkin, and the carving plate
> To bits that are too little to be heard.

whereupon he went onto the pile of potential winners. It is possible to show evidence of great intelligence and sensibility but to be lacking in the first power essential to poetry, the power to *speak*. Mr. Dickey's lines have both. . . . Again I read through them, looking for only one thing, the power to notice, the possession of what one might call uncommon common sense. This may appear either as an accurate and vivid description of some creature or object which we have all seen or as a truthful and illuminating comment upon some experience with which we are all familiar. For example, everyone carries some scar or other upon his body, but it is Mr. Dickey and not everyone who makes this observation:

> Like hasty marks on an explorer's chart:
> This white stream bed, this blue lake on my knee
> Are an angry doctor at midnight, or a girl
> Looking at the blood and trying not to see
> What we both have seen. Most of my body lives,
> But the scars are dead like the grooving of a frown,
> Cannot be changed, and ceaselessly record
> How much of me is already written down.

The capacity to notice is not, like the power to speak, essential to all poetry—there are beautiful lyrics in which it plays no part at all—but I value it very highly in this age as a *moral* virtue. (pp. viii-ix)

Having satisfied myself that the author of a manuscript can make words speak and is interested in something more than his precious little self, I now read it poem by poem, looking to see if he has learned to write a whole poem and has written enough of them to be ready to publish a book. How many is enough? Remembering that, when reading a volume by the greatest and most famous names, one almost always says of some of the poems "Why did he include that?" but that one never says this about a volume of one's own, I regard a manuscript as meriting publication if I like a third of its contents.

Like any work of art, a successful poem is a complete world with which, though it is a thing, the reader can make personal contact. But poetry is peculiar in that it is made of words; the medium of this art is the same as that of guidebooks, treatises on plumbing, business correspondence, and the *Congressional Record*. A poem therefore is, necessarily, what a painting need not be and a piece of music cannot be, a double world of things (words) and meanings. "Pure" poetry, poetry, that is to say, in which word and meaning are identical, is an impossibility; even a lyric like "Full Fathom Five" is "representational." Further, since the meaning of words depends upon common social agreement, poetry is the most "traditional" of all the arts. No poet can invent a language of his own; even the puns in *Finnegans Wake* presuppose an unchanging traditional language. Assuming that he had learned to speak French, the shade of Homer would have little difficulty, I believe, in reading the poetry of Rimbaud; he might not like it but he would know why. But a Greek musician confronted with a piece by Webern, let us say, would be unable to pass any judgment whatsoever, because he would hear no musical sounds, only noises.

Thus while in the other arts an original vision may often seem to be the result of a change of style or method, in poetry an original and in itself nonverbal vision seems the necessary precondition for a change in the handling of the language.

Most arguments about *how* poetry should be written seem to me futile because they conceal the real difference between the parties, which is their respective notions of the proper poetical subject, what poetry should be *about*.

As an example of one of Mr. Dickey's poems, let me cite **"Part Song, with Concert of Recorders."** I choose it because it is a song, and of all kinds of poetry songs are the least personal and most verbal.

This poem is a little ballad, a melodramatic dialogue between a lady and her doctor-lover, who has just murdered her husband. In each of the seven five-line stanzas, the first line ends with the word *there* or *where*, the fourth and fifth lines with the word *care*.... A lucky chance of the English language gave Mr. Dickey two rhyme words which can be used in a number of different senses, but his use of them, and of a simple, melodramatic situation which might all too easily have been ridiculous, to compose a poignant and resonant parable comes from his personal vision, not the English language.

At present, to judge from [*Of the Festivity*], Mr. Dickey's speciality is nightmare worlds described in the simplest possible diction. (pp. ix-xi)

[Mr. Dickey's poetry] satisfies the three demands I have made in my readings: the lines speak, something has been noticed, and speech and observation have become the servants of a personal vision. (p. xii)

W. H. Auden, "Foreword" (reprinted by permission of Curtis Brown, Ltd.; copyright © 1959 by Yale University Press, Inc.), in Of the Festivity *by William Dickey, Yale University Press, 1959, pp. vii-xii.*

PHILIP BOOTH

William Dickey's **"Of the Festivity"** [is] a model of modern prosody that features the required sestina, the able sonnet. Unfortunately, the emotion behind the poems is diminished in a defensive structure of carefully controlled meters and lapidary rhymes. The author's **"Exploration Over the Rim"** is not that in spite of its title. He is on the perimeter still, circling with only the formal language of educated men. But he has his claim staked out in **"Questions About a Spaniel of Eleven,"** **"Lesson of the Master"** and the moving **"Memoranda."** These are the heights, the varieties of rhythm and speech he must climb over, and beyond, to explore himself fully.

Philip Booth, "Voices That Speak in Verse," in The New York Times Book Review *(copyright © 1959 by The New York Times Company; reprinted by permission), September 6, 1959, p. 6.*

THOM GUNN

William Dickey reminds me ... of a young English poet, Gordon Wharton. Both have at present reached that important and exciting point at which they are relinquishing the influence of Auden for something of their own. As it is, there is still a good deal too much of Auden in *Of the Festivity* for one to say of it (and to say without the least condescension) more than "promising." He is particularly attracted by the Auden of "The Witnesses," but he is developing his own sense of the ridiculous, as in ... [certain] lines, from **"Questions of a Spaniel of Eleven,"** which owe nothing to Auden.... There are also some more self-consciously serious poems, some of which (among them the title-poem) are a trifle awkward, but others of which really say something in an interesting way. **"Memoranda"** and **"Twenty Years Gone, She Returns to the Nunnery"** are a good deal more than promising. Most of the book, however, is the enjoyable and competent work of an apprentice who has good chances of becoming a master. (p. 303)

Thom Gunn, "Excellence and Variety," in The Yale Review *(copyright 1959 by Yale University; reprinted by permission of the editors), Vol. XLIX, No. 2, December, 1959, pp. 295-305.*

WILLIAM STAFFORD

William Dickey's poems in *Of the Festivity* offer many patterns. He is ready, on balance, hurrying here, hesitating expressively there. His topics provide him with opportunities which he deftly picks up. For an example of pace, variety, and exploitation of what the current brings, here is the last portion of a poem entitled *Minotaur:*

> Where you will meet me first is no great matter,
> A casual leaf that flutters in your face,
> A spider or a dog. More like the latter,
> Running, and all at once it is a race,
> And where you turn, I win, and in that place
> I shall learn silence, and you will learn grace.

This fluency impresses the reader throughout the book.

W. H. Auden [see excerpt above], retiring from his job as editor of the Yale series, tells in a six-page foreword how he went about the process of selecting manuscripts. . . . About *Of the Festivity,* he provides examples to show how the book satisfies [his] three tests.

Auden is persuasive, and he carries several kinds of authority in whatever he says; but sometimes he appears to provide distinctions more absolute than actuality will sustain: "A practicing poet is never a perfect editor: if he is young, he will be intolerant of any kinds of poetry other than the kind he is trying to write himself; if he is middle aged, the greater tolerance of his judgment is offset by the decline of his interest in contemporary poetry." A sentence like this stirs up a stutter of qualifications, among them this: Might some practicing poet, instead of being tolerant of the kind of poet he himself is, be antagonistic? Might he shy away from recognizing someone doing his own job well?

William Dickey does jobs well that the later Auden approves. The earlier Auden, however, I believe might have judged differently in this certain way: he had purposes that *grooved* his talent. A young poet might do well to guard against working to get full approval of middle-aged guides, especially overwhelming middle-aged guides, and even more especially overwhelming middle-aged guides whose sense of direction depends on a kind of determined virtuosity. William Dickey shows in some later poems that he may be better than those who approve him think he is. (pp. 250-51)

> William Stafford, "Several Tongues" (© 1960 by The Modern Poetry Association; reprinted by permission of the Editor of Poetry and the author), in Poetry, Vol. XCV, No. 4, January, 1960, pp. 248-57.*

JUDSON JEROME

One might judge from [some of the remarks that Dickey has made that his] poetry would be easy-going; but it is not. There is a difference between the difficulties offered by closely textured thought, complex sentences, subtley (all of which I find in Dickey's work), and that of obscurity (which I do not, as a rule, find). That is, the answers are all clearly there, in the poem—and the imaginative leap demanded by symbols, allusions, truncated structures, sudden transitions, is not usually required. But one may not read with the inattention permitted by a murder mystery or the *World Almanac.*

"Song for Disheartened Lute," a poem so timelessly classic that one might have found it with delight in the *Greek Anthology,* is, indeed, limpid—and limpid bitter—as it records the ingrowing frigidity and final insane self-love of the aging virgin. One could not ask for a poem more direct. **"The Easy House"** is fairly easy, too, though all those messages crisscrossing create an appropriate complexity to try the nerves in the sterile, anxious cosmopolitan life, contrasted to the easy house by the productive sea where simpler messages are uttered by the seals and the tide. The image of the "circus of bright knives," laid down by the mercury lights, stands out—an excellent touch, but a kind of hard cleverness unusual in his poetry. Usually his sensibility tones it down.

"Antiquity" is a mood poem that reminds me, curiously, of Andrew Marvell's "vegetable love"—if there were world enough and time. It eases into a kind of passionless generation, like the leaving of olives and passive multiplication of the vines. Or maybe it is as though those lovers on Keats's urn just vaguely, infinitesimally, began to move. I delight in the still scene and its kinetic possibilities. **"Those Who Have Burned"** is difficult for me. I admire the piling rhetoric, the anapests surging in the endless first sentence. But I am not quite sure what I am being told. These intense types burning themselves out in contempt for life and love of death are suicidal, warrant no pity, get just what they wish, oblivion. On the other hand we admire the spectacle of their conflagration. And surely we recognize that however they deny our well-wishing, they cannot mean what they say, that the attention-getting-mechanism is a plea for love. Perhaps this complexity of response is just the point of the poem. You want death? So yours, and welcome. And we stand back at a safe distance in amazement, amusement, contempt, and inevitable respect. I wish I knew more exactly whom he is talking about. (pp. 52-3)

[**"She in Summer,"**] so far as I can tell, makes very little sense. . . . As a very sensuous apprehension of a fairly exotic erotic experience (she "cried aloud!") the poem is vivid, overwhelming. I say it "makes very little sense" only because the poet abandons reason—in sentence structure, sequence of images, even in diction, just as languidly does she. I like reason—but a good poem ought to be, as a friend once told me, "a little spooky at the core." In the domination of good sense in current poetry—both in the work and in poets' careers—there is some danger that reason might break out all over. Time was I thought that would be the salvation of us all, but reason works so well everywhere I find myself beginning again to cheer on madness. At least a touch. (p. 53)

> Judson Jerome, "Introduction to the Poems of William Dickey," in The Antioch Review (copyright © 1963 by the Antioch Review Inc.; reprinted by permission of the Editors), Vol. XXIII, No. 1, Spring, 1963, pp. 50-3.

THE TIMES LITERARY SUPPLEMENT

[William Dickey] lacks a distinctive voice and ranges uneasily from sophisticated epigram to laboured parable. At one point [in his *Interpreter's House*] he has a "Dialogue" between Jack, whose work is "bloodless with elaboration" and The Giant, who writes from "rude instinct": the Giant seems to get the best of the debate but in fact Mr. Dickey writes like Jack. . . . His vocabulary is abstract and circuitous and throughout one has the impression that he is casting around for curious subject matter. It takes only a few pages of such speculative meandering to set one growling, with Dr. Williams: "Say it! No ideas but in things."

> "No Ideas But in Things," in The Times Literary Supplement (© Times Newspapers Ltd. (London) 1964; reproduced from The Times Literary Supplement by permission), No. 3245, May 7, 1964, p. 396.*

DeWITT BELL

"Interpreter's House" by William Dickey is solidly made of the traditional forms of English poetry. Dickey is very much influenced by Yeats, but to Yeats he adds a dry dissonance.

Although the book has real moments, times of openness, they are rarely sustained; the poet assumes strict disciplines and all but asphyxiates behind them. His originality is drawn out of the manipulations of his mind, not the depths of his self.

To read **"Interpreter's House"** is to know little about the interpreter. . . . (p. 5)

DeWitt Bell, "Wonders of the Inner Eye," in The New York Times Book Review (copyright © 1964 by The New York Times Company; reprinted by permission), July 5, 1964, pp. 4-5.*

THE VIRGINIA QUARTERLY REVIEW

The love poems [in William Dickey's *The Rainbow Grocery*] are excellent—spontaneous, gentle, the mellow bittersweet tone reminiscent of Auden. Whimsical, colloquial, urbane, Dickey's voice is adaptable to many subjects and moods: myth, lyric, dramatic monologue, parody. Flat observations alternate with deft, sinister lines, identifying the ordinary with the grotesque. The poems sometimes strain to be offhanded and fanciful, detailing the confusion of his own life—but his genial posturing is still lovable.

>A review of "The Rainbow Grocery," in The Virginia Quarterly Review (copyright, 1979, by The Virginia Quarterly Review, The University of Virginia), Vol. 55, No. 2 (Spring, 1979), p. 66.

REG SANER

On the basis of hardly a shred of evidence I have wondered if poets' approaches to poetry might be encapsulated in a dyad: get/give. The writer's early phase would be bent on prying loose from the world one or two favors like love and fame. His later career would become increasingly less predatory, and aim more at giving than getting. (p. 113)

Especially in America, where "famous poet" remains an oxymoron, the maturing poet will progress from simply wanting attention to wanting to deserve it.

For example, William Dickey's *The Rainbow Grocery* renounces mere attention-getting by its nonchalant, discursive manner. Undoubtedly "to get" spurs Dickey along even in this, his fifth book; nonetheless, its poetry is deeply, humanely generous.

True, the risk of rhetorical strategy exploiting effects of "artlessness" in the longer poems entails slackness and lessened intensity. A fairly high percent of the book consists of pieces whose whimsey fails to deepen, the sort of "fun" pieces that go over well at readings. Poems like **"The Revival of Vaudeville"** or **"Show Biz"** or **"Honolulu"** kindle only amusement. If they seem just padding, Dickey's strongest work arises from the same, whimsical vein. So he can take an image like **"Sheeba the Outcast Drag Queen"** and produce an eerie novelty on death, utterly authentic and original.

Dickey's attraction to the garage-sale aspect of reality moves in the book's remarkably fine poem **"Alligators and Paris and North America"** from "Bernice Dewey hypnotizing her alligator" in the bathtub, to six-foot mushrooms and carrots flanking a healthfood store; to an outrageous prose squib about Mary Cassatt . . . and from there to a clumsy transvestite who flubs a mawkish stage-gesture while trying to toss artificial flowers out among his audience.

The assembled oddities of **"Alligators and Paris and North America"** climax with an anecdote of an old man who precedes his suicide with fireworks on which he has spent his life savings. By means of their eccentricity, Dickey meditates towards the "universal" each oddity contains. The poem's four pages amount to a beautifully compassionate elevation of the gauche and the deviant. (pp. 113-14)

As rule of thumb I've often felt a solid collection should include at least five good poems. Re-readings of *The Rainbow Grocery* yield almost double that number. Unfortunately the best poems resist piecemeal quotation—as for instance **"Telemachus," "The Raft of the Medusa," "In the Dreaming," "After Two Years of Analysis: Reactions,"** and the superb **"Die Alte Frau, Die Alte Marshallin."** Here Dickey—like Randall Jarrell, whom the latter poem seems to invoke—finds room for his colloquial "low" style to gather effect. (pp. 114-15)

Most poets would not be caught dead being so little "impressive." Only the context of *The Rainbow Grocery*'s wit, erudition-made-invisible, and its quiet depth legitimates or "earns" such flat simplicity. (p. 115)

>Reg Saner, in a review of "The Rainbow Grocery," in The Ohio Review (copyright © 1980 by the Editors of The Ohio Review), No. 25, 1980, pp. 113-19.

ROBERT B. SHAW

The Sacrifice Consenting, briefer, more luxuriously printed and bound, seems something of a spinoff of [William Dickey's earlier volume, *The Rainbow Grocery*]. In both books Dickey enjoys blurring the line between poetry and a standup comedian's routine. His satire is aimed at easy targets: bureaucracy, the media, the computer age, California. . . . Most of these poems are funny the first time, then not so funny. There are a number of pieces touching on the gay life which go about their business with a teary-eyed grinning reminiscent of *The Boys in the Band*. . . . When he is able to keep his feverish jocosity within bounds, Dickey writes a rare and enviable sort of poem, truly humorous and truly serious at once: **"The Food of Love"** is characteristic of him in this vein. . . . This poem is from *The Rainbow Grocery*, which has within its plebeian paper covers a good deal more worth reading than one can find within the choice boards that grace *The Sacrifice Consenting*. (pp. 177-78)

>Robert B. Shaw, "Fireflies and Other Animals" (© 1982 by The Modern Poetry Association; reprinted by permission of the Editor of Poetry and the author), in Poetry, Vol. CXLI, No. 3, December, 1982, pp. 170-81.*

John Gregory Dunne
1932-

American novelist, essayist, journalist, and scriptwriter.

Dunne is known for documentaries and novels usually set in California. His fictional mood is darkly humorous and his characterizations and mastery of dialect almost always elicit praise.

Dunne's first major work, *Delano: The Story of the California Grape Strike* (1967), established him as one of the New Journalists, a group of participatory reporters who evolved during the 1960s. His portrayal of the strike against the grape growers in central California centers on Cesar Chavez's efforts to organize farm workers into the National Farm Worker's Association. Most critics praised the book for its perception and objectivity. A second work of investigative journalism, *The Studio* (1969), a satirical look at the business of making movies, resulted from his on-location study of Twentieth Century-Fox.

Dunne's next book, *Vegas* (1974), conveys the decadence of Las Vegas through the composite portraits of three Las Vegas "types"—a prostitute, a second-rate entertainer, and a private investigator. Against this background he describes the emotional breakdown he himself was experiencing. Critics were impressed with Dunne's powerful and evocative writing but were reluctant to categorize the work, finding it a blend of memoir, reportage, and novel.

Dunne's novels, *True Confessions* (1977) and *Dutch Shea, Jr.* (1982), have both been well received by critics and the public. The first depicts the Irish-Catholic community in Los Angeles of the 1950s through the lives of two brothers, one a priest, the other a policeman. In Dunne's second novel the title character, Dutch Shea, Jr., is a criminal lawyer doomed by his memories and by the realities of his work. Both novels have complex, fast-moving plots with vivid characterizations and realistic settings.

(See also *Contemporary Authors,* Vols. 25-28, rev. ed. and *Dictionary of Literary Biography Yearbook: 1980.*)

Photograph by Quintana Roo Dunne; courtesy of John Dunne

MARTIN DUBERMAN

[In 1962 Cesar Chavez] founded the National Farm Worker's Association. It was the NFWA which jumped in to lead the grape pickers' strike that erupted near Delano in the spring of 1965.

John Gregory Dunne sets out in his book, *Delano,* to tell the story of that strike, a struggle which continues down to this day. (pp. 24-5)

Dunne's "objectivity" sometimes serves as an easy way of avoiding the rigors of interpretation; he settles for presenting all available points of view instead of trying to discover where, amongst them, the truth might lie. In failing to adjudicate, he dilutes his own viewpoint: though his sympathy with the strikers is clear, his willingness to admit considerable contrary—and often specious—argument, ends by maximizing the "anguish" of the growers. Where Dunne does take on the job of interpretation, he too often performs it by indirection. This is especially true of his oblique devaluation of the commitment of "outsiders" who have come to the aid of Chavez and his organization. Dunne refers to one white clergyman as "never without a folder of press clippings detailing his skirmishes with Church superiors in the past decade." And he acidly comments that most of the white college students in Delano migrated there because it "was the only game in town" after they had been drummed out of SNCC and CORE. If Dunne has a reasoned case to make against the volunteers he should spell it out. Indictment by innuendo is never very attractive.

Indeed, "sketchiness" is the book's chief defect. Dunne tries to tell a complex story, one with reference points in several cultures and with historical antecedents dating back several decades, in a mere 176 pages. It is not enough, though his spare and affecting prose does convey considerable information in limited space. But what we need and do not get, are some solid analytical passages and some of those individual case studies (à la Oscar Lewis) which help to make concrete the suffering and endurance that statistics alone cannot convey.

Dunne does not even give us a depth portrait of Chavez. Now and then he drops a clue or an off-hand comment, but there is no confrontation with Chavez' personal style or the thrust of his mind. Some of Dunne's offhand comments sound, intriguingly, rather hostile. . . . The portrayal of individuals can be legitimately ignored when an author wishes to focus instead on patterns of group behavior. But when sociological insights are likewise absent, there are grounds for complaint. (pp. 25-6)

> Martin Duberman, "Grapes of Wrath," in The New Republic (reprinted by permission of The New Republic; © 1967 The New Republic, Inc.), Vol. 157, No. 23, December 2, 1967, pp. 23-6.

GLADWIN HILL

[*Delano: The Story of the California Grape Strike*] is an exceptionally incisive report on the anatomy of the strike; a colorful, perceptive examination of its impact on the community; and an analysis of actions of both employers and labor so realistic as to make it important reading for current students of economics and public policy.

> Gladwin Hill, "'La Huelga', a Step in the Struggle," in The New York Times Book Review (copyright © 1967 by The New York Times Company; reprinted by permission), December 2, 1967, p. 58.

PAUL D. ZIMMERMAN

Anyone trapped in a movie house with a horrible three-hour spectacular as his only distraction has wondered more than once, "How did they ever make such an awful picture?" Some of the answers can be found in this fascinating study of the motion-picture business as recorded by John Gregory Dunne, who spent a year amid the infernal regions of Twentieth Century-Fox.

Not all of ["**The Studio**"] is consistently interesting, for Dunne wandered around awhile before he found his denouement, the fate of the multimillion-dollar "Dr. Dolittle." But even his meanderings are fruitful. Instead of fixing on a single film, Dunne treats us to an unhurried tour of the entire studio at work . . . always zeroing in on the decision-making process that shapes these products and on the men in control. (pp. 110, 112)

Much of [the information in the book] is familiar to anyone who has followed Hollywood since its disastrous collision with television. The real contribution of Dunne's book lies in its nicely honed portrait of the Hollywood ethos, that gothic mix of greed, hypocrisy, shrewd calculation, mad hoopla and boundless optimism that shapes American films and, through them, much of the sensibility of the American public. (pp. 112, 114)

> Paul D. Zimmerman, "The Internal Regions," in Newsweek (copyright 1969, by Newsweek, Inc.; all rights reserved; reprinted by permission), Vol. LXXIII, No. 19, May 12, 1969, pp. 110, 112, 114.

TRACY ALIG

Presumably [Dunne's purpose in *The Studio*] was to give his readers an objective look at the phenomenon we know as Hollywood. How can anything about Hollywood be objective? This book comes pretty close, and in that lies its chief merit.

Dunne begins by telling us something we should already know: that the mass media have formed many of our responses to life situations. . . .

Many of the norms provided us by movies and television have proved inadequate and inaccurate, and Dunne, through objective reporting and excellent characterization, shows us why. *The Studio* reveals a closed society. When I read some of the short-sighted opinions of these men, I wanted to laugh and cry at the same time. . . .

The author does a spectacular job of characterization of studio personnel, from Darryl and Richard Zanuck downward. There is no gossip (in a book about Hollywood!), and the impression is that these are men who work, think and talk constantly about their medium. If their personal lives are messy, it is because they have no personal lives.

Plenty of incidental information can be gleaned from these pages, too. . . .

Movies and their production represent the American phenomenon at its most vulgar and most spectacular. *The Studio* is a top notch piece of journalism describing them. Even those who don't see many movies should thoroughly enjoy this book. But the people who really should read it are the movie people, from stars to stagehands. The pity is, however, that they probably wouldn't recognize themselves without their makeup.

> Tracy Alig, in a review of "The Studio," in America (reprinted with permission of America Press, Inc.; © 1969; all rights reserved), Vol. 121, No. 1, July 5, 1969, p. 17.

A. CROCE

We know before we open Dunne's book [*The Studio*] that the people in it are going to be foolish and vulgar and, sure enough, they are—a whole cast of celebrities, studio execs and functionaries caught in the act of sweating, belching, cringing, chewing hangnails and saying things like: "We've got entertainment *and* a message in this picture, Arthur." What we hadn't expected, possibly, is to find no one to side with. Even Lillian Ross' *Picture* had its sad little hero. But no one on the Fox lot fights to make things like *Planet of the Apes, Dr. Dolittle, Star!, The Boston Strangler* and *Hello, Dolly!* Dunne's book has the built-in tedium, the moral vacancy, of a Maysles Bros. documentary. His picture people, all employees of a company that five years before stood on the edge of bankruptcy, walk through his pages like the grateful dead. Richard Zanuck, efficient and colorless, is the unquestioned architect of the Studio's survival and its champion hangnail-chewer. His father is grateful, too. Sitting in his New York office, Darryl Zanuck tells Dunne: "I was put under terrific criticism when I sent Dick out to head the Studio. What could I do? He was the only one I could trust." The corporate drama has all passed over. *The Studio* is the epilogue.

> A. Croce, in a review of "The Studio," in National Review (© National Review, Inc., 1969; 150 East 35th St., New York, NY 10016; reprinted with permission), Vol. XXI, No. 49, December 16, 1969, p. 1283.

L. J. DAVIS

John Gregory Dunne's *Vegas* begins: "In the summer of my nervous breakdown, I went to live in Las Vegas, Clark County, Nevada."

It is a miracle he survived. Las Vegas itself is a kind of nervous breakdown, a huge, tawdry pathological distortion of what we are pleased to call The American Dream. . . .

Dunne approached the place as a voyeur in search of catharsis. Thirty-seven years old and death-obsessed, burdened with an existence that, like a bad job of tie-dyeing, wouldn't come out right no matter what he did, he set himself up in an apartment near the Strip and proceeded to eat himself silly on junk food. One knows the scene so well, in literature and in life, and in literature as in life it more often fails than succeeds: the self-pity of the incipiently middle-aged, the nocturnal rambles and ceaseless brooding, the desperate, solipsistic search for some sort of parole from the prison of the spirit. Two weeks in another town, the whole bag.

Yet from this unpromising and overworked clay, Dunne has produced something very like a work of art—a minor one, it is true, but art nevertheless. He is a skillful writer, but it is more than that; it is his clear-eyed sense of the insane trap both he and the people he meets have wandered into, all unawares. . . .

Vegas is less a novel (though part of it is purportedly fiction) or a documentary (though it is that, too) than a prolonged agonized meditation on the true value of life on earth. Dunne himself is never far from its center, observer and participant, whether making the rounds of the clubs or taking steam in a Turkish bath or ruminating about sex and a Catholic boyhood or sitting in his room catatonically watching television, wishing he were someone else. His conclusions will not lift many hearts, but at least he went home in the end. It may seem odd to say it, but this is also a very funny book—or I should say comic, in the sense that comedy is tragedy gone mad. And all too horribly real.

> L. J. Davis, "Round and Round It Goes," in Book World—The Washington Post (© 1974, The Washington Post), February 3, 1974, p. 3.

JONATHAN YARDLEY

["**Vegas**"] is an exercise in journalism-as-therapy. Dunne makes no bones about that. (p. 6)

Dunne set himself up in a ticky-tacky Vegas apartment and began to roam the Strip, in search not so much of adventure as of the company that misery loves. He found plenty of it, most notably in the persons—all pseudonymous and to some degree fictitious—of a prostitute named Artha . . . ; Buster Mano, an amiably cynical private eye with a special knack for tracking down fled husbands; and Jackie Kasey, a "semi-name" comedian who grossed over $100,000 the year before, yet, in spite of that and his bluster and bustle, remained resolutely unknown and mediocre.

Their stories are funny, poignant and fascinating, and Dunne tells them with sympathy but without sentiment. He understands that no matter how sordid or desperate or even meaningless they may at first seem, there is something distinctly honorable in their dogged struggle to stay off the scrap heap. Dunne also has a marvelously keen eye for Vegas itself. . . . His portrait of the city is sharp, at times painted in acid; yet, again, there is compassion in it as well, for he recognizes that people are drawn to Vegas's tawdry tinsel in search of comforts more complex and elusive than quick gain at the gaming tables or sex in an air-conditioned hotel room.

Dunne himself was one of those people, and interwoven with the story of Vegas and its people is his own story—perhaps the most intriguing aspect of which is that this lapsed Catholic from an upper-middle-class New England background should have chosen Vegas to straighten himself out in the first place. As personal journalists tend to do, Dunne injects himself into the book more than really seems warranted—the catalogue of his sexual escapades and hangups, though frequently amusing, ultimately is wearisome—and indeed seems more interested in himself than in the other people he writes about. The problem is compounded by his admission at the outset that "**Vegas**" is "a fiction which recalls a time both real and imagined." What, one cannot help but wonder, is reportage, and what is invented to serve Dunne's private purposes?

But those are familiar complaints against personal journalism, and there is not much to be gained by dragging out all the old arguments against it. It does seem to me that Dunne indulges himself in a semi-truth when he says, "There is a therapeutic aspect to reporting that few like to admit. . . . Reporting anesthetizes one's own problems," but at least he has the candor to admit that his journalistic motives are ulterior.

What, in fact, do those motives really matter? What does matter is that Dunne has written a fine, wry, perceptive, graceful book that does as much for the dark side of the American funhouse as Hunter Thompson's "Fear and Loathing in Las Vegas" did for the manic side. Neither side is pretty, but each has produced an entertaining and disturbing book. (pp. 6-7)

> Jonathan Yardley, "Reportage As Anesthesia," in The New York Times Book Review (copyright © 1974 by The New York Times Company; reprinted by permission), February 3, 1974, pp. 6-7.

BRUCE COOK

John Gregory Dunne's [*Vegas*] is as good as it is difficult to classify. I've been trying to put a label of some sort on it ever since I finished it. He subtitles it "A Memoir of a Dark Season," and that sounds like just another arty, slightly cryptic subtitle, but in this case it is justified; the author is being helpful—and precise. Dunne has a reputation as a "new journalist" left over from a time when the phrase seemed to mean something to people. The book's subjective tone and tight, strong dialogue make it *look* like a novel, *sound* like "new journalism." Well, it's not—not, in Tom Wolfe's sense. No, *Vegas* is far more personal than that. John Gregory Dunne, in fact, has been about as frankly personal about himself as anyone ever has been in a book—and so the subtitle, a *caveat lector* discreetly warning the reader something different lies ahead. . . .

This book is—a thing of misery, an object of moral waste, an expression of despair. Dunne knows the terrain so well and describes it in such precise, measured, understated style that he makes his hell a thing of beauty, or, a very peculiar sort of beauty. . . .

Las Vegas! It is as though Dunne had set out to find an environment that was the perfect objective correlative for the misery he was carrying around inside him. And whether or not he set out to *find* it, Las Vegas was there waiting for him, waiting for a writer of his talent and perception to come along and tell us what it is really like.

He lays it all before us, with marvelous economy, chiefly by presenting three inmates of the city—Jackie Kasey (a lounge comic), Artha Ging (a prostitute), and Buster Mano (a private detective). Each of them, like Walt Whitman, contains multitudes. Through Dunne's relationship with them we come to know others in the city, we get a sense of what Las Vegas is for those who actually live there after the gamblers, the tourists and the conventioneers have come and gone. . . . The three are completely realized as characters, three-dimensional as few in novels are today: each has a personal history, a reason for being who and what he is; each is encased in his own little cocoon of responses, relationships and desires—they occupy *space*. Yet Jackie Kasey, Artha and Buster are probably composite characters rather than literal individual human beings whose names have been changed. *Vegas* is then, in this respect and a few others, a work of fiction.

Dunne, in fact, says as much in a note prefacing the text. . . . The difficulties in labeling *Vegas* become clear. If it is "a fiction," as he says it is, then is it a novel? If, as Dunne tells us, "I am more or less 'I,'" then is it a memoir—as he himself labeled it in the book's subtitle? Or has he just pushed new journalism a bit further in a direction it was already inching? Does it really matter *what* it is labeled?

To some it matters a great deal. When Gail Sheehy published a series of articles on prostitution in New York City that later became the basis for her book *Hustling*, there was a great furor when it developed that some of her portraits of hustlers and pimps were "composites"—that is (let's be frank about it), they were fictional. . . . Critics were disturbed because it blurred further the dim lines separating fiction and reporting. *Vegas* may well obliterate altogether these lines limiting the accepted "forms." As a novel, as a memoir it is unsatisfactory. But as a piece of writing, it is superb.

> Bruce Cook, "Dark Season," in The New Republic (reprinted by permission of The New Republic; © 1974 The New Republic, Inc.), Vol. 170, No. 10, March 9, 1974, p. 28.

PETER STRAUB

John Gregory Dunne's masterly account of his season of breakdown, *Vegas,* proves that emotional deadness, if intended and built into the style, can paradoxically turn up the narrative juice. *Vegas* is far closer to reportage and autobiography than to fiction, and the reportage is notably clear-eyed and perceptive. In the discount hell of losers and grifters—with steady infusions of meaty suckers with pinky rings and nametags—which is Las Vegas, Dunne chose to ride out his crack-up, just drifting through and taking notes. The book is bitter and touching at once, utterly compulsive reading. The dialogue is from the bottom of the world, spoken by people who hustle by reflex and have passed caring that the hustle is all they've got. . . .

Dunne's knowingness, his ability to intuit values coldly from the meanest elements of behaviour, make him the most valuable of guides through this weird flatland.

> Peter Straub, "Hot & Cold," in New Statesman (© 1974 The Statesman & Nation Publishing Co. Ltd.), Vol. 88, No. 2276, November 1, 1974, p. 627.*

JUDITH RASCOE

We might have known he'd do something like this. . . .

I wonder if Dunne said, "Eureka!"

That is, I wonder if he woke up in the middle of the night to find *True Confessions* all right there in his head—that priests and detectives, Irish Catholicism of the Fifties, Los Angeles (his home these days), and Harold Pugh had recombined themselves into a tale of fraternal rivalry, politics, and murder. . . .

Probably not. Writers don't have it that easy. . . . Dunne may have had to sweat blood over this book, but the result is one of those novels in which all the elements fit together so aptly and simply and apparently naturally that it seems, like vodka and orange juice, a truly inspired combination. . . .

The author of *True Confessions* is, for my money, a very funny man indeed, and if we weren't in mixed company I'd quote a few of the choicer bits. But the humor is blasphemous, scatological, and obscene. Which is perfectly appropriate to this story of a corrupt homicide detective and his brother, a priest, who share a taste for comedy, high and low; a ghetto instinct for finding the edge; and a fine Irish sense of sin. Two players in a game that includes the police, the construction business, and the archdiocese—and the grisly murder of a dumb and pathetic little hooker whom the papers celebrate as "the virgin tramp."

It's not just a murder story. It's not just funny. It reminds me a little of those novels Graham Greene is pleased to call his "entertainments." You can take them lightly or consider their dark side. Yang and yin. That fine Irish sense of sin is at bottom implacable. That's why we laugh. (p. 106)

True Confessions is about all sorts of confessions: the confessions of nuts who call the police after every big murder and the confessions of priests to other priests and the confession a petty crook makes to a cop outside the gas chamber and the dying confession of a pillar of the community.

You might say that what is at issue, finally, between Detective Lieutenant Tom Spellacy and the Right Reverend Monsignor Desmond Spellacy is who has the greater power to enforce a judgment of sin. . . .

Like George Higgins, J. F. Powers, and the late Edwin O'Connor, John Dunne has the Irish-American talent for writing about politics—in the broad sense of all exercises of power—with relish and wit. He knows how the police and the church both trade in favors and find the means for their ends. . . .

In *The Book of Kells* there's a drawing of two men who sit face to face, tugging at each others' beards; the beards curl upward to disappear into a vast, intricate knot. Only with patience can you trace the line and make out whether the two men are in fact one and the same in substance. So it is with Tom and Des—Cain the hunter and Abel who has the Lord's respect—tugging at either end of the story's thread. Bound together because of and in spite of themselves. "You and me," says Des, "we were always just a couple of harps." (p. 108)

> Judith Rascoe, "Sins of Omission" (reprinted by permission of Wallace & Sheil Agency Inc.; copyright © 1977 by Judith Rascoe), in Harper's, Vol. 255, No. 1530, November, 1977, pp. 106-08.

BENJAMIN STEIN

[In *True Confessions* a] woman has been found murdered in a rundown section of Los Angeles. She has been neatly cut in half and left in a vacant lot; the press seizes upon the murder of "The Virgin Tramp" by a "Werewolf Killer." Beginning with the police, all Irish-Americans, who work on the girl's case, John Dunne weaves a story of the entire Irish-American community in Los Angeles for a few weeks in 1946. It is a story of layer upon complex interconnected layer of venality, corruption, taint, and animal energy seen through the eyes of two of the men intimately involved in the crime and the evils that ripple from it.

The two men are brothers. One is a rapidly rising, ambitious Machiavelli of a Monsignor, bucking for Cardinal. Desmond Spellacy, the Right Reverend Monsignor, would have been perfectly at home with the Borgias. He sees every step of the diocesan chess game three moves ahead. He knows where the power is, and he knows what he wants. Tom Spellacy, his slightly older brother, is a Lieutenant of Detectives, LAPD. He took the police route as the alternative to a life as a fourth-rate prize-fighter. . . .

[The] little Irish-American world revealed in *True Confessions* is the real heart of the book. For while there is a complex and relentless plot, the plot is the vehicle to illustrate a world where human beings struggle and scheme and work to keep themselves one step ahead of their own venality, striving, unsuccessfully, for some kind of grace.

Born and bred devout Catholics, even if they have fallen away, Dunne's people are angry that the world and they are so imperfect. The only successful person in the book is the Cardinal, who has somehow made his peace with the tainted world. That peace will come to Tom and Des Spellacy, too, as they finally let out enough anger to wreck their careers and to send them both into thirty years of searching for a way to reconcile ambition, shame, reality, and salvation. (p. 1440)

[In *True Confessions* Dunne] has reached a brilliant level of literary craftsmanship. His use of ethnic dialect, his ear for the ridiculous and the revealing, yield many treasures. And his gift for recreating the poetry of certain conversational moments gives the book a lyric, elegiac quality as it laments a vanished time, the postwar world when even a lower-middle-class cop could feel some small security in his status.

Dunne has gracefully laid the mantle of humanity over all his characters. There is none so horrible that Dunne does not see in him the possibility of redemption. And this is no small thing in the detective genre wherein *True Confessions* at least partly lies. It is the first bloom of detective theology, and a fine flower. (pp. 1440-41)

Benjamin Stein, "L. A. Lace," in National Review (© National Review, Inc., 1977; 150 East 35th St., New York, NY 10016; reprinted with permission), Vol. XXIX, No. 48, December 9, 1977, pp. 1440-41.

ANTHONY BAILEY

Boston, Massachusetts is sometimes said to be the city where Irish politics found their fullest expression. According to John Gregory Dunne's novel [*True Confessions*], Los Angeles is the city where Irish-American cops and clerics were or possibly are most on the make and take. In fact, Mr Dunne does not quite name LA, though the delimiting geography is all there; and the time remains vague—a year or so after the Second World War. Tom Spellacy, a retired policeman, is looking back from now to then. . . .

There is enough plot here for several seasons of an ethnic cop television series. But Mr Dunne keeps it all jumping; he also keeps counterpointing his already pithy paragraphs with terse one-liners: "He rubbed his ass." "Tom Spellacy lit a cigarette." "The bathroom door opened."

The effect of it all has been such that in the present in which Tom recalls the long flashback that forms most of the book, his wife is in a state mental institution, praying to St Barnabas; his daughter Moira (who weighed 161lb when she was thirteen) is now Sister Angelina; and his son Kev is in "the religious supply game. . . ."

There are disadvantages to having a narrator whose sensibility and style of life are expressed in this way. But Mr Dunne gets a bit beyond Tom's diction, and what one takes at first for a routine piece of sub-Chandlery, by skilful use of his clerical characters. His reverends and right reverends run their churches as businesses, with building funds, loans and endowments, debts temporal as well as spiritual, and connections both on the golf course and in the confessional. It is a secular empire that co-exists with the criminal underworld while profitably harping on what it can do for its parishioners in the after-life. All the abuses and indulgences, of self and others, are here. . . . Possibly not a tragic situation, merely a shoddy and destructive one, which Mr Dunne catches well: the West inhabited by people who have lost their original illusions and will never be able to replace them with anything higher than Tom Spellacy's "You treat people right and they treat you right and you can retire in very nice shape. The golden rule of the police department."

And if the small and the cheap, the constant corruption and sexual ickiness, come to seem a little unvarying, Mr Dunne keeps one hooked with his double suspense: not simply who killed Lois Fazenda but how are Tom and Des going to take their final fall? *True Confessions* has a muscle-bound, dirty-talking strength which suggests that Mr Dunne—stretching his wings a little and looking at the glories as well as the detritus of creation—has it in him to write a first-rate Irish-American novel.

Anthony Bailey, "The Religion Racket," in The Times Literary Supplement (© Times Newspapers Ltd. (London) 1978; reproduced from The Times Literary Supplement by permission), No. 3968, April 21, 1978, p. 433.

SUSAN LARDNER

The very first line [of **"True Confessions"**]—"None of the merry-go-rounds seem to work anymore"—sets a cheerless scene; that line is spoken at a distance of thirty years or so from the main events and hints at happier times, but there is hardly a wisp of cheer in **"True Confessions,"** not counting a large portion of malicious humor. "This is a work of fiction," Dunne declares in a defiant paragraph of introduction. "The author is aware of the anachronisms and ambiguities in the social and cultural punctuation of this book, as he is aware of distortions of time and geography." The reader, on guard against complaining of trivial inaccuracies, gradually begins to suspect that the work of fiction has been produced mainly for the chance to commemorate a virtual antique of a minority group in its own language. The pre-Pope John American Irish are out of political and literary fashion, if not yet extinct, and Dunne has composed a most unsentimental tribute to a seamy side of their way of life.

Apparently more at ease with his characters than with the effort of steering them through a plot, he transmits the dialect in its higher and lower forms—that is, in both the clerical and the constabulary versions, which differ in recourse to polite and tactful expression, having in common an abrupt rhythm, inverted syntax . . . , and a widespread contempt for fellow men and women. . . . The epithets "moron," "dummy," "dumbbell," "numbskull," "knucklehead," and "boob" define the outlook of the novel more exactly than the more ecumenical four-letter words or the frequency of what Mencken called "opprobrious names" for outsiders, mostly directed against blacks but including "harp." . . . Dunne's impersonation falters here and there—in that first line about the merry-go-rounds, for example, which sounds more like a literary tough guy (Pete Hamill came to mind) than the harder-than-hardboiled ex-cop who turns out to be talking. And in the feeling attributed to Tom Spellacy as he investigates the murder, "that everything was connecting in some way he did not understand," which sounds more like an unsteady novelist.

What puzzled me about the book was the shift in the narration from first person to semi-detached third and back, when there seemed no reason not to have left it in first from beginning to end. Dunne doesn't take much advantage of the freedom allowed by the more objective stance. In fact, he sticks so close to the narrow mental confines of his original speaker that the technical problems of pressing the plot through that single character and of somehow representing through him the Church's side of the story might well have been manageable. A beneficial side effect would have been the need to ditch figures of speech like "It was a slum of a relationship surrounded by acres of indifference" and "The broken palm trees along the street all looked as if they had curvature of the spine." But there aren't many lines like those.

Writing about men who are social insiders, Dunne eludes a direct confrontation with the ghost of Raymond Chandler—inevitably conjured up by the subject and the locale. The emotional slum and the deformed palms indicate that Chandler isn't easy to avoid. But Dunne does hold him off. . . . Considered as a composition for voices, **"True Confessions"** is a well-cut slice of real life. As a novel, it has a stiff, uncertain quality, as though characters and ideas had been pushed into place before they had time to ripen. I suppose I am stuck with the thought that Tom Spellacy should have told the story on his own. The last line, which I won't quote, because it is worth reading up to, suggests that Dunne could have pulled it off. (pp. 157-58)

> Susan Lardner, "The Mind's Ear," in The New Yorker (© 1978 by The New Yorker Magazine, Inc.), Vol. LVIII, No. 10, April 24, 1978, pp. 157-58, 161.*

JOHN DRUSKA

About halfway through, *True Confessions* becomes an intriguing read. With the history of the Spellacy brothers' typical escape from an Irish ghetto, via seminary for one, prize-fighting and police department for the other, as backdrop, the mystery of the so-called "Virgin Tramp" murder turns into a fascinating case of detection, as well as an inevitable sequence of revelations about the network of shady and often shared connections that Des and Tom's escape has required of them. By the time the mystery ends in anticlimax, a new fix and Tom's revenge on an old boss from his bagman days, Tom has lost some friends, Des his bishopric, and the reader some of that buoyant sense of voyeurism which mystery creates and which Dunne manages to stir in the middle of his book. . . .

Tom and Des Spellacy seem just a mite more complex than *Extension* comic strip heroes; and the novel's heralded Catholic and political implications appear envisioned at times in a manner akin to a finger-paint version of J. F. Powers or a cartoon remake of *Chinatown,* another Los Angeles tale.

I don't think the simplicity of the novel is Dunne's fault so much as it is a function of his part-time narrator and full-time lead. It may be Dunne's fault that he doesn't capitalize on his character and try for a leaner, *simply* superb police story. Instead of a potboiler, Dunne might have the hardboiled kind of book that George V. Higgins has achieved several times. . . . (p. 315)

The virtues of John Gregory Dunne's non-fiction work suggest how he might have accomplished this sort of novel. Strongest among those virtues is a reportorial distance he maintains, but couples with an openness toward his subjects and the shapes of their experience. His scenes of movie moguls sweating out the previews of *Dr. Dolittle (The Studio)* or of gringo liberals bullshitting in the Delano bar during the Chavez strike (*Delano*) are effective because Dunne convinces us that he is suspending his preconceptions of the people he's depicting; and whatever his present conception, however childish or crass his characters appear, he usually conveys an affectionate interest in them, at least a reluctance to judge overtly, along with a sense of himself as impartial or part partial observer, and of his interest in discovering the truth. From his perspective Dunne is adept at focusing on telling vignettes, that at times connect to create their own significance.

Dunne's non-fiction makes me wonder how *True Confessions* might have sounded had his reportorial technique informed it more fully. Perhaps a version with a greater distancing of the narration from Tom Spellacy but no less engagement with the character and his experience, and a greater dependence on the events of the murder mystery and its aftermath as they happen, from 1946 on, rather than in retrospective frame, to locate the story's shape and ironies. As it is, the telling of *True Confessions* is more contrivance than natural fiction, maybe because Dunne has tried too hard to signify, to frame his characters for us, to explain scenes toward an end, to invent dimensions. *True Confessions* is a middling, big book. Somewhere inside it is a good small book, waiting to get let out like the truth at confession. (pp. 315-16)

> John Druska, in a review of "True Confessions," in Commonweal (copyright © 1978 Commonweal Publishing Co., Inc.; reprinted by permission of Commonweal Publishing Co., Inc.), Vol. CV, No. 10, May 12, 1978, pp. 315-16.

EVAN HUNTER

John Gregory Dunne's new novel [**Dutch Shea Jr.**] has its roots in John O'Hara's *Appointment in Samarra,* George V. Higgins' *Kennedy for the Defense,* James T. Farrell's *Studs Lonigan,* James Joyce's *Ulysses,* and any number of Ross Macdonald's "Lew Archer" mystery novels. For all that, **Dutch Shea, Jr.** is an original: a very serious, very funny, very Irish-Catholic, very suspenseful and—when all is said and done—altogether marvelous book.

Outlining its complicated plot is like trying to describe a spiral staircase without using one's hands. Dutch Shea, Jr. is a criminal lawyer. (A black burglar who breaks into his apartment calls him "some kind of pimp lawyer.") As such, his clients include a man who operates an out-call massage parlor, a woman who has run over her own granddaughter with a power mower, . . . and whichever other flotsam and jetsam of society float his way. . . .

It is the blurring of Shea's professional and *personal* lives, however, that provides the book with its impact and its weight. Three decades ago, Shea's lawyer-father was sent to prison for embezzlement, and subsequently hanged himself in his cell. Young Shea was raised by his father's closest friend, a widower with two children. (p. 3)

Shea is a man who wakes and feels "the fell of dark, not day," a haunted individual clearly at the end of his tether, lonely and desperate and doomed. When his surrogate father gives him a gun after the burglary, we know it will only be a matter of time before he uses it on himself. Why, then, should we bother reading further? Because we hope against hope that Dunne's bright, witty, sad and entirely sympathetic hero will *not* do what we dread he *might* do, and because the novel is so rich in character and detail that we are compelled to turn the pages as rapidly as our fingers can move. At one point, Shea thinks, "My life is a Chinese box full of uninvestigated mysteries." Most of these mysteries are skillfully resolved by Dunne in a style that successfully blends interior monologue with ongoing action, briskly and humorously moving the multi-layered plot forward while simultaneously chronicling Shea's gradual disintegration.

The accidental disinterment of his long-dead father, for example, serves a triple-pronged purpose: we are symbolically reminded of the resurrection of Christ; we are advised that the past is always with us; and we are clued to the fact that history is about to repeat itself. The wake of an Irish fireman, as another example, is perhaps the best such evocation I've ever read, but here again, it serves at the same time to bring Shea close to losing complete control. Similarly, the intrusion of the black burglar graphically sums up the shabby condition of Shea's present existence and—because a gun figures largely in the scene—foreshadows his self-destruction. (pp. 3, 10)

Dunne falters only once in his unraveling of the various mysteries in Shea's life, and unfortunately with the single most important plot thread. I am not giving anything away when I mention the name "Kathleen Donnelly" or when I say that although I scrupulously backtracked her alleged indiscretion through the tangled undergrowth of the past, I was not entirely convinced by Shea's conclusions. I was troubled, too, by some of Dunne's stylistic tricks: the repetition of key words, phrases, or sentences that blink on and off throughout like neon signs outside an all-night L.A. supermarket; the use of brand names to delineate character; the sometimes "Who's-On-First?" exchanges of comic dialogue; the transfer of verbal tics from one character to another, so that some of the people seem interchangeable.

These are minor flaws. Dunne has written a fine novel that examines and dissects a unique individual whom we come to know—and indeed love and admire—as the story unfolds toward its tragic end. By so movingly bringing to life this troubled and complicated man, he has illuminated our own human condition—and that, in the long run, is what good fiction is all about. (p. 10)

Evan Hunter, "The Lawyer in the Lower Depths,"
in Book World—The Washington Post (© 1982, The
Washington Post), March 28, 1982, pp. 3, 10.

GEORGE STADE

John Gregory Dunne, reporter, essayist, novelist, scriptwriter, wry observer of California mores, is best known for two of his five earlier books ["**Vegas**" and "**True Confessions**."] . . . If you liked these earlier books, you will like "**Dutch Shea, Jr.**" For one thing, the heroes of all three books are "people without illusion"—except for the illusion that they are without them.

The detectives among Mr. Dunne's characters are exemplary; like their West Coast ancestors in Hammett, Chandler and Ross MacDonald, they are people who "expected the worst" and to whom "the worst did not mean much," people who "accepted as a given the taint on human nature." Detectives imply mysteries; mysteries imply crime, sin, guilt—and there's plenty of all that in Mr. Dunne's fiction. . . . His new hero, Dutch Shea Jr., is not a detective by profession but by pressure of events, of forces as much within as around him. By profession he is a criminal lawyer "working out of L.A."

The event that turns him into a fisherman of guilt, his own included, occurs in the first sentence of Mr. Dunne's new novel. Dutch Shea's only child, an adopted daughter of 17, is the sole victim of a bomb set off by the I.R.A. . . . This horror conspires with reminders of his father's moral dismemberment and violent death to set off two reciprocal and accelerating processes in Dutch Shea. He begins to see and remember what he had put out of sight and out of mind; he begins to come apart at the seams.

At first he throws himself into his work by way of "chemotherapy for a metastasizing memory." He's known as "the city dump" to his colleagues because he takes on cases no one else will touch. Some of them are doozies. Harriet Dawson, welfare recipient, is an instance. . . . [Anxious] to take her mind off her mind by doing something, anything, she gets to work on the lawn with a power mower stolen by her son. Instead of weeds, she runs over (and kills) her namesake and only joy, her granddaughter Baby Harriet. "Her little fingers were flying all over the lawn." But that's just the beginning. Dutch Shea's interview with her is a setpiece, a little masterpiece of black comedy, the horror, pity and farce somehow increasing each other.

But Dutch Shea's examinations and cross-examinations of cops and whores . . . , are all funny, often chastening, sometimes ghastly, and always deftly handled by Dutch Shea and Mr. Dunne. The latter's knowledge of legal legerdemain, of police, of criminal and courtroom procedure, of forensic medicine and in-chambers fencing, feels like an insider's. The details are precise, unexpected, convincing and full of ironies. Dutch Shea buries his head in the grit and sand of them to hide from all that he does not want to see or remember. (pp. 1, 24)

Dutch Shea Sr. was an embezzler whose scam was exposed by a fire and who was convicted and sentenced to jail, where he hanged himself. He took the rap, however, in an honorable refusal to implicate friends, among whom, as it turns out, was his son's foster father-to-be. Dutch Shea Jr., his father's son in more than the oxymoronic name, is also an embezzler, to the tune of $200,000. Why? To pay off a debt of honor. He is also suicidal. Then a mud slide literally, and symbolically, unearths Dutch Senior's corpse. It is in pieces, like Baby Harriet and Dutch Junior's daughter.

By now some 20 characters are caught in the turns and baffles of Mr. Dunne's mazy plot. Six varieties of shyster, aspiring pols, mobsters, underhanded undertakers, professional mourners, media priests, feminist nuns, horny greenhorns from County Galway, lace-curtain prudes, a low-minded comedian, a high-minded lady judge who has sometimes a pistol under her robes and sometimes her boyfriend, Dutch Shea—all these are implicated in Dutch Shea's cases, all implicated in the mysteries of his natural father's death and his adopted daughter's birth. You won't have any trouble telling these many characters apart. They're a vivid bunch, these wits and butts, each in his own way. Each has his own manner of speaking. And the talk, as in everything Mr. Dunne writes, is music to the ear and truer than true to life—and a good thing, too. If we spoke like Mr. Dunne's characters, we would reveal ourselves entirely.

Like the characters and the dialogue, the shapely yet elaborate plot is something to be enjoyed for its own sake rather than for its implications. Its coincidences, symmetries and sudden gatherings-up of what seem like loose strands do not imply a benevolent providence, as in Dickens; or a psychological determinism, as in Kafka; or an implacable force brooding over an inscrutable intention, as in Conrad; or a paranoid epistemology, as in Pynchon; or that God is an artist, as in Nabokov; or the absurdity of existence, as in all the Vonnegutterlings and Garpists. Very shyly, the coils and recoils of the plot just manage to imply a slow return of the repressed, as in life. More boldly, Mr. Dunne's bravura plotting asserts an exhilarating mastery in the face of gratuitous risk, as with trapeze artists. That's good enough for me.

But it's not always good enough for Mr. Dunne. If the plotting, characterization and dialogue are masterly, patches of narrative and of Dutch Shea's interior monologue are derivative and artsy, as though Mr. Dunne thought that someone might take him for a mere entertainer. We get Dutch Shea's thoughts in snappy little sentence fragments. Cumulatively, however, these fragments lose much of their snap. The reason, in part, is that they are not organized by a characterizing rhythm, by the sound of someone talking to himself. Mr. Dunne seldom manages to fuse, in a single phrase, the effects of perception, memory, thought and unconscious stirrings as does his ultimate source James Joyce. As the novel goes on, eruptions of involuntary memory increasingly fill Dutch Shea's consciousness. We then get page-long stacks of sentence snips, each its own paragraph, each grabbing us by the lapels, each claiming through position and reiteration a weight we become reluctant to grant.

A resulting oddity is that of all the characters only the main one has no voice of his own. He remains in the mind as a kind of mosaic of memory bits grouted loosely together by attitudes derived from Hemingway via Raymond Chandler. Dutch Shea has less impact on us than what he sees has. We are not as moved by his grief, by his quirky integrity and hard-won lucidity as Mr. Dunne wants us to be.

But all that is to judge this book by very high standards—the kind, though, that it solicits. It may well be that its reach exceeds its grasp; just the same, this year is not likely to offer us many American novels better than **"Dutch Shea, Jr."** (p. 24)

> George Stade, "A Fisherman of Guilt," in The New York Times Book Review (copyright © 1982 by The New York Times Company; reprinted by permission), March 28, 1982, pp. 1, 24.

THOMAS M. GANNON

Like *True Confessions, Dutch Shea, Jr.* is a tale of moral decay in an Irish-American Catholic setting. Its author's gifts lie in the areas of comedy and social observation; he finds sardonic hilarity in the gritty texture of his characters' lives. Dunne is less effective, however, as creator of an adequately motivated protagonist, and his somber theme—the unendurable sadness, cruelty and capriciousness of life in our time—is neither original with him nor organic to his material here. As a result, ***Dutch Shea, Jr.,*** while a triumph of darkly comic writing, is not a wholly satisfying novel. . . .

Dunne's comic talent is on display throughout the novel. Its gamy dialogue is studded with jokes that are racial, ethnic, sexual or scatological, yet mordantly funny. Many of Dunne's characters, like the pathetic celebrity priest who conducts gourmet pilgrimages to the Catholic shrines of Europe, and the business-like pimp who dispatches the girls from his outcall massage agencies with credit card imprinters, are models of bleakly humorous invention. And his comic set-pieces—for example, Shea's confused, rambling interview with a drunken, despairing black woman who has inadvertently run over her infant granddaughter with a power mower—are grotesquely hilarious.

Dunne has a sharp eye for certain aspects of Catholic life. What Catholic has not, at one time or another, either ducked out, or wished he or she had ducked out, of a wake before the rosary began? Dutch Shea, Jr. spends his rosary time on the funeral parlor's veranda, discussing plea-bargaining with a pot-smoking colleague. Some of Dunne's perceptions are dated, though; he has Shea slip out of church before the Last Gospel. Dunne is thoroughly familiar with the grubby realities of the criminal justice system as well, and Shea is a believably skilled criminal lawyer. His dealings with clients and witnesses and judges and private detectives have an authentic ring.

As a plausibly motivated human being, however, Shea is less convincing. In that border area of the novel where character and action work on each other to determine plot development, Dunne loses his otherwise sure touch. . . . And Shea's passivity is extraordinary. In one notable instance, he has known for 30 years that the man who raised him after his father's death was somehow involved in the events that led to the suicide. Not until the end of the novel does Shea seek to learn the nature of the involvement. That is a little late.

Perhaps life is as unspeakably sad and cruel and capricious as Shea perceives it to be, but Dunne has not provided his protagonist with sufficient dramatic reason to make that judgment. And precisely because Shea's conduct lacks solid artistic justification, this novel is only a limited success. Eminently worth reading for its comedy, it is not fully believable as tragedy.

> *Thomas M. Gannon, in a review of "Dutch Shea, Jr." (reprinted with permission of America Press, Inc. and the author; © 1982; all rights reserved), in* America, *Vol. 147, No. 3, July 31, 1982, p. 58.*

JEFFREY BRODRICK

That body over there that just blew up—that's Dutch Shea Jr.'s daughter, or what's left of her. Dutch is our hero [in ***Dutch Shea, Jr.***]. Who's his favorite person? The one joy in his life? His daughter, of course, except she just blew up in the first sentence. Terrorists got her in a restaurant. Dutch made the reservation. And just so you know where we're heading—we're going *down*. Welcome to John Gregory Dunne country: Catholics, pimps, arsonists, bad fate.

As befits a book whose climax is in its first sentence, Dunne presents not so much a plot that unfolds as a character that unravels. Once the bomb goes off we do little more than follow the vibrations, the shudders, through Dutch's head. Dutch doesn't blow up, he collapses inward for the remaining 352 pages of the novel. Dutch Shea Jr. is broken from page one. He's a cooked bird and he doesn't even care.

At the same time, nonetheless, Dutch is one very cool cuke, one of the coolest, most offbeat heroes since—well, it's as if Holden Caulfield got tough and went to law school after running numbers for the mob for twenty years and working out in Harlem. Dunne's strongest character to date? That's like calling Willie Mays the best outfielder the Giants ever had. Dutch Shea Jr. is an inverted powerhouse who's in total control in the courtroom. He wins cases for absurd pimps. He dismantles prosecution witnesses effortlessly. Nothing fazes this guy: he's untouchable, he never flinches. . . .

Dutch Shea Jr. was born to take the rap just like his father. Is this why we love him? Because he acquiesces in his fate, a loser by choice, utterly resigned and without ambition or malice? Dutch remembers too much for his own good. I am a victim of memory, he says. (p. 965)

They visit him every other second, it seems, these memories, and he can't kick them out—he makes love to his girlfriend and thinks about his wife. You could make a board game out of this novel, there are so many subliminal mysteries loose in Dutch's head. Everybody is connected. Dunne has created a sinister and incestuous web.

In fact this may be one of those works more brilliant than it is entertaining or even feasible: like listening to the Sex Pistols for more than twenty seconds—genius, okay, but why hurt yourself? Dunne is playing with magnets, never letting them touch. The tension in Dutch's head over his wife is mindboggling. But it's all in his head. He never sees her. They do fight on the telephone every night. God, to have them meet—the pages would spark up.

Dutch almost spoils the novel for us. It is such a weird book: at once thriller, comedy, farce, absurdly sleazy and morose. When he released his delightful collection of essays, *Quintana & Friends* . . . , Dunne confessed to being a mimic from an early age. This talent shows up here in the form of some hip, scatological dialogue, wacky, vivid voices, and more livewire characters than in any one novel since Thackeray: underworld, underbelly riffraff to the max. A gangster just out of the slammer tells Dutch he wants to date his ex-wife. "You wouldn't have her number, would you, Dutch?" When Dutch defends a woman facing manslaughter charges for running over a baby with a power mower it's clear some contradictory instincts are at work: Dunne the Hollywood pro is unable to stop himself from turning out a little skit for us. Should we be laughing? Or comparing John Gregory Dunne to Faulkner for writing the best first 42 pages of any novel in the last ten years?

Yet ultimately Dunne just wears us down. It's not that there's too much doom, but too much interior. Unlike *True Confessions,* not enough people absorb the madness; the tensions are played out internally. As it is, it's a whole novel given to one man's ruin. (pp. 965-66)

Jeffrey Brodrick, "Doomtown," in National Review *(© National Review, Inc., 1982; 150 East 35th St., New York, NY 10016; reprinted with permission), Vol. XXXIV, No. 15, August 6, 1982, pp. 965-66.*

MARION GLASTONBURY

Early socialist fears of thought-control by business interests manipulating technology seem amply justified today. Modern American fiction is furnished with brand-names. Slogans punctuate dialogue. Dreams are peopled by celebrities. The eponymous protagonist of **Dutch Shea Jr**, a divorced lawyer with a clientele of micks and mafiosi, keeps the television on in his bedroom as a nightlight, so, when an armed intruder enters, violence in the dark mingles with a shoot-out on the screen. The staccato patter of wisecracks and gunfire in this sort of comedy often gets commended as 'gutsy'. Indeed, entrails are prominently featured throughout. Carbuncles fester; a colostomy complicates rape. A baby is dismembered by a lawnmower; a flooded cemetery disgorges the corpse of a convict, Shea's father. His daughter, blown to bits when the IRA bombs a London restaurant, lands in a sorbet dish. . . .

Why should a novelist of obvious wit and energy write as if satire were in competition with snuff movies? The traditional art of 'getting inside a character' is here taken literally, and the urge to penetrate human identity via the mucous membranes leads straight to the morgue. Among members of the cast saved from decomposition, my favourite is Clarice from the convent, whose consultancy service helps ex-nuns to package themselves for a second career. But Dunne is not consistently irreverent. Shea's last words are, 'I believe in God.' So far, intimate confessions have revealed only carnal knowledge. The stream of consciousness is a body-fluid; the health of the soul lies in the medicine cabinet: 'She had Comprazine suppositories and Septra DS for systitis and Hydro Diuril for premenstrual symptoms and Naturetin-K for bloat'. If pharmacology has coopted the inner life, what is left for literature to analyse?

Marion Glastonbury, "Plain Terms," in New Statesman *(© 1982 The Statesman & Nation Publishing Co. Ltd.), Vol. 104, No. 2686, September 10, 1982, p. 24.*

ADAM MARS-JONES

Corruption in [*Dutch Shea, Jr.*] is more than a theme; it is something of an obsession, almost an infatuation. . . . There is much mutilation and decay, plentiful autopsies and accidents, and though the life of a pimp lawyer is unlikely to be savoury in all its details, the glee behind the disgust becomes disturbing.

Even when there is no obvious occasion for revulsion, no severed nipple, no shredded baby, Dunne finds ways of letting the corruptible body know just what he thinks of it. It excretes, therefore it is. It bleeds, it farts, it develops blackheads. At funerals it sneezes, spraying the flag with mucus. It has cellulite deposits on its thighs. . . .

The reader must be quite an aficionado of mucus properly to enjoy this book. Even when there is discharge aplenty on the level of action, the book further insists upon it. . . . But is this agonized suppurating Catholicism, as advertised, or something quite different? Does this book represent a tortured view of human existence, or merely a canny view of bookbuying America?

Only in one area does the disgust let up.

Cat.

Cat is the daughter killed by the IRA. . . . When Cat died, Dutch stopped caring. He let things slide. He started using the short sentence. All the time.

Because Cat was different. She called butterflies "flybutters". She wrote her first poem at the age of seven. She called fear and death and the unknown The Broken Man. . . .

Cat, in other words, is cute, and as a focus of values in the novel she is a disaster. There must be better ways of loading a dice than applying smegma to five of its faces, and sugar to the sixth. To make his mixture of disgust and sentiment plausible, if not palatable, Dunne employs a single device: the self-lacerating wisecrack. Cat was eighteen when she died. Volvo dealers claim their car has a life expectancy of 17.9 years. So: "Who would have thought she had the life expectancy of a Volvo?" This phrase is repeated three times in two pages. You see? He feels so deeply that he must pretend to feel nothing. His, you understand, is a tragic coarseness. The book also contains a disgusting stand-up comic, Jackie Gross, intended to make Dutch seem fastidious. But every character has alienated one-liners to deliver, in the same street-wise rhythm.

The book has plenty of plot, most of it concerning the parentage of Cat, whom the Sheas adopted. As the action proceeds, Dutch makes stylized announcements about his life . . . like a hard-boiled inner-city Oedipus; but there is no feeling of unmasking or development. The cheaply ironical tone remains constant through all the legal jargon, the medical details, the lists of brand names and the never-ending wisecracks.

Once or twice, Dunne achieves an effect of some eeriness and power. One of Dutch's clients, for example, admits that he has strangled a pair of hamsters because they were "hassling" him. Perhaps it's just the refreshing change after so much hollow human horror, but those extinguished rodents are the most affecting thing in the book.

Dutch Shea, Jr. pretends to analyse corruption, political, social and moral, but its real ambitions are much humbler. Ignore the epigraphs from Hopkins and Waugh. John Gregory Dunne isn't exposing the spiritual emptiness of modern life, he isn't even strangling the hamsters that hassle him (worldly clerics, liberals). He is turning disgust into another cheap thrill, and fetishizing what he claims to denounce.

Adam Mars-Jones, "Ugliest Is Best," in The Times Literary Supplement *(© Times Newspapers Ltd. (London) 1982; reproduced from* The Times Literary Supplement *by permission), No. 4146, September 17, 1982, p. 992.*

Umberto Eco
1932-

Italian scholar, editor, and novelist.

Known primarily among scholars for his works in the field of semiotics and as a medievalist, Eco gained wider recognition with the publication of his first novel, *Il nome della rosa* (1980; *The Name of the Rose*). Set in a Benedictine abbey in Northern Italy in 1327, this work is an intricately plotted "semiotic" murder mystery that can be read on many levels. It is at once a gothic thriller, a novel of ideas, and an elaborate recreation of medieval life and political and religious thought. Eco is especially acclaimed by critics for his ability to maintain with equal effectiveness the different levels of meaning of *The Name of the Rose*. Through the creation of his ingenious plot and the portrayal of his character's spiritual and intellectual conflict, he is able to fully engage the reader's interest in his tale. The novel is unanimously praised as a beautifully constructed work of both scholarship and the imagination.

(See also *Contemporary Authors*, Vols. 77-80.)

© Jerry Bauer

MASOLINO D'AMICO

There is something of the sleuth in any scholar; small wonder, therefore, that one as flamboyantly articulate as Umberto Eco should have successfully turned his talents to the writing of a detective story, *Il nome della rosa*. But this, Eco's first novel, is no mere detective story; rather, its framework serves as a vehicle for nothing less than a *summa* of all the author knows about the Middle Ages—and all he wishes us to know. . . . Eco's rare gift for epitome has a chance to shine forth in this book and his own delight in his task is often infectious. At the same time, this very delight carries a risk: one is intermittently reminded of novels by Jules Verne such as *Around the Moon*, in which the author's desire to impart knowledge has carried him away, and leaves the reader toiling along behind, a little baffled. Still, like Verne, Eco exhibits a winning confidence in his own power to recapture our attention.

Much ingenuity has gone into the plot. The action is set in a major Benedictine abbey in Northern Italy, in the turbulent year 1327. All over Europe the Church is persecuting the so-called Fraticelli, followers of a lapsed Franciscan, fra' Dolcino who was burnt at the stake twenty years earlier, and whose advocacy of total poverty may, it is feared, cause anarchy, and undermine the secular power of the Church. For this very reason the Emperor is encouraging the movement. A Franciscan brother, an Englishman with the Holmesian name of Guglielmo da Baskerville (his Watson, called Adso, tells the story; these, and the novel's Shakespearean title, are by no means Eco's only homage to English culture) arrives at the abbey to act as mediator between the forces of tolerance and the Pope's inquisitor, the chief persecutor of the Dolcinians, who is due to stop there on his way to the South. The newcomers find the abbey in turmoil after the sudden and violent death of a monk, and Baskerville is asked to revive his once famous gift for investigation, and throw light on the crime before the notables arrive. He does solve the murder, though not before several more monks have been similarly dispatched, seemingly in keeping with a crazy pattern based on the Book of Revelations. At the end of the story the abbey itself is reduced to ashes.

The murders are all connected with the exclusive, well-defended nerve-centre of the abbey, the library. . . . It is soon apparent that the victims have all come into contact with a certain dangerous codex, whose contents are disclosed only at the end.

Eco makes it clear that he is not aiming to create suspense—indeed, the deaths and other *coups de théâtre* are announced in the chapter-headings. But the novel is cunningly constructed, especially the description of the all-important and secret layout of the forbidden library whose architecture is a representation, as it were, of all available doctrine, sacred and profane. Nightly, and by slow degrees, this labyrinth reveals its mysteries to the investigator—a modern man pitting his cool intelligence against a medieval puzzle; in the process we are given long and often absorbing insights into that age—its history, its predicaments, its intricate politics and religious wars, its philosophy, mythology, science, handicrafts, cuisine, medicine and sorcery. Faithful to medieval taste, there are also elaborate catalogues of herbs, monsters, heresies, prodigies, superstitions, and so on; sometimes compelling, sometimes entertaining, but sometimes exasperating. . . .

But no one will quarrel with the book's main point, which is to vindicate humour. While the learned dispute the question whether Jesus ever laughed, the villain of the piece goes to inordinate lengths to conceal from the world Aristotle's defence of comedy. For this is the explosive codex which must be kept hidden at all costs; the murderer believes havoc would result if it came to light. Eco's English detective takes the opposite view and like him we are inclined to blame the age's ferocity and misery on its lack of humour. Who will not side with Baskerville and his efforts to keep at least one spark of the fire of comedy alive? The final loss of the great library is sad, but perhaps no culture at all is preferable to a culture parsimoniously transmitted, and falsified in the process, by gloomy madmen.

> Masolino D'Amico, "Medieval Mirth," in The Times Literary Supplement (© Times Newspapers Ltd. (London) 1981; reproduced from The Times Literary Supplement by permission), No. 4058, January 9, 1981, p. 29.

GIAN-PAOLO BIASIN

On the cover of Eco's novel **Il nome della rosa** there is the outline of the labyrinth which one appeared on the floor of the Reims cathedral, and which was destroyed during the eighteenth century because children made a playful use of the maze and disturbed the sacred functions "for evidently perverse ends." Hence, from its very appearance, Eco's novel is posited under two signs: the labyrinth as an artistic structure, and play as transgression. Both are at the core of the book and explain its powerful appeal.

Thematically, the labyrinth is the form of the library of an abbey in northern Italy in the year of the Lord 1327, where seven consecutive murders take place in a mysterious connection with the quest for a lost (and forbidden) volume, Aristotle's second book of poetics, dealing with laughter and comedy. Almost until the end, a blind and fearsome Benedictine friar, Jorges da Burgos, defies the reasoned efforts of a Sherlock-Holmesian Dominican friar, Guglielmo da Baskerville, to trace the murders to the lost volume in the labyrinthine library. The events are faithfully recorded by another friar, the old Adso da Melck, who witnessed them as a young novice. . . . But in the process the narrator conveys an incredible mass of *medievalia*. . . . (p. 449)

Play is at the core of the plot because it is forbidden and hidden in the abbey's library, the site of serious knowledge. . . . But play should also be considered at a metanarrative level. In fact Eco, who started his scholarly career with a study of Thomas Aquinas, won many bets with his latest book: **Il nome della rosa** can be read as a gothic novel, a thriller, a novel of ideas, even an allegory. Although the author disclaims any intention of having written something that connects his fictional world with our own present, it is sufficient to go back and read an essay of his, **"Il Medioevo è già cominciato"** . . . , to see that for Eco "the model of the Middle Ages can be useful for understanding what is happening today"; just to give two examples, the reciprocal accusations between Benedictines and Dominicans are compared to those between Stalinists and Trotskyites, and medieval logic is said to be "close" to structuralism. Eco also won a linguistic bet: his novel is filled with Latin quotations, yet it is pleasant and easy to read, highly communicative; the logic of the plot with its denouements does not detract anything from pensive and poetic moments (and vice versa). For instance, here is the conclusion, which throws light on the whole book and its title: "It is cold in the scriptorium, my thumb aches. I leave my writing, I don't know for whom, I no longer know about what: stat rosa pristina nomine, nomina nuda tenemus." The words of the Latin quotation . . . seem to echo the concerns of the modern semiotician: the primeval rose stands, exists as a name, we only have bare names. That is the serious conclusion of an extended, literate, learned, labyrinthine play. (pp. 449-50)

> Gian-Paolo Biasin, in a review of "Il nome della rosa," in World Literature Today (copyright 1981 by the University of Oklahoma Press), Vol. 55, No. 3, Summer, 1981, pp. 449-50.

FRANCO FERRUCCI

Using both intelligence and flexibility, [Mr. Eco] has become the spokesman of a philosophical trend that could be labeled as a kind of "neo-enlightenment." His approach entails methodological doubting versus dogmatism, and the use of parody and irony against sectarian thought; his idea of culture is that it is mainly a channel of interdisciplinary exchange rather than a provider of certainties or a chapel for hermetic and initiatory rites.

But that description is already a beginning of an interpretation of Mr. Eco's novel. **"The Name of the Rose"** takes place in the 14th century. In some of his essays Mr. Eco has linked that century with our age, with all of its certainties weakened under the combined blows of new sciences and contradictory social events. Aptly enough, the novel is a *mystery,* the most rationalist of all literary genres, based on a determination to reach irrefutable, if partial, truth: Who is the assassin and what are his motives? And what *signs* will help to unravel the mystery?

In the novel, William of Baskerville, the protagonist, has been called to investigate a crime in a Benedictine abbey. Like Sherlock Holmes, William comes from England—not from Scotland Yard, however, but from the philosophical school of Roger Bacon and William of Occam, the founders of cognitive empiricism, a philosophy based on the exact examination of real evidence revealed by the senses and thus a perfect tool for unraveling a mystery. It is to these men that our learned and ironic monk-detective constantly refers.

The story is narrated by Adso, a novice who is young and whose admiration of William is naïve. . . . Adso speaks in the name of a faith that William has probably lost. The old biblical problem, about whether the first sin was a forbidden pursuit of knowledge or a sin of disobedience, finds no answer. Does the passion for knowledge derive from loss of faith? Or, in today's terms: Does semiotics derive from loss of certainty in unshakable truth?

The assassin himself gives us an answer when he finally confesses the reasons for his crimes. His motivations deal with a poetic and philosophic problem that I cannot reveal without being unfair to the reader. It is enough to say that wild theological discussions develop between William of Baskerville and the murderer. After the discovery of the culprit, the novel explodes with pyrotechnic inventions, literally as well as figuratively. Hold on till the end.

The narrative impulse that commands the story is irresistible. That is no mean feat for a book in which many pages describe ecclesiastical councils or theological debates, and many others analyze in detail the positions of European powers regarding the reform of the Franciscan Order. There are also frequent quotations in classic and medieval Latin. Yet Mr. Eco's delight in his narrative does not fail to touch the reader, who may or may not choose to be intrigued with the levels of interpretation crisscrossing in front of him as in a semiotic labyrinth. After all, for a semiologist like Mr. Eco, a sleuth's pursuit of the truth behind a murder mystery involves also the pursuit of meaning—in words, symbols, ideas, every conceivable sign the visible universe contains.

I shall point out just one hidden path as an example. It is certainly possible to read **"The Name of the Rose"** as a novel in which every character and event find an equivalent in today's world. In many ways this is a *roman à clef*. Those pages dedicated to heretical movements in the Middle Ages—two stories in the novel are about Brother Dolcino and Brother Michael, heretics burned alive, along with their followers, by the Inquisition—have clear references to contemporary attempts at revolution in different countries and the harsh repression of those efforts. In addition, the trial of the cellarer in this novel reveals analogies with Stalin's purges: savage self-accusations, brainwashing and all.

Different levels of meaning pervade the microcosm of the book. In New York two months ago I met a friend of Mr. Eco, a scholar who, not having published any books, cannot find an academic appointment. I am sure I recognize in him the model of a minor character of this novel—"a most voracious reader, he knew by heart all the books in the library, but he had a strange infirmity: he was unable to write. They called him Abbas agraphicus.''

Many similar games are there for the reader to discover. He may decide not to play any of the games but to be carried along instead by the élan of the narration. He will have to make a choice between Adso and William. It is almost too obvious that William is Mr. Eco himself. But he is Eco the philosopher and essayist, while the Eco who writes **"The Name of the Rose"** is Adso: a voice young and old at the same time, speaking from nostalgia for love and passion. William shapes the story with his insight; Adso gives it his own pathos. He will never think, as William does, that "books are not made to be believed but to be subjected to inquiry"; Adso writes to be believed.

I, for one, go along with Adso. After all, even if it is William who solves the mystery, it is Adso who makes possible the memory of the events. In writing this book, Mr. Eco himself may have discovered that the real memory of things lies in passion. Adso's is the only love story, an encounter with a maiden who is, in the words of the "Song of Solomon," "beautiful and terrible as an army arrayed for battle." His are the intense religious feelings evoked by the sight of the Great Door of the abbey's church. He is the one who has a great dream or vision toward the end of the book. William explains to him the philosophical meaning of all these experiences after Adso has devotedly told his friend what has happened.

There is only one event for which William would probably not give any clue. In the last page of the book Adso, grown old, foresees his own death in poetic terms: "I shall soon enter this broad desert, perfectly level and boundless, where the truly pious heart succumbs in bliss. I shall sink into the divine shadow, in a dumb silence and an ineffable union." In reading these lines there came back to me a reflection I found in one of Mr. Eco's essays: that death is the only reality for which there is no semiotic interpretation. Other than that, it seems William has always something to teach Adso. (pp. 20-1)

Franco Ferrucci, "Murder in the Monastery," in The New York Times Book Review (copyright © 1983 by The New York Times Company; reprinted by permission), June 5, 1983, pp. 1, 20-1.

MICHAEL DIRDA

The Name of the Rose [is] a novel of murder, politics and ideas that has rightly become an acclaimed European best seller.

Late in 1327 a Franciscan, William of Baskerville, accompanied by the novice Adso of Melk, journeys to an unnamed Benedictine monastery to arrange a meeting of detente between representatives of Pope John and Emperor Louis. Just as master and disciple arrive at the abbey, a young monk commits suicide under suspicious circumstances. The worldly abbot asks the Sherlock Holmes-like Franciscan—a disillusioned inquisitor and former pupil of Roger Bacon—to investigate the shadowy affair. To this end, William is granted free run of the establishment—except for the library, the finest in all Christendom. Malachi the librarian and his assistant prohibit any direct access to the fragile illuminated manuscripts. And if a man were to try to enter the locked tower rooms? "No one," replies the abbot, "even if he wished, would succeed. The library defends itself, immeasurable as the truth it houses, deceitful as the falsehood it preserves. A spiritual labyrinth, it is also a terrestrial labyrinth. You might enter and you might not emerge."

Ah, now that's the kind of demonic book room that Jorge Luis Borges might imagine. And indeed, William and Adso soon meet the ancient blind monk Jorge de Burgos, whose name and bookishness recall the Argentine fabulist (as does the novel's learned preface about how the author researched Adso's manuscript). Such homage whispers, *sub rosa*, that Eco's novel aims to be modernist as well as medieval, to reflect both the time of its action and the time of its telling. William, for example, embodies a spirit of tolerance and scientific inquiry, that of the approaching Renaissance; he consequently appears a relatively modern man surrounded by religious fanatics, many of these actual historical figures. In the course of his detecting this relentless bloodhound of Baskerville meets, for instance, the mystic Ubertino of Casale, the inquisitor Bernard of Gui, the general of the Franciscans Michael of Cesena, and followers of the Italian leveler, Fra Dolcino. Each of these believes he possesses the Truth; yet their voices and vociferations resonate in 20th-century ears with the stridency of born-again evangelicals, fascists, corporation climbers, Marxist fellow-travelers.

The mirroring of now-in-then seems peculiarly appropriate in *The Name of the Rose* for such a technique mimics the figural or typological thinking common to the Middle Ages. . . . So too this novel can be read as a poetic synthesis of the early 14th century, and as oblique commentary on the excesses of the 20th. Adso, for instance, learns about the various cults that take fire from Joachim of Flora's vision of an earthly paradise, but modern readers also learn the timeless character and appeal of a revolutionary ideology. Such rich, implicitly ironic textuality might be expected from Eco . . . , yet even his seemingly ultra-modern academic discipline finds its roots in monastic learning and patristic exegesis. The Bible and the Universe are God's two great scriptures, and in them we may read his message to the world—though their intricate symbols must first be properly understood on several levels, including the anagogical and eschatological.

Especially the eschatological. For like the theological thrillers of Charles Williams, *The Name of the Rose* returns obsessively to John's vision of apocalypse. The various heresies that the monks practice or discuss—and this is a talky novel, in the vein of Mann or Murdoch—all derive from a chiliastic foreboding that traditional hierarchies are being upset by new ideas, new ways. The theme of The World Turned Upside Down occurs pervasively: in allusions to the topsy-turvy realms of Cockaigne, Saturnalia, the *Coena Cypriani,* and Carnival, in unnatural love between monks, in the leveling character of the various heretical movements, in the triumph of inductive reasoning over a priori reliance on received authority, in Aristotle deposing the Church Fathers, even in the new-fangled inventions that William makes passing mention of: gunpowder, the compass, spectacles, paper, the sextant, flying machines. All the signs suggest that breakup of the great chain of being which will herald the Last Days. Slyly, even the novel's preface alludes to such millennial fantasies, for Eco tells us that he "translated" this manuscript in 1968—at the very time a youthful revolutionary populism was overturning the old order, hoping to forestall a fiery Armageddon and establish the new Jerusalem.

In his investigations William comes to realize that the secret of the abbey is somehow intertwined with the Biblical revelation to John. After the first death, there is a second, and a third; the murderer's modus operandi seems to derive from, almost to copy religiously, the opening of the Seven Seals. Even more disquieting, behind all the ritual killings looms a book, a book to rival the Ark of the Covenant in its awesome power. But to find that dread manuscript, William and Adso must penetrate the forbidden library, solve its riddles, and find their way to a hidden *sanctum sanctorum.*

Such Gothic hugger-mugger—part Borges, part John Dickson Carr—lightens Eco's operatic gravity, especially when the reader might begin to weary of visionary rapture or philosophical and theological wrangling. Number symbolism, alchemical secrets, the language of gems, pagan love charms, a linguistic Quasimodo, and the clockwork of a life ordered by the Benedictine rule further enhance the supernatural atmosphere. So too does the religious imagery, and the interlacing of vernacular and Vulgate. (pp. 5, 14)

In its range, *The Name of the Rose* suggests an imaginative *summa,* an alchemical marriage of murder mystery and Christian mystery. It conveys remarkably the desperation of a dying culture, while at the same time touching on perennial issues of love, religion, scholarship and politics. Even an occasional reliance on coincidence and fortuitous revelation strengthen its medieval aura, its convincing recreation of a way of life now lost. As Adso writes at the end of his chronicle—quoting a 12th-century poem about the passing of Babylon and Rome—*Stat rosa pristina nomine, nomina nuda tenemus.* The rose of yore is but a name, mere names are left to us. Yes and no, for through Umberto Eco's prodigious necromancy some of those names live again. Unforgettably. (p. 14)

> Michael Dirda, "The Letter Killeth and the Spirit Giveth Life," *in* Book World—The Washington Post *(© 1983,* The Washington Post*), June 19, 1983, pp. 5, 14.*

JEFFREY SCHAIRE

In *The Name of the Rose,* [Eco's] first work of fiction, he has bestowed his own talents lavishly on his created sleuth. William knows that "the universe is talkative . . . and it speaks not only of the ultimate things (which it does always in an obscure fashion) but also of closer things, and then it speaks quite clearly." His acumen in deciphering the secret signs of the world would be sufficient delight, but Eco's complex themes include sparkling disquisitions on the arts of the Middle Ages—its architecture, manuscript illumination, gemmology, herbarism, numerology, cuisine, and witchcraft, as well as witty and erudite depictions of its manners, morals, and intricately twined politics and theology.

Eco has done more than create a learned diversion. *The Name of the Rose* (like *One Hundred Years of Solitude* and *Pale Fire*) is a mirrored hallway; each strand of the tale is in some sense merely a reflection, a blind alley, a red herring. As the clues proliferate and William and Adso approach the heart of the labyrinth, so do the possibilities of what they may find there. Yet, as they follow one red herring after another, the riddle is nonetheless resolved, and its solution reveals Eco's novel to be an eloquent *speculum mundi* of our own age. *The Name of the Rose* is an antidetective-story detective story; as a semiotic murder mystery it is superbly entertaining; it is also an extraordinary work of novelistic art. (p. 76)

> *Jeffrey Schaire, in a review of "The Name of the Rose," in* Harper's *(copyright © 1983 by* Harper's Magazine; *all rights reserved; reprinted from the August, 1983 issue by special permission), Vol. 267, No. 1599, August, 1983, pp. 75-6.*

William (Cuthbert) Faulkner
1897-1962

(Born William Cuthbert Falkner) American novelist, short story writer, poet, scriptwriter, and essayist.

Faulkner is a seminal figure in modern American literature. Specifically, his works reflect the distinct heritage of the American South. The northern region of Mississippi where Faulkner lived all his life provided the geographical and cultural background for the Yoknapatawpha County of his novels and short stories. But only in a superficial sense can Faulkner be considered a regional writer: through their radical stylistic innovations and moral depth his works achieve a universality which places him among the major figures of world literature. Faulkner received the Nobel Prize in literature for 1949. In his acceptance speech, Faulkner stated that his basic theme was "the human heart in conflict with itself," and his exploration of this theme resulted in a variety of highly original, often difficult literary techniques expressing the full spectrum of human experience.

While Faulkner's importance rests almost solely on his fiction, his first ambition was to be a poet. His poems were published in various periodicals and collected in *The Marble Faun* (1924), Faulkner's earliest full-length book. Although the collection drew scant notice at the time, it is now considered of interest as an early display of the stylistic qualities Faulkner later developed in his fiction. For example, pastoral imagery and frequent use of symbol and image are characteristic of both his poetry and his prose. *The Marble Faun* was followed by the publication of Faulkner's first two novels, *Soldier's Pay* (1926) and *Mosquitoes* (1927), neither of which received much critical response. *Soldier's Pay* is categorized as a "lost generation" novel because it centers on a physically and emotionally scarred young soldier who returns home from war and finds only further trauma and disillusionment. *Mosquitoes* features a character type that reappears throughout Faulkner's work—the individual who lives a life of unfulfilled hope but strives to endure, even in grief. The necessity to struggle and to endure is central to Faulkner's view of human existence. In his famous Nobel Prize acceptance speech, he stated: "I believe that man will not only endure: he will prevail."

With the publication of his third novel, *Sartoris* (1929), Faulkner won greater critical attention. *Sartoris* is considered by many to be the first "typical Faulkner novel," primarily because it is set in Yoknapatawpha County and displays a full array of storytelling techniques, but also for the tragic fate of its protagonist, Bayard Sartoris. Many of Faulkner's later works develop stories that he touched upon in *Sartoris*. In 1929, Faulkner also published *The Sound and the Fury,* a novel about the disintegration of the Compson family. The story is told through four separate points of view in a seemingly disjointed narrative that gradually reveals its meaning. Critics were impressed by the complicated structure of the novel, especially the opening section told from the viewpoint of the idiot man-child Benjy. However, the difficulty of fathoming Faulkner's narrative tactics turned many readers away. Through characters like Benjy, whose memories of past events mingle with present experiences with no distinction between the two, Faulkner was able to give a more complex rendering of char-

The Bettmann Archive, Inc.

acters and events. This technique was further developed and refined in subsequent works.

With critical recognition established, Faulkner sought greater financial rewards from his writing. With an eye on the commercial market, he began composing what he called "the most horrific tale I could imagine." The result was *Sanctuary* (1931), a novel which had to be revised before final publication due to its graphic violence and the extravagant depravity of its characters. An objective study of human evil, *Sanctuary,* even in its revised form, caused a minor uproar. While it became Faulkner's best-selling novel, a number of critics disparaged the work for its sensationalistic depictions of violence. Critical studies of *Sanctuary* often focus on the character Popeye, particularly because he embodies the philosopher Henri Bergson's theory of humor—that we laugh at people who act rigidly and mechanically rather than at those capable of expressing diverse emotions. Faulkner himself acknowledged an interest in Bergson's ideas, including his theory of the fluidity of time. Faulkner stated: "There is only the present moment, in which I include both the past and the future, and that is eternity."

Faulkner's work grew increasingly complex during the 1930s, making even greater demands upon readers and eliciting mixed critical response. *As I Lay Dying* (1930), for example, is a novel composed of fifty-nine interior monologues: by this use of constantly shifting, contrasting points of view, Faulkner gradually and methodically reveals his themes and characters. In *Light in August* (1932), Faulkner examines the origins of personal identity and the roots of racial conflicts. *Light in August* begins by introducing a few characters and then turns to the plight of Joe Christmas, who is trying to uncover his true identity by piecing together bits of hearsay information. Because this story is told in an extended flashback, many critics felt that the novel suffered from faulty structure. However, defenders of the novel claim that this structure is intentional and serves to enhance the thematic scope of the narrative.

Faulkner's next major novel, *Absalom! Absalom!* (1936), has been called the work in which he is most in control of his experimental narrative techniques. At the center of this novel is the story of Thomas Sutpen, a tragic character with a monomaniacal passion for creating and controlling a self-contained world. Many of the "facts" regarding Sutpen, as well as other characters and events in the novel, are based on unreliable information, and the novel thus questions the human capacity to know the truth about anyone or anything. Upon publication of *Absalom! Absalom!*, many critics hailed Faulkner as a great artist, while others felt that his abstruse method of storytelling was confusing and ultimately ineffective. After publishing two subsequent novels that received lukewarm critical response, *The Unvanquished* (1938) and *The Wild Palms* (1939), and following a brief stint in Hollywood as a scriptwriter, Faulkner published *The Hamlet* (1940). According to some critics, this novel concludes Faulkner's "major period." *The Hamlet*, along with two later novels, *The Town* (1957) and *The Mansion* (1959), are collectively known as the "Snopes Trilogy." These novels center on Flem Snopes, whose single ambition in life is to acquire more and more property, and are a blend of tragedy and comedy. While some critics view the tragedy in these novels as both heightened and made more tolerable by its juxtaposition with comedy, others feel that the humor is detrimental to a basically tragic theme. The Snopes trilogy also highlights another prominent theme in Faulkner's work—exploitation of land and people as a source of human misery.

In the opinion of some critics, Faulkner is most effective as a short story writer. He often used short stories to fill gaps in the historical development of Yoknapatawpha County as depicted in his novels. Many characters who appear in the novels also appear in the short stories, while new characters are also introduced. Even in isolation from his novels, Faulkner's short fiction provides the complete chronological development of Yoknapatawpha from the coming of white men, who introduced the concept of private property, up to the twentieth century, when the automobile becomes a common fixture in American society. *Go Down, Moses* (1942) is a short story collection that can also be considered as a novel, with a thematic unity binding the separate sections of the work. Though Faulkner himself referred to this collection as a novel, many critics view "episodes" such as "The Bear" as fully realized short stories which are more concise and complete than many of Faulkner's novels.

During the 1950s, Faulkner spent much time traveling and lecturing both abroad and at American colleges. His novel *A Fable* (1954) won the Pulitzer Prize in fiction and the National Book Award, but received mixed reviews because of its rigidly structured prose. After completing the Snopes trilogy, Faulkner wrote his final novel, *The Reivers* (1962), which was published shortly before his death. *The Reivers* provides a final glance at Yoknapatawpha County. Although written as a tall tale in the manner of the nineteenth-century Southwestern humorists, this work, like most of Faulkner's fiction, can also be read symbolically as a moral tale. Since his death, Faulkner's work has been extensively analyzed and is now more fully appreciated. Faulkner created a body of work that is distinctly American yet reflects, on a grander scale, the universal values of human life.

(See also *CLC*, Vols. 1, 3, 6, 8, 9, 11, 14, 18; *Contemporary Authors*, Vols. 81-84; *Dictionary of Literary Biography*, Vols. 9, 11; and *Dictionary of Literary Biography Documentary Series*, Vol. 2.)

WYNDHAM LEWIS

Faulkner, unlike Hemingway, is a novelist of the old school—the actual texture of his prose-narrative is not at all 'revolutionary' or unusual. Just occasionally (as in the opening page or two of *Sartoris* and here and there in *Sanctuary* and *Light in August*) a spurious savour of "newness' is obtained by a pretended incompetence as a narrator or from a confused distraction—a 'lack of concentration' it would popularly be called if it occurred in the narrative of a police-court witness. There is, very occasionally, a clumsy slyness of this sort, of the *faux-naif* variety, but it is quite a minor thing. Just now and then—only if for a page or two—he will Joyce for a bit, but merely to the extent of innocently portmanteauing a few words just to show he is on the right side, such as 'shadowdappled' or 'downspeaking': but he has not much luck with this, as he is apt to arrive at such a result as the following: "the rank *manodor* of his sedentary . . . flesh"—which looks too like *escupidor* to be a happy conjugation. For the most part his books might have been written by a contemporary of Trollope or the early Wells. (p. 43)

There is no reason whatever why a novelist today should not use the most 'straightforward' methods of narrative—the *code napoléon* was good enough for Stendhal, and we might do far worse than model ourselves upon it—I am not at all . . . [damning] Mr. Faulkner for being 'old-fashioned': my object is to place him technically. More than half of his text belongs, as far as the *genre* of the writing is concerned, to the 'psychological' method of Conrad (or the translations of the great nineteenth-century Russian authors). (p. 44)

[There] is a lot of *poetry* in Faulkner. It is not at all good. And it has an in the end rather comic way of occurring at a point where, apparently, he considers that the *atmosphere* has run out, or is getting thin, by the passage of time become exhausted and requiring renewal, like the water in a zoological-garden tank for specimens of fish. So he pumps in this necessary medium, for anything from half a dozen to two dozen lines, according to the needs of the case. (p. 45)

His characters demand, in order to endure for more than ten pages, apparently, an opaque atmosphere of whip-poor-wills, cicadas, lilac, 'seeping' moonlight, water-oaks and jasmine—and of course the 'dimensionless' sky, from which the moonlight 'seeps.' The wherewithal to supply them with this indispensable medium is as it were stored in a *whip-poor-will tank*, as it might be called: and he pumps the stuff into his book in generous flushes at the slightest sign of fatigue or deflationary listlessness, as he thinks, upon the part of one of his characters.

To compare him with Ernest Hemingway as an artist would indeed be absurd: but actually he betrays such a deep unconsciousness in that respect as to be a little surprising. . . . If in reading a book of his you came across [the word 'sourceless']—say upon the first page of **Sanctuary** where it occurs ("a thick growth of cane and brier, of cypress and gum in which broken sunlight lay sourceless") and said to yourself "*sourceless*—what for mercy's sake is that!" you would soon find out. For a dozen pages farther on (where more poetic atmosphere was being pumped in, in due course) you would probably come across it again: and after you had encountered it half a dozen times or so you would see what he meant. (pp. 45-6)

[There] are other words (apart from such hackneyed ones common to all American books as *frustration*) which he uses so repeatedly that it would be a game for an idle person to count them—'timbrous,' 'viscid,' 'shard,' 'sibilant,' etc. No one ever had less care for the *mot juste*. (p. 46)

There is no question here of conscious repetition. It reveals the character of this slipshod and redundant artistic machine. (p. 48)

Faulkner is as full of 'passion'—of sound and fury—as Hemingway is austerely without it. He is as hot and sticky as Hemingway is dry and without undue heat. He works up and up, in a torrent of ill-selected words, to his stormy climaxes. With Hemingway the climaxes are registered by a few discreet touches here and there. The characters in Faulkner's books are as heavily *energized* as the most energetic could wish. And if they are all futilely energized and worked-up to no purpose—all 'signifying nothing'—if each and all of his stories is 'a tale told by an idiot'—that does not make his Sartorises, Popeyes, Christmases, the priest in **Mistral** or Temple Drake, any the less an impressive company, in their hysterical way. All are demented: his novels are, strictly speaking, clinics. Destiny weighs heavily upon every figure which has its being in this suffocating atmosphere of whip-poor-wills, magnolias, fireflies and water-oaks (not to mention the emanations of the *dark* and invariably *viscid* earth). And the particular form that that destiny takes is *race*. Whether it is Christmas or Sartoris, it is a matter of a fatality residing in the blood. They are driven on in a crazy and headlong career by the compulsion of their ancestry. (pp. 48-9)

Violent death . . . is a matter of such importance in Faulkner's universe, it has such a baleful attraction, for his most ordinary puppets, in expectation or in memory, that it is able, two generations away, to so paralyze the imagination of one of them as to turn him into a dream of death-on-horseback!

The Civil War, and that apparently central problem of the American soul, the Black and White (for it is rather an important issue, all said and done, whether you shall give the negro equality and a century hence have a mulatto America, or on the other hand lynch him as soon as look at him) are the shadows over every life dealt with by Faulkner. The Sartoris family is literally rotten with fatality—there the *doom* becomes deliberately comic. . . . (p. 50)

A *flash, a glare*—that is what Faulkner's books are intended to be—a very long flash, and a chronic glare, illuminating a 'doomed,' a symbolical landscape—centred in that township of the Old Dominion symbolically named *Jefferson*.

The longest flash and glare of all is **Light in August**—and that, I think, is a flash in the pan. It is full of wearisome repetitions and is long-winded to the last degree: it is hysterical and salvationist more than is necessary, and it is comical where it is not meant to be. It contains, however, a great deal of good observation and passages of considerable power. Christmas, the half-negro, supplies us with all of these. He is a quite empty little figure, like 'Popeye' in **Sanctuary**: but he carries round a big 'doom' with him all right, and he makes it sound. His doom is of course his *blood*—or rather his two bloods, the white and the black. (p. 52)

But the 'doom' in the case of Joe Christmas is complicated by a new factor, namely, the presence of a personal fate referred to as 'the Player.' This personage only turns up quite at the end of this long trail, and I am bound to say does not behave at all nicely. Here he is—moving Percy Grimm, who has tracked down the fugitive negro, and run him to earth behind the kitchen-table in the disgraced pastor's house. . . .

"It was as though he had been merely waiting for the Player to move him again, because with that unfailing certitude he ran straight to the kitchen and into the doorway, already firing, almost before he could have seen the table overturned and standing on its edge across the corner of the room, and the bright and glittering hands of the man who crouched behind it, resting upon the upper edge. . . ." (p. 53)

With this sinister Player (spelled with a capital p) we reach a further complication of Faulkner's studied amateur fatalism. We first hear of the presence of the Player while Grimm is in pursuit of Christmas before the latter reaches the shelter of the house. "He (Grimm) was moving again almost before he had stopped, with that lean, swift, blind obedience to whatever Player moved him on the Board. . . . He seemed indefatigable, not flesh and blood, as if the Player who moved him for pawn likewise found him breath."

The belief of W. B. Yeats that human life is a game of chess, in which beings of a supernatural intelligence, in another dimension, are engaged, lending us sometimes their wisdom and their strength, seems to be implied in this. But I should doubt if Faulkner is the master of any systematic notion of fatality. Evidently he took a great fancy at some time to the conception of a rigid destiny controlling human life, as exemplified in the Greek Drama: and it supplies the melodramatic backbone of his books. That is all, I think.

There can be nothing harder to define than *melodrama* in distinction to tragedy. But a too great addiction to a notion of 'fate,' and a consequent loosening and slackening of the 'realistic' web of 'chance' or 'accident,' will undoubtedly lead a writer more surely than by any other path—especially if his purposes are sensational, and mainly directed to excite and to entertain—to what would probably be described as the *melodramatic*. Faulkner seems to me to be melodramatic, distinctly. All his skies are inky black. He deals in horror as in a cherished material. Coincidence, what he would call 'fate,' does not stand on ceremony, or seek to cover itself in any fussy 'realistic' plausability, with him. When the doomed man, at long last, is to be run to earth, there is every probability (according to the law of these *improbable* narratives) that after wandering all over the world, he will be run to earth at the very door of the cottage in which dwells, quite unknown to him, his old grandmother, who, however, has never set eyes on him until that day, and who has no idea whether such a person as he exists or not until she finds him with the rope round his neck. In short, there is *no* coincidence that this robust fatalism is not prepared to admit. This certainly makes novel-writing easier.

Of course, the intellectual morale of a destiny-crank, on the grand model, is sorely tried in any case. It is enervating for him in that respect, even as it is for men at large, in its influence upon their general outlook. The conception of an all-embracing destiny has its concomitant in an obviousness of association, and imposes at once a mechanical form upon existence: as it is pre-eminently the philosophy of the pure determinist.

A man like William Faulkner discovers fatalism, or whatever you like to call it: it at once gives him something to live for, or rather gives his characters something to live for—namely a great deal of undeserved tribulation culminating in *a violent death*. That simplifies the plot enormously—it is, in fact, the great 'classical' simplification, banishing expectation. No one who knows Faulkner's work is in any doubt, in picking up a book of his, as to what will happen to the principal character; he will unquestionably die a violent death, there is no occasion to turn to the last page. He is, in fact, as dead already upon the first page, to all intents and purposes, and bloodily dead, as is the corpse at the opening of a Van Dine crime-novel. And it takes a more powerful and subtle intelligence than Faulkner's to cope with this essentially mechanical situation in such a manner as not to make it appear over-mechanical to the reader—or to prevent it from degenerating into a flabby and artificial structure, with eventually the necessary pawns practically emerging from a trap-door, or being telepathically spirited to the spot desired, blatantly in the nick of time. And where everyone knows what is going to happen the temptation merely to moralize the mechanism into *such* a preordained pattern that the march of events is a purely *ad hoc* progression, highly unreal and unconvincing, is very great. In fact, increasingly, there will be little incentive to do anything else, for such a story-teller. His attitude will tend to become like that of the doomed man himself. Why worry? A supernatural agency is at work. Miracles are the stock in trade of a supernatural agency.—Indeed, once you have admitted the existence of a supernatural agency, the unlikely and fortuitous are more 'natural' than the reverse. Indeed, it only remains a question of what quantity, if any, of non-fatalist, non-miraculous, constituents you shall include.

Since the climax is from the start in full view of *everybody*, including the figure who is destined to suffer it, the tendency must be at least to slacken the tension and conventionalize all that comes *in between*. And in **Light in August** that last of this fatal series and the best working of its working—that is just what we find. A great deal of prosy melodramatic talk does intervene, in an interminable, sultry, marking time, until the Player shall produce the carving-knife, and balefully point at the root of all the 'abomination and bitchery,' namely the sexual organs of the half-caste hero. (pp. 54-6)

I have said (not in disparagement) that Faulkner is an 'old-fashioned' writer compared with Hemingway, and this accounts for a good deal. He has gone back to the old conception of 'the novel,' or he has never emerged from it would, I suppose, be more exact. He is artistically a contemporary of Conrad or Trollope (his Hightower, for instance, is an American Mr. Crawley of Hogglestock). He is a bold and bustling romantic writer, of the 'psychological' school. That is the main thing to grasp about him. It is, in short, except for a mere handful of *shadowdappleds* and *manodors,* as if Joyce had never jingled: except for *one* little shamefaced flourish, it is as if Miss Stein had never stuttered. . . . (pp. 57-8)

All this is to say that he has to be judged according to conventional standards of romantic novel-making: the question of his success or ill-success must be subordinated to the framework of a conventional and unreal pattern. Whereas Hemingway, reporter of genius that he is, fails or succeeds largely upon whether you decide he has got the facts *dead-right*, or, on the other hand, has ever so slightly shifted and conventionalized them in the process of reporting them, Faulkner neglects or ignores that criterion of 'realistic' method. He must be judged according to romantic standards only—as, for that matter, is the case with most novelists. There are few people, who are professional novelists, able to do anything else, if they are to 'make good,' than to conform to the more conventional and romantic standards of this rather slovenly, undisciplined art. And of course it remains an open question whether such an art deserves the more exacting approach at all. (p. 58)

> Wyndham Lewis, "William Faulkner (The Moralist with a Corn Cob)," in his Men without Art (©; reprinted by permission of The Wyndham Lewis Memorial Trust), Cassell & Company, Limited, 1934 (and reprinted by Russell & Russell, Inc., 1964), pp. 42-64.

ALFRED KAZIN

The problem that faces every student of Faulkner's writing is its lack of a center, the gap between his power and its source, that curious abstract magnificence (not only a magnificence of verbal resources alone) which holds his books together, yet seems to arise from debasement or perplexity or a calculating terror. It is the gap between the deliberation of his effects, the intensity of his every conception, and the besetting and depressing looseness, the almost sick passivity, of his basic meaning and purpose. No writer, least of all a novelist so remarkably inventive and robust of imagination, works in problems of pure technique alone; and though it is possible to see in his books, as Conrad Aiken has shown [see *CLC*, Vol. 8], the marks of a writer devoted to elaboration and wizardry of form, who has deliberately sought to delay and obscure his readers so that the work may have a final and devastating effect, Faulkner's "persistent offering of obstacles, a calculated system of screens and obtrusions, of confusions and ambiguous interpolations and delays," seems to spring from an obscure and profligate confusion, a manifest absence of purpose, rather than from an elaborate but coherent aim.

For while Faulkner has brought back into the modern American novel a density of perception and elaboration of means unparalleled since Henry James, his passion for form has not been, like James's, the tortuous expression of an unusual and subtle point of view; it has been a register of too many points of view, and in its way a substitute for one. It is precisely because his technical energy and what must be called a tonal suggestiveness are so profound, precisely because Faulkner's rhetoric is so portentous, that it has been possible to read every point of view into his work and to prove them all. To a certain type of social or moralist critic, his work seems at once the product of some ineffable decadence and a reluctant commentary upon it. (pp. 457-58)

By identifying all life with the South, by giving himself so completely to it, Faulkner showed why he could see all things in it and at the same time draw no clear design from it. His absorption was too complete; it was almost a form of abnegation. Accepting the South, hating it, memorializing it, losing himself in it, Faulkner was forced into a series of improvisations; and his need for pyrotechnics and a swollen Elizabethanism of rhetoric, his delight in difficulty and random inventiveness, became the expression of his need to impose some external intensity, an almost synthetic unity, upon his novels. The nerve-jangled harshness and self-conscious grandeur of his work show only one elaboration of that inner confusion, that compulsion to brood always at polar extremes. More significant has been his need to present almost all his characters at the unwavering pitch of absolute desperation and damnation, to expand everything to a size larger than life and ambiguously more tragic, to represent everything—every life, every thought, every action—as something unutterably lost and doomed.

There is a pillar of darkness that moves between the Faulkner characters and the world—blotting out the sun, blotting out our simple and confident knowledge of their qualities and relations to each other, blotting out their normality. But if this darkness is in one sense the equivalent atmosphere of Faulkner's misanthropy and bitterness, it is also a mechanism, a stage apparatus, that provides an artificial medium within which his people move, and it suggests some secret and harried compensation for his failure. For what one always feels in even Faulkner's greatest moments is not a lack or falsity of achievement; it is a power almost grotesque in its lack of relation to the situation or characters; it is a greatness moving in a void. From this point of view the mechanical damnation of his characters is not a valid projection of some conception of damnation which must include everything that draws breath in the South; it is a simple lack of flexibility, some cardinal stiffness or agony of imagination. It is significant to note that while Faulkner's ability to create character has always been superb, his characters are not so much a succession of individuals freshly, directly visualized and created, as molds into which the same fantastic qualities have been poured. They live, they live copiously and brilliantly; but they live by the violence with which Faulkner sustains them, by the sullen, screaming intensity which he breathes into them (often with all of Faulkner's own gestures, fury, and raging confusion of pronouns), by the atmospheric terror that encloses them. They live because they are incredibilities in action, because they have been scoured by death before they reach the grave, so that one sees them always in the posture of some fantastic relinquishment and irrevocable agony, the body taut and the soul quivering with death. And if they seem forever to be watching and waiting in their own stupor, to be accumulated sensations rather than people having sensations, to be even the same extreme sensations (the doctor in *The Wild Palms*, Quentin Compson and old Mr. Coldfield in *Absalom! Absalom!*, young Bayard in *The Unvanquished*, the young teacher in *The Hamlet*, Joe Christmas and almost everyone else in *Light in August*), is it not because they are personifications rather than human beings, and is not their astounding capacity for unhappiness and perdition a confession of some final awkwardness in Faulkner—his need to write and think in monotones?

Nervously alive, his characters are fundamentally not alive at all, not acting out individual parts, but seem rather to be pure fantastic aggregates. They are multiform qualities acting out, participating in, that general myth of Faulkner's creation, the jungle South, and it is significant that the darkness in which they live, the darkness through which they must always be grasped and pieced together, makes them appear curiously distant, refractions of refractions. In the end we seem always to be reading the same story, following through the familiar formula of damnation, conscious of the same mysterious submission—extraordinarily abject—to perdition. Yet though the energy that drives them along is torrential, we do not see *them* intensely; we see everything under *conditions* of intensity. It is precisely because Faulkner's characters are charged with a vitality not their own that he is able to do everything with them except make us believe instinctively and absolutely in them. And it is precisely because Faulkner does not know too much about them himself, does not believe in them with sufficient consciousness of purpose, that he is forced into those leaping improvisations of language and incident, that nervous magnificence, which invests everything with epic grandeur that is suspiciously grandiose, that plots and strains and leaves us all too often with the mere fact of tumultuous exaggeration. (pp. 459-61)

In the end one must always return to Faulkner's language and his conception of style, for his every character and observation are lost in the spool of his rhetoric, and no more than they can be ever wind himself free. That rhetoric—perhaps the most elaborate, intermittently incoherent and ungrammatical, thunderous, polyphonic rhetoric in all American writing—explains why he always plays as great a role in his novels as any of his characters to the point of acting out their characters in himself; why he has so often appeared to be a Laocoön writhing in all the outrageous confusions of the ineffable; why he has been able, correlating the South with every imagined principle and criticism of existence, writing in many styles, to project every possible point of view, every shade or extremity of character, and to persuade us of none. In one sense, of course, Faulkner has sought to express the inexpressible, to attain that which is basically incoherent in the novel and analogous only to the most intense mysticism in poetry, where sensations contract and expand like tropical flowers. Yet his novels are not poetry or even "poetic"; they are linked together by a sensational lyricism, itself forever in extremis and gasping for breath, that, as Yeats said of rhetoric, "is an attempt of the will to do the work of the imagination." For what one sees always in Faulkner's mountainous rhetoric, with its fantastic pseudo-classical epithets and invertebrate grandeur, its merely verbal intensity and inherent motor violence, is the effort of a writer to impose himself upon that which he cannot create simply and evocatingly. It is the articulation of confusion rather than an evasion of it; force passing for directed energy. With all its occasional felicity and stabbing appropriateness of phrase, Faulkner's style is a discursive fog, and it is not strange—so clever and ready is his style the advantage taken over confusion itself—that his extremities should seem intimations of grandeur and the darkness within which his characters move an atmosphere of genuine tragedy. (pp. 462-63)

[Why] must everything in Faulkner's novels be raised to its tenth power? . . . Why is it that the Faulkner country must always appear as "a shadowy miasmic region," "amoral evil's undeviating absolute," a "quicksand of nightmare," "the seething and anonymous miasmal mass which in all the years of time has taught itself no boon of death"? For the same reason, as it must appear, that despite his extraordinary talents no writer has ever seemed so ambitious and so purposeless, so overwhelming in imaginative energy and so thwarted in his application of it. A fanatic, as Santayana once said, is a man who redoubles his effort when he has lost sight of his aim; and even if it be admitted that Faulkner's effort has been to express the inexpressible, to write the history of the unconscious, to convey some final and terrifying conception of a South that seems always to exist below water, the impression one always carries away from his novels is of some fantastic exertion of will, of that exaggeration which springs from a need to raise everything in Yoknapatawpha County, Mississippi, to its tenth (or its hundredth) power because there is not sufficient belief, or power, or ease in his conception of Yoknapatawpha County, or the South, or human existence in general.

It is not strange, then, that his scene should always be some swamp of the spirit, or that his subject should always be murder, rape, prostitution, incest, arson, idiocy (with an occasional interpolation of broad country humor almost as violent as his tragedies); or that the country of his mind should be a Mississippi county larger than life, but not visibly related to it. Faulkner's obsession has been agony, as his art has been the voice of that agony—the agony of a culture, his culture; but it has been even more the agony of his relation to that culture, the tormenting disproportion between his immersion in the South and his flinging, tumultuous efforts to project it. It has been the agony inherent in any effort to transcend some basic confusion by force of will alone. Faulkner's corn-fed, tobacco-drooling phantoms are not the constituents of a representative American epic, protagonists in a great modern tragedy; they are the tonal expression of Faulkner's own torment, the walking phantasmagoria, sensation beating against sensation, of his perpetual tension. No writer ever made so much of his failure; in no writer of his stature is the suggestion of some cardinal failure so ambiguous and yet so penetrating. (pp. 464-65)

>   Alfred Kazin, "The Rhetoric and the Agony," in his On Native Grounds: An Interpretation of Modern American Prose Literature (copyright 1942, 1970, by Alfred Kazin; reprinted by permission of Harcourt Brace Jovanovich, Inc.), Reynal & Hitchcock, 1942 (and reprinted by Harcourt Brace Jovanovich, 1963), pp. 453-84.*

CLIFTON FADIMAN

I came to every new Faulkner opus wearily determined to see in it what my betters saw. No more than the next man do I enjoy looking like a dunce. But, no matter how hard I tried, I was licked every time. Some major defect, some incurable myopia, prevented me from seeing in him more than a dazzling, though often unsuccessful technician, passionately and sincerely creating a private world whose inhabitants would be completely unrecognizable to the natives of Oxford, Mississippi, but are apparently immediately recognizable to a host of young academics and, let us be fair, to many non-specialized, average, intelligent readers.

For them there is no disproportion between Mr. Faulkner's Gothic-horrors material and the complex means used to embody it. No gap between the noble, free-floating utterances of the Nobel Prize speech and the moral chaos of most of the novels. No impatience with the violence, the humorlessness, the portentousness of his characters. No willful and, as I see it, unrewarding deformation of our English tongue. No feeling that at the heart of all his books there is, as an English critic has put it, "an abrogation of natural law, an act of violence." Nothing of the uneasy sense I get from time to time of Charles Addams trying to be Dostoevski.

If there exist, as I believe to be the case, a few other old-fashioned reactionaries who are like myself baffled by Mr. Faulkner and even more baffled by his commentators, the putting down of this record of bewilderment may not have been entirely wasted. I claim no more for it. (pp. 124-25)

>   Clifton Fadiman, "William Faulkner," in his Party of One: The Selected Writings of Clifton Fadiman (copyright © 1955 by Clifton Fadiman; reprinted by permission of Harper & Row, Publishers, Inc.), World Publishing Co., 1955, pp. 98-125.

MICHAEL MILLGATE

It is necessary to emphasise that Faulkner in his best work is not concerned with ideas in any abstract sense. His preoccupations are not intellectual but moral; what he offers is not philosophy but wisdom. At the same time, his public statements are in no sense divorced from his literary achievement. The Nobel Prize Speech has sometimes been regarded as very much a *post hoc* statement, a deliberate effort on Faulkner's part to match with his own grandiloquence the grandeur of the occasion. It should properly be seen as a distillation, necessarily couched in abstract terms, of the kind of statements and moral judgments which had been implicit in his work from the very first. As Faulkner wrote to Warren Beck in 1941: "I have been writing all the time about honor, truth, pity, consideration, the capacity to endure well grief and misfortune and injustice and then endure again . . ." Like the people of Oxford, so many of Faulkner's critics have failed to understand, in the words of "Mac" Reed, that Faulkner was "their closest friend who was trying to show them in his own peculiar way that they must appreciate the good life better."

The crucial failure of much Faulkner criticism, however, and the one which underlies so many misreadings and misjudgments of his work, has been the continuing underestimation of Faulkner as an artist. The case against Faulkner was made out by Wyndham Lewis in his book, *Men Without Art*, published in 1934. In a chapter subtitled "The Moralist with the Corn-Cob" [see excerpt above], Lewis attacked Faulkner for his presentation of "demented" characters and fiercely criticised his style, accusing him of injecting poetic effects to liven up listless passages of his prose, and arguing of his repeated use of such words as "myriad" and "sourceless" that such repetition was not deliberate but merely revealed "the character of this slipshod and redundant artistic machine." The various critics who have echoed Lewis's observations down the succeeding years have done so with little of his brilliance, much less of his justification, and nearly all of his misstatements. Meanwhile the small but distinguished body of serious Faulkner criticism has increasingly revealed the intricate structural and imagistic patterns which operate within the novels, and shown that the elaboration of the style, with its repetitions and rhetorical flourishes, possesses an organic relationship with the material of the novels and with their moral and emotional themes. The overall tendency of such criticism has been to establish Faulkner as a deliberate, conscientious, and highly sophisticated literary artist, who, though not always successful, was always fully aware of what he was doing and always absolutely in control of material, characterisation, structure, and style.

That these conclusions can continue to be ignored by critics who still adhere to Lewis's line of attack can perhaps be attributed to Faulkner's much-criticised and widely-misunderstood "provinciality," his isolation in a part of the United States which the rest of the nation has agreed to call backward. Nothing could be less illuminating than to think of Faulkner as a kind of American primitive, a sort of literary and less engaging Grandma Moses, a wild untutored genius of the backwoods. It is not helpful even to see him as self-educated, lacking in literary culture, cut off from literary tradition, suffering as an artist because of his isolation from a sophisticated milieu such as he might have found in New York, London, or Paris. . . . Faulkner was well aware of that diffusion of creative energy in talk which constitutes the seductive but fatal danger inherent in the life of literary circles, and his self-isolation in Oxford represented not a negative act of withdrawal but a positive commitment to literature, to the act of writing. That long shelf of Faulkner's books would surely have been a good deal shorter if he had not stayed at home and written with intense concentration for long periods of time: it is staggering to think, for example, that in a period of about eight years, from 1928 to 1936, Faulkner wrote four major novels (*The Sound and the Fury, As I Lay Dying, Light in August,* and *Absalom, Absalom!*), three other novels (*Sartoris, Sanctuary,* and *Pylon*), and a large number of short stories; he may also have made considerable progress towards an early version of *The Hamlet* at this time.

But if Faulkner isolated himself, and with good reason, from the contemporary literary world, he did not isolate himself from historical literary tradition. Indeed, it would seem fair to say that in certain important respects Faulkner was more actively aware of American and European literary traditions than any other important American novelist of this century, Hemingway not excluded. (pp. 287-89)

The first two novels, *Soldiers' Pay* and *Mosquitoes,* show signs of influence from T. S. Eliot, Sherwood Anderson, James Branch Cabell, James Joyce, and possibly from Aldous Huxley, Scott Fitzgerald and Thomas Beer. In *Sartoris* Faulkner first began to find a voice distinctively his own, and in *The Sound and the Fury,* despite the continuing presence of Joyce, he achieved it, with astounding abruptness and completeness. Following the all-important initial breakthrough represented by the brilliant technical success of *The Sound and the Fury,* Faulkner seems to have gone beyond the range of direct literary influences. He no longer needed to fall back on the patterns created by his contemporaries or immediate predecessors, or even to seek encouragement in their example. He moved on, with superb assurance and technical sophistication, to the multiple viewpoints of *As I Lay Dying,* the rhetorical splendour and intricate, deliberately unresolved narrative patterns of *Absalom, Absalom!*, the violent juxtapositions of *The Wild Palms,* the rich, varied, and precisely calculated stylistic and thematic patterning of *The Hamlet,* the complex interrelationships and interactions of *Go Down, Moses,* the play-within-a-novel of *Requiem for a Nun,* the austere parable of *A Fable.*

Of *The Sound and the Fury* itself it has to be said not only that it is a book of outstanding individuality which no one but Faulkner could have written, but also that Faulkner himself could not have written it if he had not been a Southerner, indeed a Mississippian, born at a particular moment in time. Yet one does not need to underrate either Faulkner's originality or his Southerness in order to see that the novel is far from what it has too often been taken to be—a series of daring and almost random experiments made in isolation from the main streams of the novel in America and in Europe. On the contrary, *The Sound and the Fury* is a deliberately conceived and superlatively executed work of great technical sophistication: it is set in the American South, but it stands in the direct tradition of the modern psychological and experimental novel. Once we accept Faulkner's awareness of other writers and their innovations—perhaps Dostoevsky, probably Flaubert and James, certainly Conrad, and most importantly Joyce (whether or not Faulkner had read the whole of *Ulysses* at the time of beginning work on his own novel)—then the experiments he makes in *The Sound and the Fury* take on a double significance, for they can be seen not as a series of blind leaps in the dark, the speculative adventures of an isolated genius, but as the result of definite choice. Well informed of experiments which previous novelists had made, Faulkner did not simply evolve homemade solutions for his own problems but chose particular solutions rather than others of which he was also aware. His explorations broke new ground because they were not groping forays but planned expeditions which took the achievements of others as their starting-point.

It is important that the influences which almost certainly lie behind *The Sound and the Fury* were primarily European, even allowing for the possibility of certain minor influences from Sherwood Anderson and John Dos Passos. . . . There are obvious dangers, in fact, in attempting to place Faulkner in any exclusively American tradition. His literary environment includes Melville, Hawthorne, and James, but it also includes—to name only the most significant for Faulkner himself—Dostoevsky, Balzac, Flaubert, Verlaine, Cervantes, Shakespeare, Keats, Shelley, Swinburne, Wilde, Joyce, Synge, Eliot, Conrad, and the King James Bible. Much has been written about Faulkner as a humorous writer in the tradition of the American Southwest, and certainly the tall tale figures largely in his work from the first sketches written in New Orleans to his last book, *The Reivers,* which might be considered as one long tall tale. Yet [we can see] in discussing *The Hamlet* that when Faulkner employs the tall tale he does so with precisely calculated literary objectives in view: he uses it with a full knowledge of its antecedents and with a sophisticated awareness of its contribution to the elaborate interplay of traditional and experimental features which constitutes the complex multiple presentation of his novels. He is not committed to the tall tale in any uncritical way, as an essential element in a literary tradition to which he owes and recognises allegiance, and it remains only one of many devices which he can deploy and manipulate at will. Further warning against taking a purely Southern or even purely American view of Faulkner is provided by his remark, in 1922, that Mark Twain was "a hack writer who would not have been considered fourth rate in Europe, who tricked out a few of the old proven 'sure fire' literary skeletons with sufficient local color to intrigue the superficial and the lazy." As time went on Faulkner came to rank Twain more highly, at least for *Huckleberry Finn,* but the early comment at least emphasises how European was Faulkner's outlook at this period. It suggests, too, that if Faulkner did later resume some of the characteristic features of Twain's work, and of the work of other American figures, he did so consciously and discriminatingly, as a viable method of treating the material offered by that corner of native earth with which he had elected to deal.

Faulkner's achievement can be adequately estimated only by our seeing him as a great novelist in the context not merely of the South, or even of the United States, but of the whole western tradition. His deep identification with his own region is one of his greatest strengths, especially as it emerges in the marvellous sense of place, whether it be the heart of the wilderness or the interior of Miss Reba's brothel, and in the rich evocation of the world of Yoknapatawpha County; and certainly the intensity of his tragic power in novels such as *The Sound and the Fury, Light in August,* and *Absalom, Absalom!* derives both from this profoundly localised sense of social reality and from a poignant awareness of the proud and shameful history of the courageous, careless, gallant and oppressive South. At the same time, to concentrate too exclusively on this aspect of his work is to be in danger of mistaking means for ends and of seeing Faulkner as a lesser figure than he really is. The solidity of Faulkner's provinciality provides the unshakable foundation for his immensely ambitious exploration of the fundamental human themes with which he is always primarily concerned, and the examples of Hardy and Emily Brontë may suggest that Faulkner is not alone among novelists in pursuing the universal in terms of the intensely local. But it is Dickens whom Faulkner most resembles, in the passionate humanity of his tragi-comic vision, in the range and vitality of his characterisation and the profusion of his social notation, in the structural complexity of his novels and their broad symbolic patterns. It is also Dickens whom Faulkner most resembles in the sheer quantity and sustained quality of his achievement, and it is alongside Dickens, the greatest of the English novelists, that Faulkner must ultimately be ranked. (pp. 290-92)

> Michael Millgate, in his The Achievement of William Faulkner (copyright © 1966 Michael Millgate; reprinted by permission of A D Peters & Co Ltd), Constable, 1966, 344 p.

ROBERT PENN WARREN

It was in the Spring of 1929 that John Gould Fletcher, on a visit to Oxford University, where I was a student, gave me a copy of **Soldiers' Pay**. I had been out of the South for a long time—in a sense, in flight from the South—and at least half of me was oriented toward Greenwich Village and the Left Bank and not toward the Cumberland Valley in Tennessee; but at the same time I was, I suppose, homesick, and was making my first serious attempt at fiction, fiction with a setting in the part of the South where I had grown up. As a novel, **Soldiers' Pay** is no better than it should be, but it made a profound and undefinable impression on me. Then came, in the order of my reading, *The Sound and the Fury, A I Lay Dying, Sanctuary,* and *These Thirteen.*

What happened to me was what happened to almost all the bookreading Southerners I knew. They found dramatized in Faulkner's work some truth about the South and their own Southerness that had been lying speechless in their experience. Even landscapes and objects took on a new depth of meaning, and the human face, stance, and gesture took on a new dignity.

If you, in spite of your own sometimes self-conscious and willed Southernness, had been alienated by the official Southern pieties, alibis, and daydreams, the novels of Faulkner told you that there was, if you looked a second time, an intense, tormented, and brutal, but dignified and sometimes noble, reality beyond whatever façade certain people tried to hypnotize you into seeing. With this fiction there was not only the thrill of encountering strong literature. There was the thrill of seeing how a life that you yourself observed and were part of might move into the dimension of art. There was, most personally, the thrill of discovering your own relation to time and place, to life as you were destined to live it.

Even the images of degradation and violence—by which Southern pride, as officially exemplified by the DAR and the Chamber of Commerce, was so often shocked—seemed added certification of the reality of the novels: a perverse and perhaps self-indulgent delight, which you yourself recognized, in the dark complications of Southern life, a reflexive response to an unidentified tension and a smouldering rage beneath the surface of Southern life. What, in other words, the fiction of Faulkner gave was a release into life, into the sense of a grand and disturbing meaningfulness beneath the crust of life, into a moral reality beneath the crust of history. (pp. 1-2)

> Robert Penn Warren, "Introduction: Faulkner, Past and Present," in Faulkner: A Collection of Critical Essays, edited by Robert Penn Warren (© 1966 by Prentice-Hall, Inc., Englewood Cliffs, New Jersey; reprinted by permission of Prentice-Hall, Inc., Englewood Cliffs, NJ 07632), Prentice-Hall, 1966, pp. 1-22.

ARTHUR F. KINNEY

Mayday is derivative in idea and technique, a product of a self-conscious affecting of Symbolist art quivering at its own fragility in a harsh and cruel world at the same time it openly parodies young passions and lusts. The setting is medieval: Sir Galwyn of Arthgyl is given a dream of death by St. Francis, and, accompanied by Pain and Hunger, he sets out on his journey of life to be united with this Little Sister. The first men who try to stop him protect Yseult whose naked bathing in a pool not only arouses Sir Galwyn but is meant to double the Little Sister Death he searches after. Naked, Yseult rises from the pool to romp and lie in the woods with her new lover until the cold darkness causes him to suggest she get dressed; at this first opportunity, as he shows Pain and Hunger, he escapes, sighing with relief. Two other princesses, representing the evening and morning stars, come to him, the first as a deer, the second carried in a chariot by dolphins, but his affairs with both are brief. In each instance the knight is lightly mocked by the vulgar colloquialism of the women he leaves behind: at the end, he welcomes not the Afterworld but Death herself. This singular journey towards embracing death obviously anticipates Quentin's section in *The Sound and the Fury,* especially in the closing lines of *Mayday,* but where the later portrait is cautious in defining Quentin's psychology and tragic in its implications, *Mayday* is romantic and parodic, the language enjoying its departures from a more serious French original: "'I am Gallwyn of Arthgyl, knight at the hand of the Constable du Boisgeclin,'" the knight tells Yseult upon surprising her, "'who, having heard the beauty of the Princess Yseult sung by many a minstrel in many a banquetting hall, must needs dare all things to see her; and who, now that he has gazed upon her. finds that all his life before this moment was a stale thing, and that all the beautiful faces upon which he has looked are as leaves in a wind; and that you are like honey and sunlight and young hyacinths have robbed him of peace and contentment as a gale strips the leaves from a tree; and because you are the promised bride of a king there is no help for it anywhere.'" ... Even the attempts to stress themes of greater depth—"'it is not the thing itself that man wants, so much as the wanting of it'" ...; "'I ... remarked once that man is a buzzing insect blundering through a strange world, seeking something he can neither name nor recognize, and probably will not want. I think now that I shall refine this aphorism to: Man is a buzzing fly beneath the inverted glass tumbler of his illusions'"—are embarrassingly if unintentionally bald. The first is the sort of sentimental indulgence that still marks *Soldiers' Pay* and much of Faulkner's poetry to which it is most clearly aligned; the second anticipates the rambling and precious comments that constitute *Mosquitoes.* In this it is recognizably Faulkner. The thick, cloying images, too—notably of hyacinths—look forward to the imagist thoughts of Benjy and Quentin, while Sir Galwyn's opening vision, with its whirling vortex of faces, will remind readers of Hightower's vision in *Light in August* and the use of the pool of visions adumbrates passages in *Sanctuary.* Yet even these observations may press too hard what is, by any account, a slight and adolescent piece of writing, however fashionable it may have been in establishing a self-portrait of the lover as a young artist. (pp. 337-38)

> Arthur F. Kinney, in a review of "Mayday," in Modern Fiction Studies (© 1980 by Purdue Research

Foundation, West Lafayette, Indiana 47907, U.S.A.), Vol. 26, No. 2, Summer, 1980, pp. 337-38.

CALVIN S. BROWN

Mayday itself is not, as one might expect, a fumbling piece of apprentice-work, but a skillful and amusing exercise in a very minor literary genre which might be described as a lightly allegorical medieval pastiche. It is the story of Sir Galwyn of Arthygal, who, accompanied by Hunger and Pain, rides forth as a new knight, kills "a small dragon of an inferior and cowardly type," seduces three beautiful princesses in three consecutive days and immediately abandons each of them, and finally, with the help of St. Francis, seeks and finds little sister Death in the river. On the way he encounters various figures, including Time, with whom he has philosophical discussions; and the whole work operates in a spirit of cheerful and unportentous nihilism. The manner and style are essentially those of Cabell, and the archaic language is remarkably well handled, especially in view of the fact that Faulkner was no scholar. Much of the amusement comes from what [Carvel Collins in his introduction] calls anachronisms, though they are not really that but are deliberate juxtapositions of the tone of high romance with everyday trivial clichés, as when Yseult, standing naked in the water, replies to a highflown speech of Sir Galwyn: "Do you really think I am beautiful? You say it so convincingly that I must believe you have said it before—I am sure you have said it to other girls. Now, haven't you? But I am sorry you saw me with my hair done this way." There is nothing unmedieval about this, as Chaucer's Criseyde shows us on occasion; but it clashes engagingly with the conventions and language of high romance.

Mayday will do nothing, of course, to increase the stature of Faulkner as one of the few really great writers of our century, but it is no disgrace to Faulkner and is worth publishing for literary as well as biographical and scholarly purposes. (p. 332)

Calvin S. Brown, "Faulkner, Criticism, and High Fashion," in The Sewanee Review (reprinted by permission of the editor; © 1980 by The University of the South), Vol. LXXXVIII, No. 4, Fall, 1980, pp. 631-41.

MALCOLM COWLEY

Faulkner himself is to blame for the long critical disparagement of **"Sanctuary,"** the fifth novel he wrote. "To me it is a cheap idea," he said in his introduction to the Modern Library edition (1932), "because it was deliberately conceived to make money.... I took a little time out, and speculated what a person in Mississippi would believe to be current trends, chose what I thought would be the right answer and invented the most horrific tale I could imagine and wrote it in about three weeks and sent it to [Harrison] Smith, who had done '**The Sound and the Fury**' and who wrote me immediately, 'Good God, I can't publish this. We'd both be in jail.'" ...

Being a "cheap idea" hastily executed to make money, **"Sanctuary"** could be brushed aside. Critics and readers didn't suspect that Faulkner mightn't be telling the complete truth about it, given his early passion for astounding the public.... It wasn't wholly invented, but was largely based on a story that Faulkner had heard from a woman in a New Orleans nightclub about her abduction by an impotent gangster. Faulkner was familiar with the various backgrounds to be presented, including the Memphis underworld (Memphis then being the murder capital of the United States). Moreover, he had on hand Horace Benbow, a character left over from **"Sartoris"** when that novel was shortened before publication; Horace might serve as his storyteller. With all this material, and with the help of his extraordinary imagination, he might somehow develop the cheap idea into a powerful novel.

Critics didn't consider that possibility, and for a long time they also failed to note what Faulkner had said at the end of that brief and—as regards public judgment—disastrous introduction. There he tells how Smith changed his mind, and how, more than a year later, the galley proofs of **"Sanctuary"** arrived in Oxford. "I saw it was so terrible," Faulkner says, "that there were but two things to do: tear it up or rewrite it.... I had to pay for the privilege of rewriting it, trying to make out of it something which would not shame '**The Sound and the Fury**' and '**As I Lay Dying**' too much, and I made a fair job and I hope you will buy it." He made more than a fair job; he transformed **"Sanctuary"** into a haunting study of evil triumphant; and the early reviewers made it a sensation. It established Faulkner as a popular (for a time) author, and the book was even sold to the movies.... What we have now, in **"Sanctuary: The Original Text,"** capably edited by [Noel] Polk, is the manuscript that Faulkner submitted to Hal Smith.... When Faulkner tore into the galleys of **"Sanctuary,"** he didn't change the original story, even if he had come to question it. He did not soften its horrors, nor did he delete the comic interludes; all of these survive unchanged in the novel as first published. His utter disgust with the original version was a craftsman's feeling. Obviously—to those who now read it—he rejected it as a story told awkwardly and ineffectively, one that confused the sequence of events and scamped its dreadful climax.

In the **"Ur-Sanctuary"**—as the critic Michael Millgate was the first to call the original version—Horace Benbow had been the central character. Much of the story had been concerned with his ineffectuality, arising from his incestuous feeling for his sister Narcissa and his stepdaughter Little Belle. The first six chapters were his stream of consciousness, with his mind leaping from one event to another without regard to chronology. Faulkner rewrote those chapters as simple but brilliant narration. He let Horace recede a little—though using him as an observer—and made the novel essentially what the 1933 movie called it, "The Story of Temple Drake." It is an appalling story, and it justifies André Malraux's often quoted remark that it "marks the intrusion of Greek tragedy into the detective story." ...

Although the revised novel is vastly better, the original **"Sanctuary"** is not at all a contemptible book, as Faulkner tried to make us believe.... I should think that the original text will be extremely useful to Faulkner students, who can now read it without making a pilgrimage to the Alderman Library. It should be of service to apprentice writers, who will profit, if they can, from learning how a brilliant technician who happened to be a genius in other ways could work with disappointing galley proofs, save all the type that could be saved and come out with a new and more effective novel. I should hesitate, however, to recommend it as a book for the general reader.

Malcolm Cowley, "Faulkner Was Wrong about 'Sanctuary'," in The New York Times Book Review (copyright © 1981 by The New York Times Company; reprinted by permission), February 22, 1981, pp. 9, 25.

SEAN O'FAOLAIN

[Faulkner] was a richly gifted writer and there are times when he writes with real genius. He is keenly observant, and when he so wishes can be stereoscopically graphic. He gives us the intimate feel of an old banker's run-down bank and an easy-going little town, its age and southern heat, by referring in passing to the gold lettering on the bank's windows as 'cracked'. He evokes idle days spent sitting on the steps of a country store by letting us catch on the wing a reference to those steps as 'heel-gnawed'. A dog nosing in a cupboard has a 'barometric tail'. The dusty, hot air is 'insect-rasped'. The frost tonight will shrink the water in a pool about 'rank bayonets of dead grass in fixed glassy ripples in the brittle darkness'. On a wet day the sounds of the guns 'linger in the air like a spreading stain'. When the sun has half-set behind hedges a horseman 'rides stirrup-deep in cold air'. And so on, his eyes and ears recording automatically, his excellent memory reevoking. He seems possessed when at work by a terrific power of concentration, to have been explosively responsive to every experience, to have been courageous whether as a woodsman, a hunter after big game, a cross-country horseman, or a writer driven by penury—one cannot say poverty because he was a spendthrift with a *folie de grandeur*—to earn writing-time by any and every means from painting roofs in his meagre and sometimes mean little home-town of Oxford (Miss.) to hack-writing under the most humiliating circumstances in Hollywood.

Gifts he had galore: so many that had this been all he had he might be known today as one of the more highly talented of American novelists. Unhappily for him, he possessed much more than talent. He had genius, upsoaring, outpouring, exultant, eloquent, capable of so lighting up his little, local world as to turn it into a great kingdom. . . . At each new venture one wonders: will he be a Daedalus or an Icarus? 'Old father, old artificer, stand me now and ever in good stead.' Like Joyce he should have said it every day, clutching his talent to guide his genius. All too often he flew too near the sun. (p. 16)

There was no firm or constant bridge between the two sides of the man. His art oscillates between civilisation and the wilderness. The impatient would dismiss him as a schizo. His talent and his genius resided in the same set of apartments, but like jailor and jailed they did not share the same room. To adapt Cyril Connolly's famous aphorism, there was in this slim, small man a great giant roaring to get out. If his genius escaped and if his talent dashed after him to sing, drink, dance, whore, hunt, to exchange dreams and memories, above all to argue with him, then we get such superb stories as *A Rose for Emily,* or *Go down Moses,* or that splendid saga *The Bear* (but firmly cutting out the addenda), or that weird, haunting half-fantasy about aboriginal Indians which I do not even pretend to understand called *Red Leaves,* or we get his three time-outlasting novels, *Light in August, As I lay dying* and the frankly romantic *Sartoris*—if only for the sake of its clean, clear, genre sequences about the MacCallum family, a possum hunt, a fox, an encounter with a nigger (always 'niggers' in Faulkner) towards the end of the book. Talent can write alone. Genius never. It was his arrogant error not to realise it.

Why did he not always write so well? Whence this division? We need no psychologist here: we need a sociologist to mark his times, his place, his education, the financial and social structures of his Mississippi, and a few examples of his style to note his resultant grammar, syntax, phraseology and especially his vocabulary. Two sentences will show what I mean.

Here is a sentence taken at random from *Absalom, Absalom!* It refers to Quentin Compson's reaction after listening for some eighteen pages to the rambling memories of an old lady who takes possession of him, and of us, for the first 25 non-stop pages of the novel:

> It (the talking, the telling) seemed (to him, to Quentin) to partake of that logic- and reason-flouting quality of a dream which the sleeper knows must have occurred, stillborn and complete, in a second, yet the very quality upon which it must depend to move the dreamer (verisimilitude) to credulity—horror or pleasure or amazement—depends as completely upon a formal recognition of elapsed and yet-elapsing time as music or a printed tale.

The sentence is a fair example of Faulkner's Plain Style, and it is quite intelligible, certainly at a second reading or even at a first if one has concentrated all one's attention on it. All he is saying is that for Quentin the old lady's talk has by this become like an illogical dream which lasted for no more than a second but which the sleeper, if he wants to get its full meaning, must pretend has lasted quite a while. Whether or not this notion makes sense is beside our point, which is that we *can* cope with Faulkner's Plain Style. I do not think, however, that anybody who reads the following sentence will deny that when the seed of obscurity in that Plain Style sprouts into his Coloured or Baroque Style, we begin to wonder whether something more ominous than just a lack of technical control is at work. The sentence comes from *Intruder in the Dust:*

> his uncle came through the door and drew it after him, the heavy steel plunger crashing into its steel groove with a thick oily sound of irrefutable finality like that ultimate cosmolined doom itself when as his uncle said man's machines had at last effaced and obliterated him from the earth and, purposeless now to themselves with nothing left to destroy, closed the last carborundum-grooved door upon their own progenitorless apotheosis behind one clockless lock responsive only to the last stroke of eternity.

Just what is going on in Faulkner's mind when this kind of prose takes over? At this point our sociologist-historian-critic must surely wish to intervene with a self-satisfied Holmes-to-Watson smile: '*Stylus virum arguit.* Style shows a fellow up. I am sure you must have noted, my dear Watson, that every writer has his own catchwords or bosswords. Take Yeats. I was reading his *Wind among the Reeds* last night. I found him using the word 'pale' twenty times in as many pages. 'Pale hands. Pale eyelids. Pale breasts.' They date him. The pale-end of a century. One could name his fellow writers, calculate his age, almost guess his address in London. Please hand me two or three volumes by this man Faulkner and let us glance at his vocabulary. In those two last sentences you have read for me we are held by the words 'irrefutable', 'doom', 'finality', 'obliterated', 'purposeless', 'progenitorless', 'clockless', 'eternity'. As I turn these pages my eye catches 'fatal', 'fatality', 'fated', 'irrevocable', 'ultimate', 'doom', 'doomed', 'doom'. He has lots of dooms, destiny, blind tragedy of human events, solitude, dream, nebulous, vast, impalpable, dissolution. And such awesome phrases. 'The apotheosis of his youth assumed a thousand avatars.' 'The gasoline roar of apotheosis'. 'A thunderous and silent solitude'. . . . This is the kind of style that might well be bred, perhaps could only be bred between the lower Ohio, the Mississippi and the Gulf by what our stylist would call irrevocable, vast, doomed, blind, final, clockless shame, guilt and total defeat. (pp. 16-17)

Stuck with the place, he looked not at it but through it, let his wild imagination rip, sublimated the actual (his biographer's excellent phrase in an excellent summary of his 'Great Discovery') and without, one feels, in the least realising what he was doing, started to create myths. Years after, Malcolm Cowley, his great admirer, defined the outcome magisterially: 'Essentially [Faulkner] is not a novelist . . . He is an epic or bardic poet in prose' [see *CLC*, Vol. 8]. As a guide to daily life in the American South at any period, his works are about as informative as *Wuthering Heights* would be to a Saudi Arabian contemplating a holiday in the Pennines.

If we are unsatisfied with these pointers from a sociologist-historian as to why he had to write as he did, let us turn to a philosopher. Asked once for his concept of Time, he said there isn't any. 'There is only the present moment in which I include the past and the future and that is eternity.' Sartre commented that Faulkner's work shows a man caught in a metaphysic of Time which by denying chronology denies freedom both to the present and the future: it embeds what we think of as an active present in an unending continuum that drowns it and us in timeless fate; castrates human potency; means that in our sense nothing ever happens, things merely recur. It is a view that would leave in any novel based on it small room for such wilful characters as we are familiar with in Balzac, or Stendhal, or Henry James, or Mark Twain. Malraux went so far as to say that Faulkner conceived his situations in a void without thinking of any character at all, pre-imagining *'l'écrasement des personnages inconnus'*. By writing in terms of myth or saga he evaded this impasse, although in all the great myths—Danae, Atalanta, Orpheus, Midas, Eve—we appreciate the parallel human theme. In his very finest novel Faulkner wedded human theme and saga theme superbly. I refer to the saga of a white-skinned mulatto, partly hating, partly priding in his invisible black hood, who corrupts a middle-aged white woman who has come south to do good among the Blacks. He desires her, perhaps loves her, arouses desire in her chaste body, but feeling his precious hate being enfeebled by her autumnal passion, fills her with the most savage lust, transforms her into a lascivious trollop, hiding from him in cupboards, lying naked in the bushes for him to smell her out. The inevitable end comes when, either not knowing or caring that he is a Black, she tries to enrol him in a campaign to uplift his wretched likes. With his razor he all but decapitates her. Naturally he is duly lynched. Has there been any other novelist except Dostoevsky who could have conceived and written *Light in August*?

'A lost soul'? The view of an intellectual. Earlier, in 1945, Sartre had reported that *'pour les jeunes en France Faulkner c'est un dieu.'* But in that exciting hour of history, its symbol de Gaulle marching down the Champs-Elysées at the head of the victorious Allied troops, French students might have said anything in praise of America. Something in between? Perhaps a lost star wandering high among the fleets of stars, seeking, losing, finding his proper station from which to view and mark that postage stamp of earth, as he called it, that was fated to be his bit of the undefeated South.

It is only when we turn for relief from him to other American writers with more control that we think, yes, these are good *but* . . . and recall his intensity, his almost savage concentration, his almost volcanic rumblings and furious groanings, that we really feel how good and how bad he was, and again ask the gods why they had to give him so much genius and so little of the talent of the simplest craftsman. But where is the use? And why should we ask? Whatever else he did or failed to do, I have the feeling that he wrote in *Light in August* the first purely American novel, owing, as far as is possible in any created thing, nothing to the traditions of any other country or continent, a tree growing of its own energy out of the black earth of the Delta. If he really did that, then he is his own myth. He had heard the Furies beating their wings. (p. 17)

Sean O'Faolain, "Hate, Greed, Lust and Doom" (copyright © by Sean O'Faolain; appears here by permission of London Review of Books, Curtis Brown, Ltd. and the author), in London Review of Books, April 16 to May 6, 1981, pp. 16-17.

CLEANTH BROOKS

[*Brooks, one of the most notable scholars of Faulkner, says of his* William Faulkner: First Encounters: *"[This book] has been written for the general reader and for the student coming to Faulkner for the first time." Brooks adds that he "limits himself" to discussions of theme, character, plot, and historical and fictional settings. The following excerpts from Brooks's introduction illustrate his main concerns throughout this lucid, informative analysis of Faulkner's major works.*]

Most of us identify Faulkner with the South, and it is natural that we should do so, for his fiction is filled with references to its history, its geography, its customs; and his prose often employs its special idiom. Though there are exceptions, most of his great fiction has a Southern setting. Yet Faulkner's identification with the South can be misleading, for his value as a writer is not at all limited to what he can tell us about a particular regional culture. He was not a mere provincial in either time or space.

Thus, Faulkner differs radically from the typical Southern local colorists who preceded him by a generation. The local colorist in his crassest form is engaged in exploiting the local scene for the amused curiosity of the outsider. He stresses the differences between the "locals" and the national norm, his tacit assumption, of course, being that his reader represents the norm.

Even when the local colorist cherishes his region's differences and does not mean to hold them up to scorn, he is usually very much aware of his typical reader's assumption that the customs and attitudes depicted are different and even quaint. (p. 1)

How, then, does a writer like Faulkner, whose fiction is suffused with references to Southern history, folk ways, and attitudes, and whose characters' natural speech is the Southern idiom, whether in its cultivated or illiterate forms—how does Faulkner differ from the local colorist? The difference can be put simply: Faulkner's use of the local material is never allowed to become an end in itself. His ultimate aim, as he often tells us in his various interviews, is to talk about people—and he evidently meant by *people,* men and women in their universal humanity. (p. 2)

Using one's own environment ("what he knows," as Faulkner put it) in order to get at universal problems and relationships is very different from using the environment that one knows for its own sake or because it differs, interestingly or shockingly, from his reader's environment. For fiction, that difference is crucial.

True, the difference is sometimes blurred, and even when distinct it can be overlooked. A hasty or an insensitive reader will be likely to miss it altogether. Nevertheless, the ability to discern that difference will have everything to do with a reader's ability to appreciate fully a given piece of fiction and to take an accurate measure of its literary worth. It will have a great deal to do with the reader's enjoyment of Faulkner's work and it will make plain why so many critics at home and abroad regard him as one of the great novelists of our century.

Even so, it may seem odd that an introductory essay on Faulkner's work should begin by insisting on a principle that obviously applies to all fiction of genuine worth. The explanation lies in Faulkner's preoccupation with a region that is still not apprehended by the rest of the country as fully "American." Thus, the South's differences—real and imagined—from the rest of the country can prove to be a distraction.

An analogy may be useful here. Though Melville's masterpiece is entitled *Moby-Dick, or the Whale,* we do not read Melville primarily to learn about whales. Though Hawthorne's greatest novels are set in the Puritan New England of earlier centuries, we do not read *The Scarlet Letter* to learn about New England Puritanism. We read Hawthorne's novels because they set forth the human predicament in its most dramatic phases, or because, as Faulkner himself once put it with regard to his own basic aims, they show the human "heart in conflict with itself." It is true that in order to experience Melville's presentation of the human drama we may have to learn something about whaling; or with Hawthorne, to learn about the Puritan mind, but we do so in order to reach a more important goal. So also with Faulkner.

In short, Faulkner's world is worth the reader's possessing because his themes are finally universal human issues and his characters have a relevance to basic humanity. Nevertheless, Faulkner's world does have its own fascination, as even European readers have testified. Among other things, it points back to an earlier America. If Faulkner's world has lagged behind industrialized America, that very fact gives it a special interest. The family is still important, whether as a sustaining or a suffocating force. (In his novels, Faulkner does full justice to the family's blessed and its baleful aspects.)

In addition, the community is still in being. There is an almost instinctive consensus about basic issues. If the community also has its darker aspect in its tendency to suppress the rebel, it provides real resistance to the rebel who means business and is not merely posturing. His attempt to assert his individuality becomes no play-act, no mere pillow fight.

Faulkner's world is furthermore a world suffused with history. In it, history is not a series of far-off events. Battles were fought on Southern soil. (pp. 2-4)

Moreover, for the world depicted in Faulkner's fiction, evil is real and tragedy is close at hand. The South was the one part of America that had suffered defeat, and smashing defeat at that. In the South the typical American optimism had for decades been in short supply. In this regard, Faulkner's world is close to the world of Thomas Hardy's imagination or that of William Butler Yeats.

Faulkner writes, and often very sympathetically, of the older order of the antebellum plantation society. It was a society that valued honor, was capable of heroic action, and believed in courtesy and good manners. It had all the virtues and also many of the faults to which such a society was prone, and Faulkner, as the reader of this discussion of his fiction will discover, does justice to both. . . .

Yet some of Faulkner's finest examples of heroism come from the ranks of his yeoman whites, most of whom neither owned slaves nor came from former slave-owning families. These yeomen are, by the way, as jealous of their honor as any of Faulkner's aristocrats, and some of them—V. K. Ratliff of *The Hamlet,* for instance—are as interesting and attractive as any characters that Faulkner ever created.

The blacks, on whose labor the older plantation system rested, are also very important in Faulkner's work. (p. 4)

Faulkner was properly cautious in trying not to impose his own ideas and sentiments on his black characters. He rarely, if ever, forgot that in describing such characters he was looking at them from the outside. But he treats them sympathetically, and fully accords them their human dignity.

Much the same might be said with regard to Faulkner's female characters. This point is worth making in view of the fact that the notion has got about that Faulkner was something of a misogynist and was really comfortable only with gray-haired matriarchs. A review of the whole of his fiction ought to dispel this illusion. . . . Faulkner admired such young women as Eula Varner in *The Hamlet,* Lena Grove in *Light in August,* Caddy Compson in *The Sound and the Fury,* and Judith Sutpen in *Absalom, Absalom!*.

Was there no period of development in Faulkner? . . . How did he learn his craft? Or did it come to him instinctively?

Faulkner possessed a great natural gift. The record shows that. His *Soldiers' Pay* (1926) is a remarkable first novel, and his first published short story, **"A Rose for Emily"** (1930), displays a brilliant fictional technique. But he definitely went through a period of growth and development which shows, among other things, a movement from a rather decadent Swinburnian romanticism to a robust acceptance of reality and a tough-minded appraisal of it. It also shows a shift from poetry, his acknowledged first love, to prose, albeit a rich and at times an even highly rhetorical prose, as his proper instrument. More than once, Faulkner called himself a "failed poet."

Yet a book which presumes to be no more than a brief introduction does not offer the possibility of providing a really useful account of Faulkner's development as a literary artist. Besides, most of us are not interested in the story of preparation and development unless we already have a lively sense of what that preparation and development came to. Hence I have limited my selections to the great achievements—what most people would regard as clearly his masterpieces. My only conscious concessions to other interests are to be found in my choice of a few of the stories, some of which I included for the sake of providing further aspects of Faulkner's world.

In limiting myself to the great works, I have been unfair to Faulkner's later career, for his career did not end in 1942 with the publication of *Go Down, Moses.* Novels were yet to come, novels such as *The Wild Palms* or *The Mansion* that contain some of Faulkner's most daring fictional experiments and some of his most accomplished writing. But if this book achieves its purpose in bringing new readers to Faulkner, such readers can explore for themselves both his later and his earlier fiction.

One further point ought to be made: is the reader to prepare himself to experience tragedy or comedy? He should not, of course, "prepare" himself for either. He should open his mind and imagination to what Faulkner is capable of providing him. He must not block out possibilities for either a tragic or a comic response by assuming in advance what response will be appropriate. Actually, the sensitive, open-minded reader will find both comedy and tragedy, and often both in the same novel. For Faulkner's vision of reality is broad enough to encompass both, and the presence of both is a testimony to the artist's honesty and integrity in presenting his characters. What the reader will not find is mawkish sentimentality or mere farce, nor will he find special pleading for a thesis or cause.

There is tragedy to be found in Faulkner, and his *Absalom, Absalom!* seems to me to approach more nearly to great tragedy than does any other twentieth-century American work. But Faulkner is also one of our great masters of comedy. The novice reader must not assume that all is somber and melancholy in Faulkner's Yoknapatawpha County. There is gusto and laughter in which he is expected to join. (pp. 5-6)

Cleanth Brooks, in his William Faulkner: First Encounters *(copyright © 1983 by Yale University), Yale University Press, 1983, 230 p.*

Roy (Broadbent) Fuller
1912-

English poet, novelist, essayist, and memoirist.

Although considered a novelist of distinction, Fuller has been best known as a poet since he first began to publish verse in the 1930s. In that decade, Fuller was active in left-wing literary and political movements and became influenced by the work of W. H. Auden and Stephen Spender. His work of this period is characteristic of much of the verse written in the 1930s in its political liberalism and concern for the effects of modern society on the individual. Although Fuller's later poetry grew increasingly personal, his work has always been shaped by a strong humanitarian conscience. Death, loss, aging, and the role of the artist in society are persistent themes.

Two of Fuller's early collections of verse, *The Middle of the War* (1942) and *A Lost Season* (1944), chronicle his perceptions of World War II and his time spent serving in the British Navy in East Africa. Described by critics as among the best collections of the "war" poetry of this era, these two books mark, in the words of George Woodcock, "the liberation of Fuller's poetic talent." In both books, Fuller writes powerfully and sensitively of his experiences. In such books as *Counterparts* (1954) and *Brutus's Orchard* (1957) he treats his subjects in a broader manner. *Collected Poems* (1962) and *The Individual and His Times* (1982) contain the bulk of Fuller's achievement as a poet. In these volumes, Fuller's shift from the emotionalism of the war years to a calmer, less formal poetry is strikingly contrasted. Critics regard Fuller's later examinations of disappointment, loss, and aging as compelling.

Fuller's concern with the relationship between the individual and society is evident in all of his novels. In such works as *The Second Curtain* (1953) and *Image of a Society* (1956), characters are portrayed as being in conflict with an organization or institution which challenges their integrity and freedom. These groups are symbolic of the society which surrounds them and the struggle of his characters against them represents the attempt of all persons to survive with dignity in a dehumanizing world. Fuller has also published two volumes of his Oxford poetry lectures and his recent work includes two volumes of memoirs, *Souvenirs* (1980) and *Vamp Till Ready* (1982).

(See also *CLC*, Vol. 4; *Contemporary Authors*, Vols. 5-8, rev. ed.; and *Dictionary of Literary Biography*, Vols. 15, 20.)

Photograph by Alan Hillyer; courtesy of Roy Fuller

THE TIMES LITERARY SUPPLEMENT

[In] contrast to most of his contemporaries, Mr. Fuller still believes in the unambiguous direct statement about immediate issues. [Many of the new poems collected in *Epitaphs and Occasions*], occasional and informal in the best sense, are concerned with the relation of the individual's integrity to the collective good; others with the positive meanings of art in a society doomed by the pressure of outside events. . . . [One] aspect of Mr. Fuller's recent development [is his] realization of the dichotomy between the role of art, making coherent and discernible the unformulated, and the enormous "death by nature, chanceless, credible." The word "art" appears almost obsessively in these poems, and Mr. Fuller uses it as a sort of final reference, Olympian but powerless, to suggest the kind of myths to which the sensitive individual holds after having discarded the cleft stick of religion and politics. Yet, although Mr. Fuller assumes defeat for the curious "dyspeptic, bookish, half-alive" figure he projects of himself, he still believes

> Confused and wrong though things have gone
> There is a side we can be on:
> Distaste for lasting bread and peace
> May thus support a King in Greece
> And trust in General Chiang Kai-shek
> Will safely lead to freedom's wreck.

It is this essential rationalism, this urgent belief in the necessity of moral action, however trivially stated, that is most notable in Mr. Fuller's poems. He has ruthlessly simplified his verse-forms to enable his writing, without change of tone, to move easily through very different kinds of theme, while the meaning remains transparent. Mr. Fuller's latest manner is perhaps over-reminiscent in style of the early Auden, possibly also of the colloquial Byron. But that, and the latter especially, is the most healthy tradition for contemporary English verse, whose greatest need is for more clarity of thought and greater preciseness in technique. Moreover, Mr. Fuller is exact where Mr. Auden is only vaguely impressive; though he is not such a sparkling writer, the lines he chooses to "throw away" contain seriously considered antitheses where Mr. Auden's tended only to arrest.

It is impossible here to suggest every aspect of a book so closely packed as this. *Epitaphs and Occasions,* as its title hints, is not ambitiously creative writing at full stretch; but its best poems are minor verse at its most accomplished. There is no other contemporary poet who reduces so much thought, socially or politically crucial in the widest sense, to so small a space as Mr. Fuller has done in this book. The form of the poems may make them seem, at first glance, rather slight, but their content is highly condensed, varied, often both moving and witty. Beneath Mr. Fuller's rather fusty cloak of minor, saddened distemper a major poet is waiting to be revealed. Of his importance there is no question.

> "Tenant of a Star," *in* The Times Literary Supplement *(© Times Newspapers Ltd. (London) 1949; reproduced from* The Times Literary Supplement *by permission), No. 2500, December 30, 1949, p. 858.*

JAMES SANDOE

["**Fantasy and Fugue**"] is at least as exciting and as disturbing as [Roy Fuller's first crime novel] "**The Second Curtain**" and by that token one of the more considerable mysteries in this or any other season. Like its predecessor it has the haunting quality of those entertainments with which Graham Greene expressed his alertness to the Thirties. But like its predecessor too Mr. Fuller's novel has its own integrity and its own expressiveness in explicating an unsettled state of mind.

Its principal is a younger brother through whose multiple awareness we recall a murder and its precedents while he goes through London carrying a great bundle of incertitude which may just possibly be a corpse. It is all a most uncommon evocation which, while never losing hold of its first objective, manages half a hundred deft, often sardonic, comments on contemporary tastes and failings. Curious, meticulous and memorable.

> James Sandoe, *in a review of* "Fantasy and Fugue," *in* New York Herald Tribune Book Review *(© I.H.T. Corporation, reprinted by permission), August 19, 1956, p. 9.*

THE NEW YORKER

[*Fantasy and Fugue* is a] study of the origin and consequences of a guilty obsession (the hero is sure he has killed a man, but why and how are mysteries to him almost to the end) [which] takes the reader into some extremely strange backwaters of literary London. Fay Lavington is a dreadful girl, and, in their separate ways, Clarence Rimmer, Charles Legge, and Bob Midwinter are pretty repulsive specimens, too. They are not, however, without their conversational charms . . . and their behavior is also moderately bizarre. Mr. Fuller is known in London as a poet of some distinction, and his book is written with a style very rare in works of this kind. In spite of an almost unendurably lurid climax, it is a remarkably exciting story as well. (pp. 175-76)

> *A review of* "Fantasy and Fugue," *in* The New Yorker *(© 1956 by The New Yorker Magazine, Inc.), Vol. XXXII, No. 31, September 22, 1956, pp. 175-76.*

THE TIMES LITERARY SUPPLEMENT

Mr. Fuller's post-war poetry has generally been that of a quiet, contemplative family man who uses the trivial happenings of domestic existence as a starting-point for an analysis of the larger horrors of modern life. His viewpoint is suburban rather than metropolitan or rural, his tone is wry, ironic and dryly critical, his mood tends to be gloomy. The experiences out of which his poetry is created are rarely beyond the reach of the ordinary commuting man: his attitude to them is deprecating, rational, closely observant. His poetry could be said to put dullness under a microscope, to restate the familiar commonplaces of human life in terms that are sometimes amused, sometimes tragic, but always to the point. His style, as befitting his subjects, is sober, neat, unadorned: the wilder passions, the deeper fantasies, the more beguiling landscapes are outside not his range, not his experience, not his awareness but simply his habit. He has chosen to explore the everyday, rather than exploit the occasional. Yet—for all this deliberate limiting of standpoint, this unemotional assessment of prospects—the passion, the horror, the sharp appetite for the crucial, are clearly there. The ambiguity has deceived many: for some reason the surface calm has apparently failed to suggest the dark, crowded war within.

It is strange that this should be so, and that Mr. Fuller's reputation has, if anything, declined since the end of the war. Certainly, there is a thirtyish quality in some of his less original poems (the first two poems in [*Brutus's Orchard*], for example, are schematically Audenesque), he is scarcely ever exuberant or overtly lyrical, and there is an occasional flatness of rhythm, an obviousness of rhyme. But, accepting all this, his true seriousness as a writer, the clarity with which he examines moral problems, the often deeply touching quality of his concern for animal or human victims, the candid steadiness of the gaze he turns on himself, are beyond question. He is, *sui generis,* the moralist among contemporary poets, and if moralists do not always seem attractive, and if they tend to morbidity, they are none the less valuable. In fact, Mr. Fuller's touch is of the lightest, his idiom pleasantly conversational. He is as far removed from ponderousness as it is possible to be.

Brutus's Orchard has not the variety, or freshness of feeling of Mr. Fuller's war poems, which gained a lot both from their sense of separation and their African setting. But he has been developing as a prose writer in the last decade and his poems, though no less serious in intention, have been rather more occasional in theme. . . .

The major achievement of this volume are the nineteen mythological sonnets that close it. Here the sustaining passions of men, as of gods—love, hate, lust, ambition, art, jealousy—are scrutinized and compared in a series of finely wrought images.

> "The Poet As Moralist," *in* The Times Literary Supplement *(© Times Newspapers Ltd. (London) 1958; reproduced from* The Times Literary Supplement *by permission), No. 2914, January 3, 1958, p. 9.*

THOM GUNN

A lot of [*Brutus's Orchard*] is taken up with occasional poems. Most short poems are occasional, I suppose, in that they take particular and possibly trivial situations as their starting points, but to be of any importance they should also expand on these situations, giving them some larger, yet definite, place in the writer's experience. Unfortunately, with a great many of Mr. Fuller's poems, we are left where we started, contemplating some either obvious or vaguely didactic comment on an ordinary occupation of no great significance.

The most surprising defect of his poetry may be connected with the nature of the didacticism—surprising in that Mr. Fuller is one of the most perceptive poetry reviewers in England. He has still not shaken off his dependence on an idiom borrowed from Auden, which he uses everywhere, from the bright slangy epithet ("the charming cyclists") to the whole conception of a poem (*The Day*). The attractive jargon partly conceals and partly accounts for the weakness of the many general statements. (pp. 378-79)

The faults of triviality, derivativeness, and facile pessimism, however, are shown up by some very real qualities: a power of accurate description, an accomplished urbanity of tone, and a sense of humor which is at its best in the **Mythological Sonnets** at the end. Too often the virtues are so mixed in with the vices that few of the poems are completely flawed or completely unflawed, but there are at least two poems which are real accomplishments: **The Ides of March,** with its fine control of irony; and (in spite of a slightly confused first stanza) **Eclipse**. . . . Roy Fuller at his best is a poet to be reckoned with, and there would be many more poems like these two if only he were to examine the general assumptions on which his despair is grounded—if he were to show us the general forces *in action,* instead of merely tagging on sententious comments about them. (pp. 379-80)

Thom Gunn, "The Calm Style" (© 1958 by The Modern Poetry Association; reprinted by permission of the Editor of Poetry *and the author), in* Poetry, *Vol. XCII, No. 6, September, 1958, pp. 378-84.**

THE TIMES LITERARY SUPPLEMENT

[In *The Ruined Boys*, published in the United States as *That Distant Afternoon,*] Mr. Roy Fuller has written a series of quiet vignettes of school life. We are subjected to no gradual gathering of momentum, to no resounding climax. The boy Bracher is taken through three terms of his life in a second-rate English boarding school, makes friends and enemies, rumbles the headmaster, and at the end learns that Mr. Percy, the master who has exercised most influence over him, will not be returning after the holidays. That is all. It does not seem much, perhaps, set against the bloodbaths and the perversions one so increasingly reads about. And yet the book, quietly ironic, unobtrusively accomplished, fully succeeds in what it purposes to do. The trickle of small incidents, each one scrupulously observed from the point of view of the boy, saps busily away at Bracher's unfledged confidence in, and respect for, an immutable ordered world. The absolute monarchy of the headmaster in the English public school system has rarely been sniped at with more murderous accuracy. . . .

Mr. Fuller's writing is admirably lucid and controlled. His Virgilian fondness for extended simile gives an illuminating stateliness to his prose.

"Nonage and Verbiage," in The Times Literary Supplement *(© Times Newspapers Ltd. (London) 1959; reproduced from* The Times Literary Supplement *by permission), No. 2977, March 20, 1959, p. 166.**

DAN WICKENDEN

"**That Distant Afternoon**" is a subtle and uncannily penetrating novel, and by the time we have reached its final, fascinating page we have observed something momentous: a young and very human being has taken several long strides toward maturity. . . .

[Although] Mr. Fuller is a wit and an ironist, he respects his characters; he knows (and irrefutably demonstrates) that a boy of fourteen or fifteen is at least as complex and as worthy of concentrated attention as any adult. He also commands a polished, supple, almost immaculate style; and part of its delight is a constant play of simile—often surprising, always original and strikingly apt—in which much of the wit and the illumination resides. "**That Distant Afternoon**" may be on a small scale, but it is first rate, an accomplished, impressive and continuously entertaining novel.

Dan Wickenden, "A Young, Very Human Being," in New York Herald Tribune Book Review *(© I.H.T. Corporation; reprinted by permission), April 12, 1959, p. 4.*

ROBERT CONQUEST

The quality of Roy Fuller's **Collected Poems** must make any honest reviewer ask himself once more what truly relevant comment he can offer. To say what sort of poetry it is is not to convey its excellences. . . .

[Fuller's] standing as a poet is one of the two or three highest of those now writing. Yet his reputation is mainly among poets and readers of poetry. The professional critics, busy with estimates of Pound, have scarcely looked at him. His name does not ring glamorously round the campuses—and this alone is enough for us to write off completely all fashionable American opinion about British verse.

This American neglect is even odder when one considers that Fuller is in effect doing what Wallace Stevens tried to do, failing because of a streak of frivolity and dilettantism, and perhaps for lack of an adequate rhythmic sense too. For Fuller's humanism arises not only from the generalities of society and the particulars of love and suffering, but also from the particulars of seeing and understanding, of man's grasp of the phenomenal world.

Fuller is (or anyhow was throughout most of the period covered by this book) a Marxist poet. It would be idle to deny that this has sometimes led him to descend from his broader vision to a ludicrous close-up: as when he maintains that support for the constitutional Greek government against the loathsome Zachariades can only have been motivated by dislike of bread and peace. To yield this facile assent to formula in a matter of political detail is objectionable poetically, regardless of the political philosophy. But such blemishes are rare. . . .

[On] the whole his Marxism is one side of a powerful and positive virtue. He is doing what Pound pretended to do—seeing the human condition in a vast social and historical perspective. It is an insult to Fuller to compare them at all: but a crucial difference is that Pound affects to work up to the grandiose from a potty little economic fiddle, while Fuller starts with the wide vision. He sees . . . a various unity forming one long human drama. This gives him what is commonly lacking in modern poets, a properly rooted tragic sense.

For his verse is not social for social's sake, but for man's. His themes, particularly in his later poems, are from the whole human sphere: all those extremities which the philosophies and religions have failed to allay. Ageing, sex, dying, pity, nostalgia, melancholy: the *lacrimae rerum,* and some of the *cach-*

innationes rerum too, played out on a grand stage. Even the comic servant in his Faust cycle, complaining of vulgar lusts which he can no longer satisfy, is essentially an adjunct and broadening of tragedy, and even tragic himself. Moreover Fuller is never really happy with anything resembling a social millennium. In the Justish City

> full of bread and wine
> I shall dream of the discipline of insomnia
> And an art of symbols, starved and saturnine.

Similarly, from the Freudian type of thought he derives not a setpiece of mechanistic concepts, but the human being, caught yet conscious, in his Condition. In fact, the moods and ideas of the Thirties are strong upon Fuller: but he wears them with a difference. It would be hard to deny that the vigour and the inventiveness of Auden and MacNeice was accompanied by a certain slapdashness, a tenuousness and sometimes frivolity of matter. I am not wanting to imply that 'density' and 'tension' are the most important criteria of poetic merit: such a notion is one of the dullest-minded of recent critical generalities, and would involve one in asserting that Crashaw was a better poet than Marlowe or Dryden. Yet Fuller has, typically, managed to combine the best effects and strengths of both types of writing. He is the heir, not only of the lucidity and power of Auden, but also of the vividness and penetration of the best in symbolism.

Fuller's phrasing is individual and unmistakable to the point sometimes of caricature; though never of contrivance. . . .

In his later poems there is often an uncertain calm. . . .

[Fuller's] resources are all the usable ones of traditional, and of 'modern,' English poetry: a rare and remarkable fusion. Moreover, although this *Collected Poems* unaccountably omits a number of fine poems from his first book, and the newest '**Meredithian Sonnets**' are not his best work, we can yet follow the development of increasing scope and mastery. Eccentricity and preconception drop off like boosters, leaving the second stage of a free personality shameless in its skill, sincerity, sanity and sensitivity.

No book by even the best of English poets is faultless, but Fuller's flaws are meagre and peripheral. Some adjectives ('enormous') are overdone. In spite of his view that 'poetry should be intelligible,' there are obscurities (what are the 'foliate five' acts?). Occasional mannerisms annoy—throwaway images justified only by rhyme; Auden or others echoing too closely; and so on. But in general his verse has that naturalness and rightness of tone, even when the language is least colloquial, which arises from an intrinsic and personal unity. It happily comprehends (as no unity prescribed by critical preconception can) lyric and rhetoric, statement and metaphor, concretion and abstraction.

> Robert Conquest, "Saturnine Daylight," in The Spectator (© 1962 by The Spectator; reprinted by permission of The Spectator), Vol. 209, No. 7001, August 31, 1962, p. 307.

MARTIN SEYMOUR-SMITH

The blurb to Mr. Fuller's *Collected Poems*—an unusually platitudinous one—implies that he is, above all, a continually developing poet. This is seriously misleading, for it neatly misses the point: he is, in the proper sense, an occasional poet—the most worthy of his time. What may have seemed like a consistent poetic development to the blurb-writer is in reality a record of the changing attitudes of a remarkably sensitive and good-hearted man. (Some modern exponents of verse would deny that good-heartedness has anything to do with poetry—they have to; but it does, and it is one of Mr. Fuller's strongest assets.) Genuinely readable and unpretentious though he is, Mr. Fuller's use of language has not undergone that change which alone can justify the word "developing": diction, texture, rhythm, tone—all these have remained more or less constant throughout his twenty-five years' work. He does many effective things to words; they seldom do anything to him. In fact, when he is "carried away" he is at his weakest.

He is a poet of public themes. Even when he is writing of himself—of his reactions to the seasons, war, sex, or metropolitan awfulness—he carefully represents himself as the civilised creature in its public, primitive, or natural environment. (p. 72)

Mr. Fuller's *Collected Poems* represents a real achievement. This is put into bold relief by the verse of those who imitate him or try to borrow his acrid, amiable tone of voice. One of the purely incidental values of this book is that it cruelly shows up the work of a new wave of poetasters: the authors of those "intelligible" verses, written in accordance with "rules," that make neat, small points. Such authors are using verse-making as a means to an end.

One values Mr. Fuller because his poems are so obviously prompted by different, less ambitious, less trivial needs. His readability does not arise from any easily acquired slickness, but from seriousness and true awareness.

Mr. Fuller expresses his position most clearly in the Horatian *Translation*. . . . Here Mr. Fuller is at his best: humorous, honest, and authoritative. It is the poetry of the civilised attitude rather than of passion; but its strength is derived from a decency, unsentimental concern, and intellectual self-effacement not to be found in the culture-marionettes who ape its urbane tone, but who lack the qualities of character that are required to achieve it.

Mr. Fuller retained his early Marxism until relatively late, and in the poems of his middle period this sometimes takes on a specious appearance. . . . But there are fewer signs of this in his latest poems, notably the *Faustian Sketches* and in the twenty-one fine *Meredithian Sonnets* that close the book. Here, one feels, Mr. Fuller is less certain of the full implications of his themes; and although his increasing and salutary awareness of the unknown has not yet got into his language, it has got into his themes, which are often complex—even recondite. One of the Sonnets (XVI) gives a clue. . . . The detail of this poem suffers from most of Mr. Fuller's linguistic weaknesses—over-use of "effect" adjectives to fill up a line, forced rhymes (such as "bare")—but here at last is a hint of a *personal* predicament, a private situation. It has been skilfully dramatised by the novelist-element in the poet, but this device only serves to communicate it more powerfully and disturbingly.

Mr. Fuller's well-deserved success as a novelist may have caused him to experience a new difficulty in writing poems; as this increases his poems may become fewer, but rewarding in an unexpected and perhaps even more valuable way. Meanwhile, this collection demands our respect and admiration. (pp. 73-5)

> Martin Seymour-Smith, in a review of "Collected Poems," in Encounter (© 1963 by Encounter Ltd.), Vol. XX, No. 1, January, 1963, pp. 72-5.

THE TIMES LITERARY SUPPLEMENT

It is rare and difficult for any poet, young or old, to find a true voice; rarer and even more difficult to adopt a new one in the notoriously barren stretches of middle age. Yet this is what Roy Fuller has splendidly done in his *New Poems*. The voice is both true and new. It speaks from recognizably the same man as that of the *Collected Poems* . . . and *Buff* . . . , but with a directness of personal reference quite unexpected from Mr. Fuller, whose sequences of *Mythological Sonnets, Meredithian Sonnets, To X* and *The Historian* seemed to be leading him farther and farther from himself, perhaps as a necessary corrective to what he has called "the tyranny of the personal lyric" in recent poetry. These sequences were extremely well done, but they did seem to hold dangers of boxing the poet too constrictingly in elegant pre-ordained structures, and of confining inspiration in future to dyspeptic reflections drawn from books or of laboriously inventing a whole range of ad hoc personae.

Mr. Fuller has turned in on himself—a successful professional man in his mid-fifties, now pulled down by ill health and disappointed with what he has achieved. Yet it would be quite wrong to imagine that the result is anything like the "confessional" poetry we have come to recognize (and—some of us—distrust). The abandonment of strict forms and ingenious rhymes has not meant a blurring of focus. Such poems by Mr. Fuller as **"In Memory of my cat Domino"** and **"Romance"** are deceptively relaxed and low-keyed, but they do not lack art. . . .

[One] must acknowledge the faults here too, of which Mr. Fuller is sometimes, though seldom, guilty: faults which are directly related to the virtues of his method. Self-revelation inevitably leads to self-dramatization, however scrupulous the admission of pose:

> Is it possible that anyone so silly can
> Write anything good?

Again, one is disarmed, but this sort of remark (from **"Last Sheet"**) nudges one into a sort of indulgence which is embarrassing. One finds it towards the end of **"Chinoiserie"**, charming, self-deprecating, honest, but diminishing too. It is the price that has to be paid for choosing to "tell all", and the fidelity of such a mirror is not to be questioned. . . . These poems force one into asking severely moral questions, of art and of oneself. That they do so in such a disquieting way is, quite apart from their great skill, a sign of their importance.

"Turning In," in The Times Literary Supplement (© Times Newspapers Ltd. (London) 1968; reproduced from The Times Literary Supplement by permission), No. 3475, October 3, 1968, p. 1134.

GEORGE WOODCOCK

[Since the publication of his first volume of verse, *Poems,* in 1939,] Fuller has published, including his *Collected Poems* [1962] (which contains items ungathered elsewhere) some eight volumes of verse, showing a continual process of development and change within clearly defined philosophic and poetic objectives. He influenced very strongly the "Movement" of the 1950's; but where those who followed him, like John Wain and Kingsley Amis, remained frozen in their attitudes, his verse developed and changed until by the end of the Sixties he had built up a body of work which gave an appropriateness as well as an inevitability to his election this year as Oxford Professor of Poetry; among the depleted ranks of contemporary English poets, he stood out in unchallenged prominence.

In some ways Fuller's career reminds one of that of Wallace Stevens. He quite deliberately avoided the pressures and perils that encompass a professional man of letters by continuing, until his recent retirement at the age of 57, the occupation as solicitor to a building society which he took up more than thirty years before. He has observed this situation with appropriate irony:

> In the event his life was split
> And half was lost bewailing it;
> Part managerial, part poetic—
> Hard to decide the more pathetic.
>   (**"Obituary of R. Fuller"**)

Yet there seems a close relationship between the kind of life Fuller chose—and there were alternatives he rejected—and the kind of *oeuvre* he has produced. His poetry can be seen as the autobiography—intellectual growing into spiritual—of a man who seeks, as he has said, "always the human in reality." It is a poetry which, being produced mainly after the great disillusionment in which the Thirties ended, lacks the ebullient idealism of the early Spender, the truculent self-righteousness of the early Day Lewis. Stoicism, but not negation, compassion but not acceptance, define its tone. Fuller combines, perhaps uniquely, an intense sense of the tragedy that lurks in all human—and animal—lives, with a profound consciousness of the part which the social environment plays in this condition; his great achievement seems to lie in the fact that he has succeeded through this combination in preserving, as no other survivor from that time has done, the best elements of the political idealism of the Thirties. (pp. 24-5)

It has not been possible for the poet in the last thirty years to speak in the tones of fresh and glittering optimism one hears in poems like Spender's "After They Have Tired." For those who in the Sixties retain radical ideas and yet look realistically at the world, there remains only what Fuller expresses in his later poems; the feeling that the search for sublime societies is "not quite in vain," the attitude of the man who, recognising all the defeats and the betrayals, cannot reconcile himself to the thought that man's hopes will not finally—by however devious a process of history and in however humble a way—triumph.

Such a faith can destroy an indifferent poet by submerging his fragment of talent in hopeful abstractions. Unaccompanied by the development of a personal and independent vision, it can turn even a potentially good poet into an archaicist of the Left. But Fuller has been much more than a survivor from a lost decade. From his early poems down to the *New Poems* which appeared twenty-nine years afterwards in 1968, there is a steady subtilising of technique, a steady opening of perception, and it is a measure of Fuller's maturity as a poet that he has not allowed a frankly sustained didacticism to loosen his grip on the world of experience; everything is referred back to the point of living in these later poems. They are poems fired by opinion, fuelled by thought and objective observation, yet they project intense and highly personal feelings, expressed sensitively yet ironically, with gravity but not without wit. The personal images, figures of dream and myth, illuminate the general philosophic stance. . . . [The] tension between the private nature of the poet's world and the public preoccupations which history forces upon him has been a constant concern for Fuller. It is a tension linked closely with a personal aloofness that has never allowed him to become totally involved in a political movement, and which at the same time has kept him uneasily aware how far his class background, his professional occupation, his personal aesthetic, his need for privacy, have all helped force him apart from those who struggle for the social hopes he himself maintains. It is the dilemma Stendhal defined a century ago when he remarked: "I love the people and detest oppressors but every moment would be a torture to me if I had to live with the people." Even in relatively recent poems Fuller expresses it in terms of an agonizing division of will. . . . This constancy of Fuller's attitudes, of withdrawal into the private self straining against the external demands of political socialism and literary realism, clarifies his development as a poet by allowing one's attention to turn often away from the basic content, which always remains within the same broadly humanist field, and towards the character of the writing itself, the bare, controlled verse, tight with meaning, of a craftsman who has spent thirty years shedding influences and avoiding easy mannerisms so as to find the voice that would speak as clearly as possible what he wanted all along to say.

A look back at the 1939 volume of *Poems* suggests how long and patiently followed was the road to the clarity and personal language of the poems of the Sixties. On its first appearance thirty years ago, the verse in *Poems* seemed at least to have novelty, but in fact it was merely fashionable; now it appears obsolete and derivative. . . . The speech is stiff, the images are awkward and musty like period slang; there is almost no invitation to involvement. These are Fuller's shyest poems, for the writer seems to be reciting a series of hieratic phrases, of secular mantras, designed to conceal rather than express his meaning, and he has a slight air of embarrassment, as if he fears a real feeling may put its unauthorized and clowning face between the curtains.

I would like to dwell a little more closely on the relationship between Fuller and Auden which is suggested by these early poems. Auden's influence, first evident in imagery and language, seems in the long and positive run to have been more important in guiding Fuller's absorption of intellectual elements into his verse. From Auden's experiments Fuller learnt how to use both Marxist and Freudian concepts as part of the material of poetry, and—since Auden's muse has long departed to more celestial regions—one can perhaps regard him as the heir who has proved by performance his claim to these particular territories. Yet the differences between the two poets are greater than the obvious links at first suggest. Both are didactic in their intent, yet Fuller in his recent verse is much more deeply and emotionally involved in human predicaments—and a great deal less involved in games of wit—than Auden. He also differs from him in nurturing a simplism resembling that of the early Romantics. Where Auden made poetry an agent of intellectual complexity, a way of saying things too involved for prose with little regard for ease of access, Fuller has always worked with the thought in mind that "poetry must be intelligible," and his shedding of Thirties mannerisms was part of a progression towards maximum clarity. (pp. 25-8)

Fuller was perhaps fortunate in the way his development coincided with changes in his world and consequent changes in his life. He developed too late in the Thirties to have to make the choice whether "To be committed or to stand apart"; he could live in the world between, more or less indefinitely, and such tensions are productive of art. Then, before his life could become completely crystallized into the pattern of the lawyer's career, came the war. And the consequent change in tone and power evident in Fuller's second volume, *The Middle of a War* (1942), is remarkable. (p. 28)

It was the release of private emotions by the public event of war that began the liberation of Fuller's poetic talent. The agony of interrupted love, and the discovery of classless comradeship; the horror of destruction, and the hope rising like rosebay in the ruins of London; above all, the enjoyment of a life which peril made at once intense and fragile: all these aspects of a world suddenly illuminated became evident in his war poems.

But mostly it is the emotion of parting that gives *The Middle of a War* its peculiar sensitivity; I can think of no collection of that period which explores more poignantly this most insidious of war's mental wounds. Through this exploration Fuller came to manhood as a poet. . . . (pp. 28-9)

If parting gives its tone to *The Middle of a War,* it is strangeness that sets the atmosphere of *A Lost Season* (1944), whose contents are inspired largely by Fuller's experiences serving with the Navy in East Africa. The regret of *The Middle of a War* is still there, but it is counterpointed by the wonder of the African hills, of their bizarre animal and human world of unreason and violence. In this environment Fuller's awakening power of observing and of selecting the right images from observation had full play, and the result was a series of poems that conveyed with exceptional pungency the physical presence of Africa.

These war poems are crucial to Fuller's development; they not merely mark the release of his individuality but also tell us much about his character as a poet. . . . [They] reveal him as a passive writer, whose powers are not spontaneously inventive, but are set into motion when they are acted upon by the great external events that perturb his personal world. At this point he becomes impressionist rather than expressionist. . . . (p. 29)

[Fuller] expresses best what he is directly involved in, and has little power of imaginative projection into a situation outside his own experience; there he becomes the observer rather than the interpreter. This explains why the little he wrote about Spain, where he went only long after the Civil War was over, was ineffectual, and why his anti-Fascist poetry, written about issues outside his direct experience, was never very convincing, while what he wrote about the war in which he did take part was good; at this point he had accepted his function as that of an autobiographical poet, taking his cues from what life gives.

Despite their bitterness against the fact of war, *The Middle of a War* and *A Lost Season* are the most romantic in tone of Fuller's books, in which emotions flower freely under the pain of parting and the fascination of strange lands. After the war, disillusionment sweeps in and the tone changes. *Epitaphs and Occasions,* which appeared in 1949 and contained poems from a period beginning in 1944, is permeated with the sour hangover feeling that came with the end of wartime uncertainty and of its enormous possibilities of Utopia or destruction. The great, grim holiday was over; one was back in one's class and one's groove, and the world did not seem to have moved forward. And in reaction, though some poems like **"Knole"** and **"The Lake"** show the emergence of a more calmly philosophic attitude, most of the pieces Fuller wrote in this period belong in a limited spectrum of tones that extends from the flippant to the sardonic. The dominant feeling of this phase is expressed in **"The Divided Life Re-Lived,"** in which Fuller remarks bitterly:

> How we innocently thought that we should be alone
>   no more,
> Linked in death or revolution as in war.
> How completely we have slipped into the same old
>   world of cod,
> Our companions Henry James or cats or God.

The thinness of an over-cerebral statement characterizes this, like other Fuller poems contemporary with it, and one wonders—as one wonders always with Swift who appears to have influenced Fuller greatly at this time—how far this kind of writing is poetry at all.

Such doubts receded with Fuller's two volumes of the Fifties, *Counterparts* [1954] and *Brutus's Orchard* [1957]. In them the sardonic quality of *Epitaphs and Occasions* departs; it is replaced by an attempt to universalise the personal consciousness of loss that had dominated *The Middle of a War.* Fuller now considers the total tragedy of human existence, but a tragedy that, as it were, leaves a Horatio surviving. Inevitably he sees it through his own experience, and the pieces that comprise these volumes are often motivated by slight events of particular significance to the poet from which the original image is selected and related, through his reactions, to a final generalising statement. (pp. 31-2)

In these volumes of the Fifties, and in the two more recent collections, *Buff* (1964) and *New Poems* (1968), one becomes aware of the reinstatement of order after the awakening experience of war and war's losses, war's incalculable gains. Not only did Fuller return to the life of the solicitor while those of his friends who continued to write took up the profession of man-of-letters. Behind this deliberate ordering of his life in a curiously repetitive pattern lay the parallel urges to seek what kind of order might be apprehended in the apparent chaos of existence, and to give an order to the expression of that search. In the latter sense, Fuller has followed the trends of the Thirties. He has seen in the traditional forms of poetry the guarantees of an ordering of thought, of emotions, that seems to him a necessary part of the poet's function, and for this reason, while he has played on the minor irregularities, he has kept to the basic verse forms, writing sonnet sequences, Hudibrastic couplets, villanelles, unrhymed hexameters; perhaps the most interesting development has come in his most recent volume, *New Poems,* in which he has virtually abandoned rhyme, and has used a great deal of syllabic rather than metrical verse, but without jettisoning the general principle of an ordered structure, so that one both encounters unrhymed sonnets and quatrains in which a more or less regular metre preserves the structure, and other poems in which the syllabic system is used quite differently from its adaptation by the disciples of William Carlos Williams. Fuller in one of his Oxford lectures points to a poem of this kind: **"Reading *The Bostonians* in Algeciras Bay."** Metrical regularity vanishes, but structural regularity does not, for the poem consists of nine stanzas, each of nine lines, each of nine syllables. So, even in abandoning such technical devices as rhyme and metre, order is preserved; indeed, perhaps made more resilient and therefore more durable by being relaxed.

These most recent poems—and this might be said of all the volumes from *Counterparts* in 1954—do not strive after the obvious and shallow wit of so many pieces in *Epitaphs and Occasions,* and they lack the weight of nostalgia and the exotic colour that attracted one in the wartime poems. They are the works of a poet who has been lucky enough to work and develop steadily into late middle age, and they reflect the wiriness and gravity of a talent that has learnt to survive. They are no longer out to entice or to surprise, but to tell; colour, wit and high emotion they use for sparing effect. Yet from the very purposiveness of their telling has emerged some of the best poetry of our generation. . . . This is verse which preserves, curiously uncorrupted, the more lasting elements of the poetry of the Thirties in which Fuller began to write, and it suggests that the continuity between that decade and ours is perhaps not so tenuous, in terms of literary inspiration, as it has recently been fashionable to assert. Fuller himself certainly looks back to that formative period with obvious regret and respect.

> But now, I feel, the thirties gone,
> The dim light's out that could have shone.

Yet perhaps his achievement is that, alone among the poets who emerged at the end of that decade, he has in fact kept its light alive, to show him the direction towards an individuality and a maturity that make him certainly the one philosophic poet of undoubted capability writing in England today. As all men bear until death the scars of childhood, so all poets bear, however they may change, the indelible mark of the time in which they first moved into consciousness of their peculiar talents. (pp. 32-4)

> George Woodcock, "Private Images of Public Ills: The Poetry of Roy Fuller" (copyright, 1969 by Wascana Review; *reprinted by permission of the publisher and the author), in* Wascana Review, *Vol. 4, No. 2, 1969, pp. 21-34.*

EDWIN MORGAN

Roy Fuller, poet as well as novelist, has in a sense pooled his resources in [*The Carnal Island*] in order to probe the range of questions thrown up by an encounter between an old poet and a young one, and the result is a very perceptive, often amusing, and at times sad and touching, novel. The narrative framework is deliberately slight. The young poet, James, has an assignment to persuade the 80-year-old poet, Daniel House, to compile an anthology for a publisher, and visits him in his house overlooking an estuary. He meets the old man's wife, his illegitimate daughter and *her* illegitimate daughter, his local friends, his 15-year-old dog. Almost the only 'action' is a swim in the sea and a fatal ferry-crossing. But the light chain of events, all ordinary except for the climactic ferry, is carefully forged to set memory and speculation free, to allow the relationship between the two writers to develop quickly and naturally from curiosity to respect and love, and also to reinforce the point the book seems to want to make, that art's job is mainly, through feeling, to transform the commonplace. This point is emphasised in James's conviction that Daniel's poetry was released not through his socialist belief that the world must be changed but through his private flashpoints of love and involvement.

Yet the necessary mundaneness, symbolised on one page by a cheap glass dish of crisps brought in with beer on a tray, cannot be separated from myth and mystery when strong human feelings, or the even stronger urges towards art, begin to emerge. The title of the novel is also the title of a sequence of erotic poems published by Daniel in the Twenties, and the 'island' is in fact the land across the estuary, where his daughter still lives. The dead mother, the reality behind the passionate affair celebrated in the poems, had ridden a horse along the beach on a misty day and been drowned, but was it suicide, or an assignation with Daniel, or an assignation with another lover as the poetry suggested? The 'sea-nymph' theme returns when the granddaughter and her girlfriend go swimming with James, and again at the end when the foundered boat is called *Sea Nymph* and the aged poet is delivered to the dangerous element he loved. In a book which for its length may seem a shade over-baggaged with quotations, Mr Fuller forbears to quote the end of Eliot's 'Prufrock', but one feels that those sea-girls, and the human voices that 'wake us and we drown', must have been very much in the author's mind.

Charlie the ferryman reminds the narrator of Charon, the estuary becomes the Styx, Daniel's dog becomes Cerberus, and Daniel himself an Orpheus who bursts into poetic recital on board. All this is done fairly lightly, but it jars, even on the level of dramatic irony. On the other hand, there are some beautifully managed moments where restraint says everything.

> *Edwin Morgan, "Private Flashpoints" (© British Broadcasting Corp. 1970; reprinted by permission of Edwin Morgan), in* The Listener, *Vol. 84, No. 2165, September 24, 1970, p. 428.**

THE TIMES LITERARY SUPPLEMENT

The themes which preoccupy Roy Fuller in his poetry are nakedly, indeed oppressively, active in [*The Carnal Island*]. Most of Fuller's verse has, in one way or another, been about the role of the poet in a society that is hostile or indifferent to him; how absurd and tragic the discrepancy between the poet's art-life and his real life, between his grand therapeutic dreams and his actual social and political impotence. Can Freud and Marx be married? That classic worry of the 1930s has continued to provide Fuller with his basic subject matter, preventing him from either retreating into the personal or from striding out into the public. If the persona of his most recent poems has been one of disappointment and exhaustion, it has also seemed rather heroic; he is, after all, the only one of those many bright young men of theory who has not either stopped writing altogether or lapsed into godliness or borrowed rusticism.

The central figure in *The Carnal Island* can offer similar credentials. A famous poet, now in his eighties, Daniel House is a veteran of the trenches as well as of the Spanish Civil War, but he is very much a 1930s figure. . . .

The Carnal Island is narrated by a young poet/publisher, an admirer of House (one who "knows" him through his work). Visiting the old poet for a weekend in order to persuade him to edit an anthology, James Ross finds himself drawn into a study of the real-life background to the art-life of the poems. The connexions and the contradictions, the facts transmuted and suppressed, evaded and enhanced—contemplating these is to contemplate the mechanics of poetic truth. Knowing the man and knowing the man's work; in one sense, they are the same thing and in another they are utterly distinct.

It is a knotty and absorbing topic and Fuller does not duck any of its intellectual demands. Unfortunately the fictional embodiment is a good deal more knotty than absorbing. The characterization is thinly utilitarian, the dramas unsurprising and a good third of the book is devoted to bald literary theorizing—cast unconvincingly as conversation. And the narrator is afflicted with a style of such excruciating pomposity that everything he touches gets bogged down in verbiage. . . . It is suggested here and there throughout the novel that this style is "Housian", and that the narrator employs it in admiring imitation of the master. There are also hints that we are supposed to find it repellently mannered and pedantic (another measure of the distance between art and life). But we cannot help noting that it is a style which has much in common with Roy Fuller's own style when writing in his own persona; we therefore have to wonder just *how* repellent we are meant to find it.

> *"The Poet at Home," in* The Times Literary Supplement *(© Times Newspapers Ltd. (London) 1970; reproduced from* The Times Literary Supplement *by permission), No. 3578, September 25, 1970, p. 1075.*

PETER WASHINGTON

Roy Fuller is a man of considerable distinction; he is not a genius. There is no need for me to disparage Mr Fuller, he does the job well enough himself: it is part of his persona as a writer. In his new book **From the Joke Shop** it produces a few moments of pathos, but nothing more.

This record of ageing, written mostly at night, when thoughts of mortality are supposed to be strong, is preoccupied with death. The prospect of dying comes to Mr Fuller as a shock, the grotesqueness of old age suddenly realised. He is only sixty-three and an operation plus retirement seem to have brought on these morbid thoughts.

But there is something embarrassing about these confessions of inadequacy; even the title disarms. The embarrassment is largely due to the fact that the poems are as awful as he leads us to expect they might be; and the constant note of "I've never been much good anyway, etc." is a receipt for flabbiness and a self-pity which ought to be surprising in a writer whose virtues have always been rightly named as reservation, courtesy and wryness, close observation and a dubious introspection. But the question is: can one write poetry out of such virtues? The answer given by this book is No.

His verse, once the pleasant and thoughtful Augustan companion of a wet afternoon, is now as tired as he says he is: civilised and dull. For unleavened sadness, wry or otherwise, is always dull. The fragments the poet uses to shore up his ruins—those lines from the *Waste Land* would make an apt epigraph—lose their native vitality in his verses. But Mr Fuller's fate, as he rightly diagnoses, is the product of timidity—not personal but artistic. Eliot was right about separating the man who suffers and the artist who creates, in the sense that the artist must recreate the man not merely represent him, as Roy Fuller does. We sympathise with his noble and generous spirit, and pity his pains; but we cannot praise his art. (pp. 314-15)

> *Peter Washington, "Doleful," in* The Spectator *(© 1975 by* The Spectator; *reprinted by permission of* The Spectator), *Vol. 235, No. 7860, September 6, 1975, pp. 314-15.**

GEORGE WOODCOCK

If being a philosophic poet means finding, in all the changing conditions of one's life, the poetic correlative—the tone and language—appropriate to one's reflections on inner and outer experience, then Roy Fuller is perhaps the best philosophic poet writing in English today, the nearest to Matthew Arnold in his time, or Wordsworth in his. Indeed, perhaps the reference to Wordsworth is more apposite than an immediate glance through Fuller's poetry might suggest, for both have the unfulfilled ambition to promote the meeting of poetry and common speech, as Fuller admits in his new book, *From the Joke Shop*: "It seems I rarely found the common touch / Though my emotions common as they come." And both move from revolutionary youths (Godwinian for Wordsworth and Marxist for Fuller) to positions unexpected in the uncritical generosity of youth. (p. 858)

From the Joke Shop is a book of contemplative verse (if one strips away from contemplation its pietistic element) written by a man in his early sixties, conscious of having slipped over the elusive bound of middle age, and in some understated way also conscious of the liberations that come from being old.

One liberation is from the obligation to be experimental. In the extreme sense—that of Cummings or the Dadaists or their recent imitators—Fuller was never notably experimentalist; he has believed that poetry must be reasonable and comprehensible and he has avoided both the technical innovations and the deliberate irrationalities that interfered with clarity of meaning. He respected, for example, the sheer abounding vitality of Dylan Thomas' poetry, but he could never have written like him. Nevertheless, in his time he has tried out many forms, from the renewed use during the thirties (when he started publishing) of traditional models—the sonnet, the quatrain, the ballad, the sestina, etc.—through *vers libre* to, more recently, syllabic verse. Now he comes back to an uncompromisingly formal pattern: a mostly regular iambic pentameter, arranged in triplets each of which pushes the thought of the poems a clearly defined step forward, and for the most part without rhyme, though occasionally it is used with Byronic sharpness. . . . [The poems in *The Joke Shop* are] largely nocturnal, the kind of works that spring out of notes jotted down on sleepless nights, when one dozes into broken dreams, reads books in a desultory way, remembers inconsequential details and incidents from the past. Yet, for all this use of the fragmented mental process of the insomniac, *The Joke Shop* is strongly unified and restricted, and the very restriction becomes a kind of symbol of the process of aging which is one of its main themes.

Spatially, it centers on the poet's house and garden on the edge of Blackheath. . . . His only excursions, so far as the poems are concerned, are to the nearby suburban shopping streets, where he uses such mundane details as the high price of bread and sausages to comment on social change. Significantly, the Blackheath of his poems is inhabited by none of the people who are important in his present life—his wife, his son, his close friends; the only friends who do appear are dead poets like Kenneth Allot, Auden, and (I suspect in one case) Randall Swingler; the family with which he lives in thought is represented by his dead father and mother, by a dead Thespian uncle, by photographs of grandpaternal gatherings before the Great War.

Even apart from its memories, *The Joke Shop* is temporally united by taking us through an autumn and a winter whose oncoming corresponds with an illness that takes the poet into hospital and brings him out. . . . [The] poet reflects on the way in which, after all the political idealism of his youth, all the high hopes for humanity, he has come to immerse himself in compassion for other kinds of being. (pp. 858-60)

Fuller, who has always been concerned with the interplay of public views and private feelings, understands how at the most personal level even history takes its shape from the individual's condition (in his case the narrowing of interests with age). (pp. 860-61)

It is a very specifically English line of poetry that runs down from the best Augustans, through Wordsworth, Edward Thomas, and Hardy, and seeks to use a selection from the functioning (though not exclusively colloquial) language for the thoughtful exploration of man's moral relation to his inner self, his outer world, the beings that share it. Roy Fuller, more than any of his contemporaries, has during the past forty years made this line his own. Hardy's heir? He might not reject the title. (p. 861)

> George Woodcock, "Common As They Come" (copyright, 1977, by George Woodcock; reprinted by permission of the author), in The Southern Review, Vol. XIII, No. 4, Autumn, 1977, pp. 858-61.

ALLAN E. AUSTIN

Literary history will almost certainly record that Roy Fuller was one of the handful of Englishmen who sustained the quality of British poetry during the relatively lean period from 1950 to 1960. George MacBeth has suggested with both humor and astuteness that Fuller was somewhat unlucky in the timing of his career. In the thirties he was too young and had written too little poetry to really be counted among the full-fledged members of Auden's army; though he wrote more first-rate poetry during the war years than any other Englishman, the war did not kill him and hence sanctify this work with an aura of great loss; and though he performed with the virtues of the Movement poetry of the fifties, he was not a fresh face and hence did not stimulate the kind of excitement which greeted the pristine Larkin, Amis, and Gunn among others. This is not the kind of record to trouble Fuller. The early thirties coloration of his earlier work has been proven to be rather deceptive; though of his time, Fuller has marched to his essentially independent beat. While many of the poets who caused a greater stir in the fifties and sixties than did Fuller have either ceased writing verse or been unable to sustain their first promise, Fuller with undiminished productivity and quality has never broken pace.

It is easy enough to note what Fuller has not done. In his period he has not written the most original poetry, nor the most lyrical, nor the profoundest, nor the most humorous, nor the most vibrant—the list could be extended—for one must take into account Ted Hughes, the venerable Robert Graves, Philip Larkin, Sir John Betjeman, and Stevie Smith among others. If it is possible to generalize about poets as diverse as those named, then it can be said these artists succeed on the whole by working a narrow and particularized approach. This is by way of identifying Fuller as a normalized generalist. Fuller's high profile representativeness is both his strength (and value) and limitation as a poet. Fuller does not lift the reader out of his being and does not afford him unusual or striking ways of apprehending experience; he does enable the reader to comprehend more penetratingly and feelingly a reality approximating his own sense of it. If he does not take the reader out of himself he permits him to more fully possess himself. Fuller has a worldliness, a flexibility, a balance, a totality of being not found in Hughes or Graves or Smith. This may make, finally, for a less impressive kind of poetry in a literary sense, but produces nonetheless moving and meaningful work in a humane one. Is it a fair kind of analogy to suggest that one would be more excited to meet Hughes or Graves than Fuller, but one would choose Fuller for extended personal friendship?

Fuller has looked out at his times with astuteness and honesty, with generosity and perspective, and anyone who considers the longevity of his career is bound to be struck by his resilience. The thirties, the war years, the aftermath, the truculent sixties—for forty years he has sustained unflagging fascination with life, essentially the "little" life surrounding him as a suburban Londoner, essentially the out-of-sight life of responses to his life in time. Some may believe the times are best reflected in the tramps of Beckett and Pinter. I see the omniverously intellectual Fuller voicing the worries and concerns, the good sense and joy-in-life-despite-everything outlook of masses of thoughtful people. And he has sustained it without the least sense of trivialization or sentimentalism. (pp. 134-35)

Of the contemporaries I have named, Larkin is of course closest to Fuller in his affinity for the commonplace. Larkin handles this largely from the inside and with great specificity and consequently his verse has an emotive force that exceeds that found or intended in Fuller's work. Fuller is detached and exploratory and accordingly cooler and inevitably ironic. As has been noted, "In common with most of the intellectual Left, Roy Fuller suffered an imaginative estrangement from those to whom he was intellectually committed." . . . [In my view], Fuller is the preeminent British ruminative poet of his age. (pp. 135-36)

Fuller has been frequently generalized as a politically oriented writer and while this description is founded on solid evidence it is too facile and delimiting. Fuller has not been different at various junctures of his career so much as capable of interchanging his concerns and attitudes at any point. He has written notable occasional or public verse; but the present survey demonstrates a very high percentage of light verse. He has been a nature poet, a spokesman for what I have termed the anagogical states, he has been an endearing voyeur, and he has been preeminent as a poet who has made poetry out of illness and not the fact so much as the process of aging. Throughout his career he has been a craftsman of a high order who has neither eschewed established poetic forms nor hesitated to experiment with such challenges as those posed by syllabic versification. (p. 136)

Allan E. Austin, in his Roy Fuller *(copyright © 1979 by Twayne Publishers; reprinted with the permission of Twayne Publishers, a Division of G. K. Hall & Co., Boston), Twayne, 1979, 146 p.*

BLAKE MORRISON

Though [*Souvenirs*] is a prose memoir and [*The Reign of Sparrows*] a book of poems, they form two halves of the same sexagenarian drama. There are the same themes: tributes to dead friends and relatives, reflections on music and poetry, and above all preoccupation with age—its destruction of the body . . . and its surprising consolations. . . . The same voice informs both volumes—a voice with many different tones (in turns it is confessional and evasive, immodest and self-deprecating, dry-as-dust and wetly sentimental), but which remains at all times relaxed and chatty, no less so in the poems than the poetry.

Fuller has been called a poet who is 'safe', 'trim', 'tidy', 'conventional' (some underhand allusion to the fact that he made his living as a solicitor often lies at the back of such adjectives), but there's actually a great deal of risk-taking in his poetry's flatness, its eschewal of grand gestures and resonances. . . . [The] charmlessness is deliberate, part of Fuller's challenge. The low-key tone and awkwardness, the mass of odd titbits and facts, the endless caution and self-qualification—these are the price you have to pay for authenticity. Fuller has always been fond of, and is nowadays almost tediously insistent on, regular and disciplined verse-forms; yet it's when he's at his most formal that he comes nearest to speaking most openly.

As this might suggest, the relatively informal mode of the autobiography isn't one that particularly suits Fuller: as a 'memoir of childhood and youth', *Souvenirs* has not a great deal of range and is not very outspoken. True, the seemingly key events of his early years are present, principal among them his father's death. . . .

Though there's plentiful detail in the account (food, clothes, musical tastes, reading habits) and extensive, indeed excessive attention to school friends and relations, much remains unsaid. For this Fuller blames a failing memory . . . but there's also a tendency to back away from the emotions surrounding family deaths like that of his father and brother. At key shy-making moments Fuller's 'I' takes refuge in the more impersonal 'one'. . . . And though in small ways self-deprecating throughout, Fuller doesn't in the end give the impression of searing honesty about painful memories or weaknesses. The faults he concedes often sound suspiciously like virtues, self-laceration like a sly pat on the back: at one point he accuses himself of being 'shy, intellectual, naive to the point of gormlessness (archetypally poetic, one might say)', and at another of 'too great a facility for seeing another's point of view, an almost morbid concern for another's feelings'.

Given that the book is concerned mainly with the early years of Fuller's life, and that he can't in any case take the matter very seriously, it would have been rash to expect from *Souvenirs* any very serious account of Fuller's political development. . . . [The] crucial passage on Fuller's politics runs as follows.

> Why one should always want to ally oneself with the underdog is not altogether clear. One is tempted to discount utterly any virtue in the matter: I mean why should trying to see that a certain one-clawed pigeon gets more than its fair share of bread on the lawn . . . reflect creditably on the bread-scatterer?

Anyone who has read more than a handful of Fuller's poems will find the bird-feeding analogy entirely in character. His poetic persona is a great taker-in of birds: whether they've fallen out of nests or are lying half-dead in the road, feathered friends have always been able to rely on Fuller to appear and relieve them of their distress. Fuller implies here that his early socialism was motivated by the same impulse of pity for the underprivileged, but the passage more properly places him within a tradition of liberal humanism, a tradition in which enlightened youthful paternalism almost invariably gives way to the disillusioned conservatism of age. Benevolence in one's back garden is better than no benevolence at all, of course, and throughout both these books Fuller emerges as a decent, thoughtful man. But it seems a pity that the more ambitious, public voice of the early work proved no more than a fad of the time.

Blake Morrison, "Despondency & Sadness," in New Statesman *(© 1980 The Statesman & Nation Pub-*

JONATHAN KEATES

A layer of glum senescence covers Roy Fuller's latest collection of poems [*The Reign of Sparrows*] like a fall of volcanic ash. There is plenty here about movement, growth and vitality, but the drift is distinctly that of an unburdened crawl towards death. . . . Almost the entire final section of the book is dedicated to the business of reckoning with the onset of old age. Being 65 is viewed, not, as in Auden's case, with quietly smirking triumph, but with a sense of tremulous astonishment at having got there at all and a distinct apprehensiveness as to going any further.

Finest of all the poems on this theme, and among the best things Fuller has ever done, is **'On His Sixty-Fifth Birthday'**, a free imitation of Arnold's 'Rugby Chapel', with a significant halfway nod in the direction of the original. More than simple skeins of curt pindarics create the Arnoldian allusion: there is the same sense here, as in the earlier poem, of hopelessness and spent energy, as the poet, collecting his pensioner's off-peak bus pass, sees in it the embodiment of something altogether more Stygian. . . . (p. 23)

Good as this, and companion poems like **'In His Sixty-Fifth Year'** are, there is still, now and then, a vestigial aura of schoolmasterly beefiness left over from the days of **'Tiny Tears'** and **'From the Joke Shop'**, when Fuller's muse was a rather saucier number. A mildly risible string of three-line stanzas describes buying a pair of trousers at the Plymouth branch of Debenham's, and there is a rueful, down-the-sleeve guffaw on the theme of the poet's dapper moustache. One doesn't, after all, ask him to eschew the jokey or the flip, but the balance here tilts heavily in favour of a moss-dampened, Hardyesque charnel gloom. Yet despite the denture-rattling authenticity of:

> Bits of me keep falling off;
> bits don't work properly

the paradox (if we go the whole way with Fuller's vision of his own decay) is that he has probably never excelled himself in sheer cohesion, resourcefulness and versatility. (pp. 23-4)

> Jonathan Keates, "Vault Echoes," in The Spectator (© 1980 by The Spectator; *reprinted by permission of* The Spectator), Vol. 244, No. 7922, May 10, 1980, pp. 23-4.*

ALAN BROWNJOHN

The Reign of Sparrows is not quite as good as either [*Brutus's Orchard* or *New Poems*], but there is plenty in it to remind [Roy Fuller's] admirers just how varied, skilful and surprising he can be. Three opening poems in his lengthy, reflective manner (a bit Hardyesque these days in **"Ghost Voice"**) remain rather arcane and uncomfortable after several readings; but **"Sloth Moth"** sees him away into a favourite later theme, the oddities and ironies of natural history; and **"Musical Offering"** takes him back again to the old preoccupation with creation and execution in the other art he most admires. I wonder when we are going to realise that Fuller in his sixties (and on the subject of his sixties) is one of the most varied, accomplished, alternately disturbing and entertaining poets we have—none the worse for the sprightly oddities his style has acquired in recent years? . . . [The] splendid centrepiece of this book [is] the set of poems written **"In his Sixty-fifth Year."** There is nothing small in these perceptions, which come in a kind of diary-sequence stretching from October 1976 to the summer of 1977—and offer a rueful, touching commentary on the concerns of the poet in his unsatisfied, un-Horatian old age. (p. 58)

Souvenirs, Roy Fuller's memoir of his childhood and youth, is in many respects a companion volume to **The Reign of Sparrows,** sharing the preoccupations of the verse. Fuller's later prose style owes much to the clipped, idiosyncratic cadences of many of the poems. It also owes more than a little to the prose style of Anthony Powell, especially the insertion of the deadpan authorial comment. . . . The book is a very funny, occasionally very moving, account of Fuller's respectable, yet reduced and itinerant lower middle-class childhood, in Lancashire (mainly Blackpool); a world of pier performers and Hallé concerts, private hotels and waning private schools, of Lawrence's *Nettles* taken into law lectures during his solicitor's training. It's a reticent book but not at all an unrevealing one: the quirks and peculiarities of distant relations, lost music-hall artistes and windswept, humble places, are cherished so delicately and recalled in such detail as to amount to a love for, and celebration of, an expansive world which the shy youth (and the man) feels guiltily he has never wholly managed to re-enter. (pp. 58-9)

> Alan Brownjohn, "A Cold Wind Blows," in Encounter (© 1980 by Encounter Ltd.), Vol. LV, Nos. 2 & 3, August-September, 1980, pp. 56-63.*

GAVIN EWART

[**'Vamp Till Ready'**] takes us, roughly, from [Fuller's] time as a solicitor's articled clerk in London in the early Thirties (Fuller was 20 in 1932) up to, more or less, the present day. That is to say, through his conscripted days in the Royal Navy ('The Andrew'), postwar solicitorship with the Woolwich, Professorship of Poetry at Oxford, Governorship of the BBC, the novels and the poems. . . .

But, as with **'Souvenirs,'** although there is a ground bass of strict chronology, the variations in time and the various themes interweave throughout without much regard for strict tempo. My musical metaphor is no doubt faulty; but nevertheless the models here are Proust and Powell. While Dicky Umfraville doesn't occur anywhere in the background, it wouldn't come as much of a surprise if he did. A lot of this, with its Soho phoneys, eccentric colleagues and nicely remembered detail, is very funny. All of it is interesting. It's a picture of a period—or, if you like to think of it that way, of three periods: Pre-War, War and Post-War. I found it more satisfying than the first book. . . .

Fuller, although a novelist of talent, is most prized for his poetry. **'The Individual And His Times'** is a selection of his verse made by Victor Lee. The poems are divided into sections (The Passage of Time, The Poet and His Art, The Poet of Everyday Life, Nature, etc) and the lines are numbered. It carries an 'autobiographical' preface by Fuller, explaining the poems in each section, and there are notes 'compiled in consultation with' him at the end. In other words, this is a book for schools. It favours short poems and neglects some of Fuller's best work of the War (**'The Photographs'** would be too 'advanced' for schoolmasters), though there are also marvellous poems included.

Since it is now 20 years since Fuller's **'Collected Poems'** appeared, when he was 50, it would certainly seem that another 'Collected' was overdue. It is, I think, a disgrace to British publishing that such a book hasn't been produced. In effect, one of our finest writers is being passed over in favour of tripe—the sentimental, the sensational, the blockbuster embryo film-epic, you name it. It's easier to name it than to think about it.

Gavin Ewart, "A Waiting Game," in The Observer *(reprinted by permission of The Observer Limited), June 27, 1982, p. 31.*

RONALD BLYTHE

Vamp Till Ready, which is the tale of a newly grown-up Fuller acquiring his Marxism, his legal career, his wife, his war and proof that he was indeed a poet, grows most naturally out of ***Souvenirs,*** which is the tale of his childhood. The tone continues to be one of laconic eloquence. The flavour of the Thirties, now so familiar to us because of its endless evocations, is given a stranger, more compelling taste because of the economical way in which he handles it. The signposts pointing from slump to call-up indicate the usual old road, but the sights and comments on the way provoke a fresh attention. Again, it has something to do with their descriptive frugality, their never going on and on. 'Poetry is, on the whole, a succinct art,' remarks Fuller, and so in his view is autobiography. The title refers to that extempory rhythmic strumming, so popular at the time with pianists, which preceded the song.

The style is one of affectionate irony, reticence and bursts of wayward colour having to contend with an amused formality. Although Fuller reminds us that the 'I' of a poem is not necessarily the poet himself, here on every page it is made absolutely plain that the 'I' speaks for his 1930-42 self as exclusively as art and memory can persuade it to. Although the 'I' of ***Obituary of R. Fuller*** is decidedly that of the poet at his most self-candid . . . the 'I' of the autobiographer has been able to speak with more justice. In poetry, says Fuller, a writer can be free with the details of his personal life, can 'give himself away as a lesson, not a confession'. In prose, as we see here, it is quite another telling of the same story. True confessions, nothing less. He rakes them out of his past with wit and civility.

Certainly, it appears to have been a life minus the traditional conflicts. That fundamental one of whether he should become a full-time writer or a lawyer, or a poet and a lawyer, or a lawyer who writes poetry, for example. To be able to recognise 'almost from the start that I should never abandon a "job" in favour of "writing"' is a type of self-knowledge which puts paid to a whole mass of struggles, confusions and hurts from the word go. He treats it simply as a basic fact and then, of course, has to describe how two such apparently opposing strands, that involving the orthodoxies of a successful legal career, and that involving an equally committed role as a poet, began, right from the start, to work in tandem.

There is no apology; that is the essence of it. He has also had to deal with the characteristics which made him conventionally attractive and acceptable, these being obvious and unavoidable. In this volume we see their emergence. Modesty, mercifully, doesn't really come into it; something more obliquely unpretentious allows Fuller to take close stock of what was clearly in most respects a fortunate being with the minimum of self-regard.

The secret seems to be to reveal himself without dwelling on himself. Hence the concise and brief form of each revelation. (p. 20)

Ronald Blythe, "'He Remembers Things Like the Psychology of Cigarettes'" (© British Broadcasting Corp. 1982; reprinted by permission of Ronald Blythe), in The Listener, *Vol. 108, No. 2773, August 12, 1982, pp. 20-1.*

ALAN BROWNJOHN

Probably no living English poet has taken up more constantly than Roy Fuller the themes of the man in the street and the poet in his society. He feels himself to be an ordinary man, a member of a mass civilization, with a job (albeit a responsible one, as solicitor to a large building society) which ties him to quotidian matters: "Builders of realms, their tenants for an hour". But as a poet, as an alert and mordantly perceptive observer with an ironic overview of human affairs and a reverence for the "glamour of unapproachable geniuses", he is really rather a special version of the man on the Woolwich omnibus. Much of his verse is about the ambiguities generated when one of these figures takes on the role of the other, and for most of his writing life he seems to have seen himself wavering uneasily between the two. Yet this dilemma has never been a disabling one. Fuller's triumph is to have made from it a poetry which has looked outwards from the experiences (including the books and the music) mulled over in reflective solitude, and provided a continuous, highly individual commentary on the malaise of the time.

The characteristic Fuller preoccupations took shape in his poetry very gradually, and in ways which V. J. Lee's selection [in ***The Individual and His Times***]—arranged under six thematic headings rather than chronologically, with no note of the separate books from which the poems come—does not easily reveal. Most of the poems in the very early volumes are graphically descriptive and immediate: in ***The Middle of a War*** (1942) things were moving with alarming speed, and there were distinctions to be made between **"August 1940"** and **"October 1940"** in poems with those titles. This, in its way, is "social reporting" and Louis MacNeice (who coined the phrase) might have approved the intention if he did not influence the style. Fuller's mood seems passively observant, not actively committed or indignant, and not nearly as "dogmatic" as he believes. The reflective note and muted romanticism suggest the influence of Stephen Spender at least as much as W. H. Auden—about whose influence Fuller is so candid as to state how lucky he feels himself to be in falling under it.

The kind of war poetry Fuller wrote was especially typical of the Second World War: that of the serviceman left waiting for something to happen, enduring tension and loneliness either in Britain or in foreign places which are seen all the more sharply for the alienation imposed by service routines. Not much of this is shown in the selection's sparse representation of the wartime Fuller; and there is no way of telling from it how he turned service experience to good account in some excellent poems about Africa in ***A Lost Season*** (1944). But what we do have are the early signs, from his first postwar book, ***Epitaphs and Occasions*** (1949) of the later and more familiar Fuller beginning to emerge.

The clues are to be found in the witty octosyllabic couplets of the **"Dedicatory Epistle"** and the **"Obituary of R. Fuller"**. The views expressed are emphatic, and pointed topical references (including literary references) abound. . . . Creative pursuits come to seem difficult to reconcile with the demands of a more mundane—but also more menacing—world. And yet from this point onwards he steadily expands his technical resources and widens the range of his themes: the poet of limits becomes the poet of a rueful humanist vision for whom man's very inadequacies have their necessity.

Such a development has to be intuited, by the reader of *The Individual and His Times,* from Fuller's idiosyncratic and entertaining introductory essay, since it cannot be seen in the arrangement of the editor's choice of poems. . . . [The selection here fails] to show the growth of this poet's mind and technique as he accumulates slim volumes and reacts to events. And it gives no sense of how Fuller's work has alternated unexpectedly between a "high" style, in which he achieves genuine power and eloquence using traditional and challenging verse forms with impressive ease, and a "low" style employed to treat details of everyday living in an engagingly bizarre fashion. In fact, the individual volumes from the 1950s onwards are indispensable; and an updating of the *Collected Poems* of 1962 is certainly overdue.

Counterparts (1954) brought the first wholly successful poems in the "high" Fuller manner; not so much with the slow **"Rhetoric of a Journey"**, or even the neat satire of **"Translation"**, which are both included here, but with the graver cadences of **"A Wet Sunday in Spring"**, which is omitted. . . . [The] poem, **"Inaction"**, is a fine example of his "low" style: here he has become the laureate of the little symbolic disturbances which break the even tenor of living with reminders of something else: the spider in the bath, the lost fountain pen, the feel of a jelly baby ("in its rigid arms / Held close against its side. / And absolute identity with others. / Its pathos and fate reside. / That else it had not died.")

None of this, however, prepared Fuller's readers for either the sustained power of the finest poems in his 1957 volume, *Brutus's Orchard,* or the verse experiments of *New Poems* in 1968, arguably his two best books. . . . For Caesar's Rome . . . read the post-war world—or perhaps even post-Suez Britain, with its conviction of a noble past and its dismal sense of impending menace or chaos in the present. The handsome format of *Brutus's Orchard* . . . allowed the poems ample room; and they seemed truly to expand, in breadth of outlook and technical confidence, developing ingenious and moving variations within the unity of this theme. . . .

New Poems is a distinguished and varied book, packed with absorbing argument concerning the role of art in human society and the status of the artist. Already there are hints of the autumnal note which prevails in Fuller's latest two volumes, *From the Joke Shop* (1975) and *The Reign of Sparrows* (1981); these are well-represented by about a quarter of the poems in this selection. It is valuable to have them; yet it tilts the balance of the choice towards the later work with an opening group, "The Passage of Time", where poems written in, and about, the poet's seventh decade predominate. This is not a tactic which is going to draw new, younger readers into Fuller's poetry; the spread might have been wider.

Nevertheless, these poems, combining self-deprecating humour and irony with meticulous recording of tiny moments . . . , convert Fuller's tendency to digress, complain, or make fastidious demands on life, into poignant—and entertaining—art.

Alan Brownjohn, "Observations of the Ordinary," in The Times Literary Supplement *(© Times Newspapers Ltd. (London) 1982; reproduced from* The Times Literary Supplement *by permission), No. 4146, September 17, 1982, p. 998.*

John (Champlin) Gardner (Jr.)
1933-1982

American novelist, short story writer, poet, critic, essayist, dramatist, and editor.

Gardner's career, although relatively short, was diverse and distinguished. He worked in nearly every genre, including children's fiction, opera libretti, and scholarly criticism, and his writings reflect the rich legacy of Western culture. Some of Gardner's fictional works are set in his birthplace of Batavia, New York, and also in New England, while others have such historical settings as ancient Greece or medieval Scandinavia, in which he recreated historical and fictional narratives as well as inventing his own. Gardner is often called a "philosophical novelist," for regardless of the setting, his works address timeless philosophical questions. For example, in *Grendel* (1971), Gardner retells the fourteenth-century Scandinavian legend of Beowulf and also explores the relationship between good and evil, the necessity of facing death, and the value of art. In his contemporary novels, Gardner often incorporates philosophical ideas from the past in order to show their relevance to the present. Gardner also made use of stylistic traits of others. He cited Chaucer as his greatest influence, yet also acknowledged the importance of William Gass and the creations of Walt Disney to his work.

Gardner was a professor of medieval literature and creative writing at several American universities before his first novels were published, and he continued teaching throughout his literary career. *The Resurrection* (1966) and *The Wreckage of Agathon* (1970) earned a modest amount of critical attention, but the publication of *Grendel* established Gardner's reputation as an important new novelist and was followed by such critical and popular successes as *The Sunlight Dialogues* (1972), *Nickel Mountain* (1973), and *October Light* (1976), which won the National Book Critics Circle Award for fiction. Gardner explained his enormous productivity during the 1970s by observing, "When you're sitting writing for fifteen years, and nobody liking you, you do build up a backlog. I've been publishing an early work, a late work, an early work. . . ." Gardner's popularity diminished somewhat in the late 1970s. *On Moral Fiction* (1978), a controversial book of critical theory, was unflattering to many of his literary colleagues and perhaps can be blamed for the largely negative reviews of his last books, *The Art of Living and Other Stories* (1981) and *Mickelsson's Ghosts* (1982). Gardner was killed in a motorcycle accident a few months after the publication of *Mickelsson's Ghosts*.

Gardner's novels and short stories follow the philosophy of art delineated in *On Moral Fiction*. Gardner believed that an artist is responsible for creating works which affirm life and present inspirational visions, and he criticized nearly all of his contemporaries for being more concerned with "technique" than "truth" and presenting the "creepy" side of life without holding out any hope to their readers. *The Art of Living and Other Stories* illustrates fictionally the critical principles espoused in *On Moral Fiction*. Characteristically, the ten stories contain a wide variety of settings and include both realistic and fantastic approaches, but nearly all of the stories treat a single theme: the value of art as a life-affirming moral force. In "Nimram," for example, a dying girl befriends an older,

© Lütfi Özkök

prestigious orchestra conductor and is uplifted when she hears his symphony. Gardner's concern with art can be seen in his earlier works as well. In some of his novels, the protagonists are professional or amateur philosophers, which allows Gardner to discuss many provocative issues. In *Grendel*, Gardner explicitly argues the primacy of art. The monster Grendel witnesses several phases in the emergence of Western civilization, but dismisses all of the various cultural innovations, with the exception of poetry, as unhealthy. Gardner calls the poet in *Grendel* "the Shaper," and Grendel realizes that the poet is the guiding force in society.

On Moral Fiction can be seen as an apologia for Gardner's earlier works. Although the protagonists in each of his first four novels face their own deaths, these works are not pessimistic. James Chandler, the terminally ill protagonist in *The Resurrection*, achieves a "resurrection" by performing a compassionate act shortly before his death. In *The Wreckage of Agathon*, a historical fantasy set in the fifth century B.C., an aging philosopher reflects upon the chances for good to triumph in an already corrupt society after he is imprisoned and sentenced to death. *The Sunlight Dialogues*, set in modern-day Batavia, parallels *Wreckage* in that the central character, The Sunlight Man, is jailed and about to be killed. The Sunlight Man is an insane visionary whose spirited personality is contrasted favorably with that of his jailer and persecutor, Fred

Clumly, to whom order is all-important. In all of these novels, Gardner presents characters who are close to death as metaphors for all humankind, and assures his readers that salvation can be found in the artistic creations of the human mind.

Although Gardner was unquestionably one of contemporary literature's most important authors, many critics complain that his novels are weighted down by philosophizing, are overly long, and do not read well. These accusations are made especially about *The Resurrection* and *Mickelsson's Ghosts*, in which the central characters are philosophy professors. Critics have often made negative use of *On Moral Fiction* in interpreting Gardner's later works. Some contend that the themes of the stories in *The Art of Living*, taken directly from *On Moral Fiction*, overpower the stories themselves. Initial reviews of *Mickelsson's Ghosts* were largely negative and sometimes hostile. Many critics saw the novel as Gardner's attempt to answer the commentaries elicited by *On Moral Fiction* and charged that he was expressing his philosophy at the expense of writing an interesting novel. *On Moral Fiction* itself was judged as arrogant, self-serving, and wrongheaded. Critics disputed Gardner's contention that art can radically change people's lives. Nevertheless, Gardner is widely respected for presenting artistically the principles in which he believed and for creating an ambitious and innovative body of work.

(See also *CLC*, Vols. 2, 3, 5, 7, 8, 10, 18; *Contemporary Authors*, Vols. 65-68, Vol. 107 [obituary]; *Something about the Author*, Vol. 31 [obituary]; *Dictionary of Literary Biography*, Vol. 2; and *Dictionary of Literary Biography Yearbook: 1982*.)

JULIAN MOYNAHAN

Most of the 10 stories in John Gardner's new collection ["**The Art of Living and Other Stories**"] develop the common theme of art and its vexed relation to life. This was also the subject of Mr. Gardner's book-length essay, "**On Moral Fiction.**" . . . There he made substantial use of Tolstoy's argument for a strictly moral art, as developed in the pamphlet "What is Art?" Some of Tolstoy's later fiction is sadly marred by his determination to make his artistic instincts conform to doctrinaire moral and religious views. Certainly it is possible that Mr. Gardner runs a comparable risk in following up his moralizing essay on fiction with stories closely related to it in theme. But before addressing that problem let's recall what "**On Moral Fiction**" had to say.

In it he argues that all good art, including prose fiction, should be moral. By this he means it should be life-enhancing, protecting human existence from the dark forces of chaos (the "trolls") pressing in from all sides and coming up from below, seeking whom they may devour. In making this argument he is quite hard on many of his fellow writers, issuing such dismissive decrees as "bad art is always basically creepy." . . . These magisterial judgments are consistent with Gardner's idea that "true art treats ideals, affirming and clarifying the Good, the True and the Beautiful," that "real art creates myths a society can live instead of die by."

While there is something of the Welsh preacher, full of righteousness, in John Gardner, perhaps even something of the upstate New York prophet in a direct line from Joseph Smith, many pages of "**On Moral Fiction**" make lively reading, and it's a positive pleasure to see various fashionable gloom spreaders and doomsday peddlers get it in the neck. Yet one wishes that Mr. Gardner gave more evidence of having deeply meditated on modern history, and that he would avoid such juvenile terms as "creepy" in assessing mature art and artists. I suppose Giacometti's sculptures are in his sense creepy, yet their contribution to modern art and life is major. On the other hand, Mr. Gardner's title story, "**The Art of Living**"—about a small-town chef slaughtering and ragouting a small black dog stolen from a pet store—is very creepy, and I believe I could survive the shock of being enjoined never to reread it.

The worst thing about this story is not its central event, or the idea that event may illustrate, but its technical ineptness. The narrator, supposedly a member of an adolescent motorcycle gang during the early years of the Vietnam War, looks back on that period from a time considerably later but never establishes any significant relation between "then" and "now." His and his companions' speech patterns of the earlier period lack flavor and verisimilitude, and the various Italian-American males connected with the restaurant where the canine feast is prepared are hard to tell apart. Also, the story lacks a consistent economy of treatment, so that we are told too much about this or that person or incident, too little about others. The thing reads like a try at a novel that didn't work out, not like a crafted short story.

Rather better is the story "**Nimram.**" The title character is a prominent conductor of late-Romantic symphonic music, much preoccupied with his own success, who finds himself next to a 16-year-old girl on a flight from the West Coast to Chicago. It turns out she is dying of an incurable disease, and this shows Nimram his vulgarity in worrying about being recognized in public or being interviewed by People magazine. In a brief epilogue, the child is brought to Orchestra Hall, where Nimram is conducting a hugely augmented Chicago Symphony in Mahler's Fifth Symphony: ". . . she had never in her life heard a sound so broad, as if all of humanity, living and dead, had come together for one grand onslaught."

Here no doubt is an instance of art's life-affirming quality, but is it truly what a young girl with an incurable disease, who has had some recent experience playing in the string section of her school orchestra, would hear in the music? I don't think so. This tiresome "humanizing" of music tends to be a vice not of the young, but of fiction writers and second-string critics meeting deadlines. (pp. 27-8)

The best story in "**The Art of Living**" is "**Come on Back.**" It is a heritage piece about rural and Welsh roots which produces pleasing variations on the theme of art through an informed, affectionate look at the Welsh passion for choral singing. By far the worst and longest story is "**Vlemk the Box-Painter**," a tedious pseudo-medieval allegory about the painting of a "speaking likeness" of a princess on a rosewood box. There is nothing to be said in its favor, except that Mr. Gardner, in conceiving it, going on with it and publishing it, shows the courage of his moral convictions. (p. 28)

Julian Moynahan, "Moral Fictions," in The New York Times Book Review (copyright © 1981 by The New York Times Company; reprinted by permission), May 17, 1981, pp. 7, 27-8.

DOUGLAS HILL

There are 10 pieces in [*The Art of Living*], in diverse modes—gothic folktale and fantasy, down-home rural comedy, evocative memoirs of childhood and adolescence in western and northern New York state. Many of the stories focus upon some crisis of artistic expression, nearly all catch a crystalline moment and refract it into a spill of glittering images or sharp-edged memories. The book is not experimental in any avant-garde manner; Gardner's too much the medievalist for that. Still, it is marked with impressive surprises at every turn. (p. 51)

Gardner is a master of the economical opening; he gives a reader just enough setting and background to slip him effortlessly into the world of each tale. With voices he's equally adept. He never seems to labor as he shifts from the stylized narrative of Vlemk to the quirky ironic recall of a misunderstood ex-hoodlum to laconic Bible Belt patois (in **The Joy of the Just**) that would do any of Flannery O'Connor's "good country people" proud.

Readers familiar with Gardner's work will recognize his primary images—light and dark, river and valley, travel and flight. There's humor in these stories, and a full measure of graceful, unstudied prose. He is never hard on his characters. In his recent critical book, **On Moral Fiction,** he speaks approvingly of moral art which "seeks to improve life, not debase it," which "seeks to hold off, at least for a while, the twilight of the gods and us." Gardner meets these standards easily.

What gives these stories their power is Gardner's interest in the connection between the moral and the possible. From first (**Nimram**, a worldly middle-aged man's perception of life and death in his encounter with a doomed young girl) to last (**The Art of Living**), Gardner is consistently a romantic moralist. His stories are like the box-painter's vivid pictures of gardens [in **Vlemk the Box-Painter**]—"accurate in their depiction of both the beauty and the sadness of the world as it is." There's considerable expertise in this book, and courage and joy. (p. 52)

Douglas Hill, "Between the Moral and the Possible," in Maclean's Magazine *(© 1981 by* Maclean's Magazine; *reprinted by permission), Vol. 94, No. 23, June 8, 1981, pp. 51-2.*

BRUCE ALLEN

If the author of such basically dissimilar books as **"Grendel," "October Light,"** and that curmudgeonly manifesto **"On Moral Fiction"** is noted for any particular qualities, they are probably his distinctively energetic and impudent variety and vitality. Some of the variety, at least, surfaces in [**"The Art of Living and Other Stories"**]. . . .

For example, there's the least typical story here, **"The Joy of the Just,"** which portrays a moralist turned avenger, an elderly woman bent on destroying her (perfectly innocent) "offenders." The conception is promising, but the development is repetitious and dull—finally, it's a pointless story, enlivened only by some combative Bible-quoting.

Whenever Morality *per se* doesn't rear its head, Art does. **"Trumpeter,"** for another example, announces itself as a picturing of "the only kingdom in the world where art reigned supreme"—but it relaxes into anthropomorphical whimsy. . . .

Several other stories (**"Nimram," "Redemption," "Stillness"**) deal with the evocative or restorative powers of art (specifically, music). **"The Music Lover"**—an acknowledged steal from Thomas Mann—contrasts the ravaged emotions of an elderly "concert devotee" against the pomposities of a satanic composer, whose music becomes in performance an avant-garde exercise in atonality and discord. Here again we feel the "moral fiction" argument stirring: an advocate of "decency" in art opposes "one of those fashionable nay-sayers."

The contours of fable are traceable elsewhere. **"Vlemk the Box-Painter"** is an interminable allegory about a painter whose creations assume their own life—thus complicating and compromising his. The idea that artistic creations enter, despite themselves and their creators, into "reality" also suffuses **"The Library Horror."**

The idea that Art is more than a match for Life also (almost) animates the title story (note the reversible nature of that title?), the silly tale of a revivifying collusion between a restaurant cook who thinks he's an artist and a gang of smalltown layabouts who yearn to be feared as "motorcycle hoods." Gardner uses the standard medieval forms of knightly quest and formal debate, setting up a dialectic between the claims of social organization and individual freedom. But the elements never cohere: arbitrary whimsy and atrocious dialogue keep us at a distance from the world of the story.

I read on, rubbing my eyes, wondering if there would be any relief from this fun-and-games obsession with those enormous cloudy abstractions Art-and-Morality, Art-and-Life; this tepid schoolmarmish medievalism.

Well, there is relief, in the splendid story **"Come on Back."** This is a loving portrait of a Welsh farming community in upstate New York, and an intimation of adulthood for the young narrator enthralled by his elders' penchant for singing and "magic." It isn't really a story (though the dying of a beloved uncle provides a narrative thread); rather, a refreshing immersion in period and local detail. Though Gardner is often a slapdash writer, he has here achieved some beautiful observations . . . and images. . . .

The art that created **"Come on Back"** doesn't need any fabulistic trimmings or joky justifications. I hope that the artist who created it will pass beyond defending and examining Art, and keep on producing it.

Bruce Allen, "From Gardner, Short Stories Dimmed by Abstractions" (reprinted by permission of the author; © 1981 The Christian Science Publishing Society), in The Christian Science Monitor, *June 24, 1981, p. 17.*

KENT THOMPSON

Arnold Deller is a practitioner of the most ephemeral of the arts. He is a cook. But because he is an artist, he knows that an artistic response is fitting when his son is killed in Vietnam. Art is love, he says. And because that son had written to him about the joys of eating an ancient Chinese dish called Imperial Dog, Arnold believes that he must prepare that meal in honour of his dead son. . . .

That's a brief summary of the title story in John Gardner's **The Art of Living and Other Stories**. It is probably the strongest story in the collection, if only because of its central image. But its point is clear: art is first of all an act of love—Arnold cooks the meal as a tribute to his dead son. It is also a continuation and extension of an ancient tradition. By preparing and serving the meal Arnold has put himself in touch with his son and all the ancient Asian traditions epitomized by the meal. And by serving it to a new audience, Arnold is enlarging the art. . . . And finally, Arnold fulfils the commercial demands of art as well as his identity as an artist. No one is an artist until someone defines him as such by buying his art. When [the motorcycle gang] The Scavengers pay $1.50 a plate they are confirming Arnold's status.

With one exception, every story in the collection is equally concerned with the various relationships between art and life. (p. 9)

These are stories that are written to be discussed. And as such, they are perhaps to serve as a corrective to Gardner's *On Moral Fiction*.... In that essay Gardner was very perceptive about the creation of art, less so about the intentions of art, and least of all about its function in society. He was in fact sometimes malicious and devious in his arguments. However, he was passionately clear about his feelings. He is an old-fashioned idealist who believes that art should provide models for right human conduct. But by the time he had shoved all the art he admired into the categories of his ideals, the categories had become so all-inclusive that he had become inconclusive.

But because Gardner is first of all a fiction writer and not an essayist, it should not be surprising that his stories are more coherent than his abstract prose. In fact it seems to me that most of these stories contradict entirely one of the chief demands he made for fiction in *On Moral Fiction,* where he wrote: "moral art holds up models of decent behavior ... characters ... whose basic goodness and struggle against confusion, error, and evil ... give firm intellectual and emotional support to our own struggle."

In *The Art of Living and Other Stories* he has done something quite different. He has not presented exemplary characters. Instead, he has written stories from which we might draw moral truths. Therefore, although the stories are often instructive, they do not necessarily illustrate good moral character. Quite the opposite. We must see that the ostensibly good old lady, admirably crusty in character, in **"The Joy of the Just,"** is actually guilty of the sin of pride. And if we are to emulate his characters, how far should we go? Arnold Deller, cook, might show the way to metaphysical connections with the dead by means of art: but if you or I should serve up cooked dog we would surely be arrested; if we served up pot roast of cocker spaniel, we would surely be lynched.

I am not being entirely facetious. The story **"Nimram"** suggests that art is an answer to the fear of death. Perhaps—but not entirely. The image of the musician and the dying girl on the airplane brought to my mind the very similar image in the farcical film *Airplane*. There the joy of musical performance is such that the passengers delight in it, ignoring the little girl—whose life-support system is disconnected—and they sing blithely on while she croaks. There's a harsh moral truth there, and an apt criticism of Gardner's point.

Many of his stories in fact invite comparisons, and few of them are flattering to Gardner. For example, the old lady of **"The Joy of the Just"** immediately invokes Flannery O'Connor's masterpiece, "A Good Man Is Hard to Find," and next to it Gardner's story seems thin and contrived—the more so when one realizes that the characters seem to be drawn from *Li'l Abner* and/or *The Beverly Hillbillies*. And perhaps the narrator of Arnold Deller's story is in fact The Fonz, from *Happy Days*. Certainly he is not a biker of the kind we recognize on the streets or in the courts. And Gardner's use of flat popular stereotypes—the absent-minded professor in **"The Music Lover,"** or the bookworm in **"The Library Horror"**—is almost certainly deliberate.

Although in *On Moral Fiction* Gardner is very hard on writers who use thin characters to promulgate or examine ideas, he is much more generous when he finds something very similar in medieval literature.... And clearly in these stories he wants to communicate a certain doctrine about art. Not surprisingly, he seems to do this best in the quasi-ancient fairy-tales of **"Trumpeter"** and **"Vlemk the Box-Painter."** He is clearly much happier with the metaphoric truths of the fairy-tale form than he is with the factual observations to which he must restrict himself in the stories of the present.

In fact it seems to me that there is a crippling contradiction at the heart of Gardner's most recent writing. On the one hand he believes in writing that illustrates or exemplifies doctrines of right conduct. On the other hand he believes that fiction is an exploration of the imagination and the intuition.... [Each] of the stories in *The Art of Living* seems scrupulously planned to prove or illustrate a particular theory about art and life.

It is perhaps this contradiction between intention and belief that makes Gardner's stories succeed as theories and fail as art. Because although it is possible to have works of art about art—examples from Keats, Browning, Yeats, and Joyce Cary spring to mind—Gardner's stories do not achieve what they set out to illustrate.

They are, in the end, illustrations of ideas. Their consequent value is therefore not in what they are, but in what they lead us to talk about. They seem to be written for professors and students, and indeed, if one were looking for a text with which to teach a course entitled "Art and Society," one could look a lot farther and do much worse than to choose Gardner's *The Art of Living and Other Stories*. But if one wanted, like Arnold Deller, to set a work of art before an audience to continue the tradition and enlarge their taste—a real feast of beast, as it were—one would be wise to choose *Grendel*—by John Gardner. (p. 10)

Kent Thompson, "Intimations of Morality" (reprinted by permission of the author), in Books in Canada, Vol. 10, No. 7, August-September, 1981, pp. 9-10.

ROBERT R. HARRIS

It is a good bet that John Gardner enjoys writing his novels far more than the public enjoys reading them. *Mickelsson's Ghosts* is dreadfully long and padded, and it often degenerates into drivel.

Gardner has striven to become America's Tolstoy, or, perhaps in this new novel, its Dostoevsky. He's failed, but has convinced a lot of critics. In a split of critical sensibilities, the National Book Critics Circle, by a single vote, conferred its 1976 fiction award on Gardner's *October Light* over Renata Adler's brilliant *Speedboat*. The majority of one was convinced that Gardner had something deep to say about bicentennial America and fiction-writing, mistaking for profundity his workmanlike ability to describe rural life and characters and his simplistic ruminations about, for example, the evils of television. It is rare to find a review of Gardner's fiction that does not respectfully dub him a "philosophical novelist."

In this new work, Gardner takes this praise literally. His protagonist is a philosophy professor. Readers are required to sit through endless classes during which they are subjected to long sophomoric discourses intended to solve, once and for all, such pressing questions as whether Plato and Aristotle were really fascists. It is a maddeningly talky book; abstractions are bandied about in a sleep-inducing dialectic. As he has done in earlier novels, Gardner ponderously tries to infuse his discussions of basic notions (order vs. freedom, nature vs. art) with originality.

Gardner's confidence that he's an originator of ideas has gotten him into trouble. He was accused of "borrowing passages" from scholars in his *The Life and Times of Chaucer;* he admitted to "paraphrasing." On the defensive, he writes in this novel's acknowledgments that he has "borrowed ideas and good lines" from Martin Luther, Friedrich Nietzsche, Ludwig Wittgenstein, Norman O. Brown, Martin Heidegger, and—if that's not enough to cover himself—from "acquaintances, friends, and loved ones." He's also effectively hidden them. The ideas in *Mickelsson's Ghosts* are so muddled that one doubts that anyone would want to claim them.

Gardner's connection with ideas has always been dilettantish. His book *On Moral Fiction* was, for the most part, a diatribe against those who write more sophisticated—better—novels than he does. An early foray into the cultural conservatives' trendy war on contemporary writing, it was a cut above the kind of literary massacre that the old regime at *Harper's* perpetrated every other year or so. (p. 70)

[In] *Mickelsson's Ghosts,* Gardner's efforts to clarify and explore moral truth turn on a muddied, ambivalent relationship between Mickelsson and Gardner himself.

Peter Mickelsson, "on the dark side of fifty," is a philosopher and author whose orderly life disintegrates when his marriage breaks up. He has left Brown University for the lowly State University of New York at Binghamton and a rundown house in nearby rural Pennsylvania. Mickelsson's son has gone underground to pursue terrorist activities against the nuclear-power industry. Mickelsson worries about him a lot. He loves his daughter, too, and wants to pay his ex-wife more in alimony than he earns. The IRS is on his trail. He has affairs with a fellow teacher and a teenage prostitute. He condescends to academic colleagues and students. And Gardner involves him in a neat little murder mystery. (Are the murders the work of local Mormons, or a sinister homosexual conspiracy, or the nuclear-power industry as representative of the evil forces of the Modern World?) This mystery holds the reader's attention; when Gardner gets around to spinning a yarn he can be quite good—at times sensitive and even funny.

And Mickelsson is haunted by ghosts—an incestuous brother and sister who did guess-what to their child. The ghosts are present to scare the bejesus out of Mickelsson and to force him to ruminate—philosophically, of course. Gardner needs the ghosts, you see, to show that although fiction aspires to tell the truth about life, that truth needn't be realistic. The fantastic happens—ghosts exist! The reader, however, might reasonably want to hear more from the ghosts and less from Mickelsson. If there is anything more insufferable than a whiny philosopher, it is a philosopher who whines about Wittgenstein.

As a philosopher about literature, Gardner holds that although fiction should be moral (i.e., that during the creative process the artist affirms what is good for man), a character may do evil. As a result, Gardner distances himself from Mickelsson, hoping his character will "get his just deserts hereafter." But because the distancing applies only to Mickelsson's acts and not to what he thinks, it is not convincing. Too often, Mickelsson is a garrulous spokesman for Gardner. When Mickelsson reflects on his own writings, one is more than a little suspicious that he is expressing Gardner's high opinion of Gardner. . . . The old claim to originality persists, even though one of the major lessons that Gardner has to offer in *Mickelsson's Ghosts* is this startling gem: "Women are people too; that was the crushing wisdom of modern love." And it isn't nit-picking to wonder if the admission of occasional carelessness sanctions the moral morass that Gardner gets into when he lets Mickelsson first call some Marxist sociologists Nazis, then later claim that it is those who run the nuclear-power plants who are Nazis. The "moral" artist would have made some distinctions.

When his teenage prostitute becomes pregnant, anti-abortionist Mickelsson robs a man to pay the girl to have the baby. To inject some moral "ambiguity" into the scene, Gardner makes the victim a former bank robber. During the robbery, the man is stricken with a heart attack, and Mickelsson watches him die. . . . Gardner does not excuse Mickelsson's actions. But he does allow Mickelsson—like Gardner, a self-appointed "ranter against sloganers and simplifiers . . . indefatigable shamer of the shallow-minded, fulminator against the frivolous and false"— to get away with the arrogant assertion that there exists a "widespread practice of aborting when the foetus is not of the parentally desired sex." *Widespread?* It is obvious that Gardner enjoys—and mostly approves—Mickelsson's clichéd view of the world, and therefore the novelist never convinces us that he himself believes that Mickelsson has "lost the ability to tell the truth." Gardner may chastise Mickelsson for what he does, but Gardner is so taken with Mickelsson's thought-processes (because they are so much his own) that he fails to make clear just how creepy Mickelsson's ideas are. (pp. 70-1)

Late in the novel, Gardner defines religious fundamentalism as "permission not to think." Some of his own fundamentalist ideas about how to write fiction seem to invite the same definition. He has attempted to equal the great Russians—to write "something obsessive and morose and no doubt philosophical"—but as a philosophical novel, *Mickelsson's Ghosts* is a sham. Stripped of its excesses, however, it does have enough substance to have made a good Raymond Carver short story. (p. 71)

> Robert R. Harris, "What's So Moral about John Gardner's Fiction?" in Saturday Review (© 1982 Saturday Review Magazine Co.; reprinted by permission), Vol. 9, No. 6, June, 1982, pp. 70-1.

ANATOLE BROYARD

There are different ways of enjoying a book. For most of **"Mickelsson's Ghosts,"** John Gardner's new novel, I felt like sprawling out in a big chair and just having a good time with it, taking the pleasure as it comes. It seemed to me to be doing just about everything a novel can do. It offered characters I liked, but who troubled me, so that I wanted to see them feeling better, doing better. It gave me the kind of sense of place that one doesn't often find in serious novels today: A thick texture of landscape, community, friendships, infatuations, intrigues, insanities.

Mickelsson, the protagonist, has a romance with a house, rebuilding and redecorating it as a preliminary or a substitute for rebuilding or redecorating himself. The house is haunted by its past, just as he is, and Mr. Gardner manages this so adroitly that one can almost regard these "ghosts" or apparitions as creatures of Jung's racial unconscious. Mickelsson's wife, Ellen, who has just thrown him out, is a fine portrait of the sort of person Mr. Gardner was opposing when he wrote **"On Moral Fiction."** She is one of those trendy people who hates every human contract or convention as an infringement on her freedom. . . .

Nothing in fiction has a stronger pull than a man with some greatness in him who is teetering between self-realization and ruin, who is frightened by the possibility of greatness, by the scope of the questions he's asking. I found myself pulling for Mickelsson, hoping he'd either make it or go to hell with himself and give up his ghosts, that he'd come to terms with his anguish either way.

Mr. Gardner is an old-fashioned novelist in the best sense—he gives you more people, places, problems and ideas to think about than you can possibly deal with. It's as if the world had suddenly become unbearably vivid again, after all our disillusionment and irony. I've often felt that people in modern fiction don't seem to want enough things, to lust after experience as they appear to do in my experience—but Mr. Gardner is surely an antidote for that trend. His people are a hotbed—what a wonderful word that is—of all kinds of desires: political, esthetic, sexual, and quite a few that baffle description.

He knows how to catch the small, sad, comical, cruel, or bland irrationalities of small-town people—and he's just as good on the pretentions and grandiosities—deserved and undeserved—of intellectuals. He knows the difference between love and sex and shows us what a fearful struggle it is not to confound one with the other. . . .

My only complaint against **"Mickelsson's Ghosts"** is that, toward the end, Mr. Gardner writes as if he were on a wild binge, as if he were determined to compensate us for all the listless or lifeless novels we've read in the last 10 years. He's like a manic host at a party who pours champagne over our heads instead of into our glasses. Mickelsson goes through so many convolutions or evolutions that I began to lose the comfortable, satisfying feeling that I knew him. It's one thing to be perplexed in the middle of a novel and another to be perplexed at the end.

Yet there's a feeling somehow of justice in it all, as if Mr. Gardner were saying, "Here, I'll give you characters! I'll give you plot! Take that! And that!" If you read **"Mickelsson's Ghosts,"** as you certainly should, I suggest that you simply lift out some of its too-muchness and paste it into some of the current novels that leave you feeling hungry or shortchanged.

Anatole Broyard, "A Scrabbling in the Soul," in The New York Times *(copyright © 1982 by The New York Times Company; reprinted by permission), June 12, 1982, p. 19.*

BENJAMIN DE MOTT

It's a rule, seemingly, that a Gardner novel will be—in at least one of its dimensions—the story of somebody's intellectual life.

And for part of its extreme length, **"Mickelsson's Ghosts"** obeys the rule. As with any novel set in academia, there's a measure of plain socializing in its pages (the inevitable stiff academic dinner party) and a good deal of caricature (the inevitable artsy-clerksy faculty musicale). But there's also—highly unusual in academic novels—a serious representation of teaching and thinking. . . .

We're offered a believable account of peaks and pits in the desk life of an academic essayist, and at intervals the novelist engages a genuinely challenging philosophical theme, namely the mind's endless—and doomed—hunt for self-knowledge. . . .

In the early going Gardner works hard and effectively to maintain a tight seal between the particulars of his hero's emotional life and the brainier flights of his fancy. What does an aging philosopher's infatuation with a corrupt teen-ager signify about man's nature? What are the roots of the soul's misgivings about abortion? What kind of solace can physical labor afford? Why is disbelief in manifestations of the supernatural both vulgar and foolish? The questions spring directly from the specifics of the hero's dailiness, and the notion that he, as a philosopher, might undertake to address them in philosophical terms seems entirely reasonable.

But as the book proceeds, the gap widens between thought and action, mental events and turns of plot. The task the author has set himself emerges as that of yoking a novel of sensibility and ideas to a mystery tale about Mormons bent on hiding seamy secrets of the saints from hostile eyes. In theory, this isn't an impossible task. A decently loose and baggy novel is supposed, after all, to be capable of accommodating everything from toothbrushes to apparitions. And links do exist between Mickelsson and Mormonism. . . .

Still, despite these efforts, the marriage of philosophy and mystery doesn't come off, largely, I think, because as Gardner thickens his plot he thins out his voice. The Mormon line of narrative in **"Mickelsson's Ghosts"** brings with it a termitelike infestation of crime-story cliché. The novelist's voice grows duller and flatter—loses variousness and flexibility. The intricate, emotion-laden questions about supernatural manifestations and the sanctity of life give way to "Then why was Thomas Sprague's house burned? Who cut his throat?" All at once we're in a world of snub-nosed pistols and eyes closed to slits, people stopped in their tracks who "shoot looks" at each other, stand up "needing to pace" or cry out, "Wait a minute!" as Solutions Dawn. The hoped-for successful mix of tones and modes doesn't materialize, and the novelist behaves as though he'd never had anything in mind in the first place except unraveling, in standard crime-story jargon, a perfectly conventional mystery.

Criticism, Gardner wrote in **"On Moral Fiction,"** gives us "art cleaned up and clarified, at worst reduced to what the critic considers its main point"; complicated emotional developments are transformed "into logical progression," and artistic vision becomes thesis. Implicit in this contention is Gardner's pride that his own art resists cleanup, and in truth it has done so on occasion—witness the remarkable blend of novelistic forms and voices in **"October Light"**—and undoubtedly will do so again. But the book at hand leaves an impression of self-dilution and diminishment. Reductively simplifying the complicated emotional and intellectual quandaries with which it begins, **"Mickelsson's Ghosts"** does to itself something more harmful, even, than what the author thinks criticism does. It transforms the stuff of its own potential vision, not into a thesis, but into canned goods—a standard-brand thriller with a queer Gothic hum in the background. (p. 26)

Benjamin De Mott, "A Philosophic Novel of Academe," in The New York Times Book Review *(copyright © 1982 by The New York Times Company; reprinted by permission), June 20, 1982, pp. 1, 26.*

SELDEN RODMAN

To judge from John Gardner's 10th novel [*Mickelsson's Ghosts*], published shortly before his death last month in a motorcycle accident at age 49, he believed in ghosts. Also in witches, hex signs and divergent spectral assemblies, such as a government-supported group of Mafia landfillers and a Mormon-affiliated SS troop called the Sons of Dan. Although Peter Mickelsson, Gardner's primary witness to these questionable incarnations, is a philosophy instructor who might well be cast as "the nutty professor," the weird phenomena are visible to more responsible friends and colleagues as well. The author thus seemed to indicate that he indeed thought them real.

But the spooks are only used to set the scene. What, if anything, they have to do with the plot is impossible to deduce. This is a novel that asks the question: Can a man who is being sued for alimony in excess of his earnings and pursued by IRS agents, criminals and spirits, a man who impregnates a teenage prostitute, harbors a terrorist son and inadvertently commits a murder, still find happiness with the woman he loves? . . .

Mickelsson is full of ruminations on Life, Death, Truth, Beauty, Meaning, and Suicide, punctuated with quotations from Plato, Kant, Aristotle, Wittgenstein, and especially Nietzsche. This is a serious work by a serious intellectual, right? Well, the nutty professor certainly displays his credentials. . .

Gardner's own curriculum vitae was quite impressive. Author of 15 books and recipient of abundant critical acclaim, he had even sought to define art. In a collection of essays, *On Moral Fiction,* he wrote: ". . . true art is moral; it seeks to improve life, not debase it. It seeks to hold off, at least for a while, the twilight of the gods and us. . . . We recognize true art by its careful, thoroughly honest search for an analysis of values. It is not didactic because, instead of teaching by authority and force it explores, open-mindedly, to learn what it should teach . . . moral art tests values and rouses trustworthy feelings about the better and the worse in human action."

Using Gardner's criteria to assess his last work, one must ask: Is Peter Mickelsson a moral man? By conventional standards, absolutely not. The first thing we see him do is kill a dog. . . . He deliberately snubs a suicide-prone student by not inviting him to a party. He ignores his children.

At the same time, he does feel responsible for the lives he touches. He is ready to give his ex-wife anything and everything—making concessions far beyond his means that she hardly seems to deserve. We wonder what horrors he must have perpetrated to feel so much guilt. (The author never tells us.) . . . [Mickelsson] worries about the suicidal young man, he worries about his children. He worries a lot. The suggestion is that concern equals morality. . . .

Mickelsson's moral stature is, at best, dubious. Nevertheless, he is a survivor. Retribution through suffering is his strongest claim to a happy ending. Anyone who gets through so much misery, Gardner seems to be saying, is entitled to whatever he can salvage.

Selden Rodman, "Gardner's Last Novel," in The New Leader (© 1982 by the American Labor Conference on International Affairs, Inc.), Vol. LXV, No. 18, October 4, 1982, p. 18.

KATHRYN VANSPANCKEREN

When one stands back to consider the shape of John Gardner's works as a whole, certain recurring "obsessive metaphors" or polysemous "figures" (in the terminology of Charles Mauron and the Russian Formalists) force themselves upon the imagination. One of the most resonant of these figures is the magician as artist or criminal. The figure involves the idea of a shaper—part magician, part storyteller—who purposely manipulates reality and therefore may either enhance or violate it.

If the shaper's medium is verbal, he becomes a fabulist, liar, or poetic visionary. The seer Agathon, with his queerly sunlit eyes, Taggert Hodge the Sunlight Man, and Jonathan Upchurch, glib Yankee fan of magicians, are compulsive talkers. They are also in several ways fictional analogues of the artist as writer (talker) and seer. Ordinary people in Gardner's books are likely to fly off the verbal handle as well, becoming temporary sybils or ranters. One thinks of James Chandler philosophizing, and of John Horne in the same book; of the shaper-skald and Grendel; of Henry Soames and Fred Clumly, whose novel resolves itself in his public speech. As the 107-year-old poetess Miss Woodworth remarks irritably in *The Sunlight Dialogues,* "yakety yakety yakety." (p. 114)

Of the great talkers in Gardner, a striking number are criminals as defined by society—hunted outlaws or prisoners. The obvious examples are Agathon, the imprisoned cynical Socratic character whose incessant and intemperate speech is a devious tool to provoke and enlighten his disciple, Peeker; Taggert Hodge, who likewise is either in jail or in hiding throughout his book, and whose talk similarly is both inadvertent compulsion and purposeful manipulation meant to deceive or instruct; and the Devil, archetypal criminal, whose powers of persuasion and magic cause the events in *Freddy's Book.* . . . The notion of words and stories as "smugglers," potent as marijuana at heightening or replacing (violating) our sense of reality, returns us through another circular path to our figure of the artist as potential criminal, at worst a Captain Fist.

Metaphoric prisons, containments and preventions abound in Gardner. Like plots or rules of conduct, they often offer the imprisoned characters a structure within which to work. Freddy's book, for example, is his only means of expressing himself from his voluntary imprisonment in his room. Another imprisonment which facilitates transcendent understanding is James Chandler's apprehension of nearing death, which urges him towards a more generous and emotional sense of human life. Chandler's death is brought about by an act of generosity: breaking the doctor's orders, Chandler leaves his house to assist a dubious Magdalene-like girl. The novel's final tableau of the dead Chandler ("candle maker") lying in a grotesque crucifixion, somewhat heavy-handedly proclaims that his gesture is an imitation of Christ that redefines a narrowly medical idea of "health" to include the spiritual. To break the doctor's law is to restore the law of humanity. (p. 115)

The virtue of laws and prisons is that, like artistic conventions, they give one something to violate or defend. Prisons and crosses not only martyrs make: they construct a reality with depth of landscape, history, and human significance. Like God, Gardner makes humanity and sets it in a walled garden (for his work is also pastoral). There is no escape except into "singing the wall," as he shows in *Grendel* and elsewhere. There is no magical short cut, no exit. . . .

Language is never neutral in Gardner. It either imprisons or liberates. Again and again an imprisoned man chooses between the language of liberation and the language of slavery. Often the languages are disguised. Grendel allows his fear to extend to language, which in turn paints a fearful landscape. "I shrieked in fear; still no one came" he wails as he hangs in the tree trunk and is charged by a bull in the Taurus chapter. (p. 116)

Yet all one has is language and its silent partners, emotion and thought. If they are solipsistic, what recourse is there? The notion of life as an unsolved question, or wall, is central in Gardner. Main characters are set the task of solving the riddle, on pain of one or another form of death. (p. 117)

The syntactic analogue of imprisonment is *enchassement* or embedding. The term, taken from traditional poetics, denotes the projection of the grammatical figure of subordination into a closed narrative structure so that one gets framed stories within stories, each ending where it began and serving to delay the action of the main tale.... Essentially it is a folk tale structure; as such embedding would appeal to Gardner the historian and medievalist. (p. 118)

Virtually all of Gardner's novels are embedded. All of them backtrack and use flashbacks to prolong reaching the end. Amazingly, all the novels except *Nickel Mountain* employ explicit frame stories or other clear framing devices which enclose or divide the works by returning to the same setting or motif. *The Resurrection* begins in the graveyard where Chandler is buried and returns to retrace his life; the whole novel is a flashback, as is *The Sunlight Dialogues,* whose prologue takes place after the events and after Clumly's wife has died. "The King's Indian" opens with the aged Upchurch qua Ancient Mariner recounting the novella as a story from his youth: it, too, is a flashback. Every few chapters Gardner brings back his reflexive frame in which Upchurch recounts his tale to the angel who sits in embarrassed judgment. *The Wreckage of Agathon,* too, starts near the ending of the chain of events in the book, with chapters alternately divided between Agathon and Peeker until the end, where a mature Peeker's vantage envelops the dead Agathon's. *Jason and Medeia*'s narrator returns periodically; his reactions frame and punctuate the tale, which like *Grendel,* is a return to the past in several senses. *October Light* and *Freddy's Book* provide obvious examples of embedding. (pp. 118-19)

Delay is a temporal analogue of imprisonment. Gardner's technique resembles the opposed story and plot movements Todorov finds in popular fiction and which appear in the form of embedding in folk stories. Gardner insists on suspense as morally necessary as well as being a cornerstone for plot (by which he means structured and hence meaningful experience which offers more than texture and stylistic felicity). His defense of suspense, which he typically achieves through embedding structures, is central to his artistic and moral purpose.... (p. 119)

Gardner repeatedly delays action on one plot line to further another line, or interrupts one with an intrusive narrative from a frame story or a different text, until the novel's main level of reality is, if not called into question (as in *Freddy's Book*), at least modified and substantially deepened. Essential to this discontinuity and the paradox or riddle Gardner means to convey is suspense, which he achieves in three ways: through flashbacks, delays in the plots (often occasioned by scenes of entrapment), and imagery. In a large sense, all are forms of embedding.

Suspense often takes the form of flashback given in characters' memories. Through flashbacks Gardner reveals his abiding concern with history and how people can come to terms with it or try to escape it. Given Gardner's commitment to character—which more than anything else sets him apart from many contemporary novelists—flashbacks are a natural way for him to show what is significant about a situation for the person living through it. (p. 120)

Both *The Sunlight Dialogues* and *The Wreckage of Agathon* are delayed by long prison scenes that occasion flashbacks. Static imprisonment scenes are given very early in both novels and are held like a long cinematic still or a strongly stated key signature. The scenes of imprisonment extend through many chapters, damming the flow of plot.... Confinements throw the alternatives each character embodies into sharp relief as people literally jostle each other under pressure; imprisonments also offer Gardner occasions to interweave alternative texts or plot lines, as in *October Light* and *Jason and Medeia*. And every time Gardner shifts his book to different sets of characters, he has a chance to delay the interrupted plot.

Through imagery Gardner also creates suspense. Attica prison looms on Batavia's skyline throughout *The Sunlight Dialogues*. Grendel lives in caves and is obsessed with existential walls. Often a delicate nostalgia hints at a vulnerable, finite humanity caught in immensity's chaotic flux. (p. 121)

Sometimes Gardner shifts scenes so rapidly that plot merges with imagery to suspend action. A description from the first chapter of *The Sunlight Dialogues*, "The Watchdog," marks time while the Sunlight Man waits in prison and Clumly and his wife sleep in their house.... The imagery evokes how the lawless life of adolescents, lovers, and hunters heedlessly breaks through a multiplicity of metaphoric confinements and how this vital chaos illuminates, and dwarfs, the small drama of Clumly and Taggert Hodge. The imagery shoots beyond the tale to paint the walls of the universe, while the sleeping actors lie suspended in their lives' cocoons. (p. 122)

Gardner's paradoxes pose characters an ethical choice: whether to attribute paradox to the world or to themselves. If, as Grendel at first does, a character gives up and assumes the world is merely relative, unintelligible, and therefore deserving no allegiance or engagement, he makes a moral choice leading, as we have seen, to mute solipsism. But to choose to accept the paradox as a mysterious wall or limitation caused by one's narrow perspective and determine to solve it by extending one's scope and reaching out into another's experience, as Clumly and the Sunlight Man do, requires a certain belief, a sense of significance about people and the world.

To embody this heightened and firm communication with outer reality, Gardner's writing depends heavily on descriptions so distinct and original that they can magically heighten the most mundane subjects. Time and again Gardner indulges us with metaphors, similes, and adjectives slipped in before nouns.... Usually the descriptions are embedded in a surrounding sentence. Interjections between dashes, parenthetical remarks, and other devices that sandwich description into sentences are numerous.... (p. 123)

More than his peers, Gardner uses frames to question fictive reality and moral vision. His more recent works, *The King's Indian* and *Freddy's Book*, and the epic poetic novel *Jason and Medeia*, increasingly draw on framing devices and odd narratives using heightened language—Spencer's description of closed novels fits them perfectly.... Frames allow Gardner three major innovations: the use of the text as a character, the deliberate placement of the reader in opposed fictive realities, and the entrapment of the reader in the narrative paradox.

Gardner uses the device of the frame, which sets off disparate texts, to make texts into analogues of characters. He opposes stories within stories as he opposes characters within the same plot line—say Taggert and Clumly, or Jason and Medeia. A text—*The Smugglers of Lost Souls' Rock* or *King Gustav & the Devil*—is made to bear ethical weight and occupy significant space (as many or more pages than the ostensibly "real" or enclosing narrative), and is elevated to the stature held by a person whose choices, in this case, must be deduced from the odd, often hidden narrator's implicitly moral, or amoral, viewpoint of the world. The text's actions and language bear on the novel's total interpretation as if they belonged to a chief character in the main line of the plot, but they exist on a higher dimension which transcends the division between text and containing novel.

The reader's placement within opposed and alternating realities is an issue in all of Gardner's recent works. In *Freddy's Book*, for example, the reader is stranded in the inset tale at the book's end somewhere in medieval Scandinavia. In **"The King's Indian"** the reader is drawn sometimes to the sympathetic listening angel, eager to be pleased but made of delicate sensibilities and easily offended by poor taste and improbable lies. Other times, during the more realistic passages, the reader obliviously inhabits Upchurch. The ability to manipulate the reader's imaginative locale makes for an effortless reflexivity; every time Gardner shifts us, the reader's dislocation is an implicit comment on what went before. When the angel balks at the great white boobylike albatross which flops on the deck of the *Jerusalem* after Upchurch downs a psychedelic given him by an avatar of Queequeg, it is hard not to think of the discriminating angel as the reader; the angel's objections are also a sly comment on the absurdities of much postcontemporary writing.

In using the frame this subtly, Gardner almost dissolves it. In his hands the metaphoric wall between fictive spaces becomes more like a door or window inviting the reader one step beyond. The wildly different texts make the novels mysterious and unresolved: there is nothing in the novels that contains all the frames and texts in a final interpretation. The reader's mind is essential as only his consciousness contains all the stories and can read the complex message of their relationships. The reader completes the novel in the process of reading and thus supplies the answer to the books' deliberate paradox. In the end it is the reader who confronts the Sphinx of the novels.

In conclusion, the magician in Gardner operates as the shaper of frames but also passes through them to gain a greater perspective on the known social structure and make forays into the unknown. The reader also participates in magic; to read him is to be creator and escape artist, to claim kin with magicians. Gardner sometimes sees himself as a mystic and will remark on his intuitions and his family's interest in magic. Yet he is also distinctly unassuming. Whether or not one draws parallels, it is evident that again and again Gardner opposes texts or characters who exemplify, in Frye's categorization, the *eiron* or self-deprecator and the *alazon* or impostor. The true magician in Gardner is the self-deprecating *eiron*: the humane, passive Agathon as opposed to the dangerous, deluded and deluding false magician Taggert, who manipulates in order to confuse. Clumly, and even more Clumly's suffering wife, are the *eirons* to Taggert's *alazon*. As text, *The Smugglers of Lost Souls' Rock* is *alazon* to the *eiron* of the surrounding novel, as a trumpet to a quiet landscape. In Gardner's balancings, appearances deceive: when a character speaks truth he is likely to sound ridiculous. If a man starts out idealistic and handsome (Taggert, Agathon) he will tend to end as an unsightly, mad wreck. Life is grim enough in Gardner. Yet—and here lies his hopefulness—suffering can ennoble. Work pays. Nothing ventured in good faith, with belief and compassion, is wholly lost. It is true that thematic resolutions and transcendences often accompany brutal accidental deaths in Gardner: Bale's death tries Soames and offers him a fatal choice—to learn or die. But if Gardner sees no good as unmixed, then (such is his humanism) an evil, once confronted, can bring good. The criminal can be society's surgeon. Even the false magician can startle insight and provoke us beyond his frame. (pp. 126-28)

> Kathryn VanSpanckeren, "Magical Prisons: Embedded Structures in the Work of John Gardner," in *John Gardner: Critical Perspectives, edited by Robert A. Morace and Kathryn VanSpanckeren (copyright © 1982 by the Board of Trustees, Southern Illinois University; reprinted by permission of Southern Illinois University Press), Southern Illinois University Press, 1982, pp. 114-29.*

Andrew M(oran) Greeley
1928-

American nonfiction writer, novelist, poet, and journalist.

Greeley is a Roman Catholic priest, an educator, and a sociologist whose numerous studies of religion within modern society have earned him the reputation as an authority on the sociology of religion. His recent ventures into novel writing reveal yet another dimension of this Irish Catholic writer.

In his nonfiction Greeley writes about Catholics and their role in American society by delving into such topics as the effectiveness of Catholic education, the presence of anti-Catholic sentiment in the United States, and the value of ethnicity. His liberal opinions concerning ordination of women, birth control, and divorce have sometimes brought him into conflict with official Catholic doctrine. Much of his writing is based on data collected by The National Opinion Research Center with which he has been connected. While critics sometimes question his conclusions, most admit that Greeley stimulates discussion of neglected issues and that he often anticipates sociological trends. *The Making of the Popes 1978* (1979), his diarylike record of the two papal elections of that year, is a revealing study of ecclesiastical politics. Critics praised the book for its lively, penetrating look behind the scenes but faulted it for its lack of focus and documentation.

Greeley's most popular novels are *The Cardinal Sins* (1981), *Thy Brother's Wife* (1982), and *Ascent into Hell* (1982). In these fast-paced, sensational narratives, Greeley fictionalizes the world of Irish Catholic politics and intrigue in Chicago.

(See also *Contemporary Authors*, Vols. 5-8, rev. ed. and *Contemporary Authors New Revision Series*, Vol. 7.)

Photograph by Alex Gotfryd

of America Press, Inc.; © 1964; all rights reserved), Vol. 110, No. 3, January 18, 1964, p. 102.

ROBERT M. BROOKS

In this impressive study of the influence of religion upon the career and graduate school plans of the nation's college graduates of June, 1961 [*Religion and Career*], Fr. Greeley documents the recent and dramatic rise in status of American Catholics. . . .

Fr. Greeley finds no evidence among the current Catholic crop of college graduates to support the oft-repeated allegations that Catholic colleges are notably inferior, that Catholics are making but a negligible contribution to the intellectual life of America, or that American Catholics are prone to undervalue economic achievement. . . .

This study has many virtues. Not only does it provide a factual base for moving ahead the "great debate" on the intellectual qualities of American Catholicism, but it should help to dispel the notion that sociologists merely count noses. The author teases out many provocative conclusions from his data, but always with the restraint and caution of the trained social scientist (let Catholic apologetes take note!). His prose is characterized by a lucidity and wit that are rare in sociological reporting.

Robert M. Brooks, "Scholars and Schools: 'Religion and Career'," in America (reprinted with permission

MICHAEL MORRISON

The multi-talented Fr. Andrew Greeley has turned his energies to the interpretation of American Catholic history. In [*The Catholic Experience*] he gives a series of intellectual biographies of the men who have tried to adapt the Catholic Church to the political and social life of the United States. . . . Fr. Greeley has a definite interpretation that he wants to get across: the struggle between Americanizers and those conservatives who did not want to make Catholicism a fully American Church.

The book is a combination of summarized secondary-source history and interpretation of the efforts to accommodate Catholicism to American life. The history is well told, interesting and informative to readers who do not know of the life of John Carroll, the controversies of the 1890's and the social doctrine of John A. Ryan. The interpretation is valuable because it brings the insights of a liberal of the present to the men and events of the American Catholic past, and also because it is a pioneer attempt in the interpretation of American Catholic history. Fr. Greeley describes the great efforts to acculturate Catholicism and Americanism; these efforts were usually frustrated. Despite these setbacks, he thinks, American Catholics of today have achieved this synthesis, though their bishops may be slow in recognizing the fact.

At times Greeley paints his "bad guys" too darkly. He seems unable to appreciate the reasons why the anti-Americanizers held their point of view. . . . The author is too quick to judge figures of the past by our present-day insights, rather than by the criteria of the times.

Fr. Greeley desires that his book be taken seriously, and it certainly should be; but the absence of footnotes, bibliography and index makes this difficult. In quite a few instances the reader would like to know the sources of Greeley's information, or the origin of the material that is found in quotation marks.

All in all, Greeley has produced an informative introduction to American Catholic history for beginners and a thought-provoking interpretation for those with more background. (pp. 297-98)

> Michael Morrison, in a review of "The Catholic Experience," in America (reprinted with permission of America Press, Inc.; © 1968; all rights reserved), Vol. 118, No. 9, March 2, 1968, pp. 297-98.

NAOMI BLIVEN

["**Why Can't They Be Like Us? America's White Ethnic Groups**"] is a short, intelligent work that its author, Andrew M. Greeley . . . , announces is both a preface to and a plea for further studies he thinks should be done about the individual natures and peculiar qualities of those American groups that still identify themselves with a European ethnicity. Some of the chapters report on surveys, some argue, some are anecdotal or impressionistic, but the theme is all one—a plea for the rights of ethnicity. The book is informative, pleasant to read, sometimes diverting, and sometimes surprising. It is also frequently perplexing, since findings about ethnic groups can be mysterious, at least to outsiders: Why do Polish-Americans and Irish-Americans get along badly? Greeley's enthusiastic espousal of ethnic nationalisms in the United States is even more puzzling, inasmuch as he admits that the European contributions to these hyphenated American cultures are not especially glorious but merely the cultures of European peasant villages that—both cultures and villages—failed to sustain themselves in nineteenth-century Europe. One of Greeley's points—the most important, perhaps—is indisputable: prejudice against members of white ethnic groups is as unjustifiable as any other prejudice. But on this matter, too, Greeley is puzzling. He keeps saying that ethnic groups dislike each other . . . , but just as often he suggests that prejudices against ethnic Americans are held only, or mainly, by left-wing intellectuals. Were this true, we could all rejoice, for it would mean that American Nativism, which was politically powerful for nearly a century (from the days of the Know-Nothings to the election of 1928), is now confined to that tiny number of Americans who consider themselves radicals or revolutionaries or intellectuals. And yet, though Greeley is witty and lively about this, he is not jubilant, possibly because he must realize that he is pushing a good argument so far that it becomes a bad one. His praise of self-created ethnic ghettos, of urban ethnic "turfs," as quasi-public and legitimate arrangements is unpersuasive. He extols pluralism and diversity, but his Americans tucked into ethnic and racial Bantustans would encounter not diversity but homogeneity. And he keeps talking of "primordial" human urges to differentiate between a "we" and a "they," of the "territorial imperative," and of similar speculative and ahistorical notions, as if we all agreed on what is "primordial" and as if what is "primordial" had precedence over what is civilized. That opens all sorts of vistas. Incest, anybody?

The philosophical implications of all this primitivism and particularism are deplorable. They are at odds with Christianity, and, for that matter, with any of the first-rate thought of the Western World, which, whether pagan or religious or secular, is universal. Ethnicity in our time has been the refuge of the second-rate: at best, nationalism; at worst, Fascism. This is probably because loyalty to one's own kind, a virtue Greeley extols, is an insufficient virtue; as Jesus noted, "For if ye love them which love you, what reward have ye?" But the main difficulty in emphasizing, perpetuating, or even having any respect for ethinc and racial differences within this country is simply that our state and federal constitutions, our public institutions, and the spirit of our laws have always been opposed to such divisions. (p. 225)

Greeley keeps referring to a past more remote than the eighteenth century, arguing that, despite changes in human society, human beings and human nature have not changed since approximately the Creation, and that ethnic communities meet the same unaltering needs that pre-industrial villages did. I wish I felt as sure about the past as Greeley does. (p. 228)

> Naomi Bliven, "E Pluribus What?" in The New Yorker (© 1971 by The New Yorker Magazine, Inc.), Vol. XLVII, No. 40, November 20, 1971, pp. 225-26, 228-29.

RAYMOND A. SCHROTH

Frankly, I would like to suggest, knowing that Fr. Greeley's other great work cannot be diminished by my criticism, that [*The Jesus Myth*] need not have been written. First of all, I don't think he's answering the right question. There's no problem demonstrating the relevance of Jesus. He has seldom been more popular or relevant. It's the Church that appears irrelevant. Perhaps Fr. Greeley should have written a book demonstrating the relevance of the Church. There's a real challenge.

Rather, we have a work that smells of scissors, paste and the tape recorder. We have long paragraphs from Scripture scholars followed by the rambling "reflections" of the author. (p. 126)

> Raymond A. Schroth, in a review of "The Jesus Myth," in America (reprinted with permission of America Press, Inc.; © 1972; all rights reserved), Vol. 126, No. 5, February 5, 1972, pp. 126-27.

THOMAS H. CLANCY

The Irish, according to George Bernard Shaw (himself a Gael), have only enough sex life to perpetuate their cantankerous species. Fr. Andrew Greeley's fleshing out of this charge is only one of the things in [*That Most Distressful Nation*] to make the Irish even more cantankerous. There are also chapters on their (or should I say "our"?) history, culture, politics, drinking, religion, family life and future to give them more excuses for both rage and amusement. Some pages might even give a boost to their fragile pride.

The story is written from the inside, for Greeley had four Irish grandparents when he was born in Irish middle-class respectability in Oak Park, Illinois, and he has lived all of his forty-odd years among the Irish of Chicago. The subtitle tells the story, "The Taming of the American Irish." . . .

With the exception of the Jews [the American Irish] have achieved the most remarkable success of any European immigrant group. They have made notable contributions to the American church, to politics and to the bar (both kinds). Contrary to one of the most widespread myths of "pop" social science, they are not bigots in the mode of Archie Bunker. On the liberalism scale they are second only to Jews among identifiable ethnic groups and way ahead of WASPs.

But in the process of climbing economically and socially they have lost their soul. They are still remarkably faithful to their religion, but they have lost "their explicit sense of distinction as a group and their consciousness of a heritage."

Part of this is due to the fatalism and a peculiar form of self-hatred that infects the breed. Like a national virus it is handed on by the females of the species, the Irish moms, who spoil their sons while at the same time cutting them down to size by nagging and sarcasm.

Yes, Greeley is Irish all right. There is more than a little Celtic melancholy in this account and even a trace of self-hatred. Fr. Greeley, it has been said, has never had an unpublished thought. Among the many attractive features of this volume is a brief explanation of why he writes so voluminously. . . .

But we can thank St. Patrick he wrote this book. It is one of few absorbing works on this mad and fascinating race. No matter that not all chapters fit together neatly and that the last one repeats things he has said twice over.

> Thomas H. Clancy, in a review of "That Most Distressful Nation," in America (reprinted with permission of America Press, Inc.; © 1972; all rights reserved), Vol. 127, No. 3, August 5, 1972, p. 73.

WILLIAM L. O'NEILL

[*That Most Distressful Nation: The Taming of the American Irish*] will come as a great relief to Irish-Americans (hereinafter known as the Irish), intellectuals especially. To be Irish has not been a handicap for some time, but neither has it seemed to offer many advantages. It is still a common impression, shared frequently by Irish liberals, that the race is notable chiefly for producing drunks, bigots and politicians. How pleasing it is to have Irishman Andrew Greeley, a sociologist (and priest) associated with the National Opinion Research Center in Chicago, tell us that the Irish are affluent, well-educated and politically liberal, and that they even value independence in their children. Greeley's book might well have been called *The Next Best Ethnic Group,* since it turns out, as he would have it, that Irishmen (and women) are second only to Jews.

Yet this is not a chauvinistic book because what Greeley aims to show is that the Irish acquired success by trading off their ancient racial virtues—mysticism, tribal passion and the like—for more suitably modern traits. The result is that on the one hand the Irish are like everyone else, and on the other more neurotic and contradictory than anyone else. . . . The poetry is gone; what remains are tension, anxiety, repression.

Greeley's argument, that the Irish have sold off their birthright (even though for a good price), is hard to accept. Greeley makes abundantly clear that the Irish who came to America did not have much left worth cherishing. Hundreds of years of savage oppression culminating in a terrible famine had destroyed the Ireland of bards, saints and heroes. The Irish emigrated because death was the alternative. They brought with them neither great gifts nor expectations, but rather defensive adaptions, some of which—political realism, loyalty, fraternity—worked very well. It seems odd, now that they have gained so much, to complain of the little that was lost. Of course the Irish paid a price for success, but so has everyone, even the Jews. Greeley does not persuade me that the psychic and cultural cost to the Irish has been excessive.

Greeley touches only briefly on the largest ethnic question of all: should immigrants "melt" or not? (p. 25)

Greeley is no help here because while he laments the loss of tribal passion and other Irish traits he never asks himself if a country can afford much ethnic variety. It is one thing to say that America could not have been built without immigrants (who were frequently treated badly); it is another to glory in ethnic distinctions that are in some respects the nation's curse. For it was ethnic division as much as anything that kept organized labor so weak for so long, condemning millions to lives of underpaid drudgery. And it was ethnicity that helped kill the Socialist party during and just after World War I, thus delaying the welfare state for a generation or more. And ethnicity remains the major barrier to equality for blacks even today, as Governor Wallace has shown. So though as an Irishman I welcome Greeley's effort to demonstrate that we are in some ways better than we thought we were, I think it sentimental and romantic of him to suggest that what makes us different should be encouraged. The country has all the diversity it can stand.

With all its faults this is a fine book, intelligent and surprising. Though its parts do not always hang together, it is full of thoughtful speculations about the Irish character and Irish family life that are stimulating even when, as I think, in error. So long as ethnicity remains a fact of American life it needs to be studied, and Greeley has approached it with real inventiveness. He is not maudlin, boastful or self-serving, and breaks new ground in ways that other historians and social scientists would do well to exploit. (pp. 25-6)

> William L. O'Neill, "The Contradictory Ethnics," in The New Republic (reprinted by permission of The New Republic; © 1972 The New Republic, Inc.), Vol. 167, No. 9, September 9, 1972, pp. 25-6.

PETER L. BERGER

Andrew Greeley possesses what is probably the sharpest tongue in American sociology. . . . [He] has for several years been busy sending out books and articles, most of them broadside attacks on prevailing views both inside and outside his own field.

Of late one of his favorite targets has been the view that religion is declining in contemporary society, a view now commonly called secularization theory. He has previously castigated its proponents in his book **"Religion in the Year 2000."** . . . [**"Unsecular Man: The Persistence of Religion"**] is mainly notable because Greeley now places his analysis of contemporary religion in a broader theoretical framework, coupling his attack on secularization theory with a general assault on the assumptions of most sociologists about modern society.

Greeley's central proposition is stated brashly on page 1: "The thesis of the book, bluntly, is that the basic human religious needs and the basic religious functions have not changed very notably since the late Ice Age; what changes have occurred make religious questions more critical rather than less critical in the contemporary world." Greeley's argument for this proposition is two-pronged. As he has done before, he marshals empirical data to show that religion continues as a vigorous reality in the contemporary world and, indeed, that it has recently gone through an upswing, especially among American campus youth.

Leaning heavily on Robert Nisbet's recent work in sociological theory, Greeley also argues that secularization theory, at least among sociologists, is the result of the distortive notion that modern society is inexorably moving from communal (*Gemeinschaft*) to impersonally abstract (*Gesellschaft*) patterns: On the contrary, Greeley tells us, the abstract structures of modernity can only keep going because they rest on the foundation of continuing communal bonds—in family, neighborhood, ethnic group, *and* religious community.

The argument is a strong one. . . . In the end, he fails to convince. He weakens his own thesis by using a definition of religion that is so broad as to include every conceivable system of overarching symbols. . . . (pp. 22, 24)

Greeley also weakens his thesis by failing to distinguish his own target (secularization theory) from Nisbet's (*Gemeinschaft/Gesellschaft* theory): It is quite possible to agree with Nisbet that there is still a lot of *Gemeinschaft* around, and still to disagree with Greeley that the religious version of this has not been doing as well as it used to.

Perhaps one reason for Greeley's overstatement of his thesis is his orientation in sociology, which is empiricist, data-oriented, and thus averse to historical evidence. There was no opinion research in the Ice Age. But we have a wealth of evidence, if not on the Ice Age then on much of later history, including evidence on the place of religion in everyday life. . . .

Greeley has a gift for overstatement, as when, in previous writings, he presented intellectuals as an ethnic group and conveyed the idea that Chicago is the best-governed city in the nation. Such overstatement is very useful. It stops the routines of the mind. It provides a chance for reassessments. For sociologists and other observers of the current scene, Greeley's book usefully puts in question one-sided generalizations about modernity and secularity.

For those with a personal stake in religion, there is the eminently useful critique of those theologians who have tried frantically to be "relevant to modern man," while all the time they did not have the slightest idea what this creature was actually like. Some of the best passages in the book deal with the high comedy now being enacted in American academia, where the religious intellectuals have desperately tried to divest themselves of every vestige of supernaturalism and now confront a constituency immersed in astrology, divination and every conceivable sort of mysticism.

The view that the modern world is less religious than most of what preceded it in human history continues to be plausible. Secularization theory, in this its central proposition, is not demolished by Greeley's argument. Greeley does make a very plausible case that this theory has been wrong about the *degree* of secularization. Even more important, he shows that most proponents of the theory have been misled by evolutionary bias to assume, without warrant in the evidence, that secularization is progressive and irreversible. (p. 24)

Peter L. Berger, in a review of "Unsecular Man," in The New York Times Book Review *(copyright © 1972 by The New York Times Company; reprinted by permission), November 19, 1972, pp. 22, 24.*

ALAN L. MINTZ

In *Unsecular Man* and in an earlier volume, *What Do We Believe?*, [Greeley] demonstrates that in the past twenty years there have been very few changes in the high degree of group affiliation and religious belief among Americans. Where most of us would expect to find significant decline Greeley shows us evidence of even more astonishing continuity. Why is this so? To explain, Greeley posits a universal and unchanging need for "meaning systems" which provide "an ultimate explanation" of the world, a need which penetrates and transcends man's rationalism and self-sufficiency precisely at critical moments: the sense of bafflement about the nature of things, the need to integrate "the troubling forces of sexuality" into the rest of man's life, the crises in the stages of the life cycle, the experience of moral outrage that goes beyond the self. No matter how far a man lives his life outside of traditional religious categories, such experiences force him to ask questions which are in fact essentially religious and prompt him to use myth in attempting to formulate and answer them.

The case is appealing, and one appreciates the clarity with which Greeley's mind cuts through the rhetoric that has been churned out about the "inexorable unfolding of modern man." But in looking closely at Greeley's thesis one discovers that his presentation succeeds only by allowing several critical qualifications. For example, he excludes from his generalizations persons who occupy important positions in government, in the media, in university faculties, and in the larger corporate businesses, for among such groups, apparently, secularity has made significant inroads. . . . To pretend to chart the state of belief while disregarding the creators of the culture in which belief must exist only reinforces a mistaken notion about the utter separation of a society from its intellectuals.

Another freedom Greeley allows himself is to be exceedingly broad in defining religion, a habit he shares with most other sociologists of religion. This is not the quibble it might seem, for to define religion as a "meaning system which offers an ultimate explanation of the world" is, in a telling way, to allow a great deal. Greeley is thus able to hedge on the crucial difference between religions as we have known them and social movements which merely evince and gratify religious needs, a confusion which often undercuts the otherwise strong arguments of the book. . . . [Greeley] leaves us to wonder if, in the end, he escapes by simply equating religion with value or world-view.

In addition to this imprecision there is the related problem of Greeley's habit of speaking about religion in general rather than about particular religions. I do not believe that he intends to grant independent reality to the abstract universal, Religion, but rather to discuss developments that are occurring in parallel yet particular ways within the various religions of America. The distinction, however, is often unclear. (pp. 84-5)

Man's new freedom to choose how to satisfy his religious needs is one of the few changes Greeley does . . . acknowledge. In the place of the fiery convert of the 19th century who stood firmly within his adopted ideology, there has emerged a more cautious type: man, in Thomas Luckmann's phrase, as a "consumer of interpretive schemes." Avoiding the limitations imposed by total systems, post-ideological man pieces together from the marketplace of traditions and values his own, self-fabricated framework. These frameworks combine to form churchless "invisible religions" such as the civil-rights movement of the 60's and the "counter-culture" of recent years. In these formations, it is important to note, one finds no special allegiance to the celebrants' birthright religions: these phenomena are heterodoxies composed of whatever materials are at hand. Greeley presents this closing picture, in which I believe there is a great deal of truth, with feelings that are obviously divided. As a sociologist he is gratified by evidence of the enduring need to form "meaning systems," but as a Catholic priest he is disturbed by the implications for the future of the Church. (p. 86)

> Alan L. Mintz, "Religion and Modern Man" (reprinted by permission of the publisher and the author; all rights reserved), in Commentary, Vol. 56, No. 2, August, 1973, pp. 83-6.

JAMES HITCHCOCK

It is a compliment to a book to say that it should have been longer, which is my main criticism of Father Greeley's [*An Ugly Little Secret: Anti-Catholicism in North America*].

Both title and subject are very apt, in that anyone who has paid even perfunctory attention to what is going on in America is aware that it has been open season on Catholics for well over a decade. Father Greeley has ample documentation, particularly in terms of newspaper articles of the How-the-Catholic-Church-Oppresses-People-and-Distorts-Their-Psyches type. . . . Father Greeley's cases are choice; each one has at least another ten standing behind it.

In an age when the molders of "enlightened" opinion are almost obsessively sensitive to signs of discrimination or prejudice, the general response to blatant anti-Catholicism has been, in the inelegant Watergate phrase, "stonewalling." The charge of anti-Catholicism is neither admitted nor denied by those in positions of influence. It is simply ignored. The title of Father Greeley's book is apt because, by tacit agreement, anti-Catholicism is perhaps the one remaining form of bigotry which is respectable in the United States, the one indulgence of this sort which the educated classes still allow themselves.

Defamation—ridicule and vituperation directed at Catholics and Catholicism in the media—is common enough. Father Greeley also ventures into the sticky area of job discrimination. . . . (p. 77)

This leads into another subject upon which Father Greeley touches—why have Catholics themselves not gotten more upset and more aggressive about discrimination? (pp. 77-8)

Father Greeley thinks it may have something to do with the fact that, according to his findings, identifiably Catholic ethnic groups are now economically quite successful in America and have thus become both complacent and loath to rock the boat. There has also been bred into them a certain inferiority complex concerning the things of the mind, a habitual attitude of deference towards the "enlightened" opinion-makers. . . .

[One] of my major criticisms of Father Greeley's book [is], namely, his generally unfriendly stance towards the anti-abortion movement, which is noticeable in some of his other writings even more. This is short-sighted because the Church's position on abortion, and the militancy of so many Catholics on the subject, has been the greatest single occasion for the resurgence of respectable anti-Catholic feeling. There has been a massive effort—in the media, in academic life, in government agencies—to deny Catholics even the right to have a position on this subject, to discredit what they say simply because it is Catholics who are saying it. Thus, in my opinion, any defense of Catholic rights in this country has to include a strong defense of the anti-abortion movement. (p. 78)

> James Hitchcock, in a review of "An Ugly Little Secret: Anti-Catholicism in North America," in The Critic (© The Critic 1978; reprinted with the permission of the Thomas More Association, Chicago, Illinois), Vol. 36, No. 3, Spring, 1978, pp. 77-9.

CHOICE

[In *An Ugly Little Secret*] Greeley has drawn upon decades of work in the sociological study of ethnics and Catholicism to present his interpretation of why anti-Catholic nativism continues to exist in America. He offers documented evidence of discrimination against Catholics, especially among the intellectual elite within the U.S., and concludes that anti-Catholic bigotry continues in subtle forms because of inattention to its possible existence, ignorance of its dynamics, and residual bias remaining from the nativism of the 19th and early 20th centuries. The chapter on Catholics and Jews is especially significant for future Catholic-Jewish dialogues. Greeley, a Roman Catholic priest, notes Catholic duplicity in the continuation of anti-Catholicism and concludes that it is due to Catholic middle-class toleration of discrimination for the sake of social acceptance and economic success. This brief volume is well written in a conversational style with great clarity. It provides a good introduction to contemporary anti-Catholicism in America but needs the support of Greeley's larger, more systematic works. . . .

> A review of "An Ugly Little Secret: Anti-Catholicism in North America," in Choice (copyright © 1978 by American Library Association; reprinted by permission of the American Library Association), Vol. 15, No. 3, May, 1978, p. 418.

RAYMOND A. SCHROTH, S.J.

["The Making of the Popes 1978" is Father Andrew Greeley's first venture] into the New Journalism.

His model, he says, is Theodore H. White, his fellow witness to history; and with his teasingly disguised sources (two, he says, for every allegation), he clearly identifies with Woodward and Bernstein. But sometimes he seems closer to Lincoln Steffens, whipping up, for Playboy serialization, "The Shame of Vatican City," discovering some of the same intrigue and disillusionment in Rome that the famous muckraker found in St. Louis and Philadelphia, but ever hopeful that his journalistic "shaming" would help inspire the city's reform.

True to the New Journalism genre, Father Greeley brings in his own intellectual and emotional baggage at every opportunity. He is depressed about the decline and drift in the church; the American bishops have ignored his sociological surveys, including his study of the priesthood and his findings on the devastating impact of the 1968 encyclical against birth control, *Humanae Vitae,* on church attendance. His own diocese, he informs us, suffers the rule of John Cardinal Cody, an incompetent, racist, bizarre tyrant whom the new Pope, if he has the nerve, ought to remove. But the writer has not given up hope; he has come to Rome with a profile of an ideal pope—"a hopeful, holy man who smiles."

"**The Making of the Popes 1978**," like many of Father Greeley's other books and columns, is filled with useful insights and information: voting tallies of previous conclaves, a long footnote on Vatican finances (the church is not really rich), his attempts to reconstruct the Cook County-style wheeling and dealing of purple-garbed conspirators. But Father Greeley, unlike Theodore H. White, has been reluctant to do the writer's work of reorganizing his raw experience.

Father Greeley can never decide whether the popes, the church or he himself is his central subject, and gives us instead a repetitious, scarcely edited tape-recorded diary about everything he thinks, hears or knows: his charges that the Vatican is trying to remove Cardinal Cody, which Cardinal Cody has publicly denied; his sideswipes at journalists who don't see what he sees (he misquotes and distorts Commonweal's editorial on John Paul I); his sinuses and migraines. At the end we share Father Greeley's new-found hope for the church; but I wish, for his sake, he had either told us more about his personal struggle so we could share it more sympathetically, or had stood back and let the larger story speak for itself. But then he wouldn't be Father Greeley. (p. 11)

Raymond A. Schroth, S.J., "The Vicars of Christ on Earth," in The New York Times Book Review (copyright © 1979 by The New York Times Company; reprinted by permission), June 24, 1979, pp. 11, 44-5.*

GARRY WILLS

[In *The Making of the Popes 1978* Greeley] rambles, tells bad jokes, blows his own horn, indulges in guess and gossip. He pretends to know what he obviously doesn't (e.g. what cardinals were thinking in their sequestration). We have to rely on his unnamed informers for the count of votes in both conclaves. But he brings to papal politics the skills and interests of a sociologist who studies voter behavior through computer models. He knows there is hard bargaining behind the hocus pocus, and he thinks the papacy needs a kind of demythologizing for its own good. I'm not sure John Paul II would disagree with him. The papacy will probably have to mean less, in terms of conventional piety, before it can mean more again.

Garry Wills, in a review of "The Making of the Popes 1978: The Politics of Intrigue in the Vatican," in The New Republic (reprinted by permission of The New Republic; © 1979 The New Republic, Inc.), Vol. 181, Nos. 3 & 4, July 7 & 14, 1979, p. 37.

GEORGE W. CORNELL

[*The Making of the Popes 1978* is] a fascinating chronicle, marvelously candid, rippling with pointed anecdotes, revealing conversations, rumors and rivalries, the sights, manners and sounds of old Rome, crisp, quick sketches of personalities and issues, fleshed out with emotional tension and relevant dashes of history. It looks like a real winner.

Because of the book's particular sequential mode and Greeley's fidelity to it before the unexpected tumble of events, the account is also essentially self-effacing. (p. 4)

The running, diary entries, recorded with the freshness of immediacy, are interspersed with subsequent, time-ripened passages set apart in boldface type. They provide fuller perspective and information gathered after the events, explaining how the unanticipated became reality, including votes in the secret conclaves.

The format makes for an unusual, charming turn-about, in which the reader has the advantage of sitting back in ex post facto wisdom and watching the author struggle and squirm with valid clues he relentlessly turns up and discards. . . .

He also offers lively summations of contemporary church issues, apt glimpses into the church's past of a less centralized papacy and open, popular elections. He sets forth the ramshackle state of Vatican finances, the bottleneck of the Vatican press office, the lack of departmental coordination. . . .

What keeps the book crackling with life are the images of Roman activity and attitudes, the dizzying traffic and finger-shaking ritual of accidents, the Roman clergy who never smile even "at one another," the rain and sun, the restaurant menus, the searchlights playing over the Sistine Chapel with its erratic smoke signals, the "beautiful vintage moon" riding low over the Via Della Conciliazione, Greeley's own fluctuating glee and despondency. (p. 5)

George W. Cornell, in a review of "The Making of the Popes 1978," in The Critic (© The Critic 1979; reprinted with the permission of the Thomas More Association, Chicago, Illinois), Vol. 38, No. 4, September, 1979, pp. 4-5, 8.

THOMAS P. FAASE

With [*Crisis in the Church: A Study of Religion in America*], Greeley fulfilled his commission from the American Bishops' Ad Hoc Committee on Evangelization, to study the phenomenon of the unchurched in America. He concludes that evangelization "would represent a misplaced emphasis." The unchurched are so by their own design, he says; religious affiliation is more complex than evangelization can itself address; and it is better to strengthen family life for the sake of greater religiosity. The greatest stumbling block to Catholic evangelization is the Church's ban on birth control.

As sociology, this work is a spotty potpourri of secondary analysis of survey data. . . . After expressing due caution about his data, Greeley goes on to provide a sometimes fascinating, sometimes strikingly insightful, sometimes trite, and sometimes petulant discussion of an array of variables and phenomena related to church affiliation in the United States. (p. 992)

The greatest contribution of this book is its emphasis on the importance of the marital relationship. "It is the family of procreation that really matters. In most cases that family accounts for more of the variance in religious behavior than all the other variables put together." But he stretches beyond that to say: "The principal cause of Catholic religious decline in the United States is sex—and the highly specific kind of sexual issue represented by the birth control prohibition encyclical." Therefore, he concludes: "Until the Church begins to develop a new agenda for intimacy, evangelization will be nothing more than occupational rehabilitation for troubled bishops, priests, and religious."

Like so much of Greeley's writing, this book is often maddening. Greeley adopts a cavalier tone that attempts to persuade by correlations stretched into thoroughgoing insistence. The paucity of citations to work other than his own and that of his friends amounts nearly to sociological solipsism. From beginning to end, he mars his professional work by pursuing personal vendettas....

Yet, as usual, Greeley's instinctive understanding and common sense leads him to some very fine assessments. His analysis of important secondary data indicates a direction that he rightly invites the sociology of religion to follow. (p. 993)

> *Thomas P. Faase, in a review of "Crisis in the Church: A Study of Religion in America," in* Social Forces *(copyright © 1980,* Social Forces*), Vol. 58, No. 3, March, 1980, pp. 992-93.*

PUBLISHERS WEEKLY

Flying from his expatriate digs in Paris, famous novelist Jimmy O'Neill lands in his home city, Chicago, and literally bumps into Lynnie, the love of his youth. Lynnie is now a businesswoman, widowed mother of five and still gorgeous. The flame between the two burns anew, leading Jimmy into a fight for her honor. Corrupt politicians are about to indict Lynnie on trumped-up charges of bribery, a threat the novelist tries to dispel by oneupmanship against the Chicago archbishop, district attorney and others. This is the heart of the plot in Greeley's novel ["**Death in April**"], hard to extract from a mass of excesses including views on modern literature, the mob, Roman Catholicism, discrimination, etc. It's even harder to care for or believe in any of the characters or the situations the author has manufactured, and the ending is simply ridiculous.

> *A review of "Death in April," in* Publishers Weekly *(reprinted from the June 20, 1980 issue of* Publishers Weekly, *published by R. R. Bowker Company, a Xerox company; copyright © 1980 by Xerox Corporation), Vol. 217, No. 24, June 20, 1980, p. 75.*

HUGH M. CRANE

Novelists usually describe the Church's impact on childhood to explain the importance of adult faith. [In ***The Cardinal Sins***] Father Greeley sins by omission, therefore, in beginning with the adolescence of his main characters. Fortunately, the author resists the temptation to make them allegorical figures. Instead, he dramatizes through their lives the course of postwar American Catholicism. Scholar-priest Kevin Brennan infrequently comforts his friends as he tells what he knows of them: fellow seminarian Patrick Cardinal Donohue, in whom zeal vies with concupiscence; rich "cousin" Maureen Cunningham, whose prophetic perception of others doesn't save her; and old flame Ellen Foley, who survives tragedy and bitterness.... If the story is "not history, biography, or (perhaps sadly) autobiography," it is partly popular journalism, ecclesiastical gossip, and (perhaps regrettably) apologia. People, not structure, sustain the Church—and this certain best-seller.

> *Hugh M. Crane, in a review of "The Cardinal Sins," in* Library Journal *(reprinted from* Library Journal, *May 15, 1981; published by R. R. Bowker Co. (a Xerox company); copyright © 1981 by Xerox Corporation), Vol. 106, No. 10, May 15, 1981, p. 1098.*

WEBSTER SCHOTT

[In "**Thy Brother's Wife**"] Greeley proposes to show us how an American Catholic bishop ... can love his brother's wife for most of a lifetime and still keep the faith as he fights for a more humane and sexually informed Catholicism.

Greeley's principal characters are a tyrannical Chicago multimillionaire named Mike Cronin; his two sons, Paul and Sean; and his adopted daughter, Nora Riley....

Mike decides things, and he has decided that someday Paul will be President of the United States and Sean will become a cardinal. (p. 7)

Trouble comes because, while everyone sets out to fulfill Mike Cronin's expectations, Sean and Nora are attracted to each other like magnets, and Paul is as faithless in marriage as he is opportunistic in politics. Paul's only redeeming quality is his devotion to his brother. Thus, in the middle of the novel, he willingly places Nora in Sean's care when he must cut short a family vacation in Italy to accept appointment as Richard Daley's aviation commissioner. During a week in Amalfi, Sean and Nora become lovers. Nine months later she gives birth to a son.

There are two major plot lines in "**Thy Brother's Wife.**" One concerns Sean's continuous love for Nora and his ambivalent attitude toward a church seething with intrigue and divided bitterly on the issue of sex and birth control. Greeley suggests that as a result of Sean's experience with Nora in Italy, his attitude turns radical. He leads the opposition against the conservatives, and that ironically propels him toward the College of Cardinals.

Greeley artfully intertwines the account of Sean's ecclesiastical problems and yearning for Nora with the story of Paul's monstrous behavior as he rises in Democratic politics. Having inherited his father's lust, he ignores his wife and exploits his mistresses....

Andrew Greeley's novel makes strong statements about important matters—love, morality, power, belief and human frailty under the pressure of animal drives. It's by design that the only loving man in his novel is a priest who has an illicit sexual relationship with his brother's wife. It's pertinent that the church, the world and the other men in Greeley's novel all treat women the same—as property or servants. Justice, like Paul's death, is self-delivered.

Finally, however, one does not respond to Greeley's book as a novel of characters or ideas. His material is so sensational that it dwarfs the fragile characters he creates to put his concepts in motion. And what we are left with, when the entertainment is over, are images of an archbishop-to-be on a beach with a naked woman, a feeble Paul VI refusing to accept reality, and a papal envoy resisting seduction. His is a novel of electrifications. (p. 22)

> *Webster Schott, "Sacred and Secular Love," in* The New York Times Book Review *(copyright © 1982 by The New York Times Company; reprinted by permission), April 11, 1982, pp. 7, 22.*

FRANK McCONNELL

[In] ***The Cardinal Sins*** and now ***Thy Brother's Wife,*** the politics is as corrupt, the priests as troubled, the sex as overwritten, and the malarkey as uncut as you could wish. And, of course, since Greeley is a priest ... the novels carry an added, albeit extraliterary thrill. A priest, after all, writing so frankly about ecclesiastical hypocrisy and about illicit sex? Writing, God help us, about sex as if it were *fun*? What must the world be coming to?

Well, rather less, actually, than Greeley himself seems to think. The big news that priests can be as horny as the rest of us should shock nobody. . . . His descriptions of political and churchly corruption are about as daring in their revelations as an average prime-time television series. And his espousal of a new, liberated Catholic theology turns out to be as inoffensive to conservatives, as basically old-fashioned and unadventurous, as Jacques Maritain himself could have desired.

Then why all the noise? (pp. 342-43)

I think it has to do with two basic things: the innate fascination of the Irish Catholic experience in America, and Greeley's own brilliant talent for self-advertising.

Faith 'n begorrah, Sodom and Gomorrah: I said a few years ago that this is the elementary formula for the Irish Romantic American novel—let's abbreviate that to the IRA—and I think it still holds true. . . . Greeley's characters, in times of severe stress or despair, tend to fall back for solace not so much on a faith or a love or even an idea, but rather on the mere fact of their Irishness. Silly, yes: but that's what the IRA is all *about:* and Greeley has grasped the formula with an accuracy that is either cynical or so innocent that it is just next door to pure cynicism.

This nonsense appeals as much as it does, I think, because—in post-Watergate, pre-nuclear, mid-Reagan America—the Irish obsession with family and with guilt and with tradition is a kind of mythic antidote for what, otherwise, seems a national crisis of jadedness. . . . And such are the ironies of history that, when we try to think ourselves back to a time of real hope and real creativity in government, most of us inevitably remember the image of the Kennedy years, of "Camelot"—a tarnished coin, to be sure, but still a brighter one than any since minted. Greeley, like Eugene Kennedy and a number of other writers of the IRA school, puts heavy stress on Camelot-nostalgia in both his novels, even introducing Robert F. Kennedy as a minor character in *Thy Brother's Wife*.

And if the Irish Americans generally are a self-hugging lot, nowhere do they embrace themselves more ferociously than in Dublin-by-the-lake, Chicago: the inevitable scene of Greeley's stories. Paul Cronin, the politician/anti-hero of *Thy Brother's Wife,* is described early on in the book as having "a devil-may-care grin and mischief-filled eyes: a black Irish warrior with the looks of a movie star." But of course, one sighs. Greeley perfectly incarnates in his characters all the arrogance, insularity, and irresponsible sentimentality of the Second City. He just doesn't, one feels, *know* that he does. And that is the difference between art and schlock, between a storyteller and a mere relayer of anecdotes.

Not that Greeley isn't fun to read. There is a set form to the IRA novel, almost as predictable as the conventions of soap opera, and both Greeley's novels fill it out to perfection. Take two strong male figures, both Irish Catholic, one dedicated to worldly success, the other dedicated to the spiritual life; make them related (e.g. father and son, best buddies from childhood, brothers); put them in conflict; put them in Chicago; stir in one, or no more than two, sexually active but guilt-ridden Irish women; and serve. (p. 343)

Those twins, fathers and sons, brothers and brothers, who inhabit the landscape of the IRA are really a dramatization—or maybe, even, a *projection*—of the deep split that cuts across

that narcissistic culture. So the attractiveness of the IRA mythology for America at the present time may be more than merely a nostalgia for a lost culture of shared values. It may be, more seriously and more distressingly, a nostalgia for a simplified world of easy solutions and unexamined bromides that was false to begin with.

This, at any rate, is the impression one gets of the culture of Irish American Catholicism from Greeley's two books. Negligible as fiction, laughable as cultural history, they are nevertheless important—and disturbing—as phenomena. They are *smug;* and they seem to advocate smugness as a rational response to life.

Why should a priest, Greeley asks in the pompous afterwords to both novels, write novels at all? "Particularly," as he says after *Thy Brother's Wife,* "a secular novel, about adultery, incest, and sacrilege?" . . . Well, because, he tells us, all the greatest religious teachers—Jesus, Mohammed, Buddha, etc.—have always used fiction as a means of getting their lessons across. Indeed, at the beginning of *The Cardinal Sins* and again at the beginning of *Thy Brother's Wife,* he thoughtfully provides us with introductory paragraphs explaining just how the story and characters to follow fit into a conventional scheme of Catholic morality. (pp. 343-44)

It is not the astonishing arrogance of this that I find so distressing, as much as the unsophistication of it all. If Greeley wants to explain his work as a fiction writer by analogy with the parables of Jesus, then by all means let him. But let him *not* have the bad taste to make the identification explicit. Any number of writers—J. F. Powers, Norman Mailer, Lawrence Sanders, and most especially Thomas Pynchon—have managed to transmute the Catholic experience in America into the stuff of real mythmaking, the stuff of real legend, the stuff of a real cultural access of consciousness. And these—*Morte D'Urban, The Third Deadly Sin, Gravity's Rainbow*—are *real* parables; they are stories that humanize us, that is, and stories that help us get through the day with something like grace. Andrew Greeley's crude cartoons are nothing of the sort. And it is, well, offensive of him to suggest that they are. In his headlong quest for scandalous storytelling, and his clumsiness on that quest, he resembles most, among recent American novelists, the unfortunate Erica Jong, whose *Fear of Flying* announced to us all what we all already should have known.

But to claim that this clumsiness is a "religious story?" Well, let me quote the famous utterance of a deposed alderman—convicted of fraud, speculation, blackmail, and embezzlement—from Greeley's beloved Chicago. As he exited, for the last time, the City Council, he turned in wrath and delivered the eloquent judgment:

"It ain't seemly." (p. 344)

Frank McConnell, "Self-Hugging Parables: Boiling the Irish Catholic Pot," in Commonweal *(copyright © 1982 Commonweal Publishing Co., Inc.; reprinted by permission of Commonweal Publishing Co., Inc.), Vol. CIX, No. 11, June 4, 1982, pp. 342-44.*

MAYO MOHS

The Cardinal Sins shocked many with its tortured, bisexual archbishop, whose encounters with women are invariably brutal. *Thy Brother's Wife* . . . is in fact a better, more hopeful book. The pace is quicker, the characters more firmly drawn, the sexual rites gentler. Greeley's turf remains Camelot West:

the Chicago of lace-curtain Irish who have pushed their way to the top. Multimillionaire Mike Cronin, who beds women faster than Joe Kennedy could say "Gloria Swanson," has set the course for his two sons. Paul, the Notre Dame boy who goes off to win a Medal of Honor in the Korean War, is going to be President. Sean is bound for the priesthood, and will of course be a Cardinal. Paul's wife is to be Nora, orphaned daughter of a family friend and a foster child in the Cronin home. Sean loves her; Paul gets her, hence the temptation of *Thy Brother's Wife*.

Everything moves fast for the Cronins—even tragedy. (p. 70)

Sean's fate seems to be Greeley's fantasy. He is ordained at St. Mary of the Lake Seminary in Mundelein, the author's alma mater, in 1956, just two years after Greeley was. Greeley remembers being "very cautious, very conservative. I kept all the rules." So does Sean. Assigned to a black parish (unlike Greeley), he works himself to near collapse. A new archbishop sends the exhausted curate off to Rome to study the history of church marital theology, and Sean finds himself on the famous papal birth control commission, where he stubbornly decides to abstain from voting. The move wins him an interview with Pope Paul VI, whom he lectures about the need for a new theology of sexual morality. Sean could use it himself: he has just spent two weeks in bed with Nora. Neither the interlude nor a brash period of liberalism prevents his rise, however, first to bishop and then, after a telephone call from Pope Paul, to Cardinal Archbishop of Chicago.

Sean's triumph is something more than diverting summer fiction for Greeley. For years he was an outspoken foe of the late, scandal-plagued Archbishop of Chicago, John Cardinal Cody.... Assuming Cody's position would be the ultimate revenge. That is a basic problem with *Thy Brother's Wife*: its mean streak. Most of the tragedies in the novel result not from too much lovemaking but too much getting even. Perhaps this is less a reflection of Greeley's art than of his anger. There are many Andrew Greeleys, and there are clearly two working at cross-purposes here: Greeley the romantic, wishing that life could be full of grace, and Greeley the realistic priest, who knows how dark human souls can be. The priest keeps trying to explain, but it is the bitter romantic who keeps getting even. (pp. 70, 72)

> Mayo Mohs, "The Luck of Andrew Greeley," in *Time* (copyright 1982 Time Inc.; all rights reserved; reprinted by permission from Time), Vol. 120, No. 2, July 12, 1982, pp. 70, 72.

PEOPLE WEEKLY

[In *Ascent Into Hell* a] handsome Irish-American lad in Chicago is promised to the priesthood at birth as his mother's life hangs in the balance. When he grows up, he dutifully takes his vows but is only partially successful in repressing his sexual feelings. This is the world of the American Catholic novel, and its subject is sex and more sex. All the characters are stereotypes, and the plot is utterly familiar: There is hanky-panky by the priest's bad-boy brother, and some silver ingots wind up at the bottom of a swimming pool. The priest goes to prison on a bum rap. But his sexy former teenage sweetie, who has become a bank president, comes to his rescue. Greeley ... tries to justify this foolishness by maintaining: "There is not a character or incident in my story, I think, without a scriptural counterpart, and not a story in scripture that would not shock us if we listened to it carefully." But the scriptures were not written to become instant best-sellers. Their purpose was moral and historical. What is shocking about *Ascent Into Hell* is that the book is so deliberately sleazy. (pp. 18, 20)

> A review of "Ascent into Hell," in People Weekly (© 1983 Time Inc.), Vol. 19, No. 24, June 20, 1983, pp. 18, 20.

JOHN B. BRESLIN

A decade ago in a capsule review of an early foray by Andrew Greeley into sexology, it was suggested that the prolific priest-sociologist had advanced from having no unpublished thoughts to having no unpublished fantasies. Had we only known! ... [Those] fantasies, now fictionalized [in *Ascent into Hell*], have multiplied the biblical hundredfold with no end in sight.

Interestingly, not all the fantasies are sexual, despite those matching, tastelessly titillating jackets with their crimson draperies and statuesque women suggestive of bishops and bordellos. The fantasies have just as much to do with that broader range of human obsessions dear to commercial fiction: power, money, status. To that already heady mix Greeley adds large dollops of religion in its Roman Catholic form, still the most mystifying and intriguing for many Americans. Like the standard protagonists of such fiction, Greeley's heroes and heroines are handsome, successful, and perceptive, as well as sexy; they are also God-haunted and/or plagued with dark secrets. (p. 3)

Character and plot come from the same never-never land of bestsellerdom as the style. Hugh Donlon is an elder son destined by parental vow for the priesthood, a vocation he dutifully accepts and follows honorably despite his red-blooded urges to bed every attractive woman he meets. His younger brother Tim, lacking clerical constraints, wenches and cheats his way through life, while their sister Marge starts out badly but ends up marrying a fabulously wealthy and entirely lovable Irish nobleman. The mother and father of this brood, in addition to enjoying a sensational sex life, are, respectively, a distinguished painter of sensual forms and a judge who turns down a seat on the Supreme Court. In short, a typical Chicago Irish Catholic family!

Hugh's problems begin with a psychotic pastor in his first parish and are compounded when he falls for a recently liberated nun in graduate school. They marry, on the strength of a supposed pregnancy, and live miserably ever after. But Hugh does become a vastly successful trader of commodities, a master of revenge, and no mean Casanova into the bargain (a mother and daughter in one case). If this all sounds familiar, it should; the plot of *Thy Brother's Wife* has many of the same building blocks, just assembled differently.

The crisis comes when Tim gambles big and loses on the silver market, implicating the absent Hugh, now a much abused ambassador to a Third World despot who is craftier, crazier, and even more dangerous than a Chicago pastor. A vindictive judge sends Hugh to jail, but he is rescued by the shrewd sleuthing of Maria, the true love of his life, who was a shapely high school beauty in Hugh's seminary days and is now a gorgeous bank president. Her naval-hero husband, a military clone of Hugh, has recently been killed in Vietnam. As fate would have it, Hugh's wife and brother die in a plane crash during an illicit tryst in the Caribbean, leaving the now rehabilitated Hugh free to return to the priesthood or to marry Maria. But let me not spoil the ending.

Is there no grand design behind all this? Indeed there is, and Greeley spells it out in assorted prefaces and afterwords, as well as in publisher's handouts. This novel along with the previous two make up a "Passover trilogy" in which the true nature of God and the role of religion are worked out in modern parables. Man's needless crucifixion of himself and God's unfailing forgiveness are at the center of this one, which concludes on Good Friday. Sexual love as a sacrament of God's love, and the woman's role as the privileged representative of that love are all part of the message.

The ideas are worthy ones, and they put Greeley's fiction several notches above a novel like *The Thorn Birds,* which may well have been his inspiration. I'd always choose Andrew Greeley's gracious Yahweh, who organizes his plane crashes and other disasters for a clearly beneficent purpose, over Colleen McCullough's vindictive Jehovah who can't seem to punish his creatures enough for their sins. But good ideas, like good intentions, do not a good novel make. What we have instead is mainline commercial fiction, as addictive as bonbons or soap operas, and equally nourishing. (pp. 3, 18)

If you're interested in Greeley's ideas without the fictional trappings, you can get them by the score in *A Piece of My Mind.* It's a classic example of a non-book, being in fact some hundred weekly newspaper columns from 1980 to 1982 arranged under nine headings including "Women," "Politics," "Priesthood," "Church," "Youth." No genre, with the possible exception of book reviews, is more ephemeral by its very nature. Moreover, topical grouping has the unfortunate effect of revealing redundancies happily concealed by serial publication.... Finally, the brief space of a column (two book pages), while ideally suited to the cut and thrust of debate, gives little scope for serious reflection.

Still, there are lots of characteristically provocative ideas tossed around, from the correlation between images of a loving God and support for pre-marital chastity among the young, to the claim that bad preaching is the American Catholic Church's number one problem. In both cases he claims clear statistical support from opinion polls. On other questions he's more intuitive but probably no less right, for example in his remarks on the need to refurbish our religious symbols, especially our images of Mary.

In the end, however, form triumphs over content, and the serious reader would be well advised to look up earlier Greeley books.... The current pair of books will not be how Greeley is remembered in 20 years, or should want to be. But amid the several score of his others there are enough sturdy monuments of varying sizes and shapes for several Andrew Greeleys. (p. 18)

John B. Breslin, "Andrew Greeley: Piety and Prurience," in Book World—The Washington Post *(© 1983, The Washington Post), July 10, 1983, pp. 3, 18.*

JOHN GUINN

Andrew Greeley is a priest-sociologist who often tangles with the Roman Catholic hierarchy. Since most of the worthwhile priests I have encountered tangle with the hierarchy from time to time, that fact has never bothered me.

What has bothered me about the good Father Greeley is that he writes novels that seem to be steamy, seamy, decidedly unpriest-like works, although I have based this knowledge only on the salacious covers of his two earlier attempts in this genre....

But since I haven't read either of Greeley's previous novels, I really had no hard evidence with which to chide him for straying so far from his anointed mission.

Now comes **"Ascent into Hell,"** Greeley's third novel.

Armed with a strong Catholic upbringing and an unyielding desire to expose the tawdry in art, I got beyond the pronounced cleavage of the blond on the cover and plowed through the book.

The experience, I'm surprised to say, has altered my attitude towards Greeley. For one thing, the novel is not salacious. For another, this Irish-American priest has a marked talent for writing fiction. His characters are well-developed, his plot has an authentic ring, his style is consistently fluid.

"Ascent into Hell" is the story of Hugh Donlon, a man the Irish would call a "spoiled priest," since he forsakes his priesthood in the midst of the spiritual cyclone that affected the church after John XXIII opened those fabled windows in the early 1960s.

But Donlon is more than a renegade from the priesthood. He is a man at odds with himself, and it is his struggle to find out who he really is that makes the novel ultimately worthwhile.

The course of Donlon's struggle is peppered with characters and situations that will be familiar to any Catholic who lived through the profound changes that swept through the church in the past two decades. There are elderly pastors who rule their parishes like feudal fiefs, swinging nuns with names like Liz and Jackie, liturgies celebrated in communes with plum pudding and wassail in place of bread and wine.

Greeley details these things with unerring wit and charm, clearly pointing out the fallacies in the simplistic attitudes that infected both conservatives and liberals during those wild, woolly days.

More importantly, though, Greeley's new novel is a reaffirmation that the real mission of the church has survived the turmoil of the Second Vatican Council, that faith and morals, although viewed in a new (and more sensible) light, are still with us, that some human beings continue to gravitate towards a compassionate, forgiving God.

There are some steamy scenes, although none of them compares to what one sees on "Days of Our Lives" most any weekday. And there are some ideas that seem a bit strained, like titling the sections of the novel with Christ's seven last words on the cross. But on the whole, Greeley has succeeded in doing what he set out to accomplish.

Exactly what that is may be open to question. "My story is only secondarily about one man's struggle with a priestly vocation," Greeley writes in an afterword. "Like all religious stories this is primarily a story of God."

Knowing that Greeley's books usually end up on the best-seller lists, I suspect there is at least one more reason: Money.

Whether one likes it or not, Greeley seems to be doing the impossible with his novels. He is serving, saints preserve us, both God and mammon.

John Guinn, "He Leadeth Us Beyond the Blond to a Priestly Drama," in Detroit Free Press, *September 4, 1983, p. 5B.*

Edward Hoagland
1932-

American essayist, travel writer, and novelist.

Hoagland is considered by many critics to be a gifted and versatile essayist. Although many of his works are factual chronicles of his travels through America and foreign lands, he writes freely, inserting many digressions and asides. His method results in essays which are individualistic, loosely structured, and which move easily from one subject to another, often within a single paragraph. Some critics find Hoagland's technique distracting, while others contend that his digressions add relevance and variety to his objective observations. Most critics admire Hoagland's virtuosity. His keen eye for details, his ability to convey a precise sense of place, and his enthusiasm for all that he encounters are revealed in his dramatic metaphors and creative phrasing.

Although his subjects vary widely, many critics believe that Hoagland writes best about animals. Whether discussing caged circus animals, as in his first novel, *Cat Man* (1956), wild creatures from the backlands of British Columbia, as in *Notes from the Century Before* (1969), trivia about turtles, as in an essay from the collection *The Courage of Turtles* (1970), or superstition and lore about bears and wolves, as in *Red Wolves and Black Bears* (1976), Hoagland deftly combines realism and romanticism in his compassionate and detailed descriptions. In addition to *Cat Man*, Hoagland has published two other novels, *The Circle Home* (1960) and *The Peacock's Tail* (1965), which are generally considered less successful than his essays.

(See also *Contemporary Authors*, Vols. 1-4, rev. ed.; *Contemporary Authors New Revision Series*, Vol. 2; and *Dictionary of Literary Biography*, Vol. 6.)

Photograph © by Gerard Malanga

WILLIAM LINDSAY GRESHAM

A circus contains three worlds—the bosses, the performers and the laborers. Up to now circus fiction has almost always dealt with performers. Yet there is a vast, living mechanism, lubricated with sweat, blood and cheap wine, without which the big top could never be torn down, loaded, moved and set up again. "Cat Man" is a chronicle of the circus laborers, told with the same microscopic detail that Melville lavished on whaling.

Structurally it is hardly a novel; it is a minute dissection of the circus' sinews. Yet the story of the shambling "winos" who hire on from town to town, who last a single jump or three or a month, only to drift away or be found dead behind the wagons, this could hardly be told by any other medium than fiction, which lets us feel the grime ground into the skin, the blood caked on the knuckles, lets us smell the reek of these "creatures that once were men." . . .

The viewpoint is that of a hobo youth, nicknamed "Fiddle." . . . It is an account of one stand of the big show in Council Bluffs, Iowa, from the first sight of the freight yards to a few minutes before "Doors" when the horde of townies surge in and the glittering pageant begins. Running counterpoint to this day are slices of other days in other towns, incidents of violence, desperation or depravity which highlight the experience of the hero.

Fiddle is a cat man—a workman who tends the big cats. And never before—to the knowledge of this reviewer—has so much vivid data been set down about the behavior of lions, tigers, leopards and cheetahs in their cramped prisons-on-wheels. Edward Hoagland writes with a sharpness of focus which suggests hyperesthesia coupled with total recall. He has the gift of the pungent simile, far-fetched at times but always memorable.

The book is crammed with incidents which could stand alone—battles between elephants, courtship of tigers, psychotic arguments among the "characters" who tote water, spread straw and rake bones. The action builds toward one overpowering scene of butchering ancient horses to provide meat for the cats, a scene which leads into the book's inevitable and swiftly drawn catastrophe.

How much the casual reader will get out of "Cat Man" is a question. For serious circus fans it is required reading; the squeamish among them may have to take it in small doses but they will want it on their shelves nevertheless.

William Lindsay Gresham, "Behind the Big Top," in The New York Times Book Review (copyright © 1956 by The New York Times Company; reprinted by permission), January 15, 1956, p. 4.

NEWSWEEK

In the modern novel's never-ending quest for madder music and stronger wine, Edward Hoagland's queasy non-hero [of **"The Peacock's Tail"**]—the unhappy, suburban-bred Ben Pringle—sounds like an old and well-worn record. Ditched abruptly by his girl, he suffers with perfect pitch in the key of Moses Herzog minor. Let down by shallow friends when he seeks commiseration, he mimes Holden Caulfield's anguished wisecracks. Checked into a swinging, madcap Harlem hotel to escape familiar memories, he runs on endlessly like Tom Wolfe—the pop-prose WOW! of middle-class discovery snapping faster than a string of penny-crackers.

Sad-sacked Ben, too tender for the wooden touch of adults, takes refuge in the company of the multiracial kids who inhabit the "Aspinwall Hotel." He drops into a comfortable infantilism of fairy tales and fun and games with this redeeming, healing bunch who, despite his ardor, seem suspiciously like an amalgam of settlement-house losers and "Our Gang." But even at face value, Ben's recuperation from a bombed-out romance is hard to take.

The more Ben's following increases, the more author Hoagland gets caught up in the whirling dervish of his own prose. Finally Ben becomes a real Pied Piper to his nimble mouse pack.... His fellow-feeling mounts until he makes his big discovery about the kids, about things like prejudice and all: "For Ben their color was almost a negligible factor, in contrast to if he had been with their parents." Suffering spitballs, a sociological revelation!

The really unfortunate thing about this book is that it is not a first novel. Hoagland's **"Cat Man"** and **"The Circle Home"** showed keener insight and hipper prose. This time he seems to be writing for the Great American Everybody all at once, and **"Peacock"** turns out to be something less proud—no fantail charmer but a risible gooney bird that flaps its wings wildly but never gets off the ground.

> "Camp Counselor," in Newsweek (copyright 1965, by Newsweek, Inc.; all rights reserved; reprinted by permission), Vol. LXVI, No. 6, August 9, 1965, p. 83.

ANNETTE GRANT

Exploring by bush plane, boat and foot, Hoagland gives an account [of the interior wilds of British Columbia in **"Notes from the Century Before"**] at once blunt and rhapsodic of this demi-paradise and its self-exiled inhabitants. Why did they go there? For gold, to be sure. But gold cloaked a more interesting, and more persistent, motive in human nature: man's need to pit himself against a savage and magnificent wilderness—and come out alive. But now, a mere three years since the author's first journey, the last frontier, or last Eden, has practically disappeared under helicopters and neon. Hoagland's lyric account, therefore, becomes all the more eloquent, for it records not only a fading ideal but is, finally, a parable—and warning—for America.

This book is as remarkable as the landscape and people that it describes. Like the Kispiox River, it is all "dazzle and slash"; it's as exuberant as a prospector who finds a five-dollar nugget lying on the ground and as full of freshness and life as the stream where any man could pull out bushels of silvery salmon with his bare hands. (p. 94)

> Annette Grant, "The Last Eden," in Newsweek (copyright 1969, by Newsweek, Inc.; all rights reserved; reprinted by permission), Vol. LXXIII, No. 22, June 2, 1969, pp. 92, 94.

MARGERIE BONNER LOWRY

Notes from the Century Before is a document unlike any I have ever read, and it has left me with a feeling of the vast country to our north that we know so little about. The title is apt, for northern British Columbia must be very much like our own frontier a century ago, except for the paralyzing cold, and, of course, except for Alaska. Edward Hoagland explains that he went to this still wild and dangerous place to get first-hand accounts, before it was too late, from the few surviving old-timers who had explored the north country. He wanted it fresh and clear and not watered down or built into legends, and he found it and has recorded it for our pleasure.

The major part of the book is in the form of a daily journal which records conversations with the people Hoagland met and talked to, and the hazardous trips he made to find them. Some of the stories are gruesome but the tone is cheerful, even ebullient. (pp. 107-08)

In his loosely casual diary style Hoagland gives us the sense and feeling of having been in this country with its mighty mountain chains, tremendous rivers, and hidden lakes. (pp. 110-11)

> Margerie Bonner Lowry, "Frontier" (copyright 1969 by Margerie Bonner Lowry; reprinted by permission of the publisher and Literistic, Ltd; all rights reserved), in Commentary, Vol. 48, No. 3, September, 1969, pp. 107-08, 110-11.

GEOFFREY WOLFF

Midway through an essay about New York rodeos and midnight cowboys, Edward Hoagland remarks that "writers can be categorized by many criteria, one of which is whether they prefer subject matter that they rejoice in or subject matter they deplore and wish to savage with ironies. Since I'm of the first type . . ." Indeed he is. Here [in **"The Courage of Turtles"**] are fifteen essays about matters that either delight Hoagland or make him curious. . . .

He is a marvelous writer. . . .

"The Courage of Turtles" is not to be taken as a collection of bits and pieces written over the years. Rather it should be read as the first look back by a man in his late 30s. . . . Hoagland remarkably combines the observer's clear sense with the self-revealing passion of a man who has been "bottled up" too long. His image is apt, for Hoagland stutters terribly, and that fact about himself finds its way into almost everything he writes now. He tells us he labors over his words when he writes, but behind the blockades to speech and prose is glee, generosity, hope. . . .

We are not used to taking optimists seriously; we do not believe them. But to read two pages of Hoagland, at random, is to know immediately that you are in the hands of a supremely tough-minded man, and a man of perfect honesty. . . .

Hoagland uses the essay form as it is very seldom used today, picking a subject that interests him rather than a subject that interests a magazine. Then he moves through it leisurely, pausing whenever he wishes to illustrate a lesson, taking what appears to be a detour till we are brought back again to the true course, enhanced by the sights we have seen, perfectly confident, as we should be, that we have been all the while in good hands.

> Geoffrey Wolff, "A Very Busy Life," in Newsweek (copyright 1971, by Newsweek, Inc.; all rights reserved; reprinted by permission), Vol. LXXVII, No. 3, January 18, 1971, p. 73.

DAN WAKEFIELD

To those of you who feel your mind slipping away when confronted by further questions and arguments about such matters as the difference between fiction and nonfiction, the alleged death of the novel, short story or drama, the contention that journalism is now the "real" kind of writing, or whether it is possible to be a writer at all any more, I recommend Edward Hoagland's essay "Books, Movies, the News" [in his book **"The Courage of Turtles"**]. In a passage I intend to quote whenever such topics arise, Mr. Hoagland explains that "prose has no partitions now. . . . No forms exist anymore, except that to work as a single observer, using the resources of only one mind, and to work with words—that is being a writer."

Mr. Hoagland is a writer. He even *believes* in being a writer, and is not in despair that his craft will become obsolete. . . .

[What] Hoagland brings to bear in this book is the writer's private vision, the "resources of only one mind" looking in on itself and outward on the world. The tone is casual, conversational, the voice of a civilized man in his late thirties "touching topics I've cared about," which range from bear hunts and circuses and tug boats to the author's own struggles in dealing with personal problems of stammering, of coming to terms with his parents, of extricating himself through marriage and a newborn child from the deadly rituals of bachelor seduction which had led him no further than "the lapping, itchy edge of love."

Mr. Hoagland has written three novels (as well as one journal-style book less easily categorized) and it is probably inevitable that the stylistic excellence of these essays will be attributed to his "novelistic eye," just as when a novelist who exhibits a grasp of meaningful detail is credited with a "journalistic eye." I think Mr. Hoagland would agree that such terminology is beside the point; the point simply being good writing. That is what is on display here. . . .

In a fascinating essay on—of all things—turtles, the author describes those creatures as "a kind of bird with the governor turned down low." As I read further, the turtle began to remind me of a certain kind of writer—inquisitive, idiosyncratic, courageous, unobtrusive. There are also writers who are more like peacocks, and if that is your preference, this collection is not for you. If you're tired, though, of flashiness and preening, and would welcome the quiet, controlled tone of a fine and ironic intelligence, then Mr. Hoagland is your man and this is your book.

> Dan Wakefield, "Turtles? Birds with the Governor Turned Down," in The New York Times Book Review (copyright © 1971 by The New York Times Company; reprinted by permission), February 7, 1971, p. 8.

ALFRED KAZIN

Hoagland is one of the best "personal essayists" in the business, a virtuoso of the reader-capsizing sentence, a splendid observer of city street, circus lot, go-go girls, freight trains, juries in the jury room plus, and especially, any and every surviving patch of North American wild he can get to moon around in—whether in British Columbia or just beyond his summer acres in Vermont.

But this much expertise, readiness, fluency of information and manner is of course to be expected these days in the magazine business, where so many people now write like a flash and with a flash, smart-smart-smart. There is so much information around, so many "personalities," so much ease of movement, so much eloquent bitterness, that as the magazines get fewer and thinner, the writing gets "better"—or at least more upsetting, more concentrated, more outdoing. . . . Only fiction writers now seem capable of satisfying our demand for "facts." Edward Hoagland is as much a whiz in this department, as subtle a stylist, as V. S. Pritchett, Norman Mailer, Truman Capote, James Baldwin, Elizabeth Hardwick.

But what has come to interest me most in Hoagland's essays is "Hoagland" himself, the person set-up behind or in front of these personal essays. Unlike the all-knowing insider looking over the stable in Stillman's Gym, the "Hemingway" correspondent coolly watching "Greek women carrying dead babies in the rain," the black militant scorning the effete decaying flesh of middle-aged white liberals, Hoagland is not afraid to sound vulnerable, excited, self-deceiving, gentle. He is openly sentimental about the father-type woodsmen and state scientists who regularly get idealized in everything Hoagland writes about trekking the wild. . . .

Perhaps some day Hoagland will write the autobiography of a handsome 40-year old Harvard Wasp brought up in Connecticut who *looks* all this but is obviously a man with interesting human difficulties. He is, for example, a writer born, a writer obsessed, whose passionately right rhythms as a writer get in the way of more ordinary communications. The true confession of Edward Hoagland would be a true and marvelous book about the writer as dissimulator, the necessary role that writers play.

In any event, the role that "Hoagland" plays in [**"Walking the Dead Diamond River"**], the stance one essayist writes from, is noteworthy and somehow endearing because it presents a man who still believes in joy and is always waiting for the rapture on the next mountain trail. And the reason this is not cloying, not sticky at all, is that like that other happily "immature" American solitary and nature-nut, Henry David Thoreau, Hoagland clearly has no other way of meeting the world than by writing about it. He, too, lives his life by writing it—in New York City. But the concentration of this is so fierce, the rhythms so dominating, that the imaginative life Hoagland clearly wants is accomplished only by nailing every detail down as if his life depended on it. As perhaps it does.

So we get "fact" writing here in the sweet, classic American style of getting closer to a bear or a bush than Thoreau ever got to a woman. . . . Hoagland's best feat in these essays is the way he catches Americans-in-the-woods-nowadays, even native Maine woodsmen and silent leather-faced guides, watching themselves play woodsman.

The main characters in Hoagland's "nature" essays, as in his fine book about British Columbia, **"Notes From the Century Before,"** are recurrently foresters, guides, trainmen, surveyors, fishermen, hermits, field scientists. Hoagland is rarely alone in wild deep country; he's always a boy released from Greenwich Village, rolling over and over with delight. . . .

The art, and business, of magazine writing consists in knowing too well what your reader will be thinking. Hoagland is very good at the sentence as deceiving drop ball . . . and especially at a sentence or two as a character's whole life. . . .

Although magazine writers more than anyone else may be flagrant examples of Kenneth Burke's dictum, "We have been sentenced to the sentence," Hoagland, though as clever as you and I, is somehow more urgent, more winsome, and even more desperate.

> Alfred Kazin, in a review of "Walking the Dead Diamond River," in The New York Times Book Review (copyright © 1973 by The New York Times Company; reprinted by permission), March 25, 1973, p. 31.

PETER S. PRESCOTT

A friend told me the other day that the last book about animals he had read was "Animal Farm," his sneer implying that animal books are best reserved for readers at the Peter Rabbit level of literacy. For those who think they agree (on alternate Tuesdays, *I* agree, having never recovered from once reading books for a publisher who sponsored an annual animal book award), let me quickly say that Edward Hoagland's essays are never wholly about animals, though some contain a lot of wildlife lore, but are often about Hoagland's attempts "to rediscover the commonality of animal and man." By losing our awareness of animals, he writes, "we sacrifice some of the intricacy and grandeur of life." Bears and wolves, the subjects of the two longest essays in ["**Red Wolves and Black Bears**"], particularly delight him because in these large predators he finds resemblances to man—our anatomy and churlishness are not unlike the bear's, and our method of hunting is so similar to the wolf's that it recognizes us as superior predators, not prey.

Hoagland spends half of each year in the wilderness, the other half in the savage literary precincts of New York. He writes with intuitive perception about both, but better about the outdoors, on which he feeds expansively, exuberantly. . . .

Watching Hoagland work his way through a long piece is like watching a hunter stalk his game. More than most writers, he seems to use everything that has ever happened to him, everything he has ever heard. He chooses his subjects well: a 70-year-old man, for instance, who dives 40 feet into 12 inches of water; in the tackiness of this low-water act, and in its supreme daring, Hoagland isolates the urge in some men to push themselves to the limits of the possible. And he is by his own insistence an optimist—but his optimism is not of the Smile button sort; it is tinged with irony and wit. "He married the same woman twice," he writes of a friend. "Although it didn't work out either time, she was well worth marrying twice, and to my way of thinking this showed that he was at once a man of fervent, rash, abiding love, and yet a man of flexibility, ready to admit an error and to act to correct it." It is hard not to be seduced by that view of what most writers would take to be a messy situation, but then few writers run on the fuel that Hoagland burns while working: joy.

> Peter S. Prescott, "Endangered Species," in Newsweek (copyright 1976, by Newsweek, Inc.; all rights reserved; reprinted by permission), Vol. LXXXVII, No. 19, May 10, 1976, p. 108.

THOMAS R. EDWARDS

Hoagland is surely one of our most truthful writers about nature, one of the few who can be counted on to avoid the distracting theatricality of preaching or blaming or apocalypse-mongering. And his truthfulness doesn't rule out the pleasures of a brilliant image . . . or of passages of sustained inventive brio.

At times the going is admittedly harder. Hoagland sometimes lapses into routine philosophizing. . . . His essays on wild animals and those who study them sometimes substitute the rehearsing of worked-up data (however fascinating . . .) for continuous thinking about such information. The tendency to take long views becomes a little too evident. And, though this gets to be rather endearing, there's a reliance for lightness on a repertory of idioms that seems to have been retrieved from a time-capsule buried several decades ago; what other writers would now use, without visible nervousness, such words as "razz," "rib" (as a verb), "gumption," "umpteen," "tizzy," "the willies," "lummoxy," "savvy," "going cattywomp," "mingy" or "flummoxed," or refer to male persons so repeatedly as "fellows"?

"**Red Wolves and Black Bears**" is an uneven volume. As a novelist as well as a nature-writer, Hoagland offers some literary commentaries that seem anxious and at least debatable. . . . And some of his meditations about being at once a city man and a country man maneuver so complexly between the two worlds as to risk organizational chaos, if not also a touch of smugness.

But the good things here are up to Hoagland's past standard. There are lengthy essays, packed with curious lore and modestly including the author in the field of vision, on wolves and bears and the strange, inarticulate, suspicious investigators—half scientist, half woodsman—who work without much support or recognition to understand and perhaps preserve them in habitats that continue to shrink. There are passages as richly informed with a sense of the strangeness and wonder of American landscapes and folkways as any I can remember. Above all, there's the welcome companionship of an unusual personality, a man determined to know the worst of us so that he can find something helpful to say, a lover of animals who will not have them sentimentalized simply because they are endangered (wolves *will* attack man, he insists, even though they haven't eaten any graduate students in the field lately), an intelligence that's quiet, speculative, sensible.

> Thomas R. Edwards, "Serious Games, Tasty Crabs and a Natural Writer: 'Red Wolves and Black Bears'," in The New York Times Book Review (copyright © 1976 by The New York Times Company; reprinted by permission), June 13, 1976, p. 7.

GEOFFREY WOLFF

"How long will these readers continue to miss walking in the woods enough to employ oddballs like me and Edward Abbey and Peter Matthiessen and John McPhee to do it for them? Not long, I suspect. We're a peculiar lot: McPhee long bent to the traces of *The New Yorker,* Matthiessen an explorer in remote regions that would hound most people into a nervous breakdown, Abbey angry, molded by what is nowadays euphemistically called 'Appalachia.' As a boy, I myself was mute for years, forced either to become acutely intuitive or to take to the woods. By default, we are the ones the phone rings for, old enough to have known real cowboys and real woods."

There's Edward Hoagland; I'd know the author of that paragraph from a mile off. It comes from the middle of an essay titled "Writing Wild," and like a wolf pissing along his trail, its author lets you know whom you're following. The breezy "oddball" is a Hoagland signature, and so is the confident placement of his own work with McPhee's, Abbey's and Matthiessen's. The outburst of candor—"As a boy, I myself was mute . . ."—is vintage Hoagland, together with the audacious transition to and from his confession.

We are speaking here of an original. . . . In the course of an essay on the literary situation, Hoagland hit upon a truth relevant to his *career* (a word he doesn't like): "There are writers' writers and readers' writers, and though each group is inclined to envy the other, the writers' writers envy the readers' writers more and cross over if they find they can. After all, writers want to be read."

Of course they do. Hoagland has written that while he could easily set limits on his appetite for fame and fortune, he'd happily have readers in their millions with their noses stuck in his pages, finding something they need or want. He deserves them: he has range, tenacity, intelligence, special knowledge, comic gifts, invention, an intimate proximity with his reader.

God knows the critical attention has been extravagant: Alfred Kazin has called Hoagland "a writer born, a writer obsessed" [see excerpt above]. Philip Roth has chimed in, Archibald MacLeish, Saul Bellow, John Berryman, many heavyweights. Hoagland's essays are accessible: about how we live, love, marry, die, divide, replicate, suffer, celebrate . . . essays about the circus, boxing, New York, bears, tugboats, turtles, country fairs, dogs, taxidermy, bad luck. One of my favorites is "A Low-Water Man," about a man who dives from an ever increasing height into an ever-decreasing depth of water, a paradigm for the "writers' writer," who continues to do what he does, like the diver, because "this is what he is good at."

When I suggested in a review that Hoagland is a kind of low-water man, he bristled; he is a *hell* of a bristler. "Why not a high-water man?" he asked me. Why not indeed? It's past time for this gorgeous writers' writer to dive deep into a great abundance of readers, who have for too long missed too much. (pp. ix-xi)

Hoagland's life is artfully balanced—or divided, depending on your perspective—between the wildness of New York and the wilderness of places unsought by most people. Sometimes he is at home either in New York or in Vermont's Northeast Kingdown, and sometimes he is torn between them, but always he's alive to the distinction, and often in his personal journalism he remarks it. (p. xv)

But wherever he fetches up, there's the immutable fact of solitude, another of his great subjects, and of all his subjects the one that has most deepened his judgment. (p. xvii)

Hoagland has the gift of fine discrimination. . . . At his best Hoagland, like anyone telling us what we didn't know, is eagle-eyed, and keen-eared, listening for peculiarities and particularities of speech. . . .

At his worst he is merely astringent, uncharitable, too quick to assume he has a stranger's number. "I have yet to like anyone who wears a string tie," he says, and I believe him, and wish I didn't. Jealous of his own privacy, he is nevertheless intrusive, a journalist, after all. (p. xix)

When Hoagland judges people fecklessly, and calls for hanging, I don't much care for him. . . . So much for Hoagland's vices, and my reservations: the rest is trumpet voluntaries. And even his occasional sourness is the fruit of a brassbound optimist's vision of the night-side of things. . . . (pp. xx-xxi)

As an essayist Hoagland is a conservative, hanging on for dear life to things still here, about to vanish. That's why he prefers old-timers to young knuckleheads; he wants to conserve their stories, the lore in the attics of their memories. . . . He feels no compulsion to record, for himself, what he has already experienced. Neither does he write, like a polemicist, to reverse the world's processes. "Lament the Red Wolf" is a long essay about a dying species: an interviewer asked Hoagland if he wrote about red wolves to save them, and Hoagland said, "No. There is absolutely no hope for red wolves, and my article didn't do a thing for them." He writes for generations to come, as all writers with reach write. . . . (p. xxii)

[The] most radical quality of his architecture—especially in his most recent work—is the detour. Like his precious wolves and bears, he needs range room; his many and often abrupt transitions cannot survive excessive constriction, which is why his longer essays seem to me so much more successful than his short performances.

Look at "Other Lives," the final essay in [**The Edward Hoagland Reader**]. It disregards commonplace syntactical, logical and epistemological transitions; Hoagland lights and flies, lights and flies again, on through an entire alphabet of postulates and preoccupations. At a first, casual reading it is impossible to know (but easy to feel) what the essay is "about." It touches on the following subjects, among others: wisdom, playfulness, vulnerability, resilience, divorce, expectation, risk, ambition, leisure time, the social efficiency that places a New York penitentiary next door to a neighborhood drug exchange. The essay is set in New York, but bound only by its author's meditation as he walks from his apartment to the waterfront, and sits on a pier, thinking of mortality, cruelty, his dog, flux, the clergy, communards, the institution of the family. (p. xxiv)

Hoagland is never impassive, sometimes uncivil, often hallucinatory. His diction, seldom gratuitously or strenuously bizarre, can, at the necessary moment, astonish like a dream. (p. xxv)

Humor, the wise wink and city shrug, runs through Hoagland's work; it's as much his style as the unexpected confession, radical locution, winding progress through the things on his mind. (p. xxvi)

Hoagland celebrates the minute detail, reporting to those who didn't know that white birch, because it is odorless, is used to make Popsicle sticks. (p. xxvii)

But the rhapsodies and celebrations are his specialty. I like them because they're felt, and because they're manageable, no rebuke to novices and stay-at-homes. (pp. xxvii-xxviii)

Perhaps best of all, I like why Hoagland goes to the circus, and why he's glad to see you and me there, too. It's because it's one of the last places left, or so he believes, where a crowd will watch someone teeter on the wire of death and not yell "Jump!" So he writes in "Splendid, with Trumpets," and so he repeats, with a variation, in "Tiger Bright": "In a day of casual death everywhere, we are rejoicing *he lives! he lives!*" (p. xxviii)

Geoffrey Wolff, "Introduction" (introduction copyright © 1979 by Geoffrey Wolff; reprinted by per-

mission of the author), in The Edward Hoagland Reader *by Edward Hoagland, edited by Geoffrey Wolff, Vintage Books, 1979, pp. ix-xxx.*

DIANE JOHNSON

Inevitably the first and most engaging effect of Edward Hoagland's two new books [*The Edward Hoagland Reader* and *African Calliope*] is to draw our interest to the writer himself. Despite his rooted WASP belief that "personality is quarrelsomeness," his personality, or rather his character, emerges and we're glad. Our estimation of it becomes essential to our appreciation of his work. One thing his admirers like most about his writing is his quite distinctive combination of subjectivity and authority. (p. 30)

Maybe the reason novels exist is to disguise human musings. The novelist, afraid his ideas may be foolish, slyly puts them into the mouth of some other fool and reserves the right to disavow them. . . . In the essays collected in *The Edward Hoagland Reader,* . . . [Hoagland] pulls off the considerable feat of being interesting without being in disguise.

There are essayists who, like anxious hosts, amuse you with confessions, as if they fear that only a bit of scandal will make you string along. Hoagland tries the riskier business of presenting thoughts. (p. 31)

With what does he concern himself? The world of nature—salmon spawning, bears—but also people and, most successfully, the frail, big subjects: a run of bad luck, or pain. "Dogs and the Tug of Life." "Other Lives." "The Courage of Turtles." With sly discursiveness he tells us how things tasted, looked and felt, and what the people said. He has a strong sense of what the life of others is like—it is perhaps this which gives him a certain air of diffidence or, as he appears (without foundation) to fear, a "lack of panache." Among the chaotic sights and smells of Africa, it is individuals who catch his ear. . . . (pp. 31-2)

The broad political issues, accordingly, do not seem to interest him as much as the particulars of ethnicity, including his own. (p. 32)

[He] has led an interesting life as naturalist, lionkeeper, wanderer and city-dweller. But the best moments in [*The Edward Hoagland Reader*] concern not actions or escapades but general matters of enduring interest—the death of a father, childbirth, the relation of man and animals, qualities of the human heart. These are subjects about which wisdom is of better use than wit, and rarer—wisdom and a lively sense of the role of the imagination in getting through life. . . . He is vivid and observant, responsive to how things grow. . . . (pp. 32-3)

It is this responsiveness that makes him a wonderful travel writer, sharing qualities with other good travel writers, and with other good travelers. . . . (p. 33)

Hoagland's only fault as a reporter, if he has one, is his discursiveness. It is a virtue in his essays and occasional pieces, but in a travel book some might prefer the facts up front: geography, political history, an explanation of the author's presence. Instead he parcels out these disorienting bits from time to time, as if, trudging across the Sudan, he occasionally feels the need to lighten the load of his pack by shedding a piece of notebook paper. His essays meander like streams, and it is part of a desired effect, but here the meandering alters the chronology and confuses the geography. The logic of this organization strains against the logic of journeys, which the reader is deeply familiar with: journeys must begin somewhere, go from here to there and then end.

While with him on the journey, however, one is merely caught up in his meticulous and wonderful descriptions of things. . . . (pp. 34-5)

Altogether, in his essays, in his fiction and in his travel books, it is against the deadness of life that Edward Hoagland writes, or at least that is the effect of his writing. Beneath the wise and faintly elegiac tone of regret for this deadness there always lies a confidence about life that is reassuring. (p. 36)

> *Diane Johnson, "One of the Best in a Risky Business," in* The New York Times Book Review *(copyright © 1979 by The New York Times Company; reprinted by permission), September 16, 1979 (and reprinted as "The Traveling Self: Edward Hoagland," in her* Terrorists and Novelists, *Alfred A. Knopf, 1982, pp. 30-6).*

ROSS WETZSTEON

Speaking for myself, I'd read Hoagland if only because (a) he has the finest sense of paragraph structure of any writer alive, and (b) he's an old friend. But since these aren't exactly qualities likely to endear his work to a wider audience, it's fortunate other things are going on as well. As a stylist, he's gifted at rescuing moribund adjectives and nursing them back to health, at combining the arcane with the colloquial, at guiding us through bewildering but suddenly gratifying digressions (like detours that turn out to save hours), and especially at jolting one's mind with abrupt, revelatory transitions. . . .

As a reporter . . . he also rescues, combines, guides, and jolts, dealing with places and subjects we know little and care less about, and revealing that the universe can be glimpsed in a turtle or a tugboat as well as in a grain of sand.

Hoagland began his career as a promising novelist. But all three of his novels were marvelously rendered settings (the circus, a box gym, a welfare hotel) in futile search of narrative, and I remember feeling at the time that it was too bad he was apparently entranced with the notion, as so many were in the '50s, that any other form of prose than fiction was a sign of timid ambition and failed artistry. Even more problematic, all three novels dealt with confrontations between unequals in narrowly confined settings, and while this allowed the novels to explore the nature of power in human relationships, their inability to achieve any kind of narrative or emotional resolution meant that their attempts at compassion too often had overtones of something close to sadism.

But an odd thing happened when Hoagland turned to nonfiction in the late '60s—the exotic settings, in moving from the background to the foreground, became paradoxically less important. In his fiction, it seemed as if he'd invented characters and stories largely as a pretext to write about his settings, but now he seemed to have chosen his settings largely as a pretext to write about characters and stories—only this time it worked, for they no longer seemed to be imposed by the author but to emerge from the material.

Observation rather than invention is Hoagland's great talent—he has the most acute peripheral vision of any writer I know—and the relationship between environment and character his great theme—not "travel" books or "nature" books, as they're usually called, but natural history in the broader sense of the interaction between nature and people. In turning from fiction to nonfiction, he was liberated to tell us not what he envisioned but what he discovered. Furthermore, loneliness and isolation, major themes of his fiction, become, in his non-fiction, states we share rather than barriers between us, and irresolution, yet another major theme, became a condition of being rather than a failure of novelistic imagination. . . .

[If] I say that when I finished his latest book [*African Calliope*] I was only marginally more interested in the Sudan, I mean it not in dispraise of his admirable reporting but in recognition of a larger achievement. Of course, he discovered a great deal about Africa in his travels. . . . (p. 39)

But to emphasize what Hoagland discovered about Africa would be to minimize what he discovered about *us*—about the role of Africa in our imagination, about the way persistence and craft compensate for our isolation, about the way customs and costumes connect us to our environment, and how the differences in centuries and civilizations only superficially veil the similarities of our characters.

Hoagland's books, ironically like fine novels, are built on details so precisely observed and so imaginatively rendered they become metaphors—*African Calliope* is about the Sudan in the same way *The Sun Also Rises* is about bullfighting. The accomplishment of his form is to bring novelistic virtues to nonfiction, to show that observation can perform the same function as imagination—detail as discovery, reporting as rhapsody, fact as revelation. (pp. 39-40)

> Ross Wetzsteon, "Up from Fiction," (reprinted by permission of The Village Voice and the author; copyright © News Group Publications, Inc., 1979), in The Village Voice, Vol. XXIV, No. 42, October 15, 1979, pp. 39-40.

DONALD HALL

Edward Hoagland has taken a place among the best living practitioners of the sentence—and like many present prose writers he concentrates not on fiction but on fact. . . . Last year he summed up a decade of his essays with two books: *The Edward Hoagland Reader* . . . collects 21 essays from four earlier books; *African Calliope,* which recounts "A Journey to the Sudan," we must, for lack of better terminology, call a travel book.

If it is clearly inadequate to call *African Calliope* a travel book, it is difficult in general to categorize Edward Hoagland. Although he uses much factual detail, he is not a writer of what *The New Yorker* calls fact-pieces, like the wonderful John McPhee. Nor is he typically an autobiographer, whose subject is endlessly himself. His writing combines world and self, or creates a self that we watch with delight as it observes and renders the world. He mostly describes or recounts matters external to himself—a tugboat, a lion tamer, a settlement on the Blue Nile—but which he observes very much in his own person. The measuring instrument, he is aware, distorts by its presence the object measured. If he is a camera, he is a camera forty years old that graduated from Harvard, that stutters badly, and that alternates its domicile between Manhattan and Vermont. . . .

Always Hoagland is *there;* we feel him, we listen to him examine himself, remember, and even think. One has the impression not of egotism but of restless self-examination—skeptical, alert, and intelligent. . . . His mind perseveres with an idea, he sticks with it, he pushes it; things are never glib or easy with Hoagland. . . .

Sometimes, in fact, Hoagland is a clumsy writer. In pursuit of the idiomatic sentence which imitates the mind's fumbling toward a perception, he can be confusing. His essay structures are sometimes awkward, long bridges to small islands, or highways that seem to end mid-paragraph, the bridge washed out. If these infelicities are annoying, they remain minor, and at times Hoagland's very clumsiness seems evidence of the energy and enthusiasm which thrusts him from page to page—as if he were too excited to be perfect. (p. 669)

Although his details are well chosen, although his metaphors are sharp, although his sentence rhythms satisfy us and resolve themselves, although his topics remain interesting, what I love most in Edward Hoagland is the character of the mind. As he improvises inside a chosen landscape—rendering it, responding, and rendering the responder—he makes discoveries, because he is *free* to speculate; and because his thought perseveres and pushes, he often discovers something astonishing. . . . Hoagland's sentences embody an enthusiasm for the dailiness of existence, an excitement over breathing, living, opening one's eyes and ears to anything at all. (pp. 669-70)

> Donald Hall, "Hoagland Was There!" in National Review (© National Review, Inc., 1980; 150 East 35th St., New York, NY 10016; reprinted with permission), Vol. XXXII, No. 11, May 30, 1980, pp. 669-70.

SPENCER BROWN

Edward Hoagland has been enormously praised, and with some justice. The quality of his huge output is consistently high. He is so good that he ought to be much better. *The Edward Hoagland Reader* and *African Calliope,* both published in 1979, show his power and his weakness.

As a good essayist he is interested in everything, his especial passions being the wilderness, animals, circuses, crowds, and the city. In all these he shows the easy familiarity of the complete With-It. He retails his wide information tirelessly but painlessly. (p. 500)

The Hoagland Reader shows the essayist as sprinter, *African Calliope* as distance runner. [The latter] is an extended account of Hoagland's travels in the Sudan. . . . *African Calliope,* like its subject, is bewildering but fascinating. The sharp phrase, the lively though characteristically gruesome simile, the eye cocked for dirt and distress and hunger and hideous ugliness and cruelty, with a cast of thousands of eccentric expatriates and natives—these make a spectacular performance. But it is clutter, with no architecture. It is like bright sophisticated conversation, or perhaps, as Sainte-Beuvé said of Voltaire, a chaos of clear ideas.

Recognizing Hoagland's undeniable skills and virtues, one feels a certain embarrassment. In a travel book one expects the writer's hardships but not his neuroses. Hoagland cherishes both, presumably as additional evidence that he is With It. . . . (pp. 501-02)

For all his confessional disclaimers, Hoagland is prone to Hemingwayize himself, to take himself seriously not only as writer but as person. An injured hero in perpetual peril because he stutters, he can view himself with occasional rueful wit, but he does not smile. His humor is sardonic.

I keep wishing he would take himself more conscientiously as writer. With all his talent he is slipshod. A paragraph will baffle, as he switches from animal to animal or person to person in a thicket of orphan pronouns. He perpetrates the phrase "a journeyman trainer, a fellow tired of it now but who knows all the jumps and moves." He uses *nauseous* for *nauseated*, *lady* everywhere for *woman*, and *intriguing* for *interesting*. He can write a brilliant account of the desertification process and its visible symptoms, or of bird songs in a tropical forest. And he can produce a passage eligible for the Department of Utter Confusion. He is so good that he should be much better. (p. 502)

Spencer Brown, "Four Essayists," in The Sewanee Review *(reprinted by permission of the editor; © 1980 by The University of the South), Vol. LXXXVIII, No. 3, Summer, 1980, pp. 498-505.**

GEOFFREY STOKES

"To live is to see," writes Edward Hoagland, and that credo has placed him consistently among this country's most distinguished essayists ever since **"The Courage of Turtles"** was published 12 years ago. In this fourth collection [**"The Tugman's Passage"**], he continues to range widely in his concerns. Bumpkin skeptic in the city, sure-footed urbanist in the woods, he sees as well as ever. . . .

There is, in Hoagland's descriptive prose, such a comforting sense of place that in the altogether distressing event that I was actually forced to walk through a bear-infested forest, I would trust him to be my guide—that is, with my life. (p. 7)

Hoagland can be very good on people, too. "The boss on a construction project in Syria will work right alongside his men, whereas in Egypt there is much bowing and salaaming to the 'doctor' in a ministry office, the 'director' of a business. . . . In fact, it's said the principal reason why Nasser's experiment at unifying the Egyptian and Syrian nations in 1958 didn't succeed was that thousands of know-it-all Egyptian civil servants suddenly turned up in Damascus, fussy and correct, to set everyone straight."

One sees the Hoagland method nicely at work in that passage. A particular observation—work relations in two different countries—leads to a generalization about the inevitable incompatibility of their politics and national personalities. The observation is critical because Hoagland's mind is so quick, his associations so quirky, that without the observed world he would float off like a balloon.

Consider, for example, sex. In the book's best essay—the wonderfully convoluted "The Ridge-Slope Fox and the Knife Thrower"—Hoagland writes as directly and brilliantly about his own sexuality as has any living male writer. Alone in the woods he is capable of being amused by his physical maleness, "futile as a club, and a Stone Age implement for all of us, which is why we love it so," but he can also be terrifyingly frank (". . . we who go into the woods nowadays are as likely to be kinky as chaste. Still waiting to get to sleep . . . I have a fantasy that at least has the virtue of logic. I am an itinerant slave dealer. . . .'").

Hoagland's reporting on sex and fantasy is honest, even touching, but the passages just quoted hint at the major stumbling block in his work. Hoagland seems genuinely to believe that his possession of a club makes his imagined right to own other humans logical. And when he shifts from close reporting—where his eyes keep him honest—to generalizations about gender in the real world, the result is predictably disastrous.

Unanchored by observation, the lengthy "Women and Men" announces early on that "Some women activists wanted men to cease to exist. Others wanted women to become like men. Others wanted women to become like men and men to become like women, in the old sense—while still others wanted everybody to become the same, somewhere in between." One is, in charity, tempted to excuse this passage as merely panicky, but I fear it is as devious as it would be to list within an otherwise credible series of what "some" and "other" Reaganites advocate, the information that certain of them feel that cannibalism might offset the increasing demand for food stamps. (pp. 7, 33)

There are 20 pages of obviously sincere fulmination along these lines. Some of them are merely curious. . . . But others are unpleasantly homophobic—the opinions he distrusts seem rather too often to be held only by "some lesbians," or the Woman's Movement's "lesbian or radical wings."

But for what seems to me to be irredeemable hostility of spirit, nothing quite equals Hoagland's portrait of an older woman, a "$60,000-a-year-executive, whose cough is unexpectedly deep-voiced in the morning, but whose soft excesses of flesh almost seem to 'ask' for cancer because they are appendices without a function now." Can this passage be serious? *Breast cancer* is what they deserve?

Such pages undermine **"The Tugman's Passage,"** for instead of yielding to what might have appeared mere eccentricities in Hoagland's vision, one is forced to consider the psychosexual strangeness behind such notions as a tugboat captain eating fried eggs with "the yolks like breasts" or a hosed-down garbage scow looking "like a vast greenish condom." Misogyny is not a lovable tic, and in its more severe manifestations—many of which Hoagland exhibits—it makes a reporter's testimony as unreliable as a Klansman's or an anti-Semite's.

Perhaps in some future book, Edward Hoagland will slow down, look into himself, and tell us what upsets him so. On the basis of "The Ridge-Slope Fox and the Knife Thrower," he is capable of it. Until then, however, though his prose may delight, his judgment will be trustworthy only when he is in the woods, alone. (p. 33)

Geoffrey Stokes, "Quick Mind, Keen Eye," in The New York Times Book Review *(copyright © 1982 by The New York Times Company; reprinted by permission), March 21, 1982, pp. 7, 33.*

Hugh (John Blagdon) Hood
1928-

Canadian novelist, short story writer, essayist, critic, and biographer.

Hood is an intellectual writer whose prose is deceptively simple. Although he has described himself as a "Catholic novelist," his views are often unorthodox and are rooted as much in philosophy as religion. The tone of his fiction shifts between the serious and the satirical, creating a fictive atmosphere at once realistic and fantastical, or as Hood has defined it, "superrealistic." Critics praise Hood's concise diction and the skillful craftsmanship which is particularly evident in his short stories. Also notable in his short fiction is his ability to convey large moral and philosophical concepts through seemingly trivial events. *Flying a Red Kite* (1962) and *Dark Glasses* (1976) contain examples of his most masterful writing.

Hood's most ambitious project is a twelve-volume novel entitled *The New Age*, which is designed to convey a comprehensive fictional representation of the Canadian experience. Hood introduces narrator Matthew Goderich in *The Swing in the Garden* (1975), the first volume of *The New Age*, and experiments in the series with the concepts of time, space, history, art, and identity. Four volumes have been published thus far; Hood has projected that the series will be completed in the year 2000.

(See also *CLC*, Vol. 15; *Contemporary Authors*, Vols. 49-52; and *Contemporary Authors New Revision Series*, Vol. 1.)

Photograph by Sam Tata; courtesy of Hugh Hood

KILDARE DOBBS

[It's] evident from the stories in [Hood's] first book, *Flying A Red Kite*, that he has knocked about a good deal in the world outside the universities. . . . One of them, **"After the Sirens"**, not the best of the stories but certainly a rigorously imagined and professionally executed vision of nuclear war, made it in the big league of *Esquire*. It is a tribute to the genuineness of Hood's talent that his work appealed just as much to ordinary educated people as to fellow academics and to more self-consciously literary readers. . . . The patient accumulation of sensuous detail induces recognition of place as well as of people. Toronto is here (**"Recollections of the Works Department"**), Montreal is here (**"Flying a Red Kite"**), and in the magnificent **"Three Halves of a House"**, set on the Canadian shore of the St. Lawrence near Gananoque, there's a continental feeling, a sense of the whole of Canada. It is this aspect of the stories that patriotic reviewers are apt to seize on, rightly feeling that our own lives are that much more real for being brought into a context of art and imagination, that our country is the more unquestionably present for having been seen by a real writer and set down forever in print. But Hood isn't writing advertising copy for the Canadian Way. His stories are about life and death and eternity. . . . (p. 72)

[Hood] writes as confidently in the third person as in the first and with as much inwardness about women as about men. In form, his stories follow the shape of a meditation rather than a plot, and he has taken pains, as he hints in one story, to master the English sentence. In this he resembles American writers like Updike rather than any Canadian predecessor. (p. 73)

<blockquote>Kildare Dobbs, "Memory Transfigured" (reprinted by permission of the author), in Canadian Literature, No. 16, Spring, 1963, pp. 72-3.</blockquote>

ROBERT FULFORD

This man is French Canadian, unmarried, middle-aged, rich, attractive, intellectual. He's a professor at the University of Montreal, and he drives fast, expensive cars. He's passionately federalist and he scorns both separatists and nationalists. Furthermore, he's just decided to go to Ottawa to save Canada.

A profile, of course, of Pierre Elliott Trudeau. Right? Wrong. The man in question is Roger Talbot, the hero—or at least one of the two heroes—of Hugh Hood's new novel, *A Game of Touch*. (p. 47)

[Few] readers will fail to notice the resemblance immediately. Indeed, *A Game of Touch* looks like the first Trudeau novel, the first sign that Trudeau may have begun to possess Canada's literary imagination as he has possessed its political imagination.

This implies a certain audacity on Hood's part, but that's nothing beside the bravado he displays by putting at the core of his book the very stuff of Canadian politics itself: federal-provincial relations. Hood's Roger is no cool above-the-battle hero, no charismatic saint of the television age: he's an untiring part-time bureaucrat whose most passionate desire is to figure out how to make Canada run more or less to everyone's satisfaction. (pp. 47, 49)

The quintessential Canadian hero comes to life at last, fighting his way to mythic stature not through Greek islands or western plains but through the thickets of federal-provincial relations. Hood's novel will stir a warmth of gratitude in the heart of every civil servant who has laboured, long and hard, to produce the precise comma and the perfect paragraph-number to hold our dear land together.

Marvelously, it isn't boring (except for a few pages at the beginning). Hood makes Roger a complex, believable character, and even if his book won't appeal to any but the obsessively Canadian he has still produced a solid achievement. The advance over his rather ponderous *White Figure, White Ground* (1964) and his superficial *The Camera Always Lies* (1967) is clear. Hood's best qualities emerge stronger than before, particularly his ability to grasp and convey a group sense of affectionate communality. His protagonist, Jake . . . , watches and observes nicely the difficult and yet loving relationships of the people who shape modern Quebec. Moreover, Roger's experience in Ottawa—paralleling, in some ways, the experiences of Favreau and Lamontagne during the Pearson years—is believable in its disillusionment. And the cityscape of Montreal has perhaps never been conveyed in a novel with such confident authenticity. (p. 49)

> Robert Fulford, "Captain Canada" (copyright © 1970 by Saturday Night; reprinted by permission of the author), in Saturday Night, Vol. 85, No. 11, November, 1970, pp. 47, 49.

ANTHONY ROBERTSON

Around the Mountain is subtitled, 'Scenes from Montreal Life'. A collection of essays, some of them apparently non-fiction fiction, about the varied aspects of life in Montreal that moves from scrub hockey leagues, to suburban development, to the old quarters of the city. Hood loves the city. He walks it, he bicycles it, he drives it. Some parts of the city foster life, some parts do not. Hood accepts both. Progress means scummed rivers, vanishing farms and sculpture on the overpass pylons of uncompleted freeways. Hood sometimes likes what replaces the farms and streams, sometimes he does not. The waterfront is filthy but active. He goes there frequently to get the feel of it; just as he goes to the top of the mountain. Both places are the city, not any city, *the* city. Perhaps if he were designing the city he would do it differently, but he's not, so he'll take it as it is. His eye is honest. He does not use his subjects as ways into himself, although the self of the observer is plainly there. The essays are not excuses for condemnation or commendation. Most of them are in one way or another mood pieces; definitive of elusive moments within the ordinary. Hood is a topographist of a particular kind. His attachment is to what moves between what he sees and his quizzical undetached self. The city and its inhabitants are alien to each other, but for Hood there is some connection between all, the things and people he describes that does not make the city a place of total alienation. However disjointed, it is a place of superb life.

> Anthony Robertson, in a review of "Around the Mountain" (copyright © June, 1971 West Coast Review Publishing Society, reprinted by permission of the publisher and the author), in West Coast Review, Vol. 6, No. 1, June, 1971, p. 53.

KENT THOMPSON

That Hugh Hood is a serious and accomplished Canadian artist of considerable significance is a fact that ought to be more widely known than it is. . . . [Some] of the best fiction in Canada is now being written in the short story form, and Hood is one of the masters of it. Furthermore, he is probably its most ambitious practitioner, demanding more of the form than almost any other writer, and he is one of the few who is concerned with the totality of a collection—seeing the collection, I think, as an entity which has its effect *in sum* and not in bits and pieces.

It seems to me, in fact, that this feeling for coherence is one of the most admirable aspects of Hood's work. All his work is of a piece, although it shifts focus, takes new directions, explores. It is not obviously *avant-garde* . . . , but it is always exploratory, always pushing on, expanding on its previous discoveries, looking more closely here and there, developing, broadening, and always deepening. Indeed, I think there is no predicting the eventual dimensions of his work—and that, I suppose, is part of the definition of an artist.

To give some idea how all this has developed, I suppose I am justified in briefly reviewing Hood's career. One ought begin with his first novel, *White Figure, White Ground* (1964), a novel of Canadian identity, history, and culture, and one which says a great deal about art. It is also a novel which deals with the relativity of space (conceptual and geographical) and time (conceptual and historical and spatial) and the artist who looks out at the universe from his own specifically individual perspective. In this case the artist is a Montreal-based painter who has married a French-Canadian beauty and returns to Nova Scotia in search of his ancestral identity. The point is made that *meaning,* in an abstractly relativistic universe, results from the individual creation and imposition of meaning. Thus, as a religion makes the universe coherent, so does an artist, and so does every man. . . . This sounds more complicated than it is (and I have reached into other parts of Hood's work to make my generalizations) because the weight of Hood's concern falls on the individual. His art deals with the individuals who live in the context just described. (pp. 116-17)

But the context is important, and the individual who ignores it does so at his peril. One has to consider one's time, place, and history in one's creation, and one has to decide if one's creation of an identity is valid and worthwhile. For example, in an early Hood story, **"O Happy Melodist!"**, the heroine tries to create herself in the world of fashion, and the result is that she becomes so ''in'' that she's ''out.'' That is, she disappears as an individual in becoming a representative of something fashionable. This is just one of the themes which Hood pursued in his second collection of stories, *Around the Mountain,* and again in his second novel, *The Camera Always Lies.* (p. 117)

In *The Fruit Man, The Meat Man & The Manager,* Hood continues his explorations within his contexts, but he seems to concentrate on a new aspect: that of morality. Hood has always been a writer of moral concerns, interested in moral difficulties and ambiguities, but in this collection he seems to me to center his focus upon the idea of the *good man.* (pp. 117-18)

[According to Hood, each man] must try to be good. If he has some measure of success, he may very well change other individuals for the better. He may even take on the dimensions of a religious metaphor, emulate the great teachers, become, nearly, a saint.

It is as difficult as that. And to my mind, this is the chief thrust of Hood's latest work. He is concerned with the individual human condition in the face of the universal human condition, and he asks the hard questions: what is a good man, and how does a good man become a saint?

Usually, of course, such an achievement comes within our own religious traditions. For example, in **"The Holy Man,"** Hood examines the growth of a Jewish boy from poet to playwright to holy man. . . . The holy man in the story becomes a teller of simple parables, making sense and goodness out of a difficult world. As the narrator says: "He made the cruel sometimes kind. People changed their lives at his entreaty. This is miraculous." The emphasis, therefore, is on the effect of the good man upon the human condition as we know it *in the individual*. Whenever a change for the better is brought about—however trivial it might seem to be—then it is possible that the man who created that change is a saint. In the Roman Catholic tradition Hood sees this in the work of the famous Montreal figure, Brother André, of **"Brother André, Père Lamarche and My Grandmother Eugenie Blagdon."** . . . Brother André is famous because of his devotion to God and the Oratory in Montreal, but he approaches saintliness because he can alter an individual for the better and alleviate suffering, the human condition.

But Hood is most of all a very coherent writer, and if some of his short stories are related to his general concerns, others are related to one another as well. (pp. 118-19)

Hood's stories are easy to read but sometimes difficult to understand. On the one hand this may well be because most of us are simply insufficiently skilled as readers. Hood—like a number of other short story writers—has developed in the little magazines, where one has a selected audience—an audience which is skilled, in fact, in dealing with the flickering implications of the contemporary short story. . . . But sometimes you have to wait a while for all the possible meanings of the story to filter through your consciousness.

And this may be due to a technique which Hood likes to use: allegory. I confess that I have always disliked allegory, but Hood is beginning to win me over. Or perhaps I have simply misunderstood the use of allegory, which I have always summed up briefly as the saying of one thing and meaning another. That's true, I think, but not true enough. For Hood, an allegory means what it says but it also means something more and sometimes something more again. The distinction is important.

Hood's characters are never simply representative. One might contrast this with Robertson Davies' characters in *Fifth Business.* Only the narrator of Davies' novel seems to me to be a real person. (pp. 122-23)

But Hood's characters are first of all what they seem to be and they maintain that identity even while gathering others. In the title story of this collection, for example, the Fruit Man, the Meat Man, and the Manager are just that. But also something more. (p. 123)

Kent Thompson, in a review of "The Fruit Man, the Meat Man & the Manager" (copyright by Kent Thompson; reprinted by permission of the author), in The Fiddlehead, *No. 92, Winter, 1972, pp. 116-23.*

EUGENE McNAMARA

[*The Fruit Man, the Meat Man & the Manager*] shows that [Hood] knows perfectly well where he is and what he is doing. The stories are carefully varied, like a bon voyage fruit basket. **"Who's Paying for This Call?"** is a stream of consciousness, lower case word portrait of the artist agonizing over his use/misuse of his craft and his public. **"Cura Pastoralis"**, about a young priest who violates his vows, **"One Owner, Low Mileage"**, about a widow left with a large new automobile she doesn't know how to drive, and **"The Singapore Hotel"**, about a bank manager's encounters with the home office's whizz kid, are three samples of a kind of workmanlike, slice-of-life story that J. F. Powers used to be good at. They are the kind of stories that set literature classes on the hunt for subtle epiphanies.

"Dog Explosion" is an actual shaggy dog story. **"Harley Talking"** is a documentary set in Moishe's Steak House that would make, I think, a very effective television play or short movie. As a short story, it seems too full of implications that are dropped too evidently. **"Places I've Never Been"** is a Joycean-Borges style story made up of cinematic (televisionistic?) elements juxtaposed to make up a nightmarish time-collapsing collage of contemporary images: a canoe trip into almost spoiled nature, a grotesque funland, a contemplated rape, an urban riot. Why?

"A Solitary Ewe" is a case in point. It is a carefully wrought piece, with a strong sense of place. ("Most of the club members knew about *Le Normand* which was not much publicized, maybe because a lot of people who did publicity ate there. The restaurant had a cluttered little window with Calvados bottles and tearsheets of ancient A. J. Liebling articles in it, a number of pictures of Canadian Troops at Caen in 1944 and a deceitful menu which was never revised.")

This sort of thing could easily become arch, coy, cute. But Hood brings it off. The story works very well as an investigation of human crossed-purposes, friendship, love, jealousy. Many of his stories come to the brink of cuteness, where the right words, the best stage properties, the exact touches, like prestige books cornered on a coffee table, threaten to overwhelm the fiction. But most of the time, the stories avoid the final pitfall and work brilliantly.

Eugene McNamara, in a review of "The Fruit Man, the Meat Man & the Manager" (copyright © 1972 by Eugene McNamara; reprinted by permission of the author), in Queen's Quarterly, *Vol. LXXIX, No. 1, Spring, 1972, p. 120.*

THE TIMES LITERARY SUPPLEMENT

[*You Can't Get There From Here*] is the story of Leofrica, an "emergent" African nation, living at or below subsistence level. There are two tribes, Ugetis and Pineals (isn't the pineal a gland?), the UN, the USSR, the USA, a giant corporation called INTERFOODS, agents, double agents, tribal myths, trained scuba divers, two currencies (nuts and UN Scrip). The local girls use an oil pipeline for ritual masturbation, believing it to be a snake god. There is intrigue, and counter-intrigue. The descriptive prose and the dialogue are both good, and include humour of an ironical kind—for this is basically a nightmare, where a tribal civil war is artificially provoked by powerful outside interests (Albania/China). The storyline is strong, though concerned mainly with politics and finance and sometimes a bit confusing: there are almost too many agents. But the novel is both exciting and intelligent . . . and contains very little of the spy-story cliché. It is written with none of the snideness with which some novelists write about Africans, and seems very much the work of somebody who knows and understands Africa. Furthermore, as a kind of parable, it has a lot of relevance to the situation there today.

"Nightmare Parable," in The Times Literary Supplement (© Times Newspapers Ltd. (London) 1973; reproduced from The Times Literary Supplement by permission), No. 3708, March 30, 1973, p. 340.

PATRICIA A. MORLEY

You Can't Get There From Here . . . [focuses on] the freedom of societies, and the problematic survival of indigenous cultures assaulted by Western technology and by the cultural package of ideas and attitudes which necessarily accompanies this technology.

You Can't Get There From Here is a very sophisticated novel. It should firmly establish Hood's place in the top rank of Canadian writers, confirming the promise in earlier novels and in short story collections such as *Flying a Red Kite* (1962) and *The Fruit Man, the Meat Man and the Manager* (1971). Hood's latest novel is simultaneously black comedy and a profound philosophical comment on human nature and societies; at once slapstick, tragic farce, and a sparkling parody of academic rhetoric and the classic disciplines of politics, economics and anthropology—a tonic, in short, for all academics. It is both a story of international intrigue and a parody of spy thrillers. All in two hundred pages.

As the plot thickens and his fortunes steadily decline, Antony Jedeb, Prime Minister of the newly created African state of Leofrica, addresses those present at a meal described as *highly symbolic:* "Nation, faction, culture, tribe, people, race, clan, family, names for different-sized groups. . . . My people, my tribe, my class, my clan, my caste, are not yours and cannot be yours. It is the exclusiveness of these notions that makes them so bloody. . . . Of these notions, only that of the family is peacefully neutral, for when we think of our family we take others in—not thinking of them as outsiders." The passage is atypical in its overt didacticism but contains the theme. The novel is about the brotherhood of man under the fatherhood of God—an ironic portrait, for the most part, of that brotherhood betrayed. (pp. 138-39)

You Can't Get There From Here is, on the surface, a grimly comic picture of the problems facing an emergent African state. But Hood has never been in Africa, and this novel is as deceptive as Leofrica itself, a land of shifting sands and perpetual mists. Leofrica, it is emphasized, is a mirage. Similarly, the novel is really about *us*, not Africans; about genuine cultures and bastard ones; about fellowship versus rape. (p. 139)

Patricia A. Morley, in a review of "You Can't Get There from Here" (copyright © 1973 by Patricia A. Morley; reprinted by permission of the author), in Queen's Quarterly, Vol. LXXX, No. 1, Spring, 1973, pp. 138-39.

PATRICIA MORLEY

The Swing in the Garden is the first of a projected series of twelve novels, a *roman fleuve* in the manner of Marcel Proust's *Remembrance of Things Past*. Proustian references recur, sometimes rather self-consciously. In the Goderich family, Sunday drives in the country alternate with trips to the docks. Matt is reminded of Proust's narrator and of his weekend choice of excursions from Combray along the Guermantes' path, or along the way to Swann's house. Proust's narrator discovered much later in life that the two ways united to form a single meaning. . . . (p. 99)

The handling of time is deceptively simple. The mind of the adult narrator, a sophisticated art-historian, is set alongside the experiences of himself as a child, rather like parallel tracks. Didactic passages for example, the nature of time and change, are validated by the narrator's scholarly interests or those of his father, a professional philosopher. As a child, Matt is vaguely aware of the elasticity of chronological time in conjunction with emotional experience. . . . (pp. 99-100)

Hood's models, besides Proust, are novelists such as George Eliot and Balzac. He obviously aspires to catch the entire social fabric in his net. His feeling for social nuance, for the ambiance of class feeling "in the by no means democratic society of English-speaking Canada in the twenties and thirties," is excellent. Matt, delivering magazines, knows the distance that separates him from classmate Bea Skaithe who lives on Highland Avenue. The curving path, the shrubbery, the heavy door with brass knocker, induce inferiority feelings of a specific flavour. Class barriers are flexible but nevertheless real. . . . (p. 100)

Hood's pace is leisurely. . . . The five parts of *Swing* take Matt Goderich from infancy to the age of nine, while Canada moves through the Depression to the brink of World War Two. His panorama takes in Spain, Maritain, Woodsworth, Sir Joseph Flavelle, Mackenzie King, and the academic socialists who could not believe that Stalin would ever co-operate with Adolph Hitler. The Goderich family move from relative affluence to poverty, when the father's radical principles drive him out of his university job, and bad weather sabotages his summer venture into the restaurant business. At the end of the novel, Canada is moving into the tragedy of war and Matt, into intimations of adolescence.

There are some memorable comic scenes. One concerns Saturday matinées at the Beverly, a neighbourhood theatre featuring a double bill for ten cents. Pandemonium is an added attraction. . . . Another scene describes a policeman on a bicycle chasing an ancient Ford across Toronto Island, where cars were forbidden. (pp. 100-01)

Despite Hood's flair for slapstick, the comic tone is frequently subtle. A remark of Matt's father, "What we have is a six room house," may not sound hilarious to the average reader but it is one of Andrew Goderich's small turns of phrase which his family love to parody, "with almost antiphonal repetition." Matt describes his father's kind of humour as "almost impossible to explain or defend before people with no ear for it." The phrase describes much of Hood's own wry sense of fun.

Hood's first four novels demonstrate a remarkable variety in technique. *White Figure, White Ground* is relatively traditional in form. Its protagonist is a painter in search of his roots. The narrative functions as metaphor. . . . *The Camera Always Lies* is a romance, a witty parody of Hollywood films, and a rollicking satire of *American* moeurs. Many reviewers seemed to miss the parody and panned it severely. In *A Game of Touch*, Hood uses the game as "a microcosm of middle-class eastern Canada" (George Woodcock's phrase). The novel is both a modern example of the picaresque form, where the interest centres in the structure of society, and an informal *kunstler-roman* with political cartoonist Jake Price as the artist-to-be-educated. *You Can't Get There From Here* is an anti-utopia, a brilliant parody of human folly and unrealistic social aspirations, set in the mythical state of Leofrica.

With nine books to his credit . . . , Hood seems to be moving into a comfortable high gear and settling down for the long haul. First of twelve: the idea might intimidate some writers. *The Swing in the Garden* is marked by the social concerns which have always been prominent in Hood's fiction, and the conscious regard for craftsmanship or *métier*, his watchword. Matt Goderich observes that there is a kind of mind among some writers of fiction which feeds, almost compulsively, upon facts; and another which lies "not in the facts themselves but in the exactions of the a priori form into which they had to be made to fit. . . . This alliance of doubled realities may, often does, issue in art of extraordinary richness." Where do we place Hood's work? I opt for the double reality. Facts transformed. (pp. 101-02)

Patricia Morley, "Where the Myth Touches Us" (reprinted by permission of the author), in Canadian Literature, No. 67, Winter, 1976, pp. 99-102.

J. R. (TIM) STRUTHERS

In his imagination Hugh Hood has outlined a twelve-book epic on Canadian life entitled *The New Age/Le nouveau siècle,* which he intends to complete by the year 2000. The first part in this extraordinary project is *The Swing in the Garden,* a fictional story of an art historian's boyhood in and near Toronto during the thirties. *The Swing in the Garden* is a novel, an extended "digressive" essay, an autobiography, a topographical map, a snapshot album or documentary film, a history book, a philosophical work, a piece of socialist rhetoric, a commentary on national economic policy, and a dream-vision allegory. *The Swing in the Garden* is all of these things; but in essence it is the beginning of an elaborate social mythology, a detailed examination of part of the Canadian style.

Hood focuses on a great social revolution in the mid-thirties [which involved a radical lengthening of the expected duration of one's formal schooling and] which eventually remade the then predominantly rural and small-town character of Canadian life. (p. 518)

What raises the personal story of Matt Goderich to the level of a national myth or epic is the fictional shaping of Hood's own autobiographical materials, seen, for example, in the dating of Matt's birth in 1930 (Hood was born in 1928) and his father's, Andrew Goderich's, birth in 1900. Hood's partial modelling of the career of Andrew Goderich on that of professor and socialist thinker Frank Underhill has the same elevating effect. Even more generally, the structuring of *The Swing in the Garden* between the Biblical archetypes of the garden and the Fall underlines the novel's universality.

The Swing in the Garden moves from microcosm to macrocosm, from Matt's relations with his family and friends to Toronto life, to Canadian life and beyond, to archetypes, though, of course, all of these seemingly outer dimensions telescope and are really contained within Matt's particular experience.

Individual situations mirror world history. The dawning consciousness of Matthew Goderich in this novel reflects the consciousness of Canadian society in the process of gaining awareness of its position in the world.

Although Matthew emphasizes that the Canadian style is interiorized, he expresses great interest in its more obvious outward manifestations or symbols, especially the successive forms of communication and transportation, which are each generation's iconography, by which we are able to judge our age. Matthew Goderich's fascination is centered initially on the garden swing, but it expands until he becomes, like Hood, an explorer and a mapmaker of the entire social mythology of Canadian life.

The grandness of Hood's conception of delineating Canada's social mythology would, in itself, qualify his project as an important achievement in modern literature. But in *The Swing in the Garden* this accomplishment is matched by a finely polished prose and a significant technical innovation. The story is presented through the expanding and contracting consciousness of Matthew Goderich, whose consciousness will shrink to record exact childhood impressions of the thirties, or momentarily widen to make a vitriolic attack on the ineptitude of the Ontario Government in the seventies. Matthew's consciousness also expands and contracts in that having evaluated different experiences it selects some for more detailed scrutiny while treating others more briefly.

This handling of narrative point of view is perfectly adapted to the view, expressed in the novel, of "the elasticity of time," a theory which insists on a "double-chronology, psychological 'felt' time and that of the calendar." This sophisticated device for the handling of time in narrative fiction might appear to resemble Margaret Laurence's use of a double narrative flow, past and present, in *The Stone Angel* and *The Diviners,* but it is more fluid, more subtle, less obviously manipulated—expanding and contracting, like the breathing of a living thing, rather than simply running parallel.

Such a wedding of conception, material, prose style, and technique is the signature of a master. (pp. 518-19)

J. R. (Tim) Struthers, in a review of "The Swing in the Garden" (copyright © 1976 by J. R. (Tim) Struthers; reprinted by permission of the author), in Queen's Quarterly, Vol. 83, No. 3, Autumn, 1976, pp. 518-19.

DAVID LATHAM

[*Dark Glasses* contains] three or four of the best examples in all of literature of how the short story works. The weaker of the twelve stories could be dismissed on the assumption that they were included because of Hood's predilection for arranging his "pieces according to complex numerologies" that provide "a scaffolding for the imagination." . . . (p. 105)

Hood's strength lies in his ability to shape what he calls the "physical form" of material as diffuse as metaphysical speculation. Thus in terms of both manner and matter Hood is like the painter Alex Colville. Neither artist can rid himself "of those four or five bloody sets of metaphysical states" that Mathew Goderich (the persona for Hood's projected twelve volume prose epic) complained about: "Permanence and change; sameness and difference; being and becoming; form and matter." . . . Both Hood and Colville react to the same dilemma by concentrating on the spirit of the shapes of things: "If you pay close enough attention to things, stare at them, concentrate on them as hard as you can, not just with your intelligence, but with your feelings and instincts, you begin to apprehend the forms in them." . . . Hood is less impressive in his fiction than in his journalism because he frequently exploits artifice to impose an extrinsic pattern on his fiction. . . . By emphasizing [a] kind of extrinsic symbolism Hood reinforces his "scaffolding of the imagination" at the expense of obscuring the more important implications of the metaphor concerning time and space. The child may be thought safe from the railroad tracks that lie beyond the garden fence but the pendulum motion of the swing suggests that the real journey from the garden is a temporal one.

At his best Hood succeeds in complementing the physical form of his stories with an inner scaffolding developed through the manipulation of metaphors which seem to emerge from within the incident. **"Going out as a Ghost"** is an excellent story that presents two strands of action which appear to be unrelated but actually are connected through the metaphor of the mask—the convincing disguises of a family's Halloween costumes and the suspected disguise of a convicted con-artist. The two story lines complement one another and then meet when the father suspiciously hangs up the phone on his desperate friend and then turns to reward the small Halloween visitor who is dressed as a ghost—the same unimaginative costume which the father had considered suitable for himself. This and the other successful stories illustrate the epigraph that Hood chose for the collection: "For now we see through a glass darkly; but then face to face." Most of Hood's characters quickly retreat from the impact of the brief moment of self-revelation. (pp. 105-06)

When Hood fails to develop an intrinsic metaphor he reveals his weakness as a story-teller and leaves himself wide open to the charge first made ten years ago by Robert Fulford that his natural medium is journalism rather than fiction. Hood can objectify his metaphysical speculations into a story through the manipulation of metaphor but when he fails with metaphor he has no skill with character or incident to fall back on. **"The Chess Match"** is the one story in which the portrayal of character is the dominant feature. The eighty-six year old Page Calverly is a match for Margaret Laurence's Hagar Shipley. His petty crankiness is comical but understandable as we see how he maintains his dignity by determining what can be endured with the least discomfort. Yet **"The Chess Match"** still demonstrates how Hood's metaphors work best when they inform the story rather than supply external scaffolding. Even the minor metaphors are well exploited here. "Tortoise-like" is an adjective that describes Calverly's walk but it also anticipates the image of the impaled spider that Calverly resembles after he has slipped and fallen which in turn raises the insolent question of why such an ugly specimen should be preserved.

In **"The Hole"** the metaphor is given no story to support. As the idle musings of a philosophy professor, **"The Hole"** is really little more than a commentary on a song by Thomas Carew. . . . **"The Pitcher"** is ostensibly a satire on the American dream in which the common man through dedication (and money) becomes an inspiration to American youth. But the satire seems no more than an excuse for some exciting sports talk. . . .

As the latest addition to Hood's canon, *Dark Glasses* makes it difficult to judge the nature of Hood's talent. Documentary fantasy is the term he has coined to describe the compromise between fiction and journalism that he is seeking to achieve. . . . (p. 107)

Personal journalism with epic intentions is a genre which Hood has not mastered. A comparison of the title essay from *The Governor's Bridge Is Closed* (Hood's personal recollection of his childhood in Toronto during the 1930s) and the first volume of his documentary fantasy, *A Swing in the Garden* (similar recollections now objectified as the gospel according to Mathew Goderich), suggests that Hood's gifts are more suited to journalism. His essay is personal, informal, and speculative. His documentary fantasy must depend on character, structure, and incident, but being weak on character and incident it is little more than a longer and less personal essay, sustained only by its structure. (pp. 107-08)

Hood could overcome the problem of his documentary fantasy by being more directly personal as he is in his essays. . . . But any wish that Hood would abandon all pretense of fictional technique must be modified by the brilliance of some of the short stories from *Dark Glasses* which proves that he is capable of producing great fiction. Still the nature of the strength of these stories, being limited to the exploitation of metaphor, reveals the problems that Hood must confront if the epic which he is devoting his life to is to serve the nation. (p. 108)

David Latham, "Optical Allusions," in Essays on Canadian Writing *(© Essays on Canadian Writing Ltd.), Nos. 7 & 8, Fall, 1977, pp. 105-08.*

HALLVARD DAHLIE

The opening paragraph of [*A New Athens*] reflects what has come to be a Hood trademark: the transformation of circumstantial detail and self into a kind of mystical entity which, for all its ontological complexities, represents finally a re-affirmation of Wordsworthian man. Hood takes us quickly into speculations about "original glory," "wild multiplicity of forms in this world," "a curious infinity," and other components of transcendentalism, all through the consciousness—and prescience—of the articulate narrator/protagonist, Matthew Goderich.

The novel, the second of a projected twelve-volume chronicle about mid-century Canada, takes up Matthew's story a generation or so after the events of the first in the series, *The Swing in the Garden*. It is to me a more successful novel than the earlier one, which suffered, I thought, from the imposition of too much overt moralizing; the pre-adolescent Matthew was not given sufficient opportunity to be himself, as it were. *A New Athens* succeeds, in my view, in resolving the components of reality and imagination—though not without effort on the part of the reader. Hood wins us over more by rational persuasion than by catering to our emotions, but our patience is rewarded by a new respect we gain for his disciplined aesthetic. (p. 138)

In *A New Athens,* Hood reflects his abiding obsession with naming places, people, and things. I suspect the places may be real places, for at least one Ontario critic has dutifully located all the little towns and railway stations on the map, in the general neighbourhood of Brockville. . . . But that the novel works even for those of us who are unfamiliar with the Brockville area is a tribute to Hood's ability to transcend place, and create an imaginative world that convinces. (pp. 138-39)

In an article published some seven years ago, Hugh Hood—unwittingly or otherwise—laid the philosophical groundwork for the project he has now embarked upon. Subtitled "The Ontology of Super-Realism," this article outlines with some precision how Hood moved from an eclectic position at the outset of his career in the mid fifties—though one in which he leaned towards what he calls "moral realism"—to a position where he could propose "the Wordsworthian account of the marriage of the mind and the thing as a model of artistic activity." Acknowledging his debt to such artists as Vermeer, Hopper, W. C. Williams, and Haydn, Hood defines his term "super-realism" as the "art which exhibits the transcendental element dwelling in living things," and argues that all art, "like every other human act, implies a philosophical stance."

Readers of his two novels in this current series will, I think, see the fictional applicability of propositions such as these, though they may quarrel with the appropriateness of the term "super-realism." It is clear in my mind that Hood is unequivocally a realist in most of his fiction I have read, one exception being *You Can't Get There From Here*, which depends largely on allegory for its impact. "Super-realism" has, however, a rarefied connotation which his own philosophy may well support, but which *A New Athens* wholly does not. The novel is thoroughly realistic and, as with the realism of Howells, James and Wiebe, Hood's realism serves as a basis on which to build a moral universe. Readers of this present novel might well interpret "super-realism" to mean "minute realism"—an excess of routine detail—and find in the process that they become less charitable about Hood's larger meaning: the spiritual transformation of self and the real world. (p. 139)

Hallvard Dahlie, "A Moral Universe," in Essays on Canadian Writing *(© Essays on Canadian Writing Ltd.), No. 11, Summer, 1978, pp. 138-41.*

LOUIS K. MacKENDRICK

Most of the 16 stories here (drawn from Hugh Hood's previous collections) don't appear in general anthologies. Since this seems to be the purpose of *Selected Stories,* one may regret the absence of **"Three Halves of a House"**, **"The Village Inside"** or **"Getting to Williamstown"**. But we are given **"Looking Down From Above"**, Hood's lovely evocation of Montreal's mountain and reflection on self-fulfilment despite the accidents of the flesh.

Hood's prose is finely controlled in several tempi, as for example in his chronicle stories where fiction and documentary meet. He has an exacting sense of location, of specific and loved places. Often he emphasizes wonder and discovery in his writing as if he were the heart-struck cicerone who can nonetheless radiate a slight but unclinical coolness. The internal connections and thematic unities of his tales are subtle because the stories are so deceptively relaxed.

This book has stories "about" the immediate present balanced against the accumulation of personal history, impermanence, vulnerability, and the oddly similar arrangements between life and art. These are stories whose revelations are paced precisely and persuasively not to an "epiphany" but to an understated point of awareness, to a compromise with mortality.

Louis K. MacKendrick, in a review of "Selected Stories," in Quill and Quire *(reprinted by permission of* Quill and Quire*), Vol. 45, No. 1, January, 1979, p. 34.*

JOHN ORANGE

Hugh Hood's style, including diction, characterization, symbolism, and tone, is very difficult to deal with in a general way. He is a very eclectic stylist and he does not seem to pay much attention to whether or not various techniques are actually suited to each other or mesh together—especially in the first two novels of **The New Age**. Since, for one thing, he is interested in ways of knowing various dimensions of reality, he incorporates the vocabularies and styles of different approaches to reality. . . . [The] reader is apt to run into lists of names of places and things which are given for their own sake. Along with this "Eaton's catalogue" style one also finds a journalistic *recording* of historical events as well as a listing of scientific data and theories, rules of games, features of old automobiles, and opinions on various and sundry local and global problems. On the one hand the diction can be very concrete. On the other hand it can suddenly become very abstract.

Mixed in with the journalistic prose is the language of metaphysics, when a narrator is in a philosophical frame of mind, and along with everything else one finds the language of "intuitive reason"—poetic imagery, descriptions of almost mystical awareness, symbolism, word play in names of characters, obscure allusions, and connections to past works of art, the Bible, and Greek mythology. This last style comes closer to more conventional techniques in contemporary fiction and Hood can use them all masterfully.

This blending of prose styles has its thematic function . . . , and when it works it can both exhilarate and instruct the reader. When it does not work, and it often does not, the reader is confused and unsatisfied, as though he has been forced to listen to a radio which keeps rapidly changing stations back and forth across the dial. Just as the reader settles into one posture demanded by the conventions of one style, he is forced to change over to a completely different one. When Hood or his narrators become garrulous they can try the reader's patience to the point of abuse. . . . [However], Hood has set himself a tremendous task—one which is far too large for one prose style or one set of stylistic conventions. Once the reader catches on to what Hood is trying to do, and accepts his style on its own terms, then it becomes easier to relax with it while at the same time remaining alert for nuances of meaning even, for example, in the middle of what seems to be a rather dull geography lesson!

If the novels often contain a mixture of styles, most of the short stories are univocal and tightly controlled. Hood's prose is more like that of the 1920-1950 generation of prose writers than it is like the more poetic prose of contemporary writers such as Buckler, Leonard Cohen, Atwood, Kroetsch, or Munro. Hood's prose is usually lean and taut and in the short stories it is economical, evenly paced, and very effective for his purposes. He is closer to MacLennan, Garner, Grove, and, particularly, Callaghan than he is to the next generation of writers. As in Callaghan's works, the tone in Hood's short stories is quiet, his humour is usually understated, and metaphors, images, and symbols are usually used only when necessary and are seldom obtrusive. This kind of prose is suited to the kinds of characters and to the daily routine which the stories describe, as well as to their parable quality. Hood's **"Flying a Red Kite"** . . . , **"Cura Pastoralis,"** **"The Fruit Man, the Meat Man and the Manager,"** **"The Good Tenor Man"** . . . , **"Socks,"** **"Boots,"** and **"An Allegory of Man's Fate"** . . . , although they are not imitations of Callaghan, certainly resemble Callaghan's stories in prose style, tone, intention, and form, and they follow from his tradition.

There are other ways in which Hood is unlike the writers around him and these ways have to do with his techniques of characterization. Most modern fiction writers have emphasized the *psychological* complexities of character and they have used techniques of irony, the theories of psychology and psychiatry, gothic imagery and episodes, stream of consciousness and interior monologue, dreamscapes, and layers of symbols from the unconscious mind to try to probe the human psyche. Hood rarely uses these things in any sustained way. His characters are mostly faceless . . . and his usual style simply gives us physical dimensions of their persons or a summary word to describe them—"pretty," "old," "wrinkled," "tall," etc.— or simply a name. For at least two reasons, Hood's purposes usually do not require the presentation of psychologically complicated characters. First, he is often writing parables, and parables usually start off "There once was an old lady who had two sons" and that is all we have to know about her for the purposes of the story and its moral. Secondly, Hood tries to get at what he calls "a completely immaterial element" in characters as he says in . . . *A New Athens*. This kind of characterization is well suited to the short story form; but it is problematical in full length novels. . . . [As a solution to this problem, Hood] tries to invent episodes in the character's life which will in a metaphorical or allusive way reveal something about the character's attitudes, development, or the quality of his or her experience. (pp. 122-24)

A related problem is Hood's use of characters who are obviously moral centres of the novels and spokesmen for the author. Their speeches tend to have neon lights around them spelling out "author's message" and the reader begins to feel manipulated. . . . The danger of using this kind of character is that either he will disintegrate as a believable character when he is being so obviously used or he will come across as a rather condescending stuffed shirt thereby undermining his/her credibility. If they impress us as being just plain dull, then the *author's* credibility is undermined too. This problem is one which Hood seems to be wrestling with constantly. It is offset usually by narrators or protagonists who are slightly naïve, unsophisticated but sensible and worth accompanying most of the time. . . . (p. 125)

Allusions to classical mythology are also used as a kind of intellectual overlay and they can become obtrusive. . . . It is as though an author who is writing moral tales or parables and who is interested in metaphysical issues has no alternative but to include somewhere in the work itself explanations of what the work is about—a technique comparable to the homiletic sections which come after the parables of Jesus.

One further aspect of style which must be considered in any discussion of Hood's place in Canadian fiction is his usual tone. One does not find in Hood's work the finely honed cynicism which one hears in the voices of so many contemporary writers. Nor does one hear the wit, nor sense the multiple layers of irony at work, which we find in so many others. There is no pervasive gloom either. In the short stories, generally, and in the early novels, the tone of the narrator's voice is one of humility and of wonder at how things *are* in his world; but often it is also a voice of confidence. . . . Still, Hood is at times witty and often ironical. Parody and irony, for example, are close associates and Hood sometimes likes to use parody in his works. . . . In the longer works this element of parody often seems to conflict with the dominant tone of the work itself. When an author is shifting to another style inside his work, he usually has to signal the reader somehow that this is happening. Often this is accomplished by a change of tone. Sometimes Hood fails to change the tone and the reader is confused. Are those descriptions of Leofrican topography in *You Can't Get There From Here* really parodies, as John Moss suggests? Is Jean-Pierre Fauré meant to be taken as an overbearing prig? How seriously are we to take Matt Goderich? How much sympathy are we supposed to have for Marie-Ange Robinson or Rose Leclair? Evidently Hood is still trying to work this out. It is, perhaps, his trickiest problem. (pp. 125-26)

> John Orange, "Lines of Ascent: Hugh Hood's Place in Canadian Fiction," in Before the Flood: Hugh Hood's Work in Progress, *edited by J. R. (Tim) Struthers (copyright © Essays on Canadian Writing Ltd., 1979), ECW Press, 1979, pp. 113-30.*

W. J. KEITH

If sensitivity is the hallmark of the artist, one wonders how he can be anything but an outsider in a crassly insensitive age.

In this new volume of interrelated short stories [***None Genuine Without This Signature***], Hood offers a clue in the first narrative, **"God Has Manifested Himself Unto Us As Canadian Tire"** (a bold title—what story could live up to it?—but this one does). Here we are confronted by A. O. and Dreamy, who seem at first sight bitterly satiric creations crudely symbolizing a consumer society run riot. Hood saturates his prose with the rhythms and slogans of advertising. The couple are surrounded by the latest buys . . . ; their culture consists of reading about the next sale . . . ; Dreamy is physically enveloped by bargains. . . . But by the end of the story they are revealed as a pathetically unfulfilled pair, babes in a commercialized artificial-*bonsai* wood, only half convinced that they must be happy since they have everything, aware of a lack but unable to name it. For careful readers, however, the pathos of a self-imposed barrenness is intimated as early as the first paragraph: "Baby Car Seat by Travl-Gard conforming to all government safety needs. We'll never need one of those." Our ultimate response is complex. Contempt is no longer possible, but we are not allowed to relinquish the responsibility of judgment. An achieved insight beyond the reach of direct statement: such is the capacity of Hood's art. (p. 27)

In prose fiction, perhaps only Margaret Atwood can rival Hood in his presentation of the modern city (and I should make clear that Hood writes in this collection about New York, the West Indies, rural Ontario and "Sweet Cream, Manitoba" as well as Toronto and Montreal). I experience the same piercing insight into otherwise unknown lives in Atwood, but neither the range of character nor the sense of full compassionate understanding. In poetry, Raymond Souster can cajole or bully me into looking at Torontonians in a new way—but the effect is only temporary. In Hood alone I find a palpable extension of my sympathies and awareness. And this is achieved partly through the technical sophistication of his art (but Atwood has that), partly through an assured and tested religious and moral position. Hood begins with a faith that the world—even megalopolis—can be redeemed.

He has recently described himself as "through and through a Catholic novelist." Although fundamentally true, this has the unfortunate effect, for those without a religious commitment, of suggesting pious sentiments, limited subject-matter and sugared pills. On the contrary he offers a joyous acceptance, a healthily positive response to the things of this world, and above all a considered, anything-but-cloistered confidence.... Hood is, I suppose, Canada's most learned, most intellectual novelist. His philosophical *credo,* as offered in a recent interview, is as follows: "I think Truth, Beauty, and Goodness are co-extensive and that they stem from the Divine Being, and I think all created being, insofar as it is being, is good and beautiful." Which leads in turn to an artistic stance: "I think of art without Hope as inoperative art. It won't work." A refreshing change from "All's shit"—and far more firmly based.

From this religious foundation, it is only a short step to the idea of literature as "a secular analogy of Scripture"—Hood's sole point of agreement with Northrop Frye. But once again this sounds too solemn, too pretentious, for Hood's own practice. Comparisons with Dante, which Hood has made himself ..., may be intellectually comprehensible but give the wrong impression. Ultimately, Hood is Hood and no one else. His viewpoint allows him to see the sacred in the profane, to turn even casual expletives back to the religious meanings which they originally defied. Set within his achieved context, religious allusions in ordinary speech regain their pristine impact.... Hood never insists on his allegorical or emblematic meanings. They are available in his fiction because he recognizes them as available also in the reality out of which his stories emerge....

The stories become increasingly intricate as the book proceeds. Inter-relations are frequent. In the name-story (it is typical of Hood that the actual human signature in the narrative should be a fake), an advertising campaign is initiated, and we are—or should be—reminded of the language of the opening tale. Three stories involve song-writers or singers, Hood's artistic equivalent in this collection to the painters in his earlier work. A "SOCIAL WORKER for God's sake" appears briefly in the first story; in **"Gone Three Days"** the phrase takes on a literal meaning. The narrator of the final story, **"Doubles,"** eschews the solemnity of Mann's *The Magic Mountain* and explores his own "magic plain"—the terrain we come to recognize as the "strange geography" of all the stories here—and, indeed, of all Hood's work.

Hood's final distinction, in my view, is one that his critics have often denied him: he has extended the boundaries of fiction. Ironically, because he is seldom conspicuously innovative in technique, his firm artistic control is always in danger of passing unnoticed. One can read a long way in *The Camera Always Lies,* for instance, before the larger meaning beyond the Hollywood routines becomes manifest. Yet so multifarious are his interests that, in his more recent work, the normal limits of narrative form, whether in novel or short story, are inadequate to contain his vision. History, philosophy, politics, sociology, art theory—these and many others are grist to his mill, and he refuses to confine fiction to the traditional elements of plot and characterization. Often (and the numerous allusions to and quotations from Wordsworth are relevant here) he employs an essentially poetic form, as in *A New Athens*—which I believe to be his masterpiece to date—where the incidents are unified by image and emblem rather than by narrative succession. He has described himself as "probably not a novelist but another kind of fiction writer," and he is doubtless referring to an encyclopedic form that remains as yet unnamed. But if he isn't a novelist, he certainly isn't a short story writer either, since, here as elsewhere, his stories lose much by being extracted and belong not only to the volume as a whole but even to the order within the volume. (p. 28)

None Genuine Without This Signature offers what we have now come to expect from Hood—precision of detail, delicacy of nuance, firmness of (albeit inconspicuous) structure, a smooth felicity of language, and warmly human compassion. It is a worthy successor to the writing that so many of us have come to read in the last few years with ever-increasing admiration. The ramifications of the title are complex, but on one level the reference is to the writer and his work. Hood's signature here is undoubtedly genuine. (p. 29)

W. J. Keith, "The Case for Hugh Hood," in The Canadian Forum, *Vol. LX, No. 703, October, 1980, pp. 27-9.*

MICHAEL BLISS

Most readers have passed judgement on Hugh Hood's great work-in-progress, *The New Age/Le nouveau siècle,* on the basis of the first three novels, *The Swing in the Garden, A New Athens,* and *Reservoir Ravine.* A number are hooked on the series, acclaiming it one of the most audacious, skilful, and satisfying literary enterprises undertaken in this country. But a larger body of readers—those who make the Atwoods, Richlers, Laurences, et al., national best sellers—have apparently been turned off by Hood's disregard for some of the conventions of narration, plotting, and character development, as well as by the extreme intellectualism of both Hood and his central characters. *Black and White Keys,* the fourth novel in the series, will utterly delight the addicted and may be the best entrée into the series for the non-believer. It is certainly the most powerful and most accessible volume so far.

There is a simple plot and structure. In 1941 Andrew Goderich, former professor of philosophy at the University of Toronto, is chosen to attempt to rescue Georg Mandel, the heir to Kant and Hegel as the voice of philosophic idealism, from Dachau. While Andrew is confronting absolute evil in Germany, his teenage son, Matthew, enjoys the near-fantastic innocence of a Toronto boyhood. He tinkers with the piano keyboard trying to become a musician, experiences the images of war only through the ritual of the movies, and witnesses evil personified on Thursday nights when the Masked Marvel performs at Maple Leaf Gardens. The European adventure reads like a political thriller; the alternating Toronto chapters like relaxed, nostalgic sketches.

The book deals with the great themes of twentieth-century and Canadian history. It is a novel about the Holocaust, about the confrontation of Christianity and Judaism, about the relevance of the Canadian experience to the agony of mankind. Hood's intellectual resolution of the themes is an elaboration of a comment uttered in *Reservoir Ravine;* one of the (so far) lesser characters says in a 1923 Hart House debate at which Lord Balfour is present: "I say to you that the Holy Land is in Manitoba and Québec, and it is the other way round too."

It is possible to quibble about Hood's treatment of some of the literary conventions in *Black and White Keys*. The dialogue and plotting in the thriller chapters sometimes seem forced. The digressions in the Toronto chapters will try many readers' patience. Hood's sense of a Christian universe permeates the novel to the point of obtrusiveness. These are Hoodisms, though; a reader who can't adjust to them had better give up on *The New Age.* (p. 54)

Not many of us any more share Hood's Catholic belief in history as the unfolding of the divine will, or even agree, since

1967, with his Pearsonian-Hegelian view of Canada as a model of racial pluralism. While differing fundamentally with Hood on these points, it is possible to share completely his feel for the structure and texture of history. He sees the universal in the particular; he sees the novelist-historian, or any artist, reaching out in a creative act of comprehending the universal-particular. Some doubts have lingered. Through the first three volumes, the Goderich family and their acquaintances have lived and moved in a fairly confined, confident, WASPish Ontario. Was *The New Age* going to be twelve volumes of nostalgia and Christian metaphysics? With *Black and White Keys* the series moves into startlingly new territory, undercutting fears that Hood's range was limited. The anticipations of darkness to come were there in the "long fall" ending *The Swing in the Garden* and Matthew's melancholy as he surveyed the covered reservoir in [*Reservoir Ravine*]. Now evil has not only been unleashed in Europe, but finally burns into Matthew's Toronto consciousness when *Life* magazine carries pictures of the Holocaust victims. In a low-key way, Hood ends Matthew's war years in Toronto by taking us toward the image Pynchon uses to begin the greatest post-war novel, *Gravity's Rainbow*, "A screaming comes across the sky." (pp. 54, 56)

Black and White Keys is rich in the allusions, epiphanies, symbols, emblems, and play that we have come to expect in the series. The analogies to the Christological drama seem heightened because Hood and heaven are mobilizing angels and apostles to try to cope with the great disturbance of the universe that genocide represents.

It's been seven years since Hugh Hood started publishing a series of novels that he wanted to be comparable to the work of Anthony Powell and Marcel Proust in their complexity and scope. Volume twelve, God willing, will appear in the year 2000. As time passes, Hood will gather increasing critical acclaim as an outstanding novelist and historian of our age. As more readers begin to come to terms with Hood's work, some of us will be passing *The New Age* to our children. These are books we will want them to read in order to know our experience. (p. 56)

Michael Bliss, "New Territory" (copyright © 1982 by Saturday Night; *reprinted by permission of the author), in* Saturday Night, *Vol. 97, No. 10, October, 1982, pp. 54, 56.*

M(ary) M(argaret) Kaye
1909?-

(Has also written as Mollie Kaye and Mollie Hamilton) Indian-born British novelist and author of books for children.

Although Kaye has written many mystery novels, she is best known for her works of historical fiction set in India. Her experiences growing up in India and, later, her travels with her husband, a major general in the British army, have enabled her to write knowledgeably about the exotic locales in which she sets her novels.

Kaye's first novel, *Death Walked in Kashmir*, was published in 1953 but her first work to achieve wide acclaim was *The Far Pavilions* (1978). Four of her novels published in the 1950s and early 1960s have recently been republished and have been better received now that *The Far Pavilions* has established Kaye's reputation as an accomplished historical novelist. Changing British attitudes towards India partially explains the different receptions accorded Kaye's work in the two time periods.

Kaye's historical dramas, *The Far Pavilions* and *Shadow of the Moon* (1956), each combine a faithful account of the era of the 1857 Sepoy Mutiny with a romantic love story. The books are thematically similar as well, both centering on the conflict between Western and Indian culture. This conflict is seen on both a political level, in Britain's failure to maintain control of India, and on a personal level, in the protagonists' struggle to reconcile elements of both cultures in their own lives. Like Kaye herself, the protagonists in both of these novels spent their childhoods in India, were brought to England to be educated, and returned to India as adults out of love for that country. *Trade Wind* (1963), another historical novel, is set in Zanzibar and also concerns a clash between cultures. The heroine of this novel goes to Zanzibar to stop slavery and discovers that her limited understanding of the culture of the people she is trying to help will interfere with her goal. This book was reissued in 1981.

Although critics have virtually ignored Kaye's mystery novels, they have praised her India books, comparing them to Margaret Mitchell's *Gone with the Wind* and Rudyard Kipling's *Kim*. They commend her ability to tell a suspenseful story and her knowledge of Indian history and culture; however, they also note that her characterizations are weak and that her lavish descriptions of the Indian countryside are overdone. Kaye's books have attained popular success in Britain, where anti-Indian sentiment has died down; in the United States, where interest in India is growing; and in India, where *The Far Pavilions* has reportedly been used as a classroom text.

(See also *Contemporary Authors*, Vols. 89-92.)

JOHN BAYLEY

Shadow of the Moon is an excellent, long historical novel about the Indian Mutiny, excellent because Miss Kaye has a real historical conscience, a sense of impartiality and a great many old mutiny records to draw upon. She cannot refrain from exploiting the amorous and horrific side of the business—dash-

ing officers with moustaches, and screaming ladies in crinolines having their heads hacked off by sepoys—but she does not let these things get out of hand and she should be read by those interested in the period as well as by addicts of the romantic past.

John Bayley, in a review of "Shadow of the Moon," in The Spectator (© 1957 by The Spectator; *reprinted by permission of* The Spectator), Vol. 198, No. 6720, April 12, 1957, p. 495.

THE TIMES LITERARY SUPPLEMENT

Shadow of the Moon is an unbiased picture of India at the time of the Mutiny, emphasizing that not only the policy of the Company but in addition the personal failings of many of its servants gave the sepoys of the Bengal Army an excuse for betraying their allegiance. The events of the war are clearly described, and the author makes the point that British garrisons in every station were hampered by the presence of women and children, who must be protected even if their protection immobilized a possible striking force. But perhaps this book would have been better as a popular history of the Mutiny, for the fictitious characters are wooden and unconvincing.

"History in Disguise," in The Times Literary Supplement (© *Times Newspapers Ltd. (London) 1957;*

DAVID TILDEN

Miss Kaye has lived in India much of her life and her forebears have distinguished themselves in service in that country for more than a century. [*Shadow of the Moon*], centered in the Indian Sepoy Mutiny, is dedicated to them.

The story beginning in a mid-Victorian setting in England that is hardly less strange by present-day standards than India itself, is the tale of a young girl, half British, half Spanish, who was born in India but reared chiefly in England after the death of her parents. Her mother, dying in India's heat, had asked to have the baby named Winter in longing for the coolness of her distant home.

The story is of Winter's journey and marriage, by circumstance ended in the carnage of the uprising, and the way out that the girl found through the reign of terror. Episodes in that story, patterned largely after the almost incredible actual events of 1857, are filled with excitement and suspense, but the story of India itself will have even greater fascination for many readers. Out of her own experience, including tales handed down in her family, Miss Kaye pictures its welter of races, religions, ideals and superstitions; its fragrances and stench, beauty and horror. Nor does she shrink from showing the shortcomings of all but a few of its British overlords.

Once one gets past a rather slow start . . . , this novel is a thriller the more thrilling because so much of it is or might have been true.

> David Tilden, "An Indian Mutiny Thriller," in New York Herald Tribune Book Review (© I.H.T. Corporation; reprinted by permission), September 1, 1957, p. 3.

THE TIMES LITERARY SUPPLEMENT

Kenya and the lingering aftermath of Mau-Mau provide the setting for Mrs. Kaye's *Later Than You Think*. A glorious farm in a golden valley beside a lake, surrounded by a garden with wonderful flowers and trees, is very well described by the author and it is hard not to feel that the Kenya scene and the love-interest of her story have not charmed her imagination more than has the detective-work necessitated by the plot. The colonial police-officers, however, are well drawn and there are some moments of lively apprehension.

> "Deck-Chair Detectives," in The Times Literary Supplement (© Times Newspapers Ltd. (London) 1958; reproduced from The Times Literary Supplement by permission), No. 2947, August 22, 1958, p. 469.*

ANTHONY BOUCHER

Price and jacket copy [for *Later than You Think*] might lead you to suspect a serious suspense story bordering on the straight novel. Don't be misled; this is a perfectly conventional whodunit of the feminine persuasion, verging on the Had-I-But-Known school, redeemed and revitalized by its setting in the Rift Valley, fifty miles from Nairobi, just after the Mau-Mau uprising—which apparently is known euphemistically in Kenya as "the Emergency." What seems to be first-hand depiction of the delicate tensions among white-settlers in this uneasy aftermath to violence manages to impart conviction and even distinction to an otherwise routine mystery-romance.

> Anthony Boucher, in a review of "Later than You Think," in The New York Times (copyright © 1958 by The New York Times Company; reprinted by permission), October 26, 1958, p. 57.

THE TIMES LITERARY SUPPLEMENT

The heroine [of *House of Shade*] is an English rose of truly startling naivety. ("Your I.Q. is probably the lowest on record," says her admirer with a rare flash of insight.) This silly girl, having been incompetently framed for a murder in London, dashes off to her mother's house in Zanzibar accompanied by a whole plane-load of suspicious characters. There is mention of Communists and buried treasure before she just escapes being pushed out a window. Miss Kaye writes pleasantly and the Zanzibar settings are agreeable, but the whole thing has a fairly old-fashioned air, reminiscent of those innocent adventure stories which filled young people's magazines in the 1930s.

> "Professional Skulduggery," in The Times Literary Supplement (© Times Newspapers Ltd. (London) 1959; reproduced from The Times Literary Supplement by permission), No. 2996, July 31, 1959, p. 445.*

JAMES SANDOE

The House of Shade . . . is in Zanzibar but Dany Ashton is in London and the police want her for questioning. So, one thing leading to another, she boards the plane as the secretary of a very tipsy young American publisher. M. M. Kaye's comic romance (with detection) takes a nimble, cooly absurd, somewhat word-heavy course, making admirable use of a handsome drench in the charms of Zanzibar. The sound of Americans (two of whom have strategic places in the plot) eludes Miss Kaye, whose range of British voices is well enough heard. It's a pleasant piece of work, striving a little hard for its thrills but keeping one diverted well enough.

> James Sandoe, in a review of "The House of Shade," in New York Herald Tribune Book Review (© I.H.T. Corporation; reprinted by permission), September 20, 1959, p. 15.

FRANCIS KING

Among the many different categories of the novel, I have created two for myself: holiday novels and hospital novels. The first must be long, absorbing and not too exacting in style or thought. The second must be also long, also absorbing and in no way productive of morbid imaginings. M. M. Kaye's *The Far Pavilions* falls into both these categories, even if its size and weight are such that to place it across the knees might easily bring a deck-chair crashing to the ground or cause a relapse in a debilitated convalescent.

An account of a young man's life in India for about twenty-five years from the Indian Mutiny to the Second Afghan War, this jumbo historical novel reminded me irresistibly of one of those elephants, slow, strong and dependable, on which I would sometimes journey during my Indian childhood. The reader has the reassuring knowledge that he is going to be carried safely and comfortably to his destination; and, from his eminence, he is going to see a great deal of the surrounding countryside on his leisurely way....

Fortunately both the author's sense of history and her gift for narrative help to redeem a book in which characterisation is fitful and feeble, in which Ash says to his beloved things like 'I never meant this to happen' after it has happened again and again, and in which the descriptions of the countryside induce the same kind of tedium as an endless showing of colour snaps from an Indian holiday. I never really believed in Ash, his half-Russian and half-Indian princess or their eventual secret marriage; but the book—especially when Ash is playing Kipling's Great Game as a British spy in Afghanistan—is extremely skilful in its evocation of place and period.

The publishers are to be congratulated on offering in one volume, at a reasonable price, a book that many another publisher might have been tempted to foist on to the public as a trilogy. The result could best be described as an Indian 'Gone with the Wind'. The obvious comparison is with J. G. Farrell's novel of the Indian Mutiny, 'The Siege of Krishnapur'. Farrell's novel has all the insight into motive, all the stylistic surprisingness and all the intellectual distinction that this one wholly lacks. But just as Edgar Wallace told a better yarn than Shakespeare, so M. M. Kaye tells a better yarn than J. G. Farrell. On that level, her book is a triumph of narrative, perseverance and hard work.

> Francis King, "Elephantine," in The Spectator (©1978 by The Spectator; reprinted by permission of The Spectator), Vol. 241, No. 7836, September 9, 1978, p. 22.

BRIGITTE WEEKS

The legendary sun has finally set on the British Empire and the India of the Raj has passed into history. In the inevitable sea-change that follows, its strengths are being remembered, its weaknesses softened by time.

Riding the crest of this revisionist wave, this Cecil B. DeMille production of a novel [*The Far Pavilions*]—15 years in the writing—brings those times close as only the most stirring fiction can. M. M. Kaye's formidable imagination, steeped in history, war and romance, conjures up sights and sounds of India, from palaces in the Himalayas to the docks of Bombay.

Ashton Pelham-Martyn, a hero worthy of the name, is the son of an eccentric British anthropologist working in India. Orphaned in a cholera epidemic at the time of the 1857 Indian Mutiny, Ash is saved by his nurse Sita, who then passes him off as her own son for his own protection in murderous times. As a teenager his true identity is revealed, but he has already grown up Indian and Hindu.

Nevertheless, British heredity is assumed to be thicker than Indian environment, and he is shipped off to England where his rich and aristocratic paternal relatives undertake to transform him into an officer and a gentleman.

When Ash returns to India as a soldier he pursues a checkered career torn constantly between his two heritages....

Ash's divided loyalties—his fierce understanding of Indian ways and his admiration for the spirit of the British army—lay the foundations for this novel's most impressive achievement: its balanced insight into the contemporary confusion and ancient order of 19th-century India. On one hand Kaye shows tremendous affection, sensitivity and understanding of the Indian people, their culture, religion and traditions, as they attempt to live in an imposed British environment with all its narrowness and blunderings. Yet at the same time she gives full credit to those colonialists, both civilian and military, who make the best of an unheroic situation, whose sense of duty—however odd in retrospect—is strong and whose courage is unfailing. (p. 1)

Because Ash is always on the move, from Bombay to Rawalpindi to Mardan to the Khyber, his perceptions give the reader a sense of being caught up in the fabric of another time, with the bonus of having an informed insider's viewpoint. The tragic role of the Guides as pawns in the Afghan conflict would be bloodchilling as pure fiction, but the knowledge that Kaye's drama is based on actual events heightens our involvement. The fanatical messianic Sir Louis Cavagnari and his superiors in Whitehall did indeed play international power games while ignoring firsthand reports from the Northwest Frontier, as actual cables and correspondence quoted in the novel plainly demonstrate.

All this historic drama is interwoven with the high romance of Anjuli-Bai, princess of Gulkote, Rani of Bhithor, lover and finally wife of Lieutenant Pelham-Martyn. Lovers crossed by race, culture, religion and heredity are irresistible. Officers of the Guides needed the permission of their commanding officer to marry in those feudal days, not to mention the fact that Juli has already been traded to a dissolute Rana (as part of a package deal with her half-sister) before she and Ash fall in love. Throw in the ill health of the said Rana and the ancient custom of *suttee* (wives immolating themselves on the funeral pyres of their husbands) and another panel is woven into the gleaming tapestry.

This intricate blending of fact and fiction would be ill-served by further summary, but Ash, Zarin, Wally and Anjuli play out an epic drama. Who cares to admit to infatuation, to having fallen for the old Dickensian virtues of storytelling? Shelves are haunted by the dusty ghosts of so many "unforgettable" sagas, yet it would be churlish as well as thoroughly craven not to admit that this novel, with its unabashed vigor, has genuine power.

A second reading relieves the intense pressure to discover the fate of the protagonists, allowing hundreds of details and transient characters previously unnoticed to fill out the huge canvas. In the simplest terms, readers of *The Far Pavilions* cannot ever feel quite the same about either the Indian subcontinent or the decrepit history of the British Empire. Few novels can claim as much, or ask for more. (p. 6)

> Brigitte Weeks, "The Romance of the Raj," in Book World—The Washington Post (© 1978, The Washington Post), September 10, 1978, pp. 1, 6.

THEON WILKINSON

The Far Pavilions follows M. M. Kaye's two highly successful historical novels *Shadows of the Moon* and *Trade Wind;* all three set in the second half of the nineteenth century in lands bordering the Indian Ocean, and all three evidence of the author's passionate involvement with India.... She writes with the conviction that events must be told in their fullness or not at all, that every facet of information touching the characters must be embraced; and *The Far Pavilions* is a great oriental pot-pourri from which nothing is left out: Indian lullabys; regimental bawdy songs; regimental history, wars and campaigns;

weddings; funerals; poisonous plants—a tribute to much painstaking research, some drawn from original diaries and journals.

It is a tale of twenty-five traumatic years in the life of a remarkable young man who epitomizes in the circumstances of his birth and upbringing the gulf between cultures and races in India. . . .

The book ends with young Ash at the Kabul massacre, disillusioned, his best friend dead, realizing that his closest English, Muslim and Hindu "brothers" are locked within their own worlds of custom and prejudice which make him a stranger. He sets out with his Hindu princess to find their own "Far Pavilions", the name of a distant snow-capped peak of the Himalayas that has been their lifelong inspiration.

The length of the book is a challenge but the effort is rewarded. Some of the adventures may be rather too melodramatic but the richness of historical and social detail more than makes up for this. . . .

> Theon Wilkinson, "Skin-deep Sahib," in The Times Literary Supplement (© Times Newspapers Ltd. (London) 1978; reproduced from The Times Literary Supplement by permission), No. 3990, September 22, 1978, p. 1056.

DAVID WEINBERGER

Shadow of the Moon is a pale shadow of M. M. Kaye's previous best seller, *The Far Pavilions*, a 1,000-page epic of 19th-century India (pronounced In-juh). Her writing was competent and professional, she conveyed the historical information painlessly, and if the plot and characters were coldly calculated to get the hero to all the important events, still it was a novel one could read with a clear conscience. The new book is again set in India, this time prior to the Sepoy Rebellion of 1857, and we learn little new. Still, the familiar landscape might be enticing is only Kaye had bothered to come up with a new plot. (p. 56)

Kaye's reliance on mutual misunderstandings as a plot device in *The Far Pavilions* becomes fatal in *Shadow of the Moon*: the protagonists fall in love early on, but to keep the story rolling Kaye has to frustrate them. For hundreds of pages all would be fine if only he would tell her that he loves her. In her first book this had a sort of Victorian charm because the lack of candor was rooted in character. Here the characters themselves are without roots or solidity. And the plot is shameless, relying on absurd coincidences. . . .

The writing is not quite clichéd, only hackneyed. . . . The dialogue is pompous and impossible, facts are over-explained, and Kaye is given to doubling phrases: "His message was less general and more specific." In a 600-page book, this is especially wearisome. Her political point of view is also suspect. Nominally she sympathizes with the Indians, but over-all her picture of them is fairly nasty and we find ourselves rooting for the British.

If an historical novel cannot be as interesting as its topic, it ought at least to be harder to put down than an encyclopedia article. (p. 57)

> David Weinberger, "A Passage to In-juh," in Maclean's Magazine; (© 1979 by Maclean's Magazine; reprinted by permission), Vol. 93, No. 39, September 24, 1979, pp. 56-7.

NICHOLAS SHRIMPTON

M. M. Kaye's *The Far Pavilions* blended lurid oriental colour with homely occidental emotions. A quarter of a million copies have been sold in hardback alone, in less than a year. *Shadow of the Moon,* from the same hand and in the same manner, seems set to repeat that extraordinary success.

It's not in fact a new novel, having first seen the light of day, in abbreviated form, in 1957. But it is an extraordinarily apt successor to *The Far Pavilions*. Like that book it is a romance set in Victorian India. Like that book, again, its plot combines a dash of *Kim* with a good deal of *Tristan und Isolde*. Winter de Ballesteros, the heroine, is the orphan daughter of an English heiress and a Spanish aristocrat. Born in Lucknow and brought up in England, she is betrothed at the tender age of eleven to a distant relative. But he is a district commissioner in far-away India and when the moment comes for him to claim his bride he is so broken down by drink and debauchery ('two things that have never yet failed to ruin those devotees who have worshipped them to excess') that he cannot face the journey to fetch her. Instead he sends his handsome, upright and courageous assistant, Alex Randle. There follow six hundred pages of aching erotic suspense as the overpowering mutual attraction of traveller and guide struggles with their feelings of honour and duty.

Amid all this emotional drama we also have the little matter of the Indian Mutiny, about which it must be said M. M. Kaye writes with conspicuous expertise. She is eager to celebrate the empire builders from whom she is descended. But she is also close enough to India to see it through the eyes of its own people. For them the Mutiny is a war of liberation and Alex is given the insight to see it as such. Intellectual argument of this kind is very welcome and it does, of course, have to be attributed to someone. The trouble is that everything else is attributed to Alex as well. When his mighty brain isn't predicting the next hundred years of Indian history, his mighty body is wrestling with sharks or saving the Raj single-handed. If you can tolerate a bionic tailor's dummy for a hero, however, the local colour is terrific.

> Nicholas Shrimpton, "A Dash of Kim," in New Statesman (© 1979 The Statesman & Nation Publishing Co. Ltd.), Vol. 98, No. 2534, October 12, 1979, p. 559.*

RAHUL SINGH

It's intriguing how certain themes and subjects can be dormant for years and then, for some uncanny reason, they suddenly catch the popular imagination. In the 1960s Africa was "in" and now, I'm glad to say, it seems to be my country, India.

Until quite recently, anybody writing on India for a Western audience was usually told, sadly but firmly, by his publisher that "India just doesn't sell." (p. 903)

[How] does one explain the change? Perhaps the 32 years since India won its independence have been a sufficiently long period for the British public to reconcile itself to the loss of Empire and to view the Raj without too much discomfort. One could go further to say, a little cruelly, that it is only after the delusions of grandeur have been shattered and Britain has accepted its place in the world as a second-rate power that an objective look into the past is possible.

Whatever the reasons, Ms M. M. Kaye is certainly right on cue with her two massive historical novels on the Indian subcontinent, one of which runs to 958 pages and the other to 612. And to emphasise the point about the sudden upsurge of . . . [interest in India], *Shadow of the Moon* was first published 22 years ago, apparently without much success. Then came the phenomenal popularity of *The Far Pavilions*—probably the biggest selling book ever of its kind on India—and the publishers smartly brought out a "revised" version of *Shadow of the Moon.* To nobody's surprise, it is already climbing the best-seller charts.

Which is not to say that Ms Kaye's achievement is due solely to the current mood. Both her novels have obviously been painstakingly researched and contain few of the kind of elementary errors that so infuriate Indians and which one associates with popular novels on India. . . .

With her lively imagination and marvellous eye for detail, [Kaye] takes us at a furious pace through the mayhem that was mid-nineteenth century India, with its sordid palace intrigues, its constantly warring communities, and its barbaric customs such as *suttee* (widow burning). It was a time for heroics, when a resourceful and brave British officer leading a handful of men could defeat a vast army and change the history of territories many times the size of Britain. But it was also a time when life could be suddenly shortened by a silent dagger-thrust in the night or by one of the many diseases that periodically cut an irresistible swathe across the land.

Ms. Kaye evokes the brutal atmosphere well and some of her descriptions are truly first rate. . . .

She fails, however, on two counts. Her main characters remain simplistic, cut-out cardboard figures who fail to come to life. Secondly, and more seriously, her narrative does not compel us to pause and reflect, so busy is she at constantly gripping our attention: the best of novels should, every now and then, make one want to put the book aside, look into space and ponder over what we have just read.

These failures are more evident in *Shadow of the Moon,* an account of the Indian Mutiny. Here, too, the central character is a young, brave, upright, far-seeing, British civil servant caught between his duty as a ruler and his unmistakable sympathy for those Indians striving for independence. Though she captures beautifully the gay and unreal life of the British just before the Mutiny, we learn little of the complexities that made 1857 a turning point of British rule in India.

But to this reviewer the significance of Ms Kaye's two books lies in her attitude towards India, which can only be characterised as healthy. Take the following passage: ". . . that other India: that mixture of glamour and tawdriness, viciousness and nobility. A land full of gods and gold and famine. Ugly as a rotting corpse and beautiful beyond belief. . . ." There is none of the romantic sentimentality that saw India as a country of snake charmers and bejewelled princes, with the faithful Gunga Din thrown in. Nor the view of it as one vast, multiplying, putrefying sewer for which there was no possible hope. Ms Kaye sees India as many Indians do, and for this one must applaud her. (p. 904)

Rahul Singh, "A View from India," in Punch (©️ 1979 by Punch Publications Ltd.; all rights reserved; may not be reprinted without permission), Vol. 277, November 14, 1979, pp. 903-04.

STAIGE D. BLACKFORD

[Molly Kaye's] love of India is equalled only by her knowledge of it. This love and knowledge help to explain the superb success of her [*The Far Pavilions* and *Shadow of the Moon*] in America. You can quickly tell that this author writes not only from the heart but also from the head, that her comprehension of things Indian is as vast as it is varied. On the pages of her works India, with its many castes and creeds, its poverty and splendor, with its appalling heat and towering mountain peaks, comes to life. Furthermore Miss Kaye has been able to make the past come alive in the present. As one critic said, she "gives the reader a sense of being caught up in the fabric of another time, with the bonus of having an informed insider's viewpoint."

That viewpoint is decidedly pro-Indian. The British protagonists in each of the novels are out of step with their colonialist countrymen. They see Indians not as "wogs" but as human beings, not as subjects but as equals. (p. 444)

Still it is not merely her sympathy for India or her ability to evoke that nation's turbulent and often tragic past that makes Molly Kaye a superb historical novelist. She has another great talent: she is a splendid storyteller. Even if her dialogue sometimes sounds as if it came right out of the worst sort of romantic penny dreadful, the pace of her plots never falters, the suspense never slackens, the surprises never cease. This is so even though her narratives have as many twists and turns as the meandering Mississippi itself.

Parenthetically one might note that, unlike some of her American counterparts, Miss Kaye does not spice her novels heavily with sex. This is not to say that there are no sexual scenes. But they are few, opportune, discreet, and tasteful. (p. 445)

If you read both books, you will discover that while their plots are quite different, they do have some notable similarities (in addition to the obvious similarity of locale). Both open with a mother's death in childbirth, followed by the father's death shortly thereafter, with the orphaned child coming under the tutelage of Indian hands before being sent back to relatives in England (in the cases of Winter and Ash respectively). Having learned the language and lived the lives of Indians, both orphans spend a miserable English childhood and, upon reaching maturity, return to India. The heroines of both books must endure an unhappy first marriage and be widowed before marrying their true loves. Both books, of course, are replete with descriptions of Indian flora and fauna, birds and beasts, and of the harrowing hardships of enduring its climate. Finally both novels have enough scenes of violent death to make the last act of *Hamlet* seem as tame as a reading of "The Children's Hour."

Of the two works *Shadow* strikes me as the more successful, perhaps because it is less ambitious. *Pavilions,* which took its author fifteen years to complete, is actually several stories in one. As the British say, it tends to go on a bit, without ever becoming boring. (pp. 445-46)

There is one final observation to be made about Molly Kaye, and that is this: if she does not rank with Tolstoy, she has every right to take a place alongside Margaret Mitchell, for she has given us India's versions of *Gone with the Wind.* (p. 446)

Staige D. Blackford, "The Great Mutiny, M. M. Kaye, and the Historical Romance," in The Sewanee Review (reprinted by permission of the editor; ©️ 1980 by The University of the South), Vol. LXXXVIII, No. 3, Summer, 1980, pp. 441-46.

ANDREA LEE SHUEY

"God is a great deviser of stratagems," writes Kaye. The stratagems devised for [*Trade Wind*] will keep the reader turning pages compulsively. Twenty-one year old Hero Athena Hollis sets out from Boston for Zanzibar in 1859 to fulfill her mission in life—to stop slave trading. On the journey she is washed overboard and rescued by Rory Frost, a piratical slave trader. Stubborn, spoiled Hero clashes with equally stubborn, overconfident, wicked Rory. Disagreements come in rapid succession about her naïve assumptions, his overbearing manner, her proposed marriage, his occupation, etc. Palace intrigue, revolution, a pirate raid on the island, and a murder lead up to Rory's kidnapping of Hero.

> Andrea Lee Shuey, in a review of "Trade Wind," in Library Journal (reprinted from Library Journal, June 15, 1981; published by R. R. Bowker Co. (a Xerox company); copyright © 1981 by Xerox Corporation), Vol. 106, No. 12, June 15, 1981, p. 1322.

WALTER SHAPIRO

[In *Trade Wind* Kaye's] theme is, as always, the collision between western values and native culture in remote corners of the world in the mid-19th century. But Kaye recognizes all the moral ambiguities raised by this titanic clash of alien cultures. Her narrative indicts hypocrisy, intolerance and the inability of many westerners to appreciate or understand local customs. But she carefully avoids blanket indictments or the shrill rhetoric of anti-colonialism.

For those who have read her earlier novels, particularly *The Far Pavilions,* an epic portrayal of colonial India, it is unnecessary to emphasize her complex moral stance. But it is important to sing the praises of M. M. Kaye for the type of reader, such as myself, who is normally put off by anything resembling genre fiction—particularly since the jacket copy for *Trade Wind* describes it as a "splendid tale of love and death in an exotic locale."

Trade Wind is, indeed, an incongruous love story linking Rory Frost with Hero Athena Hollis, a plucky, 21-year-old right-thinking abolitionist prig from Massachusetts who sails to Zanzibar determined to end the slave trade in the Sultan's domains. There is death in many forms, particularly an emotionally wrenching description of a cholera epidemic. There are few more exotic locales than Zanzibar and Kaye is painstaking in her effort to describe every nook and cranny of this small island.

But *Trade Wind* transcends such easy labels as romance or exotic historical novel. It is a sophisticated treat for those traditional readers who favor good writing, subtle character development, clever plotting and a slightly ironic narrative tone....

Trade Wind is the story of Hero Hollis' maturity as she learns that reading *Uncle Tom's Cabin* and attending a few abolitionist lectures has not prepared her for the realities of Zanzibar. Life is too complex to fit into her moral cubbyholes. With more zeal than good sense, Hero becomes the innocent pawn of French colonial interests as she takes an active part in triggering a bloody rebellion by the Sultan's brother. Her efforts to free individual slaves are comically ineffectual. Slowly she comes to chafe at the rigidity and the hypocrisy of the social mores of the small resident western community on the island. Even after her chastity has been brutally violated, Hero comes to remember fondly "a man's hard body."

Trade Wind was originally published in abbreviated form almost 20 years ago and is as much a reissue as a new novel. This tangled publishing history helps explain why in many ways it is not as mature or complex a novel as *The Far Pavilions*. Zanzibar, for all its interest as a center for slavetrading, does not provide M. M. Kaye with anything resembling the vast canvas of colonial India. The Sultan and his court generally lack the complexity of the European characters in the novel. Even a few of the Europeans come across as one-dimensional windup toys, particularly the English naval officer whose mission is to prevent native dhows loaded with slaves from reaching Zanzibar.

But these are quibbles. The novel is carefully researched and much of the action is based on actual events; even unlikely occurrences as a pirate attack on the European enclave and the elopement of the Sultan's half-sister with a German businessman are historically accurate. *Trade Wind* is a satisfying novel which provides enough action even for sensibilities jaded by television without leaving the bitter aftertaste that comes with long hours of intellectual slumming. Only when compared to the exceedingly high standards set by *The Far Pavilions* does *Trade Wind* fall short.

> Walter Shapiro, "Coming of Age in Zanzibar," in Book World—The Washington Post (© 1981, The Washington Post), July 12, 1981, p. 5.

THE NEW YORKER

[In *Trade Wind,* as usual,] Miss Kaye's heroine and hero (this time, an orphaned American socialite and an English-born, Anglophobic smuggler) are outsiders and iconoclasts; while they despise the arrogance of Victorian talk about "progress and the millennium," they cannot adopt the cold-blooded resignation of some of their Eastern friends, the difference between intervention and interference must be learned by trial and error. Miss Kaye's ideal reader would be an amateur of British colonial history with a weakness for romantic fantasy; most readers will enjoy her novels for one of her specialties and in spite of the other. (p. 87)

> A review of "Trade Wind," in The New Yorker (© 1981 by The New Yorker Magazine, Inc.), Vol. LVII, No. 23, July 27, 1981, pp. 86-7.

William Kennedy
1928-

American novelist.

Labeled a regionalist writer in a positive sense, Kennedy has succeeded in putting Albany, New York, on America's literary map. In the three novels of his Albany cycle, *Legs* (1976), *Billy Phelan's Greatest Game* (1978), and *Ironweed* (1982), Kennedy has created what Paul Gray calls a "geography of the imagination." Focusing on depression-era Albany, Kennedy sympathetically but unsentimentally portrays its politicians, journalists, gamblers, and its down-and-out "low-life" people. As a life-long resident, Kennedy knows the city well. He was a former reporter for the Albany *Times Union* and has been an English professor in that city at State University of New York.

Although most critics enthusiastically praise his fourth novel, *Ironweed*, Kennedy's earlier fiction received mixed appraisals. *The Ink Truck* (1969), a fast-paced black comedy about a newspaper strike, was considered promising by one critic in its blend of fantasy and reality, but another contended that its surrealistic elements were unnecessary. Similarly, *Legs* was denounced by some as tedious and ambiguous in its moral stand, but others viewed it as a skillful, vigorous novel. In general, however, most critics find Kennedy's characterizations and dialogue outstanding and suggest he has finally realized his potential in *Ironweed,* winner of the 1983 National Book Critics Circle Award.

(See also *CLC*, Vol. 6 and *Contemporary Authors*, Vols. 85-88.)

Photograph by Layle Silbert; © copyright 1983

SHANE STEVENS

Novels that combine reality and fantasy are not generally successful. Either the reality obtrudes to where the fantastic becomes merely ridiculous, or the fantasy dwarfs the real. But sometimes the combination works: richness of imagination does not get in the way of the storytelling. William Kennedy's first novel, *The Ink Truck,* is one of these happy few.

The Ink Truck is a work of the imagination, inventive, circular and multi-layered. Yet its characters are as real as they are symbolic, the scenes as much reality as fantasy. Normally, novels of great imaginative density, such as those of John Barth, are unreadable. As the reader sinks deeper into the author's stream of consciousness, the threads of the story unravel. Not so with *The Ink Truck*. Kennedy has been able to confine his wickedly surrealist imagination within a well-told tale. The result is a Dantesque journey through the hells of existence. . . .

The Ink Truck is a fine debut by a writer of obvious talent and much promise.

> Shane Stevens, "A Guided Tour in Hell," in Book World—The Washington Post *(© 1969 Postrib Corp.; reprinted by permission of* Chicago Tribune *and* The Washington Post*), October 5, 1969, p. 16.*

DANIEL ST. ALBIN GREENE

Don't let the title of William Kennedy's first novel mislead you. *The Ink Truck* has little to do with an ink truck; even the newspaper strike the truck symbolizes is only a framework for the wild obsessions of its central figure—a chap named Bailey, who tilts incessantly against windmills in lonely resistance to conformism. It is this character's comic recalcitrance that throbs through the book and makes it an extraordinary achievement.

Bailey is a loser of heroic dimensions. He has the irrational idealism of the Man of La Mancha, the life style of Jimmy Breslin, the indomitable bellicosity of a guerrilla fighter. An eloquent wild man of large intellect and larger spleen, he is the most intransigent of a tiny knot of diehard strikers, hapless remnants of a once-cocky Newspaper Guild local that walked out on the paper a year ago. In forlorn perseverance, they still go to the guild office every day, keep free-lance pickets walking up and down, and try to sustain the appearance of militancy—even though everybody knows if the strike were settled now, they would be worse off than before they struck. . . .

By this time, fighting the lost cause has become a way of life to Bailey and his inept colleagues. . . .

Bailey, a syndicated columnist of waning comprehensibility, is incapable of doing anything half-heartedly. He harasses and beats up scab reporters; hatches crazy espionage schemes, such as sneaking a skunk into the ad office; and finally plots a first-anniversary blow against the company that would be more than a gesture: "It would be the transfiguration of a protest."

Bailey's ultimate gesture is an attempt to bleed an ink truck serving the newspaper plant of its cargo. Typically, this fails too, so the frustrated saboteur sets fire to a company shack inhabited by a bunch of gypsies hired as company thugs. Thereafter, this story of a newspaper strike becomes something else. We follow Bailey through a weird, bizarre odyssey that reels back and forth between hilarious reality and surrealistic nightmare and climaxes in an incredible end-of-the-strike party in which the once-warring factions become a drugged herd *sans* clothes, individualism, and bothersome principles. Bailey resists even this, though, and tries to shoot the company man who planned the diabolical orgy. As an assassin, he fails again; the gun blows up in his hand. Yet through it all, he makes failure seem noble....

"It is my hope," says the author, "that *The Ink Truck* will stand as an analgesic inspiration to all weird men of good will and rotten luck everywhere."

> Daniel St. Albin Greene, "There's Nobility in a Born Loser in Mr. Kennedy's Comic 'Ink Truck'," in The National Observer *(reprinted by permission of* The National Observer; © *Dow Jones & Company, Inc. 1969; all rights reserved), October 20, 1969, p. 21.*

STANLEY REYNOLDS

I do not think one can blame the barbaric culture of the New World for ... *The Ink Truck.* The novel has the look of something typed in dull moments around a newspaper office: the first chapters of the great comic novel that Joe at the next desk is going to finish one of these days. *The Ink Truck* is about a newspaper strike, and one feels that Mr Kennedy was unfortunate to have had the free time given to him to finish his 'comic masterpiece'. In the fashionable mould of *Catch 22* or Kurt Vonnegut Jr, his novel departs from anything resembling real life before it even starts. The crazy, surrealistic antics serve no apparent purpose either, and are not as funny as they should be. Still, the novel is readable and just now and again it manages to break through the desperate hilarity to make a serious point. Mr Kennedy is, after all, a serious and successful American journalist ... and he has something to say about the way American society crushes idealism.

> Stanley Reynolds, "Cosy Souls," *in* New Statesman (© *1970 The Statesman & Nation Publishing Co. Ltd.), Vol. 80, No. 2056, August 14, 1970, p. 185.**

VALENTINE CUNNINGHAM

Forty-three years after his death the old comrades of the now legendary Jack "Legs" Diamond are reminiscing atop their bar-stools in a somewhat boozier than Conradian vein. Among them, her memory juiced-up by the drink, one Flossie recalls that Diamond "had a tan collie, could count to fifty-two and do subtraction", that he "could turn on the electric light sometimes just by snapping his fingers", that "he could tie both his shoes at once". But the story that's enclosed within this romanticizing frame [*Legs*] and told us by William Kennedy's ersatz-Marlowe—a lawyer called Marcus who's paid to bail out the boys and front the mob with a clean bib and tucker—amounts to something less fantastic but considerably more gripping. Not that the narrative is consistently exciting: it does come with longueurs and detumescences, and as is the wont of stories told in flashes back it lights up only in flashes. Still, these climaxes are certainly worth waiting for....

Above all, though, the coherence and attraction of the novel are a matter of tonality. Acidic *mots* are jerked out of the sides of bad-mouthing bad guys' mouths in the best manner of 1940s movies about 1920s gangsters. Legs has met Fitzgerald; he likes Von Sternberg films; he follows the boxing careers of Jack Sharkey and Benny Shapiro. And his world is delightfully peopled with the likes of Mendel (The Ox) Feinstein, Murray (The Goose) Pucinski, Tony (The Boy) Amapola, Edward (Fats MacCarthy) Popke, and Big Frenchy De Mange.

If only all this were all, *Legs* would make a decently engaging read, but total enjoyment is blunted by the gangster's memorialist only allowing us to have his boss when portentously trailing the heavy festoons of a thesis. Legs Diamond is not just an attractive thug, he stands for the American Dream of shooting your way to riches and glory. As a licensed killer eventually to be cathartically slain, he ensures, we are assured, the health of the social system. He is even made the prophet of the intimate interlocking of American city politics and crookery in later decades.... If it were clear that the author disconnected himself from his Marlowe all would be well (or at least better than it is). But Kennedy and his novel appear simply unperturbed by their narrating man's inevitably curious moral position as a mobsters' legal adviser: a morally and philosophically alerter fiction would certainly want more clearly to disown this narrator.

> Valentine Cunningham, "Theoretical Thuggery," *in* The Times Literary Supplement *(©* Times Newspapers Ltd. (London) 1976; reproduced from *The Times Literary Supplement* by permission), No. 3884, August 20, 1976, p. 1037.*

JONATHAN PENNER

Lemon Lewis and Daddy Big, Honey Curry and Red Tom. Spanish George—not to be confused with Georgie the Syph. Poop and Chick and Charlie Boy.

All these and more colorful characters live ... in Albany, New York, in October of 1938. William Kennedy has swept his net through that time and place—swept it at the depth inhabited by politicians and journalists, gamblers and criminals—and in [***Billy Phelan's Greatest Game,*** a] flawed but fascinating novel, he empties his catch before us.

The two chief fish are Billy Phelan and Martin Daugherty, who take turns serving as viewpoint character. Billy is a bookmaker and pool shark, a hustler with quick fists, who honors the rule he lives by: If you lose, you pay. Narrow and intense, self-centered but loyal, he is perfect both as a caricature and as a character.

Martin, unfortunately, is a very sick fish at best, and often indistinguishable from a dead one. Philosopher and part-time mystic, he seems out of place here. His preoccupations are abstract, his elocution excessively fine.

The main plot concerns the kidnapping of Mayor Patsy McCall's nephew. In one way or another it sweeps up all of the many characters. Developed artfully, paced with sure instinct, it generates the tension that holds the novel together.

But only just barely. For this is a book rife with subplots that come to nothing, flashbacks that explain what needs no explaining—an awesome wealth of invention, but invested too diversely....

Too many threads are followed too far beyond the circle's perimeter.

For instance, Martin Daugherty has ESP—a dim sort of precognition. This is firmly insisted upon, and gone into in some detail. It is also entirely unnecessary to the novel. By requiring readers to believe what many of them can't, the author needlessly estranges these many from his story.

Again: the novel is painfully overstuffed with fathers and sons and their relationships. Here the author is ponderously working out a theme. Turbid prose can give it a bogus appearance of depth....

There are other problems. One is point of view: the narration wanders too far, both in content and in tone, from what the viewpoint character knows and how he might think about it. Another problem is the slighting of women characters. Another lies in the happy ending, which requires a creaky deus ex machina.

And yet **Billy Phelan's Greatest Game** is a novel that generously rewards the reading. It creates, with total authority, a complex and interesting society. The dialogue is magnificent: so terse, idiosyncratic, and natural that Kennedy can use it even to get in background information, a technique that seems artificial in most other writers.

But certainly the rarest achievement of this novel is a persuasive account of man's nature. We are shown—we are, within the world the novel creates, convinced—that a man is by nature a *type* of man, with the instincts of his type: the politician, the hustler, the priest, the bum, the whore. He understands only his own type, and only their world. It is as though Homo sapiens were divided into subspecies, defined not morphologically but spiritually.

It is when the force of events pulls a character out of his accustomed world—demands of him what his type doesn't have to give—that he is put in conflict with himself, and suffers. In showing us this natural law, William Kennedy offers us a vision of our own histories and destinies.

As fierce Billy Phelan would put it: We owe the guy. Mark him okay.

> Jonathan Penner, "If You Lose You Pay," in Book World—The Washington Post (© 1978, The Washington Post), April 23, 1978, p. E7.

PETER S. PRESCOTT

"**Legs**" translated the career of a gangster into a shimmering, witty story that combined fact and myth to prod at our national ambivalence toward celebrity criminals. The disappointment of ["**Billy Phelan's Greatest Game**"] is not that it lacks its predecessor's magnetic core, but that its core is so weak that its author seems to disdain it: the story's depth, as someone once said, is entirely on the surface....

But it is a surface polished to a high gloss.... Kennedy's story, such as it is, concerns Albany's night people, who live on the edge of the underworld. Chief among these are Billy Phelan, a part-time bookie and gambler who is good enough at cards, pool and bowling to win more often than not, and Martin Daugherty, a failed novelist and columnist for the Albany paper, who writes admiringly of Billy's style. When a nephew of the city's political boss is kidnapped, both Billy and Martin become reluctant negotiators for the fellow's release.

I won't say any more about the plot; it seems no more to have engaged its author's interest than it did mine. From time to time Kennedy tries to impose a little form upon his story—both Martin and Billy, for instance, must come to terms with their fathers' derelictions—but the line of his narrative would have been firmer if he had let Martin tell Billy's story, and if he had not been so distracted by the details, the anecdotes, the scraps of Albany lore and legend. I must stress that I found these distractions very pleasing indeed, and expertly done; at any point in his narrative Kennedy can be seen writing with great skill and authority, but the pieces do not coalesce, the story does not really progress. We are left at the end with the impression of a great many glittering shards thrown carelessly before us; yet they are, in their disarray, more attractive than the stolid structures assembled by some of his colleagues. You will find me at the head of the line again, awaiting Kennedy's next novel. (p. 100)

> Peter S. Prescott, "Nightcrawlers," in Newsweek (copyright 1978, by Newsweek, Inc.; all rights reserved; reprinted by permission), Vol. XCI, No. 19, May 8, 1978, pp. 99-100.

PUBLISHERS WEEKLY

["**Ironweed**" is the] third in a series of novels set in Albany, N.Y., [and] this strong, authentic book bursts with black humor and stinging insights about a segment of American society. Francis Phelan, father of Billy, is a bum. He knows it and so does everyone else. It's 1938, and the landscape is thick with hobos—not just those looking for work, but those on the run. "What was it that did you in?" Francis wonders about a fellow traveler and then wonders about himself. Understanding why he's on the move is Francis's quest. Dodging the cold and taking care of his companion-in-arms, Helen, are his sacred duties. Returning to Albany 22 years after he had abandoned his family, Francis knows he never quit loving his wife, and by book's end, he is back home with plainspoken forgiveness on all sides. Wholly realistic dialogue and details of a tramp's rough life never clash with the big questions: How did I come to be what I am? And what am I? This supple, lyrical novel winds in and out of Francis Phelan's thoughts and questions, his sensitive perspective and perceptions, and creates a captivating character.

> A review of "Ironweed," in Publishers Weekly (reprinted from the October 22, 1982 issue of Publishers Weekly, published by R. R. Bowker Company, a Xerox company; copyright © 1982 by Xerox Corporation), Vol. 222, No. 17, October 22, 1982, p. 42.

CHRISTOPHER LEHMANN-HAUPT

"**Ironweed**"—which refers to a tough-stemmed member of the sunflower family—recounts a few days in the life of an Albany skid-row bum, a former major-league third baseman with a talent for running, particularly running away, although his ambition now, at the height of the Depression, has been scaled down to the task of getting through the next 20 minutes or so.

The novel is rich in plot and dramatic tension, building as it eventually does, to a violent showdown between a gang of marauding American Legionnaires and a handful of derelicts in a hobo jungle. It is almost Joycean in the variety of rhetoric it uses to evoke the texture and sociology of Albany in the 1930's, particularly the city's Irish community, which by the time of the novel is in full control of the city's politics. And the book is remarkable in its refusal either to sentimentalize or trivialize "life on the bum."

Francis Phelan, the down-and-out protagonist, has plenty of reason for being a bum. Many years earlier, as an employee of an Albany trolley line out on strike, Francis threw a stone at a strikebreaker and fatally cracked his skull, which forced him to run away from Albany for a while. Only a few years later, he picked up his 13-day-old son by the diaper—as he had often done with his two older children—only to have a safety-pin snap open and the infant fall to the floor and die of a broken neck. This led Francis to run from his family for good. Ever since, he has been doomed to kill, just as he is at the climax of **"Ironweed."**

Yet Francis's guilt over these misdeeds doesn't really account for his self-contempt and sense of having erred, which are of sufficient magnitude to universalize him as a human being doomed to sin. And conversely, no matter how low Francis sinks—no matter how drunk and foul smelling and abhorrent to the eye he becomes—Mr. Kennedy continues to grant him access to the spontaneous ecstasy that being alive entitles him to. . . .

Still, **"Ironweed"** will come as a particular pleasure to those familiar with Mr. Kennedy's previous Albany books, especially **"Billy Phelan's Greatest Game."** For the new novel represents a dramatic development both in terms of plot and artistry over the earlier ones. First of all, since **"Ironweed"** is the story of Billy Phelan's father, who disappeared when the boy was only 9, the new book repeats or expands many of the scenes that tantalize us in the second novel.

But more important, **"Ironweed"** is a streamlining and economizing of Mr. Kennedy's novelistic technique. The guilty-father-innocent-son theme is effectively elaborated without all the earlier novel's ruminations on Abraham's sacrifice of Isaac. Instead of using rhetoric to call up both Francis's and Albany's past, Mr. Kennedy relies more on the age-old device of ghosts. The result is an altogether starker, less cluttered fiction—a novel that goes straight for the throat, and the funnybone.

Christopher Lehmann-Haupt, in a review of "Ironweed," in The New York Times *(copyright © 1983 by The New York Times Company; reprinted by permission), January 10, 1983, p. C18.*

PAUL GRAY

[William Kennedy, a] lifelong resident of Albany, has shown again how certain talents flourish best in native soil. *Ironweed* dovetails with its predecessor. The scene is still Albany, the time still 1938. It is Halloween, and Billy Phelan's father Francis is back in his old haunts, meeting ghosts and goblins from his scary past.

Francis is a bum and a lush. . . .

Characters without wills of their own are usually bad bargains in fiction, able to play nothing but victims. But Kennedy shows Francis as both helpless and thoroughly responsible for his own condition. This aging drunk is quite capable of exercising volition; the problem is that his choices are crazed. He has taken on the burden of caring for an aging hobo named Helen Archer. Francis finds her warm places to sleep before looking out for himself. He would like to think of this behavior as virtuous, but honesty forces him to admit that he has bummed "not because there was a Depression but first to help Helen and then because it was easy: easier than working."

The '30s are receding into mythology, where the heroic unemployed are martyred on the altar of false and tyrannical economics. Like most myths, this one is generally plausible and specifically false. Kennedy's fiction returns dignity to the little fellow, the common man or woman, those quite capable of fouling up their lives during the best of times, not to mention the worst. *Ironweed* stands handsomely on its own, but *Legs* and *Billy Phelan's Greatest Game* are being issued in paperback to accompany its publication. Those who wish to watch a geography of the imagination take shape should read all three and then pray for more.

Paul Gray, "Imaginative Necessities," in Time *(copyright 1983 Time Inc.; all rights reserved; reprinted by permission from* Time*), Vol. 121, No. 4, January 24, 1983, p. 82.*

PETER S. PRESCOTT

A good novel announces itself on its opening page: whatever distinctiveness of vision and discipline of language its author can muster will be at once apparent. In **"Ironweed,"** William Kennedy fixes his story's tone—an elegiac tone, undercut by irony—in his opening sentence and moves immediately to set up the delicate blend of realism, myth and satire that will carry his tale to its conclusion. . . .

William Kennedy has written good fiction before, which has gone largely unnoticed. This novel, if only enough people will pay attention, should place him among the best of our current American novelists. In its refusal of sentimentality, its freshness of language and the originality with which its author approaches scenes well worn before his arrival, **"Ironweed"** has a sense of permanence about it.

Peter S. Prescott, "Albany's Mean Streets," in Newsweek *(copyright 1983, by Newsweek, Inc.; all rights reserved; reprinted by permission), Vol. CI, No. 5, January 31, 1983, p. 72.*

Tadeusz Konwicki
1926-

Polish novelist, short story writer, filmmaker, and journalist.

Konwicki has emerged as a leading literary figure in post-World War II Poland. His work reflects the grim realities of modern Polish life, including the devastating effects and lingering memories of the war and the subsequent Communist domination. Critics have especially praised Konwicki's analysis of what he has termed "the Polish complex," which he develops through characters who are bored with the present, foresee a bleak future, and are haunted by both the romantic idealism and the tragic events of the Polish past. Konwicki assesses Polish history as a series of failed attempts to gain freedom and independence. Because his writings and films project such dismal images of life in Poland, Konwicki has had difficulty having some of his work produced.

Konwicki gained critical acclaim in Poland for his initial works of socialist-realist fiction. With *Rojsty*, written in the late 1940s but not published until 1956 when state-imposed restrictions on literary content were gradually eased, Konwicki abandoned socialist-realist literature, primarily because of its tendency to portray the triumph of Communism. A satire, *Rojsty* depicts a young man who desperately wants to become a hero but who dies anonymously while attempting to impede the Soviet invasion of Poland. Konwicki later won international recognition with *Sennik współczesny* (1963; *A Dreambook for Our Time*), whose protagonist Oldster, a tormented survivor of World War II, struggles to endure his bleak, godless existence. Based on a theme of Joseph Conrad's, "we live as we dream—alone," *Dreambook* is related by flashbacks to past experiences through the blurred perception of Oldster. Nightmarish episodes and a reliance on inner monologue give the novel a surrealistic quality. Czesław Miłosz spoke for many critics by calling *Dreambook* "a major literary sensation." Some critics, however, have found the novel nihilistic and incapable of arousing sympathy.

As with *Dreambook*, Konwicki won critical acclaim in the West with *Kompleks Polski* (1977; *The Polish Complex*), a novel which was officially banned in Poland. The novel portrays a group of Poles waiting in line for a shipment of gold rings from Russia; the people represent various types of Polish personalities and their situations reflect the state of life in contemporary Poland. Critics have found the novel to be a powerful statement on the degrading effects of totalitarian government and a poignant analysis of the Polish condition. The image of the Poles waiting for gold has been read as symbolic of the Polish people anticipating the deliverance of their idealized homeland. The historical digressions in the novel, including accounts of failed uprisings in the past, reveal an unending cycle of thwarted ambitions. Most critics agree that *The Polish Complex* features Konwicki's finest literary qualities—a skillful use of surrealist techniques, distinctive Polish character types, and an ability to reveal the role of history in shaping the modern Polish psyche.

(See also *CLC*, Vol. 8 and *Contemporary Authors*, Vol. 101.)

© 1984 Thomas Victor

GEORGE GÖMÖRI

Tadeusz Konwicki is one of the best-known living Polish novelists. *Mała apokalipsa* [published in the United States as *A Minor Apocalypse*] . . . is his ninth novel and his second one published in samizdat [an "underground" system for circulating dissident literature]. . . . His previous book in samizdat, *Kompleks polski* (1977), was an amusing though somewhat chaotic account of a day and night of encounters in the Warsaw of the seventies. His new novel goes further: it is Konwicki's first attempt to portray an anti-utopia that takes place in a vaguely defined future.

And a very grim future it is: Poland is on the verge of being incorporated (with the consent of the Polish Communist Party, of course) into the Soviet Union; it is a seedy, forlorn, half-awake land steeped in drunkenness where shadows from the past live on in a social and cultural vacuum. Technology and services are breaking down, but nobody seems to care; money has completely lost its value, a simple taxi-ride costing 5,000 złotys. The state controls not only information but time as well—nobody knows the exact date; it is a top state secret, and all calendars are falsified. Most people live in a near-somnambulistic state of complete apathy, although some kind of an Opposition still keeps functioning. It is this (officially tolerated) Opposition that orders the narrator of Konwicki's story, a writer like himself, to set himself on fire in the evening as a public protest against the latest political move of the regime. The plot is in fact a description of the narrator's last day in painstaking detail.

This gives an opportunity to Konwicki to go through most of the well-known motifs and gimmicks of his previous fiction. The hero awakes with a nasty hangover, has several meaningful encounters and less meaningful conversations, is interrogated by the secret police in the lavatory of a nightclub, makes love to a young Russian girl of unusual sex appeal, talks to disenchanted old Communists, meets his ex-girlfriends and gets ready for the final act of self-immolation. As always, Konwicki is very readable, but his perception of the future is strangely pessimistic: in fact, he seems to project certain depressing facts of contemporary Poland into the not-very-distant future, blowing them up to gigantic proportions. As for the West, one character claims that "we have demoralized the West . . . by our terrible example"—peaceful coexistence has produced creeping etatism and finally a Soviet-type mess in the West as well. In other words, this is the end of the road, at least for Konwicki's generation.

Mała apokalipsa is a cynical, wry, occasionally very funny book, but it is not the masterpiece that it was rumored to be in Polish intellectual circles. For one thing, there are too many in-jokes and wisecracks decipherable only to people who know what present-day Poland is like; also, for an anti-utopia, the construction of the book is too loose and haphazard. Or is this also a stratagem, a reflection of the unreality, sometimes the irreality, of a Poland tottering now forward, now backward on its tortuous path to Communism?

> George Gömöri, in a review of "Mała apokalipsa," in World Literature Today *(copyright 1980 by the University of Oklahoma Press), Vol. 54, No. 2, Spring, 1980, p. 307.*

EVA HOFFMAN

An Eastern European writer does not have to look far to find his subject. The subject, most often, chooses him. In Poland, the Second World War, the country's turbulent history, the conditions created by an artificially imposed and often intolerably oppressive system—these are the given, the almost inevitable, matters which an author must confront if he is to understand his own and his countrymen's condition. They are matters which have preoccupied—even obsessed—Tadeusz Konwicki, one of Poland's eminent and more difficult writers. In his previous novels, such as **"The Dreambook for Our Time,"** . . . he treated "the Polish question"—or "the Polish complex"—with gingerly indirectness, often through fragments of personal and veiled memories. [In **"The Polish Complex"**], he approaches it head on, with full philosophical steam and not an ounce of rage held back. The result is a novel that has the energy and the weaknesses of obsession—and that did not pass the Polish censors.

At times the novel comes close to being a tract. But it's a powerful tract—an impassioned, furious polemic on Poland's impossible condition. Konwicki, who continues to live in Poland, forgoes all the techniques of coding—allegory, symbolism, allusion—that Polish writers critical of the system have been forced to resort to. He writes like a man who has nothing to lose—and who wants to use that freedom for the primary and urgent task of speaking the raw, unmediated truth.

But **"The Polish Complex"** is also a comedy of manners. The entire present-time action takes place in that most ubiquitous of Polish institutions, the queue. This one has formed on the day before Christmas, in front of a Warsaw jewelry store where a shipment of gold rings from the Soviet Union is supposed to arrive. The queue is made up of a motley crew of ordinary citizens, most of them intent upon pulling off some small con in the perennial Polish game of outwitting the system. There's a woman who feigns old age to get a better place in line; another who, under her peasant garb, is wearing a caracul coat and who, from her shopping bag, unearths several legs of veal for sale; there's a Government "stoolie"; a vaguely opportunist student; and a French anarchist who has come to Poland because he wants to dedicate himself to the revolution—any revolution that might come along. The line also contains three more important characters: Tadeusz Konwicki, a well-known author and the novel's narrator; Kojran, the narrator's pursuer and shadow self, who during the war fought in the same partisan resistance organization and was supposed to carry out a death sentence imposed on Konwicki by his former comrades when he changed political allegiance; and Duszek, another stoolie and Kojran's pursuer, part of whose task, it is hinted, has been to torture Kojran, the old anti-Communist. Waiting in line, in this novel, means in one sense taking one's place in the chain of victimization and oppression.

In spite of such a divisive past and a fractious present, the customers achieve a kind of grudging, sardonic camaraderie. They make wisecracks, fight, taunt Konwicki for being a boring and a pessimistic writer; Duszek delivers himself of such maxims on the Polish character as "A Pole gets sleepy when he thinks," or "When a Pole complains, he feels better right away." The electricity in the store goes off; a group of Soviet tourists arrive and are allowed to barge in ahead of the others; instead of the gold rings, a shipment of Soviet samovars is delivered.

Konwicki treats these vignettes of the tawdry daily reality with a salty, intimate, shrewd, colloquial humor that is, unfortunately, almost untranslatable. It is a humor that he sees as intrinsic to Polishness: "In our country tragedy often walks hand in hand with buffoonery," he writes. "In this I see our strength. I love that ambiguous consanguinity, that risky symbiosis, that genius of a people enchanted in two directions."

The tragedy is given its due through essayistic set pieces in which Konwicki ruminates, sometimes with detachment, sometimes with impatience and a baffled desperation, on his own and his country's human condition. The narrator, who is feeling the symptoms of a heart attack, is beset by nagging guilts—perhaps for having participated in a fratricidal conflict between the Home Army partisans and the indigenous Communist guerrillas toward the end of World War II; perhaps for temporarily turning Communist and writing in the "socialist realism" mode. He's also, as he repeatedly says, "waiting for a miracle"—the miracle which would absolve him from this haunting past, would give him peace and a full understanding, would free him from the limitations of his own situation.

But the contradictions and conflicts of the narrator's psyche are not merely his own; they are a piece, an inseparable part, of his country's collective biography. At the center of the novel is a long historical reverie in which Konwicki imagines a young soldier who in 1863 leads a small regiment in a failed uprising against the Russians. The young man returns to his native Lithuania (where Konwicki himself was born) inspired with the idea of a reborn Poland: "Just, noble, intelligent. An example for all of Europe. An uprising begun with the blood of our finest sons." He is welcomed with expressions of fraternal love—and the news that the peasant division he was promised has wandered off. The ragtag crew he manages to gather instead disappears in its first absurd encounter with the equally terrified Russians on Insurrection Hill—where Konwicki himself will fight some 80 years later. (pp. 3, 16)

In making the young soldier's story central to the novel, Konwicki seems at first to accept one standard diagnosis—which is that Poland's tragedy has been caused by romanticism, by a deep-rooted, heedless, patriotic, individualistic love of independence and freedom. But after looking at this interpretation, Konwicki angrily rejects it. . . .

Any analysis of Poland's situation has to reckon with the proximity of [its] neighbors. They, at least as much as national character, have indeed been the country's fate—relentless, absolute and unjust. Against such forces, Konwicki can only raise an anguished cry. In one of the bitterest sections of the novel, thinly disguised as a letter about another country, he lashes out with Swiftian fury at a regime that "was on its last legs from the start. It was rotting, gurgling, disintegrating, moldering, rusting, choking, dying, and yet at the same time standing firmly on its feet, enduring due to the immense power of inertia, withstanding all storms, entrenched in bedrock by the weight of its own sins"—a regime that kills with boredom as well as with betrayals, and that has turned an entire country into a no-exit prison.

Novelistically, **"The Polish Complex"** is unfinished, full of loose ends, situations that go nowhere, characters only dimly realized. In the middle of the novel, Konwicki has a minor heart attack and then experiences something like a miracle when he makes love to a fey, sexy, mysterious salesgirl. But the scene is unconvincing. In this novel, politics is the immediate, primary reality, and it is the purely personal encounter that disrupts the action like a pistol shot.

The real miracle—for Poland as much as for Konwicki—doesn't come. As a philosophical inquiry, **"The Polish Complex"** is necessarily unresolved. (p. 16)

Eva Hoffman, "Keeping a Nation in Line," in The New York Times Book Review *(copyright © 1982 by The New York Times Company; reprinted by permission), January 10, 1982, pp. 3, 16.*

JAROSLAW ANDERS

[**The Polish Complex**] moves back and forth between historical episodes from the uprising of 1863—the most misguided and tragic of Polish insurgencies of the nineteenth century—and scenes from contemporary Polish life. The modern story brings together a mixed yet typical group of Poles from the early Seventies: disenchanted intellectuals, tired workers, police informers, con men, communist upstarts—all observed by the narrator and the main character, the Polish writer Tadeusz Konwicki. . . .

As the people gradually reveal their life stories—with Konwicki as their medium, their confessor, as well as an offstage commenting voice—it becomes clear that their failures and frustrations have deeper roots than the everyday hardships and humiliations of postwar Polish life. Most of them, like the narrator, Konwicki himself, are tormented by a real or irrational sense of guilt, by feelings of utter degradation and the wish for death. (p. 16)

Something went wrong in the lives of these people—a long time ago or just recently—something involving not only individuals but the Polish community. An act of betrayal was committed—Konwicki muses—yet no one wanted to be a betrayer. A destiny was sabotaged, yet no one was clear what the destiny was. What, then, is the real source of the agony of Konwicki's characters?

The answer can be found in the historical sections of the novel, as well as in the author's personal reflections which occur throughout the book in a seemingly random way.

The two historical sections of **The Polish Complex** set in the nineteenth century—almost self-contained short stories inserted into the novel—concern two heroes of the long struggle of independence against the Russian empire. One of them is Zygmunt Mineyko, the ill-fated young soldier who toward the end of the uprising of 1863 tries to organize partisan units in Lithuania. The other is Romuald Traugutt, a Polish patriot and a former officer in the Russian army, who is appointed the leader of the same uprising in its final, hopeless phase.

Both men throw themselves into the struggle when the chances for victory are practically nil. . . . Both heroes accept their destinies with courage and with resignation, as if obeying a historical compulsion that is darker and less comprehensible than the patriotic maxims they repeat. They cannot change their fate because they feel they are not only historical figures, but also phantoms from a dream that has been sustained from generation to generation by crushed, hopeless people like those passively waiting in front of the jewelry shop.

Trapped for centuries in a political deadlock, the Polish people have lived with a sense of thwarted ambitions and political failure. Since history itself provided little hope, their will to survive took an ahistorical, apolitical form—that of a romantic dream which could be boiled down to a myth of a unique spiritual "Polishness" and to something that Konwicki himself calls a "religion of freedom." This was the unshakable belief in an ultimate liberation and the fulfillment of national longings, past, present, and future, the promise of a final national redemption that will take place in an indefinite future or in some higher, metaphysical realm.

Like most religions, the Polish "religion of freedom" proved to be a source of astonishing moral power in times of crisis, yet it also created its own orthodoxy, bound its followers by an overwhelming sense of guilt, and demanded a constant ritual of sacrifice. Nowhere was its presence more clearly demonstrated than in the tradition of Polish insurgency. The "Romantic Uprisings"—a term used by Polish historians not only for the repeated attempts at liberation during the nineteenth century but also for the Warsaw uprising against the German occupiers in 1944—usually started as military ventures based on political calculations and a sense of attainable goals. Yet after the rebels ran up against the overwhelming force of the enemy or faced a political stalemate preventing them from reaching their goal, their struggles turned into rituals of sacrifice that served to transform physical defeat into moral victory, to create a legend that would take hold of future generations. What for dispassionate observers often looked like masochism or senseless acts of desperation was perceived by Poles as the only strategy of survival.

However, the romantic dream had also a negative side. Born of a sense of failure, it included failure as a part of its mythology. It marked bold political undertakings with a certain fatalism and extremism, and tended to undermine limited, yet realistic projects. After some time the sarcophagi of national symbols started to issue the poisons of hatred and frustration. The irresistible flood of the national will rushing against a wall of historical impossibility left behind the sour heat of wasted energy and inaction, with their sediment of memory.

The modern plot of *The Polish Complex* portrays this final phase of the Polish historical cycle. The characters gathered on Christmas Eve—for Poles especially a time of remembrance and hope—represent different forms of moral decomposition and failure. Yet at the same time these people seem the crippled children of such heroes as Mineyko and Traugutt. Their thoughts and drunken confessions recall the same romantic creed, debased and caricatured as they are, like the slogans about the uniqueness of the Polish character mouthed by Duszek or the blurred words "Honor and Fatherland"—the battle cry of Polish knighthood—that are tattooed on the arm of Kojran, who dreams now only about inheriting a gas station in America.

Hence, "was it worth it?"—the inevitable question uttered by Mineyko as he is taken to be executed—resounds in the contemporary story of *The Polish Complex*. Did the tradition of resistance and sacrifice confer upon the Poles special spiritual powers—as they themselves like to believe? Or is the Polish fate ". . . a fate which causes degeneration, like every misfortune, every calamity"? The group of people waiting for gold on a December night provides evidence for the sadder of these views. Yet was there any alternative that was overlooked or ignored?

The history presented in *The Polish Complex* has a quality of *déjà vu*. It is experienced as a cycle, repeating itself with a striking regularity. (pp. 16-17)

New actors come on stage to pick up the same, familiar script. The choice of roles is, as usual, a limited one: Martyr, Skeptic, Traitor. Such a disturbing vision of history poses the question of what ultimate human or metaphysical sense it may make. This question hovers over the events presented in *The Polish Complex*. And although no answer is finally given, Konwicki the writer persists in his search: "I write because in my subconscious there stirs a spark of hope that somewhere there is something, that something endures somewhere, that, in my last instant, Great Meaning will take notice of me and save me from a universe without meaning." So do people freezing in a Warsaw street. At the end of the book the line refuses to disperse even when it becomes clear that the gold rings will not be delivered. The pointless vigil becomes a symbol of the eternal Polish wake, a wait for a miracle of understanding and rebirth.

The problem with *The Polish Complex,* like that with most contemporary Polish writing, is that it is often cryptic. Konwicki himself calls it "writing on the blackened walls of a cell." Writing on prison walls is a compulsive activity, a desperate attempt at communication with invisible partners—the person who wrote on the wall before and the one who will come later. It is a code, a language reduced to symbols easily recognizable by those who share a similar experience, but an act of disdain toward those who were lucky enough to avoid it. "I am an individual who is not understood by his fellow men on the Tiber, the Seine, or the Hudson," says the author. (p. 17)

Such a presupposition—not uncommon among contemporary Polish writers—can unnecessarily hamper the clarity of their books. The prose of *The Polish Complex* is highly allusive. References to Konwicki's own life, and to Warsaw gossip about him, as well as to little-known facts of Polish history, may puzzle anyone who was not brought up on the banks of the Vistula. The characters appear as contours to be filled in with the stuff of the reader's own experience. Unfortunately, their vivid, saturated language, which in Polish suggests their social status, and sometimes their past, sounds somehow flat and unconvincing in English translation. Nevertheless, *The Polish Complex* is a powerful and engaging book, demonstrating how in the less fortunate parts of the world history becomes a private obsession, and how the collective subconscious can determine the fates of both individuals and nations. (pp. 17-18)

Jaroslaw Anders, "The Polish Wake," in The New York Review of Books *(reprinted with permission from* The New York Review of Books; *copyright © 1982 Nyrev, Inc.), Vol. XXIX, No. 3, March 4, 1982, pp. 16-18.*

JOHN UPDIKE

"The Polish Complex" is as zany as [Benedict Erofeev's] "Moscow Circles" and as intellectual as [Milan Kundera's] "The Joke." Konwicki, born near Wilno, which is now part of Soviet Lithuania, fought as a teen-age Partisan in 1944-45, and in his early writings supported the new Communist order. A screenwriter and director as well as a productive author, he until **"The Polish Complex"** expressed his disillusions obliquely enough not to rouse the censors. Here in this banned novel, which was published in the underground Polish press in 1977, he seems to express a personal crisis as well as political exasperation; the Konwicki persona drinks too many "binoculars" (two tall hundred-gram glasses of vodka), has chronic pain in his chest, suffers a heart attack, and while recovering from the attack in a back room copulates with a voluptuous shop attendant who calls him "old man." "I've been through it all," he tells her. "I have no curiosity left, my curiosity's exhausted, or actually, it was never satisfied and now nothing will satisfy it." He sees himself as "a miserable creature with emphysema of the soul." (pp. 131-32)

The texture of the present-day, ostensibly autobiographical passages is airy, startling, disjointed, and deft—somewhat like that of Raymond Queneau, if Queneau had been a less happy man. Konwicki enjoys that easy access to the surreal noticeable in Polish writers as disparate as Lem and Witold Gombrowicz and Bruno Schulz, as Jerzy Kosinski and I. B. Singer. But our attention scatters amid these tipsy incidents and arguments; it is in two extended historical fantasies that Konwicki shows his imaginative strength and brings the reader into the continuing Polish agony. The first, over fifty pages long, describes the attempt of a twenty-three-year-old soldier, Zygmunt Mineyko, to lead, under the name Colonel Maciej Borowy, a section of the uprising of 1863, one of a number of unsuccessful nationalist rebellions in the long century (1795-1918) when Poland didn't exist on the map, having been partitioned among its three large neighbors; the second historical episode, in a later time of troubles, shows another young man, with the name of Traugutt, saying goodbye to his wife in a hotel room before going off to accept "the leadership of the People's Government" in Warsaw—an assignment certain to cost him his life. No doubt both these doomed heroes are enshrined in the collective Polish memory; for any reader the sense of circumambient oppression, of futile daring, of terror and bravery amid the details of the daily are evoked with a masterly command of such sensory realities as the noises of drunken Russian officers in the adjoining hotel room and the singing sound of sand spinning from the wheels of a carriage. Of course, Communist writers have often sought breathing space in historical fiction, where dangerous contemporary issues can be avoided or disguised, and are at home there; nevertheless, the immediacy of these "old-fashioned" pieces of Konwicki's narrative oddly overpowers the whimsical, skittish rest. A sexy strain of imagery does link the Polish past and present: the desirable women all savor of grass and herbs. Colonel Borowy admires a young wife whose eyes "shimmered with the colors of moss and heather" and whose scent is mingled of "sleep, lovage herb, and impetuous love." Traugutt's wife "gave up her warm cloak, which smelled of heather" and, when further undressed, "her damp sweat . . . smelled like herbs." And our aging author joins these warriors whose "sweetheart [was] Poland, golden-haired Poland" when, rather ignominiously couched with his shop assistant, he finds "she smelled like the wild herbs of the earth." An earth that, in the Polish complex, floats underfoot, not quite possessed, parcelled out, dominated historically and now by others.

Estrangement—from earth, sky, and the ruling powers in between—is not absent from Western contemporary literature, either, and there is no assurance that under a capitalist system Erofeev would drink less, Ludvik [the protagonist of "The Joke"] would find it easier to locate what he calls "final beauty," or Konwicki would be spared the discomforts of turning fifty. Yet all three books have been outlawed in their respective homelands, and therefore must contain words judged dangerous by the authorities. The absurd cowering by Communist governments in the face of honest and questing art is one of the wonders of the world, a fertile source of embarrassment to its enforcers and an apparent declaration of bad faith; for from such fear of the truth we can only deduce a power that believes itself to be based upon lies. (p. 132)

> *John Updike, "How the Other Half Lives" (© 1983 by John Updike), in* The New Yorker, *Vol. LIX, No. 1, February 21, 1983, pp. 126, 129-32.*

DAVID J. LEIGH, S.J.

Like Milan Kundera, the Czech novelist and critic, Konwicki has gained the attention and support of American writers like Updike and Roth for his mixture of satire, surrealism, humor, and political complexity. Despite some lapses into sentimentality and verbosity, [*A Minor Apocalypse*] shows Konwicki at his best and provides evidence of his potential for moving from the Italian Mondello Prize to greater achievements. Only his lofty popular status and the inner conflicts of the present regime seem to protect him from reprisals for his open flaunting of the communist bungling of Poland in the 1970's.

A Minor Apocalypse, composed in 1979 after the collapse of Gierek's bourgeois-socialist government, suggests why Solidarity could have risen (and as quickly fallen under the Soviet axe). The story involves a Kafkaesque hero who is told by his fellow dissident authors that he has been chosen to immolate himself that very day during a visit by the Soviet secretary to the Palace of Culture in Warsaw. In his journey around the city on his last day, the narrator encounters all the contradictory elements of Polish society—the bumbling secret police, the lapsed communists, the ambitious worker-leaders, the collaborators and dissidents, the film makers and writers, all except, oddly, the Church leaders (with only a naive but sinister young priest appearing near the end). As the narrator threads his way through these Fellini-like crowds (some from the present, others from the past), he carries on a Joycean monologue amidst the witty encounters. In this monologue, we learn of Konwicki's ambivalence about every potential for change in Poland today. The government, he learns on television, is about to offer to join the Soviet Union; the writers and film makers are either covering up a guilty past or secretly collaborating with the Party; the workers and middle-class are easily misled by power or pleasure. Even the hero himself succumbs to the sentimentality of a last minute fling of therapeutic sex with a Russian woman named Hope. He is also constantly confessing his own ambiguous motives and ends with an ersatz revelation that the only 'god' is the People.

Yet the novel fascinates the reader in the way that Orwell's *1984*, with all its flaws, fascinates. It combines the surrealistic detail of a dream with the repartee and reflection of a novel of ideas. It embraces the narrator's favorite card tricks along with his opinions on physics and philosophy. It reads in places like Dante's *Inferno*, in others like a minor league *Ulysses*. The combination of irony, disillusionment, sentiment, and Hope suggests that the contradictions of the novel are those of the Polish soul in the twentieth century. (pp. 198-99)

> *David J. Leigh, S.J., in a review of "A Minor Apocalypse," in* Best Sellers *(copyright © 1983 Helen Dwight Reid Educational Foundation), Vol. 43, No. 6, September, 1983, pp. 198-99.*

Richard (Cory) Kostelanetz
1940-

American poet, essayist, literary critic, editor, short story writer, and novelist.

Kostelanetz is one of the major supporters of avant-garde literature written during the past twenty years. His *oeuvre* consists of nontraditional creative writing in nearly every literary genre, and he also promotes and encourages young experimental artists. Kostelanetz describes these writers as "fictioneers" and has devoted several anthologies, including *The Young American Writers: Fiction, Poetry, Drama, and Criticism* (1967) and *Breakthrough Fictioneers* (1973), to their work. As an experimentalist, Kostelanetz is best known for his "visual poetry," a concept which combines elements of poetry and painting. His poems in *Visual Language* (1967) and *I Articulations* (1974) often contain the repetition of one letter or word accompanied by graphic design.

Kostelanetz's work has earned him a prominent position in small press publications. However, his reputation in mainstream literary circles is not nearly so well established, for it rests almost entirely on *The End of Intelligent Writing: Literary Politics in America* (1974). In this book Kostelanetz discusses what he perceives as a conspiracy against experimental artists by established literary groups. Although most critics dismissed this book, some applauded Kostelanetz for his insight on the state of present-day literature and publishing.

(See also *Contemporary Authors*, Vols. 13-16, rev. ed.)

Photograph by J. Nebraska Gifford; courtesy of Richard Kostelanetz

GRANVILLE HICKS

Richard Kostelanetz, a young critic who is acutely conscious of both his youth and his critical responsibilities, has edited a volume called *Young American Writers*. . . . As some of the young politicians do, he distrusts everyone who is over thirty, and therefore he has included only authors born after 1936. As it happens, several of his best writers were born in 1937, and it must grieve him to feel that within the next twelve months they will be lost to the cause. Indeed, Kostelanetz himself has only three years to go.

Older artists are always conscious of the hungry generations that come along to tread them down, but nowadays they come faster and faster. "American writers born 1937 and after," Kostelanetz says, "comprise the third literary generation of the postwar period." First there were such writers as Norman Mailer, Gore Vidal, James Jones, and John Aldridge. The second generation, which was "thoroughly disorganized," included LeRoi Jones, Philip Roth, Susan Sontag, John Updike, John Barth, and others. The third group, to which Kostelanetz devotes this volume, seems to him "a talented generation, more thoroughly educated and culturally sophisticated than earlier chronological sets; and although we are hardly cautious, the mistakes of our elders, particularly their vulgarisms, oppress us." Although he complains that most of the younger writers are neglected, he takes consolation in the fact that "by 1972 one-half of the voting population will be under thirty-two . . . the future is very much ours." But by that time Mr. Kostelanetz will belong to the unhappy minority.

It is interesting to note that four of Kostelanetz's writers have not been ignored but have a respectable record of publication: [Jerome Charyn, Joyce Carol Oates, Heather Ross Miller, and William Melvin Kelley]. . . . It may be heresy to say so, but I think that these four are the best writers represented in the book, and I will add that, of the stories by the others, there are only two or three that seem to me to have cried out for publication.

"In the literature itself," Kostelanetz says, "no theme seems as pervasive as the discontinuity of experience—the unwillingness of the writer to make what he portrays fall together into the neat linear patterns of traditional literature." He goes on: "Discontinuity, one hastens to add, does not mean incoherence." Not necessarily, I would say, but often. Awareness of the discontinuity of experience is not new, nor is the attempt to make literary use of it. T. S. Eliot, who must, by Kostelanetz's reckoning, belong to the ninth generation back, relied heavily upon it in his early work, and E. E. Cummings, who was presumably of the eighth generation, devoted his life to raising hell with "neat linear patterns." It is true that their work seemed incoherent to many of their contemporaries, yet for several decades the continuity underlying the discontinuity has been obvious. Perhaps some of the writers Kostelanetz includes will eventually emerge in the same sort of triumph. However, there are only two or three about whom I feel hopeful—Eric Felderman, for example, Kenneth Gangemi, and maybe Arno Karlen....

The poets are also much possessed with discontinuity, as many poets have been in the past. Several of them seem to me largely or even completely unintelligible. Experience warns me that the fault may be mine, but not necessarily. There are some poems that justify the effort they demand, but not many. (p. 25)

Certainly [Kostelanetz] is right about the rapidity of change, but it does not follow that the new is the better. Moreover, I should think that serious young writers, including Kostelanetz, would be disheartened by the prospect of being obsolete day after tomorrow. (p. 26)

> Granville Hicks, "Obsolete at Thirty," in Saturday Review (© 1967 Saturday Review Magazine Co.; reprinted by permission), Vol. L, No. 48, December 2, 1967, pp. 25-6.

MARGUERITE McANENY

Richard Kostelanetz, who edited *The New American Arts*..., has also written or edited several other books on literature and the arts. In [*The Theatre of Mixed Means*] he defines "mixed means" as various noises and sights—people shuffling along the street, electronic beams, even the noise of many butterflies being released from a bag—which constitute a special kind of theater when these accompany some sort of dramatic happening, no matter where it may be presented, in a street, field, hall, or theater.... The mixed means Mr. Kostelanetz describes are often used, or are happening, at the same time as the plot (if there is one), apparently distracting the audience. The modern mind seems to need to be splintered in many artistic directions at once in order to feel involved. To an old theatergoer who wants to find some meaning in a dramatic action that has a beginning, middle, and end, mixed means may not seem to be theatre at all, but another form of art. This question is among the many Mr. Kostelanetz discusses with practitioners of this new art: composers, dancers, poets, sculptors, and others.... For those with open minds about what "theater" means, this book is instructive and interesting. (pp. 1497-98)

> Marguerite McAneny, in a review of "The Theatre of Mixed Means: An Introduction to Happenings, Kinetic Environments and Other Mixed Means Performances," in Library Journal (reprinted from Library Journal, April 1, 1968; published by R. R. Bowker Co. (a Xerox company); copyright © 1968 by Xerox Corporation), Vol. 93, No. 7, April 1, 1968, pp. 1497-98.

L. J. DAVIS

Richard Kostelanetz introduces his new anthology of so-called innovative writing, **"Breakthrough Fictioneers,"** with a long, peevish preface, the gist of which is (if I read it correctly) that fiction is pretty much anything he says it is, and the only valid innovation in it is going to follow, more or less, the lines laid down between these covers. This bold statement is accompanied by the usual *pro forma* assault on the blindness of the critics and editors of the world, and is footnoted by the rather astonishing statement that if James Joyce were alive and writing today, he couldn't get "Ulysses" published in a month of Sundays. One might be more inclined to indulge the point if only the writers Mr. Kostelanetz had selected were somewhat better at their jobs than they are.

The book—hectoringly punctuated by quotations from academic theorists who happen to agree with the editor, rather as if his craving were for Establishment legitimacy rather than artistic freedom—is a kind of cross between a lobotomy, a college literary magazine and a joke book. The selections are relentlessly minor. There are no names to conjure with here, no writing that makes you either want to stand up and cheer or denounce from the nearest soapbox. The strongest emotions that I experienced were, on the one hand, a fleeting smile, and, on the other, a barely audible sigh. (p. 49)

> L. J. Davis, "Two Novels, an Anthology and an Alphabet," in The New York Times Book Review (copyright © 1973 by The New York Times Company; reprinted by permission), October 21, 1973, pp. 48-9.*

THOMAS POWERS

After a solid week of reading Richard Kostelanetz's long book about literary politicking [*The End of Intelligent Writing*], I got a bright idea of how to proceed with this review: I would start by describing "the New York literary mob," the familiar oracles of *Commentary* and *The New York Review of Books*. I would list (per Kostelanetz) their alleged abuses of literary power—log-rolling, back-scratching, puffing, touting, "white-collar mugging." Then I would consider whether there really are interlocking literary establishments that control writers' grants, fellowships, academic appointments, concluding that the answer had to be yes and no—"yes," there are constellations of writers and critics with similar attitudes and interests who write for and about each other, but "no," this likemindedness is neither corrupt nor conspiratorial.

But in any case, I would ask, what is really at stake? Which writers does Kostelanetz think have been frozen out of the literary marketplace?

And then I would quote something like the following passage from Toby MacLennan's "I Walked out of 2 and Forgot it," which Kostelanetz cites for its originality:

> He was bombarded by various memories. An
> A and an Of, the toe of a shoe, a half of an
> apple. That night as he sat down for dinner, a
> stone dropped out of his ear.

Or, perhaps, the following passage from Armand Schwerner's poem, "The Tablets," which Kostelanetz admires for its musical qulities:

> min-na-ne-ne Dingir En-lil-ra
> mun-na-nob-gi-gi
> uzu-mu-a-ki dur-an-ki-ge
> Dingir nagar Dingir nagar
> im-man-tag-en-zen
> mu-mud-e-ne nam-lu-galu
> mu-mu-e-ed

And then I would express amazed disbelief: This is the new literature Kostelanetz is worried about? This is what the New York literary mob is suppressing? This is what "our children will study with respect"?

The trouble with this approach, so appealing for low reasons, is that it unfairly ignores Kostelanetz's fine passion for writing, the strength of his case for the existence of a cultural conservatism very like (if in the end not) a conspiracy and the problem of what to make of the work of Toby MacLennan and Armand

Schwerner. His defense of their experimentalism is really the heart of his book; it's what makes the first 300 pages of socio-politico-literary polemic worth paying attention to. What Kostelanetz likes and defends is elusive to say the least, but it ought not to be dismissed out of hand.

In one of his many illuminating asides, he points out the way established critics make fun of experimental writers as if they, the critics, were the neglected, mistreated minority, when of course it is quite the other way around. (p. 97)

Still, I can't help feeling grateful that *Commentary* and *The New York Review* are at the gates, defending future generations of college freshmen from one-hour essay questions on stone symbolism in "I Walked out of 2." Kostelanetz cites 836 poets, playwrights, essayists, and "fictioners," all born since 1937, whom he considers to be the embryonic giants of the age. This makes me feel, as it does the New York literary mob, that the dams are about to burst, that literature of the heart and mind is about to be drowned by a formalist, experimental, manufactured literature of the head. So Kostelanetz is right, and something of importance is at stake.

The New York literary mob's conspiracy to keep "the young and the new" unknown and neglected is described by Kostelanetz as being of the informal sort in which no one has to mention the rules to guarantee that no one breaks them. The mob members, despite the occasional family squabble, share a common ground in their interests and intellectual style. They are passionate about politics and are well-grounded in Marx and Freud. They hold important professorial posts in and around New York; frequently publish their books with Random House, Pantheon, or Alfred Knopf; can be fiercely polemical when they see Western civilization in the balance, which is often; fight dirty; defend each other against "outsiders"; distribute such patronage as they have to their "own"; admire Saul Bellow, Robert Lowell, and Philip Roth; think modernism shot its bolt by the second world war, and are getting old.

From their positions of power as professors, editors, publishers, and writers they exert a broad if informal influence over the life of literature in America, inflating the reputations of their friends and freezing out strangers. The result, Kostelanetz says, is that the "channels of communication" between writers and readers are "clogged" and "corrupted." Old writers are overpraised and new writers ignored. Tired styles and stale controversies linger on after their time. Second-raters get promoted by their patrons and intellectual lassitude settles over literature as the giants of one age mistake their own inevitable decay for a general decline.

There is much truth in this. It is too hard for young writers to get published, and the fate of their work is too arbitrary. Reviewing is brutal and capricious. Good books get lost and bad books get more notice than they deserve. Big names get too much attention and newcomers too little. The protégés of established writers, and especially of established writers who are members of established groups, coteries, and movements, get preferential treatment. (pp. 97-8)

Perhaps Kostelanetz is right and the young writers he admires don't get into anthologies, or get reviewed, or receive academic appointments, or win grants because of the New York lit mob's indifference or opposition. The mobsters are, after all, an influential group. Kostelanetz is right to call all that politicking, right to think it is unfair, but wrong to think it much matters. The only thing outside a writer's control that makes a real difference is primary publication; all the rest is hurt feelings.

To prove a conspiracy that matters Kostelanetz must demonstrate that the mob is denying young writers publication, and this he does not do.

What he does instead is to argue that "puffing," "touting," and politicking account for Saul Bellow's literary reputation. A certain shrillness enters his voice whenever he mentions Bellow, which is often. . . . "The process of inflating his [Bellow's] reputation, as we shall see, reflected not rare critical judgment but the more common techniques of American advertising and publicity." But we do not see; or at least I don't.

Kostelanetz cites all the favorable reviews of Bellow's early novels, the interest in his career taken by certain mob critics (e.g., Lionel Trilling), and his sudden promotion to Major American Novelist with the publication of *The Adventures of Augie March*. . . . He talks about everything, in fact, except Bellow as a writer. He searches for a hidden explanation of Bellow's success and ignores the one that is most obvious.

Why are some writers "puffed" and "touted"? Kostelanetz does not examine this question, which seems to me to be at the root of the interconnectedness that alarms him. Actually, it is the same as asking why Henry James admired (and "touted") Flaubert; or Fitzgerald, Hemingway; or Roth, Lelchuk. These affinities are at the heart of literature. Writers should not have to divest themselves of their intellectual and artistic allegiances, like a banker putting his stocks into a blind trust before accepting a public appointment. If people did not have common interests, were not concerned with common questions, did not pursue common inquiries, or experiment with common styles, there would be no point in writing, or reading. Why does the New York literary mob "tout" Saul Bellow? *Because the mobsters think he's a good writer*.

Kostelanetz apparently does not. What we have here is a difference of critical opinion, not a political struggle. . . . Bellow's world does not like Kostelanetz's post-modernist experimentalism for the best and most innocent of reasons; it is alien to their experience, their sensibility, their whole intellectual style. No conspiracy is necessary to unite them in opposition; they do it instinctively. It's clear that Bellow is not a pioneer like Proust or Joyce, but his virtues are still real, and they are his own. This sort of argument only makes Kostelanetz impatient. When literature begins to look like something he's already seen he wants to chuck it out and bring in the new champions, with their weird instruments and strange music. He wants a Joyce every decade, a Renaissance twice a century, "unending innovation," a constant literary ferment something like Trotsky's permanent revolution. In effect, he wants youth to last forever. He loves the new and the different for their own sakes and does not seem at all inclined to ask what it all adds up to. (pp. 98-100)

The experiments described by Kostelanetz are endless: "novels" printed on unnumbered and interchangeable pages, "stories" that are supposed to be cut out and pasted together, "poems" that consist of a single word endlessly repeated, or the names of national parks, or sentences in which verbs and nouns are interchanged. Kostelanetz's appetite for their inventiveness (which strikes me as nervous and distracted, the restlessness of minds out of touch with their own experience) is unlimited: he has read thousands of such works and seems to admire them all, which is nice, even generous to a fault, but not exactly what we expect from a critic. He has failed to explain to me what it is that these people are doing or why I ought to make it part of my life and care about it.

This all sounds more negative than I feel. Kostelanetz is a witty, committed, engaging writer. He is not meanspirited (except where Bellow is concerned). He is tireless, informed, and often perceptive. He wants to further the cause of literature and encourage all those young writers who live a long way from and don't know how to approach the centers of literary power. It seems to me that anyone interested in literature, or in the practical business of writing, or in the creative crisis of artists to whom nothing is forbidden, ought to read his book. In *Catcher in the Rye,* Holden Caulfield says he doesn't really like a book unless it makes him feel like calling up the author. That's the way I feel about Kostelanetz; I'd like to spend all night talking with him. If I were insistent enough perhaps then he would tell me what the experimenters are doing. But until he does I will think he has missed the heart of literature. (pp. 100-01)

> Thomas Powers, "A Conspiracy of Good Taste," in Harper's *(copyright © 1974 by Harper's Magazine; all rights reserved; reprinted from the November, 1974 issue by special permission),* Vol. 249, No. 1494, November, 1974, pp. 97-101.

ROGER SALE

"The End of Intelligent Writing" isn't about that, and isn't itself as intelligently written as it could and should have been. Many will say the title should have been "Richard Kostelenetz, His Enemies and Friends," and while they would be wrong, Kostelanetz has let himself in for it. He spends the first half of the book on his enemies—he takes Jason Epstein and The New York Review of Books to be the centers of power in literary-political America, and he works from there, identifying establishments here and in-groups there. He offers his list of those who count, one that is accurate enough, one supposes, but boringly rude, and not as much news as Kostelanetz himself thinks. The second half is about his friends, the young writers who have been excluded, and he offers a list of these too, to which he attaches this caveat: "Any 'critic of contemporary writing' who cannot identify works by fifteen per cent of these should, perforce, retire into the Academy to lecture on people and periods already past."

Conveniently, my name is not on the first list, and, while I spotted more than a quarter of the young writers in two of Kostelanetz's categories, my total number of recognitions qualifies me only for the job I already have, lecturer on people and periods already past. Inconveniently, almost anything I can say about this book will be taken simply as symptomatic of my illness. Late in the proceedings we are told: "The time for cordial chatter is past. If you're not contributing to the solution, you must be part of the problem." Yes, oh dear me yes, I must be, but I'm thankful, too, that I don't think that way. (p. 12)

Kostelanetz's recital of the sins of his powerful elders, which is probably what this book will become noted for, just isn't news. His own epigraphs show similar conditions operating in earlier days. As people get older, in my experience, they grow more capable of personal sympathy and generosity, but they become less willing to grub about in unlikely places for whatever is brand new and less responsive to the programs of the young. It may be that past a certain age the process is reversed; I don't know. But these truths are close enough to being universal. Thus someone like Kostelanetz, who is interested in supporting what he takes to be radically new writing, should not be surprised when those within some establishment are less eager than he to become radicals.

The second half of **"The End of Intelligent Writing"** is much less feisty, and I found it much better. It is a rough road map of young writers, especially those Kostelanetz admires, and I'm glad he wrote it. He likes the poetry of Clark Coolidge, who seeks to have a reader's "mind turned back towards the unitary experience of words as structure,"—a clause both Kostelanetz and I can rejoice in, but one that I find incomprehensible. Twice he refers to Eugene Wildman's 1969 collection, "Experiments in Prose," as "path-breaking," though for me it opened a path not taken. He likes visual poetry, and gives examples I find mostly inconsequential. But Kostelanetz does not stop here. He recognizes that not all work of the kind he admires is equally good and offers tips as to the best. Since I more than once have found myself rejecting something because it was new, only later to find that familiarity bred appreciation, I'm glad to have his recommendations. He also is interested in all young writers, however "conventional" or "esthetically conservative," to use his most contemptuous phrases, and he writes with intelligent care about those whose persuasions are different from his own. There is, in other words, a mine of information in the second half of this book, and once one gets clear those whom Kostelanetz will speak of with highest praise, and why, one can learn a lot from it.

But "esthetically conservative" is a term Kostelanetz would eschew if he did not need it so much. It makes politics out of art, judgments based on kinds rather than individual cases. Worse, it hides a truth at least as deep as those Kostelanetz knows—that, among the hundreds of "esthetically conservative" works published every year, there are some, perhaps many, that never receive the attention they deserve. There are many reasons for this, but it is sad nonetheless, and one must therefore constantly be speaking up for those books one admires. I am entirely with Kostelanetz in believing that Philip Roth and John Updike and Norman Mailer are not now writing the best novels being written by Americans. I also know that in many American universities certain books, like Ken Kesey's "One Flew Over the Cuckoo's Nest," Kurt Vonnegut's "Slaughterhouse Five," James Dickey's "Deliverance," are constantly assigned on the ground that the kids like such books, and that is a practice, and a choice of books, which gains no support from the New York establishment, or Kostelanetz, or me.

In the last six months I've read new novels, by Frederick Buechner, Thomas Savage, James Welch, and Maureen Howard, all of which are "conventional," and better than those mentioned above and those of Kostelanetz's list of "masterpieces" that I've seen. All will gain some praise and fame, none enough, either in the classroom or among Kostelanetz's young. I wish it were otherwise, but none of us made the world, especially a world as hugely and as often mindlessly productive as ours. All the more reason to be intelligent and careful and sensible, in ways Richard Kostelanetz has not yet been. (p. 16)

> Roger Sale, in a review of "The End of Intelligent Writing: Literary Politics in America," in The New York Times Book Review *(copyright © 1974 by The New York Times Company; reprinted by permission),* December 29, 1974, pp. 12, 16.

WELCH D. EVERMAN

A book is a possibility for action. Like a musical score, it does not exist until it is performed by a reader, and, of course, some texts are more difficult to perform than others.

Mr. Kostelanetz's unique and fascinating **Recyclings,** apparently composed from earlier essays by aleatory techniques, are as difficult to review as they are to perform. In these pieces, the reader must come to terms not with plot, character, theme, or idea, but with words in themselves, devoid of connection, syntax, and guidelines. Performance is controlled by the printed page but remains infinite in interpretation, for the elements of these important texts are simply what they are: words as openness, words as freedom, words as possibility, words as words, offered up by Kostelanetz, and free and open to the play of thought. The **Recyclings** then are words in their purest form, and they are well worth the efforts of performance.

> *Welch D. Everman, in a review of "Recyclings: A Literary Autobiography Volume One 1959-67," in* Small Press Review *(© 1975 by Dustbooks), Vol. 7, No. 3, April, 1975, p. 6.*

JOHN W. ALDRIDGE

There are several remarkable features of Mr. Kostelanetz's discussion [in *The End of Intelligent Writing*], one of which is that he should find the situation he describes so terribly shocking. However vigorously we may deplore the fact, it is simply in the nature of literary groups in all times and places that they will protect and promote their own and, with one degree or another of malevolent calculation, will exclude or ignore those who are not their own. This may not be a desirable state of affairs, but it is the usual one, and reasons for it are not difficult to discover. Since as a rule the members of a literary group initially come together as a beleaguered minority fighting to be heard against the opposition of whatever establishment may be in power, they tend to go on regarding themselves as a beleaguered minority long after they have become a persecuting majority. In the course of achieving power they also inevitably come to understand the politics of power, just how necessary it is to their collective survival that they support one another individually, if only because no one outside the group can be counted on to give them support. It often happens that with the passage of time and the accretion of influence, political considerations come to outweigh and even eclipse intellectual and artistic considerations, and power for its own sake becomes the sole, if unacknowledged object of the group's existence. But whether or not they evolve to the final phase of total tyranny, all literary groups must achieve a certain measure of power, and they must use it discriminatorily—to protect and advance their own members to the exclusion of others and, in so doing, increase still further the power of the collective.

Historical precedents for this kind of activity are virtually unlimited. For as long as literature has existed writers have promoted one another and not always for purely esthetic reasons. The furtherance of self-interest, dedication to the cause of a movement, the desire to publicize the writing of a particular ethnic group or locale or even of an entire literary generation have all been strongly operative motives behind the advancement of certain writers over others, and have often determined which writers will survive long enough to be discovered by posterity and which will be forgotten completely. Highly organized self- and group-promotion had a very great deal to do with the rise to prominence of such literary cabals as the Bloomsbury group, the Paris expatriates, and more recently the New Critics, the San Francisco Beat writers, the Black Mountain poets, and of course the present New York literary establishment. (pp. 347-48)

In view of all this, one cannot help finding it remarkable that Mr. Kostelanetz would want to be allowed entry into such a sinkhole of chicanery, yet he clearly does. He even confesses that one of his compelling motivations for writing his book was resentment at being snubbed by the New York establishment. But he then proceeds to call on his young literary contemporaries who have been similarly snubbed to rise up, band together, and form another establishment, a new cabal of young talent, from which, presumably, they will have the pleasure of snubbing all writers older than thirty-five. It would seem, therefore, that like the people he attacks, Mr. Kostelanetz is dying to have power and prestige, even if he lacks the stomach for the kind of politicking currently required to obtain them. One might well admire him for this and even be tempted to join him in exhorting his generation to the barricades. But then at just the moment when he seems on the verge of winning his case, Mr. Kostelanetz destroys it calamitously and completely. He manages to do this with all earnestness and in the midst of a stalwart crusade for what would seem the most exemplary of causes. He generously appeals for recognition for the literary efforts of his contemporaries, and he does so on the ground that they represent brilliantly original work so revolutionary in form and concept that, if the establishment were not so repressive, they would surely be recognized as constituting a vital new literature. He then offers some examples of this literature, and they are so unbelievably bad, so pretentious, and so derivative of all the out-moded styles of antique modernist experimentation—Dadaism, Surrealism, Imagism, Vorticism—that one almost supposes that Mr. Kostelanetz is putting us on. But no, unfortunately he is not. (pp. 349-50)

Such experiments, when undertaken for the first time by modernist pioneers like Tristan Tzara, Francis Picabia, and Alfred Jarry during and after World War I, had their importance because they were genuine radical and innovative, and they helped to prepare the way for the revolutionary literary movement which gave us Pound, Joyce, Eliot, Cummings, and the other great writers who now constitute the modernist canon. But the only justification for an avant-garde in any of the arts is that it is truly *in advance* and represents the exploration of new modes of consciousness along with new techniques for expressing them. If it merely resembles in style and concept the formerly revolutionary effects of a past era—as Mr. Kostelanetz's avant-garde appears to do—then it is only an empty recapitulation of what has been done before and done to some meaningful purpose because done for the first time.

The problem today is that the classic modern avant-garde literature of those early years has been thoroughly institutionalized both by criticism and by university English departments. We are schooled in its characteristic effects beyond the point of intellectual surfeit and have absorbed them into our literature very much in the way that the once-radical effects of modern painting have been absorbed and finally homogenized into the stylistic cliches of decor modernism. When artists now seek to be innovative, they tend to imitate the innovative techniques of the past just because the possible choices that were first identified at the beginning of our era all seem to have been explored by the artists who had the immense good fortune to be alive at the beginning of our era.

This is clearly a serious dilemma for young artists of the present time, and in their struggles to break out of it, they deserve all the sympathy they can get. If they ultimately succeed in discovering a new consciousness and new forms for its expression, then they will eventually win an audience and a reputation—traditionally by slow degrees and through the kind of little magazines that first provided the early modernists with a channel of publication. But Mr. Kostelanetz concedes that his generation of writers have been disinclined to develop themselves through little magazines and, children of instant celebrity that they are, seem primarily interested in "making it" in the Big Time. If that is the case, there is a clear option open to them. They can learn to play the kind of politics Mr. Kostelanetz so despises and finally ingratiate themselves with the establishment, so that one day they will be invited to write for *The New York Review of Books*. As they grow older, they will come to realize the importance of sticking together and helping one another get ahead, and of course they will make very certain that no one younger than themselves is allowed into their circle—unless he has the proper respect for his elders and can be counted on to do exactly as he is told. (pp. 351-52)

>John W. Aldridge, "Unmaking It: The Politics of Literary Failure," in Michigan Quarterly Review (copyright © The University of Michigan, 1975), Vol. XIV, No. 3, Summer, 1975, pp. 346-52.

CHARLES MOLESWORTH

What a sour book [*The End of Intelligent Writing*] is—no allowance made for its "heroic" attack on entrenched elites, or its wide-eyed support of the new and the young, or its implacable earnestness will alter this central fact, and the reader will leave it frazzled and stale.... Granted that paranoia and apocalypse currently serve to authenticate artistic believeability, Kostelanetz' network of sinister, aging moguls ... are hard to recognize in their desperate power game, hell bent on conspiratorially censoring Jonathan Cott, Madeline Gins, and Clark Coolidge, thereby assuring that "serious new and young writers are publicly dead." There are, to be sure, more villains in the cast than this, and more putative heroes as well, but the outlines of the struggle are cast in such melodramatic cliches that many will find it hard to take the argument seriously. Some of the book—the chapter on the fortunes of once-quality publishers, their conglomerate godfathers, and the decline in serious fiction, for example—make tough sense and important journalism, but the bulk of its polemic sinks into whining puerility and banal repetition. (p. 107)

[The book's] fundamental errors are several, but chief among them are three: [Kostelanetz'] misunderstanding of audience, his lack of a broad historical sense, and his economic naivete. First, if Kostelanetz taught for a year in a typical American college and saw a cross-section of students struggling to comprehend even the *New York Times,* his sanguine appraisal of this nation's literacy might well be challenged. (I assume it is safe to say the literacy of the entire population falls somewhat below that of college students.) Most publishers, despite their boundless cynicism, are right in supposing that the audience for quality literature is small and virtually confined to practitioners and near-practitioners of the arts themselves. If the typical college graduate resists buying *Gravity's Rainbow* in favor of *Airport,* how can we suppose he or she will soon appreciate Clark Coolidge's concrete poems if only the *New York Times* would review them? Literature simply doesn't stand out as a "growth industry," especially in the more refined forms of concrete poems, though kitsch best sellers keep the bubble afloat. Literary texts of any degree of complexity daunt the vast majority of people in this country; the reasons for this are many and depressingly deep-rooted, and it won't do to pretend the situation is other than it is or easily altered.

Secondly, Kostelanetz' book is itself an example of the appalling tunnel-vision of the American literary scene. Any brief examination of the current state of affairs in other countries, or the history of bookselling in, say, seventeenth or eighteenth century London will show the conditions he describes are hardly endemic to America or solely the result of a network of New York literary "mobsters." No cultural establishment has ever been willing to spend but a minimal fraction of its resources on ensuring the promotion of new talent.... Publishing is not, and never has been, a democratic enterprise (one is reduced to truisms in responding to an argument as wrong-headed as Kostelanetz'), and only in America could someone feel outraged at the supposed injustice and patent inequality that results when people seek to make a profit or advance their views over others, as if equality were something you should be able to buy in the supermarket. No state, not even America, actively supports a pluralistic society; they merely tolerate it.

Which brings us to the third of Kostelanetz' weaknesses: his sense that somehow "alternative" publishing could be made profitable and hence conducive to intelligent writing.... Publishing in America mimics the structure and mores of advanced capitalism.... Kostelanetz, though sporadically aware of much of this, dreamily persists in seeing it primarily as the result of "bad will," as if editors and agents *could* escape the debilitating tentacles of the profit system but choose not to, just to taunt the young, talented writer. He envisions a "stronger, more populist distributional network," with writers publishing their own work and that of their friends, buying from each other and returning all profits to new enterprises and promising talent.... In other words, Kostelanetz wants the already existing alternative forms of little magazines, small presses, and "underground" and specialty bookstores to seize control of the larger system. I have often heard myself described as a fuzzy-headed utopian socialist, but even I blushed to read these final chapters. (pp. 110-12)

Kostelanetz' view of literature is essentially one of liberal, reformist capitalism. This view insists new markets can "rejuvenate" a dying system; distribution and packaging are key elements, it claims, not epiphenomena, and their renewal can alter the course of development. At one point, Kostelanetz glibly dismisses Herbert Marcuse as a second-class thinker, but he would do well to re-examine the notion of repressive tolerance, despite his passing rejection of it as "demonstrably untrue." For what we end with in Kostelanetz is the falsest of challenges to a system all too unignorably true. People of talent are stunted or exploited, while people of ambition inflate their own and the egos and reputations of others, and a confused "public" is badgered by a thousand spokesmen and faddists and practitioners of universal brotherhood all trying to shape taste and influence history. This unfortunately remains true in the "fields" of academic learning, pop music, pharmaceutical sales, high fashion designing, and women's liberation, as well, all fields that reflect in exaggerated and distorted ways the structure and mores of monopoly capitalism. And truly fundamental changes in each of these fields are possible only if the basic social relations are altered, and such alterations are seldom, if ever, merely the result of good faith and an idealistic vision. The faults are not simply in ourselves, or our stars, and certainly not in Jason Epstein alone or in concert with other self-serving "hatchet men." And the answer to literature's malaise won't be found in concrete poetry or a universally acclaimed avant-garde. (pp. 112-13)

Intelligent writing takes as many forms in America as does justice, and the forms are equally partial, ephemeral, doggedly fought for, and constantly threatened. The publicity surrounding this writing, however, resembles the American forms of freedom, since it is often more talk than performance, more a matter of confused and self-defeating wills than supportive actions. Intelligence, contrary to Kostelanetz' sense of "literary politics," finally isn't determined by manipulable procedures. Its fate, and that of the writing that fosters and embodies it, is both grimmer and grander than that, more solidly tied to the larger fortunes of the species, and more subject to the ubiquitous deceptions of ego than we dare admit. (p. 113)

Charles Molesworth, "Literary Politics in America," in Salmagundi (copyright © 1975 by Skidmore College; reprinted by permission of the publisher), No. 30, Summer, 1975, pp. 107-13.

MICHAEL JOSEPH PHILLIPS

Richard Kostelanetz really staggers the imagination—another publication has listed him as a sort of Renaissance figure in modern garb. After all the things Richard has accomplished as a critic, editor, and scholar, one discovers that he is also a great visual poet.... The first poem in [*Visual Language*] is a series of manifestoes done circularly and in different sizes so as to overlap—one sees "the poetry of life copies," "artistry bellies argument . . . ," and so on. The whole thing just jumps out off the page at you, and the poem is very pleasant provoking. A nice and easy to see Nymphomania work follows in the shape of a woman; then, lightly, a lollypop poem in the shape of a lollypop takes up a whole page....

Kostelanetz likes good art, Twiggy, and social issues—I am sort of reminded of Melville's short stories. Richard closes *Visual Language* with his famous **"Disintegration"**—a poem which just repeats this word time after time as it slowly fades away.... One can only shout bravo and ask for more work by this talented poet.

Michael Joseph Phillips, "Innovative," in Small Press Review (© 1976 by Dustbooks), Vol. 8, Nos. 6 & 7, June-July, 1976, p. 67.

VAL MOOREHOUSE

Kostelanetz focuses on kinetic/semantic book elements in his minimal guy-meets-gal fiction [*One Night Stood: A Minimal Fiction*] printed in contrasting formats. In 310 words he parodies the humorously familiar "rise and fall" progress of the one-night-stand. Plot's quickly done, leaving the shift in format, mini-book to tabloid, to assume the burdens of action, reaction, and relationship. The book, with one to two words per page, cultivates page-turning suspense not present in the tabloid. The tabloid, with word pairs zig-zagging down large pages, invites ironic comparison and cross-reading not possible page by page. Normally invisible, tension between design and meaning is here perceived.

Val Moorehouse, in a review of "One Night Stood: A Minimal Fiction," in Booklist (reprinted by permission of the American Library Association; copyright © 1978 by the American Library Association), Vol. 75, No. 8, December 15, 1978, p. 669.

EDWARD BUTSCHER

Kostelanetz remains a child of the 1960s—when he was in his twenties—a bad boy who refuses to grow up or be bought off, except, on occasion, by his own arrogance. His literary judgments [in *Twenties in the Sixties*] follow suit, swinging wildly from the unexpected shaft of insight to the petulant philistinism of blanket rejections. The "radical" typographical decision to print other essays and commentary alongside the main pieces is similarly both distracting and intriguing, but Kostelanetz is still essential, still fighting the "good fight" against the literary cabals and commercial barkers that have our literature by the neck.

Edward Butscher, in a review of "Twenties in the Sixties: Previously Uncollected Critical Essays," in Booklist (reprinted by permission of the American Library Association; copyright © 1979 by the American Library Association), Vol. 75, No. 17, May 1, 1979, p. 1340.

SMALL PRESS REVIEW

["*The End*" *Appendix* and "*The End*" *Essentials*] is literally two books (in reversible format, front to back, and back to front) by the most perceptive watchdog of American publishing and writing, and one of the most articulate and persistent spokesmen for the experimental, the new and the young in contemporary American literature. It is sometimes irritable, often controversial and always articulate.

"*The End*" *Appendix* is an addendum to Kostelanetz's *The End of Intelligent Writing*, a book that stirred literary controversy for months after its publication. *The End* documents, after the fact, the difficulties the author had in publishing subsequent works, and analyses the causes of his ostracism by commercial publishers.

"*The End*" *Essentials* announces its argument. Kostelanetz's thesis is that "a panoply of growing forces and fostering symptoms forecast the likely end of "intelligent writing" or "literature" as we have know those traditions. The reason for this crisis is not that such writing is no longer produced—quite the contrary is true—or that it is not read—also untrue—but that the channels of communication between the intelligent writer and intelligent reader have become clogged and corrupted." Kostelanetz uses history and an acute analysis of the current literary establishment to outline the answers to questions about how a writer is "recognized," why certain tendencies dominate in writing, or appear to, and to define the nature and sources of "literary power." Two powerful and controversial books—critical reading for any writer or reader concerned with the state of contemporary letters.

A review of "'The End' Appendix and 'The End' Essentials," in Small Press Review (© 1980 by Dustbooks), Vol. 12, No. 2, February, 1980, p. 8.

JOHN MARTONE

Although his title [*The Old Poetries and the New*] might imply an evolutionary understanding of the relationship between traditional and avant-garde poetries, Kostelanetz finds them to be engaged in a battle to the death. His dichotomous view of contemporary poetry (one often gets the feeling that a poet is either experimental or morally deficient) comes across very strong in this retrospective, and one suspects that Kostelanetz's polemical tone may in itself have significantly hindered the development of the new poetry.

Surveying the old poetries in a series of reviews and articles on American poetry since 1949, Kostelanetz expresses an almost obsessive fear of and distaste for any poetry that can be associated—if only by virtue of an anthology—with the university. To be sure, his descriptions of contemporary poetry at its worst ("a soft surrealism . . . willfully mysterious, and, of necessity, attitudinally poetic") are frequently to the point and well taken, but he is too often simply ungenerous and morally presumptuous. . . .

At his best, in essays such as **"The New Poetries"** and **"Text-Sound Art in North America,"** Kostelanetz communicates the intellectual importance and excitement that non-syntactic and a-coherent poetic strategies have for contemporary writers. But even though these essays are well written . . . , one experiences discomfort upon hearing the new poetries praised as programmatically as the old were condemned. Above all, one misses an articulation of the basis of the new poetries: what is the relationship of such art to technology? of non-syntactic poetry to the *structure* of our lives? of the art work to the self? These are questions that Kostelanetz only alludes to here. One is thankful for the allusion, though, and for his recently published anthology *Visual Literature Criticism,* which provides a context wherein those questions can be more fully addressed.

John Martone, in a review of "The Old Poetries and the New," in World Literature Today *(copyright 1981 by the University of Oklahoma Press), Vol. 55, No. 4, Autumn, 1981, p. 675.*

PETER FRANK

Fiction is the last battleground between modernism and the academy, and is the best demonstration of the alliance and pattern of succession that modernism and post-modernism have established. The "innovative fictions" sampled in **Breakthrough Fictioneers** are seen by editor Richard Kostelanetz as moving. . . . In proving his point Kostelanetz draws on the work of ninety-eight authors, the inclusion of some of whom in an anthology of "fiction" may seem far-fetched, no matter how generous the rationale. But that rationale is elucidated with convincing insight with the observation that "fictions . . . favor sequential forms (and yet remain distinct from film), or the difference between the material on one page and its successors (and predecessors) often generates the work's internal event." The presence of "straight" poetry, theater, photography, comic strip, and other orthodox forms seems justified: the category of *fiction* is strained, but it ought to be. To burst its parameters, as many of the authors do here, is not to obliterate its core but only to bring that core into conjunction with other art forms. Kostelanetz, premier anthologist of the new sensibility, has too adventurous a mind to follow the safe, shopworn selections, smorgasbord nods, or cronyism masking as aesthetic stance by which legions of hacks have discredited the notion of "anthology" and given it a status beneath that of the digest. He has assembled some tremendously provocative collections; this one—powered by his clear polemical position, which he underscores with pithy epigraphs (by Ortega y Gasset, Northrop Frye, Robbe-Grillet, Moholy-Nagy, et al)—is one of his best. (pp. 52-3)

Peter Frank, in a review of "Breakthrough Fictioneers," in his Something Else Press: An Annotated Bibliography *(reprinted by permission of the publisher, McPherson & Company, New Paltz, NY), McPherson & Co., 1983, pp. 52-3.*

Maxine (Winokur) Kumin
1925-

American poet, novelist, short story writer, essayist, and author of children's books.

Kumin is best known for her poetry, which often portrays the simple workings of day-to-day life at her New Hampshire farm. Animals, children, the seasons, and neighbors are recurring subjects. Often classified as a transcendentalist, Kumin probes the human relationship to nature and celebrates the redemptive qualities of the natural world. Her writing has been compared to that of her friend, Anne Sexton, and in some aspects to the work of Sylvia Plath. Like Sexton, Kumin writes personal poems which focus on the inner lives of her characters. Unlike Sexton or Plath, however, she does not dwell on despair.

Since the publication of *Halfway* (1961), her first collection of poetry, Kumin's verse has generally been praised by critics. Many feel that her work is impressive both technically and in its portrayal of deep feelings and emotions. Although sometimes faulted for sentimentality and forced metaphors, among other things, Kumin's poetry is often described as authentic, believable, and refreshing in its affirmation of life.

Kumin's recent collection of poetry, *Our Ground Time Here Will Be Brief* (1982), continues her exploration of the importance of personal relationships and human ties to nature. This work introduces into Kumin's poetry her increased awareness of the process of aging and death and the fleeting nature of life. Critics praise the intensity this awareness has added to her work and applaud her refusal to submit to despair. *Our Ground Time Here Will Be Brief* is assessed as the honest and mature work of a poet sure of herself and her craft.

(See also *CLC*, Vols. 5, 13; *Contemporary Authors*, Vols. 1-4, rev. ed.; *Contemporary Authors New Revision Series*, Vol. 1; *Something about the Author*, Vol. 12; and *Dictionary of Literary Biography*, Vol. 5.)

© 1984 Thomas Victor

RICHARD MOORE

Maxine Kumin is an accomplished and professional poet of what might be called the Bishop-Lowell-Sexton school. More important, when she has a subject she can write moving and memorable poems. The best of those in her second book, *The Privilege* . . . , are a series of evocations of childhood. In **"The Spell,"** for example, that enchanted garden we can all remember (and which has been popping in and out of modern verse for quite some time now) suddenly becomes startlingly real and alive with supernatural presences, including a mother who seems like the God in Genesis. (pp. 29-30)

One can see in [some of the poems collected in *The Privilege* a] witty manner which—along with striking descriptions evoking unexpected senses—is Mrs. Kumin's main way of making poems. Sometimes she seems grimly determined to be witty, and this can distract one from a good poem, as with **"The Praying Fool."** At other times her manner seems to keep her from finding her subject. In **"The Appointment,"** for example, there is vividness; there is experience behind the vividness; but the poem, one feels, is needlessly coy about that experience. In other poems the tangible part of a metaphysical conceit works loose and develops a life of its own, and again the subject tends to get lost.

But with so many fine poems (there are some excellently lush love poems in the final section that makes me think of *The Song of Songs*), one mustn't quibble too much about a few. Mrs. Kumin is a real poet. (p. 30)

Richard Moore, "A Poet Who Needs His Poem," in Saturday Review (© 1965 Saturday Review Magazine Co.; reprinted by permission), Vol. XLVIII, No. 52, December 25, 1965, pp. 29-31.*

CHOICE

[*The Privilege* contains] intensely felt poems about deep-reaching family relationships, sharply realized memories of childhood, and odd, ambiguous, and elusive emotional experiences of adulthood. Miss Kumin's clipped, nervous verse line (even when run-on), which seems unusually consonantal in sound, proves highly various and adaptable, easily meeting the demands of the sonnet form, of which the poet provides far too few since she produces a most authentic *contemporary* sonnet when she tries. She is reminiscent of Millay in a detailed knowledge of closely observed natural phenomena. Similarly, all of her imagery is clear, sharp, and concrete, including that of the final section of intimate love poems. A poetic voice as distinctive as this deserves inclusion in any collection of recent American poetry.

> A review of "The Privilege," in Choice (copyright © 1966 by American Library Association; reprinted by permission of the American Library Association), Vol. 2, No. 11, January, 1966, p. 772.

MARY CARTER

"It's like a bad dream," says a character in **"The Passions of Uxport."** "Something happening to somebody else. A soap opera on TV." And, as Maxine Kumin's second novel unrolls, its domestic crisis and rhythmic interlocutions are also sharply reminiscent of series TV.

The Davises struggle with Sukey's death-wish and suffer the loss of their only child to leukemia. The Peakeses battle reciprocal adultery, the pregnancy of an unmarried niece, the psychosomatic pain in Hallie's stomach. Such troubles compose the condition of man and are valid elements of his drama. Yet here they seem framed within a 21-inch screen, rich and full-color as it is. Introspection throbs through this long book like organ music, and eventually drowns out the action. Can the universal condition be illuminated in terms of Hallie's gut-pain and Sukey's death-wish? Can the definitive question be plumbed in two housewives' neuroses? Can a Main Current of American Thought really be, "How do we fulfill the Little Woman?"

If not, it may be because in these two women the anguish seems so arbitrary, risen not from a universal but a private source, willful, insulated and resistant. "It hurts Martin terribly when I want to die," Sukey complains. "He takes it *personally*." Aside from the clinical argument on the universality or even existence of the classic death-wish, Sukey's emerges as a personal tic, a lump palpated daily. Hallie, examining her dogged compulsions, appears more concerned with her personal psychic hygiene than with charity. Their tight friendship is bonded in the bitter In-joke that they've been somehow duped or ill used. . . .

The other characters are real and touching: Ernie, a clerk at the supermarket wrestling his own mad angel (a compulsion to scoop up animal casualties on the Interstate and give them decent burial); Adam, aflame with social commitment; Freudian Dr. Zemstvov, who moves us—in much the way we're moved by old Chaplin films—by the sadness of genius become inevitably quaint; Mellon, with his humble lechery; and Martin, who risks everything on the gamble of another child.

Mrs. Kumin's prose is graceful, inventive, informed by intelligence and wit. Unfortunately, in focusing on the dolorous hang-ups of Hallie and Sukey, she has, for the most part, limited her gifts to the small screen.

> Mary Carter, "Hallie and Sukey's Hang-ups," in The New York Times Book Review (copyright © 1968 by The New York Times Company; reprinted by permission), May 5, 1968, p. 37.

DAVID J. GORDON

[Maxine Kumin's] powers of observation, interpretation, and phrasing are as strong as Updike's and less marred by moral perversity, excessive symbolism, and fine writing. But her novel [*The Passions of Uxport*] is as preoccupied as his [*Couples*] . . . with animal decay and the struggle to conquer the fear of death. And her narrative also suggests that sexual loss, though not the whole of this fear, is central to it. Hallie's mysterious stomach pain, which sends her eventually to a psychoanalyst, is the novel's dominating fact. It is called "death," but we see that it has much to do with the fact that her husband will be away a great part of this year, that his adulteries have for the first time been discovered, that her children are growing beyond her care, that her niece's predicament arouses old resentments concerning her early marriage and hysterectomy, and above all that it disappears only when she asserts her sexuality by hurting her husband with a report of her own adultery. Mrs. Kumin is unnecessarily burdened by the idea that the analysis of Hallie's motives will cancel the moral value of her acts of rescuing and mending which her husband and doctor question. In any case we can accept Hallie's identification with Christ the prophet of social justice and the protector of outcasts. Mrs. Kumin is particularly impressive in conveying the moral bond between the insane Ernie, obsessed with his private rituals, and her more or less normal, very intelligent, and earnest heroine. Hardly less impressive is the fact that she can raise the question of individual moral commitment in connection with the Nazi holocaust without making one squirm.

The one major blemish is the ambitious portrait of Dr. Zemstvov, "the last of Freud's inner circle." Mrs. Kumin is conscientious enough to describe with some success Zemstvov's private feelings and the process of treatment. But there are crudely fitting pieces that make one uncomfortably aware of the author's own vanity and spite. Zemstvov at eighty comes out of retirement, reluctantly, to take on the fascinating Hallie, spouts jargon to the point of parody, intensifies the treatment against her wishes when he learns he is going to die, almost forces her to deny her belief that a certain dream means she wants to stop treatment (he admits he behaved badly here), dies the next day assuming "a foetal position," and is heavily mourned by Hallie with no mention of any relief at being rid of him. This won't do, and it looks worse in view of the illogicality of her two principal charges against psychoanalysis itself: first, that it wrongly tries to be a substitute religion, although it is clearly the Bible-haunted Hallie who is searching for that; and, second, that it imposes on its practitioners an Olympian detachment in contrast to Hallie's belief in "total commitment," a charge which is not only inconsistent with the first but which looks weak in itself, for the instances specified (Zemstvov advising her not to help Ernie further, another analyst advising Sukey not to have a baby) are instances of intervention, not detachment. But fortunately a sympathetic attitude toward psychoanalysis is not a requisite for insight, and *The Passions of Uxport* is often a wise and satisfying book. (pp. 120-21)

> David J. Gordon, "Some Recent Novels: Styles of Martyrdom," in The Yale Review (copyright 1968 by Yale University; reprinted by permission of the editors), Vol. LVIII, No. 1, October, 1968, pp. 112-26.*

THE VIRGINIA QUARTERLY REVIEW

One is impressed by several qualities in [the poems collected in Maxine Kumin's *The Nightmare Factory*]: depth and range, delicately controlled yet forceful emotion, and the unobtrusive presence of formal devices. Miss Kumin never settles for superficial treatment of her material although she deals with an extensive range of subjects. From her "pastoral" poems, which move beyond the idyllic to realistic cycles of birth and decay, through her "tribal" poems, in which she manages to focus on various of her familial situations without making the reader uncomfortable by the willing surrender of privacy, to her poems involving the pains dealt to body and psyche by the experiences of love, loss, sickness, uncertainty, she is always ready with the image, the insight, the detail that takes the reader into a deeper realization of the poem.

A review of "The Nightmare Factory," in The Virginia Quarterly Review *(copyright, 1971, by* The Virginia Quarterly Review, *The University of Virginia), Vol. 47, No. 2 (Spring, 1971), p. lx.*

JASCHA KESSLER

Maxine Kumin's sixth collection of poems is called **The Retrieval System,** and it is a generous gathering of 35 poems. I would characterize her work as straightforward, ruminative, prosaic, and pleasant to read: she is intelligent and thoughtful; she is also at the prime of her own life, her mid-Fifties, and in a position to speak plainly and with a kind of personal authority that convinces the reader. She is also writing a poetry of retirement, so to speak, of observation, of civility and domesticity. This is, when one thinks of her work in that way, a poetry that partakes of a very ancient and widespread tradition, in the Classical World, in the Orient, and the Middle East. That is, the poet has grown up in cities, and been educated at good schools, the poet has been cultivated in the literary life of the times, but then, towards middle age, the poet has gone into the country to live, not as a peasant or a farmer, but the life of the gentleman, or in Kumin's case, the wife of a country squire. There is no necessity involved, and there is leisure and satisfying work: the animals to be cared for, the orchard to be overseen, the kitchen garden, and the more or less easygoing life of the New England countryside, with its seasons, its woods, its excursions. I think the effects of this will always be noticeable in such poetry: a narrative form of meditation; images of domestic and rural life reflected upon; the world is there but at a distance; the immediacy, the poignant immediacy of the seasons; the sorrows and joys and hurts of association with tamed animals, the odd local characters; the fates of one's parents and friends and of one's children; all of which give the poet occasions to weep private tears, to reflect on the world's constant change and pressures; on the fact of death, others' and obviously one's own; this quiet background encourages dreaming, dreaminess and slowly-congealing judgments on the self and on life in general, judgments that are weighted by slowpassing country time, that grow and ripen like fruit or ooze from life's wounds like gum on a fruit tree, hardening slowly into a form of amber, a turgid sap from the quick of one's being, exposed on the hard bark of the outer self for all to see. Kumin's made statements intelligible; that is we can easily recognize ordinary human emotions, simple joys and deep griefs over our losses: she is not melodramatic, morbid, or sensational, as her close friend Anne Sexton was, and about whom she offers here a few intimate poems; and she is not able to excite us by her use of language or show any interesting technique. In short, the poetry in this book is the poetry of herself, of her day to day life. And that has always been the main feature of the civilized poet in the rustic life of retirement. It is a poetry that offers the reader genuine country products, organically grown, so to speak, the fruit, the berries, the walks through the four Northern seasons, the glimpses of the domestic life, glimpses both wry and sad, as befits a woman in middle age....

And as befits the poetry of ripe middle-age, and rustication, which implies that the future can hold few surprises or breakthroughs; exaltation and ecstasy are not to be looked for: most of the poems are elegies, grieving poems: mourning for the dead, one's parents and one's friends, and for one's losses, the losses of children, or their inevitable disappearance over the horizon into their own difficult lives. The title poem of the book, **"The Retrieval System,"** sets the theme for the other 34 poems. I'm not very happy with its trendy, jargonical metaphor, but the poem is a good one, a grave one, and the book elaborates on it.

Jascha Kessler, "Maxine Kumin: 'The Retrieval System'," in a radio broadcast on KUSC-FM—Los Angeles, CA, January 31, 1979.

MONROE K. SPEARS

[Maxine Kumin] is not much anthologized or discussed, and I suspect that many readers have been aware of her, as I was until recently, only as a name. At any rate, if there are such readers, I have good news for them: Kumin is very much worth discovering, and [*Our Ground Time Here Will Be Brief* and *Why Can't We Live Together Like Civilized Human Beings?*] are an excellent introduction. (p. 1)

The arrangement [of *Our Ground Time Here Will Be Brief*] is reverse chronological, beginning with the latest work and ending with the earliest; and selections from the later volumes are ... generous, including 31 poems from the most recent as against nine from the earliest. I am glad to report that this heavy emphasis on the recent work seems fully justified, on the grounds both of quality and of contemporary resonance.

Many of these later poems are very much in the mode of Robert Lowell; they capture the private and public significance of times, places, and events, and at their best they succeed in being at once personal and historical. A good example is **"Lines Written in the Library of Congress After the Cleanth Brooks Lecture,"** a meditation on Brooks' enumeration of history, time, and personal identity as "touchstones of the poem" and his description of ours as the "respectable second-best / Silver Age of Literature." Vividly evoking Washington and the contemporary scene, the poem brings together reflections on the political and cultural functions of poetry with personal history in a wry, quiet, chastened style.... (pp. 1, 11)

Much of her poetry throughout is openly autobiographical, and the reader becomes acquainted with her family from her immigrant great-grandfather Rosenberg the Tailor to her pawnbroker father, her mother who played the piano while her daughter swam, her own daughters now in Belgium and Berkeley, her female friend who committed suicide, her Frostian New Hampshire neighbor Henry Manley, her brother who recently died, and so on. These gain in power as the reader becomes more aware of the constellations and dynamics....

One of the pleasures of reading Kumin is to see the same experience appear differently in the different forms of poems, stories, and novels. Though she is not primarily a short-story writer (apparently the stories collected in *Why Can't We Live Together Like Civilized Human Beings?* constitute most of her output in that medium), she uses the form with great skill. **"The Facts of Life,"** for example, makes a sharp triple juxtaposition of a girl's entry into puberty with her mother's recollection of her own menarche which coincided with her discovery of her mother's early abortion; what is here rendered in schematic parallels and contrasts is developed more slowly and cumulatively in *The Passions of Uxport*. . . . **"The Perfect Body,"** about love among summer-camp counselors, and **"The Neutral Love Object,"** about a family dog, are more limited and sharply focused than similar material in the novels. On the other hand, some stories are so beautifully wedded to the form that it is hard to imagine any other treatment. . . .

One virtue of the stories is that they are informative: Kumin inspires trust that she is an honest reporter and that her facts are accurate, and she knows about everything from psychoanalysis to agribusiness, from rural New England to life behind the Iron Curtain. She is wonderful on animals, as pets, as individuals, and as units on factory farms; she is good on Jews, WASPs (and various combinations), hippies, children, young lovers, old people; on death and survival, the bonds of sex and love and family. She is always solid, intelligent, and compassionate; she convinces you that she knows and understands what she is talking about. . . . Clever, witty, with a remarkable range of information, awareness, and sympathy, she is never less than readable and entertaining, and often a great deal more. (p. 11)

> Monroe K. Spears, "A Gathering of Poets, Voices from Four Decades: 'Our Ground Time Here Will Be Brief: New and Selected Poems' and 'Why Can't We Live Together Like Civilized Human Beings?'" in Book World—The Washington Post (© 1982, The Washington Post), June 27, 1982, pp. 1, 11.

JULIE STONE PETERS

Maxine Kumin, who has earned a reputation for poems of such bright beatitude that she is an unlikely bard of the geriatric, has entitled her new collection *Our Ground Time Here Will Be Brief*, as if in honor of "the aging poets, old friends" she refers to in one poem.

This sprint toward the finish line wouldn't be surprising in a young poet (or young as well-known poets go) habitually prone to the death watch, a poet, say, with Galway Kinnell's inclination for the volcanic nightmare, or Louise Glück's sense of doom. But until now, Kumin has observed the simple particularities of country life and committed herself to conserving nature with an optimism that has bound her to New England transcendentalism.

Harold Bloom (never mind his Romantic biases) has often said that American poets after the mid-19th century are either Emersonian or radically anti-Emersonian, either forgiving of God and man or fundamentally unforgiving. Kumin forgave, indeed rejoiced, and she survived, unlike her friends and self-claimed sisters in poetry, Sexton and Plath, who could not refuse despair, let alone allow a place for the transcendentalist's ecstatic transformations of nature.

Now Kumin seems to have run smack into Time and his henchman, Death, and the encounter has given her poetry a new depth. . . .

[It] has finally allowed Kumin to move beyond the breathy wonder that pervaded much of her earlier work, allowed her to see beyond a world redeemed by the regenerative powers of nature into a world darkened by the unyielding passage of time. . . .

Even in the darkest of these poems, [however], the ones that veer closest to the abyss, Kumin speaks with peculiar sprightliness. This has been and continues to be her voice, so different from the voice of terror (bridled in Moore and Bishop, unleashed in Sexton, Plath, and Rich) to which we've grown accustomed in our recent women poets. . . . Kumin's voice remains, inviolably, that of the young girl so pleased by the largesse of nature that her experience, translated into language, blows lightly across the page. . . .

Kumin's best poems are simple narratives written in loose colloquial speech that falls naturally into pentameters, and are reminiscent of Frost or Bishop, but without the acrid underwash. They have a cumulative effect. . . . [But] Kumin's optimism occasionally slides into sentimentality. . . .

[In **"Rejoicing with Henry,"** for example,] Kumin makes Henry and the foal Romantic individualists: both are kinless; both overcome and persevere alone. . . . Both affirm their share in the natural and human community—a maudlin concept perhaps, but saved by Kumin's specificity. She tacks down her poem with . . . a colloquial language as weighty as things: "Worth waiting for, that filly," says Henry, and his voice becomes the glue of the poem.

When Kumin suddenly veers off into the crudely figurative, it's intrusive; the figure consumes her simple language. . . . Kumin's naive joy in the metamorphic power of figuration infects **"Peeling Fence Posts"** with a profusion of similes: The hickory "shuck[s] his watery slats / like long underwear"; the birch "spool[s] her curls / like a typewriter ribbon / loosed from its socket"; the ash's skin "comes away like a glove"; all turn "brown as a tribe." Post-Emersonians seem particularly susceptible to the pathetic fallacy, but it is difficult to excuse Kumin for such monstrous personifications as male peapods that say "do me, dangle their intricate / nuggety scrota" and female peapods that "call up a woman in a gauzy dress / young, with tendrils of hair at her neck, / leaning in a summer doorway." She should know better.

Kumin is good enough to make her better-wrought poems musically articulate as well as metaphorically subtle, but even in her rhythms she often fails. She has admitted in interviews that she feels lost in free verse, and this can be painfully obvious. . . .

Her new collection of fiction, *Why Can't We Live Together Like Civilized Human Beings?*, is plagued by . . . vocal indecision, even though Kumin clings to an unvarying point of view (a middle-aged, educated, nature-loving woman always narrates, if sometimes only implicitly). The poet is far less at home in prose, and frequently adopts, in these stories, a popular sort of wary speech. All too many contemporary writers have determined that a choppy style, glutted with sentence fragments, gives the easily distracted reader a sock in the arm. Kumin is no exception. . . . [And] Kumin cannot resist occasional outbursts of poetic profusion, verbiage that hangs just over the edge of triteness. . . .

Kumin falls into lyricism most often when she deals with the themes in her poems: the deaths of parents and friends; the ways in which these deaths remove the barriers to our own mortality; middle-aged love affairs; aging and the passage of time. "The hardest thing about old age," Martha Carpenter thinks in **"Other Nations,"** "is the ruptured synapses which sentence the elderly to repeat . . . a drudgery of unwanted anecdotes to faceless attendants." Martha writes her will as a long meditation, but decides to leave it in an airplane seat-pocket. Here and elsewhere, language is a stay against death, but it ultimately fails.

If we return to the poems from this story, it becomes clear that whenever Kumin speaks about time and death, she is also speaking of the failure of language to hold them off.... Kumin's modernism, her insistence on the failure of language in the face of time, has finally overcome her vision of a redeemable world. For if words have no connection to human existence, if they are always "freestanding but misheard," then there is little chance for redemptive transformation.

> *Julie Stone Peters, "Sprinting Toward the Finish Line" (reprinted by permission of* The Village Voice *and the author; copyright © News Group Publications, Inc., 1982), in* The Village Voice, *Vol. XXVII, No. 29, July 20, 1982, p. 39.*

CLARA CLAIBORNE PARK

One can only cook with what's in the cupboard, Mary Ellman wrote some years ago, speaking of fiction by women. And that, if not entirely true, is true enough. Fortunately, a lot accumulates in the cupboard as time goes on. Maxine Kumin's poems, like her fiction, mine a life whose elements might seem too familiar to be promising material for the storyteller or the poet—too familiar, at any rate, to (as we once used to say, instead of merely think) "people like us." People like us read *The Nation*, or at the very least *The New York Times Book Review*. They are administrators, teachers, translators and such—the kind of people who fly in planes to address meetings in distant cities. In other moods, they demonstrate at the Pentagon.... They are not carried away by passion, though they panic sometimes; their marriages last more often than not, and their adulteries are not flamboyant or destructive but decently maintained—"another form of marriage," as the title of one story [in *Why Can't We Live Together Like Civilized Human Beings*] has it. Kumin's is the fiction and poetry of maturity. It is significant that in selecting the poems for *Our Ground Time Here Will Be Brief,* she has chosen to reverse the usual chronological order, opening with twenty-nine recent poems, then working backward through six previous collections: youth is seen from the perspective of late middle age. That perspective too is familiar....

Kumin's well-made poems and stories are two ways of coming at the same immemorial preoccupations: aging and mortality—"That time of year thou may'st in me behold"—or as Frost put it, "what to make of a diminished thing." Indeed, our ground time here will be brief.

Poets are makers; they make what they can. In Kumin's work, parents age and die; brothers and childhood friends do, too; daughters and sons move far away and one cannot follow. Love flares, still, between strangers in a story titled, in Walter Pater's poignant words, **"On This Short Day of Frost and Sun,"** but it is a brief, restrained magic, based, we learn at the end, on the glowing misperceptions born of need, though no less real for that. Best to hold on to what one has. Nature abides—and home and marriage too, if they have been well made. One late poem, **"Continuum,"** is subtitled **"A Love Poem"**:

> going for grapes year
> after year we two with
> ladder and pail stained
> with the rain of grapes
> our private language

"Feeding Time" is an even simpler affirmation. (p. 89)

Yet beneath these settled, gentled transactions bad dreams lurk. The last of the recent poems leaves us "inching toward Armageddon"; an earlier collection is called *The Nightmare Factory*. The most innocent of activities turns dark in an instant.... Metaphor intensifies into sinister metamorphosis, as anger transforms its object: in **"Changing the Children,"** "the furious wish / turns the son into a crow / the daughter, a porcupine ... all arched bristle and quill." ... The poem that follows this one is called **"The Lovers Leave by Separate Planes."** Even nature's rich affirmations are deceptive, we read in **"The Poets Observe the Absence of God from the St. Louis Zoo"**—an absence which may be just as well, since in **"Heaven as Anus,"** "the sphincter of the good Lord opens wide / and he takes us all inside."

Such metaphysical speculation, however, is not typical of Kumin. The world she explores is a restricted one, limited by the familiar boundaries of class background and habit, as well as by a traditionally feminine personalism that seems less inevitable today than it did when Mary Ellman wrote about it ten years ago, and is perhaps more significant for that reason. In both Kumin's fiction and her poetry, the vistas are interior. Her stories about women professors and film makers and investment analysts are in fact stories of women as daughters, mothers, wives and lovers; that their spheres are no longer exclusively, or even chiefly, domestic seems to have made little difference to where they really live. What's in the cupboard is nourishing, however. Here [in *Our Ground Time Here Will Be Brief* and *Why Can't We Live Together Like Civilized Human Beings?*] are fourteen stories and 148 poems as accessible as life, and more shapely. (p. 90)

> *Clara Claiborne Park, "Mature Fruits," in* The Nation *(copyright 1982 The Nation magazine, The Nation Associates, Inc.), Vol. 235, No. 3, July 24-31, 1982, pp. 89-90.*

ALICIA OSTRIKER

Which of her poetic peers does Maxine Kumin resemble? Unlike Sylvia Plath and Anne Sexton, she keeps her demons bridled. Unlike Elizabeth Bishop or May Swenson, she is bawdily personal. Like Adrienne Rich, she makes us pay respectful attention to images of strong female identity, yet she avoids ideology. And is there another poet who finds or invents such a sweet male alter ego [as Henry Manley, the country neighbor who is one of the several recurring figures in **"Our Ground Time Here Will Be Brief"**]? ...

Typical of Maxine Kumin's art are the sensory weight, the play of alliteration and assonance sliding into the closing couplets, the perfectly expressive halting and crystallizing rhythms [in the poems about Henry]....

Mirroring his creator, Henry Manley is a supervisor, a capable countryperson of multiple skills. He will die before the poet does, and he is one of her many means of studying mortality. He is also what she is not, or can be only through him: an *isolé*. He is alone, not looking back. For her, not looking back would be intolerable.

"Our Ground Time Here Will Be Brief" contains selections from Maxine Kumin's first six volumes as well as 29 new poems, all but one of them gems; the book amounts to 20 years' solid work. Her Pulitzer Prize-winning **"Up Country"** comes just about halfway, both in chronology and in power;

rather like Frost's imagined wanderer to the edge of doom, she is not changed, only more sure—so that her poems become increasingly unforgettable, indispensable. What drives her throughout is attachment. If she had her way, no loved (or hated) human or animal would die unremembered. Thus she writes not only the usual kinfolk poems but **"Sperm,"** a tragicomic celebration of 17 look-alike cousins. . . .

Children, especially daughters, keep cropping up, growing as they go, from Mrs. Kumin's earliest work to her most recent. No poet writes more richly and more subtly of mother-daughter relations. Or, for that matter, of animal-human relations, since her attachment and attention extend to the forms and gestures, the detailed lives and deaths of mice, turtles, frogs, goats, beavers, cows and calves, sheep and lambs, and—most powerfully—horses. Creatures surround her; she sees and touches them; she foresees their doom. At times—see **"Woodchucks"** or **"How It Goes On"**—she is their doom's guilty agent. At times—see **"Thinking of Death and Dogfood"** or **"A Mortal Day of No Surprises"**—she contemplates the uses of horseflesh and her own potential to sweeten a crop, and wishes her mare and herself good endings. I believe that Thoreau would commend her honesty, the precision of her language and her occasional moral allegory. (p. 10)

Besides the poetry by which she is best known, Mrs. Kumin writes charming children's books and good readable fiction. Her four novels, thick with human physicality and human decency, like her poems tend to concentrate on sex and love. This is also the case in her first collection of stories, **"Why Can't We Live Together Like Civilized Human Beings?"**

The narrator of the title story, a documentary film maker who meets and loves a colleague at a film festival behind the Iron Curtain, answers the title's question, to her own unhappy satisfaction, by believing "in the infinite depravity of man." Another answer is that love sustains civilized individuals only intermittently. Almost all of Mrs. Kumin's protagonists are reasonable people in middle life, enduring situations they do not quite choose. . . .

High violence and high passion take place offstage in these stories, though never far offstage. Maxine Kumin's writing emanates from the bodies of her characters, delivering their senses and sense together as a poet's writing should, and invites us to recognize our destinies in theirs. (p. 22)

> Alicia Ostriker, "Memory and Attachment," in The New York Times Book Review (copyright © 1982 by The New York Times Company; reprinted by permission), August 8, 1982, pp. 10, 22.

DANA GIOIA

Kumin is understandably a popular poet. She is an intelligent and sensitive woman who writes on the enduring themes of life and death, place and family. Essentially a domestic poet, she takes as her material the world of her everyday life in rural New Hampshire—her home, children, neighbors, land, and animals, especially horses, which she has loved since girlhood. She is a strong woman whose independence is natural, not ideological, and the usual modesty of her tone does not hide her underlying self-assurance. She writes confidently about what she knows—the death of friends, the departures of her children, the landscape around her—and she does so honestly and directly without striking fashionable postures. (p. 652)

There is much to enjoy in Kumin's volume [*Our Ground Time Here Will Be Brief*], especially among the new poems. Her readers will be glad to see further reports on her engaging neighbor, Henry Manley, the eighty-two-year-old Yankee bachelor, whose presence has enlivened Kumin's poetry since his first appearance in *The Nightmare Factory*. There is also a very moving group of poems about her brother and his brave struggle against the crippling nervous disease which killed him, and there is an affecting elegy for her friend, Anne Sexton, written "on being interviewed by her biographer." The people in Kumin's poetry come alive. She captures their personality and makes her affection for them contagious.

Yet with all these strengths, there is a curious thinness to Kumin's verse. She uses language in a skillful but utilitarian way. It is a medium to communicate the facts of her poetry, and even in her formal poems one finds little evidence of joy in language for its own sake. The rhymes seem forced and incidental, the metrical pattern filled out rather than exploited. Even Kumin's most lyrical outbursts sound flat and perfunctory, as in the climax to **"Sunbathing on a Rooftop in Berkeley."** . . .

Perhaps it is . . . [her] dependence on "the exact truth" that sets the limits on Kumin's achievement. When her poems succeed, they do so mainly on the strength of the characters they introduce, the scenes they describe, the stories they tell. While her language presents the subject matter clearly enough, it rarely heightens it sufficiently to make the exact words definitive. Her poems are moving without being memorable. Ultimately Kumin is a writer who has applied her diligence more to exploring her own life than to the possibilities of her medium. (p. 653)

> Dana Gioia, in a review of "Our Ground Time Here Will Be Brief," in The Hudson Review (copyright © 1983 by The Hudson Review, Inc.; reprinted by permission), Vol. XXXV, No. 4, Winter, 1982-83, pp. 652-53.

John le Carré
1931-

(Pseudonym of David John Moore Cornwell) English novelist and short story writer.

Le Carré is an enormously popular writer of spy fiction. His novels are praised for their insight into human motivation and personality, and are noted for their credible plots and realistic characterizations. Le Carré's protagonist, British agent George Smiley, is considered by many critics to be a refreshing contrast to the suave, superhuman heroes of other contemporary spy fiction. Le Carré portrays Smiley as an ordinary, somewhat lonely middle-aged man who often battles his superiors and bureaucratic red tape in addition to Soviet agents.

The authenticity of le Carré's work derives from his career in the British Foreign Office. From 1960 to 1963, le Carré served as Second Secretary in the British Embassy in Bonn, West Germany, and in 1964, as Consul in Hamburg, he was involved in intelligence activities throughout West Germany. *Call for the Dead* (1961), le Carré's first novel, received positive reviews for its gritty realism and nonglamorous depiction of cold war espionage. Le Carré's third novel, *The Spy Who Came In from the Cold* (1963), was both a critical and popular success and placed him in the forefront of spy fiction. The "Smiley" trilogy—*Tinker, Tailor, Soldier, Spy* (1974), *The Honourable Schoolboy* (1977), and *Smiley's People* (1980)—are other best-selling works.

In *The Little Drummer Girl* (1983) le Carré abandons the cold war and Smiley for the Middle East conflict. *The Little Drummer Girl* is the story of an English actress who is recruited and trained by Israeli agents to help capture a high-ranking Palestinian terrorist. It is controversial because the heroine begins to sympathize with the Palestinian cause, which many equate with terrorism. In general, however, *The Little Drummer Girl* received favorable and provocative reviews and has affirmed le Carré's universal status as a powerful and entertaining novelist.

(See also *CLC*, Vols. 3, 5, 9, 15 and *Contemporary Authors*, Vols. 5-8, rev. ed.)

Stephen Cornwell/Picture Group

a novel as intense and as morally complex as the best of Graham Greene himself. (pp. 47-8)

Mark Abley, "John le Carré's Trail of Terror," in Maclean's Magazine (© 1983 by Maclean's Magazine; reprinted by permission), Vol. 96, No. 10, March 7, 1983, pp. 47-52.

MARK ABLEY

With *The Little Drummer Girl*, le Carré has abandoned the polite chess game of the Cold War. He has plunged instead into a very hot and current struggle of hand grenades and fragmentation bombs, the mutual campaign of terror waged by the Israelis and Palestinians. . . . [The central character,] Charlie, an idealistic young actress and a political innocent, has been chosen to lead an imaginative journey, one that parallels a personal journey of le Carré's: from initial sympathy for the Israelis to a sombre, bitter recognition of Palestinian oppression and pain. The plot is as labyrinthine as ever. But the passion of the writing, kindled by an overwhelming concern for peace in the Middle East, is unmatched. Out of his sorrow and fury le Carré has written a novel that rises eloquently above the politics of the Middle East. With *The Little Drummer Girl* he has transcended his fluent technique as a thriller writer, creating

WILLIAM F. BUCKLEY, JR.

The beginning of John le Carré's new book ["**The Little Drummer Girl**"] is, for a spy thriller, entirely orthodox: There is a bombing, a bombing by a terrorist. Where? Near Bonn, but the location does not matter. There have been so many others, in Zurich, in Leyden, here and there. It matters only that the victim was an Israeli. Although the reader spends time in Bonn and in Tel Aviv and in Vienna, Munich, Mykonos, London, it matters hardly at all, except that the ambiance of these places is an invitation for Mr. le Carré to use his palette. The places are simply where the terrorist strikes, or where the antiterrorists are collected.

It becomes instantly apparent that we are in the hands of a writer of great powers. (p. 1)

We are very quickly aware that we are reading not Dashiell Hammett but someone much more like Lawrence Durrell. The author does not forget his duty. There is sleuthing galore ahead of the reader; and, in the end, the Palestinian terrorist is emphatically dead. But the momentum of the story is not ended with his death. There is left—the girl. The instrument of the Israeli antiterrorists. An English actress named Charlie, she is permanently changed by the complex role imposed on her—to be faithful at once to the Israeli and the Palestinian causes. And she is in love with the most mysterious character to have appeared in recent fiction, whose flesh-and-blood reification Mr. le Carré flatly refuses to give us. His name is Joseph, and other than the Israeli superspy Schulmann, the English actress Charlie and, however briefly, the Palestinian superterrorist Khalil, there is only Joseph seriously to ponder. At first he is merely a will-o'-the-wisp, and one is not entirely certain that he actually exists. Then he is incorporated formally into the plot, his persona on the one hand central, on the other hand continuingly elusive. And when finally only he exists for Charlie, after the entrapment, after Khalil is gone, the magnetism is enormous. The emotional tension of the postlude elevates it into a full fourth act. A wonderful achievement.

Mr. le Carré's novel is certainly the most mature, inventive and powerful book about terrorists-come-to-life this reader has experienced. It transcends the genre by reason of the will and the interests of the author. The story line interests him but does not dominate him. He is interested in writing interestingly about things interesting and not interesting. Terrorism and counterterrorism, intelligence work and espionage are, then, merely the vehicle for a book about love, anomie, cruelty, determination and love of country. **"The Little Drummer Girl"** is about spies as "Madame Bovary" is about adultery or "Crime and Punishment" about crime. Mr. le Carré easily establishes that he is not beholden to the form he elects to use. This book will permanently raise him out of the espionage league, narrowly viewed. . . .

"Drummer Girl" has here and there passages that demand diligent reading. And sometimes Mr. le Carré is drawn, annoyingly, to nondeclarative narrative. Disdain for narrative rigidity is probably closer. There is something of John Fowles in his style, in the liberties he gives himself to wander about as he likes, to dwell at any length that grips him or amuses him, serenely confident as he is that we will be, respectively, gripped and amused—and if not, we should go read other people's books. But he succeeds, almost always, because he is naturally expressive, dominant and in turn dominating in his use of language. And so the liberties he takes tend to be accepted as a part of his tapestry—even if, looked at discretely, they can be, as I say, annoying and even logically dissonant. . . .

Is there a message in **"Drummer Girl"**? Yes. A quite earnest one. It is that the intensity with which the Israelis defend what they have got can only be understood if one understands the intensity with which the Palestinians resent what it is that they have lost. The Israelis triumph in the novel, even as they do in life. But Mr. le Carré is careful to even up the moral odds. I have in the past been discomfited by trendy ventures in ideological egalitarianism, such that the reader ends by finding the Communist spy and the Western spy equally weak, equally heroic; and perhaps the ambiguist in Mr. le Carré would overcome him in any exercise in which the alternative was moral polarization. But having acknowledged that this may be in John le Carré a temperamental weakness, reflecting the clutch of ambiguity rather than any ultimate fear of moral fine-tuning, one must go on to acknowledge that he permits the Palestinian point to be made with rare and convincing eloquence.

He is a very powerful writer. His entertainment is of a high order. He gives pleasure in his use of language. And his moral focus is interesting and provocative. (p. 23)

> William F. Buckley, Jr., "Terror and a Woman," in The New York Times Book Review (copyright © 1983 by The New York Times Company; reprinted by permission), March 13, 1983, pp. 1, 23.

MELVYN BRAGG

[*The Little Drummer Girl*] is the third Le Carré novel which is exceedingly well-timed. The first was *The Spy Who Came In From The Cold,* which defined the Cold War with an intensity and adult perception which came as a relief after the lockjawed propaganda of the politicians and the comic-cuts cartoons of popular fiction.

Then came Smiley who tinkered his honourable way through people in institutions so very like the institutions most of us have suffered through. Whether it was school, university, the factory, the civil service, Smiley talked about the JOB. Moles were found in every cranny; spooks in every nook.

Now, with *The Little Drummer Girl,* Le Carré has slipped away from Smiley and pitched camp in the Middle East.

It is the Middle East of espionage: in that sense Le Carré is taking his life-belt with him. It is also the Middle East of propaganda: in that sense he is walking into a fiery furnace. For as everyone knows who has ever written anything about the State of Israel, to applaud is permissible; to question is to criticise; to criticise is to ask to be pilloried. . . .

[How much] is Le Carré taking on here where the new fuse in the book is the discovery by the chief character—an English actress called Charlie and borrowed, in part, from the author's sister, the actress Charlotte Cornwell—that the Palestinians too have a case, a cause, and should have a country. . . .

The Middle East drew Le Carré on. He talked to Israeli intelligence officers. He "goofed around". Then he went to the Palestinian camps and met Arafat. His perception changed, as does that of Charlie in the novel. She is enlisted by Israeli Intelligence to act as a double agent and help the Israelis eliminate a particularly effective nexus of Palestinian opposition. . . .

Charlie then goes into the Palestinian camp, literally, and here she discovers another clever, paranoid, deeply wronged Semitic people. Her outrage on their behalf—against the Israeli bombers which, as she sees it, blast utterly defenceless villages and take massive retribution; against the publicity machine of the Diaspora which turns every Palestinian into a guerilla; against so many other grievances she hears of from those who believe their land was appropriated in order to appease the conscience of the West—springs from the page fully armed with radical indignation.

Yet, in response to a personal passion, Charlie goes ahead and does her work, acts out her betrayal, helps the story to thrive, piles up another victory against a people, the Palestinians, whom she discovers to be convinced that the Jews will "genocide us to death".

Her role in the theatre of the real is deadly and cannot be cast off. Israel routs its enemies again: Le Carré's Charlie is their chosen instrument.

Le Carré's method digs again into that seam of thriller-writing he has made so individual and so flexible. Information is given through interrogation. Information is both gold and fool's gold. Loyalty to an institution—whether it is the State of Israel or the Aspiration of Palestine—is tested and chronically distorted through loyalty to an individual. Sometimes it seems that every action is a betrayal: usually it is.

The advantages of this novelistic engine are evident. The story has drive, tension, verve, the attraction of unravelment. The possible disadvantages lie in an anxiety we might have that the characters are *too* fatally pre-determined, even predestined, by the plot. Charlie's wrack of doubts—not only her 180° swivelling between the Israelis and the Palestinians, but her doubts over her sanity in the role given to her—is felt, and well felt, but we feel the heavy breath of the plot: curious to raise a point of doubt over what is a fine gift and quality—story-telling—but the very force of the plot can appear to ride over the lives of the characters.

Which is precisely, the answer could be, what history does to the individual. And in that sense, too, the detailed and taut plotting is a valid fictional abstraction.

As we have now come to expect from Le Carré, but ought not to take for granted, there is an abundance of that kind of researched authenticity so few authors can produce, let alone match. The lyrical fall of a sentence still tempts him, thankfully. Descriptions are often highly wrought—a piquant contrast to the speed and toughness of the action.

> Melvyn Bragg, "Off Beat" (© 1983 by Melvyn Bragg; reprinted by permission of Georges Borchardt, Inc., as agents for the author), in Punch, Vol. 284, No. 7426, March 23, 1983, p. 69.

REGINALD HILL

[In *The Little Drummer Girl*] Le Carré has moved right away from Smiley-land to the Middle East, from the Cold War to the passions of the Israeli-Arab conflict, from national security to national hate. Smiley himself is no great miss, still less his tiresome wife. The fascination of the Smiley books lay increasingly in what he did rather than what it did to him, and in *Smiley's People* we were given a splendid gala performance by the espionage circus, a sort of celebratory perhaps even valedictory climax to a life of deception and make-believe. The skill was breathtaking but you didn't lie awake afterwards wondering what the performers did when they went home. We'd come a long way from the focal humanity of *The Spy Who Came In From The Cold*.

Now in *The Little Drummer Girl* the human dimension tops the bill once more, though happily not at the expense of those special effects, those shifts of shade and light, those transformation scenes, those *trompe l'oeil* backcloths, those gods out of machines, which make Le Carré's stagings of the drama of subversion so memorable. The theatrical metaphor is apt. The little drummer girl herself is an actress called Charlie. Why not? Karla, after all, was a chap. Names are where we start to know each other and in Le Carré's world, knowledge is the beginning of deceit. Who else would have called a constitutional melancholic Smiley? And the Smiley-figure here, the puppet-master, the planner, the director, the producer, but more skilful than Smiley, thinking bigger, moving further afield and faster, who spots, auditions and casts Charlie, is an Israeli first appearing as Schulmann whose real name is Kurtz, "though he used it so seldom, he might have been forgiven if one day he forgot it altogether."

Charlie is also known as 'Charlie the Red', not just for the colour of her hair. It is her unfocussed but passionately held radical beliefs that make her perfect for the part Kurtz has in mind. On the firm foundation of her known and documented sympathies with the Palestinian cause (as with every other anti-establishment capitalist/bourgeois/reactionary/Fascist cause) he can build for her an activist role which will eventually lead to a billing with Khalil, the superstar of Arab terrorism. But Charlie must accept the part willingly. It is a role too complex and too demanding to be maintained by someone simply coerced into it by threat, blackmail or bribery. It requires a twofold commitment which may tear her in half. For her to *agree* to it, she must be made to feel like an Israeli; for her to *succeed* in doing it, she must be made to feel like a Palestinian. And for the novel to succeed as a work of art, the reader must be persuaded that this is possible.

Le Carré does not belong to the with-one-mighty-leap school. He glosses over nothing in the long slow process of persuasion and preparation. And in the end we are thoroughly convinced.

> Reginald Hill, "Buy It," in Books and Bookmen (© copyright Brevet Publishing Ltd. 1983; reprinted with permission of the publisher), No. 331, April, 1983, p. 30.

MARTIN CRUZ SMITH

Writing about Le Carré is chancy. Ever since 1962, when *The Spy Who Came In from the Cold* was published, he has been the standard by which other writers of the so-called international thriller are measured. A couple of years ago I got the garland "Le Carré of the Year." The next season it was passed to the succeeding pretender. Le Carré stayed the constant. With his new novel, *The Little Drummer Girl*, he remains ahead of us, dwelling at, exploring, the very end of espionage as the analogy he helped create. . . .

In each new book, Le Carré becomes more involved and entangled in espionage as the professional technique it really is. This is the context and lesson of his work as it has developed: ever more detailed means, ever more obscure ends. . . .

This may be the best and most complete novel about espionage technique, about its psychoanalytical application, ever written. It's also the most balanced novel about Jews and Arabs, outrage for outrage and tear for tear, I've read. Still, for all that, there is no touch of Le Carré's great characters—no Leamas, no Smiley—in *The Little Drummer Girl*. While there is much to be learned about how to tear apart the psyche of a second-rate actress and remake her into a spy, there remains a vacuum for a central human. Charlie is essentially an innocent bystander, a fellow traveler, and the willing slave of love; she is shrewdly observed but so suggestible as to give us no constant person we can live in. Leamas, *Spy*'s centerpiece, has here developed into Gadi Becker, an Israeli intelligence officer, still middle-aged and scarred but smoother, handsomer, a deliberate seducer. He acts the part of a young Arab with painstaking exactness and utter denial of his own character and emotions, and he becomes more a blur the further we go into this long book. There are interesting secondary characters, but in the center no one alive. Espionage itself, with its self-deluding detail and obsession with manipulation, is the main character of *The Little Drummer Girl*.

It may be said that when espionage no longer delivers new characters, only finer gears, it has ceased to be a creative metaphor. Yet this is a bleak and daring novel for all its hollowness, because of its hollowness, and because it delivers a message with no comfort. *The Little Drummer Girl* is in part a primer on what it means to be a spy. Klaus Fuchs, the "Atomic Spy," once said he could work with, admire, and be a close friend to the people he was betraying because he operated with a "controlled schizophrenia." That schizophrenia is what Le Carré and Gadi teach; it is what all spies eventually must learn. (p. 106)

> Martin Cruz Smith, "Season of Spies" (copyright © 1983, Martin Cruz Smith; reprinted by permission of the author), in Esquire, Vol. 99, No. 4, April, 1983, pp. 106-07.*

THURSTON DAVIS

[Le Carré's] new novel, which marks a sharp break away from the tortured world of George Smiley and his colleagues at the Circus, springs from the author's complete immersion in the stream of Middle-East terror and counterterror. They spill out into many of the European cities to which the action of *The Little Drummer Girl* takes us. Le Carré entered that grim world looking for a fresh plot for Smiley, but he soon discovered that the locale demands a cast of entirely new characters. So he has given us Kurtz, Litwak, Ned Quilley, Tayeh, Salim, Khalil, the indomitable Joseph whose real name is Gadi Becker, together with a troop of subsidiary people, each drawn so as to be sharply remembered. Then, of course, there is Charmian, the girl, the drummer girl, known as "Charlie," or "Chas," or often "Charlie the Red," in deference to the color of her hair and her somewhat crazy radical stances.

Top Israeli intelligence people choose Charlie, a bright young actress from the stages of provincial England, to be their at first unwilling, then fully consenting, collaborator. This is where, for long pages of flawless tradecraft and endless attention to detail, our renowned author leads us through the thickets of an Israeli plan to ensnare and eliminate the most feared and elusive of Palestinian terrorists. As Kurtz, grizzled espionage genius who sets the plot in motion for the Israelis, explains with his "pirate's grin": "You want to catch the lion, first you tether the goat."

Frankly, it is here, where Charlie is inveigled into taking the goat's role in what her Israeli kidnappers and mentors keep telling her is a "theatre of the real," that credibility becomes definitely strained. Even this long-addicted reader of Mr. le Carré had to struggle over immense stretches of dreamlike narration, to maintain some measure of willing suspension of disbelief. To his great credit, the author won out, but it was a triumph of his writing over the implausibilities and arabesques of plot.

"Dreamlike" seems, on reflection, the best way to denominate the quality of that writing. The author has this confident, idiosyncratic way of moving from scene to scene with no sign of noting the sharp turns and yawning interstices that might, in a less fantastic setting, call for a few words of explanation. But that's the way dreams behave, don't they?

Let no one fail to see, however, that le Carré has added another worldful of unforgettable characters to the treasury of his literary imagination. But even more significant—at least, so it seems to one reader—is the powerful and assured way he has taken hold of the dilemmas faced by Israel in this dolorous year after the fateful 1982 incursion into Lebanon.

At the very end of this novel, Gadi Becker, alias Joseph, speaks out of his deep sorrow to an uncompreding Israeli official. Gadi asks a question, "a most offensive question," a question he claims he has culled from the writings of the late Arthur Koestler. "What are we to become, I wonder? A Jewish homeland or an ugly little Spartan state?" (pp. 264-66)

> Thurston Davis, in a review of "The Little Drummer Girl" (reprinted with permission of America Press, Inc. and the author; © 1983; all rights reserved), in America, Vol. 148, No. 13, April 2, 1983, pp. 264-66.

JAMES WOLCOTT

With *The Little Drummer Girl*, John le Carré has thrown off his winter cloak and let his limbs flex. Unlike the Smiley novels, which have a burrowing, circumspect determination, *The Little Drummer Girl* doesn't read as if it were written with mittens. The book feels as if it were dashed off with the zealous haste of a reporter filing for a deadline. Once the dread Karla had been flushed from his lair like a sick, shivering animal at the close of *Smiley's People* . . . , le Carré must have sensed it was time to strike down the tents of the Circus and push on to a larger, more turbulent arena—the Middle East.

Yet this novel is far from a severe break from le Carré's previous preoccupations. . . . With its secret sharers and frequent stresses on terrorism as the theater of the real, *The Little Drummer Girl* is a rugged elaboration on that moment when Smiley and Karla met as mirrors. Newsy as the novel is, it's also le Carré's go at writing a meditative adventure saga in the tradition of Joseph Conrad, and it's hardly a fluke that one of the characters here is named Joseph; another, Kurtz. A concealed bomb is this book's heart of darkness.

Not that le Carré succumbs to Conradian mystifications. *The Little Drummer Girl* is very bold colored, very pop; it pares away the brooding ruminations of a Conrad adventure to reach instead the sinews of heroic romance. . . .

Like all of le Carré's novels, *The Little Drummer Girl* abounds in well-choreographed set pieces; a description of a bomb explosion knocking flowers out of vases, and vases against the wall; an account of how the bearings of a prisoner are psychologically stripped by Israeli intelligence through the use of time distortion, white light, forged documents, and sound effects (screams, gunfire, chain rattles, even the forlorn tootle of funeral bagpipes); a tour of a Palestinian guerrilla camp, where the stone battlements suggest a set for a remake of *Beau Geste* and the figures for target practice are "brutish man-sized effigies of American marines, with painted grimaces and fixed bayonets. . . ." But the gut of the novel is the recruitment, auditioning, and rehearsing of Charlie in her new role as counterinsurgent lure—the applying of her blinkers. And it takes an awfully long time to get a secure fit. (p. 19)

For all its waywardness, *The Little Drummer Girl* carries an exhilaration because it's le Carré's firmest and most searching exploration of the dynamics of need, and how neediness is used, perverted. Love of his daughter toppled Karla, and love here is betrayal and submission, crippler and crutch. And the absence of love, le Carré seems to be saying in the novel's fade, is not hate but exhaustion. *I'm dead, I'm dead.* As in the best Smiley novels, le Carré poeticizes exhaustion in *The*

Little Drummer Girl, and leaves you feeling that there are embers in the ashes of fatigue which will spark new obsessions, new betrayals. Hungry for reckoning, his burnt-out cases never find true rest. (p. 21)

> James Wolcott, "The Secret Sharers," in The New York Review of Books *(reprinted with permission from* The New York Review of Books; *copyright © 1983 Nyrev, Inc.), Vol. XXX, No. 6, April 14, 1983, pp. 19-21.*

DAVID PRYCE-JONES

John Le Carré's thrillers have conveyed, as few others, the urgency of the struggle waged between East and West, between totalitarianism and democracy. The struggle is openly about human values, and its outcome will affect the lives of virtually everyone. Some aspects of it nevertheless are largely invisible, or at least concealed from public inspection, and it is upon them that Le Carré has focused. In order to depict the East-West struggle in fictional terms, he has blurred its moral outlines, to show that both sides use comparable means to advance their very different ends. The intensity and drive of his thrillers have derived from the ambiguity at their center, whereby good men often do evil for reasons of state.

The Little Drummer Girl is constructed upon the fraught issue of the Palestinians and the Israelis, a microcosm of the East-West struggle, to be sure, but more importantly a historical issue in its own right. The famous seductions of Le Carré's fiction, however, are not the whole story. For all the twists and turns of his plot, and the ironies and complexities of his character portraiture, this novel is about a current flesh-and-blood conflict. Here, one might have thought, is an ideal subject for moral ambiguity. Le Carré finds it clear-cut. To him, the Palestinians are good, the Israelis bad. Such tension as there is springs only from the presentation of the good as unfortunately weak, and the bad as unnaturally strong.

In this novel, the Israelis have become committed to sweeping away the whole pack of Palestinian men, women, and children. Israeli murderous intentions are posited time and again. "Nervous politicians and war-hungry generals" are accused of making the killing of innocent Palestinians the habitual practice of the armed forces. In the novel's foreground are the first-line killers, members of the Israeli secret service, repulsive characters one and all. Neither universal morality nor the laws of their country act as the slightest restraint upon their urge to power and domination, for the greater glory of Israel. (p. 27)

The willing submission of Charlie to Kurtz and Gadi is an implausibility so enormous and so central that the story collapses under it. Love is all very well, but she is risking her life every day on behalf of Israelis whom she scarcely knows, who treat her abominably, and whom she thinks wrong and wicked, in order to damage Palestinians whom she admires without reserve. Her motivation is incoherent. Manipulated in this incredible manner, she is that very old figment indeed, the nice Gentile girl who has fallen into the hands of secretive and scheming Jews who will stop at nothing.

The implausibility serves a purpose for Le Carré, however, for it allows him to express the most extreme anti-Israel passions through the mouth of a character ostensibly working for Israel. When Charlie screams that the Israelis are fascists and rotten killing bastards, these obscenities can appear to be wished upon her by exigencies of plot. Such is not the case, however. Here is a matter, which for all its twists of narrative, belongs to the dimension of agitprop. It is wretched. It is also childish in its sentimental personifications of good and evil. To reduce the complex Arab-Israeli encounter, with its weight of suffering, to this pictorial simplicity, is to ignore its history and its contemporary reality. To select some ideals for praise, or some guilts for blame, at the expense of all other ideals and guilts, is not an act of imagination, but a lie. (p. 29)

Le Carré's opinion of Israel—his participation in this campaign against it—is a matter of record. In *The Observer* of June 13, 1982, he laid the foundation for a comparison between Israelis and Nazis. The Israeli invasion of Lebanon, he wrote, was "a monstrosity, launched on speciously assembled grounds." (pp. 29-30)

Generally speaking, people of independent mind can acquire adequate information to measure agitprop against what actually happens in the Middle East. Lies and distortions, even in newspapers or on television, are open to correction. But *The Little Drummer Girl* matters very much indeed, because in it the contemporary image of Israel as an unutterable, indeed Nazi, evil is crystallized, and this portrait will go round the world with the authority of a best seller. Statements in fiction are immune to the truths of real life. A novel lives in the imagination, after all, and it is there, for the credulous, that the image of an evil Israel will be fired and sustained. And an imagination like Le Carré's, when out of control, is a thing that will impress those who want to believe in a demonological vision, or perhaps cannot judge it for themselves, and it will scarify a good many others. . . .

[The] Palestinians have seen for themselves why and how Jews arrived in their midst, not in the least as "powerful European custodians" but as pitiful survivors from a real genocide. It has not been the failure to kill more Jews that has aroused their bitterness, but the failure to make peace. Even in P.L.O. circles, they know that they and the Israelis have been inexorably trapped in the same history: that is the nature of the tragedy.

But now an author of renown and standing comes to inform the Palestinians that they have been wrong in these perceptions. They are to understand instead that they have been selected for premeditated assault by a people too powerful to be defended, but so inherently evil that peace cannot be made with them. Incited to become aggressive, they also find themselves patronized for being helpless. If Le Carré's view is correct, then the Palestinians have nothing to live for, since whatever they do in these frightening circumstances, the Jews will still be the death of them. Real enemies are not so harmful and demoralizing as friends like these. (p. 30)

> David Pryce-Jones, "A Demonological Fiction," in The New Republic *(reprinted by permission of* The New Republic; *© 1983 The New Republic, Inc.), Vol. 188, No. 15, April 18, 1983, pp. 27-30.*

MARGHANITA LASKI

[It] is not on being an excellent thriller-writer that John le Carré has gained the kind of superior acceptance that Marilyn Monroe has over Joan Blondell, but because he has come to count (as, say, Price, Gardner, Freeling, and Lyall have not) as a *good* writer, a writer worthy of more than inclusion in some forthcoming Best of British Thrillers list, a writer who can be read for vicariously authentic agony. So is *The Little Drummer Girl* a *good* book? It's hard to feel that this is a useful question as compared with the far more interesting, Is this a good thriller? And yes, it is, though with interesting flaws.

The most trying of these is a flaw that is becoming endemic in the better thriller-writers, those who are confident that they have made a world which has become an overlap with our own reality. The flaw is knowingness. The way le Carré plays it here, as he did in *Smiley's People,* is to posit the existence of his puppet world as one that abides outside and beyond the circumference of any novel carved out of it, a world whose creatures in some other time than that of the novel in question can look at what happened there and judge it: not only we, the readers, but the devoted team of Kurtz the Israeli spymaster will, as Smiley's boys did, wonder if he knew, if he foresaw, and was this the wisest way, that the finest hour?

Then, boldly and deliberately (though I am not certain that deliberately it was), le Carré has deprived himself of the most usual exercise of tension: will our man or, here, our woman, Charlie, the small-time actress, be blown, be caught, get away and even succeed? And the reason for this is that Charlie, uprooted, unplaced, untruthful young shiksa, has been turned by the Israelis, or, rather, by one Israeli, the mysterious, infinitely beguiling Joseph. What Charlie was caught for was, of course, good. 'We are decent people,' Kurtz insists to her impertinent defiance after hijacking her in Greece, the expected night of love with Joseph becoming a fantasy affair with a phantom Arab. But it is not only decent that the Israelis are: what they are too, as they have been in thrillers ever since Entebbe, is marvellous, miraculous, brilliant, unbeatable, so wonderful that the other side, the inferior if pitiable Arabs, haven't a chance.

So nothing, we know, can possibly happen to Charlie that her Israeli masters don't intend. . . . So in addition to almost knowing that, as almost always, our side, which is the Israeli side, which is the right side, is bound to triumph, we are spared, while in suspended belief, any worry about it.

Thus the tensions, if adequate, are unusually limited. (pp. 27-8)

[It] would be improper for you to learn here how Charlie ends up. But this I will tell you. Three-quarters of the way through there is an exceptionally good piece of lovemaking.

We are over-used to these in thrillers, whether inserted to fill up a few pages or to display a kind of knowingness that no writer mentioned in this review would have recourse to. This one, however, which is briefly told, minimally detailed, is as climactically necessary and as cathartic as any other I can recall in fiction. The title is excellent in all its reverberations. (p. 28)

Marghanita Laski, "Oh, the Brave Music!" (© British Broadcasting Corp. 1983; reprinted by permission of Marghanita Laski), in The Listener, *Vol. 109, No. 2805, April 21, 1983, pp. 27-8.*

RAEL JEAN ISAAC AND ERICH ISAAC

Apart from the rare scathing review, *The Little Drummer Girl* has won well-nigh universal praise. In some respects the praise is deserved, for the novel moves at a brisker pace than most Le Carré novels while retaining their characteristic virtues: it is carefully plotted, well written, has a strong sense of place, and offers a credible portrait of the mechanisms of clandestine intelligence struggle. . . .

[However, the] novel suffers from Le Carré's weakness in characterization. He makes elaborate efforts with Charlie, his first female protagonist, but the end result is a mass of contradictions. (p. 24)

But *The Little Drummer Girl* is interesting principally because in it Le Carré carries forward—and moves beyond—the themes of his previous novels. Le Carré's protagonists are usually British and Soviet (or East European) agents and spymasters, whose similarity of methods and perspectives make them into mirror images of one another. In the Smiley novels, on which Le Carré's fame rests, Smiley eventually triumphs over Karla, his Soviet antagonist, but in the process becomes the mirror image of his enemy. . . .

It is, to be sure, legitimate for a novelist to point out that there are similarities between people who fill similar roles. But by never exploring the differences between the systems Smiley and Karla represent, Le Carré conveys the impression that there is no difference between the governments for which they work or the societies they serve. Le Carré thus draws upon and feeds currents fashionable among liberals in the West who emphasize supposed correspondences and convergences between East and West, and insinuates to the reading public the idea that a determined enemy is no different from his prey.

On the surface *The Little Drummer Girl* seems to follow the same pattern. Le Carré applies his familiar mirror-imaging technique to his Israeli agents and Palestinian terrorists. (p. 25)

But these suggestions of ambiguity and correspondence are deceptive, for Le Carré sets Israel up as the villain of this novel. He ignores the broader Arab-Israel conflict and confines his focus to Israel and the Palestinians—in Le Carré's portrait a military juggernaut against a helpless, dispossessed people. The bitterest attacks on Israel are from the mouths of Israelis (there are no mirror-imaging attacks on the Palestinian cause by Palestinian Arabs). For example, Joseph, the agent who "runs" Charlie, provides a long, emotional defense of the Palestinian cause. And it is an Israeli professor's wife who compares Zionism and nazism. . . . Both Joseph's speech and that of the professor's wife can be partially defended in terms of the novel's structure. . . . But Le Carré serves as PLO propagandist well beyond the requirements of his plot. . . . Le Carré's use of the professor and his wife, the Minkels, is propagandistic because they are wholly implausible targets for an Arab terrorist. Khalil decides to eliminate Minkel because he fears the professor's moderation and willingness to acknowledge Palestinian rights will weaken Arab resolve by making it appear that the Israelis are ready to make concessions their leaders will not in fact make. (pp. 25-6)

Le Carré employs meretricious techniques to make Israel appear guilty of the vicious practices that the PLO has made famous. . . . Repeatedly Le Carré implies that Israelis make children a deliberate target. Charlie participates in a march in which children demonstrate on a playing field in the camp. She notices aircraft and the bombs fall. No one is hurt this time, but Charlie knows why. "You bastards, she thought. You rotten killing Zionist bastards. If I hadn't been here, you'd have bombed them to Kingdom Come." Even the Israeli spymaster Kurtz is horrified by his government. . . . Throughout this book Kurtz is engaged in a race against time, trying to eliminate Khalil so as to prevent "those clowns in the Knesset and Defense" from launching all-out war. When Israeli forces move into Lebanon, Kurtz is crushed: "His body seemed to shrink to half its size, his Slav eyes lost all their sparkle, he looked his age, whatever that was, at last." Joseph is also "unable to come to terms with what was being done in the name of Zion." He asked himself what Israel was to become: "A Jewish homeland, or an ugly little Spartan state?" . . .

In *The Little Drummer Girl* Le Carré has transcended the fashion that sees no difference of consequence between East and West; he has joined the still more fashionable ranks of those ranged *against* Western values and civilization. He has aligned himself with those who see virtue and vigor in the terror of "the weak" (usually backed in practice by the arms of the Soviet Union, whether in the Middle East, Central America, or elsewhere). That their targets may be representative democracy, the rule of law, and civil liberties is a matter of indifference. It is interesting in this light that, although part of the novel is set in Lebanon, there is no indication of what the PLO did to destroy the institutions of one Arab country that most closely approximated Israel in its respect for Western values. Le Carré seems to disdain European anarchists, although he portrays them accurately enough as integral to Palestinian terrorist networks. To underscore his point, Le Carré has his highly sympathetic terrorist training chief Tayeh dismiss them as "scum." Presumably, for Le Carré, middle class and affluent, they lack the experience of suffering that makes identical activities by Palestinian terrorists justifiable. (p. 26)

Le Carré has set out to undermine the common sense of the common man with what Alan Pryce-Jones aptly calls his "demonological" fiction [see excerpt above], which will reach millions through paperback editions and sway millions more through the more powerful images of the film verison now being prepared. (p. 27)

*Rael Jean Isaac and Erich Isaac, "Tinny Drum,"
in* Chronicles of Culture *(copyright © 1983 by The Rockford Institute), Vol. 7, No. 8, August, 1983, pp. 24-7.*

Elmore Leonard
1925-

(Also writes under pseudonym of Emmett Long) American novelist, short story writer, and scriptwriter.

Leonard is a crime writer whose works are usually set in Detroit. His crime novels are praised for their believable plots, authentic characterizations, and clear, effective prose style. Some critics compare Leonard's books with those of Raymond Chandler and Ross Macdonald, and Leonard himself cites Ernest Hemingway and James M. Cain as influences on his narrative style.

Leonard's early work includes several western novels and short stories published in pulp magazines during the 1950s. He also wrote the scripts for the films *Joe Kidd* (1973) and *Mr. Majestyk* (1974). Leonard's novels *Fifty-two Pickup* (1974), *Swag* (1976), and *Unknown Man No. 89* (1977) received favorable critical response for their refreshing originality and for the creation of some of the most despicable villains in crime fiction. *City Primeval: High Noon in Detroit* (1980), perhaps his most violent novel, is based on Leonard's own interviews and experiences as he accompanied a Detroit police homicide squad on its patrols. *Stick* (1983) contains humorous elements in its depiction of an ex-convict's attempt to go straight amid the drug trafficking business in southern Florida.

(See also *Contemporary Authors*, Vols. 81-84.)

Photograph by Joan Leonard

NEWGATE CALLENDAR

When Elmore Leonard's **"Fifty-Two Pickup"** appeared in 1974, it had some critics talking in terms of Raymond Chandler and Ross Macdonald. **"Swag"** in 1976 indicated that Leonard's first book was no mere accident. A new and important writer of mystery fiction had arrived. Now comes **"Unknown Man No. 89,"** and it maintains the high standard Leonard has set for himself.

But it really is wrong to talk of this writer in terms of Chandler and Macdonald. He has little in common with those two. They are "clean" writers; there is no profanity to speak of in Chandler, and Macdonald has never been an exponent of the *verísmo* school of speech. Leonard is.

The real influence on Leonard is George V. Higgins, whose "The Friends of Eddie Coyle" came out about five years ago and marked a breakthrough into the kind of language previously encountered only in paperback books with green covers. (p. 13)

Higgins was the first to take full advantage of the new permissiveness. Like Higgins's, Leonard's characters, all middle-class or criminal types, speak in a way that cannot be reproduced in a family newspaper. Leonard often cannot resist a set-piece—a lowbrow aria with a crazy kind of scatological poetry of its own—in the Higgins manner.

But that is where the similarity ends. Where Higgins wrote only about criminals, Leonard writes about basically decent, ordinary men who get into trouble and have to work their way out of it. In **"Swag,"** the decent man happens to be a criminal, but toward the end he achieves all but mythic stature. In **"Fifty-Two Pickup"** a rich industrialist commits one sexual mistake and is blackmailed. Rough and tough, he will not give in, and he finds a way to get rid of the punks. Permanently. He too emerges bigger than life at the end.

Leonard is a moralist in his way. In all three of his books, Good overcomes Evil (even in **'Swag,"** where the hero is finally undone only by a freak of fate). But Leonard is also a realist and, in an objective, matter-of-fact way, he can portray some of the most vicious, slimy villains that ever horrified a spellbound reader.

"Unknown Man No. 89" follows the pattern. It is the story of a not very admirable man who, under stress, discovers himself and becomes a whole man. The central character is a man named Ryan, formerly a drifter, now a process-server who is very good at his job. He follows Rule No. 1: Never get personally involved. But get involved he does, with a young lady about to be fleeced by an oily, dangerous crook. He gets her out of trouble at the end, in a blaze of Leonardian pyrotechnical finesse. As in the two previous books, the plotting is remarkably ingenious.

Also, as in the other two books, the locale is Detroit. . . . He knows his city, and he has observed some of the hoodlums in it. He is very good at creating figures of menace. . . . (pp. 13, 32)

Leonard bows to no one in plot construction. Yet there is never the feeling of gimmickry in his plots; events follow a natural course. Above all, there is Leonard's style. He has a wonderful ear, and his dialogue never has a false note. He avoids artiness, writes clear expository prose and has the ability to create real people. It is not High Literature, nor does it pretend to be. Leonard is primarily an entertainer. But he is one with enormous finesse, and he can write circles around almost anybody active in the crime novel today. (p. 33)

> *Newgate Callendar, "Decent Men in Trouble," in* The New York Times Book Review *(copyright © 1977 by The New York Times Company; reprinted by permission), May 22, 1977, pp. 13, 32-3.*

THE TIMES LITERARY SUPPLEMENT

In Elmore Leonard's ***The Hunted*** . . . Ed Rosen, head of a million-dollar mortgage company, is blackmailed by the Justice Department into testifying against two mobsters on indictment for murder; but both beat the rap, and Rosen leaves hurriedly for Israel. . . . [His] identity is accidentally revealed, and three hitmen arrive on the plane that is also bringing his lawyer with $200,000 severance pay from the company. On his side Rosen has a pretty Israeli girl and Davis, a Marine guard at the United States Embassy, with two Purple Hearts and a Silver Star from Vietnam, and only twenty-seven days to do in the corps. His professional instincts as an infantry-man are aroused by the situation; he takes command, and after a few inconclusive skirmishes the book comes to a climax with a siege and pitched battle in the desert near Eilat. Brilliantly written, and extremely funny at times, with some good oddball characters (such as Willard Mims, the gung-ho Marine who keeps a cache of souvenir Claymore mines in his foot-locker), ***The Hunted*** is exciting enough to warrant, for once, the adjective "unputdownable".

> *A review of "The Hunted," in* The Times Literary Supplement *(© Times Newspapers Ltd. (London) 1978; reproduced from* The Times Literary Supplement *by permission), No. 3972, May 19, 1978, p. 545.*

CONNIE FLETCHER

Leonard's style [in ***City Primeval***] is clear, crisp, and mean. He writes about a tough-guy cop, Raymond Cruz, who lights out after crooks and con artists in one of the world's toughest cities, Detroit. Cruz tracks down high-level corruption as he investigates the murder of a very abusive, very angry, very important citizen—Judge Alvin B. Guy. Guy was about to squawk, murder stopped his breath, and Cruz finds out what the judge was about to reveal. Strong stuff.

> *Connie Fletcher, in a review of "City Primeval: High Noon in Detroit," in* Booklist *(reprinted by permission of the American Library Association; copyright © 1980 by the American Library Association), Vol. 77, No. 7, December 1, 1980, p. 506.*

ROBIN WINKS

Elmore Leonard has written his toughest book in ***City Primeval: High Noon in Detroit***. . . . It's too bad Leonard felt he needed a subtitle, for the theme is obvious enough: how one vicious killer and one committed cop come to see themselves locked in a classic shootout in the OK Corral of modern America, the city in which the lone hero climbed down from his mustang to climb into his Mustang and do battle once again for the cowardly, blind populace. This is rough stuff: the language, the attitudes, and the people are all unpleasant, products of the city that has grown up over the primeval forest. Theme, plot, writing are obvious, yet compelling.

> *Robin Winks, in a review of "City Primeval: High Noon in Detroit," in* The New Republic *(reprinted by permission of* The New Republic; *© 1980 The New Republic, Inc.), Vol. 183, No. 24, December 13, 1980, p. 40.*

KEN TUCKER

Elmore Leonard strikes me as being the finest thriller writer alive primarily because he does his best to efface style, and has done this so successfully that few readers know about him at all. Since 1953, Leonard has written a remarkable series of novels, Westerns as well as thrillers, the latest of which is ***Split Images***. . . . There are no wisecrack-eloquent detectives or over-wrought similes in Leonard's writing. His characters are often lower-middle-class people who fall into crime because it's an easier way to make money than that tedious nine-to-five. Leonard's favorite plot is the revenge story—someone exploited by criminals commits a bigger, better crime that ruins his or her victimizers. . . .

[In] ***Split Images***, Walter Kouza, a 21-year veteran of the Detroit police force, leaves his job to become a chauffeur for Robbie Daniels, a demented millionaire whose hobby is planning the assassination of a larcenous Latin American fat cat. Kouza knows he's asking for trouble, but figures that being well-paid and enjoying a few upper-class comforts is worth enduring a little of his employer's madness. What he doesn't realize is that Daniels is more than a right-wing eccentric—he's a peevish killer who uses his gun collection to plug anyone who annoys him. Pretty soon, another cop—honest plodder Bryan Hurd, the hero of the tale—is on the trail of both of them.

Split Images is filled with references to recent public shootings: upon first seeing his old colleague Hurd, Walter Kouza jabbers, "You believe it? Secret Service're standing there, the guy squeezes off six rounds, empties the piece, then, *then* they're all over him . . . what's his name, Hinckle? Then this other thing, Jesus Christ, the motive, thing with the broad? What's her name, Jodie Foster? 'Gain her respect and love'—I never even heard of her. . . ." As ***Split Images*** unwinds, Leonard fills the air with violence; fact and fiction merge. After Daniels murders a parking-lot attendant, a policeman inspecting the body notes that "the one in the head very much like that press secretary, what's his name?"

More is at stake here than trendy timeliness. Leonard's references capture the way monstrous crimes enter our minds as a jumble of TV-news details, bad jokes, and nightmares—the way everyone is always burying the information, always saying, "What's his name?" Leonard never pushes for a profound analysis; he knows that violence works in superficial ways. . . .

Split Images is in many ways a companion piece to his 1980 ***City Primeval: High Noon in Detroit***. . . . Both novels feature cops as their heroes instead of thieves, and both attempt to stoke a romance between the policeman and a woman whose career is just as rough.

But romance curdles Leonad's writing. During the sticky scenes in *Split Images*, he reverts to being an ad man for the amorous: "He said I love you. He said it again and then again, trying the emphasis on a different word. He said, I'm in love with you . . . " . . . His inability to convey a complex love relationship may define his limitation as a novelist, even as it indicates the extent of his ambition.

But the failed romance doesn't ruin *Split Images*; the book has a hard, clean narrative voice that sets the scene properly before the characters begin their icy chatter. And though he's named George Higgins as a crucial exemplar, it's clear that Leonard also understands Higgins's flaw: in reducing the thriller to pure dialogue, he rendered his novels as elegantly mannered as Ivy Compton-Burnett's.

Leonard resists mannerism instinctively; it's one reason he ditches his heroes from book to book, always inventing new crooks and detectives who weight the balance between good and bad in quirky disproportion. Early on in Leonard's best novels, there's always a disorienting, exhilarating period when you can't tell where your sympathy is supposed to fall; the first few chapters not only offer up the donnée of the thriller plot, but also spend a while picking, choosing, and discarding people—a cop who looks like a pip of a fellow in chapter one gets blown away in chapter three so that a seedy hood flitting around the back alleys of the story can step into the glare of Leonard's admiring prose. The best thing about *Split Images*, in fact, is that initially it looks as if we'll have to work up a fondness for rich, twitchy Robbie Daniels; what a relief it is when Bryan Hurd, as unassuming a gumshoe as you'll find this side of Jim Rockford, comes forward to mull over Daniels's nastiness.

This lovely trick of Leonard's—the ability to keep you in the dark about not only where the story is going, but also who its hero is—adds great force to the violence that rears up regularly; it permits the author to dispatch characters you may have been convinced were central to the drama. In all of this there's a kind of wicked amorality. Thriller writers can be the cruelest of artist-gods, lopping off heads in cynical, mean ways, as if envisioning the colorful scenes they'll make in the movie version. But Leonard is much more skillful, more scarily witty, than that. The violence in his books is quick, quiet, and brutal; it's the kind that can strike you as being true and realistic even though the actions are utterly beyond your experience. Can an artist receive a higher compliment than that?

Ken Tucker, "The Author Vanishes: Elmore Leonard's Quiet Thrillers" (reprinted by permission of The Village Voice *and the author; copyright © News Group Publications, Inc., 1982), in* The Village Voice, *Vol. XXVII, No. 8, February 23, 1982, p. 41.*

JONATHAN YARDLEY

Leonard's bandwagon had left the station by the time I heard its music, and I've had to do some running to catch up. But better late than never: Leonard is the real thing. He doesn't write "literature," and I'd be astonished if he claimed to; there's nothing in his fiction to suggest that he packs even an ounce of pretentiousness. But like John D. MacDonald, whom he resembles but does not appear to imitate, he raises the hardboiled suspense novel beyond the limits of genre and into social commentary; he paints an acute, funny and sometimes very bitter picture of a world that is all too real and recognizable, yet a world that rarely makes an appearance in the kind of fiction that is routinely given serious consideration.

It is a world in which people do business; they don't often do it honestly, but in one form or another business is what they do. This is the great untouched subject in contemporary American fiction: the focus round which American life revolves, yet which American writers resolutely ignore. As a character in *Stick* puts it: "Anyway, what's my goal, the American dream. What else? Put money in some gimmick everybody *has* to have, get rich and retire. No more worries, no more looking over your shoulder." Making a buck: it's a story rooted as deeply as any other in the American tradition, yet when it comes to telling it in fiction, only a handful of suspense writers and an occasional peddler of schlock are willing to take up the challenge.

The buck-making in *Stick* takes two forms: Chucky hustles drugs, Barry engages in "investing, trading or speculating." The fellow who watches them both is named Ernest Stickley Jr., known to one and all as Stick. . . . He has just been released from prison in Michigan, where he served seven years for armed robbery. Now he is in South Florida. . . .

But that's only part of the story. As Stick goes through the process of getting back into the rhythm of life outside the penitentiary, Leonard sends him through an impressive (but in no way gratuitous) series of alarms and diversions: the tawdry underworld of the drug dealers, the tacky luxuries of the ostentatiously rich, the clash between Anglo and Latin cultures as it permeates life in South Florida. There's a rather hilarious evening during which more sexual passion is thrust at Stick than even a "real man" can handle, and several sobering encounters with unsavory fellows whose assignment is to put Stick permanently out of commission.

But if thrills and amussements are Leonard's principal stock in trade, it is also clear that *Stick* is a novel with more serious purposes. Stick, as he re-enters the world of ordinary life after seven years in the cramped, isolated world of prison, is a man trying to adjust; Leonard has Jack Henry Abbot firmly in mind as he depicts Stick's attempts to relearn the rules of the world on the outside, rather than to impose the laws of "the hole" on society. And he obviously has Abbott's literary and political accomplices in mind when he depicts Barry Stam, with his taste for assembling a retinue of the violent and notorious. . . .

Elmore Leonard has no tolerance for sham or pretense, in the prose he writes or the people he depicts. He's a funny writer—all the best suspense writers are—and an incisive, unsparing one. He does honest work, and reading it is great pleasure.

Jonathan Yardley, "Elmore Leonard: Making Crime Pay in Miami," in Book World—The Washington Post *(© 1983, The Washington Post), February 20, 1983, p. 3.*

GEORGE STADE

[Elmore Leonard] is never more entertaining than when one of his villains is stealing a scene. They are inspired hams, these bad actors, so empty inside that they only become themselves when they are playing a part, milking it for all it's worth. There is therefore something desperate about their zest, which nevertheless releases our own. (Think of Laurence Olivier playing Richard III; think of Marlon Brando playing the bounty hunter in "The Missouri Breaks"; think of Orson Welles playing anything.) They are treacherous and tricky, smart enough to outsmart themselves, driven, audacious and outrageous, capable of anything, paranoid-cunning and casually vicious—and rousing fun. Mr. Leonard's villains upstage his heroes, who are sticks, and his heroines, who are as modish and blank as the dummies in Bloomingdale's windows.

The chief villain of **"Stick"** (a book named after its hero) is Charles Lindsay Gorman III, known on the street as Chucky Buck. He is a wholesale distributor of controlled substances like grass, hash and coke. He is rich, but he is not happy.... Bucky knows that he is due to be either busted by the narcs or whacked by the wise guys. What he wants is a safe investment for all this cash he has hidden around his top-floor Fort Lauderdale condominium, looking to retire, get down off the hook....

[As] we move through swingers' bars, swanky country clubs, sumptuous estates, 60-foot yachts, we meet the supporting players, each made vivid and distinct through a single gesture, a bit of costume, a few lines of dialogue. Mr. Leonard's skills as a caricaturist and satirist are very impressive. (p. 11)

Whenever the heavies, bit players and walk-ons are performing, this novel is irresistible.

The novel, unfortunately, also has a hero and a heroine. Stick is the familiar 20-minute yegg, wary, wily, living by his wits, reputed to be laconic but garrulous in fact, touchy about his honor, quick to rescue a pretty barmaid being bothered by a drunk.... The heroine, Kyle McLaren, a super-successful investment counselor, exists mainly to magnify Stick, to show him off to us. One night this penniless and 42-year-old ex-con is bedded down by three beautiful, well-off and experienced women. There is no reason why Mr. Leonard should not enjoy himself through his hero, but the scenes between Stick and his women make for slack reading. The long bull sessions between Stick and Kyle on this and that, on life in general, are awful. They make you wonder whether Mr. Leonard's many admiring critics have not begun to make him take himself, rather than his writing, seriously.

But these scenes don't last forever (it only seems that way)—about 40 pages out of 300. For the rest, when Mr. Leonard is observing, satirizing, plotting, working up suspense, thickening the air with menace, discharging it in lightning flashes of violence, exposing the black holes behind the parts people play—when he tends to business, that is, he gives us as much serious fun per word as anyone around. (p. 41)

George Stade, "Villains Have the Fun," in The New York Times Book Review *(copyright © 1983 by The New York Times Company; reprinted by permission), March 6, 1983, pp. 11, 41.*

RAYMOND OBSTFELD

I read an article about [Elmore Leonard] in *Writer's Digest* a few months ago and went out and bought his **City Primeval: High Noon in Detroit**.... It's practically a textbook in hard-boiled cop style, without the self-consciousness that usually goes with such a style. I loved it enough to buy **Cat Chaser**, which I thought was even better. So when **Split Images** arrived in one of those cancerous tan envelopes, I was looking forward to reading it that night.

I wasn't disappointed. Mr. Leonard doesn't strain himself with character details, but somehow the characters are three-dimensional and compelling. The plot isn't complex—cop hunts down playboy killer while courting dynamic woman reporter—but its simplicity is one of its strengths. Leonard's main fault here is that he does not do a believable job in establishing the love interest, a problem in all three of the books of his I've read. The cop and the reporter fall for each other much too quickly and easily, as if the romantic angle were merely a bothersome convention to be dispensed with quickly. Still, I enjoyed the characters so much that I couldn't wait to get back to the book at night to find out what would happen to them.

Raymond Obstfeld, "Paper Crimes," in The Armchair Detective *(copyright © 1983 by The Armchair Detective), Vol. 16, No. 3, Summer, 1983, p. 296.*

NEAL JOHNSTON

The tone of Elmore Leonard's latest mystery [**"LaBrava"**] is dry and mordant, the action well paced and the voices of the riffraff convincing. I do not know if Mr. Leonard has captured the real Miami Beach in the pastel seediness of the place he describes, but his depiction is entirely convincing and should entice readers to be manipulated and led through an intricate maze.

Joseph LaBrava is the conventional omnicompetent, angst-ridden former agent. After too many months protecting Bess Truman from her piano parlor, he has left the Secret Service to take photographs of aged Jewish ladies sitting on the porches and Latin hustlers sauntering through the shadows of the Floridian Grand Concourse. (Is anyone writing about a American detective who is happily married?)

LaBrava finds himself photographing the principals of two seemingly separate extortion schemes. (p. 12)

LaBrava has been trained to observe—to sit endlessly inside the automotive equivalent of the plain brown wrapper watching for something to happen, to stand endlessly on boring campaign platforms and look for unusual activity in the audience, to wait endlessly for the daily arrival of the postman at Mrs. Truman's house. Having stumbled on the connection between the two schemes, the conventional detective would arrest the villain, but Mr. Leonard, playing games with his clichés, finds a much more arresting function for his hero. Mr. Leonard exploits and dismembers most of the clichés of the mystery genre by ingeniously combining them with the clichés of the old black-and-white movies LaBrava watched as a boy and again as a man while protecting Mrs. Truman.

The book's many surprises have nothing to do with the identities of the three different killers of the three victims scattered about the field. There is no question about who kills whom or why, nor are there questions about all the sleazy scams that are woven into the plot. Instead, the surprises concern the revelation, unraveling and reraveling of the book's devious design.

Elmore Leonard is a prolific author with a cult following.... **"LaBrava"** may be the best of Mr. Leonard's books; it is about as good as the form allows. And even in winter, it is warming to realize that next summer there will be a stock of Leonard books to substitute for the Ross Macdonald titles that won't be forthcoming. **"LaBrava"** has no more redeeming social value than any of the dozen petty criminals who people its pages, but it fills an evening well. (pp. 12, 26)

Neal Johnston, "A Maze in Miami" in The New York Times Book Review *(copyright © 1983 by The*

New York Times Company; reprinted by permission), November 27, 1983, pp. 12, 26.

ALAN CHEUSE

I was an Elmore Leonard virgin, perhaps the last one on my block. Then I picked up a copy of his new novel, **"LaBrava,"** and gave myself over to several hours of the most sustained pleasure I'd had from a crime novel since the last good Ross Macdonald, or James Crumley's "Last Good Kiss." Where had I been all these years? **"LaBrava"** is Leonard's 18th novel, and for a book to work within the genre at a level as high as this means that there have to be a half-dozen or more earlier ones just as precisely made and as satisfying to read....

We can say the same both for LaBrava's creator and the book about his cunning but romantic hero. There's the setting, first of all: the sleazy, decadent beach-front facades, mental health stations, go-go clubs and water-soaked immoralities of contemporary south Miami Beach where antique widows cross paths with young hustlers fresh out of Cuban prisons and the atmosphere is as appealing—as Norman Mailer once put it— as inhaling a rubber glove. Elmore Leonard has the feel of it; he makes us feel it—and the characters, whom we know as much by their dialogue as their actions; Leonard's got the feeling *sound* of them as well as sight. It's difficult to say, in fact, who among this novelist's contemporaries has a better ear....

Leonard's plot is superb, offering just the right vehicle for the display of the moral ambiguity and physical peril we expect in a book of this kind. It fits perfectly—like that glove in the lungs—LaBrava's notion of the perfect motion picture....

Hollywood's faded dream world, rather than the opiate of a quick million made from the drug trade, is the narcotic of choice in **"LaBrava."** Given the current tide of drug novels set in Miami, that seems to suggest Elmore is going against fashion. But his novel works in deeper waters, plumbs the possibilities of the best hard-boiled-detective fiction we've been given, and makes few concessions to fads. **"LaBrava"** is impure entertainment—it gives off too many resonances on moral themes and on the confusions we make between illusion and reality to be called "pure." It's a book for old fans and for new converts. I'm going back for more.

Alan Cheuse, "A Pleasure for the Hard-Boiled Fans" (copyright, 1983, Los Angeles Times; reprinted by permission of the author), in Los Angeles Times Book Review, *December 4, 1983, p. 3.*

Denise Levertov
1923-

English-born American poet, short story writer, essayist, editor, and translator.

Levertov is an important postmodern poet. Her career began in England, where her first collection, *The Double Image*, was published in 1946. Her early verse was influenced by the romanticism prevalent in Britain during World War II and displayed the formal, even stiff, construction and dreamlike extravagance characteristic of that period. In 1948, after marrying the American novelist Mitchell Goodman, she moved to the United States. This move was crucial to her development as a postmodern poet.

Through her husband's friendship with Robert Creeley, Levertov became involved with the Black Mountain poets. Her poetic development was heavily influenced by Charles Olson's aesthetics, by the innovative application of everyday speech patterns encouraged by poets Robert Duncan and Kenneth Rexroth, and by the immediacy and vitality characteristic of William Carlos Williams's work. *Here and Now* (1957), her first collection following her move to the United States, evidences the dramatic effect these poets had on her writing; *Collected Earlier Poems 1940-1960* (1979) charts her artistic development.

Like her contemporaries, Levertov sought to capture the "authentic experience" in verse and to develop the relation of form to content. Thematically, she combines attention to concrete daily objects with a larger personal, political, and religious awareness. While on the one hand she writes poems grounded in social reality—for example, in *The Sorrow Dance* (1967) she protests the Vietnam War—she also displays a romantic reverence for the natural world in connection with the mythical and spiritual dimensions of the human psyche. Endorsing Gerard Manley Hopkins's "inscape concept," she adds depth and relevance to her poems by applying her own inward response to extrinsic phenomena. Her recent collection, *Candles in Babylon* (1982), continues Levertov's tradition of writing graceful, powerful, and irreducible poems.

(See also *CLC*, Vols. 1, 2, 3, 5, 8, 15; *Contemporary Authors*, Vols. 1-4, rev. ed.; *Contemporary Authors New Revision Series*, Vol. 3; and *Dictionary of Literary Biography*, Vol. 5.)

CHARLES ALTIERI

When one puts pressure on postmodern poetics by asking questions about philosophical adequacy, one immediately confronts a powerful contradiction: considered as metaphysical or religious meditation, the poetry of the sixties seems to me highly sophisticated; it takes into account all the obvious secular objections to traditional religious thought and actually continues and extends the inquiries of philosophers as diverse as Heidegger, Whitehead, and Wittgenstein. This very success, however, makes it disappointing that the poetry fails so miserably in handling social and ethical issues. One cannot avoid asking why this is the case, and when he does he finds that at least one poet, Denise Levertov, has preceded his questions. . . . Miss Levertov has been one of the major voices of the new

© 1984 Thomas Victor

poetry in the 1960s, and while not very original, she is often quite a good poet devoted to developing concrete moments in which the numinous emerges out of the quotidian. Yet what interests me most about her work . . . is her experience of the inadequacy of the aesthetics of presence when in *The Sorrow Dance* (1966) and subsequent volumes she tries to adapt her poetic to pressing social concerns caused by the war in Vietnam. Miss Levertov presents a very compelling critique of that aesthetic, but even more telling is her own lack of poetic power and authority when she tries to adapt the principles that had shaped her work to social questions. In effect, her later work testifies to the most basic intellectual weaknesses of the contemporary aesthetic. . . . (p. 226)

Let me first briefly sketch her earlier objectivist celebrations of presence as plenitude. . . . From Olson, and more directly from Duncan and Creeley, she takes her objectivist ideals: verse must capture the energies of the attentive consciousness open to the event of arriving each step along the way. But like Creeley, her tone and dramatic context differ radically from Olson's bardic voice and generalizing perspective. Both poets keep the less hero-oriented dimensions of Olson's aesthetic, but use them in specific domestic contests that share O'Hara's emphases on the local, the casual, and the contingent. Finally, in her desire to correlate objectivist ideals with the mystical attitudes that sustain the "pilgrim's way," her pursuit of presence leads to meditations on the deep image and the development of techniques to render a "slip inward," or in her case a slip beyond, to a sense of the infinite depth and mystery at the horizon of what is sharply seen.

Her most characteristic image for reconciling the sense of continual arrival in a satisfying present with the "pilgrim way" is the image of ripeness, as exemplified by the last stanza of **"Under the Tree"**:

> let the oranges
> ripen, ripen above you
> you are living too, one
> among the dark multitude . . .

Presence as plenitude here is very different from Olson's energy of spring or Snyder's "Communionism." . . . Rather this stanza concentrates a slow process of satisfaction (the repeated "ripen") blending into a sense of transcendent union. The poem dwells lovingly on "one," a word at once requiring a strong pause and, because it is enjambed, a quick transition into the "dark multitude." Ripeness then functions in several ways. As a physical image it renders a sense of the scene as self-contained plenitude. But ripeness is of its very nature a transitional state; it testifies to the fact that individual perfection is not essentially an end in itself but a means for becoming a functioning and satisfying element in the total process. The tree puts forth fruit in order to nourish the seed and create new life. Moreover, from man's perspective the ripe fruit calls out to be eaten, and thus is another way to sustain life. Psychologically a similar ripening process takes place for the speaker. The stanza's initial imperative, "let," summarizes the poem's moral movement. The speaker is willing to accept process as process and to dwell with attention on the fullness of the "Here and Now." Like the fruit, she is at once fully there and gradually preparing for a new relationship to the total life process, a relationship embodied in the shift in attention from the trees to herself and then to the climactic sense of oneness. (In many of Miss Levertov's poems this movement from ripeness to union takes explicit sexual form.) Finally the sense of oneness leads in the last line to the "slip beyond" into a metaphysical vision of shared process at a deeper level of awareness. "Dark multitude" is unfortunately vague and abstract, but in a sense these qualities are necessary to get the intended feeling of the whole physical scene being carried into a level of experience where the mind itself sees its place in an all-embracing process.

How different from this satisfying enclosed space and relaxed accepting attitude is the opening poem of *Relearning the Alphabet*. . . . [In this poem every] step is no longer an arrival as she replaces confident assertion with a series of questions that set the dominant tone of the volume. This poet of place and attention now can neither stand peacefully nor follow a purposive path. Moreover, accustomed to merging her ego into a field of actions, she now feels that field breaking up into a public self merely playing roles and a genuine "I" that grows so deeply private one must fear for its continued presence. . . . Even touching and tasting, two of her most recurrent acts of celebration, now only alienate the sensitive spirit from the things of this world. . . . (pp. 226-29)

No orange will compensate for the fact that the present moment is now inextricable from the continual awareness of the senseless suffering and death created by the war in Vietnam. The psychological counterpart to this hunger is the doubt about her previous poetic stance that permeates *Relearning the Alphabet*. . . . (p. 229)

What she knows can no longer suffice because she is now confronted with two problems her aesthetics of presence cannot handle. With the war so dominant a fact of experience, especially for the poet whose sensitivity now becomes a kind of curse, she perceives in the present at least as many inescapable reminders of suffering and pain as causes for awe and religious acceptance. Second, the war brings home the poet's helplessness. What mystery she does perceive in the present is too personal and too particular to help her either judge or transform the suffering. The "dark multitude" has shown itself as a mass of isolated individuals who share only confusion. In **"The Cold Spring"** she seeks to renew her sense of the numinous sources or origins that can sustain the way of poetic affirmation, but she finds instead that at the source of the spring feeding poetic inspiration, the life-giving waters are reddened and muddied by human violence. The eye now is only a physical instrument recording ambiguities and can give no direction, no structure, to the I. . . .

"Advent 1966" is Levertov's most powerful statement of the changed landscape where the sensitive eye, which once served to unite the "I" with the numinous scene, now sees only a demonic version of incarnation. And this reversal of traditional possibilities for satisfying mythic transformations is paralleled by the fact that now the intense literal reality of the flames from napalm no longer allows the shift to mythic dimensions of fire so easily and movingly rendered in **"Eros at Temple Stream."** . . . (p. 230)

Relearning the Alphabet has a place in the modern tradition of volumes of poetry revaluing a whole poetic career and tentatively exploring new directions. Like Yeats, Eliot, and Stevens before her, she knows what she has to do, but she has considerably less at her disposal to help her realize the new goals. Her task is twofold—to awaken the sensitivity of those supporting the war so they might see its evils . . . and to formulate an ethic and an aesthetic that might help restructure the consciousness of society. The poetry of numinous presence must grow more discursive in order to propound values at once more explicitly ethical than those of immanence and more general than those bound to the now muddied objective contexts of specific moments of perception. (p. 231)

Where, however, is she to find within her sense of poetry and the poet's role, style and themes adequate to the task she sees as necessary? Where will she find an ethical basis for creating models of humane behavior? To what value structures can the poet turn when for most of her life she has rejected humanism and the early moderns' use of tradition and creative imagination as the basis of her ideals? While she recognizes that the aesthetics of presence no longer suffices, she has only its implicit ethical ideals to work with. That aesthetic is built on visions of immanence whose only ethical corollary is the command to let be and to recognize the fullness of what lies before one. Such an ideal might provide the goal for a transformed society, but it will not give much help in determining or propounding the means for creating such a society. Moreover, that aesthetic is intensely antisymbolist . . . and can provide little guidance when the poet feels that she must deal with symbolic generalizations and must transform moments of vision into the basis of discursively presented structures of value. With so much cut away in order to reach the numinous present, what has the contemporary poet left with which to build an ethical vision based on his insights?

I am now entering aspects of the crisis presented in *Relearning the Alphabet* that are no longer under Miss Levertov's self-conscious control. She wants to raise questions in order to provide at least tentative answers, but the poems giving answers only make one realize that the crisis is a deeper one than she seems to think. She tries to work out a solution by turning to the notebook form, for here she can remain faithful to the now confused present while replacing the dramatic poem of sharply realized perceptions with one loose enough to allow moral reflections. In this form she can discuss moral issues without pretending to a structured moral vision and can allow moments of moral conviction to emerge from her intense suffering and inner contradictions. If the poet cannot adequately judge her age intellectually, she can provide personal witness of what it is doing to its sensitive and reflective spirits. Moreover, unwilling and perhaps unable to construct heroic models of resistance that may be mere fictions, she can in the notebook form capture as models of humane behavior whatever acts strike her, without endangering the power of the acts themselves by either interpreting them or excessively dramatizing them. Personal example is perhaps the only ethical model for social action that makes coherent sense within an aesthetics of presence because it simply shifts attention from the numinous qualities of natural scenes to the qualities of human actors in social situations.

In theory, then, the notebook form makes a certain amount of sense, given Miss Levertov's plight. But it simply does not work, and perhaps could not work to achieve what she desires. The notebook style at best can serve as a historical document dramatizing the problems of a sensitive consciousness at given moments. But it has little reconstructive value because it provides no checks—either formal or in demands for lyric intensity—against the temptations—so strong when one is driven by moral outrage—to easy rhetoric and slack generalizations. Moreover, the form exerts very little authority: it seems only the cries of a passive victim. Here perhaps the "wise passiveness" cultivated by the poetics of presence shows its ultimate weakness. It is, of course, not easy for the poet, so lacking in real social power, to assert authority, but there are, if she will ally herself with them, moral and artistic traditions that demand and support resistance to the kind of forces oppressing Levertov. But before I get into theoretical questions about the limitations of all modern political poetry, I shall look closely at the undeniable weaknesses in Miss Levertov's efforts. Then one can hardly doubt that there are better philosophical and aesthetic foundations for public poetry, and one can see how deeply her own work is victimized by the very problems she describes in the aesthetics of presence. (pp. 231-33)

The details [in **"From a Notebook: October '68—May '69"**] are flat, often sentimental, asserting rather than manifesting value.... And loose propagandistic phrases like "the people" and "The War / comes home to us" neither create fresh insights nor bear up under intellectual analysis. More telling is the pathetic quest to make assertions of value in generalizations that seem simplistic. "Happiness / in the sun" might be a simple moment of life, but it is not an adequate model for basing so general a conclusion as, "Is it that simple, then, / to live." No, for our culture it is not, whether one accepts its vision of authentic life or whether one wants to change it in any meaningful way. And the symbolic equation of the grass revealed in its freshness when the garbage is removed with "a new testament" has a certain momentary validity, but it is too slight an event on which to hang so portentous and inclusive a symbolic referent. Here human action restores a simple natural dynamism, but that is a far cry from receiving the vision, structure, and ground of a new law as implied by the metaphor.

No wonder she does not develop this but quickly changes her perspective. Where she arrives, though, is even more problematic. Miss Levertov has a quick mind; she recognizes the irony of removing garbage only to add to the Bay-fill destroying the San Francisco harbor, and she records this both to dramatize the self-irony a revolutionary can maintain and to stave off her critics. But her clever way of dismissing the irony will not do. In fact, it makes childish and questionable the love she is trying to celebrate. It is precisely that easy praise of human virtues and the tendency to assert it in order to cover up political contradictions that has made the new calls to revolution suspect and undermined the authority of those poets celebrating it.

What bothers me most in this passage, though, is the way it exemplifies problems I suspect are endemic to a poetics of immanence. That aesthetic, in the pursuit of an unmediated sense of Being and in its attempts to make ontologically real harmonies perceived between aesthetic and natural processes, tends in social questions to confuse art and life and to misuse poetic categories of thought. Miss Levertov, as I have shown, explicitly denies a symbolic way of thinking in her pursuit of objects; numinous experiences require primarily attentive participation and not artificial interpretive acts of the reflective mind. Not terribly conscious or analytic, then, about what symbols she does use, she is likely to misuse the poet's synthesizing power by constructing problematic analogies like that between the uncovered grass and the New Testament. After encountering repeated instances of this kind of faulty thinking, the reader is likely to grow skeptical, and to replace a sympathetic openness to her work with an analytic attitude—scrutinizing language he should trust the poet has scrutinized so that he can simply respond to it.

A more elaborate misuse of aesthetic categories takes place here when she facilely extends the particular experience of cooperation at People's Park into a universal model for the new society to be created by the revolution. It takes very little skepticism to note that this group is politically homogeneous and gathered together for a short time to achieve a particular purpose that has obvious mythical values underlying it. Such a model is far removed from the problems encountered in creating or maintaining a political society, particularly in cultures that value freedom and difference. (pp. 234-35)

This social denial of the complexity and differences constitutive of modern societies is reinforced by a characteristic postmodern view of the nature of evil. The aesthetics of presence is essentially monistic, conceiving evil as basically only a privation, a failure to perceive correctly or to align one's consciousness with the latent harmonious orders of a given scene. The dream is that proper action will follow naturally from a correct understanding or, more radically, a correct positioning in which the understanding receives its "sentences" from the situation. But however appealing the metaphysics of this vision might be, the realm of politics is largely constituted by the need to correlate different visions and priorities.... Poetry, one might say, is primarily a meditative mode of consciousness that seeks to bring minds into accord with one another by dramatizing a given perspective. But politics is a mode of action, where the distribution of goods and powers requires reconciling different perspectives. It is not enough to see how others might see; people need to find forms of agreement that do not require sharing the same particular perspectives and priorities. Poetry unifies perspectives within provisional dramatic points of view; society must seek abstract agreements acceptable to dramatic positions widely separated in time, space, and quality.

Given these conditions, one must recognize the fact that no poetry is likely to have much direct impact on the social order. Still, as high modernism makes clear, in style if not in content, political poetry need not be embarrassingly simplistic. This form of poetry can profoundly engage one's sympathies, if not political allegiances. To do so, however, political poetry, and perhaps the more general category of ethical as opposed to perceptual poetry, must first of all recognize the enormous gulf between values found in meditating on nature and those explicitly developed by reflection on public themes and problems. With respect to public poetry, then, modernism is far more effective than the postmodern alternative because of the modernist reliance on tradition and the mythmaking or reconstructive imagination. First, tradition provides both a set of recurrent public and ethical problems that have been central to political debate and a series of roles and allusions that can give dignity and depth to the poet's social stance. Indeed the more fully one includes history in his work, as Yeats does for example in "Nineteen Hundred and Nineteen" and "Meditations in Time of Civil War," the more he perforce admits the complexity of political questions and achieves for himself a stance that can claim authority and universality for both its suffering and its ideals. Second, the very tension between ideals and the recalcitrance of history forces the poet to recognize the complexity of human motives and the enormous gulf, in both society and in the self, between the imagination and empirical reality.

Ideals make dualists of us all, but they need not force us to despair. The third advantage of the modernist poetic, in fact, stems directly from this gulf. For in order to reconcile desires bred by the traditions of imaginative literature with the realities societies produce in the name of these ideals, poets had to distinguish between social values and a deeper ground for values carried by the tradition but never realized. This social condition generates in turn an ethical distinction between empirical or social and ideal or best selves, and it gives the poets a powerful set of analogies between remaking the self imaginatively and reconstituting social order. In the poetry, then, social conflicts need not remain abstract nor invite self-righteous judgment. Social order becomes the parallel to the poet's remaking himself in terms of ideal images, and his struggles to establish poetic orders at once repeat and give authority to his pursuit of social order—an order dependent on correlating psychological and social materials. By making the self an analogue for redeemed society, these poets were easily tempted by elitist and authoritarian models of order, and they had their own problems in successfully distinguishing between art and politics. But because they were so aware of the ideal (not necessarily "fictive") status of their visions, their poetry maintained a sense of the difficulties and possible self-delusions involved in relating art and life, poetic tradition and political realities. And, more important, because they distinguished between perception and making or reconstructing viable social myths and images, their public poetry retained a sense of drama and conflict. They could create personae who could do more than pathetically record their hopes and confusions in the form of private notebooks. They felt that they could speak to society, not simply be overheard by it lamenting impersonal, demonic forces, and hence they articulated dignified forms of public speech as a last noble, if hopeless, model for the poet's active relationship to his society.

More than Levertov's work is at stake in this contrast, and the problems in developing an adequate postmodern public poetry are largely symptoms of psychological problems inherent in the aesthetics of presence. The quest for immanent plenitude, for example, leads readily toward quiescent passivity. Snyder and Levertov make it clear that too strong a sense of evil as mere privation and too much reliance on strategies of perception or imaginative stances as the mode for overcoming that privation leave the self helpless or pathetic in relation to social forces. Moreover, by locating most or all significant values in moments of vision, the poet has great difficulty constructing specific ethical values or moral images that are more applicable and more general than specific epistemological poses. The pursuit of immanence simply does not bring into play important rational faculties of the mind, nor does it focus the poet's attention on historical and traditional forces that might both define the contemporary situation and provide values and images from the past one can use to judge and transcend it. (pp. 235-38)

One ought finally to keep in mind that if the contrast with modernism serves to clarify the limits of the poetry of the sixties, it also helps in another way to illustrate the significance of its achievement. For in their attempts to articulate the creative powers of the imagination, even the greatest of the modernists blinded themselves to two primary needs in any society. They were unable to imagine culture except in ideal and mythic terms, and most of them could provide alternatives to what they saw as a vulgar positivist and philistine society only by returning to what now seem outmoded and indefensible forms of organicist social and metaphysical thought. The postmoderns would have performed a significant cultural role if they merely tried to right the balance. (pp. 238-39)

If they do not either reconcile us to society or lead us to want or to see how to change it, they do help reconcile us to the more general and perhaps more significant situations in which it is man's constant task to find ways of affirming his own existence. Postmodern poetry builds a temple out of nature, not a city, but that can be a considerable achievement even for those whose ultimate dream is some version of a redeemed society. History shows that man's efforts to build temples have little effect on the specific practices characterizing life in the city. Yet history also shows that without the temple, however it may be constructed, life in the city seems at best vulgar and callous, at worst a demonic force driving man back on the woeful inadequacy of endless introspection. When Lowell left Rome for Paris, the archetypal secular city, he found only the second alternative—forcing him to a more and more enervated self-consciousness and a desperate quest to locate all value in domestic experience. The other alternative, implicit in many poets and working for adequate expression in Miss Levertov's **"Relearning the Alphabet,"** requires that one first seek ontological security and then gradually try to extend the terms of that security as the elements of a moral alphabet that one can begin applying to social issues. Once identity has a fixed base, it is possible to endure the contradictions, restraints, and tentative projection of ideals that constitute the public moral life. (p. 239)

Charles Altieri, "Denise Levertov and the Limits of the Aesthetics of Presence," in his Enlarging the Temple: New Directions in American Poetry during the 1960s *(© 1979 by Associated University Presses, Inc.), Bucknell University Press, 1979, pp. 225-44.*

N. E. CONDINI

Collected Earlier Poems—a selection from Denise Levertov's earliest English book, ***The Double Image*** (1946), and her three following collections, *Here and Now* (1957), *Overland to the Islands* (1958), and *With Eyes at the Back of Our Heads* (1960)—has appropriately just come out . . . as a complement to *Life in the Forest* (1978), allowing us to trace Miss Levertov's poetic development from its nervous English beginnings to the sensitive American balance of discourse and reflection. Composed for the most part in London in the Forties, the early and uncollected poems, tightly structured, already evince a desire for solitude and a celebration of the gifts of nature that are typical of the more mature Levertov. War is seen in them not as hatred or violence, but as mere lack of love, aridity of the spirit. What disturbs the writer is the boredom, the deprivation of wonder. In her Wordsworthian intimations she endeavors to survive, opposing inertia as if it were the real culprit, the root of many social evils. Mild intimations to be sure, but Miss Levertov's poetics does indeed start here. . . . (p. 360)

In *The Double Image,* a recurrent sense of loss prompts her to extemporize on death as not a threat but a rite to be accepted gladly and honored. This germ of a personal mythology burgeons in *Here and Now* with a fable-like aura added to it. Animated by the wildest zest for life, Miss Levertov listens keenly to "the humble rhythms, the falling and rising of leaf and star," where the falling is observed and treasured as much as the rising, death as much as life. What predominates, though, is still a predilection for bright colors and a call for the restoration in us of the animal quality of wonder. The thought of black as something terse, concentrated, and final is present only in **"Ink Drawings"** and **"The Third Dimension,"** and it brings in a surprising note of honesty. As to the rest, the book is a hymn to "idiot" joy, which the poet still considers the best protection against the aridity of war and war's memories. Her weakness lies in a childish romanticism, which will be replaced later by a more substantial concision. Here the language is a bit too ornate, too flowery.

The quest for the real returns, even if feebly, in *Overland to the Islands,* together with occasional lapses into sentimentality. There is a strong, fresh presence of the maternal, best recalled in a beautiful poem on Wales, emblematic of the purity of nature. *With Eyes at the Back of Our Heads* continues this exploration. With polished style, Miss Levertov pries into things, objects, plants, to their last detail, their most hidden secret. This inward movement to the center of things, to the ultimate core, death, is her fullest achievement. There are warm intimacies here, but also meditations and Confucian analects. Most of all, there's an insistence on the need to watch nature as it incessantly recreates life. Nature is truth, says Miss Levertov, revising Keats. All the rest is false. This concept is taken up again in . . . *Life in the Forest,* where the two main themes of the previous collection—mother and the forest symbol—stand for the inevitability of death and the permanence of creation. (pp. 360-61)

N. E. Condini, "Embracing Old Gods," in National Review *(© National Review, Inc., 1980; 150 East 35th St., New York, NY 10016; reprinted with permission), Vol. XXXII, No. 6, March 21, 1980, pp. 360-61.*

DORIS EARNSHAW

Denise Levertov was fitted by birth and political destiny to voice the terrors and pleasures of the twentieth century. Granddaughter on her father's side of a Russian Hasidic Jew and on her mother's of a Welsh mystic, she has published poetry since the 1940s that speaks of the great contemporary themes: Eros, solitude, community, war. . . . How consistently she has constructed her poems of hard, solid and mysterious qualities can be seen in [*Collected Earlier Poems 1940-1960*]. (pp. 109-10)

Perhaps because she was educated by private tutors in her English childhood, Levertov seems never to have had to shake loose from an academic style of extreme ellipsis and literary allusion, the self-conscious obscurity that the Provençal poets called "closed" (*trobar clus*). Other poets—Adrienne Rich, for example—move away from an early brilliant but rigid and pedantic voice to direct and personal speech. A reading of Levertov's early work shows her to be remarkably consistent in theme and form throughout her career. A recent verse mass . . . takes up the threads of her first passion for physical beauty and emotional sincerity in human life. The tone is deeper and more tragic, naturally, as both private and public life move through these dreadful decades; yet even her first published poem, the haunting eight-line **"Listening to Distant Guns,"** sounds the message of her perceptions, senseless terror and sacred natural existence. As an "evacuated" English girl in the southern countryside, she could hear the booming of cannon across the Channel.

Many poems of these early volumes are set in Mexico; others have New York or suburban country as their locale. Levertov plays with dialects and language, though not often. Her favorite style is to use a narrative as slightly sketched background for the presentation of a state of mind. Feeling is brought to clear expression while story or dramatic element is a shadow. Always rooted in the presence of a tangible, visible reality, the poems caress objects with praise. . . . Word and object are handled with a peasant strength, direct and wise. Titles are short, only one or two words. The influence of Rilke is here. . . . In an age of sarcasm, individual and mass alienation and "double-voiced" words, as Mikhail Bakhtin shows, when few famous poets in the West are being arrested for their political views, Levertov both writes and lives her belief in the poet as bringer of praise and hope. The publication of her early work reveals the good seed from which a rich harvest has come. (p. 110)

Doris Earnshaw, in a review of "Collected Earlier Poems: 1940-1960," in World Literature Today *(copyright 1981 by the University of Oklahoma Press), Vol. 55, No. 1, Winter, 1981, pp. 109-10.*

PUBLISHERS WEEKLY

Poetry and prose are different talents, originating from opposite spheres of the brain. Not many poets have the ambidexterity to do both well, but Denise Levertov ranks high among that elect. Her essays and memoirs [in **"Light Up the Cave"**] are not only marked by the intense personal integrity of her poems; they stand alone as works of art. . . . Her memoirs of Sexton, Rukeyser, Duncan and Herbert Read are free of nostalgia and are concrete and frank in the details of Levertov's close relationships with these poets. Also included are pieces on Levertov's experiences in wartime England, first as a ballet student, subsequently as a nurse. Both are moving on account of their perspicacity, distrust of authoritarianism in all its forms and compassion for other human beings.

A review of "Light Up the Cave," in Publishers Weekly *(reprinted from the September 11, 1981 issue of* Publishers Weekly, *published by R. R. Bowker Company, a Xerox company; copyright © 1981 by Xerox Corporation), Vol. 220, No. 11, September 11, 1981, p. 70.*

INGRID RIMLAND

[In *Light Up the Cave*, Denise Levertov, a] noted poet with a fertile mind and unabashed emotions, treats her readers to a volume of prose about what it means to be, and to live as, a craftsman of language. The writing is rich, polished and complex—with insights to ponder, feelings to share, assumptions to correct and meaning to distill. A critic might object to certain statements or conclusions—that Solzhenitsyn, for example, has a "martyr complex" or that Sylvia Plath and other suicides could have done better than to confuse and complicate the independent entities of creativity and death—but the strong impression remains that here speaks a poet intensely loyal to her craft, abiding by an artist's inner rules and deserving attention and respect.

Intelligent and nourishing, her writing leaves a lingering glow long after the last page is turned. . . .

This volume is a potpourri: assorted musings, subtle insights, tender memories of youth and strength, political passions, gentle but respectful accolades to other writers. The prose is utterly free of restraints, save those demanded by a fierce, independent spirit insisting at all times on honesty.

Part I offers three short stories with cliff-hanger endings. Part II squeezes the last drop of meaning out of the subtleties of good poetic structure—and, no, it is not boring reading. The next two parts depict a goodly dose of liberal sentiment, but served up in such a way as to force a smile. Part V is perhaps the most readable section—descriptions of friendships that nourished a writer of substance, the influence of early years that shaped and honed a questing mind. Finally, the book pays tribute to other exceptional writers—some known, some not so known.

This is a book to read, then reread at leisure.

Ingrid Rimland, "A Poet Offers Prose That Glows" (copyright, 1982, Los Angeles Times; *reprinted by permission of the author*), in Los Angeles Times Book Review, *July 18, 1982, p. 8.*

JAMES FINN COTTER

Denise Levertov is a poet whose public outspokenness has not harmed her reputation as a highly private poet. *Candles in Babylon* . . . displays the same technical expertise that marked her previous dozen books; there is little in the open form that she cannot manage: nostalgia, protest, satire or story. **"The Great Wave"** catches the excitement of swimming at the shore as a child, while **"The Art of the Octopus"** is a perfect description and allegory. Levertov admits that one piece, written for an antidraft rally, really is a speech rather than a poem. Unfortunately, too many others move in the same direction, where good causes bury good poetry. Even her **"Mass for the Day of St. Thomas Didymus"** strikes me as pulpit oratory sprinkled with omnipresent "we's"—a word that the poet should use more sparingly. Poetry should entice and not force us to acceptance. (p. 75)

James Finn Cotter, "Poets Then and Now: A Review of Recent Literature" (*reprinted with permission of America Press, Inc. and the author;* © *1983; all rights reserved*), in America, *Vol. 148, No. 4, January 29, 1983, pp. 75-6.*

DANIEL BERRIGAN, S.J.

The hallmark of Denise Levertov's prose [as in *Light Up the Cave*] is something so simple and elusive as clear eyed common sense. In the nature of things, so esoteric a virtue has not been grandly rewarded. Common sense? mainline writers along with their multicorporate pushers, have stampeded toward the rainbow named Avarice; others have shown a sorrowful, even despairing obsession with the Confession That Bares All.

Levertov is aware of the implications here, destructive as they are of political understanding and writers' craft. And of life itself, as in writers who have constructed a game called despair; and played it, bullet to head.

She takes up such matters, despair, anomie, political indifference, matters which most writers today prefer to keep decently out of sight and mind. She analyzes despair and its practitioners, and those who justify it as a resource. And by a parallel right instinct, she avoids the rapacious rush to trivialize life, to bring it in line with a desperate and trivial culture.

She is that rara avis, a poet, a political writer, very much a woman. These are the poles of her art as of her existence. She stays close to essentials, and the resolve, in the best sense, has paid off. Her writing remains wonderfully contemporary, it walks with us, illumines the journey of conscience that began in civil rights days and continues on into the eighties and the antinuclear struggle.

She charts the essentials; how we grew, what mistakes we made, how we failed one another, what gains and losses percolated, boiled over. And perhaps, most important, how we've grown, and into what. . . .

There is a measure of courage required to march and be arrested. And there is another sort of courage, intelligence, and discipline implied in setting down a record of the march, the arrests, the meaning of it all. Their tone, excitement, verve! In the lives of most who take part, there is no comparable taste of the lost American art known as community.

Her essays thus hearten young and old alike; they are a diary of our neglected soul. Norman Mailer did something like this in the sixties; but since those heady days and nights, he, like most such marchers and writers, has turned to other matters. . . .

Levertov is still marching, still recording the march. There are dazzling skills here; they start in the feet, rhythmically implanted in mother earth, and make their way, mysterious, tingling, into hand, fingers, pen. It begins with courage, a continuity of courage, a cold stream in the temperate larger stream of soul. Robert Frost's contrary stream, headlong in one direction when the rivers of a given time, and the voice of those rivers, would have us believe that "all is well." . . .

She tells of that comatose decade, the seventies, almost as though it hadn't existed. She marches, keeps something alive, is personally dispassionate. There was work to be done, that was all. It little mattered that the work was despised or ignored or neglected. It was simply there, as evil was, as the world was; as hope was. She is passionate only about the issues, life or death. In this she, so to speak, turns the cultural method on its head. That is to say, American writing in the seventies, both prose and poetry, was disproportionately passionate about the self, and correspondingly numb (passion not being in large supply) toward the public weal and woe. Thus was a natural balance thrown out of kilter.

In insisting on this balance, and thus restoring it, Levertov reminds me of Paul Goodman; in political sanity, in large scope and interest, in intellectual clarity—and especially in moral unabashedness. I think of her, as I recall him, unashamed to be old fashioned and patriotic, calling the country to accounts, being (horrors!) "judgmental" toward morons and rogues in high places, linking her work to spirits like Thoreau, Emerson, Hawthorne, Melville, Mother Jones, John Brown, the Quaker chroniclers—and, in our lifetime, to the incomparable Martin Luther King and Dorothy Day. Moralists, poets, activists, pacifists, abolitionists, prolabor, propoor, prohuman, these formed her history, as ours, if we can but rise to it; living it, rising to it, testing its native decency against the manifest social indecency of war, piratical economics, hatred of the poor, racism, nouveau riche clowning, the mad mutual rhythms of waste and want.

I have not so much as mentioned the richness and scope of her literary criticism. *Multum in parvo;* the entire book is beyond praise. I think of how, in a sane time, such a book and those which preceded it, including poetry, short stories, literary essays, social criticism, would form a university course entitled something like: A Renaissance Woman of the Late Twentieth Century. But this is dreaming; it would mean crossing jealous frontiers, violating "expertise."

Meantime, for those who come on this book, there is much to ponder, much to learn. Since these essays were published, several of her themes have grown, imperceptibly and ominously, like stalactites aimed at the heart of things. The despair for instance, which she analyzes so acutely, a point of departure for a debased theory of "art at the extremes"—despair has spread, become the national mood, from sea to shining sea....

All this being our predicament, political responsibility, resistance, together with the recounting and pondering and exemplifying—these can no longer be viewed as a choice in a range of choices. Our options, as they say, are no longer large.... [We] may choose to do nothing; which is to say, to go discreetly or wildly mad, letting fear possess us and frivolity rule our days.

Or we may, along with admirable spirits like Denise Levertov, be driven sane; by community, by conscience, by treading the human crucible.

Daniel Berrigan, S.J., in a review of "Light Up the Cave," in The American Book Review *(© 1983 by The American Book Review), Vol. 5, No. 2, January-February, 1983, p. 14.*

Mina Loy
1882-1966

English-born American poet.

Although Loy is virtually unknown to most readers today, a number of important critics describe her as one of the most influential contributors to the modernist movement in America in the early 1900s. T. S. Eliot and Ezra Pound praised her poems highly and her work is often linked with and discussed in terms of that of William Carlos Williams, Marianne Moore, and Wallace Stevens. Well-acquainted with European avant-garde literary and artistic circles, she introduced the ideas and techniques of such groups as the European futurists and other experimentalists to American poets and readers. She was not, however, directly aligned with any of these movements: her life and her art were marked by a dramatic insistence on independence, privacy, and individuality.

Loy's poetry is now generally recognized as the work of an acutely perceptive and intelligent mind. However, her densely compressed lines and images, bold sexual references, and lack of punctuation led some of her initial critics to reject her work and its stark unconventionality. Other early critics found in Loy's writing a cutting and satirical wit, a precise and forceful style, and a direct yet passionate objectivity. Having remarked on these qualities, they expressed the belief that Loy was creating a unique foundation upon which all future significant poetry would be constructed.

Many of Loy's poems appeared in *Others,* a small magazine published by Conrad Arensberg and Alfred Kreymborg between 1915 and 1919, and other "little" magazines of this period dedicated to exposing new poetic forms. Her collections of poetry have until recently numbered only two—*Lunar Baedecker* (1923) and *Lunar Baedecker and Time Tables* (1958). Much of the criticism written after Loy's rise to prominence in the 1910s and 1920s speculates on the causes of her subsequent silence and obscurity, and attempts to place her in the history of American poetry. The 1982 collection of previously unpublished and reprinted poems, *The Last Lunar Baedecker,* is dedicated to the critic and poet Kenneth Rexroth, who has taught and given public readings of Loy's work.

Most critics cite Loy's slow, meticulous manner of writing, her self-imposed isolation, and the creative energy she expended in other areas of the arts, such as painting and design, as primary reasons for her sparse publication and for her lack of greater fame. Whatever the explanation, Loy now occupies the unusual position of having been "one of the most pivotal voices in the American Free Verse Movement," while she "remains today virtually the only important poet of the pre-World War I avant-garde who has neither been assimilated into the mainstream literary culture nor picked up by the small press movement."

(See also *Dictionary of Literary Biography,* Vol. 4.)

EZRA POUND

[Mina Loy and Marianne Moore] have, without exaggerated "nationalism", without waving of banners and general phrases

Photograph by Lee Miller; courtesy of Mrs. Herbert Bayer

about Columbia gem of the ocean, succeeded in, or fallen into, producing something distinctly American in quality, not merely distinguishable as Americans by reason of current national faults.

Their work is neither simple, sensuous nor passionate, but as we are no longer governed by the *North American Review* we need not condemn poems merely because they do not fit some stock phrase of rhetorical criticism. (p. 57)

In the verse of Marianne Moore I detect traces of emotion; in that of Mina Loy I detect no emotion whatever. Both of these women are, possibly in unconsciousness, among the followers of Jules Laforgue (whose work shows a great deal of emotion). It is possible, as I have written, or intended to write elsewhere, to divide poetry into three sorts; (1.) melopoeia, to wit, poetry which moves by its music, whether it be a music in the words or an aptitude for, or suggestion of, accompanying music; (2.) imagism, or poetry wherein the feelings of painting and sculpture are predominant (certain men move in phantasmagoria; the images of their gods, whole countrysides, stretches of hill land and forest, travel with them); and there is, thirdly, logopoeia or poetry that is akin to nothing but language, which is a dance of the intelligence among words and ideas and modification of ideas and characters. Pope and the eighteenth-century writers had in this medium a certain limited range. The intelligence of Laforgue ran through the whole gamut of his time. T. S. Eliot has gone on with it. Browning wrote a condensed form of drama, full of things of the senses, scarcely ever pure logopoeia.

One wonders what the devil anyone will make of this sort of thing who has not in their wit all the clues. It has none of the stupidity beloved of the "lyric" enthusiast and the writer and reader who take refuge in scenery description of nature, because they are unable to cope with the human. . . . [Mina Loy and Marianne Moore] write logopoeia. It is, in their case, the utterance of clever people in despair, or hovering upon the brink of that precipice. . . . It is a mind cry, more than a heart cry. "Take the world if thou wilt but leave me an asylum for my affection" is not their lamentation, but rather "In the midst of this desolation, give me at least one intelligence to converse with."

The arid clarity, not without its own beauty, of le tempérament de l'Americaine, is in the poems of these, I think, graduates or post-graduates. If they have not received B.A.'s or M.A.'s or B. Sc-s they do not need them.

The point of my praise, for I intend this as praise, even if I do not burst into the phrases of Victor Hugo, is that without any pretences and without clamours about nationality, these girls have written a distinctly national product, they have written something which would not have come out of any other country, and (while I have before now seen a deal of rubbish by both of them) they are, as selected by Mr. Kreymborg [in his anthology "Others"] interesting and readable. . . . (p. 58)

Ezra Pound, "A List of Books: 'Others'," in The Little Review, *Vol. IV, No. 11, March, 1918, pp. 56-8.*

YVOR WINTERS

Mr. Sacheverell Sitwell once wrote a very long poem, two lines of which stay in my memory:

My natural clumsiness was my only bar to progress
Until I conquered it by calculation.

As I go through such of Miss Loy's poems as I possess, this seems to describe her. If she has not actually conquered the clumsiness which one can scarcely help feeling in her writings, she has, from time to time, overcome it; and these occasional advantages have resulted in momentous poems. Or perhaps it is not clumsiness, but the inherently unyielding quality of her material that causes this embarrassment. She moves like one walking through granite instead of air, and when she achieves a moment of beauty it strikes one cold.

More intent on the gutter and its horrors than any of the group with which she was allied, and more intensely cerebral, perhaps, than any save one of them, her work ordinarily presents that broken, unemotional, and occasionally witty observation of undeniable facts that one came to regard as the rather uninviting norm of *Others* poetry. . . . Her unsuccessful work is easier to imitate than that of any of the three other outstanding members of her set—Miss Moore, Dr. Williams, and Mr. Stevens—and beyond a doubt has been more imitated. Rhythmically, it is elementary, whereas the metres of Miss Moore and Dr. Williams are infinitely varied and difficult, and those of Mr. Stevens are at least infinitely subtle. Emotionally, Dr. Williams is no farther from what one might regard as some sort of common denominator than Miss Loy, and he has covered—and opened to poetry—vastly more territory, so that the likelihood of his becoming the chief prophet of my own or some future generation is probably greater. . . . Of all contemporary poets, he is, I shall say, the closest in spirit to Miss Loy. Miss Moore, on the other hand, as a point of departure, is unthinkable—like Henry James, she is not a point of departure at all, but a terminus. Her work suggests nothing that she herself has not carried to its logical and utmost bounds. And Mr. Stevens, with his ethereal perversity, inhabits a region upon which one feels it would be a pity to encroach.

And yet I think that few poets of my own generation would deny that these writers as a group are more sympathetic, as well as more encouraging, than either the Vorticists or the Mid-Americans. Their advantage over the professional backwoodsmen consists in part, perhaps, in superior intellectual equipment, but mainly, I suspect, in a larger portion of simple common-sense—they have refused from the very beginning to consider themselves in any way related to Shawnee Indians or potato-beetles, and have passed unscathed through a period of unlimited sentimentality. Their advantage over the Vorticists consists not so much in their having superior brains, but in their having used their own brains exclusively. Had their own brains been unequal to the task, this would have been but little advantage, as Mr. Pound, Mr. Eliot, and H. D. are formidable rivals, and, it seems to me, genuinely great poets, but the courage of the Others group appears, by this time, to have been pretty thoroughly justified. It was a hard-headed courage, and little repaid by adulation, and is nearly as admirable as its poetic outcome. One can find little in contemporary poetry of a similar sturdiness except in the work of Messrs. Hardy and Robinson.

Of the four Mr. Stevens and Miss Moore deserve the least compassion for their struggle, if compassion is to be meted out—one suspects that they always knew they could do it; and Dr. Williams, hurling himself at the whole world with the passion of the former bantam-weight champion who bore his name, has achieved a blinding technique and magnificent prose and poetry by sheer excess of nervous power. And indeed compassion is scarcely the proper offering to bring Miss Loy— one feels timorous in bringing anything. She attacked the dirty common-place with the doggedness of a weight-lifter. Nearly any one might have written her worst poems, and innumerable small fry have written poems as good. Her success, if the least dazzling of the four, is not the least impressive, and is by all odds the most astounding. Using an unexciting method, and writing of the drabbest of material, she has written seven or eight of the most brilliant and unshakably solid satirical poems of our time, and at least two non-satirical pieces that possess for me a beauty that is unspeakably moving and profound. Satires like **The Black Virginity** and the piece on D'Annunzio need give little if any ground before the best of Pope or Dryden, and poems like **Der Blinde Junge** and the **Apology of Genius** need, in my judgement, yield ground to no one. And then there is the host of half-achieved but fascinating poems like **Lunar Baedecker**. One cons them—with the author's pardon—as one might a rosary, and is thankful if the string doesn't break, but most of the beads are at the very least spectacular. . . . (pp. 27-9)

They are images that have frozen into epigrams. It is this movement from deadly stasis to stasis, slow and heavy, that, when unified and organized, gives to her poetry its ominous grandeur, like that of a stone idol become animate and horribly aware. . . . (p. 30)

[Hers is] a genius that rises from a level of emotion and attitude which is as nearly common human territory as one can ever expect to find in a poet. Mr. Rodker once said that she wrote of the SOUL (in four capital letters, unless my memory betrays me) but the word doesn't mean much, no matter how one spells it. One might substitute the *subconscious* (which Mr. Rodker doubtless meant) but this word is nearly as frayed. Whatever tag one fastens to it, and regardless of what happens to her emotion in passing through her brain (which, being a good brain, is responsible for her being a good poet) one can scarcely help sensing at bottom a strange feeling for the most subterranean of human reactions, of a padding animal resentment, and of a laughter that is curiously physical. This habitation of some variety of common ground, although it may have no intrinsic aesthetic virtue, yet places her beside Dr. Williams as one of the two living poets who have the most, perhaps, to offer the younger American writers—they present us with a solid foundation in place of Whitman's badly aligned cornerstones, a foundation which is likely to be employed, I suspect, for a generation or two, by the more talented writers of this country, or by a rather large part of them. This suggested development is not a call to salvation, nor even a dogmatic prediction, but simply as speculation. If it materializes, Emily Dickinson will have been its only forerunner. (pp. 30-1)

> Yvor Winters, "Mina Loy" (originally published in The Dial, Vol. LXXX, No. 6, June, 1926), in his Yvor Winters: Uncollected Essays and Reviews, edited by Francis Murphy (© 1973 by Janet Lewis Winters; reprinted by permission of Ohio University Press, Athens), The Swallow Press, Inc., 1973, pp. 27-31.

ALFRED KREYMBORG

Visiting the shrines of modern art and literature in Paris and Florence, and being accepted as a coeval in the maddest circles, Miss Loy, who is an artist as well as poet, imbibed the precepts of Apollinaire and Marinnetti and became a Futurist with all the earnestness and irony of a woman possessed and obsessed with the sum of human experience and disillusion. Her first poems appeared in Alfred Stieglitz's *Camera Work,* along with some of the earliest work of Gertrude Stein. Most of Mina Loy's later work, including a whole issue of her **"Songs To Joannes,"** appeared in *Others,* and created a violent sensation. . . . Though *Others* was a private publication with a circulation of only a few hundred copies, the first number was hailed with public derision: it contained some of Miss Loy's **"Love Songs."** In an unsophisticated land, such sophistry, clinical frankness, sardonic conclusions, wedded to a madly elliptical style scornful of the regulation grammar, syntax and punctuation . . . , horrified our gentry and drove our critics into furious despair. The nudity of emotion and thought roused the worst disturbance, and the utter nonchalance in revealing the secrets of sex was denounced as nothing less than lewd. It took a strong digestive apparatus to read Mina Loy. Unhappily for her, the average critic had been fed on treacle and soda water over too long a Puritanical term in the jails of our daily papers. . . . Here are the lines which opened the overture and released the pens of Billingsgate:

> Spawn of fantasies
> Sitting the appraisable
> Pig Cupid   his rosy snout
> Rooting erotic garbage . . .

To reduce eroticism to the sty was an outrage, and to do so without verbs, sentence structure, punctuation, even more offensive. And yet, behind the abnormally scornful style, the careful reader, reading many times, might have detected genuine emotions, feelings inspired by "something the shape of a man" whose "skin-sack" packed "all the completions of my infructuous impulses" and whose hair is "a God's doormat" on the threshold of the mind. We, here in enlightened Manhattan, were simply unaccustomed to such passionate, clinical writing. . . . Certain sacrilegious references to the love of the Holy Trinity, as compared with the love of manhood and womanhood sweeping the brood clean out, were too strong even for nonconformists. Had a man written these poems, the town might have viewed them with comparative comfort. But a woman wrote them, a woman who dressed like a lady and painted charming lamp-shades. It is difficult to appraise the work of Mina Loy in perspective. Though she was original, a number of eccentricities, some of which are conscious distortions of style, hamper one's full admiration. I am certain, in reviewing the glamorous years of the poetic civil war, that a few of her best poems will survive. . . . Some of my old enthusiasms have cooled in perspective, whereas doubts I held concerning Miss Loy have vanished. Though I printed the work she gave me almost in toto, much of it puzzled me at the time. I felt that she might have made a greater effort to communicate herself more clearly. She did not have to compromise with the reader, but with a stricter artistic conscience. If some of her work still looks haphazard, the best of it remains provocative and wears well in the proverbial test of time. (pp. 488-90)

> Alfred Kreymborg, "Originals and Eccentrics," in his Our Singing Strength: An Outline of American Poetry, 1620-1930 (reprinted by permission of Coward, McCann & Geoghgan, Inc.; copyright 1929 by Alfred Kreymborg; renewed © 1957), Coward-McCann, 1929 (and reprinted as his A History of American Poetry: Our Singing Strength, Tudor Publishing Company, 1934), pp. 466-522.*

KENNETH FIELDS

At a time when "cerebral" was a pejorative term, Mina Loy was dealing with ideas. Pound's genius lay in other directions; his importance is his diversity: his mastery of various styles, his influence on the little magazines, and the fragments of a curious sort of scholarship. It may be that Williams, in a few poems only, surpasses Mina Loy stylistically, because of his extraordinary finish and precision, but the body of his work does not compare with her poems; his subjects are frequently trivial, and hers are not. And where Marianne Moore is clever and superficial, Mina Loy is profound; where Miss Moore is amusing, Miss Loy is bitterly satirical. The poets of this period tended toward a narrowness which was concerned with the image, "the thing itself," and with the technical aspects of free verse. This sort of brilliant specialization is always beneficial for the sophistication of poetic style, but it may prevent the writer from dealing with broader and more permanent areas of human experience. Thus Williams, because of his scepticism, his desire for communication, and his personal limitations, narrowly restricts his subject in his best poems and presents the isolated object with great clarity. While Pound, who lacks nothing in depth of subject, breaks his material into intractable fragments, resulting in an incoherence of which Pound is most aware. And in the poems of H. D., who cultivates effects of rhythm and sound to a high degree, subject gives way to a monotonous and private ecstasy.

Mina Loy's intelligence enables her to deal with matters of more general concern than those of her contemporaries, while her sharp perceptions and style always render the experience unique. Frequently with great brevity, she handles many of the sentimental stereotypes which had been too easily accepted for some time; and this refusal to accept the merely conventional involves a rigorous examination of states of mind and feeling, and gives to her poems a very personal quality. (pp. 598-99)

Miss Loy has written poems on D'Annunzio, Brancusi, Wyndham Lewis, and Joyce, and much of her subject matter involves a critique of many of the aesthetic commonplaces of the period and of the preceding "nineties." One of these commonplaces was the artist-as-clown, a notion which relegates art to the skillful pose and derives from an aesthetic such as Wilde's which declares that "All art is quite useless." It is art for art's sake, or art specialized to the point of excluding life. She may sympathize with the despair which is usually found behind the dandy's pose, but she satirizes the attitude which undermines artistic integrity. For style, if one takes the notion in its extreme sense, may become simply a game, and all art, a fraudulent discourse. (pp. 599-600)

In **"Lunar Baedecker,"** the moon at first emerges as a nineties effigy, the superficial artists "draped / in satirical draperies." The irony in phrases such as "posthumous parvenues" is consistent and cannot be summarized. Moreover, the figurative language of the poem controls several areas of experience, and a good deal of careful reading is required to keep them in mind. The language, for example, evokes, not only the sterile poetic commonplaces . . . but also the effete, superficially dazzling life of (presumably) New York of the period. Both aspects are brought into juxtaposition by very forceful imagery. . . . The infusoria (lines 12-18) are marvelous. A certain species of [the microscopic organisms pictured] is shaped something like a chandelier and, seen through a microscope, appears to be tremulously glowing with light. The image describes both the neon lights of Broadway . . . and the stars of this "Lunar Baedecker"; it is a controlled vision of decay in which macrocosm and microcosm, the telescopic and the microscopic, are united. It is this compression by way of imagery which is peculiar to Mina Loy. It is her own special brilliance.

Mina Loy's versification is unsophisticated and sometimes awkward. Her line resembles neither the quick, nervous line of Williams and H. D., nor the smooth, longer line of Pound, sometimes Stevens, and John Gould Fletcher. Her most serious rhythmic deficiency is a lack of unity from beginning to end of many of her poems. In **"Lunar Baedecker,"** for example, she stops and starts, moving from one subject to the next, the individual stanzas nearly becoming separable sections in themselves. Her rhythms vary in speed, but the movement of most of her verse is slow; if it is uncomplicated, it is nevertheless unpretentious. What is most impressive about her verse, finally, is the incredible energy of her language—and her intelligence. The simple movement is often accentuated by the use of unusual and unexpected rhymes and effects of alliteration. . . . But these devices may be used excessively, and **"Lunar Baedecker"** comes short of her best work because of the awkwardness and obvious redundancy of . . . [some of the lines]. (pp. 600-02)

"Apology of Genius" is better. The theme of the artist's isolation grew increasingly more common toward the end of the nineteenth century as a result of very narrow ideas about art and epistemology. Here, the experience is more universal. If poetry is a function of the intelligence, and if great poets are to be persons of genius, then their poems will be largely unintelligible to the majority of the people. I am not speaking about technical features only; many poets, I suspect, would be satisfied if the simple content of their poems were understood. This is not to say that great poems are obscure; but poetry, contrary to popular notions, is not for the enlightenment of the masses; it is available to those who possess the talent and the energy to acquire a rather specialized knowledge, and who, additionally, are willing to respect the mind of the poet of genius. Consequently, those who lack this respect are often the cause of unpleasantness for the poet; at best, his poems are misconstrued. But poets wish to have their poems understood, and the isolation, increasingly more modern as fewer ideas are commonly shared, is painful and desperate.

To the first number of *The Blind Man*, dedicated to the Independents, Mina Loy contributes a short note, evidently the transcript of a public address, on the subject of educating the public. . . . She presents ironically the split between the artist and the public. . . . In **"Apology of Genius,"** we get the public view of the artist . . . along with the poet's view, stated with the force which illustrates her genius. . . . The procedure differs from that of a "compensatory ironist" such as Laforgue in this way: while Laforgue vacillates between the sentimental cliché and its hard-boiled reverse (this is essentially the method of Cummings), Mina Loy presents the double view while maintaining the integrity of her art. The result is an unsentimental poem of great irony and satiric force, in which the bitterness is stated in precise terms. (pp. 602-04)

"Der Blinde Junge" is, I think, her best poem. . . . There is no awkwardness here. The poem has a thematic and rhythmic coherence which many of her poems lack, and its conclusion is, for me, as moving as anything in the period. Here, she deals with another, more absolute sort of isolation, in which feeling, cut off from its object, becomes a "centripetal sentience" of unfulfilled craving, objective values having been lost which might accurately inform experience. The treatment of vision in religious terminology is another example of the density of her figurative language. The black lightning of war has desecrated the retinal altar of the young boy, the purposeless eremite. By virtue of this compressed diction, she can keep before us the general and the particular situations at once, both of which are equally terrifying. The motive is World War I, and the blind youth is "Kriegsopfer," war's offering, of Bellona, the goddess of war. Though the poem may be an analogue for the bleakness of much of modern experience, and though Mina Loy is in sympathy with the blind anguish of the youth, her statement is more than the effusion of "concussive dark"; for the poem is written with great precision. . . . (p. 605)

[Mina Loy] is one of the great modern poets and, in spite of her faults, should be read in bulk. It will be slow work for the curious, carried out in rare book rooms and magazine files. But I know of no poetry in English which resembles hers; she is unique. This is the distinction, and, I suppose, the despair of the great. (p. 607)

Kenneth Fields, "The Poetry of Mina Loy" (copyright, 1967, by Kenneth Fields; reprinted by permission of the author), in The Southern Review, *n.s. Vol. III, No. 3, July, 1967, pp. 597-607.*

VIRGINIA M. KOUIDIS

[In considering the question of why Mina Loy is an *American* poet, it seems essential to consider three factors which link her to the American modernists.] First, in her awareness that the subjects and structures of English poetry in 1910 were inadequate to experience, Mina Loy anticipates the Americans in drawing upon French literature of the art-for-art's-sake tradition for the justification and practice of her poetic revolt. As justification it taught the supremacy of art and contempt for the bourgeois fear of the new. But as her satires of the tradition and her praise of artistic responsibility indicate, she condemns the pose of artistic alienation. Implicit in her poetry is the notion of the poet as seer—the poet of Emerson and Whitman—who guides the way to divine self-realization. Certainly her emphasis on the self harkens back to American romanticism although its origins are not necessarily American. In terms of the practice of literature, the French tradition emphasized the craft of poetry and encouraged experiment. It also offered a greater freedom of subject: the seamy and mundane aspects of life as well as the sexual fantasies and subconscious terrors of the self became available to the poet. Within this tradition Jules Laforgue provides Mina Loy—as he does Ezra Pound, T. S. Eliot, and Wallace Stevens—a cure for clichéd sentimentalism. The sophisticated irony of Laforgue's Pierrot serves as a model for disdaining social ritual and expressing emotion.

Laforgue of course introduces the second and perhaps the most important link between Mina Loy and the Americans: a verbalism that in some of its manifestations Pound calls logopoeia. Like the Americans she employs a compressed diction that abandons the poetic commonplace and demands the total involvement of the reader in the poem's language; indifferent to poetic eloquence, this diction reflects modes of perception and utilizes the spoken language. More at home with abstractions than some of the Americans, Mina Loy nevertheless shares their creation of (sometimes arbitrary) word-worlds that do not depend on previous explanations of experience. Among the Americans Marianne Moore employs a "crystalline structure" that conveys the integrity of her vision and of the "perceived world's multifarious otherness" in careful symmetries of language. William Carlos Williams depicts the world's processes and independent thingness—"no ideas but in things"—in words cleansed of the corrosion of habit, while Wallace Stevens, the philosopher, constructs whimsical fictions—the world's only order—from word games. Even more radical, Gertrude Stein in *Tender Buttons* liberates words from denotation to form nearly abstract word patterns. As her contribution to these experiments Loy causes words to express the movement of consciousness over and into the human quest for significance. As with the Americans her verbalism, at its best, shapes vividly fresh images and exact descriptions, finding its rhythms in the movement of the mind's eye rather than in conventional metric. In short, her poetry illustrates American modernism as René Taupin early defined it. This poetry, he says, observes even among non-Imagist poets the tenants of Imagism—conciseness and exactness, use of the image, composition by musical phrase. . . . (pp. 135-36)

Finally, Mina Loy is linked to the Americans by her translation into poetry of the techniques and structures of modern European painting, especially Futurism and Cubism. Gertrude Stein, at times a verbal Cubist, is famous for her patronage of modern art; and Marianne Moore, Stevens, and Williams were interested in painting. This interest, fed by contact in New York City with the new art, influenced their experiments with image and structure. Loy's distinction is that, as much a painter as a poet, she appears in the American little magazines of 1914 with the innovations of the painters already assimilated into her poetry. Historically she is among the first English-language poets to adopt the techniques of modern painting, especially fragmentation and collage juxtaposition, and to tie these to the age's "crisis in consciousness." Poetry had to make sense of a radically changing world and to depict new modes of perception. Hesitation would have meant a personal and artistic failure of vision.

Mina Loy's tragedy as a poet is that although she was among the first to respond innovatively to the crises of the new century, she lacked the discipline, or desire, to carry her innovations much beyond their culmination in **Lunar Baedeker** and **Anglo-Mongrels and the Rose**. Later poems portend a major development of her theme, but they do not break through to new structures for conveying the I-eye's relation to existence; in fact, they abandon some of the most daring of her early experiments. This failure may be due to her sense that poetry was but a handmaiden to the business of living. The attitude prompts the question she put to her publisher Jonathan Williams: "'But, why do you waste your time on these thoughts of mine—I was never a poet?'" The reader is unlikely to share her self-disparagement. Mina Loy may have lacked a sense of vocation but for over a decade, fired by self-awakening and the excitement of the age's artistic revolt, her poetic genius met the criterion she set for the artist of giving meaningful form to chaos.

Speculation on what direction Mina Loy might have taken had she been dedicated to poetry helps to place her in the currents of American poetry as they spill into the present. While her early poetry contains overtones of Prufrockian despair, she does not move with Eliot and his descendants among the poets and critics of the New Criticism into religious, political, and artistic conservatism. Rather, her theme of vision and her disavowal of absolutes, her depictions of consciousness, and her tolerance of experiment situate her . . . with Stein, Pound, and Williams as a precursor of postmodernism or, more specifically, of poets such as Kenneth Rexroth, the Beats, and Charles Olson and the Black Mountain poets. . . . The connection Mina Loy forges in her imagery between (female) sexuality and the unconscious looks to surrealist, confessional, and feminist poetry. Her use of collage, fragmentation, and free verse anticipates the composition by field proposed in Olson's "Projective Verse." **"The Costa San Giorgio,"** drawing upon Futurist dynamism, parallels the Projectivist depiction of a world in flux with the I become a part of the world's thingness. However, unlike many of the poets in Olson's orbit, Mina Loy gives up her attempt to place the I within the flux; she does not wish to diminish the ego, or self, but through the intuitions and cerebrations of the self to arrive at tentative explanations of existence. She strives not for "escape from the self" but for self-realization. Furthermore, the theme of the escape from time which runs throughout her poetry reflects a desire for transcendence of this world, not for oneness with it. The desire triumphs in her poems on art. Here she joins those modernists who step out of time into the fixed, spatialized realm of the work of art. But she relinquishes this dream of nirvana, for in her later poetry on common humanity she acknowledges the near impossibility of such transcendence and shares the existentialist commitment to responsible human action in the time of this world, action embodied for her in vision. On the basis of her movement in this direction an existentialist-feminist poetry employing organic forms seems best to fulfill the emphases of her poetry.

But speculation on how Mina Loy might have developed her themes and structures needs to be limited to clarifying and appreciating the achievement of the poetry she actually wrote.

What emerges is a poetry that earns our recognition partially by its original and honest response to modernity. More importantly, her poetry demonstrates the fine attunement to the possibilities for words that raises the poet above other practitioners of language. By this quality Mina Loy merits inclusion among the distinguished poets of the twentieth century. (pp. 137-40)

Virginia M. Kouidis, in her Mina Loy: American Modernist Poet *(reprinted by permission of Louisiana State University Press; copyright © 1980 by Louisiana State University Press), Louisiana State University Press, 1980, 148 p.*

ROGER L. CONOVER

For a brief period, it is fair to say that Mina Loy did as much as any woman of her generation to foster the international trafficking of avant-garde life and thought in Paris-America. She introduced Stieglitz and his circle to the work of Apollinaire, imported Futurist techniques to American theater, applied methods borrowed from the revolution in the visual arts to the new poetics, and exerted an influence on the leaders of New York Dada. Her insinuation that a rampant disease called provincialism infected the American literary scene *entre les deux guerres* and her move from total involvement to a position of detachment earned her the indifference of her colleagues and did damage to her reputation. While most of the expatriates were just beginning their exile training, shifting their allegiance from one short-lived masthead to the next and changing headquarters as fast as Jimmie the Barman switched jobs in Montparnasse, Mina Loy moved freely in World Bohemia—a land without seacoast or policy whose mythic contours were barely sensed, let alone set foot upon, by the rank-and-file visitors.

She did not write—or rather chose not to finish—her own memoirs, preferring to live life rather than record it. It is clear from her manuscripts that had she done so, however, she would have given us more of the flavor of French bohemian intellectual life and underground cabaret culture than F. Scott Fitzgerald and the American Regulars knew existed. (p. xviii)

By birth about fifteen years older than most of those who comprised the so-called Lost Generation of American poets, by residency the veteran of two earlier waves of American artistic emigrations, and by action and temperament more closely aligned with the leaders of the international avant-garde in painting than the classic modernist poets of her generation, she was viewed with admiration and fear by the new lieutenants of letters for whom poetry existed in a basically literary framework.

So Mina Loy in the Twenties was a bright star, engaging and distant. . . . She was one of the most beautiful of a beautiful generation of poets. (pp. xix-xx)

Kenneth Rexroth once compared her to "those kings whom history has always given a bad name because no one wanted to claim them." It is true that she remains singularly isolated historically. There has been no voice in the English language like hers; she has had no followers. For forty years Rexroth has been trying to get readers to look back in time to find a voice which is still out front. He, more than any other living critic, has been responsible for directing younger poets to her work. . . . In 1944 he made his case in the pages of *Circle*, ending with a mandate to James Laughlin of New Directions Press:

> Mr. Laughlin, the 'Five Young Poets' are still Eliot, Stevens, Williams, Moore, Loy—get busy.

But the most Laughlin was able to do was publish one of her poems in his anthology of 1950. (pp. xxi-xxii)

There was a time when it was common to couple the names of Mina Loy and William Carlos Williams. In 1926, Yvor Winters treated them as equals, said they were "the two living poets who have the most . . . to offer the younger generation of American writers" [see excerpt above].

> They present us with a solid foundation in place of Whitman's badly aligned cornerstones, a foundation which is likely to be employed, I suspect, for a generation or two, by the more talented writers of this country, or by a rather large part of them.

If this suggested development materializes, he went on to say, "Emily Dickinson will have been its only forerunner."

Loy had just published her first book when Winters made that speculation. Not wishing to give equal odds based on so little evidence from her, he qualified his prediction by conceding that Williams' chance of "becoming the chief prophet of my own or some future generation is probably greater." Williams wrote poems of blinding technique and extraordinary precision. Hers sometimes lacked grace. And whether through sheer stamina or nervous power, he also produced at a faster rate, at the kind of pace that was more likely to make him a major poet. Whereas Williams "hurled himself at the whole world with the passion of the former bantam-weight champion who bore his name . . . she attacked the dirty commonplace with the doggedness of a weight lifter." Loy was by far the more deliberate, and in the end, although Williams lived within the brackets of her life, Winters' hunch was correct—she would produce less. (p. xxiii)

Mina Loy wrote with almost stoic slowness for half a century, sometimes drafting a single line twenty, thirty times before she moved on. The margins of her notebooks are cramped with word-counts and manuscriptural erasure; she spent hours applying lapidary care to make lines that have the hard-cut look of crystal. Their diamond-faceted finish gave Winters the impression of "images that have frozen into epigrams," and the density of her material gave him the sensation of "walking through granite instead of air." (pp. xxiii-xxiv)

Apart from her slowness of pace, the one deterrent that might keep Loy from eventually emerging as the most influential poet of her generation, Winters reckoned, was also the source of her power. When she was fully in control, he said, she had an advantage over all of her contemporaries. What was her deficiency? A certain clumsiness, or artlessness, that he detected whenever her ideas were too complex to handle in the compressed forms she favored working in. "Or perhaps it is not clumsiness, but the inherently unyielding quality of her material that causes this embarrassment." Emily Dickinson had this problem too. The hard and direct simplicity of her forms was not always equal to the sublimity of her conceptions. Loy occasionally overcame this fault, and when she did, Winters felt, she attained an athletic grace that made "her success, if the least dazzling of the four [Williams, Stevens, Loy, Moore] . . . by all odds the most astounding. . . . More intent on the gutter and its horrors than any of the group with which she was associated, and more intensely cerebral, perhaps, than any save one of them, her work ordinarily presents that broken, unemotional, and . . . witty observation of undeniable facts" that was exemplary of "Others" poetry. (pp. xxviii-xxix)

[Mina Loy] published only ten poems in the last thirty-five years of her life, all solicited.

In 1967, a year after she died, Yvor Winters mistook her long abstinence from print for a failure to write. This implied contempt for the literary world pleased him, perhaps because it reminded him of his other great admiration, Valéry. In any case it allowed him to add a coda to his youthful prediction. "She had an unusually good mind, but it exhausted its materials early; at least she knew when to stop." Still pronouncing **"Der Blinde Junge"** and **"Apology of Genius"** her best poems, and still standing her in the company of Williams, he equivocates in his final estimate of her achievement.

> She has nowhere written a poem as successful as the best of Williams, but she has attempted more in the two poems just mentioned and she is successful to a remarkable degree. . . .

During the forty years separating his early and late assessments, Winters had taught hundreds of young poets at Stanford. Though he volte-faced on many of his opinions over the years, Mina Loy's work remained an obsession, and at least two of his students—poets Ann Stanford and Kenneth Fields—left his classroom to give her a distinguished place in writings or anthologies of their own. In his doctoral dissertation (completed under Winters' supervision in 1967), Fields reëxamines the Loy-Williams-Stevens-Moore equation and finds Loy the positive integer [see excerpt above]. . . . "In spite of her faults," he concludes, "she should be read in bulk."

The faults he refers to are mechanical—a lack of metric unity from beginning to end of her poems, a rhythm that breaks with the stanza, starting and stopping as she moves from one idea to the next. She lacks the prosodic sophistication of Moore and Williams, the grace of Stevens. Alfred Kreymborg published almost everything she ever gave him, but later admitted that much of it puzzled him at the time [see excerpt above]. "A number of eccentricities, some of them conscious distortions of style, hamper one's full admiration." Overalliteration is a problem. She goes on sound-binges, gets stuck on plosive consonants, can't stop. Initially even Kenneth Rexroth hedged: "Metrically it is sometimes difficult to discover what effects she was seeking, if any." Then he started reading her poems on KPFA radio in San Francisco, testing them on students, reciting them aloud to other poets. A few years of this, he overcame his doubts. (pp. xxx-xxxi)

While Williams was resolving emotional complexity by way of craft, Loy was examining states of mind by projecting outlines of thought onto the page. While he restricted himself to the nominal domain of *things*, she was X-raying ideas. She implied everything—including sex—through intellect. Her sensuality is something new. She gives us the skeleton, the bone structure of ideas, compels us to provide the flesh. Williams was direct, but he softened the news. Loy delivered it like an invoice. When she was obscure, she was deliberately so. (pp. xxxi-xxxii)

Besides Williams, the poet with whom she was most often compared by her contemporaries was Moore. By 1944, this comparison too was obsolete. "Today only one visible ground of this equation remains. They are both moderately difficult for the careless reader" [Kenneth Rexroth]. Despite the imparity of their reputations, Rexroth insisted that Loy's "material is self-evidently more important than Miss Moore's, and treated with great earnestness, never with Miss Moore's dehydrated levity." Others who have responded positively to Loy's work are also fond of saying that her neglect has to do primarily with her "difficulty" as a poet, thus establishing a special privilege for themselves because they can appreciate demanding texts while others scratch their heads. "She is readable," Pound said, "by me that is." (He was no potato-head.) Moonstruck critics are largely the cause of Mina Loy's eclipse. She wears their label—DIFFICULT POET—like a parasalenic halo around her head. It is this ascription, more than inexigible lines, that has kept her from being read. Textual difficulty in fact has very little to do with Mina Loy's not being understood.

The major reasons for her obscurity today are self-imposed, the result of her own intransigence and intrepidness. In her twenties and thirties, the voltage she provided by sheer force of intellect and personality was enough to attract or repel the literary worlds around her. (p. xxxii)

Briefly a member of the Futurist ring and special friend of its grand muftis, Mina Loy's infatuation with the group ended when it embraced fascism. Her disillusion gave way to a polemical hostility that is the source of most of the satires in [*The Last Lunar Baedeker*]. Poems like **"Giovanni Franchi," "The Ineffectual Marriage,"** and **"Lions' Jaws"** are only sparring pieces, however, compared to her experimental verse play, *The Pamperers*. . . . It is a scathing satire of the Futurist attitudes toward women and a dramatic restatement of the exaggerated masculinities which came to dominate the movement. In it, she indicts several of her former colleagues, who, as political lunatics and misogynists lead a phobic and paranoid movement whose aim is to teach men to bear their own children. In **"Lions' Jaws,"** she mocks herself for seeking escape in Causes and warns other women not to delude themselves into thinking they are exempt from the sexist attitudes of amorists like Gabriele D'Annunzio. . . . (pp. xxxiii-xxxiv)

For the first ten years of her publishing career, Mina Loy actively monitored critical reaction to her work. Using the tactical skills she learned from Marinetti, she turned her detractors into her publicists. When John Rodker, one of her early admirers, wrote that she seemed to have "lost her grip," she engaged him in an exchange of volleys that spanned three successive issues of *The Little Review*. Repartéeing the "jealous frog [who] wishes only he could write. . . . The most difficult thing for a Georgian poet is to say something when he has nothing to say," she eventually forced him into a retraction. When Loy heard that Amy Lowell had criticized her poems, she sortied in kind. "Scholars and Moderns thought her book on French poets second-rate—very, very poor. So is *she* a judge?" And when T. S. Eliot praised what she considered to be an inferior translation of Valéry's "Le Serpent," she confided to Van Vechten again. "I think anyhow Eliot is second-rate himself. . . . Reading the translation after reading Valéry's French is a little like falling down a vegetarian's lavatory." Repeatedly in letters to friends she objected to the pieties of Harriet Monroe and the pontifical stance of *Poetry* in the 1910s.

It was Harriet Monroe's strenuous opposition to Mina Loy's **"Love Songs"** that made Mina Loy the *cause célèbre* of *Others*. Of all those writing in America, Monroe warned, Madame Loy is the most dangerous. Calling her "an extreme otherist" and designating Loy "one of the long-to-be-hidden-moderns," Monroe wished on her a spell that still sticks. For fifty years

Mina Loy has been the lost member of the modernist generation of American poets. (pp. xxxiv-xxxv)

As Monroe's taste matured, she was later to grant compromising approval to Mina Loy, saying that she "had strangely turned understandable—and less fragmentary—though still scorning the use of punctuation marks." But she never published her, and never overcame her defensive view of the entire *Others* phenomenon. (p. xxxv)

Two years after the first four **"Love Songs"** landed like strange, unidentifiable objects in Greenwich Village, thirty more appeared. An entire issue of *Others* was devoted to the expanded cycle. Also in 1917, the second *Others* annual was issued, containing new poems by Mina Loy and Marianne Moore. A new critical constant entered the vocabulary the following year, in direct response to "this first adequate presentation of Mina Loy and Marianne Moore." Until now, Pound had successfully divided poetry into two classes: *melopoeia,* or poetry that moves by music; and *phanopoeia,* poetry that depends on image. Now [see excerpt above] he was forced to revise his taxonomy to accommodate a new utterance, and to do so he coined a third term, *logopoeia:*

> poetry that is akin to nothing but language, which is a dance of the intelligence among words and ideas and modifications of ideas and characters.

Of the two poets under review, Loy wrote a purer form of it, Pound said; hers had the true-coin ring: "In the verses of Marianne Moore I detect traces of emotion; in that of Mina Loy I detect no emotion whatever." But the work of these two women had many features in common: polysyllabic diction, precise description, collage composition. Both had a penchant for using extra-literary (especially scientific) words and elaborate sound patterns, often for ironic effect. Both poets spoke from a position of detached irony, but while Moore's stance was moral and ethical, Loy's was cosmic and abstract. Moore used convoluted syntax to assert a special and peculiarly slanted sensibility, Loy favored straightforward constructions for didactic means. Moore's subjects—presented in such a way that they are inaccessible to all but the ultramundane experiencer—were tangibles, solids. Loy sidled up to the eternal platitudes—love, sex, marriage, procreation, parturition, mortality, disaster, death—and brought them all within the scope of her poetic capability and range. Compared to Moore's sidewinding sentences, Loy's were unusually direct.

Exactly forty years later, William Carlos Williams made this point again.

> The essence of her style is its directness in which she is exceeded by no one. Her metaphors, when they can be detected, are of the quality of sunlight, they sparkle. There is no dimming of the light. . . . Her lines are short. There is no inversion of the phrase for ironic effect or to keep an imposed order. You cannot find a single instance of a measure retained to complete a conventional stanza or indeed a set pattern of any sort.

What interested both Pound and Williams was how anyone could write with such telegraphic directness and yet still achieve the distance necessary for irony. How could Mina Loy be so explicit and yet still manage the verbal flourishes that made her poems ornate? In *How to Read,* Pound refined his original definition of *logopoeia* to account for this paradoxical quality of Loy's speech. It is a method, he said, which

> employs words not only for their direct meaning but it takes count in a special way of habits of usage, of the context we expect to find with the word, its usual concomitants, of its known acceptances, and of ironical play.

Indeed, the local connotation of a Loy phrase often alleges itself against the meaning of the same locution in broader contexts. Some poets poeticize in order to be 'poetic'—when Loy evokes a poeticism, it is to achieve the contrary effect. When she uses rhetoric, she is anti-rhetorical. When she seems to be one thing, she is the opposite. Pound might have added yet a fourth term to his lexicon to describe Loy: *prosopopoeia,* or poetry whose acting voice animates the absent. (pp. xxxvii-xxxviii)

[When Pound reviewed the work of Marianne Moore and Mina Loy in *The Little Review* in 1918, he knew only the basic facts of Moore's life]; of Loy's he knew less. But he could detect enough hard-boiled courage in their texts to be pretty sure that what Harriet Monroe mistook for passing *moues* and "sardonic little cries" were in fact drops of treacle in her eyes. The voice Pound heard was not one of self-pity, but one of "clever people in despair, or hovering on the brink of that precipice." . . . They have produced "something distinctly American in quality . . . something which could not have come out of any other country." About Moore's autochthony there was, of course, no question. Loy's provenance? That was something different. She had not even set foot in the States when she wrote the poems that Pound thought were so exemplary of the American condition. From a less literal standpoint, however, Pound was correct. Mina Loy did not emerge from a single literary environment. She was a chronic itinerant, not burdened with the pieties and compensations that sometimes attend residency and birthright. Like other members of the international avant-garde who migrated to America during the war, her attraction to America and its machine-age values began abroad. America was where the Revolution of the Word was starting; Europe was where the Great Tyranny of Cultural Heritage was ending. (pp. xxxix-xl)

[Mina Loy] lived an exotic life, but in her indigent years the mundane habitat was of vital interest. Out of the jetsam she collected on her Bowery rounds, she would confect some wondrous image. One goes through her manuscripts in much the same way, trying to make some coherent exhibit out of curiosities drawn from oblivion, salvaging what may now look to us like poems, but were first encountered as strange, personal objects. Her hats, dresses, lampshades, and inventions were accessories to her literary creations. Not her indifference, but her resolute attachment to life made all of its furnishings autobiographical adjuncts. She was as interested in newspapers and fashion magazines as in literary journals. She integrated artistic, commercial, and domestic expression into one interdisciplinary condition. Her impulse was to break down existing boundaries, to go beyond fixed limits. No collection of writings can encompass all the drafts, no biography all the facts. But we keep shining our light on the margins, and occasionally we pick up something odd, and new. We think we are reading a poem. Then something glistens. Mina Loy? (p. lxi)

Roger L. Conover, "Introduction" (copyright © 1982 by Roger L. Conover and The Jargon Society, Inc.; excerpted by permission), in The Last Lunar Baedeker *by Mina Loy, edited by Roger L. Conover, Jargon, 1982, pp. xv-lxi.*

CONSTANCE HUNTING

[What] does "morality" mean to a poet? Obviously, it has little to do with behaving in accordance with a set of social standards. Nor is it necessarily concerned with the ascertainment of or instruction in what is good or evil.... It may have to do with religion, but if it does, religion is subsumed—witness T. S. Eliot and Gerard Manley Hopkins. It may have to do with patriotism, but in a subversive way—witness Siegfried Sassoon and Robert Lowell. But over and beyond these minor manifestations, morality, to a poet, means one thing and one thing only. Few poets of the 20th century came closer to it than did Mina Loy. (p. 133)

[Mina Loy's] independence was largely misunderstood and misinterpreted, although it was recognized as an essential ingredient of the peculiar power of her poetry. She could not be dismissed—though Harriet Monroe, of *Poetry,* which never published anything by Loy, tried: "The load being too heavy to talk about, she carries it as she may . . . making gay little satiric *moues* at us as she passes, and giving sardonic little cries." It was not exactly the fault of her would-be champions that they equated self-reliance with the American spirit, patriotism with moral and thus with aesthetic good, prescription with kindness. Simply, they wished to "place" Loy within their particular spheres, not realizing that she travelled with a different visa in a different orbit.

If Pound could discover "no emotion whatever" in her work, what, then, did he make of . . . [some passages in **"Love Songs"**?] . . . Pound appears ambivalent about his feelings about her seeming lack of feeling. On the intellectual level, he admires it: by clearing the underbrush from the thing in itself, Loy separates, as it were, the tree from the forest. But on a human level, he regrets it—after all, he considers that he is able both to separate and to combine. He does not perceive Loy's shaking of sense to metaphor and back again . . . , nor her use of sound to convey a physical and thus an emotional state—not her reaction to it, but the state itself. (pp. 135-36)

When Yvor Winters [see excerpt above] gave Loy credit for using "the drabbest of material," he was not referring to her Bowery poems of the 'forties, during which she engaged in a "metaphorical quest to find Christ" on Manhattan's Lower East Side, but was praising such **"Satires"** of 1916-1923 as **"Black Virginity"** and **"Lions' Jaws,"** and, by inference, **"Giovanni Franchi"** and **"O Marcel . . . Otherwise / I Also Have Been to Louise's."** It is something of a paradox that Winters should speak of the **"Satires"** as containing "seven or eight of the most brilliant and unshakably solid satirical poems of our time" and, in almost the same breath in which he compares them favorably to those of Pope and Dryden, designate their approaches and subjects as, complimentarily, dull. . . . As for Loy's "unexciting method," did Winters not notice [in **"Lions' Jaws,"** for instance] the suitably ironic mingling of slang ("get a move on," "jump the train") and artificially heightened image ("melodious magnolia," "neurotics / wince at the dusk"), the effect of which is to satirize not only the "revolutionary" situation but the strange-bedfellow language of the situation and the attitude towards it of the poet? Did he not see or hear the word-play of such ploys as "lyrical birds" / "lyrebirds," women who are poets; "amusing men" / "a-musing men," male poets seeking the Muse "in their mail," maleness, chain armor, chain letters "discover[ed]" in their maleness as "sans couvert," as spinsterish; "lurid mother" / "lured," and, in semi-holy connotation, "Lourdes"; and, amid the obvious pi-spellings of her own name, "alas" and "Helios" for "alias"? Wallace Stevens is here, with more bite because Loy is immediately engaged with the political world; Pound, cum quiddities, sans quirks; William Carlos Williams, without his occasional ponderosity.

Williams wrote that Loy's metaphors, "when they can be detected, are of the quality of sunlight, they sparkle." Both Pound and Williams use the verb "detect"; it is as though they are using those machines which pick up wedding rings and gold fillings from beach sand; as though analysis of Loy's poetry demands a special instrument. Whereas all that needs to be done is to extend the apprehension of the old, understood terms. What is a poem such as **"O Marcel . . ."** but a metaphor for the volatile, precious salon life of Paris-gone-New York in 1916? . . . In a poem like this—and **"O Marcel . . ."** is merely an extreme example—something seems to happen for Loy high up in the air, an insistent but not unpleasant clashing of sounds that make sense beyond sound, in somewhat the same way that for a musical person the clattering of dishes in a noisy restaurant will sound not *like* music but will actually be perceived *as* music. Thus **"O Marcel . . ."** becomes far more than a clever transcription of talk in Walter and Louise Arensberg's New York apartment. . . . In its comical-hysterical rhythms and its verbal disjunctives, the poem metamorphoses into a live artifact. And most of Mina Loy's poetry is able to achieve this kind of supra-creation.

Pound was on the right track when he revised his *melopoeia* and *phanopoeia* principles of classification to include, in recognition of Loy's unique utterance, *logopoeia:*

> poetry that is akin to nothing but language, which is a dance of the intelligence among words and ideas and modifications of ideas and characters.

Certainly Loy's goes beyond poetry that depends on music if by music is meant harmony, and beyond that which depends on image if by image is meant visual impression. But Pound, like William Carlos Williams and the editor of **The Last Lunar Baedeker,** persists in the notion of poetry as linear. Loy, however, writes neither in horizontals nor in attempts at verticals, but in tonal clusters. An analogy may be made with the second movement of Beethoven's Opus 110 piano sonata: if played as printed on the page, the configuration of notes in the movement's middle section appears linear; but if, for purposes of analysis of related motion or progressive memorization, the patterns are metamorphosed to chord clusters, what emerges are startling constellations of sound that leap from the 19th to the 20th century. So with Loy: not the 20th but the 21st century, in poetry, is heard. Her word-tonal clusters are ideational and emotional constellations. How could her work accommodate itself to the dicta of the acknowledged innovators of her day? For although she uses her own times and places, her concepts of time and place allow them a near-irrelevance:

> The antique way to live and express life was to . . . say it according to the rules. But the modern flings herself at life and lets herself feel what she does feel then upon the very tick of the second she snatches the images of life that fly through the brain.

The innovators turn out to be "antique"; the "modern" turns out to be ahead of time. The above passage irresistibly reminds of the celebrated words of Virginia Woolf in her essay "Modern Fiction":

> Let us record the atoms as they fall upon the mind in the order in which they fall, let us trace the pattern, however disconnected and incoherent in appearance, which each sight or incident scores upon the consciousness.

The morality of Mina Loy? Simply, *integer artis*. This is the thing, for any artist, in any age, that matters. This she has preserved. Her terms? "No surrender." (pp. 136-39)

Constance Hunting, "The Morality of Mina Loy," in Sagetrieb *(copyright © 1983 by the National Poetry Foundation), Vol. 2, No. 1, Spring, 1983, pp. 133-39.*

Norman Mailer
1923-

American novelist, essayist, filmmaker, and journalist.

Since the 1948 publication of his first novel, *The Naked and the Dead*, Mailer has been regarded as one of America's most prominent contemporary writers. A prolific and highly controversial literary figure, Mailer resists identification with current writing movements and is usually viewed independently. According to many critics, Mailer's fiction since *The Naked and the Dead* is of uneven quality. But most critics agree that he has consistently produced outstanding works of nonfiction in a style frequently referred to as New Journalism, a blend of factual and dramatic, usually highly subjective reporting, which is often unsympathetic to traditional attitudes.

In the 1950s, Mailer's work became more radical. His gravitation to a leftist philosophy began when he associated with Marxist intellectuals while studying in Europe. His novels *Barbary Shore* (1951) and *The Deer Park* (1955) began the social attack which typifies Mailer's later works. The main character in *The Deer Park* is a sociopathic hipster, a figure Mailer comes to celebrate, mythologize, and identify with in his first nonfiction works. In the late 1950s, Mailer published two works which defined and advanced the "Mailer Myth." His essay "The White Negro" (1957) defines his philosophy of "hip" as a combination of rebelliousness, violence, primitive sexuality, and existentialism. "The White Negro" appears in *Advertisements for Myself*, a 1959 collection of essays in which Mailer plays the role of an American artistic and cultural critic.

In the late 1960s, the Vietnam conflict was the focus of Mailer's most celebrated argument in the New Journalistic style. *The Armies of the Night* won both the Pulitzer Prize in fiction and a National Book Award in 1968. In this work he narrates his involvement in contemporary events from a third person viewpoint, referring to the central character as "Mailer." Leo Braudy has commented, "*The Armies of the Night* gains much of its power from the perfect melding of the public author and the private foolish individual, the public event and the limited individual perspective. All of Mailer's impotent and weak heroes culminate for a moment in the 'Norman Mailer,' whose double consciousness . . . can understand the Pentagon march, both in its immediacy and its history, its moment-to-moment nature and its ultimate meaning."

During the 1970s Mailer tended to focus on celebrated individuals whose lives were emblematic of the conflict between public and private life. Two of these books were about the late actress Marilyn Monroe: a novelized biography entitled *Marilyn* (1973) and *Of Women and Their Elegance* (1980), a fictional interview between Mailer and Monroe. His most acclaimed biographical work is *The Executioner's Song*, which received both the Pulitzer Prize in fiction and a National Book Award in 1979. While *The Executioner's Song* relates the events in the life of convicted killer Gary Gilmore, it also examines the dynamics of American society, which Mailer contends simultaneously fosters and condemns aberrant behavior.

While he was producing his biographical novels, Mailer was working on a novel which he has described as the most am-

© Jerry Bauer

bitious project of his career. This novel, *Ancient Evenings*, which is set in Egypt during the reign of the pharaohs, was the object of much critical anticipation and speculation long before its publication in 1983. Critical reception of *Ancient Evenings* has been mixed, with the majority of critics finding the work too long and unnecessarily laden with shocking sexual content. However, most critics praised Mailer's thorough historical research and evident knowledge of Egyptology.

(See also *CLC*, Vols. 1, 2, 3, 4, 5, 8, 11, 14; *Contemporary Authors*, Vols. 9-12, rev. ed.; *Dictionary of Literary Biography*, Vols. 2, 16; *Dictionary of Literary Biography Yearbook: 1980*; and *Dictionary of Literary Biography Documentary Series*, Vol. 3.)

JENNIFER BAILEY

One of the major obstacles to a proper understanding of Norman Mailer's work is his series of pronouncements on the nature of his ambitions. If these remarks are taken quite literally then Mailer's achievements can easily be distorted. Dotted throughout his writing since 1959, when *Advertisements for Myself* was published, is a thinly veiled longing to embody the conflicting currents of thought in the twentieth century just as Melville did in the nineteenth. The response to this has often been to regard Mailer's novels as noble but failed efforts and to settle for his journalism as a frequently brilliant but comparatively second-class literary activity. His forays into politics, poetry, biography, literary criticism, the theatre and filmmaking are then relegated to the amateur efforts of a versatile man. This kind of pigeonholing tends to miss the essentially innovatory nature of Mailer's talent.

In *The Armies of the Night* (1968), Robert Lowell makes the same mistake when he assures Mailer, '"I really think you are the best journalist in America".' Mailer irritably replies, '"Well, Cal, . . . there are days when I think of myself as being the best writer in America".' The point is that throughout his career, Mailer has attempted to transgress and transform the boundaries between literary genres in order to realise and maintain a major premise first defined in *Advertisements for Myself:* 'one may even attempt to reshape reality in some small way with the "fiction" as a guide'.

In order to see how a writer like Mailer engages with these polarities, it is useful to turn to the analysis by Richard Poirier, in his book *A World Elsewhere,* of the relationship between self and environment in the American imagination. Poirier considers that the categorisation of American writing into genres tends to obscure the more important issues. 'The crucial problem for the best American writers is to evade all such categorizations and to find a language that will at once express and protect states of consciousness that cannot adequately be defined by conventional formulations. . . .' By means of a richly metaphorical language, Mailer has maintained the premise, formulated in *Advertisements for Myself,* that 'There is finally no way one can try to apprehend complex reality without a "fiction".' (pp. 1-2)

Mailer declares his aesthetic artifice even as it is reaching for a reality that threatens it. But he also wants to demonstrably exercise a control over that reality—to 'reshape' it. The development of Mailer's use of metaphorical oppositions in his writing reflects a movement towards an effective appropriation of the external world in his radical 'fictions'. In his early novels, Mailer opposes politics and history in order to distinguish between collective and individual power. But as yet, this individual power is seen to be impotent, even though General Cummings in *The Naked and the Dead* (1948) hints at its subversive possibilities: '"politics have no more relation to history than moral codes have to the needs of any particular man".' Mickey Lovett, the narrator of *Barbary Shore* (1951) puts this notion into a literary context. His projected novel must give the duplicitous social reality a historical meaning. Yet this historical meaning is, as yet, uncertainly defined. In **'The White Negro'** (1957), civilised history is opposed to the personal history, or the new nervous system of the existential hipster. The essay defends the individual's independent choice to act against a society of 'conformity and depression'. . . . To stress the force of this radical rebellion, the act is always described as violent in a murderous or sexual sense. Because these actions are socially subversive, the hipster is entering an unknown realm and creating a causality to his actions that is distinct from the causality of impersonal 'civilized history . . .'. . . . (p. 2)

The status of the hipster's personal time or new nervous system, which is the precondition of this subversive action, is uncertainly figurative in the context of the essay. But in suggesting that the psychopath (and Mailer argues that the hipster possesses a psychopathic personality) seeks love that is 'Not love as the search for a mate, but love as the search for an orgasm more apocalyptic than the one which preceded it . . .' . . . , Mailer first develops a metaphor which describes the method by which the individual searches for an independent and therefore creative means of self-expression. By employing the sexual metaphor, Mailer can relinquish the term history as representing everything beyond the individual's control. The forces that threaten the creative act are found within a metaphor that is restricted to the creative life of one individual and by extension to Mailer himself. He is not forced to oscillate confusedly between literal and figurative terms of reference in order to incorporate the world into his writing. Any sexual activity that prevents conception undermines the individual's selfhood. Masturbation, buggery and contraception are therefore condemned. Mailer reiterates his views from the publication of *The Presidential Papers* (1963) onwards, while the sexual activities of Sergius O'Shaugnessy in **'The Time of Her Time'** and Stephen Rojack in *An American Dream* (1965) demonstrate these principles.

Mailer simultaneously developed another metaphorical opposition which similarly described the struggling precariousness of the individual's creativity. Although the notion of the hipster was the source of this opposition, Mailer only amplified it in a subsequent interview with Richard Stern, given in 1958 (reprinted in *Advertisements for Myself*):

> And I think there is one single burning pinpoint of the vision in Hip: it's that God is in danger of dying. In my very limited knowledge of theology, this never really has been expressed before. I believe Hip conceives of Man's fate being tied up with God's fate. God is no longer all-powerful. . . .

This enables Mailer to go on to suggest that when the hipster takes drugs, for example, 'in draining the substance of God he's exhausting Him, so that the drug-taker may be indulging an extraordinarily evil act at the instant he is filled with the feeling that he is full of God and good and a beautiful mystic'. . . . As with his sexual metaphor, Mailer is trying to define metaphysical entities within the individual in order that oppressive external forces can be incorporated into his fiction.

Until *Advertisements for Myself,* Mailer confined these metaphysical metaphors to the context of the rebellious hipster. But in a speech delivered on Vietnam Day in 1965 and reprinted in *Cannibals and Christians* (1966), Mailer argues that anyone is 'a member of a minority group if he contains two opposed notions of himself at the same time . . . as both exceptional and insignificant, marvellous and awful, good and evil'. The advantage of giving his metaphors a universal psychological relevance is that Mailer can successfully employ them in his works of fictional reporting as well as in his two novels written at this time: *An American Dream* and *Why Are We in Vietnam?* (1967). An image in the anti-Vietnam speech of 'the ego in perpetual transit from the tower to the dungeon and back again' . . . describes the satirised archetypal quest form of *An American Dream,* but it also leads Mailer towards the kind of oppositions he defines in his work at the end of the 1960s.

If Mailer's metaphorical oppositions attempt to stress the precariousness of artistic creativity, then the greatest threat will come from literal and therefore uncontrolled reality. In his sexual and metaphysical metaphors, Mailer transforms this literal and almost always oppressive reality into a dialectical entity within the individual. *The Armies of the Night, Miami and the Siege of Chicago* (1968) and Mailer's film *Maidstone*

(1970), successfully incorporate non-fictional realms without there being any threat to their aesthetic structure. In *The Armies of the Night,* Mailer reintroduces the term 'history' to signify the collective reality that modifies the individual vision of his protagonist. In the essay written about his film, *Maidstone: A Mystery* (1971), this collective reality is the force that ambiguously blurs the acted fiction of the film. But *Miami and the Siege of Chicago* is narrated by a reporter who is professionally obliged to observe and record the events he witnesses.

The function of Mailer's metaphors, however, is not just to extend the boundaries of fiction, but also explicitly to demonstrate that it can interpret the world in a social, political and cultural sense. Mailer's writing begins successfully to fulfil that claim when he controls the form of his fiction which records the struggling dialectical activity of his protagonist. Norman Mailer is, in this sense, an artist whose formal control distinguishes him from the vulnerable artist figures in his fiction.

Ihab Hassan's theory of radical irony, which he introduces and defines in the prologue to his book, *The Literature of Silence,* illuminates the nature of Mailer's achievement. Hassan initially advances the proposition that certain contemporary writers acknowledge what critics tend to ignore by providing the mirror-images of outrage and apocalypse 'that contain something vital and dangerous in our experience'. At the centre of these extreme responses is a silence which Hassan describes 'as the metaphor of a new attitude that literature has chosen to adopt toward itself'. This new attitude is one which 'compels the author to deprecate and even to spurn his activity'. Hassan's description of the silence which is achieved in this kind of literature through radical irony describes the function of Mailer's protagonists in his work after *Advertisements for Myself.* Hassan explains that radical irony is 'a term I apply to any statement that contains its own ironic denial'. When this technique is practised by fiction writers, the result is 'the paradox of art employing art to deny itself [which] is rooted in the power of human consciousness to view itself both as subject and object.' All of Mailer's protagonists after 1959 possess this power, so that the impulse to create is always fought for because it can only be expressed in the context of those forces that threaten it.

It is possible, however, to trace the development of these ideas in Mailer's fiction written before *Advertisements for Myself.* In his first three novels—*The Naked and the Dead, Barbary Shore* and *The Deer Park* (1955)—Mailer explores the discrepancy that seems to exist between the individual and the world; the discrepancy between moral choice and political expediency or between the artist and corrupt oppressive external forces. Mailer tries to resolve this dilemma by developing the idea that identity is always a fiction in so far as it depends upon a constantly changing milieu for its definition. He wanted, though, to explore the practical connotations of this theory, to synthesise fictional and literal frames of reference. Yet no matter how much the writer may want his fictional world to reflect the real one, it remains a created object. *Advertisements for Myself* was a breakthrough in that Mailer made himself a protagonist whose identity is a composite of roles that are triggered off by a variety of contexts both autobiographical and cultural. He simultaneously discovered that the reactions of a public audience was a necessary prerequisite for this form of writing. It was not an established literary reputation that he wanted, but a notoriety. (pp. 2-5)

Mailer consolidated his achievements when he discovered that the nature of improvised acting was analogous to his radical ideas on fiction. John Kennedy in **'The Superman Comes to the Supermarket'** is defined by Mailer as both a serious politician and a great box-office actor. Since Mailer characterises himself as an appreciative if bewildered spectator, his shifting perceptions dictate the actor's series of roles on the stage (in this case, a literal one, since the occasion is the 1960 Democratic National Convention in Los Angeles). In so doing, Mailer presents Kennedy as the personification of an ambiguous social reality.

From this, it was a short step to Mailer being both actor and audience in the performances of his personae which dominate his fictional reporting published in the late 1960s. The characters in *An American Dream* and *Why Are We in Vietnam?* are conceived in the same way as these personae. They shift roles, voices and points of view with the same rapidity and possess only the most conventional of physical embodiments in order that they might be mockingly dismembered by one of their many roles. Mailer has previously been underrated or ignored as a film director, yet the process of filming and the theories that he evolved from this process illuminate a period of prodigious activity.

Although it may now be possible to detect an impending creative impasse in Mailer's fiction of the shifting identity, this kind of radical fictionalising, first defined in *Advertisements for Myself,* still constitutes the foundation on which his unique talent rests. (pp. 5-6)

Jennifer Bailey, in her Norman Mailer: Quick-Change Artist *(© Jennifer Bailey 1979; by permission of Barnes & Noble Books, a Division of Littlefield, Adams & Co., Inc.), Barnes & Noble, 1979, 160 p.*

CHRISTOPHER LEHMANN-HAUPT

[There] can be little doubt that in some important respects "Ancient Evenings" is a triumph of technique over what for many writers would have proved forbiddingly intractable material. By a simple and altogether plausible use of mental telepathy, Mr. Mailer is able to compress into one narrative voice, speaking over the course of a single, albeit interminable, evening, an account not only of the 19th and 20th dynasties of ancient Egypt (1320-1121 B.C.), but also of the four lives of a heroic figure who manages to reincarnate himself three times over the course of 180 years.

What's more, by achieving this technical victory, Mr. Mailer has created a world ideally suited to many of his pet theories and fixations—psychic darts, single combat, staring contests, mindreading, vibrations of evil and virtue, all manner of magic and sorcery, the rich possibilities of sex in all its forms, the mysteries of excrement and, above all, the curious fantasy that one can literally reconceive oneself by dying in the act of sexual intercourse, and thereby defeat death and live forever. Such theories and fixations have often seemed preposterous in Mr. Mailer's writing on contemporary subjects, but they fit seamlessly into his conception of ancient Egypt, which may well explain why he was attracted to the subject in the first place.

But alas, for all the rounds he has won in this historical novel, Mr. Mailer appears not to know what every competent writer of historical novels needs to know—indeed what must be understood instinctively by any good storyteller, which is what one certainly would call Mr. Mailer, at least on the basis of his past achievements. What every good historical novelist knows is that once you've established the landscape, the culture and the precise exotic flavor of the world you're imagining, you start making them work for you instead of continuing to work for them. In short, you use them to tell your story.

But Mr. Mailer never ceases to describe and detail and seize new imaginative territory, and to do so with prose that can only be described as rich to the point of indigestibility. At some point in any novel, a reader's mind wants to relax and be borne along by the action of the story or at least by some irresistible logic that the author might be unfolding.

But all the way through **"Ancient Evenings,"** one keeps having to absorb new rituals and ceremonies and landscapes, described with prose that rarely acknowledges that it has successfully created a world. And the effort to keep taking all this in is simply exhausting. Or else it's just that Mr. Mailer's story isn't strong enough to lift us out of the prose. Or else some new cosmology he is trying to unfold is too dumbfounding.

Something has gone wrong. It may be that 10 years was too long a stretch of time to spend on the book, especially when its writing had to be interrupted by the production of three other books. Or perhaps Mr. Mailer worked with too much determination to prove that he could finally deliver the big novel he had promised for so long and thus used too much muscle when he should have relaxed.

Whatever the reason, **"Ancient Evenings"** lacks the pace and rhythm of good storytelling. It walks when one wants it to run, marches when one wants it to fly and only soars when one is at last too weary to hold on to it anymore. Somewhere there may be profundities coiling in its vast design. But if there are, my eyes just got too tired to see them.

>   Christopher Lehmann-Haupt, in a review of "Ancient Evenings," in The New York Times Book Review (copyright © 1983 by The New York Times Company; reprinted by permission), April 4, 1983, p. C17.

BENJAMIN DeMOTT

Here it is at last, more than a decade in the making, . . . Norman Mailer's long-awaited "Egyptian novel." For months the publishing trade press has hummed with reports of responses to the work, and the range of compliments already on file is striking. The most recent compliment came from Mailer's alma mater, Harvard; usually reserved in its relations with famous sons and daughters, the university put his photograph on the cover of its alumni magazine this spring and filled pages with an interview probing the meanings of **"Ancient Evenings."** Nobody doubts the newsworthiness of memoirs by government officials or biographies of film stars by their embittered children, but pre-publication interest in imaginative writing is invariably more limited. For a novel set in Egypt before the birth of Christ to rouse levels of excitement on the order of those inspired by **"Ancient Evenings"** is astonishing.

Not more astonishing, though, I found, than the excitement stirred by the book's opening chapters—an excitement unrelated to hype. Swiftly **"Ancient Evenings"** pulls its reader inside a consciousness different from any hitherto met in fiction. A soul or body entombed is struggling to burst free, desperate not alone for light and air but for prayer and story—promised comforters that have been treacherously withheld or stolen. Dwelling within this consciousness we relive the "experience" of an Egyptian body undergoing burial preparations, sense the soul's overwhelming yearnings, within an unquiet grave, for healing that no physical treatment can provide. All is strange, dark, intense, mysteriously coherent.

A second voice speaks. Offering a kind of taunting succor, it commences a story of the gods—the myth of Isis and Osiris which in this telling is made utterly new, indeed seems to have been given utterance by the strewn bones and limbs themselves. I looked up at the end of this section of the book, simultaneously moved and (I am speaking seriously) ashamed—troubled by my own habitual skepticism, my trained resistance to whatever is heavily promoted. Would it not prove impossible for a work so well begun to be anything but magnificent over all? Was not the book in my hand certain to prove the truth of its author's contention that he was capable of producing a masterpiece totally unique and incomparably splendid?

The answer to both questions is no. **"Ancient Evenings"** turns out to be neither magnificent nor a masterpiece. What is more, describing the book simply as a failure—a near-miss earning respect for noble ambitions and partial triumphs—will not do. The case is that, despite the brilliance of those first 90 pages, this 700-page work is something considerably less than a heroic venture botched in the execution. It is, speaking bluntly, a disaster, and the reasons why wants careful inquiry.

Just as one tends to be a shade slow in absorbing the evidence that a powerful imagination is working with stunning intensity at the start of this book, so one resists acknowledging that a sorry descent has begun as one moves deeper in. The opening, mythological frame of **"Ancient Evenings"** gives way, in the third through sixth of the book's seven sections, to a social drama—a dinner party at the palace of Rameses IX (circa 1100 B.C.) marking a festival called the Night of the Pig; persons of faith are required by the gods to act lewdly and speak obscenely on the occasion.

Guests at the Pharaoh's party consist of the Pharaoh's "Overseer of the Cosmetic Box" and the Overseer's family—his wife, 6-year-old son and the 6-year-old's great-grandfather. The speaker for most of the evening is Menenhetet, the great-grandfather: former general, harem-master, magician, priest, grave-robber and raconteur. . . . Menenhetet has been reincarnated three times; since he discourses knowledgeably in the book's final chapter on Greek and Roman religious beliefs, his four lives appear to span roughly 1,000 years; it's his account of his lives that speedily sinks the work. (pp. 1, 34)

Two problems beset this storytelling from its start. The first problem is that the mentality of the dynastic world, magically imagined in the book's opening pages, is replaced with fearful abruptness by the preoccupations and obsessions of a late 20th-century mind—Norman Mailer's—as soon as the narrator settles into his dinner party discourse. The second problem is that, in dramatizing those obsessions, Mailer relentlessly suppresses his own sense of the ridiculous—a deed few readers are likely to emulate.

One of Mailer's obsessions is with the need for social forms that honor the human capacity for exuberance rather than thwart it by prohibiting vulgarity and inhibiting emotional expression. This obsession is embodied in a set of characters who, though meant to be perceived as exhilaratingly free-spirited, stand forth instead as ludicrous blends of Mel Brooks and the Marquis de Sade. . . .

Another of Mailer's obsessions is with our refusals to acknowledge our animality and our need to speak our being through acts of violence. This theme—which reverberates through Menenhetet's speech on that evening 3,000 years ago—is dramatized in a series of scenes that are pitiably foolish in conception and executed at staggering length. During the postlude to the Battle of Kadesh, we're told that the Charioteer came upon the royal lion Hera-Ra "half-asleep under the full moon." The lion gave "a great broad grin" at the sight of him, "rolled over on his back, spread his legs, showed me the depths of his anus and the embrace of his front paws and invited me to roll on his belly." . . .

Thereafter pages are devoted to a battlefield constitutional during which Menenhetet learns the satisfactions of cannibalism. (p. 34)

The modern obsession most absurd in its appearance in **"Ancient Evenings"** has to do, predictably, with female sexuality as a wound. It surfaces in the extended chronicle of Menenhetet's passion for an overweight concubine named Honey-Ball, "the greatest little queen of them all," whose "hips were like the hips of a horse"—a person who once displeased the Pharaoh and, for punishment, had a toe amputated. Impossible to summarize this story in neutral tones. Powerfully drawn to each other, Honey-Ball and the Charioteer are nevertheless unhappy about their lovemaking until, by accident, a breakthrough occurs. . . . [It] emerges that the place of the missing toe is a G-spot. (pp. 34, 35)

The farther one proceeds in **"Ancient Evenings"** the longer one lingers over any page or passage bare of embarrassments. Here is a carefully researched chapter on the tactical maneuvers preceding the Battle of Kadesh: Pause, speculate about its sources. Here is a chariot charge, vigorously evoked: Pause, savor. Here the Nile rises and the river-bank folk sense the change: Stiff old school historians, such as J. H. Breasted, had their own eloquence on the subject, but Mailer's eloquence is at least not negligible. Here is the Charioteer catching his first glimpse of the Pharaoh: Concentrate on the fine phrases.

But in truth release and escape are elusive. Arguably the obsessions that control this work, considered abstractly, possess dignity. The writer who gives himself up to them is, at the minimum, a challenger—someone admirably scornful of the diminution of his humanity that arid decorum, politic timidity and the like seek to enforce. Conceivably the underlying motives deserve praise. Yet too much, far too much, is demanded of the reader for that praise to be easily granted. The early annoyances in the book—idioms like "kiss My foot" used minus irony as elevated utterance; seemingly gratuitous eruptions of late 20th-century colloquialism and so on—can be shrugged off. But from chapter to chapter episodes of pointless, painful, unintended hilarity flood ever more absurdly upon each other. Material in the Mel Brooks mode is repeatedly presented as though it were without comic dimension. The sound of epic elevation time and again is drowned by a voice resembling Howard Cosell's: "Behold, there was blood on my King's leg . . . and the look in his eye was not good." There are talking horses and women who shout in bed that: "I am the Keel . . . My Secret Name is Thigh of Isis . . . I am the Rudder . . . In My Name is Leg of the Nile."

Everywhere the assumption is that bisexuality, aphrodisiac obscenity and anxiety about whether a "member will stay firm" were key features of Eastern sensuality. . . . And, for a final epic note, we're offered portentous metaphors of human life as a tide-beaten boat, "washed by the swells of time"—echoes of the concluding sentence of a book difficult to coerce into meaningful connection with XXth Dynasty Egypt: Scott Fitzgerald's "The Great Gatsby."

"Why did Mailer write it?" the author asks himself in the interview appearing in Harvard magazine. "What is he saying that means something to him? The man we know. What is in this?"

The first answer the author returns is that he wished to write a long novel, and "to do a long book, you would want to take risks. Why not? How dignify it if large risks aren't taken?" In studying the past, moreover, "dealing with Egypt, its gold and its pharaohs," he came "to an understanding of the wealthy I've never had before" and glimpsed a teacher's mission: that of awakening others to their provinciality. "I want people to realize, my God, there are wholly different points of view that can be as interesting as our own. In other words, probably a social evening in Egypt . . . that period 3,000 years ago, was as interesting as an evening in New York today."

The ambition to teach has often been visible in Mailer's books, and it has seldom stifled either wit or self-awareness. The writer's ruling assumption has been that, regardless of subject or form, all his feeling and remembering, inventing and reporting, must be accompanied by critical activity. . . . The surprising perspective—the leap offering instant release from bondage to cliché—is what we have come to expect in even the shortest piece from this pen. But that expectation is nowhere satisfied in **"Ancient Evenings."**

Intelligence has disappeared before from Mailer's work—witness **"Maidstone."** Invariably, though, it returns, and the point warrants emphasis. In a world in which the beautiful is "decreed in the marketplace" (Ezra Pound's phrase), the jettisoning of self-criticism in a widely publicized novel written under who knows what financial pressure can not seriously be regarded as mysterious. What can be so regarded is the frequency with which this author, in dark hours of the past, has renewed his inventiveness and wit. During the decade of labor on **"Ancient Evenings"** Norman Mailer produced seven other books, including **"Marilyn," "The Fight"** and the gripping saga of Gary Gilmore. It's possible that "the Egypt book" is a darker hour than any preceding it in his career; surely the author's hold on the title that's been his for a full decade and a half—the title of America's most consistently entertaining writer—has been weakened.

But Mailer's past record of resilience, productivity and readiness to leave disaster behind makes deep gloom—the overwhelming feeling as one grasps that **"Ancient Evenings"** has collapsed—seem inappropriate. So too does the announcement that the author is already at work on a new volume of fiction, unconnected to the work at hand. (pp. 35-6)

Benjamin DeMott, "Norman Mailer's Egyptian Novel," in The New York Times Book Review (copyright © 1983 by The New York Times Company; reprinted by permission), April 10, 1983, pp. 1, 34-6.

PAUL GRAY

[*Ancient Evenings*] is hands down the most surprising work Mailer has ever offered. It really is set entirely in an alien long ago, just as the author had been promising during the decade he took to write it. Yet no amount of advance speculation proves adequate to the thing itself: an artifact of evident craftsmanship and utterly invisible significance.

A lengthy journey begins with the agonies of death ("Volcanic lips give fire, wells bubble. Bone lies like rubble upon the wound"). Surviving this fiery purgation is the ka (diminished soul) of an Egyptian named Menenhetet II. After experiencing the mummification of his discarded body, this ghost meets the kindred spirit of his great-grandfather Menenhetet I. . . .

The book is already some 230 pages old when Menenhetet I eases into this narration, and none of the characters seems in any hurry to pick up the pace. Worse, Mailer shuns the devices that can make long pieces of fiction irresistible. Suspense is banished: everything has already happened in *Ancient Evenings,* not only historically, but also in the lives of its people. Nothing is surprising, except perhaps how polymorphously perverse and consistently swinish the ancients were, according to their newest historian. . . .

Language might yet have made *Ancient Evenings* a page turner, and the novel does offer brief, poetic passages. The shimmer and heat of the Nile, the blaze of Egyptian architecture when it was new and radiant with epochal ambition, the perfume and soft light of a harem garden: all enjoy moments of intense realization. But such moods are continually broken by ludicrous sentences: "In either case, my Pharaoh's mind was now concerned with buttocks." Or: "Now, with the redolence of my nose, I watched and admired the delicacy with which the Pharaoh ate." Mailer's historical posing stalls an already leisurely narration. . . .

The sex in the book is equally droning. The penile principle predominates; it is the staff of life and the stuff of seemingly endless repetition. Pharaohs spontaneously impose themselves on the underling, male or female, who happens to be closest. Indiscriminate rutting is a sign of power, sodomy the proof of triumph. Male-on-male copulation, in particular, becomes so predictable that the nonexplicit stretches of narrative come as moments of noncomic relief.

Mailer is a member of the postwar generation of writers who still believed in the possibility of the Great American Novel. This notion always flirted with silliness, but its power to spur the ambition of young authors cannot be discounted. The paradox of Mailer's career is that his pursuit of this white whale proved the quest in his case unnecessary. He became a major writer without becoming a major novelist. His instinct to abandon fiction for long periods was, given his talents and temperament, entirely correct. His unique value among his contemporaries proved to be the witness he could bear to his age and its possible consequences. His energy and imagination have been aroused most keenly by doubt, the sense that every act, individual and civic, leads perilously into the unknown. Looking backward is not the job such a mind performs best, as *Ancient Evenings* proves. The book is a gesture of obeisance to graven images and an abstract ideal, dutifully performed by an inherently disruptive spirit.

Paul Gray, "And Now, the Book," in Time (copyright 1983 Time Inc.; all rights reserved; reprinted by permission from Time), Vol. 121, No. 16, April 18, 1983, p. 85.

HAROLD BLOOM

[In *Ancient Evenings*] Mailer has gone back to the ancient evenings of the Egyptians in order to find the religious meaning of death, sex, and reincarnation. . . .

[There is] spiritual power in Mailer's fantasy (it is not the historical novel that it masks itself as being) and there is a relevance to current reality in America that actually surpasses that of Mailer's largest previous achievement, *The Executioner's Song*. More than before, Mailer's fantasies, now brutal and unpleasant, catch the precise accents of psychic realities within and between us. *Ancient Evenings* rivals *Gravity's Rainbow* as an exercise in what has to be called a monumental sado-anarchism, and one aspect of Mailer's phantasmagoria may be its need to challenge Pynchon precisely where he is strongest. Paranoia, in both these American amalgams of Prometheus and Narcissus, becomes a climate. . . .

Thomas Mann proudly remarked of *his* Egyptian novel, *Joseph and His Brothers,* that "as the son of a tradesman I have a fundamental faith in quality. . . . The song of Joseph is good, solid work." Mann gave his life to the book for sixteen years, and its quality is durable. Mailer has given *Ancient Evenings* a decade, and it is wild, speculative work, but hard work nevertheless. Its quality is not durable, and perhaps does not attempt to be. Mailer is desperately trying to save our souls as D. H. Lawrence tried to do in *The Plumed Serpent* or even as Melville did in *Pierre*. An attentive reader ought to bring a respectful wariness to such fictions for they cannot be accepted or dismissed, even when they demand more of the reader than they can give. Mailer wishes to make his serious readers into religious vitalists, even as Lawrence sought to renew our original relationship both to the sun and to a visionary origin beyond the natural sun. Mailer's later works thus strain at the limits of art.

Mailer's readers will learn rather more ancient Egyptian mythology than they are likely to want or need, but the mythology is the book, and seems more than mythology to Mailer. Like his ancient Egyptian nobles, Mailer hunts, slays, roasts, and devours his gods, in order to increase his share in courage, sexual potency, immortality. I assume that a reading of *The Book of the Dead (The Papyrus of Ani)* first alerted Mailer to the Egyptian analogues to his own ongoing obsessions, but whether that is true or not, it is of some interest to look at the translation of the ancient text by E. A. Wallis Budge alongside Mailer's nightmare of a book.

The Book of the Dead exists in many versions. . . . But they tend to tell the same stories concerning the gods and the afterlife, stories that center upon the death, mutilation, and resurrection of the god Osiris. Even as Osiris triumphed over death, so the Egyptians hoped to emulate him, and indeed to achieve a virtual identity with that king of eternity, who in his resurrection had taken on aspects of Ra, the sun god. And even as Osiris had risen in his reassembled corporeal body, so the ancient Egyptians conceived that they would live again in more than the spirit. As resurrected gods, they would feast and love forever. . . .

What Mailer adds are his own emphases upon scatology, buggery, and the war between women and men, but the fundamental material on the wavering border between the human and the divine, and on the world of the dead, is already there in Egyptian mythology for him to develop. His book's peculiar and disturbing sincerity is its strength. The reader is likely to be numbed by the repetition of charnel-house horrors, and even the most avid enthusiasts of buggery, whether heterosexual or homosexual, may flinch at confronting Mailer's narrative exuberance in heaping up sodomistic rapes, but the religious seriousness of all these representations is rather humorlessly unquestioned and unquestionable. . . .

I don't intend to give an elaborate plot summary, since if you read *Ancient Evenings* for the story, you will hang yourself.

There is a lot less story than any summary would indicate, because this is a book in which every conceivable outrage happens, and yet nothing happens, because at the end everything remains exactly the same.

There are only two characters who matter in the book, and they not inaccurately could be termed versions of Hemingway (I mean the novelist, not one of his characters) and of Mailer himself, the heroic precursor and his vitalistic follower and son. One is the great pharaoh Ramses the Second, victor over the Hittites at the battle of Kadesh, and the other is the three-times reincarnated magician Meni the First, who fought at Kadesh as the pharaoh's first charioteer. . . .

There is an unsolved problem of form here, but that is minor compared to defects of texture, to hopelessly unresolved inconsistencies of tone and of badly mixed imagery. Mann found a style for Joseph in Egypt, but Mann's strength was irony and Mailer's strength is never ironic. There are some horribly grand set pieces, most notably the battle of Kadesh, but there are also immense stretches through which the poor reader must crawl with an unrewarded patience, including the entire **"Book of Queens,"** which occupies 135 pages of harem intrigues. (p. 3)

Why are we in Egypt? Where else could we be? Mailer's dialectics of sex and death have found their inevitable context, though the world of Usermare and Meni may not be wholly distinct from the world of Gary Gilmore. Pynchon and this newest Mailer are what Vico called "magic primitives," giant bards who try to deify themselves by the ancient praxis of devination, but Pynchon scatters himself even as he finally scatters his hero Slothrop in *Gravity's Rainbow* quite literally, by having him undergo a parody of the fate of Osiris, or as Yahweh scattered the builders of the Tower of Babel. Mailer, like his American ancestors from Poe through Hemingway, resists the scattering of his self and name. *Ancient Evenings* thus fulfills the critical prophecy of Richard Poirier's book on Mailer (1972) which found in the emphasis upon buggery a dialectic by which meaning is both de-created and restituted. Poirier argued that it is almost as though in the Kabbalah of Norman Mailer, buggery constitutes the trope of the breaking of the vessels, as a negative creation that is a prime Gnostic image.

Mailer, as a fictive theologian, has been developing a private version of an American gnosis for some time now, in the sense that Gnosticism can be a doctrine insisting upon a divine spark in each adept that cannot die because it never was any part of the creation anyway. Such a doctrine resigns history and mere nature to the demons or bad angels, and identifies what is immortal in the self with the original abyss, from which the Yahweh of Genesis stole in order to form his bad creation. Libertine and antinomian, since it identifies the law of the Torah with a catastrophic creation, such a faith is the antithesis both of normative Judaism and of orthodox Christianity. In Jewish Gnosticism or Kabbalah, the catastrophe that ruins creation is imaged as the breaking of the vessels, the shells of the cosmos and the body that becomes riddled with divine light. Consciously or not, Mailer has substituted buggery for the breaking of the vessels. . . .

Mailer had some earlier inclination toward regarding buggery as an antinomian act—a transgression of all the rules of a deeply false order that would reveal a higher truth (see the buggering of Ruta, the German maid, in *An American Dream* and **"The Time of Her Time"**). In *Ancient Evenings* he has emancipated himself, and seems to be verging upon a new metaphysic, in which heterosexual buggery might be the true norm (as it may have seemed to the Lawrence of *Lady Chatterley's Lover*), and more conventional intercourse perhaps is to be reserved for the occult operation of reincarnating oneself in the womb of the beloved. . . .

Mailer's is too formidable a case of an authentic literary drive to be dismissed, and dismissal is certainly not my intention. *Ancient Evenings* is on the road of excess, and what Karl Kraus said of the theories of Freud may hold for the speculations of Mailer also—it may be that only the craziest parts are true. Mailer probably is aware that his Egyptian obsessions are in the main tradition of American literature, carrying on from much of the imagery of the major writers of the American renaissance.

The definitive study here is John Irwin's *American Hieroglyphics: The Symbol of the Egyptian Hieroglyphics in the American Renaissance*. Irwin centers on Poe, and in particular on *The Narrative of Arthur Gordon Pym*, but much that Irwin says about Melville's *Pierre* is as relevant to *Ancient Evenings* as is Irwin's brilliant commentary on *Pym*. Irwin argues that Emerson and those he stimulated—Thoreau and Whitman positively; Poe, Hawthorne, and Melville negatively—found in ancient Egypt a vision of resurrection through reincarnation or reappearance that they could oppose to the Hebraic vision of the resurrection of the body. Certainly the attitudes toward death of the Pharisees, and of mythological Egypt, could not be more antithetical than they were, and perhaps American writers inevitably prefer the Egyptian account of personal survival, as Yeats did also. Irwin, commenting on *Pym* and on *Pierre*, sees in the Egyptian resurrection a kind of Freudian displacement of the writer's body into the writer's book, of blood into ink. As the great Western version of the *Abendland*, nineteenth- and twentieth-century American literature perhaps takes on an almost Egyptian sublimity, an exaltation of cultural belatedness as the second chance of a literal life beyond death. Mailer's *Ancient Evenings* yet may seem a work in *Pierre*'s sad class, if not quite that of *Pym*'s, an American vision of final sunset. (p. 4)

Irwin reads Poe's *Pym* and to a lesser extent Melville's *Pierre* and *Mardi* as a kind of Egyptian reversal of the Jewish and Christian understanding of death as God's revenge for our original sin against the Father. Like Poe and Melville, Pynchon and the Mailer of *Ancient Evenings* participate in this reversal which, as Irwin says, "refers not to death as revenge, but to a revenge against death, the revenge that man attempts to take, through art, against time, change, and mortality, against the things that threaten to obliterate all trace of his individual existence." Thus Melville said of his Pierre's Maileresque attempt to write a book of "unfathomable cravings" that: "He is learning how to live, by rehearsing the part of death."

Mailer too wishes us to learn how to live, in an America where he sees our bodies and spirits as becoming increasingly artificial, even "plastic" as he has often remarked. If our current realities, corporeal and psychic, manifest only lost connections, then Mailer's swarming, sex-and-death-ridden ancient Egyptian evenings are intended at once to mirror our desperation, and to contrast our evasions with the Egyptian rehearsal of the part of death. . . .

Mailer concludes his book with an enigmatic rhapsody, in which the Ka or double of Meni the First expires, and the power of the dying heart enters the Ka of Meni the Second.

That combined Ka sails toward rebirth, while Mailer-Meni declares somberly: "I do not know if I will labor in greed forever among the demonic or serve some noble purpose I cannot name." That may be a touch grandiose, but it is thoroughly American, and perfectly Gnostic also in its aspiration to join itself to an alien God. Mailer, until now, has seemed to lack invention, and so after all to resemble Dreiser more than Hemingway, a judgment that *The Executioner's Song,* an undoubted achievement, would sustain. *Ancient Evenings* is an achievement of a more mixed kind but it is also an extravagant invention, another warning that Mailer is at home on Emerson's stairway of surprise. (p. 6)

> Harold Bloom, "Norman in Egypt," in The New York Review of Books (*reprinted with permission from* The New York Review of Books; *copyright © 1983 Nyrev, Inc.*), *Vol. XXX, No. 7, April 28, 1983, pp. 3-4, 6.*

ANTHONY BURGESS

We learn, in [the 709 large pages of **"Ancient Evenings"**], a great number of things. Most of all we learn how much Egyptology Mailer has learned in the past 10 years. Gold mining, magical ceremonies, priests and eunuchs and concubines, the moods of the Nile, crocodiles, the character of Queen Nefertiti and her son Amen-khep-shu-ef—the whole of ancient Egypt is set before us, complete with its odours and its sexual ecstasies, these two last being given about equal billing. And the secret of power, which the book is chiefly about? This lies in magic, and magic is essentially control of the lower human functions. In a word, magic is anal.

The anus is here sometimes called the ass or the asshole. This is a pity. The word should be arse, which has an ancient ancestry, whereas ass is an Americanism of puritanic provenance. A pity because a novel about ancient Egypt must not sound as though it is written by an American, and this is the only verbal area where Mailer's careful stylistic neutrality breaks down. It is the most difficult thing in the world for the speaker of a new language to mimic an old one, and Mailer has, for the most part, done admirably. Never (except for ass and, I would say, cock) is there a breath of anachronism, but the timelessness of the narrative idiom, avoiding slang, Freudianisms, and various forms of hindsight knowingness, inevitably bores a little until it flares into lurid life with cannibalism and buggery. . . .

Clearly, Mailer has not spent 10 difficult years on a difficult book in order to demonstrate his skill, not previously disclosed, as a writer of historical fiction. If I can achieve a second, or third, reading of '**Ancient Evenings,**' I may be prepared to name it as the best reconstruction of an ancient world since Flaubert's *Salammbô,* but Mailer does not want that kind of praise. His concern is with the modern world, with the psychic problems of modern America above all, and he considers that these problems may find a solution through an understanding of the repressed areas of sexuality, with the reality of magic. Our own rationality has failed. Here, he seems to say, is a complex civilisation of high achievement based on the irrational, on the radial power of a magic whose centre is both decay and resurrection.

He justifies himself with an epigraph from Yeats's 'Ideas of Good and Evil,' in which the poet, always a dangerous thinker, expresses his belief in the evocation of spirits and ends by asserting 'that the borders of our mind are ever shifting, and that many minds can flow into one another, as it were, and create or reveal a single mind . . . and that our memories are part of one great memory, the memory of Nature herself.' Mailer finds his spirits in the gods of Egypt and the power of intercourse between minds in the Egyptian doctrines of death. He also finds, in his imagined world of a post-Mosaic Pharaoh, a location for his own anal obsessions. . . . Strange that, nearly 10 years ago, some of us could believe that Mailer was working on a great chronicle of exodus and diaspora. Egypt has proved to be no house of bondage for him but the terrain of the release of his fantasies.

In America this novel—which, whatever its intermittent unreadability, makes the fictional products of our own islands seem all too readably bland—has had a bad press. I don't think it has been well understood. Give it a few years and, like Thomas Pynchon's equally misunderstood 'Gravity's Rainbow,' it may well appear as one of the great works of contemporary mythopoesis. It certainly gives us a new look up the anus.

> Anthony Burgess, "Magical Droppings" (*copyright © 1983 by Anthony Burgess; reprinted by permission of the author*), *in* The Observer, *June 5, 1983, p. 30.*

RICHARD POIRIER

[*Ancient Evenings* is] the strangest of Norman Mailer's books, and its oddity does not in any important way have to do either with its Egyptian setting or with the exotic career—exotic even by ancient Egyptian standards—of Menenhetet, its protagonist-narrator whose four lives, including three reincarnations, span 180 years (1290 to 1100 BC) of the nineteenth and twentieth dynasties (1320 to 1121 BC). What is remarkable here is the degree to which Mailer has naturalized himself as an ancient Egyptian, so that he writes as if saturated with the mentality and the governing assumptions, some of which he revises rather freely, of a culture in which the idea of the human is markedly different from what it has been in the West for the last 1,500 years or so. Mailer has never before tried anything so perilous, and the prodigious demands he makes on the reader are a clue to his ambitions. This is at once his most accomplished and his most problematic work.

Of the twenty-three books Mailer has written so far, only *Ancient Evenings* achieves the magnitude which can give a retrospective order and enhancement to everything else. Up to now it has been possible to think of him as perhaps a great writer, but one who had yet to write his major book. Many commentators have mistakenly credited him here, and in his last novel *The Executioner's Song,* with a new degree of self-effacement. Looking back from the new book one can see even more clearly than before that the central condition of nearly all his writing depends not on some prior sense of self, the famous Mailer ego, but rather on self-fragmentation and dispersal. Even when, as is so often the case, Mailer is his own subject, he cannot be said to exist simply in the narrative that tells his story, but is to be found instead within a larger, expressive structure of which his voice is only one part looking for other parts. Just as it radically reduces his literary, let alone his personal identity, to assume that the voice in *Armies of the Night* refers us directly to the "real" Mailer, so it is equally mistaken to assume that because that voice is absent from *Ancient Evenings* he has thereby and suddenly become invisible.

Quite the reverse. The book comes into focus only when we are able to recognize the complicated way in which it is the most self-revealing of his works. Menenhetet, for example, carries out the implications of Mailer's more directly autobiographical writings because even as he tells stories about himself he is by that very process trying to put himself together from several different, remembered versions. This is also the case when Mailer writes about a march on the Pentagon or a championship fight. He treats the earlier Mailer who participated in those events as if he were already a soul or a spirit. The Mailer of the later time not only records but contends with earlier versions of himself, until the work is a record of the abrasions out of which will emerge, or so he hopes, a form he can call himself or his work or his career. The form his narratives achieve is what has survived of "Mailer" from the past, but the achievement is conditioned by a recognition that some of the many selves who make up a single person have been sacrificed to the making of form. Any form, especially for a believer in karmic roots, creates a longing for some possibly larger and more inclusive one. . . .

Books of sustained visionary ambition—and this is true even of *Paradise Lost* or *Moby-Dick*—are bound to have stretches of tiresome exposition, phrasings that are ludicrous, whole scenes that, as Johnson remarked, should have been not only difficult but impossible. *Ancient Evenings* has Honey-Ball's scenes of spellbinding in "The Book of Queens". Nearly anything can happen here, and does, and what is remarkable is not that the American reviewers found things to make fun of, but that the risks usually pay off: moments of subliminal ecstasy, visionary descriptions of royal personages, of pools at sunrise and gardens which bring on a kind of sexual swooning, of floatings down the Nile. Mailer seems more at home in the writing than in any of his books except for *Why Are We In Vietnam?* He luxuriates, sometimes to the limits of patience and beyond, in accounts of Egyptian low life, in the power put into play during a royal dinner party, in details of costume and what must have been at best a truly awful cuisine. Near the beginning Meni calmly tells us what it feels like, moment by moment, to be eviscerated and embalmed, and there are equally confident accounts of the practice of magic and of the wholly chaotic polytheism of the Egyptians.

Mailer has imagined a culture that gives formal, and not merely anthropological sanction to what in his other works often seems eccentric or plaintively metaphysical, like his obsessions with "psychic darts" and mind-reading, with immortality, with battles of the gods . . . , with villainous homosexuality, with magic and sorcery, and with excrement as an encoding of psychic failure or success. Having so often written as if the self had several versions, he is completely at ease with Egyptian names for the seven spirits of the self that continue to exist in different degrees of intensity after death. (p. 591)

Ancient Evenings to some extent resembles Faulkner's *Absalom, Absalom!* or those novels of Conrad such as *Nostromo*, where, as Edward Said describes them, there is "evidence of a felt need to justify in some way the telling of a story". Faulkner and Conrad are more successful than Mailer in creating suspense and expectation within the stories, and among characters vividly differentiated; though *Ancient Evenings* is not lacking in suspense of this kind—it is there in the stunning account of the battle of Kadesh, or the intrigues between the rival Queens, Nefertiri and Rama-Nefru—the design of the book as a whole refers us finally to motives which are as vague as Mailer's or any novelist's motives for writing. Mailer offers none of the illusions so brilliantly sustained by Conrad, that there is something we want to know and that we will eventually know it, that a centre will be located in a wilderness of possibility, that the true shape of a person's life will emerge out of the mysteries that have shrouded it. The disaffection or impatience which many will feel with *Ancient Evenings* is likely to result from the fact that telling and listening have less to do with a desire to get somewhere . . . but rather to get away from the loneliness, darkness, waste and dissolution which are, interestingly enough, the conditions Mailer has worried about since the mid-1950s as peculiar to the fate of the writer, especially the American writer, in the last half of this century.

It is in this context that one should consider his obsession with buggery. The obsession has in the past carried Mailer into a metaphysics of human biological creativity as a compensation for meaninglessness . . . and from there to a religion of artistic creativity. . . . Like the building of Hell in the nether regions by Milton's Satan, buggery for Mailer is a perverse response to God's invitation that we join him in the creation. . . . In nearly all his work Mailer at some point contemplates the significance of a juxtaposition concisely described by Lawrence when in "Pornography and Obscenity" he observed that "The sex functions and the excrementary functions . . . work so close together, yet they are, so to speak, so utterly different in direction. Sex is a creative flow, the excrementary flow is towards dissolution, decreation. . . ."

Though Menenhetet, like the Mailer of **"The Metaphysics of the Belly"** *(The Presidential Papers)*, offers positive theories of scatology, the anus is mostly imagined as the site of evil. But there is also for Mailer a kind of art which is a trope for buggery. Writing about Genet he has referred to those aesthetic acts which "shift from the creation of meaning to the destruction of it", offering as further examples "the therapy of the surrealist artist, of Dada, of Beat". And he continues, speaking now of his own involvement in this dilemma: "jaded, deadened, severed from our roots, dulled in leaden rage, inhabiting the centre of illness of the age, it becomes more excruciating each year for us to perform the civilizing act of contributing to a collective meaning." *Ancient Evenings* represents such an attempt, haunted by failure, to discover "collective meaning", to create spiritual (and literary) genealogies that are as strong and mysterious as biological ones.

Questions of origin soon become, for Mailer, questions also about originality and authorship. It is impossible to claim either of these, so the book will tell us, without first accepting one's incalculable obligations to a marvellous but murky antecedence. Mailer's (and our) debts to the past, it is suggested, are enormous; they are also mysteriously entangled and untraceable. It is therefore a mistake to suggest, as some reviewers have done, that because Menenhetet is given "that look of character supported by triumph which comes to powerful men when they are sixty and still strong" he is meant to represent Mailer, or that he is Hemingway, Mailer's precursor. Mailer partakes both of Meni and Menenhetet, who at the end are transformed into yet another dual figure: a triumphant Icarus-Daedalus. In the final scene Menenhetet embraces and dissolves into the young man's Ka as it tries to escape the destructive force of "the abominable onslaught of offal" and to ascend the ladder of lights, knowing it will take not goodness to get to the top, but strength.

The joining has been made possible because Meni comes at last to accept all the stories he has been listening to, and, along with these, all the burdens of the past. . . . He cannot disown any of it because he cannot even know for sure that he did not somehow father himself or father his own father, whoever that might be, as did Ra in Egyptian mythology. (pp. 591-92)

Genealogies confound one another to create a future that can call on the assembled strengths of Menenhetet, Meni, all the characters they have loved, the Egyptian gods, along with their latest manifestations in Christian mythology, and, not least, the now enriched figures of Mailer's earlier writings and earlier selves. The "I" in the last paragraphs is a composite of all these but it is also the creative spirit with whom Mailer associates himself in an apocalyptic vision that could anticipate either the coming of, in Yeats's phrase, "the fabulous, formless darkness" of Christianity, or the last phase of our own civilization. . . .

This is, then, Mailer's "portrait of the artist as a young man", but it does not allow, as Joyce's does, for much distinction between that "artist" and the author of the book. If we are reminded of Joyce it is certainly not for the ironic reservations about Stephen implied in the last chapter of *A Portrait* and the first section of *Ulysses,* or even for the moment on the sea shore when Stephen imagines that "his soul had arisen from the grave of boyhood, spurning her graveclothes. Yes! Yes! Yes! He would create proudly out of the freedom and power of his soul, as the great artificer whose name he bore, a living thing, new and soaring and beautiful, impalpable, imperishable." This is a beautiful but forever embarrassing moment in the long history of the artist *exalté,* and Joyce meant to bring into question the prospects of anyone in the twentieth century who chooses to "enter into the power of the word". Mailer has always been frighteningly naive about this "power" and especially . . . the privileges that should be accorded it, and he fully endorses Meni's grandiloquence. This is his most audacious book largely because behind it all is the desire, once and for all, to claim some ultimate spiritual and cultural status for the teller of stories, the Writer. Which is yet another ancient and perhaps pernicious story, though Mailer will always need to believe every word of it. (p. 592)

Richard Poirier, "In Pyramid and Place," in The Times Literary Supplement *(© Times Newspapers Ltd. (London) 1983; reproduced from* The Times Literary Supplement *by permission), No. 4184, June 10, 1983, pp. 591-92.*

David Malouf
1934-

Australian novelist, poet, and short story writer.

Malouf first gained attention for his poetry but has since developed a reputation as a novelist of considerable talent. His work, much of which is set in Australia, is often concerned with the relation of the past to the present and with the human desire to live in harmony with nature. Malouf's fiction and poetry are often marked by memories of childhood and are full of concrete, vivid descriptions of the natural world. Malouf is also intensely interested in the subject of individuals in search of their "hidden," or true, selves. His first novel, *Johnno* (1977), portrays the spiritual growth and coming of age of two young men who have been friends since childhood. In the novel *An Imaginary Life* (1978), which has been described as a long prose poem, Malouf speculates on how the Roman poet Ovid might have come to terms with himself and nature during his exile to a village on the Black Sea.

Malouf's poetry, which has not received the critical interest accorded his prose, reflects his belief that "poems are acts of reconciliation." In his verse, Malouf seeks to join the past and the present, the real and the imagined, and the individual with others and with life itself. In spite of mixed opinions as to how well Malouf succeeds, critics admire his ability to capture the beauty and mystique of nature and are pleased by his wit. *First Things Last* (1981), Malouf's recent collection of poetry, has received a generally favorable critical response. This volume shares with Malouf's other collections and novels an attentiveness to detail and finely drawn, elaborate backgrounds.

Courtesy of David Malouf

HELEN DANIEL

[The] narrative line in *Johnno* wavers between Johnno and Dante, uncertain of its direction, and by sometimes leaping across periods of several years that seem to have worked significant changes in Johnno or Dante, fails to sustain the development of either as a wholly convincing character. (p. 192)

In *Johnno,* the narrator is at times observer, duly recording the activities of the observed with the detachment this implies; he is at times directly engaged with Johnno so that their interaction is foremost; at other times Dante seems almost the central figure in whose experience Johnno is a striking but only periodic element. The uncertainty reflected in these different impulses works against the vigour often felt in the portrayal of Johnno himself, particularly in the sections of the novel set in Europe. Malouf does suggest the expatriate search for meaning against what Johnno and Dante both conceive as a stifling and narrow Brisbane, but this period in their lives is broken into isolated sequences and the pace slows. Dante reports increasing bitterness in Johnno, a more aimless and dissolute life, a forced quality to his exuberance. . . . The nature of the change is not fully realized because there are only glimpses of Johnno during this period, the narrative seeming more attentive to Dante here. (pp. 193-94)

The novel somewhat unsteadily moves towards Johnno's death, through Dante's musing on conventional married life and through Johnno's enigmatic explanation of his return to Australia. . . . Johnno's death is "aesthetically apt" and Dante's awareness of this overrides the subdued guilt he feels at having not cared enough for Johnno, not realized Johnno's need of him. . . . Johnno's baulking at the "narrow certainties" of an ordered, conventional world, his feeling of oppression and diminution, does not . . . emerge from an explicitly realized society that is scathingly exposed. The novel does rather focus on an attempt to distil a more meaningful existence, through fantasy. It establishes fantasy for Johnno as a defining of him and "Maybe, in the end, even the lies we tell define us. And better, some of them, than our most earnest attempts at the truth." . . . (p. 194)

Johnno himself is often a compelling figure, the portrayal of him lively and rich. When the narrative focuses on Dante, it seems to lose direction, to falter and create a kind of passivity in him. Dante's perception of the implications for him of a relationship found important in the past remain shadowy. In part, this uncertainty in the novel springs from the narrator's role that is both observer and participant, both confined to the narrator's own experience yet extended to the portrayal of Johnno himself. (p. 195)

*Helen Daniel, "Narrator and Outsider in 'Trap' and 'Johnno'" (reprinted by permission of the publisher and the author), in Southerly, No. 2, June, 1977, pp. 184-95.**

KATHA POLLITT

"How close to where I live lie the ultimate ends of the earth," Ovid wrote from Tomis, the semisavage Black Sea village to which he had been exiled by Augustus in A.D. 8. History is silent about the reason for the sudden banishment from Rome of its wittiest, gayest poet, last of the generation that included Virgil, Horace and Propertius. Ovid himself thought he was being punished for his writing. "My only fault is that I possess both talent and taste," he claimed in the "Tristia," a long, half-defiant, half-abject poem that he thought would somehow win him imperial forgiveness (it did not; he died in exile sometime after A.D. 16) and that gives a vivid picture of the many miseries of life in Tomis. (p. 10)

From this meager historical background the Australian poet David Malouf has fashioned an extraordinary novel. "**An Imaginary Life**" is just that: a kind of fantasia on what Ovid's life in exile might have been and, as time went by, become, as the quintessentially civilized man of letters was forced to come to terms with a harsh, pre-rational, thoroughly alien world.

To Mr. Malouf's Ovid, newly arrived from Rome, Tomis is raw nature, primeval mud and stone and brackish water: "Even the higher orders of the vegetable kingdom have not yet arrived among us. We are centuries from the notion of an orchard or a garden made simply to please." Yet as he learns the native language, he comes to see that his hosts have, after all, their wisdom—hunting rituals, the visions of the shaman, the secret magic practiced by the women. . . . His exile becomes a quest for his real self, lost years ago when he put his own childhood behind him and entered what he now sees as a frivolous and superficial existence.

In that long-ago childhood, Ovid had a friend, a wild child who lived in the forest and who in later years came to seem like a mysterious messenger, possibly even a god. Now, on a hunting trip he sees another wild boy, and persuades the men of Tomis, much against their better judgment, to capture him. As Ovid patiently attempts to humanize the child, it is really he who is changing, regaining his own early sense of oneness with nature. But the boy's wildness is a direct threat to the barbarians' precarious existence, and so the novel ends with the flight of the poet and the child across the Danube and into the grasslands that seem to stretch all the way to the Pole, lands upon which perhaps no human has ever set foot, and where, tenderly cared for by the child as he sinks toward death, Ovid has a final vision of the mystical union of man and the natural world.

Essentially, "**An Imaginary Life**" is a meditation on the dialectic between the human and the nonhuman, a subject that arises gracefully in connection with Ovid, whose central work, Mr. Malouf reminds us, was the "Metamorphoses." Mr. Malouf has many penetrating and even original things to say about what it means to be human—his notion that play and ornament are the essential characteristics of civilized life, for instance—so that when Ovid plants a flowerbed he is in a sense subverting the whole barbarian ethos. I must say I was sorry to have it all end in the standard modern wish to dissolve the self in blissed-out communion with the universe, and perhaps my resistance to Mr. Malouf's conclusions was what made me find the wild-child theme a bit forced; this story was already exotic enough. Moreover, Mr. Malouf's child strongly resembles the boy in François Truffaut's recent film, "L'Enfant Sauvage" (which is not surprising, because both are based on the same actual case, the 18th-century wild child of Aveyron), and thus seems from the outset oddly familiar. Certainly he is a much less compelling figure than Mr. Malouf's Ovid, whose complex Romanness is conveyed with great sensitivity.

All the same, David Malouf has produced a work of unusual intelligence and imagination, at once sensuous and quirky, full of surprising images and intriguing insights. Poets are sometimes said to write the best prose, and Mr. Malouf's is indeed fine: a spare yet evocative English that captures both the bleak monochromes of Tomis and the sunny humanized landscape of Ovid's remembered Italy, without ever losing the distinctive voice, now caustic, now dreamlike, in which Ovid tells his own story. (pp. 10-11)

<blockquote>Katha Pollitt, "Ovid and the Boys," in The New York Times Book Review (copyright © 1978 by The New York Times Company; reprinted by permission), April 23, 1978, pp. 10-11, 46.*</blockquote>

KATE ELDRED

If Lucretius was Rome's philosophical poet, and Virgil her chronicler of former glories, then Ovid was Rome's poet of decadence, the bad boy, extoller of carnal love, the avant-garde revolutionary of the last days of Glorious Rome. Not much is known for sure about his life beyond some bare facts. . . .

In [*An Imaginary Life*], David Malouf, following in the footsteps of Doctorow and Vidal and Meyer, has taken an historical figure and invented the missing part of his story. (p. 36)

[Malouf's novel] is a vehicle for expounding one of Ovid's favorite themes, transformation. Beginning with the poet's early journal of banishment, Malouf shows us the mind of a great wordsmith struck dumb in his surroundings trying to adjust to a new life. When he spots the child for the first time the poet recognizes something of himself in him, speechless, outcast, unacceptable; and in transforming the child to human, Ovid will effect his own transformation. Moreover, the poet is interested in his posthumous readers; he questions us rhetorically, asking if we have become gods by the time we read this, if we have harnessed the sun, taken the steps to transformation, stilled the elements.

There are two possible ways to read this book. One is from a position of total ignorance about Ovid, to read it as a daring and experimental novel, a novel that plays with the language and dazzles us with startling syntactical shifts and concatenations of adjectives that enrich our literate experience. And the other is from the position of a classical student, to come to it having read Ovid and knowing something of what he stood for and what the time was like.

If it's read as simply a lyrical dream novel, it has certain rewards; Malouf, an Australian poet, has a gift for phrases and an eye for the evocation of murky and mystical places. The book is oddly whimsical, taken naively, and fey and fabulistic in its subjective tone and philosophical overtones.

But read from the point of view of a classicist, it opens up a further dimension of allusion and intellectual appreciation. Malouf interplays the historical present, clumsy in English, with a narrative present and an anecdotal past tense, interweaving them so gracefully that the techniques aren't obvious, only the aftertaste of grandeur in certain passages, of a facile rhythm in others. The knowledge of Ovid's preoccupations from his writings lets us see the change occurring before he, as narrator, does; and knowing that Ovid was an iconoclast if anything, one appreciates his growing sense of omnipotence, his realization that he can become like a god and further, that it doesn't really matter.

There is, of course, a price to pay in each case. For not having to scuff through dusty collections of Ovid's writings, the unlettered reader has to settle for a one-dimensional account of a weird experience. And for being conversant with Latin history, one has to wince slightly at the portrait Malouf draws of Ovid, the bawdy agnostic.

For instance he wrote a lot about and for women; his love poems glorified them and his "metamorphoses" happened more to women than to men. But there are no women in this book, no significant women. Further, Ovid was politically inclined; it may have been only a naughty sort of pseudoanarchism that he espoused, but it was effective enough to get him banished. And there's no sign of that in this Ovid. Certainly not least, one of the most beloved aspects of his work was a line of wry and urbane humor that ran through all his poetry. Granted that a middle-aged decadent Roman plunked down among barbarians might find it difficult to laugh, a devotee of Ovid would look for at least a nod to the absurdity of the position in which Ovid found himself.

Malouf says, in his own afterword, "My purpose was to make this glib fabulist of "the changes" live out in reality what had been, in his previous existence, merely the occasion for dazzling literary display." If the reader might wish that Malouf had let Ovid take a little more of his acclaimed *chutzpah* into the wilderness, I guess that's her own problem. Malouf at least accomplishes his purpose. (pp. 36-7)

> Kate Eldred, in a review of "An Imaginary Life," in The New Republic (reprinted by permission of The New Republic; © 1978 The New Republic, Inc.), Vol. 178, No. 19, May 13, 1978, pp. 36-7.

CECIL HADGRAFT

[If] you are committed to literature and have written poems, which are shorter and do not require the persistent physical effort—among other efforts—that a novel does, then it may seem that a novel is next in the natural order of things. But a saving sophistication makes you wary of the thinly veiled autobiography. A decent camouflage of interests and themes is advisable. Instead of yourself, an acquaintance may serve as a focus. And if he is in the novel, then you yourself are naturally, even necessarily, present as well, so that you may introduce him, accompany him, and possibly farewell him. A further device should add the last touch to the disguise: enclose it as it were in a frame. (p. 214)

You can even introduce an additional refinement. To underline the fact that it is the friend, not yourself, who is the main attraction, you note some inexplicable trifle that stresses the oddity of the friend. That, indeed, that was characteristic of him, it was part of the fascination that induced you, almost in despite, to take up a reluctant pen to tell his story. As David Malouf puts it in **Johnno:** "The book I always meant to write about Johnno will get written after all . . . he had me hooked. As he had, of course, from the beginning. I had been writing my book about Johnno from the moment we met." . . . To say we don't believe Malouf is to pay him a compliment, to enter the conspiracy, to join with him in the literary jape.

The jape, however, has taken charge of the author. Johnno, the narrator's friend, is to be the lure, distracting our attention while the author enters unnoticed. But a third contestant has slipped in and occupies at frequent intervals those parts of the stage where the spotlight rests. This intruder is Brisbane. It turns out to be the book's real concern, a background against which people move and things happen. It is brought before us by appeals to sight and hearing, touch and even smell: pubs and brothels, corners and alleys, the river and its banks, gardens and backyards, wooden walls and iron roofs—the whole range of dubious items that make up an old-fashioned entirety that as child and adolescent and young man the author carries off as indelible memories. In even greater particularity there are the individual details of rooms and their contents. Indeed, furniture and food have a special place. The most lyrical passage in the book, for instance, is on lollies. . . . For any reader familiar with the reality evoked, such parts of the book are extremely effective in their nostalgic savour. They are authentic and unromanticized except for the haze of the years between, which gives them the charm that mist confers upon even an unromantic scene. (pp. 214-15)

Charming as the book is in style and vignette, and however evocative, one has to be careful not to overestimate it on this last score. Anyone who knows the period and place cannot but respond to Malouf's re-creation of parts of the overgrown country town. A name is given, of street or suburb or building, and, conjured up with a phrase, the old and sometimes vanished reality rises before the reader. Momentarily he is back where he once was, and he perforce feels a sort of gratitude for this rejuvenation. The same thing occurs in, say, poetry, where an untutored reader finds a poem effective in one way and therefore good in all ways. . . .

If Brisbane, then, is the hero or heroine of the novel, what of Johnno, the overt eponym? He need not worry any reader. Malouf has been saying: Bear with me a little, and join with me in seeing how we can ring the changes on a rather trite theme—Looking Backwards. A variation here and there, an elaboration, an omission, an altered stress and we almost have a new genre. . . . It would be an unresponsive reader who would not collaborate. In doing so, he comes to recognize that Johnno is of little consequence. Johnno appears most frequently in the schooldays, less frequently at the university, and sporadically after that. He dies at the end of the novel, whether by suicide or accident does not matter. So he bulks large when he is small, but when he grows up—if he ever does—he is minor. And this is how he should be. Malouf does his best for him, but nobody adult could find him of much attraction. (p. 216)

The only quality [Johnno] has is his honesty to himself. Hypocrisy being, as the adage goes, the tribute that vice pays to virtue, we all of us try to justify or hide our failings—we may even try to cure them. Johnno will have none of this: he is not so much shameless as indifferent. He is as he is—let them do what they like about that.

This is not endearing: it is merely surprising. We are not shocked at the natural behaviour of a leech or scorpion, but we are shocked that a human being should resemble both and apparently think this natural. So any fascination Johnno may have for us at the start evaporates as the novel progresses. We come to find him distasteful. Then we lose interest. This is a probability that Malouf must have foreseen, for he attributes to Johnno an element of mystery. He is spoken of as having some inner life, as though he concealed an enigma that would be worth solving. And near the end of the book this mystery, we are told, still resides in that fascinating figure—even his death is a mystery. Most of us will remain cheerfully unconvinced. That mystery, if ever it existed, is a bagatelle. (pp. 217-18)

> Cecil Hadgraft, "Indulgence," in Studies in the Recent Australian Novel, edited by K. G. Hamilton (© University of Queensland Press, St. Lucia, Queensland, 1978), University of Queensland Press, 1979, pp. 194-224.*

JOHN M. WRIGHT

Many of the poems in *First Things Last* . . . seem overwrought, as if Malouf were struggling to find forms in which to embody his lyricism. There is often a laboured quality to the rhetoric. 'Reading a View' is typical in this respect. . . .

Most of the *First Things Last* poems deal with only those aspects of human life that reflect the natural world. A constant stream of intricate metaphor runs through this poetry, with an occasional triumph of the literal. This juxtaposition of the abstractly rhetorical with the sharply delineated detail gives the better poems their edge. . . .

['The Crab Feast'] is a ten-page work in which the speaker digs away at what seems common to his own life and that of the crab. I find it a self-conscious poem, factitious in places. The opening, for instance, applies conventional sexual metaphors to the reality of the speaker's eating the crab. But the effect is merely bizarre. . . .

Notwithstanding the weakness of this, the poem has fine moments. . . .

'The Crab Feast' is an odd mixture of epicureanism (there being no doubt that the speaker plans to eat the crab that sits on a restaurant dinner plate as he addresses it), sharp summary imaging a whole society in landscape . . . , and a kind of abstract sentimentality where the speaker finds it too easy to see himself as a crab. . . . 'The Crab Feast' is an ambitious poem, and I may not have done it justice. Its failings, however, preclude it from being the finest in the volume. . . .

[*First Things Last* is a significant work] by an author who blessedly evades categorisation. What often comes through . . . is a lyricism about the possibilities for human life when lived in the context of an animal natural earth. (p. 59)

> John M. Wright, "David Malouf: Lyrical Epicurean," in Quadrant (reprinted by permission of Quadrant, Sydney, Australia), Vol. XXV, No. 12, December, 1981, pp. 58-9.

FLEUR ADCOCK

David Malouf is a . . . mature poet, and . . . [an] accessible one; his long looping sentences twining over their line-endings need to be followed carefully, but he is no exhibitionist: the techniques he has learnt are subordinated to the poems themselves. He has a strong visual consciousness with a sense of joyful absorption in the natural world which makes the overworked word "celebration" irresistible. The first poem in [*First Things Last*] is about lemon trees gone wild, and the second about a garden; the image of Eden recurs throughout the book, as garden or as wilderness or as landscape remembered from the past (in a fine long poem, **"Deception Bay"**, he reconstructs the surroundings of his childhood by a series of conscious acts of will shared with his readers). . . .

One of Malouf's concerns is with the relations between reality and seeming. . . . Another preoccupation is time, the interfusion of the present and the past. In an elegy for his father he writes of the dead being buried in the living and looking out through their eyes, as do the not yet born. The concept occurs again in **"Deception Bay"**. . . . Then there is his reiterated use of the word "blue", not only for sky and sea and shadows on the land but as a personal symbol, almost a verbal tic. It is the indigo of the crabs—"blue, majestic"—he lovingly pursues in **"The Crab Feast"**, in order to eat them, incorporate them and become one with them. The process of achieving a symbiotic harmony with the natural world is also at the centre of his novel, *An Imaginary Life*, which like many of these poems looks back to a prelapsarian mode of existence.

Malouf's powerful imagination allows a certain amount of surrealism, without too much self-indulgence. He uses a variety of fairly free verse forms, including prose-poetry, while retaining a commitment to normal syntax. He can be playful, and his obsession with the visual sometimes carries him away into digressions, but he is a serious poet concerned with serious things.

> Fleur Adcock, "Importing a Modern Tradition," in The Times Literary Supplement (© Times Newspapers Ltd. (London) 1982; reproduced from The Times Literary Supplement by permission), No. 4113, January 29, 1982, p. 114.*

DAVID GUY

The coupling of two so different novellas as [**"Child's Play"** and **"The Bread of Time to Come"**] seems peculiar at first: one concerns a young Australian's experiences just before and during the First World War; the other is an intensely inward first-person narration by a contemporary Italian terrorist. David Malouf, however, is a richly imagistic writer, philosophical and literary in the best sense; his terrorist is hardly the subject of a slick thriller. Though probably not written to do so, his stories do reflect and enrich one another by being together.

"The Bread of Time to Come" is the simpler and—at least for awhile—the quieter of the two. Ashley Crowther has returned to pre-World War I Australia after 12 years in England with only a vague idea of what he wants to do with himself and with the thousand acres of land he has inherited. On his land he discovers Jim Saddler, a lower-class man similarly vague about his future, who until his 20th year has been content simply to observe, alertly and patiently, the natural world around him, especially the countless varieties of birds that migrate to Australia in season. Ashley hits on the happy idea of leaving his land as a wildlife sanctuary and hiring Jim as a kind of Adam to name the beasts. . . . The situation seems too good to be true. . . .

It is too good to be true. The modern world intervenes, in the form of World War I, and Jim feels compelled to enlist simply in order to understand the changes that are taking place. Ashley soon follows. At first Jim's war is liberating and a bit of a lark, but not once it moves to the front; Malouf's descriptions of trench warfare are vivid, sickening, horrifying, and—in their last scenes—almost surreal. Men in that war and, as Ashley sees, in the world to come, are parts in a machine, interchangeable, expendable, a far cry from what a man could be in the little paradise Ashley had founded. Determined individualists in the modern world are like the peasant whom soldiers found digging a garden in a bombed-out forest: obviously mad (or, perhaps, the only sane people left).

"Child's Play" has seen this modern world evolve still further; its nameless narrator has postponed what he thinks of as his real life in order to perform a single act of political terror. He gives few details from his past, and only the vaguest reasons for wanting to pursue this course. . . .

The narrator's rather fascinating assignment is to assassinate a world-renowned man of letters, and Malouf's portrait of this writer—a man of iron discipline and deep compassion, enormous intellect and playful irony—is masterful. To the extent that we are all the children of such an artist—his voice has epitomized a previous generation—the drama is Oedipal, and thus, in one of the title's several senses, child's play. We resent the man who in some ways shaped us, who saw from his lofty eminence what we would become. His knowledge of us is insufferable, and we kill him in order to live.

In his isolation, the narrator studies the approaching event from every conceivable angle. . . . None of these meditations, however, prepares him for the event itself, which in the shock of the actual becomes, like the battle scenes of **"The Bread of Time to Come,"** almost surreal, revealing that nothing—not art, nor history, nor news, nor even dream—is a match for bare reality.

"Child's Play" is the richer of these two works, but also perhaps the less fully realized, with a few loose ends and odd episodes; still, it is a striking story whose scenes and images remain with the reader long after he has finished it. Malouf is something of a primitive narrator, rough around the edges, but he is also a deeply serious writer, not to be taken up lightly. In these two unique perspectives on the modern world, he exhibits the kind of eccentric vision that one might expect from an outsider, an Australian, say, or an isolated terrorist, or a genuine artist.

David Guy, "Coming Out of the Country," in Book World—The Washington Post *(© 1982, The Washington Post), May 2, 1982, p. 9.*

PETER KEMP

Surreally hard-edged, the world [the short novel, **Child's Play,** and the short stories, **"Eustace"** and **"The Prowler,"** project] is one where details have a hallucinatory vividness and patterns stand out with stark clarity: only significance remains creepily opaque.

Like the dreams that regularly perturb their characters, the short novel and two stories gathered here are intensely enigmatic. Though geographically a world apart—Italy is the background to the novel, Australia to the stories—all three fictions cover the same imaginative ground. Whatever the ostensible setting, Malouf's *locales* invariably turn out to be disorientating mazes, full of echoing de Chirico perspectives and *trompe l'oeil* Magritte effects. Ranged in cryptic symmetries around them, the same types recur. Particularly favoured is the threatening solitary, some ominous loner endowed with "the ambiguous gift of singularity". Central to these three pieces are, respectively, an outsider, an intruder, and an interloper. Anti-social figures, they are often cast as the shadows of respectability: dark, distorted counterparts that people in the well-lit public world are unable to shake off. . . .

Polarities . . . magnetize Malouf's attention. Conformity, community, security are repeatedly set against anarchy, loneliness, danger. Obsessively, his work juxtaposes order and disturbance, light and dark. Those positives and negatives can unexpectedly change places. And always in Malouf's stories the powerful attraction between seemingly opposed poles is used to generate some shock effects. In **"Eustace"**, a trespassing misfit slides into the dormitory of a decorous girls' school, pacing eerily round the ranged beds, fantasizing among dreaming children. When the girls awake, he is not denounced because, until menace breaks through make-believe, he satisfies "their own hunger for fairytale". Similarly, in **"The Prowler"**, a placid and affluent suburb is infiltrated by a sexual maniac. Soon, however, he comes to seem a weird externalization of disruptive urges lurking inside law-abiding citizens. Reports of his behaviour, multiplying fantastically, take on bizarre, semi-revelatory patterns. False prowlers proliferate bemusingly, as deviance is carbon-copied. Finally, the investigating officer, symbol of authority and reassurance—"a sort of prowler in reverse"—emerges as the prime suspect.

Malouf's fiction opts for dream-like stylization. Through-the-looking-glass reflections and refractions turn his work into something like a hall of mirrors. Twisted likenesses loom everywhere: doubles, doppelgängers, secret sharers, alter egos. But the high degree of similarity between the various figures is only attained by a low degree of individual characterization. In these works, even proper names are rationed. Slimmed down to the bone of type—"the woman", "the boy", "the son"— the characters are psychologically anorexic. And their undernourishment is particularly pointed up by the fact that the backgrounds they are silhouetted against are portrayed with great fullness. Here, lavish detail is stamped sharply on the mind's eye. The Italian scene especially is captured with inventive accuracy—as when, for example, Malouf writes of a piazza suddenly floodlit with sunshine after heavy rain: "the square was full of pieces of sky with pigeons sipping at them or splashing up broken glass". Mirroring the natural world in this glittering fashion, ***Child's Play*** shows a poetic talent that is at its best when trained outwards rather than diffused in shadowy reflections of the doublings of the psyche.

Peter Kemp, "The Outsider Inside," in The Times Literary Supplement *(© Times Newspapers Ltd. (London) 1982; reproduced from* The Times Literary Supplement *by permission), No. 4129, May 21, 1982, p. 549.*

JAMES TULIP

There is good reason for believing that the Australian coastline region north from Newcastle to Brisbane is one of the choicest parts of the earth, indeed in a good season a Garden of Eden. . . . David Malouf in ***Fly Away Peter*** [published in the United States as ***The Bread of Time to Come***] has . . . made one part of it his own. The South Coast of Queensland (or, as it is now known, the Gold Coast) is created in his novel of pre-World War I days as if it is a Paradise before the Fall, a world of harmony between nature and human nature. There is even an Adam and Eve. (p. 113)

The moment when [Jim Saddler and Imogen Harcourt] meet is a fine one. It is by accident. Separately, they each are observing a sandpiper, and when the photo is developed their pleasure is caught by the novel as a moment of suspension of the centrally achieved interest of the book. . . . The openness of two people—their love of nature—is richly present. It is a poetic triumph for Malouf to have found this kind of stasis and sharing. The maturity in the characters is a measure of yet another advance in his gifts as a writer.

Fly Away Peter, however, does not rest there. It attempts to move out from this centre and frame this Paradise with its Fall. Jim Saddler goes to World War I and dies there. His is no migratory pattern or cycle. Nor was Imogen's, who had come from England and settled eccentrically in Australia. Only Ashley Crowther follows the pattern of the birds in coming home from England to his property, then in going to the War and returning. The two patterns—bird and human—are held up for inspection and comparison. It is as if the myth in the birds' cycle is the superior one. A sadness envelopes the human Fall. Even Imogen's closing vision of a surfboard rider off Southport as if it were some eternal resurgence of youth does not dispel the irony. It has daunting associations for the reader with what the South (Gold) Coast has since become. Who there now thinks of sandpipers?

Malouf's novella works best as a prose poem. So much is evocatively said of nature here. The charm in Jim Saddler's response to life brings a lyric and celebrative density to the writing. (pp. 113-14)

Gratuitously, I feel, Gallipoli makes an entrance in the novel; the second half is given over to a strong but finally unconvincing account of Jim Saddler in France. His knowledge and experience grow; he keeps his morale steady with watching birds. But the effect on the novel is to increase a sense of passivity in a negative sense with regard to human nature, which touches on the overall limitation of the book. For the characters and events in *Fly Away Peter* are in some disturbing sense not real. The duality of Jim Saddler and Ashley Crowther is transparently schematic. Class consciousness, while real enough in Australian society especially of this period, has an arbitrary feel to it in *Fly Away Peter*. And even Jim Saddler seems to be a centre of consciousness more than a character. Only in Imogen Harcourt has Malouf landed on a person who is a subject in her own right. She is choric, but quirky. She has made a choice where she wants to be in life. Her answer to the conundrum of choice and doubt in the title of the book is to accept what she has done in migrating like a bird. She knows, however, that she will never return. (p. 114)

*James Tulip, "Poets and Their Novels" (reprinted by permission of the publisher and the author), in Southerly, Vol. 43, No. 1, 1983, pp. 113-18.**

Bobbie Ann Mason
1940-

American short story writer and critic.

Shiloh and Other Stories (1982), Mason's first fictional collection, is set in rural Paducah, Kentucky, where she grew up. The sixteen stories in *Shiloh* depict a changing South, a world in which characters must reconcile elements of the past, represented by the older generation, with the present. Mason's characters are introduced to the modern world primarily through television. She uses such concrete details as brand names to illustrate the effects of mass culture on the society she portrays, and many of her working-class characters are employed in chain stores rather than on farms or in family businesses. The intrusion of the present into the lives of Mason's people creates not only commercial and material changes, but also more threatening changes in societal mores. Several of the stories concern married couples who are divorced or separated; progress places the same strain on family relationships in Paducah as it does elsewhere.

Critical reaction to *Shiloh* has been overwhelmingly positive. Mason has been applauded especially for her skillful rendering of a language rich in Southern regionalisms and her often humorous dialogue, both of which help to bring her characters to life. Some critics have commented, however, that Mason's stories are weakened by the same lack of aim or resolution which characterizes much of modern fiction.

Mason has also published two works of literary criticism: *Nabokov's Garden: A Guide to Ada* (1974) and *The Girl Sleuth: A Feminist Guide* (1975), which explores and evaluates series fiction written for girls.

(See also *Contemporary Authors,* Vols. 53-56 and *Contemporary Authors New Revision Series,* Vol. 11.)

ANNE TYLER

[To say that Mason] is a "new" writer is to give entirely the wrong impression, for there is nothing unformed or merely promising about her. She is a full-fledged master of the short story, and *Shiloh and Other Stories,* her first collection, is a treasure.

Her characters are backwoods Kentuckians, for the most part, and they're so vividly and lovingly portrayed that we feel we know everything about them. We know their food: the potato and mushroom-soup casseroles, uncooked fruitcake made with graham cracker crumbs and marshmallows, and marshmallow-centered sweet-potato balls rolled in crushed cornflakes. We know their clothing: the women's pantsuits and the men's Worm-and-Germ caps from the feed mill. We know they earn their living selling Tupperware or clerking in Kroger's, the K-Mart, or J. C. Penney, and they pass their free time making latch-hook wall hangings of an Arizona sunset. (pp. 36, 38)

What they say comes through so clearly and directly that their voices ring through our living rooms. . . . Their English is often ungrammatical and filled with gangling, country-style similes, but not a one of these people is described with anything less than complete respect.

Photograph by James Baker Hall

Characters alone, of course, don't make a story, no matter how quirky or colorful; nor does an eagle eye or a perfect-pitch ear. What matters finally is that the story enlarge our view of human beings, and these do. They are extraordinarily touching, in the most delicate and apparently effortless way. They explore, usually, the sense of bewilderment and anxious hopefulness that people feel when suddenly confronted with change. It is especially poignant that the characters in these stories, having led more sheltered lives than the average reader, are trying to deal with changes most of us already take for granted.

"One day I was listening to Hank Williams and shelling corn for the chickens and the next day I was expected to know what wines went with what," Nancy Culpepper says. The women in **"Third Monday"** are throwing a traditional baby shower, but the mother-to-be is a proudly unwed thirty-seven-year-old, and since amniocentesis has divined the baby's sex the cake reads WELCOME HOLLY. In **"Graveyard Day,"** a divorcee who's considering remarriage finds herself unable to accept the idea that families should "shift membership, like clubs." A stepfather for her daughter, she thinks, would be "something like a sugar substitute," something like "a substitute host on a talk show." . . .

In **"Rookers"**—a jewel of a story . . .—a lonely father searches for a link with his modern, rather brittle college daughter.

271

Thinking she's taking a philosophy course, he struggles through *The Encyclopedia of Philosophy* until his daughter comes home and tells him it's physics she's studying. In **"A New-Wave Format,"** a middle-aged bus driver who's worried about losing the up-to-the-minute young girl he lives with "suddenly blurts out so much praise for [her] zucchini bread that Sabrina looks at him oddly."

The situations are all the more affecting because the characters try so hard, and with such optimism, to keep up with change instead of fighting against it. They have an earnest faith in progress; they are as quick to absorb new brand names as foreigners trying to learn the language of a strange country they've found themselves in. . . .

It's heartening to find male characters portrayed sympathetically, with an appreciation for the fact they can feel as confused and hurt and lonely as the female characters. These truck drivers, bus drivers, and carpenters show an endearing sensitivity and alertness to others.

And "simple" though these people may be, they are fully capable of moments of insight that are remarkably perceptive but never strained. Just watch the wife realizing suddenly why she's spent weeks painting nothing but watermelons after her husband left her; or another wife all at once comprehending what's behind her husband's compulsive calls to the weather recording; or the daughter putting her finger, with perfect accuracy, on the reason for her mother's bringing up a gruesome news story. . . .

Have I mentioned that, for all the sorrow contained in these stories, they are also hilarious? Did I neglect to say you're likely to find yourself in tears on several occasions? But you'll find that out for yourself. Go buy this book. Don't borrow it, don't look for it in the library, but buy it, as a way of casting your vote for real literature. (p. 38)

> Anne Tyler, "Kentucky Cameos," in The New Republic (reprinted by permission of The New Republic; © 1982 The New Republic, Inc.), Vol. 187, No. 17, November 1, 1982, pp. 36, 38.

DAVID QUAMMEN

For several years short stories by Bobbie Ann Mason have been turning up—rather improbably, it seemed—in The New Yorker and The Atlantic. The improbability lay in the fact that Miss Mason writes almost exclusively about working-class and farm people coping with their muted frustrations in western Kentucky (south of Paducah, not far from Kentucky Lake, if that helps you), and the gap to be bridged empathically between her readership and her characters was therefore formidable. But formidable also is Miss Mason's talent, and her craftsmanship. **"Shiloh and Other Stories,"** her first collection, shows not only how good she can be but how consistently good she remains. The most improbable thing about this volume is that not a single page lags, hardly a paragraph fails, not one among 16 stories is less than impressive. . . .

Loss and deprivation, the disappointment of pathetically modest hopes, are the themes Bobbie Ann Mason works and reworks. She portrays the disquieted lives of men and women not blessed with much money or education or luck, but cursed with enough sensitivity and imagination to allow them to suffer regrets. These are lives seen against an equally disquieted social landscape, where old grocery stores with front porches are being replaced by things called "the Convenient," where the grown daughters of ranch wives work as clerks at K Mart, where higher wisdom comes in via the Phil Donahue show. . . .

In this sad and scary moment of failing certainties it is time for the venerable tulip tree in the yard to be cut down, time for Granny to be moved to the nursing home, time for an arthritic old dog named Grover Cleveland to be put to sleep. Time too for a couple of Miss Mason's heroines to see the gynecologist about a lump in the breast. All the bad portents, all the sickening changes seem somehow connected, uniting **"Shiloh and Other Stories"** as tightly as a good novel. One elderly woman says to her grown daughter: "Did you hear about the datsun dog that killed the baby?" She means dachshund. Ominous forces of disorientation are loose in Masonland. (p. 7)

Most compellingly, Miss Mason examines in her various truck drivers and salesclerks the dawning recognition—in some cases only a vague worry—of having missed something, something important, some alternate life more fruitful than the one that's been led. For instance, Norma Jean Moffitt of the story **"Shiloh"** sells cosmetics at a Rexall and has lately, for reasons unclear to her husband Leroy, begun developing her pectorals with barbells. Because he fears she is drifting away from him (and he is right), Leroy buys her an electric organ, upon which Norma Jean proceeds to master every tune in "The Sixties Songbook." "I didn't like these old songs back then," she says. "But I have this crazy feeling I missed something." And a long deferred car picnic with Leroy to the battlefield at Shiloh is not, it transpires, what she has in mind.

The message from Bobbie Ann Mason, which by her wit and skill she makes a fascinating matter, is that inexorable changes are coming upon the plain folk of western Kentucky. (p. 33)

> David Quammen, "Plain Folk and Puzzling Changes," in The New York Times Book Review (copyright © 1982 by The New York Times Company; reprinted by permission), November 21, 1982, pp. 7, 33.

ANATOLE BROYARD

To me, the small-town Kentucky people of Bobbie Ann Mason's are stranger and more remote than the inhabitants of any French, Italian or Spanish village. I think it's because many of the men and women in **"Shiloh and Other Stories"** seem to improvise their styles of being, while the people in European towns are more likely to begin with, refer to, or depart from a recognizable tradition.

Miss Mason's people live in the spaces cleared or emptied by the movement of American life, rather than in the configurations created by time and change. They don't seem to progress from one thing to another, but to fall between one thing and another, to live in an absence bracketed by nostalgia and apprehension. To be restless or rootless in a small American town is to suffer a modern anxiety with none of the camouflaging sophistication of the big city.

A couple of these stories are about husbands who, for one reason or another, are at home alone with their wives, where they look at one another in surprise, as if they suddenly saw themselves stripped of all contexts, as if the world around them abruptly fell away and left them mercilessly exposed. One such husband feels an impulse to explain himself to his wife, as if they had forgotten who they were and what they had expected to do together.

The men in **"Shiloh and Other Stories"** are sometimes silent and transient, as if their only language was a language of place-names, and each place and each name was weighty with meaning, a definition of another kind of effort. Forced to stay behind, their women scrutinize the rejected places with disillusioned or defensive eyes.

In Miss Mason's stories, the capacity that small towns have for terrifying or mystifying outsiders appears to rebound and strike the very people who live in such towns. They are unexpectedly transfixed by the fact that they are Americans, without knowing what American means. . . .

In **"A New-Wave Format,"** my favorite story in the book, Edwin, who is 43 years old, drives a busload of mentally retarded people to training classes every day. He's had all sorts of jobs, as well as two wives whom he remembers only "by their food."

Now he lives with a 20-year-old girl named Sabrina, who makes him feel 20 years younger too. But it's as if he's lost those years somewhere and he watches Sabrina as if he could deduce from her what they would have been like. . . .

Though they are sometimes bleak, Bobbie Ann Mason's stories can be beautiful too, as in a scene of a woman standing in the dark, trying to lure her ducks out of a pond into the safety of their pen. Another woman is told by her doctor that she will have to resist chocolate cake and she feels that "somehow, this is a welcome guide for living, something certain—particular and silly."

"Shiloh and Other Stories" reminds us how much we need such certainty, and how particular and disarmingly silly its ingredients can be.

Anatole Broyard, in a review of "Shiloh and Other Stories," in The New York Times *(copyright © 1982 by The New York Times Company; reprinted by permission), November 23, 1982, p. C14.*

ROBERT TOWERS

Vision and technique come exhilaratingly together in Bobbie Ann Mason's collection of stories [*Shiloh and Other Stories*]. She is one of those rare writers who, by concentrating their attention on a few square miles of native turf, are able to open up new and surprisingly wide worlds for the delighted reader. Less tragically gloomy than Raymond Carver, Mason nonetheless resembles that fine writer in the way she lays bare the heart of a domestic drama; and like him she holds up for our inspection a whole class of unremarkable people who are seldom noticed in fiction. (p. 39)

Bobbie Ann Mason is wonderfully even-handed and nonjudgmental in the handling of her characters, male as well as female. They are what they are, she seems to say, as restless women strain against the confines of marriage, as restless men take off in pickup trucks for Texas or the Rockies, leaving their women stuck with more rent than they can afford to pay. Her interest in them is both friendly and detached—and it extends to cats and ancient, ailing dogs . . . and to mechanical objects as well: an injured truck-driver's rig "sits in the backyard, like a gigantic bird that has flown home to roost." She avoids extended descriptions, depending upon a few exactly observed details to establish her situations and scenes.

Individually effective as they are, there is a degree of sameness to the stories read as a collection. This is due partly to the rather narrow restrictions of class and circumstance and outlook within which the characters lead their untidy lives; it is due more, I think, to the fact that Mason seldom varies the form and rhythmic pattern of her pieces. She is a superb technician, but I wish she did not adhere quite so closely to the conventions that seem to apply chiefly to women writing for *The New Yorker:* i.e., the use of the present tense for narration and the avoidance of anything resembling a "closed" ending. Mason's stories are open-ended with a vengeance. Most often her conclusions swerve abruptly from the path that has been hitherto pursued and take off across the fields. A few resolutions might add some needed variety to an otherwise remarkable achievement. *Shiloh and Other Stories* is among the best of the recent good collections that have once again brought the short story to the forefront of literary interest. (p. 40)

Robert Towers, "American Graffiti," in The New York Review of Books *(reprinted with permission from* The New York Review of Books; *copyright © 1982 Nyrev, Inc.), Vol. XXIX, No. 20, December 16, 1982, pp. 38-40.*

PATRICIA VIGDERMAN

[*Shiloh and Other Stories*] has been treated to a remarkable amount of favorable critical attention for a first collection, and indeed [Mason's] appeal is undeniable. The first lines pull you in with an easy, quirky rhythm: "The former astronaut claims that walking on the moon was nothing, compared to walking with Jesus." Every story is rich with surface details, little pleasures and pains captured absolutely, of the everyday life of future shock in the provinces. Mason has really heard people speak the way her characters speak, and she has certainly watched the TV shows they watch.

When you turn the page, however, her people vanish, because their stories have no emotional gravity. Mason establishes an energetic comic distance, and then ends the stories with a little lurch of the heart, a closeness that seems tacked on. In **"Old Things,"** for example, Mason presents Cleo, a middle-aged Kentucky widow, from many angles. Cleo is a likable person who lives in a small house where the TV is almost always on. Her daughter Linda, who has left her husband, has moved in, along with her two young children. The kids are making a mess of the place, and Cleo can't believe Linda's husband has mistreated her: "It's as if she had been told some wild tale about outer space, like something on a TV show." She's uncomfortable about the way Linda seems to be enjoying her life now. It's all so newfangled the way people just do what they want.

We see Cleo looking idly through a mail-order catalogue, talking to her granddaughter, grieving over the impending death of a friend's cat. But we never get close to her. *She*'s like somebody from outer space—until the very end, when at a flea market she comes across a miniature whatnot with an idyllic train scene painted across the front. She is sure it once belonged to her husband, and the story ends in a zoom close-up of Cleo fantasizing the family all together on the train, gliding west into a perfect future.

Like most of Mason's characters, Cleo is not long off the land, and she is completely vulnerable to contemporary American culture. This vulnerability of Mason's New Southerners is never quite integrated into the plots, however. It's used—often with great humor—as local color, but the inner life it implies is not deeply imagined. Mason takes us into her characters' new

Kentucky homes and then runs a made-for-TV movie. Her people's emotions come across merely as dots on the screen. Ultimately, the stories seem idle: **"Old Things"** ends for no particular reason, which makes it seem to have been written likewise. This aimlessness is not unique to Mason, of course. It characterizes much of what passes for good fiction right now—but it disappoints all the same. (p. 345)

Patricia Vigderman, "K-Marts and Failing Farms," in The Nation *(copyright 1983* The Nation *magazine, The Nation Associates, Inc.), Vol. 236, No. 11, March 19, 1983, pp. 345-47.**

FRANCIS KING

Each story [in *Shiloh*] . . . is a recreation of life, in all its quaint, baffling, funny, pathetic inconsequentiality, in one small, obscure corner of the world. Few of her English readers will ever have visited the towns that she describes, few are likely to do so. But it is probable that they will retain the impression that they have made a visit, in some other existence or in a dream, so intense is her evocation. . . .

One of Miss Mason's constant themes is the manner in which, with no decisive snap of the thread, human relationships become unravelled. In some instances, they remain that way; in others, the fabric knits up again, with no apparent effort by either of the parties. In the title story, **'Shiloh'**, for example, a truck-driver, out of work after an accident, observes, through a haze of marijuana smoke, how his tough, independent wife is slowly receding from him, in a new-found interest first in body-building and then in English composition. When he takes her to the Civil War battlefield of Shiloh, she, in effect, vanishes out of sight, leaving him with the desolating sense that, just as he has never understood the inner workings of history that erupted in so much carnage, so he has never understood the inner workings of the marriage that is now causing his own living death.

Again, in **'Still Life with Watermelon'**, a wife, whose husband has inexplicably taken off for Texas with a buddy—is the buddy perhaps, as her closest woman friend suggests, a homosexual?—obsessively paints one amateurish picture of watermelons after another, in the hope that a rich, eccentric collector of pictures of watermelons will buy one off her. Eventually, wife and husband are reunited. The journey to Texas has been a crazy adventure for him; and she, working away at her watermelons, has been on a journey no less crazy. Now they are together once more in all their usual ordinariness; but some faint recollection of their fugues into craziness will obstinately remain with them.

Another constant theme is the persistence with which the past works like a yeast in the present. In **'Nancy Culpepper'** for example, a young woman becomes obsessed with the ancestress whose name she bears. Her nonagenarian grandmother has a hoard of family photographs, which, now that she is about to go into an old people's home, the young woman hopes to claim for herself. Eventually, there, in her hands, is the faded photograph of another young woman, in an embroidered white dress, 'her eyes fixed on something so far away'—the future containing her namesake. Photographs, as the symbols, at once shadows and powerful, of an ever-living past are used to eerie effect in stories other than this one.

As an incessant, intrusive counterpoint to the lives of these ill-educated characters, their television screens, in living-rooms, kitchens or bedrooms, project images of a world which they are doomed never to experience except at second-hand. Often, they pay more attention to the images of drama than to the actual dramas (love, bereavement, betrayal) in which they are engulfed.

Francis King, "Fantasy Lives," in The Spectator *(© 1983 by* The Spectator; *reprinted by permission of* The Spectator*), Vol. 251, No. 8093, August 20, 1983, p. 21.**

Thomas McGrath
1916-

American poet, novelist, scriptwriter, young adult writer, and editor.

Although McGrath has been cited by such noted critics as Kenneth Rexroth and Donald Hall for being a distinctive and important voice in contemporary American poetry, his readership has been surprisingly small. The themes McGrath introduced in *To Walk a Crooked Mile* (1948), his first volume of poetry, are mentioned by critics as factors which have contributed to his relative obscurity. In this book, McGrath expresses anger toward the dehumanizing effects of American life, which he views as corrupted by such elements as technology, capitalism, and social class struggle. McGrath has described his political stance as "unaffiliated far Left."

McGrath often writes about his native North Dakota, but, more than that, he strives to capture the expansiveness of the American West in his poems. Some of his techniques for broadening the scope of his poetry include kaleidoscopic surrealism and cataloging. Although McGrath's poetry is often unstructured, critics have praised its ability to lead the reader back to the main theme or image.

Letter to an Imaginary Friend, Parts I & II (1962, 1970) is considered McGrath's most important work to date. A long autobiographical poetic narrative, it is a tapestry of personal experience, history, myth, and concrete physical description held together by a powerful, masculine voice. McGrath's recent collection, *Waiting for the Angel* (1979), displays much the same technique as *Letter,* but possesses a more solemn tone and a darker vision of the loss motif which is present in all of McGrath's poetry.

(See also *Contemporary Authors*, Vols. 9-12, rev. ed. and *Contemporary Authors New Revision Series*, Vol. 6.)

Photograph by Layle Silbert; © copyright 1983

HUGH GIBB

[In *To Walk a Crooked Mile,* McGrath] has continued the tradition of the English poets of the Thirties with their deep concern for those disturbing elements of social life—poverty, injustice and war. But he does not suffer from some of their weaknesses which Virginia Woolf describes in her essay on poets of the "Leaning Tower." In the first place, when contemplating a harsh and chaotic world, he never allows his genuine pity for the oppressed to degenerate into self-pity; and secondly, he is never forced to retreat into a world of private fantasy and introspection. In consequence he has been able not only to sustain the tradition which would otherwise appear to be almost extinct, but has brought to it a new and vigorous honesty.

Most of this collection are poems of "occasion" in which McGrath uses a very great variety of vivid images. . . .

But the often surrealistic imagery is never allowed to distract the imagination by making it fly off at wild tangents and nearly always succeeds in reinforcing the main meaning of the poem. Moreover, by the subtle use of recurrent symbols which run like threads through all the poems, he contrives to bind them together as a whole.

In the central section of the book, "The Dialectics of Love," the poems still appear to be "occasional," but in point of fact they all form part of a prolonged attempt to study and resolve the rival claims of personal love and love for humanity in general. Of these, perhaps the most remarkable individual poem is an ode entitled: **"The Drowned Man: Death Between Two Rivers,"** in which the Leaning Man, symbol of indecision, discovers himself in that Waste Land which fringes all industrial civilizations. This ode, however, is not a dry statement of observations, as in T. S. Eliot's famous poem, but has all the excitement of a constantly searching intelligence.

In his wartime poems, collected under the heading **"Wounds in the Rain,"** McGrath displays much anger against the senseless forces that have produced so brutal a situation, but at the same time he succeeds in capturing with ruthless accuracy the disturbing atmosphere of war and the conflicting emotions of the active soldier. If judged by these war poems alone he would clearly have established himself as one of the more vital and significant of contemporary poets.

Hugh Gibb, "Leaning Man in the Waste Land," in The New York Times Book Review *(copyright ©*

1948 by The New York Times Company; reprinted by permission), March 7, 1948, p. 4.

GERARD PREVIN MEYER

Surrealism can be fun; it can shake us out of grooves of convention. But it cannot go ahead—or lift up, either: what momentary exultations it achieves are fast and forgettable, the effects of a jag. The "new myth" does not come.

Nevertheless, [it is apparent in **To Walk a Crooked Mile** that] Thomas McGrath, a likable and ingenious young poet very largely under the sway of two established "myths"—the Whitman-democratic and the Marxist-revolutionary—has allowed himself to be lured into the camp of the surrealists, apparently by his reading of the current English school of poetry—the same group aptly characterized by W. Y. Tindall as having "achieved a confusion of Marx with Freud." The chances are that this is only a passing allegiance. While it lasts, however, McGrath rattles off such stanzas as this:

> Remember the blind harp tethered in the bathroom?
> Or earlier the surrealist station where,
> Fenced with false faces, and brushing off the eyes
> Which stuck to our naked suits we dined upon the air.

This is rather good, of its sort; but what can one say for something like this?

> Maine is a map of Freud with feminine fine lakes
> And phallic forests wherever the blind eye looks.
> Here the last century exists on rubber crutches,
> And the hours and the enigmas multiply in hutches.

It is really painful to see a poet of real talent occupying himself with these three-finger exercises, which any reasonably fair student can turn out. McGrath has a "line" of his own, based on genuine Western folk-speech . . . ; he hardly needs to lean on such worn props as Dali's crutches. When he wants to, he can find the right words for love, or command anger and revulsion, irony and wit. (pp. 51-2)

In so far as he directs his poetry toward political action, McGrath simplifies too much (as when he exalts the pure love of vagrants above the corrupt love of the rich) and loses his grip as an artist, permitting banalities of diction ("comradeship," "brotherhood," "bourgeois," "upper class," and the like). . . .

But there is a great deal of life in this poetry, for which one can forgive the lapses into crutches or class-war. (p. 52)

Gerard Previn Meyer, "Enigmas in Hutches," in The Saturday Review of Literature (© 1948 Saturday Review Magazine Co.; reprinted by permission), Vol. XXXI, No. 16, April 17, 1948, pp. 51-2.

KENNETH REXROTH

Probably it is those distinguished blacklists, and just living in Los Angeles, where everybody is on somebody's blacklist, that has kept Thomas McGrath from his due. For all its tremendous expense of spirit, the Proletarian Thirties produced almost no verse which can be read today without a blush—Edwin Rolfe, Don Gordon, Charles Humboldt, Walter Lowenfels, that's about it. McGrath is a decade younger than most of those people, and, excepting for Lowenfels, more skilled. Further, he is a lot less "cooked." Few of these poems [in **New and Selected Poems**] are about issues—except the abiding issue of being Thomas McGrath. Poets are most effective in politics when they write-in their own names on all ballots. Whatever his opinions have been, McGrath has always known this. It is the other peoples' opinions which have kept him from being as well known as he deserves, for he is a most accomplished and committed poet.

Kenneth Rexroth, "Written in American," in The New York Times Book Review (copyright © 1965 by The New York Times Company; reprinted by permission), February 21, 1965, pp. 4, 14.*

PUBLISHERS WEEKLY

Part I of this extraordinary autobiographical poem [**Letter to an Imaginary Friend**] was first published in 1962. . . . McGrath has grown measurably since he wrote that first volume with its hairy nimbus of half-shaken memories of a Dakota youth, of friends half-forgotten or dead, of groping first-doubts stiffened by war experiences. Here the stylistic overtones are Thomas Wolfe without Wolfe's purified identity or fictional frame of reference. But Part II, here published in its entirety for the first time, shows a remarkable gain; McGrath suddenly stands "naked as a studhorse in a rhubarb patch," delivering himself with sharp, stinging certainty. He is proclaiming our lost heritage, naming our traumas—"The Indian is the first wound," and money. McGrath is a writer of long poems, labyrinthine as his life; but in many passages and in the terrible statement of desolation toward the close of Part II he merits rank with the best American poets writing today.

A review of "Letter to an Imaginary Friend, Parts I and II," in Publishers Weekly (reprinted from the March 2, 1970 issue of Publishers Weekly, published by R. R. Bowker Company, a Xerox company; copyright © 1970 by Xerox Corporation), Vol. 197, No. 9, March 2, 1970, p. 79.

THE ANTIOCH REVIEW

Trying to reconstitute and renew the soured American Dream, Thomas McGrath hopes to move, in life as well as in art, for he is a political man, "beyond history to Origin / To build that Legend where all journies [sic] are one / where Identity / Exists / where speech becomes song." This means he must replace the historical and diseased idea of manifest destiny, individual and national, which gave us Los Angeles, with the communal myth of unitary voyages that end by bringing us together. Unhappily McGrath succeeds no better than other politicians at this hard task, but not, unlike those others, for want of sincerity or passionate devotion. No, [**Letter to an Imaginary Friend**] is not hypocritical, just very hard to write; for, having chosen the autobiographical form, the poet must, given his theme, make his life the nation's, make us believe that "North Dakota [his boyhood home] *is* / Everywhere." Too often, though, the personal details do not explode into myth, so that the letter is not written to an imaginary friend but to "Those I have named and the others—flowers of a bitter season— / They'll know who I mean."

A review of "Letter to an Imaginary Friend, Parts I and II," in The Antioch Review (copyright © 1971 by the Antioch Review Inc.; reprinted by permission of the Editors), Vol. XXX, Nos. 3 & 4, Fall-Winter, 1970-71, p. 465.

CHOICE

Written mostly in long cadenced lines reminiscent of Jeffers, [*Letter to an Imaginary Friend*] constitutes a loose framework in which anything and everything can be developed as semi-autonomous sections. In a medley of memory and observation, the poet ranges back and forth over past and present. Episodes of childhood, youth, today mingle with reflections on social and political events. One moment he describes his first job or the dawning awareness of the nubility of girls, the next he narrates how "The leather priests of the hieratic dollar enclave to bless / The lushworking washing machines of the Protestant Ethic ecumenical / Laundries: to steam the blood from the bills. . . ." There is a Bunyan-sized quality about the book—its length, the vigor and vividness of the infinitely varied sections, the kaleidoscopic picture it gives of mid-century America and one man's response to the spectacle. Both as poetry and as social history, it invites fascinated browsing, and then sustained reading.

> A review of "Letter to an Imaginary Friend, Parts I and II," in Choice (copyright © 1971 by American Library Association; reprinted by permission of the American Library Association), Vol. 8, No. 4, June, 1971, p. 552.

JAMES ATLAS

Thomas McGrath is an older poet . . . and the astonishing document of his life, *Letter to an Imaginary Friend*, illuminates much of what has been forgotten by this generation. Parts I and II of what promises to be an unending chronicle are presented here in 214 wide pages. This project is astonishing, and I find it hard to believe so little attention has been drawn to it. . . . McGrath's *Letter* is an incessant, grieving lyric, obsessive and polemical, euphoric and bereaved. The long six-stress line he has chosen acts as an incantation; lines are broken up, dispersed, orchestrated. . . . It is the narrative of a joyous, terrible journey, during which the poet, like Jacob, finds himself abandoned and blessed.

Throughout, the resonance of personal history is drowned out by the larger concerns of American life during the Depression and World War II. As a boy from a desolate farm in North Dakota driving off to college, McGrath recalls the lean years, the men, his family, girls. . . . Nothing has been excluded in the telling, because nothing is irrelevant. Solipsism is absent from the *Letter* because McGrath endured an era when America seemed to be collapsing, not as now, in chaos, but in a grand apocalypse of hope and dread.

Certain things are mentioned in the *Letter*, not as expiation, but out of need; workers, Party meetings, strikes, polemics against capitalism and its ravages, the dull pathos of alienating labor, old Communist songs are mingled in a collective impulse to claim the world. Not having lived through that period, I feel tempted to search in those arduous times for a passion missing from this enervated decade. (pp. 47-8)

> James Atlas, "What Is To Be Done?" (© 1971 by The Modern Poetry Association; reprinted by permission of the Editor of Poetry and the author), in Poetry, Vol. CXIX, No. 1, October, 1971, pp. 45-51.*

JAMES N. NAIDEN

The Movie At The End Of The World, is a collection of poems written over the past three decades or so that the author wishes to preserve for a contemporary audience. As Franklin Brainard recently pointed out in his review of this book in *The Minnesota Daily*, McGrath could have profited greatly by "trimming" the contents, by weeding out the less significant poems and thereby giving the reader a leaner, but stronger, collection in terms of the over-all result. But I must agree further with Brainard's assessment that if one reads the book from cover to cover and judges it as a book, the results will be very rewarding. McGrath's efforts over this long span of time reveal a highly accomplished poet, a craftsman of hitherto unrecognized, but considerable, ability—whose reputation is confirmed as among those ten or twelve American poets writing today who should be considered "major" in import and influence. But what of the poems? . . . I can refer the reader to two poems which rendered my reading well. McGrath is above all an experimenter; he writes free verse as much as tried-and-true forms, such as the sonnet, the sestina and so forth. The poems in *Movie,* however, are written mostly in forms peculiar to McGrath's own personal idiom, the structure of which is more often than not developed by the message and import of the given poem. Such would be the poem, **"A Warrant For Pablo Neruda"**. . . .

Another poem—**"Obituary"**—is very short, only five lines, yet it shows the "Dakota experience" very well, reminding the reader of what McGrath means when he says of his North Dakota upbringing that, wherever he went and whatever he did after leaving North Dakota as a young man, he found "North Dakota is everywhere"—he could not escape it, even if he had wanted to forget it, to bury it along with a thousand other things in his past. Naturally, the poet's past pervades this book—it is a personal history rich with experiences not always explained, but revealed in essence throughout a reading of this collection. And it is in **"Obituary"** that this rich awareness of the past is brought out so well. . . .

Mention should also be made of McGrath's long epic poem, *Letter To An Imaginary Friend, Parts One and Two;* while it is not my purpose here to examine *Letter,* I highly recommend it as essential reading to anyone who wishes to understand one of the most significant long poems in recent American literary history, as well as the moving force—the personal ethos—of one of the most important poets now writing. (p. 59)

> James N. Naiden, "Minnesota Poetry—II," in North Country ANVIL (copyright © 1973 by North Country Anvil, Inc.), No. 7, August-September, 1973, pp. 59-62.*

CHARLES POTTS

any of u, lost in wundrland, or perfektly aware of wher u r, in th vicinity of a good library, a good bookstore, or a good frends stash on th intellekt, cd perhaps in thos locashns lokate, *The Movie at the End of the World* . . . for th quikest way tu th nuclear minimum essential McGrath. not tu imply that *Movie* . . . is a huge book and one u cdnt find yr way in for it is a refreshingly slendr undr 200 pages of mor than 30 years of th best short work of one mans publishing history. if u kan read [a] dozen or th entire book and remain as u wer bfor thers litl i kan du for u. i just re read them and hav red th book a fu times bfor and they remain as good as i thot them th first time i tried them. . . .

thes poems r capable of breaking out in such satirik sharpness that i'd guffaw if they hadnt taken mi breath away. . . . ther is ample musikashn in thes poems. **"Gone Away Blues"** cd b set tu musik and sung. im opposing mi desire tu quote a lot, prefering u tu go tu th text. he klaims tu c th city blinking in a neon code he reads all tu klearly, going down with all hands. i shd hope so. sumtimes i get th feeling that sum of th poetry puts unecessary formalistik yokes on itself but when its good it makes th format sing and at its best transforms it purely into McGraths own voice. . . . ther is a place in amerika for McGraths poetry, rite up front with th best of it. (p. 22)

> Charles Potts, "Thomas McGrath: Native Son," in Small Press Review (© 1974 by Dustbooks), Vol. 6, No. 2, October, 1974, pp. 21-3.

JOHN JACOB

McGrath is best known for his great long-poem *Letter to an Imaginary Friend*, a work whose epic regional, artistic, and political sweep has extremely affected American poetry. [The poems in *Open Songs: Sixty Short Poems*] lack the room McGrath sometimes needs to sweep perceptive powers about him, the sense of history that makes him great. They are valuable because they contain the lesson of how a good poet slowly and deliberately fashions the detail of a poetic world, strand by strand, word by word.

> John Jacob, in a review of "Open Songs: Sixty Short Poems," in Booklist (reprinted by permission of the American Library Association; copyright © 1978 by the American Library Association), Vol. 74, No. 16, April 15, 1978, p. 1319.

DONALD HALL

Curse and invective are strangely missing from American poetry. Poets save their invective for other poets, in hate mail that causes short circuits in post offices all over the country. After Pound slammed out at Wall Street bankers, what is there? You can find a little in Allen Ginsberg, a little in Robert Bly. But for the most part our poets are public lovers and private haters. We lack public denunciation, like this:

> And these but the stammering simulacra of the Rand
> Corpse wise men—
> Scientists who have lost the good of the intellect,
> mechanico-humanoids
> Antiseptically manufactured by the Faustian humunculus
> process.
> And how they dream in their gelded towers these demi-
> men!
> (Singing of overkill, kriegspiel, singing of blindfold
> chess—
> Sort of ainaleckshul rasslin matches to sharpen their
> fantasies
> Like a scout knife.)
>   Necrophiles.
>   Money protectors.

Thomas McGrath shows the way. This passage comes from his best book, the long autobiographical poem, *Letter to an Imaginary Friend*. There are fine poems in his collected shorter poems, *The Movie at the End of the World*. There are also bad ones: there are also many, many poems with wonderful parts and terrible parts. That's the way he is. Anybody who is put off, and runs away, because of the bad lines, is losing out; also, he is a chickenshit who is scared of anything untidy. McGrath belongs to the line of poets who are perfect in their imperfections. . . . Sometimes he uses images with an extraordinary audacity: "The sea builds instantaneous lace which rots in full motion—" This image is nearly ghastly, nearly a cliché, and nearly hype; but it leaps across the milewide chasm, strenuously and without any grace at all, and lands on all six feet, on the other side, having accomplished a prodigy. (When McGrath misses, the drop is at least three miles, and you can hear the scream from the bottom.) (pp. 51-2)

[Other] people can tell stories out of their own lives; nobody does invective the way McGrath does it. (p. 52)

I suppose there are twenty people who read the bogus populism of Kenneth Patchen, or the bogus proletarianism of Charles Bukowski, for the one man who reads the real thing, in Thomas McGrath. (p. 53)

> Donald Hall, "Notes on Poetry: McGrath's Invective," in his Goatfoot Milktongue Twinbird: Interviews, Essays, and Notes on Poetry, 1970-76 (copyright © by The University of Michigan 1978), University of Michigan Press, 1978, pp. 50-3.

FREDERICK C. STERN

Waiting for the Angel, Thomas McGrath's most recent book of poems, is about the past and about the expectation of death, among other things. It is also about an effort to "angelize the demons," as McGrath says in an as yet unpublished portion of the third part of his *Letter to an Imaginary Friend*. . . . The past as shaping force, death as personal and political fact, the horror and loneliness of living in an inhuman and dehumanizing society—all these have been the stuff of McGrath's twelve or more volumes of published poetry. In *Waiting for the Angel* these themes remain, though some new ones are added, and the effort is to make much that is demonic in the world McGrath perceives more "angelic," that is, more humanized and bearable. New in this volume is an elegiac note which I have not heard sounded in McGrath's work before, and which bespeaks the growing awareness of a personal end in the mind of a poet born in 1916. New also is an intense involvement with a boy-child, in fact McGrath's young son Tomasito, which adds to McGrath's frequent concern with his relationship with parents and siblings an extension of that concern to the future as embodied in McGrath's progeny.

This volume once again demonstrates McGrath's ongoing mastery of techniques and modes characteristic of recent poetry, as well as of the personal voice he has developed so forcefully since he first began publishing verse before World War II. . . . [One] would expect McGrath to be more widely known than he is. . . . Important contemporary poets, Robert Bly for one, proclaim his as a major voice in American poetry in the last three or four decades. His *Letter to an Imaginary Friend, Parts I and II* . . . is among the few really outstanding book-length poems published by an American, perhaps since *Paterson*. But his work is not very widely known by poetry readers and has not received the wide acclaim to which I believe it is justly entitled. It is difficult, of course, to know with any certainty why that is so, but one suspects that a large part of the reason is McGrath's ongoing and unregenerate political radicalism. . . . (pp. 108-09)

In part. . . , I suspect that McGarth's radicalism has overshadowed his outstanding qualities as a contemporary poet of the first rank, so that he has been too easily consigned to the ranks of the "reds." . . . But what is fascinating about McGrath as a "red" poet is that he is not *just* a "red" poet. In this he is comparable to a MacDiarmid, a Neruda, a Quasimodo. His image-making skills are of the first order. His ability to integrate the materials of popular and working people's culture, and the language spoken by all levels of American society, materials which come from deeply felt roots in his own North Dakota poor farm childhood and his adult life as city dweller, are outstanding qualities of his work. He uses a large variety of poetic techniques, from his most frequently employed long free verse line to couplets and other rhymed forms. His poetry is highly allusive, alluding to the classics, to the works of recent and contemporary poets, to his own earlier poetry, and to the political and social events of his times. All these attributes are among those which stamp McGrath as a contemporary poet, and especially as a poet of the generation of Karl Shapiro, Robert Lowell, and Randall Jarrell. Many of these qualities are displayed at their very best in *Waiting for the Angel*. It is a credit to McGrath's integrity and courage that he has not abated his radicalism, even though it . . . has perhaps cost him wider recognition among America's contemporary poets.

Waiting for the Angel contains a new portion of *Letter to an Imaginary Friend,* part 1 of a contemplated four-part Christmas Section of Part III of the long poem. It displays the same skilled interweaving of personal history and political history, of the mythic and the realistic, which characterizes the published portions of *Letter*. The new poem is a little difficult to follow without a clear conception of the earlier parts of the poem, and perhaps without some of the larger context I have had an opportunity to read. . . . Nevertheless, the poem is worth publishing in this partial form if for nothing else than the very funny rendition of the three kings coming through the snow, as perceived respectively and in intermingled fashion by two North Dakota farm families, one Irish and one Swedish, who are not sure if it is the Three Kings they see or "Some other lonesome deadbeat staggerin' home from the Hills . . .". . . . Such passages serve to remind us how funny McGrath often is, although his humor is usually satiric, and though funny, highly serious. There are also several graphics in this poem, integral parts of the verse itself, which enhance its humor, and an interesting new device, a kind of anti-illusionary, perhaps Brechtian, series of footnotes concerning relations between author and publisher. On the whole, this section of *Letter to an Imaginary Friend* has some portions which have about them a frenetic quality adumbrated but never quite reached in earlier parts of the poem.

The other three sections of *Waiting for the Angel* contain poems in the various forms typical of McGrath's work. Quite a few exemplify the elegiac note I have mentioned earlier. (pp. 109-10)

In the several poems involving his son Tomasito, as well in other poems, McGrath goes to some pains to make us understand that the voice of his poems is not a created persona, but the voice of the "real" Tom McGrath, as much as that is possible in so obviously fictional a medium as poetry. The comparison here with works like Lowell's *Life Studies* is inescapable. . . .

A little surprising were the several epigrammatic poems in this volume. I do not associate this format with McGrath's verse, though in retrospect I can certainly see the basis for it in earlier books. (p. 111)

Perhaps the best thing about *Waiting for the Angel* is that it provides, with all new material, such a full display of McGrath's variety and richness as a poet. Each of its four sections contains some examples of that variety. Perhaps the last poem in the volume can stand as emblem for the peculiar voice which is McGrath's. It is entitled **"The Return,"** and it tells the reader how the poet has attempted, for brief moments at least, to reenter the past as history, as myth, as record of personal passion and agony. (p. 112)

Frederick C. Stern, "Angelicizing the Demonic," in Southwest Review *(© 1980 by Southern Methodist University Press), Vol. 65, No. 1, Winter, 1980, pp. 108-12.*

ROGER MITCHELL

When I think of some of the better-known poetry of the early fifties, I think first of Dylan Thomas, E. E. Cummings, Robert Lowell, Theodore Roethke and of a poetry that was intensely, sometimes cloyingly, personal. . . .

The thirties were not just over in the fifties: they were devalidated. . . . The loss of faith in the public life and in progress in general was wide and deep, and it provided a rich ground for the cultivation of conservative social and political ideas. After the war there was an eager return to "normality" in human affairs, a normality that neatly ignored the Depression in fashioning fantasies about what was, in fact, a new sociological occurrence, the suburb. It was also a time of an intense desire to substitute moral categories for political ones. The attack did not always come from the right, though. Whatever Joseph McCarthy or J. Edgar Hoover did in those days to dampen the Left, they had a great deal of help from the Left. Its leading voices wavered, capitulated or disappeared, and they did so less out of a fear of political reprisal or a damaging appearance before HUAC than out of a fear that the whole human enterprise was fundamentally marred, that much less could be expected from it than had been hoped for in the thirties. The leading literary spokesman for the Left in the English-speaking world, W. H. Auden, left England and Marx behind in 1939 and turned his large talents toward a life with God, his friends and literature.

This broad reversal of direction or cancellation of hope in western culture comes more and more to seem like one of the primary facts of life in the twentieth century, and Thomas McGrath is one of the few writers who, in living through it, saw it and refused to give in to its compelling logic. His new book [*Waiting for the Angel*] continues and intensifies his lifelong brooding on "the generous wish" and its deferral in the latter part of our century. . . .

McGrath's career makes an interesting comment on the possibilities of a Marxist art in America. There has never been a time when any but a sentimental leftism could make the slightest dent in our consciousness. Sandburg has been the most successful American poet on the Left, but his success depended on developing the hard-working, long-suffering, and suspiciously noble side of working people. (p. 2)

Throughout the forties, McGrath's work was hard, spare, and abstract in the distantly conversational tone perfected by the Auden group. Nowhere is the manner better practiced, perhaps even by Auden himself, than in McGrath's **"The Dialectics of Love."** (pp. 2-3)

Judging from his later work, however, McGrath came to see limitations in this way of recording experience. In the early fifties he began work on the long and still unfinished ***Letter to an Imaginary Friend***. . . . In most conceivable ways, it is the opposite of his early work: long, loose in structure, extravagantly witty, emotionally varied, far less embedded in intellectual categories, local, and personal. . . . The early Audenesque manner, adopted out of understandable admiration and for lack of native models of revolutionary art, kept McGrath away from his real experience and the places in which it happened. His later ability to turn in these directions has produced one of the most unusual poems we have, a personalized history of "the generous wish" of the far Left in our country, tender and raucous, damning and hoping, a poem written in an uncongenial time in which he writhes and rages to keep the hope of "the solidarity/In the circle of hungry equals" alive. . . .

Many of the strongest poems in [*Waiting for the Angel*] are personal and traditional. **"Round Song"** is a poem of the generations. . . . The last poem, **"The Return,"** revives a Romantic longing at least as old as Keats' "Ode to a Nightingale." . . .

The most effective poems are those that seem to reflect both on McGrath personally and on the temporary failures of history. In **"After I'm Gone (Da Da Da Da Da),"** the poet imagines his wife long after his death. . . . One of the most beautiful and provocative poems in the collection is **"The End of the World."** . . . Apocalypse is thwarted by a sigh, a tinkle of music, a careless irreverent laughter. In both poems we are given images which make as clear as any writing I know the real state of revolutionary hope in our time. It is a hope preserved against immense odds; an exhalation, a laugh, an isolated, personal refusal to believe in such tormenting lies as the world's violent end or the working class's ritual suicide. These are not times, and have not been for forty years or more, to make us think that "the generous wish" could become fact, but Thomas McGrath, more than any other poet of his time and place, and with greater skill and energy than we have yet recognized, has helped keep that wish alive. (p. 3)

Roger Mitchell, "Unaffiliated Far Left," in The American Book Review *(© 1980 by* The American Book Review), *Vol. 2, No. 5, July-August, 1980, pp. 2-3.*

John (Clifford) Mortimer
1923-

English dramatist, novelist, scriptwriter, critic, and translator.

Although Mortimer began his literary career as a novelist, he has gained his greatest success as a playwright. His works make effective use of autobiographical experiences, particularly those relating to his career in the English legal system. As a lawyer, Mortimer has argued for the defense in several freedom-of-speech trials and helped to have government censorship powers over the British theater abolished in 1968. As a writer, Mortimer is partial to comedy; he believes that it is "the only thing worth writing in this despairing age, provided the comedy is truly on the side of the lonely, the neglected, the unsuccessful." While containing fantasy and humor, much of his work has at its center such serious topics as human rights, the problems experienced by society's outcasts, and corruption in the legal profession.

Mortimer unites many of his interests in *The Dock Brief* (1957). In this play, an undistinguished lawyer is chosen to defend a man accused of murder. The lawyer, who has waited all his life for this chance, rehearses his defense with his client, and fantasizes about the effect his closing argument will have on the jury. However, once in the courtroom, the attorney is dumbstruck and loses the case. Nevertheless, his client is freed because, according to the judge, the lawyer's incompetence has caused an unfair trial. Such surprise endings are typical of much of Mortimer's work.

Although most of Mortimer's dramas are traditionally constructed, they treat many of the same issues dealt with by his more experimental contemporaries. For example, the failure of communication is a prominent theme in the one-act plays *The Dock Brief* and *What Shall We Tell Caroline?* (1958), among others. Critics often praise Mortimer's one-act plays for their eloquent dialogue and for his grasp of theatrical convention. However, many find his full-length plays less successful because their plots are either too ambitious or too slight for the longer format. Mortimer is praised perhaps most of all for his ability to incorporate humorous autobiographical anecdotes in his work. For example, the play *A Voyage Round My Father* (1970) is a witty, sensitive portrait of his father, and *Clinging to the Wreckage* (1982) is an autobiographical account of his various occupations and acquaintances. Mortimer has gained recent critical acclaim for his script for *Rumpole of the Bailey* (1975) and his adaptation for television of Evelyn Waugh's novel *Brideshead Revisited* (1981).

(See also *Contemporary Authors,* Vols. 13-16, rev. ed. and *Dictionary of Literary Biography,* Vol. 13.)

© Chris Davies

THE TIMES LITERARY SUPPLEMENT

Answer Yes or No is professional in manner and closely knit. Mr. Mortimer, whose **Rumming Park** has left an agreeable impression, writes with an authority remarkable in a man under 30, and gets his story going with a verve and precision which command the reader's confidence. His hero Ransom, a young Common Law barrister, is isolated by circumstance, and is making his way by devotion to work and ability. The first chapter shows him in court, and the skill with which his nature—humane but sturdy, conscientious but not diffident—is conveyed through action, in a double sense of that word, is admirable. Mr. Mortimer has a mature conception of characters and relationships in public life, but an immature conception of private emotions and conflicts.

Ransom meets a couple called Letts and almost at once falls deeply in love with the unhappy wife, Caroline. A close parallel exists in Ransom's mind between this triangle and one in a defended divorce case in which he is appearing; the story shifts between the two without loss of impetus. It is the unfolding of Letts which causes a decline in the reader's confidence, for that white-faced mental sadist belongs in some pretentious film, and the predicament in which he involves Ransom seems false, too. He is stagey, and so is the culminating scene of violence between the two men. It is sad that Mr. Mortimer, such a persuasive guide in public places, should give private faces "blazing eyes," and make the nice genuine Caroline break out melodramatically: "I'm just a woman of flesh and blood who needs loving, that's all."

"Public and Private Lives," in The Times Literary Supplement (© Times Newspapers Ltd. (London) 1950; reproduced from The Times Literary Supplement *by permission), No. 2525, June 23, 1950, p. 385.**

WALTER ALLEN

It is time a halt was called to titles containing the words "traitor," "treachery" or "betrayal." Mr. Mortimer's novel is the choice of the Book Society, which shows again how unerring is that awesome body's sense of the contemporary: *Like Men Betrayed* is nothing if not the English Novel, Model 1953. It is a highly professional piece of work, but its modishness prevents one from taking it very seriously. Its characters, chilled by cold blasts from Greeneland, brace themselves with a little weak Sartre. In the country, the county families run their feckless riding schools while waiting for their tippling wealthy relations to die. In London, the young man, who has never known security, takes to crime, while his father, the rectitudinous solicitor (yes, as a young man he had wanted to be an artist), prepares to take on his son's guilt and its consequences. . . . In his sourly efficient way [Mr. Mortimer] gives us a brisk and vivid reshuffling of the current cliches of fiction. He writes very well except when his desire for the curt image betrays him into meaninglessness. . . .

Walter Allen, in a review of "Like Men Betrayed," in The New Statesman & Nation *(© 1953 The Statesman & Nation Publishing Co. Ltd.), Vol. XLV, No. 1164, June 27, 1953, p. 785.*

THE TIMES LITERARY SUPPLEMENT

Like Men Betrayed [seems] emotionally thin. . . . The very facility of [Mr. Mortimer's] style betrays him too often, in his neat descriptive phrases, into a cleverness of invention rather than observation which challenges the reader's acceptance. Particularly in many of his passages of scornful satire the reality beneath ceases to be recognizable. However, the exciting and complicated plot, developed rather slowly at first and relying at two vital points on the coincidence of one character receiving a telephone call intended for another, compels and holds the reader's attention and interest.

"Back to the Land," in The Times Literary Supplement *(© Times Newspapers Ltd. (London) 1953; reproduced from* The Times Literary Supplement *by permission), No. 2683, July 3, 1953, p. 425.**

ROGER PIPPETT

Before [Kennet discovers the swindle that is to change several peoples' lives and lead Kennet himself to his death in **"Like Men Betrayed"**], Mr. Mortimer has introduced us to a chain-stitched cross-section of contemporary England, embroidered with a score of richly colored and contrasting characters, kind, hateful and indifferent, greedy and generous, fantastic and familiar. He has led us through dingy London boarding-houses, cozy clubrooms, solid, middle-class homes and "sad pubs that smell of the Middle Ages." He has given us a glimpse of a bleak, remote village in the shires, where men ride to hounds three times a week while their wives "try to light, with blue fingers, paraffin lamps in stone-flagged kitchens."

But, since he is a brooding philosopher as well as a magnetic story-teller, the author never for a moment lets us lose sight of Kennet and all he symbolizes as he moves, almost willingly, to his doom. A passive, sensitive, essentially lonely man, incapable of a mean act, Kennet felt that he had failed in his responsibility to the war-shocked Kit. "Had he not known himself and his limitations so well, he might have succeeded in knowing Kit better. He had been content, perhaps, to admit that the generation which opposed him baffled him—and, when the chance of resignation came, he almost welcomed it."

Perhaps the author only meant to say that Kennet's death redressed the balance—giving his son a sense of destiny.

Roger Pippett, "His Death Redressed the Balance," in The New York Times Book Review *(copyright © 1954 by The New York Times Company; reprinted by permission), March 28, 1954, p. 22.*

LEWIS FUNKE

There are plenty of words in John Mortimer's two one-act plays, **"What Shall We Tell Caroline?"** and **"The Dock Brief,"** But they do not really signify enough.

"What Shall We Tell Caroline?" is one of those allusive and elusive plays in which Mr. Mortimer is dealing with the ineffectualness of human beings in relationship to each other, with that troubling problem of communication. A little song toward the end of the play with the line, to the effect that we are birds in the wilderness gives the clue to what the playwright is trying to say. No one on the stage truly speaks to the others.

Arthur Loudon, a stodgy headmaster, is deeply in love with his wife, but finds it impossible to say so. Instead of endearments he snorts and bellows in his conversations with her. Tony Peters only pretends to be fond of Mrs. Loudon, yet, nevertheless, in feigning affection provides her with the tonic her husband cannot give. None of the adults has any way of communicating with 18-year-old Caroline. What shall they really tell her of life and human beings?

All this Mr. Mortimer wraps in a mixture of real and stream-of-consciousness dialogue. Not all that is spoken between his characters is actually heard by them. A good bit of it is interior reaction to situations. The mixture is not always easy to fathom and one has to dig hard for meaning. It is questionable whether the effort is worth the trouble.

In **"The Dock Brief"** Mr. Mortimer starts off with a touching notion—an old, unsuccessful barrister gets his first chance to defend a criminal. He hobbles into the man's cell aglow with dreams of glory. At last he will have his chance to rise in court, confound the judge, tear at the heart strings of his client he plays out the different approaches he will use, how he will summon different witnesses and deliver the crucial bit of surprise evidence that will turn an open-and-shut case into victory and liberation.

But Mr. Mortimer does not know when to turn off the word-spigot. Although there is humor and sadness of vain dreams in this play, they are inundated. A listener must fight to ward off the stupefication. . . .

"The Dock Brief" has been done with reported success in other cities abroad. It would be interesting to know how that was accomplished.

Lewis Funke, in a review of "What Shall We Tell Caroline?" and "The Dock Brief," in The New York Times *(copyright © 1961 by The New York Times Company; reprinted by permission), November 22, 1961 (and reprinted in* The New York Times Theater

Reviews: 1960-1966, *The New York Times Company & Arno Press, 1961*).

GEORGE WELLWARTH

John Mortimer puts himself firmly on the side of the drama of protest. Like most of the current English writers, however, his protest is a severely limited one. It is not a cosmic, nihilistic protest, as in the French avant-garde drama, but a protest against the oppressiveness of society's rules. It is a protest, furthermore, that has its feet firmly and distinctly planted within the society it protests against. Mortimer is not only against—he is also *for*. He is for those who have been unable to cope with society: for the failures, the flotsam, the drifting scum of society; for the rejects and the defeated; for the hopeless and the numb; and for those who have chosen to conceal their hopelessness even from themselves in a desperate pretence. John Mortimer's plays are the glorification of the failure.

A failure is hardly a heroic figure. Mortimer's failures receive their stature by analogy: they are the antitheses of the organization men. The efficient compromisers are the villains of Mortimer's plays, even though they do not appear in them personally. They are condemned by contrast. Mortimer has no use for the survival-of-the-fittest doctrine, since, as he sees it, the terms of the survival are dictated by those who know they will triumph under those terms, the sum of which constitutes the society we live in.

Although he began his writing career as a novelist, Mortimer's talent definitely does not lie in the direction of the longer stage forms. *The Wrong Side of the Park* (1960) is interesting only as the representative of a type of play much favored by the young English writers. It is a rather clumsily told story of an incipiently schizophrenic housewife in suburban London who is saved on the brink of lunacy by her husband's sudden awakening from the torpor into which his job as a civil servant has sunk him. The interesting thing about this play is its exemplification of a syndrome that appears to afflict most of the current young English playwrights. The syndrome is the writer's need to exorcise his personal drab middle-class background by producing a work in which his origins are denigrated and ripped apart. In Mortimer's play, . . . we see the writer serving his apprenticeship with a play about family life in suburban, semi-detached houses where restless adolescent children rebel against their parents, usually a weak-willed and ineffectual husband married to a stronger but unpleasantly neurotic wife. (pp. 253-54)

The real value and originality of Mortimer's drama lies in his one-act plays. Like Jean Tardieu in France, Mortimer seems to have made the one-act form peculiarly his own. It is here that his failures come into their own—here that they become successes at last by alienating themselves completely from the society that has trodden them down through decreeing terms they have found impossible to honor.

The most successful of Mortimer's one-act plays . . . are *The Dock Brief* and *What Shall We Tell Caroline?* Both of these plays take place in Mortimer's world of the misfits and failures. . . . *The Dock Brief* and *What Shall We Tell Caroline?* are about unsuccessful lawyers, blundering schoolmasters, and families where the children grow up in silence and regret. The lawyer in *The Dock Brief* is a pathetic figure who has gone gray waiting for a "dock brief" (charity case) to show up. Now, at sixty-three years of age, he has finally been chosen to try his first case. It is a murder case, and he has no doubt at all that it will make him famous. . . . He spends most of the time allotted to him for interviewing his client in acting out his pipe dreams of success with the result that when the time comes to go to trial he is totally unprepared. The case is hopeless, anyway. In the second scene we learn that the lawyer has failed again. Instead of the brilliant two or three day address to the jury which was going to move strong men to tears and cause women to faint, he said nothing. No words would come; and so he just sat down again and gave up. His client is convicted, of course, but is immediately afterwards pardoned on the grounds that the incompetence of his lawyer rendered the trial an unfair one. Momentarily depressed, the lawyer cheers up again at the thought that his client, with whom he has become quite friendly, may need some little legal advice in the future. As the curtain falls, both men happily dance out of the cell whistling a gay tune. After a brief excursion into the cruel world of reality for which he is simply unfitted, Morgenhall, the lawyer, scampers back into the dream world where he fiddles away his existence with his crossword puzzles and his dreams of glory. . . . He simply does not have the stamina to make his way in the everyday world; and Mortimer's sympathy is entirely with him and with his kind.

In *What Shall We Tell Caroline?* the debonair pretender becomes a faded London roué who has been an assistant master at a small boys' boarding school on the bleak Norfolk coast for eighteen years. For eighteen years he has kept his spirits up by reminiscing about his days as a gay young blade on the Earl's Court Road. Accompanying himself on a banjo as he tells stories of lurid escapades that probably never happened, he brings a little light into the drab life of the school. . . . The one thing wrong with the household is that Caroline, the headmaster's daughter, has not spoken to anyone for a long time. At the end of the play she finds her voice again and announces that she is going to London. But the play is really about the aging roué who has been hiding out from the reality he constantly talks about and dreams about for eighteen years.

Mortimer's other plays, *I Spy, Call Me a Liar, Lunch Hour, David and Broccoli, Collect Your Hand Baggage,* and *Two Stars for Comfort* are all similar efforts. All of them deal with people who are unable to cope with the world and who seek refuge in their illusions. Mortimer's sympathy is entirely with these characters, for he feels that their rejection of the conditions of society—their mute rebellion as it might be called—is justified. To function in society and be a success is commendable only if we accept the conditions set up by society as correct. This there is no reason to do. The laws of society are purely arbitrary, and there is nothing wrong. Mortimer feels, in receding into an individual world of one's own. Mortimer's view of people is one of personal sympathy. . . . (pp. 255-57)

> George Wellwarth, "John Mortimer: 'The Apotheosis of Failure'," in his *The Theater of Protest and Paradox: Developments in the Avant-Garde Drama (reprinted by permission of New York University Press; copyright © 1964 by New York University), New York University Press, 1964, pp. 253-57.*

JOHN RUSSELL TAYLOR

John Mortimer sees himself as a pretty traditional sort of playwright, in whom traditional influences are at work (Dickens, Chekhov, the Russian novelists), and feels that his admiration for the plays of Pinter and Simpson, the ideas of Osborne and Wesker, does not imply any very close kinship. Many of his critics, particularly those unequivocally left of centre, have tended to agree with him, suggesting that though on a number of occasions he has been bracketed with 'new dramatists' . . . he is really an 'old dramatist' in disguise, writing 'in almost every respect typical Shaftesburiana', as a reviewer in *Encore* put it in connection with *The Wrong Side of the Park.*

Now there is something in this: certainly *The Wrong Side of the Park* in particular is nearer the sort of play which a British dramatist would be writing now if no real challenge to the supremacy of Rattigan had been heard in the theatre than almost any other new play by a writer under forty. But even here there are important differences, and when one looks more closely at Mortimer's one-act plays it rapidly becomes clear that he is after, on a more popular level, the same sort of thing as many of his contemporaries. His subject, like theirs, is more often than not the failure of communication, the confinement to and sometimes the liberation from private dream-worlds; his approach to language is not so far from that of, say, Alun Owen, involving the use of a hypersensitive ear for the way people really talk and a talent for selecting and heightening to produce a fully theatrical eloquence which yet carries the hallmark of reality. . . .

[Mortimer] applies his exploratory techniques to the middle classes in decline rather than the working classes ascendant. . . . (p. 258)

[His] plays take place entirely in a seedy middle-class world of run-down private schools, draughty seaside hotels, nine-to-five offices and the shabbier corners of the courts. *What Shall We Tell Caroline?* and *David and Broccoli* are both set in schools, *The Dock Brief, Two Stars for Comfort,* and at least one of the sketches have law in the background, and so, in a more roundabout way, does *I Spy,* though it is set in a seaside hotel; most of the rest are about office workers at work or at home in faded but 'quite nice' suburbs on the wrong side of the park. The world they present is consistent in its mixture of tragedy and comedy, the mixture being a practical expression at once of Mortimer's views on what the writer should be doing in the modern world and what the dramatist specifically should be offering audiences in the theatre. (p. 259)

Mortimer's championship of 'the lonely, the neglected, the unsuccessful' is the more telling in that it is, strictly, an elevation of them and not a degradation of 'the others'—in Mortimer's plays there are no ready-made villains on whom the blame can be put ('This man would not be lonely and unsuccessful if it were not for . . .'); instead, the seedy and downtrodden are accepted on their own terms, as human beings, mixtures inevitably of good and bad qualities, and then without glossing over or minimizing the bad qualities, Mortimer gradually unfolds the good for our inspection.

The danger in this is obvious enough: that in showing all one's characters in the best possible light one will fall imperceptibly into the sort of sentimental whimsy favoured by Frank Capra and Robert Riskin in such thirties comedies as *Mr Deeds Goes to Town, Mr Smith Goes to Washington,* and *You Can't Take it With You,* in which each character tends to be established by some 'quaint', 'lovable' peculiarity (as though for a contemporary comedy of humours), and a fantasy world of good intentions is hopefully substituted for the real world in which, even at its most comic, everybody does not mean well. Up to now Mortimer has managed to avoid falling into this particular trap, though he is often near enough the brink for his audience to be aware of the danger. Partly it is his taste for the grotesque (Dickens is the obvious parallel here) which saves him, and partly his precise ear for the way people really talk, which enables him, by a sort of sleight of hand if nothing else, to give his plays a certain stiffening of reality whenever they look like going too soft on him. (pp. 260-61)

Mortimer is at his happiest when he does not have to explain directly, but can imply as much explanation as we are entitled to expect in the action of the play as it unrolls. For despite himself Mortimer seems to be at one with other dramatists of his generation in the belief that human behaviour cannot really be explained by some simple formula which makes everything clear; you cannot turn every play into a sort of whodunit—a why-did-he-do-it, perhaps—in which the clues are planted and then just before the curtain someone explains which was the one vital clue to explain a whole personality. Life is seldom if ever as clear-cut as that: all sorts of explanations may fit the facts, and any or all of them may be true; motives are generally so mixed that even the principals in any given event do not know quite why they are acting as they are. When, as in *What Shall We Tell Caroline?* or one or two of his later plays, Mortimer is content just to show us such a situation and leave us to 'explain' it how we will, the result is far more satisfactory than in his cut-and-dried *pièces à thèse,* since then the audience's imagination is quickened instead of deadened, and the dramatist is compelled to integrate cause (what would be explained) and effect (what is actually said and done in the present) into dialogue of a fairly uniform density, instead of letting his play disintegrate into wads of aimless, if for the instant quite entertaining, chatter among which are scattered occasional hard nodules of too clinical explanation.

Several of the later one-act plays offer good examples of this less direct technique, and so do a number of the revue sketches. . . . In these, obviously, the discipline of extreme brevity precludes explanation. The situations have to carry such explanation as they need as graphically and succinctly as possible—and the same applies slightly less forcibly in the one-acters for stage and television. In *Lunch Hour,* for example, we have what is in effect an extended sketch about a couple, a fairly respectable business-man and an office-girl, trying to find somewhere where they can make love in the lunch hour. He is not very expert, chooses a respectable boarding-house near a station and spins the landlady a story about having to talk something over quietly with his wife. But the secretary, being a simple unimaginative soul, begins to act as if what he has said is true, wants to know what was the business which was so urgent she should be summoned down from Scarborough to discuss it, and wonder if she ought to have anything to do with a man who can behave so heartlessly towards his (imaginary) loved ones. The joke is prolonged and elaborated much too far, but at least the characters are permitted simply to reveal themselves in what they say and do and the explanation ('Telling the truth is often a great concealment; we are given away by what we pretend to be') is kept for the preface to the published text.

In *The Encyclopaedist* . . . , the method is similar: an encyclopaedia salesman has three encounters with the same woman and sees three faces of her in three successive phases of her marriage, phases in which the question of knowledgeability plays an important part, hence the relevance of his encyclopaedias. And in *Collect Your Hand Baggage* we have another comedy of misunderstanding when Crispin, the forties bohemian surviving bravely into the sixties, decides to bestow himself as a favour on the daughter of his landlady, plain and therefore, he believes, loveless, only to find that she does not want him, has hardly noticed him, and is about to go off to Paris with someone else altogether. (This is an odd and none-too-well-balanced piece, since the role of the young people who accompany Crispin is never made clear, though they seem to have more significance than the sort of collective straight-man to him they are here required to be. . . .) *Too Late for the Mashed Potato* is another television piece about the role of illusion in life, again very schematic in its demonstration of 'Lies for the sake of truth, infidelity for the sake of fidelity'; a husband revitalizes his marriage by pretending to flirt with a girl in a deserted Italian lakeside resort, and thus satisfying his wife's need for drama.

But arguably the most successful of all the later plays is Mortimer's second foray into the world of school, *David and Broccoli*. . . . Here the scene alternates between two of Mortimer's pet stalking-grounds, the old-fashioned, slightly disreputable private school in North London and a faded residential hotel cluttered with potted plants and tea-room wickerwork. The story is that of a timid, unathletic boy's fear of and animosity towards 'Broccoli' Smith, the rough, powerful, but slow-witted P.T. coach. He has his chance to get even with Broccoli when he discovers Broccoli's weakness—a passion for the elementary occultism of Everyman's Almanac of future events—and exploits it to such effect that he convinces Broccoli that the end of the world is due the very next Thursday, the day of the prize-giving, and thereby brings about a scene as a result of which Broccoli leaves under a cloud, with no other job open to him. Though the central premise of the plot is rather far-fetched, the play scores by the precision with which the backgrounds are evoked and the unsentimental reality of the boys, particularly David, who is a fascinatingly accurate amalgam of overdeveloped intellect and undeveloped understanding: in his terror he sees no farther than the immediate object of his terror, and sees it as something to be disposed of at all costs. But even when Broccoli is routed and thoroughly cut down to size he feels, apparently, no particular compunction about having removed the one security in his victim's pathetic life: he is a child, yet he has vanquished a man, and that is enough. About children at least Mortimer has no illusions, and the end product, though evidently more fantasticated than *What Shall We Tell Caroline?* is as far away as that minor masterpiece from the sentimentality which always tends to soften unduly the sinister and grotesque elements in Mortimer's work.

As much can hardly be said for *Two Stars for Comfort*, his second full-length play, though it does in some respects show an advance on *The Wrong Side of the Park:* it is concentrated fairly and squarely on one character and the events which lead up to his belated moment of truth, and it resists the temptation to tie everything up too neatly with a cut-and-dried explanation of him and his way of life in the last five minutes. But these improvements are counterbalanced by the recurrence in exaggerated form of other faults from Mortimer's earlier work, notably the shameless reduction of minor characters (and even some major characters) to comedy-of-humours stereotypes, each tirelessly parroting variations of his or her *idée fixe*, and the tendency to play what is basically a rather slight and sentimental plot anecdote for considerably more than it is worth. (pp. 265-69)

The most obvious miscalculation in the play is Mortimer's apparent mistaking of this story, eminently suitable as it would be for one of his more insubstantial one-act *comédies larmoyantes*, for the real stuff of tragedy. Neither of the principal characters develops, they just change: Sam right at the end, when like his namesake in *Call Me a Liar* he is persuaded by the action of the girl he is involved with to forsake illusion and embrace reality; Ann, the girl, twice, first of all when she (predictably) succumbs to Sam's advances and the charms of a twirl of the drum-sticks, and then at the end when an unkind burlesque of her relationship with Sam staged by the other young people snaps her back, rather less explicably, to the realities of the situation. But the progression of their affair and the effect it has on them both is made the central theme of the play, a position it is far too weak to sustain. To support it Mortimer has in effect devised two contrasting choruses: the quartet of young people from *Collect Your Hand Baggage,* who represent presumably iconoclastic youth and vitality (though they appear rather softened and the 'bigger and more destructive part' they were intended to play is confined to their cathartic regatta-night entertainment), and the matching quartet of old regulars (the woman whose one subject of conversation is her vanished husband; the schoolmaster obsessed with local history, and so on). For the most part, in fact, these other characters are present just to fill in any gaps in the action with amusing and characterful conversation—which they do quite efficiently, though by this stage in Mortimer's work the device is becoming rather too mechanical for comfort, an over-glib way of inflating a slight inspiration to superficially imposing proportions.

Mortimer's latest full-length stage play, *The Judge* (1966) is more problematical. A judge at the end of his career comes to hold his last assizes in his home town, which he has never returned to during the previous forty years. Evidently he has come back to deal with some unfinished business; evidently, too, he is quietly going off his rocker. He talks darkly of past crimes he has allowed to go unpunished. He expects some sort of protest in court, some challenge of his fitness to judge, and we gather that the crime must be something he has done himself, or connived at, in his youth: it is himself first and foremost that he wants judged. And little by little, from his devious allusions, we can piece together that it was a guilty liaison with a girl living in the cathedral close, that he agreed to her having an abortion, and has been haunted by this, and the wrong he feels he then did her, ever since. Now he has come to square things, to face the accusation he feels must necessarily come from the girl, now a woman in late middle age keeping a run-down antique shop as a front for a sort of casually organized and perhaps largely amateur brothel. By half-time the judge has got a couple of his old schoolmates, now a doctor and a journalist on the local paper (and both regular visitors at 'Aunt Serena's') into such a tizzy that they are ready to start a witchhunt against Serena, whom they imagine to be the object of the judge's obscure fulminations, in order to take the heat off themselves. From this arise some rather unlikely plot manoeuvres, with Serena being not only ostracized by her regulars but set upon in the streets and chased home from the off licenses. And so, finally, to the inevitable confrontation between the judge and his past (Serena), from which, in a slightly unexpected way, he gains nought for his comfort, because not enough for his discomfort.

Basically, there is a good plot here, but in its treatment Mortimer has taken on several liabilities and then loaded things still further against himself by writing the play in the particular style he does. To begin with, it is surely important, for a plot so odd, highly charged and mysterious, that all the people involved should seem at the outset very ordinary and everyday. In particular, the judge, eaten up by a hidden obsession, should seem the model of correctness and sanity, instead of being presented as an evident nutcase from the start. Similarly, it would surely be more effective if his victim were a peacable, respectable body, keeping, perhaps, lodgings for girls studying at the local teacher-training college, instead of the garrulous old bore she is here, wildly over-characterized with endless requests that others should save her life with a ciggy and chats about the Fitzroy and the Café Flore over glasses of cheap vino. It would also help if the various twists and turns of the plot were better motivated. For example, why are the judge's schoolmates so terrorized by him? What can a judge do to clean up local morals in a town where he is holding assize if the police are not playing along with him, as here they patently are not? To remove things even further from familiar reality, the play is written for much of the time in Mortimer's most flowery and picturesque vein, with a number of long addresses straight to the audience which rely on telling us (very eloquently, to be sure) about the town and its atmosphere instead of showing us in the course of the dramatic action. Clearly at long last Mortimer has hit in this play on a plot capable of going the necessary length for a whole evening's entertainment; what a pity, then, that he has not hit on the right style to make it work.

Mortimer remains in many ways an unknown quantity among the new dramatists, if only because he appears too completely knowable. There is no noticeable development between *The Dock Brief* and *The Judge:* each successive work has shown the general expertise, the amazing skill and facility with dialogue, and the thorough practical grasp of the medium for which it was originally intended which marked the first play of all, and the most we can proffer, tentatively, by way of a subsequent discovery is that the full-length play may not be his *forte* and that he should eschew the temptation to point his moral too plainly. Mortimer's world is consistent and instantly recognizable, and he knows his way round it with complete certainty: the question now is will he find it in subsequent works the trap it looks now like becoming, or see it rather as a launching-pad to the discovery of fresh worlds elsewhere? His most recent work does not begin to provide the answer. (pp. 270-72)

> John Russell Taylor, "In the Air: John Mortimer," in his The Angry Theatre: New British Drama (reprinted by permission of Hill and Wang, a division of Farrar, Straus and Giroux, Inc.; in Canada by A D Peters & Co Ltd; copyright © 1962, 1969 by John Russell Taylor), revised edition, Hill and Wang, 1969, pp. 258-72.

THE TIMES LITERARY SUPPLEMENT

John Mortimer is not alone among contemporary playwrights in being at his best in his one-act plays. The same is true of writers as diverse as Ionesco and Peter Shaffer but for very different reasons. With Mr. Mortimer it is not an inability to sustain the development of a character over three acts—he does that quite well with Sam Turner in *Two Stars for Comfort*—but his plot nearly always depends on a narrative structure very much like that of an anecdote. The pattern is a simple one and could easily be spoiled by over-elaboration. The murderer is reprieved because the barrister, so talkative in the cell, becomes too tongue-tied to defend him. The private detective who can find no evidence against the woman he is shadowing starts by dating her and ends by proposing to her. The lunch-hour lovers get so involved in arguing about the fiction the man invents for the hotel manageress that they have no time to go to bed.

In his dramatization of stories like these, Mr. Mortimer does succeed, to some extent, in capturing the flavour of some of the anachronisms of the Macmillan era the half-hearted rearguard action fought by middle-aged middle-class failures trying to pretend that everything was still going to be all right. Mr. Mortimer himself has enormous affection for these incompetent barristers, helpless private detectives, shabby schoolteachers, unloved waitresses and unsuccessful seducers—so much affection, in fact that he loads his own charm on all of them. This has the advantage of making them all lovable and entertaining and the disadvantage of making them all rather too much like each other and rather mannered in their use of words. The dialogue in his four new one-act plays, *Come As You Are,* is less self-conscious than it is in the [one-act plays collected in *Five Plays*], and the language in the latest of these, *Collect Your Hand Baggage,* is already less artificial than in the earliest, *The Dock Brief* and *What Shall We Tell Caroline?* But it is hard to see how Mr. Mortimer got his reputation for writing realistic dialogue.

> "Anecdotal Anachronisms," in The Times Literary Supplement (© Times Newspapers Ltd. (London) 1970; reproduced from The Times Literary Supplement by permission), No. 3578, September 25, 1970, p. 1096.*

CLIVE BARNES

John Mortimer's **"A Voyage Round My Father"** . . . is a rewarding but essentially trivial play. It is autobiographical, and Mr. Mortimer is telling the story of his father, a blind, curmudgeonly lawyer, who never let his disabilities get the better of him, but then, with his sour and easy wit, never got the better of his disabilities.

As a playwright Mr. Mortimer has always seemed to suffer from an inability to distinguish between a character and an eccentric. His portrait of his father is probably totaly truthful, but in dramatic terms it remains a caricature blandly begging for kindness. This father would be a bore if he had sight, and a rather nasty, self-opinionated bore at that. The fact that he was blind adds slightly to his interest, but not enough.

> Clive Barnes, "London Season," in The New York Times (copyright © 1971 by The New York Times Company; reprinted by permission), August 27, 1971 (and reprinted in The New York Times Theater Reviews: 1971-1972, The New York Times Company & Arno Press, 1971, p. 116).*

DOROTHY E. LITT

[*Will Shakespeare: The Untold Story*] is a fictionalized biography. . . . The author has created a chatty, colorful narrator, Jack Rice, a member of Shakespeare's company, to fill in the gaps in what we know of the life. Mortimer, a novelist and playwright, is delightfully imaginative as he reveals the genesis of some of Shakespeare's best lines and scenes. He has steeped himself in the period and in Shakespeareana, apocryphal as well as substantiated; he uses everything that comes to hand with intelligence, wit, and good taste. The book's charm increases in direct proportion to the amount of knowledge the reader brings to it. In the best tradition of Shakespeare-spoofery, as irreverent as Shaw's *Dark Lady of the Sonnets,* as inventive as Wilde's *Portrait of Mr. W. H.,* it is at the same time as full of action and color as a novel by Jeffrey Farnol.

Dorothy E. Litt, in a review of "Will Shakespeare: The Untold Story," in Library Journal *(reprinted from* Library Journal, *July, 1978; published by R. R. Bowker Co. (a Xerox company); copyright © 1978 by Xerox Corporation), Vol. 103, No. 13, July, 1978, p. 1436.*

STANLEY REYNOLDS

[There] is no doubt that Mortimer's Rumpole is like something out of Wodehouse in that he has become, seemingly overnight, an institution like Bertie Wooster and Jeeves. In America they even have a Rumpole Society. But Rumpole, under all that eccentricity and the oceans of wine at Pomeroy's Fleet Street wine bar, is a radical just as his maker John Mortimer is a radical. Underneath the paraphernalia Rumpole carries about—which includes his wife, She Who Must Be Obeyed; Nick, the appalling sociologist son now living happily in the even more appalling Miami, Florida; plus the sometimes very crude tricks of plots there is a continuous radical message being beamed out at us. Perhaps radical is not the best word to use. What it simply means is that Rumpole is always for the weak against the strong, for the little man against the big man and that, surprisingly enough, is a rare place to be, for most people are usually on the other side, right behind the strong against the weak every time.

Rumpole is in the genteel, upper-middle class English radical tradition and a good thing, too, because we've heard a bit too much lately from the Left-wing loonies and the braying asses on the Right. Rumpole, I suppose, when you come down to it, is a Social Democrat. . . .

[*Regina V. Rumpole*] is composed of ***Rumpole for the Defence*** and ***Rumpole's Return***. This last is novel-length and, I think, all the better for it. We are so used to Rumpole in short-story form that it takes you back a bit being confronted with an entire novel, but Mortimer actually cut his literary teeth on novels and he handles this long tale with ease.

In it the great man has been forced into retirement by the appalling Hilda, She Who Must Be Obeyed; by the dreadfully modern son, Nick, who has sunk to being head of the sociology department at a university in Miami, Florida; and by losing ten cases in a row because they were heard by the old mad Bull himself, Judge Bullingham, the curse of Rumpole's legal life.

Rumpole up against the horrors of America is everything you could wish for. Nick is married to an American girl who speaks American, saying things like "poolside" when she means by the side of the swimming pool—Rumpole calls it swimming bath and is so out of sorts with America he even puts inverted commas round "sidewalk". Not surprisingly perhaps, She Who Must Be Obeyed takes to Yankee ways, even starts, Rumpole notices, speaking American. He is in despair. Rumpole dislikes the sunshine. He is homesick for the rain outside Temple Tube station. It is perhaps some measure of Mortimer's genius that you can sit down, positively damp from just glancing out the window, with an evil English indoor gale billowing the old socks, pick up Rumpole and know just what he means about loving the rain.

A lovely little murder back in London brings him out of retirement. It is Rumpole at John Mortimer's best. (p. 1073)

Stanley Reynolds, "Rumpole SDP," in Punch *(© 1981 by Punch Publications Ltd.; all rights reserved; may not be reprinted without permission), Vol. 281, December 9, 1981, pp. 1073-74.**

DAVID PANNICK

Rumpole of the Bailey deserves to take his place among the great barristers of literature. Like Trollope's Chaffanbrass he knows nothing of the law. . . . Like Dickens's Serjeant Buzfuz he plies his trade on behalf of worthless clients by telling each new jury that never before has he approached a case with such feelings of deep emotion and heavy responsibility. . . . The stories written by John Mortimer about Rumpole are already classics of legal literature, at least in the same class as A. P. Herbert's *Uncommon Law* and Theo Mathew's *Forensic Fables*. (p. 789)

[*Regina V. Rumpole*] contains several more short tales and one longer story. It will give further satisfaction to those who know Horace Rumpole and will provide a perfect introduction for anyone who has yet to make his acquaintance.

In addition to Rumpole, the entire cast of legal London is portrayed in caricatures that are wickedly accurate. . . . John Mortimer's style enables him to deflate any ego with a well-aimed sentence. When Rumpole 'applied a torn-off page of the *Criminal Law Review* to the electric fire and lit the small cigar', the value of academic lawyers to the practitioner is effectively demonstrated.

Part of the joy of these stories is the very accurate description they present of the lower judiciary in England. If Mortimer, or anyone else, published such accounts of named judges, an action for contempt of court would be likely to ensue. Only in legal memoirs or in 'fiction' does the convention permit one to evoke the villains on the Bench. The judges before whom Rumpole appears are perverse and, often, biased; they are ignorant of the ways of the world; and they are deferential or rude to witnesses depending on the status of those who have the misfortune to give evidence before them. Only a counsel of Rumpole's experience (and lack of ambition) can afford to reply in kind to the discourtesy emanating from the Bench. The reasons for the inadequacy of those who sit in judgment are explored. Appointment to the Bench depends not on satisfying defined criteria, but on being recommended to the Lord Chancellor's Office. (pp. 789-90)

Rumpole himself remains something of an enigma. He has his failures in court, but he frequently displays remarkable powers of advocacy; he is a shrewd judge of character; and he often has judges eating out of his hand. Moreover, he exercises powers of detection that would do credit to Scotland Yard. Yet we are asked to believe that he is a hack barrister whose career has never progressed. High-class crooks should be queuing up to secure the services of such a wizard of the courts.

The world of Rumpole is partly fictitious. Although the guilty are sometimes acquitted, it is very rare for Rumpole to see the innocent convicted. Furthermore, at the end of his cases (and often well before the end, by reason of his intuition) Rumpole finds out what really happened. The adversary process of a real trial more often leaves the truth mysteriously hidden, covered over by the evasions and half-truths of competing contentions. However, if the Rumpole stories, and the advocacy of their chief protagonist, may occasionally fail to convince, they are never less than a delight. (p. 790)

David Pannick, "The Rumpole Enigma" (© British Broadcasting Corp. 1981; reprinted by permission of David Pannick), in The Listener, *Vol. 106, No. 2740, December 17 & 24, 1981, pp. 789-90.*

WILLIAM BOYD

In the final episode of *Brideshead Revisited* Charles Ryder and Julia sit on the steps in the enormous house and agree to part. They're both weeping and generally inarticulate, but one of the 'broken sentences' Charles manages to mutter between stifled sobs is 'So long to say so little'. It could serve quite nicely for the last word on this paradoxically compelling serial. Rather like [Evelyn Waugh's] book itself, I suspect that it was the first half that got us watching the second. The departure of Sebastian, leaving centre stage to Charles Ryder, consigned most of the final episodes to a level of infuriating dullness. It's a foreseeable defect, but one which scriptwriter John Mortimer seemed reluctant to avoid.

There's been much talk of Mortimer's faithfulness to the text, but in changing medium—from novel to TV series—such commendable rectitude can often be technically inept if not wrongheaded. This was particularly evident in episode six, where Julia is finally led on stage. Almost the entire episode was a sepia flashback of the courtship of Rex Mottram. In the book this largely takes the form of straightforward reported speech, but there are also some pages of direct conversation—*post facto* reminiscence by Julia and Charles. This is a clumsy device in the novel, but on the screen it comes across as sheer thoughtlessness. The voice-over renditions of this dialogue, and the clear intimacy that the interlocuters share, effectively deprive the forthcoming Charles/Julia romance of any vestige of suspense. We know from the very outset of Julia's appearance, while we're still in the process of learning about her and Rex, that she and Charles will end up together. One minute Charles is an art student in Paris, then suddenly we're presented with a view of him on an ocean liner arm in arm with Julia. To someone who doesn't know the book such methods of moving the story on must appear bafflingly amateurish.

Mortimer, of course, is simply reproducing Waugh's own struggles with the plot, and to that extent is blameless. But, while Mortimer's adaptation is by and large unobtrusive, he can't entirely escape responsibility as he does occasionally contribute material of his own.

The most notable expansion has been of the general strike episode. The strike, and the party Charles and Boy Mulcaster go to while it's on, occupy some five and a half pages in the novel. In the serial these peripheral events took up an entire episode. The party scenes in particular had to be supplied almost entirely by Mortimer. This isn't a bad thing; in fact these scenes were amusing and entertaining. The point is that if you can take these sort of liberties with the text on one occasion, then there are no grounds for not taking them on others, and the excuse of 'scrupulous adherence' is no longer viable. (p. 23)

William Boyd, "Back to Brideshead," in New Statesman *(© 1982 The Statesman & Nation Publishing Co. Ltd.), Vol. 103, No. 2650, January 1, 1982, pp. 23-4.*

LORD GOODMAN

John Mortimer's book [*Clinging to the Wreckage*] has a thoroughly misleading title. It is designed to enlist a little pathetic sympathy for someone carried along like a piece of flotsam without the courage or determination to strike out for the shore. It would be difficult—judging from the book itself—to find anyone less shipwrecked than John Mortimer and less likely to pursue this policy if shipwrecked. At every stage Mr. Mortimer demonstrates a firmness of intention which makes the title slightly fraudulent.

In the Wild West idiom, 'a man's gotta do what a man's gotta to do': but when and where a man has 'gotta' write an autobiography is a matter for debate. The interesting question is why Mr. Mortimer chose this moment of his life to write this book. One senses a motivation more pressing than the importunities of hopeful publishers. . . . [There] can be no doubt that Mr. Mortimer had a book, and an interesting book, inside him. It is unnecessary to say that his autobiography is immensely readable. He is a distinguished, if not a great dramatist; he has evolved an imaginative and immensely popular television series; he is first-class in discussion programmes on television and, presumably, radio, and is careful not to be overexposed; and he has recently developed into one of the best newspaper interviewers in the country. He writes book reviews which are usually more entertaining than the books he is reviewing. It follows that what he has to say about his life must be of interest. The book has received, in almost all quarters, unqualified and well-deserved praise for its readability. But I must confess it leaves me dissatisfied.

I can claim to be a friend of John Mortimer, although not a close friend. I have never mixed in his circles. But I know and have seen enough of him to doubt whether the book presents a full picture. Since he is an honest man, it certainly presents a true picture so far as it goes, and I am not even sure that the author is conscious of what he has left out. John Mortimer is an interesting and exciting original—a rare commodity in this country today. He is amiable (the word 'Pickwickian' struggles to emerge but he is worthy of a less cloying adjective), witty, warm-hearted, generous and humane. it is sad to say that these qualities do not emerge from the book with any great clarity. The book presents, and was clearly intended to present, the picture of a cool, dispassionate and largely uncommitted observer. Mr. Mortimer may see himself in this light, but few other people will so see him. For someone like him, it would have taken quite a feat of dissembling to achieve this result. . . .

[Although] he espouses unconventional causes he represents the essential upper-middle-class Englishman, pursuing some erratic notions. (p. 11)

The book is episodic and was obviously written at some speed. The great autobiographies of the world depend, I think, on the attention to detail with which they are written: this book is self-indulgent in that there is detail only of those matters which have retained his interest. We gather that he was—but is probably no longer—a supporter of the Labour Party. Politics are clearly not for him, although he would seem to be natural material for the SDP. The book is marred by a certain calculated crudity in some of his descriptions of his emotional life and by one absolutely nauseating jest. This does not imply any genuine coarseness of character so much as the determination to maintain an emotional nonchalance lest the reader should suspect that events have made a deeper and sharper impact than the author likes to admit.

It is in relation to his legal career that the book is most disappointing, and for two disparate reasons. Legal memoirs are in special need of detailed recollection. What the Judge actually said to the impertinent advocate and what exactly was the response; how the late F. E. Smith insulted the Judge with sufficient forensic skill to avoid evil consequences; how Marshal Hall demonstrated the pistol and how his clerk brought in an air cushion for him to sit on. It is details such as these which grip the interest, and in such details the book is notably lacking. The two main interests in his life I share. The theatre, to which he has made such a distinguished contribution, has been a love of mine, incredibly enough, for sixty years or more. . . . John Mortimer adds little of novelty in his account of his theatrical life. We do not smell grease-paint from the pages and the occasional reference to a distinguished theatrical figure is insufficient to make the book a significant one about the stage. His prominence in the law arises through his participation in a number of cases to defend the 'book' and the 'writer' against intolerable outside interference. Here he has justifiably acquired a reputation as a freedom fighter, but this, alas, does not make him a legal progressive. (pp. 11-12)

I enjoyed reading [John Mortimer's] book and recommend it warmly to those who want something to wile away the odd hour, but I have a feeling that we will one day get a more profound account of his life from this very remarkable man. That book may be less readable and sell fewer copies, but it will tell us more about the author than he is at present prepared to divulge. (p. 12)

Lord Goodman, "Aversion Theory" (appears here by permission of the London Review of Books and the author), in London Review of Books, May 20 to June 2, 1982, pp. 11-12.

V. S. PRITCHETT

The debt of autobiography to the antics of extraordinary fathers as they appear to their sons is native to English comedy. In **"Clinging to the Wreckage"** . . . , Mr. John Mortimer, who is equally distinguished as a lawyer and as a playwright, draws on this powerful source. His discursive narrative is often as hilarious, if not as innocent, as early Wodehouse; it is also often touching, warm, and wise. When he is combative, he is also tolerant of his bizarre of dubious characters. He is as tender with his pugnacious father as he is cheerfully candid about himself. The title of the book is dead right: both parties, in their differing ways, had to cling to wreckage; they did not sink, but, with dogged good humor, they clung. The stoical father's case was more desperate than the son's. A formidable barrister, the father went blind in middle age yet tapped his way to court and argued his cases to the end of his life. He was determined not to be a pitiable figure. On the contrary, he was alert; he used his blindness resourcefully. . . . A father who on his deathbed can cry out "I'm always angry when I'm dying" is a man of parts.

So is the son, in another way. He is myopic, which enables him to see things in a cheering mist. He wanted to be a poet and novelist, and turned to the law to earn his bread and butter. Very slowly, distracted eventually by a large family, he found his way to the theatre and films—scriptwriting. . . . The difficulty of reconciling a literary mind and the practices of advocacy often crops up in this book. (p. 166)

[As] a barrister-would-be-writer Mr. Mortimer faced a dilemma: "The writer cannot help exposing himself, however indecently. Every performance he gives, although cloaked in fiction, reveals his secret identity." The distinction seems to have puzzled judges in the well-known English obscenity cases of the last twenty years—such as the attempt to ban the novel "Last Exit to Brooklyn," in which Mr. Mortimer appeared for the defense. . . . In his own passionate hostility to censorship, however, Mr. Mortimer found himself in a dangerous situation as a lawyer. He had come, he says, to believe in the truth of what he was saying. He was failing to suspend disbelief.

All that he has to say about the peculiar habits of British law is amusing, and particularly the shoptalk, though it must be said that lawyers' conversation often degenerates into anecdotage. (pp. 166, 69)

After the usual public-school roughhouse at Harrow, which demanded dandified clothes, Mr. Mortimer caught Byronic notions, but at first the only girls who could attract him were boyish. At Oxford, he was the puzzled heterosexual when homosexuality was the fashion. . . . He came down during the war to dismal London to live among pacifists who had noncombatant jobs, and began his struggles to get his start at the bar, wrote a novel, and floated from pubs to bed-sitters in the gray period when sex seemed to come in like the first sight of scampi on restaurant menus, happily "off-ration." . . . Mr. Mortimer writes well of this drab bohemia. Then, suddenly, the would-be Byron turns into the family man with a vengeance. The young hack in the divorce courts and the rising dramatist becomes, perhaps by contagion, a co-respondent himself and marries a talented young novelist with four daughters. It seems that the lonely child longed for a real, ready-made family, to which he could adoringly add. (p. 170)

The marriage lasted for years. Why it broke up (though without acrimony) is not clear. There is no reason that it should be. Mr. Mortimer's narrative simply dodges into impressionistic scenes. One suspects that the classic farces of Feydeau, so intricately boxed together—and which he has translated—came to replace the cult of Byron's blend of puritan romanticism and robust common sense. In Feydeau, farce is Greek tragedy turned upside down. But, pausing for an introspective moment, Mr. Mortimer writes of the stunning sense of loneliness he felt when his father died; then of a "flight" like Gauguin's, from family life to an emotional Tahiti and in search of an adolescence he had "never enjoyed." Had he been under an arresting spell in his father's company? We must make what we can of this part of Mr. Mortimer's plea in the court of private life. (pp. 170-71)

V. S. Pritchett, "John Mortimer" (© 1982 by V. S. Pritchett; reprinted by permission of Literistic, Ltd.), in The New Yorker, Vol. LVIII, No. 36, October 25, 1982, pp. 166, 169-71.

R(asipuram) K(rishnaswami) Narayan
1906-

Indian novelist and short story writer.

Narayan is one of India's most prominent contemporary authors. He is most noted for the creation of Malgudi, a mythical town in southern India which provides the setting for most of Narayan's novels and short stories. Some see Malgudi as a composite of Madras, Narayan's birthplace, and Mysore, where he has lived most of his life. Narayan's evocation of Malgudi has been compared with William Faulkner's Yoknapatawpha County, largely due to the highly developed sense of place and the intimate descriptions of the inhabitants and their daily lives.

Malgudi is a small village peopled by the lower and middle classes. Most of the Malgudi stories center on the struggles and triumphs of seemingly insignificant people such as the title characters in *The Financial Expert* (1952), *The Guide* (1958), *The Vendor of Sweets* (1967), and *The Painter of Signs* (1976). These characters typically strive for self-identity and awareness; some rise above their situation and achieve self-fulfillment, others never quite succeed, but all of them retain a dignified, calm acceptance of fate, which is a significant aspect of the Hindu religion. Their struggles often involve a conflict between tradition and the modern world; their self-discovery and happiness are often found in a return to the past rather than an emergence into the future.

Critics frequently praise Narayan's natural and unaffected use of the English language. Although he writes in English, it has been noted that he does not write with a Western audience in mind. He captures the essence of the Indian way of life and the Indian sensibility through the unspoken assumptions and convictions of his nation, which lie at the heart of his work and are the matter from which Malgudi is formed. It is with a compassionate yet detached approach that Narayan portrays the subtleties of his major and minor characters. His success in creating a village which stands as a metaphor for both India and the human condition partly stems from his use of irony and satire while maintaining the dignity of his characters. In his understated manner, Narayan is calling for personal and social growth in modern India, while simultaneously celebrating humanity's will to survive.

(See also *CLC*, Vol. 7 and *Contemporary Authors*, Vols. 81-84.)

WILLIAM WALSH

It is odd at a time when we are beginning to pay attention to Commonwealth writers that a writer of the character and maturity of R. K. Narayan should hardly have been noticed at all. It is true that some of the more obvious motives directing us to these writers probably do not operate in respect of Narayan. His themes are not particularly contemporary, fashionable or provocative. . . . Nor does his language work with the peasant vigour which we are apt to find so attractive in the West Indians, our current novelists having elected, either from inclination or simply helplessness, to restrict themselves to very few of the language's possibilities. Narayan uses a pure and

© Joyce Ravid 1983

limpid English, easy and natural in its run and tone, but always an evolved and conscious medium, without the exciting, physical energy—sometimes adventitiously injected—that marks the writing of the West Indians. Narayan's English, in its structure and address, is a moderate, traditional instrument but one abstracted from the context in which it was generated—the history, the social condition, the weather, the racial memory—and transferred to a wholly different setting—brutal heat and hovering vultures, flocks of brilliant, glistening parrots, jackals rippling over the rubbish dumps, an utter shining clarity of light and the deadly grey of an appalling poverty. It is clear of the palpable suggestiveness, the foggy taste, the complex tang, running through every phrase of our own English. What it has instead is a strange degree of translucence. Unaffected by the opacity of a British inheritance or by the powerful, positive quality of a language which as we use it can never be completely subordinated to our private purposes, Narayan's language is beautifully adapted to communicate a different, an Indian sensibility.

By now Narayan is the author of a fairly substantial body of fiction, some eight or nine novels. . . . The world established in these novels (although 'established' is too harsh a term for the delicate skill in implication everywhere evident) impresses the reader with its coherence, its personal stamp and idiom. The action is centred in the small town of Malgudi in Mysore. . . . The detail suggests, surely and economically, the special flavour of Malgudi, a blend of oriental and pre-1914 British, like an Edwardian mixture of sweet mangoes and malt vinegar—a wedding with its horoscopes and gold-edged, elegantly printed invitation cards; tiny shops with the shopkeeper hunched on the counter selling plantains, betel-leaves, snuff and English biscuits; the casuarina and the Post Office Savings Bank; the brass pots and the volumes of Milton and Carlyle; the shaved head and ochre robes of the *sanyasi* and Messrs. Binns's catalogue of cricket bats. Especially is this true of the detail of the public life, of the shabby swarming streets and the stifling bye-lanes, the cobbles of Market Road and the sands on Sarayu bank, the banyan tree outside the Central Co-operative Land Mortgage Bank (built in 1914), the glare of Kitson lamps and the open drain down Vinayah Mudali Street. (pp. 91-2)

But although these novels convey so full and intimate a sense of place, they are not in any limiting way regional. They send out long, sensitive feelers to the villages where the inhabitants are 'innocent and unsophisticated in most matters excepting their factions and fights', and to the cities where they are 'so mechanical and impersonal'. They concern themselves too with such varied spheres of interest as business, education, journalism, filmmaking, money-lending. One mustn't, of course, exaggerate this matter of the scope of reference. Narayan does work by focusing his attention sharply. Part of his strength is never to ignore his instinct for limitation. But he has the serious artist's gift for achieving representativeness by concentration. His preoccupation is with the middle class, a relatively small part of an agricultural civilisation and the most conscious and anxious part of the population. Its members are neither too well off not to know the rub of financial worry nor too indigent to be brutalised by want and hunger. They may take their religion more easily than the passionately credulous poor but even in those with a tendency towards modernity one is always aware under the educated speech of the profound murmur of older voices, of 'Lakshmi, the Goddess of Wealth, the spouse of God Vishnu, who was the Protector of Creatures'. It is the members of the middle class who are psychologically more active, in whom consciousness is more vivid and harrowing, that Narayan chooses for his heroes—modest, unselfconfident heroes, it is true. They have some room for independent, critical existence; but there is always a tension between this and that deep source of power, the family where the women rather than the old represent 'Custom and Reason' and know 'what is and what is not proper'. The family indeed is the immediate context in which the novelist's sensibility operates, and his novels are remarkable for the subtlety and conviction with which family relationships are treated. . . . (p. 93)

It is against the presence of the town, firmly and freshly evoked, and amid a net of family relationships, each thread of which is finely and clearly elaborated, that Narayan's heroes engage in their characteristic struggles. The conditions of the struggle vary from novel to novel, the stress is highly particularised, the protagonist may be a student, a teacher, a financial expert, a fighter for emancipation. One still discerns beneath the diversity a common pattern, or predicament. What is so attractive about it is the charm and authenticity of its Indian colouring; what makes it immediately recognisable is that it seems to belong to a substantial human nature. The primary aim of all these characters to achieve, in the words of Chandran in *The Bachelor of Arts,* 'a life freed from distracting illusions and hysterics'. . . . At first the intention is obscure, buried under the habits of ordinary life, personal responsibilities and—since this is India—a heavy, inherited burden. The novels plot the rise of this intention into awareness, its recognition in a crisis of consciousness, and then its resolution, or resolutions, since there are more often than not several mistaken or frustrated efforts at a resolution.

This theme—it doesn't seem extravagant to call it the aspiration towards spiritual maturity—is sustained throughout Narayan's work. Clearly it is one with its own special dangers. How easily it could slide into formlessness or puff itself into grandiosity. It is a remarkable achievement—given such a theme and an Indian setting—that Narayan's work is singularly free of pretentiousness. A cool sympathy, a highly developed sense of human discrepancy, a rare feeling for the importance and the density of objects—these check any straining after undue significance or any tendency to lapse into a search for large truths about life. In particular each stage of the impulse towards maturity is defined with meticulous accuracy in minutely specified circumstances, so that the reader is left not with a vague scheme of some dialectical progress but the conviction of an individual living his chequered, stumbling life. Let me give an illustration of this. Here is an example of one of these young men—it is Krishna and it occurs on the first page of *The English Teacher*—at the beginning of his development when what I have called the impulse or aspiration is still too dim to be recognized and when it simply produces vague feelings of dissatisfaction and irritable moods of brooding and analysis:

> The urge had been upon me for some days past to take myself in hand. What was wrong with me? I couldn't say, some sort of vague disaffection, a self-rebellion I might call it. The feeling again and again came upon me that as I was nearing thirty I should cease to live like a cow (perhaps a cow, with justice, might feel hurt at the comparison), eating, working in a manner of speaking, walking, talking, etc.— all done to perfection, I was sure, but always leaving behind a sense of something missing.
> (pp. 94-5)

The issue from this malaise comes about through some critical event which precipitates a crisis of consciousness and a new effort of will. In *The English Teacher* the event is the illness and death of Krishna's wife, but more often it is a meeting or a series of meetings. The meetings may be disconcerting or terrifying, bewildering or exalting. In *The Financial Expert,* Margayya, perhaps Narayan's most brilliant single comic creation, gradually realises his desire for a life 'freed from illusions' (but for him this means ironically a life dedicated to the cult of money—not money which with gross simplicity is spent across the counter of a shop but money as a beautiful, living force) in a series of encounters: first with Arul Dass, the dignified peon of the Co-operative Bank who shows up Margayya's utter insignificance, then with the strangely impressive priest in the seedy temple who rehearses him in rituals for propitiating the Goddess of Wealth, then with Dr. Pal, 'journalist, correspondent and author', whose 'sociological' work, *Bed Life,* (later changed to *Domestic Harmony*) combining the Kama-Sutra with Havelock Ellis eventually makes Margayya's fortune, and finally with Mr. Lal, the large, astute, but fundamentally uncomprehending businessman. The effect of these meetings, the effect of Sriram's exalting meeting with Gandhi in *Waiting for the Mahatma* or Chandran's baffling meeting with the middle-aged rake in Madras in *The Bachelor of Arts,* is to wake the character from 'an age-old somnolence', from what he now sees to have been his illusory and hysterical past and to determine him wholly in favour of a completely new life.

If the analysis of the subject's struggle to extricate himself from the habitual, dreamy automatism of his past—and in a country like India where the influence of the given is so powerful, the severity of the effort required must be arduous and intense—if this shows Narayan's gift for serious moral analysis, then the various solutions adopted by his *personae* in the search for another, more conscious life, exhibit his remarkable comic talent. (Not of course that the fiction offers a neatly logical division just like this. The serious and the comic flow in and out of one another throughout in an intricate, inseparable alliance.) Tracts of human experience are looked at with an affectionately ridiculing eye, and with that kind of humour in which the jokes are also a species of moral insight. Such treatment brings out the note of the bizarre, of human queerness, in the activities of many sorts of people, business men, printers, teachers, holy men, press agents, money-lenders. At our most commonplace we are all exotic if scrutinised by a fresh eye. The range is impressive but it has to be said that it follows naturally on Narayan's reading of the key experience at the heart of his novels. Since it was a meeting, the intervention of human difference, human otherness, into the hero's narcissistic world which first shattered it for him, he feels in response that he has to break out of his solipsistic circle into a novel, even a deliberately alien, field of action. To evoke so much variety with such casual, convincing authority and to make it also organic and functional testify to a notable and original talent.

Sometimes these solutions end in a moment of illumination like Krishna's vision of his dead wife in **The English Teacher,** 'a moment for which one feels grateful to Life and Death', or in a total reverse like Margayya's bankruptcy, or even for Raju in *The Guide* in death. Often they show a character now more solid yet also more conscious, more finished yet more sensitive, accepting, though with misgivings and backslidings, the responsibilities of ordinary life. Always they conclude on a note of acceptance. . . . 'Accepting' indeed, is the word which best defines his attitude, not just here but Narayan's attitude generally in the face of his experience. 'Welcome' would be too shrill and hearty, 'resignation' too passive and submissive. In any case his attitude is too nimble with irony for one or the other. And that irony, it should be noted, is an irony of recognition, not an irony of correction.

Perhaps irony is too sharp a word for the calm scrutiny turned on these ardent young men and earnest old ones. Irony has a social reference and the characters in these novels seem to be tested against something deeper than conscious, formulated standards. And irony is in place in the presence of corruption, but all these people, even the seedy, the stupid and the vain, retain what Lawrence called 'a peculiar, nuclear innocence'. The naïveté of being human: that is the daring subject of this decidedly self-effacing writer.

For Narayan is not a pushing or intrusive novelist. He has no anxiety to be tugging at our sleeve or to be giving us a knowing look. He has no message, no doctrine. The half-baked is not an item in his diet. The acceptance of life which his art expresses has no doubt a root in the national condition. One feels that a more than individual sensibility, more than simply personal categories and feelings, are operating under the surface. But his acceptance, a kind of piety towards existence, isn't simply an inherited temperament with its corresponding technique of passive reflection. It is something which has to be worked towards, grown up to, gradually matured. Nor is it—as I mean to imply by calling it 'piety'—in any way rapt or mystical but altogether homely and human. It includes delight in the expressive variety of life, cognisance of its absurdities, mockery at its pretensions and acknowledgement of its difficulties. And like other kinds of piety, other sorts of tradition, it tends to focus itself in objects. Objects become hallowed with more than their own nature and invested with singular and lasting importance. This appreciation of the weight, the form, the value of *things* is both a feature of the temperament sustained throughout these novels and a device of the art employed in their construction. It pins down and solidifies the lightness and fluency of a manner that might otherwise be too evasive, too 'spiritual'. The effect of Krishna's clock, of his father's 'steel pen with a fat green wooden handle' and his ink made up by hand in a careful, yearly ceremony, or Sriram's teak and canvas chair, is to help to enclose the souls of these people in flesh, pitted, worn and ordinary flesh. Here is an example of this particularising power of objects at work, a passage from **Mr. Sampath** which gives a new meaning to the words, 'an object of sentimental value':

> He prayed for a moment before a small image of Nataraja which his grandmother had given him when he was a boy. This was one of the possessions he had valued most for years. It seemed to be a refuge from the oppression of time. It was of sandal wood, which had deepened a darker shade with years, just four inches high. The carving represented Nataraja with one foot raised and one foot pressing down a demon, his four arms outstretched, with his hair flying, the eyes rapt in contemplation, an exquisitely poised figure. His grandmother had given it to him on his eighth birthday. She had got it from her father, who discovered it in a packet of saffron they had brought from the shop on a certain day. It had never left Srinivas since that birthday. It was on his own table at home, or in the hostel, wherever he might be. It had become part of him, the little image. He often sat before it, contemplated its proportions and addressed it thus: 'Oh, God, you are trampling a demon under your foot, and you show us a rhythm, though you appear to be still. May a ray of that light illumine my mind.' He silently addressed it thus. He never started his day without spending a few minutes before this image.

The permanence of objects makes them a protection against the oppression of time. Clearly the direct reference here is to the Indian scene, to the hard agricultural tradition, the vast distances, the ruthless climate, the terrible poverty. But it seems to me to have as well, like so much in Narayan's writing, a measure of the wider validity that belongs to genuine works of art—the universal imprisoned but visible in the particular. In utterly different conditions, where nobody's grandmother could have handed down an image of Nataraja discovered by her father in a packet of saffron, we are probably like Srinivas and 'grasp the symbol but vaguely'. And yet as we contemplate its proportions we are not, I think, deceived in detecting through all the appearances of stillness and strangeness a rhythm, the common and extraordinary rhythm of life. (pp. 96-9)

William Walsh, "The Intricate Alliance: The Novels of R. K. Narayan," in A Review of English Literature *(© Longmans, Green & Co. Ltd. 1961), Vol. 2, No. 4, October, 1961, pp. 91-9.*

V. S. NAIPAUL

The virtues of R. K. Narayan are Indian failings magically transmuted. I say this without disrespect: he is a writer whose work I admire and enjoy. He seems forever headed for that *aimlessness* of Indian fiction—which comes from a profound doubt about the purpose and value of fiction—but he is forever rescued by his honesty, his sense of humour and above all by his attitude of total acceptance. He operates from deep within his society. Some years ago he told me in London that, whatever happened, India would go on. He said it casually; it was a conviction so deep it required no stressing. It is a negative attitude, part of that older India which was incapable of self-assessment. It has this result: the India of Narayan's novels is not the India the visitor sees. He tells an Indian truth. Too much that is overwhelming has been left out; too much has been taken for granted. There is a contradiction in Narayan, between his form, which implies concern, and his attitude, which denies it; and in this calm contradiction lies his magic which some have called Tchekovian. He is inimitable, and it cannot be supposed that his is the synthesis at which Indian writing will arrive. The younger writers in English have moved far from Narayan. In those novels which tell of the difficulties of the Europe-returned student they are still only expressing a personal bewilderment; the novels themselves are documents of the Indian confusion. The only writer who, while working from within the society, is yet able to impose on it a vision which is an acceptable type of comment, is R. Prawer Jhabvala. And she is European. (pp. 227-28)

V. S. Naipaul, "Fantasy and Ruins," in his An Area of Darkness *(copyright © 1964 by V. S. Naipaul; reprinted by permission of the author), A. Deutsch, 1964, pp. 197-229.**

PERRY D. WESTBROOK

The first of R. K. Narayan's three volumes of short stories, *An Astrologer's Day and Other Stories* (1947), contains thirty pieces, all of which had previously appeared in the Madras *Hindu*. Thus they had been written for, and presumably read and enjoyed by, the readership of one of India's greatest English-language newspapers. Though this readership would include most of the British, Anglo-Indians, and Americans living in South India, it would be made up overwhelmingly of true Indians. It is an important point. Narayan is an Indian writing for Indians who happen to read English. He is not interpreting India for Westerners. . . .

Paradoxically, however, though Narayan's short pieces have been welcomed in the *Hindu* for thirty years, his novels have never been popular in India. . . . (p. 41)

Any reader of Narayan is aware that his stories are cut from very much the same cloth, both in quality and in pattern, as his novels. There is no intrinsic difference to explain why in the same cities where his novels are obtainable, several thousand or more subscribers to the *Hindu* read him with gusto. (p. 42)

The newspaper origins of the short stories would tend to place them in the category of reporting on Indian life and thus make them more acceptable to readers who would ignore his longer and more ambitious works. The reportorial quality is especially marked in his second collection, *Lawley Road,* in which the selections are sketches and vignettes rather than plotted stories. In *An Astrologer's Day* the tales also accurately mirror Indian life and character, but most of them appear to have been chosen for the ingenuity of their plots. The title story, **'An Astrologer's Day'**, is a good example. The description of the astrologer pursuing his profession on the sidewalk provides an entirely typical glimpse of Indian street life. The astrologer himself, a fake driven into imposture by hard luck, is well drawn. The trickiness of the plot (its O. Henry quality) results from the coincidence of the astrologer's being requested, during a day's business, to forecast the fortune of a man he recognizes as one whom he had stabbed and left for dead years ago. . . . [More] than half the tales in *An Astrologer's Day* depend on such twists for their effect. Many of them have other merits as well, such as compelling atmosphere or a memorable character, but perhaps the most justifiable of them are those which present ghosts. **'An Accident'** vividly conjures up on a lonely mountain road the ghost of a man killed in an automobile accident who now devotes himself to helping other motorists in distress. **'Old Man of the Temple'** evokes the mystery and desolation of one of the ruined temples along the South Indian highways. **'Old Bones'** exploits the atmosphere of the more isolated of the *dak* bungalows (government-operated overnight hostels). These are skilfully told stories of pure entertainment.

But some of the stories in *The Astrologer's Day* do not depend upon coincidence or some strange circumstance. The most impressive are those that open a window on to the bleak, tedious lives of the white-collar workers of India, that large segment of the population who drag out their lives at forty or fifty rupees a month in government or business employment. Examples are **'Forty-Five a Month'** and **'Fruition at Forty'**, accounts of dreary, lifelong wage-slavery. In depicting such prisoned lives Narayan is at his best, even in stories freighted with 'surprise endings'. (pp. 42-3)

Narayan's second volume of stories appeared . . . almost ten years after *An Astrologer's Day.* It is also compiled from writings previously printed in the *Hindu*, but contains fewer elaborately contrived stories. Named *Lawley Road* after a typical thoroughfare in the typical, though fictitious, South Indian city of Malgudi, the volume is made up of sketches, character studies, and anecdotes indigenous to just such a street in such a town. They are the more powerful for the absence of gimmicks, and are marked by naturalness, by the easy pace of Narayan's novels, and the informal style of a leisurely raconteur. (p. 44)

If there is an all-pervasive theme in Narayan's work it is that human beings are human beings, not gods. Men and women can make flights toward godhood, but they always fall a bit short. (p. 45)

Narayan has said, 'My focus is all on character. If his personality comes alive, the rest is easy for me.' Certainly in the *Lawley Road* collection, the stories of character are the most absorbing, and where other considerations obtrude, character usually remains the dominant interest. Thus in **'The Martyr's Corner'** the focus is always on the *chapati* seller rather than on the rather violent action; always before the reader's eyes is the little vendor—his drab monotonous life, his comments on his customers, his manipulation of the officials who could ruin him, above all his attitude towards existence, his sense of occupying a niche in the social order, the sense of dignity and satisfaction that transforms sheer dreariness into human significance. (p. 47)

Narayan believes that modern writers, especially those of the West or under Western influence, have strayed far from their original function of providing pleasure and instruction to the masses. He is uncomfortable about recent academic interest in his own writing. 'Literature', he asserts, 'is not a branch of study to be placed in a separate compartment, for the edification only of scholars, but a comprehensive and artistic medium of expression to benefit the literate and illiterate alike.' Though far from achieving this purpose himself in his own country, where he writes in a tongue known mainly to the educated elite, perhaps he comes nearest to it in his short stories, at least those of the first two volumes, which first appeared in a widely circulated newspaper. (pp. 50-1)

> Perry D. Westbrook, "The Short Stories of R. K. Narayan" (copyright Perry D. Westbrook; by permission of Hans Zell Publishers, an imprint of K. G. Saur Verlag), in Journal of Commonwealth Literature, No. 5, July, 1968, pp. 41-51.

HARISH RAIZADA

While summing up R. K. Narayan's characteristics as an author, the first thing that strikes us most is the dispassionate manner in which he judges the Indian life of his own times. Like other great artists he also possesses artistic impersonality and serene abstraction from life. He loves humanity but does not take sides. In his novels we have no didacticism, no philosophy, no propaganda. He is an artist pure and simple and interprets Indian life aesthetically with unprejudiced objectivity. It is because of the quality of comprehending reality from the objective heights of a luminous temperament and presenting people as they are without personal bias that he is considered as the most artistic of Indian writers in English and is often compared to Jane Austen and Anton Chekhov. The comparison is not unjust also for there is a very close affinity between the methods of these writers and those of R. K. Narayan. (p. 157)

[Narayan's] primary aim is to present convincingly a scene formed in his imagination. The great social, economic and political changes that have taken place in the last few decades seem to have left him untouched. He neither denounces nor upholds any cause or takes any sides. His writings are refreshingly free from all types of ideological prejudices. By temperament and choice he holds himself aloof, not an actor, but a spectator sympathising but not sharing in the interests of the world around him. (p. 158)

But this method requires a great talent and master-mind to use it with success and effect. . . . It is virtue of Narayan's great and singular creative power that he has achieved an unusual distinction with this highly difficult method and that he has described the Indian people and the Indian way of life with an abundant measure of success without trying to moralise or to give expression to his personal views.

Though self-detached, Narayan does not lack sympathy for his characters. Like Jane Austen, sympathy with his characters he always has, though identity never. . . . He looks at human life with all its flaws and frivolities with an amused tolerance and indulgence. Depicted by a Jonathan Swift, Ramani or Margayya or Sampath or Raju or Vasu will appear a veritable demon deserving our contempt and indignation. Narayan does not find anything contemptuous or malignant about these sons of Adam, who are not very much different from other mortals, their innumerable erring brethren of this earth. In his sympathetic hands they turn into interesting and amusing figures such as make the earth very colourful if not very rich by their presence. (pp. 158-59)

Narayan's good sense and keen sensibility make him easily discern the frivolities and incongruities in the nature and actions of his characters. These frivolities and weaknesses of his characters, however, never annoy him. They simply amuse him. He is not found in the least anxious to hide or to lash the weaknesses and idiosyncrasies of his characters. He rather rejoices in them and feels decidedly more comfortable when he can have a good laugh at them. The ground quality of his mind is humour and his view of the world like that of all the great masters of universal laughter such as Aristophanes, Chaucer, Cervantes, Rabelais, Moliere and Fielding, has the immense tolerance and profound sympathy of a true humorist. Narayan is a great master of humour and all of his writings abound in it in all its rich variety. (p. 161)

[Yet, all] of his novels have an undertone of sadness hidden beneath their flashing humour. G. K. Chesterton was right when he remarked that jesters were the most serious people in the world. Charles Lamb, Charles Dickens, Thackeray and R. L. Stevenson testify to this statement for their smiles seem to tremble very often on the brink of tears. Narayan also appears to cry inwardly while he laughs outwardly. (p. 164)

Narayan feels the pathos of life very intensely and expresses it in an artistic manner. Like Thackeray he exercises moderation and restraint in describing pathetic scenes for he knows that long descriptions tend to mar the effect. But for the latter half of *The English Teacher* where the author's interest in parapsychology makes him melodramatic, pathos is never overdone in the novels of Narayan.

Though very successful in the handling of humour and pathos, it is in the delineation of characters—the chief *differentia* of the novel as distinguished not merely from the romance and the drama but also from every other kind of literature—that Narayan stands preeminent. His keen observation of men and manners and all-embracing sympathy towards them make him a skilled portrayer of characters. . . .

Unlike a dramatic novelist, however, he does not aim at depicting the interactions of various characters on one another and revealing changes that occur in their nature and temperament from the clash of relationships. It is why the characters in the novels of R. K. Narayan always remain static and unchanging. Unlike the characters of Jane Austen, they lack the capacity to surprise us. Their weaknesses, their vanities, their foibles, they possess from the beginning and never lose to the end; and what actually does change is not these but our knowledge of them. (p. 165)

Narayan has drawn his characters both as individuals and types. In reality he describes the species in terms of the individual. That is why though his characters are typical of their class, they are not typical as the puppets in a morality play are typical, by being labelled with some outstanding attribute, but as real persons are typical of their class. Their virtue or foible is only one among many attributes, only one rather striking aspect of a complete and many-sided personality. Sen is a typical journalist, Shanta Bai a typical adventuress for all time, Nataraj a typical printer, yet they are all highly individualized characters, having their own whims and idiosyncrasies, totally different from other persons of their class. Each of these characters is typical of a class without losing any of its own individuality.

Narayan has had recourse both to analytical and dramatic methods in depicting his characters. It is, however, the latter that figures most successfully in his works. His characters are presented in and by their speech and action. He is less the pure describer than Smollett, Dickens and Thackeray. Their method is rather that of the reporter, Narayan's of the dramatist. (p. 167)

One of the most important features of Narayan as a novelist is his brilliant descriptive art. It is because of his great skill in descriptive method that every scene he describes, comes out alive and realistic. The vividness and variety of his pictures are unsurpassed. He, however, eschews elaborate details in his descriptions. Description for its own sake has little interest for him. It is with a few significant and suggestive details that he gives exactness to his pictures. To him the interest does not lie in pomp and pageantry but in human emotions. It is amply evidenced by the descriptions he gives of a quarrel between husband and wife or son and mother, a procession, a function, a dance and a public meeting. In all these scenes scattered over his novels and stories, it is emotion, not action, which has interested him and caught his fancy.

Narayan's descriptions of nature are also characterized by precision, brevity and vividness. Though not a novelist of nature like Thomas Hardy or Emily Bronte, he shows a genuine love for it in his works. . . . (p. 180)

One of the great assets of Narayan as a descriptive artist is his graceful and simple style. There are very few Indian writers who are able to handle English with so much purity and elegance as he does. He is a master of excellent English prose both in narrative and dialogue. It is to the ease, the refinement and the exquisite naturalness of his prose that we owe a large part of our pleasure in reading him. . . .

Simplicity and clarity of his style is mainly the result of his use of the very language of everyday life and his scrupulous adherence to the accepted patterns of sentence structure, and choice of words. Narayan's is not an experimental but a conservative and traditional style. He never uses sentences of complicated grammatical construction with such dependent and subordinate clauses, as make the sense difficult to follow. (p. 181)

It is true that his works lack the emotional and humanitarian appeal of Victor Hugo's novels or the extensive range of themes, motives and sentiments of Balzac's human comedies. We also do not find in them the spiritual fervour and the epical representation of human life as given by Tolstoy in his chronicle novel, *War and Peace*. Narayan also does not try to go deeper into the religious or psychological roots of human behaviour or probe into the depths of the human mind and reveal the startling contradictions in men's souls and personalities as Dostoevsky does in *Crime and Punishment* and *Brothers Karamazov*. He has not the verve, exuberance, energy, wider and higher interests and deeper psychological insight of these great novelists of the world. But his greatest triumph is that like Jane Austen, he obeys what has been described as the first rule of all imaginative composition, that he stays within the range of his imaginative inspiration. He knows that he has a comedian's imagination and that he can draw only human beings in their personal relations and humorous situations. He, therefore, does not attempt to depict man in relation to God, to politics, to abstract ideas. He sees him only in relation to his family and his neighbours. He is perfect because he never steps beyond his range even once. (p. 183)

> Harish Raizada, in his R. K. Narayan: A Critical Study of His Works (copyright: © Harish Raizada; reprinted by permission of the author), Young Asia Publications, 1969, 204 p.

JOYCE CAROL OATES

R. K. Narayan is considered one of the finest of contemporary Indian writers. He is the author of **The Guide** and **The Vendor of Sweets**, novels about a mythical town called Malgudi in South India, and of a number of short stories. *A Horse and Two Goats* is made up of sketches or vignettes rather than stories; the dominant tone of the writing is casual, unthreatening, unsurprising. . . .

The most interesting of the stories, **"A Breath of Lucifer,"** which is apparently based upon a personal experience of the author's, deals with a temporarily blinded man and his dependence upon an eccentric hospital attendant. But their relationship does not reveal anything to either of them, or to the reader. One wants very much to get into the reality, the texture of Indian life, to see the contemporary Indian world through an intelligent man's eyes, but Narayan consistently frustrates us: he is an entertaining writer of anecdotes here and nothing more.

> Joyce Carol Oates, "The World of Moderation," in Book World—Chicago Tribune (© 1970 Postrib Corp.; reprinted by permission of Chicago Tribune and The Washington Post), January 18, 1970, p. 6.*

LAURENCE LAFORE

[The stories in R. K. Narayan's **"A Horse and Two Goats"**] are all very specifically Indian, richly adorned with picturesque native customs and vivid local color, so that the casual reader with a limited appetite for folklore might well form the misleading impression that this is all they are. He might also be misled by their brevity and simplicity into supposing that they belong in the category of Theophrastian vignettes.

They are, in fact, something quite different. Picturesque they may well seem to an American reader, but they are no cliché. Except in the title story, there are none of those distressing encounters between East and West that have become so dominant (and tiresome) a theme in most of the fiction written in or about India. It is also refreshing to find that Mr. Narayan, who writes in English, does so with a perfect American accent, equally free from both the Anglicisms and the brand of folkloristic archaism frequently judged appropriate by authors and translators dealing with Asian subjects.

Much more important, Mr. Narayan is not really concerned with character sketches or with anthropological particularities. He is concerned with ideas, and with dramatic structure. His stories are not particularly novel in their themes, but they are certainly universal in their application. The collection adds up to a consistent and coordinated expression of his view of the world and its inmates.

The subjects are various. . . . But the unifying theme is very strong. Mr. Narayan is dealing with the failure of people, in the word of current cant, to "communicate." But his is an original approach to the subject. He is saying that if people *do* "communicate" they destroy each other.

Men live, in short, by illusions which, being peculiar to themselves, insulate them effectively against reality and everyone else in the world as well. The illusions are widely assorted, some diabolic, some funny, some tragic. Some involve submission to traditional mythology, some are the mistakes of very ignorant people, some the fantasies of madmen, some the fecund imaginings of intelligent and educated men. But in every case they are the motive and means of staying alive and of taking action. . . .

All meanings, all beliefs, and all hopes, Mr. Narayan tells us, are insulating illusions. . . . He presents his argument in finely subtle and forceful dramatic form.

> Laurence Lafore, "At Their Back Stands Reality Ready to Undo Them," in The New York Times Book Review (copyright © 1970 by The New York Times Company; reprinted by permission), January 25, 1970, p. 5.

LAKSHMI HOLMSTROM

Narayan is a comic novelist. His attitude to comedy grows out of a whole view of man's condition in the universe, and therefore the criticism of society and the observation of the social predicament implicit in his work is only incidental. For Narayan, society is not man-made by choices but existing as part of a universal order with which it is continuous. Thus to appreciate his work, one must understand his view of man's life in a universal order which is cyclical, of man's relation to this cyclical order and attachment to the wheel of existence. This can be seen in his work at three levels: his own philosophical and metaphysical beliefs; the beliefs he puts into the minds of his characters and from which he, as the author, detaches himself; and the conscious use he makes of this view as a comic and literary device.

The cyclical construction which is the characteristic form of Narayan's novel is a universal comic device. Bergson, in his book *Laughter: an Essay on the Meaning of the Comic,* calls it the 'snowball effect'. . . . Treating the 'snowball' as one among other comic devices, Bergson describes it as 'an effect which grows by arithmetical progression so that the cause, insignificant at the outset culminates in a result as important as it is unexpected'. . . . We get comedy, he says when man acts in a mechanical or rigid way rather than in accordance with the flexibility and adaptability which are the special qualities of living beings. . . . It is easy to see how Bergson's theory of the logic of the absurd applies to many of Narayan's characters whose lives become organized around a particular obsession—it may be money, or an ambition, or love, or even an inanimate thing. (pp. 122-24)

[In a 1968 interview with Professor Walsh, Narayan] explained his view of the comic as 'that vast gap that exists within what a man thinks of his surroundings and what it happens to be'. . . . Narayan shares with Bergson this view of the comic as arising from man's illusions and obsessions which make him act in a particular way, and he sees this as an inevitable part of life. Thus his work can be seen as examples of a universal kind of comedy to which Bergson's analysis applies. (p. 124)

Bergson argues that a mechanical arrangement like the 'snowball' is funny because life is not like that: things do not really happen in an inevitable way, events are alterable. On the other hand, in Narayan's **'Engine Trouble'** or **'Lawley Road'**, the cyclical construction or inevitable sequence is really parodying a much more serious and determined order by making the solemn familiar. . . .

Bergson finds Don Quixote funny only because he acts mechanically on his illusions instead of adapting his image of the world to fit the changing circumstances of life. Don Quixote, thus, could have controlled these circumstances within realistic limits. But for Narayan while thought and experience are free, there is no possibility at all of really free action. So every man with ideals, plans and illusions is Quixotic and funny, because all these plans will come into collision with the fixed and determined. (p. 125)

The literary device that Narayan develops in his novels is really part of his material or theme: the study of an individual against the scheme of an inevitable determined cyclical order which includes the moral order. Man's attachment to things (that is, material objects, love, money, ambition) which get out of control reflects the relation between the unique individual experience and the mechanical repetition of the universe. This relation is explored in different ways in different novels. (p. 128)

In his interview with Professor Walsh, Narayan said that he is obsessed with the detail, the particular. He gave as examples from his novels, the fat green penholder that Krishna remembers his father using, and the Queen-Anne style chair that is the place of honour in Nataraj's main room. Narayan said: 'In an otherwise philosophical country, concrete evidence in continuity and mortality lies in little things'. He places great stress on the value of individual experience precisely because of this awareness of continuity and mortality at the same time. Thus material objects in his novels are given the value of things seen, felt and experienced. They are selected for this reason rather than as the external setting of a social type.

In the second place, a perception of the total scheme of which every human action is part, serves in his novels only to emphasize the loneliness of each man, his inability to avert destiny either for himself or for others. . . . Narayan states his view of the cyclically ordered universe simply and explicitly, in this differing from other recent Indian novelists such as Raja Rao and Rajan who are greatly concerned to justify their views. What is particularly valuable in his work is the exploration of the single experience in such an ordered universe, and his awareness all the time of the tension or balance between continuity and mortality. (pp. 129-30)

> Lakshmi Holmstrom, in his The Novels of R. K. Narayan (© 1973 Lakshmi Holmstrom), Writers Workshop, Calcutta, 1973, 130 p.

JOHN UPDIKE

The autobiography of a writer of fiction is generally superfluous, since he has already, in rearrangement and disguise, written out the material of his life many times. A novel like **"The Man-Eater of Malgudi,"** though its hero, Nataraj, and its author, Narayan, are not to be confused, tells us more about the India that R. K. Narayan inhabits, and more explicitly animates his opinion of what he sees, than his recent brief memoir, **"My Days."** . . . Not that Mr. Narayan's mischievous modesty does not lend an agreeable tone to this account of his rather uneventful life. Nor are his delightful gifts of caricature entirely inhibited by factuality. In **"My Days,"** as in his novels, one meets men so absorbed in self-interest that they become grotesque and wonderful: the young Narayan, seeking employment, grooms himself smartly to meet a prospective employer, who comes onto his veranda "bare-bodied and glisten[ing] with an oil-coating, as he prepared himself for a massage; he blinked several times to make me out, as oil had dripped over his eyes and blurred his vision. . . . All my best efforts at grooming were wasted, for I must have looked to him like a photograph taken with a shivering hand." The man barks a rebuff of the boy, and then paces "like a greasy bear in its cage." This sense of imprisonment within character, of each person energetically if ruinously fulfilling his dharma—his vocation, a Christian might say—reached its peak in English fiction with Dickens, and perhaps requires a religious basis. In the liberal view, character is significantly malleable, whereas the traditional character-creators fatalistically look into men for a fixed posture, an irrevocable passion.... Few writers since Dickens can match the effect of colorful teeming that Narayan's fictional city of Malgudi conveys; its population is as sharply chiselled as a temple frieze, and as endless, with always, one feels, more characters around the corner. (p. 80)

Narayan is one of a vanishing breed—the writer as citizen. His citizenship extends to calling up municipal officials about inadequate street lighting, to "dashing off virulent letters to newspapers about corruption and inefficiency." Such protests do not feel, as with so much American social consciousness, forced—a covert bid for power and self-justification. "If I have to worry, it's about things outside me, mostly not concerning me." What a wealth of material becomes accessible to a writer who can so simply assert such a sense of community! We have writers willing to be mayor but not many excited to be citizens. We have writers as confessors, shackled to their personal lives, and writers as researchers, hanging their sheets of information from a bloodless story line. But of writers immersed in their material, and enabled to draw tales from a community of neighbors, Faulkner was our last great example. An instinctive, respectful identification with the people of one's locale comes hard now, in the menacing cities or disposable suburbs, yet without it a genuine belief in the significance of humanity, in humane significances, comes not at all. (p. 82)

John Updike, "Alive and Free from Employment," in The New Yorker *(© 1974 by The New Yorker Magazine, Inc.), Vol. L, No. 28, September 2, 1974, pp. 80-2.*

M. M. MAHOOD

'It's the original violence which has started a cycle—violence which goes on in undying waves once started, either in retaliation or as an original starting-ground—the despair of Gandhi—.' These reflections which arise in the course of a small difference between husband and wife in one of R. K. Narayan's novels seem to belong to the world of the Marabar Caves rather than to the placid world of Malgudi. But then this South Indian novelist has been too easily stereotyped by many readers. It has been his misfortune that while his reputation has grown with healthy slowness over his long career as a novelist, his cult has more recently sprung up in an ivy-like fashion beside that reputation and now threatens to smother it in a luxuriant growth.

Several features of his work combine to make him a typical cult novelist. Like Jane Austen, who is similarly dogged by the Janeites, he offers his devotees a topographical security that grows from book to book. We know it all like the backs of our hands: the animated torpor of human and animal life around the fountain in Malgudi's Market Road, the well laid out respectability of the British and post-British 'Extensions', the maze of narrow streets humming with the activity of innumerable printing presses—from one of which, surely, must issue the small drab paperbacks that give us the freedom of this South Indian town. His books afford us too in lavish measure the delight offered by all cult novelists (Dickens being the most prolific example) of encounters with characters whose extraordinariness is, in the inescapable cliché, unforgettable.... (p. 92)

Many of these characters are comic in a Shakespearean way: they are encapsulated in, and nourish themselves on, inexhaustible self-delusions.... Not only the characters but also the course of the various stories remind us repeatedly of Shakespearean comedy. The movement is from order to disorder and back again; the characters enter a world of 'distracting illusions and hysterics' which seems, like Forster's world of telegrams and anger, to be real enough at the time, but in retrospect is recognized as *maya*, a dream that hath no bottom.... Narayan shares with some characters of Shakespeare's last plays the belief that the divine powers will, in their own good time, set all to rights, and that in order to grasp this and break free from the nightmare of illusory evil, 'it is required', in the words of *The Winter's Tale*, 'you do awake your faith'. At the end of the autobiographical ***The English Teacher***, the narrator's Hermione actually does return, without even a romance's pretence at plausibility, and long after the fire has consumed her body in a scene of unbearable verisimilitude.

Narayan is in short a happy novelist. In the eyes of his devotees the radiant quality of his imagination proceeds from an essentially Indian serenity and detachment; indeed the cult of the novelist is closely associated with the larger cult of oriental other-worldliness that draws Western youth in its hundreds along the overland route to India. The judicious reader, however, as distinct from the devotee, is likely to be less than happy in Narayan's happiness. Confronted by the magnitude of Indian distress, he may even wonder if Narayan does not outdo the complacency of his own characters.... Narayan's technique as a story-teller is the source of that luminous quality which to his cult-followers is so comforting a sign of his serene fatalism, and to others so uncomfortable a sign of his social unawareness. My purpose here is ... [to demonstrate, in one of Narayan's best novels, ***The Man-Eater of Malgudi***,] that the luminosity manifest through the form of the book is in fact the light of genuine social concern. Non-attachment is not indifference.... (pp. 93-4)

[The] reader of Narayan has to learn not to be distracted by solecisms and inelegancies. He is inattentive to his medium, to the colouring and connotations of English words, because his attention is focused so unswervingly on the message, the scene before his inner eye.... We are aware of the same kind of attentiveness in much Indian music, in which the performer (and incidentally Narayan is himself a skilful musician), as he improvises, has the air of receiving his music from unheard dictation. And although Narayan never wrestles with words, his method as a writer, far from being slapdash, is one of care and sensitivity. (p. 95)

Far from condoning the stagnation of traditional life, ***The Man-Eater of Malgudi*** offers a fable for the developing world. Traditional India, the novel makes plain, needs to be awakened out of its stagnation, but not by Vasu's methods nor with Vasu's intentions. Nothing but harm can come of imposing alien political philosophies and economic aims on India; what is required is growth from the grass roots. As in Julius Nyerere's fable of the centipede, all the legs need to move a little, and then the body politic will find that it is on the march.

There is no incompatibility between this appeal to 'get up and go' and the belief that the powers of social and moral disorder are self-destructive. 'Evil on itself shall back recoil / And mix no more with goodness': the seventeenth century could combine this Miltonic certainty with political radicalism. And the puritan ethic of a later generation blended surprisingly well with the Indian concept of *dharma*—which is one reason why Kipling, contrary to all Western expectation, has many Indian admirers. The educations of Gandhi and of the South Indian leader C. Rajagopalachari—like Narayan, a Tamil Brahman—were a mixture of the two traditions. Narayan himself grew up in a home 'crammed' with the works of Ruskin and Carlyle, and Ruskin's writings contributed almost as much as the Indian sacred books to Gandhi's formulation of the 'Victorian' virtues of industry, sobriety, punctuality, devotion to duty, which in the novel are embodied in the figure of Sastri.

But while Indian thought was receptive to the gospel of work, it in its turn, by virtue of its belief that men should perform right actions without seeking the fruit of action, took the strain out of puritan effort and the self-righteousness out of Victorian energy. The conviction that we need to care and not to care propels Narayan's gentle mockery of his characters' anxieties as [*The Man-Eater of Malgudi*] approaches its crisis. And the resolution of that crisis, in a way that is once again Shakespearean, puts human endeavour in its proper perspective. A serene and enlightening wisdom in the end makes *The Man-Eater of Malgudi* not a mythological romance, nor a political satire—though it has aspects of both these—but the rarest of literary forms, a true comedy. (pp. 113-14)

> M. M. Mahood, "The Marriage of Krishna: Narayan's 'The Man-Eater of Malgudi'," in his The Colonial Encounter: A Reading of Six Novels (© M. M. Mahood 1977), Roman & Littlefield, 1977, pp. 92-114.

V. S. NAIPAUL

"India will go on." This was what the Indian novelist R. K. Narayan said to me in London in 1961, before I had ever been to India. (p. 10)

[Narayan's] conviction in 1961, after fourteen years of independence, that India would go on, whatever the political uncertainties after Mr. Nehru, was like the conviction of his earliest novels, written in the days of the British, that India was going on. In the early novels the British conquest is like a fact of life. The British themselves are far away, their presence hinted at only in their institutions: the bank, the mission school. The writer contemplates the lesser life that goes on below: small men, small schemes, big talk, limited means: a life so circumscribed that it appears whole and unviolated, its smallness never a subject for wonder, though India itself is felt to be vast. (pp. 10-11)

Subjection flattened, made dissimilar places alike. Narayan's India, with its colonial apparatus, was oddly like the Trinidad of my childhood. His oblique perception of that apparatus, and the rulers, matched my own; and in the Indian life of his novels I found echoes of the life of my own Indian community on the other side of the world.

But Narayan's novels did not prepare me for the distress of India. As a writer he had succeeded almost too well. His comedies were of the sort that requires a restricted social setting with well-defined rules; and he was so direct, his touch so light, that, though he wrote in English of Indian manners, he had succeeded in making those exotic manners quite ordinary. The small town he had staked out as his fictional territory was, I knew, a creation of art and therefore to some extent artificial, a simplification of reality. But the reality was cruel and overwhelming. In the books his India had seemed accessible; in India it remained hidden. To get down to Narayan's world, to perceive the order and continuity he saw in the dereliction and smallness of India, to enter into his ironic acceptance and relish his comedy, was to ignore too much of what could be seen, to shed too much of myself: my sense of history, and even the simplest ideas of human possibility. I did not lose my admiration for Narayan; but I felt that his comedy and irony were not quite what they had appeared to be, were part of a Hindu response to the world, a response I could no longer share. And it has since become clear to me—especially on this last visit, during a slow rereading of Narayan's 1949 novel, *Mr. Sampath*—that, for all their delight in human oddity, Narayan's novels are less the purely social comedies I had once taken them to be than religious books, at times religious fables, and intensely Hindu.

Srinivas, the hero of *Mr. Sampath,* is a contemplative idler. (pp. 12-13)

Just twenty years have passed between Gandhi's first call for civil disobedience and the events of the novel. But already, in Srinivas, Gandhian nonviolence has degenerated into something very like the opposite of what Gandhi intended. For Srinivas nonviolence isn't a form of action, a quickener of social conscience. It is only a means of securing an undisturbed calm; it is nondoing, noninterference, social indifference. It merges with the ideal of self-realization, truth to one's identity. These modern-sounding words, which reconcile Srinivas to the artist's predicament, disguise an acceptance of *karma*, the Hindu killer, the Hindu calm, which tells us that we pay in this life for what we have done in past lives: so that everything we see is just and balanced, and the distress we see is to be relished as religious theater, a reminder of our duty to ourselves, our future lives.

Srinivas's quietism—compounded of *karma*, nonviolence, and a vision of history as an extended religious fable—is in fact a form of self-cherishing in the midst of a general distress. It is parasitic. It depends on the continuing activity of others, the trains running, the presses printing, the rupees arriving from somewhere. It needs the world, but it surrenders the organization of the world to others. It is a religious response to worldly defeat.

Because we take to novels our own ideas of what we feel they must offer, we often find, in unusual or original work, only what we expect to find, and we reject or miss what we aren't looking for. But it astonished me that, twenty years before, not having been to India, taking to *Mr. Sampath* only my knowledge of the Indian community of Trinidad and my reading of other literature, I should have missed or misread so much, should have seen only a comedy of small-town life and a picaresque, wandering narrative in a book that was really so mysterious.

Now, reading *Mr. Sampath* again in snatches on afternoons of rain during this prolonged monsoon, which went on and on like the Emergency itself . . . , I saw in *Mr. Sampath* a foreshadowing of the tensions that had to come to India, philosophically prepared for defeat and withdrawal (each man an island) rather than independence and action, and torn now between the wish to preserve and be psychologically secure, and the need to undo. (pp. 17-19)

What had seemed speculative and comic, aimless and "Russian" about Narayan's novel had turned out to be something else, the expression of an almost hermetic philosophical system. The novel I had read as a novel was also a fable, a classic exposition of the Hindu equilibrium, surviving the shock of an alien culture, an alien literary form, an alien language, and making harmless even those new concepts it appeared to welcome. Identity became an aspect of *karma,* self-love was bolstered by an ideal of nonviolence. (p. 19)

> V. S. Naipaul, "An Old Equilibrium," in his India: A Wounded Civilization *(copyright © 1976, 1977 by V. S. Naipaul; reprinted by permission of Alfred A. Knopf, Inc.; in Canada by V. S. Naipaul), Knopf, 1977, pp. 3-30.*

K. S. NARAYANA RAO

The Ramayana by the great sage Valmiki, running to about 28,000 verses of thirty-two syllables each and existing in seven volumes, is considered by Indians to be the first great literary work to be produced in India, and Valmiki is described as India's first great poet (*aadi kavi*). The influence of this work in other writers is to be seen not only through centuries but even in other countries, such as Ceylon, Thailand and Indonesia, where there are modified versions of this great love story. Even within India great poets like Kamban (the Tamil composer) and Tulasidas (the Hindi author) have composed epics of their own based on Valmiki's work but telling essentially the same story as the original. There have been condensed English versions too, both in prose and verse, but none really successfully captures the spirit of the original. R. K. Narayan, well known for his novels, has now tried his hand at retelling in English this epic story, using Kamban's Tamil version as his source.... (p. 521)

The Ramayana is a story of ideals—ideal king, ideal father, ideal son, ideal brother, ideal wife, et cetera—in addition to being a celebration of the ideals of monogamy and chastity for both men and women. Valmiki tells the story in an extremely poetic manner. In retelling this story, known to most Indians of all ages (for Rama is regarded as God incarnate by the Hindu), Narayan is not at his best, though he is capable of retelling epic and other religious stories well enough as demonstrated by his **Gods, Demons, and Others**. . . . Instances of awkward English and expository comment interfering with a straight narrative are not wanting. . . . Notwithstanding, the overall story is reasonably well told, and for a Western reader, though Narayan's book might appear to be simple, it is a good introduction to one of the world's greatest poems. (pp. 521-22)

> K. S. Narayana Rao, in a review of "The Ramayana," in World Literature Today *(copyright 1978 by the University of Oklahoma Press), Vol. 52, No. 3, Summer, 1978, pp. 521-22.*

GRAHAM GREENE

[*Graham Greene was directly responsible for the publication of Narayan's first novel,* Swami and Friends. *Narayan had mailed the manuscript to a friend in England who had approached several publishers. When they all promptly rejected the book Narayan, bitterly discouraged, instructed his friend not to mail the manuscript back to India, but rather to tie a stone to it and throw it into the Thames. Instead, Narayan's friend brought the manuscript to Greene, who was so impressed with the novel that he secured a publisher for it. Greene subsequently became one of Narayan's most influential proponents.*]

There are writers—Tolstoy and Henry James to name two—whom we hold in awe, writers—Turgenev and Chekhov—for whom we feel a personal affection, other writers whom we respect—Conrad for example—but who hold us at a long arm's length with their "courtly foreign grace". Narayan (whom I don't hesitate to name in such a context) more than any of them wakes in me a spring of gratitude, for he has offered me a second home. Without him I could never have known what it is like to be Indian. Kipling's India is the romantic playground of the Raj. . . . E. M. Forster was funny and tender about his friend the Maharajah of Dewas and severely ironic about the English in India, but India escaped him all the same. . . . No one could find a second home in Kipling's India or Forster's India.

Perhaps no one can write in depth about a foreign country—he can only write about the effect of that country on his own fellow countrymen, living as exiles, or government servants, or visitors. He can only "touch in" the background of the foreign land. In Kipling and Forster the English are always posturing nobly and absurdly in the foreground; in Narayan's novels, though the Raj still existed during the first dozen years of his literary career, the English characters are peripheral. They are amiable enough (Narayan, unlike Mulk Raj Anand, is hardly touched by politics), but hopelessly unimportant like Professor Brown in *The Bachelor of Arts.* How Kipling would have detested Narayan's books, even that Indian "twang" which lends so much charm to his style. (pp. v-vi)

In the eleven novels which extend from **Swami and Friends** to **The Painter of Signs** Narayan has never, I think, strayed far from Malgudi, though a character may sometimes disappear for ever into India, like Rajam, friend of the schoolboy Swami, simply by taking a train. Year by year Narayan has peopled Malgudi with characters we never forget. In his second novel—a very funny and happy book—there is Chandran, little more than a schoolboy, whom we leave at the end of **The Bachelor of Arts** in a bubble of excitement at a marriage which has been arranged with the help of a dubious, even dishonest, horoscope. In his third book, **The English Teacher,** the marriage ends in death and Narayan shows how far he has grown as a writer to encompass the sadness and loss. In **The Dark Room** the screw of unhappiness is twisted further, the killing of love more tragic than the death of love.

Narayan himself had known the death of love, and **The English Teacher** is dedicated to his dead wife. It took some years before a degree of serenity and humour returned to Malgudi with **The Financial Expert** and his "office" under a banyan tree, with Mr Sampath, the over optimistic film producer, the sweet vendor's son Mali and his novel writing machine, Raman, the sign painter who was lured by love of Daisy from his proper work to make propaganda in the countryside for birth control and sterilisation, the bullying taxidermist, Vasu, in **The Man-Eater of Malgudi**, perhaps Narayan's best comic character.

Something had permanently changed in Narayan after **The Bachelor of Arts**, the writer's personal tragedy has been our gain. Sadness and humour in the later books go hand in hand like twins, inseparable, as they do in the stories of Chekhov. (pp. viii-x)

> Graham Greene, "Introduction" *(reprinted by permission of International Creative Management; in Canada by Laurence Pollinger Limited for Graham Greene; copyright © 1978 by Graham Greene), in* The Bachelor of Arts *by R. K. Narayan, Heinemann, 1978, pp. v-x.*

GEORGE WOODCOCK

[As] a South Indian [R. K. Narayan] knew he must come to terms with the power which in his novels he shows shaping Malgudi physically, giving it the plan of streets created by the mythical Sir Frederick Lawley, the schools and colleges, the municipal government, the railways and mills and printing presses, the whole structure of a western city superimposed on a native life that, with its temples and household shrines and vegetarian Brahmin food and astrologers and untouchables and arranged marriages, had remained obstinately unchanged. In Malgudi the two worlds are shown as indissolubly linked—even though no more than three actual Englishmen appear in minor roles during the whole cycle—and linked (Narayan seems to imply) forever, since on the public level India has become as inevitably dominated by twentieth-century progress as on the private level it has remained loyal to the Hindu past, to the traditions that embody the essential genius of India and to which its people return when the world's attractions grow dim.

Swaminathan and his fellow schoolboys in *Swami and Friends* are unwitting examples of the contradictions Narayan sees entering deeply into the culturally divided lives of twentieth-century Indians. They attend a mission school oriented toward preparing them for the college in Malgudi, and in this imitation English grammar-school they become passionately devoted to the alien game of cricket; their heroes are the English cricketers Hobbs and Tate, and their special form of the quest that occurs in all Narayan novels is a comic one, the creation on Malgudi's waste lots of a Marylebone Cricket Club that will rival its English namesake. Yet when nationalist riots take place, Swaminathan participates in them and smashes school windows; and when one of his Christian teachers attacks and derides the Indian deities with a convert's zeal, Swami is moved to defend them.

Can a modern Indian reject westernization, with its political and ultimately moral implications? The only way to attempt it, Narayan suggests, is by withdrawal into one of the two Indian worlds that remained relatively untouched by the intrusion of the raj and the influences that have survived it. These are the interlocking worlds of villages, still living largely by traditional techniques as well as beliefs, and of the wandering holy men, who usually find their warmest welcome among poor and illiterate peasants. In Narayan's novels such withdrawal rarely provides a way to self-transformation, but it does often lead to self-discovery. (pp. 16-17)

On a different and political level the search for a fulfillment outside the ordinary currents of middle-class Indian life is portrayed in *Waiting for the Mahatma*. A rich immature man, Sriram, is involved in the Gandhian movement through falling in love with one of the mahatma's court of young women devotees. He and the girl, Bharati, whom Gandhi has appointed Sriram's instructor, work together until, at the mahatma's command, she courts imprisonment in the *satyagraha* campaigns preceding Indian independence. Deprived of her guidance, Sriram falls in with a violent revolutionary, Jagadish, who leads him into acts of sabotage, so that eventually he too is imprisoned. Sriram is finally released at the time of India's liberation and rejoins Bharati; they take their places in Gandhi's entourage in time to witness his assassination in 1948.

The bullets that kill Gandhi both in real life and in Narayan's novel remind one of Stendhal's dictum that politics in a novel is like a pistol shot in a concert. Gandhi and his death represent an incursion from the outside world that shakes the magic equilibrium of Malgudi and makes *Waiting for the Mahatma* one of the most interesting but also one of the most disturbing of Narayan's novels, and all the more disturbing because of the difference in grain and stature between Gandhi and the people of Malgudi. For if there is one characteristic which Narayan's characters almost without exception share, it is mediocrity. Eccentrically colorful as it may strike one on first introduction, Malgudi is a city of the petty and the unfulfilled through which Narayan's art moves, to quote Stendhal again, "like a mirror walking down a main street." Narayan resembles Chekhov in that from the very inadequacies of his characters, their weakness and their shallow pretensions, he can produce a blend of sadness and comedy that appeals irresistibly. The sickness from which all the citizens of Malgudi suffer, and which their mediocrity reflects, is the mid-twentieth-century alienation of the Indian middle class. Their traditional codes and hierarchies have become fragmented and private, so that no man can any longer fulfill himself in a traditional way except by holy withdrawal; yet the material success on the western model to which the Malgudians aspire belongs to an alien world which they rarely understand, so that here too their lives are diminished and unfulfilled.

When the inhabitants of Malgudi do seek to break out of their encircling mediocrity, they fail because their ambitions overleap their capacities. The eponymous hero of *Mr. Sampath* sets out to establish in Malgudi a film studio rivaling those of Bombay and Calcutta, but the great Hindu epic that is to be his first production is ruined by a series of farcical disasters arising out of the jealousies, passions, and sheer inadequacies of Sampath and his associates. (pp. 18-19)

Even when they seem to triumph, Narayan's characters cannot sustain their success; no citizen of Malgudi goes on to become an all-Indian celebrity. (p. 20)

Especially in his later work, from *The Guide* onward, Narayan has tended to base his novels structurally on the classic Indian myths, but to no greater extent than many western writers have used the Odysseus or the Orpheus myth; and insofar as a traditional moralism underlies the social comedy of his works, he can certainly be called—as Naipaul calls him—a Hindu fabulist. But this, it seems to me, strengthens rather than weakens his power as a writer of social comedy, for comedy is not nihilistic: it demands a tacitly accepted collective view of life and behavior. Naipaul implies [see excerpt above] that in the long run the past-oriented negation which he sees overwhelming India has also overwhelmed Narayan as India's leading novelist. Admittedly I lack Naipaul's Indian ancestry, but . . . I see in Narayan's microcosmic Malgudi a just and not despairing projection of the lasting reality of India. (p. 22)

Narayan is not primarily a satirist: the comic irony through which he sees his characters suggests no strong desire to change them. Perhaps his Hinduism emerges most strongly in this limitation: the people he describes are what their karmas made them, and in accepting their weaknesses all we hope is that by following out their destinies they may transcend them. But even such an attitude is not exclusively Hindu: the Christian visionary William Blake tacitly agreed with the anonymous poet of the *Bhagavad Gita* when he said: "If the fool would persist in his folly he would become wise." Narayan never condemns men because they are not better than they are: he merely shows how the evil they manifest may in true comic manner be diverted. (p. 23)

George Woodcock, "Two Great Commonwealth Novelists: R. K. Narayan and V. S. Naipaul" (reprinted by permission of the editor; © 1979 George

Woodcock), in The Sewanee Review, Vol. LXXXVII, No. 1, Winter, 1979, pp. 1-28.*

ASHOK AKLUJKAR

To narrate the long and involved story of the Mahābhārata in about 180 pages without giving the reader the impression that a bare skeleton is being presented is no mean achievement. Mr. Narayan has certainly succeeded in [*The Mahabharata: A Shortened Modern Prose Version of the Indian Epic*].... His narration proceeds at a comfortable pace and is enlivened by the short, simple dialogues he introduces at appropriate places. The adjectives "shortened," "modern" and "prose," appearing in the sub-title of his book, are fully justified. However, there are some difficulties which arise from the desire to present a modern version. One who seeks to do so is frequently uncomfortable with the mysterious and the miraculous elements in the original story. There is often an urge to make events follow each other logically, to gloss over the problematic turns in the original, to assign rational motives to characters, and to employ techniques of narration foreign to the original. Fortunately, Narayan's version has not suffered much from this.... [However, his] annotation should have concentrated on explaining motives and factors that are peculiar to India and its past and thus not readily intelligible to a modern reader, particularly to a Western reader. His transliteration of Sanskrit names and words does not follow the standard system and lacks consistency. (p. 182)

> Ashok Aklujkar, in a review of "The Mahabharata: A Shortened Modern Prose Version of the Indian Epic," in Pacific Affairs (copyright 1979, University of British Columbia), Vol. 52, No. 1, Spring, 1979, pp. 181-82.

PETER GREEN

Rasipuran Krishnaswami Narayan embodies in his career and writing all the necessary ambiguities of an Indian novelist who came to maturity under the British Raj.... A master of Chekhovian irony, he also moves in a world where marriage horoscopes are crucial, neighborhood temples blossom with exotic theriomorphic deities, reincarnations are taken for granted, priests bless movie cameras, and a great-grandfather's caste can make or break your social pretensions. I used to find it paradoxical that Narayan was discovered by Graham Greene and puffed by Evelyn Waugh: no longer.

"Malgudi" is the name of a fictional South Indian city which bears more than a passing resemblance to Mysore, with touches of Bangalore, Madras, and Chennapatna. It has formed the setting for all Mr. Narayan's novels and stories: one critic describes it, a trifle portentously, as "a metaphor of India." ... Malgudi belongs to that select group of fictitious localities—Macondo, Llareggub, Yoknapatawpha County—that for their devotees are more real than anywhere in this tangible, lackluster world. Albert Mission College, Lawley Extension, and Vinayah Mudali Street may have pale and quotidian originals, but it took Narayan's creative art to immortalize them.

The stories in *Malgudi Days* cover a wide slice of Narayan's career. Some are selected from two earlier volumes, *An Astrologer's Day* and *Lawley Road*, hitherto unpublished in the United States. Eight are new; and these, it's good to be able to report, easily top the rest in size, richness, depth and complexity. (p. 3)

Narayan's gentle and universal irony can get a bit wearing if taken in large doses. Obviously it is, in a sense, self-protection: he is writing about a country of such grinding poverty and rampant disease as a Western reader can barely conceive, and for an observer of his sensibilities almost the only alternative to irony would be a long sustained scream of protest and horror.... I suspect that a good deal of Mr. Narayan's success in England and America—the same applies to the early novels of V. S. Naipaul, like *A House for Mr. Biswas*—stems from a covert sense of superiority in the reader. How funny, how quaint these characters are, with their elephant gods and astrologers and exorcists! There is one story in this collection, **"Cat Within,"** that subtly panders to such sub-racist instincts: a holy man is called in to deal with what's assumed to be a noisy poltergeist, but finally emerges in the form of a cat with a pot stuck on its head. Of course, we knew better all along.

This ambivalence in the reader isn't Narayan's fault. He really believes the old proverb that to understand is to forgive; lurking behind his keen Westernized style is a whole age-old Hindu cosmos. In his best stories, like **"God and the Cobbler,"** there is an unforced universalism, that can embrace and link the quiet cobbler with attempted murder in his past and the hippie who ("in another incarnation") flew over, and blasted with napalm, people he'd never met. Sometimes the mask is dropped. Nothing could be more chilling than **"The Edge,"** in which a needy knife-grinder, with a termagant wife and dreams of a professional career for his daughter, thumbs a lift and ends up on the operating table of a government sterilization clinic. Narayan has been called an apolitical writer. This, as any reader of *Waiting for the Mahatma* will know, is nonsense; he is intensely political, but at the deep level of being involved in mankind. His methods are oblique, but none the less effective for that.

Still, it is possible for the imperceptive to read a good deal of *Malgudi Days* simply for the laughs: and the laughs are worth having.... Yet this is not a happy town. People threaten, or commit, suicide, fail examinations repeatedly, starve, get sick. Life expectancy is short, and not helped by claustrophobic family quarrels. Ultimately it's not the exotic details we remember, but the perennial human relationships. To that extent Narayan's Malgudi is a metaphor, not of India, but of the world. (pp. 3, 11)

> Peter Green, "Main Street, Malgudi: Fakirs, Beggars and Brahmins," in Book World—The Washington Post (© 1982, The Washington Post), March 7, 1982, pp. 3, 11.

JACK BEATTY

Malgudi days; not nights. There are dark moments in [the] thirty-two short stories [of *Malgudi Days*], but the tragic logic is usually broken by a spot of joy in the middle or a bit of puckishness at the end. Ambiguity? The term implies a muscularity of will foreign to Narayan. He does not strive for ambiguity, nor force the action in a tragic direction, nor in a sentimental direction. The salient virtue of his art in these miniature displays is his entire ease before the double faces of existence: the tragic / joyful, funny / sad, good / evil weave of things. If nature could write, someone has said, it would be Tolstoy. But in its calms it might also be Narayan. The sun in these Malgudi days beams from beneath his brow, and its light is generous and steady and benign....

I have two impressions of the place. First, Malgudi is mythical not only in the sense that it is made up but also in the sense that it is a projection of desire. It is in fact an Indian pastoral. Second, I demur from Narayan's judgment in his introduction that the characteristics of Malgudi are "universal." Certainly people from all over can see themselves in these characters. But the first-time visitor is more apt to be struck by the Indianness of Malgudi. The events and the characters' reactions to them: these could take place anywhere. The difference, the Indianness, lies in the structure of feeling and implication the stories exploit.

The moral ethos makes the main difference. It is a deeper and more pervasive order than any available to a modern Western writer, and its hierarchy of virtues is very different from our ideal morality. Its first principle is loyalty, which holds sway over both the human and natural worlds. The **"Blind Dog"** offers a good example of this theme. A pathetic dog with "spotty eyes and undistinguished carriage and needless pugnacity" befriends a blind beggar, and becomes his guide and sole means of life after the old woman who has looked after the beggar dies. The beggar is cruel; he treats the dog so viciously that sympathetic townspeople set him loose. Yet the dog returns, to what is surely his doom. "He simply had to stay forever at the end of that string." Loyalty is the law of his life. (p. 45)

Several other stories deal with the theme of loyalty in class terms. **"A Willing Slave"** is the most moving of these. . . . **"Leela's Friend"** is also about a servant's loyalty. Accused of stealing little Leela's missing gold chain, a servant remains silent rather than shift blame to the careless girl, who has dropped the chain in the tamarind pot. His devotion costs him his job, as well as a jail sentence.

Such irrational constancy provides the moral gravity of story after story. It is all very strange, un-Western, and moving. Loyalty in Malgudi has nothing to do with the particular qualities of persons; it is not inspired or elicited. It is simply the central pulse of this fictional world.

What can be the source of this vision? My guess is that Malgudi's moral order is an ideal projection of the Indian caste system. Caste is odious to us, a sort of totalitarianism of the spirit. Narayan's depictions, however, make the Western reader slightly uncomfortable in his condemnation. They remind us that our individualistic ethos does not encompass all values. It leaves some out. Loyalty, for example. It can hardly be held in high esteem by a culture that sets so much store by self-realization and in an economic order where the bottom line rules. Malgudi renders this awareness in human terms. This Indian idyll makes a gentle criticism of our life. . . .

[Narayan] writes a lovely prose; however, it works only in context and can't be quoted to impressive effect. Perhaps the uninflected prose is the reason these stories do not take the reader over. Instead, the reader must supply the emotion intimated but not expressed by the style. The stories are perhaps better read aloud.

A final interesting aspect of **Malgudi Days** is the unfailing dignity and moral richness with which Narayan portrays the poor. Our first thought about India is The Poor, The Wretched. Narayan writes as if this stock idea of his country were unknown to him. . . . [We] must be impressed with the way the circumambient Hinduism of India adds weight and shade and even wit to the lives of Narayan's characters. But of course it is Narayan who discovers these qualities. No living American author can compare with him in social imagination. There is no one who writes with his tact of feeling, his lack of condescension, his freedom from the falsifying pity about the people in our society comparable to his gatekeeper and servants and cobblers. . . .

The poor occupy the margin of our imaginative no less than our urban life. How different the case is with Narayan! Situated in a society that makes no pretense of being open and democratic, but where the poor are everywhere, he depicts them as interesting individuals, not as abstract objects of guilt or righteousness. He claims that his art is universal, and in its truth and beauty that is so. But the reach and intimacy of his social knowledge and the authenticity of his identification with the poor tell a different story. They mark him as a writer from a society unlike ours, where the division of labor and the apartheid of living arrangements do not separate the men of imagination from the common life of their country. (p. 46)

Jack Beatty, "Idyll of Loyalty," in The New Republic (reprinted by permission of The New Republic; © 1982 The New Republic, Inc.), Vol. 186, No. 3507, March 31, 1982, pp. 45-6.

ROBERT TOWERS

While changes on the macrocosmic scale in India have been tumultuous since R. K. Narayan's first novel, **Swami and Friends**, appeared in 1935, the imaginary South Indian town of Malgudi—the microcosm of his fiction—has undergone little transformation. . . .

The new stories in **Malgudi Days** confirm the impression that Narayan's mild and delicate craft has changed over the decades almost as little as Malgudi itself. Early in his career he found—and quickly perfected—a narrative mode that has remained untouched by all that we think of as modernism. Nowhere in his fiction do we encounter the dissonance, the structural disjunctions, the obscurity, or multilevel wordplay—indeed any of the radical techniques—by which the great writers of this century have jolted the reader from his sense of literary security.

Narayan's mode is that of a shrewd and ironic teller-of-tales whose aim is to beguile his listeners, to share with them his appreciation—sympathetic though slightly withdrawn—of the oddities of human (and animal) behavior. . . .

Storytellers appear with some frequency in Narayan's fiction: sometimes as the figure known as the Talkative Man, sometimes (as in **The Painter of Signs**) in the person of a temple *pandit* who recites to an audience of old women the fantastic tales culled from the *Ramayana*, the *Mahabharata*, and the cycle of the Lord Krishna; Narayan himself has engagingly retold episodes from this vast body of legend in **Gods, Demons, and Others**. In his own fiction, however, Narayan largely avoids the supernatural and the fantastic while retaining the classical right to *tell* rather than merely show, to manipulate rather than merely render, to propel an action and to assert an ending.

This display of a firm narrative hand works in conjunction with a perfected simplicity of style, a limpid English prose that is adequately sensuous without ever becoming lush, a prose of the sort that Graham Greene and the early Waugh achieved for their very different purposes. This combination is admirably suited to Narayan's evocation of a way of life—a way of perceiving human relations and human destinies—that has more in common with Chaucer's world than that of Jane Austen or

Proust or Saul Bellow. The inhabitants of Malgudi still partake of what might be called the "old consciousness," in which men and women define themselves (and are perceived by others) more in terms of their occupations, their roles, or stations in society than as the embodiments of individualized psyches....

[One] of the charms of Narayan's fiction for a contemporary Western reader is precisely this evocation of an older consciousness—now mostly lost to us but still recognizable, in some sense still remembered—that offers a degree of relief from the burdens of personal choice and relentless self-assessment. (p. 21)

As a narrator, Narayan remains detached, refusing to take sides in the tension between the old ways and the new and conveying his sly enjoyment of the absurdities that arise....

Narayan pays a certain price for the mildness of his fictional demeanor. I find that, because of their relatively low intensity, his stories and novels tend in retrospect to blur, to lose definition. While a strong sensory impression of Malgudi remains, the characters and situations of the individual works sink back into their collective existence—perhaps a very Hindu effect. In the near view, however, each piece has a distinct shapeliness and coloration of its own. Though some are slight, hardly more than bright flutterings quickly caught and fixed upon the page, a high proportion of the new stories are expertly wrought, full of interest and charm. (p. 22)

> Robert Towers, "The Old Country," in The New York Review of Books (reprinted with permission from The New York Review of Books; copyright © 1982 Nyrev, Inc.), Vol. XXIX, No. 5, April 1, 1982, pp. 21-2.

JOHN UPDIKE

[When] Naipaul visited India for the first time, he found that "Narayan's novels did not prepare me for the distress of India" [see excerpt above].... (p. 84)

Narayan's most recent book, a collection of short stories called **"Malgudi Days"**..., tends to illustrate [what Naipaul called a] "Hindu response to the world.".... Hinduism is not infrequently bound into the substance of [Narayan's] short stories: in one, **"Iswaran,"** a student so thoroughly immerses himself in the visions of "a Tamil film with all the known gods in it" that he allows an imaginary horse to carry him into a river and drown; in another, **"The Snake-Song,"** a man plays the flute with such inspiration that the god Naga Raja, a great black cobra, appears and compels him to play the same song all night long.... A certain benign indifference presides above these tales, causing them to flicker out inconclusively.... The older stories, especially—selected from the previous collections **"An Astrologer's Day"** (1947) and **"Lawley Road"** (1956)—have the brevity and flimsiness of fables, mixed with a certain slickness imitated, perhaps, from the fiction of those English magazines, like the *Strand* and *Mercury*, which, Narayan has told us in his memoir **"My Days,"** entranced his youth and led to his first attempts to write.

Yet it cannot be fairly said that the distress of India is absent from the pages of **"Malgudi Days,"** or that the author averts his gaze from poverty. Many of the stories deal with people to whom a few rupees—even as little as one rupee (ten cents, approximately)—a day mean the difference between starvation and survival. (pp. 84-5)

Poverty is seen but not abhorred in these stories; "dereliction and smallness" are indulged by the author, even relished, as Naipaul charges. **"Malgudi Days"** is so innocent of protest we are put in mind of Naipaul's remark, later in his searing portrait of India, that "social inquiry is outside the Indian tradition; journalism in India has always been considered a gracious form of clerkship." If anything is abhorred by the gracious clerkship of these stories, it is the new, the modern and reforming. (p. 85)

[Narayan's] charm and compassion, which no one disputes, deliver not a reality that is "cruel and overwhelming" but one that is, usually, believable. Small lives seek their own solutions within an insoluble mass that leads visiting reporters to despair. There might be a Tolstoy or Cervantes who could render India more fully, without the touch of complacence and insubstantiality that Narayan's Hindu sensibility bestows. Nevertheless, in these simple stories of poverty and failure accepted lies the implicit social protest that we feel in such classics of the short story as Chekhov's "Grief" and O. Henry's "Gift of the Magi" and Flannery O'Connor's "Artificial Nigger": to portray poverty is to cry out against it. The very poor are something of an embarrassment to the novel; not enough happens to them, their struggles are too one-sided and hopeless. But a short story, like the flare of a match, brings human faces out of darkness, and reveals depths beyond statistics. All people are complex, surprising, and deserving of a break: this seems to me Narayan's moral, and one hard to improve upon. His social range and his successful attempt to convey, in sum, an entire population shame most American authors, who also, it might be charged, "ignore too much of what could be seen." American fiction deals in the main with the amorous and spiritual difficulties of young upper-middle-class adults; a visitor arriving in New York after studying the short stories of, say, Ann Beattie and Donald Barthelme as intently as Naipaul had read Narayan would be ill prepared for the industrial sprawl of Queens and the black slums of Brooklyn, for the squalid carnival of the avenues and the sneaking dread of the side streets after dark. Perhaps some disproportionate tilt toward the genteel and the comic is intrinsic to prose fiction, which rose with the bourgeoisie and still depends upon bourgeois purchasing power; authors seeking to rectify the balance could do worse than emulate Narayan's Hindu acceptance and vital, benign fellow-feeling. (p. 86)

> John Updike, "India Going On" (© 1982 by John Updike), in The New Yorker, Vol. LVIII, No. 24, August 2, 1982, pp. 84-6.

Gloria Naylor
1950-

Black American novelist and short story writer.

Naylor, who has also published several short stories, elicited critical interest with her first novel, *The Women of Brewster Place* (1982). Subtitled *A Novel in Seven Stories*, the book concerns seven women residents of a ghetto housing project. Although their personal situations differ, they collectively share the problems of the black, urban female. Each chapter reads like a short story and focuses on one character and her interaction with the others.

Critics unanimously praise Naylor's controlled narrative ability and her lyrical, passionate prose. *The Women of Brewster Place* received the 1982 American Book Award for best first novel.

(See also *Contemporary Authors*, Vol. 107.)

PUBLISHERS WEEKLY

A remarkable first novel from a gifted black writer, ["**The Women of Brewster Place**"] marks Gloria Naylor's talent as one to watch. In an unidentified northern city Brewster Place has become a slum for blacks. Naylor tells her story through the eventually interlocking lives of seven women, old and young, who have come there in refuge, despair or defiance.... [Their] lives reflect in depth the experiences of many black women alive in this country today, from the old woman tossed out as a teenager by her self-righteous Southern father when she bore an illegitimate child, to the young woman from a rich family fascinated by her African roots and trying to persuade her sisters to fight a slum landlord. It is when two lesbians move in that all the fears and prejudices of Brewster Place rise to a terrible climax, one that leaves the reader shattered.

A review of "The Women of Brewster Place," in Publishers Weekly *(reprinted from the April 9, 1982 issue of* Publishers Weekly, *published by R. R. Bowker Company, a Xerox company; copyright © 1982 by Xerox Corporation), Vol. 221, No. 15, April 9, 1982, p. 45.*

WILLIAM BRADLEY HOOPER

[In *The Women of Brewster Place*] Naylor focuses on seven black women, residents of Brewster Place. She is concerned with the distance between their dreams and realities, problems and solutions; these women are of different ages, come from different backgrounds, react differently to their blackness and to men, and have different notions of personal accomplishment, but all are burdened by being both black and female. Naylor is not angry; she writes with conviction and beautiful language, but spares the reader any bitterness. Characters are not puppets but exist and function as well-rounded personalities.

William Bradley Hooper, in a review of "The Women of Brewster Place," in Booklist *(reprinted by permission of the American Library Association; copyright © 1982 by the American Library Association), Vol. 78, No. 19, June 1, 1982, p. 1300.*

Courtesy of George Washington University

SUSAN BOLOTIN

Imagine a sort of Catfish Row moved North. Snow and rain have replaced the buzzards as omens, and Ben, a pure-hearted janitor who drinks too much, is standing in for Porgy. Bess, Serena and Clara are now called Mattie and Etta Mae and Ciel, but the street's universe still twirls around its women—tough, caring, sexy, sometimes mean, mostly tired, often loyal. (As one of them remarks, "All the good men are either dead or waiting to be born.")

A long tradition of urban fiction and nonfiction, cinema and theater has made places like Catfish Row instantaneously recognizable—and dangerously stereotypic. Even if Gloria Naylor's first novel ["**The Women of Brewster Place**"] were not the emotionally satisfying and technically accomplished book that it is, her decision to set it on Brewster Place, a one-street "ghetto," would have been courageous. What is marvelous, however, is that she doubled her own dare by leaving in the predictable landmarks, the archetypal characters, the usual clues, and made the whole thing work....

You see, the protagonist of Miss Naylor's book is the street; the drama of its birth, development, senescence and eventual death make "**The Women of Brewster Place**" a novel and not a collection of pieces—though it is written in seven chapters that work as independent short stories. Convincing us to believe in a street's tragic flaw is not easy, and Miss Naylor occasionally falters, slipping dangerously close to bathos and rhetoric. But mostly, she achieves her purpose with a dazzling efficiency....

In **"The Women of Brewster Place"** Miss Naylor has spun those fictional maybes and a whole lot of reality into an unusually textured tapestry.

> *Susan Bolotin, in a review of "The Women of Brewster Place," in* The New York Times *(copyright © 1982 by The New York Times Company; reprinted by permission), July 13, 1982, p. C10.*

DEIRDRE DONAHUE

Gloria Naylor centers her radiant first novel, **"The Women of Brewster Place,"** not in a specific city but in the chipped concrete and stinking trash cans of any dead-end slum block. In language as intricately whorled as mahogany, Naylor sculpts profiles of seven women....

"The Women of Brewster Place" is no pallid tale of attenuated perception recollected over cappuccino; Naylor is not afraid to grapple with life's big subjects: sex, birth, love, death, grief. Her women feel deeply, and she unflinchingly transcribes their emotions....

Naylor's potency wells up from her language. With prose as rich as poetry, a passage will suddenly take off and sing like a spiritual....

Vibrating with undisguised emotion, **"The Women of Brewster Place"** springs from the same roots that produced the blues. Like them, her book sings of sorrows proudly borne by black women in America.

> *Deirdre Donahue, "The Sorrows of 7 Sisters," in* The Washington Post *(© 1982, Washington Post Co.), August 13, 1982, p. D2.*

ANNIE GOTTLIEB

Gloria Naylor's **"The Women of Brewster Place"** is set in one of those vintage urban-housing developments that black people (who are, in truth, "nutmeg," "ebony," "saffron," "cinnamon-red" or "gold") have inherited from a succession of other ethnic groups. The difference is that while the Irish and Italians used it as a jumping-off place for the suburbs, for most of its "colored daughters" Brewster Place is "the end of the line."... But the end of the line is not the end of life. With their backs literally to the wall—a brick barrier that has turned Brewster Place into a dead end—the women make their stand together, fighting a hostile world with love and humor. (p. 11)

Despite Gloria Naylor's shrewd and lyrical portrayal of many of the realities of black life (her scene of services in the Canaan Baptist Church is brilliant), **"The Women of Brewster Place"** isn't realistic fiction—it is mythic. Nothing supernatural happens in it, yet its vivid, earthy characters (especially Mattie) seem constantly on the verge of breaking out into magical powers.... Miss Naylor bravely risks sentimentality and melodrama to write her compassion and outrage large, and she pulls it off triumphantly. (p. 25)

> *Annie Gottlieb, "Women Together," in* The New York Times Book Review *(copyright © 1982 by The New York Times Company; reprinted by permission), August 22, 1982, pp. 11, 25.*

DOROTHY WICKENDEN

It won't come as a surprise to readers of contemporary fiction by black women that Gloria Naylor has few kind words to waste on members of the other sex. Yet ***The Women of Brewster Place***, like Alice Walker's extraordinary *The Color Purple*, ... is not simply a self-indulgent celebration of female solidarity. Naylor and Walker write with equal lucidity about the cruelty that poverty breeds and the ways in which people achieve redemption. Nor is there a wariness about traditional women's roles. ***The Women of Brewster Place*** is a novel about motherhood, a concept embraced by Naylor's women, each of whom is a surrogate child or mother to the next. (p. 38)

> *Dorothy Wickenden, in a review of "The Women of Brewster Place," in* The New Republic *(reprinted by permission of* The New Republic; *© 1982 The New Republic, Inc.), Vol. 187, No. 10, September 6, 1982, pp. 37-8.*

Pablo Neruda
1904-1973

(Born Ricardo Eliecer Neftali Reyes y Basoalto) Chilean poet.

Neruda is considered one of the finest poets of our time. A prolific and adventurous writer who was awarded the Nobel Prize in literature in 1971, he passed through several literary and political stages in his long career. The poetry consistently celebrates love, nature, and human experience, and was in certain periods intensely political.

Neruda's passion for writing love poetry is particularly evident in the early *Veinte poemas de amor y una cancion desesperada* (1924; *Twenty Love Poems and a Song of Despair*). In the poems of this collection, Neruda presents woman and nature as "two aspects of the same reality" and uses nature imagery to describe women. Although it is now among the best known of Neruda's works, Chile's leading publisher refused to publish the book, claiming that it was too blatantly erotic. Neruda's poetry of that time is extremely personal and characterized by a melancholy view of the world and a preoccupation with unrequited love. In *Tentativa del hombre infinito* (1925; *Venture of the Infinite Man*) Neruda employs a freer style and surreal imagery. This movement toward the surreal culminated in *Residencia en la tierra* (1933; *Residence on Earth*), one of Neruda's most acclaimed works. The poems in this collection are anguished and despairing, full of surreal images of nature. They are perhaps the result of the loneliness Neruda was experiencing at the time of their writing.

The years 1945-1952 were turbulent and productive ones for Neruda. In 1945 he joined the Communist party in Chile and was elected to the Senate. In 1946 he supported the leftist presidential candidate who, once elected, became a pawn of the nation's industrial leaders. Communism was outlawed and Neruda's arrest ordered. In 1948 Neruda fled to Mexico and lived there until his return to Chile in 1952. During his exile he wrote the poems that were published as *Canto general* in 1950; they represent, in the opinion of most critics, Neruda's most significant work. The collection expresses his outrage at the Chilean political situation in the late 1940s. The work is his attempt to analyze and interpret the political and cultural directions being taken by South America. The book was banned in Chile.

After *Canto general*, Neruda's poetry underwent an important change. Subsequently, he began to write in a clear and simple style to powerful effect. The poems in *Odas elementales* (1954; *Elemental Odes*), for instance, take as their subjects everyday, familiar objects and raise them to a point of dignity and grace. At the time of their publication, these earthy, realistic poems came under critical fire for being too simple, but they are now considered among Neruda's most significant works.

At the time of his death Neruda was working on his memoirs and several volumes of poetry, including *El mar y las campanas* (1973) and *Jardín de invierno* (1974). Although the subjects of these collections are similar to Neruda's previous works, they were written with the knowledge of his imminent death. Death and winter are the most dominant themes.

© Lütfi Özkök

(See also *CLC*, Vols. 1, 2, 5, 7, 9; *Contemporary Authors*, Vols. 19-20, Vols. 45-48 [obituary]; and *Contemporary Authors Permanent Series*, Vol. 2.)

JAMES WRIGHT AND ROBERT BLY

What is most startling about Neruda, I think, when we compare him to Eliot or Dylan Thomas or Pound, is the great affection that accompanies his imagination. Neruda read his poetry for the first time in the U.S. in June of '66 at the Poetry Center in New York, and it was clear from that reading that his poetry is intended as a gift. When Eliot gave a reading, one had the feeling that the reading was a cultural experience, and that Eliot doubted very much if you were worth the trouble, but he'd try anyway. When Dylan Thomas read, one had the sense that he was about to perform some magical and fantastic act, perhaps painting a Virgin while riding on three white horses, and maybe you would benefit from this act, and maybe you wouldn't. Pound used to scold the audience for not understanding what he did. When Neruda reads, the mood in the room is one of affection between the audience and himself.

We tend to associate the modern imagination with the jerky imagination, which starts forward, stops, turns around, switches from subject to subject. In Neruda's poems, the imagination drives forward, joining the entire poem in a rising flow of imaginative energy. In the underworld of the consciousness, in the thickets where Freud, standing a short distance off, pointed out incest bushes, murder trees, half-buried primitive altars, and unburied bodies, Neruda's imagination moves with utter assurance, sweeping from one spot to another almost magically. The starved emotional lives of notary publics he links to the whiteness of flour, sexual desire to the shape of shoes, death to the barking sound where there is no dog. His imagination sees the hidden connections between conscious and unconscious substances with such assurance that he hardly bothers with metaphors—he links them by tying their hidden tails. He is a new kind of creature moving about under the surface of everything. Moving under the earth, he knows everything from the bottom up (which is the right way to learn the nature of a thing) and therefore is never at a loss for its name. Compared to him, most American poets resemble blind men moving gingerly along the ground from tree to tree, from house to house, feeling each thing for a long time, and then calling out "House!" when we already know it is a house.

Neruda has confidence in what is hidden. The Establishment respects only what the light has fallen on, but Neruda likes the unlit just as well. He writes of small typists without scorn, and of the souls of huge, sleeping snakes.

He violates the rules for behaviour set up by the wise. The conventionally wise assure us that to a surrealist the outer world has no reality—only his inner flow of images is real. Neruda's work demolishes this banality. Neruda's poetry is deeply surrealist, and yet entities of the outer world like the United Fruit Company have greater force in his poems than in those of any strictly "outward" poet alive. Once a poet takes a political stand, the wise assure us that he will cease writing good poetry. Neruda became a Communist in the middle of his life and has remained one: at least half of his greatest work, one must admit, was written after that time. He has written great poetry at all times of his life.

Finally, many critics in the United States insist the poem must be hard-bitten, impersonal and rational, lest it lack sophistication. Neruda is wildly romantic, and more sophisticated than Hulme or Pound could dream of being. He has few literary theories. Like Vallejo, Neruda wishes to help humanity, and tells the truth for that reason. (pp. 15-17)

> *James Wright and Robert Bly, "Introduction: Refusing To Be Theocritus," in* Twenty Poems *by Pablo Neruda, translated by James Wright and Robert Bly (copyright © 1967 by The Sixties Press, Odin House, Madison, Minnesota), Sixties Press, 1967, pp. 7-17.*

NANCY WILLARD

[In the poem **"Ode to Bread,"** from his collection *Elemental Odes,*] Neruda wants to do with bread what Stevens did with his jar in Tennessee: to place it on a hill and let its presence tame the wilderness. The comparisons in the first stanza of the poem make it clear that he celebrates bread for being itself, not for being eaten. Making bread is a birth and a growing. Its shape suggests the birth of man, its growth the rebirth of spring, an "equinoctial terrestrial germination" (*equinoccial/germinación/terrestre*). It grows like a mouth, a breast, a hill, in a universe where everything is alive. Change is the sign of its life. If you cannot change, you cannot grow, and in Neruda's eyes you are less alive than the bread or the hill.

Because bread does not happen by itself, man is as much the subject of the poem as bread. But the "I" of the earlier poems has become "we," and Neruda no longer uses things to carry his private emotions. (p. 103)

In bread Neruda sees the kingdom of man. Contrary to Christian teachings, man does live by bread alone. Beauty and love have meaning nowhere but here. The pitiful spectators he sees at religious processions tell him that institutionalized religion destroys those it promises to save. The Indians are servile and abused; the hungry parochial schoolmasters, the nuns, and the clergy have lost touch with the earth. They deny life because they are afraid of death. But a salvation that asks of anyone such a denial is not for Neruda. (p. 104)

Neruda's kingdom of peace on earth is to come only when people have learned to share the gifts of the earth. It will come through sacrifice, for the meek cannot inherit the earth until the conqueror has been conquered and the treacherous arena converted into the plains of peace. If the rich hoard bread, let no man beg or pray for it; but let him and hungry men everywhere fight for justice. . . . (p. 105)

Although Neruda wants you to feel the urgent life of bread, too many explicit ideas make the whole effect rather flat. Ultimately, the poem has little to do with bread and everything to do with the government of man. The apocalypse is oversimplified, as in Neruda's least successful political poems, where the line between poetry and prose disappears altogether. Compared to those in **"From: Elephant"** . . . , the metaphors in this poem are general and the rhythms weak. Furthermore, you cannot read his promise that the simple man will conquer the earth without remembering Neruda's remarks elsewhere that no one can conquer it. Both the oppressed and the oppressor are subject to the laws of nature; here, he has already said, is the real conqueror.

The *Elemental Odes* are Neruda's hymns to being alive. But he knows that the poet of life must also be the poet of death. He has answered the question, What is man, by showing man's life as part of the bigger life of nature. But although death in nature is both a midwife and an executioner, when a man dies, that particular man does not return in any season. You cannot tell what man is until you know whether there is any way of saving that particular man without bringing in metaphysics or an afterlife.

Neruda's answer is his experience. What has happened to him cannot be refuted. In his long poem **"The Heights of Macchu Picchu"** . . . , Neruda makes it clear that our most intense experience of impermanence is not death but our own isolation among the living. . . . (p. 106)

One cause of man's loneliness is that, unlike all other creatures, he lives with the knowledge of his own death. All his life he saves time, yet at the end of his life he has saved nothing; his anxiety floods him with choices and desires . . . , he seldom fulfills his role, and he ends by setting up barriers between himself and other lives. The difference between the simple life and the treacherous arena is the difference between isolation and love. Civilization is built on the failure to love. And without love, nothing of us survives in the imaginations of those who come after us. For permanence is what can be continued. . . .

Neruda points out that we, unlike things, can die two kinds of death. The great death destroys us physically; it is natural; it is one of the changes that sustain life. The small death destroys us spiritually; it keeps us from being reborn; you find it in whatever confirms men in their isolation from one another, and then, like Neruda, it happens you are tired of being a man. For you see that men are threshed like corn in the granary of lost deeds and miserable events.... (p. 107)

When Neruda visited the relics of the ancient mountain city of Macchu Picchu, he first saw it as a monument to the permanence of nature and the impermanence of man. Not a trace of man remains. His life has disappeared along with his knives, cloth, "customs, frayed syllables, / masks of blazing light." But nature knows no such obliteration. To the waterfalls, rivers, and vegetation, pressed into coal deep in the earth, destruction is a most fruitful transformation. Of them at least, Neruda can say, even in the shadow of the vulture, "The dead kingdom still lives."

But can you say this of man? Not if you are asking for a physical survival, certainly. Neruda reminds us that our identity is not our physical presence alone but other men's response to it. Love alone rescues us from oblivion. So he calls upon the place to give up its dead, and he will resurrect them through his love.... (p. 108)

The lost deeds that make up the life of the "inconclusive man" (*hombre inconcluso*) are now the stuff of his immortality. Neruda finds that only his own life can show him the dead and make them present to him. Trying to love the solitudes, the dangers, and the weaknesses of those he could never meet joins him to their lives, and in this joining Neruda sees man's indestructible return....

If Neruda is intolerant of despair, it is because he wants nothing to sully man's residence on earth. He knows that each man must build his own, and that Eden can survive only where your love is stronger than your knowledge of death. As a poet, he dedicates himself to making this happen again and again.... (p. 109)

> Nancy Willard, "Radiant Bread for the Sun of Man," in Chelsea *(copyright © 1968 by Chelsea Associates, Inc.; reprinted by permission of the editors)*, Nos. 22 & 23, June, 1968 *(and reprinted in her* Testimony of the Invisible Man: William Carlos Williams, Francis Ponge, Rainer Maria Rilke, Pablo Neruda, *University of Missouri Press, 1970, pp. 83-109).*

JAMES WRIGHT

this time it is clear to everybody who has ever heard of him that Neruda is a very great poet.

It is the folly of Americans to assume that to say as much is to say that a man is a great man, worthy of worship, a relief to us in our frantic and temporary deaths.

But a great poet is a disturbance. If poetry means anything, it means heart, liver, and soul. If great poetry means anything, anything at all, it means disturbance, secret disturbance, that can be disposed of in public, as the pharmacist's delivery of prescription disposes of lonely midnight daydreams. But that cannot be so easily disposed of privately, as the insomniac discovers that the soporific provides him with sleep only to follow the hand of sleep into a land of secret wakening, nightmare, or illumination, that he wished to escape in the first place. It is bad enough to be miserable; but to be happy, how far beyond shock it is. To be alive, with all one's unexpected senses, and yet to face the fact of unhappiness.

There is a critic in the English language whose nobility and spaciousness allowed him to make the statement about poetry that can in turn allow us to cherish what is great. It is a statement about Shakespeare, and it applies to Neruda's poem *The Heights of Macchu Picchu*. In his preface to the works of Shakespeare, Dr. Johnson wonders why we should care about a poet after he has been dead for more than a hundred years. After all the envious reviewers are dead, something lives. How do we know it lives? We love it. It is alive. It is all we have. But why? Why do we love it? What is alive?

It combines a flowering in language with a cold pruning of form. Great poetry folds personal death and general love into one dark blossom.

I don't know why you read it, but I read it because I like it. I want poetry to make me happy, but the poetry I want should deal with the hell of our lives or else it leaves me cold. Why should I care? Why should I let it touch me?

Here is Johnson's remark on great poetry, which on this particular occasion happens to be Shakespeare:

> Nothing can please many or please long but just representations of general nature. Particular manners can be known to few, and few only can judge how nearly they are copied. The irregular combinations of fanciful invention may delight awhile, by that novelty of which the common satiety of life sends us all in quest. But the pleasures of sudden wonder are soon exhausted, and the mind can only repose on the stability of truth.

Neruda's abundance is clear in every country whose citizens care about poetry. He is too huge to handle in an essay, but I think we should try to identify his genius in a single poem.

Neruda wrote *The Heights of Macchu Picchu* in the fall of 1945. In 1943 he had returned to Chile, and it is very odd to reflect that on that return from his travels as Chilean consul-general in Mexico, a "triumphal journey, on which he found himself acclaimed in capital after capital by huge crowds" ..., he should have written this great poem. He had achieved fame, all right. And we know what fame is. Milton has told us. It is an infirmity. But Neruda responded as follows.

In a sequence of twelve poems, the poet tells how he had spent his early life wandering in the cities of his country, sick to death of his loneliness, longing for love. The love he longed for was partly sexual, and this love had already been achieved and celebrated in the *Twenty Poems* that made his poetic reputation.... But Neruda's love is human, and human love is a hell. Coming home, acclaimed, he responded by grieving over his failure to achieve a fulfillment of love with the living. And yet they were cheering him! Imagine. He is a very great poet. Instead of writing an Ode to His Readers, he composed the *Macchu Picchu*.

But how can that be? Macchu Picchu, the big city of the Incas, was dead. And the people who built it were dead.

No, they were living in the modern cities of Chile. They were also living in Cleveland, as we know. (If we are sane.)

Neruda couldn't find them in Cleveland, or in Santiago.

So he ascended.

I would paraphrase Neruda's argument as follows: Appalled by loneliness I sought my human brothers among the living; I do not really object to their death, as long as I can share with them the human death; but everywhere I go among the living I find them dying each by each a small petty death in the midst of their precious brief lives. So I ascended to the ancient ruins of the city of Macchu Picchu in the Andes; and there I found that, however the lives of my human brothers may have suffered, at least they are all now dead together. Look at the gorgeous things they have made. But wait a moment. Weren't their lives just as petty and grotesquely fragmented as the very people who die early and pointlessly in the modern cities where I have just been celebrated? Yes, they were. And therefore I love the poor broken dead. They belong to me. I will not celebrate the past for its perfect power over the imperfect living. "I come to speak for your dead mouths." The silent and nameless persons who built Macchu Picchu are alive in Santiago de Chile. The living are the living, and dead the dead must stay.

In conveying this idea, Neruda writes twelve poems that move from his despair in the living cities to his ascent to the city of the dead, and thence to his invocation of the dead who, in his poetry, are the living. As Professor Pring-Mill remarks, the poet's ascent through space is also an ascent backwards through time. In fact, that is the form of the poem; to discover the living in the past is to discover the living in the present. (pp. 191-93)

> James Wright, "'I Come to Speak for Your Dead Mouths'" (© 1968 by The Modern Poetry Association; reprinted by permission of the Editor of Poetry and Mrs. James Wright), in Poetry, Vol. CXII, No. 3, June, 1968, pp. 191-94.

FERNANDO ALEGRIA

[Neruda] will keep on dying with the movement of our century and with us: a vast and profound death of incalculable significance, dying first here, later there, and then beyond; now in me and then in other men and women, without obvious rhythm, but really with the rhythm of the seasons, of the sea, the stars and the trees, through which he keeps growing, stretching, resting from his life, breathing at last all the atmosphere and all the earth, all of time, the components of his death....

I want to write a few things down about the friend I loved and the poet, who at the end faced up to the fact of his death, clothed as always in a magical complexity and simplicity. To my mind what is significant is how Neruda, dying so quickly, transformed this moment of truth into a fascinating and delicate balancing act of reserve, allusion, boldness, shyness, vertigo and tranquility. My evidence is . . . the ten poems which Neruda published in *Crísis* in August, 1973. . . .

The first thing to be noted is the ordering of these ten poems: Neruda begins with **"Integraciones,"** ends with **"Una canción de amor"** and sends special instructions to the publisher that both poems should be printed in italics. His death testimony is thus supported by two love songs, like a medal where the front and the back, the face and its shadow, sustain an affirmation of life. (p. 42)

[There are two poems] that refer directly to the theme of death, clearly reflecting his secret speculation: **"Animal de luz"** is a recognition of his solitude, of the closed circle, and of those who can no longer touch him in his innermost being. The poet has retired, followed by his escort of ocean waves and stars, an escort determined by time. What is left is at once small and vast. Terribly weary, cities resting on his shoulders and strings of countries around his neck, he flees, but not from the others who have already said and done all, but from his own interminable inner dialogue. "There is no more deciphering to do." It's clear. "Nothing more to say." Alone, surrounded by silence but also by the sound of the ocean, he concludes simply: That's all. The enormity of this conclusion falls at the end of the poem like a stone curtain. Neruda unhesitatingly turns out the lights. Great doer that he was in life, he prepares himself to work in the great inactivity that will be his death.

"Triste conción para aburrir a cualquiera" is a solitary game, a balancing of achievement against absurdity, of hours against emptiness; the waverings of man divided, the eternal rhythm of life and death. The simple force of the *leitmotiv* slips through his fingers like the beads of a rosary, a wise and melancholy litany which can nevermore arrive at conclusions.

In **"Preguntas"** there are four clues to man's initial and ultimate curiosity: the butterfly which doesn't know the signs of its wings, the bee unaware of its path, the ant ignorant of the number of casualties in its army, and the cyclone unable to remember its name while it is quiescent. Neither love nor knowledge offers answers to man who remains "looking at buried time." Only in doubt, at the edge of death, can man sustain certain hope: "Or is it that what I see from afar / Is that which I have yet to live?"

In summing up his poetic experience Neruda becomes aware of the personal dimension he gave to words, but without forgetting what effect words had on him. At first he names things, then he delves beyond into their essences, searching for the sound and the echo, that is, the secret action which reveals the meaning of matter. A virgin sound, a name seemingly chosen at random, **"Oregano,"** is launched as the symbol of his battle against rhetoric, against the irrationality of rationalism, the vehement search for the magic word which will "not speak to anyone," but which will bring him to his destiny, an inner recess, substance in a sown-field, a flower blooming-decaying, oregano-defense, oregano-elation, oregano-revolver, a green and aromatic word brandished like a sword.

We seem to be approaching inescapable ends, affirmations that echo through a world in which old symbols open up and let their fruits fall to the ground. Both **"El héroe"** and **"La situación insostenible"** are images which represent the implacable assault of death. The hero is a man who passes through life stripped naked, an intransigent philosopher, unchanging before the claims of society, covered with black scales, civilization's last great nudist, reflecting in his nakedness the passage of history "like an old editorial—in a defunct newspaper," dead on his terrace due to the harshness of winter.

The second poem, **"La situación insostenible,"** refers to a family, a household, a world, methodically appropriated and invaded by its dead, thrown off-kilter by likenesses of man, cheeky and intrusive deceased, who first enter the living room, filling the chairs, the tables, the family larders, break into the bathrooms where they polish skulls, push the kindly and patient Ostrogodos into the farthest reaches of the garden under the shade of an orange tree, there climbing into its branches and diligently proliferating, until the Ostrogodos have no choice but to submit and deliver themselves benignly and complacently to the cemetery. (pp. 44-6)

The eight poems in *Crísis* dealing with death bear no direct relation to two of Neruda's fundamental books: *Residencia en la tierra* and *Canto general*. In the first two volumes of *Residencia*, Neruda faces a death which is an essential part of the eternal movement of life, an implacable and progressive wearing-down, a seed destroying itself in a vague search, blind, constant, for an atmosphere not to be found again, for a stalk already cut; the image of a world in the present which carries in it the dead burden of a future mirroring past destructions. Neruda sees the world disintegrate before his eyes and knows himself to be part of this ruin that grows and envelops him from without and from within. (p. 48)

What we are dealing with is a mature conception of death, not as a unique, individualized event, but as a process gauged by its material consequences and metaphysical projections: destruction and emptiness. Neruda manages two powerful symbols: the sea and time. He submits them to collective experiences of the phenomenon of alienation and to a personal state of anguish. He will search incessantly the answer to this anguish, drawing himself closer to the peaceful nature of things that remain unconscious of their attrition and their voyage toward death: stones, sacks, trees, mirrors, papers, shackles.

In *Canto general* Neruda considers death historically, not as boundless history, but a daily chronicle of the deaths in which he is routinely clothed: an autumnal tree, demises which cover him like patches, a collective death speaking to him from the fortress of Macchu Picchu or slowly spanning the abysses of the Great Ocean. His testament is a literary document with political content, the balance sheet of a life's struggle, testimony of his faith in the Communist Party. (p. 49)

I think Neruda confronted the final enigma with total consciousness and solved it in terms of love and surrender to the materialistic dynamic of the world as he conceived it. What I want to emphasize is something very simple: Neruda was, above all, a love poet and, more than anyone, an unwavering, powerful, joyous, conqueror of death. That is why he asked the editor of *Crísis* to italicize his two love poems. What does he say in them? What didn't Neruda say about love in his poetic works? . . . Time has not been, nor shall it be, anything but a fragile ring; duration through tenderness has its own will and logic, that of the sea in its wise and constant motion. He will remain in what he calls "integrations," the most important of which is Matilde and all that is within her. **"Canción de amor"** is a ballad, a tender *ritornello,* a song to the youthful glory of tenderness, music and possession. (pp. 49-50)

> Fernando Alegría, "Neruda: Reminiscences and Critical Reflections," translated by Deborah S. Bundy, in Modern Poetry Studies *(copyright 1974, by Jerome Mazzaro), Vol. V, No. 1, Spring, 1974, pp. 41-51.*

ROBERT PRING-MILL

At the time of his death in Santiago in 1973, twelve days after the military coup, [Pablo Neruda] had just seen the fourth edition of his *Obras completas* through the press, he was nearing the completion of his memoirs (*Confieso que he vivido*), and was working on the last of eight volumes of new poetry [*La rosa separado, Jardín de invierno, 2000, El corazón amarillo, Libro de las preguntas, Elegía, Defectos escogidos,* and *El mar y las campanas*]. He had planned to publish these, along with his autobiography, on his seventieth birthday. Those eight collections make up a remarkable last chapter in the life of the most varied twentieth-century poet to have written in Spanish. Two of them—*Jardín de invierno* and *El mar y las campanas*—include some poems which rank among his finest. They represent the winter of his poetry, whose autumn had begun in 1958 with the return to introspection of *Estravagario*. With this final chapter Neruda becomes at last, in death, a poet for all seasons. (p. 1154)

2000 is the shortest [of the eight volumes]: a nine-poem sequence looking forward to the next millennium, in the tones of *Fin de mundo. El corazón amarillo* is largely whimsical, after the manner of *Estravagario:* one poem, beginning "The certainty of the green tree in spring / is something proven", reads almost like a deliberately nonchalant reply to the *desengaño* of **"With Quevedo during spring"**. The *Libro de las preguntas* collects more than 300 questions without answers, like "How many bees to a day?" Some are humorous, others (the least effective) satirical or sly; a few link up with the longer poems, such as "Where does the French spring / find so many leaves?" or "How do seasons know / the time to change their shirt?"

Elegía, on Russian themes, is largely about Moscow and friends now dead; some of its thirty poems have strikingly effective lines, but most depend too much on personal associations for the poet's grief to move the reader deeply. . . . *Defectos escogidos* is somewhat of a miscellany. Though planned as a collection of people's faults (Neruda's own as well as those of others), its best poems do not fit the title and are better suited to the whimsy of *El corazón amarillo.* . . .

El mar y las campanas was the only volume not yet ready for the press. Of its forty-nine poems, thirty-two (including many of the most powerful) were still untitled when Neruda died. He often left the titling of individual poems until a volume was complete, deciding which key-texts should be italicized, and establishing the final order of contents—something to which he attached the greatest importance. The sequence of *El mar y las campanas* is Neruda's own, with one exception: the publishers have placed **"Final"**—a poem "concluded not long before [the poet] died"—at the very end. A simple farewell to Matilde, it balances the opening **"Inicial"** which sets the richly meditative mood for this last lyrical collection, and establishes the two symbolic title-images of sea and bells.

In these taut poems Neruda reaches a new kind of simplicity. Where the *Odas* had used easy words to talk of simple things, here the words themselves could not be simpler, but their associations lead the reader into an unmapped world which he can only dimly apprehend, half hinted at through punning turns of phrase and richly ambiguous syntax.

The sea had been a major theme throughout Neruda's life, and the bell a frequently recurring image. Sometimes the word *campana* is meant literally, but even then it carries overtones. The bell can have a "resonant and dying" note, in the context of a lover's voice; it is both a summons and a warning in the *Canto general,* where it belongs to the web of imagery relating man to the natural and social world that he inhabits. . . .

As his poetry became more personal again, from *Estravagario* onwards, the bell grew more mysterious—not denying its earlier associations, but rather drawing them together—till in *El mar y las campanas* it opens out into an almost cosmic symbol, inexorably ringing in the waves of the sea and the pulse of the land, and ultimately inside each man as his own bell takes up the rhythm. Yet the bells of Isla Negra were quite real: ships' bells hung high to face the sea. It is worthy of note that the two key symbols of Neruda's final poems should be so firmly rooted in reality. That is how all his best poetry had always worked.

When he returned from Paris with his wife, they found that the salt-laden winds had rotted through the lashings, and that one large bell had fallen and cracked. In one of the untitled poems, this fractured bell implicitly becomes a symbol of Neruda himself: "This broken bell"—whose "hard gold hue of bronze / is now frog-green"—still wants to sing, but can no longer summon anyone. In another untitled poem, Neruda asks to be left alone with this cleft bell beside the sea, observing a long silence, seeking fresh knowledge. This line of thought extends the marine imagery in "[**There's not that much to say**]", to give a positive reply to the bleak questions-and-answers of *Residencia en la tierra*. . . .

El mar y las campanas offers us "the tally, the tale, the sound" of life and of Neruda's own approaching death. But also of ours: each man is his own bell (as **"Inicial"** implies) waiting beside the ocean, on the land, until the time for him to sound arrives.

When he received the Nobel Prize, Neruda said that poetry involved achieving a proper balance "between solitude and solidarity, between feeling and action, between the intimacy of one's self, the intimacy of mankind, and the revelation of nature". In his own poetry, that balance between opposite or complementary concepts varied greatly, at different stages of his life. In the final serenity of that last Chilean winter in Isla Negra, when the poems of *El mar y las campanas* withdraw from action into feeling, they might seem to withdraw entirely into "solitude". Yet the insights which they give into "the intimacy of mankind"—as well as of Neruda's "self"—communicate a kind of solidarity which operates at a level deeper by far than that of mere political allegiance. This does not mean that the political poetry has been annulled, but rather that the human feelings which inspired it have found their ultimate fruition. (p. 1156)

> Robert Pring-Mill, "The Winter of Pablo Neruda," in The Times Literary Supplement (© Times Newspapers Ltd. (London) 1975; reproduced from The Times Literary Supplement by permission), No. 3838, October 3, 1975, pp. 1154-56.

RENÉ DE COSTA

In relation to Neruda's previous public posture as a writer of the people, *Estravagario* seemed very individualistic, even frivolous in its self-indulgence. What is more, the frivolity was not unintentional. (p. 175)

How is one to interpret this about-face, Neruda's sudden lack of solemnity regarding himself and his work? Only eight years before, in 1950, at the end of **Canto general**, he had piously willed his books to the poets of tomorrow. . . . Then, speaking as the collective voice of his people, he went on to claim for his own work an enduring meaning for future generations. . . . In 1958 he makes no such claim on posterity. He does not even ask that his writings be practical or utilitarian as in the elemental odes; he shrugs literature off as a light entertainment. Neruda's stance in *Estravagario* is that of an anti-poet. His subject is himself. (pp. 177-78)

Estravagario is a very personal book. For this reason some critics suggested it be compared to **Veinte poemas de amor**. Others, noting a certain hermeticism, were inclined to consider it in the context of **Residencia en la tierra**. Actually, the book refuses such pat categorizations, for it contains recognizable snatches of almost everything: the serendipity of the odes, the episodic development of the epic, even a good measure of politics. The problem is that the repertory, while recognizably Nerudian, is completely reworked; everything is treated irreverently. (p. 179)

Estravagario is important not so much for its political or personal revision of the past as for its successful adaptation of the tone and style of what has come to be called anti-poetry. In this work Neruda, utilizing many of the techniques and procedures of Parra's *Poemas y antipoemas* (1954), began a whole new stage in his own poetry and contributed to the public acceptance of a radically different type of literary expression. . . . Essentially it is a colloquial mode of literary discourse, more chatty and less reasoned than that of the elemental odes. The differences of degree and procedure reflect the author's revised attitude toward the function of his work. In *Odas elementales* Neruda confidently assumed the role of philosopher and the public responsibilities of the role; in *Estravagario* he takes a philosophic look at himself as a poet and as a man, and talks frankly to his readers as though to a circle of good friends gathered for witty after-dinner conversation. The assumption is that we share not only his concerns but his droll sense of humor as well. The poet or, rather, the anti-poet thus brings poetry down from its pedestal and, through humor, desacralizes the figure of himself as author. (pp. 180-81)

By any measure *Estravagario*, as it appeared to the reader of 1958, was a most unusual book. In it the author not only refused to take himself seriously, but he also presented his work in such a way as to challenge the reading public's sense of decorum. Readers of these poems today . . . tend to take them all very earnestly. On the other hand, the reader of the original 1958 edition was faced with an illustrated text, a book whose outlandish engravings enhanced and contradicted the literary content. True to at least one connotation of its title, the book was an extravaganza of sorts, containing a miscellany of literary texts both serious and comic, each illustrated with graphic material culled from diverse sources. . . . (p. 183)

In the interplay of text and illustration a new kind of poetry is born. And, although Neruda adopted the rhetoric of the anti-poem from Parra, Parra ultimately came to acknowledge the appropriateness of the graphic complement in his own *Artefactos* (1971), poems printed like postcards combining text and illustration. The purpose was the same: to go beyond the linguistic frame of literature. This is not to say that the anti-poem as practiced by Parra and Neruda lacks a literary form. Quite the contrary; the illustration enhances the text by playing against it. In this way the special effects of the assemblage, created for the most part with standard literary devices, are more directly noticeable. (p. 184)

One of the fundamental breakthrough concepts of Parra's anti-poetry that Neruda has made his own in *Estravagario* is the recognition that poetry, like other literary genres, need not be so solemn; it can be an entertainment. Whether printed in newspaper columns or in luxurious volumes, poetry is read primarily for aesthetic pleasure. Recognizing this literary fact of life, the author does not preach in *Estravagario*. He asks only that we allow him to work on our minds, to entertain us for a while. Thus, to read any poem in *Estravagario* requires the same "suspension of disbelief" as for a spectator at the performing arts. In a sense, each composition is a performance, requiring a flight of the imagination on the part of the reader. For each poem the point of departure for this flight into fancy is the illustration which precedes the text and serves as a kind of visual epigraph. The reader-viewer is thus guided into the total imaginative construct the author has provided. The extraordinary in this way does not take on the air of the ordinary; it is kept extraordinary. . . .

One thing above all else is evident in this book: from beginning to end it is playful. The author is performing, holding forth as though at a party, and we reader-spectators are asked to join in the fun, provided of course that we do not interrupt. The entertainer after all knows what he is up to. (p. 187)

Throughout *Estravagario* Neruda is striving for special effects. Just as the visual epigraph in each composition is carefully chosen to arouse the reader's imagination at the outset so also is each text made to conclude in a forceful way. In poem after poem the conversational rambling and colloquial informality suddenly comes to a halt; a one- or two-line variation is introduced and the closing is strikingly, often rhetorically, terse. Echo effects are sometimes created, leaving a strong and lingering impression on the reader. . . .

In some of the no-nonsense compositions the closure has a loftily resonant quality, while in the jesting poems it can be abruptly discordant. These are all calculated effects. (p. 189)

In the context of Neruda's oeuvre at the time [*Estravagario*] occupied a class by itself. Only with the passage of time has it become possible to perceive in this volume presages of the various directions his poetry was to take in the years to follow: the chattily discursive memory-poem, for example, would culminate in *Memorial de Isla Negra* (. . . 1964), a five-volume autobiography in verse; while the more capricious art of, say, "*Bestiario*" would be continued in *Arte de pájaros* (. . . 1966); and the stagey quality of certain fantasy poems . . . would later be developed into a full-fledged verse drama, *Fulgor y muerte de Joaquín Murieta* (. . . 1967). A poetry directly concerned with the here and now would also appear from time to time, coinciding with international crises: the Cuban Revolution in *Canción de gesta* (. . . 1968); Vietnam and the generally deplorable state of the world in *Fin de mundo* (. . . 1969); Nixon in *Incitación al Nixonicidio y alabanza de la Revolución Chilena* (. . . 1973). (pp. 198-99)

Estravagario marks a high point in Neruda's life and art. With this book he freed his writing from his own literary tradition, at the same time that he managed to free his person from his social, political, and literary past. Equipped with the colloquial diction of the anti-poem and the liberated attitude of the anti-poet, he was able to strike out in many diverse directions. (p. 199)

>René de Costa, in his The Poetry of Pablo Neruda (copyright © 1979 by the President and Fellows of Harvard College; excerpted by permission), Cambridge, Mass.: Harvard University Press, 1979, 213 p.

MANUEL DURÁN and MARGERY SAFIR

Neruda's career as a poet began with love poetry and ended with love poetry. One of his very last works, written only days before his death, is **"The End,"** a love poem to [his wife] Matilde. There were, of course, changes; there were deviations during the period of *Residence on Earth*, for example; there were turns and innovations during the period of political and epic poetry that began in the late thirties and culminated in 1950 with *Canto General*, but there was also a remarkable continuity. Erotic poetry and love poetry were for Neruda an important, essential part of his poetic life.

Pablo Neruda was one of the most prolific poets of our century. To trace the development of even one aspect of his poetic world is far from easy. Yet in the case of his erotic poetry and his love poetry the outline of that development is clear enough. The early Neruda, from his first published book, *Crepusculario*, and then especially in *Twenty Poems*, is a sensualist and a materialist in his approach to love and woman. . . . [In *Twenty Poems*] Neruda intensifies the complete fusion between woman and Nature. Joy and despair, like Marisol and Marisombra, mingle and alternate in this book, but whatever the emotion of the moment, the poet is constant in his identification of woman with Nature, in his use of Nature imagery to describe woman, and in his conception of woman as a vehicle for a return to Nature. In these richly sensual poems, the style is still on the whole "modern Romantic" with symbolist overtones and the first few hints of the newer, more disturbing poetic styles. Yet they remain "constructive" poems, in that they are organized around experiences in which real human beings, Neruda himself and the women he loved, provide a stabilizing platform upon which each poem is built.

The period following *Twenty Poems* is largely a time of disintegration. The intensely passionate *The Ardent Slingsman* was published in 1933, but it had been written much earlier, at about the same time as *Twenty Poems*. From 1925 to 1935 Neruda wrote very little erotic poetry. Flashes of it appear now and then, for instance, in the poems to Josie Bliss. Neruda was still a poet of sensuality, but in *Residence on Earth* the sexual imagery is primarily used in a graphic, blatantly anti-erotic form designed to show glimpses of a world in decay, without aim, collapsing of its own stench and rot.

The poetry written in the late thirties and the forties is more loving and more erotic than that of the period 1925-35. In *Canto General* the poet is, as in his youth, drunk with Nature, earth, mankind, but his passion is directed toward a continent, toward America, rather than toward any individual woman in it. This is a period of great love poetry, but one in which the primary thrust is political and epic, the erotic and love images defining the tone, sketching the hues, not providing the central impulse. Sexual elements abound in *Canto General*, but they are ancillary—they help build the whole poem; they are not the whole poem.

The Grapes and the Wind and *The Captain's Verses*, while very different from each other, form a sort of bridge between this period of public poetry and the books that were published from the late 1950s on. In both books, Neruda continues his passionate commitment to a political cause, but now a specific woman also reappears in his verses in the person of Matilde Urrutia. The first of these books is still primarily political, and the perspective is that of a travel chronicle, with Neruda's growing love for Matilde entering almost in secondary fashion. In *The Captain's Verses*, Neruda returns to the clear intention of writing love poetry; the proportions are inverted and here the political militancy defines the poet's notion of what he wants from love and from his lover, but it is Matilde and his love for her that are consciously the center of the work. The image of his lover as a "fellow combatant" in this book is markedly different from the images in Neruda's earlier love poetry or those in his later books; yet this work is linked to both the earlier and the later works by the fact that once again a particular woman is at the core of Neruda's verses.

After this period of transition where, in differing degrees, political commitment and love poetry are fused, Neruda returned in the late fifties and the sixties to a tone of clear, romantic intimacy. His love for Matilde was by then an established, publicly acknowledged fact, and with the love poetry in *Extravagaria, One Hundred Love Sonnets,* and *Barcarole,* Neruda built a new vision of love. He wrote some of his finest poetry in this period. The style has become more supple, at times full of surprises and unexpected adjectives. Yet it is still recognizably linked to the style of the young Neruda, which has been subjected to a few limbering exercises. The late poetry openly expresses joy, confidence, and optimism, with none of the anguish of the early verse. It is also monogamous—there are no distressing alternations like those between Marisol and Marisombra in *Twenty Poems*. The differences are notable. But a continuity still remains, in the Nature imagery, always the essence of Neruda's eroticism, and in the presence of the poet's romantic self and the self of the woman he loves, providing again a solid ground.

We are faced, in other words, with one essential personality, a single literary *persona*, expressing his vision through varied techniques which respond to the different changes in his life, the accumulation of experience in living and in writing, yet echoing with constancy the same fundamental voice. . . . There is a continuity in Neruda's work, and part of that continuity is to be found in the constant return to erotic love poetry, a return that encompasses different and evolving visions, but which remains at its core constant, earthy, sensual, material.

The literary importance of Neruda's erotic and love poetry has at times been overshadowed by the dazzling imagery of *Residence on Earth* and the epic political vision in *Canto General*. For the average Latin American reader, however, the reader that Neruda the committed Marxist most wanted to reach, there is no aspect of Neruda's work more significant than his love poetry. Neruda's erotic love poetry includes several indisputably brilliant masterpieces. His love poetry is a thread running through his different works, his successive styles and periods, unifying his whole poetic world and giving clues to the relationships between the parts, the books, and the total opus. Neruda's erotic poetry and his love poetry, and perhaps this is one of their single greatest contributions, have served to acclimatize an entire generation of readers to modern avant-garde styles. Many of Neruda's readers acquired their taste for innovative language and bold images from his early works, and they did not desert the poet even when he beckoned them into the subterranean labyrinths of *Residence on Earth*. Neruda gradually introduced the new styles, and his readers were still with him when, in the forties, fifties, and sixties, his style underwent a process of simplification and emerged as clearly understandable to the average reader while never sacrificing the use of bold, striking images. (pp. 28-31)

Like his love poetry, Neruda's Nature poetry runs throughout his entire career. (p. 33)

In his numerous books where Nature dominates, Neruda seems to have intuitively understood that Nature is so vast that no single angle of vision can do it justice. It is not surprising, therefore, that the poet's approach to Nature underwent significant changes through the years. In *Crepusculario*, Neruda looks at Nature in what can be called a traditional fashion: the poet contemplating the world and focusing on those aspects of it that have attracted poets for centuries—the sunsets, the sea, the wind. In *Twenty Poems* this stance changes somewhat, and a second stage of Neruda's Nature poetry is initiated. Nature does not enter for itself alone, but rather Nature and woman are seen as two aspects of the same reality. The beauty and strength—and mystery, at times terror—of Nature and the beauty, strength, and mystery of woman are but mirrors of one another. In *Twenty Poems,* nostalgia, love of Nature, and love of woman are united in a single strand and nowhere do we find the detached contemplation of Nature itself, as occurred in a number of the poems in *Crepusculario*.

A third vision begins with *Venture of the Infinite Man* and reaches its climax with the *Residence* poems. Neruda's loneliness impels him to flight, to look at the world from new angles, whether soaring as in *Venture* or immersed in the heart of darkness as in *Residence on Earth*. The poet invades matter and is in turn invaded by it. It is an uneven battle; the poet is crushed, his senses explode on the verge of delirium and madness, and yet his flight gives us a glimpse of the pure energy—and inhumanity—of the vast chaotic forces of our external environment.

A fourth approach to Nature springs forth in Neruda's epic period. . . . This is a time of commitment to interpreting the past of the poet's continent in order to understand its present. In *Canto General,* Neruda seeks original Nature. He looks to recreate the initial innocence, the lost paradise, to plunge into a primeval world in which plants and animals are still only emerging. Neruda's vision of Nature here is didactic and politically oriented; it is also colorful and sometimes spectacular. His American Genesis gives us a glimpse of creative Nature at work. In this volume Neruda defines a unique approach to Nature: the personification of Nature, on occasion its mythification, Nature poetry as narration as well as description. The poet sees not just Nature as it presents itself to us. He imposes his imagination on Nature and develops a history for each natural element from the instant of its creation. While the climactic moment for this approach is undoubtedly *Canto General,* it characterizes in differing degrees several of his later works as well: the personification and narrative history of origin in the *Odes;* the mythification in *The Stones of Chile* and in the posthumous *The Separate Rose*.

These post-*Canto* works exemplify a fifth stage that, with certain variations, also endures until the end of Neruda's life. In these books, one senses that the film of evolution has been arrested at specific frames, giving us time to examine a particular plant, a stone, a flower, a bird, an aspect of modern life, at leisure. We look at the object, handle it, turn it around, all the sides are examined with love, care, attention. This is, in many ways, Neruda as a Nature poet at his best. The close-ups are more vivid, more detailed, more refreshing than the sweeping panoramas and traveling shots of some of his early poems. This perspective, which we have sampled in the *Odes* and in *The Stones of Chile,* reappears in *The Art of Birds,* in the focus on the sea in *A House by the Shore,* in *Sky Stones,* and in *The Separate Rose*. In these books Nature poetry is again for Neruda the poetry of unity. (pp. 71-3)

Neruda's desire to share what he finds in Nature is evident in these works. And yet in the *Odes* and in *The Stones of Chile,* their public aspects notwithstanding, or in *The Art of Birds, A House by the Shore,* or *Sky Stones,* we find the poet alone, a solitary individual contemplating Nature. In this sense, these books lay the foundation as well for a sixth stage that surfaces in some of Neruda's poetry of the 1960s and that is fully developed in the posthumous works: the poet's desire for silence and solitude, his retreat into Nature, his yearning to be left alone with the sounds and smells of the natural world around him. In Nature Neruda seems to find a permanence that cannot be found in human life. This is implicit in the historical treatment given the virgin American continent in the *Canto* and the rocks in *The Stones of Chile*.

As his own death approaches, Neruda's attachment to Nature and to the continuity it represents grows. More and more he sees Nature as a life force overpowering the feeble impermanence of human existence, and in the posthumous works the poet seeks, in solitude, contact with this force. Man's life is fleeting. Nature is the source. It is the "before" and the "after" in regard to man, the enduring element that remains constant. For the poet and for his poetry Nature is the point of perpetual return. (p. 73)

[Political] militancy was regularly a part of Neruda's poetry. Moreover, it defined a role for the poet as spokesman of a people, with an obligation to employ his art for public utility. Neruda did not shirk this responsibility; he alternated between his need for personal, lyrical expression and his sense of duty as a militant poet.

Political poetry that is artistically excellent is relatively rare. The sense of actual circumstances and concrete realities of the moment often invade the poetic atmosphere and interfere with the quality of the poetic expression. In poetry there is always a delicate balance between content and expressive form, and in political poetry there is the risk of disturbing this balance by giving too much weight to content. Far more than most other contemporary poets, Neruda was able to produce clearly political poetry where this balance remains intact. This is the case with much of *Spain in My Heart* and, of course, *Canto General*. In the *Canto*, Neruda reached his peak as a public poet. He produced an ideological work that largely transcended contemporary events and became an epic of an entire continent and its people. It is a monumental work, an extraordinary achievement; but it is also an uneven work and we see in this masterpiece the potential artistic dangers that plagued his later political poetry. Where Neruda remains historical, truly epic, and mythological in the *Canto*, the work is brilliant; where he allows contemporary political events to become the central focus, as in section V or XIII, for example, the poetic quality of his song suffers.

Unfortunately, beginning with *The Grapes and the Wind*, much of Neruda's later public poetry follows the lead of the *Canto*'s weaker sections, rather than its most profound ones, and becomes primarily partisan or didactic poetry lacking the resonance of a poem such as **"Heights of Macchu Picchu."** Neruda's return to the epic form in *Chanson de Geste* or on occasion in *Ceremonial Songs* recalls certain parts of the *Canto;* the same is true for some of the Biblical overtones and cosmic vision in *The Flaming Sword*, and the political diatribes of *A Call for Nixonicide*. And in all these works Neruda adopts once more the stance of public bard, addressing himself to all mankind and to History. Neruda's definition of the poet's responsibility is evident in these works as it was in the *Canto,* and his sincerity is no less present here than in the earlier work. Yet none of these books rises to the level of the best portions of *Canto General*. The balance between content and poetic expression is not the same, and the richness, the depth, and the layers of meaning of the *Canto* are not repeated in these later works. We sense, rather, a weak echo of the original masterpiece. It is not in these works, but only in Neruda's treatment of Nature during the 1960s and 1970s, where the historical perspective and mythification of the *Canto* are at times replayed, that the profound essence touched in *Canto General* is once more revealed.

The *Canto* remains unchallenged as Neruda's outstanding accomplishment as a public poet. The vastness of its vision, tracing an entire continent from its genesis to its present reality, is virtually unique in contemporary poetry. We have insisted upon the fact that as a public poet, Neruda never ceases being at the same time a lyrical poet, expressing his own individual vision; the distinction between the two is a question of proportion, of stress, and not of mutual exclusion. Neruda's finest poems from the sixties and seventies are those where the lyrical carries the stress, those where the poet's personal "I," rather than a global public theme, is the primary focus. Neruda's commitment to public poetry was constant, and he took up his pen for public causes when he felt it was needed. Yet something seems forced in his public poetry of this period. It is as if Neruda the man, the militant, responded willingly to an external call to duty, but that the call came at a time when the urgent impulse of Neruda the poet was already moving toward contact with his own inner world. This is an observation, not a reproach. One can hardly fault Neruda for never duplicating the brilliance of *Canto General* in his subsequent public poetry. Most poets never achieve what Neruda produced in this one single work. (pp. 113-14)

The late 1950s, the 1960s, and the early 1970s were . . . for Neruda an enormously prolific period and a period of astounding variety as well. During these years he published some of the finest love poetry in *One Hundred Love Sonnets* and parts of *Extravagaria* and *Barcarole;* he produced Nature poetry that continued the movement toward close examination, almost still shots of every aspect of the external world, in the odes of *Voyages and Homecomings*, in *The Stones of Chile*, in *The Art of Birds*, in *A House by the Shore*, and in *Sky Stones*. He continued as well his role as public poet in *Chanson de Geste*, in parts of *Ceremonial Songs*, in the mythical *The Flaming Sword*, and the angry *A Call for Nixonicide and Glory to the Chilean Revolution*.

In addition to these works, . . . Neruda put forth as well an important collection of deeply personal poetry whose themes encompass virtually every subject and whose only unity can be found in their singular focus on the mind, memories, thoughts, and life of Pablo Neruda. Throughout most of Neruda's career the movement between the two poles of public and private poetry has been evident, and the period between the late 1950s and the 1970s is no exception. What is exceptional in this period is the number of works produced in which the poet's "I" dominates in a conscious fashion, in which the poet is openly recounting his life or concentrating on his own private metaphysical concerns. As Alazraki observes, with *Extravagaria* Neruda begins the "thawing out of his 'I,'" and it is a process which will continue throughout the rest of his published poems. Public works continue to appear during these years . . . , but their poetic quality is decidedly inferior to that of the personal works and they are far outnumbered by them as well. Most of the books of this period are invariably to some degree "Neruda on Neruda." In them we can see the poet's "will to return to the 'I,' the vindication of solitude and mystery as inalienable voices in his song." It is not always an easy road for Neruda. . . . [The] poet experiences at times a despair over language, a guilt over his intellectual work, he apologizes more than once for the continued intrusion of his self into his poetry: and yet the presence of that self undeniably continues to dominate the works of these years, and to define them as a unity.

What is remarkable in these works—*Extravagaria, Ceremonial Songs, Fully Empowered, Notes from Isla Negra, Barcarole,*

The Hands of Day, And Yet, World's End and *Barren Terrain*—is that within the unifying context of being very personal books of poetry, the variety among them is immense. Thematically, the books cover a staggering range, moving from the irreverent and playful satire of parts of *Extravagaria* to the autobiographical *Notes from Isla Negra* to the romantic nostalgia of *Barcarole* to the lament on his lack of manual labor in *The Hands of Day* to the focus on the events of this century in *World's End*. Stylistically as well, Neruda shows constant versatility in these books: the long verses and musical quality of *Barcarole* convey the tenderness and romanticism of that book; the 433 lines of *And Yet* are mainly short verses; the view of the twentieth century in *World's End* is communicated in a harsh rhythm of nine syllables that accords with the dark picture of the contemporary world which the poet paints. In the books of this period we see Neruda exploring not only diverse regions of his memory and of the world around him, but finding as well the poetic rhythm and style appropriate to each vision. The quality of a number of the books written during the sixties and early seventies is not always as high as Neruda's best; yet it is generally good, and the books are rich above all in what they tell us about the man himself, about Neruda inquiring into every aspect of his own being, delving into autobiographical introspection and metaphysical reflection. As Robert Pring-Mill observes, "Neruda grew earthwards till he reached the roots, and those roots proved to be his own." As we look back from the present, we see that it is these roots that Neruda excavates and exposes, making them the central core of his poetry in this autumnal period of his life and his work. (pp. 145-46)

> Manuel Durán and Margery Safir, in their Earth Tones: The Poetry of Pablo Neruda *(copyright © 1981 by Manuel Durán and Margery Safir), Indiana University Press, 1981, 200 p.*

ROBERT BLY

In 1962, Pablo Neruda began to set down some autobiographical poems centered around his house in Isla Negra, Chile. He wrote just over a hundred before he finished; it is this book ["**Isla Negra**"] Alastair Reid has now translated elegantly.

In some of the poems Neruda goes below the surface of life, with its poisoned flowers, snakes and waterfalls that he loves to describe, and talks of a mysterious "wicked King," who is allied with the terrifying jungle. It's not clear who this wicked King is, but Neruda knows that his life as a poet is associated with the jungle and that his growth resembled a jungle's. . . .

Neruda's growth *was* amazing; he does find, following Whitman's lead, the secret route that allows him to leaf out, exfoliate, become more and more moist and massive, until his work includes the poor, wristwatches, rabbits, the history of South America. (p. 9)

Neruda means this book to sum up his life in poetry, to make clear what he wanted to do. If we compare him with Akhmatova and Yeats, we could say that Akhmatova wanted to join classical form with heart feeling; Yeats wanted to help Ireland regain greatness, to embody a high and unrequited love and to get to the other world. Neruda doesn't seem to want any of the things Yeats wanted: He doesn't believe there is any other world, doesn't believe in unrequited love and declared several times that the gods are "enemies of man." What did he expect of himself? He says here:

> I believed my obligation was to sing,
> to sing as I grew and left my life behind,
> out of the pain of the struggle.
> It was my dedication, my function,
> alongside carpenters in the morning,
> drinking at night with horsemen,
> to pour out my song in writing. . . .

That is why he wrote three or four hours every morning. Singing also means paying careful attention to sound, developing arias and recitativos (as Whitman also did), elevating suffering, avoiding self-pity, giving courage to everyone alive at your time. Neruda's was basically an extroverted life task, and it doesn't suggest what he was afraid of. In a poem here called **"The Hero,"** he says he is afraid of a motionless castle with a dark-haired woman in it. He is so afraid of being caught there that whenever he comes near a castle he puts on his mask and walks on faster without looking behind. . . .

So we mustn't imagine that Neruda wears his own face or is a simple man. He is a complicated man who wears a mask in the unconscious, and he does that out of fear. There we come close to Yeats.

I thought of Yeats much while reading this book. Both took powerful political stands. Neruda wrote for years sentimental praise of Stalin, but here he talks of the horrifying side of Russian life under Stalin: "Everyone asked themselves without asking / and a poisoned life began, / day and night, no one knew why . . ." It's odd. Yeats adored spiritual love and paid little attention to matter or ordinary human suffering and ended up praising right-wing maniacs. Neruda loved matter, and the poor, was suspicious of gods and ended up praising Stalin. What can one say about that? They each fell into the ditch. It is not because "they were poets"—even though each was following a dream. Thousands of silent ones fell into the ditch too. Why should we read them then? They aren't guides to political life, but I read them because divine energy is present in the poems of both men: Each contains a moist madness that teaches us to praise and an abundant dark that each poet praises.

It's important not to ask more from Neruda than he can give. This book is rambling and loosely put together, but in the poems he gives evidence of the astonishing abundance human imagination has when mingled with memory. Neruda has sewn the secret thoughts of the imagination into his clothes, as Pascal once sewed in certain sentences he got from the spirit. (p. 26)

> Robert Bly, "Songs of Himself," *in* The New York Times Book Review *(copyright © 1982 by The New York Times Company; reprinted by permission), May 23, 1982, pp. 9, 26.*

JASCHA KESSLER

[Pablo Neruda's *Isla Negra, A Notebook,* was] written during 1962-63, and consists of about 202 pages of meditative, autobiographical poems. He seems to have written them "as a present to himself for his sixtieth birthday" (as Professor E. M. Santi observes in his *Afterword*). In this "present to himself," Neruda contemplates the various periods of his life, dividing the lyrical series into 5 sections: *Where the Rain is Born, The Moon in the Labyrinth, Cruel Fire, The Hunter after Roots,* and *Critical Sonata*. It is in the last of these, *Critical Sonata,* that the poet takes up the questions of his political belief, if not of his political acts in support of that belief, and suggests what he wanted to think of these matters himself, and what he expects the world to think of them. A man who writes such work as a present for his 60th birthday, a rather self-absorbed venture, to put it mildly, is not one capable of much guilt or remorse. And yet Neruda is not a hard man; just the opposite in fact: he is supersensitive, profoundly intuitive and sympathetic, and visionary, the quintessential lyrical poet, a poet who sees and who speaks in song. . . . [He] is a great and true poet, and his nature must be contemplated seriously, in the hope of understanding something most important about life and art.

In the pages of this private notebook of poems, informal and also meant for public scrutiny, Neruda is summing up his past, his childhood, his family, his education and his rich experience in the world, for he was a career diplomat all his life, and most of all recalling his passional life, both as a poet and as a lover of many women, for he was one who adored, as he puts it, "the entanglements of the genitals."

Some of his griefs come from his memories of at least three of the women he writes about in *Isla Negra*. One of them he gives the name of Josie Bliss, who was a Burmese woman.

[Neruda's poem about her reflects] the painful agony of memory, regret mingled with the horror of desire that is and is not. And there are many poems in this large collection as powerful and as vivid: the landscapes of Chile that nurtured the poet, his cities around the world, his friends and his enemies, and, as I said, his final strange and rather ambiguous reckoning with his political convictions. Neruda was to live on another ten years and to play a part in the events of 1970 to 1973 in Chile. And this book, titled after the place he loved most, where he lived, Isla Negra, is a powerful and beautiful testament to his undiminished powers. It offers us not only great insight into Neruda, but into poetry and history too.

Jascha Kessler, "Pablo Neruda: 'Isla Negra: A Notebook'," in a radio broadcast on KUSC-FM—Los Angeles, CA, June 16, 1982.

Marsha Norman
1947-

American dramatist and scriptwriter.

Norman's plays express a bleak view of society and human nature. Her characters are people who experience loneliness and despair. *Getting Out* (1978), her first play, brought Norman instant acclaim as a writer of intelligence and honesty. This work explores the psychological changes in a woman just released from prison. Two actresses, onstage at the same time, tell Arlene's story before and after her imprisonment. Although some critics feel this technique is merely a gimmick, Norman is usually praised for the directness of her theme and the authenticity of her dialogue.

Norman's recent play *'night, Mother* won the 1983 Pulitzer Prize for drama. The play follows the emotions and reactions of a mother and daughter from the time the daughter announces her imminent suicide until she commits the act ninety minutes later. To some critics, Norman dignifies Jessie's decision by portraying her as a woman who refuses to continue a life which has become meaningless. However, to other critics, most prominently Stanley Kauffmann, Jessie seems a neurotic, vengeful daughter who makes her announcement only to torture her mother. The play is characteristic of Norman's work in its gruelling emotions and unsparing confrontation of a painful subject.

(See also *Contemporary Authors*, Vol. 105.)

Stokley Towles/The Patriot Ledger

TERRY CURTIS FOX

[*Getting Out*] is a post-prison drama: we watch Arlene . . . make her shattered way back into the real world while Arlie . . . , Arlene's former self, is present on stage in a series of linked flashbacks. Norman is intent on describing a world that is a permanent prison and a prisoner who is not rehabilitated but gutted.

This script is weighted down with intelligence. Arlie is presented as a thoroughly dangerous and unpleasant person whose response to a brutalizing childhood is brutality; the description is one that understands both the individual and social antecedents of personality. The chaplain who is credited by Arlene with changing her life is, it turns out, the man responsible for the gravest brutality done to her, while the auxiliary characters who slowly pull the story out on stage are all a step, but only a step, away from stock. If the flashback technique seems arch at times (mention of Johnny Cash in the apartment leads to flashback of guard singing Johnny Cash songs in jail) it is descriptive of the memory process Norman wants to portray. *Getting Out* is a pretty well-made play which manages to avoid both the sentimental and the sententious.

I also found [the production] . . . rather boring. There's no exhilaration in sheer verbal power, no joy about creating a work for the stage. W. H. Auden described being approached by two kinds of aspiring writers: those who wanted to write because they felt they had something to say, and those who loved to play with words. The former he sent packing. The latter, he thought, might stand a chance. I suspect Norman wrote *Getting Out* because she thought she had something to say. It's a tame work, a respectable play which takes few chances. Since writing *Getting Out,* Norman has produced two more scripts: I'd like to see them. They should tell us whether or not Marsha Norman has learned how to play in the theatre as well as how to write a play. (p. 129)

> Terry Curtis Fox, "Early Work" (reprinted by permission of *The Village Voice and the author; copyright © The Village Voice, Inc., 1978), in* The Village Voice, *Vol. XXIII, No. 43, November 6, 1978, pp. 127, 129.*

JOHN SIMON

[*Getting Out*] is a spiny, realistic play about not exactly prepossessing people, but it is written with such a brisk, fresh, penetrating touch that sordid, brooding things take on the glow of honesty, humanity, very nearly poetry. These disturbed or at least disheveled people—some ex-convicts, and some whose lives have been interwoven with those of criminals—have intelligence, wit, and pride. They are not sentimentalized, however; not easily reformed, and perhaps never redeemed. But they are brutally, sadly, and sometimes thrillingly real, full of little surprises that play havoc with our expectations, yet, on reflection, prove devastatingly believable and, therefore, right.

The story unfurls parallelly in the past and present, with the heroine as a young girl, Arlie, going from bad to worse while, elsewhere on the stage, she is Arlene, a young woman returning after a long stretch in the penitentiary (for holdup with homicide) to her shabby Louisville apartment. Displaying the woman's past and present selves more or less simultaneously (sometimes one or the other fades temporarily out of the picture) is not mere cleverness: The two avatars of the same person, Before and After, communicate with each other through memory or through speaking to a third person, such as their mother, at the same stage time but in different chronological times. Arlene thinks that she has killed the wicked Arlie in herself but still communes with her in various, involuntary ways. And Arlie leads up to Arlene and may, even destroyed, never quite let her go.

Still more ingenious, perhaps, than bringing on these two together is the author's strategy of not bringing on at all the heroine's evil and good angels: the cabdriver father who seduced and bullied Arlie (no wonder that the man she killed was a cabby), and the prison chaplain, who with the help of the Bible and some very shrewd psychology gave her a new self—was midwife to Arlie's rebirth as Arlene. It is right that extreme badness and goodness should not be shown, only talked about; like a stage in pitch darkness or a spotlight in our eyes, their presence would merely blind us. Instead, we see various men and women who, at different points, brought relative good or bad into the heroine's life, or lives; and who, as shades of gray, constitute proper subjects of dramatic inquiry.

Getting Out is such a good play that even if I gave away every plot twist and quoted large chunks of dialogue, you could still see it and be amazed; but . . . I merely hope that you will take my word for its remarkable insights, truthfulness, and untearful compassion. The only obvious help the author has had stems from two years of hospital work with severely disturbed children. But those were four- to ten-year-olds; to have extrapolated from them (even assuming that there were mothers and elder sisters) the next twenty years of Arlie-Arlene's life is an imaginative leap so fraught with percipience, so blessed with empathy, that one feels awe in its presence. (p. 152)

> John Simon, "Free, Bright, and 31," in New York Magazine (copyright © 1984 by News Group Publications, Inc.; reprinted with the permission of New York Magazine), Vol. 11, No. 46, November 13, 1978, pp. 152, 155.

WALTER KERR

When I first saw Marsha Norman's technically accomplished and vigorously acted **"Getting Out"** . . . , I left the theater irritated with myself for having, in the end, become irritated by the play. Surely my discontent was unreasonable in the face of all that was admirable here. The author had elected to show us two facets of a girl's personality . . . by letting [two actresses] share the same stage space, with their paths crossing often enough, and intimately enough, for one to pause to light the other's cigarette. The younger, thrashing willfully about in baseball cap and sneakers, roamed the stage fitfully, now hugging the bedclothes of her childhood home in Kentucky, now tilting a chair and rocking in sassy rhythm as she gave a psychiatrist short shrift, now setting fire to the cell in which she'd landed after the fatal shooting of a gas station attendant.

The older, insisting that she was no longer the rebellious and immature Arlie but a reformed Arlene bent on a responsible new life, spent her first day on parole adrift in a grimy apartment, clutching at her own forlorn elbows, starting in fright at the first knock on the door. The psychological interplay between Arlie and Arlene was ingeniously sustained, the overlapping of past and present virtually musical in its counterpoint. (pp. 112-13)

Now that the play [has resurfaced] . . . , I think I begin to see why I balk. The evening's virtues remain virtues. . . .

But here's the problem. Sympathetic as we are to a girl who's recovered from a ramshackled childhood and summoned up the shaky strength to go it alone, we're still not prepared to suffer (for her, with her) *all* of the blows aimed at her as she takes a first step toward freedom. The guard who has so generously driven her from the "correctional facility" back to her home state is, in fact, on the make—violently so. The mother who has come to give the premises a fast wipe with a mop is actually there to tell her, bluntly and coarsely, that she can neither visit her family for a Sunday dinner nor see her own small son. The curly-headed, twitchy-fingered junkie who was once her lover and pimp arrives on the double—he's just escaped from his own prison—to lure her, or lambaste her, into resuming a profitable way of life. The only window she can look out of has bars on it: they are there to forestall thieves, but they are bars again. The bag of groceries she has so hopefully shopped for winds up scattered all over the still-filthy floor. Arlene cannot even get a lithograph of Jesus, the gift of a chaplain who has helped her, to hang straight on the wall.

I don't mean to be facetious about the girl's troubles, or to suggest that the play ever loses its earnestness. But too much is askew. The barrage of ills that assails the curiously passive Arlene is so unremitting (with the last-minute exception of a kindly, if thoroughly realistic, girl from upstairs) that we come to see some of them as gratuitous, some of them as repetitive. The pimp, for instance, appears in each of the play's two acts, slipping through the doorway on jittery feet to sneer, cajole, and, if necessary, attempt rape. But both scenes are the same scene, pursuing the same pattern of persuasion and threat. In time, we come to expect that all encounters will go badly; the badgering downhill structure becomes predictable, and leaves us restive.

Playwright Norman undoubtedly wants us to know just how rugged the straight and narrow can be; by her own rights, she's surely being honest. But honesty needn't rule out a degree of surprise, a pinch of variety, along the way. Shouldn't Arlene—with her so knowing background—anticipate the turn of events much more quickly than she does, and perhaps cope more inventively now and again? (p. 113)

> Walter Kerr, "Variety Never Hurts," in The New York Times (copyright © 1979 by The New York Times Company; reprinted by permission), June 3, 1979, pp. 112-13.*

GERALD WEALES

Marsha Norman is not the ordinary beginning playwright. Most talented neophytes display either a passionate concern about their subjects or an imaginative flair for theater. *Getting Out* may not be quite the masterpiece that this . . . lead suggests, but it scores well on both content and form. It is a substantial work and a moving one. . . .

[The] play sounds like a case study, which in one sense it is. In presentation, however, it is much more than that. In the dramatic present, we watch Arlene, docile and uncertain after years of doing what she was told to do, finding and turning to positive use some of the spirit which her earlier self (Arlie) used with such horrifying results. At the same time, often in the same acting space, we see Arlie, strutting, tough, unregenerate and, finally, broken. There are parallel scenes—Arlie's last long speech in solitary, Arlene's hysterical outburst which leads to her monologue on how she tried to kill the Arlie in her. Finally, there is the shared speech in which Arlie, caught at an earlier, happier moment of rebellion, begins a reminiscence in which, finally, Arlene speaks lines with her, laughs with her, indicates dramatically that what was best in Arlie—her vitality, her drive—has not been killed, cannot be killed if Arlene is to survive.

When I read the script last year, I was impressed by what it was attempting to do, but there was no way to be certain that the theatrical intricacies on the page could be successfully realized on stage. They are. . . .

Some of the secondary characters—the mother, the pimp—come close to caricature. . . . Some of the Arlie scenes are little more than exposition, presenting biographical information that is unnecessary since Arlie's speeches and Arlene's confrontations tell us all we need to know about the character. Despite these shortcomings, *Getting Out* is an effective theater piece which has a genuine concern for the traps of both heredity and environment and a wicked way of suggesting the ambiguities of its title. If Marsha Norman's more recent plays . . . have as much force and intelligence as *Getting Out*, she is an impressive addition to the list of good young American playwrights. (p. 559)

> Gerald Weales, "*'Getting Out': A New American Playwright*," in Commonweal (copyright © 1979 Commonweal Publishing Co., Inc.; reprinted by permission of Commonweal Publishing Co., Inc.), Vol. CVI, No. 18, October 12, 1979, pp. 559-60.

FRANK RICH

"We've got a good life here," says Thelma Cates to her daughter, Jessie, in Marsha Norman's new play, "**'Night, Mother.**" Many would agree. Thelma, who is a widow, and Jessie, who is divorced, live together in a spick-and-span house on a country road somewhere in the New South. There are no money problems. Nights are spent in such relaxed pursuits as crocheting and watching television.

But on the particular, ordinary Saturday night that we meet Thelma . . . and Jessie . . . , we learn that the good life may not be so good after all. As the daughter prepares to perform her weekly ritual of giving her mother a manicure, she says calmly, almost as a throwaway line, "I'm going to kill myself, Mama." And, over the next 90 minutes, Mama—and the rest of us—must face the fact that Jessie is not kidding. . . .

["**'Night, Mother**"] is a shattering evening, but it looks like simplicity itself. A totally realistic play, set in real time counted by onstage clocks, it shows us what happens after Jessie makes her announcement. What happens, unsurprisingly, is that the first skeptical and then terrified mother tries to cajole and talk her child out of suicide. "People don't really kill themselves," argues Thelma, "unless they're retarded or deranged."

But Jessie isn't deranged—she's never felt better in her life—and that's why "**'Night, Mother**" is more complex than it looks, more harrowing than even its plot suggests. Miss Norman's play is simple only in the way that an Edward Hopper painting is simple. As she perfectly captures the intimate details of two individual, ordinary women, this playwright locates the emptiness that fills too many ordinary homes on too many faceless streets in the vast country we live in now. . . .

Although it is likely to kindle many debates about the subject, "**'Night, Mother**" is not a message play about the choice to commit suicide. It's about contemporary life and what gives it—or fails to give it—value. We first get a sense of the Cates's existence before "**'Night, Mother**" begins. . . . [The set] is an all-American living room and kitchen, right out of a television sitcom: homey, appointed with the right appliances, conventionally tasteful. But, when . . . [the] cruelly bright lighting comes up, we see the house is colorless and dead—a pair of antiseptic model rooms, framed like a department-store window.

Miss Norman's dialogue maps the rest of the vacuum. When Thelma at first mistakes Jessie's preoccupation with guns for a fear of burglars, she says, "We don't have anything people would want." And we come to see that neither mother nor daughter do. Their lives are built on neighborhood gossip, ritualized familial obligations and housekeeping. Before tonight—when a gun is literally to their heads—they've never expressed their real feelings to one another or to anybody else. The more loneliness that is exposed the more we realize that the most horrifying aspect of "**'Night, Mother**" is not Jessie's decision to end her life but her mother's gradual awakening—and ours—to the inexorable logic of that decision.

The play would never work, never make that logic real, if Miss Norman for a second condescended to her characters by painting them as fools—or if she stuck in authorial speeches that commented on or judged their predicament. As she previously demonstrated in "**Getting Out**," Miss Norman is far too honest a writer to fall into those traps.

Jessie and Thelma are not caricatured as stupid yokels. They are not without wit. (p. 333)

There are pockets of humor—the mother even gets a laugh describing her daughter's youthful epileptic fits—and there is warmth.

But there is also the sight of . . . Thelma, a gabby "plain country woman," turning white and dumb with fear as she realizes that the daughter through whom she's lived by proxy is beyond her reach—"already gone," even though still alive. And there is the moment when the otherwise deliberate [Jessie] . . . turns away from her whimpering mother to wail defiantly, "I say *no* to hope."

Does "**'Night, Mother**" say no to hope? It's easy to feel that way after reeling from this play's crushing blow. But there can be hope if there is understanding, and it is Marsha Norman's profound achievement that she brings both understanding and dignity to forgotten and tragic American lives. (pp. 333-34)

> Frank Rich, "Suicide Talk in ''Night, Mother'," in The New York Times (copyright © 1983 by The New York Times Company; reprinted by permission), April 1, 1983 (and reprinted in New York Theatre Critics' Reviews, Vol. XXXXIV, No. 4, March 21-April 2, 1983, pp. 333-34).

JOHN SIMON

'night, Mother [is] honest, uncompromising, lucid, penetrating, well-written, dramatic, and as unmanipulatively moving

as we expected from the author of the remarkable *Getting Out*. Though there are many laughs, I cannot tell you that the play isn't, as the popular parlance has it, "depressing." But I can tell you that it gleams with wisdom, reeks of observed and comprehended reality. That it is something to feel, think, and talk about; that it will force you to examine and re-examine new and old beliefs, fresh and stale convictions. That it will relentlessly confront you with your own and other people's humanity; that it will do what only the profoundest things—philosophy, religion, and art—can do for human beings, which may not be much but is all there is.

The play combines the lucent objectivity of a case history with the sublime subjectivity of language, style, art; it does not wrest forced, factitious tears from you, and it scrupulously, fastidiously refrains from telling you what to think. The subjects are suicide, love, and the meaning of life—as huge as they come; but they are treated with the specificity of threading a needle or choosing the right breakfast for your needs. Humor and pathos pop up as naturally as wild flowers or fences by the roadside; there is devastating psychological accuracy and nothing seems contrived; and there is that bustle of minutely perceived existential details that bespeak the master. The imminent suicide, from force of habit, puts lotion on her hands after doing the dishes; the mother, told by her daughter to keep washing a dirty chocolate pan after the shot rings out from behind the locked door for as long as it takes for the police and relatives to arrive, tries to assert her independence by saying she'll just sit and wait—yet as she goes to the phone after the gunshot, she already clutches the pan.

Believers and atheists, Freudians and anti-Freudians, rationalists and idealists, Marxists and capitalists, parents and children—everyone will have his or her interpretation of *'night, Mother*. I think I know what Miss Norman really meant by it, but so will you, and your meaning, I wager, will be different. Good! Perhaps even great. . . . Miss Norman may not provide answers, but anyone who can serve up questions so brilliantly—in language that is only slightly, but finally appositely and awesomely, heightened—has more than earned that right. (pp. 56-7)

John Simon, "Journeys into Night," in New York
Magazine (copyright © 1984 by News Group Publications, Inc.; reprinted with the permission of New
York Magazine), Vol. 16, No. 15, April 11, 1983,
pp. 55-8.*

RICHARD GILMAN

The hyperbole machine is operating on Broadway again. Upon a modest two-character play with nothing flagrantly wrong with it—but not much to get excited about either—the reviewers have lavished nearly their whole stock of ecstatic adjectives, to which encomiums a Pulitzer Prize has just been added. Even before Marsha Norman's *'night, Mother* reached New York City, Robert Brustein likened it to *Long Day's Journey Into Night* [see excerpt above]. . . . Well, O'Neill's best play and Norman's do have something in common: they both bring us unpleasant news about the family.

The play takes place one evening in a house "way out on a country road" in the South. A middle-aged woman and her thirtyish daughter live here. The mother is silly, self-indulgent and totally reliant on her daughter in practical matters; the daughter is heavyset, slow-moving and morose. Early in the evening she informs her mother that she is going to kill herself that night. . . . From then on the play details the mother's frantic efforts to dissuade her daughter and the young woman's stolid insistence on carrying out her plan. . . .

Up to this point the play is moderately interesting as a moral inquiry (do we have the right to kill ourselves?) and moderately effective as a tale of suspense. But then the women begin to talk about the past, the daughter's childhood in particular, and what emerges is commonplace and predictable. I don't mean their lives are commonplace and predictable—that's a given—but dramatically the play falls into domestic cliché. The mother confesses that she and her husband, the girl's father, had no love for each other and, in response to the daughter's lament, says, "How could I know you were so alone?"

Next we learn that the daughter suffers from epilepsy. She says it's in remission and isn't the reason she's killing herself, but the fact of the illness, and especially the fact that the mother for a long time hid the truth about it from her, enters our consciousness as a diminution of mystery. So too does the daughter's admission that her own husband left her partly because she refused to stop smoking.

The effect of these revelations is that the suicide becomes explicable on the one hand—epileptics, neglected children and abandoned wives have a hard time "coping"—and ludicrous on the other—if nicotine is more important than marriage, what can you expect? The play might have had a richness, a fertile strangeness of moral and philosophical substance, had the suicide been undertaken as a more or less free act; had Norman not offered as the executor of this fascinating, dreadful decision a character with so many troubles. When the shot sounded (from behind a bedroom door) I wasn't startled, dismayed or much moved; it was all *sort of* sad, *sort of* lugubrious.

Norman writes cleanly, with wry humor and no bathos. . . . But the only way I can account for the acclaim *'night, Mother*'s been getting, besides the hunger for "important," "affecting" dramas that gnaws at our educated theatergoers, is that this domestic tragedy doesn't succumb to the occupational disease of its genre: an "uplifting" or at least a consoling denouement. But what a negative virtue that is, and what a comment on our impoverished theater! Yes, the play's *honest,* yes it's sincere; but have we reached the point where we find such minimal virtues something to rave about?

Richard Gilman, in a review of "'night, Mother,"
in The Nation (copyright 1983 The Nation magazine,
The Nation Associates, Inc.), Vol. 236, No. 18, May
7, 1983, p. 586.

STANLEY KAUFFMANN

If the hoopla about Marsha Norman's new play [*'night, Mother*] were credible, the current state of American drama would be better than it is. . . . Because the play has only two characters, is in one long act, and ends with a death, some commentators have called it classical and have invoked Aristotle. I envy their rapture; the play itself keeps me from sharing it. *'night, Mother* is certainly better written and constructed than Norman's last New York production, *Getting Out,* but like that earlier play, the new one is fundamentally a stunt. Moreover, I think it has been misconstrued by most who have written about it, and apparently by the author herself. (p. 47)

Inarguably *'night, Mother* addresses deeper themes [than *Getting Out*], is less flashy, and has a number of sharp lines; nonetheless it too is a device, a stunt, and not an authentic drama; and it fails at being even the drama that it claims to be.

The play *seems* to be about a woman in her thirties for whom life has lost savor and point and who decides to make a quick exit with one bullet: it seems to be a drama of the courage to face nullity, to recognize and reject it. Jessie is a plump, divorced country woman who lives with her widowed mother in the family home. . . . At the moment that the play begins, Jessie comes into the parlor-and-kitchen set carrying a beach towel and asks her mother whether there's a sheet of plastic around. The question is matter-of-fact, as is her question about where Daddy's gun is. She climbs to the attic, gets the pistol, and announces as she cleans it that she is going to kill herself. At the end of an hour and a half, by the clock on the wall crammed with doodads, she goes into the bedroom, locks the door, and does it. (The play could have used the same title as the last Norman work.)

After Jessie's calm announcement of intent, her mother, Thelma, goes through recurring stages of disbelief, fright, panic, near-petulance, near-acceptance, and dismay. Jessie just plows ahead through the last ninety minutes of her life, occasionally pierced by stabs of feeling, but mostly making careful preparations or informing Thelma of preparations already made, including much trivia about deliveries of groceries, milk, and candy.

The trivia are used as light background for the dark matters that are revealed. Jessie has been divorced by the husband she still loves; her teenage son is a thief and drug addict living on the loose; she has epilepsy, as her father had. She has had a year's remission of the illness, which apparently is meant to underscore that she is not committing suicide to escape it. Nor is she killing herself because of any other circumstance of her life that we learn about. Why, then, is she doing it? She is empty. She has been waiting for herself all these years, and " 'I' never got here." Her life is so unvaryingly flavorless that, she says, death will only be like getting off a bus fifty blocks before the end of the line. She is quitting life fifty years before the end because she will be in the same "place" then as she is now.

Despite her mother's increasing terror, Jessie is obdurate. "You are my child!" cries Thelma. "No," Jessie replies, "I am what became of your child." At the last, a self-determined last, she tears herself from her mother's grasp, goes into the bedroom, locks the door so that Thelma can't be suspected of murdering her, and after a moment, shoots.

Ostensibly we have been watching the last moments of a present-day spiritual aristocrat, a woman who can look on life and death with a judicious eye and can choose courageously, a woman who recognizes desolation and declines to be humiliated by it even if her choice costs her life. But is that really what we have seen?

How can we accept Jessie's statements about herself: accept her condition of emancipated despair? If these things were true, what possible reason would she have to *announce* her decision, then put her mother through those ninety minutes? She says she is doing it to spare Thelma the pain of discovery after the event. Is this a rational way to spare another person pain: to subject her mother to these ninety minutes and leave her with a memory of them in *addition* to the suicide? Could a nobly philosophic, privately resolved Jessie really come in calmly with that blanket, calmly ask for a plastic sheet and a pistol, and calmly sit there cleaning the pistol in front of her mother?

In reality, we are watching an act of vengeance. Jessie is not, as implied, our vicar in a Slough of Despond that possibly threatens us all. Jessie is a case. She is a woman haunted by an illness that may recur, a woman parted from the husband she loves because, she says, he asked her to choose between him and smoking! As for her relationship with her mother, Thelma says she got tired of watching Jessie and her father, whom Jessie loved, "going on and off like electric lights" because of their illness. This is the same Thelma who walked away from her husband's deathbed to watch *Gunsmoke* because he wouldn't talk to her.

Add up all these elements, and Jessie stands clear as a vengeful neurotic, not a tragic heroine. It's a truism that suicides are committed *at* someone, and this play, intentionally or not, dramatizes it. Jessie's last utterance, which is the title of the work, is the last twist of the knife. Instead of a woman quietly exalted by her ultra-rational choice and by her will to carry it out, we see a woman deceptively serene (as serenity often is), whose life has been made impossible by ill luck and warped values, whose buried hatred for her mother has italicized her despair, who is bent on suicide, and who comes in to torture her mother for ninety minutes before doing it. That grim, twisted Jessie is latent in the script, of course, or she couldn't be perceived; but Norman, deliberately or unwittingly, has chosen to present Jessie as a rustic female samurai who speaks implicitly to the residual nobility in us all.

Thelma, too, is contradictorily drawn. From Moment One she is almost a caricature of a self-centered old baby, with no more brain than she needs to make hot chocolate and watch TV. And what does this silly old woman do when she hears her daughter's suicide plan? She plunges into deterrent chat, in domestic light-comedy style. Instead of the hysteria we might expect from this dodo, instead of the screaming or fainting or struggle or even a transparent ruse to get the gun, she casts herself as a partner in a "clever" cat-and-mouse duet, as if she were accustomed to such crises and were competent to handle them. When she sees deterrence failing, she thinks more of the threat to herself than to Jessie, of the disturbance of her cozy life, and in childish pique she makes a mess—she throws pots on the floor. Thelma's actions result not from the complexity of a character, but from the traffic-management of a character by its author to make the play possible.

That is the pervasive flaw of the whole play: manipulation. To put it another way, if the play were true—true to Norman's characters as she wants us to think of them—it wouldn't exist. Either Jessie would shoot herself before it begins, or, as soon as she discloses her plans, Thelma would collapse. Thus, though *'night, Mother* is more subtle than **Getting Out,** it is at bottom equally a stunt, a contrivance, and the author's tyrannical governance of characters in order to flesh out a gimmicky framework: the suicide announcement at the start and the pistol shot at the finish.

Thelma's one impeccable line comes right after the shot. Against the locked bedroom door she sobs: "Forgive me. I thought you were mine." The drama that really leads to that line—of a clawing Electra complex, of the mother's mirror-image hatreds, and of the pity overarching both—has not been written. (pp. 47-8)

Stanley Kauffmann, "More Trick than Tragedy," in Saturday Review (© 1983 Saturday Review Magazine Co.; reprinted by permission), Vol. 9, No. 10, September-October, 1983, pp. 47-8.

Clifford Odets
1906-1963

American dramatist, scriptwriter, and director.

Odets was among the most prominent American playwrights of the 1930s. His play *Waiting for Lefty*, about a taxi drivers' union that is preparing to take a strike vote, became an immediate sensation when first produced in 1935 for its leftist philosophy and its powerful, realistic conflicts. As in many of his plays, *Lefty* depicts the search by working-class characters for a place in modern society. Although Odets never repeated the critical success of *Waiting for Lefty*, his best plays have historical significance for their portrayal of American life after the Great Depression.

Odets began his career as an actor and joined the Group Theatre in 1930. Founded by Harold Clurman, Cheryl Crawford, and Lee Strasberg, the Group Theatre was intended to be both a training ground for actors and an idealistic collective which would attempt to change society through the onstage presentation of alternative values. Odets gained little recognition in the organization as an actor, but his first play, *Waiting for Lefty*, became a huge success, appearing on Broadway and in many cities across the United States. *Awake and Sing!*, also produced in 1935, was also very popular, and is seen in retrospect by many critics as a more important play than *Waiting for Lefty*. *Awake and Sing!* was the last of Odets's early critical and commercial triumphs. His next full-length play, *Paradise Lost* (1935), was attacked by many critics who found fault with his stock characters and the optimistic closing speech, for which there seemed to be little justification. After the failure of *Paradise Lost*, Odets accepted an offer from Paramount Studios as a scriptwriter. Refuting charges that he was "selling out," Odets contended that he could improve his craft and also help finance the Group Theatre. He returned to the Group Theatre in 1937 after seeing only one of his scripts produced. *Golden Boy* (1937), Odets's next play, became the greatest commercial success of his career. The story of a young man trying to decide between careers as a violinist or a boxer, *Golden Boy* is generally regarded as Odets's most thoughtful and humanistic drama. Many of his later plays involve love relationships and were faulted for their lack of structural unity and social concern. Following the failure of Odets's play *Clash by Night* in 1941, the Group Theatre disbanded, and Odets returned to Hollywood. Although he continued to work in the theater, and found commercial success with *The Country Girl* (1950), his most acclaimed later works were the scripts for such films as *None but the Lonely Heart* (1944) and *Humoresque* (1946). Odets often spoke disparagingly of his film work, but he remained in Hollywood until his death.

Odets's career as a playwright is seen by many critics to fall into three distinct phases. The first and most important phase encompasses Odets's efforts as a proletarian dramatist. *Waiting for Lefty*, *Awake and Sing!*, and *Paradise Lost* are all placed in this category. Odets structured *Lefty* so that the personal problems of the characters reflect the conflict between the union and the taxi company. *Awake and Sing!* examines the aspirations of a Jewish working-class family who has become disillusioned by an oppressive economic system. In *Paradise*

Photograph by Alfredo Valente; reproduced by permission of Billy Rose Theatre Collection of The New York Public Library at Lincoln Center—Astor, Lenox and Tilden Foundations and Mrs Alfredo

Lost, a respectable middle-class businessman and his family are destroyed by a series of disasters. Each of the characters in this play represents a particular middle-class value, and the catastrophes that befall them symbolize the fall of these values during the 1930s. Odets had joined the Communist party during 1934 and wrote most of his early plays during this brief association; it is obvious that through his art he was confirming leftist principles while declaring archaic the values of middle-class America.

The second phase of Odets's career includes plays involving personal relationships rather than direct social criticism. *Golden Boy* portrays the quest for success and the tragedies suffered as a result of faulty decisions and changes in values. *Rocket to the Moon* (1938), *Night Music* (1940), and *Clash by Night* (1941) are love stories that focus more on plot and dialogue than on characterization and social commentary. These three plays were among Odets's least effective works. The final phase of Odets's career comprises semi-autobiographical dramas with psychological overtones. In *The Big Knife* (1949), a movie actor has been offered a multimillion-dollar contract but wants to escape the corruption of the film industry and return to the New York stage. *The Country Girl*, perhaps the most psychological of Odets's plays, is the story of an alcoholic actor who attempts a comeback on Broadway with the help of his wife, on whom he is emotionally dependent. Odets's last play, *The*

Flowering Peach (1954), is an adaptation of the biblical Noah legend. The play is uncharacteristic of Odets's work, for it combines elements of comedy, philosophy, and theology. Social commentary is nearly nonexistent in these late plays; the only work with a critical concern is *The Big Knife*, which attacks the film industry with unrelenting anger. However, critics find these plays superior to Odets's love stories because of their intriguing characters and suspenseful scenarios.

By the end of 1935, Odets's impressive first year as a playwright, many critics were praising him as a genius who spoke for the American people. However, even Odets's best plays are not held in such high regard today. His early works are considered simplistic propaganda, with stereotypical characters and obvious messages. Nevertheless, Odets's work is still appreciated for its moving dialogue and his belief in the nobility of humankind. His protagonists perpetually battle to maintain their individuality despite pressure from the conformist forces of society. Odets can be seen from a historical perspective as a skilled craftsman who, according to Allan Lewis, "rose splendidly as the playwright most able to dramatize an injured nation in need of hope and unity."

(See also *CLC*, Vol. 2; *Contemporary Authors*, Vols. 85-88; and *Dictionary of Literary Biography*, Vols. 7, 26.)

JOSEPH WOOD KRUTCH

The pace [of **"Waiting for Lefty"**] is swift, the characterization is for the most part crisp, and the points are made, one after another, with bold simplicity. What Mr. Odets is trying to do could hardly be done more economically or effectively.

Cold analysis, to be sure, clearly reveals the fact that such simplicity must be paid for at a certain price. The villains are mere caricatures and even the very human heroes occasionally freeze into stained-glass attitudes, as, for example, a certain lady secretary in one of the flashbacks does when she suddenly stops in her tracks to pay a glowing tribute to "The Communist Manifesto" and to urge its perusal upon all and sundry. No one, however, expects subtleties from a soap-box, and the interesting fact is that Mr. Odets has invented a form which turns out to be a very effective dramatic equivalent of soap-box oratory. (pp. 427-28)

[Mr. Odets] has made a clean sweep of the conventional form along with the conventional intentions. He boldly accepts as his scene the very platform he intends to use, and from it permits his characters to deliver speeches which are far more convincing there than they would be if elaborately worked into a conventional dramatic story. Like many of his fellows he has evidently decided that art is a weapon, but unlike many who proclaim the doctrine, he has the full courage of his conviction. To others he leaves the somewhat nervous determination to prove that direct exhortation can somehow be made compatible with "art" and that "revolutionary" plays can be two things at once. The result of his downrightness is to succeed where most of the others have failed. He does not ask to be judged by any standards except those which one would apply to the agitator, but by those standards his success is very nearly complete. . . .

However much **"Waiting for Lefty"** may owe to a Marxian formula, both the characters and the situation come within the range of the author's experience and there is a basis of concrete reality. **"Till the Day I Die"** is founded upon nothing except the printed word, and the characters are mere men of wax. In so far as we believe it at all, we do so only because we have been told that such things do happen. There is little in the play itself to carry conviction, and neither its hero nor its villains seem very much more real that those of the simplest and most old-fashioned melodramas. The acting in the two pieces is as different as they are themselves. Mr. Odets's Germans strike attitudes and declaim. His strikers are so real—perhaps so actual would be better—that when the play is over one expects to find their cabs outside. (p. 428)

> Joseph Wood Krutch, "Mr. Odets Speaks His Mind," in The Nation, *Vol. CXL, No. 3640, April 10, 1935, pp. 427-28.*

STARK YOUNG

As an active figure, conducive to sweat, clapping and partisanship, Mr. Odets may be in a short time an impressive dramatist. Already, without appearing to be middle-class and stupid, he gives the impression of convictions. And he does not give the impression of grabbing any movement or cause for its stage exploitation and jabber. I still say, I repeat, that, though to a much less degree in **"Till the Day I Die"** and **"Waiting for Lefty"** than in **"Awake and Sing,"** he needs to establish the plane, indicate the measure, of his various motivations. Taking any of his situations, there is still room for a more important interpretation. The line of living, after the jungle has been superseded and left, is not so simple as in many of the speeches it may seem to be. To take a good example, we find one of Mr. Odets' characters speaking of an aged Jewish father, a man who has read Spinoza all his life—and look what they have done to him! It would be a more profound art in Mr. Odets—I am one who believes he will come to it (and this review is written for him)—if he showed us this character, too, this Spinoza-read old man. In sum it would better convince us of the motif intended if he created this spiritual aspect against which the material tides of circumstance beat so disastrously. In sum, we should have a greater and more significant range in character creation if we saw two men between whom there is not only the force of capitalism but also of Spinoza. Otherwise, this flinging of spiritual and musical culture into the scales is much too easy. Thrown in like that, Spinoza is, as theatre argument, not much more carrying than to say that the heroine ate spinach all her life and now the factory has spoiled her liver.

Since the earliest beginnings of drama, obviously, the great motifs or abstractions built on have been pretty much the same. Their application, as bases for definite situations or subjects, depends on the dramatists' discovery of what will arouse toward them the most powerful and complete response. On this basis, in **"Till the Day I Die,"** the torturing of the Communist by the Nazis until he will be disgraced and lost, is no more than what happened, very likely, to plenty of aristocrats or bourgeois victims under the changed Russian system. You can like or not like, then, Mr. Odets' partisanships, so long as you remember that (setting aside the special appeal of his causes to this man or that) the test of his work lies in its emotional resources, its dialogue, the response it evokes. The test of his work lies in its theatrical powers and its human emotional powers, both of which are at their zeniths when one of them has been made inseparable from the other.

"Till the Day I Die" appears to lack a particularly clear development. During the final scene there is a definite drop. If the suffering Communist . . . is to get into that kind of generalized semi-noble speech, we need an emotional plane or, perhaps better, a distinct indication, that he has, through pain and strain, been brought into an exalted and not wholly cogent state of speaking. The play has, nevertheless, many good short scenes, flashes here and there into the situation's progress. The dialogue shows great talent. The instinct for getting the scene forward over the footlights is so great as to be perhaps the chief source of this new playwright's promise. . . .

"Waiting for Lefty" jerks along through resilient little scenes, sometimes remarkably graphic, secure or moving. It gains greatly over "Till the Day I Die" by its nearness and vernacular. The whole tone of it is essentially gay; which is a great compliment to it as theatre; and yet the conviction of grave reality is strong. Creation of character (realistic), if strongly achieved, is in itself so full of satisfaction for us that it rises above mere depression. The vim and sharp eyes and theatre invention of much of this play are such as to bring the whole of it up to theatre delight. And nothing is lost thereby; the progress of a zest for life, combined with a fighting spirit, is, however rousing, prophetic or passionate, not grim. The grim become theatre is very different from theatre turned grim.

> Stark Young, "Lefty and Nazi," in The New Republic, Vol. LXXXII, No. 1062, April 10, 1935, p. 247.

GRENVILLE VERNON

In ["**Awake and Sing**"] Mr. Odets showed a keen sense of dramatic values and for a young playwright an unusual mastery of theatrical technique; but far more important than these, the ability to visualize and project living men and women by means of significant action, and vivid, realistic, pungent dialogue. The characters of "**Awake and Sing**" were entirely Jewish, and Mr. Odets was evidently working in a milieu and in a spirit which he thoroughly understood. That Mr. Odets is a radical, even perhaps a Communist, might have been gathered from the play, not so much by what was definitely spoken, but what was implicit. Neither his sense of character nor his telling of the story were hobbled by the intrusion of the author speaking in his own person. And this was good art. In the two one-act plays which the Group Theatre has now presented ["**Till the Day I Die**" and "**Waiting for Lefty**"], Mr. Odets is unfortunately no longer the artist, but frankly the propagandist, and the result is far less satisfying. Moreover in these plays the characters are primarily non-Jewish, and Mr. Odets gives to them no such sense of verity either in action or dialogue as he displayed in "**Awake and Sing**". Indignation and intensity may be admirable things in the drama, but only when they are held in check; if they are left to run wild they destroy verity of character and of theme, leaving the figures of the play mere puppets, devoid of their own life, and existing only in the heated fancy of the author. This was what happened in "**Till the Day I Die**" and to a large extent in "**Waiting for Lefty**." . . .

In the course of ["**Till the Day I Die**"] are introduced a number of stock characters; the Nazis all either hysterical, degenerate, brutal or stupid; the Communists, idealistc heroes. The result is that without exception the characters are as unreal in action and speech as the figures of old-time bourgeois melodrama. Moreover, the author is forever present, striking dramatic attitudes, spouting communistic sentiments in communistic jargon. Not for a moment is there the sense of reality, and what effects are obtained are obtained through the most obvious melodramatic means. In short, Mr. Odets neither feels nor understands the people he is trying to depict. . . .

"**Waiting for Lefty**" is a much better play. Here at least Mr. Odets is dealing with a scene and with characters he has seen and known, at least superficially. When he condescends to have them speak in their own persons, they speak the language of the New York streets, the language of taxi-drivers, labor leaders, *agents provocateurs*. The main action, and by far the most interesting and vital portion of the play, takes place in the scenes representing a meeting of taxi-drivers, with the officers of the union trying to prevent a strike, and the radicals insisting on one. Speeches are made from the stage, and actors are interspersed in the audience to heckle the speakers. These scenes are exciting, and despite the overdose of communistic propaganda are on the whole true to life. But the scenes between, depicting the evils of capitalistic civilization, of what happens in the homes of the workers, in the hospitals, in theatrical offices, are stereotyped bits of communistic hokum, and not particularly good hokum. Mr. Odets hasn't taken the trouble to saturate himself with the spirit which might have informed his figures; he has simply taken age-old puppets and situations, given them a revolutionary twist, and let them go at that. That this isn't enough for a serious dramatist goes without saying; it isn't enough even for effective propaganda.

> Grenville Vernon, "Two Communist Plays," in Commonweal (copyright © 1935 Commonweal Publishing Co., Inc.; reprinted by permission of Commonweal Publishing Co., Inc.), Vol. XXI, No. 24, April 12, 1935, p. 682.*

JOSEPH WOOD KRUTCH

Clifford Odets was given every encouragement to let himself go. Unfortunately he chose to be as little critical of his work as his admirers had been, and the result is simply that his latest play seems like nothing so much as an improbable burlesque of "**Awake and Sing**." Apparently the idea was that if a play about a somewhat neurotic family in the Bronx was good, then a play about a madhouse similarly located would be very much better. And if this theory is accepted, then "**Paradise Lost**" . . . must certainly mark the uttermost reach of the author's genius.

Never in the course of more than a decade of persistent theatergoing have I seen quite so much of madness and woe, or quite such a rich variety of sins, felonies, and other torts, legal and moral, crowded into one evening. . . .

If one knew nothing of the author one might assume that the play was an unsuccessful attempt at the pure macabre, but in a statement issued to the press Mr. Odets warned all concerned that he was about to present them with a picture of the state of the middle class today, and we are left with the necessity of assuming that he asks us to believe his picture in some sense typical. Surely, if it were, even the solid foundations of the Bronx would not be standing this morning. . . .

My own faith in the reality of Mr. Odets's talents is sufficiently firm to make me quite sure that only the force of some strong delusion could make him guilty of such an atrocity, and I think that I know what that delusion is. . . . Mr. Odets has lost his reason (only temporarily, I hope) from too much brooding over the Marxian eschatology. For Marxism also does, of course, have its "science of last things," its vision of the process by which the end of the world will come about and of the portents by which the approach of the millennium will be announced. There will be wars and rumors of wars. But that is not all. The middle class, collapsing economically, will lose faith in itself. It will be seized with all sorts of neuroses, and finally it will expire miserably in the midst of its futilities, its corruptions, and its perversities—precisely as this strange family is expiring in the Bronx. . . .

I am perfectly sure that Mr. Odets is at least ahead of events, that what he professes to have discovered has not happened yet, and that what he is giving us is not a picture of anything as it now exists but an apocalyptic vision of what he feels sure will happen and of what, being an impatient millennarian, he wants to believe is happening now. But he can be answered by thousands of citizens of the Bronx who, should they see the play, would reply with one voice in terms of the American folk phrase, "Home was never like this." If it were, then the revolution would be closer than even most of Mr. Odets's fellow-believers think that it is.

Joseph Wood Krutch, "The Apocalypse of St. Clifford," in The Nation, Vol. CXLI, No. 3677, December 25, 1935, p. 752.

EDITH J. R. ISAACS

Paradise Lost is not a great play, as the Group thinks it is. But it is without doubt an important play because in material and method it marks the fresh, swift advance of a young dramatist who not only thinks and feels deeply but whose writing talents are essentially and in an unusual degree theatre talents: the power to state a situation in terms of its most dramatic elements, to observe and define character, to write active dialogue, to conquer attention.

Paradise Lost, so far as one can interpret Mr. Odets through the play and through what he has said about it in print, aims to be the story of the disintegration of the middle-class liberals in America under the capitalist system, and their hope of redemption through a new social system. This is almost exactly the theme of *Awake and Sing,* except that in the earlier play Mr. Odets chose a family in the Bronx as his protagonist, and tried to prove his thesis from his type. In *Paradise Lost* he has broadened his canvas 'to find a theatrical form with which to express the mass as hero'. (pp. 94-5)

It is good, in these cowardly days when old men are afraid to think freely, to see a young man boldly hitting out for a new paradise, convinced not only that he knows what is wrong and why, but that he can, quite surely, put us all on the real right road out of a world's unrighteousness that tortures him. 'Take it from me,' he seems to say; and whether you take it or not, you must be impressed by his earnestness and his ideals.

Such a subjective method applied to playwriting has, of course, its obvious penalties. As you watch the play, you find the playwright himself recurrently, and insistently, showing through his characters, and pretty soon you find yourself judging not the play, but the playwright, saying to yourself, 'This boy thinks the Bronx is the world'. He is not only cock-sure, but naively inexperienced. Someone should tell him that [his characters], . . . while they may be American citizens, are not in any sense representative of the middle-class, nor is there anything in their thinking or acting to indicate that they are liberal. They are the dregs of the social system, money-loving, money-starved capitalists who have gone rotten through spinelessness and the frustration of their own golden longings. No revolution would help them. They are too old—every one of them, but especially the young ones.

All of this only means that Mr. Odets has not made you accept either his first premise or his conclusion. But between the two there still stands a play of more than usual power, observation, tension. (pp. 95-6)

The special quality in Odets' playwriting . . . that is the most developed facet of his talent is related to his own acting experience—although it is by no means accounted for by that alone. His plays are made to the measure of his actors; there is nothing he demands of them, no characterization, no action, no conflict, that is beyond the reach of a fairly competent player. He knows how and why and when actors should speak, when the emphasis should be on the character who is speaking, on the immediate situation, on the play's theme. (p. 96)

Odets' speech, moreover, when it is not affected, or perhaps it is more generous to say when it is not affected by his desire to try the higher flights of poetry, almost speaks itself, it is so exactly and seems to instinctively right for the stage—even if it is not always rightly adjusted to the individual character. Half of the strength of *Waiting for Lefty* was the strength of speech, clear, simple, expressive, every word doing its work singly and as a part of a phrase, a speech, a scene. In *Paradise Lost* Odets has carried both of these marked talents—the talent for the word and for writing an actors' play—far ahead of what he did in *Awake and Sing.* (p. 97)

Edith J. R. Isaacs, "At Its Best," in Theatre Arts Monthly, Vol. XX, No. 2, February, 1936, pp. 93-7.*

KENNETH BURKE

After having been led, by the explicitly formulated objections of some dissenters, to expect that I would dislike Odets' **"Paradise Lost,"** I finally went to see it, and liked it enormously. . . . And though I had in the past complained against propagandists who compromised their cause by the depiction of people not worth saving, and had been led to believe that Odets transgressed on this score, I found on the contrary that the characters, for all their ills, possessed the ingredients of humanity necessary for making us sympathetic to their disasters. To me there was nothing arbitrary about the prophetic rebirth in Leo's final speech. And as I had witnessed, not pedestrian realism, but the idealizations of an expert stylist, I carried away something of the *exhilaration* that good art gives us when, by the ingratiations of style, it enables us to contemplate even abhorrent things with calmness.

The opportunity to examine the play in print has even heightened my admiration, by revealing the subtlety, complexity and depths of the internal adjustments. For all his conscious symbolism, the author has not merely pieced together a modern allegory. His work seems to embody ritualistic processes that he himself was not specifically concerned with. . . .

At the close of Act I, as the characters listen to Pearl playing the piano upstairs, Gus says: "And when the last day comes—by ice or fire—she'll be up there playin' away." I consider this the "informing" line of the play. "By ice or fire." . . .

Along with the "ice or fire" epigram, I should note the significant credo of Pike, who, within the conditions of the play, comes nearest to the "proletarian" philosophy: "I'm sayin' the smell of decay may sometimes be a sweet smell." And taking these two passages as seminal, I should say that the play deals with three modes of "redemption"—redemption by ice, fire or decay—and finally chooses the third. Like certain ancient heresies, it pictures the "good" arising from the complete excess of the "bad," as the new growth sprouts from the rotting of the seed.

The first act rejects "redemption by ice." In its simplest objectivization, we find the situation placed before our eyes in the form of Ben's statue on the stage. The friends, Ben and Kewpie, had been under ice together; they had been skating with a third boy, when the ice broke and their friend had drowned. The spell of this "life-in-death" is still upon them. . . .

Act II, by my analysis, considers and rejects "redemption by fire." It is in this way that I would locate the symbolic element underlying the remarkable realism of Mr. May, the professional firebug. Leo refuses to accept his impotent partner Sam's proposal that they solve their financial troubles by employing this man. But Pike, the proletarian furnace tender (who would thaw the ice), had proclaimed his belief in "redemption by decay." He is thus the bridge between Sam's fire solution and Leo's rebirth from decay. And we complete the pattern in the third act where, as the process of decay is finished, Leo's prophesy of rebirth sprouts from the rotted grain, and the curtain descends.

I might note other features of the internal organization. Thus, Pike's mere entrance at times foreshadows the "fatality" of the plot. For he knocks at the door (1) just as Julie has said, "When the time comes—" (2) when Gus has said he would like to "go far away to the South Sea islands and eat coconuts," and (3) when, Clara having asked "Is it the end?" Leo has answered, "Not yet." At these crucial moments, Pike's message is in the offing. But whereas the message remains the same throughout the play, Leo (the "father") must assimilate it in his own way, as he does by conscientiously completing the symbolism of the rotting grain. . . . (p. 283)

Approached from this angle, . . . doubts as to the play's statistical value (its actuarial truth as a survey of the bourgeoisie) may seem less relevant. If a poet happens to have the sort of imagination that revivifies an old heresy in modern details, how would he go about it to put this imaginative pattern into objective, dramatic form? At other times, he might have externalized the pattern as a struggle between angels and demons, or between Indians and settlers, or between patriot and foe, or in the "war of the sexes," etc. At present, in keeping with current emphasis, he may symbolize it with relation to an interpretation of historic trends, where its "prophetic" truth is enough. Incidentally, the *subjective* origin of the pattern need not impair the *objective* validity of the symbols used. If the bourgeoisie is oppressed by loss of certainty, one may have many good objective reasons for externalizing the pattern of his imagination in this form, particularly as the pattern itself may have been established in the individual poet precisely by the effects of the same frustrating process.

Our approach also may have bearing upon the comments of Stanley Burnshaw, who observed in The New Masses that the play erred as political strategy. Inasmuch as the proletariat must expect the petty bourgeoisie to become its allies, he asks, how could people so decayed have the vitality to assist in the tremendous work of establishing a new order? This objection is justified only if one does not believe in the Odets formula for redemption, remembering only the ash and not the Phoenix that arises from the ash. But if one follows the Odets ritual to the end, the objection is weakened. By the Marxist formula, the complete "proletarian" would require no process of rebirth. He would grow up with his morality. He and it would be one. But the bourgeois would have to "come over," dropping the morality that made him and taking another in its place. Converting the situation into drama, we should require rebirth, the ritualistic changing of identity, rather than merely a superficial matter of climbing off one bandwagon and climbing on another. And we should require the dramatist to deepen and broaden the process as greatly as possible.

Thus, I question whether we can appreciate the play by a simple "scientific" test of its truth. . . . A more integral test is to be found, I submit, in a consideration of the play as ritual. And those who respond to its ritual will be enabled to entertain drastic developments, without drawing simply upon a masochistic desire to be punished. (pp. 283-84)

Kenneth Burke, "By Ice, Fire or Decay?" in The New Republic, *Vol. LXXXVI, No. 1115, April 15, 1936, pp. 283-84.*

JOSEPH WOOD KRUTCH

[In **"Golden Boy"**] Clifford Odets has written what is certainly his best play since **"Awake and Sing."** To say this is to say that the piece exhibits unmistakable power and genuine originality, even though it is not, unfortunately, to deny that there is still in his work something which suggests imperfect mastery of a form he will probably have to invent for himself if he is ever to become completely articulate. There are moments when **"Golden Boy"** seems near to greatness; there are others when it trembles on the edge of merely strident melodrama.

Ostensibly the play deals with the career of a young Italian boy who abandons the fiddle for the prize ring because "you can't pay people back with music," and because he wants the money which will make him forget an embittered youth. Actually the theme is the same as the theme of **"Awake and Sing,"** and the power which Odets exhibits is again the power to suggest the lonely agony of souls imprisoned in their own private hells of frustrated desire and inarticulate hate. No one that I know can more powerfully suggest the essential loneliness of men and women, their inability to explain the varied forms assumed by the symbols of their desire, and the powerlessness of any one of them to help the other. His dialogue is often brilliantly suggestive, especially when he puts it into the mouths of ignorant or uncultivated people; even the vulgarest of his villains rises to the dignity of the tortured; and he involves the spectator in the agonies of his characters until the palms sweat and one goes out of the theater tense with an emotion which the author has been unwilling or unable to resolve.

I suppose that the interpretation which Mr. Odets puts upon his own play is obvious enough. It is, I assume, that suffering like this "is inevitable under capitalism," and that the fiddler turned prize fighter is the type of those in whom rebellion assumes a merely symbolic instead of an effective form. But this time, at least, Mr. Odets keeps his political theories in the background where they belong and writes a play which does not depend for its appeal upon a concern with his economic opinions. The agonies of his characters are real and affecting whatever one may think of the reasons for their existence. (p. 540)

Joseph Wood Krutch, "Two Legends," in The Nation, *Vol. 145, No. 20, November 13, 1937, pp. 539-40.**

STARK YOUNG

It seems to me the first thing about Mr. Odets' new play ["**Golden Boy**"] that we should mention is a certain quality in the dialogue. He has a sense of character drawing that exhibits the courage of outline. An unusual number of the characters in "**Golden Boy**" are set beside one another with the right bold theatre instinct, a perception of the fact, unknown to most playwrights nowadays, that character in fiction and character on the stage are two very different matters—see the fuzzy nonsense in most British plays that come to Broadway. He has an intuition of emotional impacts that make real theatre instead of mere description. The story in "**Golden Boy**" wanders for a few moments at the start but goes straight on after that. The number of motifs in personality, reactions, inheritance, hurts, secrecies, hopes, happiness, fate, bodily conditions, and so forth may seem crowded in at times, to lack a steady, or mature, distribution and proportion; but the direction is a good one nevertheless, it makes for abundance, it interweaves elements that promise a living fabric. His conception of the scenes, where to emphasize, where bring down the curtain, has grown neater and sharper. And the insistence, more or less adolescent, that once threw things in our faces is warmed now into both better persuasion and better taste.

The point I wanted to stress as where his theatre gift most appears is in the dialogue's avoidance of the explicit. The explicit, always to be found in poor writers trying for the serious, is the surest sign of lack of talent. To write in terms of what is not said, of combinations elusive and in detail, perhaps, insignificant, of a hidden stream of sequences, and a resulting air of spontaneity and true pressure—that is quite another matter. In this respect Mr. Odets is the most promising writer our theatre can show. The effect very often, and always the promise, of such a manner of dialogue is glowing, impressive and worthy of the response and applause that the audience gives it. (p. 45)

Stark Young, "Gods, Golden Lads and Girls," in The New Republic, *Vol. XCIII, No. 1198, November 17, 1937, pp. 44-5.*

EDITH J. R. ISAACS

[Even] in *Golden Boy,* which is far and away better theatre fare than any other Odets play, he is still the most personal of all playwrights, still speaking for himself and listening to himself as he speaks. He is still recording rather than creating, still not quite dramatically mature, with all of his faults as plain to see in his playwriting as white figures on a blackboard. But he has vigor, a mental and spiritual pressure of ideas against his material which does not let his story down, and he is acquiring a sure sense of form. He has, moreover, that gift of rhythmic speech which is the mark of the more-than-one-play author, a gift which most little boys on any street corner possess, and which grown men seem somehow unhappily to lose before they put their pens to the pages of a play.

This gift of speech Odets has not yet quite under control. To give it full value he must either set it free or discipline it more severely, or both. Many of the most authentic and spirited passages of his dialogue still sound like phrases carefully culled from a notebook carefully documented by a playwright with a fine ear. It is some of the lush, sentimental scenes in *Golden Boy,* overwritten but with a clear, crisp undertone, that show how well Odets will write when he once creates freely and allows his characters to speak out of their own mouths. (p. 12)

Golden Boy tells Joe Bonaparte's story concretely and well—the swift, almost unthinking plunge into the fighter's world, the first defensive fights that subconsciously protected the musician's hands from danger, the growing lust for success, the love for the girl who belonged to his boss, the separation from his family—especially from the loving, soulful father—the final victory and the death of his opponent, the disillusionment.

Only at the end of the story does the author of *Golden Boy* fail, both in ambition and attainment. Death is too easy and too false an ending. Golden boys, at the moment of empty victory, do not ride out into the dark with a beautiful maiden and crash against the heavens they thought to storm. (p. 13)

Edith J. R. Isaacs, "When Good Men Get Together," in Theatre Arts Monthly, *Vol. XXII, No. 1, January, 1938, pp. 11-13.*

JOSEPH WOOD KRUTCH

The tendency still persists to make of Clifford Odets and his plays a political issue. That, I think, is a pity from any point of view now that the facts are becoming increasingly clear. Whatever his opinions may have been or, for that matter, may still be, those opinions are shared by many, while Mr. Odets reveals a gift for characterization and a gift for incisive dialogue unapproached by any of his Marxian fellows and hardly equaled by any other American playwright.

"**Rocket to the Moon**" . . . carries him at least one step farther along the road he is traveling, and to my mind at least makes the best of the other new plays now current on Broadway seem pallid indeed. Certain crudities, though they are less conspicuous than those in any of his previous works, do remain. Moreover, the fable of "**Rocket to the Moon**," like that of both "**Awake and Sing**" and "**Golden Boy**," seems more powerful in conception than in development; so that as the story approaches its end the manipulation of events tends to become more nearly mechanical. Perhaps the play as a whole never rises above the level of its first act. But the personages are endowed with a life almost painfully intense, and the incisive thrusts of the dialogue follow one another relentlessly from the beginning to the end.

Reduced to an outline, the story may seem almost commonplace. . . . But no such outline can suggest either the solid reality of the characters or the insight exhibited into the workings of their minds. Not one of the personages is a story-book cliché; not one of the situations seems other than freshly imagined; and Mr. Odets exhibits among other things, two gifts not often combined—the gift for a kind of literal realism which makes his characters recognizable fragments of reality, and the gift for endowing these same characters with an intensity of life which lifts them into another realm. They are immediately recognized and accepted, but the sense that one has met them before is soon succeeded by the realization that the full force of what they are and what they imply is here thrust for the first time upon an awakened awareness.

Like the best scenes in previous works, "**Rocket to the Moon**" is in one sense not a "pleasant" play. The spectator is spared no ugliness and, except perhaps at the very end, permitted no romantic or sentimental evasion of the situation. The broken spirit of the middle-aged failure, the desperate gallantry of the old man trying to pretend that he can accept the emptiness of his own life, and the unconscious cruelty of the girl who cannot even imagine what it is like not to have a whole lifetime before one, are realities which nothing can explain away and nothing make other than painful in themselves. Yet the intensity which makes the play at moments almost unbearable is responsible also for the fact that it is more than a tale of frustration and rises above mere realism toward the tragic level. No desires so agonizingly intense as those which possess these people can be really trivial, and even the defeated become heroes when they fight with such desperation.

The political implications of the play, if they exist at all, are even less intrusive and less explicit than they were in **"Golden Boy,"** and seem to come down to no more than the suggestion that money or the lack of it plays some part in determining the course which our lives must take. It needs no ghost come from the grave to tell us that, and the fact is frequently recognized by writers without party affiliations. Whatever further private meanings the play may have for the author need be no concern of either the general public or the critic. Mr. Odets is welcome to any opinions he may care to hold so long as he can write as impressive a play as the present one. (pp. 600-01)

> *Joseph Wood Krutch, in a review of "Rocket to the Moon," in* The Nation, *Vol. 147, No. 23, December 3, 1938, pp. 600-01.*

TIME

Stripped to the bone, **Rocket to the Moon** is a triangle play; the story of a kindly, thin-blooded, tired dentist . . . who has accepted life at prevailing odds, surrendered to routine, "gone to sleep." His bitter nagging wife and his sinister, mocking father-in-law . . . appreciate his goodness, yet cannot help taunting him. From a romantic young girl . . . in his office who is fighting to live, do, go somewhere, and who loves him, he gets sympathy. Suddenly he finds himself in love with her. But when the showdown comes, he stays with his wife: not only because of conscience or past ties, but because he is too weary to wrench himself out of the old life and cope with the high-powered demands of the new.

Odets does not encase this eternal situation in the snug, tight frame of the well-made Broadway "domestic drama." Heaving, racked, volcanic, the play belches the hot subterranean lava of its characters' anger, helplessness, pain. It draws back their skin to leave every nerve exposed. In its best scenes **Rocket to the Moon** is blisteringly real, its dialogue forks and spits like lightning from a scornful sky.

Like **Awake and Sing!,** like **Paradise Lost,** like confusion itself, the new play does not move in a straight line. In his social-minded plays Odets has drawn people who are confused because a materialistic society pulls them one way, their instincts another. But in **Rocket to the Moon** psychological dislocations result from a clash of temperaments, a lack of drive. And Odets will not stay with his plot. He pursues a mystical theme which overrides it: the need for love to vitalize human lives. Inoculated with this virus, his characters cease to be individuals in a specific situation, turn into orators, poets, philosophers who halt the action to harpoon the cosmos.

Like **Paradise Lost, Rocket to the Moon** is full of clashing moods, windy flights, people half-real, half-symbolic. At moments the over-intense young girl and the too-sinister old man all but tumble into the whacky farce world of a *You Can't Take It With You.* The last act wobbles all over the place. This is not miscalculation on Odets' part. It springs from a pretentious side of him that wants to make every common dentist's office widen out into the universe. Sometimes he mistakes abracadabra for revelation. (pp. 44-5)

> *"White Hope," in* Time *(copyright 1938 Time Inc.; all rights reserved; reprinted by permission from* Time*), Vol. XXXII, No. 23, December 5, 1938, pp. 44-7.*

GRENVILLE VERNON

In all that has been written about the plays of Clifford Odets it is odd that little attention has been paid to the fact that first and foremost these plays are Jewish, and that Mr. Odets himself is a direct descendant of those playwrights such as Gordon and Lubin who once made the Yiddish theatre in America so extraordinarily vital. What has been impressive in Mr. Odets's plays has not been their ideas, which are usually pretty confused, or their structure, which has been pretty melodramatic, but the fact that the characterizations and the dialogue have a bite and an originality of turn which set them apart from the somewhat pallid characters and dialogue of most modern plays. It is true that Mr. Odets's people often shout at the top of their lungs, that their emotion is unrestrained, and at times they utter appalling banalities with an air of owlish wisdom. But all in all their vitality, both emotional and intellectual, is a welcome relief equally from chatterers or sophisticated nothings and from people who are all hard-boiled surface, with no intelligence underneath. Mr. Odets's people are at once primitive and intelligent, and it is this antinomy which imparts to them their color and variety. Neither of these qualities are hurt by the fact that their emotion is not strong enough to conquer their intelligence nor their intelligence deep or keen enough to kill their emotion. It is this struggle of emotion with intelligence which is the basis of much of the great drama of the world, and it is this struggle which is abundantly evident in the half-Americanized Jews of Mr. Odets.

A man familiar with the Yiddish drama told me recently that many of Odets's most pungent speeches are practically direct translations from the Yiddish, and it is this that makes the dialogue so alive and vital. It is dialogue, not created by the dramatist, but inherited by him from the speech of his people, which gives the feeling at once personal and universal which informs the talk in all his plays and notably in his latest success, **"Rocket to the Moon."** Up to the present Mr. Odets has given no sign of understanding people other than his own type of Jewish-Americans, and for this reason it is not well to hope for the great American play from him; indeed it is unfair. . . . But as a dramatist of the melting-pot he is unique and unapproached.

> *Grenville Vernon, "Clifford Odets," in* Commonweal *(copyright © 1938 Commonweal Publishing Co., Inc.; reprinted by permission of Commonweal Publishing Co., Inc.), Vol. XXIX, No. 8, December 16, 1938, p. 215.*

STARK YOUNG

Mr. Odets' **"Night Music"** has been generally taken, in so far as I have read comments on it, as a sort of Manhattan "Boy

Meets Girl," that Hollywood story, with its appealing jibe. . . . If Mr. Odets' play was taken this way, as a Manhattan idyll with et cetera trimmings, it is largely his own fault rather than the reviewers' stupidity, as some would have us believe.

It is Mr. Odets' fault for two reasons. First, there is the kind of wandering, seemingly casual, tangential quality in **"Night Music"** by which it meanders along, or seems superficially at least to do so, until at the last the Good Friend detective has—without beard or reindeer or stockings—brought the young man and the young woman to a cheerful mood, courage, sweetness, yes, and bright advance on the American future that they will share and help create. I hope I can manage to be clear at this point—to do so is difficult without the attendance at the performance assured and remembered or the full text spread out for one to read. A friendly comment tells us that the "play stems from the basic sentiment that people nowadays are affected by a sense of insecurity; they are haunted by the fear of impermanence in all their relationships; they are fundamentally homeless, and whether or not they know it, they are in search of a home, of something real, secure, dependable in a slippery, shadowy, noisy and nervous world."

This search for a home and a security genuinely human can, of course, go in many directions and take many forms, comic, tragic, what not. On the whole, as Mr. Harold Clurman, director of the play [says] . . . , **"Night Music"** tends to present "this deeply serious pursuit" in a light vein, wistful, pathetic, even farcical.

To take "this pursuit" is all very well, but taking it thus does not consist in that lively, skip-the-rope, youthful dénouement. No! Taking "this pursuit" thus demands that certain elements shall be found all through the play—such elements are as a matter of fact now and again present, delightfully and truly—and demands a tone in the conclusion of it that sustains the whole approach and impression thus intended or presupposed. As the play stands, however, this is not true: those forward-looking speeches, almost doctrinal or dogmatic, that appear from time to time are often what we might call inserted—they connect, for one instance, rather poorly with the central character, this young man that Mr. Odets writes every one of his plays around, this hero of assorted races—Jewish, Italian, Greek, but always the same. In sum the tone, the general tone, of **"Night Music"** is not either continuously or definitely or with any total unity established.

Second, in the struggling, loving and aspiring of which we hear in connection with the play, Mr. Odets' idea, or theme, apparently is that the acceptance of the struggle without bitterness or self-pity promises the possibility of growth and of a world where such characters as these in **"Night Music"** may find a home. Nowadays, that is the kind of statement that may be as good as any other, provided we are catching a train, rushing to cocktails, or to a motor car or supper club, or writing a column, or making a broadcast or listening to the radio, et cetera, et cetera: it will serve—just as one hasty counter lunch is as good as another. Otherwise it is, by default, 50-percent nonsense. Did any historian ever frankly record a civilization, or a social system, that sprang from this negative-positive condition? To stop being sour and stop feeling sorry for yourself is all very well; it is the first step, and almost to be taken for granted. But afterwards comes something else again. There must be some conception—or at least some semi-conception—to go on with. Bitterness, self-pity, the sense of disadvantage, etc., are certainly not desirable as traits that are operant in oneself, and certainly they should be corrected, dramatically or otherwise; but they are all a private disease, not the basis of a social theory.

To give up bitterness, malice and self-pity and start "seeking" may be in certain cases, if you like, a profoundly important move; but it remains, nevertheless, a matter of cases. It is a very limited procedure. It is as if socially (meaning—old style—sociologically) one had never grown up: one has merely turned away from his lamentations. Such a turning, such antistrophic vision and movement, is not enough. Its quality may be lyrical, violent, vitriolic, seething, rabid; or it may be international; or, as against some extant and resented state of things, revolutionary. But essentially it is nomadic, barbaric and without logic. Whatever the boasted tradition of intellectualism behind it may be, it is without all clarity of mind ultimately, without even any passionate mentality that could be said to exist beyond the sheerly subjective.

There is, furthermore, a question that in all fairness should be raised. Can we demand from a dramatist, in an age like ours, scattered, distracted, surging, wide, chopped-up and skimmy, that he provide his play with a background of social conceptions that are basic, sound, organized, prophetic, deep-rooted? Shall he, in sum, be asked to draw the hare of heaven from a shallow cap? The answer is no, we can scarcely demand that. In general we should remind ourselves that there is no reason to ask any theatre to surpass its epoch in solidity, depth or philosophic summation.

Could we ask, then, this everlasting young man of Mr. Odets' play—with that exhibitionism, very considerable commonness, slight hint of the pathetic, and endless resentment—to compensate us somewhat by manifesting some tangible notion of just what his philosophy of life may be, what the nature is of his passionate dream, and, in plain English, what it is he wants and if there is anything he can think of that would put him out of this stew he is in? The answer again is that this would be desirable, but not reasonably to be demanded. We can, however, ask that the dramatist himself make clear the point that the young man does not know. (pp. 377-78)

Stark Young, "Two New Failures," in The New Republic, Vol. 102, No. 12, March 18, 1940, pp. 377-78.*

DAVID BURNHAM

Hollywood has been generally blamed for Clifford Odets's failure to live up to the promise of **"Awake and Sing"** and **"Waiting for Lefty."** But the faults of **"Clash by Night"** aren't the faults of Hollywood; indeed, Mr. Odets might to advantage have borrowed more liberally from the movies' adroitness for plot mechanics and episodic elaboration, particularly in his static second act. No: **"Clash by Night"** suffers principally from a lack of direction arising from the want of any adequate frame of reference.

Odets's frame of reference in 1935 was the class struggle. What has lasted over into 1942 is principally a humanitarian intuition of the individual's private separation, which is valid background for pathos but not for tragedy. Here is a triangle of the bored wife, the insentient husband and the handsome lodger: surely no novelty in the theater and demanding the justification of a fresh approach. Or at least a special quality of perception and analysis. It is disappointing to report that Odets has given it neither. Nor has he given the familiar situation stature by relating it to any moral or social standard. Infidelity is meaningless outside the moral arena; tragedy requires a villain, whether it be a person or a society. Odets no longer indiscriminately blames Society, and doesn't recognize the Devil. He succeeds in interesting us in his characters' temperaments, but never in their tragedy.

Before he lets us down, however, Odets gives us three scenes out of his top drawer. Here he shows himself again a master of vivid colloquial dialogue—occasionally over-stylized so that single phrases stand out in epigrammatic isolation, but the stylization is in general a benefit; "lifelike" dialogue is a far more subtle affair than mere stenographic naturalism. (pp. 319-20)

> David Burnham, in a review of "Clash by Night," in Commonweal (copyright © 1942 Commonweal Publishing Co., Inc.; reprinted by permission of Commonweal Publishing Co., Inc.), Vol. XXXV, No. 13, January 16, 1942, pp. 319-20.

ROSAMOND GILDER

[The theme of **Clash by Night**] is eternal, its plot the classic formula of the *drame passionel*. Yet so vibrant, so steeped in life and passion are Mr. Odets' characters that the world he creates with them exists as solidly, more solidly indeed, than most of the aspects of the world in which we live. Mr. Odets' story is negligible. He is concerned with a quite ordinary couple living on a Staten Island water-front.... Of these everyday ingredients Odets has fashioned a poignant picture of man's loneliness, of his yearnings and frustrations, of mischievous evil, of sorrow, ungainliness, love and death. (pp. 150-51)

The first half of the play offers by far the richest material for actors and audience alike. It is warm with life and with the irrelevant and mysterious action of human beings living on this 'darkling plain'. The scene on the porch of the Wilenski's house on a hot summer night where time and the stars are suddenly close at hand; the scene in the frowzy dance hall; certain haunting moments of search and revelation throughout the play show Odets at his best. If the last half is occasionally labored and repetitious, if, taken as a whole, the play has not the completeness of, let us say, **Awake and Sing** or **Golden Boy**, it yet proves that Odets has by no means lost his power or his poetry and that he is as creative as ever when it comes to giving form and substance to character and thought. (p. 152)

> Rosamond Gilder, "Time and the Rivals: Broadway in Review" (reprinted by permission of the author), in Theatre Arts, Vol. XXVI, No. 3, March, 1942, pp. 149-60.*

HAROLD CLURMAN

Odets's work from the beginning contained "a protest that is also prophecy." There was in it a fervor that derived from the hope and expectation of change and the desire for it. But there was rarely any expression of political consciousness in it, no deep commitment to a coherent philosophy of life, no pleading for a panacea. "A tendril of revolt" runs through all of Odets's work, but that is not the same thing as a consistent revolutionary conviction. Odets's work is not even proletarian in the sense that Gorky's work is. Rather is it profoundly of the lower middle class with all its vacillation, dual allegiance, fears, groping, self-distrust, dejection, spurts of energy, hosannas, vows of conversion, and prayers for release. The "enlightenment" of the thirties, its effort to come to a clearer understanding of and control over the anarchy of our society, brought Odets a new mental perspective, but it is his emotional experience, not his thought, that gives his plays their special expressiveness and significance. His thought, the product chiefly of his four years with the Group and the new channels they led to, furnished Odets with the more conscious bits of his vocabulary, with an occasional epithet or slogan that were never fully integrated in his work. The feel of middle-class (and perhaps universal) disquiet in Odets's plays is sharp and specific; the ideas are general and hortatory. The Left movement provided Odets with a platform and a loud-speaker; the music that came through was that of a vast population of restive souls, unaware of its own mind, seeking help. To this Odets added the determination of youth. The quality of his plays is young, lyrical, yearning—as of someone on the threshold of life. (pp. 150-51)

Perhaps Odets privately harbored the belief that socialism offers the only solution for our social-economic problems. Perhaps his desire to share a comradely closeness to his fellowmen might attract him to those who hoped to bring about socialist society, but he must also have suspected that temperamentally he might prove a trial to any well-knit party. Instead of being an adherent of a fixed program, a disciplined devotee of a set strategy or system, Odets possessed a talent that always had an ambiguous character. If because of all this the regular press was misled into chatter about his "Marxism" while the Left press was frankly perplexed and troubled by him, it may also be guessed that Odets too was pretty much in the dark on this score.

On the one hand, Odets felt himself very close to the people—the great majority of Americans—even in his bent for the "good old theatre"; on the other hand, his heart was always with the rebels. But who precisely were the rebels, and what did they demand of him? Those he knew were a small minority, and they marked out a line for him that he could not altogether accept. After the first flurry of Odets's success had passed, everyone discovered a "change" in him. The conventional reviewers were glad, the Left was disconcerted. But, in the sense they had in mind, both were wrong—Odets had not changed.

Perhaps the truth is that the vast majority, to which Odets felt he belonged as much as to any rebellious few, had not yet created for itself a cultural clarity or form, not to speak of other kinds of clarity or form—had not, for example, yet made for itself a theatre in which he could function freely. Perhaps the "few" who often criticized him more harshly than anyone else did not know how much they had in common with those they professed to scorn. (pp. 151-52)

> Harold Clurman, in his The Fervent Years: The Story of the Group Theatre and the Thirties (copyright 1945 and renewed 1973 by Harold Clurman; copyright © 1957 by Harold Clurman; reprinted by permission of Alfred A. Knopf, Inc.), Knopf, 1945 (and reprinted by Harcourt Brace Jovanovich, 1975, 329 p.).*

HAROLD CLURMAN

Logic might insist that there are three kinds of plays—good, bad, indifferent—but Clifford Odets' **"The Big Knife"** is none of these. It represents the state of Odets' soul in 1949; it is exasperating and exciting.

As a mechanism for conveying a definite theme, idea or emotion, **"The Big Knife"** is misbegotten. . . .

The ostensible point of [the play] is that a good person in our society becomes the prisoner of forces that will manipulate him as a commodity. Unless he is a saint or a revolutionary he can live only by dying. Apart from any judgment as to the validity of this thesis, the play fails to demonstrate it.

The victim here is a good person because his wife says so, and because he speaks Odets' dialogue. The process of Charlie's deterioration is not dramatized. We never see him in a normal state. He has almost no history or background. When we meet him he is already a bad husband, a coward, a near drunkard and generally wrong at the top of his voice. (p. 28)

The theme cannot function within the story as Odets has seen fit to tell it. The story is largely off-stage, so that the theme becomes mostly rhetoric. Since this rhetoric is applied beyond the point of positive action, much of it is as impotent as the philosophic insults that Charlie hurls against his oppressors. But it is for these insults rather than for the story that Odets has written his play. Due to its faulty construction, much sincere feeling is wasted, many lines that might have been pithy are rendered pompous.

How then can the play be exciting? The subjective turmoil within the author blows gusts of passion through the proceedings and so sweeps the stage that story, characters, lines, no matter how incredible they may appear when isolated, shape to a form—tortured, inchoate, frustrated and rousing—the like of which no other American playwright can produce.

The lack of coördination between plot and theme in **"The Big Knife"** arises from emotional confusion in the author. It may be possible to write a clear play from a confused source, if one is honest about what actually motivates one's characters. Odets never tells the truth about Charlie Castle, which is that he *loves* Hollywood with a vicious zest, and Odets thinks this love sinful. The conflict between appetite—reinforced by society's encouragement of it—and the insistent cry of conscience creates self-loathing and conceit. The self-loathing stems from a desire to punish oneself for one's sin, the conceit from an exalted sense of one's superiority in recognizing the sin and wishing to punish oneself for it. "If I didn't love people so much," Charlie mutters, "oh, how I would hate them."

But this is Odets speaking, and one is inclined to answer that if he would stop hating himself so much he would find it easier to get closer to himself, to people, to society. He would not then have to burn himself in effigy by having his heroes kill themselves, and he would not have to cry out, like Charlie's wife at the final curtain, "Help! Help!" . . . It is much better to make the world's sorrow one's own than to try to make one's own sorrows the world's.

"The Big Knife" is not a play about Odets—it would have been better if it had been so. It is a play in which Odets' confusion about himself has unsettled the foundation of what it is supposed to be about. That is why it is difficult to praise the flashes of character perception, spiritual energy and virile quest that glint within its texture. (pp. 28-9)

    Harold Clurman, "Sins of Clifford Odets," in The New Republic, *Vol. 120, No. 11, March 14, 1949, pp. 28-9.*

JOSEPH WOOD KRUTCH

[**"The Big Knife"**] is an exposure of the movie capital which must take its place beside the exposures of the advertising business written by bright young advertising men and the exposures of the publishing business written by bright young publishers. . . .

Most of us think of Hollywood as a place where mediocrity is overpaid—in money and in fame; but to Mr. Odets it is, instead, a place where genius is prevented from expressing itself. His hero is a fabulously successful young leading man of the films whose better self we are expected to take on faith while he, languishing under a fourteen-year contract assuring him several million dollars, laments that he cannot get away from it all into some world where he can indulge his natural integrity. (p. 340)

At one point in the action he remarks, very sagely indeed, that "there is nothing so habit-forming as money"; and if Mr. Odets had not been so anxious to shift all the guilt from his hero to "the industry," he might have written a very interesting play on just that theme. Its moral would be that you cannot eat your cake if you insist on having it too. And that is the moral which, despite all the playwright's efforts to distract attention from it, keeps shouting itself out from almost every scene.

If Mr. Odets were not a man of considerable talent, the subject would hardly be worth discussing. But he is a man of considerable talent with a real gift for words, which he all too often misuses, and a real gift for writing effective scenes. As in the old days, he can still strike out a bitter wisecrack and still invent the seemingly irrelevant remark which, like the irrelevant remarks in his professed master, Chekhov, is not really irrelevant. He can also, as is here illustrated by the role of the movie magnate . . . , sketch out a grand melodramatic villain. But the tendency to blame everything on some system or other becomes obviously absurd when Hollywood and the California climate have become responsible for everything which he used to blame on capitalism. (pp. 340-41)

At one point in the play our hero remarks that "when people say, 'Be yourself,' they don't really mean, 'Be yourself'; what they really mean is, 'Be like me.'" That is Odets at his best. But when, almost at the very end, this same hero utters his final complaint, "I have always wanted a world which would bring out the best in me," that is so completely Odets at his worst as to sound almost like satire. The desire for exculpation is all too plain. Something, alas, is always preventing Odets from being what he ought to be. Sometimes it is the Hollywood system; sometimes it is just "the system." And that makes it rather too much like a woman who might say, "I always wanted a world in which I could be chaste; but the men just *will* go on asking me." (p. 341)

    *Joseph Wood Krutch, in a review of "The Big Knife,"
in* The Nation, *Vol. 168, No. 12, March 19, 1949, pp. 340-41.*

JOHN GASSNER

It is no small tribute to Clifford Odets that his return to Broadway after eight years of Hollywood peonage should have roused singular expectations. Although these were not exactly fulfilled in **"The Big Knife,"** it was a relief to learn that his talent had not been eviscerated in Southern California, that he retains his capacity for passion, and that he is still a formidable scenewright. If one could drive a team of horses through some of the gaps in his argument, if his writing was charged with subjective perversities and non sequiturs, we had reason to be concerned only over the more obvious presence of faults we had tended to overlook in his earlier work. They pertain to his habits of thought and implicate his virtues as well as his vices. They also provide an indispensable basis for any effort to discover why this gifted playwright has not fulfilled the hopes many of us entertained for him, and why his writing is so uneven. (pp. 25-6)

To assume that the author of **"The Big Knife"** is simply careless or bereft of sense, since he made his own premises, is scarcely tenable. On the contrary, he deliberately chose Hollywood as a symbol for everything deteriorative and unscrupulous in our society; he returned to the **"Golden Boy"** theme of how a materialistic, success-worshipping world corrupts the soul. He overlooked the weak character of his hero in his zeal to transfer guilt to society; he made equations without considering whether the terms were right. Everything that can be charged to faulty logic and unreality, everything that can be attributed to subjective causes in the play, is implicated in this allegorizing tendency. Odets was off his guard because his eyes were fixed on the horizon. He picked his own pocket while looking for signs above. He dropped some of the change while transferring his money from the pocket of immediate fact to the fancy wallet of social criticism. No wonder his bookkeeping didn't tally. I think that this has been his habit ever since he came to attention as a playwright, and that it is indurated in his intention of writing plays that will have large meaning.

Odets has been a writer of allegories in all his work except the underground drama **"Till the Day I Die."** This has probably passed comparatively unnoticed because allegory is no longer a popular form of writing, and its terms generally too vague today when there is no common belief out of which they can rise. Critics have always been less impressed with his conclusions than with his dramatic drive. The allegorical method was an almost inevitable procedure for a man who sought significance for his narration, vents for explosiveness of his characters, and a function for his poetic and romantic flare. Odets, who could never be content with mere realism . . . had to transfigure his particulars if he was to write at all.

His early version of **"Awake and Sing,"** under the highly personal title of **"I've Got the Blues,"** had to acquire a social rationale before the play could emerge out of its private chrysalis into the Group Theatre's repertory. A public correlate for personal experience was demanded of writers by the embattled nineteen thirties, when "social significance" was the oriflamme of art, and "the theatre is a weapon" was a slogan. (p. 26)

Odets found identification with others and release from loneliness in the cohesive life of the Group Theatre. . . . [He] made an identification with the radical and liberal elements that had by 1935 cemented a united front against the vultures of depression and fascism. He was presumably sure that his identification was with the entire working class, even if his characters were either unmistakably middle class or else pastiche; in any event this belief either real or illusory, was an outlet for the love that was in him, as it is in every creative personality. On the social canvas Odets could now draw sketches of class struggle like **"Waiting for Lefty"** or represent one phase of that struggle—the dissolution of the middle classes which Marxist theory made inevitable and the depression seemed to confirm. The Marxist vanguard proffered numerous keys to individual problems and situations for young writers who wanted to make sense of their experience. Home life was viewed as a miniature class struggle, and intramural revolt was considered a step toward revolutionary consciousness, as it is in **"Awake and Sing."** (Orthodox psychoanalysts agree, but call it "maladjustment.") The competitive system made exploiters and dealers in human flesh out of fairly decent human beings, and its materialism gave once-unspoiled young people a debased sense of values, as in **"Golden Boy."** Economic insecurity invaded sexual relations and deprived men of the energy and freedom to love, as in **"Rocket to the Moon."** The "Little Man What Now" humiliations of the dispossessed and unemployed made them susceptible to the Horst Wessel song of fascism, or disposed to blind accesses of violence as in **"Clash by Night."** Homelessness and rootlessness bedeviled the individual until he struck new roots of social purpose, as in **"Night Music."**

A creative spirit, of armed vision and a poet's susceptibility to symbolism, could easily multiply such propositions and the symbols that sustained them. . . . Odets' commitment to allegory (which was only a perfunctory engagement in **"Awake and Sing"**) became a marriage in **"Paradise Lost"** and **"Golden Boy."** The bonds frayed in **"Rocket to the Moon." "Clash by Night,"** and **"Night Music,"** but were still strong enough to hold him in uneasy marriage. In **"The Big Knife"** he is still wedded—but more uncomfortably than ever.

Particulars reveal the allegorical design. In **"Waiting for Lefty"** a taxicab strike became synonymous with, among other things, the overthrow of economic exploitation, betrayal by labor bosses, poison-gas manufacture, racial discrimination in medicine, and unemployment in the theatre. . . . Both the rigid Marxist and the ordinary labor leader could raise an eyebrow at Odet's peculiar orchestration of this song of revolution, in which the trumpets were blown by a doctor, a chemist, and an actor. Skeptics could also question whether low standards of living, corruption of leadership, racialism, and military preparations were exclusively capitalistic indulgences. The overall effect was nevertheless contagious theatre, in which no small part was played by the animated structure of vignettes for the pro-strike delegates' moments of conversion, by the inflammatory device of turning the theatre into a strike meeting with actors planted in the audience. The sketchy characterization was not a felt shortcoming in this one-acter, and symbol and fact were so explicitly one that it occurred to neither the author nor his critics to call **"Waiting for Lefty"** an allegory.

Nor was **"Awake and Sing"** so patently allegorical that critics could not accept it as a remarkably vivid story of family life, ignoring the explicit conclusion as a dispensable genuflection to the left. . . . The family was treated as the breeding ground of revolt, stalemate was predicated for the wool-gathering father who lacked force as well as social understanding: the anguish and suicide were assigned to the man of good will, the old Socialist grandfather who had allowed himself to be trapped into compromise. The working-class family with middle-class pretensions was wrecked after the mother's unscrupulous effort to safeguard its respectability. The only thriving individuals were the capitalist Uncle Morty and the racketeer Moe Axelrod.

In **"Awake and Sing"** Odets already showed the difficulty that was to dog him in all his later playwriting, the discrepancy between the facts he gives us and the interpretation he derives from them. **"Awake and Sing"** was neither airtight allegory nor completely integrated drama. On neither count were the relations he expressed completely tenable. It was, for instance, much clearer that Hennie's affairs with Moe Axelrod and a second man were attributable to the libido acting up in an intense girl unmarried at twenty-six than to anything in her immediate environment or "the system." . . . It did not follow either that Ralph's great sorrow, his inability to marry his girl, was more than puppy love, and it made a weak example of frustration by the villain Economics when he was so ready to put her out of mind after his grandfather's death provided him with an inheritance with which he could have located and married her. For Ralph, moreover, to applaud his sister's abandonment of her child and flight with Moe as an awakening does not speak well for his own awakening. As impressionism and as a drama of chaos, stalemate, and fumbling toward self-expression, **"Awake and Sing"** was the best piece of new writing of its time, without possessing either inevitability or force of argument. It was probably the intent of allegorizing a particular slice of life that made Odets so cavalier with his deductions and valuations. There is a certain arbitrariness in making *x* equal *y*, or in saying that if *x* equals *y* and *y* equals *z* then *x* equals *z*. The mathematician can do that freely because all his work is tautology, his system a closed one; because he deals with quantities, not qualities. A writer is not in that fortunate position: his system is entirely open and his human material is qualitative, unfixed and incalculable. It has been fortunate for Odets that he has sometimes written better than he knew. The characters engendered by his considerable creative impulse have often broken the molds prepared for them by his intellect.

In his next two plays, **"Paradise Lost"** and **"Golden Boy,"** the calculations appear to have been present from the beginning, not the afterthoughts of **"Awake and Sing."** The first of these was acceptable drama, in fact, only when taken as a poetic parable whose large assortment of catastrophes and blunderings serve an allegorical purpose and represent the social chaos that Odets felt. **"Paradise Lost"** failed for most people who saw it, since the allegorical scheme used people instead of being used by them, drained their vitality instead of enhancing it. The symbolism lacked an objective coordinate, except by poetic or Marxist license, when it made Leo Gordon's schematically deviled family stand for the doldrums and errors of the American middle class. . . . [The] son, a glorified Olympic runner who counted on connections to launch his career, is the impersonation of the American ideal of athletic prowess, and he is adrift in the cold world of economic fact: he contracts a weak heart, loses his wife, drifts into crime, and courts death by policemen's bullets. The trustful liberal Leo Gordon loses his business and his home. The desperate partner Katz, who contributed to the catastrophe by stealing money from the business, is the rugged individualist who has no future. . . . When the Gordon family has to leave its foreclosed home, its situation is Paradise Lost for the bourgeoisie. These and other symbolic situations comprise a social whole, according to Odets and those whose beliefs he shared. That these disasters should all happen to one single family made the jeremiad look like a fabricated play and a fulsome contrivance.

In **"Golden Boy,"** on the contrary, symbolism and fact were sufficiently close, and allegory sufficiently fused with reality, to make it Odets' most successful play. Odets had found in his prizefight saga a fable recognizably rooted in American life, and therefore amenable to allegorical explication. He did not have to employ esoteric detail to vaporize characterization, to warp reality, to strain simple credibility after starting with the hypothesis that a boy who had the hands and soul of a violinist could become a champion boxer. (Hypotheses at the start, as we have found ever since "Oedipus Rex," do not destroy convictions as do far-fetched assumptions in the body of a play.) The drama progressed clearly and relentlessly until the last scene, even if in that Odets used a somewhat less acceptable hypothesis: that his hero and heroine, Joe and Lorna, having found themselves and their love at last, decide to commit suicide. Those who cared to trace social significance in the parable could do so without ambiguity, and those who cared only for the personal story and character drama could find sufficient satisfaction on that level. The rise and fall of Joe Bonaparte in the context of the prizefighting business made a self-contained story, and anyone was welcome to make as much as he wished of the playwright's references to the corruption of values by economic insecurity. In **"Golden Boy"** Odets was singularly fortunate. Dealing with a piece of Americana for which a common understanding existed, Odets did not have to force too many parallels outside the realistic context of the work. Never again did he light upon another fable that would serve him nearly as well.

His next play, **"Rocket to the Moon,"** with its simple story of a married dentist's inability to win freedom from an unhappy marriage and to enjoy the love of his secretary, seemed to achieve no more than a minor-key variation on men's ineffectual striving for happiness. Odets found himself in the position of dealing with an essentially undramatic character and a tepid situation, which may explain why the play runs downhill after an excellent first act. He tried to make it run uphill by giving self-realization to the girl, who renounces the weak-spirited dentist who could only nibble at love, and rejects the advances of an old man (and an admirably drawn one) who offers her only financial security. But neither the personal drama nor the gospel of liberation could climb with sufficient conviction for anyone not implicated in the author's strategy as director or actor. The girl was simply too unimportant for significant or exciting action and too commonplace a person to represent a theme or ideal. . . . Written with real sensitivity and vividness, as well as with more restraint and balance than any of the other plays, **"Rocket to the Moon"** failed to advance a promising career at precisely the point where it should have reaped the best harvest.

Thereafter the author seemed rattled and unsure. Personal problems, we assume, and unsteady weather in the Marxist bailiwick as well as in the nation, were unfavorable to righting the keel of his dramaturgy. **"Night Music,"** with its theme of homelessness in the modern world, was a fugue with variations that went off in too many directions. It proved to be more bewildering than enlightening, although a creative imagination attempted some of its boldest strokes in this work. The allegory was slipshod and the symbolism sometimes miniscule, sometimes esoteric. **"Clash by Night,"** in 1941, emerged as a rather febrile triangle, and again some laudable intentions went by the board. Even more regrettably, good writing went to waste as Odets invited obtuseness with his fable of adultery, and skepticism by the earnestness with which he sought to impose significance on the banal plot. Most recently, **"The Big Knife"** cut the throat of its argument almost as thoroughly as the life-thread of its Hollywood hero, even though once more Odets reminded us that only two young writers since his emergence, Williams and Miller, can write with such animation.

Odets can find comfort that his talent is intact, and we may still expect much when matter and the significance he intends for it can meet. It may be unreasonable to expect that he will some day take the fact and let the symbol go, for his ambition is of a higher order and compulsive. All the division in his writing, all the breach between intention and execution, is attributable to that ambition. The largeness of his spirit, as well as his artist's need to impose unity upon the disordered raw material of observation, cries out against easy victories in the theatre. Like other men of original talent, he must do things the hard way or not undertake them at all. Like other driven spirits, he can find no sure middle ground between the sublime and the ridiculous, between exalted feeling and mere patter. It is either a major encounter or no encounter. Alignment with a body of values, with a critique of society and dreams for it, has been a creative necessity for Odets. (pp. 27-8, 30)

> John Gassner, "The Long Journey of a Talent" (reprinted by permission of the Literary Estate of John Gassner), in Theatre Arts, Vol. XXXIII, No. 6, July, 1949, pp. 25-30.

WALTER KERR

Clifford Odets has taken a very small and very familiar situation ["**The Country Girl**"] and, by the simple process of being patient with it, found it to contain more dramatic interest than anyone could have supposed. His story is that of the actor who has drunk himself downhill and of the wife of the director who pulls him back into shape for a performance. The trouble with clichés is that people treat them as clichés; they slap them onto a stage in their baldest outlines, without taking the trouble to think them through again. Odets has thought this one through, down to the last detail, and it comes out with the reality it must have had the first time someone used it. He has been particularly successful with his actor: the man's moral weakness, superimposed aggressiveness, and natural talent are blended in a dimensional character which is not at all attractive, but is commanding because it is true. (pp. 196-97)

The play is well balanced: passages of quiet, careful motivation are followed by inevitable and satisfying flareups; nothing is tacked on; everything moves with easy confidence. (p. 197)

> Walter Kerr, in a review of "The Country Girl," in Commonweal (copyright © 1950 Commonweal Publishing Co., Inc.; reprinted by permission of Commonweal Publishing Co., Inc.), Vol. LIII, No. 8, December 1, 1950, pp. 196-97.

HAROLD CLURMAN

"**The Country Girl**" is lightweight Odets. That the least meaty of his plays should prove to be almost the most popular is significant of the press, not of the author.

No more gifted playwright has appeared in the past fifteen years. I doubt whether any American playwright at all has a greater talent for living dramatic speech, for characterization, for intensity of feeling. Above all, Odets is a true theatre poet: he is never literal, and his power with words does not represent verbal proficiency but a blood tie with the sources from which sound literature and dramatic action spring.

Apart from a certain romantic afflatus, which is at times an easily discernible defect but more often a virtue, the strength of Odets' work lies in his main theme and the particular quality of its statement. The question Odets constantly asks is: What helps a man *live*? Since we are citizens of the twentieth century, we may translate this as: What today injures man's spirit? What enhances or diminishes the creatively human in him? (pp. 29-30)

Odets' art has an immediacy and an *intimacy* equaled by no other dramatist of our generation. His plays strike home; they touch us where we live. Though they often shout, they are powerful because, in fact, they speak quietly to our hearts. They are moving because beneath their occasional bluster they sigh and weep with our own unadvertised and non-literary anguish. Their tone sometimes has a slight aura of portentousness, but at bottom they are unabashedly homey.

When at first he emphasized economic pressure as the deterrent to man's development, Odets was considered new, bold and "revolutionary," and his name became consonant with a big social noise. But this was partly due to the mood of the thirties and our foolish appetite for novelty. Later, when he began to explore the depressive effect of the wounded ego on man's soul, he no longer seemed so "new," though in fact he had become subtler and more valuable. The truth is that even "the economic interpretation" of man's unhappiness in Odets' first plays was only an indirect statement of one of the ways Americans feel the injury to their egos.

This confusion in understanding Odets results in part from his immaturity of judgment in regard to his own feeling. Corresponding to the conflict between his inadequate plot structures and his swarming emotion, there has always been a discrepancy between what he is and what he thinks he is, a breach between his consciousness and his actual experience. The most visible dramatic symptom of this was the clash between the story line in some of his later plays and what he expected us to gather from them. This produced an increasing emotional and artistic turmoil which reached its most distressing state in "**The Big Knife**."

To evade this dilemma, Odets has written "**The Country Girl**," in which he pretends to do nothing but tell a "human-interest" story as effective stage ware. But he is so subjective a writer that he must disclose something of his true feeling. In "**The Country Girl**" he tells us that the faltering and enfeebled artist (or man) may be restored by the staunch love of a woman if it is combined with the steady assistance of a friend.

To my mind the play is thin in characterization, meager in authentic feeling, shallow in invention. It is by no means dull, because Odets can never be uninteresting. Even his least vital effort smolders unmistakably with the black burn of his not-so-secret hurt—and there are always those flashes of humor and warm understanding that make us realize that we are in the presence of a *person*, not just a showman. This play, then, is a victory by default. By giving up some of his complexity, Odets has, for the moment, ceased to trouble us, even as he has failed to inspire. The negative discipline Odets has here imposed on himself may prove useful to his future even as it has proved profitable to his present. (p. 30)

> Harold Clurman, "The First 15 Years," in The New Republic, Vol. 123, No. 24, December 11, 1950, pp. 29-30.

RICHARD HAYES

Mr. Clifford Odets' ["**The Flowering Peach**"] is a work of secular piety, imperfect and somewhat arid, but nonetheless, luminously touched with the imagination of reverence. To his recasting of the Biblical tale of Noah, Mr. Odets brings a discreet humanism which shapes the experience beautifully, constantly points but never presses its contemporary reference. He was not, I think, wise to include among his dramatic baggage on the Ark so many rancorous family disputes: they do not illumine, rather they rasp and fatigue. They are, moreover, the remains of a moral intention exhausted in the more "activist" plays of Mr. Odets' youth, and as such have a somewhat gratuitous, calculated air. The same uncertainty of tone mars Mr. Odets' drawing of the important roles of Rachel and Japheth: these characters seem like intrusions from an alien world—their anguished self-regard is too conscious, too articulate, and dwarfed by the massive, obliterating humanity of Noah and Esther. Yet beyond these flaws, how vivifying it is to hear the Jewish idiom transmuted by tact and wit into art; how wonderful, above all, to find in this time of noisy commitments and harassing coercion a serious statement about human life which never says *must* or *should*, never imposes, sets up programs, announces, prescribes—only draws from the neglected well of our common pieties the small, permanent manifestations of tenderness and affection, of pleasure and reverence and a faith rich enough to nourish the seeds of the world. (p. 502)

> Richard Hayes, in a review of "The Flowering Peach," in Commonweal (copyright © 1955 Commonweal Publishing Co., Inc.; reprinted by permission of Commonweal Publishing Co., Inc.), Vol. LXI, No. 19, February 11, 1955, pp. 502-03.

GERALD WEALES

[In *The Flowering Peach* it] was Odets's apparent decision to make of the Biblical story a modern Jewish folk play.... The pattern of Noah's family is that of many lower-middle-class Jewish families in New York. The old folks, who speak with a Yiddish accent, hold close the tradition of the family; they demand of the sons and their wives, who are Americanized (i.e., modernized) in speech and thought, a loyalty that cannot easily be given. (p. 74)

[It is] to such an environment that Odets tries to wed the Noah legend. He fails for two reasons. First, his setting sounds surprisingly phony, even to an outsider; second, there is a good chance that Noah could not fit into such a setting even if it were presented with authenticity. All of the familiar devices for the stage recognition of Jewish family life are in the play: there is the mixture of practical wisdom and semi-philosophic foolishness, which in this case should be inspiration, in Noah and his wife; there are the loud, pointless arguments; there is the emphasis on getting ahead; there are the recurrent references to food. The desultory chatter that weaves in and out of these identification marks is written and read in the inverted singsong that characterizes and caricatures English-Yiddish speech, but Odets vulgarizes the whole process.... As often as not Odets sounds as though he is writing an extended dialect joke, a friendly one of course. There are occasional funny lines, but for the most part the cheapness goes beyond the rhythm of the speech and takes in the content as well. (pp. 74-5)

It may be that *Awake and Sing* was no more authentic, that it was, in fact, consciously arty in its transmutation of a family in the Bronx to a family on the stage. Yet the vigor of the language and the relevance of the setting to the theme gave the play a reality that *The Flowering Peach* cannot hope to duplicate....

[Even if Odets had] managed to bring to *The Flowering Peach* the vitality of *Awake and Sing,* it is doubtful that the Noah legend could have become a modern Jewish folk play. (p. 75)

[The] story of Noah, even though it is a Jewish legend, seems to have little relation to the only two possible forms for a modern Jewish folk play. Neither Odets nor Noah could be comfortable in the European Yiddish folk tradition represented by Sholom Aleichem and Y. L. Peretz.... This kind of writing is inevitably marked by the situation of the European Jews out of whom it grew; it is tinged with the deprecating laughter of survival that is sometimes called "ghetto humor." Odets, as an American Jew, could not write this kind of literature and Noah, as a pre-Diaspora patriarch, could not fit comfortably into it. Any new tradition would have to lie where Odets, in his earlier plays, vaguely sees it, in the communities with a Jewish population dense enough to allow its members to retain a group personality even while they absorb everything that is more widely American. (pp. 75-6)

One might, at least, have supposed that Odets undertook his attempt at folk art because he had something important that he hoped to say in this new guise. *The Flowering Peach* does not offer even that consolation. Just as the play cuts Noah down in stature, it reduces God to a series of lighting effects.... This is perhaps understandable because Odets is ordinarily more interested in men than he is in God. Yet the message of the play, if it has a message, is one that we have had from Odets before. When, shortly before the final curtain, Noah cocks his head and looks inquiringly toward the Lord, he comes up only with the news that the Flood was God's last bit of interference, that from now on the earth is in the hands of men. What Noah is actually telling us to do is to awake and sing—individually, not collectively this time—but, still to awake and sing. There is also the idea that Japheth spells out heavily, before he and his wife go off to repopulate the world, the new truth that he and Noah and all the brothers have learned on the voyage, that no man is always right, and that humility is more useful as a social weapon than self-righteousness. Even this idea is not totally new to Odets, for Dr. Stark has a glimmer of this truth at the end of *Rocket to the Moon.* The trouble with Odets's ideas, however, does not lie in the fact that he has said them before; they seem pointless here largely because they have no dramatic validity. Japheth says that everyone has changed on the voyage, but there has been no evidence of the changes on stage, except that Noah does let two of the sons swap wives, which he certainly would not have done at the beginning of the play. Noah's last conference with God is even more plainly outside the action of the play.

There were a few imaginative touches, one of which was the mouselike animal that Odets invented, which sang to indicate the presence of God. Another was his depiction of Ham.... In the play Ham's own predilection for liquor at any price and his lack of interest in anything beyond the immediate possibilities give an interesting twist to the sentence from Genesis; Shem makes the connection quite clear by shouting in a moment of anger that Ham will always work for him, for he will always have something that Ham needs. But because Odets has nothing very new or very exciting to say and because he chooses to cheapen the vessel that carries his old wine, *The Flowering Peach* is an extremely disappointing play. Because, this time at least, he has written badly and at some length, *The Flowering Peach* is a very tiresome play. (p. 76)

> Gerald Weales, "'Bronx Ararat': Mr. Odets's Folk Drama" (copyright 1983 by Gerald Weales; re-

printed by permission of the publisher and the author; all rights reserved), in Commentary, *Vol. 20, No. 1, July, 1955, pp. 74-6.*

MARY McCARTHY

Golden Boy again demonstrates the lesson of the Odets' *Paradise Lost:* that this author appears to be psychically glued to the material of his first play. He cannot advance beyond *Awake and Sing:* he can only revive it with different costumes, scenery, and (sometimes) accents. That the refurbishing of the material implies its adulteration seems not to concern Mr. Odets, who perhaps imagines that he is exploring genuinely new horizons; but to those who have admired *Awake and Sing,* each new play seems a more shocking caricature of the first. (p. 9)

The narrowness of his invention, the monotony of his subject matter have anaesthetized [Mr. Odets] to a point where he must wade in blood and tears in order to feel that he is writing a play.... (p. 10)

Thus the simple Bronx apartment dwellers of *Awake and Sing* appear in *Golden Boy* dressed up as gangsters, prizefighters, and tarts. Mr. Odets has taken a collection of types out of any underworld film, and on them he has grafted the half-ludicrous, half-touching cultural aspirations, the malapropisms, the pride in material possessions, the inarticulate longing for a sunny life, that make up the Odets formula of frustration. The Chekhovian baggage of middle-class futility with which Mr. Odets equips these low-life stereotypes is, of course, fearfully inappropriate to the milieu of lust, murder, crime and perversion in which they must travel. The voices are the dreamy, ineffectual voices of the little people of the world; the deeds are the deeds of the headliners. This contradiction between form and substance gives the play the aspect of a fancy-dress ball; there is the same grotesquerie, the same stridency, the same laughable yet indecent incongruity.

Golden Boy is a much more popular play than *Awake and Sing.* The melodramatic nature of the characters and events would alone guarantee its success at the box office. But Mr. Odets has taken out double insurance against the failure of his work by stuffing it with familiar Jewish low-comedy jokes and ancient wheezes out of vaudeville. Yet, though the stale luridity of characters and plot and the stale gag-comedy of the lines have been sufficient to keep audiences in the alternate shivers and stitches to which the underworld films have habituated them, it is not these qualities which have commanded the deferential attention of both critics and playgoers. Serious people have sat unflinchingly through this play, because they knew or thought they knew that Mr. Odets had Something To Say, that somewhere in this theatrical grab bag there lay a treasure.

Mr. Odets has a theme which in the last century would have been stated as Money Does Not Bring Happiness. But Mr. Odets conceives of it in more modern terms. He would summarize it, I suppose, by saying that the struggle for financial success which the capitalist system tends to impose on the individual is detrimental to personal happiness and to culture. Stated thus abstractly, the theme does Mr. Odets credit. Concretely visualized as a choice between playing the violin and fighting in the prize ring, it already becomes a little ridiculous. But, granting Mr. Odets the virtue of this rather simple-minded antithesis, one finds that here it has been distorted out of all truth and vulgarized out of all nobility. In the selection of a superman for a hero lies the essential hollowness of the play, for the choice between culture and money cannot be valid for a character who possesses two such remarkable gifts. If Mr. Odets' hero were a potentially great violinist, he could have become rich or at least prosperous via the concert stage, and he need never have considered prize-fighting as an alternative career. If he were not, then his abandonment of the violin was surely no tragedy. But Mr. Odets' juggling of his theme does not stop with this original false alternative; it eats deeper into the plot. What is the cause of Bonaparte's downfall and death? His greed for money, his selection of prizefighting as a life work? Not at all. A purely *accidental,* non-social circumstance: the fact that the girl he loved felt pity, loyalty, and tenderness for another man. One assumes that, were it not for the girl, Mr. Odets' hero would have been as successful and as long-lived as Jack Dempsey, Mickey Walker, Gene Tunney, or any other well-known fighter.... Mr. Odets' social theme, like his formula for the manufacture of characters, is a carry-over from his first and most sincere play. It is clearly inoperative in the world of macabre melodrama into which he has imported it. That he was forced to use a fortuitous, melodramatic device to dissolve the elements of his play and bring it to its falsely tragic curtain is itself an exposé of the play's "serious" pretentions. (pp. 10-12)

    Mary McCarthy, "Odets Deplored" (copyright 1938 by Mary McCarthy; reprinted by permission of the author; originally published in a slightly different form in Partisan Review, *Vol. IV, No. 2, January, 1938), in her* Sights and Spectacles: 1937-1956, *Farrar, Straus and Cudahy, 1956, pp. 9-12.*

STANLEY KAUFFMANN

Odets's new film, in terms of its script, lives up to its advance defense; it is not a prostituted work. But the author has stoutly defended the wrong portal, or not enough portals. The picture may be uncompromised but it is also undistinguished, pointless, and dull....

We look for positive achievements, and of these *The Story on Page One* has virtually none. It is an utterly routine courtroom drama, devoid of rewarding characters and development, even of superficial plot twist and, what is most disheartening, with hardly a trace of the arresting pungency that has been a hallmark of Odets dialogue. The picture plods along until it is finished, at which moment we ask ourselves why Odets bothered to write and direct it. The only intrinsic lure for him could have been the contrast between the mothers of the two protagonists—the heroine's hard-working mother ... and the hero's silkily domineering rich mother.... If so, it was a small and trite return on a large investment.

The theme of all this is meant to be regret and stubborn hope. American films certainly can use what Odets, at his best, can give them. The theater misses desperately the slash and thrust of his usually faulty but always exciting plays. "I'm 53 years old," he says, "a professional writer, and there's never been any loss or shrinkage of integrity." But there has, alas, been some shrinkage in intensity and relevance. What we badly need at this time is a 53-year-old edition of the Clifford Odets that was.

    Stanley Kauffmann, "Is Artistic Integrity Enough?" (reprinted by permission of Brandt & Brandt Literary Agents Inc.; copyright © 1960 by The New Republic*), in* The New Republic, *Vol. 142, No. 6, February 8, 1960, p. 22.*

MICHAEL J. MENDELSOHN

Odets' motion picture career can be roughly divided into three periods: 1936-38, 1943-47, and 1955-61. His name finally appeared on only seven produced films, but he estimated the output of those years variously from fifteen or twenty scripts to "dozens." The Hollywood practice of script-doctoring explains the disparity. He told an interviewer in 1944 that though he had written many scripts, he had taken credit only for *The General Died at Dawn*. "'The others were rewritten . . . after I left town, by four or five hacks to each script,' he says, 'and rather than share credit for what they churned out between gin-rummy games, I decided to pass up fame and keep my self-respect.'" (p. 31)

[Few of Odets' films are] of more than routine interest, except *The Story on Page One*, which he originated and directed. It is unquestionably the purest finished product of any task Odets attempted in Hollywood. The entire work, from its conception as a story idea to its actual filming, may safely be credited to him.

It is unfortunate, then, that the net result of his tremendous effort as author-director is not more satisfying. *The Story on Page One* is a rather ordinary courtroom melodrama in which, true to tradition, the defense is clever, vigorous, occasionally taken by surprise by a prosecution maneuver, but never in doubt as to ultimate victory. The prosecution team is clearly the villain of the piece. Viewers conditioned by several years of watching the unconquerable Perry Mason on television would easily forecast the jury's verdict. Odets' script does not save the unraveling until the end; the viewers are let in on the entire story almost from the beginning. The adulterous love affair that leads to the husband's death is thin plot material. The characters involved in it are hardly engrossing: Mike Morris, a crass, unfeeling detective; Jo, his attractive wife; Larry, a vacuous, mother-dominated accountant. The theme, at least from the viewpoint of the central character, would seem to be that adultery is acceptable, given the proper set of circumstances.

It is safe to assume that Odets, recognizing all the weaknesses of his script, wished his emphasis on another facet of the film, a typical social protest—equal justice. Early in the screen play, the young defense attorney, approached by Mrs. Brown to defend her daughter in court, makes a ringing speech about the inequality of justice. He explains to the mother that the state is willing to commit unlimited resources to gain a conviction, while poor Mrs. Brown can't afford even a single trained investigator. Oddly, though, this is the last the audience hears of this theme. With echoes of Zola rushing to the aid of Dreyfus, Vic Santini takes the case; from that point on, the state, with all its trained experts and unlimited bankroll, does not stand a chance for conviction.

In spite of such disheartening drawbacks, there are moments to admire in *The Story on Page One*. Odets wisely places nearly three quarters of the action in the courtroom. Vic Santini for the defense and Phil Stanley for the state are cunning, ruthless, worthy opponents. Though the necessity of making Stanley the heavy tends to cause Odets to exaggerate his disagreeable side, he is nonetheless, a brilliantly drawn courtroom tiger. Aided by some well-drawn minor characters, its vigorous dialogue, and its frequent moments of veracity, *The Story on Page One*, though a long way from the best of Odets' plays, is a workmanlike script. (pp. 33-4)

Odets tended to separate his playwriting from his film and television writing, though he frequently asserted that he was not ashamed of anything he wrote. To the end of his life he was filled with grandiose plans; something big was always in the immediate offing. Much as he wished to outgrow his reputation as the playwright of the Thirties, Odets was never granted more. Hollywood was not the answer. (p. 34)

> Michael J. Mendelsohn, "Odets: The Artist in Wonderland" (reprinted by permission of the author), in Drama Critique, Vol. IX, No. 1, Winter, 1966, pp. 31-4.

EDWARD MURRAY

The structure of Odets' plays has been misinterpreted. To some extent the playwright himself is responsible for this critical confusion. "I was influenced a little by Chekhov," Odets told Mendelsohn in 1963. "Not by Ibsen, because you see my forms are not Ibsen's. But my chief influence as a playwright was the Group Theater acting company. . . ." Invariably, critics and scholars of the drama refer to Odets' plays as Chekhovian in structure. The truth of the matter, however, is that the basic structure of an Odets play is Ibsenite; that is, one can perceive in it a single rising line of action which can be analyzed in terms of a point of attack, a turning point, and a resolution composed of a crisis, climax and conclusion. Chekhov's plays do not have this single action structure. . . . It was Odets' achievement to integrate a basic Ibsenite action with certain structural techniques of a Chekhov play, and thus assure his work a rising line of tension while simultaneously enriching the piece by counterpoint and the indirect expression of emotion and feeling. In short, Odets avoided, on the one hand, reducing the Ibsenite structure to a bald, straight-forward thesis play, and, on the other, fashioning a static genre study in the alleged Russian manner. It is necessary to add, however, that Odets' recourse to Chekhovian devices is much more apparent in *Awake and Sing!* than in his other plays. Finally, Odets has sometimes been dubbed a "scenewright" by critics; but as I hope to show throughout this study the structure of an Odets play is generally much more unified than some critics have allowed. In short, Odets is very much a "playwright." (pp. 33-4)

[*Awake and Sing!*] is far more unified than critics generally allow. John Howard Lawson was one of the first critics to attack the structure of Odets's play. According to the author of *Theory and Technique of Playwriting* the turning point in the piece looks back to the scene in Act One in which Jacob entertains Moe by playing Caruso records . . . ; but, says Lawson, Jacob's death "has no organic connection with the play as a whole." Lawson misses the point of attack—his analytical approach fails to include such a point—and hence he does not account for the total action of the play. Furthermore, contrary to what Lawson maintains, Ralph does show signs of development as a result of Jacob's death: he is able to choose social idealism in favor of Blanche—something he was not able, or willing, to do before—and, moreover, this change is dramatized when Ralph breaks with his girl, when he reads Jacob's books, and when he asserts himself with Bessie. True, Ralph will remain at home, but his situation will not be the same as it had been with the family. Finally, Ralph's motivation is clear because the basic dramatic conflict was focused at the point of attack and logically developed throughout the action of the play.

Nevertheless, there *is* a structural defect in *Awake and Sing!*. Lawson says that Jacob's death does not make Hennie's flight with Moe "inevitable." One should add that the grandfather's death does not make Ralph's choice of revolution "inevitable" either. Nor *should* Jacob's death make either choice "inevitable": for that way lies contrivance and determinism. What the turning point in the action makes "inevitable" is a decision of *some* kind: either girl or revolution—either self or society. Jacob's death, however, does not influence Hennie's escape in the same terms, for Hennie has not been involved in the main structure of the play. Yet one might be willing to accept Hennie's action if Odets presented it as a credible response to the situation enacted in the play. . . . Ralph, who is supposed to be socially "mature" now, announces the dawn of a new world—but how will Hennie's irresponsible behavior usher in that new world? What of her child? Is leaving the child in the keeping of Bessie a wise thing to do? What of Sam? Won't he become another Schlosser? People may act like Hennie in our society, but why the idealistic Marxist Ralph should applaud such action remains a mystery. One might argue that Ralph's new love of action—"DO!"—has gotten the better of him; this would be credible. It would not square entirely, however, with Odets' evident approval of Ralph standing "full and strong in the doorway" as the curtain falls. . . . One is forced to conclude that Odets remained somewhat confused about the significance of his play's ending. There is also a suggestion of an agitprop conversion in the last act which runs counter to the more realistic elements in the piece. Furthermore, *Awake and Sing!*, like some other plays and novels of the period, poses an "either-or" dramatic question. But why must it be *either* Blanche *or* the revolution? Wasn't Marx married? Wasn't Lenin? Apparently Odets anticipated such objections, and consequently endeavored to downgrade Blanche by emphasizing her cowardice and lack of sympathy. It is a weakness in the play, however, that the audience is never permitted to see Blanche. After all, she is the counterweight to Jacob's dream and as such she should be palpably on view to sharpen the dramatic conflict. Had she been on stage, though, the logical weakness in Odets's "either-or" construction would have been more clearly manifest. This is not to say, of course, that all "either-or" situations in drama are to be censured. After all, life itself occasionally poses "either-or" questions. It *is* to say, though, that in *Awake and Sing!* the dramatic question seems unrealistic.

The crude Marxist thrust of *Awake and Sing!* makes embarrassing reading today. . . . It is only the warmth of Odets' compassion and characterization that saves his first important play from the oblivion deserved by other less genuinely conceived works. "*Waiting for Lefty* had a functional value," Odets was quoted as saying in the *New York World-Telegram* on March 19, 1935. "This is sometimes called the propaganda angle in writing. But the important thing about *Awake and Sing!* is the fact that the play stems first from real character, life and social background of these people.". . . The years have not diminished the power and realism of *Awake and Sing!*, qualities which endure in spite of Odets' "ideology." Not even the romanticism that at the end degenerates into a mindless irresponsibility as the lovers escape causes any great harm to the piece. It would be a mistake, then, to put *Waiting for Lefty* and *Awake and Sing!* in the same category. As Charles Kaplan recently pointed out, *Awake and Sing!* "is less a play dealing with the class struggle than one embodying the vague dissatisfactions of the lower middle class at the thwarting of normal human desires." Indeed, few works in American drama reveal so well what happens to a family when natural relations are perverted.

Bessie Berger has usurped control in the household . . . , and as a result all the male characters are warped, impotent and crippled in some way. (pp. 40-3)

The characters in *Awake and Sing!* are extremely frustrated in their social relations, their normal development is blocked, and as a consequence they seem to regress to primitive, or infantile, modes of desire and expression. It is striking how often Odets' characters reveal what the psychoanalyst calls an "oral orientation." "Every other day to sit around," says Ralph, "with the blues and mud in your mouth.". . . "In a minute I'll get up from the table," Bessie declares. "I can't take a bite in my mouth no more.". . . Clearly, then, Marxist and Freudian motivation, which for some critics are like oil and water, appear to mix here, making *Awake and Sing!* one of the most complex plays in the American drama.

As a result of their pervasive frustration on both the personal and the social level, the characters in *Awake and Sing!* evince strong aggressive drives and a preoccupation with death. It is still another mark of Odets' skill as a playwright that he is able to fuse the death imagery of his language with the resurrection motif in the play. Analysis of dialogue reveals an astonishing number of references to violent action and death. (pp. 45-6)

[The] resurrection motif, the references to Ralph as "boychick," Hennie's name, and lines like the following: "Mom can mind the kid. She'll go on forever, Mom," says Moe. "We'll send money back, and *Easter eggs*" . . .—all are part of a thematic pattern of imagery. A study of the language in *Awake and Sing!*, then, reveals a high degree of verbal unity in the play.

Note, furthermore, how subtly Odets integrates structure, imagery and theme in his characterization of Moe. The following exchange takes place in Act One:

MOE. Didn't I go fight in France for democracy? Didn't I get my goddam leg shot off in that war the day before the armistice? Uncle Sam give me the Order of the Purple Heart, didn't he? What'd you mean, a no-good?

JACOB. Excuse me.

MOE. If you got an orange I'll eat an orange.

JACOB. No orange. An apple.

MOE. No oranges, huh?—what a dump!

(p. 48)

Here Odets' "Chekhovian" technique is brilliantly rendered. As Stark Young once said: "[Odets'] theater gift most appears . . . in the dialogue's avoidance of the explicit. . . . To write in terms of what is not said, of combinations elusive and in detail, perhaps, insignificant, of a hidden stream of sequences, and a resulting air of spontaneity and true pressure—that is quite another matter." The orality that I discussed earlier is also evident in [this same scene in Act One], which indicates that Moe's oblique expression of emotion is part of a thematic pattern. Furthermore, the structure of the scene anticipates the end of Act One and the turning point of the play.

Later in the scene just discussed, Odets orchestrates his themes:

MOE. Ever see oranges grow? I know a certain place—One summer I laid under a tree and let them fall right in my mouth.

JACOB. (*off, the music is playing; the card game begins*). From "L'Africana" . . . a big explorer comes on a new land—"O Paradiso." From act four this piece. Caruso stands on the ship and looks on a Utopia. You hear? "Oh paradise on earth! Oh blue sky, oh fragrant air—"

MOE. Ask him does he see any oranges?

(p. 49)

The counterpoint here is more than merely humorous, for Odets juxtaposes Jacob's Marxist "Utopia" with Moe's version of "Paradise.". . . . Whereas Jacob opts for the Marxist gospel, Moe seeks a romantic apotheosis. When Hennie remarks: "Oh God, I don't know where I stand," Moe tells her: "Don't look up there. Paradise, you're on a big boat headed south. . . . The whole world's green grass and when you cry it's because you're happy.". . . It is interesting to observe that Moe identifies Hennie with "oranges": "Gone big time, Paradise? Christ, it's suicide! Sure, kids you'll have, gold teeth, get fat, big in the tangerines.". . . Hence, "oranges" equal "tangerines" equal "breasts." If one recalls that Moe has said: "One summer I laid under a tree and let [oranges] fall in my mouth". . . , one can see that this imagery in *Awake and Sing!* runs counter to the basic structure of social awakening, for Moe and Hennie, like Myron and Morty, are attempting to solve adult problems in an oral, or infantile, manner. This fact would seem to undercut Odets' confidence in Hennie's attempt to make a new life and appears to be further proof of a certain amount of confusion in the playwright's conception of his material. A search for womb-like security and oral passivity seems plain when Moe informs Hennie: "Come away. A certain place where it's moonlight and roses. We'll lay down, count stars. Hear the big ocean making noise. You lay under the trees. Champagne flows like—". . . . Which contrasts sharply with the image of Ralph at the end of the play: "Spit on your hands and get to work," he says, and Moe remarks of Ralph: "The kid's a fighter!". . . . The tensions within *Awake and Sing!* no doubt spring from polarities in Odets himself.

Finally, I should like to point out how pervasive verbal echoes are in the play and how they knit together its various motifs. Perhaps some of the imagery already discussed was not consciously contrived by Odets, but it seems likely that the greater part of his language, with its various levels of significance, was deliberately wrought. Take, for example, the conclusion of the opening act:

MYRON. I remember that song . . . beautiful. Nora Bayes sang it at the old Proctor's Twenty-third Street—"When It's Apple Blossom Time in Normandy."

MOE. [Hennie] wantsa see me crawl—my head on a plate she wants! A snowball in hell's got a better chance. (*Out of sheer fury he spins the quarter in his fingers.*)

MYRON (*as his eyes slowly fill with tears*). Beautiful . . .

MOE. Match you for a quarter. Match you for any goddam thing you got. (*Spins the coin viciously.*) What the hell kind of house is this it ain't got an orange!!

(pp. 49-50)

Myron's reference to the song, "When It's Apple Blossom Time in Normandy" looks back to Hennie's line, "Wake me up when it's apple blossom time in Normandy" . . . , and, what is more important, both lines underscore the resurrection motif. Myron's dialogue also anticipates the end of the play when Hennie escapes with Moe. (p. 51)

Odets maintains his control [of language] when, at the end of [Act two], he reveals, through a sensitive extension of Chekhovian technique, the deeper feelings of Moe after the death of Jacob is announced:

BESSIE. [Jacob] slipped. . . .

MOE (*deeply moved*). Slipped?

BESSIE. I can't see the numbers. Make [the call to Morty], Moe, make it. . . .

MOE. Make it yourself. (*He looks at her and slowly goes back to his game of cards with shaking hands.*)

BESSIE. Riverside 7- . . . (*Unable to talk she dials slowly. The dial whizzes on.*)

MOE. Don't . . . make me laugh. . . . (*He turns over cards.*) . . .

Moe and Morty have both learned how to exist in the jungle, but Moe "fights against his own sensitivity" while Morty has no sensitivity against which to fight. . . . Moe's tag: "Don't make me laugh," contrasts with the hollow, wooden, inhuman tag of Morty: "Ha, ha, ha!"—which suggests that Moe means: "Don't make me laugh *like Morty!*" *Awake and Sing!* is full of such subtle touches of characterization and language.

With all its faults, then, *Awake and Sing!* is a powerful drama and one of the most impressive achievements in the modern theater. An absorbing enactment, told with anger and pity, with humor and love—and above all with verbal brilliance—of people caught in a moment of time, it nevertheless transcends the thirties to reveal the human being in the agony and longing that represents the continuing spiritual plight of man in the twentieth century. (p. 52)

Edward Murray, in his Clifford Odets: The Thirties and After *(copyright © 1968 by Frederick Ungar Publishing Co., Inc.), Ungar, 1968, 229 p.*

ALLAN LEWIS

The most acclaimed writer of the thirties was Clifford Odets. He rose out of the Depression to give voice to a world in crisis. He put the Bronx Jewish middle class on stage and gave them courage, dignity, and stature. (p. 109)

Paradoxically, Odets was the playwright least able to maintain persuasive drama in the sixties. His exodus to Hollywood, together with many members of the Group Theatre, removed him from his natural nourishment. When he returned to Broadway ten years later with *The Big Knife,* he no longer was a man of social anger. Success had deprived him of identification with the downtrodden. Of the next plays, *The Country Girl* (1950) was an outright attempt at a superficial success, and *The Flowering Peach* (1954), a drama that never focused precisely on what it had to say.

The human dislocation caused by the Depression supplied Odets with his strength as an artist. He rallied a nation to action and hope. . . . The result is theatre in its oldest form, an Epic theatre technique involving the audience and propelling them into open participation. *Waiting for Lefty* has a hard-hitting, bare, cumulative power, very much like a tribal war dance.

The members of a thug-dominated, taxi-drivers' union belong, for the most part, to the middle class that has fallen socially— the American dream in reverse. No longer do they have hopes of rising beyond their station. To Odets, as to Bernard Shaw, the greatest crime is poverty. Not psychopathic disturbances, but failure to support the family, turns men to desperate actions or makes them submit to failure. In *Awake and Sing* and *Paradise Lost,* a disintegrating family is held together momentarily by a courageous mother. (p. 110)

The language Odets used was fresh and invigorating—twisted, torn images of rare strength, a poetry of the people often excessive and at times brilliant. (pp. 110-11)

Though *Waiting for Lefty* is expressionist in form, its content is realistic, as is all of Odets' work. The small people crushed by economic forces and pictured magnificently as they give way or rise in dignity. Too often, the final affirmation is tagged on mechanically. In *Waiting for Lefty,* the rank-and-file voice of Agate shouts out like a Communist leader on the barricades. (p. 111)

[The] final exhilarating but inconsistent affirmations [as in *Awake and Sing*] were requirements of the play of the Depression, for actuality was full of heartbreak and terror. Pain and suffering make up the substance of the Depression play. Lives are destroyed, but there is hope for a better world, if people fight for it, a world in which people will be able to "awake and sing." In an interview published in *Theatre Arts Magazine,* Odets said of Leo's speech that he did believe in the possibilities expressed in this theme, and that it was a logical outgrowth of the text. "I believe that older and more crushed human beings can pass on some lifting values to the younger generation."

In Odets' plays, the Depression, as a special moment in American life, is evident in every scene. Today, the working class has risen to middle-class comfort, and Odets' former Bronx characters now live more comfortably in the suburbs. Audiences no longer have the same identification, save for the underprivileged and the oppressed minorities. Lorraine Hansberry's *A Raisin in the Sun* is an Odets drama with Negro replacements. In his own day, Odets was a man with a mission, and his plays burned with furious intensity. He gave vitality to the theatre of an era and established a memorable place in our history, but today his early plays are rarely revived. A production of *Waiting for Lefty* at Williams College was greeted with loud applause by the sons of the wealthy, all of whom shouted at the end, with playful enthusiasm, "Strike!" The work has become a museum piece, a sociological document.

When Odets returned to Broadway with *The Big Knife,* his first play after many years of financial success in Hollywood, he retreated to the personal drama. Charley Castle seeks to escape from Hollywood's erosion of his artistic integrity, but he really wants the physical comfort that Hollywood offers. The drama never reached beyond Odets' own dilemma. Everyone attacks Hollywood, particularly those who have been its best-paid hirelings. No one yet has made the attack significant. Satire would be a more effective weapon.

Odets seemed troubled by success and his desertion of a cause. *Golden Boy* is his own story, raising the question of whether art and commerce mix. Odets wanted big money, but his voluntary submission to its code became the big knife. No one else was particularly concerned. (pp. 111-12)

Odets' technique kept him afloat in the less demanding medium of the motion picture, but he longed to return to the theatre with another try at socially significant drama. Before his death in 1963, however, he was back in Hollywood preparing a television series for Richard Boone's acting company, which encouraged serious work. Only two scripts were completed.

Odets betrayed his own talent. He was a sensitive man who believed in a better world to come, but he was unable to sustain that belief under difficult and changing social conditions. He was a lonely writer, but too weak to become a great one. In the thirties, however, he rose splendidly as the playwright most able to dramatize an injured nation in need of hope and unity. (p. 113)

> Allan Lewis, "The Survivors of the Depression—Hellman, Odets, Shaw," in his American Plays and Playwrights of the Contemporary Theatre *(copyright © 1970 by Allan Lewis; used by permission of Crown Publishers, Inc.), revised edition, Crown, 1970, pp. 99-115.*

GERALD WEALES

Mr. Bonaparte was wrong and so was Marion Castle. No man is so simply made that he has a single nature which a wrong turn can violate. The violation, too, is in his nature. Both fist and fiddle were natural to Joe; both Hollywood and the escape from it were necessary to Charlie. The observer in Odets knew this; the idealist, the idealogue did not want to know. Alter the circumstances, rearrange the environment, brick off the false choices, said the latter, and the natural man will flower; home, love, happiness will become possible. This assumption had personal and artistic consequences for Odets.

He was a restless man. In his work and in his life, we can see the vacillation between a home which turns out to be a trap and a promised land that fails to keep its promises. That comic figure, the radical playwright in the fashionable Hollywood restaurant, is an oblique image for the artist who never found consolation in his art. The idealist in Odets could point Ralph toward the future, but the observer in him, who could see the self-pity and the weakness in the character, also knew that the making of *Awake and Sing!* did not bring peace. Odets did what was "in [his] nature to do" and it was not enough. He ran, in disappointment, to Hollywood and ran back, in guilt, to the stage. "A job is a home to a homeless man," says Bernie in *The Country Girl,* but he is looking around for a real home or its equivalent in Georgie. Odets was still coping with the homelessness of art at the end of his life. . . . In an odd piece he wrote for *Show,* half fiction, half sociology, the profile of a mythical movie star, Odets quoted his friend Jean Renoir. The lines are aimed at the actor, but since he is Odets's invention, it is safe to assume that they were at some time spoken to the inventor himself: "Maybe, my friend, when you were given so many other gifts, you must grow used to the fact that happiness is not among them."

The artistic consequences of Odets's ideational approach to man are less conjectural than the personal ones. The plays are their own testimony. "I believe in the vast potentialities of mankind . . ." Odets wrote to John Mason Brown back in 1935. "I want to find out how mankind can be helped out of the animal kingdom into the clear sweet air." The rhetoric may be a little heady (Odets was only twenty-nine), but the line contains a statement of artistic intentions that can be tested in all of Odets's plays. The "how" is finally less important than that there be a way into the "clear sweet air." From the certainty of *Waiting for Lefty* to the uncertainty of *The Flowering Peach,* Odets has organized his plays to make a specific point about human possibility; he has manipulated his characters to let one or more of them reach the moment of change, of recognition that will allow the play to look into a better future. A propagandist, first and last, he has always held out hope of the happy land. It is this quality that makes Odets such a likable playwright, since a happy ending (even if it is a tragic one) is hard to resist. The same quality limits him as a playwright, threatens to reduce him to the simplicity of his ideas, his themes. Yet the observer in Odets never let the preacher run free, the pessimist hobbled the optimist, the realist partnered the idealist. . . . [In Odets's plays] the characters, the dramatic situations, the lines slip their traces and escape their functions within the ideational drama. From Bessie Berger to Noah, the characters refuse to stay nailed down. Villains start charming us, heroes turn into milksops, minor characters stroll across stage and walk off with the play. I sort out the symbols in *Golden Boy* only to discover that my mind's eye is on Roxy in I, 3, where, having made a mess of things as usual by shooting off his mouth, he says, "What's the matter? What happened?" and shrugging, "I think I'll run across the street and pick up an eight-cylinder lunch." I satisfy myself about the use of the Washington-Lincoln motif in *Night Music,* but the concept is upstaged by the hot-fur salesman in I, 2: "Take it for ten plus ten—that's what I'll do—two ten spots an' you can't go wrong." The contrast between the simplicity of concept and the complexity of creation which in the man himself must have caused pain and unrest, in the plays brought richness. Odets's plays have a way of being less than what the perfectionist in us wants them to be, but they are a great deal more than they seem to the jaundiced eye. (pp. 187-89)

Gerald Weales, in his Clifford Odets: Playwright *(© 1971; reprinted by permission of the author), Bobbs-Merrill—Pegasus, 1971, 205 p.*

Toby Olson
1937-

(Born Theodore Olson) American poet and novelist.

Olson writes simple, clear, and direct poetry. He gently yet relentlessly penetrates the "things" of his life to extract an ironic but sympathetic vision of the world. He claims that "it is through writing about what I can see, hear, and feel that I can best touch the nature that I believe is common in all of us." His attempt to do this produces work in which concrete observations are colored by meditative speculations. Many of the poems from his previous volumes have been collected in *Changing Appearance: Poems 1965-70* (1975).

In addition to his poetry, Olson has published two novels, *The Life of Jesus* (1976) and *Seaview* (1982). Both novels are experimental in structure: realistically detailed descriptions merge with surreal manipulations of plot and poetic passages are interspersed with standard narrative techniques. *The Life of Jesus* uses the mystical symbolism of Catholicism to explore the psychology of the protagonist who views his life in terms of the life of Jesus.

(See also *Contemporary Authors*, Vols. 65-68 and *Contemporary Authors New Revision Series*, Vol. 9.)

Photograph by Layle Silbert; © copyright 1983

PUBLISHERS WEEKLY

[Toby Olson's first novel "*The Life of Jesus*"] is a mystical mixture of autobiography and the religious legend shaped by his Catholic school upbringing. The author poetically fulfills his need to make the holy family his own, recounting his life as the life of Jesus—not pretentiously, but dreamfully. . . . A deeply symbolic work that explores at a most basic level the mind of Catholicism.

> A review of "*The Life of Jesus*," in Publishers Weekly (reprinted from the October 4, 1976 issue of Publishers Weekly, published by R. R. Bowker Company, a Xerox company; copyright © 1976 by Xerox Corporation), Vol. 210, No. 14, October 4, 1976, p. 71.

PHILIP MILNER

The focus of [*The Life of Jesus*] is not on religious faith nor on Jesus, but on an unnamed California boy who identifies completely with the Jesus of his Catholic education. He works as a carpenter, tells parables in a spare prose that resembles that of the Gospels, heals the sick, offers communion, dies, and is resurrected. The miraculous dimension is always understated. . . . Since he is completely merged with Jesus, we learn little about him that does not have a parallel in the life of Jesus. The symbolic structure has more reality than the hero's experiences in 20th-Century America.

> Philip Milner, in a review of "*The Life of Jesus*," in Library Journal (reprinted from Library Journal, October 15, 1976; published by R. R. Bowker Co. (a Xerox company); copyright © 1976 by Xerox Corporation), Vol. 101, No. 18, October 15, 1976, p. 2195.

ROBERT VAS DIAS

Changing Appearance assembles the work of Toby Olson's five previous small-press books plus material unpublished in book form, from the period 1965-70. . . . (p. 50)

The means by which Olson gets at central concerns—and his poetry deals always with the essentials—is well-illustrated in *Maps* (1969), the first book in *Changing Appearance*. Taking as occasion various kinds of maps . . . he explores the difference between what is measured and represented graphically, and a state of being which cannot be measured. The analogue is to that which sets up tensions between formal attempts at representation—in art, in literature—and experience. . . . The "reading" of a map becomes a means toward establishing connections between events and objects and the makeup of the human psyche—a way of perceiving the self both as individual and as part of an organic process. Though the occasion may at first glance seem literary, the poetry is the poetry of experience and conveys always a strong sense of place and circumstance. In fact, this is the source of the poetry's power. . . . The language of the poems is also "natural"—not casual or sloppy, but the language of a man talking to you or thinking aloud, having paced himself and concentrating on particulars.

The movement of these poems, as in most of Olson's work, is most often inductive: he casts a line with a hook on it, and you are drawn immediately into the world of the poem. Starting with what can be described as the generative particular—the assertion or image expressed indicatively which requires illumination or extension—he builds the poem deftly out of the materials supplied by autobiographical reflection and the concrete, sensual image.... (pp. 50-1)

Making the conceptual statement which is realised perceptually involves the loss of innocence, a penetration at once carnal and imaginative. It is this process which gives the poem its momentum. The poems of *Maps* proceed by the collaging of one perception "instanter, on another," done rather carefully and formally in **"The Globe,"** and with greater flexibility in the best poem in this section—and one of the best poems in the book—, the longer **"The Mapping of the Currents."** ... The casual ingathering proceeds more from Whitman, the carefulness from the shorter poems of W. C. Williams and from Robert Creeley, the flexibility from Charles Olson (no relation) and Paul Blackburn, and the contemplative, philosophical rhetoric from William Bronk—diverse poets in a by now well-recognised American tradition. But almost from the beginning, Toby Olson has had his own voice—rigorous, familiar, tough and meditative by turns.

He is a poet for whom the language needs continual renewing: he takes it as he finds it. But our language is always more than we find it. The poem **"Hair"** in *Worms into Nails,* also published originally in 1969, is a good example of the way Olson deals with the inputs that make our language a living one. (p. 51)

Starting with a locution typical of the proverb, Olson sets up a range of expectations stemming from its rhythms and constructs, though making it new. The poetics of the proverb has to do with fulfilling its rhythms, with wit in the use of metaphor—to place the dissimilar in apposition with the similar, in such a way that the idiosyncratic quality instead of sounding strange, appears inevitable, and even in the best examples, worth committing to memory.... There is in Olson's work a clarity, a directness, even simplicity of vision more characteristic of American Objectivists such as George Oppen, though again, the voice is typically Olson's. It is a voice that speaks of the love of the world, that supplies no ready and facile answers to the emotional turmoil of human relationships, that speaks with humour and candour of sexuality, that is not condescending to any form of human experience, that acknowledges doubt and confusion, that deals uncompromisingly with the difficulties of living as it does with its joys.

Part of my great pleasure on reading and hearing Olson's poetry arises from the recognition that concerns of process underly most of the poems but that these concerns move in one's consciousness—recede and gather strength—so that they are never dominant but always exist in a state of tension. Concern with process reveals a poet who has a serious attitude towards the materials and therefore a poet who repays serious attention, but these poems are never written to exemplify a poetic.... **"From A Window,"** one of the longer poems in *Changing Appearance,* has an impressive range and flexibility while at the same time the concentration and unity of the tightly-constructed, more delimited work. It represents Olson at his best. The language is supple and relaxed, and the materials are handled unobtrusively and surely. The poet allows objects, images, conclusions their own space and time to shape the construct.... (pp. 52-3)

Other longer poems in addition to **"From A Window"** which should receive equal mention ... are **"The Brand,"** printed as a book ... in 1969, **"The House"** (1968-69), and **"Provincetown: Short-Suite"** (1970).

Pig/s Book (1970) is a dense, strange, metaphysical bestiary in which the animals are described from Pig's point of view. But Pig is more than a dispassionate observer, he is also an actor in a series of small, sometimes deadly encounters....

The tone of *Pig/s Book* is generally ironic, but not heavily so. The traditional method of the bestiary—to speak of human qualities under the guise of animal ones—is employed in a manner in which the allegorical teaching does not expound conventional morality.... (p. 54)

What one learns from this bestiary is not always relevant to a sense of what one feels one should be learning, which is the source of much of the humour in these poems; the intent is, after all, not overtly didactic, as in the medieval form, but to use the form to avoid judgmental statements about behaviour.

The poems of *Pig/s Book* represent a change of pace: they are generally shorter, more pungent, less personal, more philosophical and hermetic, and funnier, but Olson's skills in making the form suit the content are hardly less evident in these curious and provoking poems. *Pig/s Book* also is evidence of Olson's abilities in constructing the poem-sequence—better unified than the slightly earlier *Maps* poems, with an accordingly sharper focus and a more consistent tone amongst the various poems of the sequence.

The penultimate poem in *Changing Appearance* is "Crazy," one that combines the tight construction of those in *Pig/s Book* (and the allegorical animals) with a more direct manner of presentation, prefiguring the method of the poems in *Home.* (p. 55)

The images in this impressive poem are more overtly archetypal than is usual in most of Olson's poetry ... and the poem [speaks] ... in almost Freudian terms of the death-wish. But having said this, one recognises at the same time that the poem does not by any means depend on mythic, literary or clinical allusions. It is a self-contained construct in which the archetypal figures enter the contemporary ground of the psyche, as in dreams. This poem reveals Olson's interest in the psychic and metaphysical energies represented by such figures as Jesus, and which he explores in his brilliant and poetic first novel, *The Life of Jesus* (1976).... (pp. 55-6)

The poems of *Home* (1976), Olson's most ambitious and outstanding poem-sequence to date, are plainsongs or variations on the theme "That each poem written derives from love". They concern the marital state, the domestic circumstances, relationships with women, the spaces in one's life and home occupied by friends, the pleasures and difficulties of love. Though the impression is one of simplicity and directness, they must not have been easy poems to write ... ; they grapple with attempts to define the undefinable.... *Home* is a work of great achievement. It exemplifies Olson's abilities to perceive himself, others and the world with a clarity, depth and toughness seldom achieved in contemporary poetry. There is no "apparatus of the persona" behind which the poet lurks in his need to adopt disguises, as in Berryman's *Dream Songs* or Hughes' *Crow,* and though these poems are often intimate and personal, there is no striking of histrionic poses in the effort to come to terms with the self, as in Plath, Sexton or Lowell. The poems of *Home* share with some of William Bronk's and Creeley's work a general willingness to forgo metaphor in an effort to "talk straight". Olson's voice has developed into an instrument capable of giving shape in an extended form to the range of the experience of living with others (and himself).... (p. 56)

Robert Vas Dias, "Toby Olson" (copyright by Robert Vas Dias; reprinted by permission of the author),

CHOICE

[*The Life of Jesus*] is a daring and perceptive work of the imagination, which throws new light on the Gospel legends while offering witty and profound insights about growing up. The boy, for example, sees his mother as the Virgin, his father as an interloper, and himself as a divine and miraculous being. As the book progresses, it becomes less fairy tale and more autobiography, until one sees the point—learning from his trials that he is neither all-God or all-man, the protagonist can accept death and return to the hitherto alien father. An interesting, at times beautiful, book which says through surrealism and poetry what cannot be said directly.

> *A review of "The Life of Jesus," in* Choice *(copyright © 1977 by American Library Association; reprinted by permission of the American Library Association), Vol. 14, No. 2, April, 1977, p. 202.*

THOMAS MEYER

I couldn't describe [Toby Olson] nor do I know his age, even so he seems almost a brother, so moved am I this April morning reading and rereading *The Florence Poems*.

So what does one do? Praise, point out, explain? Jerome Rothenberg prefaces the poems saying they respond to "the death by sickness that a friend must live through." *Festina lente*, make haste slowly, a woman is dying. The urgency of address is part of the book's occasion, yet with courage and great honesty Olson lets himself linger over moments like this:

> And down the sandy path from the parking lot
> a tall young woman in a large red hat
> maneuvers a wheel chair
>   containing a thin old man
> in a blue swimming suit
> & comes to the water's edge

One after another, such details enter the penumbra of Florence's dying almost as soon as her poet elegantly and carefully records them. The gravity of this illness, cancer, both personal and cultural, releases Olson's focus. Clearly everything will be drawn into its field without him exercising too boldly any scheme of his own. No one specific emotion itself sets up that force field.... Thus lifted into an urgent, public realm, the immediate emotional charge of the poems uncovers something precious: a rare articulation of thinking's most beautiful act, its power of arrival rather than resolution. A young woman in a red hat stands beside an old man in blue trunks at the edge of some water. No one dies of cancer, they die when they can no longer support a second life overtaking their own. They die of circumstances. They die when all the pieces are in place, when each blue is complemented by a red. Death is finality. Ironic, isn't it, that cancer is the disease of new beginnings, the fatal result of a few cells trying to start up all over again.

Stanza upon stanza, Olson draws new breath against the resonance of their breaks. On the upbeat, unexpectedly, each subsequent cluster of lines carries the poem forth. The attention is generous but relentless. The thin old man is lowered into the surf by the tall young woman and he swims out "to where the gulls sit." The details are narrative, yet their accumulation describes no story, each stanza seems to be all there is to tell, but is never quite that. In the longest poem, "**Whales**," Olson allows himself to go inside a whale, inside a photograph of beached whales, inside the view before a window, telling us all the while what is eventually happening. He hides nothing, unlike a good story teller. Finally, he brings us to himself and Florence, side by side ... with no division between body and head.

Throughout a second recent Olson book, not primitive unity, but twentieth-century separation abounds. *Aesthetics* is a succession of twenty-eight poems, each of whose stanzas crack, revealing planes of a crystallography unseen in *The Florence Poems*.... The sequence is a philosophical consideration of "style," and like the songs of troubadours these poems are eager to depict their audience's recently acquired intelligence, wealth and sophistication. Each remark, each image is propped up like a cutout by the self-conscious lack of sentimentality style demands and high art dictates. Each of the poems becomes a cardboard *mise en scène* displayed one after the other upon the stage of a Victorian child's miniature theater. Depth is an illusion created by a series of receding, sensual planes, rather than a plastic, emotional phenomenon. One imagines these settings falling into acts, then perhaps a drama.

Behind the scenes money, sex, and power proffer in the glare of an amyl nitrite rush.... (pp. 8-9)

Distance remains a crucial factor. While none intervenes between us and style, the expanse separating us from art is wider than the Atlantic....

As Americans we suffer from a sore lack of middle distances, without which it is impossible to perceive or maintain anything that doesn't depend for its being upon raw nerve and ambition. U.S. aesthetics so far results in the Shakers on one hand and Las Vegas on the other....

Aesthetics and *The Florence Poems* provide their reader with a rich study in serious intent. How I admire their language, its cadence and self-assured grammatical vigor, its bid for permanence. But what do I mean by permanence? I mean that I admire the meaningfulness of the language, which I take to be a human expression of trust in the content each poem contains (or may conceal). And too, I praise and value their occasion. When these things are said in both books is equal in worth to the act of saying them. These are all early concerns, appropriate to the beginning of an enterprise and that is where I put American poetry today. Our language has just begun to develop a sense of space and perspective which allows for recognition as well as speculation. In other words, we're on our way out from under the burden of territory and frontier.

It is my pleasure to commend and hail these books by Toby Olson as they appear, not upon our horizon, but within ear range. (p. 9)

> *Thomas Meyer, in a review of "The Florence Poems" and "Aesthetics," in* The American Book Review *(© 1980 by The American Book Review), Vol. II, No. 3, February, 1980, pp. 8-9.*

KIRKUS REVIEWS

Though certainly a failure—ponderous, unpaced, lurching, implausible—poet Olson's second work of fiction [*Seaview*] ... nonetheless has about it an imagistic, visionary hunger that's striking, that sets it apart.... [Seaview, a Cape Cod golf course,] is built on Indian tribal land—and it's here that the book concludes on a note of apocalypse: Indians staging a siege of the course, Richard stalking Allen in revenge for being burned, a nude-beach protest, Melinda meanwhile dying. True, such ungainliness—if speeded up—would deliver comedy. But Olson slows it down instead. And though certain scenes are just awful—Allen and Melinda making love while the Laetrile drips intravenously into her arm, a symbol-laced game of miniature golf, the climax—a few are spookily clear and magical: Bob White's explanation of what immortality actually involves; and the explanation of golf as a model for the invisibly drawn lines of everyday human effort.... Indeed, this golf imagery—despite the pawky golf scenes themselves—is a distinct poetic achievement. Unfortunately, however, the disastrous overload of the rest—with Olson attempting to put Indians, cancer, golf, and drugs in one lumpy narrative package—means that only intrepid, boredom-tolerant readers will come upon the genuinely fine moments here.

A review of "Seaview," in Kirkus Reviews *(copyright © 1982 The Kirkus Service, Inc.), Vol. L, No. 1, January 1, 1982, p. 30.*

JAMIE JAMES

In *Seaview,* his second novel, Toby Olson has written half a good book. What is good about this novel is so good, so smart and so beautifully realized, that one instinctively resists the harsh judgment that the other half of the book deserves....

Seaview is the story of Allen, a golf player, and Melinda, his wife, who is dying of cancer. Accompanied by a sententious old Indian man named Bob White, they are driving across the United States, living out of motels and their automobile, making their way to Cape Cod, Melinda's home, where she wants to die....

It is Olson's sensitive portrayal of Allen and Melinda's relationship that makes the novel work as well as it does. He goes beyond the conventional assertion of contemporary fiction that there are unbridgeable spaces between lovers, and defines those spaces, giving them contours as sharp and clear as the sculptures of Brancusi. The uncommunicable is expressed as surely as is the blatant. Olson, the author of thirteen books of poetry, creates scenes of powerful beauty in his descriptions of the Western landscape, as when he juxtaposes the rugged magnificence of desert and mountain with the weary commonplaceness of a motel coffee shop.

Olson's most effective images are simple and naturalistic; when he constructs elaborate metaphors, they come off as labored. A scene in the middle of the novel, a twilight game at a ruined miniature golf course, contains what is clearly intended to be a central symbol for the book, the freshly severed head of a snake in the process of eating a baby bird. Presented as a hermetical emblem, the image seems merely contrived. Occasionally Olson indulges a passion for precise, endlessly detailed physical descriptions, telling us far more than we want to know about the exact spatial relationships of buildings, or the workings of mechanical contraptions, passages which are confusing and muddle the narrative flow. And there are a few disconcerting bits of lazy writing: a minor character is introduced with the name of George Wall, but six pages later he is called Fred Wall.

A strong credit to the novel—and there is no way to express it that doesn't sound left-handed—is that Olson makes golf not only interesting but powerfully suspenseful. I know very little about the sport, and always considered it rather silly, but I found the long narratives of golf games in *Seaview* as breathlessly engrossing as the best trashy thriller. Olson uses these scenes well, blending in philosophical and psychological insights about the game. He tells us more about a character in the way he putts than many a novelist is able to convey in pages of interior monologue.

The novel is a pleasure to read (when it is) because it does so many things. Olson successfully pulls off a sophisticated multiple-point-of-view structure in the first part of the book, slipping pages of first-person introspection into the omniscient narration in a way that doesn't seem "stuck in." Dream sequences, so often maddening distractions in ambitious fiction, here are well executed and fit, in an appropriately dreamlike way, into the scheme of the novel. The sex scenes are strange but altogether convincing, giving us significant insights into the characters.

The first half of *Seaview,* in short, does an impressive job of what the first half of a novel is supposed to do: interesting characters are drawn, suspenseful situations are created for them, thoughtful themes are introduced. The reader is captive, an eager believer, settled in for the rest of the ride. Then the book falls apart. Olson, inexplicably, jettisons everything he has done and starts over.

The action moves forward to the Seaview Links, a golf course on Cape Cod, which will be the final destination of Allen and Melinda. An entirely new cast of characters, vapid and cartoonish, is introduced, and a clutch of flimsy subplots is invented for them to walk through. Most dismaying, the tone shifts to one of comic fantasy which is completely at odds with what has come before. The golf sequences, with characters we don't care about, become excruciatingly dull. When scenes involving Allen and Melinda are spliced in, they stand up only by association with the earlier book, but nothing is gained by apposition with the lifeless Cape Cod whimsies.

It is difficult to imagine what compelled Olson to undercut his work in this way, unless it was to conform to the current fashion for fantasy, as seen in the novels of John Irving, what one might call creeping *Garp*-ism, which dictates that whenever fiction begins to be believable, the bizarre must be gratuitously injected, the reader must be bludgeoned into an awareness that "it's only make-believe."...

[There is] a ridiculous scene (reminiscent of the movie *It's A Mad Mad Mad Mad World*) which brings together in riotous confusion radical-activist Indians, Hell's-Angels-style bikers, a pod of whales, the press corps, police, militant nudists, golfers, the armed forces, and hang-glider snipers.... When Olson finally gets around to winding up his main story, he has lost us. If it's all only make-believe, what do we care about Allen and Melinda?

The comic-fantasy episodes in Cape Cod, on their own, might have been credible, but the effect here might be compared to taking a copy of, say, *The Scarlet Letter* and shuffling it playing-card fashion with an "Archie" comic book. The result is disconcerting in the extreme and—one must say it—a failure. But the strong passages in the first part of the novel survive; they stay with you. It is worth reading the book for them.

Jamie James, in a review of "Seaview," in The American Book Review *(© 1982 by The American Book Review), Vol. 5, No. 1, November-December, 1982, p. 22.*

Cynthia Ozick
1928-

American short story writer, novelist, essayist, poet, and translator.

Ozick's works generally treat ethnic and language problems unique to the Jewish artist. She treats Judaism as a religious as well as an ethnic and social characteristic, and her work displays an overt reverence for her heritage. Concerned with the creation of a distinctively Jewish literature, Ozick has conceived of a "new Yiddish" which would be comprehensible to speakers of English yet preserve the inflections and tone of the waning Jewish language.

After her first novel, *Trust* (1966), the story of a young woman's search for identity, Ozick turned to shorter forms in her next three books: *The Pagan Rabbi and Other Stories* (1971), *Bloodshed and Three Novellas* (1976), and *Levitation: Five Fictions* (1982). In an interview, Ozick explained that she writes novellas because she cannot write anything short enough to be a short story and no longer has the ambition to write anything so long as *Trust,* which was six hundred pages long and took six years to write. She said, "I will never again write so well . . . will never again have that kind of high ambition or monastic patience or metaphysical nerve and fortitude." She did, however, write another novel, *The Cannibal Galaxy* (1983). She has also recently compiled twenty-three of her previously published critical essays into a collection entitled *Art and Ardor* (1983). Ozick's critical reputation has grown steadily over the years, and she is now both well known and highly respected by critics. She frequently contributes book reviews, poetry, and short stories to a variety of periodicals and also translates works of Yiddish literature.

In Ozick's short fiction collections, most of the stories revolve around similar themes. The stories in *The Pagan Rabbi* concern the predicament of the transplanted Jew in America, which Ozick typically presents through a character's struggle with two opposing forces. In the title story, the rabbi is caught between love of religion and scholarship and also between love of nature and magic. "Envy: Yiddish in America" concerns one Yiddish author's attempt to save his language from extinction in America, and contrasts him with another author who has achieved fame in America by being translated. This story expresses the conflict which Ozick feels confronts her and other Jewish-American writers—that of being true to one's heritage yet desiring to be understood in a foreign land. In "Virility," Ozick confronts assimilation and sexism and also introduces the issue of authorial borrowing, which is developed more fully in the later novella, "Usurpation (Other People's Stories)" from her collection *Bloodshed and Three Novellas.* As the subtitle of "Usurpation" suggests, it is composed of fragments of stories by other writers. Her point in this story is that the writer is always borrowing material from other writers and, more importantly, from God. Ozick's religious concern is that by creating a story, a writer breaks the second commandment which prohibits idol worship, the making of graven images, and adoration of magic. According to Ozick, stories, like statues, are graven images. Thus, there is a conflict inherent in being both a Jew and a writer: "Whoever sets up

© 1984 Thomas Victor

an image-making shop is in competition with the Maker of the world."

In *Art and Ardor,* Ozick addresses Jewish, literary, and feminist questions. In the process, she criticizes many of her fellow writers, especially those Jewish writers who use religious background to add ethnic color to their stories while writing essentially secular works. Where feminism is concerned, she is adamant in her contention that separatism should not be tolerated in literature and that such categories as "women's literature" are dangerous. Her ideas about literature are traditional, and she opposes what she calls "self-indulgent" fiction. The quality of her own writing, in these essays and elsewhere, reveals that she believes that ideas should never be so important as to excuse poor writing. *Art and Ardor* includes two essays which are personal rather than critical. In one of these, "Lesson From a Master," she writes of her obsession with Henry James early in her writing career, pointing out the danger of being too influenced by someone else.

With the exception of *Trust,* Ozick's work has always been extremely well received by critics. A major problem with *Trust,* critics contend, is that the language is so opaque that it obscures the world Ozick tries to portray. In her subsequent work, Ozick controls her treatment of language so that, while it remains a dominant feature of her work, it does not get in the way of the story itself. In general, critics seem to feel that characterization and emotive qualities are the weak points of her work, while words and ideas are the strong ones. *Art and Ardor,* her nonfiction work, is her most controversial. To many critics, she was too severe with other writers and made unreasonable pronouncements. Katha Pollitt and others find a contradiction between Ozick's desire for a uniquely Jewish literature, on the one hand, and her abhorrence of a uniquely feminine literature, on the other. But nearly all consider her handling of language superb and her intellectual prowess stimulating.

(See also *CLC*, Vols. 3, 7; *Contemporary Authors*, Vols. 17-20, rev. ed.; and *Dictionary of Literary Biography Yearbook: 1982*.)

SARAH BLACHER COHEN

A Jewish writer not preoccupied with her characters' gender identity and more sure of her artistic identity is Cynthia Ozick. Finding the designation "woman writer" too confining and essentially discriminatory, she regards the entire range of human experience as the fit subject matter for her fiction. Exploring the consciousness of both male and female characters, she doesn't mind being considered a betrayer to the feminist cause or a trespasser in male territory. What does concern Cynthia Ozick is that her fiction retain an authentically Jewish nature. At the American-Israel Dialogue of 1970, she described the characteristics of a genuine Jewish literature in the American diaspora. Its language, though written in English, will be "New Yiddish." "Centrally Jewish in its concerns," the literature will be "liturgical in nature." By "liturgical" she does not mean "didactic or prescriptive," but "Aggadic, utterly freed to invention, discourse, parable, experiment, enlightenment, profundity, humanity." (pp. 179-80)

Cynthia Ozick's [short story] **"Envy; or, Yiddish in America,"** is an excellent illustration of this liturgical "New Yiddish," since it is a parabolic comedy in which morality and humor are inextricably linked. Edelshtein, the central figure of the story, is a sixty-seven-year-old Yiddish poet desperately striving for forty years to have his talents recognized in America. In one respect he is still the fearful little man of the *shtetl* who has a Chaplinesque sense of himself as the accidental and insignificant creature barely surviving in the hostile world. In another respect he has the hauteur of the high priest of Yiddish culture, censuring superficial Jewish-American writers and a slickly translated Yiddish author, Yankel Ostrover, who have made financial killings in the literary marketplace. Edelshtein's feelings of extreme inferiority and extreme superiority incur Ozick's humorous treatment. When he is the insecure *shtetl* figure, she compassionately views him as a saintly fool in his valiant efforts to keep Yiddish alive for American Jews.... But she also harshly mocks Edelshtein when he becomes the supercilious Yiddish purist. This is not to suggest that Ozick totally disagrees with his assessment of American Jewish literature. With the exception of Saul Bellow, whom she respects as the "most purely and profoundly ideational" of the Jewish-American novelists, she generally shares Edelshtein's belief that they are largely ignorant of their Jewish heritage, yet reviewers praise them for their ethnic wit and perception. Indeed, much of the story's amusement stems from the fact that Edelshtein acts as the stringent literary critic who, often expressing Ozick's views, employs the quaint accent and syntax of Yiddishized English to pronounce his unkind judgments. He deplores, for example, the cheap way Jewish-American novelists add Yiddish local color to their work.... (pp. 180-81)

What Ozick finds most objectionable and worthy of satire about Edelshtein is his hypocrisy. Much as he mocks Ostrover, he prefers to be like him. He, too, would like to escape from the "prison of Yiddish" . . . , if he could achieve fame. He pretends to lament the waning of Yiddish when he actually laments the waning of an audience to appreciate his creativity. His hypocrisy is attacked, however, not by the author but by a twenty-three-year-old Yiddish-reading woman whom Edelshtein implores to be his translator, though she is a devotee of Ostrover. . . . We are not to side with the young woman, however. Her diatribe shows the limitations of American-born Jewish youth who would readily sacrifice the parochial for the universal and, in so doing, lose their claim to any distinctiveness. Because Yiddish is an indigenous part of Edelshtein, and because Christians and anti-Semitic Jews alike won't allow him to forget this fact, he can't give up Yiddish. . . . Ozick sympathizes with his desire to communicate and be understood in an alien land. She can even forgive his envy of those who achieve a spurious kind of communication.

Satiric indictment and sympathetic acquittal of petty Yiddish writers is not Ozick's primary concern in **"Envy."** The story allows her to express her affection for Yiddish, the *mama-loshen*, the mother tongue, in which childhood endearments, *shtetl* solidarity, and a closeness with God are conveyed. Moreover, she laments the American Jews' abandonment of Yiddish for English, a language they consider more secular and thus more aesthetic. Abandonment of the Jewish sources for creativity in pursuit of more worldly fame is also the theme of **"Virility,"** the next short story Ozick wrote after **"Envy."** On the surface, **"Virility"** appears to be a feminist comedy of literary manners revealing the double standard in the world of letters. Edmund Gate, born Elia Gatoff, has come to America from Czarist Russia via Liverpool to make his literary fortune. His first attempts at poetry are marred by contrived alliteration and polysyllabic diction. Though his work is continually rejected, he is a confident male and still believes in his talent. After several years of persistence, his poems miraculously improve and appear in the best magazines. Promoted by a married woman with whom he has had two illegitimate children, he publishes five volumes of poetry, each entitled *Virility*. The critics, more impressed with the title of the poetry than with its substance, single out what they consider its masculine virtues and overpraise them. . . . (pp. 182-83)

It turns out, however, that Edmund Gate is not the author of these poems. They have been written by Tante Rivka, his spinster aunt who cared for him in Liverpool. . . . Three years after her death, he has nearly exhausted the supply of her poetry and faces artistic sterility. A Jamesian mentor convinces him to confess his plagiarism and do right by Tante Rivka. Her remaining poems, which were to comprise Gate's *Virility VI*, are published under her own name as *Flowers from Liverpool*. This collection contains Tante Rivka's finest poetry, yet the reviewers are unimpressed. Employing phallic criticism, they find her book to be "Thin feminine art." . . . (p. 183)

"Virility," however, is not exclusively an attack upon male parasites and male supremacists. Ozick includes an element of the ludicrous within Edmund Gate's treachery for the purpose of jest and symbolic import. Since he has appropriated a woman's talents, Ozick has him fear he has acquired a female's gender as well. Clutching his genitals to confirm his sex, his last words to the narrator are: "I'm a man." . . .

Gate's uneasiness about his anatomy is symptomatic of his uneasiness about being a Jew. He readily saps the creativity of Tante Rivka, Ozick's allegorical figure representing Judaism, but he is reluctant to acknowledge his indebtedness to her. Once in America he ceases to communicate with her and lets her starve to death. If he had provided nourishment for her, she would have survived many more years and prolonged Gate's poetic career. Instead, Tante Rivka, productive until the end, died with dignity, whereas Edmund Gate, disaffected Jew and poet manqué, committed suicide.

In a recent novella, **"Usurpation (Other People's Stories),"** Cynthia Ozick mocks herself as author for pilfering other writers' fiction. That the novella's narrator-protagonist is a woman writer who has plagiarized from the works of male writers is not at issue. Her prime concern is not the invasion of the males' literary domain to redress the wrongs perpetrated against her sister writers. Rather, she is an asexual spinner of tales who jests about the snags in her narrative technique and the literary larceny she commits. (p. 184)

One of the purposes of **"Usurpation,"** other than providing the true confessions of a story thief, is to ridicule the writing of fiction itself. It is revealed not as a miraculous process whereby the finished product emerges fault-free from the divinely inspired head of the creator. Rather, it is shown to be a suspect art, relying on counterfeit experience, dubious techniques, and contrived language to achieve its lifelike effects. Ozick also mirthfully punctures the inflated position of the writer. Her narrator-protagonist is a vain, short-tempered opportunist who values public renown over the perfection of her craft. For her, no edifying relationship exists between tradition and the individual talent. She is too busy exploiting the talent of others to appreciate tradition and to cultivate her own creativity.

Ozick disapproves of the art of fiction not only on aesthetic and ethical grounds. For the Jewish writer, fashioning a make-believe reality through words is an idolatrous act, in direct violation of the Second Commandment. . . . But her greatest objection to story-telling is its usurpation, since the author appropriates from God the role of creator. (pp. 184-85)

[Ozick] suggests that as long as the Jewish storyteller writes in this world, where he is exposed to an alien culture and must employ a secular language, he will be an idolatrous fiction-monger. And if he chooses to write about the heathen rather than the holy in the next world, then the pagan inhabitants of Paradise, like Hitler in this world, will not allow him to forget that he is a Jew. He will be caged and instructed: "All that is not Law is levity." . . .

Fortunately, Cynthia Ozick has not been caged, and she writes about levity and Law. . . . She has not taken refuge in the hackneyed jokes of Jewish masochism or mocked things Jewish with a self-advertising bravado. Her humor does not confine itself to stereotypes, nor does she exploit ethnic externals for ready laughter. Steeped in the Jewish tradition and aware of its conflicting viewpoints, she deftly reveals its wry paradoxes. A comedienne of ideas, she transforms the farcical into the philosophical. But because of her wit and imagination, her "philosophical stories" do not "make excellent lullabies." They keep her readers awake and amused. (p. 186)

Sarah Blacher Cohen, "The Jewish Literary Comediennes," in Comic Relief: Humor in Contemporary American Literature, edited by Sarah Blacher Cohen (© 1978 by the Board of Trustees of the University of Illinois; reprinted by permission of the author and the University of Illinois Press), University of Illinois Press, 1978, pp. 172-86.*

EDWARD ALEXANDER

In 1969 and 1970, Cynthia Ozick published, within a period of a few months, a short story and an essay that defined two American Jewish responses to the Holocaust and the relation between them. The story, a small masterpiece, was entitled **"Envy; or, Yiddish in America."** In it she ironically but affectionately re-created the ambience of American Yiddish writers, for whom continuation of Yiddish, the language of the majority of the victims of the Holocaust, constitutes the most meaningful form of Jewish survival. . . . The story conveys its author's profound dissatisfaction with what one of the characters archly refers to as "so-called Amer.-Jewish writers." It conveys too the sense that Yiddish and Hebrew have now, because of the Holocaust and the establishment of the State of Israel, exchanged their traditional roles within Jewish life, with Yiddish, now the language of martyrdom, acquiring a sacred status, and Hebrew, used (often badly) by bus-drivers and peddlers of unkosher meat in Tel Aviv, becoming the language of the folk and the street. Yet this very transformation and elevation of Yiddish into the language of a coterie, who seek meaning and salvation through continuing to write in it, would itself seem the final confirmation that Yiddish language and literature, which for centuries actually did perform many of the functions of a homeland for people who had none, can no longer do so. The elegiac note in this mainly comic story can be deeply moving: "'In Talmud if you save a single life it's as if you saved the world. And if you save a language? Worlds maybe. Galaxies. The whole universe.'" But how can a language itself in need of salvation save others?

Cynthia Ozick sought an answer to this question in her lecture/essay of 1970 entitled **"America: Toward Yavneh."** Yavneh traditionally and literally, of course, refers to the place in which, in the year 70, following the fall of Jerusalem to the Romans, the sage Yohanan ben Zakkai established an academy that became the spiritual center of Judaism after the nation ceased to be an independent political entity. (pp. 138-39)

By applying, however tentatively, the term *Yavneh* to America, Ozick does not, like some subsequent exploiters of this metaphor, intend to congratulate American Jewry on a moral or intellectual character superior to that of Israeli Jews. On the contrary, she makes clear that American Jews for the most part remain in their corner of the Exile because they love to be flattered for having those very traits that are so easily (and often fraudulently) claimed by people without power or responsibility, their devotion to "Mankind" (rather than to Jews), their pacific character, their widespreading, indiscriminate philanthropy. . . . Indeed, her whole thrust up to this point in her essay is that when the Jews went into Exile their capacity for literature seemed to abandon them, especially when they chose to address, as most American Jewish writers still do address, the principle of "Mankind" rather than the culture and problems of their own people. Nevertheless, she finally expresses the hope that just as Spain was for a time in the Middle Ages a sort of Jerusalem Displaced, so can America be.

"'Yavneh,'" she says, "is an impressionistic term, a metaphor suggesting renewal. The original Academy at Yavneh was founded after the destruction of the Temple; the new one in prospect coincides with the restoration of Zion." She expresses the hope that the Yavneh of America can share responsibility for Jewish destiny with the Jews of Israel. (pp. 139-40)

The main instrument of this reconstruction will be a creative union between Yiddish and English that Ozick labels New Yiddish, and that she hopes will become, just as "old" Yiddish was, "the language of multitudes of Jews, spoken to Jews by Jews, written by Jews for Jews." If doubters ask who is to invent such a language, her answer is that it has already been invented, that her essay itself is written in it, that Norma Rosen's *Touching Evil* and Saul Bellow's *Mr. Sammler's Planet* are novelistic examples of it. Just as a dialect of Middle High German was once changed into Yiddish by being made the instrument of Jewish peoplehood, Jewish necessities, so too can English be transformed into New Yiddish by Jewish writers who have found their proper subject—the Holocaust and Jewish fate—and can transmute the characteristic rhythms and intonations of Yiddish into English.

Although few readers have failed to be impressed by Cynthia Ozick's brilliance of mind and style, many come away from the essay feeling that she is something like the magician who puts eggs into a hat and brings forth—eggs. Her procedure is similar to that of the Gothic revivalists of the nineteenth century who thought to recreate the civilization of the Middle Ages by imitating its architecture, even as they maintained that all architecture was inevitably an index of the ethical values of the civilization that produced it. But if criticism cannot create a new culture, perhaps it can, as Matthew Arnold believed, create a new literature. Cynthia Ozick's call for American Jewish culture to assume, alongside Israeli Jewish culture, responsibility for the reconstruction of Jewish life, has already stirred a response among younger writers.... (p. 141)

> Edward Alexander, "The Holocaust in American Jewish Fiction: A Slow Awakening," in his *The Resonance of Dust: Essays on Holocaust Literature and Jewish Fate (copyright © 1979 by the Ohio State University Press; all rights reserved), Ohio State University Press, 1979, pp. 121-48.*

ROBERT R. HARRIS

Self-consciousness about writing fiction can lead to overindulgent prose and the substitution of egoism for ideas. Cynthia Ozick is the most self-conscious writer I know of. Yet she steadfastly shuns overindulgence of any sort, and instead does what too few contemporary fiction writers do on a regular basis—think. Ozick is obsessed with the words she puts on paper, with what it means to imagine a story and to tell it, with what fiction is. The result is a body of work at once as rich as Grace Paley's stories, as deeply rooted in Jewish folklore as Isaac Bashevis Singer's tales, as comically ironic as Franz Kafka's nightmares....

She debates what fiction should strive to embrace: "incident versus event; experience versus consequence; deed versus outcome; feeling versus connecting; seeing versus seeing-into...." These tensions are ever-present for Ozick.

A perfectionist, she has written just one novel, *Trust*, and three collections of short works: *The Pagan Rabbi and Other Stories, Bloodshed and Three Novellas,* and now *Levitation: Five Fictions.* Yet she is one of the best. Because she deals with ideas—many of them steeped in Jewish law and history—her stories are "difficult." But by difficult I mean only that they are not in the least bit fluffy. No word, emotion, or idea is wasted. They are weighty, consequential tales, lightened and at the same time heightened by their visionary aspects.

Ozick writes magically about magical events. But she distrusts sorcery, the stock in trade of fiction writing. This irony gives her work a thought-provoking dialectical quality. Her stories are elusive, mysterious, and disturbing. They shimmer with intelligence, they glory in language, and they puzzle.

In the title story, two writers, husband and wife, seemingly live a serene existence, sharing "premises." [Each] has published a novel. They think of themselves as "literary friends and lovers, like George Eliot and George Henry Lewes." Yet they realize—but can't accept—that they are "secondary-level" people, with secondary-level friends, "not the fiercely cold-hearted literary critics, but those wan and chattering daily reviewers of film." (p. 58)

To a party they invite Philip Roth, Norman Mailer, William Styron, and other guiding lights of literature. None shows up. Husband and wife are resentful. The husband—bitterly obsessed by the atrocities committed against the Jews throughout history—joins with some fellow Jews to begin a trance-like discussion of the Holocaust. From the sidelines, the wife, a convert to Judaism, observes the room rising into the air, carrying the "real" Jews away from her. She "decides it is possible to become jaded by atrocity. She is bored by the shootings and the gas and the camps, she is not ashamed to admit this." She is bitter because she does not share "the glory of their martyrdom." Both husband and wife avoid confronting the palpable bitterness of their unfulfilled lives. And it is bitterness that they share, and bitterness that separates them.

In **"Puttermesser: Her Work History, Her Ancestry, Her Afterlife,"** we first meet Ruth Puttermesser—34, an unmarried lawyer, something of a feminist—while she is living in her family's apartment in the Bronx.... Ruth is assistant corporation counsel in New York's Department of Receipts and Disbursements, "not quite a civil servant and not quite *not* a civil servant—one of those amphibious creatures hanging between base contempt and bare decency." She dreams of an Eden where she eats fudge and reads "Non-Fiction into eternity; and there is still time for Fiction!" Twice a week she visits Uncle Zindel the Stingy for Hebrew lessons. Ozick intrudes to note that Zindel died before Puttermesser was born. "But Puttermesser must claim an ancestor," writes Ozick. "She demands a connection—surely a Jew must own a past." Her illusion provides her with a history, in effect, creates her. And Ozick warns us not to examine her "as an artifact but as an essence." (pp. 58-9)

"Puttermesser and Xanthippe," the longest of the five fictions, is an almost perfect novella. Ozick's character, Puttermesser, now 46, is still single. She is still working for the city government.... When the mayor ousts her boss, political appointees take over.... Patronage is in; Puttermesser is out; the city is falling apart.

Puttermesser, pushed beyond fantasy, creates a golem—an artificial creature of cabalist lore—out of the earth in her potted plants. When Puttermesser is fired, the golem, who insists on being called Xanthippe after Socrates's shrewish wife, gets her elected mayor of New York.

Under Puttermesser's rule, the city is transformed....

Again Ozick returns to the theme of creation that runs through her stories:

> Puttermesser made Xanthippe; Xanthippe did not exist before Puttermesser made her: that much is clear enough. But Xanthippe made Puttermesser Mayor, and Mayor Puttermesser too did not exist before. And that is just as clear.

Puttermesser sees that she is the golem's golem.

Golems turn on their makers. Xanthippe, who like all golems has not stopped growing, discovers sex, becomes insatiable, and thereby, in hilarious fashion, destroys Puttermesser's administration. Puttermesser—disgraced, unmade—unmakes Xanthippe. New York is delivered back unto chaos.

Like Ozick, Puttermesser is an intelligent rationalist. Puttermesser makes a golem; Ozick makes up stories. Ozick equates the magic in her stories with the magical process of writing fiction. So writing about rooms levitating and golems becomes writing about writing, about making magic. For Ozick, fiction *is* magic. (p. 59)

>Robert R. Harris, "The Complex Magic of Cynthia Ozick," in Saturday Review (© 1982 Saturday Review Magazine Co.; reprinted by permission), Vol. 9, No. 2, February, 1982, pp. 58-9.

LESLIE EPSTEIN

The prospect of reviewing a new book by Cynthia Ozick gave me great pleasure, since I believe her two previous collections—**"The Pagan Rabbi and Other Stories"** and **"Bloodshed and Three Novellas"**—to be perhaps the finest work in short fiction by a contemporary writer; certainly it is the work in that genre that has most appealed to me. Then the bound galleys of **"Levitation"** arrived, subtitled **"Five Fictions."** Immediately a voice whispered, "On guard! Why *fictions*? Why not stories, why not novellas, as the subtitles of the two earlier volumes plainly declared their contents to be? What is a *fiction*, anyway?" A quick glance through the galleys provided a calming, commonsensical answer. Some of these five pieces seemed to be stories, while others, although made up and works of the imagination, were not what we think of as tales. But a closer reading has proved unsettling. *Each* of these works, however dazzling, original and even beauteous, does shy crucially from the kind of resolution we rightly demand from imaginative fiction. I'll attempt, in what follows, to explain.

The two works in the middle of the book are the furthest from story form. **"From a Refugee's Notebook"** consists of two fragments supposedly left in a rented room by a European or South American refugee. The first is a meditation on the subject of Freud's room, the burden of which seems to be that Freud, in his attraction to the cauldron of the unconscious, to the irrational, wished to become a god. . . .

The second fragment discusses the fad of Sewing Harems "on the planet Acirema." These were women who sewed up their vaginas but occasionally managed to conceive anyway when they rented themselves out, en masse, for the pleasure of wealthy businessmen. Most of this Swiftian exercise focuses upon the unfortunate children, who band together in Momist sects, produce offspring of their own and in time come to spread their totems, "great stone vulvae," over the surface of the globe. This "fiction" is less sterile and recondite than it is private—by which I mean it reveals nothing of the personality or situation of the refugee, its putative author. We are refused entrance to a fictional world. (p. 11)

The two [Puttermesser] stories are the best in the book—often humorous, wonderfully quirky and possessed of a Dickensian delight in depicting the cracks and crannies in the Municipal Building and the Kabbala. And yet, I fear, my thesis holds. For example, the finest moment in the first Puttermesser story occurs when she travels to the run-down flat of her Uncle Zindel for a Hebrew lesson. Here is a character! Here is a voice! . . .

Yet no sooner does Uncle Zindel take shape before us than he is vaporized. "Stop, stop! Puttermesser's biographer, stop!" In that halt we are told the old man has been dead for decades, the lesson never happened, the meeting never occurred. Could there be a plainer instance of how our text, our "biographer," quails before the demands of, the power of, imagination? Let us put it another way: Puttermesser is not to be examined as an artifact but as an essence. No wonder the ending is but a cry for help: "Hey! Puttermesser's biographer! What will you do with her now?" . . .

It is time to call a halt, time to determine—perhaps we can only speculate—what is going on. The clue to this turn in Cynthia Ozick's work is her concentration upon language, upon sheer words—lists, syllables, names, letters. There is hardly a page of this book not, to one degree or another, obsessed by the magical power of writing. The golem is assembled after Puttermesser has held the Sunday Times (a world of woe in print) in her arms, just as Feingold and friends began to levitate only after the same edition of the paper had been burnt in the fireplace. Every golem is made of holy syllables, and some from 221 alphabetical combinations; each may be undone by reciting the same formula backwards. . . . In broad terms, I think the issue here is again one of translation—how to turn our secular language into holy script; how, in a sense, Puttermesser's list of Russian bureaucrats (who hinder Jewish emigration) or former mayors can be simultaneously translated into, let us say, Hebrew incantations or the names of the Rabbis of Baghdad, of Prague, of Worms. There is great danger for a writer here. At the end of the list is the Name of Names, which of course is ineffable, which is silence.

Our author knows her dilemma and has addressed it before. In her preface to **"Bloodshed"** she speaks of her frustration at not being able to write in a Jewish language instead of profane, biased English. And more: in that preface, as well as in a remarkable essay, she writes of the blasphemy of the imagination as if the impulse to create were a violation of the Second Commandment, "as if ink were blood," as if her stories were the idols themselves. So there ought to be no doubt what the golem (like the camera, like the shabby novels of the Feingolds, and perhaps even Freud's cauldron) represents. It is her art, by which we may be purified and saved; by which we may be engulfed and even destroyed. It is awesome to watch this great and generous talent turn with such intensity upon itself. One longs, in spite of the impertinence, in spite of the risk of blasphemy, to cry out! Cynthia Ozick! Walk counterclockwise! Make seven circles! Undo what you are doing! God is—as one of your own characters tells us—in details. (p. 25)

>Leslie Epstein, "Stories and Something Else," in The New York Times Book Review (copyright © 1982 by The New York Times Company; reprinted by permission), February 14, 1982, pp. 11, 25.

ADAM MARS-JONES

Cynthia Ozick is a woman, and Jewish, and a New Yorker; these conditions in combination might be expected to produce a narrow art, if any at all. And certainly there are few men in [the stories which make up *Levitation*], fewer gentiles, and hardly a single out-of-towner, but the result is anything but narrow; the absentees are hardly noticed.

Cynthia Ozick has the enviable knack of moving, with impressive speed, in opposite directions at the same time; her specialities are prose poetry, intellectual slapstick, meticulous detail, and wild rhetorical fantasy. The result at its best is an audacious and unorthodox balancing of forces, both within the story and within the sentence. Within the story, there is tension between a carefully rendered milieu and the wildly elaborated fantasy which arrives to transform it. Within the sentence, there is a running battle between a realism that describes things as they are, and a rhetoric that takes constant liberties with the appearances....

The story of Puttermesser and her creature (**"Puttermesser and Xanthippe"**) takes up over half the book and contains most of its high points; the fantastical elaboration, ballasted by an intimate knowledge of bureaucracy, of Puttermesser's rise to worldly power (Mayor of New York, inevitably, given the book's priorities) is oddly balanced by a matter-of-fact account of her progressive gum disease.

The pair of sketches entitled **"From A Refugee's Notebook"** are by far the weakest in the volume. The first portentously analyzes the décor of Freud's house in Vienna; the second is a surprisingly leaden fantasy about a craze, on the planet Acirema (which no doubt should be read backwards), for Sewing Harems: groups of women who can be hired to sew themselves together. These fragments contain the ingredients of Cynthia Ozick's successful fiction, but wilfully separate them into one piece of non-fiction and one aimless improvisation.

When the materials are properly combined, the results are formidable; the text flushes with the idea of Jewishness and the idea of New York. The sense of history and the sense of place become resources of fact and feeling for an entirely new enterprise, and the whole unlikely rocket takes off, trailing sparks and coloured rain. After a vivid and exhilarating flight, admittedly, all that comes clattering down through the trees is a scorched stick; but with very little more discipline and expertise Cynthia Ozick will produce fireworks that can carry passengers.

> Adam Mars-Jones, "Fantastic Flushes," in The Times Literary Supplement (© Times Newspapers Ltd. (London) 1982; reproduced from The Times Literary Supplement by permission), No. 4125, April 23, 1982, p. 456.

A. ALVAREZ

Ezra Pound once divided writers into carvers and molders. The molders—Balzac, Lawrence, Whitman—work fast, not much worried by detail or repetition or precision, impatient to get down the shape and flow of their inspiration, while the carvers—Flaubert, Eliot, Beckett—work with infinite slowness, painstakingly writing and rewriting, unable to go ahead until each phrase is balanced, each detail perfect.

Cynthia Ozick is a carver, a stylist in the best and most complete sense: in language, in wit, in her apprehension of reality and her curious, crooked flights of imagination. She once described an early work of hers, rather sniffily, as "both 'mandarin' and 'lapidary,' every paragraph a poem." Although there is nothing stiff or overcompacted about her writing now, she still has the poet's perfectionist habit of mind and obsession with language, as though one word out of place would undo the whole fabric....

Miss Ozick is very much a New York intellectual, like Puttermesser, the heroine of two of the five stories in **Levitation,** who "had the habit of flushing with ideas as if they were passions," and whose idea of paradise is an eternity of books and candy . . . [and time to read].

[The pair of Puttermesser stories] is a witty, elegant, and invigorating fable, but Miss Ozick is not kidding. For her, redemption is racial and religious: it lies in Jewish conscience, Jewish history, Jewish magic, and the Hebrew language. In the preface to an earlier book, **Bloodshed,** this most subtle of stylists paradoxically confessed to a profound unease in writing English while remaining so intensely Jewish in her apprehension of the world.... (p. 22)

Certainly, she is too authentic an artist to go running after immigrant rhythms or Hester Street kitsch. The English she writes is pure and controlled and, in a wholly twentieth-century way, classical. Yet she seems, nevertheless, to hanker after Bashevis Singer's *shtetl* with its superstitious peasants and dybbuks and what she has recently called "the centripetal density and identity of a yeshiva society." So Puttermesser . . . creates for her salvation a golem, as though all her cosmopolitan intelligence and sensibility were a secret source of guilt. In the same way, Miss Ozick bends her subtle, beautifully controlled prose and strange imagination to the service of folk magic. It is, in the end—despite the brilliance, despite the humor—an odd and uneasy displacement, like the Chagalls in Lincoln Center. (pp. 22-3)

> A. Alvarez, "Flushed with Ideas," in The New York Review of Books (reprinted with permission from The New York Review of Books; copyright © 1982 Nyrev, Inc.), Vol. XXIX, No. 8, May 13, 1982, pp. 22-3.*

ANATOLE BROYARD

The ardor in Cynthia Ozick's **"Art and Ardor"** is for dissent. She is a brilliant disagreer whose analysis is so penetrating that in this collection of literary essays it often passes right through the book under discussion. Whether this should be called transcending the author's limitations or missing her point may be a matter of taste.

Miss Ozick polices modern literature and tries to arrest what she sees as self-indulgence. She seems to be morally insatiable, to want every author to wrestle with his book, like Jacob wrestling with the angel, until it blesses him, or us. She is the antidote to all the soft reviews, the easy forgiveness. As she points out, sympathy can be an offense against the truth.

She is terribly smart, to the point where it is just a little dehumanizing. Each time you think you have understood her, after considerable labor, she refines her analysis once again, climbing one more rung on her ladder to some ultimate perspective. One wonders, if she were to have her way, whether fiction could survive her demands, whether she might not intimidate it out of existence....

She wonders why, in his novel "The Tenants," Bernard Malamud could not have had a sophisticated black novelist like Ralph Ellison in place of the furious literary primitive called Willie. Then the Jewish novelist Lesser might have had a more balanced exchange with the other tenant in Malamud's house of fiction. This is almost like saying, "Why didn't Hamlet sit down and have a sensible talk with his mother?"

In the same way, the ardent Miss Ozick asks why, in his first Bech book, John Updike refused to "theologize" his Jewish protagonist. He theologizes all of his other major characters, she argues. Why is Bech alone "wholly untouched by the transcendental"? To this, Mr. Updike might reply, "Because I am not you." Or, "Because that's the way Bech *is*." Miss Ozick admits that she knows lots of Bechs; what she will not admit is that Mr. Updike has sufficient reasons for portraying him.

As a reader of one of these essays said in a letter to Miss Ozick, she is not sufficiently grateful to authors for what they do, as opposed to what they might have done. When a critic becomes too ungrateful, then he or she becomes a reformer with a different set of values. Yet—there is usually a "yet" in speaking of Miss Ozick—isn't it also true that Bech lacks a tragic dimension and that to deny a man a tragic dimension is, on some sublime level, to discriminate against him, to refuse to let him join your club? . . .

There is something relentless, something humorless, in **"Art and Ardor,"** which also includes essays on Edith Wharton, Henry James, Harold Bloom, Gershom Scholem, I. B. Singer and Truman Capote. Still, Miss Ozick might say that we have had enough of relenting, of humoring our writers. She appears to have chosen for herself, in literary criticsm, the role of the anxious mother who wants only the best for her children, who expects them to be serious. When we don't try for the best in our fiction, she warns, time "dies around a book; and then the book lies there, a shaming thing because it shows us how much worse we once were to have liked it."

"More often than not," Miss Ozick says in one of her many perorations, "the Zeitgeist is a lie." What she doesn't say is that, more often than not, it's a necessary lie.

Anatole Broyard, in a review of "Art and Ardor," in The New York Times *(copyright © 1983 by The New York Times Company; reprinted by permission), April 27, 1983, p. C23.*

KATHA POLLITT

We may be living in "an era when the notion of belles-lettres is profoundly dead," as Miss Ozick says in her foreword, but it's thriving in **"Art & Ardor,"** which is by turns quarrelsome, quirky, unfair, funny and brilliant.

Looked at one way, these essays, though originally published in magazines as divergent as Ms. and Commentary, are a unified and magisterial continuation of Miss Ozick's short stories by other names. Admirers of her three story collections . . . will recognize at once her yeasty, extravagant prose, her intellectual preoccupations (jeremiads against violations of the Second Commandment, for instance—that's the one about worshiping idols) and some of her characters too. . . .

Looked at another way, though, **"Art & Ardor"** is the work not of one Cynthia Ozick but three: a rabbi, a feminist and a disciple of Henry James. Among them, this trio—old classmates, perhaps, or relatives, but hardly friends—have co-authored a fascinating and very odd anthology of essays about Judaism, women and literature.

As rabbi, Miss Ozick's chief target is idol worship, whose ramifications, she argues, include the Holocaust, Jewish assimilation and much modern literature, all of which are the result of substituting "aesthetic paganism" for moral seriousness. "When a Jew becomes a secular person he is no longer a Jew," she writes in **"Toward a New Yiddish"**; he's merely a neuter, an "envious ape" of gentile culture. It follows that Miss Ozick regards most of the writers we think of as Jewish—Proust, Kafka, Heine, not to mention Philip Roth and Norman Mailer—as Christians *manqués,* the main exception being Saul Bellow, for reasons I couldn't quite catch. (Actually, the writer who best fits Miss Ozick's criteria is Miss Ozick herself, whose fiction does indeed answer her call for "a new Yiddish," that is, a culturally Jewish-American literature informed by a "sacral imagination" and an engagement with history.) . . . At her gloomiest, Miss Ozick wonders if "Jewish writer" is not a contradiction in terms.

The feminist Ozick, a more cheerful sort, takes on Anatomy as Destiny. "If anatomy were destiny, the wheel could not have been invented; we would have been limited by legs," she snaps in **"The Hole/Birth Catalogue,"** a masterly demolition of Freud on women. She's outraged by sentimentalists who patronize women by comparing housekeeping or pregnancy to artistic creation. . . .

Miss Ozick reserves particular scorn for the "Ovarian Theory of Literature," whose proponents include feminist literary scholars, the author's own college students . . . and most book reviewers: "I think I can say in good conscience that I have never—repeat, *never*—read a review of a novel or, especially, of a collection of poetry by a woman that did not include somewhere in its columns a gratuitous allusion to the writer's sex and its supposed effects," she wrote in 1971. (p. 7)

At this point, the Jamesian Ozick takes over. For her, the imagination is a holy mystery and the writing of fiction the only thing that matters. The Jamesian knows precisely what was wrong with W.R.B. Lewis's biography of Edith Wharton—it left out her life as a writer. She's devastating on Truman Capote's arch early novels—perhaps too devastating, for she denounces "Other Voices, Other Rooms" like someone going after a hummingbird with a chain saw. The Jamesian even knows that worshiping James is a trap: Art may be all that matters, but one can't be an artist if one lives as though that were true. As I'm trying to indicate, Cynthia Ozick has a complicated mind.

All three Ozicks love a good fight, which is one of the reasons **"Art & Ardor"** is so much fun to read. They share some less attractive qualities too—a tendency to seize irrelevant moral high ground, and to present Ozick as a beleaguered minority of one (to read her on other feminists, you'd think she was the only woman writer who hasn't retired to a lesbian commune to write prose poems about the Great Mother). She draws wild inferences from ideas she opposes and then uses her extrapolations as a club. How could Harold Bloom possibly answer her charge that his theory of strong and weak poets is a covert defense of human sacrifice?

The problem is not that there is a polemic at the heart of most of these essays, but that Miss Ozick's true targets are not always fully acknowledged. Would she have slammed quite so hard into poor Mr. Capote had he not, as she reminds us in a casual aside, once complained of a "Jewish Mafia" in American letters? . . . Perhaps, but she does favor hit-and-run tactics, as when she drops into a discussion of the late Israeli scholar Gershom Scholem the suggestion that "the seeds of the Inquisition somehow lie even in the Sermon on the Mount." They do? Where? If she wants to say that Christianity is innately murderous, let her stand her ground and produce her evidence, not deliver a one-liner and move on.

Miss Ozick is fond of grand pronouncements, and she delivers them with such confidence one might almost not notice that many of them are flatly invalid.... To help her praise moral fiction, she denies morality to poetry, dismissing it as a "decoration of the heart" and ultimately evil. Forget the religious, social, political and moral visions of Milton, Blake, Dickinson, Frost, Lowell. We go in one paragraph from "Tintern Abbey" to the Hitler Youth.

Such sweeping overstatements may be pardoned as a byproduct of exuberance. A more serious difficulty, at least for me, was a growing sense that Cynthia Ozick's three selves were not very well acquainted with each other. How, I found myself wondering, does she square her commitment to sexual egalitarianism with her passionately traditional Judaism (for needless to say, she has nothing but contempt for Reform Judaism, the only branch that would let her be a rabbi for real). There are those who argue that Conservative and Orthodox Judaism offer separate but equal spheres for men and women, but I doubt that Miss Ozick is one of them, and anyway, separate but equal is not what she wants. Why is it incumbent upon Jews to write as Jews, even if they must first acquire a whole religious and historical education to do so (not to mention learn Hebrew) but anathema for women to write as women? And if biology is irrelevant to a writer's work, why does Miss Ozick discuss the childlessness of Woolf and Wharton at all, let alone bring in moralistic terms like "solipsistic"? She doesn't tell us which of the male writers she discusses were fathers (although we do learn which ones were homosexual). If it matters that Woolf and Wharton were free from household chores, it ought also to matter that John Updike and I. B. Singer are too. Contradictions and excluded middles of this sort are the reasons why my copy of **"Art & Ardor"** is as heavily scored with question marks and irritated cross-references as it is with passages underlined for saving. (pp. 7, 35)

I suspect that Cynthia Ozick's three selves do not try harder to make peace with each other because they sense it can't be done. The secular drift she castigates as a religious Jew is, after all, exactly what gives her the freedom to reexamine traditional notions of women, and to posit the imagination as sovereign. All the same, it would be interesting to see what she would come up with if she set herself the task of synthesis. For now, though, it's enough that she has given us this wonderful, if sometimes frustrating book—among whose gems, I must not forget to mention, is a childhood memoir, **"A Drugstore in Winter,"** that is as rich and dense as the best of her fiction. The book it so splendidly concludes deserves a wide readership among women and men, Jews and gentiles, lovers of fiction and lovers of ideas. (p. 35)

> Katha Pollitt, "The Three Selves of Cynthia Ozick," in The New York Times Book Review (copyright © 1983 by The New York Times Company; reprinted by permission), May 22, 1983, pp. 7, 35.

VICTOR STRANDBERG

If we postulate that the "scene" in fiction corresponds to the image in poetry, we may say that Ozick's interplay of fictional devices consistently develops scenes answering to Ezra Pound's Imagist Manifesto of 1913: they "transmit an intellectual and emotional complex in an instant of time." The pagan motifs converging into the night of Tilbeck's apotheosis; the Pagan Rabbi's breathtaking consummation of love with the dryad; Puttermesser chanting her beloved golem back to a pile of mud;

Tchernikhovsky insolently at ease in Zion; Lushinski in Africa contemplating his buried self in Warsaw; the many dramatic verbal battles rendered with a perfect ear for speech patterns: Edelshtein versus the evangelist, Bleilip versus the rebbe, German versus Jew in **"The Suitcase"**—such scenes bespeak a gift of the first order of talent. Even if not outstandingly abundant in the fashion of Joyce Carol Oates or Saul Bellow, Ozick's stream of creativity has been outstandingly pure.

Although her ensconcement within a minority subculture may initially seem to limit her appeal to a larger audience, I (though not Jewish) have found that the obstacles to understanding her work have little to do with her Jewish materials. They result, rather, from her willful adherence to basic aesthetic principles. A holdover from the Modern Period—the Age of Eliot, Faulkner, Joyce—she is no more inclined to simplify her complex art, so as to ease her reader's task, than she is to falsify her view of reality, so as to thrive in the marketplace. Her Jewish heritage, for the most part, is not more constrictive than Hawthorne's or Faulkner's regionalism.

What matters in the end is the imaginative power to elevate local materials toward universal and timeless significance. By that standard, I judge Ozick's work to be memorably successful. Her variety and consistent mastery of styles; her lengthening caravan of original and unforgettably individualized characters; her eloquent dramatization through these characters of significant themes and issues; her absorbing command of dialogue and narrative structure; her penetrating and independent intellect undergirding all she writes—these characteristics of her art perform a unique service for her subject matter, extracting from her Jewish heritage a vital significance unlike that transmitted by any other writer. In the American tradition, Cynthia Ozick significantly enhances our national literature by so rendering her Jewish culture. (pp. 310-11)

> Victor Strandberg, "The Art of Cynthia Ozick," in Texas Studies in Literature and Language (copyright © 1983 by the University of Texas Press), Vol. 25, No. 2, Summer, 1983, pp. 266-312.

PHYLLIS ROSE

In *Art & Ardor,* Ozick's perfectionist, self-critical habits produce a book which surprises and delights on every line, a model—except that her prose is inimitable—of the play of mind over matters of life and literature....

Cynthia Ozick puts everything she has into her essays—and that's a lot: wit, fierce intelligence, supple writing, and an absence of hackneyed opinion. Her subjects include literature, Judaism, feminism. Beginning one of her essays, you don't know where it will end up or what strange points she will make along the way. An essay on Truman Capote produces an ironic reminiscence of studying literature at NYU in the post-war years, along with unappreciative Army vets....

Ozick's positions are unequivocal and often unfashionable. She dislikes the new feminism which celebrates women's separateness. A "classic" feminist herself, she hates the term "woman writer" and opposes the idea of a female nature, calling it "the Great Lie." She thinks Jewish writers will last only if they write as Jews and for Jews. Norman Mailer will one day be no more than "a small Gentile footnote." Her deeply religious nature attacks what she calls "idolatry," the worship of anything other than God. And that includes Art. The book concludes with two masterpieces of autobiographical essay, "The Lesson of the Master" and "A Drugstore in Winter," which make very personal the point about idolatry. Her sterile and premature obsession with Henry James postponed her own growth as a writer. She herself was a worshiper of art, an idolater. Her conversion came late, which explains the virulence of her dislike of idolatry.

> Phyllis Rose, "Oates and Ozick: Essays on Art and Culture," in Book World—The Washington Post (© 1983, The Washington Post), July 3, 1983, p. 9.*

PUBLISHERS WEEKLY

Ozick's first novel in more than 15 years [*The Cannibal Galaxy*] displays a complex, elegant style and deep sensitivity to the eternal difficulties of the human condition. Her story of a school principal who becomes aware of the pinched nature of his life through the unexpected blossoming of a student he had considered dull manages to combine brilliantly detailed individual character portraits with a more general philosophical consideration of the unpredictability of life. Ozick's technique is elliptical. She builds characters and delineates ideas bit by bit, dropping each additional mosaic . . . into place in her larger design with deceptively casual aplomb. Characteristically permeated by Jewish thought and folklore, her novel is universal in its warning against "stopping too soon"—fencing ourselves and others in by timidity and shortsightedness.

> A review of "The Cannibal Galaxy," in Publishers Weekly (reprinted from the July 8, 1983 issue of Publishers Weekly, published by R. R. Bowker Company, a Xerox company; copyright © 1983 by Xerox Corporation), Vol. 224, No. 2, July 8, 1983, p. 58.

BARBARA KOENIG QUART

[Even] if one wants to argue with Ozick every step of the way—and I only want to argue with her every third step—one must start by noting how very well she writes. [The twenty-three essays collected in *Art and Ardor*], on subjects ranging from Edith Wharton to John Updike to Gershom Scholem, with stops in between for mulling over what art should be doing and what Jewishness is, are a pleasure to read for their vividness of thought and language. . . .

Ozick is a writer of passionately held beliefs and values asserted with great confidence and verve, a fierce moralist who often sees herself as the solitary caretaker of truths everyone else is too wrongheaded to understand. Her opposition to contemporary feminism is a case in point. For Ozick, the women's movement has given itself over to "separatism," when it should be tearing down the whole idea of gender difference. In view of the fertility and vitality of contemporary feminism, the rich body of scholarship from women's studies and the generally liberating effect of acknowledging that women indeed have a different—and enormously valuable and interesting—experience, it seems almost perverse for her to argue that separate necessarily means inferior, means the old lists of derogatory stereotypes of women's natures and disparagements by male critics of "lady writers." Ozick argues that in a world of "women writers" (as opposed to writers), "individuality of condition and temperament do not apply"—as if all feminism were a crude Judy Chicago tableau with V. Woolf and E. Dickinson all porcelain genitalia together—but surely she is too intelligent to call the worst case the whole. Her stance is particularly odd in view of her enormous concern for Jewish identity, and her scorn for "universalists" (mainly Jews who insist they are just like everyone else). How can she, of all people, insist that women and men are all just human beings? (p. 87)

[One] feels that buried under the literary sophistication, high intelligence and stylish prose are the values of one's Brooklyn aunt (and I don't mean Park Slope)—the kinds of parental injunctions that Philip Roth's heroes do intense though ambivalent battle against. Ozick, with no ambivalence (but often not quite overtly), promotes those values—prime among them the centrality of blood ties, marital loyalty no matter what and childbearing. They often intrude on literary discussions, as when she finds E. M. Forster's gentle humanism discredited by his childless, homosexual life (she says it in a qualified and complex way but that's what she means). The Wharton essay, ostensibly written to bring her belated justice, instead reproaches her—for finally terminating her miserable twenty-eight-year marriage (Ozick's sympathy is all with husband Teddy); for caring more about the deaths of two longtime servants than about the illness of a brother; for having been attached to dogs rather than children. . . .

Such moralizing is the lower level of Ozick's larger insistence that art must be morally engaged—which for her is a Jewish quality. She notes that while the New Critics were sealing literature off from history and biography, Jewish critics like Trilling, Rahv, Howe and Kazin "put humanity back in." She finds it significant that Bellow, Malamud and Roth continue to write fairly traditional novels about recognizable worlds, although she also finds those worlds *too* real and scorns them—excepting Bellow's—as gross sociology. With such doctrinaire and restrictive notions about fiction, no wonder she sees herself sitting alone on a "wastepile of discarded artists." And yet, she is indeed different: she holds her Judaism in an ideological embrace that has no equivalent among male Jewish American writers. . . .

Ultimately, Ozick's intense morality rests on religion. The words that recur through the essays, invested with suggestive meaning, are "Covenant," "liturgy," "idols" and "redemption." Although she writes that "as a Jew I am an autodidact," and that "print is all my Judaism," she still upholds Jewishness like a female Moses, giving out commandments straight from God: Rashi and Yehudah Halevi will live on, but Norman Mailer will not. "When a Jew is a secular person, he is no longer a Jew," she declares, unblinkingly disqualifying the vast majority of Jews. Yet because she takes that stance jokingly, obliquely, stylishly, its full severity is rarely apparent.

She is unfailingly eloquent on the subject of non-American Jewish writers, for whom she feels a generosity she rarely extends to other writers. . . .

Finally, after one has argued with one position, admired another and differed with but respected a third, the fact is that summaries suggest a narrower and cruder response than one has when reading the book. Ozick talks a lot about idols, by which she means esthetics (or any other delight of the world) taken as an end in itself. Perhaps she warns against idols so much because she herself is an idolmaker, an anomalous mixture of the esthete and the moralist, obviously in love with style and form, with art. And a good thing too. The polemic edge keeps yielding to the elegance of prose, to the intensity of its engagement with art, with writers and with Jewishness—to an ardor (just the right word) for ideas and books and two cultures. (p. 88)

Barbara Koenig Quart, "An Esthete in Spite of Herself," in The Nation (copyright 1983 The Nation magazine, The Nation Associates, Inc.), Vol. 237, No. 3, July 23-30, 1983, pp. 87-9.

MICHIKO KAKUTANI

When we first meet the middle-aged bachelor named Joseph Brill [in **"The Cannibal Galaxy"**], he is presiding as the rather sour principal of a small primary school in the Middle West. Like so many of Cynthia Ozick's characters, he spends much of his time alone, and he is alone because he is guilty of hubris. He has not only allowed intellectual pretensions to calcify his heart, but he has also committed what Miss Ozick seems to regard as one of the worst sins of all—in creating a rigid, self-referential system of education and worshiping something other than God, he has broken the Second Commandment: he is guilty of idolatry.

Idolatry and the complicated relationship between the creator and the thing created has been a favorite subject of Miss Ozick's fiction and essays; and in her new novel, **"The Cannibal Galaxy,"** she examines its implications in terms of both art and human relationships. Although she once wrote that "it is insulting to a poet to compare his titanic and agonized strivings with the so-called 'creativity' of childbearing, where—consciously—nothing happens," she appears to be fascinated by people's continual attempts to "create" their children, to turn them into flesh-and-blood works of art, invested with their own hopes and expectations. . . .

Dense with ideas and philosophic speculation, **"The Cannibal Galaxy"** is also an organic and beautifully told story of one teacher's attempts to discover his place in history and the meaning of his vocation.

Miss Ozick has a distinctive, idiomatic voice, at once elliptical and allusive; and her moral intelligence uncovers parables in contemporary American life with casualness and sometimes even humor. Because that humor is often directed toward her deluded heros, however, a certain coldness can result; one feels that she not only disapproves of her characters but often actively dislikes them as well. . . .

[Brill is a] French Jew who grew up in Paris . . . , he attends the Sorbonne where he learns to worship "serenity, absorption, civilization, intellect, imagination." During World War II, Brill is saved from history by a group of nuns who hide him in the basement of their convent. There, in his damp, smelly dungeon, he discovers a cache of books, and the books—a motley assortment that includes everything from catechisms to Corneille—give him an inspiration. If he survives the war, Brill thinks, he will found a school based on a marriage of Hebrew and European Enlightenment cultures. . . .

Brill establishes his school on the banks of one of the Great Lakes. . . .

Instead of achieving a synthesis of two great cultures [Jewish and secular European], however, his school seems to specialize in mediocrity. . . . Frustrated in his attempts to find a prodigy—that one special child whose talents he can nurture and mold—Brill himself begins to decline. . . .

Then, one day, Hester Lilt, a formidable woman who has achieved intellectual celebrity as an "imagistic linguistic logician," arrives in Brill's life and enrolls her daughter, Beulah, in his school. Infatuated with the mother's air of seriousness and disdain, Brill remains oblivious to the daughter's gifts. She falls through a hole in his school's carefully constructed system, and he dismisses her as ordinary, as dim, as remarkably unexceptional. In doing so, of course, he makes a great mistake—a mistake, as Miss Ozick reveals through several swift cranks of the narrative machinery, that will reveal the narrow solipsism of Brill's own life and mind.

Michiko Kakutani, in a review of "The Cannibal Galaxy," in The New York Times (copyright © 1983 by The New York Times Company; reprinted by permission), August 29, 1983, p. 14.

PATRICIA BLAKE

The Cannibal Galaxy, Cynthia Ozick's first full-scale novel in 17 years, comes as a welcome reminder of her commanding powers as a storyteller. Her previous book, **Art and Ardor**, a collection of essays published last spring, revealed her to be one of the most vigorously intellectual of contemporary American authors. Still, no other fiction writer except Isaac Bashevis Singer has succeeded so brilliantly in harnessing what Ozick has called "the steeds of myth and mysticism" in the Jewish tradition. The wonder is that her style has remained as disciplined and supple as it was in her first novel, *Trust*. . . .

The premise of Ozick's new novel is the uneasy condition of the Jewish heritage in the prevailing Gentile culture, a subject that can be fully viewed only in the shadow cast by the Holocaust. The book's governing metaphor is the cannibal galaxy—in astronomy, one of the vast colonies of stars that devour smaller galaxies. The cannibal stands for Europe, devouring its Jewish citizens. Such out-of-the-way images spring naturally from Ozick's prodigious erudition. This novel, like her earlier short stories and novellas (*The Pagan Rabbi, Levitation, Bloodshed*), is dense with metaphor, often drawn from the rich Jewish resources at her command: the Hebrew Bible, the *Midrashim*, or Jewish homilies, and the mystic texts of the Kabbalah. At the same time, as *The Cannibal Galaxy* demonstrates, she navigates the currents of other world cultures with the surehandedness of a true lover of ideas. . . .

The Cannibal Galaxy seems to suggest that it is all but impossible for Jews to break into the surrounding culture with their heritage intact. Their loss, and the world's, of such a vast and distinctive tradition would be a tragedy. As Ozick has warned, "The annihilation of idiosyncrasy assures the annihilation of culture." But we may take heart: the sense of her commanding novel is that Cynthia Ozick has prevailed, as ever more readers are attracted by the universal appeal of her Jewishness. Hers is a triumph for the idiosyncrasy that animates all art.

Patricia Blake, "A New Triumph for Idiosyncracy," in Time (copyright 1983 Time Inc.; all rights reserved; reprinted by permission from Time), Vol. 122, No. 10, September 5, 1983, p. 64.

RICHARD EDER

Cynthia Ozick has stood immortality on its head. What fails and dies in her clenched and scintillating parable is learning and knowledge. What lives is life.

The publishers call **"The Cannibal Galaxy"** a novel; perhaps novella is more like it, because it is a single sunset, not a chain of days. The sunset is for Principal Joseph Brill of the Edmond Fleg School, set beside an unnamed Great Lake....

Brill has studied astronomy, but he can't quite give himself to the galaxies. He is too cunning for the stars—and too middling. "Middling" is a key word; it is Ozick's word for the mortal Philistinism of knowledge, for the academy, for the critic....

Ozick writes with irony and wit, but her book is not one more satire of academic life. Beyond her wit is a flinty metaphysical poetry. And Brill's school stands for something much more than itself: the deadness of that which seeks to endure through preserving itself. Brill feels an access of foreboding: the perpetual youthful renewal attributed to teaching is a sham, really....

The foreboding is the first eddy before the storm arrives, in the person of a parent. Hester Lilt is a frumpy eminence, a scholar whose works bear such titles as "Metaphor as Exegesis." (p. 1)

[Brill] has presented himself to her, with wry self-disparagement, as a failed thinker, but she will have none of it. It is not that he has failed, she says; it is that he has stopped too soon. Stopping too soon, turning back to secure what is achieved instead of pressing on, it is her pronouncement upon him, and it is the book's pronouncement upon the myriad sinecures that infest our world of intellect and turn it into a vast and rigid bureaucracy.

But there is more to **"The Cannibal Galaxy"** than the duel between a live intellect and a stratified one. It is the life itself that Ozick is after; and beyond Hester Lilt there is her daughter, Beulah. If Hester humbles Brill, Beulah unseats him.

Beulah is mute and vacant—an underachiever. Brill struggles to arouse her but Beulah won't be aroused.

Hester refuses to treat her daughter as a problem to be worked upon. Instead, she sends Brill her latest paper, an essay on the fertile and significant properties of silence.

And Brill telephones her, in furious triumph. So all her brilliant theories and metaphors are no more than an effort to explain her daughter. Hester hangs up.

Years later, a kind of answer comes. Beulah has become an avant-garde painter, a Parisian sensation. Asked about her childhood education in America, she says she doesn't remember it.

Ozick has made her meaning plain. If Beulah's muteness was the seed of Hester's brilliance, it is a glory, not a shame. It is life, the willingness to respond to it, that preserves the intellect from its own corruption. *Ars,* in other words, *brevis; vita lunga.* (p. 7)

Richard Eder, "The Principal Import As a Porsche," in Los Angeles Times Book Review *(copyright, 1983, Los Angeles Times; reprinted by permission), September 18, 1983, pp. 1, 7.*

JOSEPH COHEN

Cynthia Ozick's new novel, **"The Cannibal Galaxy"** ... is so rich in its tapestries it can be read variously as an incisive though ironic evaluation of the American private school system, as a commentary on the problems of assimilation increasingly faced by Jewish day schools, as a wry report on the aggressiveness of Jewish mothers asserting the educational prerogatives of their children; or as a book dealing with Jewish marginality, power and powerlessness, and generational conflict; or as a study in the "second lives" of Holocaust survivors, who have lost one family, created another, and breathe always the tragedy of the past with the hope of the future in the monomania of the present.

To drive her point home about the dangers of allowing Western culture to supplant Covenant and Commandment, Ozick has borrowed from the world of physics the concept of larger "cannibal" galaxies swallowing smaller ones whole. This concept she turns into a metaphor for the threat facing the survival of Diaspora Judaism, and develops from the metaphor an illuminating and entertaining parable which will likely be one of the best books of the year.

Joseph Cohen, "'Cannibal Galaxy' by No Ordinary Teacher," in The Jewish News *(copyright © The Jewish News Publishing Co.), October 21, 1983, p. 2.*

Bette Pesetsky
1932-

American short story writer and novelist.

Pesetsky's fiction focuses on the dispirited lives of female protagonists whose ennui can usually be attributed to unstable or failed relationships. Isolation, estrangement, and hopelessness are themes which permeate and connect the stories of the author's first work, *Stories Up to a Point* (1982).

Though similar to the stories in its dark themes and cutting humor, Pesetsky's first novel, *Author from a Savage People* (1983), ostensibly offers the possibility of escaping despair through action. Rather than accept her underpaid position as a ghostwriter, May Alto, the protagonist, blackmails her famous client. The ironic result is that May, angered by oppression, becomes oppressive.

Pesetsky is generally regarded as a skillful writer. While her stylistic economy has at times been seen as a deficiency, most critics praise Pesetsky's unadorned prose style as being reflective of her characters' bleak lives.

Courtesy of Bette Pesetsky

CHRISTOPHER LEHMANN-HAUPT

"One day it came to me that I was neither adopted nor the illegitimate daughter of the King of Rumania and Magda Lupescu. Everything, of course, has run downhill since then." So begins **"Offspring of the First Generation,"** the eighth of the 15 brief stories in this collection. But the notes sounded here of humor, disillusionment and cheerful resignation in the face of loss are typical of Bette Pesetsky's infectious first work of fiction, **"Stories Up to a Point."**

For all, or most, of these stories are about middle-aged women whose lives have broken up, whose parents have died or divorced, whose husbands or lovers have left them, or vice versa, whose children have turned out badly, who do not wish to remember anymore, who cannot find anything to remember or who realize that the only continuity that remains is, as the narrator of one story concludes, "All things that happen to everybody will someday happen to my children."

Yet they go on looking desperately for continuity, these women do, and take it wherever they can find it. . . .

In the fifth story, my favorite, **"The Hobbyist,"** . . . the narrator searches for continuity by cleaning out her grandparents' apartment, her grandfather having died at 82 and her grandmother having gone to live in Venice, Calif. She discovers her grandfather's lifelong hobby, which "was collecting dust." He would put dust samples in bottles and label them: "The store on Essex Street. 1923." The story of his life is collecting dust. This is a witty play on words, but it's also more. At the end, the narrator's husband tells her, "although I am tolerant, I want that dust out of this house. I'm warning you." The past is dangerous.

But so is the lack of a past. The woman in the first story whose life has "run downhill" since she discovered she was neither adopted nor the offspring of royalty, has "noticed that many people do not like me," not her children, her husband, her lovers or even her analyst. . . . Since there is no other explanation . . . , one can only think that the clue to why she's spurned is in the title—the woman is the offspring of immigrants, a fish out of water.

Not all of Bette Pesetsky's verbal tricks are so resonant. . . .

But the best stories, like **"The Hobbyist,"** or **"From P Forward,"** about the loss of magic in growing up, or the title story, in which a father burns all his daughter's belongings and makes his wife swear to be cold to her if she telephones—these have the power to rearrange the space inside one's head with their strong mood of urban paranoia. And what is the point that these stories are "up to"? Sometimes it's that the point is yet to be made. Sometimes it's that it's not worth making. But mostly it's that there simply is no point anymore.

Christopher Lehmann-Haupt, in a review of "Stories Up to a Point," in The New York Times *(copyright © 1982 by The New York Times Company; reprinted by permission), January 15, 1982, p. 21.*

DAVID QUAMMEN

With their compactness, their flat tone, their arresting elisions and juxtapositions, Bette Pesetsky's **"Stories Up to a Point"** read like telegraphic dispatches from the battlefield of modern life. The telegrapher is in almost every case a woman, anonymously reflecting upon her failures and disappointments as

357

wife, mother, lover, friend, urbanite. Generally these women sound shellshocked. But the messages are clear. They carry, some of them, important news from the front.

The news is all bad. . . . The only relief Miss Pesetsky offers, throughout her dispiriting reports on the state of human relations, are deft writing and flashes of hilarious pessimism. A testament to these strengths—her craftsmanship and her mordant humor—is that the volume is, against all odds, enjoyable.

This is still more surprising in that **"Stories Up to a Point"** is her first book. . . . [The stories] show a controlled originality, a distinctive and consistent vision. Ironically, the book's chief flaw is that very consistency of vision. In the weaker stories, the endless succession of injuries-numbly-adapted-to molds into a blur, and the mood of cool despair seems programmatic or facile. Yet even these few, which don't work well as whole stories, fail interestingly and contain at least touches that do work.

Of the rest, some are terrific. **"The Person Who Held the Job Before You"** is a small wry parable about the psychic toll of work in a dull office, compressing into four pages and a punch line much of what Joseph Heller pursued throughout "Something Happened." **"Moe, Nat, and Yrd,"** about a self-confessed student of radio call-in shows and the people who make them possible, at first seems to promise only rambling and eccentric comedy, but then snaps closed at the end like a high quality strongbox. Both **"Dyslexia"** and **"The Theory of Sets"** are ingeniously constructed and emotionally potent, the sort of short story for other short-story writers to look at and envy.

Social disjunction, dislocation and discontinuity (especially as they afflict women) are the main themes of all these stories, and so the author's use of narrative disjunction, dislocation and discontinuity is apt; at its best her off-rhythm, quirky technique is impressive. (pp. 11, 34)

David Quammen, "Women in Crisis," in The New York Times Book Review (copyright © 1982 by The New York Times Company; reprinted by permission), February 14, 1982, pp. 11, 34.*

MARY SOETE

When a character in the title story [of **"Stories Up to a Point"**] declares that "misery is specific," he could be stating this collection's epigraph. These are first-person tales narrated in a sardonic, slightly depressed voice with the hatchet-edged impact of simple declarative sentences. They have the sort of disarming artifice that seizes attention: shocking misfortunes announce themes that are not pursued; stories of dissecting satire carry titles like **"Ulcer,"** **"Scratch,"** and **"Dyslexia."** Pesetsky's people collect and document dust; write pamphlets, graphs, business letters of regret, threat, or supplication; are victimized by anonymous commuter abuse, city crazies, their own disconnected families. Funny, absurd, and troubling—the most refreshing challenge to the traditional boundaries of the short story since Barthelme.

Mary Soete, in a review of "Stories Up to a Point," in Library Journal (reprinted from Library Journal, February 15, 1982; published by R. R. Bowker Co. (a Xerox company); copyright © 1982 by Xerox Corporation), Vol. 107, No. 4, February 15, 1982, p. 474.

BILL GREENWELL

Care by Women, the best of Bette Pesetsky's **Stories up to a Point** is . . . a skeletal sketch of a marriage, the arrival, adolescence and later life of three daughters, their relationship with their mother, their father's desertion—he'd wanted a son. It is but nine neat pages long (sorry, *short*). That it could so easily be decked with flesh, knocked into an excellent novel, is irrelevant. The scratches on its surface are exceptionally skilful. This first collection, with its admirably ambiguous title, contains fifteen tight, slightly antiseptic snippets, concerned with the loss of a lover, love, or both. **Care by Women** is significantly the most striking, as one of only two told in the third person. Pesetsky's speakers, cool, almost emotionless, sound too improbably similar, too mannered to be individual. Fractured in form, some pieces are maddeningly insubstantial. To snatch at a point and miss is agreeably tantalising: not to glimpse one is, well, pointless.

Bill Greenwell, "Novel Tales," in New Statesman (© 1982 The Statesman & Nation Publishing Co. Ltd.), Vol. 104, No. 2685, September 3, 1982, p. 22.*

DAVID MONTROSE

Bette Pesetsky assembles short declarative sentences into very short stories, the kind that are now usually called fictions, their traditional "story" elements having been minimized. . . . [Pesetsky] reflects the influence of Donald Barthelme, revered in creative writing classes for his apparent imitability. All fifteen stories in this first collection incorporate Barthelme's early "see-Jane-run" manner and his "fragmentary" method of construction. Typically, Pesetsky's narrator (always a woman) presents a mosaic of autobiographical episodes linked thematically or by association (the title story, an exception, comprises six *récits* in no particular order). If the resulting arrangement appears to skip inconsequentially between two points, this is because it is designed only, in Barthelme's words, to "supply a kind of 'sense' of what is going on".

Pesetsky has borrowed Barthelme's method, but not his madness, eschewing the surreal for a firm attachment to the quotidian. . . . Her world, though, is the familiar made strange: second-hand echoes of Kafka—as distilled, that is, through Barthelme—permeate these stories. Their heroines are anonymous inhabitants of anonymous places; when familiar locations *are* named, they have no more substantiality than that of words on the page; other people exist only as one-dimensional shadows. Neurotic, lonely, sad, Pesetsky's women endure lives of quiet desperation and write anxious, jerky prose. But they occupy no world apart; theirs is the one we inhabit, with the same phone-in shows, Wedgwood china, muggers, Danish pastries, spastic children. . . . The point, presumably, is that life is in the angle of vision of the beholder: every individual creates a subjective reality. For Pesetsky's casualties, it will be as it appears in her stories: a bleak, directionless trial.

A number of stories are catalogues of misfortune that lack distinctiveness almost to the point of interchangeability. The standard heroine is cursed with broken relationships. . . . The most successful stories are those farthest removed from the formula—and these are also the most "story"-like. The heroine of **"Dyslexia"** departs from the norm by having too many, rather than too few, personal involvements. . . .

"Dyslexia" is the story nearest to Barthelme's unique comedy. Elsewhere, Pesetsky's attempts at fashionably grim humour achieve only grimness relieved by odd amusing passages. Throughout, one suspects that Pesetsky has chosen the wrong master, and this feeling hardens into conviction whenever she utilizes family history. As far as one can divine from recurrent motifs, Pesetsky's ancestors were Polish Jews; her grandparents brought the family to America. Unsurprisingly, quiet resonances of Isaac Bashevis Singer can be detected wherever she draws on this background. Then one realizes how much better a more traditional master, such as Singer, would have served her. The vicissitudes of Pesetsky's wounded are strikingly similar to those endured by comparable characters in Singer's "American" stories, but there is a wide gap between their portrayals. Barthelme's kind of minimalism is simply too detached and impressionistic to suggest a full spectrum of human predicaments; in his own work, of course, it is not meant to. Pesetsky may write as she does precisely in order to avoid comparisons with Singer, or perhaps in order to be modish. Whatever the reason, she will have to resolve this incompatibility between form and content.

> David Montrose, "Life in a Bottle-Full of Dust," in The Times Literary Supplement (© Times Newspapers Ltd. (London) 1982; reproduced from The Times Literary Supplement by permission), No. 4145, September 10, 1982, p. 965.

DORIS GRUMBACH

I admire the strong silences that exist among the words, between the sentences, and hover everywhere over the events in Bette Pesetsky's *Stories Up to a Point*. . . . These are original and unusual stories . . . [in which we notice both] the bleakness of her vision and her barren prose. The only difficulty I had with these poignant pieces is that her prose leaves large air holes through which, if one happens to put the book down in mid-story, memory escapes. Then there is no shortcut back into the story: you must start over. . . .

[Pesetsky's] is wholly a feminine vision. . . . She is preoccupied with women's lives, their particular brand of hopelessness, their acceptance of their hopeless futures. Her women are shadowy, silhouettes rather than rounded and developed, and her situations sketched in with the thinnest lines. Before you have time to grow comfortable in them, you are out at the end. Your tenure has been too short to permit the people and their circumstances to stick in memory. (p. 672)

> Doris Grumbach, "The Extra Skin That Language Can Give: Recent Collections of Short Stories," in The Georgia Review (copyright, 1982, by the University of Georgia), Vol. XXXVI, No. 3, Fall, 1982, pp. 668-74.*

THE NEW YORKER

["**Author From a Savage People**" is a] darkly humorous novel about a brilliant ghostwriter who is other than overjoyed when an eminent client of hers wins, with "his" first book, the Nobel Prize. The ghostwriter could easily expose the fraud—she larded the text with scenes from the lives of her mother and her aunt—but she would prefer to see the book praised and reprinted rather than discredited and remaindered. Mrs. Pesetsky's novel, which covers about three weeks of tense negotiations before the ceremony in Sweden (the ghostwriter wants the prize money and a hefty monthly stipend; her client wants to buy her silence with one lump sum), is larded with some telling scenes from the life of the ghostwriter, a victim turned victimizer. It begins in a hospital emergency room, where she has just been patched up after a mugging; she returns home to cook and clean for a batch of bratty children; and her second ex-husband drops by for free meals and for money (he has already made off with her car). These scenes are effective because Bette Pesetsky makes them move; and they help explain the ghostwriter's edgy glee, which peaks in a concluding scene that will appease all but the most vengeful readers. (pp. 135-36)

> A review of "Author from a Savage People," in The New Yorker (© 1983 by The New Yorker Magazine, Inc.), Vol. LIX, No. 8, April 11, 1983, pp. 135-36.

CHRISTOPHER LEHMANN-HAUPT

Women are the "savage people" in the title of Bette Pesetsky's effective first novel, "**Author From a Savage People**"—at least according to the book's epigraph, which reads "'You're savages,' the politician said. 'Women are savages. I've always known that Civilization has never reached women.'"

As for the "author" in the title: it obviously refers to the story's protagonist, May Alto, who is both a writer and a woman, and thus an "author from a savage people." But it also could refer to an author that the "savage people" as a class are addressing—a male writer, possibly, who, the women might feel, was exploiting them and thus would need to be petitioned in a letter sent to the "author from a savage people," as it were.

These ambiguous meanings of "author" are mostly captured in Mrs. Pesetsky's novel, which follows by about a year the publication of her impressive collection of short fiction, "**Stories Up to a Point**." . . .

[The plot may] sound a bit far-fetched, especially the idea of awarding the Nobel Prize to a two-book author who sounds like a cross between Kahlil Gibran and Lewis Mumford. But in the world created by Mrs. Pesetsky's mordant, hallucinatory prose, such extremes seem not only possible but also downright plausible.

> Christopher Lehmann-Haupt, in a review of "Author from a Savage People," in The New York Times (copyright © 1983 by The New York Times Company; reprinted by permission), April 18, 1983, p. C15.

BARBARA KOENIG QUART

In Bette Pesetsky's awkwardly titled but inventive novel, *Author From a Savage People*, women are the "savage people" and the heroine, May Alto, is the "author," a much put-upon ghostwriter. . . . [Its] central emotion is its heroine's intense ambition, her anger and the pleasure she takes in wreaking vengeance, in feeling powerful for a change. May is an uncredited "helper": to her many clients; to her two former husbands, who used her and deceived her, one shamelessly continuing to do so; to her three children. (p. 738)

May is guided throughout by advice (often banal) from her mother and aunt, both long dead—a nice fictional equivalent of the mother-mentor voice we carry in our heads. . . . May's glee mounts over her power to make the now famous Quayle quail; and her demands grow ever more outrageous, until she's telling him she wants everything that's his—not only his Nobel Prize and his money but his wife, his house. All the while Pesetsky makes us aware of the stab wound in May's arm that won't heal properly, an emblem of vulnerability and guilt to accompany her aggression.

For all that, the novel never feels polemical. It has its own vision, and its own large ambitions and skills. It keeps making surprising leaps and yet it has a strong narrative, at least until—fairly late in the book—it runs out of material. Central devices misfire, particularly May's repeated use in her ghost-writing inventions of an early family triumvirate—mother Sonya, aunt Giselle, uncle Trasker. (Actually, the novel is as much about literary invention as it is about anything else—along with a bitterness toward the hyper-rewarded celebrity writers who bask in applause while the less favored scratch away in harassed obscurity.) May's use of those three family names in every kind of writing she does—even if it can be explained by saying that all fiction draws on one's early experiences—is irritating and pointless. Other devices also don't come off: an endlessly repeated motif of a man chasing a boy, for example. Pesetsky, perhaps influenced to go beyond psychological realism by such exciting recent attempts at narrative enlargement as E. L. Doctorow's *Ragtime* and D. M. Thomas's *The White Hotel,* seems not to have known quite what to do with those self-conscious techniques. Nonetheless, she is a serious and skillful writer, and the novel is well worth reading. (p. 739)

> *Barbara Koenig Quart, "First, the Bad News," in* The Nation *(copyright 1983* The Nation *magazine, The Nation Associates, Inc.), Vol. 236, No. 23, June 11, 1983, pp. 738-39.**

Robert (Schaeffer) Phillips
1938-

American poet, short story writer, critic, and editor.

Phillips has written three volumes of poetry: *Inner Weather* (1966), *The Pregnant Man* (1978), and *Running on Empty* (1981). Critics consider his poetry witty and inventive and laud Phillips for his masterful wordplay. Although writing poetry is a favorite interest, Phillips also wrote the short story collection *The Land of Lost Content* (1970) and the critical study *The Confessional Poets* (1973). In addition to his writing, Phillips has pursued a full-time career in advertising. He has also been a contributing editor to the *Paris Review* and *The Ontario Review* and a book review editor for *Modern Poetry Studies*.

(See also *Contemporary Authors*, Vols. 17-20, rev. ed. and *Contemporary Authors New Revision Series*, Vol. 8.)

WILLIAM VAN O'CONNOR

I think from here on one might chance it that Robert Phillips is going to have a place among the young poets. His *Inner Weather* is a thoughtful book. Much of the writing is very skillful. . . .

If one could read the poem ["**Weird Sister**"] through, one could see that not only are there Shakespearean echoes here, Keatsian echoes, and echoes from Coleridge because we're dealing with what Graves calls the white goddess. What struck me in going through the poem was the way in which Mr. Phillips had modified the Yeatsian idiom. I suppose, if there is one influence here that seems to me to be at least conscious, it would be from Yeats. (p. 44)

Another thing that struck me in reading Mr. Phillips was how the post World War II generation has assimilated its literary heritage. It looks at Eliot, Dylan Thomas, Yeats, but from a new position. The poets who were writing in the thirties and early forties didn't turn and look over their shoulders at the work of Eliot or Dylan Thomas. These poets following World War II do just that. They take the writing seminar for granted; they like to do poems about pictures, particularly zany pictures, and melodramas. They can go back and pick up verse form such as Haiku. They look on the world as beaten from the oppressions of World War II. They are in a sense down to rock bottom in a way that poets in the 1920's and 30's were not. The bomb as we say may have something to do with it.

But I think there is another consideration, namely, that each generation stands on the shoulders of its predecessor; in this case I think there are two predecessors—one composed of the 1920's and secondly Dylan Thomas. One must admit I think that the ironies of Eliot and Pound are in the true sense of the word, sensational. The wasteland image is sensational. The cantos reach in all directions for arcane learning. Then in the thirties we have Thomas with his ocean rhythms which no one should try to repeat because they are peculiar to him. And in Auden the poet who protects himself by ironies, by being a wiseacher. But with these new poets like Phillips, the irony is there but it is reined in, in control. This sort of poetry is being written in England and I suppose some of it is being written in America but this poem is the one that most struck me from Mr. Phillips' poetry.

If this volume is indicative, then we can rest in the assurance that Mr. Phillips' contribution to the American literary scene in the next generation may be considerable. (pp. 44-5)

William Van O'Connor, "Comer," in The North American Review *(reprinted by permission from* The North American Review; *copyright © 1966 by the University of Northern Iowa), Vol. 3, No. 6, November, 1966, pp. 44-5.*

ANDREW CURRY

[*Inner Weather*]—designed ". . . to smash a witch who could not / fly . . ."—is more curious than interesting. The quote is from *"The Weird Sister"* which opens this series of poems authored by one of the most consistent of the young poets. Phillips is 30ish; but in *"Rosedale Afternoon"* he is as death and insanity. The poems appear to have been written between 1958-1965, constituting, perhaps, Phillips' "early work." Phillips knows the craft well—perhaps too well. His sense of humor is apparent and tastefully used.

The image of flying is Phillips' explicit focus here. He defines poetry as "flight, rising on its strength." But the majority of these poems never pulled me into that promised flight. I never flew and when I wanted to structure, tradition, technical devices . . . simply prevented me from doing so. Perhaps it *is* true that one concentrates on a poem's externals when he doesn't know what else to say. Fortunately, Phillips is his own best critical reviewer—

> Sleight of hand must be outgrown.
> Mere magic cannot stay the mind.
> The boy becomes a man of shop-worn tricks
> in a world with no trap door.

Andrew Curry, in a review of "Inner Weather," in Small Press Review *(© 1968 by Dustbooks), Vol. 1, No. 4, December, 1968, p. 71.*

ROBERT EMMET LONG

[*The Land of Lost Content*] comprises fifteen related stories about present or former inhabitants of Public Landing, an Eastern Shore community some 100 miles below the Mason-Dixon line and apparently based on Phillips's boyhood home in Sussex County, Delaware. A prologue called **"The Happy Highway"** introduces us to the area: the dreary stretches of flat, sandy fields and chicken farms; the crumbling colonial estates along the highway that have been converted into neon-lighted "fudge palaces"; the revival camp on the outskirts of town; the Baptist Church with its spire surmounted by an angel, lavishly illuminated at night; the fertilizer plant of "Mr. Sam," a local tycoon vigilant in keeping new industry out and wages down; the Bijou theater, with its balcony divided down the middle by a plywood wall—one half for white patrons, the other for blacks. It also appears that Public Landing has a scandalously high rate of alcoholism. Bleak as this community is (H. L. Mencken would have loved and applauded Phillips's depiction of the aridities of the New South), it is only a foretaste of the barren lives of its citizens.

Take, for example, Mr. Sam's widow (**"A Lady of Fashion"**), whose pathetic attempts to retain her youth end in painful self-recognition. Take Fulton Oldfield (**"The Angel of the Church"**), whose dignity conceals an inner sordidness, or the wife in **"The Death of a Good Man,"** whose illusions about her husband are cruelly dispelled at his funeral. Other characters are outright grotesques—Nathan Fooks in **"Obsession,"** Nora Lee in **"The Lost Child."** Phillips's characters grapple with destinies that are too much for them. He looks on with detachment, at times even with mocking amusement. One wonders which side of Phillips will prevail in the novel about Public Landing that he has completed but not yet published—the observer or the satirist. (pp. 42-3)

Robert Emmet Long, in a review of "The Land of Lost Content," in Saturday Review *(© 1971 Saturday Review Magazine Co.; reprinted by permission), Vol. LIV, No. 18, May 1, 1971, pp. 42-3.*

L. S. DEMBO

As a description of a general tendency in post World War Two American poetry, the term "confessional" is probably useful enough. Robert Lowell casually applied it to his own work in a *Paris Review* interview several years ago and M. L. Rosenthal succeeded in giving it currency in *The New Poets* (1967). Now [in *The Confessional Poets*] Mr. Phillips has come along with a whole book on the subject, seeking to establish the emergence of a "movement" or "school" or, at the very least, a "mode."

Robert Lowell, W. D. Snodgrass, and possibly Anne Sexton are the cofounders . . . and John Berryman, Theodore Roethke, and Sylvia Plath are among the chief practitioners. Mr. Phillips summarizes their work thus:

> It is highly subjective.
> It is an expression of personality, not an escape from it.
> It is therapeutic and/or purgative.
> Its emotional content is personal rather than impersonal.
> It is most often narrative.
> It portrays unbalanced, afflicted, or alienated protagonists.

—and so forth. . . . He then devotes a chapter to each poet in which, as he says, he serves as a reader's guide.

All in all, it is a tedious business, and it is so precisely because Mr. Phillips never gets beyond the kind of general description to which the term "confessional" is limited. His explications usually being little more than paraphrases, he tells us what any literate reader of the poetry can discover well enough for himself. To make matters worse, Phillips is not always a trustworthy guide. In his treatment of Lowell, for example, he implies that it was not until *Life Studies* that Lowell "abandoned his reserve and passionately cried out, 'Grandpa! Have me, hold me, cherish me!'" (Thus, we are told, *Life Studies* ushered in an age of emotion in American poetry.) Correspondingly, he dismisses *Lord Weary's Castle*, whose style he calls "constipated." The fact is, of course, that the outcry just mentioned is virtually the only one of such intensity in the whole of *Life Studies*, a collection that for all its autobiographical material is characterized by understatement and oblique presentation of feeling. On the other hand, *Lord Weary's Castle*, for all its so-called Christian dogma, is so obviously infused with personal anguish and despair that one is wholly at a loss to understand how Phillips could so blithely ignore it.

Actually, *The Confessional Poets* is not so pretentious a study as this discussion suggests. It really does not aspire to be much more than an introduction and its style is informal rather than polemical. This does not, however, excuse a book which, at best, is hopelessly competent. (pp. 415-16)

L. S. Dembo, in a review of "The Confessional Poets," in American Literature *(reprinted by permission of the Publisher; copyright © 1974 by Duke University Press, Durham, North Carolina), Vol. 46, No. 3, November, 1974, pp. 415-16.*

JOYCE CAROL OATES

[In *The Pregnant Man*, Robert Phillips is] idiosyncratic, rather wildly inventive . . . speaking with a wry, sad humor of the sort of pregnancy a man must endure. . . . In **"The Married Man," "The Cultivated Man"** . . . , **"The Invisible Man,"** and **"Hand Poem"** Phillips presents a compelling alternative vision to Rich's oppressive "male god"; feminists should read *The Pregnant Man* if for no other reason than to see, to be forced to see, that "feminine" sensitivity (and, indeed, suffering) is hardly the exclusive lot of women. In a fantasy, **"The Skin Game,"** the poet acquires a wet-suit to protect him . . . and in **"The Stone Crab: A Love Poem,"** he establishes a rather frightful identity with a creature whose giant claw is broken from him to be eaten (the crab itself is thrown back into the sea so that he can grow another claw). How many losses can he endure?, Phillips inquires.

The first section of *The Pregnant Man* is called **"Body Icons,"** and is prefaced by a statement by Dylan Thomas: "All thoughts and actions emanate from the body. Every idea, intuitive or intellectual, can be imaged and translated in terms of the body, its flesh, blood, sinews, veins, glands, organs, cells, or senses." Phillips's poems on various body organs or bodily predicaments—poems on the skin, on the heart, on the head, the penis, the hand, the foot, and on the recurring metaphor of male pregnancy—are wittily accomplished, and might be misread as satirical verse just as Steinberg's art is often misread as cartoon art. Elsewhere in the volume Phillips is more conventionally "serious": his poems on Picasso, Giacometti, Burchfield . . . , Carson McCullers, Delmore Schwartz, and Shirley Jackson are simply very good poems. *The Pregnant Man* seems a slimmer volume than it really is, perhaps because one wishes it longer. (pp. 27-8)

> Joyce Carol Oates, in a review of "The Pregnant Man," in The New Republic (reprinted by permission of The New Republic; © 1978 The New Republic, Inc.), Vol. 179, No. 24, December 9, 1978, pp. 27-8.

JEROME MAZZARO

Most readers will be delighted by the surface wit of *The Pregnant Man*. Robert Phillips is a very entertaining poet and a master of the double-take. Not only are words given double duty in terms of puns, but line breaks do double duty, images and statements recur, and poems have two movements or become new looks at subjects treated first by painters or other writers. Even the epiphanies of this attempt at "male consciousness raising/razing" force new looks. One immediate reaction is laughter in that perceptions that are momentarily disappointing still prove pleasurable. . . . A second result is a search for resolution and transcendence in the wisdom that comes of dual perspective. Divided into three stages, the search moves from the individual (**"Body Icons"**) to intersubjectivity (**"In Clown Clothes"**) to community (**"The Sacred and the Suburban"**), and more often than the speaker of **"Foot Notes,"** readers discover that they, too, have "one foot / in the door of the future, / [and] one in the grave." They must revise their idea of the female as "fecund vessel" in **"The Tenant"** and, in **"The Cultivated Man,"** learn to live with an image of the Earth Father. But in doing so, they expand their lives, for challenging socio-sexual myths precedes the greater effort to frame more accurately the truths underlying racial myths; and since challenging does not always imply overturning, in this area serious readings of *The Pregnant Man* are likely to collect.

Phillips comes to the "intra" conflicts of *The Pregnant Man* from the commoner "inter" conflicts of *Inner Weather* (1966). There, in the manner of early Auden, "us" opposed "them" or "you," and the lines of demarcation followed what Søren Kierkegaard calls "ethical" rather than "aesthetic" choice. One made lifetime rather than momentary decisions because choice seemed always to involve the "either/or" of things "out there," and the process of choosing implicated the personality, if not the salvation, of the chooser in consequences. . . . But what if the notion of choice were itself illusory and momentary? If, like myth, ambiguity resided in articulation and perception, and choices were susceptible to pun and double entendre? What sort of personality would then be framed? **"Vital Message"** provides one answer. A "message" is vital neither to the sender (who is now without it) nor to the receiver (who thus far has existed without it). A "vital message" is vital only to itself and may, as in this case, also be a message about vitality. What is "vital" to the speaker—heart, watch, soul, attention, friendship, affection, nourishment—is ambiguously perceived because attempts at separated scientific perception wrongly reduce significance to single meanings and render the perceiver somehow transparent. Phillips would prefer extended, "humanistic" multiplicity and visibility.

In registering this preference, Phillips relies—as he does in **"Penis Poem"**—on distinctions that Carl Jung makes concerning "male" and "female" identity myths. Jung associates the "male" myth with succession and linear history and the "female" myth with simultaneity and natural cycles of return. Yet, as *The Pregnant Man* demonstrates, men, too, think dually, and certainly, readers feel men are healthier psychologically and aesthetically for doing so. Such a feeling may disarm believers of *Civilization and Its Discontents*, for it challenges the "male" power of sublimation by which Freud had society and civilization ordered. But it should delight believers in poetry who have too long tolerated dreary quests for "sincerity" whose only virtues seem to be an exoticism of direct or vicarious victimization. If, as critics like Delmore Schwartz and Randall Jarrell maintained, poetry reflects the tensions of Freudian psychology, these victimizations—including that by the poet—reflect the kinds of fierce suppression Freud associates with order. Like late Auden, Phillips would avoid these tensions by rooting his approach squarely in the joys, exasperations, and opportunities inherent in words, where simultaneity negates Necessity and, hence, ethical sequence. **"The Skin Game,"** for example, elaborates "onion skin"—derma, epidermis, and paper—into a process of imaginative and actual uncoverings and coverings without forcing these actions into some final "male" irony or *discordia concors*. (pp. 109-10)

Much as the **"Body Icons"** section of the volume presents Phillips's most serious challenges to conventional male/female identity myths in the ambiguities of such excellent poems as **"Vital Message," "The Head," "Hand Poem," "The Tenant," "The Invisible Man,"** and **"The Married Man,"** the **"In Clown Clothes"** section offers conventional postures in its reexaminations of art by Picasso, Giacometti, and Burchfield and its recourse to art/life, inner/outer, and self/other dualities. Ambiguities of language persist in lines like "who have nothing at all in their nakedness" and themes of inner thinness and difference, but the very partitive nature of intersubjectivity demands real opposites and, hence, choices. The motivation of the section's best poem **"Books"** resides not in words like "binding" and "type," from which movement seems to come, so much as on a duality of "open life" and "closed art" on which the poem ends, reasserting an ability of life to move beyond art. The wisdoms of the third section, **"The Sacred and the Suburban,"** are similarly less revolutionary. In two of the volume's finest poems—**"Soft and Hard"** and **"The Stone Crab: A Love Poem,"** speakers take up the "lessons" of nature and the stone crab to face setback. In their positive returns to nature and cycle, the poems challenge again conventional successive linear "male" roles that **"Transfer of Title," "Jimmy's Chicky-Run,"** and **"Jonah"** uphold. Once more, simultaneity and succession do not reliably identify myths of sexual identity so much as reflect society's needs to handle breakdown. One accepts (simultaneity) or transcends (succession). **"The European Scene"** negates this choice by rising to that spiritual realm of traditionally wed simultaneities and transcendences.

"The Married Man," "Soft and Hard," and **"The Stone Crab"** must be numbered among the tenderest and best recent love poems, and the volume's insistence that properly selected words can be precise, enriching, and baffling is a refreshing change from poets who think truthful language need be dull. "Onion skin" does exist as paper and onion. "Mickey Mouse" is a watch and dull routine. A balloon can be said to "moon" outside a window, prompting the poem's "Gothic" violation of "a virgin / sheaf of paper." Poetic intelligence exists in seizing these correspondences as much as in getting down Heidegger, Sartre, or Roussel. Poems can proceed from such springboards as well as from the pre-existing molds of pre-packaged thought, end-rhyme, pentameter, quatrain, and sonnet. Yet, Phillips preserves enough echoes of the old to afford easy recognition and allow readers to come away finding multiple meaning and problems in the most ordinary things about them. The volume thus has that characteristic of extending a reader's perception at the same time it asserts the opacity of the poems' personae and art's function not as a mirror but as a means for understanding, accepting, enjoying, and using multiplicity. As such, *The Pregnant Man* will be beneficial to women as well as men—a situation that will doubtlessly also contribute to its being among the year's most cherished, troubling, and influential books of poetry. (pp. 110-11)

Jerome Mazzaro, "'Male Consciousness Raising/Razing'," in The Ontario Review (copyright © 1979 by The Ontario Review), No. 9, Fall-Winter, 1978-79, pp. 109-11.

ALAN WILLIAMSON

Robert Phillips's poetry has the surface virtues of clarity, verbal gamesmanship, descriptive grace. But the substance of the theme-and-variations poems that make up most of *The Pregnant Man* too often reminds me of the exercises given out in slightly trendy or "experimental" writing workshops. Take a myth, give it a more cynical—or more psychoanalytic—moral than it usually has, then write it up in slang, mentioning diaphragms, Forest Hills, and Truman Capote. Take a dead metaphor involving a part of the body . . . and literalize it. . . . Phillips's relentless reliance on cliché in these poems will doubtless strike some readers as purposeful, a rueful commentary on the inescapable banality of our true feelings. For me, it mainly adds an unpleasing brittleness of tone to what remains—even when touched with lyric grace, as in **"The Head"**—a poetry written to formula, with an almost indecently built-in claim to extreme levels of psychic pain. Joyce Carol Oates has recommended this book to feminists—a recommendation the title rather solicits—as an instance, assuming one is needed, of "'feminine' sensibility (and, indeed, suffering)" in men [see excerpt above]. In fact, the book has little to say about whether, and how, "sensibility" is related to gender; what Oates seems—to me, rather appallingly—to class as "feminine" is Phillips's indulgence in feelings of helplessness, allegorized rather than explored or tested in terms of reality.

When the resistance of reality is felt, to whatever degree, Phillips's work almost invariably becomes more agreeable in tone, and his technical resources come to the fore. The small group of poems I really enjoyed in this book would include **"Transfer of Title," "Corn Flakes," "Happenings," "Giacometti's Race"** . . . , and—best of all, despite a conspicuous theft from Williams's "The Dance"—the exuberant **"Burchfield's World"**. . . . (pp. 348-49)

Alan Williamson, "In a Middle Style," in Poetry (© 1980 by The Modern Poetry Association; reprinted by permission of the Editor of Poetry), Vol. CXXV, No. 6, March, 1980, pp. 348-54.*

JAMES FINN COTTER

If the measure of a poet is, as Keats thought, the ability to give up self and become other beings, then Robert Phillips is as close to being a poet as anyone writing today. Not birds and clouds, but giraffes and crabs are the subject of his metamorphoses, and his quest is more classical than romantic. In his third collection of poems, *Running on Empty,* Phillips explores the sensations of being the other (even the child once oneself) by dramatizing the experience of both losing a sense of the ego and filling the void. The title poem describes the process by a perfect allegory: a teen-ager's defiant ability to drive with the fuel gauge reading empty and below, "riding on nothing but fumes."

"The Silent Man" spells out the same sensation of blankness (a true tabula rasa) when Phillips concludes: "there simply is nothing / to say worth breaking / this white silent web."

Why then write at all? Because the other, the loved one, gives a voice to the void and makes the silent one a poet. The price is often misunderstanding, like the child thinking that, when his father said he would prune a tree, he meant to decorate it with prunes, not cut down its limbs. . . . Even though it blossomed again, the loss could not be repaired. Only words remain to tell the parable.

The poems are divided into five sections that trace different kinds of metamorphosis: **"Middle Age Nocturnes," "Ninety Miles From Nowhere," "Modern Gallery," "A Bestiary,"** and **"Survival Songs."** I enjoyed most the biographical series of the second section with its memories of childhood, the losses his mother endured and the cruelties his father thoughtlessly allowed himself. The cellar where his father worked out of the reach of the family becomes a symbol of hell and the unconscious where all the demons dwell. Phillips recreates the loneliness of an ordinary boyhood with striking accuracy and an economy of imagery and language. His restraint adds to the tension of telling secrets out of home, of breaking the painful silence after long years, and of confessing now to the present emptiness that will not disappear.

Phillips is comic, however, even when hurt, and hopeful in the face of despair. He grows eloquent in an encounter with a woodchuck, an adversary he refuses to kill, or with a severed hand or a beardless Allen Ginsberg. Imagining himself as "Miss Crustacean," a beauty queen winner at the Crab Derby, he is funny and cunning. He makes you feel zero at the bone, but it is the crazy bone at that. You can get lost reading him, but you know that there is method in his madness and he still holds on to the map of his poetry. (pp. 156-57)

James Finn Cotter, "The Poet's Food Is Love and Fame" (reprinted with permission of America Press, Inc. and the author; © 1982; all rights reserved), in America, Vol. 146, No. 8, February 27, 1982, pp. 156-60.*

G. E. MURRAY

Running on Empty takes a significantly different direction from that set forth in earlier work, notably *The Pregnant Man*. There Phillips displayed an appetite for literary decorum. Erudite, polished, technically accomplished, those poems seemed not as fine as the craftsmanship that formed them. Happily, this new work, taken in its breadth, achieves a greater emotional consistency by relinquishing some of composition's ornament.

It also should be noted that Phillips' new title is derived from pop composer Jackson Browne's upbeat California country-rock anthem. It should be further clarified that Phillips' patient causes strike no relationship to Browne's pulsating lyrics, and indeed are about as trendy as a hoola-hoop. What does emerge at first inspection from Phillips' borrowed title is a tentative and occasionally clumsy performance—one seemingly predisposed to dabbling in minor events or "bluffing our way / through Kool-Aid afternoons." To be sure, Phillips could be faulted for posturing as an oracle of the obvious, dwelling on the insignificant, and applauding his own forced cleverness. . . . (p. 151)

Yet the book at large is presumably after larger issues, namely, an evaluation of the poet's life tumbling toward middle-age with all its "weather marks, / stretch marks, traumas of all sorts." In this Phillips is more compelling, depicting a blatantly normal world with the illogic of associative memory. For Phillips, past tends to be present, as he recalls bittersweet snatches from adolescence and family history in Laurel, Delaware. This is particularly the case with the twelve-part sequence **"Ninety Miles from Nowhere,"** which depends mainly upon accumulation for its final effect. Phillips risks most when seizing upon the odd and the trivial—a fenceless gate, the importance of beans, holiday disappointments—but this is more a means of working by indirection to establish the poet's key theme in this work: belonging in terms of dislocation. It's a life-heightening premise.

Certainly, too, "the lure of chicanery" remains with Phillips, adept at lulling readers into contentment with an ice cream-social style, only to conclude that "The boy becomes a man of shopworn tricks, / in a world with no trapdoor." At last, Phillips is a survivor with a sense of humor and purpose, well-equipped to speak to such realities as cancer's threat (**"Lump"**) or the world as vibrant artifact. . . . (pp. 151-52)

On such dear subjects Phillips seldom falters. His quirky point of view combines the serious and the silly, anguish and doubt, the tender and mundane. In *Running on Empty*, cloudy dreamscapes eventually give way to moments of inexplicable, if sometimes naively stated, clarity. He sees things and manages to reproportion them into aspects of meaningful life. (p. 152)

> G. E. Murray, "Two Poets," in The Hudson Review (copyright © 1982 by The Hudson Review, Inc.; reprinted by permission), Vol. XXXV, No. 1, Spring, 1982, pp. 151-53.*

DAVID SANDERS

My single dominant first reaction to Robert Phillips' *Running on Empty* . . . was "I like this man." The personality behind the voice makes the impression here, not the poet's way of dealing with ideas or exploring new techniques.

In fact, I would not be surprised to hear certain critics rather unfairly refer to this book as *Running on Emptyheaded* for its lack of intellectual content. Phillips' is the kind of poetry which may be at once the delight of readers and the bane of critics. Intellectual it does not attempt to be. More important to Phillips are his personal reactions to such things as the seasons, flowers, small animals, childhood, aging, and numerous contemporaries. He is fascinated by oddities and incongruities; he is enamored of the trivial. As the opening poem of his volume indicates, he thinks of a poem as a little leaf offered to mother by child heedless of her mother's (and by implication the critics') reaction. So he writes little poems about flatworms, beans . . . , his old cat named Pekoe, Miss Crustacean (the winner of the annual Crisfield, Md., Hard Crab Derby). Each poem conveys its meaning easily without needing explication. Each is touched by a tone of light whimsy, neither fully cynical nor truly humorous.

Phillips' most noteworthy techniques rely on whimsy. His favorite poetic device has to be the pun—he supplies dozens. . . . Phillips also likes paradox, split words, and sound-play. That he can bring a smile to the reader's lips using these well-worn devices in such an unsubtle way must say something about the success of their combination in the poem.

The stock employment of such devices may seem uncharacteristic of a 45-year-old man who has published three collections of poetry . . . , in addition to anthologies, criticism, reviews, and works of fiction; who is Associate Editor of *Paris Review*, has spent years in advertising, and is the recipient of awards from Puchcart, Yaddo Corporation, and the State of New York. But his main strength lies elsewhere—in his ability to ingratiate his personality through his poems. This is a man you have to like and with whom a part of you identifies: he has been cheated out of his space in the family plot, gets his kicks seeing how far the car will go on empty, feels unsafe around fur coats, has lived in a monotonous flatland like that in eastern North Carolina, worries about every larger-than-normal pimple. . . . His willingness to reveal his fears and vulnerabilities keeps his cuteness from being cloying. The reader comes away from the book knowing more about the Phillips' persona than he does many of his own acquaintances—from his being an unhappy, shy child (one of four) who loved magic and whose father beat him . . . to his marrying, living in Germany, having two children, and divorcing. Auden, who "understood so much of this world," was wrong, he believes, about our lack of concern for Icarus falling; people care. So he invites his readers to tarry and share in the human condition.

There is something lonely and pained at the heart of these poems . . . , but Phillips by philosophic bent and poetic design manages to cast a ray of humor in the darkest of settings. Even a poem on the accidental blinding of a friend from childhood is topped off with a whimsical "Let there be light." Phillips' combination of sadness, humor, and fancifulness is thoroughly reminiscent of Robert Herrick, the seventeenth century poet of *carpe diem* fame (unfortunately without Herrick's wonderful scatological excesses). Perhaps Phillips' most attractive quality is that he, like Herrick, doesn't pretend to be more than he is. (pp. 38-40)

> David Sanders, "Divers Crossroads of Earth and Mind," in Tar River Poetry (copyright © 1983 by East Carolina University), Vol. 22, No. 2, Spring, 1983, pp. 38-46.*

Katha Pollitt
1949-

American poet and critic.

Pollitt's first collection of poetry, *Antarctic Traveller* (1982), received the National Book Critics Circle Award. She is a "visual" poet, one whose lyric and free verse poems are composed of vivid and compelling images. She is also, in the words of one critic, a poet "of essences." Pollitt's verse explores the relationship of life to art and portrays moments of transformation in the lives of her characters. Pollitt has an ability to effectively convey diverse settings: some of her poems recreate stark urban landscapes, others celebrate places and things of great pastoral beauty.

Critics acclaim Pollitt's clearmindedness and economy of style. She is said to communicate thoughts and feelings with a poise, grace, and directness not commonly found in the work of poets of her age. Her development as a poet, critics feel, will be both of interest and importance.

ROBERTA BERKE

In Katha Pollitt's work there is a continual counterpoint between romance and disillusionment, between transcendence and skepticism. In the fourth of "Five Poems on Japanese Paintings," **"Moon and Flowering Plum,"** she reveals this dilemma.... (p. 171)

This is not Katha Pollitt's quandary alone but the mood of many poets as the eighties begin: they're not as optimistic as in the romantic sixties ("ya can do anything if your head is right"), but neither are they as cynical and detached as were the academic poets of the fifties. Katha Pollitt's reversals are not always from the sublime to the ridiculous: sometimes, as in **"Nettles,"** she shows that the unattractive nettle can still nourish butterfly caterpillars. She carries this contrast between idealized and everyday reality further in another poem about a Japanese painting, **"A Screen Depicting the Fifty-Four Episodes of the Tale of Genji on a Background of Gold Leaf."** As he appears on the screen, Genji is a prince, a legendary lover, who progresses triumphantly from woman to woman in his glittering court. Real life, however, is different:

© 1984 Thomas Victor

A tea merchant of Kyoto commissioned this screen for
    his wife.
At night as they lay on their uncomfortable mats
she stared at it and sighed.
He, however, concluded
that the difference between his own life and Prince Genji's
was that he lacked an artist
to blot discreetly all but fifty-four moments
with a dazzle of golden clouds.

It is the artist who screens off uncomfortable reality from his golden fiction, and Pollitt is well aware both of the artist's deceit and of his or her genius. Pollitt herself is a miniaturist who captures elusive subjects with great delicacy and concision.

In contrast to some recent poems, Katha Pollitt's poems are unabashedly intelligent and often metaphysical. She majored in philosophy at Radcliffe and is intrigued by complexities and paradoxes, "the monochromatic / landscape of an ambiguous season: / hills neither gray nor green, / sky neither blue nor gray." Although her poems are cerebral, they are firmly grounded in specific subjects, such as potatoes and onions. Indeed the number of her pastoral poems is surprising, since she grew up in Brooklyn and lives in Manhattan working as a freelance writer. Her lines are graceful and quieter than those of many of her contemporaries, as if she were striving for a Japanese painter's "reticence, calm, clarity of mind." So well-constructed are her poems that it is difficult to quote only a few lines without quoting the entire poem.

Pollitt combines her awareness of contraries and her intelligence with a vivid imagination that impels her best work toward that "Supreme Fiction" which was Wallace Stevens's goal. In the short space of **"A Turkish Story"** she creates not only the setting of a distant culture, but also the contrasting emotions of those who live there.... (pp. 171-73)

In the future, hopefully, Katha Pollitt will succumb to her imagination even more, like the cultivated flowers she writes about in **"Wild Escapes,"** which seed themselves over the wall, where "a darker seed / drove on a starker, more essential white." (p. 173)

Roberta Berke, "'We Say, Today. This Day': New Poets," in her Bounds Out of Bounds: A Compass for Recent American and British Poetry *(copyright © 1981 by Roberta Berke; reprinted by permission of Oxford University Press, Inc.), Oxford University Press, New York, 1981, pp. 150-76.*

BRUCE BENNETT

Like Wallace Stevens, whom she sometimes echoes, Katha Pollitt contrasts life and art. Process, especially aging and decay, haunts her; "longing" is practically the first word in **"Antarctic Traveller."** Yet art, for all its transcendence, is not a solution; it may even be illusion. . . .

Moreover, life, for all its mundaneness, provides opportunity for celebration. Thus, **"Five Poems From Japanese Paintings"** are followed by five **"Vegetable Poems."** . . .

Whatever the reservations about art in them, these poems are beautiful objects. Stately, dignified, slightly aloof, they exult in polished diction and elegant surface. They delineate nuance. . . .

Most important, they are a culmination; they are that country the poet-archeologist, evoked in **"Archaeology,"** has devoted a lifetime to constructing. . . . (p. 17)

Bruce Bennett, "The Work of Four Poets," in The New York Times Book Review *(copyright © 1982 by The New York Times Company; reprinted by permission), March 14, 1982, pp. 12, 16-17.*

RICHARD HOWARD

Not since Robert Hass's first book have I encountered a debut so seductive as Katha Pollitt's [*Antarctic Traveller*], poems so determined to be beguiled by the world that we cannot peer between them to the sour scrawling self that writes, an inky revenge. What Pollitt wants, what she creates, is the alternative life, unconditioned, eagerly espousing all that is unknown. . . . But she is shrewd, too, and passionately disabused by moments, intervals of chagrin "when suddenly 'choices' / ceased to mean 'infinite possibilities' / and became instead 'deciding what to do without' . . ." So there is a wariness about these ecstasies, so readily bestowed, so rashly withdrawn. It can be anything—any delight of physical recognition is enough to set Pollitt off, to light her up like an electric field, wherein any correspondence takes her into other minds, other worlds, back country, desertion of the usual. . . .

Stevens is here . . . , and Elizabeth Bishop, at "Seal Rock" . . . , and even Strand and Simic serve her turn. (p. 343)

What gives the distinction, the special twist of idiom we call style, is the perception of delight in the world entertained on its own terms, as in **"Five Poems from Japanese Paintings."** Readers who came upon these in *The New Yorker* were the first to know what is dramatized for us all here, that the decorative is the decisive moment, indulged only to be twitched away from us with a teasing laugh, tragic—as Oscar Wilde says pleasure is tragic, has more tragic possibilities than happiness. . . . As [**"Moon and Flowering Plum"** reveals], there is just enough decorum in the decor to keep the poems together. The frogs are real and the gardens too; what is imaginary is the will, "the ego glinting at the heart of things," as she calls it in the title poem. Startling, in this rapturous first book, to find the poet willing to entrust herself so readily and so richly to the appearances, the worldly arrangements "not understanding what it was she'd seen / but trusting it, a mystery that would keep." Miranda's account, unmonitored by Prospero or Ferdinand. (pp. 343-44)

Richard Howard, "Poetry Unyoked," in The Nation *(copyright 1982 The Nation magazine, The Nation Associates, Inc.), Vol. 234, No. 11, March 20, 1982, pp. 342-45.*

JAY PARINI

At her best, Katha Pollitt writes vividly in her own idiom of cultivated poise and reflection. . . . I admire [the simplicity of **"Blue Window,"** the opening poem of *Antarctic Traveller*], which comes from steadiness of mind, and the deft use of the impersonal "you" to distance the author from her "self"— the illusion of which is, after all, the subject of the poem.

Not all her poems are so good. She makes heavy use of the "you," which has become an irritating mannerism passed around the various M.F.A. programs like the German measles. She has also picked up the most common, and boring, mannerism of all: beginning poems with a vaguely mysterious indefinite nominative pronoun. . . . Nevertheless, poets should be judged by their successes, and Pollitt accumulates enough of these in *Antarctic Traveller* to make its publication an occasion. In **"Composition in Black and White,"** for instance, she speaks engagingly in the lyric "I." . . . Pollitt depends rather too much on familiar metaphors. . . . Yet she can be quite original. . . .

By turns wistful, sorrowing, or tough, Pollitt recreates the affections of her masters—Lowell and Bishop, especially—in poems of domesticity (**"Vegetable Poems"**), confession (**"Turning Thirty"**), and close natural description (**"Sea Graces"**). I prefer her descriptive vein, in which she seizes and holds her often urban landscapes in order to repossess them imaginatively, as in **"Night Blooming Flowers."** . . . Her best poems are what D. H. Lawrence called "acts of attention," meticulous and bright, and there is every reason to look forward to her next book. (p. 38)

Jay Parini, "A New Generation of Poets," in The New Republic *(reprinted by permission of The New Republic; © 1982 The New Republic, Inc.), Vol. 186, No. 15, April 14, 1982, pp. 37-9.*

PETER STITT

[That the] objective mode of lyric poetry has not died is demonstrated convincingly by [*Antarctic Traveller*]. . . . (p. 439)

[Pollitt's] primary technique is the image (not the metaphor, not the symbol) gently used to suggest meaning. Her best poems have a spare delicacy reflective of a rigorous sense of decorum—everything that wouldn't contribute directly to the primary point of the poem, one feels, has been excised from it. A good example is **"Failure,"** which describes a person settling into a new room in the poorer part of town. . . .

Pollitt is primarily a visual poet; the entire second part of this book is accurately subtitled **"Five Poems from Japanese Paintings."** And part III begins with another set of five sketches collectively called **"Vegetable Poems."** . . . It may be that poems [like **"Tomato"**] demand greater complexity of form, given the absence of complex meaning; there are times when just a sequence of simple images is not enough. In **"Thinking of the World as Idea,"** Pollitt again tries to use a visual element to carry meaning. . . . The idea or theme here is simply too much for the method; the image of the ferry boat (anachronistic and confused) is unequal to its intellectual cargo. Pollitt's best poems show verbal skill and a good eye for imagery, but they challenge neither the mind nor the emotions. (p. 440)

> Peter Stitt, "The Objective Mode in Contemporary Lyric Poetry," in The Georgia Review (copyright, 1982, by the University of Georgia), Vol. XXXVI, No. 2, Summer, 1982, pp. 438-48.*

DANA GIOIA

Katha Pollitt has an extraordinarily good ear. Her lines are almost always exactly right, and there is a sense of finish and finality to her work one rarely sees nowadays in poets young or old—the diction clean and precise, the rhythms clear and effective. One can hear all of these virtues in **"Blue Window,"** the opening poem of her *Antarctic Traveller*. (p. 644)

Pollitt is also refreshing in that she is not afraid to write beautifully. She has a fine sensibility and does not try to hide it under a hard or aggressive mask. She is original enough to shun the predictable clichés of "beautiful" description and carefully avoids sentimentality when presenting emotions. As a result she can create bewitchingly effective scenes when she chooses, as in **"Moon and Flowering Plum"** from her **"Five Poems from Japanese Paintings."** . . . (p. 645)

One needn't remember Marianne Moore's definition of poetry as "imaginary gardens with real toads in them" to know that **"Moon and Flowering Plum"** is the genuine article. This poem, however, not only illustrates Pollitt's style but also her aesthetic. For her, poetry is primarily the recreation and examination of those small epiphanies which suddenly illuminate one's life. . . . *Du musst dein Leben ändern,* the silent imperative of Rilke's archaic torso of Apollo, "You must change your life," seems echoed throughout Pollitt's work. But it is only in . . . [her] imagined poems, however, that she can translate illumination into action. In those poems which seem to be more directly based on her personal experience she can feel the unexpected moments of enlightenment but they find no release, only a transitory heightening of awareness for the world around her. The epiphany diminishes into an *aperçu,* and her poems become brilliantly fluid renditions of a passive imagist aesthetic. At these times one suspects that Pollitt undersells her conspicuous talent by not pursuing the perceptions further—wherever they may lead.

This latent strain of aestheticism dictates the nature of Pollitt's successes. She is at her enviable best in those poems which she can treat as closed systems—musical compositions sealed off from the world which she can perfect measure by measure, bringing every word or image into resolution with some underlying harmony. Her striking poem, **"Of the Scythians,"** for instance, literally approaches the conditions of music and could profitably be analyzed in strictly musical terms independent of its meaning. Likewise her five beautiful poems on Japanese paintings present Pollitt's skillful transposition from one closed system to another. . . . When Pollitt's poems do not work, it is usually because some foreign elements intruded which she could not control. In **"Failure"** a wonderful beginning is undermined by a few lines in the second half which destroy the tone. But if this perfectionism and quest for control limits Pollitt's range, it is also the source of her strength. She is an exceptionally accomplished young poet who has mastered her craft. She is a poet to watch. . . . (pp. 645-46)

> Dana Gioia, in a review of "Antarctic Traveller," in The Hudson Review (copyright © 1983 by The Hudson Review, Inc.; reprinted by permission), Vol. XXV, No. 4, Winter, 1982-83, pp. 644-46.

RICHARD TILLINGHAST

Antarctic Traveller by Katha Pollitt possesses a winning quality that Robert Fitzgerald has aptly characterized as "serious charm." . . . Pollitt's posture [in the first stanza of the opening poem, **"Blue Window"**] and elsewhere in this fine collection is romantic, full of emotion and delicate sensibility, yet convincing.

By convincing I partially mean that here I am able to accept the presumption behind the poet's use of what Jonathan Holden (in *The Rhetoric of the Contemporary Lyric*) calls the "blurred you": a use of the second-person pronoun midway in meaning between the ordinary second-person form of address, the French pronoun *on,* and a suggestion that the speaker is talking about herself or himself. The blurred you is essentially a device of rhetorical persuasion, because the writer is asking the reader to blend his experience with a description of hers. . . . [In **"Blue Window"**] I gladly assent to being included in the poem. In other poems by Pollitt and by other poets, I bridle. When I read "You wanted to see / your life as a rope of diamonds: permanent, flashing," I simply respond No, I never wanted to see my life as a rope of diamonds. Hence the limitations of this rhetorical device. Its current vogue surely has something to do with the abuse of the pronoun *I* by confessional poets such as Anne Sexton.

The overuse of this device is a minor flaw in this rope of diamonds. Pollitt manages equally well in free and in formal verse. She also writes charmingly of New York City, with a sense of excitement about being a young person on the rise in life, in a way that used to be a lot more common; but that excitement has faded as we have become disillusioned with the city, and as it has become uglier and more dangerous. (pp. 476-77)

> Richard Tillinghast, "Ten New Poets," in The Sewanee Review (reprinted by permission of the editor; © 1983 by The University of the South), Vol. XCI, No. 3, Summer, 1983, pp. 473-82.*

Manuel Puig
1932-

Argentinian novelist.

Puig is one of the leaders of the recent Latin American literary development known as the Boom. Like the work of his contemporaries José Donoso, Carlos Fuentes, Severo Sarduy, Mario Vargas Llosa, and Gabriel García Márquez, Puig's fiction is stimulated by the political and social tensions in Latin America. These writers are linked by their experimentation with literary form, their concern with unconscious and irrational forces in human life, and their pioneering portrayal of the lower classes of Latin America. Puig has received special critical attention for his innovative narrative style. By interlocking his characters' dialogues and internal monologues with fragments of newspaper and magazine articles, conversations from soap operas, Hollywood movies, trivial novels, and lyrics from mundane popular songs, Puig suggests that individuals supplant spontaneous emotion and reaction with their hackneyed counterparts portrayed in popular art forms. His plots, which resemble those of serials and detective stories, rely heavily on sentimentality and cliché, but most critics agree that the demand on the reader to assimilate a montage of information and the irony created by the gaps between the characters' real and imagined lives give Puig's work the status of serious literature.

In his initial works, *La traicion de Rita Hayworth* (1968; *Betrayed by Rita Hayworth*) and *Boquitas pintadas* (1969; *Heartbreak Tango*), Puig depicts the poor inhabitants of the Argentinian pampas who fantasize about the glamorous lives of movie and dance idols rather than confronting their own emotionally weak relationships. The financially successful Leo and Gladys of his third and more complex work, *The Buenos Aires Affair* (1973), are ostensibly closer to a glorified media image, yet in imitating stereotypical male and female roles they are unable to achieve spiritual satisfaction, and the romantic ideal is revealed to be even more of an illusion than in his earlier novels. Somewhat similar are the imprisoned characters in *El beso de la mujer arana* (1976; *The Kiss of the Spider Woman*), who recount movie plots as a means of avoiding boredom and loneliness. However, since the sharing of the plots engenders communication and understanding between these ideologically opposed cellmates, popular art is here shown to be a positive, unifying force.

Because Puig's characters allow the world of attractive images to replace a dull reality, critics find implicit in all his works the theme of subjective truth. *Maldicion eterna a quien lea estas paginas* (1982; *Eternal Curse on the Reader of These Pages*) treats this issue directly. Told almost entirely through dialogue, the shifting factual information and confused time frames of the novel create a tense aura of uncertainty. Although the clarification of facts with the presentation at the novel's end of letters and documents is criticized as anticlimactic, Puig's continued experimentation with technique is praised.

Puig's treatment of such complex issues as politics, sexual power, homosexuality, and violence is seen by some critics as superficial, but is generally regarded as insightful and moving. These issues have aroused enough controversy in Argentina to cause Puig's books to be banned, and Puig has left his country to live in the United States.

© Jerry Bauer

(See also *CLC*, Vols. 3, 5, 10; *Contemporary Authors*, Vols. 45-48; and *Contemporary Authors New Revision Series*, Vol. 2.)

RONALD DE FEO

The appearance of Manuel Puig's new novel, *The Buenos Aires Affair,* is especial cause for celebration, not only because the book makes for fascinating reading, but also because it demonstrates that its already highly accomplished author continues to take chances and to grow as an artist.

In his two previous novels, ***Betrayed by Rita Hayworth*** and ***Heartbreak Tango,*** Puig explored, in a somewhat campy, comic manner, the dreams and obsessions of a host of provincial Argentine characters whose speech and lives often seemed to have been influenced by popular movies of the Thirties and Forties. His characters recalled, in a way, Nathanael West's dreaming, unfulfilled, hopeless Hollywood souls, but Puig's people were much more down-to-earth, and Puig, unlike the unsparing West, treated them affectionately, even at times sentimentally. For the most part, he allowed them to speak for themselves, recording their conversations, interior monologues, letters, and diary entries.

In ***The Buenos Aires Affair,*** Puig again concentrates on the blandness of middle-class Argentine existence, but this time he focuses on cosmopolitan rather than on provincial types. The nostalgia for the past is absent here; the characters live in a harsh, alienating contemporary world where dreams are quickly trampled upon. Though brief excerpts from various old movie tear-jerkers and melodramas serve as epigraphs for each chapter, the protagonists, the discontented sculptress Gladys D'Onofrio and her lover, the haunted, seriously disturbed art critic Leo Druscovich, aren't the movie dreamers that previous Puig people have been. Pop romance can hardly exist in their world. In fact, the contrived, inflated romance reflected in the little movie scenes contrasts sharply with the blunt and colorless reality Gladys and Leo know so well. (pp. 1194-95)

Though Puig's approach is very objective, almost clinical, and though in this novel we are kept at a distance from his characters, the people still manage to hold us and affect us. Occasionally this book reads like a parody of a French *nouveau roman* or a German investigative work, but Puig's humanity and wit still shine through.

The facts in "the case" of Gladys and Leo carry us on, and every so often we are reminded of the other violence, both criminal and political, that is occurring in their world. We expect the facts eventually to point to a significant conclusion, a meaning of some sort, but they don't, really. Both lives, in very different ways, lead nowhere. That, Puig seems to be saying, is the real crime in the novel. In a long, brilliantly rendered scene, Gladys finds herself in the apartment of a very typical, happily married young mother. It is ironic that the lonely and troubled Gladys should be left here, in an atmosphere she has rarely known in her own life, and it is equally ironic that this warm, happy place should prove so horribly bland.

The Buenos Aires Affair is neither as purely entertaining as Puig's previous novels nor as accessible to the general reader. Sometimes the author's stylistic methods are a shade too inventive, and we are not always convinced that they are necessary. But the book is more intense, serious, and disturbing than the other novels, and it is a welcome departure for this searching, gifted writer. (p. 1195)

Ronald De Feo, "Laying Out the Evidence," in National Review (© National Review, Inc., 1976; 150 East 35th St., New York, NY 10016; reprinted with permission), Vol. XXVII, No. 41, October 29, 1976, pp. 1194-95.

RONALD CHRIST

In his three novels, *Betrayed by Rita Hayworth, Heartbreak Tango* and *The Buenos Aires Affair,* Puig has shown an incrementing skill, range of perception and control of varying emotions.... If the promise of these books is kept by Puig's next novel, and if he continues to be productive, Puig will show himself not only as a good writer getting better but as a major author.

Puig's novels exhibit their growth in a double sense. First of all, the maturation is evident in the subject matter. His books have progressed from a central focus on the formation of a latently homosexual child (*Rita Hayworth*), to the adolescence and early adulthood of a pampas Don Giovanni, to the adult catastrophe of a couple who emerge from the background established in the preceding books to inherit the fearful, sadomasochistic side of romantic love carried to its extreme in a contemporary society. Puig says that the novels are displaced "investigations" or "researches" into his own past, so the novels also offer a version of the growth of a writer's mind.

More remarkable still, they embody the development of his formal accomplishment because Puig is never content to tell things as they were—the criterion for much of Latin American fiction for so many years—but always aims at rigorous subordination of the data from his memory to an esthetic code....
Weakly apparent in *Rita Hayworth,* the imposition of Puig's esthetic will comes to the fore in *Heartbreak Tango* and *The Buenos Aires Affair,* where he invents an exterior skeleton for the soft flesh of his narrative, in the former by shaping the narrative as a magazine or radio serial with a climax in every chapter; in the latter, according to the more rigid requirements of the detective story *à la* Hitchcock. This is not to say that Puig writes serials or detective stories. Far from it. Rather, he uses those forms as molds to cast his corny, bathetic material in a form displaying a witty, ironic attitude toward that material. The result is that Puig has solved a major problem of all autobiographical subject matter: how to present it as the experience of another so that both writer and reader can have a perspective wider than the egotistical.

The Buenos Aires Affair simultaneously imposes this strict form on the narrative and undermines the form in order to present a doubly ironic picture. Early in his career, Puig began eliminating much that we ordinarily expect in a novel. Not with the tight-lipped intention of Hemingway, who divided writers into the takers-out and the putters-in, but for the expressive voice of the absent, the silent. For example, in *Rita Hayworth*'s fourth chapter, there is a striking, extended monologue printed as a telephone conversation where we hear only one voice. A brilliant development of Strindberg's device in *The Stronger* as well as a borrowing from the conventions of radio and the movies, the monologue is similarly most expressive in its blanks. Carrying this device to the point of vision in *The Buenos Aires Affair,* Puig writes a detective story that has, in the conventional sense, neither detective nor corpse and whose climax is an anti-climax. Of course there are police investigators in the novel and a murder victim, but they are not central. This further displacement results in a book that conforms to the elegant esthetic of the doughnut: it is what it is precisely for what has been left out, and for the way it has been left out. (pp. 412-13)

Puig presents us with the case of two people who have achieved careers in the urban world only dreamed of by the provincial, unsuccessful characters in his previous work. Gladys and Leopoldo, however, lead lives which take no substance from their success because both, like those other characters, are still victims of the myth of the weak woman and the strong man.

The complex metaphor of the essential void in these lives—typified by Gladys's missing eye—surrounded by an inappropriate abundance—emblematized in Leopoldo's oversize penis—is everywhere evident in the novel. The neutral, often didactic narrator is attentive to all the things the characters *don't* see, the people they *don't* meet, the newspapers they read *without* paying attention. Puig's constant attention to what is lacking or unnoticed recalls films where the camera often shows more of a scene than the actors could be aware of and thus fits in nicely with the epigraphs for his chapters, all of which are taken from sentimental movies and supply the everpresent but invisible romantic ethos of the book.

No mere parody then, these epigraphs show Puig's further opening up to the social conditioning of his characters. Similarly, there is an off-center attention to the political envelope of the fiction notably in a serving woman's grief over the ousting of Peron. In this respect, Puig has taken major strides toward integrating the individual motivation of his characters with the political and economic tensions informing them. What was implicit social criticism in the previous novels here comes to be explicit in the telling of the story but without any recourse to *engagé* or agit-prop prose.

The balance between presenting a unified picture of the world these people live in (and create) and a mere talking about the world is preserved through the reserve of the narrator's voice, which is mannered in its neutrality. For example, when Gladys is masturbating, we get the substance of her fantasy in the text proper—in a diction appropriate to her mind—and we get the gestures in matter-of-fact footnotes. . . . The full irony of this technique transcends its humorous effect to include the nature of narrative itself.

In such a poised narrative, the diction is, if not everything, then the thing on which everything else depends. The distinction between the narrator's and the characters' voices must be preserved with exquisite delicacy if the book is not to become heavy-handed or confused. For us, the problem is all the more interesting because what we read is a collaboration between Puig and his translator, Susanne Jill Levine, a combination that Puig refers to as an "experimental authorship" that brought off *Rita Hayworth* and *Heartbreak Tango* with grace and wit. But in *The Buenos Aires Affair,* where the risks are more subtle, the English text frequently goes flat. (pp. 413-14)

>Ronald Christ, in a review of "The Buenos Aires Affair," in Commonweal (copyright © 1977 Commonweal Publishing Co., Inc.; reprinted by permission of Commonweal Publishing Co., Inc.), Vol. CIV, No. 13, June 24, 1977, pp. 412-14.

ROBERT COOVER

If [the] insistent use of unedited dialogue tends to make ["**Kiss of the Spider Woman**"] read a bit like a radio script . . . , it is Mr. Puig's fascination with old movies that largely provides its substance and ultimately defines its plot, its shape. What we hear are the voices of two suffering men, alone and often in the dark, but what we see are panther women and zombies, exquisite Nazi heroines and radical racing drivers, exotic settings (a lot of finely perceived detail, especially about fashion) and fabulous metamorphoses, all the iconographic imagery, magic and romance of the movies.

Not that there's anything very innovative about the way this is accomplished. The homosexual is simply an old movie buff who entertains his young, somewhat unimaginative cellmate—especially after lights-out, as a kind of lullaby, and later to get the student's mind off his agony when the police are weakening him with food poisoning—with the plots of fanciful and sentimental old films, seducing him, as it were, with story.

There are five of these films, plus a sixth remembered but (during a lovers' quarrel) not told, and they all touch on the novel's themes of repression and liberation, beauty and (or versus) goodness, strange or unusual women, somnambulism and heroism, love, fear, change and a desire for "Hollywood endings," prefiguring many elements of the novel's plot (the homosexual becomes a kind of tragic film heroine, for example, the student one of the living dead). (p. 15)

But other than these film synopses, there's not much here. A few ambiguous hints about the two men's lives outside of prison. . . , the footnote lecture on homosexuality and a few radical slogans . . . , and a laborious seduction in which the seducer is in effect seduced.

The translation by Thomas Colchie, while adequate, seems stiff and hasty, needing a relaxed revision. It fails to capture Mr. Puig's easy colloquial flow, and the voices of the two very different protagonists are not distinguished. (pp. 15, 31)

>Robert Coover, "Old, New, Borrowed, Blue," in The New York Times Book Review (copyright © 1979 by The New York Times Company; reprinted by permission), April 22, 1979, pp. 15, 31.

CLARA CLAIBORNE PARK

Puig is a master of narrative craftsmanship, but [*Kiss of the Spider Woman*] is no mere concoction. Every subtlety of character and situation—and there are many, as the relationship between the two men develops and changes—is conveyed by dialogue, and conveyed fully. The economy of means mirrors the cell's constriction. There is no exposition at all; the police documents we are given in the middle of the book only confirm what we have inferred already. Yet except for Molina's stories we have heard only the brief, inarticulate exchanges of those who in other circumstances would not have become friends.

The dialogue must work hard. Puig has not only characters to develop, but a story to tell. It is not for nothing that Molina's films are about love and betrayal. The delicate changes that take place in both men as the days pass and they learn from each other lead to a climax; they are ratified by as violent an event as concludes any of Molina's stories. In a paradoxical rebuke to all us snobs of culture, the tawdry, sentimental art is seen to have nourished not only the life of the imagination, but real affection, and, at length, heroic self-sacrifice. The relationship which has made Valentin more of a woman has made Molina more of a man, and we recognize both changes as gain. (pp. 575-77)

>Clara Claiborne Park, in a review of "Kiss of the Spider Woman," in The Hudson Review (copyright © 1979 by The Hudson Review, Inc.; reprinted by permission), Vol. XXXII, No. 4, Winter, 1979-80, pp. 575-77.

MICHAEL WOOD

[Recent Latin American fiction is] constantly in search of new stances, angles, tones, twists, and modes of narrative, but it asks these discoveries to lead it back to a shared world, not off into a region of pure play or dream.

The work of Manuel Puig is a good example, since in his four novels he evokes or simulates, among other things, soap operas, school essays, sentimental letters, police reports, the novels of Robbe-Grillet, newspaper items, film scripts, tapes of telephone conversations, the later chapters of *Ulysses,* an application form for an art competition, a psychiatrist's notes, a report on an autopsy, and the testimony a certain character would have given if he were asked—to say nothing of the "principal imaginary actions" of another character. All this may sound like a set of gags, or even like naturalism gone wild, yet the point is neither wit nor verisimilitude but formal variety, which is itself a fidelity to the shifting relations between experience and its representations.

Movies play a large part in all of Puig's novels. . . . (p. 43)

The movies, for Puig, are true not to the thin dreams of glamour we usually associate with them, but to the emptiness and solitude the dreams are supposed to disguise. [In *The Buenos Aires Affair*] Gladys acquires a certain amount of sexual experience in America—enough to allow her to masturbate in the footnotes while the flow of her thoughts is recorded on the rest of the page—but none of her men will stay with her, and Puig suggests that her upbringing and her favorite movies, listed above, have helped to make things difficult for her. She wants good financial prospects *and* romantic love *and* a satisfactory physical relation. Finally she breaks down in New York, and is taken home by her mother.

Gladys, like everyone else in her world, is lulled and charmed by movies, songs, poems, and political promises which hide their truths even as they tell them. The point, of course, is not only that such consolations are part of the problem, but that they are the only consolations going. The poor comforts of culture begin to resemble those of religion: we cannot live with them, and have a hard time without them.

Kiss of the Spider Woman is a slightly more cheerful work concentrating on hidden truths rather than acts of hiding.... The occasional footnotes to the narrative carry on a rather elementary symposium on homosexuality.... But then they also offer a splendid pastiche of a press-book for a Nazi movie showing the conversion of a slinky French singer to love for the Führer and disgust for the degradations her cherished France is suffering at the hands of the villainous Jews. The result of this activity at the foot of the page, in conjunction with what goes on higher up, is not a simple equation between sexual and political repressions, but an intimation of the complicated lure of prejudice, whether political or sexual.

Puig is especially interested in the notion that many homosexuals of both sexes, until recently, imitated, in reverse, the defects of heterosexuality. Luis Molina, the homosexual in the novel, wants to be treated not only as a woman, but as grotesque old stereotype of a woman, submissive, anxious to please, lovable, flirtatious, kind, and the rest. Clearly, a politics of sexuality is involved here, freedoms are to be fought for. But how are they related to other freedoms? Puig poses the question by making Arregui a political prisoner; but he pursues it by having Molina turn out to be an informer, planted in Arregui's cell by the warden of the prison. Then Molina falls for Arregui, doesn't want to leave the prison even when he is paroled, and is shot while trying to get a message to Arregui's friends. He dies for the cause, in a fashion, but Arregui himself sees Molina's death differently: "he let himself be killed because that way he could die like some heroine in a movie."

It is a measure of what has happened to Arregui in the course of the novel that this thought is a compliment, not a dismissal. Throughout the book, illustrating every theme, giving structure to the whole narrative, Molina has been telling Arregui the plots of movies he remembers, expertly evoking actors and actresses, sets and lighting.... Arregui understands, as Molina doesn't, that these films deal in sexual terror, that they conjure up a universe ruled by the mutual fear of the sexes, but blurred by images of doting sacrifice and incursions of the supernatural.

But then Arregui has to learn to enjoy the movies as Molina does. He comes to see the rags of humanity hanging to these stilted tales, something his stern Marxism could not have taught him. Even Nazi junk, as Arregui correctly identifies the film about the French singer, corresponds to genuine desire as well as to the instructions of a vicious propaganda. When Arregui at last tries to invent a movie himself and makes Molina the star—"You're the spider woman, that traps men in her web"—he is revoking the implications of the first movie Molina recounted, the one about the panther woman. And from the kiss that Arregui and Molina then exchange, if from nowhere else, terror has been banished. This begins to sound like one of Molina's movies, but Puig manages to end his novel before sentimentality, coming round again, knocks over the precarious truth he has rescued from the eager arms of romance. (pp. 43-4)

>   Michael Wood, "The Claims of Mischief," in The New York Review of Books (*reprinted with permission from* The New York Review of Books; *copyright © 1980 Nyrev, Inc.), Vol. XXVI, Nos. 21 & 22, January 24, 1980, pp. 43-7.*

ELIZABETH B. MARSHALL

[*Pubis Angelical*] is a collage of the human, subhuman, and superhuman, through which characters pass without achieving full dimension. During the course of the book Puig manages to set before the reader all the dubious enrichments of the age: computers, robots, ESP, occult prophecies, assassinations, terrorism, espionage, drugs, prostitution, movie-making, munitions-making, and feminism versus the myth of male superiority. His people are a mixed lot, and most of them come to rather unpleasant ends.

Two interrelated stories could be said to represent exposition and resolution. One focuses on a mad scientist and his offspring, the other on an Argentine expatriate divorcée confined to a cancer ward in Mexico City. The cancer patient, Ana, survives her operation and is humbled by her cure to the point where she wishes to resume her relationship with her mother and daughter, on a more loving basis....

Despite its unearthly flummery, blatant vulgarity, and a concluding burst of sentimentality, **Publis Angelical** is worthy of respect as an honest confrontation between the writer and his circumstances, but compared with Puig's truly innovative first novel, **Betrayed by Rita Hayworth,** it seems woefully derivative. Puig mirrors a lamentable period in history whose weaknesses he gives regrettable prominence. His final message takes form as an outcry against violence.

>   Elizabeth B. Marshall, "A World Where Man Is Prey," in Américas (*reprinted by permission from* Américas, *a magazine published by the Organization of American States in English, Spanish, and Portuguese*), Vol. 32, No. 5, May, 1980, p. 48.

RAYMOND L. WILLIAMS

Readers aware of *La traición de Rita Hayworth* and *El beso de la mujer araña* will find similar sexual and political considerations in [*Pubis angelical*]. Mexico City is the setting; the female Argentine protagonist Ana, who is in a hospital there, suffers the psychological and political repercussions of having experienced most of her life in contemporary Argentina. The substance of the novel consists of her discussions with two other characters concerning this past, her diary and her private fantasies.

Puig has employed his now standard formal construction: sixteen chapters divided into two equal parts. The development of Ana's series of conversations is chronological, providing a general structural unity. Most chapters, however, contain brief narratives seemingly unrelated to her immediate circumstance; they take place in a variety of times and places: elegant and nostalgic Vienna, Mexico of the 1930s and 40s, a plastic futuristic twenty-first century. The novel opens with one of these fantasy sections; they appear regularly throughout it, and three chapters are entirely such narratives. They can be read as Ana's projections of worlds she has been unable to find in her past, or perhaps as ideal escapes from the harsh reality that surrounds her. The traditional sex roles played out in these sections exemplify ideals articulated by Ana in her dialogue and diary. The activization of the reader in the process of integrating these narratives is one of the novel's successful and attractive features.

As in *El beso de la mujer graña,* Puig deals with the sexuality of politics and the politics of sex, and the relations between the two. Ana's discussions with a political exile and her personal relationship with him are one evident exposition of this matter. Despite her ostensible desire to be apolitical, all aspects of her life are influenced, if not determined, by the political realities of her life in both Argentina and Mexico. Although more a continuation than an innovation in Puig's writing, *Publis angelical* is perhaps his best novel.

> Raymond L. Williams, in a review of "Pubis angelical," in World Literature Today (copyright 1981 by the University of Oklahoma Press), Vol. 55, No. 1, Winter, 1981, p. 70.

CHARLES CHAMPLIN

Technically, ["**Eternal Curse on the Reader of These Pages**"] is a tour de force. Except for a handful of letters at the end to sew up the plot, it consists entirely of dialogue between its only two speaking characters.

They are Juan Jose Ramirez, an old and ailing Latin-American political leader in exile in Manhattan, and Lawrence John, a cynical young New York graduate student (a sort of careerist grad student) who has been hired to push Ramirez on wheelchair outings in the city.

The speech is presented in what is, I guess, the international style:

—How are you?

—I am fine.

Occasionally one of them does not respond. . . .

Occasionally they exchange silences. . . .

It is maddening because they sound rather alike and unless they call each other by name from time to time you find yourself counting back to see whose voice is saying what.

A further difficulty is that Ramirez speculates constantly about Larry's life, inventing parents, a past, a wife, situations that may exist in whole, part or, probably, not at all. Ramirez also likes to be evasive and contradictory about his own life, speaking in panic of enemies who still pursue him. (He apparently escaped a bomb blast that killed his wife and family in their home country.)

Beyond his problems of paranoia, Ramirez appears to have lost his memory for the meaning of words and indeed of the realities they represent, although this is probably only a device to make Larry talk more. Ramirez in his unidentified pain and his querulous fears is nothing if not fluent. . . .

It is true that Ramirez, who is in his 70s, seems the carrier of an international intellectual idealism, however spent or demoralized he is, and is both fascinated and horrified by the cynicism and opportunism he finds in Larry.

For the reader, it is remarkable (a grudging admission) how much information can be conveyed only through printed speech, without a stage direction or any descriptions of time, place, weather or interior states beyond what the men care to say to each other.

But the reader, struggling through 230 pages that are very slow going indeed, may well ask if form and substance are ideally matched: whether a technical exercise, however clever, was the best way to get at this study of conflicting cultures and the ambiguities in the relationship.

It is not that nothing happens, or that the relationship does not change; Ramirez has health failing fast, is ever more dependent on Larry, and Larry is more dependent on the old man, if only as a way around the present impasse in his own life.

Still, there is a kind of sterility in the cleverness, a sense of game-playing that denies or at least undermines the emotional weight Puig does seem to have felt in the relationship and particularly in the forlorn old man.

I found myself thinking of one and another of the Latin-American novelists (Gabriel Marquez most notably) in their fable-making richness but also of Georges Simenon in his non-Maigret psychological novels, hardly less spare in style than Puig but in the end going far deeper into character.

As an experiment, "**Eternal Curse on the Reader of these Pages**," even stingier with illuminating detail than a scenario, is interesting but not, I feel, interesting enough, and frustrating.

The title, I'm not even going to think about.

> Charles Champlin, "Novel Voices, Nowhere Rooms," in Los Angeles Times Book Review (copyright, 1982, Los Angeles Times; reprinted by permission), June 20, 1982, p. 3.

WILLIAM HERRICK

Manuel Puig is a Marxist and the United States is, after all, the major stronghold of world capitalism, its inhabitants stupefied and/or morally decayed, the rich by too much and the poor by too little; everyone is a victim in some sense. Still, Puig is also a Freudian. He knows—as the protagonist [of *Eternal Curse on the Reader of These Pages*], a 74-year-old Argentine expatriate named Juan José Ramirez, tells his interlocutor, 36-year-old Larry John—that "There's a particular danger involved in Marxism, for young people. Aside from the moral coherence and the voice it gives to so many feelings and sentiments. It's such a total critique of society, and the mission it sets itself so overshadows other concerns that young people who embrace Marxism often find within it their means to deny the necessity for any further exploration of their own psyche."

The conflict between Marx's theory of alienation and Freud's incessant probing of our psyche motivates and gives life to this brilliant *tour de force*. . . .

The narrative is told entirely in dialogue between the two men. Not until the very end, the dénouement, is the story carried by a series of letters. Ramirez, an invalid with a fragile heart and high blood pressure, lives in a home for the aged and the sick. Several times a week he is wheeled about Greenwich Village by Larry John, born Giovanagelo, an impoverished, unemployed history professor. (p. 19)

The two men probe each other's past like duelists—parrying, lunging, seeking out the vulnerable center. (To make a point? To delve into a mystery that will make life a little easier once it is revealed?) Their battle is at times heart-rending, at other times frustrating. They catch each other in lies, in harsh truths; they are guileful, they are ferociously candid, they are soon enmeshed in fantasies, conspiring in their invention.

All this lays bare the struggles in their lives, in the lives of their families—husband and wife, mother and son, father and son, worker and employer. Fiction or truth? We don't know. It doesn't matter. Fiction exposes truth—and truth fabricates a curtain to hide behind. Ramirez and Larry are metaphorically father and son. Sometimes they are interchangeable. We have to backtrack on the unfolding dialogue to remind ourselves who is speaking. It is confusing—deliberately so. Again, it doesn't matter. Our inner and external lives are being scrutinized, suddenly spotlighted, just as suddenly enveloped in darkness.

Larry tells us about his sometimes violent father—whose brutality explodes spasmodically from a silent passivity—about his loving mother, and about his Oedipal desires, soon translated into various (not many) amorous adventures. Sex is withheld, given, thwarted, passionate. Ramirez, the aged amnesiac, now becomes a voyeur, constantly pushing at Larry to reveal more and more explicitly his sexual desires for his mother and his intimacies in his sundry affairs with young women.

From Ramirez we discover little. He was a political dissident in Argentina, led a general strike, was imprisoned, tortured, finally released and permitted to leave his country under the auspices of the human rights organization that subsidizes him. He had a wife and a son, both of whom were murdered by the Argentine authorities—or have they disappeared, or did they never exist? He has a rich brother, he says, who gave money for his own release from prison. He ignored his wife and child in the past because of his commitment to the fight for trade union independence—or is that also fantasy? The old man's fantasy or Larry's? (pp. 19-20)

By the time we reach the concluding exchange of letters, we realize that we have been through a series of psychoanalytic forays (I hesitate to use the word sessions) between the old man and the younger one—that each is responsible for his own trauma, his own neuroses, yet also that both are casualties of history.

Whether one accepts Freud's Oedipal theory or Marx's theory of alienation is of course up to the reader. Puig is an artist, though, and his portrait of two men grappling with their suffering is exceedingly moving and brilliantly done. Strangely, the more space I put between the book and myself, the more tragic I find it. It sticks to the mind. Like one cursed, I cannot find peace, cannot escape from its pain. (p. 20)

> William Herrick, "Alienated within and without," in The New Leader (© 1982 by the American Labor Conference on International Affairs, Inc.), Vol. LXV, No. 13, June 28, 1982, pp. 19-20.

ALLEN JOSEPHS

As in Puig's previous experiments, [in **"Eternal Curse on the Reader of These Pages"**] things are not as simple as they first seem. The only way Mr. Ramirez can recover a sense of his own life is to plumb Larry's past and his fantasies. What Mr. Ramirez is really seeking is some key to his own subconscious. At first the self-serving Larry is reluctant to indulge his often exasperating patient except when humoring him appears to be expedient. Gradually, though, Larry becomes caught up in Mr. Ramirez's psychological game, and the two of them begin exploring a mélange of fantasy, sex, guilt and dreams, all the therapeutic stuff of everyday post-Freudian reality.

These strange conversations between an old man who has suppressed his memory and a young man who obeys only the law of self-gratification are sometimes funny, but in general Puig has chosen to investigate the serious side of their relationship. In **"Kiss of the Spider Woman,"** an aging homosexual and a political activist, cellmates in a Buenos Aires prison, carry on a dialogue in which the recounting of old movies creates a bond of invention between them. Similarly in **"Eternal Curse on the Reader of These Pages,"** mutual fantasies, and in several episodes mutual dreams, begin to create a tentative subconscious bridge between these unlikely psychic castaways. And when Larry starts decoding Mr. Ramirez's prison journal, which opens with the title phrase, so that we (and they) begin piecing together some of Mr. Ramirez's secrets as well, their relationship becomes even more bizarre. (p. 9)

"Eternal Curse on the Reader of These Pages" has the unusual effect of a morbid radio play that you only listen to with your mind's ear. Puig spins a fascinating web of words, capturing the reader's attention with his uncanny ability to develop plot and character solely through dialogue. Overhearing these pathetic but sometimes riveting conversations turns one into a kind of blind voyeur listening to the twin soliloquies of two characters bent on symbiotic disintegration.

Puig's characteristic virtuosity has not failed him in this English-language experiment, which devotees of psychological fiction will no doubt appreciate; but the novel has a pared-down and displaced quality. Its reliance on psychology and its occasionally ferocious dialogue are more reminiscent of the theater of the absurd than of Puig's passionately Latin early novels. It is surely one of the vagaries of history that a noted Argentine novelist should give us a book set in New York precisely when we would like to know more about affairs in his own country. That irony is, of course, no fault of Puig, who, like so many Latin American writers, must work in exile. Seen in that context, Larry and Mr. Ramirez are dispossessed souls whose very rootlessness reveals, perhaps inadvertently, the sad truth about life in Argentina. (p. 12)

> Allen Josephs, "Negative Symbiosis," in The New York Times Book Review (copyright © 1982 by The New York Times Company; reprinted by permission), July 4, 1982, pp. 9, 12.

GILBERT SORRENTINO

Eternal Curse on the Reader of These Pages is, like Manuel Puig's *Kiss of the Spider Woman*, developed almost entirely as a splintered colloquy between two unlikely companions. It is also, like the earlier novel, a structural failure, and for much the same reason: the conclusion, disastrously, comments on and "explains" an otherwise richly ambivalent and mysterious text. It is as if Puig lost his nerve and decided, for whatever reason, to serve that famous "general audience," an audience that is already grandly served by what Blanchot has called "the nonliterary book," the book that has, "before it is read by anyone . . . been read by everyone." Puig's natural readership, the readers of literary books, could comfortably fit into Madison Square Garden, but in this book he seems to be reaching out to snare the same people who think of, say, John Gardner as pretty complex. It's too bad, because Puig *has* something, most obviously a wonderful sense that the essential elements of life, life's serious "things," are precisely the elements of soap opera, sit-coms, and B-movies. Both *Kiss of the Spider Woman* and this new novel *almost* set these two planes one atop the other, so that they look like one plane. But both novels fail, and the failure is one of form; or, to be clearer, the novels fail because Puig holds his content to be somehow more than just materials, to be a set of ideas.

This novel's two characters are by turns (and turns!) dull, narrow, crude, envious, misinformed, and politically boring and ingenuous—and at times, disingenuous. Larry, the younger man, an American, even speaks of revolutionary "struggle"— here in the land of flabby unions, pots, and looms: the author's ironic sense of dopiness here is brilliant.

We are almost immediately aware that Puig is aware of the fact that he is writing an ambiguous comedy in which the deepest feelings about sex, love, family, marriage, patriotism, loneliness, and on and on, are proved to be also the "deepest feelings" of those who turn these things into the corrupt products of the market and national politics, those products that keep us dozing in the face of their familiar, pleasant, and undisturbing selves. All the dialogue is vapid, its "themes" but a weird reflection of things long ago debased. Puig has set himself a tough problem: to criticize cultural enervation in the same language that has helped bring that enervation to pass. So we read on. (pp. 1-2)

[Larry and Mr. Ramirez] have convoluted talks in the most hopelessly bad dialogue this side of comic books, the pulp magazines of my youth, and B-movies, in which one or the other of them plays the roles of victim, hero, betrayer, etc. It is delicious. Larry's life is taken over selectively by Mr. Ramirez, and, in part, the converse is true. Whole swatches of dialogue are repeated verbatim in different contexts, serving to change the "meaning" of the words—words that are already almost completely drained of meaning, so that language becomes a shadow of a shadow. It is very interesting work.

Even more interesting is that one slowly comes to suspect that Larry may not exist at all, but is an invention of Mr. Ramirez's, someone onto whom he can project his own misery and sadness, through whose talk Ramirez's ruined life can become that of another man, a fantasy American to take the heat of Ramirez's bad conscience. On the other hand, Mr. Ramirez may be Larry's invention: we have no true evidence for anything, since the text, which can be, as in all fiction, verified only by itself, gives us none. Even the places in the book are carefully restricted to names, words—nothing is described.

But then: The last eight pages of the novel are made up of a series of letters that serve to "explain" it, to tell us that Larry is indeed real (and worse, that he is the lout we were not sure he was); that Ramirez is noble and good, though mentally ill (we were not sure of any of these things either); and that the book has a "subject" after all, something like "appearances are deceiving." The effect is catastrophic, and the textual strength, the *risk* of the novel, disintegrates. The complex deployment of what Barthes calls the "middle voice" (in this case one should perhaps say "voices"), through which Puig permitted himself no authorial intrusion, is subverted at the very end of the novel, damaging its wholeness irremediably. This is terribly depressing, at least to me, since it is clear that Puig is a writer of luminous talents. (p. 2)

Gilbert Sorrentino, "South American Fantasy, Obsession, and Soap Opera: 'Eternal Curse on the Reader of These Pages'," in Book World—The Washington Post *(© 1982, The Washington Post), August 1, 1982, pp. 1-2.*

James (Amos) Purdy
1923-

American novelist, short story writer, poet, and dramatist.

Purdy is a gifted author whose subject is human estrangement and whose style blends the real and the surreal. Basic to Purdy's bleak vision of contemporary life is his belief that American culture is destructive to the individual and to family relationships. Postwar urban society as represented by New York City is Purdy's example of all that is wrong with a culture that places material gain above spiritual enrichment. Purdy's negative outlook affects his characterizations. His protagonists are desperate, alienated, and unhappy; his antagonists are often cruel, greedy, and manipulative.

Purdy's early works, including *63: Dream Palace* (1957) and *Malcolm* (1959), focus on the exploitation of innocents by adults who attempt to buy love rather than earn it. The principal character in these stories is the adolescent male searching for love in his life but who, knowing nothing of its nature, can neither give nor receive it. He is often orphaned or abandoned, and has known no normal relationships. He is thus at the mercy of deceivers and victimizers. The physically or emotionally absent father is also a central character, and the mother is frequently depicted as immature, narcissistic, or sadistic. Most of Purdy's characters are married for the wrong reasons, and children are born into loveless homes. All his characters are removed in some way from the mainstream of society. Purdy believes that in their "otherness" they typify the alienation of contemporary life.

As with many of his works, *Cabot Wright Begins* (1964) is a statement on the failures of society. Here Purdy proposes that technical advancement and affluence have not eliminated the need to connect with other human beings. He believes that those who cannot communicate often resort to criminal or other unacceptable behavior. *Eustace Chisholm and the Works* (1967) and *Narrow Rooms* (1978) concern homosexuality. In these stories Purdy attempts to portray the lonely and isolated lives of homosexuals as being merely other forms of empty love. *The Nephew* (1960) and *In a Shallow Grave* (1976) are the closest of Purdy's works to an acknowledgment that life may yet hold some kind of hope and meaning. The characters suffer the tortures of love and become more spiritually aware. Communication leads to a discovery of self and an appreciation of others. Critics think that Purdy developed this more positive view of life in *Jeremy's Vision* (1970), one volume of a planned trilogy entitled *Sleepers in Moon-Crowned Valleys*. In this book he turns his attention towards the midwestern American past, where life is based on the founding morals and virtues of this country. This is in contrast to the decline of those same values in present-day society.

Purdy's strengths lie in his use of language, especially the patterns and dialects of his native Ohio, skillfully employed in dialogues between characters. He has been compared to many great writers, yet attempts to classify him have resulted in such diverse labels as naturalist, realist, black humorist, and satirist. However, he has been accused of writing from bitterness, petulance, and an inability to grow beyond the deprivations and disappointments of his early life.

© Kelly Wise

(See also *CLC*, Vols. 2, 4, 10; *Contemporary Authors*, Vols. 33-36, rev. ed.; and *Dictionary of Literary Biography*, Vol. 2.)

HERBERT GOLD

James Purdy began to make his reputation with some stories first successfully published in England, where the praise for him had that overripe odor that characterizes a peculiar subdepartment of British enthusiasm for minor American writers.... But the stories themselves, when they finally appeared in this country in the collection *Color of Darkness,* emanated a hard harsh radiance....

Purdy, like Kafka, tells dreams which turn out to be stories and at the same time retain their fretful, oppressive dream quality. With all their subdividing and subtlety of mood and observation, wit and document, they are very close to the origins of literature in dreamlife. Purdy seems to cross over into the dream world and carry back his booty into consciousness.

The Nephew, like *Malcolm,* Purdy's earlier novel, has a farcical surface, but his picture of life in "Rainbow Center" ... is pervaded beneath the comic accuracy of speech by a deep despair and boredom. The plot concerns the unravelling of the life, or rather, its meaning, of the nephew, Cliff, the "boy missing in Korea," and of his connections with his ancient aunt and uncle and the other people of a stagnant Midwestern town.

But the plot is a mere excuse for a curious parody of a Norman Rockwell illustration or an Edgar Lee Masters poem. Talk of custard pies . . . is succeeded by talk of the great issue of life in the American Midwest now that the dust bowl and farm price supports seem to have receded in the American imagination. . . . Knitted together of interlocked anecdotes and archetypical figures, there are the foreign professor, formerly concupiscent, now senile, the real estate dealer, the unhappy school teacher skinnified by lost love, and a host of grumbling old folks; there is secret alcoholism, Christian Science, and class resentment; there is young Cliff, hiding in the wings, with his life both banal and mysterious. An accident occurs while hanging up "Old Glory" on Decoration Day. Hands are pressed together in silent understanding. Vladimir Nabokov seems to have been translating Edgar Lee Masters from the original Swedish into his native American.

Although the manifest action has to do with digging up the real life of Cliff, the dialogue, observation, and even more, the dreamy horror of the prose provide the actual subject. Like Nabokov in *Lolita,* Purdy is pervaded by a hopeless, witty, intelligent nostalgia. He *expects,* but does not dare define just what it is he expects from life. He only finds that "we, none of us, know anybody or know one another."

This familiar insight is not enough, and the sudden revelation of "love" is not enough, and the flash of oddball satire is not really enough, either. Of talent and prose pressure James Purdy has enough. Now he needs to find a compelling action for all this devilled-away feeling.

Herbert Gold, "Dame Edith Was Right," in The New Republic *(reprinted by permission of* The New Republic; © *1960 The New Republic, Inc.), Vol. 143, No. 15, October 3, 1960, p. 17.*

MARTIN TUCKER

A problem novel in which the problem is never solved, Purdy's latest book [**The Nephew**] is in many ways a departure from the fey and fantastic humor for which he has become celebrated. If he mystified people and won many fans by **Malcolm,** he may gain some dissenters with this relatively simple novel of compassion and small-town humors. The nephew, unlike Malcolm, has few adventures, and the only one he has which is of dramatic consequence remains shrouded in Purdy's dialectical ambivalence.

In an unfair but accurate summary, the central problem is whether the nephew is a homosexual. His old-maid aunt and widowed uncle, who live together in a big, stuffed house, have taken care of the nephew from the time he enters the army. When they are informed that Cliff is missing in action, their world collapses. In an attempt to keep Cliff's presence alive, the aunt decides to write a memorial about him. But in trying to write down on paper the things that made up Cliff, she discovers she knows almost nothing about the only person she has loved.

In her search for the knowledge of Cliff's identity, the aunt begins to learn compassion through the discovery of many damning facts, or suggestions which might be facts. . . . The old-maid aunt, who used to be a bossy grade school teacher, is, in Purdy's eyes, discovering life.

Such a theme—self-discovery through understanding of friend or lover—is as old and valid as the first novel written. Where Purdy fails this time is in employing only sincerity and an extraordinary writing style in which every sentence seems the result of centuries of meditation. People also are needed for a novel. The plain fact is that the central character, Aunt Alma, is just not very interesting in the manner Purdy presents her. If she were a better woman, she would gain sympathy; if she were worse, she might exact a vulgar and lusty fascination. Remaining a narrow-minded, naive, lonely old woman, she is only pitiable. It is not so much that Aunt Alma is simple; the trouble is that Purdy simplifies her. She is closer to a type than an individual; her distance and mystery come not from complexity but from a lack of specific motivations. . . .

Vagueness, in all of Purdy's short stories and novels, is at the center of experience, and Purdy's literary tactics are always to skirt the center, where pain and nothingness lie in wait. Instead, Purdy tells his story through the sidelines, just as most of his characters live their lives, or the most important moments in their lives, when they are reflecting on what others are doing. In this novel, the nephew is never seen, and the reader finds out little about him. Is he a homosexual? Purdy doesn't say. Did he love his aunt or hate her? Purdy doesn't say. But the novel is concerned with these questions, and the structure of the novel is as much a wandering journey as *Ulysses.* Only, unlike Joyce's book, there is no Daedalus, and Bloom is old Aunt Alma.

Also, what Purdy lacks is a conclusion, a Molly Bloom episode, some way of gathering up the shells picked up on the trip. He tries for this in a final scene between Alma and the richest woman in town—two characters separated by personality who are reconciled by the desire to understand the need for and the course of love. This scene is probably the most emotionally engaging in the book, but it is not a statement or a conclusion. It is a further investigation, and the center, the issue of the nephew's identity, remains nebulous.

Yet this technique—the search for understanding—worked wonders in **Malcolm** where the hero was looking for his father, or fathers. . . . In that book, however, Purdy exploited his fey sense of fantastic humor to make the improbable and absurd reveal perceptions about more mundane matters. In **The Nephew,** he tries for compassion and high seriousness with such earnestness that he verges on sentimentality one moment and on vagueness the next. As a matter of fact, his generous attempt to portray the commonplaces of life (including homosexuality) may earn him the dubious distinction of making the commonplace seem odd, and the queer, ordinary.

Martin Tucker, "All Ambivalent," in Commonweal *(copyright © 1960 Commonweal Publishing Co., Inc.; reprinted by permission of Commonweal Publishing Co., Inc.), Vol. LXXIII, No. 4, October 21, 1960, p. 99.*

WINFIELD TOWNLEY SCOTT

There is a double edge to the quite remarkable talent of James Purdy. The simplest view of this may be taken by looking at the two novels he has so far published. . . . Yet the simple view of Purdy is not easily maintained, for he is more likely to blend what I think we may call the realistic and the surrealistic visions. He is rather complex and special. This was evident in the arresting short stories, eventually collected as **Color of Darkness,** which brought him such high praise several years ago; we have it again in [*Children Is All,* a] new collection of nine stories and two brief plays. (p. 25)

The shorter of the two [plays], "**Cracks,**" presents a very old lady, her nurse-companion, and a small child. It consists largely of the musings of the old lady on life and death. Then when we have the old lady solo in darkness a Figure appears and they converse also of life and death. But the Figure, close-wrapped and half-shadowed in darkness, identifies himself as the Creator and says the world has come to an end. Nevertheless the vision concludes—or the old lady wakens from a dream?—and we are back with nurse, child, morning and an affirmation of ever-continuing creation.

"**Children Is All,**" the longer play, is one of those "waiting for" situations which we have had at least from "Lefty" to "Godot." Here the regional atmospherics compare to *The Nephew.* We await with a middle-aged, middle-class woman the return after fifteen years in the Pen of her son who, perhaps unfairly, had been jailed for stealing bank funds. We are asked to believe (1) that in all those years she has never visited Billy and (2) that when he arrives in the night, wounded, and quickly dies in her arms she does not recognize him—though her house companion and a neighboring child know perfectly well it is Billy. Thus the play moves into symbols of human dissociation, of human estrangement or nonrecognition, and thus we have another dimension.

That James Purdy can—almost always—blend these strata of real and surreal effectively there is no doubt. It is this that gives so much of his writing an air of strangeness. For one thing, he never assumes the role of omniscient author: his characters enact the episode; and we are teased—not told—into some knowledge beyond what they know. . . . Purdy, line for line, is a master of living speech, but with utterly real speech he more often than not creates a bizarre situation.

Almost any story in *Children Is All* illustrates what I mean. A girl has an undefined but tension-building encounter with a swimming instructor. Two young men are rooming together, and one asserts terrifying, utter power over the other. A naked and aging school teacher, after being raped wanders across town to the home of a former student, now a pathetic teacher of music who has just lost his mother, and he takes her into his house with trepidation but finally, impotently, beside him into his bed. A man, also aging, wants to possess his daughter-in-law.

And so on. Always the vigor of creative talk (it is not surprising, from the stories, that Purdy is attracted to plays) building, to put it mildly, the special drama.

All this would add up really to tricks only, if it were not conceived in such penetrating compassion. In the second play the child reads from a book, "I felt the zephyrs of death blowing from the cracks in my surroundings." Such zephyrs blow chilly through these stories. The basic themes are loneliness and separateness. Where lives touch, or almost touch, there is terror. The author, as I say, is never on stage. But we know him by what attracts him and by the brooding wonder with which he probes it. So Purdy continues to be the exciting writer he has been from the very first. (pp. 25-6)

Winfield Townley Scott, "The Zephyrs of Death," in The New Republic (reprinted by permission of The New Republic; © 1962 The New Republic, Inc.), Vol. 147, No. 20, November 17, 1962, pp. 25-6.

IHAB HASSAN

In the last five years James Purdy has published two novels, "**Malcolm**" and "**The Nephew,**" and a collection of stories, "**Color of Darkness.**" These very nearly established him as one of the most important American writers to appear since the war. The judgment, which in the mind of crusty critics was rendered suspect by a certain voguishness that attended his sudden appearance on the scene, is now confirmed by the present collection ["**Children Is All**"].

Like Salinger, Purdy is a writer of love, "pure and complicated." But there all analogies end. For Purdy is a true original within the area where, neither windswept nor entirely claustral, his sensibility dwells. The area, as in so many works of Kafka, is sharply defined in its details and weirdly ambiguous in outline. His focus in human relations is the paradox of love and loneliness in our age, illuminated time and again by terror and humor. This is why Purdy's language, precise, simple, and spare as it seems, often glows in a surreal haze. The originality of Purdy may finally rest in his profound insight that language and feeling, in our day, have severed their connections. Dominated by dialogue, both incremental and repetitive (Purdy seldom describes, never editorializes), his work presents characters who can never say what they are most desperate to communicate. The casual, chatty surface of each narrative covers a cauldron of unappeased desires.

The present volume contains ten stories and two short plays. These fall generally into two categories: gossipy pieces, full of feminine intuition and sharp observation, and surrealistic parables written in an entirely credible manner. I confess to my preference for the latter genre, which seems to strike deeply at the origins of our perplexity. The best is "**Daddy Wolf,**" about a man, whose wife has deserted him, waiting to be connected with a stranger over the phone. . . . Also among the best: "**The Lesson,**" about a teen-age girl speaking to a swimming instructor about nothing and everything; "**Encore,**" about a mother and her son; "**Goodnight Sweetheart,**" about a gentle school-teacher raped at the age of sixty; and "**Sermon,**" a masterpiece about everything and nothing, in which the preacher says to his audience: "I have talked here tonight in the hope you would not hear, because if you didn't you might not so thoroughly disgust yourselves, and therefore me." Indeed, that message may be what the fine and unholy art of Purdy disguises from his readers. . . .

The uncanny technical skill of Purdy brings his material to terrible life because it is backed by an authentic vision of love, anguish, and incongruity. When the vision falters, the work becomes fussy, nasty, or narrow. But this so seldom occurs that we can rejoice again in the possession of this new work by one of America's best writers.

Ihab Hassan, "Of Anguish and Incongruity," in Saturday Review (© 1962 Saturday Review Magazine Co.; reprinted by permission), Vol. XLV, No. 46, November 17, 1962, p. 29.

RICHARD HORCHLER

[In] *Children Is All,* Purdy displays once more the talents, quirks and compulsions that have, in the few short years he has been publishing, moved his readers to almost equal extravagance of praise and exasperation.

What is best in this volume is unmistakably Purdy. Perhaps the same is true of what is worst in it, but that is at least a less obvious conclusion. "**Daddy Wolf,**" for instance, the first story in the collection, is a totally successful *tour de force*—a semihysterical monologue by a Negro whose wife and child have abandoned him and their rat-infested tenement flat. Dialogue has always been a Purdy strength, and in **"Daddy Wolf"** the speech is exactly right. It is funny, sad, realistic and poetic, conveying a story that slides imperceptibly from the closely observed commonplace to the hallucinatory and symbolic.

In Purdy's stories, of course, the hallucinatory and symbolic *are* the commonplace, or at least they make themselves felt in the sense of doom and strangeness, of impending revelation, which is attached in Purdy's world to every human situation. So it is in **"Encore,"** another of the more successful stories in the book. As in most of Purdy's narratives, nothing much happens in **"Encore,"** except that a despairing mother eats some "jello" and her grown son plays his harmonica. But in the "ordinary," albeit pain-filled, mother-son encounter, the meaninglessness of their conversation, the *non sequiturs,* the arrested gestures, the silences—everything, no matter how inconsequential, is charged with an almost unbearable weight of *significance.* Invariably in Purdy's stories the nature of that significance remains mysterious, but always it is threatening and tragic.

Such stories have been praised, and rightfully, for their "insights," their perceptions of the madness or horror or agony that lurks beneath the surface of all our lives. This is Purdy's great gift—to be able to hear the thunderclap of significance in the merest word, to see the presences which are felt by all, but denied by those who live in the "clear light of every day." Often enough, though, Purdy's visions are so obscure, so tremulous and fragmentary that they signify nothing except that they are visions. Often the strangeness of his imaged world makes it impossible to believe in, impossible to be moved by anything so remote, so blurred and shapeless.

These are standard objections to fiction like this, and they are real. Most basically, an epiphany must show forth *something;* Purdy's revelations tend to be as incoherent as the life he depicts. But the most surprising observation to be made about *Children Is All* is that its stories are perhaps worse, not better, when their author seems to have heeded the suggestions implicit in this kind of criticism. That is, the stories which are least vague and least incredible, which turn from the world of irrationality and dream in favor of tangible reality and "normal people in normal situations," are at least as bad in their way as the most unfortunate of Purdy's grotesqueries. Without the surrealistic twist, the hint of hysteria which gives point to the other stories, Purdy's more "realistic" narratives—**"Mrs. Benson,"** for instance, which is a labyrinthine conversation between two women in a tea shop—succeed only in being at the same time trivial and pretentious. (pp. 393, 395)

The plays in this collection—**"Children Is All"** and, especially, **"Cracks"**—prove only that Purdy is no playwright. They are static, clumsy, self-consciously oracular, as the stories seldom are, as well as murky and diffuse, as the stories not so seldom are. That is not to deny, of course, that they have flashes of poignance, memorable images and gems of language.

But as a volume, *Children Is All* is weak and faltering. Some of the stories in it are masterful; most of them are impressive. Even at their best, however, they add up, for me, to little more than a sudden wrench of pain, a shudder, a glimpse of the moving darkness. Brilliant and rare as these displays may be, I am afraid there is little in them to engage us very long. (p. 395)

Richard Horchler, "Impending Revelations," in *Commonweal* (copyright © 1963 Commonweal Publishing Co., Inc.; reprinted by permission of Commonweal Publishing Co., Inc.), Vol. LXXVII, No. 15, January 4, 1963, pp. 393, 395.

HENRY CHUPACK

In the three decades since the end of World War II—a period when American affluence and technological impersonality grew to astronomical heights and appeared to many Americans to be the be-all and end-all of human existence—Purdy dared to tell them the truth: behind the facade of great material wealth lay a vast spiritual wasteland of loveless lives and hellish marriages; from such barren marriages came children who, as a rule, were treated cruelly by their parents or by other adults; rape and homosexuality were engaged in by those who, denied love in their own lives, sought it in antisocial actions; and most ironic of all, the quest for wealth and the possession of it did not result in happiness. (p. 126)

In fiction delineating such malaises, Purdy has resorted to shock devices, but certainly not for the sake of mere shock; rather, he has employed them, we think, to awaken his readers from the torpor into which many of them have fallen, lulled as they have been by the innumerable material satisfactions and pleasures easily available and by the ennui and boredom that accompany a surfeit of pleasures. If shock is effected by subject matter in which one homosexual is shown severing the genitals of another homosexual, or in which rape is as casually committed as the smoking of a cigarette, shock is not Purdy's purpose: he is intent upon showing us that these actions are simply the ugly results that occur in a society in which, despite a cornucopia of wealth and mountains of material goods, very little love is expressed by Americans for one another. Indeed, a person in Purdy's fiction does not so much die of love as he does from a lack or betrayal of this life-giving and life-animating quality; therefore, the lack of love in the lives of those so affected leads them to seek love in what would be considered antisocial actions.

Still, Purdy's forte is not his choice of subject matter and its shock effect, for all of us know that shocks resident in subject matter soon cease to be effective; it is rather in the shock of style that Purdy excels. For, in narrating his tales of blighted lives, he manages to portray scenes in which the extremely abnormal is linked to the so-called normal ways that have a degree of verisimilitude not previously thought of; in which unexpected aspects of character surface when least expected; in which the lovelessness of modern marriages is set forth in a minimum of dialogue but with such vividness and horror that the reader knows instinctively that he has never before experienced these terrors in print.

This shock of style never ceases to be effective and startling and applies to practically all of his fiction, with *63: Dream Palace,* **"Color of Darkness,"** and **"Daddy Wolf"** as immediate examples. This power is seen in the use of such technical devices as jostling contradictions, the mixing of the banal and the wise, and the juxtaposition of the grotesque and the normal—all in absolutely new ways. In fact, Purdy's major strength lies in his ability to take so-called repellent subject matter and so work with it that he turns it into a true work of art.... All this is accomplished in a style that is not only unique in its simplicity, but which is also characterized by clarity, force and beauty—the three chief qualities of good writing. In addition to Purdy's ability to write unforgettable parables of the way Americans have lived in the past two decades, Purdy's loveless view of life is rich in humor of various kinds—zany, "black," surreal or quietly reflective. We all remember how the drunken porter's humor in Shakespeare's *Macbeth* serves as a contrast to Duncan's murder; as a result, this swinish humor helps set this ghastly deed in stark relief. In Purdy's case, his humor does not serve as a contrast to the dour actions that he usually narrates; instead, his humor is warp and woof of his style; and an example of the humor of the quietly reflective kind illustrates this point. In **"Plan Now To Attend,"** the reader notes that Fred, who normally drinks heavily to bury his sense of emptiness, is shown listening very carefully and soberly to his friend Ezra Hightower, the converted atheist, who is muttering in his drunken stupor that Fred will ultimately be saved. Such a scene reveals Purdy's ability to intertwine aspects of humor with the elements of tragedy but to keep uppermost the tragic sense.

Purdy's talent is a many sided one; for, in addition to being an instinctive portrayer of the dark underside of human nature, he is also an excellent regionalist, as is seen in **The Nephew** and a crack fantasist, as in **Malcolm**. . . . **Eustace Chisholm and The Works** reveals his strength as a Realist who depicts the tragic world of homosexuality. But Purdy has, in fact, created many worlds; and each with its own discernible and distinct features. Each of these worlds is populated with a host of characters: orphans, thoughtless and cruel parents, failed artists, budding writers and actors, spinsters, grand ladies, teachers and professors, widowers and widows, financiers, homosexuals, and invalids—all of whom form a veritable gallery of typical figures of and for our time. (pp. 126-28)

However much Purdy has been on target in depicting the malaises of contemporary society, and however faithfully and stylistically he delineates these problems, his portrait of contemporary America nonetheless lacks balance in certain respects. First, not a single character in his fiction can be said to be a truly happy person, in the sense that the character's potentialities have to a degree been fulfilled. Second, no Jews are presented in his works—a glaring omission in an age when these people have played such important roles in American life and have also filled the pages of so many contemporary novelists. Third, there is a scarcity of good people in his fiction—people who would perform an unselfish act merely for the pleasure such an act would provide. Fourth—and here Purdy can be scored—there are many marriages that are really a union of hearts, and there are the children of these marriages who grow up to become loving parents themselves. Fifth, in his humor, an area where Purdy excels, never once do we find a play of wit; this omission is probably due to the lack of intellectuals in his works.

Because of his consistently dour vision, we would say that Purdy has an affinity with the Naturalists. But where such earlier writers as Theodore Dreiser, James Farrell, and John Dos Passos fashioned characters who were shown as scrambling for survival and buffeted by an indifferent universe, Purdy's characters, on the other hand, are not so circumstanced. Rather, their emotional deficiencies—their inability to give or receive love in any meaningful way—subjects them to our careful scrutiny and finally arouses our compassion for their disability. (pp. 128-29)

In conclusion, we could forecast Purdy's future as a writer to be a promising one; however, he is at a crucial point in his career. Should he continue to write about orphans, failed and miserable marriages, rape, and homosexuality, readers will soon conclude that Purdy has run out of material for his fiction. On the other hand, should he grow and use new and different source material for his fiction, readers will eagerly seek to see what a fundamentally honest craftsman has fashioned that is fresh. . . . Should he, however, not develop new themes but adhere to his former ones, he will still remain important as an author who wrote about Americans and the way they were in the 1950s and the 1960s. With his many characters who suffer so deeply and lamentably because of a lack or betrayal of love, Purdy has fashioned several works of art out of the dark interiors of the human soul. With his satirical treatment of many aspects of American life, he has portrayed a way of life, which apparently is materially successful, but at rock bottom is characterized in many instances by spiritual bankruptcy and has caused us many of our current problems.

All told, Purdy is a writer of marvelous power, who has made us think deeply and seriously about the human condition, which he regards woefully. . . . In short, Purdy's power and style are two positive virtues in a period when many writers simply lack one or another of these ingredients in their works. (pp. 129-30)

> *Henry Chupack, in his* James Purdy *(copyright © 1975 by Twayne Publishers; reprinted with the permission of Twayne Publishers, a Division of G. K. Hall & Co., Boston), Twayne, 1975, 144 p.*

STEPHEN D. ADAMS

[Purdy's] originality and extraordinary talents cannot be neatly inventoried and . . . to portray him as the author of an eccentric body of fiction, as a part of some movement or fashionable literary trend, or as a novelist who essentially mocks the capacities of art, is to deny the complexities of his individual voice. His own description of his work as an exploration of the American soul conveyed in a style based on the rhythms and accents of American speech runs contrary to such categories and is a claim that merits examination.

The author's distinctive formal and philosophic preoccupations need to be seen in a broader, more tentative perspective. Although it has an urgent bearing upon the present day, there is a timeless quality to his work. The avowed concern for the world of the spirit and its relation to language evokes the native tradition of Melville and Hawthorne with their passion for metaphysics and command of symbolist techniques. As might be expected, there is also an evident fascination with the hellenic age when speculations on human destiny were at an intense pitch. Purdy sees modern America as the enemy of the soul and would subvert the suffocating patterns its culture imposes upon the individual self by his own exemplary fictions. Thus his families and miniature societies are simultaneously the vehicles for an exploration of the national psyche. At another level he re-tells, in his own special idiom, the Christian story of how a being charged with life's spiritual or divine possibilities is denied kinship in the larger world. It is misleading, then, to insist on measuring the characters in such a drama by the criteria of social realism or by those of a strict psychological verisimilitude. They are projections of the inner life, put forward as hypotheses about existence and endowed with the reality of the author's innermost convictions. Regarded in this light, art is accorded the highest functions—it keeps alive the memory of those ingredients that have been excluded from everyday existences and Purdy might more profitably be seen as the 'memorialist' of the qualities that have gone missing from his native culture. He is the self-styled prophet and chronicler of its omissions.

The philosophic basis of his work might loosely be described as that of the Christian existentialist. The difficulty of the individual's quest for an authentic selfhood in a society whose commercial forces, in particular, are pitted in opposition, is imaged in that pervasive feeling of being alone in an alien, absurd world. Characters are mysteriously orphaned and cut off from the source of their spiritual identity, in exile from some heavenly home. Their 'homelessness' is captured in those moments when the everyday fabric of life is suddenly shot through by radical doubts as they become aware of an essence that cannot be fulfilled within the terms of an earthly existence. A typical reaction is to abdicate the painful struggle, to refuse to live in the present and to conjure up idealised realms within the past or future. Though Purdy is fond of alluding to Platonic doctrines to comment on these inner yearnings, he is also acutely aware of the dangers associated with attempts to arrest life in forms that simulate such ideals. His vision has affinities with that expounded by Unamuno in his book *The Tragic Sense of Life*, for both articulate in their different ways the sense that it is the dialectic of faith and doubt itself, with its roots in the paradox of suffering, that offers an authentic mode of being. This religious dimension is responsible for that elusive manner in which highly individualised characters seem inseparably involved in some mythological drama or mystery play, in which life discourses upon its own possibilities and failings. This is not to suggest we are presented with dimly veiled allegories, but that the author's focus is upon the minute interactions of different levels of being.

These interactions are communicated by subtle formal strategies as distinct layers or patterns of meaning are brought into contact. Purdy resembles Faulkner in the sheer quantity of narrators he employs. But now the narrative act has turned in upon itself and instead of dramatising a search for meaning, it more frequently exemplifies the author's notion that real life has been reduced to the texture of a fiction. His characters typically aspire to an omniscience over the raw materials of their destiny and of those around them. Yet the stultifying consequences of such attempts to superimpose a story upon the actual world of love and suffering are constantly exposed by the subversive artistry of Purdy himself. Their elaborate constructions are caused to perform a slow dance of death, to spell out the 'inside story' as we are brought to read 'between the lines'. (pp. 8-10)

Stephen D. Adams, in his James Purdy *(© 1976 by Stephen D. Adams; by permission of Barnes & Noble Books, a Division of Littlefield, Adams & Co., Inc.), Barnes & Noble, 1976, 166 p.*

JULIA M. KLEIN

In *Mourners Below*, Purdy's latest demonstration that "terrible events are the order of the universe," a dead brother dictates the destiny of his grieving family. The novel focuses on Duane Bledsoe, 17, whose two older half-brothers, Douglas and Justin, have been killed in war. Duane's parents are divorced, and in his father, Eugene, with whom he lives, Duane encounters only "deep wells of silence" and a refusal to mourn their common loss. Alone in his grief, Duane welcomes the company of his brothers' ghosts, particularly that of his beloved Justin.

The first third of *Mourners Below* is Purdy's account of the costs of repression—a skillful psychological portrait of a father whose profound emotional inhibitions cripple those around him. But this psychological realism explodes into something wilder and more comic—and finally more terrible—once Duane receives an invitation to a costume ball from the luscious Estelle Dumont.

Estelle is another of Purdy's irresistible, devouring women, kin to Elvira Summerlad in *Jeremy's Version* and Madame Girard in *Malcolm*. Once Justin's mistress, she will not be content until she recaptures Justin in Duane. The costume ball is wonderfully metaphorical; before it begins, each of the novel's characters . . . is comically intent on finding the pliable Duane just the right costume to cloak his identity.

The rites of passage for a Purdy adolescent are never easy. They entail the twinned savagery of sex and violence, neither executed without blood. Before Duane can come into his own, he must survive an all-night orgy with Estelle and a brutal rape by two ruffians who—like just about everyone else in the book—confuse him with Justin.

The narrative pace quickens and the improbability of events mounts as *Mourners Below* speeds to a conclusion. Plot revelations are few; revealed instead are the passionate depths to which these characters, at first so vacant and bloodless, can descend.

Mourners Below recapitulates many of Purdy's concerns—with small-town families in crisis, the explosiveness of contained emotion, the marriage between the dead and the living. Purdy sees to the heart of relations between the sexes, mourning the dreadful chasm between them. He celebrates the bonds between brothers, between father and son, even as he underlines the near impossibility of intimacy. Creating a world where the supernatural merges with the real, he illuminates a reality whose core, if not its contours, matches our own.

Julia M. Klein, in a review of "Mourners Below," in The New Republic *(reprinted by permission of The New Republic; © 1981 The New Republic, Inc.), Vol. 185, No. 3, July 18, 1981, p. 39.*

JEROME CHARYN

The story [of *Mourners Below*] is deceptively simple. It's a kind of battlefield where the living play dead, and the dead begin to warp those "mourners below." Most of the novel exists in that lost hour "between very late and very early." This has always been the strength of Mr. Purdy's writing. He cuts below the skin and doesn't become involved with the sociology of any particular time or place. He uses locale to isolate hysteria and deal with that terrible anger of being unloved. The rhythms of his prose have nothing to do with mimicry, or the rendering of American speech. He has never sought to be a caricaturist, to parody the best or the worst of our lives. That slight awkwardness of Mr. Purdy's corrosive style, the deadpan electricity his characters speak with is the crazy jumping sound of the heart's own music.

James Purdy is one of the very best writers we have. He exists in some strange limbo between adoration and neglect. His books are "noticed," but they are rarely celebrated the way they should be. Perhaps this is because Mr. Purdy doesn't play the peacock in his books or strut around with his talents. You have to peek under the feathers to catch the wildness of his prose.

Jerome Charyn, "Unloved and Angry," in The New York Times Book Review *(copyright © 1981 by The New York Times Company; reprinted by permission), July 26, 1981, p. 8.*

GARY KRIST

Mourners Below, which appeared this past summer, is Purdy's tenth full-length novel, and the book appears likely to share the same fate as its immediate predecessors. If critics can be likened to rock climbers, then *Mourners Below* is a sheer scree slope, offering countless apparent critical footholds, but none which is strong enough to bear the weight of complete interpretation. The book seems to call out for all manner of critical approaches—psychoanalytic, archetypal, even phenomenological—yet it cannot be made to cohere in any of these systems. The book remains elusive, and this fact, while certainly inconvenient for the critic, is perhaps the novel's greatest strength. Unlike many works that fit neatly into the syntax of a specific critical language, *Mourners Below* is a work that cannot be easily assimilated intellectually. It retains its mysteries to the very end....

[The plot] sounds very bleak and melodramatic on the surface, and more than one critic has been fooled into thinking that Purdy's intentions are gloomy drama and symbolic tragedy. But, while the grief in *Mourners Below* is very real indeed, it is touched by an inimitable quality of absurdity and deadpan excess. The morbid background of silence and death is only an instrument of Purdy's essentially comic vision. Every obsession—silence, love, sexuality—is pushed to an extreme, and the effect is as unsettling as it is indescribable.

Purdy achieves comedy principally through his use of language. Although the author likes to think that he accurately renders colloquial American speech, the words that issue from his characters' mouths are comic for their very awkwardness and oddness—for their very distance, in other words, from natural speech....

Purdy's narrative voice . . . serves to magnify [the] impression of a world slightly askew: "On learning of Duane's predicament, Aileen had a mild heart attack"; "Nothing was ever quite the same after Duane's fall through the railing of the staircase"; "Had he returned unexpectedly he would have been baffled but perhaps gratified to hear the savage cries of weeping coming from the billiard-hall operator as he pressed his face against the cheap green paint of the wall, and presently beat with his two fists against it." This is hardly melodrama. Nor, however, is it parody. While Purdy's language resembles the flat prose of an Ann Beattie or a Raymond Carver carried to its extreme, it is imbued with an archaic formality quite unlike anything else in contemporary fiction. It is the language of no world I am familiar with outside of Purdy's novels.

James Purdy is, in short, an unusual and remarkable writer. He may even be an important one, and *Mourners Below,* one of his best novels will do nothing to hurt his reputation. If we are ever to appreciate the true value of his body of work, however, it is imperative that we stop viewing him as either embarrassing cult idol or neglected genius, and begin seeing him for what he is—a compassionate storyteller and an original stylist of the very first order.

Gary Krist, in a review of "Mourners Below," in The American Book Review *(© 1982 by The American Book Review), Vol. 4, No. 4, May-June, 1982, p. 11.*

Ruth Rendell
1930-

English mystery novelist and short story writer.

Since the publication of her first novel, *From Doon with Death*, in 1964, Rendell has become one of England's most popular mystery writers. Her work features Reginald Wexford, a Scotland Yard inspector who solves homicide cases by revealing in his suspects the emotions and motivations usually overlooked by other detectives. Critics praise Rendell's realistic portrayal of Wexford, who, in each novel, is allowed to change and to grow as a human being. Her accounts of Wexford's private life are considered refreshing and entertaining subplots.

Rendell has also written several novels outside the traditional mystery genre. In such works as *The Face of Trespass* (1974) and *A Demon in My View* (1976), she combines elements of the crime novel with insightful character studies. For example, the latter is a psychological thriller about a mentally disturbed man who "strangles" store mannequins in order to repress his homicidal tendencies.

(See also *Contemporary Authors*, Vol. 109.)

© Jerry Bauer

ALLEN J. HUBIN

Ruth Rendell's **"The Best Man to Die"** . . . is a sturdy representative of the genus *Britannicus detectivus*. Charlie Hatton is not well loved—except by Jack Pertree, who wants him to stand up at his wedding. The would-be best man is also too bemoneyed for a lorry driver, and the woods seem flush with suspects for Chief Inspector Wexford of the Kingsmarkham police when Charlie fatally encounters a blunt object one moonlit night. Separating the killer from the merely guilty becomes more perplexing with passing days. Added complications include a curious car accident case and a carnivorous elevator.

> Allen J. Hubin, in a review of "The Best Man to Die," in The New York Times Book Review (copyright © 1970 by The New York Times Company; reprinted by permission), August 23, 1970, p. 24.

NEWGATE CALLENDAR

["**One Across, Two Down**"] is a bleak study of what used to be known as the lower classes, done with the dispassionate air of a surgeon in an operating room. A nagging mother-in-law, living with her daughter and a rat of a son-in-law, is bound to create trouble, especially as she has some money and they do not. . . .

Most of the people in this book are unlovely specimens, and it is hard to work up much interest in them. But Rendell is so acute an observer, and has such an ear for speech patterns, that she has created something resembling a case history. There is a horrid air of truth in **"One Across, Two Down,"** that cements her position as an outstanding realist of the genre.

> Newgate Callendar, in a review of "One Across, Two Down," in The New York Times Book Review (copyright © 1971 by The New York Times Company; reprinted by permission), November 7, 1971, p. 26.

THE TIMES LITERARY SUPPLEMENT

Ruth Rendell is really first-class, easy, natural and gemütlich in her writing, unhampered in her invention, a natural storyteller who uses crime as conveniently as the Victorian novelists used to, as a tensing part of stories about people. In [*No More Dying Then*], a provincial policeman has lost his wife and is suffering agonies of deprivation, and a child disappears, not the first to go in this town. Among many good characters, the creation of the destructively indolent Ivor Swan is especially worth praise.

> A review of "No More Dying Then," in The Times Literary Supplement (© Times Newspapers Ltd. (London) 1971; reproduced from The Times Literary Supplement by permission), No. 3644, December 31, 1971, p. 1638.

NEWGATE CALLENDAR

Primarily ["**Murder Being Once Done**"] is a novel of police routine, traditional in its plotting, full of false clues and leads that peter out. Secondarily it is a novel of character exploration, sensitively written, full of the deft touches one comes to expect from the author of **"One Across, Two Down"** and **"No More Dying Then."**

Newgate Callendar, in a review of "Murder Being Once Done," in The New York Times Book Review *(copyright © 1972 by The New York Times Company; reprinted by permission), December 10, 1972, p. 56.*

NEWGATE CALLENDAR

[Ruth Rendell] is a sensitive writer who is at her best in **"Some Lie and Some Die."** . . . This book enters the world of rock and pop. A body is found during a pop festival at which some 80,000 young people are in attendance. The murder, however, occurred before the start of the festival. There is not much to go on. But, slowly, the trail leads to a rock star. Clearly he is involved. But to how great an extent?

Rendell, in her quiet way, can shake mountains. Like all good writers, she has a keen insight into character. In **"Some Lie and Some Die"** she has created in her rock star a monster of a human being. To balance this, there is a civilized, middle-aged chief inspector who understands people and—rarer—even understands himself. At the end of the book there is the usual showdown, but even here there is a different element in the denouement. In none of her books has Rendell taken the easy way out, and she doesn't here.

Newgate Callendar, in a review of "Some Lie and Some Die," in The New York Times Book Review *(copyright © 1973 by The New York Times Company; reprinted by permission), December 16, 1973, p. 18.*

THE TIMES LITERARY SUPPLEMENT

[*The Face of Trespass*] is the story of Gray, a failed writer and nearly alienated man, sick with infatuation for a corrupt, rich, married girl, whom he dare not see for fear of her terrible demands. Ruth Rendell conveys the derelict half-dream, half-nightmare life Gray is leading in an Essex hovel far better than a crime-writer need, and through this, and his sad, unsatisfied love for a dog and for his ridiculous French stepfather, makes credible the blindness that allows him to be led to total disaster—or, rather, to disaster that would have been total had it not been for the conventional crime-writer's beginning and end.

A review of "The Face of Trespass," in The Times Literary Supplement *(© Times Newspapers Ltd. (London) 1974; reproduced from* The Times Literary Supplement *by permission), No. 3761, April, 1974, p. 375.*

PATRICK COSGRAVE

A "favourite" crime or thriller writer is, to me, one the whole corpus of whose work I sit down and re-read every now and again. Next in line to the favourites—or, as I would call them, the classics—are the writers the whole *oeuvre* of whom I can imagine myself re-reading in five or ten years time. The essence of the character of a near-favourite is, of course, that one cannot be certain of that future pleasure: one can only hope for it. . . .

In Ruth Rendell's **Shake hands for ever** . . . the dyspeptic Inspector Wexford is called to a curious murder scene. A much loved, but sluttish second wife is found murdered in an immaculately clean house by her implacably hostile mother-in-law. Wexford knows that the husband is the killer (I am betraying no secrets that Mrs Rendell does not give away, and there is a twist I have not revealed) but is hauled off the investigation after over-eagerness, and pursues it privately for more than a year with the aid of his superior copper son-in-law, with whom he came to terms in the last adventure. . . . [The book is not vintage, but it is gripping.] Mrs Rendell's special gift is for tying the stubborn and intuitive personality of Wexford into the fascinating detail of the best *romans policier*. . . . In the new Rendell, Wexford is not quite deep enough a personality for the obsessiveness of the Simenon novels—which is needed—to come across; but to Simenon she must now be compared.

Patrick Cosgrave, "Crime Compendium," in The Spectator *(© 1975 by The Spectator; reprinted by permission of* The Spectator*), Vol. 234, No. 7668, June 14, 1975, p. 717.*

MARGHANITA LASKI

For most writers, the compulsive strangler would be the centre of only a deliberately nasty book. For Ruth Rendell, he, like her previous misfits, is part of a larger life where health surges but needs defence. The setting of **A Demon in my View** is very prettily made: a North London lodging-house where everyone is waiting hopefully for life to change, except for the strangler, who hopes only that the girl waiting in the cellar will go on being ready to die and save him from seeking new victims. (p. 29)

Marghanita Laski, "Good Crimes" (© British Broadcasting Corp. 1976; reprinted by permission of Marghanita Laski), in The Listener, *Vol. 96, No. 2465, July 8, 1976, pp. 29-30.*

T. J. BINYON

[*A Demon in My View*] is set in the seedy, rundown west London suburb of Kenbourne Vale. The large Victorian houses on streets and terraces which bear the names of Oxford colleges have been converted into flats and bedsitters; some have been demolished, others boarded up. . . . Into a room on the ground floor of 142 Trinity Road moves Anthony Johnson, who is writing a thesis entitled "Some Aspects of the Psychopathic Personality"; in an immaculately clean flat on the top floor lives Arthur Johnson, a psychopath who has in the past strangled two young girls: almost too neat a juxtaposition, but in the event justified by its successful handling. The paths of the two Johnsons intertwine; a series of minor, seemingly insignificant events drives Arthur, once more, towards murder. A deeply satisfying and subtly ironic plot, and a good, depressing picture of west London.

T. J. Binyon, in a review of "A Demon in My View," in The Times Literary Supplement *(© Times Newspapers Ltd. (London) 1976; reproduced from* The Times Literary Supplement *by permission), No. 3890, October 1, 1976, p. 1260.*

T. J. BINYON

Although most of the eleven stories in Ruth Rendell's new collection [*The Fallen Curtain*] have a crime as their subject, its detection is not the object in any of them. Instead she sets out to create a mood—ranging from the domestic to the mildly macabre—and then suddenly, in the last few pages, whisks away the veil to reveal a situation which startles the reader as much as the characters. The method could become mechanical, but it is never so here: each story has its own individual and different jolt. The best are **"A Bad Heart"**, which works the method in reverse, and **"The Vinegar Mother"**, a child's-eye view of adult intrigue.

> T. J. Binyon, "Criminal Proceedings," in The Times Literary Supplement (© Times Newspapers Ltd. (London) 1976; reproduced from The Times Literary Supplement by permission), No. 3896, November 12, 1976, p. 1437.*

NEWGATE CALLENDAR

From the beginning [of **"A Judgement in Stone"**] we know the details of a multiple murder and who was responsible. But Miss Rendell is a master at bringing horror to ordinary situations. She takes an illiterate housekeeper—really illiterate—with a shady past, puts her into a nice family, then starts applying pressure. The way Miss Rendell gets into the woman's mind is a tour de force. Little by little a chip is added, with well-meaning people contributing to their own doom. This is one of Ruth Rendell's best.

> Newgate Callendar, in a review of "A Judgement in Stone," in The New York Times Book Review (copyright © 1978 by The New York Times Company; reprinted by permission), February 26, 1978, p. 34.

JANE S. BAKERMAN

Ruth Rendell is hailed by her publishers as "The New First Lady of Mystery." The fact is that, publishers' enthusiasm aside, Rendell is worth serious critical attention because she has not only created a series of ingenious and clever plots, but has, above all, explored human nature effectively and with genuine insight.

The appeal of the Rendell novels is diversified and full; she uses such interest-generating devices as social criticism, brief comments upon the detective story, and short but striking glimpses of setting (the base of operations is a town called Kingsmarkham in Sussex) to lend depth and strength to her stories. Other elements of style—foreshadowing, simile, metaphor, dialogue, and irony, for instance—are equally well handled, lifting the works above the level of much detective fiction.

Perhaps her most useful device is her treatment of the characterizations of Chief Detective Inspector Reg Wexford and his aide, Detective Inspector Mike Burden. The friendship between the two men is a workable device for maintaining continuity, and the character of Wexford, himself, is developed in such a way as to provide a sane and solid framework of understanding and compassion for her real center of interest: a varied and compelling examination of friendship and love—and their too frequent companion, selfishness. These explorations of two of the most powerful of human relationships are readily perceivable in [her novels] . . . *From Doon With Death*, 1964; *The Best Man to Die*, 1969; *A Guilty Thing Surprised*, 1970; *No More Dying Then*, 1971; *Murder Being Once Done*, 1972; and *Some Lie and Some Die*, 1973.

In the Rendell novels, friendship is clearly viewed as an important kind of love, though the author acknowledges the difficulty with which contemporary human beings handle the relationship. Wexford, himself, is developed, in part, through his friendships with Dr. Crocker, the local physician, as well as with his deputy, Mike Burden.

The relationship with Crocker is continuing, but, in the natural course of events, occupies less of Rendell's—and the Inspector's—attention. Although Wexford and the doctor abrade one another, chiefly over the question of Wexford's health, the medico does occasionally prevail, when it suits Wexford's fancy. . . . Even though in one novel (*Murder*), the doctor's professional and friendly judgment almost destroys the Inspector by protecting him too completely—Wexford has suffered a minor stroke and Crocker's injunctions to the family to keep his patient away from all work demolish Wexford's sense of himself for a time—the relationship is steady, always based upon understanding and affection, and occasionally useful for casting a nostalgic yearning for bygone days, a fairly frequent Rendell device. (pp. 139-40)

In the Burden relationship also, there is sometimes tension between the two men, as when, both upset by their jobs, they annoy one another. . . . The fact that Burden is much younger than Wexford allows their relationship a certain elasticity; Wexford is sometimes able to abort Burden's tendency to be over-protective toward his son . . . , and he often urges Burden to make allowances for both his children. . . . The steady normality between the two men, their ability to balance affection and tension in a realistic fashion, greatly help to offset the horror of the ultimate rejection, the final non-affection, murder, around which each book is organized. (pp. 140-41)

Familial love is another Rendell interest, and once again, the Wexford and Burden families are used as foils and frames. Burden's children, a boy and a girl, are growing up in the course of the novels, and despite the loss of their mother, they are doing so in a vigorous, scrappy way. For a time, their father's preoccupation over his own loss is an alienating factor . . . , but the situation is resolved healthfully, even though Burden remains overanxious. . . . (p. 141)

During the period of Burden's alienation, when he is leaving the children largely to the care of his sister-in-law . . . , his neglect, based on suffering and loss, is clearly contrasted with the seemingly benign but actually devastating neglect that another child has undergone. Rendell contrasts the Burden family with the Swans; Ivor and Rosalind Swan are so preoccupied with one another that the disappearance, some two years before, of her child by an earlier marriage has hardly made a ripple in their relationship. . . . In both households, the point is made; a totally selfish preoccupation is damaging, even deadly. For the Swans, happiness will be easy to achieve; neither is mature or sensitive enough to suffer, and their emotional handicap, acceptable to themselves, is, to the reader—and to Rendell—a fearful irony. Burden *is* mature; he is able to come to terms with his grief and return to the task of parenting his children.

This return is thanks not only to Wexford's ultimate understanding and steady friendship . . . , but also to the lessons Mike Burden learns [in *No More Dying Then*] from the head of the plot's . . . third major household, Gemma Lawrence, whose child has been kidnapped. For Gemma, the loss of her child is, as one would expect, almost unbearable . . . , but when he is returned to her, she is able to save his abductor, a former friend, from loneliness and despair. . . . Gemma's incredible largess of love and Burden's ultimate balance of love are striking contrasts to the Swans' inability to extend their love to children.

Wexford's daughters are grown, one married and one attending drama school. In *The Best Man to Die,* his relationship with Sheila, the drama student, is used to offset the essential selfishness which is the operational center of another family. Wexford and Sheila are close and loving; this relationship is symbolized by the fact that although the Inspector is homely and

Sheila is beautiful, they resemble one another.... The two are not always in accord..., but the steady affection is there, if not always articulated.... (pp. 141-42)

In contrast, the Fanshawe family is presented. In the course of a complicated investigation, Wexford meets Nora Fanshawe, whom he finds to be cold and unfeeling about her father, recently killed in an auto accident. As the story unfolds, the girl tells the Inspector that her view of her father was formed because of the constant string of mistresses he kept.... The end result is not only a loss of love among the family members but also a sort of crippling of Nora to the point where she, too, settles for a life of "purchased" love, a lesson which, in her view, she's learned only too well from her parents. (p. 142)

In every Rendell novel, sexual love, as well as friendship and familial love, is an important concern. In some, however, it is a central motif and an important motivational force. The lovers are sometimes redemptive forces in one another's lives, and sometimes destructive. In the case of Burden and Gemma Lawrence, the movement is toward redemption.

The most difficult adjustment Burden has to make is the loss of his physical relationship with his wife....

Both sick with loneliness, Gemma Lawrence and Burden turn to one another for love and comfort..., and she teaches him that loving is giving. Their affair not only goes a long way toward healing his sense of loss and filling his physical needs, but also teaches him the lesson Wexford has, for years, been trying to get across—tolerance....

In the instances when sexual love is a destructive force, the genesis of that destruction lies in the selfish nature of the bond, even when the lovers are engaged in affairs outside the accepted norms of society. This evenhandedness, always reenforced by Wexford's refusal to be condemnatory or judgmental, lends balance and grace to the novels. (p. 143)

Wexford himself perceives his dispassion as professional preoccupation.

> Wexford knew that look. He had seen it hundreds of times on the faces of people who fancied that they had said too much to him, opened their hearts too wide. Presumably they imagined their confidences led him to regard them with disgust or pity or contempt. If only they knew that to him their revelations were but bricks in the house he was building, rungs on the ladder of discovery, twisting curve-edged pieces in the current puzzle....

The puzzles are fascinating to the reader, it is true, and Rendell's skill in developing them is exciting; but there is more. The careful portrayal of the shrewd but sensitive Inspector is central to the value of the novels, and the examination of his sane, redemptive relationships with the characters close to him provide a vital and workable framework for Rendell's compelling, wise, and insightful explorations of love. (p. 144)

Jane S. Bakerman, "Explorations of Love: An Examination of Some Novels by Ruth Rendell," in The Armchair Detective (copyright © 1978 by The Armchair Detective), Vol. 11, No. 2, April, 1978, pp. 139-44.

PATRICK COSGRAVE

The appearance of any novel by Ruth Rendell is a cause for celebration. But I am particularly pleased by *A Sleeping Life* ... because it sees the return of Chief Inspector Wexford, investigating, this time, the unfathomable death of an apparently respectable, well-heeled, middle-aged woman who appears, once the investigation has begun, to have had no past and, indeed, no existence. The resolution is a little disappointing and rather obvious (the same trick was used years ago by Josephine Tey in *To Love And Be Wise* ...) but that, to me, is little when weighed against the greater humour and humanity that Wexford produces in his creator: I can do with a rest from Mrs Rendell's grimmer (though brilliant) recent forays into criminal psychopathology.

Patrick Cosgrave, in a review of "A Sleeping Life," in The Spectator (© 1978 by The Spectator; reprinted by permission of The Spectator), Vol. 241, No. 7833, August 19, 1978, p. 22.

NEWGATE CALLENDAR

[In **"Make Death Love Me"**], ordinary, middle-class people do an unusual thing once in their lives. Miss Rendell gives us a bank clerk, a milquetoast type, poor, with an unlovely family and, withal, a yen to lead a life of romance. The poor guy actually reads poetry and has a private interior life of his own. He is on hand when two punks rob his bank, and in the ensuing excitement he skips away with £3000. It is not a big sum, but then the clerk is not asking for much from life.

Miss Rendell is an ironist. There is no free will. Men are puppets manipulated by outside forces, and as often as not the only reward in life is a poke in the eye with a sharp stick. There is a concurrent story in **"Make Death Love Me,"** and the two stories, of course, mesh at the end, to the grief of most of the characters.... Miss Rendell is extremely skillful at this kind of psychological suspense story, and while she never forgets the genre in which she is writing (her plotting almost always is very ingenious), there also are strong novelistic aspects to her work.

Newgate Callendar, in a review of "Make Death Love Me," in The New York Times Book Review (copyright © 1979 by The New York Times Company; reprinted by permission), October 14, 1979, p. 26.

NEWGATE CALLENDAR

Miss Rendell, a prolific writer, usually centers her books on commonplace people who find themselves in unusual situations. But the five short stories in **"Means of Evil"** are in the traditional British mainstream. Yet, competent as they are, they lack the special quality that Miss Rendell is able to get in her full-length novels. There is something gray about the writing; characters are not developed; even Wexford seems a stereotype. Short mysteries take a certain kind of explosive quality that is missing from the skillful Miss Rendell's arsenal. (pp. 30-1)

Newgate Callendar, in a review of "Means of Evil," in The New York Times Book Review (copyright © 1980 by The New York Times Company; reprinted by permission), February 24, 1980, pp. 30-1.

HARRIET WAUGH

Ruth Rendell is as English as Simenon is French. In *The Lake of Darkness* ... she does not make the mistake of attempting to cross the cultural borders. Instead of playing spot-the-murderer as in the traditional detective novel, the excitement and tension of her story derive, as with Patricia Highsmith, probably the most notable exponent of this form of thriller, from spotting the victim and watching as disparate strands come together to make an unexpectedly terrible combustion resulting in death. . . . The killer of the story is a very enjoyable creation; a young man who as a teenager caused poltergeistly manifestations and as an adult is able to levitate, while meditating, to the ceiling. Miss Rendell writes particularly well and I have not often enjoyed a thriller more than this well-constructed and deftly executed story.

> *Harriet Waugh, in a review of "The Lake of Darkness," in* The Spectator *(© 1980 by The Spectator; reprinted by permission of* The Spectator*), Vol. 244, No. 7926, June 7, 1980, p. 21.*

NEWGATE CALLENDAR

Ruth Rendell is at it again in **"The Lake of Darkness."** . . . As in so many of her books, this one concerns middle-class Londoners faced with unusual situations, coping as well as they can. . . .

Many of Miss Rendell's books have an O. Henry ending, with an unexpected twist. But where O. Henry was always light-hearted, Miss Rendell is grim, and **"The Lake of Darkness"** ends with a combination of irony and horror. Her writing style is muted, purposely so, and that makes the extraordinary situations all the more biting. She has worked out a special field for herself, and she continues to pursue it with ingenuity.

> *Newgate Callendar, in a review of "The Lake of Darkness," in* The New York Times Book Review *(copyright © 1980 by The New York Times Company; reprinted by permission), November 9, 1980, p. 26.*

FRANCIS WYNDHAM

With twenty-two books written over eighteen years, Ruth Rendell has established a double eminence in two separate categories of crime fiction: the classic puzzle, with a stable background and a recurring cast headed by a mildly eccentric detective and his more conventional subordinate; and the novel of pure suspense, in which a blundering innocent and a haunted psychopath become fatally entangled in a paranoid atmosphere of cross purposes and sinister coincidence. In both fields success is difficult, but for opposite reasons: the first has been so thoroughly mined, by a brilliant team stretching from Agatha Christie to P. D. James, that its resources are in danger of being exhausted; and the second, pioneered by the lone figure of Patricia Highsmith, is all the more daunting because comparatively unexplored. Combining a masterly grasp of plot construction with a highly developed faculty for social observation, Ruth Rendell's remarkable talent has been able to accommodate the rigid rules of the reassuring mystery story (where a superficial logic conceals a basic fantasy) as well as the wider range of the disturbing psychological thriller (where an appearance of nightmare overlays a scrupulous realism). . . .

Put On By Cunning continues the chronicles of Kingsmarkham, that murder-prone Sussex village protected by Chief Inspector Wexford and Inspector Burden, as neatly paired a couple in their way as the two Ronnies. When first met in 1964 (***From Doon With Death***) Wexford was fifty-two years old, "thickset without being fat"; six years later (***A Guilty Thing Surprised***) he "looked more mountainous than ever"; by 1972 (***Murder Being Once Done***) a thrombosis had been diagnosed; and in 1979 (***Means Of Evil***) he is described as "a tall, ungainly, rather ugly man who had once been fat to the point of obesity but had slimmed to gauntness for reasons of health". He has a rather irritating addiction to literary quotations (often reflected in his creator's oddly unmemorable titles) which he exchanges competitively with his nephew, Detective Superintendent Howard Fortune of the Kenbourne Vale CID, but which tend to go over Burden's head. He is happily married to the understanding Dora, although in 1975 (***Shake Hands For Ever***) he only just resisted infidelity with the frankly sensual Nancy Lake. His eldest daughter Sylvia is married with two sons; in 1978 (***A Sleeping Life***) she briefly left her husband as a feminist protest, but soon returned. The younger daughter is his favourite: Sheila Wexford of the Royal Shakespeare Company, who has played Jessica at the National, and starred in a revival of Maugham's *The Letter,* and is now a household name after appearing for five years as Stewardess Curtis, the most beautiful of the air hostesses in the successful TV serial *Runway*.

Twenty years younger than his chief, Burden is prim, handsome, a natty dresser. After his adored wife Jean died in 1971 (***No More Dying Then***) and he was left to bring up John and Pat alone, everyone thought he would marry Jean's nice sister Grace; instead, he had a passionate affair with an equivocal waif named Gemma Lawrence. This experience left him a little less prudish than before; and since his second marriage, to Jenny Ireland, whose brother Amyas works for the publishing firm of Carlyon Brent, he is slightly less of a philistine. There are even signs in ***Put On By Cunning*** that he may one day be able to match some of Wexford's more accessible literary references. Other developments of a domestic nature revealed in the new novel include Sheila's wedding to a rich young businessman named Andrew Thorveton and Dora's decorous reunion with a former admirer, Rex Newton.

Why does one dwell so obsessively on these trivial marginalia which have nothing to do with the substance of Ruth Rendell's work? Partly because to reveal only a minor detail of the central plot is to risk spoiling the fun of potential readers by inadvertently defusing a surprise (in thrillers all material is classified and any comment can be a leak); and partly because obsessive dwelling on trivial marginalia is an indulged pursuit of the registered addict. Of the book itself, there is little more to say than that the scene shifts twice away from Kingsmarkham, to California and to the South of France; that the plot is as elaborate as usual; and that I had the satisfaction of failing to guess its solution.

> *Francis Wyndham, "Deadly Details," in* The Times Literary Supplement *(©* Times Newspapers Ltd. *(London) 1981; reproduced from* The Times Literary Supplement *by permission), No. 4079, June 5, 1981, p. 626.*

HARRIET WAUGH

Ruth Rendell's new detective novel ***Put on by Cunning*** [is very pleasurable to read]. She is England's premier detective-thriller writer. . . . She excels in both fields, although personally I think her thrillers have individual standing that her highly accomplished detective fiction lacks.

Chief Inspector Wexford, Miss Rendell's familiar detective, is drawn into a case of accidental death when aged widower, Sir Manuel Camargue, a great flautist, dies ostensibly from falling into his pond one snowy night shortly before he is to marry a girl 50 years his junior. Foul play is not suspected by anyone except the bereaved fiancée. However, Wexford begins to think that the flautist's long estranged daughter might be other than what she seems and finds her repellently attractive. His superiors think he is wrong-headed and obsessive but Wexford bloodhounds his way out to California in the quest for truth. There is a marvellous surprise twist three-quarters of the way through involving an unexpected death that turn everything on its head. Although Miss Rendell does not cheat on the plotting—the clues are present to be picked up if you can (I could not)—there was little satisfaction for this reader in the identity of the murderer when unmasked.

*Harriet Waugh, in a review of "Put On by Cunning,"
in* The Spectator *(© 1981 by* The Spectator; *reprinted by permission of* The Spectator), *Vol. 246, No. 7981, June 27, 1981, p. 25.*

HARRIET WAUGH

Crime novels, once a name is established, should be a dream to sell as, on the whole, the writers are an unusually consistent bunch. A reader approaching that section in a shop can put out a confident hand to a familiar name. . . . The quality of the book may vary a little within the *oeuvre* of a writer but the kind of crime and the style of the novel rarely do. Ruth Rendell, however, is an exception to this rule because there is Ruth Rendell the detective writer and Ruth Rendell the psychological thriller writer, and there is no relationship between the two. I am pleased to announce that her new novel, ***Master of the Moor,*** is one of the latter.

The story opens with our central character, Stephen Whalby, finding the body of a strangled girl with a shorn head on his beloved Vangmoor. The moor is part of a group of bleak hills dominated by a warren of disused mines. Stephen, a good-looking man of 30, with a pretty, nervous wife and a melancholia-ridden father, still inhabits the emotional and physical world of his childhood. In that world he was King of Vangmoor. When the moor delivers up a second victim the police's attention fixes on him.

Although I was never in much doubt as to who the murderer was, the author is less interested in that aspect than in the effect of the killings on Stephen. There are two excellent, macabre twists in the tale, although the final confrontation, which the reader awaits with some expectation, is slightly skimped.

*Harriet Waugh, in a review of "Master of the Moor,"
in* The Spectator *(© 1982 by* The Spectator; *reprinted by permission of* The Spectator), *Vol. 248, No. 8022, April 10, 1982, p. 23.*

M(acha) L(ouis) Rosenthal
1917-

American poet, critic, and editor.

Rosenthal is a well-respected critic and scholar of British and American poetry. His independence from any particular "school" of criticism and his passion and respect for "the poem itself" are significant elements of his critical method. Rosenthal treats each of the poems he examines as a unique and important expression, and he is noted for his ability to point up the subtle complexity and depth of a work. Among his most influential studies are *The Modern Poets* (1960) and *The New Poets* (1967), which analyze the verse of some of the most important poets of the twentieth century. Like all of Rosenthal's critical works, these books are shaped by his desire to make poetry accessible to the average reader. They provide perceptive readings of individual poems and also place them within the general context of modern literature.

In addition to his critical studies, Rosenthal has published five volumes of his own verse. Although some critics find these poems overly academic and lacking in emotional impact, others admire Rosenthal's ability to use a wide range of forms and styles to explore traditional themes. His collection *She* (1977) is evidence of his great interest in the poetic sequence. Within his sequences as well as his individual poems, Rosenthal's style ranges from traditionally metered lyrics to free verse and prose poems. *Poems 1964-1980* (1981) displays these different styles and reveals various tones. This collection contains poems that are light and sardonic as well as ones that are deeply emotional and philosophical.

(See also *Contemporary Authors*, Vols. 1-4, rev. ed.; *Contemporary Authors New Revision Series*, Vol. 4; and *Dictionary of Literary Biography*, Vol. 5.)

© 1984 Thomas Victor

JOHN HOLMES

The first assertion M. L. Rosenthal makes [in **"The Modern Poets"**] is that "the most marked stylistic break between past and present is not, as is commonly assumed, a break from forthrightness to riddle-making. It is from relative formality to simplicity and directness; an unpretentious intimacy, and awareness of everyday life, has been brought into poetry more emphatically than before." He points out that Yeats, Pound, and Eliot, from whom the most powerful impulses in our poetry today derive, are grounded in tradition, and concerned with continuity. At the same time, our poetry since the twenties has made every effort to use whatever in the past is "myth-making, wonder-contemplating, and strength-giving, and to discover widened, fresher meanings."

This effort, he makes us see, in long and lucid outlines of modern poems, is energetic in invention and experiment, but always sensitive to the voices of the past. Mr. Rosenthal is not defensive, however. He states more clearly and reasonably than any other literary historian of the time, what exactly goes on in the poetry of our time. His view is in sharp focus at a decade's length, and in a single poem's length.

"The Modern Poets" is divided into seven chapters. In the first, Mr. Rosenthal describes the widening of sensibility, and the continuity of tradition, then makes a bridge of Hopkins and Hardy, to reach the modern period. That Yeats is the first great poet of the period, he leaves no doubt. "Ezra Pound: the Poet as Hero," which is the third chapter, also leaves no doubt in the reader's mind as to the importance of this poet, to Mr. Rosenthal, at any rate. His treatment is full, detailed, and commanding, when he discusses the Cantos, and this is a valuable chapter. With Eliot, he pictures the displaced sensibility; this fourth chapter establishes the dominating effect of such displacement on modern poetry.

Having set forth the great trio, Mr. Rosenthal in his fifth chapter groups Robinson, Frost, Williams, Stevens, MacDiarmid, Muir, Moore, Cummings, Sandburg, and Jeffers as "Rival Idioms: the Great Generation." His admiration and respect is mixed, for any one of these figures, as compared with his feeling for Yeats, Pound, and Eliot, to whom he devotes a full chapter each. In some respects, one is convinced against his will; there is also ample room for disagreement.

D. H. Lawrence, Hart Crane, Auden and others, are discussed in the sixth chapter "New Heaven and Earth." The total structure of Mr. Rosenthal's book builds steadily and strongly, as he moves forward, and he unfailingly traces recurrent themes, styles, and language as he goes.

John Holmes, "Not Riddle-Making but Simplicity," in The Christian Science Monitor *(reprinted by permission from* The Christian Science Monitor; *© 1961 The Christian Science Publishing Society; all rights reserved), January 12, 1961, p. 7.*

ROBERT LANGBAUM

[*The Modern Poets*] is for those who know modern poetry as well as for serious beginners. I say serious because M. L. Rosenthal . . . conducts his discussion on the highest level. His book is an introduction in the sense that he writes with admirable lucidity, does not assume a specialized knowledge on the part of the reader, and treats each poet briefly, indicating the direction of his work. It is the best introduction to modern poetry since Lloyd Frankenberg's "Pleasure Dome" in 1949.

Mr. Rosenthal tries to give a comprehensive view of British and American poetry all the way from Hopkins and Yeats to such young contemporaries as W. S. Merwin and Denise Levertov, and to explain what is distinctively modern in the revelations of modern poetry. To rationalize the poetic landscape, he tries to make a chronological arrangement coincide with an arrangement of the poets according to style and subject matter. He combines Marianne Moore, e. e. cummings, Carl Sandburg and Robinson Jeffers in order to suggest that Americans run to both extremes of a maximum and a minimum commitment to style. Especially illuminating is the pairing of William Carlos Williams with Wallace Stevens by way of Williams' four-line "El Hombre" and Stevens' "Nuances of a Theme by Williams" which is based on it. The comparison shows where the two poets are alike and different; for they both write about the otherness or transcendent impersonality of nature, but Stevens in his wittily embroidered treatment makes explicit an analogy between the self-containment of nature and art. This is first-rate criticism, and it shows how through close readings of a few selected poems Mr. Rosenthal can chart a path through the whole of a poet's work. . . .

The title, "Exquisite Chaos," under which Mr. Rosenthal treats Dylan Thomas and the other poets of the Forties and Fifties, will make everyone nervous. But it does force us to ask the right questions about these poets. "Chaos" obviously tells us a great deal about them and their world. But "exquisite"? For Thomas, whose euphuistic love of language has behind it such physical vitality? Or for Robert Lowell who, as Mr. Rosenthal points out, emerged in last year's "Life Studies" as our best confessional poet? The title suits perfectly one of the two groups into which Mr. Rosenthal divides contemporary American poets. It suits the poets who are inside "the new academy" (the others are outside), of whom he writes: "If only we could settle for 'appreciation' alone, the great poets of any time would be the [Elizabeth] Bishops and the [Richard] Wilburs. . . . After the stormy inventors of new rhythmic idioms and new imaginative horizons had done their work, the gifted exquisites would take over—remolding, improving, getting the nuances not of a new artistic problem but of an established tradition."

We have, in other words, to judge by the quality of the revelation. This does not mean that Mr. Rosenthal wants moral lessons in poetry. On the contrary, he criticizes Frost for taking refuge in easy moral reflections that are not adequate to his hard observation of natural phenomena. "Sententiousness and a relative absence of formal daring are his main defects." The quality of the revelation is determined by the energy with which the poet pursues all the implications of his vision both in content and form. That is the critical assumption throughout, and the reason Mr. Rosenthal gives the primacy to Yeats, Pound and Eliot. For while their vision is so intense that it leads toward commitment, they never sacrifice the vision or the self to the commitment. Yeats, for all his politics and occultism, remained "the unconsenting spirit": "In the deepest sense he believed in nothing yet spoke for belief." Pound made the mistake of trying to "politicalize" an esthetic vision, but as an esthetic vision his poetry remains valid. Eliot, for all his Christian faith, "interests us most as he explores the limits of sensibility and conveys the sense of what it is to be alive today."

Mr. Rosenthal does not sufficiently distinguish among commitments—Hopkins' and Frost's for example—but his criteria, which would not work for all poetry, are right for modern poetry. His strength as a critic comes from the consistency of his criteria, from the theoretical power behind the flexible judgments of individual poems and poets. It is only because one wants more of a good thing that one wishes the book had an epilogue to tie together the general ideas on modern poetry which have now to be gathered from brief and scattered statements.

Robert Langbaum, "A Critic Surveys Modern Poetry, and Poets Speak Their Minds: 'The Modern Poets: A Critical Introduction'," in Lively Arts and Book Review *(© I.H.T. Corporation; reprinted by permission), May 14, 1961, p. 33.*

ROBIE MACAULEY

The fact may be as deplorable as Randall Jarrell once insisted, but nevertheless it is true: the direct reader of poetry scarcely exists in this country any longer. Nearly everyone who reads the new poets arrives at them by way of a critical initiation of some kind and our understanding of poetry written today is inseparable from poetry-pedagogy. Thus, the taste and acumen shown by the introducer-critic is probably more essential to the persistence of the art than it has been in any other time. Both readers and writers, then, should be grateful for the mediatory excellence of M. L. Rosenthal, professor of English at New York University and a critic of real talent.

His two new books, taken together, make up a very sensible kind of strategy. **"The New Poets"** is . . . "an attempt to characterize . . . in depth the range . . . of British and American poetry" since 1946. Mr. Rosenthal limits his study (with one special exception) to the writers who began in that period, and he examines the work of such people as Robert Lowell, John Berryman, Sylvia Plath, Allen Ginsberg and Robert Duncan among the Americans; Ted Hughes, Philip Larkin and Thom Gunn among the British; and Austin Clarke, Patrick Kavanagh and Thomas Kinsella among the Irish. **"The New Modern Poetry"** is an anthology containing poems by nearly all those discussed in the critical volume, plus many other poets of the postwar generation. . . . The books supplement each other nicely. The result is the first broad view of the new poetry and at the same time the first study that distinguishes and examines the major trends in a satisfactory way.

One of the most prominent modes of the era is of course "confessional" poetry. Mr. Rosenthal sees this as a Romantic inheritance, yet one that has become highly intensified in our time, to a "literally self-exposing vulnerability." Its marks are "sexual candor, frankness about family life, and confession of private humiliations of varying psychological kinds." Some of this poetry is in the tone of cool, self-analyzing devastation and some of it is agonized but, as Mr. Rosenthal points out, the voice is very definitely that of a victim....

Mr. Rosenthal takes Robert Lowell's "Life Studies" as possibly the leading and most influential book of confessional poetry—though he makes clear that this is no more than one strand in the work of a varied and extremely resourceful poet....

Mr. Rosenthal, however, sees confessional poetry as a style already on the wane: "As a startlingly new factor in our art [it] may be just about played out, or . . . may be absorbed and taken for granted as a part of the . . . new poetic scene." He very neatly isolates the most tiresome thing about confessional poetry when he remarks on "the danger that its practitioners may be over-indulging themselves if they think that every nuance of suffering brought out on the couch or in reverie is a mighty flood of poetic insight or the key to a new aesthetic." Those golden words of warning deserve a wide publicity.

As for poetic theory, Mr. Rosenthal finds little that is distinctly new or productive in this period—he finds it "raggedly improvisational" for the most part. He does discuss the theory of "Projective Verse" as described by Charles Olson and as applicable to a number of poets . . . associated with him; and the idea of "Concretist" verse held by Ian Hamilton Finlay and other British poets. Though the discussion is conscientious, Mr. Rosenthal remains unconvinced that this period has brought forth any new theory of form powerful enough to shape very much poetry. He finds the ideas expressed by Olson, Finlay and Donald Davie interesting largely in a post-facto way—at one point he describes Mr. Olson as a kind of "literary Casey Stengel," whose theory is made up of separate references to points of poetic action.

The section of **"The New Poets"** dealing with British writers is a report on an interesting minority; Rosenthal remarks that "English talent was, and still is, concentrated into fairly genteel and conventional channels." . . .

Possibly the most interesting discovery—or rediscovery—of this book is the Irish poet Austin Clarke, a contemporary of Yeats, who is still writing ably at 71. Here Mr. Rosenthal has broken one of his own rules—Mr. Clarke is not a "new" poet in any way, though he is a good one, and I am moved to regret the exclusion of several poets now stout and middle-aged who write verse with a newer feel than much in **"The New Modern Poetry."** . . .

Still, I should say that these two books, on balance, do such a wise and worthy job of surveying American, Irish and British poetry in the past 21 years that they will easily survive any minor disappointments.

> Robie Macauley, "Voices of Victims," in The New York Times Book Review (copyright © 1967 by The New York Times Company; reprinted by permission), September 10, 1967, p. 6.

THE TIMES LITERARY SUPPLEMENT

Dutiful, accommodating, mild, eager to fit in even when not eager to be generous, Mr. Rosenthal is . . . rather like a slightly dim war correspondent, sending his copious despatches out of the fury and the mire; and at the end of it all the battle is not much clearer. To make sense of Mr. Rosenthal's book [**The New Poets**], one has to accept early on (page 7) a sentence which—if one can negotiate the shrill metaphor he has chosen—seems to encapsulate what all his favourite new poets are up to: "If there is, in fact, one distinctively modern quality in literature, it lies in the centrifugal spin toward suicide of the speaking voice." It is evident that this is not the "high-pitched scream" with which Stephen Spender characterized the reaction of the 1930s poets to the events they saw looming up on their horizon, but a histrionic way of isolating and making vivid the phenomenon known as "confessional" poetry. By and large, in fact, Mr. Rosenthal's book is concerned with this kind of poetry.

This means, of course, that Robert Lowell and Sylvia Plath bulk large in Mr. Rosenthal's pages, . . . while Theodore Roethke, oddly enough, is recruited but then dismissed, apparently because he "absorbed so little of the concerns of his age into his nerve-ends": in a way this may be true, but it is hardly a perceptive or just judgment on Roethke's poems. Mr. Rosenthal is a bit of a literalist, and the tone of his strictures against Roethke, who seems in so many ways to be the sort of poet he values, is apparently a reaction against some possibly ill-considered but typically honest and forthright remarks Roethke made here and there in prose. If you are going to have confessional poets, you must put up with their confessions, even when they do not suit your pattern of the confessional.

Mr. Rosenthal's general method is one of extended explication, usually quite decently done, though without much imagination and with a tendency to underline the plodding platitude. . . . Mr. Rosenthal is . . . [warm towards] Edwin Brock (remorselessly given as "Bronk" throughout the book, bibliography and index included), enthusiastic about Christopher Middleton, Charles Tomlinson and George MacBeth, dismisses Peter Porter and Anthony Thwaite in one sentence, mentions Elizabeth Jennings so much in passing that one wonders whether he has ever read her, and does not even mention R. S. Thomas, Geoffrey Hill, and Jon Silkin. This leaves room for a lengthy consideration of modern Irish poets, and an epilogue which runs itself into the ground with that stutter of proper names which seems endemic to this sort of roundup. Yes, on reflection, . . . [this is a] long but only mildly rewarding book.

> "Suicidal Spin," in The Times Literary Supplement (© Times Newspapers Ltd. (London) 1967; reproduced from The Times Literary Supplement by permission), No. 3424, October 12, 1967, p. 963.

THOMAS LASK

[Although M. L. Rosenthal's second book of poems, **"Beyond Power,"**] is in its way an extension of the first, it is marked by a deeper and more enriched tone. His wry attitude, his sense of limits in man's relations to nature and to history are still present. His unwillingness to strike rhetorical poses gives his work that playfulness and surface lightness that characterized the earlier, **"Blue Boy on Skates."** Some of the new poems are infectiously funny. **"Homage to Matthew Arnold"** may ruin "Dover Beach" for you forever. **"Love in the Luncheonette"** redeems a dreary piece of Americana by its wit and humorous empathy. . . . But for the most part, these poems are the expression of a thoughtful and deeply moved man before the majesty and impersonality of nature and the equal impersonality of history. He acknowledges without understanding the evil that lies in men's hearts. He faces death and loss without seeking transcendental solace, knowing that death is part of living. The ease and flexibility of his lines hide his technical assurance. A highly satisfying book by one for whom all show, all pretense have been burned away in the cauldron that is our age.

> Thomas Lask, in a review of "Beyond Power," in The New York Times (copyright © 1969 by The New York Times Company; reprinted by permission), August 29, 1969, p. 27.

THE TIMES LITERARY SUPPLEMENT

M. L. Rosenthal's services to modern poetry are important and well known. But his new book, **Beyond Power,** does not match in distinction his work as a scholar or anthologist. The poems are adventurous and in good taste; they convey the impression of a charming, tolerant man, blessed with humour and wisdom. But they do not possess the strength of language, the coherence of vision, or the marks of individual character that one demands from writers who stir up more than a murmur of polite appreciation.

> "Falling Water and Fading Flames," in The Times Literary Supplement (© Times Newspapers Ltd. (London) 1970; reproduced from The Times Literary Supplement by permission), No. 3589, December 11, 1970, p. 1436.*

THE TIMES LITERARY SUPPLEMENT

Mr Rosenthal has a good many thoughts, metaphysical or otherwise, as the prose-poems which intersperse [**The View from the Peacock's Tail**] show in particular; but he has a problem in shaping them into coherent verse and blending them with the lyrical romanticism which represents the other side of his sensibility. His imagery is full-bloodedly aggressive . . . , his tone invariably high-pitched; and although the book shows a vein of ironic comedy, it tends not to run through those poems which need its prudent deflating effect most.

> "Nature As She Is," in The Times Literary Supplement (© Times Newspapers Ltd. (London) 1973; reproduced from The Times Literary Supplement by permission), No. 3730, August 31, 1973, p. 996.*

ROBERT B. SHAW

In **The View from the Peacock's Tail** M. L. Rosenthal writes what most readers would call a critic's poetry. In consideration of Rosenthal's eminence as a critic this may seem to follow naturally, but upon examination it seems peculiar. Shouldn't a critic, of all people, be wary of leaning too heavily on the poets he has studied? Rosenthal isn't. He gives us a poem (free verse) about Williams, another (rhymed) about Yeats, another directed to a revolutionary that begins:

> Rhetorician of your own agony, scooping
> the pain of the world into the cornucopia of
>   your particular pleasure
> (emperor of that particular sort of ice-cream) . . .

The great poems of the past are thus brought into embarrassing collocation with Rosenthal's own, which come disastrously short of the models they invoke. When the book is not about poets it is often about politics, and there (especially in some prose passages in the sequence **His Present Discontents**) the thought is incredibly clichéd:

> I am for Revolution, though I believe that, at
> the same time, I am impossibly apart. It is
> impossibly apart to hate rudeness, violence,
> grossness, overstatement. And these seem inseparable from Revolution . . .

> Yeats was too bound by the sense of *some* meaningful order, however incommensurate with man's needs, to see the true arbitrariness of our choices. The pity of our loss, yes—those dearly bought "many ingenious lovely things" that are gone forever. But the full horror of statistical man was hidden from him, statistical man with his "random" behavior. . . .

Many of us are similarly confused, but few of us would feel obliged to document our confusion in a book of verse. It is as if confusion were being presented as a virtue; but fuzziness in itself is no more praiseworthy than fanaticism, and it can be just as dangerous. This prose, and a lot of these poems, sound as if they were written by Statistical Man. Everything in them is second-hand. (p. 347)

> Robert B. Shaw, "No Strokes of Lightning" (© 1973 by The Modern Poetry Association; reprinted by permission of the Editor of Poetry and the author), in Poetry, Vol. CXXII, No. 6, September, 1973, pp. 344-50.*

SAMUEL HUX

One must admire the intention behind M. L. Rosenthal's **Poetry and the Common Life** . . . : the attempt to sway to love of poetry the "common reader," who, no matter how elusive, is precisely the person scholars and university presses should seek. But I find I admire the intention somewhat more than the book itself. I think it misleading to say that "the greatest poetry is closest to the common life" without emphasizing a great deal more than Rosenthal does uncommon genius and the fierce artifice that transmutes the common.

Rosenthal loves a line because it shows "how much poetry is present in the voices of people to whom it would hardly occur that this could be so"—which makes sense to me as well. But to build the case for our need of poetry on how much like us it is instead of asking us to move outside ourselves toward something else is a kind of pandering to passivity. Not that Rosenthal ignores that a poem is a thing made and worthy of active wonder—some of his readings are beautifully appreciative of rhythm and image—but his emphasis is steadily on the test of familiarity, often of the most naturalistic sort. . . .

Most of the poems he discusses resist his method. Sure they are of the stuff of life, but they ask the reader to extend himself instead of simply complimenting him on being the stuff. The view of poetry this book assumes doesn't really need an apologist. Our most popular "serious poetry" of the moment, Erica Jong's for instance, depends for its success on providing us with self- (ours and hers) aggrandizing images of the ordinary. And it's a far cry from that poetry most directly related to the common life: folk ballad, with its frank artifice.

> Samuel Hux, in a review of "Poetry and the Common Life," in Commonweal (copyright © 1975 Commonweal Publishing Co., Inc.; reprinted by permission of Commonweal Publishing Co., Inc.), Vol. CII, No. 5, May 23, 1975, p. 150.

WILLIAM HEYEN

Poetry and the Common Life ranges wide to explode all sorts of traditional classroom assumptions about what poetry is supposed to be and do for us. The entire book is a collection of variations on how a poem does mean, on what to many may be the radical idea that poetry "brings out the actual quality of what our senses perceive and what our hearts feel about the perception." Even while the impulses of his discussion lead him to detailed examination of poems or passages from Whitman or Williams or Paul Blackburn, Rosenthal never loses sight of the fact that paraphrase and summary and statement are pale versions of the many communications that go on between reader and poem. Rosenthal engages us by pointing out what he describes as "the shape and suggestion of the language as it flows and erupts and shifts direction in the poem." There are no statics in this book, the critic himself realizing at the end that his conclusions are only beginnings, that the subject's proliferations, as those of any poem, are endless.

If this book never loses sight of the poem's text, it is at the same time often personal, telling us where the readings of poems come from. . . .

[In reading *Poetry and the Common Life* we] sense a thoughtful man behind the words, someone whose experiences have been transmuted into the understanding and sympathy necessary for an ample reading of any worthwhile poem. His feelings about poems are rooted in his own life, one he would hold to be, in the most important senses, representative, for, as he says in many different ways, "The thought I am insisting on here is that an essential ingredient of poetic vision and genius is present in all minds. . . . Poetry draws deeply on experiences we have all had." The book's personalism grows naturally from this belief. *Poetry and the Common Life* has grown from a sensibility that sees and absorbs and considers, and M. L. Rosenthal has written it, not a critical persona.

Rosenthal is such a convincing advocate of the excellences of certain poems that I sometimes have the feeling—though this is probably my own failure of taste as a reader—that he is making them into more than they are, that they are not as good as his readings of them and his delight suggest. It seems to me that Paul Blackburn's "The Once-Over," Williams' "Love Song," George Barker's "To My Mother," and Paul Goodman's "Long Lines," for example, are finally unimportant, even uninteresting pieces, their language too easy to forget. Rosenthal cares a great deal for some poems that bore me. Why, I often wondered unfairly, didn't he turn to work by David Ignatow and William Stafford, to name two poets of subtle power who have always explored the poetry of the quotidian? At the same time, Rosenthal's discussions of Stevens' "Sunday Morning," of the incident of the stolen boat in Wordsworth's "The Prelude," of sections of Whitman's "Song of Myself," of Blake's "London," of Wyatt's "They Flee from Me," of Plath's "Ariel" have made me know and feel anew the undeniable power of poems I have dwelled on and loved, or feared. (p. 725)

Because it is so easy and even fashionable to be a relativist these days, we can easily feel the intellectual courage behind this book. Rosenthal knows what happened in the Nazi death camps, says that the voice of Baraka's poem ["Black Art"] comes out of the world that shaped those camps, and *still*, as he condemns this poem, as it sickens him, recognizes its "clearly conscious voice for one side of things in the modern world." This is not a man who will burn texts, but one who hopes to help us to read that we may come to disavow rhetoric, perhaps even as Eldridge Cleaver has recently regretted his own early rhetoric.

As we read this book, we have the feeling that the critic's words become discoveries for him as well as for us. We sense a flow, one that bends the chapter boundaries. The voice here is that of one of our best readers, a poet coming to realize what he knows and what his memory and imagination insist on as he writes. This is the book of a whole man. In *Poetry and the Age* Randall Jarrell describes what he sees to be the best criticism, criticism "written by a reader for readers, by a human being for human beings." *Poetry and the Common Life* is such a book, one with none of the "institutional magnificence" Jarrell despised, but an important appreciation and defense of an art that reaches out to share its earth, water, and air with all of us. (p. 726)

> William Heyen, "Rosenthal: 'Poetry and the Common Life'," in The Nation (copyright 1975 The Nation magazine, The Nation Associates, Inc.), Vol. 220, No. 23, June 14, 1975, pp. 725-26.

WILLIAM E. STAFFORD

M. L. Rosenthal, in attempting to share an understanding of what is valuable in poetry, faces the barrier of having to assume some of that understanding in order to identify that value. A remark attributed to Louis Armstrong comes to mind: "If you gotta ask you'll never know," or in Wordsworth's translation, speaking of the poet: ". . . you must love him, ere to you / He will seem worthy of your love."

In this instance, a result of this complexity is a book [*Poetry and the Common Life*] that is probably too good to achieve its aim.

The poetry of common life is hardly ever identified by common people in actual poems; yet it is in poems that poets and their like ordinarily seek it. Mr. Rosenthal does so, and his book comes alive in discussions of favorite poems. At one point he catches himself: "But my purpose in quoting . . . was not really to criticize . . . in detail." It is a charming and a revealing passage—Mr. Rosenthal is so enthusiastic that he cannot restrain himself to language that might reach the unliterary. He shows a zest like that he identifies in a quote about Mayakovsky, "'. . . a man for whom truth held an almost animal attraction.'" (p. 426)

In the spirit of liking this book and the impulse behind it, I want to identify two hovering issues. One is just a reverting to the issue of the relation between the poetry found in common life and that found in *poems,* in which adepts find an embodiment of that poetry. I would welcome more caution in linking poetry to poems.

Second, I wonder if more caution is needed in assuming that a poet uses language in order to define an experience: it may be that the language itself is the experience. Mr. Rosenthal carefully handles this issue, but I believe most of his book implicitly assumes a *using* of language to *express* something already achieved.

Finally, though, Mr. Rosenthal has gallantly attempted to overcome what he sees as an "unconscious conspiracy" "to keep the people from their poetry." In making his book he manifests a generous impulse he finds in the best of poets: "The impulse of which I have been speaking, the need to follow through on a quite private insight until it completes itself in a poem that is both a world unto itself and a window into everyone's secret mind, is doubtless the chief link between poetry and the common life. I half believe that it underlies all communication and all rhetoric, and that it is far more important than any overt system of principles and beliefs.'' (pp. 426-27)

> William E. Stafford, in a review of "Poetry and the Common Life," in American Literature (reprinted by permission of the Publisher; copyright © 1976 by Duke University Press, Durham, North Carolina), Vol. 48, No. 3, November, 1976, pp. 426-27.

SALLY M. GALL

> Did you ever imagine, as a child,
> these silences falling away
> from where death watched us for a moment
> and then the mockingbird's manic medley
> wild with the morning, wild for heaven to notice.

So ends the epilogue to M. L. Rosenthal's masterly new sequence, *She,* his finest achievement and in my estimation a leading candidate for the best love poem in English since William Carlos Williams' "Asphodel, That Greeny Flower." These closing lines, with their imagery of ardent song flung forth on the brink of the abyss, are suggestive of Rosenthal's practice as a whole: this situation is a recurring one in his poems. Also, the phrase "manic medley" is apt for his intensely energetic poetry with its quick shifts of focus and tone. Just in the brief space of five lines, for example, the speaking voice moves from conversational, nostalgic reverie to appalled confrontation of disaster to triumphant yet dismayed song in an effort to overcome death's ultimate silences. In **"To His Other Spirit,"** the key poem of the sequence **"His Present Discontents,"** Rosenthal uses the phrase "stormy, volatile, tentative as all living thought." His thought and poetry live precisely in this volatile, energetic fashion; and the shifting points of attention in his poetry—its volatility and the high degree of craftsmanship make for intelligent, varied, passionate poems. There are few if any barren or dull stretches in Rosenthal's books of poems (or, for that matter, in his extensive criticism of modern poetry). (p. 119)

In his first book . . . Rosenthal showed how much he had learned from such masters as W. B. Yeats about the art of integrating quite varied poems into a coherent, satisfying whole. ***Blue Boy on Skates*** is an engaging collection of thirty-four lyrics and the prose-poem **"Footnote." "Psalm"** and **"Footnote"** provide a frame for lyrics that range from the humorous and whimsical to the nostalgic, elegiac, philosophical, celebratory, satirical, or politically anguished. The underlying theme is the need to keep an intensely loving stance not only toward family and friends but toward strangers and "enemies" as well. . . . (p. 120)

Love—not so incidentally, the word appears in the first and last lines of the book—is the all-important counter to the violence of the twentieth century, a violence engendered in part by historical hatreds, by the "sick Memory" and "foolish History" that made schoolboy enemies of the Polish Catholic Raymond and the "Jewish kid" the poet once was. In **"The Enemy,"** the mock-epic battle by the bakery is treated humorously enough, but the implications are, of course, deadly serious and treated so elsewhere. (p. 121)

The two sequences in ***Blue Boy,*** **"Three Conversations"** and **"Liston Cows Patterson and Knocks Him Silly,"** differ in structure and length from the later sequences—**"Beyond Power"** in the book of that name; the three sections of ***The View from the Peacock's Tail;*** and ***She***—yet they offer a similar blend of personal and political notes. I should stress that Rosenthal's poetry is not "political" in the obvious sense of being written to support a political position; he is no Imamu Amiri Baraka whipping up racial hatred or Vladimir Mayakovsky lauding the Soviet state—not, fortunately, the only modes of poetry practiced by these poets. Rather, Rosenthal's poetry is "saturated with political consciousness," a condition of much modern poetry, as he points out in the "Politics" chapter of ***Poetry and the Common Life.*** . . . Both sequences suggest how impregnated with violence and terror the modern experience is and how vulnerable and helpless average human beings are. . . . (pp. 121-22)

The title sequence of ***Beyond Power*** is longer and the individual poems more independent than either **"Three Conversations"** or **"Liston Cows Patterson."** The book as a whole—also closely organized—is informed with a deeper despair; the poet's state of mind is evidently linked to the worsening world situation during the late 1960s, as Vietnam came to dominate our politics. But as the poems make clear, there is a more personal reason for the elegiac cast. Rosenthal's mother and others near and dear to him had recently died. Surely in this book the frequent mirror images are an emblem of loneliness, of his isolation from those other beings with whom he was once in intimate touch. Not all the poems are bleak, however. There are comic poems—**"Love in the Luncheonette"** is one of his best in this vein—as well as more philosophical and lyrical ones. **"Love Wrapped Me in Darkness,"** adapted from a poem by Baqir, is sweetly happy. **"Returning"** anticipates poems in *Peacock* and *She* in its linking of love-awareness and the disastrous aspects of existence. . . . (pp. 122-23)

"Beyond Power: A Sequence" is the most developed of Rosenthal's political poems in the first two books. The four poems, **"Paris, 1968," "The Radiance," "Three Poets,"** and **"Beyond Power,"** provide complementary perspectives on the revolutionary dream of world brotherhood. (p. 123)

[***The View from the Peacock's Tail*** demands a longer treatment than can be given it here.] Divided into three separate but related sections, **"His Present Discontents," "Notations of Love,"** and **"Like Morning Light,"** each of which is quite carefully orchestrated, *Peacock* becomes a sequence of sequences. But I must confine myself to a few observations on the first two sections, **"His Present Discontents,"** which is the most explicitly political of any of the sequences, short or long; and **"Notations of Love,"** which shows the poet shifting in the direction that will make the poems of *She* possible. (Both, of course, are much longer than the sequences in *Blue Boy* and *Beyond Power,* and *She* is longer yet. The second section includes among its twelve poems a five-poem sequence, also called **"Notations of Love,"** which could be compared profitably with **"Three Conversations," "Liston Cows Patterson,"** and **"Beyond Power."** For in its renewed awareness of intimate communion and love, this fourth short sequence shows the distance the poet has come from the desolation of **"Beyond Power."**)

In his effort to explore the "ocean" of revolution in connection with his own private intensities, Rosenthal resorts to six prose poems in **"His Present Discontents,"** intermingling them with an equal number of lyrics. The result is that the work as a whole reads better than it sounds, since the long prose passages ("long" relative to the lyrics), even the most rhythmical ones, slow the sequence too much. Despite this structural problem, the sequence is extremely interesting; for the varied lyrics include some of Rosenthal's best work, and the prose-poems are among his most passionate. (pp. 124-25)

"**To His Other Spirit**" [is] probably Rosenthal's best single poem. The anguished intensity with which the speaker focuses on a young man who has retreated from the stormy and volatile atmosphere of the Vietnam era to the "womb bliss of needles" is matched only in the key poem of *She*, "**Through Streets Where Smiling Children**," with its comparable effort at delving the female spirit. The last stanza is a magnificent expression of the speaker's "abundant, political emotion." . . . In the last two lines Rosenthal conveys with magnificent economy the agony and ecstasy of life, man's unlimited aspiration joined to his mortality. It is hard to find a poem in this generalizing mode with a comparably powerful close. Rosenthal's language stays concrete but does not narrow down to a single image in the manner, for example, of the closing stanza of Wallace Stevens' "Sunday Morning." . . . (pp. 125-26)

The penultimate section of "**His Present Discontents**," the prose-poem "'**To Bodies Gone': Pygmalion Remembering**," expands on the images of the earlier poem "**Returning**." In this act of love "everything flowers in one moment," for the "world within world" of love bears with it the outside world's violence—the "waves that come storming towards the shore to shock and engulf us forever." The most compressed and powerful statement of the awareness of violence at the peak of ecstasy, however, comes near the end of "**Notations of Love**." . . . (p. 126)

Also in "**Notations of Love**" is a translation of Rainer Maria Rilke's "Schlaflied," the first line of which —"Some day, when I lose you"—sparked two variations, one published here and one in *She*, where it becomes one of the main motifs of the sequence. Another key transition poem is "**Late at Night**." . . . The poem recapitulates the poet's psychological journey from *Beyond Power* to the moment when empathy with other beings again seems possible. . . . The tone is quite different from the earlier book, however, in its breezy, colloquial, humorous attitude. . . . (p. 127)

The image from the closing stanza of the title poem of *She* of the "battered pinnace" riding the abyss is a key one for the sequence as a whole. Throughout *She* the speaker's sensibility sinks and rises on waves of love, anguish, desolation, joy. (p. 128)

Framed by a prologue and epilogue, the twenty-six poems of *She* form loose clusters. The title poem introduces motifs that will be preoccupations of the speaking sensibility throughout the sequence—separation, war, love—and, equally important, sets the tonal key of sensuous reverie. The next three poems touch on reawakening to love, with certain notes of the difficulty of breaking with the old life and realizing the new fully. Four poems centering on separation follow, and the ninth poem, "**Compleynte, etc.**" serves as transition to a group of six poems that focus concretely on the more ecstatic side of the relationship, although certain dark notes are heard as well. This section consciously invokes the whole lyric tradition, with allusions to Elizabethan poets, Longfellow, and Pablo Neruda—the twelfth poem is an excellent translation of Neruda's "Fable of the Mermaid and the Drunks." The sixteenth poem, "**Once**," is also a transition poem, this time to a dark group—with some glimmerings of light—that merge personal distress with certain terrible aspects of existence in the twentieth century.

The sequence then surges upward in the last three poems, with the humble yet firm assertiveness of "**Saint**," the ecstatic repossession of a moment of union in "**Joy**," and the remarkable poem "**Through Streets Where Smiling Children**." Published here for the first time, this climactic poem is the longest in the sequence. In it the poet focuses for the first time on the real woman alive. Yet he keeps his dual perspective, so that she is both real and imagined, carrying within herself on ordinary city streets as much potential for arousing his poetic imagination as any legendary or mythical being.

She is considerably longer than Rosenthal's other sequences. Indeed, if we exclude the prose-poems in the earlier books, *She* is of comparable book length. The major difference is, of course, the device of using a central love relationship to focus his deepest preoccupations, giving *She* a more sustained effect than the other books. (pp. 128-29)

"**Through Streets Where Smiling Children**" contains much of the essence of *She*, with the addition of certain physical details that serve to demonstrate that this "She" obviously exists other than in the speaker's mind. The poem thus has an anchoring function for the sequence as a whole, the way "**To His Other Spirit**," with its focus on one young man, anchors "**His Present Discontents**." That poem ended with all-encompassing imagery of combined hope and despair; this one ends with the vision of one loved human face, embodying similar complexities. This vision—the beloved of "**Joy**" made concrete, the mermaid made fully human—allows the speaker to hold steady despite his constant awareness of the violence and cruelty threatening young and old. (Another link with "**His Present Discontents**" is the stress on childhood violence; these vicious smiling children are much like those described in the "**Cruelty**" section of the earlier sequence.)

"**Through Streets Where Smiling Children**" offers the kind of medley that the sequence as a whole does, moving among many points of attention. The tonal range is wide as well: cries of "Bullshit" are as much a part of the poem's texture as the lovely closing celebration; the sensuous language of the love scene in the first stanza fits seamlessly with the violent language of the street scene in the second. So the phrase "manic medley" in the epilogue comes at a particularly apt moment. *She* is a medley—as volatile as this man's own sensibility, yet always under the steady control of a poet who knows a great deal about the art of making sequences work. The result is a wonderfully encompassing love poem, a paean to the ability of the human spirit to change despair and desolation into song, and a major addition to the genre of the modern lyric sequence. (p. 133)

Sally M. Gall, "'Wild with the Morning': The Poetry of M. L. Rosenthal," in Modern Poetry Studies *(copyright 1977, by Media Study, Inc.), Vol. VIII, No. 2, Autumn, 1977, pp. 119-33.*

GREGORY A. SCHIRMER

The description of a literary critic that M. L. Rosenthal offers in the foreword to his new book [*Sailing Into the Unknown: Yeats, Pound, and Eliot*] strikes a refreshingly poetic note in this day of increasing enchantment with elaborately theoretical and often decidedly unpoetic approaches to literature. For Rosenthal, who is a poet as well as a critic, the interpreter of a literary work should be thought of as an adventurer, someone who, like the poet himself, journeys into "the unknown realm where fantasy and keenest observation and volatile emotions unite to create a reality of a thousand dimensions."

If this description also strikes a somewhat romantic note, the criticism that springs from it is thoroughly practical. It is also generally perceptive, undogmatic, and, above all, empathic.... It is to "the poems themselves" that Rosenthal directs his considerable critical abilities, proving that close and sensitive attention to texts, even to those of three poets who have generated at least as much criticism as have any writers this side of Milton, still has something to teach us.

All this is not to say, however, that Rosenthal's book lacks a thesis. In following his dictum, stated in the title to Chapter One, that "The Poets Are Their Poems," Rosenthal does advance an argument, and one that grows naturally out of his view of the critic as an empathic adventurer. What makes the adventure worthwhile, Rosenthal says, what really counts in poetry is the intensity of experience, or, more specifically, the intensity of feeling, that good poems offer, and what distinguishes the work of Yeats, Pound, and Eliot, and what makes them so important to poets writing after them, is that they wrote poetry built around distinct centers of emotional intensity, points of heightened awareness that dominate and control a given poem, sometimes regardless of what the poem seems to be saying on a strictly rational level. Rosenthal calls this a "poetry of open process," and describes it as loosely structured, "largely presentative," and, far from being didactic, directed at "a balancing of volatile emotional states." (p. 364)

Rosenthal is ... less convincing on Yeats than on Pound and Eliot, and his failings here reveal important shortcomings in his subjective critical approach and in his thesis about controlling emotional centers. For one thing, one reader's notion of a poem's controlling center may not be another's. Rosenthal argues, for example, that the main thrust of "Sailing to Byzantium" is the poet's desire, frustrated though it may be, to join the sensual world described in the opening stanza.... But it could as readily be argued that ... the poem's main thrust is the desire to transcend the sensual world of death and generation. (pp. 365-66)

Rosenthal runs into similar problems in trying to rescue *A Vision* from the unpoetic realms of philosophy and mysticism to which it usually is consigned. His argument that "The Phases of the Moon," one of Yeats's poems that first appeared in this book, deserves to be admired in its own right and not merely as a verse crib on *A Vision* is, on the whole, convincing. But when he takes on the considerably taller order of demonstrating that "All Souls' Night," a poem of much less lyric intensity, "may be the most original and moving poem" in *The Tower* (a volume containing, to name just a few, such poems as "Sailing to Byzantium," "The Tower," "Leda and the Swan," and "Among School Children"), the reader surely is justified in demanding some strong evidence. Unfortunately, this is precisely where Rosenthal's usually specific criticism fails him, and he falls back on such summary and subjective statements as "The poignancy of each of the three lives is developed with tender sympathy" and, in reference to the poem's decidedly unexalted closing image, "... the language reaches another plane: a state of ultimate readiness—that 'ecstasy of pure sensibility.'"

Nevertheless, a book that announces that criticism should concern itself with "the idiosyncratic life and form of individual poems—something to be explored one poem at a time, and again and again" deserves to be judged, to a significant extent, on the quality of its readings of individual poems. And here, with some important exceptions (the discussion of "All Souls' Night" being one, and an unconvincing reading of "Nineteen Hundred and Nineteen" being another), *Sailing Into the Unknown* is to be recommended. In fact, if this book does nothing else, it demonstrates once again that poets of the calibre of Yeats, Pound, and Eliot—however much they seem to have been exhausted by hordes of scholars and critics, including those eager to apply complex theoretical systems to works of art—still reward the close and sensitive textual attention that Rosenthal's brand of criticism can give. (p. 366)

> Gregory A. Schirmer, in a review of "Sailing into the Unknown: Yeats, Pound, and Eliot," in Western Humanities Review (copyright, 1978, University of Utah; reprinted by permission), Vol. XXXII, No. 4, Autumn, 1978, pp. 364-67.

THEODORE WEISS

A number of English poets and critics, some of the best among them, have understandably long resented Pound, Eliot, and Yeats as well....

A similar reaction has occurred in the United States. A number of poets and critics have deprecated Yeats and Eliot (if not so much Pound). (p. 124)

But the detractors of Yeats, Pound, and Eliot, especially the more vehement among them, may be doing these poets a service. They are voicing the inevitable human reaction to success: our tiring of the triumphant, in itself and in our applause of it. This would-be dethronement—the reasonable desire of new poets to throw off the past and to find their own voices notwithstanding—may help to preserve and eventually restore our three poets.

After a time readers and writers, young ones particularly, needing to react to their present's fix, may seek out Yeats and Eliot again. To prosper, literature requires hindrances, oppositions.

It is all this that makes M. L. Rosenthal's *Sailing into the Unknown: Yeats, Pound and Eliot* sharply pertinent. During the years that he has had the work in mind, books about these poets have appeared in swarms. Consequently, one might think his volume belated. However, the time and its havocs have ripened Rosenthal's powers and afforded him an important perspective.... Moreover, it is precisely at this moment, when we are in danger of discarding these three poets, that we need a reassertion of their relevance. Rosenthal's book reminds us of what we are always inclined to forget: how much a poem can come to. He urges us not to settle for too little, not to be too easily satisfied. Out of his respect for poetry's basic significance to our lives and his refusal to allow critical theorizing to eclipse poems themselves, he is ideally prepared to demonstrate the pertinacy of Yeats, Pound and Eliot in the only way that matters—through their work. We must esteem the intensity of his involvement and, his direct but highly discriminating love of that work.

His book offers an accurately bifocal view: Yeats, Pound and Eliot in their poems and in their appositeness to us. He emphasizes their innovativeness, their great Odyssean daring, their ability to exploit and make prominent "the implicitly presentative and improvisatory character of poetry", or structure and process, the structure frequently made of and by the process.

However, he does not blink his poets' weaknesses, their programmatic impulses that sometimes weighed upon their imaginative powers. He prizes them for their part in establishing a new genre, perhaps the most significant in modern times, the poetic sequence, which enables the poet to exercise his whole being. Rosenthal's experience in writing sequences himself, most recently his moving *She,* enables him to respond to them with special rapport. It is something like Elizabethan completeness he is after, a recovery of the total human condition.

Undertaking his journey through the work of his three poets, he proposes that we try to read them "with mind entire", in the way they read their lives and the work of their great predecessors, in the way they wrote their poems. By this proposal Rosenthal means the reverse of a removal from society or life itself. Plunging into Canto 47 as it "directly acts out that communion of past and present which, felt at the pitch of experience is nothing less than our human meaning in process", he enlightens us on the brilliant experimental use Pound made of traditional or archaic materials, on the mystery and the energy he released in bringing Odysseus up to date. . . .

Rosenthal considers *The Cantos* "a sequence of sequences". Because of the half century in which the work accumulated and because of its improvisatory nature he thinks it absurd—and I agree—to expect the poem to have a single integrity. . . .

The Cantos constitute a texture, the weaving and reweaving, like Penelope's endless industry, of a most extraordinary poetic mind. Or rather, like Odysseus himself, one twisting in and out and back and forth on its long journey. And Rosenthal is most helpful in following the intricate movements of Pound's imagination. In his examination of the first *A Draft of XVI Cantos* he establishes the pacing of the process and, at the same time, the emergent moments of ecstatic yet completely lucid loveliness; these, like imagism itself, stabilize the poem and focus, even while they underwrite, its riotous energies.

Rosenthal recognizes the "tendentious" material that invades the later *Cantos* and the mechanical that now and then overtakes the organic. However, sympathetic to what he calls their "found poetry", he applauds Pound's "genius in deploying documentary quotations and other data". Pound, it is true, almost persuades us to share his enthusiasm for his sources, as important to him in their original utterance as the unique moments in the languages he admired. Despite his aversion for abstractions, the fact of his documents, their very literalness, saved them from being mere ideas to Pound. Rosenthal reads *The Pisan Cantos* with great, delicate sympathy. So much so that one might feel some uneasiness before statements like "change the names [here Mussolini and company] and a few specific details, and the same passage could be used to memorialize a political martyrdom or defeat in a cause cherished by more of us. . . ." No doubt, but surely the names and the specific details, especially to anyone as sensitive to them as Rosenthal, make a fundamental difference?

With Yeats's "Civil War Sequences" Rosenthal pauses briefly to discuss the poetic sequence itself. He finds it a natural outgrowth of the modern sensibility. Whatever diverse elements it may include, he concludes that "its ordering is finally lyrical, a succession of effects . . . openly improvisational and tentative in structure. . . ." Indeed the lyrical is the core of modern poetry, out of the person of the poet. . . .

In his chapter "Uncomfortable Choices" Rosenthal suggests that Eliot, falling somewhere between Yeats and Pound, was less rooted than Yeats but, his greater "orbit of association" notwithstanding, "always more deliberate" than Pound. The uncomfortable choice, as Rosenthal sees it, was Eliot's deciding increasingly that his didactic Christian message must be openly expressed; for Rosenthal this tendentiousness mars the work: Eliot ". . . took the risk of bringing the whole baggage of his mind along, cluttering the aesthetic field of action as he went". Certainly the religious and philosophical matters in the poems can constitute a problem. But Eliot's tendency to elaborate his ideas, one might observe, did find great precedence in Dante, who never hesitated to bring the whole baggage of his mind along, especially in the purgatorial cantos. And, of course, Pound stuffed his *Cantos* with all kinds of recalcitrant materials. In his wariness before ideas as ideas, his suspicion of abstractions, Rosenthal seems closer to Pound, despite his actual practice, than to Eliot or Yeats—closer, that is, to the more recent prevailing attitude.

In spite of such reservations Rosenthal, impressed with Eliot's precocity, says that, from the start of his writing, "Everything Eliot does is experimental in some genuine sense". At the same time he examines Eliot's gradual (sometimes years-long) building of a poem, occasionally cut of seemingly discrete, separately published sections. And he admires the depth and extent of feeling such building elicits (and requires) to make a whole poem. . . .

In his last chapter, "Continuities: Lessons of the Masters", Rosenthal stresses the three poets' continuing presence. Deftly and briefly, commenting on other poets, mostly more recent ones, from Lowell and Creely to Ashbery and Snyder, he remarks their debt to Yeats, Pound, and Eliot, but their lesser stature for exercising only a small part of the earlier poets' mastery. . . .

Returning, finally to his initial image of the Odyssean model that Pound employed, Rosenthal accents the past, its use, as a vital presence and reassurance, a source of strength rather than anxiety. "The normal poetic position—from a poet's point of view—is that communion with the sensibilities of the past is necessary both to self-location and to learning what it is to explore the hitherto unknown." But the normal poetic position does not seem to be so normal today. It is ironical that for almost diametrical reasons many poets and critics concur in distrusting the past. The poets shy away from it out of their gainsaying its worth, its relevancy, and out of their desire to be themselves, wholly here and now. . . .

Rosenthal is to be commended for pointing out that [William Carlos] Williams, an immense influence on recent poets, was, especially in *Paterson,* much closer to Eliot, Pound and Yeats than he or his followers have recognized. Convincingly, Rosenthal compares elements of *Paterson* Book I with the much-earlier *The Waste Land.* Then he suggests the vast reach of the three poets' influence, and in England the impact of Yeats (not Hardy) on Auden, Empson, Larkin, and Hughes—though not one of these, Rosenthal contends, possesses their model's manysidedness. But, Rosenthal judiciously concludes, what poets after Yeats and Eliot have done and are doing helps, like more news of Odysseus, to reveal additional facets of the latter's great, still richly living art, helps us also to realize more than ever the breadth of their poems. New poems help us, and so do books of criticism as astute as this one. (p. 125)

Theodore Weiss, "The Many-Sidedness of Modernism," in The Times Literary Supplement *(© Times*

Newspapers Ltd. (London) 1980; reproduced from The Times Literary Supplement by permission), No. 4010, February 1, 1980, pp. 124-25.

JOSEPH A. LIPARI

Rosenthal displays impressive range and intelligence in [*Poems 1964-1980*], which includes poems from four previous books and new pieces. Rosenthal is not afraid to tackle major themes (nature and the imagination, memory and desire, the violence of our time, the redemption which is love), and he does so with suppleness and wit. Still, his limitations as a poet are apparent here. At his best, Rosenthal fuses the personal and universal in a lucid yet suggestive rhetoric. At times, though, stridency and ironic undercutting, mythological and literary allusions, and archaic diction ("you're borne / whithersoever the torrent lists") are poor substitutes for vivid emotion.

Joseph A. Lipari, in a review of "Poems 1964-1980," in Library Journal *(reprinted from* Library Journal, *October 1, 1981; published by R. R. Bowker Co. (a Xerox company); copyright © 1981 by Xerox Corporation), Vol. 106, No. 17, October 1, 1981, p. 1930.*

JOHN PARISI

The variety of subjects and tones, the technical skills, the fine perceptions, but also the faults of the poet are well represented in [*Poems, 1964-1980*], especially in his rightly acclaimed love lyrics. Rosenthal has a special gift for locating the peculiar nexus where human duality results in dilemma. He is probably at his best in witty verses that contract complexities into pithy paradoxes. Too often, however, his heart gets the better of his head—an understandable occupational hazard for one so immersed in amatory matters—and the poet veers toward merely facile remarks, sentimental tags, or pseudoprofound aphorisms, especially in disappointing closing lines that betray the strengths and originality of those preceding them. Still, this is a most enjoyable, and accessible, collection from a poet of many tastes and talents.

John Parisi, in a review of "Poems, 1964-1980," in Booklist *(reprinted by permission of the American Library Association; copyright © 1981 by the American Library Association), Vol. 78, No. 5, November 1, 1981, p. 366.*

Mari (Susette) Sandoz
1896-1966

(Also wrote under pseudonym of Mari Macumber) American nonfiction writer, novelist, short story writer, and historian.

Sandoz is widely considered an outstanding historian of the American West, as well as an accomplished regional novelist. Although she was not formally trained as a historian, her work has been praised for its accuracy in describing the development and settling of the Great Plains. Believing that earlier books on the Old West had relied on romanticism and had grossly distorted historical fact, Sandoz became known as an exceptional authority on the West because of her candid realism and strong narrative skill.

Sandoz was born in northwest Nebraska and raised by Swiss immigrant parents. Her childhood was typical of many frontier children. As the eldest of six children, she bore the burden of tending to her younger brothers and sisters as well as performing heavy physical chores. While in her teens, Sandoz was sent out in a blizzard to retrieve the family's livestock that had strayed. As a result of the exposure to the sun and snow during that incident, she was permanently blinded in her left eye. At seventeen Sandoz completed the eighth grade and became a teacher at a nearby rural school. She later attended the University of Nebraska.

Sandoz's father had a significant impact on her life and writing career. Her first book, *Old Jules* (1935), is a narrative based on the life of her father. Jules Sandoz was the quintessential pioneer. He was one of the original immigrants to settle along the Niobrara river in Nebraska during the 1880s and had vigorously recruited many families to migrate near his homestead. He became a dominant figure in the region. Sandoz was often the victim of her father's violent temper and their relationship was strained, yet she saw his compassionate side in his relationship with the Indians who lived on a nearby Sioux reservation. These Indians were frequent guests of the Sandoz family. During their visits Sandoz heard many colorful stories of past Indian wars and such historical figures as Chief Sitting Bull and General George A. Custer. These stories influenced her use of idioms and enabled her to employ the symbolic language patterns of the Sioux. After the publication of *Old Jules* Sandoz spent the remainder of her career researching and writing about the Western frontier.

Sandoz's nonfiction is collectively known as *The Great Plains Series* or *The Trans-Missouri Series*. *Crazy Horse* (1942), the first book published in this series, is a picturesque biography of Chief Crazy Horse. Sandoz researched his life through government files and included Indian folktales she had heard as a child. Critical reception to the book was generally positive, although some critics maintained that Sandoz's method of writing from the point of view of an Indian made the book difficult to read. *Cheyenne Autumn* (1953) is an epic chronicle of a group of Cheyennes and their two-thousand-mile march from an Oklahoma reservation back to their Montana homeland. Although most critics praised Sandoz for the book's authenticity and scholarship, some questioned her objectivity, charging that she was overly sympathetic toward the Indians. The remaining three books of the *Great Plains Series*, *The Buffalo Hunters* (1954), *The Cattlemen* (1958), and *The Beaver Men* (1964), are also historical studies of the American West.

Caroline Pifer for Mari Sandoz Estate

Sandoz has also written several novels for both adult and juvenile readers. Her adult novels never received the critical attention accorded her nonfiction. However, her first novel, *Slogum House* (1937), became notorious for its plot and strong language. Set in a mythical Nebraska county, *Slogum House* is about a ruthless woman and her quest for power and wealth. To achieve her goal, she offers her daughters to influential men in exchange for political and business favors, and openly encourages her sons to murder anyone who opposes her. This book was banned in Omaha and in several other Nebraska libraries. *Capital City* (1939) is an allegorical novel about the threat of fascism in modern American society. Although critics compared this book with Sinclair Lewis's *It Can't Happen Here*, they found its message too sensational to be credible.

Sandoz's keen sense of history is prevalent throughout her work. She eloquently explored the conflict between the Plains Indians and the settlers, and recorded the Indian's demise in journalistic, yet lyrical prose. Having grown up on the prairie, Sandoz was attuned to nature and recognized the need to protect and preserve it. Although she deeply regretted the ways in which the West was finally conquered by the white man, critics believe that her vibrant love of the land and of America itself prevail in her work.

(See also *Contemporary Authors*, Vols. 1-4, rev. ed., Vols. 25-28, rev. ed. [obituary]; *Something about the Author*, Vol. 5; and *Dictionary of Literary Biography*, Vol. 9.)

WILLIAM ALLEN WHITE

[*Old Jules*] is the story of a pioneer in the high plains of the trans-Missouri country—western Nebraska. To understand Old Jules thoroughly and to get the sap out of him, to see him in his rugged beauty, one must understand his habitat. The trans-Mississippi country rises, an inclined plane, from the Father of Waters. In six hundred miles the plane is tilted from five hundred feet above sea level to five thousand feet, at the base of the Rocky Mountains. The land along the valley through the eastern Dakotas, Minnesota, Iowa, Missouri, Nebraska, and eastern Kansas is much like that from the Mississippi east to the base of the Alleghenies, rich alluvial soil, loam mostly, where corn grows wherever there is adequate rainfall. There crops are fairly certain. But after the land has risen more than 2500 feet into the thin, dry air, rainfall is never predictable. It is a land of strong contrasts, floods and drouths. Here the buffalo and the horse Indians of the high plains roamed in the sixties and seventies until the late eighties, the last stand of the red man. Here the regular army after the Civil War appeared as a defender of the settler, and the Indian, the soldier, and the pioneer made a unique and colorful civilization. Spread fairly thin, this rather gaudy pattern of American life covered those high plains in the western Dakotas, Nebraska, Kansas, and Texas, eastern Colorado and Wyoming. This was the area which geographers of the first half of the nineteenth century called 'The Great American Desert.' It was then and is still semi-arid, a land of tremendous variations—forty below sometimes in winter, one hundred and twenty above sometimes in the summer; a land of floods and withering hot winds; a land that dried up men and discouraged women.

Here Old Jules, the subject of this biography, came in the early eighties. He was a Swiss. He met the soldier and the Indian and looked them both in the eye without fear. He proposed to make an Eden out of those blanched plains. And this story, which is a definitive, documented, carefully verified account of his fifty years' battle with the elements, is a most remarkable tale. The author has painted Old Jules warts and all, a coarse, strong, unwashed, passionate, contentious, domineering, amorous old male. He seems to have derived from the vanishing buffalo some of his tenacious traits. But this book is more than the story of Old Jules. It is the story of three successive charges of pioneers who rushed up the long slanting plain from the lush fields of the lower valley toward the mountain, and who fell under the merciless fire of the wind, the dust, the floods, the grasshoppers, and all the inclement and terrible forces of nature in that bleak wilderness. (pp. 16, 18)

The writing of this story is as rough and raw as Old Jules himself. There is a sort of native twang and flavor to the telling that no one could put there who did not have in his blood something of the militant, dogged, gorgeous zest of life that marked Old Jules.

In this chronicle which is earthy but never dirty, one sees and feels the pioneer life, enjoys its food gradually expanding from simple bread, meat, and potatoes into a wide bill of fare as the fruit trees Old Jules loved to propagate came into bearing. A thesis on pioneer sophisticated country cooking could be made up from this book. Also one might write another thesis about the evolution of folk furniture; another about the growth of folk decorations in pioneer homes. Half a dozen Master's theses might be collected from this story of Old Jules, a really great folk tale. (p. 18)

William Allen White, "A Prize Winner," in The Atlantic Book Shelf, *November, 1935, pp. 16, 18.*

STANLEY T. WILLIAMS

Distrustful of Leatherstocking and of the vast body of sentimental literature of the frontier, some of us have long suspected that the true conqueror of the land was a hero as brutal as its icy winters but, at times, as picturesque as the sunflowers along its sand trails. . . . Romanticists have tinted the stark fact of such men, and realists have dimmed their romance, until in our present attempts to relive the life of the West we encounter either the Rousseauesque natural man, ennobled beyond all probability, or the free trapper with his ax and rifle, keeping his bare journal, too sterile, too colorless to be the true mirror of the explorer's life. The extraordinary power of [*Old Jules*] appears to be in conveying truth of event and scene on the frontier in the medium of a style so vital and imaginative that instead of fiction or a trader's diary we read the very minds of these pioneer men and women. (pp. 391-92)

The story of Old Jules himself is absorbing. So are the glimpses of the frontier women, as authentic as those in the untutored pages of St. John de Crèvecoeur of the eighteenth century. I think the story itself a valuable bit of Americana: how Jules Sandoz quarrelled with his father; how he came out of the East in the spring over the pale green prairie to found his home and race. Two passions moved him, to obtain a woman for his home, and to subdue the land. To fulfil the first aim he had four wives, one of whom became insane. For the latter he fought, setting out claims, developing townships, growing orchards, and, with the aid of a medical book, delivering babies. So he lived, until at the end of the road, where the signpost read FORTY MILES TO OLD JULES, he lay dying and bade farewell at the age of seventy-one to this world. . . . Perhaps this story is enough, but two other elements are the true gold of the book. Throughout the turmoil of Old Jules's life may be heard the deeper murmur of the nation's battle with the frontier. Familiar figures pass for a moment and are gone—a youthful doctor named Walter Reed, a young lawyer called Bryan, a hunter known as Theodore Roosevelt, and a lad, of the same surname, known as Franklin Delano. We look down over the terrible aftermath of the massacre of Wounded Knee; we hear the new railroad, and Old Jules learning to use the telephone. In brief, the march of civilization westward is the ground-tone of the book. But, most of all, we are conscious of the land, the terrible, the beautiful land, with its grass, yellow or green, its magnesia white bluffs, its haze on the horizon, its naked knolls and canyons, its silver ribbon of the Niobrara. Surely never, save perhaps in the novels of Miss Willa Cather, has the sinister enchantress, the frontier, seemed so real as in this narrative of the Swiss frontiersman Old Jules. (pp. 392-93)

Stanley T. Williams, "A Nebraska Outpost," in The Yale Review *(copyright 1935 by Yale University; reprinted by permission of the editors), Vol. XXV, No. 2, December, 1935, pp. 391-93.*

ROSE C. FELD

["*Slogum House*"] is a book that none but Mari Sandoz could have written. No other woman would have dared attempt such a background and such a story and no man possesses the intimate knowledge of a feminine mind as strong and corrosive and ruthless as that of Gulla Slogum. "**Slogum House**" is a brutal book written for strong stomachs, and its author in her strength casts a shadow tall and deep.

Pioneer life—its trials, its hardships, its color—has been the magnet that has drawn the steel of many a novelist. It is an important part of the heritage of the nation, nearer to this generation, as this volume shows, than most persons realize. The years have cast a glamour about it, made up of covered wagons, of strong silent men, of splendid brave women who made fine mates and good mothers. There is truth in this picture but not the whole truth.

"**Slogum House**" tells the story of pioneer strength divorced from goodness, of greed for land that knows no law and no kindness, of motherhood that uses its power for evil and for gain. It is as though Mari Sandoz, incapable of longer retaining her impatience with the pretty stories of a life she has known and heard about at first hand, had come to the conclusion that the reading world is old enough and mature enough to face the facts of life. It is possible that in her devotion to integrity of fact and scene she has crowded the canvas beyond artistic proportions, but hers is a compulsion that knows no conventional measurements. Like the principal character she depicts, she is ruthless in attaining her desire and, like her, succeeds in becoming a person unique among her kind. . . .

The four hundred pages of this novel are packed with violence of action and emotion. There is no crime too low or too vicious that Gulla cannot contemplate to attain her ends. Moving heavily through a secret passage in the walls of Slogum House, she hears everything that goes on, listens to the talk of the men who come to spend the night, and gleans from their gossip the news that gives direction to her plans. One neighbor is killed because he knows too much about the disappearance of horses, another is unspeakably outraged for daring to put a decent thought in the head of an indecent daughter, others are robbed, intimidated, or run out of the country. And Gulla, fearsome, large, heavy, works at her map and moves her boundaries ever wider.

The novel moves to its end with the beat of crashing doom. [Gulla's brother] Butch is murdered by the hand of the gentle Ruedy to protect the virtue of a daughter who had none, one son is driven to death by the man whom he destroyed, another is strangled in his hour of triumph. These are some of the fruits of Gulla's sowing but inconsequential to her as compared to the greater harvest of land. She is an incredible creature made monstrously credible by Mari Sandoz. She runs a bawdy house but will not have liquor in the house, she ruins her neighbors but cooks them a dinner when prairie fires destroy their homes, she uses her daughters for no good purposes but insists that the cattlemen talk respectfully to them.

Mari Sandoz writes with a sweep and power as strong as a tornado and as devastating. Just as she has no fear of piling horror upon horror and outrage upon outrage, she has no fear of using language that gives integrity to the picture she presents. It is the language of the frontier, of the saloon and the fancy house. Coming from a woman, many may find it shocking, but with these Mari Sandoz will have small patience and little concern. For men and women with stronger tastes "**Slogum House**" is an unforgettable book and Gulla Slogum an unforgettable character.

> Rose C. Feld, "Pioneer Strength Divorced from Goodness," in New York Herald Tribune Books (© I.H.T. Corporation; reprinted by permission), November 28, 1937, p. 7.

MARGARET WALLACE

It is not altogether unusual, in these literate days, to come upon a first novel of artistic merit. But it is always bound to be something of an event when a first novel not only proves to be admirable on the score of craftmanship but also introduces to the ranks of contemporary novelists a new and original and arresting personality. This is what "**Slogum House**" does. While it is a first novel, and one to review with surprise and remember with pleasure, it is not a first book. Mari Sandoz's story of her father, "**Old Jules**," won a non-fiction prize award in 1935. Geographically the two narratives are similar. . . . Mari Sandoz shows herself so closely informed of the life of her own country—its history, its physical aspect, its economic roots and political necessities—that a reader even slightly acquainted with the literature of the Middle West could identify not only the scene of her story but the very decade in which any given action must have occurred. Thus, among other things, "**Slogum House**" is a fine piece of reporting.

There are dozens of scenes which will stick in the reader's mind like burrs in a saddle blanket. The dusty little court room at Dumur, where the Slogum boys come to trial, first for a matter of colt stealing and later for the murder of the principal witness against them. The parlor at Slogum House, where the pretty daughters entertain the county officialdom and the "upstairs girls" are sold off to console the cowhands and teamsters. Gulla Slogum's office, the center of her spider-web, with its map of her projected rangeland empire. The crow's nest on top of the house, where lurks an occasional fugitive from justice, holding his gun steady out of sheer desperation whenever the trapdoor is lifted. . . .

The whole intricate plot, the whole sprawling and vastly populated scene of "**Slogum House**," is integrated in [a] single figure. Gulla is the rugged individualist—the very archetype of the unscrupulous builders of empire to whom the West offered, in the past century, such golden opportunity. Moreover, Gulla had suffered a serious slight back in Ohio. She had succeeded in her intention of marrying Rudy Slogum. But when she went to call on his sisters she had been sent around to the back door, where she was offered a cup of tea in the kitchen and a ten-dollar bill.

This was the springboard of Gulla's soaring ambition. Definitely she meant to wring a fortune out of the cattle country, by foul means if fair proved inefficient, and to show those sisters of Rudy's a thing or two before she was through. But it ought to be explained, in justice to Mari Sandoz, that this is no childish tale of obsession and spite. It is a remarkably sweeping and ironic picture of America's last frontier during a period of half a century. Gulla's ambition, like all authentic urges of the kind, ends by outstripping and losing sight of its original object. In the most vivid sense she grows up with the country.

It is clearly no part of Mari Sandoz's intention in this novel to express a political or social philosophy, although she permits her characters their convictions and programs and panaceas. These are bound to arise, she would seem to say, whenever the going gets particularly rough. She brings her story to 1933, through all the catch-phrases of the recent depression, but never without a backward glance at the hard times of the Nineties—when, as we always seem apt to forget, similar philosophies flourished.

If "**Slogum House**" itself has a conclusion to express, it is concerned rather with human character than with any principle of collective action. Laws may be passed and economies planned, but the strong and insensitive still have a natural advantage in dealing with the weak and vulnerable.

This may not be a pretty conclusion. But "**Slogum House**" could not be described as a pretty book. On the contrary, it may be attacked in some quarters as a sordid book.... It is neither sordid nor obscene, however, because it is free of any gratuitous intention in these respects. Mari Sandoz has included nothing here which is not a necessary and legitimate part of her picture.

> Margaret Wallace, "Mari Sandoz, Author of 'Old Jules', Writes Again of the Nebraska Cow Country," in The New York Times Book Review (copyright © 1937 by The New York Times Company; reprinted by permission), November 28, 1937, p. 6.

CLIFTON FADIMAN

The design on the jacket of Mari Sandoz's novel, "**Capital City,**" suggests a bursting bomb. While the book's materials are potentially explosive, I doubt that its final effect on the reader will be more than that of a mild concussion. For one thing, Miss Sandoz is too obviously out to shock: her very sentences show the strain. For another, though the journalistic value of "**Capital City**" is high, it is simply not a very good novel.

Miss Sandoz aims to pin down with the brass tacks of fact the picture of American Fascism that Sinclair Lewis drew so tellingly in "It Can't Happen Here." In the not-so-imaginary Midwestern State of Kanewa is the not-so-imaginary capital city of Franklin. Things are going on today in Franklin, and in a hundred Franklins throughout the land, if we are to trust Miss Sandoz's angry eye and pen. Gold Shirts, college-boy Storm Troopers, mysterious deaths of people with names like Greenspan; demagogues and new democratic leaders rising in opposition to the demagogues; the town's "best people" scared into violence by fear, desperate with the knowledge that they are not the men and women their pioneer forefathers were; the loose-enders, the intellectual outcasts uniting around social issues instead of aesthetic issues as in Carol Kennicott's day; newspapers, puzzlingly subsidized, with names like the *Christian Challenger,* printing open incitements to pogroms. In brief, not Fascism but the possible setup for Fascism.

That's what "**Capital City**" is about. All the material is real enough, perhaps even yanked out of newspaper files, and yet "It Can't Happen Here," which was based on a mere hypothesis, has greater solidity, as both art and propaganda, than Miss Sandoz's book. In "**Capital City**" the town itself has a certain vividness, but the characters have none.... The author has plenty of hardbitten talent, as "**Old Jules**" and "**Slogum House,**" her previous books, testify, but I think "**Capital City**" makes very little use of them.

The message of "**Capital City**" is not one American citizens can lightly disregard. It seems too bad that it has not been clothed in more convincing form. Indignation alone does not make novels. (pp. 94, 96)

> Clifton Fadiman, "Sandburg Finishes Lincoln—Setup for Fascism—Why We Travel" (copyright © 1939, 1967 by The New Yorker Magazine, Inc.; reprinted by permission of Lescher & Lescher, Ltd.), in The New Yorker, Vol. XV, No. 42, December 2, 1939, pp. 94, 96-7.*

STANLEY WALKER

Miss Sandoz, that unusual and powerful writer who is best remembered for her story of her lusty father, "**Old Jules,**" now turns her hand to the life and times of the great warrior of the Oglala Sioux, the quiet and deadly one known as Crazy Horse. Her regard for the man is deep, amounting almost to adoration. And this is understandable. For among all those remarkable Plains Indians none was braver than Crazy Horse, and none more steadfast.

The research that obviously has gone into ["**Crazy Horse**"] is downright astounding. Miss Sandoz has dug into every old report she could find, the government files, faded letters, and in addition she has interviewed scores of persons who might contribute something to the lore of Crazy Horse and the story of his people during the tragic years of their gradual and inevitable dissolution. She has brought to the task an indefatigable spirit and an understanding heart. As a child, in the southern part of what once was the hunting grounds of the Sioux, she knew the Indians, and all her life the stories of these people have been all about her. As any one must who has become at all familiar with the history of these people, she has much sympathy for them....

There seems little doubt that Crazy Horse was the most outstanding of the many eminent Sioux warriors—and that noble confederation produced many good ones. Sitting Bull, of course, has had more publicity than Crazy Horse, but when there was fighting to be done it was usually Crazy Horse who was in the thick of things, although this is not to cast any aspirations on Sitting Bull's courage, of which the old boy was well supplied. But this Crazy Horse—what a fighter!...

The story of Crazy Horse is eminently worth doing. Miss Sandoz writes with vigor and feeling. For these reasons it is probable that many persons will greet this book as a masterpiece of its sort. Those who fancy they have insight into the ordinarily inscrutable soul of the Indian will doubtless be delighted with this performance. But not every one will feel this way. This reviewer, for example, who yields to no one, not even Miss Sandoz, in admiration for the Plains Indians and in fascination at their history, found it exceedingly tough going. To be blunt about it, the book is hard to read. The reason for this is that the gifted Miss Sandoz tries to write and think as a Sioux of the period of Crazy Horse would think and write.

Many readers are sure to find it an awkward device. To say that there are no "white man words" for certain things is, of course, true enough but the question arises whether the author hasn't carried this theory pretty far. The point is debatable. Some will find her attempt at Indian rhythm, and her constantly recurring imagery, entrancingly beautiful; others will wish that she had set down a simple, clear, factual, objective and yet understanding account, in the King's English. The daughter of old Jules knows her Indians, all right, but when she tries to write like an Indian it all becomes a bit thick....

Perhaps she has succeeded, notwithstanding the enormity of the assignment which she set for herself. Certainly her tale is worth telling, and it does have passages of great beauty, and much strength, for all its convolutions. Here, as reconstructed by Miss Sandoz, is what Crazy Horse did, said and thought throughout his eventful career. She is scrupulously careful to adhere to the main known outlines of the record, and her poetic imagination has supplied the rest.

> Stanley Walker, "Greatest of the Buffalo Hunters," in New York Herald Tribune Books (© I.H.T. Corporation; reprinted by permission), November 29, 1942, p. 4.

CLIFTON FADIMAN

[Mari Sandoz] has been carrying on a fervent historico-literary affair with a dead Indian, the consequence of which is a curious, half-interesting, uneven book called **"Crazy Horse: The Strange Man of the Oglalas."** (p. 84)

The author has gone to enormous trouble not merely to get at the tangled truth of our own somewhat shameful relations with the Indians of the region but to project her imagination backward in such a manner as practically to identify herself with the Indian mind. The result is a book that is half history, half heroic epic, and not entirely successful as either. Crazy Horse was doubtless a great, if inevitably doomed, leader, but his story is told so completely from his own point of view that it seems to belong as much to the literature of apologetics as to the literature of biography.

Whenever she is able to extricate herself from the quagmire of detail (in which students of the period will doubtless take considerable pleasure), Miss Sandoz writes with great drive and passion—more, perhaps, than the average reader will think the theme deserves. Unquestionably, her book, the product of studious labor, will rank among the important records of the history of the American Indian. (pp. 84, 86)

> Clifton Fadiman, "Nemetskies" (copyright © 1942, 1970 by The New Yorker Magazine, Inc.; reprinted by permission of Lescher & Lescher, Ltd.), in The New Yorker, Vol. XV, No. 42, December 5, 1942, pp. 82, 84, 86.*

W. R. BURNETT

Because of my bias in favor of all accounts and stories of the Old West, I hesitate to state categorically that [**"Cheyenne Autumn"**] is a great book, but I have a deep suspicion that it is. And I say this in spite of the fact that at times the author annoys and irritates me with her wild partisanship in favor of the Cheyennes. The Indians are shown throughout as high-minded and well-intentioned—even when they are looting, killing and burning. And, with few exceptions, the whites are shown as cowardly, treacherous, drunken and generally repulsive and ridiculous. And yet this very understandable partisanship, particularly in a woman, is part of the strength of this Indian epic. Miss Sandoz . . . writes of the Cheyennes with deep insight, complete sympathy, and great knowledge.

If you are interested in the history of your own country, don't miss this excellent book.

> W. R. Burnett, "The Frozen Flight of Little Wolf and His People," in The New York Times Book Review (copyright © 1953 by The New York Times Company; reprinted by permission), November 22, 1953, p. 6.

J. FRANK DOBIE

Let no one regard **"Cheyenne Autumn"** as one of those customary attempts by historians to rescue an episode or a figure from oblivion. The episode did not change history, any more than the march of 10,000 Greeks under Xenophon out of Persia changed history, but it has all the elements of that drama. Miss Sandoz has made it into a Lear-like tragedy of displaced persons.

The story begins in the fall of 1878 and ends in the following winter. The place is along 2,000 harsh miles between a guarded reservation camp in Oklahoma and the mouth of Powder River on the Yellowstone. The main actors are Dull Knife and Little Wolf, who fulfilled the conception of a great chief: "Forget himself and remember only the people."

A few of the people in the cast with those great chiefs are warriors, from 13 years old up, more with bows and arrows than with rifles, some as hostile to discipline as to "the spiders" (white men). The impersonators of love, jealousy and murder act their parts. The presence of a boy, seldom seen and always silent, has the power of the Voice of Kurtz in Conrad's "Heart of Darkness." (pp. 1, 14)

Superstition, hunger, lack of horses, and not understanding the minds of their conquerors pressed as hard against the hiding homeseekers as the soldiers. And the mind of Mari Sandoz is inside these Cheyennes as sensitively as it is inside her outlooking self. She seldom comments. She pictures constantly with economy. Without one word of analysis concerning the deep spiritual content of Plains Indians, she stands on Bear Butte with Little Wolf "to fast and meditate," seeking wisdom for the guidance of his people. She is there by a campfire with Spotted Deer feeding broth to his old grandmother, "who has been so homesick for the North that his Southern parents sent him to take her there." In cold so deep that it froze grouse stone dead, she is with a lone little girl that soldiers found in a rocky crevice fingering some cards—and refusing to tell where other Indians hid.

Nobody can read this moving book, along with George Bird Grinnell's noble volumes on "The Fighting Cheyennes" and Captain John G. Bourke's noble "On the Border with Crook" without considering again the tragic failure of the United States to incorporate into its Melting Pot the great tribes of the West. . . . (p. 14)

> J. Frank Dobie, "When the Cheyennes Went Home," in New York Herald Tribune Book Review, December 13, 1953, pp. 1, 14.

W. R. BURNETT

The fate of the Plains Indian was inextricably bound up with the fate of the buffalo; they fell together. This is the story Miss Sandoz has to tell [in **"The Buffalo Hunters"**], and she tells it beautifully, forcefully, epically. She knows what she is writing about to the minutest detail; she knows the Great Plains country and loves it—not as a tourist but as a native, well aware of its drawbacks and dangers.

A procession of interesting frontier figures, red and white, passes through the narrative, briefly but sharply characterized: Wild Bill Hickok, one of the most controversial figures of the time—they are still arguing about him in some sections of the West; pompous Buffalo Bill, part charlatan, part authentic frontiersman; Phil Sheridan, Bat Masterson, Custer and his wild-headed brother, and the great Indian chiefs Roman Nose, Yellow Wolf, Spotted Tail and Sitting Bull. There are battles, massacres, cowtown gunfights, but no violence for the sake of violence. This is history, and the reading of it is both saddening and exhilarating. . . .

In conclusion I'd like to repeat what I said about **"Cheyenne Autumn,"** an earlier book of Miss Sandoz [see excerpt above]: "Because of my bias in favor of all accounts and stories of the Old West I hesitate to state categorically that this is a great book, but I have a deep suspicion that it is."

> W. R. Burnett, "The Passing of a Great Race," in The New York Times Book Review (copyright © 1954 by The New York Times Company; reprinted by permission), August 22, 1954, p. 3.

W. R. BURNETT

Mari Sandoz has written one good book after another, including **"Old Jules," "Cheyenne Autumn"** and **"Buffalo Hunters."** These are solid studies of the Old West, displaying not only great knowledge of an area and a period but a great sympathy and an intuitive understanding; at times this has seemed almost a personal involvement, as if the author had actually lived through the times she described and experienced them at first hand. These books, though listed as fiction, hardly seem like novels at all, but more like memoirs of the time. The story is allowed to take care of itself while incident follows incident—chaotic, seemingly pointless at times, but all contributing to a vivid, naturalistic, almost hallucinatory picture of the times.

In **"Miss Morissa, Doctor of the Gold Trail,"** Miss Sandoz has tried to write a more conventional type of fiction. I am sorry to say that, in my opinion, she has failed.

The story she has to tell is a simple one: an intelligent young girl (discovering, under the most embarrassing circumstances, that she is illegitimate) leaves the man she is to marry, buries herself in studies, emerges as a pioneer woman doctor, and goes West to the then remote frontier of the North Platte River in Nebraska. . . . This was the time of the great gold rush to the new Eldorado called Deadwood Gulch, the gathering of "great wagon trains of mine machinery and equipment, trains of whisky too, and mahogany bars and roulette tables, guns and ammunition, mirrors and couches for the fancy houses." With Miss Morissa, we watch these bizarre pioneers cross the rugged buttes and the timber-flanked mountains, where the trails were "lined by tents and low buildings, mostly log and sod, and little taller than the bearded, sunburnt, waiting men."

So far, so good. We become interested in the problems of a woman doctor mingling with cutthroats and bandits, involved with Sioux and Cheyenne, and the war between settlers and cattlemen. Unfortunately, as she faces this plethora of material, Miss Sandoz reverts to her normal method of writing, memoir-style. The potentially interesting story of the young woman doctor gets lost completely, while one unrelated, or barely related, incident after another is told, about freighters, cattle thieves, Wild Bill Hickok, Buffalo Bill, even Calamity Jane.

It was Sainte-Beuve, I think, who wrote that in Flaubert's "Salammbo" the pedestal was too big for the statue. In **"Miss Morissa"** there is hardly any statue at all—but the pedestal is enormous. . . . Like all of Miss Sandoz' books, it is beautifully written and full of striking images and masterful descriptions. As a novel it doesn't succeed.

W. R. Burnett, "The Lady Was a Medic," in The New York Times Book Review *(copyright © 1955 by The New York Times Company; reprinted by permission), November 20, 1955, p. 49.*

J. FRANK DOBIE

"The Cattlemen," by Mari Sandoz, is another essay, following Paul Wellman's "The Trampling Herd," at summing up the whole drama of cows and cow people—women excluded—on the ranges of western America. It begins with a good deal of fancifulness over the first Spanish cattle and ends with the contemporary "ritual" of rodeo riding and roping. The best part of the book is laid in the part of the country with which, despite dutiful reading, Mari Sandoz is most familiar—Nebraska, the Dakotas, Wyoming, Montana—the setting for the stronger parts of her books on Crazy Horse, the buffalo hunters, the Cheyennes, and Old Jules, her masterpiece.

Miss Sandoz uses the word *dedicated* over and over in subtitles and as a kind of Homeric epithet for certain cowmen. In her sense, Silas Marner could be called a "dedicated" man. She herself seems particularly dedicated to killings in Kansas cow towns and to the lot of smoke and comparatively little bloodletting of the so-called Johnson County War (by big cowmen and politicians against homesteaders and thieves) in Wyoming. Some of her chapters are easily recognizable rewrites of standard books on the range. It would be interesting to have the sources specified for a rather extended account of Print Olive—a tough cowman from Texas who got tougher in Nebraska. I don't think any authority could be cited for statements that Texas granted a syndicate 500,000 acres (actually 40,000 acres) to survey what became the 3,000,000-acre XIT Ranch, and that brush poppers in lower Texas leap from horses to bulldog outlaw steers in the way Bill Pickett bulldogged for the 101 Ranch Wild West Show. Although she uses the word, Miss Sandoz surely knows that "cowpoke" is recent journalistic jargon. No real range man has ever called himself a cowpoke. . . .

"The Cattlemen" is uneven both historically and stylistically. One of the high spots is the description of the big die-up of 1886-1887, some of the best of the description taken without a thank you from Granville Stuart's "Forty Years on the Frontier," though that excellent book is listed in a Mother Hubbard kind of bibliography. Maybe I have read too many books about cows and cow people. I'm looking for something fresh in treatment. I'm tired of the same old dance to the same old tune.

J. Frank Dobie, "Battle of the Beef," in The Saturday Review, New York *(© 1958 Saturday Review Magazine Co.; reprinted by permission), Vol. XLI, No. 26, June 28, 1958, p. 30.*

ALVIN M. JOSEPHY, JR.

There is really nothing new in [Mari Sandoz's telling of **"The Battle of the Little Bighorn"**], save the quality of the telling itself, and this rises above all previous accounts. This is the author of **"Old Jules,"** bringing the same creative power and style to a great historic theme, enfolding in top-drawer literature what should have been there long ago. It is almost as if this were properly the climactic work of Miss Sandoz's career. . . .

Buffs may disagree with some of Miss Sandoz's interpretations and conclusions, but to the white man that is the basis of the continuing lure of the battle: no one but Indians knew exactly what happened to Custer, and no one will ever know for sure why Custer did what he did. Miss Sandoz makes no mention of something that old Indians had told her about, but of which she was unsure: that some of Custer's men had gotten down to the bank of the Little Bighorn, but had been driven back after a sharp fire-fight. Now, new evidence secured with metallic detectors (and as yet unpublicized) seems to confirm the Indians' story. On the other hand, the author is quite uninhibited in using the testimony of Arikara Indians concerning Custer's hope of winning a battle and being nominated for the Presidency to explain his motives that tragic June. Her Custer is deaf and brooding, riding in a trance, committed to an appointment. (p. 6)

Alvin M. Josephy, Jr., "Soldiers and Indians," in The New York Times Book Review *(copyright © 1966 by The New York Times Company; reprinted by permission), July 3, 1966, pp. 6, 18.**

SCOTT L. GREENWELL

Mari Sandoz was a didactic writer. Because of her tendency toward instruction, she found much of American fiction—particularly romantic western novels—thin, "without anything of the push and throb of life, totally inconsequential." She liked bone and muscle in literature. She blamed what she considered the poor quality of domestic fiction on the American writers' tendency to conform to the commercial market, and waged a continuous battle herself against what she termed "eastern editorial rewriting and pressure to recast [her works] on popular western notions." With few exceptions, Sandoz wrote to please herself and considered the market later. In this way she sought to achieve something more lasting, more permanent, in her work. (p. 133)

Sandoz is best known for her nonfiction, particularly the six volumes of history and biography which comprise her Great Plains or Trans-Missouri series. Yet Sandoz began her career writing fiction and, prior to her death in 1966, she published a total of eight books which are generally described as fiction and more than a dozen short stories. For the most part, however, her fiction has not received the same wide acclaim as her nonfiction. . . . [The] author herself was aware of certain shortcomings in her fiction writing. She viewed herself primarily as a historian who only aspired to be a literary artist, and was struck again and again by the inadequacy of much of her fiction.

Although it is true that Mari Sandoz' fiction is less effective than her nonfiction, her novels—particularly the early, more serious ones—are interesting and make a valid contribution to an understanding of the times about which they were written and of the author herself. (pp. 133-34)

Believing that serious writers, particularly beginners, "do their best work in material with which they have an emotional identity," Sandoz found in the story of her father and the community he helped to establish some of the most promising material to start with. In the long and difficult process of writing *Old Jules,* Sandoz became acutely aware of the drama of human conflict, especially when it resulted from greed and the lust for power, and this awareness influenced her thinking and helped mark the future direction of her career. By taking a locale as familiar to her as her own hands, the Sand Hills of western Nebraska, and introducing into it an egocentric young Swiss of some will-to-power, certain questions were inevitably raised in the author's mind. What if Old Jules had been devoid of a social conscience? What if his first thoughts had not been to make a contribution to the larger community? While those around her talked of the shortcomings of other nations and of other peoples during the early 1930s, Sandoz wondered if some of the same faults might not exist among our pioneer ancestors.

About the time the *Old Jules* manuscript was being gathered into a whole, Sandoz came across a book that disturbed her as almost nothing had since childhood. The book, *Mein Kampf,* came to her in a German edition of 1927. She later recalled that the book was written in the kind of German she understood most readily, "bad German." What made the book so disturbing to her was that unlike Old Jules, its author appeared to be a true will-to-power individual. (pp. 134-35)

Out of the combined experience of writing *Old Jules* and learning about Hitler, Sandoz decided to write another book, a protest novel against the will-to-power individual and his system. The selection of the novel as a form for the book at once freed her from certain kinds of accountability, and allowed her to present her own views by manipulating both plot and character. The use of the novel for a didactic purpose was perfectly compatible with Sandoz' concept of fiction. She believed that the novelist is free to play God. . . . She also believed that novels could be used as a means of social criticism, and, although she believed that propaganda was always inartistic, she did not see that as a serious flaw if the book were written with sufficient forcefulness.

According to Sandoz, will-to-power individuals can rise to prominence only within a society in flux. For setting, she drew upon her own experience in the upper Niobrara country of western Nebraska during the early settlement period when land titles were not yet fixed. To disguise the setting she simply inserted an oxbow in the river, made up a few counties, and peopled them with fictitious characters. And because she recognized that in the animal kingdom the female is frequently the aggressor with an instinct for acquisitiveness, she decided to make the main character in the first novel a woman—one "masculine" enough to control lawlessness and to overcome opposition to her empire. The result was Gulla Slogum of Slogum House, a composite of the villainous types who sometimes operated the road ranches along the main arteries of the trans-Mississippi West, and one of the most repellent female characters in all of western American literature.

Because she believed that the will-to-power individual prostitutes the beautiful around him, she gave Gulla a beautiful daughter, and one not quite so beautiful, to pacify local officials. In addition, she supplied Gulla with the instruments she needed to carry out her programs of lawlessness, her *Schwarze Korps,* who could kill or emasculate anyone threatening her growth or expanse of power. For those who could not be corrupted or destroyed she needed someone who could be friendly and provide decent treatment, someone who could accommodate them for the time being. So she gave Gulla another daughter "who had no truck with the activities of her sisters of the bedroom, or the upstairs girls imported for the common customer." This daughter kept the freighters' beds clean, cooked meals with light biscuits and plum jam, and saw to it that they got away on time, their goods and their bodies intact.

But Sandoz did not feel her story was complete without the disarming aspect of weakness, of gentleness too, so she created Ward, the youngest son. And because "the set up must always look legal," she gave Gulla a husband, Ruedy, an ineffectual man who could not countenance the activities of Slogum House and so took up a separate homestead "across the hogback" and cared for such victims of the system as he could—"The charities of Slogum House" as Sandoz called them. (pp. 135-37)

At first the book brought only disappointment to the author. Although it was viewed as a work of genius by some, it was carried gingerly to the ashcan by others, especially in her own state. The objection was raised that the book slandered the pioneers, who, in the minds of many, so diligently tamed the wilderness. Then, too, Sandoz had defied tradition by giving a house of prostitution an agrarian setting. As a result, the author was hissed on the streets of the state's capital. . . . In addition, the book was banned from several libraries around the state, including the Omaha Public Library. (p. 138)

But the real source of disappointment to Sandoz was not that the book became a source of controversy; rather it was the fact that, like *Old Jules* before, this book fell short of her initial conception.

On the surface, *Slogum House* is the simple story of violence in the struggle for wealth in a small portion of the West. . . .

On another level, however, the book is intended as an allegorical study of the will-to-power individual or nation that uses force to overcome opposition, and willingly foregoes justice and truth in the process. The presentation of a society where violence is untrammeled was intended to disturb its readers. As a trained observer, Sandoz tried to visualize the methods a person like Hitler might employ in an attempt to dominate the world, and to duplicate them on a smaller scale in her story. (p. 139)

When the book came out, however, practically no one said anything about its larger purpose or meaning. Perhaps this was the author's fault. Writing as much for posterity as for her own generation, Sandoz tried to avoid the over-obvious. Her terseness of expression may have put the book beyond the grasp of most readers. In any event, Sandoz felt as though people were hissing her for the wrong reasons, and for a while it seemed to her as if she were drifting about in darkness. Then a letter came to her from a man in Winnipeg who saw its meaning. It was followed by another letter written by a lawyer in Washington, D.C. . . . It helped reassure her that this, one of her favorite books, had not been a complete failure. Since Sandoz did not believe that serious writers should expect too much, the fact that two widely separated people saw the meaning was compensation enough. (pp. 139-40)

[In *Capitol City*] Sandoz did not focus exclusively on Lincoln. . . . She decided to create a composite capital city, a sort of universal portrait of midwestern state capitals, just as she had made a composite road ranch in *Slogum House*. In *Capital City* the city itself becomes a major character, making it necessary to limit her usual treatment of years (forty in each of her two previous books) to a matter of weeks—from the September state fair to election time in November. (p. 141)

In *Capital City* the author deals with the same destructive forces as in *Slogum House,* only this time the evils do not result from individual avarice isolated on the frontier. Instead, they occur within a highly organized community where nothing is done to prevent the will-to-power individual from rising. The result is a microcosmic study of how the author thought the modern world gets led into fascism.

This time there were apparently not even two people who seemed to understand what the book was about. Again, although many people professed to like the novel, it fell far short of her expectations. Then came Norway, the Low Countries, and the fall of France. Finally, late one evening, Sandoz received a phone call from a man who confessed: "It looks like we have Capital City all over the world." From that point on she began to receive more and more letters from people who recognized *Capital City* as a serious book, an allegorical novel with broad implications. (pp. 142-43)

Mari Sandoz is not an outstanding novelist. . . . But because Sandoz was not an acknowledged expert in some of the areas that concerned her, she had to turn to the novel form or remain silent. In an effort to get her message across in fiction, however, she manipulated plots and characters excessively. As a result, her books fail to radiate a sense of discovery. But they do remain interesting experiments—attempts to portray aspects of fascism in western American garb. (p. 143)

> Scott L. Greenwell, "*Fascists in Fiction: Two Early Novels of Mari Sandoz,*" in Western American Literature *(copyright, 1977, by the Western Literature Association), Vol. XII, No. 2, Summer, 1977, pp. 133-43.*

HELEN WINTER STAUFFER

Mari Sandoz is recognized as a novelist, historian, and biographer, as well as an authority on the Indians of the Great Plains. Her work varies in quality, her novels usually considered least successful, and her histories, particularly her biographies, most trenchant. In the latter she has fused her skill as a writer, her mastery of historical research, and her empathy for her subjects to create works of unique and lasting value. (p. 1)

Mari seemed to make little conscious distinction between methods of writing fiction and those of writing nonfiction. She spoke of using the same techniques for biography and for fiction, except that in biography one must keep as close to the actual story, the actual people, and the actual times as possible. Her nonfiction written as narrative history used facts and was faithful to them, but she concentrated on specific events and characters to bring out the drama. Mari's interest, and the theme of all her books, was in the relationship of man and the land. (pp. 1-2)

On her chosen landscape, the trans-Missouri basin, certain memorable men appeared from time to time, and it is their experiences she relates in her biographies and histories. Her subjects are significant because of their unique qualities as human beings, but also because in their individual lives they exhibit certain universal qualities. They respond and react to the force of events on the Great Plains, caught in a historical moment when one culture supersedes another.

Mari Sandoz also felt a strong need to preserve the past, seeing it as a guide to the future. Someday, she believed, man will learn that the same mistakes need not be made over and over, nor will each generation need to learn once more man's goodness, generosity, and courage. Her themes are the working of fate, the re-creation of the past, the importance of nature, the rhythm of life, the strength of evil as manifested in man's inhumanity to man, and, paradoxically, man's essential nobility. These themes shape her writing. Although Mari Sandoz left no written evidence of a consciously formulated philosophy of life, throughout her writing career her epic vision was remarkably consistent. She saw man romantically, larger than life, a creature who could occasionally display characteristics of grandeur. In her biographies, histories, and novellas, Mari Sandoz hoped to recreate the culture and virtues she found in the Plains societies of the past. (p. 2)

However, Mari Sandoz did not allow her sympathy for the cultures and the heroes of the past to stand in the way of what André Maurois has called the "indefatigable search for the truth." She worked constantly to correct false historical notions, as is attested by her frequent arguments with those who venerated such figures as Buffalo Bill Cody. Her quarrel was with history and biography that perpetuated the old, incorrect information. She combined her sympathy for her heroes with solid historical research, much of it in primary sources, some never used by other historians. (p. 3)

It has been charged that western writers are too close to their material, that their personal involvement prevents objectivity. On the other hand, these writers have the inestimable advantage of writing from inside their subject, an asset that no outsider, no matter how skilled or sympathetic, can acquire. Although Mari Sandoz aimed for truth and objectivity, she could not, of course, achieve it completely, any more than can any other historian or biographer. Whatever her purpose in writing beyond simply presenting the facts, that purpose directed her use of the raw material. She recognized this when she acknowledged that every event in *Old Jules* could be authenticated but the interpretation of the action was hers, and that she tried to make the book artistically and philosophically as well as historically true. She agreed with those who believe that writing is both an ethical and aesthetic problem.

Something of a mystic, Mari shared with most western American writers the classical view of myth and tragedy, emphasizing the importance of intuition rather than logic. Relying too heavily on reason could leave one out of tune with nature, she believed; response to the natural environment should be through emotion and the senses rather than through intellect. Her proclivity toward the occult encouraged her belief in fate as a force greater than the individual. She saw the death of Crazy Horse, for example, as fated.... Agreeing with the theory of the collective unconscious, she was strongly attracted to the use of image, myth, and symbol. The concrete images of her childhood included the guns of her father and the cattlemen he opposed; the smoky kitchen of her childhood home, Indian Hill; the Niobrara that flowed past the farm; and the sandhills. There was also, constantly, her intense awareness of nature. (pp. 3-4)

As a writer, she enjoyed working with both old and new forms. Allegory, one of the oldest and most didactic forms of storytelling, is recognizable in *Winter Thunder, Slogum House, Capital City,* and *The Tom-Walker.* Her nonfiction is less obviously allegorical, but the elements are there, stressing the author's belief in the absolute necessity of development through struggle, and, particularly in the Indian books, the loss the white civilization had inflicted upon itself because of its discrimination. She felt that the United States would always have on its conscience the sin of what it had done to the Indians, and for that reason would never be what it could have been. In her use of allegory she felt close to Faulkner and Hemingway. (p. 5)

With the exception of John G. Neihardt, western writers seem not to have influenced Mari Sandoz directly. She seldom discussed them individually in her letters, and when she did, or when she reviewed their books, she judged them primarily on the basis of the amount of research undertaken and the accuracy of their historical re-creation. She approved or disapproved of authors according to how well they presented history, since she thought of herself as a historian. The writers she felt worthwhile were those who had a sense of responsibility to world society as well as to that of their own locale, who understood their obligation to see the present and future implications of their material wholly and clearly and who presented it as honestly as possible. The trans-Missouri region was the one with which she had strong emotional ties and the one she knew best, but her writing was, she hoped, universal in scope. (pp. 5-6)

By conventional literary standards, Mari Sandoz's nonfiction measures up well. Strongly affected by her sense of history, of time and of place, she wrote powerful and effective histories when working with protagonists whom she could identify with her own region. She mastered the art of recreating a man and his culture, emphasizing the moral issues involved when one culture destroys another, and illustrating her own romantic view that man has dignity and worth. She adhered closely to carefully researched information, and the strength of her artistic imagination lay in creating a verisimilitude of actual events, rather than in creating imaginary scenes. In her biographies particularly she succeeds in re-creating the living past. (p. 7)

The re-creation of early settler life abounds in Plains literature, but Mari Sandoz's *Old Jules* is so unusual it has few imitations. Her ability to fuse Jules's importance to the region with scenes from his domestic life, while involving herself, is rare.... In 1935, *Old Jules* shocked people, not only because of the domestic scenes but because it showed the public a stark, unromantic view of the frontier. The strong language, the sometimes brutal realism, the frankness were all criticized vigorously, but they made the book powerful.... The conflicts described best in *Old Jules, Crazy Horse,* and *Cheyenne Autumn* still hold significance, although the specific incidents are well in the past. The West is now tamed, and the Indians are, legally at least, freer to move about as they please, but the emotions engendered by those conflicts are universal. Mari's people experience love, hate, ambition, jealousy, sorrow, fear, satisfaction and joy. Some are caught by forces too large for them to control—by a government gigantic and relentless and sometimes apparently mindless. Some learn their fate is controlled by men too small for their responsibilities, too ignorant or too greedy to value human life. And some fight back. (pp. 7-8)

Those books of her Great Plains series using an animal as the protagonist and humans as antagonists—*The Buffalo Hunters, The Cattlemen,* and *The Beaver Men*—have a less clear-cut focus, primarily because her efforts to cram a large amount of information into them make the works seem disjointed. Although the many minor characters, together with the vast amount of time and space involved, make these books less easily controlled by the author and sometimes a challenge to the reader's memory, they are stimulating, useful, and in most instances well written. Mari uses in these books the skills of the storytellers she heard and admired in her childhood to develop the many and disparate episodes making up the variegated thread of western history.

Mari Sandoz's prose, often lyrical and lovely, appears to be standing the test of time. Much of the timelessness is achieved through her use of images and symbols, the word-pictures by which she describes the geography of the Great Plains. Of special note is the language form she created for her narration of the Indian way of life. While other writers had stressed the Indian point of view, the language of the white author almost always interfered with the atmosphere of the Indian culture portrayed in the story. It is by means of her particular use of language in her Indian books that Mari Sandoz brings the reader to greater understanding and perhaps even identification with her Indian heroes.

It may be too soon to make serious critical judgments of Mari Sandoz's canon, but her work is impressive in both quantity and quality. (pp. 8-9)

Helen Winter Stauffer, in her Mari Sandoz: Story Catcher of the Plains *(reprinted by permission of University of Nebraska Press; © 1982 by the University of Nebraska Press), University of Nebraska Press, 1982, 322 p.*

Peter (Francis) Straub
1943-

American novelist and poet.

Straub's novels of horror and suspense are characterized by the relentless influence of supernatural forces upon unsuspecting human victims. The resulting violence is recounted in unsparing detail. Unreal elements are placed in ordinary settings, thereby enhancing the atmosphere of horror.

Julia (1975) was Straub's first attempt at horror in a career which began with two volumes of poetry and a mainstream novel. It is a ghost story, full of ambiguities, unanswered questions, appearances without realities, and similar Gothic twists. The graphic scenes of evil and violence in this novel have become common throughout his subsequent works: *If You Could See Me Now* (1977), *Ghost Story* (1979), *Shadowland* (1980), and *Floating Dragon* (1982). Murder and mutilation are standard and evil often triumphs.

Critics acknowledge Straub's narrative skill and credit the appeal of his stories to the popular fascination with the supernatural. Some note, however, his over-detailed, at times repetitive style and his frequently slow pace.

(See also *Contemporary Authors*, Vols. 85-88.)

© Jerry Bauer

THE TIMES LITERARY SUPPLEMENT

[In **Open Air** Peter Straub] writes a poetry of assured, slow-moving, resonant statement, which is at best potent and at worst ponderous. Technically he is extremely competent, well able to exploit (sometimes over-consciously) dramatic shifts and pauses, working for the most part in drastically cramped and abbreviated units but capable, too, of some expansive imaginative flights. Some of the poems are *Crow*-like metaphysical musings centred on animals and tinged with a whimsical brand of irony; but the sardonic tone involved in this enterprise can slide too easily into a stilted and mannered language, too knowingly remote from the subject-matter it deals with.

"The State of Ireland," in The Times Literary Supplement (© Times Newspapers Ltd. (London) 1973; reproduced from The Times Literary Supplement by permission), No. 3702, February 16, 1973, p. 183.*

RONALD BRYDEN

Marriages is the other side of the Jamesian tradition: an American chronicle of the quest for European richness, complexity and depth. For Owen, the Middle Western businessman who narrates it, these are all embodied in the blonde, unnamed Englishwoman with whom he betrays his wife on a hyper-educated trip . . . to Paris and Provence. Their love-affair is skilfully told, in a cunning mosaic of shifting flashbacks, but like most such it has to struggle by over-writing against cliché, not wholly successfully. One has drunk this incredible Southern light, tasted these perfect meals *à deux*, seen these slumbrous, leonine post-coital looks before. Where Straub shows himself a real writer is in evoking the sallow foreground and aftermath to love's exaltations: the sharp, disappointed, comradely wife who falls back on her bitchy sister for company; the lakeshore picnic where Owen first seduced her; their drunken Middle-Western wedding, presided over by a former bootlegger.

Ronald Bryden, "American Scenes" (© British Broadcasting Corp. 1973; reprinted by permission of Ronald Bryden), in The Listener, Vol. 89, No. 2294, March 15, 1973, p. 348.*

THE TIMES LITERARY SUPPLEMENT

[*Marriages*] is a pastiche of almost every notable American novel written about Europe, from J. P. Donleavy's Ireland to Henry James's Paris, but [Mr Straub] anticipates any criticism of overliterariness or derivativeness by using those qualities as a conscious and essential ingredient. . . .

With so many echoes and resonances, it is remarkable that Mr Straub retains a distinctive voice in the story. His story of an American businessman living in Europe, and his love affairs with his wife and mistress, is intricately controlled and focused; the complex series of flashbacks and time-cuts coheres because every time, place, or emotion is fully evoked. Everything is named and labelled, from Dublin streets to London restaurants, with the exception of "the woman" at the very centre of it.

Owen's affair with this woman forms the central thread of the book, but a whole cloth of other marriages and relationships has been woven round it. An accidental tug on the central thread causes all the others to vibrate, as Owen recalls his courtship of his wife, their wedding presided over by an ominous criminal, the various marriages of her relations, and his strange life in London.

Mr Straub has already published two books of poetry, and he is what is commonly called "a poetic novelist", with the fine sense of the weight of words which every novelist should have, and which many poets lack. It may be this skill which enables him to place so securely the sense of gesture, and the texture of atmosphere, which characterize *Marriages*.

> "Poet's Prose," in The Times Literary Supplement (© Times Newspapers Ltd. (London) 1973; reproduced from The Times Literary Supplement by permission), No. 3707, March 23, 1973, p. 313.

JOHN MELLORS

Peter Straub's highly ingenious tale of Kensington gore [*Julia*] excited me only to sceptical comment. . . . Julia is American, married to an English barrister, Magnus, who even at the age of three 'had an ancient, powerful soul'. Julia and Magnus had attempted an emergency tracheotomy on their nine-year-old daughter, Kate, when she choked on a piece of meat, and the child bled to death before the ambulance arrived. Julia leaves Magnus and buys a house near Holland Park; it turns out to be haunted by Olivia, another nine-year-old who had met a violent death. Olivia seeks revenge, and is bloodily successful.

It is the clumsily imprecise writing that lets the story down. On one page 'the air in the bathroom felt silkily warm to her facial skin', and a page later 'she could nearly feel the blood beating in her facial skin'. What's wrong with 'face'? And how do you *nearly* feel blood beating? A man 'applies the flame to the tip of the cigarette'. Where else would he light it? Within six pages Julia's vagina 'throbs' twice and 'aches' once. Her heart 'thrums' and 'thunders', and 'food bounced in her stomach like an angry ant'. An overcooked and indigestible blood-pudding of a book: good ingredients spoiled.

> John Mellors, "Kensington Gore" (© British Broadcasting Corp. 1976; reprinted by permission of John Mellors), in The Listener, Vol. 95, No. 2446, February 26, 1976, p. 254.*

MICHAEL MASON

It is very disheartening to come across the following phrase in the second sentence of Peter Straub's *Julia*: "his customer was precipitous and eccentric". . . . This will strike some people as an extravagant reaction, and not worth voicing. But if you fail to notice or fail to remember that "precipitous" and "precipitate" are not the same you are likely to make other kinds of mistake to do with other parts of a fiction—in setting, character, theme, and so forth. *Julia* is set in London, and much of the action unfolds in a house in Kensington. These settings are adequately realized (though Mr Straub, who is an American, makes some errors about British institutions), but the characters are dizzyingly inconsistent. There is also a considerable vagueness in the plotting and a vicious circle ensues. It is not clear who does what, but the characters' dispositions cannot be called in as evidence because these are so indefinite, which is partly a result of the uncertainty about their actions—and so on. . . .

In the last resort *Julia* . . . [succeeds] in the brutal business of delivering supernatural thrills. . . . [Mr Straub] has thought of a nasty kind of haunting, and he presses it upon the reader to a satisfying point of discomfort. And he has, quite wittily, made the nice world which the nastiness subverts a colour-supplement one of beautiful people living in Chelsea and Bayswater.

> Michael Mason, "Nasty and Nastier," in The Times Literary Supplement (© Times Newspapers Ltd. (London) 1976; reproduced from The Times Literary Supplement by permission), No. 3859, February 27, 1976, p. 213.*

JONATHAN KEATES

Wild-eyed backwoods weirdness indeed dominates *If You Could See Me Now*. Peter Straub's third novel initially deceives by the familiarity of its opening formula: the bourgeois narrator is pitched against a conspiracy of silence among inhabitants of a farming community rocked by a sequence of killings. Apple-pie cosiness on every level, however, is quickly eroded. Miles Teagarden, steeped in useless campus apprehensions, is tossed with dour brutality round a circle of folk whose cult of the normal is interestingly offset by a tendency to maul and harry their wretchedly obtuse victim at every turn. His cousin Alison's childhood promise to 'come after' him, made minutes before her murder, reaches sinister fulfilment when Miles's Eng. Lit. sophistications crumble against a barrage of impenetrable surliness and suspicion, and the valley reverberates with death.

Straub is good at slick manipulation of pace, punctuating the story with chunks of police statement (whose unlettered authenticity doesn't come without a rueful laugh or two), and he has an equally nifty way with rustic grotesques. In a place where everyone is either broodily insane or explicitly nasty, Miles preserves a paradoxical equanimity, as Alison's spooking reaches its height. Crisp, classy buggaboo, this, full of neatly managed understatements and chillingly calculated surprises.

> Jonathan Keates, "Furtively Twitching," in New Statesman (© 1977 The Statesman & Nation Publishing Co. Ltd.), Vol. 93, No. 2414, June 24, 1977, p. 863.*

PETER ACKROYD

If You Could See Me Now works rather well. Its setting, a small farming community in the mid-West, is a great help. All Gothic novels must now streak against that particularly garish backdrop . . . , and specifically against those small immigrant communities which retain their indigenous customs while apparently adopting what is known as the American 'way of life'. This sense of 'passing', of remaining an alien while being ostensibly American, is central to American culture. . . .

In Peter Straub's novel, the alien is merely a rational East-Coast academic, Miles Teagarden, who is returning to the small town which no longer needs him or wants him back. Despite all the possibilities for cliché in a situation like this, possibilities which someone like Thomas Tryon or even Saul Bellow could use to the hilt, Peter Straub stays disarmingly distant from his material and handles it without any undue straining toward portentousness. (p. 23)

Straightforward novelists are slowly realising that nothing is straightforward any more; and that the 'reality' which they have carefully assembled doesn't actually seem very real to anyone. In this book Peter Straub has to constantly nudge and hint that his narrative is not what it seems to be, that there are in fact several separate realities all at work in the same context, and that it would be wilfully blind to concentrate upon one at the expense of all the others. The book quite carefully evokes the real world of everyday folk, while at the same time intimating—through dreams, metaphors and analogies—the existence of a superior reality which can occasionally be understood. . . .

[The novel is] filmic. There was a time when film-makers were quite happy to adopt a number of novelistic devices as a way of constructing plots or stories; now everything is quite reversed. It is the novelists, and especially those who aspire to 'realism' in any of its forms, who are acquiring the mannerisms of film. *If You Could See Me Now* makes great play, for example, with contrasts of speech and silence, of crowd scenes and empty landscapes, and of the ways in which a written 'close-up' can be employed to suggest deep 'emotion.' Some of the book's scenes, in fact, can only be understood in visual terms. . . . But the resemblance must end somewhere. A novel which relies for its main effects on suspense and upon horror is at a considerable disadvantage because it doesn't have the immediate, consistent sensory presence which such effects require and which film provides. That is why the most shocking moments in this novel emerge as melodrama, and why the book's ending—when the dazed survivors drive away into freedom—seems somehow abrupt and inconclusive. The ending ties matters up perfectly well both imaginatively and thematically, but it isn't physically or emotionally satisfying. Reality is now something which, in cultural terms, can only be experienced in direct and sensory ways; the novel, this novel, any novel, cannot offer that. It has to be oblique, or rhetorical. Or, as in *If You Could See Me Now* it has to simply tell a story—that is, it eventually has to admit to being unrealistic. (p. 24)

> Peter Ackroyd, "Vasty Deep," in The Spectator (© 1977 by The Spectator; reprinted by permission of The Spectator), Vol. 239, No. 7774, July 9, 1977, pp. 23-4.

JACK SULLIVAN

According to Straub, he wrote *Ghost Story* out of a desire to "take the classic elements as far as they could go" in a contemporary setting. It is frequently worthy of its heritage, for when he wants to, Straub can write superb horror. Although the plot—involving the invasion of a small town by a demonic entity called "the shapeshifter"—is not exactly auspicious, many of the individual apparition scenes are frightening enough to jolt the most jaded ghost-story addict. There is a dream sequence set in an abandoned house, for example, that is simply hair-raising. The dread it conjures is cumulative and the climax it reaches has, like a revelation in a real dream, elements of both inevitability and surprise.

Ghost Story is filled with bows to earlier tales. The main characters themselves are expert ghost-story tellers who meet ritualistically to spook each other; this conceit, as well as the ambiguity of stories within stories, was a favorite device of Sheridan Le Fanu. And resonances of Arthur Machen can be found in the novel's string of ominous, alluring female characters who look alike and have similar names. As for Henry James, Straub seems to admire him with little restraint. (p. L1)

Although Straub's "affection" for the proven devices of his betters is estimable, many of these allusions seem rather pedantic and pointless. The more obvious ones—such as having two of the main characters named James and Hawthorne—smack of the self-conscious cuteness that has given science fiction and horror "fandom" such a deservedly bad name.

However, the fundamental problem with *Ghost Story* is its wordiness. Straub either so distrusts (or else is so enamored of the effect of) his own images that he continually explains and repeats them. Often he eschews images altogether and substitutes repetitious descriptive labels. . . .

The same problem afflicts the larger structure of the novel. Despite the council of earlier writers (M. R. James, even Poe) on the wisdom of stylistic economy, Straub rarely knows when to stop. Although the first third of *Ghost Story* is ghoulish fun, the remainder becomes cluttered with too many subplots, too many mutilated corpses, too many ghosts, and too many words. After a while, one apparition looks pretty much like another, especially since the author commits the fatal 18th-century Gothic error of having his ghosts talk. And not only do they talk—thereby undermining their own mystery and menace—but they give away the novel's gimmick so early in the game that they have little to do for the last couple of hundred pages but butcher people and animals in increasingly violent ways.

Peter Straub tells us that his ambition was "to write a literary ghost story in the Henry James manner," but surely James, of all writers, would be appalled by the monotonous brutality, the fuzzy hyperbole, the silly italics, and the B-movie dialogue that disfigure so much of the novel's second half. These are the very cliches which the writers Straub admires attempted to exorcise from the ghostly tale.

If one suspends the high expectations set up by Straub's statement of his intentions, it is possible to savor the many unnerving moments in *Ghost Story*. According to H. P. Lovecraft, a supernatural horror novel which has genuinely terrifying passages—even if the whole doesn't work—should automatically be counted a success. Lovecraft knew all too well that the ghostly novel was a notoriously difficult form and that most writers in the genre shrewdly limited themselves to short stories and novelettes. Even *Dracula*, perhaps the greatest scary novel of all, falls apart near the end. With its praiseworthy intentions and partial success, *Ghost Story* at least falls apart in good company. (p. L4)

> Jack Sullivan, "Night Crawlers," in Book World—The Washington Post (© 1979, The Washington Post), April 8, 1979, pp. L1, L4.

GENE LYONS

[In writing **"Ghost Story"**] Peter Straub quite clearly wishes to have it both ways: to make a hit at the checkout counter and in the English department as well. For besides nightmares, apparitions, werewolves, blood-letting viragos and hosts of the undead, Mr. Straub has summoned up the literary shades of Hawthorne, Poe and Henry James in an attempt to dignify and provide a respectable context for his long and complicated book.

Up to a point, Mr. Straub succeeds in both ways. Academic fashion these days seems to favor narrative gamesmanship and irony, and **"Ghost Story"** delivers plenty of both. Parts of the novel, indeed, read like a series of illustrations to scholar Wayne Booth's "The Rhetoric of Fiction," utilizing multiple narrators and points of view, stories within stories within stories, and more flashbacks than the Odyssey. (p. 14)

Most of the novel . . . is melodramatic and convincing by turns. But Mr. Straub makes what I think are two critical errors. So convoluted a narrative must keep moving along; Mr. Straub's pace is at times glacial, as the reader anticipates and draws obvious conclusions chapters ahead of the characters. Then too, unlike the masters of the genre . . . Mr. Straub becomes entirely too literal and particular about the nature of the horror his characters are facing, so that the last third of the novel ceases being mysterious and turns into a kind of supernatural thriller, the outcome of which, to this reader at least, was somewhat predictable. Even so, **"Ghost Story"** is a quite sophisticated literary entertainment. . . . (pp. 14, 23)

Gene Lyons, "Horror Shocker," in The New York Times Book Review *(copyright © 1979 by The New York Times Company; reprinted by permission), April 8, 1979, pp. 14, 23.*

BARBARA MATTHEWS

New Englander Peter Straub, like New Englander Stephen King, is capable of writing stark cold horror—the kind worshippers of the genre love to spirit away and read quickly, inhaling fright and holding it in their lungs until it becomes brittle enough to shatter if so much as a telephone rings. Straub's last novel, **Ghost Story,** was a classic horror tale so reminiscent of King's *'Salem's Lot* that it seemed almost to have been written by the master himself. With **Shadow Land** Straub tries to go one better, forsaking the classic elements of horror for a convoluted, *Magus*-like nothing-is-quite-what-it-seems form of trickery complete with images piled so high and so haphazardly that finding a meaning is like trying to find your coat on a bed at a party. . . .

Straub does manage a scare occasionally. . . . But to hold a reader enthralled, a book about a magician should be magical. Straub's imagery—"A man with a face like a run-over dog and a woman whose head was a charred stump. . . ."—is anything but. "At the beginning it was even fun in a way. I kept trying to figure out what it was all about," says Tom in summation. No one could blame the reader who simply gave up.

Barbara Matthews, "Much Less Here than Meets the Eye," in Maclean's Magazine *(© 1981 by Maclean's Magazine; reprinted by permission), Vol. 94, No. 1, January 12, 1981, p. 44.*

THOMAS SUTCLIFFE

Like [Stephen] King, Peter Straub has a string of creepy best-sellers behind him, but he knows that he is a new arrival and knows, too, which club he wants to join—the one to which Hawthorne, Poe and Henry James belong. In fact **Shadowland** takes as its principle a remark of Hawthorne's which is quoted approvingly in Straub's previous novel **Ghost Story:** "I have sometimes produced a singular and not unpleasing effect, so far as my own mind is concerned, by imagining a train of incidents in which the spiritual mechanism of faery legend should be combined with the characters and manners of everyday life."

It is one of the faults of **Shadowland** that it is too bound up with the mechanism of the faery legend to recreate convincingly the second half of that combination. . . .

Straub deals well with the bizarre *son et lumière* of spectral effects, but the best moments in the book stem from his jokey recognition of the limitations of his genre. His demons are far less pofaced than some. They make jokes though they probably can't take them, and there is a convincing sense of bathetic surprise about some of his other manifestations. . . .

In the end it is hard to avoid the feeling that Straub is embarrassed by his material; and it is easy to see why. The naturalistic novel, intent on the characters and manners of everyday life, cannot readily cope with a scene in which one of those characters is turned into a sparrow. Such an event, in the blind, spare prose of a fairy tale, at least retains a certain dignity through its explicitness: its promise of an imminent meaning is plausible. By invoking the ghosts of Perrault and the Brothers Grimm (in the case of the latter, literally—they turn up in one of the forbidden rooms, busily working on further archetypes) and by a voguish, self-referential emphasis on the connection between magic and storytelling, Straub suggests a similar dignity for his own tale.

Hawthorne's prescription brings Straub down, however, and **Shadowland** ultimately has neither the gnomic simplicity of the fairy-tale nor the eery sense of a grossly interrupted reality, which he caught more successfully in **Ghost Story**.

Thomas Sutcliffe, "Getting the Wind Up," in The Times Literary Supplement *(© Times Newspapers Ltd. (London) 1981; reproduced from* The Times Literary Supplement *by permission), No. 4072, April 17, 1981, p. 430.*

BARBARA RIGHTON

[In **Floating Dragon**] Peter Straub has returned to the same ground of his acclaimed **Ghost Story**. Once again he has created four main characters who are linked, albeit tenuously, by a murder. But unlike his earlier tale, in which a well-defined spirit was motivated by revenge, Straub has conjured up a pervasive "wrongness" that haphazardly destroys for wanton pleasure. "Hampstead's always been rotten as a bucket of month-old oysters," says an old newspaper compositor. But this is at best a vague explanation for the series of ghastly occurrences—earthquakes, fires, suicides—dating back to 1645 when a mean Englishman named Gideon Winter tried to wrest the town from its founders.

Like the spirit of Eva Galli, the murdered beauty in **Ghost Story, Floating Dragon**'s amorphous demon is insidiously malevolent. It takes as much pleasure in toying with its victims as it does in viciously murdering them. . . .

Unfortunately, Straub undercuts the real horror as competently as his devil slices up its victims—first by drawing in a host of secondary characters and then by delving into the mundane details of their personal lives. "Nothing is ever isolated, nothing is ever random, everything is connected," Straub warns, much as he did in **Ghost Story**. Yet here inventions are left dangling. A mirror in an antique shop clouds over, emits lightning bolts and visions of carnage, only to disappear from the book. Straub has created some of the most incongruous, laughable images: bats in white face and red hair; a shotgun that changes into a glowing sword; and a pervasive evil that becomes embodied in a fire-breathing dragon. Only the most patient of readers will put up with the annoying flashbacks and flash-forwarding—as many as 17 times in one 19-page passage. . . .

Lovers of this genre are ever willing to suspend disbelief; they are even willing to slog through 623 pages to solve a mystery or nail a villain. Unfortunately, at the end of *Floating Dragon,* the reader is no wiser. The evil remains ephemeral, the ghost nameless.

Barbara Righton, "Snuff the Tragic Dragon," in Maclean's Magazine *(© 1983 by Maclean's Magazine; reprinted by permission), Vol. 96, No. 11, March 14, 1983, p. 50.*

Jun'ichirō Tanizaki
1886-1965

Japanese novelist, short story writer, translator, essayist, and dramatist.

Tanizaki ranks among the greatest Japanese writers of the twentieth century. He began his long career in the Meiji period (1868-1912) with the magazine publication of several short stories; he continued to write throughout the Taishō period (1912-1926) and into the modern Shōwa period. His novels and short fiction are marked by their combination of Western and classical Japanese literary influences and by their sensuous, almost pornographic subject matter.

The most significant of the Western writers by whom Tanizaki was influenced were Edgar Allan Poe and Oscar Wilde. Like these authors, Tanizaki displayed an interest in the relation of the grotesque to the beautiful. He also shared their emphasis on plot and the creation of a fictional world based on fantasy and subconscious obsessions. Tanizaki's works differed from the Japanese literature of his time, which was dominated by naturalism and the confessional "I-novels." Nearly all of his fiction explores the sexual obsessions and perversions of the protagonist. The typical male hero is obsessed by the beauty of an unattainable woman and he suffers acutely because of this obsession. For Tanizaki, beauty is never far from pain; humiliation, rejection, and masochism often form the base of the protagonist's erotic pleasure. The theme of the yearning for unattainable beauty is developed through the hero's quest for the ideal mother-figure, as in *Arrowroot* (1932), a recently translated novella.

Sasameyuki (1948; *The Makioka Sisters*) explores the theme of beauty through the lives of four sisters and has been called Tanizaki's greatest contribution to literature. When Tanizaki tried to publish this novel during World War II, he encountered resistance because the novel neither mentions nor offers support for the Japanese war effort.

In his later years Tanizaki began to reject much of the Western influence on Japanese culture. In the novel *Inei raisan* (1934; *In Praise of Shadows*), for example, he bemoans the loss of purity and the subtle, suggestive beauty characteristic of traditional Japan. His respect for and sensitivity to the Japanese language is reflected in his modern rendition of the eleventh-century classic, *The Tale of Genji*, by Lady Murasaki.

(See also *CLC*, Vols. 8, 14 and *Contemporary Authors*, Vols. 93-96, Vols. 25-28, rev. ed. [obituary].)

The Granger Collection, New York

MAKOTO UEDA

For all his emphasis on the subconscious, Tanizaki himself was a very self-conscious technician. Perhaps he thought a novel must have a form designed to engage the reader's conscious mind precisely because its contents made their appeal at a different level. In any case, his own novels are characterized by skillfully constructed plot and persuasive rhetoric, in sharp contrast to the uncanny, indefinable nature of their central themes and characters. (p. 71)

Tanizaki's concept of structure, as it emerges from the controversy [between himself and Akutagawa Ryūnosuke] is quite clear: a novel should have a tightly knit, skillfully woven plot. "Its components," he observed elsewhere, "should embrace each other so tightly that if one were to be removed the whole would collapse." Not many Japanese literary theorists have shared this approach. Japanese readers have always liked a loose, episodic kind of plot—if plot it can be called—far removed from what Tanizaki had in mind; they especially detested a plot that was constructed geometrically, like a classic French comedy. Tanizaki's notion of plot was also unusual in its preference for grandeur; plot, he thought, should be not only tightly knit but constructed on the grand scale. It should be like a long-distance runner with strong legs; it should demonstrate the writer's staying power.

Tanizaki's idea of plot thus turns out to be almost deterministic. Plot construction, ostensibly the fruit of the writer's conscious efforts, is determined willy-nilly by his physique. By his own criteria, Tanizaki's preference for a long, complicated story was instinctive, and his argument with Akutagawa had to end at this point because constitutional differences could never be reconciled. Once again, Tanizaki gave the subconscious an important role.

By and large, Tanizaki seems to have followed his own theoretical precepts about plot construction. His major works have plots that are considerably more complicated and more tightly woven than most Japanese novels. Few indeed of the latter have plots as complex as Tanizaki's *The Whirlpool*. Skillful storytelling contributes much to the charm of *A Blind Man's Tale,* **"The Portrait of Shunkin,"** and *The Mother of Captain Shigemoto*. What Tanizaki termed the grandeur of a far-extending mountain range is seen in the plots of such works of his as *An Idiot's Love* and *The Makioka Sisters*. *A Tale of Disarrayed Chrysanthemums* reads like a popular adventure story; in fact, Tanizaki amused himself by calling it "a popular novel," apparently in reference to Akutagawa's charge that any work of fiction that tries to attract readers by an ingenious plot is a "popular" novelist not a "genuine" one. Some of his early tales—**"The Thief," "Devils Talk in Broad Daylight,"** and **"In the Street,"** among others—are plotted as carefully as detective stories; indeed, they are usually assigned to that genre. (pp. 72-3)

As a storyteller, Tanizaki was always extremely sensitive to the use of language. . . . His desire to do something to improve the quality of Japanese writing led him to produce *The Composition Reader,* a comprehensive guidebook to good prose. While intended for a broad range of readers, the book reveals a good deal about his own literary practice.

What was distinctive about Tanizaki's approach to the language of literature was his denial that any such thing existed. He even said: "I believe there is no difference between practical and artistic language." By practical language, however, he meant language that efficiently carries out its practical purpose, which is to make the reader understand the writer. The most practical language is therefore the most artistic. "If you think there is some art of speaking or writing reserved exclusively for the novel," he said, "read any one of our contemporary novels. You will immediately discover that it contains no sentence that cannot be used for a practical purpose, and that any sentence serving a practical purpose well is also useful in literary composition." More than anything else, Tanizaki believed, the language of literature had to be persuasive; to be beautiful or euphonious was of secondary importance. (p. 74)

According to Tanizaki, good style was a matter of two rules, both of them quite relevant to his general conception of literature. The first was not to be too concerned with the rules of grammar. The reason for this, as he explained, was that the Japanese language in its very nature was not very grammatical. The writer could turn this to advantage by cultivating a certain ambiguity, which Tanizaki found elegant; indeed, he compared the effect of a passage written with no ambiguity to that of rudely exposed thighs and knees. A passage that omitted as many words as possible, even to the point at which a strict grammarian would object to it, was at once graceful in impression and provocative in meaning.

The second piece of advice Tanizaki had for beginning writers was that they should cultivate their literary taste. In order to become a good writer, one had to be able to distinguish good writing from bad. But this was like distinguishing between good and bad wines; one had only one's own taste to rely on. Here Tanizaki was retreating to subjectivism, and he knew it. He still insisted, however, that there would emerge a semblance of objectivity if the reader had developed a refined taste. . . . Education had little to do with it; inborn taste, polished by experience, was all. Here again Tanizaki's distrust of intellect was apparent.

The Composition Reader also classified prose styles in terms of two main categories. The first included the "flowing style," the "laconic style," the "calm style," the "airy style" (a light, casual, unconventional style . . .), and the "craggy style" (a deliberately rugged, uneven style; Tanizaki compared it to the surface of a crag); it referred, as these terms imply, both to the mode of sentence construction and to the way in which one sentence followed from another. The second referred to vocabulary and idiom; it comprised the "lecture style" (normal written style; professors often used it in their lectures so that students could copy them verbatim), the "military style" (more polite than the lecture style; so called because typically a serviceman used it in addressing his superior), the "salutatory style" (even more polite than the military style; used on highly ceremonial occasions), and the "conversational style" (used in normal conversations). Though in both instances the classification involved no value judgment, Tanizaki made sufficiently clear which styles he favored. In the first category, Tanizaki seems to have had a natural predilection for the "flowing style," a style that, with its long sentences and carefully but inconspicuously engineered continuity, was like a smoothly flowing stream. . . . He was fond of it because he thought it suited the genius of the Japanese language better than any other. . . . In the second category, he seems to have been most attracted to the "conversational style." He liked it because, as he pointed out, this style had four main strengths: (1) expression was freer; (2) sentences could end in a greater variety of sounds; (3) the reader could feel the tone of the writer's speech and almost see his feelings and facial expressions; (4) the reader could tell whether the speaker was a man or a woman. Tanizaki seems to have especially liked this last fact. He observed that as a rule a male reader read a book in a male voice even when he was not reading aloud, but that if the book was written in the conversational style he would read it in either a male or a female voice, whichever the sense required. For this reason, Tanizaki recommended that writers use the conversational style more frequently.

Tanizaki's predilection for the flowing and conversational styles is clearly seen in his own writings. Though he was a very versatile writer, who could command a variety of styles with consummate skill, these two styles underlie most of them. The flowing style is the one in which he wrote many of his novels and short stories in his mature years; the most notable example of it is *The Makioka Sisters*. It is also conspicuous in *The Cat, Shōzō, and Two Women,* **"Ashikari"** (in which many quotation marks are deliberately omitted in order not to interrupt the flow of words), and **"The Portrait of Shunkin"** (in which most of the punctuation is omitted, for the same reason). Some parts of *The Diary of a Mad Old Man* are written in the "craggy style," and *Chronicles of Our Peaceful Kitchen* inclines somewhat toward the "airy style"; yet in both instances the overriding tone of voice is unmistakably that of the flowing style. The same style is latent in his earlier works, too—in **"The Clown,"** for instance.

As for Tanizaki's use of the conversational style in his fiction, examples are too numerous to cite. The most striking one is *The Whirlpool,* which is told entirely in the peculiarly feminine vernacular of a woman brought up in the Osaka area. (pp. 75-7)

It has often been claimed that Tanizaki's style went through drastic changes during his long literary career. But his basic style does not seem to have changed much, when judged in the light of his classification of styles, since it always inclined toward the flowing and the conversational. Many of his readers would be willing to concede that there is a good deal of stylistic difference between "Tattoo" and *The Makioka Sisters*. Yet how many of them would be ready to say of the former that it approaches the "laconic style," the opposite of the "flowing style" in which the latter is written? . . . Likewise, Tanizaki's fondness for the conversational style was lifelong. If one thinks this style is not often used in his early works of fiction, one has only to be reminded that the young Tanizaki wrote a good many plays. Among his early stories, too, there are those that, like **"Creation"** and **"From a Certain Protocol,"** consist solely of dialogue. It does not appear, then, that Tanizaki ever attempted to change his basic stylistic preferences, or that the attempt would have made any sense to him, since he saw style as a natural product of physique. (p. 78)

Despite all . . . [his] emphasis on the idea that literature is play—and play for a very large number of people—Tanizaki seems to have secretly harbored a belief in literature's didactic function. This can be seen, for instance, in the passage . . . where he said that beauty of form is ultimately the same as beauty of content, that physical beauty is essentially no different from spiritual beauty. Tanizaki seems to be implying here that art at its highest level is as capable as religion of bringing spiritual enlightenment to its devotees—more capable, in fact, since visible beauty is more readily appreciated than spiritual beauty. (p. 82)

Again, this is hardly a novel idea. But when we consider Tanizaki's daemonic ideal of beauty, it takes on some very strange applications. Can an admirer of one of Tanizaki's she-devils be led thereby to the realm of religious enlightenment? Tanizaki's answer was emphatically in the affirmative. In his opinion, art was valuable precisely because it had that function. In most Oriental religions, the worshiper had as a rule to be a good man to be saved, but art could redeem even a bad man, a worshiper of evil beauty. "I believe," he said, "that art is the only way by which an evil man can attain a realm of perfect liberation without becoming an entirely different person. While religion spurns evil men . . . art permits them to enter its realm, as long as they believe in it. This is so because evil is only of this world; in the other world there is neither good nor evil; all there is is beauty."

The argument gains in force if "this world" is equated with the conscious mind, and "the other world" with the subconscious. Religion teaches man to be good in this world; it wants him to discipline himself by his conscious effort. A good man in religious terms is a person whose conscious mind has complete control over his behavior, so complete that he follows the religious codes automatically. But some people (everybody, potentially) are more faithful to the subconscious; they follow its commands because they come from a deeper level and speak to deeper needs. Religion would label such people wayward and refuse to save them unless they reformed. Art, in contrast, would both accept and save them, because it understands these needs.

A characteristic instance of art functioning as redeemer is cited by Tanizaki in a short polemic piece called **"The Censor."** The literary work being censored here is a play called *First Love,* and the playwright (modeled after Tanizaki himself), summoned before the censor, vigorously defends himself by insisting that the play is not at all immoral, that in fact it serves a didactic purpose. The hero of the play is a young student who falls in love with a maidservant in his father's household. She, however, loves another man, and these two scheme to murder the student and grab the family estate. The student, well aware of the woman's evil design, willingly meets his death. "The flame that was burning in this boy's heart cannot be explained away by the logic of this world," the playwright remarks. "Nevertheless, the play does not give the spectators the impression that he met an unfortunate destiny. Or, even if some spectators should feel he was unfortunate, they will not believe his death was meaningless. They will be convinced that something remains after his death." The young student, Tanizaki is saying, is "saved" in the sense that he has been awakened to something higher than death, something that makes him readily meet his death. In this sense, though the object of his passion was unworthy, the play is didactic, even highly moral, since death is overcome as truly by passion as by religion.

Some of Tanizaki's novels are "religious" in the same sense, but more plainly so. Plainest of all is his last novel, **The Diary of a Mad Old Man,** in which the aged hero worships his young and beautiful daughter-in-law like a female Buddha. Keenly aware of approaching death, the old man buys a lot for his grave and prepares a plan for his tombstone, on which are to appear the young woman's footprints carved in the manner of the Buddha's. Once the plan is set, the old man is no longer afraid of death, since he can dream of his departed soul lying at peace under her feet. A similar identification of a beautiful woman with a female Buddha is suggested in **The Whirlpool:** here, too, her admirers are not at all afraid of dying when they dream of being with her after their death. A more pathetic case is that of Captain Shigemoto's father, in the novel named after his wife. This old man is robbed of his beautiful wife, whom he worshiped. In deep grief and agony, he tries every means of salvation available to him—he reads the poetry of Po Chü-i, he drinks wine, he devotes himself to the practice of esoteric Buddhism—but to no avail. It is only his wife that can save him. His futile search for peace is awe-inspiring, and it is with relief that one finally reads of his son, Captain Shigemoto, being reunited with his mother, and so saving the old man's soul. However strange, even perverse, these emotions, they ennoble the characters who are driven by them. If the reader, too, is momentarily ennobled, perhaps he has gained from literature the best that Tanizaki thought it had to offer. (pp. 82-4)

Makoto Ueda, "Tanizaki Jun'ichirō," in his Modern Japanese Writers and the Nature of Literature *(reprinted with the permission of the publishers, Stanford University Press; © 1976 by the Board of Trustees of the Leland Stanford Junior University), Stanford University Press, 1976, pp. 54-84.*

GWENN BOARDMAN PETERSEN

Many of Tanizaki's contemporaries ended their stories with a question: "When and where will these two meet again?"—or as in the play by Fujimori Seikichi flashing a sign that reads "What made her do it?" But Tanizaki's questions are unvoiced, though often related to specific incidents. Just what *did* the prostitute do to the author in *Itansha no Kanashimi*? Who poured the scalding water on Shunkin and why? What is the nature of the "snake" in the untranslated *Shōnen* (where critics tend to focus on the presence of another cruel female—Mitsuko, the girl who frightens the other children)? Only marginally of Freudian significance, this focus of horror ultimately leaves the reader, like the boy, uncertain as to the nature of the threat. Was the snake real or carved from wood? And was the terror any less real or the domination more perverse if the beast's only life was in the imagination of a frightened boy?

Tanizaki's ambiguities may be poetic in the Japanese tradition or prosaic in the manner of a mystery story. His perceptive psychological studies are rendered with great artistry and always leave room for the reader to exercise imagination. His careful delineation of the past implies—but never makes explicit—a judgment of those who are merely fanciers of tradition. At the same time, Tanizaki fashions from the past a commentary on the distance between dream and reality: between our hopes and "the way things are."

It might be tempting to read the voice of **Ashikari**'s narrator as Tanizaki's, "trying to embody the idea of my sense of loss that all these days are past," recognizing that many of his words seem "nothing but whimsical fancy to a young man," yet hinting that they are an essential means by which older people can endure the present. Tanizaki, however, has a full appreciation of modern ways and conveniences—though he continually exposes the weaknesses of those who use the modern marvels not because they are superior but simply because they are new. Again he implies a criticism of false values and superficial judgment.

But Tanizaki's fiction of ambiguity, his mastery of point of view, his understanding of both past and present, and his psychological insight illuminate the *in-yō* (yin and yang) of twentieth-century Japan without attempting to award the prize to either of the elements that must eventually settle into proper harmony. Tanizaki's essay **"Kyoto: Her Nature, Food . . . and Women"** demonstrates attitudes that provide clues to this balance and to his theory of fiction.

His aesthetic of shadows—his preference for vague language and meanings hinted at rather than specified—is one aspect of Kyoto, as his essay **"In Praise of Shadows"** revealed. He finds "art, tradition, elegance, and sophistication" in Kyoto's women now. But he also recalls the jolly custom of *zakone*, that occasion when customers, geisha, and *maiko* (young apprentice geisha) spread their bedding on the floor and "all jumped in together," sleeping happily in one room. A jolly custom, indeed, although "one would often wake up the next morning with a splitting headache."

That headache should remind us of the outstanding quality, the realistic touches, that help to maintain the balance in Tanizaki's chronicles of Japan. Recognizing the exquisite past and enjoying the often confusing (although convenient) present, he hints at the need for *values* upon which the future can depend. If Tanizaki's reflective, tentative tone seems reminiscent of Buddhist "acceptance" on some occasions, on others it is an intensely modern irony not to be confined within national attitudes but having a universal appeal.

Viewing tradition objectively, while gently mocking all empty conventions of word and gesture, Tanizaki illuminates a world that is, in final analysis, still the intensely Japanese home of Meiji Man's sons and grandsons. The Western reader needs some footnotes on the social and psychological context, of course. Often Tanizaki provides all the necessary clues—as in his carefully inserted perspectives on a time that valued Beauty in terms of a painful tattoo, an artist who produced exquisite sounds by following a tradition that included many cruel masters and suffering pupils, or a marriage that must consider family ahead of personal feelings. We can appreciate Tanizaki's role as chronicler in his recording of the minutiae of these unfamiliar worlds. At the same time, appreciating his craftsmanship, we can come to recognize his true role in recording the paradoxical ways of modern Japan.

The actors in Tanizaki's fictions are trained in a tradition—just as ninth-generation Kabuki actors proudly carry on the art of their ancestors. They are related, however tenuously, to Saikaku's amusing Men (and Women) Who Loved Love. But they are not so closely tied to time and place as Saikaku's seventeenth-century heroes. Their actions are sometimes linked with attitudes that differ from those in the West. Their eye for beauty is still more apt to be focused on the exquisite line of the back of the neck or on the delicate foot than on the curves of Western breasts. Telling detail, rich in connotation for the Japanese, may seem only tiresome cataloguing to the uninitiated. At the same time, words and gestures may seem impossibly vague to the Westerner demanding familiar conciseness and logic. Yet in the final analysis, Tanizaki has succeeded in the seemingly impossible. In his finely constructed chronicles he has set the universal Human Comedy upon a truly Japanese stage. (pp. 110-13)

> Gwenn Boardman Petersen, "Tanizaki Jun'ichirō," in her The Moon in the Water: Understanding Tanizaki, Kawabata, and Mishima (copyright © 1979 by The University Press of Hawaii), University Press of Hawaii, 1979, pp. 44-120.

NORIKO MIZUTA LIPPIT

[The Taisho period (1912-1926) in Japan] was one of reaction to naturalism and to the confessional I-novels; it was characterized by two dominant literary movements, one of the Shirakaba group and the other the so-called aesthetic school. These movements—and the philosophic and aesthetic ideas underlying them—were almost diametrically opposed. The Shirakaba group sought a new sense of life in the limitless expansion of the self and of human possibilities, while the aesthetic school was committed to the pursuit of the beautiful, even to the point of sacrificing social and moral integrity. Yet they were in agreement that literature is an art form and that style, structure, words, and images are at least as important as the content of literary works. Perfection in a work as art, together with or in place of philosophic depth, was a professed goal of most of the writers of this period; this was especially true of the writers of the aesthetic school who were most strongly influenced by [Edgar Allen] Poe. Among them Sato Haruo, Hagiwara Sakutaro, Akutagawa Ryūnosuke, and Tanizaki Junichiro openly acknowledged their indebtedness to Poe, and their works show the depth of his influence. (pp. 83-4)

Students of Tanizaki usually agree that, like other Taisho writers, he began his career under the spell of the West: the influence of Poe, Baudelaire, and Oscar Wilde, among others, is reflected in many of his early works. It is agreed, however, that the influence of the Japanese literature of the seventeenth and eighteenth centuries, especially the erotic and sadistic stories in Kusazoshi and Kabuki plays, was also strong. According to the orthodox view, the influence of the Western writers became superficial by the end of the Taisho period. Drawn to both East and West, Tanizaki, after a period of severe internal conflict between the two attractions, turned completely to the world of classical Japanese literature and made a conscious artistic endeavor to link his later works with his Japanese heritage. My purpose here is to consider whether the Western influences were indeed superficial and to examine Poe's influence on Tanizaki's later development, when he attempted to create his Japanese Byzantium. (p. 84)

Most of [Tanizaki's works] . . . were controversial, and critics do not agree in their assessment of them or of Tanizaki himself as a writer; they do agree, however, on the perfection of his novelistic skills in creating a self-sufficient, polished world of beauty. In most of his works, especially those of his middle period, Tanizaki fastidiously excluded the social, economic, and political life of Japan, creating a literary space untouched by the forces of life in modern Japan. Often drawing material from Japanese history or old Japanese legends, he created a "pleasure dome" which is "out of space, out of time."

It is only natural that proletarian writers and such existentialist writers as Oe Kenzaburo criticize the lack of basic ideology and relevance to modern existence in Tanizaki's works. On the other hand, critics like Ito Sei argue that to regard the conditions of the flesh, such as erotic desire for life, as a determining factor in human life is an ideology in its own right, and defend Tanizaki as a writer whose major theme was man's struggle to attain the sense of life at the risk of moral and social integrity. (p. 85)

Tanizaki's creative works can be divided roughly into three periods; the first ends with *Some Prefer Nettles* in 1928, and the third starts with *The Key* in 1956. It is in the first period, from the forty-third year of Meiji to the third year of Showa (1910-1928), that Western influences, including that of Poe, were most evident; we can find many themes, expressions, descriptions, and stories reminiscent of Poe and of such writers as Baudelaire, Wilde, Zola, and Thomas Hardy.

Some critics have emphasized the influence of Wilde on Tanizaki, underestimating that of Poe. The importance of Wilde's influence is undeniable. Tanizaki tries to separate art from life, placing art above life. Because of his characters' antimoralistic and antisocial pursuit of sensual pleasure, justified for the sake of artistic creation, the term "diabolism" has been widely applied to Tanizaki's early works. Yet Tanizaki's diabolic aesthetes do not suffer from the severe remorse or pangs of conscience experienced by Dorian Gray. In Tanizaki's works, there is no struggle against conscience, against a firmly established social and religious orthodoxy. (pp. 85-6)

Tanizaki's heroes' diabolic pursuit of sensuous pleasure proves to be a distorted effort to attain a sense of life through the pursuit of unattainable feminine beauty, the pursuit of the absolute. Throughout Tanizaki's works, the search for a sense of life through the masochistic pursuit of an unattainable woman is a major theme. Tanizaki's heroes feel a deep sense of alienation that spurs them to perverted efforts to recover from it. Tanizaki's grotesque expresses these efforts to overcome alienation: it is not merely an exercise in decadent aestheticism. Indeed, the grotesque that expresses the heroes' pursuit is an appropriate style. In Tanizaki, as well as in Poe, the grotesque does not refer merely to this perverted pursuit, but also to the narrative form or perspective, which is ironic and tragicomic. Furthermore, Tanizaki developed, in his later period, his own myth of eternal woman, a myth that justifies the heroes' grotesque efforts at self-recovery. By developing his own myth, Tanizaki created his own world of romanticism. In these respects, Tanizaki's works are fundamentally similar to Poe's.

The major themes of Tanizaki's early works are the fear of death, the sadomasochistic pursuit of feminine beauty, the discovery of perversity or cruelty in human nature, and the relation of art to these themes. . . . In many of his tales, he describes a fear of persecution, a fear of madness and death. The narrator of **"Kyofu" (The Fear,** 1913) explains that his heart starts beating rapidly the minute he enters a moving vehicle. The drumming of his heart increases in speed and intensity, and he feels as if all his blood was rushing to his head, with his body about to burst into pieces or his brain into madness. This immediately reminds us of the descriptions in Poe's "The Imp of the Perverse" and "The Tell-Tale Heart," where the narrators burst out into self-destructive confessions of their crimes, urged on by the ever-growing sound of their hearts.

In **"Seishun monogatari" (My Adolescent Days,** 1932), Tanizaki says that he could not exalt death or madness as did Takayama Chogyu, a romantic writer of a decade earlier; instead, when he read Poe, Baudelaire, Strindberg, and Gorki, anxiety and fear permeated his nervous system, distorting his senses and his emotional responses to things. The fear of the explosion of his body and brain could be ignited at any time and place by the slightest sensory stimulus, for it had no concrete external source. He calls the period in which he suffered from this fear a period of inferno. In many of his tales he describes it in terms of the dizziness felt when standing at the verge of an abyss, a sensation of extreme fear and pain that might culminate in the total loss of his sanity.

The fear is clearly that of death and persecution, yet Tanizaki, unlike Poe, gives death itself a very small role in his works. Furthermore, the fear of death is actually the fear of his own urge toward self-destruction. The fear, therefore, can be called a "pleasurable pain," and its source is entirely internal. The hero's urge toward self-destruction is indeed the work of what Poe called the "imp of the perverse." In fact, to evoke this state of pleasurable pain, of the abysmal terror of self-destruction, is the purpose of the protagonists' diabolic actions in almost all of Tanizaki's works and is their major theme.

This sensation of pleasurable pain is directly related to the other themes of this period, the discovery of the perversity or cruel love of destruction in human nature and the sadomasochistic pursuit of feminine beauty. Many of Tanizaki's tales were obviously inspired by Poe's crime and detective stories, tales in which the heroes commit, with the utmost cruelty, crimes that are almost gratuitous. These tales include **"Gold and Silver," "The Criminal," "An Incident at Yanagiyu,"** and **"The Cursed Play."**

Many devices and techniques used by Poe appear in these tales. (pp. 86-8)

In most cases, the heroes' extreme sadism, the analytical precision with which they murder and hide the corpse, and their observations on criminal psychology vividly reveal their fascination with evil and gratuitous cruelty and their concern with making murder a work of art. (p. 88)

Yet the sadism of the heroes is often masochistic. . . . **"Hokan" (A Harlequin,** 1911), a masterpiece of the early period, is the story of a man who takes uncontrollable pleasure in humiliating himself and in pleasing others by allowing them to control and manipulate him. His effort to exist only in the consciousness of others, in which condition the pain he feels gives him a strong sense of his own self and body, is a classic case of masochism. (pp. 88-9)

The act of evil for evil's sake is as masochistic as it is diabolic: the [hero's] pure evil is directed against himself, to vex his own soul so that he can be immersed in the immediacy of pain and terror. In the spontaneous experience of pain and terror, the nonreflecting consciousness kills the reflecting consciousness and thus the hero is immersed in the sense of himself, of his immediate body and subjectivity. (p. 89)

In [Poe's] "The Premature Burial" and "The Pit and the Pendulum," the heroes, by their own imagination, induce sensations of the utmost terror and pain of death. "A Descent into the Maelström" and "MS. Found in a Bottle" also describe the heroes' experience of the ecstasy and terror of self-annihilation, their experience of an abysmal descent into nothingness. Thus, both in Poe and Tanizaki, the diabolism is actually directed toward the heroes themselves as a method of inducing pain and ecstasy and of intoxicating the reflecting consciousness in the immediacy of pain.

In Tanizaki, the themes of the discovery of perversity in human nature and the masochistic desire for self-destruction are intertwined and are, furthermore, related to his other major theme, the pursuit of the *femme fatale*. **"Bushu-ko hiwa" (Secrets of Lord Bushu,** 1931), set in medieval Japan, is the most successful dramatization of the relations among these themes. (p. 90)

In all of Tanizaki's stories in which the fatal woman is the main theme, the heroes are involved in drawing out the diabolic nature of beautiful women, thus molding them into ideal women, black-widow spiders which devour males after sexual ecstasy. The creation of the cruel, beautiful woman is the externalization of the hero's inner desire, and in actuality, she is his puppet. This can be seen most readily in **"Chijin no ai" (A Fool's Love,** 1924). (p. 91)

The hero of the novel falls in love with a Western-looking waitress and encourages her to be more bold in displaying her beauty and sexual attraction. She begins to have many love affairs, yet the more cruel her treatment of him becomes, the more ecstatic the pleasure he finds in being with her. The creation of the fatal woman in order to be tortured by her is also the main theme of such other major works of the early period as **"Shisei" (Tattoo), "Jyotaro"** and **"Suterareru Made" (Until Forsaken).** In the latter period, such works as **"Shunkinsho" (A Portrait of Shunkin), "Ashikari"** and *Futen rojin nikki* **(The Diary of a Mad Old Man)** are only extensions of these early works.

Tanizaki's heroes, however, do not pursue beautiful women for the sake of erotic fulfillment. Rather, they pursue an unattainable absolute, the symbolic essence of feminine beauty. In the early period, the beauty is typically revealed in human flesh, but it is human flesh as an *objet d'art* which refuses normal erotic communication: Tanizaki's heroes find the essence of feminine beauty in women's feet. (pp. 91-2)

The heroes long for the beauty that rejects them absolutely as ugly and weak, precluding any possibility of normal human relationships. Thus, beauty is elevated to the position of an absolute, an almighty existence... Tanizaki's characters are involved in such fetishism, besides the involvement in women's feet, as licking a handkerchief dirtied by the woman's mucous, drinking a loved one's urine, and so forth. The pursuit of the unattainable beauty and the pursuit of the ugly are essentially the same...

The fear of death described by Tanizaki's heroes is based on their psychic dread of life, their sense of alienation; their masochism is a means of objectifying their fear. Yet Tanizaki's hero is the creator of the sadistic persecutor; she is the externalization of his inner desire and is almost his double. Thus he is the schemer responsible for the whole situation: he is the persecutor as well as the victim. In this sense, Tanizaki's hero becomes a god, the creator of his own, self-contained world. (p. 92)

[Both] Poe and Tanizaki frequently use the uninvolved, third-person narrator to describe the hero's grotesque effort. In Poe's stories the uninvolved narrator becomes involved. Thus, at the climax, the hero's drama is experienced by the narrator as his inner experience. In the works in which Poe uses a first-person narrator, the hero is split between a rational self and an irrational one; the narrator-hero, representing the rational self, describes the grotesque drama of the irrational self, a drama which the narrator-hero says that he himself finds difficult to comprehend. This skillful use of the narrator is a device to express the ironic, dual perspective inherent in Poe's grotesque; the serious and rational appear comical and absurd, while the mad and perverted appear tragic.

Although Tanizaki uses the uninvolved third-person narrator with great skill, the tales narrated by the hero himself do not always maintain the ironic point of view successfully. The reader is called upon to take the hero's grotesque drama seriously and with sympathy, which immediately raises the question of the drama's social, moral, and ideological relevance. It is only in **The Diary of a Mad Old Man** that Tanizaki, dramatizing man's tragicomic struggle for life, uses the ironic perspective successfully. In this work he reveals an almost terrifying spirit of irony and self-mockery. In his middle period, however, Tanizaki turned to the world of dream and imagination in his effort to create a self-sufficient romantic world, one that could give structure to his hero's grotesque pursuit of a sense of life.

While Poe had a myth that justified the poet's grotesque endeavor at destructive transcendence through his art, Tanizaki had no such cosmic myth. Tanizaki's heroes, therefore, are not transcendental heroes, but mad aesthetes who indulge in sensuous ecstasy to the point of death. Poe was a romantic who perceived the deterioration of the isomorphic relations between the order of mind and that of the body and who believed in the power of imagination to transcend the phenomenal world to reach a higher level of reality where the split between subject and object is eliminated.

Tanizaki, on the other hand, did not yet have his own myth to explain metaphorically his view of the universe—his view of the source of man's alienation and of the life and task of the artist and his vision of the ideal reality. Although in his youth he defined himself as a romantic writer who believed in the "poetic intuition" which perceives the world beyond phenomenal reality (a world he grasped in Platonic terms), it is difficult to call Tanizaki's early works romantic in the absence of a myth which creates a self-sufficient world of dream and legitimizes the theme of grotesque recovery from alienation. While Poe's mythopoeic thrust to create his own universe resulted in the creation of the beautiful, mathematically balanced universe of Eureka in which the poet is finally absorbed, Tanizaki had to depend on his skill of expression to convince the reader of the validity of his hero's grotesque endeavor. Asking the reader to hold in abeyance the question of morality, Tanizaki sought to appeal only to the reader's aesthetic sense. In this endeavor, the novel was not quite an appropriate form, and in the middle period his works gradually moved toward the world of romance.

While Poe's exploration of the sadomasochistic attempt to attain a sense of life and of the endeavor in grotesque art to induce dreaming consciousness presents features of human experience that are meaningful and interesting from the existential-phenomenological point of view, Poe dramatized them in his own fantasy world. He also had a myth that justified them externally as legitimate endeavors for man's return to Original Unity.

Tanizaki's middle period starts with his awareness of the need to create a self-sufficient world of dream and beauty in which the question of morality and relevance to reality will be temporarily suspended. Without such a world, his exploration of grotesque eroticism might prove to be merely sensational.

This problem concerned all of the writers of the grotesque. Until the middle of the nineteenth century, the grotesque had been considered pejoratively, for it explored the realm of the ugly, the fantastic, and the subconscious, including man's fears and secret desires. During the romantic age, when artists saw the grotesque aspects of objective reality, the grotesque came to be regarded as closely related to the artist's reaction to and conception of reality. Even then, the grotesque was approved only half-heartedly; it was only in the modern period that the grotesque became recognized, through the works of Dostoevski, Kafka, Faulkner, Pinter, and Beckett, among others, as a highly significant symbol, style, form of imagination, and structural basis for literary works. (pp. 95-7)

Tanizaki's turning to the world of classical Japanese culture reflects the same concern as that of the writers of the grotesque with the legitimacy of the grotesque world he creates. It is, like Coleridge's adoption of the medieval ballad form, a device to draw a magic circle around the hero and his exploration. It also reflects his mythopoeic desire to create his own dreamworld, which first became evident at this time.

Some Prefer Nettles, the novel that marks the end of Tanizaki's first period, already presents his effort to draw a magic circle, to create a myth of ideal feminine beauty that would enable him to pursue the theme of the masochistic search for a sense of life as the theme of man's search for unattainable ideal beauty. (p. 97)

Tanizaki came to identify ideal beauty with the beauty of the classical Japanese court lady.... Glimpsed only momentarily, she is inaccessible, a dream woman existing only in one's imagination and separated in time and space. Although the essence of her beauty is also whiteness, it is no longer white flesh, but whiteness itself. Tanizaki's fatal woman thus emerges as an archetypal Japanese court lady as well as an archetypal mother.

There is no doubt that Tanizaki rediscovered the beauty of Japanese culture and literature, yet the claim that Tanizaki, abandoning his Western influences, returned to the classical world is misleading. Instead, Tanizaki created his own dreamworld and eternal woman, as exotic to him as their Western counterparts, out of classical Japanese culture. The court life he presents in **"The Mother of Captain Shigemoto"** (1949) and the medieval life in **"Secrets of Lord Bushu"** are distinctively Tanizaki's own creations rather than historically accurate representations. Tanizaki himself explains enviously in **"Ave Maria"** (1923) that the myth of the eternal woman and the worship of woman do not exist in Japanese culture. Thus he creates his own goddess to rule over his self-sufficient dreamworld, a mythical world or one which functions as a substitute for myth. The eternal mother as goddess, as the symbolic essence of his dreamworld, is most vividly expressed in **"The Mother of Captain Shigemoto,"** the masterpiece of his middle period. Captain Shigemoto's mother, who has lived in his dream, finally appears at the end of the novel shining faintly in the darkness with a circle of light around her. Tanizaki's return was not to classical Japanese culture but to the primordial and infantile area of human consciousness, to the realm of the subconscious and dreams. (pp. 98-9)

Some Prefer Nettles is often considered a dramatization of the conflict between Tanizaki's attraction to the beauty and culture of the West and those of the East. With this novel, the period of Western influence on Tanizaki appears to end, and since his major works all explore the world of classical beauty, critics argue that the Western influence on Tanizaki was not lasting. Rather, however, the novel dramatizes the shift of the hero's pursuit of white flesh to whiteness itself, a shift from the world of reality to the world of romance, to the self-sufficient world of romantic dream. Poe's influence on Tanizaki appears, then, not merely in Tanizaki's early choice of the themes that were to characterize his literary career, but also in the creation of the romantic world that began with this shift. (p. 101)

Tanizaki's early exposure to Poe's world of "negative romanticism," with its central concept of grotesque transcendence, cannot be irrelevant to the ultimate development of his own world of romanticism in the Japanese literary tradition. While Tanizaki's Japanese romantic world is unique, it is not incompatible with the Western romantic tradition. Thus Tanizaki emerges not as a "pagan outcast," but as the legitimate heir to both the Japanese literary tradition and to the Western tradition of romanticism, in both of which the grotesque plays an essential role. (pp. 102-03)

> Noriko Mizuta Lippit, "Tanizaki and Poe: The Grotesque and the Quest for Supernal Beauty," in Comparative Literature (© copyright 1977 by University of Oregon; reprinted by permission of Comparative Literature), Vol. XXIX, No. 3, Summer, 1977 (and reprinted in a slightly revised form in his Reality and Fiction in Modern Japanese Literature, M. E. Sharpe Inc., 1980, pp. 82-103).*

GEOFFREY O'BRIEN

The long career of Junichiro Tanizaki ... offers a spectacle of unity in the utmost diversity. From his early "diabolist" tales through the traditionalist underpinnings of his middle period to the erotic realism of his last novels, Tanizaki's preoccupations remain the same: the secret ritual, the obsessive desire, the nostalgia so profound that it defines an entire existence. Oddly, he is also the most objective of writers. Never judging, he turns his subjects around and inside out, proposing motives, contradicting them. He rarely hesitates to make jokes of the grotesque figures his characters cut as they attempt to reconstruct the world according to the laws of fetishism.

Of the many fetishes that crop up in Tanizaki's books, few are as bizarre as that of Terukatsu, the Lord of Musashi [the protagonist of *The Secret History of the Lord of Musashi*], who responds only to the sight of noseless male heads caressed by young female hands....

Tanizaki's novella is on one level a burlesque of heroic feudal sagas—loyal retainers commit suicide by leaping into toilets, and far more space is devoted to the hero's sexual proclivities than to his prowess in battle. But beyond that, it is an analysis of the ways in which Terukatsu's secret sexual agenda determines his role in history. In the end he will topple a powerful clan solely to bring about the desired conjunction of a lovely woman and a noseless face.

The generally humorous tone of the story in no way diminishes the terrifying intensity of Terukatsu's obsession; but, as always in Tanizaki's work, a sexual compulsion is part of the natural world. It is born in a moment of time . . . and takes root in the watcher, forcing him to recreate the instant again and again. Tanizaki's groveling masochists and ingenious voyeurs are like the demon-possessed protagonists of Noh plays, and he compels us to admire them as we would an interestingly deformed plant.

In *Arrowroot,* by contrast, Tanizaki puts the kinks to one side and contemplates a remote mountainous region in central Japan. This is the author's traditionalist mode, familiar to readers of *The Makioka Sisters* and *In Praise of Shadows.* Rather than universalize, he immerses himself in a specific location and all the associations it summons up. The place names and recipes and song lyrics distill a quintessentially local spirit. . . . But the inner structure of Tanizaki's world remains constant. The central character here is haunted, like the Lord of Musashi, by a mysteriously powerful image—in this case the "chapped and cracked" fingers of the women in a family of papermakers.

> Geoffrey O'Brien, in a review of "The Secret History of the Lord of Musashi and Arrowroot" (reprinted by permission of The Village Voice and the author; copyright © News Group Publications, Inc., 1982), in The Village Voice, Vol. XXVII, No. 17, April 27, 1982, p. 47.

EDMUND WHITE

Junichiro Tanizaki may well prove to be the outstanding Japanese novelist of this century, rivaled only by Yasunari Kawabata. . . . Both writers presided over the obsequies of traditional Japan, and both responded to its demise with a strong but ironic nostalgia. . . .

For Tanizaki, **"Arrowroot"** (1932) and **"The Secret History of the Lord of Musashi"** (1935), now admirably translated into English for the first time, mark the period when, after 20 years of writing novels in a fairly orthodox style, he fused two interests—traditional Japanese storytelling and experimental narrative—into a unique style. But their themes are mirrored in many of his other stories. . . .

Sadism—or more exactly sexual coercion, quietly engineered and often taking place among members of the same family—is a theme that fascinated Tanizaki. He managed to exclude it altogether only from **"The Makioka Sisters,"** as though he had determined not to mar his masterpiece with anything too recherché. But even in those pages, the grim relish with which diseases, operations and natural disasters are described seems a bit suspect. . . .

[Many of Tanizaki's] plots, if baldly summarized, sound merely pornographic. But what must be kept in mind is that the erotic maneuvers in a Tanizaki novel are performed in a tight, almost claustrophobic society based on filial deference and an equally strong parental sense of responsibility for children. If such roles form the tight mesh of the backdrop, the "lighting" of the scenes is always esthetic. We are never far from the powerful Buddhist response to nature (thus time in **"The Bridge of Dreams"** is marked by the flowering of seasonal plants) nor from Tanizaki's taste for whatever is old, shadowy, rustic, tarnished, even filthy—that constellation of qualities summed up by the Japanese word *wabi*. That quality is explicated by Tanizaki in his essay, **"In Praise of Shadows,"** which he starts off by rejecting the Western bathroom, of all things, for its harsh light and shiny tiles and fixtures. He goes on to praise light-absorbing Japanese paper and the "muddy" Japanese complexion. He ends by stating: "I would call back at least for literature this world of shadows we are losing. In the mansion called literature I would have the eaves deep and the walls dark, I would push back into the shadows the things that come forward too clearly, I would strip away the useless decoration."

Virtually all the elements of Tanizaki's vision—its sexual kinkiness, its swift narrative thrust, its gaudy display of violence against a muted grisaille of nature—appear in **"The Secret History of the Lord of Musashi."** The book purports to be a reconstruction, based on "secret documents," of a 16th-century warrior's intimate life.

Anyone who has ever contemplated writing a historical novel will admire Tanizaki's serious solutions to the real (as opposed to the routine) problems of the genre. The greatest temptation and the one almost always succumbed to is to put new wine into old bottles, modern psychology into period costume. The second most common sin is to make historical characters perpetually conscious of their high destinies, to make them breathe at all times the ozone of purpose, of will, of heroism. Tanizaki avoids both mistakes. His men and women are quite palpably different from whatever their modern counterparts would be. These characters are more impulsive, more mettlesome, more aware of their rank and dignity and more adult at an early age. (p. 8)

[What Terukatsu, the Lord of Musashi,] most longs to see is a sadistic woman make love to a noseless man. The origin of this strange taste is carefully explained, and within the confines of the tale the explanation is believable. Indeed, the function of obsessive sexuality in this book is to lend credibility to the entire story. For if most historical novels seem unreal because the characters are too conscious of their noble destinies, these characters are convincing because they are motivated by thirst for revenge and lust, the two most systematic emotions, which find their clues and spin their designs everywhere.

In no sense is **"The Secret History"** pornographic. It is not written out of prurience or for the reader's delectation. Both the writer and reader stand back in solemn amazement at the characters' demonic energy and aristocratic freedom from guilt.

"Arrowroot" explores another aspect of Tanizaki's psychology—his search for the lost mother. Tanizaki first sounded this note in his 1919 story **"Reminiscence of My Beloved Mother."** . . . In **"Arrowroot,"** a young man named Tsumura searches for the relatives of his deceased mother and finally finds them in the rustic mountain fastness of Yoshino. He even marries a distant relative who resembles his mother. Thus the dead mother once again merges with the figure of the beloved.

This drama occurs in a cold, luminous mountainscape where, centuries before, a pretender to the throne had taken refuge: "He was always accompanied by two doubles, so that no one could tell which was the real King. The pursuers asked an old village woman who chanced to come by. She told them, 'That one, whose breath is white, is the King.'" It is through that sort of detail, plain in language but poetic in conception, that the blood of Tanizaki's rich and mysterious art pulses. (pp. 8, 22-3)

> Edmund White, "Shadows and Obsessions," in The New York Times Book Review (copyright © 1982 by The New York Times Company; reprinted by permission), July 18, 1982, pp. 8, 22-3.

RICHARD HOWARD

[With *The Secret History of the Lord of Musashi* and *Arrowroot*] we begin to discern the coastline of that other Japanese archipelago, the works of Junichiro Tanizaki. The tale and the meditation . . . were written fifty years ago, after the publication of the author's first **"Collected Works"**—the twelve volumes of novels, stories, plays and essays of his first twenty years of writing. Even so, they predate the books by which he is known in the West—*Some Prefer Nettles, Seven Japanese Tales, The Makioka Sisters.* They stand—*Arrowroot* mild and maieutic, a kind of prolegomenon to any future storytelling, *Secret History* almost comic in its excruciating violence—as flags staking claim to a still unexplored continent, or, given the nature of the case, *in*continent. Coprophilia, a curiously lyrical theme sounded in all of Tanizaki's works, constitutes one of our clues. It is hinted at in the famous last sentence of his 1949 family chronicle, the Turgenev-like *Makioka Sisters* ("Yukiko's diarrhoea persisted, and was a problem on the train to Tokyo"). In *Secret History* it is given astonishing scope:

> Ladies born into a daimyo family were not only ignorant of money, they never allowed anyone to see their excretory matter, nor did they ever see it themselves. . . . There is a story of the beautiful Heian court lady who tantalized a suitor with a copy of her feces fashioned out of cloves. Discretion of this order was shared by all high-born ladies. In contrast, the modern flush toilet, while satisfying the requirements of hygiene, lays everything bare before your very eyes, and so, it must be said, is an ill-mannered, vulgar device, the designer of which must have forgotten that there is such a thing as decorum even when one is alone.

This is one of the mocking asides which accumulate, like the terrible series of severed heads and lopped noses, in this archive of imaginary documents in which horror story nests within horror story like a set of glistening Japanese boxes. But the violence, like Tanizaki's obsessive pursuit of an Ideal Mistress in her fecal prime, is offered as a kind of bribe to attend to the writer's real concern. It is the sensational sop to get past the Cerberus of amusement and into the region of Tanizaki's authentic preoccupation: how can a story be told? If there is no story, if there is only the prestige of an overpowering past and a prostrate present, how do you make one up? (p. 183)

The year before he wrote *Secret History,* Tanizaki gave us his program:

> I am basically uninterested in politics, so I have concerned myself exclusively with the way people eat, dress, live, the standards of feminine beauty and the program of recreational facilities.

Not even such a determined aesthete as Tanizaki could suppose that he might *escape* politics, given such concerns. It is evident, however, that politics are going to be part of the presentation, not the "subject"—rather in the fashion of Borges, another nostalgic imperialist helplessly beguiled by violence.

In the beginning was the Parody: that might be Tanizaki's motto. In *Arrowroot,* a double journey—of a writer searching the wild mountains southeast of Kyoto for scraps of information about an imperial court that hid out there in the fifteenth century; of a failed scholar exploring the same region in quest of his mother and his eventual bride—is beautifully unrolled as a sort of epitome of all those scroll-romances. The perfectly placed episodes lead us further and further into the wilderness of bygones. (pp. 183-84)

Arrowroot, with its twin delvings into the vestiges of dynasty and of family, is a quiet hymn to mythmaking. Always . . . it is the *writing* which is left over, which therefore triumphs when mere truth gives out. *Arrowroot* ends with the inevitable confession of failure: that the truths of history (unless remade) are worthless, and that only the imagined—or imaginary—"life-truths" come to anything. . . . These fictions, subversive and self-referential, join the already dazzling canon of Tanizaki's work in English, one so convulsive, the other so murmurous, but both wonderfully alike in their insistence that we know of the past only what we can imagine, just as we endure of the present only what we can connect. I believe they are masterpieces. (p. 184)

Richard Howard, "Japanese Master," in The Nation *(copyright 1982* The Nation *magazine,* The Nation Associates, Inc.), *Vol. 235, No. 6, September 4, 1982, pp. 183-84.*

Paul Theroux

1941-

American novelist, travel writer, short story writer, critic, and poet.

Theroux's growing reputation derives from his steady production of highly commended fiction and travel books. An American expatriate himself, Theroux often focuses in his novels and short stories on strangers in strange lands and the resulting cultural conflicts. His travel books are among the best in the genre.

After graduating from University of Massachusetts, Amherst, Theroux joined the Peace Corps and was sent to Malawi in eastern Africa as a lecturer in English. He subsequently lived and taught in Uganda and Singapore before settling in England. He still travels extensively. His first travel book, *The Great Railway Bazaar* (1975), contains the impressions and insights gained on a four-month train journey through Turkey, Iran, and the Far East. *The Old Patagonia Express* (1979) recounts his trip by train from his birthplace in Massachusetts down through the tip of South America. His recent excursion around the coast of England added a third travel book, *The Kingdom by the Sea* (1983).

Much of Theroux's fiction centers on characters whose experience of a foreign culture has disillusioned them, giving them an unfavorable perspective on the values of their own society. The anthropologist of *Black House* (1974) is reluctant to return to a British village where the inhabitants seem to him more malicious, violent, and petty than those of the tribal societies he grew to respect. Similarly, the Peace Corps volunteer in *Girls at Play* (1969) and the insurance salesman in *Jungle Lovers* (1971) are shaken by the discovery that the standards of conduct they set out to dispense are in fact morally inadequate and potentially destructive. Many of the short stories in *The Consul's File* (1977) and *World's End* (1980) feature protagonists who gain comparable insights. Displacement, alienation, and the shifting identity experienced by foreigners are related topics in most of Theroux's work. The most developed of Theroux's emigrant characters is Allie Fox, the "epic hero" of his highly acclaimed novel, *The Mosquito Coast* (1981). This story of an American who, angered by his country's emphasis on materialism, moves his family to South America portrays the romantic American ideal of starting anew. However, although Allie is well intentioned, his actions are intrusive and harmful to the native culture.

Notable novels outside the realm of cultural conflict are Theroux's first novel, *Waldo* (1967), *The Family Arsenal* (1976), and *Picture Palace* (1978). They explore the themes of creativity and the artist's vicarious role as observer and recorder.

(See also *CLC*, Vols. 5, 8, 11, 15; *Contemporary Authors*, Vols. 33-36, rev. ed.; and *Dictionary of Literary Biography*, Vol. 2.)

Photograph by Mark Gerson

RODERICK COOK

[*Waldo* is a] good funny novel. It starts, appropriately enough, with the hero's getting a cream pie flung in his face and ends with his becoming a star cabaret turn, as a sort of Writer in Residence—the Residence being a glass bubble in the middle of a dance floor. While Waldo is inside, pecking away at the typewriter, the subject of his prize article stands outside, reciting the story that made them both rich and famous: "Dying Mother Tells All." Thousands cheer.

Waldo's progress is like some kind of Mod Candide. We see him through college, in a home for delinquent boys, in running fights with his parents, and in bed for weeks on end with an aging, nympomaniac starlet. . . . His disintegration is made quite literal (all his hair falls out) and it is a pity that, toward the end, the scenes get so grotesque and surreal. We get the fact that there is a scream behind the laughter without the author's turning up the volume.

But there is a lot of wit and laughter in the book, and Mr. Theroux has such a wild flair for dialogue and the vivid scene that, if he is not careful, he may end up, as rich and famous as Waldo, in the glass bubble of a movie or TV studio, turning out scripts. (pp. 117-18)

Roderick Cook, in a review of "Waldo" (copyright © 1967 by Harper's Magazine; all rights reserved; reprinted by permission of the author), in Harper's Magazine, Vol. 234, No. 1404, May, 1967, pp. 117-18.

THE NEW YORKER

[In Paul Theroux's *Waldo* the hero] is a shadowy, passive young man, who moves from one intensely symbolic site to another until he has turned into a slightly older shadowy, passive young man.... The novel is introduced with a quotation from Tristan Tzara, a founding father of Dadaism, which is an omen of the bizarre turns in the road ahead rather than a clue to where it is leading. The conclusion—"It didn't have anything to do with love"—is as good a conclusion as any to the collection of flashy insights and observations and snatches of overheard conversations that mark Waldo's development. These are presented in an unending procession of flat declarative sentences, most of which are not bad taken one at a time.

> A review of "Waldo," in The New Yorker (© 1967 by The New Yorker Magazine, Inc.), Vol. XLIII, No. 38, November 11, 1967, p. 246.

THE TIMES LITERARY SUPPLEMENT

Paul Theroux has set his novel [*Girls at Play*] in East Africa, and the country is every bit as important as the characters. Its effect is pernicious; its principal weapon, dilapidation—both physical and spiritual. The action centres almost exclusively on a girls' school and the women who teach there....

Even in its smaller aspects, the novel is unremittingly depressing. The domestic guerrilla warfare waged between Miss Poole and Heather has not the slightest element of farce about it. Like their endless verbal bitchery, it is singlemindedly cruel and they take a good deal of pleasure in each other's discomfort. The Africans (disliked by most of the whites) are presented either as petty bureaucrats or as oafish, scrawny inhabitants of villages littered with cigarette wrappings and Coca-Cola bottles.

Rape and murder provide the novel with a climax, but they come as no surprise. Indeed, they seem inevitable; and the book's power lies in Mr. Theroux's ability to instil an aura of seediness and decay, and a resultant tension, in which violence is a constant possibility.

> A review of "Girls at Play," in The Times Literary Supplement (© Times Newspapers Ltd. (London) 1969; reproduced from The Times Literary Supplement by permission), No. 3511, June 12, 1969, p. 643.

LAURENCE LAFORE

"Girls at Play" is a horror story—not in the usual sense, but in the way that "King Lear" is a horror story. It is, more precisely, a novel of interlocking horrors: of lonely women exiled from society by their own peculiarities; of an isolated girls' boarding school; of Europeans (with their obsolete convictions about white superiority) in an African land recently emancipated; of the Africans, proud, bitter, tempestuous and full of elemental hatred; of the collision between American goodwill, with its callow certainty that love can conquer primordial violence, and the stupid, sometimes sadistic, loathing with which the British respond to it; and, most of all, the horror of people lost in fear in a world turned upside down by invaders and their alien ideas.

Five schoolteachers—an Afro-Indian, an American girl from the Peace Corps, and three British women who cannot face life in England—find themselves thrown together in an isolated school for African girls in the Kenyan bush....

[Paul Theroux] tells his tale of terror and cruelty with cold detachment dressed in wit and irony, and his cold-bloodedness is so relentless that it becomes in itself a sort of cruelty inflicted on the reader. He is out to instruct us in the ways that life and death can be horrible, and he does so with such persuasiveness that quite trivial details become nightmares....

[The teachers'] common fear of Africa sustains them as a group, but it is not strong enough to prevent them from trying to destroy one another.

Only the American girl, tormented in an endless quest for an earthly Eden where her own silly ideals of peace and the brotherhood of man may be realized, tries to bridge the awful chasms that surround her. She defends the Indian and the Africans and tries to make friends with them. She is sure that, with a little goodwill, everything will turn out happily, but there is no goodwill, and in the end her folly destroys them all, and the school with them.

Her efforts break down the thin crust of inhibitions and ritual courtesies that insulate the whites from each other and from the Africans; her clumsy effort to bring them together releases their murderous hatred of one another. The novel ends, as "Lear" and "Hamlet" end, in an orgy of gore—a murder, two rapes, a catalogue of treacheries, and the suicide of the American. The bloodbath seems excessive, but that is precisely the point. Excess is the core and key of the situation.

The book is very convincing. The punctilious realism of the details, the strange, haunting ubiquity of the African landscape, the plausibility of characters divested of the straitjackets of their own conventional worlds, are lessons in a course in the high cost of sudden social change. Mr. Theroux's intellectual edifice is stunningly logical and eerily lit by the appalling certainty of approaching doom. The horrors are both engrossing and clinging. The reader, dreading tragedy to come, will stay up half the night in avid eagerness for its fulfillment, and then he will have nightmares until he wakes.

> Laurence Lafore, "Terror and Cruelty, Dressed in Wit and Irony," in The New York Times Book Review (copyright © 1969 by The New York Times Company; reprinted by permission), September 28, 1969, p. 5.

SHANE STEVENS

In *Heart of Darkness*, Joseph Conrad brilliantly evoked the sense of isolation that white interlopers feel in Africa: the indescribable loneliness and physical languor that eventually bring on moral collapse. In the person of Kurtz, Conrad seems to be saying that Africa is no place for whites unless they have extraordinary strength of will.

In the deceptively titled *Girls at Play*, Paul Theroux returns to this haunting theme with a vengeance. His people, three white women—teachers in a girls' school in the East African bush—are not extraordinarily strong-willed, but women without men, hapless creatures set in an alien land at a wrong time in history. Today's Africa is for Africans and whites are, at best, tolerated. The women are strangers and have no business being here at all....

Girls at Play has the right feel to it. Yes, Conrad was right and nothing has really changed. Africa does have an imbalance lurking in the bush that is deadly to the Western psyche, and that will corrupt and destroy it.

This novel is well worth reading, perhaps more for its mood than for its story. But that should be more than enough.

> Shane Stevens, "Strangers in Africa," in Book World—Chicago Tribune (© 1970 Postrib Corp.; reprinted by permission of Chicago Tribune and The Washington Post), February 8, 1970, p. 13.

SUSAN HILL

Jungle Lovers invites comparison with Graham Greene. The setting might certainly have been his, the serio-comic situations in which the characters find themselves frequently made me speculate as to whether Greene could have handled them any better. This is a Black—and a black—Comedy. I was reminded forcefully both of *The Comedians* and *Travels with my Aunt*, which is not to say that Mr Theroux sets out to imitate either, or that he is as good a novelist as Greene—yet. His use of language is never so cool and masterly, there is the occasional fuzziness in style. But, judged on its own terms, the novel is assured, mature and compassionate, the author has a fine eye for the ludicrous and he gives us a brilliant feeling of the stratification of life—something novelists of the 20th century seem to find harder and harder to do....

Unless one is intimately concerned in them, all the revolutionary struggles in smaller African countries can appear ludicrous but while Mr Theroux pinpoints the truth of this, he goes far beyond it, to the heart of the matter. Mullet [the protagonist] is as convincing a character as I have found in a novel for years; we continue to discover new facets of him as the book unfolds, so that by the end he is like a real person, both truly understood and essentially mysterious. Mr Theroux is a novelist of power and distinction and this is a fine, rich book.

> Susan Hill, "Jungle Book," in New Statesman (© 1971 The Statesman & Nation Publishing Co. Ltd.), Vol. 81, No. 2099, June 11, 1971, p. 815.*

THE TIMES LITERARY SUPPLEMENT

Paul Theroux's comic and disturbing fifth novel, *Jungle Lovers* [is] set in the brilliantly, and sometimes maliciously, realized Malawi of today. His fable, with roots in satiric caricature and documentary terror, uses the linguistic complexity to underscore the wavering relationships between lingering British, Africans, and the two American protagonists, a genial insurance salesman, Calvin Mullet, and a tough, often brutal, revolutionary, Marais, the dissolution of whose interlinked ideals forms the central theme of the book....

The fable has a circularity which passes through so many degrees of the chillingly terrible, and so many of the humanly amusing, before it comes full-circle when Marais takes out one of the few policies Calvin sells and makes the as yet unborn son of Calvin and his Black wife his beneficiary before going to his death in the so-called "liberated" area. This clinches the point but has a slightly irritating air of contrivance; and yet it is the same cool, sometimes cold-blooded, control that guarantees the success of so much of the book. The background is mercilessly accurate, with the littered rejects and incongruous assimilations of post-colonial "culture contact" that have their antecedents in the absurd, decaying machinery of *Heart of Darkness*.... Some are originally observed, some the stock-in-trade of every expatriate reminiscence.... Some seem the throwaways of an irresistible brightness, as when his African trainee tells Calvin that "Thomas Hobbies" [sic] was right: "Life in Africa is nasty, British and short." All in all, though, there is the same brilliance of detail that distinguished this young author's other African novel, *Girls at Play*.

> "New Out of Africa," in The Times Literary Supplement (© Times Newspapers Ltd. (London) 1971; reproduced from The Times Literary Supplement by permission), No. 3617, June 25, 1971, p. 725.

L. J. DAVIS

Paul Theroux has chosen to measure himself against a very tall ghost indeed: Joseph Conrad. *Jungle Lovers* is an audacious attempt to tell the other half of *The Heart of Darkness*, to reveal precisely what it was about Africa that drove the humanitarian trader, Kurtz, out of his mind and reduced him to a raving savage with human skulls impaled atop his palisade.

The novel's setting is the Central African peanut republic of Malawi, a country that is in actual fact at least half fictitious—one of those arbitrary creations of European colonialism that bears little relation to any economic, geographical, ethnic, or other observable reality. It is a figment of the imperial imagination that has been converted, by the stroke of a pen and the hoisting of a flag, into a modern political illusion. The place is ideal for Theroux's purposes; he could scarcely have invented a better one. It is a black country with a white past, a present that is both arbitrary and impoverished, and a future that is bleak. Torn by conflicting cultural forces, its population has been reduced to living out a compulsive parody of Anglo-South African civilization.... Yet as Theroux is at some pains to show, this seemingly slavish and degrading mimicry of an alien white culture has less to do with ideas than with things. It is a kind of cargo cult that really works in a sporadic way.

In Theroux's view, to be African is to deal with the particularized and the immediate, whereas to be Western is to be abstract, having to do with words, postures, dogma, and time. Malawi itself is just such a Western abstraction and so, for that matter, is anything pertaining to politics in the accepted Western sense. In the African cultural climate, Westerners tend to become abstractions of themselves, types rather than men, like Major Beaglehole, Theroux's best creation, who contrives to scale heights of Britannic fatuity, ignorance, charm, childishness, and decency that have seldom been reached by an Englishman in an American novel. If the Africans are living out a parody of someone else, Beaglehole and his fellow Britons have become parodies of themselves. It is either that or be destroyed; for as Theroux realizes, they are not parodying their weaknesses, but their strengths.

Theroux's protagonists, like Kurtz, are humanitarians: Calvin Mullet, a sincere young boob of an insurance man from Massachusetts, and the Canadian guerrilla, Marais, who leads a small, all-native band in an attempt to bring down the government. Each has come to save the African, Mullet with American insurance, Marais with the Cuban revolution. In the manner of all missionaries, they have come, not to learn, but to teach. Both fail....

Both sociologically and politically, *Jungle Lovers* is a first-rate performance—informative, colorful, and insightful. As a piece of cross-culture fiction, it is the best thing of its kind to come along since Ghanaian novelist Ayi Kwei Armah's *Fragments*, and Paul Theroux is much the better novelist of the two. His portrait of modern Malawi is as good as one could want, and the book deserves a wide readership on the basis of his insights alone. Throughout the book one seems to hear the echoes of Conrad's voice and that most extraordinary of tales, that begins: "And this also . . . has been one of the dark places of the earth."

L. J. Davis, "In One of the Dark Places of the Earth," in Book World—Chicago Tribune (© 1971 Postrib Corp.; reprinted by permission of Chicago Tribune and The Washington Post), August 8, 1971, p. 8.

MORDECAI RICHLER

I am unfamiliar with Paul Theroux's highly-praised earlier novels, and only wish I could like **"Jungle Lovers"** more. There is so much that is admirable in the novel, and deeply-felt; it distresses me to have to say that I, for one, found it ultimately unsatisfying. Forced in the ideological hothouse. Even so, **"Jungle Lovers"** abounds with virtues. It is genuinely perceptive. Mr. Theroux's ear for the absurd, for the nuances of British and African dialogue, is convincing, subtle. He also writes exceedingly well about the taste and feel of tropical Africa.

Put baldly, **"Jungle Lovers"** is about the folly of preconceived American ideas about Africa. On the one hand, the clumsily capitalist (Africa, the last commercial frontier, candidate for the American way) and, on the other, the presumptuously revolutionary. The ultimate Play-Pen U, for a would-be Che. . . .

[The novel teeters] uneasily between Waugh-like distance and the intensity of Graham Greene. **"Jungle Lovers"** suffers from double vision, the lack of a consistent viewpoint. . . .

"Jungle Lovers" is filled with incidental delights, some very funny set-pieces. It is also enriched by a clean, ironic prose style and a powerful narrative drive. The novel's architecture is undeniably intelligent, but, alas, the beams show through clearly, the author's hand ever-present. I couldn't believe in the metamorphosis of Mullet from clumsy Babbittry to a character whose perceptions about Africa, though they do his maker credit, rest uneasily on his fragile shoulders. Marais's undoing, I fear, also owes more to ideological geometry than to life. There is too much that is superimposed, too little that flows with inner life.

Mordecai Richler, in a review of "Jungle Lovers," in The New York Times Book Review (copyright © 1971 by The New York Times Company; reprinted by permission), August 8, 1971, p. 6.

BENJAMIN DeMOTT

Travelers, truants and transplants—Paul Theroux's favorite people since the start of his writing career—are the central figures in **"World's End,"** his new collection of stories. . . .

Impressive as much of **"World's End"** is . . . , the book's preoccupation with uprootedness does become wearing before the end. In Mr. Theroux's work in longer forms, no single preoccupation ever tyrannizes. A travel jotting in a novel stands adjacent to and competes with, say, a cameo appearance by a celebrity living or dead (Graham Greene, D. H. Lawrence, Che Guevara, whom you will)—or with a penetrating passage of art criticism, or a witty parody, or a splendid joke about science that one hasn't heard before, or a subtle probe of an artist's mind on the verge of discovering a subject. And all the while, shuttling from interest to interest, entertainment to entertainment, we're immersed (I'm describing **"Picture Palace,"** actually) in a family chronicle extending over generations and having a haunting incestuous relationship at its core. The impression is of brave abundance, a lively mind and tonic improvisatory energy.

But when, as in the short story, space doesn't permit this kind of exuberance, some other kind is needed. Thematic variety is the obvious possibility; yet, to repeat, there's not much of that in **"World's End."**

Benjamin DeMott, "Englishmen & Americans," in The New York Times Book Review (copyright © 1980 by The New York Times Company; reprinted by permission), August 24, 1980, p. 7.

ALAN HOLLINGHURST

Paul Theroux's short stories [in **World's Fair**] avoid . . . problems of commitment by their comedy and brevity; when he expands in the longer form of 'The Greenest Island' (some 50pp) the attempt at seriousness and psychological interest becomes dogged and unconvincing. His natural gift for place is a means of capitalising on his passion for travel, and the short story with its emphasis on plot and its need for quick and shapely resolution is an ideal form for him. A restlessness of movement testifies to a disinclination to dig deep. A whole vein of comic writing exploits the relishedly superficial, reflecting the tactics rather than the neuroses of life, and Theroux sometimes has a ring of pure Lifemanship, for instance in 'Algebra', a story about an insignificant man making friends with the famous through a policy of reckless lying. He displays a hilarious callousness and a pleasure in showing up a particular world—diplomatic, literary, commercial—in all its fraudulence. Literary life is the most frequent target, for its vacuity and pretension; an American professor steals a poet's worksheets in a bid for fame, and there are other sardonic developments of the International Theme, the hazards and absurdities of British and Americans abroad. In 'White Lies' there is real horror, narrated by a bloodless entomologist, who draws a gloatingly distorted moral. It is immaculately manipulated.

Alan Hollinghurst, "First-Rate," in New Statesman (© 1980 The Statesman & Nation Publishing Co. Ltd.), Vol. 100, No. 2588, October 24, 1980, p. 26.*

JONATHAN RABAN

One needs energy to keep up with the extraordinary, productive restlessness of Paul Theroux. . . .

He is as busy as a jackdaw in the way he scavenges for forms and styles. In earlier novels he has taken conventional popular molds, like the ghost story (**The Black House**), the thriller (**The Family Arsenal**), the celebrity memoir (**Picture Palace**), and made them over for his own thoroughly original purposes. The geographic locations of his tales now make an almost unbroken ring around the globe. His train journeys (**The Great Railway Bazaar, The Old Patagonian Express**) are best read as freewheeling, impromptu fictions—the adventures of a picaresque hero who happens to bear the same name as his author and who shares his author's chronic cabin fever.

Theroux is 40 now—the most gifted, most prodigal writer of his generation. . . . He has moved in skips and bounds, never staying long enough in one place for the moss of a mannered style to grow on his writing. Even in the most trivial ways, he ducks classification. . . .

Yet with *The Mosquito Coast* he has arrived at a temporary summation. This is not just his finest novel so far. It is—in a characteristically hooded way—a novelist's act of self-definition, a midterm appraisal of his own resources. It is a wonderful book, with so many levels to it that it feels bottomless.

In Allie Fox, Theroux has created his first epic hero. If one can imagine an American tradition that takes in Benjamin Franklin, Captain Ahab, Huey Long, and the Reverend Jim Jones, then Allie Fox is its latest, most complete incarnation. (p. 55)

To his wife and children, and to a bedraggled cluster of starving sidekicks in both Americas, Allie Fox, devout atheist, is little short of God Himself. And *The Mosquito Coast* is the gospel according to his son, Charlie. The novel tells two perfectly interwoven stories. The first is of how Allie Fox leads his little flock up to the precipice of madness and beyond. The second is of how Charlie slowly emerges from the shadow of his father's divinity into the cold, frightening light of skepticism and sorrow. Out of the twin stories, Theroux has made a novel that has the richness, simplicity, and power of myth.

Even in the barest outline, *The Mosquito Coast* sets up a whole series of suggestive ripples. Jonestown is there, of course: the foul clearing, the loudspeakers in the trees, the piled cadavers, the spools of recording tape. Beyond that, there is *the* original American story: the stale Old World, the sea crossing, the Indians, the "first Thanksgiving" as Allie Fox himself names it. Then there is a universal fable about the nature of godhead and belief. Finally, and much the most important, there is a tale here about the limits and possibilities of the creative imagination. Allie Fox is very like a novelist. He is an inventor. He makes and populates a world with an artist's totalitarian joy in his creation, bending everything and everyone in it to the requirements of his aesthetic design. At the end, it turns on him and he is literally consumed by it, as vultures tear out the very brains that set the world in motion. Fox's great imaginative enterprise both mirrors and mocks the creations of Theroux the novelist: The overreaching hero and the writer are one and the same man.

I mustn't mislead here. These big themes (and one could hardly imagine bigger ones) are never proclaimed in the novel. They run deep, like subterranean rivers, nourishing the life of the book's surface. For, reading *The Mosquito Coast,* one is engrossed in a marvelously told realistic story. It is a measure of the obsessive exactitude of Theroux's writing that there is not a page in the book in which one doesn't know the particular color of the sky, the texture of the earth underfoot, the cast of a face, the rhythm of a voice. In simile after simile, these physical details spring from the print. . . . This is an invented world that one can live in, smell, see, touch, and a style of writing so easy and precise that one reads through it like a transparent pane of glass.

The same loving particularity is what makes Allie Fox such an enthralling creation. Geniuses are notoriously hard to depict, but Fox—a cursed genius if ever there was one—is so solidly done that you can catch the stink of his armpits. . . . One believes him, too. When he builds his ice machine, or rights a listing ship, his schemes always have the ring of authority and good sense. He is obstreperously plausible. He has a thing or two to teach every reader of this book. And so one finds oneself submitting, like Charlie Fox, to Allie's extraordinary capacity to spellbind and bludgeon.

That is part of Theroux's secret. He has rooted his story deep in the reasonable—in sense impressions that we can all share, in knowledge we can ascertain. All the nuts and bolts are secure. And from that stable platform, the novel is able to take off like a rocket into the empyrean. From the dingy familiarity of a hardware store in Northampton, Massachusetts, to a grotesque and tragic climax in the jungle, Theroux leads the reader cunningly on, step by reasonable step, reaching the exotic by means of the ordinary.

Here, too, the writer and his hero are in collusion. For that, of course, is just what Allie Fox does. (pp. 55-6)

The Honduran hell that is Allie Fox's last act of invention is only a modest magnification of the commonplace social world he leaves behind in Massachusetts. Allie Fox himself is a magnification, no more, of the inventor who made him, Paul Theroux. If one bass-line runs consistently through *The Mosquito Coast,* it warns that to possess an imagination is to have a very dangerous faculty indeed. It brings one uncomfortably close to being both a god and a madman. (p. 56)

Jonathan Raban, "Theroux's Wonderful, Bottomless Novel," in Saturday Review *(© 1982 Saturday Review Magazine Co.; reprinted by permission), Vol. 9, No. 2, February, 1982, pp. 55-6.*

FREDERICK BUSCH

The Mosquito Coast has already been greeted in England as a denunciation of America's failures, and it may well be so greeted here. Paul Theroux, who lives in England but knows his native America, has surely decried, through his central figure Allie Fox, some of what is said to ail us. . . . (p. 1)

While indicting our aerosol cheese goop and excessive imports (Allie hates decaying America from both left-and-right-wing viewpoints) what he *really* hates is the world's imperfections. Maddened, in the jungle, he will cry: "It's savage and superstitious to accept the world as it is. Fiddle around and find a use for it." What a fine articulation of Americanness from this anti-American character.

And what an excellent way of calling America a Frankenstein's monster, and Allie something of a Frankenstein. For, yes, this surely *is* a gothic novel. . . . It is possible that some readers have forgotten, that many haven't read, *The Black House* and *The Family Arsenal.* I mention these because each is an exercise in aspects of the gothic—buried sexuality, frightening eruptive violence, labyrinthine settings (*Arsenal* is brilliant on "cockney" London). Theroux has an affinity for the gothic, which is often available to us as a metaphor for the forbidden—whether in terms of forbidden sexual urges, or lustings after forbidden powers.

And in *The Mosquito Coast,* where sex is mentioned only with regard to the narrator's hesitant stepping into adolescence—Charlie, the son of Allie Fox, a psychically-battered boy in love with a selfish father, turns 14 in the course of the novel—the gothic elements are very much about power. Instead of a Creature or Mad Scientist pursuing a virginal woman through dark halls, we have a father terrorizing his innocent son with dares, danger, and tests of loyalty.

Allie Fox, handyman and inventor in Massachusetts, usually called Father, takes Mother, Charlie, his younger son Jerry and two even younger twins, and makes his escape from an America he says is disintegrating. In Honduras, wonderfully described—Theroux can describe the feathers off a bird, the leaves off a tree—Allie settles his family in a soggy, itchy Eden. He is going to fail, and we know it. His mission is to carry ice, made in one of his inventions to this hot iceless world. He and Charlie name his machine "Fat Boy." The bomb that destroyed Hiroshima was called "Little Boy"; the bomb that destroyed Nagasaki was called "Fat Man." Put them all together, and they spell gothic comeuppance.

Early in the novel, Allie's death is also foreshadowed. Charlie dreams of his father's death in a crucifixion, the man later revealed to be a scarecrow. Sure enough, at the novel's end, after Jerry and Charlie have plotted to kill their father, just as Freud told in *Moses and Monotheism* the primitive Jews plotted to kill *their* endangerment, father-figure and Oedipal adversary, Allie is by accident killed. As he dies, he cries, "Christ is a scarecrow!" Which is all too well-plotted, symmetrical, and plain *neat* for a shaggy reader such as I. While I complain, let me add that Mother, who is once or twice an active figure, remains essentially what Theroux wants in a tale of people returning to primitive, idyllic patterns: she is pedagogue, soother, obedient though sometimes caustic helpmate, currently sexless and almost never persuasive as a person in the book.

But *The Mosquito Coast* is an interesting working-out of gothic patterns. In Father, we have the philosopher-scientist who, since *Dr. Faustus* (1593), and surely since *Frankenstein* (1818), has been our character-of-choice for gothic fiction. He wishes to rival God, whose creation he sees as imperfect, or of whose realm he wants too large a share. (pp. 1-2)

The problem with Allie Fox is that he's hypnotic to Mother and Charlie, and the brilliant Dickensian minor characters of this novel (they are its supreme achievements), only because Theroux says he is. He commands no loyalty in us; we cannot see why he does so in the narrator, Charlie. To us he remains a bully, a cruel parent, a mouthpiece who speaks not to the other characters, much of the time, but over their shoulders *at* us. When his downfall is guiltily mourned by Charlie, we are not saddened. He doesn't serve to remind us of the perils of unlimited ambition. He is not a cautionary figure.

He *is* a literary invention, and you can smell the furnaces working to cook him up. He is surrounded by fragments of several Graham Greene figures. He is part *Herzog* in his declarations of middle-aged *angst*, he is part *Henderson the Rain King* in his journeying exuberance; he is part Mr. Kurtz of *Heart of Darkness;* he is a shadow of Lewis Moon in Peter Matthiessen's *At Play in the Fields of the Lord;* he strives for the magic of *One Hundred Years of Solitude*. In a way, he reminds me of the mad Americans at the frontier whom Dickens invented for *Martin Chuzzlewit*—all the secondary cultural characteristics were got right, and yet they weren't living people: they were abstractions.

Surrounding this abstraction are some first-rate writing, a true professional's ability to move an entire family from New England to Honduran jungles convincingly, and marvelous descriptions of the people and conditions with which the Fox family meets. Discomfort is brilliantly evoked; a child's terror of the father he loves is often moving (the book's best drama, I think). Theroux can write nearly anything smoothly and smartly. Many readers will appreciate Allie's sometimes-funny causticisms about America, and his entanglements in a plot that overwhelms, for me, the unfinished character of Allie himself. . . .

Gothic fiction ought to be tragic fiction. This tragedy is not sufficiently faced by Theroux, who prefers surface, here, to interior exploration. He adopts the form, but not enough substance, of the gothic. When Father is making plans to drag ice through the jungles of Honduras, a lightning bolt actually flashes upon his face as he actually declaims, "You feel a little like God." Theroux might perhaps have trusted us more. (p. 2)

> Frederick Busch, "Dr. Faustus in the Jungle," in Book World—The Washington Post (© 1982, The Washington Post), February 14, 1982, pp. 1-2.

JACK BEATTY

The Mosquito Coast is a seemingly straightforward adventure story which ends with a splotch of *Lord of the Flies*-like horror and which trails clouds of dark parable behind it. I think children would like it; the whole novel, which is told by a 13 year old, would enact their fantasies, and they would be agreeably scared by the gruesome end. As for adults, they can enjoy it on a more complex level, since there is an ambiguous interpretive distance between the tale and its young teller. In fact, the novel is made to order for a structuralist analysis of the tension between its story and its narrative commentary, which is to say the contrast between our perspective on the events and that of Charlie Fox, the young narrator.

Like anything by Paul Theroux, moreover, *The Mosquito Coast* is a delight to read. Theroux is a master storyteller. . . . And he writes uncommonly well. There are wonderfully exotic words here, as well as familiar words in fresh contexts, and metaphors you want to savor. Theroux tries to make the narrative voice that of a 13-year-old, but you have only to compare Charlie Fox's prose persona to Huck Finn's to see how far he fails. Charlie is a touch literary. But if his voice isn't credible, his innocence is, and that is the main thing. . . .

To the adult reader, Allie Fox is a crazed bore and know-it-all, who tells a ship's captain how to sail and the natives how to survive in the jungle (whose every slither and shriek Theroux captures with astonishing ease). But to Charlie, his father is brave, tireless, and inexhaustibly clever, a figure of towering and total authority. After Allie comes a cropper in the jungle, however, a reversal of sympathies takes place, with Charlie starting to see him as fallible, and even pitiable, just as we come to admire the way trouble steels his stubborn will. His failure makes him moving to us, a Lear without his kingdom, and though it shocks his son, it also gives him room to be himself.

Beneath its adventure story surface, *The Mosquito Coast* has big things on its mind. At home with paradox, it is about civilization as a savage will to dominance (and yet it defends civilization against nature, red in tooth and claw), about order as anarchy, about the admirable energy and malign motives of invention, about fantasy as tyranny and fiction as spurious power. It is about the way fathers hide their real purposes from their sons, and sons hide their wishes from themselves.

The Mosquito Coast is, I think, finally more interesting than affecting, but then I expect its real force is reserved for teenagers. For, professing his innocence every step of the way, Charlie Fox pushes his father aside—this modern *Swiss Family Robinson* is a displaced dream of parricide. The kids should love it.

> Jack Beatty, in a review of "The Mosquito Coast," in The New Republic (reprinted by permission of The New Republic; © 1982 The New Republic, Inc.), Vol. 186, No. 8, February 24, 1982, p. 40.

ROBERT TOWERS

There is so much to marvel at in *The Mosquito Coast*—Theroux's orchestration of his story, his marshaling of technological knowledge, the easy authority with which he establishes and exploits the Honduran setting—that I wish I liked it as wholeheartedly as I admire many of its parts. But I found myself from time to time backing away, as though it were a bully with a club coercing my response.

By concentrating so exclusively upon the almighty Father, Theroux leaves little breathing space for the other characters. While Charlie is a sensitive and observant narrator, perceptive beyond his years, he is scarcely allowed a thought that is not centered on his old man. Mother (she has no other name) has hardly any existence at all; she seems not only subservient to the point of extinction but stupid as well. Jerry's rebelliousness toward the novel's end comes as a relief, but until that point he too has hardly existed. While graphically sketched in, the various Creoles, Indians, marauders, and missionaries appear and disappear, leaving no real mark upon the reader. Megalomania, when relentlessly depicted, has a way of using up all the available air.

I am left finally with the sense that **The Mosquito Coast** is a brilliant display-piece, the latest and most spectacular of Theroux's performances. Perhaps we should think of him as the Paganini of contemporary novelists and stop worrying about the coherence of his authorial identity.

Robert Towers, "Moby-Dad," in The New York Review of Books *(reprinted with permission from The New York Review of Books; copyright © 1982 Nyrev, Inc.), Vol. XXIX, No. 6, April 15, 1982, p. 37.*

STANLEY REYNOLDS

The title of Paul Theroux's new book [**The London Embassy**] is rather misleading. The anonymous narrator indeed works at the American Embassy but his work takes him out of that grotesque building in Grosvenor Square and allows him to wander all round London. In fact London at times seems to be the real hero of this collection of short stories. The city is always present. Sometimes it is a rather strange, foreign city—not so much a capital of an Empire but a far off, distant colonial outpost. This is because Mr Theroux is, like his unnamed hero, an American. It is also one of the pleasures of the book, seeing such a familiar city seem somehow strange and foreign.

The London Embassy is a collection of short stories . . . but it can be read as a novel if one begins at the beginning and carries on. The hero appears in all the stories. It is the same man who narrated Mr Theroux's highly successful **The Consul's File**. . . . (p. 601)

[Theroux's] ability to look into the lives of people is what makes **The London Embassy** so fascinating. The background here is not exotic Asia, as in **The Consul's File**, but hum-drum, every day London, albeit a London tinged with espionage—the hero is a sort of spy—corruption, and the Brixton Riots.

The author is a New Englander, and although he has lived for many years in London he is still able to look at the city as if it were new and foreign. Some readers may dislike the lack of an exotic setting but it is a far more difficult job to look under your own nose at the ordinary and come up with something different. (p. 602)

Stanley Reynolds, "Passing Theroux," in Punch *(© 1982 by Punch Publications Ltd.; all rights reserved; may not be reprinted without permission), Vol. 283, No. 7404, October 13, 1982, pp. 601-02.*

CHRISTOPHER LEHMANN-HAUPT

"There is an English dream of a warm summer evening on a branch-line train," writes the novelist and travel writer Paul Theroux in one of the many evocative passages in **"The Kingdom by the Sea: A Journey Around Great Britain."** . . .

[One] of the challenges that confronted Mr. Theroux in writing about Britain was to penetrate the English dream and find the reality. Another was more practical—how to find a systematic route, for in "choosing a route, one was choosing a subject." And then a marvelous solution presented itself. He would travel around the entire coast clockwise. . . .

[It] may sound monotonous to read about the three-month trip that Mr. Theroux finally made in 1982 by rail, wheel, foot and thumb. After all, a coast is a coast; there's the sea and the land and the people doing whatever they do along a coast. Yet just as the author found that "Every British bulge is different and every mile has its own mood," a reader is continually surprised by what Mr. Theroux turns up along his way.

He copies down unusual graffiti; "Wogs ought to be hit about the head with the utmost severity," he read at St. Ives Station. He thumbnails every sort of unusual character he encountered, from the female tramp in Liverpool who asked him to pull her heavy cart for a bit, to a young man named Fuggle who told him that he'd once dyed his hair purple—"aubergine, actually"—to draw attention to the fact that "deep down" "I'm just not like other blokes."

He records all manner of amusing and revealing dialogues he overheard. . . .

The book is filled with history, insights, landscape, epiphanies, meditations, celebrations and laments. . . .

[There is a] depressing aspect of reading **"The Kingdom by the Sea."** Almost everywhere Mr. Theroux went along the coast, he saw poverty, unemployment, retrenchment. The great branch railway system—the machine that had been set down in the garden and left it undefiled—was shutting down. You could no longer "get there from here." England was reverting to its pre-industrial condition and the people seemed to lack the energy or will to do anything about it. . . .

Reading **"The Kingdom by the Sea"** has many compensations, both practical and inspirational. Mr. Theroux's evocation of northern Scotland is breathtaking. Following his entire route with a good atlas—the book's endpaper maps are unsatisfactory—is an ideal way to get much of Great Britain's geography straight in one's mind. But a reader isn't left with much desire to follow the author's route. On the whole, one prefers to go on dreaming the English dream.

Christopher Lehmann-Haupt, in a review of "The Kingdom by the Sea," in The New York Times *(copyright © 1983 by The New York Times Company; reprinted by permission), October 13, 1983, p. C25.*

Anne Tyler
1941-

American novelist, short story writer, and critic.

Tyler is noted as a writer of finely crafted fiction which is straightforward and realistic, yet lyrical. She achieves subtle, sometimes somber, effects of pathos or comedy through her precise choice of words. Tyler is especially adept at depicting tense family situations that result in lonely, confused members who long for meaning and understanding. Critics point out that she is representative of a new generation of Southern writers. Tyler tends toward restrained rather than dramatic effects and her characters do not react in bizarre or grotesque ways to their emotional isolation. Like the characters of William Faulkner and Flannery O'Connor, Tyler's people are heavily influenced by the past, but it is a personal, familial history, rather than a social one, which shapes them.

With her first two novels, *If Morning Ever Comes* (1964) and *The Tin Can Tree* (1965), Tyler established a reputation as a young novelist with an unusual command of her craft. Critics were especially impressed with her ability to describe setting, to characterize, and to create realistic dialogue while maintaining a spare and polished prose style. In subsequent works she has grown increasingly ambitious, creating more eccentric and imaginative characters and extending the time span of her stories to include several generations. In all of her works, Tyler's major concern is with the difficulties of human relationships and she focuses on individuals within large families whose members feel alienated from each other. Many critics have praised Tyler for examining the effects that family members have on each other's lives. Others suggest that Tyler has limited herself by not exploring the role that society plays in the shaping of personality.

Tyler's recent novel, *Dinner at the Homesick Restaurant* (1982), has been acclaimed as her most accomplished work. Many critics maintain that it clearly establishes her as a major figure in American literature. As insightful, sensitive, and well-made as her previous works, this novel achieves greater depth through the complexity of its narrative structure. By juxtaposing the personalities of her six central characters and their outlooks on the present and the past, Tyler makes poignant observations on the benefits and limitations of family life.

(See also *CLC*, Vols. 7, 11, 18; *Contemporary Authors*, Vols. 9-12, rev. ed.; *Contemporary Authors New Revision Series*, Vol. 11; *Something about the Author*, Vol. 7; *Dictionary of Literary Biography*, Vol. 6; and *Dictionary of Literary Biography Yearbook: 1982.*)

ROLLENE W. SAAL

In her first novel, "*If Morning Ever Comes*," 22-year-old Anne Tyler has written a subtle and surprisingly mature story about the lack of communication between human beings, of a man's essential isolation from the world—and especially and more poignantly from his own family.

Ben Joe Hawkes returns to his North Carolina hometown from New York—where, as a law student at Columbia University, he has been suffering the chills of the city's loneliness. Not

© Helen Marcus

that the emotional climate in Carolina is much warmer. Though he enjoys feeling responsible for his family, a widowed mother, a grandmother, six sisters (one of whom, the bright and flirtatious Joanne, has left her husband and returned home), they are astonishingly self-contained. From Susannah, who works in the library, to 10-year-old Tessie, the Hawkes women are as cool and crisp as starched petticoats and as able to stand by themselves. One can assume they inherit their restraint from their mother, whose own chilling ways led her husband to set up another household on the wrong side of town. . . .

Why Ellen Hawkes froze her husband from her house remains a mystery, since she never comments on the past. Indeed, she steadily refuses to involve herself even in the affairs of her children—when, like Ben Joe, they cry out for some sign of love, a token of caring. When he inquires about Joanne's shattered marriage, his mother brusquely warns him against meddling in another's life. Though no reason is offered for her coldness, its effects are clear. Ben Joe's sisters bear the scars of her detachment, just as he is marked with a lack of commitment to life. "I don't guess you're hardly *alive* if you're as reversible as I am," says Ben Joe to his high-school sweetheart, Shelley, with whom he renews his acquaintance. Shelley, plain, pinched, the girl no football player ever asked for a date, has no one to care for her. For all his bustling family,

Ben Joe finally comes to realize that his own situation is identical.

In a touching finale, they prepare to make a life for themselves in New York. Although he can foresee the limitations of a future with Shelley, he can also savor the warmth and constancy of her affection. . . .

Miss Tyler, who grew up in North Carolina, writes well, selecting with care the details which distill small-town life. **"If Morning Ever Comes"** is written in a minor key about minor characters. Nothing momentous happens; there's scarcely a raised tone in the book. The pace is far too slow: scenes take too long to evolve, and when they do they reveal only incompletely the story yet to be told. For all this, Miss Tyler has written a meaningful book. She has brought to it a delicate sense of emotional isolation—and a hero who, however blighted by his past, proceeds with dignity to count for something in somebody's life.

Rollene W. Saal, "Loveless Household," in The New York Times Book Review *(copyright © 1964 by The New York Times Company; reprinted by permission), November 22, 1964, p. 52.*

JOHN ALLAN LONG

Several Southern novels have come out in the past year or so which bear little resemblance to earlier literary legends of the South.

These novels are not about the Tobacco Roads of 40 years ago. Nor do they dwell consciously on the dynamics of Negro-white relationships. Instead they reflect a South not so very different from small-town society anywhere in the United States. As the old agrarian South has become part of the past, life since World War II has grown to be more and more middle-class.

Significantly, these "new" Southern novels are written by the younger, post-war generation. Anne Tyler is a product of this generation. Her first novel [**"If Morning Ever Comes"**] is set in fictitious Sandill in busily industrializing North Carolina. . . .

The reader must discard any romanticized picture of the South. There is no abject poverty here. Neither is there any remnant of aristocracy. Sitting quietly, unsensationally in their place is the family of Ben Joe Hawkes—the kind of small-town life Miss Tyler knows well.

With poignancy and humor, this young novelist conveys the responses of a college student living among a sea of women—a flock of independent sisters, a proud mother, and an incorrigible grandmother. The head of the household, feeling somehow responsible for the women, Ben Joe leaves Columbia University to make an impulsive trip home. . . .

Who handles the family's finances? Who does the shopping? Why are the sisters up all times of night, wandering outside and inside the house? One sister has just left her husband. Father left mother years back for another woman.

Yet in all this confusion—or is it really?—the women are not only surviving but persevering, caught up in the business of day-to-day living.

His long weekend exhausted, realizing his uselessness, Ben Joe returns to college. With a sweet touch of irony, he takes with him a remnant of his youth.

This small book is certainly not wrought with the drama or melodrama of earlier Southern novels. But its simplicity and rare sensitivity to the everyday make Anne Tyler's novel worth reading.

John Allan Long, "'New' Southern Novel," in The Christian Science Monitor *(reprinted by permission from* The Christian Science Monitor; *© 1965 The Christian Science Publishing Society; all rights reserved), January 21, 1965, p. 9.*

MILLICENT BELL

The fact that 24-year-old Anne Tyler . . . grew up in Raleigh, N.C., must seem to her significant enough to make her publishers note on the jacket of [**"The Tin Can Tree"**] that she "considers herself a Southerner." And this novel, in so far as it goes in for regional subject matter, does report upon life in still another rural Southern pocket. Her characters are the eight inhabitants of a three-family house on the edge of backwater tobacco fields—two bachelor brothers, two spinster sisters and the Pike family, whose small daughter has just been killed in a tractor accident when the book opens.

There are, indeed, some fine scenes and sounds of a regional sort, especially in one chapter in which a group of women talk over the Pike tragedy while tying tobacco. Here, as elsewhere in the book, she makes use of a nice specificity of local detail and neatly captures the casual and yet complex movement of Southern rural speech with its indirections and interruptions, its reticences and awkwardnesses which manage to express emotion.

Yet rurality and Southernism are not really Miss Tyler's chief interest. Despite some obvious debts to the tradition of the Southern novel, she has none of the Faulknerian anguish over a present rooted in past wrongs. Nor does she share the late Flannery O'Connor's sense of a religious soil out of which characters are thrust forth into the withering present, taking grotesque and tragic shape—though Miss O'Connor's style, with its austere notation of scene and dialogue, may have taught her to make an eloquence of sparenoss. If she reminds me of anyone, it may be the Carson McCullers of 25 years ago—who, then as young as Miss Tyler, also wrote of human disconnection and the need for love in a stagnant community.

Carson McCullers herself, of course, was only in part a regional writer. Her gothic tales of loneliness and inchoate longing carried on the mood and themes of Sherwood Anderson among the older generation of American writers. Thinking back that far we discover the significant precursor for Miss Tyler's story. More a vignette than a novel, it glances at lives twisted by inhibition and loneliness, gnarled like frostbitten apples (Anderson's metaphor) because the sap of community has grown thin. . . .

Like [Anderson's] Winesburg stories, **"The Tin Can Tree"** shows us human beings frozen into fixed postures. And James, it happens, is a photographer whose snapshots have a way of capturing people in characteristic single attitudes—Ansel reclining on a couch, his hand idly playing with the window shade, Jane in a dust storm which makes her look like a ghost. . . .

Life, this young writer seems to be saying, achieves its once-and-for-all shape and then the camera clicks. This view, which brings her characters back on the last page to where they started, does not make for that sense of development which is the true novel's motive force. Because of it, I think, her book remains a sketch, a description, a snapshot. But as such, it still has a certain dry clarity. And the hand that has clicked its shutter has selected a moment of truth.

> Millicent Bell, "Tobacco Road Updated," in The New York Times Book Review (copyright © 1965 by The New York Times Company; reprinted by permission), November 21, 1965, p. 77.

CHRISTOPHER LEHMANN-HAUPT

Writers are rare who can swiftly generate a story with instantly distinguishable characters and the prospect of development. Rarer still is the fiction artist who controls his material with such subtle dexterity that his presence is barely felt. To do so is essentially the dramatist's craft, normally mastered in middle age, when the artist is exhausted of illusions that any part of the world spins at the lashing of his single will and when he is ripe in his understanding of the inherent mechanism of things. It requires an eye, an ear and a knowledge of character. Remarkably, Anne Tyler, at the age of 24, has now produced two novels ["**If Morning Ever Comes**" and "**The Tin Can Tree**"] that display her understanding of the dramatic mode, as distinct from the lyrical.

Her second book, "**The Tin Can Tree**" tells a story that seems unpromisingly slight in summary. Janie Rose Pike, a plump, strong-willed 10-year-old girl, has been killed in a tractor accident just before the novel begins. The waves of this barely audible "plunk" in the universe wash over the members of her family and the people of a small Southern community whose emotional lives are intertwined with theirs.

Janie Rose's mother submerges herself in numb grief. The vacuum she creates sucks her husband and Joan, a niece who lives with them, out of their accustomed channels, and leaves her son Simon alone, perplexed and foundering. The changes in Simon and Joan disorient Ansel and James Green, two brothers who inhabit the same three-family dwelling. And further from the vortex, the entire community in which the Pikes live detects the change, and alters its course.

Simon, half from a child's distressed need to regain his mother's attention and half from an adolescent desire to exploit the opportunity to explore new oceans, runs away from home to a town half an hour away. His disappearance draws Mrs. Pike back to the surface, and the balance of emotional dependencies is restored.

Equilibrium, disruption, crisis, response, equilibrium restored: a time-worn dramatic formula. But Miss Tyler's simple descriptive passages, her spare but telling dialogue and her deft touches of characterization are so effortless, so even in perspective, so jointlessly integrated, that the landscape and people of her novel are virtually palpable. . . .

In "**The Tin Can Tree**," Miss Tyler has selected material slight enough to be controlled completely, and squeezed more emotional power from it than one would have thought it contained. One hopes that her grasp of material will grow and that her power to squeeze will grow proportionally. She will then surely avoid the fate of the growing band of Southern writers adept at staging the dramas of grown-up children, who are enjoyed as charming entertainers and dismissed as such.

> Christopher Lehmann-Haupt, "A Small Pebble with a Big Splash," in The New York Times (copyright © 1965 by The New York Times Company; reprinted by permission), December 23, 1965, p. L25.

SARA BLACKBURN

[**The Clock Winder** seems to have] many of the virtues that we associate with "southern" writing—an easy, almost confidential directness, fine skill at quick characterization, a sure eye for atmosphere, and a special nostalgic humor—and none of its liabilities—sentimentality, a sometimes cloying innocence wise beyond its pretense, a tendency toward over-rich metaphor. The title character is 20-year-old Elizabeth, a strong figure who is both oddly timeless and perfectly contemporary; she arrives vaguely from Ellington, North Carolina, to manage and eventually become a loving part of the lives of an eccentric but not very unusual Baltimore family who have enormous and even agonizing trouble relating to one another. . . .

If the result smacks of a group of hurt and inept people propping one another up to live a bearable, cozy life—another quality, come to think of it, of "southern" writing—it's neither sentimental nor intrusive enough to detract from the strength of its delightful heroine: Elizabeth, in her ashamed passivity, her struggle against it, her bursts of energy and what prevents them, her wry, open humor, is a recognizable and even memorable character who encompasses many of the contradictions that women are seeking to resolve today. And the author has created a group of minor characters to surround her who ring absolutely true. Anne Tyler has a special talent; she is a solid writer with real skill, but modest about her reach.

> Sara Blackburn, in a review of "The Clock Winder," in Book World—The Washington Post (© 1972 Postrib Corp.; reprinted by permission of Chicago Tribune and The Washington Post), May 14, 1972, p. 13.

PAUL A. DOYLE

[Anne Tyler] writes of lonely, unhappy, confused individuals who seek meaning, comfort, and a bit of human understanding and contact. Her closest progenitor is Carson McCullers, but I find Miss Tyler's work to be more wistful, delicate, and touching.

In ["**The Clock Winder**"] one can not only witness and understand the incredible difficulty of human relationships but also the ambivalent burdens of family life. Parents cannot understand their children, and children cannot understand their parents. "Why," asks the aged Mrs. Emerson, "are my children always leaving?" and "Why are they always coming *back*?" Advancing age on all sides further complicates the situation. Miss Tyler has probed this puzzle maturely and carefully and continually conveys much of the mystery, the loneliness, and the aloneness of existence. Her art is quiet, delicate, sensitive, and acutely tender. She is not cheaply sensational and artificially flamboyant, and in this day and age I could pay no higher compliment. Readers who appreciate depth of perception, thoughtful analysis of life and people, and a graceful, fresh prose style will enjoy and meditate. "**The Clock Winder**" is one of Miss Tyler's best novels which is to say that it is one of the most perceptive novels written in America in several years. (p. 149)

> Paul A. Doyle, in a review of "The Clock Winder," in Best Sellers (copyright 1972, by the University of

Scranton), Vol. 32, No. 6, June 15, 1972, pp. 148-49.

BENJAMIN DeMOTT

New work by a young writer who's both greatly gifted and prolific often points readers' minds toward the future. You finish the book and immediately begin speculating about works to come—achievements down the road that will cross the borders defined by the work at hand. Anne Tyler's books have been having this effect on me for nearly a decade. Repeatedly they've been brilliant—"wickedly good," as John Updike recently described one of them. **"Dinner at the Homesick Restaurant"** is Anne Tyler's ninth novel; her career began in 1964 with a fully realized first novel (the title was **"If Morning Ever Comes,"** and there are piquant links between it and her latest book); everything I've read of hers since then—stories, novels and criticism (Anne Tyler is a first-rate critic, shrewd and self-effacing)—has been, at a minimum, interesting and well made. But in recent years her narratives have grown bolder and her characters more striking, and that's increased the temptation to brood about her direction and destination, her probable ultimate achievement.

The time for such brooding is over now, though—at least for a while. **"Dinner at the Homesick Restaurant"** is a book to be settled into fully, tomorrow be damned. Funny, heart-hammering, wise, it edges deep into truth that's simultaneously (and interdependently) psychological, moral and formal—deeper than many living novelists of serious reputation have penetrated, deeper than Miss Tyler herself has gone before. It is a border crossing.

The setting, as in many of this author's fictions, is Baltimore. The focus at first is Pearl Tull, 85 and dying, whose ruminations on her sickbed center partly on a moment 35 years before, when her husband, Beck Tull, a traveling salesman, announced he was clearing out for good; partly on the years of ferocious labor that followed this catastrophe ("an out-of-date kind of woman, frail boned, deep bosomed," more or less gently bred, Pearl went to work as a grocery-store checkout clerk, toughened her provisioning skills, struggled to nurture and civilize the three children she'd had with her husband in her late 30's); partly on the mystery of the character of those youngsters, persons who are approaching middle age as their mother approaches her end. (pp. 1, 14)

On its face **"Dinner at the Homesick Restaurant"** is a book about the costs of parental truancy (a subject that surfaces in Miss Tyler's first novel and elsewhere frequently in her *oeuvre*). None of the three Tull children manages to cut loose from the family past; each is, to a degree, stunted; each turns for help to Pearl Tull in an hour of desperate adult need; and Pearl's conviction that something's wrong with each of them never recedes from the reader's consciousness. But no small measure of the book's subtlety derives from its exceptional—and exceptionally *wise*, the word bears repeating—clarity about the uselessness of cost accounting in human areas such as these. Cody Tull suffers from obscure guilt (was it something I said, something I did that made my father go away?). Ezra Tull suffers from want of desire. Jenny Tull suffers from fear of connection. And the behavior and feelings of all three are linked somehow with the terrible, never-explained rupture: their father's disappearance.

But it's also the case that what is best in each of these people, as in their mother, has its roots in the experience of deprivation that they jointly despise. Jenny's outward exuberance flows from instinctive knowledge of how overwhelming the need for cheer can be among young or old. Ezra's movingly unconsidered kindness and generosity have a similar source. Even Cody, who for much of the story is perceived as an enemy of light, emerges at the end as a man elevated by what he's obliquely learned from his father's irresponsibility.

Adversity teaches? We advance well beyond that truism in **"Dinner at the Homesick Restaurant."** We arrive at an understanding that the important lessons taught by adversity never quite make themselves known to the consciousness of the learners—remain hidden, inexpressible. Outsiders stumble on them sometimes, and behave in their innocence as though the lessons couldn't be missed—but oh yes they can. . . .

Much as I've admired Miss Tyler's earlier books, I've found flaws in a few—something excessively static in the situation developed in **"Morgan's Passing,"** for instance, something arbitrary in the plotting of **"Earthly Possessions."** But in the work at hand Miss Tyler is a genius plotter, effortlessly redefining her story questions from page to page, never slackening the lines of suspense. There are, furthermore, numberless explosions of hilarity, not one of which (I discover) can be sliced out of its context for quotation—so tightly fashioned is this tale—without giving away, as they say, a narrative climax. There are scenes that strike me as likely to prove unforgettable: Pearl Tull attempting, after years of silence on the matter, to explain to her adamantly inattentive children that their father isn't coming back; Jenny Tull revising and revising, as though aiming at a masterpiece in the mode of the laconic-sublime, a letter accepting a marriage proposal; Cody Tull declaring his suspicion to his wife that his brother is the father of their son; and many more. . . .

Seriousness does insist, in the end, that explicit note be taken of the facts of this career. Anne Tyler turned 40 just last year. She's worked with a variety of materials, established her mastery of grave as well as comic tones. Her command of her art is sure, and her right to trust her feeling for the complications both of our nature and of our nurturing arrangements stands beyond question. Speculating about this artist's future is, in short, a perfectly natural movement of mind. But, as I said before, I'm reluctant to speculate, and I expect other readers, in quantity, will share my reluctance. What one wants to do on finishing such a work as **"Dinner at the Homesick Restaurant"** is maintain balance, keep things intact for a stretch, stay under the spell as long as feasible. The before and after are immaterial; nothing counts except the knowledge, solid and serene, that's all at once breathing in the room. We're speaking, obviously, about an extremely beautiful book. (p. 14)

Benjamin DeMott, "Funny, Wise and True," in The New York Times Book Review *(copyright © 1982 by The New York Times Company; reprinted by permission), March 14, 1982, pp. 1, 14.*

VIVIAN GORNICK

Good writers often have preoccupations. Sets of characters or pieces of experience repeat themselves in book after book because an idea of life is being obsessed over. If a reader is responsive to the preoccupation, each new book deepens the tale being told. If a reader is not responsive, the writer is silently instructed: "Tell another story, you've told this one already."

Anne Tyler is a writer with a preoccupation. Writing in a time and place that is stimulated by the idea of the separately maturing self, Tyler's novels are relentlessly devoted to the idea of never growing up, never leaving home. Not only do her characters refuse to leave their parents' houses, they inevitably marry surrogate brothers or sisters whom they pull into the house as well—whereupon they become their parents without even becoming men or women. In Tyler's world there is neither terror nor rapture because there is no sex. Instead, there is an endless child-parent interchange prolonged into listless adulthood: the only refuge is in a kind of acted-out fantasy commonly referred to as making magic.

Tyler has real feeling for the condition she describes, and sympathizes keenly with her characters as they burrow back into childhood. It is this sympathy, above all, that makes her such a fine writer. Her gift for dialogue and narration is prodigious—she skillfully stitches her prose from a single, mysteriously lengthening thread into landscape, densely made, fully peopled—but it is the sympathy that allows her to achieve genuine pathos. Pathos is the dominant color in each of her novels, woven strongly through the design of her writing—warm, repetitious, predictable, somewhat like the comforting familiarity of an ironic home sampler.

Dinner at the Homesick Restaurant is Anne Tyler's ninth novel in 18 years. The character of its prose, the quality of its invention, the inevitability of its conclusion can easily be traced to her early work—that's how stable the inner experience in Tyler's writing is. As the years pass, this experience seems to dig in, insist upon itself, and here, in *The Homesick Restaurant* it stands its ground, weighted and immovable, achieving a curious self-command through the integrity of its stubbornness.

Most of Tyler's novels are set in or near an unreal city called Baltimore (a cardboard backdrop; it could be Anytown, USA). On a residential street in a once-good section of town, in a shabby frame house whose foundations are settling and whose paint is peeling, there lives a family named Peck or Gower or Emory. There are many people in the family—mothers, fathers, in-laws and grandparents, aunts and uncles, children growing up, others grown and returned home—pack rats every one of them. The house is piled floor to ceiling with books, toys, furniture, clothing, objects of every size, description, and meaning; physical dishevelment alone makes life inside the house a three-ring circus.

At the same time that they collect everything in sight, Tyler families seem always to be drifting. The tension, of course, is between staying put and running off, and in every Tyler novel one character or another *does* run off—a traveling-salesman husband who deserts the family, a brother who leaves to become a jazz musician, a mother who elopes with an inappropriate relative. Fairs, carnivals, circuses, traveling shows abound; people endlessly try to recapture that last moment before life got hopelessly bogged down. Meanwhile, the ones who remain behind eat the most amazing amount of junk food. I know of no other novelist whose 45-year-old men and women are forever eating Fritos and Baby Ruths and drinking Yoo-hoos.

Inevitably, one of those who stay put will detach from the group, adopt a narrative voice of dazed and slightly fantastical confusion, and guide us through a 300-page Tyler happening: a picaresque chronicle of the satisfying sadnesses of family life invariably described as warm, magical, funny, and wise. (p. 40)

Dinner at the Homesick Restaurant is the best of Anne Tyler's novels. It is free of "magical" invention and strikingly direct in communicating the depression behind the adopted whimsy of her middle books. No longer young, but not yet free from her preoccupation of 20 years, Tyler now stares openly into the emotional arrest that is her true, her only subject.

Again Baltimore, again a family, again one who ran off and many who stayed. Pearl Tull lives on in a seedy frame house with her three children (Cody, Ezra, Jenny) after Beck, her traveling salesman husband, leaves—informing her one night that he doesn't want to be married any longer. Pearl has always been angry: now she'll be in a rage until she dies. Her children, traumatized by their need for her love, will flinch before that rage for the rest of their lives, but not one of them will walk away. Tyler makes this inability to leave seem moving and inevitable. . . .

Anne Tyler is held spellbound before the hopeless loss of childhood her characters refuse to accept. She feels the dull pain of that lifelong desire for the normal family no one ever had, understands the psychic bondage in which people far into middle age are held. But Tyler mythicizes the inability to give up the family, and because she does her novels do not achieve depth.

A hundred years ago novelists wrote successfully about family life. A writer could take a group of people, set them down in a country house, move them about from the drawing room to the garden to the upstairs parlor for 30 years, and every time the door closed on two or three of them, pages of charged thought and feeling flowed from the writer's pen. A microcosm of self-discovery was locked up inside those framed, landscaped lives. There are, it seems to me, not many ways a contemporary novel can duplicate that action, insist successfully on that gestalt. Today, if a novel is to dive down into the experience that gives us back to ourselves its people must be up and about in the alien world, struggling to become men and women. The energy that ignites them is sexual in character, not filial.

Tyler's prose is sexually anesthetized—in fact, mass sexual coma prevails in her books—and so the energy it gives off feels fabricated. The warmth is shallow; it is nostalgia being burned, not immediate experience. Ironically, she is beloved precisely because her writing skill invests the ordinary infantilism of American family life with a tender glamour. She allows the middle-brow middle class to love itself for all its poignant insufficiency. A pity: A good writer being rewarded for making a virtue out of the fear of experience. (p. 41)

    Vivian Gornick, "Anne Tyler's Arrested Development" (reprinted by permission of The Village Voice *and the author; copyright © News Group Publications, Inc., 1982), in* The Village Voice, *Vol. XXVII, No. 13, March 30, 1982, pp. 40-1.*

R. Z. SHEPPARD

Every other year or so since 1964, loyal readers pick up their new Anne Tyler novel as they would buy a favored brand of sensible shoe. Each of her nine books is solidly constructed from authentic and durable materials. Yet traditional style and comfort do not necessarily mean dullness. Tyler's characters have character: quirks, odd angles of vision, colorful mean streaks and harmonic longings. They usually live in ordinary settings, like Baltimore, the author's current home, and do not seem to have been overly influenced by the 7 o'clock news. An issue in a Tyler novel is likely to mean a new child; a cause, the reason behind a malfunction in an appliance or a marriage.

Tyler does not trivialize motives with rationalizations. She launches her imagined lives and describes their trajectories with an unpretentious sense of fate. No explanations are necessary when Beck Tull, a retired traveling salesman, attends the funeral of the wife he left 35 years before and acts as if he has been on a long business trip. This occurs at the end of **Homesick Restaurant,** and the reader is not surprised. The scene has had careful preparation, and Tull has been well defined by his absence. He is the black hole around which his wife Pearl and children Cody, Jenny and Ezra have had to exist. The novel opens with Pearl Tull, 85, dying and remembering. It then turns effortlessly into a series of chapters about her children that can almost be read as self-contained stories. (p. 77)

Ezra is the dreamer who nurtures the novel's most enduring illusion. He runs a restaurant as if his soups and stews could cure loneliness and disappointment. The permutations of food and woe inspire him: "Why not a restaurant full of refrigerators, where people came and chose the food they wanted? . . . Or maybe he could install a giant fireplace, with a whole steer turning slowly on a spit. You'd slice what you liked onto your plate and sit around in armchairs eating and talking with the guests at large. Then again, maybe he would start serving only street food. Of course! He'd cook what people felt homesick for."

Ezra's homesick restaurant is not very profitable. It does manage to survive on its owner's terms, which, if one reads Tyler correctly, are worth more than the print-outs of an efficiency expert. Cody, in fact, hates Ezra for his wise foolishness and steals his fiancée. She is a scrawny country girl who unhappily ends up in expensive boxy suits and fancy automobiles. But Ezra is not deterred. A would-be wife turned sister-in-law is still family, and a family should eat together.

The amusing motif of the novel is Ezra Tull's persistent efforts to prepare feasts for his family. They are acts of faith at which courses go untouched. The clan gathers only to eat and run. Even old Beck, sitting down with his children after 35 years, says, "I plan to leave before that dessert wine's poured." Everything has changed; nothing has changed. It is the special satisfaction one gets from Anne Tyler, a writer who knows exactly what to do with leftovers. (p. 78)

> R. Z. Sheppard, "Eat and Run," in Time (copyright 1982 Time Inc.; all rights reserved; reprinted by permission from Time), Vol. 119, No. 14, April 5, 1982, pp. 77-8.

HERMIONE LEE

'Dinner at the Homesick Restaurant' is redeemed by its singularity from being yet another three-generation 'Depression to Post-Vietnam' American family saga. True, its coy title smacks of Carson McCullers ('Ballad of the Sad Café'), and the structure—a section for each member of the family, beginning with the ailing, reminiscing mother ('Dying, you don't get to see how it all turns out')—owes something to Faulkner's 'As I Lay Dying.' But the writing, like the restaurant's cooking, is deliciously idiosyncratic, enough to make one wish that Anne Tyler were better known over here [in England].

Beck Tull, travelling salesman, runs away from his oppressive wife Pearl, who leads a 'stunted' life, terrorising her three children, 'always wearing her hat when out walking, keeping her doors tightly shut when at home.' The three respond differently to this travesty of 'home.' Saintlike Ezra gives up his girl to his competitive brother Cody, stays with Pearl and runs his Baltimore restaurant like a home, where guests are offered, not what they ask for, but what's good for them. Cody, though he travels farthest from home, is the most locked in rivalry with his vanished father and passive brother; like Iago, he wants revenge on people who are 'just naturally nicer' than he is. Jenny (the least interesting) acquires, as consolation, a warm extended family.

'How plotless real life was!' Ezra says. But, though a random, scatty air is maintained, the novel is almost too neatly ordered, like Pearl's bureau drawers. The dinner that Ezra has throughout been trying to give his family finally takes place, suggesting that 'family life' is inescapable, even life-giving. The flaws, though, aren't fatal: this is a vigorous, funny, original novel.

> Hermione Lee, "Heart of Urban Darkness," in The Observer (reprinted by permission of The Observer Limited), October 3, 1982, p. 33.*

JOHN UPDIKE

Anne Tyler, [like John Cheever], has sought brightness in the ordinary, and her art has needed only the darkening that would give her beautifully sketched shapes solidity. So evenly has her imagination moved across the details of the mundane that the novels, each admirable, sink in the mind without leaving an impression of essential, compulsive subject matter—the phobia portrayed in **Celestial Navigation** being something of an exception. Now, in [**Dinner at the Homesick Restaurant**], she has arrived, I think, at a new level of power, and gives us a lucid and delightful yet complex and somber improvisation on her favorite theme, family life. **Searching for Caleb** is the earlier book it most resembles, in its large cast and historical reach, and even in the perky monosyllabic name assigned the central family: Peck in the first case, Tull in this. Both novels play with the topic (a mighty one, and not often approached in fiction) of heredity—the patterns of eye color and temperamental tic as they speckle the generations. But genetic comedy, in **Dinner at the Homesick Restaurant,** deepens into the tragedy of closeness, of familial limitations that work upon us like Greek fates and condemn us to lives of surrender and secret fury. (p. 296)

The Tulls . . . present a not untypical American family history, marred by abandonment and scattering but redeemed by a certain persisting loyalty and, after early privation, respectable success. And the telling of the Tull saga is soaked through, you may be sure, with all the deft geographical, topical, professional, and cultural specifics required to make it stick, from 1903 to 1979, to the landscape of the upper South and to the curve of national life as glimpsed in its wars and fads and fashions. This type of authenticity Anne Tyler has provided consistently; what she has not shown before, so searchingly and grimly, are the violences, ironies, and estrangements within a household, as the easy wounds given dependent flesh refuse to heal and instead grow into lifelong purposes. A bitter *narrowness* of life is disclosed through all the richness of detail as the decades accumulate, to claustrophobic and sad effect.

The novel leaves Pearl Tull's mind, and chapter by chapter gives us Cody's, Jenny's, Ezra's, and even young Luke's view of the branching consequences of the primal event—Beck Tull's abandonment, as abrupt and mysterious as his courtship, of his wife. In her own mind a doting and heroic mother, Pearl is seen by Cody as a "witch," a terrible-tempered mother who "slammed us against the wall and called us scum and vipers, said she wished us dead, shook us till our teeth rattled, screamed in our faces." Cody's own violences to his placid and harmless younger brother follow suit. Jenny, too, has seen how her mother's "pale hair could crackle electrically from its bun and her eyes could get small as hatpins," has felt her stinging slaps, has dreamed that her mother is raising her to eat her. Even on her deathbed, Pearl calls her children "duckers and dodgers." A perfectionist, a fanatic laundress and housekeeper, she strives to keep her bare clean house free of contamination. She disapproves of her children's friends and has few friends herself; the isolation of this embattled family, in its Baltimore row house, is dreadfully well felt. Of course, all children are somewhat embarrassed by their parents and their homes; Pearl is a witch but also our authentic heroine, and the novel ends with Cody's adolescent vision of her beauty, "his mother's upright form along the grasses, her hair lit gold, her small hands smoothing her bouquet." The paradoxes of the family, *Dinner at the Homesick Restaurant* suggests, include love that must for survival flee its object, and daily communication that masks silence—that deep resentful silence of those who live together. Ezra, the most loving of Pearl's children, yet turns cold-hearted when she falls sick, because, it is explained, "he had trusted his mother to be everything for him. When she cut a finger with a paring knife, he had felt defeated by her incompetence. How could he depend on such a person?" When Luke runs away from home, he is given rides by three persons who all have a horror story of family life uppermost in their minds—infants who die, daughters who are ingrates, wives who leave. The family, that institution meant to shelter our frailty, in fact serves as a theatre for intimate cruelties, and brims with the cruellest of invisible presences, time. As Pearl's memories accumulate in the course of the novel, we become dizzied by the downward perspective into a well of personal history wherein hereditary traits reverberate and snapshots and frozen memories gleam amid the blackness of loss. Pearl, blind in her last years, directs Ezra to describe old photos and read aloud her girlhood diaries. At last, near the bottom of the well, she finds what she has been looking for, the diary entry:

> Early this morning I went out behind the house to weed. Was kneeling in the dirt by the stable with my pinafore a mess and the perspiration rolling down my back, wiped my face on my sleeve, reached for the trowel, and all at once thought, Why I believe that at just this moment I am absolutely happy. The Bedloe girl's piano scales were floating out her window, and I saw that I was kneeling on such a beautiful green little planet. I don't care what else might come about, I have had this moment. It belongs to me.

The plot holds a number of such epiphanies and moves its extensive cast agilely along, with flashback and side glance, through ten chapters that are each rounded like a short story. Miss Tyler, whose humane and populous domestic novels have attracted (if my antennae are tuned right) less approval in the literary ether than the sparer offerings of Ann Beattie and Joan Didion, is sometimes charged with the basic literary sin of implausibility. To me, her characters seem persuasive outgrowths of landscapes and states of mind that are familiar and American. The principal characters in *Dinner at the Homesick Restaurant* have their tics but also real psychologies, which make their next moves excitingly unpredictable. It is true, no writer would undertake to fill a canvas so broad without some confidence that she can invent her way across any space, and some of Miss Tyler's swoops, and the delayed illuminations that prick out her tableaux, have not quite the savor of reality's cautious grind. But any reader who picks up a work of fiction enters into a contract whereby he purchases with credulity satisfactions of adventure and resolution that his lived life denies him. This novel does not abuse the terms of that contract; its entertainments become our recognitions. (pp. 297-99)

John Updike, "Bellow, Vonnegut, Tyler, Le Guin, Cheever," in his Hugging the Shore: Essays and Criticism *(copyright © 1983 by John Updike; reprinted by permission of Alfred A. Knopf, Inc.), Knopf, 1983, pp. 247-99.*

Miriam Waddington
1917-

Canadian poet, dramatist, and editor.

Waddington's reputation as a poet is well established in Canada. Although she has read widely and expresses special fondness for formal poets such as W. H. Auden and Hart Crane, Waddington has demonstrated considerable eclecticism in her own writing and adheres to no fixed poetic style. For Waddington, poetry is a natural outpouring into the world of the artist's existence, or as she states, "a bridging of the inner and the outer." This view of poetry makes theories of poetic form a secondary consideration to her. Consequently, over the span of nearly forty years of publication, Waddington's work has shown considerable flexibility in form and content.

Waddington's first collection, *Green World* (1945), contains many of the themes and subjects which dominate her poetry over the next twenty years. As the title of this work suggests, she is extremely conscious of nature, especially its rejuvenative processes. Waddington's lyrics in this volume express faith in the solace provided by nature as opposed to the frustrations caused by modern industrial society. Waddington's experience as a social worker provides much of the subject matter for her poetry. Many of the poems in her second book, *The Second Silence* (1955), demonstrate her familiarity with social problems and individual suffering. Waddington's poetry also manifests her strong political awareness, which can be traced to her childhood years when she was exposed to many social and political controversies through her intellectual Russian-Jewish parents and their associates.

In her later poetry, Waddington has moved away from social and political subjects. Instead, her recent books *The Price of Gold* (1976) and *The Visitants* (1981) include poems which focus on basic human concerns: loss, aging, death, and, ultimately, the primal joy of being alive.

(See also *Contemporary Authors,* Vols. 21-24, rev. ed.)

Photograph by Paul Orenstein, Toronto; reproduced by permission of Miriam Waddington

DESMOND PACEY

[Miriam Waddington is a] quiet and unspectacular poet . . . , but she has a persuasive sincerity that is very winning.

[Her first book, *Green World* (1945),] established quite clearly the general outlines of her work. The book's dominant theme was the beauty and goodness of the natural world, expressed by recurring images of greenness and growth, and the ugliness and evil of contemporary industrial society, evoked by images of angles, coils, tunnels, walls and "tangles of hot streets". Within human society, the one positive liberating force was seen as love, whether love in the sense of charity or "lovingkindness" or love in the sense of sexual attraction and union. Unlike most of her Canadian contemporaries at that time, Mrs. Waddington did not speak in terms of socialist doctrine, nor indeed of any dogma, and although there were occasional references to the hope for a better social order there was no attempt to be specific about the causes of social chaos or the means of social amelioration. These early poems were simple, colourful, melodic and easy; they had spontaneity and verve, a youthful affirmation and exuberance modified only slightly by twinges of pity, anger or disgust.

In *The Second Silence* (1955) the themes remained much the same. Nature and love were still the main positive attractions, and the sufferings of modern industrial man the main sources of discontent. A decade of experience had, however, broadened the scope of her poetry. Love, especially sexual love, was given more complex treatment, revealed as a source of frustration and pain as well as of satisfaction and pleasure. The discussion of social evils was more specific, being related frequently to the plight of individuals whom Mrs. Waddington had encountered in the course of her duties as a social worker; and the experience of maternity provided her with material for poems on childbirth and the child's view of the world. But if there was a gain in breadth there was something of a loss in verve: there was occasionally a note of weariness or of querulousness. The technique had developed in a similarly paradoxical way: the verse forms were more intricate and skilful, there was more technical sophistication, but at the same time there was a faintly artificial air, a hint of contrivance, in some of the poems. The best poems in this second volume, however, retained the directness of her earlier volume and exhibited a richer sensibility.

Mrs. Waddington's third volume, *The Season's Lovers* (1958), did not mark a spectacular change in either her themes or her techniques. Nature played a slightly less prominent part, but meadows and flowers were still her chief symbols of happiness and of the creative freedom which she finds so sadly lacking in the life of our large cities. She still celebrated love in both its sexual and non-sexual forms as the chief value in human life and, indeed, in several of the poems including the title poem, as a truly miraculous force which transforms the world. She continued to pour out her compassion for those victims of our social disorder whom she encounters in her social work. The only new theme was that of art, seen as another of the forces that can at least temporarily liberate man from suffering.

In technique, there was a more conspicuous development. She has obviously become convinced that the simple free verse technique which she used almost exclusively in her first two volumes needed the disciplines of rhyme and rhetoric. Her use of rhyme is often advantageous, but her attempts at a more sophisticated rhetoric, at metaphysical ingenuity of image and syntax and epigram, often seem merely laboured.

In her poem **"The City's Life"** Mrs. Waddington writes of herself:

> All she has are her own human channels,
> Eyes that observe, a pulse that beats,
> A heart that moves to other troubled hearts.

and in these lines she has clearly expressed both the strengths and limitations of her poetry. The honest self-evaluation of the passage is symptomatic of the directness with which at her best she responds to the world about her. She is an accurate observer of nature and society, and her pictures of persons and places are frequently the most memorable passages of her verse.... The chief desideratum in her poetry is a set of original or strongly-held ideas: there is something passive about her poetry, a lack of passionate conviction and assurance. For this lack, however, she largely atones by the quickness and sensitivity of her emotional responses. (pp. 167-70)

> Desmond Pacey, "Modern Canadian Poetry (1920-1950)," in his Creative Writing in Canada (copyright © McGraw-Hill Ryerson Limited, 1952 and 1961; reprinted by permission), revised edition, Ryerson Press, 1961, pp. 125-85.*

MARVIN BELL

In a poem entitled **Losing Merrygorounds,** Miriam Waddington regrets that loss as well as "... the careful prose / of growing up". Indeed, throughout The Glass Trumpet, one feels that Miss Waddington is willing to abandon care entirely to avoid writing "prose". The battle against prose is exhausting, finding its expression in run-on syntax and sentimental attitudes. It includes lots of crying, wishing, dreaming, and singing. Half of everything seems to be blinded or blinding.

None of this would be quite as bothersome if Miss Waddington would exploit the best of the metaphors she so casually picks up, instead of dropping each for abstractions in those places where she is led to significant thought by her materials. The language is not without a talented urgency—quite deserving of care, even at the cost of the infiltration of "prose". As it is, all that this technique allows to be clear is the most general of feelings.

The best of Miss Waddington's poems seem to me those which arise from her harshest attitudes.... (p. 326)

> Marvin Bell, "Nine Canadian Poets" (© 1968 by The Modern Poetry Association; reprinted by permission of the Editor of Poetry and the author), in Poetry, Vol. CXI, No. 5, February, 1968, pp. 323-28.*

D. G. JONES

[Waddington's language in Say Yes is close to the conventional lyric, appears fresh,] surprises with sudden illumination, touches us with her gaiety and convinces us of her gravity. Her language enlivens the dark. Acutely aware of the loss of love, of language, of a familiar world, she confronts it directly and articulates it honestly. With a possible hint from Dr. Williams she has devised a rather baroque, run-on form made up of lines of two to four feet into which the most prosaic sentences may be fitted, in a potentially endless series.... In the country, in the city, in art or in nature, everywhere the dark appears. In **"Shakedown"** we read:

> Time like a raftered roof has
> shaken us down like grain or
> brickdust into the lowest bin
> of the dark world.

One poem is entitled **"Swallowing darkness is swallowing dead elm trees."** And swallow it Mrs. Waddington does. The dark is not simply an alien dark; it is our own.... The dark is the home of the inarticulate "other." Moving into the dark with affection, she retains her language and enlarges it, rediscovering her world in the bleakest times and the most unpromising places. Iron bridges fold their wings like swans; construction cranes like colourful amphibious animals bring her a breakfast basket of helmeted workers and bricks by the ton.... Despite the strangeness of cities, the "black leather police," empty libraries, empty rooms, Eros survives. It survives to inform the imagination and the control of the language, and with it survives the capacity for song. (pp. 73-4)

> D. G. Jones, "Voices in the Dark" (reprinted by permission of the author), in Canadian Literature, No. 45, Summer, 1970, pp. 68-74.*

TOM WAYMAN

I think most of Miriam Waddington's poems in her recent collection of new and selected poems, **Driving Home,** are boring. But as this collection spans thirty years of work, boredom here is perhaps not entirely her fault: the worst poems reflect the fashions of times they were written in. It is difficult not to be bored with intricate little home-made myths and texts designed to fill up with sentiment the empty prairies or an empty life. And it is difficult now not to be bored with the careful encapsulating into rhyme of the passions and anguish of a social worker in the 40's and 50's, and of the lives of those she was in contact with.

But I wonder if Waddington doesn't share these views. The best of the poems in **Driving Home** are mostly in the section of new poems (since 1969). Here she is able sometimes to get inside her present life and show it to the reader in a convincing way. (p. 85)

Some hint of the powerful poems Waddington might have written out of her social work in clinics, jails and as a welfare official can be seen in **"Investigator"** (1942) where she captures for a moment something of the inside of the homes and lives of the poor. . . . But too often the emotion is lost in the prison of rhyme. . . . This poem clunks along to the stunning insight of:

> I haven't heard much that was new to me
> or brought any word that was new to you;
> it seems our separate selves must curve
> wide from the central pulsing nerve
> which ought to unite us, you and me . . .

Waddington's poems such as this one fail to let any particular emotion break out, to transcend the confines of rhyme in any way so that the poem is more than reporting in verse. Or maybe there *was* no further emotion? (p. 86)

My lack of complete belief in what Waddington is saying appears even in the new poems of this collection. Something is missing, for me, in a poem like **"Transformations"** when she says she wants to spend her life in Gimli listening to the silence. . . . Similarly, in **"Dead lakes"**:

> I look down
> in the dead waters
> of Sudbury and
> I think of Flaubert . . .

I lose the poem entirely when leaps like this are too large for me. Something else must be going on in the poet's mind, I keep thinking, to make these images mean more to her than she has conveyed to me. (pp. 87-8)

And disconnectedness appears in more of the early poems. In some sort of try to give Canada a veneer of European mythical and traditional history, Waddington has lines like (from **"Lullaby"** (1945)):

> and night's sweet gypsy now
> fiddles you to sleep
> far from snows of winnipeg
> and seven sisters lakes.

Images of gypsies, or Elizabethan rhetoric in poems like **"Thou didst say me"** (1945), **"Sea bells"** (1964) or **"The mile runner"** (1958), appear slightly incongruous in the Canadian reality, to say the least—like the pseudo-gothic Houses of Parliament rising over the sawmills of Hull.

Just how Waddington herself fits into the Canadian reality is the question dealt with in some of the better poems of this collection. In **"Fortunes"** (1960), Waddington considers how luck and chance finally don't alter her own specific historical being:

> I went out into the autumn night
> to cry my anger to the stone-blind fields
> just as I was, untraditional, North American
> Jewish, Russian, and rootless in all four,
> religious, unaffiliated, and held
> in a larger-than-life seize of hate.

In a poem about her travels (1966) she describes how around the world she finds both beautiful things and hatred of Jews. Her response here is to suddenly feel that there is nowhere she can be at home. But in **"Driving Home"** (1968) she seems to find home where she *is,* under the huge signs of the corporations. . . . (p. 88)

The finest of the older poems in ***Driving Home*** to me are the poems about love. In **"Interval"** (1943) Waddington shows a man who has idealized women being forced at last to recognize their humanity. . . . There are also poems that speak of the men that fail her, however: the poignant **"Remembering you"** (1965):

> When you kissed you
> kissed like a young man
> filled with greeting and gaiety;
>
> when you loved you
> loved like an old man
> filled with slowness and ceremony;
>
> when you left you
> left like a man of no age
> filled with fear that ceremony
>
> had given me something
> to keep more lasting than ritual
> richer and brighter than darkness.

Despite such betrayals, Waddington can celebrate another relationship in **"The lonely love of middle age"** (1966). And in **"Icons"** (1969), she says she carries with her the idea and memory of love, to hold out against the darkness of her age and our age. (pp. 88-9)

Celebrations like this of the dilemmas of Waddington's recent existence seem to me the best and most interesting work she has ever done. These poems speak more directly and openly of her predicament than her earlier work does, and thus the recent poems give me the impression of greater accuracy. I like Waddington's work of the last seven years or so so much better than her previous poems that I find it difficult in my mind not to think of her as a new talent: emerging strong and mature in middle age with a lot to say about that time of life in her social position in modern Canada. (p. 89)

Tom Wayman, "Miriam Waddington's New Talent" (reprinted by permission of the author), in Canadian Literature, *No. 56, Spring, 1973, pp. 85-9.*

L. R. RICOU

When Miriam Waddington writes of the exhaustion of language, that inevitable subject for poets, she speaks first of the lost language of nature. . . . But for Waddington the sense of a lost language is only momentary. She turns again and again to writing of the ineffable wind, and of whatever grows, in a language "light / and quick" through which she makes it possible, in the words of another poem, for "trees [to] yield up their wordless therapy."

Waddington declared this direction for her poetry in her first book, *Green World* (1945). Its title poem, later called **"Green world one,"** is a good place to begin because it focusses on a subject—the green world—which defines Waddington's outlook, because it uses a metaphor—the growth of a plant—central to her vision, and because, more generally, it shows her ability to build a poem both rhythmically and aurally beautiful, and rich with meaning. . . . (pp. 144-45)

"Green world one" is an intense and subtle consideration of the process of becoming and growing, of transforming energy, of turning dream into vision, of finding meaning in image. The poem is not anecdotal, but slightly elusive in its playing with correspondences; it is not colloquial, but charged with alliterative rhythms; its images are relatively general, and do not serve to locate a specific experience or landscape; it begins with "I" and ends with "me," emphasizing the contours of the personal response. It is not difficult to find Waddington poems which do not fit this description, but I find that the characteristics of **"Green world one"** mark the fundamental direction of her poetry, and its fundamental strength. (p. 146)

A poem like **"Runners"** gives a more relaxed and casual expression of the fusion of man's spirit with the rhythms of the natural world. . . . Back of the poem there seems to lie an image of children romping through fields at dawn. The poem expresses a receptiveness both to the small rhythms of nature (''the closing flower'') and the large (''the sun''). With childlike energy and randomness the flower, sun, wind and rainbow combine to create a generalized landscape which is the very happiest fantasy world: ''the enchanted land / of ourselves.''

A poet becoming the enchanted land of herself. Such lyrical terms, resonant but perhaps vague, seem more suited to describing the poetry of Miriam Waddington than pseudo-precise critical terminology. Not willing to be aligned closely with particular movements or schools, Waddington places herself in these general terms: ''In poetry I disliked rhetoric, intellectual word play, and T. S. Eliot, which made me native rather than cosmopolitan (according to A.J.M. Smith's famous classification), and realist-physical rather than metaphysical.'' Suitable as this description is it seems to need immediate qualification: **"Green world one"** seems to derive much of its effectiveness from metaphysical word-play, and the extensive influence of Yiddish and European poetry . . . adds a strong cosmopolitan note.

The difficulty of placing Waddington is compounded by her casual indifference to poetic form. My remarks should not be misinterpreted: I don't mean that Waddington isn't attentive to her craft . . . , but I do mean that she is unconcerned with poetic theory as something which might govern her own verse. The ''bridging of the inner and outer,'' she writes, ''the artist expresses through form.'' Thus, form in the artistic work is the attainment of psychic unity and equilibrium between the individual artist and a collective ideology. This concept of form as a sort of psychological ordering, of form as a selection of elements from the outer world neither conscious nor voluntary, is primarily an emphasis on the naturalness of poetry and the inevitability of form. There is no literary dogma here about rhyme being essential to expressing a certain world view, or the short line being apt only to a particular kind of content.

Insofar as Miriam Waddington has a theory of poetry, it is expressed in one of her favourite books, Stanley Burnshaw's *The Seamless Web*. Burnshaw's book, for all its scholarship, is convincing for making a theory of having no theory of poetry. Burnshaw argues for the biological necessity of poetry—''Poetry begins with the body and ends with the body''—an approach especially congenial to a poet interested in the interconnections of body, spirit and green world. (pp. 147-48)

The Seamless Web celebrates the unique enlargement of the mind possible through poetry. . . . I simplify and risk trivializing an intricate and fascinating argument when I say that Burnshaw sees metaphor and condensation as keys to the pluralistic totality of poetry; he apologizes for his ''inevitably static term 'metaphoric totality,''' which he uses to describe a poem as that ''all-enclosing metaphor that produces a new relationship out of elements hitherto existing apart, one that is memorable and meaningful in the way that individual poetic metaphors are meaningful: by 'saying one thing and meaning another.''' (pp. 148-49)

Yet, the many poems rising out of [Waddington's] career and sensibility as a social worker seem, perhaps because of their subject matter, more likely to ignore the new relationships which can be established within Burnshaw's 'metaphoric totality.' **"The bond,"** for example, is an early poem in which Waddington expresses her discovery of the situation which is ultimately shared by ''the Jewish me on Adelaide,'' and ''the Jewish whore'' on Jarvis Street. There is little metaphorical resonance in this poem: when she states ''woman you are kin to me'' she says one thing and means the same thing. No matter what the variety of metaphor brought to bear on the kinship— the sleep of the whore and the sleep of death, the evil of the noonday sun, ''the slippered creep / of famine through the surplus grain''—the result is not further ''extensions into infinity,'' but more strainings toward the same point, that they are ''joint heirs to varied low estate.'' Again, at the end of the poem, with night ''closing in,'' the poet promises to ''recognize your face.'' What this ''salute'' means is unclear: it seems to be a final expression of sisterhood, but the promise must be cold comfort indeed either to poet or whore. (pp. 151-52)

Though many of Waddington's poems on social themes tend to declaim, she is seldom specifically political. The legacy of her father's socialism, and her own education in a ''socialist Yiddish school'' is rarely made explicit in the poetry. One well-known poem that does take up this particular background is **"The nineteen-thirties are over."** The three sections of the poem discuss her memories of childhood, her memories of adolescence, and her present reality as a middle-aged professor living in Don Mills. . . . [The] memories here are of connections with the international workers' movement. She says ''we survived / the depression'' though there is nothing else in the poem to describe personal hardship. The preoccupation of that era, she remembers, was ''keeping / one eye on the revolution''; her heroes were Sacco and Vanzetti, Tom Mooney, Eugene Debs, all celebrated figures regarded as martyrs to socialist, labour principles and as victims of unjustified persecution. . . . The poem is Waddington's exploration of the Depression and a statement of her personal relationship to it. She feels the deep pain of the revolutions that have been crushed, but the pain is coloured by green-gold memories of a happy childhood. Consistent with this sense of the nineteen-thirties it does not seem clear at the end of the poem whether she is making a renewed dedication to the war of revolution, or she is guiltily thinking how easy it was, and is, for her to live enjoying the benefits gained through her ''father's old war.''

Most of Waddington's better social poems move in the direction of **"The nineteen-thirties are over"**—toward a personal meaning, toward a statement about the ''I,'' rather than to a political statement or a call to social action. (pp. 153-54)

Green World, Waddington's first book, is itself defiantly titled to declare her rejection of the wasteland, the fragmentation, and the greyness in modern poetry. The title of her most recent collection, *The Price of Gold*, suggests the green finding fruition, ripening into gold. The titles point to central motifs whose associations place Waddington in the lineage of Dylan Thomas, deeply nourished by the world of ''children green and golden,'' yet never completely forgetting that ''time held me green and dying.''

Echoes of Dylan Thomas, things green and golden, the voice of the awestruck provincial, the fanciful dream—these have led to a commonplace among reviewers that Waddington has a particular liking for the perspective of the child, that she sees things with the simple clarity of youth. . . . Yet her frequent inclination toward childhood makes Waddington neither hopelessly nostalgic, nor resolutely naïve. The typical spirit is caught in one of her own phrases, "blazing innocence," a quality she attained, she writes in **"Things of the world,"** during her Winnipeg childhood. This is an innocence neither flimsy nor unconsidered, but a passionate, convinced, robust, determined innocence which pervades her strongest poetry. (p. 156)

Even the infamous Canadian winter is readily absorbed in the green world.... The reader, abroad in Waddington's green world, shares [her] spirit of imaginative playfulness in a world filled with light. It is a spirit so central to Waddington's poetry that a poem in which she expresses her amusement with the poet and the repetitiveness of his subject matter, also can be read as a bemused comment on her own green world. The poem is irreverently titled **"Poets are still writing poems about spring and here is mine: Spring."** In it Waddington dances light-heartedly with the possible analogies for spring.... The second half of the poem leaps to the more distant possibilities of the metaphors, so that eventually the poet and reader, all men, become the essence of spring in a buoyant conclusion typical of Waddington's cavorting through the green world:

> and we'll be
> dyed green by the
> crowds of wildly
> cheering fern fans
> sitting in the packed
> high galleries of summer.

Some comparisons with modern American poetry provide a way to summarize the distinctive place of this dyed-green poet in Canadian poetry. Clearly she is no Whitman (or, in the Canadian context, Pratt) with sprawling lines and epic visions; just as certainly she is no Sylvia Plath (or Margaret Atwood) with brittle language and nervous intensity; nor is she a determined innovator of language and syntax like e.e. cummings (or bill bissett, or joe rosenblatt). No, the American poet whom she most resembles is Theodore Roethke. There is much of the same love of nature and greenhouse/garden, the same use of nature as a psychic landscape which can expand consciousness, the same tendency to "think by feeling," the same continual *persona* of the naif, the child, whatever the personal tortures or social commitment, the same linking of a spiritual self with the green world, with water and light, the same love, in sum, of leaf-language. (pp. 159-60)

> L. R. Ricou, "Into My Green World: The Poetry of Miriam Waddington," in Essays on Canadian Writing (© Essays on Canadian Writing Ltd.), No. 12, Fall, 1978, pp. 144-61.

MARK ABLEY

Reading *The Visitants,* I was struck by the absence of something I couldn't exactly place: some quality, some attitude that these 40 poems simply didn't contain. Anger? Sorrow? Bitterness? No, because in a few public lyrics, a few civil elegies, Miriam Waddington does express these dark emotions. What was it, this absence? It took me a while to realize that I was missing all sense of fear, and that *The Visitants* is a fearless book. Its main preoccupations are death, old age, and solitude—all of which are usually tackled with regret, unease, or the kind of boisterous swagger that seems a poor disguise for fear. But Waddington is undaunted at the prospect of death, and unafraid of direct feeling. She can, in consequence, write with warmth about the cold.

The rich texture of her language arises partly from another sort of courage. When the mood and the occasion are right, she's happy to use simple rhymes and verse-forms that more "sophisticated" poets might scorn.... Waddington is particularly adept at using internal rhymes to knit the various elements of a poem together. Embedded in a poem called **"When the Shoe Is on the Other Foot for a Change"** are the phrases "old bread," "spidery red," and "unleavened as lead"—but the natural linkword, the underlying rhyme of *dead,* is never uttered. She often directs her energies to the nurture of a simple lyricism that will be able, if necessary, to carry complex emotions. In the 40 years that she has been writing poetry, Waddington's vision of life has probably changed less than the means by which she expresses it.

Perhaps the title poem of the new book is as close as she gets to personal despair. It describes things that have been lost, things that are no more: friends, her father, Gabriel Dumont, ancient stories, and so on. Unusually, she uses the term "emptiness," and the dead friends who come to her are "anguished." But these visitants bring with them gifts of music and light.... Not only the images but the very rhythms suggest acceptance, even delight. Her words flow like galvanized honey. Two of the poems in this collection, **"Crazy Times"** and **"Prairie"** ..., use not a single word of more than two syllables. If you think that's easy, try it!

Most of her work is written in long meandering sentences—a delta of words, giving her images and thoughts enough time to develop through time. Waddington has never been a poet of broken, isolated fragments of ideas. In some of her poems a sweet sense of narrative underlies the lyric form, keeping us in touch with an oral, story-telling tradition. When you scan the lines with your eyes, and neglect to listen for the sound of her words, you miss at least half the effect. She is essentially a poet who connects. Canada with the Eastern Europe of her Jewish forebears, the Prairies with Toronto and Montreal, our lives with other generations, and our language with the speech of the dead.

This suggests one reason why her longer-than-usual poem **"Real Estate"** comes as such a surprise: for here the connections are snapped, and the twining familiar voice is broken constantly by brutal injunctions from another mouth: WE COULDN'T CARE LESS, SO LET THEM EAT GRASS, HURRY UP TIME IS MONEY, and so on. To this second voice everything is material, and everything is profane. Waddington's own vision takes things from this world (late flowers, lost languages, even the hard-working earthworms) and makes them into a sacrament. Her poems teem with things that are somehow ordinary, sacred, doomed, and eternal.... The words sing, the world gleams. The danger is easy lushness, a vice to which she occasionally, but only occasionally, succumbs. (p. 21)

> Mark Abley, in a review of "The Visitants" (reprinted by permission of the author), in Books in Canada, Vol. 11, No. 2, February, 1982, pp. 21-2.

René Wellek
1903-

Austrian-born American critic and essayist.

Wellek's reputation as an important critic is based largely on the theories propounded in his two most significant works: *Theory of Literature,* with Austin Warren (1949) and *A History of Modern Criticism* (1955, 1966). At the center of Wellek's theories lies a differentiation between an "intrinsic" and an "extrinsic" approach to critical analysis. Wellek maintains the necessity of viewing a work of art as an entity in and of itself rather than as the result of properties extrinsic to the work, such as the social or cultural environment in which it is created. Wellek examines qualities intrinsic to the work, relying on qualitative judgments which are based on what he calls "an internal history of the art and tradition of literature," which in turn assumes an intrinsic structure of value or "literariness" of the text. These critical viewpoints, expounded most notably in *Theory of Literature,* have evoked heated controversy among Wellek's contemporaries, many of whom believe that a work of literature cannot be studied without examining the sociopolitical conditions under which it was written.

A History of Modern Criticism, an ambitious, four-volume set, traces the history of literary theory from the mid-eighteenth century through the middle of the twentieth century. In this work Wellek displays his erudition by recounting and evaluating the views of numerous international critics.

(See also *Contemporary Authors,* Vols. 5-8, rev. ed. and *Contemporary Authors New Revision Series,* Vol. 8.)

Courtesy of René Wellek

W. K. WIMSATT, JR.

["**Theory of Literature**"] discusses aims and methods in the expansive field of literary study. It observes and assesses both "extrinsic" and "intrinsic" avenues of approach to literature, the ways of getting at a poem, novel, or play for its own sake or for something else.

The peculiar success of the book lies in a harmony of powers often mutually restrictive: clear theoretical vision and diverse learning. There is a sense in which **"Theory of Literature"** may be said to recapitulate an era of revolutionary scholarship and criticism, but it is a sense which may easily be overstressed, for if properly used the book should be less a chronicle than a charter. The authors make the justifiable claim that it "lacks any close parallel." Certainly none in English comes to mind. (p. 180)

Obviously [Wellek and Warren's] book transcends the immediate needs of that perhaps mythical person, the "ordinary reader" of serious literature. The authors address themselves to theory of literature as a form of knowledge the worth of which is not to be reckoned by its simplicity or its easy applications. The no doubt difficult inquiries of literary philosophy, the whole undertaking asserts, are desirable and admirable in themselves. The ultimate bearing of these inquiries on the ordinary reader—or at least their ideal and possible bearing—will scarcely be questioned by anybody who believes that reading is an intellectual activity rather than an aid to day-dreaming.

Wellek and Warren are able to see literature from any number of angles and yet realize that if the term "literature" has any meaning, there must be one angle which is definitive of what we mean by the term and which is hence in a very real sense the proper angle of approach for literary students. We may read literature for a number of purposes, but we ought to know in what department of studies a given reading falls, and whether there is any way of distinguishing literature from the Newgate Calendar or of deciding under what circumstances we ought to make the distinction.

It is difficult to lay adequate stress upon the authors' range of learning or upon their steeltrap faculties of defining and categorizing. The book seems destined to be widely used as a reasoned encyclopedia of literary and scholarly method. It will supply for the speculative student of general critical problems something like the orientation and checks which have heretofore been far less available for him than for the purely historical inquirer. Here we find our favorite theories of mimesis or of escape, our perceptions of verbal orchestration, our entrenched fallacies of method, neatly set forth under their correct names and key phrases and placed accurately among the serried ranks of their approximates and alternatives. (p. 181)

The criterion of literary excellence made more or less explicit throughout the book and at length developed in the chapter on evaluation is that of complexity and coherence—a criterion which if not always easy to manage appears at least to be the unavoidable implication of any effort at critical analysis. The chief embarrassment to this criterion may lie, not in its thinness, as those who use the term "formalist" pejoratively seem to believe, but in the apparently rival claims of what has traditionally been called "simplicity" in poetry—Wordsworth and the Psalms. The same chapter affirms the unity of exegesis and evaluation, though at earlier stages of the book there has been a certain, no doubt practical and inevitable, willingness "to postpone the problem of evaluative criticism." The related problems of evaluation and of complex coherence (Does not coherence in a system of verbal signs always reflect some external relation of correspondence?) are central literary problems to which **"Theory of Literature"** may not offer a triumphant solution but which at least it places in a very special focus. (p. 182)

> W. K. Wimsatt, Jr., "A Charter for Literary Studies," in The Yale Review (copyright 1949 by Yale University; reprinted by permission of the editors), Vol. XXXIX, No. 1, September, 1949, pp. 180-82.

ELISEO VIVAS

[*Theory of Literature* contains a discussion of the quarrel between scholarship and criticism which] leaves nothing to be desired; it makes clear the way in which each is relatively autonomous and yet dependent on the other. On the conflict between the "extrinsic" and the "intrinsic" interests in literature it throws a good deal of light. The upshot cannot be an irrefragable solution of these problems, for each of them would require a book to explore with adequacy; but it is a well balanced statement of the points at issue. If the book had no other virtues its authors could justly claim to have made an important contribution. But it does more: the book is equipped with a very extensive bibliography which represents the catholic erudition of the writers. And above all, the learning displayed is controlled by a discriminating taste.

Given these virtues, why does the book fail to sustain upon study the excellent impression that it makes on first reading? The reason is, I suggest, that the authors do not really have a fully worked out and consistent aesthetic of their own. Just as the critic needs a consistent "theory of literature" if his work is to stand up under scrutiny, so do the proponents of a "theory of literature" need a controlling aesthetic. It does not seem unfair to ask that theorists be theoretical. I do not mean that they ought to have made their aesthetic explicit any more than the critic or scholar needs to make his theory of literature explicit every time that he practices his art. It could have functioned as a set of deeply implicit, perhaps even instinctive presuppositions, controlling their speculation unconsciously. All I mean is that somehow they ought to have avoided mutually incompatible assumptions and ought to have based their speculations on defensible and coherent foundations. Unfortunately limitations of space do not allow me to do more than present a rough sketch of a few of the important points at which the absence of a coherent aesthetic betrays them.

The authors' conceptions of the nature and function of literature seem to me intrinsically bewildering although I am in sympathy with the purpose that controls them and with the conclusions that they reach. The nature of literature—or "poetry" in its widest sense—is defined in terms of the poetic use of language, as distinguished from the scientific and the every-day use. And the function or use of poetry is defined in terms of its nature. This would cause no genuine difficulty if the authors had shown that poetic language involves the employment of certain devices or elements which are not found either in ordinary or in scientific language. In Chapter II, entitled **"The Nature of Literature,"** expression, exploitation of medium, lack of practical purpose and fictionality are said to mark the distinction between poetry and non-poetry. Part IV, entitled **"The Intrinsic Study of Literature"** studies euphony, rhythm and meter in one chapter, image, metaphor, symbol and myth in another, and the genres of literature in a third. Now I do not doubt that these analyses constitute valuable efforts to approach the nature of poetry. But it is not sufficient to point out that we find these elements or devices in poetry. Since they are to some extent also found in practical language, in rhetoric and in the inexact sciences, it is necessary to show also that they function in poetry in a unique way, or the distinction breaks down. . . . What is needed in addition to what we are given is a study of the way in which the elements discriminated interpenetrate to endow the object with the organic integration and the artistic intensity that, according to the authors, give the poem its intrinsic poetic value.

Lack of fundamental coherence also vitiates the important distinction which the authors correctly draw between "the intrinsic study of literature" and "the extrinsic approach." . . . The authors do not deny in advance the legitimacy of the extrinsic claims, but examine them each fairly on its own merits. However, the distinction between the intrinsic and extrinsic approaches probably involves the most important, the most controversial, and the most difficult problem of contemporary aesthetics, and therefore one can demand of the writers that at least they indicate where a detailed elucidation of its solution can be found. How do the authors meet the arguments of the "extrinsicalist"—as I beg leave to call him? For what the latter claims is that literature, since it uses language, must point beyond itself. The Aristotelian says that it involves "an object of imitation," and the contemporary aesthetician prefers to say that it "expresses" something. A bitter controversy rages as to whether it expresses emotion, or the neuroses of the writer or of his age, or the social values and attitudes of his class, or more or less persistent "ideas" or, of course, a number of these in combination. But if literature expresses something not itself, to insist that "its prime and chief function is fidelity to its own nature" is to say something which seems to be either banal or false and morally noxious. It seems banal if what it prescribes is that the reader ought to attend to what literature imitates or expresses—for that is precisely what the "extrinsicalist" insists on. Or it is false, or at least confusing, if it implies without qualification that poetry has an "autotelic" function, since, as we have seen, the referential function of language gives us grounds to argue that the nature of poetry is to imitate or to express something not itself. And to make such a statement seems also morally wrong since it constitutes an invitation to turn attention from the valuable content of poetry to "mere" form. This is indeed what the authors appear to be saying when they conclude a chapter with this sentence: "poetry of ideas is like other poetry, not to be judged by the value of the material but by its degree of integration and aesthetic intensity." And the source of the difficulty is that the writers have not clearly worked out, at the theoretical level, how it is possible for a poem both to embody values and ideas of any kind whatever and yet, *at the same time,* to function as a non-referential aesthetic object. For it either does both or the authors are gored by one of the two horns of the dilemma—intrinsicalism which is "merely" formalistic or extrinsicalism which is non-aesthetic. The problem is not insoluble, since it can be shown that an object in an aesthetic transaction both embodies content while it functions "intransitively" and yet, outside of the experience, becomes retrospectively fully operative in practical life. But to arrive at some such solution the discussion would have to be controlled by a coherent conception of the aesthetic transaction as both distinct from other modes of human experience and yet interrelated with it.

Study of the book will also reveal that the claim made by Wellek and Warren that they are not eclectic cannot be sustained. They are opposed to any kind of subjectivism, since it denies that the values discovered by criticism, and which presumably are at least part of the intrinsic values whose possession is the end of literary study, are "really or potentially present in the art object—not 'read into it' or associatively attached to it, but with the advantage of a special incentive to insight, seen in it." I believe that a lesser claim would turn all effort to correct taste into mere arbitrary substitution of one irrational response for another. Yet when we ask why the authors believe in objectivity we find ourselves embarrassed by two mutually incompatible answers. We are told that a work of literature is "a structure of norms which is perhaps never realized in the actual experience of its many readers." For a justification of this doctrine we are sent to an article by the Polish philosopher Ingarden, who arrives at his solution by using the methods of Husserl's "Phenomenology." Nothing more can legitimately be asked of the authors, although the reference to Ingarden is a bit esoteric for our public. But in the chapter on "Evaluation" the phenomenological mode of existence of a work of art is forgotten and the objectivity of value is defended in terms of "objective relativism," or of "perspective realism." Leaving aside the fact that these terms refer to mutually exclusive epistemologies it can be shown that neither position saves the judgment of value from subjectivism. This is not difficult to see by turning critically to the article, "The Aesthetic Judgment," to which the authors refer favorably as backing their position. But even if this were not the case, in neither of these two formulations is the position in respect to method, assumptions and implications, at all compatible with Husserl's phenomenological method.

I do not believe that these defects (and others which could be mentioned were there space) rob the book of its immediate practical utility. We have nothing like it in English that I know of, and it points the way to what can be done and what is urgently needed. But it will not be done until the writer or writers rear their structure on a solid foundation. (pp. 162-65)

Eliseo Vivas, "Theorists without Theory," in The Kenyon Review *(copyright 1950 by Kenyon College), Vol. XII, No. 1, Winter, 1950, pp. 161-65.*

MARK SCHORER

In these first two volumes of his projected four-volume history ["**A History of Modern Criticism: 1750-1950**"], René Wellek, Professor of Comparative Literature at Yale, has undertaken an enormous project for which every literary student has long felt the need but which no other has had the courage to attempt.

The only work of comparable range on this subject is George Saintsbury's three-volume "History of Criticism and Literary Taste in Europe," and the limitations of that book have, after fifty years, rendered it nearly useless. It is a work that criticism, scholarship and literary education could hardly have done without, but it is no longer so much a history of criticism as it is a part of the history of criticism.

In the fifty years since Saintsbury's work an enormous amount of European and American scholarship has gone into the exploration of the details of this whole large subject. What has been needed is a man with the linguistic skill, intellectual scope, scholarly discipline and independence of mind necessary to bring all this material together, to correct it where he should and use it when he could, and then to frame it all within his method, his interpretation and the "international perspective." Even in an age of great scholars such a man is not commonly come by. . . .

The intellectual challenge is not only to a thorough knowledge of world literature but to that of history, esthetics and philosophy; more pressingly, to an ability to see all this material as a whole, to hold in the mind the full picture, in which every detail falls into its relationship with all the other details that comprise the whole. The scholarly discipline reveals itself not only in the mastery of "the history of ideas." It reveals itself also in the skill with which the method is modulated in order to take account of the independent character of particular critics, and in the ease with which "causality" is eschewed ("All causal explanation leads to an infinite regress, back to the origins of the world"). Knowledge, method, independence and the benefit of the "international perspective"—all work together to give us a book that will serve as standard reference to the whole subject or to the work of any individual within it for many decades to come.

Mark Schorer, "Roots of the Modern Literary Critic," in The New York Times Book Review *(copyright © 1955 by The New York Times Company; reprinted by permission), July 10, 1955, p. 6.*

DAVID DAICHES

The first two volumes of René Wellek's projected four-volume "**History of Modern Criticism**" carries the story from the later eighteenth century through the Romantic Age. By "modern" Mr. Wellek means criticism which is close enough to us still to have some relevance to our present way (or ways) of looking at literature. (p. 24)

I can think of no one better qualified than Mr. Wellek for the task of writing the history of modern European criticism. In the first place, he knows the languages and the literatures at first hand, and he is at home in the whole European literary scene in a way that few contemporary English or American scholars can claim to be. Whether he quotes from Wackenroder, Chateaubriand, or Manzoni, we know he has read them in their original languages, and is not dependent on summaries in works of reference. Secondly, he has devoted many years to research and reflection both on the most fruitful ways of discussing and exploring a work of literary art (the record of this is in **"Theory of Literature"** . . .) and on the development throughout the centuries of a critical and methodological apparatus adequate for the writing of literary history (recorded in his **"Rise of English Literary History"**).

Perhaps, indeed, Mr. Wellek is too well qualified. He has lived for years in a world of critical theory; he has crossed swords with other critics and scholars in debating such questions as: "Was there really a Romantic movement?"; he has scratched his head over the question of the mode of existence of a work of literary art; he has observed, recorded, classified, corrected, blessed, and at the same time participated in that enormous mass of modern critical discussion which has not only given us the so-called "New Criticism" but has made ours the critical age *par excellence,* unprecedented for the abundance, complexity, subtlety, and professional specialization of its literary criticism. He is by temperament a theorist, and patently enjoys discussing and recording the theories of others.

Mr. Wellek is thus committed to modern criticism, to the view of literature elaborated in **"Theory of Literature."** And this means that his new history is written from the point of view of a benevolent (but sometimes, in spite of himself, irascible) observer on the summit, watching the struggles of climbers below as they endeavor to climb upwards.... [Those who] laudably move upwards but are prevented by fatigue from reaching the summit ... are praised for moving in the right direction and indicating the true path to those behind.

There are advantages in this. George Saintsbury, whose monumental "History of Criticism" is the only rival to the present work, and will certainly, as far as the period from 1750 goes, be superseded by it, had to guide him only a post-romantic impressionism and a general sense that liberation from neo-classic rules and the development of a critical relativism was a Good Thing; as a result, he found it impossible to keep his history from degenerating into a series of extended notes, some of them based on hasty and careless reading of the sources. Mr. Wellek knows better than that. Whenever one of the critics he is discussing shows signs of extending the meaning of poetry into some vague, all-inclusive amalgam of art and life, philosophy and religion, he is sternly reproved.... This is the history of criticism written from a clearly defined standpoint: the author is continually assessing the degree to which a particular critic contributed to our mature modern view of literature, and he gives praise or blame according to whether his man points forward to or leads away from—shall we say Wellek and Warren?

Sometimes we feel that Wellek has not done a particular critic justice; that he is so concerned to relate him to the modern movement, either positively or negatively, or to place him in the context of "neo-classic" or "romantic" thought, that he has not sufficiently considered what the critical position being discussed really amounts to. I cannot help feeling that he misunderstands Shelley's "Defense of Poetry" quite radically, because he is looking at it in a wrong context, and that he misses the significance of Wordsworth's having shifted critical attention from the relation of the work of art to the nature which it professes to imitate to the relation between the work of art and the state of mind of the artist who begets it. (pp. 24-5)

One may make minor reservations, but there can be no doubt of the importance of this work. The combination of scholarly and critical apparatus is formidable. There is no other history of criticism like it, none which combines its scope with its sense of contemporary relevance. The next two volumes (which we are told are in active preparation) should be even more useful and interesting. We await them with eagerness. (p. 25)

> David Daiches, "A Century of Critical Thought," in The Saturday Review, New York (© 1955 Saturday Review Magazine Co.; reprinted by permission), Vol. XXXVIII, No. 29, July 16, 1955, pp. 24-5.

SVEN ERIC MOLIN

Professor René Wellek's *A History of Modern Criticism: 1750-1950* ... stands fair to become an important history of criticism, replacing its now half-century old predecessor by George Saintsbury which has long been felt to be inadequate on a number of grounds, including its excessive impressionism and its undue neglect of Continental critics. Both of these faults Professor Wellek abundantly corrects by his own practice, which is true to its announced intention of being written from a consistent point of view and which, if it errs, does so, perhaps, in the opposite direction by giving almost total credit for originality to the Continental—particularly German—critics. In addition to Professor Wellek's great range ..., he also exhibits an admirable knowledge and apportionment of minor critics and an awesome thoroughness with the major critics. Whatever equipment one would expect an historian of criticism to bring to his task, Professor Wellek has brought. (p. 156)

There would seem to be at least two directions in which one is led by reading a particular literary critic. When we ask what kind of job a particular critical theory enables us to do in understanding and evaluating diverse works of literature, we are led directly from that theory to those diverse works. We are led by Coleridge to Shakespeare and Wordsworth, by Dr. Johnson to Shakespeare, Milton, Pope, Thomson, *et al.* This, one would expect, is as it should be, for, in the first place ..., a literary theory is related, however indirectly or obliquely, to literary practice; and in the second, the *point* of criticism is the understanding and evaluation of diverse works.

But this direction is exactly one that Professor Wellek is explicit in rejecting. Early in his Introduction he sets as his aim the middle ground between "a history of abstract aesthetics and [a history] of concrete taste," ... and in his first chapter he spells out in detail the limitations he has imposed to achieve this aim. The first limitation is a dissociation of literary criticism ("a topic which has its own inherent interest") from literary practice.... Another acknowledged limitation is an avoidance of "the casual explanation of the changes we shall describe," ... and still another, the removal of literary criticism from a direct relationship "with particular social or historical changes." ... (p. 157)

The limitations which Professor Wellek accepts, in short, are those he had to accept to write his "internal history" with "its own inherent interest," and the direction in which he leads us is from critic to critic, and not from critic to poetry. What he does is to do—with different standards, emphases, and judgments—what Saintsbury did before him, namely, to pass from one critic to another critic and to another, until all have been put into place. Thus, while his undoubted superiority to Saintsbury lies in his breadth of coverage, and while his standards are more clearly revealed and hence more discussable than are Saintsbury's, his aims are essentially the same. His book is criticism *in vacuo,* a history of modern critical ideas discussed in their relationship to each other.

Professor Wellek's means of keeping these ideas in hand and of avoiding an undigested relativism is his own firmly developed point of view, a point of view I do not propose to dispute. The self-imposed limitations, however, are more questionable. For example, to admit the "new and difficult question" of the relationship between poetic theory and poetic practice, while admittedly new and difficult, perhaps may be not to confuse the "internal history of criticism," but rather necessary to define that history in the first place. I am not suggesting that Professor Wellek should have written a history of concrete taste (similar in ways, perhaps, to Saintsbury's histories of literature), for to do this would be only to continue the dichotomy, but that a history of concrete taste is not a true alternative to his own historical practice. In examining a critic (whether to "place" him historically or to glean from him his contributions to modern theory), one cannot avoid examining the critic's own examples. No matter how great the difference may seem to be between a contemporary theory and practice, it is by a critic's own examples that we define his critical terms from context. We define Dr. Johnson's famous *discordia concors,* for example, not only by his statements, but by the particular lines he wants us to see as discordant. Coleridge's argument with Wordsworth and Wordsworth's problems with himself are both defined in Wordsworth's specific practice. We know these critics by their understanding and evaluation of diverse works of literature.

What happens when one considers criticism *in vacuo,* moving from critic to critic instead of from criticism to poetry, can be seen in Professor Wellek's chapter on Dr. Johnson. It is by looking at Johnson merely as one in a long line of literary critics, as related only to his predecessors, and successors, that Professor Wellek is able to make his "sensational" opening charge against Johnson: "he is . . . one of the first great critics who has almost ceased to understand the nature of art, and who, in central passages, treats art as life." Professor Wellek later in his chapter seems to give Johnson more credit. He labels several tendencies of Johnson's criticism as realism, moralism, and abstractionism, and he states:

> Dr. Johnson's criticism . . . is not defeated by the conflicting theories of realism, moralism, and what is here called abstractionism. The three strands were no doubt reconcilable in his own mind . . . The three motifs here analyzed are kept in balance and stressed according to context, alternating by turns, apparently without a clear consciousness that these criteria lead to very different conclusions about the nature of art and the value of particular works of art.

The fact that Johnson worked "apparently without a clear consciousness that these criteria lead to very different conclusions about the nature of art," and that Johnson's conception of metaphor seems to us in some ways an incomprehension is not what one concludes about Johnson, but where one begins. It is just what makes Johnson a critic worth studying. (pp. 157-59)

The danger of Professor Wellek's approach can be stated in other terms. To delimit his subject, he has sharply restricted the "history" of which he will talk, and he has omitted the object of criticism, namely, literature. The dialectical chain-reaction has its effects on the third term of his entity, criticism. If we can laud him for the breadth of his knowledge and for his emphatic attack on the existing provincialism of modern English-language criticism, we must nevertheless say that criticism *in vacuo* ignores some of the most pressing problems of criticism itself: for example, its place in society—which is to say, the language that critics can validly use to understand and evaluate diverse works of art. What we are left with is Professor Wellek's own point of view, honestly labelled *a* history. But, to reapply words he uses in his preface, the history he writes is one that illuminates and interprets our present situation in rather oblique ways. It is a history that is not "comprehensible *only* in the light of a modern literary theory." (pp. 159-60)

> Sven Eric Molin, "Criticism in Vacuo," in The Kansas City Review *(copyright University of Kansas City, 1957), Vol. XXIV, No. 2, December, 1957, pp. 156-60 [revised by the author for this publication].*

LAURENCE LERNER

Professor Wellek is perhaps the most learned man now writing on literature—he has read, it seems, all European literature (in the original languages) and all the criticism on it—and it is humiliating to read his [*Concepts of Criticism*]. You may have thought, for instance, that you knew what 'baroque' meant—but you didn't. After you've read his essay **'The Concept of Baroque in Literary Scholarship'** you will know about the history of the term (it appears there are two separate etymologies: *baroco,* a type of syllogism in scholastic logic, as well as the better known suggestion of *barroco,* an odd-shaped pearl); the sense in which every important critic has used it; and the arguments for and against each definition. Stylistic definitions will not do: if they merely mention the use of conceits they cover too wide a field, and Sydney, Shakespeare, even Montaigne become baroque writers; but if they limit the concept to certain kinds of 'metaphysical' conceit they become too narrow, and Marino ceases to be baroque. Ideological definitions will not do either, since they have to be so general that they lead us away from the baroque poets and even from the seventeenth century. Professor Wellek argues for a concept that will correlate the two, and though he is forced to recognise two forms of baroque (the intimate and the public), he insists that the term is worth preserving against these nominalists who are sceptical of period terms in literary history.

When we have got over our first awe, we demand that the scholar, descending from his mountain tops, bring us back something that was worth the climb. Does Professor Wellek? There is nothing else as good as the baroque article: two similar and equally learned pieces treat the concepts of 'romantic' and 'realist' (he is a great believer in period terms), but though they survey the ground as thoroughly, they are disappointing when they begin to sort out the clashing meanings. Professor Wellek's mind, we realise, is lucid and well-stocked, but not very exciting; he does not grab hold of ideas direct. As for the rest of the essays, most of them are simply surveys of modern criticism and critical terms, that read like encyclopædia articles.

> Laurence Lerner, "The Critical Heights," in The Spectator *(© 1963 by The Spectator; reprinted by permission of The Spectator), No. 7068, December 13, 1963, p. 799.*

MONROE K. SPEARS

[For] more than a quarter-century Mr. Wellek has been both teacher and intellectual physician for critics, theorists, and historians of literature. Most Americans who aspire to criticism have learned from him, and many of us feel that literary studies would be in a healthier condition if we had learned more. His role has been unique and indispensable. As critic of critics, he has striven not to propagate any dogma in terms of which other dogmas are to be judged, but rather to remind those who practice criticism that their vision of the truth is partial, their assumptions and methods not forever valid but limited and imperfect. Against all varieties of parochialism, patriotism, and dogmatic complacency, he has maintained the rigorous ideal of literary criticism, theory, and history as distinct yet indissoluble, and as part of a common culture, a potential European intellectual community. His principal aim has been, with this ideal in mind, not to accept some doctrines and reject others, but to reconcile and synthesize the various doctrines in the hope of arriving at a consensus, if not on answers to ultimate questions, at least on which approaches are likely to be most fruitful. Mr. Wellek not only upholds this ideal but, happily, exemplifies it: a genuine polymath, widely and deeply read not only in the literatures of a dozen languages, but in their philosophy and history, and most comprehensively of all, in their criticism and scholarship, he does not let his central concern for literary theory become exclusive, but practices and discusses equally the other two disciplines of literary history and criticism of specific works. He is academic in learning, poise, and rigor, but without the academic vices of dullness, superficiality, and pretentiousness; he has a shrewdness and common sense and scepticism that do not desert him in dealing with complex abstractions or seas of facts. (pp. 321-22)

[*Concepts of Criticism*], which has been edited by [Stephen G. Nichols, Jr.] as a tribute to Mr. Wellek on his 60th birthday, contains 14 essays, three of them new and the others published originally in widely scattered books and periodicals between 1946 and 1962. . . . The essays are very much worth preserving: some of them develop, with more detail and documentation, ideas presented briefly in *Theory of Literature* or other works; some expand and bring up to date Mr. Wellek's analyses of various controversial matters; and some break new ground. Since the essays are not revised, there is a good deal of repetition in the book; but most of it seems justified because the same issues are seen in different perspectives in different essays. This varied context also explains many points that Mr. Wellek's earlier treatments may have left in some obscurity: for example, the Russian formalists and the Linguistic Circle of Prague who keep turning up in *Theory of Literature* like King Charles's head, to the incredulous bafflement of most American students. In the present volume these exotic references are seen to be justified on the ground that Mr. Wellek was himself a member of the Prague circle for many years and thus speaks from first-hand knowledge, and, more importantly, that the references are a part of Mr. Wellek's demonstration that the "New Criticism" is not provincial or eccentric but is part of a worldwide movement.

The heart of the book is the three famous essays on the concepts of Baroque, Romanticism, and Realism; the first two of these, which first appeared in the late 1940's, are now brought up to date by extensive postscripts. Protesting against the extreme nominalism and pragmatism of many scholars, Wellek defends the use of such "period terms," though he wishes to re-examine and define them most scrupulously. His position is remote from a naive traditionalism or a Teutonic worship of abstractions; in command of the facts he is easily a match for the "tough-minded" scholars who would abolish the terms, while in philosophical awareness and dexterity he is clearly their superior. To simplify drastically, his basic contention is that we cannot talk meaningfully about literature in its historical or theoretical aspects without using such concepts, because, whatever the difficulties of definition, they do point to distinctive and massive phenomena. To despair before the complexity of the task and simply abandon the terms is, he suggests, an evasion of responsibility. (pp. 322-23)

There are also several very penetrating surveys of recent trends in criticism, American and European, with the kind of wide-ranging synoptic view that only Wellek can give. One of these, "Philosophy and Postwar American Criticism," is specially noteworthy as an example of the kind of thing Wellek, with his philosophical training and aptitude, is uniquely qualified to do. . . . [His] principal effort is, as we have seen, toward synthesis and reconciliation. This approach is rare, since most critics whose range of learning is comparable to Wellek's use

it to buttress a doctrine of their own; and it is immensely useful. Wellek is keenly aware of the larger world outside the literary one, of the relation of literature to philosophy and other modes of discourse, and to the other arts, and of the relation of literary study to other disciplines, both in and outside the academy. By precept and example, he shows the importance of wide and deep learning, of philosophical and historical training and awareness, of rigorous definition of premises, aims, and methods. American literary students, misled by our British cousins, are all too prone to dismiss these as Teutonic requirements which do not apply to cultivated and artistic souls. But Wellek will not let us evade our responsibilities in any such fashion. There is an important sense in which the special virtue of his work may be called moral: he practices and teaches a discipline of humility among the prophets, aesthetes, and hanging judges who dominate the critical scene.

In this respect, as in most others, Wellek is at the opposite pole from Dr. F. R. Leavis. . . . (pp. 323-24)

[Where] Leavis offers a temptation to pride, Wellek gives the critic a lesson in humility. One must choose among imperfect alternatives and be aware of the premises and consequences of the choice, Wellek says again and again; no approach is perfect and no reader ideal, and therefore the critic must strive to be conscious of his assumptions and motives and methods, must seek philosophical and historical perspective. Leavis, on the other hand, would separate literary theory and history from criticism and would deny them any real significance; obviously he thinks the critical approach is the *only* way to deal with literature: the ideal reader is the critic, and vice versa, and it is dangerous for the critic to know too much of theory or history. Wellek, in contrast, insists that all three approaches are indispensable, and that they are distinct but inseparable. His ideal is a collaborative one, and sometimes he seems to hope for more disinterested collaboration than is ever likely to take place; but the ideal is as healthy morally as it is rigorous intellectually. His influence on critics and scholars has been wholesome, clarifying, and inspiring; long may it flourish and increase! (pp. 325-26)

> Monroe K. Spears, "Doctor for Critics," in The Sewanee Review *(reprinted by permission of the editor;* © *1964 by The University of the South), Vol. LXXII, No. 2, Spring, 1964, pp. 321-26.*

WOLFGANG BERNARD FLEISCHMANN

[*Confrontations: Studies in the Intellectual and Literary Relations between Germany, England, and the United States during the Nineteenth Century,* a] miscellany from the study of a very great scholar, has all the virtues which collections of a similar nature tend often to lack: a lucid and readable style artfully concealing mountainous learning, consistent evidence of original thought, and, in spite of being a collection of essays and reviews written over a thirty-five year period, real organic unity.

Reading *Confrontations* means encountering René Wellek as a literary historian at important focal points mid-way between his work in the history of ideas, as exemplified by *Immanuel Kant in England 1793-1838*, and his monumental *History of Modern Criticism,* the mid-way focus being visualized as intellectual rather than chronological transition. For it is in essays like **"Carlyle and German Romanticism (1929)," "Emerson and German Philosophy (1943),"** and **"De Quincey's Status in the History of Ideas (1944)"** that Wellek deals critically with individual writers and with their texts, a welcome extension of intellectual history *per se* and a necessary foreshadowing of any knowledgeable history of literary criticism. The masterful **"German and English Romanticism: A Confrontation (1963)"** presents the sort of synthetic statement along paradoxical lines which can illuminate a historical account but cannot, because of the demands for definitive rhetoric in historiography, be part of it. The thesis of this essay, that "a common core of Romantic thought and art throughout Europe . . ." is offset, for the cases of German and English Romanticism, both by a wide generic and formal differentiation among literary phenomena and by a singular lack of dialogue among writers in the two countries looks back to the discussions of individual Romanticists published in *Confrontations* and forward to the account of Romantic writers as literary critics in Wellek's *History of Modern Criticism*. More than this, the lead essay on German and English Romanticism furnishes insight into an intellectual attitude which binds *Confrontations* together: In example after example throughout the book, René Wellek demonstrates that membership in a historically authenticated "species" of Romantic authors does not by any means imply, from writer to writer, similarity in individual casts of mind, in preferred modes of literary expression, or in political and theological stance. Thus Carlyle and De Quincey, as they deal with Kant, are shown to do this in very different ways: Carlyle, in a scholarly manner inhibited somewhat by Calvinistic Christianity; De Quincey, in an erratic and highly subjective way. (pp. 398-99)

Indeed it may paradoxically be said that the scholarly tenor of *Confrontations* is at its strongest when René Wellek demonstrates a lack of confrontation between a given writer and a set of works and ideas. For it is in these non-confrontations, and in the reasons shown for these, that certain clear individual traits of authors manifest themselves. . . .

[It is] perhaps not altogether surprising that some minor theses stated in *Confrontations* which this reviewer considers open to debate may be found either where a lack of confrontation is asserted too dogmatically or where acknowledged lines of intellectual encounter are too narrowly and exclusively drawn. Shelley may, as René Wellek points out . . . , have been differentiated from music-loving German Romantic poets through musical insensitivity; still, Shelley's *Defense of Poetry* includes music explicitly as one "expression of the imagination" akin to poetry. . . . This is not to question Professor Wellek's demonstration . . . that the *Defense* could hardly have been representative of German influence on Shelley, but to wonder whether a lack of sympathy for music should be invoked as a specific point of differentiation between Shelley and the German Romantics. (p. 399)

Yet [this is only an example of] minor questions addressed to a major book. *Confrontations* will long serve as an example of how a retrospective collection of essays ought to be organized so as to give readers a chance not only to get acquainted with a scholar's work but to become aware of his intellectual dimensions. (p. 400)

>Wolfgang Bernard Fleischmann, in a review of "Confrontations: Studies in the Intellectual and Literary Relations between Germany, England, and the United States during the Nineteenth Century," in The Modern Language Journal, Vol. XLIX, No. 6, October, 1965, pp. 398-400.

ROBIE MACAULEY

Is [**"A History of Modern Criticism"**] possible? Can even such a brave and erudite man as René Wellek put the vast and heterogeneous writings of modern literary criticism from 1750 to 1950 in an orderly historical form? Certain critics, for instance, belong more to the history of esthetics than anything else; others border on sociology, psychology, politics, or general cultural observation; and—most baffling of all—literary theory seems to coincide seldom with the kind of literature actually being written in its own time.

It is even difficult to find very many critics who will agree on what criticism is or what purpose it is supposed to serve. . . .

Whatever the critics have lacked in common purpose, however, they have made up in industriousness and numbers. Mr. Wellek's four volumes thus far published (**"Volume 1: The Later Eighteenth Century,"** and **"Volume 2: The Romantic Age"** appeared in 1955) take cognizance of over 500 books in five languages by some 93 critics—plus attention to a good many essays and numerous lesser critics. (p. 6)

Therefore it was a remarkable accomplishment on Wellek's part to find a procedure flexible enough to account for all the variety of criticism and yet coherent enough to bind it together in a work of historiography. He decided to treat the subject, in its widest scope, as a branch of the history of ideas yet giving a generous account of the individuality of each author. At the same time he avoided the fallacy of thinking that criticism and literature are very closely synchronized—"a loose relationship," he calls it, "which should not be confused with the internal history of criticism."

The broad movement of 19th-century critical thought was from idealism early in the century through realism or naturalism to symbolism at the close (though, of course, not in any sort of strictly chronological development). Wellek . . . has a fine capacity for relating individual critics to the general configuration of ideas and idea-themes. On the other hand, he is equally good at close range, when he tries to show the critic actually engaging with specific works of literature.

He takes each critic, one by one, and proceeds to give a succinct account and appraisal of all his significant work. These accounts, in many cases masterpieces of compression and essence, are almost invariably both shrewd and generous. Criticism, like any other large body of writing, has a great deal of repetition and a high nonsense-content, but Wellek tends to cut it short without exasperation. Only very rarely does he permit himself a little mild sarcasm—chiefly at the expense of some Americans. (pp. 6-7)

Perhaps one of the best effects of **"A History of Modern Criticism"** will be to give American readers a balanced view of a number of the great European critics who are little-known in this country or who have dropped out of favor. . . .

Nevertheless, no reputations are revived merely for the sake of revival, and no one is overrated. Wellek is always clear in distinguishing between the critics whose ideas remain more or less stalled in the fashions of their period . . . and the greater critics who have continued to contribute something to the eternal debate on literary art.

Another virtue of **"A History of Modern Criticism"** is that it gives due attention to a number of the poets and novelists who were only incidentally and unofficially literary critics. Flaubert—whose posthumously published correspondence contains most of his critical ideas—is probably the extreme example of an imaginative writer with an enormous influence on theory. (p. 7)

It is the very inclusion of these writers that raises again—for me, at least—the nagging question of criticism's relevance to actual contemporary practice. Wellek has deliberately limited it to a "sub-theme" of his book—and yet it is very difficult to subordinate, especially in trying to arrive at some valuation of the function of literary criticism as a whole. That "loose relationship" often seems entirely too loose. Is the critic really doing his whole job when he writes admirably about Milton or Dante and yet has nothing very intelligent to contribute to contemporary literary judgment?

"A History of Modern Criticism" shows that some critics could operate ably in their own milieux, but it also shows a great many examples of fallibility or stupidity. Matthew Arnold was harsh on "Madame Bovary" and thought "Anna Karenina" no work of art. Emerson thought Jane Austen, "vulgar in tone, sterile in artistic invention . . . without genius, wit, or knowledge of the world." Carlyle speaks of Keats as a "horrible" man with "a weak-eyed maudlin sensibility." Ruskin despised Dickens, Thackeray and George Eliot. Nietzsche considered Ibsen a moral poisoner. Saintsbury thinks we could well "have done without" Dostoevsky.

Contrast such obtuse contemporary judgments by official critics with the advancing, future-relevant ideas of Flaubert, Mallarmé or Baudelaire and we are faced with some striking questions. How much criticism has any dynamic relationship to written art? How much of it is merely scholarship flavored with opinion, pertinent only to its own game, "the internal history of criticism"? Is criticism too important—in relation to the living writer and his audience—to be left to the official critics?

The author says that, as a historian, it is not his job to discuss these matters and, in terms of the book, he is probably right. Still, they are questions that arise from its pages again and again. It seems to me that any complete history of literary criticism ought, eventually, to give an assessment of the whole subject's rationale. Criticism, by its nature, is an activity that operates only because art exists to set it in motion. Thus it is highly artificial to pretend—in the long run—that criticism has its own autonomous "internal history." Wellek, who is quite as capable a critic as he is a historian of critics, ought not to decline his final responsibility. Perhaps the final, forthcoming volume of this work, **"The Twentieth Century,"** will offer an opportunity to take up the subject of interaction between the critic and the world in which he lives—the world of the writer and the literary audience. (pp. 7, 27)

> Robie Macauley, "Never So Much from So Many for So Few," in The New York Times Book Review (copyright © 1966 by The New York Times Company; reprinted by permission), January 2, 1966, pp. 6-7, 27.

RONALD HAFTER

René Wellek's massive study [*A History of Modern Criticism*] has already gained wide acceptance as the best survey of its kind to be produced in our century; despite its narrow scope it is far superior to George Saintsbury's erudite but rambling *History of Criticism*, the only work by a single author with which it might be legitimately compared, in its incisive analysis of the grounds on which literary judgments have been made and in its dispassionate appraisals of individual critics and movements. But if it is an essential text for the student of literature it is no less so for one interested in the history of ideas, for Wellek discusses criticism within the wider context of the movement of ideas and social forces which have left their imprints on European and American culture. The formulation of concepts and judgments about literature, as he clearly sees, is premised upon a host of underlying assumptions which are not purely aesthetic but also psychological, philosophical, ideological, and social; and these in turn are conditioned by the period and nation in which the critic lives. Thus, Whitman conceived the duty of the American poet to be "to define his nation, give it 'moral identity', help to unify it after the ordeal of the Civil War." Dostoevsky's socio-political views also coloured his aesthetic vision; he "attacked Tolstoy openly . . . for his views on the Southern Slavs, voiced by Levin at the end of *Anna Karenina*." Such remarks may seem today exasperatingly simplistic and doctrinaire; we have grown accustomed to more formal, professedly disinterested technical analysis, but it is tonic to be reminded, even if in a relatively unsophisticated way, that part of the critic's function is judging, and a whole judgment always involves more than aesthetic criteria alone. The many original source quotations with which Wellek saturates the pages of his *History* continually keep us aware of this truth.

Wellek does more, however, than relate the critic to the concern of his time; he also focuses on the network of ideals and beliefs and attitudes which link together seemingly diverse figures. He writes: "The common denominator between Wordsworth and Tolstoy is their Rousseauism, their enmity toward urban civilization, their concern for the effect of literature on the masses of humanity, their hope for literature as an instrument of unification in a spirit of love." Despite the suspicious neatness of such comparisons, they do illuminate the connection between minds existing in vastly different worlds. This is as Wellek intends, for one of his cardinal although unstated tenets is that the history of criticism, like the history of any intellectual discipline, implies a sense of spatial and temporal continuity. The questions that men ask about literature—what is its relation to society? to objective truth? to the individual? what should literature *do*?—and the solutions they propose are recurrent ones, though necessarily restated for every culture. One of the things Wellek has attempted to do, and succeeded very well in doing, is to examine the ways in which a multitude of English, European, and American critics have consciously or unconsciously borrowed from or parallelled one another. His attention is always more closely fixed on the interdependence of critics, on the philosophic roots which they mutually share, than on that which sets one man off from his fellows. Any particular chapter devoted to an individual or a small cohesive group thus invariably involves a complex of other figures, schools, movements, so that in structure the chapter resembles a waggon wheel with spokes gravitating outwards from the hub and leading to a wider referential circumference. (pp. 400-01)

This is not one of those all too common modern exercises in inflated jargon which brightly gild over banalities and inchoate perceptions. Wellek's material is weighty, but his style is not. (p. 401)

There are occasional typographical errors. For example, perhaps in compensation for his neglect of the contemporary scene, Wellek offers a glance into the future: the date of Leslie Stephen's *Samuel Johnson* is given as 1978. Such minor flaws, however, detract very little from the significance of his achievement. Wellek has given us the most comprehensive and balanced account of the history of criticism in the modern age. (p. 403)

Ronald Hafter, in a review of "A History of Modern Criticism," in The Dalhousie Review, Vol. 46, No. 3, Autumn, 1966, pp. 400-01, 403.

ROGER SALE

In the last fifteen years, René Wellek has become established as the premier historian of modern literary criticism. Before this, though he always spoke mildly and judiciously, Wellek seemed to have an eager eye out for enemies of his favorite ideas: that criticism needs a coherent philosophical base from which to work, that impressionistic criticism and historical relativism are dangerous, and that extrinsic material is usually irrelevant in the understanding of a given work. But since he began work on his massive *A History of Modern Criticism,* the third and fourth volumes of which are now at hand, Wellek has slowly become convinced that he is really unopposed, and so he has ascended to a height from which he is able to view contemporary criticism as though it were ancient scroll work and still receive increased adulation rather than scorn as his reward. He calls Earl Wasserman's books "turgid," he speaks of M. H. Abrams's *The Mirror and the Lamp* as a "booklet," he blandly announces that the aims of Northrop Frye's "Polemical Introduction" to *Anatomy of Criticism* are "doomed to failure." It seems that heresy, even when it speaks the truth, can be received in the scholastic establishment with equanimity—when uttered from very high elevations.

Wellek has achieved this eminence almost exclusively by one method: knowing more than anyone else. Blessed with a prose style no one would describe as better than adequate, equipped with a literary sensibility that strikes few as being superior to their own, possessed of an intelligence that reveals no originality and seldom more than judiciousness, he has simply blown competitors from the field with erudition. He is conversant in at least seven modern languages and commands a staggering knowledge of their respective literatures. In the *History,* he quotes in English, provides the original in the notes, and does almost all his own translating. These notes also contain large bibliographies of their subjects while the text itself ranges over history and literature of the last two centuries without pausing for breath. In the sweeping reviews of modern scholarship now included in *Concepts of Criticism* he handles up to four major authors per page. If anyone can claim to have read everything literary and philosophical written since 1750, Wellek is the man. The *History* was originally announced in four volumes, but four have now appeared and the twentieth century is still untouched; maybe it can be finished in two more. It is a huge mine of a work, ranging almost as widely as anyone could wish yet spending much of its time scrutinizing the major figures. Beside it, Brooks's and Wimsatt's *Short History of Criticism* seems both narrow and narrow-minded, and many more specialized literary histories do not do as well as Wellek in surveying and examining the assumptions of a critic's work. A number of the individual treatments of separate authors are the most sensible these authors have yet received, at least in English. With all this, no one could possibly claim the *History* is a bad book. But it certainly is a very disappointing one. One finishes the fourth volume with the feeling that amidst the great concern to cover and do right by everything, Wellek has not asked the relevant questions about literature and criticism.

There is, first of all, the theoretical inflexibility. Wellek means this to be here, to be sure, but it hurts nonetheless. . . . Readers of the earlier volumes will remember that Wellek takes Dr. Johnson to task for "misunderstanding the nature of literature." We have all been here before: the genius of English literature and criticism is not congenial to a Continental philosopher like Wellek. Wellek thinks the words "coherent" and "consistent" are synonyms, and one need be no Arnoldian to see how much English criticism will be distorted under the weight of *that.* The critics in the generation after 1830 are Carlyle, De Quincey, Hunt, Mill, and Ruskin; only Hunt is well handled while the important ones, Mill and Ruskin, are wrestled into contorted positions and then pronounced inadequate. Mill's early and extravagant "What Is Poetry?", written shortly after the crisis, is laid out elaborately and then refuted. But the really interesting literary fact about Mill is his constant mediation between his Benthamite training and his love of Wordsworth, and this is passed over, presumably because it appears to best advantage in *Dissertations and Discussions,* "non-literary" essays that reveal on every page that Mill did not "misunderstand literature." The instance of Ruskin is worse, for Wellek knows Ruskin is a great writer, yet he is also sure he is "the most obsolete and remote of all the Victorian 'sages.'" Ruskin is a scattered and derivative theorist, something hardly worth showing again at this late date; yet Wellek can comment exasperatedly:

> Much of *Modern Painters* does not concern itself with works of art at all, but for long stretches discusses cloud formations, tree shapes, rock surfaces, etc. quite apart from pictures. . . .

As though that were the end of the matter, as though some of these descriptions were not magnificent and did not contain in them a striking "theory" of vision. Wellek can say Ruskin has "little use for Dickens" and ignore the wonderful note on *Hard Times* in *Unto This Last.* He can refer to Ruskin's famous assertion that the great scenes of nature are "all done for us, and intended for our perpetual pleasure," as "naïve," as though the passage came not from *Modern Painters* but perhaps from the *The World as Will and Idea.* Again and again Wellek distorts as he finds "positions" for his authors and attempts to hold them in some timeless solution, as he shakes his head at the refusal of the English to know what they were doing.

But the objection must be made more deeply. Wellek is opposed to treating his subjects biographically, and, given the limitations of space and the usual irrelevance of such biographical work, the choice is perhaps wise. But, beyond this, he seems not even to conceive of them as men that were or writers that are. That these critics ever struggled with the world, that the mind may grasp fitfully yet wonderfully, that understanding literature is a precious and difficult occupation, that readers may find these nineteenth-century monsters both exasperating and fascinating—one can look in vain through hundreds of pages without finding more than fitful recognition of these things. Wellek is a large-minded and sympathetic man, yet there is something fundamentally disrespectful about his habit—it amounts almost to an insistence—of never quoting a writer at length and then discussing the quotation, of almost never going through a piece of writing to locate not only its outlines but its motion and sense of motion, its characteristic twists and turns. Wellek, hunting for theoretical assumptions, quotes only words and phrases and sentences, and often these are gathered from different works written years apart. We are told each critic's preferences in literature, we learn what everyone thought of Goethe or Shakespeare, but seldom do we get a description of the constellation of this taste or the pressures and contradictions at work in a given writer that formed the taste. Quite a few are denigrated as impressionistic with only passing worry given to the question of the excellence or tastelessness of these impressions. (pp. 129-32)

Wellek does not look freshly because he places his authors rather than seeks them out. There is, more generally, a certain complacency in Wellek about his own taste. He says, for instance, that Courbet's paintings "appear to us conventional and mediocre"; that "nowadays" Keats, Shelley, and Coleridge "seem much greater poets than Byron"; that "it is hard to believe Stephen's criticism can be made to speak to our time"; that Robert Buchanan's attack on Rossetti has "arrogant moral pretentions." That these judgments seem extremely nearsighted is not quite as important as the way they show Wellek's refusal to find merit in anything flamboyantly vulgar or solemnly moral, which means, in effect, that Wellek is left with very little genuinely to admire in the nineteenth century.

This brings us to Wellek's whole idea of historical study, but before considering that, we should mention some smaller matters. First, the Continental writers tend to be better handled than the English and American, and the reason seems to be that they fall more often into the class of the fully theoretical, like Dilthey and DeSanctis, or the fully untheoretical, like Heine, Flaubert, and Anatole France. On both groups Wellek is excellent—on the first because he is very good at laying out a system, on the second (Heine, by the way, called Hugo's *Les Burgraves* "versified sauerkraut") because the absence of theory throws Wellek back on those native sensibilities he so seldom trusts otherwise. Even better, or at least more surprising, are the fine sections on Taine and Pater, with neither of whom Wellek agrees but both of whom he explains delicately and carefully. Finally, it should be added that throughout both volumes he is consistently good on the really minor writers who do not demand elaborate treatment; he can allow himself to say what he finds good about them without worrying about their shortcomings.

But the result *is* an encyclopedia, not a history. At one point Wellek describes Ludvig Uhland's idea of literary history: "Mere description of work according to genres, or explanation of the conditions and influences from which the works arose, or even critical appraisal, is not sufficient." Wellek seems to approve, but does not see he has in fact here described his own method. It is the result, almost certainly, of his need to discredit something he variously calls "historicism" and "historical relativism," which seems to mean anything from genuine historical insight such as that of François Brunetière to belle-lettristic sinking of writer and work into "period." Wellek can speak highly of Brunetière's idea that

> "At all times, in literature as in art, it is the past which presses with heaviest weight upon the present." What is to be established is the inner causality. In literature—after the influence of the individual—"the greatest operating force is that of works on works."

Yet he cannot see that his own volumes have almost no sense of "inner causality" or "the operating force" of "works on works." The nearest he comes to understanding is in a rather pathetic "Postscript" to the fourth volume. "Is it correct to say," he asks, "that we have written a history?" He then, really, gives it all away by showing what he thinks a history would be if it sought to be "beyond the chronological order of exposition." He says he has attended to external influence:

> The change from the idealistic Hegelian atmosphere of the early 19th century to the prevalence of empirical positivistic, or materialistic allegiances and terminologies is too obvious to be missed. The profound impact of science. . . .

That, for Wellek, is history: an endless flow of *isms* within and across boundaries of countries and disciplines: an eternal fountain of psychologism, organicism, historicism, conceptualism, intellectualism, comparativism; a profound aversion to treating human beings as the unit of historical description and analysis. Finally, for Wellek, history is either "the chronological order of exposition" or "a reflection of the social, political, philosophical or even literary-historical conditions of a time." That such a position is terribly impoverished, in fact and probably in theory, let one instance attempt to show. (pp. 133-34)

[One] needs an idea of history more responsive to relevance than is Wellek's; one has to see writers not just being "influenced" in some unreal thematic way, but also invented, as Shelley and Keats invented Wordsworth. What these younger men were doing with their master is what Eliot did with LaForgue and Donne, what James did with Hawthorne, George Eliot, and Turgenev. It is what Eliot meant by tradition, what Brunetière meant by history, what Wellek does not see and therefore cannot use to save his book from the reference shelf. (pp. 135-36)

> Roger Sale, "René Wellek" (originally published as "René Wellek's History," in The Hudson Review, Vol. XIX, No. 2, Summer, 1966), in his On Not Being Good Enough: Writings of a Working Critic (copyright © 1979 by Roger Sale; reprinted by permission of Oxford University Press, Inc.), Oxford University Press, New York, 1979, pp. 129-36.

DENIS DONOGHUE

The new volumes [of *A History of Modern Criticism 1750-1950,* Vol. III: *The Age of Transition* and Vol. IV: *The Later Nineteenth Century*] are even wider in scope than the old, annexing America and Russia as countries of the critical mind. There is the same evidence of erudition, intelligence, concern. There is also evidence of great structural power. The new volumes are organised according to nationality: criticism in France, Italy, England, America, Germany, Russia, and Denmark (Georg Brandes the Great Dane). (p. 80)

Mr. Wellek is the most patient of scholars, but he is often irritated, it seems, by the fumbling critics, their gaucherie, playing games without learning the rules. When he writes of De Quincey, he implies that Thomas would have been protected against his worst excesses by taking a few decent courses at Yale. The trouble is that Mr. Wellek is right: the major figures in *The Age of Transition* are a bunch of amateurs. If you insist that criticism be professional, academic, and intellectually coherent, the 20th century is your period, France and America are your fields. Mr. Wellek says that in the 19th century the greatest critics after Coleridge are Taine, Baudelaire, De Sanctis, Nietzsche, Dilthey, and James. But none of these can vie with Mr. Wimsatt: that is, if criticism means what it means to Mr. Wellek.

The problem is that critics are not willing to write criticism. Or criticism is always flying off to become something else: autobiography (Sainte-Beuve), history (Carlyle), psychology (De Sanctis), philosophy (Mill), morality (Ruskin), sociology (Taine), theology (Dallas), propaganda (Brandes), philosophy of history (Nietzsche). Critics will not learn their trade. The easy way out is to let each man go his own way. If the mind is good enough, the way is likely to be vivid. Mr. Wellek is not willing to concede this. In the new volumes he describes the emergence of certain concepts of criticism in the 19th century. These are often notes toward the definition of taste, realism, form, tradition, truth, culture, style, value, and imagination. But Mr. Wellek thinks many of these notes are off the point, the science too gay by half. So the reader of the *History* must allow for Mr. Wellek's idea of criticism, unless it is identical with his own. It is not Everyman's idea. (pp. 80-1)

[The] first point to make about 19th century critics is that many of them had no interest in arriving at a coherent theory of literature. Much of their criticism is "related pursuits." Mr. Wellek's book is really a history of theoretical criticism. If it finds the critics engaged in other activities, it disapproves and often scolds.... Mr. Wellek is so keen on criticism as a systematic body of knowledge that he is impatient with the amateur. The amateur is a drop-out. My own feeling is that most of the illuminating things in criticism have been said by fumbling poets, your truest amateurs. Mr. Wellek sometimes quotes an observation of this kind, but he does not rejoice in the impurity of a criticism which allows it. If an amateur says something good, it is merely beginner's luck. Much better to isolate your object, establish your subject matter. (pp. 81-2)

True, an activity is not justified by the brilliance of its malice, but a defence of criticism might well remark the plenitude of the error it accommodates. Mr. Wellek seems to say: get it right, or give it up. I would prefer to say: *etiam peccata*. In criticism many a *culpa* is *felix*. In the volumes at hand Mr. Wellek is a little hard, almost totalitarian, with his great fools. So he tends to overlook those occasions on which an amateur does something of real value. He does not mention Hallam's 1831 review of Tennyson, but it has been argued (and I agree with the arguers, Yeats and McLuhan) that it is a fundamental text in the elucidation of modern poetry. Even Henry James comes off poorly in Mr. Wellek's hands.... The rhetorical aim of the *History* is to make theory the cause and end of criticism, and to fend off other claimants, those related pursuits, literary history, practical criticism, history of ideas, rhetoric, and linguistics....

Indeed, [Mr. Wellek] implies that the title of his own *History of Modern Criticism* was forced upon him by Continental usage and that he accepts it most reluctantly. He should not have allowed himself to be intimidated. His book is, in fact, a *History of Literary Theory*, and it should be so called. (p. 82)

[There is] a special problem in Mr. Wellek's *History*. It goes somewhat like this. Criticism aspires to a theory of literature. The most erudite and accomplished theorists are our own modern critics, the professional men in the universities. Therefore it follows as night the day that Truth resides in them; hence in "us." Mr. Wellek spurns the ideal of a neutral History, and indeed he is right. But he implies that 19th-century criticism is interesting and important because it leads to 20th-century criticism, and only then; setting up our exhilarating problems. So the old critics who get high marks are those who anticipate the terms of 20th-century discussion.... Mr. Wellek also implies that with all our faults we have most of the answers. Or at least we know the real, permanent questions. We have found out the issues that are relevant; we know a blind alley when we see one....

I make these remarks because Mr. Wellek's *History* is now moving toward its last Volume with intimations of a corresponding climax. He is to engage the criticism of the present century. And even if all roads lead to New Haven or Toronto I hope he will find an honourable place for the quirky mavericks of criticism who have said true things without benefit of theory. It is difficult to write a fair History because it is impossible. The maverick refutes the herd.... But what I miss in Mr. Wellek's book is a care for the underground man, the man in solitary pursuit of true judgment. If this marginal figure is a critic rather than a theorist, and if he is not a full Professor, he is likely to be ignored. Mr. Wellek has a powerful mind, enormous learning, and an unequivocal voice. It is good to hear him defending Zola and De Sanctis, citing just cause. But he often speaks like the March of Time and occasionally like the Voice of Doom as he directs the weakest to the wall.

This is to ask (an inordinate request) that Mr. Wellek, who has already excelled other historians of literary theory, should now excel himself. (p. 84)

> Denis Donoghue, "The Gay Science," in Encounter (© 1967 by Encounter Ltd.), Vol. XXVIII, No. 6, June, 1967, pp. 80-2, 84.

J. D. O'HARA

"There is no exercise of the intellect which is not, in the final analysis, useless." The stoic, melancholy tone is that of Jorge Luis Borges, of course....

We live in a terminal ward; the air our minds breathe is sighed out by dying ideas. Ecology demands that they be sanitarily interred; piety prays that we revere them. In the history of ideas, especially literary ideas, no embalmer is more industrious than René Wellek. *Discriminations* is the latest in his collection of amber-tinted antiques: It includes essays on the terms *comparative literature, classicism,* and *symbolism,* and surveys of Kant's aesthetics, of English literary historiography, of genre theory, and of Dostoevsky criticism. Almost inevitably the approach is historical; Wellek goes as far back toward Genesis as possible and then tracks an idea doggedly through the ages....

An idea or term so tracked emerges into the present looking rather tattered and scarcely fit for further use, but with an air of fallen grandeur about it. Wellek praises Leo Spitzer because "he could focus on the learned key-words of our civilization and write word history within a general history of thought, combine lexicography with the history of ideas." The aim is Wellek's too, and the achievement. The result is a wake on a large scale, as after a massacre, but without whiskey or music.

In the words of Nabokov's poet John Shade . . . , Wellek is "a preterist: one who collects cold nests." The living birds have long left most of the nests in Wellek's display; the nests have become mere chapters—if not paragraphs or names—in the history of ideas; and the musing reader can invent no thought, no feeling, no cry of dismay that does not immediately take its place with the others, classified and labeled. "All is relative!" he cries, and the ancient holiday fear of relatives mounts the spine.

The title *Discriminations* is an awkward one for this collection. When Wellek attempts precision, he is shaky: "Style in this sense is identical with great art. It is a critical concept, a criterion of excellence." When he makes a discriminating judgment we wince: Dostoevsky, he tells us, is "a novelist, a supreme creator of a world of imagination, an artist with a deep insight into human conduct and the perennial condition of man." At his best Wellek is a collector—and yet human too, as he reveals in discussing Georg Lukács' *Aesthetik:* "I have counted the phrase 'Wiederspiegelung der Wirklichkeit' in the first volume; it appears 1,032 times. I was too lazy or bored to count it in Volume Two."

J. D. O'Hara, "Large-Scale Wake," in Book World—Chicago Tribune *(© 1970 Postrib Corp.; reprinted by permission of* Chicago Tribune *and* The Washington Post), *August 2, 1970, p. 7.*

EMERSON R. MARKS

Wellek's book [*Discriminations*] is admirably named. Here again, as so often before, his astonishing erudition is put to the service of discrimination, of elucidating terms and ideas and making needed distinctions, not as a lexicographical exercise but to the end of sounder literary history and theory than we have generally had. Given such an aim, much of Wellek's reasoning is necessarily in refutation of other theorists, whose views he is at pains to expose as partial or extreme, views usually involving one or another misconception of the literary work. Among such are the attempts of some comparatists to divorce history and criticism, or to set barriers between the study of past and contemporary literature. (p. 135)

To his earlier discussions of romanticism and the baroque Wellek now adds essays on the terms classicism and symbolism. He first sketches the history of their usage, a process enlightening in itself but in Wellek's procedure mainly preparatory to judging their fitness as historiographical tools. Neither "dead" nor neutral, terms for Wellek have consequences; they clarify or obfuscate. His concern with labeling and distinguishing literary periods manifests his career-long interest in literary history and, beyond that, his even profounder concern with order. Wellek's attack on disorder and indiscrimination in literary study is an old one which has long motivated his unremitting opposition to critical relativism, to theories confounding life and art (here in the guise of *Erlebnis*), and to various post-Kantian attempts to dissolve the esthetic category into the terms of psychologistic theory.

Wellek is alarmed, now more than ever, and with reason. "The whole enterprise of esthetics and art is being challenged today." It is in the context of this sense of crisis that we should read his masterly essay on Kant's esthetics, his tribute, discerning and generous, to Leo Spitzer, as well as his survey of **"Stylistics, Poetics, and Criticism,"** richly informed and sympathetic but containing, as its chief "discrimination," a protest against the reduction of the literary work to a mere verbal construct, a *Wortkunstwerk,* currently urged by those who would subsume the whole of literary study within the admittedly fruitful field of linguistics.

Wellek's topics are not easy ones, nor is he one to shun the risks of clarifying complex and elusive issues. . . . [He] distinguishes between symbolism and romanticism by broadly philosophic criteria. The Romantics are essentially Rousseauistic believers in nature and human perfectibility; the symbolists, from Baudelaire on, distrust inspiration, dislike nature, and, though generally atheistic, see man as "fallen." Yet the difficulties of such distinctions appear when he declares elsewhere that Baudelaire's esthetics is mainly romantic, celebrating the creative imagination, and thus "incompatible" with Mallarmé's. A conceptualization enforcing so harsh a split between the credo of *L'Art romantique* and the "symbolist" *Weltanschauung* of *Fleurs du mal* may give us pause.

But of course no nomenclature can remove doubtful cases, and the soundness of Wellek's discriminations on the whole vexed question of period labels becomes clear when he advocates a "multiple scheme of periods." Like his literary ontology (elaborated in the influential **"Mode of Existence of a Literary Work"**), Wellek's conception of a literary period fosters fruitful analysis and debate because it resolutely avoids the opposite dead ends of Platonic abstraction and the blank nominalism of arbitrary labels. A period, he argues, "should be understood as a 'regulative idea,' as a system of norms, conventions, and values which can be traced in its rise, spread, and decline, in competition with preceding and following norms, conventions, and values." (pp. 135-36)

Emerson R. Marks, "A Conjunction of Critics," in The Yale Review *(copyright 1971 by Yale University; reprinted by permission of the editors), Vol. LX, No. 4, June, 1971, pp. 135-38.*

MARTIN BUCCO

[While] René Wellek called for intense critical exploration of the text, he never abandoned the historical method embodied in his ***Kant in England*** and ***The Rise of English Literary History.*** His synthesis of theory, criticism, and history reflects a passionate dedication to literary studies as a humane discipline, its standards derived not from "personal" taste or "impersonal science," but from the norms of history. For Wellek, the literary work is no simple verbal construct and no mere reflection of society: it is a phenomenological aesthetic object. Thus criticism means concern for values and qualities. Understanding—adequate analysis, interpretation, and evaluation—requires theory. Adequate theory requires a history of criticism. And adequate history requires an international perspective.

Envisioning the distant ideal of universal literary history and scholarship, Wellek in ***A History of Modern Criticism*** richly contributes to what Aldo Scaglione calls "an ecumenical republic of letters.". . . [Wellek's] historical imagination and critical intelligence vivify not only high-ranking and familiar critics, but also the unfashionable, the forgotten, the unknown. His work enlarges one's awareness of criticism as a discipline, of modern literary theory as growing out of the past, of German innovation in shaping the New Criticism, and of the New Criticism in relation to wider European currents. Though Wellek failed to devise an "evolutionary" scheme, ***Theory of Literature*** informs ***A History of Modern Criticism.*** Formed out of critical chaos, so to speak, the coherent ***Theory*** reenters that chaos, imparting to a substantial time sequence a reasonable unity, making the diverse episodes of the critical epic—the ***History***—hang together.

The twentieth-century revolt against positivism and impressionism generated not only critics and critics of critics, but critics of critics of critics. (pp. 155-56)

To characterize *the* critic of critics, reviewers have drawn images from such areas as sports, medicine, law, and politics. Amusingly enough, René Wellek has been likened to a universal umpire, to an observer on a mountaintop, to an intellectual physician, to a firm but kindly traffic policeman, to a tireless United Nations man going around ascertaining justice. For all his decisiveness and outspokenness, however, Wellek follows the sane middle path. He is never doctrinaire or rancorous. . . . Even his trenchant and balanced book reviews— for which he seems often to turn over many other books—

exemplify the art and craft of criticism in a small compass. (pp. 156-57)

What makes his influence so wholesome is that over the years he has reminded his students and his readers . . . that our vision of truth is only partial, that our assumptions are limited, that consensus might be fruitful. René Wellek has asserted: "Men can correct their biases, criticize their presuppositions, rise above their temporal and local limitations, aim at objectivity, arrive at some knowledge and truth." In pursuing knowledge and truth in Europe and America, he has struggled to maintain his critical independence and integrity. . . . "The world may be dark and mysterious,"—so writes this American from Central Europe—"but it is surely not completely unintelligible." Whatever else is obscure, clearly the world's greatest living historian of literary criticism is himself a signal part of that history. (pp. 157-58)

> *Martin Bucco, in his* René Wellek *(copyright © 1981 by Twayne Publishers; reprinted with the permission of Twayne Publishers, a Division of G. K. Hall & Co., Boston), Twayne, 1981, 186 p.*

A. R. LOUCH

Literature, you might think, is to be enjoyed, and criticism concerned with the quality and criteria of that enjoyment. Wellek's critics will have none of that. Their perspective is totally different. For them books, pictures, compositions, like the phenomena of biological speciation or the refraction of light, are objects to subsume under theory. It is not surprising that a critic with such a motive will sooner or later attack literature. After all, the exciting business is theorizing, mere imaginative writing is only the matter on which critics build. Does one remember a particular light beam, or does one celebrate Planck, Einstein, Rutherford? So, who should remember poets and novelists? But alas, critics discover that people do remember writers without having heard of the critics at all. So there is a motive of revenge in the attack on literature, pique that the *hoi polloi* recognize the names of Dante, Shakespeare, or Tolstoy, while Northrop Frye draws a blank. Somehow the reduction of the world to the reputation of the scientist has not worked out in the case of books. So the critic attacks what we might have thought was the point of his existence.

In [the title essay of his *The Attack on Literature and Other Essays*] Wellek distinguishes with fine irony and splendid detachment the various brigades in this critical army. First come the political critics, who see art as one of the instruments of exploitation of class by class. (p. 100)

Then come those who mistrust language. Wellek catalogues them like so many outlandish mesozoic beasts: the advocates of silence who continue writing; those like Barthes, who think every word a lie because it is not, as it cannot be, a thing . . . ; the apocalyptics, like Maurice Blanchot, who looks forward to the day when libraries and museums will be burned, and only silence speaks; and the McLuhanites who in promoting electronic successors to books deliberately confuse "visibility and legibility." . . . These genera belong to a class of critics defined by their common refusal to discriminate between "trivial and sublime" acts of writing. . . . (pp. 100-01)

Other genera of critics develop more flexible digestions, adapted to a more generalized ecological niche. They consume any word out of the mouth or on paper. This is the Northrop Frye genre, in which the critic looks at writing in an ingeniously ambivalent way, at once as literature and as behavior. (p. 101)

I wish that at this stage of his exposition Wellek had dwelt more on the equivocation in critics' abuse of literature, and how they have used that device to gain academic respectability. It seems particularly appropriate for him to do so, given the final sentences of the last essay in this collection: "The lawyer knows or thinks he knows what is right and what is wrong; the scientist knows what is true and what is false; the physician knows what is health and what is disease; only the poor humanist is floundering, uncertain of himself and his calling instead of proudly asserting the life of the mind which is the life of reason." He has in his hands the diagnosis of the absurdities he treats with such gentle irony. But, though it occurs to him to think the critics he has chosen to describe do perhaps overdo it, it does not lead him to the plain conclusion of what he so neatly and ironically observes. Criticism has learned to adapt to a scientific age, by the simple expedient of denying literature. But its pretense, like the fierce appearance affected by some defenseless creatures, is a sham, and so seen, is mere clownish posturing, so oddly at variance with Wellek's sweet reasonableness. It is in consequence, like the speeches of politicians, a resource for satire, fair game for farce, but not the subject of serious inquiry. (pp. 101-02)

Wellek reaffirms again and again in this volume his faith in those intuitions that require him to take Tolstoy, but not the pulp mystery, seriously. At the same time, he wants to offer a sober and scholarly account of the genres of criticism (or is it the criticism of genres?), the assumption justifying this labor being that a reputable branch of inquiry is in his sights, and will repay his study. Much of the labor comes across in this volume as a veritable blizzard of bibliographical citation, useless unless you are hunting a lost reference. . . . In between we catch occasional glimpses of these odd beasts, the critics. But one may wonder whether there is a proper study of literature-denying criticism of the ambitious sort Wellek proposes or whether, like the foibles of baseball players on and off the field, anecdote is not the appropriate level of response. Surely it is not reasonable to write a multi-volume heavily footnoted history of everything.

I hasten to add that at least one essay in this collection, **"The Fall of Literary History,"** is devoted to just such misgivings. Wellek introduces the topic with another of his many bibliographical summaries. In this case he counters the overwhelming vote of critics against the possibility of literary history, and counters it with a veritable telephone directory of practitioners of that discipline, most of them continental, including a few that some of his readers may even have heard of. But he acknowledges that names alone do not dispel doubts, or refute skepticism. Literary historians, he concedes, tend toward "inconsequential antiquarianism." They commonly inflate coincidence into causality, linking episodes in life with the characters of the work. . . . They suffer "from a lack of focus," unable to mark out an area that falls short of general history, but incompetent to take on the task of the general historian.

This observation is the occasion for another laundry list, this time of philosophers of history, whose disagreements are symptomatic of the difficulties of doing history at all. The problem, one begins to think, is not that literary history is literary, but that it is history.

And at some level this is right. Still one wonders whether there is not some more particular difficulty. Historians generally have trouble distilling causality out of coincidence, but that is not the complaint in Wellek's remark that "What the attempts at social explanation fail to achieve is the causal explanation of a specific work of literature, its individuality, its pattern and value." . . . He does not balk at social history, which embeds literary styles and themes in their social, political or economic context. He questions the relevance of such theories to the *literariness* of a work. Do we comprehend better the extraordinary quality of the *Tempest* knowing that it comes at the end of Shakespeare's stage career or that it may have been stimulated by accounts of a shipwreck in Bermuda? Does the question seem perverse? One has the impulse to say any new association enriches our understanding. And that it is a later, probably the last of his plays may, like contemplating in the same valedictory way the late quartets of Beethoven or the B-flat Piano Sonata of Schubert, add some dimension to one's perception of such works. But there are exceptions. Does it add to one's sense of the music to know that Wagner was an anti-semite, or that his conversations, recently revealed, have all the tawdriness and banality of any nineteenth-century bourgeois with an inflated ego? Sometimes the setting enriches, at other times it dissipates that particular way in which one apprehends a work of this kind—as something to be read or seen or heard. The problem with literary history turns out to be an instance of the problem of literary research. These methods press us toward an objective view of texts, which we come to see as objects with origins outside themselves, and having consequences that may, or may not, have to do with literature. At the same time, our interest in following up these lines of inquiry springs from our appreciation of the text—at least it does so for Wellek, and I for one will not want to fault him for it. So I want to say: There are in a sense literary histories of each generation's doggerel verse and pulp mysteries, but they are somehow uninteresting, just as there may be uncounted stories to be told about Adolf Adam, but who cares? Well, no, that is not quite right. For the historian, without the literary preoccupations, may find pulp food for his particular thought. In the case of Shakespeare or Schubert, on the other hand, if one has a literary or musical mind, one begins with its unaccountability, which is part of one's seeing and hearing it, part, one might say more pompously, of its aesthetics. One wants information about the days and nights over which the labor of creation occurred, the events in the life of the person who wrote such masterpieces, and the external circumstances in which they came into being. The motive to this inquiry is perhaps no more than gossip, details of lives and times that acquire an interest because the thing created is taken as having such an importance. Research of this kind acquires a discipline of its own—independent of the peculiar attitude that stimulates inquiry in the first place. We want to be more deeply acquainted with marvels, though at the same time we cannot expect that our discoveries will explain them. Miracles are by definition unaccountable. But the elevation of anecdote about great artists into the disciplines of critical history and biography takes on a life of its own. The stimulus of the miraculous is replaced by the impulse to tell such stories, appropriately documented of course, about any scribbler, any writing. Of course one loses the interest that, when one studies the great artist, rubs off on the facts of his history. And at the same time one's inquiries do not acquire the intrinsic interest of explaining anything that really puzzles us. Much history, Lord Acton said, is a burden to the memory and not an illumination to the mind.

Perhaps that is why literary history fails, or why much criticism comes to have the level of interest of anything pointless. In any case literary history seems to share with contemporary criticism that characteristic rejection of the literary. . . . Could it be, do you suppose, that critics have simply fallen out of love with literature? . . . But critics, as Wellek remarks, go on writing. But that in itself is not surprising; they must earn a living, it's too late to change . . . all that sort of thing. Familiar answers—familiar to philosophers as well as critics. It is as if whole disciplines—philosophy and criticism—turn to scavenge their own dead and decaying selves. They keep saying, my field consists in saying there is no field, except to point out with dreary repetitiveness how absurd anyone could be to think there might have been fields like metaphysics, epistemology, ethics, aesthetics.

But there are *objects*. *War and Peace* is a book containing ever so many printed pages and bearing a date. So, as a phenomenon, it must come within the clutches of some aspiring theory. One may have become bored with literature, but alive to the possibilities of pseudo-science. Psychologists and social scientists did it, and got away with it. Why not critics? (pp. 102-04)

Is it merely because critics fancy a role as scientist that they come to deny literature? Wellek does not say. Perhaps he has been too instrumental in acquainting Americans with continental fashions in the peculiar enterprises of criticism to set it aside as the incoherent ambitions of the envious. Still, though too gentle with the antics of those who assault literature, he remains firm in his conviction that what makes writing interesting is that it is literature. But it follows, does it not, that in denying literature, the modern fashion in criticism simply becomes uninteresting. (p. 105)

A. R. Louch, in a review of "The Attack on Literature and Other Essays," in Philosophy and Literature *(copyright © 1983 by The Johns Hopkins University Press), Vol. 7, No. 1, Spring, 1983, pp. 99-105.*

KATHLEEN BURKE

Wellek is the kind of critic and theorist to whom one listens closely, even when not always agreeing; usually there is little to disagree about, because Wellek is the paramount example of a critic who's intent upon explaining simply and disinterestedly others' criticism. He takes his own positions, but only after a fair account of the subject. My particular fondness for Wellek lies in his introducing me to the Russian Formalists in his *Concepts of Criticism*. Not only did he discuss the Formalists, and not only did he record their views accurately, but he also agreed with much of what they said. Only a handful of critics can be found about whom the same might be said. Wellek saw the Formalists' thought as still something to be dealt with, rather than a minor note in literary history.

Everything in [*The Attack on Literature and Other Essays*] is worth reading. In some of the essays, however, Wellek is more contentious than he appears in, for instance, his on-going *A History of Modern Criticism*. One position, which is perhaps the basis for all the others, is his view that the relevant questions for literature are aesthetic ones, while at the same time "Literature . . . says something about the world, and makes us see and know the external world and that of our own and other minds." That is, the great works of literature *say something*, have meaning, have value, etc., etc. Wellek does not disguise his humanist bias, regardless of its lack of fashion. Arguing with a popularist like Fiedler, Wellek insists that the comic book and *Hamlet* do *not* exist on the same plane of literature; and, of course, he launches his own attack on the poststructuralists et al because they draw the curtain between life and art, or because they turn over the matter of "value" to the individual reader. . . . (p. 245)

The group that Wellek has the most sympathy for is, God save us, the New Critics. Indeed, he argues their case better than they did. His attachment to these critics is, I think, two-fold: first, their general orientation towards aesthetic criteria in judging literature; and second, that they did judge it. . . . [The New Critics] did argue that literature—particularly the poem—is self-contained; did argue that the basis for criticism was aesthetic, though they had a narrow aesthetic view; and did argue that literature had "value" and that one work could be shown to be "better" than another. What always struck me as a paradox, if not a contradiction, was that they thought that literature could be autonomous and yet still be so tied to moral and ethical questions and values. I finally realized that these critics *did* see a separation between life and art; or rather, they saw art *as* life. The poem became the new world's order, though usually it was an old order that the New Critics were trying to reestablish. In other words, art took the place of the world; or the world was contained in the art, or however you want to describe this. This sense of autonomy is quite distinct from that of the Russian Formalists whose view was that art existed as one object in a world of objects; it didn't reflect other objects, didn't "talk about" them, didn't compete with them. The Russians devoted themselves to describing this art, to seeing it as it is, and if possible, to formulating the laws by which it seemed to work. For the New Critics, art became the receptacle for all that was lacking in the modern world—values, meaning, order, morals, and so on. And, as one might expect and as the New Critics proceeded to demonstrate, a certain kind of art was better equipped to perform this act than were others. (pp. 245-46)

Wellek's treatment of the Russians here is generally similar to what it has been at other times, though he is more cautious about them now. . . . Since Russian Formalism went nowhere except into the underground, jails, or exile, we will never know what may have happened to criticism if the Russians had exerted their due influence. But what seems clear to me is that the Russians deposited absolute values in art, did discriminate between the good and the bad, and finally "humanized" art by placing so much emphasis upon it as a "thing made," an act of the will and imagination, thereby restoring it to its proper place in human activity rather than subordinating it to history, biography, sociology, psychology, or whatever other sphere of disciplines and thought to which art is usually subjugated.

Enough of this wrangling. Read Wellek's book. (p. 246)

Kathleen Burke, in a review of "The Attack on Literature and Other Essays," in The Review of Contemporary Fiction *(copyright, 1983, by The Review of Contemporary Fiction), Vol. III, No. 1, Spring, 1983, pp. 245-46.*

Charles Wright
1935-

American poet and translator.

Wright is widely regarded as one of America's most important living poets. Although Wright's poetry has been strongly influenced by his Southern upbringing and contains many personal details about his home in Tennessee, it conveys a sense of universal connections to the past, rather than employing a confessional stance. Wright's poetry is marked by strong internal rhythms which contribute to an overall musicality of language. A typical Wright poem is filled with objects which give it the illusion of immediacy and concreteness. Wright's poems transcend traditional religious definitions of spirituality and move toward embracing mysticism of natural forces. The combination of a sustained, detached vision and abundant images and objects gives his poetry a painterly quality. His use of personal scenes and anecdote contribute to a sense of self-portraiture, but without subjectivity or intimacy. Helen Vendler has used the term "the transcendent I" to refer to Wright's impersonal perspective.

Wright's career has steadily gained momentum since the publication of his first major collection, *The Grave of the Right Hand,* in 1970. *China Trace* (1977), Wright's fourth major volume, clearly shows his individuality and poetic range. In this work, Wright models some poems after Chinese poetry and incorporates a catalogue-like rush of photographic imagery. Many critics consider *The Southern Cross* (1981) to be Wright's best volume of poetry. Its subject matter is closely connected to his home and past, and the celebration of the physical world emerges as its major theme. Wright combines first-hand experience and personal subjects to convey a sense of spiritual yearning for what has been lost in the past.

In 1983, Wright received an American Book Award for *Country Music* (1982). Richard Tillinghast described the poetry in this book as "austere and somewhat difficult of access," but possessing the same musically rhythmic language and imagery which makes reading Wright's poetry such a rewarding experience.

(See also *CLC,* Vols. 6, 13; *Contemporary Authors,* Vols. 29-32, rev. ed.; and *Dictionary of Literary Biography Yearbook: 1982.*)

© 1984 Thomas Victor

HELEN VENDLER

Because Wright's poems, on the whole, are unanchored to incident, they resist description; because they are not narrative, they defy exposition. They cluster, aggregate, radiate, add layers like pearls. Often they stop in the middle, with a mixed yearning and premonition, instead of taking a resolute direction backward or forward. It may be from the Italian poet Eugenio Montale . . . that Wright learned this pause which looks before and after; Wright recently issued his translation, done in the sixties, of Montale's powerful 1956 volume entitled *La Bufera e altro (The Storm and Other Poems).*

The translation offers an occasion for a glance at both Montale and Wright; the conjunction helps to define what sort of poet Wright has become. Montale wrote *La Bufera* during the postwar years, and his pauses in the midst of event come as often as not in the midst of nightmare: "The Prisoner's Dream" shows a speaker imprisoned in a time of political purges, tempted, like everyone else, to "give in and sign," but instead waiting out the interminable trial, addressing from prison his fixed point of reference—a dreamed-of woman who represents beauty, justice, truth. . . . This poetry, though it implies a better past and an uncertain future, incorporates them in the burning-glass of the present. It renounces, as forms of articulation, narrative, the succession of events, the sequence of action and reaction. The spatial form, one of many in Montale, is for Wright the most natural. . . . [Arrested Motion], taking thought, though it is congenial to Wright, requires nevertheless certain sacrifices.

The first sacrifice is autobiography. The autobiographical sequence **"Tattoos,"** which appeared in ***Bloodlines,*** solved the problem of reference by appending, at the end of twenty poems, a single note on each one: a sample note reads "Automobile wreck; hospital; Baltimore, Maryland." Instead of a first-person narrative of the crash and its surgical aftermath, Wright produces a montage of sensations. . . . In ***Bloodlines*** these verses are encountered with no title, no explanation; the note is to be read later, and then the poem reread, from the crash to the hospital. . . . It is easy to see how interminable, predictable, and boring a plain narrative might appear after this "jump-cut" (Wright's words) monitoring of sensation. The problem of affixing closure to sensation and perception . . . has bothered Wright a good deal. The automobile wreck finds closure in sententious question-and-answer, with echoes of Williams and Berryman. . . . (pp. 277-79)

His next experiment, in the second sequence in *Bloodlines* (a wonderful poem called **"Skins"**), was to abandon the three equal pieces—presentation, complication, and conclusion—of **"Tattoos"** for a set of seamless meditations, each fourteen lines long. Though these have of course affinities with sonnets, they are sonnets that go nowhere, or end where they began: either the second half of the poem repeats the first, or the last line reenters the universe where the first line left it. Even the poems which seem to evolve in a linear way show only a moment in a life-cycle itself endlessly repeated; they are therefore more fated than free, as in the case of the sixth and most beautiful meditation, about the metamorphosis of a mayfly. . . . The mind of the reader is delayed by the felicities of the slate wings on the slate water-film, by the dun detritus of chrysalis played off against the watershine, by the flesh flush on the surface, by the conjugation of drift and force, compression and incipience, and by the brief cycle of wings drying, rising, dropping. This sensual music precludes thought, almost; but the subject of metamorphosis is so old and so noble, the flesh as chrysalis so perennial a metaphor, that the conceptual words—image, self, imago, destiny—work their own subsidiary charm in the long run. In spite of the ephemeral nature of the cycle, Wright rescues by his vocabulary a form of transcendence. (pp. 280-81)

Wright's aim in translating Montale has been to be idiomatic, within his own idiom as well as within Montale's. . . . Montale—compressed, allusive, oblique, full of echoing sound—is relatively untranslatable; his poems swell awkwardly as they take on English under anyone's hands, and his infinitely manipulable Italian syntax begins to hobble, hampered by stiff English clauses. Wright's translations, as he says, taught him things:

> I feel I did learn . . . how to move a line, how to move an image from one stage to the next. How to create imaginary bridges between images and stanzas and then to cross them, making them real, image to image, block to block.

These are not—though they may appear to be—idle concerns. If conclusions are not the way to get from A to B, if discursiveness itself is a false mode of consciousness, if free-association in a surrealist mode (to offer the opposite extreme) seems as irresponsible as the solemn demonstrations of the discursive, what form of presentation can recreate the iconic form of the mind's invention? It is really this question that Wright takes up in *China Trace* and subsequent poems. Chinese poetry, as it entered twentieth-century literature through Waley and Pound, came to stand for an alien but immensely attractive combination of sensation and ethics, both refined from crudeness by their mutual interpenetration. Suggestion and juxtaposition seemed adequate to replace statement, as Pound's petal-faces on the Métro-bough would claim. Wright's trace—*vestigium*—of China is in part a homage to Pound, but it also pursues, yet once more, the problem of the potential complacency of stanzas, especially of repeated stanzas. (pp. 281-83)

This problem is less superficial than it may seem. Aside from light verse, gnomes, or riddles, poems in English often have either two or three stanzas, chiefly because thought and feeling often proceed either by comparison or antithesis (resulting in two stanzas) or by statement, complication or amplification, and resolution (yielding three stanzas or divisions). Perception, unsupported by reflection, tends to seem truncated, unfinished, uncommented upon. That analytic restlessness which causes the second, and even the third, stanzas to be written is absent in the Chinese lyrics—compact, single, coherent—favored by Waley, and hovering over *China Trace*. But in spite of Wright's deliberate variety of form, a principle of repetition has its way in the design of the book: each of its halves is prefaced by the same citation from Calvino's *Invisible Cities,* envisaging the day when, knowing all the emblems, one becomes an emblem among emblems. This Yeatsian notion stands side by side with a Chinese epigraph, about the ambition "to travel in ether by becoming a void," or, failing that, to make use of a landscape to calm the spirit and delight the heart. In these epigraphs Wright reveals his own disembodied ethereality in coexistence with his pure visual sense.

The poems in *China Trace* are frosty, clear, descriptive, seemingly dispassionate, wintry even in spring. . . . Throughout the volume Wright persistently imagines himself dead, dispersed, re-elemented into the natural order. . . . In focusing on earth, in saying that "salvation doesn't exist except through the natural world," Wright approaches Cézanne's reverence for natural forms, geometrical and substantial ones alike. *China Trace* is meant to have "a journal-like, everyday quality," but its aphorisms resemble *pensées* more than diary jottings, just as its painters and poets (Morandi, Munch, Trakl, Nerval) represent the arrested, the composed, the final, rather than the provisional, the blurred, or the impressionistic. *China Trace* is in fact one long poem working its desolation by accretion; it suffers in excerpts. Its mourning echoes need to be heard like the complaint of doves—endless, reiterative, familiar, a twilight sound. . . . (pp. 283-84)

Wright is not innocent of influence; one recognizes Whitman, Pound, and Stevens, as well as Berryman and Williams, among his predecessors. On the other hand, he is obsessed with sound rather more than they were. Sound adds to his poems that conclusiveness which logic and causality confer on the poetry of others. . . . Wright's poems would be endangered if they were constructed on a more casual base, but he seems to work with infrastructures which are powerfully organized. . . . These sub-scaffoldings may in the long run drop away, but they keep the poems from being at the mercy of whims of sound.

If *China Trace* can be criticized for an unrelenting elegiac fixity, nonetheless its consistency gives it incremental power. Its deliberateness, its care in motion, its slow placing of stone on stone, dictate our reading it as construction rather than as speech. It is not surprising that as a model Wright has chosen Cézanne, that most architectural of painters. . . . (p. 285)

Wright's eight-poem sequence **"Homage to Cézanne"** builds up, line by line, a sense of the omnipresent dead. Wright's unit here is the line rather than the stanza, and the resulting poem sounds rather like the antiphonal chanting of psalms. . . . Wright does this poetry of the declarative sentence very well, but many poets have learned this studied simplicity, even this poetry of the common noun. What is unusual in Wright is his oddity of imagery within the almost too-familiar conventions of quiet, depth, and profundity. As he layers on his elemental squares and blocks of color, the surprising shadow or interrupting boulder emerge as they might in a Cézanne. . . . To Wright, death is as often ascent as burial; we become stars, like Romeo, after death, as often as roses. The modern unsheeted mirror reveals the Tennysonian twist of the constellations round the pole-star, in this Shakespearean image of the posthumous—or so we might say if we look at Wright for his inheritances as well as for his originality. (pp. 285-86)

The hunger for the purity of the dead grows, in these poems, almost to a lust. . . . The eternal and elemental world is largely unrelieved, in **China Trace** and after, by the local, the social, the temporary the accidental, the contingent. Some very good poetry has incorporated riotous, and occasionally ungovernable, irruptions of particularity; the "purer" voice of finely ascetic lyric has a geniune transmitter in Wright. His synoptic and panoramic vision, radiating out from a compositional center to a filled canvas, opposes itself to the anthropocentric, and consequently autobiographical or narrrative, impetus of lyrics with a linear base. If there is nowehre to go but up from making the unsupported line your unit, the dead your measure of verity, and the blank canvas meticulously layered with single cubes of color your creative metaphor, Wright's poetry is bound to change. As it stands, it is engaged in a refutation of the seductions of logic, of religion, and of social roles. By its visionary language it assumes the priority of insight, solitude, and abstraction, while remaining beset by a mysterious loss of something that can be absorbed and reconstituted only in death.

The spiritual yearning in Wright is nowhere rewarded, as it sometimes is in Montale, by a certain faith in an absolute—damaged no doubt, elusive surely, disagreeable often, but always unquestioned and recoverable. The difference in part may be historical. Montale, who fought in World War I and saw the shambles of post-war Italy give rise to Mussolini, faced pressing social evils that demanded a choice of sides; he refused to join the Fascist party and lost his job in consequence. Virtue made visible by its denunciation of the evils of of Pandemonium can appear emblematic, allegorical, winged, embattled. Without a historical convulsion, tones of poetry subside into perplexity, sadness, elegy. Wright's debt to Montale, attested to by original poems as well as by these early translations, is more than stylistic: the disciple exhibits that desire and hopelessness we associate with Montale at his most characteristic. (p. 287)

Wright's verse is the poetry of the transcendent "I" in revolt against the too easily articulate "I" of social engagement and social roles. Whether one "I" can address his word to other, hidden "I"s across the abyss of daily life without using the personal, transient, and social language of that life is the question Wright poses. . . . I would hope to see in Wright's future poetry a more vivid sense of the social and familial landscape in which the soul struggles. (p. 288)

> Helen Vendler, "The Transcendent 'I'" (originally published in The New Yorker, Vol. LV, No. 37, October 29, 1979), in her Part of Nature, Part of Us: Modern American Poets (copyright © 1980 by the President and Fellows of Harvard College; excerpted by permission), Cambridge, Mass.: Harvard University Press, 1980, pp. 277-88.

DAVID ST. JOHN

Charles Wright's stunning new book, **The Southern Cross** . . . , is full of the familiar verbal iconographies and textural chromatics that have made his earlier books so distinctive and powerful. Wright's palpably physical sense of language—of language as sensual, supple *material*—invites us to see him in terms one usually reserves for the visual arts. Yet Wright's poems are clearly aware of and delighted by their own painterly and sculptural qualities; their architectures are simultaneously intellectual and spiritual. . . . Though Wright has always spoken of the profound influence Pound and Montale . . . have had upon his work, **The Southern Cross**—even its title—shows the enormously rich resource the poetry of Hart Crane has become for him. (pp. 230-31)

In many of the poems in **The Southern Cross,** Wright's concerns revolve around the idea of self-portraiture—not autobiography, with its implication of self-absorption and completeness, but self-portraiture. The distinction is important to Wright, as a quality of self-objectification details all of his poems. Just as each of the emblematic and imagistic strokes (of each poem's lines) in each self-portrait serves to approximate the figure, so the sequence of self-portraits in **The Southern Cross** serves to give us perhaps a less literal but more vivid and multidimensional reading of the poet.

For Wright, it is always language, its textures and music, that reclaims and collates all of the images of the self, all of the moments lost to the freeze frame of the blinked eye. Self, in Wright's poems, is the necessarily constant but web-cracked lens through which the world and the body are seen in their decomposition and regeneration. Self is that zero, that perfect circle of consciousness, through which all elemental shiftings—the blown dust, the drowned flame—and all spiritual aspirations are, for better or worse, to be regarded. (p. 231)

> David St. John, "Raised Voices in the Choir: A Review of 1981 Poetry Selections," in The Antioch Review (copyright © 1982 by the Antioch Review Inc.; reprinted by permission of the Editors), Vol. XL, No. 2, Spring, 1982, pp. 225-34.*

PETER STITT

The Southern Cross is surely Charles Wright's best book, the one he has been preparing for through all his earlier volumes. Like Bin Ramke and Robert Penn Warren, Wright is a Southerner, a fact which has a profound relevance to the texture of his verse. His poems throb with stylistic richness, most palpably in a lushness of image and word; one needs a delicate touch indeed to feel the subtle modulations of theme that lie just beneath this surface. (p. 188)

[The] spiritual setting of this entire volume has much in common with the *Purgatorio* of Dante, from which Wright has chosen a comprehensive epigraph: the concluding seven lines of Canto XXI. . . . Wright in this book is always aware of and searching for evidence of the spiritual within the real, always aware of the possibility of angels.

Time is the most serious and pervasive theme in **The Southern Cross,** and appears both in a preoccupation with death and in a preoccupation with memory and the burden of the past. The best poems here are the two long ones—**"Homage to Paul Cézanne"** (eight pages), which opens the volume, and **"The Southern Cross"** (seventeen pages), which closes it. That these are also probably the strongest poems this outstanding poet has yet written indicates that his talent is both meditative and expansive—he works best in extended forms. **"Homage to Paul Cézanne"** is an intimate meditation on the dead. . . . (p. 189)

"The Southern Cross" is less concerned with death than with memory and the burdens of a personal past, just as the title refers less to the constellation than to Wright's Tennessee heritage and his preoccupation with Italy, both of which define him, establishing the "cross" he carries through life. The poem is rich in image and incident, with interspersed passages of a more abstract nature. (p. 190)

There is a conceptual similarity between this poem and much of the work of Robert Penn Warren; here it is the quality of the remembered scene and the generalized notion of human life that remind us of Warren. A bit later the resemblance is even more striking:

> Time is the villain in most tales,
> and here, too,
> Lowering its stiff body into the water.
> Its landscape is the resurrection of the word,
> No end of it,
> the petals of wreckage in everything.

The handling of imagery is different, though the ideas are nearly the same. Wright twice turns from abstract statement to metaphor in this passage, as is the general method of his generation of poets. Warren would either stay at the abstract level or extend his earlier narrative . . . a bit further. Charles Wright is a marvelous writer, as profoundly suggestive in content as he is entertaining in style. *The Southern Cross* is an important book that reaches to depths of significance and cohesion new even to an artist as serious as this one. (p. 191)

> *Peter Stitt, "Problems of Youth . . . and Age," in* The Georgia Review *(copyright, 1982, by the University of Georgia), Vol. XXXVI, No. 1, Spring, 1982, pp. 184-93.**

MARY KINZIE

[With *The Southern Cross,* Charles Wright creates] two new kinds of environment, civilization as manifest in gem-like labyrinths like Venice, and lush quasi-savage blossoming vegetation of the sort that flourishes in latitudes where the southern cross is prominent in the night sky. Furthermore, Wright could be said to depend absolutely on place, to work from it, in his crucial journeys, traced in so many poems, from rest to intense engagement with ethereal thresholds, tints of light, floating gestures—"an incandescent space," he says in one poem, "where nothing distinct exists, / And nothing ends, the days sliding like warm milk through the clouds." I quote these lines because they make explicit the poet's preference for the hazy, the milky, the upper-atmospheric; these are the trappings of his transcendent states of infancy.

I use the term "infancy" advisedly. Charles Wright's apotheoses are characteristically visions of a presexual, light-suffused mist, the matrix of dreams and the medium of serenity and soaring, of effortless floating, a rising-upwards that is very much more pleasant but far less emotionally pressing than the sultry risings and impassioned upwellings and poolings in the poetry of Louise Gluck. Whereas she clearly returns to the profound tensions and jealousies of childhood, Wright explores an almost fetal suspended state just prior to birth. . . . The desire to return to the softer outline he had at the beginning before experience marked him with choices and errors and the simple banalities of repetition emerges over and over again in Wright's new volume. As he travels backward in time toward his origins, he is also preparing for his death, expressed as a return to infant dependency. . . .

One of the voices Wright invokes is Dante's, from those two books of the *Comedy* whose imagery and exempla are paler and less violent than the *Inferno*'s. As epigram to *The Southern Cross,* Wright quotes Statius's homage to Vergil from the twenty-first canto of *Purgatory,* who ruefully admits that his love of the Master had enflamed him to treat a shade as a solid thing. . . .

Wright reads Dante with the same selective lens he uses for Eugenio Montale and for the third great mentor of the current poems, William Blake; that is, he is intrigued by the tissues of their imagery at its softest, and by their treatment of nostalgia, but not by their anagogy. It is a very selective reading of both Dante and Blake that would ignore both allegories and discourses; and without the earnest attention of an elegist like Montale to other human beings, nostalgia becomes sentimental. In Wright, however, the anagoge is always self—one who happens to be a sensitive lover of beauty, to be sure; and a maker of elegant artifacts, without question; but occasionally an artist, possibly among false spirits (this I can't judge), with decidedly false professions and poses.

The long failed sequence **"Homage to Paul Cézanne"** so abounds in misjudgments in tone and in tact that the reader is apt to forget that the painter Cézanne is supposed to be central, although there is little in his paintings that the mediumistic dramatizations of these eight poems have touched. Wright posits a community of dead; unlike Dante's or Montale's dead, these are specific neither to history nor to the poet's own life, they are a vague body, with no will or direction, that can be made to function like rain, like color, like darkness, like moods, like clothing, like sounds, like premonition. Hence the dead are the collective noun for lugubrious poetic feeling. Some of the personifications are quite funny: "Spring picks the locks of the wind"; "spaces / In black shoes, their hands clasped"; "The dead are constant in / The white lips of the sea." Some of the stage props the dead must carry around are also awkwardly amusing: "We filagree and we baste. / But what do the dead care for the fringe of words, / Safe in their suits of milk?" . . . But there is the more general problem of framework and intention raised by the **"Homage"** and applicable to other poems as well; the poet fails to make his choices of subject, diction, and tone seem always necessary; at times they do not even sound deliberate. On occasion I have considered that Wright as a craftsman with words, tropes, and sentences is without a built-in censor. He inflates his poetics into mere shapeless benevolence. Nothing is judged, nothing rejected, nothing refused admittance to the poem.

What William Blake offered in 1789 as a negative representation of timidity . . . Charles Wright exports, two centuries later, as a positive and strong representation of life, I think because for him behavior does not count, nor is religion a living possibility. Hence he can devote himself to the composition of emphemeral structures about ephemeral tints and passing, filmy, essentially solitary manifestations. . . . (p. 40)

I [suggest] that Charles Wright may lack a self-censoring mechanism for his poetry; that he needs to apply standards for determining when a metaphor or colloquialism is or is not apropos; that in consequence of failing to do so, and given his interest in ghostly landscapes and a consciousness entranced, his poems are sometimes apt to be indiscriminately hospitable, undiscerning, childlike. (pp. 40-1)

> *Mary Kinzie, "Haunting" (copyright © 1982 by World Poetry, Inc.; reprinted by permission of Mary Kinzie), in* The American Poetry Review, *Vol. 11, No. 5, September-October, 1982, pp. 37-46.**

RICHARD TILLINGHAST

"**Country Music**" (poems originally published between 1970 and 1977) is . . . [a] substantial selection from a poet in his middle 40's. The title, though it playfully alludes to the music of the American South, where [Wright] was born and brought up, more accurately refers to the silent "music" of the landscape. (p. 14)

Mr. Wright's Tennessee boyhood provides the subject matter of many of these poems, but . . . he is no literalist. Rejecting plot and naturalistic detail, he would draw our attention, in his finely crafted poems, to subtler essences. (pp. 14, 31)

In contrast to many of his contemporaries who might say, with Jim Harrison, "In our poetry we want to rub our nose hard / into whatever is before it," Mr. Wright has a distinctly different purpose: "I write poems to untie myself, to do penance and disappear / Through the upper right-hand corner of things, to say grace." To avoid the problem of literal reference in "**Tattoos**" and "**Skins**," two poetic sequences from his third book, "**Bloodlines**" (1975), he simply appends a list of brief notes to the poems, a few words for each; for instance: "Recurrent dream," "The Naxian lions; Delos, Greece," etc. The result of this distancing is often disorienting and at times disturbing: One wishes Mr. Wright would step into his own poems more often.

But the impersonality of his approach is a quite conscious choice, and in "**The Southern Cross**" (1981) there are five poems entitled "**Self-Portrait**" that are the opposite of what a "confessional" poet would write in the same context. . . . Mr. Wright's poems make a statement about that indeterminacy of the artist's personality which has been familiar since Keats's assertion of "negative capability" but which is rare in its actual appearance in poetry. This "country music" is austere and somewhat difficult of access, but its rhythms and images are exquisite and fully reward the reader's effort. Charles Wright is among a handful of contemporary poets carrying the art to its outermost limits. (p. 31)

Richard Tillinghast, "From Michigan and Tennessee," in The New York Times Book Review *(copyright © 1982 by The New York Times Company; reprinted by permission), December 12, 1982, pp. 14, 31.*

JASCHA KESSLER

Country Music, Wright's Selected Poems, . . . , offers the poems that the poet would suggest convey his best thoughts over twenty years. It contains 153 pages of work, and a good idea of his career so far is furnished by it. There is a blank verse sonnet sequence of 20 poems in it, entitled "**Skins,**" and they trace from first to last something of Wright's flat, hard declaration, his closed, and bitter ruminations, his unhappiness with his lot, and perhaps with ours, as his human relatives, if not his personal relations. . . . Along the route of this sequence, Wright looks at the world as he knows it, this natural world, and puzzles about the promises religion once made to him, for it was that Tennessee, middle-class upbringing, church and dogmatic, its indoctrination of him to what he now sees is illusion and vanity of belief and superstitious hope, that pains him most. . . . In fact, bitterly, Wright, in many of his poems, ends with the celebration of the process of nature's ceaseless cycling of the particles everything is made of, and everything is, of course, insentient, unfeeling, and unknowing, as we must be as we dissolve into it. I say *bitterly,* because often enough this commonplace is put forward by Wright with an energy that shows that he is quarreling with the voices of his past, with those beliefs that made up his childhood and youth, and which his whole life is no more than a unremitting struggle to overcome. (pp. 5-6)

Not that Wright ever shows us much of any world but that of plants and small animals and insects; the greater human world of many histories, of arts and sciences, of conquests and defeats, of passions and infamies, indeed of great mystical traditions and disciplines, far more challenging than his childhood, Christianity, all that is absent from his lyrical imagination, which is fixed on his own sad plight. In *Southern Cross* . . . , there are some faintly sardonic poems that he calls "**Self-Portraits,**" and there is a fine, long introductory poem, again about the dead who color this world of our perceptions, called "**Homage to Paul Cezanne.**" Often enough, Wright desires to fly outward on the lights of the world, outward forever, or dissolve in dust below. The longest poem is "**Southern Cross**" an autobiographical meditation, at the outset of which he declares that there is, nonetheless, "No trace of a story line." The almost complete self-absorption of this poet while frankly thus engaged in picturing his picturesque, and picturable memories of himself in Europe, Tennessee, and California, may not be to everyone's liking, but it does express itself in firm, choice, clear writing, for it is not simply vain or merely solipsistic work. Quite the contrary, it is full of a deep pathos, full of sorrows that ring plangently from the page. Why those sorrows, and wherefore? is as troubling to the poet as to the reader. To Wright's credit, he never quite accepts the doleful, nor quite rationalizes it away. On the other hand, he can never do what his greater models, Dino Campana, Eugenio Montale, or Dante, for that matter, do: he can never establish or justify his personal sorrow in terms that might be common to us all. (pp. 8-9)

Jascha Kessler, "Charles Wright: 'The Southern Cross' and 'Country Music: Selected Early Poems'," in a radio broadcast on KUSC-FM—Los Angeles, CA, September 14, 1983.

James (Arlington) Wright
1927-1980

American poet and translator.

Wright, who ranks among the most esteemed poets of his generation, was a significant contributor to the "deep image" school of poetry that emerged in the 1960s and 1970s. Reacting against the limits of traditional verse, the writers of the deep image school wrote emotional, subjective poetry and relied primarily on image to convey meaning. They called for an intimacy between the poem and the reader and a direct relationship between human experience and its poetic expression. Before becoming involved with this group, Wright wrote in the formalist tradition of such writers as John Crowe Ransom. His poetry in this early period was characterized by formal construction and by a precise use of rhythm, meter, and rhyme. Wright's first two volumes of verse, *The Green Wall* (1957) and *Saint Judas* (1959), were written in this mode and were well received by critics. *The Green Wall* won the Yale Series of Younger Poets Award in 1957. Wright's writing nevertheless underwent a drastic change.

In the early 1960s, while writing and teaching English at universities in Minnesota, Wright became influenced by his contemporary, Robert Bly. Through Bly, Wright became aware of the highly subjective, surrealist poetry of Pablo Neruda, César Vallejo, and others. *The Branch Will Not Break* (1963), Wright's third volume, is the first to be written in this later style. This collection displays both a relaxing of his previous formal control and a change from the exalted visions of his earlier work. Wright became more concerned with contemporary society, and his poems were often marked by despair. Prostitutes, murderers, and social outcasts peopled his writing. Whether Wright was expressing joy found in the mundane—one poem, for instance, celebrates the beauty of a sewage drain—or anguishing over the encroachment of technology and the spoiling of landscape, his hometown of Martin's Ferry, Ohio, often provided the backdrop.

When Wright died, he had completed the manuscript for *This Journey* (1982), a collection of poems concerned with his journey through life and his contemplations of death. An acutely emotional poet, Wright wrote with compassion about human suffering and helped bring about the heightened immediacy and impact of deep image poetry, which is the basis for his importance to contemporary poetry.

(See also *CLC*, Vols. 3, 5, 10; *Contemporary Authors*, Vols. 49-52, Vols. 97-100 [obituary]; *Contemporary Authors New Revision Series*, Vol. 4; and *Dictionary of Literary Biography*, Vol. 5.)

W. H. AUDEN

One of the problems for a poet living in a culture with a well-developed technology is that the history of technology is one of perpetual revolution, whereas genuine revolutions in the history of art (or society) are few and far between. He is tempted to imagine that, unless he produces something completely novel, he will be unoriginal. The reading public, too,

© Thomas Victor 1984

may be similarly misled and attach undue importance to the individual differences between one poet and another, which, of course, exist and matter, ignoring that which is characteristic of them all, though this may really be of greater interest.

For example, Mr. Wright uses as an epigraph to [*The Green Wall*] the well-known medieval carol "Adam Lay Ibounden." It is as impossible to imagine a poet of the twentieth-century writing this as to imagine a fifteenth-century poet writing . . . lines by Mr. Wright. . . . (p. 43)

A modern poet might perfectly well be a Catholic, believing in the divine plan for human redemption of which the medieval carol sings, but his consciousness of historical earthly time is so different that he could never strike the same note of naive joy in the present; should he attempt it, the note struck would almost certainly be false, expressing not Christian hope but a sort of Rotarian optimism. (p. 44)

One way of perceiving the characteristics of an age is to raise certain fundamental questions which human beings have always asked and then see how the poets of that age answer them, such questions, for example, as: "What is the essential difference between man and all the other creatures, animal, vegetable, and mineral?" "What is the nature and human significance of time?" "What qualities are proper to the hero or sacred person who can inspire poets to celebrate him and what is lacking in the churl or profane person whom poetry ignores?" A man in the Middle Ages would have said that the difference between man and other creatures is that only man has an immortal soul eternally related to God. He has, therefore, a goal, salvation or damnation, but this goal is not in time nor is reaching it a matter of time. A baby who has been baptized and an old man who repents after a lifetime of crime die and both are saved; their ages are irrelevant.

On the other hand, so far as his temporal existence, individual or social, was concerned, like anyone who lives in a predominantly rural culture without machinery, he would be conscious of little difference between himself and other creatures, that is to say, he would be mainly aware of their common subjection to biological time, the endless cycle of birth, growth, and decay. Of man as creating irreversible historical time so that the next generation is never a repetition of the last, he would be scarcely, if at all, conscious. But to a modern man, whether or not he believes in an immortal soul, this is the great difference, that he and his society have a self-made history while the rest of nature does not. He is anxious by necessity because at every moment he has to choose to become himself. His typical feelings about nature, therefore, are feelings of estrangement and nostalgia. In **"A Fit against the Country"** Mr. Wright sees nature as a temptation to try and escape human responsibility by imitating her ways, in **"The Seasonless"** he contrasts the rotation of the seasons with a human figure to whom no season can ever return, in **"The Horse"** and **"On the Skeleton of a Hound"** he contrasts the "poetical" animal and its unchanging identity with the "unpoetical" man who can never say who he is.

Poets have always reflected on the passage of time, comparing the present and the past, but before the modern period this usually meant expressing a sorrow because the present was less valuable than the past, what was once strong is now weak, what was beautiful has faded, and so forth, but past and present were felt to be equally real. But in Mr. Wright's poems, as in nearly all modern poetry, the present is not unhappy but unreal, and it is memories, pleasant or unpleasant, which are celebrated for their own sake as the real past. The present can only be celebrated, as in **"A Girl in a Window"** or **"To a Hostess Saying Good Night,"** by showing it as pure chance; what makes the present moment poetical is an awareness that it is related to nothing so that nothing can come of it. (pp. 44-5)

Given the circumstances of modern life, the feeling that only memories are real is to be expected. When a man usually lived in the house where his father and grandfather had lived before him, the past still existed in the present, not just in his memories but objectively about him. Today when men change not only their house but their part of the world every few years, their present circumstances become more and more impersonal, subjective memories more and more important.

Even more striking than its attitude toward nature and time is the kind of person whom modern poetry chooses to speak of. Aside from love poems and poems addressed to relatives, the persons who have stimulated Mr. Wright's imagination include a lunatic, a man who has failed to rescue a boy from drowning, a murderer, a lesbian, a prostitute, a police informer, and some children, one of them deaf. Common to them all is the characteristic of being social outsiders. They play no part in ruling the City nor is its history made by them, nor, even, are they romantic rebels against its injustices; either, like the children (and the ghosts), they are not citizens or they are the City's passive victims.

His one poem to a successful citizen is, significantly, to a singer, that is to say, to someone whose social function is concerned with the play of the City, not with its work.

Mr. Wright is not alone in his imaginative preferences. It is difficult to find a modern poem, unless it be a satire, which celebrates a contemporary equivalent of Hector or Aeneas or King Arthur or the Renaissance prince. To the poetic imagination of our time, it would seem that the authentically human, the truly strong, is someone who to the outward eye is weak or a failure, the only exception being the artist or the intellectual discoverer, the value of whose achievements is independent of his contemporary fame.

There are many reasons for this change, and everyone will be able to think of some for himself. One, obviously, is the impersonal character of modern public life which has become so complex that the personal contribution of any one individual is impossible to identify and even the greatest statesman seems more an official than a man. Another, I think, is the change effected by modern methods of publicity in the nature of fame. Formerly a man was famous *for* something, for this great deed or that which he had done; that is to say, the deed was the important thing and the name of the doer was, in a sense, an accident. Today a famous man is a man whose name is on everybody's lips. Their knowledge of what he has done may be very vague and its value, whether it was noble or shameful, matters very little. (pp. 45-6)

We should not be surprised, then, if modern poets should be drawn to celebrate persons of whom nobody has heard or whom, at least, everybody has forgotten.

I have not said anything about the quality of Mr. Wright's poems because assertions have no point without proofs, and the only proof in this case is reading. (p. 47)

> W. H. Auden, "Foreword" (reprinted by permission of Curtis Brown, Ltd, and Mrs. James Wright; copyright © 1957 by Yale University Press, Inc.), in The Green Wall by James Wright, Yale University Press, 1957 (and reprinted in The Pure Clear Word: Essays on the Poetry of James Wright, edited by Dave Smith, University of Illinois Press, 1982, pp. 43-8).

CRUNK [PSEUDONYM OF ROBERT BLY]

Despite [the faults of his poetry], it is clear James Wright is an amazingly good poet. His lines are not stiff like sticks, but flexible like a living branch. Some emotion, rising very close to the surface, always seems to keep the words alive. In thought, his words, underneath, are in touch with something infinite. Another way of saying this is to say that his personality as a man drives forward, disregarding the consequences. Deep in his personality is the plower who does not look back. Everyone recognizes this in his work instinctively, and it is probably one reason for the great affection people have for his work. His instinct is to push everything to extremes, to twist away and go farther. It is obvious that out of devotion to poetry, he would leave any job in the world, with no notice, or live in any way. Men like Whittemore or Nemerov can never write anything new because they are on-the-other-hand men. If you say, "The Christian Church is corrupt," they would say, "On the other hand. . . ." If you say, "John Foster Dulles was as close to being crazy as most statesmen get," they would say,

"On the other hand. . . ." Wright's tendency is the opposite—to follow an idea until it flies, or turns back into a fish. What he admires about the Chinese poets is their ability to get drunk without remorse, to write short poems for a whole lifetime without apology, to ride out of a gate into the desert without looking back.

His work shows an unusual intellectual enthusiasm. Behind the pleasant sense of something new in language lies a conscious and deliberate rejection of an entire structure of thought, which is very well understood. Behind the subtle language, which seems all emotion and fragrance, lies intellectual energy, in this case, extremely powerful intellectual energy.

He goes long distances when he starts, and gives the impression of someone obeying ancient instincts, like some animal who spends all summer with his herd, then migrates alone, traveling all night, drinking from old buffalo wallows. (pp. 97-8)

> Crunk [pseudonym of Robert Bly], "The Works of James Wright," in The Sixties (copyright © 1966 by The Sixties Press; reprinted by permission of the editors), No. 8, Spring, 1966 (and reprinted as an essay by Robert Bly in The Pure Clear Word: Essays on the Poetry of James Wright, edited by Dave Smith, University of Illinois Press, 1982, pp. 78-98).

ROBERT HASS

I have been worrying the bone of this essay for days because, in an issue of *Ironwood* honoring James Wright, I want to say some things against his poems. The first of his books that I read was *The Branch Will Not Break*. It is supposed to have broken ground by translating the imagery of surrealist and expressionist poetics into American verse. That was not what I responded to. What mattered to me in those poems was that their lean, clear, plain language had the absolute freshness of sensibility. They made sensibility into something as lucid and alert as intelligence. . . . I can give you an example from *Shall We Gather at the River:*

> Along the sprawled body of the derailed
>   Great Northern freight car,
> I strike a match slowly and lift it slowly.
> No wind.
>
> Beyond town, three heavy white horses
> Wade all the way to their shoulders
> In a silo shadow.
>
> Suddenly the freight car lurches.
> The door slams back, a man with a flashlight
> Calls me good evening.
> I nod as I write good evening, lonely
> And sick for home.

Those last two lines are what I mean. They were not written by the poet who is lonely and sick for home, they were written by the man who noticed that the poet, sitting in his room alone, recalling a scene outside Fargo, North Dakota, nods when he writes down the greeting of his imagined yardman, and catches in that moment not the poet's loneliness but a gesture that reveals the aboriginal loneliness of being—of the being of the freight cars, silos, horses, shadows, matches, poets, flashlights. And that man, the man who wrote those lines, is not lonely. At least that is not quite the word for it. There is a poem by Basho that gets at this:

> Not my human
>   sadness, cuckoo,
>   but your solitary cry.

The cuckoo, or hototogisu, is the nightingale of Japanese poetry. Its evening song has all the automatic associations with loneliness and beauty, and Basho is correcting that tradition. He is not, he says, talking about our plangent human loneliness but about the solitariness of being, of beings going about their business. The business of singing, if you are a bird, of feeling lonely, if you are a human. This is a distinction and it is the function of intelligence to make distinctions, but this one has been felt toward, with an absolute clarity of feeling, and that is what I mean by sensibility. It is a quality that flashes out from time to time in Wright's poems and it made *The Branch Will Not Break* an enormously important book for me. So I should probably rephrase my first sentence in the manner of *Two Citizens*: I want to say some things against James Wright's poems, which I love. (pp. 196-97)

Someone has calculated that the words *dark, darkness,* and *darkening* appear over forty times in the twenty-six pages *The Branch Will Not Break* occupies in the *Collected Poems. Green* must appear at least as often. And the book is full of those Wordsworthian words that no one is supposed to be able to get away with: *lovely, terrible, beautiful, body,* and *lonely* run like a threnody through all his books. I don't care how often James Wright uses any word, but I do care how he uses them and why. The early poems have helped me to think about this, particularly **"On Minding One's Own Business"** in *Saint Judas*. . . . The poem ends, like many of Wright's poems, with a prayer:

> From prudes and muddying fools,
> Kind Aphrodite, spare
> All hunted criminals,
> Hoboes, and whip-poor-wills,
> And girls with rumpled hair,
> All, all of whom might hide
> Within that darkening shack.
> Lovers may live, and abide.

Maybe the worst thing about American puritanism is the position it forces its opponents into. If the puritan can't distinguish a hobo from a hunted criminal, a little nighthawk from a girl who does the sorts of things that rumple hair, the poet won't. Hunted criminal, in fact, equals hobo equals bird equals girl. The puritan can't tell one from another and knows they are all bad; the poet can't tell either, only he knows they belong to the dark and are good. When he agrees to disagree with the puritan on his own terms, he gives away will, force, power, weight because they are bad American qualities and he settles for passivity and darkness. This explains why the grown man's dream is the beginning of a dark hair under an illiterate girl's ear. (pp. 199-200)

Wright has often been praised, to use the curious language of *The Norton Anthology of Modern Poetry,* for his "compassionate interest in social outcasts." That has never seemed to me to be the way to say it. What has always been a remarkable, almost singular, fact about his poetry is the way in which the suffering of other people, particularly the lost and the derelict, is actually a part of his own emotional life. It is what he writes from, not what he writes about. He has a feeling in his own bones for what a cold and unforgiving place the social world is. More than that, he has a feeling, almost Calvinist, for how unforgiving the universe is. . . . He is fascinated by defeat the way some men are fascinated by money, as the intelligible currency of our lives. His poems return and return to this theme, to the unformed hopes growing in the warm dark and the cold dark to which they return, until loneliness and death seem like the price exacted for living. (pp. 200-01)

Over and over again in American writing, [we find the] theme or discovery, that the inner life has no place, that it makes outlaws of us. Whether it is Huck deciding to go to hell or the hell of West's *Miss Lonelyhearts,* or Gatsby thinking the rich with their good teeth and fast cars can transform the ugly midwestern body of the world or poor Clyde Griffith, who rises from the squalor of his childhood when he glimpses velvet curtains in a Kansas City hotel, or Robinson's loyalty to Luke Havergal and the boozy moon, there is always this sense of a radical division between the inner and outer worlds and the hunger for a magic which will heal it, a sanctification or election. It gives a kind of drama to Wright's search for a style, but it also gives me the uneasy feeling that the way of posing the problem is the problem.

These themes persist through all the later work: a poetry that aims at beauty of feeling, a continuous bone-aching loneliness, a continuous return to and caressing of the dark, a terror of the cold dark, a compassion for whoever suffers it, a desire to escape from the body. The new manner of *The Branch Will Not Break* doesn't signal a change in theme, but a different rhetorical strategy. The more relaxed rhythms, with pauses at line end, feel like a man taking a deep breath. . . . And the playfulness of the titles insists on the fact of imagination. So do the plain words from romantic poetry, *lovely, beautiful, terrible,* that don't describe anything but tell you that someone is feeling something. And the images let go of the known configurations so that they can look inward and try to name the agency of transformation. . . . This is the freshness of the book and it helps me to understand why I responded to it so deeply and why I end by gnashing my teeth over so many of the poems:

> . . . Only two boys
> Trailed by the shadow of rooted police,
> Turn aimlessly in the lashing elderberries.
> One cries for his father's death,
> And the other, the silent one,
> Listens into the hallway
> Of a dark leaf.

The means, this style that is to make transformation possible, keeps wanting to be the end, the transformation itself, the beauty by which we are justified. There is no ground in these lines between the violent outer world and the kid listening poetically down the hallway of a dark leaf. There must be a Yiddish joke somewhere or a story by Peretz in which the poet appears before the recording angel who asks him what he's done and he says I listened down the hallway of a dark leaf or the long dream of my body was the beginning of a dark hair, etc. And one of the angels, maybe Raphael whom Rilke called the terrible one, says, this guy has got to be kidding.

Wright knows this most of the time, that the "one wing" of beauty won't take him very far. But again and again in *The Branch Will Not Break* he tries to see what can be made to happen by saying beautiful things, by repeating his talismanic nouns and adjectives of the discovery of the inner world. . . . (pp. 203-05)

In 1963, the year in which *The Branch Will Not Break* appeared, Robert Bly printed in *Choice* a passionate, ragged, very contradictory and very important essay called "A Wrong Turning in American Poetry." He attacked the modernist movement, especially imagism, as a kind of pictorialism, mesmerized by things, frightened of the spirit, preoccupied with technique, a replica of American culture. A great deal of what Bly had to say is true. He wanted a poetry that was inward, fresh, alive to its own impulse. "When the senses die, the sense within us that delights in poetry dies." "In a poem, as in the human body, what is invisible makes all the difference." But much of it read like an evangelical tract. It distrusts the mind and it insists on the radical and permanent division between the inner and the outer, believing only in the election of inward illumination: "A man cannot turn his face at the same moment toward the inward world and the outer world: he cannot face both north and south." Imagination is the source of election and, as in Wright, the world is its enemy. "The imagination *out of its own resources* creates a poem as strong as the world which it faces." And, as in Wright, the world is a jail in which the soul is imprisoned. Bly translates Rilke's "die Befreiung der dicterish Figur" as "the releasing of the image from jail," and adds, "the poet is thinking of a poem in which the image is released from its imprisonment among objects." But what is an object? A horse? The round white stone on my desk? The old curled postcard of a still life by Georgia O'Keefe? It is when the imagination withdraws from things that they become objects, when it lets the world go. This is a Calvinist and solipsistic doctrine. No wonder that the poetry of the deep image is preoccupied with loneliness. (p. 206)

Galway Kinnell has said some [things similar to Robert Bly's account of the role intelligence plays in the life of the imagination] with less polemical distortion. "We have to feel our own evolutionary roots and to know that we belong to life in the same way that other animals do and the plants and the stones. . . . The real nature poem will not exclude man and deal only with animals and plants and stones, a connection deeper than personality, a connection that resembles the attachment one animal has for another." This seems to me to say many of the things that are valuable in Bly's essay without hauling in a Manichean dualism, if we add to it that the poem has to be made out of the whole being and not out of assent to the idea.

Wright is both a more literary and less theoretical poet than Bly or Kinnell. If Bly seems sometimes to apply his ideas about imagination to the activity of writing, Wright suffers the tenor of a style as if it were the temperament of a lover. He lives inside it, feels through it. That's why his poems reflect, with desperate force, the lameness of the isolated inner world, "the sight of my blind man," its mere sensitivity which issues so often in the same nouns and adjectives, the same verbal constructions, the same will to be beautiful. Against the defense economy, we place—as plea and touchstone—little boys wondering, wondering. Against Moloch, as Allen Ginsberg said in a moment of lovely impatience, the whole boatload of sensitive bullshit.

Aestheticism is what I am talking about, decadence. It's a cultural disease and it flourishes when the life of the spirit, especially the clear power of imagination and intelligence, retreats or is driven from public life, where it ought, naturally, to manifest itself. The artists of decadence turn away from a degraded social world and what they cling to, in their privacy, is beauty or pleasure. The pleasures are esoteric; the beauty is almost always gentle, melancholy, tinged with the erotic, tinged with self-pity. Pound and Eliot, Joyce and Lawrence grew up in a period of decadence in poetry. They did not put down the aesthetes who ought to have been their fathering generation; they honored them. (pp. 207-08)

The issue seems to me urgent and I want to say the whole thing against these poems, this tone, in Wright because his struggle with it belongs so much to our culture, to American ugliness, to every kid who wanders into every public library Carnegie built in every devastated American town and, glimpsing the dim intuited features of his own inwardness in some book of poems he has picked up, is, when he emerges into the sunlight of drug store, liquor store, gas station, an outcast and a fugitive. *The Branch Will Not Break* is a book vivid with inward alertness, but it also brings us up against the limitations behind the aesthetic that informs it.

Wright's subject, like Wordsworth's, is the discovery of his own inwardness and the problem of what it can mean, what form it can take in the world. A large part of Wordsworth's struggle had to do with the fact that, in his time, there was no coherent psychological or philosophical accounting for the intensity and reality of his own experience, so he labored in *The Prelude* both to make it visible and to find a form for it in thought. Wright's problem is different in crucial ways. For one thing, he was born a convicted sinner in southern Ohio. For another, his experience is closer to the erotic. For that reason, it seems to me, by some measure, truer because it is through the erotic that one body turns to another and social life, in which the intensity of human inwardness has to find a form, begins. (p. 208)

[Wright's poem] **"Autumn Begins in Martins Ferry, Ohio"** is about a form the inner life takes in the world. (p. 209)

[The] Friday night football games [in that poem] are in one way a deeper order than either the political or the economic systems of which Blake is thinking [in his poem "London"], because their necessity is entirely imaginative. This is a harvest festival and a ritual. Ritual form is allied to magic, as it is in every community, and magic is allied to the seasons and the sexual potency of the earth.

Because this festival is American and puritan, it is an efficient transmutation of lovelessness into stylized violence. "Gallop terribly": or changing chickens into horses. It is a way of describing and evoking the animal beauty in the violence of the dying year, the explosive beauty of boys who are heroes because they imagine they are heroes and whose cells know that it will be their turn to be ashamed to go home. Even the stanzaic structure of the poem participates in the ritual. The first two stanzas separate the bodies of the men from the bodies of the women and the third stanza gives us the boys pounding against each other, as if they could, out of their wills, effect a merging. Insofar as this is a political poem, it is not about the way that industrial capitalism keeps us apart, but the way it brings us together.

This is, in other words, the poem Wright has always been writing:

> Sick of the dark, he rose
> For love, and now he goes
> Back to the broken ground.

Everything about those fall nights is brought to bear here, even the harsh artificial light in which they occur and the cold and darkness that surround them. . . . Later again, in **"A Mad Fight Song for William S. Carpenter,"** he will make the connection . . . between the beauty of football and the beauty of war. Saying that, we are in the territory of *The Iliad* and the territory of tragedy. Beyond any social considerations, what the fall of the year tells us is that we are all going down to the dark, one way or another. It is Homer who describes battle as the winds of autumn sweeping the leaves, terribly, from the trees and it is Homer's Apollo who watches the battle and says, with a god's luminous contempt, "Men, they are like leaves, they flourish a little and grow warm with life, and feed on what the ground gives, and then they fade away." Suicidally beautiful: that adverb is not there to nudge us into feeling. It means what it says. It tries to describe what happens when the inner life can't find its way out of the dark and it also describes, illuminates that tendency in James Wright's art. (pp. 209-11)

Suicidally beautiful: the poems [in *The Branch Will Not Break*] have suffered from that temptation and the poems from this point on, the best of them I think, reflect a determination to face "the black ditch of the Ohio" and not be killed by it. This is announced—in another place by another river—in **"The Minneapolis Poem,"** the second poem in *Shall We Gather at the River,* that utterly painful book. . . . [Wright's] response to . . . suicidal beauty matters to me because it introduces that odd comic tone which will continue into some very desperate poems . . . and because what he places over against that death is the life of the imagination. (p. 212)

A strange thing, a wonderful and strange act of imagination occurs in *Shall We Gather at the River.* It is the appearance of Jenny. She is the secret inside the word *secret* which appears so often in the book: the discovery of his spirit and of the beauty of the body and of the desire for love which grew up in Ohio and was maimed there. She is probably also the young girl in the earlier poem **"Beginning"** who lifts up the lovely shadow of her face and disappears wholly in the air. *Shall We Gather at the River* is dedicated to her. . . . (p. 213)

In the new poems at the end of the *Collected Poems,* Jenny is **"The Idea of the Good,"** and as she emerges, her name echoing all those sentimental midwestern songs, Wright returns again and again to the terror of the river down home. . . . (p. 216)

What emerges from [the] birth and death [portrayed in the new poems at the end of *Collected Poems*] was not possible in the diction of the early poems or in the willful beauty of *The Branch Will Not Break*—the poems about Uncle Willie, Uncle Shortie, Emerson Buchanan, Aunt Agnes, Wright's teacher Charles Coffin, the poems of the people of Ohio, his own Winesburg. Much of this is in *Two Citizens,* where Jenny is identified as "the Jenny sycamore" who had been "the one wing, the only wing." But it isn't only Ohio that emerges in these poems. There is also a more open insistence by Wright on his art and the traditions of his art. And this has required him, once again, to find a new language, a style that can accommodate what he has learned and gather it to the spoken language of his childhood. The way he has achieved this is, I think, intensely artificial, even a little weird, and I think it is meant to be. At its best it's very funny and playful. . . . (pp. 216-17)

At other times its artfulness consists in rendering peculiarities of diction exactly. (p. 217)

Here and there in the artifice is something like boozy insistence, that strange pride that dares you to contradict. . . . (p. 218)

Sometimes the manner blusters through difficulty, but at their best these poems do make a wholeness. Especially **"Prayer to the Good Poet"** in which he links his own father to Horace, one of his fathers in poetry, and the poems to his Ohio teacher, and the unmannered fluidity and assurance (and amazed gratitude) of some of the love poems. And . . . Jenny becomes the sycamore, his first rising and discovery of poetry. That is why **"October Ghosts"** is the most crucial poem in the book, for me. It's a poem in which Wright makes a kind of peace with the terror and loneliness of **"To the Muse"**:

> Jenny cold, Jenny darkness,
> They are coming back again.
> We came so early,
> But now we are shovelled
> Down the long slide.
> We carry a blackened crocus
> In either hand.

And then these lines in which Wright seems to have, at last, two wings. One of them is Jenny who is beauty, loneliness, death, the muse, the idea of the good, a sexual shadow, a whore, the grandmother of the dead, the lecherous slit of the Ohio, an abandoner of her child, a "savage woman with two heads . . . the one / Face broken and savage, the other, the face dead," the name carved under a tree in childhood close to the quick, a sycamore tree, a lover, the first time he ever rose. The other wing is his art, and with both of them he returns to his native place. The lines are a four-verse summary of "The Heights of Macchu Picchu" and, because they gather—at the river—the whole struggle of James Wright's poetry, I think they are among the most beautiful and simple lines he has written:

> I will walk with you and Callimachus
> Into the gorges
> Of Ohio, where the miners
> Are dead with us.

This is the poem that ends, "Now I know nothing, I can die alone." Which is what has to be, and did not seem possible before. (pp. 218-19)

> Robert Hass, "James Wright," in Ironwood, Special Issue: James Wright, 10 (copyright © 1977 by Ironwood Press; reprinted by permission of the editors), 1977 (and reprinted in The Pure Clear Word: Essays on the Poetry of James Wright, edited by Dave Smith, University of Illinois Press, 1982, pp. 196-219).

WILLIAM S. SAUNDERS

Wright's *The Branch Will Not Break* (1963) came out a year after [Robert Bly's] *Silence in the Snowy Fields* and resembles it too much for critical comfort. The poems in ***The Branch***, although much more personal and forceful than Wright's earlier efforts, seemed to borrow not so much Bly's honesty as Bly's emotions and subjects. As in *Silence*, one found the love of mysticism, of abrupt leaps between apparently unconnected material, of solitude, of the instant of extraordinary perception, of playful, scene-setting titles (**"As I Step Over a Puddle . . ."**), of dusk and small plains towns, and of animals and nature. Occasionally, however, Wright's differences from Bly emerged and clashed with the Bly adaptations: Wright did not share Bly's Whitmanesque attraction to death; Midwestern bleakness was just that for him; solitude was often as painful as it was exquisite; and the Midwest was not only the locale of Minnesota farms where Wright awkwardly felt Bly's sort of ecstacy . . . , it was also the scene of his brutalized working class youth in Martins Ferry, Ohio, where his father's vitality was crushed in factory work. . . . Often, Wright seemed confused about his feelings in ***The Branch***; his dominantly joyful response to Midwestern realities seemed forced. (pp. 353-54)

Since ***Shall We Gather at the River*** (1968), however, Wright's poetic independence, sincerity, and power have steadily increased. By being original, he has more profoundly learned from Bly. In ***Shall We Gather***, Wright . . . found his voice. . . . His new honesty after ***The Branch*** resulted in a shift in subject matter, from rural scenes to people and urban scenes, and, more crucially, a shift in feelings, from ecstacy to anger and misery. . . . Even Bly saw that the happiness of ***The Branch*** was willed: "tired of his own vision of the hostility of things, Wright assumes in animals a gentleness that is not there." Recently, however, especially in ***Two Citizens***, Wright has become our most scrupulously honest, our least pretentious poet.

There is, however, an aspect of Wright's determined honesty that can be, in its own way, artificial. Often Wright is strangely aggressive about his supposedly humble straight-talking, as if he were saying, at one and the same time, "I'm just a simple man, not all that bright or special, in fact quite thoroughly ordinary and vulnerable," yet also "There is more value in an ordinary man's honest emotions than in any elaborate, self-conscious thinking. So here is my emotion and you can take it or leave it. You'd better take it." Mark Twain without the hidden smile. Wright's aggressiveness about the value and validity of all his emotions leads him, at times, into blundering impulsiveness and embarrassing sentimentality. He has always felt and demonstrated, with intense preoccupation, the value of mercy and tenderness. But in at least two poems of ***Two Citizens***, he seems to be not so much loving someone as loving love. . . . Immersed in his emotion, Wright has no awareness of its wishfulness. In his new book, ***To a Blossoming Pear Tree*** (1977), Wright again occasionally refuses to do any hard thinking in order to keep a desired emotion unsullied.

When Wright is not just blusteringly direct or uncritically wishful but is aware of his aggression and raises the possibility that his simplicity is sentimental, when he hears how others might hear him, as he does more and more in his recent work, his affirmed emotions, underpinned by intellect, have double the power and weight. **"Well, What Are You Going to Do?"** . . . , quite obviously in its very title, conveys this self-awareness. It is a love poem about a cow. Wright knows his readers might think deep and tender love for a cow absurd, but it is against that thought that the poem squarely places itself. Wright splits himself in two: he is half identified with himself as a boy watching his pet cow give birth and half an adult watching, questioning, and finally justifying that boy's awe-filled tenderness. . . . The boy watches the cow's suffering for two hours and then finally helps the birth along. The event is presented as one which is as frightening, intense and exposing as a boy's first sexual love. The cow is called "a beautiful woman," whose "problem" the boy knows nothing about. . . . [This] sense of witnessing a sacred event from profane life suffuses James Wright as a boy. But another James Wright occasionally emerges and finally dominates the poem. This Wright asks us "What was I going to do?" and "What was I supposed to do there . . . ?" half to convey awe, but also to assert that he was right to feel tender rather than indifferent or afraid or disgusted. This is the Wright who deliberately brings in details that are hardly romantic or sentimental. . . . This Wright is boldly challenging his readers to find fault with his love. The unpleasant aspects of the experience seem insignificant for someone capable of empathizing with the animals. . . . Wright is an extremist when it comes to love, but usually he avoids the shrillness and defensiveness of this poem. My main point here is that Wright is focusing not only on his experience but also on his response to that experience. Wright's best recent work is similarly self-conscious and similarly asserting the interdependence of love and indignation: if you love, you will hate all that threatens the loved object; if you hate it is because you love. Thus Wright frees himself from both dreamy, soft love and consuming hatred. (pp. 354-57)

>William S. Saunders, "Indignation Born of Love: James Wright's Ohio Poems," in The Old Northwest (copyright © Miami University 1978), Vol. 4, No. 4, December, 1978, pp. 353-69.

EDWARD HIRSCH

[James Wright] was a poet of enormous verbal resources and skills engaged in a complex and deeply human quest to write—in his own terms—"the poetry of a grown man" in the style of "the pure clear word." He was one of our great poets of the lost and desolate, feeling his way emotionally into the lives of the cheated, the drunk, the lunatic. He was also a Horatian craftsman for whom craftsmanship was never itself enough, continually struggling for clarity and against glibness in his work, and somehow capable of revealing what Robert Hass calls "the aboriginal loneliness of being." But if Wright was an explorer of our specifically human social darkness, he was also a poet of lyric ecstasy and radiant natural light. Over the years his work increasingly evoked the external natural world. Now in his last, posthumous collection—virtually completed before his death—Wright returns to his primary concerns, particularly exploring the terrible harshness and beauty of nature, but with a luminous depth and intensity.

"This Journey" takes Wright through the temples and cemeteries of Italy, where he is continually surprised by his own life and the lives of others. . . . [His] sense of astonishment at being alive and at the way things disappear and change is one of the leitmotifs of the volume, whether he is contemplating the ruined Temple of Apollo, where the frightened men who "cowered here" are now long dead, or the Forum, where the pitted statue of a girl is slowly dissolving into someone he can "almost name." This strange, double metamorphosis—humans turning to stone, statues becoming humanlike—is a subject the book returns to again and again.

The transforming moments in Wright's work are characteristically either moments of human exchange or moments of the isolated self's ecstatic communion with nature. "This Journey" is the study of a man bringing himself into harmony with the natural world before his death. . . .

[It] is the book of a man stepping lightly through the ruins, trying not to brood about the dead but brooding anyway, amazed by the transformations of time. It is appropriate that Wright's final journey ends with him watching a new day breaking over Venice, telling himself that he has to believe in his life because it is the only one he has, somehow still living inside his body, "sitting here strangely / On top of the sunlight." (p. 15)

>Edward Hirsch, "Stepping through the Ruins," in The New York Times Book Review (copyright © 1982 by The New York Times Company; reprinted by permission), April 18, 1982, pp. 15, 37.

JASCHA KESSLER

I think it is fair to suggest that a poem like [the title poem of his collection *This Journey*] speaks of Wright's understanding of his situation, which is the mortal situation, common to all of us, of course, but mortal in the extraordinary sense of the word too, in the sense of his own imminent mortality, and the reconciliation of the poet that already-passed sentence of doom. It is also fair to observe about that poem that it contains not only some of the themes of this book, but also the echoes of much of Wright's past work too: a verbal reticence or quietness, a gentle kind of toughness, a patient tenderness and tenderheartedness, and a stoic strength. . . .

Most of this book offers poems about places in Italy and France, for Wright spent a good deal of time in the Mediterranean region in his last period, and wrote a lot of poems, verses and prose poems about his contemplation of nature, a rather subdued, sometimes philosophically pious sort of contemplation at that. He did not write many "touristic" poems, however: monuments and history, contemporary life and politics and so on are hardly ever presented. And in this last volume, where several poems deal with what he knew was his last season of spring in Europe, the poet meditated on some Classical objects and themes, on Diana especially, the Virgin goddess, the huntress who killed, the bringer of death, the inviolable maiden, whom he seems to have regarded, implicitly, as his Muse. Which is hardly surprising, given his situation. I am sure he was deeply pondering the paradox that April is, as Eliot put it, "the cruellest month," and perhaps knew that there is a most ancient tradition, from quite pre-Christian roots too, in which the attendance upon the goddess of love, Venus, or Aphrodite, not Diana or Artemis, as in Wright, is a sad and dangerous nocturnal observance. And Wright surely changed his goddess to Diana the Huntress because he knew her fatal arrow had already struck him. Wright places the opening poem of this book ["**Entering the Temple in Nimes**"] squarely in that awareness.

That poem, grave and quiet, a prayer, not for salvation, but for a moment's respite in which to see a sign, a bare sign, . . . that would be all the grace the poet asks for, the promise of life's continuity, for others, if not for him, is not only a motif that runs through the book, but one that conveys much of Wright's characteristic poetic voice. For, from the beginning, James Wright's poetry is full of lamentation and sorrowing, full of pity for those who suffer.

I think, in short, of Wright as a Weeper, a poet overflowing with tears. But not a simply lachrymose poet, in the 19th Century mode, the sort of poet Mark Twain satirizes in *Huckleberry Finn*. It's a bit chancy to risk showing a heart and mind always weeping, in this society of ours that respects power, speed, strength, and winning at whatever cost; and it risks being misunderstood as merely sentimental and soft . . . but Wright was not really all that soft, and he was no whimperer. If one recalls Castaneda's odd stereotypes, in his *Don Juan*, namely Don Juan who is the Warrior, and the other wizard who is a Dancer, and the witch who is a Killer, then one can think of the essential Wright as what I have called A Weeper. It seems to have been his nature, and it certainly is his hallmark as a poet: a fountain of flowing tears.

In a culture like ours today, when it seems that so few even know how to weep, when indeed it almost seems to be forbidden to weep, and when grieving is a forgotten emotion, when loss and failure are denied, a poet who weeps is an important phenomenon, and someone to be considered very seriously.

> *Jascha Kessler, "James Wright: 'This Journey: Poems',"* in a radio broadcast on KUSC-FM—Los Angeles, CA, June 30, 1982.

ROBERT B. SHAW

Wright's stylistic odyssey is paradigmatic for his generation of American poets. His first two books, *The Green Wall* (1957) and *Saint Judas* (1959), are the work of a 1950s formalist chafing against formal disciplines. Strained, high-flown diction only occasionally relaxes, as though with a sigh of relief, into the plainness of everyday speech. The syntax is extended, convoluted—a snare in which the poet thrashes, gamely but helplessly. More than once the reader may have the disconcerting experience of coming to the bottom of a page and thinking a poem is over, only to turn the page and discover another two or three stanzas yet to go. The movement of such poems is like the galvanism that keeps a corpse's limbs twitching for some moments after the last breath has been drawn.

The milieu of these early poems—the industrial wasteland of southern Ohio— . . . is incongruous with the mandarin style they employ. Wright's wasteland, like Eliot's, features a once beautiful river polluted by human rapacity. But Wright's cast of characters is as quintessentially American as Eliot's is cosmopolitan. His small-town whores, ne'er-do-wells, drunks and wage slaves in mines and mills are belated versions of those portrayed by poets like Edgar Lee Masters and Edwin Arlington Robinson. The great difference is in point of view. Robinson, who certainly provided one model for Wright's intricate stanzas, scanned his characters from a clinical distance, rehearsing their disasters with a tone of stoic irony. Irony is not a tone Wright often reaches for; when he does, it eludes his grasp. In poem after poem he seeks imaginative identification with outcasts. . . . He is obsessed with the sufferings of victims, with his own sufferings and with the guilt of having suffered less than others he has known. It is the obsessiveness of feeling in the poems, just as much as their mechanically elaborate rhetoric, which often prolongs them beyond their natural span into exhausted anticlimax. In all manner of ways, the early Wright was overwrought.

Having grown disillusioned with his awkward and faltering devices, Wright looked outside his own literary tradition. Like a number of other poets near him in age—Bly, Merwin, Kinnell—he found a new voice through translating foreign poets and adapting some aspects of their styles. For Wright the new models included Trakl, Neruda and Vallejo, all of whom he translated, as well as certain Chinese poets to whom he paid a more remote yet discernible homage.

The Branch Will Not Break (1963) exhibited the new approach, which governed his work from then on. It is hard to recall how startling these poems were when they first appeared, so thoroughly have their once venturous strategies been assimilated over the last twenty years. Wright's near-abandonment of rhyme and meter was bound to make a difference, but a more striking innovation in these poems is his use of language as a seemingly immediate transmitter of perception. His words no longer smother what they seek to describe; they depict objects with the entranced accuracy of Chinese painting. And in a way which seemed jarring to some of the first readers of these poems, Wright often abruptly couples passages of calm, objective description with expressions of feeling that may or may not have an evident link to the scene. (p. 118)

One's reaction to [the last lines in the anthology piece **"Lying in a Hammock at William Duffy's Farm in Pine Island, Minnesota"**] is a test of one's taste for the later Wright. If one thinks the last line a self-indulgent non sequitur, one will not get far with this poetry. But if one appreciates the threads of intuition, at once as tenuous and as strong as a spider's web, which hold imagery and statement together, one will find much to admire in Wright's later books.

Sometimes even a fan may feel the new method misfires. Wright is capable of a tone of faux naïveté that is cloying in large doses. And his experimentalism occasionally has about it that wide-eyed American spit-and-rubberband quality, the self-applause of an auto mechanic seeking a patent on the wheel. But his successes outnumber his lapses.

He never stopped writing about the American Gothic dinginess of Martins Ferry, Ohio; but he managed in time to master his emotions in dealing with his past, subduing them to the rule of a contemplative spirit. He aspired, in Stevens's phrase, to write "profound poetry of the poor and of the dead." This he did, on more than one occasion. And yet it is not so much in these laments that his most lasting work appears as in his steady views of the enduring forms of nature that provide a serene backdrop for human perturbation. By drawing together the lasting and transient aspects of existence, Wright achieved an elegiac tone as complex as Hardy's. As his voice gained in flexibility, his settings took on variety. To his stark vignettes of the Midwest he added others of landscapes far afield. A great many of the poems in *This Journey,* as in his previous volume, *To a Blossoming Pear Tree* (1977), come out of Wright's travels in Europe. They eloquently continue the line in American literature that seeks to come to terms imaginatively with the old world. Perhaps surprisingly, what comes through most vividly is the poet's sense of being at home. (pp. 18-19)

Wright's awareness of approaching death can be discerned in these poems—not in any cadaverous quality but rather in a heightened sensitivity to the pulse of vitality everywhere around him. . . .

Two words that turn up time and again in these poems are especially suggestive of the nature of Wright's last phase; they are "light" and "gather." He had come to see life as both radiant and fragile: "light" in both senses. And without renouncing the local and tragic themes he began with, he made it his final business to integrate, to "gather," a wider range of scenes and tones than many poets master in longer careers. This last book gives the lie to his most famous line: his life was not wasted. (p. 119)

> *Robert B. Shaw, "Exploring the Ruins," in* The Nation *(copyright 1982 The Nation magazine, The Nation Associates, Inc.), Vol. 235, No. 4, August 7-14, 1982, pp. 118-19.*

WILLIAM HARMON

[Although James Wright] was an extraordinarily sophisticated and erudite poet, he kept plenty of room in his heart for the humble virtues. A concordance will show that he was never too lofty to make frequent use of *good* and *bad*—words that have become members of an endangered verbal species. *Bad* has come to mean *good,* while *good* has slipped down to the C-minus range, above *fair* but below *excellent* and other hyperbolic superlatives. (p. 612)

So when I say that James Wright was a good poet, I am using his characteristic vocabulary and saying two things about goodness: Wright was a good man and he wrote well.

Those nine monosyllables are so easy for me to put down that there is some danger of our forgetting how hard it is to be good and to work well. Wright's books seem to bear the scars, stretch-marks, and trophies of much struggle and even some defeat. He had a certain kind of good poem in mind, but he never achieved it, not quite. It was a vexing, perplexing problem of making ends meet. Here I am tempted to revise Blake and claim that, yes, extremes do indeed meet, but not until you introduce them. For Wright the extremes were *ends,* in many senses, of subject and technique. Wright's Democratic Vistas embraced so much that they make Whitman's look Republican. Wright wanted to canonize Judas and all the nameless sinners and pariahs. His outcast and downtrodden people were not the picturesque peasantry of the Liberal Imagination, not the eloquent Joads of Steinbeck, not the entertaining Snopeses of Faulkner. Wright's "people" were scum, the dregs, the horrible and disgusting filth of gutter, slum, and a richly deserved death row. Wright seems not only to have smooched lepers but also to have rejoiced in their leprosy. At the same time he rejoiced in the beautiful things of nature and culture: love among people, great art, the masterpieces and royalty of the plant and animal kingdoms. The glory of Wright's *To a Blossoming Pear Tree* is only partly a function of the pear's unilateral beauty; the glory depends also on the horrible presence of a shameless queer old derelict. Both tree and man—terminal extremes of health and disease—do what they do in passionate response to a biological summons to love in one way or another. Courageously Wright launched poem after poem in the direction of this indulgent democratic ideal, and it can be a thrilling enterprise to witness. (p. 613)

To include Judas, Harding, Daley, murderers, and drooling winos in lyric poems requires much more talent than Whitman's practice of sanctimonious slumming. The struggle to memorialize the aristocrats of squalor, the world-class crooks alongside the no-class losers, drew Wright to a correspondingly forked aesthetic. He seemed to want to embrace both James Whitcomb Riley and Rainer Maria Rilke in one hug: to keep faith with the corniest midwestern vernacular (a faith rather like Orson Welles's respect for Booth Tarkington, or Eliot's for Mark Twain) and at the same time to respond to the hypermodern voices of continental symbolist and surrealist poets whose primordial archetypal languages may lie even deeper in the soul than one's native vulgate. . . . Wright's effort to celebrate splendor while honestly recognizing the squalor inside and outside oneself, along with the parallel effort to honor conventional verse-verities, as registered in Robinson and Frost, while comprehending Rilke and Neruda—these labors resulted in nine volumes of poetry published over a twenty-five-year period. . . . The nine make up a corpus that is the most inconsistent known to me and is also among the most distinguished. The transition from *The Branch Will Not Break* . . . to *Shall We Gather at the River* . . . seems relatively smooth, but the other items in the series represent swerves, leaps, experiments, feints, backslidings, divagations, miscues, and even episodes of repudiation. (pp. 613-14)

This Journey, which cannot be called a culmination, is simply the last book by a poet who died too soon. It contains some very fine poems and some that seem inchoate or perfunctory. (But Wright at his most perfunctory could be far superior to many another poet at his most brilliant.) **"Wherever Home Is"** impresses me as a poem in Wright's most convincing voice. . . . In a few poems like **"Lament: Fishing with Richard Hugo"** Wright treats his own sharp tongue to a banquet of mockery. . . . One can speculate that Wright could have put all his voices and talents in a book-length poem or sustained sequence. He could not handle plots, and most of his characters reduce to one persona called "James Arlington Wright"; but that persona has enough depth and richness, and his experience takes in enough time (from classical antiquity to this century's Hardings, Eisenhowers, and Mayor Daleys; from Sappho to Doris Day and Barbra Streisand) and covers enough ground (China, Hawaii, Ohio, Italy) to have generated a great long poem. Instead we must be content with the pieces that we have. (pp. 614-15)

Of the seventy poems in *This Journey,* almost a third are in prose. Most of these are all right, I suppose, and a few (preeminently **"Honey"**) are as good as anything of this sort that I know of. But "this sort" in itself somehow fails to satisfy. Mixed in with ordinary verse, as in *This Journey,* the prose poems have a chance of pleasing; but, in a work like Wright's *Moments of the Italian Summer* . . . , in which all the so-called poems are prose, the total effect is unsettling and frustrating. (p. 615)

Wright commanded a range of poetic devices adequate to provide all the relief and variety that a book may need. Without the prose poems, *This Journey* stands as the work of a good man who wrote well. (p. 617)

William Harmon, "James Wright, the Good Poet," in The Sewanee Review *(reprinted by permission of the editor; © 1982 by The University of the South), Vol. XC, No. 4, Fall, 1982, pp. 612-23.*

DAVE SMITH

[James Wright is] at least in part a representative man whose poetics demonstrate what we mean by *contemporary* as both an extension of and a rebellion against modernism. . . .

We live in a time when critical theory has called into question not merely the function of art but the very existence of art. Theorists deny there can be an author. From Derrida to Culler to Fish, the talk is of the *text,* an impersonal object neither story nor poem. The desire of such criticism . . . is to bring to literature the objectivity of scientific inquiry; that is, to codify what and how literature *knows*. This is the direction and legacy of New Criticism in part, of modernist rebellion in part—but it is largely the temperament of the industrial world. While criticism fabricates objectivity and impersonality, becoming at last not a way of experiencing art but a kind of parodic extension of Robert Frost's remark about free verse—that is, a game played without net, racket, or balls—poetry has gone in the opposite direction. To understand and to follow James Wright's development as a poet we have to search for the man in the poems. (p. xii)

When W. B. Yeats spoke about the need to choose between perfection of the art and perfection of the life, he touched upon the central issue in poetry since the emergence of romanticism. If he seemed to echo modernist doctrine, to take the side of art's perfection, Yeats's poems moved always toward the inseparability of life and art that seems and is particularly contemporary. His act, the contemporary act, is that of the personality of a man rising symbolically to become the personality of men. We can see exactly this process in the poetry of James Wright.

Wright began with poems remarkable for their facility in verse elegance and for their implicit homage to the modernist obsession with an ideal and an impersonal music which might create an art, as Flaubert had said, apparently about nothing at all. Wright's first book, *The Green Wall,* appeared in 1957. . . . [It] made far less splash that year than did the Russian satellite Sputnik. *The Green Wall* carried into the space age the approving introduction of the last major modernist, W. H. Auden. In style and in attitude it echoed Robert Frost and E. A. Robinson, Thomas Hardy and Edward Thomas. It was the kind of poetry that Wright has referred to as "quietist" but it did not entirely conform to Donald Hall's survivor's description of poetry in the 1950s: "Here was the ability to shape an analogy, to perceive and develop comparisons, to display etymological wit, and to pun six ways at once. It appealed to the mind because it was intelligent, and to the sense of form because it was intricate and shapely. It did not appeal to the passions and it did not pretend to." Wright's was most unlike this paradigmatic poetry in that within his acceptance and practise of modernist restraint, decorum, and structure more received than evolved, he brought great passion to contend against historical constrictions. . . . The poet of *The Green Wall* is capable primarily of conventional language and pastoral scenes of bruised beauty. Wright learned to call this glib. Even so he gave us a surprising mix of poems about mad girls, black prostitutes, George Doty the murderer, and Sappho the Lesbian. Sappho? From a Martins Ferry boy? That was the college influence, the books. The others were Wright's true subject, and his subject was the ghostly debris of the American promise. (pp. xii-xiii)

James Wright understood the American promise to be life, liberty, and the pursuit of happiness. It was a vision of possibility, sometimes utopian but ordinarily practical. It was the vision of a small farm, a decently fed family, and the right to be responsible for one's self and one's own. . . . Wright's subject was heroism, promise and failure and evidence. Even in the slicked-up poems of *The Green Wall* there are hints of the blunt, aggressive poetry he will come to, of the dream life he will dramatize, and of the fearful privation of the human spirit that will be his battleground. Yet, the poet who speaks *The Green Wall* is the composite voice of Wright's literary fathers. Wright himself is scarcely to be seen.

Saint Judas, published just two years after the first book, continues the neo-Georgian style, though there is a new urgency of personality. The book's initial poem, **"Lunar Changes,"** suggests not so much an alteration in the way the poems will comport themselves—and indeed **"Complaint"** exhibits the smooth couplets of iambic pentameter which look backward in time—as the presence of deeper, more subtle changes. Wright had begun to abandon the pastoral hymn to Nature as the perfect Emersonian mirror. He had decided to know the reality of nature as he is in it and it is in him. As yet the attempt was rough and sporadic, but it was there. It was there stuttering through personality. Implicit in his lunar changes were the questions of what a poet knows and how he knows; that is to say, of facing the problem of what authority poetry might have in a post-*Wasteland* and post-Holocaust world. When poets or critics talk about the problem of form and content they are inevitably talking about the poet's *authority,* that which allows poetry to *do* anything or, as Auden says, "to make nothing happen."

The interjection of personality as the fundamental force of contemporary poetics drove against the cultural and critical lust for objective knowledge. To describe and evaluate the new poetry, criticism called it "confessional." . . . Confessionalism meant the recording and presentation of the raw data of biographical existence, the evidence of naturalistic decay. Everyone pointed out the extreme subjectivity and lack of shapeliness. It was, of course, a further rebellion against passionless modernism and the art about nothing. The poetry of personality, which had to have a confessional dimension but which might not be confessional, imagined that the details of the individual life might be drawn to a coherence and meaning that extended beyond the one life. (pp. xiii-xv)

With *Saint Judas* Wright began the invention of himself, his place, and of a poetry that would dramatize the life he had known, the American promise and the American nightmare. He began to feel that what he wrote and the way he wrote were historical lies. He wanted truth in his life and life in his poems. His poems underwent lunar changes and more. His titles pointed at guilt and innocence, purity and impurity. . . . Speaking of shame and humiliation, of revelation and accusation, Wright was a poet passing through learned abstractions toward finite places and things, what he called "secrets," that might constitute and define the individual life apart from and yet within a community. In **"At the Executed Murderer's Grave,"** Wright believed that "We are nothing but a man." This theme, Donne's and Coleridge's, of obligation and responsibility to man and being, which displaces the modernist obligation only to art, welled up. Wright had begun to allow his Ohio mythology to gleam forth from the details of his life, to allow his life to shape what was both immediately, verifiably true and also historically, mythically accurate. (pp. xv-xvi)

Sylvia Plath and others would join Wright in portraying art as the instructor of how to die. Wright's employment of biographical details which are verifiable, the confessional element, was obvious and demonstrated the poetry of personality. However, the syntactical skill and suppleness, the suspensions and juxtapositions, the rigorous cadence and tight rhymes drove against the poem's spontaneity. Wright created a character in whom we could place trust, a mature and sympathetic and ironic voice. . . . Wright's lunar changes and those of his contemporaries were directed at discovering, assembling, and giving cohesive authority to their secret lives. It is not difficult to see that the poets were regarding poetry as more nearly inspired than confessional. Their poet, logically, was an extension of the romantic corrective agent, though an agent virtually without power because their secret lives remained too often *merely* personal. (pp. xvi-xvii)

Wright's lunar changes did not happen in a vacuum. The contemporary movement toward personality is a romantic impulse, though it is an impulse finally as characteristic of modernism as of nineteenth-century art, with perhaps a renewed emphasis on a naked style capable of expressing experience in a world which had overnight hurtled into the space age. Of course Sputnik is only an image for a world spinning geometrically faster from its Cartesian birth. . . . Pastoral visions and melodious verses were, in the new age, as unreal as bogeymen, and what life was there in seamless artifacts? Poetry, it seemed, was beyond passion, rather than made of passion. The contemporary poets responded by beginning to write what Donald Hall described as "the poetry of a man in the world, responding to what he sees: with disgust, with pleasure, in rant and in meditation." If the result was art it would be the art of personal experience from which might rise a forged self, an empirical wisdom, a more tested vision of the real. The choice is, in retrospect, clear: the art about nothing at all or the life-roughened poem.... James Dickey had said in *The Suspect in Poetry,* published by Wright's friend Robert Bly in 1964, that "The secret does not, of course, reside in a complete originality, which does not and could not exist. It dwells, rather, in the development of personality, with its unique weight of experience and memory, as a writing instrument, and in the ability to give literary influence a new dimension which has the quality of this personality as informing principle." From within and from without, James Wright was under pressure to bring his life, or an invented life, forth in his poetry.

Following the publication of *Saint Judas,* Wright wrote a letter to his publisher in which he said he would not do that kind of poetry again. His third book, *The Branch Will Not Break,* showed radical stylistic changes but not a complete break with the past.... The changes in Wright are ... the predictable steps taken by literary history away from modernist orthodoxy.... In general, the change is from a dispassionate, ironic, closed-form poetry to Hall's poem in the world, to open form as it had been appearing to Wright and others through non-English models. The usual argument is that Wright was transformed by the influence of Robert Bly and through readings outside of the Anglo-American tradition of poetry. While this is a valid argument, we might be reminded that Wright no more abandoned his native traditions in poetry than he abandoned his Ohio Valley.

Nevertheless, Wright's poetry was now marked by a turn toward a private vision generally characterized by a juxtaposition of vivid and disparate images, an abjuring of narrative or linear progression in favor of an elliptical and spatial movement, and an economy of adjective, adverb, or qualifying phrase, all of which produced a resonance from the particular as it was baldly felt. William Carlos Williams had said "no ideas but in things," but he had not said *no ideas*. Wright did not abandon thought or thing in his new poems; he put them in a different balance. (pp. xvii-xviii)

The critics called Wright a surrealist and an imagist. He thought himself neither. In time we are going to get what academics call the definitive examination of what Wright was. We may get one after another and we may actually learn something about his lunar changes—but it will be a small something. Critics are not very good at understanding something any poet knows, which is that he contains multitudes because he lives by the imagination. Wright was more and less than any label. Nevertheless he created a visible character, a personality, and a coherent art in which his individual poems function as pieces of a mosaic.

In 1971 Wright published his *Collected Poems*.... It contained, in addition to most of his previous work and a section of translations, thirty-one new poems under the title **"New Poems."** This work showed Wright had come far from his early conventional poetry, but it also showed that he had moved away from the dream and nightmare image poems of his middle career. There was a renewed interest in narrative, or at least narrativelike, poems. He did not abandon rhetoric or image, private or public consciousness, screech or song, but he recombined these elements with an increasingly colloquial diction and an abruptly modulating tone. He tried to speak forcefully and plainly within the constraints of poetry, a poetry now identified with loosened rhythms, circling syntax, repetitions of image and phrase, anecdotes daringly dramatized and punctuated by authorial intrusion. In other words, he tried to stretch his expectations for and his accomplishments in poetry and he stepped even closer to the personal: he demanded the right to speak not as persona or mask but as himself, a man in the midst of chaotic experience who means to achieve a cohesive view of the real.... The foundation of Wright's vision of man being, as he said, that most of us are selfish sons of bitches, he still believed that no one was wholly without the evidence of hope and possibility. Wright was, we should remind ourselves, making these poems in an era of terrible racial struggles, of apparent social fragmentation, and of the daily news delivered icily in body counts. Yet Wright's testimony was finally quite clear: life is good. (pp. xix-xx)

Wright's awareness of the American dream of possibility, a dream which subsumes all other dreams, led him to rant and sing of kinsmen, waste, violence, betrayal, destruction, and love.... There was in **"New Poems"** and subsequently in *Two Citizens* ... a more raggedly personal style than ever. And in *Two Citizens,* which he came to reject, there was an open argument with country and kin. A surprising, shocking book, *Two Citizens* has been widely regarded as evidence of Wright's and contemporary poetry's failure to make art, a failure inherent in the exchange of art's distance for personal authority. Certainly there was an extension of Wright's decision not only to front the people, places, and ideas nearest to him but also to front his reader. Time will, of course, judge Wright's choice and the value of his writing but it is not irrelevant that his private argument has been felt by many to possess significant public resonance. (p. xx)

[In a preface Wright provided in 1963 for a book of poems by Hy Sobiloff, he] identified the fundamental task of modern art: the attempt to give coherence and objectivity to the subjectively real and all but ungraspable design of human experience. He moreover reveals the large and primary figure of his poetry by evoking the ubiquitous wandering exile whose journey is first shadowed in the Christian image of the lost garden and then echoed in the contemporary exile who is technocratically and industrially victimized. Wright has evoked Thoreau's fear of being ground up in the machine, processed, lost, made anonymous and irresponsible. In such a world, Wright knew, we belong not to the dead or the living but to the undead mass. How then shall we live—not merely survive as naturalistic motes—when to live is to see, to be fully conscious, able as Thoreau said to look another man in the face, to recall what the American promise was and to understand what it has come to? From this perspective it seems not surprising but predictable that Wright would woo a poetry of prosaic character and the emotional range of a Dickens, who not incidentally was the subject of James Wright's doctoral dissertation. Wright is devoted to Horace and the demands of Horatian craft, restraint, distance, humility, elegance—but it is the anger, humor, indignation, love, and ragged passion of Dickens in contention with that Horatian ghost that most identifies Wright's late poetry and his citizenship. (pp. xxii)

[Few] American poets have become so ruthlessly local, regional, and willing to address their arguments so directly as James Wright. In *Two Citizens* the mythical and real Ohio River Valley are one in contrast with Wright's adopted Italy, the country of Horace. His two citizens are himself and his wife

Annie, but they are also America and Italy. Wright claims he loves Italy and hates America but he spits and blusters and does not believe that himself.... Neither in memory nor in poetry could he abandon the source of his dreams.... He understood that the artist cannot perfect life or art but must settle for a ragged interpenetration of both. When he wrote of his Appalachian country of steel mills, mines, factories, farms, and river towns, Wright showed us the suffering and horror and ugliness that Dickens had known, but after Horace the last words of Wright's **Collected Poems** are "I am so happy." And the last words of **Two Citizens** are "I love you so." Beyond all the false starts, for Wright, there had to be the journey homeward, the inside journey, where there would be courage and, more than courage, joy. (pp. xxii-xxiii)

We hear of nothing so frequently in his poems as the glint of ... joy, the flash of happiness, the blossoming of beauty.... James Wright never thought of himself as a morbid or death-haunted poet, though some of his readers did. He was keenly aware of what it felt like to live in perhaps the most turbulent, confusing, painful, absurd, and incomprehensible time man has ever known. He had survived the hell of the Ohio River Valley and he had experienced firsthand the hell of destruction that the Atomic Age was in Japan. But he believed, as he wrote, that the branch would not break, that a man might lie still enough to watch a blue jay on that branch "abandon himself / To entire delight."

Wright's poems are counters to the fear and the ugliness that attack us all. The world of his poetry is one in which we may discover the heroic in ourselves, the secret life we hadn't known about. His poems tell only one story, the great story of finding the way home, and on the right terms. This is most significantly the American story, but it is not only the American story. We find him again and again standing in the place of darkness where the dream had died. Trying always to assume his individual responsibility for life, he leans like a compass needle toward the true place which is inside but which in the poems is Ohio, the place named after the river that is life itself. (pp. xxiii-xxiv)

In 1976 James Wright published what is commonly referred to as a collection of prose poems, **Moments of the Italian Summer.** He regarded these pieces as prose fragments but he also felt that the distinction between prose and poetry was irrelevant. The pieces, however defined, are reveries, testimonies to a joy immanent in the natural world. His language pours out like water from a broken dam and in contrast we become aware, as he must have, of how fitful and choked his poetry had sometimes been. In retrospect there is an impression that Wright spoke in spite of himself, that there was a joy in him he could not hide.... Wright had learned that for the writer every life and every piece of creation was no less than the image of all creation. Through the struggle with language and for language, he had been given the gift of life that is the self. He had understood that he had to break down and scrape away the dead expression that sealed him from the living presence of the past in its pastness and from himself, from the actual world in which he and all men walked. Wright had discovered that history was not merely style; it was memory and power as the evidence of and the stimulus to ordinary human responsibility. The living past, shown forth by all that debris of the American promise, cries out to the poet. When he answers it is with poems. When the poems are true and strong they return us all to the dream of possibility. (p. xxv)

I said earlier that James Wright was not death-haunted. Still, Death is the main character in our fictions. Wright was like most of us God-haunted and self-isolated. This risked the refusal of life and the debasement of creation which he had described. Wright allows us to see that if we choose not to undertake our destiny and choose not to front life, which the choice to employ habitual language and gesture means, we effectively ignore communal responsibility. This is the responsibility each bears to all. It is the responsibility of courage. Wright's courage consists in his willingness to communicate the truth of his feelings at the risk not only of public failure but of failure before his masters, Dickens and Horace. Wright continuously praised writers for telling the truth boldly and powerfully but shied away from such claims for himself. The irony, though it is not very ironic, is that the more he brought his life into his poems, his emotional and ethical and biographical and mythical life, the more truth he made us feel in ourselves, the more courage he gave us. The one story he tells proceeds from the conviction to which he was always faithful, that however tragic life may be there is the beauty of joy within it and we must seek tirelessly for it. (p. xxvi)

> Dave Smith, "Introduction," in The Pure Clear Word: Essays on the Poetry of James Wright, edited by Dave Smith (© 1982 by the Board of Trustees of the University of Illinois; reprinted by permission of the author and the University of Illinois Press), University of Illinois Press, 1982, pp. xi-xxviii.

ALAN WILLIAMSON

[James Wright] was a poet of emotional extremes. Certain of his feelings—his overflowing compassion, and his lifelong loving preoccupations with his working-class origins—appealed to readers so strongly as to rule out a purely aesthetic judgment. At the same time, Wright was an exceedingly private poet, whose impulse was often to protect the object of his feeling even against the intrusion of his own words.... He probably changed the possibilities of American poetry more than any other poet of his generation except Ashbery and Ginsberg. The style which he, and his friend Robert Bly, invented—at once emotionalist and secretive, with its simple sentences, forbidden nineteenth-century words like "lovely," and opalescent, mysterious nature imagery—became for more than a decade the dominant mode of the American brief lyric. Yet it remains a conspicuously mannered style, derived neither from speech nor from traditionally fluent writing. Poignant though it can be, it is perhaps too limiting, in its exclusion of complex thought and resonant music, to yield poetry of the very greatest impact. Wright himself—though showered with easy and, often, implicitly anti-intellectual praise—continued, rather endearingly, to suggest that, judged by the standards of the dead poets he loved best, he was "minor."

He also continued to change, in a way that makes one think of Yeats, Eliot, Lowell—poets not at all "minor" in their ambitions. In **Two Citizens** . . . , he largely turned away from the imagistic, to make poetry out of the inarticulate violence of American masculine speech when it tries to deal with intense emotion. It was a confusing, disquieting kind of poetry. The poet's feelings seemed to veer to opposite extremes from line to line, or to protect themselves behind inscrutable sarcasms.... [In] his next book, **To a Blossoming Pear Tree,** he often seemed to be ironing out the new style's subtlety along with its prickliness, while remaining indulgent toward its worst real fault, the Hemingwayesque mannerism of sentimental toughness.

Wright's posthumous volume, *This Journey,* is a much better book than *To a Blossoming Pear Tree,* though there is no return to the drastic originality of *Two Citizens. This Journey* is probably the least mannered of any of Wright's books. Something happened to the poet in the advance aura of his dying (as it happened to Williams, to Roethke, to Lowell) to produce both an unusual transparency toward the world as it is, and an unprecedented power of direct statement. . . . Never before had he spent so much poetic time calmly looking at things, without making them preternaturally "lovely" or sad. . . . (pp. 36-7)

This Journey might be a good place for the uninitiated reader to begin with Wright—and then work back into the labyrinth of intention, risk, and talent in the earlier books. It is also a good place to see what a remarkable ear Wright had, even though for a while he almost worked to suppress it, in the grammatically determined free verse linebreaking he shared with Bly. (p. 37)

Alan Williamson, "An American Lyricist," in The New Republic *(reprinted by permission of* The New Republic; © 1983 The New Republic, Inc.), Vol. 188, No. 4, January 31, 1983, pp. 36-7.*

Appendix

THE EXCERPTS IN *CLC*, VOLUME 28, WERE REPRINTED FROM THE FOLLOWING PERIODICALS:

America
The American Book Review
American Humor: An Interdisciplinary Newsletter
American Literature
The American Poetry Review
Américas
The Antioch Review
Arizona Quarterly
The Atlantic Book Shelf
Best Sellers
Book World—Chicago Tribune
Book World—The Washington Post
Booklist
Books and Bookmen
Books in Canada
Broom
The Canadian Forum
Canadian Literature
Carolina Quarterly
Catholic World
Choice
The Christian Century
The Christian Science Monitor
Chronicles of Culture
The Classical World
The Colorado Quarterly
Commentary
Commonweal
Contemporary Literature
The Critic
Dalhousie Review
Detroit Free Press
The Dial
Drama Critique

Educational Theatre Journal
Encounter
English Journal
Esquire
Essays on Canadian Writing
The Fiddlehead
The Georgia Review
Harper's
Harper's Magazine
Hispania
The Hudson Review
The Jewish News
Journal of Commonwealth Literature
The Kenyon Review
Kirkus Reviews
Library Journal
The Listener
The Literary Review
The Little Review
Lively Arts and Book Review
London Review of Books
Los Angeles Times Book Review
Maclean's Magazine
Michigan Quarterly Review
Modern Fiction Studies
Modern Language Journal
Modern Poetry Studies
The Nation
The National Observer
National Review
The New Leader
The New Republic
New Statesman
The New Statesman & Nation
New York Herald Tribune Book Review

New York Herald Tribune Books
New York Herald Tribune Weekly Book Review
New York *Magazine*
The New York Review of Books
The New York Times
The New York Times Book Review
The New Yorker
Newsweek
The North American Review
North Country ANVIL
The Observer
The Ohio Review
The Ontario Review
Pacific Affairs
Parnassus: Poetry in Review
Partisan Review
People Weekly
Philosophy and Literature
Poetry
Publishers Weekly
Punch
Quadrant
Queen's Quarterly
Quill and Quire
The Review of Contemporary Fiction
A Review of English Literature
Sagetrieb
Salmagundi
Saturday Night
Saturday Review
The Saturday Review, *New York*
The Saturday Review of Literature
The Sewanee Review
Small Press Review

Social Forces
Southerly
The Southern Review
Southwest Review
The Spectator
Tar River Poetry
Texas Studies in Literature and Language
Theatre Arts

Theatre Arts Monthly
Time
The Times Literary Supplement
The University of Kansas City Review
The Village Voice
Virginia Kirkus' Service
The Virginia Quarterly Review
VLS

Wascana Review
The Washington Post
West Coast Review of Books
Western American Literature
Western Humanities Review
World Literature Today
World Literature Written in English
The Yale Review

APPENDIX

THE EXCERPTS IN *CLC*, VOLUME 28, WERE REPRINTED FROM THE FOLLOWING BOOKS:

Adams, Stephen D. James Purdy. *Barnes & Noble, 1976.*

Alexander, Edward. The Resonance of Dust: Essays on Holocaust Literature and Jewish Fate. *Ohio State University Press, 1979.*

Altieri, Charles. Enlarging the Temple: New Directions in American Poetry during the 1960s. *Bucknell University Press, 1979.*

Auden, W. H. Foreword to Of the Festivity, *by William Dickey. Yale University Press, 1959.*

Austin, Allan F. Roy Fuller. *Twayne, 1979.*

Bailey, Jennifer. Norman Mailer: Quick-Change Artist. *Barnes & Noble, 1979.*

Bowen, Zack. Padraic Colum: A Biographical-Critical Introduction. *Southern Illinois University Press, 1970.*

Bowden, J. H. Peter De Vries. *Twayne, 1983.*

Boyd, Ernest. Ireland's Literary Renaissance. *Knopf, 1922, Barnes & Noble, Inc., 1968.*

Brooks, Cleanth. William Faulkner: First Encounters. *Yale Univeristy Press, 1983.*

Bucco, Martin. René Wellek. *Twayne, 1981.*

Cabrera, Vincente. Juan Benet. *Twayne, 1983.*

Cain, James M. Preface to Three of a Kind, *by James M. Cain. Knopf, 1943, The Blackiston Company, 1944.*

Chupack, Henry. James Purdy. *Twayne, 1975.*

Clurman, Harold. The Fervent Years: The Story of the Group Theatre and the Thirties. *Knopf, 1945, Harcourt Brace Jovanovich, 1975.*

Cohen, Sarah Blacher, ed. Comic Relief: Humor in Contemporary American Literature. *University of Illinois Press, 1978.*

Conover, Roger L. Introduction to The Last Lunar Baedeker, *by Mina Loy. Edited by Roger L. Conover. Jargon, 1982.*

De Costa, René. The Poetry of Pablo Neruda. *Harvard University Press, 1979.*

Durán, Manuel, and Safir, Margery. Earth Tones: The Poetry of Pablo Neruda. *Indiana University Press, 1981.*

Fadiman, Clifton. Party of One: The Selected Writings of Clifton Fadiman. *World Publishing Co., 1955.*

Fitts, Dudley. Foreword to The Breaking of the Day and Other Poems, *by Peter Davison. Yale University Press, 1964.*

Greene, Graham. Introduction to The Bachelor of Arts, *by R. K. Narayan. Heinemann, 1978.*

Hadgraft, Cecil. Studies in the Recent Australian Novel. *Edited by K. G. Hamilton. University of Queensland Press, 1979.*

Hall, Donald. Goatfoot Milktongue Twinbird: Interviews, Essays, and Notes on Poetry, 1970-1978. *University of Michigan Press, 1978.*

Herzberger, David. The Novelistic World of Juan Benet. *American Hispanist, 1976.*

Holmstrom, Lakshmi. The Novels of R. K. Narayan. *Writers Workshop, 1973.*

James, Louis. Introduction to The Islands in Between: Essays on West Indian Literature. *Edited by Louis James. Oxford University Press, 1968.*

Johnson, Diane. Terrorists and Novelists. *Alfred A. Knopf, 1982.*

Kouidis, Virginia M. Mina Loy: American Modernist Poet. *Louisiana State University Press, 1980.*

Kazin, Alfred. On Native Grounds: An Interpretation of Modern American Prose Literature. *Reynal & Hitchcock, 1942, Harcourt Brace Jovanovich, 1963.*

Kreymborg, Alfred. A History of American Poetry: Our Singing Strength. *Tudor Publishing Company, 1934.*

Lee, L. L. Critical Essays on the Western American Novel. *Edited by William T. Pilkington. G. K. Hall & Co., 1980.*

Lerner, Max. Public Journal: Marginal Notes on Wartime America. *The Viking Press, 1945.*

Lewis, Allan. American Plays and Playwrights of the Contemporary Theatre. *Rev. ed. Crown, 1970.*

Lewis, Wyndham. Men without Art. *Cassell & Company, Limited, 1934, Russell & Russell, Inc., 1964.*

Lippit, Noriko Mizuta. Reality and Fiction in Modern Japanese Literature. *M. E. Sharpe, Inc., 1980.*

Mahood, M. M. The Colonial Encounter: A Reading of Six Novels. *Roman & Littlefield, 1977.*

McCarthy, Mary. Sights and Spectacles: 1937-1956. *Farrar, Straus and Cudahy, 1956.*

Millgate, Michael. The Achievement of William Faulkner. *Constable, 1966.*

Milton, John R. The Novel of the American West. *University of Nebraska Press, 1980.*

Morris, Mervyn. Critics on Caribbean Literature: Readings in Literary Criticism. *Edited by Edward Baugh. St. Martin's Press, 1978.*

Murray, Edmund. Clifford Odets: The Thirties and After. *Ungar, 1968.*

Naipaul, V. S. An Area of Darkness. *A. Deutsch, 1964.*

Naipaul, V. S. India: A Wounded Civilization. *Knopf, 1977.*

Nettleford, Rex. Introduction to Jamaica Labrish, *by Louise Bennett. Sangster's Book Stores, 1966.*

The New York Times Theatre Reviews: 1920-1980. *13 vols. The New York Times Company, 1975-83.*

Orange, John. Before the Flood: Hugh Hood's Work in Progress. *Edited by J. R. (Tim) Struthers. ECW Press, 1979.*

Pacey, Desmond. Creative Writing in Canada. *Rev. ed. Ryerson Press, 1961*

Petersen, Gwenn Boardman. The Moon in the Water: Understanding Tanizaki, Kawabata, and Mishima. *University Press of Hawaii, 1979.*

Raizada, Harish. R. K. Narayan: A Critical Study of His Works. *Young Asia Publications, 1969.*

Sale, Roger. On Not Being Good Enough: Writings of a Working Critic. *Oxford University Press, 1979.*

Smith, Dave, ed. The Pure Clear Word: Essays on the Poetry of James Wright. *University of Illinois Press, 1982.*

Stauffer, Helen Winter. Mari Sandoz: Story Catcher of the Plains. *University of Nebraska Press, 1982.*

Stegner, Wallace. One Way to Spell Man. *Doubleday, 1982.*

Taylor, John Russell. The Angry Theatre: New British Drama. *Rev. ed. Hill & Wang, 1969.*

Ueda, Makoto. Modern Japanese Writers and the Nature of Literature. *Stanford University Press, 1976.*

Updike, John. Hugging the Shore: Essays and Criticism. *Knopf, 1983.*

VanSpanckeren, Kathryn. John Gardner: Critical Perspectives. *Edited by Robert A. Morace and Kathryn VanSpanckeren. Southern Illinois University Press, 1962.*

Warren, Robert Penn. Introduction to Faulkner: A Collection of Critical Essays. *Edited by Robert Penn Warren. Prentice-Hall, 1966.*

Weales, Gerald. Clifford Odets: Playwright. *Bobbs-Merrill-Pegasus, 1971.*

Wellwarth, George. The Theater of Protest and Paradox: Developments in the Avant-Garde Drama. *New York University Press, 1964.*

Willard, Nancy. Testimony of the Invisible Man: William Carlos Williams, Francis Ponge, Rainer Maria Rilke, Pablo Neruda. *University of Missouri Press, 1970.*

Wilson, Edmund. Classics and Commercials: A Literary Chronicle of the Forties. *Farrar, Straus and Giroux, 1950.*

Winters, Yvor. Yvor Winters: Uncollected Essays and Reviews. *Edited by Francis Murphy. The Swallow Press, Inc., 1973.*

Wolfe, Tom. Introduction to Cain X 3: Three Novels, *by James M. Cain. Alfred A. Knopf, Inc., 1969.*

Wolff, Geoffrey. Introduction to The Edward Hoagland Reader, *by Edward Hoagland. Edited by Geoffrey Wolff. Vintage Books, 1979.*

Wright, James, and Bly, Robert. Introduction to Twenty Poems, *by Pablo Neruda. Translated by James Wright and Robert Bly. Sixties Press, 1967.*

Cumulative Index to Authors

This index lists all author entries in the Gale Literary Criticism Series and includes cross-references to other Gale sources. References in the index are identified as follows:

- **AITN:** *Authors in the News*, Volumes 1-2
- **CA:** *Contemporary Authors* (original series), Volumes 1-110
- **CANR:** *Contemporary Authors New Revision Series*, Volumes 1-11
- **CAP:** *Contemporary Authors Permanent Series*, Volumes 1-2
- **CA-R:** *Contemporary Authors* (revised editions), Volumes 1-44
- **CLC:** *Contemporary Literary Criticism*, Volumes 1-28
- **CLR:** *Children's Literature Review*, Volumes 1-6
- **DLB:** *Dictionary of Literary Biography*, Volumes 1-26
- **DLB-DS:** *Dictionary of Literary Biography Documentary Series*, Volumes 1-4
- **DLB-Y:** *Dictionary of Literary Biography Yearbook*, Volumes 1980-1982
- **LC:** *Literature Criticism from 1400 to 1800*, Volume 1
- **NCLC:** *Nineteenth-Century Literature Criticism*, Volumes 1-6
- **SATA:** *Something about the Author*, Volumes 1-34
- **TCLC:** *Twentieth-Century Literary Criticism*, Volumes 1-12
- **YABC:** *Yesterday's Authors of Books for Children*, Volumes 1-2

A. E. 1867-1935............TCLC 3, 10
See also Russell, George William
See also DLB 19

Abé, Kōbō 1924-.............CLC 8, 22
See also CA 65-68

Abell, Kjeld 1901-1961..........CLC 15

Abish, Walter 1931-............CLC 22
See also CA 101

Abrahams, Peter (Henry) 1919-....CLC 4
See also CA 57-60

Abrams, M(eyer) H(oward)
1912-.......................CLC 24
See also CA 57-60

Abse, Dannie 1923-..............CLC 7
See also CANR 4
See also CA 53-56

Achebe, Chinua
1930-..........CLC 1, 3, 5, 7, 11, 26
See also CANR 6
See also CA 1-4R

Acorn, Milton 1923-.............CLC 15
See also CA 103
See also AITN 2

Adamov, Arthur 1908-1970.....CLC 4, 25
See also CAP 2
See also CA 17-18
See also obituary CA 25-28R

Adams, Alice (Boyd) 1926-......CLC 6, 13
See also CA 81-84

Adams, Douglas (Noel) 1952-......CLC 27
See also CA 106

Adams, Henry (Brooks)
1838-1918..................TCLC 4
See also CA 104
See also DLB 12

Adams, Richard (George)
1920-.....................CLC 4, 5, 18
See also CANR 3
See also CA 49-52
See also SATA 7
See also AITN 1, 2

Adamson, Joy (-Friederike Victoria)
1910-1980...................CLC 17
See also CA 69-72
See also obituary CA 93-96
See also SATA 11
See also obituary SATA 22

Adler, Renata 1938-..............CLC 8
See also CANR 5
See also CA 49-52

Ady, Endre 1877-1919..........TCLC 11
See also CA 107

Agee, James 1909-1955...........TCLC 1
See also CA 108
See also DLB 2, 26
See also AITN 1

Agnon, S(hmuel) Y(osef Halevi)
1888-1970.............CLC 4, 8, 14
See also CAP 2
See also CA 17-18
See also obituary CA 25-28R

Ai 1947-......................CLC 4, 14
See also CA 85-88

Aiken, Conrad (Potter)
1899-1973............CLC 1, 3, 5, 10
See also CANR 4
See also CA 5-8R
See also obituary CA 45-48
See also SATA 3, 30
See also DLB 9

Ajar, Emile 1914-1980
See Gary, Romain

Akhmatova, Anna
1888-1966...............CLC 11, 25
See also CAP 1
See also CA 19-20
See also obituary CA 25-28R

Aksakov, Sergei Timofeyvich
1791-1859..................NCLC 2

Aksenov, Vasily (Pavlovich)
1932-.......................CLC 22
See also CA 53-56

Aksyonov, Vasily (Pavlovich) 1932-
See Aksenov, Vasily (Pavlovich)

Alain-Fournier 1886-1914........TCLC 6
See also CA 104

Alarcón, Pedro Antonio de
1833-1891..................NCLC 1

Albee, Edward (Franklin III)
1928-.....CLC 1, 2, 3, 5, 9, 11, 13, 25
See also CANR 8
See also CA 5-8R
See also DLB 7
See also AITN 1

Alberti, Rafael 1902-.............CLC 7
See also CA 85-88

Alcott, Amos Bronson
1799-1888..................NCLC 1
See also DLB 1

Alcott, Louisa May 1832-1888.....NCLC 6
See also CLR 1
See also YABC 1
See also DLB 1

Aldiss, Brian (Wilson) 1925-....CLC 5, 14
See also CANR 5
See also CA 5-8R
See also SATA 34
See also DLB 14

Aleichem, Sholom 1859-1916...... **TCLC 1**
See also CA 104

Aleixandre, Vicente 1898- ....**CLC 9**
See also CA 85-88

Alepoudelis, Odysseus 1911-
See Elytis, Odysseus

Algren, Nelson 1909-1981 ...... **CLC 4, 10**
See also CA 13-16R
See also obituary CA 103
See also DLB 9
See also DLB-Y 81, 82

Allen, Heywood 1935-
See Allen, Woody
See also CA 33-36R

Allen, Woody 1935-.................**CLC 16**
See also Allen, Heywood

Allingham, Margery (Louise)
1904-1966....................**CLC 19**
See also CANR 4
See also CA 5-8R
See also obituary CA 25-28R

Allston, Washington
1779-1843..................**NCLC 2**
See also DLB 1

Almedingen, E. M. 1898-1971......**CLC 12**
See also Almedingen, Martha Edith von

Almedingen, Martha Edith von 1898-1971
See Almedingen, E. M.
See also CANR 1
See also CA 1-4R
See also SATA 3

Alonso, Dámaso 1898-.............**CLC 14**

Alta 1942-........................**CLC 19**
See also CA 57-60

Alther, Lisa 1944-..................**CLC 7**
See also CA 65-68

Altman, Robert 1925-...............**CLC 16**
See also CA 73-76

Alvarez, A(lfred) 1929-......... **CLC 5, 13**
See also CANR 3
See also CA 1-4R
See also DLB 14

Amado, Jorge 1912- ....**CLC 13**
See also CA 77-80

Ambler, Eric 1909- .... **CLC 4, 6, 9**
See also CANR 7
See also CA 9-12R

Amichai, Yehuda 1924- .... **CLC 9, 22**
See also CA 85-88

Amiel, Henri Frédéric
1821-1881................... **NCLC 4**

Amis, Kingsley (William)
1922-....**CLC 1, 2, 3, 5, 8, 13**
See also CANR 8
See also CA 9-12R
See also DLB 15
See also AITN 2

Amis, Martin 1949-.............. **CLC 4, 9**
See also CANR 8
See also CA 65-68
See also DLB 14

Ammons, A(rchie) R(andolph)
1926- ...... **CLC 2, 3, 5, 8, 9, 24**
See also CANR 6
See also CA 9-12R
See also DLB 5
See also AITN 1

Anand, Mulk Raj 1905-...........**CLC 23**
See also CA 65-68

Anaya, Rudolfo A(lfonso)
1937-......................**CLC 23**
See also CANR 1
See also CA 45-48

Anderson, Jon (Victor) 1940- ....**CLC 9**
See also CA 25-28R

Anderson, Lindsay 1923-..........**CLC 20**

Anderson, Maxwell 1888-1959 .... **TCLC 2**
See also CA 105
See also DLB 7

Anderson, Poul (William)
1926-......................**CLC 15**
See also CANR 2
See also CA 1-4R
See also DLB 8

Anderson, Robert (Woodruff)
1917-......................**CLC 23**
See also CA 21-24R
See also DLB 7
See also AITN 1

Anderson, Roberta Joan 1943-
See Mitchell, Joni

Anderson, Sherwood
1876-1941................ **TCLC 1, 10**
See also CA 104
See also DLB 4, 9
See also DLB-DS 1

Andrade, Carlos Drummond de
1902-......................**CLC 18**

Andrews, Cecily Fairfield 1892-
See West, Rebecca

Andreyev, Leonid (Nikolaevich)
1871-1919................... **TCLC 3**
See also CA 104

Andrić, Ivo 1892-1975 ....**CLC 8**
See also CA 81-84
See also obituary CA 57-60

Angell, Roger 1920-................**CLC 26**
See also CA 57-60

Angelou, Maya 1928- ....**CLC 12**
See also CA 65-68

Anouilh, Jean (Marie Lucien Pierre)
1910-..............**CLC 1, 3, 8, 13**
See also CA 17-20R

Anthony, Florence 1947-
See Ai

Antoninus, Brother 1912-
See Everson, William (Oliver)

Antonioni, Michelangelo 1912- .....**CLC 20**
See also CA 73-76

Antschel, Paul 1920-1970
See Celan, Paul
See also CA 85-88

Apollinaire, Guillaume
1880-1918................. **TCLC 3, 8**
See also CA 104

Appelfeld, Aharon 1932- ....**CLC 23**

Apple, Max (Isaac) 1941-..........**CLC 9**
See also CA 81-84

Aquin, Hubert 1929-1977.........**CLC 15**
See also CA 105

Aragon, Louis 1897-1982....... **CLC 3, 22**
See also CA 69-72
See also obituary CA 108

Arbuthnot, John 1667-1735..........**LC 1**

Archer, Jeffrey (Howard)
1940-......................**CLC 28**
See also CA 77-80

Archer, Jules 1915-................**CLC 12**
See also CANR 6
See also CA 9-12R
See also SATA 4

Arden, John 1930-..........**CLC 6, 13, 15**
See also CA 13-16R
See also DLB 13

Arguedas, José María
1911-1969.................**CLC 10, 18**
See also CA 89-92

Armah, Ayi Kwei 1939- ....**CLC 5**
See also CA 61-64

Armatrading, Joan 1950-..........**CLC 17**

Arnim, Achim von 1781-1831..... **NCLC 5**

Arnold, Matthew 1822-1888 ...... **NCLC 6**

Arnow, Harriette (Louisa Simpson)
1908-....................**CLC 2, 7, 18**
See also CA 9-12R
See also DLB 6

Arp, Jean 1887-1966................**CLC 5**
See also CA 81-84
See also obituary CA 25-28R

Arquette, Lois S(teinmetz)
See Duncan (Steinmetz Arquette), Lois
See also SATA 1

Arrabal, Fernando 1932- ..... **CLC 2, 9, 18**
See also CA 9-12R

Artaud, Antonin 1896-1948....... **TCLC 3**
See also CA 104

Arthur, Ruth M(abel)
1905-1979....................**CLC 12**
See also CANR 4
See also CA 9-12R
See also obituary CA 85-88
See also SATA 7
See also obituary SATA 26

Arundel, Honor (Morfydd)
1919-1973....................**CLC 17**
See also CAP 2
See also CA 21-22
See also obituary CA 41-44R
See also SATA 4
See also obituary SATA 24

Asch, Sholem 1880-1957......... **TCLC 3**
See also CA 105

Ashbery, John (Lawrence)
1927-..... **CLC 2, 3, 4, 6, 9, 13, 15, 25**
See also CANR 9
See also CA 5-8R
See also DLB 5
See also DLB-Y 81

Ashton-Warner, Sylvia (Constance)
1908-......................**CLC 19**
See also CA 69-72

Asimov, Isaac
1920-............ **CLC 1, 3, 9, 19, 26**
See also CANR 2
See also CA 1-4R
See also SATA 1, 26
See also DLB 8

Asturias, Miguel Ángel
1899-1974............... CLC 3, 8, 13
See also CAP 2
See also CA 25-28
See also obituary CA 49-52

Atheling, William, Jr. 1921-1975
See Blish, James (Benjamin)

Atherton, Gertrude (Franklin Horn)
1857-1948.................... TCLC 2
See also CA 104
See also DLB 9

Atwood, Margaret (Eleanor)
1939-........CLC 2, 3, 4, 8, 13, 15, 25
See also CANR 3
See also CA 49-52

Auchincloss, Louis (Stanton)
1917-.................CLC 4, 6, 9, 18
See also CANR 6
See also CA 1-4R
See also DLB 2
See also DLB-Y 80

Auden, W(ystan) H(ugh)
1907-1973........ CLC 1, 2, 3, 4, 6, 9, 11, 14
See also CANR 5
See also CA 9-12R
See also obituary CA 45-48
See also DLB 10, 20

Austen, Jane 1775-1817.......... NCLC 1

Avison, Margaret 1918-......... CLC 2, 4
See also CA 17-20R

Ayckbourn, Alan 1939-....... CLC 5, 8, 18
See also CA 21-24R
See also DLB 13

Aymé, Marcel (Andre)
1902-1967....................CLC 11
See also CA 89-92

Ayrton, Michael 1921-1975.......CLC 7
See also CANR 9
See also CA 5-8R
See also obituary CA 61-64

Azorín 1874-1967.................CLC 11
See also Martínez Ruiz, José

Azuela, Mariano 1873-1952...... TCLC 3
See also CA 104

"Bab" 1836-1911
See Gilbert, (Sir) W(illiam) S(chwenk)

Babel, Isaak (Emmanuilovich)
1894-1941.................. TCLC 2
See also CA 104

Bacchelli, Riccardo 1891-.......CLC 19
See also CA 29-32R

Bach, Richard (David) 1936-.......CLC 14
See also CA 9-12R
See also SATA 13
See also AITN 1

Bagnold, Enid 1889-1981..........CLC 25
See also CANR 5
See also CA 5-8R
See also obituary CA 103
See also SATA 1, 25
See also DLB 13

Bagryana, Elisaveta 1893-.........CLC 10

Baillie, Joanna 1762-1851 .... NCLC 2

Bainbridge, Beryl
1933-.......CLC 4, 5, 8, 10, 14, 18, 22
See also CA 21-24R
See also DLB 14

Baker, Elliott 1922-.................CLC 8
See also CANR 2
See also CA 45-48

Bakshi, Ralph 1938-...............CLC 26

Baldwin, James (Arthur)
1924-......CLC 1, 2, 3, 4, 5, 8, 13, 15, 17
See also CANR 3
See also CA 1-4R
See also SATA 9
See also DLB 2, 7

Ballard, J(ames) G(raham)
1930-.................... CLC 3, 6, 14
See also CA 5-8R
See also DLB 14

Balmont, Konstantin Dmitriyevich
1867-1943.................... TCLC 11
See also CA 109

Balzac, Honoré de 1799-1850 ..... NCLC 5

Bambara, Toni Cade.............CLC 19
See also CA 29-32R

Banks, Lynne Reid 1929-..........CLC 23
See also Reid Banks, Lynne

Baraka, Imamu Amiri
1934-............. CLC 2, 3, 5, 10, 14
See also Jones, (Everett) LeRoi
See also DLB 5, 7, 16

Barbey d'Aurevilly, Jules Amédée
1808-1889.................... NCLC 1

Barbusse, Henri 1873-1935 .... TCLC 5
See also CA 105

Barfoot, Joan 1946-.................CLC 18
See also CA 105

Baring, Maurice 1874-1945 .... TCLC 8
See also CA 105

Barker, George (Granville)
1913-........................CLC 8
See also CANR 7
See also CA 9-12R
See also DLB 20

Barnes, Djuna
1892-1982.............CLC 3, 4, 8, 11
See also CA 9-12R
See also obituary CA 107
See also DLB 4, 9

Barnes, Peter 1931-.................CLC 5
See also CA 65-68
See also DLB 13

Baroja (y Nessi), Pío
1872-1956.................... TCLC 8
See also CA 104

Barondess, Sue K(aufman) 1926-1977
See Kaufman, Sue
See also CANR 1
See also CA 1-4R
See also obituary CA 69-72

Barrett, William (Chistopher)
1913-........................CLC 27
See also CANR 11
See also CA 13-16R

Barrie, (Sir) J(ames) M(atthew)
1860-1937.................... TCLC 2
See also CA 104
See also YABC 1
See also DLB 10

Barry, Philip (James Quinn)
1896-1949.................... TCLC 11
See also CA 109
See also DLB 7

Barth, John (Simmons)
1930-......CLC 1, 2, 3, 5, 7, 9, 10, 14, 27
See also CANR 5
See also CA 1-4R
See also DLB 2
See also AITN 1, 2

Barthelme, Donald
1931-...... CLC 1, 2, 3, 5, 6, 8, 13, 23
See also CA 21-24R
See also SATA 7
See also DLB 2
See also DLB-Y 80

Barthes, Roland 1915-1980 ....CLC 24
See also obituary CA 97-100

Bassani, Giorgio 1916-..............CLC 9
See also CA 65-68

Baudelaire, Charles
1821-1867.................... NCLC 6

Baum, L(yman) Frank
1856-1919.................... TCLC 7
See also CA 108
See also SATA 18
See also DLB 22

Baumbach, Jonathan 1933-..... CLC 6, 23
See also CA 13-16R
See also DLB-Y 80

Baxter, James K(eir)
1926-1972....................CLC 14
See also CA 77-80

Bayer, Sylvia 1909-1981
See Glassco, John

Beagle, Peter S(oyer) 1939-.........CLC 7
See also CANR 4
See also CA 9-12R
See also DLB-Y 80

Beardsley, Aubrey 1872-1898 ..... NCLC 6

Beattie, Ann 1947-...........CLC 8, 13, 18
See also CA 81-84
See also DLB-Y 82

Beauvoir, Simone de
1908-............ CLC 1, 2, 4, 8, 14
See also CA 9-12R

Becker, Jurek 1937-............ CLC 7, 19
See also CA 85-88

Becker, Walter 1950-
See Becker, Walter and Fagen, Donald

Becker, Walter 1950- and **Fagen, Donald**
1948-........................CLC 26

Beckett, Samuel (Barclay)
1906-......CLC 1, 2, 3, 4, 6, 9, 10, 11, 14, 18
See also CA 5-8R
See also DLB 13, 15

Beckman, Gunnel 1910-............CLC 26
See also CA 33-36R
See also SATA 6

Becque, Henri 1837-1899........ NCLC 3

Beddoes, Thomas Lovell
 1803-1849.................. NCLC 3

Beecher, John 1904-1980.......... CLC 6
 See also CANR 8
 See also CA 5-8R
 See also obituary CA 105
 See also AITN 1

Beerbohm, (Sir Henry) Max(imilian)
 1872-1956.................. TCLC 1
 See also CA 104

Behan, Brendan
 1923-1964............ CLC 1, 8, 11, 15
 See also CA 73-76
 See also DLB 13

Behn, Aphra 1640?-1689 .... LC 1

Belasco, David 1853-1931........ TCLC 3
 See also CA 104
 See also DLB 7

Belcheva, Elisaveta 1893-
 See Bagryana, Elisaveta

Belinski, Vissarion Grigoryevich
 1811-1848.................. NCLC 5

Belitt, Ben 1911- .... CLC 22
 See also CANR 7
 See also CA 13-16R
 See also DLB 5

Bell, Acton 1820-1849
 See Brontë, Anne

Bell, Currer 1816-1855
 See Brontë, Charlotte

Bell, Marvin 1937-.................. CLC 8
 See also CA 21-24R
 See also DLB 5

Bellamy, Edward 1850-1898 ...... NCLC 4
 See also DLB 12

Belloc, (Joseph) Hilaire (Pierre)
 1870-1953.................. TCLC 7
 See also CA 106
 See also YABC 1
 See also DLB 19

Bellow, Saul
 1915-..... CLC 1, 2, 3, 6, 8, 10, 13, 15,
 25
 See also CA 5-8R
 See also DLB 2
 See also DLB-Y 82
 See also DLB-DS 3
 See also AITN 2

Belser, Reimond Karel Maria de 1929-
 See Ruyslinck, Ward

Bely, Andrey 1880-1934.......... TCLC 7
 See also CA 104

Benary-Isbert, Margot
 1889-1979.................. CLC 12
 See also CANR 4
 See also CA 5-8R
 See also obituary CA 89-92
 See also SATA 2
 See also obituary SATA 21

Benavente (y Martínez), Jacinto
 1866-1954.................. TCLC 3
 See also CA 106

Benchley, Peter (Bradford)
 1940-.................... CLC 4, 8
 See also CA 17-20R
 See also SATA 3
 See also AITN 2

Benchley, Robert 1889-1945 ...... TCLC 1
 See also CA 105
 See also DLB 11

Benedikt, Michael 1935-........ CLC 4, 14
 See also CANR 7
 See also CA 13-16R
 See also DLB 5

Benet, Juan 1927- .... CLC 28

Benét, Stephen Vincent
 1898-1943.................. TCLC 7
 See also CA 104
 See also YABC 1
 See also DLB 4

Benn, Gottfried 1886-1956........ TCLC 3
 See also CA 106

Bennett, (Enoch) Arnold
 1867-1931.................. TCLC 5
 See also CA 106
 See also DLB 10

Bennett, George Harold 1930-
 See Bennett, Hal
 See also CA 97-100

Bennett, Hal 1930-.................. CLC 5
 See also Bennett, George Harold

Bennett, Louise (Simone)
 1919-...................... CLC 28
 See also Bennett-Coverly, Louise Simone

Bennett-Coverly, Louise Simone 1919-
 See Bennett, Louise (Simone)
 See also CA 97-100

Benson, Sally 1900-1972.......... CLC 17
 See also CAP 1
 See also CA 19-20
 See also obituary CA 37-40R
 See also SATA 1
 See also obituary SATA 27

Bentley, E(dmund) C(lerihew)
 1875-1956.................. TCLC 12
 See also CA 108

Bentley, Eric (Russell) 1916- .... CLC 24
 See also CA 5-8R

Berger, John (Peter) 1926-...... CLC 2, 19
 See also CA 81-84
 See also DLB 14

Berger, Melvin (H.) 1927- .... CLC 12
 See also CANR 4
 See also CA 5-8R
 See also SATA 5

Berger, Thomas (Louis)
 1924-............. CLC 3, 5, 8, 11, 18
 See also CANR 5
 See also CA 1-4R
 See also DLB 2
 See also DLB-Y 80

Bergman, (Ernst) Ingmar
 1918-...................... CLC 16
 See also CA 81-84

Bergstein, Eleanor 1938- .... CLC 4
 See also CANR 5
 See also CA 53-56

Bernanos, (Paul Louis) Georges
 1888-1948?................. TCLC 3
 See also CA 104

Bernhard, Thomas 1931- .... CLC 3
 See also CA 85-88

Berrigan, Daniel J. 1921-.......... CLC 4
 See also CANR 11
 See also CA 33-36R
 See also DLB 5

Berry, Chuck 1926-................ CLC 17

Berry, Wendell (Erdman)
 1934-................ CLC 4, 6, 8, 27
 See also CA 73-76
 See also DLB 5, 6
 See also AITN 1

Berryman, John
 1914-1972..... CLC 1, 2, 3, 4, 6, 8, 10,
 13, 25
 See also CAP 1
 See also CA 15-16
 See also obituary CA 33-36R

Bertolucci, Bernardo 1940- .... CLC 16
 See also CA 106

Besant, Annie (Wood)
 1847-1933.................. TCLC 9
 See also CA 105

Bessie, Alvah 1904-................ CLC 23
 See also CANR 2
 See also CA 5-8R
 See also DLB 26

Beti, Mongo 1932-................ CLC 27

Betjeman, John 1906-........ CLC 2, 6, 10
 See also CA 9-12R
 See also DLB 20

Betti, Ugo 1892-1953............. TCLC 5
 See also CA 104

Betts, Doris (Waugh)
 1932-.................. CLC 3, 6, 28
 See also CANR 9
 See also CA 13-16R
 See also DLB-Y 82

Bienek, Horst 1930-............. CLC 7, 11
 See also CA 73-76

Bierce, Ambrose (Gwinett)
 1842-1914?................. TCLC 1, 7
 See also CA 104
 See also DLB 11, 12, 23

Bioy Casares, Adolfo
 1914-.................... CLC 4, 8, 13
 See also CA 29-32R

Bird, Robert Montgomery
 1806-1854.................. NCLC 1

Birdwell, Cleo 1936-
 See DeLillo, Don

Birney (Alfred) Earle
 1904-.................. CLC 1, 4, 6, 11
 See also CANR 5
 See also CA 1-4R

Bishop, Elizabeth
 1911-1979........ CLC 1, 4, 9, 13, 15
 See also CA 5-8R
 See also obituary CA 89-92
 See also obituary SATA 24
 See also DLB 5

Bishop, John 1935-................ CLC 10
 See also CA 105

Bissett, Bill 1939-..................CLC 18
See also CA 69-72

Biyidi, Alexandre 1932-
See Beti, Mongo

Bjørnson, Bjørnstjerne (Martinius)
1832-1910.................. TCLC 7
See also CA 104

Blackburn, Paul 1926-1971........CLC 9
See also CA 81-84
See also obituary CA 33-36R
See also DLB 16
See also DLB-Y 81

Blackmur, R(ichard) P(almer)
1904-1965.............. CLC 2, 24
See also CAP 1
See also CA 11-12
See also obituary CA 25-28R

Blackwood, Algernon (Henry)
1869-1951................... TCLC 5
See also CA 105

Blackwood, Caroline 1931-...... CLC 6, 9
See also CA 85-88
See also DLB 14

Blair, Eric Arthur 1903-1950
See Orwell, George

Blais, Marie-Claire
1939-............. CLC 2, 4, 6, 13, 22
See also CA 21-24R

Blake, Nicholas 1904-1972
See Day Lewis, C(ecil)

Blasco Ibáñez, Vicente
1867-1928.................. TCLC 12

Blatty, William Peter 1928-........CLC 2
See also CANR 9
See also CA 5-8R

Blish, James (Benjamin)
1921-1975....................CLC 14
See also CANR 3
See also CA 1-4R
See also obituary CA 57-60
See also DLB 8

Blixen, Karen (Christentze Dinesen)
1885-1962
See Dinesen, Isak
See also CAP 2
See also CA 25-28

Blok, Aleksandr (Aleksandrovich)
1880-1921................... TCLC 5
See also CA 104

Bloom, Harold 1930-..............CLC 24
See also CA 13-16R

Blume, Judy (Sussman Kitchens)
1938-........................CLC 12
See also CLR 2
See also CA 29-32R
See also SATA 2, 31

Blunden, Edmund (Charles)
1896-1974....................CLC 2
See also CAP 2
See also CA 17-18
See also obituary CA 45-48
See also DLB 20

Bly, Robert 1926-..... CLC 1, 2, 5, 10, 15
See also CA 5-8R
See also DLB 5

Bødker, Cecil 1927-.................CLC 21
See also CA 73-76
See also SATA 14

Boell, Heinrich (Theodor) 1917-
See Böll, Heinrich
See also CA 21-24R

Bogan, Louise 1897-1970...........CLC 4
See also CA 73-76
See also obituary CA 25-28R

Bogarde, Dirk 1921-..............CLC 19
See also Van Den Bogarde, Derek (Jules
Gaspard Ulric) Niven
See also DLB 14

Böll, Heinrich (Theodor)
1917-........... CLC 2, 3, 6, 9, 11, 15
See also Boell, Heinrich (Theodor)

Bolt, Robert (Oxton) 1924-........CLC 14
See also CA 17-20R
See also DLB 13

Bond, Edward 1934-.....CLC 4, 6, 13, 23
See also CA 25-28R
See also DLB 13

Bonham, Frank 1914-............CLC 12
See also CANR 4
See also CA 9-12R
See also SATA 1

Bonnefoy, Yves 1923-.......... CLC 9, 15
See also CA 85-88

Bontemps, Arna (Wendell)
1902-1973.................. CLC 1, 18
See also CLR 6
See also CANR 4
See also CA 1-4R
See also obituary CA 41-44R
See also SATA 2
See also obituary SATA 24

Booth, Martin 1944-...............CLC 13
See also CA 93-96

Booth, Philip 1925-................CLC 23
See also CANR 5
See also CA 5-8R
See also DLB-Y 82

Booth, Wayne C(layson) 1921-......CLC 24
See also CANR 3
See also CA 1-4R

Borchert, Wolfgang 1921-1947 .... TCLC 5
See also CA 104

Borges, Jorge Luis
1899-.......CLC 1, 2, 3, 4, 6, 8, 9, 10,
13, 19
See also CA 21-24R

Borowski, Tadeusz 1922-1951..... TCLC 9
See also CA 106

Bourget, Paul (Charles Joseph)
1852-1935.................. TCLC 12
See also CA 107

Bourjaily, Vance (Nye) 1922-........CLC 8
See also CANR 2
See also CA 1-4R
See also DLB 2

Bowen, Elizabeth (Dorothea Cole)
1899-1973...... CLC 1, 3, 6, 11, 15, 22
See also CAP 2
See also CA 17-18
See also obituary CA 41-44R
See also DLB 15

Bowering, George 1935-...........CLC 15
See also CANR 10
See also CA 21-24R

Bowers, Edgar 1924-...............CLC 9
See also CA 5-8R
See also DLB 5

Bowie, David 1947-...............CLC 17
See also Jones, David Robert

Bowles, Jane (Sydney)
1917-1973....................CLC 3
See also CAP 2
See also CA 19-20
See also obituary CA 41-44R

Bowles, Paul (Frederick)
1910-................... CLC 1, 2, 19
See also CANR 1
See also CA 1-4R
See also DLB 5, 6

Boyd, William 1952-..............CLC 28

Boyle, Kay 1903-............ CLC 1, 5, 19
See also CA 13-16R
See also DLB 4, 9

Boyle, Patrick....................CLC 19

Bradbury, Edward P. 1939-
See Moorcock, Michael

Bradbury, Ray (Douglas)
1920-.................CLC 1, 3, 10, 15
See also CANR 2
See also CA 1-4R
See also SATA 11
See also DLB 2, 8
See also AITN 1, 2

Bradley, David (Henry), Jr.
1950-........................CLC 23
See also CA 104

Bragg, Melvyn 1939-..............CLC 10
See also CANR 10
See also CA 57-60
See also DLB 14

Braine, John (Gerard) 1922-..... CLC 1, 3
See also CANR 1
See also CA 1-4R
See also DLB 15

Brancati, Vitaliano
1907-1954................. TCLC 12
See also CA 109

Brand, Millen 1906-1980..........CLC 7
See also CA 21-24R
See also obituary CA 97-100

Brandes, Georg (Morris Cohen)
1842-1927.................. TCLC 10
See also CA 105

Branley, Franklyn M(ansfield)
1915-.......................CLC 21
See also CA 33-36R
See also SATA 4

Brathwaite, Edward 1930-.........CLC 11
See also CANR 11
See also CA 25-28R

Brautigan, Richard
1935-.............. CLC 1, 3, 5, 9, 12
See also CA 53-56
See also DLB 2, 5
See also DLB-Y 80

Brecht, (Eugen) Bertolt (Friedrich)
1898-1956.................. TCLC 1, 6
See also CA 104

Brennan, Maeve 1917-..............CLC 5
See also CA 81-84

Brentano, Clemens (Maria)
1778-1842.................. NCLC 1

Breslin, James (E.) 1930-
See Breslin, Jimmy
See also CA 73-76

Breslin, Jimmy 1930- ....CLC 4
See also Breslin, James (E.)
See also AITN 1

Bresson, Robert 1907-.............CLC 16

Breton, André 1896-1966..... CLC 2, 9, 15
See also CAP 2
See also CA 19-20
See also obituary CA 25-28R

Breytenbach, Breyten 1939-........CLC 23

Bridgers, Sue Ellen 1942-..........CLC 26
See also CANR 11
See also CA 65-68
See also SATA 22

Bridges, Robert 1844-1930........ TCLC 1
See also CA 104
See also DLB 19

Bridie, James 1888-1951 .... TCLC 3
See also CA 104
See also DLB 10

Brink, André (Philippus) 1935-.....CLC 18
See also CA 104

Brinsmead, H(esba) F(ay)
1922-........................CLC 21
See also CANR 10
See also CA 21-24R
See also SATA 18

Brittain, Vera (Mary)
1893?-1970..................CLC 23
See also CAP 1
See also CA 15-16
See also obituary CA 25-28R

Brodsky, Iosif Alexandrovich 1940-
See Brodsky, Joseph
See also CA 41-44R
See also AITN 1

Brodsky, Joseph 1940- .... CLC 4, 6, 13
See also Brodsky, Iosif Alexandrovich

Brodsky, Michael (Mark)
1948-.......................CLC 19
See also CA 102

Bromell, Henry 1947-..............CLC 5
See also CANR 9
See also CA 53-56

Bromfield, Louis (Brucker)
1896-1956.................. TCLC 11
See also CA 107
See also DLB 4, 9

Broner, E(sther) M(asserman)
1930-.......................CLC 19
See also CANR 8
See also CA 17-20R

Bronk, William 1918-..............CLC 10
See also CA 89-92

Brontë, Anne 1820-1849.......... NCLC 4
See also DLB 21

Brontë, Charlotte 1816-1855...... NCLC 3
See also DLB 21

Brooke, Henry 1703?-1783 .... LC 1

Brooke, Rupert (Chawner)
1887-1915................. TCLC 2, 7
See also CA 104
See also DLB 19

Brooks, Cleanth 1906- ....CLC 24
See also CA 17-20R

Brooks, Gwendolyn
1917-.............. CLC 1, 2, 4, 5, 15
See also CANR 1
See also CA 1-4R
See also SATA 6
See also DLB 5
See also AITN 1

Brooks, Mel 1926-.................CLC 12
See also CA 65-68
See also DLB 26

Brophy, Brigid (Antonia)
1929-..................... CLC 6, 11
See also CA 5-8R
See also DLB 14

Brosman, Catharine Savage
1934-........................CLC 9
See also CA 61-64

Broughton, T(homas) Alan
1936-.......................CLC 19
See also CANR 2
See also CA 45-48

Broumas, Olga 1949-..............CLC 10
See also CA 85-88

Brown, Dee (Alexander) 1908- .....CLC 18
See also CANR 11
See also CA 13-16R
See also SATA 5
See also DLB-Y 80

Brown, George Mackay 1921-.......CLC 5
See also CA 21-24R
See also DLB 14

Brown, Rita Mae 1944- ....CLC 18
See also CANR 2, 11
See also CA 45-48

Brown, Sterling A(llen)
1901-..................... CLC 1, 23
See also CA 85-88

Brown, William Wells
1816?-1884.................. NCLC 2
See also DLB 3

Browne, Jackson 1950-............CLC 21

Browning, Elizabeth Barrett
1806-1861................... NCLC 1

Browning, Tod 1882-1962 ....CLC 16

Bruce, Lenny 1925-1966...........CLC 21
See also Schneider, Leonard Alfred

Brunner, John (Kilian Houston)
1934-..................... CLC 8, 10
See also CANR 2
See also CA 1-4R

Bryant, William Cullen
1794-1878................... NCLC 6
See also DLB 3

Bryusov, Valery (Yakovlevich)
1873-1924.................. TCLC 10
See also CA 107

Buchheim, Lothar-Günther
1918-........................CLC 6
See also CA 85-88

Buck, Pearl S(ydenstricker)
1892-1973............. CLC 7, 11, 18
See also CANR 1
See also CA 1-4R
See also obituary CA 41-44R
See also SATA 1, 25
See also DLB 9
See also AITN 1

Buckler, Ernest 1908-.............CLC 13
See also CAP 1
See also CA 11-12

Buckley, William F(rank), Jr.
1925-.................... CLC 7, 18
See also CANR 1
See also CA 1-4R
See also DLB-Y 80
See also AITN 1

Buechner, (Carl) Frederick
1926-.................CLC 2, 4, 6, 9
See also CANR 11
See also CA 13-16R
See also DLB-Y 80

Buell, John (Edward) 1927-........CLC 10
See also CA 1-4R

Buero Vallejo, Antonio 1916- .....CLC 15
See also CA 106

Bukowski, Charles 1920- ...... CLC 2, 5, 9
See also CA 17-20R
See also DLB 5

Bulgakov, Mikhail (Afanas'evich)
1891-1940................... TCLC 2
See also CA 105

Bullins, Ed 1935-.............. CLC 1, 5, 7
See also CA 49-52
See also DLB 7

Bulwer-Lytton, (Lord) Edward (George Earle Lytton) 1803-1873 .... NCLC 1
See also SATA 23
See also DLB 21

Bunin, Ivan (Alexeyevich)
1870-1953................... TCLC 6
See also CA 104

Bunting, Basil 1900- ....CLC 10
See also CANR 7
See also CA 53-56
See also DLB 20

Buñuel, Luis 1900- ....CLC 16
See also CA 101

Burgess, Anthony
1917-..... CLC 1, 2, 4, 5, 8, 10, 13, 15, 22
See also Wilson, John (Anthony) Burgess
See also DLB 14
See also AITN 1

Burke, Kenneth (Duva)
1897-.................... CLC 2, 24
See also CA 5-8R

Burns, Tex 1908?-
See L'Amour, Louis (Dearborn)

Burnshaw, Stanley 1906- ...... CLC 3, 13
See also CA 9-12R

Burr, Anne 1937-..................CLC 6
See also CA 25-28R

Burroughs, Edgar Rice
1875-1950................... TCLC 2
See also CA 104
See also DLB 8

Burroughs, William S(eward)
1914- .... CLC 1, 2, 5, 15, 22
See also CA 9-12R
See also DLB 2, 8, 16
See also DLB-Y 81
See also AITN 2

Busch, Frederick 1941- ...... CLC 7, 10, 18
See also CA 33-36R
See also DLB 6

Butler, Samuel 1835-1902 .... TCLC 1
See also CA 104
See also DLB 18

Butor, Michel (Marie François)
1926- .... CLC 1, 3, 8, 11, 15
See also CA 9-12R

Byatt, A(ntonia) S(usan Drabble)
1936- .... CLC 19
See also CA 13-16R
See also DLB 14

Byrne, David 1953?- .... CLC 26

Byrne, John Keyes 1926-
See Leonard, Hugh
See also CA 102

Byron, George Gordon (Noel), Lord Byron
1788-1824 .... NCLC 2

Cabell, James Branch
1879-1958 .... TCLC 6
See also CA 105
See also DLB 9

Cable, George Washington
1844-1925 .... TCLC 4
See also CA 104
See also DLB 12

Cabrera Infante, G(uillermo)
1929- .... CLC 5, 25
See also CA 85-88

Cain, G. 1929-
See Cabrera Infante, G(uillermo)

Cain, James M(allahan)
1892-1977 .... CLC 3, 11, 28
See also CANR 8
See also CA 17-20R
See also obituary CA 73-76
See also AITN 1

Caldwell, Erskine 1903- ...... CLC 1, 8, 14
See also CANR 2
See also CA 1-4R
See also DLB 9
See also AITN 1

Caldwell, (Janet Miriam) Taylor (Holland)
1900- .... CLC 2, 28
See also CANR 5
See also CA 5-8R

Calisher, Hortense 1911- ...... CLC 2, 4, 8
See also CANR 1
See also CA 1-4R
See also DLB 2

Callaghan, Morley (Edward)
1903- .... CLC 3, 14
See also CA 9-12R

Calvino, Italo 1923- .... CLC 5, 8, 11, 22
See also CA 85-88

Campbell, (Ignatius) Roy (Dunnachie)
1901-1957 .... TCLC 5
See also CA 104
See also DLB 20

Campbell, (William) Wilfred
1861-1918 .... TCLC 9
See also CA 106

Camus, Albert
1913-1960 .... CLC 1, 2, 4, 9, 11, 14
See also CA 89-92

Canby, Vincent 1924- .... CLC 13
See also CA 81-84

Canetti, Elias 1905- .... CLC 3, 14, 25
See also CA 21-24R

Cape, Judith 1916-
See Page, P(atricia) K(athleen)

Čapek, Karl 1890-1938 .... TCLC 6
See also CA 104

Capote, Truman
1924- .... CLC 1, 3, 8, 13, 19
See also CA 5-8R
See also DLB 2
See also DLB-Y 80

Capra, Frank 1897- .... CLC 16
See also CA 61-64

Carey, Ernestine Gilbreth 1908-
See Gilbreth, Frank B(unker), Jr. and
Carey, Ernestine Gilbreth
See also CA 5-8R
See also SATA 2

Carleton, William 1794-1869 ...... NCLC 3

Carman, (William) Bliss
1861-1929 .... TCLC 7
See also CA 104

Carpentier (Y Valmont), Alejo
1904-1980 .... CLC 8, 11
See also CANR 11
See also CA 65-68
See also obituary CA 97-100

Carr, John Dickson 1905-1977 ...... CLC 3
See also CANR 3
See also CA 49-52
See also obituary CA 69-72

Carrier, Roch 1937- .... CLC 13

Carroll, Lewis 1832-1898 .... NCLC 2
See also CLR 2
See also YABC 2
See also DLB 18

Carroll, Paul Vincent
1900-1968 .... CLC 10
See also CA 9-12R
See also obituary CA 25-28R
See also DLB 10

Carruth, Hayden
1921- .... CLC 4, 7, 10, 18
See also CANR 4
See also CA 9-12R
See also DLB 5

Carter, Angela 1940- .... CLC 5
See also CA 53-56
See also DLB 14

Carver, Raymond 1938- .... CLC 22
See also CA 33-36R

Cary, (Arthur) Joyce
1888-1957 .... TCLC 1
See also CA 104
See also DLB 15

Casares, Adolfo Bioy 1914-
See Bioy Casares, Adolfo

Casey, John 1880-1964
See O'Casey, Sean

Casey, Michael 1947- .... CLC 2
See also CA 65-68
See also DLB 5

Casey, Warren 1935-
See Jacobs, Jim and Casey, Warren
See also CA 101

Cassavetes, John 1929- .... CLC 20
See also CA 85-88

Cassill, R(onald) V(erlin)
1919- .... CLC 4, 23
See also CANR 7
See also CA 9-12R
See also DLB 6

Cassity, (Allen) Turner 1929- ...... CLC 6
See also CANR 11
See also CA 17-20R

Castaneda, Carlos 1935?- .... CLC 12
See also CA 25-28R

Castro, Rosalía de 1837-1885 ..... NCLC 3

Cather, Willa (Sibert)
1873-1947 .... TCLC 1, 11
See also CA 104
See also DLB 9
See also DLB-DS 1

Causley, Charles (Stanley)
1917- .... CLC 7
See also CANR 5
See also CA 9-12R
See also SATA 3

Cavafy, C(onstantine) P(eter)
1863-1933 .... TCLC 2, 7
See also CA 104

Cavanna, Betty 1909- .... CLC 12
See also CANR 6
See also CA 9-12R
See also SATA 1, 30

Cayrol, Jean 1911- .... CLC 11
See also CA 89-92

Cela, Camilo José 1916- .... CLC 4, 13
See also CA 21-24R

Celan, Paul 1920-1970 .... CLC 10, 19
See also Antschel, Paul

Céline, Louis-Ferdinand
1894-1961 .... CLC 1, 3, 4, 7, 9, 15
See also Destouches, Louis Ferdinand

Cendrars, Blaise 1887-1961 .... CLC 18
See also Sauser-Hall, Frédéric

Césaire, Aimé (Fernand) 1913- ...... CLC 19
See also CA 65-68

Chabrol, Claude 1930- .... CLC 16

Challans, Mary 1905-
See Renault, Mary
See also CA 81-84
See also SATA 23

Chambers, James 1948-
See Cliff, Jimmy

Chandler, Raymond
1888-1959 .... TCLC 1, 7
See also CA 104

Chaplin, Charles (Spencer)
1889-1977 .... CLC 16
See also CA 81-84
See also obituary CA 73-76

Chapman, Graham 1941?-
See Monty Python

Chapman, John Jay
1862-1933................... TCLC 7
See also CA 104

Char, René (Emile)
1907-.................. CLC 9, 11, 14
See also CA 13-16R

Charyn, Jerome 1937- .... CLC 5, 8, 18
See also CANR 7
See also CA 5-8R

Chase, Mary Ellen 1887-1973 .... CLC 2
See also CAP 1
See also CA 15-16
See also obituary CA 41-44R
See also SATA 10

Chateaubriand, François René de
1768-1848.................... NCLC 3

Chatwin, (Charles) Bruce
1940-........................ CLC 28
See also CA 85-88

Chayefsky, Paddy 1923-1981 .... CLC 23
See also CA 9-12R
See also obituary CA 104
See also DLB 7
See also DLB-Y 81

Chayefsky, Sidney 1923-1981
See Chayefsky, Paddy

Cheever, John
1912-1982...... CLC 3, 7, 8, 11, 15, 25
See also CANR 5
See also CA 5-8R
See also obituary CA 106
See also DLB 2
See also DLB-Y 80, 82

Cheever, Susan 1943-............. CLC 18
See also CA 103
See also DLB-Y 82

Chekhov, Anton (Pavlovich)
1860-1904................. TCLC 3, 10
See also CA 104

Chernyshevsky, Nikolay Gavrilovich
1828-1889................... NCLC 1

Chesnutt, Charles Waddell
1858-1932.................... TCLC 5
See also CA 106
See also DLB 12

Chesterton, G(ilbert) K(eith)
1874-1936................. TCLC 1, 6
See also CA 104
See also SATA 27
See also DLB 10, 19

Ch'ien Chung-shu 1910-............ CLC 22

Child, Lydia Maria 1802-1880 .... NCLC 6
See also DLB 1

Child, Philip 1898-1978 .... CLC 19
See also CAP 1
See also CA 13-14

Childress, Alice 1920-........ CLC 12, 15
See also CANR 3
See also CA 45-48
See also SATA 7
See also DLB 7

Chitty, (Sir) Thomas Willes 1926-
See Hinde, Thomas
See also CA 5-8R

Chomette, René 1898-1981
See Clair, René
See also obituary CA 103

Chopin, Kate (O'Flaherty)
1851-1904................... TCLC 5
See also CA 104
See also DLB 12

Christie, Agatha (Mary Clarissa)
1890-1976.............. CLC 1, 6, 8, 12
See also CANR 10
See also CA 17-20R
See also obituary CA 61-64
See also DLB 13
See also AITN 1, 2

Christie, (Ann) Philippa 1920-
See Pearce, (Ann) Philippa
See also CANR 4

Ciardi, John (Anthony) 1916-...... CLC 10
See also CANR 5
See also CA 5-8R
See also SATA 1
See also DLB 5

Cimino, Michael 1943?-............ CLC 16
See also CA 105

Clair, René 1898-1981 .... CLC 20
See also Chomette, René

Clark, Eleanor 1913-........... CLC 5, 19
See also CA 9-12R
See also DLB 6

Clark, Mavis Thorpe 1912?- .... CLC 12
See also CANR 8
See also CA 57-60
See also SATA 8

Clark, Walter Van Tilburg
1909-1971...................CLC 28
See also CA 9-12R
See also obituary CA 33-36R
See also SATA 8
See also DLB 9

Clarke, Arthur C(harles)
1917-................. CLC 1, 4, 13, 18
See also CANR 2
See also CA 1-4R
See also SATA 13

Clarke, Austin 1896-1974........ CLC 6, 9
See also CAP 2
See also CA 29-32
See also obituary CA 49-52
See also DLB 10, 20

Clarke, Austin C(hesterfield)
1934-........................ CLC 8
See also CA 25-28R

Clarke, Shirley 1925- .... CLC 16

Claudel, Paul (Louis Charles Marie)
1868-1955................ TCLC 2, 10
See also CA 104

Clavell, James (duMaresq)
1924-..................... CLC 6, 25
See also CA 25-28R

Cleese, John 1939-
See Monty Python

Clemens, Samuel Langhorne 1835-1910
See Twain, Mark
See also CA 104
See also YABC 2
See also DLB 11, 12, 23

Cliff, Jimmy 1948-................CLC 21

Clifton, Lucille 1936-............CLC 19
See also CLR 5
See also CANR 2
See also CA 49-52
See also SATA 20
See also DLB 5

Clutha, Janet Paterson Frame 1924-
See Frame (Clutha), Janet (Paterson)
See also CANR 2
See also CA 1-4R

Coburn, D(onald) L(ee) 1938-......CLC 10
See also CA 89-92

Cocteau, Jean (Maurice Eugene Clement)
1889-1963.......... CLC 1, 8, 15, 16
See also CAP 2
See also CA 25-28

Coetzee, J(ohn) M. 1940-..........CLC 23
See also CA 77-80

Cohen, Arthur A(llen) 1928- ......CLC 7
See also CANR 1
See also CA 1-4R

Cohen, Leonard (Norman)
1934-....................... CLC 3
See also CA 21-24R

Cohen, Matt 1942-.................CLC 19
See also CA 61-64

Colette (Sidonie-Gabrielle)
1873-1954................. TCLC 1, 5
See also CA 104

Collins, Hunt 1926-
See Hunter, Evan

Collins, (William) Wilkie
1824-1889................... NCLC 1
See also DLB 18

Colman, George 1909-1981
See Glassco, John

Colum, Padraic 1881-1972........CLC 28
See also CA 73-76
See also obituary CA 33-36R
See also SATA 15
See also DLB 19

Colvin, James 1939-
See Moorcock, Michael

Colwin, Laurie 1945- .... CLC 5, 13, 23
See also CA 89-92
See also DLB-Y 80

Comfort, Alex(ander) 1920-........CLC 7
See also CANR 1
See also CA 1-4R

Compton-Burnett, Ivy
1892-1969..........CLC 1, 3, 10, 15
See also CANR 4
See also CA 1-4R
See also obituary CA 25-28R

Condon, Richard (Thomas)
1915-................CLC 4, 6, 8, 10
See also CANR 2
See also CA 1-4R

Connell, Evan S(helby), Jr.
1924-..................... CLC 4, 6
See also CANR 2
See also CA 1-4R
See also DLB 2
See also DLB-Y 81

Connelly, Marc(us Cook)
1890-1980................CLC 7
See also CA 85-88
See also obituary CA 103
See also obituary SATA 25
See also DLB 7
See also DLB-Y 80

Conrad, Joseph 1857-1924...... TCLC 1, 6
See also CA 104
See also SATA 27
See also DLB 10

Constant (de Rebecque), (Henri) Benjamin
1767-1830.................. NCLC 6

Cook, Robin 1940-................CLC 14
See also CA 108

Cooke, John Esten 1830-1886..... NCLC 5
See also DLB 3

Cooper, James Fenimore
1789-1851.................. NCLC 1
See also SATA 19
See also DLB 3

Coover, Robert (Lowell)
1932-..................... CLC 3, 7, 15
See also CANR 3
See also CA 45-48
See also DLB 2
See also DLB-Y 81

Copeland, Stewart (Armstrong) 1952-
See The Police

Coppard, A(lfred) E(dgar)
1878-1957..................... TCLC 5
See also YABC 1

Coppola, Francis Ford 1939-........CLC 16
See also CA 77-80

Corcoran, Barbara 1911-..........CLC 17
See also CANR 11
See also CA 21-24R
See also SATA 3

Corman, Cid 1924-.................CLC 9
See also Corman, Sidney
See also DLB 5

Corman, Sidney 1924-
See Corman, Cid
See also CA 85-88

Cormier, Robert (Edmund)
1925-.......................CLC 12
See also CANR 5
See also CA 1-4R
See also SATA 10

Cornwell, David (John Moore) 1931-
See le Carré, John
See also CA 5-8R

Corso, (Nunzio) Gregory
1930-..................... CLC 1, 11
See also CA 5-8R
See also DLB 5, 16

Cortázar, Julio
1914-.........CLC 2, 3, 5, 10, 13, 15
See also CA 21-24R

Corvo, Baron 1860-1913
See Rolfe, Frederick (William Serafino Austin Lewis Mary)

Ćosić, Dobrica 1921-..............CLC 14

Costello, Elvis 1955-..............CLC 21

Coward, Noel (Peirce)
1899-1973................ CLC 1, 9
See also CAP 2
See also CA 17-18
See also obituary CA 41-44R
See also DLB 10
See also AITN 1

Cox, William Trevor 1928-
See Trevor, William
See also CANR 4
See also CA 9-12R

Cozzens, James Gould
1903-1978................CLC 1, 4, 11
See also CA 9-12R
See also obituary CA 81-84
See also DLB 9
See also DLB-DS 2

Crane, (Harold) Hart
1899-1932................. TCLC 2, 5
See also CA 104
See also DLB 4

Crane, R(onald) S(almon)
1886-1967....................CLC 27
See also CA 85-88

Crane, Stephen 1871-1900....... TCLC 11
See also DLB 12
See also YABC 2

Craven, Margaret 1901-1980.......CLC 17
See also CA 103

Crayencour, Marguerite de 1913-
See Yourcenar, Marguerite

Creasey, John 1908-1973..........CLC 11
See also CANR 8
See also CA 5-8R
See also obituary CA 41-44R

Crébillon, Claude Prosper Jolyot de (fils)
1707-1777...................... LC 1

Creeley, Robert (White)
1926-.......... CLC 1, 2, 4, 8, 11, 15
See also CA 1-4R
See also DLB 5, 16

Crews, Harry 1935-............ CLC 6, 23
See also CA 25-28R
See also DLB 6
See also AITN 1

Crichton, (John) Michael
1942-...................... CLC 2, 6
See also CA 25-28R
See also SATA 9
See also DLB-Y 81
See also AITN 2

Crispin, Edmund 1921-1978 ....CLC 22
See also Montgomery, Robert Bruce

Cristofer, Michael 1946-..........CLC 28
See also CA 110
See also DLB 7

Cross, Amanda 1926-
See Heilbrun, Carolyn G(old)

Crowley, Aleister 1875-1947 ...... TCLC 7
See also CA 104

Crumb, Robert 1943-.............CLC 17
See also CA 106

Cryer, Gretchen 1936?-..........CLC 21

Cullen, Countee 1903-1946 .... TCLC 4
See also CA 108
See also SATA 18
See also DLB 4

Cummings, E(dward) E(stlin)
1894-1962........ CLC 1, 3, 8, 12, 15
See also CA 73-76
See also DLB 4

Cunningham, J(ames) V(incent)
1911-........................CLC 3
See also CANR 1
See also CA 1-4R
See also DLB 5

Cunningham, Julia (Woolfolk)
1916-......................CLC 12
See also CANR 4
See also CA 9-12R
See also SATA 1, 26

Dąbrowska, Maria (Szumska)
1889-1965....................CLC 15
See also CA 106

Dahl, Roald 1916-........... CLC 1, 6, 18
See also CLR 1
See also CANR 6
See also CA 1-4R
See also SATA 1, 26

Dahlberg, Edward
1900-1977................CLC 1, 7, 14
See also CA 9-12R
See also obituary CA 69-72

Daly, Maureen 1921-..............CLC 17
See also McGivern, Maureen Daly
See also SATA 2

Dannay, Frederic 1905-1982
See Queen, Ellery
See also CANR 1
See also CA 1-4R
See also obituary CA 107

D'Annunzio, Gabriele
1863-1938.................... TCLC 6
See also CA 104

Danziger, Paula 1944-............CLC 21
See also SATA 30

Darío, Rubén 1867-1916........ TCLC 4
See also CA 104

Darley, George 1795-1846 .... NCLC 2

Daryush, Elizabeth
1887-1977................ CLC 6, 19
See also CANR 3
See also CA 49-52
See also DLB 20

Daudet, (Louis Marie) Alphonse
1840-1897................... NCLC 1

Davenport, Guy (Mattison), Jr.
1927-..................... CLC 6, 14
See also CA 33-36R

Davidson, Donald (Grady)
1893-1968.............CLC 2, 13, 19
See also CANR 4
See also CA 5-8R
See also obituary CA 25-28R

Davidson, Sara 1943- ....CLC 9
See also CA 81-84

Davie, Donald (Alfred)
1922-.................... CLC 5, 8, 10
See also CANR 1
See also CA 1-4R

Davies, Ray(mond Douglas)
1944-.......................CLC 21

Davies, Rhys 1903-1978 ....CLC 23
See also CANR 4
See also CA 9-12R
See also obituary CA 81-84

Davies, W(illiam) H(enry)
1871-1940.................. TCLC 5
See also CA 104
See also DLB 19

Davies, (William) Robertson
1913-................CLC 2, 7, 13, 25
See also CA 33-36R

Davis, Rebecca (Blaine) Harding
1831-1910.................. TCLC 6
See also CA 104

Davison, Frank Dalby
1893-1970................CLC 15

Davison, Peter 1928-..............CLC 28
See also CANR 3
See also CA 9-12R
See also DLB 5

Davys, Mary 1674-1732 .... LC 1

Dawson, Fielding 1930-.............CLC 6
See also CA 85-88

Day, Thomas 1748-1789.............. LC 1
See also YABC 1

Day Lewis, C(ecil)
1904-1972................ CLC 1, 6, 10
See also CAP 1
See also CA 15-16
See also obituary CA 33-36R
See also DLB 15, 20

Dazai Osamu 1909-1948........ TCLC 11
See also Tsushima Shūji

Defoe, Daniel 1660?-1731............ LC 1
See also SATA 22

De Hartog, Jan 1914-..............CLC 19
See also CANR 1
See also CA 1-4R

Deighton, Len 1929 ....CLC 4, 7, 22
See also CA 9-12R

De la Mare, Walter (John)
1873-1956.................. TCLC 4
See also SATA 16
See also DLB 19

Delany, Samuel R(ay, Jr.)
1942-....................CLC 8, 14
See also CA 81-84
See also DLB 8

De la Roche, Mazo 1885-1961......CLC 14
See also CA 85-88

Delbanco, Nicholas (Franklin)
1942-...................CLC 6, 13
See also CA 17-20R
See also DLB 6

Delibes (Setien), Miguel
1920-.....................CLC 8, 18
See also CANR 1
See also CA 45-48

DeLillo, Don 1936- .... CLC 8, 10, 13
See also CA 81-84
See also DLB 6

De Lisser, H(erbert) G(eorge)
1878-1944.................. TCLC 12
See also CA 109

Deloria, Vine (Victor), Jr.
1933-.....................CLC 21
See also CANR 5
See also CA 53-56
See also SATA 21

Dennis, Nigel (Forbes) 1912-.......CLC 8
See also CA 25-28R
See also DLB 13, 15

De Palma, Brian 1940-............CLC 20
See also CA 109

De Quincey, Thomas
1785-1859................... NCLC 4

Deren, Maya 1908-1961............CLC 16

Derrida, Jacques 1930-............CLC 24

Desai, Anita 1937-...............CLC 19
See also CA 81-84

De Saint-Luc, Jean 1909-1981
See Glassco, John

De Sica, Vittorio 1902-1974........CLC 20

Destouches, Louis Ferdinand 1894-1961
See Céline, Louis-Ferdinand
See also CA 85-88

Deutsch, Babette 1895-1982........CLC 18
See also CANR 4
See also CA 1-4R
See also obituary CA 108
See also SATA 1
See also obituary SATA 33

De Vries, Peter
1910-........... CLC 1, 2, 3, 7, 10, 28
See also CA 17-20R
See also DLB 6
See also DLB-Y 82

Dick, Philip K(indred)
1928-1982....................CLC 10
See also CANR 2
See also CA 49-52
See also obituary CA 106
See also DLB 8

Dickens, Charles 1812-1870....... NCLC 3
See also SATA 15
See also DLB 21

Dickey, James (Lafayette)
1923-........... CLC 1, 2, 4, 7, 10, 15
See also CANR 10
See also CA 9-12R
See also DLB 5
See also DLB-Y 82
See also AITN 1, 2

Dickey, William 1928-.......... CLC 3, 28
See also CA 9-12R
See also DLB 5

Dickinson, Peter 1927- ....CLC 12
See also CA 41-44R
See also SATA 5

Didion, Joan 1934- ....CLC 1, 3, 8, 14
See also CA 5-8R
See also DLB 2
See also DLB-Y 81
See also AITN 1

Dillard, Annie 1945-...............CLC 9
See also CANR 3
See also CA 49-52
See also SATA 10
See also DLB-Y 80

Dillard, R(ichard) H(enry) W(ilde)
1937-......................CLC 5
See also CANR 10
See also CA 21-24R
See also DLB 5

Dillon, Eilis 1920- ....CLC 17
See also CANR 4
See also CA 9-12R
See also SATA 2

Dinesen, Isak 1885-1962...........CLC 10
See also Blixen, Karen (Christentze Dinesen)

Disch, Thomas M(ichael) 1940-......CLC 7
See also CA 21-24R
See also DLB 8

Disraeli, Benjamin 1804-1881..... NCLC 2
See also DLB 21

Dixon, Paige 1911-
See Corcoran, Barbara

Dobrolyubov, Nikolai Alexandrovich
1836-1861................... NCLC 5

Dr. A 1933-
See Silverstein, Alvin and Virginia B(arbara Opshelor) Silverstein

Doctorow, E(dgar) L(aurence)
1931-.............CLC 6, 11, 15, 18
See also CANR 2
See also CA 45-48
See also DLB 2
See also DLB-Y 80
See also AITN 2

Dodgson, Charles Lutwidge 1832-1898
See Carroll, Lewis

Donleavy, J(ames) P(atrick)
1926-..................CLC 1, 4, 6, 10
See also CA 9-12R
See also DLB 6
See also AITN 2

Donoso, José 1924- .... CLC 4, 8, 11
See also CA 81-84

Doolittle, Hilda 1886-1961
See H(ilda) D(oolittle)
See also CA 97-100
See also DLB 4

Dorn, Ed(ward Merton)
1929-.................... CLC 10, 18
See also CA 93-96
See also DLB 5

Dos Passos, John (Roderigo)
1896-1970.....CLC 1, 4, 8, 11, 15, 25
See also CANR 3
See also CA 1-4R
See also obituary CA 29-32R
See also DLB 4, 9
See also DLB-DS 1

Dostoevski, Fedor Mikhailovich
1821-1881................... NCLC 2

Dourado, (Waldomiro Freitas) Autran
1926-.....................CLC 23
See also CA 25-28R

Dowson, Ernest (Christopher)
1867-1900.................. TCLC 4
See also CA 105
See also DLB 19

Doyle, (Sir) Arthur Conan
1859-1930 . . . . TCLC 7
See also CA 104
See also SATA 24
See also DLB 18

Drabble, Margaret
1939- . . . . CLC 2, 3, 5, 8, 10, 22
See also CA 13-16R
See also DLB 14

Dreiser, Theodore (Herman Albert)
1871-1945 . . . . TCLC 10
See also CA 106
See also DLB 9, 12
See also DLB-DS 1

Drexler, Rosalyn 1926- . . . . CLC 2, 6
See also CA 81-84

Dreyer, Carl Theodor
1889-1968 . . . . CLC 16

Droste-Hülshoff, Annette Freiin von
1797-1848 . . . . NCLC 3

Drummond de Andrade, Carlos 1902-
See Andrade, Carlos Drummond de

Duberman, Martin 1930- . . . . CLC 8
See also CANR 2
See also CA 1-4R

Du Bois, W(illiam) E(dward) B(urghardt)
1868-1963 . . . . CLC 1, 2, 13
See also CA 85-88

Dubus, Andre 1936- . . . . CLC 13
See also CA 21-24R

Duclos, Charles Pinot 1704-1772 . . . . . LC 1

Dudek, Louis 1918- . . . . CLC 11, 19
See also CANR 1
See also CA 45-48

Dudevant, Amandine Aurore Lucile Dupin
1804-1876
See Sand, George

Dugan, Alan 1923- . . . . CLC 2, 6
See also CA 81-84
See also DLB 5

Duhamel, Georges 1884-1966 . . . . CLC 8
See also CA 81-84
See also obituary CA 25-28R

Duke, Raoul 1939-
See Thompson, Hunter S(tockton)

Dumas, Henry (L.) 1934-1968 . . . . CLC 6
See also CA 85-88

Du Maurier, Daphne 1907- . . . . CLC 6, 11
See also CANR 6
See also CA 5-8R
See also SATA 27

Dunbar, Paul Laurence
1872-1906 . . . . TCLC 2, 12
See also CA 104
See also SATA 34

Duncan (Steinmetz Arquette), Lois
1934- . . . . CLC 26
See also CANR 2
See also CA 1-4R
See also Arquette, Lois S(teinmetz)

Duncan, Robert
1919- . . . . CLC 1, 2, 4, 7, 15
See also CA 9-12R
See also DLB 5, 16

Dunlap, William 1766-1839 . . . . NCLC 2

Dunn, Douglas (Eaglesham)
1942- . . . . CLC 6
See also CANR 2
See also CA 45-48

Dunne, John Gregory 1932- . . . . CLC 28
See also CA 25-28R
See also DLB-Y 80

Dunsany, Lord (Edward John Moreton Drax Plunkett) 1878-1957 . . . . TCLC 2
See also CA 104
See also DLB 10

Durang, Christopher (Ferdinand)
1949- . . . . CLC 27
See also CA 105

Duras, Marguerite
1914- . . . . CLC 3, 6, 11, 20
See also CA 25-28R

Durrell, Lawrence (George)
1912- . . . . CLC 1, 4, 6, 8, 13, 27
See also CA 9-12R
See also DLB 15

Dürrenmatt, Friedrich
1921- . . . . CLC 1, 4, 8, 11, 15
See also CA 17-20R

Dylan, Bob 1941- . . . . CLC 3, 4, 6, 12
See also CA 41-44R
See also DLB 16

Eastlake, William (Derry) 1917- . . . . . CLC 8
See also CANR 5
See also CA 5-8R
See also DLB 6

Eberhart, Richard 1904- . . . . CLC 3, 11, 19
See also CANR 2
See also CA 1-4R

Echegaray (y Eizaguirre), José (María Waldo) 1832-1916 . . . . TCLC 4
See also CA 104

Eckert, Allan W. 1931- . . . . CLC 17
See also CA 13-16R
See also SATA 27, 29

Eco, Umberto 1932- . . . . CLC 28
See also CA 77-80

Edgeworth, Maria 1767-1849 . . . . . NCLC 1
See also SATA 21

Edmonds, Helen (Woods) 1904-1968
See Kavan, Anna
See also CA 5-8R
See also obituary CA 25-28R

Edson, Russell 1905- . . . . CLC 13
See also CA 33-36R

Edwards, G(erald) B(asil)
1899-1976 . . . . CLC 25

Ehle, John (Marsden, Jr.)
1925- . . . . CLC 27
See also CA 9-12R

Ehrenbourg, Ilya (Grigoryevich) 1891-1967
See Ehrenburg, Ilya (Grigoryevich)

Ehrenburg, Ilya (Grigoryevich)
1891-1967 . . . . CLC 18
See also CA 102
See also obituary CA 25-28R

Eich, Günter 1907- . . . . CLC 15
See also obituary CA 93-96

Eigner, Larry 1927- . . . . CLC 9
See also Eigner, Laurence (Joel)
See also DLB 5

Eigner, Laurence (Joel) 1927-
See Eigner, Larry
See also CANR 6
See also CA 9-12R

Eiseley, Loren (Corey)
1907-1977 . . . . CLC 7
See also CANR 6
See also CA 1-4R
See also obituary CA 73-76

Ekeloef, Gunnar (Bengt) 1907-1968
See Ekelöf, Gunnar (Bengt)
See also obituary CA 25-28R

Ekelöf, Gunnar (Bengt)
1907-1968 . . . . CLC 27
See also Ekeloef, Gunnar (Bengt)

Ekwensi, Cyprian (Odiatu Duaka)
1921- . . . . CLC 4
See also CA 29-32R

Eliade, Mircea 1907- . . . . CLC 19
See also CA 65-68

Eliot, George 1819-1880 . . . . NCLC 4
See also DLB 21

Eliot, T(homas) S(tearns)
1888-1965 . . . . CLC 1, 2, 3, 6, 9, 10,
 13, 15, 24
See also CA 5-8R
See also obituary CA 25-28R
See also DLB 7, 10

Elkin, Stanley L(awrence)
1930- . . . . CLC 4, 6, 9, 14, 27
See also CANR 8
See also CA 9-12R
See also DLB 2
See also DLB-Y 80

Elliott, George P(aul)
1918-1980 . . . . CLC 2
See also CANR 2
See also CA 1-4R
See also obituary CA 97-100

Ellis, A. E. . . . . CLC 7

Ellison, Harlan 1934- . . . . CLC 1, 13
See also CANR 5
See also CA 5-8R
See also DLB 8

Ellison, Ralph (Waldo)
1914- . . . . CLC 1, 3, 11
See also CA 9-12R
See also DLB 2

Elman, Richard 1934- . . . . CLC 19
See also CA 17-20R

Éluard, Paul 1895-1952 . . . . TCLC 7
See also CA 104

Elvin, Anne Katharine Stevenson 1933-
See Stevenson, Anne
See also CA 17-20R

Elytis, Odysseus 1911- . . . . CLC 15
See also CA 102

Emecheta, (Florence Onye) Buchi
1944- . . . . CLC 14
See also CA 81-84

Emerson, Ralph Waldo
1803-1882 . . . . NCLC 1
See also DLB 1

Empson, William 1906- . . . . CLC 3, 8, 19
See also CA 17-20R
See also DLB 20

Endo, Shusaku 1923- .... CLC 7, 14, 19
See also CA 29-32R

Enright, D(ennis) J(oseph)
1920- .... CLC 4, 8
See also CANR 1
See also CA 1-4R
See also SATA 25

Ephron, Nora 1941- .... CLC 17
See also CA 65-68
See also AITN 2

Epstein, Daniel Mark 1948- .... CLC 7
See also CANR 2
See also CA 49-52

Epstein, Jacob 1956- .... CLC 19

Epstein, Leslie 1938- .... CLC 27
See also CA 73-76

Erdman, Paul E(mil) 1932- .... CLC 25
See also CA 61-64

Erenburg, Ilya (Grigoryevich) 1891-1967
See Ehrenburg, Ilya (Grigoryevich)

Eseki, Bruno 1919-
See Mphahlele, Ezekiel

Esenin, Sergei (Aleksandrovich)
1895-1925.................... TCLC 4
See also CA 104

Eshleman, Clayton 1935- .... CLC 7
See also CA 33-36R
See also DLB 5

Espriu, Salvador 1913- .... CLC 9

Evans, Marian
See Eliot, George

Evans, Mary Ann
See Eliot, George

Evarts, Esther 1900-1972
See Benson, Sally

Everson, R(onald) G(ilmour)
1903- .... CLC 27
See also CA 17-20R

Everson, William (Oliver)
1912- .... CLC 1, 5, 14
See also CA 9-12R
See also DLB 5, 16

Evtushenko, Evgenii (Aleksandrovich) 1933-
See Yevtushenko, Yevgeny

Ewart, Gavin (Buchanan)
1916- .... CLC 13
See also CA 89-92

Ewers, Hanns Heinz
1871-1943.................... TCLC 12

Ewing, Frederick R. 1918-
See Sturgeon, Theodore (Hamilton)

Exley, Frederick (Earl)
1929- .... CLC 6, 11
See also CA 81-84
See also DLB-Y 81
See also AITN 2

Fagen, Donald 1948-
See Becker, Walter and Fagen, Donald

Fagen, Donald 1948- and **Becker, Walter**
1950-
See Becker, Walter and Fagen, Donald

Fair, Ronald L. 1932- .... CLC 18
See also CA 69-72

Fallaci, Oriana 1930- .... CLC 11
See also CA 77-80

Fargue, Léon-Paul 1876-1947 .... TCLC 11
See also CA 109

Farigoule, Louis 1885-1972
See Romains, Jules

Fariña, Richard 1937?-1966 .... CLC 9
See also CA 81-84
See also obituary CA 25-28R

Farley, Walter 1915- .... CLC 17
See also CANR 8
See also CA 17-20R
See also SATA 2
See also DLB 22

Farmer, Philip José 1918- ...... CLC 1, 19
See also CANR 4
See also CA 1-4R
See also DLB 8

Farrell, J(ames) G(ordon)
1935-1979.................... CLC 6
See also CA 73-76
See also obituary CA 89-92
See also DLB 14

Farrell, James T(homas)
1904-1979............. CLC 1, 4, 8, 11
See also CANR 9
See also CA 5-8R
See also obituary CA 89-92
See also DLB 4, 9
See also DLB-DS 2

Fassbinder, Rainer Werner
1946-1982.................... CLC 20
See also CA 93-96
See also obituary CA 106

Fast, Howard (Melvin) 1914- .... CLC 23
See also CANR 1
See also CA 1-4R
See also SATA 7
See also DLB 9

Faulkner, William (Cuthbert)
1897-1962....... CLC 1, 3, 6, 8, 9, 11,
14, 18, 28
See also CA 81-84
See also DLB 9, 11
See also DLB-DS 2
See also AITN 1

Fauset, Jessie Redmon
1884?-1961.................... CLC 19
See also CA 109

Faust, Irvin 1924- .... CLC 8
See also CA 33-36R
See also DLB 2
See also DLB-Y 80

Federman, Raymond 1928- .... CLC 6
See also CANR 10
See also CA 17-20R
See also DLB-Y 80

Feiffer, Jules 1929- .... CLC 2, 8
See also CA 17-20R
See also SATA 8
See also DLB 7

Feldman, Irving (Mordecai)
1928- .... CLC 7
See also CANR 1
See also CA 1-4R

Fellini, Federico 1920- .... CLC 16
See also CA 65-68

Felsen, Gregor 1916-
See Felsen, Henry Gregor

Felsen, Henry Gregor 1916- .... CLC 17
See also CANR 1
See also CA 1-4R
See also SATA 1

Ferber, Edna 1887-1968.......... CLC 18
See also CA 5-8R
See also obituary CA 25-28R
See also SATA 7
See also DLB 9
See also AITN 1

Ferlinghetti, Lawrence (Monsanto)
1919?- .... CLC 2, 6, 10, 27
See also CANR 3
See also CA 5-8R
See also DLB 5, 16

Feuchtwanger, Lion
1884-1958................... TCLC 3
See also CA 104

Fiedler, Leslie A(aron)
1917- .... CLC 4, 13, 24
See also CANR 7
See also CA 9-12R

Field, Eugene 1850-1895 .... NCLC 3
See also SATA 16
See also DLB 21

Fielding, Henry 1707-1754.......... LC 1

Fielding, Sarah 1710-1768 .... LC 1

Finch, Robert (Duer Claydon)
1900- .... CLC 18
See also CANR 9
See also CA 57-60

Findley, Timothy 1930- .... CLC 27
See also CA 25-28R

Fink, Janis 1951-
See Ian, Janis

Firbank, (Arthur Annesley) Ronald
1886-1926.................... TCLC 1
See also CA 104

Firbank, Louis 1944-
See Reed, Lou

Fisher, Roy 1930- .... CLC 25
See also CA 81-84

Fisher, Rudolph 1897-1934 ...... TCLC 11
See also CA 107

Fisher, Vardis (Alvero)
1895-1968..................... CLC 7
See also CA 5-8R
See also obituary CA 25-28R
See also DLB 9

Fitzgerald, F(rancis) Scott (Key)
1896-1940.................. TCLC 1, 6
See also DLB 4, 9
See also DLB-Y 81
See also DLB-DS 1
See also AITN 1

Fitzgerald, Penelope 1916- .... CLC 19
See also CA 85-88
See also DLB 14

FitzGerald, Robert D(avid)
1902- .... CLC 19
See also CA 17-20R

Flanagan, Thomas (James Bonner)
1923- .... CLC 25
See also CA 108
See also DLB-Y 80

Flaubert, Gustave 1821-1880 ...... NCLC 2

Fleming, Ian (Lancaster)
1908-1964......................CLC 3
See also CA 5-8R
See also SATA 9

Follett, Ken(neth Martin)
1949-..........................CLC 18
See also CA 81-84
See also DLB-Y 81

Forbes, Esther 1891-1967..........CLC 12
See also CAP 1
See also CA 13-14
See also obituary CA 25-28R
See also DLB 22
See also SATA 2

Forché, Carolyn 1950- ....CLC 25
See also CA 109
See also DLB 5

Ford, Ford Madox 1873-1939..... TCLC 1
See also CA 104

Ford, John 1895-1973..............CLC 16
See also obituary CA 45-48

Forman, James D(ouglas)
1932-..........................CLC 21
See also CANR 4
See also CA 9-12R
See also SATA 8

Forrest, Leon 1937-................CLC 4
See also CA 89-92

Forster, E(dward) M(organ)
1879-1970....... CLC 1, 2, 3, 4, 9, 10,
13, 15, 22
See also CAP 1
See also CA 13-14
See also obituary CA 25-28R

Forsyth, Frederick 1938- .... CLC 2, 5
See also CA 85-88

Fosse, Bob 1925- ....CLC 20

Fouqué, Friedrich (Heinrich Karl) de La Motte 1777-1843............ NCLC 2

Fournier, Pierre 1916- ....CLC 11
See also CA 89-92

Fowles, John
1926-...... CLC 1, 2, 3, 4, 6, 9, 10, 15
See also CA 5-8R
See also SATA 22
See also DLB 14

Fox, Paula 1923- .... CLC 2, 8
See also CLR 1
See also CA 73-76
See also SATA 17

Fox, William Price (Jr.) 1926-......CLC 22
See also CANR 11
See also DLB 2
See also DLB-Y 81

Frame (Clutha), Janet (Paterson)
1924-.................CLC 2, 3, 6, 22
See also Clutha, Janet Paterson Frame

France, Anatole 1844-1924 .... TCLC 9
See also CA 106

Francis, Dick 1920-............ CLC 15, 22
See also CANR 9
See also CA 5-8R

Francis, Robert (Churchill)
1901-.........................CLC 15
See also CANR 1
See also CA 1-4R

Franklin, (Stella Maria Sarah) Miles
1879-1954.................. TCLC 9
See also CA 104

Fraser, George MacDonald
1925-..........................CLC 7
See also CANR 2
See also CA 45-48

Frayn, Michael 1933- ....CLC 3, 7
See also CA 5-8R
See also DLB 13, 14

Freeman, Douglas Southall
1886-1953.................. TCLC 11
See also CA 109
See also DLB 17

Freeman, Mary (Eleanor) Wilkins
1852-1930................... TCLC 9
See also CA 106
See also DLB 12

French, Marilyn 1929- .... CLC 10, 18
See also CANR 3
See also CA 69-72

Freneau, Philip Morin
1752-1832.................... NCLC 1

Friedman, B(ernard) H(arper)
1926-..........................CLC 7
See also CANR 3
See also CA 1-4R

Friedman, Bruce Jay 1930-...... CLC 3, 5
See also CA 9-12R
See also DLB 2

Friel, Brian 1929- ....CLC 5
See also CA 21-24R
See also DLB 13

Friis-Baastad, Babbis (Ellinor)
1921-1970....................CLC 12
See also CA 17-20R
See also SATA 7

Frisch, Max (Rudolf)
1911-....................CLC 3, 9, 14, 18
See also CA 85-88

Frost, Robert (Lee)
1874-1963...... CLC 1, 3, 4, 9, 10, 13,
15, 26
See also CA 89-92
See also SATA 14

Fry, Christopher 1907-...... CLC 2, 10, 14
See also CANR 9
See also CA 17-20R
See also DLB 13

Frye, (Herman) Northrop
1912-.........................CLC 24
See also CANR 8
See also CA 5-8R

Fuchs, Daniel 1909-............CLC 8, 22
See also CA 81-84
See also DLB 9, 26

Fuentes, Carlos
1928-............ CLC 3, 8, 10, 13, 22
See also CANR 10
See also CA 69-72
See also AITN 2

Fugard, Athol 1932- ......CLC 5, 9, 14, 25
See also CA 85-88

Fuller, Charles (H., Jr.) 1939- .....CLC 25
See also CA 108

Fuller, (Sarah) Margaret
1810-1850................. NCLC 5
See also DLB 1
See also Ossoli, Sarah Margaret (Fuller marchesa d')

Fuller, Roy (Broadbent)
1912-..................... CLC 4, 28
See also CA 5-8R
See also DLB 15, 20

Gadda, Carlo Emilio
1893-1973....................CLC 11
See also CA 89-92

Gaddis, William
1922-............ CLC 1, 3, 6, 8, 10, 19
See also CA 17-20R
See also DLB 2

Gaines, Ernest J. 1933- ..... CLC 3, 11, 18
See also CANR 6
See also CA 9-12R
See also DLB 2
See also DLB-Y 80
See also AITN 1

Gale, Zona 1874-1938............ TCLC 7
See also CA 105
See also DLB 9

Gallagher, Tess 1943-.............CLC 18
See also CA 106

Gallant, Mavis 1922-........... CLC 7, 18
See also CA 69-72

Gallant, Roy A(rthur) 1924- ....CLC 17
See also CANR 4
See also CA 5-8R
See also SATA 4

Gallico, Paul (William)
1897-1976.....................CLC 2
See also CA 5-8R
See also obituary CA 69-72
See also SATA 13
See also DLB 9
See also AITN 1

Galsworthy, John 1867-1933...... TCLC 1
See also CA 104
See also DLB 10

Galt, John 1779-1839 .... NCLC 1

Gann, Ernest K(ellogg) 1910- ..... CLC 23
See also CANR 1
See also CA 1-4R
See also AITN 1

García Lorca, Federico
1899-1936................. TCLC 1, 7
See also CA 104

García Márquez, Gabriel
1928-.......... CLC 2, 3, 8, 10, 15, 27
See also CANR 10
See also CA 33-36R

Gardner, John (Champlin, Jr.)
1933-1982....... CLC 2, 3, 5, 7, 8, 10,
18, 28
See also CA 65-68
See also obituary CA 107
See also obituary SATA 31
See also DLB 2
See also DLB-Y 82
See also AITN 1

Garfield, Leon 1921-..............CLC 12
See also CA 17-20R
See also SATA 1, 32

Garland, (Hannibal) Hamlin
1860-1940 .... TCLC 3
See also CA 104
See also DLB 12

Garner, Alan 1935- .... CLC 17
See also CA 73-76
See also SATA 18

Garner, Hugh 1913-1979 .... CLC 13
See also CA 69-72

Garnett, David 1892-1981 .... CLC 3
See also CA 5-8R
See also obituary CA 103

Garrett, George (Palmer)
1929- .... CLC 3, 11
See also CANR 1
See also CA 1-4R
See also DLB 2, 5

Garrigue, Jean 1914-1972 .... CLC 2, 8
See also CA 5-8R
See also obituary CA 37-40R

Gary, Romain 1914-1980 .... CLC 25
See also Kacew, Romain

Gascar, Pierre 1916-
See Fournier, Pierre

Gaskell, Elizabeth Cleghorn
1810-1865 .... NCLC 5
See also DLB 21

Gass, William H(oward)
1924- .... CLC 1, 2, 8, 11, 15
See also CA 17-20R
See also DLB 2

Gautier, Théophile 1811-1872 ..... NCLC 1

Gaye, Marvin 1939- .... CLC 26

Gelbart, Larry (Simon) 1923- ...... CLC 21
See also CA 73-76

Gelber, Jack 1932- .... CLC 1, 6, 14
See also CANR 2
See also CA 1-4R
See also DLB 7

Gellhorn, Martha (Ellis) 1908- ..... CLC 14
See also CA 77-80
See also DLB-Y 82

Genet, Jean 1910- ..... CLC 1, 2, 5, 10, 14
See also CA 13-16R

George, Stefan (Anton)
1868-1933 .... TCLC 2
See also CA 104

Gerhardi, William (Alexander) 1895-1977
See Gerhardie, William (Alexander)

Gerhardie, William (Alexander)
1895-1977 .... CLC 5
See also CA 25-28R
See also obituary CA 73-76

Gessner, Friedrike Victoria 1910-1980
See Adamson, Joy(-Friederike Victoria)

Ghelderode, Michel de
1898-1962 .... CLC 6, 11
See also CA 85-88

Ghiselin, Brewster 1903- .... CLC 23
See also CA 13-16R

Giacosa, Giuseppe 1847-1906 ..... TCLC 7
See also CA 104

Gibbon, Lewis Grassic
1901-1935 .... TCLC 4
See also Mitchell, James Leslie

Gibran, (Gibran) Kahlil
1883-1931 .... TCLC 1, 9
See also CA 104

Gibson, William 1914- .... CLC 23
See also CANR 9
See also CA 9-12R
See also DLB 7

Gide, André (Paul Guillaume)
1869-1951 .... TCLC 5, 12
See also CA 104

Gilbert, (Sir) W(illiam) S(chwenck)
1836-1911 .... TCLC 3
See also CA 104

Gilbreth, Ernestine 1908-
See Carey, Ernestine Gilbreth

Gilbreth, Frank B(unker), Jr. 1911-
See Gilbreth, Frank B(unker), Jr. and
  Carey, Ernestine Gilbreth
See also CA 9-12R
See also SATA 2

Gilbreth, Frank B(unker), Jr. 1911- and
  Carey, Ernestine Gilbreth
1908- .... CLC 17

Gilliam, Terry (Vance) 1940-
See Monty Python
See also CA 108

Gilliatt, Penelope (Ann Douglass)
1932- .... CLC 2, 10, 13
See also CA 13-16R
See also DLB 14
See also AITN 1

Gilman, Charlotte (Anna) Perkins (Stetson)
1860-1935 .... TCLC 9
See also CA 106

Gilroy, Frank D(aniel) 1925- .... CLC 2
See also CA 81-84
See also DLB 7

Ginsberg, Allen
1926- .... CLC 1, 2, 3, 4, 6, 13
See also CANR 2
See also CA 1-4R
See also DLB 5, 16
See also AITN 1

Ginzburg, Natalia 1916- .... CLC 5, 11
See also CA 85-88

Giono, Jean 1895-1970 .... CLC 4, 11
See also CANR 2
See also CA 45-48
See also obituary CA 29-32R

Giovanni, Nikki 1943- .... CLC 2, 4, 19
See also CLR 6
See also CA 29-32R
See also SATA 24
See also DLB 5
See also AITN 1

Giovene, Andrea 1904- .... CLC 7
See also CA 85-88

Giraudoux, (Hippolyte) Jean
1882-1944 .... TCLC 2, 7
See also CA 104

Gironella, José María 1917- .... CLC 11
See also CA 101

Gissing, George (Robert)
1857-1903 .... TCLC 3
See also CA 105
See also DLB 18

Glanville, Brian (Lester) 1931- ...... CLC 6
See also CANR 3
See also CA 5-8R
See also DLB 15

Glasgow, Ellen (Anderson Gholson)
1873?-1945 .... TCLC 2, 7
See also CA 104
See also DLB 9, 12

Glassco, John 1909-1981 .... CLC 9
See also CA 13-16R
See also obituary CA 102

Glissant, Edouard 1928- .... CLC 10

Glück, Louise 1943- .... CLC 7, 22
See also CA 33-36R
See also DLB 5

Godard, Jean-Luc 1930- .... CLC 20
See also CA 93-96

Godwin, Gail 1937- .... CLC 5, 8, 22
See also CA 29-32R
See also DLB 6

Goethe, Johann Wolfgang von
1749-1832 .... NCLC 4

Gogol, Nikolai (Vasilyevich)
1809-1852 .... NCLC 5

Gold, Herbert 1924- .... CLC 4, 7, 14
See also CA 9-12R
See also DLB 2
See also DLB-Y 81

Goldbarth, Albert 1948- .... CLC 5
See also CANR 6
See also CA 53-56

Golding, William (Gerald)
1911- .... CLC 1, 2, 3, 8, 10, 17, 27
See also CA 5-8R
See also DLB 15

Goldman, William (W.) 1931- .... CLC 1
See also CA 9-12R

Goldmann, Lucien 1913-1970 ...... CLC 24
See also CAP 2
See also CA 25-28

Gombrowicz, Witold
1904-1969 .... CLC 4, 7, 11
See also CAP 2
See also CA 19-20
See also obituary CA 25-28R

Gómez de la Serna, Ramón
1888-1963 .... CLC 9

Goncharov, Ivan Alexandrovich
1812-1891 .... NCLC 1

Goodman, Paul
1911-1972 .... CLC 1, 2, 4, 7
See also CAP 2
See also CA 19-20
See also obituary CA 37-40R

Gordimer, Nadine
1923- .... CLC 3, 5, 7, 10, 18
See also CANR 3
See also CA 5-8R

Gordon, Caroline
1895-1981 .... CLC 6, 13
See also CAP 1
See also CA 11-12
See also obituary CA 103
See also DLB 4, 9
See also DLB-Y 81

Gordon, Mary (Catherine)
1949- .... CLC 13, 22
See also CA 102
See also DLB 6
See also DLB-Y 81

Gordon, Sol 1923- .... CLC 26
See also CANR 4
See also CA 53-56
See also SATA 11

Gordone, Charles 1925- .... CLC 1, 4
See also CA 93-96
See also DLB 7

Gorenko, Anna Andreyevna 1889?-1966
See Akhmatova, Anna

Gorky, Maxim 1868-1936 .... TCLC 8
See also CA 105

Goryan, Sirak 1908-1981
See Saroyan, William

Gotlieb, Phyllis (Fay Bloom)
1926- .... CLC 18
See also CANR 7
See also CA 13-16R

Gould, Lois 1938?- .... CLC 4, 10
See also CA 77-80

Goyen, (Charles) William
1915- .... CLC 5, 8, 14
See also CANR 6
See also CA 5-8R
See also DLB 2
See also AITN 2

Goytisolo, Juan 1931- .... CLC 5, 10, 23
See also CA 85-88

Grabbe, Christian Dietrich
1801-1836 .... NCLC 2

Gracq, Julien 1910- .... CLC 11

Grade, Chaim 1910-1982 .... CLC 10
See also CA 93-96
See also obituary CA 107

Graham, Winston (Mawdsley)
1910- .... CLC 23
See also CANR 2
See also CA 49-52

Granville-Barker, Harley
1877-1946 .... TCLC 2
See also CA 104

Grass, Günter (Wilhelm)
1927- .... CLC 1, 2, 4, 6, 11, 15, 22
See also CA 13-16R

Grau, Shirley Ann 1929- .... CLC 4, 9
See also CA 89-92
See also DLB 2
See also AITN 2

Graves, Robert 1895- ...... CLC 1, 2, 6, 11
See also CANR 5
See also CA 5-8R
See also DLB 20

Gray, Francine du Plessix
1930- .... CLC 22
See also CANR 11
See also CA 61-64

Gray, Simon 1936- .... CLC 9, 14
See also CA 21-24R
See also DLB 13
See also AITN 1

Greeley, Andrew M(oran)
1928- .... CLC 28
See also CANR 7
See also CA 5-8R

Green, Hannah 1932- .... CLC 3
See also Greenberg, Joanne
See also CA 73-76

Green, Henry 1905-1974 .... CLC 2, 13
See also Yorke, Henry Vincent
See also DLB 15

Green, Julien (Hartridge)
1900- .... CLC 3, 11
See also CA 21-24R
See also DLB 4

Greenberg, Ivan 1908-1973
See Rahv, Philip
See also CA 85-88

Greenberg, Joanne (Goldenberg)
1932- .... CLC 7
See also Green, Hannah
See also CA 5-8R
See also SATA 25

Greene, Gael .... CLC 8
See also CANR 10
See also CA 13-16R

Greene, Graham
1904- .... CLC 1, 3, 6, 9, 14, 18, 27
See also CA 13-16R
See also SATA 20
See also DLB 13, 15
See also AITN 2

Gregor, Arthur 1923- .... CLC 9
See also CANR 10
See also CA 25-28R

Gregory, Lady (Isabella Augusta Persse)
1852-1932 .... TCLC 1
See also CA 104
See also DLB 10

Greve, Felix Paul Berthold Friedrich
1879-1948
See Grove, Frederick Philip
See also CA 104

Grey, (Pearl) Zane
1872?-1939 .... TCLC 6
See also CA 104
See also DLB 9

Grieg, (Johan) Nordahl (Brun)
1902-1943 .... TCLC 10
See also CA 107

Grieve, C(hristopher) M(urray) 1892-1978
See MacDiarmid, Hugh
See also CA 5-8R
See also obituary CA 85-88

Griffiths, Trevor 1935- .... CLC 13
See also CA 97-100
See also DLB 13

Grigson, Geoffrey (Edward Harvey)
1905- .... CLC 7
See also CA 25-28R

Grillparzer, Franz 1791-1872 ..... NCLC 1

Grimm, Jakob (Ludwig) Karl 1785-1863
See Grimm, Jakob (Ludwig) Karl and
Grimm, Wilhelm Karl

Grimm, Jakob (Ludwig) Karl 1785-1863
and **Grimm, Wilhelm Karl**
1786-1859 .... NCLC 3
See also SATA 22

Grimm, Wilhelm Karl 1786-1859
See Grimm, Jakob (Ludwig) Karl and
Grimm, Wilhelm Karl

Grimm, Wilhelm Karl 1786-1859 and
Grimm, Jakob (Ludwig) Karl
1785-1863
See Grimm, Jakob (Ludwig) Karl and
Grimm, Wilhelm Karl

Grove, Frederick Philip
1879-1948 .... TCLC 4
See also Greve, Felix Paul Berthold
Friedrich

Grumbach, Doris (Isaac)
1918- .... CLC 13, 22
See also CANR 9
See also CA 5-8R

Grundtvig, Nicolai Frederik Severin
1783-1872 .... NCLC 1

Guare, John 1938- .... CLC 8, 14
See also CA 73-76
See also DLB 7

Gudjonsson, Halldór Kiljan 1902-
See Laxness, Halldór (Kiljan)
See also CA 103

Guest, Judith 1936- .... CLC 8
See also CA 77-80

Guillén, Jorge 1893- .... CLC 11
See also CA 89-92

Gunn, Bill 1934- .... CLC 5
See also Gunn, William Harrison

Gunn, Thom(son William)
1926- .... CLC 3, 6, 18
See also CANR 9
See also CA 17-20R

Gunn, William Harrison 1934-
See Gunn, Bill
See also CA 13-16R
See also AITN 1

Guthrie, A(lfred) B(ertram), Jr.
1901- .... CLC 23
See also CA 57-60
See also DLB 6

Guy, Rosa (Cuthbert) 1928- .... CLC 26
See also CA 17-20R
See also SATA 14

Haavikko, Paavo (Juhani)
1931- .... CLC 18
See also CA 106

Hacker, Marilyn 1942- .... CLC 5, 9, 23
See also CA 77-80

Haggard, (Sir) H(enry) Rider
1856-1925 .... TCLC 11
See also CA 108
See also SATA 16

Haig-Brown, Roderick L(angmere)
1908-1976 .... CLC 21
See also CANR 4
See also CA 5-8R
See also obituary CA 69-72
See also SATA 12

Hailey, Arthur 1920- .... CLC 5
See also CANR 2
See also CA 1-4R
See also DLB-Y 82
See also AITN 2

Haley, Alex (Palmer) 1921- ..... CLC 8, 12
See also CA 77-80

Hall, Donald (Andrew, Jr.)
1928- .... CLC 1, 3
See also CANR 2
See also CA 5-8R
See also SATA 23
See also DLB 5

Hall, (Marguerite) Radclyffe
1886-1943 .... TCLC 12

Halpern, Daniel 1945- .... CLC 14
See also CA 33-36R

Hamburger, Michael (Peter Leopold)
1924- .... CLC 5, 14
See also CANR 2
See also CA 5-8R

Hamill, Pete 1935- .... CLC 10
See also CA 25-28R

Hamilton, Edmond 1904-1977 .... CLC 1
See also CANR 3
See also CA 1-4R
See also DLB 8

Hamilton, Gail 1911-
See Corcoran, Barbara

Hamilton, Mollie 1909?-
See Kaye, M(ary) M(argaret)

Hamilton, Virginia 1936- .... CLC 26
See also CLR 1
See also CA 25-28R
See also SATA 4

Hammett, (Samuel) Dashiell
1894-1961 .... CLC 3, 5, 10, 19
See also CA 81-84
See also AITN 1

Hammon, Jupiter
1711?-1800? .... NCLC 5

Hamner, Earl (Henry), Jr.
1923- .... CLC 12
See also CA 73-76
See also DLB 6
See also AITN 2

Hampton, Christopher (James)
1946- .... CLC 4
See also CA 25-28R
See also DLB 13

Hamsun, Knut 1859-1952 .... TCLC 2
See also CA 104

Handke, Peter 1942- ..... CLC 5, 8, 10, 15
See also CA 77-80

Hanley, James 1901- ..... CLC 3, 5, 8, 13
See also CA 73-76

Hannah, Barry 1942- .... CLC 23
See also CA 108
See also DLB 6

Hansberry, Lorraine
1930-1965 .... CLC 17
See also CA 109
See also obituary CA 25-28R
See also DLB 7
See also AITN 2

Hanson, Kenneth O(stlin)
1922- .... CLC 13
See also CANR 7
See also CA 53-56

Hardwick, Elizabeth 1916- .... CLC 13
See also CANR 3
See also CA 5-8R
See also DLB 6

Hardy, Thomas 1840-1928 ..... TCLC 4, 10
See also CA 104
See also SATA 25
See also DLB 18, 19

Harper, Michael S(teven)
1938- .... CLC 7, 22
See also CA 33-36R

Harris, Christie (Lucy Irwin)
1907- .... CLC 12
See also CANR 6
See also CA 5-8R
See also SATA 6

Harris, Joel Chandler
1848-1908 .... TCLC 2
See also CA 104
See also YABC 1
See also DLB 11, 23

**Harris, John (Wyndham Parkes Lucas)
Beynon** 1903-1969
See Wyndham, John
See also CA 102
See also obituary CA 89-92

Harris, MacDonald 1921- .... CLC 9
See also Heiney, Donald (William)

Harris, Mark 1922- .... CLC 19
See also CANR 2
See also CA 5-8R
See also DLB 2
See also DLB-Y 80

Harris, (Theodore) Wilson
1921- .... CLC 25
See also CANR 11
See also CA 65-68

Harrison, James (Thomas) 1937-
See Harrison, Jim
See also CANR 8
See also CA 13-16R

Harrison, Jim 1937- .... CLC 6, 14
See also Harrison, James
See also DLB-Y 82

Harte, (Francis) Bret(t)
1836?-1902 .... TCLC 1
See also CA 104
See also SATA 26
See also DLB 12

Hartley, L(eslie) P(oles)
1895-1972 .... CLC 2, 22
See also CA 45-48
See also obituary CA 37-40R
See also DLB 15

Hartman, Geoffrey H. 1929- .... CLC 27

Hašek, Jaroslav (Matej Frantisek)
1883-1923 .... TCLC 4
See also CA 104

Hass, Robert 1941- .... CLC 18

Hauptmann, Gerhart (Johann Robert)
1862-1946 .... TCLC 4
See also CA 104

Havel, Václav 1936- .... CLC 25
See also CA 104

Hawkes, John (Clendennin Burne, Jr.)
1925- ...... CLC 1, 2, 3, 4, 7, 9, 14, 15, 27
See also CANR 2
See also CA 1-4R
See also DLB 2
See also DLB-Y 80

Hawthorne, Nathaniel
1804-1864 .... NCLC 2
See also SATA 2
See also DLB 1

Hayden, Robert (Earl)
1913-1980 .... CLC 5, 9, 14
See also CA 69-72
See also obituary CA 97-100
See also SATA 19
See also obituary SATA 26
See also DLB 5

Haywood, Eliza (Fowler)
1693?-1756 .... LC 1

Hazzard, Shirley 1931- .... CLC 18
See also CANR 4
See also CA 9-12R
See also DLB-Y 82

H(ilda) D(oolittle)
1886-1961 .... CLC 3, 8, 14
See also Doolittle, Hilda

Head, Bessie 1937- .... CLC 25
See also CA 29-32R

Heaney, Seamus
1939- .... CLC 5, 7, 14, 25
See also CA 85-88

Hearn, (Patricio) Lafcadio (Tessima Carlos)
1850-1904 .... TCLC 9
See also CA 105
See also DLB 12

Hébert, Anne 1916- .... CLC 4, 13
See also CA 85-88

Hecht, Anthony (Evan)
1923- .... CLC 8, 13, 19
See also CANR 6
See also CA 9-12R
See also DLB 5

Hecht, Ben 1894-1964 .... CLC 8
See also CA 85-88
See also DLB 7, 9, 25, 26

Heidegger, Martin 1889-1976 ...... CLC 24
See also CA 81-84
See also obituary CA 65-68

Heidenstam, (Karl Gustaf) Verner von
1859-1940 .... TCLC 5
See also CA 104

Heifner, Jack 1946- .... CLC 11
See also CA 105

Heilbrun, Carolyn G(old)
1926- .... CLC 25
See also CANR 1
See also CA 45-48

Heine, Harry 1797-1856
See Heine, Heinrich

Heine, Heinrich 1797-1856 .... NCLC 4

Heiney, Donald (William) 1921-
See Harris, MacDonald
See also CANR 3
See also CA 1-4R

Heinlein, Robert A(nson)
1907- .... CLC 1, 3, 8, 14, 26
See also CANR 1
See also CA 1-4R
See also SATA 9
See also DLB 8

Heller, Joseph 1923- .... CLC 1, 3, 5, 8, 11
See also CANR 8
See also CA 5-8R
See also DLB 2
See also DLB-Y 80
See also AITN 1

Hellman, Lillian (Florence)
1906- .... CLC 2, 4, 8, 14, 18
See also CA 13-16R
See also DLB 7
See also AITN 1, 2

Helprin, Mark 1947- .... CLC 7, 10, 22
See also CA 81-84

Hemingway, Ernest
1899-1961 ...... CLC 1, 3, 6, 8, 10, 13, 19
See also CA 77-80
See also DLB 4, 9
See also DLB-Y 81
See also DLB-DS 1
See also AITN 2

Henley, Beth 1952- .... CLC 23
See also Henley, Elizabeth Becker

Henley, Elizabeth Becker 1952-
See Henley, Beth
See also CA 107

Henley, William Ernest
1849-1903................... TCLC 8
See also CA 105
See also DLB 19

Hennissart, Martha
See Lathen, Emma
See also CA 85-88

Henry, O. 1862-1909? .... TCLC 1
See also Porter, William Sydney
See also YABC 2

Hentoff, Nat(han Irving) 1925- ..... CLC 26
See also CLR 1
See also CANR 5
See also CA 1-4R
See also SATA 27

Heppenstall, (John) Rayner
1911-1981.................. CLC 10
See also CA 1-4R
See also obituary CA 103

Herbert, Frank (Patrick)
1920- .... CLC 12, 23
See also CANR 5
See also CA 53-56
See also SATA 9
See also DLB 8

Herbert, Zbigniew 1924- .... CLC 9
See also CA 89-92

Hergesheimer, Joseph
1880-1954.................. TCLC 11
See also CA 109
See also DLB 9

Herlagñez, Pablo de 1844-1896
See Verlaine, Paul (Marie)

Herlihy, James Leo 1927- .... CLC 6
See also CANR 2
See also CA 1-4R

Herriot, James 1916-................ CLC 12
See also Wight, James Alfred

Hersey, John (Richard)
1914-................. CLC 1, 2, 7, 9
See also CA 17-20R
See also SATA 25
See also DLB 6

Herzog, Werner 1942- .... CLC 16
See also CA 89-92

Hesse, Hermann
1877-1962...... CLC 1, 2, 3, 6, 11, 17, 25
See also CAP 2
See also CA 17-18

Heyen, William 1940- .... CLC 13, 18
See also CA 33-36R
See also DLB 5

Heyerdahl, Thor 1914- .... CLC 26
See also CANR 5
See also CA 5-8R
See also SATA 2

Heym, Georg (Theodor Franz Arthur)
1887-1912................... TCLC 9
See also CA 106

Heyse, Paul (Johann Ludwig von)
1830-1914................... TCLC 8
See also CA 104

Hibbert, Eleanor (Burford)
1906-.......................CLC 7
See also CANR 9
See also CA 17-20R
See also SATA 2

Higgins, George V(incent)
1939-.................CLC 4, 7, 10, 18
See also CA 77-80
See also DLB 2
See also DLB-Y 81

Highsmith, (Mary) Patricia
1921-................... CLC 2, 4, 14
See also CANR 1
See also CA 1-4R

Highwater, Jamake 1942-.......... CLC 12
See also CANR 10
See also CA 65-68
See also SATA 30, 32

Hill, Geoffrey 1932-.......... CLC 5, 8, 18
See also CA 81-84

Hill, George Roy 1922-.............CLC 26

Hill, Susan B. 1942- ....CLC 4
See also CA 33-36R
See also DLB 14

Hilliard, Noel (Harvey) 1929- ...... CLC 15
See also CANR 7
See also CA 9-12R

Himes, Chester (Bomar)
1909-...............CLC 2, 4, 7, 18
See also CA 25-28R
See also DLB 2

Hinde, Thomas 1926-......... CLC 6, 11
See also Chitty, (Sir) Thomas Willes

Hine, (William) Daryl 1936- .... CLC 15
See also CANR 1
See also CA 1-4R

Hippius (Merezhkovsky), Zinaida
(Nikolayevna) 1869-1945 ..... TCLC 9
See also CA 106

Hiraoka, Kimitake 1925-1970
See Mishima, Yukio
See also CA 97-100
See also obituary CA 29-32R

Hitchcock, (Sir) Alfred (Joseph)
1899-1980....................CLC 16
See also obituary CA 97-100
See also SATA 27
See also obituary SATA 24

Hoagland, Edward 1932- ....CLC 28
See also CANR 2
See also CA 1-4R
See also DLB 6

Hoban, Russell C(onwell)
1925-..................... CLC 7, 25
See also CLR 3
See also CA 5-8R
See also SATA 1

Hobson, Laura Z(ametkin)
1900-..................... CLC 7, 25
See also CA 17-20R

Hochhuth, Rolf 1931- .... CLC 4, 11, 18
See also CA 5-8R

Hochman, Sandra 1936-......... CLC 3, 8
See also CA 5-8R
See also DLB 5

Hocking, Mary (Eunice) 1921- .....CLC 13
See also CA 101

Hodgins, Jack 1938- ....CLC 23
See also CA 93-96

Hoffman, Daniel (Gerard)
1923-..................CLC 6, 13, 23
See also CANR 4
See also CA 1-4R
See also DLB 5

Hoffman, Stanley 1944- ....CLC 5
See also CA 77-80

Hoffmann, Ernst Theodor Amadeus
1776-1822................. NCLC 2
See also SATA 27

Hofmannsthal, Hugo (Laurenz August
Hofmann Edler) von
1874-1929.................. TCLC 11
See also CA 106

Hogg, James 1770-1835 .... NCLC 4

Holden, Ursula 1921- ....CLC 18
See also CA 101

Holland, Isabelle 1920-............CLC 21
See also CANR 10
See also CA 21-24R
See also SATA 8

Holland, Marcus 1900-
See Caldwell, (Janet Miriam) Taylor
(Holland)

Hollander, John 1929- .....CLC 2, 5, 8, 14
See also CANR 1
See also CA 1-4R
See also SATA 13
See also DLB 5

Hollis, Jim 1916-
See Summers, Hollis (Spurgeon, Jr.)

Holt, Victoria 1906-
See Hibbert, Eleanor (Burford)

Holub, Miroslav 1923- ....CLC 4
See also CA 21-24R

Hood, Hugh (John Blagdon)
1928- .... CLC 15, 28
See also CANR 1
See also CA 49-52

Hope, A(lec) D(erwent) 1907- ....CLC 3
See also CA 21-24R

Hopkins, John (Richard) 1931-......CLC 4
See also CA 85-88

Horgan, Paul 1903- .... CLC 9
See also CANR 9
See also CA 13-16R
See also SATA 13

Horwitz, Julius 1920- .... CLC 14
See also CA 9-12R

Household, Geoffrey (Edward West)
1900- .... CLC 11
See also CA 77-80
See also SATA 14

Housman, A(lfred) E(dward)
1859-1936 .... TCLC 1, 10
See also CA 104
See also DLB 19

Housman, Laurence
1865-1959 .... TCLC 7
See also CA 106
See also SATA 25
See also DLB 10

Howard, Elizabeth Jane 1923- ...... CLC 7
See also CANR 8
See also CA 5-8R

Howard, Maureen 1930- .... CLC 5, 14
See also CA 53-56

Howard, Richard 1929- .... CLC 7, 10
See also CA 85-88
See also DLB 5
See also AITN 1

Howard, Robert E(rvin)
1906-1936 .... TCLC 8
See also CA 105

Howells, William Dean
1837-1920 .... TCLC 7
See also CA 104
See also DLB 12

Howes, Barbara 1914- .... CLC 15
See also CA 9-12R
See also SATA 5

Hrabal, Bohumil 1914- .... CLC 13
See also CA 106

Hueffer, Ford Madox 1873-1939
See Ford, Ford Madox

Hughes, (James) Langston
1902-1967 .... CLC 1, 5, 10, 15
See also CANR 1
See also CA 1-4R
See also obituary CA 25-28R
See also SATA 4, 33
See also DLB 4, 7

Hughes, Richard (Arthur Warren)
1900-1976 .... CLC 1, 11
See also CANR 4
See also CA 5-8R
See also obituary CA 65-68
See also SATA 8
See also obituary SATA 25
See also DLB 15

Hughes, Ted 1930- .... CLC 2, 4, 9, 14
See also CLR 3
See also CANR 1
See also CA 1-4R
See also SATA 27

Hugo, Richard F(ranklin)
1923-1982 .... CLC 6, 18
See also CANR 3
See also CA 49-52
See also obituary CA 108
See also DLB 5

Hugo, Victor Marie
1802-1885 .... NCLC 3

Hunt, E(verette) Howard (Jr.)
1918- .... CLC 3
See also CANR 2
See also CA 45-48
See also AITN 1

Hunt, (James Henry) Leigh
1784-1859 .... NCLC 1

Hunter, Evan 1926- .... CLC 1
See also CANR 5
See also CA 5-8R
See also SATA 25
See also DLB-Y 82

Hunter, Mollie (Maureen McIlwraith)
1922- .... CLC 21
See also McIlwraith, Maureen Mollie Hunter

Hurston, Zora Neale 1901-1960 ..... CLC 7
See also CA 85-88

Huston, John (Marcellus)
1906- .... CLC 20
See also CA 73-76
See also DLB 26

Huxley, Aldous (Leonard)
1894-1963 .... CLC 1, 3, 4, 5, 8, 11, 18
See also CA 85-88

Huysmans, Joris-Karl
1848-1907 .... TCLC 7
See also CA 104

Hyde, Margaret O(ldroyd)
1917- .... CLC 21
See also CANR 1
See also CA 1-4R
See also SATA 1

Ian, Janis 1951- .... CLC 21
See also CA 105

Ibsen, Henrik (Johan)
1828-1906 .... TCLC 2, 8
See also CA 104

Ibuse, Masuji 1898- .... CLC 22

Ichikawa, Kon 1915- .... CLC 20

Idle, Eric 1941?-
See Monty Python

Ignatow, David 1914- .... CLC 4, 7, 14
See also CA 9-12R
See also DLB 5

Immermann, Karl (Lebrecht)
1796-1840 .... NCLC 4

Inge, William (Motter)
1913-1973 .... CLC 1, 8, 19
See also CA 9-12R
See also DLB 7

Innaurato, Albert 1948- .... CLC 21

Innes, Michael 1906-
See Stewart, J(ohn) I(nnes) M(ackintosh)

Ionesco, Eugène
1912- .... CLC 1, 4, 6, 9, 11, 15
See also CA 9-12R
See also SATA 7

Irving, John (Winslow)
1942- .... CLC 13, 23
See also CA 25-28R
See also DLB 6
See also DLB-Y 82

Irving, Washington 1783-1859 .... NCLC 2
See also YABC 2
See also DLB 3, 11

Isherwood, Christopher (William Bradshaw)
1904- .... CLC 1, 9, 11, 14
See also CA 13-16R
See also DLB 15

Ishiguro, Kazuo 1954?- .... CLC 27

Ivask, Ivar (Vidrik) 1927- .... CLC 14
See also CA 37-40R

Jackson, Jesse 1908-1983 .... CLC 12
See also obituary CA 109
See also CA 25-28R
See also SATA 2, 29

Jackson, Laura (Riding) 1901-
See Riding, Laura
See also CA 65-68

Jackson, Shirley 1919-1965 .... CLC 11
See also CANR 4
See also CA 1-4R
See also obituary CA 25-28R
See also SATA 2
See also DLB 6

Jacob, (Cyprien) Max
1876-1944 .... TCLC 6
See also CA 104

Jacobs, Jim 1942-
See Jacobs, Jim and Casey, Warren
See also CA 97-100

Jacobs, Jim 1942- **and Casey, Warren**
1935- .... CLC 12

Jacobson, Dan 1929- .... CLC 4, 14
See also CANR 2
See also CA 1-4R
See also DLB 14

Jagger, Mick 1944-
See Jagger, Mick and Richard, Keith

Jagger, Mick 1944- **and Richard, Keith**
1943- .... CLC 17

James, Henry (Jr.)
1843-1916 .... TCLC 2, 11
See also CA 104
See also DLB 12

James, M(ontague) R(hodes)
1862-1936 .... TCLC 6
See also CA 104

James, P(hyllis) D(orothy)
1920- .... CLC 18
See also CA 21-24R

Jarrell, Randall
1914-1965 .... CLC 1, 2, 6, 9, 13
See also CLR 6
See also CANR 6
See also CA 5-8R
See also obituary CA 25-28R
See also SATA 7

Jarry, Alfred 1873-1907 .... TCLC 2
See also CA 104

Jeffers, (John) Robinson
1887-1962 .... CLC 2, 3, 11, 15
See also CA 85-88

Jellicoe, (Patricia) Ann 1927- ..... CLC 27
See also CA 85-88
See also DLB 13

Jennings, Elizabeth (Joan)
1926- .... CLC 5, 14
See also CANR 8
See also CA 61-64

Jennings, Waylon 1937- .... CLC 21

Jerrold, Douglas 1803-1857 ...... NCLC 2

Jewett, Sarah Orne 1849-1909 .... TCLC 1
See also CA 108
See also SATA 15
See also DLB 12

Jhabvala, Ruth Prawer 1927- .... CLC 4, 8
See also CANR 2
See also CA 1-4R

Jiles, Paulette 1943- .... CLC 13
See also CA 101

Jiménez (Mantecón), Juan Ramón
1881-1958 .... TCLC 4
See also CA 104

Joel, Billy 1949- .... CLC 26
See also Joel, William Martin

Joel, William Martin 1949-
See Joel, Billy
See also CA 108

Johnson, B(ryan) S(tanley William)
1933-1973 .... CLC 6, 9
See also CANR 9
See also CA 9-12R
See also obituary CA 53-56
See also DLB 14

Johnson, Charles 1948- .... CLC 7

Johnson, Diane 1934- .... CLC 5, 13
See also CA 41-44R
See also DLB-Y 80

Johnson, Eyvind (Olof Verner)
1900-1976 .... CLC 14
See also CA 73-76
See also obituary CA 69-72

Johnson, James Weldon
1871-1938 .... TCLC 3
See also CA 104
See also SATA 31

Johnson, Marguerita 1928-
See Angelou, Maya

Johnson, Pamela Hansford
1912-1981 .... CLC 1, 7, 27
See also CANR 2
See also CA 1-4R
See also obituary CA 104
See also DLB 15

Johnson, Uwe 1934- .... CLC 5, 10, 15
See also CANR 1
See also CA 1-4R

Johnston, Jennifer 1930- .... CLC 7
See also CA 85-88
See also DLB 14

Jones, D(ouglas) G(ordon)
1929- .... CLC 10
See also CA 29-32R

Jones, David
1895-1974 .... CLC 2, 4, 7, 13
See also CA 9-12R
See also obituary CA 53-56
See also DLB 20

Jones, David Robert 1947-
See Bowie, David
See also CA 103

Jones, Diana Wynne 1934- .... CLC 26
See also CANR 4
See also CA 49-52
See also SATA 9

Jones, Gayl 1949- .... CLC 6, 9
See also CA 77-80

Jones, James 1921-1977 ...... CLC 1, 3, 10
See also CANR 6
See also CA 1-4R
See also obituary CA 69-72
See also DLB 2
See also AITN 1, 2

Jones, (Everett) LeRoi 1934- .... CLC 1
See also Baraka, Imamu Amiri
See also CA 21-24R

Jones, Madison (Percy, Jr.)
1925- .... CLC 4
See also CANR 7
See also CA 13-16R

Jones, Mervyn 1922- .... CLC 10
See also CANR 1
See also CA 45-48

Jones, Preston 1936-1979 .... CLC 10
See also CA 73-76
See also obituary CA 89-92
See also DLB 7

Jones, Robert F(rancis) 1934- .... CLC 7
See also CANR 2
See also CA 49-52

Jones, Terry 1942?-
See Monty Python

Jong, Erica 1942- .... CLC 4, 6, 8, 18
See also CA 73-76
See also DLB 2, 5
See also AITN 1

Jordan, June 1936- .... CLC 5, 11, 23
See also CA 33-36R
See also SATA 4

Josipovici, G(abriel) 1940- .... CLC 6
See also CA 37-40R
See also DLB 14

Joyce, James (Augustine Aloysius)
1882-1941 .... TCLC 3, 8
See also CA 104
See also DLB 10, 19

Just, Ward S(wift) 1935- .... CLC 4, 27
See also CA 25-28R

Justice, Donald (Rodney)
1925- .... CLC 6, 19
See also CA 5-8R

Kacew, Romain 1914-1980
See Gary, Romain
See also CA 108
See also obituary CA 102

Kacewgary, Romain 1914-1980
See Gary, Romain

Kafka, Franz 1883-1924 .... TCLC 2, 6
See also CA 105

Kaiser, (Friedrich Karl) Georg
1878-1945 .... TCLC 9
See also CA 106

Kallman, Chester (Simon)
1921-1975 .... CLC 2
See also CANR 3
See also CA 45-48
See also obituary CA 53-56

Kaminsky, Melvin 1926-
See Brooks, Mel

Kane, Paul 1941-
See Simon, Paul

Kanin, Garson 1912- .... CLC 22
See also CANR 7
See also CA 5-8R
See also DLB 7
See also AITN 1

Kaniuk, Yoram 1930- .... CLC 19

Kantor, MacKinlay 1904-1977 ...... CLC 7
See also CA 61-64
See also obituary CA 73-76
See also DLB 9

Karamzin, Nikolai Mikhailovich
1766-1826 .... NCLC 3

Karapánou, Margaríta 1946- .... CLC 13
See also CA 101

Kassef, Romain 1914-1980
See Gary, Romain

Kaufman, Sue 1926-1977 .... CLC 3, 8
See also Barondess, Sue K(aufman)

Kavan, Anna 1904-1968 .... CLC 5, 13
See also Edmonds, Helen (Woods)
See also CANR 6

Kavanagh, Patrick (Joseph Gregory)
1905-1967 .... CLC 22
See also CA 25-28R
See also DLB 15, 20

Kawabata, Yasunari
1899-1972 .... CLC 2, 5, 9, 18
See also CA 93-96
See also obituary CA 33-36R

Kaye, M(ary) M(argaret)
1909?- .... CLC 28
See also CA 89-92

Kaye, Mollie 1909?-
See Kaye, M(ary) M(argaret)

Kazan, Elia 1909- .... CLC 6, 16
See also CA 21-24R

Kazantzakis, Nikos
1885?-1957 .... TCLC 2, 5
See also CA 105

Keaton, Buster 1895-1966 .... CLC 20

Keaton, Joseph Francis 1895-1966
See Keaton, Buster

Keller, Gottfried 1819-1890 .... NCLC 2

Kelley, William Melvin 1937- ...... CLC 22
See also CA 77-80

Kellogg, Marjorie 1922- .... CLC 2
See also CA 81-84

Kemal, Yashar 1922- .... CLC 14
See also CA 89-92

Kemelman, Harry 1908- .... CLC 2
See also CANR 6
See also CA 9-12R
See also AITN 1

Keneally, Thomas (Michael)
1935- .... CLC 5, 8, 10, 14, 19, 27
See also CANR 10
See also CA 85-88

Kennedy, John Pendleton
1795-1870 .... NCLC 2
See also DLB 3

Kennedy, Joseph Charles 1929-
See Kennedy, X. J.
See also CANR 4
See also CA 1-4R
See also SATA 14

Kennedy, William 1928- .... CLC 6, 28
See also CA 85-88

Kennedy, X. J. 1929- .... CLC 8
See also Kennedy, Joseph Charles
See also DLB 5

Kerouac, Jack
1922-1969......... CLC 1, 2, 3, 5, 14
See also Kerouac, Jean-Louis Lebrid de
See also DLB 2, 16
See also DLB-DS 3

Kerouac, Jean-Louis Lebrid de 1922-1969
See Kerouac, Jack
See also CA 5-8R
See also obituary CA 25-28R
See also AITN 1

Kerr, Jean 1923- .... CLC 22
See also CANR 7
See also CA 5-8R

Kerr, M. E. 1927- .... CLC 12
See also Meaker, Marijane

Kerrigan, (Thomas) Anthony
1918- .... CLC 4, 6
See also CANR 4
See also CA 49-52

Kesey, Ken (Elton)
1935- .... CLC 1, 3, 6, 11
See also CA 1-4R
See also DLB 2, 16

Kessler, Jascha (Frederick)
1929- .... CLC 4
See also CANR 8
See also CA 17-20R

Kettelkamp, Larry 1933- .... CLC 12
See also CA 29-32R
See also SATA 2

Kherdian, David 1931- .... CLC 6, 9
See also CA 21-24R
See also SATA 16

Kielland, Alexander (Lange)
1849-1906................... TCLC 5
See also CA 104

Kiely, Benedict 1919- .... CLC 23
See also CANR 2
See also CA 1-4R
See also DLB 15

Kienzle, William X(avier)
1928- .... CLC 25
See also CANR 9
See also CA 93-96

Killens, John Oliver 1916- .... CLC 10
See also CA 77-80

King, Francis (Henry) 1923- .... CLC 8
See also CANR 1
See also CA 1-4R
See also DLB 15

King, Stephen (Edwin)
1947- .... CLC 12, 26
See also CANR 1
See also CA 61-64
See also SATA 9
See also DLB-Y 80

Kingman, (Mary) Lee 1919- .... CLC 17
See also Natti, (Mary) Lee
See also CA 5-8R
See also SATA 1

Kingston, Maxine Hong
1940- .... CLC 12, 19
See also CA 69-72
See also DLB-Y 80

Kinnell, Galway
1927- .... CLC 1, 2, 3, 5, 13
See also CANR 10
See also CA 9-12R
See also DLB 5

Kinsella, Thomas 1928- .... CLC 4, 19
See also CA 17-20R

Kinsella, W(illiam) P(atrick)
1935- .... CLC 27
See also CA 97-100

Kipling, (Joseph) Rudyard
1865-1936.................. TCLC 8
See also CA 105
See also YABC 2
See also DLB 19

Kirkup, James 1927- .... CLC 1
See also CANR 2
See also CA 1-4R
See also SATA 12

Kirkwood, James 1930- .... CLC 9
See also CANR 6
See also CA 1-4R
See also AITN 2

Kizer, Carolyn (Ashley) 1925- ..... CLC 15
See also CA 65-68
See also DLB 5

Klein, A(braham) M(oses)
1909-1972................... CLC 19
See also CA 101
See also obituary CA 37-40R

Kleist, Heinrich von
1777-1811................... NCLC 2

Klinger, Friedrich Maximilian von
1752-1831................... NCLC 1

Knebel, Fletcher 1911- .... CLC 14
See also CANR 1
See also CA 1-4R
See also AITN 1

Knowles, John 1926- ...... CLC 1, 4, 10, 26
See also CA 17-20R
See also SATA 8
See also DLB 6

Koch, Kenneth 1925- .... CLC 5, 8
See also CANR 6
See also CA 1-4R
See also DLB 5

Koestler, Arthur
1905-1983......... CLC 1, 3, 6, 8, 15
See also CANR 1
See also CA 1-4R
See also obituary CA 109

Kohout, Pavel 1928- .... CLC 13
See also CANR 3
See also CA 45-48

Konrád, György 1933- .... CLC 4, 10
See also CA 85-88

Konwicki, Tadeusz 1926- .... CLC 8, 28
See also CA 101

Kopit, Arthur (Lee) 1937- ...... CLC 1, 18
See also CA 81-84
See also DLB 7
See also AITN 1

Kops, Bernard 1926- .... CLC 4
See also CA 5-8R
See also DLB 13

Kornbluth, C(yril) M.
1923-1958................... TCLC 8
See also CA 105
See also DLB 8

Kosinski, Jerzy (Nikodem)
1933- .... CLC 1, 2, 3, 6, 10, 15
See also CANR 9
See also CA 17-20R
See also DLB 2
See also DLB-Y 82

Kostelanetz, Richard (Cory)
1940- .... CLC 28
See also CA 13-16R

Kotlowitz, Robert 1924- .... CLC 4
See also CA 33-36R

Kotzwinkle, William 1938-...... CLC 5, 14
See also CLR 6
See also CANR 3
See also CA 45-48
See also SATA 24

Kozol, Jonathan 1936- .... CLC 17
See also CA 61-64

Krasiński, Zygmunt
1812-1859.................. NCLC 4

Kraus, Karl 1874-1936........... TCLC 5
See also CA 104

Kristofferson, Kris 1936- .... CLC 26
See also CA 104

Krleža, Miroslav 1893-1981........ CLC 8
See also CA 97-100
See also obituary CA 105

Kroetsch, Robert 1927- .... CLC 5, 23
See also CANR 8
See also CA 17-20R

Krotkov, Yuri 1917- .... CLC 19
See also CA 102

Krumgold, Joseph (Quincy)
1908-1980.................... CLC 12
See also CANR 7
See also CA 9-12R
See also obituary CA 101
See also SATA 1
See also obituary SATA 23

Krutch, Joseph Wood
1893-1970................... CLC 24
See also CA 1-4R
See also obituary CA 25-28R

Krylov, Ivan Andreevich
1768?-1844.................. NCLC 1

Kubrick, Stanley 1928- .... CLC 16
See also CA 81-84
See also DLB 26

Kumin, Maxine (Winokur)
1925- .... CLC 5, 13, 28
See also CANR 1
See also CA 1-4R
See also SATA 12
See also DLB 5
See also AITN 2

Kundera, Milan 1929-........ CLC 4, 9, 19
See also CA 85-88

Kunitz, Stanley J(asspon)
1905-................. CLC 6, 11, 14
See also CA 41-44R

Kunze, Reiner 1933-.............CLC 10
See also CA 93-96

Kuprin, Aleksandr (Ivanovich)
1870-1938................. TCLC 5
See also CA 104

Kurosawa, Akira 1910-...........CLC 16
See also CA 101

Kuttner, Henry 1915-1958....... TCLC 10
See also DLB 8

Kuzma, Greg 1944-................CLC 7
See also CA 33-36R

Labrunie, Gérard 1808-1855
See Nerval, Gérard de

Laclos, Pierre Ambroise François Choderlos de 1741-1803.............. NCLC 4

Laforgue, Jules 1860-1887........ NCLC 5

Lagerkvist, Pär (Fabian)
1891-1974............. CLC 7, 10, 13
See also CA 85-88
See also obituary CA 49-52

Lagerlöf, Selma (Ottiliana Lovisa)
1858-1940.................. TCLC 4
See also CA 108
See also SATA 15

La Guma, (Justin) Alex(ander)
1925-..........................CLC 19
See also CA 49-52

Lamming, George (William)
1927-..................... CLC 2, 4
See also CA 85-88

LaMoore, Louis Dearborn 1908?-
See L'Amour, Louis (Dearborn)

L'Amour, Louis (Dearborn)
1908-.......................CLC 25
See also CANR 3
See also CA 1-4R
See also DLB-Y 80
See also AITN 2

Landis, John 1950- ....CLC 26

Landolfi, Tommaso 1908-..........CLC 11

Landwirth, Heinz 1927-
See Lind, Jakov
See also CANR 5

Lane, Patrick 1939-...............CLC 24
See also CA 97-100

Lang, Fritz 1890-1976 ....CLC 20
See also CA 77-80
See also obituary CA 69-72

Lanier, Sidney 1842-1881......... NCLC 6
See also SATA 18

Larbaud, Valéry 1881-1957....... TCLC 9
See also CA 106

Lardner, Ring(gold Wilmer)
1885-1933.................. TCLC 2
See also CA 104
See also DLB 11, 25

Larkin, Philip (Arthur)
1922-............ CLC 3, 5, 8, 9, 13, 18
See also CA 5-8R

Latham, Jean Lee 1902-............CLC 12
See also CANR 7
See also CA 5-8R
See also SATA 2
See also AITN 1

Lathen, Emma ....CLC 2
See also Hennissart, Martha
See also Latsis, Mary J(ane)

Latsis, Mary J(ane)
See Lathen, Emma
See also CA 85-88

Lattimore, Richmond (Alexander)
1906-.......................CLC 3
See also CANR 1
See also CA 1-4R

Laurence, (Jean) Margaret (Wemyss)
1926-................. CLC 3, 6, 13
See also CA 5-8R

Lavin, Mary 1912-............. CLC 4, 18
See also CA 9-12R
See also DLB 15

Lawrence, D(avid) H(erbert)
1885-1930............. TCLC 2, 9
See also CA 104
See also DLB 10, 19

Laxness, Halldór (Kiljan)
1902-.......................CLC 25
See also Gudjonsson, Halldór Kiljan

Laye, Camara 1928-1980...........CLC 4
See also CA 85-88
See also obituary CA 97-100

Layton, Irving (Peter) 1912- .... CLC 2, 15
See also CANR 2
See also CA 1-4R

Leacock, Stephen (Butler)
1869-1944................... TCLC 2
See also CA 104

Lear, Edward 1812-1888 .... NCLC 3
See also CLR 1
See also SATA 18

Lear, Norman (Milton) 1922- ......CLC 12
See also CA 73-76

Leavis, F(rank) R(aymond)
1895-1978.....................CLC 24
See also CA 21-24R
See also obituary CA 77-80

Lebowitz, Fran 1951?-.............CLC 11
See also CA 81-84

Le Carré, John
1931-............ CLC 3, 5, 9, 15, 28
See also Cornwell, David (John Moore)

Leduc, Violette 1907-1972 ....CLC 22
See also CAP 1
See also CA 13-14
See also obituary CA 33-36R

Lee, Don L. 1942-.................CLC 2
See also Madhubuti, Haki R.
See also CA 73-76

Lee, (Nelle) Harper 1926-..........CLC 12
See also CA 13-16R
See also SATA 11
See also DLB 6

Lee, Manfred B(ennington) 1905-1971
See Queen, Ellery
See also CANR 2
See also CA 1-4R
See also obituary CA 29-32R

Lee, Stan 1922- ....CLC 17
See also CA 108

Lee, Vernon 1856-1935........... TCLC 5
See also Paget, Violet

Leet, Judith 1935-.................CLC 11

Leffland, Ella 1931-...............CLC 19
See also CA 29-32R

Léger, (Marie-Rene) Alexis Saint-Léger
1887-1975
See Perse, St.-John
See also CA 13-16R
See also obituary CA 61-64

Le Guin, Ursula K(roeber)
1929-................. CLC 8, 13, 22
See also CLR 3
See also CANR 9
See also CA 21-24R
See also SATA 4
See also DLB 8
See also AITN 1

Lehmann, Rosamond (Nina)
1901-.......................CLC 5
See also CANR 8
See also CA 77-80
See also DLB 15

Leiber, Fritz (Reuter, Jr.)
1910-.......................CLC 25
See also CANR 2
See also CA 45-48
See also DLB 8

Leithauser, Brad 1953-.............CLC 27
See also CA 107

Lelchuk, Alan 1938-................CLC 5
See also CANR 1
See also CA 45-48

Lem, Stanislaw 1921- .... CLC 8, 15
See also CA 105

L'Engle, Madeleine 1918-...........CLC 12
See also CLR 1
See also CANR 3
See also CA 1-4R
See also SATA 1, 27
See also AITN 2

Lennon, John (Ono) 1940-1980
See Lennon, John (Ono) and McCartney, Paul
See also CA 102

Lennon, John (Ono) 1940-1980 and
McCartney, Paul 1942- ....CLC 12

Lenz, Siegfried 1926- ....CLC 27
See also CA 89-92

Leonard, Elmore 1925-.............CLC 28
See also CA 81-84
See also AITN 1

Leonard, Hugh 1926- ....CLC 19
See also Byrne, John Keyes
See also DLB 13

Lerman, Eleanor 1952-.............CLC 9
See also CA 85-88

Lermontov, Mikhail Yuryevich
1814-1841.................. NCLC 5

Lessing, Doris (May)
1919-........CLC 1, 2, 3, 6, 10, 15, 22
See also CA 9-12R
See also DLB 15

Lester, Richard 1932-..............CLC 20

Levertov, Denise
1923- ....CLC 1, 2, 3, 5, 8, 15, 28
See also CANR 3
See also CA 1-4R
See also DLB 5

Levin, Ira 1929- ....CLC 3, 6
See also CA 21-24R

Levin, Meyer 1905-1981............CLC 7
See also CA 9-12R
See also obituary CA 104
See also SATA 21
See also obituary SATA 27
See also DLB 9
See also DLB-Y 81
See also AITN 1

Levine, Philip 1928- .... CLC 2, 4, 5, 9, 14
See also CANR 9
See also CA 9-12R
See also DLB 5

Levitin, Sonia 1934- ....CLC 17
See also CA 29-32R
See also SATA 4

Lewis, Alun 1915-1944........... TCLC 3
See also CA 104
See also DLB 20

Lewis, C(ecil) Day 1904-1972
See Day Lewis, C(ecil)

Lewis, C(live) S(taples)
1898-1963........ CLC 1, 3, 6, 14, 27
See also CLR 3
See also CA 81-84
See also SATA 13
See also DLB 15

Lewis, (Harry) Sinclair
1885-1951............ TCLC 4
See also CA 104
See also DLB 9
See also DLB-DS 1

Lewis, (Percy) Wyndham
1882?-1957................ TCLC 2, 9
See also CA 104
See also DLB 15

Lezama Lima, José
1910-1976................ CLC 4, 10
See also CA 77-80

Li Fei-kan 1904-
See Pa Chin
See also CA 105

Lie, Jonas (Lauritz Idemil)
1833-1908................ TCLC 5

Lieber, Joel 1936-1971.............CLC 6
See also CA 73-76
See also obituary CA 29-32R

Lieber, Stanley Martin 1922-
See Lee, Stan

Lieberman, Laurence (James)
1935-........................CLC 4
See also CANR 8
See also CA 17-20R

Lightfoot, Gordon 1938-..........CLC 26
See also CA 109

Lima, José Lezama 1910-1976
See Lezama Lima, José

Lind, Jakov 1927-........CLC 1, 2, 4, 27
See also Landwirth, Heinz
See also CA 9-12R

Lipsyte, Robert (Michael)
1938-......................CLC 21
See also CANR 8
See also CA 17-20R
See also SATA 5

Livesay, Dorothy 1909-........ CLC 4, 15
See also CA 25-28R
See also AITN 2

Llewellyn, Richard 1906-...........CLC 7
See also Llewellyn Lloyd, Richard (Dafydd Vyvyan)
See also DLB 15

Llewellyn Lloyd, Richard (Dafydd Vyvyan)
1906-
See Llewellyn, Richard
See also CANR 7
See also CA 53-56
See also SATA 11

Llosa, Mario Vargas 1936-
See Vargas Llosa, Mario

Lloyd, Richard Llewellyn 1906-
See Llewellyn, Richard

Lockhart, John Gibson
1794-1854................... NCLC 6

Logan, John 1923-.................CLC 5
See also CA 77-80
See also DLB 5

London, Jack 1876-1916 .... TCLC 9
See also SATA 18
See also DLB 8, 12
See also AITN 2

Long, Emmett 1925-
See Leonard, Elmore

Longfellow, Henry Wadsworth
1807-1882................... NCLC 2
See also SATA 19
See also DLB 1

Lord, Bette Bao 1938-............CLC 23
See also CA 107

Lorde, Audre 1934-...............CLC 18

Loti, Pierre 1850-1923 .... TCLC 11
See also Viaud, (Louis Marie) Julien

Lovecraft, H(oward) P(hillips)
1890-1937................... TCLC 4
See also CA 104

Lowell, Amy 1874-1925 .... TCLC 1, 8
See also CA 104

Lowell, James Russell
1819-1891................... NCLC 2
See also DLB 1, 11

Lowell, Robert (Traill Spence, Jr.)
1917-1977...... CLC 1, 2, 3, 4, 5, 8, 9, 11, 15
See also CA 9-12R
See also obituary CA 73-76
See also DLB 5

Lowndes, Marie (Adelaide Belloc)
1868-1947................... TCLC 12
See also CA 107

Lowry, (Clarence) Malcolm
1909-1957................... TCLC 6
See also CA 105
See also DLB 15

Loy, Mina 1882-1966 ....CLC 28
See also DLB 4

Lucas, George 1944-..............CLC 16
See also CA 77-80

Lucas, Victoria 1932-1963
See Plath, Sylvia

Ludlum, Robert 1927-.............CLC 22
See also CA 33-36R
See also DLB-Y 82

Ludwig, Otto 1813-1865.......... NCLC 4

Lu Hsün 1881-1936.............. TCLC 3

Lukács, Georg 1885-1971.........CLC 24
See also Lukács, György

Lukács, György 1885-1971
See Lukács, Georg
See also CA 101
See also obituary CA 29-32R

Lurie, Alison 1926-..........CLC 4, 5, 18
See also CANR 2
See also CA 1-4R
See also DLB 2

Luzi, Mario 1914-................CLC 13
See also CANR 9
See also CA 61-64

Lytle, Andrew (Nelson) 1902- ......CLC 22
See also CA 9-12R
See also DLB 6

Lytton, Edward Bulwer 1803-1873
See Bulwer-Lytton, (Lord) Edward (George Earle Lytton)

Macaulay, (Dame Emile) Rose
1881-1958................... TCLC 7
See also CA 104

MacBeth, George (Mann)
1932-....................CLC 2, 5, 9
See also CA 25-28R
See also SATA 4

MacDiarmid, Hugh
1892-1978............CLC 2, 4, 11, 19
See also Grieve, C(hristopher) M(urray)
See also DLB 20

Macdonald, Cynthia 1928-..... CLC 13, 19
See also CANR 4
See also CA 49-52

MacDonald, George
1824-1905................... TCLC 9
See also CA 106
See also SATA 33
See also DLB 18

MacDonald, John D(ann)
1916-..................... CLC 3, 27
See also CANR 1
See also CA 1-4R
See also DLB 8

Macdonald, Ross
1915-..................CLC 1, 2, 3, 14
See also Millar, Kenneth

MacEwen, Gwendolyn 1941-.......CLC 13
See also CANR 7
See also CA 9-12R

Machado de Assis, (Joaquim Maria)
1839-1908................... TCLC 10
See also CA 107

Machado (y Ruiz), Antonio
1875-1939................... TCLC 3
See also CA 104

Machen, Arthur (Llewellyn Jones)
1863-1947.................... TCLC 4
See also CA 104

MacInnes, Colin 1914-1976..... CLC 4, 23
See also CA 69-72
See also obituary CA 65-68
See also DLB 14

MacInnes, Helen 1907-............CLC 27
See also CANR 1
See also CA 1-4R
See also SATA 22

Mackenzie, (Edward Montague) Compton
1883-1972....................CLC 18
See also CAP 2
See also CA 21-22
See also obituary CA 37-40R

MacLean, Alistair (Stuart)
1922-..................... CLC 3, 13
See also CA 57-60
See also SATA 23

MacLeish, Archibald
1892-1982................ CLC 3, 8, 14
See also CA 9-12R
See also obituary CA 106
See also DLB 4, 7
See also DLB-Y 82

MacLennan, (John) Hugh
1907-..................... CLC 2, 14
See also CA 5-8R

MacNeice, (Frederick) Louis
1907-1963............... CLC 1, 4, 10
See also CA 85-88
See also DLB 10, 20

Macpherson, (Jean) Jay 1931-......CLC 14
See also CA 5-8R

Macumber, Mari 1896-1966
See Sandoz, Mari (Susette)

Madden, (Jerry) David
1933-..................... CLC 5, 15
See also CANR 4
See also CA 1-4R
See also DLB 6

Madhubuti, Haki R. 1942-..........CLC 6
See also Lee, Don L.
See also DLB 5

Maeterlinck, Maurice
1862-1949.................... TCLC 3
See also CA 104

Mahon, Derek 1941-..............CLC 27

Mailer, Norman
1923-......CLC 1, 2, 3, 4, 5, 8, 11, 14, 28
See also CA 9-12R
See also DLB 2, 16
See also DLB-Y 80
See also DLB-DS 3
See also AITN 2

Mais, Roger 1905-1955........... TCLC 8
See also CA 105

Major, Clarence 1936-......... CLC 3, 19
See also CA 21-24R

Major, Kevin 1949-................CLC 26
See also CA 97-100
See also SATA 32

Malamud, Bernard
1914-......CLC 1, 2, 3, 5, 8, 9, 11, 18, 27
See also CA 5-8R
See also DLB 2
See also DLB-Y 80

Mallarmé, Stéphane
1842-1898.................... NCLC 4

Mallet-Joris, Françoise 1930-.......CLC 11
See also CA 65-68

Maloff, Saul 1922-..................CLC 5
See also CA 33-36R

Malouf, David 1934-...............CLC 28

Malraux, (Georges-) André
1901-1976......... CLC 1, 4, 9, 13, 15
See also CAP 2
See also CA 21-24R
See also obituary CA 69-72

Malzberg, Barry N. 1939-..........CLC 7
See also CA 61-64
See also DLB 8

Mamet, David 1947-.......... CLC 9, 15
See also CA 81-84
See also DLB 7

Mamoulian, Rouben 1898-........CLC 16
See also CA 25-28R

Mandelstam, Osip (Emilievich)
1891?-1938?............... TCLC 2, 6
See also CA 104

Manley, Mary Delariviere ?-1724..... LC 1

Mann, (Luiz) Heinrich
1871-1950................... TCLC 9
See also CA 106

Mann, Thomas 1875-1955...... TCLC 2, 8
See also CA 104

Manning, Olivia 1915-1980..... CLC 5, 19
See also CA 5-8R
See also obituary CA 101

Mano, D. Keith 1942-......... CLC 2, 10
See also CA 25-28R
See also DLB 6

Mansfield, Katherine
1888-1923.................. TCLC 2, 8
See also CA 104

Marcel, Gabriel (Honore)
1889-1973....................CLC 15
See also CA 102
See also obituary CA 45-48

Marchbanks, Samuel 1913-
See Davies, (William) Robertson

Marinetti, F(ilippo) T(ommaso)
1876-1944................... TCLC 10
See also CA 107

Markandaya, Kamala (Purnaiya)
1924-........................CLC 8
See also Taylor, Kamala (Purnaiya)

Markfield, Wallace (Arthur)
1926-.......................CLC 8
See also CA 69-72
See also DLB 2

Markham, Robert 1922-
See Amis, Kingsley (William)

Marks, J. 1942-
See Highwater, Jamake

Marley, Bob 1945-1981 ....CLC 17
See also Marley, Robert Nesta

Marley, Robert Nesta 1945-1981
See Marley, Bob
See also CA 107
See also obituary CA 103

Marquand, John P(hillips)
1893-1960................. CLC 2, 10
See also CA 85-88
See also DLB 9

Márquez, Gabriel García 1928-
See García Márquez, Gabriel

Marquis, Don(ald Robert Perry)
1878-1937.................... TCLC 7
See also CA 104
See also DLB 11, 25

Marryat, Frederick 1792-1848 .... NCLC 3
See also DLB 21

Marsh, (Edith) Ngaio
1899-1982....................CLC 7
See also CANR 6
See also CA 9-12R

Marshall, Garry 1935?-..........CLC 17

Marshall, Paule 1929-.............CLC 27
See also CA 77-80

Marsten, Richard 1926-
See Hunter, Evan

Martínez Ruiz, José 1874-1967
See Azorín
See also CA 93-96

Martínez Sierra, Gregorio 1881-1947
See Martínez Sierra, Gregorio and Martínez Sierra, María (de la O'LeJárraga)
See also CA 104

Martínez Sierra, Gregorio 1881-1947 and
Martínez Sierra, María (de la O'LeJárraga) 1880?-1974 .... TCLC 6

Martínez Sierra, María (de la O'LeJárraga)
1880?-1974
See Martínez Sierra, Gregorio and Martínez Sierra, María (de la O'LeJárraga)

Martínez Sierra, María (de la O'LeJárraga)
1880?-1974 and **Martínez Sierra, Gregorio** 1881-1947
See Martínez Sierra, Gregorio and Martínez Sierra, María (de la O'LeJárraga)

Martinson, Harry (Edmund)
1904-1978....................CLC 14
See also CA 77-80

Masefield, John (Edward)
1878-1967....................CLC 11
See also CAP 2
See also CA 19-20
See also obituary CA 25-28R
See also SATA 19
See also DLB 10, 19

Mason, Bobbie Ann 1940- ....CLC 28
See also CANR 11
See also CA 53-56

Masters, Edgar Lee
1868?-1950................... TCLC 2
See also CA 104

Mathews, Harry 1930-.............CLC 6
See also CA 21-24R

Matthias, John (Edward) 1941-......CLC 9
See also CA 33-36R

Matthiessen, Peter 1927- ..... CLC 5, 7, 11
See also CA 9-12R
See also SATA 27
See also DLB 6

Maturin, Charles Robert
1780?-1824 .... NCLC 6

Matute, Ana María 1925- .... CLC 11
See also CA 89-92

Maugham, W(illiam) Somerset
1874-1965 .... CLC 1, 11, 15
See also CA 5-8R
See also obituary CA 25-28R
See also DLB 10

Maupassant, (Henri René Albert) Guy de
1850-1893 .... NCLC 1

Mauriac, Claude 1914- .... CLC 9
See also CA 89-92

Mauriac, François (Charles)
1885-1970 .... CLC 4, 9
See also CAP 2
See also CA 25-28

Maxwell, William (Keepers, Jr.)
1908- .... CLC 19
See also CA 93-96
See also DLB-Y 80

May, Elaine 1932- .... CLC 16

Mayakovsky, Vladimir (Vladimirovich)
1893-1930 .... TCLC 4
See also CA 104

Maynard, Joyce 1953- .... CLC 23

Mayne, William (James Carter)
1928- .... CLC 12
See also CA 9-12R
See also SATA 6

Mayo, Jim 1908?-
See L'Amour, Louis (Dearborn)
See also CA 109

Maysles, Albert 1926-
See Maysles, Albert and Maysles, David
See also CA 29-32R

Maysles, Albert 1926- and **Maysles, David**
1932- .... CLC 16

Maysles, David 1932-
See Maysles, Albert and Maysles, David

Mazer, Norma Fox 1931- .... CLC 26
See also CA 69-72
See also SATA 24

McBain, Ed 1926-
See Hunter, Evan

McCaffrey, Anne 1926- .... CLC 17
See also CA 25-28R
See also SATA 8
See also DLB 8
See also AITN 2

McCarthy, Cormac 1933- .... CLC 4
See also CANR 10
See also CA 13-16R
See also DLB 6

McCarthy, Mary (Therese)
1912- .... CLC 1, 3, 5, 14, 24
See also CA 5-8R
See also DLB 2
See also DLB-Y 81

McCartney, Paul 1942-
See Lennon, John (Ono) and McCartney, Paul

McClure, Michael 1932- .... CLC 6, 10
See also CA 21-24R
See also DLB 16

McCourt, James 1941- .... CLC 5
See also CA 57-60

McCrae, John 1872-1918 .... TCLC 12

McCullers, (Lula) Carson
1917-1967 .... CLC 1, 4, 10, 12
See also CA 5-8R
See also obituary CA 25-28R
See also SATA 27
See also DLB 2, 7

McCullough, Colleen 1938?- .... CLC 27
See also CA 81-84

McElroy, Joseph 1930- .... CLC 5
See also CA 17-20R

McEwan, Ian 1948- .... CLC 13
See also CA 61-64
See also DLB 14

McGahern, John 1935- .... CLC 5, 9
See also CA 17-20R
See also DLB 14

McGinley, Phyllis 1905-1978 .... CLC 14
See also CA 9-12R
See also obituary CA 77-80
See also SATA 2
See also obituary SATA 24
See also DLB 11

McGivern, Maureen Daly 1921-
See Daly, Maureen
See also CA 9-12R

McGrath, Thomas 1916- .... CLC 28
See also CANR 6
See also CA 9-12R

McGuane, Thomas (Francis III)
1939- .... CLC 3, 7, 18
See also CANR 5
See also CA 49-52
See also DLB 2
See also DLB-Y 80
See also AITN 2

McHale, Tom 1941-1982 .... CLC 3, 5
See also CA 77-80
See also obituary CA 106
See also AITN 1

McIlwraith, Maureen Mollie Hunter 1922-
See Hunter, Mollie
See also CA 29-32R
See also SATA 2

McIntyre, Vonda N(eel) 1948- ...... CLC 18
See also CA 81-84

McKay, Claude 1889-1948 .... TCLC 7
See also CA 104
See also DLB 4

McKuen, Rod 1933- .... CLC 1, 3
See also CA 41-44R
See also AITN 1

McManus, Declan Patrick 1955-
See Costello, Elvis

McMurtry, Larry (Jeff)
1936- .... CLC 2, 3, 7, 11, 27
See also CA 5-8R
See also DLB 2
See also DLB-Y 80
See also AITN 2

McNally, Terrence 1939- .... CLC 4, 7
See also CANR 2
See also CA 45-48
See also DLB 7

McPherson, James Alan 1943- ..... CLC 19
See also CA 25-28R

Meaker, Marijane 1927-
See Kerr, M. E.
See also CA 107
See also SATA 20

Medoff, Mark (Howard)
1940- .... CLC 6, 23
See also CANR 5
See also CA 53-56
See also DLB 7
See also AITN 1

Megged, Aharon 1920- .... CLC 9
See also CANR 1
See also CA 49-52

Meltzer, Milton 1915- .... CLC 26
See also CA 13-16R
See also SATA 1

Melville, Herman 1819-1891 ...... NCLC 3
See also DLB 3

Mercer, David 1928-1980 .... CLC 5
See also CA 9-12R
See also obituary CA 102
See also DLB 13

Meredith, William (Morris)
1919- .... CLC 4, 13, 22
See also CANR 6
See also CA 9-12R
See also DLB 5

Mérimée, Prosper 1803-1870 ...... NCLC 6

Merrill, James (Ingram)
1926- .... CLC 2, 3, 6, 8, 13, 18
See also CANR 10
See also CA 13-16R
See also DLB 5

Merton, Thomas (James)
1915-1968 .... CLC 1, 3, 11
See also CA 5-8R
See also obituary CA 25-28R
See also DLB-Y 81

Merwin, W(illiam) S(tanley)
1927- .... CLC 1, 2, 3, 5, 8, 13, 18
See also CA 13-16R
See also DLB 5

Mew, Charlotte (Mary)
1870-1928 .... TCLC 8
See also CA 105
See also DLB 19

Mewshaw, Michael 1943- .... CLC 9
See also CANR 7
See also CA 53-56
See also DLB-Y 80

Meynell, Alice (Christiana Gertrude Thompson) 1847-1922 .... TCLC 6
See also CA 104
See also DLB 19

Michaels, Leonard 1933- .... CLC 6, 25
See also CA 61-64

Michaux, Henri 1899- .... CLC 8, 19
See also CA 85-88

Michener, James A(lbert)
1907- .... CLC 1, 5, 11
See also CA 5-8R
See also DLB 6
See also AITN 1

Mickiewicz, Adam 1798-1855 ..... NCLC 3

Middleton, Christopher 1926- ...... CLC 13
See also CA 13-16R

Middleton, Stanley 1919- .... CLC 7
See also CA 25-28R
See also DLB 14

Miguéis, José Rodrigues 1901- ..... CLC 10

Miles, Josephine 1911- .... CLC 1, 2, 14
See also CANR 2
See also CA 1-4R

Millar, Kenneth 1915-
See Macdonald, Ross
See also CA 9-12R
See also DLB 2

Millay, Edna St. Vincent
1892-1950 .... TCLC 4
See also CA 104

Miller, Arthur
1915- .... CLC 1, 2, 6, 10, 15, 26
See also CANR 2
See also CA 1-4R
See also DLB 7
See also AITN 1

Miller, Henry (Valentine)
1891-1980 .... CLC 1, 2, 4, 9, 14
See also CA 9-12R
See also obituary CA 97-100
See also DLB 4, 9
See also DLB-Y 80

Miller, Jason 1939?- .... CLC 2
See also CA 73-76
See also DLB 7
See also AITN 1

Miller, Walter M(ichael), Jr.
1923- .... CLC 4
See also CA 85-88
See also DLB 8

Millhauser, Steven 1943- .... CLC 21
See also CA 108
See also DLB 2

Milne, A(lan) A(lexander)
1882-1956 .... TCLC 6
See also CLR 1
See also CA 104
See also YABC 1
See also DLB 10

Miłosz, Czesław 1911- .... CLC 5, 11, 22
See also CA 81-84

Miró (Ferrer), Gabriel (Francisco Víctor)
1879-1930 .... TCLC 5
See also CA 104

Mishima, Yukio
1925-1970 .... CLC 2, 4, 6, 9, 27
See also Hiraoka, Kimitake

Mistral, Gabriela 1889-1957 ...... TCLC 2
See also CA 104

Mitchell, James Leslie 1901-1935
See Gibbon, Lewis Grassic
See also CA 104
See also DLB 15

Mitchell, Joni 1943- .... CLC 12

Mitchell (Marsh), Margaret (Munnerlyn)
1900-1949 .... TCLC 11
See also CA 109
See also DLB 9

Mitchell, W(illiam) O(rmond)
1914- .... CLC 25
See also CA 77-80

Mitford, Mary Russell
1787-1855 .... NCLC 4

Modiano, Patrick (Jean) 1945- ..... CLC 18
See also CA 85-88

Mohr, Nicholasa 1935- .... CLC 12
See also CANR 1
See also CA 49-52
See also SATA 8

Mojtabai, A(nn) G(race)
1938- .... CLC 5, 9, 15
See also CA 85-88

Momaday, N(avarre) Scott
1934- .... CLC 2, 19
See also CA 25-28R
See also SATA 30

Monroe, Harriet 1860-1936 ...... TCLC 12
See also CA 109

Montague, John (Patrick)
1929- .... CLC 13
See also CANR 9
See also CA 9-12R

Montale, Eugenio
1896-1981 .... CLC 7, 9, 18
See also CA 17-20R
See also obituary CA 104

Montgomery, Marion (H., Jr.)
1925- .... CLC 7
See also CANR 3
See also CA 1-4R
See also DLB 6
See also AITN 1

Montgomery, Robert Bruce 1921-1978
See Crispin, Edmund
See also CA 104

Montherlant, Henri (Milon) de
1896-1972 .... CLC 8, 19
See also CA 85-88
See also obituary CA 37-40R

Monty Python .... CLC 21

Mooney, Ted 1951- .... CLC 25

Moorcock, Michael (John)
1939- .... CLC 5, 27
See also CANR 2
See also CA 45-48
See also DLB 14

Moore, Brian
1921- .... CLC 1, 3, 5, 7, 8, 19
See also CANR 1
See also CA 1-4R

Moore, George (Augustus)
1852-1933 .... TCLC 7
See also CA 104
See also DLB 10, 18

Moore, Marianne (Craig)
1887-1972 ...... CLC 1, 2, 4, 8, 10, 13, 19
See also CANR 3
See also CA 1-4R
See also obituary CA 33-36R
See also SATA 20

Moore, Thomas 1779-1852 .... NCLC 6

Morante, Elsa 1918- .... CLC 8
See also CA 85-88

Moravia, Alberto
1907- .... CLC 2, 7, 11, 18, 27
See also Pincherle, Alberto

Morgan, Berry 1919- .... CLC 6
See also CA 49-52
See also DLB 6

Morgan, Frederick 1922- .... CLC 23
See also CA 17-20R

Morgan, Robin 1941- .... CLC 2
See also CA 69-72

Morgenstern, Christian (Otto Josef Wolfgang)
1871-1914 .... TCLC 8
See also CA 105

Morris, Steveland Judkins 1950-
See Wonder, Stevie

Morris, William 1834-1896 .... NCLC 4
See also DLB 18

Morris, Wright 1910- ...... CLC 1, 3, 7, 18
See also CA 9-12R
See also DLB 2
See also DLB-Y 81

Morrison, James Douglas 1943-1971
See Morrison, Jim
See also CA 73-76

Morrison, Jim 1943-1971 .... CLC 17
See also Morrison, James Douglas

Morrison, Toni 1931- .... CLC 4, 10, 22
See also CA 29-32R
See also DLB 6
See also DLB-Y 81

Morrison, Van 1945- .... CLC 21

Mortimer, John (Clifford)
1923- .... CLC 28
See also CA 13-16R
See also DLB 13

Mortimer, Penelope (Ruth)
1918- .... CLC 5
See also CA 57-60

Moss, Howard 1922- .... CLC 7, 14
See also CANR 1
See also CA 1-4R
See also DLB 5

Motley, Willard (Francis)
1912-1965 .... CLC 18
See also obituary CA 106

Mott, Michael (Charles Alston)
1930- .... CLC 15
See also CANR 7
See also CA 5-8R

Mowat, Farley 1921- .... CLC 26
See also CANR 4
See also CA 1-4R
See also SATA 3

Mphahlele, Es'kia 1919-
See Mphahlele, Ezekiel

Mphahlele, Ezekiel 1919- .... CLC 25
See also CA 81-84

Mrożek, Sławomir 1930- .... CLC 3, 13
See also CA 13-16R

Mueller, Lisel 1924- .... CLC 13
See also CA 93-96

Muir, Edwin 1887-1959 .... TCLC 2
See also CA 104
See also DLB 20

Mull, Martin 1943- .... CLC 17
See also CA 105

Munro, Alice 1931- .... CLC 6, 10, 19
See also CA 33-36R
See also SATA 29
See also AITN 2

Munro, H(ector) H(ugh) 1870-1916
See Saki
See also CA 104

Murdoch, (Jean) Iris
1919- ...... CLC 1, 2, 3, 4, 6, 8, 11, 15, 22
See also CANR 8
See also CA 13-16R
See also DLB 14

Musgrave, Susan 1951- .... CLC 13
See also CA 69-72

Musil, Robert (Edler von)
1880-1942................ TCLC 12
See also CA 109

Nabokov, Vladimir (Vladimirovich)
1899-1977...... CLC 1, 2, 3, 6, 8, 11, 15, 23
See also CA 5-8R
See also obituary CA 69-72
See also DLB 2
See also DLB-Y 80
See also DLB-DS 3

Nagy, László 1925- .... CLC 7

Naipaul, V(idiadhar) S(urajprasad)
1932- .... CLC 4, 7, 9, 13, 18
See also CANR 1
See also CA 1-4R

Narayan, R(asipuram) K(rishnaswami)
1907- .... CLC 7, 28
See also CA 81-84

Nash, (Frediric) Ogden
1902-1971.................. CLC 23
See also CAP 1
See also CA 13-14
See also obituary CA 29-32R
See also SATA 2
See also DLB 11

Natsume, Sōseki
1867-1916................ TCLC 2, 10
See also CA 104

Natti, (Mary) Lee 1919-
See Kingman, (Mary) Lee
See also CANR 2

Naylor, Gloria 1950- .... CLC 28
See also CA 107

Nelson, Willie 1933- .... CLC 17
See also CA 107

Nemerov, Howard 1920- .... CLC 2, 6, 9
See also CANR 1
See also CA 1-4R
See also DLB 5, 6

Neruda, Pablo
1904-1973........ CLC 1, 2, 5, 7, 9, 28
See also CAP 2
See also CA 19-20
See also obituary CA 45-48

Nerval, Gérard de 1808-1855 ..... NCLC 1

Nervo, (José) Amado (Ruiz de)
1870-1919................ TCLC 11
See also CA 109

Neufeld, John (Arthur) 1938- ...... CLC 17
See also CANR 11
See also CA 25-28R
See also SATA 6

Neville, Emily Cheney 1919- .... CLC 12
See also CANR 3
See also CA 5-8R
See also SATA 1

Newbound, Bernard Slade 1930-
See Slade, Bernard
See also CA 81-84

Newby, P(ercy) H(oward)
1918-....................... CLC 2, 13
See also CA 5-8R
See also DLB 15

Newlove, Donald 1928- .... CLC 6
See also CA 29-32R

Newlove, John (Herbert) 1938- ..... CLC 14
See also CANR 9
See also CA 21-24R

Newman, Charles 1938- .... CLC 2, 8
See also CA 21-24R

Newman, Edwin (Harold)
1919-........................ CLC 14
See also CANR 5
See also CA 69-72
See also AITN 1

Ngugi, James (Thiong'o)
1938- .... CLC 3, 7
See also Wa Thiong'o, Ngugi
See also CA 81-84

Ngugi Wa Thiong'o 1938-
See Ngugi, James
See Wa Thiong'o, Ngugi

Nichol, B(arne) P(hillip) 1944- ...... CLC 18
See also CA 53-56

Nichols, Peter 1927- .... CLC 5
See also CA 104
See also DLB 13

Niedecker, Lorine 1903-1970....... CLC 10
See also CAP 2
See also CA 25-28

Nietzsche, Friedrich (Wilhelm)
1844-1900................ TCLC 10
See also CA 107

Nightingale, Anne Redmon 1943-
See Redmon (Nightingale), Anne
See also CA 103

Nin, Anaïs
1903-1977........ CLC 1, 4, 8, 11, 14
See also CA 13-16R
See also obituary CA 69-72
See also DLB 2, 4
See also AITN 2

Nissenson, Hugh 1933- .... CLC 4, 9
See also CA 17-20R

Niven, Larry 1938- .... CLC 8
See also Niven, Laurence Van Cott
See also DLB 8

Niven, Laurence Van Cott 1938-
See Niven, Larry
See also CA 21-24R

Nixon, Agnes Eckhardt 1927- ...... CLC 21

Norman, Marsha 1947-............ CLC 28
See also CA 105

Norris, Leslie 1921-................ CLC 14
See also CAP 1
See also CA 11-12

North, Andrew 1912-
See Norton, Andre

North, Christopher 1785-1854
See Wilson, John

Norton, Alice Mary 1912-
See Norton, Andre
See also CANR 2
See also CA 1-4R
See also SATA 1

Norton, Andre 1912-............... CLC 12
See also DLB 8

Nossack, Hans Erich 1901-1978 ..... CLC 6
See also CA 93-96
See also obituary CA 85-88

Nova, Craig 1945-................... CLC 7
See also CANR 2
See also CA 45-48

Nowlan, Alden (Albert) 1933- ...... CLC 15
See also CANR 5
See also CA 9-12R

Noyes, Alfred 1880-1958 .... TCLC 7
See also CA 104
See also DLB 20

Nye, Robert 1939-................. CLC 13
See also CA 33-36R
See also SATA 6
See also DLB 14

Nyro, Laura 1947-................. CLC 17

Oates, Joyce Carol
1938-..... CLC 1, 2, 3, 6, 9, 11, 15, 19
See also CA 5-8R
See also DLB 2, 5
See also DLB-Y 81
See also AITN 1

O'Brien, Darcy 1939-............... CLC 11
See also CANR 8
See also CA 21-24R

O'Brien, Edna 1932-........ CLC 3, 5, 8, 13
See also CANR 6
See also CA 1-4R
See also DLB 14

O'Brien, Flann
1911-1966.......... CLC 1, 4, 5, 7, 10
See also O Nuallain, Brian

O'Brien, Richard 19?- .... CLC 17
See also CA 73-76

O'Brien, Tim 1946-............. CLC 7, 19
See also CA 85-88
See also DLB-Y 80

O'Casey, Sean
1880-1964........ CLC 1, 5, 9, 11, 15
See also CA 89-92
See also DLB 10

Ochs, Phil 1940-1976 ....CLC 17
See also obituary CA 65-68

O'Connor, Edwin (Greene)
1918-1968................... CLC 14
See also CA 93-96
See also obituary CA 25-28R

O'Connor, (Mary) Flannery
1925-1964 ...... CLC 1, 2, 3, 6, 10, 13, 15, 21
See also CANR 3
See also CA 1-4R
See also DLB 2
See also DLB-Y 80

O'Connor, Frank
1903-1966 .... CLC 14, 23
See also O'Donovan, Michael (John)

Odets, Clifford 1906-1963 ...... CLC 2, 28
See also CA 85-88
See also DLB 7, 26

O'Donovan, Michael (John) 1903-1966
See O'Connor, Frank
See also CA 93-96

Ōe, Kenzaburō 1935- .... CLC 10
See also CA 97-100

O'Faolain, Julia .... CLC 6, 19
See also CA 81-84
See also DLB 14

O'Faoláin, Seán 1900- .... CLC 1, 7, 14
See also CA 61-64
See also DLB 15

O'Flaherty, Liam 1896- .... CLC 5
See also CA 101

O'Grady, Standish (James)
1846-1928 .... TCLC 5
See also CA 104

O'Hara, Frank
1926-1966 .... CLC 2, 5, 13
See also CA 9-12R
See also obituary CA 25-28R
See also DLB 5, 16

O'Hara, John (Henry)
1905-1970 .... CLC 1, 2, 3, 6, 11
See also CA 5-8R
See also obituary CA 25-28R
See also DLB 9
See also DLB-DS 2

Okigbo, Christopher (Ifenayichukwu)
1932-1967 .... CLC 25
See also CA 77-80

Olesha, Yuri (Karlovich)
1899-1960 .... CLC 8
See also CA 85-88

Oliver, Mary 1935- .... CLC 19
See also CANR 9
See also CA 21-24R
See also DLB 5

Olivier, (Baron) Laurence
1907- .... CLC 20

Olsen, Tillie 1913- .... CLC 4, 13
See also CANR 1
See also CA 1-4R
See also DLB-Y 80

Olson, Charles (John)
1910-1970 .... CLC 1, 2, 5, 6, 9, 11
See also CAP 1
See also CA 15-16
See also obituary CA 25-28R
See also DLB 5, 16

Olson, Theodore 1937-
See Olson, Toby

Olson, Toby 1937- .... CLC 28
See also CANR 9
See also CA 65-68

Ondaatje, (Philip) Michael
1943- .... CLC 14
See also CA 77-80

O'Neill, Eugene (Gladstone)
1888-1953 .... TCLC 1, 6
See also AITN 1
See also DLB 7

Onetti, Juan Carlos 1909- ...... CLC 7, 10
See also CA 85-88

O'Nolan, Brian 1911-1966
See O'Brien, Flann

O Nuallain, Brian 1911-1966
See O'Brien, Flann
See also CAP 2
See also CA 21-22
See also obituary CA 25-28R

Oppen, George 1908- .... CLC 7, 13
See also CANR 8
See also CA 13-16R
See also DLB 5

Orlovitz, Gil 1918-1973 .... CLC 22
See also CA 77-80
See also obituary CA 45-48
See also DLB 2, 5

Ortega y Gasset, José
1883-1955 .... TCLC 9
See also CA 106

Orton, Joe 1933?-1967 .... CLC 4, 13
See also Orton, John Kingsley
See also DLB 13

Orton, John Kingsley 1933?-1967
See Orton, Joe
See also CA 85-88

Orwell, George 1903-1950 ..... TCLC 2, 6
See also CA 104
See also SATA 29
See also DLB 15

Osborne, John (James)
1929- .... CLC 1, 2, 5, 11
See also CA 13-16R
See also DLB 13

Oshima, Nagisa 1932- .... CLC 20

Ossoli, Sarah Margaret (Fuller marchesa d')
1810-1850
See Fuller, (Sarah) Margaret
See also SATA 25

Otero, Blas de 1916- .... CLC 11
See also CA 89-92

Owen, Wilfred (Edward Salter)
1893-1918 .... TCLC 5
See also CA 104
See also DLB 20

Owens, Rochelle 1936- .... CLC 8
See also CA 17-20R

Owl, Sebastian 1939-
See Thompson, Hunter S(tockton)

Oz, Amos 1939- .... CLC 5, 8, 11, 27
See also CA 53-56

Ozick, Cynthia 1928- .... CLC 3, 7, 28
See also CA 17-20R
See also DLB-Y 82

Ozu, Yasujiro 1903-1963 .... CLC 16

Pa Chin 1904- .... CLC 18
See also Li Fei-kan

Pack, Robert 1929- .... CLC 13
See also CANR 3
See also CA 1-4R
See also DLB 5

Padgett, Lewis 1915-1958
See Kuttner, Henry

Page, Jimmy 1944-
See Page, Jimmy and Plant, Robert

Page, Jimmy 1944- **and Plant, Robert**
1948- .... CLC 12

Page, P(atricia) K(athleen)
1916- .... CLC 7, 18
See also CANR 4
See also CA 53-56

Paget, Violet 1856-1935
See Lee, Vernon
See also CA 104

Palamas, Kostes 1859-1943 .... TCLC 5
See also CA 105

Palazzeschi, Aldo 1885-1974 ...... CLC 11
See also CA 89-92
See also obituary CA 53-56

Paley, Grace 1922- .... CLC 4, 6
See also CA 25-28R
See also AITN 1

Palin, Michael 1943-
See Monty Python
See also CA 107

Parker, Dorothy (Rothschild)
1893-1967 .... CLC 15
See also CAP 2
See also CA 19-20
See also obituary CA 25-28R
See also DLB 11

Parker, Robert B(rown) 1932- ...... CLC 27
See also CANR 1
See also CA 49-52

Parks, Gordon (Alexander Buchanan)
1912- .... CLC 1, 16
See also CA 41-44R
See also SATA 8
See also AITN 2

Parra, Nicanor 1914- .... CLC 2
See also CA 85-88

Pasolini, Pier Paolo 1922-1975 ..... CLC 20
See also CA 93-96
See also obituary CA 61-64

Pasternak, Boris
1890-1960 .... CLC 7, 10, 18

Pastan, Linda (Olenik) 1932- .... CLC 27
See also CA 61-64
See also DLB 5

Patchen, Kenneth
1911-1972 .... CLC 1, 2, 18
See also CANR 3
See also CA 1-4R
See also obituary CA 33-36R
See also DLB 16

Paterson, Katherine (Womeldorf)
1932- .... CLC 12
See also CA 21-24R
See also SATA 13

Paton, Alan (Stewart)
1903- .... CLC 4, 10, 25
See also CAP 1
See also CA 15-16
See also SATA 11

Paulding, James Kirke
1778-1860.................. NCLC 2
See also DLB 3

Pavese, Cesare 1908-1950 .... TCLC 3
See also CA 104

Paz, Octavio 1914-..... CLC 3, 4, 6, 10, 19
See also CA 73-76

Peake, Mervyn 1911-1968 .... CLC 7
See also CANR 3
See also CA 5-8R
See also obituary CA 25-28R
See also SATA 23
See also DLB 15

Pearce, (Ann) Philippa 1920-....... CLC 21
See also Christie, (Ann) Philippa
See also CA 5-8R
See also SATA 1

Pearl, Eric 1934-
See Elman, Richard

Peck, John 1941-.................. CLC 3
See also CANR 3
See also CA 49-52

Peck, Richard 1934- .... CLC 21
See also CA 85-88
See also SATA 18

Peck, Robert Newton 1928-........ CLC 17
See also CA 81-84
See also SATA 21

Peckinpah, (David) Sam(uel)
1925-...................... CLC 20
See also CA 109

Péguy, Charles (Pierre)
1873-1914.................. TCLC 10
See also CA 107

Percy, Walker
1916-........... CLC 2, 3, 6, 8, 14, 18
See also CANR 1
See also CA 1-4R
See also DLB 2
See also DLB-Y 80

Perelman, S(idney) J(oseph)
1904-1979......... CLC 3, 5, 9, 15, 23
See also CA 73-76
See also obituary CA 89-92
See also DLB 11
See also AITN 1, 2

Perse, St.-John 1887-1975 ...... CLC 4, 11
See also Léger, (Marie-Rene) Alexis Saint-Léger

Pesetsky, Bette 1932-............... CLC 28

Peters, Robert L(ouis) 1924- .... CLC 7
See also CA 13-16R

Petrakis, Harry Mark 1923- .... CLC 3
See also CANR 4
See also CA 9-12R

Petry, Ann (Lane) 1912-...... CLC 1, 7, 18
See also CANR 4
See also CA 5-8R
See also SATA 5

Phillips, Jayne Anne 1952-......... CLC 15
See also CA 101
See also DLB-Y 80

Phillips, Robert (Schaeffer)
1938-...................... CLC 28
See also CANR 8
See also CA 17-20R

Piccolo, Lucio 1901-1969 .... CLC 13
See also CA 97-100

Piercy, Marge
1936-........... CLC 3, 6, 14, 18, 27
See also CA 21-24R

Pincherle, Alberto 1907-
See Moravia, Alberto
See also CA 25-28R

Pinero, Miguel (Gomez) 1947?-...... CLC 4
See also CA 61-64

Pinget, Robert 1919-........... CLC 7, 13
See also CA 85-88

Pinsky, Robert 1940-........... CLC 9, 19
See also CA 29-32R
See also DLB-Y 82

Pinter, Harold
1930-........ CLC 1, 3, 6, 9, 11, 15, 27
See also CA 5-8R
See also DLB 13

Pirandello, Luigi 1867-1936....... TCLC 4
See also CA 104

Pirsig, Robert M(aynard)
1928-..................... CLC 4, 6
See also CA 53-56

Plaidy, Jean 1906-
See Hibbert, Eleanor (Burford)

Plant, Robert 1948-
See Page, Jimmy and Plant, Robert

Plante, David 1940-............ CLC 7, 23
See also CA 37-40R

Plath, Sylvia
1932-1963....... CLC 1, 2, 3, 5, 9, 11, 14, 17
See also CAP 2
See also CA 19-20
See also DLB 5, 6

Platt, Kin 1911-.................. CLC 26
See also CA 17-20R
See also SATA 21

Plomer, William (Charles Franklin)
1903-1973.................. CLC 4, 8
See also CAP 2
See also CA 21-22
See also SATA 24
See also DLB 20

Poe, Edgar Allan 1809-1849 ...... NCLC 1
See also SATA 23
See also DLB 3

Pohl, Frederik 1919-.............. CLC 18
See also CANR 11
See also CA 61-64
See also SATA 24
See also DLB 8

Poirier, Louis 1910-
See Gracq, Julien

Poitier, Sidney 1924?-.............CLC 26

Polanski, Roman 1933-............CLC 16
See also CA 77-80

Police, The.......................CLC 26

Pollitt, Katha 1949-...............CLC 28

Pomerance, Bernard 1940-........CLC 13
See also CA 101

Ponge, Francis (Jean Gaston Alfred)
1899-..................... CLC 6, 18
See also CA 85-88

Poole, Josephine 1933-..............CLC 17
See also CANR 10
See also CA 21-24R
See also SATA 5

Popa, Vasko 1922-................CLC 19

Porter, Katherine Anne
1890-1980..... CLC 1, 3, 7, 10, 13, 15, 27
See also CANR 1
See also CA 1-4R
See also obituary CA 101
See also obituary SATA 23
See also DLB 4, 9
See also DLB-Y 80
See also AITN 2

Porter, Peter (Neville Frederick)
1929-..................... CLC 5, 13
See also CA 85-88

Porter, William Sydney 1862-1909?
See Henry, O.
See also CA 104
See also YABC 2
See also DLB 12

Potok, Chaim 1929-.......CLC 2, 7, 14, 26
See also CA 17-20R
See also SATA 33
See also AITN 1, 2

Pound, Ezra (Loomis)
1885-1972..... CLC 1, 2, 3, 4, 5, 7, 10, 13, 18
See also CA 5-8R
See also obituary CA 37-40R
See also DLB 4

Powell, Anthony (Dymoke)
1905-.............. CLC 1, 3, 7, 9, 10
See also CANR 1
See also CA 1-4R
See also DLB 15

Powers, J(ames) F(arl)
1917-..................... CLC 1, 4, 8
See also CANR 2
See also CA 1-4R

Pownall, David 1938- .... CLC 10
See also CA 89-92
See also DLB 14

Powys, John Cowper
1872-1963............... CLC 7, 9, 15
See also CA 85-88
See also DLB 15

Powys, T(heodore) F(rancis)
1875-1953.................. TCLC 9
See also CA 106

Pratt, E(dwin) J(ohn)
1883-1964.................... CLC 19
See also obituary CA 93-96

Preussler, Otfried 1923-........... CLC 17
See also CA 77-80
See also SATA 24

Prévert, Jacques (Henri Marie)
1900-1977.................... CLC 15
See also CA 77-80
See also obituary CA 69-72
See also obituary SATA 30

Prévost, Abbé (Antoine Francois)
1697-1763..................... LC 1

Price, (Edward) Reynolds
1933-................... CLC 3, 6, 13
See also CANR 1
See also CA 1-4R
See also DLB 2

Price, Richard 1949-.......... CLC 6, 12
See also CANR 3
See also CA 49-52
See also DLB-Y 81

Priestley, J(ohn) B(oynton)
1894-...................... CLC 2, 5, 9
See also CA 9-12R
See also DLB 10

Prince, F(rank) T(empleton)
1912-........................ CLC 22
See also CA 101
See also DLB 20

Pritchett, V(ictor) S(awdon)
1900-................... CLC 5, 13, 15
See also CA 61-64
See also DLB 15

Procaccino, Michael 1946-
See Cristofer, Michael

Prokosch, Frederic 1908-.......... CLC 4
See also CA 73-76

Proust, Marcel 1871-1922 .... TCLC 7
See also CA 104

Pryor, Richard 1940- .... CLC 26

Puig, Manuel 1932-....... CLC 3, 5, 10, 28
See also CANR 2
See also CA 45-48

Purdy, A(lfred) W(ellington)
1918-..................... CLC 3, 6, 14
See also CA 81-84

Purdy, James (Amos)
1923-................. CLC 2, 4, 10, 28
See also CA 33-36R
See also DLB 2

Pushkin, Alexander (Sergeyevich)
1799-1837................... NCLC 3

Puzo, Mario 1920-.......... CLC 1, 2, 6
See also CANR 4
See also CA 65-68
See also DLB 6

Pym, Barbara (Mary Crampton)
1913-1980............... CLC 13, 19
See also CAP 1
See also CA 13-14
See also obituary CA 97-100
See also DLB 14

Pynchon, Thomas
1937-.......... CLC 2, 3, 6, 9, 11, 18
See also CA 17-20R
See also DLB 2

Quasimodo, Salvatore
1901-1968.................... CLC 10
See also CAP 1
See also CA 15-16
See also obituary CA 25-28R

Queen, Ellery 1905-1982 .... CLC 3, 11
See also Dannay, Frederic
See also Lee, Manfred B(ennington)

Queneau, Raymond
1903-1976................. CLC 2, 5, 10
See also CA 77-80
See also obituary CA 69-72

Quin, Ann (Marie) 1936-1973....... CLC 6
See also CA 9-12R
See also obituary CA 45-48
See also DLB 14

Quinn, Simon 1942-
See Smith, Martin Cruz

Quoirez, Françoise 1935-
See Sagan, Françoise
See also CANR 6
See also CA 49-52

Rabe, David (William) 1940-..... CLC 4, 8
See also CA 85-88
See also DLB 7

Radcliffe, Ann (Ward)
1764-1823................... NCLC 6

Rado, James 1939-
See Ragni, Gerome and Rado, James
See also CA 105

Radomski, James 1932-
See Rado, James

Radvanyi, Netty Reiling 1900-
See Seghers, Anna
See also CA 85-88

Ragni, Gerome 1942-
See Ragni, Gerome and Rado, James
See also CA 105

Ragni, Gerome 1942- and **Rado, James**
1939-........................ CLC 17

Rahv, Philip 1908-1973 .... CLC 24
See also Greenberg, Ivan

Raine, Kathleen (Jessie) 1908-....... CLC 7
See also CA 85-88
See also DLB 20

Rand, Ayn 1905-1982............... CLC 3
See also CA 13-16R
See also obituary CA 105

Randall, Dudley (Felker) 1914-...... CLC 1
See also CA 25-28R

Ransom, John Crowe
1888-1974......... CLC 2, 4, 5, 11, 24
See also CANR 6
See also CA 5-8R
See also obituary CA 49-52

Rao, Raja 1909-.................CLC 25
See also CA 73-76

Raphael, Frederic (Michael)
1931-.................... CLC 2, 14
See also CANR 1
See also CA 1-4R
See also DLB 14

Rattigan, Terence (Mervyn)
1911-1977..................... CLC 7
See also CA 85-88
See also obituary CA 73-76
See also DLB 13

Raven, Simon (Arthur Noel)
1927-....................... CLC 14
See also CA 81-84

Rawlings, Marjorie Kinnan
1896-1953................... TCLC 4
See also CA 104
See also YABC 1
See also DLB 9, 22

Ray, Satyajit 1921- .... CLC 16

Read, Herbert (Edward)
1893-1968....................CLC 4
See also CA 85-88
See also obituary CA 25-28R
See also DLB 20

Read, Piers Paul 1941-...... CLC 4, 10, 25
See also CA 21-24R
See also SATA 21
See also DLB 14

Reade, Charles 1814-1884 .... NCLC 2
See also DLB 21

Reaney, James 1926-.............CLC 13
See also CA 41-44R

Rechy, John (Francisco)
1934-.................CLC 1, 7, 14, 18
See also CANR 6
See also CA 5-8R
See also DLB-Y 82

Redgrove, Peter (William)
1932-........................CLC 6
See also CANR 3
See also CA 1-4R

Redmon (Nightingale), Anne
1943-....................... CLC 22
See also Nightingale, Anne Redmon

Reed, Ishmael 1938- .... CLC 2, 3, 5, 6, 13
See also CA 21-24R
See also DLB 2, 5

Reed, John (Silas) 1887-1920...... TCLC 9
See also CA 106

Reed, Lou 1944-...................CLC 21

Reid Banks, Lynne 1929-
See Banks, Lynne Reid
See also CANR 6
See also CA 1-4R
See also SATA 22

Reiner, Max 1900-
See Caldwell, (Janet Miriam) Taylor (Holland)

Remark, Erich Paul 1898-1970
See Remarque, Erich Maria

Remarque, Erich Maria
1898-1970.................... CLC 21
See also CA 77-80
See also obituary CA 29-32R

Renault, Mary 1905-....... CLC 3, 11, 17
See also Challans, Mary

Rendell, Ruth 1930- ....CLC 28
See also CA 109

Renoir, Jean 1894-1979 .... CLC 20
See also obituary CA 85-88

Resnais, Alain 1922-............... CLC 16

Rexroth, Kenneth
1905-1982......... CLC 1, 2, 6, 11, 22
See also CA 5-8R
See also obituary CA 107
See also DLB 16
See also DLB-Y 82

Reyes y Basoalto, Ricardo Eliecer Neftali
1904-1973
See Neruda, Pablo

Reymont, Wladyslaw Stanislaw
1867-1925.................. TCLC 5
See also CA 104

Reynolds, Jonathan 1942?- ....CLC 6
See also CA 65-68

Reznikoff, Charles 1894-1976 ....CLC 9
See also CAP 2
See also CA 33-36
See also obituary CA 61-64

Rezzori, Gregor von 1914- ....CLC 25

Rhys, Jean
1894-1979......... CLC 2, 4, 6, 14, 19
See also CA 25-28R
See also obituary CA 85-88

Ribeiro, João Ubaldo (Osorio Pimentel)
1941- ....CLC 10
See also CA 81-84

Ribman, Ronald (Burt) 1932- ....CLC 7
See also CA 21-24R

Rice, Elmer 1892-1967 ....CLC 7
See also CAP 2
See also CA 21-22
See also obituary CA 25-28R
See also DLB 4, 7

Rice, Tim 1944-
See Rice, Tim and Webber, Andrew Lloyd
See also CA 103

Rice, Tim 1944- and **Webber, Andrew Lloyd** 1948- ....CLC 21

Rich, Adrienne (Cecile)
1929- .... CLC 3, 6, 7, 11, 18
See also CA 9-12R
See also DLB 5

Richard, Keith 1943-
See Jagger, Mick and Richard, Keith

Richards, I(vor) A(rmstrong)
1893-1979................ CLC 14, 24
See also CA 41-44R
See also obituary CA 89-92

Richards, Keith 1943-
See Richard, Keith
See also CA 107

Richardson, Dorothy (Miller)
1873-1957.................... TCLC 3
See also CA 104

Richardson, Ethel 1870-1946
See Richardson, Henry Handel
See also CA 105

Richardson, Henry Handel
1870-1946.................... TCLC 4
See also Ethel Richardson

Richardson, Samuel 1689-1761 .... LC 1

Richler, Mordecai
1931- .... CLC 3, 5, 9, 13, 18
See also CA 65-68
See also SATA 27
See also AITN 1

Riding, Laura 1901- .... CLC 3, 7
See also Jackson, Laura (Riding)

Riefenstahl, Berta Helene Amalia 1902-
See Riefenstahl, Leni
See also CA 108

Riefenstahl, Leni 1902- ....CLC 16
See also Riefenstahl, Berta Helene Amalia

Rilke, Rainer Maria
1875-1926...............TCLC 1, 6
See also CA 104

Rimbaud, (Jean Nicolas) Arthur
1854-1891.................... NCLC 4

Ritsos, Yannis 1909- .... CLC 6, 13
See also CA 77-80

Rivers, Conrad Kent 1933-1968 .....CLC 1
See also CA 85-88

Robbe-Grillet, Alain
1922-.........CLC 1, 2, 4, 6, 8, 10, 14
See also CA 9-12R

Robbins, Harold 1916- ....CLC 5
See also CA 73-76

Robbins, Thomas Eugene 1936-
See Robbins, Tom
See also CA 81-84

Robbins, Tom 1936- ....CLC 9
See also Robbins, Thomas Eugene
See also DLB-Y 80

Robbins, Trina 1938- ....CLC 21

Roberts, (Sir) Charles G(eorge) D(ouglas)
1860-1943................... TCLC 8
See also CA 105

Roberts, Kate 1891- ....CLC 15
See also CA 107

Roberts, Keith (John Kingston)
1935-......................CLC 14
See also CA 25-28R

Robinson, Edwin Arlington
1869-1935................... TCLC 5
See also CA 104

Robinson, Jill 1936-................CLC 10
See also CA 102

Robinson, Marilynne 1944- ....CLC 25

Robinson, Smokey 1940- ....CLC 21

Robinson, William 1940-
See Robinson, Smokey

Roddenberry, Gene 1921- ....CLC 17

Rodgers, Mary 1931- ....CLC 12
See also CANR 8
See also CA 49-52
See also SATA 8

Rodgers, W(illiam) R(obert)
1909-1969.....................CLC 7
See also CA 85-88
See also DLB 20

Rodriguez, Claudio 1934-..........CLC 10

Roethke, Theodore (Huebner)
1908-1963......... CLC 1, 3, 8, 11, 19
See also CA 81-84
See also DLB 5

Rogers, Sam 1943-
See Shepard, Sam

Rogers, Will(iam Penn Adair)
1879-1935................... TCLC 8
See also CA 105
See also DLB 11

Rogin, Gilbert 1929-................CLC 18
See also CA 65-68

Rohmer, Eric 1920- ....CLC 16

Roiphe, Anne (Richardson)
1935- .... CLC 3, 9
See also CA 89-92
See also DLB-Y 80

Rolfe, Frederick (William Serafino Austin Lewis Mary) 1860-1913..... TCLC 12
See also CA 107

Romains, Jules 1885-1972 ....CLC 7
See also CA 85-88

Rooke, Leon 1934-..................CLC 25
See also CA 25-28R

Rosa, João Guimarães
1908-1967....................CLC 23
See also obituary CA 89-92

Rosenberg, Isaac 1890-1918...... TCLC 12
See also CA 107
See also DLB 20

Rosenblatt, Joe 1933- ....CLC 15
See also Rosenblatt, Joseph
See also AITN 2

Rosenblatt, Joseph 1933-
See Rosenblatt, Joe
See also CA 89-92

Rosenthal, M(acha) L(ouis)
1917-......................CLC 28
See also CANR 4
See also CA 1-4R
See also DLB 5

Ross, (James) Sinclair 1908- ....CLC 13
See also CA 73-76

Rossetti, Christina Georgina
1830-1894................... NCLC 2
See also SATA 20

Rossetti, Dante Gabriel
1828-1882................... NCLC 4

Rossetti, Gabriel Charles Dante 1828-1882
See Rossetti, Dante Gabriel

Rossner, Judith (Perelman)
1935-....................... CLC 6, 9
See also CA 17-20R
See also DLB 6
See also AITN 2

Rostand, Edmond (Eugène Alexis)
1868-1918................... TCLC 6
See also CA 104

Roth, Henry 1906-............CLC 2, 6, 11
See also CAP 1
See also CA 11-12

Roth, Philip (Milton)
1933-...... CLC 1, 2, 3, 4, 6, 9, 15, 22
See also CANR 1
See also CA 1-4R
See also DLB 2
See also DLB-Y 82

Rothenberg, Jerome 1931-..........CLC 6
See also CANR 1
See also CA 45-48
See also DLB 5

Rourke, Constance (Mayfield)
1885-1941................... TCLC 12
See also CA 107
See also YABC 1

Rovit, Earl (Herbert) 1927-.........CLC 7
See also CA 5-8R

Rowson, Susanna Haswell
1762-1824................... NCLC 5

Roy, Gabrielle 1909-.......... CLC 10, 14
See also CANR 5
See also CA 53-56

Różewicz, Tadeusz 1921- ..... CLC 9, 23
See also CA 108

Ruark, Gibbons 1941-...............CLC 3
See also CA 33-36R

Rubens, Bernice 1927- .... CLC 19
See also CA 25-28R
See also DLB 14

Rudkin, (James) David 1936- ...... CLC 14
See also CA 89-92
See also DLB 13

Rudnik, Raphael 1933- .... CLC 7
See also CA 29-32R

Ruiz, José Martínez 1874-1967
See Azorín

Rukeyser, Muriel
1913-1980 .... CLC 6, 10, 15, 27
See also CA 5-8R
See also obituary CA 93-96
See also obituary SATA 22

Rule, Jane (Vance) 1931- .... CLC 27
See also CA 25-28R

Rulfo, Juan 1918- .... CLC 8
See also CA 85-88

Runyon, Damon 1880-1946 ...... TCLC 10
See also CA 107
See also DLB 11

Rushdie, (Ahmed) Salman
1947- .... CLC 23
See also CA 108

Rushforth, Peter (Scott) 1945- ...... CLC 19
See also CA 101

Russ, Joanna 1937- .... CLC 15
See also CANR 11
See also CA 25-28R
See also DLB 8

Russell, George William 1867-1935
See A. E.
See also CA 104

Russell, (Henry) Ken(neth Alfred)
1927- .... CLC 16
See also CA 105

Ruyslinck, Ward 1929- .... CLC 14

Ryan, Cornelius (John)
1920-1974 .... CLC 7
See also CA 69-72
See also obituary CA 53-56

Rybakov, Anatoli 1911?- .... CLC 23

Ryga, George 1932- .... CLC 14
See also CA 101

Sabato, Ernesto 1911- .... CLC 10, 23
See also CA 97-100

Sachs, Nelly 1891-1970 .... CLC 14
See also CAP 2
See also CA 17-18
See also obituary CA 25-28R

Sackler, Howard (Oliver)
1929-1982 .... CLC 14
See also CA 61-64
See also obituary CA 108
See also DLB 7

Sade, Donatien Alphonse François, Comte de
1740-1814 .... NCLC 3

Sadoff, Ira 1945- .... CLC 9
See also CANR 5
See also CA 53-56

Safire, William 1929- .... CLC 10
See also CA 17-20R

Sagan, Françoise 1935- ..... CLC 3, 6, 9, 17
See also Quoirez, Françoise

Sainte-Beuve, Charles Augustin
1804-1869 .... NCLC 5

Sainte-Marie, Beverly 1941-
See Sainte-Marie, Buffy
See also CA 107

Sainte-Marie, Buffy 1941- .... CLC 17
See also Sainte-Marie, Beverly

Saint-Exupéry, Antoine (Jean Baptiste Marie Roger) de 1900-1944 .... TCLC 2
See also CA 108

Saki 1870-1916 .... TCLC 3
See also Munro, H(ector) H(ugh)

Salama, Hannu 1936- .... CLC 18

Salamanca, J(ack) R(ichard)
1922- .... CLC 4, 15
See also CA 25-28R

Salinger, J(erome) D(avid)
1919- .... CLC 1, 3, 8, 12
See also CA 5-8R
See also DLB 2

Salter, James 1925- .... CLC 7
See also CA 73-76

Saltus, Edgar (Evertson)
1855-1921 .... TCLC 8
See also CA 105

Samarakis, Antonis 1919- .... CLC 5
See also CA 25-28R

Sánchez, Luis Rafael 1936- .... CLC 23

Sanchez, Sonia 1934- .... CLC 5
See also CA 33-36R
See also SATA 22

Sand, George 1804-1876 .... NCLC 2

Sandburg, Carl (August)
1878-1967 .... CLC 1, 4, 10, 15
See also CA 5-8R
See also obituary CA 25-28R
See also SATA 8
See also DLB 17

Sandoz, Mari (Susette)
1896-1966 .... CLC 28
See also CA 1-4R
See also obituary CA 25-28R
See also SATA 5
See also DLB 9

Saner, Reg(inald Anthony)
1931- .... CLC 9
See also CA 65-68

Sansom, William 1912-1976 ...... CLC 2, 6
See also CA 5-8R
See also obituary CA 65-68

Santos, Bienvenido N(uqui)
1911- .... CLC 22
See also CA 101

Sarduy, Severo 1937- .... CLC 6
See also CA 89-92

Saroyan, William
1908-1981 .... CLC 1, 8, 10
See also CA 5-8R
See also obituary CA 103
See also SATA 23
See also obituary SATA 24
See also DLB 7, 9
See also DLB-Y 81

Sarraute, Nathalie
1902- .... CLC 1, 2, 4, 8, 10
See also CA 9-12R

Sarton, (Eleanor) May
1912- .... CLC 4, 14
See also CANR 1
See also CA 1-4R
See also DLB-Y 81

Sartre, Jean-Paul
1905-1980 ...... CLC 1, 4, 7, 9, 13, 18, 24
See also CA 9-12R
See also obituary CA 97-100

Saura, Carlos 1932- .... CLC 20

Sauser-Hall, Frédéric-Louis 1887-1961
See Cendrars, Blaise
See also CA 102
See also obituary CA 93-96

Sayers, Dorothy L(eigh)
1893-1957 .... TCLC 2
See also CA 104
See also DLB 10

Sayles, John (Thomas)
1950- .... CLC 7, 10, 14
See also CA 57-60

Schaeffer, Susan Fromberg
1941- .... CLC 6, 11, 22
See also CA 49-52

Schevill, James (Erwin) 1920- ...... CLC 7
See also CA 5-8R

Schisgal, Murray (Joseph)
1926- .... CLC 6
See also CA 21-24R

Schneider, Leonard Alfred 1925-1966
See Bruce, Lenny
See also CA 89-92

Schnitzler, Arthur 1862-1931 ..... TCLC 4
See also CA 104

Schorer, Mark 1908-1977 .... CLC 9
See also CANR 7
See also CA 5-8R
See also obituary CA 73-76

Schrader, Paul (Joseph) 1946- ..... CLC 26
See also CA 37-40R

Schreiner (Cronwright), Olive (Emilie Albertina) 1855-1920 .... TCLC 9
See also CA 105
See also DLB 18

Schulberg, Budd (Wilson) 1914- ..... CLC 7
See also CA 25-28R
See also DLB 6
See also DLB-Y 81

Schulz, Bruno 1892-1942 .... TCLC 5

Schulz, Charles M(onroe)
1922- .... CLC 12
See also CANR 6
See also CA 9-12R
See also SATA 10

Schuyler, James (Marcus)
1923- .... CLC 5, 23
See also CA 101
See also DLB 5

Schwartz, Delmore
1913-1966 .... CLC 2, 4, 10
See also CAP 2
See also CA 17-18
See also obituary CA 25-28R

Schwarz-Bart, André 1928- ...... CLC 2, 4
See also CA 89-92

Schwarz-Bart, Simone 1938-........CLC 7
See also CA 97-100

Sciascia, Leonardo 1921-........ CLC 8, 9
See also CA 85-88

Scoppettone, Sandra 1936-........CLC 26
See also CA 5-8R
See also SATA 9

Scorsese, Martin 1942-............CLC 20

Scott, Duncan Campbell
1862-1947................... TCLC 6
See also CA 104

Scott, F(rancis) R(eginald)
1899-.......................CLC 22
See also CA 101

Scott, Paul (Mark) 1920-1978.......CLC 9
See also CA 81-84
See also obituary CA 77-80
See also DLB 14

Seelye, John 1931-.................CLC 7
See also CA 97-100

Seferiades, Giorgos Stylianou 1900-1971
See Seferis, George
See CANR 5
See also CA 5-8R
See also obituary CA 33-36R

Seferis, George 1900-1971 ...... CLC 5, 11
See also Seferiades, Giorgos Stylianou

Segal, Erich (Wolf) 1937-........ CLC 3, 10
See also CA 25-28R

Seghers, Anna 1900-...............CLC 7
See Radvanyi, Netty

Seidel, Frederick (Lewis) 1936-.....CLC 18
See also CANR 8
See also CA 13-16R

Selby, Hubert, Jr.
1928-...................CLC 1, 2, 4, 8
See also CA 13-16R
See also DLB 2

Sender, Ramón (José)
1902-1982....................CLC 8
See also CANR 8
See also CA 5-8R
See also obituary CA 105

Seton, Cynthia Propper
1926-1982...................CLC 27
See also CANR-7
See also CA 5-8R
See also obituary CA 108

Settle, Mary Lee 1918-............CLC 19
See also CA 89-92
See also DLB 6

Sexton, Anne (Harvey)
1928-1974....... CLC 2, 4, 6, 8, 10, 15
See also CANR 3
See also CA 1-4R
See also obituary CA 53-56
See also SATA 10
See also DLB 5

Shaara, Michael (Joseph)
1929-.......................CLC 15
See also CA 102
See also AITN 1

Shaffer, Anthony 1926-............CLC 19
See also DLB 13

Shaffer, Peter (Levin)
1926-.................CLC 5, 14, 18
See also CA 25-28R
See also DLB 13

Shalamov, Varlam (Tikhonovich)
1907?-1982..................CLC 18
See also obituary CA 105

Shamlu, Ahmad 1925- ....CLC 10

Shange, Ntozake 1948- .... CLC 8, 25
See also CA 85-88

Shapiro, Karl (Jay) 1913-..... CLC 4, 8, 15
See also CANR 1
See also CA 1-4R

Shaw, (George) Bernard
1856-1950................ TCLC 3, 6
See also CA 104, 109
See also DLB 10

Shaw, Irwin 1913-.............. CLC 7, 23
See also CA 13-16R
See also DLB 6
See also AITN 1

Shaw, Robert 1927-1978 ....CLC 5
See also CANR 4
See also CA 1-4R
See also obituary CA 81-84
See also DLB 13, 14
See also AITN 1

Sheed, Wilfrid (John Joseph)
1930-..................CLC 2, 4, 10
See also CA 65-68
See also DLB 6

Shepard, Sam 1943- .... CLC 4, 6, 17
See also CA 69-72
See also DLB 7

Sheridan, Richard Brinsley
1751-1816................... NCLC 5

Sherman, Martin ....CLC 19

Sherwin, Judith Johnson
1936-..................... CLC 7, 15
See also CA 25-28R

Sherwood, Robert E(mmet)
1896-1955................... TCLC 3
See also CA 104
See also DLB 7, 26

Shiel, M(atthew) P(hipps)
1865-1947................... TCLC 8
See also CA 106

Shimazaki, Tōson 1872-1943 ...... TCLC 5
See also CA 105

Sholokhov, Mikhail (Aleksandrovich)
1905-..................... CLC 7, 15
See also CA 101

Shreve, Susan Richards 1939-......CLC 23
See also CANR 5
See also CA 49-52

Shulman, Alix Kates 1932-...... CLC 2, 10
See also CA 29-32R
See also SATA 7

Shuster, Joe 1914-
See Siegel, Jerome and Shuster, Joe

Shuttle, Penelope (Diane) 1947-......CLC 7
See also CA 93-96
See also DLB 14

Siegel, Jerome 1914-
See Siegel, Jerome and Shuster, Joe

Siegel, Jerome 1914- and **Shuster, Joe**
1914-......................CLC 21

Sienkiewicz, Henryk (Adam Aleksander Pius)
1846-1916.................. TCLC 3
See also CA 104

Sigal, Clancy 1926-................CLC 7
See also CA 1-4R

Silkin, Jon 1930-................ CLC 2, 6
See also CA 5-8R

Silko, Leslie Marmon 1948-.....CLC 23

Sillanpää, Franz Eemil
1888-1964...................CLC 19
See also obituary CA 93-96

Sillitoe, Alan 1928- .... CLC 1, 3, 6, 10, 19
See also CANR 8
See also CA 9-12R
See also DLB 14
See also AITN 1

Silone, Ignazio 1900-1978...........CLC 4
See also CAP 2
See also CA 25-28
See also obituary CA 81-84

Silver, Joan Micklin 1935-.........CLC 20

Silverberg, Robert 1935- ....CLC 7
See also CANR 1
See also CA 1-4R
See also SATA 13
See also DLB 8

Silverstein, Alvin 1933-
See Silverstein, Alvin and Silverstein,
Virginia B(arbara Opshelor)
See also CANR 2
See also CA 49-52
See also SATA 8

Silverstein, Alvin 1933- and **Silverstein,
Virginia B(arbara Opshelor)**
1937-.......................CLC 17

Silverstein, Virginia B(arbara Opshelor)
1937-
See Silverstein, Alvin and Silverstein,
Virginia B(arbara Opshelor)
See also CANR 2
See also CA 49-52
See also SATA 8

Simak, Clifford D(onald) 1904-......CLC 1
See also CANR 1
See also CA 1-4R
See also DLB 8

Simenon, Georges (Jacques Christian)
1903-.............. CLC 1, 2, 3, 8, 18
See also CA 85-88

Simic, Charles 1938-........ CLC 6, 9, 22
See also CA 29-32R

Simms, William Gilmore
1806-1870................... NCLC 3
See also DLB 3

Simon, Carly 1945-...............CLC 26
See also CA 105

Simon, Claude 1913-........ CLC 4, 9, 15
See also CA 89-92

Simon, (Marvin) Neil 1927- ..... CLC 6, 11
See also CA 21-24R
See also DLB 7
See also AITN 1

Simon, Paul 1941-.................CLC 17

Simpson, Louis (Aston Marantz)
1923- .... CLC 4, 7, 9
See also CANR 1
See also CA 1-4R
See also DLB 5

Sinclair, Andrew (Annandale)
1935- .... CLC 2, 14
See also CA 9-12R
See also DLB 14

Sinclair, May 1865?-1946. ..... TCLC 3, 11
See also CA 104

Sinclair, Upton (Beall)
1878-1968. .... CLC 1, 11, 15
See also CANR 7
See also CA 5-8R
See also obituary 25-28R
See also SATA 9
See also DLB 9

Singer, Isaac Bashevis
1904- .... CLC 1, 3, 6, 9, 11, 15, 23
See also CLR 1
See also CANR 1
See also CA 1-4R
See also SATA 3, 27
See also DLB 6
See also AITN 1, 2

Singh, Khushwant 1915- .... CLC 11
See also CANR 6
See also CA 9-12R

Sinyavsky, Andrei (Donatevich)
1925- .... CLC 8
See also CA 85-88

Sissman, L(ouis) E(dward)
1928-1976. .... CLC 9, 18
See also CA 21-24R
See also obituary CA 65-68
See also DLB 5

Sisson, C(harles) H(ubert) 1914- ..... CLC 8
See also CANR 3
See also CA 1-4R

Sitwell, (Dame) Edith
1887-1964. .... CLC 2, 9
See also CA 9-12R
See also DLB 20

Sjoewall, Maj 1935-
See Wahlöö, Per
See also CA 65-68

Sjöwall, Maj 1935-
See Wahlöö, Per

Skelton, Robin 1925- .... CLC 13
See also CA 5-8R
See also AITN 2

Skolimowski, Jerzy 1938- .... CLC 20

Skolimowski, Yurek 1938-
See Skolimowski, Jerzy

Škvorecký, Josef (Victor)
1924- .... CLC 15
See also CANR 10
See also CA 61-64

Slade, Bernard 1930- .... CLC 11
See also Newbound, Bernard Slade

Slavitt, David (R.) 1935- .... CLC 5, 14
See also CA 21-24R
See also DLB 5, 6

Slesinger, Tess 1905-1945. .... TCLC 10
See also CA 107

Slessor, Kenneth 1901-1971. .... CLC 14
See also CA 102
See also obituary CA 89-92

Smith, A(rthur) J(ames) M(arshall)
1902-1980. .... CLC 15
See also CANR 4
See also CA 1-4R
See also obituary CA 102

Smith, Betty (Wehner)
1896-1972. .... CLC 19
See also CA 5-8R
See also obituary CA 33-36R
See also SATA 6
See also DLB-Y 82

Smith, Dave 1942- .... CLC 22
See also Smith, David (Jeddie)
See also DLB 5

Smith, David (Jeddie) 1942-
See Smith, Dave
See also CANR 1
See also CA 49-52

Smith, Florence Margaret 1902-1971
See Smith, Stevie
See also CAP 2
See also CA 17-18
See also obituary CA 29-32R

Smith, Lee 1944- .... CLC 25

Smith, Martin Cruz 1942- .... CLC 25
See also CANR 6
See also CA 85-88

Smith, Martin William 1942-
See Smith, Martin Cruz

Smith, Patti 1946- .... CLC 12
See also CA 93-96

Smith, Sara Mahala Redway 1900-1972
See Benson, Sally

Smith, Stevie 1902-1971 ...... CLC 3, 8, 25
See also Smith, Florence Margaret
See also DLB 20

Smith, William Jay 1918- .... CLC 6
See also CA 5-8R
See also SATA 2
See also DLB 5

Snodgrass, W(illiam) D(e Witt)
1926- .... CLC 2, 6, 10, 18
See also CANR 6
See also CA 1-4R
See also DLB 5

Snow, C(harles) P(ercy)
1905-1980. ...... CLC 1, 4, 6, 9, 13, 19
See also CA 5-8R
See also obituary CA 101
See also DLB 15

Snyder, Gary 1930- .... CLC 1, 2, 5, 9
See also CA 17-20R
See also DLB 5, 16

Snyder, Zilpha Keatley 1927- ...... CLC 17
See also CA 9-12R
See also SATA 1, 28

Sokolov, Raymond 1941- .... CLC 7
See also CA 85-88

Sologub, Fyodor 1863-1927. ...... TCLC 9
See also CA 104

Solwoska, Mara 1929-
See French, Marilyn

Solzhenitsyn, Aleksandr I(sayevich)
1918- .... CLC 1, 2, 4, 7, 9, 10, 18, 26
See also CA 69-72
See also AITN 1

Sommer, Scott 1951- .... CLC 25
See also CA 106

Sontag, Susan 1933- ...... CLC 1, 2, 10, 13
See also CA 17-20R
See also DLB 2

Sorrentino, Gilbert
1929- .... CLC 3, 7, 14, 22
See also CA 77-80
See also DLB 5
See also DLB-Y 80

Souster, (Holmes) Raymond
1921- .... CLC 5, 14
See also CA 13-16R

Southern, Terry 1926- .... CLC 7
See also CANR 1
See also CA 1-4R
See also DLB 2

Soyinka, Wole 1934- .... CLC 3, 5, 14
See also CA 13-16R

Spacks, Barry 1931- .... CLC 14
See also CA 29-32R

Spark, Muriel (Sarah)
1918- .... CLC 2, 3, 5, 8, 13, 18
See also CA 5-8R
See also DLB 15

Spencer, Elizabeth 1921- .... CLC 22
See also CA 13-16R
See also SATA 14
See also DLB 6

Spender, Stephen (Harold)
1909- .... CLC 1, 2, 5, 10
See also CA 9-12R
See also DLB 20

Spicer, Jack 1925-1965. .... CLC 8, 18
See also CA 85-88
See also DLB 5, 16

Spielberg, Peter 1929- .... CLC 6
See also CANR 4
See also CA 5-8R
See also DLB-Y 81

Spielberg, Steven 1947- .... CLC 20
See also CA 77-80
See also SATA 32

Spillane, Frank Morrison 1918-
See Spillane, Mickey
See also CA 25-28R

Spillane, Mickey 1918- .... CLC 3, 13
See also Spillane, Frank Morrison

Spivack, Kathleen (Romola Drucker)
1938- .... CLC 6
See also CA 49-52

Springsteen, Bruce 1949- .... CLC 17

Staël-Holstein, Anne Louise Germaine Necker, Baronne de
1766-1817. .... NCLC 3

Stafford, Jean 1915-1979 ..... CLC 4, 7, 19
See also CANR 3
See also CA 1-4R
See also obituary CA 85-88
See also obituary SATA 22
See also DLB 2

Stafford, William (Edgar)
1914- .... CLC 4, 7
See also CANR 5
See also CA 5-8R
See also DLB 5

Stanton, Maura 1946- .... CLC 9
See also CA 89-92

Stead, Christina (Ellen)
1902- .... CLC 2, 5, 8
See also CA 13-16R

Stegner, Wallace (Earle) 1909- ..... CLC 9
See also CANR 1
See also CA 1-4R
See also DLB 9
See also AITN 1

Stein, Gertrude 1874-1946 ...... TCLC 1, 6
See also CA 104
See also DLB 4

Steinbeck, John (Ernst)
1902-1968 .... CLC 1, 5, 9, 13, 21
See also CANR 1
See also CA 1-4R
See also obituary CA 25-28R
See also SATA 9
See also DLB 7, 9
See also DLB-DS 2

Steiner, George 1929- .... CLC 24
See also CA 73-76

Stephens, James 1882?-1950 ...... TCLC 4
See also CA 104
See also DLB 19

Stern, Richard G(ustave) 1928- ...... CLC 4
See also CANR 1
See also CA 1-4R

Sternberg, Jonas 1894-1969
See Sternberg, Josef von

Sternberg, Josef von
1894-1969 .... CLC 20
See also CA 81-84

Sternheim, (William Adolf) Carl
1878-1942 .... TCLC 8
See also CA 105

Stevens, Wallace
1879-1955 .... TCLC 3, 12
See also CA 104

Stevenson, Anne (Katharine)
1933- .... CLC 7
See also Elvin, Anne Katharine Stevenson
See also CANR 9

Stevenson, Robert Louis
1850-1894 .... NCLC 5
See also YABC 2
See also DLB 18

Stewart, J(ohn) I(nnes) M(ackintosh)
1906- .... CLC 7, 14
See also CA 85-88

Stewart, Mary (Florence Elinor)
1916- .... CLC 7
See also CANR 1
See also CA 1-4R
See also SATA 12

Sting 1951-
See The Police

Stoker, Bram (Abraham)
1847-1912 .... TCLC 8
See also CA 105
See also SATA 29

Stolz, Mary (Slattery) 1920- .... CLC 12
See also CA 5-8R
See also SATA 10
See also AITN 1

Stone, Irving 1903- .... CLC 7
See also CANR 1
See also CA 1-4R
See also SATA 3
See also AITN 1

Stone, Robert 1937?- .... CLC 5, 23
See also CA 85-88

Stoppard, Tom
1937- .... CLC 1, 3, 4, 5, 8, 15
See also CA 81-84
See also DLB 13

Storey, David (Malcolm)
1933- .... CLC 2, 4, 5, 8
See also CA 81-84
See also DLB 13, 14

Storm, Hyemeyohsts 1935- .... CLC 3
See also CA 81-84

Storm, (Hans) Theodor (Woldsen)
1817-1888 .... NCLC 1

Storni, Alfonsina 1892-1938 ...... TCLC 5
See also CA 104

Stout, Rex (Todhunter)
1886-1975 .... CLC 3
See also CA 61-64
See also AITN 2

Stow, (Julian) Randolph 1935- ..... CLC 23
See also CA 13-16R

Stowe, Harriet (Elizabeth) Beecher
1811-1896 .... NCLC 3
See also YABC 1
See also DLB 1, 12

Strachey, (Giles) Lytton
1880-1932 .... TCLC 12

Strand, Mark 1934- .... CLC 6, 18
See also CA 21-24R
See also DLB 5

Straub, Peter (Francis) 1943- ...... CLC 28
See also CA 85-88

Strauss, Botho 1944- .... CLC 22

Streatfeild, Noel 1897- .... CLC 21
See also CA 81-84
See also SATA 20

Stribling, T(homas) S(igismund)
1881-1965 .... CLC 23
See also obituary CA 107
See also DLB 9

Strindberg, (Johan) August
1849-1912 .... TCLC 1, 8
See also CA 104

Strugatskii, Arkadii (Natanovich) 1925-
See Strugatskii, Arkadii (Natanovich) and
Strugatskii, Boris (Natanovich)
See also CA 106

Strugatskii, Arkadii (Natanovich) 1925-
and **Strugatskii, Boris (Natanovich)**
1933- .... CLC 27

Strugatskii, Boris (Natanovich) 1933-
See Strugatskii, Arkadii (Natanovich) and
Strugatskii, Boris (Natanovich)
See also CA 106

Strugatskii, Boris (Natanovich) 1933- and
Strugatskii, Arkadii (Natanovich) 1925-
See Strugatskii, Arkadii (Natanovich) and
Strugatskii, Boris (Natanovich)

Stuart, (Hilton) Jesse
1907- .... CLC 1, 8, 11, 14
See also CA 5-8R
See also SATA 2
See also DLB 9

Sturgeon, Theodore (Hamilton)
1918- .... CLC 22
See also CA 81-84
See also DLB 8

Styron, William
1925- .... CLC 1, 3, 5, 11, 15
See also CANR 6
See also CA 5-8R
See also DLB 2
See also DLB-Y 80

Sue, Eugène 1804-1857 .... NCLC 1

Sukenick, Ronald 1932- ...... CLC 3, 4, 6
See also CA 25-28R
See also DLB-Y 81

Suknaski, Andrew 1942- .... CLC 19
See also CA 101

Summers, Andrew James 1942-
See The Police

Summers, Andy 1942-
See The Police

Summers, Hollis (Spurgeon, Jr.)
1916- .... CLC 10
See also CANR 3
See also CA 5-8R
See also DLB 6

Sumner, Gordon Matthew 1951-
See The Police

Susann, Jacqueline 1921-1974 .... CLC 3
See also CA 65-68
See also obituary CA 53-56
See also AITN 1

Sutcliff, Rosemary 1920- .... CLC 26
See also CLR 1
See also CA 5-8R
See also SATA 6

Sutro, Alfred 1863-1933 .... TCLC 6
See also CA 105
See also DLB 10

Sutton, Henry 1935-
See Slavitt, David (R.)

Svevo, Italo 1861-1928 .... TCLC 2
See also CA 104

Swados, Elizabeth 1951- .... CLC 12
See also CA 97-100

Swados, Harvey 1920-1972 .... CLC 5
See also CANR 6
See also CA 5-8R
See also obituary CA 37-40R
See also DLB 2

Swenson, May 1919- .... CLC 4, 14
See also CA 5-8R
See also SATA 15
See also DLB 5

Swift, Jonathan 1667-1745 .... LC 1
See also SATA 19

Swinburne, Algernon Charles
1837-1909 .... TCLC 8
See also CA 105

Symons, Arthur (William)
1865-1945.................. **TCLC 11**
See also CA 107
See also DLB 19

Symons, Julian (Gustave)
1912-..................... **CLC 2, 14**
See also CANR 3
See also CA 49-52

Synge, (Edmund) John Millington
1871-1909.................. **TCLC 6**
See also CA 104
See also DLB 10, 19

Tabori, George 1914- .... **CLC 19**
See also CANR 4
See also CA 49-52

Tagore, (Sir) Rabindranath
1861-1941.................... **TCLC 3**
See also CA 104

Tamayo y Baus, Manuel
1829-1898................... **NCLC 1**

Tanizaki, Jun'ichirō
1886-1965......... **CLC 8, 14, 28**
See also CA 93-96
See also obituary CA 25-28R

Tarkington, (Newton) Booth
1869-1946.................... **TCLC 9**
See also SATA 17
See also DLB 9

Tate, (John Orley) Allen
1899-1979...... **CLC 2, 4, 6, 9, 11, 14, 24**
See also CA 5-8R
See also obituary CA 85-88
See also DLB 4

Tate, James 1943- .... **CLC 2, 6, 25**
See also CA 21-24R
See also DLB 5

Tavel, Ronald 1940- .... **CLC 6**
See also CA 21-24R

Taylor, C(ecil) P(hillip)
1929-1981................... **CLC 27**
See also CA 25-28R
See also obituary CA 105

Taylor, Eleanor Ross 1920- .... **CLC 5**
See also CA 81-84

Taylor, Elizabeth 1912-1975 ..... **CLC 2, 4**
See also CANR 9
See also CA 13-16R
See also SATA 13

Taylor, Kamala (Purnaiya) 1924-
See Markandaya, Kamala (Purnaiya)
See also CA 77-80

Taylor, Mildred D(elois) .... **CLC 21**
See also CA 85-88
See also SATA 15

Taylor, Peter (Hillsman)
1917-..................... **CLC 1, 4, 18**
See also CANR 9
See also CA 13-16R
See also DLB-Y 81

Taylor, Robert Lewis 1912- .... **CLC 14**
See also CANR 3
See also CA 1-4R
See also SATA 10

Teasdale, Sara 1884-1933........ **TCLC 4**
See also CA 104
See also SATA 32

Tegnér, Esaias 1782-1846........ **NCLC 2**

Teilhard de Chardin, (Marie Joseph) Pierre
1881-1955.................. **TCLC 9**
See also CA 105

Tennant, Emma 1937- .... **CLC 13**
See also CANR 10
See also CA 65-68
See also DLB 14

Terry, Megan 1932- .... **CLC 19**
See also CA 77-80
See also DLB 7

Tertz, Abram 1925-
See Sinyavsky, Andrei (Donatevich)

Thackeray, William Makepeace
1811-1863.................. **NCLC 5**
See also SATA 23
See also DLB 21

Thelwell, Michael (Miles)
1939-..................... **CLC 22**
See also CA 101

Theroux, Alexander (Louis)
1939-..................... **CLC 2, 25**
See also CA 85-88

Theroux, Paul
1941- .... **CLC 5, 8, 11, 15, 28**
See also CA 33-36R
See also DLB 2

Thiele, Colin (Milton) 1920-....... **CLC 17**
See also CA 29-32R
See also SATA 14

Thomas, Audrey (Callahan)
1935-..................... **CLC 7, 13**
See also CA 21-24R
See also AITN 2

Thomas, D(onald) M(ichael)
1935-..................... **CLC 13, 22**
See also CA 61-64

Thomas, Dylan 1914-1953 ..... **TCLC 1, 8**
See also CA 104
See also DLB 13, 20

Thomas, Edward (Philip)
1878-1917.................. **TCLC 10**
See also CA 106
See also DLB 19

Thomas, John Peter 1928-
See Thomas, Piri

Thomas, Piri 1928- .... **CLC 17**
See also CA 73-76

Thomas, R(onald) S(tuart)
1913-..................... **CLC 6, 13**
See also CA 89-92

Thompson, Francis (Joseph)
1859-1907................... **TCLC 4**
See also CA 104
See also DLB 19

Thompson, Hunter S(tockton)
1939-..................... **CLC 9, 17**
See also CA 17-20R

Thurber, James (Grover)
1894-1961................. **CLC 5, 11, 25**
See also CA 73-76
See also SATA 13
See also DLB 4, 11, 22

Thurman, Wallace 1902-1934 ..... **TCLC 6**
See also CA 104

Tieck, (Johann) Ludwig
1773-1853................... **NCLC 5**

Tindall, Gillian 1938- .... **CLC 7**
See also CANR 11
See also CA 21-24R

Tolkien, J(ohn) R(onald) R(euel)
1892-1973......... **CLC 1, 2, 3, 8, 12**
See also CAP 2
See also CA 17-18
See also obituary CA 45-48
See also SATA 2, 32
See also obituary SATA 24
See also DLB 15
See also AITN 1

Toller, Ernst 1893-1939 .... **TCLC 10**
See also CA 107

Tolstoy, (Count) Leo (Lev Nikolaevich)
1828-1910.............. **TCLC 4, 11**
See also CA 104
See also SATA 26

Tomlin, Lily 1939-................ **CLC 17**

Tomlin, Mary Jean 1939-
See Tomlin, Lily

Tomlinson, (Alfred) Charles
1927-................. **CLC 2, 4, 6, 13**
See also CA 5-8R

Toole, John Kennedy
1937-1969................... **CLC 19**
See also CA 104
See also DLB-Y 81

Toomer, Jean
1894-1967........... **CLC 1, 4, 13, 22**
See also CA 85-88

Tournier, Michel 1924- .... **CLC 6, 23**
See also CANR 3
See also CA 49-52
See also SATA 23

Townshend, Peter (Dennis Blandford)
1945-..................... **CLC 17**
See also CA 107

Trakl, Georg 1887-1914 .... **TCLC 5**
See also CA 104

Traven, B. 1890-1969 .... **CLC 8, 11**
See also CAP 2
See also CA 19-20
See also obituary CA 25-28R
See also DLB 9

Trevor, William
1928-................. **CLC 7, 9, 14, 25**
See also Cox, William Trevor
See also DLB 14

Trilling, Lionel
1905-1975............. **CLC 9, 11, 24**
See also CANR 10
See also CA 9-12R
See also obituary CA 61-64

Trollope, Anthony 1815-1882 ..... **NCLC 6**
See also SATA 22
See also DLB 21

Troyat, Henri 1911- .... **CLC 23**
See also CANR 2
See also CA 45-48

Trudeau, G(arretson) B(eekman) 1948-
See Trudeau, Garry
See also CA 81-84

Trudeau, Garry 1948-............CLC 12
See also Trudeau, G(arretson) B(eekman)
See also AITN 2

Truffaut, François 1932-..........CLC 20
See also CA 81-84

Trumbo, Dalton 1905-1976........CLC 19
See also CANR 10
See also CA 21-24R
See also obituary CA 69-72
See also DLB 26

Tryon, Thomas 1926-..........CLC 3, 11
See also CA 29-32R
See also AITN 1

Ts'ao Hsüeh-ch'in 1715?-1763........LC 1

Tshushima Shūji 1909-1948
See Dazai Osamu
See also CA 107

Tunis, John R(oberts)
1889-1975.................CLC 12
See also CA 61-64
See also SATA 30
See also DLB 22

Turco, Lewis (Putnam) 1934-......CLC 11
See also CA 13-16R

Tutuola, Amos 1920-..........CLC 5, 14
See also CA 9-12R

Twain, Mark 1835-1910.......TCLC 6, 12
See also Clemens, Samuel Langhorne

Tyler, Anne 1941-.......CLC 7, 11, 18, 28
See also CANR 11
See also CA 9-12R
See also SATA 7
See also DLB 6
See also DLB-Y 82

Tyler, Royall 1757-1826..........NCLC 3

Tynan (Hinkson), Katharine
1861-1931..................TCLC 3
See also CA 104

Unamuno (y Jugo), Miguel de
1864-1936.................TCLC 2, 9
See also CA 104

Underwood, Miles 1909-1981
See Glassco, John

Undset, Sigrid 1882-1949.........TCLC 3
See also CA 104

Ungaretti, Giuseppe
1888-1970..............CLC 7, 11, 15
See also CAP 2
See also CA 19-20
See also obituary CA 25-28R

Updike, John (Hoyer)
1932-......CLC 1, 2, 3, 5, 7, 9, 13, 15,
                                         23
See also CANR 4
See also CA 1-4R
See also DLB 2, 5
See also DLB-Y 80, 82
See also DLB-DS 3

Uris, Leon (Marcus) 1924-..........CLC 7
See also CANR 1
See also CA 1-4R
See also AITN 1, 2

Ustinov, Peter (Alexander)
1921-........................CLC 1
See also CA 13-16R
See also DLB 13
See also AITN 1

Vaculík, Ludvík 1926-............CLC 7
See also CA 53-56

Valera (y Acalá-Galiano) Juan
1824-1905.................TCLC 10
See also CA 106

Valéry, Paul (Ambroise Toussaint Jules)
1871-1945..................TCLC 4
See also CA 104

**Valle-Inclán (y Montenegro), Ramón (María)
del** 1866-1936..............TCLC 5
See also CA 106

Vallejo, César (Abraham)
1892-1938..................TCLC 3
See also CA 105

**Van Den Bogarde, Derek (Jules Gaspard
Ulric) Niven** 1921-
See Bogarde, Dirk
See also CA 77-80

Van der Post, Laurens (Jan)
1906-........................CLC 5
See also CA 5-8R

Van Doren, Mark
1894-1972................ CLC 6, 10
See also CANR 3
See also CA 1-4R
See also obituary CA 37-40R

Van Druten, John (William)
1901-1957..................TCLC 2
See also CA 104
See also DLB 10

Van Duyn, Mona 1921-.........CLC 3, 7
See also CANR 7
See also CA 9-12R
See also DLB 5

Van Itallie, Jean-Claude 1936-......CLC 3
See also CANR 1
See also CA 45-48
See also DLB 7

Van Peebles, Melvin 1932-......CLC 2, 20
See also CA 85-88

Van Vogt, A(lfred) E(lton)
1912-........................CLC 1
See also CA 21-24R
See also SATA 14
See also DLB 8

Varda, Agnès 1928-.............CLC 16

Vargas Llosa, (Jorge) Mario (Pedro)
1936-............ CLC 3, 6, 9, 10, 15
See also CA 73-76

Vassilikos, Vassilis 1933-........CLC 4, 8
See also CA 81-84

Verga, Giovanni 1840-1922......TCLC 3
See also CA 104

Verhaeren, Émile (Adolphe Gustave)
1855-1916.................TCLC 12
See also CA 109

Verlaine, Paul (Marie)
1844-1896..................NCLC 2

Verne, Jules (Gabriel)
1828-1905..................TCLC 6
See also SATA 21

Vian, Boris 1920-1959 ....TCLC 9
See also CA 106

Viaud, (Louis Marie) Julien 1850-1923
See Loti, Pierre
See also CA 107

Vicker, Angus 1916-
See Felsen, Henry Gregor

Vidal, Gore
1925-........CLC 2, 4, 6, 8, 10, 22
See also CA 5-8R
See also DLB 6
See also AITN 1

Viereck, Peter (Robert Edwin)
1916-........................CLC 4
See also CANR 1
See also CA 1-4R
See also DLB 5

**Villiers de l'Isle Adam, Jean Marie Mathias
Philippe Auguste, Comte de,**
1838-1889..................NCLC 3

Visconti, Luchino 1906-1976......CLC 16
See also CA 81-84
See also obituary CA 65-68

Vittorini, Elio 1908-1966.....CLC 6, 9, 14
See also obituary CA 25-28R

Vliet, R(ussell) G. 1929-............CLC 22
See also CA 37-40R

Voinovich, Vladimir (Nikolaevich)
1932-........................CLC 10
See also CA 81-84

Vonnegut, Kurt, Jr.
1922-...... CLC 1, 2, 3, 4, 5, 8, 12, 22
See also CANR 1
See also CA 1-4R
See also DLB 2, 8
See also DLB-Y 80
See also DLB-DS 3
See also AITN 1

Voznesensky, Andrei 1933-...... CLC 1, 15
See also CA 89-92

Waddington, Miriam 1917-........CLC 28
See also CA 21-24R

Wagman, Fredrica 1937-..........CLC 7
See also CA 97-100

Wagoner, David (Russell)
1926-................... CLC 3, 5, 15
See also CANR 2
See also CA 1-4R
See also SATA 14
See also DLB 5

Wahlöö, Per 1926-1975...........CLC 7
See also CA 61-64

Wain, John (Barrington)
1925-................CLC 2, 11, 15
See also CA 5-8R
See also DLB 15

Wajda, Andrzej 1926-.............CLC 16
See also CA 102

Wakefield, Dan 1932-..............CLC 7
See also CA 21-24R

Wakoski, Diane
1937-............ CLC 2, 4, 7, 9, 11
See also CANR 9
See also CA 13-16R
See also DLB 5

Walcott, Derek (Alton)
1930-............ CLC 2, 4, 9, 14, 25
See also CA 89-92
See also DLB-Y 81

Waldman, Anne 1945-.............CLC 7
See also CA 37-40R
See also DLB 16

Waldo, Edward Hamilton 1918-
See Sturgeon, Theodore (Hamilton)

Walker, Alice
1944-............ CLC 5, 6, 9, 19, 27
See also CANR 9
See also CA 37-40R
See also SATA 31
See also DLB 6

Walker, David Harry 1911-........CLC 14
See also CANR 1
See also CA 1-4R
See also SATA 8

Walker, Joseph A. 1935- ....CLC 19
See also CA 89-92

Walker, Margaret (Abigail)
1915-..................... CLC 1, 6
See also CA 73-76

Walker, Ted 1934-.................CLC 13
See also CA 21-24R

Wallace, Irving 1916-.......... CLC 7, 13
See also CANR 1
See also CA 1-4R
See also AITN 1

Wallant, Edward Lewis
1926-1962................. CLC 5, 10
See also CA 1-4R
See also DLB 2

Walpole, (Sir) Hugh (Seymour)
1884-1941................. TCLC 5
See also CA 104

Walser, Martin 1927-..............CLC 27
See also CANR 8
See also CA 57-60

Wambaugh, Joseph (Aloysius, Jr.)
1937-........................ CLC 3, 18
See also CA 33-36R
See also DLB 6
See also AITN 1

Ward, Douglas Turner 1930-........CLC 19
See also CA 81-84
See also DLB 7

Warhol, Andy 1928- ....CLC 20
See also CA 89-92

Warner, Francis (Robert le Plastrier)
1937-........................CLC 14
See also CANR 11
See also CA 53-56

Warner, Sylvia Townsend
1893-1978.................. CLC 7, 19
See also CA 61-64
See also obituary CA 77-80

Warren, Robert Penn
1905-........CLC 1, 4, 6, 8, 10, 13, 18
See also CANR 10
See also CA 13-16R
See also DLB 2
See also DLB-Y 80
See also AITN 1

Washington, Booker T(aliaferro)
1856-1915................... TCLC 10
See also SATA 28

Wassermann, Jakob
1873-1934................... TCLC 6
See also CA 104

Wa Thiong'o, Ngugi 1938-.........CLC 13
See Ngugi, James (Thiong'o)

Waugh, Auberon (Alexander)
1939-......................CLC 7
See also CANR 6
See also CA 45-48
See also DLB 14

Waugh, Evelyn (Arthur St. John)
1903-1966...... CLC 1, 3, 8, 13, 19, 27
See also CA 85-88
See also obituary CA 25-28R
See also DLB 15

Waugh, Harriet 1944-...............CLC 6
See also CA 85-88

Webb, Charles (Richard) 1939-......CLC 7
See also CA 25-28R

Webb, James H(enry), Jr.
1946-......................CLC 22
See also CA 81-84

Webb, Phyllis 1927- ....CLC 18
See also CA 104

Webber, Andrew Lloyd 1948-
See Rice, Tim and Webber, Andrew Lloyd

Weber, Lenora Mattingly
1895-1971....................CLC 12
See also CAP 1
See also CA 19-20
See also obituary CA 29-32R
See also SATA 2
See also obituary SATA 26

Wedekind, (Benjamin) Frank(lin)
1864-1918.................. TCLC 7
See also CA 104

Weidman, Jerome 1913-............CLC 7
See also CANR 1
See also CA 1-4R
See also AITN 2

Weir, Peter 1944- ....CLC 20

Weiss, Peter (Ulrich)
1916-1982................. CLC 3, 15
See also CANR 3
See also CA 45-48
See also obituary CA 106

Weiss, Theodore (Russell)
1916-................... CLC 3, 8, 14
See also CA 9-12R
See also DLB 5

Welch, James 1940-........... CLC 6, 14
See also CA 85-88

Weldon, Fay 1933- ....CLC 6, 9, 11, 19
See also CA 21-24R
See also DLB 14

Wellek, René 1903-................CLC 28
See also CANR 8
See also CA 5-8R

Weller, Michael 1942-..............CLC 10
See also CA 85-88

Weller, Paul 1958-.................CLC 26

Welles, (George) Orson 1915-......CLC 20
See also CA 93-96

Wells, H(erbert) G(eorge)
1866-1946.................TCLC 6, 12
See also SATA 20

Wells, Rosemary...................CLC 12
See also CA 85-88
See also SATA 18

Welty, Eudora
1909-........... CLC 1, 2, 5, 14, 22
See also CA 9-12R
See also DLB 2

Werfel, Franz (V.) 1890-1945..... TCLC 8
See also CA 104

Wergeland, Henrik Arnold
1808-1845................. NCLC 5

Wertmüller, Lina 1928-...........CLC 16
See also CA 97-100

Wescott, Glenway 1901-..........CLC 13
See also CA 13-16R
See also DLB 4, 9

Wesker, Arnold 1932-........... CLC 3, 5
See also CANR 1
See also CA 1-4R
See also DLB 13

Wesley, Richard (Errol) 1945-.......CLC 7
See also CA 57-60

West, Jessamyn 1907-......... CLC 7, 17
See also CA 9-12R
See also DLB 6

West, Morris L(anglo) 1916-........CLC 6
See also CA 5-8R

West, Nathanael 1903?-1940 ..... TCLC 1
See also CA 104
See also DLB 4, 9

West, Paul 1930-................ CLC 7, 14
See also CA 13-16R
See also DLB 14

West, Rebecca 1892-............ CLC 7, 9
See also CA 109
See also CA 5-8R

Westall, Robert (Atkinson)
1929-......................CLC 17
See also CA 69-72
See also SATA 23

Westlake, Donald E(dwin)
1933-......................CLC 7
See also CA 17-20R

Whalen, Philip 1923-...............CLC 6
See also CANR 5
See also CA 9-12R
See also DLB 16

Wharton, Edith (Newbold Jones)
1862-1937................. TCLC 3, 9
See also CA 104
See also DLB 4, 9, 12

Wharton, William 1925-...........CLC 18
See also CA 93-96
See also DLB-Y 80

Wheelock, John Hall
1886-1978..................CLC 14
See also CA 13-16R
See also obituary CA 77-80

White, Edmund III 1940-..........CLC 27
See also CANR 3
See also CA 45-48

White, E(lwyn) B(rooks) 1899- .....CLC 10
See also CLR 1
See also CA 13-16R
See also SATA 2, 29
See also DLB 11, 22
See also AITN 2

White, Patrick (Victor Martindale)
1912-............ CLC 3, 4, 5, 7, 9, 18
See also CA 81-84

Whitehead, E(dward) A(nthony)
1933- .... CLC 5
See also CA 65-68

Whitman, Walt 1819-1892 .... NCLC 4
See also SATA 20
See also DLB 3

Whittemore, (Edward) Reed (Jr.)
1919- .... CLC 4
See also CANR 4
See also CA 9-12R
See also DLB 5

Wicker, Thomas Grey 1926-
See Wicker, Tom
See also CA 65-68

Wicker, Tom 1926- .... CLC 7
See also Wicker, Thomas Grey

Wideman, J(ohn) E(dgar) 1941- .... CLC 5
See also CA 85-88

Wiebe, Rudy (H.) 1934- ..... CLC 6, 11, 14
See also CA 37-40R

Wieners, John 1934- .... CLC 7
See also CA 13-16R
See also DLB 16

Wiesel, Elie(zer) 1928- .... CLC 3, 5, 11
See also CANR 8
See also CA 5-8R
See also AITN 1

Wight, James Alfred 1916-
See Herriot, James
See also CA 77-80

Wilbur, Richard (Purdy)
1921- .... CLC 3, 6, 9, 14
See also CANR 2
See also CA 1-4R
See also SATA 9
See also DLB 5

Wild, Peter 1940- .... CLC 14
See also CA 37-40R
See also DLB 5

Wilde, Oscar (Fingal O'Flahertie Wills)
1855-1900 .... TCLC 1, 8
See also CA 104
See also DLB 10, 19

Wilder, Billy 1906- .... CLC 20
See also Wilder, Samuel
See also DLB 26

Wilder, Samuel 1906-
See Wilder, Billy
See also CA 89-92

Wilder, Thornton (Niven)
1897-1975 .... CLC 1, 5, 6, 10, 15
See also CA 13-16R
See also obituary CA 61-64
See also DLB 4, 7, 9
See also AITN 2

Wilhelm, Kate 1928- .... CLC 7
See also CA 37-40R
See also DLB 8

Willard, Nancy 1936- .... CLC 7
See also CLR 5
See also CANR 10
See also CA 89-92
See also SATA 30
See also DLB 5

Williams, Charles (Walter Stansby)
1886-1945 .... TCLC 1, 11
See also CA 104

Williams, (George) Emlyn
1905- .... CLC 15
See also CA 104
See also DLB 10

Williams, John A(lfred)
1925- .... CLC 5, 13
See also CANR 6
See also CA 53-56
See also DLB 2

Williams, Jonathan (Chamberlain)
1929- .... CLC 13
See also CANR 8
See also CA 9-12R
See also DLB 5

Williams, Paulette 1948-
See Shange, Ntozake

Williams, Tennessee
1914-1983 .... CLC 1, 2, 5, 7, 8, 11,
15, 19
See also CA 5-8R
See also obituary CA 108
See also DLB 7
See also DLB-DS 4
See also AITN 1, 2

Williams, Thomas (Alonzo)
1926- .... CLC 14
See also CANR 2
See also CA 1-4R

Williams, William Carlos
1883-1963 .... CLC 1, 2, 5, 9, 13, 22
See also CA 89-92
See also DLB 4, 16

Willingham, Calder (Baynard, Jr.)
1922- .... CLC 5
See also CANR 3
See also CA 5-8R
See also DLB 2

Wilson, Angus (Frank Johnstone)
1913- .... CLC 2, 3, 5, 25
See also CA 5-8R
See also DLB 15

Wilson, Brian 1942- .... CLC 12

Wilson, Colin 1931- .... CLC 3, 14
See also CANR 1
See also CA 1-4R
See also DLB 14

Wilson, Edmund
1895-1972 .... CLC 1, 2, 3, 8, 24
See also CANR 1
See also CA 1-4R
See also obituary CA 37-40R

Wilson, Ethel Davis (Bryant)
1888-1980 .... CLC 13
See also CA 102

Wilson, John 1785-1854 .... NCLC 5

Wilson, John (Anthony) Burgess 1917-
See Burgess, Anthony
See also CANR 2
See also CA 1-4R

Wilson, Lanford 1937- .... CLC 7, 14
See also CA 17-20R
See also DLB 7

Wilson, Robert (M.) 1944- .... CLC 7, 9
See also CANR 2
See also CA 49-52

Winters, (Arthur) Yvor
1900-1968 .... CLC 4, 8
See also CAP 1
See also CA 11-12
See also obituary CA 25-28R

Wiseman, Frederick 1930- .... CLC 20

Witkiewicz, Stanislaw Ignacy
1885-1939 .... TCLC 8
See also CA 105

Wittig, Monique 1935?- .... CLC 22

Wittlin, Joseph 1896-1976 .... CLC 25
See also Wittlin, Józef

Wittlin, Józef 1896-1976
See Wittlin, Joseph
See also CANR 3
See also CA 49-52
See also obituary CA 65-68

Wodehouse, P(elham) G(renville)
1881-1975 .... CLC 1, 2, 5, 10, 22
See also CANR 3
See also CA 45-48
See also obituary CA 57-60
See also SATA 22
See also AITN 2

Woiwode, Larry (Alfred)
1941- .... CLC 6, 10
See also CA 73-76
See also DLB 6

Wojciechowska, Maia (Teresa)
1927- .... CLC 26
See also CLR 1
See also CANR 4
See also CA 9-12R
See also SATA 1, 28

Wolf, Christa 1929- .... CLC 14
See also CA 85-88

Wolfe, Gene (Rodman) 1931- ..... CLC 25
See also CANR 6
See also CA 57-60
See also DLB 8

Wolfe, Thomas (Clayton)
1900-1938 .... TCLC 4
See also CA 104
See also DLB 9
See also DLB-DS 2

Wolfe, Thomas Kennerly, Jr. 1931-
See Wolfe, Tom
See also CANR 9
See also CA 13-16R

Wolfe, Tom 1931- .... CLC 1, 2, 9, 15
See also Wolfe, Thomas Kennerly, Jr.
See also AITN 2

Wolitzer, Hilma 1930- .... CLC 17
See also CA 65-68
See also SATA 31

Wonder, Stevie 1950- .... CLC 12

Wong, Jade Snow 1922- .... CLC 17
See also CA 109

Woodcott, Keith 1934-
See Brunner, John (Kilian Houston)

Woolf, (Adeline) Virginia
1882-1941 .... TCLC 1, 5
See also CA 104

Woollcott, Alexander (Humphreys)
1887-1943 .... TCLC 5
See also CA 105

Wouk, Herman 1915- .... **CLC 1, 9**
See also CANR 6
See also CA 5-8R
See also DLB-Y 82

Wright, Charles 1935- ...... **CLC 6, 13, 28**
See also CA 29-32R
See also DLB-Y 82

Wright, James (Arlington)
1927-1980............ **CLC 3, 5, 10, 28**
See also CANR 4
See also CA 49-52
See also obituary CA 97-100
See also DLB 5
See also AITN 2

Wright, Judith 1915- .... **CLC 11**
See also CA 13-16R
See also SATA 14

Wright, Richard (Nathaniel)
1908-1960....... **CLC 1, 3, 4, 9, 14, 21**
See also CA 108
See also DLB-DS 2

Wright, Richard B(ruce) 1937- ...... **CLC 6**
See also CA 85-88

Wurlitzer, Rudolph
1938?- .... **CLC 2, 4, 15**
See also CA 85-88

Wylie (Benét), Elinor (Morton Hoyt)
1885-1928................... **TCLC 8**
See also CA 105
See also DLB 9

Wyndham, John 1903-1969 .... **CLC 19**
See also Harris, John (Wyndham Parkes
Lucas) Beynon

Yanovsky, Vassily S(emenovich)
1906- .... **CLC 2, 18**
See also CA 97-100

Yates, Richard 1926- .... **CLC 7, 8, 23**
See also CANR 10
See also CA 5-8R
See also DLB 2
See also DLB-Y 81

Yeats, William Butler
1865-1939................ **TCLC 1, 11**
See also CANR 10
See also CA 104
See also DLB 10, 19

Yehoshua, Abraham B. 1936- ...... **CLC 13**
See also CA 33-36R

Yerby, Frank G(arvin)
1916- .... **CLC 1, 7, 22**
See also CA 9-12R

Yevtushenko, Yevgeny (Aleksandrovich)
1933- .... **CLC 1, 3, 13, 26**
See also CA 81-84

Yglesias, Helen 1915- .... **CLC 7, 22**
See also CA 37-40R

Yorke, Henry Vincent 1905-1974
See Green, Henry
See also CA 85-88
See also obituary CA 49-52

Young, Al 1939- .... **CLC 19**
See also CA 29-32R

Young, Andrew 1885-1971......... **CLC 5**
See also CANR 7
See also CA 5-8R

Young, Neil 1945- .... **CLC 17**

Yourcenar, Marguerite 1913- ...... **CLC 19**
See also CA 69-72

Yurick, Sol 1925- .... **CLC 6**
See also CA 13-16R

Zamyatin, Yevgeny Ivanovich
1884-1937.................... **TCLC 8**
See also CA 105

Zappa, Francis Vincent, Jr. 1940-
See Zappa, Frank
See also CA 108

Zappa, Frank 1940- .... **CLC 17**
See also Zappa, Francis Vincent, Jr.

Zaturenska, Marya
1902-1982................. **CLC 6, 11**
See also CA 13-16R
See also obituary CA 105

Zelazny, Roger 1937- .... **CLC 21**
See also CA 21-24R
See also DLB 8

Zimmerman, Robert 1941-
See Dylan, Bob

Zindel, Paul 1936- .... **CLC 6, 26**
See also CLR 3
See also CA 73-76
See also SATA 16
See also DLB 7

Zinoviev, Alexander 1922- .... **CLC 19**

Zola, Émile 1840-1902 .... **TCLC 1, 6**
See also CA 104

Zorrilla y Moral, José
1817-1893.................... **NCLC 6**

Zuckmayer, Carl 1896-1977 .... **CLC 18**
See also CA 69-72

Zukofsky, Louis
1904-1978....... **CLC 1, 2, 4, 7, 11, 18**
See also CA 9-12R
See also obituary CA 77-80
See also DLB 5

Cumulative Index to Critics

Aalfs, Janet
Jane Rule **27**:422

Aaron, Daniel
Thornton Wilder **15**:575

Aaron, Jonathan
Tadeusz Rózewicz **23**:363

Aaron, Jules
Michael Cristofer **28**:96
Jack Heifner **11**:264

Abbey, Edward
Robert M. Pirsig **6**:421

Abbott, James H.
Juan Benet **28**:21

Abbott, John Lawrence
Isaac Bashevis Singer **9**:487
Sylvia Townsend Warner **7**:512

Abeel, Erica
Pamela Hansford Johnson **7**:185

Abel, Elizabeth
Jean Rhys **14**:448

Abel, Lionel
Samuel Beckett **2**:45
Jack Gelber **6**:196
Jean Genet **2**:157
Yoram Kaniuk **19**:238

Abernethy, Peter L.
Thomas Pynchon **3**:410

Abicht, Ludo
Jan de Hartog **19**:133

Ableman, Paul
Brian Aldiss **14**:14
Beryl Bainbridge **22**:45
Jurek Becker **19**:36
William Boyd **28**:39
William S. Burroughs **22**:85

J. M. Coetzee **23**:125
Len Deighton **22**:116
William Golding **17**:179
Mary Gordon **13**:250
Mervyn Jones **10**:295
Michael Moorcock **27**:351
Piers Paul Read **25**:377
Mary Renault **17**:402
Anatoli Rybakov **23**:373
Andrew Sinclair **14**:489
Scott Sommer **25**:424
D. M. Thomas **22**:419
Gore Vidal **22**:438

Abley, Mark
Margaret Atwood **25**:65
Harry Crews **23**:136
John le Carré **28**:226
William Mitchell **25**:327
Agnès Varda **16**:560
Miriam Waddington **28**:440

Abraham, Willie E.
William Melvin Kelley **22**:249

Abrahams, Cecil A.
Bessie Head **25**:236

Abrahams, William
Elizabeth Bowen **6**:95
Hortense Calisher **2**:97
Herbert Gold **4**:193
Joyce Carol Oates **2**:315
Harold Pinter **9**:418
V. S. Pritchett **5**:352

Abrahamson, Dick
Sue Ellen Bridgers **26**:92
John Knowles **26**:265
Norma Fox Mazer **26**:294

Abrams, M. H.
M. H. Abrams **24**:18
Northrop Frye **24**:209

Abramson, Doris E.
Alice Childress **12**:105

Abramson, Jane
Peter Dickinson **12**:172
Christie Harris **12**:268
Rosemary Wells **12**:638

Acheson, James
William Golding **17**:177

Acken, Edgar L.
Ernest K. Gann **23**:163

Ackerman, Diane
John Berryman **25**:97

Ackroyd, Peter
Brian Aldiss **5**:16
Martin Amis **4**:19
Miguel Ángel Asturias **8**:27
Louis Auchincloss **6**:15
W. H. Auden **9**:56
Beryl Bainbridge **8**:36
James Baldwin **5**:43
John Barth **5**:51
Donald Barthelme **3**:44
Samuel Beckett **4**:52
John Berryman **3**:72
Richard Brautigan **5**:72
Charles Bukowski **5**:80
Anthony Burgess **5**:87
William S. Burroughs **5**:92
Italo Calvino **5**:100; **8**:132
Richard Condon **6**:115
Roald Dahl **6**:122
Ed Dorn **10**:155
Margaret Drabble **8**:183

Douglas Dunn **6**:148
Bruce Jay Friedman **5**:127
John Gardner **7**:116
Günter Grass **4**:207
MacDonald Harris **9**:261
Joseph Heller **5**:179
Mark Helprin **10**:261
Russell C. Hoban **7**:160
Elizabeth Jane Howard **7**:164
B. S. Johnson **6**:264
Pamela Hansford Johnson **7**:184
G. Josipovici **6**:270
Thomas Keneally **10**:298
Jack Kerouac **5**:215
Francis King **8**:321
Jerzy Kosinski **10**:308
Doris Lessing **6**:300
Alison Lurie **4**:305
Thomas McGuane **7**:212
Stanley Middleton **7**:220
Michael Moorcock **5**:294;
 27:350
Penelope Mortimer **5**:298
Iris Murdoch **4**:368
Vladimir Nabokov **6**:358
V. S. Naipaul **7**:252
Joyce Carol Oates **6**:368
Tillie Olsen **13**:432
Grace Paley **6**:393
Frederik Pohl **18**:411
Davi Pownall **10**:418, 419
J. B. Priestley **9**:441
V. S. Pritchett **5**:352
Thomas Pynchon **3**:419
Frederic Raphael **14**:437
Simon Raven **14**:442
Peter Redgrove **6**:446
Keith Roberts **14**:463
Judith Rossner **9**:458

May Sarton 4:472
David Slavitt 5:392
Wole Soyinka 5:398
David Storey 4:529
Peter Straub 28:409
Paul Theroux 5:428
Thomas Tryon 11:548
John Updike 7:488; 9:540
Gore Vidal 8:525
Harriet Waugh 6:559
Jerome Weidman 7:518
Arnold Wesker 5:483
Patrick White 4:587
Roger Zelazny 21:469

Aczel, Tamas
Heinrich Böll 27:63

Adam, G. F.
Rhys Davies 23:143

Adamowski, T. H.
Simone de Beauvoir 4:47

Adams, Agatha Boyd
Paul Green 25:197

Adams, Alice
Lisa Alther 7:14
Cynthia Propper Seton 27:429

Adams, Franklin P.
James M. Cain 28:43

Adams, George R.
Lorraine Hansberry 17:190
Ann Petry 18:403

Adams, J. Donald
Erich Maria Remarque 21:327

Adams, Jacqueline
Al Young 19:479

Adams, James Truslow
Esther Forbes 12:206

Adams, John
Roy A. Gallant 17:131

Adams, Laura
Norman Mailer 11:340

Adams, Leonie
John Crowe Ransom 4:428

Adams, M. Ian
Juan Carlos Onetti 10:376

Adams, Percy
James Dickey 7:81

Adams, Phoebe-Lou
Chinua Achebe 26:11, 13
Richard Adams 18:2
Joy Adamson 17:3
Beryl Bainbridge 5:40
Ann Beattie 18:38
David Bradley, Jr. 23:81
André Brink 18:68
Robert Cormier 12:133
Margaret Craven 17:80
Roald Dahl 18:109
Peter Davison 28:100
G. B. Edwards 25:151
John Ehle 27:105
John Fowles 15:234
Dick Francis 22:150
Günter Grass 22:196
Dashiell Hammett 5:161

James Herriot 12:282
George V. Higgins 18:234
Jamake Highwater 12:285
Bohumil Hrabal 13:290
P. D. James 18:275
David Jones 7:189
Garson Kanin 22:232
Jerzy Kosinski 6:285
William Kotzwinkle 14:311
Halldór Laxness 25:292, 300
Harper Lee 12:341
Yukio Mishima 9:385
N. Scott Momaday 19:317
Berry Morgan 6:340
Joyce Carol Oates 6:374
Tillie Olsen 13:433
Sylvia Plath 17:352
Reynolds Price 6:426
Jean Rhys 19:394
João Ubaldo Ribeiro 10:436
Philip Roth 15:452
Françoise Sagan 17:419
Khushwant Singh 11:504
Jean Stafford 19:431
Christina Stead 8:500
R. G. Vliet 22:441
Joseph Wambaugh 18:532

Adams, Richard
Robert Newton Peck 17:338

Adams, Robert M.
Adolfo Bioy Casares 13:87
R. V. Cassill 23:105
John Cheever 25:121
Eleanor Clark 19:105
Edward Dahlberg 7:63
Peter Matthiessen 11:361
Mary McCarthy 14:362
Alberto Moravia 18:348
Robert M. Pirsig 4:404
Severo Sarduy 6:485
Mary Lee Settle 19:409
Edmund Wilson 24:469

Adams, Robert Martin
John Barth 10:24
Samuel Beckett 14:74
Jorge Luis Borges 10:66
Richard Brautigan 12:61
Anthony Burgess 10:90
Lawrence Durrell 13:185
T. S. Eliot 10:171
William Faulkner 11:201
Carlo Emilio Gadda 11:215
William H. Gass 2:154
José Lezama Lima 10:321
Vladimir Nabokov 11:393
Flann O'Brien 10:363
Thomas Pynchon 11:453
Alain Robbe-Grillet 10:437
J.R.R. Tolkien 12:586
Angus Wilson 2:472

Adams, Robin
Frank Herbert 12:279
Roger Zelazny 21:470

Adams, S. J.
Ezra Pound 13:453

Adams, Stephen D.
James Purdy 28:380

Adams, Timothy Dow
Leon Rooke 25:394

Adcock, Fleur
John Berryman 13:83
Robert Lowell 11:331
David Malouf 28:268
Peter Porter 13:453

Adelman, Clifford
John Berryman 3:71

Adelman, George
Frank B. Gilbreth, Jr. and Ernestine Gilbreth Carey 17:156

Adereth, M.
Louis Aragon 22:36

Adkins, Laurence
Eilís Dillon 17:96
Farley Mowat 26:336

Adler, Bill
Marvin Gaye 26:132

Adler, Dick
Ross Macdonald 1:185

Adler, Joyce
Wilson Harris 25:207

Adler, Renata
Mel Brooks 12:75
Francis Ford Coppola 16:232
Joan Micklin Silver 20:346

Adler, Thomas P.
Edward Albee 11:13
Harold Pinter 15:424
Sam Shepard 17:446

Aers, Lesley
Philippa Pearce 21:284

Agar, John
Jonathan Baumbach 6:32
Laurie Colwin 5:107

Agee, James
Frank Capra 16:156
Charles Chaplin 16:193
Maya Deren 16:251
Carl Theodor Dreyer 16:256
Alfred Hitchcock 16:339, 342
John Huston 20:158, 160
Buster Keaton 20:188
Laurence Olivier 20:234
Billy Wilder 20:456

Agee, Joel
Aharon Appelfeld 23:38

Agena, Kathleen
Charles Wright 13:613

Aggeler, Geoffrey
Anthony Burgess 2:86; 5:85; 13:123; 22:69

Aghazarian, Nancy
Milton Meltzer 26:304

Agius, Ambrose, O.S.B.
Edward Dahlberg 7:64

Ahearn, Kerry
Wallace Stegner 9:509

Ahokas, Jaakko A.
Paavo Haavikko 18:206
Frans Eemil Sillanpää 19:418

Ahrold, Robbin
Kurt Vonnegut, Jr. 3:501

Aiken, Conrad
William Faulkner 8:206
St.-John Perse 11:433
I. A. Richards 24:370
Karl Shapiro 15:475

Aiken, David
Flannery O'Connor 10:365

Aiken, William
David Kherdian 6:281

Aithal, Rashmi
Raja Rao 25:373

Aithal, S. Krishnamoorthy
Raja Rao 25:373

Aitken, Will
Carlos Saura 20:319

Aklujkar, Ashok
R. K. Narayan 28:301

Alazraki, Jaime
Jorge Luis Borges 19:45
Pablo Neruda 2:309; 7:261

Albers, Randall
Ai 14:8

Albert, Walter
Blaise Cendrars 18:90

Albertson, Chris
Laura Nyro 17:313
Stevie Wonder 12:662

Aldan, Daisy
Phyllis Gotlieb 18:193

Alderson, Brian W.
Leon Garfield 12:226
William Mayne 12:395, 401

Alderson, S. William
Andre Norton 12:464, 466, 470

Alderson, Sue Ann
Muriel Rukeyser 10:442

Alderson, Valerie
E. M. Almedingen 12:6
Noel Streatfeild 21:412

Aldiss, Brian
J. G. Ballard 3:33
Frank Herbert 12:272

Aldiss, Brian W.
Isaac Asimov 26:38
Robert A. Heinlein 26:162

Aldrich, Nelson
Piri Thomas 17:497

Aldridge, John W.
James Baldwin 4:42
Donald Barthelme 2:39
Saul Bellow 2:49, 50
Louis-Ferdinand Céline 7:47
John Cheever 3:105
John Dos Passos 4:131
James T. Farrell 4:157
William Faulkner 3:150
William Gaddis 3:177; 6:193
Joseph Heller 5:177
Ernest Hemingway 3:231, 233

James Jones 3:261
Jerzy Kosinski 2:231
Richard Kostelanetz 28:216
Alison Lurie 5:260
Norman Mailer 1:193; 2:258
Mary McCarthy 3:327, 328
Wright Morris 3:342; 18:352
John O'Hara 2:323
Katherine Anne Porter 3:392
Philip Roth 4:459
Alan Sillitoe 3:447
William Styron 3:472
John Updike 2:439
Gore Vidal 22:431
Robert Penn Warren 1:356
Eudora Welty 2:461
Colin Wilson 3:536
Edmund Wilson 2:474
P. G. Wodehouse 2:478

Aldridge, Judith
Ruth M. Arthur 12:27
Honor Arundel 17:14, 15, 18

Alegria, Fernando
Jorge Luis Borges 2:71
Pablo Neruda 28:309

Aletti, Vince
Marvin Gaye 26:130, 131, 132
Laura Nyro 17:312
Smokey Robinson 21:342, 345
Stevie Wonder 12:656, 660

Alexander, Alex E.
Stephen King 26:234

Alexander, Edward
Cynthia Ozick 28:348
Isaac Bashevis Singer 11:503

Alexander, Jean
Richard Peck 21:296

Alexander, John R.
Robinson Jeffers 2:215

Alexander, Michael
Donald Davie 5:113
Ezra Pound 7:336

Alexander, William
Carl Sandburg 4:463

Alexandrova, Vera
Mikhail Sholokhov 7:420

Alfonso, Barry
Van Morrison 21:239

Alford, Steven E.
Doris Betts 28:34

Algren, Nelson
Clancy Sigal 7:424

Ali, Ahmed
Raja Rao 25:366

Ali, Tariq
Jules Archer 12:19

Alig, Tracy
John Gregory Dunne 28:121

Allen, Blaine
Monty Python 21:223

Allen, Bob
Waylon Jennings 21:206
Willie Nelson 17:305

Allen, Bruce
Richard Adams 5:6
David Bradley, Jr. 23:81
Julio Cortázar 5:110
Stanley Elkin 6:168
John Gardner 8:236; 28:162
Mary Gordon 13:250
Thomas Keneally 5:212
Kenneth Koch 5:219
Peter Matthiessen 7:211
Wright Morris 18:354
Iris Murdoch 6:347
Joyce Carol Oates 6:369
Manuel Puig 5:355
John Sayles 10:460
Isaac Bashevis Singer 6:509
Paul West 7:524
Patrick White 5:485

Allen, Bruce D.
Jane Rule 27:417

Allen, Carol J.
Susan Fromberg Schaeffer 11:491

Allen, Dexter
Mary Lee Settle 19:408

Allen, Dick
Margaret Atwood 2:20
Wendell Berry 6:61
Hayden Carruth 7:40
Paul Goodman 2:169
Thom Gunn 6:221
Richard F. Hugo 6:245
Philip Levine 2:244
Lisel Mueller 13:400
George Oppen 7:281
Judith Johnson Sherwin 7:414

Allen, Don
François Truffaut 20:397

Allen, Gay Wilson
Carl Sandburg 10:447

Allen, Henry
Robert M. Pirsig 4:403

Allen, John A.
Eudora Welty 14:564

Allen, John Alexander
Daniel Hoffman 13:288

Allen, L. David
Arthur C. Clarke 18:106

Allen, Louis
Shusaku Endo 14:161

Allen, Merritt P.
Walter Farley 17:116
Andre Norton 12:455

Allen, Patricia H.
Zilpha Keatley Snyder 17:469

Allen, Ralph G.
Eric Bentley 24:51

Allen, Steve
S. J. Perelman 23:335

Allen, Tom
Ralph Bakshi 26:73
Vittorio De Sica 20:97
Rainer Werner Fassbinder 20:115
Kon Ichikawa 20:186
Yasujiro Ozu 16:450
Pier Paolo Pasolini 20:270
Sidney Poitier 26:361
Carlos Saura 20:321
Jerzy Skolimowski 20:354

Allen, Tom, S. C.
Mel Brooks 12:81

Allen, Walter
A. Alvarez 5:17
Kingsley Amis 1:5
Riccardo Bacchelli 19:31
Saul Bellow 1:30
Elizabeth Bowen 1:40
Paul Bowles 1:41
Truman Capote 1:55
Ivy Compton-Burnett 1:61
James Gould Cozzens 1:66
Edward Dahlberg 1:71
John Dos Passos 1:79; 8:181
Margaret Drabble 22:120
Lawrence Durrell 1:85
James T. Farrell 1:98; 8:205
William Faulkner 1:101
E. M. Forster 1:104
John Fowles 4:170
William Golding 1:120
Henry Green 2:178
Graham Greene 1:132
L. P. Hartley 2:181; 22:211
Ernest Hemingway 1:142
Richard Hughes 1:149
Aldous Huxley 1:150
Christopher Isherwood 1:155
Pamela Hansford Johnson 1:160; 27:217
Doris Lessing 1:173
Richard Llewellyn 7:206
Bernard Malamud 1:197
Olivia Manning 19:300
John P. Marquand 2:271
Carson McCullers 1:208
Henry Miller 1:221
Wright Morris 1:231
John Mortimer 28:282
Iris Murdoch 1:234
P. H. Newby 2:310
Flannery O'Connor 1:255
John O'Hara 1:260
William Plomer 4:406
Anthony Powell 1:277
Henry Roth 2:377; 11:487
J. D. Salinger 1:298
William Sansom 2:383
C. P. Snow 1:316
John Steinbeck 1:325
William Styron 1:330
Allen Tate 2:427
Gore Vidal 22:434
Robert Penn Warren 1:355
Evelyn Waugh 1:358
Glenway Wescott 13:592
Rebecca West 7:525
Angus Wilson 2:471

Allen, Ward
Donald Davidson 2:112

Allen, Woody
S. J. Perelman 15:419

Alley, Phillip W.
Franklyn M. Branley 21:18

Allott, Miriam
Graham Greene 18:193

Allsop, Kenneth
J. P. Donleavy 6:139
Thomas Hinde 6:238

Alm, Richard S.
Betty Cavanna 12:99
Maureen Daly 17:89
Mary Stolz 12:548

Alma, Roger
Philippa Pearce 21:291

Almansi, Guido
Alan Ayckbourn 18:27
Italo Calvino 22:90
Mario Luzi 13:354

Alonso, J. M.
Rafael Alberti 7:11
Jorge Luis Borges 9:117

Alpert, Hollis
Vincent Canby 13:131
Howard Fast 23:156
Daniel Fuchs 8:220
William Kotzwinkle 14:311
Olivia Manning 19:300
Ernesto Sabato 23:375
Budd Schulberg 7:402
Melvin Van Peebles 20:410

Altbach, Philip G.
Jonathan Kozol 17:252

Alter, Robert
S. Y. Agnon 4:11
Yehuda Amichai 9:23
John Barth 9:71
Donald Barthelme 8:49
Saul Bellow 3:48, 49
Heinrich Böll 27:68
Jorge Luis Borges 2:76; 6:94
R. V. Cassill 23:104
Leslie Epstein 27:130
Leslie A. Fiedler 13:212
John Hollander 8:298
Jerzy Kosinski 2:232
Doris Lessing 22:285
Norman Mailer 3:312; 11:342
Bernard Malamud 3:30, 321; 27:299, 305
Claude Mauriac 9:366
Elsa Morante 8:402
Alberto Moravia 18:346
Vladimir Nabokov 2:302; 8:414
Hugh Nissenson 4:380
Flann O'Brien 7:269
Manuel Puig 10:420
Thomas Pynchon 9:443
Raymond Queneau 10:429
Philip Rahv 24:353
Alain Robbe-Grillet 6:468
Earl Rovit 7:383
André Schwarz-Bart 4:480
Isaac Bashevis Singer 11:501; 15:507
J.I.M. Stewart 7:465
William Styron 15:527
John Updike 2:444
Kurt Vonnegut, Jr. 8:531
Elie Wiesel 3:526
Abraham B. Yehoshua 13:618

Alterman, Loraine
 Ray Davies **21**:96
 Jesse Jackson **12**:291
 Gordon Lightfoot **26**:279
 Carly Simon **26**:408
 Andrew Lloyd Webber and Tim Rice **21**:428

Altieri, Charles
 Robert Creeley **2**:107
 Robert Duncan **15**:191
 Denise Levertov **28**:238
 Robert Lowell **15**:345

Altman, Billy
 Elvis Costello **21**:75
 Ray Davies **21**:102
 Peter Townshend **17**:537, 539
 Brian Wilson **12**:652

Alvarez, A.
 Aharon Appelfeld **23**:38
 John Berryman **2**:58; **3**:65
 Albert Camus **4**:89
 William Empson **19**:154
 E. M. Forster **1**:109
 Carlos Fuentes **22**:165
 Dashiell Hammett **3**:218
 Seamus Heaney **25**:247
 Zbigniew Herbert **9**:271
 Russell C. Hoban **25**:266
 Miroslav Holub **4**:233
 Dan Jacobson **14**:289
 Philip Larkin **3**:275
 Robert Lowell **3**:300
 Hugh MacDiarmid **4**:309
 Norman Mailer **3**:312
 Cynthia Ozick **28**:351
 David Plante **23**:346
 Sylvia Plath **2**:335; **3**:388
 Jean Rhys **4**:445
 Jean-Paul Sartre **4**:475
 Edith Sitwell **9**:493
 Aleksandr I. Solzhenitsyn **7**:436
 Robert Stone **23**:428
 Patrick White **3**:521
 Elie Wiesel **3**:527
 Yvor Winters **4**:589

Alvia, Sister
 Robert Newton Peck **17**:339

Amacher, Richard E.
 Edward Albee **1**:5

Amado, Jorge
 João Ubaldo Ribeiro **10**:436
 João Guimarães Rosa **23**:348

Amanuddin, Syed
 James Welch **14**:559

Amberg, George
 Jean Cocteau **16**:229

Ambrose, Stephen E.
 Cornelius Ryan **7**:385

Ambrosetti, Ronald
 Eric Ambler **9**:20

Ames, Alfred C.
 Joy Adamson **17**:5

Ames, Carol
 John Berryman **25**:96

Ames, Evelyn
 J. B. Priestley **5**:351

Ames, Katrine
 Gordon Parks **16**:460

Amiel, Barbara
 Margaret Atwood **15**:37
 Jack Hodgins **23**:228
 Chaim Potok **14**:429
 A. W. Purdy **14**:435
 Jane Rule **27**:422

Amis, Kingsley
 Ray Bradbury **10**:68
 Arthur C. Clarke **13**:155
 Ivy Compton-Burnett **1**:60
 Ilya Ehrenburg **18**:132
 Leslie A. Fiedler **4**:159
 Christopher Isherwood **14**:278
 Philip Roth **1**:293
 Arnold Wesker **3**:517

Amis, Martin
 J. G. Ballard **6**:27
 Peter De Vries **7**:77
 Bruce Jay Friedman **5**:127
 Ernest J. Gaines **3**:179
 John Hawkes **7**:141
 Philip Larkin **13**:337
 Iris Murdoch **4**:367
 Vladimir Nabokov **8**:412
 Roman Polanski **16**:472
 Philip Roth **6**:475
 Fay Weldon **11**:565

Ammons, A. R.
 Mark Strand **18**:514

Amory, Cleveland
 Rod McKuen **1**:210

Amprimoz, Alexandre
 Joe Rosenblatt **15**:448

Amy, Jenny L.
 Robert Newton Peck **17**:343

Anders, Jaroslaw
 Tadeusz Konwicki **28**:209

Anderson, A. J.
 Jeffrey Archer **28**:11

Anderson, David
 Albert Camus **4**:89, 90
 William Golding **3**:197, 198
 Jean-Paul Sartre **4**:477

Anderson, David C.
 L. E. Sissman **9**:491

Anderson, Elliott
 Vladimir Nabokov **3**:354

Anderson, George
 Piri Thomas **17**:499

Anderson, H. T.
 Herbert Gold **14**:208
 Erich Segal **10**:467

Anderson, Isaac
 Agatha Christie **12**:114
 Joseph Krumgold **12**:316

Anderson, Jack
 Philip Levine **4**:286
 George MacBeth **2**:252

Anderson, Jervis
 James Baldwin **8**:41
 Michael Thelwell **22**:415

Anderson, Joseph L.
 Akira Kurosawa **16**:396

Anderson, Lindsay
 Luis Buñuel **16**:129
 Vittorio De Sica **20**:84
 John Ford **16**:305, 306
 Elia Kazan **16**:362
 Fritz Lang **20**:205
 Yasujiro Ozu **16**:447

Anderson, Michael
 Edward Bond **6**:85
 Tennessee Williams **11**:577

Anderson, Patrick
 Ward Just **4**:266

Anderson, Poul
 Poul Anderson **15**:14
 Fritz Leiber **25**:303

Anderson, Quentin
 Vladimir Nabokov **3**:351

Anderson, Reed
 Juan Goytisolo **10**:244; **23**:184

Anderson, Robert W.
 Helen MacInnes **27**:279

André, Michael
 Robert Creeley **2**:107

Andrews, Nigel
 John Cassavetes **20**:47
 Sam Peckinpah **20**:277
 Jerzy Skolimowski **20**:350

Andrews, Peter
 Michael Crichton **6**:119
 Peter De Vries **28**:108
 Ken Follett **18**:157
 Arthur Hailey **5**:157
 Martin Cruz Smith **25**:413
 Irving Stone **7**:471

Andrews, Sheryl B.
 Barbara Corcoran **17**:70
 James D. Forman **21**:119
 Virginia Hamilton **26**:149
 Isabelle Holland **21**:148
 Mollie Hunter **21**:158
 Andre Norton **12**:460

Angell, Roger
 Brian De Palma **20**:80
 Bob Fosse **20**:126
 Gene Roddenberry **17**:413
 Paul Schrader **26**:395
 Lina Wertmüller **16**:600

Angier, Carole
 Stevie Smith **25**:421

Angle, Paul M.
 Milton Meltzer **26**:299

Angogo, R.
 Chinua Achebe **11**:2

Annan, Gabriele
 Aharon Appelfeld **23**:37
 Simone de Beauvoir **4**:47
 Heinrich Böll **9**:111
 Laurie Colwin **23**:129
 Anita Desai **19**:133
 Iris Murdoch **11**:388
 Jean Rhys **19**:391

 Sylvia Townsend Warner **19**:459

Annan, Noel
 E. M. Forster **4**:166

Anozie, Sunday O.
 Christopher Okigbo **25**:350

Anselm, Felix
 Hermann Hesse **17**:194

Ansen, David
 George Roy Hill **26**:208
 Stephen King **26**:243
 Sidney Poitier **26**:362

Ansorge, Peter
 Trevor Griffiths **13**:256
 Sam Shepard **6**:495

Anthony, Robert J.
 Isaac Asimov **26**:38

Appel, Alfred, Jr.
 Fritz Lang **20**:211
 Vladimir Nabokov **1**:240; **2**:300

Apple, Max
 John Gardner **10**:222

Aptheker, Herbert
 W.E.B. Du Bois **13**:180

Araújo, Virginia de
 Carlos Drummond de Andrade **18**:4

Arbuthnot, May Hill
 Frank Bonham **12**:53
 Franklyn M. Branley **21**:18
 Julia W. Cunningham **12**:164
 Maureen Daly **17**:91
 Jesse Jackson **12**:290
 Joseph Krumgold **12**:320, 321
 Madeleine L'Engle **12**:350
 Emily Cheney Neville **12**:452
 Alvin Silverstein and Virginia B. Silverstein **17**:455
 Mary Stolz **12**:553
 Noel Streatfeild **21**:412
 Rosemary Sutcliff **26**:436
 Jade Snow Wong **17**:566

Archer, Eileen A.
 Diana Wynne Jones **26**:228

Archer, Eugene
 Ingmar Bergman **16**:46
 Bernardo Bertolucci **16**:83
 Federico Fellini **16**:271
 John Huston **20**:164, 165
 Sam Peckinpah **20**:272

Archer, Marguerite
 Jean Anouilh **13**:18

Arendt, Hannah
 W. H. Auden **6**:21

Argus
 Josef von Sternberg **20**:370

Arias, Ron
 Rudolfo A. Anaya **23**:25

Aristarco, Guido
 Satyajit Ray **16**:474

Arkhurst, Joyce E.
 Mildred D. Taylor **21**:419

Arland, Marcel
Françoise Sagan 17:416

Arlen, Michael J.
Alex Haley 12:254

Armes, Roy
Michelangelo Antonioni 20:38
Robert Bresson 16:114
Claude Chabrol 16:170
Jean Cocteau 16:228
Federico Fellini 16:284
Pier Paolo Pasolini 20:265
Alain Resnais 16:505
Alain Robbe-Grillet 4:449
Agnès Varda 16:556

Armour, Robert A.
Fritz Lang 20:214

Armstrong, Judith
Philippa Pearce 21:292

Armstrong, Marion
Fletcher Knebel 14:308

Armstrong, William A.
Sean O'Casey 1:252; 9:407

Arnason, David
Amos Tutuola 14:540

Arnett, Janet
Roderick L. Haig-Brown 21:146

Arnez, Nancy L.
Alex Haley 12:250

Arnheim, Rudolf
Maya Deren 16:253

Arnold, A. James
Aimé Césaire 19:99

Arnold, Armin
Friedrich Dürrenmatt 15:193

Arnold, Gary
Woody, Allen 16:4

Arnold, Marilyn
John Gardner 18:177

Arnolt, Vicki
Hermann Hesse 17:215

Aronowitz, Alfred G.
John Lennon and Paul McCartney 12:364
Peter Townshend 17:526

Aronson, James
Donald Barthelme 1:18
Saul Bellow 1:33
James Dickey 1:73
John Fowles 1:109
John Knowles 1:169
John Updike 1:345
Eudora Welty 1:363

Aros, Andrew
Christopher Fry 14:189

Arpin, Gary Q.
John Berryman 10:48

Arthos, John
E. E. Cummings 12:146

Arthur, George
Monty Python 21:226

Arthur, George W.
Judy Blume 12:47
Robert Crumb 17:85

Artinian, Robert W.
Jean-Paul Sartre 24:411

Arvedson, Peter
Roy A. Gallant 17:131

Asahina, Robert
Woody Allen 16:12
Mel Brooks 12:80
Brian De Palma 20:82
Athol Fugard 25:175
Jean-Luc Godard 20:153
Werner Herzog 16:334
George Roy Hill 26:208
Pier Paolo Pasolini 20:270
Eric Rohmer 16:538
Joan Micklin Silver 20:346
Steven Spielberg 20:366

Ascherson, Neal
Beryl Bainbridge 14:38
Leslie Epstein 27:129
Rolf Hochhuth 18:256
György Konrád 10:304
Tadeusz Konwicki 8:327
Milan Kundera 4:278
Tadeusz Różewicz 9:465
Yevgeny Yevtushenko 1:382

Aschkenasy, Nehama
Amos Oz 27:361

Asein, Samuel Omo
Alex La Guma 19:276
Ezekiel Mphahlele 25:342
Derek Walcott 25:451

Ashbery, John
A. R. Ammons 2:13
Elizabeth Bishop 9:89
Philip Booth 23:75
James Schuyler 23:390

Ashcroft, W. D.
Janet Frame 22:146

Ashley, L. F.
Rosemary Sutcliff 26:433

Ashlin, John
William Mayne 12:390

Ashton, Dore
Octavio Paz 10:392

Ashton, Thomas L.
C. P. Snow 4:504

Asimov, Isaac
Roy A. Gallant 17:127, 128

Asinof, Eliot
Pete Hamill 10:251

Asnani, Shyam M.
Mulk Raj Anand 23:21

Aspel, Alexander
Ivar Ivask 14:286

Aspler, Tony
William F. Buckley, Jr. 7:36
William Gaddis 8:226
Josef Škvorecký 15:510

Astrachan, Anthony
Agnes Eckhardt Nixon 21:246
Vladimir Voinovich 10:509

Atchity, Kenneth
Stephen King 26:241

Atchity, Kenneth John
Jorge Luis Borges 2:71
James Jones 3:261
Robert Penn Warren 4:581

Athanason, Arthur N.
Pavel Kohout 13:326

Atheling, William, Jr.
Isaac Asimov 3:17
Arthur C. Clarke 1:58
Harlan Ellison 1:93
Robert A. Heinlein 1:139; 3:227

Atherton, J. S.
Anaïs Nin 11:398

Atherton, Stan
Margaret Laurence 6:290

Atkins, Anselm
Robert Bolt 14:90

Atkins, John
L. P. Hartley 2:182

Atkinson, Brooks
Robert Anderson 23:30
Enid Bagnold 25:76
Sally Benson 17:49
Paddy Chayefsky 23:112
William Gibson 23:174, 175
Paul Green 25:195
Lorraine Hansberry 17:182
Garson Kanin 22:230
Jean Kerr 22:254, 255
Arthur Miller 26:315
Elmer Rice 7:361
Irwin Shaw 23:397

Atkinson, Joan L.
Sue Ellen Bridgers 26:92

Atkinson, Michael
Robert Bly 10:58

Atlas, Jacoba
Mel Brooks 12:78
Joni Mitchell 12:436

Atlas, James
Samuel Beckett 6:37
Marie-Claire Blais 6:82
Raymond Carver 22:102
J. V. Cunningham 3:122
Peter Davison 28:102
Alan Dugan 6:144
Paul Goodman 4:198
Graham Greene 27:172
Mark Harris 19:206
John Irving 23:248
Randall Jarrell 6:261
Galway Kinnell 5:217
Thomas McGrath 28:277
W. S. Merwin 5:287
John O'Hara 6:386
Kenneth Rexroth 6:451
Laura Riding 7:375
Delmore Schwartz 4:478
L. E. Sissman 9:490
James Tate 2:431

Richard Yates 23:482

Attebery, Brian
James Thurber 25:437

Atwell, Lee
Michelangelo Antonioni 20:39
George Roy Hill 26:199

Atwood, Margaret
Ann Beattie 18:38
Marie-Claire Blais 6:80
E. L. Doctorow 18:126
Janet Frame 22:148
Susan B. Hill 4:227
Erica Jong 6:267
A. G. Mojtabai 5:293
Tillie Olsen 13:432
Marge Piercy 14:420; 27:381
Sylvia Plath 11:451
A. W. Purdy 14:430
James Reaney 13:472
Adrienne Rich 3:429; 11:478
Cynthia Propper Seton 27:425
Audrey Thomas 7:472

Aubert, Rosemary
Patrick Lane 25:288

Auchincloss, Eve
Vera Brittain 23:93
Bruce Chatwin 28:71
Mavis Gallant 18:171
R. K. Narayan 7:257
Gilbert Rogin 18:457

Auchincloss, Louis
Katherine Anne Porter 7:316

Aucouturier, Michel
Aleksandr I. Solzhenitsyn 7:432

Auden, W. H.
Joseph Brodsky 4:77
Cleanth Brooks 24:101
Kenneth Burke 24:121
William Dickey 28:116
Loren Eiseley 7:90
Daniel Hoffman 23:237
Christopher Isherwood 14:281
Chester Kallman 2:221
C. S. Lewis 27:261
J.R.R. Tolkien 1:336; 12:564
Andrei Voznesensky 1:349
James Wright 28:461

Auriol, Jean-George
René Clair 20:57

Auster, Paul
John Ashbery 6:14
John Hollander 8:300
Laura Riding 7:375
Giuseppe Ungaretti 7:484

Austin, Allan E.
Elizabeth Bowen 22:61
Roy Fuller 28:155

Auty, Martyn
John Landis 26:273

Avant, John Alfred
Eleanor Bergstein 4:55
Gail Godwin 5:142
Gayl Jones 6:266
José Lezama Lima 4:291
Carson McCullers 12:427

Joyce Carol Oates 6:371, 373
Tillie Olsen 4:386
Patrick White 5:486

Averill, Deborah
Frank O'Connor 14:395

Avery, Evelyn Gross
Richard Wright 14:597

Axelrod, George
Gore Vidal 4:556

Axelrod, Rise B.
Anne Sexton 15:471

Axelrod, Steven
Robert Lowell 2:249

Axelrod, Steven Gould
Saul Bellow 6:60

Axhelm, Peter M.
Saul Bellow 13:66
William Golding 10:232

Axthelm, Pete
Robert Lipsyte 21:210
Gilbert Rogin 18:457

Ayd, Joseph D., S.J.
Louis Auchincloss 18:26

Ayer, A. J.
Albert Camus 9:152

Ayling, Ronald
Sean O'Casey 11:409; 15:405

Ayo, Nicholas
Edward Lewis Wallant 10:515

Ayre, John
Austin C. Clarke 8:143
Mavis Gallant 7:110
V. S. Naipaul 13:407
Mordecai Richler 5:378

Baar, Ron
Ezra Pound 1:276

Babbitt, Natalie
Paula Danziger 21:85
Lois Duncan 26:106
William Mayne 12:395
Katherine Paterson 12:403, 486
Robert Westall 17:559

Babenko, Vickie A.
Yevgeny Yevtushenko 13:620

Bach, Alice
Sandra Scoppettone 26:400

Bachman, Charles R.
Sam Shepard 17:442

Bachmann, Gideon
Shirley Clarke 16:215
Federico Fellini 16:283
Jean Renoir 20:290
Luchino Visconti 16:572

Backscheider, Nick
John Updike 5:452

Backscheider, Paula
John Updike 5:452

Bacon, Leonard
Eric Bentley 24:43

Bacon, Martha
Walter Farley 17:118

Bacon, Terry R.
Robert Creeley 11:137

Bader, Julia
Vladimir Nabokov 23:303

Baer, Barbara L.
Harriette Arnow 7:16
Christina Stead 5:403

Bagshaw, Marguerite
Farley Mowat 26:337

Bailey, Anthony
James Baldwin 17:38
John Gregory Dunne 28:124
David Plante 23:342

Bailey, Bruce
George Ryga 14:474

Bailey, James
Andrei Voznesensky 15:553

Bailey, Jennifer
Norman Mailer 28:255

Bailey, Nancy I.
Roch Carrier 13:142

Bailey, O. L.
Eric Ambler 6:2
Dick Francis 2:142
George V. Higgins 4:223
Maj Sjöwall 7:501
Mickey Spillane 3:469
Per Wahlöö 7:501

Bailey, Paul
James Baldwin 15:43
Gabriel García Márquez 3:180
Nadine Gordimer 10:239
Kazuo Ishiguro 27:202
P. D. James 18:274
Yasunari Kawabata 2:223
Louis L'Amour 25:278
Brian Moore 3:341
Alberto Moravia 11:384
James Purdy 2:351
Philip Roth 3:437
Muriel Spark 5:400
David Storey 2:426
Paul Theroux 11:531
Gore Vidal 6:550
Tennessee Williams 7:544

Bailey, Peter
Nikki Giovanni 2:165
Melvin Van Peebles 2:447

Bair, Deirdre
Samuel Beckett 6:43

Baird, James
Djuna Barnes 8:49

Baker, A. T.
A. R. Ammons 5:30

Baker, Carlos
Truman Capote 19:79
Ernest Hemingway 6:234
Elizabeth Spencer 22:401
John Steinbeck 21:366
Jessamyn West 17:546

Baker, Charles A.
Robert Altman 16:25

Baker, Donald W.
Edward Dahlberg 7:63

Baker, Houston A., Jr.
James Baldwin 1:16
Arna Bontemps 1:37
Gwendolyn Brooks 15:92
Sterling A. Brown 1:47
W.E.B. Du Bois 1:80
Ralph Ellison 1:95; 3:145
Leon Forrest 4:163
Langston Hughes 1:149
LeRoi Jones 1:163
Ann Petry 1:266
Ishmael Reed 2:369; 6:449
Jean Toomer 1:341
Richard Wright 1:380

Baker, Howard
Caroline Gordon 6:206
Katherine Anne Porter 1:273

Baker, James R.
William Golding 3:200; 17:169, 175

Baker, John Ross
Wayne C. Booth 24:94

Baker, Kenneth
Walter Abish 22:18
Leon Rooke 25:391

Baker, Nina Brown
Madeleine L'Engle 12:344

Baker, Peter
Lindsay Anderson 20:12
Vittorio De Sica 20:89

Baker, Rob
Albert Innaurato 21:196

Baker, Roger
Poul Anderson 15:11
Beryl Bainbridge 4:39
James Blish 14:83
John Buell 10:81
Paula Fox 8:217
Janet Frame 3:164
John Hawkes 1:139
Jerzy Kosinski 1:172
Alistair MacLean 13:359
Larry McMurtry 3:333
Harold Robbins 5:378
Herman Wouk 9:580
Rudolph Wurlitzer 2:483
Helen Yglesias 7:558
Roger Zelazny 21:466

Baker, Ruth
Frank B. Gilbreth, Jr. and Ernestine Gilbreth Carey 17:152

Baker, Sheridan
Alan Paton 25:358

Baker, William
William Carlos Williams 13:606

Baker, William E.
Jacques Prévert 15:437

Bakerman, Jane S.
Toni Morrison 22:318
Ruth Rendell 28:385
May Sarton 14:481

Bakker, J.
William Gaddis 19:189

Bakshy, Alexander
Frank Capra 16:153
Charles Chaplin 16:188
René Clair 20:57, 58
Rouben Mamoulian 16:418, 419

Balakian, Anna
Louis Aragon 22:42
André Breton 9:132; 15:90
René Char 9:164
Monique Wittig 22:472

Balakian, Nona
Taylor Caldwell 28:58

Baldanza, Frank
Alberto Moravia 2:293
Iris Murdoch 1:235
James Purdy 2:350; 4:424; 10:421

Baldeshwiler, Eileen
Flannery O'Connor 1:255

Balducci, Carolyn
M. E. Kerr 12:297

Baldwin, James
Alex Haley 8:259
Norman Mailer 8:364
Richard Wright 21:438

Bales, Kent
Richard Brautigan 5:71

Ballard, J. G.
Philip K. Dick 10:138
Harlan Ellison 13:203
Frederik Pohl 18:410
Robert Silverberg 7:425

Balliett, Whitney
James Baldwin 17:44
Ann Beattie 18:40
R. V. Cassill 23:103
Richard Condon 4:105
Pamela Hansford Johnson 27:218
William Melvin Kelley 22:247
Clancy Sigal 7:424

Ballif, Gene
Jorge Luis Borges 6:87
Vladimir Nabokov 6:351
Sylvia Plath 11:449
Alain Robbe-Grillet 6:464
Nathalie Sarraute 8:469

Ballstadt, Carl
Earle Birney 6:78

Balm, Trixie A.
David Bowie 17:63

Baltensperger, Peter
Robertson Davies 25:129

Bambara, Toni Cade
Gwendolyn Brooks 2:81
June Jordan 23:256
Ntozake Shange 25:396

Bamborough, J. B.
F. R. Leavis 24:300

Band, Arnold J.
S. Y. Agnon 14:2

Bander, Edward J.
 Jules Archer **12**:16

Bandler, Michael J.
 Chaim Potok **14**:430; **26**:369
 Elie Wiesel **11**:570

Banfield, Beryle
 Rosa Guy **26**:143

Bangs, Lester
 Chuck Berry **17**:51
 David Bowie **17**:63
 David Byrne **26**:97
 Jimmy Cliff **21**:64
 Mick Jagger and Keith Richard
  17:225, 226, 236
 John Lennon and Paul
  McCartney **12**:381
 Bob Marley **17**:270, 271
 Joni Mitchell **12**:437
 Jim Morrison **17**:289, 290, 292
 Van Morrison **21**:234, 238
 Jimmy Page and Robert Plant
  12:474, 476
 Lou Reed **21**:306, 310, 317
 Bruce Springsteen **17**:481
 Lily Tomlin **17**:523
 Peter Townshend **17**:536
 Frank Zappa **17**:586, 587, 591

Banks, Joyce
 Ruth M. Arthur **12**:28

Banks, R. Jeff
 Mickey Spillane **13**:527

Banks, Russell
 Joyce Carol Oates **19**:355

Bann, Stephen
 Lawrence Durrell **27**:99

Bannerman, David
 Allan W. Eckert **17**:104

Bannikov, Nikolai
 Anna Akhmatova **25**:29

Banning, Charles Leslie
 William Gaddis **10**:210

Barber, Michael
 Simon Raven **14**:443
 Gore Vidal **4**:557

Barber, Raymond W.
 Jean Lee Latham **12**:324

Barbera, Jack Vincent
 John Berryman **8**:88

Barbour, Douglas
 Matt Cohen **19**:111
 Louis Dudek **11**:160
 Ursula K. Le Guin **22**:265
 Gwendolyn MacEwan **13**:358
 B. P. Nichol **18**:368
 Michael Ondaatje **14**:407
 Joe Rosenblatt **15**:446
 Rudy Wiebe **6**:566
 Gene Wolfe **25**:472
 Roger Zelazny **21**:466

Barbour, Joan
 Anne McCaffrey **17**:282

Barclay, Pat
 Robertson Davies **7**:72
 Farley Mowat **26**:344

Bardeche, Maurice
 René Clair **20**:61

Bargad, Warren
 Yehuda Amichai **22**:29
 Amos Oz **8**:436
 Abraham B. Yehoshua **13**:617

Bargainnier, E. F.
 Agatha Christie **12**:126

Barge, Laura
 Samuel Beckett **10**:34; **11**:39

Bargen, Doris G.
 Stanley Elkin **27**:122

Barghoorn, Frederick C.
 Aleksandr I. Solzhenitsyn **4**:508

Barish, Jonas A.
 Jean-Paul Sartre **24**:408

Barker, A. L.
 Edna O'Brien **5**:311

Barker, Frank Granville
 Margaret Drabble **10**:163
 J. B. Priestley **9**:442

Barker, George
 Brian Aldiss **5**:14

Barkham, John
 Alan Paton **25**:359

Barksdale, Richard K.
 Gwendolyn Brooks **5**:75
 Langston Hughes **15**:294

Barnard, Caroline King
 Sylvia Plath **17**:361

Barnes, Anne
 Laurie Colwin **23**:128

Barnes, Clive
 Enid Bagnold **25**:78
 John Bishop **10**:54
 Alice Childress **12**:104, 105
 Michael Cristofer **28**:96
 Gretchen Cryer **21**:77, 78, 80
 Lawrence Ferlinghetti **2**:134
 Athol Fugard **25**:176
 Larry Gelbart **21**:126, 127
 Jack Gelber **14**:193
 Simon Gray **9**:240
 Lorraine Hansberry **17**:191
 Jack Heifner **11**:264
 Arthur Kopit **1**:170
 Mark Medoff **23**:292
 Monty Python **21**:226
 John Mortimer **28**:286
 Richard O'Brien **17**:322
 Gerome Ragni and James Rado
  17:378, 380, 383, 386, 387
 Anthony Shaffer **19**:413
 Sam Shepard **17**:436, 437, 438, 441
 Tom Stoppard **1**:328
 Elizabeth Swados **12**:556
 Lily Tomlin **17**:517
 Andrew Lloyd Webber and Tim
  Rice **21**:425, 427, 430, 432
 Michael Weller **10**:525
 Lanford Wilson **7**:547

Barnes, Harper
 James Tate **2**:431

Barnes, Howard
 Irwin Shaw **23**:396

Barnes, Julian
 Richard Brautigan **5**:72; **9**:124
 Vincent Canby **13**:131
 Agatha Christie **12**:120
 James Clavell **6**:114
 Len Deighton **7**:76
 B. S. Johnson **6**:264
 Pamela Hansford Johnson **7**:184
 G. Josipovici **6**:270
 Richard Llewellyn **7**:207
 Alistair MacLean **13**:359
 Vladimir Nabokov **6**:359
 Joyce Carol Oates **9**:402
 Chaim Potok **26**:373
 Richard Price **12**:490

Barnes, Peter
 John Huston **20**:162

Barnes, Regina
 James T. Farrell **4**:158
 Geoffrey Household **11**:277

Barnett, Abraham
 John Ehle **27**:102

Barnett, Ursula A.
 J. M. Coetzee **23**:121
 Ezekiel Mphahlele **25**:336

Barnouw, Dagmar
 Elias Canetti **14**:120
 Doris Lessing **6**:295

Barnstone, William
 Jorge Luis Borges **6**:93

Barnstone, Willis
 Jorge Luis Borges **9**:120

Baro, Gene
 R. V. Cassill **23**:103
 Carolyn Kizer **15**:308
 Henri de Montherlant **19**:324
 Auberon Waugh **7**:512

Barolini, Helen
 Lucio Piccolo **13**:441

Baron, Alexander
 Bernard Malamud **2**:268

Barr, Alan P.
 Akira Kurosawa **16**:405

Barr, Donald
 Mary Renault **17**:392
 George Tabori **19**:435

Barrenechea, Ana María
 Jorge Luis Borges **1**:38

Barrett, Gerald
 Jerzy Kosinski **10**:305

Barrett, William
 Samuel Beckett **2**:48
 Albert Camus **2**:99
 Arthur C. Clarke **4**:105
 William Faulkner **3**:154
 Leslie A. Fiedler **24**:188
 Romain Gary **25**:186
 William Golding **17**:168
 Martin Heidegger **24**:271
 Ernest Hemingway **3**:238
 Hermann Hesse **2**:191
 Fletcher Knebel **14**:308

Halldór Laxness **25**:292
Yukio Mishima **27**:336
Philip Rahv **24**:358
Alain Robbe-Grillet **2**:377
Françoise Sagan **17**:423
Leon Uris **7**:491

Barrow, Craig Wallace
 Madeleine L'Engle **12**:351

Barrow, Geoffrey R.
 Blas de Otero **11**:425

Barry, Elaine
 Robert Frost **26**:125

Barry, Iris
 Fritz Lang **20**:200, 201

Barry, John Brooks
 T. S. Eliot **6**:165

Barry, Kevin
 John Berryman **6**:65

Barsam, Richard Meran
 Leni Riefenstahl **16**:522

Barson, Anthony
 Chaim Potok **26**:371

Bartelme, Elizabeth
 Alice Walker **27**:454

Barthelme, Donald
 Werner Herzog **16**:334

Barthes, Roland
 Raymond Queneau **5**:357

Bartholomay, Julia A.
 Howard Nemerov **6**:360

Bartholomew, David
 Larry McMurtry **11**:371
 Lina Wertmüller **16**:597

Bartkowech, R.
 Alain Robbe-Grillet **14**:462

Bartlett, Lee
 Lawrence Ferlinghetti **27**:137

Barton, Mrs. G. V.
 H. F. Brinsmead **21**:28

Barzun, Jaques
 Lionel Trilling **11**:539

Baskin, Barbara H.
 Virginia Hamilton **26**:156

Bassan, Maurice
 Flannery O'Connor **21**:261

Basso, Hamilton
 Paul Green **25**:195
 Halldór Laxness **25**:291
 Andrew Lytle **22**:292

Bassoff, Bruce
 William H. Gass **8**:244

Batchelor, John Calvin
 Ann Beattie **18**:39
 William Golding **17**:179
 Mark Helprin **10**:262
 Steven Millhauser **21**:220
 Joyce Carol Oates **19**:355
 Walker Percy **18**:400
 David Plante **23**:344
 Peter Rushforth **19**:407

Batchelor, R.
André Malraux **9**:353

Bates, Ernest Sutherland
T. S. Stribling **23**:445

Bates, Evaline
Ezra Pound **3**:397

Bates, Gladys Graham
Sally Benson **17**:48
Laura Z. Hobson **25**:268

Bates, Graham
Pär Lagerkvist **7**:198

Bates, Lewis
E. M. Almedingen **12**:2

Bateson, F. W.
W. H. Auden **6**:24
John Gardner **2**:151

Bati, Anwer
Ken Russell **16**:551

Battcock, Gregory
Andy Warhol **20**:415

Bauer, Arnold
Carl Zuckmayer **18**:555

Bauer, William
John Buell **10**:82

Baugh, Edward
Derek Walcott **25**:450

Bauke, J. P.
Jakov Lind **4**:292

Bauke, Joseph P.
Heinrich Böll **27**:60

Baum, Alwin L.
Alain Robbe-Grillet **14**:458

Baum, Betty
Robert Westall **17**:556

Baumann, Michael L.
B. Traven **8**:520; **11**:535, 537

Baumbach, Elinor
Sylvia Ashton-Warner **19**:22

Baumbach, Jonathan
Robert Bresson **16**:117
Truman Capote **8**:132
R. V. Cassill **23**:106
Ralph Ellison **1**:95
John Hawkes **4**:212
Stanley Kubrick **16**:377
Norman Mailer **4**:318
Bernard Malamud **1**:197, 199
Mary McCarthy **5**:275
Wright Morris **1**:232
Flannery O'Connor **1**:256
Grace Paley **6**:393
J. D. Salinger **1**:299
Scott Sommer **25**:424
William Styron **1**:330
Peter Taylor **1**:333
Edward Lewis Wallant **10**:511
Robert Penn Warren **1**:355

Baumgarten, Murray
Jorge Luis Borges **19**:52

Bauska, Barry
Dick Francis **22**:151

Baxter, Charles
J. R. Salamanca **15**:464

Baxter, John
John Ford **16**:312
Josef von Sternberg **20**:375

Baxter, Ralph C.
Allan W. Eckert **17**:104

Bayley, John
Anna Akhmatova **11**:9
W. H. Auden **2**:27, 28
Anthony Burgess **4**:85
D. J. Enright **8**:203
E. M. Forster **22**:136
M. M. Kaye **28**:197
Robert Lowell **4**:296
Amos Oz **11**:428
Vasko Popa **19**:375
Anthony Powell **10**:417
Varlam Shalamov **18**:479
Stevie Smith **25**:420
Aleksandr I. Solzhenitsyn
 4:511; **7**:444; **10**:479; **18**:499
Alexander Zinoviev **19**:486

Baylis, Jamie
Edmund White III **27**:481

Bazarov, Konstantin
Ivo Andrić **8**:20
Heinrich Böll **3**:76
James A. Michener **1**:214
Aleksandr I. Solzhenitsyn
 2:411; **10**:483

Bazelon, David T.
Dashiell Hammett **19**:193

Bazin, André
Robert Bresson **16**:111
Luis Buñuel **16**:131
Charles Chaplin **16**:200
Orson Welles **20**:435

Bazzdlo, Gretchen
Lee Kingman **17**:246

Beach, Joseph Warren
John Dos Passos **25**:137

Beacham, Walton
Erskine Caldwell **8**:124
Paul West **14**:568

Beagle, Peter S.
J.R.R. Tolkien **12**:567

Bean, Robin
Bob Fosse **20**:121
Pier Paolo Pasolini **20**:258, 259
Carlos Saura **20**:313

Beards, Virginia K.
Margaret Drabble **3**:128

Beardsley, Monroe C.
Wayne C. Booth **24**:99

Beatie, Bruce A.
J.R.R. Tolkien **3**:477

Beattie, Munro
Daryl Hine **15**:282
Irving Layton **15**:323
Dorothy Livesay **15**:341
A.J.M. Smith **15**:516

Beatty, Jack
Ann Beattie **18**:39
George V. Higgins **18**:235
Ward S. Just **27**:230
William Maxwell **19**:308
Alice Munro **19**:346
V. S. Naipaul **18**:362
R. K. Narayan **28**:301
Alexander Theroux **25**:432
Paul Theroux **15**:534; **28**:427
William Trevor **25**:443

Beatty, Jerome, Jr.
Larry Kettelkamp **12**:305

Beatty, Richmond C.
Donald Davidson **13**:166

Beauchamp, Gorman
E. M. Forster **10**:183

Beauchamp, William
Elizabeth Taylor **4**:541

Beaufort, John
Martin Sherman **19**:416
Elizabeth Swados **12**:560
Tennessee Williams **19**:473

Beauman, Sally
Julia O'Faolain **19**:359
Leon Rooke **25**:390
Monique Wittig **22**:473

Beaupre, Lee
Ralph Bakshi **26**:67

Beauvoir, Simone de
Violette Leduc **22**:260
Henri de Montherlant **19**:322

Beaver, Harold
William S. Burroughs **15**:112
Daniel Fuchs **22**:161
Allen Ginsburg **13**:241
Joyce Carol Oates **11**:404
Flannery O'Connor **21**:278

Bechtel, Louise S.
Margot Benary-Isbert **12**:31, 32
Franklyn M. Branley **21**:16
Walter Farley **17**:117
Henry Gregor Felsen **17**:121, 122
Margaret O. Hyde **21**:171
Mary Stolz **12**:546
Noel Streatfeild **21**:399, 400, 401
Rosemary Sutcliff **26**:425, 426
John R. Tunis **12**:596
Lenora Mattingly Weber **12**:632

Beck, Alfred D.
Franklyn M. Branley **21**:16
Margaret O. Hyde **21**:172

Beck, Marilyn
Rod McKuen **1**:210

Beck, Richard
Frans Eemil Sillanpää **19**:417

Beck, Warren
William Faulkner **11**:197; **14**:171

Becker, Brenda L.
Mary Gordon **22**:187

Becker, George J.
John Dos Passos **15**:183
Upton Sinclair **15**:500
T. S. Stribling **23**:446

Becker, Lucille Frackman
Louis Aragon **3**:14
Michel Butor **11**:80
Henri de Montherlant **19**:325
Georges Simenon **2**:398, 399; **8**:488; **18**:481

Becker, May Lamberton
Betty Cavanna **12**:97, 98
Maureen Daly **17**:88
Walter Farley **17**:115
Henry Gregor Felsen **17**:119
Esther Forbes **12**:207
Jesse Jackson **12**:289
Noel Streatfeild **21**:397, 398, 399
John R. Tunis **12**:594, 595
Leonora Mattingly Weber **12**:631, 632

Becker, Stephen
Jerome Siegel and Joe Shuster **21**:355

Beckett, Samuel
Václav Havel **25**:230
Sean O'Casey **11**:405

Beckham, Barry
Piri Thomas **17**:499

Beckman, Susan
Jack Hodgins **23**:234

Beddow, Reid
Iris Murdoch **22**:328

Bedford, William
Robert Lowell **15**:342
Eugenio Montale **18**:342

Bedient, Calvin
A. R. Ammons **8**:13
John Ashbery **15**:29
W. H. Auden **2**:27
Samuel Beckett **1**:24
Leonard Cohen **3**:110
Edward Dahlberg **7**:67
Donald Davie **10**:120
Richard Eberhart **11**:178
T. S. Eliot **13**:196
Louise Glück **7**:119
John Hawkes **4**:215
Seamus Heaney **25**:242
Anthony Hecht **19**:209
Joseph Heller **5**:178
Geoffrey Hill **5**:184
Daniel Hoffman **6**:243
Ted Hughes **2**:202; **4**:235
David Ignatow **7**:182
Donald Justice **19**:236
Thomas Kinsella **4**:271; **19**:256
Philip Larkin **5**:228
Robert Lowell **3**:303
George MacBeth **5**:264
James Merrill **8**:381
Joyce Carol Oates **2**:314; **3**:362
Octavio Paz **4**:398
Sylvia Plath **14**:426
Jon Silkin **6**:498
Dave Smith **22**:386
Stevie Smith **25**:416

Mark Strand **18**:520
James Tate **25**:429
R. S. Thomas **6**:532
Charles Tomlinson **4**:545, 547
Mona Van Duy **7**:499
Robert Penn Warren **10**:523;
  18:534, 538
John Hall Wheelock **14**:571
Richard Wilbur **9**:568
James Wright **5**:520

Bednarczyk, Tony
Edmund Crispin **22**:111
William X. Kienzle **25**:274

Beer, John
E. M. Forster **22**:131

Beer, Patricia
W. H. Auden **6**:19
Beryl Bainbridge **18**:33
Christopher Fry **14**:188
Seamus Heaney **14**:241
Eleanor Hibbert **7**:156
Lisel Mueller **13**:400
Alice Munro **10**:357
Peter Redgrove **6**:447

Beerman, Hans
Hermann Hesse **17**:199

Beesley, Paddy
Horst Bienek **11**:48

Begley, John
Oriana Fallaci **11**:191

Begnal, Michael
Vladimir Nabokov **23**:309

Behar, Jack
T. S. Eliot **13**:198

Beichman, Arnold
Arthur Koestler **1**:170
Anthony Powell **3**:400

Beidler, Peter G.
Leslie Marmon Silko **23**:407

Beja, Morris
Lawrence Durrell **4**:145
William Faulkner **3**:153
Nathalie Sarraute **4**:466

Belben, Rosalind
David Plante **23**:347

Belgion, Montgomery
André Malraux **4**:334
I. A. Richards **24**:373

Belitt, Ben
Jorge Luis Borges **2**:75
Robert Lowell **4**:297
Pablo Neruda **1**:247

Belkind, Allen
Amos Oz **27**:361
Ishmael Reed **13**:480
Kurt Vonnegut, Jr. **22**:447

Bell, Anthea
Otfried Preussler **17**:377

Bell, Bernard
William Styron **3**:473

Bell, Bernard W.
Jean Toomer **4**:550; **22**:427

Bell, David
Joyce Carol Oates **19**:356

Bell, De Witt
William Dickey **28**:118

Bell, Frederick J.
Ernest K. Gann **23**:162

Bell, Gene H.
Jorge Luis Borges **9**:118
Alejo Carpentier **8**:135
Vladimir Nabokov **6**:360

Bell, Ian F. A.
Ezra Pound **10**:404

Bell, Lisle
Frank B. Gilbreth, Jr. and
  Ernestine Gilbreth Carey
  17:152
Ogden Nash **23**:316

Bell, Marvin
F. R. Scott **22**:375
Dave Smith **22**:387
Miriam Waddington **28**:437

Bell, Millicent
Margaret Atwood **2**:19
Lynne Reid Banks **23**:40
Peter De Vries **2**:113
Janet Frame **22**:144
Eugenio Montale **7**:231
John O'Hara **2**:325
Anne Tyler **28**:430

Bell, Pearl K.
Martin Amis **4**:20
John Ashbery **6**:12
Beryl Bainbridge **4**:39
James Baldwin **4**:40; **15**:42
William Barrett **27**:24
Ann Beattie **18**:40
Saul Bellow **8**:70
Marie-Claire Blais **6**:81
Louise Bogan **4**:69
William F. Buckley, Jr. **7**:35
Anthony Burgess **22**:77
John Cheever **15**:130
Eleanor Clark **5**:106
Arthur A. Cohen **7**:51
Len Deighton **7**:76
William Faulkner **6**:177
Paula Fox **2**:140
Nadine Gordimer **5**:146
Juan Goytisolo **5**:149
Günter Grass **4**:206
Graham Greene **3**:214
Joseph Heller **5**:180
Mark Helprin **22**:222
George V. Higgins **7**:157
Maureen Howard **5**:189
John Irving **13**:293
Ruth Prawer Jhabvala **8**:311
Charles Johnson **7**:183
Diane Johnson **5**:199
Uwe Johnson **10**:284
James Jones **10**:291
Milan Kundera **4**:277; **19**:270
Philip Larkin **13**:337
John le Carré **5**:232
Alison Lurie **4**:307
Bernard Malamud **18**:321
Peter Matthiessen **5**:275
Mary McCarthy **14**:360
John McGahern **5**:281
Steven Millhauser **21**:217
A. G. Mojtabai **9**:385
Toni Morrison **22**:323
V. S. Naipaul **7**:254
Amos Oz **5**:335
Cynthia Ozick **7**:288
Walker Percy **8**:438
Marge Piercy **18**:409
Anthony Powell **3**:403
J. F. Powers **8**:447
Ishmael Reed **6**:448
Adrienne Rich **6**:459
Jill Robinson **10**:439
Philip Roth **15**:455
J. R. Salamanca **15**:463
Susan Fromberg Schaeffer
  22:367
Anne Sexton **6**:494
Alix Kates Shulman **10**:475
Stephen Spender **5**:402
D. M. Thomas **22**:421
Mario Vargas Llosa **6**:546
Patrick White **3**:523
Edmund Wilson **24**:483

Bell, Robert
Honor Arundel **17**:12
H. F. Brinsmead **21**:27
Robert Cormier **12**:137
Eilís Dillon **17**:95, 96
Mollie Hunter **21**:163
Madeleine L'Engle **12**:350
William Mayne **12**:390, 399
Robert Westall **17**:555, 557

Bell, Vereen M.
E. M. Forster **1**:107
Ted Hughes **9**:281
Richard F. Hugo **18**:260

Bellamy, Joe David
Donald Barthelme **13**:60
Sam Shepard **4**:490
Kurt Vonnegut, Jr. **4**:564

Bellman, Samuel Irving
Saul Bellow **8**:81
Jorge Luis Borges **6**:91
Jerome Charyn **5**:103
Leonard Cohen **3**:109
Stanley Elkin **6**:169
William Faulkner **3**:152
Leslie A. Fiedler **4**:160, 161
Bruce Jay Friedman **3**:165
William H. Gass **15**:258
Ernest Hemingway **3**:234
Yoram Kaniuk **19**:239
Jack Kerouac **3**:263, 264
Meyer Levin **7**:205
Bernard Malamud **1**:197; **3**:320,
  325
Saul Maloff **5**:271
Wallace Markfield **8**:380
James A. Michener **5**:288
Harry Mark Petrakis **3**:382
Philip Roth **3**:435
John Updike **3**:487
Elie Wiesel **5**:490

Belloc, Hilaire
P. G. Wodehouse **22**:479

Bellow, Saul
Camilo José Cela **13**:144
Ilya Ehrenburg **18**:131

Bellows, Silence Buck
Frank B. Gilbreth, Jr. and
  Ernestine Gilbreth Carey
  17:155
Zilpha Keatley Snyder **17**:471

Bell-Villada, Gene H.
Gabriel García Márquez **15**:254

Beloff, Max
Paul Scott **9**:477

Beloof, Robert
Stanley J. Kunitz **6**:285
Marianne Moore **4**:360

Belton, John
Claude Chabrol **16**:177

Benchley, Nathaniel
Robert Newton Peck **17**:337

Bendau, Clifford P.
Colin Wilson **14**:585

Bender, Marylin
Alix Kates Shulman **2**:395

Bender, Rose S.
Babbis Friis-Baastad **12**:214

Bender, William
Andrew Lloyd Webber and Tim
  Rice **21**:423

Bendiner, Elmer
Piri Thomas **17**:498

Bendow, Burton
Grace Paley **4**:393

Benedikt, Michael
David Ignatow **14**:276
Galway Kinnell **2**:230
Charles Simic **22**:379
Richard Wilbur **3**:532

Benestad, Janet P.
M. E. Kerr **12**:300

Benet, Rosemary
Enid Bagnold **25**:74

Benét, William Rose
Alvah Bessie **23**:60
Sterling A. Brown **23**:95
Agatha Christie **12**:111
Robert Francis **15**:235
Ogden Nash **23**:316

Benham, G. F.
Friedrich Dürrenmatt **11**:174

Benjamin, Cynthia
Madeleine L'Engle **12**:351

Benjamin, David A.
John D. MacDonald **27**:274

Benn, M. B.
Michael Hamburger **14**:234

Bennett, Bruce
Brad Leithauser **27**:240
Katha Pollitt **28**:367

Bennett, C. S.
Rosemary Sutcliff **26**:427

Bennett, Joseph
Philip Booth **23**:75
Anthony Hecht **8**:266

Bennett, Spencer C.
John Lennon and Paul McCartney 12:365

Bennett, Virginia
Truman Capote 19:80

Bennett, Wendell C.
Thor Heyerdahl 26:190

Benson, C. David
P. G. Wodehouse 22:484

Benson, Gerard
Leon Garfield 12:229

Benson, Jackson J.
Ernest Hemingway 6:232
John Steinbeck 9:517

Benson, Mary
Athol Fugard 14:189

Benson, Sheila
Jerzy Skolimowski 20:355

Benson, Thomas W.
Wayne C. Booth 24:89

Benstock, Bernard
William Gaddis 3:177
Flann O'Brien 7:270
Sean O'Casey 5:317

Benston, Alice N.
W. S. Merwin 2:276

Bentley, Allen
Morris L. West 6:564

Bentley, Eric
Robert Anderson 23:29
Sally Benson 17:50
Truman Capote 19:81
Charles Chaplin 16:205
I. A. Richards 24:388
Robert Penn Warren 8:536
Orson Welles 20:434
Herman Wouk 9:579

Bentley, Joseph
Aldous Huxley 1:152

Bentley, Phyllis
Pearl S. Buck 11:69
Noel Streatfeild 21:394

Benton, Michael
Alan Garner 17:146

Berendt, John
Phil Ochs 17:333

Berets, Ralph
Saul Bellow 15:47
John Fowles 3:163

Berg, Beatrice
Agnes Eckhardt Nixon 21:243

Berger, Arthur Asa
Robert Crumb 17:85
Stan Lee 17:257
Monty Python 21:228
Charles M. Schulz 12:529
Jerome Siegel and Joe Shuster 21:360

Berger, Charles
Olga Broumas 10:77
James Merrill 18:331
Frederick Seidel 18:474

Berger, Harold L.
Frank Herbert 12:278

Berger, John
Lindsay Anderson 20:11

Berger, Matt
Roger Zelazny 21:474

Berger, Peter L.
Andrew M. Greeley 28:171

Bergin, Thomas G.
Aldo Palazzeschi 11:432
Lucio Piccolo 13:440
Salvatore Quasimodo 10:429
João Guimarães Rosa 23:349

Bergman, Andrew
Frank Capra 16:159
Isaac Bashevis Singer 11:499

Bergman, Andrew C. J.
Peter Benchley 4:53
Guy Davenport, Jr. 6:124

Bergmann, Linda Shell
Ishmael Reed 13:479
Ronald Sukenick 4:531

Bergonzi, Bernard
Kingsley Amis 2:6, 9
W. H. Auden 6:22
John Barth 3:39
Heinrich Böll 27:60
Paul Bowles 2:79
Anthony Burgess 2:85
R. V. Cassill 23:106
Donald Davie 10:123
Nigel Dennis 8:173
Ilya Ehrenburg 18:135
Richard Fariña 9:195
John Fowles 2:138
Paula Fox 2:139
Geoffrey H. Hartman 27:189
B. S. Johnson 6:262
Doris Lessing 3:283
William Maxwell 19:307
Iris Murdoch 2:297
Flann O'Brien 4:383
Anthony Powell 3:400
Thomas Pynchon 3:408
Alain Robbe-Grillet 4:447
Andrew Sinclair 2:401
C. P. Snow 4:501; 13:508
Evelyn Waugh 1:357; 3:510
Angus Wilson 2:473; 25:461

Berke, Roberta
John Ashbery 25:55
Katha Pollitt 28:366

Berkson, Bill
Frank O'Hara 2:320
Jerome Rothenberg 6:477

Berkvist, Margaret
Babbis Friis-Baastad 12:213

Berkvist, Robert
Isaac Asimov 26:36
Allan W. Eckert 17:105
Earl Hamner, Jr. 12:258
Robert A. Heinlein 26:161
Farley Mowat 26:337
Andre Norton 12:456, 457
Kin Platt 26:348, 352
Mary Rodgers 12:493

Berlin, Isaiah
Aldous Huxley 3:254

Berlin, Normand
Roman Polanski 16:469

Berman, Bruce
Rainer Werner Fassbinder 20:105

Berman, Jeffrey
E. M. Forster 22:129

Berman, Michael
Milan Kundera 19:267

Berman, Neil
Robert Coover 15:143

Berman, Paul
Isaac Bashevis Singer 11:501

Berman, Ronald
William F. Buckley, Jr. 18:81

Berman, Susan K.
Fredrica Wagman 7:500

Bermel, Albert
Ed Bullins 1:47
Jean Genet 10:227
Christopher Hampton 4:211
Megan Terry 19:439

Bermel, Joyce
Hilma Wolitzer 17:562

Bernays, Anne
Alice Adams 6:1
Adrienne Rich 11:474

Berner, Robert L.
André Brink 18:68
Bessie Head 25:233
Alan Paton 10:388

Berner, Steve
Louis L'Amour 25:281

Bernetta (Quinn), Sister Mary, O.S.F.
Allen Tate 4:539
See also Quinn, Sister Mary Bernetta, O.S.F.

Bernhardt, William
François Truffaut 20:380

Bernikow, Louise
A. S. Byatt 19:77
Muriel Rukeyser 6:479

Berns, Walter
Daniel J. Berrigan 4:57

Bernstein, Burton
George P. Elliott 2:131

Bernstein, Paul
James Clavell 25:127

Bernstein, Samuel J.
Robert Anderson 23:33

Bernstein, Theodore M.
Isaac Asimov 26:36

Berrigan, Daniel, S.J.
Horst Bienek 7:28
Denise Levertov 28:243
Thomas Merton 11:373

Berry, Mabel
Maureen Daly 17:91

Berry, Margaret
Mulk Raj Anand 23:12

Berry, Wendell
Hayden Carruth 4:94

Berryman, Charles
Gore Vidal 22:435

Berryman, John
Saul Bellow 10:37
T. S. Eliot 13:197
Ernest Hemingway 10:270
Randall Jarrell 13:299
Ezra Pound 13:460

Bersani, Leo
Julio Cortázar 2:104
Jean Genet 2:158
Norman Mailer 8:364
Henri de Montherlant 19:328
Alain Robbe-Grillet 1:288
Robert Wilson 7:551

Berthoff, Warner
Alex Haley 12:245
Norman Mailer 3:313
Iris Murdoch 3:345
Vladimir Nabokov 3:352
Muriel Spark 3:464
Edmund Wilson 2:475; 3:538

Bespaloff, Rachel
Albert Camus 9:139

Bessai, Diane
Austin C. Clarke 8:142

Besser, Gretchen R.
Julien Green 3:205

Bessie, Alvah
Norman Mailer 3:319

Bester, Alfred
Isaac Asimov 3:16
Robert A. Heinlein 3:227

Bester, John
Masuji Ibuse 22:225, 226
Kenzaburō Ōe 10:372

Beston, John B.
Patrick White 18:544

Bethell, Nicholas
Aleksandr I. Solzhenitsyn 7:441

Betsky, Celia B.
A. Alvarez 5:19
Max Apple 9:32
Harriette Arnow 7:15
Don DeLillo 10:135
Margaret Drabble 2:119
John Hawkes 4:217
Doris Lessing 10:315
Iris Murdoch 4:370
Tim O'Brien 19:358
Marge Piercy 14:419

Bettelheim, Bruno
Lina Wertmüller 16:599

Bettersworth, John K.
Milton Meltzer 26:300

Betts, Whitney
Winston Graham 23:192

Bevan, A. R.
Mordecai Richler **5**:377

Bevan, David G.
Pier Paolo Pasolini **20**:268

Bevan, Jack
Arthur Gregor **9**:253

Bevington, Helen
Peter Davison **28**:101
Louis Simpson **4**:500

Bewick, E. N.
H. F. Brinsmead **21**:28

Bewick, Elizabeth
Josephine Poole **17**:371

Bewley, Marius
A. R. Ammons **2**:11
John Berryman **2**:56
Kenneth Burke **24**:124
C. Day Lewis **6**:128
Thomas Kinsella **4**:270
Hugh MacDiarmid **2**:253
Sylvia Plath **2**:335
Herbert Read **4**:440
Charles Tomlinson **2**:436

Bezanker, Abraham
Saul Bellow **1**:32
Isaac Bashevis Singer **3**:454

Bianco, David
James Purdy **10**:426

Biasin, Gian-Paolo
Umberto Eco **28**:131
Carlo Emilio Gadda **11**:211
Leonardo Sciascia **8**:473

Bibby, Geoffrey
Thor Heyerdahl **26**:192

Bick, Janice
Christie Harris **12**:269

Bickerton, Dorothy
Melvin Berger **12**:41

Bidart, Frank
Robert Lowell **9**:336

Bien, Peter
Yannis Ritsos **6**:462

Bienstock, Beverly Gray
John Barth **3**:41

Bier, Jesse
James Thurber **5**:434

Bierhaus, E. G., Jr.
John Osborne **11**:423

Bigger, Charles P.
Walker Percy **8**:440

Bigsby, C.W.E.
Edward Albee **9**:6, 9; **13**:4
James Baldwin **13**:51; **17**:33
Imamu Amiri Baraka **14**:43
Lorraine Hansberry **17**:185
Arthur Miller **10**:342; **26**:321
Willard Motley **18**:357

Bilan, R. P.
Margaret Atwood **25**:62
F. R. Leavis **24**:310
Rudy Wiebe **14**:574

Bilik, Dorothy Seidman
Bernard Malamud **27**:296

Bill, Rise
Richard Peck **21**:301

Billman, Carol W.
Arthur Kopit **18**:290

Binder, Lucia
Cecil Bødker **21**:12

Binding, Paul
Jurek Becker **19**:36
Rolf Hochhuth **18**:256
Brian Moore **19**:334

Binham, Philip
Paavo Haavikko **18**:207, 208
Hannu Salama **18**:460

Binns, Ronald
John Fowles **4**:171

Binyon, T. J.
Eric Ambler **9**:21
William Boyd **28**:40
Peter Dickinson **12**:175, 176
Paul E. Erdman **25**:154
Ruth Rendell **28**:384

Birbalsingh, F. M.
Mordecai Richler **13**:485

Birch, Ian
David Byrne **26**:95

Bird, Caroline
Milton Meltzer **26**:299

Bird, Christopher
Colin Wilson **14**:584

Birkerts, Sven
Blaise Cendrars **18**:97
Brad Leithauser **27**:241

Birmingham, Mary Louise
Jesse Jackson **12**:289

Birnbaum, Henry
Gil Orlovitz **22**:332

Birnbaum, Larry
Frank Zappa **17**:595

Birnbaum, Milton
Aldous Huxley **3**:255; **4**:239

Birney, Earle
A.J.M. Smith **15**:513

Birrell, Francis
René Clair **20**:59
Rouben Mamoulian **16**:420

Birstein, Ann
Iris Murdoch **4**:370
David Plante **23**:343
Sylvia Plath **17**:352

Bishop, Christopher
Buster Keaton **20**:189

Bishop, Claire Huchet
Joseph Krumgold **12**:316
Noel Streatfeild **21**:401

Bishop, Elizabeth
Flannery O'Connor **15**:408

Bishop, Ferman
Allen Tate **2**:428

Bishop, John Peale
E. E. Cummings **12**:142

Bishop, Lloyd
Henri Michaux **8**:390

Bishop, Michael
Stephen King **26**:238
Ursula K. Le Guin **22**:275
Fritz Leiber **25**:307

Bishop, Morris
Ogden Nash **23**:323

Bishop, Tom
Jean Cocteau **8**:145
Julio Cortázar **2**:103
Raymond Queneau **5**:359
Claude Simon **9**:482

Biskind, Peter
Elia Kazan **16**:371
Sam Peckinpah **20**:278
Lina Wertmüller **16**:588

Bissell, Claude T.
Hugh Garner **13**:234

Bissett, Donald J.
Colin Thiele **17**:493

Black, Campbell
Mary Renault **17**:400
Isaac Bashevis Singer **6**:507

Black, Cyril E.
André Malraux **1**:203

Black, Susan M.
Pamela Hansford Johnson **27**:219
Elizabeth Spencer **22**:400

Blackburn, Sara
Lynne Reid Banks **23**:41
Marie-Claire Blais **22**:58
R. V. Cassill **4**:95
Don DeLillo **27**:77
Peter Dickinson **12**:169
Rosalyn Drexler **2**:120
Jim Harrison **6**:225
Maxine Hong Kingston **12**:313
Alan Lelchuk **5**:244
David Madden **5**:266
Michael McClure **6**:316
Toni Morrison **4**:365
Marge Piercy **3**:384
Alix Kates Shulman **2**:395
Elizabeth Spencer **22**:402
Gillian Tindall **7**:473
Anne Tyler **28**:431
David Wagoner **5**:474
Fay Weldon **6**:562

Blackburn, Thomas
Sylvia Plath **17**:344

Blackburn, Tom
Kingsley Amis **2**:6

Blackford, Staige D.
M. M. Kaye **28**:201

Blackman, Ruth
Sylvia Ashton-Warner **19**:20

Blackmur, R(ichard) P.
Cleanth Brooks **24**:102
E. E. Cummings **8**:154; **12**:140
T. S. Eliot **24**:159
Archibald MacLeish **14**:336
Marianne Moore **13**:393
John Crowe Ransom **5**:363
I. A. Richards **24**:389
Allen Tate **4**:536
Lionel Trilling **24**:450

Blackwood, Caroline
Ingmar Bergman **16**:49

Blades, Joe
Bob Fosse **20**:123

Blaha, Franz G.
J. P. Donleavy **4**:125

Blair, Karin
Gene Roddenberry **17**:408, 411

Blair, Walter
Ogden Nash **23**:320

Blais, Marie-Claire
Elizabeth Bishop **13**:88

Blaise, Clark
Salman Rushdie **23**:365

Blake, George
John Cowper Powys **9**:439

Blake, Nicholas
Margery Allingham **19**:12
Agatha Christie **12**:113

Blake, Patricia
Cynthia Ozick **28**:355
Aleksandr I. Solzhenitsyn **1**:319; **7**:439
Andrei Voznesensky **1**:349

Blake, Percival
Leonardo Sciascia **8**:474

Blake, Richard A.
Norman Lear **12**:331
George Lucas **16**:411
Monty Python **21**:224

Blakeston, Oswell
Michael Ayrton **7**:19
Gabriel García Márquez **3**:180
Paul Theroux **15**:535
P. G. Wodehouse **2**:480

Blamires, David
David Jones **2**:216, 217; **4**:260; **13**:308

Bland, Peter
Derek Walcott **25**:457

Blanford, S. L.
Honor Arundel **17**:13

Blaser, Robin
Jack Spicer **18**:506

Blassingame, Wyatt
Harriette Arnow **7**:15

Blaydes, Sophia B.
Simon Gray **9**:242

Blazek, Douglas
Robert Creeley **2**:107
W. S. Merwin **5**:286
Diane Wakoski **4**:573

Bleikasten, André
Flannery O'Connor 10:366

Bleiler, E. F.
Isaac Asimov 26:58

Blicksilver, Edith
Leslie Marmon Silko 23:409

Blindheim, Joan Tindale
John Arden 13:26

Blish, James
Poul Anderson 15:11
John Brunner 10:77
Theodore Sturgeon 22:411
Roger Zelazny 21:465

Blishen, Edward
Alan Garner 17:150
William Golding 27:159
William Mayne 12:391, 394

Bliss, Michael
Hugh Hood 28:195

Bliss, Shepherd
Frederick Wiseman 20:477

Bliven, Naomi
Marie-Claire Blais 22:58
Louis-Ferdinand Céline 4:103
Agatha Christie 12:125
Andrea Giovene 7:117
Andrew M. Greeley 28:170
Eugène Ionesco 6:257
Anthony Powell 7:343
Emlyn Williams 15:578
Monique Wittig 22:471

Bloch, Adèle
Michel Butor 8:120
Pär Lagerkvist 7:200

Blodgett, E. D.
D. G. Jones 10:285
Sylvia Plath 3:388

Blodgett, Harriet
Colin MacInnes 23:285
V. S. Naipaul 4:375

Blomster, W. V.
Christa Wolf 14:594

Blomster, Wes
Siegfried Lenz 27:256

Bionski, Jan
Czesiaw Miiosz 11:377

Bloom, Harold
A. R. Ammons 5:25; 8:14; 9:26
John Ashbery 4:23; 9:41; 13:30;
   15:26, 33
W. H. Auden 6:16
Saul Bellow 6:50
Jorge Luis Borges 6:87
James Dickey 10:141
Northrop Frye 24:226
Allen Ginsberg 6:199
Seamus Heaney 25:246
Anthony Hecht 13:269
Daryl Hine 15:282
John Hollander 8:301, 302;
   14:264
Philip Levine 9:332
Robert Lowell 8:355
Archibald MacLeish 8:363

Norman Mailer 28:260
James Merrill 8:388
Howard Moss 7:249; 14:375
Robert Pack 13:439
W. D. Snodgrass 10:478
Mark Strand 18:517
Robert Penn Warren 8:539;
   18:535
Charles Wright 13:614

Bloom, J. Don
Alvin Silverstein and Virginia
   B. Silverstein 17:454

Bloom, Janet
Linda Pastan 27:368

Bloom, Robert
W. H. Auden 1:10; 11:13

Blotner, Joseph L.
Cleanth Brooks 24:116
J. D. Salinger 1:295

Blow, Simon
Julia O'Faolain 19:360
Sylvia Plath 11:451
Isaac Bashevis Singer 6:510

Blue, Adrianne
Buchi Emecheta 14:160
Henri Troyat 23:461

Bluefarb, Sam
Leslie A. Fiedler 13:213
Bernard Malamud 1:196; 9:350
Chaim Potok 26:370
John Steinbeck 5:407
Richard Wright 3:546

Bluestein, Gene
Bob Dylan 12:189
Richard Fariña 9:195

Bluestone, George
Nelson Algren 10:5

Blum, David
Peter Handke 15:268

Blum, Morgan
Peter Taylor 18:522

Blumenberg, Richard M.
Alain Resnais 16:510

Blumenfeld, Yorick
John Berger 19:37
Yevgeny Yevtushenko 1:382

Blundell, Jane Boyarin
Maya Angelou 12:14

Bly, Robert
A. R. Ammons 5:28
Carlos Castaneda 12:94
Gunnar Ekelöf 27:111, 115
David Ignatow 14:274
Robert Lowell 4:297
Pablo Neruda 28:306, 315
Francis Ponge 18:419

Blythe, Ronald
Roy Fuller 28:158
William Golding 17:178
Erica Jong 6:267
Alice Munro 6:341
Joyce Carol Oates 6:368
Jean Rhys 19:391
David Storey 8:506

Boak, Denis
André Malraux 4:330

Boardman, Gwenn R.
Yasunari Kawabata 2:222
Yukio Mishima 2:286

Boatwright, James
Harry Crews 23:132
John Ehle 27:104
Paul Horgan 9:278
James McCourt 5:278
Gore Vidal 6:549
Robert Penn Warren 1:356

Boatwright, John
Walker Percy 8:438

Boatwright, Taliaferro
Ernest K. Gann 23:165
Emily Cheney Neville 12:450

Bobbie, Walter
Stephen King 12:309

Bobbitt, Joan
James Dickey 15:173
William Price Fox 22:140

Bochner, Jay
Blaise Cendrars 18:93

Bochtler, Stan
Cecil Bødker 21:12

Bocock, Maclin
Donald Barthelme 23:44

Bodart, Joni
Frank Herbert 12:272
Rosemary Wells 12:638

Bode, Carl
Katherine Anne Porter 7:318

Bodo, Maureen
Gore Vidal 10:504

Boe, Eugene
Christina Stead 2:421

Boek, Jean K.
Vine Deloria, Jr. 21:113

Boeth, Richard
Len Deighton 22:114
John O'Hara 2:324

Bogan, Louise
W. H. Auden 1:9
Richard Eberhart 19:140
Barbara Howes 15:289
Patrick Kavanagh 22:235
Marianne Moore 13:396; 19:338
W. R. Rodgers 7:377
Muriel Rukeyser 15:456
Frederick Seidel 18:474

Bogart, Gary
Sol Gordon 26:137
Robert Newton Peck 17:340

Bogdanovich, Peter
Alfred Hitchcock 16:343

Bohn, Chris
Bob Marley 17:272

Bohner, Charles H.
Robert Penn Warren 1:354

Bok, Sissela
Vladimir Nabokov 1:245

Boland, John
Brian Aldiss 5:15
John Dickson Carr 3:101
Richard Condon 4:106
Harry Kemelman 2:225
Michael Moorcock 5:293

Bold, Alan
Robert Graves 1:130

Boles, Paul Darcy
Truman Capote 19:81

Bolger, Eugenie
Hortense Calisher 8:125
José Donoso 4:130

Bollard, Margaret Lloyd
William Carlos Williams 9:571

Bolling, Doug
John Barth 27:30

Bolling, Douglass
E. M. Forster 9:206
Doris Lessing 3:290
Clarence Major 19:296
Rudolph Wurlitzer 4:598;
   15:588
Al Young 19:478

Bolotin, Susan
Gloria Naylor 28:304

Bolton, Richard R.
Herman Wouk 9:580

Bond, Kirk
Carl Theodor Dreyer 16:260

Bondy, François
Günter Grass 2:173

Bone, Robert
William Melvin Kelley 22:247
Paule Marshall 27:309
Jean Toomer 22:425

Bone, Robert A.
James Baldwin 1:15; 17:29
Arna Bontemps 1:37
W.E.B. Du Bois 1:80
Ralph Ellison 1:95; 3:142
Jessie Redmon Fauset 19:170
Langston Hughes 1:147
Zora Neale Hurston 7:171
Willard Motley 18:357
Ann Petry 1:266
Jean Toomer 1:341
Richard Wright 1:378
Frank G. Yerby 1:381

Bongiorno, Robert
Carlo Emilio Gadda 11:209

Boni, John
Kurt Vonnegut, Jr. 5:465

Boniol, John Dawson, Jr.
Melvin Berger 12:40, 41

Bonner, Joey
Bette Bao Lord 23:279

Bontemps, Arna
Ann Petry 18:403
Jean Toomer 13:551

Booth, Martin
Ted Hughes 14:272
John Matthias 9:361
Gilbert Sorrentino 14:500
Yevgeny Yevtushenko 26:469

Booth, Philip
Hayden Carruth 18:87
William Dickey 28:117
Richard Eberhart 11:176;
  19:140
Randall Jarrell 1:159
Maxine Kumin 13:327
Mary Oliver 19:361
Louis Simpson 7:426

Booth, Rosemary
Marilynne Robinson 25:388

Booth, Wayne C.
M. H. Abrams 24:13
Kenneth Burke 24:133
Susan Fromberg Schaeffer
  22:367
Hunter S. Thompson 17:507

Borden, Diane M.
Ingmar Bergman 16:78

Bordewich, Fergus M.
Agnes Eckhardt Nixon 21:246

Bordwell, David
Charles Chaplin 16:199
François Truffaut 20:389
Orson Welles 20:445

Borg, Mary
Bessie Head 25:232
Françoise Sagan 17:426

Borges, Jorge Luis
Adolfo Bioy Casares 4:63
Orson Welles 20:453

Boring, Phyllis Zatlin
Miguel Delibes 18:117

Borinsky, Alicia
Manuel Puig 5:355

Borkat, Robert F. Sarfatt
Robert Frost 9:222

Borland, Hal
John Ehle 27:103
Farley Mowat 26:333, 335

Boroff, David
R. V. Cassill 23:104, 105
William Melvin Kelley 22:247

Boroff, David A.
John A. Williams 13:598

Borroff, Marie
John Hollander 2:197
Denise Levertov 2:243
William Meredith 4:348
James Merrill 2:274

Borrus, Bruce J.
Saul Bellow 15:57

Bosley, Keith
Eugenio Montale 7:229

Bosmajian, Hamida
Louis-Ferdinand Céline 3:103

Boston, Howard
Eilís Dillon 17:93, 94
Jean Lee Latham 12:323
Farley Mowat 26:333

Bosworth, David
Robert Stone 23:430
Kurt Vonnegut, Jr. 12:629

Botsford, Judith
Franklyn M. Branley 21:19

Boucher, Anthony
Margery Allingham 19:13
Taylor Caldwell 28:65
Agatha Christie 12:115, 116,
  117
John Creasey 11:134
Edmund Crispin 22:109, 110
C. Day Lewis 6:128
Jan de Hartog 19:131
Len Deighton 22:113, 114
Eilís Dillon 17:95
Howard Fast 23:158
Timothy Findley 27:140
Dick Francis 22:150
Winston Graham 23:193, 194
Patricia Highsmith 2:193
P. D. James 18:272
M. M. Kaye 28:198
Harry Kemelman 2:225
Colin MacInnes 23:282
Mary Lee Settle 19:409
Anthony Shaffer 19:413
Mary Stewart 7:467
Julian Symons 2:426; 14:523

Bouise, Oscar A.
Allan W. Eckert 17:103
Eleanor Hibbert 7:155
Per Wahlöö 7:501

Boulby, Mark
Hermann Hesse 11:272; 17:207

Boulton, James T.
Harold Pinter 6:406

Bouraoui, H. A.
Nathalie Sarraute 2:385

Bourdillon, Jennifer
Otfried Preussler 17:374

Bourjaily, Vance
Kay Boyle 19:66
David Bradley, Jr. 23:80
Roald Dahl 18:109
Jim Harrison 14:235
Philip Roth 9:460
John Sayles 14:483
George Tabori 19:436

Bourne, Mike
Jimmy Page and Robert Plant
  12:476
Frank Zappa 17:588

Bourneuf, Roland
Hubert Aquin 15:17

Boutelle, Ann E.
Hugh MacDiarmid 2:253

Boutrous, Lawrence K.
John Hawkes 3:223

Bova, Benjamin W.
Franklyn M. Branley 21:17

Bowden, J. H.
Peter De Vries 28:112

Bowe, Clotilde Soave
Natalia Ginzburg 11:228

Bowen, Barbara C.
P. G. Wodehouse 10:538

Bowen, Elizabeth
Henri de Montherlant 19:322

Bowen, John
Arthur Kopit 1:171
Randolph Stow 23:433

Bowen, Robert O.
Andrew Lytle 22:293
Flannery O'Connor 21:259

Bowen, Roger
Philip Larkin 18:297

Bowen, Zack
Padraic Colum 28:90

Bowering, George
Milton Acorn 15:9
Margaret Atwood 2:19
Margaret Avison 2:29
Earle Birney 4:64
D. G. Jones 10:288
Margaret Laurence 3:278
Denise Levertov 15:336
Gwendolyn MacEwan 13:357
John Newlove 14:377
A. W. Purdy 6:428
Mordecai Richler 5:374
Audrey Thomas 7:472; 13:538

Bowering, Marilyn
Patrick Lane 25:285

Bowering, Peter
Aldous Huxley 4:237

Bowers, A. Joan
Gore Vidal 8:526

Bowers, Marvin
L. E. Sissman 9:491

Bowie, Malcolm
Yves Bonnefoy 9:114

Bowles, Gloria
Diane Wakoski 7:505

Bowles, Jerry G.
Craig Nova 7:267

Bowra, C. M.
Rafael Alberti 7:7

Boxer, David
Raymond Carver 22:98

Boyce, Burke
Esther Forbes 12:205

Boyd, Blanche M.
Renata Adler 8:5

Boyd, Celia
Honor Arundel 17:16

Boyd, Ernest
Padraic Colum 28:86, 87

Boyd, John D.
Theodore Roethke 11:483

Boyd, Malcolm
Andrew Lloyd Webber and Tim
  Rice 21:425

Boyd, Robert
James Purdy 2:350

Boyd, William
Margaret Drabble 22:126
Gabriel García Márquez 15:252
Penelope Gilliatt 13:238
William Golding 27:162
Steven Millhauser 21:221
John Mortimer 28:288
Irwin Shaw 23:399
Kurt Vonnegut, Jr. 22:451

Boyer, Robert H.
Roger Zelazny 21:473

Boyers, Robert
Saul Bellow 3:57
Ingmar Bergman 16:79
Alan Dugan 6:143
Louise Glück 22:173
Witold Gombrowicz 7:125;
  11:241
Robinson Jeffers 2:214; 3:258
Arthur Koestler 6:281
Robert Lowell 8:349; 9:336
Sylvia Plath 11:447
Adrienne Rich 7:364
Theodore Roethke 8:457
W. D. Snodgrass 2:406
Gary Snyder 2:406
Richard Wilbur 6:569

Boyle, Kay
James Baldwin 1:15
Tom Wicker 7:534

Boyle, Ted E.
Kingsley Amis 2:6
Brendan Behan 1:26

Boylston, Helen Dore
Betty Cavanna 12:97
Henry Gregor Felsen 17:120
Lee Kingman 17:243

Bozek, Phillip
Hugh MacDiarmid 19:285

Bracher, Frederick
John Cheever 15:127
James Gould Cozzens 11:127

Brackman, Jacob
Robert Crumb 17:84
Melvin Van Peebles 20:411

Bradbrook, M. C.
T. S. Eliot 1:91; 2:130

Bradbury, John M.
Allen Tate 24:446

Bradbury, Malcolm
J. G. Ballard 14:40
A. S. Byatt 19:75
Ivy Compton-Burnett 10:109
John Dos Passos 8:181
E. M. Forster 4:167; 10:180
John Fowles 3:162; 4:172
William Gaddis 8:227
Thomas Hinde 6:240
Aldous Huxley 4:244
Michael Mott 15:379

Iris Murdoch **4**:367; **11**:388
John O'Hara **11**:413
Piers Paul Read **25**:378
C. P. Snow **4**:505
Gilbert Sorrentino **14**:501
Muriel Spark **2**:418
Lionel Trilling **9**:531
Evelyn Waugh **8**:543
Angus Wilson **5**:513

Bradbury, Maureen
Phyllis Gotlieb **18**:193

Bradbury, Ray
Ray Bradbury **15**:86

Bradford, Melvin E.
Donald Davidson **2**:111, 112; **13**:167
William Faulkner **1**:102; **3**:155; **18**:149
Walker Percy **3**:381
Allen Tate **2**:429

Bradford, Richard
A. B. Guthrie, Jr. **23**:199
M. E. Kerr **12**:300
James Kirkwood **9**:319

Bradford, Tom
Ray Bradbury **10**:69

Bradley, Sculley
Robert Frost **3**:169

Bradlow, Paul
Frederick Wiseman **20**:469

Brady, Ann P.
T. S. Eliot **15**:213

Brady, Charles A.
David Kherdian **6**:281
C. S. Lewis **14**:322

Brady, Owen
Richard Wright **21**:460

Brady, Patrick
Albert Camus **9**:147

Brady, Veronica
Thomas Keneally **19**:245

Braestrup, Peter
James H. Webb, Jr. **22**:454

Bragg, Melvyn
Kingsley Amis **13**:14
Saul Bellow **25**:84
William F. Buckley, Jr. **18**:82
E. M. Forster **2**:136
John le Carré **28**:227

Bragg, Pamela
Frank Bonham **12**:52

Bragin, John
Jean-Luc Godard **20**:133
Jean Renoir **20**:297

Braine, John
Richard Llewellyn **7**:207
Fay Weldon **9**:559

Braithwaite, William Stanley
T. S. Stribling **23**:439

Bramwell, Gloria
Richard Wright **21**:439

Brander, Laurence
E. M. Forster **15**:224
Aldous Huxley **18**:269

Brandriff, Welles T.
William Styron **11**:514

Brandt, G. W.
John Arden **13**:23

Brasillach, Robert
René Clair **20**:61

Brater, Enoch
Samuel Beckett **6**:42; **9**:81; **14**:78; **18**:51
Harold Pinter **27**:389

Braudy, Leo
John Berger **2**:54
Thomas Berger **3**:63
Bernardo Bertolucci **16**:90
Richard Condon **4**:107
Alfred Hitchcock **16**:347
Norman Mailer **1**:193; **8**:368
Jean Renoir **20**:301

Braudy, Susan
Nora Ephron **17**:112

Braun, Devra
Lillian Hellman **18**:225

Braun, Eric
John Landis **26**:273
Elaine May **16**:433

Braun, Julie
Philip Roth **4**:453

Braver-Mann, Barnet G.
Charles Chaplin **16**:188

Braybrooke, Neville
Graham Greene **1**:130
François Mauriac **4**:337

Brazier, Chris
David Byrne **26**:94
Mick Jagger and Keith Richard **17**:239
Bruce Springsteen **17**:482
Paul Weller **26**:443

Brée, Germaine
Louis Aragon **3**:12
Marcel Aymé **11**:21
Samuel Beckett **10**:27
Stanley Burnshaw **13**:128
Albert Camus **1**:54; **11**:93
Louis-Ferdinand Céline **1**:57
Jean Cocteau **1**:59
Georges Duhamel **8**:186
Jean Giono **4**:183
Julien Green **3**:203
André Malraux **1**:202
François Mauriac **4**:337
Raymond Queneau **2**:359
Jules Romains **7**:381
Jean-Paul Sartre **1**:306; **7**:397

Breen, Jon L.
Robert Lipsyte **21**:210

Bregman, Alice Miller
Milton Meltzer **26**:301

Breit, Harvey
James Baldwin **2**:31

Breitrose, Henry
Shirley Clarke **16**:215

Brench, A. C.
Mongo Beti **27**:41

Brendon, Piers
Donald Barthelme **5**:53
Rosalyn Drexler **2**:119
Daphne du Maurier **6**:146
Robert Penn Warren **4**:582

Brennan, Anthony
W. P. Kinsella **27**:235
Jane Rule **27**:420

Brennan, Anthony S.
Samuel Beckett **14**:80

Brereton, Geoffrey
Lucien Goldmann **24**:239

Breschard, Jack
Billy Joel **26**:213

Breskin, David
Sterling A. Brown **23**:100

Breslin, James E.
T. S. Eliot **6**:166

Breslin, Jimmy
Gore Vidal **8**:525

Breslin, John B.
Andrew M. Greeley **28**:177
C. S. Lewis **6**:308
Phyllis McGinley **14**:368
Tom McHale **5**:281
Wilfrid Sheed **10**:474
Susan Sontag **13**:516

Breslin, Patrick
Miguel Ángel Asturias **8**:25
Romain Gary **25**:189
Paul Theroux **15**:534

Breslin, Paul
Philip Booth **23**:77
Michael S. Harper **22**:209
Geoffrey Hill **18**:239
Daniel Hoffman **23**:242
William Meredith **22**:303
James Schuyler **23**:391

Bresnick, Paul
James Purdy **10**:425

Breton, André
Luis Buñuel **16**:152

Brew, Claude C.
Tommaso Landolfi **11**:321

Brewer, Joan Scherer
Sol Gordon **26**:138

Brewster, Ben
Yasujiro Ozu **16**:455

Brewster, Dorothy
Doris Lessing **1**:173

Brickell, Herschel
Harriette Arnow **7**:15

Bricker, Karin K.
Mavis Thorpe Clark **12**:131

Brickner, Richard P.
Anthony Burgess **2**:86
Jerome Charyn **8**:136
Frederick Exley **11**:186
Frederick Forsyth **2**:137
Herbert Gold **7**:120
William Kotzwinkle **14**:309
Cormac McCarthy **4**:341
Vladimir Nabokov **3**:355
Harry Mark Petrakis **3**:383
Muriel Spark **3**:465
Richard B. Wright **6**:581

Bridges, Les
Mickey Spillane **3**:469

Bridges, Linda
Donald Barthelme **5**:55
Alistair MacLean **13**:359
Georges Simenon **8**:487

Brien, Alan
Kingsley Amis **2**:6
Alan Ayckbourn **8**:34
Trevor Griffiths **13**:255
Ann Jellicoe **27**:205
John Osborne **5**:333
Harold Pinter **6**:418
Wole Soyinka **14**:505
Tennessee Williams **8**:547

Brien, Dolores Elise
Robert Duncan **15**:188

Brigg, Peter
Arthur C. Clarke **13**:148

Briggs, Julia
Leon Garfield **12**:234
Diana Wynne Jones **26**:227
Philippa Pearce **21**:290

Brignano, Russell Carl
Richard Wright **4**:594

Brink, André P.
Breyten Breytenbach **23**:83, 84

Brinnin, John Malcolm
John Ashbery **6**:12
Ben Belitt **22**:49
Allen Ginsberg **6**:201
Galway Kinnell **1**:168
William Meredith **13**:372
Sylvia Plath **1**:269
Muriel Rukeyser **27**:404
William Jay Smith **6**:512

Brinsmead, H. F.
H. F. Brinsmead **21**:28

Brinson, Peter
Jean Renoir **20**:289

Bristol, Horace
Pearl S. Buck **7**:33

Britt, Gwenneth
Vittorio De Sica **20**:94

Brivic, Sheldon
Richard Wright **9**:585

Brockway, James
Beryl Bainbridge **10**:16
Angela Carter **5**:102
J. P. Donleavy **4**:126
Mavis Gallant **7**:111
Penelope Gilliatt **10**:230

Julien Green **3**:205
Susan B. Hill **4**:228
Ursula Holden **18**:257
Frederic Raphael **14**:438
Piers Paul Read **10**:435
Muriel Spark **5**:399; **8**:495
Emma Tennant **13**:537

Broderick, Dorothy M.
H. F. Brinsmead **21**:27
Lois Duncan **26**:101
James D. Forman **21**:119
Nat Hentoff **26**:185
Jesse Jackson **12**:655
Stephen King **26**:239

Brodin, Dorothy
Marcel Aymé **11**:22

Brodrick, Jeffrey
John Gregory Dunne **28**:127

Brodsky, Arnold
Stevie Wonder **12**:655

Brodsky, Joseph
Anna Akhmatova **25**:26
Czeslaw Miiosz **11**:376
Eugenio Montale **9**:388

Brody, Patricia Ann
Joan Armatrading **17**:9

Brogan, Hugh
Mervyn Peake **7**:301

Bromberg, Pam
Lillian Hellman **18**:229

Brombert, Victor
St.-John Perse **4**:398

Bromell, Nicholas
Derek Walcott **25**:456

Bromwich, David
Conrad Aiken **5**:10
A. R. Ammons **9**:2
John Ashbery **15**:34
Ben Belitt **22**:54
Hayden Carruth **10**:100
Leslie Epstein **27**:127
Robert Frost **9**:266
John Hawkes **4**:216
John Hollander **5**:187
Richard Howard **7**:167
Thomas Kinsella **19**:253
Doris Lessing **3**:288
Jay Macpherson **14**:346
Penelope Mortimer **5**:299
Michael Mott **15**:380
Iris Murdoch **3**:348; **6**:347
Howard Nemerov **9**:394
Robert Pinsky **9**:416
Eric Rohmer **16**:532
Anne Sexton **10**:467
Charles Simic **9**:479
Stevie Smith **8**:492
Muriel Spark **3**:465
Paul Theroux **5**:427
Robert Penn Warren **13**:572
Elie Wiesel **3**:528
Charles Wright **13**:615

Broner, E. M.
Maxine Hong Kingston **19**:250

Bronowski, J.
Kathleen Raine **7**:352

Bronson, A. A.
Joe Rosenblatt **15**:448

Bronstein, Lynne
Trina Robbins **21**:338

Brooke, Jocelyn
Elizabeth Bowen **1**:39

Brooke, Nicholas
Anne Stevenson **7**:462

Brooke-Rose, Christine
Ezra Pound **7**:328

Brookner, Anita
Ursula Holden **18**:259
Colleen McCullough **27**:320
Fay Weldon **19**:469

Brooks, Anne
Maureen Daly **17**:87
Mary Stolz **12**:548

Brooks, Cleanth
William Empson **19**:152
William Faulkner **18**:148; **28**:144
Randall Jarrell **1**:159
Marianne Moore **10**:347
Walker Percy **6**:399
I. A. Richards **24**:396
Allen Tate **4**:539; **11**:522

Brooks, Ellen W.
Doris Lessing **3**:284

Brooks, John
Ernest K. Gann **23**:163

Brooks, Peter
Louis Aragon **22**:39
Roland Barthes **24**:28
Violette Leduc **22**:262
Alain Robbe-Grillet **1**:287

Brooks, Rick
Andre Norton **12**:467

Brooks, Robert M.
Andrew M. Greeley **28**:169

Brooks, Taye
Cecil Bødker **21**:12

Brooks, Thomas R.
Muriel Spark **18**:506

Brooks, Valerie
Beryl Bainbridge **22**:47

Brooks, Van Wyck
Upton Sinclair **15**:497

Broome, Peter
Robert Pinget **7**:306

Brophy, Brigid
Kingsley Amis **2**:5
Simone de Beauvoir **2**:42
Hortense Calisher **2**:95
Ivy Compton-Burnett **3**:111
William Faulkner **1**:102
Ernest K. Gann **23**:167
Jean Genet **2**:157
Shirley Hazzard **18**:213
Patricia Highsmith **2**:192
W. Somerset Maugham **1**:204
Henry Miller **2**:281
Françoise Sagan **3**:443; **6**:482
Georges Simenon **2**:397

Elizabeth Taylor **2**:432
Evelyn Waugh **3**:509

Brophy, James D.
W. H. Auden **11**:15

Brose, Margaret
Giuseppe Ungaretti **11**:558; **15**:538

Brosman, Catharine Savage
Jean-Paul Sartre **13**:503

Brosnahan, John
Stephen King **26**:236
Larry McMurtry **27**:333

Brothers, Barbara
Elizabeth Bowen **15**:79

Brotman, Sonia
Margaret O. Hyde **21**:176, 177

Broughton, Glenda
Hilma Wolitzer **17**:563

Broughton, Panthea Reid
William Faulkner **6**:175
Carson McCullers **4**:345

Brown, Alan
Marie-Claire Blais **22**:59
Ernest Hemingway **19**:217

Brown, Ashley
Caroline Gordon **6**:204, 206; **13**:241
Allen Tate **2**:428

Brown, Calvin S.
Conrad Aiken **3**:4
William Faulkner **18**:149; **28**:142

Brown, Clarence
Jorge Luis Borges **19**:48
Czeslaw Milosz **5**:292
Vladimir Nabokov **1**:242

Brown, Constance A.
Laurence Olivier **20**:239

Brown, Cynthia
Barbara Corcoran **17**:75

Brown, Dee
Vine Deloria, Jr. **21**:112

Brown, Deming
Alexander Zinoviev **19**:487

Brown, E. K.
Louis Dudek **19**:136
E. J. Pratt **19**:382

Brown, Edward Hickman
Doris Lessing **22**:279

Brown, Edward J.
Ilya Ehrenburg **18**:136

Brown, F. J.
Arthur Koestler **3**:271
Alberto Moravia **2**:293
Mario Puzo **1**:282
Muriel Spark **2**:417

Brown, Frederick
Louis Aragon **3**:13
Jean Cocteau **1**:60

Brown, Geoff
Woody Allen **16**:8
Walter Becker and Donald Fagen **26**:79
Jackson Browne **21**:35
Marvin Gaye **26**:132
Satyajit Ray **16**:495
Smokey Robinson **21**:345, 350
Joan Micklin Silver **20**:342
Peter Weir **20**:425
Brian Wilson **12**:648

Brown, Harry
Hollis Summers **10**:494

Brown, Ivor
J. B. Priestley **2**:346

Brown, Jennifer
Richard Peck **21**:300

Brown, John L.
Helen MacInnes **27**:281
Marguerite Yourcenar **19**:484

Brown, John Mason
Eric Bentley **24**:46
Paul Green **25**:193
Laura Z. Hobson **25**:270

Brown, John Russell
John Arden **6**:8
John Osborne **5**:332
Harold Pinter **6**:408, 413
Arnold Wesker **5**:482

Brown, Kenneth R.
Sam Peckinpah **20**:275

Brown, Lloyd W.
Imamu Amiri Baraka **3**:35
Wilson Harris **25**:212
Langston Hughes **10**:281
Paule Marshall **27**:313

Brown, Margaret Warren
Jean Lee Latham **12**:323

Brown, Merle E.
Kenneth Burke **2**:88
Geoffrey Hill **18**:236
Philip Larkin **18**:295

Brown, Pam
Billy Joel **26**:215

Brown, Ralph Adams
Henry Gregor Felsen **17**:121
Andre Norton **12**:455
John R. Tunis **12**:595

Brown, Richard
Douglas Adams **27**:14
John Kennedy Toole **19**:443

Brown, Robert
Stanley Elkin **14**:157

Brown, Robert McAfee
Elie Wiesel **5**:493

Brown, Rosellen
Margaret Atwood **8**:28; **15**:39
Marilyn French **18**:158
Toni Morrison **22**:321
Tim O'Brien **7**:272
May Sarton **4**:471
Judith Johnson Sherwin **7**:414
Diane Wakoski **4**:572

Brown, Royal S.
Brian De Palma **20**:78

Brown, Russell M.
Robert Kroetsch **5**:221
Leon Rooke **25**:392

Brown, Ruth Leslie
John Gardner **2**:151
Gilbert Rogin **18**:457

Brown, Slater
Jerome Siegel and Joe Shuster **21**:353

Brown, Spencer
Edward Hoagland **28**:185

Brown, Steve
Arthur C. Clarke **18**:107

Brown, T.
Louis MacNeice **10**:323

Brown, Terence
Kingsley Amis **2**:6
Seamus Heaney **25**:240
Derek Mahon **27**:288

Brown, William P.
John Brunner **10**:78

Browne, Joseph
Larry McMurtry **27**:334

Browne, Ray B.
Irving Wallace **13**:569

Browne, Robert M.
J. D. Salinger **12**:511

Browning, Dominique
Susan Cheever **18**:101

Browning, Preston M., Jr.
Flannery O'Connor **3**:367; **21**:275

Brownjohn, Alan
Dannie Abse **7**:1
Elizabeth Daryush **19**:120
Donald Davie **5**:115
C. Day Lewis **6**:128
Roy Fisher **25**:157, 159
Roy Fuller **28**:157, 158
Geoffrey Grigson **7**:136
Thom Gunn **18**:199
Seamus Heaney **7**:148
Hermann Hesse **17**:215
Geoffrey Hill **18**:239
Elizabeth Jennings **14**:292
Thomas Kinsella **4**:270
Philip Larkin **5**:226
George MacBeth **9**:340
Derek Mahon **27**:287
Leslie Norris **14**:388
Linda Pastan **27**:370
Kenneth Patchen **18**:393
Anthony Powell **7**:341
Marilynne Robinson **25**:388
Alan Sillitoe **19**:420
Louis Simpson **7**:428
D. M. Thomas **13**:541
Ted Walker **13**:567
Yevgeny Yevtushenko **26**:467

Brownjohn, Elizabeth
Philip Larkin **5**:227

Broyard, Anatole
Walter Abish **22**:17
William Barrett **27**:19
Saul Bellow **2**:52
William F. Buckley, Jr. **18**:83
Frederick Busch **18**:84
Elias Canetti **25**:113
John Cheever **25**:119
Laurie Colwin **23**:129
Len Deighton **22**:119
Peter Dickinson **12**:176
José Donoso **8**:179
Lawrence Durrell **27**:97
Nora Ephron **17**:111
Jules Feiffer **8**:217
Ken Follett **18**:156
John Gardner **28**:164
Penelope Gilliatt **10**:229
Herbert Gold **14**:208
Günter Grass **2**:172
Lillian Hellman **18**:227
Mark Helprin **22**:221
Garson Kanin **22**:232
Yoram Kaniuk **19**:239
Benedict Kiely **23**:266
Jerzy Kosinski **10**:307
Helen MacInnes **27**:283
Bernard Malamud **2**:266
Bobbie Ann Mason **28**:272
A. G. Mojtabai **15**:378
Wright Morris **18**:353
Edna O'Brien **13**:415
Michael Ondaatje **14**:410
Cynthia Ozick **28**:351
Robert B. Parker **27**:367
Marge Piercy **14**:420
V. S. Pritchett **15**:442
Anne Redmon **22**:342
Jean Rhys **19**:393
Marilynne Robinson **25**:387
Philip Roth **3**:436; **22**:356
Françoise Sagan **9**:468; **17**:427
Nathalie Sarraute **8**:473
Mark Schorer **9**:473
Georges Simenon **8**:488
Peter Taylor **18**:527
William Trevor **25**:445
Anne Tyler **11**:553
John Updike **2**:440; **9**:539; **15**:545
Hilma Wolitzer **17**:563

Bruccoli, Matthew J.
James Gould Cozzens **11**:131
John O'Hara **3**:370

Bruchac, Joseph
Chinua Achebe **26**:21

Brudnoy, David
James Baldwin **2**:33
Robin Cook **14**:131
Bob Fosse **20**:123

Bruell, Edwin
Harper Lee **12**:342

Brukenfeld, Dick
Joyce Carol Oates **3**:364

Brumberg, Abraham
Aleksandr I. Solzhenitsyn **4**:514; **18**:498

Brummell, O. B.
Bob Dylan **12**:183

Brunette, Peter
Archibald MacLeish **14**:338

Bruning, Peter
Ward Ruyslinck **14**:472

Brustein, Robert
Edward Albee **3**:6, 7; **25**:37
Jean Anouilh **1**:6
Enid Bagnold **25**:77
James Baldwin **4**:40; **17**:28
Brendan Behan **1**:26
Robert Bolt **14**:88
Christopher Durang **27**:89, 91
Federico Fellini **16**:278
Athol Fugard **25**:178
Jack Gelber **1**:114
Jean Genet **1**:115
William Gibson **23**:175
Joseph Heller **3**:228
Rolf Hochhuth **4**:230
William Inge **1**:153
Eugène Ionesco **1**:154
Arthur Kopit **18**:287
Stanley Kubrick **16**:378
Mark Medoff **23**:294
Arthur Miller **6**:330
John Osborne **5**:332
Harold Pinter **1**:266; **3**:385, 386; **15**:426; **27**:392
Gerome Ragni and James Rado **17**:379
Ronald Ribman **7**:357
Jean-Paul Sartre **4**:476
Murray Schisgal **6**:489
Peter Shaffer **5**:386
Sam Shepard **17**:442
Martin Sherman **19**:416
Tom Stoppard **3**:470; **15**:524
Ronald Tavel **6**:529
C. P. Taylor **27**:447
Jean-Claude Van Itallie **3**:492
Gore Vidal **4**:552, 553
Peter Weiss **3**:514
Arnold Wesker **5**:482
Tennessee Williams **19**:470

Brutus, Dennis
Alan Paton **25**:361

Bruun, Geoffrey
Marguerite Yourcenar **19**:480

Bryan, C.D.B.
Jonathan Baumbach **23**:54
Julio Cortázar **2**:103
Craig Nova **7**:267

Bryant, J. A., Jr.
Allen Tate **14**:530
Eudora Welty **1**:361; **5**:480

Bryant, Jerry H.
James Baldwin **8**:41
John Barth **2**:36
Saul Bellow **2**:52
William S. Burroughs **2**:91
Ronald L. Fair **18**:140
Ernest J. Gaines **18**:165
Nikki Giovanni **19**:191
Joseph Heller **3**:228
James Jones **3**:261
Norman Mailer **2**:260
Bernard Malamud **2**:266
Carson McCullers **4**:344
Toni Morrison **4**:366

Flannery O'Connor **2**:317
Walker Percy **2**:333
Thomas Pynchon **2**:353
Ayn Rand **3**:423
John Updike **2**:441
Kurt Vonnegut, Jr. **2**:452
John A. Williams **5**:497

Bryant, Nelson
James Herriot **12**:282

Bryant, Rene Kuhn
Thomas Berger **8**:83
Heinrich Böll **6**:84
John Fowles **6**:187
Paula Fox **8**:219
John Hersey **7**:154
Doris Lessing **10**:316
James A. Michener **5**:291

Bryden, Ronald
Peter Barnes **5**:49
Doris Lessing **6**:299
Peter Nichols **5**:306
Françoise Sagan **17**:421
David Storey **4**:529
Peter Straub **28**:408
Paul West **7**:525

Buache, Freddy
Luis Buñuel **16**:138

Bucco, Martin
René Wellek **28**:452

Buchanan, Cynthia
Norman Mailer **2**:263

Buchen, Irving H.
Carson McCullers **10**:334

Buchsbaum, Betty
David Kherdian **6**:280

Buck, Philo M., Jr.
Jules Romains **7**:378

Buck, Richard M.
Andre Norton **12**:457

Buckle, Richard
John Betjeman **2**:60

Buckler, Ernest
Hugh Hood **15**:283

Buckler, Robert
Elia Kazan **6**:274
Thomas Williams **14**:582

Buckley, Kathryn
Joan Barfoot **18**:36

Buckley, P. L.
Helen MacInnes **27**:282

Buckley, Peter
Lily Tomlin **17**:522
Andy Warhol **20**:420

Buckley, Priscilla L.
Eric Ambler **6**:4

Buckley, Tom
Michael Cimino **16**:212
Irving Wallace **13**:570

Buckley, Vincent
T. S. Eliot **3**:138

Buckley, Virginia
Katherine Paterson **12**:487

Buckley, William F., Jr.
William F. Buckley, Jr. **7**:35
Len Deighton **22**:118
Lillian Hellman **14**:257
John le Carré **28**:226
Monty Python **21**:229
Gerome Ragni and James Rado **17**:381
Aleksandr I. Solzhenitsyn **4**:511
Hunter S. Thompson **17**:513
Garry Trudeau **12**:590
Tom Wolfe **2**:481

Buckmaster, Henrietta
Maxine Hong Kingston **19**:250
Paule Marshall **27**:310
Barbara Pym **19**:387

Bucknall, Barbara J.
Ursula K. LeGuin **13**:349

Budgen, Suzanne
Jean Renoir **20**:299

Budrys, Algis
Isaac Asimov **26**:52
Robert A. Heinlein **26**:174
Fritz Leiber **25**:307
Frederik Pohl **18**:412
Keith Roberts **14**:464
Arkadii Strugatskii and Boris Strugatskii **27**:435
Gene Wolfe **25**:473, 475
Roger Zelazny **21**:479

Buechner, Frederick
Annie Dillard **9**:178

Buell, Ellen Lewis
E. M. Almedingen **12**:3
Isaac Asimov **26**:35
Margot Benary-Isbert **12**:31
Betty Cavanna **12**:97, 98
Maureen Daly **17**:90
Walter Farley **17**:115
Henry Gregor Felsen **17**:120, 122
Esther Forbes **12**:207
Roderick L. Haig-Brown **21**:134
Lee Kingman **17**:243
Joseph Krumgold **12**:317
Jean Lee Latham **12**:32
Madeleine L'Engle **12**:345
William Mayne **12**:389
Andre Norton **12**:456
Otfried Preussler **17**:374
Mary Stolz **12**:545, 546, 547, 548, 549, 550, 551, 552
Noel Streatfeild **21**:396, 397, 398, 399
John R. Tunis **12**:593, 594, 595, 596
Lenora Mattingly Weber **12**:631
Maia Wojciechowska **26**:451

Buell, Frederick
A. R. Ammons **8**:17

Bueno, J.R.T., Jr.
Roderick L. Haig-Brown **21**:136

Buffalohead, W. Roger
Vine Deloria, Jr. **21**:110

Buffington, Robert
Wayne C. Booth **24**:92
Cleanth Brooks **24**:111
Frederick Busch **18**:85
Donald Davidson **2**:112
John Crowe Ransom **4**:430, 437

Bufithis, Philip H.
Norman Mailer **11**:342

Bufkin, E. C.
Iris Murdoch **2**:297
P. H. Newby **2**:310

Buford, Bill
Gabriel García Márquez **27**:151

Buitenhuis, Peter
Harry Mathews **6**:314
William Trevor **7**:475
Richard Yates **23**:479

Bukoski, Anthony
W. P. Kinsella **27**:237

Bullins, Ed
Alice Childress **12**:106

Bullock, Florence Haxton
John Ehle **27**:102
Laura Z. Hobson **25**:268

Bulman, Learned T.
Henry Gregor Felsen **17**:122
Margaret O. Hyde **21**:171
Jean Lee Latham **12**:323, 325
Andre Norton **12**:456

Bumpus, Jerry
Mario Vargas Llosa **15**:552

Bunnell, Sterling
Michael McClure **6**:321

Bunting, Basil
Hugh MacDiarmid **4**:313

Bunting, Charles T.
Elizabeth Spencer **22**:403

Bunting, Josiah, III
James H. Webb, Jr. **22**:453

Burbank, Rex
Thornton Wilder **1**:364

Burch, Noel
Alain Resnais **16**:496

Burg, Victor
Richard Elman **19**:150

Burger, Marjorie
Walter Farley **17**:116, 117

Burger, Nash K.
Elizabeth Spencer **22**:400

Burger, Otis Kidwell
Lynne Reid Banks **23**:40

Burgess, Anthony
Kingsley Amis **1**:6; **2**:8
James Baldwin **1**:16
Samuel Beckett **1**:23; **3**:44
Saul Bellow **1**:31
Elizabeth Bowen **1**:40; **3**:82
Bridgid Brophy **6**:99
William S. Burroughs **1**:48
Italo Calvino **22**:92
Albert Camus **1**:54
Louis-Ferdinand Céline **7**:46
Agatha Christie **1**:58
J. M. Coetzee **23**:126
Ivy Compton-Burnett **1**:62
Don DeLillo **13**:178
Peter De Vries **28**:109
E. L. Doctorow **18**:125
Lawrence Durrell **1**:87
T. S. Eliot **3**:139
E. M. Forster **1**:107
Carlos Fuentes **13**:231
Gabriel García Márquez **27**:156
Jean Genet **1**:115
Penelope Gilliatt **2**:160
William Golding **1**:121
Günter Grass **1**:125; **11**:251
Henry Green **2**:178
Graham Greene **3**:207
Joseph Heller **1**:140
Ernest Hemingway **1**:143; **3**:234
Aldous Huxley **1**:151
Christopher Isherwood **1**:156
Pamela Hansford Johnson **1**:160
Erica Jong **18**:278
Arthur Koestler **1**:169; **3**:270
John le Carré **9**:326
Colin MacInnes **4**:314
Norman Mailer **1**:190; **28**:262
Bernard Malamud **1**:199; **3**:322
Olivia Manning **19**:301
Mary McCarthy **1**:206; **24**:345
Henry Miller **1**:224
Iris Murdoch **1**:235
Vladimir Nabokov **1**:244; **3**:352
Flann O'Brien **1**:252
Lucio Piccolo **13**:440
Reynolds Price **13**:464
J. B. Priestley **2**:347
Alain Robbe-Grillet **1**:288
J. D. Salinger **1**:299
William Sansom **2**:383
Alan Sillitoe **1**:307
C. P. Snow **1**:317
Muriel Spark **2**:416
Paul Theroux **11**:528
John Wain **2**:458
Evelyn Waugh **1**:359; **3**:510
Angus Wilson **2**:472
Edmund Wilson **3**:538

Burgess, Charles E.
William Inge **8**:308

Burgess, Jackson
Robert Altman **16**:22
Stanley Kubrick **16**:380

Burgess, John
Satyajit Ray **16**:476

Burgin, Richard
Isaac Bashevis Singer **23**:420

Burhans, Clinton S., Jr.
Joseph Heller **3**:230
Ernest Hemingway **8**:283
Kurt Vonnegut, Jr. **8**:530

Burian, Jarka M.
Václav Havel **25**:223

Burke, Frank
Federico Fellini **16**:298

Burke, Jeffrey
Carolyn G. Heilbrun **25**:256
Thomas Keneally **19**:248
Ted Mooney **25**:330
Alberto Moravia **18**:349
Jayne Anne Phillips **15**:420
Richard Price **12**:492

Burke, Kathleen
René Wellek **28**:454

Burke, Kenneth
Wayne C. Booth **24**:90
Clifford Odets **28**:325
John Crowe Ransom **24**:363
Theodore Roethke **11**:479
James Thurber **25**:435
Glenway Wescott **13**:590

Burke, Susan E.
Cynthia Propper Seton **27**:424

Burke, William M.
John A. Williams **5**:497

Burkman, Katherine H.
Harold Pinter **27**:384

Burkom, Selma R.
Doris Lessing **1**:174

Burnett, Constance Buil
Frank B. Gilbreth, Jr. and Ernestine Gilbreth Carey **17**:153

Burnett, Michael
James Thurber **5**:440

Burnett, W. R.
Mari Sandoz **28**:403

Burnham, David
Clifford Odets **28**:329
Emlyn Williams **15**:577

Burns, Alan
Michael Moorcock **27**:348
Ann Quin **6**:442
C. P. Snow **1**:317

Burns, Gerald
W. H. Auden **4**:33
John Berryman **6**:62, 63
Austin Clarke **9**:169
Seamus Heaney **7**:147
Donald Justice **19**:236
Robert Lowell **5**:256
Frank O'Hara **5**:324
Charles Olson **5**:328
Ezra Pound **5**:348
Gary Snyder **5**:393
William Stafford **4**:520
Diane Wakoski **11**:564

Burns, J.
Noel Hilliard **15**:280

Burns, Landon C., Jr.
Mary Renault **17**:395

Burns, Martin
Kurt Vonnegut, Jr. **12**:608

Burns, Mary M.
Cecil Bødker **21**:14
Alice Childress **12**:107
Barbara Corcoran **17**:77
Peter Dickinson **12**:171
Lois Duncan **26**:102

Jamake Highwater **12**:287
Isabelle Holland **21**:154
Mollie Hunter **21**:164
Diana Wynne Jones **26**:230
M. E. Kerr **12**:297, 298
Lee Kingman **17**:247
Jean Lee Latham **12**:325
Norma Fox Mazer **26**:290
Anne McCaffrey **17**:282
Nicholasa Mohr **12**:445
Andre Norton **12**:471
Robert Newton Peck **17**:340, 342
Noel Streatfeild **21**:410
Maia Wojciechowska **26**:457

Burns, Stuart L.
Jean Stafford **4**:517

Burns, Wayne
Alex Comfort **7**:52, 53

Burnshaw, Stanley
James Dickey **10**:141

Burroughs, Franklin G.
William Faulkner **3**:157

Burrow, J. W.
Aldous Huxley **3**:254
J.R.R. Tolkien **3**:482

Burroway, Janet
James Leo Herlihy **6**:235
Mary Hocking **13**:284
Masuji Ibuse **22**:227
Paule Marshall **27**:310

Burt, Struthers
Kay Boyle **19**:62

Burton, Dwight L.
Betty Cavanna **12**:99
Maureen Daly **17**:88

Burton, Thomas
Alfred Hitchcock **16**:338

Busch, Frederick
J. G. Farrell **6**:173
John Hawkes **7**:140
Alice Munro **10**:356
Paul Theroux **28**:426
Paul West **7**:523

Bush, Kent
Thor Heyerdahl **26**:190

Bush, Roland E.
Ishmael Reed **3**:424

Busi, Frederick
Alain Resnais **16**:513

Butkiss, John F.
Lee Kingman **17**:246

Butler, Christopher
I. A. Richards **24**:401

Butler, Colin
Hermann Hesse **17**:214

Butler, Florence W.
Henry Gregor Felsen **17**:120

Butler, G. P.
Siegfried Lenz **27**:251
Martin Walser **27**:466

Butler, Geoff
Rolf Hochhuth **18**:256

Butler, Michael
Heinrich Böll **11**:58

Butler, Rupert
Laurence Olivier **20**:239

Butler, William Vivian
John Creasey **11**:135

Butscher, Edward
John Berryman **3**:67
Shusaku Endo **14**:162
John Gardner **3**:185
Jerzy Kosinski **6**:282
Richard Kostelanetz **28**:218
John Sayles **14**:483
James Wright **5**:519
Rudolph Wurlitzer **4**:598

Butt, John
Carlos Fuentes **10**:208

Buttel, Robert
Seamus Heaney **25**:241

Butterick, George
Ed Dorn **18**:129

Butwin, Joseph
Richard Brautigan **12**:62

Byars, Betsy
Kin Platt **26**:350

Byatt, A. S.
Penelope Fitzgerald **19**:174
Diane Johnson **13**:305
Pamela Hansford Johnson **27**:221
Amos Oz **11**:429
V. S. Pritchett **15**:440
C. P. Snow **13**:514

Byer, Kathryn Stripling
Carolyn Kizer **15**:309

Byers, Margaret
Elizabeth Jennings **5**:197

Byers, Nancy
Jean Lee Latham **12**:324

Byrd, James W.
Willard Motley **18**:357

Byrd, Max
Jorge Luis Borges **6**:93
Peter DeVries **10**:136

Byrd, Scott
John Barth **1**:17

Byrom, Thomas
Frank O'Hara **13**:423

Byron, Stuart
Woody Allen **16**:12

Cabrera, Vincente
Juan Benet **28**:23

Cadogan, Mary
William Mayne **12**:404
Noel Streatfeild **21**:143

Cahill, Daniel J.
E. L. Doctorow **18**:121
Jerzy Kosinski **2**:232

Caidin, Martin
Ernest K. Gann **23**:166

Cain, James M.
James M. Cain **28**:45

Cain, Joan
Camilo José Cela **13**:147

Cain, William E.
Wayne C. Booth **24**:97

Cairns, Scott C.
Michael S. Harper **22**:209

Calas, Nicholas
André Breton **9**:125

Calder, Angus
T. S. Eliot **2**:128
Alex La Guma **19**:273

Calder, Robert L.
W. Somerset Maugham **15**:369

Caldwell, James R.
Muriel Rukeyser **27**:407

Caldwell, Joan
Margaret Laurence **13**:344
Audrey Thomas **7**:472

Caldwell, Stephen
D. Keith Mano **2**:270

Calisher, Hortense
Yukio Mishima **2**:289
Vladimir Nabokov **1**:246
Raja Rao **25**:365
Christina Stead **5**:403

Callaghan, Linda Ward
Gene Roddenberry **17**:414

Callahan, John
Michael S. Harper **7**:138

Callahan, John F.
Alice Walker **5**:476

Callahan, Patrick
Wendell Berry **27**:33

Callahan, Patrick J.
C. S. Lewis **3**:297
George MacBeth **2**:251
Alan Sillitoe **1**:308
Stephen Spender **2**:420

Callan, Edward
W. H. Auden **1**:9, 11; **14**:30
Alan Paton **4**:395; **25**:363

Callan, Richard J.
José Donoso **11**:147
Octavio Paz **19**:364

Callenbach, Ernest
Ingmar Bergman **16**:60
Charles Chaplin **16**:198
Shirley Clarke **16**:218
John Ford **16**:309
Alfred Hitchcock **16**:342, 344
Elia Kazan **16**:367
Satyajit Ray **16**:482
Andy Warhol **20**:418
Orson Welles **20**:438

Callendar, Newgate
Eric Ambler **4**:18
Isaac Asimov **9**:49
William Peter Blatty **2**:64
William F. Buckley, Jr. **18**:81, 83
Robert Cormier **12**:136
John Creasey **11**:135
Edmund Crispin **22**:111
Rhys Davies **23**:147
Peter Dickinson **12**:170, 171, 177
Paul E. Erdman **25**:153, 154
Howard Fast **23**:160, 161
Dick Francis **22**:152
Carolyn G. Heilbrun **25**:252, 254
Evan Hunter **11**:279, 280
P. D. James **18**:272
James Jones **3**:262
Harry Kemelman **2**:225
William X. Kienzle **25**:275, 276
Emma Lathen **2**:236
Elmore Leonard **28**:233
Robert Ludlum **22**:289
Ross Macdonald **14**:336
Helen MacInnes **27**:284
Robert B. Parker **27**:363, 364
Ellery Queen **11**:458
Ruth Rendell **28**:383, 384, 385, 386, 387
Georges Simenon **2**:399
Martin Cruz Smith **25**:412
Mickey Spillane **3**:469
J.I.M. Stewart **14**:512
Vassilis Vassilikos **8**:524
Gore Vidal **22**:434
Donald E. Westlake **7**:528, 529

Callow, Philip
Andrew Sinclair **2**:400

Caltabiano, Frank P.
Edward Albee **25**:39

Cambon, Glauco
Michael Hamburger **14**:234
Robert Lowell **8**:348
Eugenio Montale **7**:224
Giuseppe Ungaretti **7**:482; **11**:555; **15**:536
Elio Vittorini **14**:543

Cameron, Ann
Tom Robbins **9**:454

Cameron, Barry
A. W. Purdy **14**:432

Cameron, Ben
Edward Albee **25**:38

Cameron, Eleanor
Julia W. Cunningham **12**:164
Leon Garfield **12**:226
Alan Garner **17**:138
Nat Hentoff **26**:184
Mollie Hunter **21**:159, 160
Joseph Krumgold **12**:320
William Mayne **12**:393
Emily Cheney Neville **12**:452
Philippa Pearce **21**:283
Rosemary Sutcliff **26**:434

Cameron, Elspeth
Margaret Atwood **13**:4
Timothy Findley **27**:145

Cameron, Ian
Michelangelo Antonioni **20**:20
Nagisa Oshima **20**:247

Cameron, Julia
Judith Rossner **6**:469

Camp, Raymond R.
Roderick L. Haig-Brown
21:135

Camp, Richard
Leon Garfield **12**:221

Campbell, Barbara
Henry Gregor Felsen **17**:124

Campbell, Colin
Muriel Rukeyser **27**:408

Campbell, Gregg M.
Bob Dylan **6**:157

Campbell, James
William S. Burroughs **22**:84
Kazuo Ishiguro **27**:202
Vladimir Nabokov **23**:314

Campbell, Josie P.
E. L. Doctorow **18**:123

Campbell, Mary Jo
Isaac Asimov **26**:51

Campbell, Patricia
Kin Platt **26**:353

Campbell, Patty
Sol Gordon **26**:138, 139
Stan Lee **17**:262
Norma Fox Mazer **26**:292
Kin Platt **26**:353, 355
Sandra Scoppettone **26**:402

Canary, Robert H.
Robert Graves **11**:256

Canby, Henry Seidel
Pearl S. Buck **18**:75

Canby, Peter
Randolph Stow **23**:438

Canby, Vincent
Lindsay Anderson **20**:16
Ralph Bakshi **26**:66, 68, 72, 76
Shirley Clarke **16**:218
Brian De Palma **20**:72, 74, 75, 79, 80
Vittorio De Sica **20**:95, 97
Marguerite Duras **20**:99
Rainer Werner Fassbinder
20:113, 120
Federico Fellini **16**:290
Bob Fosse **20**:123
George Roy Hill **26**:205, 207
Alfred Hitchcock **16**:359
John Landis **26**:273
Nagisa Oshima **20**:249
Pier Paolo Pasolini **20**:262, 265
Sam Peckinpah **20**:276
Sidney Poitier **26**:357, 359
Richard Pryor **26**:380
Carlos Saura **20**:316
Paul Schrader **26**:391, 394
Martin Scorsese **20**:323, 330

Jerzy Skolimowski **20**:348
François Truffaut **20**:393
Peter Weir **20**:428

Candlin, Enid Saunders
Bette Bao Lord **23**:280

Cannella, Anthony R.
Richard Condon **10**:111

Cannon, JoAnn
Italo Calvino **11**:92

Cansler, Ronald Lee
Robert A. Heinlein **3**:227

Cantarella, Helene
Jules Archer **12**:15

Cantor, Peter
Frederic Raphael **2**:367

Cantwell, Mary
Alan Sillitoe **19**:421

Cantwell, Robert
Erskine Caldwell **14**:94
Upton Sinclair **15**:498

Capers, Charlotte
Mary Lee Settle **19**:409

Capey, A. C.
William Golding **17**:177

Capitanchik, Maurice
E. M. Forster **2**:135
Yukio Mishima **6**:338
Michael Moorcock **27**:348

Caplan, Brina
John Gardner **18**:176
Lillian Hellman **18**:226
Larry McMurtry **27**:331

Caplan, Lincoln
Frederick Buechner **6**:103

Caplan, Pat
Colleen McCullough **27**:319

Caplan, Ralph
Kingsley Amis **1**:6

Capouya, Emile
Albert Camus **2**:98
Camilo José Cela **13**:145
Robert Coover **7**:57
Howard Fast **23**:158
Paul Goodman **7**:129
James Leo Herlihy **6**:234
Ignazio Silone **4**:493
Aleksandr I. Solzhenitsyn **1**:320
Robert Stone **23**:425
Dalton Trumbo **19**:445

Capp, Al
Charles Chaplin **16**:194
Mary McCarthy **5**:276

Capps, Benjamin
Christie Harris **12**:262

Caprio, Betsy
Gene Roddenberry **17**:411

Caputi, Jane E.
Steven Spielberg **20**:363

Caputo, Philip
Thomas McGuane **18**:322

Caputo-Mayr, Maria Luise
Peter Handke **8**:261

Caram, Richard
Anne Stevenson **7**:463

Card, Orson Scott
Roger Zelazny **21**:472

Cardinal, Roger
André Breton **15**:86

Cardullo, Robert J.
Robert Altman **16**:37

Carduner, Art
Ingmar Bergman **16**:69

Carens, James F.
Evelyn Waugh **27**:472

Carew, Jan
John Irving **13**:292
George Lamming **2**:235

Carey, John
Richard Bach **14**:35
Lawrence Durrell **4**:147
Richard Eberhart **3**:135
William Empson **8**:201
D. J. Enright **4**:155
Doris Lessing **6**:292
John Updike **7**:489

Carey, Julian C.
Langston Hughes **10**:278

Cargill, Oscar
Pearl S. Buck **7**:32

Cargin, Peter
Michael Cimino **16**:208

Carleton, Joyce
Patrick Modiano **18**:338

Carleton, Phillips D.
Halldór Laxness **25**:290
Frans Eemil Sillanpää **19**:417

Carls, Alice-Catherine
Tadeusz Różewicz **23**:363

Carlsen, G. Robert
Frank Herbert **12**:273

Carlson, Dale
M. E. Kerr **12**:296
Rosemary Wells **12**:638

Carmer, Carl
A. B. Guthrie, Jr. **23**:197

Carmody, Rev. Francis R., S.J.
Roy A. Gallant **17**:129

Carne-Ross, D. S.
John Gardner **3**:185
Eugenio Montale **7**:222

Carollo, Monica
Margaret O. Hyde **21**:177

Carpenter, Bogdana
Zbigniew Herbert **9**:274

Carpenter, Frederic I.
William Everson **14**:163
Robinson Jeffers **2**:212; **11**:311; **15**:300
Carson McCullers **12**:417
Jessamyn West **17**:547

Carpenter, John R.
Zbigniew Herbert **9**:274
Greg Kuzma **7**:196
John Logan **5**:255
James Schevill **7**:401
Gary Snyder **2**:407
Diane Wakoski **2**:459
Peter Wild **14**:581
Charles Wright **6**:580

Carpenter, Richard C.
Kay Boyle **19**:63, 64

Carpio, Rustica C.
Bienvenido N. Santos **22**:363

Carpio, Virginia
Andre Norton **12**:464

Carr, John
George Garrett **3**:190

Carr, Patrick
Peter Townshend **17**:540
Neil Young **17**:580

Carr, Roy
John Lennon and Paul
McCartney **12**:379

Carroll, David
Chinua Achebe **1**:1
Jean Cayrol **11**:107

Carroll, Paul
John Ashbery **2**:16
Robert Creeley **2**:106
James Dickey **2**:116
Allen Ginsberg **2**:163
Frank O'Hara **2**:321
W. D. Snodgrass **2**:405
Philip Whalen **6**:565

Carruth, Hayden
Ai **14**:9
A. R. Ammons **9**:30
W. H. Auden **1**:11
John Berryman **2**:56
Earle Birney **6**:75
Robert Bly **15**:68
Edward Brathwaite **11**:67
Charles Bukowski **5**:80
Cid Corman **9**:170
Robert Creeley **8**:153
J. V. Cunningham **3**:121
Babette Deutsch **18**:119
Annie Dillard **9**:177
Robert Duncan **2**:122
Loren Eiseley **7**:91
Clayton Eshleman **7**:97, 98
Robert Frost **10**:198
Tess Gallagher **18**:169
Jean Garrigue **8**:239
Arthur Gregor **9**:251
H. D. **8**:256
Marilyn Hacker **9**:257
Jim Harrison **14**:235
William Heyen **18**:230
John Hollander **8**:301
Richard Howard **7**:166
David Ignatow **7**:174, 175, 177; **14**:275
June Jordan **11**:312
Denise Levertov **8**:346
Philip Levine **2**:244
Audre Lorde **18**:309
Robert Lowell **4**:299; **9**:338

Archibald MacLeish 14:337
W. S. Merwin 8:390
Josephine Miles 2:278
Frederick Morgan 23:297
Howard Nemerov 2:306
Charles Olson 9:412
Robert Pinsky 9:417
J. F. Powers 1:280
Kenneth Rexroth 2:370
Reg Saner 9:468
Anne Sexton 2:390; 4:484
Judith Johnson Sherwin 15:480
Leslie Marmon Silko 23:406
W. D. Snodgrass 18:492
Gilbert Sorrentino 7:448
Raymond Souster 14:502
R. G. Vliet 22:443
David Wagoner 15:559
Diane Wakoski 2:459; 4:574
Theodore Weiss 8:545
Louis Zukofsky 2:487

Carson, Dale
Gunnel Beckman 26:87

Carson, Katharine W.
Claude Simon 9:485

Carson, Neil
Arthur Miller 26:327
George Ryga 14:472, 473

Carson, Tom
Van Morrison 21:239
The Police 26:363
Richard Pryor 26:378
Lou Reed 21:315
Paul Simon 17:467
Paul Weller 26:446
Brian Wilson 12:653
Neil Young 17:582
Frank Zappa 17:594

Cart, Michael
Virginia Hamilton 26:148

Carter, Albert Howard, III
Italo Calvino 8:126
Thomas McGuane 7:213

Carter, Angela
John Hawkes 27:197
Thomas Keneally 5:210

Carter, Anne
Eilís Dillon 17:100
Josephine Poole 17:373

Carter, Lin
J.R.R. Tolkien 1:339

Carter, Mary
Maxine Kumin 28:221

Carter, Paul
Eugenio Montale 9:387

Carter, Robert A.
Arthur Gregor 9:253

Carter, Steven R.
Isaac Asimov 19:28
Julian Symons 14:523

Carver, Ann Cathey
Lucille Clifton 19:109

Cary, Joseph
Eugenio Montale 7:223; 9:386
Giuseppe Ungaretti 7:482
Louis Zukofsky 18:558

Casari, Laura E.
Adrienne Rich 11:479

Casebeer, Edwin F.
Hermann Hesse 3:245

Caserio, Robert L.
Gilbert Sorrentino 7:449

Casey, Carol K.
Eleanor Hibbert 7:156

Casey, Daniel J.
Benedict Kiely 23:260

Casey, Jane Barnes
Peter Taylor 18:527

Casey, John
T. Alan Broughton 19:73
John D. MacDonald 27:275

Cashin, Edward J.
Walker Percy 14:411

Caspary, Sister Anita Marie
François Mauriac 4:337, 338

Casper, Leonard
Flannery O'Connor 6:375
Bienvenido N. Santos 22:361, 362, 365

Cassada, Jackie
Jeffrey Archer 28:14

Cassal, Gould
Irwin Shaw 23:395

Cassidy, T. E.
Jessamyn West 17:545

Cassill, R. V.
Mavis Gallant 7:110
Thomas Hinde 6:241
James Alan McPherson 19:309
Irwin Shaw 7:413
Wilfrid Sheed 2:393
Christina Stead 2:422
Thomas Williams 14:581

Cassirer, Thomas
Mongo Beti 27:43

Casson, Lionel
Mary Renault 17:399

Castor, Gladys Crofoot
Betty Cavanna 12:98

Catania, Susan
Alvin Silverstein and Virginia B. Silverstein 17:452

Catanoy, Nicholas
Mircea Eliade 19:147, 148

Cate, Curtis
Romain Gary 25:185

Catinella, Joseph
Christopher Isherwood 1:157
Joel Lieber 6:311
Bernard Malamud 1:201

Catling, Patrick Skene
William Trevor 25:447

Causey, James Y.
Camilo José Cela 4:95

Caute, David
Breyten Breytenbach 23:86
Jean Genet 5:137
Lucien Goldmann 24:236, 242
Lionel Trilling 9:531

Cavan, Romilly
Derek Walcott 4:574

Caviglia, John
José Donoso 11:149

Cavitch, David
William Stafford 4:521

Cawelti, John G.
Dashiell Hammett 19:195
Mario Puzo 6:430
Mickey Spillane 3:468

Cawley, Joseph A., S.J.
Isabelle Holland 21:150

Caws, Mary Ann
André Breton 2:81; 9:125
Yves Bonnefoy 9:113
Blaise Cendrars 18:92

Cecchetti, Giovanni
Eugenio Montale 7:221

Cecil, David
Aldous Huxley 3:252

Cederstrom, Lorelei
Doris Lessing 22:281

Ceplair, Larry
Alvah Bessie 23:61

Cerf, Bennett
John O'Hara 2:324

Cerf, Cristopher
Peter De Vries 28:105

Cevasco, G. A.
Pearl S. Buck 18:77

Chabot, C. Barry
Frederick Exley 11:187

Chabrol, Claude
Alfred Hitchcock 16:357

Chace, William M.
Ezra Pound 4:415

Chaillet, Ned
Athol Fugard 9:232
Hugh Leonard 19:281

Chamberlain, Ethel L.
E. M. Almedingen 12:8

Chamberlain, John
James Gould Cozzens 11:131
Mary McCarthy 3:326

Chamberlin, J. E.
Margaret Atwood 8:28
George MacBeth 5:265
W. S. Merwin 3:338
Charles Tomlinson 4:547; 6:535, 536
David Wagoner 5:475

Chambers, Aidan
Alan Garner 17:145, 147
William Mayne 12:404
Philippa Pearce 21:293
Robert Westall 17:555

Chambers, Colin
Peter Shaffer 18:477

Chambers, D. D.
Alan Paton 25:359

Chambers, D.D.C.
Matt Cohen 19:111

Chambers, Robert D.
Ernest Buckler 13:120
Sinclair Ross 13:492

Chambers, Ross
Samuel Beckett 9:77

Chametzky, Jules
Edward Dahlberg 14:134
Isaac Bashevis Singer 1:313

Champagne, Roland A.
Roland Barthes 24:32
Marguerite Duras 11:167
Romain Gary 25:188

Champlin, Charles
Don DeLillo 27:84
John Hawkes 27:196
Manuel Puig 28:373
Evelyn Waugh 27:476

Chandler, D. G.
Len Deighton 22:117

Chang, Charity
Barbara Corcoran 17:74

Changas, Estelle
Elia Kazan 16:368

Chankin, Donald O.
B. Traven 8:517

Chapin, Katherine Garrison
Allen Tate 4:536

Chaplin, William H.
John Logan 5:253

Chapman, Raymond
Graham Greene 1:133

Chapman, Robert
Anthony Burgess 4:83
Ivy Compton-Burnett 3:112

Chappell, Fred
George Garrett 3:191
Richard Yates 7:554

Chappetta, Robert
Bernardo Bertolucci 16:88
Roman Polanski 16:466

Charnes, Ruth
M. E. Kerr 12:303

Charters, Ann
Charles Olson 5:326

Charters, Samuel
Robert Creeley 4:117
Robert Duncan 4:142
Larry Eigner 9:180
William Everson 5:121
Lawrence Ferlinghetti 6:182
Allen Ginsberg 4:181
Charles Olson 5:329
Gary Snyder 5:393
Jack Spicer 8:497

Charyn, Jerome
Kōbō Abé 8:1
Martin Amis 9:26
David Bradley, Jr. 23:79
T. Alan Broughton 19:72
R.H.W. Dillard 5:116
Elizabeth Jane Howard 7:165
Margaríta Karapánou 13:314
William Kotzwinkle 14:311
Richard Price 12:492
James Purdy 10:424; 28:381
Judith Rossner 9:457
Luis Rafael Sánchez 23:383
Joseph Wambaugh 18:533
Jerome Weidman 7:518
Kate Wilhelm 7:538

Chase, Edward T.
Nat Hentoff 26:181

Chase, Gilbert
Louis Aragon 22:35

Chase, Richard
Saul Bellow 1:27
Philip Rahv 24:351

Chasin, Helen
Laurie Colwin 23:128
Alan Dugan 6:144
May Sarton 4:472

Chaskel, Walter B.
Robert Lipsyte 21:208

Chassler, Philip I.
Meyer Levin 7:205

Chatfield, Hale
Gil Orlovitz 22:334

Chatfield, Jack
William F. Buckley, Jr. 18:83

Chatham, Margaret L.
Isaac Asimov 26:50
Roy A. Gallant 17:133

Chazen, Leonard
Anthony Powell 3:402

Cheatwood, Kiarri T-H
Ayi Kwei Armah 5:32

Cheever, John
Saul Bellow 10:43

Chelton, Mary K.
Anne McCaffrey 17:281

Chemasi, Antonio
Christopher Durang 27:88

Cheney, Brainard
Donald Davidson 2:112
Flannery O'Connor 1:254; 21:261

Chernaik, Judith
Beryl Bainbridge 14:39
Amos Oz 27:360

Cherry, Kelly
John Betjeman 10:53

Cherry, Kenneth
Vladimir Nabokov 8:413

Cheshire, Ardner R., Jr.
William Styron 11:518

Chesnick, Eugene
John Cheever 7:48
Nadine Gordimer 7:133
Michael Mewshaw 9:376

Chester, Alfred
Terry Southern 7:454

Cheuse, Alan
Alejo Carpentier 11:100
Carlos Fuentes 13:231
John Gardner 5:132
Stephen King 26:241
Jerzy Kosinski 15:317
Elmore Leonard 28:237
André Schwarz-Bart 4:480
B. Traven 11:534

Chevigny, Bell Gale
Toni Cade Bambara 19:32
Julio Cortázar 15:148
Paule Marshall 27:311
Tillie Olsen 4:387

Chew, Shirley
Wilson Harris 25:211

Chiari, Joseph
Jean Anouilh 8:23
Jean Cocteau 8:144

Chiaromonte, Nicola
Eric Bentley 24:45

Child, Ruth C.
T. S. Eliot 24:169

Childs, E. Ira
Peter Townshend 17:534

Chinn, Nick
Trina Robbins 21:338

Chomsky, Noam
Saul Bellow 8:81

Christ, Carol P.
Doris Lessing 22:283
Ntozake Shange 25:401

Christ, Ronald
Chinua Achebe 26:13
Jorge Luis Borges 2:70, 73; 4:75
José Donoso 8:178
Gabriel García Márquez 3:179
Leonard Michaels 25:315
Pablo Neruda 5:301; 7:260
Octavio Paz 3:375; 4:397; 6:398
Manuel Puig 5:354; 28:370
Luis Rafael Sánchez 23:384
Mario Vargas Llosa 9:542

Christensen, Paul
Ed Dorn 18:128

Christgau, Georgia
Joan Armatrading 17:8
Bob Marley 17:273

Christgau, Robert
Chuck Berry 17:54
Richard Brautigan 9:124
Jimmy Cliff 21:62
Mick Jagger and Keith Richard 17:225, 237
John Lennon and Paul McCartney 12:358

Carly Simon 26:407
Patti Smith 12:539
Peter Townshend 17:525
Stevie Wonder 12:658, 659

Christie, Ian Leslie
Ken Russell 16:541

Christon, Lawrence
Monty Python 21:229

Chrzanowski, Joseph
Jorge Luis Borges 19:49
Carlos Fuentes 22:167

Chupack, Henry
James Purdy 28:379

Church, D. M.
Arthur Adamov 25:16

Church, Richard
Robert Frost 26:113
Erich Maria Remarque 21:324

Churchill, David
Peter Dickinson 12:175
Mollie Hunter 21:161

Churchill, R. C.
John Cowper Powys 15:433
P. G. Wodehouse 10:537

Churchill, Winston
Charles Chaplin 16:189

Ciardi, John
Robert Frost 13:223
Stanley Kunitz 14:312
Richard Wilbur 14:576
William Carlos Williams 13:602

Cifelli, Edward
John Ciardi 10:106

Cioffi, Frank
Gilbert Sorrentino 22:397

Ciplijauskaité, Biruté
Gabriel García Márquez 3:182

Cismaru, Alfred
Simone de Beauvoir 2:43
Albert Camus 11:95
Aimé Césaire 19:96
Marguerite Duras 6:149; 11:164
Eugène Ionesco 9:289
Robert Pinget 13:442

Cixous, Helen
Severo Sarduy 6:485

Claire, Thomas
Albert Camus 9:150

Claire, William F.
Stanley Kunitz 11:319
Sylvia Plath 17:347
Allen Tate 9:521
Mark Van Doren 6:541

Clancy, Cathy
Piri Thomas 17:502

Clancy, Thomas H.
Andrew M. Greeley 28:170

Clancy, William P.
Carson McCullers 12:413
Brian Moore 7:235

Clapp, Susannah
Caroline Blackwood 9:101
Penelope Fitzgerald 19:172
Ursula Holden 18:257
Margaríta Karapánou 13:315
Seán O'Faoláin 7:274
George MacBeth 9:340
David Plante 7:308
Barbara Pym 19:386
Cynthia Propper Seton 27:427, 428
Hilma Wolitzer 17:562

Clare, Anthony
Susan Sontag 13:518

Clarens, Carlos
Eric Rohmer 16:530, 531

Clareson, Thomas D.
James Blish 14:83
Gene Wolfe 25:475, 477

Clark, Barrett H.
Paul Green 25:192

Clark, Gerry
Bernice Rubens 19:405

Clark, J. Michael
Jean Toomer 22:426

Clark, John R.
Doris Betts 6:69
Alan Sillitoe 1:308

Clark, Katerina
Vasily Aksenov 22:28

Clark, Walter Van Tilburg
A. B. Guthrie, Jr. 23:198

Clarke, Gerald
Edward Albee 25:37
Larry Gelbart 21:126
Gore Vidal 2:449
P. G. Wodehouse 2:480

Clarke, Henry Leland
Melvin Berger 12:38

Clarke, Jane H.
Jesse Jackson 12:289

Clarke, Kenneth
Jesse Stuart 14:516

Clarke, Loretta
Paul Zindel 6:587

Clarke, Pauline
Rosemary Sutcliff 26:437

Clarkson, Paul R.
Robert Kroetsch 23:269

Claudel, Alice Moser
David Kherdian 9:317

Clausen, Christopher
T. S. Eliot 10:171

Clayton, John
Richard Brautigan 12:63

Clayton, John Jacob
Saul Bellow 6:50

Clements, Bruce
Robert Cormier 12:137
Richard Peck 21:297

Clements, Robert J.
Pablo Neruda 2:308
Irving Stone 7:469
Vassilis Vassilikos 4:551

Clemons, Walter
Lisa Alther 7:12
James Baldwin 5:43
Saul Bellow 6:55
Peter Benchley 8:82
G. Cabrera Infante 5:96
E. L. Doctorow 6:133
Nora Ephron 17:113
J. G. Farrell 6:173
Joseph Heller 5:176, 182
George V. Higgins 7:158
Maureen Howard 5:189
Erica Jong 4:263
Milan Kundera 4:276
Doris Lessing 6:302
Alison Lurie 4:305
Ross Macdonald 1:185
James McCourt 5:278
Carson McCullers 1:210
Vladimir Nabokov 6:354
Donald Newlove 6:364
Joyce Carol Oates 2:316; 3:363
Flannery O'Connor 2:317
Grace Paley 4:391
Robert M. Pirsig 4:403
Manuel Puig 5:354
Adrienne Rich 6:458
Isaac Bashevis Singer 3:456
Martin Cruz Smith 25:412
Raymond Sokolov 7:430
Tom Wicker 7:534
Richard B. Wright 6:582

Clever, Glenn
E. J. Pratt 19:383

Clifford, Gay
Staley Middleton 7:221
Bernice Rubens 19:403

Clifford, Paula M.
Claude Simon 9:485

Clifford, William
Walter Farley 17:116

Clinton, Craig
John Arden 15:24

Clinton, Dana G.
Sue Ellen Bridgers 26:91

Clinton, Farley
William Safire 10:447

Cloonan, William
André Malraux 13:368

Cloutier, Pierre
Hugh Hood 15:285

Clouzot, Claire
John Cassavetes 20:45
Andy Warhol 20:419

Clucas, Humphrey
Philip Larkin 5:227

Clum, John M.
Paddy Chayefsky 23:115
Peter Shaffer 14:487

Clurman, Harold
Edward Albee 2:2; 5:14; 25:37
Robert Anderson 23:28
Jean Anouilh 3:12
Fernando Arrabal 2:15; 9:41
Alan Ayckbourn 5:37; 8:35; 18:30
Samuel Beckett 2:47; 6:33
Lenny Bruce 21:52
Ed Bullins 1:47; 5:83
Alice Childress 12:106
D. L. Coburn 10:108
Padraic Colum 28:88
E. E. Cummings 8:160
Christopher Durang 27:89
Brian Friel 5:129
Jean Genet 2:158
William Gibson 23:174
Trevor Griffiths 13:256
John Guare 14:220
Bill Gunn 5:153
Christopher Hampton 4:211, 212
Lorraine Hansberry 17:190
Lillian Hellman 18:226
Rolf Hochhuth 4:230
William Inge 8:308
Eugène Ionesco 4:250
Ann Jellicoe 27:209
Preston Jones 10:296
Jean Kerr 22:254
Arthur Kopit 18:287, 291
David Mamet 15:355, 356
Terrence McNally 4:347; 7:217, 218
Mark Medoff 6:322
Arthur Miller 1:218; 6:335
Jason Miller 2:284
Yukio Mishima 27:337
Sławomir Mrożek 13:399
Clifford Odets 2:320; 28:330, 334
John Osborne 5:330
Miguel Piñero 4:402
Harold Pinter 6:405, 410, 415, 419; 15:426
David Rabe 4:426; 8:450, 451
Terence Rattigan 7:355
Eric Rohmer 16:537
Tadeusz Różewicz 23:361
Anthony Shaffer 19:413
Peter Shaffer 5:388
Sam Shepard 6:496, 497; 17:437, 442
Neil Simon 11:496
Bernard Slade 11:508
John Steinbeck 5:408
Tom Stoppard 1:327; 4:526; 5:411; 8:501; 15:521
David Storey 5:417; 8:505
Elizabeth Swados 12:557
George Tabori 19:437
Megan Terry 19:438
Gore Vidal 2:450
Joseph A. Walker 19:454, 455
Richard Wesley 7:519
Thornton Wilder 6:573
Tennessee Williams 2:465; 5:500, 504; 7:545
Lanford Wilson 7:549; 14:592

Clute, John
Douglas Adams 27:13
Isaac Asimov 26:58
Samuel R. Delany 14:147
Fritz Leiber 25:308
Gene Wolfe 25:478

Cluysenaar, Anne
László Nagy 7:251
Jon Silkin 6:498

Coady, Matthew
Monty Python 21:223

Coale, Samuel
Donald Barthelme 23:49
John Cheever 25:118
Jerzy Kosinski 3:273; 6:284
Alain Robbe-Grillet 6:468

Coates, John
Patrick White 18:545

Coates, Ken
Aleksandr I. Solzhenitsyn 18:500

Cobb, Jane
Taylor Caldwell 28:61
Betty Cavanna 12:97
Henry Gregor Felsen 17:120
Frank B. Gilbreth, Jr. and Ernestine Gilbreth Carey 17:154, 155
Lee Kingman 17:243
James Schuyler 23:387
Mary Stolz 12:547

Cobb, Richard
René Clair 20:68

Cockburn, Alexander
P. G. Wodehouse 22:480

Cocks, Geoffrey
Thomas Pynchon 18:437

Cocks, Jay
Mel Brooks 12:77
Michael Cimino 16:208
Werner Herzog 16:326
Richard Lester 20:231
Gordon Parks 16:460
Harold Pinter 3:388
Lou Reed 21:316
Bruce Springsteen 17:480
François Truffaut 20:383
Frank Zappa 17:587

Cocks, John C., Jr.
Federico Fellini 16:274

Cockshott, Gerald
John Ford 16:307

Coe, Richard L.
Lily Tomlin 17:521

Coe, Richard N.
Jean Genet 1:117
Eugène Ionesco 6:251

Coelho, Joaquim-Francisco
Carlos Drummond de Andrade 18:4

Coffey, Barbara
François Truffaut 20:393

Coffey, Warren
Flannery O'Connor 21:262
Kurt Vonnegut, Jr. 3:494

Cogell, Elizabeth Cummins
Ursula K. LeGuin 13:348

Coggeshall, Rosanne
Lee Smith 25:408, 409

Cogley, John
Dan Wakefield 7:502

Cogswell, Fred
Earle Birney 1:34
Phyllis Gotlieb 18:191
Joe Rosenblatt 15:446

Cohen, Arthur A.
Joseph Brodsky 4:77
Cynthia Ozick 3:372
Marguerite Yourcenar 19:483

Cohen, Dean
J. P. Donleavy 1:76

Cohen, Debra Rae
Anne McCaffrey 17:283
The Police 26:365
Carly Simon 26:413

Cohen, F.
Romain Gary 25:189

Cohen, George
Robin Cook 14:131

Cohen, Henry
Aimé Césaire 19:96

Cohen, J. M.
Yevgeny Yevtushenko 13:619

Cohen, Joseph
Cynthia Ozick 28:356

Cohen, Larry
Jules Feiffer 2:133

Cohen, Mitchell
David Byrne 26:98
Smokey Robinson 21:351
Brian Wilson 12:652
Neil Young 17:578

Cohen, Mitchell S.
Elaine May 16:433

Cohen, Nathan
Mordecai Richler 5:371

Cohen, Phyllis
Kin Platt 26:349

Cohen, Robert
Farley Mowat 26:336

Cohen, Sarah Blacher
Cynthia Ozick 28:347

Cohen, Stephen F.
Aleksandr I. Solzhenitsyn 18:497

Cohn, Dorrit
Alain Robbe-Grillet 1:289

Cohn, Ellen
Lily Tomlin 17:517

Cohn, Jeanette
Hilma Wolitzer 17:564

Cohn, Nik
Mick Jagger and Keith Richard 17:234
Paul Simon 17:465
Bruce Springsteen 17:480

Cohn, Ruby
Edward Albee 1:4; 2:4
Fernando Arrabal 18:20
James Baldwin 2:32
Imamu Amiri Baraka 2:35
Djuna Barnes 4:43
John Dos Passos 4:133
Lawrence Ferlinghetti 2:134
John Hawkes 4:215
Robinson Jeffers 11:310
Kenneth Koch 5:219
Robert Lowell 11:324
Arthur Miller 2:279
Harold Pinter 6:405
Kenneth Rexroth 11:472
Thornton Wilder 15:569
Tennessee Williams 2:465

Cohn-Sfetcu, Ofelia
Hubert Aquin 15:15

Colby, Elbridge
James D. Forman 21:119

Colby, Harriet
Enid Bagnold 25:72

Colby, Rob
Olga Broumas 10:76

Colby, Thomas E.
Hermann Hesse 17:206

Coldwell, Joan
Marie-Claire Blais 13:96

Cole, Barry
Ann Quin 6:442

Cole, Laurence
Jean Rhys 2:372

Cole, Sheila R.
Julia W. Cunningham 12:166

Cole, Terry M.
Sonia Levitin 17:263

Cole, William
Charles Causley 7:42
Alex Comfort 7:54
Richard Condon 10:111
Louis Simpson 7:429
R. S. Thomas 6:531

Coleby, John
E. L. Doctorow 15:180
Robert Nye 13:413
David Rudkin 14:471
George Tabori 19:438
Francis Warner 14:553

Colegate, Isabel
Susan B. Hill 4:227
Joyce Carol Oates 6:369

Coleman, Alexander
Alejo Carpentier 11:99
José Donoso 11:145
Pablo Neruda 2:309
Nicanor Parra 2:331
João Guimarães Rosa 23:350, 352
Marguerite Yourcenar 19:484

Coleman, Sister Anne Gertrude
Paul Vincent Carroll 10:95

Coleman, Arthur Prudden
Joseph Wittlin 25:466

Coleman, John
Chinua Achebe 26:12
Robert Altman 16:44
Mel Brooks 12:79
Marguerite Duras 20:102
George Roy Hill 26:201
Kon Ichikawa 20:180
Garson Kanin 22:231
Elia Kazan 16:367
Jack Kerouac 2:227
Pier Paolo Pasolini 20:266
Sidney Poitier 26:361
Simon Raven 14:439
Satyajit Ray 16:487
Jerzy Skolimowski 20:354
Leon Uris 7:490
Orson Welles 20:452

Coleman, Ray
Joan Armatrading 17:8
Billy Joel 26:215
Bob Marley 17:268, 269

Coleman, Sidney
Roger Zelazny 21:467

Coles, Don
Graham Greene 27:174

Coles, Robert
Shirley Ann Grau 4:208
Nat Hentoff 26:182
Kenneth Koch 8:324
Jonathan Kozol 17:249
Cormac McCarthy 4:343
Milton Meltzer 26:298
Tillie Olsen 13:432
Walker Percy 14:415
William Stafford 7:461
William Styron 1:331
Frederick Wiseman 20:467
James Wright 3:544

Colley, Iain
John Dos Passos 25:140

Collier, Carmen P.
Pearl S. Buck 7:32

Collier, Christopher
Esther Forbes 12:212

Collier, Eugenia
James Baldwin 2:33
Melvin Van Peebles 2:447

Collier, Michael
Delmore Schwartz 10:463

Collier, Peter
Earl Rovit 7:383

Collings, Rex
Wole Soyinka 5:397

Collins, Anne
James Clavell 25:126
Stephen King 12:311

Collins, Bob
Gene Wolfe 25:478

Collins, Harold R.
Amos Tutuola 5:443

Collins, J. A.
Christopher Fry 14:185

Collins, Michael
Tom Wolfe 15:584

Collins, Ralph L.
Elmer Rice 7:360

Collins, Robert G.
George Lucas 16:412

Colmer, John
Shirley Hazzard 18:215

Colombo, John Robert
B. P. Nichol 18:366

Colum, Mary M.
Vera Brittain 23:89

Colum, Padraic
Patrick Kavanagh 22:234
Rosemary Sutcliff 26:433

Columba, Sister Mary, P.B.V.M.
Rosemary Wells 12:638

Combs, Richard
Woody Allen 16:4
Robert Altman 16:24
John Cassavetes 20:48, 53
Claude Chabrol 16:182
Brian De Palma 20:76
Rainer Werner Fassbinder 20:107, 117, 120
Werner Herzog 16:322, 323, 333
Elaine May 16:431
Gordon Parks 16:459
Sidney Poitier 26:361, 362
Paul Schrader 26:388, 396, 399
Martin Scorsese 20:330, 331, 332
Jerzy Skolimowski 20:353
François Truffaut 20:393
Peter Weir 20:425, 427
Orson Welles 20:453

Commager, Henry Steele
Esther Forbes 12:209
MacKinlay Kantor 7:194

Compton, D. G.
Samuel Beckett 3:47
Frederick Buechner 2:84
John Gardner 2:151
Bernard Kops 4:274
Vladimir Nabokov 6:352
Frederic Prokosch 4:422

Compton-Burnett, Ivy
Ivy Compton-Burnett 15:139

Conarroe, Joel
John Berryman 8:91; 13:76
Stanley Elkin 27:124
Richard Howard 7:167
Brad Leithauser 27:240
Howard Nemerov 2:307
Anne Sexton 2:391
W. D. Snodgrass 2:405

Condini, N. E.
Denise Levertov 28:241

Condini, Nereo
Eugenio Montale 7:230
Octavio Paz 19:368
David Plante 23:345
Isaac Bashevis Singer 6:511
Tom Wolfe 9:579

Condon, Richard
John le Carré 15:324

Conley, Timothy K.
William Faulkner 9:200

Conn, Stewart
Anne Stevenson 7:463

Connell, Evan
Carlos Fuentes 22:170

Connell, Evan S., Jr.
Simone de Beauvoir 2:43
James Dickey 2:116
Gilbert Rogin 18:459
Wilfrid Sheed 2:392

Connelly, Kenneth
John Berryman 1:34

Connelly, Robert
Luchino Visconti 16:565

Conner, John W.
E. M. Almedingen 12:5
Honor Arundel 17:15, 16
Judy Blume 12:44
Frank Bonham 12:53
James D. Forman 21:118
Nikki Giovanni 4:189
Jesse Jackson 12:290
Madeleine L'Engle 12:348, 349, 350
Robert Lipsyte 21:209
John Neufeld 17:309
Lenora Mattingly Weber 12:635
Maia Wojciechowska 26:455, 456

Connole, John M.
Thor Heyerdahl 26:191
Margaret O. Hyde 21:172

Connolly, Cyril
Ernest Hemingway 6:225
Louis MacNeice 4:315
Ezra Pound 4:408, 414

Conover, Roger L.
Mina Loy 28:250

Conquest, Robert
Roy Fuller 28:149
Ezra Pound 7:334
Aleksandr I. Solzhenitsyn 2:413; 4:513

Conrad, George
Helen MacInnes 27:280

Conrad, Peter
Beryl Bainbridge 22:46
F. R. Leavis 24:307

Conrad, Randall
Luis Buñuel 16:145

Conrad, Robert C.
Heinrich Böll 27:65

Conradi, Peter J.
Harold Pinter 27:391

Conron, Brandon
Alice Munro 19:343

Conroy, Jack
Charles Bukowski 2:84

Consiglio, Alberto
Rouben Mamoulian **16**:421

Contoski, Victor
Robert Duncan **2**:123
David Ignatow **7**:175
David Kherdian **6**:281
W. S. Merwin **18**:334
Czesiaw Miiosz **11**:376
Marge Piercy **6**:403; **18**:405; **27**:374
Charles Simic **9**:480

Conway, John D.
Paul Vincent Carroll **10**:98

Coogan, Tim Pat
Brian Moore **19**:332

Cook, Albert
Djuna Barnes **4**:43
André Malraux **4**:327

Cook, Bruce
Kingsley Amis **8**:11
James Baldwin **3**:32; **17**:39
Heinrich Böll **6**:84
William S. Burroughs **1**:49
Evan S. Connell, Jr. **4**:109
Gregory Corso **1**:64
Robert Duncan **1**:83
John Gregory Dunne **28**:122
Allen Ginsberg **1**:118
Lillian Hellman **8**:281
Marjorie Kellogg **2**:224
Thomas Keneally **5**:211
Jack Kerouac **1**:166
Jerzy Kosinski **1**:171
Ross Macdonald **2**:256
Norman Mailer **1**:193
Brian Moore **7**:235
Charles Olson **1**:263
Ezra Pound **1**:276
Budd Schulberg **7**:403
Irwin Shaw **7**:413
Georges Simenon **2**:399
Gary Snyder **1**:318
Dalton Trumbo **19**:446, 448
Arnold Wesker **5**:484
William Carlos Williams **1**:372

Cook, Carole
Janet Frame **22**:149
V. S. Pritchett **15**:443
Eudora Welty **14**:565

Cook, David
Roald Dahl **18**:108
Camara Laye **4**:283

Cook, John
Robert Kroetsch **23**:274
Patrick Lane **25**:286

Cook, Martha E.
Donald Davidson **19**:128

Cook, Reginald L.
Robert Frost **1**:111

Cook, Richard M.
Carson McCullers **12**:429
Edmund Wilson **24**:486

Cook, Roderick
Harry Mathews **6**:314
Berry Morgan **6**:340
Paul Theroux **28**:422

Cook, Stanley
William Golding **17**:173
Mollie Hunter **21**:168

Cooke, Alistair
C. S. Lewis **27**:260

Cooke, Judy
Peter Rushforth **19**:406
John Updike **23**:477

Cooke, Michael G.
Ronald L. Fair **18**:141
Alex Haley **12**:246, 252
Gayl Jones **9**:308
Margaríta Karapánou **13**:314
George Lamming **4**:279
Michael Mott **15**:381
Joyce Carol Oates **9**:403
Jean Rhys **4**:445
William Styron **1**:331
John Updike **2**:443
Alice Walker **9**:558
Robert Penn Warren **4**:581

Cookson, William
David Jones **4**:260
Hugh MacDiarmid **4**:310

Cooley, Peter
Daniel Halpern **14**:231
Daniel Hoffman **13**:286
Ted Hughes **2**:201
David Ignatow **14**:275
Peter Wild **14**:581

Coombs, Orde
James Baldwin **8**:40

Coon, Caroline
Joan Armatrading **17**:8

Cooper, Arthur
Richard Adams **5**:5
Ralph Bakshi **26**:70
Richard Condon **6**:115
Michael Crichton **2**:109
J. P. Donleavy **6**:142
Ward S. Just **4**:266; **27**:228
John le Carré **3**:281
James A. Michener **5**:290
Wright Morris **7**:245
Gordon Parks **16**:459
Ishmael Reed **6**:450
Philip Roth **2**:378
Irwin Shaw **7**:414
David Storey **5**:417
Gore Vidal **6**:549
Fay Weldon **6**:563

Cooper, Carolyn
Louise Bennett **28**:30

Cooper, Ilene
Norma Fox Mazer **26**:294

Cooper, Jane
Muriel Rukeyser **15**:456

Cooper, Keith B.
Milton Meltzer **26**:306

Cooper, Nina
Gabriel Marcel **15**:362

Cooper, Philip
Robert Lowell **4**:300

Cooper, Susan
Mollie Hunter **21**:160
Mildred D. Taylor **21**:419
Colin Thiele **17**:494, 495

Cooper, William
C. P. Snow **19**:427

Cooperman, Stanley
W. S. Merwin **1**:212
Philip Roth **3**:438
Marguerite yourcenar **19**:481

Coover, Robert
José Donoso **4**:127
Carlos Fuentes **8**:224
Gabriel García Márquez **15**:253
Manuel Puig **28**:371
Ernesto Sabato **23**:381

Copland, R. A.
Noel Hilliard **15**:279

Coppage, Noel
David Bowie **17**:66
Jackson Browne **21**:42
Janis Ian **21**:184
Mick Jagger and Keith Richard **17**:233
Waylon Jennings **21**:202, 203, 204, 205
Kris Kristofferson **26**:266, 270
Gordon Lightfoot **26**:279, 280, 281, 282, 283
Joni Mitchell **12**:439
Willie Nelson **17**:304
Laura Nyro **17**:314
Phil Ochs **17**:334
Buffy Sainte-Marie **17**:431
Carly Simon **26**:407
Neil Young **17**:583

Corbin, Louise
Jean Renoir **20**:293

Cordell, Richard A.
Taylor Caldwell **28**:56, 59

Cordesse, Gérard
William S. Burroughs **15**:110

Core, George
Andrew Lytle **22**:293
Edna O'Brien **8**:429
Seán O'Faoláin **7**:273
John Crowe Ransom **2**:364; **5**:366
Jean Rhys **14**:447
William Styron **1**:331
Allen Tate **4**:537
William Trevor **9**:529

Coren, Alan
James Thurber **25**:440

Corke, Hilary
Isaac Asimov **26**:37
John Cheever **3**:106

Corliss, Richard
Ingmar Bergman **16**:58
Larry Gelbart **21**:128
Stephen King **26**:243
Richard Lester **20**:224
Garry Marshall **17**:277

Corman, Cid
Kon Ichikawa **20**:179
George Oppen **13**:433

Corn, Alfred
Elizabeth Bowen **15**:78
John Hollander **8**:302
Czesiaw Miiosz **22**:310
Eugenio Montale **18**:339
Frederick Morgan **23**:299
Boris Pasternak **7**:300
Reg Saner **9**:469
James Schuyler **23**:390
L. E. Sissman **18**:489

Cornell, George W.
Andrew M. Greeley **28**:174

Cornwell, Ethel F.
Samuel Beckett **3**:45
Nathalie Sarraute **8**:471

Corodimas, Peter
Ira Levin **6**:305
Françoise Sagan **17**:425

Corr, Patricia
Evelyn Waugh **1**:356

Corrigan, Mary Ann
Tennessee Williams **11**:571, 575

Corrigan, Matthew
Charles Olson **5**:328

Corrigan, Robert W.
Edward Albee **5**:11
John Arden **6**:9
Saul Bellow **6**:51
Robert Bolt **14**:89
Friedrich Dürrenmatt **8**:196
Michel de Ghelderode **6**:197
Arthur Miller **1**:218
John Osborne **5**:332
Harold Pinter **6**:417
Thornton Wilder **5**:494

Corrigan, Sylvia Robinson
Sylvia Plath **17**:350

Corrington, John William
James Dickey **1**:73
Marion Montgomery **7**:233

Cort, David
Jules Archer **12**:16

Cort, John C.
Helen MacInnes **27**:279

Cortázar, Julio
Jorge Luis Borges **8**:102

Cortínez, Carlos
Octavio Paz **10**:393

Corwin, Phillip
Kay Boyle **5**:67
Siegfried Lenz **27**:249

Cosgrave, Mary Silva
Maya Angelou **12**:13
Robert Lipsyte **21**:208
Paul Zindel **26**:472

Cosgrave, Patrick
Kingsley Amis **3**:8
Robert Lowell **4**:300
Ruth Rendell **28**:384, 386
Georges Simenon **3**:452
Julian Symons **14**:523

Cosman, Max
Sylvia Ashton-Warner **19**:21

Cott, Jonathan
  Bob Dylan **6**:156
  Mick Jagger and Keith Richard **17**:234
  John Lennon and Paul McCartney **12**:356
  Jim Morrison **17**:287
  Van Morrison **21**:236
  Patti Smith **12**:542
  Andrew Lloyd Webber and Tim Rice **21**:423

Cotter, James Finn
  Robert Bly **10**:62
  Philip Booth **23**:76
  Peter Davison **28**:104
  William Everson **14**:167
  Nikki Giovanni **19**:192
  Thom Gunn **18**:204
  Daniel Hoffman **23**:243
  Denise Levertov **28**:243
  Frederick Morgan **23**:298, 300
  Robert Phillips **28**:364
  Robert Pinsky **19**:371
  May Sarton **14**:482
  Barry Spacks **14**:511
  James Tate **25**:429
  Mark Van Doren **6**:542
  David Wagoner **15**:559
  John Hall Wheelock **14**:571

Cottrell, Robert D.
  Simone de Beauvoir **8**:58

Coughlan, Margaret N.
  E. M. Almedingen **12**:4

Coult, Tony
  Edward Bond **23**:65

Cournos, John
  R. V. Cassill **23**:102

Courtivron, Isabelle de
  Violette Leduc **22**:263

Couto, Maria
  Salman Rushdie **23**:367

Covatta, Anthony
  Elio Vittorini **6**:551

Coveney, Michael
  Athol Fugard **5**:130
  Sam Shepard **6**:496

Cowan, Louise
  Caroline Gordon **13**:243
  John Crowe Ransom **5**:363
  Allen Tate **2**:431
  Robert Penn Warren **6**:555

Cowan, Michael
  Norman Mailer **8**:371

Cowan, Paul
  Edmund White III **27**:480

Cowan, Robert
  Billy Joel **26**:214

Cowasjee, Saros
  Mulk Raj Anand **23**:19

Cowen, Robert C.
  Margaret O. Hyde **21**:174

Cowie, Peter
  Michelangelo Antonioni **20**:24
  Ingmar Bergman **16**:50, 65
  Nagisa Oshima **20**:249, 256
  Satyajit Ray **16**:480
  Jean Renoir **20**:294, 296
  Eric Rohmer **16**:531
  Jerzy Skolimowski **20**:353
  Orson Welles **20**:451

Cowley, Malcolm
  Conrad Aiken **10**:3
  Louis Aragon **22**:34, 35
  Cleanth Brooks **24**:116
  Pearl S. Buck **7**:31; **11**:71
  Erskine Caldwell **14**:93
  E. E. Cummings **3**:118
  John Dos Passos **4**:135
  Howard Fast **23**:154
  William Faulkner **8**:210; **28**:142
  Robert Frost **4**:173
  Ernest Hemingway **13**:270; **19**:212
  Doris Lessing **6**:303
  John O'Hara **2**:325
  Ezra Pound **4**:407
  Upton Sinclair **15**:500
  Allen Tate **24**:439
  James Thurber **5**:430

Cox, C. B.
  James Baldwin **17**:27
  William Golding **17**:163

Cox, David
  Wilfrid Sheed **4**:489

Cox, James M.
  Robert Frost **26**:118

Cox, Kenneth
  Hugh MacDiarmid **4**:311
  Ezra Pound **4**:413
  C. H. Sisson **8**:490
  Louis Zukofsky **7**:562; **11**:582

Cox, Terrance
  W. P. Kinsella **27**:238

Coxe, Louis
  David Jones **2**:217
  Mary McCarthy **24**:344
  Anne Sexton **2**:391

Coy, Jane
  Norma Fox Mazer **26**:291

Coyle, Cathy S.
  Paula Danziger **21**:83
  Diana Wynne Jones **26**:224

Coyne, John R., Jr.
  Frederick Forsyth **5**:125
  Dick Francis **2**:142
  E. Howard Hunt **3**:251
  Ward Just **4**:266
  Robert Lipsyte **21**:211
  Donald E. Westlake **7**:528
  Tom Wolfe **2**:481

Coyne, Patricia S.
  Kingsley Amis **3**:10
  Erica Jong **4**:265
  Joyce Carol Oates **9**:402
  Wilfrid Sheed **2**:395
  Elizabeth Spencer **22**:402
  Morris L. West **6**:564

Crabtree, Paul
  Louis Auchincloss **18**:27

Cracroft, Richard H.
  A. B. Guthrie, Jr. **23**:199

Craft, Robert
  Aldous Huxley **5**:193

Craft, Wallace
  Eugenio Montale **7**:230

Crago, Hugh
  Andre Norton **12**:460
  J.R.R. Tolkien **12**:573

Craib, Roderick
  Bernard Malamud **3**:322

Craig, Barbara J.
  Sandra Scoppettone **26**:405

Craig, David
  Piers Paul Read **25**:375

Craig, George
  Michel Butor **15**:115

Craig, Patricia
  Beryl Bainbridge **18**:33
  Joan Barfoot **18**:36
  Elizabeth Bowen **22**:67
  Carolyn G. Heilbrun **25**:257
  William Mayne **12**:404
  Edna O'Brien **8**:429
  Frank O'Connor **23**:330
  Julia O'Faolain **19**:360
  Katherine Paterson **12**:485
  Frederic Raphael **14**:438
  Noel Streatfeild **21**:413
  Fay Weldon **19**:468

Craig, Randall
  Jean Genet **2**:160
  Bernard Pomerance **13**:444
  Robert Shaw **5**:390
  Sam Shepard **4**:489
  E. A. Whitehead **5**:489

Crain, Jane Larkin
  Alice Adams **13**:1
  Caroline Blackwood **9**:101
  André Brink **18**:66
  E. M. Broner **19**:72
  William F. Buckley, Jr. **18**:81
  Sara Davidson **9**:175
  Lawrence Durrell **6**:153
  Leslie Epstein **27**:129
  Bruce Jay Friedman **5**:126
  John Gardner **5**:134
  Gail Godwin **8**:248
  Shirley Ann Grau **9**:240
  Milan Kundera **4**:276
  Alan Lelchuk **5**:244
  Doris Lessing **6**:299
  Grace Paley **4**:394
  Walker Percy **6**:401
  Kathleen Raine **7**:353
  C. P. Snow **6**:518
  Muriel Spark **5**:398
  Mario Vargas Llosa **6**:545
  Gore Vidal **4**:555
  David Wagoner **5**:474
  Frederick Wiseman **20**:474
  Sol Yurick **6**:583

Crane, Hugh M.
  Andrew M. Greeley **28**:175

Crane, Lucille
  Winston Graham **23**:194

Crane, Peggy
  Joy Adamson **17**:6
  Jean Rhys **14**:446

Crane, R. S.
  Cleanth Brooks **24**:104

Crankshaw, Edward
  Yuri Krotkov **19**:264
  Aleksandr I. Solzhenitsyn **1**:319

Cranston, Mechthild
  René Char **14**:126

Crawford, Pamela
  Andy Warhol **20**:418

Creagh, Patrick
  Giuseppe Ungaretti **7**:484

Creeley, Robert
  Robert Duncan **4**:141
  William Everson **5**:121
  Robert Graves **6**:210
  Charles Olson **5**:326
  Ezra Pound **3**:395
  William Stafford **4**:519
  William Carlos Williams **5**:507
  Louis Zukofsky **4**:599; **18**:559

Creighton, Joanne V.
  Joyce Carol Oates **19**:348

Creighton, Luella
  Dalton Trumbo **19**:444

Crew, Gary
  Wilson Harris **25**:217

Crews, Frederick
  Geoffrey H. Hartman **27**:187

Crews, Frederick C.
  E. M. Forster **13**:219
  Shirley Ann Grau **4**:207
  Philip Roth **2**:379

Crews, Harry
  Elliott Baker **8**:39

Crichfield, Grant
  E. M. Forster **22**:135
  Barry Hannah **23**:210

Crichton, Michael
  Frederick Forsyth **2**:136
  Kurt Vonnegut, Jr. **3**:495

Crick, Francis
  Michael McClure **6**:319

Crick, Joyce
  Michael Hamburger **5**:159
  Botho Strauss **22**:408

Crider, Bill
  Stephen King **12**:310

Crinklaw, Don
  John Gardner **3**:186

Crinkley, Richmond
  Edward Albee **2**:3

Crisp, Quentin
  Graham Greene **18**:198
  Stevie Smith **25**:422

Crist, Judith
Lindsay Anderson **20**:17
Mel Brooks **12**:81
John Cassavetes **20**:52
Julia W. Cunningham **12**:163
George Roy Hill **26**:196
Harry Kemelman **2**:225
Jean Kerr **22**:256
Richard Lester **20**:231
Laurence Olivier **20**:241
Nagisa Oshima **20**:249
Sidney Poitier **26**:358
Satyajit Ray **16**:488
Alain Resnais **16**:514
Ken Russell **16**:547

Croce, A.
John Gregory Dunne **28**:121

Croce, Arlene
Ingmar Bergman **16**:47
Shirley Clarke **16**:217
Vittorio De Sica **20**:88
Jean-Luc Godard **20**:128
John Huston **20**:163
Stanley Kubrick **16**:377
Satyajit Ray **16**:475
François Truffaut **20**:381

Croft, Julian
Robert D. FitzGerald **19**:182

Croft, L. B.
Yevgeny Yevtushenko **13**:620

Cromelin, Richard
Walter Becker and Donald Fagen **26**:79
David Bowie **17**:58

Crompton, D. W.
William Golding **17**:171

Croome, Lesley
Diana Wynne Jones **26**:225

Cross, Michael S.
Frank Herbert **12**:279

Cross, Richard K.
Richard Eberhart **19**:143

Crouch, Marcus
Ruth M. Arthur **12**:28
Margot Benary-Isbert **12**:34
Cecil Bødker **21**:13
H. F. Brinsmead **21**:32
Peter Dickinson **12**:175
Leon Garfield **12**:228
Alan Garner **17**:144
Diana Wynne Jones **26**:229, 230, 231, 232
Andre Norton **12**:464
Philippa Pearce **21**:289
Noel Streatfeild **21**:403
Rosemary Sutcliff **26**:432, 438, 440

Crouch, Stanley
James Baldwin **17**:42
Marvin Gaye **26**:134
Ishmael Reed **13**:480

Crouse, Timothy
Carly Simon **26**:406

Crow, John
Harlan Ellison **13**:203

Crowder, Richard H.
Carl Sandburg **1**:300; **15**:467

Crowe, Linda
Honor Arundel **17**:13

Crowson, Lydia
Jean Cocteau **8**:148

Crowther, Bosley
Jean Cocteau **16**:222, 223, 227
Carl Theodor Dreyer **16**:256
Federico Fellini **16**:270
John Ford **16**:305, 309
John Huston **20**:157, 158, 159, 161
Kon Ichikawa **20**:178
Elia Kazan **16**:360, 363
Norman Lear **12**:326
Laurence Olivier **20**:234
Alain Resnais **16**:498
Carlos Saura **20**:314
Josef von Sternberg **20**:375
Agnès Varda **16**:554
Andrzej Wajda **16**:577
Jessamyn West **17**:548
Billy Wilder **20**:455, 457, 462

Crozier, Andrew
Ed Dorn **18**:128

Cruickshank, John
Patrick Lane **25**:289

Crump, G. B.
Tom Stoppard **15**:519

Crunk
See also Robert Bly
James Wright **28**:462

Cruse, Harold W.
W.E.B. Du Bois **2**:120

Cruttwell, Patrick
Sylvia Ashton-Warner **19**:23
Adolfo Bioy Casares **4**:63
Jerzy Kosinski **3**:274
Iris Murdoch **2**:296
I. A. Richards **24**:392
Patrick White **7**:529

Cuddon, J. A.
Peter De Vries **2**:114
James Purdy **4**:423
Frederic Raphael **2**:367
Claude Simon **4**:497

Culbertson, Diana
Alberto Moravia **7**:243

Cullen, Elinor S.
Ruth M. Arthur **12**:26

Cullen, John B.
Len Deighton **22**:114

Culler, Jonathan
Harold Bloom **24**:75
Wayne C. Booth **24**:96
Geoffrey H. Hartman **27**:184
Walker Percy **8**:439
George Steiner **24**:433

Culligan, Glendy
Rosa Guy **26**:140

Culpan, Norman
Mollie Hunter **21**:167
Andre Norton **12**:470, 471
Roger Zelazny **21**:464, 465, 472

Cumare, Rosa
Flann O'Brien **5**:317

Cumming, Joseph B., Jr.
Richard O'Brien **17**:325

Cummings, Peter
Northrop Frye **24**:225

Cunliffe, Marcus
Irving Stone **7**:469

Cunliffe, W. Gordon
Heinrich Böll **11**:57
Günter Grass **1**:126
Uwe Johnson **10**:283

Cunningham, John
Isabelle Holland **21**:150

Cunningham, Laura
Richard Price **6**:427

Cunningham, Valentine
Jeffrey Archer **28**:12
Louis Auchincloss **6**:15
John Barth **5**:51
Donald Barthelme **3**:43
Richard Brautigan **12**:70
Pearl S. Buck **18**:80
Alejo Carpentier **8**:134
Margaret Craven **17**:79
Len Deighton **4**:119
Don DeLillo **13**:179
Ilya Ehrenburg **18**:137
Buchi Emecheta **14**:159
Shusaku Endo **7**:96; **14**:161
Penelope Fitzgerald **19**:172
Frederick Forsyth **5**:125
Mervyn Jones **10**:295
Anna Kavan **5**:206
William Kennedy **28**:204
William Kotzwinkle **5**:220
Mary Lavin **4**:282
Colin MacInnes **4**:314
Stanley Middleton **7**:220
Yukio Mishima **4**:358
Vladimir Nabokov **3**:355
Hans Erich Nossack **6**:364
David Plante **7**:307
Bernice Rubens **19**:404
Salman Rushdie **23**:366
Ward Ruyslinck **14**:471
Françoise Sagan **9**:468
William Sansom **6**:484
Randolph Stow **23**:437
Emma Tennant **13**:536
Paul Theroux **8**:513
Gillian Tindall **7**:474
Ludvík Vaculík **7**:495
Kurt Vonnegut, Jr. **22**:450
Harriet Waugh **6**:559
Arnold Wesker **5**:483
Patrick White **4**:587

Cuppy, Will
Agatha Christie **12**:112, 113

Curley, Thomas
Laura Z. Hobson **25**:272

Curley, Thomas F.
Pamela Hansford Johnson **27**:218

Curran, Charles
Vera Brittain **23**:93

Curran, Thomas M.
Shusaku Endo **19**:161

Current-Garcia, Eugene
George Seferis **11**:494

Currie, William
Kōbō Abé **8**:2

Curry, Andrew
Robert Phillips **28**:361

Curtis, Anthony
Alan Ayckbourn **18**:30
W. Somerset Maugham **15**:365
J. B. Priestley **5**:351

Curtis, C. Michael
Sara Davidson **9**:175
Annie Dillard **9**:179

Curtis, Charlotte
Bette Bao Lord **23**:279

Curtis, Jerry L.
Jean Genet **10**:224

Curtis, Penelope
Katherine Paterson **12**:485

Curtis, Simon
Donald Davie **5**:113
Seamus Heaney **7**:151

Curtius, E. R.
William Goyen **14**:209

Cuscuna, Michael
Jim Morrison **17**:289

Cushman, Jerome
Jascha Kessler **4**:270

Cushman, Kathleen
Kurt Vonnegut, Jr. **12**:610

Cushman, Keith
Roger Angell **26**:28
Marilyn French **18**:157
Mark Schorer **9**:474

Cushman, Robert
Edward Bond **23**:71

Cusimano, Jim
Lou Reed **21**:309

Cutler, Bruce
Louis Simpson **7**:428

Cutter, William
S. Y. Agnon **4**:15

Cutts, John
Frank Capra **16**:157
Carl Theodor Dreyer **16**:258
Lorraine Hansberry **17**:184

Cyclops
Larry Gelbart **21**:126, 127
Garry Marshall **17**:275

Czajkowska, Magdalena
Tadeusz Różewicz **9**:463

Czarnecki, Mark
W. P. Kinsella 27:238

Dabney, Lewis H.
William Faulkner 6:174

Dabney, Lewis M.
Edmund Wilson 24:482

Dacey, Philip
Arthur Gregor 9:255

Daemmrich, Horst S.
Eugène Ionesco 11:289

Dahlie, Hallvard
Hugh Hood 28:192
Brian Moore 1:225; 7:237
Alice Munro 10:357

Daiches, David
W. H. Auden 1:8
Saul Bellow 3:55
Elizabeth Bowen 1:39
Anthony Burgess 22:71
Ivy Compton-Burnett 1:60
Elizabeth Daryush 19:119
C. Day Lewis 1:72
T. S. Eliot 1:89
William Empson 3:147
Christopher Fry 2:143
Robert Graves 1:126
Henry Green 2:178
Aldous Huxley 1:149
Hugh MacDiarmid 2:252
Louis MacNeice 1:186
Bernard Malamud 3:323
I. A. Richards 24:384
Henry Roth 6:473
Edith Sitwell 2:403
Stephen Spender 1:322
Evelyn Waugh 1:356
René Wellek 28:443

Daiker, Donald A.
Hugh Nissenson 4:381

Dale, Peter
John Berryman 2:58
Basil Bunting 10:84
Stanley Burnshaw 13:128,129

Daley, Robert
Mark Harris 19:200
John R. Tunis 12:597

Dalgliesh, Alice
Margaret O. Hyde 21:173
Madeleine L'Engle 12:346, 347

Dallas, Karl
Jimmy Cliff 21:63
Janis Ian 21:185
Joni Mitchell 12:435
Jim Morrison 17:287
Phil Ochs 17:330
Frank Zappa 17:593

Dalton, David
Mick Jagger and Keith Richard 17:239
Jim Morrison 17:292
Lou Reed 21:314
Smokey Robinson 21:347
Paul Simon 17:466

Dalton, Elizabeth
E. M. Broner 19:71
Vladimir Nabokov 1:245
John Updike 1:344

Dalton, Margaret
Yevgeny Yevtushenko 26:461

Daltry, Patrice M.
Lee Kingman 17:245

Daly, Jay
Roger Zelazny 21:470

Daly, Maureen
Mary Stolz 12:551

Daly, Mike
Ray Davies 21:90

Dame, Enid
Chaim Potok 7:322

D'Amico, Masolino
Umberto Eco 28:130

Dana, Robert
Yukio Mishima 2:286

Dangerfield, George
Taylor Caldwell 28:55
Rayner Heppenstall 10:272
Compton Mackenzie 18:313
Carson McCullers 12:410
Noel Streatfeild 21:397

Daniel, Glyn
Thor Heyerdahl 26:191

Daniel, Helen
David Malouf 28:265

Daniel, John
Ann Quin 6:441
Isaac Bashevis Singer 6:507

Daniel, Lorne
Andrew Suknaski 19:432

Daniel, Mary L.
João Guimarães Rosa 23:354

Daniel, Robert D.
Walker Percy 14:414

Daniel, Robert W.
W. D. Snodgrass 10:478

Daniels, Jonathan
T. S. Stribling 23:440

Daniels, Les
Trina Robbins 21:338
Jerome Siegel and Joe Shuster 21:359

Daniels, Robert V.
Larry Woiwode 10:540

Danielson, J. David
Simone Schwarz-Bart 7:404

Danischewsky, Nina
Ruth M. Arthur 12:26
Peter Dickinson 12:167

Danner, G. Richard
Eugène Ionesco 15:298

D'Arazien, Steven
Hunter S. Thompson 9:528

Dardess, George
Jack Kerouac 5:213

Darling, Frances C.
Henry Gregor Felsen 17:120

Darrach, Brad
George V. Higgins 4:224
Joyce Carol Oates 2:313
Ezra Pound 7:336
Irving Stone 7:471

Das Gupta, Chidananda
Satyajit Ray 16:481

Dasgupta, Gautam
Albert Innaurato 21:191

Datchery, Dick
Agatha Christie 12:120

Dathorne, O. R.
Mongo Beti 27:45
Christopher Okigbo 25:347

Dauenhauer, Richard
Paavo Haavikko 18:206

Dault, Gary Michael
Joe Rosenblatt 15:447, 448

Dauster, Frank
Gabriel García Márquez 3:182

Davenport, Basil
Daphne du Maurier 11:162
Carson McCullers 12:409

Davenport, G.
J.R.R. Tolkien 3:482

Davenport, Gary
Seán O'Faoláin 14:406

Davenport, Gary T.
E. M. Almedingen 12:4
Matt Cohen 19:113
Timothy Findley 27:142
Frank O'Connor 23:326
Seán O'Faoláin 7:275

Davenport, Guy
E. M. Almedingen 12:4
Michael Ayrton 7:17
Beryl Bainbridge 8:36
Thomas Berger 8:82
Wendell Berry 8:85
Richard Brautigan 12:58
Frederick Buechner 2:82
Paul Celan 10:101
Louis-Ferdinand Céline 3:104
John Cheever 25:116
Evan S. Connell, Jr. 4:110
Harry Crews 23:132
Joan Didion 1:75
J. P. Donleavy 4:124
G. B. Edwards 25:151
Günter Grass 22:197
Donald Hall 13:260
Miroslav Holub 4:233
Benedict Kiely 23:267
Frederick Morgan 23:296
Michael Mott 15:379
Charles Olson 6:388; 9:412
Nicanor Parra 2:331
Chaim Potok 2:338
James Purdy 2:350
Gilbert Sorrentino 22:394
J.I.M. Stewart 7:466
Harriet Waugh 6:560
Eudora Welty 14:564
Richard Wilbur 6:569
Louis Zukofsky 2:487; 4:599; 7:560

Davey, Frank
Margaret Atwood 25:68
Bill Bissett 18:58
E. J. Pratt 19:380
Joe Rosenblatt 15:446

David, Jack
B. P. Nichol 18:369

Davidon, Ann Morrissett
Simone de Beauvoir 8:57
Grace Paley 4:391
Gore Vidal 4:557

Davidson, Michael
Jack Spicer 18:509

Davidson, Peter
Sylvia Plath 17:346

Davidson, Richard B.
Christie Harris 12:266

Davie, Donald
A. R. Ammons 5:30
John Berryman 8:87
Austin Clarke 6:112
Elizabeth Daryush 19:120
T. S. Eliot 15:210
Thom Gunn 18:202
Michael Hamburger 5:159
Anthony Hecht 8:267
John Hollander 8:299
Galway Kinnell 5:217
John Peck 3:377
Ezra Pound 13:456
F. T. Prince 22:339
Andrew Sinclair 14:488
Paul Theroux 11:529
J.R.R. Tolkien 12:572

Davies, Brenda
René Clair 20:65
Jean Renoir 20:296

Davies, Brian
Robert Bresson 16:103
Claude Chabrol 16:168

Davies, R. R.
Joanne Greenberg 7:135
Diane Johnson 5:198
William Sansom 6:482

Davies, Ray
Ray Davies 21:88

Davies, Robertson
Marie-Claire Blais 22:57
William Golding 27:160
John Irving 23:248

Davies, Russell
Richard Condon 8:150
Joan Didion 8:177
Michael Hamburger 14:234
Thomas Hinde 11:273
Francis King 8:321
S. J. Perelman 15:418
Harold Pinter 27:386
Kate Roberts 15:445
Josef Škvorecký 15:511
C. P. Snow 19:429
William Trevor 9:528
John Updike 23:477

Davis, Arthur P.
Arna Bontemps 18:64
Ann Petry 18:404

Davis, Charles T.
　Robert Hayden **5**:68

Davis, Cheri Colby
　W. S. Merwin **13**:383; **18**:332

Davis, Christopher
　Diana Wynne Jones **26**:225

Davis, Deborah
　Julio Cortázar **5**:109

Davis, Elrick B.
　A. B. Guthrie, Jr. **23**:197

Davis, Fath
　Toni Morrison **4**:366

Davis, George
　George Lamming **2**:235
　Clarence Major **3**:320

Davis, Gladys
　Vera Brittain **23**:90

Davis, Hope Hale
　John Cheever **8**:140
　Oriana Fallaci **11**:190

Davis, James
　Gretchen Cryer **21**:78

Davis, Jorja
　Sandra Scoppettone **26**:405

Davis, Jorja Perkins
　Sol Gordon **26**:139

Davis, L. J.
　Richard Brautigan **12**:71
　Anthony Burgess **22**:71
　Richard Condon **4**:106
　Peter De Vries **7**:78
　John Gregory Dunne **28**:121
　Stanley Elkin **4**:153
　Leon Forrest **4**:163
　Lois Gould **4**:200
　Hannah Green **3**:202
　A. B. Guthrie, Jr. **23**:200
　John Hersey **2**:188
　Stanley Hoffman **5**:184
　James Jones **10**:291
　Ward S. Just **27**:226, 227
　William Kennedy **6**:274
　Richard Kostelanetz **28**:213
　Ira Levin **6**:307
　Colin MacInnes **23**:284
　Larry McMurtry **27**:326
　John O'Hara **2**:324
　J. F. Powers **8**:448
　Philip Roth **2**:379
　Françoise Sagan **6**:481
　Ronald Sukenick **4**:531
　Paul Theroux **28**:424
　J.R.R. Tolkien **8**:516
　Vassilis Vassilikos **8**:524
　Richard B. Wright **6**:582

Davis, Lavinia
　Margot Benary-Isbert **12**:31
　Maureen Daly **17**:90

Davis, Lavinia R.
　Rosemary Sutcliff **26**:425, 426

Davis, M. E.
　José María Arguedas **10**:10

Davis, Mary Gould
　Betty Cavanna **12**:98
　Esther Forbes **12**:207
　John R. Tunis **12**:595, 596

Davis, Ossie
　Lorraine Hansberry **17**:184

Davis, Paxton
　Eric Ambler **9**:18
　George Garrett **3**:189
　Paul Zindel **26**:480

Davis, Richard
　Woody Allen **16**:2
　Claude Chabrol **16**:169
　Larry Gelbart **21**:126
　Ken Russell **16**:541

Davis, Richard A.
　Sam Shepard **17**:439

Davis, Rick
　Richard Brautigan **9**:125
　Richard Condon **10**:111

Davis, Robert Gorham
　Saul Bellow **2**:49
　Paul Bowles **19**:57
　John Dos Passos **1**:78
　A. B. Guthrie, Jr. **23**:197
　Halldór Laxness **25**:291
　Irwin Shaw **23**:396
　William Styron **3**:472

Davis, Robert Murray
　John Steinbeck **21**:387
　Evelyn Waugh **1**:359

Davis, Stephen
　Jimmy Cliff **21**:63, 64
　Bob Marley **17**:267
　Jimmy Page and Robert Plant **12**:480
　Lou Reed **21**:307
　Carly Simon **26**:407
　Brian Wilson **12**:645

Davis, Thurston
　John le Carré **28**:229

Davis, William V.
　Robert Bly **15**:63, 67

Davison, Peter
　Robert Creeley **8**:151
　Robert Frost **4**:175
　Tess Gallagher **18**:169
　Doris Grumbach **13**:257
　Robert Hass **18**:209
　John Hollander **8**:298
　Galway Kinnell **2**:229
　Denise Levertov **8**:345
　Sylvia Plath **2**:337
　Anne Sexton **8**:482
　William Stafford **7**:460

Davy, Charles
　René Clair **20**:61
　Rouben Mamoulian **16**:422

Davy, John
　Arthur Koestler **1**:169

Dawson, Dorotha
　Walter Farley **17**:115
　Noel Streatfeild **21**:399

Dawson, Helen
　David Storey **4**:529

Dawson, Jan
　Robert Altman **16**:20, 21
　Rainer Werner Fassbinder **20**:116, 118
　Werner Herzog **16**:328
　Roman Polanski **16**:470
　Jerzy Skolimowski **20**:349
　François Truffaut **20**:392
　Andrzej Wajda **16**:583

Dawson, Margaret Cheney
　Noel Streatfeild **21**:395

Dawson, Rosemary
　Betty Smith **19**:422

Day, A. Grove
　James A. Michener **1**:214

Day, Doris M.
　Peter Shaffer **14**:487

Day, Douglas
　Robert Graves **1**:127

Day, James M.
　Paul Horgan **9**:278

Daymond, Douglas M.
　Mazo de la Roche **14**:150

Deal, Borden
　Doris Betts **28**:33

Dean, Joan F.
　Peter Shaffer **18**:475

Dean, Leigh
　Lois Duncan **26**:108

Deane, Seamus
　Seamus Heaney **7**:150
　Thomas Kinsella **19**:253
　Derek Mahon **27**:289

Deas, Malcolm
　Bruce Chatwin **28**:70

Debicki, Andrew P.
　Dámaso Alonso **14**:15
　Claudio Rodríguez **10**:439

De Bolt, Joe
　John Brunner **8**:110

Debrix, Jean R.
　Jean Cocteau **16**:223

DeBuys, William
　Paul Horgan **9**:279

Decancq, Roland
　Lawrence Durrell **8**:191

De Charmant, Elizabeth
　Giorgio Bassani **9**:74

Deck, John
　Harry Crews **6**:17
　Henry Dumas **6**:145
　J. G. Farrell **6**:173
　Michael Moorcock **5**:294
　John Seelye **7**:406

de Costa, René
　Pablo Neruda **28**:311

Dector, Midge
　Leon Uris **7**:491

DeCurtis, Anthony
　Leonard Michaels **25**:316

Deedy, John
　J. P. Donleavy **4**:123
　Nora Ephron **17**:114
　Upton Sinclair **11**:498

Deemer, Charles
　Renata Adler **8**:7
　James Baldwin **17**:38
　John Cheever **3**:108
　Peter Handke **5**:165
　Bernard Malamud **3**:324

Deen, Rosemary F.
　Randall Jarrell **6**:259
　Galway Kinnell **3**:268

Deer, Harriet
　Stanley Kubrick **16**:387

Deer, Irving
　Stanley Kubrick **16**:387

De Feo, Ronald
　Martin Amis **4**:21
　Beryl Bainbridge **8**:37
　Thomas Bernhard **3**:65
　William S. Burroughs **2**:93
　José Donoso **4**:128
　Frederick Exley **11**:187
　William Gaddis **6**:195
　Gabriel García Márquez **2**:149; **10**:216
　John Gardner **5**:131, 134
　Graham Greene **6**:219
　John Hawkes **1**:138
　Richard Hughes **11**:278
　Dan Jacobson **4**:255
　Jerzy Kosinski **1**:172
　Iris Murdoch **6**:345
　Howard Nemerov **6**:360
　Sylvia Plath **1**:270
　Anthony Powell **3**:404
　Manuel Puig **28**:369
　James Salter **7**:388
　Gilbert Sorrentino **3**:461
　William Trevor **7**:477
　John Updike **5**:460
　Angus Wilson **5**:514

Deford, Frank
　Martin Scorsese **20**:334

Degenfelder, E. Pauline
　Larry McMurtry **7**:213

Degnan, James P.
　Kingsley Amis **2**:10
　Roald Dahl **1**:71
　John Knowles **26**:258
　Wilfrid Sheed **2**:394

Degnan, James P., Jr.
　Betty Smith **19**:424

Deitz, Paula
　Frederick Busch **18**:84

De Jonge, Alex
　Dick Francis **22**:151
　Robert A. Heinlein **26**:165
　Frank Herbert **23**:219
　Frederik Pohl **18**:413
　Aleksandr I. Solzhenitsyn **9**:506
　D. M. Thomas **22**:417
　Roger Zelazny **21**:471, 472

Dekker, George
　Donald Davie **8**:166

Dekle, Bernard
  Saul Bellow **1**:32
  E. E. Cummings **1**:69
  John Dos Passos **1**:80
  William Faulkner **1**:102
  Robert Frost **1**:111
  Langston Hughes **1**:148
  John P. Marquand **2**:271
  Arthur Miller **1**:219
  John O'Hara **1**:262
  J. D. Salinger **1**:300
  Upton Sinclair **1**:310
  Thornton Wilder **1**:366
  Tennessee Williams **1**:369
  William Carlos Williams **1**:371

Delahanty, Thornton
  Rouben Mamoulian **16**:419

Delamater, Jerome H.
  Jean-Luc Godard **20**:145

Delaney, Marshall
  See Fulford, Robert

Delany, Paul
  A. Alvarez **5**:19
  Margaret Atwood **4**:24
  John Berger **19**:39
  Vera Brittain **23**:93

Delap, Richard
  Fritz Leiber **25**:306

De la Roche, Catherine
  Jean Renoir **20**:288

De la Torre Bueno, J. R., Jr.
  Roderick L. Haig-Brown
    21:134, 135, 137

Delattre, Genevieve
  Françoise Mallet-Joris **11**:355

De Laurentis, Teresa
  Italo Calvino **8**:127

De Laurot, Edouard L.
  Paddy Chayefsky **23**:111
  Federico Fellini **16**:270

Delbanco, Nicholas
  Frederick Busch **10**:93
  Graham Greene **9**:251
  Doris Grumbach **13**:257

Deligiorgis, Stavros
  David Kherdian **9**:318

Delius, Anthony
  Breyten Breytenbach **23**:86
  Alan Paton **25**:361

Della Fazia, Alba
  Jean Anouilh **1**:7

Dellar, Fred
  Smokey Robinson **21**:345

Delong-Tonelli, Beverly J.
  Fernando Arrabal **9**:36

Del Rey, Lester
  Frederik Pohl **18**:412
  Roger Zelazny **21**:471

De Luca, Geraldine
  Mollie Hunter **21**:168
  J. D. Salinger **12**:517
  Sandra Scoppettone **26**:403

De Man, Paul
  Harold Bloom **24**:72
  Georg Lukács **24**:323

DeMara, Nicholas A.
  Italo Calvino **11**:87

Demarest, Michael
  Michael Crichton **6**:119

DeMaria, Robert
  Diane Wakoski **2**:459

Dembo, L. S.
  Charles Olson **2**:327
  George Oppen **7**:283
  Robert Phillips **28**:362
  Louis Zukofsky **2**:488

Demetz, Peter
  Lucien Goldmann **24**:241
  Rolf Hochhuth **18**:250
  Georg Lukács **24**:328

De Mille, Richard
  Carlos Castaneda **12**:95

Demorest, Stephen
  David Byrne **26**:95
  Lou Reed **21**:313
  Neil Young **17**:579

Demos, E. Virginia
  Larry Kettelkamp **12**:307

Demos, John
  Gunnar Ekelöf **27**:113

DeMott, Benjamin
  Margaret Atwood **2**:20
  James Baldwin **2**:32
  John Barth **14**:58
  Jorge Luis Borges **2**:70
  Lenny Bruce **21**:49
  Anthony Burgess **13**:126
  Vincent Canby **13**:132
  Truman Capote **19**:84
  Eleanor Clark **19**:107
  Robert Coover **15**:142
  E. L. Doctorow **18**:124
  T. S. Eliot **2**:127
  John Gardner **28**:165
  Barry Hannah **23**:210
  Nat Hentoff **26**:183
  Russell C. Hoban **7**:162; **25**:266
  John Irving **23**:250
  Doris Lessing **2**:240
  Norman Mailer **28**:258
  Mary McCarthy **14**:357
  Henry Miller **2**:283
  Philip Roth **9**:462
  Josef Škvorecký **15**:512
  William Styron **15**:526
  Alexander Theroux **25**:433
  Paul Theroux **28**:425
  William Trevor **14**:537
  Anne Tyler **28**:432
  John Updike **5**:459
  Kurt Vonnegut, Jr. **2**:453
  John Wain **15**:562
  Derek Walcott **14**:550
  Patrick White **18**:547
  Maia Wojciechowska **26**:456

DeMott, Robert
  Mary Oliver **19**:362
  Judith Johnson Sherwin **15**:480

Dempsey, David
  Patrick Boyle **19**:67
  James M. Cain **28**:48
  R. V. Cassill **23**:103
  Janet Frame **22**:143
  Ernest K. Gann **23**:162
  Martha Gellhorn **14**:195
  Willard Motley **18**:357
  Terry Southern **7**:454

Dempsey, Michael
  Robert Altman **16**:20
  Lindsay Anderson **20**:14
  Francis Ford Coppola **16**:248
  John Huston **20**:171
  Richard Lester **20**:226
  George Lucas **16**:408
  Ken Russell **16**:546
  Paul Schrader **26**:387

Demuth, Philip
  Jerome Siegel and Joe Shuster
    21:363

Denby, David
  Woody Allen **16**:2
  John Cassavetes **20**:55
  Francis Ford Coppola **16**:237,
    241, 245
  Brian De Palma **20**:81
  Bob Fosse **20**:126
  Werner Herzog **16**:334
  John Landis **26**:272, 274
  Richard Lester **20**:232
  Richard Pryor **26**:380
  Paul Schrader **26**:392, 396, 398
  Martin Scorsese **20**:325
  Joan Micklin Silver **20**:345
  Steven Spielberg **20**:366, 367
  Andy Warhol **20**:419

Deneau, Daniel P.
  Hermann Hesse **3**:249
  Jakov Lind **1**:178
  Amos Oz **27**:360
  Alain Robbe-Grillet **4**:449

Denham, Paul
  Louis Dudek **11**:159

Denham, Robert D.
  Northrop Frye **24**:227

Denison, Paul
  Ward S. Just **27**:227

Denne, Constance Ayers
  Joyce Carol Oates **6**:372

Denney, Reuel
  Conrad Aiken **1**:3

Dennis, Sr. M., R.S.M.
  E. M. Almedingen **12**:1

Dennis, Nigel
  Louis-Ferdinand Céline **1**:57
  William Golding **17**:167
  Günter Grass **11**:253
  Robert Pinget **7**:305
  E. B. White **10**:531

Dennis, Patrick
  Françoise Sagan **17**:422

Dennison, George
  Paul Goodman **4**:197

Denuel, Eleanor P.
  Laura Z. Hobson **25**:273

DeRamus, Betty
  Joyce Carol Oates **3**:364

Deredita, John
  Pablo Neruda **7**:257
  Juan Carlos Onetti **7**:278

Deren, Maya
  Maya Deren **16**:252

Der Hovanessian, Diana
  David Kherdian **6**:280

Derman, Lisa
  Ken Follett **18**:156

Desai, Anita
  Salman Rushdie **23**:365

De Santana, Hubert
  Brian Moore **19**:332

Desilets, E. Michael
  Frederick Wiseman **20**:471

Desmond, Harold F., Jr.
  Melvin Berger **12**:38

Des Pres, Terrence
  Geoffrey H. Hartman **27**:186
  Peter Matthiessen **11**:360
  Czesiaw Miiosz **22**:308

Dessner, Lawrence Jay
  Mario Puzo **6**:429

De Teresa, Mary
  Laura Nyro **17**:318

Detweiler, Robert
  John Updike **2**:442

Deutsch, Babette
  W. H. Auden **2**:21
  Ben Belitt **22**:49
  Louise Bogan **4**:68
  E. E. Cummings **3**:116
  Richard Eberhart **11**:176
  T. S. Eliot **2**:125
  William Empson **8**:201
  Robert Frost **3**:171
  Jean Garrigue **8**:239
  H. D. **3**:217
  Robinson Jeffers **15**:300
  Stanley Kunitz **11**:319
  Marianne Moore **2**:290
  St.-John Perse **4**:398
  Ezra Pound **2**:339
  Kathleen Raine **7**:351
  John Crowe Ransom **2**:361;
    24:363
  Theodore Roethke **3**:432
  Carl Sandburg **4**:463
  Edith Sitwell **2**:402
  Stephen Spender **2**:419
  Allen Tate **2**:427
  Richard Wilbur **9**:568
  William Carlos Williams **2**:466
  Marya Zaturenska **11**:579

Deutsch, Herbert
  Margaret O. Hyde **21**:173

De Van, Fred
  Janis Ian **21**:187
  Billy Joel **26**:214
  Richard Pryor **26**:378

DeVault, Joseph J.
  Mark Van Doren **6**:541

Dever, Joe
Edna Ferber 18:151

Devert, Krystyna
Hermann Hesse 2:189

DeVitis, A. A.
Graham Greene 1:133

Devlin, John
Ramón Sender 8:478

DeVoto, Bernard
Erich Maria Remarque 21:327

De Vries, Daniel
Stanley Kubrick 16:387

De Vries, Peter
James Thurber 5:429

Devrnja, Zora
Charles Olson 9:412
Charles Simic 9:478

Dewart, Leslie
William Barrett 27:18

Dewsnap, Terence
Christopher Isherwood 1:156

Dey, Susnigdha
Octavio Paz 19:368

Dial, John E.
José María Gironella 11:237

Díaz, Janet Winecoff
Fernando Arrabal 18:17
Miguel Delibes 18:111
Ana María Matute 11:363

Dick, Bernard F.
Michelangelo Antonioni 20:41
William Golding 1:120
John Hersey 2:188
Iris Murdoch 6:342; 22:331
Mary Renault 3:426
I. A. Richards 14:454
Stevie Smith 8:492
Gore Vidal 4:558

Dick, Kay
Simone de Beauvoir 4:48

Dickens, Anthony
E. M. Forster 22:137

Dickens, Byrom
T. S. Stribling 23:444

Dickens, Monica
Colin Thiele 17:495

Dickenson, Peter
P. G. Wodehouse 22:485

Dickey, Chris
Kurt Vonnegut, Jr. 5:470

Dickey, James
Conrad Aiken 1:3
John Ashbery 2:16
John Berryman 1:33
Philip Booth 23:74
Kenneth Burke 2:87
Stanley Burnshaw 3:91
Hayden Carruth 4:93
E. E. Cummings 1:68
J. V. Cunningham 3:120
Robert Duncan 1:82

Richard Eberhart 3:133
Ronald G. Everson 27:133
William Everson 1:96
Robert Frost 1:111
Allen Ginsberg 1:118
David Ignatow 4:247
Robinson Jeffers 2:214
Galway Kinnell 1:167
James Kirkup 1:169
John Logan 5:252
Louis MacNeice 1:186
William Meredith 4:347
James Merrill 2:272
W. S. Merwin 1:211
Josephine Miles 1:215
Marianne Moore 1:226
Howard Nemerov 2:305
Mary Oliver 19:361
Charles Olson 1:262; 2:327
Kenneth Patchen 1:265
Sylvia Plath 2:337
Herbert Read 4:439
I. A. Richards 14:452
Theodore Roethke 1:290
May Sarton 4:470
Frederick Seidel 18:474
Anne Sexton 2:390
Louis Simpson 4:497
William Jay Smith 6:512
William Stafford 4:519
Allen Tate 6:527
Derek Walcott 14:548
Robert Penn Warren 1:352; 18:538
Theodore Weiss 3:515
John Hall Wheelock 14:571
Reed Whittemore 4:588
Richard Wilbur 3:531
William Carlos Williams 1:370
Yvor Winters 4:590

Dickey, R. P.
Lawrence Ferlinghetti 6:183
Robert Lowell 5:258

Dickey, William
Daniel J. Berrigan 4:56
John Berryman 13:75
Hayden Carruth 7:40
James Dickey 2:115
William Everson 5:121
W. S. Merwin 2:277
George Oppen 7:281
Richard Wilbur 14:577

Dickins, Anthony
Vladimir Nabokov 2:304

Dickinson, Hugh
Eugène Ionesco 6:250

Dickinson-Brown, R.
Barry Spacks 14:510
Lewis Turco 11:551

Dickstein, Lore
Gail Godwin 8:247
Judith Guest 8:254
Sue Kaufman 3:263
Judith Rossner 6:469
Susan Fromberg Schaeffer 22:369
Cynthia Propper Seton 27:426
Isaac Bashevis Singer 3:456
Botho Strauss 22:408

Dickstein, Morris
John Barth 7:24
Donald Barthelme 6:29
R. P. Blackmur 2:61
John Cassavetes 20:55
Daniel Fuchs 8:220
John Gardner 3:184
Günter Grass 11:252
Bernard Malamud 27:300
Philip Roth 4:454
Hunter S. Thompson 17:509
Richard Wright 21:458
Rudolph Wurlitzer 2:484

Didion, Joan
Woody Allen 16:13
John Cheever 8:137
Elizabeth Hardwick 13:265
Doris Lessing 2:240
Norman Mailer 14:352
V. S. Naipaul 18:365
J. D. Salinger 12:511

Dienstag, Eleanor
Sylvia Ashton-Warner 19:22
Lee Kingman 17:246

Dietemann, Margaret
Arthur Adamov 25:16

Dietrichson, Jan W.
Daniel Hoffman 23:239

Diez, Luys A.
Juan Carlos Onetti 7:280

Dillard, Annie
Evan S. Connell, Jr. 4:109

Dillard, R.H.W.
William S. Burroughs 22:83
W. S. Merwin 8:389
Wright Morris 18:351
Vladimir Nabokov 2:304
Colin Wilson 3:537

Diller, Edward
Friedrich Dürrenmatt 11:171

Dillingham, Thomas
Susan Fromberg Schaeffer 6:488

Dillon, David
William Goyen 14:211
John Hawkes 4:218
Edwin O'Connor 14:393
Tillie Olsen 13:433
Wallace Stegner 9:509

Dillon, George
Gil Orlovitz 22:332

Dillon, Michael
Thornton Wilder 6:571

Dimeo, Steve
George Roy Hill 26:197

Dimeo, Steven
Ray Bradbury 3:85

Dimock, Edward C.
Raja Rao 25:366

Di Napoli, Thomas
Günter Grass 11:247

Dinnage, Rosemary
A. S. Byatt 19:77
Isak Dinesen 10:152
E. M. Forster 22:137
Elizabeth Hardwick 13:264
Doris Lessing 6:303
Iris Murdoch 22:328
Fay Weldon 19:468

Dinoto, Andrea
Walter Farley 17:118

Di Piero, W. S.
John Ashbery 4:22
John Hawkes 9:269
Seamus Heaney 25:250
Philip Levine 14:321
Sam Peckinpah 20:282
R. G. Vliet 22:442

Dirda, Michael
James Dickey 15:177
Umberto Eco 28:132
Henry Green 13:251
Russell C. Hoban 25:266
John Knowles 10:303
Vladimir Nabokov 23:310
Gilbert Sorrentino 14:500
Alice Walker 19:452

Disch, Thomas M.
William S. Burroughs 22:84
Arthur C. Clarke 18:106
Philip José Farmer 19:168
Piers Paul Read 25:378
Anne Tyler 18:529
Gene Wolfe 25:474

Ditlea, Steve
Willie Nelson 17:302

Ditsky, John
Richard Brautigan 12:69
John Hawkes 2:186
Erica Jong 8:313
Joyce Carol Oates 2:316

Dix, Carol
Martin Amis 4:20

Dix, Winslow
William X. Kienzle 25:274

Dixon, Bob
Gunnel Beckman 26:89
Alan Garner 17:149
Noel Streatfeild 21:416

Dixon, John W., Jr.
Elie Wiesel 3:527

DiZazzo, Raymond
Robert L. Peters 7:303

Djilas, Milovan
Aleksandr I. Solzhenitsyn 2:408

Djwa, Sandra
Margaret Laurence 13:341
E. J. Pratt 19:381
F. R. Scott 22:376

Dobbs, Kildare
Hugh Hood 28:187
Margaret Laurence 3:278
Alice Munro 6:341

Dobie, Ann B.
Muriel Spark 2:416

Dobie, J. Frank
Mari Sandoz **28**:403, 404

Dobrez, L.A.C.
Jean Genet **14**:205

Dobson, Joan L.
Margaret O. Hyde **21**:180

Dobyns, Stephen
James Tate **25**:427

Doctorow, E. L.
E. L. Doctorow **15**:179
Mary Lee Settle **19**:411

Dodd, Wayne
Madeleine L'Engle **12**:350

Dodsworth, Martin
Robert Bly **2**:65
Donald Davie **8**:163
James Dickey **2**:115
Marianne Moore **2**:291

Doerksen, Daniel W.
Margaret Avison **4**:36

Doerner, William R.
James Herriot **12**:282

Doherty, Andy
Frank Zappa **17**:592

Dohmann, Barbara
Jorge Luis Borges **2**:69
Julio Cortázar **2**:101
Gabriel García Márquez **2**:147
Juan Carlos Onetti **7**:276
João Guimarães Rosa **23**:350
Juan Rulfo **8**:461
Mario Vargas Llosa **3**:493

Dollard, Peter
Wendell Berry **27**:37

Dollard, W.A.S.
Winston Graham **23**:191

Dollen, Charles
William Peter Blatty **2**:64
Paul Gallico **2**:147
Ernest K. Gann **23**:167
N. Scott Momaday **2**:289

Dombroski, Robert S.
Carlo Emilio Gadda **11**:208

Domowitz, Janet
Alice Adams **13**:3

Donadio, Stephen
John Ashbery **2**:19
James Baldwin **17**:33
Richard Fariña **9**:195
Sandra Hochman **3**:250

Donaghue, Denis
Donald Barthelme **13**:62

Donahue, Deirdre
Gloria Naylor **28**:305

Donahue, Francis
Antonio Buero Vallejo **15**:96
Camilo José Cela **4**:97; **13**:147

Donahue, Walter
Sam Shepard **4**:491

Donahugh, Robert H.
Allan W. Eckert **17**:104
John Knowles **26**:257

Donald, David Herbert
Alex Haley **12**:246

Donald, Miles
Alexander Theroux **25**:431
John Updike **23**:465

Donaldson, Scott
Ernest Hemingway **13**:276
Philip Roth **1**:293

Donavin, Denise P.
John Ehle **27**:106
Howard Fast **23**:161

Donelson, Kenneth L.
James D. Forman **21**:123
Rosa Guy **26**:145
Paul Zindel **26**:472

Donnard, Jean-Hervé
Eugène Ionesco **6**:249

Donnelly, Brian
Derek Mahon **27**:289, 291

Donnelly, Dorothy
Marge Piercy **3**:384

Donner, Jorn
Ingmar Bergman **16**:52

Donoghue, Denis
A. R. Ammons **9**:27
John Ashbery **15**:34
W. H. Auden **3**:24
Saul Bellow **2**:51
Elizabeth Bishop **13**:95
R. P. Blackmur **24**:58, 67
Marie-Claire Blais **2**:63
Wayne C. Booth **24**:90
Kenneth Burke **2**:88
Austin Clarke **9**:167
C. Day Lewis **6**:129
Jacques Derrida **24**:152
Margaret Drabble **22**:127
Richard Eberhart **11**:175
T. S. Eliot **2**:126
Thomas Flanagan **25**:165
John Fowles **10**:188
William H. Gass **11**:225
William Golding **3**:196
Shirley Ann Grau **4**:209
Graham Greene **9**:250; **27**:173
Geoffrey H. Hartman **27**:182, 186
Seamus Heaney **14**:245
Anthony Hecht **8**:269
Paul Horgan **9**:278
Randall Jarrell **1**:160
Robert Lowell **4**:295
James Merrill **2**:274; **18**:331
W. S. Merwin **2**:277
Marianne Moore **2**:291
Frank O'Connor **23**:331
Robert Pinsky **19**:370
David Plante **23**:341
Ezra Pound **2**:340
Philip Rahv **24**:357
I. A. Richards **24**:400
Philip Roth **6**:476
Frederick Seidel **18**:475
Christina Stead **2**:422
Mark Strand **18**:515
Allen Tate **6**:527; **9**:521; **11**:526
Charles Tomlinson **2**:437

Lionel Trilling **9**:530; **11**:543; **24**:452
Derek Walcott **2**:460; **25**:451
Anne Waldman **7**:507
Robert Penn Warren **4**:579; **13**:581
René Wellek **28**:450
Rebecca West **7**:525
William Carlos Williams **2**:467
Angus Wilson **25**:464

Donoghue, Susan
Joni Mitchell **12**:435, 436

Donohue, Agnes McNeill
Jessamyn West **17**:553

Donohue, John W.
Earl Hamner **12**:259

Donovan, Diane C.
Sue Ellen Bridgers **26**:92

Donovan, Josephine
Sylvia Plath **3**:390

Dooley, D. J.
Earle Birney **6**:71

Dooley, Dennis M.
Robert Penn Warren **10**:517

Doreski, William
Louise Glück **22**:175
Charles Simic **22**:383

Dorfman, Ariel
Miguel Ángel Asturias **13**:39

Dorian, Marguerite
Mircea Eliade **19**:147

Dorsey, David
Alex La Guma **19**:277

Dorsey, Margaret A.
Gunnel Beckman **26**:86
Babbis Friis-Baastad **12**:214
Larry Kettelkamp **12**:305
Andre Norton **12**:458, 459

Dos Passos, John
E. E. Cummings **12**:139

Doubrovsky, J. S.
Eugène Ionesco **6**:247

Doubrovsky, Serge
Albert Camus **11**:93

Dougherty, Dru
Juan Goytisolo **23**:189

Doughtie, Edward
James Dickey **15**:176

Douglas, Ann
James T. Farrell **11**:196

Douglas, Ellen
Flannery O'Connor **6**:381
May Sarton **4**:471

Douglas, George H.
Edmund Wilson **2**:477

Douglas, Marjory Stoneman
Noel Streatfeild **21**:400

Dowd, Nancy Ellen
Frederick Wiseman **20**:468

Dowell, Bob
Flannery O'Connor **21**:264

Dowie, William
Sylvia Plath **17**:364

Dowling, Gordon Graham
Yukio Mishima **6**:337

Downer, Alan S.
Thornton Wilder **5**:495

Downing, Robert
Orson Welles **20**:433

Doxey, William S.
Ken Kesey **3**:267
Flannery O'Connor **3**:368

Doyle, Charles
James K. Baxter **14**:60
See also Doyle, Mike

Doyle, Jacqueline
Sean O'Casey **15**:406

Doyle, Mike
Irving Layton **2**:236
A. W. Purdy **6**:428
Raymond Souster **5**:395, 396
See also Doyle, Charles

Doyle, Paul A.
Pearl S. Buck **11**:71
Paul Vincent Carroll **10**:96
R. V. Cassill **23**:104
James T. Farrell **8**:205
MacKinlay Kantor **7**:195
Seán O'Faoláin **1**:259; **7**:273
Anne Tyler **28**:431
Evelyn Waugh **1**:359

Drabble, Margaret
Michael Frayn **3**:164
John Irving **13**:295
Philip Larkin **8**:333; **9**:323
Iris Murdoch **4**:367
Muriel Spark **8**:494
John Updike **15**:544

Dragonwagon, C.
Stevie Wonder **12**:663

Drake, Robert
Carson McCullers **12**:426
Flannery O'Connor **21**:264, 273
Reynolds Price **3**:405
Eudora Welty **5**:478

Draper, Charlotte W.
Andre Norton **12**:471

Draudt, Manfred
Joe Orton **13**:436

Draya, Ren
Tennessee Williams **15**:579

Drew, Fraser
John Masefield **11**:356

Drexler, Rosalyn
Anaïs Nin **14**:387

Dries, Linda R.
Allan W. Eckert **17**:105

Driver, Christopher
Yukio Mishima **4**:357

Driver, Sam N.
Anna Akhmatova **11**:6

Driver, Tom F.
 Jean Genet **1**:115
 Lorraine Hansberry **17**:182
 Arthur Miller **1**:215; **2**:279

Druska, John
 John Beecher **6**:49
 John Gregory Dunne **28**:125

Dryden, Edgar A.
 John Barth **5**:52

Duberman, Martin
 Ed Bullins **1**:47
 Laura Z. Hobson **7**:163
 Albert Innaurato **21**:197
 David Mamet **15**:355

Duberman, Martin B.
 John Gregory Dunne **28**:120
 Nat Hentoff **26**:180

Duberstein, Larry
 Joel Lieber **6**:312

Dubois, Larry
 William F. Buckley, Jr. **7**:34
 Walker Percy **8**:445

Du Bois, W. E. Burghardt
 Arna Bontemps **18**:62
 Richard Wright **21**:434

Du Bois, William
 James M. Cain **28**:45
 Howard Fast **23**:158
 Laura Z. Hobson **25**:269

Dubro, Alec
 Kris Kristofferson **26**:267
 Jim Morrison **17**:288
 Laura Nyro **17**:313

Duchêne, Anne
 Beryl Bainbridge **22**:45
 Bruce Chatwin **28**:73
 Francine du Plessix Gray
  22:200
 Mark Helprin **22**:221
 Alberto Moravia **18**:347
 Rosemary Sutcliff **26**:441
 D. M. Thomas **22**:419

Duddy, Thomas A.
 Louis Zukofsky **11**:581

Dudek, Louis
 Daryl Hine **15**:281
 Irving Layton **15**:320
 Alden Nowlan **15**:399
 James Reaney **13**:474
 Raymond Souster **14**:501

Dufault, Peter Kane
 Philip Booth **23**:73

Duffey, Bernard
 W. H. Auden **4**:3
 Jack Kerouac **1**:66

Duffus, R. L.
 Richard Wright **21**:435

Duffy, Dennis
 Philip Child **19**:102
 Matt Cohen **19**:111

Duffy, Martha
 James Baldwin **4**:41
 Jean Cocteau **1**:59
 Joan Didion **1**:75
 Nikki Giovanni **2**:164
 Gail Godwin **22**:180
 Lillian Hellman **4**:221
 D. Keith Mano **10**:328
 Tom McHale **5**:281
 Grace Paley **4**:393
 Walker Percy **2**:334
 Sylvia Plath **2**:336
 Judith Rossner **6**:470
 Bernice Rubens **19**:404
 Patrick White **3**:523

Duffy, Michael
 Walter Becker and Donald
  Fagen **26**:84

Duguid, Lindsay
 Ursula K. Le Guin **22**:274

Duhamel, P. Albert
 Flannery O'Connor **1**:253
 Paul Scott **9**:477

Dukas, Vytas
 Vasily Aksenov **22**:26, 28

Dukes, Ashley
 Emlyn Williams **15**:577

Dukore, Bernard F.
 Harold Pinter **27**:393

Dullea, Gerard J.
 Gregory Corso **11**:123

Dumas, Bethany K.
 E. E. Cummings **12**:159

Dunbar, Ernest
 Jules Archer **12**:21

Duncan, Erika
 William Goyen **8**:251
 Anaïs Nin **8**:425

Duncan, Robert
 Richard Pryor **26**:378
 John Wieners **7**:536
 Frank Zappa **17**:591

Dunham, Vera S.
 Yevgeny Yevtushenko **26**:461

Dunlap, John R.
 Martin Cruz Smith **25**:414

Dunlea, William
 Richard Wright **21**:437

Dunlop, John B.
 Vladimir Voinovich **10**:509

Dunn, Douglas
 Giorgio Bassani **9**:77
 John Berryman **4**:62
 George Mackay Brown **5**:78
 Donald Davie **5**:115
 Lawrence Durrell **4**:147
 D. J. Enright **4**:156; **8**:203
 Gavin Ewart **13**:209
 Geoffrey Grigson **7**:136
 John Hawkes **7**:141
 Seamus Heaney **7**:150
 Dan Jacobson **14**:290
 Erica Jong **6**:268
 Derek Mahon **27**:287

Christopher Middleton **13**:388
 Leslie Norris **14**:387
 Sylvia Plath **5**:339
 William Plomer **4**:407
 Peter Porter **13**:452
 Peter Redgrove **6**:446
 Kenneth Rexroth **11**:473
 Jon Silkin **6**:499
 Anne Stevenson **7**:463
 Charles Tomlinson **6**:534
 Andrew Young **5**:25

Dunning, Jennifer
 Albert Innaurato **21**:195

Dunson, Josh
 Phil Ochs **17**:330, 333

Dupee, F. W.
 Kenneth Koch **5**:218
 Robert Lowell **3**:299
 Norman Mailer **11**:339
 Bernard Malamud **3**:321
 W. S. Merwin **3**:338
 John Osborne **5**:330
 J. F. Powers **4**:418

DuPlessis, Rachel Blau
 Edward Albee **13**:6
 H. D. **14**:229
 Muriel Rukeyser **27**:412

Dupree, Robert S.
 Caroline Gordon **13**:245
 Allen Tate **6**:525

Duprey, Richard A.
 Edward Albee **25**:32
 William Gibson **23**:178
 Arthur Miller **26**:318

Durán, Manuel
 Pablo Neruda **28**:312

Durand, Laura G.
 Monique Wittig **22**:475

Durbin, Karen
 Eleanor Clark **5**:107

Duree, Barbara Joyce
 Lenora Mattingly Weber **12**:633

Durgnat, Raymond
 Robert Bresson **16**:110
 Tod Browning **16**:122
 Luis Buñuel **16**:142, 150
 John Cassavetes **20**:44, 45
 Claude Chabrol **16**:168
 René Clair **20**:66
 Shirley Clarke **16**:216
 Rainer Werner Fassbinder
  20:119
 Federico Fellini **16**:273
 Jean-Luc Godard **20**:129
 John Huston **20**:168
 Kon Ichikawa **20**:177
 Richard Lester **20**:219
 Roman Polanski **16**:163, 468
 Ann Quin **6**:442
 Jean Renoir **20**:291, 304
 François Truffaut **20**:382
 Lina Wertmüller **16**:587

Durham, Frank
 Elmer Rice **7**:363
 T. S. Stribling **23**:447

Durham, Philip
 Dashiell Hammett **3**:218;
  19:194

Duroche, L. L.
 Martin Heidegger **24**:261

Durrant, Digby
 Caroline Blackwood **6**:80
 Penelope Fitzgerald **19**:174
 Julia O'Faolain **6**:383

Durrell, Gerald
 Joy Adamson **17**:2

Durrell, Lawrence
 Odysseus Elytis **15**:219
 George Seferis **5**:385

Dust, Harvey
 Jules Archer **12**:17

Dutton, Robert R.
 Saul Bellow **25**:86

Duvall, E. S.
 Ann Beattie **13**:66

Duvall, Elizabeth
 Helen Yglesias **22**:493

Du Verlie, Claude
 Claude Simon **4**:497

Dworkin, Susan
 Gretchen Cryer **21**:80

Dwyer, David J.
 Mary Renault **3**:426

Dyck, J. W.
 Boris Pasternak **18**:381

Dyer, Peter John
 René Clair **20**:64
 Jean Cocteau **16**:227
 Pier Paolo Pasolini **20**:260
 Jean Renoir **20**:291
 Luchino Visconti **16**:563
 Billy Wilder **20**:459

Dyson, A. E.
 Jorge Luis Borges **19**:50
 Ted Hughes **14**:269
 Sylvia Plath **11**:446

Dyson, Claire M.
 Kin Platt **26**:354

Dyson, William
 Ezra Pound **1**:276

Dzwonkoski, F. Peter, Jr.
 T. S. Eliot **6**:163

Eagle, Herbert
 Aleksandr I. Solzhenitsyn **9**:504
 Ludvík Vaculík **7**:495

Eagle, Robert
 Thomas Hinde **11**:274
 Alberto Moravia **7**:244
 Flann O'Brien **4**:385

Eagleton, Terry
 George Barker **8**:45
 John Berger **19**:39
 Donald Davie **8**:162
 Thom Gunn **6**:221
 Seamus Heaney **7**:150
 Hermann Hesse **11**:272

Elizabeth Jennings **14**:293
William Plomer **8**:447
Stevie Smith **8**:491
Maura Stanton **9**:508
Charles Tomlinson **6**:535
John Wain **11**:561
Andrew Young **5**:525

Eakin, Mary K.
Mary Stolz **12**:553

Earl, Pauline J.
Frank B. Gilbreth, Jr. and Ernestine Gilbreth Carey **17**:156

Early, Len
Bill Bissett **18**:59

Earnshaw, Doris
Denise Levertov **28**:242

Eastlake, William
A. B. Guthrie, Jr. **23**:198

Eastman, Fred
Marc Connelly **7**:55

Eastman, Max
I. A. Richards **24**:374

Easton, Tom
Stephen King **26**:238

Eaton, Anne T.
Sally Benson **17**:47
John R. Tunis **12**:593

Eaton, Charles Edward
Robert Frost **9**:225

Eaton, Walter Prichard
Padraic Colum **28**:88
Joseph Wood Krutch **24**:285

Eberhart, Richard
Djuna Barnes **8**:48
William Empson **19**:152
Robert Frost **13**:227
Allen Ginsberg **13**:239
Archibald MacLeish **3**:310
Ezra Pound **7**:324
Kenneth Rexroth **2**:370
Muriel Rukeyser **27**:409

Ebert, Roger
Charles Chaplin **16**:199

Eby, Cecil
Vine Deloria, Jr. **21**:109

Eccleshare, Julia
Diana Wynne Jones **26**:227

Echevarría, Roberto González
Alejo Carpentier **11**:101
Julio Cortázar **10**:114; **13**:158
Carlos Fuentes **10**:209
Severo Sarduy **6**:486

Eckley, Grace
Benedict Kiely **23**:259
Edna O'Brien **5**:312

Eckley, Wilton
Harriette Arnow **18**:10

Eckman, Martha
Colin Wilson **14**:583

Eddins, Dwight
John Fowles **10**:183

Eddy, Elizabeth M.
Jonathan Kozol **17**:250

Edel, Leon
Lawrence Durrell **1**:85
William Faulkner **1**:100
Ernest Hemingway **10**:265
Alain Robbe-Grillet **1**:286
Nathalie Sarraute **1**:303

Edelberg, Cynthia Dubin
Robert Creeley **15**:151

Edelheit, S. J.
Anthony Burgess **13**:126

Edelman, Sarah Prewitt
Robert Lowell **15**:344

Edelstein, Arthur
William Faulkner **1**:102
Janet Frame **6**:190
Jean Stafford **7**:458
Angus Wilson **2**:472

Edelstein, J. M.
Patricia Highsmith **2**:193
Doris Lessing **22**:279

Edelstein, Mark G.
Flannery O'Connor **6**:381

Edenbaum, Robert I.
Dashiell Hammett **3**:219
John Hawkes **2**:185

Eder, Richard
Gretchen Cryer **21**:81
Athol Fugard **14**:191
Albert Innaurato **21**:194
Hugh Leonard **19**:283
Edna O'Brien **8**:430
Cynthia Ozick **28**:355
Bernard Pomerance **13**:445
Gerome Ragni and James Rado **17**:388
Ntozake Shange **25**:397, 398
Lanford Wilson **14**:590

Edinborough, Arnold
Earle Birney **6**:70
Robertson Davies **25**:129
Robert Kroetsch **23**:269
Jay Macpherson **14**:345

Edman, Irwin
Ogden Nash **23**:322

Edmiston, Susan
Maeve Brennan **5**:72

Edmonds, Walter D.
Esther Forbes **12**:204

Edwards, C. Hines, Jr.
James Dickey **4**:121

Edwards, Clifford
Andrew Lloyd Webber and Tim Rice **21**:423

Edwards, Henry
David Bowie **17**:60
Jackson Browne **21**:35
Monty Python **21**:224
Lou Reed **21**:304
Bruce Springsteen **17**:479

Edwards, K. Anthony
Henry Gregor Felsen **17**:125

Edwards, Margaret A.
Betty Cavanna **12**:99
Maureen Daly **17**:89
Mary Stolz **12**:546

Edwards, Mary Jane
Paulette Jiles **13**:304
Susan Musgrave **13**:401

Edwards, Michael
René Char **14**:130
Donald Davie **5**:114
Charles Tomlinson **4**:547

Edwards, Paul
Amos Tutuola **14**:540

Edwards, Sharon
Jessamyn West **7**:522

Edwards, Thomas R.
Lisa Alther **7**:14
Kingsley Amis **8**:12
James Baldwin **4**:41
Donald Barthelme **8**:49
Thomas Berger **18**:56
Richard Brautigan **12**:73
Frederick Buechner **2**:83
Charles Bukowski **2**:84
Anthony Burgess **5**:88
Raymond Carver **22**:96
John Cheever **7**:48
Evan S. Connell, Jr. **4**:108
Don DeLillo **27**:76
Stanley Elkin **4**:153
Leslie A. Fiedler **4**:161
Timothy Findley **27**:142
Paula Fox **2**:140
John Gardner **2**:151; **5**:133
Gail Godwin **8**:248
Herbert Gold **4**:193
James Hanley **8**:266
Edward Hoagland **28**:182
Diane Johnson **13**:306
James Jones **10**:293
Yoram Kaniuk **19**:239
Jerzy Kosinski **2**:233
George Lamming **2**:235
Norman Mailer **2**:264
Harry Mathews **6**:616
Peter Matthiessen **7**:211
Mary McCarthy **14**:363
Thomas McGuane **3**:330
Leonard Michaels **6**:324
Brian Moore **7**:237
Alice Munro **19**:347
Tim O'Brien **19**:358
Ishmael Reed **2**:368
Mordecai Richler **18**:454
Philip Roth **3**:437
André Schwarz-Bart **2**:389
Hubert Selby, Jr. **2**:390
Wilfrid Sheed **4**:488
Gilbert Sorrentino **14**:500
John Updike **5**:460; **23**:469
Derek Walcott **4**:576
Tom Wolfe **1**:375
Richard Yates **23**:482

Edwards, William D.
Jules Archer **12**:18

Eggenschwiler, David
Flannery O'Connor **6**:378
William Styron **5**:419

Egoff, Sheila A.
Julia W. Cunningham **12**:165
Leon Garfield **12**:218
Roderick L. Haig-Brown **21**:140
Christie Harris **12**:265
Farley Mowat **26**:338, 339
Rosemary Sutcliff **26**:433, 440

Egremont, Max
Anna Kavan **13**:317
Seán O'Faoláin **7**:276
Anthony Powell **7**:341; **9**:438
Gillian Tindall **7**:474
Ludvík Vaculík **7**:496

Egudu, Romanus N.
Christopher Okigbo **25**:348, 355

Ehre, Milton
Aleksandr I. Solzhenitsyn **2**:412

Ehrenpreis, Irvin
A. R. Ammons **25**:45
John Ashbery **6**:13
W. H. Auden **9**:58
T. S. Eliot **13**:200
Donald Hall **13**:260
Anthony Hecht **13**:269
Geoffrey Hill **8**:293
Donald Justice **6**:272
Robert Lowell **1**:180; **8**:353
George Oppen **7**:285
John Updike **5**:455
Robert Penn Warren **18**:537

Eidelman, M.
Anatoli Rybakov **23**:370

Einarsson, Stefán
Halldór Laxness **25**:291

Eiseley, Loren
J.R.R. Tolkien **12**:566

Eiseman, Alberta
Betty Cavanna **12**:100
Maureen Daly **17**:89
William Mayne **12**:390
Lenora Mattingly Weber **12**:633

Eisen, Dulcie
Ronald Tavel **6**:529

Eisenberg, J. A.
Isaac Bashevis Singer **1**:310

Eisinger, Chester E.
Carson McCullers **12**:421
Arthur Miller **6**:331

Eisinger, Erica M.
Marguerite Duras **11**:165
Georges Simenon **18**:484

Eisner, Bob
Smokey Robinson **21**:344

Eisner, Lotte H.
René Clair **20**:64
Fritz Lang **20**:210, 213

Eksteins, Modris
Erich Maria Remarque **21**:336

Eldred, Kate
David Malouf **28**:266

Eldridge, Richard
Jean Toomer **22**:425

Eley, Holly
Laurie Colwin **23**:130
Virginia Hamilton **26**:155, 157

Eliade, Mircea
Mircea Eliade **19**:146

Elias, Robert H.
James Thurber **5**:431

Eliot, T. S.
Marianne Moore **13**:392; **19**:336
I. A. Richards **24**:371

Elizondo, Salvador
Octavio Paz **3**:376

Elkin, Judith
Diana Wynne Jones **26**:230

Elkin, Sam
Robert Lipsyte **21**:208

Elkin, Stanley
Frederick Forsyth **2**:136

Elledge, Scott
Wayne C. Booth **24**:89

Elleman, Barbara
Melvin Berger **12**:42
Barbara Corcoran **17**:77
Paula Danziger **21**:86
Madeleine L'Engle **12**:351
Sonia Levitin **17**:265
Anne McCaffrey **17**:282, 284
Katherine Paterson **12**:485
Zilpha Keatley Snyder **17**:475

Ellestad, Everett M.
Pär Lagerkvist **13**:333

Elley, Derek
Mel Brooks **12**:79
Werner Herzog **16**:324
Yasujiro Ozu **16**:455
Pier Paolo Pasolini **20**:266, 269
Ken Russell **16**:549
Carlos Saura **20**:315
François Truffaut **20**:404

Ellin, Stanley
Robert Cormier **12**:138
Richard Elman **19**:151

Elliott, David
Roman Polanski **16**:470

Elliott, George P.
Jean Giono **4**:187
Robert Graves **2**:176
Norman Mailer **3**:317
Milton Meltzer **26**:305
Susan Sontag **10**:485
David Wagoner **3**:507

Elliott, Janice
Lynne Reid Banks **23**:41
Patricia Highsmith **2**:193
Michael Moorcock **27**:347
Aleksandr I. Solzhenitsyn **1**:321

Elliott, Robert C.
Ursula K. LeGuin **8**:341

Elliott, Susan
Billy Joel **26**:215, 216

Elliott, William I.
Shusaku Endo **7**:95

Ellis, James
John Knowles **1**:169; **26**:248

Ellison, Harlan
Barry N. Malzberg **7**:208
Roman Polanski **16**:464

Ellison, Ralph
Richard Wright **9**:583; **21**:441

Ellmann, Mary
John Barth **2**:39
Vladimir Nabokov **1**:244
Joyce Carol Oates **3**:364
Sylvia Plath **17**:350
Richard Price **12**:490
Aleksandr I. Solzhenitsyn **1**:321
J.R.R. Tolkien **12**:571
Michel Tournier **6**:538
Rebecca West **7**:526
Vassily S. Yanovsky **2**:485

Ellmann, Richard
W. H. Auden **9**:55
Giorgio Bassani **9**:76
Samuel Beckett **2**:47
Elizabeth Daryush **19**:119

Elman, Richard
William Bronk **10**:73
Frederick Busch **10**:91
Daniel Fuchs **22**:160
Thomas McGuane **18**:323
Richard Price **12**:490
Françoise Sagan **17**:426
Zilpha Keatley Snyder **17**:471

Elman, Richard M.
Charles Bukowski **9**:137
Hannah Green **3**:202
Jack Spicer **8**:497
Hunter S. Thompson **9**:526
Rudolf Wurlitzer **2**:482

Elon, Amos
Yehuda Amichai **9**:22

Elsaesser, Thomas
Rainer Werner Fassbinder **20**:110

Elsom, John
Alan Ayckbourn **5**:35
Samuel Beckett **6**:43
Edward Bond **6**:85
Michael Frayn **7**:108
Arthur Miller **15**:376
David Rudkin **14**:470
Sam Shepard **6**:496
Tom Stoppard **5**:412
E. A. Whitehead **5**:488

Elstob, Peter
Len Deighton **4**:119

Elston, Nina
Susan Richards Shreve **23**:403

Emanuel, James A.
Langston Hughes **1**:147

Emblidge, David
E. L. Doctorow **11**:143

Emerson, Donald
Carson McCullers **12**:420

Emerson, Gloria
Michael Cimino **16**:213

Emerson, Ken
David Bowie **17**:61
David Byrne **26**:97
Ray Davies **21**:95, 103
Van Morrison **21**:235
Smokey Robinson **21**:345
Bruce Springsteen **17**:477
Paul Weller **26**:443
Stevie Wonder **12**:657

Emerson, O. B.
Marion Montgomery **7**:232

Emerson, Sally
Douglas Adams **27**:13
Hermann Hesse **25**:261
William Mayne **12**:404
Piers Paul Read **25**:379

Emerson, Stephen
Gilbert Sorrentino **7**:450

Emmons, Winfred S.
Katherine Anne Porter **1**:273

Empson, William
Wayne C. Booth **24**:92
Cleanth Brooks **24**:103

Endres, Robin
Milton Acorn **15**:10

Engel, Bernard F.
Marianne Moore **1**:227

Engel, Eva J.
Hermann Hesse **17**:202

Engel, Howard
Morley Callaghan **14**:102

Engel, Marian
Penelope Gilliatt **2**:160
Margaret Laurence **3**:278
Françoise Mallet-Joris **11**:356
Joyce Carol Oates **6**:372
Françoise Sagan **6**:481
Michel Tournier **6**:537

England, David A.
Garry Marshall **17**:278

Engle, Gary
Robert Altman **16**:22

Engle, Paul
Charles M. Schulz **12**:531

English, Raymond
Carl Zuckmayer **18**:553

Enright, D. J.
John Ashbery **9**:49
Simone de Beauvoir **14**:66
Heinrich Böll **3**:74; **11**:52
Anthony Burgess **4**:80; **15**:103; **22**:75
Stanley Burnshaw **3**:90
James Clavell **6**:114
Lawrence Durrell **6**:151
Witold Gombrowicz **4**:195
Günter Grass **2**:271; **4**:202
Robert Graves **2**:175
Hermann Hesse **3**:243
Randall Jarrell **9**:296
Yasunari Kawabata **5**:206; **9**:316
Thomas Keneally **14**:302; **27**:233

Carolyn Kizer **15**:308
Milan Kundera **9**:321
Philip Larkin **3**:276
Doris Lessing **3**:282
Czesław Miłosz **5**:291
Yukio Mishima **4**:353; **27**:336
Vladimir Nabokov **3**:352
V. S. Naipaul **4**:371
Ezra Pound **3**:395
Stevie Smith **3**:460
C. P. Snow **9**:496
Muriel Spark **3**:463
George Steiner **24**:429
John Updike **2**:439

Enslin, Theodore
George Oppen **7**:281

Ensslen, Klaus
Alice Walker **27**:451

Eoff, Sherman H.
Jean-Paul Sartre **1**:303
Ramón Sender **8**:477

Ephron, Nora
Erich Segal **3**:447
Garry Trudeau **12**:589

Epps, Garrett
Thomas Berger **11**:47
Nicholas Delbanco **13**:174
John Sayles **14**:483
Susan Fromberg Schaeffer **22**:368
Alan Sillitoe **19**:421
Gilbert Sorrentino **22**:394
Elizabeth Spencer **22**:406

Epstein, Helen
Isaac Bashevis Singer **23**:422

Epstein, Joseph
Jonathan Baumbach **23**:55
E. M. Forster **4**:165
Gabriel García Márquez **27**:154
Nadine Gordimer **18**:188
Mark Harris **19**:205
Joseph Heller **5**:174
John Irving **23**:253
Alan Lelchuk **5**:241
Bernard Malamud **27**:301
Aleksandr I. Solzhenitsyn **2**:409
Stephen Spender **5**:402
Edmund Wilson **2**:477; **8**:551

Epstein, Lawrence J.
Elie Wiesel **5**:493

Epstein, Leslie
Cynthia Ozick **28**:350
D. M. Thomas **22**:420

Epstein, Seymour
Saul Bellow **13**:72
Jerome Charyn **18**:99

Erickson, Peter
Alice Walker **19**:451

Ericson, Edward, Jr.
Thornton Wilder **10**:533

Ericson, Edward E., Jr.
C. S. Lewis **6**:310
Aleksandr I. Solzhenitsyn **4**:509; **26**:422

Erlich, Nancy
Ray Davies **21**:94

Erlich, Richard
Harlan Ellison 13:203

Erlich, Victor
Joseph Brodsky 6:96

Ermolaev, Herman
Mikhail Sholokhov 15:481

Ernst, Margaret
Andre Norton 12:455

Eron, Carol
John Hawkes 4:218

Eskin, Stanley G.
Nicholas Delbanco 6:130

Esmonde, Margaret P.
Ursula K. Le Guin 22:270
Zilpha Keatley Snyder 17:474

Esposito, Joseph J.
Larry McMurtry 27:332

Esslin, Martin
Arthur Adamov 4:5
Edward Albee 2:4; 9:10
John Arden 6:5
Samuel Beckett 1:24; 4:52;
  6:33, 44
Edward Bond 13:98
Friedrich Dürrenmatt 4:139
Max Frisch 3:167
Jack Gelber 1:114
Jean Genet 1:117
Günter Grass 4:201
Graham Greene 9:250
Václav Havel 25:222
Rolf Hochhuth 4:231
Eugène Ionesco 1:154; 4:252
Arthur Kopit 1:170
Sławomir Mrozek 3:344
Robert Pinget 7:306
Harold Pinter 1:268; 6:407,
  414; 27:392
Peter Shaffer 18:477
Neil Simon 6:506
Wole Soyinka 14:505
Peter Weiss 3:515

Estes, Sally C.
Sol Gordon 26:138

Estess, Sybil
Elizabeth Bishop 9:95

Estess, Ted L.
Samuel Beckett 11:41

Estrin, Barbara L.
Adrienne Rich 18:450

Esty, William
James Baldwin 17:21
Flannery O'Connor 21:255

Ettin, Andrew V.
James Merrill 2:273

Evanier, David
Saul Bellow 25:85
Leonard Michaels 25:319
John Updike 15:547

Evans, Ann
Judy Blume 12:46
Rosemary Sutcliff 26:438

Evans, Don
Ed Bullins 5:82

Evans, Donald T.
Alice Childress 12:105

Evans, Eli N.
James Dickey 7:86

Evans, Ernestine
Jessamyn West 17:544
Jade Snow Wong 17:565

Evans, Fallon
J. F. Powers 1:279

Evans, Gareth Lloyd
Edward Albee 25:34
Harold Pinter 11:444

Evans, Gwyneth F.
Christie Harris 12:267

Evans, Oliver
Paul Bowles 1:41
Babette Deutsch 18:119
Carson McCullers 12:425

Evans, Robley
J.R.R. Tolkien 3:478

Evans, T. Jeff
Peter De Vries 28:106

Evans, Timothy
Isaac Bashevis Singer 11:499

Evans, William R.
Edmund White III 27:478

Evarts, Prescott, Jr.
John Fowles 2:138

Everman, Welch D.
Richard Kostelanetz 28:215

Everson, Edith A.
E. E. Cummings 15:157

Evett, Robert
Terrence McNally 7:219
Lanford Wilson 7:548

Ewart, Gavin
Roy Fuller 28:157
William Sansom 2:383
Sylvia Townsend Warner
  19:461

Ewen, David
Gerome Ragni and James Rado
  17:385

Ewers, John C.
Jamake Highwater 12:286

Ewing, Dorothy
Miguel Delibes 18:110

Exner, R.
Botho Strauss 22:407

Eyles, Allen
Francis Ford Coppola 16:231
John Huston 20:169
Ken Russell 16:541

Eyre, Frank
H. F. Brinsmead 21:30
Peter Dickinson 12:170
Eilís Dillon 17:98
Leon Garfield 12:223
Alan Garner 17:142
William Mayne 12:396
Philippa Pearce 21:287

Colin Thiele 17:494

Eyster, Warren
James Dickey 1:74

Faase, Thomas P.
Andrew M. Greeley 28:174

Faber, Nancy W.
Frank Bonham 12:50

Faber, Roderick Mason
Tennessee Williams 19:474

Fabio, Sarah Webster
Nikki Giovanni 19:190

Fabre, Michel
James Baldwin 3:31
Chester Himes 2:195

Fadiman, Anne
Fran Lebowitz 11:322

Fadiman, Clifton
Taylor Caldwell 28:56, 57
Walter Van Tilburg Clark 28:76
Howard Fast 23:155
William Faulkner 28:139
Carson McCullers 12:409
Mari Sandoz 28:402

Fadiman, Edwin
Laura Z. Hobson 7:163

Faery, Rebecca B.
Richard Wilbur 9:570

Fager, Charles E.
Bob Dylan 12:185

Fahey, James
Evan S. Connell, Jr. 4:109

Fahey, Joseph J.
William Barrett 27:21

Fairchild, B. H., Jr.
Steven Spielberg 20:364

Faith, Rosamond
Rosemary Wells 12:638

Falck, Colin
A. Alvarez 5:16
John Berryman 2:55
William Empson 3:147
Geoffrey Grigson 7:136
Thom Gunn 6:220
Seamus Heaney 7:149
Ted Hughes 9:280
Philip Larkin 3:275, 276
Robert Lowell 2:245; 5:256
George MacBeth 9:340
Anne Sexton 8:483
Charles Tomlinson 2:436

Falk, Doris V.
Lillian Hellman 14:258

Falk, Signi
Tennessee Williams 1:367

Falke, Wayne
Kenzaburō Ōe 10:372
Jun'ichirō Tanizaki 14:525
John Updike 5:453

Falkenberg, Betty
Walter Abish 22:21
Beryl Bainbridge 18:34
Marge Piercy 18:408
Patrick White 18:549

Fallis, Laurence S.
Ruth Prawer Jhabvala 4:259

Fallowell, Duncan
Giorgio Bassani 9:77
John Berger 2:54
William Peter Blatty 2:64
Richard Brautigan 12:72
Taylor Caldwell 28:66
Robert Coover 3:114
Mark Helprin 7:152
Ruth Prawer Jhabvala 8:312
Anna Kavan 13:316
Jerzy Kosinski 3:274
Iris Murdoch 4:368
Tim O'Brien 7:272
Seán O'Faoláin 7:274
Mervyn Peake 7:303
David Plante 7:308
Françoise Sagan 9:468
James Salter 7:388
Hubert Selby, Jr. 2:390
Terry Southern 7:454
Muriel Spark 3:465; 8:493
Auberon Waugh 7:514

Fallows, James
George V. Higgins 18:233

Fandel, John
E. E. Cummings 3:120

Fandray, David F.
David Bowie 17:62

Fanger, Donald
Aleksandr I. Solzhenitsyn 1:319

Fanning, Peter
Alan Garner 17:149
Nat Hentoff 26:185
Paul Zindel 26:478

Fantoni, Barry
S. J. Perelman 15:418
Brian Wilson 12:60

Farber, Manny
Maya Deren 16:251
John Ford 16:305
Alfred Hitchcock 16:338, 339
John Huston 20:159
Akira Kurosawa 16:394
Paul Schrader 26:386

Farber, Marjorie
Laura Z. Hobson 25:269

Farber, Stephen
Lindsay Anderson 20:15
Francis Ford Coppola 16:231,
  232, 235
Michael Cristofer 28:94
George Roy Hill 26:196
Richard Lester 20:225
Sam Peckinpah 20:274
Ken Russell 16:548
Martin Scorsese 20:327
Steven Spielberg 20:358
François Truffaut 20:396
Luchino Visconti 20:569
Orson Welles 20:446
Billy Wilder 20:461, 464, 465

Farmer, Betty Catherine Dobson
Donald Barthelme 13:58

Farmer, Penelope
Alan Garner **17**:147
Diana Wynne Jones **26**:226, 229
William Mayne **12**:401
Philippa Pearce **21**:289

Farmiloe, Dorothy
Hugh MacLennan **14**:341

Farnsworth, Emily C.
Robert Newton Peck **17**:343

Farrell, Diane
Sol Gordon **26**:136
Andre Norton **12**:459
Paul Zindel **26**:470

Farrell, James T.
James M. Cain **11**:84
John Dos Passos **25**:139
Ben Hecht **8**:269
Frank O'Connor **14**:395

Farrell, John P.
Richard Wilbur **3**:532

Farrelly, John
Andrew Lytle **22**:293

Farrison, W. Edward
Lorraine Hansberry **17**:191

Farwell, Harold
John Barth **5**:50

Farwell, Ruth
George Mackay Brown **5**:77

Farzan, Massud
Ahmad Shamlu **10**:469

Fasick, Adele M.
Roderick L. Haig-Brown **21**:139

Fassbinder, Rainer Werner
Claude Chabrol **16**:181

Faulkner, Peter
Angus Wilson **25**:464

Faulkner, William
Erich Maria Remarque **21**:326

Faulks, Sebastian
Yasunari Kawabata **9**:316

Fawcett, Anthony
Jackson Browne **21**:41

Fawcett, Graham
Anthony Burgess **8**:111

Fay, Eliot G.
Jacques Prévert **15**:437

Feagles, Anita MacRae
Maia Wojciechowska **26**:455

Fearing, Kenneth
George Tabori **19**:435

Featherstone, Joseph
Katherine Anne Porter **3**:392
Frederick Wiseman **20**:468

Feaver, Vicki
Sylvia Townsend Warner **19**:460

Feaver, William
Michael Ayrton **7**:19

Feder, Lillian
Conrad Aiken **5**:8
W. H. Auden **4**:33, 34, 35
George Barker **8**:43
Samuel Beckett **6**:37
T. S. Eliot **6**:160
Robert Graves **6**:210
Ted Hughes **9**:281
Robert Lowell **4**:301
Ezra Pound **3**:396; **4**:414

Federman, Raymond
Samuel Beckett **9**:79

Feeney, Joseph J., S.J.
Jessie Redmon Fauset **19**:171
Isabelle Holland **21**:150

Feied, Frederick
John Dos Passos **1**:80
Jack Kerouac **1**:166

Feifer, George
Aleksandr I. Solzhenitsyn **7**:444

Feiffer, Jules
Richard Lester **20**:223
Jerome Siegel and Joe Shuster **21**:356

Fein, Richard J.
Robert Lowell **3**:304

Feingold, Michael
Dannie Abse **7**:2
E. L. Doctorow **15**:179
Athol Fugard **9**:235
John Guare **8**:252, 253
Peter Handke **8**:263
Beth Henley **23**:216, 217
John Hopkins **4**:234
Albert Innaurato **21**:192, 194
Jim Jacobs and Warren Casey **12**:294
Ira Levin **3**:294
Miguel Piñero **4**:401
Sam Shepard **17**:444, 445, 447
Elizabeth Swados **12**:557, 561
Tennessee Williams **7**:544

Feinstein, Elaine
Gail Godwin **8**:247
William Golding **2**:169
Nadine Gordimer **3**:202
George MacBeth **5**:265
Olivia Manning **19**:301
Mary McCarthy **3**:329
Grace Paley **6**:339
Christina Stead **5**:403

Feirstein, Frederick
Robert Graves **2**:177

Feld, Michael
Richard Brautigan **12**:63
John Updike **2**:445

Feld, Rose C.
Sally Benson **17**:47
Agatha Christie **12**:114
Ernest K. Gann **23**:162
Madeleine L'Engle **12**:345
Helen MacInnes **27**:278, 279
Farley Mowat **26**:333
Mary Renault **17**:389
Françoise Sagan **17**:420
Mari Sandoz **28**:400

Jack Spicer **8**:497

Feld, Ross
Paul Blackburn **9**:98
Laurie Colwin **13**:156
William H. Gass **11**:225
Eudora Welty **14**:566
Tom Wolfe **9**:578

Feldman, Anita
Irwin Shaw **7**:412

Feldman, Hans
Stanley Kubrick **16**:391

Feldman, Irma P.
Helen Yglesia **7**:558

Feldman, Morton
Frank O'Hara **2**:322

Felheim, Marvin
Ben Hecht **8**:272
Lillian Hellman **14**:255
Carson McCullers **1**:208
Eudora Welty **1**:361

Fell, John L.
Rainer Werner Fassbinder **20**:117

Fellows, Jo-Ann
Mazo de la Roche **14**:150

Felsen, Henry Gregor
Henry Gregor Felsen **17**:123

Felstiner, John
Pablo Neruda **1**:247; **2**:309; **5**:302

Felton, David
Richard Pryor **26**:379
Lily Tomlin **17**:519

Fender, Stephen
Jacob Epstein **19**:162
Richard Price **12**:491
John Sayles **10**:462

Fenin, George N.
Vittorio De Sica **20**:86
Billy Wilder **20**:457, 458

Fenton, Edward
Mollie Hunter **21**:157
Maia Wojciechowska **26**:454

Fenton, James
W. H. Auden **6**:18
Lynne Reid Banks **23**:41
Giorgio Bassani **9**:76
Douglas Dunn **6**:148
Gavin Ewart **13**:210
Josephine Poole **17**:372
George Steiner **24**:435
Charles Tomlinson **6**:534

Ferguson, Alan
Ivo Andrić **8**:20

Ferguson, Frances
Randall Jarrell **13**:301
Robert Lowell **4**:302

Ferguson, Otis C.
Frank Capra **16**:154, 155, 156
Charles Chaplin **16**:190, 192
John Ford **16**:303, 304
Alfred Hitchcock **16**:337
Rouben Mamoulian **16**:420

Irwin Shaw **23**:395
Orson Welles **20**:432

Ferguson, Suzanne
Djuna Barnes **3**:36
Randall Jarrell **2**:209

Fergusson, Francis
René Clair **20**:59

Fernandez, Doreen G.
Bienvenido N. Santos **22**:365

Fernandez, Jaime
Jun'ichirō Tanizaki **8**:511

Ferrari, Margaret
Colleen McCullough **27**:317
Marge Piercy **6**:402
Hilma Wolitzer **17**:561

Ferrer, José M.
Garry Marshall **17**:274

Ferrer, Olga Prjevalinskaya
Eugène Ionesco **6**:256

Ferres, John H.
Arthur Miller **26**:324

Ferretti, Fred
Norman Lear **12**:326

Ferrier, Carole
Sylvia Plath **17**:369
Diane Wakoski **7**:505

Ferris, Ina
Rudy Wiebe **11**:567

Ferris, Sumner J.
Flannery O'Connor **21**:257

Ferris, William H.
W.E.B. Du Bois **13**:180

Ferrucci, Franco
Umberto Eco **28**:131

Ferry, David
Theodore Roethke **1**:291

Fetherling, Doug
Hugh Garner **13**:235, 236
Patrick Lane **25**:283
A. W. Purdy **14**:435
Mordecai Richler **3**:431
Robin Skelton **13**:506

Fetz, Gerald A.
Martin Walser **27**:463

Feuer, Kathryn B.
Aleksandr I. Solzhenitsyn **7**:445

Feuser, Willfried F.
Chinua Achebe **7**:6

Fialkowski, Barbara
Maxine Kumin **13**:326

Fiamengo, Marya
Susan Musgrave **13**:400

Fickert, Kurt J.
Friedrich Dürrenmatt **4**:139
Hermann Hesse **17**:201

Fiedler, Leslie A.
John Barth **3**:38
Saul Bellow **1**:27, 31; **3**:48
Truman Capote **19**:79
Leonard Cohen **3**:109
Bob Dylan **3**:130

Philip José Farmer 19:164
William Faulkner 1:101; 3:149
Allen Ginsberg 2:162; 3:193
John Hawkes 3:221
Ernest Hemingway 1:143; 3:232, 33
John Hersey 7:153
Randall Jarrell 1:160
Robert Lowell 2:246
Norman Mailer 3:311
Bernard Malamud 9:341, 351
Henry Miller 2:282
Alberto Moravia 2:293
Wright Morris 1:232
Vladimir Nabokov 1:239
Ezra Pound 7:329
John Crowe Ransom 2:363
Mordecai Richler 5:375
Henry Roth 6:470
J. D. Salinger 12:512
Jerome Siegel and Joe Shuster 21:361
Kurt Vonnegut, Jr. 12:603
Robert Penn Warren 4:579
Richard Wilbur 3:530
Herman Wouk 1:376

Field, Andrew
Vladimir Nabokov 1:242
Yevgeny Yevtushenko 1:382

Field, Carol
Paule Marshall 27:308

Field, Colin
H. F. Brinsmead 21:26
Eilís Dillon 17:98
William Mayne 12:392

Field, George Wallis
Hermann Hesse 1:147

Field, Joyce
Bernard Malamud 9:348

Field, Leslie
Bernard Malamud 9:348

Field, Louise Maunsell
Alvah Bessie 23:59
Taylor Caldwell 28:57
Edna Ferber 18:150
Noel Streatfeild 21:396

Field, Trevor
Julien Green 11:261

Fields, Beverly
Anne Sexton 2:391

Fields, Kenneth
J. V. Cunningham 3:121
Robert Lowell 4:299
Mina Loy 28:247
N. Scott Momaday 2:290
Marya Zaturenska 6:585

Fiess, Edward
Edmund Wilson 24:466

Fifer, Elizabeth
Maxine Hong Kingston 12:314

Figes, Eva
Edward Bond 23:72

Filer, Malva E.
Julio Cortázar 10:117

Finch, John
E. E. Cummings 12:144

Fincke, Gary
Ben Hecht 8:271

Fincke, Kate
Isabelle Holland 21:153

Fine, Dennis
Neil Young 17:573

Finel-Honigman, Irène
Albert Camus 11:96

Finger, Louis
John Le Carré 9:326

Finholt, Richard
James Dickey 10:142
Ralph Ellison 11:184

Fink, Rita
Alvah Bessie 23:61

Finkelstein, Sidney
Louis Aragon 22:36

Finkle, David
John Fowles 9:215
Mordecai Richler 18:459

Finlay, John
Elizabeth Daryush 19:122

Finlayson, Iain
Peter Rushforth 19:405

Finley, M. I.
Michael Ayrton 7:17

Finn, James
James Baldwin 17:23, 24
François Mauriac 4:339
P. G. Wodehouse 2:480

Firchow, Peter
Lawrence Durrell 27:96
Aldous Huxley 8:305

Firchow, Peter E.
W. H. Auden 11:17
Aldous Huxley 18:266

Fireside, Harvey
Andrei Sinyavsky 8:489, 490

Firestone, Bruce M.
Anthony Burgess 10:89

Firmat, Gustavo Pérez
Dámaso Alonso 14:24

First, Elsa
Carlos Castaneda 12:91

Fisch, Harold
Aharon Megged 9:374

Fischer, John Irwin
Catharine Savage Brosman 9:135

Fischer, Lucy
René Clair 20:67

Fischer, Marjorie
Margot Benary-Isbert 12:30
Joseph Krumgold 12:317

Fischer, Michael
Wayne C. Booth 24:99

Fischler, Alexander
Eugène Ionesco 15:297

Fisher, Dorothy Canfield
A. B. Guthrie, Jr. 23:195

Fisher, Elizabeth
Jessamyn West 17:553

Fisher, Emma
Beryl Bainbridge 18:32
John Berryman 10:47
Anaïs Nin 14:386
Peter Porter 13:452
R. S. Thomas 13:544
Yevgeny Yevtushenko 26:468

Fisher, Margery
E. M. Almedingen 12:6
Ruth M. Arthur 12:25, 26
Honor Arundel 17:14, 16
Gunnel Beckman 26:88
Judy Blume 12:47
Cecil Bødker 21:11
H. F. Brinsmead 21:27, 28, 29, 30, 33
Mavis Thorpe Clark 12:130, 131, 132
Robert Cormier 12:135, 137
Julia W. Cunningham 12:164, 165
Maureen Daly 17:91
Peter Dickinson 12:169, 174, 177
Eilís Dillon 17:95, 96, 97
Walter Farley 17:118
Esther Forbes 12:211
Leon Garfield 12:216, 217, 218, 223, 227, 231, 233, 234
Alan Garner 17:135, 136, 148
Mollie Hunter 21:156, 160, 170
Diana Wynne Jones 26:224, 225, 226, 228, 231, 232
William Mayne 12:389, 405
Emily Cheney Neville 12:450
Andre Norton 12:469, 470
Katherine Paterson 12:485
Philippa Pearce 21:281, 282, 287, 288, 290, 291
Richard Peck 21:298
Josephine Poole 17:373
Otfried Preussler 17:375, 376
Zilpha Keatley Snyder 17:474
Noel Streatfeild 21:403, 409, 410, 416
Rosemary Sutcliff 26:437, 441
Mildred D. Taylor 21:421
Colin Thiele 17:493, 494, 495, 496
J.R.R. Tolkien 12:586
Rosemary Wells 12:638
Robert Westall 17:555, 556, 559
Paul Zindel 26:481

Fisher, Maxine
Paul Zindel 26:477

Fisher, William J.
William Saroyan 8:466

Fishman, Charles
A. R. Ammons 25:47

Fiske, Minnie Maddern
Charles Chaplin 16:187

Fisketjon, Gary L.
Raymond Carver 22:97
Thomas McGuane 18:323

Fison, Peter
C. P. Snow 13:511

Fitts, Dudley
Peter Davison 28:99
Mary Renault 17:394, 398

Fitzgerald, Edward J.
Howard Fast 23:156
Mark Harris 19:200

Fitzgerald, Judith
Margaret Atwood 25:66

Fitzgerald, Penelope
Barbara Pym 19:388
Stevie Smith 25:420

Fitzgerald, Robert
Seamus Heaney 7:151
Robert Lowell 11:325; 15:345
Flannery O'Connor 15:409

Fitzlyon, Kyril
Aleksandr I. Solzhenitsyn 1:321

Fitzpatrick, Marjorie A.
Marie-Claire Blais 22:60

Fitzsimmons, Thomas
Elizabeth Hardwick 13:264

Fiut, Aleksander
Czesław Miłosz 11:379

Fixler, Michael
Isaac Bashevis Singer 1:311

Flagg, Nancy
Jorge Amado 13:11

Flaherty, Joe
Richard Brautigan 9:124
James M. Cain 28:54
Edwin Newman 14:379

Flamm, Dudley
Robert M. Pirsig 4:404

Flanagan, John T.
Jessamyn West 17:551, 552

Flanagan, Kate M.
Sue Ellen Bridgers 26:91

Flanagan, Thomas
Aharon Appelfeld 23:36
Benedict Kiely 23:265

Flanders, Jane
James Dickey 15:177
Katherine Anne Porter 10:396; 27:400

Flanner, Janet
André Malraux 4:326

Flatto, Eric
Stanley Kubrick 16:382

Flaxman, Seymour L.
Hermann Hesse 17:196

Fleckenstein, Joan S.
Edward Albee 11:13

Fleischer, Leonard
Woody Allen 16:6
John A. Williams 5:496

Fleischer, Leonore
Nora Ephron 17:110

Fleischmann, Mark
Ray Davies 21:105

Fleischmann, Wolfgang Bernard
René Wellek 28:446

Fleishman, Avrom
John Fowles 9:210

Fleming, Alice
Zilpha Keatley Snyder 17:471

Fleming, Robert E.
Ronald L. Fair 18:140
John A. Williams 5:496

Fleming, Thomas J.
Ira Levin 6:305
Emily Cheney Neville 12:450
Michel Tournier 23:451

Fleshman, Bob
David Madden 15:350

Fletcher, Angus
Northrop Frye 24:219

Fletcher, Connie
Elmore Leonard 28:234

Fletcher, John
Arthur Adamov 25:18
Uwe Johnson 5:201
Kamala Markandaya 8:377
Jean-Paul Sartre 7:398

Fletcher, Peggy
Joe Rosenblatt 15:447

Flexner, James Thomas
Esther Forbes 12:209

Flint, R. W.
A. R. Ammons 8:15; 9:29
Irving Feldman 7:102
Anthony Hecht 8:267
Randall Jarrell 1:159
Karl Shapiro 8:486
Charles Tomlinson 13:550

Flippo, Chet
Waylon Jennings 21:201
Kris Kristofferson 26:268
Willie Nelson 17:302, 303, 304, 305
Sam Shepard 17:445

Floan, Howard R.
William Saroyan 1:301

Flood, Jeanne
Brian Moore 5:294

Flora, Joseph M.
Vardis Fisher 7:103
Günter Grass 6:209
J. E. Wideman 5:490
Nancy Willard 7:539

Flower, Dean
Raymond Carver 22:97
Dan Jacobson 14:291
Vladimir Nabokov 15:393
Marge Piercy 14:421
Frederic Raphael 14:438
Hubert Selby, Jr. 8:477
Helen Yglesias 7:559
Al Young 19:479

Flowers, Ann A.
Barbara Corcoran 17:78
Lois Duncan 26:108
Leon Garfield 12:239
Norma Fox Mazer 26:291
Katherine Paterson 12:486

Flowers, Betty
Isaac Asimov 26:37
Donald Barthelme 5:56

Flowers, Paul
John Ehle 27:101

Flowers, Sandra Hollin
Ntozake Shange 25:403

Fludas, John
Rita Mae Brown 18:73
Richard Price 12:491

Foell, Earl W.
Romain Gary 25:183

Fogelman, Phyllis J.
Mildred D. Taylor 21:421

Folejewski, Zbigniew
Maria Dabrowska 15:165, 167
Joseph Wittlin 25:467

Foley, Barbara
E. L. Doctorow 18:121

Folsom, James K.
Larry McMurtry 27:326

Folsom, L. Edwin
W. S. Merwin 13:384

Fong, Monique
Vittorio De Sica 20:95

Fontenla, Cesar Santos
Carlos Saura 20:320

Fontenot, Chester J.
Alex Haley 8:260
Alice Walker 19:450

Fontenrose, Joseph
John Steinbeck 21:372

Foose, Thomas T.
Jean Renoir 20:287

Foote, Audrey C.
Anthony Burgess 4:81
Nathalie Sarraute 2:386
Christina Stead 5:404
Mary Stewart 7:468

Foote, Jennifer
Richard O'Brien 17:325

Foote, Timothy
W. H. Auden 3:26; 6:24
Anthony Burgess 5:89
Peter De Vries 2:114
John Gardner 3:187
John le Carré 5:232
V. S. Pritchett 5:352
Aleksandr I. Solzhenitsyn 4:516
Tom Stoppard 4:525
Tom Wolfe 2:481

Forbes, Alastair
Lawrence Durrell 13:189

Forbes, Cheryl
Ralph Bakshi 26:73

Forbes, Jill
René Clair 20:66
Rainer Werner Fassbinder 20:116
Joan Micklin Silver 20:341

Forche, Carolyn
Ai 14:8

Ford, Nick Aaron
Harper Lee 12:341
Willard Motley 18:356
Frank G. Yerby 22:488

Ford, Richard J.
Hermann Hesse 2:189

Ford, Thomas W.
A. B. Guthrie, Jr. 23:202

Forman, Jack
Jules Archer 12:18, 20
Frank Bonham 12:51
Nat Hentoff 26:184, 185
Norma Fox Mazer 26:290
Katherine Paterson 12:485, 486
Richard Peck 21:300
Kin Platt 26:352, 354
Paul Zindel 26:477

Fornatale, Peter
Laura Nyro 17:314
Brian Wilson 12:646

Forrest, Alan
W. H. Auden 3:27
Mario Puzo 2:352

Forrey, Robert
Ken Kesey 11:316
Andrew Sinclair 14:488

Forster, E. M.
Mulk Raj Anand 23:11

Forster, Leonard
Günter Grass 15:262

Fortin, René E.
Boris Pasternak 7:296

Foster, David William
Jorge Luis Borges 3:78; 6:89
Camilo José Cela 4:96
Julio Cortázar 10:118
Ernesto Sabato 10:445

Foster, Isabel
Robert Francis 15:234

Foster, John Wilson
Seamus Heaney 5:170
Brian Moore 1:225

Foster, Richard
R. P. Blackmur 24:61
Norman Mailer 1:190; 8:365
I. A. Richards 24:393
Allen Tate 24:444

Foster, Richard J.
Arthur Miller 26:315

Foster, Roy
Brian Moore 19:333

Foster, Ruel E.
Jesse Stuart 1:328

Fotheringham, Hamish
William Mayne 12:388

Fowler, Alastair
Michael Moorcock 27:351
Charles M. Schulz 12:532

Fowler, Douglas
Thomas Pynchon 18:438

Fowler, F. M.
Günter Eich 15:203

Fowles, John
G. B. Edwards 25:149

Fowlie, Wallace
Ben Belitt 22:50
Michel Butor 8:119
René Char 9:158
Jean Cocteau 15:133
Jean Genet 5:135
Julien Green 11:258
Henri Michaux 8:392
Anaïs Nin 4:378; 11:398
Jules Romains 7:379

Fox, Charles
Akira Kurosawa 16:396

Fox, Gail
Phyllis Webb 18:542

Fox, Geoff
Rosa Guy 26:144
Nat Hentoff 26:187

Fox, Hank
Janis Ian 21:183

Fox, Hugh
William Carlos Williams 5:509

Fox, Terry Curtis
Rita Mae Brown 18:73
Marguerite Duras 20:103
Max Frisch 18:162
Athol Fugard 14:192
Jean-Luc Godard 20:152
Simon Gray 14:215
John Guare 14:221
Beth Henley 23:214
George V. Higgins 18:235
George Lucas 16:415
Marsha Norman 28:317
Harold Pinter 15:425
Martin Scorsese 20:333

Fox-Genovese, Elizabeth
Susan Cheever 18:102
William Gaddis 8:226
Gail Godwin 22:183

Fraenkel, Heinrich
Leni Riefenstahl 16:521

Fraiberg, Louis
Kenneth Burke 24:130
Joseph Wood Krutch 24:287
Lionel Trilling 24:454
Edmund Wilson 24:476

Frakes, J. R.
Robert Ludlum 22:288

Frakes, James R.
Nelson Algren 4:17
Wendell Berry 4:59
E. M. Broner 19:70
R. V. Cassill 23:108
Bruce Jay Friedman 5:127
Patricia Highsmith 2:194

Stanley Hoffman 5:185
Julius Horwitz 14:266
Evan Hunter 11:280
Diane Johnson 5:198
Michael Mewshaw 9:376
Ezekiel Mphahlele 25:332
Muriel Spark 2:418
Richard G. Stern 4:522

France, Arthur
Lorraine Hansberry 17:185

France, Peter
Anne Hébert 13:267

Francescato, Martha Paley
Julio Cortázar 10:116

Francis, William A. C.
William Price Fox 22:139

Francis, Wynne
Louis Dudek 19:137

Frane, Jeff
Fritz Leiber 25:310

Frank, Armin Paul
Kenneth Burke 2:89

Frank, Joseph
Djuna Barnes 8:47
R. P. Blackmur 24:64
Yves Bonnefoy 15:74
André Malraux 4:327
Aleksandr I. Solzhenitsyn 7:443
Lionel Trilling 24:453

Frank, Mike
Joseph Heller 11:266

Frank, Peter
Richard Kostelanetz 28:219

Frank, Sheldon
T. Alan Broughton 19:72
Margaret Laurence 6:289
Steven Millhauser 21:218
Hans Erich Nossack 6:365
Al Young 19:480

Frankel, Bernice
Mary Stolz 12:547

Frankel, Charles
William Barrett 27:17

Frankel, Haskel
Jonathan Baumbach 23:53
Bruce Jay Friedman 3:165
Muriel Spark 2:417
Peter Ustinov 1:346
Charles Webb 7:514

Frankenberg, Lloyd
Marianne Moore 19:337
Ogden Nash 23:321

Franklin, Allan
Jorg Luis Borges 9:116

Franklin, H. Bruce
J. G. Ballard 3:32
Robert A. Heinlein 26:175, 179

Fraser, G. S.
Basil Bunting 10:86
Robert Creeley 1:67
C. Day Lewis 6:127
Nigel Dennis 8:172
Lawrence Durrell 4:145; 13:184

Jean Garrigue 2:153
Randall Jarrell 9:296
Robert Lowell 2:249; 11:325
Hugh MacDiarmid 11:337
W. S. Merwin 1:214
C. P. Snow 4:502
Gary Snyder 1:318
Andrei Voznesensky 15:552
Louis Zukofsky 1:385

Fraser, John
Louis-Ferdinand Céline 1:56; 4:102
F. R. Leavis 24:298
Yvor Winters 4:592; 8:552

Fraser, Kathleen
Adrienne Rich 3:429

Fraser, Keath
Alden Nowlan 15:398
Sinclair Ross 13:492

Fraser, Russell
Eugenio Montale 18:341

Fratz, D. Douglas
Frank Herbert 23:222

Frayne, John P.
John Ford 16:320

Frazer, Frances M.
Christie Harris 12:268

Frazer, Mary
Frederick Wiseman 20:477

Fredeman, W. E.
Earle Birney 6:72

Frederick, Linda J.
Ray Davies 21:100

Fredericks, Claude
Brewster Ghiselin 23:169

Fredericks, Pierce
Ernest K. Gann 23:165

Fredrick, E. Coston
Barbara Corcoran 17:75

Free, William J.
Federico Fellini 16:284
Tennessee Williams 15:581

Freed, Donald
Alberto Moravia 27:353

Freedberg, Mike
Smokey Robinson 21:348

Freedberger, Peter
Stan Lee 17:261

Freedman, Morris
Sylvia Ashton-Warner 19:23

Freedman, Ralph
Saul Bellow 1:29
Hermann Hesse 1:146; 17:203

Freedman, Richard
A. Alvarez 13:10
Taylor Caldwell 28:69
Hortense Calisher 2:96
Dick Francis 2:142
Lois Gould 4:199
Robert Ludlum 22:290
Tim O'Brien 19:356

S. J. Perelman 9:416; 23:337
George Steiner 24:432
Henri Troyat 23:460
P. G. Wodehouse 5:517

Freedman, William
Henry Roth 11:487

Freeman, Anne Hobson
Reynolds Price 13:463

Freeman, Gillian
Robert Nye 13:412

Freeman, Suzanne
Joyce Maynard 23:290
Norma Fox Mazer 26:296
Susan Richards Shreve 23:404

Frein, George H.
Vine Deloria, Jr. 21:112

Fremantle, Anne
W. H. Auden 1:10
Auberon Waugh 7:513
Vassily S. Yanovsky 18:551

Fremont-Smith, Eliot
Richard Adams 4:6
Martin Amis 4:20
Max Apple 9:33
Louis Auchincloss 4:31
Laurie Colwin 13:156
E. L. Doctorow 6:132
Lawrence Durrell 6:152
Gael Greene 8:252
Barry Hannah 23:211
Joseph Heller 5:173; 11:268
Lillian Hellman 4:221
John Irving 13:294; 23:247
Marjorie Kellogg 2:223
Jascha Kessler 4:269
Arthur Koestler 3:271
Jerzy Kosinski 1:172
John le Carré 9:327
Alan Lelchuk 5:243
Norman Mailer 4:322
Colleen McCullough 27:318
James A. Michener 5:289
Chaim Potok 26:368
Richard Price 6:426; 12:490
Philip Roth 4:453, 455
Alix Kates Shulman 10:476
John Updike 23:468
Gore Vidal 6:54
Irving Wallace 7:510
Patrick White 3:524

French, Allen
Esther Forbes 12:206

French, Janet
Sue Ellen Bridgers 26:92
Otfried Preussler 17:375

French, Marilyn
Margaret Atwood 15:39

French, Ned
William H. Gass 15:255

French, Philip
Bernardo Bertolucci 16:101
Jorge Luis Borges 4:75
Truman Capote 8:132
Eleanor Clark 19:107
Graham Greene 3:212; 6:220
Richard Lester 20:219

S. J. Perelman 23:340

French, Roberts W.
Wendell Berry 27:32
Philip Booth 23:75
Joyce Carol Oates 1:251

French, Warren
William Goldman 1:123
R. K. Narayan 7:254
James Purdy 2:349
J. D. Salinger 1:297; 12:514
John Steinbeck 1:324; 5:406
Thornton Wilder 1:366
Richard Wright 21:447

Fretz, Sada
Julia W. Cunningham 12:165
John Neufeld 17:308

Friar, Kimon
Margaríta Karapánou 13:314
Yannis Ritsos 6:463
Vassilis Vassilikos 8:524

Fricke, David
David Byrne 26:99
Mick Jagger and Keith Richard 17:242
Paul Weller 26:447
Frank Zappa 17:592

Fried, Lewis
James T. Farrell 11:191

Friedberg, Maurice
Aleksandr I. Solzhenitsyn 1:319; 7:435

Friedenberg, Edgar Z.
James Baldwin 17:24
Mark Harris 19:201
Hermann Hesse 2:190
Frederick Wiseman 20:472

Friedman, Alan
William S. Burroughs 5:93
John Gardner 7:112
John Hawkes 27:198
Erica Jong 18:279
Yukio Mishima 4:357
Amos Oz 8:435
John Rechy 18:442
Ishmael Reed 2:367
André Schwarz-Bart 2:389
John Kennedy Toole 19:443
Elie Wiesel 3:528

Friedman, Alan J.
Thomas Pynchon 6:434

Friedman, Alan Warren
Saul Bellow 8:69
Lawrence Durrell 1:87
Bernard Malamud 8:375

Friedman, Jack
Wendell Berry 4:59
José Lezama Lima 4:290

Friedman, John
William Eastlake 8:200

Friedman, Melvin J.
Bruce Jay Friedman 5:127
Carolyn G. Heilbrun 25:252
Eugène Ionesco 6:256
André Malraux 4:333
R. K. Narayan 7:255

Flannery O'Connor **1**:253
Isaac Bashevis Singer **1**:313

Friedman, Norman
E. E. Cummings **1**:69; **12**:149; **15**:153
David Ignatow **7**:174

Friedman, Richard
The Police **26**:365

Friedrichsmeyer, Erhard
Uwe Johnson **15**:302

Frieling, Kenneth
Flannery O'Connor **13**:416

Friesem, Roberta Ricky
Lenora Mattingly Weber **12**:635

Friesen, Gordon
Phil Ochs **17**:329, 330

Frith, Simon
Elvis Costello **21**:68
Mick Jagger and Keith Richard **17**:240
Bob Marley **17**:272
Smokey Robinson **21**:346
Patti Smith **12**:543
Peter Townshend **17**:538
Paul Weller **26**:445
Neil Young **17**:580

Fritz, Jean
Ruth M. Arthur **12**:24
Barbara Corcoran **17**:73
Rosa Guy **26**:144
Virginia Hamilton **26**:153, 155
Joseph Krumgold **12**:318
Norma Fox Mazer **26**:293
Milton Meltzer **26**:297
Zilpha Keatley Snyder **17**:472
Mary Stolz **12**:553
Mildred D. Taylor **21**:418
Maia Wojciechowska **26**:457

Frohock, W. M.
James M. Cain **11**:84
Erskine Caldwell **1**:51
James Gould Cozzens **4**:113
John Dos Passos **1**:77
James T. Farrell **1**:97
William Faulkner **1**:99
Ernest Hemingway **1**:141
André Malraux **4**:324; **13**:366
John Steinbeck **1**:323
Robert Penn Warren **1**:351

Frost, Lucy
John Hawkes **3**:223

Fruchtbaum, Harold
Loren Eiseley **7**:90

Frye, Northrop
Charles Chaplin **16**:192
R. S. Crane **27**:71
Louis Dudek **11**:158; **19**:136, 137
Northrop Frye **24**:222
Daryl Hine **15**:280
Dorothy Livesay **15**:339
E. J. Pratt **19**:376, 379
A.J.M. Smith **15**:516
Allen Tate **24**:443

Fryer, Jonathan H.
Christopher Isherwood **9**:292

Fuchs, Daniel
Saul Bellow **3**:62

Fuchs, Vivian
Thomas Keneally **10**:299

Fuchs, Wolfgang
Charles M. Schulz **12**:528

Fuentes, Carlos
Luis Buñuel **16**:137

Fugard, Athol
Athol Fugard **14**:189

Fulford, Robert
George Bowering **15**:81
Michael Cimino **16**:214
Mavis Gallant **18**:172
Hugh Hood **28**:187
Kevin Major **26**:285
Brian Moore **3**:340
Mordecai Richler **3**:429
Philip Roth **3**:435
Raymond Souster **14**:504

Fuller, Edmund
Paul Bowles **1**:41
Frederick Buechner **4**:80
James Gould Cozzens **1**:65
Jan de Hartog **19**:130
John Ehle **27**:106
James D. Forman **21**:116
Pamela Hansford Johnson **27**:220
James Jones **1**:161
Thomas Keneally **19**:248
Jack Kerouac **1**:165
Bernard Malamud **27**:299
Alan Paton **4**:395; **25**:360
Mary Renault **17**:392
Mary Lee Settle **19**:408
J.R.R. Tolkien **1**:335
Herman Wouk **1**:375

Fuller, Elizabeth Ely
Isak Dinesen **10**:150

Fuller, Hoyt W.
Milton Meltzer **26**:299

Fuller, John
Anna Akhmatova **11**:9
Peter Davison **28**:102
Thom Gunn **3**:215
Michael Hamburger **14**:234
Randall Jarrell **2**:208
Diana Wynne Jones **26**:225
Leslie Norris **14**:387
Robert Pinsky **19**:370
William Plomer **4**:406
Ann Quin **6**:441
Kathleen Raine **7**:353
Jon Silkin **6**:499
Andrew Young **5**:523

Fuller, John G.
Colin MacInnes **23**:282

Fuller, Roy
W. H. Auden **3**:25
Aldous Huxley **5**:192
A.J.M. Smith **15**:513
C. P. Snow **19**:427
Stephen Spender **2**:420
Allen Tate **14**:532
Lionel Trilling **9**:530

Fulton, Robin
Pär Lagerkvist **10**:313

Funke, Lewis
John Mortimer **28**:282

Funsten, Kenneth
Derek Walcott **25**:456

Furbank, P. N.
Margaret Drabble **22**:120
E. M. Forster **4**:165, 168
William Golding **17**:176
Elizabeth Jennings **14**:291
Uwe Johnson **10**:284
Derek Mahon **27**:287
Gore Vidal **4**:556

Furlong, Vivienne
Honor Arundel **17**:18

Fussell, B. H.
Peter Taylor **4**:543

Fussell, Edwin
Wendell Berry **6**:61
Hayden Carruth **7**:40

Fussell, Paul
Graham Greene **27**:171
Thomas Keneally **8**:318
Paul Theroux **15**:533
Evelyn Waugh **27**:475, 477

Fussell, Paul, Jr.
Karl Shapiro **4**:486

Fyne, Robert
Aharon Appelfeld **23**:37

Fytton, Francis
Paul Bowles **2**:78

Fyvel, T. R.
Ilya Ehrenburg **18**:133

Gabbard, Krin
Tess Gallagher **18**:170

Gabel, Lars
Marvin Gaye **26**:133

Gabree, John
Mick Jagger and Keith Richard **17**:223
John Lennon and Paul McCartney **12**:364

Gadney, Reg
George V. Higgins **7**:158
Patricia Highsmith **2**:194
Ross Macdonald **2**:257
Alistair MacLean **3**:309

Gaev, A.
Vasily Aksenov **22**:25

Gagné, Sarah
Melvin Berger **12**:42
Larry Kettelkamp **12**:307
Alvin Silverstein and Virginia B. Silverstein **17**:456

Gaillard, Dawson
Harry Crews **23**:134

Gaillard, Frye
Willie Nelson **17**:304

Gaines, Richard H.
Chester Himes **2**:196

Gaiser, Carolyn
Gregory Corso **1**:63

Gaither, Frances
Esther Forbes **12**:210

Galassi, Jonathan
John Berryman **6**:63
Robert Duncan **2**:123
Robert Graves **6**:212
Seamus Heaney **7**:147
Randall Jarrell **9**:297
Czesław Miłosz **22**:309
Eugenio Montale **7**:231
Howard Nemerov **9**:396
George Oppen **13**:434

Galbraith, John Kenneth
Robertson Davies **25**:135
Edwin O'Connor **14**:389
William Safire **10**:446

Gall, Sally M.
Kenneth O. Hanson **13**:263
Eleanor Lerman **9**:329
M. L. Rosenthal **28**:394
Charles Wright **6**:580

Gallagher, Bob
Smokey Robinson **21**:347

Gallagher, D. P.
Adolfo Bioy Casares **8**:94; **13**:83
Jorge Luis Borges **6**:88
G. Cabrera Infante **5**:96
Gabriel García Márquez **8**:230
Pablo Neruda **7**:257
Octavio Paz **6**:394
Manuel Puig **10**:420
Mario Vargas Llosa **6**:543

Gallagher, David
G. Cabrera Infante **5**:95
Manuel Puig **3**:407

Gallagher, Michael
Shusaku Endo **7**:95

Gallant, Mavis
Simone de Beauvoir **4**:48
Louis-Ferdinand Céline **7**:46
Günter Grass **4**:205
Vladimir Nabokov **2**:303

Galler, David
Peter Davison **28**:100
Ted Hughes **2**:198
Howard Nemerov **2**:307

Galligan, Edward L.
Georges Simenon **1**:309

Galloway, David
William Melvin Kelley **22**:251

Galloway, David D.
Saul Bellow **3**:51, 55
Stanley Elkin **4**:152
Dan Jacobson **4**:253
J. D. Salinger **3**:445
William Styron **3**:473
John Updike **3**:486

Gambaccini, Paul
Smokey Robinson **21**:342

Gambaccini, Peter
Billy Joel **26**:217

Gannon, Edward, S.J.
André Malraux 4:326

Gannon, Thomas M.
David Bradley, Jr. 23:82
John Gregory Dunne 28:127

Gant, Lisbeth
Ed Bullins 5:82

Ganz, Arthur
Harold Pinter 6:416

Ganz, Earl
John Hawkes 1:139
Flannery O'Connor 2:318

Garcia, Irma
Nicholosa Mohr 12:447

Gard, Roger
Shirley Hazzard 18:214

Gardiner, Harold C.
Robert Cormier 12:134

Gardner, Averil
William Empson 19:156

Gardner, Erle Stanley
Meyer Levin 7:203

Gardner, Harvey
Jimmy Breslin 4:76

Gardner, John
Saul Bellow 10:44
Anthony Burgess 2:84
Italo Calvino 8:129; 22:90
John Cheever 25:117
E. L. Doctorow 15:178
John Fowles 9:215
William H. Gass 1:114
John Knowles 4:271
Brian Moore 8:395
Charles Newman 8:419
Joyce Carol Oates 19:354
Walker Percy 8:442
Philip Roth 2:379
John Steinbeck 21:387
William Styron 15:525
J.R.R. Tolkien 12:585
Patrick White 9:567
Thomas Williams 14:582
Larry Woiwode 6:578

Gardner, Marilyn
Barbara Corcoran 17:69
Virginia Hamilton 26:149
Mary Stolz 12:554
Maia Wojciechowska 26:457

Gardner, Peter
Allan W. Eckert 17:108
John Hersey 9:277

Gardner, Philip
William Empson 19:156
D. J. Enright 4:155
Roy Fisher 25:160
Philip Larkin 5:230; 18:293

Gardner, R. H.
William Inge 19:228
Arthur Miller 26:319

Garebian, Keith
Patrick White 9:563

Garfield, Brian
Ernest K. Gann 23:166

Garfield, Evelyn Picon
Julio Cortázar 13:163

Garfield, Leon
William Mayne 12:395

Garfitt, Roger
George Barker 8:46
James K. Baxter 14:60
Martin Booth 13:103
Joseph Brodsky 6:96
Robert Creeley 4:118
Eilís Dillon 17:99
Douglas Dunn 6:148
Geoffrey Grigson 7:136
Donald Hall 13:259
Anthony Hecht 19:209
Anna Kavan 5:206
Reiner Kunze 10:310
Philip Larkin 8:332
George MacBeth 5:263
László Nagy 7:251
Leslie Norris 14:388
Julia O'Faolain 6:383
Vasko Popa 19:375
Peter Porter 5:346
Thomas Pynchon 3:418
Peter Redgrove 6:445
Bernice Rubens 19:403
Ward Ruyslinck 14:471
C. H. Sisson 8:490
Anne Stevenson 7:462
Derek Walcott 4:575

Garis, Leslie
Doris Lessing 6:302

Garis, Robert
Herbert Gold 4:191
Anthony Powell 3:400

Garland, Phyl
Marvin Gaye 26:135
Smokey Robinson 21:348, 349

Garner, Alan
Leon Garfield 12:219

Garnet, Eldon
B. P. Nichol 18:367

Garnick, Vivian
Toni Morrison 10:355

Garrard, J. G.
Aleksandr I. Solzhenitsyn 2:411; 9:503

Garrett, George
John Cheever 3:107
Babette Deutsch 18:119
Gail Godwin 22:180
Sue Kaufman 8:317
Wright Morris 3:342; 18:351
Leon Rooke 25:391

Garrett, John
Edmund Crispin 22:109
Northrop Frye 24:207

Garrigue, Jean
Romain Gary 25:183
Mary McCarthy 14:357
Marianne Moore 1:228

Garside, E. B.
Farley Mowat 26:335

Garson, Helen S.
Truman Capote 19:85
John Hawkes 9:268; 27:192

Garvey, Michael
William Trevor 25:444

Garvin, Larry
Piri Thomas 17:501

Gascoigne, Bamber
Ann Jellicoe 27:207

Gasparini, Len
Ronald G. Everson 27:135
Patrick Lane 25:284, 286

Gasque, Thomas J.
J.R.R. Tolkien 1:337

Gass, William H.
Donald Barthelme 3:43
Jorge Luis Borges 3:76
Robert Coover 3:113
Gabriel García Márquez 27:153
William H. Gass 15:257
Vladimir Nabokov 3:351
J. F. Powers 1:281
Philip Roth 3:437
Isaac Bashevis Singer 3:454
Susan Sontag 10:484

Gassner, John
Edward Albee 3:6, 7
Robert Anderson 23:30
Jean Anouilh 3:11, 12
Samuel Beckett 3:44, 45
Brendan Behan 8:63
Eric Bentley 24:47
William Gibson 23:177
Lillian Hellman 4:220
William Inge 8:307
Eugène Ionesco 4:250
Joseph Wood Krutch 24:286
Archibald MacLeish 3:310
Mary McCarthy 24:342
Arthur Miller 6:330; 26:310
Clifford Odets 28:331
John Osborne 5:330
Harold Pinter 3:386
Thornton Wilder 5:495
Tennessee Williams 5:498, 500

Gaston, Karen C.
Gail Godwin 22:182

Gaston, Paul M.
John Ehle 27:103

Gates, David
Samuel Beckett 9:83

Gates, Henry Louis, Jr.
Sterling A. Brown 23:100

Gathercole, Patricia M.
Tommaso Landolfi 11:321

Gathorne-Hardy, J.
Vladimir Nabokov 3:354

Gatt-Rutter, John
Italo Calvino 11:89; 22:89

Gauch, Patricia Lee
Robert Newton Peck 17:343

Gaudon, Sheila
Julien Gracq 11:245

Gaull, Marilyn
E. E. Cumming 12:156

Gault, John
Stephen King 26:234

Gaurilović, Zoran
Dobrica Ćosić 14:132

Gavin, Willam
Auberon Waugh 7:514

Gayle, Addison, Jr.
Gwendolyn Brooks 1:46
Ernest J. Gaines 18:167
Ezekiel Mphahlele 25:334

Gealy, Marcia B.
Bernard Malamud 18:317

Gearing, Nigel
Pier Paolo Pasolini 20:266

Geary, Joyce
Jade Snow Wong 17:566

Gebhard, Ann
Barbara Corcoran 17:75

Geddes, Gary
Raymond Souster 5:395

Geduld, Harry M.
Woody Allen 16:8

Geering, R. G.
Shirley Hazzard 18:216
Christina Stead 2:42

Geherin, David
John D. MacDonald 27:276
Robert B. Parker 27:364

Geherin, David J.
Joan Didion 8:173

Gehrz, Robert D.
Franklyn M. Branley 21:21

Geis, Richard E.
Peter Dickinson 12:172

Geismar, Maxwell
Nelson Algren 4:16
John Beecher 6:48
Saul Bellow 1:27
Cleanth Brooks 24:107
Camilo José Cela 13:145
James Gould Cozzens 1:66
John Dos Passos 1:77
William Faulkner 1:100
William Gaddis 19:185
Nadine Gordimer 5:146
Ernest Hemingway 1:142
John Hersey 1:144
Norman Mailer 1:187
Henry Miller 4:350
Erich Maria Remarque 21:332
Henry Roth 6:471
J. D. Salinger 1:295
William Styron 1:329
Leon Uris 7:490
Herman Wouk 1:376

Gelb, Arthur
Alice Childress 12:104

Geldrich-Leffman, Hanna
Siegfried Lenz 27:256

Geldzahler, Henry
Andy Warhol 20:414

Gelfant, Blanche H.
Yasunari Kawabata 9:316
Jack Kerouac 5:213
Jean Stafford 7:459
James Welch 14:558

Gellatly, Peter
C. Day Lewis 6:128

Gelpi, Albert J.
Philip Booth 23:74
William Everson 14:164
Adrienne Rich 6:457

Geltman, Max
Arthur Koestler 8:325
Ezra Pound 5:349; 7:338

Gemmil, Janet P.
Raja Rao 25:367

Genêt
Françoise Sagan 17:422, 423

Geng, Veronica
Francis Ford Coppola 16:246
Paula Danziger 21:83
Nadine Gordimer 5:148

George, Diana L.
Lionel Trilling 9:532

George, Michael
J. B. Priestley 5:350

Georgiou, Constantine
James D. Forman 21:118
Philippa Pearce 21:283

Gerald, John Bart
Robert Lowell 3:302
Robert Stone 5:11

Gerhardt, Lillian N.
Betty Cavanna 12:101
Mollie Hunter 21:159

Geringer, Laura
Toni Cade Bambara 19:34
Norma Fox Mazer 26:293

Gerlach, John
Robert Bresson 16:118

German, Howard
Iris Murdoch 15:383

Gerould, Daniel C.
Vasily Aksenov 22:26
Tadeusz Różewicz 9:463

Gerrard, Charlotte F.
Eugène Ionesco 9:286

Gerrity, Thomas W.
Jakov Lind 27:272

Gerrold, David
Gene Roddenberry 17:403

Gerson, Ben
David Bowie 17:59
Kris Kristofferson 26:267
John Lennon and Paul
  McCartney 12:366, 377

Gerson, Villiers
Isaac Asimov 26:35
Robert A. Heinlein 26:161
John Wyndham 19:474

Gersoni-Edelman, Diane
Paul Zindel 26:471

Gersoni-Stavn, Diane
See Stavn, Diane Gersoni

Gerstein, Evelyn
Fritz Lang 20:201

Gersten, Russell
Smokey Robinson 21:343

Gerstenberger, Donna
Iris Murdoch 6:348

Gertel, Zunilda
José Donoso 4:128
Juan Carlos Onetti 7:278

Gervais, Marc
Pier Paolo Pasolini 20:260

Getz, Thomas H.
Geoffrey Hill 18:241

Giacoman, Helmy F.
Alejo Carpentier 11:97

Gianakaris, C. J.
Arthur Miller 15:376

Giannaris, George
Vassilis Vassilikos 8:524

Giannetti, Louis D.
Federico Fellini 16:295

Giannone, Richard
Kurt Vonnegut, Jr. 12:620;
  22:447

Giard, Robert
Claude Chabrol 16:169, 175

Gibb, Hugh
Thomas McGrath 28:275

Gibbons, Boyd
James A. Michener 11:374

Gibbons, Reginald
Robert Hayden 14:241
Theodore Weiss 14:553

Gibbs, Beverly J.
Juan Carlos Onetti 10:374

Gibbs, Robert
Margaret Avison 2:29
Ronald G. Everson 27:134

Gibbs, Vernon
Jimmy Cliff 21:62

Gibbs, Wolcott
Robert Anderson 23:29
Sally Benson 17:50
Garson Kanin 22:229
Emlyn Williams 15:576

Gibian, George
Varlam Shalamov 18:478
Aleksandr I. Solzhenitsyn 7:447

Gibson, Arthur
Ingmar Bergman 16:62

Gibson, Donald B.
James Baldwin 3:32
Imamu Amiri Baraka 5:46
Ralph Ellison 3:143
Langston Hughes 5:19
Jean Toomer 13:551

Gibson, Kenneth
Roch Carrier 13:143

Gibson, Margaret
Judith Wright 11:578

Gibson, Morgan
Kenneth Rexroth 22:343

Gibson, Shirley Mann
Marie-Claire Blais 22:59

Giddings, Paula
Nikki Giovanni 19:191
Margaret Walker 1:351

Giddins, Gary
James M. Cain 28:53
Elias Canetti 25:114

Gide, André
Hermann Hesse 11:270
Pär Lagerkvist 7:199

Gidley, Mick
William Faulkner 3:156

Gies, Judith
Frederick Busch 18:86
Francine du Plessix Gray
  22:201
Susan Fromberg Schaeffer
  22:368

Gifford, Henry
Joseph Brodsky 13:117
Marianne Moore 4:361

Gifford, Thomas
Stephen King 26:240

Gilbert, Elliot L.
Leonard Michaels 25:315

Gilbert, Harriett
Ntozake Shange 25:397

Gilbert, Sandra M.
Maya Angelou 12:13
Jean Garrigue 8:239
Sandra Hochman 8:297
Diane Johnson 5:200
Kenneth Koch 8:323
Eleanor Lerman 9:329
Audre Lorde 18:308
Sylvia Plath 17:361
Anne Sexton 4:484
Kathleen Spivack 6:521
Diane Wakoski 9:554

Gilbert, W. Stephen
Peter Handke 5:163
Richard O'Brien 17:322, 324
J. B. Priestley 5:350
David Storey 5:416

Gilbert, Zack
Leon Forrest 4:164

Gilder, Joshua
Dee Brown 18:71
Jerzy Kosinski 15:316
Alberto Moravia 27:356

Gilder, Rosamond
Garson Kanin 22:229
Clifford Odets 28:330

Giles, Dennis
Jean-Luc Godard 20:151

Giles, James R.
Richard Wright 21:452

Giles, Mary E.
Juan Goytisolo 10:243

Gilkes, Michael
Wilson Harris 25:210, 211, 218

Gill, Brendan
Edward Albee 5:12; 25:36
Alan Ayckbourn 5:36; 8:34;
  18:29
John Bishop 10:54
Anne Burr 6:104
D. L. Coburn 10:107
Noel Coward 9:172, 173
James Gould Cozzens 11:126
Michael Cristofer 28:96
Christopher Durang 27:93
Athol Fugard 5:174, 178
Ernest K. Gann 23:165
Larry Gelbart 21:128
William Gibson 23:180
Charles Gordone 1:125
John Guare 14:221
Bill Gunn 5:152
Lorraine Hansberry 17:189
Lillian Hellman 18:227
Beth Henley 23:216
John Hopkins 4:233
Preston Jones 10:296
Jean Kerr 22:259
James Kirkwood 9:319
Pavel Kohout 13:323
Ira Levin 6:306
David Mamet 9:360
Terrence McNally 7:219
Mark Medoff 23:293
Arthur Miller 6:334
Peter Nichols 5:307
Clifford Odets 2:319
John O'Hara 6:385
Dorothy Parker 15:414
Harold Pinter 15:425
Roman Polanski 16:464
Gerome Ragni and James Rado
  17:388
Ronald Ribman 7:358
William Saroyan 8:468
Murray Schisgal 6:490
Peter Shaffer 5:386
Sam Shepard 17:437
Martin Sherman 19:416
Neil Simon 6:505; 11:495
Isaac Bashevis Singer 15:509
Elizabeth Spencer 22:399
John Steinbeck 5:408
Tom Stoppard 4:526; 5:413;
  8:504; 15:521
David Storey 2:424
C. P. Taylor 27:446
Lily Tomlin 17:518
Gore Vidal 2:449
Andy Warhol 20:419
Tennessee Williams 5:503;
  8:548
Lanford Wilson 7:547
Robert Wilson 7:550

Gill, Richard T.
Frank O'Connor 23:325

Gillen, Francis
Donald Barthelme 2:40

Gillespie, Beryl C.
  Barbara Corcoran 17:78

Gillespie, John
  Kin Platt 26:350

Gillespie, John T.
  Frank Bonham 12:51, 55
  Alice Childress 12:107

Gillespie, Robert
  Eric Ambler 6:2
  Jorge Luis Borges 6:91
  John le Carré 9:326

Gillett, Charlie
  Jimmy Cliff 21:60

Gillett, John
  Kon Ichikawa 20:178, 180
  Fritz Lang 20:209
  Yasujiro Ozu 16:446
  Satyajit Ray 16:477
  Josef von Sternberg 20:374
  Billy Wilder 20:458

Gilliatt, Penelope
  Woody Allen 16:2, 7
  Robert Altman 16:30
  Ralph Bakshi 26:70
  Samuel Beckett 4:49
  Claude Chabrol 16:179
  Shirley Clarke 16:216
  Noel Coward 9:172
  Brian De Palma 20:76
  Rainer Werner Fassbinder
    20:108, 112, 114, 115
  Jean-Luc Godard 20:141
  Werner Herzog 16:326
  John Huston 20:173
  Buster Keaton 20:195
  John Landis 26:272
  Richard Lester 20:230
  Monty Python 21:224
  Joe Orton 4:387
  Roman Polanski 16:472
  Satyajit Ray 16:487
  Ken Russell 16:550
  Carlos Saura 20:317
  Melvin Van Peebles 20:409, 412
  Lina Wertmüller 16:589, 595
  Vassily S. Yanovsky 18:550

Gillis, William
  Friedrich Dürrenmatt 11:170

Gilman, Harvey
  Howard Nemerov 6:362

Gilman, Richard
  Richard Adams 4:7
  Edward Albee 5:10
  John Arden 6:6
  James Baldwin 15:41; 17:35, 44
  Imamu Amiri Baraka 5:44
  Donald Barthelme 2:40
  Saul Bellow 6:49
  Heinrich Böll 27:67
  J. P. Donleavy 6:140
  Bruce Jay Friedman 5:126
  Carlos Fuentes 22:163
  William H. Gass 2:154
  Jack Gelber 1:114; 6:196
  Graham Greene 6:214
  Rolf Hochhuth 11:274

Eugène Ionesco 6:249
  Kenneth Koch 5:218
  Norman Mailer 2:260; 8:367
  Bernard Malamud 18:320
  William Maxwell 19:307
  Michael McClure 10:331
  Arthur Miller 6:326, 327
  Marsha Norman 28:320
  Sean O'Casey 5:319
  Walker Percy 18:399
  Harold Pinter 6:405, 406, 410
  Reynolds Price 6:424
  John Rechy 7:356
  Philip Roth 3:438; 22:358
  Howard Sackler 14:478
  Irwin Shaw 23:398
  Robert Shaw 5:390
  Neil Simon 6:502
  George Steiner 24:425
  John Updike 2:440
  Tennessee Williams 5:499
  Edmund Wilson 24:478
  Richard Wright 21:440

Gilmore, Mikal
  Bob Marley 17:269, 270
  Lou Reed 21:316, 320
  Bruce Springsteen 17:486
  Stevie Wonder 12:660

Gilroy, Harry
  Frank B. Gilbreth, Jr. and
    Ernestine Gilbreth Carey
    17:153
  Thor Heyerdahl 26:189

Gilsdorf, Jeanette
  Robert Creeley 4:118

Gindin, James
  Kingsley Amis 2:4
  Saul Bellow 3:54
  Truman Capote 3:100
  Margaret Drabble 10:165
  E. M. Forster 3:160
  John Fowles 10:189
  William Golding 2:165; 3:198
  Rosamond Lehmann 5:238
  Doris Lessing 2:238; 22:278
  Iris Murdoch 2:295; 3:347
  John Osborne 2:327
  Philip Roth 3:436
  Alan Sillitoe 3:447, 448
  David Storey 2:423; 4:528
  John Wain 2:457
  Angus Wilson 2:470; 3:534

Gingell, S.
  William Mitchell 25:325

Gingher, Robert S.
  John Updike 5:454

Gingrich, Arnold
  Chester Himes 2:196

Ginsberg, Allen
  Gregory Corso 11:123
  Jack Kerouac 2:228; 14:306
  Ezra Pound 18:420

Gioia, Dana
  John Ashbery 25:56
  Margaret Atwood 25:69
  Maxine Kumin 28:225
  Frederick Morgan 23:301
  Katha Pollitt 28:368

Giovanni, Nikki
  Virginia Hamilton 26:149
  Alice Walker 5:476

Gipson, Carolyn
  W.E.B. Du Bois 2:120

Girson, Rochelle
  Peter S. Beagle 7:25

Gish, Robert F.
  A. B. Guthrie, Jr. 23:200

Gitlin, Todd
  James Baldwin 2:32
  Robert Bly 2:66
  Bob Dylan 4:150
  Paul Goodman 7:130
  Denise Levertov 2:243
  Marge Piercy 3:383

Gitzen, Julian
  Robert Bly 10:56
  Seamus Heaney 5:172
  Ted Hughes 4:237
  Denise Levertov 5:250
  Peter Redgrove 6:446
  R. S. Thomas 6:531
  Charles Tomlinson 2:437; 4:548
  Ted Walker 13:566

Giuliano, William
  Antonio Buero Vallejo 15:98

Givner, Joan
  Katherine Anne Porter 7:319;
    10:398; 13:450; 15:432
  Eudora Welty 5:479

Glaessner, Verina
  François Truffaut 20:404

Glassco, John
  Jane Rule 27:418

Glasser, William
  J. D. Salinger 8:464

Glassman, Peter
  Shirley Ann Grau 9:240
  R. G. Vliet 22:441

Glastonbury, Marion
  Lynne Reid Banks 23:43
  John Gregory Dunne 28:128
  Russell C. Hoban 25:264
  Thomas Keneally 27:233
  Martin Walser 27:467

Glatstein, Jacob
  Marianne Moore 4:358

Glauber, Robert H.
  Mary Oliver 19:361

Gleason, George
  Sonia Levitin 17:266
  Robert Newton Peck 17:342

Gleason, Judith
  Aimé Césaire 19:95

Gleason, Judith Illsley
  Chinua Achebe 7:3

Gleason, Ralph J.
  Nelson Algren 10:7
  Lenny Bruce 21:43
  Bob Dylan 6:156; 12:181
  Martin Mull 17:299
  Paul Simon 17:459

Gleicher, David
  Margaret Atwood 3:19

Glen, Duncan
  Hugh MacDiarmid 4:311

Glendinning, Victoria
  Margaret Atwood 15:38
  Elizabeth Bowen 22:64
  Melvyn Bragg 10:72
  Anthony Burgess 5:87
  Angela Carter 5:101
  Bruce Chatwin 28:72
  Roald Dahl 6:122
  Anita Desai 19:134
  Penelope Fitzgerald 19:173
  Thomas Flanagan 25:164
  Doris Grumbach 13:258
  James Hanley 13:262
  Chester Himes 7:159
  Russell C. Hoban 7:160; 25:264
  Ursula Holden 18:258
  Elizabeth Jane Howard 7:164
  Alison Lurie 18:310
  Olivia Manning 19:303
  Joyce Carol Oates 11:404
  Edna O'Brien 13:416
  Barbara Pym 13:471
  Jane Rule 27:418
  Françoise Sagan 9:468
  Alan Sillitoe 6:500
  Stevie Smith 25:420
  J.I.M. Stewart 7:466
  Fay Weldon 11:565
  Eudora Welty 14:565

Glenn, Jerry
  Paul Celan 10:102, 104; 19:89

Glenn, Jules
  Anthony Shaffer 19:414

Glick, William
  Walter Farley 17:115

Glicksberg, Charles I.
  Arthur Adamov 4:6
  Kenneth Burke 24:119
  Albert Camus 1:52
  Jean Genet 5:136
  Hermann Hesse 3:244
  Aldous Huxley 3:254
  Eugène Ionesco 9:288; 11:290
  Robinson Jeffers 3:260
  Joseph Wood Krutch 24:281
  André Malraux 1:201
  Kenneth Patchen 18:392
  Edmund Wilson 24:464

Glimm, James York
  Thomas Merton 3:337; 11:372

Gloster, Hugh M.
  Arna Bontemps 18:63
  Jessie Redmon Fauset 19:170
  Frank G. Yerby 22:487

Glover, Al
  Michael McClure 6:320

Glover, Elaine
  John Fowles 6:188
  Nadine Gordimer 7:131
  Joseph Heller 8:279
  Tim O'Brien 7:271

Glover, Tony
Chuck Berry 17:53
Waylon Jennings 21:202
Patti Smith 12:534

Glover, Willis B.
J.R.R. Tolkien 1:340

Goatley, James L.
Roy A. Gallant 17:132

Gobeil, Madeleine
Marie-Claire Blais 22:60

Godard, B.
Audrey Thomas 13:540

Goddard, Donald
Lothar-Günther Buchheim 6:102

Goddard, Rosalind K.
Milton Meltzer 26:301

Godden, Rumer
Carson McCullers 12:418

Godfrey, Dave
Joan Barfoot 18:35
Hugh MacLennan 14:343

Godshalk, William L.
Kurt Vonnegut, Jr. 3:500

Godwin, Gail
Beryl Bainbridge 5:39
Ann Beattie 13:64
Julien Green 3:205
Doris Grumbach 13:258
Shirley Hazzard 18:220
Vassily S. Yanovsky 18:552

Goetz, Ronald
Larry Gelbart 21:128

Goetz-Stankiewicz, Marketa
Václav Havel 25:225, 229

Going, William T.
T. S. Stribling 23:448

Goitein, Denise
Nathalie Sarraute 10:457

Gold, Herbert
Mel Brooks 12:78
Richard Condon 10:111
John Dos Passos 4:136
Doris Grumbach 22:205
Alistair MacLean 13:364
James Purdy 28:376
Aleksandr I. Solzhenitsyn 2:409
Terry Southern 7:454
Gore Vidal 6:550

Gold, Ivan
R. V. Cassill 23:106
John Ehle 27:107
Shusaku Endo 14:162
George V. Higgins 10:273
Paul Horgan 9:279
Jerzy Kosinski 15:316
Frederic Raphael 14:437
Susan Fromberg Schaeffer 22:369
Robert Stone 23:424
John Updike 2:440
John A. Williams 13:599
Helen Yglesias 7:558

Gold, Pat
Taylor Caldwell 28:68

Gold, Peter
José María Arguedas 18:5

Gold, Renee
Marge Piercy 27:378

Goldberg, Steven
Bob Dylan 6:154

Goldberg, Vicki
Paul Theroux 11:530

Golden, Robert E.
Thomas Pynchon 3:409

Goldensohn, Lorrie
Ben Belitt 22:54
Ira Sadoff 9:466
Maura Stanton 9:508

Goldfarb, Clare R.
Aleksandr I. Solzhenitsyn 7:443

Goldhurst, William
John Steinbeck 21:378

Goldknopf, David
Kurt Vonnegut, Jr. 12:600

Goldman, Albert
Lenny Bruce 21:45, 53
Bob Dylan 3:130; 12:186
John Lennon and Paul McCartney 12:367

Goldman, Eric F.
John Steinbeck 21:370
Dalton Trumbo 19:445

Goldman, Mark
Bernard Malamud 1:197

Goldman, Merle
Jules Archer 12:19

Goldman, Michael
Joyce Carol Oates 3:361

Goldman, Vivien
Jimmy Cliff 21:64

Goldman, William
Ross Macdonald 1:185

Goldmann, Lucien
Witold Gombrowicz 11:239
Georg Lukács 24:324

Goldsmith, Arnold L.
Leslie A. Fiedler 24:203
John Steinbeck 9:515

Goldsmith, Claire K.
Alvin Silverstein and Virginia B. Silverstein 17:455

Goldsmith, David H.
Kurt Vonnegut, Jr. 4:562

Goldstein, Eric
Susan Cheever 18:102

Goldstein, Laurence
Robert Frost 13:230
David Ignatow 4:248
Adrienne Rich 7:372
James Wright 3:541

Goldstein, Malcolm
Thornton Wilder 1:365

Goldstein, Marilyn
Milton Meltzer 26:298

Goldstein, Patrick
Elvis Costello 21:69

Goldstein, Richard
Bob Dylan 3:130; 12:182
John Lennon and Paul McCartney 12:357
Edmund White III 27:480

Goldstein, Toby
Jonathan Kozol 17:252
Jim Morrison 17:294

Goldstone, Richard H.
Thornton Wilder 6:574

Goldwasser, Noë
Smokey Robinson 21:345

Golffing, Francis
Salvatore Quasimodo 10:429

Gomez, Joseph A.
Ken Russell 16:550

Gömöri, George
Tadeusz Konwicki 28:207
László Nagy 7:251

Goodfriend, James
Laura Nyro 17:314

Goodheart, Eugene
F. R. Leavis 24:311
Cynthia Ozick 3:372
Theodore Roethke 1:292
John Seelye 7:405
William Carlos Williams 5:510

Goodman, Charlotte
Joyce Carol Oates 15:400

Goodman, Ellen
Maureen Daly 17:91

Goodman, Henry
Elia Kazan 16:367

Goodman, James
George Seferis 5:385

Goodman, Jan M.
Lois Duncan 26:107

Goodman, Lord
John Mortimer 28:288

Goodman, Paul
James Baldwin 17:23
Ernest Hemingway 1:144

Goodman, Robert L.
David Kherdian 6:280

Goodman, Walter
Thomas Berger 8:83

Goodrich, Norma L.
Jean Giono 4:187; 11:230

Goodrick, Susan
Robert Crumb 17:86

Goodsell, James Nelson
Jules Archer 12:18
Allan W. Eckert 17:106, 107
Piri Thomas 17:498

Goodstein, Jack
Alain Robbe-Grillet 2:376

Goodwin, Michael
Chuck Berry 17:51
John Brunner 10:80
Samuel R. Delany 14:143
Joanna Russ 15:461
Andy Warhol 20:420

Goodwin, Polly
Honor Arundel 17:12
Eilís Dillon 17:94
James D. Forman 21:117
Lee Kingman 17:245
Emily Cheney Neville 12:450

Goodwin, Stephen
Eleanor Clark 19:108
Ella Leffland 19:280
Leonard Michaels 25:317
Walker Percy 2:335
Peter Taylor 1:334
John Kennedy Toole 19:442

Goodwyn, Larry
Larry McMurtry 27:328

Gordimer, Nadine
Chinua Achebe 3:2
Simone de Beauvoir 14:67
V. S. Naipaul 4:372
James Ngugi 3:358
Alan Paton 25:359, 362

Gordon, Andrew
Ishmael Reed 2:368

Gordon, Caroline
Flannery O'Connor 15:411; 21:255

Gordon, Cecelia
Ruth M. Arthur 12:27

Gordon, David
Margaret Drabble 22:121

Gordon, David J.
Herbert Gold 4:192
William Golding 1:122
Uwe Johnson 5:200
Maxine Kumin 28:221
Brian Moore 1:225
Vladimir Nabokov 1:245
Tom Stoppard 1:328

Gordon, Jan B.
Richard Adams 5:4
John Braine 3:86
Doris Lessing 6:292
Iris Murdoch 3:349

Gordon, Lenore
Sandra Scoppettone 26:402

Gordon, Leonore
Norma Fox Mazer 26:293

Gordon, Lois
Donald Barthelme 23:49
Arthur Miller 26:322

Gordon, Mary
Diane Johnson 13:306
Maxine Hong Kingston 19:249
Mary McCarthy 14:359
Edna O'Brien 13:416
Walker Percy 18:401
David Plante 23:346

Gorman, Herbert
Taylor Caldwell 28:57

Gornick, Vivian
Paula Fox 2:140
Nadine Gordimer 18:190
Doris Grumbach 22:205
Lillian Hellman 8:282; 18:227
Jonathan Kozol 17:253
Alberto Moravia 18:347
Grace Paley 4:391
Marge Piercy 18:407
Anne Tyler 28:432
Gregor von Rezzori 25:384
Helen Yglesias 22:494

Gose, Elliot
Marie-Claire Blais 13:96
Gwendolyn MacEwan 13:357

Goskowski, Francis
Rosa Guy 26:146

Gossett, Louise Y.
William Goyen 14:209
Flannery O'Connor 1:256

Gossman, Ann
Lawrence Durrell 1:87
Iris Murdoch 15:387

Gostnell, David
Alvin Silverstein and Virginia B. Silverstein 17:456

Gott, Richard
Carlos Castaneda 12:86

Gottfried, Martin
Enid Bagnold 25:78
Gretchen Cryer 21:79
Charles Fuller 25:180
William Gibson 23:179
John Guare 14:222
Lorraine Hansberry 17:189
Jean Kerr 22:257
Bernard Pomerance 13:445
Howard Sackler 14:479
Ntozake Shange 25:396
Sam Shepard 17:436
George Tabori 19:438
Andrew Lloyd Webber and Tim Rice 21:425, 431
Lanford Wilson 7:547

Gottlieb, Annie
Maya Angelou 12:11
Henry Bromell 5:74
Louis-Ferdinand Céline 4:104
Lois Gould 10:241
Nat Hentoff 26:186
Charles Johnson 7:183
Joyce Maynard 23:288
Gloria Naylor 28:305
Tillie Olsen 4:386
Sandra Scoppettone 26:401, 404
Lee Smith 25:408

Gottlieb, Elaine
Isaac Bashevis Singer 6:507

Gottlieb, Gerald
John R. Tunis 12:599
Maia Wojciechowska 26:452

Gottschalk, Jane
Ralph Ellison 11:181

Gould, Gerald
Edna Ferber 18:150

Gould, Jack
John Lennon and Paul McCartney 12:354

Gould, Jean
Elmer Rice 7:363

Gould, Lois
Paddy Chayefsky 23:119

Goulianos, Joan Rodman
Lawrence Durrell 8:193

Gow, Gordon
Lindsay Anderson 20:18
Michelangelo Antonioni 20:40
John Cassavetes 20:45
Claude Chabrol 16:170
René Clair 20:66
Vittorio De Sica 20:88, 91
Bob Fosse 20:125
George Roy Hill 26:200, 204
Alfred Hitchcock 16:353
John Huston 20:168
Elia Kazan 16:374
Nagisa Oshima 20:246
Sidney Poitier 26:358
Satyajit Ray 16:479
Alain Resnais 16:510
Ken Russell 16:542, 543
Jerzy Skolimowski 20:352
Steven Spielberg 20:359
C. P. Taylor 27:442
Agnès Varda 16:555
Peter Weir 20:428
Orson Welles 20:439, 452

Gower, Herschel
Peter Taylor 18:525

Goyen, William
Truman Capote 19:81
Anaïs Nin 4:379

Goytisolo, Juan
Carlos Fuentes 10:204

Grace, Sherrill
Margaret Atwood 25:64

Grady, Wayne
Matt Cohen 19:116
Farley Mowat 26:347

Graff, Gerald
Geoffrey H. Hartman 27:185

Graff, Gerald E.
Donald Barthelme 6:30
Saul Bellow 6:54
Stanley Elkin 6:169
Norman Mailer 8:372
I. A. Richards 24:394

Graham, Desmond
Jorge Luis Borges 8:103
Breyten Breytenbach 23:84
James Hanley 13:262
Anthony Hecht 13:269
Philip Larkin 5:229
Robert Lowell 11:329
John Montague 13:392
Eugenio Montale 9:388
Linda Pastan 27:370
Peter Porter 13:453

Graham, John
John Hawkes 3:221
Ernest Hemingway 3:236
Gibbons Ruark 3:441

Graham, Kenneth
Richard Adams 5:5
Pamela Hansford Johnson 27:221
Laurens Van der Post 5:463

Graham, Maryemma
Frank G. Yerby 22:491

Graham-Yooll, Andrew
Gabriel García Márquez 15:253

Grahn, Judy
Alta 19:19

Granahan, Paul
Gene Wolfe 25:477

Grande, Brother Luke M., F.S.C.
Marion Montgomery 7:232

Granetz, Marc
Donald Barthelme 13:61
John Gardner 18:183

Granfield, Linda
Kevin Major 26:286

Grange, Joseph
Carlos Castaneda 12:86

Grant, Annette
Shirley Ann Grau 4:209
Edward Hoagland 28:180

Grant, Damian
W. H. Auden 6:17
Seamus Heaney 5:172
Sylvia Plath 2:337
Peter Porter 5:347

Grant, Judith Skelton
Robertson Davies 13:173

Grant, Patrick
Robert Graves 11:257

Grant, Steve
C. P. Taylor 27:441

Grau, Shirley Ann
William Goyen 8:250
Marion Montgomery 7:233

Grave, Elizabeth F.
Franklyn M. Branley 21:16

Graver, Lawrence
Samuel Beckett 6:40
Doris Lessing 2:242
Carson McCullers 1:209
Iris Murdoch 3:347
Gilbert Sorrentino 22:392
Muriel Spark 2:417
Paul Theroux 8:513
William Trevor 7:475

Graves, Elizabeth Minot
Lee Kingman 17:246
Sonia Levitin 17:263
Zilpha Keatley Snyder 17:471

Graves, Peter
Jurek Becker 19:36
Christa Wolf 14:595

Graves, Peter J.
Friedrich Dürrenmatt 15:196

Graves, Robert
Robert Frost 26:121
Yevgeny Yevtushenko 1:382

Grawe, Christian
Botho Strauss 22:407

Gray, Francine du Plessix
Oriana Fallaci 11:190
Max Frisch 14:184
Mary Gordon 22:184

Gray, Hildagarde
Gunnel Beckman 26:89
Lois Duncan 26:105
Norma Fox Mazer 26:289
Katherine Paterson 12:485

Gray, J. Glenn
Martin Heidegger 24:263

Gray, James
Pearl S. Buck 7:32
Jules Roains 7:381
Henri Troyat 23:459

Gray, John
Paul Bowles 2:79

Gray, Mrs. John G.
Jules Archer 12:20
M. E. Kerr 12:298

Gray, Larry
John Knowles 26:262

Gray, Paul
Lisa Alther 7:12
Roger Angell 26:30
Samuel Beckett 6:44
Adolfo Bioy Casares 8:94
Vance Bourjaily 8:104
Jimmy Breslin 4:76
William F. Buckley, Jr. 7:35
Alex Comfort 7:54
Evan S. Connell, Jr. 6:116
Peter De Vries 7:78
Thomas M. Disch 7:86
Carolyn Forché 25:170
John Gardner 5:132
William H. Gass 8:246
Russell C. Hoban 7:160
Maureen Howard 5:189
Elia Kazan 6:274
William Kennedy 28:206
Stephen King 26:242
Maxine Hong Kingston 12:312
Norman Mailer 28:259
Bernard Malamud 27:307
Peter Matthiessen 5:274
Ted Mooney 25:329
V. S. Naipaul 7:253
Seán O'Faoláin 7:274
Cynthia Ozick 7:288
Reynolds Price 6:425
Gregor von Rezzori 25:385
Marilynne Robinson 25:386
Robert Stone 5:409
John Updike 5:457
Sylvia Townsend Warner 19:459
James Welch 6:561
Fay Weldon 6:562

Gray, Paul Edward
Eleanor Clark 19:106
John Fowles 1:109
Iris Murdoch 1:236
Joyce Carol Oates 1:251
Eudora Welty 1:363

Gray, Richard
Erskine Caldwell 14:96
Donald Davidson 19:124
William Faulkner 11:202
Carson McCullers 12:430
John Crowe Ransom 11:469
William Styron 11:520
Tennessee Williams 11:577

Gray, Ronald
Heinrich Böll 9:112

Grayden, Robin
Waylon Jennings 21:204
Kris Kristofferson 26:270

Greacen, Robert
W. H. Auden 3:25
Samuel Beckett 4:50
Margaret Drabble 2:117
Bernard Kops 4:274
Doris Lessing 3:287
Harold Robbins 5:378
Isaac Bashevis Singer 3:457
Vassilis Vassilikos 4:551

Grealish, Gerald
Gilbert Sorrentino 14:498

Grebanier, Bernard
Thornton Wilder 1:365

Grebstein, Sheldon Norman
Ernest Hemingway 3:235
Bernard Malamud 11:348
John O'Hara 1:261

Greco, Mike
Ralph Bakshi 26:75

Greeley, Andrew M.
Richard Bach 14:36
William X. Kienzle 25:276
Francine du Plessix Gray 22:199

Green, Alan
Peter De Vries 3:126
Michael Frayn 3:164

Green, Benny
John Fowles 6:186
Compton Mackenzie 18:316
Brian Moore 7:238
V. S. Naipaul 18:359
John O'Hara 6:383
S. J. Perelman 15:417
Charles M. Schulz 12:533
Noel Streatfeild 21:417

Green, Calvin
Pier Paolo Pasolini 20:264
Eric Rohmer 16:529

Green, Gerald
Thomas Berger 3:63

Green, Harris
Jim Jacobs and Warren Casey 12:293

Green, James L.
John Hawkes 14:237

Green, Jim
Ray Davies 21:103

Green, Kate
Anne Sexton 15:473

Green, Laurence
Joan Micklin Silver 20:342

Green, Marc
Robert Altman 16:43

Green, Martin
E. L. Doctorow 6:138
B. S. Johnson 6:263
Doris Lessing 15:333
Philip Roth 15:449
J. D. Salinger 1:298

Green, Michelle
Joyce Maynard 23:289

Green, Paul
Eric Bentley 24:47

Green, Peter
William Golding 17:162
R. K. Narayan 28:301
Gore Vidal 22:433

Green, Philip
E. E. Cummings 12:147

Green, Randall
John Hawkes 4:217
Aleksandr I. Solzhenitsyn 4:512

Green, Robert J.
Roch Carrier 13:141
Athol Fugard 9:233

Green, Robin
Stan Lee 17:257

Green, Roger Lancelyn
Alan Garner 17:135

Green, Roland
Isaac Asimov 26:58
Roger Zelazny 21:478

Green, Timothy
W. H. Auden 14:27

Greenberg, Joanne
Colleen McCullough 27:321

Greenberg, Judith L.
Patrick Modiano 18:338

Greenberg, Martin
Reiner Kunze 10:310

Greenberg, Martin Harry
Robert A. Heinlein 26:170

Greenblatt, Stephen Jay
Evelyn Waugh 13:585

Greene, Daniel
Don L. Lee 2:237

Greene, Daniel St. Albin
William Kennedy 28:203

Greene, Douglas G.
Edmund Crispin 22:111

Greene, George
Paul West 7:522

Greene, Graham
Sally Benson 17:47
Frank Capra 16:154, 155
R. K. Narayan 28:299

Greene, James
Eugenio Montale 9:388

Greene, Robert W.
René Char 14:124
Francis Ponge 18:417
Raymond Queneau 10:430

Greenfeld, Josh
Emily Cheney Neville 12:451
Philip Roth 2:378
Paul Zindel 6:586

Greenfield, Jeff
Jonathan Kozol 17:255
John Lennon and Paul McCartney 12:378
Dan Wakefield 7:503

Greenlaw, M. Jean
John Knowles 26:265

Greenman, Myron
Donald Barthelme 6:29

Greenspan, Miriam
Maxine Hong Kingston 12:313

Greenspun, Roger
Bernardo Bertolucci 16:94
Brian De Palma 20:74
Marguerite Duras 20:98
Federico Fellini 16:283
Bob Fosse 20:122
Alfred Hitchcock 16:354
Akira Kurosawa 16:404
Fritz Lang 20:211
Jean Renoir 20:303
Carlos Saura 20:314, 315
Jerzy Skolimowski 20:349, 353
Melvin Van Peebles 20:411

Greenstein, Michael
Dorothy Livesay 15:342

Greenway, John
Norman Mailer 2:262
Joseph Wambaugh 18:532

Greenwell, Bill
John Cheever 25:122
Bette Pesetsky 28:358

Greenwell, Scott L.
Mari Sandoz 28:405

Greenya, John R.
Ronald L. Fair 18:139
Budd Schulberg 7:403

Greggs, R.
Robert Westall 17:559

Gregor, Ian
William Golding 27:165
Graham Greene 6:214

Gregor, Ulrich
Leni Riefenstahl 16:521

Gregory, Charles
Robert Altman 16:27

Gregory, Helen
Betty Cavanna 12:103

Gregory, Hilda
Joyce Carol Oates 1:251; 2:315
Mark Strand 6:522
Nancy Willard 7:540

Gregory, Horace
Morley Callaghan 14:99
Laura Riding 7:373

Greider, William
William Safire 10:447

Greiling, Franziska Lynne
John Knowles 26:256

Greiner, Donald J.
Djuna Barnes 8:48
Frederick Busch 10:91
Robert Frost 26:127
John Hawkes 1:138; 4:213; 7:145; 27:192
John Updike 23:472
Kurt Vonnegut, Jr. 3:499

Grella, George
Ian Fleming 3:158
Dashiell Hammett 19:197

Grene, Marjorie
Jacques Derrida 24:135
Martin Heidegger 24:270

Grenier, Cynthia
Satyajit Ray 16:476

Gresham, William Lindsay
Edward Hoagland 28:179

Gretlund, Jan Nordby
Katherine Anne Porter 27:402

Grier, Edward F.
Jonathan Williams 13:600

Griffin, Bryan
John Irving 13:27

Griffin, Robert J.
Cid Corman 9:169

Griffith, Albert J.
Carson McCullers 1:209
Peter Taylor 1:334; 4:542; 18:526
John Updike 5:455

Grigsby, Gordon K.
Kenneth Rexroth 1:284

Grigsby John L.
Frank Herbert 23:222

Grigson, Geoffrey
G. B. Edwards 25:152
Yasunari Kawabata 18:280
Robert Lowell 3:302
Kathleen Raine 7:351
George Steiner 24:431

Grimes, Ann
Joyce Maynard 23:289

Grimwood, Michael
William Faulkner 14:174

Griswold, Jerry
Ken Kesey 3:268

Groberg, Nancy
Mark Harris 19:199

Groden, Michael
William Faulkner 9:198

Gropper, Esther C.
Hermann Hesse 2:189; 3:244

Grosholz, Emily
Richard F. Hugo 18:264
Mary Oliver 19:363
Dave Smith 22:388

Gross, Amy
Lily Tomlin 17:516

Gross, Barry
Arthur Miller 10:344

Gross, Beverly
John Barth 14:49
Jonathan Baumbach 6:32
Saul Bellow 2:52
B. H. Friedman 7:109
Peter Spielberg 6:514

Gross, Harvey
T. S. Eliot 6:161
André Malraux 4:335
Ezra Pound 4:414

Gross, John
V. S. Pritchett 15:441
George Steiner 24:426

Gross, Leonard
Michael Cristofer 28:97

Gross, Michael
David Bowie 17:62

Gross, Theodore L.
J. D. Salinger 1:300

Grosskurth, Phyllis
Margaret Atwood 2:20
Mary McCarthy 24:349
Gabrielle Roy 14:463

Grossman, Edward
Simone de Beauvoir 2:44
Saul Bellow 8:80
Thomas Berger 3:63
Heinrich Böll 3:75
Joseph Heller 5:181
Doris Lessing 3:287
Vladimir Nabokov 3:355
Kurt Vonnegut, Jr. 5:466

Grossman, Jan
Václav Havel 25:219

Grossman, Joel
Philip Roth 9:459

Grossman, Loyd
Peter Townshend 17:536

Grossman, William L.
João Guimarães Rosa 23:349

Grossvogel, David I.
Agatha Christie 12:127
Julio Cortázar 10:112
Jean Genet 14:196

Groth, Janet
John Cheever 8:136

Groves, Margaret
Nathalie Sarraute 4:470

Grumbach, Doris
Maya Angelou 12:12
Simone de Beauvoir 4:49
Kay Boyle 5:66
Frederick Busch 18:85
Hortense Calisher 8:124
R. V. Cassill 23:109
Arthur A. Cohen 7:50
Joan Didion 8:175
E. L. Doctorow 6:131
Daphne du Maurier 11:164

Stanley Elkin 4:154; 14:158
Leslie A. Fiedler 13:214
Nadine Gordimer 18:188
Francine du Plessix Gray 22:201
Susan B. Hill 4:288
Maureen Howard 5:188
Ward S. Just 27:228
Garson Kanin 22:232
Alison Lurie 4:307
Cormac McCarthy 4:342
Mary McCarthy 5:276
A. G. Mojtabai 9:385
Brian Moore 5:297
Penelope Mortimer 5:299
Tim O'Brien 19:357
Julia O'Faolain 6:383
Aldo Palazzeschi 11:431
Bette Pesetsky 28:359
Jayne Anne Phillips 15:421
Judith Rossner 9:457
J. R. Salamanca 4:461
May Sarton 4:471; 14:480
Clancy Sigal 7:425
Henri Troyat 23:458
Anne Tyler 7:479
John Updike 15:546
Nancy Willard 7:538, 539
Hilma Wolitzer 17:561, 564
Helen Yglesias 22:492
Sol Yurick 6:584

Grunfeld, Frederick V.
John Lennon and Paul McCartney 12:361

Grunwald, Beverly
Maureen Daly 17:90

Gubar, Susan
H. D. 14:225

Gubbins, Bill
Brian Wilson 12:648

Guerard, Albert, Jr.
C. S. Lewis 27:259

Guerard, Albert J.
Donald Barthelme 5:53
Jerome Charyn 5:103
John Hawkes 2:183; 3:222; 15:278; 27:190

Guereschi, Edward
Joyce Carol Oates 15:403

Guernsey, Otis L., Jr.
Sally Benson 17:49

Guerrard, Philip
Mervyn Peake 7:301

Guggenheim, Michel
Françoise Sagan 17:421

Guicharnaud, Jacques
Arthur Adamov 25:13
Fernando Arrabal 18:16
Michel de Ghelderode 11:226
Eugène Ionesco 6:254
Henri de Montherlant 19:326
Jean-Paul Sartre 1:304
Claude Simon 15:485

Guicharnaud, June
Michel de Ghelderode 11:226

Guidry, Frederick H.
Thor Heyerdahl 26:193

Guild, Nicholas
Paul Theroux 11:530
Richard Yates 23:480

Guimond, James
Gilbert Sorrentino 3:461

Guinn, John
Andrew M. Greeley 28:178

Guiton, Margaret Otis
Louis Aragon 3:12
Marcel Aymé 11:21
Albert Camus 1:54
Louis-Ferdinand Céline 1:57
Jean Cocteau 1:59
Georges Duhamel 8:186
Jean Giono 4:183
Julien Green 3:203
André Malraux 1:202
François Mauriac 4:337
Raymond Queneau 2:359
Jules Romains 7:381
Jean-Paul Sartre 1:306

Gullason, Thomas A.
Carson McCullers 4:344
Flannery O'Connor 1:259

Gullette, David
Mark Strand 18:518

Gullon, Agnes
Pablo Neruda 7:260

Gunn, Edward
Djuna Barnes 4:44

Gunn, James
Isaac Asimov 19:29; 26:59, 63
Gene Wolfe 25:474

Gunn, Thom
William Dickey 28:117
Roy Fuller 28:148
Barbara Howes 15:289
David Ignatow 7:173
Donald Justice 19:232
W. S. Merwin 13:383
Christopher Middleton 13:387
Howard Nemerov 9:393
Charles Olson 11:414
Louis Simpson 7:426, 427

Gunston, David
Leni Riefenstahl 16:520

Guralnick, Peter
Waylon Jennings 21:205
Willie Nelson 17:304

Gurewitsch, M. Anatole
William Gaddis 6:195

Gurian, Jay
Thomas Berger 18:55

Gurko, Leo
Ernest Hemingway 6:226
John P. Marquand 10:331
John Steinbeck 21:383
Edward Lewis Wallant 5:477

Gussow, Mel
Ed Bullins 1:47
Michael Cristofer 28:95, 97
Christopher Durang 27:87
Charles Fuller 25:180
Charles Gordone 1:125
Albert Innaurato 21:190, 191, 193
Howard Sackler 14:480
Ntozake Shange 25:399
Sam Shepard 17:438
Elizabeth Swados 12:558

Gustafson, Ralph
Ronald G. Everson 27:134

Gustafson, Richard
Reg Saner 9:469

Gustainis, J. Justin
Stephen King 12:311
Steven Millhauser 21:217
Amos Oz 11:429

Gutcheon, Beth
Doris Betts 28:35
Agnes Eckhardt Nixon 21:245

Gutowski, John A.
Joan Micklin Silver 20:345

Guttenplan, Don David
Arna Bontemps 18:65

Gutteridge, Don
Patrick Lane 25:289

Guy, David
Virginia Hamilton 26:158
David Malouf 28:268

Guzman, Richard R.
Raja Rao 25:370

Gwynn, Frederick L.
J. D. Salinger 1:295

Gysin, Fritz
Jean Toomer 13:552

Gyurko, Lanin A.
Julio Cortázar 5:108; 10:112; 13:159
Carlos Fuentes 22:165

Haas, Diane
Judy Blume 12:46

Haas, Joseph
Bob Dylan 12:180
Jerome Weidman 7:517

Haberl, Franz P.
Max Frisch 9:218; 14:184
Botho Strauss 22:408
Peter Weiss 15:565

Haberland, Jody
Jane Rule 27:417

Hack, Richard
Kenneth Patchen 2:332
Colin Wilson 3:537

Hackett, C. A.
Henri Michaux 19:311

Hackney, Louise Wallace
John Ford 16:303

Hadas, Moses
Mary Renault 17:392
Marguerite Yourcenar 19:481

Hadas, Pamela White
Marianne Moore 10:348

Hadas, Rachel
Yannis Ritsos 13:487
Robert Penn Warren 18:534

Hadgraft, Cecil
David Malouf 28:267

Haenicke, Diether H.
Heinrich Böll 6:83
Paul Celan 10:101
Friedrich Dürrenmatt 8:194
Günter Eich 15:204
Max Frisch 9:217
Günter Grass 6:207
Uwe Johnson 5:201
Reiner Kunze 10:310
Anna Seghers 7:408
Martin Walser 27:460
Carl Zuckmayer 18:553

Haffenden, John
John Berryman 10:45
Robert Lowell 11:330

Haft, Cynthia
Aleksandr I. Solzhenitsyn 7:435

Hafter, Ronald
René Wellek 28:448

Hagan, Candace
Philip Roth 15:453

Hagan, Patti
Barbara Corcoran 17:73

Haglin, Donna
Henry Gregor Felsen 17:123

Hagopian, John V.
James Baldwin 1:15
William Faulkner 3:157
J. F. Powers 1:282

Hague, René
David Jones 7:189

Hahn, Claire
William Everson 5:122
Carolyn Forché 25:170
Jean Garrigue 8:239
Audre Lorde 18:309

Hahn, Emily
Martha Gellhorn 14:196

Haight, Amanda
Anna Akhmatova 25:26

Hainsworth, J. D.
John Arden 13:24

Hájek, Igor
Bohumil Hrabal 13:291

Hajewski, Thomas
Siegfried Lenz 27:254

Halderman, Marjorie
Larry Kettelkamp 12:304

Hale, Nancy
Jessamyn West 7:522; 17:552, 554

Hale, Thomas A.
Aimé Césaire 19:97

Hales, David
Berry Morgan 6:340

Haley, Beverly A.
Paul Zindel 26:472

Halio, Jay L.
Lawrence Durrell 27:95
William Gaddis 10:212
John Gardner 10:220
Ernest Hemingway 6:230
John Knowles 26:246
Mary McCarthy 5:276
Chaim Potok 26:373
Reynolds Price 13:464
Isaac Bashevis Singer 1:314; 6:509
C. P. Snow 6:517
Aleksandr I. Solzhenitsyn 7:434
Alice Walker 5:476
Paul West 14:569

Hall, Donald
Roger Angell 26:31
Russell Edson 13:191
Allen Ginsberg 3:195
Thom Gunn 18:202
Mark Harris 19:205
Seamus Heaney 14:242, 245
Geoffrey Hill 18:241
Edward Hoagland 28:185
Richard F. Hugo 18:263
Robert Lowell 15:344
Peter Matthiessen 11:361
Thomas McGrath 28:278
Rod McKuen 3:333
Marianne Moore 4:362
Kenneth Rexroth 22:349
David Wagoner 15:559
Thomas Williams 14:583

Hall, Elizabeth
Frank Herbert 12:275
Stephen King 12:309

Hall, James
Saul Bellow 3:50
Elizabeth Bowen 3:82
William Faulkner 3:152
Graham Greene 3:207
Iris Murdoch 2:296
J. D. Salinger 3:444
Robert Penn Warren 4:577

Hall, James B.
Mario Puzo 1:282

Hall, Joan Joffe
Wendell Berry 4:59
Marie-Claire Blais 6:81
Shirley Ann Grau 4:210
Ursula K. LeGuin 8:342
Robert Stone 5:410
John Updike 5:458
Jessamyn West 17:550

Hall, John
Gary Snyder 1:318

Hall, Linda B.
Carlos Fuentes 8:222
Gabriel García Márquez 10:214
Maxine Hong Kingston 12:314

Hall, Mordaunt
Tod Browning 16:121
Frank Capra 16:153

Hall, Richard
Breyten Breytenbach 23:86
Bruce Chatwin 28:73

Hall, Richard W.
Ezra Pound 5:348

Hall, Stephen
R. H. W. Dillard 5:116

Hall, Vernon, Jr.
Paule Marshall 27:309

Hall, Wade
Jesse Stuart 11:511

Hallberg, Peter
Halldór Laxness 25:293

Halle, Louis J.
William Golding 17:157

Haller, Robert S.
Martin Booth 13:104
Alan Sillitoe 6:500

Haller, Scot
Beth Henley 23:214
John Irving 23:248

Halliday, Mark
Eleanor Lerman 9:329

Halman, Talat Sait
Yashar Kemal 14:299, 300, 301

Halpern, Daniel
David Wagoner 5:475

Halpern, Joseph
Jean-Paul Sartre 24:416

Halsey, Martha T.
Antonio Buero Vallejo 15:99

Haltrecht, Monty
Chaim Potok 26:376

Hamalian, Leo
Jean-Luc Godard 20:141

Haman, A. C.
Margaret O. Hyde 21:176

Hamblen, Abigail Ann
Flannery O'Connor 21:270

Hamburger, Michael
Wendell Berry 27:36
Paul Celan 19:93
Martin Heidegger 24:255
Siegfried Lenz 27:247
Robert Pinsky 19:370

Hamel, Guy
William Mitchell 25:328

Hamill, Pete
Seán O'Faoláin 7:272
Leon Uris 7:492

Hamill, Sam
Greg Kuzma 7:197

Hamilton, Alice
Samuel Beckett 10:31
John Updike 2:443; 5:449

Hamilton, Daphne Ann
Melvin Berger 12:41, 42
Franklyn M. Branley 21:22
Roy A. Gallant 17:132

Hamilton, Ian
Kingsley Amis 2:6
John Landis 26:273
Robert Lowell 2:246; 4:303
Louis MacNeice 4:317
Christopher Middleton 13:387

Hamilton, James Shelley
René Clair 20:58, 61
John Ford 16:303
Rouben Mamoulian 16:420
Jean Renoir 20:286

Hamilton, Kenneth
Samuel Beckett 10:31
John Updike 2:443; 5:449

Hamilton, Mary
Paul Vincent Carroll 10:98

Hamilton, William
Albert Camus 1:52
Paul Goodman 7:128

Hamilton-Paterson, James
Anne McCaffrey 17:281

Hamley, Dennis
H. F. Brinsmead 21:32
Diana Wynne Jones 26:229

Hamlin, William C.
Leonard Michaels 25:315

Hammond, Graham
Diana Wynne Jones 26:227

Hammond, John G.
Robert Creeley 8:151

Hammond, Jonathan
Athol Fugard 9:229

Hammond, Kristin E.
Kin Platt 26:351

Hamner, Robert D.
V. S. Naipaul 13:402
Derek Walcott 25:453

Hampshire, Stuart
Christopher Isherwood 11:296

Hampson, John
Edmund Crispin 22:108

Hanckel, Frances
Isabelle Holland 21:150

Handa, Carolyn
Conrad Aiken 10:1

Handlin, Oscar
Yuri Krotkov 19:264
Hunter S. Thompson 17:503

Handy, William J.
John Crowe Ransom 24:365

Handzo, Stephen
Michelangelo Antonioni 20:36
Frank Capra 16:160

Haney, Robert W.
Erich Maria Remarque 21:333

Hanley, Clifford
Martin Walser 27:455

Hanna, Thomas L.
Albert Camus 9:143

Hannabuss, C. Stuart
Leon Garfield 12:230, 234
Andre Norton 12:463
Josephine Poole 17:372
J.R.R. Tolkien 12:575

Hannah, Barry
William Eastlake 8:200

Hanne, Michael
Elio Vittorini 9:551

Hansen, Arlen J.
Richard Brautigan 3:90

Hansen, Arthur G.
Richard Bach 14:35

Hansen, I. V.
Maia Wojciechowska 26:458

Hansen, Olaf
Peter Handke 10:259

Hansen, Ron
Stephen King 26:239

Harada, Violet H.
Barbara Corcoran 17:77

Harcourt, Joan
Roch Carrier 13:141

Harcourt, Peter
Ingmar Bergman 16:50, 72
Luis Buñuel 16:141
Federico Fellini 16:290
Jean-Luc Godard 20:143
Richard Lester 20:221
Jean Renoir 20:292, 305
Alain Resnais 16:511

Hardee, Ethel R.
Robert Newton Peck 17:337

Harder, Worth T.
Herbert Read 4:443

Hardie, Alec M.
Edmund Blunden 2:65

Hardin, Nancy Shields
Margaret Drabble 3:129
Doris Lessing 6:297

Harding, D. W.
Roy Fuller 4:178
F. R. Leavis 24:292
I. A. Richards 24:377

Hardison, O. B., Jr.
Paul Bowles 19:59
Larry McMurtry 7:215

Hardré, Jacques
Jean-Paul Sartre 24:403

Hardwick, Elizabeth
Renata Adler 8:6
Lillian Hellman 14:257
Doris Lessing 3:285
Flannery O'Connor 15:408
Marge Piercy 3:383
Sylvia Plath 17:355
Aleksandr I. Solzhenitsyn 10:480

Hardwick, Mollie
Roald Dahl 18:108
Penelope Fitzgerald 19:174

Hardy, Barbara
A. Alvarez 5:18

Hardy, John Edward
Cleanth Brooks 24:107
Katherine Anne Porter 15:428

Hardy, Melody
Arthur C. Clarke 4:105
Howard Fast 23:159

Hare, David
Ngaio Marsh 7:209

Hargrove, Nancy D.
T. S. Eliot 6:165

Harker, Jonathan
Roman Polanski 16:462
Satyajit Ray 16:475

Harker, Ronald
Mary Renault 17:401

Harlow, Robert
Jack Hodgins 23:231

Harmon, Daniel
Waylon Jennings 21:201

Harmon, Elva
Eilís Dillon 17:96
William Mayne 12:392

Harmon, William
James Wright 28:468
Louis Zukofsky 18:560

Haro, Robert P.
Piri Thomas 17:498

Harold, Brent
William Faulkner 11:199
Vladimir Nabokov 6:356

Harper, Howard M., Jr.
John Barth 1:18
Saul Bellow 1:33
Jerzy Kosinski 1:172
Vladimir Nabokov 1:245
Philip Roth 1:293

Harper, Michael S.
Sterling A. Brown 23:100
Robert Hayden 9:269; 14:241
Ntozake Shange 25:398

Harper, Ralph
Eric Ambler 4:18

Harper, Robert D.
Wright Morris 18:349

Harper, Roy
Jimmy Page and Robert Plant 12:481

Harrigan, Brian
Paul Weller 26:442

Harrington, Curtis
Josef von Sternberg 20:371

Harrington, Michael
Czesław Miłosz 22:305
Theodore Roethke 3:433

Harrington, Stephanie
Norman Lear 12:327, 334
Agnes Eckhardt Nixon 21:242

Harris, Bertha
Rita Mae Brown 18:72
John Hawkes 27:196
Jane Rule 27:418

Harris, Bruce
John Lennon and Paul McCartney 12:371
Jimmy Page and Robert Plant 12:475
Carly Simon 26:406
Neil Young 17:569

Harris, Helen
Penelope Gilliatt 13:239
Ian McEwan 13:371

Harris, Jane Gary
Boris Pasternak 10:382

Harris, Janet
June Jordan 11:312

Harris, John
Robertson Davies 25:134

Harris, Karen
Barbara Corcoran 17:78

Harris, Karen H.
Virginia Hamilton 26:156

Harris, Leo
Ngaio Marsh 7:209
Julian Symons 2:426

Harris, Lis
Truman Capote 3:100
Amos Oz 11:429
Grace Paley 4:392
Georges Simenon 18:486

Harris, Marie
Marge Piercy 6:403

Harris, Mark
Roger Angell 26:33
E. L. Doctorow 18:125
Mordecai Richler 18:455
Isaac Bashevis Singer 23:422

Harris, Michael
Thomas Berger 5:60
Andre Dubus 13:183
John Gardner 5:133

Harris, Robert R.
John Gardner 28:163
Cynthia Ozick 28:349
William Wharton 18:542
Richard Yates 23:483

Harris, Wilson
George Lamming 4:279
V. S. Naipaul 4:374

Harrison, Barbara Grizzuti
Joan Didion 14:153
Ruth Prawer Jhabvala 4:257
Iris Murdoch 6:343
Adrienne Rich 18:448

Harrison, Bernard
Muriel Spark 18:502

Harrison, Jim
Barry Hannah 23:207
Peter Matthiessen 11:360
Larry McMurtry 2:272
Farley Mowat 26:340

Harrison, Joseph G.
Mary Renault 17:395

Harrison, Keith
Margot Benary-Isbert 12:34
John Berryman 3:69
Marge Piercy 14:422

Harrison, M. J.
Henri Troyat 23:461

Harrison, Tony
Lorine Niedecker 10:360

Harron, Mary
Joan Armatrading 17:10

Harsent, David
Joe Orton 13:437

Harss, Luis
Jorge Luis Borges 2:69
Julio Cortázar 2:101
Gabriel García Márquez 2:147
Juan Carlos Onetti 7:276
João Guimarães Rosa 23:350
Juan Rulfo 8:461
Mario Vargas Llosa 3:493

Hart, Henry
Carlos Saura 20:314
Billy Wilder 20:457, 458, 459

Hart, Jane
Carson McCullers 12:416

Hart, Jeffrey
E. L. Doctorow 6:136
Robert Frost 15:243
Auberon Waugh 7:514

Hart, John E.
Jack Kerouac 3:264

Hart, Johnny
Charles M. Schulz 12:527

Hart, Marc
William X. Kienzle 25:276

Hart-Davis, Rupert
Agatha Christie 12:114

Harte, Barbara
Janet Frame 3:164

Harth, Erica
Simone de Beauvoir 14:68

Hartley, George
Philip Larkin 5:230

Hartley, Lodwick
Katherine Anne Porter 13:446

Hartley, Lois
Raja Rao 25:366

Hartman, Charles
Shirley Clarke 16:218

Hartman, Geoffrey
Kenneth Burke 24:132
Ross Macdonald 2:257

Hartman, Geoffrey H.
A. R. Ammons 2:13
Harold Bloom 24:76
Jacques Derrida 24:153
Northrop Frye 24:216
André Malraux 9:358
Lionel Trilling 24:457

Hartshorne, Thomas L.
Kurt Vonnegut, Jr. **22**:444

Hartt, Julian N.
Mary Renault **3**:426

Hartung, Charles V.
Cleanth Brooks **24**:103

Hartung, Philip T.
John Ford **16**:304
Laurence Olivier **20**:238
Gordon Parks **16**:458
Budd Schulberg **7**:402

Harvey, David D.
Herbert Read **4**:440

Harvey, G. M.
John Betjeman **10**:52

Harvey, James
Jonathan Baumbach **23**:53

Harvey, John
F. R. Leavis **24**:313
V. S. Pritchett **15**:442

Harvey, Lawrence E.
Samuel Beckett **9**:80

Harvey, Robert D.
Howard Nemerov **2**:306

Haskell, Molly
Woody Allen **16**:6
Marguerite Duras **20**:100
Elaine May **16**:434, 436
François Truffaut **20**:397

Hasley, Louis
Peter De Vries **1**:72
Joseph Heller **5**:173
S. J. Perelman **3**:381
James Thurber **11**:532
E. B. White **10**:526

Hass, Robert
Robert Lowell **9**:336
James Wright **28**:463

Hass, Victor P.
Rosa Guy **26**:141

Hassall, Anthony J.
Randolph Stow **23**:433

Hassan, Ihab
John Barth **2**:36
Samuel Beckett **1**:23
Saul Bellow **1**:29
Thomas Berger **18**:53
André Breton **2**:81
Frederick Buechner **4**:79
William S. Burroughs **2**:91
Truman Capote **1**:55
J. P. Donleavy **1**:75
Ralph Ellison **1**:94
Jean Genet **2**:159
Allen Ginsberg **2**:164
Herbert Gold **4**:190
Ernest Hemingway **3**:237
Norman Mailer **1**:188, 189; **4**:319
Bernard Malamud **1**:195, 196
Carson McCullers **1**:207, 208
Henry Miller **1**:222
Vladimir Nabokov **1**:239
James Purdy **28**:378

Alain Robbe-Grillet **2**:375
J. D. Salinger **1**:296; **3**:446
Nathalie Sarraute **2**:385
Jean Stafford **7**:455
William Styron **1**:330; **11**:514
Kurt Vonnegut, Jr. **12**:610

Hassett, John J.
José Donoso **4**:129

Hassler, Donald M.
Theodore Sturgeon **22**:412

Hatch, James V.
Alice Childress **12**:106

Hatch, Robert
Ralph Bakshi **26**:67
Anne Burr **6**:104
Francis Ford Coppola **16**:234
Rainer Werner Fassbinder **20**:115, 119
Federico Fellini **16**:300
Larry Gelbart **21**:130
Werner Herzog **16**:326
Alfred Hitchcock **16**:340
Fletcher Knebel **14**:307
George Lucas **16**:412
Nagisa Oshima **20**:257
Richard Pryor **26**:382
Carlos Saura **20**:317
François Truffaut **20**:408
Orson Welles **20**:439
Lina Wertmüller **16**:597
Frederick Wiseman **20**:467
Richard Wright **21**:436

Hatfield, H. C.
George Tabori **19**:435

Hatfield, Henry
Günter Grass **2**:173; **22**:189, 195

Hattman, John W.
Wendell Berry **27**:32

Hauck, Richard Boyd
Kurt Vonnegut, Jr. **5**:465

Haugaard, Kay
Betty Cavanna **12**:102

Haugh, Robert
John Updike **7**:489

Haugh, Robert F.
Nadine Gordimer **18**:184

Hauptman, Ira
John Buell **10**:81

Hauser, Frank
Ogden Nash **23**:322

Hausermann, H. W.
Herbert Read **4**:438, 439

Havard, Robert G.
Jorge Guillén **11**:262

Haverstick, S. Alexander
John Knowles **4**:271

Havighurst, Walter
Allan W. Eckert **17**:105
Edna Ferber **18**:152
William Mitchell **25**:321
Betty Smith **19**:423

Haviland, Virginia
E. M. Almedingen **12**:5
Ruth M. Arthur **12**:25
Margot Benary-Isbert **12**:30
Betty Cavanna **12**:100
Mavis Thorpe Clark **12**:130, 131
Barbara Corcoran **17**:70
Julia W. Cunningham **12**:165
Eilís Dillon **17**:93
Leon Garfield **12**:218
Virginia Hamilton **26**:147
Christie Harris **12**:264
Jamake Highwater **12**:287
Margaret O. Hyde **21**:173
Larry Kettelkamp **12**:304
Joseph Krumgold **12**:317
Jean Lee Latham **12**:323
John Neufeld **17**:307
Andre Norton **12**:456, 466
Philippa Pearce **21**:288
Josephine Poole **17**:372
Mary Rodgers **12**:494
Zilpha Keatley Snyder **17**:472
Mary Stolz **12**:546, 550, 555
Colin Thiele **17**:494

Hawkes, David
Ch'ien Chung-shu **22**:105

Hawkes, John
John Barth **10**:21
John Hawkes **15**:277
Flannery O'Connor **1**:254

Hawkins, Desmond
Pamela Hansford Johnson **27**:214

Hawkins, Robert F.
Vittorio De Sica **20**:85

Haworth, David
Bernice Rubens **19**:402
Morris L. West **6**:563

Hay, John
Eleanor Clark **19**:104

Hay, Samuel A.
Ed Bullins **5**:83

Hay, Sara Henderson
Brewster Ghiselin **23**:169

Hayakawa, S. Ichiyé
E. E. Cummings **12**:144
T. S. Eliot **24**:162

Haycraft, Howard
Agatha Christie **12**:118

Hayden, Brad
Richard Brautigan **12**:72

Hayes, Alfred
Ernesto Sabato **23**:375

Hayes, Brian P.
Joyce Carol Oates **1**:252

Hayes, E. Nelson
J. R. Salamanca **4**:461

Hayes, Harold
Joy Adamson **17**:6

Hayes, Noreen
J.R.R. Tolkien **1**:336

Hayes, Richard
Robert Anderson **23**:28
Sally Benson **17**:50
Paul Bowles **19**:57
Truman Capote **19**:80
William Gibson **23**:176
Mary McCarthy **24**:342
Clifford Odets **28**:334

Hayes, Sarah
Rosemary Sutcliff **26**:437

Hayman, David
Samuel Beckett **11**:34
Louis-Ferdinand Céline **7**:42

Hayman, Ronald
Robert Duncan **7**:88
Roy Fisher **25**:158
Robert Frost **4**:174
Allen Ginsberg **6**:198
Arthur Miller **6**:331
Charles Olson **5**:327
Anne Sexton **4**:482
Peter Shaffer **14**:485
David Storey **5**:414
Charles Tomlinson **4**:544
Tom Wolfe **15**:586

Haynes, Elizabeth
Andre Norton **12**:459

Haynes, Muriel
Shirley Ann Grau **4**:208
Lillian Hellman **4**:222
Thomas Keneally **5**:210

Hays, Peter L.
Henry Miller **9**:379

Hayward, Henry S.
James Clavell **25**:127

Hayward, Max
Andrei Voznesensky **1**:349

Hazelton, Lesley
Amos Oz **27**:359

Hazo, Samuel
John Berryman **2**:57
Philip Booth **23**:74
Linda Pastan **27**:369

Hazzard, Shirley
Jean Rhys **2**:371
Patrick White **3**:522

Headings, Philip R.
T. S. Eliot **1**:91

Heald, Tim
Brian Moore **19**:333

Healey, James
Catharine Savage Brosman **9**:135
Michael Casey **2**:100
Leonard Cohen **3**:110

Healey, Robert C.
Chinua Achebe **26**:12
Gregor von Rezzori **25**:381

Heaney, Seamus
David Jones **7**:187

Hearne, Betsy
Virginia Hamilton **26**:157
Robert Lipsyte **21**:212
Kin Platt **26**:352

Hearne, John
  Wilson Harris **25**:205

Hearron, Thomas
  Richard Brautigan **5**:68

Heath, Jeffrey M.
  Evelyn Waugh **8**:543

Heath, Melville
  Howard Fast **23**:156

Heath, Stephen
  Nagisa Oshima **20**:251, 252

Heath, Susan
  Martin Amis **9**:25
  John Hersey **7**:154
  Yasunari Kawabata **5**:208
  John Knowles **4**:272
  Yukio Mishima **6**:337
  Anaïs Nin **4**:379
  Richard Price **12**:489
  V. S. Pritchett **5**:353
  Kurt Vonnegut, Jr. **3**:503

Heath, William
  Paul Blackburn **9**:100

Hecht, Anthony
  W. H. Auden **2**:22
  Ted Hughes **2**:198
  James Merrill **2**:273
  Marianne Moore **2**:291
  Howard Nemerov **2**:306
  L. E. Sissman **9**:489
  Richard Wilbur **9**:570

Heck, Francis S.
  Marguerite Duras **11**:166

Heckard, Margaret
  William H. Gass **8**:244

Heckman, Don
  John Lennon and Paul McCartney **12**:358

Hector, Mary Louise
  Margot Benary-Isbert **12**:32, 33
  Mary Stolz **12**:552

Heffernan, Michael
  Albert Goldbarth **5**:143
  Gibbons Ruark **3**:441
  Dave Smith **22**:384

Heffernan, Thomas Farel
  Robert Newton Peck **17**:339

Heffernan, Tom
  Norma Fox Mazer **26**:290

Hegel, Robert E.
  Ch'ien Chung-shu **22**:106

Heidenry, John
  Agatha Christie **6**:110
  Robert M. Pirsig **4**:405

Heifetz, Henry
  Bernardo Bertolucci **16**:84

Heilbrun, Carolyn
  Nat Hentoff **26**:182

Heilbrun, Carolyn G.
  Christopher Isherwood **14**:279
  C. P. Snow **19**:428
  Noel Streatfeild **21**:407

Heilbut, Anthony
  Stanley Elkin **9**:191

Heilman, Robert B.
  Edward Albee **5**:11
  Max Frisch **3**:168
  Harold Pinter **3**:386
  Katherine Anne Porter **15**:426

Heimberg, Martha
  Shirley Hazzard **18**:220
  John Updike **15**:547
  Tom Wolfe **15**:586

Heims, Neil
  Paul Goodman **4**:198

Heineman, Alan
  Janis Ian **21**:183
  Frank Zappa **17**:586

Heiney, Donald
  Jean Anouilh **8**:22
  Natalia Ginzburg **11**:227
  Alberto Moravia **2**:294
  Elio Vittorini **9**:546, 548

Heins, Ethel L.
  Ruth M. Arthur **12**:24
  Barbara Corcoran **17**:70
  Julia W. Cunningham **12**:166
  Peter Dickinson **12**:177
  Eilís Dillon **17**:97
  Lois Duncan **26**:104
  Leon Garfield **12**:231
  Rosa Guy **26**:141, 144
  Virginia Hamilton **26**:157
  Isabelle Holland **21**:148
  Lee Kingman **17**:246, 247
  Joseph Krumgold **12**:318
  Norma Fox Mazer **26**:292
  Emily Cheney Neville **12**:451
  Katherine Paterson **12**:487
  Zilpha Keatley Snyder **17**:469, 471

Heins, Paul
  Frank Bonham **12**:50
  Robert Cormier **12**:136
  Julia W. Cunningham **12**:164, 166
  Peter Dickinson **12**:171
  James D. Forman **21**:116
  Alan Garner **17**:142
  Rosa Guy **26**:143
  Mollie Hunter **21**:164
  Madeleine L'Engle **12**:347
  William Mayne **12**:398, 402
  Milton Meltzer **26**:303, 308
  Nicholasa Mohr **12**:446
  Philippa Pearce **21**:289
  Zilpha Keatley Snyder **17**:471
  Colin Thiele **17**:496

Heiserman, Arthur
  J. D. Salinger **12**:496

Heldman, Irma Pascal
  Robert Ludlum **22**:289

Helfgott, Barbara
  Sue Ellen Bridgers **26**:90

Heller, Amanda
  Max Apple **9**:32
  John Cheever **8**:138
  Don DeLillo **8**:171
  Joan Didion **8**:175
  William Gaddis **6**:194
  Mary Gordon **13**:249
  Mark Helprin **7**:152
  Colleen McCullough **27**:319
  Leonard Michaels **6**:325
  Fay Weldon **11**:566
  Larry Woiwode **6**:579

Heller, Erich
  Martin Heidegger **24**:269

Heller, Michael
  William Bronk **10**:75
  Cid Corman **9**:170
  George Oppen **7**:284; **13**:434
  Charles Reznikoff **9**:449

Hellmann, John
  Mick Jagger and Keith Richard **17**:226
  Hunter S. Thompson **17**:511

Helm, Thomas E.
  Colleen McCullough **27**:322

Helms, Alan
  John Ashbery **2**:18
  Robert Bly **10**:61
  Richard F. Hugo **18**:261
  Galway Kinnell **13**:321
  Philip Levine **4**:287
  William Meredith **13**:373

Helms, Randel
  J.R.R. Tolkien **12**:578

Hemenway, Leone R.
  Melvin Berger **12**:39

Hemenway, Robert
  Zora Neale Hurston **7**:170

Hemming, John
  Bruce Chatwin **28**:72
  Thor Heyerdahl **26**:194

Hemmings, F.W.J.
  Mary Stewart **7**:467

Henault, Marie
  Peter Viereck **4**:559

Henderson, Alice Corbin
  Padraic Colum **28**:85

Henderson, Stephen E.
  Sterling A. Brown **23**:96, 99

Henderson, Tony
  Patricia Highsmith **4**:226

Hendin, Josephine Gattuso
  John Barth **3**:42
  Donald Barthelme **6**:28
  Richard Brautigan **1**:45
  William S. Burroughs **5**:92
  Janet Frame **2**:142
  John Hawkes **15**:276
  John Hersey **2**:188
  Marjorie Kellogg **2**:224
  Robet Kotlowitz **4**:275
  Doris Lessing **3**:286
  Michael McClure **6**:316
  Joyce Carol Oates **6**:371; **9**:404
  Flannery O'Connor **6**:375; **13**:421; **21**:274
  Thomas Pynchon **6**:436
  Hubert Selby, Jr. **1**:307; **4**:482
  Paul Theroux **5**:427
  John Updike **9**:536
  Kurt Vonnegut, Jr. **4**:569

Hendrick, George
  Mazo de la Roche **14**:148
  Jack Kerouac **2**:227
  Katherine Anne Porter **1**:273

Hendricks, Flora
  Jessamyn West **17**:544

Hendricks, Sharon
  Melvin Berger **12**:42

Henighan, T. J.
  Richard Hughes **1**:149

Henkel, Wayne J.
  John Knowles **4**:272

Henkels, Robert M., Jr.
  Robert Pinget **13**:443, 444
  Raymond Queneau **10**:430

Henkin, Bill
  Richard O'Brien **17**:325

Henniger, Gerd
  Francis Ponge **18**:416

Henninger, Francis J.
  Albert Camus **4**:93

Henry, Avril
  William Golding **10**:237

Henry, Gerrit
  Russell Edson **13**:190
  W. S. Merwin **5**:287

Hentoff, Margaret
  Paul Zindel **6**:586

Hentoff, Margot
  Joan Didion **8**:174

Hentoff, Nat
  Lenny Bruce **21**:44, 47, 51
  Bob Dylan **12**:180
  Paul Goodman **4**:197
  Alex Haley **12**:243
  Jonathan Kozol **17**:250
  Robert Lipsyte **21**:207
  Colin MacInnes **4**:314

Henze, Shelly Temchin
  Rita Mae Brown **18**:74

Hepburn, Neil
  Rayner Heppenstall **10**:273
  Patricia Highsmith **14**:260
  Mary Hocking **13**:285
  Ursula Holden **18**:257
  Thomas Keneally **5**:211; **10**:299
  Tim O'Brien **7**:272
  David Plante **7**:308
  Frederic Raphael **14**:437
  William Sansom **6**:484
  William Trevor **7**:477
  John Updike **7**:489
  Elio Vittorini **14**:547
  Fay Weldon **9**:559

Hepner, Arthur
  John R. Tunis **12**:594

Herbert, Cynthia
  Hilma Wolitzer **17**:562

Herbert, Kevin
  Mary Renault **17**:394

Herbert, Rosemary
Roger Zelazny 21:479

Herbold, Tony
Dannie Abse 7:2
Michael Hamburger 5:159

Herman, Gary
Peter Townshend 17:528

Herman, Gertrude B.
Maia Wojciechowska 26:458

Hermann, John
J. D. Salinger 12:510

Hern, Nicholas
Peter Handke 15:265

Hernández, Ana María
Julio Cortázar 13:162

Hernlund, Patricia
Richard Brautigan 5:67

Herr, Marian
Otfried Preussler 17:374

Herr, Paul
James Purdy 2:347

Herrera, Philip
Daphne du Maurier 6:147

Herrick, Robert
T. S. Stribling 23:440

Herrick, William
Manuel Puig 28:373

Herron, Ima Honaker
William Inge 19:228

Hershinow, Sheldon J.
Bernard Malamud 27:295

Hertz, Peter D.
Hermann Hesse 17:212

Hertzel, Leo J.
J. F. Powers 1:281

Herzberger, David K.
Juan Benet 28:15

Heseltine, Harry
Frank Dalby Davison 15:170

Hess, John
Botho Strauss 22:407

Hesse, Eva
Ezra Pound 7:329

Hesseltine, William B.
MacKinlay Kantor 7:194

Hewes, Henry
Edward Albee 2:2; 13:3
Robert Anderson 23:32
Robert Bolt 14:91
Ed Bullins 5:84
Truman Capote 19:81
William Gibson 23:177
Günter Grass 2:173
Jim Jacobs and Warren Casey 12:293
Garson Kanin 22:230
Jean Kerr 22:257
Terrence McNally 7:216
Alan Paton 25:361
David Rabe 4:425

Gerome Ragni and James Rado 17:379
Anthony Shaffer 19:413
Peter Shaffer 5:388
Tom Stoppard 4:524
Melvin Van Peebles 2:447
Gore Vidal 2:450
Joseph A. Walker 19:454
Tennessee Williams 2:465

Hewison, Robert
Jeffrey Archer 28:13
Ursula K. Le Guin 22:275

Hewitt, M. R.
Rosa Guy 26:142

Hewitt, Nicholas
Louis-Ferdinand Céline 15:125

Hewitt, Paulo
Paul Weller 26:444, 446, 447

Heyen, William
Robert Bly 5:61
Louise Bogan 4:68
John Cheever 3:106
E. E. Cummings 3:118
James Dickey 2:117
Richmond Lattimore 3:278
Denise Levertov 1:177
Hugh MacDiarmid 2:253
Arthur Miller 6:336
Frederick Morgan 23:296
Theodore Roethke 3:433
M. L. Rosenthal 28:393
Anne Sexton 6:491
W. D. Snodgrass 6:513
William Stafford 4:520
Lewis Turco 11:550
John Updike 3:485
Richard Wilbur 3:533
William Carlos Wiliams 2:468

Heymann, Hans G.
Horst Bienek 7:29

Heywood, Christopher
Peter Abrahams 4:1

Hibberd, Dominic
William Mayne 12:406

Hibbett, Howard
Kōbō Abé 22:12

Hichens, Gordon
Shirley Clarke 16:217

Hickey, Dave
B. H. Friedman 7:108

Hickman, Janet
Mollie Hunter 21:169

Hicks, Granville
Louis Auchincloss 4:28, 30; 9:52, 53; 18:24
James Baldwin 2:31
Peter S. Beagle 7:25
James M. Cain 28:49
Taylor Caldwell 28:60
Truman Capote 19:80
R. V. Cassill 23:102
James Clavell 25:124
James Gould Cozzens 1:66
Leslie A. Fiedler 24:189
Herbert Gold 4:189

Shirley Ann Grau 4:207
Mark Harris 19:200
Dan Jacobson 14:290
Elia Kazan 6:273
Ken Kesey 6:277
John Knowles 26:254
Richard Kostelanetz 28:212
Jonathan Kozol 17:248
Meyer Levin 7:204
Bernard Malamud 1:200; 11:345
Harry Mathews 6:314
Czesław Miłosz 22:305
Flannery O'Connor 1:258
Katherine Ann Porter 7:312
Reynolds Price 3:404, 405
Ann Quin 6:442
Mary Renault 17:397
J. D. Salinger 12:502
Upton Sinclair 15:499
Robert Stone 23:424
Randolph Stow 23:432
John Updike 23:463
Kurt Vonnegut, Jr. 2:451; 12:602
Auberon Waugh 7:514
Eudora Welty 14:561
Glenway Wescott 13:590
Herman Wouk 1:376
Richard Wright 21:435, 440

Hicks, Lorne
Patrick Lane 25:284

Hieatt, Constance B.
John Fowles 15:231

Hiesberger, Jean Marie
Charles M. Schulz 12:533

Higgins, Bertram
Fritz Lang 20:200

Higgins, James
Jonathan Kozol 17:255

Higham, Charles
Alfred Hitchcock 16:342
Andrzej Wajda 16:578
Orson Welles 20:443

Highet, Gilbert
Henry Miller 1:224
Ezra Pound 1:276

Highsmith, Patricia
Georges Simenon 2:398

Highwater, Jamake Mamake
Joan Armatrading 17:7

Hilburn, Robert
Chuck Berry 17:54
Waylon Jennings 21:200

Hildick, Wallace
William Mayne 12:390

Hill, Art
Roger Angell 26:32

Hill, Donald L.
Richard Wilbur 3:530

Hill, Douglas
Margaret Atwood 25:61
Joan Barfoot 18:35
John Gardner 28:161

Hill, Frank Ernest
Erich Maria Remarque 21:325

Hill, Gladwin
John Gregory Dunne 28:121

Hill, Helen G.
Norman Mailer 4:321

Hill, Reginald
John le Carré 28:228

Hill, Susan
Daphne du Maurier 6:146
Bruce Springsteen 17:486
Paul Theroux 28:424

Hill, William B.
Peter De Vries 10:137

Hill, William B., S.J.
Taylor Caldwell 28:65
Robert Cormier 12:133
Paul Gallico 2:147
Bernard Malamud 5:269
Anthony Powell 10:417
Muriel Spark 2:418

Hilliard, Stephen S.
Philip Larkin 9:323

Hillman, Martin
Len Deighton 22:118

Hilton, James
Jan de Hartog 19:130

Hilton, Robert M.
Henry Gregor Felsen 17:124

Hilty, Hans Rudolf
Odysseus, Elytis 15:218

Himmelblau, Jack
Miguel Ángel Asturias 8:25

Hinchcliffe, P. M.
Ethel Davis Wilson 13:610

Hinchliffe, Arnold P.
John Arden 13:28
Edward Bond 6:86
T. S. Eliot 13:195
Harold Pinter 1:267

Hinden, Michael
John Barth 3:41

Hindus, Milton
Louis-Ferdinand Céline 1:56; 15:122
Isaac Bashevis Singer 23:413

Hines, Theodore C.
Isaac Asimov 26:37

Hingley, Ronald
Anna Akhmatova 25:30
Aleksandr I. Solzhenitsyn 1:319; 4:515; 7:445
Andrei Voznesensky 1:349

Hinton, David B.
Leni Riefenstahl 16:525

Hinz, Evelyn J.
Doris Lessing 6:293
Anaïs Nin 1:248; 4:377

Hipkiss, Robert A.
Ernest Hemingway 3:242

Hippisley, Anthony
Yuri Olesha 8:433

Hirsch, Corinne
Isabelle Holland 21:151

Hirsch, Edward
Geoffrey Hill 8:296
Isaac Bashevis Singer 11:499
Charles Tomlinson 13:546
James Wright 28:467

Hirsch, Foster
Federico Fellini 16:295
Ernest Hemingway 1:144
Mary McCarthy 3:328
Laurence Olivier 20:242
Tennessee Williams 5:505;
19:471

Hirt, Andrew J.
Rod McKuen 3:332

Hislop, Alan
Richard Elman 19:150
Jerzy Kosinski 2:233
Wright Morris 3:344
Frederic Prokosch 4:422

Hiss, Tony
Patti Smith 12:536

Hitchcock, George
Diane Wakoski 7:503

Hitchcock, James
Andrew M. Greeley 28:173

Hitchens, Gordon
Vittorio De Sica 20:91
Orson Welles 20:437

Hitrec, Joseph
Ivo Andrić 8:19

Hjortsberg, William
Angela Carter 5:101
Rosalyn Drexler 2:120
Steven Millhauser 21:215

Hoag, David G.
Melvin Berger 12:40
Franklyn M. Branley 21:18, 19, 20, 22
Roy A. Gallant 17:132

Hoagland, Edward
Roger Angell 26:31
Erskine Caldwell 8:123
Peter Matthiessen 11:359
William Saroyan 8:468; 10:454
Kurt Vonnegut, Jr. 22:449

Hoare, Ian
Smokey Robinson 21:346

Hoban, Russell
Leon Garfield 12:232
William Mayne 12:403

Hobbs, Glenda
Harriette Arnow 18:14, 16

Hobbs, John
Galway Kinnell 13:318

Hobbs, Mary
Gunnel Beckman 26:88

Hoberman, J.
Jean-Luc Godard 20:155
Georg Lukács 24:338
Nagisa Oshima 20:256
Pier Paolo Pasolini 20:270
Satyajit Ray 16:495
Martin Scorsese 20:333

Hobsbaum, Philip
F. R. Leavis 24:308
Sylvia Plath 17:353

Hobson, Harold
Christopher Fry 14:188
Simon Gray 14:215

Hobson, Laura Z.
Norman Lear 12:327

Hochman, Baruch
S. Y. Agnon 4:12
Isaac Bashevis Singer 1:312

Hodgart, Matthew
Kingsley Amis 5:23
Heinrich Böll 27:60
V. S. Pritchett 5:353
J.R.R. Tolkien 12:568

Hodgart, Patricia
Paul Bowles 2:78

Hodges, Elizabeth
Rosemary Sutcliff 26:426

Hodgson, Maria
Dirk Bogarde 19:42

Hoeksema, Thomas
Ishmael Reed 3:424

Hoellering, Franz
Alfred Hitchcock 16:338

Hoerchner, Susan
Denise Levertov 5:247

Hofeldt, Roger L.
Larry Gelbart 21:129

Hoffa, William Walter
Ezra Pound 2:343

Hoffman, Barbara
Nora Ephron 17:112

Hoffman, Daniel
A. R. Ammons 2:11
W. H. Auden 2:25
Richard Eberhart 3:133, 134
Ted Hughes 2:198
Robert Lowell 2:247
Carl Sandburg 15:468
Robin Skelton 13:507

Hoffman, Eva
Tadeusz Konwicki 28:208
Anne Tyler 18:529

Hoffman, Frederick J.
Conrad Aiken 1:2
James Baldwin 1:15
Samuel Beckett 1:21
Saul Bellow 1:30
John Dos Passos 1:79
Jaes T. Farrell 4:157
William Faulkner 1:100
John Hawkes 4:212
Ernest Hemingway 1:142
Aldous Huxley 11:281

Flannery O'Connor 15:410
Katherine Anne Porter 1:272
Theodore Roethke 3:434
Philip Roth 4:451
John Steinbeck 1:325
William Styron 15:524
Robert Penn Warren 1:353

Hoffman, Lyla
James D. Forman 21:123
Milton Meltzer 26:304, 306

Hoffman, Michael J.
Henry Miller 1:224

Hoffman, Nancy Y.
Anaïs Nin 4:380
Flannery O'Connor 3:369

Hoffman, Stanley
Paul Zindel 26:475

Hoffman, Stanton
John Rechy 14:443

Hofstadter, Marc
Yves Bonnefoy 15:73

Hogan, Lesley
Leon Rooke 25:392

Hogan, Paula
Margaret O. Hyde 21:178

Hogan, Randolph
Larry Kettelkamp 12:305

Hogan, Richard
Kris Kristofferson 26:269
Paul Weller 26:445

Hogan, Robert
Paul Vincent Carroll 10:97
Hugh Leonard 19:280
Arthur Miller 1:216
Elmer Rice 7:361

Hogan, William
Jessamyn West 17:548

Hoggart, Richard
W. H. Auden 1:9
Graham Greene 6:217
Carolyn G. Heilbrun 25:252

Hokenson, Jan
Louis-Ferdinand Céline 9:152

Holahan, Susan
Frank O'Hara 5:324

Holbert, Cornelia
Kenzaburō Ōe 10:373

Holberton, Paul
Mary Renault 17:401

Holden, Anthony
Rayner Heppenstall 10:272
Daniel Hoffman 13:286

Holden, David
Piers Paul Read 4:445

Holden, Jonathan
John Ashbery 15:30
Nancy Willard 7:540

Holden, Stephen
Jackson Browne 21:35
Bob Dylan 12:191
Marvin Gaye 26:133
Janis Ian 21:187
Billy Joel 26:213, 222

Kris Kristofferson 26:268
John Lennon and Paul McCartney 12:372
Gordon Lightfoot 26:279, 280
Joni Mitchell 12:438
Van Morrison 21:234
Martin Mull 17:298
Laura Nyro 17:319
The Police 26:366
Lou Reed 21:304
Smokey Robinson 21:349, 351
Buffy Sainte-Marie 17:431
Carly Simon 26:408, 409, 412
Paul Simon 17:463, 464, 467
Patti Smith 12:535
Elizabeth Swados 12:561
Lily Tomlin 17:522
Neil Young 17:572

Holder, Alan
Robert Lowell 5:256

Holder, Stephen C.
John Brunner 8:107

Holditch, W. Kenneth
Tennessee Williams 19:471

Holland, Bette
Eleanor Clark 5:106

Holland, Isabelle
Isabelle Holland 21:148, 154

Holland, Jack
Derek Mahon 27:292

Holland, Laurence B.
Wright Morris 18:353

Holland, Norman N.
Federico Fellini 16:272
Stanley Kubrick 16:377
Alain Resnais 16:497

Holland, Philip
Leon Garfield 12:236

Holland, Robert
Elizabeth Bishop 13:95
Marilyn Hacker 9:258
Richard F. Hugo 18:263
Cynthia Macdonald 13:356
David Slavitt 14:491
James Welch 14:559

Hollander, John
A. R. Ammons 2:12
Howard Moss 7:247
S. J. Perelman 15:419

Hollindale, Peter
Mollie Hunter 21:164

Hollinghurst, Alan
William Boyd 28:37
Donald Justice 19:236
Paul Theroux 28:425
Michel Tournier 23:455
Gore Vidal 22:439
Edmund White III 27:482

Hollington, Michael
Günter Grass 11:250

Hollingworth, Roy
Ray Davies 21:92
Jim Jacobs and Warren Casey 12:295
Andrew Lloyd Webber and Tim Rice 21:428

Hollis, Christopher
Evelyn Waugh 19:461

Hollis, James R.
Harold Pinter 11:439

Holloway, John
Northrop Frye 24:211

Hollowell, John
Truman Capote 19:82

Holman, C. Hugh
John P. Marquand 10:328
Robert Penn Warren 4:576

Holmes, Carol
Joseph McElroy 5:279

Holmes, Charles M.
Aldous Huxley 11:283

Holmes, Charles S.
James Thurber 5:439, 441

Holmes, H. H.
Isaac Asimov 26:36
Roy A. Gallant 17:126
Robert A. Heinlein 26:161
Fritz Leiber 25:301
Andre Norton 12:456
John Wyndham 19:474

Holmes, John
M. L. Rosenthal 28:389

Holmes, John Clellon
Jack Kerouac 2:227

Holmes, Kay
Emma Lathen 2:236

Holmstrom, Lakshmi
R. K. Narayan 28:296

Holroyd, Michael
William Gerhardie 5:139

Holsaert, Eunice
Madeleine L'Engle 12:344

Holt, John
Jonathan Kozol 17:249

Holte, James Craig
Ralph Bakshi 26:74

Holtz, William
Joseph Wood Krutch 24:289

Holtze, Sally Holmes
Sue Ellen Bridges 26:90
Sonia Levitin 17:266
Mildred D. Taylor 21:419
Paul Zindel 26:478

Holzapfel, Tamara
Ernesto Sabato 23:377

Holzhauer, Jean
Jean Kerr 22:256

Holzinger, Walter
Pablo Neruda 9:396

Homberger, Eric
Kurt Vonnegut, Jr. 22:446

Honig, Edwin
Edmund Wilson 24:475

Hood, Eric
Rosemary Sutcliff 26:426

Hood, Robert
James D. Forman 21:118
Emily Cheney Neville 12:449

Hood, Stuart
Josef Škvorecký 15:510
Aleksandr I. Solzhenitsyn 1:319

Hook, Sidney
Eric Bentley 24:44
Martin Heidegger 24:257

Hooper, William Bradley
Paule Marshall 27:314
Gloria Naylor 28:304

Hoops, Jonathan
Ingmar Bergman 16:58
Agnès Varda 16:558

Hope, Christopher
Nadine Gordimer 5:147; 18:187
V. S. Naipaul 18:361
Louis Simpson 9:486
Derek Walcott 9:556

Hope, Francis
Mary McCarthy 24:346
Sylvia Plath 17:345

Hope, Mary
Richard Brautigan 12:74
Brigid Brophy 11:68
Bruce Chatwin 28:72
Eilís Dillon 17:100
Martha Gellhorn 14:195
James Hanley 13:261
Benedict Kiely 23:265
Fay Weldon 11:566

Hope-Wallace, Philip
Orson Welles 20:433

Hopkins, Crale D.
Lawrence Ferlinghetti 10:174

Hopkins, J.G.E.
Maureen Daly 17:87

Hopkins, Jerry
Jim Morrison 17:288

Hopkinson, Shirley L.
E. M. Almedingen 12:3

Horak, Jan-Christopher
Werner Herzog 16:330

Horchler, Richard
John Neufeld 17:307
James Purdy 28:378

Horia, Vintila
Mircea Eliade 19:144

Horn, Carole
Caroline Blackwood 6:80

Horn, Richard
Henry Green 13:253

Hornak, Paul T.
G. Cabrera Infante 25:104
Colin Wilson 14:585

Horner, Patrick J.
Randall Jarrell 13:303

Hornyansky, Michael
F. R. Scott 22:376

Horovitz, Carolyn
Esther Forbes 12:210
Joseph Krumgold 12:318
Madeleine L'Engle 12:347
Rosemary Sutcliff 26:428

Horowitz, Michael
Jack Kerouac 5:214

Horowitz, Susan
Ann Beattie 8:54

Horton, Andrew
James Welch 14:560

Horton, Andrew S.
Ken Kesey 6:278
John Updike 7:487

Horvath, Violet M.
André Malraux 4:332

Horwitz, Carey
Donald Barthelme 23:47

Horwood, Harold
E. J. Pratt 19:377

Hosking, Geoffrey
Aleksandr I. Solzhenitsyn 18:499
Vladimir Voinovich 10:507
Alexander Zinoviev 19:488

Hoskins, Cathleen
Leon Rooke 25:394

Hough, Graham
Alan Paton 25:362
John Crowe Ransom 24:365

Hough, Lynn Harold
Joseph Wood Krutch 24:281

Houston, Beverle
Bernardo Bertolucci 16:92
John Cassavetes 20:50
Roman Polanski 16:466

Houston, Penelope
Michelangelo Antonioni 20:23, 29
Charles Chaplin 16:197
Paddy Chayefsky 23:115
John Ford 16:308
Alfred Hitchcock 16:341, 342, 344
Elia Kazan 16:362
Buster Keaton 20:189, 193
Richard Lester 20:223
Laurence Olivier 20:239
Satyajit Ray 16:480
Alain Resnais 16:498
Eric Rohmer 16:528
Orson Welles 20:434, 435
Billy Wilder 20:456

Houston, Robert
Raymond Carver 22:103
Luis Rafael Sánchez 23:385
Mary Lee Settle 19:411

Houston, Stan
Isaac Bashevis Singer 15:509

Howard, Ben
Michael Benedikt 14:81
Ed Dorn 18:129
Loren Eiseley 7:92
Marilyn Hacker 5:155
F. T. Prince 22:339

Anne Sexton 6:494
John Wain 15:560

Howard, Esther
Edmund Crispin 22:109

Howard, Ivor
Larry Gelbart 21:125

Howard, Jane
Maxine Kumin 5:222

Howard, Joseph Kinsey
A. B. Guthrie, Jr. 23:196

Howard, Lawrence A.
Robert Newton Peck 17:340

Howard, Leon
Wright Morris 1:232

Howard, Maureen
Donald Barthelme 8:50
Samuel Beckett 11:43
Jorge Luis Borges 1:38
Paul Bowles 2:79
Isak Dinesen 10:150
Margaret Drabble 2:117; 10:163, 165
Mary Gordon 13:249
Peter Handke 8:261
Lillian Hellman 8:281
P. D. James 18:275
Doris Lessing 6:301
Toni Morrison 10:356
Joyce Carol Oates 15:402
Philip Roth 1:292
Isaac Bashevis Singer 11:502
Paul Theroux 15:533
John Updike 9:537
Kurt Vonnegut, Jr. 1:347
Eudora Welty 22:458
Tennessee Williams 1:369

Howard, Michael
Len Deighton 22:116
Evelyn Waugh 27:474

Howard, Philip
Douglas Adams 27:12

Howard, Richard
Walter Abish 22:16
A. R. Ammons 2:12; 5:24
John Ashbery 2:17, 18; 13:30
W. H. Auden 2:26; 3:23
Imamu Amiri Baraka 10:18
Donald Barthelme 13:61
Roland Barthes 24:28
Marvin Bell 8:67
Robert Bly 5:61
Millen Brand 7:29
Gregory Corso 1:63
Robert Creeley 15:150
James Dickey 7:79
Irving Feldman 7:102
Louise Glück 22:173
Paul Goodman 7:128
Daryl Hine 15:281
Daniel Hoffman 6:244; 23:238
John Hollander 5:185
Uwe Johnson 5:201
Galway Kinnell 5:215
Kenneth Koch 5:219
Denise Levertov 5:245
Philip Levine 5:251
John Logan 5:252, 254

William Meredith 4:348;
  13:372; 22:301
James Merrill 2:274
W. S. Merwin 2:277; 5:284
Howard Moss 7:249
Frank O'Hara 5:323
Sylvia Plath 5:338
Katha Pollitt 28:367
Adrienne Rich 3:428
Raphael Rudnik 7:384
Gary Snyder 5:393
William Stafford 7:460
Mark Strand 18:515
Jun'ichirō Tanizaki 28:420
Allen Tate 4:538
Peter Taylor 18:523, 524
Mona Van Duyn 3:491
David Wagoner 5:473
Robert Penn Warren 6:557
Theodore Weiss 3:516
James Wright 5:518; 10:547
Vassily S. Yanovsky 2:485

Howard, Thomas
Frederick Buechner 2:82

Howarth, David
Gavin Ewart 13:209

Howarth, R. G.
Frank Dalby Davison 15:170

Howe, Fanny
Clarence Major 19:299

Howe, Irving
James Baldwin 3:31; 17:21
Jurek Becker 19:36
Saul Bellow 3:49, 60; 8:79
Louis-Ferdinand Céline 3:101
James Gould Cozzens 4:111
Ralph Ellison 3:141
William Faulkner 3:151
Leslie A. Fiedler 24:190
Paula Fox 2:139
Robert Frost 3:170
Daniel Fuchs 8:221; 22:155, 156
Henry Green 13:252
James Hanley 8:265
Ernest Hemingway 3:232
Arthur Koestler 15:312
György Konrád 4:273
Jerzy Kosinski 1:171
Georg Lukács 24:337
Norman Mailer 3:311
Bernard Malamud 8:376
Czesław Miłosz 22:311
Octavio Paz 3:377
Sylvia Plath 1:270; 3:391
Ezra Pound 2:344
V. S. Pritchett 13:467
Philip Rahv 24:360
Ishmael Reed 13:477
Philip Roth 2:380; 3:440
Delmore Schwartz 10:466
Varlam Shalamov 18:479
Ignazio Silone 4:492, 494
Isaac Bashevis Singer 1:311; 23:413
Lionel Trilling 9:533
Edmund Wilson 3:538; 24:489
Richard Wright 3:545; 9:585; 21:437

Howe, Parkman
Jim Harrison 14:235

Howe, Russell Warren
Alex Haley 12:247

Howell, Christopher
Harry Martinson 14:356

Howell, Elmo
Flannery O'Connor 3:369
Eudora Welty 22:456

Howes, Victor
Peter Davison 28:100
Howard Fast 23:159
Robert Francis 15:236
Kenneth Rexroth 22:349
Muriel Rukeyser 15:457
May Swenson 14:521
James Tate 25:427

Howlett, Ivan
John Osborne 5:333

Howley, Edith C.
Isabelle Holland 21:147
Robert Newton Peck 17:338

Howley, Veronica
Barbara Corcoran 17:76

Hoy, David
Jacques Derrida 24:155

Hoy, David Couzens
Lucien Goldmann 24:251

Hoyem, Andrew
Larry Eigner 9:180

Hoyenga, Betty
Kay Boyle 1:42

Hoyt, Charles Alva
Bernard Malamud 1:196
Muriel Spark 2:414
Edward Lewis Wallant 5:477

Hubbard, Henry W.
Roy A. Gallant 17:128

Hubbell, Albert
Farley Mowat 26:329

Hubbell, Jay B.
John Hall Wheelock 14:570

Hubert, Renée Riese
André Breton 2:80
Alain Robbe-Grillet 4:449
Nathalie Sarraute 4:470

Hubin, Allen J.
Michael Crichton 6:119
Edmund Crispin 22:110
Peter Dickinson 12:168, 169
Harry Kemelman 2:225
Ruth Rendell 28:383
Julian Symons 14:523

Huck, Charlotte S.
Julia W. Cunningham 12:164
Joseph Krumgold 12:320

Huddy, Mrs. D.
Eilís Dillon 17:98

Hudson, Charles
Wendell Berry 27:38

Hudson, Christopher
John Montague 13:390

Hudson, Liam
William H. Gass 15:256

Hudson, Peggy
Earl Hamner, Jr. 12:259
Norman Lear 12:330

Hudson, Theodore R.
Imamu Amiri Baraka 14:44

Huebner, Theodore
Anna Seghers 7:408

Huff, Theodore
Charles Chaplin 16:194

Huffman, James R.
Andrew Lloyd Webber and Tim Rice 21:427

Huggins, Nathan Irvin
Arna Bontemps 18:65

Hugh-Jones, Stephen
Len Deighton 22:114

Hughes, Carl Milton
Chester Himes 4:229
Willard Motley 18:355
Ann Petry 1:266
Richard Wright 1:377
Frank G. Yerby 1:381

Hughes, Catharine
Edward Albee 2:3; 9:6
Robert Anderson 23:33
Samuel Beckett 2:47
Daniel J. Berrigan 4:57
Ed Bullins 5:82
D. L. Coburn 10:108
Allen Ginsberg 2:164
Charles Gordone 4:199
Rolf Hochhuth 4:232
Albert Innaurato 21:192
James Kirkwood 9:320
Carson McCullers 12:419
Mark Medoff 6:323
David Rabe 4:427
Robert Shaw 5:391
Sam Shepard 17:438
Neil Simon 11:496
Megan Terry 19:439
Michael Weller 10:526
Tennessee Williams 2:466; 5:502
Lanford Wilson 14:590

Hughes, Catharine R.
Anthony Shaffer 19:413
Megan Terry 19:440
Douglas Turner Ward 19:457

Hughes, Daniel
John Berryman 3:70

Hughes, David
Gabriel García Márquez 27:152

Hughes, Dorothy B.
Donald E. Westlake 7:528

Hughes, Douglas A.
Elizabeth Bowen 15:77

Hughes, James
Louis Auchincloss 9:53

Hughes, John W.
Dannie Abse 7:1
Joy Adamson 17:4
John Ashbery 2:17
W. H. Auden 2:26
John Ciardi 10:106

Hughes, Langston
James Baldwin 17:21

Hughes, Olga R.
Boris Pasternak 7:297

Hughes, R. E.
Graham Greene 1:131

Hughes, Riley
Taylor Caldwell 28:60, 62
Robert Cormier 12:133
Ernest K. Gann 23:164

Hughes, Robert
Elia Kazan 16:363

Hughes, Roger
Monty Python 21:226

Hughes, Ted
Joy Adamson 17:3
Yehuda Amichai 22:30
Leon Garfield 12:219
Sylvia Plath 1:270
Clancy Sigal 7:423
Isaac Bashevis Singer 15:503

Hughes-Hallett, Lucy
Thomas Keneally 14:302
Bernard Slade 11:508

Hughson, Lois
John Dos Passos 4:136

Hugo, Richard
Theodore Roethke 8:458

Hulbert, Ann
Ann Beattie 13:65
John Cheever 25:120
Eleanor Clark 19:107
Joan Didion 14:152
Mavis Gallant 18:172
Patrick White 18:548

Hulbert, Debra
Diane Wakoski 4:572

Hulcoop, John
Phyllis Webb 18:540

Hull, Elizabeth Anne
Robert Heinlein 14:254

Hull, Robert A.
Lou Reed 21:321

Hull, Robot A.
David Byrne 26:98
Lou Reed 21:305
Smokey Robinson 21:350

Hulse, Michael
Roy Fisher 25:161

Hume, Kathryn
C. S. Lewis 6:308

Humes, Walter M.
Robert Cormier 12:137

Humphrey, Robert
William Faulkner 1:98

Humphreys, Hubert
  Jules Archer **12**:19

Hungerford, Alice N.
  Henry Gregor Felsen **17**:122, 123

Hungerford, Edward B.
  Robert Lipsyte **21**:207

Hunt, Albert
  John Arden **6**:5

Hunt, David
  Lillian Hellman **14**:257

Hunt, George W., S. J.
  John Updike **15**:543

Hunt, Peter
  Peter Dickinson **12**:176
  Leon Garfield **12**:233
  William Mayne **12**:406

Hunter, Evan
  John Gregory Dunne **28**:125
  George V. Higgins **18**:234
  Irwin Shaw **23**:401

Hunter, Jim
  Anne Tyler **11**:552

Hunter, Kristin
  Ann Beattie **8**:55
  Virginia Hamilton **26**:152

Hunter, Mollie
  Mollie Hunter **21**:161

Hunter, Tim
  Stanley Kubrick **16**:382

Hunter, William
  Charles Chaplin **16**:189
  Fritz Lang **20**:202

Hunting, Constance
  Mina Loy **28**:253

Huntington, John
  Arthur C. Clarke **18**:105
  Ursula K. Le Guin **22**:268

Hurd, Pearl Strachan
  Philip Booth **23**:73

Hurren, Kenneth
  Samuel Beckett **6**:43
  Christopher Fry **2**:144
  John Hopkins **4**:234
  Peter Nichols **5**:306
  Harold Pinter **6**:418
  Peter Shaffer **5**:388
  Neil Simon **6**:505
  Tom Stoppard **4**:527
  David Storey **5**:415
  James Thurber **11**:534

Hush, Michele
  Brian Wilson **12**:645

Huss, Roy
  Michelangelo Antonioni **20**:37

Hussain, Riaz
  Philip K. Dick **10**:138

Hutchens, John
  Carl Theodor Dreyer **16**:256

Hutchens, John K.
  Jessamyn West **17**:546
  P. G. Wodehouse **2**:481

Hutchings, W.
  Kingsley Amis **13**:12

Hutchinson, Joanne
  Ivy Compton-Burnett **15**:139

Hutchinson, Tom
  Douglas Adams **27**:14

Hutchison, Alexander
  Luchino Visconti **16**:571

Hutchison, David
  Robert Altman **16**:20

Hutchison, Joanna
  Peter Dickinson **12**:172

Huth, Angela
  John Irving **13**:297
  Piers Paul Read **25**:380
  Michel Tournier **23**:456

Hutman, Norma L.
  John Gardner **18**:173

Hutton, Muriel
  Noel Streatfeild **21**:410

Hux, Samuel
  John Dos Passos **8**:182
  M. L. Rosenthal **28**:392

Huxley, Elspeth
  Joy Adamson **17**:5

Huxley, Julian
  Joy Adamson **17**:4
  Aldous Huxley **3**:253

Hyde, Austin T., Jr.
  Alvin Silverstein and Virginia B. Silverstein **17**:456

Hyde, Lewis
  Vicente Aleixandre **9**:18

Hyde, Virginia M.
  W. H. Auden **3**:23

Hyman, Stanley Edgar
  W. H. Auden **2**:22
  James Baldwin **2**:32
  Djuna Barnes **3**:36
  John Barth **2**:35
  R. P. Blackmur **24**:56
  Kenneth Burke **24**:126
  James M. Cain **28**:45
  Truman Capote **3**:99
  James Gould Cozzens **11**:124
  E. E. Cummings **3**:117
  T. S. Eliot **6**:159
  William Faulkner **3**:152
  Janet Frame **2**:141
  Bruce Jay Friedman **3**:165
  William Golding **2**:168
  Ernest Hemingway **3**:234
  Norman Mailer **2**:258
  Bernard Malamud **2**:265
  Wallace Markfield **8**:378
  Henry Miller **2**:283
  Marianne Moore **2**:291
  Vladimir Nabokov **2**:299
  Flannery O'Connor **1**:257
  Seán O'Faoláin **7**:273
  J. F. Powers **4**:419
  James Purdy **2**:348
  Thomas Pynchon **2**:353
  John Crowe Ransom **2**:363
  I. A. Richards **24**:389
  Alain Robbe-Grillet **2**:374
  J. D. Salinger **3**:444
  Isaac Bashevis Singer **3**:452
  John Steinbeck **5**:405
  Jun'ichiro Tanizaki **8**:510
  John Updike **2**:440
  Edmund Wilson **24**:472
  Yvor Winters **4**:589
  Joseph Wittlin **25**:467
  Herman Wouk **9**:579

Hyman, Timothy
  Federico Fellini **16**:288

Hynes, Joseph
  Graham Greene **9**:244
  Evelyn Waugh **3**:511

Hynes, Samuel
  W. H. Auden **1**:11; **3**:24
  C. Day Lewis **10**:130, 131
  T. S. Eliot **10**:172
  E. M. Forster **3**:161
  William Golding **1**:122; **27**:169
  Graham Greene **6**:219; **27**:177
  Louis MacNeice **4**:317; **10**:326
  Jean Rhys **19**:393
  Stephen Spender **5**:401; **10**:488
  J.I.M. Stewart **7**:464
  Vassily S. Yanovsky **18**:550

Ianni, L. A.
  Lawrence Ferlinghetti **2**:133

Ianzito, Ben
  Margaret O. Hyde **21**:175

Idol, John
  Flannery O'Connor **3**:366

Ignatow, David
  Wendell Berry **27**:35
  Michael S. Harper **22**:209
  Denise Levertov **8**:347
  George Oppen **7**:282
  Gil Orlovitz **22**:333
  Charles Simic **22**:380
  Diane Wakoski **7**:506

Inge, M. Thomas
  Donald Davidson **13**:168

Ingram, Phyllis
  Betty Cavanna **12**:102

Innaurato, Albert
  Albert Innaurato **21**:197

Innes, C. D.
  Martin Walser **27**:464

Innis, Doris
  Jesse Jackson **12**:289

Irby, James E.
  Julio Cortázar **15**:146

Irele, Abiola
  Chinua Achebe **7**:3

Iribarne, Louis
  Czesław Miłosz **22**:307

Irving, John
  John Cheever **11**:121
  Toni Morrison **22**:321
  Jayne Anne Phillips **15**:420

Irwin, Colin
  Billy Joel **26**:214, 220
  Kris Kristofferson **26**:268
  Gordon Lightfoot **26**:281, 282
  Carly Simon **26**:410
  Paul Simon **17**:466

Irwin, John T.
  George P. Elliott **2**:131
  William Faulkner **14**:168
  William Heyen **13**:281
  David Ignatow **7**:177
  Louis MacNeice **1**:187
  Thomas Merton **3**:336
  William Jay Smith **6**:512
  David Wagoner **3**:508
  Theodore Weiss **3**:517

Irwin, Michael
  A. S. Byatt **19**:76
  Isak Dinesen **10**:149
  Chaim Potok **26**:373
  V. S. Pritchett **13**:467
  Paul Theroux **11**:528
  John Updike **9**:539

Isaac, Dan
  Rainer Werner Fassbinder **20**:119
  Isaac Bashevis Singer **3**:453
  Elie Wiesel **5**:493

Isaac, Erich
  John le Carré **28**:231
  Chaim Potok **26**:374

Isaac, Rael Jean
  John le Carré **28**:231

Isaacs, Edith J. R.
  Clifford Odets **28**:325, 327

Isaacs, Harold R.
  Lorraine Hansberry **17**:183

Isaacs, Hermine Rich
  Orson Welles **20**:431

Isaacs, James
  Jimmy Cliff **21**:60
  Lou Reed **21**:309

Isaacs, Neil D.
  George Roy Hill **26**:200

Isbell, Harold
  John Logan **5**:253

Isherwood, Christopher
  Katherine Anne Porter **13**:446

Ishiguro, Hidé
  Yukio Mishima **9**:384

Isler, Scott
  David Byrne **26**:95, 98
  Jim Morrison **17**:294
  Lou Reed **21**:316, 320

Isola, Carolanne
  Anne McCaffrey **17**:283

Israel, Callie
  Roderick L. Haig-Brown **21**:139

Italia, Paul G.
  James Dickey **10**:139

Itzin, Catherine
  Jack Gelber **6**:197

Iverson, Lucille
Judith Leet **11**:323

Ives, John
Sonia Levitin **17**:265
Josephine Poole **17**:372
Roger Zelazny **21**:465

Iwamoto, Yoshio
Yasunari Kawabata **18**:281
Yukio Mishima **9**:381

Iwasaki, Akira
Akira Kurosawa **16**:397

Izard, Anne
Babbis Friis-Baastad **12**:213
John R. Tunis **12**:597

Jack, Peter Monro
Ogden Nash **23**:318

Jackel, David
Matt Cohen **19**:112
James Reaney **13**:476
Robin Skelton **13**:508
Raymond Souster **14**:505

Jackson, Al
Andre Norton **12**:463

Jackson, Angela
Lucille Clifton **19**:109
Henry Dumas **6**:145

Jackson, Blyden
Gwendolyn Brooks **5**:75
Sterling A. Brown **23**:98
Robert Hayden **5**:169
Langston Hughes **5**:191
Margaret Walker **6**:554

Jackson, Brian
Philippa Pearce **21**:283

Jackson, Esther Merle
Tennessee Williams **7**:540

Jackson, Jane B.
Richard Peck **21**:300

Jackson, Joseph Henry
Howard Fast **23**:154
Roderick L. Haig-Brown **21**:135
Irving Stone **7**:468

Jackson, Miles M.
Rosa Guy **26**:141

Jackson, Paul R.
Henry Miller **14**:370, 374

Jackson, Richard
Robert Pack **13**:439
Robert Penn Warren **13**:578
Charles Wright **13**:614

Jackson, Richard L.
Ramón Gómez de la Serna **9**:239

Jackson, Robert Louis
Aleksandr I. Solzhenitsyn **7**:446

Jackson, Seán Wyse
Dirk Bogarde **19**:43
D. M. Thomas **22**:418

Jacob, Gilles
Robert Bresson **16**:110
François Truffaut **20**:383

Jacob, John
Thomas McGrath **28**:278
Jonathan Williams **13**:601

Jacobs, Barry
Halldór Laxness **25**:292

Jacobs, Diane
Claude Chabrol **16**:178
Lina Wertmüller **16**:592

Jacobs, Lewis
Charles Chaplin **16**:191
Rouben Mamoulian **16**:422

Jacobs, Nicolas
David Jones **4**:261

Jacobs, Rita D.
Saul Bellow **10**:42

Jacobs, Ronald M.
Samuel R. Delany **8**:168

Jacobs, William Jay
John R. Tunis **12**:598

Jacobsen, Josephine
Peter Davison **28**:100
Arthur Gregor **9**:256
Daniel Hoffman **6**:242
David Ignatow **4**:249
Denise Levertov **3**:293
Howard Moss **14**:375
James Schevill **7**:401
Mona Van Duyn **7**:498

Jacobson, Dan
S. Y. Agnon **14**:1
James Baldwin **17**:22
D. J. Enright **4**:155
Andrei Sinyavsky **8**:490

Jacobson, Irving
Arthur Miller **6**:333; **10**:345

Jacobus, John
Charles M. Schulz **12**:531

Jacobus, Lee A.
Imamu Amiri Baraka **5**:46

Jacoby, Susan
Gore Vidal **22**:435

Jacoby, Tamar
Athol Fugard **25**:174
Maxine Hong Kingston **19**:250

Jaehne, Karen
Werner Herzog **16**:329

Jaffe, Daniel
A. R. Ammons **2**:12
John Berryman **2**:57
Philip Booth **23**:76
William Melvin Kelley **22**:248
Sylvia Plath **17**:346
Gary Snyder **2**:406
Hollis Summers **10**:493
R. G. Vliet **22**:441

Jaffe, Harold
Peter S. Beagle **7**:26
Kenneth Rexroth **2**:369

Jaffee, Cyrisse
Betty Cavanna **12**:102
Paula Danziger **21**:84
Lois Duncan **26**:106
Stan Lee **17**:261
Hilma Wolitzer **17**:563

Paul Zindel **26**:478

Jahiel, Edwin
Marguerite Duras **6**:150
Antonis Samarakis **5**:381
Vassilis Vassilikos **4**:552

Jahn, Janheing
Camara Laye **4**:282

Jahn, Mike
Chuck Berry **17**:53
Mick Jagger and Keith Richard **17**:229
Jim Morrison **17**:291
Paul Simon **17**:464

Jahner, Elaine
Leslie Marmon Silko **23**:408

Jamal, Zahir
Gail Godwin **22**:181
Olivia Manning **19**:302
Alberto Moravia **11**:384
William Trevor **14**:535
John Wain **15**:561

James, Caryn
Stanley Elkin **27**:124

James, Clive
W. H. Auden **3**:28
John Berryman **25**:89
John Betjeman **6**:66
Lillian Hellman **8**:280
Philip Larkin **5**:225, 229
John le Carré **9**:327
Norman Mailer **3**:317
Aleksandr I. Solzhenitsyn **7**:436
Evelyn Waugh **19**:465
Edmund Wilson **24**:481
Yvor Winters **8**:553
Alexander Zinoviev **19**:490

James, D. G.
I. A. Richards **24**:381

James, Jamie
Toby Olson **28**:345

James, Kathryn C.
Christie Harris **12**:263

James, Louis
Louise Bennett **28**:30
Wilson Harris **25**:210
Jean Rhys **14**:447
Derek Walcott **25**:449

James, Stuart
James A. Michener **5**:290

Jameson, Fredric
Larry Niven **8**:426
Jean-Paul Sartre **24**:412, 421

Janeway, Elizabeth
Sylvia Ashton-Warner **19**:22
Pamela Hansford Johnson **7**:184; **27**:217
Jean Kerr **22**:255, 256
Françoise Sagan **17**:417, 420
Elizabeth Spencer **22**:399
John Steinbeck **21**:369
Jessamyn West **7**:519

Janeway, Michael
Anne Tyler **7**:479
Tom Wicker **7**:533

Janiera, Armando Martins
Kōbō Abé **8**:1
Jun'ichirō Tanizaki **8**:510

Jannone, Claudia
Philip José Farmer **19**:166

Janson, Michael
Alta **19**:19

Jarrell, Randall
Conrad Aiken **3**:3
W. H. Auden **2**:21
Ben Belitt **22**:49
John Berryman **13**:75
Elizabeth Bishop **1**:34; **4**:65
R. P. Blackmur **2**:61
Alex Comfort **7**:54
R. S. Crane **27**:70
E. E. Cummings **3**:116
Robert Frost **1**:109; **3**:169
Robert Graves **1**:126; **2**:174
David Ignatow **7**:173
Robinson Jeffers **2**:213
Robert Lowell **1**:178; **2**:246
Josephine Miles **1**:215
Marianne Moore **1**:226; **2**:290; **19**:338
Ezra Pound **2**:340
John Crowe Ransom **2**:361
Theodore Roethke **3**:432
Muriel Rukeyser **6**:478
Carl Sandburg **4**:462
Karl Shapiro **4**:485
Christina Stead **2**:420
Richard Wilbur **3**:530
William Carlos Williams **1**:369; **2**:467

Jarrett-Kerr, Martin
F. R. Leavis **24**:295

Jaspers, Karl
Czesław Miłosz **22**:304

Jaszi, Peter
Stanley Kubrick **16**:382

Jayne, Edward
Roland Barthes **24**:39

Jeanneret, F.
Adolfo Bioy Casares **13**:87

Jeavons, Clyde
Sidney Poitier **26**:359

Jebb, Julian
Bernardo Bertolucci **16**:91
Alison Lurie **5**:259
François Truffaut **20**:406
Evelyn Waugh **27**:471

Jefferson, Margo
Beryl Bainbridge **5**:39
James Baldwin **17**:43
Rosalyn Drexler **6**:142
Nadine Gordimer **7**:133
Jack Heifner **11**:264
Carolyn G. Heilbrun **25**:254
Elizabeth Jane Howard **7**:164
Gayl Jones **6**:265
V. S. Naipaul **7**:253
Juan Carlos Onetti **7**:280

Jeffords, Ed
Jim Morrison **17**:289

Jeffrey, David L.
Jack Hodgins **23**:230

Jelenski, K. A.
Witold Gombrowicz **7**:123

Jelliffe, R. A.
Robert A. Heinlein **26**:161

Jellinck, Frank
Rex Stout **3**:472

Jenkins, Alan
Lawrence Durrell **27**:95
Derek Walcott **25**:457

Jenkins, Cecil
André Malraux **4**:336

Jenkins, David
A. R. Ammons **5**:28
Patrick Boyle **19**:68

Jenkins, J. S.
Eilís Dillon **17**:97

Jenkins, Peter
Simon Gray **14**:215

Jennings, Elizabeth
Robert Frost **3**:171

Jerome, Judson
John Ciardi **10**:105
William Dickey **28**:118
Marge Piercy **27**:376

Jervis, Steven A.
Evelyn Waugh **1**:359

Jochmans, Betty
Agatha Christie **8**:142

Joe, Radcliffe
Gerome Ragni and James Rado **17**:388

John, Roland
Stanley J. Kunitz **6**:287

Johnson, Abby Ann Arthur
Penelope Gilliatt **10**:229

Johnson, Albert
Lindsay Anderson **20**:14
John Cassavetes **20**:44, 45
Shirley Clarke **16**:217

Johnson, Alexandra
Isaac Bashevis Singer **15**:507

Johnson, Ann S.
David Garnett **3**:188

Johnson, Carolyn
Hilma Wolitzer **17**:562

Johnson, Colton
Anthony Kerrigan **6**:276

Johnson, Curtis
Guy Davenport, Jr. **6**:125

Johnson, Cynthia
Margaret O. Hyde **21**:177

Johnson, Diane
Beryl Bainbridge **14**:37
Donald Barthelme **13**:59
Saul Bellow **25**:83
Don DeLillo **8**:172
Joan Didion **8**:176
Nadine Gordimer **5**:147
Edward Hoagland **28**:184
Erica Jong **8**:315
Maxine Hong Kingston **12**:313
Doris Lessing **3**:286; **10**:316
Norman Mailer **14**:354
James Alan McPherson **19**:310
Toni Morrison **10**:355
Joyce Carol Oates **3**:361
Jean Rhys **6**:453
Muriel Spark **3**:465
Alexander Theroux **25**:431
Gore Vidal **10**:502
Paul West **7**:524

Johnson, Douglas
Louis-Ferdinand Céline **7**:45
Claude Mauriac **9**:367

Johnson, Ernest A., Jr.
Miguel Delibes **18**:109

Johnson, Greg
Joyce Carol Oates **15**:401
John Updike **9**:538

Johnson, Halvard
Gary Snyder **1**:318

Johnson, Helen Armstead
Joseph A. Walker **19**:454

Johnson, Ira D.
Glenway Wescott **13**:592

Johnson, James Weldon
Sterling A. Brown **23**:95

Johnson, James William
Katherine Anne Porter **7**:311

Johnson, Kenneth
Richard Wilbur **6**:570

Johnson, Lee R.
Eilís Dillon **17**:99

Johnson, Manly
David Ignatow **14**:277

Johnson, Marigold
Lynne Reid Banks **23**:43
Pamela Hansford Johnson **27**:223
Bernard Malamud **3**:324

Johnson, Nora
Jeffrey Archer **28**:13
Laura Z. Hobson **25**:272
Garson Kanin **22**:233
Darcy O'Brien **11**:405

Johnson, Pamela Hansford
Winston Graham **23**:192
Doris Lessing **22**:277
Colin MacInnes **23**:281
Olivia Manning **19**:302
Mary McCarthy **24**:343
Françoise Sagan **17**:419

Johnson, R. E., Jr.
Agnes Eckhardt Nixon **21**:248

Johnson, Richard
W. H. Auden **2**:26

Johnson, Richard A.
Turner Cassity **6**:107
Anthony Hecht **8**:268
Delmore Schwartz **2**:387

Johnson, Robert K.
Francis Ford Coppola **16**:244

Johnson, Rosemary
John Ashbery **13**:35
May Swenson **14**:520

Johnson, Sidney M.
Hermann Hesse **17**:197

Johnson, Thomas S.
Bob Dylan **12**:194

Johnson, Tom
Archibald Macleish **14**:338

Johnson, Wayne L.
Ray Bradbury **15**:85

Johnson, William
Robert Altman **16**:20
Kon Ichikawa **20**:179, 184
Eric Rohmer **16**:532
Martin Scorsese **20**:326
Jerzy Skolimowski **20**:354
Orson Welles **20**:439, 442

Johnston, Albert H.
Nora Ephron **17**:110
Patti Smith **12**:541

Johnston, Ann
Kevin Major **26**:287

Johnston, Arnold
William Golding **3**:198

Johnston, Clarie
Nagisa Oshima **20**:250

Johnston, Dillon
Austin Clarke **6**:111
Albert Goldbarth **5**:143
Seamus Heaney **7**:147

Johnston, Kenneth G.
William Faulkner **11**:199

Johnston, Neal
Elmore Leonard **28**:236

Johnstone, J. K.
E. M. Forster **3**:160

Joly, Jacques
Jean Renoir **20**:294

Jonas, George
Margaret Atwood **3**:19
Gwendolyn MacEwan **13**:357
Raymond Souster **14**:504

Jonas, Gerald
Douglas Adams **27**:12
Poul Anderson **15**:14
Isaac Asimov **9**:49; **19**:27; **26**:59
Arthur C. Clarke **13**:155
Samuel R. Delany **8**:168, 169; **14**:148
Harlan Ellison **13**:203
Robert A. Heinlein **26**:174
Frank Herbert **12**:278, 279; **23**:221
Ursula K. LeGuin **8**:343
Stanislaw Lem **15**:330
Barry N. Malzberg **7**:209
Vonda N. McIntyre **18**:326
Larry Niven **8**:426
Andre Norton **12**:470
Frederik Pohl **18**:412
Keith Roberts **14**:464
Joanna Russ **15**:461, 462
Arkadii Strugatskii and Boris Strugatskii **27**:438
Kate Wilhelm **7**:538
Gene Wolfe **25**:473
Roger Zelazny **21**:469

Jones, A. R.
James Baldwin **17**:27
Sylvia Plath **9**:430

Jones, Allan
David Bowie **17**:63, 65
Elvis Costello **21**:66, 68, 69, 74, 75
Ray Davies **21**:100, 101, 102
Mick Jagger and Keith Richard **17**:235
Laura Nyro **17**:315, 317, 319
Richard O'Brien **17**:324
Lou Reed **21**:308, 312, 314
Carly Simon **26**:410
Neil Young **17**:576, 577, 580

Jones, Alun R.
Rhys Davies **23**:148
Philip Larkin **13**:335
Eudora Welty **1**:362; **2**:460

Jones, Bedwyr Lewis
Kate Roberts **15**:445

Jones, Bernard
John Cowper Powys **9**:441

Jones, Brian
Howard Nemerov **2**:306

Jones, Chris
Athol Fugard **25**:173

Jones, D. A. N.
Marie-Claire Blais **22**:58
Dirk Bogarde **19**:41
William Boyd **28**:37
Ed Bullins **1**:47
John Fowles **6**:184
Julius Horwitz **14**:266
Mervyn Jones **10**:295
Yoram Kaniuk **19**:239
Milan Kundera **19**:267
Colin MacInnes **23**:286
John Wain **11**:564
Fay Weldon **11**:565
Vassily S. Yanovsky **18**:551

Jones, D. Allan
John Barth **5**:52

Jones, D. G.
Earle Birney **6**:76; **11**:49
Philip Child **19**:102
Phyllis Gotlieb **18**:192
Anne Hébert **4**:219
Irving Layton **2**:237
Miriam Waddington **28**:437

Jones, Daniel R.
Edward Bond **23**:70

Jones, David R.
Saul Bellow **13**:69

Jones, Du Pre
Sam Peckinpah **20**:272

Jones, E.B.C.
Noel Streatfeild **21**:395

Jones, Edward T.
John Updike **3**:487

Jones, Ernest
William Maxwell **19**:306
Aldo Palazzeschi **11**:431
Budd Schulberg **7**:403
Elizabeth Spencer **22**:398

Jones, Granville H.
Jack Kerouac **2**:226

Jones, Howard Mumford
Alvah Bessie **23**:58
Olivia Manning **19**:299
Philip Rahv **24**:352

Jones, John Bush
Harold Pinter **9**:418

Jones, John M.
Kate Roberts **15**:445

Jones, LeRoi
Robert Creeley **15**:149

Jones, Louisa E.
Raymond Queneau **10**:431

Jones, Madison
Andrew Lytle **22**:295

Jones, Margaret E. W.
Ana María Matute **11**:362, 365

Jones, Patricia
June Jordan **23**:257

Jones, Rhodri
Leon Garfield **12**:227, 235

Jones, Rhonda
Ezekiel Mphahlele **25**:335

Jones, Richard
Graham Greene **14**:218
L. P. Hartley **2**:182
Anthony Powell **7**:346

Jones, Robert F.
James Jones **3**:262

Jones, Roger
Saul Bellow **10**:39

Jones, Sumie
Jun'ichirō Tanizaki **14**:527

Jong, Erica
Sara Davidson **9**:174
Doris Lessing **3**:287
Marge Piercy **27**:373
Anne Sexton **4**:483; **8**:484
Eleanor Ross Taylor **5**:425

Joost, Nicholas
T. S. Eliot **9**:190
Ernest Hemingway **19**:217

Jordan, Alice M.
Henry Gregor Felsen **17**:120
Esther Forbes **12**:207
Lee Kingman **17**:243
Andre Norton **12**:455
John R. Tunis **12**:593

Jordan, Clive
Martin Amis **4**:19
Masuji Ibuse **22**:226
Dan Jacobson **4**:253
G. Josipovici **6**:271
Milan Kundera **19**:266

Yukio Mishima **4**:356
Thomas Pynchon **6**:432
Gillian Tindall **7**:473
Ludvík Vaculík **7**:494
Kurt Vonnegut, Jr. **4**:567

Jordan, Francis X.
Gore Vidal **10**:51

Jordan, June
Maya Angelou **12**:13
Millen Brand **7**:30
Nikki Giovanni **2**:165
Zora Neale Hurston **7**:171
Gayl Jones **9**:306
Marge Piercy **6**:402
Richard Wright **14**:595

Jose, Nicholas
Noel Hilliard **15**:280

Joseph, Gerhard
John Barth **1**:17

Joseph, Michael
Margery Allingham **19**:12
John Wyndham **19**:475

Josephs, Allen
Juan Benet **28**:22
Manuel Puig **28**:374

Josephy, Alvin M., Jr.
Mari Sandoz **28**:404

Josipovici, Gabriel
Saul Bellow **3**:54; **25**:85
William Golding **27**:168
Vladimir Nabokov **3**:353

Joye, Barbara
Ishmael Reed **13**:476
John A. Williams **13**:598

Joyner, Nancy
Andrew Lytle **22**:297

Judd, Inge
Martin Walser **27**:467

Juhasz, Suzanne
Alta **19**:18
Marge Piercy **27**:380

Jumper, Will C.
Robert Lowell **1**:178

Jürma, Mall
Ivar Ivask **14**:287

Jury, Floyd D.
Margaret O. Hyde **21**:180

Justus, James H.
John Berryman **4**:60
John Crowe Ransom **4**:431
Karl Shapiro **4**:487
Robert Penn Warren **4**:578, 582

Kabakoff, Jacob
Aharon Megged **9**:375

Kabatchnik, Amnon
William F. Buckley, Jr. **7**:36

Kadish, Doris Y.
Jean Genet **14**:203

Kael, Pauline
Woody Allen **16**:4
Robert Altman **16**:23, 28
Michelangelo Antonioni **20**:30, 38
Ingmar Bergman **16**:70
Bernardo Bertolucci **16**:89
Mel Brooks **12**:76
Luis Buñuel **16**:137
John Cassavetes **20**:46, 48
Jimmy Cliff **21**:59
Francis Ford Coppola **16**:233, 240
Brian De Palma **20**:75, 77, 79, 81, 83
Marguerite Duras **20**:102
Federico Fellini **16**:280, 282
Bob Fosse **20**:122
Larry Gelbart **21**:130
Jean-Luc Godard **20**:137, 138, 154
Werner Herzog **16**:325
George Roy Hill **26**:205
John Huston **20**:170, 173
Elia Kazan **16**:364, 373
Stanley Kubrick **16**:378, 393
John Landis **26**:275
Richard Lester **20**:226, 229
George Lucas **16**:409
Norman Mailer **3**:315
Elaine May **16**:432
Sam Peckinpah **20**:281
Sidney Poitier **26**:360
Richard Pryor **26**:381
Satyajit Ray **16**:485, 488
Jean Renoir **20**:296
Erich Rohmer **16**:537
Ken Russell **16**:543
Paul Schrader **26**:389, 394, 399
Martin Scorsese **20**:335
Steven Spielberg **20**:357, 360, 366
François Truffaut **20**:383, 384, 385, 392, 404
Agnès Varda **16**:559
Luchino Visconti **16**:570, 575
Peter Weir **20**:429
Lina Wertmüller **16**:591
Frederick Wiseman **20**:469

Kaeppler, Adrienne
Thor Heyerdahl **26**:193

Kagan, Norman
Stanley Kubrick **16**:385

Kagan, Shel
Frank Zappa **17**:593

Kahn, Lothar
Arthur Koestler **3**:271
Siegfried Lenz **27**:251
Jakov Lind **4**:293
André Schwarz-Bart **4**:479
Isaac Bashevis Singer **23**:416
Peter Weiss **3**:515
Elie Wiesel **3**:527

Kahn, Roger
Robert Lipsyte **21**:211

Kaiser, Walter
George Seferis **11**:493

Kakish, William
Peter Hundke **10**:260

Kakutani, Michiko
William Boyd **28**:41
Peter De Vries **28**:111
Cynthia Ozick **28**:355

Kalb, Marvin L.
Aleksandr I. Solzhenitsyn **26**:414

Kalem, T. E.
Edward Albee **2**:2; **5**:12
Kingsley Amis **3**:8
Samuel Beckett **2**:47
Ed Bullins **5**:84
Anne Burr **6**:104
Friedrich Dürrenmatt **4**:141
Jules Feiffer **8**:216
Robert Graves **2**:177
Bill Gunn **5**:152
John Hopkins **4**:234
Albert Innaurato **21**:192
Ira Levin **3**:294
Terrence McNally **7**:217
Jason Miller **2**:284
Peter Nichols **5**:307
Sean O'Casey **5**:319
Murray Schisgal **6**:490
Neil Simon **6**:506
Isaac Bashevis Singer **6**:511
Aleksandr I. Solzhenitsyn **1**:321
Tom Stoppard **4**:526
David Storey **2**:424, 425; **4**:530
C. P. Taylor **27**:446
Thornton Wilder **6**:572
Tennessee Williams **7**:545
Robert Wilson **7**:550

Kalstone, David
A. R. Ammons **2**:12
John Ashbery **2**:17; **13**:31
John Berryman **3**:69
Elizabeth Bishop **13**:95
A. D. Hope **3**:250
Philip Levine **5**:250
Robert Lowell **11**:326
James Merrill **2**:273, 275; **13**:378
Robert Pinsky **19**:371
Adrienne Rich **11**:475
James Schuyler **5**:383

Kameen, Paul
Daniel J. Berrigan **4**:57
Robert Lowell **3**:303

Kamin, Ira
Charles Bukowski **9**:137

Kaminsky, Stuart M.
Elaine May **16**:435

Kamla, Thomas A.
Hermann Hesse **25**:259

Kane, B. M.
Christa Wolf **14**:594

Kane, Patricia
Chester Himes **7**:159

Kanfer, Stefan
Truman Capote **19**:85
Jerzy Kosinski **6**:285
Terrence McNally **7**:218
Brian Moore **7**:237
Paul Simon **17**:458
Isaac Bashevis Singer **3**:453; **6**:510

John Steinbeck **5**:408
Dalton Trumbo **19**:447
Gore Vidal **22**:438

Kanon, Joseph
Robert Altman **16**:29
Louis Auchincloss **4**:29
Carlos Castaneda **12**:88
Daphne du Maurier **6**:147
Penelope Gilliatt **2**:160
Steven Millhauser **21**:216
Jacqueline Susann **3**:475
Hunter S. Thompson **17**:505
John Updike **2**:444

Kantra, Robert A.
Samuel Beckett **3**:46

Kapai, Leela
Paule Marshall **27**:311

Kaplan, Abraham
John Ford **16**:306

Kaplan, Fred
Francis Ford Coppola **16**:239
Bob Fosse **20**:125
Roman Polanski **16**:470
François Truffaut **20**:381

Kaplan, George
Alfred Hitchcock **16**:349

Kaplan, Johanna
Dan Jacobson **4**:254
Cynthia Ozick **7**:287
Chaim Potok **26**:374

Kaplan, Samuel
John Neufeld **17**:311

Kaplan, Stephen
Stanley Kubrick **16**:382

Kaplan, Sydney Janet
Doris Lessing **6**:296

Kapp, Isa
Thomas Berger **18**:57
John Cheever **11**:120
Oriana Fallaci **11**:189
Jascha Kessler **4**:269
Grace Paley **4**:394
Philip Roth **4**:459; **22**:356
Eudora Welty **22**:458

Kappel, Lawrence
Thomas Pynchon **18**:439

Karanikas, Alexander
Donald Davidson **19**:123

Kardokas, Christine
Zilpha Keatley Snyder **17**:475

Kareda, Urjo
Alice Munro **19**:345

Karimi-Hakkak, Ahmad
Ahmad Shamlu **10**:470

Karl, Frederick R.
Samuel Beckett **1**:20
Elizabeth Bowen **1**:40
John Braine **1**:43
Ivy Compton-Burnett **1**:60
Lawrence Durrell **1**:83
E. M. Forster **1**:103
William Golding **1**:119
Henry Green **2**:178

Graham Greene **1**:132
L. P. Hartley **2**:181
Joseph Heller **1**:140
Aldous Huxley **1**:150
Christopher Isherwood **1**:155
Pamela Hansford Johnson **1**:160
Doris Lessing **1**:173, 175
Iris Murdoch **1**:233
P. H. Newby **2**:310
Anthony Powell **1**:277
William Sansom **2**:383
C. P. Snow **1**:314, 315, 316
Muriel Spark **2**:414
Evelyn Waugh **1**:357
Angus Wilson **2**:471

Karlen, Arno
Edward Dahlberg **7**:62

Karlinsky, Simon
Vladimir Nabokov **1**:241; **2**:305
John Rechy **7**:357
Aleksandr I. Solzhenitsyn **2**:408
Edmund White III **27**:478
Yevgeny Yevtushenko **1**:382

Karp, David
James Baldwin **17**:21
Meyer Levin **7**:203

Kasack, Wolfgang
Aleksandr I. Solzhenitsyn **7**:434

Kasindorf, Martin
Christopher Hampton **4**:212
Norman Lear **12**:335

Kass, Judith M.
Robert Altman **16**:38, 40

Katope, Christopher G.
Jessamyn West **17**:548

Kattan, Naim
Mordecai Richler **5**:373

Katz, Bill
Roderick L. Haig-Brown **21**:138

Katz, Claire
Flannery O'Connor **6**:379, 380

Katz, Donald R.
Thomas McGuane **18**:325

Katz, Jonathan
Albert Goldbarth **5**:144

Kauffmann, Stanley
Kōbō Abé **22**:11
Edward Albee **2**:3; **5**:11, 14; **25**:38
Robert Altman **16**:29, 44
Lindsay Anderson **20**:16
Fernando Arrabal **2**:15; **9**:41
Alan Ayckbourn **5**:37
Ralph Bakshi **26**:67, 69, 71
Ingmar Bergman **16**:57
John Berryman **3**:69
Bernardo Bertolucci **16**:90, 94, 100
Mel Brooks **12**:80
Ed Bullins **7**:36
Luis Buñuel **16**:135
Anthony Burgess **2**:86
John Cassavetes **20**:47, 49
Charles Chaplin **16**:203, 206

Michael Cimino **16**:213
D. L. Coburn **10**:108
Francis Ford Coppola **16**:234
Vittorio De Sica **20**:95, 96
E. L. Doctorow **6**:133
Carl Theodor Dreyer **16**:262
Rainer Werner Fassbinder **20**:109, 113
Federico Fellini **16**:279, 281, 283
Bob Fosse **20**:122, 124, 127
Athol Fugard **5**:130; **9**:230
Larry Gelbart **21**:128
Jean-Luc Godard **20**:139, 140
John Guare **14**:220
Peter Handke **5**:164
Lorraine Hansberry **17**:184
Beth Henley **23**:217
James Leo Herlihy **6**:234
Werner Herzog **16**:327, 334
George Roy Hill **26**:202, 209
John Huston **20**:175
Buster Keaton **20**:194
James Kirkwood **9**:319
Jerzy Kosinski **1**:171; **2**:233
Stanley Kubrick **16**:382, 383, 390
Richard Lester **20**:224, 228, 231
George Lucas **16**:407, 408, 411
Elaine May **16**:435
Albert Maysles and David Maysles **16**:439
Arthur Miller **2**:280
Henry Miller **4**:350
Henri de Montherlant **19**:326
Monty Python **21**:225
Peter Nichols **5**:307
Hugh Nissenson **9**:399
Marsha Norman **28**:320
Edna O'Brien **3**:365
Clifford Odets **28**:336
John O'Hara **2**:325
Nagisa Oshima **20**:255
Yasujiro Ozu **16**:448
Pier Paolo Pasolini **20**:260
Miguel Piñero **4**:402
Harold Pinter **3**:386, 387; **6**:417; **15**:421
Roman Polanski **16**:464
Bernard Pomerance **13**:446
Richard Pryor **26**:379, 382
David Rabe **4**:425, 426; **8**:450
Terence Rattigan **7**:356
Satyajit Ray **16**:486
Jean Renoir **20**:300, 302
Gregor von Rezzori **25**:383
Eric Rohmer **16**:531, 537
Ken Russell **16**:543, 547
Françoise Sagan **17**:424
James Salter **7**:387
Carlos Saura **20**:317
Paul Schrader **26**:385, 389
André Schwarz-Bart **2**:388
Martin Scorsese **20**:325, 335
Irwin Shaw **7**:412
Sam Shepard **17**:434, 446
Joan Micklin Silver **20**:341
Elizabeth Spencer **22**:401
Steven Spielberg **20**:360, 367
John Steinbeck **5**:408
Tom Stoppard **4**:527; **15**:524
Elizabeth Swados **12**:560

François Truffaut **20**:386, 389
Melvin Van Peebles **20**:410
Gore Vidal **2**:450
Luchino Visconti **16**:567, 570
Kurt Vonnegut, Jr. **2**:452
Andrzej Wajda **16**:584
Joseph A. Walker **19**:455
Orson Welles **20**:453
Lina Wertmüller **16**:587, 591, 598
Billy Wilder **20**:465
Tennessee Williams **5**:504; **7**:545
Lanford Wilson **14**:593
Robert Wilson **9**:576

Kaufman, Donald L.
Norman Mailer **2**:263

Kaufman, Marjorie
Thomas Pynchon **18**:432

Kaufmann, R. J.
F. R. Leavis **24**:299

Kavanagh, Julie
Marilynne Robinson **25**:387

Kavanaugh, Patrick
Frank O'Connor **14**:400

Kaveney, Roz
Doris Lessing **15**:332
Frederik Pohl **18**:412

Kay, George
Eugenio Montale **18**:340

Kaye, Frances W.
W. P. Kinsella **27**:237

Kaye, Yvor Winters
4 593:Kaye, Lenny
Jimmy Cliff **21**:59
Mick Jagger and Keith Richard **17**:224, 239
Jim Morrison **17**:292
Jimmy Page and Robert Plant **12**:475
Lou Reed **21**:303, 314
Smokey Robinson **21**:347
Paul Simon **17**:446
Peter Townshend **17**:532
Stevie Wonder **12**:656

Kaye, Marilyn
Franklyn M. Branley **21**:23
Isabelle Holland **21**:154

Kaysen, Xana
Jerzy Kosinski **10**:309

Kazin, Alfred
Renata Adler **8**:7
James Baldwin **1**:13; **13**:52
Donald Barthelme **13**:54
Brendan Behan **1**:25
Saul Bellow **1**:28; **3**:61
R. P. Blackmur **24**:55
Jane Bowles **3**:84
Paul Bowles **1**:41
William S. Burroughs **5**:91
Albert Camus **2**:97
Elias Canetti **25**:113
Louis-Ferdinand Céline **9**:158
John Cheever **3**:108
James Gould Cozzens **4**:116

E. E. Cummings 8:155
Joan Didion 3:127
Lawrence Durrell 1:83
Ralph Ellison 1:93; 3:146
Frederick Exley 6:170
William Faulkner 28:137
Gabriel García Márquez 2:149
William H. Gass 8:240
Paul Goodman 4:195
Graham Greene 1:131
Joseph Heller 11:265
Ernest Hemingway 3:242
Edward Hoagland 28:181
Maureen Howard 14:268
David Ignatow 4:249
Jack Kerouac 1:165
Alan Lelchuk 5:241
Robert Lowell 1:179
Georg Lukács 24:321
Norman Mailer 1:187
Bernard Malamud 1:194; 3:326
Wallace Markfield 8:379
John P. Marquand 2:271
Mary McCarthy 3:329
Carson McCullers 4:345
Vladimir Nabokov 3:356; 8:418
V. S. Naipaul 4:373; 9:393
Joyce Carol Oates 2:313; 3:363
Flannery O'Connor 1:259; 3:370
Julia O'Faolain 19:359
John O'Hara 1:260; 3:371
Alan Paton 25:357
Walker Percy 2:334
Ann Petry 1:266
Thomas Pynchon 3:419
Kenneth Rexroth 1:284
Philip Roth 1:292
J. D. Salinger 1:295, 296; 3:446, 458
Karl Shapiro 4:484
Isaac Bashevis Singer 1:310; 3:457; 9:487
C. P. Snow 1:314
Aleksandr I. Solzhenitsyn 2:410; 4:515
Susan Sontag 13:515
John Steinbeck 13:530
Allen Tate 24:440
Peter Taylor 4:543
Paul Theroux 8:514
John Updike 3:488; 9:538; 23:471
Kurt Vonnegut, Jr. 3:505
Robert Penn Warren 1:352; 4:582
Edmund Wilson 2:475; 24:475
Abraham B. Yehoshua 13:618

Keane, Patrick
Galway Kinnell 5:216

Kearns, Edward
Richard Wright 1:379

Kearns, George
Walter Abish 22:23
Elizabeth Bowen 22:68
Athol Fugard 25:176
Luis Rafael Sánchez 23:385

Kearns, Lionel
Earle Birney 6:77

Keates, Jonathan
Gunnel Beckman 26:88
Dirk Bogarde 19:42
Jorge Luis Borges 6:94
John Fowles 10:187
Roy Fuller 28:157
Anthony Hecht 19:208
John Hersey 7:155
Ursula Holden 18:257
Peter Straub 28:409

Keating, H.R.F.
Robert B. Parker 27:364

Keating, L. Clark
Marie-Claire Blais 22:58

Keating, Peter
Erica Jong 8:315

Kee, Robert
Enid Bagnold 25:75
Agatha Christie 12:115

Keefe, Joan
Flann O'Brien 10:362

Keeley, Edmund
Odysseus Elytis 15:221
George Seferis 11:492

Keen, Sam
Carlos Castaneda 12:93

Keenan, Hugh T.
J.R.R. Tolkien 1:336

Keene, Donald
Yukio Mishima 2:287; 4:354
Jun'ichirō Tanizaki 8:509

Keene, Frances
Françoise Sagan 17:417

Keeney, Willard
Eudora Welty 1:361

Keffer, Charles J.
Jeffrey Archer 28:11
Robin Cook 14:131

Keils, R. M.
Vladimir Nabokov 11:391

Keith, Philip
J. E. Wideman 5:489

Keith, W. J.
Louis Dudek 19:138
Robert Frost 26:128
Roderick L. Haig-Brown 21:141
Hugh Hood 28:194
Rudy Wiebe 14:573

Kelleher, Ed
David Bowie 17:58
Carly Simon 26:408

Kelleher, Victor
Muriel Spark 13:523

Kellen, Konrad
Lina Wertmüller 16:596

Keller, Jane Carter
Flannery O'Connor 3:365

Keller, Marcia
Agatha Christie 12:117

Kellman, Steven
Max Frisch 14:184

Kellman, Steven G.
Aharon Megged 9:374
Iris Murdoch 15:385
Robert Pinget 13:442

Kellogg, Gene
Graham Greene 3:208
François Mauriac 4:339
Flannery O'Connor 3:365
J. F. Powers 4:419
Evelyn Waugh 3:511

Kelly, Aileen
Henri Troyat 23:462

Kelly, Ernece B.
Maya Angelou 12:9

Kelly, Frank
David Madden 15:350

Kelly, James
Rhys Davies 23:146
Ernest K. Gann 23:165
Pamela Hansford Johnson 27:216
Irwin Shaw 7:411

Kelman, Ken
Carl Theodor Dreyer 16:259
Leni Riefenstahl 16:522

Kemball-Cook, Jessica
Andre Norton 12:465

Kemme, Tom
Shusaku Endo 19:161

Kemp, Barbara
Françoise Sagan 17:427

Kemp, John C.
Robert Frost 15:245

Kemp, Peter
Douglas Adams 27:11
Frederick Busch 18:84
Roald Dahl 18:108
Lawrence Durrell 13:189
Buchi Emecheta 14:160
John Hawkes 27:200
Thomas Keneally 27:231
Doris Lessing 22:286
David Malouf 28:269
Iris Murdoch 22:326
Barbara Pym 19:387
Scott Sommer 25:424
D. M. Thomas 22:417
William Trevor 25:444
Fay Weldon 19:468

Kemper, Robert Graham
Robert Anderson 23:31

Kempton, Murray
Gore Vidal 4:554

Kempton, Sally
John Knowles 26:258

Kendle, Burton
John Cheever 15:128

Kendle, Judith
Morley Callaghan 14:102

Keneas, Alex
Ira Levin 6:305

Kenefick, Madeleine
Gayl Jones 6:265
Cynthia Ozick 7:290

Kennard, Jean E.
Anthony Burgess 10:86
William Golding 10:233
Joseph Heller 8:275
James Purdy 10:421
Kurt Vonnegut, Jr. 12:611

Kennaway, James
Simon Raven 14:439

Kennebeck, Edwin
Heinrich Böll 27:55
James Schuyler 23:387
Terry Southern 7:453
Marguerite Yourcenar 19:482

Kennedy, Andrew K.
John Arden 6:10
Samuel Beckett 6:46
T. S. Eliot 6:166
John Osborne 11:422
Harold Pinter 6:419

Kennedy, Dorothy Mintzlaff
Raymond Federman 6:181
Howard Nemerov 6:363

Kennedy, Eileen
Penelope Gilliatt 10:230
Susan Richards Shreve 23:402

Kennedy, Harlan
Michelangelo Antonioni 20:42
Federico Fellini 16:300
Werner Herzog 16:330

Kennedy, John S.
John Steinbeck 1:323; 13:532

Kennedy, Ray
Joseph Wambaugh 3:509

Kennedy, Raymond
Richard Wright 21:435

Kennedy, Sighle
Arthur Miller 26:311

Kennedy, Susan
Rita Mae Brown 18:75
Susan Cheever 18:101
Anne Redmon 22:342
J.I.M. Stewart 14:512

Kennedy, William
Jorge Amado 13:11
Thomas Bernhard 3:64
Carlos Castaneda 12:92
Robertson Davies 2:113
Don DeLillo 10:134
Gabriel García Márquez 8:232
John Gardner 7:111
Joseph Heller 5:179
Elia Kazan 6:273
Jerzy Kosinski 15:316
William Kotzwinkle 5:219
Peter Matthiessen 7:211
Steven Millhauser 21:219
Mordecai Richler 5:378
Piri Thomas 17:500

Kennedy, X. J.
A. R. Ammons 2:13
Edward Dahlberg 7:62
Eleanor Lerman 9:328
James Merrill 2:275
Robert Pack 13:438

David Wagoner 15:558

Kennelly, Brendan
Patrick Kavanagh 22:236

Kennely, Patricia
Jim Morrison 17:288, 289

Kenner, Hugh
W. H. Auden 2:29
Samuel Beckett 11:43
Ben Belitt 22:54
Saul Bellow 25:81
R. P. Blackmur 24:60
Robert Bly 10:62
Guy Davenport, Jr. 14:142
John Dos Passos 8:182
Leslie A. Fiedler 24:196
Ernest Hemingway 8:285
Irving Layton 15:319
Marianne Moore 4:360; 13:397; 19:340
Vladimir Nabokov 6:357
George Oppen 7:283, 285
Sylvia Plath 17:366
Ezra Pound 2:345; 4:412; 7:325
Mary Renault 11:472
W. D. Snodgrass 18:492
Richard G. Stern 4:522
William Carlos Williams 2:469; 13:605
James Wright 10:546
Louis Zukofsky 7:561, 562

Kennerly, Sarah Law
Lois Duncan 26:104
Kin Platt 26:349, 350

Kenney, Edwin J., Jr.
Elizabeth Bowen 11:61
Iris Murdoch 6:345

Kenney, Harry C.
Farley Mowat 26:335

Kenny, Kevin
Kin Platt 26:356

Kenny, Mary
Benedict Kiely 23:265

Kent, Cerrulia
Laura Z. Hobson 7:164

Kent, George E.
James Baldwin 1:15
Gwendolyn Brooks 1:46; 15:94
Nikki Giovanni 19:192
Chester Himes 4:229
Ishmael Reed 13:477

Kent, Heddie
Franklyn M. Branley 21:20

Kerans, James
Jean Renoir 20:289

Kermode, Frank
W. H. Auden 2:25; 14:33
Beryl Bainbridge 8:37; 22:46
Roland Barthes 24:25
Samuel Beckett 2:46
T. S. Eliot 2:126, 128
E. M. Forster 10:178
Northrop Frye 24:208, 213
William Golding 2:167, 169; 17:161, 167; 27:164
Nadine Gordimer 10:240

Graham Greene 6:215
Peter Handke 5:165
Christopher Isherwood 11:296
Stanley Kunitz 14:312
C. S. Lewis 27:264
Henry Miller 2:282
Iris Murdoch 2:298
Philip Rahv 24:355
I. A. Richards 14:453
Philip Roth 3:440
J. D. Salinger 12:497
Muriel Spark 2:414, 415, 418; 18:500
Edmund Wilson 24:478
Marguerite Yourcenar 19:483

Kern, Anita
Buchi Emecheta 14:159

Kern, Edith
Samuel Beckett 2:47; 14:70

Kern, Gary
Aleksandr I. Solzhenitsyn 26:420

Kern, Robert
Richard Brautigan 12:71
Gary Snyder 9:500

Kernan, Alvin B.
Bernard Malamud 27:303
Philip Roth 4:453
Evelyn Waugh 1:358

Kernan, Margot S.
Claude Chabrol 16:172

Kerr, Baine
N. Scott Momaday 19:318

Kerr, Elizabeth M.
William Faulkner 14:178

Kerr, John Austin, Jr.
José Rodrigues Miguéis 10:341

Kerr, Walter
Edward Albee 25:33
Enid Bagnold 25:75, 76
Sally Benson 17:50
Alice Childress 12:106
Michael Cristofer 28:95
Gretchen Cryer 21:79, 80, 82
Charles Fuller 25:182
Jan de Hartog 19:130
William Gibson 23:173, 174
Charles Gordone 1:124
Lorraine Hansberry 17:184, 190
Beth Henley 23:215, 217
Jim Jacobs and Warren Casey 12:292
Marsha Norman 28:318
Clifford Odets 28:334
Harold Pinter 1:267
Gerome Ragni and James Rado 17:386, 387
Martin Sherman 19:415
Neil Simon 6:503
Megan Terry 19:440
Kurt Vonnegut, Jr. 12:605
Douglas Turner Ward 19:458
Andrew Lloyd Webber and Tim Rice 21:426, 432
Michael Weller 10:526
Tennessee Williams 19:473

Kerrane, Kevin
Robert Coover 7:59

Kerridge, Roy
Colin MacInnes 23:286

Kerrigan, Anthony
Jorge Luis Borges 4:74; 9:115; 13:109
Camilo José Cela 13:145

Kerr-Jarrett, Peter
Octavio Paz 6:397

Kertzer, Jon
Matt Cohen 19:114

Kessler, Edward
Daniel Hoffman 6:242
Charles Wright 6:580

Kessler, Jascha
Yehuda Amichai 22:31
A. R. Ammons 5:28
Imamu Amiri Baraka 2:34
Sterling A. Brown 23:101
Charles Bukowski 5:79
James Dickey 7:79
Loren Eiseley 7:91
Irving Feldman 7:101
Lawrence Ferlinghetti 10:174
Robert Graves 2:176
Sandra Hochman 8:297
Ted Hughes 2:201
June Jordan 5:203
Yoram Kaniuk 19:241
Anthony Kerrigan 4:269
György Konrád 10:304
Maxine Kumin 28:222
Don L. Lee 2:238
Thomas Merton 3:335
Pablo Neruda 28:315
Robert Pack 13:438
Kenneth Patchen 18:394
Octavio Paz 10:388
John Crowe Ransom 11:467
Muriel Rukeyser 15:460
Karl Shapiro 8:485; 15:478
Muriel Spark 8:492
May Swenson 14:521
John Wain 11:561, 563
Robert Penn Warren 4:578
Charles Wright 28:460
James Wright 28:467
Louis Zukofsky 7:560

Ketterer, David
Ursula K. Le Guin 22:267
Theodore Sturgeon 22:411

Kettle, Arnold
John Berger 2:55
Ivy Compton-Burnett 3:111
E. M. Forster 3:159
Graham Greene 3:206
Aldous Huxley 3:252

Keyes, Mary
Phyllis Gotlieb 18:192

Keyser, Barbara Y.
Muriel Spark 8:494

Keyser, Lester J.
Federico Fellini 16:294

Kherdian, David
Philip Whalen 6:565

Kibera, Leonard
Alex La Guma 19:275

Kibler, Louis
Alberto Moravia 11:382; 18:344

Kidder, Rushworth M.
E. E. Cummings 8:161; 15:155, 158

Kidel, Mark
Bob Dylan 12:198
The Police 26:364

Kieffer, Eduardo Gudiño
Jorge Luis Borges 9:117

Kieley, Benedict
Brendan Behan 11:44
John Montague 13:391

Kiely, Robert
Richard Adams 18:2
Louis Auchincloss 18:26
Maeve Brennan 5:73
Frederick Busch 18:85
Hortense Calisher 2:96
Susan Cheever 18:101
Michael Frayn 7:106
Gabriel García Márquez 2:148
William H. Gass 2:155
Bernard Malamud 3:323
Joyce Carol Oates 19:356
Anne Redmon 22:342
Angus Wilson 25:463

Kieran, Margaret Ford
Walter Farley 17:117
Mary Stolz 12:547

Kiernan, Robert F.
John Barth 3:42

Kilgore, Kathryn
Juan Benet 28:22

Killam, G. D.
Chinua Achebe 1:1; 26:22

Killinger, John
Fernando Arrabal 9:37

Kilroy, Thomas
Samuel Beckett 3:45

Kimball, Arthur G.
Yasunari Kawabata 9:309
Jun'ichirō Tanizaki 14:526

Kimmel, Eric A.
Emily Cheney Neville 12:452

Kimzey, Ardis
Leslie Norris 14:388

Kinder, Marsha
Michelangelo Antonioni 20:31
Ingmar Bergman 16:75
Bernardo Bertolucci 16:92
Luis Buñuel 16:144
John Cassavetes 20:50, 52
Richard Lester 20:223
Roman Polanski 16:466
Carlos Saura 20:320
Peter Weir 20:429

Kindilien, Glenn A.
Saul Bellow 10:44

King, Bruce
Chinua Achebe 26:19, 25
Nadine Gordimer 10:240
Ruth Prawer Jhabvala 8:312
V. S. Naipaul 9:392
Derek Walcott 25:452

King, Cameron
Derek Walcott **25**:449

King, Charles L.
Ramón Sender **8**:479

King, Dolores
Margaret O. Hyde **21**:177

King, Edmund L.
Jorge Guillén **11**:263

King, Francis
Louis Auchincloss **18**:26
William Boyd **28**:39
Bruce Chatwin **28**:74
Rhys Davies **23**:148
Margaret Drabble **22**:125
Lawrence Durrell **27**:98
Shusaku Endo **14**:161
Herbert Gold **14**:208
Graham Greene **18**:195
Aldous Huxley **5**:193
John Irving **23**:253
Kazuo Ishiguro **27**:203
M. M. Kaye **28**:198
Bobbie Ann Mason **28**:274
Iris Murdoch **11**:388
Barbara Pym **19**:388
Muriel Spark **13**:525
Robert Stone **23**:430
Fay Weldon **19**:469

King, James
F. R. Scott **22**:373

King, Larry L.
Kurt Vonnegut, Jr. **12**:602

King, Thomas M.
Jean-Paul Sartre **7**:394

Kingsbury, Mary
M. E. Kerr **12**:298

Kingston, Carolyn T.
Margot Benary-Isbert **12**:35
Emily Cheney Neville **12**:453

Kingston, Maxine Hong
Bienvenido N. Santos **22**:366

Kinkead, Gwen
Penelope Gilliatt **2**:161

Kinkead-Weekes, Mark
William Golding **27**:165

Kinnamon, Keneth
James Baldwin **13**:52
Richard Wright **21**:451

Kinney, Arthur F.
William Faulkner **28**:141
Dorothy Parker **15**:415

Kinney, Jeanne
Carson McCullers **4**:344; **12**:427

Kinsella, Anna M.
Alberto Moravia **7**:242

Kinsella, Thomas
Austin Clarke **6**:111

Kinsey, Helen E.
Margot Benary-Isbert **12**:33

Kinzie, Mary
Jorge Luis Borges **2**:73
Marilyn Hacker **23**:206
Ted Hughes **14**:271
Charles Wright **28**:459

Kirby, David
A. R. Ammons **25**:44

Kirby, Emma
Lenora Mattingly Weber **12**:633

Kirby, Martin
Walker Percy **8**:440

Kirby-Smith, H. T., Jr.
Elizabeth Bishop **4**:66
Arthur Gregor **9**:254

Kirk, Elizabeth D.
J.R.R. Tolkien **1**:341

Kirk, John M.
Mario Vargas Llosa **15**:549

Kirk, Ron
Michael Moorcock **27**:349

Kirk, Russell
Ray Bradbury **10**:68

Kirke, Ron
D. M. Thomas **22**:418

Kirkham, Michael
Charles Tomlinson **4**:543

Kirkpatrick, Stephen
James Tate **25**:428

Kirsch, Robert
Jascha Kessler **4**:270

Kirton, Mary
Roderick L. Haig-Brown **21**:142

Kish, A. V.
Mark Helprin **22**:221
Helen Yglesias **22**:493

Kish, Anne V.
Jim Harrison **14**:237

Kisner, Sister Madeleine
T. S. Eliot **15**:216

Kissel, Howard
Andrew Lloyd Webber and Tim Rice **21**:433

Kissel, Susan
Robert Coover **15**:145

Kitchen, Paddy
J. M. Coetzee **23**:122
Bessie Head **25**:238

Kitchin, Laurence
John Arden **13**:24
Arnold Wesker **5**:481

Kitching, Jessie B.
E. M. Almedingen **12**:3

Kitman, Marvin
Larry Gelbart **21**:131
Garry Marshall **17**:277
Arthur Miller **26**:326

Kitses, Jim
Elia Kazan **16**:369

Kittrel, William
Edna Ferber **18**:151

Kizer, Carolyn
Ted Hughes **2**:201

Klaidman, Stephen
Juan Goytisolo **5**:150

Klappert, Peter
Daniel Mark Epstein **7**:97
Kathleen Spivack **6**:520

Klarmann, Adolf D.
Friedrich Dürrenmatt **11**:168

Klein, A. M.
A.J.M. Smith **15**:512

Klein, Gillian Parker
François Truffaut **20**:398

Klein, Julia M.
Marilyn French **18**:159
Erica Jong **18**:279
James Purdy **28**:381

Klein, Marcus
Saul Bellow **1**:29
Stanley Elkin **27**:121
Ralph Ellison **1**:94

Klein, Theodore
Albert Camus **11**:95

Kleinberg, Seymour
Isaac Bashevis Singer **3**:458

Klemtner, Susan Strehle
John Fowles **15**:232
William Gaddis **10**:212

Kley, Ronald J.
Margaret O. Hyde **21**:175

Kliman, Bernice W.
Philip Roth **3**:438

Klin, George
Yoram Kaniuk **19**:240

Kline, T. Jefferson
André Malraux **15**:353

Kling, Vincent
Rainer Werner Fassbinder **20**:111

Klinkowitz, Jerome
Walter Abish **22**:22
Imamu Amiri Baraka **5**:45
Donald Barthelme **3**:43; **5**:52; **6**:29; **13**:60; **23**:46
Jonathan Baumbach **6**:32
Erica Jong **6**:269
Jerzy Kosinski **3**:272
Clarence Major **19**:294, 295
Flann O'Brien **7**:269
Gilbert Sorrentino **3**:462; **22**:392
Steven Spielberg **20**:365
Ronald Sukenick **3**:475; **4**:530
Hunter S. Thompson **17**:510
Kurt Vonnegut, Jr. **1**:348; **3**:500; **4**:563
Thomas Williams **14**:583

Klockner Karen M.
Madeleine L'Engle **12**:352

Kloman, William
Laura Nyro **17**:312
Gerome Ragni and James Rado **17**:380

Klotman, Phyllis R.
Ronald L. Fair **18**:142
Langston Hughes **15**:292
Toni Morrison **22**:314

Klug, M. A.
Saul Bellow **15**:50

Kluger, Richard
Jerome Siegel and Joe Shuster **21**:357

Kmetz, Gail Kessler
Muriel Spark **8**:493

Knapp, Bettina Liebowitz
Jean Anouilh **8**:24
Jean Cocteau **8**:145
Georges Duhamel **8**:187
Marguerite Duras **6**:151
Jean Genet **1**:116
Yukio Mishima **27**:343
Anna Kavan **13**:317
Robert Pinget **7**:305
Nathalie Sarraute **8**:469

Knapp, James F.
T. S. Eliot **6**:163
Ken Kesey **11**:317
Delmore Schwartz **2**:387

Knapp, John V.
John Hawkes **7**:145

Knelman, Martin
W. Somerset Maugham **11**:370
William Mitchell **25**:326
Harold Pinter **9**:421
Mordecai Richler **5**:377

Knickerbocker, Brad
Allan W. Eckert **17**:108

Knieger, Bernard
S. Y. Agnon **8**:8

Knight, Arthur
Woody Allen **16**:1
Gordon Parks **16**:457

Knight, Damon
Brian Aldiss **14**:10
Isaac Asimov **3**:16
Ray Bradbury **3**:84
Robert A. Heinlein **3**:224

Knight, G. Wilson
Sean O'Casey **11**:406
John Cowper Powys **7**:347

Knight, Karl F.
John Crowe Ransom **4**:428

Knight, Susan
Frederick Busch **7**:38
John Gardner **3**:186
József Lengyel **7**:202

Knittel, Robert
Riccardo Bacchelli **19**:31

Knobler, Peter
Jackson Browne **21**:39
Bob Dylan **12**:189
Van Morrison **21**:237
Phil Ochs **17**:333
Bruce Springsteen **17**:476, 484

Knoll, Robert E.
Kay Boyle 19:64
Wright Morris 18:351, 355
Ezra Pound 3:398

Knoll, Robert F.
Ken Russell 16:542

Knopf, Terry Ann
Agnes Eckhardt Nixon 21:243, 245

Knopp, Josephine
Elie Wiesel 5:491

Knorr, Walter L.
E. L. Doctorow 11:142

Knowles, A. Sidney, Jr.
Marie-Claire Blais 2:63
Frederic Prokosch 4:421

Knowles, Dorothy
Eugène Ionesco 11:290

Knowles, George W.
Marie-Claire Blais 13:96

Knowles, John
Pamela Hansford Johnson 27:221
Françoise Sagan 17:423

Knowlton, James
Walter Abish 22:21

Knox, George
Kenneth Burke 24:129

Knox, Wendy
Carolyn Forché 25:168

Knudsen, Erika
Elisaveta Bagryana 10:11

Kobler, John
Jerome Siegel and Joe Shuster 21:353

Kobler, Turner S.
Rebecca West 7:526

Koch, Christopher
Richard Elman 19:149

Koch, Kenneth
Frank O'Hara 2:322
James Schuyler 23:387

Koch, Stephen
Hermann Hesse 3:243
Reynolds Price 6:425
Nathalie Sarraute 8:472
Christina Stead 5:404
Gore Vidal 4:554
Andy Warhol 20:420

Kodjak, Andrej
Aleksandr I. Solzhenitsyn 18:495

Koenig, Peter William
William Gaddis 10:209

Koenig, Rhoda
Roald Dahl 18:108
Peter De Vries 28:110
Mark Helprin 22:220
Paul Theroux 15:535

Koepf, Michael
Raymond Carver 22:102

Koester, Rudolf
Hermann Hesse 17:205

Koethe, John
John Ashbery 2:17; 3:15
Sandra Hochman 3:250
James Schuyler 23:388
Theodore Weiss 3:517

Kofsky, Frank
Lenny Bruce 21:56
Mick Jagger and Keith Richard 17:220

Kogan, Rick
Richard Price 12:489

Kohler, Dayton
Carson McCullers 12:413
Jesse Stuart 14:513

Kohn, Hans
E. M. Almedingen 12:2

Kolb, Muriel
Lois Duncan 26:102
Alvin Silverstein and Virginia B. Silverstein 17:451

Kolker, Robert Phillip
Robert Altman 16:30
Ken Russell 16:545
Martin Scorsese 20:336

Kolodin, Irving
Buffy Sainte-Marie 17:430

Kolodny, Annette
Thomas Pynchon 3:412

Kolonosky, Walter F.
Vasily Aksenov 22:27
Vladimir Voinovich 10:508

Koltz, Newton
Wright Morris 3:343
Patrick White 3:524

Koniczek, Ryszard
Andrzej Wajda 16:584

Koning, Hans
Jerzy Kosinski 15:315
Aleksandr I. Solzhenitsyn 18:498

Koningsberger, Hans
John Huston 20:171

Koon, William
William Price Fox 22:140

Koper, Peter T.
Ursula K. Le Guin 22:271

Kopkind, Andrew
Lenny Bruce 21:57

Koprowski, Jan
Joseph Wittlin 25:471

Korenblum, Toba
Thor Heyerdahl 26:194

Korg, Jacob
Bernard Malamud 2:269

Korges, James
Erskine Caldwell 1:51

Korn, Eric
Philip K. Dick 10:138
G. B. Edwards 25:150
Harlan Ellison 13:203
Rayner Heppenstall 10:272
John Irving 23:252
Jack Kerouac 14:307
Richard O'Brien 17:323
Judith Rossner 9:457
Claude Simon 9:482
Gore Vidal 10:502
Fay Weldon 11:566
William Wharton 18:543
Tom Wolfe 15:587
Roger Zelazny 21:470

Kornfeld, Matilda
Zilpha Keatley Snyder 17:473

Kornfeld, Melvin
Jurek Becker 7:27

Kosek, Steven
Kurt Vonnegut, Jr. 4:569

Kostach, Myrna
Rudy Wiebe 6:566

Kostelanetz, Richard
R. P. Blackmur 2:61
Ralph Ellison 3:141
Ezra Pound 2:344

Kostis, Nicholas
Julien Green 11:259

Kostolefsky, Joseph
Frank Capra 16:156

Kotin, Armine
Jean Arp 5:33

Kotlowitz, Robert
Gerome Ragni and James Rado 17:382
Howard Sackler 14:479

Kott, Jan
Andrei Sinyavsky 8:488

Kouidis, Virginia M.
Mina Loy 28:248

Kountz, Peter
Thomas Merton 11:372
Frank Zappa 17:589

Kovács, Katherine Singer
Jorge Luis Borges 19:49

Kovar, Helen M.
Christie Harris 12:261

Kozak, Ellen M.
Gene Roddenberry 17:413

Kozloff, Max
Agnès Varda 16:557

Kozol, Jonathan
Marjorie Kellogg 2:223

Kracauer, Siegfried
Fritz Lang 20:202
Leni Riefenstahl 16:519
Josef von Sternberg 20:370

Kraemer, Chuck
Frederick Wiseman 20:475

Kramer, Aaron
Stanley J. Kunitz 6:287

Kramer, Hilton
William Barrett 27:22
Donald Barthelme 8:50
Bruce Chatwin 28:71
E. L. Doctorow 6:137
Robert Lowell 8:357
Archibald MacLeish 8:362
Mary McCarthy 5:276
Marianne Moore 19:342
L. E. Sissman 9:492
Allen Tate 11:527; 14:530
Robert Penn Warren 8:538

Kramer, Jane
Maxine Hong Kingston 12:312
V. S. Naipaul 18:363

Kramer, Nora
Betty Cavanna 12:99

Kramer, Peter G.
William Goyen 5:149

Krance, Charles
Louis-Ferdinand Céline 9:153

Krasso, Nicolas
George Steiner 24:430

Kraus, Elisabeth
John Hawkes 7:146

Krause, Walter
James D. Forman 21:121

Kreidl, John Francis
Alain Resnais 16:514

Kreitzman, Ruth
Bernardo Bertolucci 16:86

Krensky, Stephen
Frank Bonham 12:55
Robert Lipsyte 21:212

Kresh, Paul
Isaac Bashevis Singer 23:417

Kreyling, Michael
Eudora Welty 22:459

Kreymborg, Alfred
Mina Loy 28:247

Krickel, Edward
James Gould Cozzens 1:67
William Saroyan 1:302

Kridl, Manfred
Maria Dabrowska 15:165

Kriegel, Harriet
Nora Ephron 17:112

Kriegel, Leonard
T. S. Eliot 6:166
James T. Farrell 11:193
Günter Grass 2:172
James Jones 10:293
Iris Murdoch 1:234
Ezra Pound 7:333
Harvey Swados 5:423
Edmund Wilson 2:475

Krieger, Murray
Northrop Frye 24:223
I. A. Richards 24:391

Krim
James Jones 10:290

Krim, Seymour
William Barrett **27**:23
Leslie A. Fiedler **24**:193
Ernest Hemingway **19**:219
Jack Kerouac **14**:303

Krispyn, Egbert
Günter Eich **15**:202

Krist, Gary
James Purdy **28**:381

Kroll, Ernest
Peter Viereck **4**:559

Kroll, Jack
Edward Albee **2**:1
Jean Anouilh **3**:12
W. H. Auden **3**:27
Alan Ayckbourn **5**:36
Saul Bellow **6**:55
Mel Brooks **12**:80
Ed Bullins **1**:47
Anne Burr **6**:103, 104
Rosalyn Drexler **2**:119
Frederick Exley **6**:171
Jules Feiffer **8**:216
Jean Genet **2**:158
John Guare **8**:253
Bill Gunn **5**:152
Ted Hughes **2**:200
Stanley J. Kunitz **6**:286
John Landis **26**:276
Ira Levin **6**:306
David Mamet **9**:360
Terrence McNally **7**:218
Mark Medoff **6**:322
Arthur Miller **2**:280; **6**:334
Jason Miller **2**:284
Rochelle Owens **8**:434
Miguel Piñero **4**:402
Terence Rattigan **7**:355
Jonathan Reynolds **6**:451
Ronald Ribman **7**:358
Tadeusz Różewicz **23**:362
Murray Schisgal **6**:490
Neil Simon **6**:504
Tom Stoppard **5**:414
David Storey **2**:424, 426
Elizabeth Swados **12**:559
Lily Tomlin **17**:518
Kurt Vonnegut, Jr. **2**:452
Andrew Lloyd Webber and Tim Rice **21**:426, 433
Lanford Wilson **7**:548

Kroll, Judith
Sylvia Plath **17**:359

Kroll, Steven
Irvin Faust **8**:215
Thomas McGuane **3**:330
Dan Wakefield **7**:503
Irving Wallace **7**:510

Kronenberger, Louis
Babette Deutsch **18**:118
Edna Ferber **18**:150
Henri de Montherlant **19**:322
Erich Maria Remarque **21**:325

Krouse, Agate Nesaule
Agatha Christie **12**:119
Robert B. Parker **27**:364
J.I.M. Stewart **14**:512
Fay Weldon **19**:466

Krumgold, Joseph
Joseph Krumgold **12**:319

Krupka, Mary Lee
Margot Benary-Isbert **12**:33, 34

Krupnick, Mark L.
Philip Rahv **24**:354

Krutch, Joseph Wood
Brigid Brophy **11**:67
Erskine Caldwell **8**:122
Paul Green **25**:194, 195
Mary McCarthy **24**:341
Clifford Odets **28**:323, 324, 326, 327, 331
Erich Maria Remarque **21**:326
Elmer Rice **7**:360
Irwin Shaw **23**:394
Emlyn Williams **15**:576, 577

Krynski, Magnus Jan
Tadeusz Różewicz **23**:359

Krysl, Marilyn
Marilyn Hacker **23**:204

Krzyzanowski, Jerzy R.
Tadeusz Konwicki **8**:325

Kubal, David
Raymond Carver **22**:104
G. B. Edwards **25**:152

Kucewicz, William
Len Deighton **22**:117

Kuczkowski, Richard
Anthony Burgess **13**:125
Don DeLillo **13**:179
Susan Sontag **10**:485

Kuehl, Linda
Doris Lessing **3**:282
Iris Murdoch **3**:345; **15**:381
Marge Piercy **3**:384
Muriel Spark **2**:417
Eudora Welty **5**:479
Thomas Williams **14**:582

Kuehn, Robert E.
Aldous Huxley **11**:284

Kuhn, Doris Young
Julia W. Cunningham **12**:164
Joseph Krumgold **12**:320

Kuhn, Ira
Uwe Johnson **15**:304

Kuhn, Reinhard
Henri Michaux **19**:312, 313

Kulshrestha, Chirantan
Mulk Raj Anand **23**:21

Kuncewicz, Maria
Maria Dąbrowska **15**:166

Kunitz, Isadora
Margaret O. Hyde **21**:174
Alvin Silverstein and Virginia B. Silverstein **17**:454

Kunitz, Stanley
John Berryman **8**:86
Robert Creeley **8**:152
Carolyn Forché **25**:168
Robert Frost **9**:223
Jean Garrigue **8**:240
H. D. **8**:255
Robert Lowell **9**:334
Marianne Moore **8**:397; **10**:346
John Crowe Ransom **11**:467
Theodore Roethke **8**:458

Kunz, Don
James Welch **14**:559

Kunzle, David
Stan Lee **17**:258

Kupferberg, Herbert
Yoram Kaniuk **19**:238

Kustow, Michael
Jean-Luc Godard **20**:130
Arnold Wesker **3**:519

Kuzma, Greg
Barry Spacks **14**:510

Kyle, Carol A.
John Barth **9**:65

LaBarre, Weston
Carlos Castaneda **12**:88

Laber, Jeri
Ilya Ehrenburg **18**:132
Aleksandr I. Solzhenitsyn **2**:411; **4**:514

Labrie, Ross
Thomas Merton **11**:373

La Charité, Virginia
René Char **9**:167; **11**:113; **14**:128
Henri Michaux **19**:314

Lachtman, Howard
Martin Cruz Smith **25**:414

Lacy, Allen
William Barrett **27**:20
Harry Crews **23**:136
Gilbert Sorrentino **14**:501

La Faille, Eugene
Isaac Asimov **26**:58

La Farge, Oliver
Howard Fast **23**:153
Robert Lewis Taylor **14**:534

Lafore, Laurence
Rhys Davies **23**:146
Shirley Hazzard **18**:214
William Maxwell **19**:307
James Alan McPherson **19**:309
R. K. Narayan **28**:295
Paul Theroux **28**:423
Irving Wallace **7**:509
Jessamyn West **17**:550

LaFrance, Marston
Evelyn Waugh **1**:358

LaHood, M. J.
William S. Burroughs **22**:85

Lahr, John
Edward Bond **13**:103
Arthur Kopit **1**:171
Darcy O'Brien **11**:405
Joe Orton **4**:388; **13**:435, 436
John Osborne **11**:422
Harold Pinter **6**:411
Richard Price **12**:489
Mordecai Richler **18**:454
Sam Shepard **4**:491; **17**:447

Laidlaw, Marc
Stephen King **12**:311

Laing, Alexander
Esther Forbes **12**:208

Laitinen, Kai
Paavo Haavikko **18**:205
Hannu Salama **18**:460

Lake, Steve
Ray Davies **21**:96
Gordon Lightfoot **26**:280
Phil Ochs **17**:332
Lou Reed **21**:307
Patti Smith **12**:536

Lalley, Francis A.
Vine Deloria, Jr. **21**:112

Lalley, J. M.
A. B. Guthrie, Jr. **23**:195

Lally, Michael
Charles Bukowski **9**:138
Larry Eigner **9**:182
Kenneth Koch **8**:323
Howard Moss **7**:249
Anne Sexton **6**:493

Lambert, Gavin
Lindsay Anderson **20**:11
Robert Bresson **16**:102
Luis Buñuel **16**:129
Charles Chaplin **16**:195
Agatha Christie **8**:142
René Clair **20**:63, 64
John Huston **20**:160, 161, 162
Stanley Kubrick **16**:376, 377
Fritz Lang **20**:205
John O'Hara **6**:384
Jean Renoir **20**:288

Lambert, J. W.
Edward Albee **2**:4
Alan Ayckbourn **5**:35
Peter Barnes **5**:50
Edward Bond **4**:70; **6**:84
A. E. Ellis **7**:95
Michael Frayn **7**:108
Athol Fugard **5**:130
Trevor Griffiths **13**:256
John Osborne **2**:328
Sam Shepard **6**:496
Bernard Slade **11**:508
Tom Stoppard **3**:470; **5**:413
David Storey **2**:425; **4**:530
Arnold Wesker **3**:518

Lamie, Edward L.
John Brunner **8**:110

Lamming, George
Ishmael Reed **3**:424
Derek Walcott **4**:574

Lamont, Rosette C.
Fernando Arrabal **9**:35
Eugène Ionesco **1**:155; **6**:252, 256; **9**:287
Boris Pasternak **18**:387

Lamott, Kenneth
Siegfried Lenz **27**:244

Lamport, Felicia
Laura Z. Hobson **25**:272
S. J. Perelman **5**:337

Lancaster, Bruce
Halldór Laxness 25:291

Landau, Deborah
Van Morrison 21:233

Landau, Elaine
Virginia Hamilton 26:150

Landau, Jon
Bob Dylan 12:190
Marvin Gaye 26:131
George Roy Hill 26:202
Mick Jagger and Keith Richard 17:221, 224, 233
John Lennon and Paul McCartney 12:377
Joni Mitchell 12:438
Van Morrison 21:231, 232
Jimmy Page and Robert Plant 12:475
Sam Peckinpah 20:278
Martin Scorsese 20:324
Paul Simon 17:461
Bruce Springsteen 17:478
Andrew Lloyd Webber and Tim Rice 21:429
Stevie Wonder 12:655, 657

Landess, Thomas
Thomas Merton 1:211

Landess, Thomas H.
John Berryman 2:60
Caroline Gordon 6:205; 13:247
Andrew Lytle 22:294
William Meredith 4:349
Marion Montgomery 7:234
William Jay Smith 6:512
Allen Tate 4:540
Mona Van Duyn 3:491
Eudora Welty 1:363
James Wright 3:541

Landis, Joan Hutton
Ben Belitt 22:52

Landy, Francis
A. Alvarez 13:9

Lane, Helen R.
Carlos Fuentes 22:165

Lane, James B.
Harold Robbins 5:379
Piri Thomas 17:499

Lane, John Francis
Michelangelo Antonioni 20:38
Vittorio De Sica 20:90

Lane, Patrick
Andrew Suknaski 19:433

Lanes, Selma G.
Richard Adams 4:9
Paula Danziger 21:84

Lang, Doug
Donald Justice 19:233
Cynthia MacDonald 19:291

Lang, Olga
Pa Chin 18:371

Langbaum, Robert
Samuel Beckett 9:85
E. M. Forster 1:107
Galway Kinnell 13:321
M. L. Rosenthal 28:390

Lange, Victor
Heinrich Böll 27:62
Martin Heidegger 24:279

Langer, Elinor
Marge Piercy 18:408

Langer, Lawrence L.
Paul Celan 19:91

Langford, Paul
Leon Garfield 12:233

Langlois, Walter
Pearl S. Buck 18:77
André Malraux 9:355

Langton, Jane
Paula Danziger 21:85
Virginia Hamilton 26:151
William Mayne 12:402
Richard Peck 21:301
Mary Rodgers 12:493
Zilpha Keatley Snyder 17:472, 473, 474
Rosemary Wells 12:637

Lant, Jeffrey
Jonathan Kozol 17:253

Lanyi, Ronald Levitt
Trina Robbins 21:339

Laqueur, Walter
Anatoli Rybakov 23:370

Lardner, David
Alfred Hitchcock 16:339

Lardner, John
Irwin Shaw 7:409

Lardner, Rex
Winston Graham 23:191

Lardner, Susan
Toni Cade Bambara 19:34
John Gregory Dunne 28:124
Mary Gordon 22:186
György Konrád 10:305
Thomas McGuane 18:324
Joyce Carol Oates 9:404
Wilfrid Sheed 2:393

Larkin, Joan
Rita Mae Brown 18:73
Hortense Calisher 4:88
June Jordan 23:256
Audre Lorde 18:307

Larkin, Philip
Dick Francis 22:153
Barbara Pym 19:386

LaRocque, Geraldine E.
Madeleine L'Engle 12:348

Larrabee, Eric
Cornelius Ryan 7:385

Larrieu, Kay
Larry Woiwode 10:542

Larsen, Anne
Lisa Alther 7:11
William Kotzwinkle 14:310
Leonard Michaels 6:325

Larsen, Eric
Charles Newman 8:419

Larsen, Ernest
Jerome Charyn 18:100
Gilbert Sorrentino 14:499

Larson, Charles
Hyemeyohsts Storm 3:470

Larson, Charles R.
Peter Abrahams 4:2
Chinua Achebe 5:1
Rudolfo A. Anaya 23:25
Ayi Kwei Armah 5:31
J. M. Coetzee 23:122
Leslie A. Fiedler 4:163; 13:211
Bessie Head 25:235, 239
Camara Laye 4:284
Kamala Markandaya 8:377
Peter Matthiessen 7:210
V. S. Naipaul 7:253; 18:359
R. K. Narayan 7:255
James Ngugi 7:263
Raja Rao 25:369
Simone Schwarz-Bart 7:404
Leslie Marmon Silko 23:406
Raymond Sokolov 7:430
Wole Soyinka 5:396
Jean Toomer 13:556
Amos Tutuola 5:445
Ngugi Wa Thiong'o 13:583, 584
James Welch 6:561

Larson, James
Gunnar Ekelöf 27:118

Lasagna, Louis
Michael Crichton 2:108
Margaret O. Hyde 21:174

LaSalle, Peter
J. M. Coetzee 23:124
J. F. Powers 8:448
Cynthia Propper Seton 27:426

Lasansky, Terry Andrews
W. P. Kinsella 27:236

Lasdun, James
Pamela Hansford Johnson 27:223

Lask, I. M.
S. Y. Agnon 4:10

Lask, Thomas
Franklyn M. Branley 21:15
Richard Brautigan 12:60
Kenneth O. Hanson 13:263
Bohumil Hrabal 13:291
David Ignatow 7:177
P. D. James 18:273
Ross Macdonald 1:185
Clarence Major 19:294
Frederick Morgan 23:298
Linda Pastan 27:368
M. L. Rosenthal 28:391
John Sayles 14:484
Georges Simenon 8:486
Josef Škvorecký 15:510
W. D. Snodgrass 2:405
Piri Thomas 17:502

Laska, P. J.
Imamu Amiri Baraka 10:21

Laski, Marghanita
Patricia Highsmith 14:260
John le Carré 28:230
Ruth Rendell 28:384

Lassell, Michael
Tennessee Williams 11:573

Lasson, Robert
Mario Puzo 2:352

Latham, Aaron
Jack Kerouac 2:228

Latham, David
Hugh Hood 28:191

Lathen, Emma
Agatha Christie 12:123

Latiak, Dorothy S.
Jules Archer 12:17

Latimer, Jonathan P.
Francis Ford Coppola 16:236

Latrell, Craig
Harold Pinter 9:421

Latshaw, Jessica
Christie Harris 12:268

Lattimore, Richmond
John Berryman 2:59
Philip Booth 23:76
Jorge Luis Borges 2:73
Edgar Bowers 9:121
Joseph Brodsky 6:97
Michael Casey 2:100
Alan Dugan 6:144
Daniel Hoffman 6:243
John Hollander 14:265
Galway Kinnell 13:318
Vladimir Nabokov 8:407
Adrienne Rich 7:364
I. A. Richards 14:453
L. E. Sissman 9:491
Andrei Voznesensky 15:557

Lattin, Vernon E.
N. Scott Momaday 19:320

Lauder, Robert E.
Ingmar Bergman 16:77
John Cassavetes 20:52, 328
Christopher Durang 27:91
Jean-Paul Sartre 24:405

Laughlin, Rosemary M.
John Fowles 2:138

Laughner, Peter
Lou Reed 21:310

Laurence, Margaret
Chinua Achebe 7:3
William Mitchell 25:322
Wole Soyinka 14:507
Amos Tutuola 14:538

Laut, Stephen J., S.J.
R. V. Cassill 23:105
John Gardner 10:220

Lavender, Ralph
Alan Garner 17:150
Diana Wynne Jones 26:227
Otfried Preussler 17:375
Robert Westall 17:557

Lavers, Annette
Sylvia Plath 9:425

Lavers, Norman
John Hawkes 2:186

Lavine, Stephen David
Philip Larkin 8:336

Law, Richard
Robert Penn Warren 13:570

Lawall, Sarah N.
Yves Bonnefoy 9:113; 15:72
Francis Ponge 18:413

Lawhead, Terry
Lois Duncan 26:108
Milton Meltzer 26:309

Lawler, Daniel F., S.J.
Eleanor Hibbert 7:156

Lawler, James R.
René Char 11:117

Lawless, Ken
J. P. Donleavy 10:155

Lawrence, D. H.
Edward Dahlberg 7:61
Ernest Hemingway 10:263

Lawrence, Isabelle
Lee Kingman 17:244

Lawrence, Peter C.
Jean Lee Latham 12:324

Laws, Frederick
Sally Benson 17:47

Laws, Page R.
Uwe Johnson 15:307

Lawson, Lewis A.
William Faulkner 3:153
Flannery O'Connor 1:255
Eudora Welty 14:567

Lawton, A.
Yevgeny Yevtushenko 13:620

Lazarus, H. P.
Budd Schulberg 7:401

Lazenby, Francis D.
Milton Meltzer 26:300

Lazere, Donald
Albert Camus 14:107

Lea, Sydney
Philip Levine 14:319
Frederick Morgan 23:299

Leach, Edmund
Carlos Castaneda 12:85

Leader, Zachary
Garson Kanin 22:233

Leaf, David
Brian Wilson 12:652

Leahy, Jack
David Wagoner 5:474

Leak, Thomas
Michael Shaara 15:474

Leal, Luis
Juan Rulfo 8:462

Leaming, Barbara
Rainer Werner Fassbinder 20:114

Lear, Norman
Norman Lear 12:328

Learmont, Lavinia Marina
Hermann Hesse 2:191

Leary, Lewis
Lionel Trilling 9:534

Leary, Timothy
Bob Dylan 12:193

Leavell, Frank H.
Jesse Stuart 14:514

Leavis, F. R.
John Dos Passos 11:152
T. S. Eliot 24:171
C. P. Snow 13:512

Leavitt, Harvey
Richard Brautigan 5:67

Leb, Joan P.
Laura Z. Hobson 25:272

Lebel, J.-P.
Buster Keaton 20:190

Leber, Michele M.
Jane Rule 27:417
Sandra Scoppettone 26:404

Lebowitz, Alan
Ernest Hemingway 1:144

Lebowitz, Naomi
Stanley Elkin 4:152
E. M. Forster 4:166
J. F. Powers 1:279

Lechlitner, Ruth
Ben Belitt 22:48

Lecker, Robert
Jack Hodgins 23:233
Hugh Hood 15:286

LeClair, Thomas
Isaac Asimov 26:51
John Barth 7:23
Saul Bellow 6:53
Anthony Burgess 1:48
R. V. Cassill 23:109
Carlos Castaneda 12:95
Jerome Charyn 5:103; 8:135
Don DeLillo 10:135; 13:179
J. P. Donleavy 1:76; 4:124; 6:141; 10:154
Stanley Elkin 6:170; 9:190; 27:125
John Gardner 8:236; 18:179, 183
John Hawkes 7:141, 144
Joseph Heller 8:278
Flannery O'Connor 13:420
Walker Percy 6:400; 14:412
David Plante 7:307
Thomas Pynchon 6:435
Tom Robbins 9:454
Marilynne Robinson 25:389
Michael Shaara 15:474
Ronald Sukenick 6:523
Harvey Swados 5:420

LeClercq, Diane
Patricia Highsmith 2:194
Susan B. Hill 4:226
William Sansom 6:483

Ledbetter, J. T.
Galway Kinnell 13:320
Mark Van Doren 6:542

Lee, A. Robert
Chester Himes 18:249

Lee, Alvin
James Reaney 13:472

Lee, Brian
James Baldwin 17:35

Lee, Charles
Taylor Caldwell 28:60, 62
Ernest K. Gann 23:163
Earl Hamner, Jr. 12:257
Laura Z. Hobson 25:271
Mary Renault 17:391

Lee, Dennis
Paulette Giles 13:304
A. W. Purdy 6:428

Lee, Don L.
Nikki Giovanni 4:189
Conrad Kent Rivers 1:285

Lee, Dorothy
Joseph A. Walker 19:455

Lee, Dorothy H.
Harriette Arnow 18:13

Lee, Hermione
J. G. Ballard 14:40
Jurek Becker 19:36
Elizabeth Bowen 11:65; 22:63
Penelope Fitzgerald 19:173
Nadine Gordimer 18:189
Thomas Keneally 14:302
Flannery O'Connor 15:413
Julia O'Faolain 19:360
Marilynne Robinson 25:387
Andrew Sinclair 14:490
J.I.M. Stewart 14:513
Anne Tyler 28:434

Lee, James W.
John Braine 1:43

Lee, Judith Yaross
Philip Roth 22:354

Lee, L. L.
Thomas Berger 18:54
Walter Van Tilburg Clark 28:79

Lee, Lance
Thom Gunn 18:201

Lee, Robert A.
Alistair MacLean 13:359

Lee, Stan
Stan Lee 17:261

Leech, Margaret
Esther Forbes 12:206

Leedom-Ackerman, Joanne
Howard Fast 23:160

Leeds, Barry H.
Ken Kesey 6:278
Norman Mailer 1:191
D. Keith Mano 2:270

Leeming, Glenda
John Arden 6:9

Leer, Norman
Bernard Malamud 8:374

Lees, Gene
John Lennon and Paul McCartney 12:358
Gerome Ragni and James Rado 17:383

Leet, Herbert L.
Frank B. Gilbreth and Ernestine Gilbreth Carey 17:155

Leet, Judith
May Sarton 14:482

Leffland, Ella
Lois Gould 10:242

Legates, Charlotte
Aldous Huxley 11:287

Le Guin, Ursula K.
Italo Calvino 22:89
John Gardner 18:181
Doris Lessing 15:334
Arkadii Strugatskii and Boris Strugatskii 27:435

Lehan, Richard
Walker Percy 2:332
Wilfrid Sheed 2:392
Susan Sontag 1:322

Lehman, David
W. H. Auden 11:20
Michael S. Harper 22:208
David Ignatow 7:182
Charles Reznikoff 9:449
Ira Sadoff 9:466

Lehmann, A. G.
Georg Lukács 24:333

Lehmann, John
W. Somerset Maugham 11:370
Edith Sitwell 2:403

Lehmann, Rosamond
Mary Renault 17:390

Lehmann-Haupt, Christopher
Roger Angell 26:28
Aharon Appelfeld 23:35
Louis Auchincloss 18:25
Thomas Berger 18:56
Italo Calvino 22:92
Truman Capote 19:85
Jerome Charyn 18:99
Susan Cheever 18:100
James Clavell 25:126
Michael Crichton 2:109
Robert Crumb 17:82
Don DeLillo 27:80
Rosalyn Drexler 2:119
Stanley Elkin 14:157
William Price Fox 22:139
Marilyn French 18:159
John Gardner 18:180
Francine du Plessix Gray 22:200
Graham Greene 27:172
Pete Hamill 10:251
Barry Hannah 23:210
George V. Higgins 18:234
P. D. James 18:276
William Kennedy 28:205
John Knowles 26:262
Ella Leffland 19:277, 278

Siegfried Lenz **27**:248
Hugh Leonard **19**:282
Bette Bao Lord **23**:280
Robert Ludlum **22**:291
Norman Mailer **28**:257
Clarence Major **19**:291
Ted Mooney **25**:330
Farley Mowat **26**:345
Iris Murdoch **22**:329
Charles Newman **2**:311
Robert Newton Peck **17**:336
Bette Pesetsky **28**:357, 359
Chaim Potok **26**:372
Richard Price **12**:488
Piers Paul Read **25**:376, 378
Gregor von Rezzori **25**:382
Mordecai Richler **18**:452
Peter Rushforth **19**:406
Irwin Shaw **23**:399
Lee Smith **25**:407
Martin Cruz Smith **25**:412
Paul Theroux **28**:428
Hunter S. Thompson **17**:504
Anne Tyler **28**:431
Kurt Vonnegut, Jr. **22**:450
Helen Yglesias **22**:492
Al Young **19**:479

Lehrmann, Charles C.
Romain Gary **25**:185

Leib, Mark
Sylvia Plath **3**:389

Leiber, Fritz
Fritz Leiber **25**:304

Leiber, Justin
Fritz Leiber **25**:309

Leibowitz, Herbert
Elizabeth Bishop **13**:91
Robert Bly **2**:66
Edward Dahlberg **14**:136
Jean Garrigue **2**:153
Philip Levine **14**:320
Robert Lowell **4**:297
Josephine Miles **2**:278
Kenneth Rexroth **6**:451
Theodore Roethke **3**:434
Delmore Schwartz **2**:388
Judith Johnson Sherwin **15**:479
Isaac Bashevis Singer **3**:453
W. D. Snodgrass **2**:405
Gary Snyder **5**:395
Mona Van Duyn **3**:492
Jonathan Williams **13**:600
William Carlos Williams **9**:574; **22**:468
Edmund Wilson **3**:540

Leibowitz, Herbert A.
Frank O'Hara **2**:321

Leichtling, Jerry
Jackson Browne **21**:35

Leigh, David J., S.J.
Ernest Hemingway **6**:233
Tadeusz Konwicki **28**:211

Leitch, David
Romain Gary **25**:187

Leiter, Robert
Janet Frame **6**:190
Nadine Gordimer **7**:132
Cormac McCarthy **4**:342
Jean Rhys **6**:453
Clancy Sigal **7**:424
Larry Woiwode **10**:541

Leiter, Robert A.
William Maxwell **19**:308

Leith, Linda
Hubert Aquin **15**:17
Marie-Claire Blais **22**:59
Matt Cohen **19**:112

Leithauser, Brad
Marianne Moore **19**:340
Jean Stafford **19**:431
Evelyn Waugh **19**:465

Lejeune, Anthony
Agatha Christie **12**:117
Paul Gallico **2**:147
Anthony Powell **7**:345
P. G. Wodehouse **2**:480

Lejeune, C. A.
René Clair **20**:59
Jean Cocteau **16**:224
Elia Kazan **16**:360

Lekachman, Robert
William F. Buckley, Jr. **18**:83
Richard Elman **19**:151
Paul E. Erdman **25**:156
Ken Follett **18**:156
Robert Ludlum **22**:290
Martin Cruz Smith **25**:413

Lelchuk, Alan
Bernard Malamud **27**:298
Isaac Bashevis Singer **11**:500

Lellis, George
Rainer Werner Fassbinder **20**:107
Martin Scorsese **20**:324

Lelyveld, Joseph
Buchi Emecheta **14**:160

Lem, Stanislaw
Arkadii Strugatskii and Boris Strugatskii **27**:436

LeMaster, J. R.
Jesse Stuart **8**:507; **11**:509

Lemay, Harding
John Knowles **26**:246
J. R. Salamanca **4**:461

Lembeck, Carolyn S.
Kevin Major **26**:286

Lemmons, Philip
Brian Moore **8**:396
William Trevor **7**:478

Lemon, Lee T.
Kenneth Burke **2**:87, 89
Louis-Ferdinand Céline **3**:105
Guy Davenport, Jr. **6**:124
Judith Guest **8**:254
Jack Kerouac **5**:213
Jerzy Kosinski **10**:306
Joyce Carol Oates **6**:369
John Rechy **1**:283
Andrew Sinclair **14**:488
C. P. Snow **4**:503
Patrick White **5**:485
Yvor Winters **4**:591

Lenardon, Robert J.
Mary Renault **17**:401

L'Engle, Madeleine
James D. Forman **21**:115
Mary Stolz **12**:552

Lennox, John Watt
Anne Hébert **13**:266

Lensing, George
James Dickey **4**:120
Robert Lowell **1**:183
Louis Simpson **4**:498
Louis Zukofsky **1**:385

Lenski, Branko
Miroslav Krleža **8**:329

Lent, Henry B.
John R. Tunis **12**:596

Lentfoehr, Sister Therese
David Kherdian **6**:281

Lentricchia, Frank
Northrop Frye **24**:229

Leonard, John
Lisa Alther **7**:12
Louis Auchincloss **18**:25
Saul Bellow **6**:56
John Berger **19**:41
E. M. Broner **19**:71
T. Alan Broughton **19**:73
Anthony Burgess **22**:75
Jerome Charyn **18**:98
John Cheever **3**:107; **8**:139; **25**:120
Anita Desai **19**:135
Joan Didion **1**:74; **14**:151
Nora Ephron **17**:113
Thomas Flanagan **25**:166
Dick Francis **22**:153
Max Frisch **18**:162
Francine du Plessix Gray **22**:201
Shirley Hazzard **18**:218
Carolyn G. Heilbrun **25**:256
Frank Herbert **23**:219, 221
Maxine Hong Kingston **19**:249
Doris Lessing **3**:285
Jakov Lind **27**:271
Robert Ludlum **22**:289
Alison Lurie **4**:306
Larry McMurtry **2**:271
V. S. Naipaul **18**:361
Joyce Carol Oates **19**:355
Marge Piercy **27**:372
Thomas Pynchon **3**:414
Wilfrid Sheed **2**:393
Gilbert Sorrentino **14**:499
Alexander Theroux **25**:433
Anne Tyler **18**:529
Joseph Wambaugh **18**:532
Alexander Zinoviev **19**:486

Leonard, Vickie
Marge Piercy **27**:380

Leonard, William J.
Hugh Leonard **19**:283

Leonberger, Janet
Richard Peck **21**:298

Leonhardt, Rudolf Walter
Martin Walser **27**:456

LePellec, Yves
John Updike **15**:540

Le Pelley, Guernsey
William F. Buckley, Jr. **18**:82
G. B. Edwards **25**:150

Lerman, Leo
Enid Bagnold **25**:74

Lerman, Sue
Agnès Varda **16**:559

Lerner, Laurence
Geoffrey H. Hartman **27**:179
René Wellek **28**:445

Lerner, Max
James M. Cain **28**:47

Lernoux, Penny
Mario Vargas Llosa **9**:544

LeSage, Laurent
Roland Barthes **24**:25
Marie-Claire Blais **22**:57
Robert Pinget **7**:305
Françoise Sagan **17**:423

Le Shan, Eda J.
Sol Gordon **26**:136

Leslie, Omolara
Chinua Achebe **3**:2
Christopher Okigbo **25**:353

Lesser, Rika
Paul Celan **19**:94

Lessing, Doris
Kurt Vonnegut, Jr. **2**:456

Lester, Julius
Henry Dumas **6**:146
Lorraine Hansberry **17**:192

Lester, Margot
Dan Jacobson **4**:256
Hugh Nissenson **9**:400

Le Stourgeon, Diana E.
Rosamond Lehmann **5**:235

Letson, Russell
Philip José Farmer **19**:167

Leung, Paul
Margaret O. Hyde **21**:179

Levensohn, Alan
Christina Stead **2**:422

Levenson, Christopher
Patrick Lane **25**:287

Levenson, J. C.
Saul Bellow **1**:29

Levenson, Michael
Herbert Gold **7**:121
Tom McHale **5**:282
John Updike **5**:460

Leventhal, A. J.
Samuel Beckett **11**:32

Lever, Karen M.
John Fowles 15:234

Leverence, John
Irving Wallace 13:567

Levertov, Denise
Imamu Amiri Baraka 14:42
Russell Edson 13:190
H. D. 14:223
David Ignatow 7:173
Gilbert Sorrentino 22:391
John Wieners 7:535

Levey, Michael
William Faulkner 1:102
W. Somerset Maugham 1:204

Levi, Peter
David Jones 4:261; 13:307
F. T. Prince 22:338
George Seferis 5:384
Yevgeny Yevtushenko 1:381

Leviant, Curt
S. Y. Agnon 4:12
Jakov Lind 4:292
Chaim Potok 26:369
Isaac Bashevis Singer 3:453
Elie Wiesel 3:530

Levin, Bernard
Howard Fast 23:157
Aleksandr I. Solzhenitsyn 7:436

Levin, Betty
Virginia Hamilton 26:155

Levin, Dan
Yasunari Kawabata 2:223

Levin, David
James Baldwin 17:26

Levin, Elena
Yevgeny Yevtushenko 1:382

Levin, Irene S.
Elizabeth Swados 12:558

Levin, Martin
Brian Aldiss 5:14
Jeffrey Archer 28:13
J. G. Ballard 14:39
Patrick Boyle 19:67
A. S. Byatt 19:75
James M. Cain 28:49
Taylor Caldwell 2:95; 28:63, 67
Austin C. Clarke 8:143
James Clavell 25:125
Robert Cormier 12:134
Margaret Craven 17:79
Harry Crews 23:131
Don DeLillo 27:76
Allan W. Eckert 17:107
John Ehle 27:105
William Price Fox 22:139
George MacDonald Fraser 7:106
Paul Gallico 2:147
Ernest K. Gann 23:166
Natalia Ginzburg 5:141
Winston Graham 23:192
Doris Grumbach 22:204
Earl Hamner, Jr. 12:258
Fletcher Knebel 14:309
William Kotzwinkle 5:220
Richard Llewellyn 7:207

Robert Ludlum 22:288
John McGahern 5:280
Alice Munro 6:341
Leslie Norris 14:388
Craig Nova 7:267
Marge Piercy 27:372
J. B. Priestley 2:347
Ann Quin 6:441
Frederic Raphael 14:437
Jean Rhys 2:371
Judith Rossner 6:468
Susan Richards Shreve 23:402
David Slavitt 14:491
Lee Smith 25:406
Terry Southern 7:452
David Storey 4:530
Jesse Stuart 8:507
Hollis Summers 10:493
Elizabeth Taylor 4:541
Fredrica Wagman 7:500
David Harry Walker 14:552
Thomas Williams 14:581
P. G. Wodehouse 2:479; 5:516
Hilma Wolitzer 17:561
John Wyndham 19:475
Louis Zukofsky 2:487

Levin, Meyer
Elmer Rice 7:358
Henry Roth 6:472

Levin, Milton
Noel Coward 1:64

Levine, Bernice
Maia Wojciechowska 26:454

Levine, George
John Gardner 7:113
Paul Goodman 2:171
Juan Carlos Onetti 7:279
Thomas Pynchon 3:414

Levine, Joan
Franklyn M. Branley 21:20

Levine, Joan Goldman
Richard Peck 21:297

Levine, June Perry
Vladimir Nabokov 6:352; 11:396

Levine, Paul
Truman Capote 1:55; 3:99
J. D. Salinger 12:498

Levine, Suzanne Jill
Severo Sarduy 6:486
Mario Vargas Llosa 6:547

Levinson, Daniel
Walter Abish 22:17

Levitas, Gloria
Frank Bonham 12:54
Lois Duncan 26:103
Sonia Levitin 17:263

Levitas, Mitchel
James D. Forman 21:117

Levitin, Alexis
J.R.R. Tolkien 12:574

Levitin, Sonia
Sonia Levitin 17:264

Levitt, Morton P.
Michel Butor 3:92
Claude Simon 4:495

Levitt, Paul M.
Brendan Behan 11:45
Jorge Luis Borges 9:116
Michel de Ghelderode 11:226

Levitzky, Sergei
Aleksandr I. Solzhenitsyn 4:507

Levy, Eric P.
Samuel Beckett 18:49

Levy, Francis
Thomas Berger 3:64
Ruth Prawer Jhabvala 4:257
Megan Terry 19:441

Levy, Frank
Norman Lear 12:330

Levy, Jacques
Sam Shepard 17:435

Levy, Paul
Kingsley Amis 13:14
James Baldwin 15:41
A. S. Byatt 19:77
Roald Dahl 6:122
E. L. Doctorow 11:141
Doris Lessing 6:301
William Styron 15:529

Levy, William Turner
Padraic Colum 28:90

Lewald, H. Ernest
Ernesto Sabato 10:446; 23:376

Lewis, Alan
David Bowie 17:59
Marvin Gaye 26:131
Neil Young 17:569, 570, 571

Lewis, Allan
Robert Anderson 23:32
Paddy Chayefsky 23:114
William Gibson 23:180
William Inge 19:227
Clifford Odets 28:339

Lewis, C. S.
J.R.R. Tolkien 1:336; 12:563

Lewis, Caroline
Bob Fosse 20:124

Lewis, Constance
Ivy Compton-Burnett 15:141

Lewis, Janet
Caroline Gordon 6:206

Lewis, Maggie
W. P. Kinsella 27:239

Lewis, Marshall
Leni Riefenstahl 16:520

Lewis, Marvin A.
Rudolfo Anaya 23:26

Lewis, Naomi
Leon Garfield 12:217
Alan Garner 17:134
Noel Streatfeild 21:399, 401
Rosemary Sutcliff 26:425

Lewis, Paula Gilbert
Gabrielle Roy 10:440

Lewis, Peter
Horst Bienek 11:48
J. M. Coetzee 23:124
Autran Dourado 23:152

Lewis, Peter Elfed
Marvin Bell 8:65
Ruth Prawer Jhabvala 8:313

Lewis, R.W.B.
R. P. Blackmur 24:57
Graham Greene 1:131
André Malraux 4:328
John Steinbeck 9:512
Lionel Trilling 24:449

Lewis, Robert W.
Edward Lewis Wallant 10:516

Lewis, Robert W., Jr.
Ernest Hemingway 1:142

Lewis, Robin Jared
E. M. Forster 22:132

Lewis, Sinclair
P. G. Wodehouse 22:478

Lewis, Stuart
Bruce Jay Friedman 3:166

Lewis, Theophilus
Gretchen Cryer 21:78
Gerome Ragni and James Rado 17:382
Neil Simon 6:502, 503
Douglas Turner Ward 19:457

Lewis, Tom J.
Stanislaw Lem 8:344

Lewis, Wyndham
William Faulkner 28:135
Ezra Pound 7:322

Ley, Charles David
Vicente Aleixandre 9:10

Leyda, Jay
Akira Kurosawa 16:395

Lhamon, W. T., Jr.
Anthony Burgess 5:89
Bob Dylan 6:158; 12:192
John Gardner 3:187
William Kennedy 6:275
Joseph McElroy 5:280
Robert M. Pirsig 4:405
Thomas Pynchon 3:412; 18:430
Kurt Vonnegut, Jr. 4:568

L'heureux, John
Bernard Malamud 27:306

Libby, Anthony
Robert Bly 15:62
Theodore Roethke 11:484
William Carlos Williams 2:470

Libby, Margaret Sherwood
Margot Benary-Isbert 12:33
Franklyn M. Branley 21:16
Betty Cavanna 12:100
Maureen Daly 17:90
Eilís Dillon 17:93
James D. Forman 21:115
Leon Garfield 12:215
Christie Harris 12:261
Margaret O. Hyde 21:174
Jean Lee Latham 12:323

Philippa Pearce **21**:281
Noel Streatfeild **21**:402
Rosemary Sutcliff **26**:426, 427

Libby, Marion Vlastos
Margaret Drabble **5**:117

Liberman, M. M.
Katherine Anne Porter **1**:274; **7**:318
Jean Stafford **4**:517

Libhart, Byron R.
Julien Green **11**:260

Librach, Ronald S.
Ingmar Bergman **16**:81

Lichtenberg, Jacqueline
Gene Roddenberry **17**:407

Lichtheim, George
Lucien Goldmann **24**:234
Georg Lukács **24**:319

Liddell, Robert
Ivy Compton-Burnett **15**:135

Lieber, Joel
Richard Elman **19**:150
Lois Gould **4**:199

Lieber, Todd M.
Ralph Ellison **3**:144
Robert Frost **9**:221
John Steinbeck **5**:406

Lieberman, Laurence
Rafael Alberti **7**:10
A. R. Ammons **2**:11
John Ashbery **9**:44
W. H. Auden **2**:28
John Berryman **1**:33
Edward Brathwaite **11**:67
James Dickey **1**:73; **2**:115
Arthur Gregor **9**:252
Michael S. Harper **22**:207
Anthony Hecht **8**:268
Zbigniew Herbert **9**:271
Richard Howard **7**:165
Richard F. Hugo **18**:259
Galway Kinnell **1**:168
Stanley J. Kunitz **6**:286
W. S. Merwin **1**:212; **3**:338
Leonard Michaels **25**:314
Frederick Morgan **23**:296
Howard Moss **7**:248
Howard Nemerov **2**:307
Kenneth Patchen **18**:394
John Peck **3**:378
Kenneth Rexroth **2**:371
Muriel Rukeyser **27**:409
W. D. Snodgrass **2**:405
William Stafford **4**:520, 521
Mark Strand **6**:521
Ted Walker **13**:565
Theodore Weiss **3**:517
Reed Whittemore **4**:588

Lifton, Robert Jay
Albert Camus **2**:99
Masuji Ibuse **22**:224
Kurt Vonnegut, Jr. **2**:455

Light, Carolyn M.
Madeleine L'Engle **12**:347

Lima, Robert
Jorge Luis Borges **6**:88
Ira Levin **6**:306
Colin Wilson **3**:538

Lindabury, Richard V.
Philip Booth **23**:73

Lindberg-Seyersted, Brita
Bernard Malamud **9**:343

Lindblad, Ishrat
Pamela Hansford Johnson **27**:223

Lindborg, Henry J.
Doris Lessing **6**:299

Lindegren, Eric
Gunnar Ekelöf **27**:109

Lindeman, Jack
Robert Francis **15**:235

Lindfors, Bernth
Chinua Achebe **7**:4

Lindner, Carl M.
Robert Frost **3**:175
James Thurber **5**:440

Lindop, Grevel
John Berryman **3**:66
Bob Dylan **4**:148

Lindquist, Jennie D.
Margot Benary-Isbert **12**:32
Walter Farley **17**:116
Lee Kingman **17**:244
William Mayne **12**:387
Mary Stolz **12**:546, 550
Lenora Mattingly Weber **12**:633

Lindsey, Almont
Milton Meltzer **26**:299

Lindsey, Byron
Joseph Brodsky **13**:116

Lindsey, David A.
Jules Archer **12**:22

Lindskoog, Kathryn Ann
C. S. Lewis **27**:262

Lindstrom, Naomi
Bob Dylan **12**:191

Linehan, Eugene J., S.J.
Taylor Caldwell **2**:95
James Herriot **12**:283
Irving Wallace **7**:509

Lingeman, Richard R.
Richard Bach **14**:36
James Herriot **12**:283
Mary McCarthy **14**:362
Charles M. Schulz **12**:531
Erich Segal **10**:466
Garry Trudeau **12**:590

Lipari, Joseph A.
M. L. Rosenthal **28**:398

Lipking, Lawrence
R. S. Crane **27**:72

Lippit, Noriko Mizuta
Yukio Mishima **27**:345
Jun'ichirō Tanizaki **28**:416

Lipsius, Frank
Herbert Gold **7**:121
Bernard Malamud **2**:268
Henry Miller **2**:283
Thomas Pynchon **6**:434

Lipson, Eden Ross
Larry McMurtry **27**:333
Robert Newton Peck **17**:339

Lipsyte, Robert
Robert Lipsyte **21**:213

Lisca, Peter
John Steinbeck **21**:380

Lissner, John
Janis Ian **21**:185

Listri, Pier Francesco
Allen Tate **6**:525

Litsinger, Kathryn A.
Andre Norton **12**:465

Litt, Dorothy E.
John Mortimer **28**:286

Littell, Robert
Howard Fast **23**:154
Robert Frost **15**:240
Jean Toomer **13**:550

Little, Roger
St.-John Perse **4**:400; **11**:433, 436

Littlejohn, David
James Baldwin **5**:40
Imamu Amiri Baraka **5**:44
Samuel Beckett **2**:45
Jorge Luis Borges **2**:68
Cleanth Brooks **24**:108
Gwendolyn Brooks **5**:75
Lawrence Durrell **4**:144
Ralph Ellison **11**:179
Jean Genet **2**:157
John Hawkes **2**:183
Robert Hayden **5**:168
Joseph Heller **3**:229
Chester Himes **7**:159
Langston Hughes **5**:190
Robinson Jeffers **2**:214
John Oliver Killens **10**:300
Henry Miller **2**:281, 283
Ann Petry **7**:304
Jean Toomer **13**:551
J. E. Wideman **5**:489
Richard Wright **9**:583

Littler, Frank
Nigel Dennis **8**:173

Litwak, Leo E.
Hunter S. Thompson **17**:503

Liv, Gwen
Barbara Corcoran **17**:70

Lively, Penelope
Penelope Fitzgerald **19**:175
Russell C. Hoban **25**:265
Kazuo Ishiguro **27**:204
Doris Lessing **22**:287
Michael Moorcock **27**:352
D. M. Thomas **22**:422
Angus Wilson **25**:461

Livesay, Dorothy
Milton Acorn **15**:8
Louis Dudek **11**:159
E. J. Pratt **19**:378

Livingstone, Leon
Azorín **11**:25

Llorens, David
Nikki Giovanni **19**:190

Llosa, Mario Vargas
José María Arguedas **18**:9

Lloyd, Peter
Leonardo Sciascia **9**:476

Lobb, Edward
T. S. Eliot **24**:185

Locke, Richard
Donald Barthelme **8**:52
Ann Beattie **18**:37
Thomas Berger **8**:83
Heinrich Böll **3**:73
John Cheever **8**:139
Joan Didion **8**:175
Barry Hannah **23**:209
Joseph Heller **11**:268
John le Carré **5**:233
Vladimir Nabokov **2**:303; **8**:418
Thomas Pynchon **2**:356
John Updike **1**:345; **9**:540

Lockerbie, D. Bruce
C. S. Lewis **1**:177

Locklin, Gerald
Richard Brautigan **12**:67

Lockwood, William J.
Ed Dorn **10**:159

Lodge, David
Kingsley Amis **2**:10
William S. Burroughs **2**:92
Mary Gordon **13**:250
Graham Greene **1**:134; **3**:206
Ted Hughes **2**:199
Doris Lessing **15**:332
Norman Mailer **4**:321
Alain Robbe-Grillet **4**:447
Wilfrid Sheed **2**:394
Muriel Spark **13**:525

Loewinsohn, Ron
Richard Brautigan **12**:59

Logan, John
E. E. Cummings **3**:117

Logan, William
Gabriel García Márquez **15**:253
Robert Hayden **14**:240
Michael Ondaatje **14**:410
James Tate **25**:428
Derek Walcott **14**:548

Lohrke, Eugene
Rhys Davies **23**:140

Lomas, Herbert
Roy Fuller **4**:179
John Gardner **7**:115
Paul Goodman **4**:196
John Hawkes **7**:143
Robert M. Pirsig **6**:421
Ezra Pound **3**:398

Londré, Felicia Hardison
Mark Medoff 23:294

Long, John Allan
Anne Tyler 28:430

Long, Margo Alexander
John Neufeld 17:311

Long, Robert Emmet
Ernest Hemingway 3:237
Robert Phillips 28:362
Edmund Wilson 8:550

Longley, Edna
Douglas Dunn 6:147
Seamus Heaney 5:170
Thomas Kinsella 19:256
Marge Piercy 18:409

Longley, John Lewis, Jr.
Robert Penn Warren 1:355

Longstreth, T. Morris
Frank B. Gilbreth and
 Ernestine Gilbreth Carey
 17:154
Jean Lee Latham 12:322
Farley Mowat 26:330

Longsworth, Polly
Madeleine L'Engle 12:349

Lopez, Daniel
Bernardo Bertolucci 16:97

Loprete, Nicholas J.
William Saroyan 10:457

Lorch, Thomas M.
Edward Lewis Wallant 10:512

Lord, James
Henri Troyat 23:460

Lorich, Bruce
Samuel Beckett 6:34

Losinski, Julie
Christie Harris 12:263

Lothian, Helen M.
Christie Harris 12:262

Lotz, Jim
Farley Mowat 26:334

Loubère, J.A.E.
Claude Simon 15:490

Louch, A. R.
René Wellek 28:453

Lourie, Richard
Joseph Brodsky 13:114

Loveman, Amy
William Maxwell 19:305

Low, Alice
Isabelle Holland 21:147

Lowell, Amy
Robert Frost 13:222

Lowell, Robert
W. H. Auden 1:9
John Berryman 2:57
Randall Jarrell 2:207; 13:298
Stanley J. Kunitz 6:285
Sylvia Plath 17:347
I. A. Richards 14:452

Allen Tate 4:535

Lowenkron, David Henry
Samuel Beckett 6:40

Lowenthal, Lawrence D.
Arthur Miller 15:374

Lowrie, Rebecca
Maureen Daly 17:88

Lowrey, Burling
S. J. Perelman 23:336

Lowry, Beverly
D. M. Thomas 22:421

Lowry, Margerie Bonner
Edward Hoagland 28:180

Lubbers, Klaus
Carson McCullers 12:423

Lubow, Arthur
Michael Cimino 16:211
George Lucas 16:414

Lucas, Alec
Roderick L. Haig-Brown
 21:142
Farley Mowat 26:341

Lucas, John
Ezra Pound 7:332
William Trevor 25:442

Luccock, Halford E.
Taylor Caldwell 28:55

Lucey, Beatus T., O.S.B.
Daphne du Maurier 6:146

Luchting, Wolfgang A.
José María Arguedas 10:9
José Donoso 4:126, 127
Gabriel García Márquez 2:150
Alain Resnais 16:499
Mario Vargas Llosa 10:496

Lucid, Luellen
Aleksandr I. Solzhenitsyn
 10:480

Lucid, Robert F.
Ernest Hemingway 6:232
Norman Mailer 4:323

Lucie-Smith, Edward
Sylvia Plath 9:424

Luckett, Richard
Lenny Bruce 21:51
Anthony Powell 7:339
Robert Penn Warren 6:555
Edmund Wilson 3:540

Luckey, Eleanore Braun
Honor Arundel 17:19

Ludlow, Colin
David Mamet 15:356
Tom Stoppard 15:520

Ludwig, Jack
Bernard Malamud 2:269
Mordecai Richler 18:452

Ludwig, Linda
Doris Lessing 6:301

Lueders, Edward
Jorge Luis Borges 2:72
George MacBeth 2:252

Lugg, Andrew M.
Andy Warhol 20:417

Lukács, Georg
Aleksandr I. Solzhenitsyn
 26:416

Lukacs, John
Aleksandr I. Solzhenitsyn 7:438

Lukacs, Paul
Anthony Burgess 13:125

Lukas, Betty
Jeffrey Archer 28:13

Lukens, Rebecca J.
Mavis Thorpe Clark 12:132
Madeleine L'Engle 12:351

Lumley, Frederick
Terence Rattigan 7:354

Lumport, Felicia
Jessamyn West 7:520

Lundquist, James
J. D. Salinger 12:518
Kurt Vonnegut, Jr. 12:615

Lunn, Janet
Kevin Major 26:286

Lupack, Alan C.
Gwendolyn Brooks 15:95

Lupoff, Richard
Kurt Vonnegut, Jr. 12:629

Lurie, Alison
Richard Adams 5:7
Peter Davison 28:101
Iris Murdoch 3:348

Lurie, Nancy Oestreich
Vine Deloria, Jr. 21:108

Luschei, Martin
Walker Percy 3:378

Lustig, Irma S.
Sean O'Casey 9:411

Luttwak, Edward
Bernard Malamud 3:325

Lyall, Gavin
Edmund Crispin 22:110

Lydenberg, Robin
Jorge Luis Borges 13:111, 113

Lydon, Michael
Chuck Berry 17:52

Lydon, Susan
Leslie Epstein 27:132
John Lennon and Paul
 McCartney 12:362
Toni Morrison 22:322

Lye, John
A. W. Purdy 14:433

Lyell, Frank H.
Harper Lee 12:340

Lyles, Jean Caffey
Richard Bach 14:35

Lyles, W. H.
Stephen King 12:310

Lynch, Dennis Daley
William Stafford 7:462

Lynch, Josephine E.
Noel Streatfeild 21:399

Lynch, Michael
Richard Howard 7:168
Michael McClure 10:332

Lynd, Helen Merrell
Muriel Rukeyser 27:409

Lyne, Oliver
Ted Hughes 9:282

Lynen, John F.
Robert Frost 1:110

Lynes, Carlos, Jr.
Arthur Adamov 25:11

Lyon, George W., Jr.
Allen Ginsberg 3:194

Lyon, James K.
Paul Celan 19:87

Lyon, Laurence Gill
Jean-Paul Sartre 18:463

Lyon, Melvin
Edward Dahlberg 1:72

Lyons, Bonnie
Margaret Atwood 8:33
Henry Roth 2:378; 6:473
Delmore Schwartz 10:463

Lyons, Donald
Luchino Visconti 16:574

Lyons, Eugene
Walker Percy 6:399
John Updike 3:486

Lyons, Gene
Jeffrey Archer 28:11
Peter Benchley 8:82
Len Deighton 7:75
John Hersey 9:277
John Irving 23:249
Elia Kazan 6:274
George MacBeth 9:340
Peter Straub 28:410
Hunter S. Thompson 17:515
John Updike 13:562; 23:470
Irving Wallace 7:510
Robert Penn Warren 8:540
Richard Yates 7:555

Lyons, John O.
Vladimir Nabokov 1:241

Lytle, Andrew
Allen Tate 4:535

MacAdam, Alfred J.
G. Cabrera Infante 25:102
Thomas Pynchon 11:455
João Guimarães Rosa 23:356

MacAndrew, Andrew R.
Yuri Olesha 8:430

Macaulay, Jeannette
Camara Laye 4:285

Macauley, Robie
Toni Cade Bambara 19:33
R. P. Blackmur 2:61
Shirley Hazzard 18:214
James Alan McPherson 19:310
Jean Rhys 14:446

M. L. Rosenthal **28**:390
René Wellek **28**:447
Patrick White **9**:566

MacBeth, George
Robert Nye **13**:412

MacBride, James
James M. Cain **28**:48
Helen MacInnes **27**:279
Jessamyn West **17**:544

MacBrudnoy, David
George MacDonald Fraser **7**:106

MacCabe, Colin
Jean-Luc Godard **20**:146

MacCarthy, Desmond
T. S. Eliot **24**:161

Maccoby, Hyam
Ezra Pound **18**:420

MacDiarmid, Hugh
Ezra Pound **4**:413

Macdonald, Dwight
Charles Chaplin **16**:199
James Gould Cozzens **4**:111
Federico Fellini **16**:274
Rouben Mamoulian **16**:424
Czesław Miłosz **22**:305
Philip Roth **1**:293

MacDonald, John D.
James M. Cain **11**:87

Macdonald, Rae McCarthy
Alice Munro **10**:357

Macdonald, Ross
Nelson Algren **10**:8
Dashiell Hammett **5**:160

MacDonald, S. Yvonne
Christie Harris **12**:266

MacDonald, Scott
Erskine Caldwell **14**:96

Macdonald, Susan
Pier Paolo Pasolini **20**:262

MacDuffie, Bruce L.
Milton Meltzer **26**:299

MacFadden, Patrick
Albert Maysles and David Maysles **16**:438, 440
Pier Paolo Pasolini **20**:260

Macfarlane, David
Margaret Atwood **25**:65

MacInnes, Colin
James Baldwin **1**:14; **17**:25
Brendan Behan **15**:44
Alex Haley **12**:244

MacIntyre, Alasdair
Arthur Koestler **1**:170

MacIntyre, Jean
Barbara Corcoran **17**:77

Maciuszko, George J.
Czesław Miłosz **5**:292

Mackay, Barbara
Imamu Amiri Baraka **10**:19
Ed Bullins **7**:37
James Kirkwood **9**:319

MacKay, L. A.
Robert Finch **18**:154

MacKendrick, Louis K.
Hugh Hood **28**:193
Robert Kroetsch **23**:272

MacKenzie, Nancy K.
Babette Deutsch **18**:120

MacKenzie, Robert
Norman Lear **12**:337

MacKethan, Lucinda H.
Lee Smith **25**:409

MacKinnon, Alex
Earle Birney **6**:79

Macklin, F. Anthony
Robert Altman **16**:34
Stanley Kubrick **16**:381
Gore Vidal **2**:449

MacLaren, I. S.
A.J.M. Smith **15**:517

Maclean, Alasdair
Elizabeth Jennings **14**:292
D. M. Thomas **13**:541

MacLean, Kenneth
William Heyen **18**:229

MacLeish, Archibald
Ezra Pound **3**:399

MacLeish, Roderick
Eric Ambler **6**:3
Richard Condon **8**:150
Len Deighton **7**:74
Ken Follett **18**:155
George V. Higgins **4**:224

MacManus, Patricia
Shirley Hazzard **18**:214
Françoise Sagan **17**:424

Macmillan, Carrie
Jane Rule **27**:421

Mac Namara, Desmond
Jessamyn West **17**:550

Macnaughton, W. R.
Ernest Hemingway **8**:286

MacPike, Loralee
Cynthia Propper Seton **27**:429
Fay Weldon **19**:470

MacQuown, Vivian J.
Mary Stolz **12**:552

MacShane, Frank
Jorge Luis Borges **2**:76
Italo Calvino **22**:93
Edward Dahlberg **1**:71; **14**:138
Barbara Howes **15**:290
Clarence Major **19**:292
W. S. Merwin **1**:212
Alberto Moravia **18**:348
Pablo Neruda **9**:399
Leslie Marmon Silko **23**:407

MacSkimming, Roy
Jack Hodgins **23**:228

MacSween, R. J.
Ivy Compton-Burnett **10**:110
Evelyn Waugh **19**:462

MacTaggart, Garaud
Jimmy Cliff **21**:65

MacWillie, Joan
Noel Streatfeild **21**:396

Madden, David
James M. Cain **3**:96; **11**:86
William Gaddis **1**:113
Wright Morris **1**:230; **3**:343
Sam Shepard **17**:434

Maddocks, Melvin
Richard Adams **4**:7
Kingsley Amis **2**:7, 8
John Beecher **6**:48
Heinrich Böll **3**:75
Paul Bowles **2**:78
Padraic Colum **28**:89
J. P. Donleavy **6**:142
Ernest J. Gaines **3**:179
John Gardner **2**:152
Mark Harris **19**:201
Joseph Heller **5**:176
Thomas Keneally **5**:209, 212
Doris Lessing **2**:239; **6**:298, 303
Jakov Lind **27**:271
Bernard Malamud **2**:267
S. J. Perelman **23**:337
Thomas Pynchon **2**:354
Piers Paul Read **4**:444
Erich Maria Remarque **21**:333
Philip Roth **4**:456
Cornelius Ryan **7**:385
Angus Wilson **3**:536

Madison, Charles A.
Isaac Bashevis Singer **23**:414

Madsen, Alan
Andre Norton **12**:457

Madsen, Axel
Jerzy Skolimowski **20**:347

Madsen, Børge Gedsø
Kjeld Abell **15**:1

Maes-Jelinek, Hena
Wilson Harris **25**:212

Magalaner, Marvin
E. M. Forster **1**:103
Aldous Huxley **1**:150

Magee, Bryan
Martin Heidegger **24**:271

Magee, William H.
Philip Child **19**:100

Magid, Nora L.
Mordecai Richler **9**:450; **18**:456
Françoise Sagan **17**:416

Magliola, Robert
Jorge Luis Borges **10**:68

Magner, James E., Jr.
John Crowe Ransom **4**:431

Magnússon, Sigurđur A.
Halldór Laxness **25**:299

Magny, Claude-Edmonde
John Dos Passos **15**:182
William Faulkner **18**:143
André Malraux **15**:351

Maguire, Clinton J.
Farley Mowat **26**:337

Maguire, Robert A.
Tadeusz Różewicz **23**:359

Mahlendorf, Ursula
Horst Bienek **7**:28

Mahon, Derek
Patrick Boyle **19**:68
Austin Clarke **9**:168
Donald Davie **10**:125
Frederick Exley **11**:186
John le Carré **5**:233
József Lengyel **7**:202
Hugh MacDiarmid **19**:289
John Montague **13**:390
Brian Moore **8**:394
Edna O'Brien **8**:429

Mahon, Vincent
Marilyn French **18**:157

Mahood, M. M.
R. K. Narayan **28**:297

Maida, Patricia D.
Flannery O'Connor **10**:364

Mailer, Norman
Bernardo Bertolucci **16**:92

Mairowitz, David Zane
Edward Bond **6**:86

Maitland, Jeffrey
William H. Gass **11**:224

Maitland, Sara
Flann O'Brien **5**:314

Majdiak, Daniel
John Barth **1**:17

Majeski, Jane
Arthur Koestler **8**:324

Majkut, Denise R.
Bob Dylan **4**:148

Major, Clarence
Ralph Ellison **3**:146
Rudolph Wurlitzer **15**:588

Malabre, Alfred L., Jr.
Paul E. Erdman **25**:153

Malamut, Bruce
Jimmy Cliff **21**:63
Lou Reed **21**:312
Peter Townshend **17**:536

Malanga, Gerard
Anne Waldman **7**:508

Malcolm, Donald
James Baldwin **17**:22
Mark Harris **19**:200

Malcolm, Janet
Maia Wojciechowska **26**:453

Malin, Irving
Kōbō Abé **22**:15
Walter Abish **22**:18
Jonathan Baumbach **23**:52, 55
Saul Bellow **13**:70
Paul Bowles **19**:61
Frederick Busch **7**:39
Hortense Calisher **4**:87

Jerome Charyn **18**:98
Eleanor Clark **5**:105
B. H. Friedman **7**:109
John Hawkes **4**:217
Joseph Heller **5**:182
Ken Kesey **6**:278
Carson McCullers **4**:344
Flannery O'Connor **2**:317
Walker Percy **8**:445
James Purdy **2**:347
Philip Roth **15**:449
Isaac Bashevis Singer **23**:415
Muriel Spark **5**:398; **8**:496
Peter Spielberg **6**:519
Harvey Swados **5**:421
Elie Wiesel **5**:490

Malkin, Lawrence
Harold Pinter **6**:418

Malko, George
Frederick Buechner **4**:80

Malkoff, Karl
Robert Duncan **15**:189
Kenneth Rexroth **1**:284
Theodore Roethke **1**:291
May Swenson **4**:533

Mallalieu, H. B.
John Gardner **7**:116
Pablo Neruda **7**:261
David Pownall **10**:419

Mallerman, Tony
Satyajit Ray **16**:479

Mallet, Gina
Iris Murdoch **1**:237
Tennessee Williams **7**:545

Malley, Terrence
Richard Brautigan **3**:88

Malmfelt, A. D.
Brian De Palma **20**:73

Malmström, Gunnel
Pär Lagerkvist **13**:330

Maloff, Saul
Nelson Algren **4**:18
Louis Auchincloss **4**:30
James Baldwin **17**:23
Heinrich Böll **9**:110
Frederick Busch **7**:38
Edward Dahlberg **7**:68
Carlos Fuentes **22**:164
Ernest Hemingway **3**:236
Nat Hentoff **26**:188
Ward S. Just **27**:226
Milan Kundera **9**:321
Norman Mailer **2**:264
Milton Meltzer **26**:303
Vladimir Nabokov **6**:356
Flannery O'Connor **3**:365
Clifford Odets **2**:319
Sylvia Plath **2**:336; **17**:358
Philip Roth **3**:435; **4**:455
Alan Sillitoe **1**:307
Josef Škvorecký **15**:512
Calder Willingham **5**:512
Maia Wojciechowska **26**:450

Malone, Michael
Thomas Berger **18**:57
Ernest K. Gann **23**:168
Barry Hannah **23**:209
Kurt Vonnegut, Jr. **22**:449

Maloney, Douglas J.
Frederick Exley **6**:171

Maloney, Russell
Ogden Nash **23**:320

Maltin, Leonard
Woody Allen **16**:5

Malzberg, Barry N.
Ursula K. LeGuin **13**:349

Mamber, Stephen
Albert Maysles and David Maysles **16**:441, 442
Frederick Wiseman **20**:470, 473, 476

Mandel, Eli
Andrew Suknaki **19**:432

Mandel, Siegfried
Uwe Johnson **5**:200
Mary Renault **17**:393

Mandelbaum, Allen
Giuseppe Ungaretti **7**:481

Mandelbaum, Bernard
Elie Wiesel **11**:570

Mander, Gertrud
Peter Weiss **15**:566

Mander, John
Günter Grass **6**:208

Mandić, Oleg
Lucien Goldmann **24**:235

Manfred, Freya
Erica Jong **18**:277

Mangelsdorff, Rich
Michael McClure **6**:318

Mangione, Jerry
Andrea Giovene **7**:116

Manguel, Alberto
Lawrence Durrell **27**:100

Manheimer, Joan
Margaret Drabble **22**:123

Mankiewicz, Don
Jessamyn West **17**:546

Mankiewicz, Don M.
Laura Z. Hobson **25**:271

Manlove, C. N.
J.R.R. Tolkien **12**:580

Mann, Charles W., Jr.
Jonathan Kozol **17**:248

Mann, Elizabeth C.
Mary Stolz **12**:551

Mann, Golo
W. H. Auden **3**:29

Mann, Jeanette W.
Jean Stafford **7**:458

Mann, Thomas
Hermann Hesse **11**:270

Mannes, Marya
Françoise Sagan **17**:422

Manning, Olivia
Louis Aragon **22**:36
Beryl Bainbridge **14**:36
Sylvia Townend Warner **7**:511

Mano, D. Keith
Richard Adams **4**:9
J. G. Ballard **3**:34
Thomas Berger **5**:60
Daniel J. Berrigan **4**:58
Jorge Luis Borges **2**:71
John Cheever **3**:108
Evan S. Connell, Jr. **6**:117
Peter DeVries **10**:136
J. P. Donleavy **4**:125
Richard Elman **19**:151
Irvin Faust **8**:214
Gabriel García Márquez **27**:157
William Gerhardie **5**:140
James Hanley **3**:221
Joseph Heller **5**:180
George V. Higgins **4**:224
B. S. Johnson **6**:263, 264
Erica Jong **8**:315
Ward S. Just **27**:229
Yuri Krotkov **19**:264
Siegfried Lenz **27**:250
James A. Michener **11**:376
Vladimir Nabokov **2**:301
Hugh Nissenson **9**:400
Richard O'Brien **17**:325
John O'Hara **2**:325
Philip Roth **4**:458
William Saroyan **10**:456
Alexander Theroux **2**:433
John Updike **2**:444; **5**:456
Patrick White **3**:525
Tennessee Williams **7**:546

Mansbridge, Francis
Rudy Wiebe **14**:573

Mansell, Mark
Isaac Asimov **26**:50
Harlan Ellison **13**:208

Mansfield, Katherine
Enid Bagnold **25**:71

Manso, Susan
Anaïs Nin **8**:424

Manthorne, Jane
Frank Bonham **12**:50, 51
Mavis Thorpe Clark **12**:130
Allan W. Eckert **17**:106
James D. Forman **21**:117
James Herriot **12**:283
Andre Norton **12**:457
Maia Wojciechowska **26**:455

Manuel, Diane Casselberry
Chaim Potok **26**:375

Manvell, Roger
René Clair **20**:63
Fritz Lang **20**:204
Jean Cocteau **16**:227
Leni Riefenstahl **16**:521
Agnès Varda **16**:554
Andrzej Wajda **16**:577
Orson Welles **20**:433, 447

Mao, Nathan K.
Pa Chin **18**:373

Maples, Houston L.
Joseph Krumgold **12**:318
William Mayne **12**:392
Maia Wojciechowska **26**:451

Marafino, Elizabeth A.
Sonia Levitin **17**:265

Marcello, J. J. Armas
Mario Vargas Llosa **10**:499

Marciniak, Ed
Frank Bonham **12**:50

Marcorelles, Louis
René Clair **20**:65
Elia Kazan **16**:373
Eric Rohmer **16**:528

Marcotte, Edward
Alain Robbe-Grillet **6**:467

Marcus, Adrianne
Anna Kavan **13**:316
Jon Silkin **2**:395
William Stafford **4**:520

Marcus, Greil
Wendell Berry **8**:85
E. L. Doctorow **6**:134
Bob Dylan **12**:197
John Irving **13**:294, 295, 296
John Lennon and Paul McCartney **12**:382
Richard Price **12**:490
John Sayles **10**:460
Patti Smith **12**:535
Raymond Sokolov **7**:431
Robert Wilson **9**:576

Marcus, Mordecai
William Everson **1**:96
Robert Frost **9**:224
Ted Hughes **2**:203
Bernard Malamud **1**:199

Marcus, Steven
William Golding **2**:165
Dashiell Hammett **10**:252
Bernard Malamud **2**:265
Irving Stone **7**:470
Evelyn Waugh **27**:470

Marder, Joan V.
Rosemary Sutcliff **26**:434

Maremaa, Thomas
Robert Crumb **17**:84

Margolies, Edward
John Ehle **27**:103
Chester Himes **18**:244
Richard Wright **21**:443

Margolis, John D.
Joseph Wood Krutch **24**:290

Marguerite, Sister M., R.S.M.
Eleanor Hibbert **7**:155

Mariani, John
Aleksandr I. Solzhenitsyn **7**:440

Mariani, Paul
Robert Penn Warren **8**:536
William Carlos Williams **9**:572

Marill-Albérès, René
Jean-Paul Sartre **1**:304

Marine, Gene
Lenny Bruce **21**:49

Marinucci, Ron
Isaac Asimov **19**:29

Marius, Richard
Frederick Buechner **4**:79

Mark, M.
Carly Simon 26:411
Bruce Springsteen 17:483

Mark, Rachel
Tom Wolfe 15:587

Marken, Jack W.
N. Scott Momaday 19:320

Marker, Frederick J.
Kjeld Abell 15:3

Markmann, Charles Lam
Julien Green 3:205
Joyce Carol Oates 2:313

Markos, Donald
Hannah Green 3:202

Markos, Donald W.
James Dickey 1:74

Markow, Alice Bradley
Doris Lessing 6:297

Marks, Emerson R.
René Wellek 28:452

Marks, Mitchell
Frederick Busch 7:38

Marnham, Patrick
Paul Theroux 15:535

Marowitz, Charles
John Arden 13:23
Ed Bullins 1:47
John Osborne 5:331
Tom Stoppard 1:327
Tennessee Williams 11:576

Marquard, Jean
André Brink 18:69
Bessie Head 25:237

Marranca, Bonnie
Peter Handke 8:261; 10:256

Mars-Jones, Adam
John Gregory Dunne 28:128
Cynthia Ozick 28:350

Marsden, Michael T.
Louis L'Amour 25:277, 278

Marsh, Dave
Jackson Browne 21:38
Jimmy Cliff 21:61
Bob Dylan 12:192
Marvin Gaye 26:135
Van Morrison 21:233
Jimmy Page and Robert Plant 12:480
Patti Smith 12:539
Bruce Springsteen 17:486
Peter Townshend 17:527, 531, 533, 535, 541
Paul Weller 26:443, 444
Brian Wilson 12:654
Neil Young 17:574

Marsh, Fred T.
Andrew Lytle 22:292
Carson McCullers 12:409

Marsh, Irving T.
Jean Lee Latham 12:323

Marsh, Meredith
Raymond Carver 22:101
Ted Mooney 25:330

Marsh, Pamela
Agatha Christie 1:58
Jan de Hartog 19:131
Ronald L. Fair 18:140
Romain Gary 25:186
Joseph Krumgold 12:317
Robert Newton Peck 17:336
Josephine Poole 17:372
Mary Stolz 12:552

Marshak, Sondra
Gene Roddenberry 17:407

Marshall, Donald
Geoffrey H. Hartman 27:184
Stanislaw Lem 8:343

Marshall, Donald G.
Jacques Derrida 24:151

Marshall, Elizabeth B.
Manuel Puig 28:372

Marshall, Margaret
René Clair 20:60
A. B. Guthrie, Jr. 23:196
Josef von Sternberg 20:370

Marshall, Megan
Thornton Wilder 15:575

Marshall, Tom
Margaret Atwood 8:29; 25:63
William Heyen 13:282
Gwendolyn MacEwen 13:358
P. K. Page 7:292
Leon Rooke 25:393

Marten, Harry
Paul Bowles 19:60
Stanley Kunitz 14:313
Denise Levertov 15:338
Muriel Rukeyser 15:457

Martin, Allie Beth
Walter Farley 17:118

Martin, B. J.
Noel Streatfeild 21:412

Martin, Brian
Bruce Chatwin 28:72
Alan Sillitoe 19:422
D. M. Thomas 22:418

Martin, Bruce K.
Philip Larkin 13:338
John Steinbeck 21:376

Martin, Dolores M.
G. Cabrera Infante 25:103

Martin, Gerald
Miguel Angel Asturias 13:37

Martin, Graham
Roy Fuller 4:177
Robert Pinget 13:444

Martin, James
May Sarton 14:480

Martin, Jane
Rhys Davies 23:143
Pamela Hansford Johnson 27:215

Martin, Jay
Robert Lowell 1:181

Martin, Judith
Erica Jong 18:278

Martin, Mick
Edward Bond 23:71

Martin, Robert A.
Arthur Miller 10:346

Martin, Robert K.
Richard Howard 10:274

Martin, Ruby
Mildred D. Taylor 21:419

Martin, Sandra
Hugh Garner 13:237
Jane Rule 27:419

Martin, Terence
Ken Kesey 11:314

Martin, Wallace
D. J. Enright 8:204

Martineau, Stephen
Susan Musgrave 13:401
James Reaney 13:475

Martinez, Z. Nelly
José Donoso 8:178

Martins, Wilson
Carlos Drummond de Andrade 18:5
João Guimarães Rosa 23:355

Martinson, Steven D.
Günter Eich 15:205

Martone, John
Richard Kostelanetz 28:218

Martz, Louis L.
Robert Creeley 1:67
Phyllis Gotlieb 18:192
John Hollander 14:261
X. J. Kennedy 8:320
Robert Lowell 1:181
Lisel Mueller 13:400
Joyce Carol Oates 9:403
Robert Pinsky 9:417
Ezra Pound 1:276
Reg Saner 9:469
Jon Silkin 2:396
William Stafford 4:521
Mark Strand 18:515
John Wain 2:458
Al Young 19:477

Martz, William J.
John Berryman 1:34

Marwell, Patricia McCue
Jules Archer 12:22

Marz, Charles
John Dos Passos 25:147

Masing-Delic, Irene
Boris Pasternak 18:389

Masinton, Charles G.
J. P. Donleavy 10:153

Maskell, Duke
E. M. Forster 1:108; 9:203

Maslin, Janet
Elvis Costello 21:72
Ray Davies 21:105
Marguerite Duras 20:103
Rainer Werner Fassbinder 20:114
Alex Haley 12:254
Werner Herzog 16:328
John Landis 26:274, 276
Gordon Lightfoot 26:278
Joni Mitchell 12:440, 443
Laura Nyro 17:318
Mary Rodgers 12:495
Buffy Sainte-Marie 17:431
Carly Simon 26:411
Paul Simon 17:466
Bruce Springsteen 17:480
Lina Wertmüller 16:589
Neil Young 17:573

Mason, Ann L.
Günter Grass 4:204; 11:247

Mason, Clifford
William Melvin Kelley 22:249

Mason, Michael
Donald Barthelme 8:53
John Cheever 15:131
Robert Coover 15:143
George V. Higgins 10:273
Colin MacInnes 23:286
Peter Straub 28:409

Massey, Ian
Ray Davies 21:96

Massie, Allan
David Harry Walker 14:552

Massingham, Harold
George Mackay Brown 5:76

Mast, Gerald
Buster Keaton 20:194

Masterman, Len
Roman Polanski 16:468

Masters, Anthony
David Rudkin 14:470
C. P. Taylor 27:444

Match, Richard
Ernest K. Gann 23:163
Winston Graham 23:191

Mathes, Miriam S.
Kin Platt 26:348

Matthews, Barbara
Peter Straub 28:411

Mathews, F. X.
P. H. Newby 13:408, 410

Mathews, Laura
James Hanley 13:261
Richard Price 12:491

Mathews, Richard
Brian Aldiss 14:10
Anthony Burgess 22:72

Mathewson, Joseph
J.R.R. Tolkien 12:566

Mathewson, Rufus W., Jr.
Boris Pasternak 7:299
Mikhail Sholokhov 7:421
Aleksandr I. Solzhenitsyn 7:441

Mathewson, Ruth
Alejo Carpentier **8**:134
Joan Didion **8**:176
J. P. Donleavy **10**:154
Margaret Drabble **8**:184
Paula Fox **8**:219
James Hanley **13**:260
Colleen McCullough **27**:320
Leslie Marmon Silko **23**:407
Christina Stead **8**:500
Robert Penn Warren **8**:540

Matlaw, Myron
Alan Paton **10**:387

Matson, Marshall
Margaret Atwood **15**:36

Matthews, Anne E.
Margaret O. Hyde **21**:177

Matthews, Charles
John Hawkes **2**:183

Matthews, Dorothy
J.R.R. Tolkien **12**:583

Matthews, J. H.
André Breton **2**:80

Matthews, James H.
Frank O'Connor **14**:396; **23**:329

Matthews, Nancie
Isaac Asimov **26**:35
Noel Streatfeild **21**:401

Matthews, Pete
Walter Becker and Donald Fagen **26**:83

Matthews, Robin
Robin Skelton **13**:507

Matthews, T. S.
Edmund Wilson **8**:551

Matthews, Virginia H.
Betty Cavanna **12**:98

Matthias, John
Elizabeth Daryush **6**:123
Michael Hamburger **5**:158
Elizabeth Jennings **14**:293
David Jones **7**:189
Anne Stevenson **7**:463
D. M. Thomas **13**:542
R. S. Thomas **6**:530

Maunder, Gabrielle
Ruth M. Arthur **12**:27
Alvin Silverstein and Virginia B. Silverstein **17**:450

Maurer, Robert
A. Alvarez **5**:17
Robertson Davies **7**:73
José Donoso **8**:180
Stanley Elkin **27**:120
Leslie A. Fiedler **24**:198
MacDonald Harris **9**:258
Pablo Neruda **9**:398
Clancy Sigal **7**:425

Maurer, Robert E.
E. E. Cummings **8**:155

Mauriac, Claude
Roland Barthes **24**:22
Samuel Beckett **2**:44
Albert Camus **2**:97
Henry Miller **2**:281
Alain Robbe-Grillet **2**:373
Nathalie Sarraute **2**:383
Georges Simenon **2**:396

Maurois, André
Aldous Huxley **3**:253
Jules Romains **7**:381

Maury, Lucien
Pär Lagerkvist **7**:198

Maxwell, D. E. S.
Brian Friel **5**:128

Maxwell, Emily
Isaac Asimov **26**:36
Maia Wojciechowska **26**:449

Maxwell, Gavin
Farley Mowat **26**:336

May, Charles Paul
Joy Adamson **17**:1

May, Derwent
Nadine Gordimer **5**:145
Alfred Hitchcock **16**:340
Ted Hughes **14**:270
Alison Lurie **4**:305
Tadeusz Różewicz **9**:463
Louis Simpson **9**:485

May, Jill P.
Robert Newton Peck **17**:341

May, John R.
Kurt Vonnegut, Jr. **2**:455

May, Keith M.
Aldous Huxley **4**:242

May, Yolanta
Emma Tennant **13**:536

Mayberry, George
Howard Fast **23**:155

Mayer, David
Thornton Wilder **15**:574

Mayer, Glenn
Taylor Caldwell **28**:67

Mayer, Hans
Friedrich Dürrenmatt **4**:140
Witold Gombrowicz **4**:193
Günter Grass **4**:202
Jean-Paul Sartre **4**:473

Mayer, Peter
Vine Deloria, Jr. **21**:111

Mayer, Thomas
Maya Deren **16**:253

Mayhew, Alice
Graham Greene **1**:134
Claude Mauriac **9**:363

Maynard, Robert C.
Alex Haley **8**:259
Garry Trudeau **12**:588

Mayne, Richard
Saul Bellow **8**:70
J.I.M. Stewart **7**:465

Mayne, William
Eilís Dillon **17**:95

Mayo, Clark
Kurt Vonnegut, Jr. **12**:617

Mayoux, Jean-Jacques
Samuel Beckett **18**:41

Mays, Milton A.
Wayne C. Booth **24**:84

Mazrui, Ali A.
Alex Haley **12**:249

Mazzaro, Jerome
Elizabeth Bishop **9**:88
Brewster Ghiselin **23**:172
David Ignatow **7**:175, 178
Randall Jarrell **6**:259
Robert Lowell **4**:295, 298
Cynthia Macdonald **19**:291
Joyce Carol Oates **3**:359
Robert Phillips **28**:363
Marge Piercy **27**:375
Ezra Pound **4**:417
John Crowe Ransom **2**:366
W. D. Snodgrass **6**:514
R. G. Vliet **22**:443
William Carlos Williams **5**:508

Mazzocco, Robert
John Ashbery **3**:15
Chester Kallman **2**:221
Philip Levine **5**:251
Mario Luzi **13**:354
William Meredith **4**:348
Anne Sexton **6**:492
Eleanor Ross Taylor **5**:426
Gore Vidal **6**:548
Derek Walcott **14**:551

McAleer, John J.
MacKinlay Kantor **7**:195
Alain Robbe-Grillet **10**:438

McAllister, H. S.
Carlos Castaneda **12**:92

McAllister, Mick
Michael McClure **6**:319

McAneny, Marguerite
Richard Kostelanetz **28**:213

McArthur, Colin
Roman Polanski **16**:464
Andrzej Wajda **16**:579

McAuley, Gay
Jean Genet **10**:225
Peter Handke **10**:254

McBride, James
Frank Bonham **12**:49

McBride, Joseph
John Ford **16**:310, 314
Alfred Hitchcock **16**:348
Sidney Poitier **26**:358
Orson Welles **20**:447, 450
Billy Wilder **20**:462, 463, 464

McCabe, Bernard
Jonathan Baumbach **23**:52, 54
Wilfrid Sheed **10**:474

McCaffery, Larry
Donald Barthelme **5**:55
William H. Gass **8**:242

McCahill, Alice
Elizabeth Taylor **2**:432

McCall, Dorothy
Jean-Paul Sartre **7**:388; **13**:498

McCalla, Nelle
Maureen Daly **17**:89

McCandlish, George
Jan de Hartog **19**:132

McCann, John J.
Arthur Adamov **25**:21

McCann, Sean
Brendan Behan **15**:46

McCarten, John
Robert Bolt **14**:88
Alfred Hitchcock **16**:339
Jean Kerr **22**:256
Douglas Turner Ward **19**:456

McCarthy, Abigail
Cynthia Propper Seton **27**:428
John Updike **15**:546

McCarthy, Colman
P. G. Wodehouse **5**:516

McCarthy, Dermot
Bill Bissett **18**:62

McCarthy, Harold T.
Henry Miller **9**:377
Richard Wright **3**:545

McCarthy, Mary
Alvah Bessie **23**:59
William S. Burroughs **2**:90
Ivy Compton-Burnett **3**:112
Mary McCarthy **14**:361
Vladimir Nabokov **2**:301
Clifford Odets **28**:336
J. D. Salinger **3**:444
Nathalie Sarraute **2**:384
Monique Wittig **22**:472

McCarthy, Paul
John Steinbeck **21**:389

McCartney, Barney C.
Ezekiel Mphahlele **25**:333

McCarty, John Alan
Roman Polanski **16**:467

McCawley, Dwight L.
Theodore Roethke **19**:401

McClain, Harriet
Paula Danziger **21**:86

McClain, John
Larry Gelbart **21**:124
Jean Kerr **22**:255

McClain, Ruth Rambo
Toni Morrison **4**:365

McClanahan, Ed
Richard Brautigan **12**:64

McClatchy, J. D.
A. R. Ammons **5**:31
Lawrence Durrell **27**:97
Louise Glück **7**:119; **22**:177
Marilyn Hacker **23**:205
Anthony Hecht **19**:210
Richard Howard **7**:167

Donald Justice **19**:237
Robert Lowell **8**:355
James Merrill **6**:324
Howard Moss **14**:376
Robert Pinsky **9**:417
Sylvia Plath **5**:346
Ira Sadoff **9**:466
Anne Sexton **15**:471
Charles Simic **22**:383
W. D. Snodgrass **18**:490
Maura Stanton **9**:507
Diane Wakoski **7**:504
Robert Penn Warren **6**:557
Theodore Weiss **8**:546
Edmund White III **27**:479
Charles Wright **6**:581

McCleary, Dorothy
Eilís Dillon **17**:94

McClellan, Edwin
Yukio Mishima **6**:338

McClelland, David
Flann O'Brien **5**:315
Patti Smith **12**:536

McCloskey, Mark
Robert Francis **15**:235

McClure, Michael
Sam Shepard **17**:441

McCluskey, John
James Baldwin **17**:39

McComas, J. Frances
Frank Herbert **12**:270

McConnell, Frank
John Barth **7**:25; **14**:57
Saul Bellow **6**:54
John Gardner **7**:115
Andrew M. Greeley **28**:175
Graham Greene **14**:217; **18**:198
Norman Mailer **14**:353

McConnell-Mammarella, Joan
Carlo Emilio Gadda **11**:210

McConville, Edward
John Sayles **10**:461

McCord, David
Ogden Nash **23**:321

McCorkle, Elizabeth
Milton Meltzer **26**:305

McCormack, W. J.
Elizabeth Bowen **22**:66

McCormick, E. H.
James K. Baxter **14**:59

McCormick, Lynde
Bruce Springsteen **17**:479

McCormick, Ruth
Nagisa Oshima **20**:249, 252

McCourt, James
Eric Rohmer **16**:538

McCown, Robert, S. J.
Flannery O'Connor **21**:255

McCue, Michael
Margaret Craven **17**:80
Anne McCaffrey **17**:283
John Neufeld **17**:310

McCullers, Carson
Carson McCullers **12**:417

McCullough, Frank
George Garrett **3**:189

McCutcheon, R. S.
Alvin Silverstein and Virginia
B. Silverstein **17**:455

McDaniel, Richard Bryan
Chinua Achebe **7**:6

McDiarmid, Matthew P.
Hugh MacDiarmid **11**:334

McDonald, Edward R.
Friedrich Dürrenmatt **15**:199

McDonald, Henry
William Price Fox **22**:142

McDonald, James L.
John Barth **2**:38
John Knowles **26**:255

McDonald, Marcia
John Crowe Ransom **24**:367

McDonald, Susan S.
Harriet Waugh **6**:560

McDonnell, Christine
Roy A. Gallant **17**:133
Noel Streatfeild **21**:417

McDonnell, Jane Taylor
Galway Kinnell **2**:230

McDonnell, John V.
William Barrett **27**:18

McDonnell, Peter J.
Noel Streatfeild **21**:400

McDonough, Jack
Jackson Browne **21**:36

McDowell, Danièle
Michel Tournier **23**:452

McDowell, Frederick P. W.
John Braine **1**:43
Lawrnce Durrell **1**:87
E. M. Forster **1**:107; **10**:181
Doris Lessing **1**:175
Iris Murdoch **1**:236
Frederic Raphael **2**:366
Muriel Spark **2**:416

McDowell, Myles
Leon Garfield **12**:228
William Mayne **12**:404

McDowell, Robert
Chinua Achebe **26**:14
A. R. Ammons **25**:42
Thomas Merton **11**:374

McDowell, Robert E.
Thomas Keneally **10**:298

McElroy, Joseph
Samuel Beckett **2**:48
Italo Calvino **5**:99
Vladimir Nabokov **2**:304

McElroy, Wendy
Gabriel García Márquez **10**:217

McEvilly, Wayne
Anaïs Nin **1**:248

McEvoy, Ruth M.
Henry Gregory Felsen **17**:121

McEwen, Joe
Smokey Robinson **21**:350

McFadden, George
Wayne C. Booth **24**:91
Robert Lowell **9**:333

McFee, Michael
Dave Smith **22**:389

McFee, William
Edna Ferber **18**:151

McFerran, Douglas
Carlos Castaneda **12**:93

McGann, Jerome
Robert Creeley **2**:106; **8**:151
David Jones **7**:188
X. J. Kennedy **8**:320
Eleanor Lerman **9**:331

McGann, Jerome J.
Michael Benedikt **14**:81
Harold Bloom **24**:70
Turner Cassity **6**:107
Daniel Mark Epstein **7**:97
A. D. Hope **3**:251
Donald Justice **6**:272
Galway Kinnell **13**:320
Muriel Rukeyser **6**:479
Judith Johnson Sherwin **7**:415

McGee, David
Kris Kristofferson **26**:269
Bruce Springsteen **17**:479

McGeehin, R.
Mary Renault **17**:402

McGerr, Celia
René Clair **20**:69

McGhan, Barry
André Norton **12**:459

McGilchrist, Iain
W. H. Auden **9**:57

McGinley, Karen
Sandra Scoppettone **26**:401

McGinley, Phyllis
Margery Allingham **19**:13

McGinnis, Wayne D.
Roman Polanski **16**:471
Kurt Vonnegut, Jr. **8**:529

McGinniss, Joe
Nora Ephron **17**:113
George V. Higgins **4**:222

McGovern, Hugh
Rhys Davies **23**:146
George Tabori **19**:436

McGowan, Sarah M.
Don DeLillo **27**:79

McGrath, Joan
Gwendolyn MacEwen **13**:358

McGregor, Craig
Bob Dylan **4**:148

McGrory, Mary
Taylor Caldwell **28**:59
Helen MacInnes **27**:280

McGuane, Thomas
Richard Brautigan **1**:44
John Hawkes **2**:185

McGuinness, Arthur E.
Seamus Heaney **14**:242

McGuinness, Frank
Kingsley Amis **1**:6
Andrew Sinclair **2**:400

McGuire, Alice Brooks
Betty Cavanna **12**:98
Jean Lee Latham **12**:322

McHale, Tom
Diane Johnson **5**:198
D. Keith Mano **2**:270
J. F. Powers **8**:447

McHargue, Georgess
Barbara Corcoran **17**:71, 74
Nicholasa Mohr **12**:447
John Neufeld **17**:308
Zilpha Keatley Snyder **17**:473

McHenry, Susan
June Jordan **23**:256

McInerney, John
John Knowles **10**:303

McInerny, Ralph
Anthony Burgess **4**:80

McIntyre, Jean
Sue Ellen Bridgers **26**:91

McKay, Nellie Y.
Jean Toomer **22**:428

McKegney, Michael
Claude Chabrol **16**:171

McKenna, Andrew J.
Patrick Modiano **18**:338

McKenzie, Alan T.
John Updike **5**:452

McKenzie, Barbara
Mary McCarthy **24**:344

McKillop, Alan D.
Wayne C. Booth **24**:88

McKinley, Hugh
Anthony Kerrigan **6**:275

McKinnon, William T.
Louis MacNeice **10**:324

McLachlan, Ian
Timothy Findley **27**:144

McLane, Daisann
Laura Nyro **17**:320
Neil Young **17**:579

McLatchie, Ian B.
W. P. Kinsella **27**:238

McLaughlin, Pat
Charles M. Schulz **12**:533

McLay, C. M.
Margaret Laurence **3**:278
Ethel Davis Wilson **13**:609

McLay, Catherine
William Mitchell **25**:324

McLean, David G.
Lewis Turco **11**:551

McLellan, Joseph
Richard Adams **18**:1
Richard Bach **14**:36
Donald Barthelme **8**:52
John Berryman **8**:90
Dee Brown **18**:70
Max Frisch **18**:163
Arthur Hailey **5**:156
Robert Heinlein **8**:275
George V. Higgins **10**:274
John le Carré **15**:324
John Sayles **7**:399
J.R.R. Tolkien **8**:515

McLennan, Winona
Alvin Silverstein and Virginia B. Silverstein **17**:453

McLeod, A. L.
Thomas Keneally **19**:248
Patrick White **7**:531

McLeod, Alan L.
Thomas Keneally **19**:243

McLuhan, H. M.
F. R. Leavis **24**:294

McLuhan, Herbert Marshall
John Dos Passos **11**:154

McMahon, Erik S.
Günter Grass **22**:197

McMahon, Joseph H.
Jean-Paul Sartre **7**:389
Michel Tournier **23**:451, 453

McMahon, Patricia
Alan Garner **17**:151

McMahon-Hill, Gillian
Russell C. Hoban **7**:161

McMichael, James
May Sarton **4**:471

McMullen, Roy
Nathalie Sarraute **2**:385

McMurray, George R.
Gabriel García Márquez **27**:147

McMurtry, Larry
Vardis Fisher **7**:103
Ernest J. Gaines **11**:217
Ward Just **4**:265
Wright Morris **18**:353
Susan Richards Shreve **23**:404

McNally, John
Carson McCullers **12**:429

McNamara, Eugene
Hugh Hood **28**:189

McNeil, Helen
Mary Gordon **22**:186
Olivia Manning **19**:304
Jean Rhys **19**:392
Philip Roth **15**:454
Colin Wilson **14**:584

McNeil, Nicholas J., S.J.
Eleanor Hibbert **7**:156

McNeill, William H.
Charles M. Schulz **12**:524

McNelly, Willis E.
Ray Bradbury **10**:70
Robert Heinlein **8**:274
Frank Herbert **12**:277
Kurt Vonnegut, Jr. **2**:452

McNevin, Tom
George V. Higgins **18**:235

McNulty, Faith
Paula Danziger **21**:85
Isabelle Holland **21**:150

McPheeters, D. W.
Camilo José Cela **4**:98

McPheron, Judith
Jamake Highwater **12**:287

McPherson, Hugo
Morley Callaghan **14**:99
Mordecai Richler **5**:374
Gabrielle Roy **14**:465

McPherson, James
Richard Pryor **26**:377

McPherson, Sandra
William Heyen **13**:283

McPherson, William
Margaret Atwood **8**:30
Paula Fox **8**:218
John Gardner **8**:235
Günter Grass **11**:252
Maxine Hong Kingston **12**:312
Maxine Kumin **5**:222
Ross Macdonald **14**:328
John Updike **5**:457; **13**:563

McRobbie, Kenneth
Seamus Heaney **14**:242

McSweeney, Kerry
Brian Moore **19**:330
V. S. Naipaul **9**:391
Anthony Powell **9**:435
Simon Raven **14**:439

McVay, Douglas
Claude Chabrol **16**:182
Vittorio De Sica **20**:91
Satyajit Ray **16**:475

McWilliams, Dean
Michel Butor **3**:94; **15**:115
Marguerite Duras **3**:129; **20**:100

McWilliams, Donald E.
Frederick Wiseman **20**:471

McWilliams, Nancy R.
John Steinbeck **5**:405

McWilliams, W. C.
Mary Renault **11**:472

McWilliams, Wilson C.
John Steinbeck **5**:405

Meades, Jonathan
Simone de Beauvoir **2**:43
Jorge Luis Borges **1**:39; **3**:77; **4**:74
Louis-Ferdinand Céline **3**:105
Iris Murdoch **2**:297
Vladimir Nabokov **2**:302; **3**:354
Alain Robbe-Grillet **1**:289; **2**:376; **4**:448
Keith Roberts **14**:463

Kurt Vonnegut, Jr. **2**:455

Meckier, Jerome
Aldous Huxley **11**:285; **18**:267
Evelyn Waugh **3**:512; **19**:462

Medawar, Peter
Arthur Koestler **6**:281; **8**:324

Medjuck, Joe
Monty Python **21**:223

Mednick, Liz
Rita Mae Brown **18**:73
Susan Sontag **13**:518

Medvedev, R. A.
Mikhail Sholokhov **15**:483

Meehan, Thomas
Peter De Vries **28**:112
Bob Dylan **12**:180
Monty Python **21**:227

Meek, Margaret
Peter Dickinson **12**:175
Alan Garner **17**:138, 148, 149, 150
Mollie Hunter **21**:170
William Mayne **12**:391, 394, 399, 405
Rosemary Sutcliff **26**:428
Robert Westall **17**:559

Meeter, Glenn
Kurt Vonnegut, Jr. **4**:566

Megaw, Moira
W. H. Auden **6**:24

Megged, Aharon
S. Y. Agnon **4**:14

Mehrer, Sophia B.
Milton Meltzer **26**:297

Meiners, R. K.
James Dickey **7**:81
Robert Lowell **1**:182
Delmore Schwartz **2**:387
Allen Tate **4**:536; **24**:447

Meinke, Peter
W. H. Auden **6**:20
John Beecher **6**:48
John Dos Passos **4**:136
H. D. **8**:256
Marilyn Hacker **5**:155
Ted Hughes **4**:236
Philip Levine **5**:250
William Meredith **13**:372
Howard Nemerov **2**:307
Muriel Rukeyser **6**:478
Anne Sexton **4**:483
Diane Wakoski **7**:504
Robert Penn Warren **6**:555
Charles Wright **6**:579

Meisel, Perry
Joni Mitchell **12**:440

Meisler, Stanley
Howard Fast **23**:157

Mekas, Jonas
Andy Warhol **20**:415

Melanson, Jim
Richard O'Brien **17**:322

Mellard, James M.
Bernard Malamud **1**:198; **27**:296
François Mauriac **9**:367
Kurt Vonnegut, Jr. **3**:504; **4**:565

Mellen, Joan
Ingmar Bergman **16**:71
Luis Buñuel **16**:135
Jean-Luc Godard **20**:142
Kon Ichikawa **20**:185
Akira Kurosawa **16**:403
Elaine May **16**:434
Nagisa Oshima **20**:253, 255
Eric Rohmer **16**:533
Carlos Saura **20**:314

Mellers, Wilfrid
Bob Dylan **12**:187
John Lennon and Paul McCartney **12**:374

Mellor, Isha
Sol Yurick **6**:583

Mellors, John
Martin Amis **4**:20
Louis Auchincloss **6**:15
Beryl Bainbridge **10**:17
Lynne Reid Banks **23**:42
Thomas Berger **5**:60
Caroline Blackwood **9**:101
Dirk Bogarde **19**:43
Elizabeth Bowen **22**:64
Melvyn Bragg **10**:72
Angela Carter **5**:102
Peter De Vries **7**:77
Shusaku Endo **7**:96; **14**:160
Penelope Fitzgerald **19**:173
John Fowles **6**:188
Athol Fugard **25**:173
Herbert Gold **14**:208
John Hawkes **7**:141
Bessie Head **25**:237
Mark Helprin **10**:260
Rolf Hochhuth **18**:256
Ursula Holden **18**:258
Dan Jacobson **4**:253
Ruth Prawer Jhabvala **8**:312
G. Josipovici **6**:270
Bernard Malamud **5**:269
Olivia Manning **19**:303
Ian McEwan **13**:370
Stanley Middleton **7**:219
Yukio Mishima **4**:357
Brian Moore **19**:334
Alberto Moravia **7**:244
Iris Murdoch **4**:369
Julia O'Faolain **6**:382; **19**:360
Seán O'Faoláin **14**:407
V. S. Pritchett **5**:353
Frederic Raphael **14**:438
Piers Paul Read **4**:444; **10**:435; **25**:379, 380
J. R. Salamanca **15**:464
William Sansom **6**:484
Nathalie Sarraute **10**:460
Penelope Shuttle **7**:422
Alan Sillitoe **6**:499; **19**:420
Wole Soyinka **5**:398
Richard G. Stern **4**:523
David Storey **8**:504
Peter Straub **28**:409
Ludvík Vaculík **7**:495

John Wain **15**:561
Charles Webb **7**:516
Patrick White **5**:48

Mellown, Elgin W.
Jean Rhys **2**:373
John Wain **2**:458

Melly, George
Jean Arp **5**:33

Melnyk, George
Andrew Suknaski **19**:432

Meltzer, R.
John Lennon and Paul McCartney **12**:382
Jim Morrison **17**:290
Patti Smith **12**:538

Melville, Robert
Herbert Read **4**:438
Susan Sontag **13**:515

Melzer, Annabelle Henkin
Louis Aragon **22**:41

Mendelsohn, John
Walter Becker and Donald Fagen **26**:80

Mendelsohn, John Ned
David Bowie **17**:57, 58
Ray Davies **21**:91
Jimmy Page and Robert Plant **12**:473, 474
Peter Townshend **17**:527
Neil Young **17**:570

Mendelsohn, Michael J.
Clifford Odets **28**:337

Mendelson, David
Eugène Ionesco **6**:255

Mendelson, Edward
John Berryman **4**:61
Thomas Pynchon **3**:415; **6**:439

Mengeling, Marvin E.
Ray Bradbury **1**:42

Menkiti, Ifeanyi A.
Chinua Achebe **26**:20

Mephisto
Maya Deren **16**:252

Mercer, Peter
John Barth **9**:61

Merchant, W. Moelwyn
R. S. Thomas **13**:542

Mercier, Jean F.
Ruth M. Arthur **12**:27
Melvin Berger **12**:42
Betty Cavanna **12**:103
Jamake Highwater **12**:288
M. E. Kerr **12**:300
Madeleine L'Engle **12**:352
Katherine Paterson **12**:484, 486
Rosemary Wells **12**:637

Mercier, Vivian
Samuel Beckett **6**:38; **14**:79
Michel Butor **11**:78
Padraic Colum **28**:89
Harry Crews **6**:118
J. P. Donleavy **4**:125
Thomas Flanagan **25**:163

E. M. Forster **2**:135
George V. Higgins **4**:222
Aldous Huxley **5**:193
Iris Murdoch **4**:368
Raymond Queneau **5**:360
Alain Robbe-Grillet **6**:465
Nathalie Sarraute **4**:466
Claude Simon **4**:496

Meredith, William
John Berryman **2**:59; **3**:68; **25**:88
Anthony Hecht **8**:268
Robert Lowell **2**:248
Muriel Rukeyser **10**:442

Merguerian, Karen
James D. Forman **21**:122

Merideth, Robert
Norman Mailer **1**:192

Meritt, Carole
Alex Haley **12**:250

Merivale, Patricia
Vladimir Nabokov **1**:242

Merkin, Daphne
Ann Beattie **13**:65
André Brink **18**:68
Michael Brodsky **19**:69
A. S. Byatt **19**:77
Vincent Canby **13**:132
Joan Didion **14**:152
Jacob Epstein **19**:162
Romain Gary **25**:188
Penelope Gilliatt **13**:239
Thomas Keneally **14**:302
Ella Leffland **19**:278
A. G. Mojtabai **15**:378
Vladimir Nabokov **23**:311
Jayne Anne Phillips **15**:421
Chaim Potok **7**:321
V. S. Pritchett **15**:443
Philip Roth **15**:452
John Updike **13**:559; **15**:546
Angus Wilson **25**:463

Mermier, G.
Romain Gary **25**:189, 190

Mermier, Guy
Françoise Sagan **17**:424

Mernit, Susan
June Jordan **23**:255

Merriam, Eve
Jacques Prévert **15**:440

Merrick, Gordon
Truman Capote **19**:82

Merrill, Anthony
Paul Green **25**:196

Merrill, George
Isaac Asimov **26**:37

Merrill, James
Francis Ponge **18**:415

Merrill, Reed B.
William H. Gass **8**:245

Merrill, Robert
Vladimir Nabokov **15**:396
Kurt Vonnegut, Jr. **8**:534

Merrill, Thomas F.
Allen Ginsberg **1**:118
Charles Olson **11**:417

Merry, Bruce
Mario Luzi **13**:352
Elio Vittorini **14**:544

Mersand, Joseph
Elmer Rice **7**:359

Mersmann, James F.
Robert Bly **5**:62
Robert Duncan **4**:142
Allen Ginsberg **4**:182
Denise Levertov **5**:247
Diane Wakoski **7**:507

Merton, John Kenneth
Pamela Hansford Johnson **27**:214

Merton, Thomas
Roland Barthes **24**:37
Albert Camus **1**:52
J. F. Powers **1**:281
John Crowe Ransom **24**:362

Meserve, Walter
James Baldwin **17**:36

Mesher, David R.
Bernard Malamud **9**:346; **11**:353

Mesic, Michael
James Dickey **4**:121
Chester Kallman **2**:221

Mesic, Penelope
Russell C. Hoban **25**:267

Meškys, Edmund R.
Franklyn M. Branley **21**:18, 19

Mesnet, Marie-Béatrice
Graham Greene **3**:210

Messer, Bill
Peter Dickinson **12**:171

Metcalf, Paul
Charles Olson **9**:413

Metzger, C. R.
Lawrence Ferlinghetti **10**:176

Metzger, Norman
Franklyn M. Branley **21**:24

Mews, Siegfried
Carl Zuckmayer **18**:553, 557

Mewshaw, Michael
Jeffrey Archer **28**:14
Jonathan Baumbach **6**:31
Doris Betts **3**:73
Robertson Davies **7**:74
William Eastlake **8**:200
B. H. Friedman **7**:108
Graham Greene **18**:195
Jack Hodgins **23**:230
Robert F. Jones **7**:192
Stephen King **12**:310
David Slavitt **5**:391
Raymond Sokolov **7**:430
Peter Spielberg **6**:519
Robert Lewis Taylor **14**:534
Paul Theroux **5**:427

Meyer, Ellen Hope
Erica Jong **4**:264
Joyce Carol Oates **2**:315

Meyer, Gerard Previn
Thomas McGrath **28**:276

Meyer, Karl E.
Garry Marshall **17**:278
Frederick Wiseman **20**:475

Meyer, Marianne
Joan Armatrading **17**:10

Meyer, Michael
Harry Martinson **14**:356

Meyer, Thomas
Lorine Niedecker **10**:360
Toby Olson **28**:344

Meyers, Jeffrey
E. M. Forster **3**:162; **4**:169
Doris Lessing **2**:241
André Malraux **4**:333

Meyers, Robert B.
Robert Altman **16**:26

Mezan, Peter
Ken Russell **16**:544

Mezey, Robert
Jerome Rothenberg **6**:478
Gary Snyder **9**:498

Micciche, Pauline F.
Roger Zelazny **21**:464

Michaels, Leonard
John Barth **2**:37
Samuel Beckett **11**:43
Thomas Berger **11**:46
Jorge Luis Borges **2**:77
Dashiell Hammett **5**:160
Peter Handke **8**:264
Joseph Heller **11**:269
Erica Jong **8**:314
Bernard Malamud **3**:324
Peter Matthiessen **11**:361
Vladimir Nabokov **8**:417
Robert Stone **23**:427

Michaels, Robert G.
Woody Allen **16**:3

Michalczyk, John J.
Fernando Arrabal **18**:23

Michałek, Bolesław
Andrzej Wajda **16**:581

Michel, Sonya
Joan Micklin Silver **20**:342

Michelson, Aaron I.
Martha Gellhorn **14**:196

Michelson, Bruce
Richard Wilbur **14**:579

Michelson, Peter
Leslie A. Fiedler **24**:199

Michener, Charles
Albert Maysles and David Maysles **16**:444

Michener, Charles T.
Anthony Powell **3**:402; **7**:343

Mickelson, Anne Z.
Toni Morrison 22:315

Middlebrook, Diane
Allen Ginsberg 6:199

Middleton, Christopher
Herman Hesse 25:258

Miesel, Sandra
Poul Anderson 15:11

Mihailovich, Vasa D.
Miroslav Krleža 8:330
Vasko Popa 19:373, 375

Miklitsch, Robert
Robert Hass 18:211

Milano, Paolo
Riccardo Bacchelli 19:32

Milbauer, Jerry
The Police 26:364

Milch, Robert J.
Chaim Potok 2:338

Milder, Robert
Flannery O'Connor 13:417

Mileck, Joseph
Hermann Hesse 17:198

Miles, G. E.
Betty Smith 19:423

Miles, Keith
Günter Grass 15:259

Miles, William
Langston Hughes 1:148

Milford, Nancy
Louise Bogan 4:69

Millar, Daniel
Jean Renoir 20:297

Millar, Gavin
Robert Altman 16:42
Lindsay Anderson 20:13
Ingmar Bergman 16:80
Claude Chabrol 16:172, 184
Michael Cimino 16:210

Millar, Margaret
Daphne du Maurier 6:146

Millar, Neil
David Harry Walker 14:552

Millar, Sylvia
Erskine Caldwell 14:95
Carlos Saura 20:315

Miller, Adam David
Alex Haley 12:249

Miller, Alice
Rosemary Wells 12:637

Miller, Baxter
Langston Hughes 10:282

Miller, Charles
Chinua Achebe 26:13

Miller, Charles L.
Joy Adamson 17:4

Miller, Dan
Roger Zelazny 21:469

Miller, David
Michael Hamburger 5:158

Miller, Faren
Gene Wolfe 25:478

Miller, Gabriel
Alvah Bessie 23:61
Daniel Fuchs 22:157
Alfred Hitchcock 16:353

Miller, Henry
Luis Buñuel 16:127
Blaise Cendrars 18:91
Anaïs Nin 14:379

Miller, James E.
John Berryman 25:98

Miller, James E., Jr.
William Faulkner 6:180
J. D. Salinger 1:298; 12:496

Miller, Jane
Ursula Holden 18:257
Julius Horwitz 14:267
Alain Robbe-Grillet 14:462
Simone Schwarz-Bart 7:404

Miller, Jeanne-Marie A.
Imamu Amiri Baraka 2:35
Gwendolyn Brooks 1:46; 4:78
Charles Gordone 4:198

Miller, Jim
Ray Davies 21:94
Van Morrison 21:236
Jimmy Page and Robert Plant 12:477
Smokey Robinson 21:350
Bruce Springsteen 17:482, 485
Brian Wilson 12:644, 648
Neil Young 17:571

Miller, Jim Wayne
Jesse Stuart 11:513

Miller, Jonathan
Lenny Bruce 21:44

Miller, Jordan Y.
Lorraine Hansberry 17:188

Miller, Karl
Kingsley Amis 13:14
Martin Amis 4:21
Beryl Bainbridge 22:44
James Baldwin 17:28
John Berger 19:38
Paula Fox 8:218
Ted Hughes 4:236
Dan Jacobson 4:256
Hugh MacDiarmid 2:254
Flann O'Brien 5:316
Barbara Pym 13:470
Anne Roiphe 9:456
Emma Tennant 13:537
Paul Theroux 11:530
Michel Tournier 6:538

Miller, Marjorie Mithoff
Isaac Asimov 26:39

Miller, Mark
Sam Peckinpah 20:279

Miller, Mary Jane
Harold Pinter 27:385

Miller, Michael H.
Rosa Guy 26:142

Miller, Neil
Julio Cortázar 2:103

Miller, Nolan
Henry Bromell 5:73
Tillie Olsen 13:433

Miller, R. Baxter
Langston Hughes 15:293

Miller, Sara
Sue Ellen Bridgers 26:91
Anne McCaffrey 17:283

Miller, Stephen
Saul Bellow 25:84
Zbigniew Herbert 9:272

Miller, Tom P.
William Stafford 4:521

Miller, Vincent
T. S. Eliot 9:182
Ezra Pound 13:462

Millgate, Michael
James Gould Cozzens 4:114
John Dos Passos 4:133
William Faulkner 28:139

Millichap, Joseph R.
Carson McCullers 12:428

Milliken, Stephen F.
Chester Himes 18:247

Mills, James
George V. Higgins 4:222

Mills, John
John Arden 13:26
Leon Rooke 25:391
Kurt Vonnegut, Jr. 22:450

Mills, Nicolaus
Joan Micklin Silver 20:344

Mills, Ralph J., Jr.
Yves Bonnefoy 9:112
René Char 9:160
Lucille Clifton 19:109
Richard Eberhart 3:134, 135
David Ignatow 7:174, 179
Maxine Kumin 5:222
Denise Levertov 2:243; 3:293
Philip Levine 4:287
Kathleen Raine 7:351
Theodore Roethke 1:291
Anne Stevenson 7:462
Jonathan Williams 13:600

Millstein, Gilbert
Lenny Bruce 21:43
Irvin Faust 8:215
Milton Meltzer 26:304
John R. Tunis 12:598

Milne, Tom
Robert Altman 16:42
Ingmar Bergman 16:54, 55
Robert Bresson 16:112, 119
Mel Brooks 12:79
Claude Chabrol 16:175, 178
René Clair 20:68
Francis Ford Coppola 16:232
Vittorio De Sica 20:97
Bob Fosse 20:121
Jean-Luc Godard 20:129, 131
George Roy Hill 26:197, 205
Kon Ichikawa 20:179, 181, 183
Stanley Kubrick 16:379
Akira Kurosawa 16:404
Rouben Mamoulian 16:424
John Osborne 5:330
Yasujiro Ozu 16:447
Gordon Parks 16:459
Sam Peckinpah 20:273
Roman Polanski 16:463
Satyajit Ray 16:483, 487, 488, 495
Jean Renoir 20:292, 293
Martin Scorsese 20:330, 331
Steven Spielberg 20:357, 358
Josef von Sternberg 20:377
Andrzej Wajda 16:578
Peter Weir 20:425
Orson Welles 20:442

Milne, W. Gordon
John Dos Passos 4:134

Milner, Joseph O.
Sue Ellen Bridgers 26:93

Milner, Philip
Toby Olson 28:342

Milner-Gulland, Robin
Andrei Voznesensky 1:349
Yevgeny Yevtushenko 1:381

Milosh, Joseph
John Gardner 10:220

Miłosz, Czesław
Tadeusz Różewicz 23:358

Milton, Edith
Beryl Bainbridge 10:17
Frederick Buechner 9:136
Leslie Epstein 27:131
Gail Godwin 22:181
Nadine Gordimer 18:190
Kazuo Ishiguro 27:203
Alison Lurie 18:311
Olivia Manning 19:303
V. S. Naipaul 18:361
Jane Rule 27:420
Alan Sillitoe 10:477
William Styron 15:528
D. M. Thomas 22:420

Milton, John R.
Walter Van Tilburg Clark 28:82
Vardis Fisher 7:105
A. B. Guthrie, Jr. 23:201
N. Scott Momaday 2:290
James Welch 14:558

Milton, Joyce
Jules Feiffer 8:217
Virginia Hamilton 26:156
Isabelle Holland 21:151
Norma Fox Mazer 26:291
Richard Peck 21:299
Kin Platt 26:355
Paul Zindel 26:476

Milun, Richard A.
William Faulkner 6:177

Milward, John
David Bowie 17:65
Billy Joel 26:222
The Police 26:364

Mindlin, M.
Yehuda Amichai 9:22

Miner, Earl
Kōbō Abé 22:11
Yukio Mishima 27:337

Miner, Robert G., Jr.
Charles M. Schulz 12:529

Minogue, Valerie
Michel Butor 11:82
Alain Robbe-Grillet 10:437
Nathalie Sarraute 10:458

Mintz, Alan L.
Andrew M. Greeley 28:172
Yoram Kaniuk 19:240

Miroff, Bruce
Neil Young 17:569

Mirsky, Mark J.
John Hawkes 7:145

Mirsky, Mark Jay
Samuel Beckett 6:38
Anthony Burgess 4:83
Günter Grass 4:205
Flann O'Brien 5:314
Manuel Puig 3:407

Mishima, Yukio
Yasunari Kawabata 18:280

Mitchell, A.C.W.
Kenneth Slessor 14:497

Mitchell, Chuck
Walter Becker and Donald Fagen 26:79

Mitchell, Deborah
Roy Fisher 25:159

Mitchell, Gregg
Paul Simon 17:460
Bruce Springsteen 17:476, 478

Mitchell, Henry
S. J. Perelman 23:338

Mitchell, Judith N.
Rosa Guy 26:146
Paul Zindel 26:481

Mitchell, Julian
Ivy Compton-Burnett 10:110

Mitchell, Juliet
Norman Mailer 1:192

Mitchell, Lisa
Stevie Smith 25:421

Mitchell, Loften
Alice Childress 12:104

Mitchell, Louis D.
Virginia Hamilton 26:150

Mitchell, Marilyn L.
John Steinbeck 9:516

Mitchell, Penelope M.
Roy A. Gallant 17:128, 130
Christie Harris 12:263

Mitchell, Roger
Thomas McGrath 28:279

Mitchell, W.J.T.
Hubert Selby, Jr. 4:481

Mitchison, Naomi
W. H. Auden 9:57
Mildred D. Taylor 21:421

Mitgang, Herbert
Giorgio Bassani 9:75
John Ehle 27:102
Michael Mott 15:379
Carl Sandburg 15:468
Leonardo Sciascia 9:475

Mittleman, Leslie B.
Kingsley Amis 8:11

Mitton, Pat
Christie Harris 12:265

Mitz, Rick
Larry Gelbart 21:132

Mix, David
Gordon Lightfoot 26:282

Miyoshi, Masao
Yasunari Kawabata 9:311
Yukio Mishima 27:338

Mizejewski, Linda
James Dickey 15:174

Mizener, Arthur
James Gould Cozzens 4:115
John Dos Passos 4:133
Anthony Hecht 8:266
F. R. Leavis 24:294
Anthony Powell 10:408
J. D. Salinger 12:501
James Thurber 5:439
Edmund Wilson 2:475

Mo, Timothy
Jennifer Johnston 7:186
John le Carré 5:234
Colin MacInnes 4:35
Wilfrid Sheed 4:489
Harriet Waugh 6:559

Moeller, Hans-Bernhard
Peter Weiss 15:563

Moers, Ellen
Lillian Hellman 2:187
Adrienne Rich 18:447

Moffett, Judith
Daniel Hoffman 13:287
James Merrill 13:376; 18:329

Mohs, Mayo
Andrew M. Greeley 28:176

Mojtabai, A. G.
Yasunari Kawabata 5:208
Thomas Keneally 5:211
Joyce Carol Oates 15:402
Amos Oz 27:358
Anne Tyler 18:530
Richard Yates 8:555

Mok, Michael
Aleksandr I. Solzhenitsyn 2:409

Mole, John
Ted Hughes 14:271
Derek Mahon 27:293
Louis Simpson 7:428
R. S. Thomas 6:530; 13:545
Theodore Weiss 14:555

Molesworth, Charles
John Ashbery 15:26
John Berryman 2:56; 8:89
Robert Bly 15:64
Hayden Carruth 18:89
Ronald G. Everson 27:135
Leslie A. Fiedler 24:200
Louise Glück 22:175
Marilyn Hacker 23:205
Robert Hass 18:210
Ted Hughes 4:236
Erica Jong 18:278
Donald Justice 19:233
Galway Kinnell 3:269
Richard Kostelanetz 28:217
Leslie Norris 14:387
Michael Ondaatje 14:410
Marge Piercy 14:421
Robert Pinsky 19:369
Anne Sexton 8:483
Charles Simic 22:381
Charles Tomlinson 4:548

Molin, Sven Eric
René Wellek 28:444

Molina, Ida
Antonio Buero Vallejo 15:103

Molloy, F. C.
John McGahern 9:370

Molnar, Thomas
Françoise Sagan 17:419

Moloney, Michael F.
François Mauriac 4:337

Momaday, N. Scott
Dee Brown 18:70
Vine Deloria, Jr. 21:110
Jamake Highwater 12:288
Leslie Marmon Silko 23:411

Momberger, Philip
William Faulkner 6:179

Monaco, James
Woody Allen 16:15
John Cassavetes 20:54
Claude Chabrol 16:182
Francis Ford Coppola 16:248
Jean-Luc Godard 20:148
Richard Lester 20:228
Gordon Parks 16:460
Alain Resnais 16:511
Martin Scorsese 20:333
Andrew Sinclair 14:489
Steven Spielberg 20:359, 365
François Truffaut 20:399
Melvin Van Peebles 20:412

Monagan, John S.
Anthony Powell 7:342

Monas, Sidney
Ilya Ehrenburg 18:134
Aleksandr I. Solzhenitsyn 4:511; 26:415
Andrei Voznesensky 15:552

Mondello, Salvatore
Stan Lee 17:259

Monegal, Emir Rodríguez-
See Rodríguez-Monegal, Emir

Monet, Christina
Mark Medoff 6:323

Monguió, Luis
Rafael Alberti 7:8

Monheit, Albert
Roy A. Gallant 17:126

Monk, Patricia
Robertson Davies 25:132, 136

Monley, Keith
Frederick Busch 18:86
Ella Leffland 19:279

Monogue, Valerie
Harold Pinter 6:404

Monroe, Harriet
Robert Frost 26:112
Marianne Moore 19:335

Monsman, Gerald
J.R.R. Tolkien 1:339

Montagnes, Anne
Phyllis Gotlieb 18:192
Brian Moore 5:297
Audrey Thomas 13:538

Montague, John
Thomas Kinsella 19:251
Hugh MacDiarmid 11:333

Monteiro, George
Bob Dylan 4:149
Robert Frost 4:174; 10:199
Ernest Hemingway 6:231

Montgomery, Marion
T. S. Eliot 6:163
Robert Frost 10:195
Flannery O'Connor 1:258

Montgomery, Niall
Flann O'Brien 7:269

Montrose, David
William Golding 27:164
Bette Pesetsky 28:358

Moody, Christopher
Aleksandr I. Solzhenitsyn 26:418

Moody, Jennifer
Lois Duncan 26:108

Moody, Michael
Mario Vargas Llosa 9:544

Moody, Richard
Lillian Hellman 18:221

Moon, Eric
Colin MacInnes 23:283
Frederic Raphael 14:436

Mooney, Bel
Doris Lessing 22:286

Mooney, Philip
Albert Camus 14:115

Mooney, Stephen
Josephine Miles 14:368

Moorcock, Michael
Angus Wilson 3:535

Moore, Anne Carroll
Margot Benary-Isbert 12:30

Moore, Brian
Robertson Davies 2:113

Moore, D. B.
Louis MacNeice 4:316

Moore, David W.
Isaac Asimov 26:58

Moore, Emily R.
Mildred D. Taylor 21:419

Moore, Gerald
Chinua Achebe 11:1
Ezekiel Mphahlele 25:343

Moore, Harry T.
Arthur Adamov 4:5
Kay Boyle 5:65
John Dos Passos 4:132
E. M. Forster 1:106
Herbert Gold 4:190
Rolf Hochhuth 18:250
Eugène Ionesco 4:252
James Jones 3:262
Meyer Levin 7:204
Henry Miller 4:350
Alain Robbe-Grillet 2:374
Nathalie Sarraute 2:384
Georges Simenon 2:397
Claude Simon 4:494
John Steinbeck 5:405

Moore, Honor
Marilyn Hacker 5:156
June Jordan 5:203

Moore, Hugo
Hugh MacDiarmid 4:311

Moore, Jack B.
Carson McCullers 12:425
Frank Yerby 7:556

Moore, John Rees
James Baldwin 2:31
Samuel Beckett 10:29
J. P. Donleavy 1:76; 4:124
Robert Penn Warren 6:558

Moore, L. Hugh
Robert Stone 23:425

Moore, Marianne
E. E. Cummings 12:141
Ezra Pound 7:322
Edith Sitwell 9:493
William Carlos Williams 13:601

Moore, Maxine
Isaac Asimov 9:49

Moore, Michael
William Wharton 18:543

Moore, Rayburn S.
Elizabeth Spencer 22:402

Moore, Richard
George Garrett 3:192
Maxine Kumin 28:220

Moore, Stephen C.
John Cheever 7:49
Robert Lowell 3:301

Moore, T. Inglis
Kenneth Slessor 14:495

Moorehead, Caroline
Joyce Maynard 23:291
David Plante 23:347
Martin Cruz Smith 25:414

Moorehouse, Val
Richard Kostelanetz 28:218

Moorman, Charles
C. S. Lewis 14:323
J.R.R. Tolkien 1:337

Moramarco, Fred
John Ashbery 4:22; 9:42
Robert Creeley 1:67
David Ignatow 7:181
Galway Kinnell 2:229
W. S. Merwin 1:213
Frank O'Hara 13:424
Ezra Pound 18:425
James Schevill 7:401

Moran, Ronald
Wendell Berry 4:59
Robert Creeley 4:117
David Ignatow 4:248
Marge Piercy 6:402
Louis Simpson 4:498
James Tate 6:528

Moravia, Alberto
Truman Capote 13:132

Mordas, Phyllis G.
Melvin Berger 12:40

Morel, Jean-Pierre
André Breton 15:88

Morello-Frosch, Marta
Julio Cortázar 2:104
Gabriel García Márquez 3:183

Morgan, Constance
Helen MacInnes 27:280

Morgan, Edwin
John Berryman 10:47
James Blish 14:83
Anthony Burgess 15:104
Ilya Ehrenburg 18:137
Roy Fuller 28:153
Halldór Laxness 25:292
Hugh MacDiarmid 11:338
Eugenio Montale 9:387
Piers Paul Read 25:376
Rudolph Wurlitzer 15:587
Yevgeny Yevtushenko 26:468

Morgan, Ellen
Doris Lessing 3:288

Morgan, John
Günter Grass 6:209

Morgan, Robert
Geoffrey Hill 8:294

Morgan, Speer
Wendell Berry 27:33
Dan Jacobson 4:256

Morgan, Ted
Harry Crews 23:136
Norman Mailer 14:354
Farley Mowat 26:346
Alice Munro 19:346

Morgenstern, Dan
Andrew Lloyd Webber and Tim Rice 21:426
Frank Zappa 17:587

Morgenstern, Joseph
Gordon Parks 16:458
Melvin Van Peebles 20:410

Moritz, A. F.
Andrew Suknaski 19:433

Moritz, Albert
Robert Kroetsch 23:276

Morley, Christopher
Enid Bagnold 25:72, 73
Ogden Nash 23:321

Morley, Patricia A.
Margaret Atwood 13:41
Hugh Hood 28:190
Patrick White 7:529

Morley, Sheridan
Terence Rattigan 7:354

Morner, Claudia
Douglas Adams 27:13

Morrell, A. C.
Jean Rhys 19:390

Morris, Alice
Christina Stead 2:422

Morris, C. B.
Rafael Alberti 7:9
Vicente Aleixandre 9:12

Morris, Christopher D.
John Barth 7:23

Morris, George
Paddy Chayefsky 23:117
Brian De Palma 20:82
Eric Rohmer 16:539
Martin Scorsese 20:329
Billy Wilder 20:466

Morris, H. H.
Dashiell Hammett 10:253

Morris, Harry
Louise Bogan 4:68
James Dickey 1:73
Jean Garrigue 2:154
John Hollander 2:197
George MacBeth 2:251
Louis Simpson 4:498
John Steinbeck 21:370

Morris, Ivan
Yasunari Kawabata 2:222

Morris, Jan
Laurens van der Post 5:464

Morris, Jeff
Robert Francis 15:238

Morris, John N.
Ai 14:7
Kenneth O. Hanson 13:263
Donald Justice 6:271
Adrienne Rich 7:370
Mark Strand 6:521
Nancy Willard 7:539
Charles Wright 6:580; 13:612

Morris, Mervyn
Louise Bennett 28:26

Morris, Robert K.
Anthony Burgess 4:81; 5:86
Lawrence Durrell 4:146
John Fowles 6:189
James Hanley 5:167
Doris Lessing 6:290
Olivia Manning 5:271

Anthony Powell 1:278; 3:404; 7:345
V. S. Pritchett 5:354
C. P. Snow 6:515
Thornton Wilder 6:578

Morris, Wesley
John Crowe Ransom 4:433

Morris, Wright
Ernest Hemingway 1:141

Morrison, Blake
Beryl Bainbridge 14:37
William Boyd 28:40
André Brink 18:69
J. M. Coetzee 23:121
Donald Davie 10:124
Jacob Epstein 19:162
Roy Fuller 28:156
Gabriel García Márquez 15:252
Patricia Highsmith 14:261
Thomas Keneally 14:301
Eugenio Montale 18:343
Anaïs Nin 14:386
Robert Pinsky 19:370
Frederic Raphael 14:438
Andrew Sinclair 14:489
Derek Walcott 25:457
Yevgeny Yevtushenko 13:620

Morrison, Harriet
Frank Bonham 12:53

Morrison, J. Allan
Leon Garfield 12:226, 234

Morrison, J. M.
Hugh MacDiarmid 2:254

Morrison, John W.
Jun'ichiro Tanizaki 8:509

Morrison, Lillian
Eilís Dillon 17:93
Mary Stolz 12:549, 551

Morrison, Michael
Andrew M. Greeley 28:169

Morrison, Philip
Franklyn M. Branley 21:17
Roy A. Gallant 17:129
Christie Harris 12:262
Thor Heyerdahl 26:191
Larry Kettelkamp 12:304

Morrison, Phylis
Franklyn M. Branley 21:17
Roy A. Gallant 17:129
Christie Harris 12:262
Larry Kettelkamp 12:304

Morrison, Theodore
Robert Frost 1:111

Morrison, Toni
Jean Toomer 22:428

Morrissette, Bruce
Alain Robbe-Grillet 1:27; 14:455

Morrissey, Daniel
John Updike 7:488

Morrow, Lance
John Fowles **6**:187
Erica Jong **8**:314
Yasunari Kawabata **5**:208
James A. Michener **5**:290
Yukio Mishima **4**:356, 358

Morse, David
Smokey Robinson **21**:344

Morse, J. Mitchell
Kingsley Amis **2**:6
James Baldwin **2**:32
Richard Elman **19**:150
Bruce Jay Friedman **3**:165
Joanne Greenberg **7**:134
Jakov Lind **2**:245
Mary McCarthy **1**:207
Vladimir Nabokov **2**:299
Peter Weiss **3**:514

Morse, John
Gilbert Sorrentino **22**:395

Morse, Jonathan
John Dos Passos **11**:156

Morse, Samuel French
W. H. Auden **6**:18
Margaret Avison **2**:29
John Berryman **3**:65
Brewster Ghiselin **23**:170
Robert Lowell **3**:301
Louis Zukofsky **1**:385

Morthland, John
Jimmy Cliff **21**:63
Waylon Jennings **21**:204
Bob Marley **17**:269

Mortifoglio, Richard
Marvin Gaye **26**:133
Laura Nyro **17**:320

Mortimer, John
James Thurber **5**:433

Mortimer, Penelope
Elizabeth Bishop **9**:89
Nadine Gordimer **7**:132
Fay Weldon **6**:562
Tom Wolfe **15**:586

Mortimer, Peter
C. P. Taylor **27**:444

Mortimer, Raymond
Enid Bagnold **25**:72

Mortimore, Roger
Carlos Saura **20**:315

Morton, Desmond
Thomas Flanagan **25**:166

Morton, Donald E.
Vladimir Nabokov **15**:390

Morton, Frederic
Richard Elman **19**:149
Romain Gary **25**:184
Erich Maria Remarque **21**:331
Henri Troyat **23**:459

Moscoso-Gongora, Peter
José Lezama Lima **10**:319

Moser, Gerald M.
José Rodrigues Miguéis **10**:340

Moses, Carole
Ernest Hemingway **19**:220

Moses, Edwin
Albert Camus **9**:148

Moses, Joseph
E. L. Doctorow **11**:140

Moses, Robbie Odom
Edward Albee **11**:12

Moses, Wilson J.
W.E.B. DuBois **13**:182

Mosher, Harold F., Jr.
Paul Simon **17**:462

Mosher, John
Alfred Hitchcock **16**:338

Moskowitz, Moshe
Chaim Grade **10**:248

Moskowitz, Sam
Fritz Leiber **25**:301
Theodore Sturgeon **22**:410
John Wyndham **19**:474

Mosley, Nicholas
J. P. Donleavy **10**:155

Moss, Mrs. E. D.
Philippa Pearce **21**:282

Moss, Elaine
Margaret Craven **17**:80
Diana Wynne Jones **26**:231
Madeleine L'Engle **12**:347
Rosemary Sutcliff **26**:438

Moss, Howard
W. H. Auden **6**:20
Elizabeth Bishop **1**:35; **9**:91
Elizabeth Bowen **1**:41; **3**:84
Graham Greene **6**:217
Flann O'Brien **1**:252
Katherine Anne Porter **1**:272
Jean Rhys **6**:454
Nathalie Sarraute **1**:302
Eudora Welty **2**:463

Moss, Leonard
Arthur Miller **1**:217

Moss, Robert F.
John Berryman **13**:76
Paddy Chayefsky **23**:119
Lawrence Durrell **6**:153
John O'Hara **6**:384
Richard Wright **14**:596

Moss, Stanley
Stanley J. Kunitz **6**:286

Mossman, Elliott
Boris Pasternak **10**:382

Motion, Andrew
William Boyd **28**:38
Buchi Emecheta **14**:159
Roy Fisher **25**:157
John Hollander **14**:265
Thomas Keneally **19**:247
Derek Mahon **27**:292
Seán O'Faoláin **14**:407
Piers Paul Read **25**:380
James Schuyler **23**:390
D. M. Thomas **22**:418
Yevgeny Yevtushenko **26**:467

Motley, Joel
Leon Forrest **4**:164

Mott, Michael
A. R. Ammons **8**:15
Geoffrey Grigson **7**:135
Elizabeth Jennings **14**:292
David Jones **7**:186
D. M. Thomas **13**:541
Charles Tomlinson **13**:545

Mottram, Eric
Fielding Dawson **6**:126
Roy Fisher **25**:157
Carolyn Kizer **15**:309
Michael McClure **6**:317
Arthur Miller **1**:218
Gilbert Sorrentino **7**:449
Diane Wakoski **4**:572
Jonathan Williams **13**:601

Moulton, Priscilla L.
E. M. Almedingen **12**:1
Christie Harris **12**:262
Lee Kingman **17**:245
Mary Renault **17**:397

Mount, Ferdinand
Harry Crews **23**:133
Peter Handke **10**:257
Bernice Rubens **19**:403

Movius, Geoffrey H.
William Carlos Williams **9**:575

Mowbray, S. M.
David Plante **23**:345

Moyer, Charles R.
Jonathan Kozol **17**:250

Moyer, Kermit
Robert Altman **16**:34

Moyles, R. G.
Kevin Major **26**:284

Moynahan, Julian
Louis Auchincloss **9**:54
Frederick Buechner **9**:137
Anthony Burgess **8**:113
R. V. Cassill **23**:109
J. P. Donleavy **4**:126
Thomas Flanagan **25**:163
Ernest J. Gaines **11**:218
John Gardner **28**:161
Francine du Plessix Gray **22**:200
John Irving **13**:293
Jack Kerouac **2**:228
Ken Kesey **6**:277
John Knowles **26**:264
John le Carré **15**:326
Tom McHale **3**:331
A. G. Mojtabai **15**:378
Brian Moore **3**:341; **8**:394
Seán O'Faoláin **7**:274; **14**:404
Philip Rahv **24**:353
Anne Roiphe **9**:455
Karl Shapiro **15**:477
Wilfrid Sheed **10**:472
Susan Richards Shreve **23**:404
James Tate **2**:431
John Wain **15**:562
William Wharton **18**:542

Moynihan, Julian
Alan Sillitoe **19**:421
C. P. Snow **19**:428
James Thurber **11**:532

Mozejko, Edward
Elisaveta Bagryana **10**:13

Muchnic, Helen
Ilya Ehrenburg **18**:137
Mikhail Sholokhov **7**:418, 421
Aleksandr I. Solzhenitsyn **9**:507

Mudrick, Marvin
Donald Barthelme **2**:39
Harold Bloom **24**:82
William S. Burroughs **2**:90
E. M. Forster **2**:135
John Fowles **2**:137
Jerzy Kosinski **2**:231
Doris Lessing **2**:239
Norman Mailer **1**:192
Bernard Malamud **1**:200
Vladimir Nabokov **3**:355
Joyce Carol Oates **2**:314
Nathalie Sarraute **2**:384; **4**:468
David Wagoner **3**:508

Mudrovic, Mike
Claudio Rodríguez **10**:440

Mueller, Lisel
Robert Bly **1**:37
Louise Glück **7**:118; **22**:174
Michael S. Harper **7**:138
Jim Harrison **6**:223
Anthony Hecht **8**:268
W. S. Merwin **1**:212
Marge Piercy **6**:401
Peter Viereck **4**:559
Alice Walker **6**:553
Reed Whittemore **4**:588

Mugerauer, Robert
Martin Heidegger **24**:266

Muggeridge, Malcolm
Paul Scott **9**:478
P. G. Wodehouse **22**:483

Muir, Edwin
T. S. Eliot **24**:158

Mulhallen, Karen
Robert Kroetsch **23**:273
Audrey Thomas **13**:538

Mulkeen, Anne
L. P. Hartley **22**:215

Mullen, Patrick B.
E. E. Cummings **12**:157

Mullen, R. D.
Roger Zelazny **21**:468, 470

Mullen, Richard D.
James Blish **14**:82

Muller, Gilbert H.
William Faulkner **8**:212

Muller, H. J.
R. P. Blackmur **24**:54

Müller-Bergh, Klaus
G. Cabrera Infante **25**:102, 104
José Lezama Lima **4**:288

Mullin, Michael
Orson Welles **20**:451

Mumford, Olive
  Larry Kettelkamp 12:304

Munk, Erika
  Martin Duberman 8:185
  Peter Handke 15:268
  David Rudkin 14:471
  Elizabeth Swados 12:560, 561
  Lanford Wilson 14:591

Murch, A. E.
  Edmund Crispin 22:110

Murch, Anne C.
  Arthur Kopit 18:287

Murchison, John C.
  Jorge Luis Borges 2:71, 75

Murchison, W., Jr.
  John Dickson Carr 3:101

Murchland, Bernard
  Albert Camus 2:97
  Jean-Paul Sartre 7:396

Murdoch, Brian
  Heinrich Böll 15:68
  Siegfried Lenz 27:252

Murdoch, Charles
  John Glassco 9:236

Murdoch, Iris
  A. S. Byatt 19:76
  Elias Canetti 25:106

Murdock, Kenneth B.
  Esther Forbes 12:203

Murillo, L. A.
  Jorge Luis Borges 4:70

Murphy, Brian
  Luis Buñuel 16:134
  Eric Rohmer 16:529

Murphy, Catherine A.
  Mary Lavin 18:306

Murphy, Mrs. J. M.
  Honor Arundel 17:14

Murphy, Reverend James M.
  Carlos Fuentes 13:232

Murphy, Joan
  Colin Thiele 17:495

Murphy, L. J.
  Isaac Asimov 26:59

Murphy, Richard
  Thom Gunn 18:203
  Patrick Kavanagh 22:235
  Philip Larkin 5:231

Murphy, Robert
  Allan W. Eckert 17:104

Murr, Judy Smith
  John Gardner 10:219

Murra, John V.
  Amos Tutuola 14:537

Murray, Atholl C.C.
  David Jones 7:188

Murray, Charles Shaar
  Peter Townshend 17:533

Murray, Donald C.
  James Baldwin 13:53

Murray, Edward
  Samuel Beckett 6:35
  William Faulkner 6:176
  Ernest Hemingway 6:229
  Eugène Ionesco 6:251
  Arthur Miller 6:327, 332
  Clifford Odets 28:337
  Alain Robbe-Grillet 6:466
  Tennessee Williams 5:501

Murray, G. E.
  Ai 14:9
  Anthony Hecht 13:269
  Howard Moss 14:376
  Michael Ondaatje 14:410
  Robert Pack 13:439
  Robert Phillips 28:364
  Derek Walcott 14:550

Murray, Jack
  Alain Robbe-Grillet 1:287

Murray, John J.
  Robert Penn Warren 4:579

Murray, Michael
  Edward Albee 2:3
  Lenny Bruce 21:52

Murray, Michele
  Robert Cormier 12:134
  Paula Fox 2:140
  Doris Grumbach 22:204
  Susan B. Hill 4:227
  William Melvin Kelley 22:246
  Robert Kotlowitz 4:275
  Pär Lagerkvist 7:200
  Mary Lavin 4:282
  William Mayne 12:399
  Grace Paley 4:392

Murray, Philip
  Aldous Huxley 3:256

Murray, Thomas J.
  Mary Lavin 18:302

Murray, William J.
  Melvin Berger 12:38

Murry, John Middleton
  I. A. Richards 24:372

Murtaugh, Daniel M.
  Marie-Claire Blais 4:67
  Eilís Dillon 17:100
  Wilfrid Sheed 2:393
  John Updike 23:470

Murtaugh, Kristen
  Italo Calvino 22:94

Mus, David
  T. S. Eliot 2:129

Musher, Andrea
  Diane Wakoski 7:505

Muske, Carol
  Jon Anderson 9:31
  Lucille Clifton 19:110
  Adrienne Rich 18:448
  Charles Wright 13:613

Mutiso, Gideon-Cyrus M.
  Alex La Guma 19:272

Myers, Andrew B.
  Alan Garner 17:137

Myers, David A.
  Kurt Vonnegut, Jr. 22:446

Myers, Robert J.
  Lothar-Günther Buchheim 6:100

Myers, Tim
  Arthur C. Clarke 18:107
  Nicholas Delbanco 13:175

Myles, Lynda
  George Lucas 16:416

Myrsiades, Kostas
  Yannis Ritsos 6:463; 13:487, 488

Nadeau, Maurice
  Louis Aragon 3:13
  Simone de Beauvoir 1:19
  Samuel Beckett 1:22
  Michel Butor 1:49
  Albert Camus 1:54
  Louis-Ferdinand Céline 1:56
  Jean Genet 1:115
  Jean Giono 4:185
  Raymond Queneau 2:359
  Alain Robbe-Grillet 1:288
  Françoise Sagan 3:444
  Nathalie Sarraute 1:303
  Jean-Paul Sartre 1:305
  Claude Simon 4:495

Nadeau, Robert L.
  Djuna Barnes 11:29
  Don DeLillo 27:80

Nadel, Norman
  Irwin Shaw 23:398

Naha, Ed
  The Police 26:363
  Monty Python 21:225

Naiden, James N.
  Thomas McGrath 28:277
  Lorine Niedecker 10:360

Naik, M. K.
  Mulk Raj Anand 23:18

Naipaul, Shiva
  Miguel Ángel Asturias 8:27
  José Donoso 4:130

Naipaul, V. S.
  Jorge Luis Borges 2:77
  R. K. Narayan 28:293, 298
  P. H. Newby 13:407
  Jean Rhys 2:372
  Françoise Sagan 17:422

Nalley, Richard
  Donald Hall 13:259

Namjoshi, Suniti
  Jay Macpherson 14:347
  P. K. Page 18:377

Nance, William L.
  Truman Capote 13:133

Nance, William L., S.M.
  Katherine Anne Porter 7:314

Napolin, Leah
  E. M. Broner 19:71

Nardi, Marcia
  Babette Deutsch 18:118

Nardin, Jane
  Evelyn Waugh 8:544

Nardo, A. K.
  C. S. Lewis 14:325

Naremore, James
  John Huston 20:172
  Philip Larkin 5:226

Nassar, Eugene Paul
  Ezra Pound 7:335

Natanson, Maurice
  Jean-Paul Sartre 24:407

Nathan, George Jean
  Noel Coward 9:171
  Lillian Hellman 18:220
  Arthur Miller 26:314
  Terence Rattigan 7:353
  Elmer Rice 7:359
  George Tabori 19:437

Nathan, Leonard
  Gunnar Ekelöf 27:118

Natov, Roni
  Leon Garfield 12:239

Naughton, John
  A. Alvarez 13:9
  Jeffrey Archer 28:12
  Beryl Bainbridge 18:33
  John Berger 19:38
  Cecil Bødker 21:13
  Autran Dourado 23:152
  Romain Gary 25:188
  Ursula Holden 18:258

Navarro, Carlos
  Jorge Luis Borges 3:79

Navasky, Victor S.
  Jules Archer 12:21
  Meyer Levin 7:204

Navone, John J.
  Federico Fellini 16:273

Nazareth, Peter
  James Ngugi 7:266

Nebecker, Helen E.
  Shirley Jackson 11:302

Necker, Walter
  Joy Adamson 17:2

Needleman, Ruth
  Octavio Paz 3:375

Neil, J. Meredith
  Jack Kerouac 14:306

Neimark, Paul G.
  Agatha Christie 1:58

Neiswender, Rosemary
  E. M. Almedingen 12:4
  Yevgeny Yevtushenko 26:462

Nekrich, Alexsandr
  Alexander Zinoviev 19:485

Nelsen, Don
  Beth Henley 23:215
  Ntozake Shange 25:397

Nelson, Alix
Nora Ephron **17**:111
Richard Peck **21**:298
Kin Platt **26**:351
Mary Rodgers **12**:494

Nelson, Anne
Jonathan Kozol **17**:254

Nelson, Donald F.
Martin Walser **27**:456

Nelson, Dorothy H.
Esther Forbes **12**:211

Nelson, Howard
Robert Bly **10**:54
Robert Francis **15**:237

Nelson, Hugh
Harold Pinter **6**:413

Nelson, John A.
Nat Hentoff **26**:186

Nelson, Joyce
Frank Capra **16**:161
Kurt Vonnegut, Jr. **4**:562

Nelson, Paul
David Bowie **17**:64
Jackson Browne **21**:40
Janis Ian **21**:186
Billy Joel **26**:221
John Lennon and Paul
 McCartney **12**:378
Willie Nelson **17**:303
Lou Reed **21**:310, 311
Paul Simon **17**:465
Patti Smith **12**:538
Bruce Springsteen **17**:484
Neil Young **17**:576, 581

Nelson, Raymond
Chester Himes **2**:196

Nelson, Robert C.
Vine Deloria, Jr. **21**:111

Nemerov, Howard
Conrad Aiken **3**:4
Kingsley Amis **2**:5
Djuna Barnes **3**:36
Ben Belitt **22**:50
Kenneth Burke **2**:89
James Dickey **4**:120
Daniel Hoffman **13**:286
Harry Mathews **6**:315
Marianne Moore **4**:359
Howard Moss **7**:247
Kathleen Raine **7**:353

Nesbitt, Bruce
Earle Birney **11**:49

Nesbitt, John D.
Louis L'Amour **25**:279, 281

Nesin, Jeff
Lou Reed **21**:321

Ness, David E.
Lorraine Hansberry **17**:191

Nettelbeck, Colin W.
Louis-Ferdinand Céline **3**:103

Nettleford, Rex
Louise Bennett **28**:28

Neubauer, John
Georg Lukács **24**:335

Neufeld, John
Maia Wojciechowska **26**:455

Neufeldt, Leonard
David Wagoner **15**:560

Neumark, Victoria
Carlos Fuentes **13**:232

Nevans, Ronald
Barry Hannah **23**:212
Bette Bao Lord **23**:278

Neves, John
Martin Walser **27**:466

Neville, Robert
Helen MacInnes **27**:281

Nevins, Allan
Howard Fast **23**:155

Nevins, Francis M., Jr.
Ellery Queen **3**:421; **11**:458
Rex Stout **3**:471

Nevius, Blake
Ivy Compton-Burnett **1**:62

New, W. H.
Ethel Davis Wilson **13**:608

New, William H.
Margaret Avison **4**:36
Robertson Davies **7**:73
Simon Gray **9**:241
Hugh Hood **15**:286
William Mitchell **25**:322, 323
Alden Nowlan **15**:399

Newberry, Wilma
Ramón Gómez de la Serna
 9:237

Newby, P. H.
Penelope Fitzgerald **19**:174

Newcomb, Horace
Larry Gelbart **21**:127

Newfield, Jack
Bob Dylan **12**:183

Newlin, Margaret
H. D. **14**:225
Sylvia Plath **3**:389

Newlove, Donald
Peter Benchley **4**:53
Joseph Brodsky **4**:78
Howard Fast **23**:159
Günter Grass **22**:195
Thomas Kinsella **4**:271
W. S. Merwin **5**:287
J. D. Salinger **8**:463

Newman, Anne R.
Elizabeth Bishop **15**:59

Newman, Barbara
Jamake Highwater **12**:288

Newman, Charles
James Baldwin **13**:48
Donald Barthelme **23**:48
Saul Bellow **6**:59
Sylvia Plath **9**:421
Philip Roth **4**:457

Newman, Christina
Brian Moore **8**:395

Newman, Michael
W. H. Auden **6**:25

Newton, David E.
Isaac Asimov **26**:57
Franklyn M. Branley **21**:22, 23
Roy A. Gallant **17**:130, 133

Newton, Francis
John Lennon and Paul
 McCartney **12**:353

Neyman, Mark
Allan W. Eckert **17**:108

Nichol, B. P.
Earle Birney **6**:76

Nicholas, Brian
Graham Greene **6**:214

Nicholas, Charles A.
N. Scott Momaday **19**:317

Nicholas, Robert L.
Antonio Buero Vallejo **15**:97

Nicholaus, Charles
Van Morrison **21**:236

Nicholls, Peter
Gene Wolfe **25**:476

Nichols, Bill
Bernardo Bertolucci **16**:85

Nichols, Kathleen L.
Ernest Hemingway **19**:221

Nichols, Lewis
Irwin Shaw **23**:396

Nichols, Ruth
Diana Wynne Jones **26**:228

Nichols, Stephen G., Jr.
John Hawkes **3**:221

Nicholson, C. E.
Theodore Roethke **11**:486

Nicholson, Kris
Neil Young **17**:575

Nickerson, Edward A.
Robinson Jeffers **15**:301

Nickerson, Susan L.
Anne McCaffrey **17**:282, 283, 284

Nicol, Charles
Kingsley Amis **5**:22
Brigid Brophy **6**:100
Anthony Burgess **5**:90
John Cheever **11**:121; **25**:116
Peter De Vries **7**:77
Dashiell Hammett **5**:162
John Hawkes **4**:218; **7**:144
John Irving **13**:293; **23**:252
Milan Kundera **9**:320; **19**:268
Norman Mailer **4**:323
Vladimir Nabokov **1**:244
Kurt Vonnegut, Jr. **3**:504;
 8:534; **12**:602

Niemeyer, Gerhart
Aleksandr I. Solzhenitsyn **7**:439

Niester, Alan
Frank Zappa **17**:590

Nightingale, Benedict
Alan Ayckbourn **5**:35; **18**:30
Edward Bond **4**:70
A. E. Ellis **7**:93
Michael Frayn **7**:107
John Hopkins **4**:234
David Mercer **5**:284
Slawomir Mrozek **13**:399
Peter Nichols **5**:305, 306
Joe Orton **13**:435
John Osborne **5**:333
J. B. Priestley **5**:350
Gerome Ragni and James Rado
 17:382
Anthony Shaffer **19**:415
Neil Simon **6**:504
Tom Stoppard **5**:412
David Storey **5**:415
C. P. Taylor **27**:443
E. A. Whitehead **5**:488

Nilsen, Alleen Pace
Maya Angelou **12**:14
Gunnel Beckman **26**:89
Judy Blume **12**:44
James D. Forman **21**:123
Rosa Guy **26**:145
M. E. Kerr **12**:300
Norma Fox Mazer **26**:291
Nicholasa Mohr **12**:447
Sandra Scoppettone **26**:401
John R. Tunis **12**:599

Nimmo, Dorothy
Judy Blume **12**:45
Diana Wynne Jones **26**:233
Philippa Pearce **21**:290

Nissenson, Hugh
Chaim Potok **2**:338; **7**:321;
 26:368

Nist, John
Carlos Drummond de Andrade
 18:3, 4

Nitchie, George W.
Robert Lowell **8**:350
George MacBeth **2**:251
Marianne Moore **8**:397

Nixon, Agnes Eckhardt
Agnes Eckhardt Nixon **21**:241, 244

Nkosi, Lewis
André Brink **18**:68
Alex La Guma **19**:272

Nnolim, Charles E.
Mongo Beti **27**:47

Noble, David W.
James Baldwin **4**:40

Nokes, David
Michael Mewshaw **9**:377

Nolan, Paul T.
Marc Connelly **7**:55

Noland, W. Richard
Elliott Baker **8**:38

Nolen, William A.
Colleen McCullough **27**:321

Nomad, Max
Ignazio Silone 4:493

Noonan, Tom
Rainer Werner Fassbinder 20:118

Nordberg, Robert B.
Ward S. Just 27:226
Jonathan Kozol 17:252

Nordell, Roderick
John Ehle 27:105
William Golding 17:172
Mark Harris 19:201
Nat Hentoff 26:185
Jerome Siegel and Joe Shuster 21:357

Nordyke, Lewis
Robert Lewis Taylor 14:533

Norman, Albert H.
Richard Brautigan 12:58

Norman, Doreen
Otfried Preussler 17:375

Norman, Gurney
Richard Brautigan 12:64

Norman, Mary Anne
Dee Brown 18:71

Norris, Jerrie
Rosa Guy 26:144

Norris, Ken
George Bowering 15:81

Norris, Leslie
Andrew Young 5:525

Norrish, P. J.
Henri de Montherlant 19:329

Norsworthy, James
Kin Platt 26:353

Norsworthy, James A.
Cecil Bødker 21:14
Jamake Highwater 12:286
Zilpha Keatley Snyder 17:474

North, R. J.
Andre Malraux 13:367

Northey, Margot
Matt Cohen 19:115
Mordecai Richler 18:451

Norton, Dale
Alex Haley 12:248

Norton, Elliot
Lily Tomlin 17:517

Norwood, Gilbert
Agatha Christie 12:113

Norwood, W. D., Jr.
C. S. Lewis 1:177

Noth, Dominique Paul
Garry Trudeau 12:589

Notley, Alice
James Schuyler 23:391

Nott, Kathleen
Graham Greene 14:217

Nouryeh, Christopher
Ben Belitt 22:54

Novak, Michael
Norman Lear 12:338

Novak, Michael Paul
Robert Hayden 5:169

Novak, William
Grace Paley 6:391
Susan Fromberg Schaeffer 6:488

Novick, Julius
Edward Albee 9:10
John Bishop 10:54
Gretchen Cryer 21:81
Charles Fuller 25:181
Simon Gray 9:242
Albert Innaurato 21:199
Hugh Leonard 19:284
David Mamet 9:360
Sean O'Casey 11:411
David Rabe 4:425
Howard Sackler 14:478
Neil Simon 11:496
Isaac Bashevis Singer 15:509
Tom Stoppard 4:525; 8:504
David Storey 8:505
Tennessee Williams 8:548
Lanford Wilson 14:592

Nowell-Smith, Geoffrey
Michelangelo Antonioni 20:27
Bernardo Bertolucci 16:100
Luis Buñuel 16:131
Richard Lester 20:218
Pier Paolo Pasolini 20:259
Luchino Visconti 16:573

Nowlan, Alden
Hugh Hood 15:283

Nugent, Frank S.
Tod Browning 16:121
John Ford 16:304
Jean Renoir 20:287

Nugent, Robert
René Char 11:111

Nwoga, Donatus I.
Christopher Okigbo 25:350

Nyabongo, V. S.
Alice Walker 6:554

Nye, Robert
Brigid Brophy 6:98
E. M. Forster 3:162
David Garnett 3:189
Graham Greene 3:214
Hermann Hesse 17:218
Mollie Hunter 21:159
Bernard Malamud 5:269
Michael Moorcock 27:347
Anthony Powell 3:402
John Cowper Powys 7:349
William Sansom 6:483
Penelope Shuttle 7:422

Nye, Russel
John Lennon and Paul McCartney 12:366

Nygaard, Anita
Joy Adamson 17:5

Nyren, D.
Marie-Claire Blais 13:97

Nyren, Dorothy
Russell Edson 13:190

Oakley, Helen
Lenora Mattingly Weber 12:633

Oates, Joyce Carol
Harriette Arnow 2:14
James Baldwin 5:42
Paul Bowles 19:60
Frederick Busch 7:38
James M. Cain 3:95
Carlos Castaneda 12:88
John Cheever 11:120
Laurie Colwin 23:129
Robert Coover 7:58
Robert Creeley 8:152
Roald Dahl 1:177
Robertson Davies 25:132
James Dickey 7:83
Joan Didion 8:175
Margaret Drabble 2:118; 5:117
Andre Dubus 13:183
James T. Farrell 4:158
Carolyn Forché 25:170
Janet Frame 2:141
Tess Gallagher 18:170
Gail Godwin 5:142; 22:179
William Golding 17:180
William Goyen 8:250
Jim Harrison 6:224
Anne Hébert 13:268
Carolyn G. Heilbrun 25:252
David Ignatow 14:276
Maxine Kumin 5:222
Philip Larkin 8:337
Mary Lavin 4:282
Stanislaw Lem 15:328
Doris Lessing 2:241
Philip Levine 4:286, 288
Alison Lurie 18:310
Norman Mailer 11:341
Bernard Malamud 3:323
Leonard Michaels 25:314
Berry Morgan 6:339
Alice Munro 6:342; 19:346
Iris Murdoch 1:237; 11:389
Vladimir Nabokov 2:304
R. K. Narayan 28:295
Charles Newman 2:312; 8:419
Flannery O'Connor 1:258
Mary Oliver 19:362
Robert Phillips 28:362
Sylvia Plath 2:338; 5:340
Gilbert Rogin 18:458
Philip Roth 4:454
J. R. Salamanca 15:463
Anne Sexton 6:492
Stevie Smith 25:422
Jean Stafford 19:430
Elizabeth Taylor 2:433
Peter Taylor 1:335
Paul Theroux 8:512
William Trevor 9:529
John Updike 2:441; 13:561
Kurt Vonnegut, Jr. 12:603
Fay Weldon 9:559
Eudora Welty 1:363
Richard Yates 7:554

Oberbeck, S. K.
Kingsley Amis 2:7
Frederick Forsyth 5:125
John Hawkes 1:137
John Hersey 7:154
John Irving 13:293
Norman Mailer 2:264
Joyce Carol Oates 2:315
Georges Simenon 2:398
Kurt Vonnegut, Jr. 3:502
Stevie Wonder 12:655

Oberg, Arthur
John Berryman 4:66; 25:93
Galway Kinnell 3:270
Greg Kuzma 7:197
Philip Levine 2:244
John Matthias 9:362
Josephine Miles 14:369
Joyce Carol Oates 6:367
Robert Pack 13:438
Sylvia Plath 14:422; 17:349
Anne Sexton 4:482
Mona Van Duyn 7:498
Derek Walcott 9:556

Oberhelman, Harley D.
José Donoso 11:146
Ernesto Sabato 23:378

O'Brien, Conor Cruise
See also **O'Donnell, Donat**
Jimmy Breslin 4:76
Thomas Flanagan 25:166
Graham Greene 3:214
Seamus Heaney 7:149

O'Brien, Darcy
Patrick Kavanagh 22:241

O'Brien, Edna
Françoise Sagan 17:428

O'Brien, Geoffrey
Jun'ichirō Tanizaki 28:419

O'Brien, James H.
Liam O'Flaherty 5:321

O'Brien, John
Clarence Major 19:293
Gilbert Sorrentino 7:450

O'Brien, Kate
Elias Canetti 14:118
Rhys Davies 23:142

O'Brien, Tom
Farley Mowat 26:346

Obstfeld, Raymond
Elmore Leonard 28:236

Obuchowski, Chester W.
Pierre Gascar 11:220

Obuchowski, Mary Dejong
Yasunari Kawabata 9:316

Occhiogrosso, Frank
Georges Simenon 18:481

O'Connell, Margaret F.
Franklyn M. Branley 21:18

O'Connell, Robert W.
Margaret O. Hyde 21:174

O'Connell, Shaun
Harry Crews **23**:134
Seamus Heaney **25**:248
Marjorie Kellogg **2**:224
Gilbert Sorrentino **7**:447

O'Connor, Flannery
Flannery O'Connor **21**:254

O'Connor, Garry
Jean Anouilh **8**:24

O'Connor, Gerald
J.R.R. Tolkien **12**:576

O'Connor, John J.
Larry Gelbart **21**:126
Earl Hamner, Jr. **12**:258
Norman Lear **12**:333, 334, 337
Garry Marshall **17**:275, 276
Lanford Wilson **7**:547

O'Connor, Mary
Caroline Gordon **6**:203

O'Connor, William Van
Kingsley Amis **1**:5
Donald Davie **5**:113
D. J. Enright **4**:154
Leslie A. Fiedler **24**:189
Elizabeth Jennings **5**:197
Philip Larkin **3**:275
Iris Murdoch **1**:234
Robert Phillips **28**:361
Ezra Pound **1**:275
John Wain **2**:458

O'Daniel, Therman B.
Ralph Ellison **1**:95

Odell, Brian Neal
Arna Bontemps **18**:64

O'Doherty, Brian
Flann O'Brien **5**:314

O'Donnell, Donat
Seán O'Faoláin **14**:402
George Steiner **24**:424

O'Donnell, Patrick
John Hawkes **27**:199

O'Donnell, Thomas D.
Michel Butor **11**:81
Claude Simon **15**:495

O'Faolain, Julia
Margaret Atwood **25**:69
Beryl Bainbridge **10**:15; **18**:33
Mark Helprin **10**:260
Alice Munro **19**:346
Edna O'Brien **5**:311
Isaac Bashevis Singer **9**:489

O'Faoláin, Seán
Daphne du Maurier **11**:162
William Faulkner **28**:143
Ernest Hemingway **13**:272

Offerman, Sister Mary Columba
Gunnel Beckman **26**:87

Offit, Sidney
H. F. Brinsmead **21**:28

O'Flaherty, Patrick
Farley Mowat **26**:338

Ogilvie, John T.
Robert Frost **26**:116

Oglesby, Leora
Frank Bonham **12**:50

Ogunyemi, Chikwenye Okonjo
Toni Morrison **10**:354
Amos Tutuola **14**:542

O'Hara, J. D.
Kingsley Amis **8**:11
Donald Barthelme **5**:54
Ann Beattie **8**:54
Samuel Beckett **6**:39; **14**:73
Jorge Luis Borges **2**:77
Kay Boyle **5**:66
Richard Brautigan **12**:58
Anthony Burgess **5**:86, 88
Italo Calvino **22**:93
Louis-Ferdinand Céline **4**:103
John Cheever **15**:129
Laurie Colwin **13**:156
Robert Crumb **17**:82
Roald Dahl **6**:121
Edward Dahlberg **7**:71
Don DeLillo **13**:178; **27**:78, 79
William Gaddis **19**:186
Lawrence Durrell **6**:152
William Golding **17**:170
Peter Handke **15**:268
George V. Higgins **4**:223
José Lezama Lima **4**:288
Steven Millhauser **21**:216, 218
Vladimir Nabokov **1**:246
Judith Rossner **6**:469
C. P. Snow **9**:498
Gore Vidal **22**:436
Kurt Vonnegut, Jr. **12**:608
René Wellek **28**:451
Paul West **14**:569

O'Hara, T.
Derek Walcott **4**:575

O'Hara, Tim
Ronald Sukenick **4**:531

O'Hearn, Walter
Farley Mowat **26**:333

Ohmann, Carol B.
Alex Haley **12**:244
J. D. Salinger **12**:516
Muriel Spark **2**:414

Ohmann, Richard M.
Pär Lagerkvist **7**:199
J. D. Salinger **12**:516

Oka, Takashi
Yukio Mishima **27**:336

Okam, Hilary
Aimé Césaire **19**:98

O'Keeffe, Timothy
Patrick White **3**:521

Okri, Ben
Mongo Beti **27**:53
Anita Desai **19**:134

Okun, Milton
Phil Ochs **17**:330
Buffy Sainte-Marie **17**:430

Olander, Joseph D.
Robert A. Heinlein **26**:170

Olderman, Raymond M.
John Barth **3**:40
Peter S. Beagle **7**:26
Stanley Elkin **4**:153; **27**:121
John Hawkes **3**:222
Joseph Heller **3**:229
Ken Kesey **3**:266
Thomas Pynchon **3**:411
Kurt Vonnegut, Jr. **3**:505

Oldfield, Michael
Jim Morrison **17**:291
Jimmy Page and Robert Plant **12**:477
Carly Simon **26**:408

Oldham, Andrew
Brian Wilson **12**:640

Oldsey, Bernard S.
William Golding **2**:167

Oliphant, Dave
Albert Goldbarth **5**:143

Oliva, Leo E.
Vine Deloria, Jr. **21**:112

Oliver, Edith
Ed Bullins **5**:83; **7**:36
Anne Burr **6**:103
Alice Childress **12**:105
Gretchen Cryer **21**:78, 81
Christopher Durang **27**:88, 90
Athol Fugard **14**:191
Charles Fuller **25**:181
Jack Gelber **14**:193
Simon Gray **14**:214, 215
John Guare **8**:253; **14**:220, 221
Christopher Hampton **4**:211
Beth Henley **23**:214
Albert Innaurato **21**:194
Jim Jacobs and Warren Casey **12**:292
Arthur Kopit **18**:286
David Mamet **15**:355, 358
Mark Medoff **6**:322
Rochelle Owens **8**:434
Gerome Ragni and James Rado **17**:379
Terence Rattigan **7**:355
Jonathan Reynolds **6**:451
Sam Shepard **6**:497; **17**:435, 442
Tom Stoppard **3**:470; **4**:525
Elizabeth Swados **12**:557, 559
George Tabori **19**:437
Megan Terry **19**:440
Kurt Vonnegut, Jr. **12**:605
Derek Walcott **2**:460; **14**:551
Joseph A. Walker **19**:455
Douglas Turner Ward **19**:457, 458
Richard Wesley **7**:518
Lanford Wilson **14**:591

Oliver, Raymond
Arthur Gregor **9**:255
George Steiner **24**:434

Oliver, Roy
Arthur A. Cohen **7**:51

Olivier, Edith
Esther Forbes **12**:203

Olmert, Michael
Philip Roth **4**:452

Olney, James
Chinua Achebe **1**:2
Loren Eiseley **7**:92

Olsen, Gary R.
Hermann Hesse **6**:238

Olsen, Miken
Norma Fox Mazer **26**:291

Olshen, Barry N.
John Fowles **9**:210

Olson, Carol Booth
A. G. Mojtabai **15**:377

Olson, David B.
Robert Penn Warren **10**:518

Olson, Lawrence
Yukio Mishima **2**:288

Olson, Toby
Diane Wakoski **7**:505

O'Malley, Michael
Erich Maria Remarque **21**:334

O'Meally, Robert G.
Sterling A. Brown **23**:98
Robert Hayden **14**:240
Michael Thelwell **22**:416

O'Neal, Susan
Robert Lipsyte **21**:208

O'Neill, Kathleen
Michel Butor **11**:80

O'Neill, Tom
Giuseppe Ungaretti **11**:557; **15**:537

O'Neill, William L.
Andrew M. Greeley **28**:171

Onley, Gloria
Margaret Atwood **4**:25; **13**:42

Onyeama, Dillibe
Alex Haley **12**:252

Opdahl, Keith
Saul Bellow **3**:51; **15**:55
Jim Harrison **14**:236

Oppenheim, Jane
Len Deighton **22**:114

Oppenheim, Shulamith
Leon Garfield **12**:230

Oppenheimer, Dan
Paul Weller **26**:442

Oppenheimer, Joel
Robert Creeley **15**:153
Lawrence Ferlinghetti **27**:136
Anthony Hecht **19**:208
Philip Roth **4**:457
William Saroyan **10**:456
L. E. Sissman **18**:489
Andrei Voznesensky **15**:557

Orange, John
Hugh Hood **28**:193

Ordóñez, Elizabeth
Ana María Matute **11**:366

O'Reilly, Timothy
Frank Herbert **12**:279; **23**:224

Orenstein, Gloria Feman
Fernando Arrabal 18:20

Orgel, Doris
Emily Cheney Neville 12:453

Oriard, Michael
Don DeLillo 13:175

Orme, John
Bob Marley 17:273

Ormerod, Beverley
Édouard Glissant 10:230

Ormerod, David
V. S. Naipaul 4:371

Ornstein, Jacob
Camilo José Cela 4:95

O'Rourke, William
Rosalyn Drexler 2:120
Craig Nova 7:267

Orr, Leonard
Richard Condon 4:107

Orr, Nancy Young
Barbara Corcoran 17:69

Ortega, Julio
José María Arguedas 18:7, 8

Orth, Maureen
Bob Dylan 3:130
Stevie Wonder 12:657

Ortiz, Alfonso
Vine Deloria, Jr. 21:111

Ortiz, Gloria M.
Pablo Neruda 7:260

Ortiz, Miguel A.
Alice Childress 12:108
Nicholosa Mohr 12:448

Ortiz, Simon J.
Leslie Marmon Silko 23:412

Ortmayer, Roger
Federico Fellini 16:286

Orton, Gavin
Eyvind Johnson 14:294

Orwell, George
Alex Comfort 7:52
Graham Greene 6:216
P. G. Wodehouse 22:480

Osborn, John Jay, Jr.
George V. Higgins 18:234

Osborn, Neal J.
Kenneth Burke 2:87

Osborne, Charles
William Faulkner 1:102
W. Somerset Maugham 1:204

Osborne, David
Albert Camus 2:99

Osborne, Linda B.
Sylvia Ashton-Warner 19:24
Ella Leffland 19:278

Osborne, Trudie
Madeleine L'Engle 12:345

Osgood, Eugenia V.
Julien Gracq 11:244

Osler, Ruth
Roderick L. Haig-Brown 21:139

Osnos, Peter
Martin Cruz Smith 25:413

Ostriker, Alicia
Ai 4:16
Cid Corman 9:170
Alan Dugan 2:121
Paul Goodman 7:131
John Hollander 14:262
Maxine Kumin 28:224
Sylvia Plath 17:348
May Swenson 14:518
Anne Waldman 7:508

Ostroff, Anthony
Donald Justice 6:271
Kathleen Spivack 6:520
Mark Van Doren 6:542

Ostrom, Alan
William Carlos Williams 1:370

Ostrovsky, Erika
Louis-Ferdinand Céline 4:98

O'Toole, Lawrence
Werner Herzog 16:335
John Landis 26:274
Paul Schrader 26:398

Ott, Bill
Stephen King 26:240

Ottaway, Robert
John Cheever 25:122

Otten, Anna
Heinrich Böll 2:66
Michel Butor 8:120; 15:120
Alain Robbe-Grillet 6:467; 8:453
Nathalie Sarraute 2:386
Claude Simon 4:497

Ottenberg, Eve
Erskine Caldwell 14:95
Vonda N. McIntyre 18:327
James Schuyler 23:389
Alexander Theroux 25:432

Overbey, David L.
Luis Buñuel 16:151
Claude Chabrol 16:178
Werner Herzog 16:324, 333
Fritz Lang 20:212
Richard Lester 20:227

Överland, Orm
Arthur Miller 15:371

Oviedo, José Miguel
Mario Vargas Llosa 10:497, 500

Owen, Carys T.
Louis-Ferdinand Céline 9:155

Owen, I. M.
Robertson Davies 7:72
Thomas Flanagan 25:164
Mavis Gallant 18:173

Owen, Ivon
Robertson Davies 13:171

Owens, Brad
Mark Harris 19:205
John Kennedy Toole 19:442

Owens, Iris
Lois Gould 4:200

Owens, Rochelle
Diane Wakoski 7:505

Owens, Tony J.
William Faulkner 18:145

Ower, John
Frank Herbert 12:273
Mordecai Richler 9:451
Edith Sitwell 9:494

Ower, John B.
Edith Sitwell 2:404

Ownbey, Steve
George V. Higgins 10:273
Georges Simenon 8:486

Owomoyela, Oyekan
Chester Himes 7:159

Oxenhandler, Neal
Jean Cocteau 16:225
Jean Genet 14:203

Oxley, Brian
Geoffrey Hill 18:240

Ozick, Cynthia
Saul Bellow 10:43
Frederick Buechner 2:83
Mark Harris 19:202
Bernard Malamud 11:346
Hugh Nissenson 4:380

Pa Chin
Pa Chin 18:371

Pace, Eric
Paul E. Erdman 25:154
Joseph Wambaugh 3:508

Pacernick, Gary
Millen Brand 7:30

Pacey, Desmond
F. R. Scott 22:371
Miriam Waddington 28:436

Pachter, Henry
Paul Goodman 7:129

Pachter, Henry M.
Hermann Hesse 6:236

Pacifici, Sergio J.
Elio Vittorini 14:543

Pack, Robert
James Schevill 7:400
Mark Strand 18:514

Packard, Nancy H.
Grace Paley 6:393

Packard, William
Kenneth Patchen 18:394

Paddock, Lisa
William Faulkner 18:147

Page, James A.
James Baldwin 3:32
Ralph Ellison 3:145
Richard Wright 3:546

Page, Malcolm
John Arden 13:25

Pagès, Irène M.
Simone de Beauvoir 14:68

Palandri, Angela Jung
Ch'ien Chung-shu 22:107

Palencia-Roth, Michael
Günter Grass 22:191

Palevsky, Joan
Isak Dinesen 10:148

Paley, Bruce
Waylon Jennings 21:205

Paley, Maggie
Laura Nyro 17:313

Palley, Julian
Azorín 11:25

Palmer, Eustace
Chinua Achebe 7:5
Mongo Beti 27:49
James Ngugi 7:265

Palmer, James W.
Francis Ford Coppola 16:242

Palmer, Penelope
Charles Tomlinson 6:536

Palmer, R. Roderick
Haki R. Madhubuti 6:313
Sonia Sanchez 5:382

Palmer, Robert
Ray Davies 21:92, 93
Smokey Robinson 21:346, 349
Sam Shepard 17:445

Palmer, Tony
Bob Dylan 12:196
Jimmy Page and Robert Plant 12:481

Pancella, John R.
Robert Newton Peck 17:340

Paniagua, Lita
Luis Buñuel 16:134

Panichas, George A.
F. R. Leavis 24:306

Pannick, David
John Mortimer 28:287

Pannick, Gerald J.
R. P. Blackmur 24:68

Panshin, Alexei
Robert A. Heinlein 3:224
Fritz Leiber 25:305

Panshin, Cory
Fritz Leiber 25:305

Panter-Downes, Mollie
Robert Bolt 14:91
John Le Carré 9:327

Paolucci, Anne
Federico Fellini 16:278

Papatzonis, Takis
Giuseppe Ungaretti 11:557

Parachini, Allan
Waylon Jennings 21:202
Garry Trudeau 12:589

Parameswaran, Uma
Derek Walcott **9**:557

Pareles, Jon
Joan Armatrading **17**:9
Walter Becker and Donald Fagen **26**:84
David Byrne **26**:96, 98
Elvis Costello **21**:70
Ray Davies **21**:104
Bob Dylan **12**:197
Mick Jagger and Keith Richard **17**:240
Kris Kristofferson **26**:269
Joni Mitchell **12**:443
William Trevor **25**:446
Frank Zappa **17**:593, 594

Parente, Diane A.
James Dickey **10**:142
Isabelle Holland **21**:149

Parente, William J.
Alexsandr I. Solzhenitsyn **10**:479

Parham, Sidney F.
Peter Weiss **15**:568

Parini, Jay
Peter Davison **28**:103
Louise Glück **22**:176
Daniel Halpern **14**:232
Seamus Heaney **25**:244
Brad Leithauser **27**:241
Christopher Middleton **13**:388
Katha Pollitt **28**:367

Parisi, John
M. L. Rosenthal **28**:398

Parisi, Joseph
X. J. Kennedy **8**:320
Susan Fromberg Schaeffer **11**:491
Mark Van Doren **6**:543
Robert Penn Warren **18**:536

Park, Clara Claiborne
Brigid Brophy **6**:99
Maxine Kumin **28**:224
James Merrill **13**:377; **18**:330
Manuel Puig **28**:371
Richard Wilbur **9**:568

Park, John G.
Shirley Jackson **11**:302

Park, Sue Simpson
Gwendolyn Brooks **15**:94
Joyce Carol Oates **11**:400

Parke, Andrea
Mary Stolz **12**:548

Parker, Dorothy
S. J. Perelman **23**:335
P. G. Wodehouse **22**:478

Parker, Dorothy L.
Pamela Hansford Johnson **27**:221

Parker, John M.
Autran Dourado **23**:151

Parkes, K. S.
Martin Walser **27**:463

Parkes, Stuart
Martin Walser **27**:462

Parkhill-Rathbone, James
C. P. Snow **1**:317; **6**:518

Parkinson, Robert C.
Frank Herbert **12**:271

Parkinson, Thomas
Robert Lowell **1**:179, 180
Gary Snyder **1**:317

Parr, J. L.
Calder Willingham **5**:510

Parrinder, Patrick
Philip K. Dick **10**:138
B. S. Johnson **9**:302
V. S. Naipaul **18**:360
Frederik Pohl **18**:411

Parris, Robert
Françoise Sagan **17**:418

Parrish, Anne
Esther Forbes **12**:202

Parrish, Paul A.
Elizabeth Bowen **11**:59

Parry, Idris
Elias Canetti **25**:108
Hermann Hesse **25**:261

Parsons, Ann
William Carlos Williams **2**:469

Parsons, Gordon
Ruth M. Arthur **12**:27
Leon Garfield **12**:231, 241
Mollie Hunter **21**:156, 158, 167

Parsons, I. M.
Agatha Christie **12**:112

Parsons, Thornton H.
John Crowe Ransom **2**:364

Parton, Margaret
Timothy Findley **27**:140

Partridge, Marianne
Patti Smith **12**:538

Partridge, Ralph
Agatha Christie **12**:113, 114
Edmund Crispin **22**:108, 109

Partridge, Robert
Willie Nelson **17**:304

Pascal, Roy
Georg Lukács **24**:332

Pascal, Sylvia
Stephen King **26**:239

Paschall, Douglas
Theodore Roethke **3**:434

Pasinetti, P. M.
Eleanor Clark **19**:105

Pasolli, Robert
Sam Shepard **17**:434

Paterson, Gary H.
Kevin Major **26**:285
Norma Fox Mazer **26**:296

Paterson, Katherine
Anita Desai **19**:135
Virginia Hamilton **26**:158
Bette Bao Lord **23**:278
Rosemary Wells **12**:639

Patrouch, Joseph F., Jr.
Isaac Asimov **19**:24

Patten, Brian
Isaac Asimov **3**:17
Kurt Vonnegut, Jr. **3**:504

Patten, Frederick
Stephen King **12**:310
Andre Norton **12**:471
Roger Zelazny **21**:468

Patten, Karl
Graham Greene **1**:131

Patterson, Patricia
Paul Schrader **26**:386

Patterson, Rob
Martin Mull **17**:300

Pattison, Barrie
Brian De Palma **20**:77

Pattow, Donald J.
Dashiell Hammett **19**:198

Paul, Jay S.
William Goyen **14**:211, 212

Paul, Louis
John Steinbeck **21**:365

Paul, Sherman
Paul Goodman **1**:123
Charles Olson **11**:420
Boris Pasternak **7**:295
Edmund Wilson **1**:373

Paulin, Tom
Kingsley Amis **13**:15
Robin Cook **14**:131
Robert Coover **15**:145
Thomas Flanagan **25**:167
John Fowles **10**:189
Patricia Highsmith **14**:261
Dan Jacobson **14**:290
Benedict Kiely **23**:264
Jerzy Kosinski **10**:308
Seán O'Faoláin **14**:406
William Trevor **14**:536
Ian McEwan **13**:370
Barbara Pym **13**:469

Pauls, Ted
Roger Zelazny **21**:464

Pauly, Rebecca M.
Kurt Vonnegut, Jr. **12**:609

Pauly, Thomas H.
John Ford **16**:313

Pavletich, Aida
Joan Armatrading **17**:11
Janis Ian **21**:188
Laura Nyro **17**:321
Buffy Sainte-Marie **17**:431

Pawel, Ernst
Heinrich Böll **2**:67; **9**:109
Hermann Hesse **2**:192
Jakov Lind **2**:245
Martin Walser **27**:467

Paxford, Sandra
Noel Streatfeild **21**:410

Payne, James Robert
Imamu Amiri Baraka **14**:48

Payne, Jocelyn
David Slavitt **14**:491

Payne, Margaret
Mildred D. Taylor **21**:421

Payne, Robert
Winston Graham **23**:193
Yuri Olesha **8**:432
Boris Pasternak **7**:292
Mary Renault **17**:397
Rosemary Sutcliff **26**:432

Paz, Octavio
Elizabeth Bishop **9**:89
André Breton **9**:129
Alexsandr I. Solzhenitsyn **10**:478
William Carlos Williams **5**:508

Peabody, Richard, Jr.
Scott Sommer **25**:426

Peacock, Allen
Frederick Busch **18**:86

Peacock, R.
T. S. Eliot **24**:184

Pearce, Howard D.
Paul Green **25**:198, 199

Pearce, Philippa
Alan Garner **17**:136
Philippa Pearce **21**:288

Pearce, Richard
Saul Bellow **8**:72
John Dos Passos **8**:181
John Hawkes **9**:266
Henry Roth **6**:473
William Styron **11**:515

Pearce, Roy Harvey
Robert Frost **26**:120

Pearlman, Sandy
Ray Davies **21**:89
Jim Morrison **17**:287
Lou Reed **21**:302

Pearson, Alan
Joe Rosenblatt **15**:447

Pearson, Carol
Joseph Heller **11**:265

Pearson, Gabriel
John Berryman **2**:55
T. S. Eliot **13**:192
Leslie A. Fiedler **24**:202

Pearson, Haydn S.
Roderick L. Haig-Brown **21**:137, 138

Pearson, Ian
W. P. Kinsella **27**:238

Pearson, Norman Holmes
Ezra Pound **2**:340

Pease, Howard
Henry Gregor Felsen **17**:121
John R. Tunis **12**:596

Peavy, Charles D.
  Larry McMurtry **27**:324
  Hubert Selby, Jr. **1**:306
  Melvin Van Peebles **20**:410

Pechter, William S.
  Lindsay Anderson **20**:16
  Ingmar Bergman **16**:48
  Frank Capra **16**:158
  John Cassavetes **20**:49
  Francis Ford Coppola **16**:234, 238
  Federico Fellini **16**:282
  Elaine May **16**:432
  Satyajit Ray **16**:482, 494
  Jean Renoir **20**:298
  Andrew Lloyd Webber and Tim Rice **21**:429
  Orson Welles **20**:448
  Lina Wertmüller **16**:589

Peck, Richard
  Robert Cormier **12**:135
  Lois Duncan **26**:104
  Katherine Paterson **12**:485
  Richard Peck **21**:30

Peckham, Morse
  Wayne C. Booth **24**:98

Peden, William
  James Baldwin **8**:40
  Doris Betts **6**:70; **28**:33
  Paul Bowles **19**:58
  Ed Bullins **7**:37
  John Cheever **7**:49
  Laurie Colwin **5**:108
  James T. Farrell **8**:205
  Ernest J. Gaines **11**:217
  Mavis Gallant **18**:170
  Shirley Ann Grau **9**:240
  Chester Himes **7**:159
  Langston Hughes **10**:281
  Grace Paley **6**:392
  Ann Petry **7**:305
  William Saroyan **8**:468
  Mary Lee Settle **19**:409
  Irwin Shaw **7**:411
  Isaac Bashevis Singer **6**:509
  Jesse Stuart **8**:507
  Peter Taylor **18**:523
  Tennessee Williams **5**:502
  Richard Wright **14**:596

Peel, Marie
  John Osborne **2**:329
  Peter Redgrove **6**:445, 446
  Penelope Shuttle **7**:423
  Alan Sillitoe **3**:448
  David Storey **2**:425
  R. S. Thomas **6**:531

Peet, Creighton
  Franklyn M. Branley **21**:15
  Robert A. Heinlein **26**:160

Pekar, Harvey
  Robert Crumb **17**:82
  Frank Zappa **17**:585

Pelham, Philip
  Dick Francis **22**:151

Pelli, Moshe
  S. Y. Agnn **8**:8

Pelorus
  Judy Blume **12**:45
  Robert Cormier **12**:135
  Alan Garner **17**:147

Peltier, Ed
  Peter Weir **20**:424

Pemberton, Clive
  Leon Garfield **12**:219

Pendergast, Constance
  Mavis Gallant **18**:171

Penner, Allen R.
  Alan Sillitoe **1**:308

Penner, Dick
  Vladimir Nabokov **15**:395

Penner, Jonathan
  Margaret Atwood **25**:69
  Carlos Fuentes **22**:171
  Graham Greene **18**:196
  William Kennedy **28**:204
  V. S. Pritchett **15**:443
  Philip Roth **15**:450
  Susan Richards Shreve **23**:483
  Richard Yates **23**:480

Pennington, Lee
  Jesse Stuart **11**:508

Penta, Anne Constance
  Jane Rule **27**:417

Peppard, Murray B.
  Friedrich Dürrenmatt **1**:81

Pepper, Nancy
  Anaïs Nin **11**:399

Perazzini, Randolph
  Robert Frost **13**:229

Percy, Walker
  Walter M. Miller, Jr. **4**:352
  Marion Montgomery **7**:232
  Jean-Paul Sartre **13**:506
  John Kennedy Toole **19**:441
  Eudora Welty **1**:362

Percy, William
  Joy Adamson **17**:2

Perebinossoff, Phillipe R.
  Jean Renoir **20**:308

Perera, Victor
  Miguel Ángel Asturias **3**:18

Pérez, Genaro J.
  Juan Goytisolo **23**:185

Perez, Gilberto
  Beryl Bainbridge **10**:16
  Ingmar Bergman **16**:81
  Werner Herzog **16**:335
  Yuri Krotkov **19**:266
  Alan Sillitoe **10**:477
  Anne Tyler **11**:553

Pérez Firmat, Gustavo
  José Lezama Lima **10**:319

Perkins, David
  W. H. Auden **11**:19
  Richard Eberhart **11**:179
  Ezra Pound **3**:397
  Carl Sandburg **10**:449

Perkins, Huel D.
  John A. Williams **13**:599

Perlberg, Mark
  Larry Eigner **9**:181
  Michael S. Harper **7**:138
  George Oppen **7**:285

Perloff, Marjorie G.
  John Berryman **2**:59
  Ed Dorn **10**:156
  Clayton Eshleman **7**:99
  Thom Gunn **3**:216
  Seamus Heaney **25**:250
  Ted Hughes **2**:204; **4**:235
  Richard F. Hugo **6**:244
  Erica Jong **6**:270
  Galway Kinnell **2**:230
  Denise Levertov **2**:243
  Robert Lowell **1**:181
  Frank O'Hara **2**:322; **5**:325; **13**:425
  Charles Olson **11**:415
  Sylvia Plath **9**:432; **17**:368
  Ezra Pound **10**:400
  Adrienne Rich **7**:369
  Françoise Sagan **6**:482
  May Sarton **14**:481
  Mark Van Doren **10**:496
  Mona Van Duyn **3**:492
  Diane Wakoski **7**:504
  John Wieners **7**:537
  James Wright **3**:542, 544

Perrick, Eve
  Ira Levin **3**:294

Perrin, Noel
  James Gould Cozzens **11**:132

Perrine, Laurence
  John Ciardi **10**:105

Perry, Charles
  Andrew Lloyd Webber and Tim Rice **21**:431

Perry, R. C.
  Rolf Hochhuth **11**:276

Perry, Ruth
  Doris Lessing **15**:330

Peter, John
  Edward Bond **13**:102
  William Golding **17**:158

Peterkiewicz, Jerzy
  Witold Gombrowicz **4**:195
  Alain Robbe-Grillet **4**:447

Peterkin, Julia
  Paul Green **25**:194

Peterman, Michael A.
  Farley Mowat **26**:340

Peters, Daniel James
  Thomas Pynchon **3**:412

Peters, Jonathan
  Chinua Achebe **26**:25

Peters, Julie Stone
  Maxine Kumin **28**:223

Peters, Margot
  Agatha Christie **12**:119
  Robert B. Parker **27**:364
  J.I.M. Stewart **14**:512

Peters, Robert
  Charles Bukowski **5**:80
  Clayton Eshleman **7**:99
  Michael McClure **6**:317
  W. D. Snodgrass **18**:492
  Anne Waldman **7**:508

Peters, Robert L.
  Hollis Summers **10**:493

Petersen, Carol
  Max Frisch **18**:160

Petersen, Clarence
  Nora Ephron **17**:110
  Charles M. Schulz **12**:527
  Wilfrid Sheed **2**:392

Petersen, Fred
  Ernesto Sabato **23**:376

Petersen, Gwenn Boardman
  Yukio Mishima **27**:341
  Jun'ichirō Tanizaki **28**:415

Petersen, Levi S.
  A. B. Guthrie, Jr. **23**:200

Peterson, Mary
  Jayne Anne Phillips **15**:419

Peterson, Maurice
  Sidney Poitier **26**:360

Peterson, Richard F.
  Mary Lavin **18**:303

Peterson, Virgilia
  Sylvia Ashton-Warner **19**:22
  Jan de Hartog **19**:131
  Betty Smith **19**:424
  George Tabori **19**:436
  Henri Troyat **23**:458
  Jessamyn West **17**:548
  Monique Wittig **22**:471

Petit, Christopher
  Peter Townshend **17**:539

Petric, Vlada
  Carl Theodor Dreyer **16**:266

Petrie, Graham
  Jean Renoir **20**:302
  Eric Rohmer **16**:529
  François Truffaut **20**:386

Petrie, Paul
  A. Alvarez **5**:16

Petroski, Catherine
  Penelope Gilliatt **13**:237

Petrović, Njegoš M.
  Dobrica Ćosić **14**:132

Petticoffer, Dennis
  Richard Brautigan **12**:73

Pettingell, Phoebe
  John Ashbery **25**:54
  Donald Hall **1**:137
  Anthony Hecht **19**:207
  John Hollander **14**:266
  Barbara Howes **15**:289
  Brad Leithauser **27**:241
  Philip Levine **9**:332; **14**:320
  Robert Lowell **8**:353
  James Merrill **13**:382
  John Wain **11**:563

Pettit, Arthur G.
Sam Peckinpah 20:280

Pettit, Michael
Paul Bowles 19:59

Pettit, Philip
J.R.R. Tolkien 3:483

Petts, Margo
H. F. Brinsmead 21:32

Pevear, Richard
A. R. Ammons 3:10
Wendell Berry 27:38
Charles Causley 7:42
Guy Davenport, Jr. 14:139
Richmond Lattimore 3:277
Denise Levertov 3:292
Hugh MacDiarmid 4:313
James Merrill 3:334
Pablo Neruda 5:301
George Oppen 7:286
Peter Porter 13:452
Ezra Pound 2:343
Louis Zukofsky 7:563

Peyre, Henri
Marcel Aymé 11:21
Simone de Beauvoir 1:19
Albert Camus 1:53; 14:106
Louis-Ferdinand Céline 1:57
René Char 9:162
Georges Duhamel 8:186
Romain Gary 25:184, 186
Jean Giono 4:185
Julien Green 3:203
Violette Leduc 22:261
André Malraux 1:201
François Mauriac 4:338
Henri de Montherlant 19:324
Raymond Queneau 5:358
Alain Robbe-Grillet 4:446
Jules Romains 7:383
Nathalie Sarraute 4:464
Jean-Paul Sartre 1:305
Claude Simon 4:494
Henri Troyat 23:458, 459, 460

Pfeffercorn, Eli
Abraham B. Yehoshua 13:616

Pfeiffer, John
Franklyn M. Branley 21:16

Pfeiffer, John R.
John Brunner 8:105

Pfeil, Fred
John Berger 19:40
Luis Rafael Sánchez 23:385

Pfeiler, William K.
Erich Maria Remarque 21:329

Phelps, Donald
Fielding Dawson 6:125
Gilbert Sorrentino 7:451

Phelps, Paul B.
Bienvenido N. Santos 22:366

Phelps, Robert
Helen MacInnes 27:280
Dan Wakefield 7:502

Philip, Neil
Diana Wynne Jones 26:230
Rosemary Sutcliff 26:440, 441

Phillips, Allen W.
Octavio Paz 3:376

Phillips, Cassandra
Raymond Carver 22:98

Phillips, Delbert
Yevgeny Yevtushenko 3:547

Phillips, Frank Lamont
Maya Angelou 12:12

Phillips, Gene D.
Ken Russell 16:551

Phillips, James A.
Vine Deloria, Jr. 21:109

Phillips, James E.
Laurence Olivier 20:237

Phillips, Klaus
Jurek Becker 19:35

Phillips, Michael Joseph
Richard Kostelanetz 28:218

Phillips, Norma
Alan Sillitoe 6:501

Phillips, Robert
A. R. Ammons 25:45
John Berryman 25:90
Philip Booth 23:77
Hortense Calisher 8:125
Arthur A. Cohen 7:52
James T. Farrell 4:158
Allen Ginsberg 6:199
William Goyen 5:148, 149;
14:213
William Heyen 18:231
Richard Howard 10:275
Robert Lowell 4:303
Bernard Malamud 3:325
Carson McCullers 4:345;
12:432
James Alan McPherson 19:310
Brian Moore 7:239
Joyce Carol Oates 11:404
Anne Sexton 15:470
Patrick White 4:586
Marya Zaturenska 11:579

Phillips, Steven R.
Ernest Hemingway 3:241

Phillips, William
Edmund Wilson 24:474

Phillipson, John S.
Vine Deloria, Jr. 21:109
Howard Fast 23:161

Phillipson, Michael
Lucien Goldmann 24:250

Piacentino, Edward J.
T. S. Stribling 23:449

Piazza, Paul
Christopher Isherwood 14:281
John Knowles 26:263

Picard, Raymond
Roland Barthes 24:23

Piccarella, John
David Byrne 26:96
Smokey Robinson 21:351

Piccoli, Raffaello
Riccardo Bacchelli 19:30

Pichaske, David R.
John Lennon and Paul
McCartney 12:373

Pick, Robert
Erich Maria Remarque 21:329
Frank Yerby 7:556

Pickar, G. B.
Martin Walser 27:461

Pickar, Gertrud B.
Max Frisch 14:181

Pickar, Gertrud Bauer
Martin Walser 27:458

Pickering, Felix
Benedict Kiely 23:264

Pickering, James S.
Alvin Silverstein and Virginia
B. Silverstein 17:450

Pickering, Sam, Jr.
Anthony Powell 7:338
P. G. Wodehouse 5:517

Pickering, Samuel
Alan Garner 17:151

Pickering, Samuel F., Jr.
Joyce Carol Oates 6:369

Pickrel, Paul
Heinrich Böll 27:54
L. P. Hartley 22:211
Aldo Palazzeschi 11:431
Sylvia Townsend Warner 7:511

Picon, Gaëtan
Jean Anouilh 13:21
Michel Butor 8:119
Albert Camus 9:144
Henri Michaux 8:392

Pierce, Hazel
Isaac Asimov 26:41

Piercy, Marge
Alta 19:18
Margaret Atwood 3:20
Margaret Laurence 6:289
Joanna Russ 15:461
Alice Walker 9:557

Pifer, Ellen
Vladimir Nabokov 23:312

Pigaga, Thom
John Hollander 2:197

Piggott, Stuart
David Jones 4:261

Pike, B. A.
Margery Allingham 19:13, 14,
15, 16, 17, 18

Pike, C. R.
Arkadii Strugatskii and Boris
Strugatskii 27:437

Pilger, John
Michael Cimino 16:211

Pinchin, Jane Lagoudis
Lawrence Durrell 13:186
E. M. Forster 13:220

Pinckney, Darryl
James Baldwin 17:44
Imamu Amiri Baraka 14:48
Jacob Epstein 19:163
Gayl Jones 9:307
June Jordan 23:257
Paule Marshall 27:315
Toni Morrison 22:322
John Rechy 18:442
Michael Thelwell 22:415
Jean Toomer 22:429
Richard Wright 9:585

Pincus, Richard Eliot
Theodore Sturgeon 22:412

Pinkerton, Jan
Peter Taylor 1:333

Pinsker, Sanford
Leslie A. Fiedler 24:204
Bernard Malamud 3:322;
18:321
Joyce Carol Oates 11:402
Isaac Bashevis Singer 3:454
John Updike 7:489

Pinsky, Robert
John Berryman 8:93
Elizabeth Bishop 15:61
Seamus Heaney 25:249
Ted Hughes 9:282
Philip Levine 9:332
Cynthia MacDonald 13:355
Theodore Roethke 8:461
Raphael Rudnik 7:384
Mark Strand 18:517

Pippett, Aileen
Julia W. Cunningham 12:163

Pippett, Roger
John Mortimer 28:282

Pirie, Bruce
Timothy Findley 27:142

Pit
Richard O'Brien 17:323

Pitou, Spire
Jean Cayrol 11:110

Pittock, Malcolm
Ivy Compton-Burnett 10:108

Pivovarnick, John
Louis L'Amour 25:282

Plaice, S. N.
Siegfried Lenz 27:255

Planchart, Alejandro Enrique
John Lennon and Paul
McCartney 12:359

Plant, Richard
Heinrich Böll 27:58
Eleanor Clark 19:105
Gregor von Rezzori 25:381
Henri Troyat 23:457

Plater, William M.
Thomas Pynchon 18:433

Plumb, Robert K.
Roy A. Gallant 17:126

Plumly, Stanley
Carolyn Forché **25**:169
Marilyn Hacker **23**:205
Lisel Mueller **13**:399
Charles Simic **22**:381
James Tate **25**:428

Plummer, William
Jerome Charyn **18**:99
Stanley Elkin **14**:157
Jerzy Kosinski **10**:306

Poague, Leland A.
Frank Capra **16**:162
Bob Dylan **6**:156

Pochoda, Elizabeth
Djuna Barnes **11**:30
Milan Kundera **19**:268
Tim O'Brien **19**:357

Pochoda, Elizabeth Turner
Anna Kavan **13**:316
Tadeusz Konwicki **8**:327
Alan Lelchuk **5**:245
Joyce Carol Oates **6**:373

Podhoretz, Norman
James Baldwin **1**:13, 14
Saul Bellow **1**:28
Albert Camus **1**:52
J. P. Donleavy **1**:75
George P. Elliott **2**:130
William Faulkner **1**:98
William Golding **17**:160
Paul Goodman **1**:123
Joseph Heller **1**:139
Thomas Hinde **6**:239
Jack Kerouac **1**:165
Norman Mailer **1**:188
Bernard Malamud **1**:194
Mary McCarthy **1**:205
John O'Hara **1**:260
Philip Roth **1**:292
Nathalie Sarraute **1**:302
John Updike **1**:343
Edmund Wilson **1**:372, 373

Poger, Sidney
T. S. Eliot **15**:212

Poggi, Gianfranco
Luchino Visconti **16**:563

Poggioli, Renato
Eugenio Montale **7**:221

Pogrebin, Letty Cottin
Laurie Colwin **23**:130
Richard Peck **21**:295

Poirier, Richard
John Barth **3**:40
Saul Bellow **8**:74
Jorge Luis Borges **3**:77
T. S. Eliot **3**:140
Robert Frost **4**:176; **9**:226
Geoffrey H. Hartman **27**:180
Lillian Hellman **4**:221
John Hollander **14**:264
Jonathan Kozol **17**:251
John Lennon and Paul McCartney **12**:368
Norman Mailer **2**:263, 265; **3**:314; **4**:322; **14**:349; **28**:262
Vladimir Nabokov **6**:354
Thomas Pynchon **2**:355; **3**:409; **18**:429

Robert Stone **23**:429
William Styron **3**:474
Gore Vidal **4**:553
Rudolph Wurlitzer **2**:482; **4**:597

Polacheck, Janet G.
Jules Archer **12**:18
James D. Forman **21**:120
Milton Meltzer **26**:300

Poland, Nancy
Margaret Drabble **5**:118

Polar, Antonio Cornejo
José María Arguedas **18**:7

Polishook, Irwin
Allan W. Eckert **17**:107

Politzer, Heinz
Jerome Siegel and Joe Shuster **21**:355

Polk, James
Leslie Marmon Silko **23**:411

Pollack, Pamela D.
Gunnel Beckman **26**:88
Rosa Guy **26**:143
Norma Fox Mazer **26**:291
Richard Peck **21**:299
Maia Wojciechowska **26**:455

Pollak, Richard
Jan de Hartog **19**:132

Pollitt, Katha
Alice Adams **13**:1, 2
Margaret Atwood **8**:30
Saul Bellow **25**:82
Anita Desai **19**:133
Leslie Epstein **27**:128
Carolyn Forché **25**:171
Gail Godwin **22**:180
Carolyn G. Heilbrun **25**:257
Sandra Hochman **8**:298
Maureen Howard **14**:268
Dan Jacobson **14**:291
Yashar Kemal **14**:300
William X. Kienzle **25**:275
Ella Leffland **19**:279
David Malouf **28**:266
Cynthia Ozick **28**:352
Marge Piercy **27**:377
James Purdy **10**:425
Françoise Sagan **17**:428
Susan Richards Shreve **23**:402
Lee Smith **25**:409
Anne Tyler **7**:479
Alice Walker **27**:448
William Wharton **18**:542

Pollock, Bruce
Mick Jagger and Keith Richard **17**:235
Paul Simon **17**:465

Pollock, Zailig
A. M. Klein **19**:262

Polt, Harriet
Ralph Bakshi **26**:69
Bernard Malamud **18**:322

Polt, Harriet R.
René Clair **20**:66

Pond, Steve
Paul Weller **26**:447

Ponnuthurai, Charles Sarvan
Chinua Achebe **5**:3

Pontac, Perry
Miguel Piñero **4**:401

Pool, Gail
Anne Sexton **10**:468

Poore, C. G.
Ogden Nash **23**:317, 318

Poore, Charles
Erich Maria Remarque **21**:330
Wilfrid Sheed **2**:392
Jessamyn West **17**:549

Popkin, Henry
Albert Camus **9**:145
Arthur Miller **26**:319

Porsild, A. E.
Farley Mowat **26**:332

Portch, Stephen R.
Flannery O'Connor **15**:412

Porter, Carolyn
Lina Wertmüller **16**:593

Porter, Katherine Anne
Kay Boyle **19**:61
Ezra Pound **7**:325

Porter, M. Gilbert
Saul Bellow **2**:54; **8**:72

Porter, Michael
Horst Bienek **11**:48

Porter, Peter
W. H. Auden **14**:31
Gavin Ewart **13**:208
Roy Fisher **25**:161
Seamus Heaney **14**:244
Ted Hughes **14**:273
Derek Mahon **27**:291
Sylvia Plath **17**:352
Stevie Smith **3**:460
Judith Wright **11**:578

Porter, Raymond J.
Brendan Behan **8**:64

Porter, Robert
Milan Kundera **4**:276

Porter, Thomas E.
John Ehle **27**:103

Porterfield, Christopher
Kingsley Amis **2**:8
Christopher Fry **2**:143
Ted Hughes **2**:199
Donald E. Westlake **7**:528

Poss, Stanley
John Hollander **8**:301
Philip Larkin **13**:337
Cynthia Macdonald **13**:355
P. H. Newby **2**:310
Adrienne Rich **7**:370
Theodore Roethke **8**:460
Nancy Willard **7**:539

Postell, Frances
Christie Harris **12**:263

Postlewait, Thomas
Samuel Beckett **18**:46

Potamkin, Harry Allan
Carl Theodor Dreyer **16**:255

Potok, Chaim
Paul West **7**:523

Potoker, Edward Martin
Michael Mott **15**:379
Judith Rossner **9**:456
Ronald Sukenick **6**:524

Potts, Charles
Thomas McGrath **28**:277

Potts, Paul
George Barker **8**:43

Potts, Stephen W.
Stanislaw Lem **15**:330

Pouillon, Jean
William Faulkner **8**:208

Pound, Ezra
Robert Frost **15**:239
Mina Loy **28**:245
Marianne Moore **19**:335
William Carlos Williams **13**:602

Povey, John
Chinua Achebe **26**:20

Povey, John F.
Chinua Achebe **1**:1; **7**:6
Cyprian Ekwensi **4**:151
Wole Soyinka **14**:506

Powell, Anthony
Evelyn Waugh **3**:513

Powell, Bertie J.
Lorraine Hansberry **17**:193

Powell, Dilys
Elia Kazan **16**:361

Powell, Meghan
Stan Lee **17**:262

Powell, Michael
Martin Scorsese **20**:340

Powell, Neil
Thom Gunn **3**:216

Power, K. C.
Michael McClure **6**:321

Power, Victor
Hugh Leonard **19**:281

Powers, Thomas
Richard Kostelanetz **28**:213
Tom Wolfe **15**:583

Pratt, Annis
Doris Lessing **3**:288; **6**:292

Pratt, John Clark
John Steinbeck **1**:326

Pratt, Linda Ray
Sylvia Plath **3**:390

Pratt, Sarah
V. S. Pritchett **13**:468

Pratt, William
John Berryman **10**:45
Joseph Brodsky **6**:97
Daniel Halpern **14**:232
Ezra Pound **18**:427
Andrei Voznesensky **15**:554

Prendergast, Christopher
Roland Barthes 24:36

Prendowska, Krystyna
Jerzy Kosinski 15:313

Prescott, Orville
Michael Ayrton 7:17
James Clavell 25:125
Earl Hamner, Jr. 12:257
Erich Maria Remarque 21:330
Betty Smith 19:422
J.I.M. Stewart 7:466
Robert Penn Warren 8:543

Prescott, Peter S.
Alice Adams 6:1
Richard Adams 4:7
Eric Ambler 6:3
Kingsley Amis 3:8
Martin Amis 4:20
Donald Barthelme 5:54
William Peter Blatty 2:64
Vance Bourjaily 8:104
Kay Boyle 5:65
Richard Brautigan 5:71
Lothar-Günther Buchheim 6:101
Anthony Burgess 5:85
Agatha Christie 12:120
Michael Crichton 6:119
Robertson Davies 7:73
Len Deighton 7:75
Don DeLillo 8:171
Peter De Vries 7:78
John Dos Passos 4:137
Lawrence Durrell 6:151
Leslie A. Fiedler 4:161
John Fowles 6:186
Michael Frayn 3:165
Nadine Gordimer 5:146
Graham Greene 3:213
Lillian Hellman 4:221
George V. Higgins 4:223
Edward Hoagland 28:182
Russell C. Hoban 7:161
Geoffrey Household 11:277
Dan Jacobson 4:254
Diane Johnson 5:198
Robert F. Jones 7:193
Thomas Keneally 8:318
William Kennedy 6:275; 28:205, 206
John Knowles 26:265
Jerzy Kosinski 6:285
John Le Carré 5:232, 234
Doris Lessing 2:241
Peter Matthiessen 5:274
Cormac McCarthy 4:341
John McGahern 5:280
A. G. Mojtabai 9:385
Brian Moore 7:236
Toni Morrison 4:365
Penelope Mortimer 5:299
Joyce Carol Oates 6:374
Flann O'Brien 5:314
Robert B. Parker 27:367
Reynolds Price 6:425
Philip Roth 2:378; 4:455; 6:475
Cynthia Propper Seton 27:425
Isaac Bashevis Singer 3:458
Aleksandr I. Solzhenitsyn 4:516
Muriel Spark 5:399
Robert Stone 5:409

Harvey Swados 5:422
Paul Theroux 5:428
Michel Tournier 6:537
William Trevor 7:478
John Updike 5:455, 458
Gore Vidal 4:554
Alice Walker 27:449
Jessamyn West 7:521
Patrick White 3:524
P. G. Wodehouse 5:515
Larry Woiwode 6:579
Richard Yates 7:555

Presley, Delma Eugene
John Fowles 3:163
Carson McCullers 4:346

Press, John
John Betjeman 6:67
Philip Larkin 8:339
Louis MacNeice 4:316

Preston, Don
Agnes Eckhardt Nixon 21:252

Prestwich, J. O.
Rosemary Sutcliff 26:426

Price, Derek de Solla
John Brunner 10:80
Ursula K. LeGuin 8:343

Price, James
Martin Amis 9:26
Beryl Bainbridge 8:37
Caroline Blackwood 9:101
Frank Capra 16:157
Margaret Drabble 8:184

Price, John D.
St.-John Perse 11:434

Price, L. Brian
Jean Genet 14:203

Price, Martin
Robert Bolt 14:87
Mavis Gallant 18:171
Marjorie Kellogg 2:224
Iris Murdoch 1:236; 3:349
Joyce Carol Oates 1:251
Nathalie Sarraute 4:469
C. P. Snow 1:317
David Storey 4:530
Angus Wilson 5:514

Price, R.G.G.
Kingsley Amis 2:7
Paul Bowles 2:78
L. P. Hartley 2:182
Robert Kroetsch 23:270
Josephine Poole 17:371
Elizabeth Taylor 2:432

Price, Reynolds
Cleanth Brooks 24:107
Lucille Clifton 19:110
William Faulkner 1:102; 3:151
Francine du Plessix Gray 22:202
Graham Greene 3:212
Mark Helprin 22:220
Toni Morrison 10:355
Walker Percy 8:442
Elizabeth Spencer 22:405
James Welch 6:560
Eudora Welty 2:463

Priebe, Richard
Wole Soyinka 3:463

Priestley, J. B.
T. S. Eliot 3:135
William Faulkner 3:150
Ernest Hemingway 3:232
F. R. Leavis 24:296
Ezra Pound 3:394

Priestley, Michael
John Irving 23:244

Prigozy, Ruth
Larry McMurtry 3:333

Primeau, Ronald
John Brunner 8:109

Prince, Peter
Martin Amis 4:19
Charles Bukowski 5:80
Anthony Burgess 4:84
John Fowles 6:184
Thomas Hinde 11:273
Yashar Kemal 14:299
Thomas Keneally 5:210
Larry McMurtry 27:333
Patrick Modiano 18:338
Alice Munro 6:341
David Pownall 10:419
Piers Paul Read 4:444; 25:377
Philip Roth 3:439

Pring-Mill, Robert
Pablo Neruda 28:310

Pringle, David
J. G. Ballard 14:40

Pringle, John Douglas
Hugh MacDiarmid 4:312

Pritchard, R. E.
L. P. Hartley 22:219

Pritchard, William H.
Dannie Abse 7:1
Margaret Atwood 3:19
Wendell Berry 8:85
John Berryman 3:72; 8:90
Henry Bromell 5:74
Anthony Burgess 1:48; 4:84
Jerome Charyn 18:99
Donald Davie 8:162, 163
John Fowles 9:214; 10:189
Allen Ginsberg 3:195
Robert Graves 2:177
Marilyn Hacker 9:257
Seamus Heaney 14:242
John Hollander 5:187
Ted Hughes 9:281
Richard F. Hugo 6:244; 18:260
Alan Lelchuk 5:245
Denise Levertov 2:242; 15:338
Philip Levine 2:244
Robert Lowell 1:184
Louis MacNeice 4:316
Wright Morris 18:354
Iris Murdoch 8:406
Vladimir Nabokov 3:353
Howard Nemerov 6:363
Anthony Powell 7:339
Thomas Pynchon 3:418
Piers Paul Read 25:379
Kenneth Rexroth 2:369
Adrienne Rich 3:427; 6:459

Susan Fromberg Schaeffer 6:489
Cynthia Propper Seton 27:428
Anne Sexton 15:473
L. E. Sissman 18:488
Aleksandr I. Solzhenitsyn 4:510
Kathleen Spivack 6:520
Richard G. Stern 4:523
Robert Stone 5:410
May Swenson 4:532
James Tate 25:429
Elizabeth Taylor 2:433
Paul Theroux 11:531
John Updike 3:487
Richard Wilbur 6:571
James Wright 3:544
Rudolph Wurlitzer 4:597
Richard Yates 7:556

Pritchett, V. S.
Kingsley Amis 13:15
Simone de Beauvoir 4:48; 14:67
Samuel Beckett 4:50
Saul Bellow 25:80
Heinrich Böll 27:64
Bruce Chatwin 28:74
Rhys Davies 23:141
Max Frisch 14:183
Ernest K. Gann 23:166
William Golding 2:168; 17:160, 166
Juan Goytisolo 5:151; 10:245
Patrick Kavanagh 22:234
Arthur Koestler 15:309
Mary Lavin 18:301
John le Carré 15:326
Compton Mackenzie 18:313
Norman Mailer 2:262
Carson McCullers 12:415
William Maxwell 19:305
John Mortimer 28:289
Vladimir Nabokov 6:356
Flann O'Brien 10:364
Flannery O'Connor 21:267
Frank O'Connor 14:395
John Cowper Powys 15:435
Gregor von Rezzori 25:382
Aleksandr I. Solzhenitsyn 1:320
Paul Theroux 8:513
James Thurber 5:433
William Trevor 14:536
Henri Troyat 23:461
John Updike 23:471
Gore Vidal 8:529
Evelyn Waugh 27:475

Procopiow, Norma
Marilyn Hacker 5:155
Eleanor Lerman 9:329
Anne Sexton 4:483

Proffer, Carl R.
Aleksandr I. Solzhenitsyn 9:506

Pronko, Leonard Cabell
Arthur Adamov 25:12
Jean Anouilh 13:16
Jean Genet 14:201
Eugène Ionesco 1:154

Proteus
Agatha Christie 12:112
Edna Ferber 18:151

Prothro, Laurie
  May Sarton 14:482

Prouse, Derek
  Elia Kazan 16:364
  Laurence Olivier 20:237

Prucha, Francis Paul
  Vine Deloria, Jr. 21:113

Pryce-Jones, Alan
  Michael Ayrton 7:16
  John Betjeman 6:69
  Italo Calvino 5:98
  John le Carré 28:230
  Vladimir Nabokov 1:246

Pryce-Jones, David
  Siegfried Lenz 27:250

Pryor, Thomas M.
  Sally Benson 17:49

Pryse, Marjorie
  Helen Yglesias 7:558; 22:493

Puckett, Harry
  T. S. Eliot 10:167

Puckette, Charles McD.
  T. S. Stribling 23:439

Puetz, Manfred
  John Barth 9:72
  Thomas Pynchon 6:434

Pugh, Anthony R.
  Alain Robbe-Grillet 4:450

Pulleine, Tim
  Woody Allen 16:9
  Claude Chabrol 16:184
  Carlos Saura 20:319
  Peter Weir 20:428

Punnett, Spencer
  Edwin Newman 14:378

Purcell, H. D.
  George MacDonald Fraser 7:106

Purcell, J. M.
  Carolyn G. Heilbrun 25:255

Purdy, A. W.
  Earle Birney 6:73

Purdy, Al
  Bill Bissett 18:59

Purdy, Strother
  Luis Buñuel 16:133

Purdy, Theodore, Jr.
  William Maxwell 19:304

Purtill, Richard
  J.R.R. Tolkien 12:577

Putney, Michael
  Hunter S. Thompson 17:504

Puzo, Mario
  James Baldwin 17:34

Pye, Michael
  George Lucas 16:416

Pym, Christopher
  Julian Symons 14:522

Pym, John
  René Clair 20:69
  John Landis 26:277

Pyros, J.
  Michael McClure 6:320

Quacinella, Lucy
  Lina Wertmüller 16:596

Quammen, David
  Bobbie Ann Mason 28:272
  Bette Pesetsky 28:357
  Leon Rooke 25:392

Quance, Robert A.
  Miguel Delibes 18:115

Quant, Leonard
  Robert Altman 16:35

Quart, Barbara Koenig
  Cynthia Ozick 28:354
  Bette Pesetsky 28:359

Quennell, Peter
  Robert Graves 6:210

Quigly, Isabel
  Robert Bresson 16:104
  Frank Capra 16:157
  Claude Chabrol 16:168
  Natalia Ginzburg 11:230
  Jean-Luc Godard 20:130
  Pamela Hansford Johnson 1:160
  Noel Streatfeild 21:411
  Elio Vittorini 14:547
  Paul Zindel 26:474

Quinn, Sister Bernetta, O.S.F.
  Alan Dugan 2:121
  David Jones 4:259
  Ezra Pound 4:416; 7:326
  William Stafford 7:460
  Allen Tate 4:539
  Derek Walcott 2:460
    See also Bernetta (Quinn), Sister Mary, O.S.F.

Quinn, James P.
  Edward Albee 5:11

Quinn, Michael
  William Golding 17:164

Quinn, Vincent
  H. D. 14:224

Quinton, Anthony
  William Barrett 27:21

R
  David Jones 4:259
  Arthur Koestler 6:281
  Aleksandr I. Solzhenitsyn 4:506

Raban, Jonathan
  A. Alvarez 5:18
  Kingsley Amis 8:11
  Beryl Bainbridge 5:40
  John Barth 1:17
  Saul Bellow 1:32
  E. L. Doctorow 11:141
  Stanley Elkin 6:169
  Nadine Gordimer 5:145
  Erica Jong 4:265
  Mary McCarthy 1:207
  Ian McEwan 13:369
  John McGahern 9:369
  Stanley Middleton 7:220
  Brian Moore 1:225
  Iris Murdoch 4:369
  Vladimir Nabokov 6:359
  Jean Rhys 6:456
  Richard G. Stern 4:523
  Paul Theroux 28:425
  Hunter S. Thompson 17:505
  William Trevor 7:476
  Angus Wilson 25:458

Rabassa, Gregory
  Alejo Carpentier 11:99
  Julio Cortázar 15:147
  Gabriel García Márquez 3:180; 27:148
  João Guimarães Rosa 23:353
  Gilbert Sorrentino 22:392
  Mario Vargas Llosa 15:551

Rabinovitz, Rubin
  Kingsley Amis 5:20
  Samuel Beckett 6:40, 41
  Norman Mailer 5:267
  Iris Murdoch 1:235; 2:297
  C. P. Snow 4:500
  Angus Wilson 5:512

Rabinowitz, Dorothy
  Beryl Bainbridge 8:36
  Elliott Baker 8:40
  Giorgio Bassani 9:77
  Maeve Brennan 5:72
  Anthony Burgess 5:88
  Hortense Calisher 4:87; 8:124
  John Cheever 3:107
  Laurie Colwin 23:128
  Lois Gould 4:201
  Peter Handke 5:165
  Mark Helprin 7:152
  Dan Jacobson 4:254
  Ruth Prawer Jhabvala 4:256, 257; 8:311
  Robert Kotlowitz 4:275
  Mary Lavin 4:281
  Doris Lessing 2:241
  Meyer Levin 7:205
  Larry McMurtry 11:371
  Brian Moore 7:237
  Wright Morris 3:344
  Edna O'Brien 5:312
  John O'Hara 6:384
  Grace Paley 4:392
  S. J. Perelman 5:337
  Philip Roth 3:437
  Anne Sexton 10:468
  John Updike 2:445
  Gore Vidal 4:553
  Dan Wakefield 7:503
  Joseph Wambaugh 3:509
  Harriet Waugh 6:560
  Arnold Wesker 5:482

Rabinowitz, Morris
  James D. Forman 21:121

Rabkin, David
  Alex La Guma 19:273

Rabkin, Eric S.
  Donald Barthelme 13:58
  Robert A. Heinlein 26:166
  Frederik Pohl 18:410

Rabkin, Gerald
  Paul Green 25:198
  Derek Walcott 9:556

Rachewiltz, Boris de
  Ezra Pound 7:331

Rachleff, Owen S.
  Woody Allen 16:9

Rachlis, Kit
  Jackson Browne 21:41
  Elvis Costello 21:70, 72
  Neil Young 17:582

Rackham, Jeff
  John Fowles 2:138

Radcliff-Umstead, Douglas
  Alberto Moravia 11:381

Rader, Dotson
  Hubert Selby, Jr. 4:481
  Yevgeny Yevtushenko 3:547

Radford, C. B.
  Simone de Beauvoir 4:45, 46

Radin, Victoria
  Sara Davidson 9:175

Radke, Judith J.
  Pierre Gascar 11:221

Radley, Philippe
  Andrei Voznesensky 15:554

Radner, Rebecca
  Lenora Mattingly Weber 12:635

Radu, Kenneth
  Christie Harris 12:264

Rae, Bruce
  John R. Tunis 12:593

Raeburn, John
  Frank Capra 16:163

Rafalko, Robert
  Eric Ambler 9:22

Rafalko, Robert J.
  Philip K. Dick 10:138

Raff, Emanuel
  Henry Gregor Felsen 17:124

Raffel, Burton
  J.R.R. Tolkien 1:337
  Louis Zukofsky 11:580

Ragusa, Olga
  Italo Calvino 22:91
  Alberto Moravia 2:292

Rahv, Betty T.
  Albert Camus 9:148
  Alain Robbe-Grillet 8:451
  Nathalie Sarraute 8:469
  Jean-Paul Sartre 7:395

Rahv, Philip
  Louis Aragon 22:34
  Saul Bellow 2:50
  Richard Brautigan 12:57
  T. S. Eliot 2:126
  Leslie A. Fiedler 24:195
  Ernest Hemingway 3:231
  F. R. Leavis 24:304
  Arthur Miller 2:278
  Delmore Schwartz 10:462
  Aleksandr I. Solzhenitsyn 2:411; 26:422

Raidy, William A.
Sam Shepard 17:449

Raine, Craig
Geoffrey Hill 18:237
Ted Hughes 14:272
Harold Pinter 6:419
Ted Walker 13:566

Raine, Kathleen
Brewster Ghiselin 23:170
David Jones 2:216; 7:191
St.-John Perse 4:399
Herbert Read 4:440

Rainer, Dachine
Rebecca West 7:525

Raizada, Harish
R. K. Narayan 28:294

Rama Rau, Santha
Khushwant Singh 11:504

Rambali, Paul
Elvis Costello 21:67

Rampersad, Arnold
Alex Haley 12:247

Ramras-Rauch, Gila
S. Y. Agnon 4:14
Yehuda Amichai 22:32
Yoram Kaniuk 19:241

Ramsey, Jarold
Leslie Marmon Silko 23:411

Ramsey, Nancy
Margaret Atwood 25:70

Ramsey, Paul
Robert Bly 5:62
Edgar Bowers 9:121
Hayden Carruth 10:100
Larry Eigner 9:181
John Hollander 14:265
Eleanor Lerman 9:328
W. S. Merwin 5:286
N. Scott Momaday 19:318
Michael Mott 15:380
Howard Nemerov 9:394
Linda Pastan 27:369
Richard Wilbur 14:577

Ramsey, R. H.
Robert Kroetsch 23:271

Ramsey, Roger
Friedrich Dürrenmatt 4:140
Pär Lagerkvist 10:311

Ramsey, S. A.
Randolph Stow 23:438

Ranbom, Sheppard J.
Philip Roth 15:453

Rand, Richard A.
John Hollander 5:187

Randall, Dudley
Robert Hayden 5:168
Audre Lorde 18:307
Margaret Walker 6:554

Randall, Francis B.
Ch'ien Chung-shu 22:105
Yevgeny Yevtushenko 26:468

Randall, Julia
Howard Nemerov 2:308
Gabrielle Roy 10:441

Randall, Margaret
Judith Johnson Sherwin 15:479

Ranjbaran, Esmaeel
Ahmad Shamlu 10:469

Rank, Hugh
Edwin O'Connor 14:390

Ranly, Ernest W.
Kurt Vonnegut, Jr. 2:453

Ransom, John Crowe
Kenneth Burke 24:122
Donald Davidson 13:167
T. S. Eliot 24:165
Randall Jarrell 1:159
Marianne Moore 19:337
I. A. Richards 24:382, 385
Allen Tate 4:535

Ransom, W. M.
Galway Kinnell 3:268

Rao, K. B.
Salman Rushdie 23:367

Rao, K. S. Narayana
R. K. Narayan 28:299

Raphael, Frederic
James Baldwin 17:41
Michael Frayn 7:107
Jakov Lind 4:293

Rascoe, Judith
Laurie Colwin 5:107
John Gregory Dunne 28:123
Dick Francis 22:150

Rasi, Humberto M.
Jorge Luis Borges 2:74

Raskin, A. H.
Milton Meltzer 26:298

Rasso, Pamela S.
William Heyen 13:284

Ratcliff, Michael
Thomas Keneally 14:303

Rathbone, Richard
Breyten Breytenbach 23:86

Rathburn, Norma
Margot Benary-Isbert 12:32

Ratner, Marc L.
John Hawkes 14:237
William Styron 5:418

Ratner, Rochelle
Yehuda Amichai 22:33
Clayton Eshleman 7:100
Carolyn Forché 25:171
Susan Fromberg Schaeffer 22:370
Patti Smith 12:541

Rave, Eugene S.
Barbara Corcoran 17:78

Raven, Simon
Alvah Bessie 23:60
Dan Jacobson 14:289
John Knowles 26:245

Ravenscroft, Arthur
Chinua Achebe 11:1
Bessie Head 25:233

Rawley, James
James Baldwin 15:43
Donald Barthelme 13:63

Ray, David
E. E. Cummings 12:151

Ray, Robert
James Baldwin 2:34
J.I.M. Stewart 7:466

Ray, Sheila G.
E. M. Almedingen 12:7

Rayme, Anne C.
Larry Kettelkamp 12:307

Raymond, John
Daphne du Maurier 11:163
Pamela Hansford Johnson 27:216
Françoise Sagan 17:417
Georges Simenon 3:449

Raynor, Henry
Laurence Olivier 20:236

Raynor, Vivien
Evan S. Connell, Jr. 6:115
Iris Murdoch 3:348
Edna O'Brien 3:364

Rayns, Tony
Shirley Clarke 16:219
Elvis Costello 21:71
Maya Deren 16:253
Rainer Werner Fassbinder 20:107, 108
Werner Herzog 16:321, 322
Richard O'Brien 17:323
Nagisa Oshima 20:251

Raysor, Thomas M.
M. H. Abrams 24:11

Rea, Dorothy
Auberon Waugh 7:514

Read, Esther H.
Melvin Berger 12:40

Read, Forrest, Jr.
Ezra Pound 7:327

Read, Herbert
Georg Lukács 24:317
Allen Tate 4:535

Read, Malcolm
Siegfried Lenz 27:252

Read, S. E.
Robertson Davies 13:172

Reagan, Dale
Robert Kroetsch 23:273

Real, Jere
Peter Shaffer 5:388

Reaney, James
Jay Macpherson 14:345

Reardon, Betty S.
James D. Forman 21:122
Jessamyn West 17:554

Rebay, Luciano
Alberto Moravia 7:239

Rechnitz, Robert M.
Carson McCullers 1:209

Reck, Rima Drell
Louis-Ferdinand Céline 7:44
Françoise Mallet-Joris 11:355

Reck, Tom S.
James M. Cain 28:50

Redding, Saunders
John Ehle 27:105
Shirley Ann Grau 4:208
Ezekiel Mphahlele 25:333
Richard Wright 1:377

Redfern, W. D.
Jean Giono 4:186

Redman, Ben Ray
Vera Brittain 23:91
Erich Maria Remarque 21:328
Dalton Trumbo 19:444
Marguerite Yourcenar 19:482

Redman, Eric
André Brink 18:69

Redmon, Anne
Judy Blume 12:45

Redmond, Eugene B.
Clarence Major 19:293

Reed, Bill
Frank Zappa 17:586

Reed, Diana
J. G. Ballard 6:28
John Wyndham 19:476

Reed, Henry
Rhys Davies 23:142
Mary Renault 17:391

Reed, Ishmael
Chester Himes 2:195

Reed, John
Arthur Hailey 5:156
Ngugi Wa Thiong'o 13:583

Reed, John R.
William Dickey 3:127
D. J. Enright 4:155
William Heyen 18:233
Daniel Hoffman 6:243
John Hollander 8:302
Richard Howard 7:169; 10:276
Judith Leet 11:323
James Merrill 8:388
Charles Reznikoff 9:450
David Wagoner 3:508
Philip Whalen 6:566

Reed, Peter J.
Kurt Vonnegut, Jr. 3:495; 12:626

Reed, Rex
Laura Nyro 17:313
Gordon Parks 16:460
Tennessee Williams 2:464

Reedy, Gerard
C. S. Lewis 6:308
Walker Percy 18:402

Reedy, Gerard C.
Richard Price **12**:490

Rees, David
Rhys Davies **23**:147
Rosa Guy **26**:145
Piers Paul Read **25**:375
Paul Zindel **26**:478

Rees, David L.
Philippa Pearce **21**:285
Otfried Preussler **17**:375
Colin Thiele **17**:494

Rees, Goronwy
Rhys Davies **23**:146
Richard Hughes **11**:278
Erich Maria Remarque **21**:328

Rees, Samuel
David Jones **13**:309

Reeve, Benjamin
Grace Paley **4**:393

Reeve, F. D.
Joseph Brodsky **6**:98
Aleksandr I. Solzhenitsyn **1**:319
Alexander Zinoviev **19**:489

Regan, Robert Alton
John Updike **5**:454

Regier, W. G.
W. H. Auden **3**:22
Michael Benedikt **4**:54
Kenneth O. Hanson **13**:263
Howard Moss **14**:375
Howard Nemerov **9**:395
Pablo Neruda **5**:305
Francis Ponge **6**:423

Rehder, Jesse
Randolph Stow **23**:432

Reibetanz, John
Philip Larkin **8**:334

Reichek, Morton A.
Chaim Grade **10**:249

Reid, Alastair
Jorge Luis Borges **2**:73
Hayden Carruth **18**:89
Bruce Chatwin **28**:71
Pablo Neruda **5**:302
John Updike **13**:561

Reid, Alfred S.
Karl Shapiro **15**:476

Reid, B. L.
V. S. Pritchett **13**:465

Reid, Beryl
Barbara Corcoran **17**:74
Lee Kingman **17**:246
Sonia Levitin **17**:264

Reid, Christopher
Ted Hughes **14**:272

Reid, David
Leonard Michaels **25**:318

Reigo, Ants
A. W. Purdy **14**:434

Reilly, Alayne P.
Yevgeny Yevtushenko **26**:463

Reilly, John H.
Arthur Adamov **25**:19

Reilly, John M.
Chester Himes **18**:245
B. Traven **11**:538

Reilly, Peter
Joan Armatrading **17**:10
Jimmy Cliff **21**:61
Ray Davies **21**:101
Janis Ian **21**:184, 185, 186, 187, 188
Billy Joel **26**:213, 214, 215, 216, 217, 221
Kris Kristofferson **26**:269
Joni Mitchell **12**:436
Monty Python **21**:227
Lou Reed **21**:312
Smokey Robinson **21**:345, 346
Carly Simon **26**:410, 411, 412, 413
Paul Simon **17**:460
Frank Zappa **17**:592

Reilly, Robert J.
C. S. Lewis **3**:298
J.R.R. Tolkien **1**:337; **3**:477

Reinhardt, Max
Charles Chaplin **16**:187

Reisz, Karel
Vittorio De Sica **20**:86
Elia Kazan **16**:361

Reitberger, Reinhold
Chares M. Schulz **12**:528

Reiter, Seymour
Sean O'Casey **5**:319

Reitman, David
Frank Zappa **17**:588

Reitt, Barbara B.
John Steinbeck **21**:392

Remini, Robert V.
Gore Vidal **8**:526

Renault, Mary
William Golding **17**:161

Rendle, Adrian
Sam Shepard **17**:433
Tom Stoppard **3**:470

Renek, Morris
Erskine Caldwell **8**:123

Renner, Charlotte
John Barth **27**:29

Rennie, Neil
Robin Skelton **13**:507

Renoir, Jean
Charles Chaplin **16**:194

Renshaw, Robert
J.R.R. Tolkien **1**:336

Resnik, Henry S.
Jonathan Baumbach **23**:54
Nora Ephron **17**:110
Richard Fariña **9**:195
John Irving **13**:292
William Melvin Kelley **22**:248
Wilfrid Sheed **2**:392
J.R.R. Tolkien **12**:566

Restivo, Angelo
Rudolfo A. Anaya **23**:26

Rexine, John E.
Vassilis Vassilikos **4**:552

Rexroth, Kenneth
Philip Booth **23**:74
Robert Creeley **4**:116
Robert Duncan **1**:82; **2**:123
T. S. Eliot **2**:127
William Everson **1**:96; **14**:162
Leslie A. Fiedler **24**:197
Carolyn Forché **25**:169
Allen Ginsberg **2**:164; **3**:193, 194
William Golding **3**:196
Paul Goodman **2**:169
Robinson Jeffers **2**:211
Pär Lagerkvist **13**:334
Denise Levertov **1**:175; **2**:243; **3**:292
Thomas McGrath **28**:276
W. S. Merwin **2**:278; **3**:338
Henry Miller **1**:219
Marianne Moore **2**:292
Kenneth Patchen **2**:332
Laura Riding **3**:432
Muriel Rukeyser **6**:478; **27**:407, 414
Carl Sandburg **1**:300; **4**:463
Isaac Bashevis Singer **3**:452
Edith Sitwell **2**:403
Gary Snyder **2**:407
Jean Toomer **4**:548
Philip Whalen **6**:565
William Carlos Williams **1**:371; **2**:469
Yvor Winters **4**:594

Reynal, Eugene
Margery Allingham **19**:11

Reynolds, Gary K.
Anne McCaffrey **17**:284

Reynolds, Horace
Olivia Manning **19**:299

Reynolds, Quentin
Erich Maria Remarque **21**:330

Reynolds, R. C.
Larry McMurtry **7**:215

Reynolds, Stanley
Frederick Exley **11**:186
Wilson Harris **25**:209
Anna Kavan **5**:205
William Kennedy **28**:204
Violette Leduc **22**:262
John Mortimer **28**:287
Chaim Potok **26**:369
Paul Theroux **28**:428
Robert Penn Warren **4**:582

Rezos, Ray
Kris Kristofferson **26**:266

Rheuban, Joyce
Josef von Sternberg **20**:375

Rhoads, Kenneth W.
William Saroyan **10**:455

Rhode, Eric
James Baldwin **17**:40
Robert Bresson **16**:105, 113
Vittorio De Sica **20**:89
Satyajit Ray **16**:477, 479
François Truffaut **20**:381

Rhodes, Joseph, Jr.
W.E.B. Du Bois **2**:120

Rhodes, Richard
Chester Himes **2**:194
MacKinlay Kantor **7**:196
Paule Marshall **27**:310
Michael Shaara **15**:474
Wilfrid Sheed **2**:394

Riasanovsky, Nicholas N.
Henri Troyat **23**:462

Ribalow, Harold U.
Meyer Levin **7**:205
Henry Roth **6**:471
Arnold Wesker **3**:518

Ribalow, Menachem
S. Y. Agnon **4**:10

Ribe, Neil
C. S. Lewis **27**:266

Rice, Edward
Thomas Merton **3**:337

Rice, Elmer
Howard Fast **23**:155

Rice, Julian C.
Ingmar Bergman **16**:76
LeRoi Jones **1**:163
Martin Scorsese **20**:327

Rice, Susan
Gordon Parks **16**:457

Rich, Adrienne
Hayden Carruth **18**:87
Jean Garrigue **8**:239
Paul Goodman **2**:170
Robert Lowell **3**:304
Robin Morgan **2**:294
Eleanor Ross Taylor **5**:425

Rich, Alan
Alan Ayckbourn **8**:34
Enid Bagnold **25**:79
Jules Feiffer **8**:216
Jack Gelber **14**:194
Simon Gray **9**:241
John Guare **8**:253
Albert Innaurato **21**:191, 193
Preston Jones **10**:297
Tom Stoppard **8**:501, 503
Elizabeth Swados **12**:558
Tennessee Williams **7**:545
Lanford Wilson **7**:549

Rich, Frank
Christopher Durang **27**:90
Athol Fugard **25**:177
Charles Fuller **25**:181
Albert Innaurato **21**:198
Jean Kerr **22**:258
Hugh Leonard **19**:284
Garry Marshall **17**:276, 278
Marsha Norman **28**:319
Ntozake Shange **25**:400
C. P. Taylor **27**:445

Rich, Nancy B.
Carson McCullers 10:336

Richards, I. A.
E. M. Forster 13:215

Richards, Jeffrey
Frank Capra 16:160

Richards, Lewis A.
William Faulkner 3:153

Richards, Marily
Vine Deloria, Jr. 21:114

Richardson, D. E.
Wendell Berry 27:35
Catharine Savage Brosman 9:135

Richardson, Jack
John Barth 3:39
Saul Bellow 8:71
T. S. Eliot 9:182
Trevor Griffiths 13:257
Jack Kerouac 2:227
Arthur Miller 2:280
Vladimir Nabokov 2:300
Peter Shaffer 5:389
Tom Stoppard 4:527
Megan Terry 19:438

Richardson, Maurice
Vasily Aksenov 22:25
Bruce Chatwin 28:70
John Knowles 26:246
Randolph Stow 23:432
J.R.R. Tolkien 12:565

Richardson, Tony
Luis Buñuel 16:128
John Huston 20:163
Akira Kurosawa 16:395
Jean Renoir 20:288
Josef von Sternberg 20:373
Orson Welles 20:433

Richart, Bette
Phyllis McGinley 14:364

Richie, Donald
Kon Ichikawa 20:177
Akira Kurosawa 16:396, 398
Yukio Mishima 2:288; 4:357
Nagisa Oshima 20:246
Yasujiro Ozu 16:450

Richie, Mary
Penelope Mortimer 5:300

Richler, Mordecai
Daniel Fuchs 22:156
Ken Kesey 3:267
Bernard Malamud 2:267
Mordecai Richler 18:458
Jerome Siegel and Joe Shuster 21:361
Isaac Bashevis Singer 15:508
Alexander Theroux 2:433
Paul Theroux 28:425

Richman, Robert
John Ashbery 25:57
John Gardner 18:180

Richman, Sidney
Bernard Malamud 1:198

Richmond, Al
Alvah Bessie 23:60

Richmond, Jane
E. L. Doctorow 6:131
Thomas McGuane 3:329

Richmond, Velma Bourgeois
Muriel Spark 3:464

Richter, David H.
Jerzy Kosinski 6:283

Richter, Frederick
Kenzaburō Ōe 10:373

Rickey, Carrie
Sidney Poitier 26:361

Ricks, Christopher
Giorgio Bassani 9:75
Samuel Beckett 2:48
Harold Bloom 24:80
Charles Causley 7:41
Robert Creeley 2:108
William Golding 17:169
Nadine Gordimer 7:131
Marilyn Hacker 5:155
Geoffrey H. Hartman 27:178
Anthony Hecht 19:207
Geoffrey Hill 8:293
Richard Howard 7:167
Galway Kinnell 5:217
Robert Lowell 1:181; 9:335
Louis MacNeice 1:186
Reynolds Price 6:423
Christina Stead 8:499
Peter Taylor 18:524
John Updike 1:346
Robert Penn Warren 6:556
Patrick White 4:586

Ricou, L. R.
Miriam Waddington 28:438

Ricou, Laurence
Jack Hodgins 23:230
Robert Kroetsch 23:270

Ricou, Laurie
Andrew Suknaski 19:434

Riddel, Joseph N.
C. Day Lewis 10:125
Jacques Derrida 24:146
T. S. Eliot 13:195
Geoffrey H. Hartman 27:179

Rideout, Walter B.
John Dos Passos 4:131
Howard Fast 23:157
Randall Jarrell 2:207
Norman Mailer 4:318
Henry Roth 2:377
Upton Sinclair 11:497

Ridington, Edith Farr
Taylor Caldwell 28:65

Ridley, Clifford A.
Julian Symons 2:426

Riefenstahl, Leni
Leni Riefenstahl 16:521

Rieff, David
Anthony Burgess 13:124
Ilya Ehrenburg 18:138

Riemer, Jack
Chaim Potok 14:430
Elie Wiesel 11:570

Riera, Emilio G.
Luis Buñuel 16:130

Ries, Frank W. D.
Jean Cocteau 15:134

Ries, Lawrence R.
William Golding 10:239
Ted Hughes 9:283
John Osborne 11:424
Anthony Powell 9:439
Alan Sillitoe 10:476
John Wain 11:561

Riesman, Paul
Carlos Castaneda 12:87

Righter, William
André Malraux 4:329

Righton, Barbara
Peter Straub 28:411

Riley, Brooks
Lina Wertmüller 16:593

Riley, Clayton
Charles Gordone 1:124
Melvin Van Peebles 20:412

Riley, Jocelyn
Cynthia Propper Seton 27:428

Riley, Peter
Jack Spicer 18:512

Rimanelli, Giose
Alberto Moravia 18:343

Rimer, J. Thomas
Shusaku Endo 19:160
Masuji Ibuse 22:227
Yasunari Kawabata 18:283

Rimland, Ingrid
Denise Levertov 28:243

Rimmon-Kenan, Shlomith
Jorge Luis Borges 19:54

Rinear, David L.
Arthur Kopit 18:289

Ringel, Fred J.
Vera Brittain 23:88

Ringel, Harry
Alfred Hitchcock 16:352

Ringer, Agnes C.
John Knowles 26:263

Rinsler, Norma
Louis Aragon 22:40

Rinzler, Alan
Bob Dylan 12:198

Rinzler, Carol Eisen
Judith Rossner 6:469

Ripley, Josephine
Frank B. Gilbreth, Jr. and Ernestine Gilbreth Carey 17:155

Risdon, Ann
T. S. Eliot 9:190

Ritchie, Barbara
Milton Meltzer 26:301

Ritholz, Robert E.A.P.
Martin Mull 17:299

Ritter, Jess
Kurt Vonnegut, Jr. 4:563

Ritter, Karen
Virginia Hamilton 26:152
Lee Kingman 17:247
Norma Fox Mazer 26:294

Ritterman, Pamela
Richard Brautigan 12:57

Riva, Raymond T.
Samuel Beckett 1:25

Rivas, Daniel E.
Romain Gary 25:191

Rivera, Francisco
José Donoso 4:129

Rivers, Cheryl
Susan Cheever 18:102

Rivers, Elias L.
G. Cabrera Infante 25:102

Rizza, Peggy
Elizabeth Bishop 4:66

Rizzardi, Alfredo
Allen Tate 4:538

Robbe-Grillet, Alain
Samuel Beckett 10:25

Robbins, Henry
Stanley Elkin 14:158

Robbins, Ira A.
David Bowie 17:66
Elvis Costello 21:72, 74, 75

Robbins, Jack Alan
Louis Auchincloss 4:28
Herbert Gold 4:189
Bernard Malamud 1:200
Flannery O'Connor 1:258

Roberts, Cecil
W. Somerset Maugham 11:370

Roberts, David
R. V. Cassill 4:94; 23:106

Roberts, Mark
Wayne C. Booth 24:86

Roberts, Paul
William Mitchell 25:327

Roberts, Philip
Edward Bond 23:67

Roberts, R. Ellis
Pamela Hansford Johnson 27:215

Roberts, Sheila
Breyten Breytenbach 23:86
J. M. Coetzee 23:123
Athol Fugard 25:176

Roberts, Thomas J.
Italo Calvino 8:129

Robertson, Anthony
Hugh Hood 28:188

Robertson, P.
Otfried Preussler 17:375

Robertson, R. T.
Mulk Raj Anand 23:20

Robins, Corinne
Leonard Michaels 25:319

Robins, Wayne
Joni Mitchell 12:438
Neil Young 17:574

Robinson, Beryl
Virginia Hamilton 26:150
Milton Meltzer 26:301
Andre Norton 12:462
Robert Newton Peck 17:337, 340
Mary Rodgers 12:494

Robinson, Christopher
Odysseus Elytis 15:219

Robinson, David
Robert Altman 16:19
Luis Buñuel 16:130
Orson Welles 20:434

Robinson, Debbie
Roy A. Gallant 17:130

Robinson, Hubbell
Gordon Parks 16:459

Robinson, James K.
Robert Francis 15:239
John Hollander 14:263
David Ignatow 14:275
Archibald MacLeish 14:338
Josephine Miles 14:370
David Wagoner 15:559

Robinson, Jill
Alice Adams 6:2
Anna Kavan 5:206
Fran Lebowitz 11:322
Larry McMurtry 11:371

Robinson, Louie
Norman Lear 12:332

Robinson, Robert
Saul Bellow 6:54

Robinson, Spider
Frank Herbert 23:223
Frederik Pohl 18:413
Roger Zelazny 21:479

Robinson, Ted
Ogden Nash 23:317

Robinson, W. R.
George Garrett 3:190

Robson, Jeremy
W. H. Auden 4:33
Leonard Cohen 3:110

Rockett, W. H.
George Ryga 14:473

Rocks, James E.
T. S. Stribling 23:448

Rockwell, John
Ray Davies 21:106
Peter Handke 5:164
Gerome Ragni and James Rado 17:384
Lou Reed 21:306
Patti Smith 12:537
Bruce Springsteen 17:478
Stevie Wonder 12:661

Rodgers, Audrey T.
T. S. Eliot 6:162, 166

Rodgers, Bernard F., Jr.
Philip Roth 22:350

Rodman, Selden
Carlos Fuentes 10:207
Gabriel García Márquez 27:157
John Gardner 28:166
Derek Walcott 14:551

Rodrigues, Eusebio L.
Saul Bellow 3:56; 6:52

Rodríguez-Monegal, Emir
Adolfo Bioy Casares 13:84
Jorge Luis Borges 2:72; 3:80
Gabriel García Márquez 3:183
Juan Carlos Onetti 7:276, 279

Rodriguez-Peralta, Phyllis
José María Arguedas 10:8

Rodway, Allan
Samuel Beckett 4:51
Tom Stoppard 8:502

Roe, Shirley
Roy A. Gallant 17:131

Roethke, Theodore
Ben Belitt 22:48

Rogan, Helen
Maeve Brennan 5:73
John Gardner 5:134
Jennifer Johnston 7:186
Irving Wallace 7:510

Rogers, D.
I. A. Richards 14:455

Rogers, Deborah C.
J.R.R. Tolkien 12:584

Rogers, Del Marie
Reynolds Price 6:423

Rogers, Ivor A.
Robert Heinlein 14:251

Rogers, Linda
Margaret Atwood 4:27
Paulette Jiles 13:304
Susan Musgrave 13:400
Angus Wilson 5:515

Rogers, Michael
Peter Benchley 4:54
Richard Brautigan 12:70
Bob Dylan 12:187
John Gardner 3:188
Richard Price 12:489
Piers Paul Read 4:445

Rogers, Norma
Alice Childress 12:106

Rogers, Pat
Daphne du Maurier 11:163

Rogers, Philip
Chinua Achebe 11:3

Rogers, Thomas
R. V. Cassill 23:107
Vladimir Nabokov 6:358
Tom Stoppard 1:328

Rogers, Timothy
Alan Garner 17:135

Rogers, W. G.
Pearl S. Buck 7:33
James Clavell 25:125
Joanne Greenberg 7:134
Irwin Shaw 23:398

Rogge, Whitney
Cecil Bødker 21:13

Roginski, Ed
Peter Weir 20:426

Rogoff, Gordon
David Mamet 9:361

Rogoff, Leonard
Lee Smith 25:406

Rohlehr, Gordon
V. S. Naipaul 4:372

Rohmer, Eric
Ingmar Bergman 16:45
Alfred Hitchcock 16:357

Rohter, Larry
Carlos Fuentes 8:223
Yashar Kemal 14:300

Roiphe, Anne
Earl Hamner, Jr. 12:259

Rolens, Linda
Margaret Atwood 25:70

Rollins, Ronald G.
Sean O'Casey 9:409

Rolo, Charles J.
Marcel Aymé 11:21
William Gaddis 19:185
Romain Gary 25:185
Martha Gellhorn 14:195
Pär Lagerkvist 7:198
Françoise Sagan 17:420
Irwin Shaw 7:411

Roman, Diane
Paul Vincent Carroll 10:98

Romano, John
James Baldwin 17:42
Donald Barthelme 23:47
Ann Beattie 8:56
Thomas Berger 11:47
Frederick Busch 10:92
Laurie Colwin 13:156
John Gardner 18:182
Graham Greene 18:196
Barry Hannah 23:212
Ella Leffland 19:279
Mary McCarthy 24:347
Joyce Carol Oates 9:406
Alan Paton 25:363
Walker Percy 18:398
Sylvia Plath 5:342
John Updike 15:544
Gore Vidal 10:501

Rome, Florence
Muriel Spark 3:465

Romer, Samuel
Alvah Bessie 23:59

Rompers, Terry
Jim Morrison 17:294

Ronge, Peter
Eugène Ionesco 6:249

Rooke, Constance
P. K. Page 18:380
Katherine Anne Porter 15:430

Roosevelt, Karyl
Diane Johnson 13:304

Root, William Pitt
Sonia Sanchez 5:382
Anne Sexton 4:483
Peter Wild 14:580

Rorabacher, Louise E.
Frank Dalby Davison 15:171

Rorem, Ned
Paul Bowles 2:79
Tennessee Williams 5:502

Rorty, Richard
Jacques Derrida 24:143

Roscoe, Adrian
Ezekiel Mphahlele 25:341

Roscoe, Adrian A.
Chinua Achebe 26:17

Rose, Ellen Cronan
Margaret Drabble 22:125
Doris Lessing 6:300

Rose, Ernst
Hermann Hesse 1:145

Rose, Frank
David Byrne 26:95
Lou Reed 21:312
Peter Townshend 17:540

Rose, Karel
Norma Fox Mazer 26:292

Rose, Kate
Richard Brautigan 12:59

Rose, Lois
J. G. Ballard 3:33
Arthur C. Clarke 4:104
Robert A. Heinlein 3:226
C. S. Lewis 3:297
Walter M. Miller, Jr. 4:352

Rose, Marilyn
Julien Green 3:204

Rose, Marilyn Gaddis
Robert Pinget 13:441

Rose, Phyllis
Margaret Drabble 22:126
Cynthia Ozick 28:353
Jean Rhys 19:394

Rose, Stephen
J. G. Ballard 3:33
Arthur C. Clarke 4:104
Robert A. Heinlein 3:226
C. S. Lewis 3:297
Walter M. Miller, Jr. 4:352

Rose, Willie Lee
Alex Haley 8:260

Rosen, Carol
Sam Shepard 17:448

Rosen, Charles
M. H. Abrams 24:12

Rosen, Marjorie
Elaine May **16**:433
Albert Maysles and David Maysles **16**:444

Rosen, Norma
Paula Fox **8**:218
Françoise Sagan **17**:425

Rosen, R. D.
S. J. Perelman **23**:339
James Tate **6**:528

Rosen, Winifred
Richard Peck **21**:299

Rosenbaum, Jean
Marge Piercy **18**:404; **27**:373

Rosenbaum, Jonathan
Robert Altman **16**:31, 39
Robert Bresson **16**:118
John Cassavetes **20**:50
Carl Theodor Dreyer **16**:268
Rainer Werner Fassbinder **20**:108
Yasujiro Ozu **16**:454
Sidney Poitier **26**:360
Roman Polanski **16**:472
Richard Pryor **26**:383
Jean Renoir **20**:304

Rosenbaum, Olga
Bernice Rubens **19**:404

Rosenbaum, Ron
Richard Condon **4**:106

Rosenbaum, S. P.
E. M. Forster **22**:130

Rosenberg, Harold
Stanley Kubrick **16**:390
André Malraux **4**:334
Muriel Rukeyser **27**:403
Anna Seghers **7**:407

Rosenberg, Ross
Philip José Farmer **19**:168

Rosenberger, Coleman
John Ehle **27**:101
Ernest K. Gann **23**:164
Carson McCullers **12**:412

Rosenblatt, Jon
Sylvia Plath **17**:364

Rosenblatt, Roger
Renata Adler **8**:5
Norman Lear **12**:332
Ludvík Vaculík **7**:496
Thornton Wilder **6**:572

Rosenblum, Michael
Vladimir Nabokov **15**:394

Rosenfeld, Alvin H.
Saul Bellow **15**:52
Herbert Gold **7**:122
Jakov Lind **4**:293
Nelly Sachs **14**:476
William Styron **15**:529

Rosenfeld, Paul
Ernest Hemingway **19**:210

Rosenfeld, Sidney
Elias Canetti **14**:124

Rosengarten, Herbert
Margaret Atwood **8**:33
William Mitchell **25**:323

Rosenman, John B.
Ray Bradbury **15**:84

Rosenstone, Robert A.
Frank Zappa **17**:585

Rosenthal, David H.
Louis-Ferdinand Céline **7**:45
Austin C. Clarke **8**:143
Nicanor Parra **2**:331

Rosenthal, Lucy
Hortense Calisher **2**:96
Richard Llewellyn **7**:207
Sylvia Plath **2**:336
Cynthia Propper Seton **27**:425
Alix Kates Shulman **2**:395

Rosenthal, M. L.
Yehuda Amichai **9**:25
A. R. Ammons **2**:13
Imamu Amiri Baraka **2**:34; **10**:19
John Berryman **2**:56
John Betjeman **2**:60
Kay Boyle **1**:42
John Ciardi **10**:105
Austin Clarke **6**:110
Robert Creeley **2**:105
E. E. Cummings **1**:68
James Dickey **2**:115; **7**:81
Robert Duncan **2**:122
Richard Eberhart **11**:178
T. S. Eliot **2**:125
D. J. Enright **4**:155
Robert Frost **1**:110
Allen Ginsberg **1**:118; **2**:162
Paul Goodman **1**:124; **4**:196
Thom Gunn **18**:203
Michael Hamburger **14**:234
Jim Harrison **6**:223
Daniel Hoffman **23**:237
Ted Hughes **2**:197; **9**:280
Randall Jarrell **13**:299
X. J. Kennedy **8**:320
Galway Kinnell **1**:168
Thomas Kinsella **4**:270; **19**:254
Philip Larkin **3**:275, 277
Denise Levertov **2**:242
Robert Lowell **1**:179; **2**:247
George MacBeth **2**:251
Hugh MacDiarmid **2**:253
W. S. Merwin **1**:211
Marianne Moore **1**:226
Charles Olson **2**:326
Robert L. Peters **7**:304
Sylvia Plath **2**:335
Ezra Pound **1**:274; **7**:332
Kenneth Rexroth **1**:283
Theodore Roethke **3**:432
Delmore Schwartz **2**:387
Anne Sexton **2**:391
Karl Shapiro **4**:484
Charles Tomlinson **2**:436
Reed Whittemore **4**:588
Richard Wilbur **14**:577
William Carlos Williams **1**:370

Rosenthal, R.
Paula Fox **2**:139

Rosenthal, Raymond
Edward Dahlberg **7**:66
Tennessee Williams **8**:547

Rosenthal, Stuart
Tod Browning **16**:123

Rosenthal, T. G.
Michael Ayrton **7**:20
Colin MacInnes **23**:283

Rosenzweig, A. L.
Peter Dickinson **12**:169

Rosenzweig, Paul
William Faulkner **14**:176
John Hawkes **27**:194

Roshwald, Miriam
S. Y. Agnon **8**:9

Ross, Alan
Kingsley Amis **2**:7
Alberto Moravia **7**:244
Satyajit Ray **16**:486

Ross, Alec
David Bowie **17**:66, 67

Ross, Catherine
Jane Rule **27**:422

Ross, Catherine Sheldrick
Hugh MacLennan **14**:344

Ross, Gary
Margaret Atwood **4**:27

Ross, James
Reynolds Price **6**:426

Ross, Jerome
Paddy Chayefsky **23**:111

Ross, Joan
Alberto Moravia **27**:353

Ross, Mary
Vera Brittain **23**:91
R. V. Cassill **23**:102
Madeleine L'Engle **12**:344

Ross, Morton L.
Norman Mailer **1**:192

Ross, Nancy Wilson
Sylvia Ashton-Warner **19**:20
Yukio Mishima **27**:335

Ross, Robert
Tess Gallagher **18**:168, 169

Rossi, Louis R.
Salvatore Quasimodo **10**:427

Rossman, Charles
F. R. Leavis **24**:309

Rosten, Norman
Lucille Clifton **19**:109
James Tate **2**:431

Roston, Murray
Aldous Huxley **18**:270

Roszak, Theodore
Paul Goodman **2**:170

Roth, Philip
Edward Albee **9**:1
James Baldwin **17**:27
Saul Bellow **6**:52
Norman Mailer **5**:268
Bernard Malamud **5**:269; **8**:376

J. D. Salinger **8**:464
Fredrica Wagman **7**:500

Rotha, Paul
Buster Keaton **20**:189

Rothberg, Abraham
Graham Greene **3**:211
Gary Snyder **9**:499
Aleksandr I. Solzhenitsyn **4**:507; **7**:437

Rothchild, Paul
Jim Morrison **17**:285

Rothenbuecher, Bea
Roman Polanski **16**:469

Rother, James
Vladimir Nabokov **11**:391
Thomas Pynchon **11**:453

Rothery, Agnes
Frans Eemil Sillanpää **19**:418

Rothman, Nathan L.
Kay Boyle **19**:63
Jessamyn West **17**:543
Frank Yerby **7**:556

Rothschild, Elaine
Elaine May **16**:431

Rothstein, Edward
Agatha Christie **8**:141
Philip Roth **22**:359

Rotondaro, Fred
Robert Kroetsch **23**:269
Robert Lipsyte **21**:211

Rottenberg, Annette T.
Taylor Caldwell **28**:63

Rottensteiner, Franz
Philip José Farmer **19**:165

Roud, Richard
Michelangelo Antonioni **20**:19
Bernardo Bertolucci **16**:86
Marguerite Duras **20**:101
Jean-Luc Godard **20**:132
François Truffaut **20**:382, 405
Luchino Visconti **16**:566

Roudiez, Leon S.
Louis Aragon **22**:35
Michel Butor **8**:114
Jean Cocteau **15**:132
Claude Mauriac **9**:363

Rout, Kathleen
Flannery O'Connor **15**:412

Routh, Michael
Graham Greene **9**:246

Rovit, Earl
Leslie A. Fiedler **24**:205

Rovit, Earl H.
Saul Bellow **1**:31; **8**:71; **13**:71
Kay Boyle **19**:66
Ralph Ellison **1**:93
John Hawkes **2**:184
Norman Mailer **8**:372
Bernard Malamud **1**:195

Rowan, Diana
Heinrich Böll **11**:58

Rowan, Louis
Diane Wakoski 7:506

Rowan, Thomas
J. F. Powers 1:281

Rowell, Charles H.
Sterling A. Brown 23:96

Rowland, Richard
Carl Theodor Dreyer 16:257

Rowley, Brian A.
Erich Maria Remarque 21:334

Rowley, Peter
Paula Fox 2:139
John Knowles 4:272

Rowse, A. L.
Vladimir Nabokov 23:309
Flannery O'Connor 2:318
Barbara Pym 13:469

Roy, Emil
John Arden 15:18
Sean O'Casey 15:403

Roy, Joy K.
James Herriot 12:284

Ruark, Gibbons
Andrei Voznesensky 1:349

Ruark, Robert
Lenny Bruce 21:45

Ruben, Elaine
Maureen Howard 5:189

Rubens, Linda Morgan
Vine Deloria, Jr. 21:114

Rubenstein, Joshua
Anatoli Rybakov 23:373

Rubenstein, Roberta
Robert Altman 16:21
Margaret Atwood 8:31
Paddy Chayefsky 23:119
Gail Godwin 22:182
Bessie Head 25:232
Doris Lessing 6:303; 10:316

Rubin, Louis, Jr.
William Melvin Kelley 22:246

Rubin, Louis D., Jr.
Donald Davidson 19:126
William Faulkner 1:101
Carson McCullers 10:338
John Crowe Ransom 4:428; 5:365
Carl Sandburg 10:450
Susan Sontag 10:484
William Styron 3:473
Allen Tate 9:523; 14:533
Robert Penn Warren 1:353; 4:577
Eudora Welty 1:361

Rubin, Steven J.
Richard Wright 21:461

Rubins, Josh
Brigid Brophy 11:69
Agatha Christie 6:108
Don DeLillo 27:86
Jacob Epstein 19:162
Helen MacInnes 27:282
Gilbert Sorrentino 22:396

William Trevor 14:537

Rubinstein, E.
Buster Keaton 20:195

Ruby, Kathryn
Linda Pastan 27:369

Ruby, Michael
Charles M. Schulz 12:528

Ruddick, Sara
Carolyn G. Heilbrun 25:254

Rudin, Ellen
Emily Cheney Neville 12:449

Rudman, Mark
James Tate 25:429

Rudolf, Anthony
Yehuda Amichai 22:32

Rueckert, William
Wright Morris 7:245

Ruegg, Maria
Jacques Derrida 24:149

Ruffin, Carolyn F.
Sylvia Ashton-Warner 19:23
Vonda N. McIntyre 18:327

Rugoff, Milton
Irwin Shaw 23:397

Rukeyser, Muriel
Gunnar Ekelöf 27:113
John Crowe Ransom 11:466

Rule, Jane
Rita Mae Brown 18:72

Rumens, Carol
Colleen McCullough 27:322
Leonard Michaels 25:319
Alice Walker 27:449

Ruoff, A. LaVonne
Leslie Marmon Silko 23:408

Rupp, Richard H.
John Updike 1:343

Ruppert, Peter
Max Frisch 18:161

Rushdie, Salman
Gabriel García Márquez 27:150
Günter Grass 22:197
Siegfried Lenz 27:255
Ernesto Sabato 23:382
Michel Tournier 23:453

Rushing, Andrea Benton
Audre Lorde 18:309

Ruskamp, Judith S.
Henri Michaux 8:392

Russ, C.A.H.
Siegfried Lenz 27:244

Russ, Joanna
Poul Anderson 15:15
Isaac Asimov 19:28
Ursula K. Le Guin 22:274
Adrienne Rich 18:447
Robert Silverberg 7:425
Kate Wilhelm 7:537
Gene Wolfe 25:472

Russ, Lavinia
Ruth M. Arthur 12:25
Judy Blume 12:44
M. E. Kerr 12:298

Russell, Charles
John Barth 7:22
Richard Brautigan 9:123
Jerzy Kosinski 6:284
Vladimir Nabokov 6:353
Ronald Sukenick 6:523

Russell, J.
Honor Arundel 17:18

Russell, John
André Malraux 9:357
Anthony Powell 3:402

Russell, Julia G.
Honor Arundel 17:15
Virginia Hamilton 26:148

Rutherford, Anna
Janet Frame 22:145

Ryan, Allan A., Jr.
Robert Ludlum 22:289

Ryan, Frank L.
Daniel J. Berrigan 4:56
Anne Hébert 4:220
Françoise Sagan 17:426

Ryan, Marjorie
Diane Johnson 5:198

Ryan, Richard W.
Isaac Asimov 26:37
Anne McCaffrey 17:281

Ryan, Stephen P.
Leslie A. Fiedler 24:190

Rybus, Rodney
Seamus Heaney 25:250

Ryf, Robert S.
Henry Green 2:179
B. S. Johnson 9:299
Doris Lessing 10:313
Vladimir Nabokov 6:353
Flann O'Brien 7:268

Ryle, John
John Berger 19:40
Penelope Fitzgerald 19:173
Mark Helprin 10:261

Rysten, Felix
Jean Giono 11:232

Rzhevsky, Leonid
Aleksandr I. Solzhenitsyn 26:417

Saal, Hubert
Mary Renault 17:393
Irwin Shaw 7:411

Saal, Rollene W.
Anne Tyler 28:429

Sabin, Edwin L.
Lenora Mattingly Weber 12:631

Sabiston, Elizabeth
Philip Roth 6:475
Ludvík Vaculík 7:497

Sabor, Peter
Ezekiel Mphahlele 25:345

Sabri, M. Arjamand
Thomas Pynchon 3:417

Sacharoff, Mark
Elias Canetti 3:98

Sachner, Mark J.
Samuel Beckett 14:71

Sachs, Marilyn
Nicholasa Mohr 12:445, 446
Robert Newton Peck 17:338

Sack, John
Ward S. Just 27:225

Sackville-West, Edward
Ivy Compton-Burnett 15:137

Saddler, Allen
Ann Jellicoe 27:210
C. P. Taylor 27:442

Sadler, Frank
Jack Spicer 18:508

Sadoff, Dianne F.
Gail Godwin 8:247

Sadoff, Ira
Tess Gallagher 18:168
Robert Hass 18:210
Philip Levine 14:315

Sáez, Richard
James Merrill 6:323

Safir, Margery
Pablo Neruda 28:312

Sagalyn, Raphael
James H. Webb, Jr. 22:453

Sagan, Carl
Paul West 14:568

Sagar, Keith
Ted Hughes 2:203

Sage, Lorna
Brian Aldiss 14:14
John Barth 27:28
Olga Broumas 10:76
Bruce Chatwin 28:74
John Hawkes 27:201
Patricia Highsmith 14:261
Erica Jong 6:267
Thomas Keneally 27:232
Iris Murdoch 11:384
Vladimir Nabokov 8:412
Sylvia Plath 11:450
Philip Roth 15:455
Françoise Sagan 17:429

Sage, Victor
David Storey 8:505

Said, Edward W.
R. P. Blackmur 2:61
Jacques Derrida 24:140
Lucien Goldmann 24:238
Paul Goodman 2:169
V. S. Naipaul 18:364

Sailsbury, M. B.
Franklyn M. Branley 21:16

Sainer, Arthur
Martin Duberman 8:185
Max Frisch 18:163
Jack Gelber 14:194
Simon Gray 9:242
Michael McClure 6:317

Miguel Piñero 4:401

St. John, David
Charles Wright 28:458

St. John-Stevas, Norman
C. S. Lewis 6:308

St. Martin, Hardie
Blas de Otero 11:424

Sakurai, Emiko
Kenzaburō Ōe 10:374
Kenneth Rexroth 11:474

Salamon, Lynda B.
Sylvia Plath 17:350

Salamone, Anthony
Howard Fast 23:160

Sale, Roger
Richard Adams 18:2
E. M. Almedingen 12:3
A. Alvarez 13:10
Kingsley Amis 5:22
Saul Bellow 6:61
Thomas Berger 8:84
Richard Brautigan 12:70
Frederick Buechner 2:83; 6:103
Anthony Burgess 5:87
Frederick Busch 10:94
Agatha Christie 8:141
Richard Condon 8:150
Robertson Davies 7:72
E. L. Doctorow 6:135
Margaret Drabble 2:118, 119; 8:183; 22:122
George P. Elliott 2:131
Frederick Exley 6:172
Leslie A. Fiedler 4:162
B. H. Friedman 7:109
Paula Fox 2:141
Herbert Gold 7:121
Witold Gombrowicz 7:122
Dashiell Hammett 5:161
John Hawkes 4:214
Mark Helprin 10:261
Maureen Howard 5:188; 14:267
Ken Kesey 6:278
Richard Kostelanetz 28:215
John Le Carré 5:234
Alan Lelchuk 5:240
Doris Lessing 2:239, 242; 6:299, 304
Alison Lurie 4:306
Ross Macdonald 2:255
David Madden 5:266
Norman Mailer 2:261; 4:319
Peter Matthiessen 7:212
Iris Murdoch 8:404
Tim O'Brien 7:271
Grace Paley 6:392
J. F. Powers 8:447
Richard Price 6:427
Judith Rossner 6:470
Philip Roth 2:381; 6:476
Andrew Sinclair 2:400
Isaac Bashevis Singer 9:487
Robert Stone 5:410
Paul Theroux 5:428
J.R.R. Tolkien 1:338
Lionel Trilling 24:458
Anne Tyler 11:553
John Updike 23:467
Mario Vargas Llosa 6:547

Kurt Vonnegut, Jr. 8:532
David Wagoner 5:475
James Welch 14:558
René Wellek 28:449
Monique Wittig 22:474
Larry Woiwode 10:541

Salemi, Joseph S.
William Gaddis 19:187

Salisbury, David F.
Ernest K. Gann 23:168

Salisbury, Harrison E.
Aleksandr I. Solzhenitsyn 4:511

Salisbury, Stephan
Howard Fast 23:159

Salkey, Andrew
Ngugi Wa Thiong'o 13:584

Salmans, Sandra
Scott Sommer 25:425

Salmon, Sheila
Barbara Corcoran 17:77

Salomon, I. L.
Robert Duncan 4:142

Salomon, Louis B.
Carson McCullers 12:408

Salter, D.P.M.
Saul Bellow 2:53

Salter, Denis
Jack Hodgins 23:229

Salvatore, Caroline
Chaim Potok 26:368

Salvesen, Christopher
Jane Rule 27:416

Salway, Lance
Robert Cormier 12:136
Peter Dickinson 12:168
Alan Garner 17:147
Robert Westall 17:556

Salzman, Eric
David Byrne 26:99
Andrew Lloyd Webber and Tim Rice 21:431
Frank Zappa 17:591

Salzman, Jack
John Dos Passos 4:138
Jack Kerouac 2:229
Tillie Olsen 4:386

Samet, Tom
Henry Roth 11:488

Sammons, Jeffrey L.
Hermann Hesse 11:271

Sampley, Arthur M.
Robert Frost 1:112

Sampson, Edward C.
E. B. White 10:529

Samuels, Charles Thomas
Richard Adams 4:7
Michelangelo Antonioni 20:33
Donald Barthelme 3:43
Robert Bresson 16:115
Lillian Hellman 2:187
Alfred Hitchcock 16:348

Stanley Kubrick 16:384
Christina Stead 2:421
John Updike 1:344; 2:442
Kurt Vonnegut, Jr. 2:454

Samuelson, David N.
Arthur C. Clarke 18:103
Robert A. Heinlein 26:164, 167

Sanborn, Sara
Anthony Burgess 4:84
Rosalyn Drexler 6:143
Alison Lurie 4:305
Joyce Carol Oates 3:363

Sandars, N. K.
David Jones 4:260

Sandeen, Ernest
R. P. Blackmur 2:62

Sander, Ellen
Mick Jagger and Keith Richard 17:223
John Lennon and Paul McCartney 12:364
Joni Mitchell 12:435
Paul Simon 17:459
Neil Young 17:569
Frank Zappa 17:585

Sanders, Charles
Theodore Roethke 19:402

Sanders, Charles L.
Norman Lear 12:330

Sanders, David
John Hersey 1:144; 7:153
Frederick Morgan 23:300
Robert Phillips 28:365

Sanders, Ed
Allen Ginsberg 4:181

Sanders, Frederick L.
Conrad Aiken 3:5

Sanders, Ivan
Dobrica Ćosić 14:132
György Konrád 4:273; 10:304
Milan Kundera 4:278
József Lengyel 7:202
Amos Oz 8:436

Sanders, Peter L.
Robert Graves 2:176

Sanders, Ronald
Richard Wright 21:442

Sanderson, Ivan
Farley Mowat 26:334

Sanderson, Stewart F.
Compton Mackenzie 18:315

Sandhuber, Holly
Lois Duncan 26:107

Sandler, Linda
Margaret Atwood 8:29, 30
Ernest Buckler 13:123

Sandoe, James
Margery Allingham 19:13
Roy Fuller 28:148
M. M. Kaye 28:198

Sandow, Gregory
Michael Moorcock 27:352

Sandrof, Ivan
Jean Lee Latham 12:324

Sands, Douglas B.
Franklyn M. Branley 21:19

Sandwell, B. K.
Mazo de la Roche 14:148

Sandy, Stephen
Peter Davison 28:104

Saner, Reg
William Dickey 28:119

Sanfield, Steve
Michael McClure 6:320

Santí, Enrico-Mario
G. Cabrera Infante 25:100

Sargeant, Winthrop
Vittorio De Sica 20:87
Robert Lewis Taylor 14:534

Sargent, David
Robert Wilson 9:576

Sargo, Tina Mendes
Luchino Visconti 16:566

Sarland, Charles
William Mayne 12:402

Sarlin, Bob
Chuck Berry 17:54
Janis Ian 21:186
Mick Jagger and Keith Richard 17:229
Van Morrison 21:235
Laura Nyro 17:316
Neil Young 17:572

Sarotte, Georges-Michel
William Inge 19:229
John Rechy 18:442

Saroyan, Aram
Kenneth Koch 8:323
Frank O'Hara 13:424
Anne Waldman 7:508

Saroyan, William
Flann O'Brien 10:362

Sarratt, Janet P.
Milton Meltzer 26:302

Sarris, Andrew George
Woody Allen 16:7, 11
Robert Altman 16:36, 38, 43
Ralph Bakshi 26:68
Mel Brooks 12:75
Michael Cimino 16:209
Francis Ford Coppola 16:245
Brian De Palma 20:80
Rainer Werner Fassbinder 20:115
Federico Fellini 16:271, 297
John Ford 16:308
Bob Fosse 20:127
Jean-Luc Godard 20:137, 153
Werner Herzog 16:333
George Roy Hill 26:203, 206, 208
Alfred Hitchcock 16:341, 357
John Huston 20:174
Elia Kazan 16:364, 366
Buster Keaton 20:196
Stanley Kubrick 16:380

Akira Kurosawa 16:406
John Landis 26:275
Richard Lester 20:231, 232
Norman Mailer 3:315
Sam Peckinpah 20:282
Roman Polanski 16:473
Jean Renoir 20:308
Alain Resnais 16:504, 518
Carlos Saura 20:318
Paul Schrader 26:390, 393, 396
Wilfrid Sheed 4:487
Joan Micklin Silver 20:344
Jerzy Skolimowski 20:354
François Truffaut 20:383, 404, 406, 407
Lina Wertmüller 16:599
Billy Wilder 20:461, 466

Sartre, Jean-Paul
Albert Camus 14:104
John Dos Passos 11:153
William Faulkner 9:197
Jean Genet 2:155

Saunders, Charles
May Swenson 14:522

Saunders, Mike
Ray Davies 21:92, 93

Saunders, William S.
James Wright 28:466

Sauvage, Leo
Charles Fuller 25:182
Beth Henley 23:217

Sauzey, François
Jean-Paul Sartre 18:473

Savage, D. S.
E. M. Forster 13:216
Christopher Isherwood 14:286
Pamela Hansford Johnson 27:215
Mary Renault 17:391

Savage, Jon
Lou Reed 21:316

Savage, Lois E.
Noel Streatfeild 21:412

Savvas, Minas
Yannis Ritsos 13:487

Sawyer, Roland
Thor Heyerdahl 26:190

Sayre, Henry M.
John Ashbery 15:31

Sayre, Joel
Garson Kanin 22:231

Sayre, Nora
Enid Bagnold 25:77
Marguerite Duras 20:99
Iris Murdoch 1:236
Richard O'Brien 17:325
Anne Roiphe 3:434
Elizabeth Taylor 2:432
James Thurber 25:439
Kurt Vonnegut, Jr. 3:502

Sayre, Robert
Lucien Goldmann 24:246

Sayre, Robert F.
James Baldwin 1:15

Scaduto, Anthony
Bob Dylan 4:148

Scammell, William
John Berger 19:40
Patrick White 18:547

Scanlan, Margaret
Iris Murdoch 15:387

Scanlon, Laura Polla
Maia Wojciechowska 26:454

Scannell, Vernon
Martin Booth 13:103
Randall Jarrell 9:298
George MacBeth 9:341
Piers Paul Read 25:375

Scarbrough, George
Babette Deutsch 18:119
James Schevill 7:400

Scarf, Maggie
Lillian Hellman 18:228
Susan Sontag 10:487

Schaap, Dick
Mario Puzo 2:351

Schacht, Chuck
Mollie Hunter 21:169
Diana Wynne Jones 26:229

Schaefer, J. O'Brien
Margaret Drabble 5:119

Schafer, William J.
Mark Harris 19:202
David Wagoner 3:507

Schaffner, Nicholas
Ray Davies 21:107
John Lennon and Paul McCartney 12:385

Schaire, Jeffrey
Umberto Eco 28:133

Schakne, Ann
Roderick L. Haig-Brown 21:136

Schamschula, Walter
Václav Havel 25:223

Schapiro, Leonard
Aleksandr I. Solzhenitsyn 7:440

Schatt, Stanley
Langston Hughes 10:279
Isaac Bashevis Singer 3:459
Kurt Vonnegut, Jr. 1:348; 4:560; 12:614

Schaub, Thomas Hill
Thomas Pynchon 18:430

Schechner, Mark
Lionel Trilling 11:540

Schechner, Richard
Edward Albee 11:10
Eugène Ionesco 6:253

Scheerer, Constance
Sylvia Plath 9:432

Schein, Harry
Carl Theodor Dreyer 16:258

Scherman, David E.
Milton Meltzer 26:305

Schevill, James
Peter Davison 28:99
Kenneth Patchen 18:395

Schickel, Richard
Woody Allen 16:3
Robert Altman 16:24
Michelangelo Antonioni 20:30
Louis Auchincloss 9:54
Ingmar Bergman 16:58, 63
John Cassavetes 20:47
Charles Chaplin 16:202
Francis Ford Coppola 16:236
Joan Didion 1:75
Jean-Luc Godard 20:143
John Landis 26:271
Norman Lear 12:333
Alan Lelchuk 5:242
Richard Lester 20:227
Ross Macdonald 1:185
Garry Marshall 17:276
Monty Python 21:228
Thomas Pynchon 2:358
Satyajit Ray 16:481
Alain Resnais 16:504
Eric Rohmer 16:530
Carlos Saura 20:318
Peter Shaffer 5:387
Luchino Visconti 16:567
Andy Warhol 20:420
Frederick Wiseman 20:470, 475

Schickele, Peter
John Lennon and Paul McCartney 12:355

Schieder, Rupert
Jack Hodgins 23:232, 235

Schier, Donald
André Breton 2:81

Schiff, Jeff
Mary Oliver 19:362

Schillaci, Peter P.
Luis Buñuel 16:140

Schiller, Barbara
Brigid Brophy 11:68

Schiller, Jerome P.
I. A. Richards 24:395

Schirmer, Gregory A.
Seamus Heaney 25:243
M. L. Rosenthal 28:395

Schjeldahl, Peter
Paul Blackburn 9:100
André Breton 2:80; 9:129
Russell Edson 13:191
Gerome Ragni and James Rado 17:384
James Schevill 7:400
Diane Wakoski 11:564

Schlant, Ernestine
Christa Wolf 14:593

Schlesinger, Arthur, Jr.
Woody Allen 16:11
Michael Cimino 16:209
Bob Fosse 20:127
Mary McCarthy 24:343
Paul Schrader 26:391

Schlueter, June
Samuel Beckett 18:43
Peter Handke 15:269
Arthur Miller 10:346
Tom Stoppard 15:522

Schlueter, Paul
Pär Lagerkvist 7:201
Doris Lessing 1:174; 3:283
Mary McCarthy 1:205
Gabrielle Roy 14:469
Robert Lewis Taylor 14:535

Schmering, Chris
Satyajit Ray 16:494

Schmerl, Rudolf B.
Aldous Huxley 3:255

Schmidt, Arthur
Joni Mitchell 12:437
Brian Wilson 12:641, 645
Frank Zappa 17:589

Schmidt, Elizabeth
Margaret Craven 17:80

Schmidt, Michael
Donald Davie 8:165
Philip Larkin 18:300
George MacBeth 2:252
Jon Silkin 2:396
Stevie Smith 25:419
Charles Tomlinson 13:548
Yevgeny Yevtushenko 26:466

Schmidt, Pilar
Lenora Mattingly Weber 12:634

Schmidt, Sandra
James D. Forman 21:116

Schmitz, Eugenia E.
Isabelle Holland 21:153

Schmitz, Neil
Donald Barthelme 1:19
Richard Brautigan 3:90
Robert Coover 3:113; 7:58
Thomas Pynchon 6:435
Ishmael Reed 5:368; 6:448
Al Young 19:478

Schneck, Stephen
Richard Brautigan 1:44
LeRoi Jones 1:162

Schneckloth, Tim
Frank Zappa 17:592

Schneidau, Herbert N.
Ezra Pound 4:408

Schneider, Alan
Edward Albee 11:10

Schneider, Duane
Anaïs Nin 1:248; 11:396

Schneider, Duane B.
Gilbert Sorrentino 22:391

Schneider, Elisabeth
T. S. Eliot 3:140

Schneider, Harold W.
Muriel Spark 13:519

Schneider, Isidor
Kenneth Burke 24:118

Schneider, Mary W.
Muriel Spark 18:504

Schneider, Richard J.
William H. Gass 8:240

Schoeck, R. J.
Allen Tate 24:442

Schoenbrun, David
Francine du Plessix Gray 22:199
Cornelius Ryan 7:385

Schoenstein, Ralph
Garry Trudeau 12:590

Schoenwald, Richard L.
Ogden Nash 23:322

Scholes, Robert
Jorge Luis Borges 10:63
Lawrence Durrell 8:190
Gail Godwin 22:179
John Hawkes 9:262; 15:273
Robert A. Heinlein 26:166
Frank Herbert 12:276
Ursula K. Le Guin 22:266
Iris Murdoch 22:324
Sylvia Plath 17:351
Frederik Pohl 18:410
Ishmael Reed 5:370
Kurt Vonnegut, Jr. 2:451; 4:561

Schopen, Bernard A.
John Updike 23:464

Schorer, Mark
Truman Capote 3:98
Walter Van Tilburg Clark 28:77
Martha Gellhorn 14:195
Lillian Hellman 4:221
Carson McCullers 4:344
Katherine Anne Porter 7:312
John Steinbeck 21:367
René Wellek 28:443

Schott, Webster
Richard Adams 5:6
Louis Auchincloss 4:31
W. H. Auden 2:25
Donald Barthelme 2:41
Saul Bellow 8:69
William Peter Blatty 2:63
Vance Bourjaily 8:103
Vincent Canby 13:131
R. V. Cassill 23:107, 108
James Clavell 6:113; 25:126
J. M. Coetzee 23:126
Robert Coover 7:57
Michael Crichton 2:108
John Gardner 10:223
Shirley Hazzard 18:219
John Knowles 26:261
Ira Levin 6:305
David Madden 15:350
Colleen McCullough 27:319
Larry McMurtry 2:272
Ted Mooney 25:329
Toni Morrison 22:320
Sylvia Plath 2:338
Raymond Queneau 10:432
Philip Roth 3:436
Susan Fromberg Schaeffer 11:492
Georges Simenon 2:398

Harvey Swados 5:421
Thomas Tryon 11:548
Elio Vittorini 6:551
Jessamyn West 7:520
Patrick White 18:549
Tennessee Williams 5:506

Schott, Webster
Andrew M. Greeley 28:175

Schow, H. Wayne
Günter Grass 11:248

Schrader, George Alfred
Norman Mailer 14:348

Schrader, Paul
Robert Bresson 16:115
Brian De Palma 20:72
Carl Theodor Dreyer 16:263
Albert Maysles and David Maysles 16:440
Yasujiro Ozu 16:449
Sam Peckinpah 20:273

Schraepen, Edmond
William Carlos Williams 9:575

Schraibman, Joseph
Juan Goytisolo 23:188, 189

Schramm, Richard
Philip Levine 2:244
Howard Moss 7:248

Schrank, Bernice
Sean O'Casey 11:411

Schraufnagel, Noel
Frank G. Yerby 22:491

Schreiber, Jan
Elizabeth Daryush 6:122

Schreiber, Le Anne
Jerome Charyn 8:135
Marilynne Robinson 25:386

Schreiber, Ron
Marge Piercy 27:379

Schroeder, Andreas
Michael Ondaatje 14:408

Schroth, Raymond A., S.J.
Andrew M. Greeley 28:170, 173
Norman Mailer 2:261; 3:312

Schruers, Fred
Joan Armatrading 17:9
Ray Davies 21:98
Neil Young 17:576

Schulberg, Budd
Laura Z. Hobson 25:270

Schulder, Diane
Marge Piercy 3:385

Schuler, Barbara
Peter Taylor 1:333

Schulman, Grace
Jorge Luis Borges 13:110
Richard Eberhart 3:134
Pablo Neruda 5:302
Octavio Paz 6:395
Adrienne Rich 3:427
Mark Van Doren 6:541
Richard Wilbur 9:569

Schulps, Dave
Elvis Costello 21:67
Ray Davies 21:106
Van Morrison 21:238
Peter Townshend 17:537

Schulz, Charles M.
Charles M. Schulz 12:527

Schulz, Max F.
John Barth 9:68
Norman Mailer 1:190
Bernard Malamud 1:199
Kurt Vonnegut, Jr. 1:347

Schumacher, Dorothy
Margaret O. Hyde 21:171

Schusler, Kris
Robert Lewis Taylor 14:534

Schuster, Arian
Richard Brautigan 12:74

Schuster, Edgar H.
Harper Lee 12:341

Schwaber, Paul
Robert Lowell 1:184

Schwartz, Alvin
Jerome Siegel and Joe Shuster 21:362

Schwartz, Barry N.
Eugène Ionesco 15:296

Schwartz, Delmore
R. P. Blackmur 24:53
John Dos Passos 15:180
T. S. Eliot 24:166
Randall Jarrell 1:159
Robinson Jeffers 11:304
Edmund Wilson 24:468

Schwartz, Edward
Katherine Anne Porter 7:309

Schwartz, Howard
Yehuda Amichai 22:31
David Ignatow 7:178

Schwartz, Julius
Roy A. Gallant 17:127

Schwartz, Kessel
Vicente Aleixandre 9:15
Juan Benet 28:21
Adolfo Bioy Casares 8:94
Antonio Buero Vallejo 15:96
Gabriel García Márquez 10:215
Juan Goytisolo 23:182, 183
Juan Rulfo 8:462

Schwartz, Lloyd
Elizabeth Bishop 9:93, 97

Schwartz, Lynne Sharon
Beryl Bainbridge 5:40
Eleanor Clark 19:107
Natalia Ginzburg 5:141
Susan Fromberg Schaeffer 11:491
Alix Kates Shulman 10:475
Anne Tyler 11:552
Fay Weldon 9:560

Schwartz, Nancy Lynn
E. M. Broner 19:72
Jill Robinson 10:438

Schwartz, Paul J.
Samuel Beckett 6:41
Alain Robbe-Grillet 8:453

Schwartz, Ronald
Miguel Delibes 8:169
José María Gironella 11:234
Juan Goytisolo 23:181

Schwartz, Sanford
Milton Meltzer 26:302

Schwartz, Sheila
E. M. Broner 19:72

Schwartz, Wendy
Marge Piercy 27:379

Schwarz, Alfred
Jean-Paul Sartre 18:469

Schwarz, Egon
Hermann Hesse 17:211

Schwarzbach, F. S.
Thomas Pynchon 9:443

Schwarzchild, Bettina
James Purdy 2:349

Schweitzer, Darrell
Roger Zelazny 21:474, 478

Schwerer, Armand
Diane Wakoski 7:506

Scobbie, Irene
Pär Lagerkvist 10:312
Leon Rooke 25:393

Scobie, Stephen
Bill Bissett 18:59
John Glassco 9:237
John Newlove 14:377
B. P. Nichol 18:366, 368
Michael Ondaatje 14:408
Leon Rooke 25:393

Scobie, Stephen A. C.
F. R. Scott 22:375

Scobie, W. I.
Melvin Van Peebles 2:448
Derek Walcott 2:459

Scofield, Martin
T. S. Eliot 9:186

Scoggin, Margaret C.
Walter Farley 17:116
Henry Gregor Felsen 17:120
Mary Stolz 12:547, 549, 550, 552
John R. Tunis 12:594

Scoppa, Bud
Walter Becker and Donald Fagen 26:79
Jackson Browne 21:34
Mick Jagger and Keith Richard 17:228
John Lennon and Paul McCartney 12:366
Jimmy Page and Robert Plant 12:479
Neil Young 17:572, 575

Scott, Alexander
Hugh MacDiarmid 4:310

Scott, Carolyn D.
  Graham Greene 1:130

Scott, Helen G.
  Alfred Hitchcock 16:346

Scott, J. D.
  Gil Orlovitz 22:334
  Andrew Sinclair 2:400

Scott, John
  Ch'ien Chung-shu 22:106

Scott, Lael
  Mary Stolz 12:554

Scott, Malcolm
  Jean Giono 11:232

Scott, Nathan A., Jr.
  Charles M. Schulz 12:522
  Lionel Trilling 24:460
  Richard Wright 1:378

Scott, Peter Dale
  John Newlove 14:377
  Mordecai Richler 5:372

Scott, Tom
  Hugh MacDiarmid 4:309
  Ezra Pound 4:413

Scott, Winfield Townley
  David Ignatow 7:173
  James Purdy 28:377
  Louis Simpson 7:426

Scott-James, R. A.
  Edith Sitwell 9:493

Scouffas, George
  J. F. Powers 1:280

Scruggs, Charles W.
  Jean Toomer 4:549

Scruton, Roger
  Lucien Goldmann 24:254
  Marge Piercy 27:381
  Harold Pinter 27:396
  Sylvia Plath 5:340

Scrutton, Mary
  Vera Brittain 23:92

Sculatti, Gene
  Brian Wilson 12:642

Scupham, Peter
  W. H. Auden 6:16
  Elizabeth Daryush 19:121
  Robert Graves 6:211
  H. D. 8:257
  Elizabeth Jennings 14:293
  David Jones 4:262
  D. M. Thomas 13:542

Sealy, Douglas
  Benedict Kiely 23:265

Searle, Leroy
  Dannie Abse 7:2
  Erica Jong 4:264

Searles, Baird
  Anna Kavan 5:205
  Andre Norton 12:459

Searles, George J.
  Joseph Heller 8:279

Seaver, Richard
  Louis-Ferdinand Céline 1:57

Seay, James
  James Wright 3:543

Sedgwick, Ellery
  Esther Forbes 12:208

Seebohm, Caroline
  Isaac Asimov 19:29
  Dirk Bogarde 19:42
  Kamala Markandaya 8:377

Seed, David
  Isaac Bashevis Singer 9:487

Seelye, John
  Donald Barthelme 2:41
  Richard Lester 20:218, 219
  Norman Mailer 3:316
  Marge Piercy 3:383
  Charles M. Schulz 12:531
  James Thurber 5:439
  David Wagoner 5:474

Segal, Erich
  Robert Lowell 15:348

Segal, Lore
  Joan Didion 1:75
  James D. Forman 21:116

Segel, Harold
  Gregor von Rezzori 25:384

Segel, Harold B.
  Vasily Aksenov 22:27
  Czesław Miłosz 22:312

Segovia, Tomás
  Octavio Paz 3:376

Seib, Kenneth
  Richard Brautigan 1:44

Seibles, Timothy S.
  James Baldwin 15:43

Seiden, Melvin
  Vladimir Nabokov 2:302

Seidensticker, Edward
  Kōbō Abé 22:12
  Yukio Mishima 27:337

Seidlin, Oskar
  Hermann Hesse 17:216

Seidman, Hugh
  Denise Levertov 15:338
  Mary Oliver 19:362
  Linda Pastan 27:371

Seidman, Robert
  John Berger 19:39

Seitz, Michael
  Luchino Visconti 16:574

Seitz, Michael H.
  Richard Pryor 26:383

Selby, Herbert, Jr.
  Richard Price 6:427

Seldes, Gilbert
  Charles Chaplin 16:188

Seligson, Tom
  Piri Thomas 17:500
  Hunter S. Thompson 9:527

Sellick, Robert
  Shirley Hazzard 18:218

Sellin, Eric
  Samuel Beckett 2:47

Seltzer, Alvin J.
  William S. Burroughs 22:80

Selz, Thalia
  Jonathan Baumbach 23:55

Selzer, David
  Peter Porter 5:346

Semkow, Julie
  Joan Micklin Silver 20:341

Sena, Vinad
  T. S. Eliot 6:159

Senna, Carl
  Piers Paul Read 25:376

Sennwald, Andre
  Rouben Mamoulian 16:421

Servodidio, Mirella D'Ambrosio
  Azorín 11:24

Sesonske, Alexander
  Jean Renoir 20:309

Seton, Cynthia Propper
  Marilyn French 18:158
  Doris Grumbach 22:206
  Barbara Pym 19:387
  Muriel Spark 18:505

Severin, Timothy
  Thor Heyerdahl 26:193

Sewell, Elizabeth
  Muriel Rukeyser 15:458

Seybolt, Cynthia T.
  Jules Archer 12:21, 22

Seydor, Paul
  Sam Peckinpah 20:283

Seymour-Smith, Martin
  J. M. Coetzee 23:126
  Roy Fuller 28:150
  Robert Graves 1:128

Sgammato, Joseph
  Alfred Hitchcock 16:351

Shadoian, Jack
  Donald Barthelme 1:18

Shaffer, Dallas Y.
  Jules Archer 12:16
  Frank Bonham 12:53

Shah, Diane K.
  Richard O'Brien 17:325

Shahane, Vasant Anant
  Khushwant Singh 11:504

Shands, Annette Oliver
  Gwendolyn Brooks 4:78, 79
  Don L. Lee 2:238

Shannon, James P.
  J. F. Powers 1:279

Shapcott, Thomas
  Frank O'Hara 2:323
  W. R. Rodgers 7:377

Shapiro, Charles
  Meyer Levin 7:203
  David Madden 5:265
  Joyce Carol Oates 3:363
  Anthony Powell 1:277
  Harvey Swados 5:420
  Jerome Weidman 7:517

Shapiro, David
  John Ashbery 25:49
  Elizabeth Bishop 15:60
  Hayden Carruth 10:100
  X. J. Kennedy 8:320
  Josephine Miles 14:370
  Eric Rohmer 16:539

Shapiro, Jane
  Rosalyn Drexler 6:143

Shapiro, Karl
  W. H. Auden 1:8; 3:21
  T. S. Eliot 3:136
  Rod McKuen 1:210
  Henry Miller 4:349
  Chaim Potok 26:367
  Ezra Pound 3:394
  William Carlos Williams 5:506

Shapiro, Laura
  Elizabeth Swados 12:560

Shapiro, Lillian L.
  Rosa Guy 26:145

Shapiro, Marianne
  Elio Vittorini 14:546

Shapiro, Paula Meinetz
  Alice Walker 6:553

Shapiro, Susin
  Joan Armatrading 17:7
  Jimmy Cliff 21:61
  Janis Ian 21:184
  Lou Reed 21:315
  Carly Simon 26:409

Shapiro, Walter
  M. M. Kaye 28:202

Sharma, P. P.
  Arthur Miller 15:370

Sharp, Christopher
  Ntozake Shange 25:397

Sharp, Sister Corona
  Friedrich Dürrenmatt 15:201
  Eugène Ionesco 15:297

Sharp, Jonathan
  Alvah Bessie 23:61

Sharpe, Patricia
  Margaret Drabble 10:162

Sharrock, Roger
  T. S. Eliot 24:179

Shattan, Joseph
  Saul Bellow 8:80

Shattuck, Roger
  Jean Arp 5:32
  Saul Bellow 6:57
  Alain Robbe-Grillet 2:376
  Octavio Paz 19:365

Shaughnessy, Mary Rose
  Edna Ferber 18:152

Shaw, Arnold
Chuck Berry 17:53

Shaw, Bob
Michael Moorcock 27:350

Shaw, Evelyn
Melvin Berger 12:37

Shaw, Greg
Monty Python 21:224
Brian Wilson 12:647

Shaw, Irwin
James Jones 10:290

Shaw, Peter
Robert Lowell 8:351
Hugh Nissenson 9:400
Ezra Pound 18:422

Shaw, Robert B.
A. R. Ammons 3:11
W. H. Auden 2:26
Wendell Berry 8:85
Stanley Burnshaw 3:91
Peter Davison 28:101
Babette Deutsch 18:120
James Dickey 2:117
William Dickey 28:119
Robert Duncan 7:88
Robert Francis 15:238
Brewster Ghiselin 23:171
Allen Ginsberg 6:201
John Glassco 9:236
Richard Howard 7:166
Barbara Howes 15:289
David Ignatow 4:248
Stanley Kunitz 14:313
Philip Larkin 8:338
Brad Leithauser 27:242
William Meredith 4:348
Frederick Morgan 23:299
Adrienne Rich 6:457
M. L. Rosenthal 28:392
Raphael Rudnik 7:384
Charles Simic 6:501; 9:479; 22:381
Allen Tate 2:430
Mark Van Doren 6:541
Eudora Welty 14:566
James Wright 28:468
Marya Zaturenska 6:585

Shawe-Taylor, Desmond
Pamela Hansford Johnson 27:212

Shayon, Robert Lewis
Norman Lear 12:329
Gene Roddenberry 17:403

Shea, Robert J.
Budd Schulberg 7:403

Shear, Walter
Bernard Malamud 1:197

Shechner, Mark
Tadeusz Konwicki 8:328
Philip Rahv 24:356
Mordecai Richler 18:453
Philip Roth 15:451
Isaac Bashevis Singer 15:508

Shedlin, Michael
Woody Allen 16:2

Sheean, Vincent
Alvah Bessie 23:59

Sheed, Wilfrid
Edward Albee 1:4
Roger Angell 26:33
James Baldwin 1:16; 8:42
Robert Coover 7:58
Robert Frost 1:110
William Golding 1:121
Joseph Heller 5:182
James Jones 1:162
Norman Mailer 1:193; 4:320
Terrence McNally 7:216
Arthur Miller 1:217
Alberto Moravia 2:292
Iris Murdoch 1:236
P. H. Newby 13:409
John Osborne 1:263
Walker Percy 2:332
S. J. Perelman 23:339
Neil Simon 6:503
William Styron 1:330
James Thurber 25:436
John Updike 1:343
Kurt Vonnegut, Jr. 1:347
Douglas Turner Ward 19:456
Evelyn Waugh 3:512
Arnold Wesker 3:518
Tennessee Williams 1:369
P. G. Wodehouse 22:482
Tom Wolfe 2:481

Sheehan, Donald
John Berryman 1:34
Richard Howard 7:166
Robert Lowell 1:181

Sheehan, Edward R. F.
Edwin O'Connor 14:392

Sheehan, Ethna
E. M. Almedingen 12:1
Lois Duncan 26:101
Christie Harris 12:261
Mollie Hunter 21:156
Philippa Pearce 21:281

Shelton, Austin J.
Chinua Achebe 7:4

Shelton, Frank W.
Robert Coover 7:60
Harry Crews 23:137
Ernest Hemingway 10:269

Shelton, Robert
Joan Armatrading 17:10
Bob Dylan 12:179

Shepard, Paul
Peter Matthiessen 5:273

Shepard, Ray Anthony
Alice Childress 12:107
Nicholasa Mohr 12:446

Shepard, Richard F.
Lois Duncan 26:102
Sam Shepard 17:433

Shepherd, Allen
Harry Crews 23:133
Reynolds Price 3:405, 406
Robert Penn Warren 1:355

Shepherd, Naomi
S. Y. Agnon 14:1

Shepherd, R.
Raja Rao 25:368

Shepley, John
Alberto Moravia 27:356

Sheppard, R. Z.
Louis Auchincloss 4:30
Saul Bellow 6:55
William Peter Blatty 2:64
Lothar-Günther Buchheim 6:101
Anthony Burgess 5:85
Peter De Vries 2:114
E. L. Doctorow 6:133
Nora Ephron 17:113
Paul E. Erdman 25:154
Alex Haley 8:260
Frank Herbert 12:270
James Leo Herlihy 6:235
Dan Jacobson 4:254
Bernard Malamud 2:266
S. J. Perelman 5:338
Ishmael Reed 5:370
Harvey Swados 5:422
Michel Tournier 6:537
Anne Tyler 28:433
Mario Vargas Llosa 6:545
Gore Vidal 6:548
Paul West 7:523
Hilma Wolitzer 17:561

Sheps, G. David
Mordecai Richler 13:481

Sheridan, Martin
Jerome Siegel and Joe Shuster 21:354

Sheridan, Robert N.
Henry Gregor Felsen 17:124

Sherman, Beatrice
Margery Allingham 19:13
Sally Benson 17:48
Dalton Trumbo 19:445

Sherman, Bill
Trina Robbins 21:341

Sherrard-Smith, Barbara
Zilpha Keatley Snyder 17:472

Sherrell, Richard E.
Arthur Adamov 25:15

Sherry, Vincent B., Jr.
W. S. Merwin 18:335

Sherwood, Martin
Isaac Asimov 26:39
Roger Zelazny 21:468

Sherwood, R. E.
Buster Keaton 20:188

Sherwood, Terry G.
Ken Kesey 1:167

Shetley, Vernon
A. R. Ammons 25:45
John Ashbery 25:59
James Schuyler 23:392

Shewey, Don
Joan Armatrading 17:11
Janis Ian 21:188
Billy Joel 26:216, 221
Lou Reed 21:319
Frank Zappa 17:594

Shideler, Ross
Gunnar Ekelöf 27:117

Shifreen, Lawrence J.
Henry Miller 14:372

Shinn, Thelma J.
Flannery O'Connor 6:375
Ann Petry 7:304
William Saroyan 10:452

Shipp, Randy
Robert Lewis Taylor 14:535

Shippey, T. A.
Samuel R. Delany 14:147
Robert Nye 13:414
Frederik Pohl 18:410
Mary Lee Settle 19:410
John Steinbeck 13:535
Arkadii Strugatskii and Boris Strugatskii 27:432
Roger Zelazny 21:469

Shippey, Tom
Fritz Leiber 25:305

Shippey, Thomas
Lothar-Günther Buchheim 6:100

Shiras, Mary
William Meredith 22:301

Shivers, Alfred S.
Jessamyn West 7:520

Shockley, Martin
John Steinbeck 21:368

Shoemaker, Alice
William Faulkner 14:175

Shore, Rima
Yevgeny Yevtushenko 13:619

Shores, Edward
George Roy Hill 26:210

Shorris, Earl
Donald Barthelme 2:42
John Gardner 3:184
William H. Gass 2:155
Thomas Pynchon 3:414

Short, Robert L.
Charles M. Schulz 12:522, 525

Shorter, Eric
Alan Ayckbourn 5:36; 18:29
Agatha Christie 12:118
Hugh Leonard 19:282
Thornton Wilder 15:574

Shorter, Kingsley
Siegfried Lenz 27:249

Shoukri, Doris Enright-Clark
Marguerite Duras 3:129

Showalter, Dennis E.
Robert Heinlein 14:246

Showalter, Elaine
Mary McCarthy 3:329

Showers, Paul
Peter De Vries 2:114
James Herriot 12:283
John Seelye 7:407
Alvin Silverstein and Virginia B. Silverstein 17:454

Shrapnel, Norman
Marge Piercy 18:406

Shrimpton, Nicholas
J. M. Coetzee 23:124
M. M. Kaye 28:200
Bernice Rubens 19:405
Irwin Shaw 23:401
C. P. Snow 19:428
D. M. Thomas 22:417

Shub, Anatole
Paddy Chayefsky 23:113

Shuey, Andrea Lee
M. M. Kaye 28:202

Shuman, R. Baird
William Inge 1:153
Clifford Odets 2:318, 320

Shuttleworth, Martin
Christina Stead 2:421

Shuttleworth, Paul
Leon Uris 7:492

Siaulys, Tony
Sonia Levitin 17:266

Sibbald, K. M.
Jorge Guillén 11:263

Sibley, Francis M.
Chinua Achebe 26:22

Sicherman, Barbara
Taylor Caldwell 28:67

Sicherman, Carol M.
Saul Bellow 10:37

Siconolfi, Michael T., S.J.
Audre Lorde 18:309

Sidnell, M. J.
Ronald G. Everson 27:133

Siebert, Sara L.
Maureen Daly 17:89

Siegal, R. A.
Judy Blume 12:47

Siegel, Ben
Saul Bellow 8:78
Bernard Malamud 1:195
Isaac Bashevis Singer 1:313

Siegel, Eve
Margaret Atwood 25:68

Siegel, Joel E.
Robert Altman 16:33
Albert Maysles and David Maysles 16:445

Siegel, Paul N.
Norman Mailer 5:266

Siegel, Robert
Philip Booth 23:76
Al Young 19:480

Siemens, William L.
Julio Cortázar 5:110

Sigal, Clancy
Kingsley Amis 3:9; 5:22
Patrick Boyle 19:67
Melvyn Bragg 10:72
E. L. Doctorow 18:127
Piers Paul Read 25:376

Alan Sillitoe 3:448
James Thurber 25:440

Sigerson, Davitt
Brian Wilson 12:653

Siggins, Clara M.
Taylor Caldwell 2:95
Alan Garner 17:146
Lillian Hellman 4:221
Saul Maloff 5:270

Signoriello, John
Mollie Hunter 21:157

Šilbajoris, Rimvydas
Boris Pasternak 10:387

Silber, Irwin
Bob Dylan 12:181

Silber, Joan
Cynthia Propper Seton 27:430
Scott Sommer 25:426

Silbersack, John
Fritz Leiber 25:308

Silenieks, Juris
Édouard Glissant 10:231

Silet, Charles L. P.
David Kherdian 9:317, 318

Silkin, Jon
Geoffrey Hill 5:183

Silko, Leslie Marmon
Dee Brown 18:71

Silver, Adele Z.
E. M. Broner 19:70

Silver, Charles
Orson Welles 20:446

Silver, David
Peter Townshend 17:527

Silver, George A.
John Berger 19:37

Silver, Linda
Lois Duncan 26:103

Silver, Linda R.
Sandra Scoppettone 26:402

Silver, Philip
Dámaso Alonso 14:22

Silverman, Hugh J.
Jean-Paul Sartre 18:472

Silverman, Malcolm
Jorge Amado 13:11
Autran Dourado 23:149

Silverman, Michael
Nagisa Oshima 20:253

Silverstein, Norman
James Dickey 7:81
Buster Keaton 20:195

Silvert, Conrad
Peter Matthiessen 7:210

Silverton, Pete
Elvis Costello 21:73

Silvey, Anita
Gunnel Beckman 26:86
Milton Meltzer 26:303
Otfried Preussler 17:377
Mildred D. Taylor 21:418

Simels, Steve
Jackson Browne 21:40
Jimmy Cliff 21:64
Ray Davies 21:95, 100
Billy Joel 26:223
Monty Python 21:230
Martin Mull 17:300
Jimmy Page and Robert Plant 12:476
The Police 26:365
Lou Reed 21:305, 308
Gene Roddenberry 17:414
Patti Smith 12:537
Bruce Springsteen 17:485
Peter Townshend 17:535
Brian Wilson 12:651
Neil Young 17:579

Simenon, Georges
Georges Simenon 3:451

Simic, Charles
Vasko Popa 19:374

Simmons, Ernest J.
Mikhail Sholokhov 7:416, 420

Simmons, John S.
Robert Lipsyte 21:209

Simmons, Ruth J. S.
Aimé Césaire 19:97

Simmons, Tom
Richard F. Hugo 18:263

Simon, John
Edward Albee 2:1; 5:13; 11:11; 13:3, 4; 25:36
Woody Allen 16:7, 13
Robert Altman 16:33, 36
Lindsay Anderson 20:14
Jean Anouilh 13:22
Michelangelo Antonioni 20:40
Alan Ayckbourn 8:34; 18:29
Ralph Bakshi 26:70, 72
James Baldwin 17:40
Peter Barnes 5:49
Samuel Beckett 3:47
Ingmar Bergman 16:77
Bernardo Bertolucci 16:100
Robert Bolt 14:88
Mel Brooks 12:80
Ed Bullins 5:84; 7:36
Anne Burr 6:104
John Cassavetes 20:51
Claude Chabrol 16:179
Francis Ford Coppola 16:240
Michael Cristofer 28:96, 97
Brian De Palma 20:74, 76
Martin Duberman 8:185
Christopher Durang 27:89, 92
Marguerite Duras 20:98
Rainer Werner Fassbinder 20:112
Jules Feiffer 2:133
Federico Fellini 16:289, 297, 300
Lawrence Ferlinghetti 2:134
Bob Fosse 20:124

Athol Fugard 9:230; 14:191; 25:177
Frank D. Gilroy 2:161
Jean-Luc Godard 20:135
Charles Gordone 1:124
Günter Grass 11:252
Simon Gray 14:215
John Guare 14:222
Bill Gunn 5:153
Christopher Hampton 4:211
Joseph Heller 11:265
Lillian Hellman 8:281; 18:226
Beth Henley 23:216
George Roy Hill 26:203, 210
Alfred Hitchcock 16:353
Rolf Hochhuth 11:275
Bohumil Hrabal 13:290
William Inge 8:308
Albert Innaurato 21:197, 198
Ann Jellicoe 27:210
Jean Kerr 22:259
Pavel Kohout 13:323
Arthur Kopit 1:171; 18:291
Stanley Kubrick 16:390
Richard Lester 20:230, 231
Denise Levertov 15:336
Ira Levin 3:294
Robert Lowell 4:299; 11:324
Norman Mailer 2:259; 3:316
David Mamet 15:356, 358
Elaine May 16:436
Albert Maysles and David Maysles 16:444
Terrence McNally 4:347; 7:217, 218, 219
Mark Medoff 6:321, 322; 23:293
Christopher Middleton 13:387
Arthur Miller 2:279, 280; 6:335
Jason Miller 2:284, 285
Czesław Miłosz 22:310
Vladimir Nabokov 23:314
Marsha Norman 28:317, 319
Joyce Carol Oates 11:400
Joe Orton 4:387
John Osborne 2:328; 11:421
Nagisa Oshima 20:245, 256
Rochelle Owens 8:434
Gordon Parks 16:460
Pier Paolo Pasolini 20:262
Sam Peckinpah 20:274
S. J. Perelman 5:337
Harold Pinter 3:386, 387; 11:443; 15:425
Sylvia Plath 17:345
Roman Polanski 16:471
Bernard Pomerance 13:446
David Rabe 8:449, 451
Gerome Ragni and James Rado 17:381, 388
Satyajit Ray 16:489
Jean Renoir 20:307
Jonathan Reynolds 6:452
Eric Rohmer 16:538
Howard Sackler 14:478
Carlos Saura 20:318
Murray Schisgal 6:490
Peter Shaffer 5:387, 389
Ntozake Shange 8:484; 25:398, 399
Sam Shepard 6:497; 17:435, 449
Martin Sherman 19:415

Joan Micklin Silver **20**:343
Neil Simon **6**:506; **11**:495, 496
Isaac Bashevis Singer **15**:509
Bernard Slade **11**:507
Steven Spielberg **20**:361
John Steinbeck **5**:408
George Steiner **24**:427
Tom Stoppard **3**:470; **4**:525, 526; **5**:412; **8**:504
David Storey **4**:528; **5**:415, 417
Elizabeth Swados **12**:559, 562
Ronald Tavel **6**:529
C. P. Taylor **27**:446
François Truffaut **20**:385, 405
Melvin Van Peebles **2**:448
Gore Vidal **2**:450; **4**:554; **10**:503
Andrzej Wajda **16**:578
Derek Walcott **2**:460; **14**:550
Andrew Lloyd Webber and Tim Rice **21**:430
Peter Weiss **3**:513
Michael Weller **10**:526
Lina Wertmüller **16**:590, 598
Billy Wilder **20**:460
Thornton Wilder **10**:535
Tennessee Williams **2**:464; **5**:501; **7**:544; **8**:549; **11**:571
Lanford Wilson **14**:591, 592
Robert Wilson **7**:550, 551

Simon, John K.
Michel Butor **15**:112

Simon, Kate
Rhys Davies **23**:145

Simonds, C. H.
Joan Didion **1**:74

Simonds, Katharine
Sally Benson **17**:47

Simpson, Allen
Albert Camus **11**:96

Simpson, Clinton
Ilya Ehrenburg **18**:130

Simpson, Elaine
Andre Norton **12**:456

Simpson, Louis
Robert Bly **2**:65
Allen Ginsberg **13**:241
James Merrill **8**:380
Kenneth Rexroth **2**:370
W. D. Snodgrass **2**:405

Sinclair, Dorothy
Erich Segal **10**:467
David Slavitt **14**:491

Sinclair, Karen
Ursula K. LeGuin **13**:350

Siner, Robin
Margaret O. Hyde **21**:179

Singer, Alexander
René Clair **20**:63

Singer, Isaac B.
Otfried Preussler **17**:376

Singer, Marilyn
Frank Bonham **12**:54

Singer, Marilyn R.
Paul Zindel **26**:471

Singh, G.
Eugenio Montale **7**:223, 226
Ezra Pound **2**:342, 344; **7**:334

Singh, Rahul
M. M. Kaye **28**:200

Singleton, Mary Ann
Doris Lessing **22**:280

Sinha, Krishna Nandan
Mulk Raj Anand **23**:15

Sinyavsky, Andrei
Anna Akhmatova **25**:24
Robert Frost **4**:174
Yevgeny Yevtushenko **26**:465

Sire, James W.
C. S. Lewis **1**:177

Sisco, Ellen
Jamake Highwater **12**:286

Sisk, John P.
Mark Harris **19**:200
J. F. Powers **1**:280
Philip Rahv **24**:354

Sissman, L. E.
Kingsley Amis **2**:7; **5**:22
Martin Amis **4**:21
Jimmy Breslin **4**:76
Michael Crichton **6**:119
J. P. Donleavy **4**:126
J. G. Farrell **6**:174
Natalia Ginzburg **5**:141
Joseph Heller **8**:278
Dan Jacobson **4**:255
Thomas McGuane **3**:329
Tom McHale **3**:332; **5**:282
Brian Moore **7**:237
Gilbert Rogin **18**:458
Anne Roiphe **3**:434
John Updike **2**:441
Evelyn Waugh **3**:513
Fay Weldon **6**:563
Emlyn Williams **15**:578
Edmund Wilson **2**:478
Al Young **19**:477

Sisson, C. H.
H. D. **8**:257

Sitterly, Bancroft W.
Roy A. Gallant **17**:127

Sjöberg, Leif
Gunnar Ekelöf **27**:111, 113, 115
Eyvind Johnson **14**:296, 297
Harry Martinson **14**:355, 356

Skau, Michael
Lawrence Ferlinghetti **10**:177

Skelton, Robin
Patrick Kavanagh **22**:236
Anthony Kerrigan **6**:276
Dorothy Livesay **4**:294
Derek Mahon **27**:286
John Newlove **14**:378
Jane Rule **27**:417

Skerrett, Joseph T., Jr.
Ralph Ellison **11**:182

Skiles, Don
Jonathan Baumbach **23**:56

Skirius, A. John
Carlos Fuentes **22**:168

Sklar, Robert
J.R.R. Tolkien **12**:568

Skloot, Floyd
Thomas Kinsella **19**:255

Skodnick, Roy
Gilbert Sorrentino **7**:448

Skoller, Don
Carl Theodor Dreyer **16**:262

Skow, Jack
John Gardner **5**:132
Robert Graves **2**:176

Skow, John
Richard Adams **5**:5
Richard Brautigan **3**:86
Arthur A. Cohen **7**:52
Richard Condon **4**:107; **6**:115
Julio Cortázar **5**:109
Robertson Davies **2**:113
Lawrence Durrell **6**:152
Barry Hannah **23**:208
Charles Johnson **7**:183
Robert F. Jones **7**:193
Sue Kaufman **3**:263
Yasunari Kawabata **5**:208
Milan Kundera **4**:277
John D. MacDonald **3**:307
Iris Murdoch **4**:370
Vladimir Nabokov **6**:354
Harold Robbins **5**:379
Susan Fromberg Schaeffer **6**:488
Irving Stone **7**:471
Kurt Vonnegut, Jr. **4**:568
Morris L. West **6**:564
Patrick White **3**:525

Škvorecký, Josef
Pavel Kohout **13**:325

Slade, Joseph W.
James T. Farrell **11**:192

Slansky, Paul
Martin Mull **17**:300

Slater, Candace
Elizabeth Bishop **13**:88
Salvatore Espriu **9**:193

Slater, Jack
Stevie Wonder **12**:662

Slater, Joseph
Nelly Sachs **14**:475

Slaughter, Frank G.
Millen Brand **7**:29
Margaret O. Hyde **21**:172

Slavitt, David R.
George Garrett **11**:220
Maureen Howard **14**:267
Ann Quin **6**:441

Slethaug, Gordon E.
John Barth **2**:38

Sloan, James Park
Alice Childress **15**:131
David Madden **15**:350

Sloman, Larry
Lou Reed **21**:306

Slonim, Marc
Ilya Ehrenburg **18**:133
Mikhail Sholokhov **7**:415, 418
Aleksandr I. Solzhenitsyn **1**:320
Arkadii Strugatskii and Boris Strugatskii **27**:432
Henri Troyat **23**:458
Yevgeny Yevtushenko **26**:460
Marguerite Yourcenar **19**:482

Sloss, Henry
Richard Howard **10**:276
James Merrill **8**:381, 384
Reynolds Price **3**:406
Philip Roth **1**:293

Slung, Michele
P. D. James **18**:273
Stephen King **26**:237
Helen MacInnes **27**:284

Slusser, George Edgar
Arthur C. Clarke **13**:151
Samuel R. Delany **14**:143
Harlan Ellison **13**:204
Robert Heinlein **14**:246
Ursula K. LeGuin **13**:345

Smeltzer, Sister Mary Etheldra
Larry Kettelkamp **12**:306

Smith, A.J.M.
Earle Birney **6**:74
Stanley Kunitz **14**:312
Irving Layton **15**:318
P. K. Page **7**:291
F. R. Scott **22**:373
A.J.M. Smith **15**:515

Smith, Barbara
Ishmael Reed **6**:447
Alice Walker **6**:553

Smith, Bradford
Roderick L. Haig-Brown **21**:136

Smith, C.E.J.
Mavis Thorpe Clark **12**:130
Leon Garfield **12**:231

Smith, Dave
Philip Booth **23**:77
Harry Crews **6**:118
Brewster Ghiselin **23**:171
Albert Goldbarth **5**:144
Daniel Halpern **14**:232
William Heyen **18**:232
Cynthia Macdonald **19**:290
Linda Pastan **27**:370
Louis Simpson **7**:429
Barry Spacks **14**:511
Robert Penn Warren **13**:581
James Wright **28**:469

Smith, David E.
E. E. Cummings **8**:158

Smith, Dinitia
Alice Walker **27**:451

Smith, Ethanne
Franklyn M. Branley **21**:21

Smith, Eleanor T.
Jessamyn West **17**:547

Smith, F. C.
Henry Gregor Felsen **17**:121

Smith, Grover
T. S. Eliot **15**:206
Archibald MacLeish **8**:359

Smith, H. Allen
Jacqueline Susann **3**:476

Smith, Harrison
Taylor Caldwell **28**:61
Ilya Ehrenburg **18**:132
Madeleine L'Engle **12**:345
Mary Renault **17**:392
Elizabeth Spencer **22**:398
Jessamyn West **17**:546

Smith, Iain Crichton
Hugh MacDiarmid **11**:336

Smith, Irene
Noel Streatfeild **21**:398

Smith, Jack
Josef von Sternberg **20**:373

Smith, Janet Adam
Richard Adams **4**:8
Farley Mowat **26**:331
J.R.R. Tolkien **2**:435

Smith, Jennifer Farley
Margaret Craven **17**:79
Allan W. Eckert **17**:108

Smith, Joan
Piri Thomas **17**:502

Smith, Larry
Lawrence Ferlinghetti **27**:138

Smith, Leslie
Edward Bond **23**:68

Smith, Liz
Truman Capote **8**:133

Smith, Martin Cruz
John le Carré **28**:228

Smith, Mason
Richard Brautigan **12**:60

Smith, Maxwell A.
Jean Giono **4**:184
François Mauriac **4**:340

Smith, Michael
Rosalyn Drexler **2**:119
Anthony Kerrigan **6**:275
Tom Stoppard **1**:327
Robert Wilson **7**:549

Smith, Patti
Lou Reed **21**:308

Smith, Phillip E., II
Charles Olson **11**:420

Smith, Raymond J.
James Dickey **10**:141

Smith, Robert
Jimmy Page and Robert Plant **12**:481

Smith, Robert P., Jr.
Mongo Beti **27**:46, 53

Smith, Robert W.
Varlam Shalamov **18**:479

Smith, Roger H.
John D. MacDonald **3**:307

Smith, Sherwin D.
Charles M. Schulz **12**:530

Smith, Sidonie Ann
Maya Angelou **12**:10

Smith, Stan
Sylvia Plath **17**:357

Smith, Stephen
Michel Tournier **23**:456

Smith, Stevie
Edna Ferber **18**:152

Smith, William James
Frank O'Connor **23**:325
Kurt Vonnegut, Jr. **12**:601

Smith, William Jay
Elizabeth Bishop **13**:89
Louis MacNeice **4**:315
Frederick Seidel **18**:474
Sylvia Townsend Warner **19**:459

Smyth, Pat
William Mayne **12**:395

Smyth, Paul
Derek Walcott **4**:575

Sniderman, Stephen L.
Joseph Heller **3**:230

Snodgrass, W. D.
Theodore Roethke **8**:455

Snow, C. P.
Norman Mailer **4**:322

Snow, George E.
Aleksandr I. Solzhenitsyn **4**:507

Snow, Helen F.
Pearl S. Buck **7**:33

Snow, Philip
Thor Heyerdahl **26**:193

Snowden, J. A.
Sean O'Casey **9**:406

Snyder, Emine
Ezekiel Mphahlele **25**:334

Snyder, Stephen
Pier Paolo Pasolini **20**:271

Snyder-Scumpy, Patrick
Martin Mull **17**:297, 298

Soares, Manuela
Agnes Eckhardt Nixon **21**:251

Sobejano, Gonzalo
Dámaso Alonso **14**:20

Sobran, M. J., Jr.
Norman Lear **12**:338

Socken, Paul G.
Anne Hébert **13**:268
Gabrielle Roy **14**:469

Soderbergh, Peter A.
Upton Sinclair **11**:497

Sodowsky, Alice
George Lucas **16**:409

Sodowsky, Roland
George Lucas **16**:409

Soete, Mary
Bette Pesetsky **28**:358

Soile, Sola
Chinua Achebe **11**:4

Sokel, Walter Herbert
Heinrich Böll **9**:102

Sokolov, Raymond A.
André Brink **18**:67
E. L. Doctorow **6**:132
Julius Horwitz **14**:267
Dan Jacobson **4**:254
Gayl Jones **6**:265
Thomas Keneally **8**:319
József Lengyel **7**:202
John Sayles **7**:400
Hilma Wolitzer **17**:563

Solecki, Sam
Earle Birney **11**:50
Robertson Davies **25**:133
Doris Lessing **22**:286

Solnick, Bruce B.
George Garrett **11**:220

Solomon, Barbara Probst
Juan Goytisolo **5**:151
João Ubaldo Ribeiro **10**:436
Mario Vargas Llosa **10**:500

Solomon, Linda
David Bowie **17**:61

Solomon, Norman
Jonathan Kozol **17**:253

Solomon, Philip H.
Louis-Ferdinand Céline **15**:123

Solomon, Stanley J.
Francis Ford Coppola **16**:244

Solotaroff, Ted
Roger Angell **26**:29
William Trevor **25**:446

Solotaroff, Theodore
Saul Bellow **1**:33
Paul Bowles **1**:41
Anthony Burgess **1**:48
William S. Burroughs **1**:48
Albert Camus **9**:146
Alex Comfort **7**:54
George P. Elliott **2**:130
John Fowles **6**:185
Herbert Gold **7**:120
Paul Goodman **1**:123
Günter Grass **1**:125
Stanislaw Lem **8**:344
Bernard Malamud **1**:196, 200
Henry Miller **1**:219
Flannery O'Connor **1**:256
Katherine Anne Porter **1**:271
V. S. Pritchett **5**:352
James Purdy **2**:348
Philip Roth **4**:451
Jean-Paul Sartre **1**:304
Hubert Selby, Jr. **8**:474
Susan Sontag **1**:322
George Steiner **24**:427
Vladimir Voinovich **10**:508
Richard Wright **1**:377
Richard Yates **7**:553

Solzhenitsyn, Alexander
Mikhail Sholokhov **15**:480

Somer, John
Kurt Vonnegut, Jr. **4**:566

Somers, Paul P., Jr.
Ernest Hemingway **8**:283

Sommer, Sally R.
Alice Childress **12**:108

Sommers, Joseph
Miguel Ángel Asturias **13**:39

Sonkiss, Lois
Jamake Highwater **12**:286

Sonnenfeld, Albert
Heinrich Böll **9**:107

Sonntag, Jacob
Amos Oz **8**:435
Isaac Bashevis Singer **3**:456
Arnold Wesker **3**:519

Sontag, Susan
James Baldwin **4**:40
Roland Barthes **24**:26
Ingmar Bergman **16**:56
Robert Bresson **16**:106
Albert Camus **4**:88
Elias Canetti **25**:110
Paul Goodman **2**:170
Rolf Hochhuth **4**:230
Eugène Ionesco **4**:251
Alain Resnais **16**:501
Nathalie Sarraute **4**:465
Jean-Paul Sartre **4**:475
Peter Weiss **15**:564

Sonthoff, Helen W.
Phyllis Webb **18**:540
Ethel Davis Wilson **13**:606

Sorban, M. J., Jr.
Woody Allen **16**:8

Sorenson, Marian
Allan W. Eckert **17**:103
Lee Kingman **17**:245

Sorrentino, Gilbert
Paul Blackburn **9**:99
Richard Brautigan **12**:57
Italo Calvino **22**:94
Robert Creeley **2**:106
Robert Duncan **2**:122
William Gaddis **8**:227
Charles Olson **2**:327
Manuel Puig **28**:374
Luis Rafael Sánchez **23**:383
John Wieners **7**:535, 536
Louis Zukofsky **7**:563

Soskin, William
James M. Cain **28**:44
Taylor Caldwell **28**:59
Esther Forbes **12**:204

Sotiron, Michael
Hugh Garner **13**:237

Soule, Stephen W.
Anthony Burgess **5**:90

Soupault, Philippe
René Clair **20**:60

Sourian, Peter
Albert Camus 2:98
Eleanor Clark 5:105
Jack Kerouac 2:227
Norman Lear 12:336
Eric Rohmer 16:535
William Saroyan 8:468
Vassilis Vassilikos 4:552

Southerland, Ellease
Zora Neale Hurston 7:171

Southern, David
Michael McClure 6:320

Southern, Jane
Helen MacInnes 27:281

Southern, Terry
William Golding 17:165
John Rechy 1:283
Kurt Vonnegut, Jr. 12:601

Southron, Jane Spence
Enid Bagnold 25:73
Pamela Hansford Johnson 27:213, 214

Southworth, James G.
E. E. Cummings 3:115
Robert Frost 3:168
Robinson Jeffers 3:257
Archibald MacLeish 3:309
Laura Riding 7:373

Souza, Raymond D.
G. Cabrera Infante 25:100
Octavio Paz 10:392
Ernesto Sabato 10:444; 23:381

Sowton, Ian
Patrick Lane 25:288
F. R. Scott 22:373

Soyinka, Wole
Mongo Beti 27:48

Spacks, Patricia Meyer
Kingsley Amis 5:24
Nicholas Delbanco 6:130
Hannah Green 3:202
Joseph Heller 5:183
Jennifer Johnston 7:186
D. Keith Mano 10:328
Alberto Moravia 2:294
Iris Murdoch 6:347
J. R. Salamanca 15:463
Anne Sexton 8:483
Andrew Sinclair 2:402
Muriel Spark 2:419; 5:400
Peter Spielberg 6:520
J.R.R. Tolkien 1:336
Elio Vittorini 6:551
Eudora Welty 2:464
Paul West 7:524
Patrick White 4:587

Spain, Francis Lander
Margot Benary-Isbert 12:31

Spann, Marcella
Ezra Pound 4:413

Spanos, William V.
Martin Heidegger 24:277
Yannis Ritsos 6:460
Jean-Paul Sartre 18:466

Sparshott, Francis
Northrop Frye 24:231

Spaulding, Martha
Laurie Colwin 13:156
Kamala Markandaya 8:377
J.R.R. Tolkien 8:516

Spears, Monroe K.
W. H. Auden 2:22
John Berryman 2:57
Cleanth Brooks 24:114
James Dickey 2:116
T. S. Eliot 2:127
Robert Graves 11:254
Daniel Hoffman 23:242
Ted Hughes 2:199
David Jones 2:217
Madison Jones 4:263
Maxine Kumin 28:222
Ursula K. Le Guin 22:269
Robert Lowell 2:248
Ezra Pound 2:342
John Crowe Ransom 2:366
Karl Shapiro 4:487
Allen Tate 2:430; 24:441
John Kennedy Toole 19:443
Robert Penn Warren 1:355; 4:579; 18:539
René Wellek 28:445

Spector, Ivar
Mikhail Sholokhov 7:420

Spector, Robert D.
William Bronk 10:73
Len Deighton 22:114
Robert Duncan 7:87
D. J. Enright 4:156
Louise Glück 22:173
David Ignatow 7:174
Carolyn Kizer 15:308
Halldór Laxness 25:293
Kenneth Rexroth 2:371

Speer, Diane Parkin
Robert Heinlein 8:275

Spence, Jon
Katherine Anne Porter 7:320

Spence, Jonathan
Kazuo Ishiguro 27:204

Spencer, Benjamin T.
Edward Dahlberg 7:70

Spencer, Elizabeth
Elizabeth Spencer 22:403

Spencer, Jack
André Schwarz-Bart 2:388

Spencer, Sharon
Djuna Barnes 3:38
Jorge Luis Borges 3:77
Julio Cortázar 3:114
Carlos Fuentes 3:175
Anaïs Nin 4:376; 14:381
Alain Robbe-Grillet 4:448

Spendal, R. J.
James Wright 10:546

Spender, Stephen
A. R. Ammons 2:12
W. H. Auden 3:25, 27
James Baldwin 17:25
T. S. Eliot 24:163
Günter Grass 22:196
Robert Graves 2:177

Thom Gunn 3:216
Ted Hughes 2:200
Aldous Huxley 3:253; 5:192; 8:304
David Jones 13:312
Arthur Koestler 15:311
F. R. Leavis 24:293
Philip Levine 4:287
James Merrill 3:335
W. S. Merwin 3:340
Eugenio Montale 7:225
Elsa Morante 8:403
Alberto Moravia 27:356
Sylvia Plath 9:429
William Plomer 4:406
Nelly Sachs 14:475
James Schuyler 5:383; 23:389
Gore Vidal 2:450; 8:527
James Wright 3:541

Spicer, Edward H.
Carlos Castaneda 12:85

Spiegel, Alan
Stanley Kubrick 16:392
Jean-Paul Sartre 7:398

Spiegelman, Willard
John Betjeman 10:53
Richard Howard 7:169
James Merrill 8:384
Adrienne Rich 7:370

Spieler, F. Joseph
Robert Wilson 9:577

Spilka, Mark
Ernest Hemingway 10:263
Doris Lessing 6:300
Erich Segal 3:446
John Steinbeck 21:385

Spina, James
Jimmy Page and Robert Plant 12:482

Spitz, David
William Golding 17:172

Spitz, Robert Stephen
Pete Hamill 10:251

Spitzer, Nicholas R.
Waylon Jennings 21:202

Spitzer, Susan
Margaret Drabble 22:122

Spivack, Kathleen
Robert Lowell 2:248

Spivey, Herman E.
William Faulkner 6:176

Spivey, Ted R.
Conrad Aiken 5:9
Romain Gary 25:189
Flannery O'Connor 1:255

Spiwack, David
Jackson Browne 21:36

Spraggins, Mary Beth Pringle
Monique Wittig 22:476

Sprague, Rosemary
Marianne Moore 4:362

Sprague, Susan
Mavis Thorpe Clark 12:132
Barbara Corcoran 17:77

Springer, Cole
Frank Zappa 17:593

Spurling, Hilary
Anthony Powell 10:417

Spurling, John
Peter Barnes 5:50
Samuel Beckett 6:42
Peter Benchley 4:54
Anna Kavan 13:315
Francis King 8:322
David Mercer 5:284
Yukio Mishima 9:384
Peter Nichols 5:308
David Plante 7:307
Anne Redmon 22:341
Peter Shaffer 5:388
Elie Wiesel 5:491

Squires, Radcliffe
Brewster Ghiselin 23:169
Caroline Gordon 6:204
Randall Jarrell 6:260
Robinson Jeffers 11:305
Mario Luzi 13:353
Frederic Prokosch 4:420
Allen Tate 2:429; 4:540; 11:524
Robert Penn Warren 18:537

Sragow, Michael
Brian De Palma 20:83
George Roy Hill 26:209
Stephen King 26:243

Srivastava, Narsingh
W. H. Auden 14:26

Stabb, Martin S.
Jorge Luis Borges 19:44
José Donoso 11:149

Stableford, Brian M.
Douglas Adams 27:15
James Blish 14:84

Stade, George
Kingsley Amis 8:10
E. E. Cummings 3:119
Guy Davenport, Jr. 14:142
Don DeLillo 27:78
E. L. Doctorow 6:132; 18:126
John Gregory Dunne 28:126
Leslie Epstein 27:131
Max Frisch 18:163
John Gardner 3:186
Robert Graves 1:129
Jerzy Kosinski 3:272
Alan Lelchuk 5:243
Elmore Leonard 28:235
Doris Lessing 15:331
Joseph McElroy 5:279
Henry Miller 14:371
Steven Millhauser 21:219
Iris Murdoch 22:328
Jean Rhys 6:452
Wilfrid Sheed 4:488
Muriel Spark 2:416
John Updike 5:458
Kurt Vonnegut, Jr. 3:501

Stafford, I. Elizabeth
Lee Kingman 17:244

Stafford, Jean
Harry Crews 23:132
M. E. Kerr 12:296, 298
James A. Michener 5:289
Jessamyn West 17:552
Paul West 7:523

Stafford, William E.
Millen Brand 7:29
William Dickey 28:117
Richard Eberhart 19:142
Loren Eiseley 7:93
Barbara Howes 15:289
David Kherdian 6:280
Kenneth Rexroth 2:370
M. L. Rosenthal 28:393
Louis Simpson 7:427
May Swenson 14:518
Theodore Weiss 8:546

Staley, Thomas F.
Margaret Drabble 22:127

Stallings, Sylvia
Doris Betts 28:33

Stallknecht, Newton P.
Amos Tutuola 5:445

Stallman, Robert W.
Ernest Hemingway 13:271; 19:212

Stambolian, George
Sam Shepard 4:490

Stamelman, Richard
Yves Bonnefoy 15:75
Francis Ponge 18:415

Stamford, Anne Marie
Taylor Caldwell 28:68
Leslie Epstein 27:127
Isabelle Holland 21:149

Stamm, Rudolf
Harold Pinter 27:388

Stampfer, Judah
Saul Bellow 6:60
Philip Roth 6:476

Standard, Elinore
Virginia Hamilton 26:147

Staneck, Lou Willet
John Neufeld 17:310

Stanford, Alfred
Thor Heyerdahl 26:189

Stanford, Ann
May Swenson 4:533

Stanford, Derek
A. Alvarez 13:9
Earle Birney 4:64
Robert Creeley 2:106
C. Day Lewis 1:72
Lawrence Durrell 4:147
Geoffrey Hill 18:238
Aldous Huxley 5:192
Elizabeth Jennings 5:197
Patrick Kavanagh 22:244
Hugh MacDiarmid 4:313
Louis MacNeice 1:187
Robert Nye 13:413
William Plomer 4:406
Carl Sandburg 15:470
Stephen Spender 1:322; 2:419
Yevgeny Yevtushenko 3:547

Stanford, Donald E.
Elizabeth Daryush 19:122
Caroline Gordon 6:202
Marianne Moore 4:364
Katherine Anne Porter 27:402
Ezra Pound 10:407
Allen Tate 2:430
Yvor Winters 4:591

Stange, Maren
Susan Sontag 10:486

Stankiewicz, Marketa Goetz
Pavel Kohout 13:323
Sławomir Mrożek 3:345

Stanleigh, Bertram
Frank Zappa 17:584

Stanlis, Peter L.
Robert Frost 3:174

Stannard, Martin
Evelyn Waugh 13:588

Stanton, Michael N.
E. M. Forster 22:135

Staples, Hugh B.
Randall Jarrell 6:261
Robert Lowell 2:246

Stark, Freya
Paul Bowles 19:58

Stark, John O.
John Barth 7:22
Jorge Luis Borges 8:94
E. L. Doctorow 6:131
William Gaddis 8:228
Vladimir Nabokov 8:407

Stark, Myra
Adrienne Rich 11:477

Starr, Carol
John Neufeld 17:310

Starr, Kevin
James M. Cain 28:52
E. L. Doctorow 6:136
John Dos Passos 8:181

Starr, Roger
Anthony Powell 3:403

Stasio, Marilyn
Anne Burr 6:105
John Hopkins 4:234
Terrence McNally 4:346, 347
Jason Miller 2:284
David Rabe 4:426
Murray Schisgal 6:491
Melvin Van Peebles 2:448

States, Bert O.
R. S. Crane 27:74
Harold Pinter 6:412

Stathis, James J.
William Gaddis 19:186

Stauffer, Helen Winter
Mari Sandoz 28:406

Stavin, Robert H.
Alvin Silverstein and Virginia B. Silverstein 17:450

Stavn, Diane G.
Nat Hentoff 26:183

Stavn, Diane Gersoni
Frank Bonham 12:51
Barbara Corcoran 17:72
Mollie Hunter 21:157
M. E. Kerr 12:297
Joseph Krumgold 12:320
Emily Cheney Neville 12:451

Stavrou, C. N.
Edward Albee 5:12

Steck, Henry J.
Jules Archer 12:20

Steck, John A.
Al Young 19:480

Steegmuller, Francis
Patrick Modiano 18:338

Steel, Ronald
Pavel Kohout 13:323

Steele, Timothy
W. S. Merwin 18:336

Steene, Birgitta
Ingmar Bergman 16:54, 59, 64

Stefanile, Felix
William Bronk 10:73
Lewis Turco 11:552

Stegner, Page
Vladimir Nabokov 1:239

Stegner, Wallace
Walter Van Tilburg Clark 28:81
N. Scott Momaday 19:318

Stein, Benjamin
Joan Didion 8:177
John Gregory Dunne 28:123

Stein, Charles
Jerome Rothenberg 6:477

Stein, Elliott
Andrzej Wajda 16:584

Stein, Howard F.
Alex Haley 12:251

Stein, Robert A.
J. V. Cunningham 3:122

Stein, Robert J.
Margaret O. Hyde 21:176, 179

Stein, Ruth M.
Jamake Highwater 12:287
Norma Fox Mazer 26:293
Anne McCaffrey 17:283, 284
Robert Newton Peck 17:342

Steinbeck, Nancy
Kin Platt 26:356

Steinberg, Karen
Martin Cruz Smith 25:414

Steinberg, Karen Matlaw
Yuri Krotkov 19:265
Anatoli Rybakov 23:372

Steinberg, M. W.
John Arden 15:23
Robertson Davies 7:72
A. M. Klein 19:258, 261
Arthur Miller 1:215

Steiner, Carlo
Giuseppe Ungaretti 7:483

Steiner, George
Jorge Luis Borges 2:70
Anthony Burgess 22:78
C. Day Lewis 6:126
Lawrence Durrell 4:144
Paul Goodman 7:127
Graham Greene 6:220
Martin Heidegger 24:275
Aldous Huxley 5:194
Thomas Keneally 8:318; 10:298
F. R. Leavis 24:303
Georg Lukács 24:318
Robert M. Pirsig 4:403
Sylvia Plath 11:445
Jean-Paul Sartre 7:397
Aleksandr I. Solzhenitsyn 4:516
John Updike 5:459
Patrick White 4:583

Stendahl, Brita
Gunnar Ekelöf 27:116

Stengel, Richard
Brian Moore 19:333

Stenson, Leah Deland
Sol Gordon 26:137

Stepanchev, Stephen
John Ashbery 2:16
Imamu Amiri Baraka 2:34
Elizabeth Bishop 4:65
Robert Bly 2:65
James M. Cain 28:47
Robert Creeley 2:105
James Dickey 2:115
Alan Dugan 2:121
Robert Duncan 2:122
Jean Garrigue 2:153
Allen Ginsberg 2:162
Randall Jarrell 2:208
Robert Lowell 2:247
W. S. Merwin 2:276
Charles Olson 2:325
Kenneth Rexroth 2:369
Karl Shapiro 4:485
Irwin Shaw 23:397
Louis Simpson 4:498
William Stafford 4:519
May Swenson 4:532
Richard Wilbur 6:568

Stephen, Sidney J.
A. M. Klein 19:260

Stephens, Donald
Dorothy Livesay 4:294
Sinclair Ross 13:490
Rudy Wiebe 6:567

Stephens, Martha
Richard Wright 1:379

Stephens, Robert O.
Ernest Hemingway 3:239

Stephenson, Edward R.
John Hawkes 15:277

Stephenson, William
James Dickey 4:122

Stepto, Robert B.
Michael S. Harper 7:139
Richard Wright 21:455

Sterling, Dorothy
Virginia Hamilton 26:148

Stern, Daniel
James Baldwin 17:33
Paul Bowles 2:79
Margaret Drabble 22:120
Joanne Greenberg 7:134
Marjorie Kellogg 2:223
Jakov Lind 4:292
Bernard Malamud 3:324
Chaim Potok 2:339
Ann Quin 6:441
Piri Thomas 17:497
Paul West 7:523
Elie Wiesel 3:529

Stern, David
Robert Kotlowitz 4:275
Amos Oz 5:334

Stern, Frederick C.
Thomas McGrath 28:278

Stern, Gerald
Gil Orlovitz 22:335

Stern, J. P.
Günter Grass 22:192
Eric Rohmer 16:537

Stern, James
William Golding 17:158

Stern, Margaret
Helen MacInnes 27:278

Sterne, Richard C.
Octavio Paz 10:391

Sterne, Richard Clark
Jerome Weidman 7:517

Stetler, Charles
Richard Brautigan 12:67
James Purdy 4:423

Stevens, George
T. S. Stribling 23:443

Stevens, Georgiana G.
Vera Brittain 23:90

Stevens, Mark
David Byrne 26:94

Stevens, Peter
A. R. Ammons 8:14
Margaret Atwood 4:24
Patrick Lane 25:283
Dorothy Livesay 15:339
A. W. Purdy 3:408

Stevens, Shane
Ronald L. Fair 18:139
William Kennedy 28:203
John Rechy 7:356
Paul Theroux 28:423

Stevens, Wallace
Marianne Moore 10:347

Stevenson, Anne
Elizabeth Bishop 1:35
Peter Davison 28:103
Michael Hamburger 14:235
Seamus Heaney 25:242
Barbara Howes 15:290
Elizabeth Jennings 14:292, 293
Marge Piercy 27:376

David Plante 23:343
Peter Porter 13:453
F. T. Prince 22:338
Muriel Rukeyser 15:457
May Swenson 14:521
R. S. Thomas 13:544
Charles Tomlinson 13:548

Stevenson, David L.
James Jones 3:260
Jack Kerouac 2:226
William Styron 1:329

Stevenson, Drew
Lois Duncan 26:105
Kin Platt 26:355

Stevenson, Patrick
W. R. Rodgers 7:377

Stevenson, Warren
Hugh MacLennan 14:343

Stevick, Philip
John Barth 14:57
Donald Barthelme 8:53
Wayne C. Booth 24:93
William S. Burroughs 5:93
William H. Gass 8:247
Jerzy Kosinski 6:283
Jan Stafford 4:518
Kurt Vonnegut, Jr. 5:465

Stewart, Alastair
Kon Ichikawa 20:176

Stewart, Corbet
Paul Celan 10:102

Stewart, David H.
George Steiner 24:437

Stewart Douglas
Robert D. FitzGerald 19:175

Stewart, Garrett
Buster Keaton 20:197
Steven Spielberg 20:361

Stewart, Harry E.
Jean Genet 10:225; 14:201

Stewart, Ian
Françoise Sagan 17:428

Stewart, J.I.M.
Compton Mackenzie 18:316

Stewart, John L.
John Crowe Ransom 2:362; 24:367

Stewart, Robert Sussman
Heinrich Böll 2:67

Stewart, Ruth Weeden
William Mayne 12:387

Stiller, Nikki
Louis Simpson 9:486

Stilwell, Robert L.
A. R. Ammons 3:10
Sylvia Plath 1:269
Jon Silkin 2:395
James Wright 3:540

Stimpson, Catharine R.
Thom Gunn 18:199
Tillie Olsen 13:432
Marge Piercy 6:403
J.R.R. Tolkien 1:338
Edmund White III 27:481

Stineback, David C.
Allen Tate 9:525

Stinnett, Caskie
S. J. Perelman 15:419

Stinson, John J.
Anthony Burgess 4:82

Stitt, Peter
A. R. Ammons 25:41
Wendell Berry 27:35
Linda Pastan 27:370
Katha Pollitt 28:367
Dave Smith 22:387
Charles Wright 28:458

Stitt, Peter A.
John Ashbery 13:34
John Berryman 10:46
Daniel Halpern 14:232
William Heyen 13:282; 18:232
David Ignatow 14:277
James Merrill 18:330
Louis Simpson 7:429
Mark Strand 18:521
Robert Penn Warren 10:519
Charles Wright 13:614
James Wright 10:542

Stock, Irvin
Saul Bellow 2:50
Mary McCarthy 1:206

Stock, Robert
Theodore Weiss 14:555

Stocking, Marion Kingston
Galway Kinnell 1:168
Gary Snyder 1:318

Stoelting, Winifred L.
Ernest J. Gaines 18:165

Stokes, Eric
Kamala Markandaya 8:378

Stokes, Geoffrey
John Cheever 25:120
Len Deighton 22:117
Stanley Elkin 14:158
Edward Hoagland 28:186
John le Carré 15:325
Phil Ochs 17:335
Frank O'Connor 23:332
Robert Stone 23:428
Richard Yates 23:482

Stoler, Peter
Douglas Adams 27:15

Stoltzfus, Ben F.
Ernest Hemingway 13:279
Alain Robbe-Grillet 1:285; 14:456

Stolz, Herbert J.
Larry Kettelkamp 12:307

Stone, Chuck
Garry Trudeau 12:590

Stone, Elizabeth
John Fowles 9:213
John Gardner 8:234
Cynthia Macdonald 13:355; 19:290
Joan Micklin Silver 20:344
Lily Tomlin 17:520

Stone, Laurie
Margaret Atwood 15:38
Max Frisch 9:217
Elizabeth Hardwick 13:266
Shirley Hazzard 18:219
Mary McCarthy 24:348
Anaïs Nin 8:423
Anne Roiphe 9:455
Dalton Trumbo 19:447
Tom Wolfe 15:584

Stone, Robert
William Kotzwinkle 14:309
Peter Matthiessen 5:274

Stone, Rochelle K.
Tadeusz Różewicz 23:362

Stone, Wilfred
E. M. Forster 15:229

Stone, William B.
Alice Munro 19:347

Stoneback, H. R.
William Faulkner 8:213

Stonehill, Brian
Vladimir Nabokov 23:310

Stones, Rosemary
Virginia Hamilton 26:152
Philippa Pearce 21:291

Stonier, G. W.
Charles Chaplin 16:187

Storch, R. F.
Harold Pinter 6:409

Storey, Mark
Stevie Smith 25:418

Storey, Robert
David Mamet 15:357

Storr, Catherine
Eilís Dillon 17:98
Leon Garfield 12:221

Story, Jack Trevor
C. P. Snow 6:517

Stothard, Peter
Lawrence Durrell 13:188

Stott, Jon C.
Kevin Major 26:288

Stouck, David
Marie-Claire Blais 2:63
Hugh MacLennan 2:257

Stourton, James
Monty Python 21:228

Stout, Janis P.
Larry McMurtry 27:329

Stout, Rex
Laura Z. Hobson 25:270

Stover, Leon E.
Frank Herbert 12:276

Stowers, Bonnie
Hortense Calisher 4:88
Saul Maloff 5:271

Strachan, W. J.
Sylvia Townsend Warner 19:460

Stracley, Julia
Rhys Davies **23**:142

Strakhovsky, Leonid I.
Anna Akhmatova **25**:23

Strandberg, Victor H.
Cynthia Ozick **28**:353
John Updike **13**:557
Robert Penn Warren **13**:573

Stratford, Philip
Graham Greene **6**:212

Straub, Peter
Michael Ayrton **7**:19
Beryl Bainbridge **8**:36
James Baldwin **4**:43
J. G. Ballard **3**:35
Donald Barthelme **3**:44
John Gregory Dunne **28**:123
Brian Glanville **6**:202
Hermann Hesse **6**:237
Julius Horwitz **14**:266
Jack Kerouac **3**:266
Francis King **8**:321
Margaret Laurence **6**:290
Olivia Manning **5**:273
Thomas McGuane **7**:213
Michael Mewshaw **9**:376
James A. Michener **5**:291
Anaïs Nin **8**:419
Joyce Carol Oates **9**:402
Flann O'Brien **4**:385
Simon Raven **14**:442
Simone Schwarz-Bart **7**:404
Isaac Bashevis Singer **6**:509
Richard G. Stern **4**:523
John Updike **5**:457
Morris L. West **6**:563

Strauch, Carl F.
J. D. Salinger **12**:505

Strauss, Harold
James M. Cain **28**:44
Taylor Caldwell **28**:56
Rhys Davies **23**:141
Dalton Trumbo **19**:44

Strauss, Theodore
Rouben Mamoulian **16**:424

Strawson, Galen
Michel Tournier **23**:454

Strawson, P. F.
George Steiner **24**:436

Strebel, Elizabeth Grottle
Jean Renoir **20**:309

Street, Douglas O.
Lawrence Ferlinghetti **6**:183

Strehle, Susan
John Gardner **10**:218

Stresau, Hermann
Thornton Wilder **15**:571

Strick, Philip
Ingmar Bergman **16**:80
Werner Herzog **16**:330
Kon Ichikawa **20**:182
Nagisa Oshima **20**:246
Pier Paolo Pasolini **20**:264
Jerzy Skolimowski **20**:348
Andrzej Wajda **16**:580

Peter Weir **20**:424

Strong, Jonathan
David Plante **23**:342

Strong, L.A.G.
John Masefield **11**:356

Stroupe, John H.
Jean Anouilh **13**:22

Strouse, Jean
Bob Dylan **12**:185
Joyce Maynard **23**:290

Strout, Cushing
William Styron **5**:420

Strozier, Robert M.
Peter De Vries **7**:78
S. J. Perelman **5**:337
P. G. Wodehouse **5**:517

Struthers, J. R. (Tim)
Jack Hodgins **23**:235
Hugh Hood **28**:191

Struve, Gleb
Ilya Ehrenburg **18**:131
Vladimir Nabokov **1**:241

Struve, Nikita
Aleksandr I. Solzhenitsyn **7**:433

Stuart, Alexander
Ralph Bakshi **26**:72
Richard O'Brien **17**:323
Pier Paolo Pasolini **20**:266

Stuart, Dabney
Ted Hughes **2**:201

Stubblefield, Charles
Sylvia Plath **1**:270

Stubbs, G. T.
Rosemary Sutcliff **26**:433

Stubbs, Harry C.
Isaac Asimov **26**:51
Melvin Berger **12**:38
Franklyn M. Branley **21**:20, 21, 23
Roy A. Gallant **17**:129, 131, 132
Alvin Silverstein and Virginia B. Silverstein **17**:451, 454

Stubbs, Helen
William Mayne **12**:399

Stubbs, Jean
Julio Cortázar **2**:102
Daphne du Maurier **6**:147
George Garrett **3**:193
Elizabeth Hardwick **13**:265
Eleanor Hibbert **7**:155
Anaïs Nin **8**:421

Stubbs, John C.
John Hawkes **1**:138

Stubbs, Patricia
Muriel Spark **3**:466

Stubing, John L.
Len Deighton **22**:119

Stuckey, Sterling
Sterling A. Brown **23**:98

Stuckey, W. J.
Pearl S. Buck **18**:76

Stuewe, Paul
Joan Barfoot **18**:35
Ernest K. Gann **23**:167
Stephen King **26**:237
Ted Mooney **25**:330
Ernesto Sabato **23**:382

Stull, William L.
William S. Burroughs **15**:111

Stumpf, Thomas
Hayden Carruth **7**:41
Daniel Mark Epstein **7**:97
Ishmael Reed **5**:368
Muriel Rukeyser **6**:479

Stupple, A. James
Ray Bradbury **10**:69

Sturgeon, Ray
Joni Mitchell **12**:443

Sturgeon, Theodore
Poul Anderson **15**:10
Isaac Asimov **3**:16
Michael Crichton **2**:108
Harlan Ellison **13**:202
Robert A. Heinlein **26**:178
Frank Herbert **12**:276
Barry N. Malzberg **7**:208

Sturm, T. L.
Robert D. FitzGerald **19**:180

Sturrock, John
Jorge Amado **13**:12
Roland Barthes **24**:33
Jorge Luis Borges **13**:105
Peter De Vries **3**:125
Gabriel García Márquez **8**:233; **10**:217
Alain Robbe-Grillet **8**:454
Claude Simon **15**:486
Michel Tournier **23**:453
Monique Wittig **22**:476

Styron, William
Terry Southern **7**:453

Subramani
W. Somerset Maugham **15**:368

Sucharitkul, Somtow
Gene Wolfe **25**:476

Suczek, Barbara
John Lennon and Paul McCartney **12**:369

Suderman, Elmer F.
John Updike **2**:443; **3**:488

Sugg, Alfred R.
Richard Lester **20**:222

Sugrue, Thomas
Riccardo Bacchelli **19**:31
Rhys Davies **23**:145
Ogden Nash **23**:318, 319
Mary Renault **17**:390

Suhl, Benjamin
Jean-Paul Sartre **24**:410

Sukenick, Lynn
Maya Angelou **12**:12
Doris Lessing **3**:288
Anaïs Nin **8**:421
Robert L. Peters **7**:303

Sukenick, Ronald
Carlos Castaneda **12**:89
Rudolph Wurlitzer **2**:483

Suleiman, Jo-Ann D.
Thor Heyerdahl **26**:194

Sullivan, Anita T.
Ray Bradbury **3**:85

Sullivan, Dan
Edward Albee **25**:40
Charles Fuller **25**:179

Sullivan, Jack
Richard Condon **8**:150
Robin Cook **14**:131
Guy Davenport, Jr. **14**:142
Paul Horgan **9**:279
Stephen King **12**:309
John Knowles **26**:263
Wright Morris **18**:354
J. B. Priestley **9**:442
Susan Richards Shreve **23**:404
Peter Straub **28**:410
Julian Symons **14**:524

Sullivan, Kevin
Thomas Kinsella **19**:251
Flann O'Brien **5**:316
Sean O'Casey **5**:320
Frank O'Connor **23**:326
Gil Orlovitz **22**:333

Sullivan, Mary
B. S. Johnson **6**:262
William Sansom **6**:483
Fay Weldon **6**:562

Sullivan, Nancy
May Swenson **4**:534

Sullivan, Patrick
Frederick Wiseman **20**:473

Sullivan, Peggy
Gunnel Beckman **26**:87
Barbara Corcoran **17**:72
Lois Duncan **26**:101, 102
Lee Kingman **17**:244
Richard Peck **21**:295

Sullivan, Richard
Harper Lee **12**:340
Colin MacInnes **23**:282
William Maxwell **19**:306
William Mitchell **25**:321
Piers Paul Read **25**:376
Betty Smith **19**:423
Mary Stolz **12**:547

Sullivan, Rosemary
Marie-Claire Blais **6**:81
Patrick Lane **25**:286
P. K. Page **18**:378
Theodore Roethke **19**:398

Sullivan, Ruth
Ken Kesey **6**:278

Sullivan, Tom R.
William Golding **8**:249
Michel Tournier **6**:538

Sullivan, Victoria
Saul Bellow **8**:76

Sullivan, Walter
Donald Barthelme 1:19
Saul Bellow 8:81
Elizabeth Bowen 11:64
Eleanor Clark 19:106
Harry Crews 23:131
Guy Davenport, Jr. 6:124
Margaret Drabble 8:184
Andre Dubus 13:182
George Garnett 11:219
William Golding 2:166, 168
Graham Greene 6:219
Richard Hughes 11:278
Bernard Malamud 1:200
William Maxwell 19:309
Joyce Carol Oates 6:368; 9:405
Flannery O'Connor 2:317; 21:268
John O'Hara 6:385
Reynolds Price 13:464
V. S. Pritchett 13:465
Jean Rhys 6:456
Alan Sillitoe 6:501
William Trevor 14:535
Anne Tyler 11:553

Sullivan, Wilson
Irving Stone 7:470

Sullivan, Zohreh Tawakuli
Iris Murdoch 6:346; 11:386

Sullivan-Daly, Tess
Michael Mott 15:380

Sultan, Stanley
Ezra Pound 7:331

Sultanik, Aaron
E. L. Doctorow 18:120
Lina Wertmüller 16:595

Suplee, Curt
Thomas Berger 11:46

Surette, Leon
George Bowering 15:84

Sussex, Elizabeth
Lindsay Anderson 20:15
Satyajit Ray 16:482
Agnès Varda 16:555
Lina Wertmüller 16:586
Billy Wilder 20:460

Sutcliffe, Thomas
Robert Stone 23:430
Peter Straub 28:411

Suter, Anthony
Basil Bunting 10:83, 84

Suther, Judith D.
Eugène Ionesco 11:292

Sutherland, Donald
Rafael Alberti 7:10
Octavio Paz 10:389
St.-John Perse 4:399
Francis Ponge 6:422

Sutherland, Fraser
Elizabeth Spencer 22:405

Sutherland, J. A.
Philip José Farmer 19:168

Sutherland, John
Len Deighton 22:118
Robert Finch 18:153
P. K. Page 18:376
Anatoli Rybakov 23:374

Sutherland, Ronald
Roch Carrier 13:140
Hugh MacLennan 14:342

Sutherland, Sam
Elvis Costello 21:67

Sutherland, Stuart
A. Alvarez 13:8
Peter De Vries 10:137; 28:107

Sutherland, Zena
E. M. Almedingen 12:3, 4, 7
Honor Arundel 17:13
Gunnel Beckman 26:87
Melvin Berger 12:39, 40, 41
Judy Blume 12:44
Frank Bonham 12:49, 50, 51, 52, 53, 54, 55
H. F. Brinsmead 21:26
Betty Cavanna 12:102
Alice Childress 12:107
Mavis Thorpe Clark 12:132
Barbara Corcoran 17:74, 76, 78
Paula Danziger 21:84, 85
Lois Duncan 26:101, 103, 106, 108
Babbis Friis-Baastad 12:214
Roy A. Gallant 17:132
Sol Gordon 26:137
Rosa Guy 26:142, 144, 145
Virginia Hamilton 26:149
Nat Hentoff 26:184
Isabelle Holland 21:148, 149, 153, 154
Mollie Hunter 21:157
Margaret O. Hyde 21:178, 179, 180
Jesse Jackson 12:290, 291
Diana Wynne Jones 26:226
M. E. Kerr 12:298
Larry Kettelkamp 12:305, 306, 307
Lee Kingman 17:247
Joseph Krumgold 12:318, 321
Madeleine L'Engle 12:350
Sonia Levitin 17:264, 265
Robert Lipsyte 21:212
Anne McCaffrey 17:282, 284
Milton Meltzer 26:298, 302, 307
Nicholosa Mohr 12:447
John Neufeld 17:308, 310
Emily Cheney Neville 12:450, 451, 452
Katherine Paterson 12:484, 486
Richard Peck 21:296, 298, 299, 300
Robert Newton Peck 17:338, 339, 340, 342
Kin Platt 26:350, 351, 352, 353, 354, 356
Josephine Poole 17:373
Alvin Silverstein and Virginia B. Silverstein 17:451, 454, 455
Zilpha Keatley Snyder 17:470, 473, 475
Mary Stolz 12:551, 553, 554, 555
Noel Streatfeild 21:403, 408, 409, 412, 415
Rosemary Sutcliff 26:436
Mildred D. Taylor 21:419
Colin Thiele 17:495, 496
John R. Tunis 12:599
Lenora Mattingly Weber 12:634
Rosemary Wells 12:639
Jessamyn West 17:552
Hilma Wolitzer 17:563
Paul Zindel 26:470, 472, 474

Sutton, Graham
W. Somerset Maugham 11:367

Sutton, Horace
S. J. Perelman 23:335

Sutton, Martyn
Joan Armatrading 17:10

Sutton, Walter
Allen Ginsberg 4:181
Robert Lowell 4:303
Thomas Merton 3:336
Marianne Moore 4:364
Ezra Pound 3:395

Suvin, Darko
Eric Bentley 24:49
Arkadii Strugatskii and Boris Strugatskii 27:432

Svensson, Frances
Vine Deloria, Jr. 21:114

Swados, Harvey
Walter Van Tilburg Clark 28:78
Howard Fast 23:156
David Ignatow 4:249

Swanbrow, Diane J.
John Knowles 26:263

Swann, Brian
Theodore Roethke 19:396

Swartley, Ariel
Joan Armatrading 17:8
Walter Becker and Donald Fagen 26:85
Joni Mitchell 12:442
Bruce Springsteen 17:490

Swartney, Joyce
Charles M. Schulz 12:533

Swayze, Walter E.
Robertson Davies 25:131

Sweeney, Patricia Runk
M. E. Kerr 12:301

Sweet, Louise
Frederick Wiseman 20:477

Sweeting, Adam
Paul Weller 26:447

Swenson, John
Ray Davies 21:99
Willie Nelson 17:303
Peter Townshend 17:533, 540
Frank Zappa 17:591

Swenson, May
Ben Belitt 22:49
Robin Morgan 2:294
Muriel Rukeyser 27:408
Anne Sexton 2:392
W. D. Snodgrass 2:406

Swift, John N.
John Cheever 15:129

Swift, Jonathan
Gerome Ragni and James Rado 17:385

Swift, Pat
George Barker 8:44

Swigg, Richard
E. M. Forster 9:209
Philip Larkin 9:324

Swigger, Ronald T.
Raymond Queneau 2:359

Swinden, Patrick
C. P. Snow 4:503

Swing, Raymond
John R. Tunis 12:596

Swingewood, Alan
Lucien Goldmann 24:244

Swink, Helen
William Faulkner 3:154

Swiss, Thomas
Donald Justice 19:234

Sykes, Christopher
Aldous Huxley 4:244; 8:303

Sykes, Gerald
Jessie Redmon Fauset 19:169
William Gibson 23:173
Pamela Hansford Johnson 27:219, 220

Sykes, S. W.
Claude Simon 9:483

Sylvester, R. D.
Joseph Brodsky 13:114

Sylvester, William
Daniel Hoffman 23:239

Symons, Julian
Eric Ambler 4:18
W. H. Auden 2:28
Beryl Bainbridge 18:34
John Berryman 2:59
Edward Brathwaite 11:66
John Dickson Carr 3:101
John Cheever 8:140
Agatha Christie 6:107; 8:140; 12:121, 126
John Creasey 11:134
C. Day Lewis 6:129
Len Deighton 4:119
Friedrich Dürrenmatt 4:141
Ian Fleming 3:159
Dick Francis 22:154
Roy Fuller 4:178
Graham Greene 27:175
Dashiell Hammett 3:219
Lillian Hellman 4:222
Patricia Highsmith 2:193; 4:225
Chester Himes 4:229
Evan Hunter 11:279

P. D. James 18:276
Eliabeth Jennings 14:292
Pamela Hansford Johnson
 27:222
John le Carré 3:282
John D. MacDonald 3:307
Ross Macdonald 3:307
Mary McCarthy 3:326
Henry Miller 2:281
Ellery Queen 3:421
Simon Raven 14:442
Kenneth Rexroth 11:473
Laura Riding 3:431
Tadeusz Różewicz 23:358
Georges Simenon 3:451; 8:487;
 18:485
Louis Simpson 4:498
Maj Sjöwall 7:501
C. P. Snow 4:500
Mickey Spillane 3:469
J.I.M. Stewart 14:511
Rex Stout 3:471
William Styron 15:528
Per Wahlöö 7:501
Robert Penn Warren 4:577
Patrick White 3:523
Angus Wilson 3:536
Yevgeny Yevtushenko 26:462

Syrkin, Marie
Henry Roth 6:472

Szanto, George H.
Alain Robbe-Grillet 1:288

Szogyi, Alex
Lillian Hellman 2:187
Isaac Bashevis Singer 11:501

Szporluk, Mary Ann
Vladimir Voinovich 10:504

Szuhay, Joseph A.
Sandra Scoppettone 26:405

Tabachnick, Stephen E.
Conrad Aiken 5:9

Taëni, Rainer
Rolf Hochhuth 18:252

Tagliabue, John
Muriel Rukeyser 27:414

Tait, Michael
James Reaney 13:472

Takiff, Jonathan
Lily Tomlin 17:521

Talbot, Emile J.
Marie-Claire Blais 22:60
Roch Carrier 13:144

Talbott, Strobe
Aleksandr I. Solzhenitsyn 4:516

Taliaferro, Frances
Frederick Busch 18:85
Laurie Colwin 13:157
Andre Dubus 13:184
Stanley Elkin 27:125
Nadine Gordimer 5:147
Maureen Howard 14:268
Tom McHale 5:283

Tallant, Robert
Doris Betts 28:32
Elizabeth Spencer 22:399

Tallenay, J. L.
Charles Chaplin 16:195

Tallman, Warren
Earle Birney 11:50
Ernest Buckler 13:118
Robert Creeley 11:135
Robert Duncan 15:187
Jack Kerouac 14:304
John Rechy 14:445
Mordecai Richler 3:430
Sinclair Ross 13:490

Tambling, Jeremy
Brian Aldiss 14:15
J.I.M. Stewart 14:513

Tamkin, Linda
Anaïs Nin 14:387

Tanner, Alain
Luchino Visconti 16:561

Tanner, Stephen L.
Ernest Hemingway 8:288

Tanner, Tony
Walter Abish 22:19
John Barth 1:17; 2:37; 14:55
Donald Barthelme 2:40
Richard Brautigan 12:66
William S. Burroughs 2:92
William Gaddis 3:177
John Gardner 2:152
John Hawkes 2:185; 7:143
Ernest Hemingway 10:266
Norman Mailer 1:189
Bernard Malamud 2:267
James Purdy 2:351; 4:422
Thomas Pynchon 6:430, 432
Philip Roth 22:357
Susan Sontag 1:322
John Updike 2:445
Kurt Vonnegut, Jr. 12:606

Taplin, Oliver
Edward Bond 23:67

Tapply, Robert S.
Roy A. Gallant 17:128

Tapscott, Stephen
Friedrich Dürrenmatt 11:173
Hugh MacDiarmid 19:288
Stevie Smith 25:417

Tarantino, Michael
Marguerite Duras 20:100, 101
Elaine May 16:437

Targan, Barry
Scott Sommer 25:425

Tarkka, Pekka
Hannu Salama 18:461

Tarn, Nathaniel
William H. Gass 1:114

Tarratt, Margaret
Nagisa Oshima 20:246
Gordon Parks 16:459
Luchino Visconti 16:568
Frederick Wiseman 20:474

Tarshis, Jerome
J. G. Ballard 3:34

Tate, Allen
Edward Dahlberg 14:134
Donald Davidson 13:167
John Crowe Ransom 2:363;
 5:364
I. A. Richards 24:387
T. S. Stribling 23:443
Eudora Welty 1:362

Tate, George S.
Halldór Laxness 25:299

Tate, J. O.
Flannery O'Connor 13:421
Alexander Theroux 25:434

Tate, Robert S., Jr.
Albert Camus 1:54

Tatham, Campbell
John Barth 1:18
Raymond Federman 6:181
Thomas Pynchon 2:354

Tatum, Charles M.
José Donoso 11:146

Taubman, Howard
Enid Bagnold 25:77
James Baldwin 17:27, 31
Larry Gelbart 21:125
William Gibson 23:179
Garson Kanin 22:230
Arthur Kopit 18:286
Gerome Ragni and James Rado
 17:379

Taubman, Robert
John Barth 27:29
Patrick Boyle 19:67
William S. Burroughs 22:85
Cynthia Ozick 7:287
Sylvia Plath 17:345
D. M. Thomas 22:419
John Updike 23:477

Taus, Roger
William Everson 14:167

Tavris, Carol
Kate Wilhelm 7:538

Taylor, Clyde
Imamu Amiri Baraka 5:47

Taylor, D. W.
Eilís Dillon 17:99

Taylor, David
John Rechy 18:443

Taylor, Eleanor Ross
Elizabeth Bishop 15:59
Sylvia Plath 17:347

Taylor, F. H. Griffin
George Garrett 3:192; 11:219
Robert Lowell 1:181
Theodore Weiss 3:516

Taylor, Gordon O.
Mary McCarthy 14:358

Taylor, Harry H.
William Golding 17:170

Taylor, Henry
Ben Belitt 22:50
Marvin Bell 8:64
Irving Feldman 7:103
X. J. Kennedy 8:319
William Meredith 13:373
Howard Nemerov 6:363
Flannery O'Connor 1:258
John Hall Wheelock 14:570
James Wright 5:521

Taylor, Jane
Galway Kinnell 1:168

Taylor, John Russell
Lindsay Anderson 20:17
Robert Anderson 23:32
Michelangelo Antonioni 20:28
John Arden 6:4
Alan Ayckbourn 5:34
Brendan Behan 11:44
Ingmar Bergman 16:50
Edward Bond 4:69
Robert Bresson 16:108
Mel Brooks 12:78
Luis Buñuel 16:132
Claude Chabrol 16:180
Vittorio De Sica 20:90
Marguerite Duras 20:99
Federico Fellini 16:274, 281,
 288
Alfred Hitchcock 16:344
John Huston 20:170, 171
Ann Jellicoe 27:207
Stanley Kubrick 16:388
Fritz Lang 20:208
Hugh Leonard 19:282
David Mercer 5:283
John Mortimer 28:283
Peter Nichols 5:305
Joe Orton 4:388
Pier Paolo Pasolini 20:266
Harold Pinter 11:436
Terence Rattigan 7:354
Satyajit Ray 16:490
Alain Resnais 16:502
Peter Shaffer 14:484, 485;
 18:477
Ntozake Shange 25:399
Robert Shaw 5:390
Tom Stoppard 4:524
David Storey 4:528
C. P. Taylor 27:440, 442
Andy Warhol 20:423
E. A. Whitehead 5:488
Billy Wilder 20:461

Taylor, Joseph H.
Milton Meltzer 26:298

Taylor, Katharine
Sylvia Ashton-Warner 19:21

Taylor, Lewis Jerome, Jr.
Walker Percy 6:399

Taylor, Mark
W. H. Auden 3:27
John Berryman 3:72
Tom McHale 5:282
Walker Percy 3:378
Earl Rovit 7:383
Edmund Wilson 8:550
Richard Yates 8:555

Taylor, Michael
Timothy Findley 27:141
Leon Rooke 25:391
Gillian Tindall 7:474

Taylor, Mildred D.
Mildred D. Taylor 21:419

Taylor, Nora E.
Isabelle Holland 21:149, 151
Noel Streatfeild 21:404

Taylor, Rhoda E.
Margaret O. Hyde 21:178

Taylor, Stephen
John Huston 20:169

Taylor, William L.
J.R.R. Tolkien 12:569

Tchen, John
Milton Meltzer 26:307

Tearson, Michael
Janis Ian 21:187

Tebbel, John
Charles M. Schulz 12:527

Téchiné, André
Carl Theodor Dreyer 16:268

Teich, Nathaniel
Pier Paolo Pasolini 20:267

Temple, Joanne
John Berryman 3:72

Temple, Ruth Z.
C. S. Lewis 14:321
Nathalie Sarraute 1:303; 2:386

Templeton, Joan
Sean O'Casey 11:406

Tenenbaum, Louis
Italo Calvino 5:97

Tennant, Catherine
Joyce Maynard 23:289

Tennant, Emma
J. G. Ballard 6:28
Italo Calvino 5:100
Thomas Hinde 6:242
Penelope Mortimer 5:298

Teo, Elizabeth A.
Jade Snow Wong 17:567

Terbille, Charles I.
Saul Bellow 6:52
Joyce Carol Oates 6:371

Teresa, Vincent
Mario Puzo 2:352

Terrien, Samuel
Fernando Arrabal 2:15

Terris, Susan
Rosemary Wells 12:639

Terris, Virginia R.
Muriel Rukeyser 27:410

Terry, Arthur
Vicente Aleixandre 9:17
Salvador Espriu 9:192
Octavio Paz 10:393

Terry, C. V.
Frank B. Gilbreth, Jr. and Ernestine Gilbreth Carey 17:154

Terry, Sara
Helen MacInnes 27:283

Tessitore, John
Francis Ford Coppola 16:247

Testa, Bart
Gordon Lightfoot 26:281
Frank Zappa 17:591

Testa, Daniel
Rudolfo A. Anaya 23:22

Tetlow, Joseph A.
William X. Kienzle 25:274

Teunissen, John T.
Doris Lessing 6:293

Thale, Jerome
C. P. Snow 19:425

Thatcher, A.
Paul Zindel 26:481

Thelwell, Mike
James Baldwin 17:36

Therese, Sister M.
Marianne Moore 1:229

Theroux, Paul
Breyten Breytenbach 23:85
Frederick Buechner 2:83
Anthony Burgess 5:89
John Cheever 7:48
Peter De Vries 3:126; 7:76
Lawrence Durrell 6:151
George MacDonald Fraser 7:106
Nadine Gordimer 5:147
Shirley Ann Grau 4:209
Graham Greene 3:213
Ernest Hemingway 6:229
Susan B. Hill 4:226
Erica Jong 4:264
Yashar Kemal 14:299
John Knowles 4:272
Milan Kundera 4:276
Mary McCarthy 5:277
Yukio Mishima 4:356
Brian Moore 3:341; 7:236
V. S. Naipaul 4:373, 374; 7:252
Christopher Okigbo 25:349
Cynthia Ozick 7:288
S. J. Perelman 9:415
Jean Rhys 2:372
Georges Simenon 18:487
Gilbert Sorrentino 22:391
David Storey 4:529
Peter Taylor 4:542
John Updike 13:563
Gore Vidal 22:437
Kurt Vonnegut, Jr. 5:470

Theroux, Phyllis
Jean Kerr 22:258

Thesen, Sharon Fawcett
Gilbert Sorrentino 14:498

Thiher, Allen
Fernando Arrabal 9:33
Luis Buñuel 16:149
Louis-Ferdinand Céline 4:101
Henri de Montherlant 19:328
François Truffaut 20:402

Thody, Philip
Roland Barthes 24:30
Albert Camus 4:91; 14:116
Jean-Paul Sartre 4:476; 24:407

Thomas, Brian
P. G. Wodehouse 22:485

Thomas, Carolyn
David Jones 7:191

Thomas, Clara
Margaret Laurence 3:281; 13:342

Thomas, D. M.
Anna Akhmatova 25:29
Martin Booth 13:103
Francine du Plessix Gray 22:202
Yuri Krotkov 19:265
John Matthias 9:362

Thomas, David
James Baldwin 5:43

Thomas, David P.
Christopher Isherwood 1:157

Thomas, John
Bernardo Bertolucci 16:84
Tod Browning 16:122
Jean-Luc Godard 20:134

Thomas, John Alfred
Josef von Sternberg 20:369

Thomas, M. Wynn
Katherine Anne Porter 10:394

Thomas, Michael M.
Paul E. Erdman 25:155

Thomas, Noel L.
Martin Walser 27:464

Thomas, Paul
Rainer Werner Fassbinder 20:109
Lina Wertmüller 16:593

Thomas, Peter
John Betjeman 6:65
Robert Kroetsch 5:220; 23:275

Thomas, Ross
Herbert Gold 14:209

Thomas, S. L.
John R. Tunis 12:592

Thompson, Craig
Vera Brittain 23:91

Thompson, Dody Weston
Pearl S. Buck 18:78

Thompson, Eric
Matt Cohen 19:112
T. S. Eliot 2:125; 24:172

Thompson, Howard
Robert Altman 16:19
Gretchen Cryer 21:79
Brian De Palma 20:73
Garry Marshall 17:274
Martin Scorsese 20:324
Jerzy Skolimowski 20:347
Andy Warhol 20:417

Thompson, John
James Baldwin 17:34
John Berryman 3:71
Bruce Chatwin 28:73
Irving Feldman 7:102
Daniel Fuchs 22:156
Natalia Ginzburg 5:141
Nadine Gordimer 18:191
Joseph Heller 5:176
Robert Lowell 9:338
Amos Oz 5:335
John Updike 13:560
Richard Yates 23:480

Thompson, Kent
John Gardner 28:162
Hugh Hood 15:284; 28:188

Thompson, Lawrence
Robert Frost 13:224

Thompson, Leslie M.
Stephen Spender 10:487

Thompson, Mildred
June Jordan 23:255

Thompson, R. J.
John Hawkes 4:214
Mary Lavin 4:282

Thompson, Robert B.
Robert Frost 13:230

Thompson, Toby
Bruce Jay Friedman 5:126

Thompson, Tyler
Vine Deloria, Jr. 21:109

Thomsen, Christian Braad
Rainer Werner Fassbinder 20:105

Thomson, David
Paddy Chayefsky 23:118
Fritz Lang 20:213

Thomson, George H.
J.R.R. Tolkien 1:335

Thomson, Jean C.
H. F. Brinsmead 21:28
Barbara Corcoran 17:72
Eilís Dillon 17:97
James D. Forman 21:117
Leon Garfield 12:216
Madeleine L'Engle 12:347
John Neufeld 17:307, 308
Philippa Pearce 21:282

Thomson, Peter
Harold Pinter 15:422

Thomson, R.D.B.
Andrei Voznesensky 15:554

Thorburn, David
Renata Adler 8:7
Ann Beattie 8:57
Judith Guest 8:254
Norman Mailer 3:315
Thomas Pynchon 3:416

Thorp, Katherine
Isaac Asimov 26:57

Thorp, Willard
W. D. Snodgrass 2:404

Thorpe, Michael
Doris Lessing 3:291

Thurley, Geoffrey
Charles Simic 22:379

Thurman, Judith
Joyce Carol Oates 6:374
Jean Rhys 6:456
Laura Riding 7:374
Susan Fromberg Schaeffer 22:368
Agnès Varda 16:560

Thurston, Robert
Fritz Leiber 25:304

Thwaite, Ann
E. M. Almedingen 12:5

Thwaite, Anthony
Kōbō Abé 22:14
W. H. Auden 6:24
Charles Causley 7:41
Douglas Dunn 6:148
Shusaku Endo 19:160
Geoffrey Grigson 7:136
Seamus Heaney 7:147; 25:249
David Jones 7:187
Yashar Kemal 14:301
Thomas Keneally 19:242
Philip Larkin 13:335
Derek Mahon 27:287
R. K. Narayan 7:256
Darcy O'Brien 11:405
Sylvia Plath 14:426
C. P. Snow 4:503

Tibbetts, John
Frank Capra 16:165
Josef von Sternberg 20:377

Tickell, Paul
Frank Zappa 17:595

Tiessen, Hildegard E.
Rudy Wiebe 14:572

Tiffin, Chris
Thomas Keneally 19:243

Tiger, Virginia
William Golding 27:166

Tilden, David
M. M. Kaye 28:198

Tillinghast, Richard
Sterling A. Brown 23:101
James Merrill 2:274
Frederick Morgan 23:300
Katha Pollitt 28:368
Adrienne Rich 3:427
Charles Wright 28:460

Tilton, John W.
Anthony Burgess 15:104
Kurt Vonnegut, Jr. 12:614

Timmerman, John H.
C. S. Lewis 14:324

Timms, David
Philip Larkin 5:223

Timpe, Eugene F.
Hermann Hesse 17:210

Tindal, Gillian
Louis-Ferdinand Céline 7:45
Leon Garfield 12:227

Tindall, William York
Samuel Beckett 1:22

Tinkle, Lon
Jean Lee Latham 12:324
Hollis Summers 10:493

Tintner, Adeline R.
Philip Roth 22:355
François Truffaut 20:406

Tipmore, David
Joyce Maynard 23:288

Tisdale, Bob
John Hawkes 4:215

Tiven, Jon
Monty Python 21:226
The Police 26:363, 364

Tobias, Richard
Thomas Kinsella 19:256

Tobias, Richard C.
James Thurber 5:435

Tobin, Patricia
William Faulkner 3:155

Tobin, Richard L.
Lothar-Günther Buchheim 6:101

Todd, Richard
Renata Adler 8:4
Louis Auchincloss 9:54
Donald Barthelme 8:49
Saul Bellow 6:55, 61
Thomas Berger 3:64
Eleanor Bergstein 4:55
Vance Bourjaily 8:104
E. L. Doctorow 6:138
Andre Dubus 13:183
Bruce Jay Friedman 5:126
John Hawkes 4:216
Sue Kaufman 8:317
William Kotzwinkle 5:220
Cormac McCarthy 4:343
Robert Newton Peck 17:337
Walker Percy 8:443
Marge Piercy 6:402
Robert M. Pirsig 6:420
Judith Rossner 6:470
John Updike 7:489
Kurt Vonnegut, Jr. 3:501
Richard Yates 7:555

Todisco, Paula
James D. Forman 21:122

Toeplitz, Krzysztof-Teodor
Jerzy Skolimowski 20:348
Andrzej Wajda 16:579

Toerien, Barend J.
Breyten Breytenbach 23:83, 84
J. M. Coetzee 23:122

Toliver, Harold E.
Robert Frost 4:175

Tolkien, J.R.R.
C. S. Lewis 27:259

Tolomeo, Diane
Flannery O'Connor 21:276

Tolson, Jay
Jakov Lind 27:272

Tomalin, Claire
Beryl Bainbridge 10:15
Charles Newman 2:311
Paul Theroux 5:427

Tonks, Rosemary
Adrienne Rich 3:428

Took, Barry
Monty Python 21:228

Toolan, David S.
Tom Wicker 7:535

Toomajian, Janice
Isaac Asimov 26:59

Torchiana, Donald T.
W. D. Snodgrass 2:404

Tosches, Nick
Mick Jagger and Keith Richard 17:240
Waylon Jennings 21:204, 205
Jim Morrison 17:293
Lou Reed 21:304
Andrew Lloyd Webber and Tim Rice 21:423

Totton, Nick
Beryl Bainbridge 8:37
J. G. Ballard 14:39
Heinrich Böll 9:111
Patrick Boyle 19:68
André Brink 18:67
Gail Godwin 8:249
James Hanley 8:265
Mary Hocking 13:285
Francis King 8:322
Alistair MacLean 13:364
Michael Moorcock 27:349
Iris Murdoch 8:405
Vladimir Nabokov 8:417
David Pownall 10:419
Frederic Raphael 14:437
Piers Paul Read 10:434

Tovey, Roberta
William Kotzwinkle 14:311
Tadeusz Różewicz 23:361

Towers, Robert
Renata Adler 8:4
Donald Barthelme 13:59
Ann Beattie 18:38
William Boyd 28:41
Michael Brodsky 19:69
Anthony Burgess 22:76
Raymond Carver 22:101
John Cheever 8:138; 11:122
Don DeLillo 27:84
E. L. Doctorow 18:127
Stanley Elkin 9:191
John Gardner 8:233
Graham Greene 18:197
Lillian Hellman 18:228
Mark Helprin 22:222
John Irving 23:251
Diane Johnson 13:305
Doris Lessing 15:335
Bernard Malamud 18:319
Bobbie Ann Mason 28:273
Ian McEwan 13:371
Larry McMurtry 7:214
Leonard Michaels 25:317
R. K. Narayan 28:302
Flannery O'Connor 13:422

Walker Percy 8:444; 18:401
Anthony Powell 9:435
V. S. Pritchett 15:444
Philip Roth 9:461; 15:451
Salman Rushdie 23:366
James Salter 7:387
Wilfrid Sheed 10:473
Scott Sommer 25:425
Paul Theroux 8:512; 28:427
John Updike 13:559
Kurt Vonnegut, Jr. 8:533
Alice Walker 27:451
Rebecca West 9:562
William Wharton 18:543

Townley, Rod
Agnes Eckhardt Nixon 21:247

Towns, Saundra
Gwendolyn Brooks 15:93

Townsend, John Rowe
Honor Arundel 17:18
H. F. Brinsmead 21:31
Peter Dickinson 12:172
Esther Forbes 12:211
Leon Garfield 12:222, 224
Alan Garner 17:143
Virginia Hamilton 26:153
Jesse Jackson 12:291
Madeleine L'Engle 12:350
William Mayne 12:397
Andre Norton 12:460
Philippa Pearce 21:289
Rosemary Sutcliff 26:435
Paul Zindel 26:471

Townsend, R. C.
William Golding 17:168

Townshend, Peter
Peter Townshend 17:534

Toynbee, Philip
Arthur Koestler 1:170
Mary Renault 17:399
Mordecai Richler 5:375

Trachtenberg, Alan
Henry Miller 4:351
Tom Wolfe 9:578

Tracy, Honor
Janet Frame 22:144
Graham Greene 3:206

Tracy, Phil
Kingsley Amis 3:9

Tracy, Robert
Benedict Kiely 23:267

Trakin, Roy
Lou Reed 21:321

Traschen, Isadore
William Faulkner 9:201
Robert Frost 26:122

Traub, James
Evelyn Waugh 27:476

Traubitz, Nancy Baker
Tennessee Williams 15:578

Traum, Happy
Van Morrison 21:231

Trease, Geoffrey
  H. F. Brinsmead 21:26
  Leon Garfield 12:216, 217
  William Mayne 12:390

Treece, Henry
  Herbert Read 4:437

Treglown, Jeremy
  Brian Aldiss 14:14
  Brigid Brophy 11:68
  Anthony Burgess 22:75
  Len Deighton 22:116
  Parel Kohout 13:325
  Olivia Manning 19:302
  Joyce Carol Oates 11:403
  Barbara Pym 13:470
  Tom Robbins 9:454
  J.I.M. Stewart 14:512

Trensky, Paul I.
  Václav Havel 25:220

Trevor, William
  Elizabeth Bowen 22:64
  Margaret Drabble 22:122
  Frank O'Connor 23:331

Trewin, J. C.
  Robert Bolt 14:89
  Agatha Christie 12:125

Trickett, Rachel
  Olivia Manning 19:302
  James Purdy 2:349
  Andrew Sinclair 2:401
  Wallace Stegner 9:508
  Angus Wilson 2:473

Trilling, Diana
  Margery Allingham 19:12
  Ilya Ehrenburg 18:131
  Esther Forbes 12:209
  Martha Gellhorn 14:194
  Aldous Huxley 8:304
  Frank O'Connor 14:395
  Jean Rhys 19:392
  Irwin Shaw 7:410
  Betty Smith 19:422

Trilling, Lionel
  E. M. Forster 1:104
  Robert Graves 2:174

Trilling, Roger
  Bob Marley 17:270

Trimbur, John
  Lawrence Ferlinghetti 27:137

Trimpi, Helen P.
  Edgar Bowers 9:121, 122

Trodd, Kenith
  Andrew Sinclair 2:400

Trombetta, Jim
  Lou Reed 21:314

Trotsky, Leon
  André Malraux 13:364

Trotter, Stewart
  Jean Genet 5:137
  Graham Greene 6:220

Trowbridge, Clinton
  John Updike 2:442

Troy, William
  Carl Theodor Dreyer 16:256
  Fritz Lang 20:202
  Josef von Sternberg 20:370

True, Michael D.
  Daniel J. Berrigan 4:58
  Robert Francis 15:236
  Paul Goodman 2:169
  Flannery O'Connor 13:422; 21:271
  Karl Shapiro 15:477

Trueblood, Valerie
  Margaret Atwood 13:43
  Tess Gallagher 18:168
  Gilbert Sorrentino 14:499
  Derek Walcott 14:548

Trueheart, Charles
  John Barth 27:25

Truffaut, François
  Ingmar Bergman 16:70
  Luis Buñuel 16:136
  Frank Capra 16:161
  Charles Chaplin 16:198
  John Ford 16:314
  Alfred Hitchcock 16:341, 346
  Elia Kazan 16:366
  Fritz Lang 20:208
  Agnès Varda 16:553
  Billy Wilder 20:457

Trumbull, Robert
  Thor Heyerdahl 26:193

Truscott, Lucian K.
  Bob Dylan 3:131

Trussler, Simon
  John Arden 15:19

Tsuruta, Kinya
  Shusaku Endo 7:96

Tsvetaeva, Marina
  Boris Pasternak 18:386

Tube, Henry
  Vasily Aksenov 22:26
  Masuji Ibuse 22:226

Tuch, Ronald
  Charles Chaplin 16:204

Tucker, Carll
  Imamu Amiri Baraka 10:19
  Ed Bullins 7:37
  Jules Feiffer 8:216
  Richard Howard 7:169
  Albert Innaurato 21:191
  Robert Lowell 9:338
  Archibald MacLeish 8:363

Tucker, Chris
  Kurt Vonnegut, Jr. 22:451

Tucker, James
  Anthony Powell 7:338; 10:409

Tucker, Kenneth
  Joan Armatrading 17:9
  Walter Becker and Donald Fagen 26:83
  David Byrne 26:96
  Waylon Jennings 21:203
  Elmore Leonard 28:234
  Carly Simon 26:410, 413
  Patti Smith 12:543
  Neil Young 17:576, 580

Tucker, Martin
  Chinua Achebe 3:1
  André Brink 18:67
  Cyprian Ekwensi 4:152
  Nadine Gordimer 3:201
  Jan de Hartog 19:131, 132
  Ernest Hemingway 3:234
  Jerzy Kosinski 1:172
  Bernard Malamud 3:322
  Ezekiel Mphahlele 25:346
  James Ngugi 3:357
  Cynthia Ozick 7:287
  Alan Paton 4:395
  William Plomer 4:406
  James Purdy 28:377
  Raja Rao 25:365
  Ishmael Reed 13:477
  Wole Soyinka 3:462
  Amos Tutuola 5:443
  Laurens van der Post 5:463

Tucker, Nicholas
  Honor Arundel 17:16
  Judy Blume 12:45
  Virginia Hamilton 26:151

Tulip, James
  David Malouf 28:269

Tunis, John R.
  Maia Wojciechowska 26:449, 454

Tunney, Gene
  Budd Schulberg 7:402

Tunstall, Caroline
  Taylor Caldwell 28:61

Tuohy, Frank
  Nadine Gordimer 18:188
  Patrick Kavanagh 22:244
  Jakov Lind 27:270
  Seán O'Faoláin 14:405
  Randolph Stow 23:437

Turan, Kenneth
  Gene Roddenberry 17:414
  Elie Wiesel 11:570

Turco, Lewis
  Edward Brathwaite 11:67
  Robert Hayden 9:270
  Donald Justice 19:232

Turin, Michele
  Alix Kates Shulman 10:476

Turkington, Kate
  Chinua Achebe 26:16

Turnbull, Colin M.
  Christie Harris 12:262

Turnbull, Martin
  François Mauriac 4:340

Turnell, Martin
  Graham Greene 1:134

Turner, Alice K.
  Jamake Highwater 12:285
  Colleen McCullough 27:318

Turner, Darwin T.
  Ishmael Reed 13:477
  Alice Walker 9:558
  Richard Wright 21:450
  Frank G. Yerby 22:488, 489, 490

Turner, E. S.
  Jeffrey Archer 28:11
  Mircea Eliade 19:148
  Daphne du Maurier 11:164
  Monty Python 21:223

Turner, Gil
  Bob Dylan 12:179

Turner, R. H.
  Claude Chabrol 16:167

Turner, Steve
  Peter Townshend 17:537

Turoff, Robert David
  Milton Meltzer 26:306

Tuska, Jon
  Louis L'Amour 25:279

Tuttle, Lisa
  Douglas Adams 27:11

Tuttleton, James W.
  Louis Auchincloss 4:29

Tvardovsky, Alexander
  Aleksandr I. Solzhenitsyn 26:415

Twichell, Ethel R.
  Norma Fox Mazer 26:295
  Milton Meltzer 26:308

Tyler, Anne
  Richard Adams 18:2
  Toni Cade Bambara 19:33
  John Cheever 11:121
  Anita Desai 19:134
  Joan Didion 14:151
  Lawrence Durrell 27:99
  Jacob Epstein 19:162
  Marilyn French 10:191
  Mavis Gallant 18:172
  Penelope Gilliatt 13:238
  Lois Gould 10:241
  John Irving 23:244
  Sue Kaufman 8:317
  Thomas Keneally 10:299
  Maxine Hong Kingston 19:250
  Paule Marshall 27:315
  Bobbie Ann Mason 28:271
  Joyce Maynard 23:289
  Ian McEwan 13:370
  Leonard Michaels 25:318
  Bernice Rubens 19:404
  Mary Lee Settle 19:410
  Alix Kates Shulman 10:475
  Susan Sontag 13:516
  Paul Theroux 11:529
  William Trevor 7:478
  Angus Wilson 25:462

Tyler, Parker
  Charles Chaplin 16:196
  Laurence Olivier 20:235
  Agnès Varda 16:554
  Andy Warhol 20:416
  Orson Welles 20:438

Tyler, Ralph
  Richard Adams **5**:5
  Agatha Christie **6**:109
  S. J. Perelman **9**:416
  Jean Rhys **6**:455

Tyler, Tony
  John Lennon and Paul
    McCartney **12**:379

Tymn, Marshall B.
  Roger Zelazny **21**:473

Tyms, James D.
  Langston Hughes **5**:191

Tynan, Kenneth
  Enid Bagnold **25**:76
  Lenny Bruce **21**:47
  William Gibson **23**:175, 177
  Roman Polanski **16**:463
  Tom Stoppard **15**:518

Tyrmand, Leopold
  Witold Gombrowicz **7**:124

Tyrrell, Connie
  Franklyn M. Branley **21**:23

Tyrrell, William Blake
  Gene Roddenberry **17**:407

Tytell, John
  William S. Burroughs **22**:86
  Jack Kerouac **3**:264

Ueda, Makoto
  Jun'ichirō Tanizaki **28**:413

Ugarte, Michael
  Juan Goytisolo **23**:187

Uglow, Jennifer
  Russell C. Hoban **25**:264
  Marge Piercy **18**:408

Uhelski, Jaan
  Jimmy Page and Robert Plant
    12:478

Uibopuu, Valev
  Ivar Ivask **14**:287

Ulam, Adam
  Agatha Christie **12**:120

Ulfers, Friedrich
  Paul Celan **19**:92

Ullman, Montague
  Melvin Berger **12**:42
  Larry Kettelkamp **12**:308

Unger, Arthur
  Alex Haley **12**:253

Unger, Leonard
  T. S. Eliot **1**:90

Unsworth, Robert
  Mavis Thorpe Clark **12**:131
  James D. Forman **21**:122
  Rosa Guy **26**:144
  Sonia Levitin **17**:265

Unterecker, John
  Lawrence Durrell **1**:84
  Ezra Pound **4**:415
  Kenneth Rexroth **2**:370

Untermeyer, Louis
  Robert Francis **15**:235
  Robert Frost **13**:223; **15**:239
  Ogden Nash **23**:319
  Muriel Rukeyser **27**:403

Updike, John
  Walter Abish **22**:16
  Michael Ayrton **7**:20
  Roland Barthes **24**:29
  Ann Beattie **8**:55
  Samuel Beckett **6**:45
  Saul Bellow **6**:56
  Heinrich Böll **27**:68
  Jorge Luis Borges **8**:100
  William S. Burroughs **22**:83
  Italo Calvino **5**:101; **8**:130
  Albert Camus **9**:149
  Bruce Chatwin **28**:75
  John Cheever **7**:50; **25**:121
  Julio Cortázar **5**:109
  Don DeLillo **10**:135
  Margaret Drabble **8**:183
  Shusaku Endo **19**:160, 161
  Daniel Fuchs **8**:221
  Witold Gombrowicz **7**:124
  Günter Grass **2**:172; **4**:206
  Barry Hannah **23**:207
  Ernest Hemingway **8**:285
  Ruth Prawer Jhabvala **8**:312
  Gayl Jones **6**:266; **9**:307
  Erica Jong **4**:263
  Tadeusz Konwicki **28**:210
  Jerzy Kosinski **6**:282
  Milan Kundera **19**:269
  Alex La Guma **19**:275
  Ursula K. Le Guin **22**:275
  Stanislaw Lem **15**:329
  Alberto Moravia **7**:243
  Wright Morris **7**:245
  Iris Murdoch **6**:344; **22**:330
  Vladimir Nabokov **2**:301;
    3:351; **6**:355; **8**:414, 415,
    416, 417; **11**:395
  V. S. Naipaul **13**:407
  R. K. Narayan **7**:256; **28**:296,
    303
  Flann O'Brien **7**:269, 270
  Tim O'Brien **19**:358
  John O'Hara **11**:414
  Robert Pinget **7**:306
  Harold Pinter **15**:423
  Raymond Queneau **5**:359, 362
  Jean Rhys **19**:395
  Alain Robbe-Grillet **8**:452
  Françoise Sagan **6**:481
  J. D. Salinger **12**:513
  Simone Schwarz-Bart **7**:405
  L. E. Sissman **18**:487
  Wole Soyinka **14**:509
  Muriel Spark **5**:400
  Christina Stead **8**:499, 500
  James Thurber **5**:433
  William Trevor **25**:444
  Anne Tyler **7**:479; **18**:530;
    28:434
  Sylvia Townsend Warner
    7:512; **19**:460
  Edmund Wilson **8**:551

Uphaus, Robert W.
  Kurt Vonnegut, Jr. **5**:469

Urang, Gunnar
  C. S. Lewis **3**:298
  J.R.R. Tolkien **2**:434

Urbanski, Marie Mitchell Oleson
  Joyce Carol Oates **11**:402

Urbas, Jeannette
  Gabrielle Roy **14**:468

Uroff, Margaret D.
  Sylvia Plath **3**:391; **17**:354

Ury, Claude
  Jules Archer **12**:17

Usborne, Richard
  MacDonald Harris **9**:261

Uscatescu, George
  Mircea Eliade **19**:145

Usmiani, Renate
  Friedrich Dürrenmatt **8**:194

Uys, Stanley
  Breyten Breytenbach **23**:85

Vaizey, John
  Kingsley Amis **5**:22

Valdéz, Jorge H.
  G. Cabrera Infante **25**:105
  Julio Cortázar **13**:165

Valentine, Dean
  Albert Innaurato **21**:195

Valgemae, Mardi
  Sławomir Mrozek **13**:398
  Jean-Claude Van Itallie **3**:493

Vallee, Lillian
  Czesław Miłosz **22**:305

Valley, John A.
  Alberto Moravia **7**:243

Vallis, Val
  Judith Wright **11**:578

Van Brunt, H. L.
  Jim Harrison **6**:224

Van Buren, Alice
  Janet Frame **2**:142

Vance, Joel
  Chuck Berry **17**:56
  David Bowie **17**:63
  Jimmy Cliff **21**:63
  Marvin Gaye **26**:132
  Bob Marley **17**:268
  Monty Python **21**:225
  Lou Reed **21**:313
  Paul Simon **17**:467

Vande Kieft, Ruth M.
  Flannery O'Connor **1**:258
  Eudora Welty **1**:360

Vandenbroucke, Russell
  Athol Fugard **9**:230

Van den Haag, Ernest
  William F. Buckley, Jr. **7**:34

Van den Heuvel, Cor
  James Wright **10**:545

Vanderbilt, Kermit
  Norman Mailer **3**:319
  William Styron **3**:474

Vanderwerken, David L.
  Richard Brautigan **5**:69

Van Doren, Carl
  Esther Forbes **12**:205, 208

Van Doren, Mark
  René Clair **20**:62
  E. E. Cummings **12**:139
  Robert Frost **13**:223; **15**:241
  Robinson Jeffers **11**:304
  John Cowper Powys **7**:346

Van Duyn, Mona
  Margaret Atwood **2**:19
  Adrienne Rich **3**:427
  Anne Sexton **2**:391

Van Dyne, Susan R.
  Adrienne Rich **18**:445

Van Gelder, Lawrence
  Charles Fuller **25**:179
  John Landis **26**:271
  Nagisa Oshima **20**:250

Vanjak, Gloria
  Jim Morrison **17**:290

Van Matre, Lynn
  Lily Tomlin **17**:517

Vanocur, Sander
  Fletcher Knebel **14**:307

Vansittart, Peter
  Lawrence Durrell **13**:189
  Winston Graham **23**:193
  Piers Paul Read **10**:436

Van Spanckeren, Kathryn
  John Gardner **28**:166

Van Wert, William F.
  Kōbō Abé **22**:14
  Marguerite Duras **20**:103
  Alain Resnais **16**:516

Vardi, Dov
  Aharon Appelfeld **23**:35
  Abraham B. Yehoshua **13**:617

Vargas Llosa, Mario
  Gabriel García Márquez **3**:181

Vargo, Edward P.
  John Updike **7**:486

Vas, Robert
  Lindsay Anderson **20**:12
  Robert Bresson **16**:105

Vas Dias, Robert
  Toby Olson **28**:342

Vásquez Amaral, José
  Julio Cortázar **13**:157

Vassal, Jacques
  Janis Ian **21**:183
  Phil Ochs **17**:331
  Buffy Sainte-Marie **17**:431

Vassallo, Carol
  Virginia Hamilton **26**:151

Vaughan, Alden T.
  Maia Wojciechowska **26**:451

Vaughan, Dai
  Carl Theodor Dreyer **16**:265

Vaughan, Stephen
Thomas Keneally 14:302

Veidemanis, Gladys
William Golding 17:169

Velie, Alan R.
James Welch 14:561

Venable, Gene
Fletcher Knebel 14:309
James H. Webb, Jr. 22:453

Venclova, Tomas
Aleksandr I. Solzhenitsyn 18:497

Vendler, Helen
A. R. Ammons 2:14; 25:46
John Ashbery 25:51
Margaret Atwood 8:29
John Berryman 3:68; 10:46
Elizabeth Bishop 9:90
Harold Bloom 24:81
Olga Broumas 10:77
Hayden Carruth 7:41
Lucille Clifton 19:109
E. E. Cummings 3:119
D. J. Enright 8:203
Allen Ginsberg 2:163; 3:195
Louise Glück 7:118; 22:174, 177
Seamus Heaney 7:152
John Hollander 5:187
Richard F. Hugo 6:245
Randall Jarrell 9:295
Erica Jong 4:263
Maxine Kumin 13:326
Brad Leithauser 27:242
Audre Lorde 18:308
Haki R. Madhubuti 6:313
Mary McCarthy 3:328
James Merrill 2:275; 18:328
W. S. Merwin 18:332
Josephine Miles 14:369
Marianne Moore 19:341
Howard Moss 7:250
Joyce Carol Oates 3:361
Frank O'Hara 5:323
Octavio Paz 4:397
Sylvia Plath 17:353
Adrienne Rich 7:367; 18:444
I. A. Richards 14:454
Irwin Shaw 7:414
David Slavitt 14:490
Dave Smith 22:384, 387
Allen Tate 2:429
Charles Tomlinson 6:535
Diane Wakoski 7:504
Derek Walcott 25:455
Robert Penn Warren 10:525; 18:533
Charles Wright 6:581; 28:456

Ventimiglia, Peter James
Albert Innaurato 21:196

Venturi, Lauro
Jean Renoir 20:288

Verani, Hugo J.
Juan Carlos Onetti 7:277

Vernon, Grenville
Clifford Odets 28:324, 328

Vernon, John
Michael Benedikt 4:54
William S. Burroughs 15:108
James Dickey 7:82
Richard F. Hugo 18:264
David Ignatow 4:247
James Merrill 3:334
W. S. Merwin 1:213
Thomas Pynchon 11:452

Verschoyle, Derek
Rayner Heppenstall 10:271

Vesselo, Arthur
Laurence Olivier 20:235

Vickery, John B.
John Updike 5:451

Vickery, Olga W.
John Hawkes 4:213

Vickery, R. C.
Jules Archer 12:23

Vidal, Gore
Louis Auchincloss 4:31
John Barth 14:51
Italo Calvino 5:98
John Dos Passos 4:132
William H. Gass 11:224
E. Howard Hunt 3:251
Doris Lessing 15:333
Norman Mailer 2:265
Carson McCullers 12:418
Henry Miller 2:282
Yukio Mishima 2:287
Vladimir Nabokov 23:304
Anaïs Nin 4:376
John O'Hara 2:323
Thomas Pynchon 11:452
Alain Robbe-Grillet 2:375
Aleksandr I. Solzhenitsyn 4:510
Susan Sontag 2:414
Tennessee Williams 7:546

Vidal-Hall, Judith
Leon Garfield 12:230

Viereck, Peter
Robert Frost 26:114

Vigderman, Patricia
Bobbi Ann Mason 28:273

Viguers, Ruth Hill
E. M. Almedingen 12:2
Ruth M. Arthur 12:24
Margot Benary-Isbert 12:33
Betty Cavanna 12:100
Eilís Dillon 17:95
Lois Duncan 26:100, 101
Leon Garfield 12:218
Christie Harris 12:261, 262
Isabelle Holland 21:147
Lee Kingman 17:244, 245
Joseph Krumgold 12:320
Madeleine L'Engle 12:345, 346
William Mayne 12:393
Emily Cheney Neville 12:450, 451
Philippa Pearce 21:283
Josephine Poole 17:370
Zilpha Keatley Snyder 17:469, 470
Mary Stolz 12:553
Noel Streatfeild 21:404, 408
Lenora Mattingly Weber 12:632

Vilhjalmsson, Thor
Gabriel García Márquez 2:150

Viljanen, Lauri
Frans Eemil Sillanpää 19:417

Villani, Sergio
Romain Gary 25:190

Vince, Thomas L.
Rosa Guy 26:140

Vincent, Celeste H.
Franklyn M. Branley 21:18

Vincent, Emily
Isabelle Holland 21:153

Vine, Richard
Stanley Kunitz 11:319

Vining, Mark
Smokey Robinson 21:344

Vinson, Joe
Isabelle Holland 21:151

Vintcent, Brian
Marie-Claire Blais 4:67
Roch Carrier 13:143
Anne Hébert 4:220

Vinton, Iris
Robert A. Heinlein 26:160

Viorst, Judith
Lois Gould 10:243

Vivas, Eliseo
F. R. Leavis 24:297
I. A. Richards 24:379
George Steiner 24:432
Allen Tate 24:443
René Wellek 28:442

Vogel, Dan
William Faulkner 6:177, 178
Arthur Miller 6:333
John Steinbeck 21:369
Robert Penn Warren 6:556
Tennessee Williams 5:504

Volpe, Edmond L.
James Jones 1:162

Vonalt, Larry P.
John Berryman 3:66; 4:60
Marianne Moore 1:230

Von Hallberg, Robert
Charles Olson 6:386
W. D. Snodgrass 18:495
William Carlos Williams 22:464

Vonnegut, Kurt, Jr.
Robert Altman 16:32
Heinrich Böll 27:61
Joseph Heller 5:175
Hermann Hesse 17:219
Stanislaw Lem 15:328
Hunter S. Thompson 17:506

Von Obenauer, Heidi
Noel Streatfeild 21:412

Von Tersch, Gary
Buffy Sainte-Marie 17:431

Voorhees, Richard J.
P. G. Wodehouse 1:374

Vopat, Carole Gottlieb
Jack Kerouac 3:265

Voss, Arthur
James T. Farrell 11:191
John O'Hara 11:413
Dorothy Parker 15:414
Jean Stafford 19:430

Wachtel, Nili
Isaac Bashevis Singer 15:504

Waddington, Miriam
Joan Barfoot 18:35
Hugh Garner 13:234
A. M. Klein 19:258

Wade, Barbara
Leon Rooke 25:394

Wade, David
J.R.R. Tolkien 2:434

Wade, Michael
Peter Abrahams 4:2

Wade, Rosalind
Lynne Reid Banks 23:42
L. P. Hartley 22:215

Waelti-Walters, Jennifer R.
Michel Butor 15:113

Wagenaar, Dick
Yasunari Kawabata 18:281

Waggoner, Diana
William Mayne 12:406

Waggoner, Hyatt H.
E. E. Cummings 3:117
Robert Duncan 2:122
T. S. Eliot 2:127
Robert Frost 3:173
H. D. 3:217
Robinson Jeffers 2:214
Robert Lowell 3:300
Archibald MacLeish 3:310
Marianne Moore 2:292
Ezra Pound 2:341
John Crowe Ransom 2:363
Theodore Roethke 3:432
Carl Sandburg 4:463
Karl Shapiro 4:485
Lewis Turco 11:549
Richard Wilbur 3:532
William Carlos Williams 2:468

Wagner, Dave
Robert L. Peters 7:303

Wagner, Dick
Yukio Mishima 9:381

Wagner, Geoffrey
R. P. Blackmur 2:61
Jerome Siegel and Joe Shuster 21:354
Josef von Sternberg 20:372

Wagner, Jean
Jean Toomer 22:423

Wagner, Linda W.
Margaret Atwood 25:66
John Dos Passos 25:142
Louise Glück 22:176

Wagner, Linda Welshimer
William Faulkner **1**:103
Robert Hass **18**:208
Ernest Hemingway **6**:231; **19**:215
Denise Levertov **1**:176; **5**:247
Philip Levine **9**:332
Phyllis McGinley **14**:365
W. S. Merwin **13**:383
Joyce Carol Oates **19**:349
Diane Wakoski **9**:554, 555

Waidson, H. M.
Heinrich Böll **11**:55; **27**:56

Wain, John
Sylvia Ashton-Warner **19**:20
William Barrett **27**:19
R. P. Blackmur **24**:62
William S. Burroughs **5**:91
Eleanor Clark **19**:105
Edward Dahlberg **7**:66
C. Day Lewis **6**:127
Günter Grass **2**:173; **4**:202
Michael Hamburger **5**:158
Ben Hecht **8**:270
Ernest Hemingway **3**:233
Aldous Huxley **5**:192
C. S. Lewis **27**:261
Archibald MacLeish **14**:336
Flann O'Brien **4**:383
Sylvia Plath **17**:345
I. A. Richards **24**:390
C. P. Snow **4**:500
Edmund Wilson **24**:476

Wainwright, Andy
Earle Birney **6**:77

Wainwright, Jeffrey
Ezra Pound **7**:332

Wakefield, Dan
Edward Hoagland **28**:181
Garson Kanin **22**:232
Agnes Eckhardt Nixon **21**:250
J. D. Salinger **12**:500
Harvey Swados **5**:422
John R. Tunis **12**:597
Leon Uris **7**:490

Wakoski, Diane
Clayton Eshleman **7**:98
David Ignatow **4**:248
John Logan **5**:255
Robert Lowell **4**:304
Anaïs Nin **4**:377
Jerome Rothenberg **6**:477
Charles Simic **22**:379

Walcott, James
Leonard Michaels **25**:318

Walcott, Ronald
Hal Bennett **5**:57, 59
Charles Gordone **4**:199

Walcutt, Charles Child
James Gould Cozzens **4**:114
John O'Hara **1**:262

Waldeland, Lynne
John Cheever **25**:118

Waldemar, Carla
Anaïs Nin **11**:399

Waldmeir, Joseph
John Updike **5**:450

Waldron, Edward E.
Langston Hughes **15**:291

Waldron, Randall H.
Norman Mailer **3**:314

Waldrop, Rosemary
Hans Erich Nossack **6**:365

Walkarput, W.
Vladimir Nabokov **11**:392

Walker, Alice
Ai **4**:16
Alice Childress **15**:132
Buchi Emecheta **14**:159
Rosa Guy **26**:141
Virginia Hamilton **26**:148
Flannery O'Connor **6**:381
Derek Walcott **4**:576

Walker, Carolyn
Joyce Carol Oates **3**:360

Walker, Cheryl
Richard Brautigan **12**:68
Adrienne Rich **3**:428
Robert Penn Warren **6**:558

Walker, David
Anne Hébert **13**:268

Walker, Greta
Babbis Friis-Baastad **12**:214

Walker, Jim
Clarence Major **19**:292

Walker, Keith
John Rechy **14**:445

Walker, Martin
Robert Ludlum **22**:291

Walker, Michael
Claude Chabrol **16**:173
Jerzy Skolimowski **20**:350

Walker, Robert G.
Ernest Hemingway **8**:287

Walker, Stanley
Mari Sandoz **28**:402

Walker, Ted
Andrew Young **5**:523

Wall, James M.
Andrew Lloyd Webber and Tim Rice **21**:429

Wall, Richard
Behan, Brendan **15**:46

Wall, Stephen
P. H. Newby **13**:408

Wallace, Herbert W.
Alvin Silverstein and Virginia B. Silverstein **17**:455

Wallace, Irving
Irving Wallace **13**:568

Wallace, Margaret
Dee Brown **18**:70
Roderick L. Haig-Brown **21**:135
Mari Sandoz **28**:401

Wallace, Michele
Ntozake Shange **8**:485

Wallace, Ronald
John Hawkes **15**:274
Vladimir Nabokov **23**:304

Wallace, Willard M.
Robert Newton Peck **17**:340

Wallace-Crabbe, Chris
Kenneth Slessor **14**:492

Wallenstein, Barry
James T. Farrell **11**:195
Ted Hughes **2**:200

Waller, Claudia Joan
José Lezama Lima **10**:317

Waller, G. F.
Joyce Carol Oates **19**:350
Paul Theroux **8**:514

Waller, Gary F.
T. Alan Broughton **19**:74
William Maxwell **19**:309

Walley, David G.
Peter Townshend **17**:526
Frank Zappa **17**:585, 588

Wallis, Bruce
Katherine Anne Porter **15**:430

Wallis, C. G.
Jean Cocteau **16**:220

Wallrich, William J.
Franklyn M. Branley **21**:16

Walsh, Chad
Robert Bly **2**:66
Stanley Burnshaw **13**:129
Robert Graves **6**:212
Ted Hughes **2**:197
Fletcher Knebel **14**:308
Philip Larkin **5**:228
C. S. Lewis **27**:265
Cynthia Macdonald **13**:355
Archibald MacLeish **3**:311
Frederick Morgan **23**:298
Howard Nemerov **2**:306
Jerome Weidman **7**:517

Walsh, Jill Paton
H. F. Brinsmead **21**:30
Mollie Hunter **21**:160
Diana Wynne Jones **26**:225
Norma Fox Mazer **26**:289
Rosemary Sutcliff **26**:437

Walsh, Moira
Gordon Parks **16**:458

Walsh, Nina M.
Alvin Silverstein and Virginia B. Silverstein **17**:452

Walsh, Thomas F.
Katherine Anne Porter **13**:449

Walsh, William
Earle Birney **6**:78
Robert Finch **18**:155
A. M. Klein **19**:261
F. R. Leavis **24**:301
R. K. Narayan **7**:254; **28**:290
Thomas Tryon **11**:548
Patrick White **3**:521; **4**:583, 584; **7**:532; **9**:567; **18**:546

Walsten, David M.
Yukio Mishima **2**:286

Walt, James
Jean Cayrol **11**:110
Ward Just **4**:266
Violette Leduc **22**:262
John O'Hara **6**:385
J. R. Salamanca **4**:462

Walter, James F.
John Barth **10**:22

Walter, Sydney Schubert
Sam Shepard **17**:435

Walters, Jennifer R.
Michel Butor **3**:93

Walters, Margaret
Brigid Brophy **6**:99

Walton, Alan Hull
Colin Wilson **3**:537; **14**:585

Walton, Edith H.
Enid Bagnold **25**:73
Sally Benson **17**:46, 48
Maureen Daly **17**:87
Esther Forbes **12**:204
Pamela Hansford Johnson **27**:213
Mary Renault **17**:390

Walton, Richard J.
Jules Archer **12**:20

Walton, Todd
Scott Sommer **25**:426

Walzer, Judith B.
Marge Piercy **18**:407

Walzer, Michael
J. D. Salinger **12**:503

Wanamaker, John
Joy Adamson **17**:6

Wand, David Hsin-Fu
Marianne Moore **13**:396

Ward, A. C.
W. H. Auden **1**:8
Samuel Beckett **1**:21
Edmund Blunden **2**:65
Ivy Compton-Burnett **1**:62
Noel Coward **1**:64
T. S. Eliot **1**:90
E. M. Forster **1**:104
Christopher Fry **2**:143
Robert Graves **1**:128
Graham Greene **1**:132
Aldous Huxley **1**:150
W. Somerset Maugham **1**:204
Iris Murdoch **1**:234
J. B. Priestley **2**:346
Edith Sitwell **2**:403
C. P. Snow **1**:316
Evelyn Waugh **1**:358
Arnold Wesker **3**:518
P. G. Wodehouse **1**:374

Ward, Allen
John Ehle **27**:102

Ward, Andrew
Bob Dylan **12**:197

Ward, David E.
Ezra Pound **1**:275

Ward, Ed
  Jimmy Cliff **21**:60
  Bob Marley **17**:268
  Paul Weller **26**:444

Ward, J. A.
  S. J. Perelman **9**:414

Ward, Jeff
  Lou Reed **21**:307

Ward, Leo
  Harper Lee **12**:341

Ward, Margaret Joan
  Morley Callahan **3**:97

Ward, P.
  N. Scott Momaday **19**:318

Ward, Robert
  Bruce Springsteen **17**:479
  Lily Tomlin **17**:523

Wardle, Irving
  Ann Jellicoe **27**:209, 210
  Hugh Leonard **19**:282
  Richard O'Brien **17**:324

Warkentin, Germaine
  A. W. Purdy **3**:408
  F. R. Scott **22**:377

Warme, Lars G.
  Eyvind Johnson **14**:297

Warner, Alan
  Patrick Kavanagh **22**:238
  Ken Russell **16**:543

Warner, Edwin
  Jorge Luis Borges **2**:71

Warner, John M.
  John Hawkes **3**:223

Warner, Jon M.
  George MacBeth **5**:263

Warner, Rex
  E. M. Forster **1**:105

Warnke, Frank J.
  Heinrich Böll **27**:61
  William Golding **17**:166
  Richard Yates **7**:553

Warnock, Mary
  Brigid Brophy **6**:98
  Lawrence Durrell **27**:94
  Iris Murdoch **8**:404

Warren, Austin
  T. S. Eliot **24**:177
  E. M. Forster **15**:223

Warren, Robert Penn
  James Dickey **10**:140
  William Faulkner **28**:141
  Robert Frost **26**:114
  Alex Haley **12**:243
  Andrew Lytle **22**:296
  Katherine Anne Porter **13**:447; **27**:401
  T. S. Stribling **23**:440
  Eudora Welty **1**:362; **14**:562

Warrick, Patricia S.
  Isaac Asimov **26**:53
  Frank Herbert **23**:219

Warrick, Ruth
  Agnes Eckhardt Nixon **21**:252

Warsh, Lewis
  Richard Brautigan **3**:86
  B. P. Nichol **18**:366

Warshow, Paul
  Buster Keaton **20**:197

Warshow, Robert
  Arthur Miller **1**:215; **26**:312

Washburn, Martin
  Richard Adams **4**:7
  Anthony Burgess **4**:84
  Nicholas Delbanco **6**:129
  John Gardner **3**:187
  Lois Gould **4**:200
  Juan Goytisolo **5**:150
  Günter Grass **4**:206
  Dan Jacobson **4**:255
  György Konrád **4**:273
  Denise Levertov **3**:293
  Alison Lurie **4**:306

Washington, Mary Helen
  Arna Bontemps **18**:66
  David Bradley, Jr. **23**:80
  Alice Walker **6**:554; **19**:452

Washington, Peter
  Roy Fuller **28**:154
  Seamus Heaney **7**:149
  Peter Porter **13**:451
  Stevie Smith **8**:491
  R. S. Thomas **13**:544

Wasilewski, W. H.
  Theodore Roethke **11**:486

Wasserman, Debbi
  Murray Schisgal **6**:490
  Sam Shepard **4**:489
  Tom Stoppard **4**:525
  Richard Wesley **7**:519

Wasserman, Jerry
  Leon Rooke **25**:393

Waterhouse, Keith
  Lynne Reid Banks **23**:40
  Harper Lee **12**:341
  Doris Lessing **22**:277
  Colin MacInnes **23**:282

Waterhouse, Michael
  William Golding **27**:161

Waterman, Andrew
  Daniel Hoffman **13**:286
  John Matthias **9**:361

Waterman, Arthur
  Conrad Aiken **3**:5

Waters, Chris
  Tim O'Brien **7**:271

Waters, Harry F.
  Larry Gelbart **21**:131
  Norman Lear **12**:335, 338
  Garry Marshall **17**:276
  Agnes Eckhardt Nixon **21**:242

Waters, Kate
  Sandra Scoppettone **26**:404

Waters, Michael
  Robert Hass **18**:209

Waterston, Elizabeth
  Irving Layton **2**:236

Watkins, Floyd C.
  Robert Frost **9**:219
  Ernest Hemingway **3**:239

Watkins, Mel
  James Baldwin **2**:33
  David Bradley, Jr. **23**:79
  Ernest J. Gaines **11**:218
  Robert Lipsyte **21**:213
  Simone Schwarz-Bart **7**:404
  Michael Thelwell **22**:416
  Alice Walker **5**:476; **27**:450
  Al Young **19**:479

Watkins, Tony
  Alan Garner **17**:141, 150

Watson, Edward A.
  James Baldwin **17**:31

Watson, George
  T. S. Eliot **24**:181

Watson, Ian
  Elias Canetti **14**:119

Watson, J. P.
  J.R.R. Tolkien **2**:434

Watson, Wilbur
  Henri Troyat **23**:458

Watt, Donald
  Isaac Asimov **26**:45

Watt, Donald J.
  Aldous Huxley **18**:266

Watt, Douglas
  Lenny Bruce **21**:48
  Gretchen Cryer **21**:80
  Andrew Lloyd Webber and Tim Rice **21**:424

Watt, F. W.
  A. M. Klein **19**:260
  Raymond Souster **14**:504

Watt, Ian
  John Fowles **2**:137

Watt, Roderick H.
  Uwe Johnson **15**:305

Watts, Harold H.
  Robert Frost **15**:241
  Aldous Huxley **1**:151
  Gabriel Marcel **15**:359
  Ezra Pound **7**:323

Watts, Michael
  Walter Becker and Donald Fagen **26**:81, 83
  David Bowie **17**:60
  Jackson Browne **21**:35
  Ray Davies **21**:98
  Mick Jagger and Keith Richard **17**:230, 242
  Waylon Jennings **21**:201, 202
  Jim Morrison **17**:290
  Van Morrison **21**:237
  Martin Mull **17**:299
  Lou Reed **21**:306
  Carly Simon **26**:409
  Paul Simon **17**:460
  Bruce Springsteen **17**:478
  Neil Young **17**:571, 575

Watts, Richard
  Jean Kerr **22**:257
  Lanford Wilson **7**:548

Watts, Richard, Jr.
  Robert Anderson **23**:30, 31
  Enid Bagnold **25**:76
  Paddy Chayefsky **23**:114

Waugh, Auberon
  Kōbō Abé **22**:13
  Michael Ayrton **7**:18
  Romain Gary **25**:187
  James Leo Herlihy **6**:235
  Elizabeth Jane Howard **7**:164
  Tom Robbins **9**:453
  Gillian Tindall **7**:474
  William Trevor **7**:476
  P. G. Wodehouse **5**:516

Waugh, Coulton
  Jerome Siegel and Joe Shuster **21**:354

Waugh, Evelyn
  Graham Greene **14**:216
  Aldous Huxley **11**:281
  Christopher Isherwood **14**:278

Waugh, Harriet
  Ruth Rendell **28**:386, 387, 388
  Emma Tennant **13**:536

Way, Brian
  Edward Albee **9**:2

Wayman, Tom
  Miriam Waddington **28**:437

Weales, Gerald
  Edward Albee **9**:4
  Beryl Bainbridge **4**:39
  Eric Bentley **24**:48
  Elizabeth Bowen **6**:95
  Ivy Compton-Burnett **1**:63
  J. P. Donleavy **4**:123
  Christopher Durang **27**:92, 93
  Charles Fuller **25**:181
  Lorraine Hansberry **17**:183, 187
  John Hawkes **1**:139; **4**:213
  John Huston **20**:168
  William Inge **19**:226
  Robert Lowell **4**:299
  Norman Mailer **3**:319; **4**:319
  Bernard Malamud **1**:201
  Mark Medoff **6**:322; **23**:294
  Arthur Miller **1**:218
  Marsha Norman **28**:318
  Clifford Odets **28**:335, 340
  Harold Pinter **9**:420
  James Purdy **2**:348; **4**:422
  David Rabe **4**:427
  Gerome Ragni and James Rado **17**:380
  Ronald Ribman **7**:357
  Peter Shaffer **5**:390
  Sam Shepard **4**:489; **17**:436
  Wole Soyinka **3**:463
  Tom Stoppard **1**:327; **8**:502
  David Storey **2**:424
  James Thurber **5**:430
  Douglas Turner Ward **19**:456
  Robert Penn Warren **1**:356
  Thornton Wilder **10**:536
  Tennessee Williams **1**:368; **2**:466; **19**:470

Weatherby, Harold L.
Andrew Lytle 22:298

Weatherhead, A. Kingsley
Robert Duncan 1:82; 7:88
Marianne Moore 4:360
Charles Olson 1:263
Stephen Spender 1:323
William Carlos Williams 1:371

Weathers, Winston
Par Lägerkvist 7:200

Weaver, John D.
Lenny Bruce 21:47

Weaver, Mike
William Carlos Williams 13:603

Webb, Phyllis
D. G. Jones 10:285

Weber, Brom
Thomas Berger 5:60
Edward Dahlberg 7:69
Bernard Kops 4:274
C. P. Snow 4:503
John Updike 2:442

Weber, Robert C.
Robert Duncan 15:189

Weber, Ronald
Saul Bellow 1:32
John Knowles 26:249

Webster, Grant
Allen Tate 2:427

Webster, Harvey Curtis
James Baldwin 17:20
L. P. Hartley 22:212
Maxine Kumin 13:329
Bernice Rubens 19:404
C. P. Snow 13:514

Webster, Ivan
James Baldwin 4:43
Gayl Jones 6:266

Weeks, Brigitte
Judy Blume 12:46
Marilyn French 10:191
M. M. Kaye 28:199
M. E. Kerr 12:301
Iris Murdoch 8:405

Weeks, Edward
Margaret Atwood 4:25
Jorge Luis Borges 1:39
Lothar-Günther Buchheim 6:102
Pearl S. Buck 7:33
Len Deighton 22:115
Daphne du Maurier 6:147; 11:163
Loren Eiseley 7:91
Howard Fast 23:155
Edna Ferber 18:152
Esther Forbes 12:208
Frank B. Gilbreth, Jr. and Ernestine Gilbreth Carey 17:153
James Herriot 12:283
Garson Kanin 22:231
Yasunari Kawabata 5:208
Madeleine L'Engle 12:344

Peter Matthiessen 5:273, 275
Iris Murdoch 6:344
Vladimir Nabokov 6:357
May Sarton 14:480
André Schwarz-Bart 4:480
Michael Shaara 15:474
Irwin Shaw 7:413
Mikhail Sholokhov 7:418
Joseph Wambaugh 3:509
Jessamyn West 7:519; 17:545
Herman Wouk 1:377

Weeks, Ramona
Lucille Clifton 19:108

Weeks, Robert P.
Ernest Hemingway 19:214

Weesner, Theodore
Robert Cormier 12:134

Wegner, Robert E.
E. E. Cummings 12:153

Weibel, Kay
Mickey Spillane 13:525

Weigel, John A.
Lawrence Durrell 1:86

Weightman, John
Alan Ayckbourn 5:37
Simone de Beauvoir 4:49
Albert Camus 2:98
Louis-Ferdinand Céline 4:100
Marguerite Duras 6:149
A. E. Ellis 7:94
Romain Gary 25:191
Jean Genet 5:136, 139
Jean-Luc Godard 20:140
André Malraux 9:359
Peter Nichols 5:308
Francis Ponge 6:422
Gerome Ragni and James Rado 17:382
Alain Robbe-Grillet 2:377
Nathalie Sarraute 4:468, 469
Jean-Paul Sartre 9:473
Tom Stoppard 5:412
David Storey 5:416
Michel Tournier 23:454
Gore Vidal 4:555
Monique Wittig 22:473

Weil, Dorothy
Arna Bontemps 18:63

Weil, Henry
Philip Roth 22:358

Weiland, Steven
Wendell Berry 27:36

Weiler, A. H.
Jean Cocteau 16:223
Werner Herzog 16:321
Elia Kazan 16:362
Alain Resnais 16:496
Maia Wojciechowska 26:453

Weinberg, Helen
Saul Bellow 2:53
Ralph Ellison 11:180
Herbert Gold 4:192
Norman Mailer 2:261
Philip Roth 4:452

Weinberg, Herman G.
Josef von Sternberg 20:374

Weinberger, David
M. M. Kaye 28:200
Farley Mowat 26:345

Weinberger, Deborah
Adolfo Bioy Casares 13:86

Weinberger, Eliot
Robert Bly 15:63

Weinberger, G. J.
E. E. Cummings 8:160

Weinfield, Henry
Gilbert Sorrentino 7:448, 449

Weingarten, Sherwood L.
Monty Python 21:224

Weinkauf, Mary S.
Fritz Leiber 25:307

Weinstein, Shirley
Maia Wojciechowska 26:458

Weintraub, Stanley
William Golding 2:167
C. P. Snow 9:497, 498

Weir, Dana
Dave Smith 22:386

Weisberg, Robert
Stanley Burnshaw 3:92
Randall Jarrell 2:211
Richmond Lattimore 3:277

Weiskopf, F. C.
Joseph Wittlin 25:467

Weisman, Kathryn
Margaret O. Hyde 21:179
Larry Kettelkamp 12:308

Weiss, Jonathan M.
Gabrielle Roy 14:470

Weiss, Nancy Quint
H. F. Brinsmead 21:26

Weiss, Paulette
Jim Morrison 17:294

Weiss, Peter
Peter Weiss 15:563

Weiss, Theodore
Cleanth Brooks 24:111
Donald Davie 5:115
Ezra Pound 10:405
M. L. Rosenthal 28:396

Weiss, Victoria L.
Marguerite Duras 6:150

Weissenberger, Klaus
Paul Celan 19:93

Weixlmann, Joe
John Barth 14:54
Ronald L. Fair 18:142

Weixlmann, Sher
John Barth 14:54

Welburn, Ron
Imamu Amiri Baraka 2:35
Don L. Lee 2:237
Clarence Major 19:291
Dudley Randall 1:283

Welch, Chris
David Bowie 17:64
Jimmy Page and Robert Plant 12:476, 478
Peter Townshend 17:524, 538

Welch, Elizabeth H.
Jules Archer 12:19

Welcome, John
Dick Francis 22:152, 153
P. D. James 18:272

Welding, Pete
Chuck Berry 17:52
Jimmy Cliff 21:62
Gordon Lightfoot 26:278

Wellek, René
R. P. Blackmur 2:62
Cleanth Brooks 24:111
Kenneth Burke 2:89
F. R. Leavis 24:302
I. A. Richards 24:395

Weller, Richard H.
Margaret O. Hyde 21:175

Weller, Sheila
Ann Beattie 8:55
Gael Greene 8:252
Diane Wakoski 7:507

Wells, John
Bob Dylan 12:200

Wellwarth, George
Arthur Adamov 4:5
Edward Albee 2:1
John Arden 6:8
Samuel Beckett 2:46
Brendan Behan 8:63
Friedrich Dürrenmatt 4:138
Max Frisch 3:166
Jean Genet 2:157
Michel de Ghelderode 6:197
Eugène Ionesco 4:251
Arthur Kopit 18:287
Bernard Kops 4:274
John Mortimer 28:283
John Osborne 2:327
Harold Pinter 3:385
Arnold Wesker 3:518

Welsh, Mary
Noel Streatfeild 21:401

Welty, Eudora
Margery Allingham 19:12
Elizabeth Bowen 6:94; 22:65
Annie Dillard 9:175
E. M. Forster 3:161
Ross Macdonald 2:255
S. J. Perelman 23:334, 337
Katherine Anne Porter 27:398
V. S. Pritchett 13:467
Jessamyn West 17:544
Patrick White 5:485

Welz, Becky
Betty Cavanna 12:101

Wendell, Carolyn
Vonda N. McIntyre 18:326

Werner, Alfred
Hermann Hesse 17:195

Werner, Craig
Tom Stoppard 15:520

Wernick, Robert
Wright Morris 3:343

Wersba, Barbara
Julia W. Cunningham 12:164, 165, 166
Leon Garfield 12:222
Norma Fox Mazer 26:290
Philippa Pearce 21:283
Noel Streatfeild 21:409

Wertham, Fredric
Jerome Siegel and Joe Shuster 21:355

Wertime, Richard A.
Guy Davenport, Jr. 14:139
Hubert Selby, Jr. 8:475

Weschler, Lawrence
Mel Brooks 12:82

Wescott, Glenway
Katherine Anne Porter 7:313

Wesker, Arnold
William Styron 15:531

Wesling, Donald
Ed Dorn 10:157

Wesolek, George
E. E. Cummings 12:152

West, Anthony
Jorge Amado 13:11
Yehuda Amichai 9:22
Enid Bagnold 25:74
James Baldwin 17:20
Heinrich Böll 27:55
Paul Bowles 19:58
Carlos Fuentes 22:164
Yukio Mishima 27:336
Edwin O'Connor 14:389
Leonardo Sciascia 9:474
Elizabeth Spencer 22:398
Sylvia Townsend Warner 7:512

West, David S.
Robert Kroetsch 23:275

West, Martha Ullman
Lee Smith 25:409

West, Paul
Walter Abish 22:20
Miguel Ángel Asturias 3:18
Michael Ayrton 7:18
Samuel Beckett 2:48
Earle Birney 6:72
Heinrich Böll 3:74
Michel Butor 8:113
Alejo Carpentier 11:99
Camilo José Cela 13:146
Louis-Ferdinand Céline 1:57
Jean Cocteau 15:132
Evan S. Connell, Jr. 4:108
Julio Cortázar 2:103
Guy Davenport, Jr. 6:123
Len Deighton 22:115
José Donoso 4:127
Richard Elman 19:151
Howard Fast 23:158
Gabriel García Márquez 10:215
John Gardner 2:150
William H. Gass 11:224
William Golding 1:122
Peter Handke 5:166

MacDonald Harris 9:261
Wilson Harris 25:202
Uwe Johnson 5:202
Robert Kroetsch 23:270
Jakov Lind 2:245
Charles Newman 2:311
Robert Nye 13:413
Sylvia Plath 1:271
André Schwarz-Bart 2:389
Gilbert Sorrentino 22:394
Allen Tate 11:526
Robert Penn Warren 1:353

West, Ray B.
Katherine Ann Porter 1:272

West, Richard
Michael Cimino 16:211

Westall, Robert
Robert Westall 17:557

Westbrook, Max
Saul Bellow 1:30
William Faulkner 1:101
Ernest Hemingway 1:143
J. D. Salinger 1:299
John Steinbeck 1:326
Robert Penn Warren 1:355

Westbrook, Perry D.
Mary Ellen Chase 2:100
R. K. Narayan 28:293

Westbrook, Wayne W.
Louis Auchincloss 4:30

Westburg, Faith
Adolfo Bioy Casares 4:64
Jerzy Kosinski 3:274

Westerbeck, Colin L., Jr.
Robert Altman 16:42
Lindsay Anderson 20:17
Ralph Bakshi 26:76
Mel Brooks 12:76, 77
Charles Chaplin 16:204
Vittorio De Sica 20:96
Bob Fosse 20:123
Werner Herzog 16:327, 336
Sidney Poitier 26:357, 359
Richard Pryor 26:383
Paul Schrader 26:397
Steven Spielberg 20:359
Lina Wertmüller 16:587

Westervelt, Linda A.
John Barth 14:52

Westfall, Jeff
Theodore Roethke 19:401

Westhuis, Mary G.
Robert Newton Peck 17:342

Westlake, Donald E.
Gael Greene 8:252

Weston, Jeremy
Roger Zelazny 21:470

Weston, John
Nat Hentoff 26:183
Paul Zindel 6:586

Weston, John C.
Hugh MacDiarmid 11:335

Weston, Robert V.
Andrew Lytle 22:299

Wetzsteon, Ross
Charles Gordone 1:124
Edward Hoagland 28:184
Albert Innaurato 21:192
May Sarton 4:472
Irwin Shaw 23:399
Lily Tomlin 17:518

Weyant, Jill
William Melvin Kelley 22:250

Whedon, Julia
Judy Blume 12:46
Lois Duncan 26:104
Penelope Gilliatt 2:160

Wheeler, Charles
Jeffrey Archer 28:12
Paul E. Erdman 25:155
William Safire 10:447

Wheelock, Carter
Jorge Luis Borges 2:76; 3:81; 4:72; 6:90; 13:104
Julio Cortázar 5:109

Wheelock, John Hall
Allen Tate 4:536

Whelan, Gloria
Margaret Laurence 13:342

Whelton, Clark
Joan Micklin Silver 20:343

Whichard, Nancy Winegardner
Patrick White 4:583

Whicher, George F.
Ogden Nash 23:319

Whicher, Stephen E.
E. E. Cummings 3:116

Whipple, T. K.
Erskine Caldwell 14:93
Robert Frost 26:110

Whissen, Thomas R.
Isak Dinesen 10:144, 149

Whitaker, Jennifer Seymour
Alberto Moravia 7:243

Whitaker, Muriel
Kevin Major 26:288

Whitaker, Thomas R.
Conrad Aiken 3:3

White, Charles, S. J.
Mircea Eliade 19:147

White, David A.
Martin Heidegger 24:274

White, E. B.
James Thurber 5:432

White, Edmund
John Ashbery 6:11; 15:33
James Baldwin 17:41
Edward Dahlberg 7:65
Thomas M. Disch 7:87
Lawrence Durrell 6:153
Jean Genet 5:138
Russell C. Hoban 7:161
Eugène Ionesco 11:290
Yasunari Kawabata 5:207
Marjorie Kellogg 2:224
Fran Lebowitz 11:322

José Lezama Lima 4:290
Harry Mathews 6:315
William Maxwell 19:308
James Merrill 18:328
Yukio Mishima 4:355
Howard Moss 7:248
Vladimir Nabokov 2:304
James Schuyler 5:383
Muriel Spark 18:505
Jun'ichirō Tanizaki 28:420
Gore Vidal 8:527
Paul West 14:569
Tennessee Williams 5:503

White, Gavin
Farley Mowat 26:336

White, Gertrude M.
W. D. Snodgrass 10:477; 18:494

White, Jean M.
Dick Francis 2:143
Carolyn G. Heilbrun 25:256
P. D. James 18:272
Ross Macdonald 3:308
George Simenon 2:398
Maj Sjöwall 7:502
Per Wahlöö 7:502
Donald E. Westlake 7:529

White, John
Michael Ayrton 7:18

White, John J.
MacDonald Harris 9:259

White, Jon Manchip
Gore Vidal 22:437

White, Patricia O.
Samuel Beckett 1:25

White, Ray Lewis
Gore Vidal 2:448

White, Robert J.
Pier Paolo Pasolini 20:269

White, Ted
Jerome Siegel and Joe Shuster 21:358

White, Timothy
Jackson Browne 21:37
Billy Joel 26:222
Bob Marley 17:268, 269, 271, 272

White, Victor
Thornton Wilder 10:536

White, William Allen
Mari Sandoz 28:400

White, William Luther
C. S. Lewis 3:295

Whitebait, William
Jean Cocteau 16:226

Whitehall, Richard
George Roy Hill 26:196
John Huston 20:168
Jean Renoir 20:291

Whitehead, James
Jim Harrison 6:224
Stanley J. Kunitz 6:287
Adrienne Rich 3:427
Gibbons Ruark 3:441

Whitehead, John
  Louis MacNeice 1:186
Whitehead, Peter
  Pier Paolo Pasolini 20:263
Whitehead, Phillip
  Vera Brittain 23:93
Whitehead, Ralph, Jr.
  Hunter S. Thompson 17:514
Whitehead, Ted
  Woody Allen 16:9
  Michael Cimino 16:210
  Peter Townshend 17:539
Whitehead, Winifred
  Eilís Dillon 17:100
Whitlock, Pamela
  Eilís Dillon 17:93
Whitman, Alden
  Norman Mailer 14:353
Whitman, Ruth
  Adrienne Rich 6:459
  Anne Sexton 6:494
Whitney, Phyllis A.
  Mary Stolz 12:551
Whittemore, Bernice
  Ilya Ehrenburg 18:130
Whittemore, Reed
  Allen Ginsberg 2:163
  James Kirkwood 9:320
  Larry McMurtry 27:329
  Ogden Nash 23:323
  Charles Olson 2:326
  Tom Robbins 9:453
Whittington-Egan, Richard
  Truman Capote 8:133
  Rayner Heppenstall 10:272
Whitton, Kenneth S.
  Friedrich Dürrenmatt 15:198
Whitty, John
  Tennessee Williams 11:575
Wickenden, Dan
  Brigid Brophy 11:68
  Roy Fuller 28:149
  Jessamyn West 17:545
Wickenden, Dorothy
  Ella Leffland 19:280
  Gloria Naylor 28:305
  Susan Fromberg Schaeffer 22:369
Wickes, George
  Henry Miller 1:221
  Anaïs Nin 1:247
Wideman, John
  Toni Cade Bambara 19:34
  Richard Wright 14:596
Widmer, Kingsley
  John Dos Passos 4:133
  Leslie A. Fiedler 4:160
  Allen Ginsberg 13:239
  Herbert Gold 4:191
  Jack Kerouac 14:305
  Henry Miller 1:220

Wiegand, William
  J. D. Salinger 1:295
  Jerome Weidman 7:516
Wiegner, Kathleen
  Michael Benedikt 14:82
  Judith Leet 11:323
  Diane Wakoski 9:555
Wier, Allen
  Laurie Colwin 23:129
Wiersma, Stanley M.
  Christopher Fry 2:144; 10:202
Wiesel, Elie
  Richard Elman 19:148
  Chaim Grade 10:246
  Anatoli Rybakov 23:372
Wieseltier, Leon
  Yehuda Amichai 9:24
  Harold Bloom 24:79
  Gregor von Rezzori 25:383
  Isaac Bashevis Singer 11:502
  Elie Wiesel 3:529
Wiggins, William H., Jr.
  John Oliver Killens 10:300
Wilbur, Richard
  Barbara Howes 15:288
Wilce, Gillian
  Beryl Bainbridge 18:32
  Pamela Hansford Johnson 27:222
Wilcher, Robert
  Samuel Beckett 11:35
Wilcox, Barbara
  Joyce Maynard 23:290
Wilcox, Thomas W.
  Anthony Powell 7:341
Wild, John
  William Barrett 27:16
Wilde, Alan
  Donald Barthelme 13:55
  Christopher Isherwood 1:156; 9:290
Wilder, Virginia
  M. E. Kerr 12:301
Wildgen, Kathryn E.
  François Mauriac 9:368
Wilding, Michael
  L. P. Hartley 2:182
  Jack Kerouac 5:215
  Christina Stead 2:422, 423
Wildman, John Hazard
  Mary Lavin 4:281
  Joyce Carol Oates 6:367
  Reynolds Price 6:423
  Muriel Spark 13:520
Wilentz, Amy
  Frederick Busch 18:85
Wiley, Marion E.
  Elias Canetti 25:108
Wilhelm, James J.
  Ezra Pound 4:418

Wilkes, G. A.
  Robert D. FitzGerald 19:178
Wilkes, Paul
  Shusaku Endo 14:162
Wilkinson, Burke
  Ernest K. Gann 23:164
Wilkinson, Doris Y.
  Chester Himes 7:159
Wilkinson, Theon
  M. M. Kaye 28:199
Will, Frederic
  Martin Heidegger 24:258
Willard, Nancy
  Pierre Gascar 11:222
  Pablo Neruda 1:246; 28:307
  J.R.R. Tolkien 8:515
Willbanks, Ray
  Randolph Stow 23:434
Willett, Holly
  Nat Hentoff 26:186
Willett, Ralph
  Clifford Odets 2:319
Willey, Basil
  I. A. Richards 24:399
Williams, A. R.
  Diana Wynne Jones 26:232
Williams, Anne
  Richard Wilbur 14:578
Williams, David
  Kon Ichikawa 20:183
  Christina Stead 2:423
  John Wyndham 19:476
Williams, Forrest
  Federico Fellini 16:279
Williams, Gary Jay
  Jean Kerr 22:258
Williams, Gladys
  Leon Garfield 12:226
Williams, Hugo
  Horst Bienek 7:29
  Richard Brautigan 12:60
  William S. Burroughs 5:92
  James Schuyler 23:392
  Derek Walcott 25:448
Williams, John
  Henry Miller 1:223
Williams, Jonathan
  Richard Brautigan 3:87
  Rod McKuen 3:333
  Anne Sexton 4:482
Williams, Linda L.
  Bernardo Bertolucci 16:99
Williams, Liz
  Sandra Scoppettone 26:404
Williams, Lloyd
  James Ngugi 7:262
Williams, Martin
  Lenny Bruce 21:44

Williams, Miller
  Donald Davidson 2:111
  John Crowe Ransom 4:434
  Hollis Summers 10:493
  Andrei Voznesensky 1:349
Williams, Oscar
  Muriel Rukeyser 27:407
Williams, Paul
  Ray Davies 21:88, 90
  Mick Jagger and Keith Richard 17:231
  Jim Morrison 17:285
  Bruce Springsteen 17:482
  Brian Wilson 12:641
  Neil Young 17:568, 577
Williams, R. V.
  James Clavell 25:128
Williams, Raymond L.
  Manuel Puig 28:372
  Aleksandr I. Solzhenitsyn 2:407
Williams, Regina
  Rosa Guy 26:143
Williams, Richard
  Joan Armatrading 17:7
  Chuck Berry 17:52
  Allen Ginsberg 6:201
  Van Morrison 21:232
  Laura Nyro 17:313
  Lou Reed 21:303, 304
  Smokey Robinson 21:343, 344, 348
  Carly Simon 26:407
  Paul Simon 17:461
  Bruce Springsteen 17:477
  Andrew Lloyd Webber and Tim Rice 21:422
  Richard Wilbur 6:568
  Brian Wilson 12:644, 646, 650
  Neil Young 17:569
Williams, Robert V.
  Ogden Nash 23:324
Williams, Sherley Anne
  James Baldwin 3:32
  Imamu Amiri Baraka 3:35; 10:20
  Ralph Ellison 3:144
  Haki R. Madhubuti 6:313
Williams, Stanley T.
  Mari Sandoz 28:400
Williams, Tennessee
  Paul Bowles 19:56
  William Inge 8:307
  Carson McCullers 12:412
Williams, William Carlos
  David Ignatow 14:274
  Marianne Moore 10:348
  Kenneth Patchen 18:391
  Carl Sandburg 15:466
Williamson, Alan
  Jon Anderson 9:31
  Robert Bly 5:65; 15:68
  Robert Creeley 15:153
  Louise Glück 22:176
  Galway Kinnell 5:216
  Robert Lowell 4:304
  Robert Phillips 28:364

Charles Simic **22**:380
L. E. Sissman **18**:489
Gary Snyder **5**:394
Barry Spacks **14**:510
Allen Tate **14**:528
James Wright **3**:541; **5**:519, 521; **28**:472

Williamson, Chilton, Jr.
Norman Lear **12**:331

Williamson, Jack
Robert A. Heinlein **26**:170

Willis, Don
Fritz Lang **20**:215
Josef von Sternberg **20**:378

Willis, Donald C.
Luis Buñuel **16**:151
Frank Capra **16**:161
Yasojiro Ozu **16**:455

Willis, Ellen
David Bowie **17**:59
Bob Dylan **3**:131; **12**:183, 186
Lou Reed **21**:317
Paul Simon **17**:459
Stevie Wonder **12**:658

Willis, J. H., Jr.
William Empson **3**:147

Wills, Garry
James Baldwin **17**:25
Andrew M. Greeley **28**:174
Thomas Keneally **5**:210
James A. Michener **11**:375
Vladimir Nabokov **3**:356
Hunter S. Thompson **17**:514

Wilmer, Clive
Czesław Miłosz **22**:310

Wilmington, Michael
John Ford **16**:310, 314
Billy Wilder **20**:462, 463

Wilms, Denise Murko
Jules Archer **12**:23
Cecil Bødker **21**:13
Frank Bonham **12**:55
Betty Cavanna **12**:103
Barbara Corcoran **17**:78
Roy A. Gallant **17**:133
Margaret O. Hyde **21**:180
Larry Kettelkamp **12**:306
Sonia Levitin **17**:266
Noel Streatfeild **21**:415
Piri Thomas **17**:502

Wilner, Eleanor
Adrienne Rich **7**:369

Wilson, A. N.
Thomas Keneally **27**:234
Barbara Pym **19**:388

Wilson, Angus
Kingsley Amis **3**:9
L. P. Hartley **2**:181
Christopher Isherwood **11**:294
John Cowper Powys **15**:433

Wilson, Barbara Ker
Noel Streatfeild **21**:404

Wilson, Bryan
Kenneth Rexroth **11**:473

Wilson, Carter
Rudolfo A. Anaya **23**:24

Wilson, Clifford
Farley Mowat **26**:330

Wilson, Colin
Jorge Luis Borges **3**:78
Christopher Isherwood **11**:297

Wilson, David
Dirk Bogarde **19**:43
Garson Kanin **22**:232
Nagisa Oshima **20**:248
Salman Rushdie **23**:364
Ken Russell **16**:547
François Truffaut **20**:389
Joseph Wambaugh **18**:533

Wilson, Douglas
Ernest Hemingway **3**:241

Wilson, Edmund
W. H. Auden **2**:21; **4**:33
Marie-Claire Blais **2**:62; **4**:66
Kay Boyle **19**:62
James M. Cain **28**:48
Morley Callaghan **3**:97
Agatha Christie **12**:114
Walter Van Tilburg Clark **28**:77
John Dos Passos **4**:130
T. S. Eliot **24**:160
Anne Hébert **4**:219
Joseph Wood Krutch **24**:286
Hugh MacLennan **2**:257
André Malraux **13**:365
William Maxwell **19**:305
Carson McCullers **12**:410
Katherine Anne Porter **7**:309
Aleksandr I. Solzhenitsyn **2**:407
John Steinbeck **13**:529
J.R.R. Tolkien **2**:433
Evelyn Waugh **13**:584; **27**:469
Angus Wilson **2**:470

Wilson, Edwin
Mark Medoff **23**:293

Wilson, Evie
Margaret Craven **17**:80
Anne McCaffrey **17**:283
John Neufeld **17**:310

Wilson, Frank
Françoise Sagan **17**:427
Susan Sontag **13**:519

Wilson, George
Fritz Lang **20**:213

Wilson, J. C.
Wright Morris **7**:246

Wilson, Jane
Andrew Sinclair **2**:401

Wilson, Jason
Octavio Paz **19**:365

Wilson, Jay
Andy Warhol **20**:416

Wilson, Keith
David Kherdian **6**:280

Wilson, Milton
Milton Acorn **15**:8
Earl Birney **6**:74, 75
A.J.M. Smith **15**:514

Wilson, Raymond J.
Isaac Asimov **19**:26

Wilson, Reuel K.
Tadeusz Konwicki **8**:328
Stanislaw Lem **15**:326

Wilson, Robert
Mark Harris **19**:206
Richard Yates **23**:483

Wilson, Robley, Jr.
Daniel J. Berrigan **4**:56
Richard Howard **7**:165
Philip Levine **4**:285

Wilson, William E.
Jessamyn West **17**:545

Wilton, Shirley
Isabelle Holland **21**:151

Wimble, Barton
Allan W. Eckert **17**:108

Wimsatt, Margaret
Margaret Atwood **3**:19
Robertson Davies **13**:173
Graham Greene **3**:208

Wimsatt, W. K.
Northrop Frye **24**:214

Wimsatt, W. K., Jr.
René Wellek **28**:441

Winch, Terence
Jonathan Baumbach **23**:56
Ann Beattie **13**:64
Benedict Kiely **23**:267
W. S. Merwin **8**:388, 390
Flann O'Brien **10**:363
William Trevor **25**:443

Winchell, Mark Royden
Robert Penn Warren **13**:579

Windsor, Philip
Josef Škvorecký **15**:511
Aleksandr I. Solzhenitsyn **7**:441

Winegarten, Renee
Ruth Prawer Jhabvala **4**:258
Bernard Malamud **3**:324; **8**:375
André Malraux **1**:203
Grace Paley **6**:392

Winehouse, Bernard
Conrad Aiken **10**:2

Winfrey, Carey
James H. Webb, Jr. **22**:454

Wing, George Gordon
Octavio Paz **3**:376

Winks, Robin W.
William F. Buckley, Jr. **18**:82
Len Deighton **7**:75
Howard Fast **23**:160
P. D. James **18**:273
Elmore Leonard **28**:234
Robert B. Parker **27**:363, 364
David Harry Walker **14**:552

Winner, Viola Hopkins
R. P. Blackmur **24**:66

Winnington, Richard
Vittorio De Sica **20**:85
Alfred Hitchcock **16**:340

Winston, Joan
Gene Roddenberry **17**:407

Winston, Richard
Mary Renault **17**:393, 399

Winter, Thomas
Anthony Burgess **4**:81

Winterich, John T.
Frank B. Gilbreth, Jr. and Ernestine Gilbreth Carey **17**:152, 154

Winters, Yvor
Elizabeth Daryush **19**:119
Robert Frost **10**:192
Mina Loy **28**:246
John Crowe Ransom **24**:364

Wintz, Cary D.
Langston Hughes **10**:279

Wirth-Nesher, Hana
Amos Oz **11**:427

Wisse, Ruth R.
Saul Bellow **8**:68
Leslie Epstein **27**:128
Chaim Grade **10**:246
Cynthia Ozick **7**:289
Chaim Potok **26**:375

Wistrich, Robert
A. E. Ellis **7**:93

Witcover, Jules
Hunter S. Thompson **17**:507

Witemeyer, Hugh
Guy Davenport, Jr. **14**:141

Witherington, Paul
John Knowles **26**:252
Bernard Malamud **11**:352

Witt, Harold
Conrad Aiken **1**:4

Witte, Stephen
George Lucas **16**:409

Wixson, Douglas Charles, Jr.
Thornton Wilder **10**:531

Wohlers, H. C.
Melvin Berger **12**:40

Wohlgelernter, Maurice
Frank O'Connor **23**:327

Woiwode, L.
John Cheever **3**:107

Woiwode, Larry
Wendell Berry **27**:37

Wojciechowska, Maia
Maia Wojciechowska **26**:451

Wojnaroski, Janet B.
Margaret O. Hyde **21**:180

Wolcott, James
John Barth **27**:26
William F. Buckley, Jr. **7**:35
Peter De Vries **28**:110
Mary Gordon **22**:185
Alex Haley **12**:253
Peter Handke **10**:255
John Hawkes **27**:197
Norman Lear **12**:333, 337, 338

John le Carré **28**:229
Norman Mailer **14**:351
Laura Nyro **17**:319
Jimmy Page and Robert Plant
 12:480
Mordecai Richler **18**:456
Wilfrid Sheed **10**:472
Lily Tomlin **17**:516
Anne Tyler **18**:530
Gore Vidal **8**:528
Frederick Wiseman **20**:476

Wolf, Barbara
Yukio Mishima **2**:288; **6**:338

Wolf, Manfred
Brigid Brophy **11**:68

Wolf, William
Ralph Bakshi **26**:73
Gordon Parks **1**:265

Wolfe, Don M.
Shirley Hazzard **18**:213

Wolfe, G. K.
Kurt Vonnegut, Jr. **3**:495

Wolfe, George H.
William Faulkner **9**:203

Wolfe, H. Leslie
Laurence Lieberman **4**:291

Wolfe, Morris
Matt Cohen **19**:111

Wolfe, Peter
Richard Adams **5**:6
A. Alvarez **5**:20
Maeve Brennan **5**:72
Laurie Colwin **5**:108
Dashiell Hammett **19**:199
John Knowles **26**:258
Jakov Lind **1**:177
Ross Macdonald **14**:329
Walker Percy **2**:333
Mary Renault **3**:425
Georges Simenon **18**:487
Charles Webb **7**:515
Patrick White **3**:522

Wolfe, Tom
James M. Cain **28**:49
John Lennon and Paul
 McCartney **12**:355, 363
S. J. Perelman **23**:338

Wolff, Ellen
Kris Kristofferson **26**:268

Wolff, Geoffrey
John Barth **14**:56
Frederick Buechner **2**:83
Raymond Carver **22**:96
Arthur A. Cohen **7**:52
Julio Cortázar **3**:115
J. P. Donleavy **6**:140
George P. Elliott **2**:131
Paula Fox **8**:217
John Gardner **2**:152
Barry Hannah **23**:212
Edward Hoagland **28**:180, 182
James Jones **3**:261
Jerzy Kosinski **1**:171; **3**:272;
 6:282
D. Keith Mano **2**:270
Peter Matthiessen **5**:273

Wright Morris **7**:247
Donald Newlove **6**:363
Ezra Pound **2**:342
Thomas Pynchon **2**:356
Isaac Bashevis Singer **3**:456

Wolfley, Lawrence C.
Thomas Pynchon **9**:444

Wolitzer, Hilma
Richard Yates **8**:556

Wolkenfeld, J. S.
Isaac Bashevis Singer **1**:311

Wolkoff, Lewis H.
Anne McCaffrey **17**:281
Roger Zelazny **21**:470, 471

Woll, Josephine
Varlam Shalamov **18**:480

Wollen, Peter
John Ford **16**:310

Wollheim, Donald A.
Isaac Asimov **1**:8
Ray Bradbury **1**:42
Arthur C. Clarke **1**:59
Harlan Ellison **1**:93
Philip Jose Farmer **1**:97
Edmond Hamilton **1**:137
Robert A. Heinlein **1**:139
Andre Norton **12**:466
Clifford D. Simak **1**:309
A. E. Van Vogt **1**:347
Kurt Vonnegut, Jr. **1**:348

Wong, Jade Snow
Jade Snow Wong **17**:566

Wong, Sharon
John Ehle **27**:105

Wood, Adolf
Louis Auchincloss **18**:25

Wood, Anne
Leon Garfield **12**:232

Wood, Charles
Kurt Vonnegut, Jr. **4**:565

Wood, Gayle
Margaret Atwood **15**:37

Wood, Karen
Kurt Vonnegut, Jr. **4**:565

Wood, Michael
Miguel Ángel Asturias **3**:18
J. G. Ballard **14**:39
John Barth **2**:37; **27**:27
Donald Barthelme **2**:41
John Betjeman **6**:66
Adolfo Bioy Casares **4**:63
Elizabeth Bishop **9**:95
Harold Bloom **24**:74
Jorge Luis Borges **2**:72
Anthony Burgess **8**:112
Italo Calvino **8**:131; **22**:95
Elias Canetti **25**:109
Alejo Carpentier **11**:101
Evan S. Connell, Jr. **6**:116
Francis Ford Coppola **16**:246
Julio Cortázar **2**:105
Jacques Derrida **24**:138
Lawrence Durrell **6**:153
T. S. Eliot **10**:169

Stanley Elkin **4**:154
William Empson **8**:201
Ken Follett **18**:156
Carlos Fuentes **8**:225; **22**:171
Gabriel García Márquez **15**:254
John Gardner **5**:131; **8**:235
Juan Goytisolo **5**:150
Judith Guest **8**:253
Barry Hannah **23**:209
John Hawkes **4**:219
Seamus Heaney **7**:147
John Hollander **14**:263
Erica Jong **4**:264
William Melvin Kelley **22**:249
John le Carré **15**:324
Violette Leduc **22**:263
Stanislaw Lem **8**:345
John Lennon and Paul
 McCartney **12**:365
José Lezama Lima **4**:289
Ross Macdonald **14**:328
Norman Mailer **3**:316
Thomas McGuane **3**:330
A. G. Mojtabai **9**:385
Brian Moore **8**:395
Alberto Moravia **27**:355
Berry Morgan **6**:340
Vladimir Nabokov **2**:303
Pablo Neruda **5**:303
Hans Erich Nossack **6**:365
Robert Nye **13**:413
Joyce Carol Oates **2**:316
Grace Paley **4**:392
Octavio Paz **4**:396
Peter Porter **13**:451
Ezra Pound **2**:345
Anthony Powell **3**:403
Manuel Puig **3**:407; **28**:371
Thomas Pynchon **2**:357
Raymond Queneau **10**:432
Jean Rhys **14**:446
Philip Roth **4**:456
Luis Rafael Sánchez **23**:386
Severo Sarduy **6**:487
Isaac Bashevis Singer **3**:459
Susan Sontag **13**:517
Muriel Spark **5**:399; **8**:495
Robert Stone **23**:426
J.R.R. Tolkien **12**:570
Charles Tomlinson **6**:534
John Updike **2**:445
Mario Vargas Llosa **6**:546
Gore Vidal **8**:525
Kurt Vonnegut, Jr. **3**:503
Eudora Welty **2**:463
Angus Wilson **3**:535
Rudolph Wurlitzer **2**:483
Roger Zelazny **21**:468

Wood, Peter
Peter De Vries **2**:114
Alberto Moravia **2**:293

Wood, Robin
Robert Altman **16**:31
Michelangelo Antonioni **20**:34
Ingmar Bergman **16**:60
Frank Capra **16**:164
Claude Chabrol **16**:173
Carl Theodor Dreyer **16**:264
John Ford **16**:311
Alfred Hitchcock **16**:354
Rouben Mamoulian **16**:428
Pier Paolo Pasolini **20**:268

Satyajit Ray **16**:483

Wood, Scott
Rudolfo A. Anaya **23**:22

Wood, Susan
Alice Adams **13**:2
Margaret Atwood **15**:36
T. Alan Broughton **19**:74
Penelope Gilliatt **10**:230
Robert Hass **18**:210
David Plante **23**:343
John Wain **11**:564

Wood, William C.
Wallace Markfield **8**:380

Woodbery, W. Potter
John Crowe Ransom **11**:467

Woodcock, George
Margaret Atwood **25**:65
Earle Birney **6**:71, 75; **11**:51
Camilo José Cela **13**:145
Louis-Ferdinand Céline **9**:158
Matt Cohen **19**:113
Robert Finch **18**:154
Roy Fuller **28**:151, 154
Hugh Garner **13**:236
Jean Genet **5**:138
Jack Hodgins **23**:229, 232
W. P. Kinsella **27**:235
Patrick Lane **25**:284
Irving Layton **15**:321
Denise Levertov **5**:246
Hugh MacDiarmid **2**:255
Hugh MacLennan **14**:339
Brian Moore **1**:225; **3**:341
R. K. Narayan **28**:300
Alden Nowlan **15**:399
A. W. Purdy **14**:431
Herbert Read **4**:441
Kenneth Rexroth **2**:70, 371
Mordecai Richler **5**:375
Gabrielle Roy **14**:469
A.J.M. Smith **15**:515
Andrew Suknaski **19**:432
Rudy Wiebe **11**:569

Woodfield, James
Christopher Fry **10**:200; **14**:187

Woodhouse, J. R.
Italo Calvino **22**:87

Woodruff, Stuart C.
Shirley Jackson **11**:301

Woods, Crawford
Ross Macdonald **3**:308
Isaac Bashevis Singer **3**:457
Hunter S. Thompson **9**:526

Woods, George A.
Margaret O. Hyde **21**:172

Woods, Katherine
Henri Troyat **23**:457

Woods, William C.
Lisa Alther **7**:13
Leon Uris **7**:492

Woods, William Crawford
Jim Harrison **6**:225

Woodward, C. Vann
William Styron **3**:473

Woodward, Helen Beal
Vera Brittain 23:93
Frank B. Gilbreth, Jr. and Ernestine Gilbreth Carey 17:155
Jean Kerr 22:255

Woodward, Kathleen
William Carlos Williams 22:464

Wooldridge, C. Nordhielm
Norma Fox Mazer 26:295

Woolf, Virginia
E. M. Forster 15:222
Ernest Hemingway 19:211

Woollcott, Alexander
Dorothy Parker 15:414

Wooten, Anna
Louise Glück 7:119

Wordsworth, Christopher
Thor Heyerdahl 26:192

Worsley, T. C.
Ann Jellicoe 27:206
Stephen Spender 10:488
Martin Walser 27:455

Worth, Katharine J.
Edward Bond 13:99

Worthen, John
Edward Bond 23:63

Worton, Michael J.
René Char 11:115

Wrenn, John H.
John Dos Passos 1:77

Wright, Barbara
Romain Gary 25:188
Michel Tournier 23:452

Wright, Basil
Luis Buñuel 16:129
Charles Chaplin 16:192

Wright, Cuthbert
Compton MacKenzie 18:313

Wright, David
C. Day Lewis 6:126
Seamus Heaney 25:249
Hugh MacDiarmid 19:289

Wright, Elsa Gress
Carl Theodor Dreyer 16:262

Wright, George T.
W. H. Auden 1:10
T. S. Eliot 3:137

Wright, Hilary
Rosemary Sutcliff 26:439

Wright, James
Richard F. Hugo 6:244
Pablo Neruda 28:306, 308

Wright, John M.
David Malouf 28:268

Wright, Judith
Robert D. FitzGerald 19:176
Kenneth Slessor 14:493

Wright, Richard
Arna Bontemps 18:63
Carson McCullers 12:408

Wunderlich, Lawrence
Fernando Arrabal 2:16

Wyatt, David M.
Ernest Hemingway 8:288; 19:223
Robert Penn Warren 8:541

Wyatt, E.V.R.
Jade Snow Wong 17:566

Wylder, Delbert E.
William Eastlake 8:198

Wylie, Andrew
Giuseppe Ungaretti 11:556

Wylie, John Cook
Earl Hamner, Jr. 12:257

Wylie, Philip
Sally Benson 17:49

Wyllie, John Cook
John Ehle 27:103
Earl Hamner, Jr. 12:257

Wymard, Eleanor B.
Annie Dillard 9:177
John Irving 23:246

Wyndham, Francis
Caroline Blackwood 6:79
Elizabeth Bowen 15:78
Agatha Christie 12:120
Aldous Huxley 18:265
Ruth Rendell 28:387

Yacowar, Maurice
Woody Allen 16:16
Alfred Hitchcock 16:351

Yagoda, Ben
Margaret Drabble 10:164
Henry Green 13:254
Tom Wolfe 15:585

Yakir, Dan
Peter Weir 20:428

Yamanouchi, Hisaaki
Kōbō Abé 22:13
Yasunari Kawabata 18:285
Yukio Mishima 27:339

Yamashita, Sumi
Agatha Christie 12:117

Yannella, Philip R.
Pablo Neruda 5:301
Louis Zukofsky 18:557

Yardley, Jonathan
Chinua Achebe 3:2
Kingsley Amis 2:8
Roger Angell 26:30, 32
Hal Bennett 5:59
Wendell Berry 4:59; 6:62
Doris Betts 3:73; 28:34, 35
Frederick Buechner 6:102
Harry Crews 6:117, 118
Don DeLillo 27:83
Peter De Vries 7:77; 28:111
James Dickey 2:116
John Gregory Dunne 28:122
John Ehle 27:106
Frederick Exley 6:171
William Faulkner 3:158
Leslie A. Fiedler 13:213
Brian Glanville 6:202
James Hanley 5:167, 168
Barry Hannah 23:208
Jim Harrison 6:224
John Hersey 9:277
George V. Higgins 7:157
Diane Johnson 5:199
Madison Jones 4:263
Ward Just 4:266; 27:228, 229
Thomas Keneally 8:319; 10:299
John Knowles 4:271; 10:303
Elmore Leonard 28:235
Robert Lipsyte 21:210
John D. MacDonald 27:275
Bernard Malamud 2:267
Saul Maloff 5:271
Cormac McCarthy 4:342
James A. Michener 11:375
A. G. Mojtabai 5:293
Toni Morrison 4:365
Robert Newton Peck 17:337
Walker Percy 3:381
David Plante 23:342, 345
Piers Paul Read 4:444
J. R. Salamanca 4:462
John Seelye 7:406
Wilfrid Sheed 2:394; 4:488
Robert Stone 23:428
James Thurber 25:438
Thomas Tryon 3:483
Jerome Weidman 7:518
Eudora Welty 2:462
Tom Wicker 7:533
Calder Willingham 5:511, 512

Ya Salaam, Kalumu
Nikki Giovanni 4:189

Yates, Donald A.
Jorge Amado 13:11
John Dickson Carr 3:100
Autran Dourado 23:149
Carlos Fuentes 13:232
João Guimarães Rosa 23:352

Yates, John
Francis Ford Coppola 16:241

Yates, Norris W.
Günter Grass 4:203
James Thurber 5:433

Yenser, Stephen
Ai 14:9
A. R. Ammons 25:43
Philip Levine 14:315
Robert Lowell 3:305
James Merrill 3:335
Robert Pinsky 19:372
Adrienne Rich 11:479
James Schuyler 23:390
W. D. Snodgrass 18:493
Robert Penn Warren 8:537, 540

Yglesias, Helen
Cynthia Propper Seton 27:427
Ludvík Vaculík 7:494

Yglesias, Jose
Christina Stead 2:421
Mario Vargas Llosa 6:547

Yglesias, Luis E.
Pablo Neruda 7:262; 9:398
Kenneth Rexroth 22:348

Yoder, Edwin M.
MacKinlay Kantor 7:195

Yoder, Jon A.
Upton Sinclair 15:501

Yohalem, John
Richard Brautigan 5:70
James McCourt 5:277
Charles Webb 7:516
Edmund White III 27:479

Yoke, Carl B.
Roger Zelazny 21:474

Yolen, Jane
Jamake Highwater 12:287
Mollie Hunter 21:158
Zilpha Keatley Snyder 17:470

York, David Winston
Chaim Potok 26:374

Young, Alan
Donald Justice 19:236
Christopher Middleton 13:389
James Schuyler 23:388

Young, Alan R.
Ernest Buckler 13:118, 119

Young, Charles M.
Mel Brooks 12:83
Patti Smith 12:543

Young, Colin
Kon Ichikawa 20:177

Young, David
John Ashbery 25:54
Robert Francis 15:236

Young, Dora Jean
Katherine Paterson 12:484

Young, Dudley
Carlos Castaneda 12:84

Young, Israel G.
Bob Dylan 12:180

Young, J. R.
Waylon Jennings 21:201

Young, James O.
Jessie Redmon Fauset 19:170

Young, Jon
Joan Armatrading 17:10
Chuck Berry 17:55
Carly Simon 26:411

Young, Kenneth
Compton Mackenzie 18:314

Young, Marguerite
Carson McCullers 12:411
Mark Van Doren 10:495

Young, Peter
Andrei Voznesensky 1:348

Young, Philip
Ernest Hemingway 13:273

Young, Scott
Farley Mowat 26:331

Young, Stark
Eric Bentley 24:45
Paul Green 25:196
Clifford Odets 28:323, 327, 328
Irwin Shaw 23:395
Emlyn Williams 15:576

Young, Thomas Daniel
Donald Davidson 13:168
Andrew Lytle 22:298
John Crowe Ransom 4:433, 436

Young, Tracy
Lily Tomlin 17:520

Young, Vernon
Woody Allen 16:10
Yehuda Amichai 22:31
W. H. Auden 2:28
Ingmar Bergman 16:66
Wendell Berry 27:35
George Mackay Brown 5:77
Charles Chaplin 16:197
Walter Van Tilburg Clark 28:78
J. V. Cunningham 3:121
Peter Davison 28:102
Vittorio De Sica 20:86, 90
William Dickey 3:126
Gunnar Ekelöf 27:116
Odysseus Elytis 15:220
Lawrence Ferlinghetti 6:183
Brewster Ghiselin 23:171
William Heyen 18:231
John Hollander 2:197
Richard F. Hugo 6:245
John Huston 20:172
Donald Justice 19:232
Galway Kinnell 13:320
Akira Kurosawa 16:397
Laurence Lieberman 4:291
Robert Lowell 5:258
Cynthia Macdonald 19:291
William Meredith 22:303
W. S. Merwin 13:384
Josephine Miles 14:369
Michael Mott 15:380
Pablo Neruda 1:247
Robert Pack 13:439
Nicanor Parr 2:331
Roman Polanski 16:469
Yannis Ritsos 6:464
Carlos Saura 20:319
Martin Scorsese 20:329
Frederick Seidel 18:475
Jon Silkin 2:396
Charles Simic 22:382
David Slavitt 14:490
Maura Stanton 9:508
James Tate 2:432
Diane Wakoski 2:459; 4:573
Ted Walker 13:566
Peter Weir 20:429

Youngblood, Gene
Stanley Kubrick 16:391

Younge, Shelia F.
Joan Armatrading 17:8

Youree, Beverly B.
Melvin Berger 12:41

Yourgrau, Barry
William Price Fox 22:141
Mordecai Richler 18:452
Peter Rushforth 19:406

Yucht, Alice H.
Richard Peck 21:296

Yuill, W. E.
Heinrich Böll 11:52

Yurieff, Zoya
Joseph Wittlin 25:468

Zabel, Morton Dauwen
Glenway Wescott 13:591

Zacharias, Lee
Truman Capote 13:139

Zahorski, Kenneth J.
Roger Zelazny 21:473

Zaiss, David
Roy Fisher 25:158

Zak, Michele Wender
Doris Lessing 6:294

Zaller, Robert
Bernardo Bertolucci 16:94
Anaïs Nin 4:377

Zarookian, Cherie
Barbara Corcoran 17:71

Zatlin, Linda G.
Isaac Bashevis Singer 1:312

Zaturenska, Marya
Laura Riding 7:373

Zavatsky, Bill
Ed Dorn 10:157

Zebrowski, George
Arkadii Strugatskii and Boris Strugatskii 27:436

Zehender, Ted
Tod Browning 16:123

Zehr, David E.
Ernest Hemingway 8:286

Zeik, Michael
Thomas Merton 3:337

Zelenko, Barbara
Nora Ephron 17:111

Zeller, Bernhard
Hermann Hesse 2:190

Zeman, Marvin
Jean Renoir 20:300

Zern, Ed
Roderick L. Haig-Brown 21:136

Zetterberg, Bettijane
Hilma Wolitzer 17:562

Zeugner, John F.
Gabriel Marcel 15:364
Walker Percy 18:396

Zibart, Eve
Penelope Gilliatt 13:238

Ziegfeld, Richard E.
Kurt Vonnegut, Jr. 22:447

Ziff, Larzer
Leslie A. Fiedler 24:205
Edmund Wilson 24:488

Zilkha, Michael
Mark Medoff 6:323

Zimbardo, Rose A.
Edward Albee 13:3

Zimmerman, Eugenia N.
Jean-Paul Sartre 9:472

Zimmerman, Paul
R. K. Narayan 7:256

Zimmerman, Paul D.
John Gregory Dunne 28:121
E. M. Forster 2:135
Lois Gould 4:199
Stanley Kubrick 16:383
Robert Lipsyte 21:211
Leni Riefenstahl 16:524
Melvin Van Peebles 20:412

Zimmerman, Ulf
Rolf Hochhuth 18:255
Martin Walser 27:463, 464, 466

Ziner, Feenie
Frank Bonham 12:53
Rosemary Sutcliff 26:437

Zinnes, Harriet
Robert Bly 1:37
Robert Duncan 1:83
Anaïs Nin 4:379; 8:425
Ezra Pound 3:399
May Swenson 4:533, 534
Mona Van Duyn 7:499

Zinsser, William
James Thurber 25:439

Ziolkowski, Theodore
Heinrich Böll 2:67; 6:83
Günter Grass 22:195
Hermann Hesse 1:145, 146; 3:248; 17:209; 25:260
Hans Erich Nossack 6:364

Zipes, Jack D.
Christa Wolf 14:593

Zivanovic, Judith
Jean-Paul Sartre 9:470

Zivkovic, Peter D.
W. H. Auden 3:23

Zivley, Sherry Lutz
Sylvia Plath 9:431

Zolf, Larry
Mordecai Richler 5:376

Zorach, Cecile Cazort
Heinrich Böll 15:70

Zoss, Betty
Jesse Jackson 12:290

Zucker, David
Delmore Schwartz 10:464

Zuckerman, Albert J.
Vassilis Vassilikos 4:551

Zuger, David
Adrienne Rich 7:372

Zukofsky, Louis
Charles Chaplin 16:190

Zunser, Jesse
Akira Kurosawa 16:394

Zvirin, Stephanie
Lois Duncan 26:108
Sol Gordon 26:138
Nat Hentoff 26:187
Norma Fox Mazer 26:295

Zweig, Paul
Richard Adams 5:6
A. R. Ammons 5:29
John Ashbery 2:18
James Dickey 15:178
William Dickey 3:126
Clayton Eshleman 7:100
Allen Ginsberg 13:240
Günter Grass 11:254
John Hollander 5:186
David Ignatow 7:181
Thomas Keneally 27:232
Kenneth Koch 8:322
Violette Leduc 22:263
Philip Levine 4:286
Jakov Lind 27:272
Peter Matthiessen 11:358
Leonard Michaels 6:325
Czesław Miłosz 5:292; 22:312
Vladimir Nabokov 3:354
Pablo Neruda 5:303
Joyce Carol Oates 15:402
Frank O'Hara 13:424
George Oppen 7:284
Charles Simic 6:502
William Stafford 7:461
Diane Wakoski 4:571
James Wright 3:542

Library
Western Wyoming Community College